Africa

Anthony Ham

Kate Armstrong, James Bainbridge, Tim Bewer, Stuart Butler, Jean-Bernard Carillet, Paul Clammer, Lucy Corne, Emilie Filou, Matthew D Firestone, Mary Fitzpatrick, Katharina Lobeck Kane, Adam Karlin, Nana Luckham, Tom Masters, Alan Murphy, Helen Ranger, Nicola Simmonds, Kate Thomas, Donna Wheeler

LUXOR, EGYPT (p110)
Discover Luxor's temples and tombs close to the banks of the Nile

LALIBELA, ETHIOPIA (p692)
Explore the rock-hewn churches and spiritual atmosphere of medieval Ethiopia frozen in stone

ASSEKREM, ALGERIA (p77)
Watch the sun rise and set, deep in the Sahara

MARRAKESH, MOROCCO (p177)
Immerse yourself in Morocco at its most clamorous and exotic

DOGON COUNTRY, MALI (p412)
Trek down the escarpment and into an utterly timeless world

SIERRA LEONE (p505)
Visit Africa's most surprising country with its primate populations and deserted palm-fringed beaches

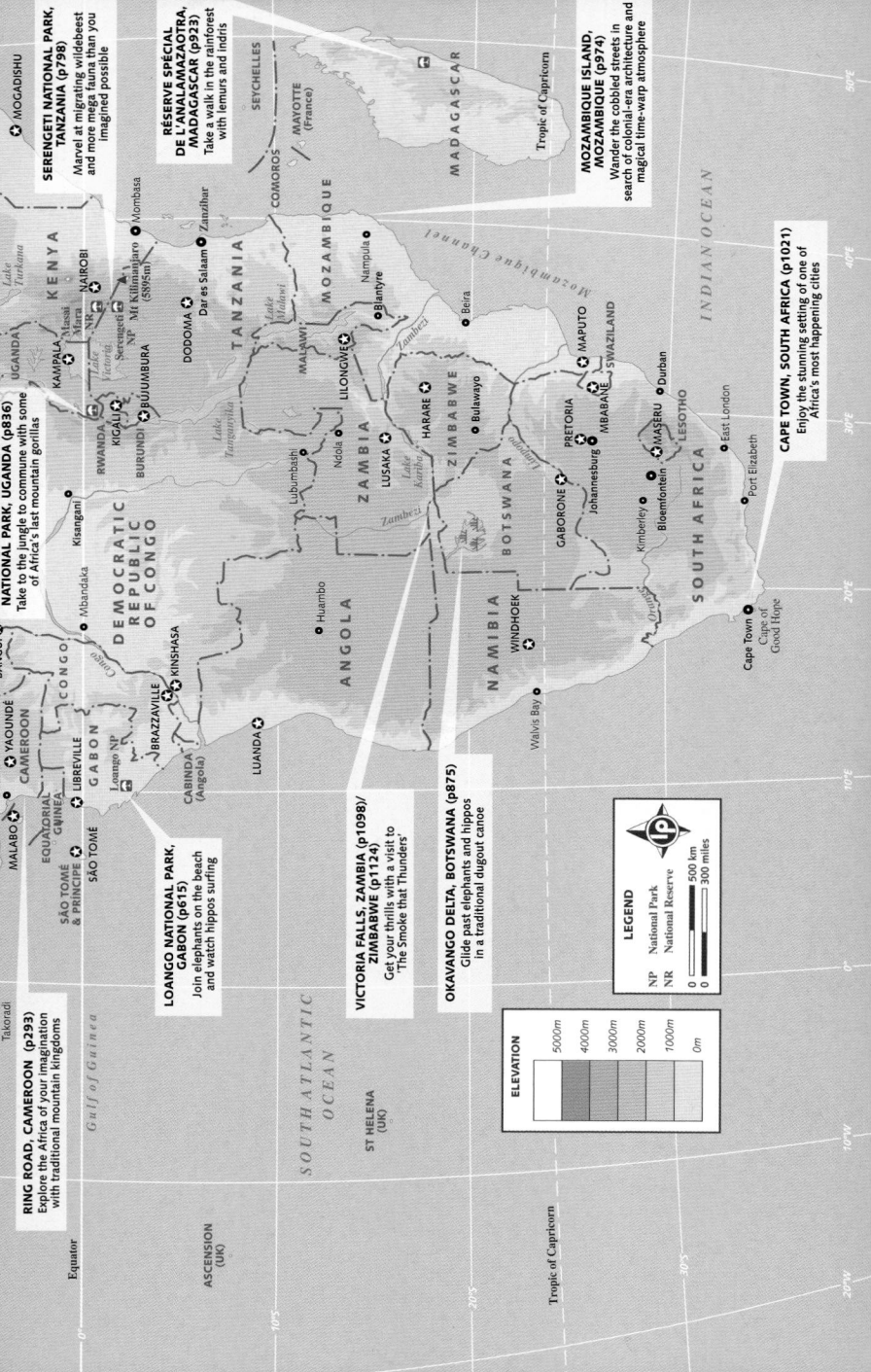

RING ROAD, CAMEROON (p293)
Explore the Africa of your imagination with traditional mountain Kingdoms

LOANGO NATIONAL PARK, GABON (p615)
Join elephants on the beach and watch hippos surfing

VICTORIA FALLS, ZAMBIA (p1098)/ZIMBABWE (p1124)
Get your thrills with a visit to 'The Smoke that Thunders'

OKAVANGO DELTA, BOTSWANA (p875)
Glide past elephants and hippos in a traditional dugout canoe

SERENGETI NATIONAL PARK, TANZANIA (p798)
Marvel at migrating wildebeest and more mega fauna than you imagined possible

RÉSERVE SPÉCIAL DE L'ANALAMAZAOTRA, MADAGASCAR (p923)
Take a walk in the rainforest with lemurs and indris

MOZAMBIQUE ISLAND, MOZAMBIQUE (p974)
Wander the cobbled streets in search of colonial-era architecture and magical time-warp atmosphere

CAPE TOWN, SOUTH AFRICA (p1021)
Enjoy the stunning setting of one of Africa's most happening cities

NATIONAL PARK, UGANDA (p836)
Take to the jungle to commune with some of Africa's last mountain gorillas

LEGEND

NP National Park
NR National Reserve

ELEVATION

5000m
4000m
3000m
2000m
1000m
0m

0   500 km
0   300 miles

Africa Highlights

Here's an impossible task: choosing the highlights of all of Africa. The sights, activities and experiences of Africa are as varied as the continent itself. From the northern beaches of Tunisia all the way down to Cape Town at South Africa's southern tip, the options that await are almost limitless. To get you started, here are some of our authors' favourites. What will your African highlight be?

MASON FLO

① PYRAMIDS OF GIZA, EGYPT

Although they're Egypt's most iconic images, nothing can prepare you for the sense of awe and wonderment you'll feel when you first lay eyes on the Pyramids of Giza and the Sphinx (p91). Towering over both the urban sprawl of Giza and the desert plains beyond, these ancient monuments are at the top of every traveller's itinerary, and they never fail to amaze. Bring lots of water, an empty memory card, and a lot of patience! Although you'll have to fend off touts to enjoy this ancient funerary complex in peace, no trip to Egypt is complete without a visit to Giza.

Matthew D Firestone, Lonely Planet Author

SERENGETI NATIONAL PARK, TANZANIA

Dusk fell over the Serengeti (p798), day melted seamlessly into night, and time seemed to stand still. We sat silently around our campfire, listening to wildebeest snorting nearby and recalling images from the day – a large lion sitting on a rock yawning lazily, giraffes and zebras grazing on the plains, crocodiles, a solitary secretary bird. We sensed how small we were amidst the surrounding vastness and felt privileged for each moment in this magnificent wildness.

Mary Fitzpatrick,
Lonely Planet Author

2

ARIADNE VAN ZANDBERGEN

OKAVANGO DELTA, BOTSWANA

Slipping into the Okavango Delta (p875) on a *mokoro* (dugout canoe) isn't just relaxing – it can almost make you comatose, and there are times you just want to doze off. Not because the land is boring – but because that sweet ripple of boat on reeds is as soothing as a lullaby in the crib.

Adam Karlin,
Lonely Planet Author

RICHARD I'ANSON

3

TONY WHEELER

4

VICTORIA FALLS, ZAMBIA & ZIMBABWE

When you stand before Victoria Falls (p1098 & p1124) the clichés abound, for this is the mighty Mosi-oa Tunya (the Smoke that Thunders). Unfortunately, visiting the falls during the peak of the heaviest rainy season in decades results in an entirely different experience. Wrapped in layers of plastic, clutching my water-logged camera with a kung-fu action grip, I am engulfed by sheets of mist and gusts of spray that pay fitting tribute to the fury of the falls.

Matthew D Firestone,
Lonely Planet Author

MATT FLETCHER

WALKING SOUTH LUANGWA, ZAMBIA

A walking safari in South Luangwa National Park (p1091) is a unique and special way to experience the African bush. If you were ever under the misapprehension that the parks are like zoos, it will be blown away once you've trod the same ground as the animals. It's exhilarating and slightly intimidating wondering what's behind the next corner, up a tree or under the water…

**Alan Murphy,
Lonely Planet Author**

5

QUIRIMBAS ARCHIPELAGO, MOZAMBIQUE

No matter how many beautiful beaches and islands you've seen, there are few coastal stretches that compare with the northern Mozambique coastline around the Quirimbas Archipelago (p976). The waters are the requisite turquoise, the sand is fine and white, and life here seems to have changed little over the centuries. We happened to arrive on sleepy, sunbaked Ibo Island during a holiday festival and were treated to a morning of dancing and singing under the shade of a huge, spreading mango tree.

Mary Fitzpatrick, Lonely Planet Author

6

DAVID

JANE SW

7

FROM TOGO TO BENIN ON THE ROAD LESS TRAVELLED

There is something exciting about crossing a border without going through a checkpoint: it's a reminder of how arbitrary borders can be when everything in the landscape and the culture talks of continuity. Driving along the red tracks of the Atakora mountains (p257) is a fine example of that; just get your passport stamped at the police station in Nadoba or Kanté in Togo or Boukoumbé in Benin, and away you go.

Emilie Filou, Lonely Planet Author

TREKKING THROUGH DOGON COUNTRY, MALI

Villages colonising the cliff face. Intricate cultural traditions that survived the onslaughts of the modern world. A landscape of rare beauty that rises from the plains of the Sahel like an apparition. Welcome to Mali's Dogon Country (p412), an extraordinary outpost of Old Africa.

Anthony Ham, Lonely Planet Author

8

DAVID ELSE

SWAZILAND

Swaziland (p1068) is a highlight in itself. Don't let the country's compact size fool you. This tiny place has the lot, all spread over extraordinary landscapes. Nowhere else in Africa can you so readily access such varied experiences: mountain wildernesses and plains, superb handicrafts and fun outdoor adventures. For genuine cultural activities, the festivals here are top of the (ceremonial) pops.

**Kate Armstrong,
Lonely Planet Author**

10

ARIADNE VAN ZANDBERGEN

9

ARIADNE VAN ZANDBERGEN

GAMBIA RIVER NATIONAL PARK, THE GAMBIA

The first flicker of sunlight sparks a symphony of baboon barks, bird calls and the morning shrieks of the chimps on the river in Gambia River National Park (p332). The cool water of the outdoor shower trickles down my spine and I'm convinced that those cheeky red colobus monkeys are debating this curious creature who has come to join their treetop haven.

Katharina Lobeck Kane, Lonely Planet Author

TRANS-KAROO EXPRESS, SOUTH AFRICA

Catch the trans-Karoo tourist-class train (p1067) from Johannesburg to Cape Town to see South Africa in all its blotchy glory. Leaving Jo'burg's razor wire behind, the train passes through tiny North-West Province towns, where denim suits and peroxide-blond hair are de rigueur, and the train porters greet cohorts: 'Howzit! Izzit? Shame!' The 27-hour journey passes so easily that you only realise you're delayed when you notice you've been waving at some school children for an hour.

James Bainbridge, Lonely Planet Author

11

ANDREW EAMES/GUAR

TONY W

12

CLIMBING KILIMANJARO, TANZANIA

On the final night of our trek up Mt Kilimanjaro (p789) we couldn't get to sleep – partly the effects of altitude, partly knowing that in a few hours we would set off for the final ascent to try to reach Uhuru Peak by dawn. It was raw, cold and damp once we were walking, and, as the night wore on, each step up the soft scree slope became more laboured. After what seemed like far too long, we reached Gilman's Point, and stopped to take in sunrise over the plains far below. On the final stretch to Uhuru Peak, we picked our way slowly over rocks and snow, fighting fatigue at every step and, suddenly, we were at the summit of Africa.

Mary Fitzpatrick, Lonely Planet Author

TODD

13

SCORCHED EARTH, NAMIBIA

Alone in the middle of Sossusvlei (p995), you get the sense of what a day at the beach must be like in hell. Sand permeates everything, from your eyes and ears to your shoes and rucksack, and the only water in sight is the few drops left at the bottom of your canteen. The world can at times be a cruel and unforgiving place.

Matthew D Firestone, Lonely Planet Author

Contents

Destination Africa

There's nowhere on earth quite like Africa. Yes, to speak of Africa as a single entity can be profoundly misleading – Africa is the unwieldy sum total of around 50 countries, tens of thousands of ethnic groups, and landscapes that span the full spectrum of the natural world's repertoire. But if we could distil Africa's appeal to its essence it would be this: wherever you go, and more than any other continent, human and natural history come together in Africa with rare power. This is a place where all the world's beauty and tragedy seem to be concentrated in one (albeit vast) corner of the earth, a diverse continent that is soulful, deeply troubled and profoundly uplifting all at once. In short, there's something special about Africa, and whether you're a hardened African veteran or a wide-eyed first timer, this is a continent that cannot fail to get under your skin.

The canvas upon which Africa's epic story is written is itself astonishing, and reason enough to visit. From the tropical rainforests of Central Africa to the endless dune scapes and waterless tracts of the Sahara, from the signature savannah of the east to jagged mountains and green-tinged highlands all across the continent, Africa has few peers when it comes to natural beauty. It is sunset on the Serengeti, and the sunrise at Assekrem, deep in the Algerian Sahara, whose name means the 'End of the World'; it is scaling the Mountains of the Moon in Uganda, and standing where sand dunes meet the sea in Namibia; or it is the deserted palm-fringed beaches of Mozambique, São Tomé & Príncipe, Guinea-Bissau and Sierra Leone, and a slow boat journey through the blissful solitude of Botswana's Okavango Delta. Exploring these stirring wilderness areas could easily occupy a lifetime and you would still scarcely have touched the surface.

Inhabiting these wilderness areas, and often living just beyond the flimsy fence of the African farmer, Africa's wildlife brings these landscapes to life, a tangible and sometimes profoundly mysterious presence that adds so much personality to the wild. The list of Africa's megafauna reads like a who's who of the animal kingdom, and so many of the great beasts, whose existence we learned about as children, call Africa home. Elephants, gorillas, lions, leopards, cheetahs, giraffes, zebras, rhinos, hippos and chimpanzees all roam free in Africa, often in massive herds, but just as often as small, precarious outposts in a sea of humanity that cling to life as wars rage around them. Going on an African safari may be something of a travellers' cliché, but we're yet to find a traveller who has watched the wildlife world in motion in the Masai Mara, stumbled upon the paradise that is the Ngorongoro Crater, or communed with gorillas in Uganda's Bwindi Impenetrable Forest, and has not been reduced to an ecstatic state of childlike wonder.

But there's so much more to Africa than nature's considerable bounty. On this continent where human beings first came into existence, customs, traditions and ancient rites tie Africans to generations past and to the collective memory of myriad people. In many rural areas, it can feel as though the modern world might never have happened, and old ways of doing things – a certain grace and civility, hospitality and a community spirit – survive. Welcome to Old Africa.

And yet, even as the past retains its hold over the lives of many Africans, just as many have embraced the future, bringing creativity and sophistication to the continent's cities and urban centres. Sometimes this New Africa is expressed in a restless search for solutions to the continent's problems, or in an eagerness to break free of the restrictive chains of the past. But just as

FAST FACTS

Population: 1 billion

Most populous country: Nigeria (146 million)

Total area: 30.2 million sq km

Largest/smallest country: Sudan/Gambia

Proportion of population living in rural areas: around 60%

Number of African countries ranked among the lowest 24 in the UN's 2009 Human Development Index: 22

Highest life expectancy at birth: Libya and Tunisia (73.8 years)

Lowest life expectancy at birth: Zambia (44.5 years)

Countries with highest proportion of national parks and other protected areas: Zambia (41.8%) and Tanzania (38.4%)

Proportion of Africa covered by deserts/rainforests: 60%/20%

often, modern Africans are taking all that is new and fusing it onto the best of the old. Leading the way have been Africa's endlessly talented musicians, who give voice in equal measure to a continent yearning for a return to the past and for a better future – the fruits of their labours provide a constantly evolving playlist to the continent's diversity and an unforgettable sound-track to your African journey. The results can be stunning and are always unmistakeably African.

'once Africa has you in its thrall, it very rarely lets go'

For all this talk of past and future, there's no denying that the African present is plagued with difficulties that read like a catalogue of human and environmental calamity. Corruption is widespread (though by no means universal) among Africa's rulers, diseases kill Africans at an unconscionable rate, wars and lawlessness continue to blight the lives of millions, and the continent's staggering wealth of natural resources has more often meant misery than a better life for people from Nigeria to Congo. Such problems are exacerbated by deserts eating away at the land and livelihoods of millions, and by deforestation, drought, loss of biodiversity and land degradation. Little wonder, then, that Africa remains the poorest continent on earth.

At the same time, Africa has an impressive array of good news stories and most of them are, by their very nature, rarely considered newsworthy by the international media. Democracy and good governance have taken hold from Benin to Botswana and countries formerly at war – Sierra Leone, Liberia, Côte d'Ivoire and Angola for example – have taken the first tentative steps along the road to peace and stability. Even Zimbabwe, that exemplifica-tion of African potential gone to ruin, has new, if fragile, reasons to hope. When it comes to environmental issues, the continent's problems can seem overwhelming, but governments, as well as local and international conser-vation groups, have had some stunning successes, from the stabilisation of once-threatened elephant, rhino and primate populations, to Gabon's ground-breaking creation of a slew of national parks, which protect some of Central Africa's most pristine wilderness. And then there are the millions of small but significant successes engineered daily by Africans themselves. Whether it's an overworked mother who puts food on the table for her children against the odds or a community-based conservation program that puts power and prosperity into the hands of a local community, these are the real African success stories.

And one final thing: travel African-style can be hard travel. While you can see Africa in five-star luxury, the African road can be a long and dusty one, particularly in areas less trammelled by tourists. In such places, and even in countries where you'd least expect it, infrastructure is often poor or nonexistent, transport is slow and uncomfortable, and the frustrations of African bureaucracy and border-crossing politics can confound even the best-laid plans. But in Africa, the journey in all its complexity will put you in close proximity with Africans who live with such difficulties on a daily basis. We can think of no people on earth with whom we'd rather share the ride. And when, in spite of it all, they smile and begin to dance, you'll find it hard to resist joining in. It's at moments like these that you begin to understand why so many travellers are passionate about Africa: once Africa has you in its thrall, it very rarely lets go.

Getting Started

By visiting Africa, you're embarking on a major expedition that requires careful planning and, for many travellers, involves setting out into the unknown. Addressing both elements – the practical and the stuff of dreams – should occupy most of your pre-departure planning. The following section is only intended to give you a mix of general and inspirational information that might be useful before you set off. For more specific titbits, flip to the Africa Directory on p1132, while for advice on travelling responsibly, turn to p54. No matter how prepared you are, however, nothing will quite prepare you for the overwhelming sensory and cultural experience that is a first visit to Africa. But isn't that why you're going?

WHEN TO GO

Most tourists tie in their trip with Africa's dry seasons – dirt tracks become a sea of mud when it rains. There are regional variations, but essentially it goes like this: East Africa has two dry seasons – December to February/March and June to October – with rainy seasons in between; by around January or February, East African wildlife is concentrated around diminishing water sources and is therefore easier to spot. In southern Africa it's dry from May/June, gets really hot in October, then rains November to April/May. In West Africa the dry season is October/November to April/May, and it gets very hot at the end of this period. In Central Africa, June to September is the dry time. In North Africa, rain isn't the main issue – it's temperature. The best time to travel is the cooler period from October to March.

For climate information about each country, see the relevant country chapters. General climate information is given on p1137.

Although dry seasons are usually the popular times, don't automatically avoid the rainy season everywhere. In some countries it only rains for a few hours each day (often at night) and then the air is crystal clear and views go on forever. It's also a good time for birdwatching, hotel rates are cheaper and popular tourist haunts are much quieter. And generally the local people are also happier because good rains mean good crops, so traditional festivals are often held at this time.

Other elements to consider when planning your trip include the continent's fascinating festivals (see p17 and the individual country chapters for details), or local holiday periods (see p1140 and the individual country chapters for details). In the case of holidays, for example, you may want to avoid travelling in Islamic countries during Ramadan.

COSTS & MONEY

Africa can be as cheap or expensive as you want it to be. Travelling around like a maniac is going to cost much more than taking time to explore a small region slowly and in depth.

The actual cost of living (food, transport etc) varies greatly around the continent, and travellers commonly blow big chunks of their budget on car hire (US$30 to US$150 per day), internal flights, adrenaline sports and organised safaris or treks (at least $100 a day in East/southern Africa). Prevailing petrol prices will have a major impact on your costs, whether you're hiring a car or buying food. Sometimes it costs the same as in Europe, but in Libya, for example, it costs as little as US$0.10 per litre.

Apart from being expensive, African visa requirements are one of the most irritating hurdles for the traveller. Accept that they are a form of retaliation for the obstacles the West puts in the way of Africans migrants; go armed with photos, and cultivate a sense of humour.

Africa is thought of as expensive among some budget travellers, but you can still scrape by for under US$30 per day. If you'd like a few more

WHAT TO TAKE?

- Cash – you can't go wrong with a wad of US dollars or euros in your pocket (or, better, strapped about your person). ATM cards are good too, but not always viable.

- Memory cards – bring more than you think you'll need as they'll come in handy if one gets damaged

- Photocopies of important documents – photocopy your passport data pages (and those with relevant visas), tickets and travellers cheques, and pack them separately from the originals

- Water purifier – bottled water is available almost everywhere, but the plastic bottles are an environmental nightmare

- Sealable plastic bags – to protect your belongings from moisture and dust

- Travel insurance (p1140) – accidents do happen

- One smart set of clothes – advisable for visa applications, crossing borders or if you're invited to somebody's house

- Basic medical kit (see p1165)

- Mosquito net and repellent

- Light sleeping bag (for cold desert nights) or a sleeping sheet (for less-than-clean hotels)

- Sunglasses, hat and sunscreen (as essential in the Sahara as on the beach)

- Torch (flashlight) and spare batteries – electricity can be a stop-start affair

- Universal washbasin plug and length of cord for drying clothes

- Sanitary towels or tampons

- Condoms

- An emergency stash of toilet paper

- Frisbee or small (size-three) football – a great way to meet local kids

- Contact-lens-cleaning-and-soaking solutions and a pair of prescription glasses as a back-up

- Patience – most transport does leave eventually

comforts (such as an in-room shower), reckon on US$40, plus a slush fund of, say, US$100 to US$150 a month for unexpected expenses. Beyond that, the scope for spending money is limited only by your bank account or credit limit...

For more on money issues, see p1141. The Fast Facts boxes in the country chapters provide more specific country budgets.

TOP AFRICAN READS

The following selection of books should give you a starting point for travel literature that covers the broader geographical spectrum. We also cover reading matter about Africa on opposite, p39 and p1135.

The Tree Where Man Was Born, by Peter Matthiessen, dates from the early '60s, but it's beautifully written and remains for many the definitive African travelogue. His *African Silences* and *Sand Rivers* are also outstanding.

Shadow of the Sun, by Ryszard Kapuściński, gets under the skin of Africa like few other books with illuminating anecdotes garnered during decades as a foreign correspondent in Africa.

The Zanzibar Chest, by Aidan Hartley, is a searing, no-holds-barred memoir of the author's time as a foreign correspondent in the war zones of Africa.

TOP 10

UNESCO WORLD HERITAGE–LISTED SITES

- **Pyramids of Giza** (Egypt, p91) The pharaohs' extraordinary gift to the world
- **Dogon Country** (Mali, p412) Dramatic scenery and intriguing traditional villages
- **Serengeti National Park** (Tanzania, p798) The largest collection of wildlife on the planet
- **Victoria Falls** (Zambia, p1098; Zimbabwe, p1124) One of Africa's most spectacular sights, with activities to match
- **Churches of Lalibela** (Ethiopia, p692) An other-worldly, ancient and deeply spiritual place with churches hewn from the rock
- **Bwindi Impenetrable National Park** (Uganda, p836) Home to half of the world's mountain gorillas and rainforest
- **Ghadames** (Libya, p135) Ancient and labyrinthine Saharan caravan town
- **Medina of Fez** (Morocco, p169) Islamic city that seems to spring from the imagination
- **Coastal forts and castles** (Ghana, p349) The oldest colonial buildings in Africa with echoes of the slave-trading past
- **Robben Island** (South Africa, p1023) Follow Nelson Mandela's (and South Africa's) walk to freedom

NOVELS

- *The Famished Road* (Ben Okri) Extraordinary magic realism epic from Nigeria
- *Petals of Blood* (Ngũgĩ wa Thiong'o) A whodunnit underpinned by biting political satire
- *Disgrace* (JM Coetzee) Confronting tale of post-apartheid South Africa
- *Things Fall Apart* (Chinua Achebe) Classic tragedy by the Nigerian master
- *Little Boys Come from the Stars* (Emmanuel Dongala) Comic yet heart-breaking Congolese story through a child's eyes
- *Half of a Yellow Sun* (Chimamanda Ngozi Adichie) Masterful storytelling set during Nigeria's Biafran War
- *The Cairo Trilogy* (Naguib Mahfouz) Sweeping family drama set in 1940s Egypt
- *Abyssinian Chronicles* (Moses Isegawa) Accomplished evocation of Idi Amin's Uganda
- *In the Country of Men* (Hisham Matar) Harrowing drama in Colonel Qaddafi's Libya
- *Waiting for the Wild Beasts to Vote* (Ahmadou Kourouma) Fantastical tale following the sweep of West African history

FESTIVALS

- **La Cure Salée** (p456) World-famous annual celebration by Fula herders, near In-Gall in Niger; September
- **Festival of the Dhow Countries** (www.ziff. or.tz; p807) Film and music festival held in Zanzibar; July
- **Festival in the Desert** (www.festival-au-desert.org; p418) Tuareg culture meets rock music near Timbuktu in Mali; early January
- **Festival Sur Le Niger** (p407) Performances along the Niger riverbank in Ségou by Mali's leading musicians; late January/early February
- **Kano Durbar** (p473) Spectacular traditional parade of horsemen, held annually in Kano, Nigeria; end of Ramadan
- **Tabaski** (p294) The festivities surrounding Eid al-Adha are celebrated throughout Muslim West Africa, but the mix of Islamic and local traditions is at its best in Foumban, Cameroon
- **Fespaco** (www.fespaco.bf, in French; p265) Africa's biggest film fest, held in odd years in Ouagadougou, Burkina Faso; February/March
- **Timkat Ethiopian Epiphany celebration** (p697) Colourful and ceremonial celebration of Ethiopia's Christian heritage;19 January
- **Umhlanga** (p1079) One of southern Africa's most vibrant spectacles; August/September
- **Sauti za Busara** (www.busaramusic.com; p807) Swahili and world-music festival in Zanzibar; February

Journey Without Maps, by Graham Greene, is a wonderful narrative by one of the 20th century's best writers as he travelled through the forests of Liberia and Sierra Leone in 1935.

Dark Star Safari, by Paul Theroux, chronicles one of the author's returns to Africa (he was a Peace Corps volunteer in Malawi in the 1960s) as he travels from Cairo to Cape Town.

Blood River – A Journey to Africa's Broken Heart, by Tim Butcher, follows HM Stanley's route into the African interior and reads like a thriller, combining gripping suspense with an engaging writing style.

The Lost Kingdoms of Africa, by Jeffrey Taylor, is a highly readable account of a modern journey through the Sahel, especially northern Nigeria, Niger and Mali; it was published in the US as *Angry Wind.*

If you can't get enough of African literature, check out the website of literary magazine *The African Review of Books* (www.africanreviewofbooks.com), which has a Top 100 list as well as reams of news, reviews and book gossip.

Travels in the White Man's Grave, by Donald MacIntosh, is a little-known classic by a writer who spent much of his working life in the forests of Liberia, Nigeria, Côte d'Ivoire and Cameroon.

INTERNET RESOURCES

For specific country overviews and hundreds of useful links, including Thorn Tree, Lonely Planet's online forum, head to lonelyplanet.com. For good news websites covering Africa, see p35. Information on Africa can also be found at the following websites:

African Studies Center (www.africa.upenn.edu//Home_Page/Country.html) Extensive links from the University of Pennsylvania's Africa program.

Bootsnall (www.bootsnall.com) Although its information about Africa varies in usefulness, the Africa message board is indispensable.

Norwegian Council for Africa (www.afrika.no) A comprehensive site with 'Index on Africa' links for each country, chat forums and more.

Sahara Overland (www.sahara-overland.com) The best practical guide for travellers to the Sahara, with useful forums, route information and book reviews.

The Africa Guide (www.africaguide.com) An all-purpose, all-Africa site with everything from extensive background information to NGOs and travel links.

Travel Africa (www.travelafricamag.com) The best print magazine on Africa, with articles on every corner of the continent and a useful 'Safari Planner' on its website.

Itineraries
CLASSIC ROUTES

TOP TO BOTTOM
One Year/Tunisia to Cape Town

Begin in **Tunisia** (p213), then cross the border into Libya where cosmopolitan **Tripoli** (p130) serves as a launch pad for a foray into the **Libyan Sahara** (p135). Stop off in **Leptis Magna** (p133) and **Cyrene** (p134) en route to **Egypt** (p82) where ancient sites and a felucca trip down the Nile await. Continue south across Lake Nasser into Sudan where the glorious **Meroe Sites** (p204) and the rest of **northern Sudan** (p204) are the highlights. **Ethiopia** (p675) has some exceptional sites, especially **Lalibela** (p692), before you journey down to **Nairobi** (p707).

The wildlife-sprinkled plains of **Kenya** (p700) and **Tanzania** (p768) form the centrepiece of many classic African journeys, but don't neglect the warm and welcoming villages of **Malawi** (p935), with a detour to **Mozambique** (p961) en route to **Zambia** (p1082); in the latter, **Victoria Falls** (p1096) is breathtaking. From here, it's back into wildlife territory with Botswana's **Okavango Delta** (p875) and Namibia's **Etosha National Park** (p1000), before reaching the very bottom of Africa in stunning **Cape Town** (p1021), South Africa.

Cairo to the Cape may be the best-known north–south African odyssey, but why not take in a bit of North Africa and travel from the very top to the very bottom?

SOUTHERN AFRICA SMORGASBORD

Three Months/ Cape Town to Cape Town

Start in South Africa's mother city, vibrant **Cape Town** (p1021), then head north into Namibia to take in the spectacular landscapes of **Fish River Canyon National Park** (p1005), the endless sand dunes of Namibia in **Namib-Naukluft Park** (p995), and the high-adrenaline activities of **Swakopmund** (p992). Continue north to **Etosha National Park** (p1000), then east along the Caprivi strip to **Kasane** (p882), the gateway to Botswana's **Chobe National Park** (p883) and its amazing concentration of elephants. Fly to **Maun** (p879) for a few days poling through the swampy maze of the **Okavango Delta** (p875). Back in Kasane, it's a short hop into Zambia's **Livingstone** (p1096), for some high-speed thrills and the spectacular **Victoria Falls** (p1098).

From Zambia, cross into Malawi, then head south to the white Lake Malawi beaches of **Cape Maclear** (p955), **Blantyre** (p948) and **Liwonde National Park** (p953) for an up-close encounter with elephants.

Once across the border in Mozambique, take the train from Cuamba to **Nampula** (p974), the jumping-off point for trips to the unforgettable **Mozambique Island** (p974). Take a trip to the lost-in-time **Quirimbas Archipelago** (p976) then head south via the sleepy towns of **Quelimane** (p973), **Beira** (p972), **Vilankulo** (p971), for the **Bazaruto Archipelago** (p972), and **Inhambane** (p970). Next stop is beguiling **Maputo** (p965) for a fiesta of seafood and caipirinhas. Then it's on to **Swaziland** (p1068) en route to **Johannesburg** (p1048), South Africa's hustling, bustling commercial capital. From here you can head to the **Kruger National Park** (p1046) or venture south to the **Drakensberg Mountains** (p1044), for great hiking, even across the border into **Lesotho** (p890). Drop down to the coast at **Durban** (p1037) before following the trail all the way back to Cape Town.

This itinerary takes in nine countries and the best southern Africa has to offer – most places are easily accessible, English is widely spoken and the countries are well set up for foreign visitors.

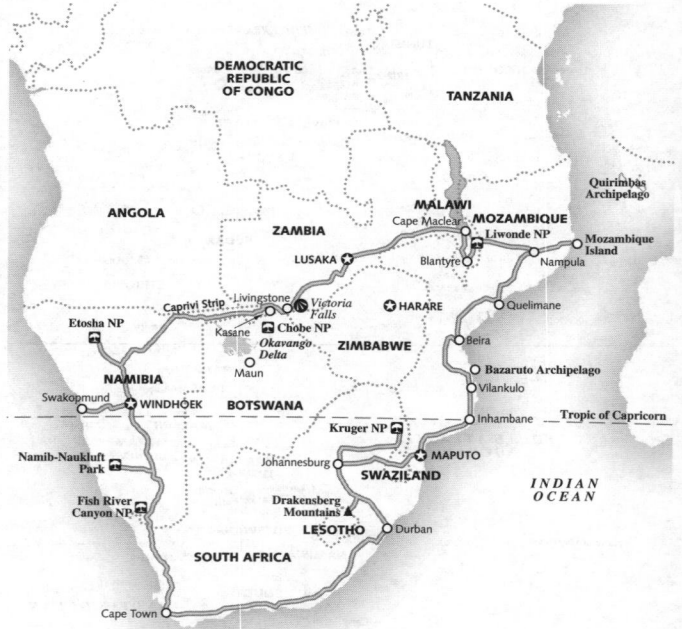

EAST AFRICAN EXTRAVANGANZA

**Three Months/
Nairobi to Addis Ababa**

Fly into Kenya's **Nairobi** (p707) and explore the Central Highlands around **Mt Kenya** (p715), then head east via **Mombasa** (p721) to the palm-fringed beaches and coral reefs of the **Lamu archipelago** (p727).

Head south into Tanzania to **Arusha** (p791), from where you can arrange 4WD safaris to the **Ngorongoro crater** (p798) or **Serengeti National Park** (p798), and trekking trips up **Mt Kilimanjaro** (p789). From **Dar es Salaam** (p773), hop offshore to drink in the Swahili history and culture of **Zanzibar** (p778) and **Pemba** (p785). From Dar es Salaam head northwest into Rwanda where soulful **Kigali** (p745) is worth seeing before you detour to the silverback gorillas of **Parc National des Volcans** (p750). Cross into western Uganda, stopping off at stunning **Lake Bunyonyi** (p838) before searching for mountain gorillas in **Bwindi Impenetrable National Park** (p836). Also possible is the chance to kick back for a few days at the **Crater Lakes** (p833) or **Ssese Islands** (p840), or go white-water rafting at **Jinja** (p828); in the north, **Murchison Falls National Park** (p841) is a gem.

From Uganda travel east into Kenya to remote **Loyangalani** (p718), before heading north into Ethiopia. In Ethiopia's south, the **Lower Omo Valley** (p695) is one of East Africa's most underrated wilderness areas, while the north is home to the castles of **Gonder** (p688), the rock churches of **Lalibela** (p692), the ancient city of **Aksum** (p690) and fantastic hiking in the **Simien Mountains National Park** (p690). After a detour to the fascinating walled city of **Harar** (p694), head to **Addis Ababa** (p681) for your flight back to Nairobi.

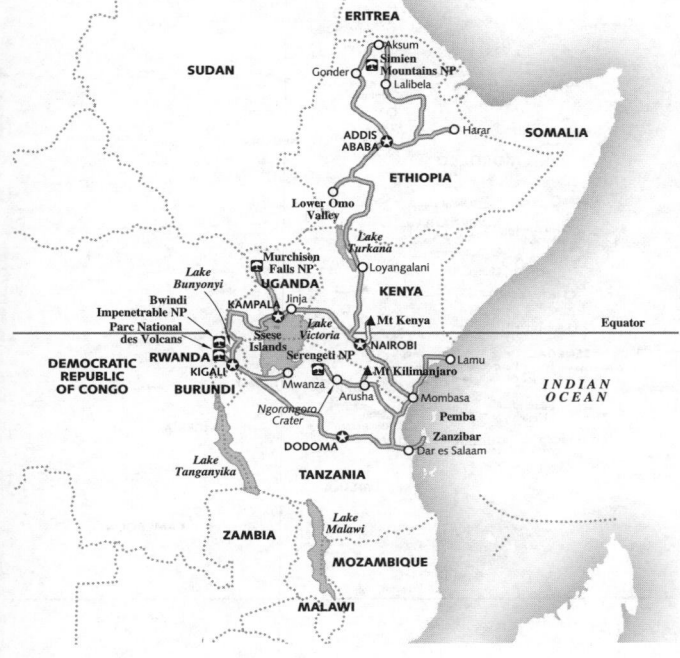

The wildlife of Kenya and Tanzania, and the island of Zanzibar, are well known, but there's so much more to East Africa, including gorillas in Rwanda and Uganda, and the other-worldly natural and cultural attractions of Ethiopia.

ROADS LESS TRAVELLED

FRENCH FOOTSTEPS

Begin in Morocco in the cities of **Marrakesh** (p177) and **Fez** (p169), with excursions to **Essaouira** (p165), the **High Atlas Mountains** (p182) and the **Drâa Valley** (p185). The long journey south through the Western Sahara, via Dakhla, takes you to **Nouâdhibou** (p434) in Mauritania. After desert detours to **Ben Amira** (p436), **Chinguetti** (p436) and **Ouadâne** (p437), head back to the coast, via **Terjît** (p436), to **Nouakchott** (p431), then across the border to **Saint-Louis** (p493) in Senegal. **Dakar** (p484) is one of West Africa's cultural capitals, with great live music and nightlife, while the bird-rich **Siné-Saloum Delta** (p492) couldn't be quieter, with pirogues drifting quietly through the mangroves. Out east, the **Parc National de Niokolo-Koba** (p497) is a worthwhile stop en route to Guinea, where the **Fouta Djalon highlands** (p371) offer fine hiking in stunning country.

Across the border in Mali, **Bamako** (p401) has terrific live music. The vast, ornate mud mosque and Monday market in **Djenné** (p408), trekking in the fascinating **Dogon Country** (p412), and a boat trip up the **Niger River** (see the boxed text, p412) to the legendary desert outpost of **Timbuktu** (p416), are Mali's stand-out attractions. In Burkina Faso, **Bobo-Dioulasso** (p269) and the **Sindou Peaks** (p272) are the highlights of this friendly country. Niger's capital **Niamey** (p446) is an agreeable base for the wonderful Sunday market in **Ayorou** (p450) and an excursion to the Sahel's last giraffes at **Kouré** (p450). In the north, **Agadez** (p454) is Niger's premier ancient city and, if the security situation permits, the gateway to some of the Sahara's most beautiful scenery.

Pack a French phrasebook and hone your sign language for this trip that takes you through the fascinating human and cultural landscape of Sahara and Sahel.

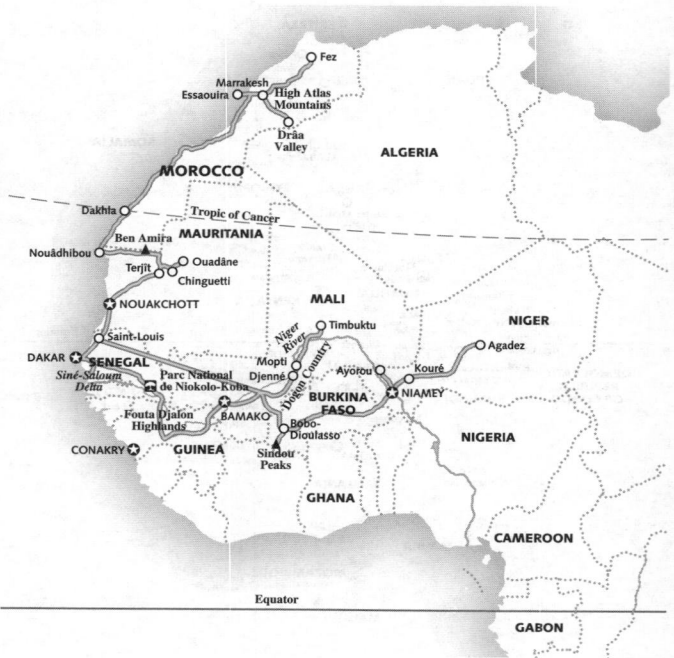

ATLANTIC WEST AFRICA

From the arid coastlines of the northwest to the palm-fringed tropics of Cameroon, West Africa's coastline has it all. Senegal's capital, **Dakar** (p484), with its African sophistication, serves both as a starting point and a base for the first part of your journey. To the north, **Saint-Louis** (p493) is like stepping back into pre-colonial Africa. From Dakar, head south via **The Gambia** (p318), **Guinea-Bissau** (p376) and **Guinea** (p361) to Sierra Leone (p505), a country very much on the rebound, with some of Africa's best **beaches** (p513). From **Freetown** (p509), consider flying to agreeable **Accra** (p341) in Ghana, from where excursions to the old **coastal forts** (p347) and stunning beaches at **Kokrobite** (p347) and **Busua & Akwidaa** (p349) never disappoint. Don't fail to detour north to **Kumasi** (p350) in the Ashanti heartland, or even further north to elephant-rich **Mole National Park** (p355). There's plenty of onward transport to the fascinating markets and fine museum of **Lomé** (p524) and don't miss an inland hiking detour around **Kpalimé** (see the boxed text, p529) or the clay-and-straw fortresses of **Koutammakou** (p532) in the far north. Not far away is Benin, with **Ouidah** (p253), the evocative former slaving port and home of voodoo; the history-rich town of **Abomey** (p255); the stilt-villages of **Ganvié** (p252); and the **Parc National de la Pendjari** (p257). **Cotonou** (p247) has all the steamy appeal of the tropics; from here fly to **Yaoundé** (p282) in Cameroon, which has a distinctive Central African feel. After a circuit of the **Ring Road** (p293) through the traditional kingdoms of Cameroon's northwestern highlands, head north to **Maroua** (p298) and the **Mandara Mountains** (p300).

For much of this route along coastal West Africa, you're likely to be the only Western traveller. In the process, you'll discover an Africa every bit as beautiful as more famous destinations.

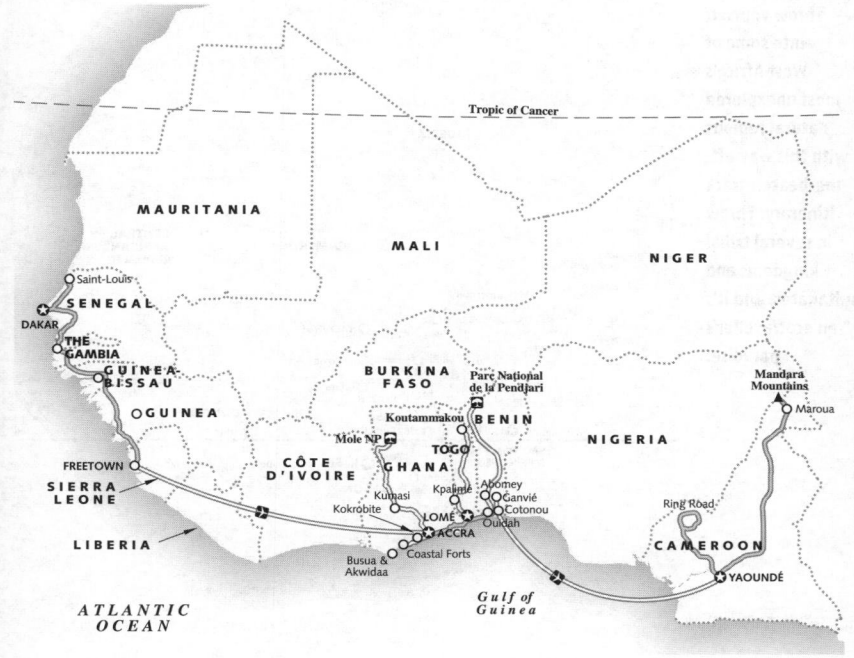

SURFING HIPPOS & NESTING TURTLES

Fly into Cameroon's capital, **Yaoundé** (p282), then head west to the lazy, chocolate-coloured beaches around **Limbe** (p289), where the Limbe Wildlife Centre is home to rescued gorillas, chimps and drills, all refugees from Cameroon's thriving bushmeat trade. After exploring **Mt Cameroon** (p289) head south to the lovely white-sand beaches of **Kribi** (p295). Even better for wildlife enthusiasts, continue down the coast to **Ebodjé** (p296) with its nesting turtles and impressive ecotourism project. From **Ebolowa** (p295), you leave behind well-travelled paths and venture across the Gabon border to **Bitam** (p614). From Gabon's capital, **Libreville** (p608), a number of outstanding wildlife-watching experiences are possible in the country's many pristine and newly created national parks. If you could choose just two, watch the surfing hippos and strolling elephants on the beaches at **Loango National Park** (p615), and more elephants and the vibrant mandrill troupes of **Réserve de la Lopé** (p617) in eastern Gabon. Most of these unique ecotourism opportunities are only accessible by plane from Libreville, so you may have to base yourself there and shuttle back and forth – it's not cheap, but it's worth it for the chance to see some of Africa's quietest wilderness areas before mass tourism takes hold. Accessible by road is **Lambréné** (p614), the site of Albert Schweizer's famous hospital. Finish the trip with a jaunt to one of Africa's smallest countries, **São Tomé & Príncipe** (p621), where the highlights include watching nesting turtles at Praia Jalé, snorkelling with dolphins and watching whales at Lagoa Azul, and the deserted and generally perfect Banana Beach.

Throw yourself into some of West Africa's most unexplored natural regions with this way-off-the-beaten-track itinerary. Throw in several tribal kingdoms and sultanates, and it's an ecotraveller's paradise.

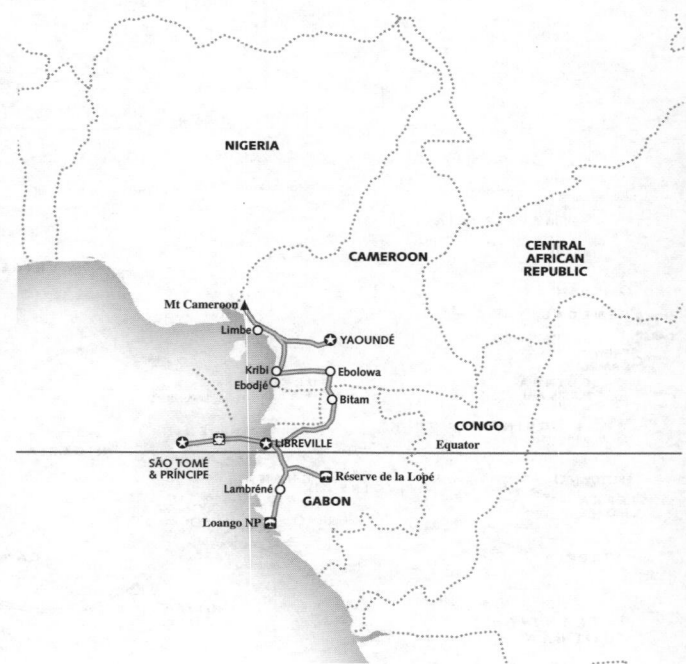

TAILORED TRIPS

GETTING ACTIVE

Many travellers are drawn to Africa by the lure of high-adrenaline thrills. If you're among them, you'll want to make a beeline for **Victoria Falls** (p1098 and p1124), where just about anything's possible from both the Zambian and Zimbabwean sides. Also in southern Africa, **Swakopmund** (p992) in Namibia is becoming world famous for its chances to get sweaty and breathless, while tiny **Swaziland** (see the boxed text, p1076) is gaining a following among discerning white-water rafters. Not to be outdone by southern Africa's more famous adventure sports capitals, Uganda's **Jinja** (see the boxed text, p831), combines the Source of the Nile with white-water rafting, kayaking, mountain biking and quad bikes. If you're an experienced climber, **La Main de Fatima** (p420) in Mali is renowned for its challenging climbs (British grades around E4, French grades around 7A).

More sedate perhaps, but diving and snorkelling in Africa is some of the best in the world. Egypt's **Red Sea** (p97 and p102) ranks among the elite. Elsewhere, the waters off southern Mozambique, especially the **Bazaruto Archipelago** (p972), and relatively untrammelled **São Tomé & Príncipe** (see the boxed text, p626) are quieter but stunning. **Zanzibar** (p781) is also popular, while there's considerable novelty about the freshwater options beneath **Lake Malawi** (p956).

THE WILDEST SHOWS ON EARTH

If you're the type who spent their childhood glued to the TV watching BBC nature documentaries, it's time to make your wildest dreams come true. In Tanzania the **Serengeti National Park** (p798) is the venue for the great wildebeest migration and epic collections of other large mammals, while the **Ngorongoro Conservation Area** (p798) is another iconic wildlife-watching experience. Kenya's most prolific wildlife concentrations are found at **Masai Mara National Reserve** (p719) and **Amboseli National Park** (p730). Uganda's **Bwindi Impenetrable Forest** (p836) and Rwanda's **Parc National des Volcans** (p750) are home to mountain gorillas. Across Central Africa to the west, Congo's **Parc National Nouabalé-Ndoki** (p571) and Central African Republic's **Dzanga-Sangha Reserve** (p546) are remote, scarcely visited by tourists, and home to western lowland gorillas as well as other large mammals. Down in southern Africa, a sunset river cruise in Botswana's **Chobe National Park** (p883) allows you to see hundreds of elephants drinking and romping in the water within metres of your boat. Other southern highlights include South Africa's **Kruger National Park** (p1046), Namibia's **Etosha National Park** (p1000), and Zambia's **South Luangwa National Park** (p1091) and **Lower Zambezi National Park** (p1095). Over in **Madagascar** (p903), get up early to hear the eerie shriek of the indri.

TREKKING TALES

There are world-class hiking trails all across Africa. The arduous, rewarding climb to the snowy summit of Tanzania's **Mt Kilimanjaro** (p789), Africa's highest point, never disappoints, not least for its unforgettable view of the Serengeti at sunrise. Nearby **Mt Meru** (p796) offers some lovely (and much cheaper) hiking. In neighbouring Kenya, **Mt Kenya** (p715) crowns some wonderful hiking country, while **Mt Elgon National Park** (p830) and **Rwenzori Mountains National Park** (p835), both in Uganda, rank among Africa's most beautiful trails. Away to the northeast, Ethiopia's challenging **Simien Mountains** (p690) are simply breathtaking. In South Africa, the magical milkwood forests of the **Otter Trail** (p1034) drop down to wild and windy beaches, while the **Southern Drakensberg Wilderness Area** (p1045) climbs up South Africa's highest point and down into Lesotho.

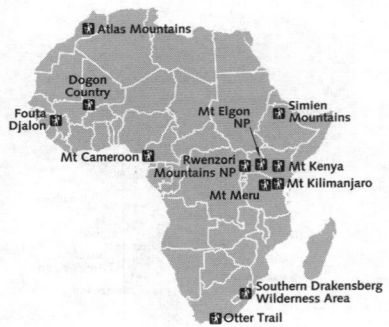

West Africa's trails are far less frequented than those in the east, but they're every bit as spectacular. Trails climb **Mt Cameroon** (p289), West Africa's highest peak, while hiking the Bandiagara Escarpment in Mali's **Dogon Country** (p412) combines natural beauty with fascinating culture – if you make one hike in West Africa, make it here. Far quieter but nonetheless wonderful is Guinea's **Fouta Djalon** (see the boxed text, p371). In Morocco's **Atlas Mountains** (p183), you can climb steep paths past flatroofed, earthen Berber villages, terraced gardens and walnut groves.

PUT YOUR FEET UP

The rigours of travelling in Africa mean that many travellers looking to rest from life on the road end up on a beach. And what beaches!

Most East African travellers choose to do their R & R in Tanzania's **Zanzibar** (p778), a spicy heaven of perfume plantations, endless white beaches and whispering palm trees. For somewhere even quieter, head to Kenya's **Lamu** (p727), where the hardest decision you'll make all day is when to take the next nap. Southern Africa's best-loved beach hang-out is the shore of turquoise **Lake Malawi** (p955) with its fresh waters, laid-back locals and reggae bars. Further south, the **Bazaruto** (p972) and **Quirimbas** (p976) islands of Mozambique have a Latin vibe and generally feel like paradise.

But don't neglect West Africa in your search for the perfect beach. Cameroon's **Kribi** (p295) and nearby **Ebodjé** (p296) are simply gorgeous, as are the beaches of **São Tomé & Príncipe** (p621). Elsewhere, Senegal's **Cap Skiring** (p501) is less popular than it deserves to be, while the beaches of **Sierra Leone** (p513), Guinea-Bissau's **Arquipélago dos Bijagós** (p381) and **Assinie** (p312) in Côte d'Ivoire rank among Africa's most beautiful (and most deserted). The beaches in **Ghana** (p347) are busier but every bit as beautiful.

History

African history is a vast and epic tale. What follows is intended as a general overview that offers a taste of the world-shaking events that have shaped the continent's past. The history of Africa is also, however, the fascinating sum total of the stories of the 49 countries and countless cultures covered in this book. You'll find more localised and detailed coverage in each individual country chapter.

HUMAN ORIGINS & MIGRATIONS

Africa has seen pretty much everything – from proto-bacteria to dinosaurs and, finally, around five to 10 million years ago, a special kind of ape called *Australopithecines* that branched off (or rather let go of the branch) and walked on two legs down a separate evolutionary track. This radical move led to the development of various hairy, dim-witted hominids (early men) – *Homo habilis* around 2.4 million years ago, *Homo erectus* some 1.8 million years ago and finally *Homo sapiens* (modern humans) around 200,000 years ago. Around 50,000 years later, somewhere in Tanzania or Ethiopia, a woman was born who has become known as 'mitochondrial Eve'. Every single human alive today is descended from her: at a deep genetic level, we're all Africans.

The break from Africa into the wider world occurred around 100,000 years ago, when perhaps as few as 50 people migrated out of North Africa, along the shores of the Mediterranean, and into the Middle East. From this small beginning came a population that would one day cover almost every landmass on the globe.

The first moves away from the nomadic hunter-gatherer way of life came between 14,000 BC and 9500 BC, a time when rainfall was high and the Sahara and North Africa became verdant. By 2500 BC the rains began to fail and the sandy barrier between North and West Africa became the Sahara we know today. People began to move southwest into the rainforests of Central Africa, most notably a group of people speaking the same family of languages. Known as the Bantu, the group's population grew as it discovered iron-smelting technology and developed new agricultural techniques. By 100 BC, Bantu peoples had reached East Africa; by AD 300 they were living in southern Africa, and the age of the African empires had begun.

AFRICAN EMPIRES

Victorian missionaries liked to think they were bringing the beacon of 'civilisation' to the 'backward' Africa, but the truth is that Africans were developing commercial empires and complex urban societies while Europeans were still running after wildlife with clubs.

For a highly readable account of millennia of African history, from Africa's human origins to the Rwandan genocide (no small task), pick up a copy of John Reader's *Africa – A Biography of the Continent* (2005).

TIMELINE

200,000 years ago	From 5000 BC	146 BC
The first 'humans' (*Homo sapiens*) begin to definitively diverge from other similar species (such as *Homo erectus,* which persists for millennia) in Africa, marking the continent as the birthplace of humanity.	Rains become infrequent and the Sahara begins the millennia-long process of becoming a desert. Africa is sparsely populated, but the drying climate prompts people to settle around waterholes, to rely on agriculture and to move south.	After a century-long struggle for Mediterranean supremacy, Carthage falls to the Romans, who utterly destroy the city. Its people are sold into slavery and the site is symbolically sprinkled with salt and damned forever.

Pyramids of Power

Arguably the greatest of the African empires was the first: ancient Egypt. Formed through an amalgamation of already organised states in the Nile Delta around 3100 BC, Egypt achieved an amazing degree of cultural and social sophistication. The Pharaohs, kings imbued with the power of gods, sat at the top of a highly stratified social hierarchy, and the annual flooding of the Nile kept the lands of the Pharaohs fertile and fed their legions of slaves and artisans, who in turn worked to produce some of the most amazing public buildings ever constructed. Many of these, like the Pyramids of Giza, are still standing today. During the good times, which lasted nearly 3000 years, Egyptians discovered the principles of mathematics and astronomy, invented a written language and mined gold. Ancient Egypt was eventually overrun by the Nubian Empire, then by the Assyrians, Persians, Alexander the Great and finally the Romans.

Phoenician & Roman North Africa

Established in Tunisia by the Phoenicians, a seafaring people with their origins in Tyre in modern Lebanon, the city-state of Carthage filled the power vacuum left by the decline of ancient Egypt. By the 6th century BC, Carthage was an empire in its own right and controlled much of the Mediterranean sea trade. Back on land, scholars were busy inventing the Phoenician alphabet, from which Greek, Hebrew and Latin are all thought to derive. It all came to an abrupt end with the arrival of the Romans, who razed Carthage and enslaved its population in 146 BC.

The Romans built some of Africa's most beautiful ancient cities in what are now Libya, Algeria and Morocco, and African-born Septimius Severus (r AD 193–211), went on to become Emperor of Rome. But the Romans, like the Carthaginians before them and the Byzantines who came after, had their control over Africa effectively restricted to the Mediterranean coastal strip. It was swept away by the Arabs who arrived in North Africa, bearing Islam, around AD 670.

The Kingdom of Sheba

Aksum was the first truly African indigenous state – no conquerors from elsewhere arrived to start this legendary kingdom, which controlled much of Sudan and southern Arabia at the height of its powers. Aksum's heart was the hilly, fertile landscape of northern Ethiopia. The Aksumites traded with Egypt, the eastern Mediterranean and Arabia, developed a written language, produced gold coins and built imposing stone buildings. In the third century AD, the Aksumite king converted to Christianity, founding the Ethiopian Orthodox church. Legend has it that Ethiopia was the home of the fabled Queen of Sheba and the last resting place of the mysterious Ark of the Covenant.

> Respected African-American scholar Henry Louis Gates Jr has spent a lifetime refuting perceptions of Africa's precolonial backwardness. The result is the compelling *Wonders of the African World* (1999).

100 BC	AD 670	Around AD 1000
The Bantu people arrive in East Africa from the west and northwest. They will later continue into southern Africa, completing what is arguably the most enduringly influential mass movement of peoples in Africa's history.	Islam sweeps across North Africa, where it remains the dominant religion today. A century later, it arrived on the East African coast and first crossed the Sahara into West Africa around AD 900.	The city of Timbuktu is founded as a seasonal encampment for Tuareg nomads where the Niger River meets the Sahara; it would later become a centre of scholarship and be home to 100,000 people.

Golden Kingdoms

The area centred on present-day Mali was home to a hugely wealthy series of West African empires that flourished over the course of more than 800 years. The Ghana Empire lasted from the 4th to 11th centuries, and was followed by the fabulously wealthy Mali Empire (around AD 1250 to 1500), which once stretched all the way from the coast of Senegal to Niger. The extravagant, gold-laden pilgrimage to Mecca by Mali's King Kankan Musa in 1324 is often credited with sparking Europe's interest in Africa and its riches. The Songhaï Empire (AD 1000–1591), with its capital at Gao in modern-day Mali, was the last of Africa's golden empires, which, at their peak covered areas larger than Western Europe, and whose wealth was founded on the salt from Saharan mines which was traded ounce for ounce with West African gold. Organised systems of government and Islamic centres of scholarship – the most famous of which was Timbuktu – flourished in the kingdoms of West Africa, but conversely, it was Islam that led to their downfall when the forces of Morocco invaded in 1591.

Swahili Sultans

While West African kings were trading their way to fame and fortune, a similar process was occurring on Africa's east coast. As early as the 7th century AD, the coastal areas of modern-day Tanzania, Kenya and Mozambique were home to a chain of vibrant, well-organised city-states, whose inhabitants lived in stone houses, wore fine silks and decorated their gravestones with artisanal ceramics and glass. Merchants from as far afield as China and India came to the East African coast, then set off again, their holds groaning with trade goods, spices, slaves and exotic beasts. The rulers of these city-states were the Swahili sultans – kings and queens who kept a hold on their domains via their control over magical objects and knowledge of secret religious ceremonies. The Swahili sultans were eventually defeated by Portuguese and Omani conquerors, but the rich cultural melting pot they presided over gave rise to the Swahili language, a fusion of African, Arabic and Portuguese words that still thrives. The Omani sultans who replaced the Swahili rulers made the fabled island of Zanzibar their headquarters, cementing the hold of Islamic culture on the East African coast.

THE AGE OF THE EXPLORERS

By the 15th century, with gold and tales of limitless wealth making their way across the Sahara and Mediterranean, European royalty became obsessed with Africa. At the precise moment when West Africa's empires went into decline and began to fragment, Europe began to turn its attention to Africa.

In 1434, a Portuguese ship rounded the infamous Cape Bojador (in present-day Morocco), the first seagoing vessel to do so since the Phoenicians in 613 BC. By 1482, the Portuguese had built a fortified trading post, the

When Ethiopian rebel forces rolled into Addis Ababa in 1991 they were navigating with photocopies of the Addis Ababa map found in Lonely Planet's *Africa on a Shoestring*!

8th century AD	AD 900	1137–1270
Arabic, Indian, Persian and Chinese merchants begin arriving along what is now the Kenyan coast, drawing Africa into the global spice trade and laying the foundations for the prosperous Swahili trading centres of East Africa.	Islam reaches the Sahel via trans-Saharan camel caravans, almost 250 years after it swept across North Africa; it would later become the predominant religion of West Africa.	The Zaghwe dynasty of Ethiopia builds some of Africa's most sacred and enduring monuments – Lalibela's rock-hewn churches. The dynasty was overthrown by Yekuno Amlak, who traced his ancestry to King Solomon and the Queen of Sheba.

earliest European structure in sub-Saharan Africa, along today's Ghanaian coast. By the early 16th century, French, British and Dutch ships had joined the Portuguese along the coast, building forts as they went. But unlike the Carthaginians and Romans, the European powers were never content with mere coastal footholds.

Victorian heroes such as Richard Burton and John Speke captured the public imagination with their hair-raising tales from the East African interior, while Mungo Park and the formidable Mary Wesley battled their way through fever-ridden swamps, and avoided charging animals while 'discovering' various parts of West Africa. Most celebrated was missionary-explorer David Livingstone, who was famously encountered by Henry Morton Stanley on the shores of Lake Tanganyika. Livingstone spent the best years of his life attempting to convert the 'natives' to Christianity and searching for the source of the Nile.

THE EUROPEAN SLAVE TRADE

There has always been slavery in Africa (slaves were common by-products of intertribal warfare, and the Arabs and Shirazis who dominated the East African coast took slaves by the thousands). But the slave trade took on a whole new dimension after the European arrival. The Portuguese in West Africa, the Dutch in South Africa and other Europeans who came after them saw how African slavery worked and, with one eye on their huge American sugar plantations, saw the potential for slavery to fuel agricultural production. They were helped by opportunistic African leaders who used slavery and other trade with Europeans as a means to expand their own power.

Exact figures are impossible to establish, but from the end of the 15th century until around 1870, when the slave trade was abolished, up to 20 million Africans were enslaved. Perhaps half died en route to the Americas; millions of others perished in slaving raids. The trans-Atlantic slave trade gave European powers a huge economic boost, while the loss of farmers and tradespeople, as well as the general chaos, made Africa an easy target for colonialism.

COLONIAL AFRICA

To understand the horrors of the European slave trade and its ultimate abolition, look no further than Adam Hochschild's definitive 2006 book, *Bury the Chains*.

Throughout the 19th century, the region-by-region conquest of the continent by European powers gathered pace and became known as the 'Scramble for Africa'. This was formalised at the Berlin Conference of 1884–5, when Europe's governments divided Africa between them. That Africans had no say in the matter, and that Europeans had never set foot in many of the territories claimed, scarcely seemed to register. France and Britain got the biggest swathes, with Germany, Portugal, Italy, Spain and Belgium picking up the rest. The resulting boundaries, determined more by colonial expediency than the complex realities on the ground, remain in place today.

1638	1652	1870
The French set up their first permanent trading post in Africa, at Saint-Louis in modern Senegal. Twenty-two years later, the British establish a base at the mouth of the Gambia River.	The Dutch East India Company establishes the first European settlement in South Africa at the Cape of Good Hope. Their descendants, known as Boers, would play a pivotal role in the region's history even into the present day.	The slave trade is abolished. Britain's parliament had abolished the trade in slaves in 1807, but it took decades for the law to be enforced and other countries to follow suit.

Forced labour, heavy taxation, and vengeful violence for any insurrection were all commonplace in colonial Africa. African territories were essentially organised to extract cheap cash crops and natural resources for use by the colonial powers. To facilitate easy administration, tribal differences and rivalries were exploited to the full, and industrial development, social welfare and education were rarely policy priorities. The effects of the colonial years, which in some cases only ended a few decades ago, continue to leave their mark on the continent (see p62).

AFRICA FOR THE AFRICANS

African independence movements existed throughout the colonial period, but organised political resistance gained momentum in the 1950s and '60s. Soldiers who had fought in both world wars on behalf of their colonial masters joined forces with African intellectuals who had gained their education through missionary schools and universities; their catchcry became 'Africa for the Africans'. Many African countries became independent in the 1960s – some peacefully, others only after years of bloodshed and struggle – and by the 1970s, most African countries had become masters of their own destinies, at least on paper.

It is impossible to overstate the euphoria that gripped Africa in the post-independence period. The speeches of bright young leaders like Kwame Nkrumah (Ghana), Jomo Kenyatta (Kenya) and Patrice Lumumba (Congo) had Africans across the continent dreaming of a new African dawn. For the most part, they were disappointed.

Thanks to colonial neglect of local education and their policies of ethnic favouritism, most African countries were woefully unprepared for independence, ruled over by an ill-equipped political class. The situation worsened when fledgling African nations became pawns in the Cold War machinations of foreign powers, and factors such as drought, economic collapse and ethnic resentment led many to spiral down into a mire of corruption, violence and civil war.

AFRICA TODAY

In May 2000, the cover of the respected *Economist* magazine declared Africa to be 'the hopeless continent' and this remains a widely held view. The continent's problems are, it is true, legion and widespread. African countries fill 31 of the bottom 33 places of the UN's 2009 Human Development Index, which is based on a range of quality-of-life indicators. The so-called 'resource curse' has also ensured that ordinary Africans still rarely enjoy the benefits of the continent's lucrative natural resources. And civil war, corruption and dictatorship continue to stalk some corners of the continent.

But to talk about 'Africa' (as opposed to its 49 diverse countries) in the context of the current situation can be misleading. That's partly because good

Even covering Africa's post-independence period alone is a monumental task, but Richard Dowden, former Africa editor of the *Economist*, carries it off with aplomb in *Africa – Altered States, Ordinary Miracles* (2008).

A mere 1% increase in world trade from Africa (Mozambique alone loses US$130 million annually due to restrictions on importing into Europe) would be the equivalent of five times the foreign aid currently received by Africa.

1884–5	**1931**	**1960**
The Berlin Conference divides Africa among colonial powers. France gets almost one-third of the entire continent (mostly in West and Central Africa), while Great Britain claims Ghana, Nigeria and much of Southern and East Africa.	Apart from Liberia (which became independent in 1847) and Ethiopia (which was never colonised save for an Italian occupation during WWII), South Africa becomes Africa's first independent country, followed by Libya in 1951.	Seventeen African countries gain independence from European colonial rule. Most are former French colonies, but include Congo (from Belgium), Somalia (from Italy and Britain) and Nigeria (from Britain).

news about Africa rarely makes headlines, even though the continent has its share of success stories. Sierra Leone, Liberia, Côte d'Ivoire, Mozambique and Rwanda have disappeared from the international headlines for all the right reasons, with impressive transformations to peace and relative stability, while both Libya and South Africa have returned to the international fold after decades of isolation. Ghana, Senegal, Mali and Botswana among others have also quietly acquired a reputation for good governance and for building stable democracies.

1990	1993	2009
Nelson Mandela is released after almost three decades in prison. Two years later, a whites-only referendum approved the dismantling of apartheid and, in 1994, Mandela becomes South Africa's president after multi-racial elections.	Eritrea gains independence from Ethiopia and becomes Africa's newest independent state, following Namibia's independence from South Africa in 1990. The last country to become independent from European rule was Zimbabwe in 1980.	Gabon's Omar Bongo dies and Libya's Colonel Qaddafi, who seized power in 1969, becomes Africa's longest-serving leader, followed by Angola's Eduardo Dos Santos (1979), Zimbabwe's Robert Mugabe (1981) and Egypt's Hosni Mubarak (1981).

The Culture

An estimated one billion people live in Africa, speaking well over 1000 different languages. Together, they make up the most culturally and ethnically diverse group of people on the planet. Many parts of Africa are also home to significant Asian, European and Middle Eastern populations.

DAILY LIFE

Such is the continent's diversity that it is difficult to speak of Africa as a whole without descending into meaningless generalisations. Life for a villager in remote Central African Republic has little to do with the daily experience of an affluent Moroccan in Casablanca; the latter's daily life will likely have far more in common with that of Europeans than with most of his or her fellow Africans.

That said, for the overwhelming majority of African societies, life has changed beyond recognition in the last 100 years. Colonialism, globalisation, technological advances and foreign influences have all been factors in this social revolution.

Perhaps the key change in African daily life, however, has been the move to the cities. By some estimates, Africa's rate of urbanisation is the fastest in the world and the population of urban centres is growing at twice the rate of rural areas. At the beginning of the 20th century, around 5% of Africans lived in cities. Now, over 40% of Africans are found in urban areas and, according to the UN, by 2025 more than half of Africa's population will be comprised of city dwellers. The reasons for this epochal demographic shift are legion: growing populations due to improved health care, environmental degradation leading to shrinking grazing and agricultural land, and poor rural infrastructure, are among the most important.

Unfortunately, urban population growth has far outpaced job creation; unemployment in many African cities is rife. One UN study found that, in 38 African countries, more than 50% of the urban population lives in slums. At the same time, many African cities have a growing and increasingly influential and sophisticated middle class.

So how does the other half live? Thanks to urbanisation, a whole generation of Africans is growing up with no connection to the countryside, its lores and traditions, and, in many cases, urbanisation has led to the breakdown of traditional social values such as respect for elders, and the loosening of family structures. Urbanisation has also caused critical labour shortages in rural areas, and has accelerated the spread of HIV (see the boxed text, p34).

In spite of these daunting challenges, rural life remains a pillar of African society, a place where the continent's historical memory survives. Family bonds are still much stronger than in many First World societies, with the concepts of community and shared responsibility deeply rooted. These values retain a deep hold over many Africans, even those who long ago left for the cities.

SPORT

Football (soccer) is the most popular of Africa's sports, and you'll never have to go far before you find someone kicking a ball (or a bundle of plastic bags tied together with string) around on a dusty patch of ground.

West African and North African countries are Africa's footballing powerhouses. Ever since Cameroon stormed to the quarter finals of the 1990 World Cup finals in Italy, West Africa has been touted as an emerging

For an exhaustive list of UN socio-economic data (ranging from literacy and life expectancy to income and infant mortality) for African countries, visit the website of the UN Development Programme (http://hdr.undp.org/en/countries).

Africa's least urbanised countries are Burundi (11%), Uganda (13.3%) and Niger (16.7%), while Djibouti (88.1%) Gabon (86%), and Libya (77.9%) are way above the African average when it comes to city dwellers.

The average British household pays over £800 a year in extra grocery bills due to the European Union subsidy system, which has been criticised by NGOs such as Oxfam for denying African farmers a fair price for their goods.

AIDS

It's difficult to overstate the impact that HIV/AIDS is having on Africa. The figures are mind-boggling: an estimated 22.4 million sub-Saharan Africans live with HIV/AIDS, including 5.7 million in South Africa, and close to 20 million Africans have died from HIV/AIDS since the epidemic began. An estimated 1.4 million Africans died from HIV/AIDS in 2008.

There are many reasons why HIV/AIDS has taken such a hold in Africa. Collective denial of the problem, migration in search of work and to escape wars and famine, a general lack of adequate health care and prevention programs, and social and cultural factors – in particular the low status of women in many African societies – are all believed to have played a role in the rapid spread of the disease.

The personal, social and economic costs associated with the disease are devastating. HIV/AIDS predominantly hits the most productive members of society – young adults. This has a huge impact on family income, food production and local economies in general, and large parts of Africa face the loss of a significant proportion of entire generations. Employers, schools, factories and hospitals have to train other staff to replace those at the workplace who become too ill to work, setting economic and social development back by decades. The numbers of HIV/AIDS orphans – an estimated 20 million in Africa by 2010, with one in four Zambian children said to be without both parents – is at once an enduring human tragedy and a massive societal problem. Average life expectancy in sub-Saharan Africa is now 47 years; without AIDS it would have been 62.

Antiretroviral drug treatments, available in the West to increase the life span of AIDS sufferers and reduce the risk of HIV-infected women passing the infection on to their unborn babies, are still out of the reach of most Africans (according to the World Health Organization, Brazil has managed to halve AIDS deaths by making such drugs free). Although things are improving, fewer than two out of every 10 Africans who need antiretroviral treatment are receiving it.

There are, however, small signs of hope. According to the 2008 report by the joint UN program on HIV/AIDS (UNAIDS), the situation has stabilised in most African countries, thanks in part to vigorous education programs in countries like Senegal and Uganda, and free antiretroviral drugs in Botswana where, according to the World Health Organization, HIV/AIDS–related deaths have fallen by 50% over the past five years. According to the same report, new HIV/AIDS infections in sub-Saharan Africa have fallen by 15% since 2001. For more information on the situation in Botswana, see the boxed text, p869.

For all its international prominence, HIV/AIDS is by no means Africa's only killer: malaria kills around 3000 Africans a day and more than half a million die annually from tuberculosis.

world power in the sport. Cameroon built on its success by winning the football gold medal at the 2000 Sydney Olympics. But apart from Senegal reaching the World Cup quarter finals in 2002, and Ghana's team winning the 2009 U-20 World Cup in Cairo, further success has proved elusive. For the moment, all hopes are directed towards the 2010 World Cup, to be held in South Africa. Perhaps, the argument goes, an African crowd can lift an African team to victory.

The African Cup of Nations, held every two years in January, also stirs great passions across the continent. Almost two years of qualifying rounds culminate in the 16 best teams playing it out for the crown of Africa's champions. Cameroon won the 2002 event in Mali, but North African sides (Tunisia in 2004, and Egypt in 2006, 2008 and 2010) have dominated the event ever since. Egypt's 2010 victory raised its tally to an unrivalled seven titles; Ghana and Cameroon (four titles) are the other most successful teams. The last country from outside West or North Africa to win the continental crown was Zaïre (now the Democratic Republic of Congo) in 1974. The 2010 Cup of Nations was held in Angola and was designed to showcase the country's return to peace. Days before the tournament was due to begin, however, an armed attack on the Togolese team bus in the northern Cabinda region saw three people killed; Togo subsequently withdrew from the tournament.

But the success or otherwise of national teams is only part of the story. West African footballers in particular have enjoyed phenomenal success in European leagues, in the process becoming the focal point for the aspirations of a generation of West African youngsters dreaming of becoming the next Samuel Eto'o (Cameroon and Inter Milan), Didier Drogba (Côte d'Ivoire and Chelsea) or Emmanuel Adebayor (Togo and Manchester City). And it's not just the kids: every weekend from September to May, Africans crowd around communal TV sets to follow the fortunes of teams in Spain, Italy, the UK and France, especially those games involving African players. There is a sense that the success of Africans in Europe is something in which they can all share with pride, something which reflects well on the continent as a whole.

Other popular African sports include marathon running (at which Kenya and Ethiopia dominate the world) and boxing. Basketball is becoming increasingly popular with the arrival of American TV channels.

Seven African nations appear in the Top 50 of FIFA's world rankings for football: Cameroon (14th), Côte d'Ivoire (19th), Egypt (28th), Algeria (29th), Nigeria (32nd), Ghana (38th) and Gabon (45th).

MEDIA

Although no one doubts the potential of mass media such as newspapers, radio stations or TV to be a tool for development in Africa, the media industry on the continent is beset by many problems. Access is one, as many people still live in rural areas, with little or no infrastructure. Many corrupt governments also ruthlessly suppress all but state-controlled media. A good barometer of press freedom in the region is to be found in the annual Press Freedom Index compiled by **Reporters Without Borders** (www.rsf.org), which ranks 173 countries according to the freedoms enjoyed by the independent media. In 2008, Eritrea came in last at 173rd, while Libya (159th), Equatorial Guinea (156th), Somalia (153rd) and Zimbabwe (151st) also fared badly. Namibia (23rd – equal with the UK and higher than Australia), Mali (31st) and South Africa (36th) performed much more creditably.

At the same time, many Africans feel that much reporting on the continent by the international media paints an unfair portrait of Africa as a hopeless case, beset by war, famine and corruption.

Internet

Africa currently has around 67 million internet users (or 6.8% of the population, as compared to 50.1% of Europeans and 73.9% of North Americans), with this number growing by 1392% in the decade to 2009. The real figures, however, are probably considerably higher, as many Africans get online via shared PCs in internet cafes or schools.

Africans are now using the internet to bypass the often unreliable reporting of the state-funded media, while groups such as rural women, who have in the past been denied access to information on health care and human rights, are empowered by their access to online education resources. Many such grass-roots cyber-education projects are still in their infancy, but exciting times are ahead.

For good English-language news sites on the region, try **AllAfrica.com** (www.allafrica.com), **Reuters Africa** (http://af.reuters.com), **Afrol News** (www.afrol.com), **BBC** (www.bbcnews.com/africa), **IRINNews** (www.irinnews.org/IRIN-Africa.aspx), **West Africa News** (www.westafricanews.com) and **Media Foundation for West Africa** (www.mediafound.org). In French, **APA** (www.apanews.net), **Afrik** (www.afrik.com, in French) and **Afrique Index** (www.afriqueindex.com, in French). Some of the publications listed under Newspapers & Magazines (p36), Radio (p36) and Television (p36) also have good websites.

Newspapers & Magazines

With 40% of Africa's population over 15 years old unable to read, the usefulness of print media as an information tool for Africans is limited. The BBC's *Focus on Africa* magazine has a devoted African following and is also the best English-language print source of information for the continent as a whole. It's available worldwide on subscription from www.bbc.co.uk and from bookshops in many African countries. Other current-affairs mags include monthly *New African* and **Africa Today** (www.africatoday.com). The **East African** (www.theeastafrican.co.ke) is good for an overview of what's happening in Kenya, Tanzania and Uganda. If you're in West Africa and your French is well oiled, **Jeune Afrique** (www.jeuneafrique.com, in French) is a highly regarded weekly news magazine.

For links to a range of websites and local newspapers for most countries in Africa, as well as a handful of pan-African sites, head to world-newspapers.com (www.world-newspapers.com/africa).

Radio

With TV out of the reach of many, radio remains by far the most popular medium of communication in Africa, with even the most remote rural villagers gathering around a crackling radio to listen to the latest news and music. A recent report suggests an explosion in private radio stations, often in languages not catered for by government stations. Uganda alone has over 150 stations (up from 42 in 2001), which broadcast in 38 languages.

For continental coverage, however, locals and travellers tune into international broadcasters; most have dedicated Africa slots. As well as the trusty BBC World Service's Focus on Africa (also available in some cities on FM), **Voice of America** (www.voanews.com) and **Radio France Internationale** (www.rfi.fr, in French) are perennial favourites. If you'd rather hear African news from Africans, try **Channel Africa** (www.channelafrica.org), the international radio service of the South African Broadcasting Corporation.

TV

To find out how to listen to BBC World Service's *Focus on Africa* radio programs, visit www.bbc.co.uk/worldservice/programmeguide and type in the country where you are. In most countries you'll be given a range of locations from which to choose.

TV ownership in Africa is much lower than elsewhere in the world and televisions remain luxury items, unavailable to most of Africa's poorer inhabitants. Walk around many African towns and villages after dark, however, and you're likely to come across the dim blue glow of a TV set, often set in a doorway so that an audience of 20 or 30 can gather around it to watch the latest episode of a local soap or a football match. In September 2008, **A24** (www.a24media.com), a pan-African TV station, the brainchild of Kenyan photojournalist Salim Amin and inspired by Al-Jazeera, began broadcasting from Nairobi.

RELIGION

Most Africans are deeply religious, with religious values informing every aspect of their daily life. Generally speaking, a majority of the population in North Africa, West and Central Africa close to the Sahara, together with much of the East African coast, is Islamic; East and southern Africa, and the rest of the continent, is predominantly Christian. Accurate figures are hard to come by, but roughly 40% of Africans are Muslim and 40% Christian (including a burgeoning evangelical Christian movement), leaving around 20% who follow traditional African beliefs. These figures should be taken with a pinch of salt, however, as many Africans see no contradiction at all in combining their traditional beliefs with Islam or Christianity. Hindus and Sikhs are found in places where immigrants arrived from Asia during the colonial era, particularly in East African countries such as Kenya, Tanzania and Uganda.

WOMEN IN AFRICA

Women form the bedrock of African society, especially in rural areas where they bear the burden of child-rearing and most agricultural work. Their task

RELIGION AFRICAN STYLE

Africa's traditional religions are generally animist, believing that objects such as trees, caves or ritual objects such as gourds or drums are endowed with spiritual powers. Thus a certain natural object may be sacred because it represents, is home to, or simply *is* a spirit or deity. Several traditional religions accept the existence of a supreme being or creator, alongside spirits and deities.

Most African religions centre on ancestor veneration, the idea that the dead remain influential after passing from the physical into the spiritual world. Ancestors must therefore be honoured in order to ensure that they intervene positively with other spiritual beings on behalf of their relatives on earth.

The practice of traditional medicine is closely intertwined with traditional religion. Practitioners (often derogatively referred to as 'witch doctors' by foreigners) use divining implements such as bones, prayers, chanting and dance to facilitate communication with the spirit world. Patients are cured with the use of herbal preparations or by exorcist-style interventions to drive out evil spirits that have inhabited the body. Not all magical practitioners are benign – some are suspected of being paid to place curses on people, causing bad luck, sickness or even death.

Although traditional religious practices can be a force for social good within a community, and herbalists are often very skilled in their craft, there's a flip side: some religious practitioners discourage their patients from seeking conventional medical help at hospitals or clinics, and someone who considers themselves cursed will very often give up the will to live entirely. In some parts of Southern and East Africa, killings occasionally take place, in which children or adults are abducted and murdered in order to gain body parts for use in magic rituals. Albinos in Tanzania and Burundi have come under particular threat in recent years.

is made more difficult by the HIV/AIDS epidemic and in the absence of men who move to the cities as migrant industrial workers.

In some countries sexual equality is enshrined in law. African women made history in 2005 when a legal protocol came into force that specifically protects women's human rights in the 17 countries that ratified it. These countries have pledged to amend their laws to uphold a raft of women's rights, including the right to property after divorce, the right to abortions after rape or abuse, and the right to equal pay in the workplace, among many others.

The reality is, however, somewhat different, and in many places women are treated as second-class citizens. Families sometimes deny girls schooling, although education is valued highly by most Africans. More serious still are reports of female infanticide, forced marriages, female genital mutilation and honour killings.

Female genital mutilation (FGM), often euphemistically termed 'female circumcision' or 'genital alteration', is widely practised in West and North Africa. The term covers a wide range of procedures, from a small, mainly symbolic, cut, to sewing up a girl's vagina to leave just a tiny hole or the total removal of the external genitalia (known as infibulation). Although outsiders often believe that FGM is associated with Islam, it actually predates the religion and has far more to do with longstanding cultural traditions than religious doctrine. The World Health Organization estimates that three million African girls are at risk from the procedure annually. In Egypt, Sudan, Somalia, Ethiopia and Mali, around 95% of young girls undergo FGM.

ARTS

Traditional African art and craft consist of ceremonial masks, figures related to ancestral worship, fetishes (which protect against certain spirits), weapons,

Niger has the lowest female literacy rate (15.1%) in Africa, followed by Guinea (18.1%) and Mali (18.2%). At the other end of the scale are Lesotho (90.3%), Namibia (87.4%), South Africa (87.2%) and Botswana (82.9%).

Gogo Mama: A Journey into the Lives of Twelve African Women, by Sally Sara, includes illuminating chapters on a Liberian former child soldier, Zanzibari diva, and HIV/AIDS-fighting grandmother in South Africa.

FEMALE GENITAL MUTILATION – AN INTERVIEW

In January 2009, Lonely Planet author Anthony Ham interviewed Menidiou Kodio who, along with his wife Maryam Dougnon, works in Mali's Dogon Country to end the practice of female genital mutilation. **What proportion of young girls undergo female genital mutilation (FGM)?** In some traditional Dogon villages, it is every girl. **What made you start this work?** We do it because we have six daughters. **Do you meet much resistance when trying to stop the practice?** It is very difficult to convert people, so when I visit a village I organise a free concert and the lyrics of the songs speak against FGM, and then I make a speech. I tell people that I respect traditional culture, but that not everything in tradition is good. As one of my songs says, 'You don't have to listen to everything that the Ana Sara [Europeans] say and you shouldn't change all of your traditions for them. But in this case, we should listen to them.' **What reasons do you give for stopping the practice?** First we explain to them that their daughters run a very high risk of contracting HIV, because the knife use[d] in some places is 40 years old. Tetanus is another risk. Then we tell them that it is a very risky procedure and that if the girls lose too much blood, they can die. We also tell them that childbirth is more difficult for a woman who has been cut. And finally we tell them that they are cutting the bodies of their daughters, the bodies that God gave to them. **And do people listen?** Many people don't. Many men also still believe that it is bad to marry a woman who has not been cut, because they worry that the woman will be stronger than him. But some people are starting to listen and some villages have promised to stop the practice. The truth is, we won't know whether they have kept their promise until 15 years from now, when these girls start to have children. **What will it take for this practice to end?** FGM will continue until all the old people, especially the old women, have died.

---

furnishings and everyday utensils. All kinds of materials are used (including bronze casting in some regions) and great skill can also be seen in the production of textiles, basketry and leatherwork. Contemporary African artists now use traditional as well as modern media to express themselves, with many now making an impact on the international art scene. Nowhere is this more evident than with African music – see p43 for a detailed overview.

The creation of many African arts and crafts is often the preserve of distinct castes of blacksmiths and weavers who rely almost exclusively on locally found or produced materials. Tourism has, however, greatly affected African art and craft, with considerable effort now going into producing objects for sale rather than traditional use. Some art forms, such as the Tingatinga paintings of Tanzania, evolved entirely out of demand from tourists. Although it causes a departure from art's role in traditional society, tourism can ensure artisans remain employed in their traditional professions and many pieces retain their power precisely because they still carry meaning for Africa's peoples.

Moolade, the powerful 2004 film by the Senegalese director Ousmane Sembène, is one of the few mass release artistic endeavours to tackle head-on the taboo issue of female genital mutilation.

West Africa has arguably Africa's most extraordinary artistic tradition. The mask traditions of Côte d'Ivoire, Mali and elsewhere are world famous, and Picasso, Matisse and others found inspiration in its radical approach to the human form. Nigeria and Benin have long been associated with fine bronze sculptures and carvings, and the Ashanti people of Ghana are renowned for fine textiles and gold sculptures. In Central Africa, Congo is another renowned centre for masks and sculpture.

In North Africa, ancient Arabic and Islamic traditions have produced some beautiful artworks (ceramics and carpets are particularly refined), as well as some phenomenal architecture; in the Sahara, Tuareg silver jewellery is unique and beautiful.

Throughout East and southern Africa the Makonde people of Mozambique and the Shona of Zimbabwe produce excellent and widely copied sculptures.

In recent years, recycled art has become popular, with artists from South Africa to West Africa producing sculpture and textiles created entirely from discarded objects such as tin cans and bottle tops.

Literature

Sub-Saharan Africa's rich, multilayered literary history was almost entirely oral. Folk tales, poems, proverbs, myths, historical tales and (most importantly) ethnic traditions were passed down through generations by word of mouth. Some societies have specific keepers of history and storytelling, such as the *griots* of West Africa, and in many cases stories are sung or tales performed in a form of theatre. As a result, little of Africa's rich literary history was known to the outside world until relatively recently.

Modern-day and 20th-century African literature has been greatly influenced by colonial education and Western trends. Some African authors have nonetheless made an effort to employ traditional structures and folk tales in their work; others write of the contemporary hardships faced by Africans and their fight to shake off the shackles of colonialism, using Western-influenced narrative methods (and penning their works in English, French or Portuguese).

Nigerian authors dominate the English-speaking African literature scene and some, like Amos Tutuola, adapt African folklore into their own works. Penned by Tutuola, *The Palm-Wine Drunkard* is a rather grisly tale of a man who enters the spirit world in order to find his palm-wine supplier! *Things Fall Apart* by Chinua Achebe is a more contemporary but deeply symbolic tale about a man's rise and fall at the time colonialism arrived in Africa. Another Nigerian writer, Ben Okri, found worldwide fame with his novels *The Famished Road* and *Starbook*, which draw heavily on folk traditions.

FOOD & DRINK

Whether it's a group of Kenyans gathering in a *nyama choma* (barbecued meat) shop to consume hunks of grilled meat washed down with cold lager, or Ghanaians dipping balls of *foufou* (pounded yam or cassava with a doughlike consistency) into a steaming communal bowl of stew, there are two things all Africans have in common – they love to eat and it's almost always a social event. Folk tales and traditions from all over the continent feature stories about cooking and consuming food, a process that is the focus of almost all social and family activities. African food is generally bold and colourful, with

The international availability of works by African novelists owes much to the Heinemann African Writers Series (www.africanwriters.com), which publishes 71 novels that would otherwise be out of print or hard to find.

In 1952, Dylan Thomas described Amos Tutuola's *The Palm-Wine Drunkard* as 'brief, thronged, grisly and bewitching' and a 'nightmare of indescribable adventures'.

TOP 10 AFRICAN NOVELS BY NON-AFRICANS

For our pick of the best novels by African writers, see the boxed text, p17.

- Joseph Conrad, *Heart of Darkness* (1899)
- Graham Greene, *The Heart of the Matter* (1948)
- VS Naipaul, *A Bend in the River* (1979)
- JMG Le Clézio, *Desert* (1980)
- William Boyd, *A Good Man in Africa* (1981)
- Ronan Bennett, *The Catastrophist* (1997)
- Giles Foden, *The Last King of Scotland* (1998)
- Barbara Kingsolver, *The Poisonwood Bible* (1999)
- Andreï Makine, *Human Love* (2006)
- Ed O'Loughlin, *Not Untrue and Not Unkind* (2009)

its rich, earthy textures and strong, spicy undertones showing influences from Arab traders, European colonists and Asian slaves.

Staples & Specialities

Each region has its own key staples: in East and southern Africa, the base for many local meals is a stiff dough made from maize flour, called – among other things – *ugali, sadza, pap* and *nsima*. In West Africa millet is also common, and served in a similar way, while staples nearer the coast are root crops such as yam or cassava (*manioc* in French), served as a near-solid glob called *foufou*. In North Africa, bread forms a major part of the meal, while all over Africa rice is an alternative to the local specialities. In some countries, plantain (green banana) is also common, either fried, cooked solid or pounded into *foufou*. A sauce of meat, fish, beans or vegetables is then added to the carbo base. If you're eating local style, you grab a portion of bread or dough or pancake (with your right hand, please!), dip it in the communal pot of sauce and sit back, beaming contentedly, to eat it.

Drinks

Tea and coffee are the standard drinks, and countries seem to follow the flavours of their former colonisers. In (formerly British) East Africa, tea and coffee tends to be weak, grey and milky. In much of (formerly French) West Africa, tea is usually served black, while the coffee from roadside stalls contains enough sugar and sweetened condensed milk to keep you fully charged for hours. In North Africa and some Sahel countries (the Sahel is a semi-arid region, which stretches from Mauritania, Gambia and Senegal to Chad), mint tea and strong Arab-style coffee are the local hot beverages of choice. Other variations include chai or coffee spiced up with lemongrass or cardamom in East Africa, or flavoured with a woody leaf called *kinkiliba* in West Africa.

International soft drinks are widely available, while many countries have their own brands that are cheaper and just as good (although often owned by the big multinationals, too). You can also get locally made soft drinks and fruit juices, sold in plastic bags, or frozen into 'ice-sticks', but avoid these if you're worried about your stomach, as the water they're made from is usually unpurified. Alcohol allegedly kills the bugs…

In bars, you can buy local or imported beer in bottles. Excellent wines and liqueurs, from South Africa or further afield, may be available in more upmarket establishments. Traditional beer is made from millet or maize, and drunk from huge communal pots with great ceremony at special events, and with less pomp in everyday situations.

West Africa's most popular brew is palm wine. The tree is tapped and the sap comes out mildly fermented. In other parts of the continent, alcohol is made using bananas, pineapples or other fruit, sometimes fermented overnight. This homemade alcohol is often outrageously strong, can lead to blindness or mental illness, and is often illegal in some places. You have been warned!

Habits & Customs

In Islamic countries, food is always eaten, passed and touched with the right hand only (the left hand is reserved for washing your bottom, and the two are understandably kept separate). Water in a basin is usually brought to wash your hands before you start eating – hold your hands out and allow the person who brings it to pour it over, then shake your hands dry. It's also customary in some parts of Africa for women and men to eat separately, with the women eating second after they've served the food. In some countries, lunch, rather than dinner, is the main meal

Ever wondered how to make a pizza oven out of a termite mound? Or prepare bacon and eggs on a shovel? Check out *The African Kitchen* by Josie Stow and Jan Baldwin, a sumptuous cookbook that reveals the secrets of a safari chef.

The Africa Cookbook: Tastes of a Continent by food historian Jessica Harris is a perfect companion for those interested in creating traditional African dishes in a non-African kitchen.

TASTES LIKE CHICKEN...

In many parts of Africa you'll find the locals chomping with gusto on some unusual foods. If you're brave in heart and stomach, why not try some of these more adventurous snacks:

- **Giant rat** – The agouti, a ratlike rodent about the size of a rabbit, frequently turns up in West African stews. Avoid this one though – it's under threat in the wild. If you really can't do without rodent, try a skewer of baby grasscutters (cane rats) roasted over coals and served up in West African markets...

- **Land snails** – Described as having a texture like 'stubborn rubber', giant land snails are eaten in parts of Nigeria.

- **Mopane worms** – These are actually not worms but caterpillars – the emperor moth's green and blue larvae, which make their home in the mopane trees of southern Africa. These protein-rich critters are boiled and then dried in the sun before being eaten.

---

of the day, and everything stops for a couple of hours while a hot meal is cooked and prepared.

Celebrations

In much of Africa, a celebration, be it a wedding, coming-of-age ceremony or even a funeral, is an excuse to stuff yourself until your eyes pop out and you beg for mercy. In non-Islamic countries, this eating-fest could well be accompanied by a lot of drinking, followed mostly by falling down. Celebration food of course varies widely from country to country, but vegetarians beware – many feasts involve goats, sheep, cows or chickens being slaughtered and added to the pot.

If you're lucky enough to be invited to a celebration while you're in Africa, it's polite to bring something (litre bottles of fizzy drink often go down well), and be prepared for a lot of hanging around – nothing happens in a hurry. The accepted wisdom is that it's considered very rude to refuse any food you're offered, but in practice it's probably perfectly acceptable to decline something politely if you really don't want to eat it, as long as you eat something else with gusto!

Where to Eat & Drink
FOOD STALLS & STREET FOOD
Most towns all over Africa have a shacklike stall or 10 serving up cheap local staples. Furniture is usually limited to a rough bench and a couple of upturned boxes, and hygiene is rarely a prime concern. However, this is the place to save money and meet the locals. Good places to seek out these no-frills joints include bus stations or markets. Lighter snacks include nuts sold in twists of newspaper, hardboiled eggs (popular for long bus journeys), meat kebabs, or, in some places, more exotic fare like fried caterpillars or baobab fruits. Street food rarely involves plates or knives – it's served on a stick, wrapped in paper, or in a plastic bag.

RESTAURANTS
For something more comfortable, most towns have cheap restaurants where you can buy traditional meals, as well as smarter restaurants with facilities such as tablecloths, waiters and menus. If you're eating in cheaper restaurants, you can expect to be served the same food as the locals, but more upmarket, tourist-oriented establishments serve up more familiar fare, from the ubiquitous chicken and chips, to pizzas, pasta dishes and toasted sandwiches.

West Africa (Festivals & Food), by Ali Brownlie Bojang, is a simply told look at some of West Africa's most interesting festivals and the foods (with recipes) with which they are celebrated.

First Catch Your Eland: A Taste of Africa, by Laurens van der Post, is a fascinating, if dated, collection of memoirs and observations about food in Africa. Well worth trawling the secondhand bookshops for.

Colonial influences remain important: you can expect croissants for breakfast in Madagascar, or to pick up Portuguese custard tarts in the bakeries of Mozambique. Africa also has its share of world-class dining, with the best restaurants brilliantly fusing African culinary traditions with those of the rest of the world. Less impressively, even smaller towns are now succumbing to the fast-food craze, with greasy burger and chicken joints springing up frequently.

Vegetarians & Vegans

Many Africans may think a meal is incomplete unless half of it once lived and breathed, but across Africa many cheap restaurants serve rice and beans and other meals suitable for vegans simply because it's all the locals can afford. For vegetarians, eggs are usually easy to find – expect to eat an awful lot of egg and chips – and, for pescetarians, fish is available nearer the coast. Be aware that in many places chicken is usually not regarded as meat, while even the simplest vegetable sauce may have a bit of animal fat thrown in. Expect to meet with bemusement when you announce that you don't eat meat – the idea of voluntarily giving up something that's seen as an aspirational luxury is hard to understand for many people.

African Music

They don't call Africa the Motherland for nothing. The continent has a musical history that stretches back further than any other, a history as vast and varied as its range of rhythms, melodies and overlapping sources and influences. Here, music – traditional and contemporary – is as vital to communication and storytelling as the written word. It is the lifeblood of communities, the solace of the nomad, the entertainment of choice. It can be a political tool – perceived as a threat (France and South Africa are full of exiled African artists) or a campaign winner (African leaders are forever trying to cash in on popular musicians, many of whom have their own record labels and charitable foundations). Its biggest acts are treated as celebrities, followed wherever they go. Oh, and despite the world music boom, some are relatively unknown in the West. If in doubt, ask a local.

Artists who are popular in the West – such as Mali's Oumou Sangaré or Senegal's Baaba Maal – work in a double market, making different mixes of the same songs for home and abroad, or recording cassette-only albums for local consumption. (Their home-town performances are wildly different, too: most start late and run all night.) Cassettes, rather than CDs, proliferate across Africa, and government pledges to address the gargantuan problem of cassette piracy have so far remained precisely that. Still, if you're looking for a gig or club sans tourists, ask a cassette-stall holder. They might send you to a hotel or a dingy club in the suburbs, but it will be an experience.

Africa Hit Music TV (www.africahit.com) is the first internet TV station that plays African music videos 24/7. Each month it features thousands of music videos from a host of artists and genres.

Without African music there would be no blues, reggae or – some say – rock, let alone Brazilian samba, Puerto Rican salsa, Trinidadian soca or any of a wide array of genres with roots in Africa's timeless sounds. And it works both ways: colonialism saw European instruments such as saxophone, trumpet and guitars integrated into traditional patterns. Independence ushered in a golden

TEN AFRICAN ALBUMS

- Ali Farke Touré, *Savane* (World Circuit) – Desert blues from the late, great Malian guitar maestro.
- Cesaria Evora, *Miss Perfumado* (Lusafrica) – Classic *morna* (Creole-language form of blues) from a Cape Verdean treasure.
- Toumani Diabate, *The Mande Variations* (World Circuit) – Visionary instrumentals from the Malian *kora* player.
- Youssou N'Dour, *Immigrés* (Sterns/Earthworks) – Frentic *mbalax* and soaring vocals from Dakar's finest.
- Khaled, *Khaled* (Barclay/Universal) – In which Khaled shows why he's the king of rai.
- Miriam Makeba, *Best of Miriam Makeba and the Skylarks* (BMG) – Vintage stuff from the South African diva and her backing group.
- Fela Kuti, *The Black President* (Universal) – Nigeria's Afrobeat hero gives his all.
- Salif Keita, *Soro* (Sterns) – Mande music and world beats from a West African superstar.
- Bassekou Kouyate and Ngoni Ba, *I Speak Fula* (Out Here) – Power-packed Ngoni riffs from a burgeoning big name.
- Baaba Maal, *Djam Leeli* (Yoff/Earthworks) – Acoustic album from the Senegalese star and his family *griot* and mentor, Mansour Seck.

era; a swath of dance bands in 1970s Mali and Guinea spawned West African superstars such as Salif Keita and Mory Kante. Electric guitars fuelled Congolese rumba and soukous and innumerable other African genres (including Swahili rumba). Ghana's guitar-based highlife (urban dance music) blended with American hip hop to become hiplife; current faves include D'Black, Kwaku-T and Okyeame Kwame. Jazz, soul and even classical music helped form the Afrobeat of late Nigerian legend Fela Kuti (which carries on through his sons, Femi and Seun, and a host of others today).

Homegrown: Hiplife in Ghana, directed by Eli Jacobs-Fantauzzi, is a 2009 documentary abut the group VIP (Vision in Progress), and traces its formation in a ghetto in Accra to its first international tour.

There is no pan-African music. The Motherland is simply way too big for that. But there are distinct musical trends too important to ignore. Looking north: in Algeria it's the trad-rock genre, rai (think Khaled, Houari Benchenet, the late grand dame Cheikha Rimitti), and the street-style pop known as *chaabi* (Arabic for 'popular'). Many of Algeria's Paris-based musicians are starting to perform at home again: check out rocker Rachid Taha; folk chanteuse Souad Massi; and DJ 'scientist' Cheb i Sabbah. In Egypt the stern presence of late diva Oum Kalthoum, the Arab world's greatest 20th-century singer, is everywhere; scratch the surface for a thrumming industry that includes gypsy band The Musicians of the Nile, the sprawling collective El Tanbura and master percussionist Hossam Ramzy.

www.afropop.org has a database of articles on African music and musicians, searchable by artist, style, and country. Includes radio shows, reviews and interviews. www.africanmusic.org is an online encyclopaedia of African music with links and a glossary.

There is also *chaabi* in Egypt and Morocco, along with the Arabic techno pop called *al-jil* and a wealth of other influences. The Berber shepherdess blues of Cherifa, the Maghreb's very own Aretha, have made her a singer-sheika (or popular artist) to be reckoned with. The pentatonic healing music of the Gnaoua – chants, side drums, metal castanets, the throbbing *guimbri*-lute (long-necked lute) – hijacks Essaouira each June during the huge Gnaoua & World Music festival; celebrity faces spotted in the thronging 20,000-strong crowd have included Mick Jagger and Robert Plant. There's nomad desert blues to be had, from guitar bands such as Tinariwen, to current music-festival darlings Etran Finatawa, whose members are drawn from Niger's Toureg and Wodaabe tribes. In the Côte D'Ivoire, Abidjan remains a hugely influential centre for music production (if you can make it here, you'll probably make it in Paris), while the percussive, melodious and totally vacuous *coupé-décale* (dance music; see p309) sound fills stadiums. Seek out the likes of reggae legend Alpha Blondy and fusionist Dobet Gnahoré – the latter in charisma and vocal power not unlike Beninese diva Angélique Kidjo.

Across West Africa the haunting vocals of the *griots* and *jalis,* the region's oral-historians-cum-minstrels, are ubiquitous. In Mali, the deep-voiced *jelimuso* (female *griot*) Kandia Kouyate rules; Mauritania's best-known *griot* is the rotund diva Dimi Mint Abba, who sings the praises of the Prophet and her country while accompanying herself on the *ardin*, a long-necked string instrument. Mali's Arabic-flavoured *wassoulou* rhythms have their most famous champion in songbird Oumou Sangaré, just as one of the *griot/jali's* traditional instruments, the 21-string *kora*, is closely linked to Toumani Diabaté. Others are making their mark: Guinea's electric *kora* master Ba Cissoko is pushing the envelope, and blind musician Madina N'Diaye is shaping up as Mali's first female *kora* iconoclast.

Africa Live: The Roll Back Malaria Concert, directed by Mick Csáky (2006), has footage of Africa's biggest ever concert, held at the Iba Mar Diop Stadium in Dakar, Senegal. The likes of Youssou N'Dour, Salif Keita, Angélique Kidjo, Baaba Maal, Orchestra Baobab and Tinariwen brought the catastrophic malaria crisis to the world's attention.

The mighty Youssou N'Dour kickstarted Senegal's pervasive *mbalax* rhythms when he mixed traditional percussion with plugged-in salsa, reggae and funk – though today it's Wolof-language rap groups that really appeal to the kids (there's a natural rap vibe to the country's ancient rhythmic poetry, *tasso*). Carlou D – a compelling singer-songwriter and former member of infamous hip-hop outfit Positive Black Soul – is challenging the pre-eminence of the N'Dour/Maal old guard. Hip-hop hybrids are creating musical revivals in countries such as Tanzania, Kenya, Angola and Guinea; elsewhere, militant artists such as Côte d'Ivoire reggae star Tiken Jah Fakoly, former Sudanese child soldier-turned-rapper Emmanuel Jal, and Somalia's 'Dusty Foot Philosopher', rapper and poet K'Naan (his country's first MTV star) are telling it like it is.

With the passing of Ali Farke Touré in 2006, his son Vieux Farke Touré is – along with ex-Super Rail Band axeman Djelimady Tounkara et al – continuing the Malian guitar blues legacy. Guitar heroes abound throughout Africa: the Congo's Diblo Dibala, Malagasy originator Jaojoby and South African axeman Louis Mhlanga among them. In the islands of Cape Verde they're singing the wistful, Creole-language blues known as *morna,* and a slew of new talent including Lura and Mayra Andrade. Over in Cameroon they're whooping it up to the guitar-based *bikutsi* or the brass-heavy sound of *makossa* while the polyphonic voices of that country's pygmies have struck a chord with the Western world.

In the often musically overlooked East Africa, bongo flava (that's Swahili rap and hip hop) is thriving; as is *taarab,* the Arab/Indian-influenced music of Zanzibar and the Tanzanian-Kenyan coastal strip. Ethiopian jazz – particularly that of guru–band leader Mulatu Atsatke – is enjoying an international renaissance. Mozambique sways to the sound of *marrabenta* – Ghorwane and Eyuphuro are two such roots-based urban dance bands – and the marimba style known as *timbila.* Down in Zimbabwe they're listening to the *tuku* (swinging, rootsy, self-styled) music of Oliver

> In a few short years Sauti za Busara (Sounds of Wisdom) Swahili Music Festival in Stonetown, Zanzibar, has become one of East Africa's finest annual events: a five-day extravaganza of music, theatre and dance before a horizon dotted with dhow boats.

CESÁRIA ÉVORA

Cesária Évora takes a thoughtful drag of her full-strength cigarette and smiles. 'You don't need to have suffered to sing *morna*', says the sexagenarian, waving away fumes with a fleshy hand. 'But okay, it helps.' Évora sings *morna,* the bluesy music of her beloved Cape Verde, a group of volcanic islands off the coast of West Africa, with a silken voice that has won her a Grammy (and five nominations) and captured the imagination of millions.

Her 2009 album *Nha Sentimento* doesn't concentrate on *morna,* the style that made her famous, but on her homeland's faster-paced *coladera* rhythms – here backed, intriguingly, by Egyptian string arrangements. Her Creole lyrics, which tell of loss and longing, separation and hardship, are still delivered with *saudade,* a particularly Cape Verdean emotion that combines a yearning for a better life elsewhere with the hope of returning to loved ones. But here, too, is the spirit of *morabeza,* the warm welcome Cape Verdeans are known give to visitors to their homes and country.

Having overcome poverty, a revolution and even a recent stroke, Évora rarely thinks of herself when she sings. 'I close my eyes and picture my people, my islands. I remember everything we have been through. Our droughts. Our history of slavery. Our 500 years as a Portuguese colony. Sometimes,' she adds, 'I can even hear the waves lapping on the shore.'

Whether singing in New York, Moscow or a ramshackle bar in her home town, Mindelo, on the island of Sao Vincente, Évora always performs barefoot. 'Where I come from, it's hot, so you don't need to wear shoes.' Her on-stage cigarette breaks are equally legendary. 'I like to have a rest in the middle of a set', says this boss-eyed grandmother. 'And if I don't smoke, I get twitchy.'

Her family was musical, 'but it wasn't until I turned 15 that I realised I had a beautiful voice'. Évora quit her strict religious school and began singing in bars, building a passionate local following and captivating the sailors who cruised into Sao Vincente's deep, blue port. Having been 'discovered' by French–Cape Verdean producer Jose da Silva, her international career began with an album, *La Diva Aux Pied Nus* (The Barefoot Diva), in 1988.

Each Cesária Évora album – including 1992's legendary *Miss Perfumado* – makes Cape Verde, out there in a corner of the Atlantic Ocean, seem closer, less mythical. Her government has put her likeness on the national stamp by way of thanks. 'It's another way for me to travel', she quips, exhaling.

KINSHASA COOL: KONONO NO 1/STAFF BENDA BILILI

You can hear it, at night, in the suburbs of Kinshasa (capital of the Democratic Republic of Congo). Trancelike rhythms – tribal, timeless, primal – bolstered by the ringing sounds of the *likembe*, the region's spiky metal thumb piano. Voices shouting and chanting, calling and responding. Whistles trilling, samba-style. The insistent beat of hand-tooled drums, the rat-a-tat of scrap metal. All of it fizzing through microphones fashioned from old car parts, warping and bulging through homemade amps and colonial-era speakers on stands. The DRC's electro-traditional grooves are always very, very loud.

The combination of traditional trance music – much of it brought into sprawling Kinshasa by displaced, war-scarred bush men – with heavily distorted DIY amplification has transformed the contemporary scene. It's been doing so for some time: 12-member collective Konono No 1 have been together for over 25 years. Comprising Bazombo people from the Congo side of the artificial DRC–Angolan border, Konono No 1 adapted the ancient Massikulu rhythms their ancestors once played on ivory horns.

'We were the first', insists Konono No 1 founder Mawangu 'Papa' Mingiedi, 70, sitting dressed in flat cap, pink shirt and braces. 'Many have borrowed from us. It's simply the music of our ancestors, sped up.'

Thanks to visionary Belgian record label Crammed, Konono No 1 are a cult hit in the West. Their self-titled album was the first release in Crammed's Congotronics series; a folkloric outfit back home, they've become the epitome of left-field club-floor cool everywhere else.

As indeed have fellow Kinshasans and Crammed label mates Staff Benda Bilili ('look beyond appearances'), a group of street musicians – some of them disabled – who live in the grounds of Kinshasa Zoo. Their vibrant vocals, rumba-rooted grooves and infectious guitar-like solos – performed by teenaged prodigy Roger Landu on a one-string electric lute-cum-tin can – have won them celebrity fans and accolades including the 2009 WOMEX Artist Award, world-music's equivalent of an Oscar. Their acclaimed debut album *Très Très Fort* was recorded outdoors using a dozen microphones, a laptop and a mains cable connected to a deserted refreshment bar; song lyrics in the Lingala language tell of hardship and suffering, and triumph over adversity.

'We always knew we'd make it in the West', says Ricky Likabu, one of Staff Benda's three vocalists. 'We're a band. It's what we do.'

www.africmusic.com has three webstreaming African channels, featuring the latest hot hits.

Mutukudzi or, in secret, the *chimurenga* (struggle) music of their self-exiled Lion, Thomas Mapfumo. Down in South Africa, where the ever-popular kwaito rules supreme (think slowed-down, rapped-over house music). The country's giant recording industry continues to rival that of Europe and America, embracing everything from the Zulu *iscathimiya* call-and-response singing as popularised by Ladysmith Black Mambazo, to jazz, funk, gospel, reggae, soul, pop, rap and all points in between.

In Africa music is more than a way of life. It is a force. Get ready to feel it.

Environment

Africa is the oldest and most enduring land mass in the world. When you stand on African soil, 97% of what's under your feet has been in place for more than 300 million years. Atop this foundation sits an astonishing breadth of landscapes, from the world's biggest desert to some of the largest rivers, lakes and tracts of rainforests on the planet, not to mention stirring mountains and the iconic savannah that tells you that you could only be in Africa. Inhabiting these epic landscapes is the world's largest collection of wildlife, which is so extraordinary in its diversity that we've given it its own chapter – see p55. For these and many more reasons, in Africa, as in no other inhabited continent on earth, the natural world will take centre stage wherever you go.

Africa: Atlas of Our Changing Environment (2008), from the United Nations Environment Programme (UNEP), is the definitive study of Africa's environment, with country statistics and before-and-after satellite photos. Available from Earthprint (www.earthprint.com).

THE LAND

Africa is the world's second-largest continent, after Asia, covering 30 million sq km and accounting for 23% of the total land area on earth. From the most northerly point, Cap Blanc (Ra's al Abyad) in Tunisia, to the most southerly point, Cape Agulhas in South Africa, is a distance of approximately 8000km. The distance between Cape Verde, the westernmost point in Africa, and Raas Xaafuun in Somalia, the continent's most easterly point, is 7440km. Such are the specs of this vast continent when taken as a whole. But zoom in a little closer and that's when the story really gets interesting.

For more on what these landscapes mean for Africa's wildlife, see p55.

Mountains & the Great Rift Valley

East and southern Africa is where the continent really soars. It's here that you find the great mountain ranges of the Drakensberg in South Africa (p1044) and Rwenzori (the fabled Mountains of the Moon; see p835) that straddle the borders of Uganda and Democratic Republic of Congo (DRC, formerly Zaïre), as well as classic, stand-alone, dormant volcanoes such as Mt Kenya (5199m; p715) and Mt Kilimanjaro (5895m; p789). The latter is the continent's highest peak and climbing it to the 'roof of Africa' is one of the region's great journeys. And then there's Ethiopia, Africa's highest country, which lies on a plateau between 2000m and 3000m above sea level – in the space of a few hundred kilometres, the country rises to the Simien Mountains (p690) and Ras Dashen (4543m), then drops to 120m below sea level in the Danakil Depression.

Geologists believe that if the process that created the rift continues, the Horn of Africa may one day break away from the African mainland and become an island, just as Madagascar did in the distant past.

North and West Africa also have plenty of topographical drama to call their own. In the far northwest of the continent, the Atlas Mountains of Morocco – formed by the collision of the African and Eurasian tectonic plates – run like a spine across the land, scaling the heights of Jebel Toubkal (4167m), North Africa's highest peak. In West Africa, Mt Cameroon (4095m) is the highest point, while other notable high-altitude landmarks include the Fouta Djalon plateau of Guinea (p371) and the massifs of the Aïr (Niger; p456) and Hoggar (Algeria; p77) in the Sahara.

The African earth deep beneath your feet is being slowly pulled apart by the action of hot currents, resulting in a gap, or rift. This action over thousands of years has formed what's known as the Great Rift Valley, which begins in Syria and winds over 5000km before it peters out in southern Mozambique. The valley is flanked in many places by sheer escarpments and towering cliffs, the most dramatic of which can be seen in Ethiopia, Kenya, and along DRC's border with Uganda and Rwanda. The valley's floor contains the legendary

The continent's highest point is the perpetually (for now) snow-capped Kilimanjaro (5895m) in Tanzania, and the lowest is Lake Assal (153m below sea level) in Djibouti.

KILIMANJARO'S MELTING ICE CAP

Glittering white like a mirage behind its veil of cloud, Mt Kilimanjaro's perfect white cap of ice is one of Africa's most iconic images. It has also become a cause célèbre in the debate over global warming. According to the UN, Kilimanjaro's glaciers have shrunk by 80% since the early 20th century and the mountain has lost over a third of its ice in the last 20 years alone. The causes are complex and not solely attributable to rising temperatures, with deforestation also to blame – the upper limit of the mountain's forests has descended significantly and overall forest cover has, thanks to fire, decreased by 15% since 1976. Whatever is to blame, some estimates suggest that Kilimanjaro's ice could disappear completely by 2020.

---

wildlife-watching habitats of the Serengeti and Masai Mara in Tanzania and Kenya, alkaline lakes such as Bogoria and Turkana, and some of Africa's largest freshwater lakes.

Rivers

Africa's waterways are more than stunning natural phenomena. They also serve as the lifeblood for millions of Africans who rely on them for transport, fishing, irrigation and water supplies. The Nile (6650km) and Congo (4700km) Rivers dominate Africa's hydrology, but it's the Niger River (4100km), Africa's third-longest, that is the focus of most environmental concern.

The Niger's volume has fallen by 55% since the 1980s due to climate change, drought, pollution and population growth. Fish stocks have fallen, water hyacinth is a recurring problem and the growth of sand bars has made navigation increasingly difficult. Given that an estimated 110 million people live in the Niger's basin, problems for the Niger could cause a catastrophic ripple well beyond the river's shoreline. The alarming signs of a river in distress prompted nine West African countries in 2008 to agree on a US$8 billion, 20-year rescue plan to save the river.

Rivers also provide the focal point of some of Africa's most enjoyable activities for travellers. White-water rafting is possible on the Zambezi River below Victoria Falls in Zambia (p1096) and Zimbabwe (p1124), on the Nile at Jinja in Uganda (see boxed text, p831), and in Swaziland (see boxed text, p1076). For something more sedate, slow trips up the Niger (see boxed text, p412) or Congo (see boxed text, p586) are also signature African river journeys.

Lakes & Wetlands

Africa has its share of famous lakes, which in turn have their share of environmental problems. Lake Victoria, which lies across parts of Uganda, Tanzania and Kenya, is Africa's largest freshwater lake (and the second largest by area in the world after North America's Lake Superior). Pollution, shrinking water levels and invasive aquatic plant species are all issues here, although a late-1990s program to combat water hyacinth has been judged a success. Lake Tanganyika, with a depth of 1471m, is the world's second-deepest lake after Lake Baikal in Russia and faces similar problems, while Lake Malawi, which borders Malawi, Mozambique and Tanzania and is reportedly home to more fish species (over 1000) than any other lake on earth, has a serious problem with algal blooms. But these problems pale in comparison to the threats to Lake Chad, which once straddled the borders of Chad, Niger, Nigeria and Cameroon and whose waters are essential to the lives of 20 million people living around its shores and in its hinterland. This was once the sixth-largest lake in the world and Africa's second-largest wetland, supporting a rich variety of wildlife. But falling rainfall, a growing population (and hence increased water

Africa's highest road is found in one of its smallest countries – Lesotho. Its Tlaeng Pass climbs to a dizzying 3275m above sea level in the northeast of the country.

After its initial descent, the Niger River has an extremely low gradient and is highly susceptible to fluctuations in rainfall: in 1972 and 1984, the river almost dried up completely.

consumption) and a notoriously shallow average depth (around 4m) have taken their toll: Lake Chad has shrunk by 95% over the past 35 years.

Less a lake than the world's largest inland delta, the Okavango Delta (p875) is home to a stunning array of wildlife, with over 2000 plant and 450 bird species. The delta's 130,000-strong elephant population is believed to be close to capacity, with increasing conflict between elephants and farmers around the delta's boundaries.

Apart from the opportunity of being poled in a dugout canoe past the elephants of the Okavango swamps, Lake Malawi (p956) is widely held to offer the best freshwater diving and snorkelling in Africa.

Deserts

Deserts or arid lands cover 60% of Africa. Much of this is the Sahara, the world's largest desert at over 9 million sq km, which is comparable in size to the continental United States. The Sahara occupies 11 countries, including more than half of Mauritania, Mali and Chad, 80% of Niger and Algeria and 95% of Libya. Contrary to popular misconceptions, sand covers just 20% of the Sahara's surface and just one-ninth of the Sahara rises as sand dunes. More typical of the Sahara are the vast gravel plains and plateaus such as the Tanezrouft of northeastern Mali and southwestern Algeria. The Sahara's other signature landform is the desert massif, barren mountain ranges of sandstone, basalt and granite such as the Hoggar (or Ahaggar) Mountains (p77) in Algeria, Aïr Mountains in Niger (p456) and Mali's Adrar des Iforas. By one estimate, the Sahara is home to 1400 plant species, 50 species of mammal and 18 species of bird.

Another little-known fact about the Sahara is that this is the youngest desert on earth. As recently as 8000 years ago, the Sahara was a fertile land, made up of savannah grasslands, forests and lakes watered by relatively regular rainfall, and home to abundant wildlife. Around 7000 years ago, rains became less frequent and by 400 BC, the Sahara was the desert we know today, albeit on a smaller scale.

Much of the Sahara is off limits to travellers in Niger, Mauritania and Mali – check the individual country chapters for details – but it's definitely possible to visit in Algeria (p77) and Libya (p138).

If the Sahara is a relatively recent phenomenon, the Namib Desert in Namibia is one of the world's oldest – a staggering 55 million years old. It was created (and is sustained) by cold-air convection that sucks the moisture from the land and creates an arid landscape of rolling sand dunes with its own unique ecosystem. Even larger than the Namib, the Kalahari Desert spans Botswana, Namibia and South Africa and is around the size of France and Germany combined.

Forests

African forests include dry tropical forests in eastern and southern Africa, humid tropical rainforests in western and central regions, montane forests and subtropical forests in northern Africa, as well as mangroves in the coastal zones. Despite the myth of the African 'jungle', Africa actually has one of the lowest percentages of rainforest cover in the world – one-fifth of Africa is covered by forests, with over 90% of what's left found in the Congo basin. Not surprisingly, the countries of Central Africa – Gabon (84.5%), Congo (65.6%), DRC (58.9%) and Equatorial Guinea (58.2%) – have the highest proportion of their territory covered by forest, although Guinea-Bissau (73.7%) is a rare West African exception.

The rainforests of Central Africa in particular are havens for gorilla, chimpanzee and other primate species. See p55 for more details.

Sahara: A Natural History, by Marq de Villiers and Sheila Hirtle, covers the natural and human history of the Sahara like no other recent book, and the lively text makes it a pleasure to read.

Forty million metric tonnes of Saharan sand reaches the Amazon annually, replenishing mineral nutrients depleted by tropical rains. Half of this dust comes from the Bodele Depression on the Niger–Chad border.

Sahara Fragile (www.saharafragile.org) is dedicated to sustainable Saharan tourism with tips for minimising your impact on Saharan environments.

Savannah

The savannah is a quintessentially African landform, covering an estimated two thirds of the African land mass. Savannah is usually located in a broad swath surrounding tropical rainforest and its sweeping plains are home to some of the richest concentrations of wildlife on earth, especially in East Africa. The term itself refers to a grasslands ecosystem. While trees may be (and usually are) present, such trees do not, under the strict definition of the term, form a closed canopy, while wet and dry seasons (the latter often with regenerating and/or devastating wildfires) are also typical of Africa's savannahs. The Serengeti (p798) is probably the continent's most famous savannah region.

> Up to 38% of Africa's coastline is considered to be under a high degree of threat from developments that include cities, ports, road networks and pipelines.

Coastal Africa

Along the coasts of East Africa and the Red Sea, warm currents provide perfect conditions for coral growth, resulting in spectacular underwater coral reefs. Off the west coast, the Benguela current, which shadows Angola, Namibia and South Africa, consists predominantly of nutrient-rich cold water and is home to one of the world's most biologically diverse marine environments. For information on how to explore these extraordinary underwater worlds from Egypt to São Tomé & Príncipe, see p1133.

Coral reefs are the most biologically diverse marine ecosystems on earth, rivalled only by tropical rainforests on land. Corals grow over geologic time – ie over millennia rather than the decades that mammals etc live – and have been in existence for about 200 million years. The delicately balanced marine environment of the coral reef relies on the interaction of hard and soft corals, sponges, fish, turtles, dolphins and other life forms.

> Of the 49 countries covered in this book, 33 have coastal frontage. Madagascar (4828km) and Somalia (3330km) have the longest coastlines, while the DRC (37km) and Gambia (80km) have the shortest.

Coral reefs also rely on mangroves, the salt-tolerant trees with submerged roots that form a nursery and breeding ground for birds and most of the marine life that migrates to the reef. Mangroves trap and produce nutrients for food and habitat, stabilise the shoreline, and filter pollutants from the land base. Both coral reefs and the mangrove colonies that support them are under threat from factors such as oil exploration and extraction, coastal degradation, deforestation and global warming. The mangrove forests of West Africa, particularly in Guinea, Nigeria and Senegal, are regarded by the United Nations Environment Programme (UNEP) as critically endangered, while Mozambique has Africa's largest area of coastal mangroves – almost 5000 sq km – followed by Madagascar (3000 sq km).

NATIONAL PARKS

Africa's protected areas range from world-class national parks in eastern and southern Africa to barely discernible wildlife reserves in West Africa; there are very few national parks in North Africa.

> Tanzania has the second-largest network of coral reefs in Africa (after Egypt), at 3580 sq km, and its waters are home to 150 different species of coral.

As such, the record of African countries is extremely mixed. Zambia (with 41.5% of its territory protected in some form) and Tanzania (38.4%) lead the way, with more than a quarter of Botswana (30.2%), São Tomé & Príncipe (28.4%) and Uganda (26.3%) also impressive. In West Africa, Benin (23%) is the star performer. At the other end of the scale, Libya (0.1%), Lesotho (0.2%), Somalia (0.7%) and Morocco (1.2%) are barely protected at all.

You can find details of the best national parks in each of the individual country chapters, but Africa also has numerous examples of transfrontier national parks that stand out as shining examples of neighbourly cooperation. There are more than a dozen of these spread around the continent; among the ones you're most likely to encounter are the Park Regional du W, which spans the Niger, Benin and Burkina Faso borders; the Masai Mara, which encompasses Kenya's Masai Mara National Reserve and Tanzania's

Serengeti National Park; and the Great Limpopo Transfrontier Park, which links South Africa's Kruger and Mozambique's Limpopo National Parks. With the exception of the Great Limpopo Transfrontier Park, however, remember that just because animals can move freely across these borders it doesn't mean that people can.

ENVIRONMENTAL ISSUES

Africa has some extraordinarily beautiful (and intact) natural areas. It also has a list of environmental concerns that read like a precursor to an apocalypse. At one level, the threats to Africa's environment seem magnified by the fact that few continents can boast so many examples of surviving natural wilderness. But these won't exist for much longer unless drastic action is taken.

According to the UN, deforestation is a serious issue in 31 African countries, followed closely by land degradation and soil erosion (29 countries), loss of biodiversity (24), coastal degradation (18), water scarcity (18) and desertification (17).

And no discussion of the African environment is complete without addressing the human element, not only because of human impact on the environment, but also because environmental changes impact first upon Africans, due to poverty and reliance on the land. Africa is the second-most populous continent after Asia, and the UN estimates that Africa's population growth rate will be almost double the world average in the first half of the 20th century.

It is as simple and as complicated as that: Africa faces some of the most pressing environmental issues of our time.

> Gabon has protected 16.2% of its territory (up from 4.7% in 1990), Equatorial Guinea 14.3% (up from 4.9% in the same period) and Congo 14.1% (up from 6.4%).

Deforestation

Rainforests are one of the richest habitats on earth – a single hectare of tropical rainforest may contain more than 600 species of tree – but also one of the most threatened. And it's not just rainforest that's under threat: pockets of temperate forest are getting the chop all over Africa, not only for timber, but also for firewood and charcoal, and to be cleared for agriculture.

A 2009 report by international forest-policy group the Rights and Resources Initiative (www.rightsandresources.org) found that African forests are disappearing at a rate four times faster than forests anywhere else in the world. The reason, according to the study, is that less than 2% of the continent's forests are under the control of local communities – over half of the rainforests of the Congo basin are already under commercial-logging leases – compared to around a third in Latin America and Asia.

East and Central Africa have the most to lose and the signs there aren't good – Burundi is losing around 5% of its forest cover every year, with massive deforestation issues in Congo, Central African Republic, Cameroon, Kenya, Tanzania and Zambia. West Africa is faring little better. Over 90% of West Africa's original forest has been lost, while Nigeria and Ghana in particular are losing forest cover at an alarming rate.

Internationally, these dire figures raise concern over the effect such large-scale deforestation may have on global warming. At a local level, soil erosion (with its devastating impact on agriculture), loss of biodiversity and an increase in the amount of wildlife hunted for bushmeat as new roads and accompanying settlements penetrate the forests, rank among the major side effects.

> In 1950 there were, on average, 13.5 hectares of land for every person in Africa. By 2050, that figure will have shrunk to 1.5 hectares.

Desertification

As forest cover diminishes, all too often the desert moves in. Desertification is one of the most serious forms of land degradation and it's one to which

GREENING NIGER: A SUCCESS STORY

Forests are considered to be an important buffer against desertification. Take, for example, the case of Niger, which has lost a third of its meagre forest cover since 1990. Although just 1% of Niger is now forested, it's not all bad news.

Satellite images show that three of Niger's southern provinces (especially around Tahoua) now have between 10 and 20 times more trees than they did in the 1970s. According to UNEP, this is 'a human and environmental success story at a scale not seen before in the Sahel'.

The secret to the success has been giving farmers the primary role in regenerating the land. Faced with arid soil that made agriculture almost impossible, farmers constructed terraces and rock bunds to stem erosion, trap rainfall and enable the planting of trees. Trees planted by the farmers now serve as windbreaks against the desert and, for the first time in a generation, agriculture (millet, sorghum and vegetables) is almost possible year-round, even in the dry season, thanks to improved water catchments and soil quality. Farmers no longer uproot trees to plant crops, instead ploughing around them, and crop yields have increased. The region's groundwater table has also risen, in some places from a depth of 20m to 3m. In some areas, pockets of desert now resemble agricultural parklands, with more than 200 trees per hectare. Even in years of drought when crops fail, the trees, a small proportion of which can be sold for cash, serve as a bastion against starvation; in the 2005 food crisis, death rates from hunger in the three southern provinces were much lower than elsewhere in the country.

the countries of the West African Sahel and North Africa are particularly vulnerable. Desertification has reached critical levels in Niger, Chad, Mali and Mauritania, each of which some believe could be entirely consumed by the Sahara within a generation; up to 80% of Morocco is also considered to have a high risk of desertification. The Sahara's southward march is by no means a uniform process (and some scientists even doubt its existence), but the Sahel in particular remains critically vulnerable to short-term fluctuations in rainfall.

Below-average rainfall 1980 to 1984 (one of the driest years on record) caused the Sahara to grow by 15%, increasing its coverage by 1.3 million sq km and temporarily pushing its boundary south by 240km.

Desertification is also a problem for countries beyond the Sahelian danger zone: a high to moderate risk of desertification exists in numerous West African countries, as well as Botswana, Namibia, DRC, Central African Republic, Kenya, Ethiopia, Sudan and Somalia.

The major causes of desertification are easy to identify – including drought, deforestation, overgrazing and agricultural practices (such as cash crops that require intensive farming) that have led to the overexploitation of fragile soils on the desert margin – and are the result of both human activity and climatic variation. But one of the most significant causes in West Africa is the use of deliberately lit fires. Such fires are sometimes necessary for maintaining soil quality, regenerating savannah grasslands and ecosystems, enabling livestock production and as a form of pest control. But when the interval between fires is insufficient to allow the land to recover, the soil becomes exposed to wind and heavy rains and can be unravelled beyond the point of recovery.

Loss of Biodiversity

In 2008 the UN Secretary-General's Special Adviser on Conflict, Jan Egeland, described West Africa's Sahel region as the world's 'ground zero' for vulnerable communities struggling to adapt to climate change.

African wildlife accounts for almost a third of global biodiversity and its statistics alone tell the story – a quarter of the world's 4700 mammal species are found in Africa, as are a fifth of the world's bird species and more fish species than on any other continent. Discoveries in the 1990s in Madagascar alone increased the numbers of the world's known amphibian and reptile species by 25% and 18% respectively. When it comes to biodiversity, South Africa has few peers, home as it is to almost 10% of the world's plant species, 16% of its marine fish species and 8% of bird species. The equatorial ecosystems of Central Africa are especially prolific.

But Africa's astonishing biodiversity is under threat, and it is home to eight of the world's 34 biodiversity hot spots, as defined by Conservation International. To qualify, a region must contain at least 1500 species of vascular plants (ie more than 0.5% of world's total) and have lost at least 70% of its original habitat. Three of these touch on South Africa (where 34% of terrestrial ecosystems and 82% of river ecosystems are considered threatened), with others in West Africa, Madagascar, the Horn of Africa, the coastal forests of East Africa and the Great Rift Valley.

Community-Based Conservation

While the history of environmental protection in Africa is one that often saw Africans evicted from their land to make way for national parks, the future lies in community-based conservation. This local, as opposed to large-scale, approach is based on the tenet that in order for the African environment to be protected, ordinary Africans must have the primary stake in its preservation. Tourism has played a pivotal role in ensuring that conservation can greatly benefit local communities, and the number of community-run lodges, tour companies and other tourism-related projects is burgeoning. Most of the gains have been made in East and southern Africa, but even West Africa is joining the party, with everything from locally run wildlife sanctuaries in Ghana to the growing ecotourism trend in Benin. For our list of businesses and activities committed to environmentally, socially, culturally or economically sustainable travel, turn to p1216.

In 2005, British scientists surveyed over 2400 plant species in Cameroon's Kupe-Bakossi region, finding a 10th that were completely new to science, making this Africa's top location for plant biodiversity.

Perfect armchair-travel fodder, the BBC's *Wild Africa* series consists of six stunningly filmed documentaries entitled *Jungle, Coasts, Mountains, Deserts, Savannahs* and *Rivers & Lakes*.

Responsible Travel

At one level, the impact of tourism in Africa can be positive: it can provide an incentive for locals to preserve environments and wildlife by generating employment, while enabling them to maintain their traditional lifestyles. However, the negative impacts of tourism can be substantial and contribute to the gradual erosion of traditional life. Please try to keep your impact as low as possible by considering the following tips:

- Try to give people a balanced perspective of life in developed countries and point out the strong points of local culture (eg strong family ties, openness to outsiders).
- Try not to waste water. Switch off lights and air conditioning when you go out.
- Many precious cultural objects are sold to tourists – you should only buy newly carved pieces to preserve Africa's history and stimulate the local carving industry.
- Question any so-called ecotourism operators for specifics about what they're really doing to protect the environment and the people who live there.
- Support local enterprise, whether it's a locally owned hotel or locally made souvenirs.
- Resist the local tendency of being indifferent to littering.
- Always, always ask permission before taking photos. Don't offer to send photos back unless you're really prepared to do it.

'Your social gaffes are usually forgiven and are more likely to cause confusion and amusement than offence'

By and large, Africans are easy-going and polite. Your social gaffes are usually forgiven and are more likely to cause confusion and amusement than offence. At the same time, good manners are respected and many people will think you most rude if you don't say hello and enquire after their health before asking them when the next bus is going to leave. That's why it's useful to learn a few local greetings.

When it comes to dress, African society is generally conservative in outlook. Put simply, it's inappropriate to wear immodest and revealing clothes anywhere except tourist-only beaches. Extra care is needed in rural areas and Muslim countries, where women should keep shoulders and midriffs covered and wear long skirts or loose trousers. See p1148 for more information.

Be very careful when distributing gifts to locals. Visitors handing out freebies to locals (especially candy, pens and coins to children) can have a detrimental effect on social networks, and create communities of people likely to greet travellers with their hands outstretched. If you want to help the people you meet, donate to a charity or go via community leaders, schools and hospitals. If you're offered a gift, don't feel guilty about accepting it; to refuse may bring shame on the giver. If you're invited to someone's home, taking a gift is appropriate.

UK-based organisation **Tourism Concern** (☎ 020-7133 3800; www.tourismconcern. org.uk; Stapleton House, 277-281 Holloway Rd, London N7 8HN) is primarily concerned with tourism and its impact upon local cultures and the environment. It has a range of publications and contacts for community organisations, as well as further advice on minimising the impact of your travels. Also worth checking out are **Responsible Travel** (www.responsibletravel.com) and **Open Africa** (www.openafrica.org).

To see our list of businesses and activities committed to environmentally, socially, culturally or economically sustainable travel, turn to p1216.

Africa's Wildlife

Welcome to the greatest wildlife show on earth. Africa is home to more than 1100 mammal species and some 2400 bird species, and throughout the continent, wildlife brings drama and life to the beauty of the African wilds, from the great wildebeest migration across the savannah to the gravitas of encountering a gorilla family deep in the forest. Your first sight of elephants in the wild, of chimpanzees high in the forest canopy, or the exhilaration of seeing a lion or cheetah on the hunt – these, too, will rank among the most unforgettable experiences of your trip.

East and southern Africa are the undoubted highlights for the sheer diversity of mammals and other species, and the professionalism of their safari operators. The rainforests of Central African countries may be more complicated as traveller destinations, but the rewards rival those to the east and south. West Africa is at once a world-class destination for birders and an underrated region for spotting large mammals if you know where to look. North Africa is something of a wildlife wasteland, but if southern Sudan ever becomes safe, its Sudd region along the White Nile could come to rival the Serengeti in Tanzania as the world's most dramatic wildlife spectacle; see the boxed text, p199 for more information.

For detailed coverage of Africa's signature habitats for wildlife, see p47; you'll also find wildlife-themed itineraries on p25 and p24.

J Kingdon's *Field Guide to African Mammals* is an excellent and authoritative guide to all the continent's land mammals. *Island Africa*, also by Kingdon, is a beautifully illustrated explanation of Africa's extraordinary biodiversity.

ELEPHANTS

The African elephant, the largest living land animal, is for many travellers the continent's most charismatic mammal. Elephants are plentiful in many areas of Africa and their survival is one of world conservation's most enduring success stories.

In the 1970s and 1980s, the numbers of African elephants plummeted from an estimated 1.3 million to around 500,000. The slaughter ended only in 1989 when the trade in ivory was banned under the Convention for International Trade in Endangered Species (CITES). Illegal poaching continues to feed demand in Asia, and may even be on the rise, but the ivory ban remains an overwhelming success. In some areas, elephant populations have recovered to such an extent that some African governments have called for the ban to be relaxed to allow the culling of elephants in areas where herds have grown beyond the land's capacity to cope, and where conflict between elephants and humans is growing as a result. As such, the future of elephants remains uncertain, but it's a far cry from the desperate situation just a few decades ago.

Seeing the 'Big Five' has become a mantra for African wildlife-watchers, but few know it was coined by white hunters for those five species deemed most dangerous to hunt: elephant, lion, leopard, rhino and buffalo.

Where to See Elephants

In East Africa, Tanzania has elephants in abundance, with Serengeti National Park (p798), Ngorongoro Conservation Area (pp798) and Ruaha National Park (p804) the picks among many. In Kenya, it just has to be Masai Mara National Reserve (p719) or Amboseli National Park (p730). To the north, in Uganda, elephants are found in greatest numbers at the remote Kidepo Valley National Park (p843) in the country's northeast.

South Africa's Kruger National Park (p1046) is perhaps southern Africa's most famous elephant sanctuary, but Botswana is also an elephant-watcher's paradise, most notably in the Okavango Delta (p875) and Chobe National Park (p883). In Namibia, the desert elephants of the Namib can be seen in Damaraland (p997) and along the Skeleton Coast (p997), but

---

WILDLIFE-WATCHING – THE BASICS

When to Go

Much of East Africa offers exceptional wildlife-viewing year-round, but, although visitor numbers can be high, wildlife is generally easier to spot during dry seasons, when waterholes become a focus for activity. Wildlife usually disperses during wet seasons and denser vegetation can make observation more difficult, but you may be rewarded with 'private' viewings and breeding activity.

How to Look

Most animals are naturally wary of people, so to minimise their distress (or aggression) keep as quiet as possible, avoid sudden movements and wear subdued colours when in the field. Try to avoid direct eye contact, particularly with primates, as this is seen as a challenge and may provoke aggressive behaviour. Good binoculars are an invaluable aid to observing wildlife at a distance and are essential for birdwatching. When on foot, stay downwind of animals wherever possible – they'll smell you long before they see or hear you.

Living with Wildlife

In Africa you are rarely at the top of the food chain – never get out of your vehicle unless it's safe to do so. Always obey park regulations, including traffic speed limits; thousands of animals are needlessly killed on African roads every year. Follow your guide's instructions at all times – it may mean the difference between life and death on a walking safari. *Never* get between a mother and her calves or cubs. Exercise care when boating or swimming, and be particularly aware of the dangers posed by crocodiles and hippos. And *never* feed wild animals – it encourages scavenging, may adversely affect their health and can cause animals to become aggressive towards each other and humans.

In 1970, Chad had 300,000 elephants; by 2006, there were just 10,000. Angola's 1981 elephant population of 12,000 has fallen to barely 250 today. And despite its name, Côte d'Ivoire now has fewer than 300.

Etosha National Park (p1000) is also prolific. Elsewhere, Malawi's Liwonde National Park (p953), Zambia's South Luangwa (p1091) and Lower Zambezi (p1095) National Parks, and Zimbabwe's Hwange National Park (p1124) are also outstanding.

The national parks of Central Africa are home to the smaller forest (rather than savannah) elephants and are deliciously remote. In Gabon, elephants wander along the beach in Loango National Park (p615), while elephants are also common in the Réserve de la Lopé (p617) and Ivindo National Park (p617). Other prime elephant areas include Central African Republic's Dzanga-Sangha Reserve (p546) and Congo's Parc National Nouabalé-Ndoki (p571).

In West Africa, elephant sightings are mostly hard-won, with the best places being Ghana's Mole National Park (p355), Burkina Faso's Ranch de Nazinga (see the boxed text, p273) and Cameroon's Parc National de Waza (p300).

PRIMATES

Secrets of the Savanna, by Mark and Delia Owens, lays bare the difficulties of protecting Africa's elephants from poachers in Zambia's North Luangwa National Park.

They may not be part of the 'Big Five', but the chance to see Africa's primates is alone worth the trip. Our obvious kinship with these always engaging animals has spawned various forms of 'primate tourism', whereby troops of monkeys or apes are habituated to human presence so visitors can observe them in their natural habitat. Central Africa's rainforests are particularly rich in primate species, although West and East Africa also have considerable populations. Although gorillas and chimpanzees get most of the attention (and rightfully so), you'll also come across colobus monkeys, mangabeys, drills, beautiful and strikingly marked guenons and forest baboons, among others.

Gorillas

Gorillas are the world's largest living primate. Their last refuges in Central Africa have too often occupied war zones and, in the Democratic Republic of Congo (DRC), the gorilla's forest habitat has often come under the control of rebel armies; in the first half of 2007, seven gorillas were shot execution-style in DRC's Parc National des Virunga. Poaching, the Ebola and Marburg viruses and even the trade in bushmeat have all contributed to the vulnerability of gorillas.

But there's also plenty of good news. A census report released in early 2009 found that, despite years of war, the population of mountain gorillas in the DRC's Parc National des Virunga had risen by 12.5%; 81 gorillas live permanently within the park, with over 200 present at any given time. Across the other side of Africa, a staggering 125,000 western lowland gorillas were discovered in 2008 in the swamps of northern Congo, almost doubling previous projections.

WHERE TO SEE GORILLAS

The most accessible gorillas in Africa are eastern mountain gorillas, of which 720 are believed to survive. Half of these are found in Uganda's southwest, with an estimated 320 inhabiting the Bwindi Impenetrable National Park (p836), and the remainder in Mgahinga Gorilla National Park (p839). Neighbouring Rwanda's Parc National des Volcans (p750) is another prime place to see mountain gorillas. They're also present in eastern DRC at the Parc National des Virunga (p585) and Parc National de Kahuzi-Biéga (p586), but security is more of an issue here.

Across the other side of Central Africa, the two best places to see the western lowland gorillas are the Central African Republic's Dzanga-Sangha Reserve (p546) and Congo's Parc National Nouabalé-Ndoki (p571). Gabon is also gearing itself up for gorilla tourism with a number of families being habituated to the human presence. There are also gorillas in Cameroon and possibly southeastern Nigeria.

Chimpanzees & Other Primates

Chimpanzees are the animal world's closest living relative to humans, with whom they share 99% of their genetic make-up. You'll find these sometimes playful, sometimes cranky creatures throughout Africa and they're usually more accessible (and cheaper to see) than gorillas.

WHERE TO SEE CHIMPS & OTHER PRIMATES

In East Africa, Tanzania is terrific for chimp tracking, especially Mahale Mountains (p802) and Gombe Stream (p803) National Parks near Lake Tanganyika. Every bit as good is Uganda's Kibale Forest National Park (p833), home to Africa's highest density of primates; Queen Elizabeth National Park (p835), Murchison Falls National Park (p841) and Toro-Semliki Wildlife Reserve (p834) are also good. In Rwanda, the Parc National de Nyungwe (p752) is the best place for chimpanzees, and you may also see colobus monkeys. Ethiopia's Simien Mountains National Park (p690) is home to a small population of gelada baboons.

In Central Africa, Central African Republic's Dzanga-Sangha Reserve (p546), Congo's Parc National Nouabalé-Ndoki (p571), DRC's Okapi Wildlife Reserve (p587) and Equatorial Guinea's Monte Alen National Park (p601) are good for a range of primate species. More accessible are the primate-rich national parks of Gabon, including Réserve de la Lopé (p617), home to some of the world's largest mandrill troupes, and Ivindo National Park (p617). Closely related to the chimpanzee, the notoriously peace-loving

---

In 2008, Cameroon announced the creation of the new Takamanda National Park, close to the Nigerian border, to protect 115 Cross River gorillas, of which only 300 are thought to survive in the wild.

Watching gorillas in the wild doesn't come cheap. In Uganda and Rwanda, gorilla permits cost US$500 per person, while it costs around US$615 in Congo. It's slightly cheaper in the Democratic Republic of Congo (US$400) and Central African Republic (around US$235).

For up-to-date coverage of a whole range of wildlife, www.africanconservation.org is the website of the nonprofit African Conservation Foundation, with links to countries, projects and info on how to get involved.

MADAGASCAR – A WORLD APART

In any discussion of African wildlife, Madagascar rates a separate mention for its unique treasure trove of endemic wildlife that has remained virtually unchanged since the island split from the mainland 165 million years ago. Most of Madagascar's wildlife exists nowhere else on earth, including 98% of its land mammals, 92% of its reptiles, and 41% of bird species. Most famous are its lemurs, a group of primates that have followed a separate evolutionary path. Lemurs have adapted to nearly every feeding niche, and range in size from tiny pygmy mouse lemurs (at 85g, the world's smallest primate) to the 2.5kg ring-tailed lemur. Perhaps the most curious, however, is the indri, which looks like a cross between a koala and a giant panda, and has a voice like a police siren. The best wildlife-watching in Madagascar is to be found at Réserve Spécial Analamazaotra (p922), Parc National de l'Isalo (p920) and Parc National de Ranomafana (p919).

bonobo is highly endangered and survives only in the DRC; seeing one in the wild is almost impossible, but you can catch a glimpse at the Lola Ya Bonobo Sanctuary (p584) near Kinshasa.

Primates are West Africa's most easily observed mammals, with a wide range of species in the countries along the region's coast. Sierra Leone's Tiwai Island Wildlife Sanctuary (p515) probably offers the best primate-viewing in West Africa. Other highlights include the chimpanzees in Côte d'Ivoire's Parc National de Taï (p313) and Guinea-Bissau's Parque Nacional do Catanhez (p384), the most westerly home of Africa's chimpanzees. For other primate species, Nigeria's Gashaka-Gumti National Park (p475), Cameroon's Parc National de Campo-Ma'an (p296) and Ghana's Kakum National Park (p348) are excellent.

> Primate conservation is about far more than gorillas and chimps – 37% of primate species in mainland Africa are considered endangered, with the figure at 43% in Madagascar.

Primate Refuges

Small sanctuaries set up to provide a haven for primates rescued from poachers and traffickers play a critical role in primate conservation. They include: Chifunshi Wildlife Orphanage (p1094), a chimpanzee sanctuary; Congo's Lésio Louna Gorilla Reserve (p570), for orphaned gorillas; and Congo's Parc National Conkouati Douli (p571), where chimpanzees are being prepared for their reintroduction into the wild. In West Africa, the best places are the Drill Ranch and Afi Mountain Drill Ranch (p471) in Nigeria; the Limbe Wildlife Centre (p289) in Cameroon; Sierra Leone's Tacugama Chimpanzee Sanctuary (p514); and River Gambia National Park (p332) in The Gambia.

CATS

> Sahara Conservation Fund (www.saharaconservat ion.org) is one of few sources of information on the wildlife of the Sahara, and the efforts being undertaken to protect it.

Some of Africa's most memorable wildlife-watching moments come from the great cats – lions, leopards and cheetahs – hunting prey, although these can be among the most elusive of Africa's megafauna. Spotting one of the smaller cat species, such as the caracal, serval, African wild cat or sand cat of the Sahara, is even more difficult.

Lions

Despite having been anointed as the 'king of the jungle', lions inhabit not forests but the savannah. Lions, probably the easiest to spot of the big cats, are found predominantly in East and parts of southern Africa, with isolated populations dotted around West Africa. Your best chance of seeing lions is probably in Kenya or Tanzania, and the lurking presence of lions is one of the great sideshows of the annual wildebeest migration. In Kenya, Masai Mara National Reserve (p719), Amboseli National Park (p730) and Hell's Gate National Park (p714) offer the best chances for sighting lions. In Tanzania, it's Serengeti National Park (p798), Ngorongoro Conservation

Area (p798) and Lake Manyara National Park (p797). Uganda's Murchison Falls National Park (p841) and Toro-Semliki Wildlife Reserve (p834) are also possibilities. Elsewhere, you might encounter lions in South Africa, Botswana, Zambia, Malawi and Namibia.

Leopards

Leopards are present throughout sub-Saharan Africa and, unlike lions, are at home in most African landscapes, from the semidesert to tropical rainforest. In addition to those places mentioned under Lions (opposite), leopards can be spotted in East Africa in Kenya's Lake Nakuru (p715) and Tsavo West (p731) National Parks. In southern Africa, try Zambia's South Luangwa National Park (p1091), South Africa's Kruger National Park (p1046), Malawi's Nyika National Park (p944) and Namibia's Namib-Naukluft National Park (p995). In West Africa, leopards are found in Niger's Parc Regional du W (p451).

There is no finer resource on Africa's wild cats than *Cats of Africa*, by L Hunter, an authoritative but highly readable book covering their behaviour, conservation and ecology, with superb photos by G Hinde.

HOOFED ANIMALS

Africa has the most diverse range of hoofed animals (also known as ungulates) on earth and, given their numbers, they're often the easiest of all large mammals to spot on the continent. Counted within their ranks are numerous signature African species such as the hippo, rhino, giraffe, wildebeest, zebra and numerous antelope species.

Rhinoceros

Rhinos rank among Africa's most endangered large mammals. These inoffensive vegetarians are armed with impressive horns that have made them the target of both white hunters and poachers – rhino numbers plummeted to the brink of extinction during the 20th century. There are two species of rhino, black and white, both of which are predominantly found in savannah regions.

Africa's rarest hoofed creature is the okapi. Just 20,000 of this zebra-giraffe hybrid survive. You can catch a rare glimpse in the breeding centre in DRC's Okapi Wildlife Reserve (p587).

The survival of the white rhino is an environmental-conservation success story, having been brought back from the brink of extinction in South Africa through captive breeding. As a result, it is now off the endangered list. Black rhinos are thought to now number around 3600, with small but encouraging gains made in recent years. The West African Black Rhino was declared extinct in 2006.

CURIOUS CHEETAHS

The fastest land animal on earth – it can reach speeds of 75km/h in the first two seconds of its pursuit and at full speed may reach 115km/h – the cheetah in full flight is one of the most thrilling sights in the African wild. And yet their survival is nothing short of a miracle.

Cat biologists believe that around 10,000 years ago, only a single pregnant female cheetah (or at most a single family) survived an unknown catastrophe. As a result, cheetahs have the lowest genetic variation of all cat species and should therefore suffer from a high proportion of birth defects and be exceptionally vulnerable to disease and environmental change. But they survive. Their secret lies in the dimensions of their bodies, the most remarkable features of which include the longest legs of any cat (enabling a stride of up to 10m), unretractable claws that act like sprinters' spikes, a long, powerful tail that enables swift changes in direction, and a long, flexible spine.

Cheetahs inhabit mostly open country, from the savannah to the desert, and they're most easily spotted in the major national parks of Kenya, Tanzania, Namibia, South Africa and Zambia. A small number of cheetahs are also believed to survive in the Sahara.

WHERE TO SEE RHINOS

The black rhino is most easily seen in Tanzania's Ngorongoro Crater (p799) or in Malawi's Liwonde National Park (p953). White rhinos can be sighted in Ziwa Rhino Sanctuary (p840) in Uganda, while both species are present in Namibia's Etosha National Park (p1000) and Waterberg Plateau Park (p1003), and in Botswana's Khama Rhino Sanctuary (p885). Rhinos are also present in South Africa and Zimbabwe.

White rhinos aren't white at all – the name comes from the Dutch word wijd *which means wide and refers to the white rhino's wide lip (the black rhino has a pointed lip).*

Hippopotamus

Hippos, the third-heaviest land mammal on earth (after the elephant and white rhino), are found throughout sub-Saharan Africa, with the largest numbers in Tanzania, Zambia and Botswana. They're usually seen wallowing in shallow water in lakes, ponds and rivers, although the wave-surfing hippos in Gabon's Loango National Park (p615) are international celebrities. They're also one of the most dangerous animals in Africa, thanks to their aggression towards humans and propensity for attacking boats.

Zebras & Giraffes

Zebras (of which Burchell's zebra is the most widespread) and giraffes may be found in small populations elsewhere, but they are especially plentiful in the open and lightly wooded savannah of East Africa, where you'll see them in most of the major national parks and reserves. Africa's most remarkable giraffes are perhaps those of Kouré (p450) in Niger, which are making a stirring comeback after coming close to extinction.

Wildebeest

The annual migration of more than a million wildebeest, the largest single movement of herd animals on earth, is one of the grandest wildlife spectacles you could imagine. It all takes place in Kenya's Masai Mara National Reserve (p719) and Tanzania's Serengeti National Park (p798) from June to October.

The vulnerable mountain zebra of southwestern Africa was saved by one farsighted farmer, who protected the last 11 surviving zebras on his farm; the species has since recovered to number several hundred individuals.

Antelope

Antelope range from the tiny, knee-high dik-dik and duiker, through the graceful gazelle, impala and springbok, to giants such as the buffalo, eland and kudu. Many of these will be seen on a typical East or southern African safari.

West Africa also has its share of antelope species, including bushbucks, reedbucks, waterbucks, kobs, roans, elands, oribis, and various gazelles and duikers. The Sahel-dwelling dama gazelle is the largest gazelle species in Africa, but is now close to extinction, and the red-fronted gazelle may still survive in Mali's remote far east. Buffalos in West Africa inhabit forest regions, and are smaller and redder than the East African version.

BIRDS

Birds of Western Africa, by Nik Borrow and Ron Demey, is a must for birders who want to know what species are present and where they're most likely to see them.

Even if you're not into birdwatching, Africa's abundant and incredibly varied birdlife could turn you into an avid birder. In most sub-Saharan countries, you're likely to see hundreds of different species without looking too hard, and a bit of preparation – there are some excellent field guides – before you set out can greatly enhance your visit. Birds reach their highest profusion in the Congo rainforests, but are easier to see in habitats such as rainforest, savannah and wetland. Several bird families, such as the ostrich, secretary bird, touracos, shoebill, hamerkop and mousebird are unique to Africa. Apart from endemic species, hundreds more species flood into the continent on migration during the northern winter.

Where to See Birds

Any of East Africa's major national parks are good for birdwatching. Kenya has recorded 1200 bird species and, in particular, Kakamega Forest Reserve (p719), Lake Naivasha (p714) and the flamingos of Lake Nakuru National Park (p715) stand out. Tanzania, with over 1000 species, isn't far behind – Lake Manyara National Park (p797) is a good choice. Southern Ethiopia is also prime birding country, especially the Rift Valley Lakes (p695) and Bale Mountains National Park (p696).

In southern Africa, Malawi's Nyika National Park (p944), Liwonde National Park (p953) and Vwaza Marsh Wildlife Reserve (p945) are prime birders' destinations. Madagascar, too, has plenty of interest, especially in Parc National Ranomafana (p919) and Réserve Spécial Analamazaotra (p922), as does Namibia at Swakopmund (p992) and Namibia's Etosha National Park (p1000). Elsewhere, Botswana's Okavango Delta (p875) and Zimbabwe's Hwange National Park (p1124) won't disappoint.

West Africa lies along one of the busiest bird migratory routes between Europe and Africa, and more than 1000 species have been recorded in the region. Tiny Gambia has a devoted following in the birding community. Good places include Abuko Nature Reserve (p330), Tanji Bird Reserve (p330) and Kiang West National Park (p331). Senegal also offers excellent birding, particularly in Parc National des Oiseaux du Djoudj (p496) and Parc National de la Langue de Barbarie (p496); both are famous for vast pelican and flamingo flocks. Sierra Leone is also good; notably, Outamba-Kilimi National Park (p515) supports more than 250 species, including the spectacular great blue turaco.

It is estimated that 500 million birds from Europe and Asia migrate to tropical Africa every year, a journey of up to 11,000km – fewer than half make it home, either dying en route or preferring to remain in Africa.

Africa & Development

In an article entitled 'How to Write about Africa', award-winning Kenyan author Binyavanga Wainaina once offered a potted summary of Western clichés that was as funny as it was scathing:

'Never have a picture of a well-adjusted African on the cover of your book', recommended Binyavanga, tongue firmly in cheek. 'An AK-47, prominent ribs, naked breasts: use these.' Treat Africa as one country, he urged – don't get bogged down in detail. Taboo subjects included 'ordinary domestic scenes, love between Africans, references to African writers or intellectuals, mention of school-going children who are not suffering from yaws or Ebola'. Last, but not least, 'readers will be put off if you don't mention the light in Africa… There is always a big sky'.

It's true that few regions have been more sloppily written about than Africa, still viewed as a destination for the adventurous, altruistic or nonconformist, those out to test themselves, save others or escape the humdrum. 'People go to Africa and confirm what they already have in their heads', wrote Nigeria's Chinua Achebe, 'they fail to see what is there in front of them'. The continent, in the Western mind, still represents 'otherness' at its most intense.

As with all clichés, such attitudes only exist because they are part-rooted in reality. How many other regions, after all, can claim the dubious distinction of having US State Department travel warnings – at time of writing – out on 12 of its 53 nations? How many other areas have introduced the modern world to such medieval horrors as Ebola or Marburg Fever? Where else does the whisper of cannibalism regularly surface in connection with some rebel movement or militia chief? And whatever Binyavanga may say, anyone who fails to notice the light has something wrong with either their eyes or their soul.

The point is not that the fly-blown refugee or psychopathic warlord don't exist, it is that they don't represent the full picture. After only a few days in Africa first-time visitors will realise that ordinary life goes on; that those they meet fret about taxes, gossip about Manchester United, tell bad jokes and surf the web just like them. They will note that Africans, too, work in high-rise office blocks and shop in malls. They will leave wanting to know more about the facets of life that never make the headlines, yet encapsulate our common humanity.

If, curious to understand trends and causes, they bother to dig deeper, they're likely to emerge confused. Because just as no other continent has been the target of such misleading hyperbole, no other has been subjected to such indulgent wishful thinking. Whether prompted by liberal guilt, political correctness or unacknowledged racism, analysis comes in extremes, ranging from the All-We-Need-Is-One-Last-Heave school of thought to the Armageddon-Is-Approaching variety.

The upbeat view runs something like this: it took its time, but the 1989 collapse of the Berlin Wall sounded the death knell for a generation of corrupt 'dinosaur' presidents propped up by Washington or Moscow. The days when Colonel Chanceyourluck seized the radio station and executed the cabinet on the beach are also – despite a recent rash of West African coups – gradually fading. More than two-thirds of African nations have now held multiparty elections. From Angola to Sudan and the Democratic Republic of Congo (DRC), the players in Africa's most devastating conflicts have been cajoled to the negotiating table. With a new generation of progressive leaders at the reins, the world's richest nations have something to work with: hence the promise to double aid at the G8 meeting in Gleneagles in

Pick up any guidebook from the '60s, '70s or '80s and one fact strikes you: Africa has got less, not more, accessible. Roads once used by ordinary cars now need four-wheel drive, popular air routes have been scrapped, hotels no longer exist, ferries are a distant memory.

2005. Africa's crippling debt burden, now widely viewed as indefensible, is being whittled away and the West has also registered a moral imperative to correct trade terms tilted against the developing world. Domestically, the liberalisation of the media and advent of modern technology are ending the continent's long isolation, with even remote villages boasting mobile phones and internet cafes. As the mixed-race son of a Kenyan economist – leader of the world's only current superpower – told an audience on his first official visit to Africa: 'The 21st century will be shaped by what happens not just in Rome or Moscow or Washington, but by what happens in Ghana'.

The pessimist's view runs as follows. Yes, multiparty elections have become the norm, but that's only because an entrenched political elite has learned to play the game, rigging polls, co-opting opposition leaders and rewriting constitutions to remain indefinitely at the helm. Democracy's arrival, hungered for by so many Africans, has often proved to come with a chilling side serving – a resurgence of ethnic chauvinism. Nigeria, Kenya and South Africa, all once regarded as vital regional linchpins, now look shockingly fragile. Cold War manipulation has simply given way to a new distortion – the 'either you're with us or against us' of the Bush era, a litmus test arguably still being applied, albeit couched in less abrasive language, by Barack Obama. US policy towards key African states – Ethiopia, Kenya and Uganda are prime examples – is now determined by whether they are seen as 'onside' in the war against Islamic extremism. While some conflicts are running out of steam, new ones have an uncanny habit of erupting and others threaten to imminently reignite. Darfur (see p198) showed that despite all the 'never again' statements voiced after Rwanda's genocide, the outside world still stands by as a regime commits massive human-rights abuses against its citizens, and Mugabe's pauperisation of Zimbabwe exposed how reluctant African leaders were to police one of their own. Despite an estimated $580 billion in Western aid since most countries gained their independence in the 1960s, Africa remains the poorest and least industrialised continent on the globe. Its share of world trade has fallen to under 2%, average life expectancy has sunk to 1950s levels and, according to the UN, the number of poor is set to rise to 404 million in 2015.

Which version to embrace? The answer, of course, is that both are true. For, as Binyavanga highlights, one of Africa's biggest handicaps when it comes to convincing analysis has always been the basic fact of its geographical shape. So neat, so apparently self-contained, it lends itself to simplifications which cannot do justice to a continent of 1800 languages; a vast land mass that holds both snow-tipped mountains and green meadowlands, freezing coastlines and crusty deserts; nomads who love their camels and farmers who lust after soil; and mosques, holy trees, animist shrines, Masonic lodges and vast cathedrals modelled on St Peter's. In reality, the French-speaking Maghreb states have far more in common with one another than Angola or Kenya; South Africa's chronicle of apartheid is emphatically not the story of the rest of the continent; few Africans consider Egypt, which they regard as an extension of the Middle East, as belonging to the continent; Ethiopia, with its 3000-year-old Queen of Sheba myth, inhabits a cultural universe all its own; while the average Nigerian has as much in common with an Eritrean as a Swiss villager has with a Native American. Anyone trying to trace historical themes and pick out future prospects is forced to do what we do here – warn against the folly of generalisation, while generalising like crazy.

'Between me and the other world there is ever an unasked question', wrote American civil rights activist and Pan-Africanist WEB Dubois in 1897. 'How does it feel to be a problem?' Dubois was talking about the 'Negro problem', but the question accurately captured the outside world's stance on Africa. Today, the question usually comes framed as a blunt: 'Tell me, why is Africa still such a

Websites provide Africa's diaspora with a way to keep in touch and let off steam, but often seem offputtingly strident to outsiders. For a general overview of the continent, try www.allafrica.com. You can also read most African newspapers online.

mess?' Now, just as then, those who pose it are suffering from a form of selective amnesia, for the continent did not reach its current predicament alone.

SLAVERY

If Africa sometimes seems like a continent suffering from post-traumatic stress disorder, one of the least thoroughly digested of its many traumas was the slave trade. What is striking is how deep in the continent's subconscious this terrible episode has been buried. Some academics estimate that, had it not been for the slave trade, Africa's mid-19th-century population would have been double its 25 million figure. Yet, with the exception of the Swahili coast's old markets, Ghana's castles and Senegal's Goree Island, one rarely stumbles upon its traces. The complicity of African rulers of the day may explain a reluctance to engage with the issue. As Senegalese President Abdoulaye Wade, whose ancestors were slave owners, told African delegates campaigning for reparations: 'If one can claim reparations for slavery, the slaves of my ancestors or their descendants can also claim money from me.' The other complicating factor may be awareness of the time it took many African states to outlaw slavery – Emperor Haile Selassie, for example, only set about it in the 1920s – and embarrassment at the knowledge that it still quietly persists in countries such as Sudan, Mauritania and Niger.

LEGACY OF COLONIALISM

Africa's second whammy was a network of national borders, imposed from outside, which ignored salient geographical features and divisions of tribe, language and religion. Until the Berlin Conference of 1884–5, Africa's distinctive contribution to history had been the art of living fairly peacefully together while not in states. When the Scramble for Africa began (see p30), South Africa and Algeria were the only areas of the continent settled by Europeans. By the time it concluded in 1914, only Ethiopia and Liberia remained unspared by a rush for land enthusiastically supported by Europe's missionary societies. As Archbishop Desmond Tutu, the Nobel Prize winner, jokes: 'When whites arrived in South Africa, they had the Bible and the blacks had the land. The whites told the blacks to close their eye and pray. When they opened their eyes, they had the Bible and the whites had the land.'

By introducing the monetary economy, colonialism effectively propelled rural communities into the industrialised age. Alarmed by the implications of former Ghanaian leader Kwame Nkrumah's Pan-African credo, Africa's post-independence leaders attempted to set those artificial frontiers in stone in 1963 with the doctrine of *uti possidetis* (boundaries shall stay as they are). But much of Africa's postcolonial turmoil can be seen as a straining against them. In Somalia (which now contains unrecognised Somaliland and Puntland), Sudan, Congo and Cote d'Ivoire, the nation state is under pressure as never before.

The scramble's other poisonous gift was to fix the continent's gaze towards the West. Under colonialism, Africa's economic role was to provide Western markets with primary commodities for processing elsewhere. Railways and roads were designed to link the interior with coastal ports, not African nations with their neighbours. Today, it is still easier to fly from Zambia to Britain, from Togo to France, than it is to travel east–west across Africa. For Frantz Fanon, that orientation formed the basis of a morale-sapping inferiority complex. 'What is often called the black soul is a white man's artefact', he wrote. If true, it may explain why 70,000 of Africa's brightest head abroad each year to join the diaspora, or why 40% of African savings are held outside the continent. Even today, despite attempts by writers such as Chinua Achebe and Ngugi Wa Thiongo to re-establish a proud African

Martin Meredith's *The State of Africa* is a clear and concise run-through of Africa's post-independence history, taking the reader from colonial withdrawal up to the present day.

identity, Africans often seem more interested in the antics of their former colonial masters than in events across the border.

COLD WAR INTERFERENCE

Africa had barely extricated itself from colonialism when it was bound in an even tighter straitjacket. Drained by WWII, Europe's powers withdrew from their colonies, only to see their place taken by the superpowers of the US and the Soviet Union, whose behaviour would be dictated by the principle of 'my enemy's enemy is my friend'. Fighting a proxy third world war, both countries plotted the assassination of elected African leaders (Patrice Lumumba being the most infamous example), funded dictators such as Zaïre's Mobutu Sese Seko and Ethiopia's Mengistu Haile Mariam, and supported atrocity-prone rebel movements like the National Union for the Total Independence of Angola (UNITA) and Namibia's South West Africa People's Organization (SWATO). The massive arming of Africa that resulted – Mengistu, for example, received at least US$9 billion in Soviet hardware – transformed the nature of conflict. It also taught a generation of leaders that, as long as they sang the appropriate ideological tune, applications for World Bank and IMF loans (in the case of the pro-US contingent) and Warsaw Pact funding (in the case of the pro-Communists) would be regarded favourably. 'The Cold War,' wrote Ryszard Kapuściński, 'was one of the most disgraceful pages in contemporary history, and everyone ought to be ashamed.'

Angola, Congo and the Horn of Africa probably bear the deepest scars of this cynicism, which encouraged a numb passivity amongst citizens who realised the future would be decided not by them, but in Washington and Moscow. While perestroika eventually concentrated the minds of South Africa's white rulers, helping to pave the way for Nelson Mandela's release, many of the continent's worst despots succeeded in clinging to power despite the shrivelling of superpower support. The danger today is that, after a period in which good governance topped foreign donors' agendas, Washington's campaign against Islamic extremism has become the new conditionality. Somalia has become the latest glaring example of Vietnam-style 'blowback', with US policy tending to exacerbate the very extremism it fears by propping up a barely credible transitional government.

HOPES & FEARS

Barack Obama's inauguration sent a wave of tearful jubilation across Africa, where he is seen as a local boy done good. But despite expectations that the US will source a quarter of its oil there by 2015, and the establishment of Africom, a military command dedicated to the continent, the bond with the US will arguably not be the one that matters. The key relationship will be with China, an economic behemoth hungry for Africa's minerals, oil and timbers. Beijing's readiness to provide much-needed infrastructure, which Western aid doesn't cover and local governments cannot afford, is already having a transformative impact. Bilateral trade has multiplied 50-fold since the 1980s, over 900 Chinese companies already operate on African soil and nearly a million Chinese live on the continent. China's arrival holds out the potential of a Pax Sinica, as African nation states are finally linked together by modern infrastructure. But sceptics warn that Beijing's relationship with Africa often bears a depressing resemblance to those of the colonial era, despite all the talk of fresh paradigms. Crowing at the prospect of 'no-strings-attached' loans, African governments have sold assets cheaply, signing deals that leave their workforces twiddling their thumbs and undermining local manufacturing.

The Western media largely missed the fact that more than 30 African countries grew at a rate of 4% or more in 2006 and 2007, the greatest expansion of

The Scramble for Africa, by Thomas Pakenham, is a wHopping doorstop of a book. But it's also a great, scintillating read, full of ruthless and eccentric characters, tracing the European greed for territory that shaped today's continent.

global wealth in history. Africa's very underdevelopment initially seemed to shield it from the impact of the international credit crunch, but by the end of the decade, shrinking remittances from the diaspora, cuts in exports and falls in tourism earnings had taken a measurable toll. Above all, the global economic crisis threatens to dry up the generosity of industrialised nations, who have already proved reluctant to fulfil pledges made at Gleneagles. With more and more African thinkers stepping forward to voice their disquiet over aid dependency and many of the administrations once deemed 'donor darlings' showing their authoritarian colours, compassion fatigue is in the air. The 'give us your money'–type messages broadcast in the 1980s and '90s by the likes of Bob Geldof and Bono seem, in retrospect, naively simplistic. Even the rock stars now temper their message with calls for good governance and warnings about corruption. The irony is that just when low-income countries could most do with help – the World Bank estimates the financial crisis jeopardises US$11.6 billion of core spending in education, health and social protection– they are least likely to get it.

Another surprise for Westerners is the revelation that Africa, at the turn of the century, was becoming a far less lethal place to live. Statistics showed that the popular image of the continent as constantly prey to war, pillage and rape was less and less rooted in reality. The Human Security Centre in British Columbia found that, between 1999 and 2006, the number of state-based armed conflicts dropped by 46%, while those between rebel groups fell by 54%. The annual number of deaths in battle actually diminished by two-thirds between 2002 and 2006. Sadly, this encouraging trend recently appears to have ended and policymakers rightly fret about the likely explosion of a new war between south and north Sudan, the total fragmentation of Somalia, a crisis in Ethiopia and the possible implosion of Kenya and Nigeria, knowing all the while that Africa's worst horrors usually come as complete surprises.

> Like iron filings around a magnet, the intellectual debate over aid has polarised around two figures, arguing that only massive injections of cash can jumpstart Africa, stands US economist Jeffrey Sachs. On the other, convinced aid corrupts and emasculates her continent, stands Zambian Dambisa Moyo.

But it may well be that the greatest threat to African livelihoods comes from the global environmental crisis. Sir Nicholas Stern's 2005 report on climate change pointed to Africa as likely to pay an unfairly high price for the West's carbon footprint, and many would say that the evidence is already visible on the ground. Temperatures in southern and northern Africa, Stern predicted, would rise by almost double the global average, causing severe water shortages. His vision of an increasingly sick continent, with malaria, dengue fever and cholera all set to spread, has huge implications for the rest of the world, as it also predicts massive population movements. Nobel prize winner Norman Borlaug, credited with Asia's green revolution, died with his ambition of engineering the same boost in crop yields in Africa still unfulfilled. It will take more than the adoption of genetically modified crops to bring that about.

For newcomers, perhaps the best advice they can heed is to resist the insidious notion that they are somehow duty-bound to rescue Africa from itself. It is ironic that a continent that has had so much harm done to it by outsiders is so often perceived as demanding some form of moral reaction from its visitors.

The truth is that Africa's future will be decided not by outsiders but by its own citizens. Extending feelers across the continent, South Africa's business-people are bringing new dynamism to industries shackled by state intervention and graft. The continent's vast, supremely well-qualified diaspora awaits the moment when its talents can be put to use back home. Terrifyingly, yet exhilaratingly, more than half Africa's population is under the age of 17. Urbanised, ill-at-ease with the ethnic loyalties of yesteryear, harbouring little respect for the leaders who sabotaged Africa's independence, and familiar with the spreadsheet, podcast and MP3 player, they currently have no say over the continent's direction. When that changes, Africa will find its way.

North Africa

Separated from the rest of Africa by the Sahara, the world's largest hot desert, North Africa is at once a world apart and the continent's bridge between Europe and the Middle East. The great civilisations of the Mediterranean and, later, Islam all left their mark here and from this stirring geographical and historical story come North Africa's most alluring attractions.

Nowhere else in Africa do the sophisticated cities of antiquity survive with such grace and splendour. The glories of ancient Egypt are the most famous, but extraordinary Roman and Greek cities are found all along the North African coast and its hinterland, while remote pyramids peer out from beneath the sand in Sudan.

The sound of North Africa is also the muezzin's call to prayer ringing out across ancient cities that have changed little in centuries. Whether in Marrakesh, Fez, Algiers, Tripoli or Cairo, you'll find yourself surrounded by the best of Arab-Islamic culture, from the soaring mosques and exquisite architecture to the warm hospitality for which the region is famous.

But visiting North Africa is also about epic natural landscapes. In the Sahara there are vast sand seas, desert massifs of rare beauty, and oasis towns that bring life to the great emptiness. The Sahara in Algeria and Libya is the stuff of dreams, while more accessible desert expeditions are possible in Egypt, Tunisia and Morocco. In the last, you can drop down from the epic Atlas Mountains, with their fortress-studded valleys, into the dunes that stretch deep into Africa.

And one final word of warning: if you plan to travel across North Africa, you'll need to plan carefully. Obtaining visas can be complicated for Libya, Algeria and Sudan, and some sections of northern Algeria may be off limits, so be prepared to fly some legs of your journey.

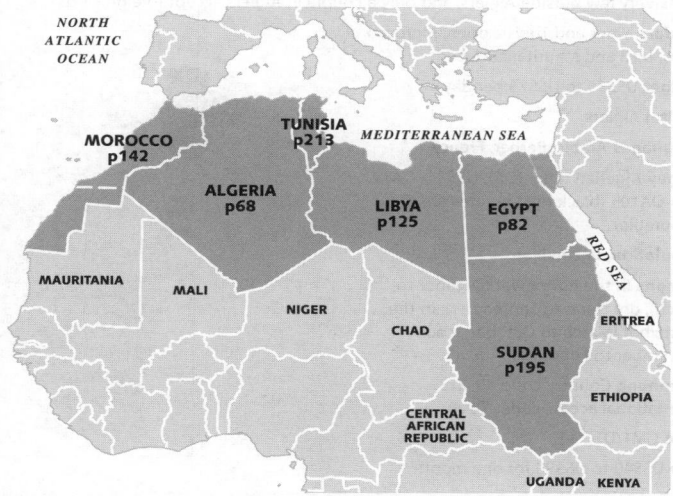

Algeria

Some of Africa's most exciting travel experiences await you in the sands of Algeria, just a short hop from Europe. The North African nation is once again welcoming independent travellers to its myriad sights, having spent the last 20 years being largely off limits due to a brutal civil war in the 1990s and subsequent problems of violence and kidnapping. Now again considered safe, Algeria is an incredible destination where tourists still remain a novelty and almost anywhere is off the beaten path.

Africa's second-largest country has attractions as varied as they are pristine. The capital, Algiers, is one of North Africa's most charismatic cities, a mix of colonial French and modern socialist architecture, with an ancient medina at its heart. The north of the country also offers some stunning Roman cities, including Djemila, where you're likely to be one of the only visitors. But the country's trump card is its Saharan region: the largest slice of the world's greatest desert is contained within Algeria's borders. Whether you skirt the sand seas in the ancient towns of Ghardaïa, or plunge headlong into its depths in the Saharan 'capital' of Tamanrasset, the Algerian Sahara offers arguably the best desert landscapes on earth.

While Algeria's tourist infrastructure remains fairly basic, it's still a breeze to get around compared with much of the rest of Africa. Affordable flights connect you to everywhere in the country, the road network is well maintained and infrastructure is decades ahead of its southern neighbours. For accessible adventure, unforgettable vistas and a taste of the Maghreb without the tour groups of Morocco, head for Algeria now.

FAST FACTS

- **Area** 2.3 million sq km
- **ATMs** Very few outside Algiers, and only a couple in Algiers accept foreign cards
- **Borders** Niger and Tunisia open; Morocco, Libya, Mali and Mauritania closed
- **Budget** US$35 to US$75 per day
- **Capital** Algiers
- **Languages** Arabic, Berber, French
- **Money** Algerian dinar (DA); US$1 = DA72, €1 = DA105 (black market rates are more favourable)
- **Population** 34.2 million
- **Seasons** In the north: wet (October to March), dry (June to September); in the south: hot (March to October), cool (November to February)
- **Telephone** Country code ☎ 213; international access code ☎ 00
- **Time** GMT/UTC +1
- **Visa** US$40 to US$90 for one month

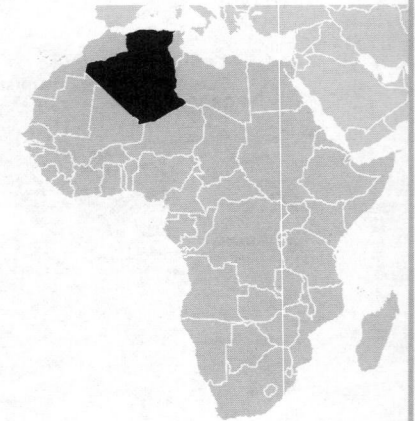

HOW MUCH?

- **Cup of tea** DA50
- **Newspaper** DA100
- **Antique tin box** DA300
- **Large quality carpet** from DA12,000
- **Tuareg taguelmoust** DA400

LONELY PLANET INDEX

- **1L petrol** DA110
- **1L bottled water** DA25
- **Bottle of beer** DA150
- **Souvenir T-shirt** DA300
- **Shared taxi in Algiers** DA100

HIGHLIGHTS

- **Algiers** (p72) Modern and traditional Algeria meet in 'la Blanche' – the country's fascinating capital.
- **The Algerian Sahara** (p77) Sleep under the stars in the Tassili du Hoggar and see some of the world's greatest desert scenery.
- **Assekrem** (p77) Watch the sun set beyond a sea of mountains, before getting up to see the sun rise again.
- **Ghardaïa** (p76) Bargain for a technicolour carpet, before peeking inside the ancient Muslim town of Beni Isguen.

CLIMATE & WHEN TO GO

Algeria has a Mediterranean climate along the coast, with mild, wet winters, and hot, dry summers. The coastal area is best visited in spring and summer months. The Sahara desert has famously ferocious summer temperatures, so visiting this part of Algeria is best done between late autumn and early spring (November to April). Despite daytime temperatures seldom falling below 25°C, desert nights can be cold, even in the height of summer. Rainfall ranges from more than 1000mm per year in the northern mountains, to zero in the Sahara. Some places go decades without a drop.

ITINERARIES

- **One Week** Fly to Algiers (p72) for a couple of nights to explore the chaotic capital before flying south to Tamanrasset (p77) for a desert expedition trip, sleeping under the stars for five days and taking in Assekrem (p77) and the Tassili du Hoggar.
- **Two Weeks** Follow the one-week itinerary, then fly on from Tamanrasset to Ghardaïa (p76), where you can take in the beauties of this ancient town in one day, with its market, colourful carpets and the daily souq (market), then visit the nearby ultraconservative town of Beni Isguen (p76), where women only ever expose one eye. Back in Algiers, make an overnight trip to Djemila (p76), and a day trip to Tipaza (p76).

HISTORY

The modern state of Algeria is a relatively recent creation. The name was coined by the Ottoman Turks in the 16th century to describe the territory controlled by the regency of Algiers – initially a Turkish colony. The regency broke free of the Ottoman Empire and founded a military republic of unusual stability. This endured almost 300 years until spurious diplomatic problems prompted the French to invade in the 19th century.

The Barbary Coast

Before the arrival of the French, Algeria was known to Europeans as the Barbary (a corruption of Berber) Coast, whose notorious pirates preyed on Christian shipping. The dreaded Khayr al-Din, going under the chilling pseudonym of Barbarossa, was the first regent of Algiers during this period, and at one point held no fewer than 25,000 Christians captive in the city. Piracy sent shivers down many a spine until the US Navy defeated a Barbary fleet off Algiers in 1815. Despite this, the feared pirates were not entirely beaten until the French attacked Algiers in 1830 and forced the ruling *dey* (commander or governor) to capitulate. It took another 41 years for total French domination of the country.

The main opposition came from Emir Abdelkader, ruler of western and central inland Algeria and the great hero of Algeria's nationalist movement. His forces resisted the French for almost six years before they were defeated near Oujda in 1844. Abdelkader himself finally surrendered in 1846 and

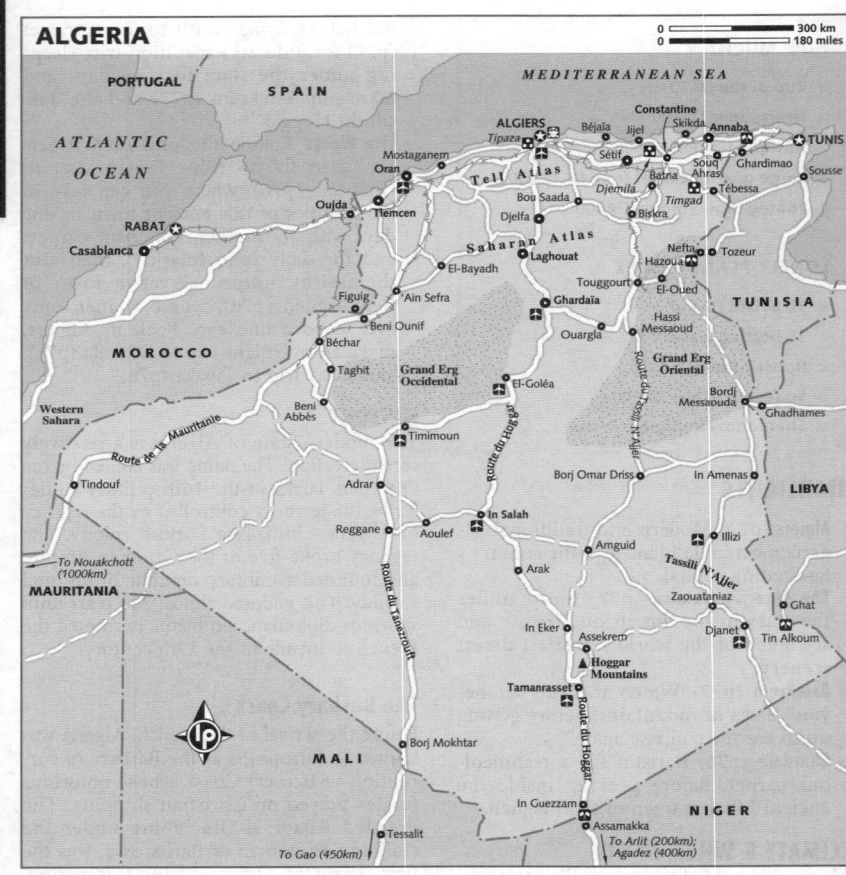

spent the rest of his life in exile. He died in Damascus in 1883.

French Rule

The French colonial authorities set about changing the face of Algeria by eliminating anything that was previously thought of as Algerian: local culture was destroyed, mosques were converted into churches and the old medinas were pulled down and replaced with streets laid out in neat grids. The greatest symbol of the change was the conversion of the Great Mosque of Algiers to the Cathedral of St Philippe. The French also distributed large parts of prime farming land to European settlers (known as *pieds-noirs*) – Italian, Maltese and Spanish families as well as French.

Algeria's war of independence, led by the newly formed Front de Libération Nationale (FLN; National Liberation Front), began on 31 October 1954 in Batna, east of Algiers. The fighting lasted seven years, with terror campaigns led by both native Algerians and *pied-noir* settlers, costing at least a million Algerian lives. The French president, Charles de Gaulle, aware of the impossibility of continued French rule, agreed to a referendum on independence in March 1962. The result was a resounding six million in favour and only 16,000 against. Independence was declared on 5 July 1962.

Socialism & Democracy

FLN candidate Ahmed ben Bella, who robbed a bank to fund a revolutionary group, became

Algeria's first president. He pledged to create a 'revolutionary Arab-Islamic state based on the principles of socialism and collective leadership at home and anti-imperialism abroad'. He was quickly overthrown in 1965 by former colleague Colonel Houari Boumédienne, who effectively returned the country to military rule.

Boumédienne's emphasis on industrial development at the expense of the agricultural sector was to have a major impact in later years, when the country became heavily dependent on food imports and migrant workers. Boumédienne died in December 1978 and the FLN replaced him with Colonel Chadli Benjedid, who was re-elected in 1984 and 1989.

There was very little political change under Boumédienne and Chadli. The FLN was the sole political party, pursuing basically secular, socialist policies. There was little evidence of opposition until October 1988, when thousands of people took to the streets in protest against government austerity measures and food shortages. The army was called in to restore order, and between 160 and 600 people were killed.

The government reacted by pledging to relax the FLN monopoly on political power and work towards a multiparty system. The extent of the opposition became clear at local government elections held in early 1990, which produced landslide victories for the previously outlawed fundamentalist group Front Islamique du Salut (FIS; Islamic Salvation Front).

The initial round of Algeria's first multiparty parliamentary elections, held in December 1991, produced another landslide win for the FIS. The FLN was left looking like a political irrelevance, taking only 15 of the 231 seats. Chadli's apparent acceptance of this prompted the army to step in, replacing the president with a five-person Haut Conseil d'Etat (HCE; High Council of State) headed by Mohammed Boudiaf, a former leader of the Algerian revolution. The second round of elections was cancelled, and FIS leaders Abbas Madani and Ali Belhadj were arrested, while others fled into exile.

Civil War

Boudiaf lasted six months before he was assassinated amid signs of a growing guerrilla offensive led by the Groupe Islamique Armé (GIA; Armed Islamic Group). He was replaced by former FLN hardliner Ali Kafi,

---

WARNING

While Algeria is now generally a safe country for independent travel, check the latest situation before finalising your itinerary. At the time of writing only one area was still considered unsafe to travel in – the Kabylie region in the country's northwest, although for this book we visited Djemila by car from Algiers with no problems. By law in Algeria, all travel to the desert needs to be done with an official guide, and as such it's very safe these days, as guides will avoid areas where problems might arise.

---

who oversaw the country's rapid descent into civil war before he was replaced by a retired general, Liamine Zéroual, in January 1994. Zéroual attempted to defuse the situation by holding fresh elections in 1995, but Islamic parties were barred from the poll and Zéroual's sweeping victory came amid widespread claims of fraud.

Hopes for peace went unfulfilled; instead, the war became even more brutal, with Amnesty International accusing both sides of massacres and war atrocities. The GIA, angered by French aid to the government, extended the war to French soil with a series of bombings and hijackings.

Eventually, government security forces began to gain the upper hand, and at the beginning of 1999 Zéroual announced that he would be stepping down. New elections held in April that year resulted in a controversial victory for the establishment candidate Abdelaziz Bouteflika, a former foreign minister, who was elected unopposed after the rest of the candidates in the field claimed fraud and withdrew.

Bouteflika moved quickly to establish his legitimacy by calling a referendum on a plan to offer amnesty to the rebels. War-weary Algerians responded overwhelmingly with a 98% 'yes' vote, and by the end of 1999 many groups had responded and laid down their weapons. However, elements within the GIA remained defiant, and, in an attempt to derail the peace process, were the key suspects in the October 1999 assassination of FIS leader Abdelkader Hachani.

Algeria Today

In April 2004, Bouteflika secured a second landslide election victory and promised to seek a 'true national reconciliation' during his second term. The military – traditionally a key player in Algerian politics – pledged neutrality during the poll. January 2005 saw the government make a deal with Berber leaders, promising more investment in the Kabylie region and enhanced recognition of Tamazight dialect. A referendum for reconciliation was held in September 2005, with voters supporting the government's plans to give amnesty to many of those involved in the 1990s conflict, and a six-month period of amnesty began in March 2006. According to the reconciliation plan, fugitive militants who surrendered were to be pardoned, except for those guilty of the most serious of crimes, and some jailed Islamic militants were set free during the first part of the year. Despite the 'yes' vote at the referendum, many relatives of the victims killed in the civil war continue to ask for those involved in the killings to be tried at the national courts and for war crimes to be investigated.

Bouteflika was again returned to power in 2009 with a large majority, having managed to change the country's constitution to allow him a third five-year term. While opposition groups (many of whom boycotted the election in protest at the constitutional change) criticised the amendment, the powerbrokers in Algiers, not to mention the population at large, seem generally content with the status quo, preferring Bouteflika's ability to deliver peace, national unity and some form of development to the nightmare of violence and anarchy that until so recently was everyday life in Algeria.

CULTURE

An estimated 99% of Algeria's population are Sunni Muslims; the majority are ethnically Arab-Berber and live in the north of the country. Berber traditions are best preserved in the Kabylie region, east of Algiers, where people speak the local Berber (Tamazight) dialect as their first language, Arabic as their second and French as their third. After sustained protests and rioting, Berber was finally recognised as an official language in 2002. The Tuareg people of the Sahara are also Berbers but speak their own tribal language, Tamashek.

The most interesting traditional crafts are those of the southern Saharan Tuareg, who are known for their intricate leatherwork and silver jewellery. In the north of Algeria, as in Morocco, carpets are big business (par-

ticularly in Ghardaïa), but because there's less tourist custom the selling process is much less pressured.

Music is a big part of life here too, and few road journeys are complete without a constant accompaniment of distinctive wailing vocals. Algeria's contribution to world music culture is rai, a genre that started out as subversive underground protest pop and has now spread around the Arab world. A notable rai star is the excellent Cheb Mami. Egyptian pop is also massively popular.

As very few people depend on tourism for their income, the constant Moroccan-style street hassle you might expect to find in Algeria is very rare – anyone who does accost you will usually be genuinely interested in where you come from and what you're doing. Invitations to tea can be regarded with far less suspicion than elsewhere!

ENVIRONMENT

Algeria is Africa's second-largest country after Sudan. About 85% of the country is taken up by the Sahara, and the mountainous Tell region in the north makes up the balance.

The Tell consists of two main mountain ranges: the Tell Atlas, which runs right along the north coast into Tunisia, and the Saharan Atlas, about 100km to the south. The area between the two ranges is known as the High Plateaus. The Sahara covers a great range of landscapes, from the classic S-dunes of the great ergs (sand seas) to the rock-strewn peaks of the Hoggar Mountains in the far south.

ALGIERS

☎ 021 / pop 3.6 million

Algiers (Al-Jazaïr) will impress anyone who visits with its sheer geography. The precipitous city tumbles down steep hillsides onto the giant Bay of Algiers, and is always alive with bright lights and noisy traffic. The Algerian capital is a mix of tradition and modernism, reflecting the country's colonial past in its wide boulevards and elegant white and blue French houses, while keeping its traditional heart hidden deep inside the maze of the medina. It's a city of steps and labyrinthine uphill streets, with fezzed old men watching the changing world go by, as youngsters stroll, comfortable with their modern attire and lifestyle. Most points of interest are found in and around the medina, and wandering through this part of the city is a lovely experience, although you should exercise caution at night. Though most people spend just enough time in Algiers to organise their onward journey, it's a fascinating city well worth a couple of days' exploration.

ORIENTATION

The harbour is an obvious landmark; four main streets run parallel to the waterfront, changing names every 500m or so. The medina lies between Blvd de la Victoire and Rue Ahmed Bouzrina.

INFORMATION

There are banks all over the city centre, but almost none have international ATMs, so cash or travellers cheques are the best way to go. One ATM that works for international credit cards is in the lobby of the Hôtel el-Aurassi. For medical emergencies, call ☎ 115. You'll need good French and/or Arabic to get medical help here.

Cyber Casbah (Rue Aoua Abdelkader; ☼ 10am-midnight) Internet access per hr DA60.

Fire ☎ 14

Main post office (Pl de la Grande Poste)

MSN Cyber Café (Rue Kheldoun Khaled; internet access per hr DA60; ☼ 10am-1am) Basement web cafe.

ONT (Office National du Tourisme; ☎ 71 29 81; www.ont-dz.com; 2 Smail Kerrar; ☼ 8am-4.30pm Sat-Wed) Friendly staff speak English here, and can help with booking tours in the Sahara.

Police ☎ 17

Telephone office (cnr Rue Asselah Hocine & Blvd Colonel Amirouche) A block from the post office.

SIGHTS

Algiers is rather short on sights – much of the enjoyment to be had here comes from wandering the steep streets, strolling in the parks and taking in the numerous views over the Bay of Algiers. That said, there's plenty to keep you busy for a day or two.

The heart of the city is its ancient Casbah, a steep and narrow maze of streets just west of the Pl des Martyrs. Inside you'll see several magnificent **Turkish palaces**, most of which are concentrated around the **Ketchaoua Mosque** at the end of Rue Ahmed Bouzrina; the finest is the **Dar Hassan Pacha** palace (no admission to the interior). Above the medina is the city's **Citadel**, currently undergoing major renovation works and therefore closed to visitors,

though it's still possible to wander around its rambling exterior, just follow the streets up the hillside from the medina.

The distinctive abstract monolith that dominates the skyline south of the centre is the **Martyrs' Monument**, opened in 1982 on the 20th anniversary of Algeria's independence. There are some great views over the city from here, though little else to do. The museum under the monument houses an exhibit of martyrs to the cause of Algerian independence, but will be of little interest to most visitors.

A second landmark is the enormous, modernist **Hôtel el-Aurassi** that overlooks the city centre proudly from the hillside above and will usually incite either love or hatred in anyone who sees it.

The city's best museum is the **Bardo Museum of Prehistory & Ethnography** (☎ 74 76 41; www.musee-bardo.art.dz; 3 Ave FD Roosevelt; adult/child DA20/10; ☼ 9am-noon & 2-5pm Sun-Thu, 2-5pm Sat) where the collection runs from a superb display of fossils to Neolithic pottery, rock carvings and paintings from the Sahara. There's also a more modern collection, showcasing mosaics and furniture.

The iconic **Notre Dame d'Afrique** (☼ 11am-12.30pm & 3-5.30pm) is one of the city's most famous buildings, a Catholic church that still celebrates mass at 6pm daily, despite the dwindling number of Catholics in Algiers since independence. It was being restored at the time of writing, but was still open to visitors who flock here for the incredible interior, striking neo-Byzantine basilica and great views from the summit of a cliff overlooking the capital. Take a taxi here from the city centre, as it's hard to get to otherwise – the cable car from the sea front was not working at the time of research.

SLEEPING

Cheap accommodation can be found around Pl Port Said on the edge of the medina, though the pickings on offer are fairly insalubrious in most cases. Hotel beds can be hard to find at the last minute, so it's well worth booking ahead.

Budget

Hôtel Terminus (☎ 73 78 17; 2 Rue Rachid Ksentini; s from DA1000-2000, d DA1800-3500) Excellently located in the heart of the city, the Terminus is just moments from the train station. Rooms vary

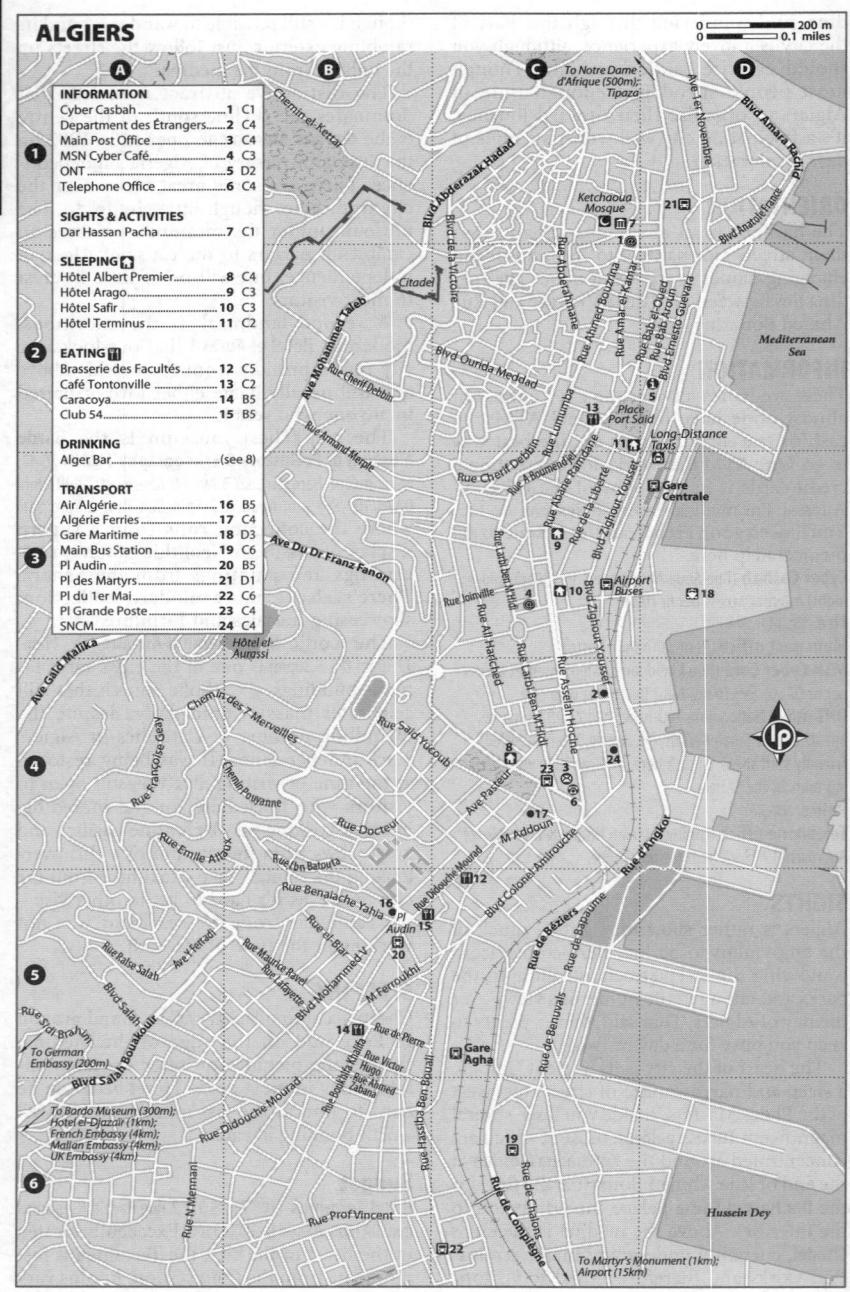

ALGIERS

| 0 | 200 m |
| 0 | 0.1 miles |

INFORMATION
Cyber Casbah..........................1 C1
Department des Étrangers......2 C4
Main Post Office.....................3 C4
MSN Cyber Café......................4 C3
ONT...5 D2
Telephone Office....................6 C4

SIGHTS & ACTIVITIES
Dar Hassan Pacha...................7 C1

SLEEPING
Hôtel Albert Premier...............8 C4
Hôtel Arago.............................9 C3
Hôtel Safir.............................10 C3
Hôtel Terminus.....................11 C2

EATING
Brasserie des Facultés..........12 C5
Café Tontonville...................13 C2
Caracoya..............................14 B5
Club 54.................................15 B5

DRINKING
Alger Bar..........................(see 8)

TRANSPORT
Air Algérie...........................16 B5
Algérie Ferries.....................17 C4
Gare Maritime......................18 D3
Main Bus Station.................19 C6
Pl Audin...............................20 B5
Pl des Martyrs......................21 D1
Pl du 1er Mai.......................22 C6
Pl Grande Poste...................23 C4
SNCM...................................24 C4

Mediterranean Sea

Hussein Dey

To Notre Dame d'Afrique (500m); Tipaza

To German Embassy (200m)

To Bardo Museum (300m); Hôtel el-Djazaïr (1km); French Embassy (4km); Malian Embassy (4km); UK Embassy (4km)

To Martyr's Monument (1km); Airport (15km)

enormously from windowless boxes with shared facilities to rooms with good views and private bathrooms.

Hôtel Arago (☎ 73 94 95; Rue Haffaf Nafaa; s DA1000-1300, d DA2100-2400) Handily located, this place could be great – the rooms are large and many have balconies and original features such as ceiling mouldings and marble fireplaces. Sadly, though, the rooms are rather rundown and the bathrooms are not properly closed off from the rest of the room. Despite this, it's an OK deal.

Midrange

Hôtel Albert Premier (☎ 73 65 06, 73 74 41; hotelalbert@yahoo.fr; 5 Ave Pasteur; s from DA4580, d from 5310; P 🕸 🎧) This white colonial building oozes history and charm – from the outside at least. The rooms are less exciting, but still good value, in the heart of the city and equipped with free wireless. Book ahead.

Hôtel Safir (☎ 73 50 40; safirhot@yahoo.fr; 2 Rue Asselah Hocine; s from DA5300, d from 5950; P 🕸 🎧) This large, functional hotel in the centre of Algiers has great views of the harbour from many rooms, and is generally a comfortable place to stay, though some of the older rooms are in need of a renovation. There's free wireless.

Top End

Hôtel el-Djazaïr (☎ 69 21 21, 23 09 33; www.hoteleldjazair.dz; 24 Ave Souidani Boudjemma; s/d DA19,500/21,500; 🕸 🖫 🖳) This classic old five-star hotel may live more off its past glories than its present reality (Kipling, Gide, Churchill and Eisenhower are all former guests, while it's actually more like a good three-star hotel today), but there's no denying the place has charm. There are four restaurants, a bar, a nightclub, a pool and sports facilities. This is definitely the place to go for an atmospheric stay.

EATING & DRINKING

There's no shortage of eateries around town, and you'll find cheap fast food on every corner, good pastries at the ubiquitous bakeries and plenty of fresh produce on sale in shops and at markets.

Café Tontonville (☎ 74 86 61; 7 Pl Port Said; mains DA150-250) This Algiers institution is a great place for breakfast and coffee on the terrace, or for a full meal. The thin-crust pizza is excellent, and more elaborate dishes are available inside the restaurant proper.

Club 54 (Rue Didouche Mourad; mains DA250-500; 🕑 7am-9pm Sun-Thu) This is a great place for lunch or dinner with the young and trendy of Algiers. Pizzas, grills, salads and soups are served up in a modern two-floor venue with cosy booths and friendly service. There's no alcohol.

Brasserie des Facultés (☎ 64 40 53; 1 Rue Didouche Mourad; mains DA1000) This excellent place offers superb meals in cosy premises on Algiers' main drag. Good service, top-quality seafood and a good selection of Algerian wine make this one of our favourite eateries in the city.

Caracoya (☎ 73 39 44; 3 Rue de Pierre; mains DA1000-1500; 🕑 noon-3pm & 7-11pm Sat-Thu, 7-11pm Fri) This curious place feels like a bit of a step back in time with its bow-tied waiters, panelled rooms and formal service. But the food is excellent, with a wonderful selection of freshly caught fish and well-realised French cuisine paired with a large wine list.

Algiers is not a hard place to find a drink, although bars are rarely a pleasant experience. Both Brasserie des Facultés and Caracoya serve alcohol, as does the bar at the Hôtel el-Djazaïr. Less refined options include **Alger Bar** (1 Ave Pasteur) in the city centre.

GETTING THERE & AWAY
Air

Air Algérie (☎ 74 24 28, 65 33 40; www.airalgerie.dz; 1 Pl Maurice Audin) covers destinations throughout the country. Routes include Tamanrasset (DA28,000 return, 2½ hours, daily) and Ghardaïa (DA9500 return, one hour, daily).

From the airport there are regular buses into town (DA50), but it's better to take a private taxi (DA1000). Spaces in shared taxis into town cost DA400.

Bus

The main intercity bus station is south of Pl Grande Poste on Rue de Compiègne. For some prices for internal bus routes, see p80.

Train

The Algiers **train station** (☎ 71 15 10) is on the lower level of the waterfront. Surviving services include Oran (DA900, six hours, four daily) and Constantine (DA940, 6½ hours, two daily).

GETTING AROUND

The four major city bus stations are at Pl des Martyrs, Pl Grande Poste, Pl Audin and Pl du 1er Mai.

There are taxis everywhere that can be hired by you alone, or shared (perfectly safe). Sample prices are DA400 per passenger to the airport from the city centre, or DA1000 for the entire car. Short trips across town cost DA100 (shared) or DA500 for the car.

NORTHERN ALGERIA

Northern Algeria's two stand-out attractions are the Roman cities of **Tipaza** (admission DA20; ☾ 9am-5pm), a short day trip from Algiers, and **Djemila** (admission DA20; ☾ 8am-5pm), a much larger and more impressive site adjacent to a small town of the same name in the stunning area around **Sétif**. To get to Tipaza, you can either take a bus for Tipaza or one to Cherchell and get off at Tipaza (1½ hours, DA150) from the *gare routière* at the Agha train station. A taxi one way will cost you DA1500. At Djemila, which is best reached by car or on a guided tour, it's necessary to spend the night due to its distance from Algiers. The rundown but friendly **Hôtel Belle Vue** (☎ 036-94 51 10, 070-92 05 29; r DA2000) is the best option for both bed and some food. It's right next to the **ruins** (☎ 036-94 51 01; adult/student DA20/10; ☾ 8am-5pm) that demand several hours of your time. Travelling to the ancient Roman settlement of **Timgad**, the country's most spectacular ruin, was considered unsafe at the time of writing, though this may change in the near future.

Other attractions in this area include **Oran**, the modern but fascinating port town made famous by Albert Camus; **Batna**, a charming town in an area known for its Roman ruins; and **Tlemcen**, the beautifully preserved gateway city for Morocco and former capital of the central Maghreb region. It's possible to fly (DA3700, four or five daily) or take the train (DA900, four daily) to Oran.

CENTRAL ALGERIA

Here you'll find the mysterious M'zab region, where life remains frozen in time. The M'zab region is home to a conservative Muslim sect known as the Ibadites, which broke from mainstream Islam some 900 years ago, and is, some say, a country unto itself. In the river valley of the Oued M'zab is Ghardaïa, a cluster of five towns –

Ghardaïa, Melika, Beni Isguen, Bou Noura and El-Ateuf.

GHARDAÏA
☎ 029 / pop 340,000

Ghardaïa is a collection of ancient towns whose sand-coloured houses enliven a long valley on the edge of the Sahara. The area is famous for its **carpets** and this is the best place to buy them in the country – head for the market square.

To enter Ghardaïa proper or the neighbouring town of **Beni Isguen**, you'll need to engage the services of a guide at the old town entrance and be dressed modestly. Here Islam is so rigorously enforced that local women, who are draped in white shawls from head to toe, are allowed to have only one eye showing (they apparently alternate the eye to keep their vision from weakening).

The best-value hotel in town is the midrange **Hôtel el Karama** (☎ 88 68 72, fax 88 32 84; Ave Ahmed Talbi; s/d DA2400/2800; ☒) near the bus station, which has 11 simple rooms with beautifully tiled walls and private bathrooms. The best budget option is the **Hôtel Atlantide** (☎ 83 29 21; Ave Ahmed Talbi; s/d DA1200/1800; ☒) on the same street, which was undergoing progressive renovation at the time of research. Don't miss the excellent **Restaurant Palmier** (☎ 83 92 89; Ave du 1er Novembre; ☾ noon-2pm & 7.30pm-midnight Sat-Thu; set meals DA1500) where you'll get some of the best food in the country (not to mention a drink!). A more affordable option is **Les Deux Palmiers** (Ave du 1er Novembre; ☾ 9am-9pm Sat-Thu; mains DA150-300).

Air Algérie flies from Ghardaïa to Algiers (one hour, daily) and Tamanrasset (2½ hours, several times a week). Regular buses run from Ghardaïa to Algiers (DA600, eight hours, 10 daily) and to Tamanrasset (DA2000, 20 hours, four daily).

SOUTHERN ALGERIA

Southern Algeria is taken up by the vast and stunning expanses of the Sahara and is by far the country's biggest drawcard. As well as the Saharan 'capital' Tamanrasset, home to a large Tuareg population, there's also **Djanet**, home to some of the best prehistoric rock art in the Sahara; and **Beni Abbès**, a springwatered town on an escarpment overlooking an oasis in the west of the country. This is also the area from which most desert trekking expeditions start.

TAMANRASSET
☎ 029 / pop 62,500

Tamanrasset is Algeria's dusty Saharan capital and is the gateway to exploring the fantastical landscapes of both Assekrem and the Tassili du Hoggar Mountains. As the last major town on the road south to Niger, Tam (as it's affectionately known) is a surprisingly busy place with plenty of modern amenities, including several banks, two Air Algérie offices, innumerable travel agencies (see p79) and an ONAT branch. The travel agencies and ONAT organise tours to Assekrem and the Tassili du Hoggar, costing anything between €50 and €100 per day depending on your numbers (note that nearly all agencies prefer to be paid in cash in euros), the time of year and type of trip you want. Almost everything can be found on the main street, Ave Emir Abdelkader and the main square, Pl du 1er Novembre.

Internet access is available at **Cyber Centre Tam** (per hr DA70; ☾ 8am-4am) and **Cyber Café Donia Soft** (per hr DA70; ☾ 10am-midnight), both on the main road. The consulates of Mali and Niger are next to each other on Rue Fougani, towards the southern end of town.

There are some good camping grounds and plenty of hotels in Tamanrasset. **Camping 4x4** (☎ 34 22 58; agence4x4tam@hotmail.com; campsites per person DA500, car/truck DA100/200, s/d DA1400/2300), near the village of Adriane, is popular with foreigners. It's a peaceful, decent place with basic facilities.

Hôtel Tinhinane (☎ 34 75 21, 73 43 85; Ave Emir Abdelkader; s DA500-2500, d DA800-3000; ☒) is a good choice if you want to stay in town, with a large selection of rooms ranging from extremely basic to perfectly comfortable, all housed in a pleasant courtyard hotel.

Head to the busy main street for food at any time of day. Our favourite place is **Restaurant Tassili** (Ave Emir Abdelkader; mains DA180; ☾ 7am-10pm), a friendly spot making a stab at interior design and serving up a large menu of Algerian food. The **Hôtel Tahat** (☎ 34 42 72; Ave Emir Abdelkader) and the Hôtel Bournane on the *oued* (dry river bed) have the only two bars in town.

Air Algérie flies between Tamanrasset and the major northern towns – Algiers, Oran, Constantine, Djanet and Ghardaïa. The French company **Point-Afrique** (www.point-afrique. com, in French) also has very convenient weekly flights to Paris and Marseille.

The bus station is on the road to the north of town. By bus it takes around 20 hours to Ghardaïa (DA2000), or 30 hours to Algiers (DA2500). For details of travelling to Niger from here, see p80.

ASSEKREM

Watching the sun set and rise across the sea of mountains from Assekrem, in the Hoggar range, is an unmissable Algerian experience. Assekrem is about 80km northeast of Tamanrasset, and hard to get to without your own vehicle. The many travel agencies in Tamanrasset operate tours to Assekrem, with some good deals available for groups. Expect to pay around €80 per person for the overnight trip including meals, accommodation and transport. There is a basic **refuge** (per person incl dinner & breakfast DA2000) here, where you can join in some fun card games or checkers with the Tuaregs. Take warm clothes; it gets chilly at night.

ALGERIA DIRECTORY

ACCOMMODATION

Hotels in Algeria tend to be either expensive state-run tourist hotels with good facilities, or cheap, rundown places intended for local visitors and budget travellers. There are some excellent campsites in the south, particularly in Tamanrasset.

BUSINESS HOURS

Most businesses in Algeria work approximately from 8am or 9am in the morning until 4pm or 5pm in the afternoon, Sunday to Thursday. While some businesses and most shops are open on Saturday, everything closes on Friday. While shops usually remain open all day in the north of the country, in the south businesses will usually close around midday and reopen from 4pm as people take to their shade during the heat of the day.

DANGERS & ANNOYANCES

Algeria has improved its safety immensely in recent years, but there's still every reason to exercise caution and check the latest information before finalising your itinerary. Foreigners are not usually targets of violence,

ALGERIA

PRACTICALITIES

■ Newspapers: El Khabar (www.elkhabar.com), private, Arabic-language daily; Le Quotidien d'Oran (www.lequotidien-oran.com), El Watan (www.elwatan.com), Liberté (www.liberte-algerie.com), La Tribune (www.latribune-online.com) are private, French-language dailies. French El Moudjahid (www.elmouudjahid.com) and Arabic Ech Chaab (www.ech-chaab.com) are state-run.

■ Algerian Radio (www.radioalgerie.dz) is operated by state-run Radio-Television Algerienne, and runs national Arabic, Berber and French networks and local stations; BBC World Service is available on shortwave (15485kHz and 12095kHz).

■ Enterprise Nationale de Television (ENTV) is the state-run TV station; BRTV is the Berber station, transmitted via satellite from France.

■ Electricity is 220V, with two-pin, European-style wall plugs.

■ Algeria uses the metric system.

---

but indiscriminate bombings have been common in the past, so vigilance is advised. Driving in the countryside is not advisable after dark, and at the time of writing the northwest Kabylie region was considered particularly unsafe.

Driving alone in the desert has been made illegal for travellers after some tourists were kidnapped there in 2003, so you'll need to travel with an officially accredited Algerian tour company to undertake any trips from Tamanrasset. The best way to get around is to travel by air – an affordable and well-run network of flights covers the entire country.

EMBASSIES & CONSULATES

Countries with diplomatic representation in Algiers include the following:

Canada (☎ (0)770 083 000; 18 rue Mustapha Khalef, Ben Aknoun) Also provides consular assistance to Australians.

France (☎ 98 17 17; www.ambafrance-dz.org; 25 Chemin Gadouche, Hydra)

Germany (☎ 741956, (0)770 880 023; 165 Chemin Sfindja)

Italy (☎ 92 25 50, 922330; 18 rue Ouidir Amellal, El-Biar)

Libya (☎ 92 15 02; 15 Chemin Cheikh Bachir el-Ibrahimi, El-Biar)

Mali (☎ 54 72 14; Cité DNC, Villa No 15, Hydra)

Mauritania (☎ 93 71 09; 107 Lot Baranès, Bouzaréah)

Morocco (☎ 69 14 08; 8 Rue des Cèdres, Parc de la Reine)

Niger (☎ 93 71 89; 54 Rue du Vercors)

Spain (☎ 92 27 13; 46 Bis rue Mohamed Chabane)

Tunisia (☎ 69 13 88; 11 rue du Bois de Bologne)

UK (☎ (0)770 085 000; 3 Chemin Capitaine Hocine Slimane, Hydra)

USA (☎ (0)770 082 000; 4 Chemin Cheikh Bachir Ibrahimi, El-Biar)

GAY & LESBIAN TRAVELLERS

Homosexual sex is illegal for both men and women in Algeria, and incurs a maximum penalty of three years in jail and a stiff fine. You're unlikely to have any problems as a tourist, but discretion is advised.

HOLIDAYS

Algeria observes Islamic holidays (p1140) as well as the following national holidays:
Labour Day 1 May
Revolutionary Readjustment (1965) 19 June
Independence Day 5 July
National Day (Revolution Day) 1 November

INTERNET ACCESS

Access is widely available, though connections vary. Prices are reasonable (around DA60–70 per hour).

MONEY

Some Algerians, especially in rural areas, might give prices in centimes rather than dinars (there are 100 centimes in a dinar). To confuse matters further, they might also drop the thousands, so a quote of '130' means 130,000 centimes (ie DA1300). Note that the black-market rate is significantly better than that you'll get at banks. Ask locals where to change (many shops in residential areas of Algiers offer this under-the-counter service). This is perfectly safe, though not officially legal. You can also change dinars back to euros or dollars on the black market, so don't get caught short with lots of dinars in your hand when you leave the country – there'll be nowhere to exchange them.

Travellers cheques are accepted in Algiers and other major towns; credit cards can be used only in big hotels and at car-hire companies. You'll need dinars for day-to-day expenses, although tourist-oriented businesses (hotels, airlines, tour companies etc) will often accept euros.

POST & TELEPHONE

The postal system in Algeria is very slow, so it's advisable to send mail from a major town. For anything important, use an international delivery service. International phone calls can be made from any of the public Taxiphone offices found in most towns. SIM cards for local networks can be bought for next to nothing and used to make calls from any unlocked handset.

TOURIST INFORMATION

Tourist offices can be found in many southern towns and are generally pretty helpful. The Algiers office of the state-run travel agency, **ONT** (Office National du Tourisme; Map p74; ☎ 021-71 29 81; www.ont-dz.com, in French; 2 Smail Kerrar; ☿ 8am-4.30pm Sat-Wed), organises excursions and is handy for lone travellers wanting to join a tour.

TRAVEL AGENCIES

Anyone wanting to visit the Sahara will need to organise a trip through a travel agency in Tamanrasset, which will then send an invitation to the country that you'll need to obtain your visa. There are many agencies in Tamanrasset, but the following are recommended.
Akar Akar (☎ 029-34 60 09; akarakartam@hotmail.com)
Hoggar Soleil (☎ 029-34 69 72; www.hoggarsoleil .com)
Tarakeft (☎ 029-34 20 07; www.tarakeft.com)

VISAS

Everyone except Moroccan and Tunisian nationals needs a visa to enter Algeria. Nationals of Israel, Malawi and Tunisia are not allowed into the country, and if you have a stamp in your passport from any of these countries your application might be rejected.

If you're getting an Algerian visa before leaving home, you need a letter from your employer or university to say you'll be coming back after your holiday, plus an 'invitation' to visit the country from an Algerian contact or tourist agency (the latter is available from several travel agencies in Tamanrasset). Getting a visa en route is usually pretty straightforward in Niger, Chad and Mali, though for anyone travelling to the Sahara you'll need a letter of invitation from your travel agency in Tamanrasset.

A 30-day visa costs anywhere between US$40 and US$90, with costs varying between embassies around the world and depending on your own nationality. Ideally, apply in plenty of time, as Algerian bureaucrats work slowly even by the standards of the region. Visas are not available at Algiers airport, or at any of the country's border posts.

Visa Extensions

Visa extensions can be obtained in Algiers from the **Department des Etrangers** (Map p74; 19A Blvd Zighout Youssef, Algiers) but are not easy to obtain.

Visas for Onward Travel

Visas for the following countries are available from embassies in Algiers (see opposite) and, in the case of Mali, a consulate in Tamanrasset. In general, though, Algiers isn't a great place to pick up visas for onward travel, simply as low tourist numbers mean that most embassies aren't used to dealing with tourist visa requests.
Mali One-month visas cost €10 to €20 depending on your nationality and are usually issued the same day. You'll need two photos.
Niger One-month visas are issued the same day, costing between US$35 and US$50. Three photos and three application forms are required. Note that in late 2009 the Niger consulate in Tamanrasset was no longer issuing visas to non-Algerians. This may change, however.

TRANSPORT IN ALGERIA

GETTING THERE & AWAY

Air

Air Algérie (Map p74; ☎ 021-74 24 28, 021-65 33 40; www.airalgerie.dz; 1 Pl Maurice Audin, Algiers) serves destinations throughout North and West Africa, including Tripoli (Libya), Casablanca (Morocco), Dakar (Senegal) and Bamako (Mali). It also flies daily to Paris, three times a week to London, two or three times weekly to Dubai and two to five times weekly to Germany. Other major European airlines, including Air France, Lufthansa and Iberia also have regular flights to Algiers from their respective hubs. Many tourists fly into Algeria on charter flights direct to Tamanrasset.

Land

LIBYA

The Libyan–Algerian border was closed at the time of writing and most travellers either fly between Algiers and Tripoli or cross overland via Tunisia.

MALI & MAURITANIA

Algeria's southwestern borders with Mali and Mauritania are currently closed to all traffic.

MOROCCO

The border with Morocco has been closed for some time due to ongoing political disputes, though it is possible to fly between the two countries.

NIGER

Travelling south into Niger is a bureaucratic and time-consuming route, but one that is still possible, though you'll need to be supported by a Tamanrasset travel agency. The official crossing point is between the sandy outposts of In Guezzam (Algeria) and Assamakka (Niger), on the main overland route from Tamanrasset to Agadez.

From Tamanrasset, trucks and battered old 4WDs run to the Algeria border post at In Guezzam (DA15,000 per vehicle, nine to 12 hours), where you can complete most formalities. From here you can hitch on a truck to the lonely checkpoint on the actual border and then to the chaotic Niger border post at Assamakka. Lifts on trucks between the border posts cost about DA500, but this is not uniform. From Assamakka, numerous trucks and 4WDs head to Arlit (CFA3000) and Agadez (CFA4000).

TUNISIA

There are numerous border-crossing points between Tunisia and Algeria, but the main one is just outside Hazoua on the route between El-Oued and Tozeur. This is used by *louages* (shared taxis), travellers driving their own vehicle and the odd overland truck.

Sea

It's possible to arrive in Algiers by ferry from Europe, though it's far from the cheapest option. The ferry terminal is near the main train station. The French company **SNCM** (Map p74; ☎ 021-71 81 15; 28 Blvd Zighout Youssef, Algiers) operates ferry services between Marseille and Algiers once a week, and less frequently to Alicante (Spain). **Algérie Ferries** (☎ 021-63 53 88; 6 Rue Khemisti, Algiers) connects Algiers to Marseille (twice a week) and Alicante (approximately twice a month). Tickets between Algiers and Marseille (the most common route) cost around DA32,500 for a seat, while a seat to Alicante costs DA21,050. The voyage to Marseille takes about 20 hours, and about 10 hours to Alicante.

GETTING AROUND
Air

Air Algérie (Map p74; ☎ 021-74 24 28, 021-65 33 40; www.airalgerie.dz; 1 Pl Maurice Audin, Algiers) offers extensive and reasonably priced domestic services. Popular domestic routes are from Algiers to Tamanrasset and Ghardaïa (see p75).

Bus

Long-distance buses are run by various regional companies, mainly in the north but also as far south as Tamanrasset. It's best to go to the bus station and buy your ticket at least a day ahead, as demand can be very high on less-frequently-serviced routes, such as those connecting remote Saharan towns. Fares include the following: Algiers to Tamanrasset (DA2500), Algiers to Ghardaïa (DA600), Ghardaïa to Tamanrasset (DA2000) and Ghardaïa to Timimoun (DA7200).

Car & Motorcycle

Driving around the Sahara by yourself has been illegal for tourists since 2003, so you'll need to hire a guide to drive your vehicle, or hire a guide with his own transport. You can easily rent a car in Algiers and drive around the north of country, though traffic is heavy and police checks frequent. Always check the latest security situation before heading off to the Kabylie region in Algeria's northwest, however.

Hitching

Independent travel in all parts of Algeria is risky because of the current political situation. However, the Sahara has long been a popular region for adventurers in their own vehicles, so backpackers have traditionally hitched rides. A great deal of patience is often required before securing a lift, especially now, as there are relatively few visitors. Most tourist vehicles are already full of passengers and kit, so drivers might be unwilling to take an extra load. You might be lucky, however, and meet a loner who's happy to offer a spare seat in return for help digging when the car gets stuck in the sand and possibly a contribution towards fuel.

The main route across the Sahara is the Route du Hoggar, which runs from Ghardaïa via El-Goléa and In Salah to Tamanrasset (and then on to the border and Arlit in Niger). The road is tar all the way to Tamanrasset. Other less-used roads include the eastern Route du Tassili N'Ajjer, which runs from Hassi Messaoud to Tamanrasset across the Grand Erg Oriental, and the Route du Tanezrouft, which runs from Adrar to Borj Mokhtar near the Mali border. The latter two routes include sections of sandy track (known as *piste* in all the Sahara countries).

Local Transport

Trucks and 4WDs carrying paying passengers are more common than buses as means of transport in the south. Prices for 4WD transport are negotiable, but you should figure on around DA2000 for a full day's driving (eg Tamanrasset to In Guezzam).

Louages operate only in the north of the country. They run when full and are more expensive than buses.

Train

The northern train line connects Oran, Algiers, Constantine and Annaba and is an efficient and fast way to get around. Additional lines run south from Oran to Béchar and from Constantine to Touggourt. International services, including to Tlemcen (for Morocco) and Tunis (Tunisia), were suspended at the time of research.

Egypt

A land of magnificent World Heritage Sites and a thousand tourist clichés, Egypt was enticing visitors millennia before Mr Thomas Cook sailed his first steamers up the Nile. It was in Egypt that the Holy Family sheltered, Alexander conquered and Mark Anthony flirted. Napoleon stopped long enough to pilfer a few obelisks, the Ottomans paused to prop up the great and barbarous pasha Mohammed Ali, and the British stayed around to get the train system running and furnish every spare nook of the British Museum. And all this was long, long after Menes united the two states of Upper and Lower Egypt, and set the stage for the greatest civilisation the world has ever known.

Lingering over coffee in one of Alexandria's cosmopolitan cafes or sipping a calming glass of *shai* (tea) after a frenzied shopping episode in Cairo's Khan al-Khalili are activities as popular today as they were back in the 19th century, when tourists started arriving en masse. Magnificent monuments are everywhere – the pointed perfection of the pyramids, the soaring minarets of Cairo's skyline and the majestic tombs and temples of Luxor are just a few of the wonders that generations of visitors have admired during their city sojourns, jaunts up and down the Nile and expeditions through spectacularly stark desert landscapes.

FAST FACTS

- **Area** 997,739 sq km
- **ATMs** In most large towns
- **Borders** Libya, Sudan, Israel and the Palestinian Territories
- **Budget** US$50 per day
- **Capital** Cairo
- **Language** Arabic
- **Money** Egyptian pound; US$1 = E£5.50, €1 = E£7.80
- **Population** 81.7 million
- **Seasons** Winter/high (October to April); summer/low (May to September)
- **Telephone** Country code ☎ 20; international access code ☎ 00
- **Time** GMT/UTC +2
- **Visa** Required for citizens of most countries

HOW MUCH?

- **Local newspaper** US$0.25 to US$0.50
- **Cup of tea** US$0.05
- **Small inlaid box** US$5
- **Camel ride** US$6 per hour
- **Museum admission** US$12

LONELY PLANET INDEX

- **1L petrol** US$1
- **1L bottled water** US$0.50 to US$0.75
- **Bottle of Stella** US$2 to US$3
- **Souvenir T-shirt** US$6 to US$8
- **Full sandwich** US$0.10

HIGHLIGHTS

- **Cairo** (p86) Witness life and death in epic proportions in this timeless city of pyramids.
- **Luxor** (p110) Explore the temples and tombs of the ancient city of Thebes.
- **Alexandria** (p103) Admire colonial grandeur through a cloud of *sheesha* (water pipe) smoke at a period cafe.
- **Abu Simbel** (p118) Sense Pharaoh Ramses II's vanity in the monumental Great Temple.
- **Dahab** (p99) Kick back at this backpackers' paradise on the shores of the Red Sea.

CLIMATE & WHEN TO GO

From December to February, Lower Egypt (Cairo and north) is often overcast and chilly, with regular downpours of rain in Alexandria, and below-zero temperatures at night in Sinai, while Upper Egypt (south of Cairo) is warm with clear, blue skies.

Between June and September, temperatures range from 31°C on the Mediterranean coast to an unbearable 50°C in Aswan.

The best time to visit is in spring (March to April) or autumn (October and November) when you should pack for hot weather in the south and include a light jacket for the north.

ITINERARIES

- **Three Days** Be seduced by the pyramids at the sound-and-light show (p91); chart the origins of ancient Egypt in Saqqara and Dahshur (p97); go swapping old lamps for new in Islamic Cairo (p91) and flex the ocular muscles at a belly-dancing venue (p96).
- **Two Weeks** When you've exhausted Cairo, take the overnight train to Luxor (p110) and wake up in ancient Egypt (p110) for three days of archaeological exploration. Then lounge on a boat to Aswan (p115) visiting Edfu (p115) and Kom Ombo (p115) en route, and make time to savour Abu Simbel (p118) by night.
- **One Month** Fly back to Luxor and retrace the old caravan route through the oases of the Western Desert (p107), allowing three days to chill in the coffeehouses of Alexandria (p103), or swim with angel fish at the Red Sea resort of Dahab (p99). There's also time to listen for commandments on Mt Sinai (p101), become a boat spotter by the Suez Canal (p101) and sample dates in the Siwa Oasis (p107).

HISTORY
Life on the Nile

Most of Egypt's landmass consists of deserts, with the nation's lifeblood, the Nile River, a green band shivering along the length of the country, drawing to it the nation's settlements, including the disproportionately large capital, Cairo. Charismatic rivers flow through many cities in the world, but few govern the ebb and flow of a country's fortunes quite as significantly as the Nile has shaped Egypt and its shifting capitals of the delta.

From at least the year 4000 BC, small settlements clung together in loose affiliations along the Nile, developing into two important states. The delta area in the north became known as Lower Egypt, and the area upstream of the delta was called Upper Egypt. The unification of these two states – around 3100 BC by the Pharaoh Menes – sowed the seeds for the flowering of ancient Egyptian civilisation.

Old, Middle & New Kingdoms

Ancient Egyptian history comprises three principal kingdoms. The pyramids date from the Old Kingdom (2670–2150 BC), when lively trade made ambitious building projects possible. Ruling from the nearby capital of Memphis, Pharaoh Zoser and his

EGYPT

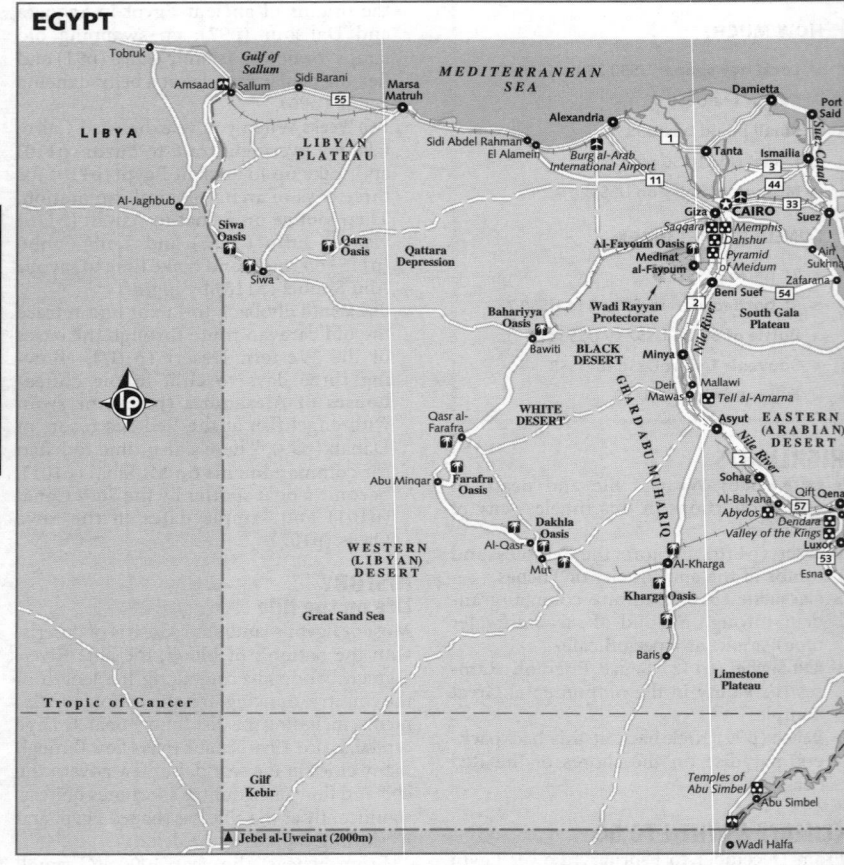

EGYPT

chief architect, Imhotep, built the pyramid at Saqqara. Subsequent pharaohs constructed ever larger temples and pyramids, which eventually culminated in the mighty pyramids of Giza, built for Cheops, Chephren and Mycerinus.

The Middle Kingdom (2056–1650 BC) was marked by the rise of a new and illustrious capital at Thebes (Luxor). It was during the period of the New Kingdom (1550–1076 BC), however, that ancient Egyptian culture blossomed. Wonders such as the Temple of Karnak and the West Bank tombs were the visible expression of a rich culture that established Egypt, under the great dynasties of Tuthmosis and Ramses, as the greatest regional power.

From Alexander to Independence

From the year 1184 BC, Egypt disintegrated into local principalities, and it wasn't until Alexander the Great arrived in the 4th century BC that the country was reunited. For the next 300 years, Egypt was ruled from Alexandria by the descendants of his general, Ptolemy. The Romans arrived in 31 BC, leaving behind little to show for their occupation except the introduction of Christianity in AD 2.

In AD 640, Arab armies brought Islam to Egypt. With it came a cultural revival and the foundation of Cairo in AD 969 by the Fatimid dynasty. The arts and sciences flourished, and trade brought much wealth into the country. The Turks found the prize irre-

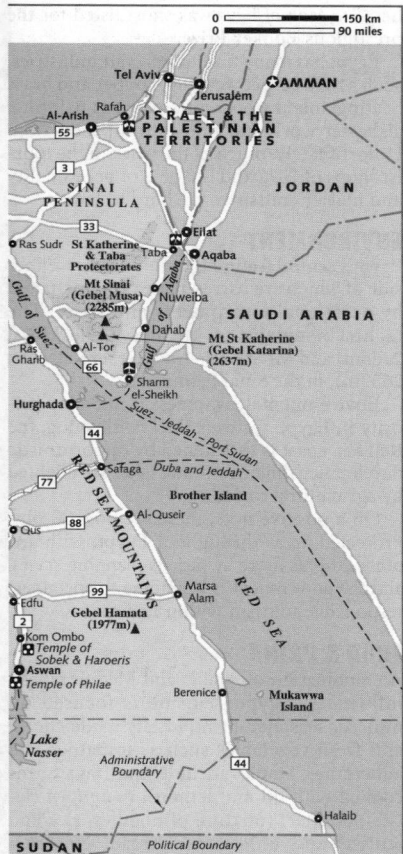

Life After Sadat

Sadat's assassin was a member of Islamic Jihad, a terrorist organisation aiming to establish an Islamic state in Egypt. Sadat's successor, Mubarak, retaliated against the extremists, declaring a state of emergency that continues until today.

While Mubarak has been canny in rehabilitating Egypt's relations with Arab states without abandoning the treaty with Israel, he has not been so successful in domestic policy. The 1980s were marked by violence, partly in response to the country's dismal economic situation. Between 1993 and 1997, Egypt's largest Islamist opposition group targeted foreign travellers in its campaign to overthrow the government, culminating in the massacre of 58 holidaymakers at the Funerary Temple of Hatshepsut in Luxor.

Egypt Today

The Luxor massacre destroyed grassroots support for militant groups, and a period of calm ensued until October 2004, when a bomb at Taba, on the border with Israel, killed 34. Mubarak introduced some democratic measures, but not enough to appease militant groups. After sporadic violence in Cairo, three bombs at Sharm el-Sheikh killed 64 people, mostly Egyptians. Various groups claimed responsibility and tourism suffered temporarily. In April 2006, three further bombs claimed 23 lives in Dahab, and in February 2009, another bomb in Cairo killed a French teenage girl, proving that the situation is far from resolved.

Egypt is in serious economic turmoil and, with an ever-growing population, rising unemployment and a decline in tourism resulting from continuing violence, and its future looks precarious.

CULTURE

Egyptians are often teased by neighbouring nationals for their 'inshallah' (God willing) mentality, which in practice translates as 'Why do today what you can put off until tomorrow?' Emphasis is placed instead on quality family and social experience, rather than on the secondary task of earning a living. Nonetheless, the country functions, crops are harvested and the great building projects throughout the ages, from Saqqara to Suez, show that the industry of some more than compensates for the lethargy of others.

sistible, and in the early 16th century, Egypt became part of the Ottoman Empire. The French followed suit during the 19th century under Napoleon, and the British made Egypt a protectorate during WWI.

After nearly 2000 years of colonisation, revolution resulted in self-rule in 1952. Gamal Abdel Nasser became Egypt's first president in 1956, and established his authority by buying out French and British claims to the Suez Canal. He did, however, lose the 1967 war with Israel. His successor, Anwar Sadat, who came to power in 1970, concluded the second war with Israel with the controversial 1979 Camp David Agreement. Widely blamed for betraying pan-Arabist principles, Sadat was assassinated in 1981.

Despite the emancipated lifestyles depicted in popular Cairo soaps, most families in Egypt live a conservative life based on traditional Islamic values. It may not look like it, but for most urban households, women rule the roost. They are expected to keep house and govern children, but men are kept in abeyance on a wish and a promise and are very often seen as a resource. Women who work are entitled to keep their money rather than share it with their husbands.

People

Egypt has the second-highest population in Africa. Growing at a rate of 2% annually, it places enormous strain on infrastructure and the national economy. Unemployment is officially 10%; unofficially it's much higher.

There are three main racial groups: the Hamito-Semites of the Nile (including the Berbers of Siwa in the Western Desert); Bedouin Arab nomads, who migrated from Arabia and live mostly in Sinai; and the Nubians, who inhabit the Aswan area.

About 94% of Egypt's population is Muslim, with Coptic Christians being the largest minority, though the two communities peacefully coexist.

Arts & Crafts

Thirty years after her death, Umm Kolthum is still the classical voice of Egypt.

Ahmed Adawiyya is the founding father of *al-jeel* (the generation) and *shaabi* (popular), both forms of repetitive, disposable pop made internationally likeable by his successor, Hakim. Amr Diab is an equally popular male star, with sophisticated production and accessible rhythms that have helped bring Arabic music to a wider audience.

Somewhat ignored locally, but feted abroad, Nubian music has a warm sound with simple melodies. The most famous exponent is Ali Hassan Kuban.

The work of the late Nobel prize winner Naguib Mahfouz is revered in Arabic literature for its profound expression of Egyptian life and language. His works include *The Cairo Trilogy* and *Children of the Alley,* still banned in Egypt as blasphemous.

Nawal al-Saadawi's works include *Woman at Point Zero* and *The Hidden Face of Eve* (banned in Egypt). Ahdaf Soueif also tackles taboo subjects; she writes in English and her *The Map of Love* was short listed for the prestigious Booker Prize.

Egypt has many traditional craft industries, such as silk carpet weaving, copper and brass beating, inlaid woodwork, papyrus painting, alabaster work and fine cotton production. Unfortunately, much of the work in the tourist shops of Giza and Luxor is of poor quality and master craftsmen are hard to locate.

ENVIRONMENT

Egypt's central feature is the Nile Valley, either side of which are barren plateaus punctuated by occasional escarpments and oases. The highest mountains are Mt Sinai (Gebel Musa; 2285m) and Mt St Katherine (Gebel Katarina; 2637m), in the Sinai Peninsula.

Environmental awareness is not a top priority in Egypt: Cairo is thick with smog; the Red Sea coast is threatened by opportunistic development and freshwater lakes are blighted by agricultural toxins.

On a positive note, there are now 20-plus protected areas throughout Egypt, with another 20-plus more in various planning stages, and the government is beginning to encourage responsible tourism within its borders.

FOOD & DRINK

A combination of Arabic and Mediterranean influences, Egypt's cuisine is focused on minced, seasoned meat, locally made cheese and fresh vegetables such as tomatoes and aubergines. Staples include *fuul* (fava beans cooked with oil and lemon), *ta'amiyya* (felafel), *kushari* (mixture of noodles, rice and lentils) and unleavened bread. Not surprisingly, fish (such as Nile perch and sea bream) is an important part of the diet.

Birds (as you'll note from the dovecotes) form an integral part of Egyptian culture, and pigeon – stuffed with rice and raisins – is a popular delicacy.

Although beer and arak are produced locally, fresh fruit juices are the favoured drink. Sweet mint tea and Turkish coffee are indispensable punctuations to any social interaction.

CAIRO

☎ 02 / pop 20 million

Let's address the drawbacks first. The crowds on a Cairo footpath make Manhattan look like a ghost town. You will be hounded by papyrus sellers at every turn. Your life will flash before your eyes each time you venture across a street. And your snot will run black from the smog.

But it's a small price to pay to visit the city Cairenes call Umm ad-Dunya – the Mother of the World. This city has an energy – palpable even at three in the morning – like no other. It's the product of its 20 million inhabitants waging a battle against the desert and winning (mostly), of 20 million people simultaneously crushing the city's infrastructure under their collective weight and lifting the city's spirit up with their uncommon graciousness and humour.

One taxi ride can span millennia, from the resplendent mosques and mausoleums built at the pinnacle of the Islamic empire, to the 19th-century palaces and grand avenues (which earned the city the nickname 'Paris on the Nile'), to the brutal concrete blocks of the Nasser years – then all the way back to the days of the pharaohs, as the Pyramids of Giza hulk on the western edge of the city.

So blow your nose, crack a joke and learn to look through the dirt to see the city's true colours. If you love Cairo, she will love you back.

HISTORY

In terms of Egypt's history, Cairo is a relatively modern capital, founded in AD 969 by the Islamic Fatimid dynasty over the ruins of earlier Roman and Islamic settlements. Much of the Fatimid city remains today: the great mosque and university of Al-Azhar are still important Islamic resource centres, while the gates of Bab an-Nasr, Bab al-Futuh and Bab Zuweila straddle the city's main thoroughfares.

Despite spilling beyond its walls, Cairo remained a medieval city at heart for 900 years. It wasn't until the mid-19th century that it started to change significantly.

Before the 1860s, Cairo extended west as far as what is today Midan Opera, surrounded by a swampy plain flooded annually by the Nile. In 1863 French-educated Ismail came to power, inviting architects from Europe to design a modern Cairo beside the old Islamic city. The building boom set in place continues today, with the city's boundaries constantly expanding into the surrounding desert.

Although the pyramids are now almost engulfed by the city, they more properly belong to the capital of ancient Egypt at Memphis, 22km to the south.

ORIENTATION

It may be vast, but Cairo is surprisingly easy to navigate. Midan Tahrir is the centre. Northeast of Tahrir is Downtown, a busy commercial district centred on Midan Talaat Harb. This is where most budget hotels and restaurants are clustered. Midan Ramses, the location of the city's main train station, marks the northern end of Downtown.

The eastern end of Downtown is Midan Ataba, on the edge of Islamic Cairo. With Khan al-Khalili bazaar at its core, this is the ebullient, medieval heart of Cairo.

In the middle of the Nile is the island of Gezira, home to the neighbourhood of Zamalek, historically favoured by ruling colonials and still a relatively upmarket enclave with foreign residents, midrange hotels and interesting restaurants and bars.

Heavy on concrete and light on charm, the west bank of the Nile is mostly residential. Giza stretches 20km either side of Pyramids Rd (Sharia al-Haram) that ends, as expected, at the foot of the Pyramids.

Maps

The American University in Cairo Press publishes *Cairo Maps: the Practical Guide* (E£30), a collection of 40 street maps with index.

INFORMATION

Bookshops

American University in Cairo (AUC) Bookshop (Map pp94–5; ☎ 2797 5370; Sharia Mohammed Mahmoud, Downtown; ☾ 9am-6pm Sat-Thu)

Diwan (Map pp88-9; ☎ 2736 2578; 159 Sharia 26th of July, Zamalek; ☾ 9am-11.30pm)

Lehnert & Landrock (Map pp94–5; ☎ 2392 7606; 44 Sharia Sherif, Downtown; ☾ 9.30am-2pm & 4-7.30pm Mon-Fri, 9.30am-2pm Sat) There's also a convenient branch opposite the Egyptian Museum (Map pp94–5).

Emergencies

Ambulance (☎ 123)
Fire department (☎ 180)
Police (☎ 122)
Tourist police (☎ 126)

EGYPT

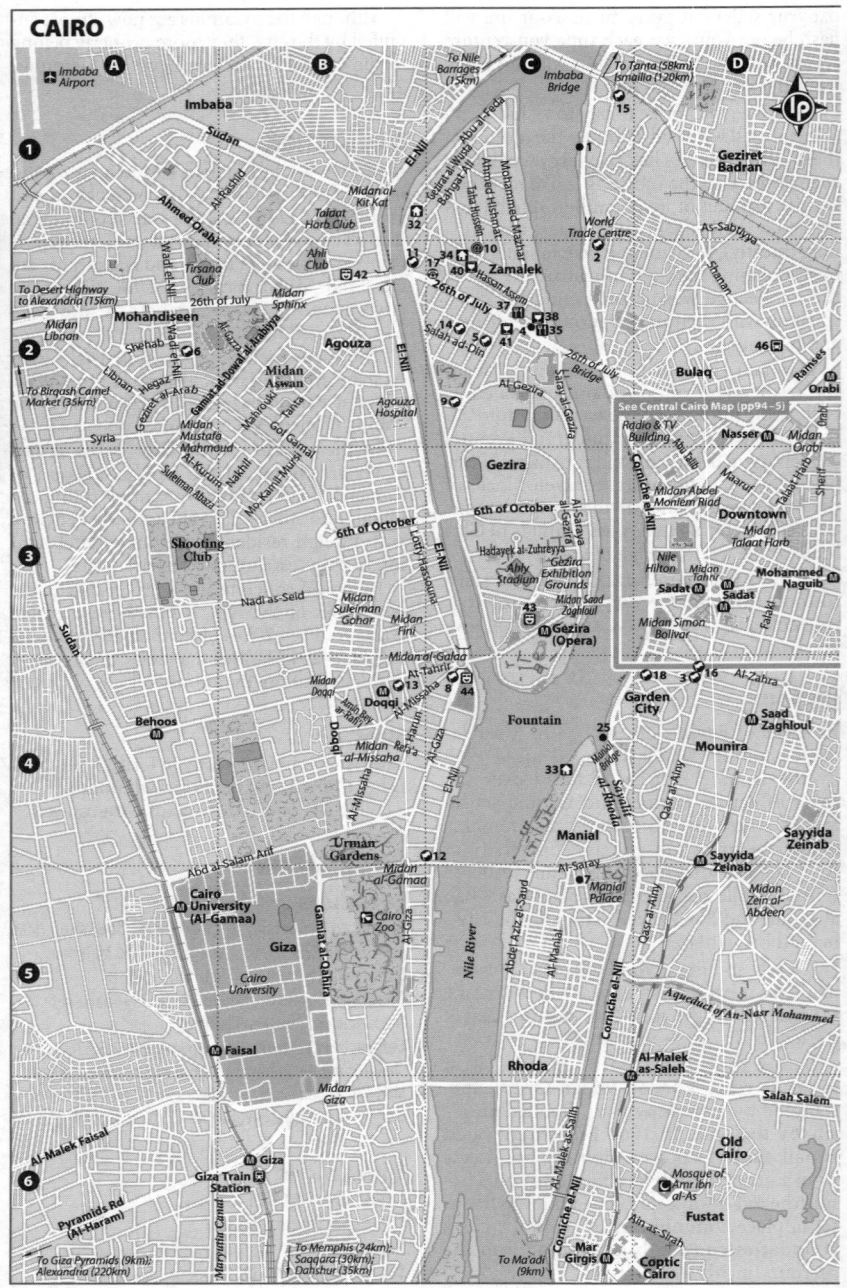

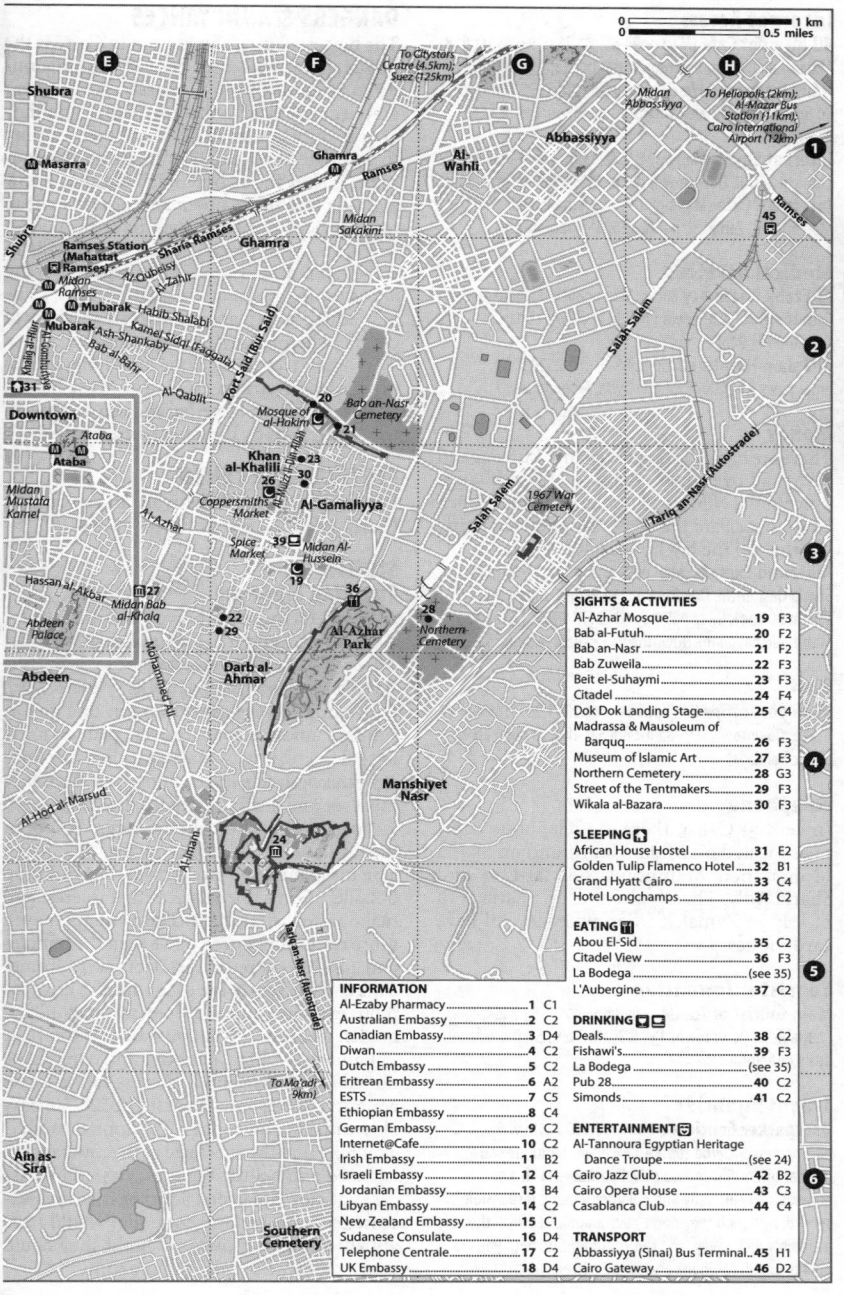

EGYPT

SIGHTS & ACTIVITIES
Al-Azhar Mosque	**19**	F3
Bab al-Futuh	**20**	F2
Bab an-Nasr	**21**	F2
Bab Zuweila	**22**	F3
Beit el-Suhaymi	**23**	F3
Citadel	**24**	F4
Dok Dok Landing Stage	**25**	C4
Madrassa & Mausoleum of Barquq	**26**	F3
Museum of Islamic Art	**27**	E3
Northern Cemetery	**28**	G3
Street of the Tentmakers	**29**	F3
Wikala al-Bazara	**30**	F3

SLEEPING
African House Hostel	**31**	E2
Golden Tulip Flamenco Hotel	**32**	B1
Grand Hyatt Cairo	**33**	C4
Hotel Longchamps	**34**	C2

EATING
Abou El-Sid	**35**	C2
Citadel View	**36**	F3
La Bodega	(see 35)	
L'Aubergine	**37**	C2

DRINKING
Deals	**38**	C2
Fishawi's	**39**	F3
La Bodega	(see 35)	
Pub 28	**40**	C2
Simonds	**41**	C2

ENTERTAINMENT
Al-Tannoura Egyptian Heritage Dance Troupe	(see 24)	
Cairo Jazz Club	**42**	B2
Cairo Opera House	**43**	C3
Casablanca Club	**44**	C4

TRANSPORT
Abbassiyya (Sinai) Bus Terminal	**45**	H1
Cairo Gateway	**46**	D2

INFORMATION
Al-Ezaby Pharmacy	**1**	C1
Australian Embassy	**2**	C2
Canadian Embassy	**3**	D4
Diwan	**4**	C2
Dutch Embassy	**5**	C2
Eritrean Embassy	**6**	A2
ESTS	**7**	C5
Ethiopian Embassy	**8**	C4
German Embassy	**9**	C2
Internet@Cafe	**10**	C2
Irish Embassy	**11**	B2
Israeli Embassy	**12**	C4
Jordanian Embassy	**13**	B4
Libyan Embassy	**14**	C2
New Zealand Embassy	**15**	C1
Sudanese Consulate	**16**	D4
Telephone Centrale	**17**	C2
UK Embassy	**18**	D4

Internet Access

4U Internet Café (Map pp94-5; ☎ 2575 9304; 1st fl, 8 Midan Talaat Harb, Downtown; per hr E£5; ☒ 24hr)

Hany Internet Cafe (Map pp94-5; ☎ 2395 1985; 16 Sharia Abdel Khalek Sarwat, Downtown; per hr E£5; ☒ 24hr)

Internet Egypt (Map pp94-5; Nile Hotel Shopping Mall, Corniche el-Nil, Downtown; per hr E£5; ☒ 9am-midnight)

Internet@Cafe (Map pp88-9; 25 Sharia Ismail Mohammed, Zamalek; per hr E£5; ☒ 9am-1am)

Medical Services

Al-Ezaby Pharmacy Bulaq (Map pp88-9; Arcadia Mall, Corniche el-Nil); Heliopolis (☎ 2414 8467; 1 Sharia Tayseer; ☒ 24hr)

Al-Salam Hospital (Map pp88-9; ☎ 2524 0250, emergency 2524 0077; Sharia Syria, Mohandiseen)

Money

There are banks, foreign exchange bureaus and ATMs all over town. Banque Misr exchange office at the Nile Hotel on the corniche is open 24 hours, as are the airport money-changing booths. All the big hotels have ATMs.

American Express (Map pp94-5; ☎ 2574 7991; 15 Sharia Qasr el-Nil, Downtown; ☒ 9am-4.30pm)

Thomas Cook (Map pp94-5; ☎ 2574 3955; 17 Sharia Mahmoud Bassiouni, Downtown; ☒ 9am-4.30pm Sat-Thu)

Post

Main post office (Map pp94-5; ☎ 2391 2615; Midan Ataba, Downtown; ☒ 8am-6pm Sat-Thu, to noon Fri & public holidays)

Telephone

In central Cairo, there are telephone centrales located on Midan Tahrir and on Sharia Mohammed Mahmoud, Bab al-Luq and Sharia Adly. There's also one on Sharia 26th of July in Zamalek (Map pp88–9). All have cardphones.

Tourist Information

Main tourist office (Map pp94-5; ☎ 2391 3454; 5 Sharia Adly, Downtown; ☒ 8.30am-7pm) Staff are notoriously unhelpful.

Travel Agencies

Backpacker Concierge (☎ 016 350 7118; www.backpackerconcierge.com) An excellent boutique start-up that offers customised travel packages with a strong emphasis on culturally and environmentally responsible service. Although they don't have an official office, they are incredibly tech savvy, and can communicate with you via phone, email, Facebook and even Twitter!

DANGERS & ANNOYANCES

The biggest source of irritation in Cairo is the bogus guide who uses remarkable ingenuity to steer you into 'no-hassle, government emporiums'. Scams include telling you they are off-duty guides from your hotel wanting to improve their English; insisting the museum is shut for a conference but they know a good place that's open; and offering cheap taxi services to places they have no permit to go. In some places, it can be difficult to walk more than a few metres without being accosted aggressively for such 'services'. The best advice is to plan where to go and how to get there before leaving the hotel.

Women travelling alone are vulnerable to unwanted attention in Cairo. Most hassle, however, tends to be verbal and can be avoided to some extent by dressing conservatively.

FESTIVALS & EVENTS

For a full listing of festivals and events in Cairo – and the rest of Egypt – see p120.

SIGHTS
Egyptian Museum

A bewildering number of exhibits (over 100,000) are housed in the **Egyptian Museum** (Map pp94-5; ☎ 2579 6748; www.egyptianmuseum.gov.eg; Midan Tahrir, Downtown; adult/student E£60/30; ☒ 9am-6.45pm). Don't hope to see everything in one go – it simply cannot be done. Instead, plan on making at least two visits, maybe tackling one floor at a time, or decide on the things you absolutely must see and head straight for them.

To gain a purchase on the magnificence of the museum's collection, consider picking up a pictorial museum guide from the bookshop outside, select a dozen pieces that interest and make a beeline for those. The museum is even more rewarding once you've seen the temples and tombs where the artefacts were found. This is particularly the case with the most famous exhibits of the museum, the magnificent golden treasures of Tutankhamen's tomb.

Guides cost E£60 per hour and congregate outside the ticket booth. Access to the Royal Mummy Room costs an extra E£100/50, payable outside the room's 1st-floor entrance. You may find the spectacle of the unwrapped, exposed and belittled bodies, viewed in glass cases at close quarters, a rather intrusive experience – it's certainly one that would have appalled the kings, who thought they could count on some dignity in perpetuity.

THE PYRAMIDS: IN & OUT OF FAVOUR

The pyramids of Giza are so iconic as to defy description. They have been puzzled over and plundered, visited and studied for 4000 years and yet their attraction continues unabated. Not that all spectators have been equally admiring of them. 'Just compare', wrote Frontinus, superintendent of Roman aqueducts, 'this vital aqueduct network [with] those useless pyramids.'

If the Romans were bemused by the apparent redundancy of the pyramids, 16th-century Islamic caliphs understood their spiritual power…and tried to tear them down. Napoleon two centuries later understood their political power…and used them for target practice. The 19th-century traveller ED Clarke understood their aesthetic power, declaring that 'no-one ever approached them under other emotions than those of terror'…and then raced his friend to the top of Cheops.

The changing and dynamic relationship of spectator and pyramid over the centuries – the theories about why and wherefore, the speculations of divine intervention and apocalyptic foreboding – ensure that the pyramids fulfil their function of keeping alive the names of a father (Khufu), his son (Kahfre) and grandson (Menkaure). This is the real wonder of these remarkable mausoleums.

Islamic Cairo

Islamic Cairo is the medieval heart of the capital. For a comprehensive walking tour of its splendid sights, begin at Cairo's most historic institution, **Al-Azhar Mosque** (Map pp88–9; admission free; 24hr). One of Cairo's earliest mosques, Al-Azhar is also the world's oldest surviving university. The campus recently moved to Nasser City but the university grounds still function as an Islamic resource centre.

Opposite Al-Azhar Mosque is the great bazaar **Khan al-Khalili** (Map pp88–9) and *midan* (city square). Before you dip into its myriad alleyways, however, walk north up Sharia al-Gamaliyya, a once-important medieval thoroughfare and home to fine clusters of Mamluk-era mosques, *madrassas* (traditional Muslim schools) and *caravanserais* (merchant's inns). Visit **Wikala al-Bazara** (Map pp88-9; Sharia al-Tombakshiyya; adult/student E£20/10; 10am-5pm), a beautifully restored *caravanserai* and head for the old **northern wall**. The square-towered **Bab an-Nasr** (Gate of Victory; Map pp88–9) and the rounded **Bab al-Futuh** (Gate of Conquests; Map pp88–9) were built in 1087. Returning to the bazaar via Sharia al-Muizz li-Din Allah, don't miss the spectacular **Beit el-Suhaymi** (Darb al-Asfar; Map pp88-9; adult/student E£25/12; 9am-5pm), a beautifully restored complex of three houses tucked down an alley. This part of Islamic Cairo is home to the city's most historic prayer-schools, including the **Madrassa & Mausoleum of Barquq** (Map pp88-9; 6am-9pm), off Bein-al Qasreen.

Walk east from Al-Hussein, which is the name of both the *midan* and the mosque at the mouth of the bazaar, along Sharia al-Azhar,

bear right at the top of the hill, and walk under the overpass to reach the **Northern Cemetery** (Map pp88–9). Commonly known as the 'City of the Dead', it is home to a sorry city of the living, too.

South of Khan al-Khalili, a busy market street runs past other exquisite *madrassa* complexes to the twin minarets of **Bab Zuweila** (Map pp88–9), the only surviving gate in the city's southern wall. Continuing south from Bab Zuweila, enter the **Street of the Tentmakers** (Map pp88–9), a covered bazaar specialising in appliqué work. Turn right to reach the celebrated **Museum of Islamic Art** (Map pp88–9; currently closed), or turn left for the Citadel (a long walk uphill that will take at least 40 to 50 minutes and will feel longer in summer).

Commenced by Saladin (Salah ad-Din) in the 12th century, the **Citadel** (2512 1735; Midan al-Qala'a; adult/student E£50/25; 8am-5pm) houses an assortment of mosques and indifferent military museums. A visit is worthwhile, however, for the panoramic city view.

Returning to the bazaar, shelter from the mayhem in one of Khan el-Khalili's many restaurants with their Moorish-style interiors or pay a visit to Fishawi's, the bazaar's most famous coffeehouse (see p96 for details).

The Pyramids & Sphinx at Giza

Built on a desert plateau encroached upon by the modern city of Cairo, the pyramids here are the last remaining wonder of the ancient world. They were built as the mausoleums of pharaohs to help their souls on the path to heaven. Representing more a celebration of life (and a desire for life to continue) than

EGYPT

a preoccupation with death, they were constructed by thousands of artisans (not slaves as previously imagined) mindful of their part in the creation of something extraordinary.

Completed around 2600 BC, the **Great Pyramid of Khufu** (Cheops) is the oldest pyramid at Giza, and the largest (146.5m high). Although there isn't much to see inside, climbing the steep, narrow passage to the heart of the pyramid is an unforgettable, if intensely claustrophobic, experience. The neighbouring **Pyramid of Khafre** (Chephren) was built by Khufu's son. In deference to his father, he built a slightly smaller pyramid but located it on higher ground, giving the impression of greater size. Part of the original smooth limestone cladding, which once covered the entire structure, still remains. At a height of 62m, the **Pyramid of Menkaure** (Mycerinus) is the smallest of the three pyramids; it was built by Khafre's son, Menkaure, from blocks of granite floated along the Nile from Aswan.

Known in Arabic as Abu al-Hol (Father of Terror) and guarding the Pyramid of Khafre, the **Sphinx** is carved from a single piece of wind-eroded limestone. It has the face of a man – perhaps that of Khafre – and the body of a lion. It was buried by sand several times since it was built in 2500 BC, and Napoleon's army shot off its nose (now in the British Museum) in the 19th century. Despite these 'mishaps', the Sphinx remains one of the most evocative monuments of the ancient world.

The necropolis of Giza, which includes valley temples, causeways and satellite pyramids, is open from 7am to 7.30pm daily. There's a general admission fee of E£50/25 per adult/student, and extra charges to enter the pyramids. Entry to the Great Pyramid costs E£100/75 per adult/student, payable in Egyptian pounds. Only 300 tickets are sold per day. These go on sale at 8am and 1pm at the ticket box in front of the pyramid and the queue forms early. Entry to the Pyramid of Khafre costs E£30/15 (tickets are obtained at the booth in front of the pyramid), while the Pyramid of Menkaure is closed to the general public. Useful background information is available at www.guardians.net/hawass, an official antiquities website.

Horses, donkeys or camels are available for rides near the pyramids, with official rates around E£35 per hour (you are nevertheless still expected to bargain).

Beside the Great Pyramid are five pits that once contained the Pharaoh's funerary barques. One of these wooden vessels was unearthed in 1954 and forms the centrepiece of the **Solar Barque Museum** (adult/student E£50/25; 9am-4pm).

The nightly **sound and light show** (3385 2880; www.soundandlight.com.eg; adult E£75) provides a magical introduction to the pyramids, despite the crowds. Three performances in a variety of languages take place nightly below the Sphinx. Check the website for the schedule.

Bus 355/357 runs from Heliopolis to the Pyramids via central Cairo every 20 minutes. It picks up from the road (not the island) under the overpass at Midan Abdel Moniem Riad. There's no sign, so you'll have to ask a local where to stand. Be alert, as you'll probably have to flag the bus down. It also passes through Tahrir, and can usually be flagged down from the bus shelter near the northwestern metro stairs. The bus is a white one, with 'CTA' on its side. A ticket costs E£2 and the trip takes about 45 minutes.

By far the most straightforward way to go is in a yellow metered taxi from the rank on Midan Tahrir. It's usually about E£20, the same price you'd be lucky to bargain a black-and-white-cab driver down to – plus you get air conditioning.

ACTIVITIES

A lovely way to enjoy sunset is to take a ride on a felucca (traditional Nile sailing vessel), which comes complete with captain and first mate. It costs about E£30 per hour per person, but bargain hard and expect to pay baksheesh. The captains wait by the mooring point (Map pp94–5) by the Semiramis Intercontinental on the corniche, or at the Dok Dok landing stage (Map pp88–9), just short of the bridge to Le Meridien Hotel.

SLEEPING
Budget

Wake UP! Cairo Hostel (Map pp94-5; 2636 3325; www.wakeupcairohostel.com; 33 A Ramsis St, Marouf Tower, Downtown; dm E£45, d/tr without bathroom E£110/150, d E£140;) A new downtown hostel where the dorm rooms are a steal if you're not fussy about privacy, though slightly more expensive rooms are still cheap and fairly cheerful.

African House Hostel (Map pp88-9; 2591 1744; www.africanhousehostel.com; 3rd fl, 15 Sharia Emad ad-Din; s/d/tr without bathroom US$12/18/24;) The

African House offers an affordable way to stay in one of the city's most gorgeous mid-19th-century buildings.

Pension Roma (Map pp94–5; ☎ 2391 1088; www.pensionroma.com.eg; 4th fl, 169 Sharia Mohammed Farid; s/d without bathroom E£60/96, d/tr with shower E£123/162) Run by a French-Egyptian woman with impeccable standards, the Roma brings dignity, even elegance, to the budget-travel scene.

Merames Hostel (Map pp94–5; ☎ 2396 2518; http://merameeshotel.net; 32 Sharia Sabri Abou Alam; s/d without bathroom E£75/110; ✕ ▣) This well-positioned hostel is relaxed and easy-going, and the rooms themselves have high ceilings, wooden floorboards, large windows and French doors leading onto balconies.

Midrange

Windsor Hotel (Map pp94–5; ☎ 2591 5277; www.windsorcairo.com; 19 Sharia Alfy; s/d with shower & hand basin US$37/48, s/d from US$46/59; ✕ ▣) The rooms are dim, but with the beautifully maintained elevator, worn marble stairs and a hotel restaurant where the dinner bell chimes every evening at 7.30pm, the place is hard for nostalgia buffs to resist.

Hotel Longchamps (Map pp88–9; ☎ 2735 2311; www.hotellongchamps.com; 5th fl, 21 Sharia Ismail Mohammed; s US$54–62, d US$78–89; ✕) Rooms are spacious and well maintained, and guests gather to chat on the peaceful, greenery-covered rear balcony around sunset or lounge in the restaurant.

Golden Tulip Flamenco Hotel (Map pp88–9; ☎ 2735 0815; www.flamencohotels.com; 2 Sharia Gezirat al-Wusta; s US$76–86, d US$86–96; ✕ ▣) This popular business-class place is comfortable and well equipped, and serves as a more fiscally reasonable alternative to Zamalek's five-star heavyweights.

Talisman Hotel (Map pp94–5; ☎ 2393 9431; www.talisman-hotel.com; 5th fl, 39 Sharia Talaat Harb; s/d from US$85/95; ✕ ▣) Thanks to double-pane windows, Downtown traffic is a distant memory once you're inside this luxurious cocoon, one of the only real boutique hotels in the city.

Top End

Grand Hyatt Cairo (Map pp88–9; ☎ 2365 1234; http://cairo.grand.hyatt.com; Corniche el-Nil, Rhoda; s/d from US$200/225; ✕) The Hyatt has by far the best Nileside terrace in town, as well as a gargantuan rooftop pool. Rooms are minimalist chic, with brushed-gold trim and large marble bathrooms even in the standard layout.

EATING
Budget

El-Abd Bakery (Map pp94–5; 35 Sharia Talaat Harb; pastries E£1–6; ◷ 8am–midnight) For pastries and sweets head for Cairo's most famous bakery, easily identified by the crowds of people outside tearing into their Oriental sweets and savoury pies.

Abu Tarek (Map pp94–5; 40 Sharia Champollion; dishes E£3–10; ◷ 8am–midnight) This veritable *kushari* palace has expanded, decade by decade, into the upper storeys of its building, and held onto the unofficial Best Kushari title.

Gad (Map pp94–5; ☎ 2576 3583; 13 Sharia 26th of July; dishes E£4–12; ◷ 9am–2am) This fast-food eatery is usually packed to the rafters with a constant stream of young Cairenes sampling its fresh and well-priced food.

Midrange

Citadel View (Map pp88–9; ☎ 2510 9151; Al-Azhar Park; entrées E£10–20, mains E£30–75; ◷ noon–1am) Eating at this gorgeous restaurant – on a vast multilevel terrace, with Cairo's elite seated around you and the whole city sprawled below – feels almost like visiting a luxury resort.

our pick Abou El Sid (Map pp88–9; ☎ 2735 9640; 157 Sharia 26th of July; mezze E£12–25, mains E£25–70; ◷ noon–2am) Cairo's first hipster Egyptian restaurant, Abou El Sid is as popular with tourists as it is with upper-class natives looking for a taste of their roots. Diners swoon over dishes such as roasted chicken drizzled with *molokhiyya* (leafy green soup), but you can also enjoy a sugar-cane-and-tequila cocktail at the big bar, or a postprandial *sheesha*. It's all served amid hanging lamps, kitschy gilt 'Louis Farouk' furniture and fat pillows.

L'Aubergine (Map pp88–9; ☎ 2738 0080; 5 Sharia Sayyed al-Bakry; entrées E£14–25, mains E£30–70; ◷ noon–2am) This white-walled candlelit bistro devotes half its menu to vegetarian dishes such as blue-cheese ravioli and aubergine moussaka.

Sabaya (Map pp94–5; ☎ 2795 7171; Semiramis Intercontinental, Corniche el-Nil; mezze E£15–30, mains E£50–110; ◷ 7.30pm–1am) Lebanese cuisine is Egypt's most common 'ethnic' food, but it's rarely done as well as it is here, where the diverse and delicate mezze come with fresh-baked pillows of pita, and mains such as *fatteh* are served in individual cast-iron pots.

Top End

La Bodega (Map pp94–5; ☎ 2735 6761; 1st fl, Baehler's Mansions, 157 Sharia 26th of July, Zamalek; mains E£70–135;

EGYPT

CENTRAL CAIRO

INFORMATION		
4U Internet Café	1	D3
American Express	2	C4
American University in Cairo Bookshop	3	C5
Banque Misr Exchange Office	4	B4
French Embassy	5	E3
Hany Internet Café	6	E2
Internet Egypt	7	B4
Lehnert & Landrock	8	E2
Lehnert & Landrock	9	B4
Main Post Office	10	H3
Main Tourist Office	11	F2
Mogamma	12	B6
Telephone Centrale	13	F2
Telephone Centrale	14	C4
Telephone Centrale	15	D5
Telephone Centrale	16	E5
Thomas Cook	17	C4
US Embassy	18	B6

SIGHTS & ACTIVITIES		
Egyptian Museum	19	B4
Felucca Mooring Point	20	A6

SLEEPING		
Meramees Hostel	21	D4
Pension Roma	22	F2
Talisman Hotel	23	E2
Wake UP! Cairo Hostel	24	B2
Windsor Hotel	25	F1

EATING		
Abu Tarek	26	C3

El-Abd Bakery	27	E2
Gad	28	E2
Sabaya	29	A5

DRINKING		
Cilantro	30	C5

ENTERTAINMENT		
After Eight	31	C4
Haroun El-Rashid Nightclub	(see 29)	

TRANSPORT		
Airport Bus	32	B3
EgyptAir	33	F2
Local Buses & Minibuses	34	B3
Maspero River Bus Terminal	35	A2
Pyramids Bus	36	B3

Foreign Ministry

To Zamalek (1.8km)

Radio & TV Building

Corniche el-Nil

6th of October Bridge

To Zamalek (1.6km)

Nile River

Qasr el-Nil (Tahrir) Bridge

To Gezira (500m); Doqqi (1.6km); Giza (4km)

Ramses

Abdel Hamid Said

Maaruf

Abdel Khalek Sarwat

6th of October Overpass (Galaa)

Midan Abdel Moniem Riad

Mahmoud Bassiouni

Champollion

Talaat Harb Complex

Downtown

Bursa al-Gadida

19 Egyptian Museum

Nile Hilton

Midan Talaat Harb

Qasr el-Nil

Qasr el-Nil

El Kadi El Fadel

Al-Bustan

Arab League Building

Talaat Harb

Al-Bustan Centre

Yousef al-Guindi

Midan Falaki

Sadat

Midan Tahrir

Sadat

Sadat

Tahrir

Souq Bab al-Luq

Falaki

Omar Makram Mosque

Sony Gallery

Mohammed Mahmoud

Mansour

Abd al-Magid ar-Rimali

Sabaya

Midan Simon Bolivar

Kamal ad-Din Salah

Abdel Kader Hamza

American University in Cairo

Sheikh Rihan

Latin America

Qasr al-Ainy

Al-Zahra

To Garden City (300m); Coptic Cairo (4km)

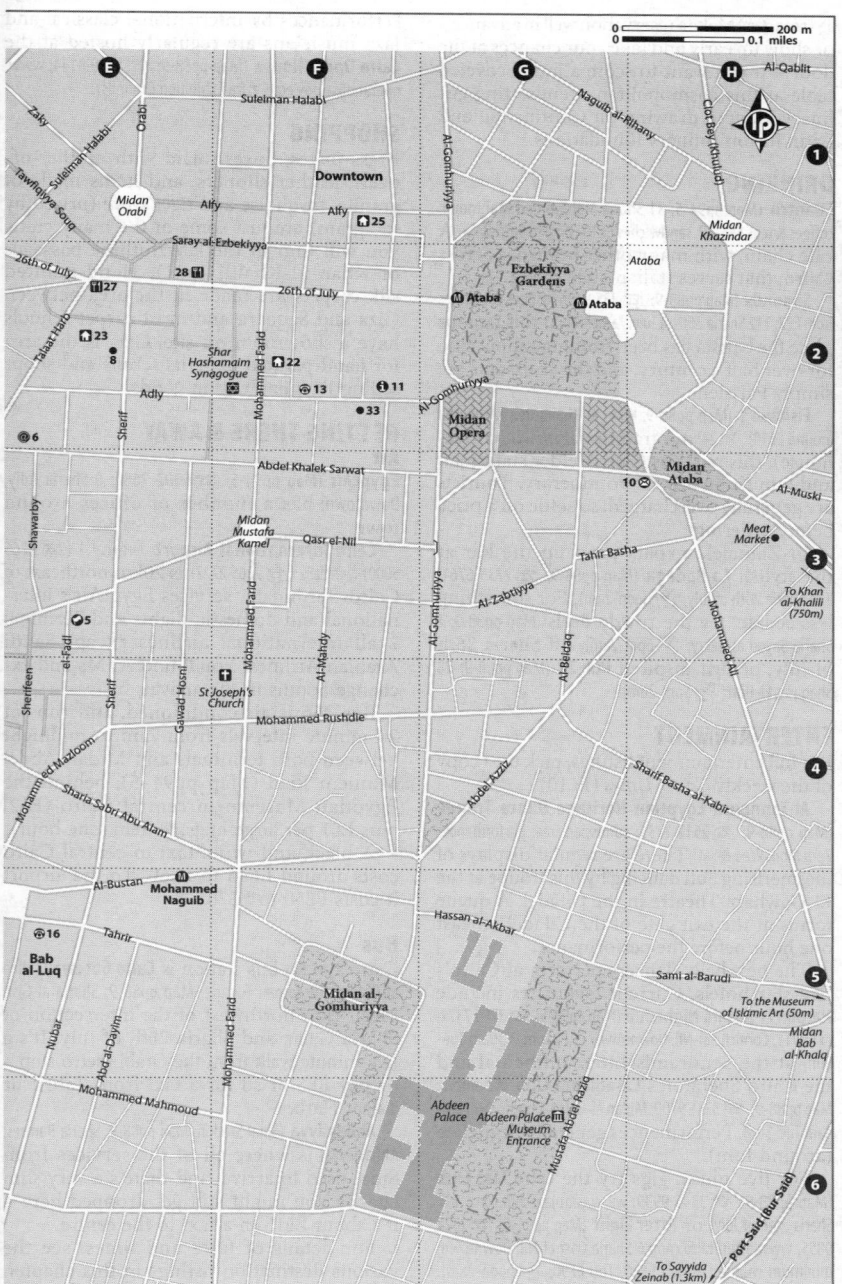

EGYPT

(🕑 noon-2am) Make a reservation well in advance – or show up early and take your chances at the door – if you want to score a much coveted table at this cosmopolitan, trendsetting culinary kingpin drawing on Continental and Latin fusion culinary foundations.

DRINKING

Cilantro (Map pp94-5; 31 Sharia Mohammed Mahmoud; coffees & teas E£5-20, sandwiches E£10-35; 🕑 9am-2am) A cafe chain, with many other branches across Cairo, that serves Italian-style coffee.

Simonds (Map pp88-9; ☎ 735 9436; coffees & pastries from E£7; 112 Sharia 26th of July, Zamalek) At this famous place the barista has been frothing cappuccino for over half a century, and the croissants are simply Parisien.

Fishawi's (Map pp88-9; Khan al-Khalili; tea & sheesha around E£10; 🕑 24hr) A traditional *ahwa* (coffeehouse), this ranks as Cairo's elder statesman and a must on any Cairo itinerary. Tourists are generally overcharged, so settle on a price before ordering.

In Zamalek, expats prop up the bar at the stylish **La Bodega** (Map pp88-9; ☎ 2735 6761; 157 Sharia 26th of July; 🕑 noon-2am). For something less sedate, try the rowdy **Deals** (Map pp88-9; 2 Sharia Sayed al-Bakry; 🕑 6pm-2am), off Sharia 26th of July, or Brit-inspired **Pub 28** (Map pp88-9; 28 Shagarat El-Dorr; 🕑 5pm-2am).

ENTERTAINMENT

For full entertainment listings, pick up a copy of the weekly *Cairo Times* (E£10).

Al-Tannoura Egyptian Heritage Dance Troupe (Map pp88-9; ☎ 2512 1735; admission free; performances 7pm Mon, Wed & Sat) There are regular displays of mesmerising Sufi dancing by this troupe at the El-Gawhara Theatre in the Citadel. A queue forms at the exit gate of the Citadel at least one hour before the performance.

The best belly dancers perform at Cairo's five-star hotels. Current favourites include **Haroun El-Rashid Nightclub** (Map pp94-5; ☎ 3795 7171, ext 8011; Corniche el-Nil, Downtown; 🕑 11pm-3.30am Tue-Sun) at the Semiramis Intercontinental and the Cairo Sheraton's **Casablanca Club** (Alhambra; Map pp88-9; ☎ 3336 9700; Midan al-Galaa, Doqqi; 🕑 7pm-4am Tue-Sun). Performances generally begin late (around 1am).

For live music gigs try the **Cairo Jazz Club** (Map pp88-9; ☎ 3345 9939; www.cairojazzclub.com; 197 Sharia 26th of July) or **After Eight** (Map pp94-5; ☎ 2574 0855; www.after8cairo.com; 6 Sharia Qasr el-Nil, Downtown; minimum charge Fri-Wed E£60, Thu E£90; 🕑 noon-2am).

Performances by international classical and jazz musicians are regularly hosted at the **Cairo Opera House** (Map pp88-9; ☎ 2739 8144; www.operahouse.gov.eg; Gezira Exhibition Grounds).

SHOPPING

Brass plates, boxes inlaid with mother-of-pearl, leather slippers, and items made of granite, turquoise and tiger's-eye (priced by the gram) are just some of the many crafts you will find in the labyrinthine passages of Khan al-Khalili (p91). Hand-knotted silk carpets are made in the area between Giza and Saqqara and most carpet schools have a showroom on site. Giza is the area for hand-painted papyrus scrolls and shops selling Egyptian cotton goods.

GETTING THERE & AWAY
Air

EgyptAir (Map pp94-5; ☎ 2392 7680; 6 Sharia Adly, Downtown) has a number of offices around town.

Cairo International Airport Terminal 1 (☎ 2265 5000) Terminal 2 (☎ 2265 2222) is 20km northeast of Cairo. Terminal 1 services EgyptAir's international and domestic flights and Terminal 2 all international airlines except Saudi Arabian Airlines. You'll find ATMs and exchange booths in the arrivals halls.

Bus 356 is air conditioned, and runs at 20-minute intervals from 7am to midnight between both terminals and Midan Abdel Moniem Riad (Map pp94–5), behind the Egyptian Museum in central Cairo (E£2, plus E£1 per large luggage item, one hour).

A black-and-white taxi to central Cairo costs around E£45 to E£60. To the airport it costs E£50 to E£70.

Bus

Cairo's main bus station is **Cairo Gateway** (Mina al-Qahira, Turgoman Garage; Map pp88-9; Sharia al-Gisr, Bulaq), 1km northwest of the intersection of Sharia Galaa and Sharia 26th of July. It's a five-minute walk from the Orabi metro stop – or pay E£5 or so for a taxi from Tahrir or Talaat Harb.

Abbassiyya (Sinai Station; Map pp88-9; Sharia Ramses, Abbassiyya) is where all of the services from Sinai used to arrive, and there's a very slim chance you might still get dropped here – it's about E£15 in a taxi to the centre.

For details of fares and times, see the various destination listings in this chapter.

For international bus services from Cairo, see p122.

Train

Characterful and colonial, **Ramses train station** (Mahattat Ramses; Map pp88-9; ☎ 2575 3555; Midan Ramses, Downtown) is Cairo's main terminus. It has a left-luggage office charging E£2.50 per piece per day and a **tourist information office** (🕙 9am-7pm).

The train is particularly recommended for the journey to Luxor/Aswan, which, with its Nile views, is something of a classic.

The **Abela Egypt Sleeping Train** (☎ 2574 9274; www.sleepingtrains.com) leaves at 8pm, arriving in Luxor at 5.05am the next morning, and Aswan at 8.15am. Tickets to either destination cost US$60/80 per person one way in a double/single cabin. Tickets must be paid for in US dollars (cash only). The price includes dinner and breakfast and the experience is enjoyably old-fashioned.

Aside from the sleeping train, foreigners can travel to Luxor and Aswan only on train 980, departing Ramses daily at 7.30am; train 996, at 10pm; and train 1902, at 12.30am. To Luxor, 1st-/2nd-class fares are E£79/41; to Aswan, E£94/47. The trip to Luxor takes 10 hours; to Aswan, around 12.

You must buy tickets at least a couple of days in advance.

GETTING AROUND

Bus & Minibus

Cairo's main local bus and minibus stations, serving all parts of the city, are at Midan Abdel Moniem Riad (Map pp94–5).

Metro

The Metro system is startlingly efficient, and the stations are surprisingly clean. A short-hop ticket (up to nine stations) costs 50pt. The first carriage is reserved for women only.

River Bus

On the corniche in front of the Radio & TV Building you'll find the Maspero river bus terminal (Map pp94–5). From here boats depart every 15 minutes between 7am and 10pm for Doqqi, Manial, Giza and Misr al-Qadima (Old Cairo). The trip takes 50 minutes and the fare is 50pt.

Taxi

The easiest way of getting around is by taxi, with average fares between E£5 and E£20 for a short jaunt, though the lack of meters necessitates bargaining.

AROUND CAIRO

SAQQARA & DAHSHUR

At **Saqqara** (adult/student E£50/25; 🕙 8am-4pm) you'll find a massive necropolis strewn with pyramids, temples and tombs where pharaohs, generals and sacred animals were interred. The star attraction is the Step Pyramid of Zoser, the world's oldest stone monument.

Ten kilometres south of Saqqara is **Dahshur** (adult/student E£25/15; 🕙 8am-4pm), a 3.5km-long field of pyramids, including the Bent Pyramid (unfortunately closed) and the mystical Red Pyramid.

If you're looking to escape Cairo for the day, organised tours can be easily arranged through your accommodation, and it's not hard to find a cab driver willing to offer their services for the day. A private car should cost between E£150 and E£250 for the day (around seven hours), excluding entry fees and the obligatory baksheesh.

SINAI

Sinai, a region of stark beauty, has been a place of refuge, conflict and curiosity for thousands of years. Wedged between Africa and Asia, it is an intercontinental crossroads par excellence – prophets, nomads, exiles and conquerors have all left their footprints here.

SHARM EL-SHEIKH & NA'AMA BAY
☎ 069

Known simply as Sharm by package travellers the world over, Sinai's largest and most famous beach town has undergone a miraculous transformation in recent years. What was once a small village that attracted mainly hard-core divers is now commonly described as Egypt's answer to Las Vegas, drawing in wave upon wave of primarily British and European holidaymakers in search of sun and sea. Here along the much-touted 'Red Sea Riviera', high-rise block hotels and dense condo developments stretch down the coastline, all the while jockeying for highly prized beachfront property.

Information

There are numerous ATMs in Na'ama Bay, and most major banks have branches in Sharm. There are many internet outlets in the mall opposite Sharm's Old Market. The **post office** (8am-3pm Sat-Thu) is on the hill in Sharm and there's a **telephone centrale** (24hr) nearby.

Sights & Activities

RAS MOHAMMED

Declared a **national park** (admission per person €5) in 1988, the headland of Ras Mohammed is 30km west of Sharm el-Sheikh, at the southern tip of the peninsula. Home to some of the world's most spectacular coral reefs, the park is teeming with most of the Red Sea's 1000 species of fish.

Diving is the area's star attraction. The following clubs in Na'ama Bay are recommended:

Oonas Dive Centre (☎ 360 0581; www.oonasdivers.com)

Red Sea Diving College (☎ 360 0145; www.redseacollege.com)

Sinai Divers (☎ 360 0697; www.sinaidivers.com)

Subex (☎ 360 0122; www.subex.org)

Sleeping

Shark's Bay Umbi Diving Village (☎ 360 0942; www.sharksbay.com; sea-view huts s/d/tr E£14/17/21, beach cabins s/d/tr E£22/33/43; village room s/d/tr E£32/43/52;) This long-standing Bedouin-owned camp has a relaxed ambience, simple but clean huts with shared bathrooms up on the cliff, and pricier huts down below with air-con and bathroom, and a recently constructed village-style block of furnished rooms To reach the camp, just tell the taxi driver 'Shark's Bay Umbi'; expect to pay about E£25 from Na'ama Bay and E£50 from the port at Sharm.

Oonas Hotel (☎ 360 0581; www.oonasdivers.com; s/d/tr from €45/60/85;) One of the best bargains in Sharm is this combination hotel and Scuba club, which has a 20-year history of certifying divers from around the world.

Amar Sina (☎ 366 2222/9; www.minasegypt.com; Hadaba; r from US$85;) With soaring domes, graceful arches and whitewashed walls adorned with brick ornaments, this *Arabian Nights*–styled hotel upholds Sharm's renowned kitsch factor.

Four Seasons Sharm el-Sheikh (☎ 360 3555; www.fourseasons.com/sharmelsheikh; r from US$325;) From the towering whitewashed walls and intricate geometric lattice workings to the ornate bronze fixtures and richly dyed Persian rugs, the Four Seasons is a model of perfection straight down to the last detail.

Eating

Mashy Café (Sanafir Hotel; dishes E£35-75) Lebanese is the undisputed king of the Middle Eastern gastronomic world, and this low-key open-air spot outside the Sanafir Hotel is as good a place as any to sample the full bounty of this refined cuisine.

La Rustichella (pizza E£25-40, mains E£40-75;) This Sharm institution serves a variety of delectable meals, including Italian-style seafood dishes, brick-oven roasted pizzas, and a good variety of chicken and beef dishes – stop by in the afternoon and cool off with an iced coffee and a creamy gelato.

Al-Fanar (Ras Um Sid; dishes E£40-150; 10am-10.30pm;) This upscale restaurant boasts an excellent seafront location at the base of the lighthouse, cosy alcoves overlooking the water, Bedouin-influenced decor, indoor and outdoor dining, and a large Italian menu featuring thin-crust pizza and homemade pasta dishes.

Drinking & Entertainment

Popular venues include the ubiquitous **Hard Rock Café** (☎ 360 2664; www.hardrock.com), in the mall at Na'ama Bay; the pricey but glamorous **Little Buddha** (☎ 360 1030; Na'ama Bay; 1pm-3am), and the **Pirates' Bar** (☎ 360 0137; Hilton Fayrouz Village, Na'ama Bay), with a popular happy hour from 5.30pm to 7.30pm.

Getting There & Around

Daily flights to Cairo, Luxor and Alexandria are available with **EgyptAir** (☎ 366 1056; www.egyptair.com; Sharm al-Maya; 9am-9pm), though prices tend to fluctuate wildly depending on the season and availability. Microbuses charge E£2 between the airport and Na'ama Bay or Sharm el-Sheikh; taxis charge E£20/40.

A high-speed ferry (one way/round trip E£250/400 or US$40/70; one to two hours) operates between Sharm el-Sheikh and Hurghada four times a week. Tickets can be bought from travel agencies or the port ferry office, two hours before departure. Taxis to

Na'ama Bay cost E£25 from outside the port compound. Inside the compound, they cost double.

The bus station is between Na'ama Bay and Sharm el-Sheikh. There are frequent services to Cairo (E£65 to 75, five to six hours) and Dahab (E£15 to E£20, one to two hours).

DAHAB
☎ 069

Long hailed as the Koh Samui of the Middle East, Dahab has a long history of luring travellers – and trapping them for days or weeks on end – with its cheap ocean-side camps, golden beaches and rugged mountain backdrop. In recent years Dahab has expanded beyond its humble origins, and now boasts a smooth fusion of hippie mellowness and resort chic. The banana pancakes, moonlight spliffs and hard-core backpackers still remain, though they now coexist with upscale restaurants, boutique hotels and holidaying European families. However, while the vast majority of Sinai is being packaged and sold for mainstream consumption, Dahab is a place where individual travellers are still the rule rather than the exception.

Orientation

There are two parts to Dahab: Dahab City has five-star hotels and the bus station; Assalah, once a Bedouin village, is about 2.5km north and is divided into two sections, Masbat and Mashraba.

Information

Internet access is available at **Download.Net** (per hr E£5; ☀ 24hr), next to the Nesima Resort, and **Felopater Internet** (per hr E£5; ☀ 10am-midnight), both in Mashraba.

The **National Bank of Egypt** (☀ 9am-10pm), on the corniche in Masbat, has an ATM and changes cash and travellers cheques. The post office and **telephone centrale** (☀ 24hr) are in Dahab City.

Activities
SNORKELLING & DIVING

Other than just lounging around, snorkelling and diving are the most popular activities in Dahab. Nearly all of the town's accommodation offers diving safaris, though the following are particularly recommended:

Desert Divers (☎ 364 0500; www.desert-divers.com; Masbat)

Fantasea Dive Centre (☎ 364 0483; www.fantasea diving.net; Masbat)

Inmo Divers Home (☎ 364 0370; www.inmodivers.de; Inmo Hotel, Mashraba)

Nesima Dive Centre (☎ 364 0320; www.nesima-resort .com; Nesima Hotel, Mashraba)

Penguin Divers (364 1047; www.penguindivers.com; Penguin Village, Mashraba)

CAMEL & JEEP SAFARIS

Dahab is one of the best places in Sinai to arrange camel safaris into the dramatic mountains lining the coast, especially the spectacular Ras Abu Gallum Protectorate. When choosing who to go with, try to find a Bedouin – or at least an operator that works with the Bedouin. Expect to pay from E£75 to E£100 per person for an evening trip into the mountains with dinner at a Bedouin camp, and from about E£300 to E£400 per person per day for a safari including all food and water.

Centre for Sinai (☎ 364 0702; www.centre4sinai. com.eg) is one organisation that tries to promote knowledge of the local culture. **Man & the Environment Dahab** (MATE; ☎ 364 1091; www. mate-info.com) is an environmental education group that helps arrange treks with Bedouin guides. Contact both organisations via telephone or email in order to arrange tours around Sinai.

Sleeping
BUDGET

Bishbishi Garden Village (☎ 364 0727; www.bishbishi. com; Mashraba; s €5-13, d €10-19, tr €21-23; ✖ 🖳) Set back from the sea on the street parallel to the waterfront is this classic backpacker spot, where guests congregate in several cushion-strewn and palm-shaded public spaces.

Penguin Village (☎ 364 1047; www.penguindivers .com; Mashraba; s €7-20, d €10-25, tr €22-30; ✖ 🖳) Another enduring backpacker favourite, the Penguin serves up its own brand of Bedouin chic, complete with pillow lounges overlooking the sand and sea that are best appreciated with several friends and a towering hookah.

MIDRANGE

New Sphinx Resort (☎ 548 8708; www.sphinxdahab.com; Mashraba; d from US$55; ✖ 🖳 🖳) Somewhat akin to an upmarket backpacker spot, this perennially popular mini-resort offers a slightly more refined take on the Bedouin camp theme that dominates Dahab's budget scene.

EGYPT

Alf Leila (☎ 364 0595; www.alfleila.com; Mashraba; r from US$60; ✂ ⊟ ☎) At long last, Dahab finally has a boutique hotel that pays tribute to the distinct architectural design elements that have emerged over the centuries from the Arab world.

Nesima Resort (☎ 364 0320; www.nesima-resort.com; Mashraba; s/d €55/65, ste €90; ✂ ⊟ ☎) Overlooking the beach in Mashraba, this modest resort is a compromise for those who want resort living without feeling as if they're isolated from the town.

TOP END

Hilton Dahab Resort (☎ 364 0310; www.hilton.com; Resort Strip; r from US$125; ✂ ⊟ ☎) The five-star Hilton is the big boy on the block and easily the swankiest hotel in the Dahab area. Though it's more subdued than some of its flashier cousins around the world, the whitewashed, domed two-storey villas strewn along the resort strip are still a class act.

Eating & Drinking

Jay's Restaurant (Masbat; dishes E£25-55) A Dahab institution serving a mixture of Egyptian and Western fare at very reasonable prices.

Tota Restaurant (Masbat; dishes E£25-60) This unique boat-shaped bar in the heart of Assalah also serves decent Italian cuisine.

Carm Inn (Masbat; dishes E£30-70) This waterfront place has a varied menu of Western, Indian and Indonesian dishes served in mellow surroundings with a hint of the South Pacific.

Blue Beach (Masbat; dishes E£35-85) Blue Beach contributes to the Thai-beach-party flair that characterises much of Dahab by offering authentic Southeast Asian–style curries.

Al Capone (at the bridge; dishes E£40-95) The impressive seafood offering, bridge-side location, and the occasional live music and belly dancing makes the strangely named Al Capone an obligatory stop.

Getting There & Around

The **bus station** (☺ 7.30am-11pm) is located in Dahab City. There are frequent services travelling to Cairo (E£60 to E£70, nine hours) and Sharm el-Sheikh (E£15 to E£20, one to two hours). There is also a 9.30am bus to St Katherine (E£20 to E£25, two to three hours), though it's much more convenient to organise a service taxi or private vehicle in the late afternoon.

ST KATHERINE'S MONASTERY
☎ 069

A place of pilgrimage for Christians since the Middle Ages, St Katherine's Monastery, at the foot of Mt Sinai, was built in the 6th century by Emperor Justinian. In residence are around two-dozen Greek Orthodox monks whose order was founded in the 4th century AD by the Byzantine empress Helena. She built the **monastery** (☎ in Cairo 02-2482 8513; admission free; ☺ 9am-noon Mon-Wed, Fri & Sun, except religious holidays) beside the burning bush (still thriving) from which God allegedly spoke to Moses.

The monastery is dedicated to St Katherine, the 4th-century martyr of Alexandria, who was tortured to death on a spiked wheel. According to legend, her body posthumously appeared on top of the highest mountain in Egypt, near Mt Sinai, which was renamed Gebel Katarina in her honour. Along with Mt Sinai, the monastery is protected by the 4350-sq-km **St Katherine Protectorate** (per person US$5), which is open to pilgrims and hikers the world over.

In the village of Al-Milga, about 3.5km from the monastery, there's a post office, a telephone centrale, a bank, shops and cafes. The **Banque Misr** (☺ 10am-1pm & 5-8pm Sat-Thu) changes cash and gives Visa and MasterCard advances. There are no ATMs or internet cafes, though you can stock up on supplies at the local shops and markets.

The friendly **El-Malga Bedouin** (☎ 010-641 3575; www.sheikhmousa.com; per person campsites E£10, per person r E£30-60; ⊟), a 10-minute walk from the bus station, offers mattresses on straw floors in stone buildings.

For those wishing to savour the sanctity of the monastery once the tour parties have departed, the **Monastery Guesthouse** (☎ 347 0353; St Katherine's Monastery; dm per person half board US$25, s/d/tr incl bathroom & half board US$40/60/75) offers plain but adequate rooms.

There is a daily bus to Cairo (E£60, six to seven hours), and another to Dahab at 1pm (E£20 to E£25, two to three hours).

Service taxis usually wait at the monastery for people coming down from Mt Sinai in the morning, and then again around noon when visiting hours end. A lift to the village costs E£10 to E£15. Plan on paying about E£30/45 per person to get to Dahab/Sharm el-Sheikh. To Cairo, expect to pay about E£400 per vehicle.

CLIMBING MT SINAI

There are two well-defined routes up to the summit – the **camel trail** and the **Steps of Repentance** – that meet about 300m below the summit at a plateau known as Elijah's Basin. Here, everyone must take a steep series of 750 rocky and uneven steps to the top, where there is a small chapel containing paintings and ornaments. Both the climb and the summit offer spectacular views of nearby plunging valleys and of jagged mountain chains rolling off into the distance, and it's usually possible to see the even higher summit of Gebel Katarina in the distance. Most people make the climb in the pre-dawn hours to see the magnificence of the sun rising over the surrounding peaks, and then arrive back at the base before 9am, when the monastery opens for visitors.

The camel trail is the easier route, and takes about two hours to ascend, moving at a steady pace. The trail is wide, clear and gently sloping as it moves up a series of switchbacks, with the only potential difficulty – apart from sometimes fierce winds – being gravelly patches that can be slippery on the descent. Most people walk up, but it's also possible to hire a camel for a negotiable price at the base, just behind the monastery, to take you all or part of the way to where the camel trail meets the steps.

The alternative path to the summit, the taxing 3750 Steps of Repentance, was laid by one monk as a form of penance. The steps – 3000 up to Elijah's basin and then the final 750 to the summit – are made of roughly hewn rock, and are steep and uneven in many places, requiring strong knees and concentration in placing your feet. If you want to try both routes, it's best to take the path on the way up and the steps – which afford impressive views of the monastery – on the way back down.

SUEZ CANAL

The Suez Canal severs Africa from Asia and links the Mediterranean with the Red Sea. Watching supertankers gliding through the desert as they ply the narrow channel is a bizarre spectacle. A hotly contested triumph of modern engineering, the canal opened in 1869 and remains one of the world's busiest shipping lanes. If you're transiting the canal, the best way to view this engineering wonder is by taking the free ferry from Port Said to the suburb of Port Fuad.

PORT SAID

☎ 066 / pop 570,000

At Port Said, watching enormous ships and tankers lining up to pass through the canal's northern entrance is an impressive sight to behold. Although heavily damaged in the 1967 and 1973 wars with Israel, much of the city has been rebuilt along its historic lines. Today, Port Said exudes a prosperous and bustling air, particularly its historic waterfront of late-19th-century colonial buildings.

Information

Banque du Caire and National Bank of Egypt have ATMs and you can change travellers cheques at **Thomas Cook** (☎ 322 7559; ☾ 8am-4.30pm), next to the petrol station. On Sharia Palestine you'll find **Amex** (☾ 9am-2pm & 6.30-8pm Sun-Thu), the **main post office** (☾ 8.30am-2.30pm), **telephone centrales** (☾ 24hr) and a helpful **tourist office** (☎ 323 5289; ☾ 9am-6pm Sat-Thu, to 2pm Fri). Internet access is available from **Compu.Net** (per hr E£3; ☾ 9am-midnight), opposite the main post office.

Sights & Activities

TOWN CENTRE

The heart of Port Said is located along the edge of the canal, on and around Sharia Palestine. Here, the waterfront is lined with late-19th-century five-storey buildings complete with wooden balconies, louvered doors and high verandahs in grand *belle époque* style.

PORT FUAD

Across the canal from Port Said is the genteel suburb of Port Fuad, founded in 1925. The streets near its quay invite a stroll, with the sprawling residences, lush gardens and sloping tiled roofs that recall the one-time European presence in the area. Free ferries from Port Said to Port Fuad offer impressive views of the canal, and leave about every 10 minutes throughout the day from the terminal at the southwestern end of Sharia Palestine.

Sleeping & Eating

Hotel de la Poste (☎ 322 4048; 42 Sharia al-Gomhuriyya; s/d from E£75/100) Port Said's best budget option, this faded classic still manages to maintain a hint of its original charm.

New Regent Hotel (☎ 323 5000; off Sharia al-Gomhuriyya; s/d from E£220/245; 🅧 🖳) A drab concrete highrise with a surprisingly smart interior, rooms here are a bit on the smallish side, but they're kept in spotless shape.

Helnan Port Said (☎ 332 0890; www.helnan.com; Sharia Atef as-Sadat; s/d from US$200/400; 🅧 🖳 🅡) Overlooking the Mediterranean at the north end of town, the five-star Helnan offers low-key luxury rather than opulent pleasure.

El Borg (☎ 332 3442; Sharia Atef as-Sadat; dishes E£10-25; 🕑 10am-3am) A local favourite, with an Arabic-only menu, and serve-yourself seafood grills.

Getting There & Away

The bus station is about 3km from the town centre at the beginning of the road to Cairo (about E£3 to E£5 in a taxi). From here, there are twice-hourly buses to Cairo (E£25, three hours) and a bus to Alexandria (E£30, four hours) at 4.30pm daily.

RED SEA COAST

Arguably the world's most famous stretch of coast, it was here that Moses allegedly parted a great sea and set free the Hebrew slaves. For independent travellers weary of package tourism, the Red Sea Coast can be a frustrating place to visit, though it remains a decent destination for families and divers in search of a cheap holiday.

HURGHADA

☎ 065

Once an isolated and modest fishing village, Hurghada has metamorphosed into a sprawling collection of more than 100 hotels, and is today Egypt's most popular resort destination for foreign travellers. Despite its immense popularity, a good number of travellers in the know tend to shun Hurghada's frightful mix of rampant construction and largely unchecked environmental degradation.

To be fair, Hurghada was put on the map because of its superb diving, and there are some incredible sites here that remain in

reasonable health. Hurghada is also a good stop if you want to combine a diving holiday with a visit to Luxor, or if you're looking for an alternative route to Sinai from the Nile Valley.

Orientation & Information

Most budget hotels are in Ad-Dahar, which is north of the resorts. The port is at Sigala. South of Sigala is the 15km upmarket 'resort strip'.

Most banks in Hurghada have ATMs.

Speed.Net (Sharia Al-Hadaba, Sigala; per hr E£10; 🕑 10am-midnight; 🅧)

Main post office (Sharia an-Nasr, Ad-Dahar)

Telephone centrale (Sharia an-Nasr, Ad-Dahar; 🕑 24hr)

Thomas Cook (☎ 354 1870/1; Sharia an-Nasr, Ad-Dahar; 🕑 9am-2pm & 6-10pm).

Tourist office (☎ 344 4421; 🕑 8am-8pm) On the resort strip.

Activities

SNORKELLING & DIVING

Although there is some easily accessible coral at the southern end of the resort strip, the best reefs are offshore, and the only way to see them is to take a boat and/or join a snorkelling or diving excursion. The following is a list of recommended operators:

Aquanaut Red Sea (☎ 065-354 9891; www.aquanaut. net; Corniche, Ad-Dahar, Hurghada)

Jasmin Diving Centre (☎ 065-346 0475; www.jasmin -diving.com; resort strip, Hurghada)

Easy Divers (☎ 065-354 7816; www.easydivers-redsea. com; Corniche, Ad-Dahar, Hurghada)

Subex (☎ 065-354 7593; www.subex.org; Ad-Dahar)

Sleeping

El-Arosa Hotel (☎ 354 8434; elarosa hotel@yahoo.com; off Corniche; s/d from E£115/165; 🅧 🅡) El-Arosa is one of the best deals in town – rooms are equipped with modern amenities, and there's even a pool (even if it is in the dining room).

Sea Garden (☎ 344 7493; www.seagarden.com.eg; off Sharia Sheraton; s/d from US$65/70; 🅧 🖳 🅡) The Sea Garden is a discernible step-up in quality – with a three-star rating, you can expect well-cared-for rooms and a reasonably professional level of service.

Le Pacha Resort (☎ 344 4150; www.lepach aresort.com; Sharia Sheraton; s/d incl all meals from US$75/115; 🅧 🖳 🅡) If you're looking for a comparatively cheap all-inclusive, this centrally located Sigala hotel offers outdoor pools, a private beach and an on-site shopping mall.

Jasmine Village (☎ 346 0460; www.jasminevillage. com; s/d all-inclusive from US$65/85; ✖ 🖳 🖭) Guests stay in one of 400-plus bungalow-style rooms, which look out onto a proper beach, a stunning coral reef and the open ocean.

Oberoi Sahl Hasheesh (☎ 344 0777; www.oberoiho tels.com; Sahl Hasheesh; ste from €200; ✖ 🖭 🖳 🖭) Peaceful, exclusive and opulent beyond your imagination, the Oberoi features palatial suites decorated in minimalist Moorish style.

Eating & Drinking

Felfela Restaurant (Sharia Sheraton; dishes E£15-55; ☽ 8.30am-midnight) Sitting on a gentle bend in the coastline, and overlooking the turquoise sea, this branch of the Felfela chain wins a prize for vistas.

Rossi Restaurant (Sharia Sheraton; mains E£20-45) This popular hang-out for divers and expats serves a variety of pizza toppings on crispy crusts, and pasta dishes.

Little Buddha (Village Rd; mains E£45-75) One of Hurghada's most well-known Asian restaurants. The cuisine at Little Buddha is a fusion of sushi spreads, Chinese-style seafood dishes and plenty of rice and noodle concoctions.

Papas Bar (www.papasbar.com; Sharia Sheraton, Sigala) This popular Dutch-run bar is the centre of nightlife in Hurghada, and deservedly popular with local expats.

Getting There & Around

EgyptAir (☎ 344 3592/3; www.egyptair.com; Resort Strip) has daily flights to Cairo and Sharm el-Sheikh; prices tend to fluctuate wildly depending on the season and availability.

The ferry to Sharm el-Sheikh departs from Hurghada at 9.30am on Monday, Tuesday, Thursday and Saturday (E£250/US$40 one way, E£450/US$70 round trip, 90 minutes). Note that departure times of the Sharm el-Sheikh ferry don't correspond with bus arrivals from Luxor, so you'll need to spend at least one night in Hurghada.

There are frequent buses to Cairo (E£70, six hours) and Luxor (E£30 to E£35, five hours), in addition to a daily bus service to Alexandria (E£90, nine to 10 hours).

ALEXANDRIA

☎ 03 / pop 4.1 million

The city of Alexandria (Al-Iskendariyya) is the stuff that legends are made of: the city was founded by none other than Alexander the Great, and sassy queen Cleopatra made this the seat of her throne. During the 19th century, a cosmopolitan renaissance had Alexandria flirting with European-style decadence, however, this was cut short in the 1950s by Gamal Abdel Nasser's wave of change.

Today, modern Alexandria feels like a teenager eager to forge its own identity. The daring new library of Alexandria signalled a brave leap into modernity, the first tentative steps of a city ready to revamp itself for the future. This town is also swooping in on the role of Egypt's culture vulture – legions of young artists and writers are finding their voices and new cutting-edge venues are providing a stage for their prolific output.

HISTORY

Established in 332 BC by Alexander the Great, the city became a major trade centre and focal point of learning for the entire Mediterranean. Its ancient library held 500,000 volumes and the Pharos lighthouse was one of the Seven Wonders of the Ancient World. Alexandria continued as the capital of Egypt under the Roman and Byzantine Empires until the 4th century. The city thereafter went into decline until the 19th century, when Napoleon revived Alexandria as a major port. Despite the 1952 Revolution, during which the nationalistic mood of the moment expelled the majority of foreign interests and stripped the city of its expatriate contingency, much of the city's cosmopolitan character remains.

ORIENTATION

Nearly 20km long from east to west and only about 3km wide, Alexandria is a true waterfront city. The focal point is Midan Ramla, also known as Mahattat Ramla (Ramla station), the terminus for the city's tramlines. Immediately adjacent is Midan Saad Zaghloul, a large square running to the seafront. Most traveller amenities are centred on these two *midan*s.

EGYPT

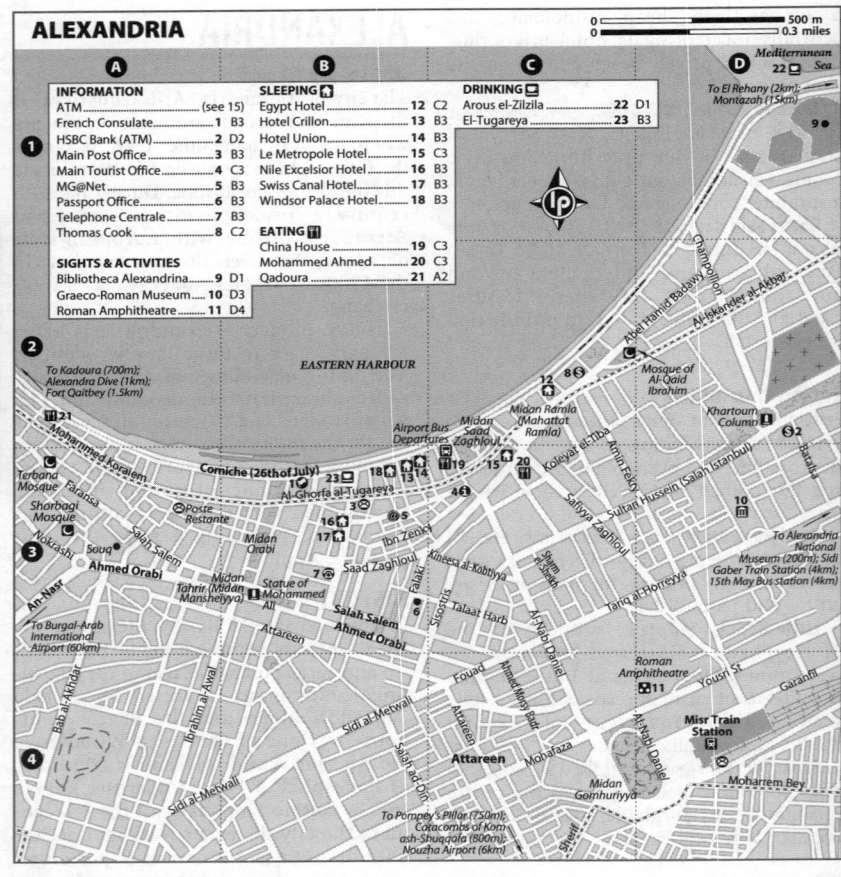

ALEXANDRIA

INFORMATION	
ATM	(see 15)
French Consulate	1 B3
HSBC Bank (ATM)	2 D2
Main Post Office	3 B3
Main Tourist Office	4 C3
MG@Net	5 B3
Passport Office	6 B3
Telephone Centrale	7 B3
Thomas Cook	8 C2

SIGHTS & ACTIVITIES	
Bibliotheca Alexandrina	9 D1
Graeco-Roman Museum	10 D3
Roman Amphitheatre	11 D4

SLEEPING	
Egypt Hotel	12 C2
Hotel Crillon	13 B3
Hotel Union	14 B3
Le Metropole Hotel	15 C3
Nile Excelsior Hotel	16 B3
Swiss Canal Hotel	17 B3
Windsor Palace Hotel	18 B3

EATING	
China House	19 C3
Mohammed Ahmed	20 C3
Qadoura	21 A2

DRINKING	
Arous el-Zilzila	22 D1
El-Tugareya	23 B3

INFORMATION

There are many exchange bureaus between Midan Ramla and the corniche and along Sharia Talaat Harb.

HSBC Bank (47 Sharia Sultan Hussein) There's an ATM here and another in the foyer of Le Metropole Hotel.

Main post office Two blocks east of Midan Orabi.

Main tourist office (☎ 485 1556; Midan Saad Zaghloul; ⊗ 8.30am-6pm) This helpful place is beneath the tourist police station.

MG@Net (per hr E£2; ⊗ 10am-midnight) Internet access, near Midan Saad Zaghloul.

Passport office (28 Sharia Talaat Harb; ⊗ 8am-1.30pm Sat-Thu) For visa extensions; it's off Sharia Salah Salem.

Telephone centrale (Midan Gomhurriya; ⊗ 24hr)

Thomas Cook (☎ 484 7830; 15 Sharia Saad Zaghloul; ⊗ 8am-5pm) The best option for cashing travellers cheques.

SIGHTS

Relics retrieved from the seabed are displayed at the **Alexandria National Museum** (Sharia Tariq al-Horreyya; adult/student E£35/20; ⊗ 9am-4pm), just east of the city centre.

The marble terraces of the only **Roman Amphitheatre** (Sharia Yousef; adult/student E£20/15; ⊗ 9am-5pm) in Egypt were discovered in 1964. Also worth seeing is the 'Villa of the Birds' **mosaic** (adult/student E£10/5) in the grounds.

Dating from the 2nd century AD, the honeycomb **Catacombs of Kom ash-Suqqafa** (Carmous; adult/student E£35/20; ⊗ 8am-5pm) once housed 300 corpses – and a rather macabre funereal dining chamber used for wakes. The principal tomb combines Egyptian, Greek and Roman iconography.

NAUTICAL ARCHAEOLOGY

Alexandria has sunk between 6m and 8m since antiquity, so most of what remains of the ancient city lies hidden beneath the modern city or the waters of the Mediterranean. So far, exploration has been concentrated around the fortress of Qaitbey where the Pharos is believed to have stood, the southeastern part of the Eastern Harbour, where parts of the submerged Ptolemaic royal quarter were found, and Abu Qir, where remains of the two sunken cities of Herakleion and Menouthis were found.

The Qaitbey dive has recorded hundreds of objects, including sphinx bodies, columns and capitals, and fragments of obelisks. Divers also discovered giant granite blocks broken as if by a fall from a great height, and more recently, pieces of stone believed to have formed the frame of a massive gateway – all more circumstantial evidence for the likely end of the Pharos.

Some recovered treasures can be seen in the city's museums, and there are tentative plans for the world's first underwater museum. For now, it's possible to explore the submerged harbour sites through **Alexandra Dive** (☎ 483 2045; www.alexandra-dive.com; Corniche, Anfushi), where a two-dive package costs US$100, with equipment rental an extra US$20. Another, newer company is **Blue Spot Divers** (☎ 961 1601; www.bluespotdivers.com; Sidi Bishr), which organises similar trips. Several divers have reported that poor visibility in the bay (as little as 1m depending on the time of year) affected their enjoyment of the harbour dives.

The catacombs are a five-minute walk from the famed and misnamed **Pompey's Pillar** (adult/student E£20/15; ⏰ 8am-5pm), the top of which once hosted a party of 22. Louis XIV of France nearly took it home as a plinth for his own statue.

Fort Qaitbey (adult/student E£25/15; ⏰ 9am-4pm), at the end of the corniche, was built on the foundations of the destroyed Pharos lighthouse in 1480.

Inspired by the original library, founded in the early 3rd century BC and hailed as the greatest of all classical institutions, **Bibliotheca Alexandrina** (☎ 483 9999; www.bibalex.org; Corniche al-Bahr; adult/student main library E£10/5, antiquities museum E£20/10, manuscript collection E£20/10; ⏰ 11am-7pm Sun, Mon, Wed & Thu, 3-7pm Fri & Sat) is an attempt to put the city back on the world's cultural map. Note the external frieze in letters, pictograms, hieroglyphs and symbols from every known alphabet.

Objects of interest in the **Graeco-Roman Museum** (☎ 483 6434) include a carved head of Cleopatra and terracotta lanterns depicting the ancient Pharos lighthouse. Unfortunately, the museum has been closed for several years for renovations, and it's unlikely it will open during the shelf life of this book.

SLEEPING

Hotel Crillon (480 0330; 3rd fl, 5 Sharia Adib Ishaq; s/d incl breakfast E£72/99) Smack dab on the corniche, this place has oodles of character but is a little rough around the edges. It boasts high ceilings, cream-and-white painted walls, and balconies with cane furniture.

Hotel Union (☎ 480 7312; 5th fl, 164 Sharia 26th of July; s E£70-140, d E£90-160; ❄) The smallish rooms are still quite charming, relatively well maintained and come in a bewildering mix of bathroom/view/air-con options and rates.

Egypt Hotel (☎ 481 4483; 1 Degla; incl breakfast s US$40-63, d US$47-68) The Egypt single-handedly fills a desperate need for decent midrange digs. A noticeable step up from the budget choices, it's set in a renovated 100-year-old Italian building right on the corniche.

Nile Excelsior Hotel (☎ 480 0799; nile_hotel@yahoo.com; 16 Sharia al-Bursa al-Qadima; s/d E£60/100, with air-con E£100/180; ❄) A very central hotel on the same street as the Spitfire bar (handy for stumbling to bed). The stairs up to the hotel are rather dirty and uninviting, but the small rooms have high ceilings and fly the 'clean and comfortable' flag with pride.

Swiss Canal Hotel (☎ 480 8373; 14 Sharia al-Bursa al-Qadima; s/d with fan E£78/90, with air-con E£90/113) The walls here are an iridescent shade of pink that really has to be seen to be believed, but if you look past that the rooms are generally clean, with towering ceilings, mammoth wooden doors, spongy soft beds, en suite bathrooms, and windows overlooking a reasonably quiet souq area. In summer, the rooms with air-con (takeef) are better value.

Le Metropole Hotel (☎ 486 1467; www.paradiseinnegypt.com; 52 Sharia Saad Zaghloul; s/d US$100/150) Once you're past the magnificently tacky lobby with its fake Parthenon-style friezes, the lushly carpeted hallways lead to tasteful rooms with gigantic gilded doors.

Windsor Palace Hotel (☎ 480 8123; www.paradise innegypt.com; 17 Sharia ash-Shohada; s/d sea view US$150) This bejewelled Edwardian gem is an institution unto itself, towering over the corniche and keeping a watchful eye on the Med since 1907.

EATING

Mohammed Ahmed (☎ 483 3576; 17 Sharia Shakor Pasha; dishes E£2-5) The undisputed king and still champion of *fuul* and *ta'amiyya*, Mohammed Ahmed is filled day and night with locals downing small plates of spectacularly good and cheap Egyptian standards.

China House (☎ 487 7173; Cecil Hotel, 16 Midan Saad Zaghloul; mains E£30-50; ☽ 11am-11.30pm) Atop the Cecil Hotel, this highly recommended restaurant serves scrumptious Asian food beneath a tent with dangling lanterns and stunning views over the harbour.

Qadoura (☎ 480 0405; 33 Sharia Bairam at-Tonsi; meals E£35-80; ☽ 9am-3am) Pick your fish from a huge ice-packed selection, which usually includes sea bass, red and grey mullet, bluefish, sole, squid, crab and prawns, and often a lot more.

DRINKING

Alexandria is famous for its cafes and coffee shops, where an accompanying pastry is *de rigueur*.

ourpick Arrous el Zilzila (Shatby Beach, across from the Bibliotheca Alexandrina; ☽ 24hr) This fantastic *ahwa* is practically the only one in Alexandria – you can sip tea and sheesha to the sound of waves rolling in, smelling sea air instead of petrol fumes. Directly on the water, it has rustic open-air tables and palm trees with cheerful coloured lights, set around a small curving beach where you can hardly hear the traffic.

El Rehany (☎ 590 5521; corniche, Camp Chesar, cnr Ismail Fangary St) Sheesha here is served with a flourish by attentive boys in smart two-toned waistcoats while waiters in black-and-white bring tea in silver urns.

El Tugareya (corniche; ☽ 9am-late) Although it may not look like much to the uninitiated (it doesn't even sport a sign), this 90-year-old institution is one of the most important *ahwa*s in town.

GETTING THERE & AWAY
Air
Alexandria is served by several major international carriers.

The airport infrastructure is undergoing significant change. There are two airports; the larger, **Burg al-Arab** (☎ 459 1483), is 60km west of the city and, at the time of writing, was closed for a major overhaul and extension. While the work is ongoing, all air traffic is being routed to the smaller airport at **Nouzha** (☎ 425 0527), much closer to the city.

Once Burg al-Arab reopens, it will become the city's primary airport and most or all flights to Nouzha will cease. This is scheduled for 2010, but delays are standard practice in Egypt, so check on the situation locally.

Bus
The 15th of May bus station is behind Sidi Gaber train station. The tram trip from Midan Ramla takes 30 minutes. There are services to Cairo (E£25, two to three hours) every 30 minutes from 5.30am to 10pm. Other daily services go to Siwa (E£33 to 35, eight to nine hours), Port Said (E£30, four hours) and Hurghada (E£90, nine to 10 hours).

Train
There are more than 15 trains daily between Cairo and Alexandria, from 6am to 11pm. There are three train types: the special (*turbini*), Spanish (*espani*), and French (*faransawi*). Special and Spanish trains (1st/2nd class E£50/35; 2½ hours) are much better, as they make fewer stops. The French train (1st/2nd class E£35/22; 3½-four hours) makes multiple stops. First class (ula) is well worth the additional cost, as you get a roomier seat and cleaner bathroom, though both classes have well-functioning *takeef* (air conditioning). Seats are reserved, and your assigned car and seat should be printed on the ticket – ask a conductor for help finding it if needed.

GETTING AROUND
As a visitor to Alexandria, you'll rarely use the buses, and while the tram is fun, it's painfully slow. Taxis are generally the best options for getting around. Some sample fares are Midan Ramla to Mihattat Misr station E£5 to E£7; Midan Saad Zagloul to Fort Qaitbey E£5; Midan Saad Zagloul to the Library E£5; Hotel Cecil to Montazah or Mamoura from E£22 to E£25.

> ### RESPECTING LOCAL TRADITION
>
> Siwans are very proud of their traditions, which are part of what makes the place so unique. They are particularly sensitive where female modesty is concerned. The least visitors can do to help preserve Siwa's culture is to respect local sensibilities and act accordingly. Modest dress is appreciated and women travellers in particular should make sure they cover their upper arms and their legs, and wear baggy T-shirts over bathing suits when taking a dip in any of the numerous springs. Do not, as the tourist office puts it, show 'displays of affection' in public.

WESTERN DESERT

It's more ancient than the Pyramids, more sublime than any temple. Nearly as vast as your imagination, Egypt's Western Desert stretches from the Nile and the Mediterranean to the Sudanese and Libyan borders, rolling far into Africa oblivious to any lines drawn on the map.

SIWA OASIS
☎ 046

Ringed by salt lakes, dunes and desert escarpment, Siwa is a haven of date plantations and olive groves. It has a distinctive Berber culture, preserved due to its relative isolation – an asphalt road to the coast was only constructed in the 1980s. With the 13th-century *shali* (fortress) at its core, there's plenty to potter round while relaxing into the rhythm of life in the slow lane.

Information
North of the main square, **El Negma Internet Centre** (☎ 460 0761; per hr E£10; ☿ 9am-midnight) is located near the *shali*. **Banque du Caire** (☿ 8.30am-2pm & 5-8pm) has an ATM and there's also a post office and helpful **tourist office** (☿ 9am-5pm Sat-Thu).

Sights & Activities
Siwa's attractions include **springs** where you can swim, the remains of the **Temple of the Oracle**, where Alexander came to confirm his divinity, and some Graeco-Roman **tombs**. At the edge of town are the towering dunes of the **Great Sand Sea**.

DESERT TRIPS
All desert trips require permits, which cost US$5 plus E£11 and are usually obtained by your guide from the tourist office. Prices and itineraries vary, but one of the most popular trips takes you to the desert hot spring at Bir Wahed, on the edge of the Great Sand Sea. Here you can have a simple meal or tea, then move on to the nearby spring-fed lake, where, in the summer, you can take a dip. Usually you will do a spot of dune driving, stop at fossil sites and see some fantastic desert vistas before returning to Siwa. This half-day trip costs about E£80 per person plus permission costs.

Other popular half-day itineraries include a tour of the springs Ain Qurayshat, Abu Shuruf, Az-Zeitun and Ain Safi (E£50 per person); and a tour of Siwa Town and its environs (Temple of the Oracle, Gebel al-Mawta, Cleopatra's Bath, Shali fortress and Fatnas; E£30). Overnight trips vary in length according to destination but a popular one-night trip is to Qara Oasis (E£300 to E£500 per vehicle, depending on whether asphalt or desert track is taken).

Sleeping & Eating
Desert Rose (☎ 012-440 8164; ali_siwa@hotmail.com; s/d/tr without bathroom E£80/150/180, s/d/tr E£120/200/280; ☒) Overlooking the magnificent dunes that stretch out to the southeast of Siwa, this friendly and cosy little hotel has creatively decorated, spotless rooms in a funky octagonal building.

Taziry Ecolodge (☎ 02-3337 0842, 012-340 8492; reservation@taziry.com; Gaary; s/d/ste incl full board US$180/225/345; ☒) This lovely hotel was designed and built by its friendly owners, an artist and an engineer, to be tranquil and laid back, with no electricity, and a natural spring pool overlooking the lake.

[our pick] Adrère Amellal (☎ 02-2736 7879, 02-2738 1327; www.adrereamellal.net; Sidi Jaafar, White Mountain; s/d/ste incl all meals, drinks & desert excursions US$415/550/ from 750; ☒) This impeccable desert retreat lies coddled in its own oasis, with stunning views over the salt lake of Birket Siwa and the dunes of the Great Sand Sea beyond. It is a truly unique place, built by environmentalist Munir Neamatallah out of *kershef* (large chunks of salt mixed with rock), and using revived traditional building techniques.

Tanta Waa Coffeeshop & Restaurant (☎ 010-472 9539; meals E£10-30; ☿ 8am-late) This superchilled and creatively clad mudbrick cafe at Cleopatra's Bath is the perfect place for a cool drink or tasty meal in between splashes in the spring.

Getting There & Around

There are three daily buses to (and from) Alexandria (E£33 to £35, eight to nine hours). Buses are often full, so buy a ticket in advance from West Delta Bus Co near the sports centre.

Donkey carts within town cost E£5. Bone-rattling bikes from the main square cost E£10 per day.

BAHARIYA OASIS

☎ 011

Bahariya is one of the more fetching of the desert circuit oases, and at just 365km from Cairo is also the most accessible. Surrounded on all sides by towering ridges, much of the oasis floor is covered by verdant plantations of date palms and pockmarked with dozens of refreshing springs.

The **tourist office** (☎ 847 3039; Main St, Bawiti; ☺ 8am-2pm & 7-9pm Sat-Thu) has official opening hours, but is open at whim. The **National Bank of Development** (☺ 8am-2pm Sun-Thu), near the tourist office, changes money but not travellers cheques.

Attractions include the **Temple of Alexander**, tombs at **Qarat Qasr Salim**, and 10 of the 10,000 famous Graeco-Roman **mummies**, which are on show near the **Antiquities Inspectorate Ticket Office** (admission to all local sites adult/student E£45/25; ☺ 8.30am-4pm).

Sleeping & Eating

New Oasis Hotel (☎ 02-3847 3030; max_rfs@hotmail.com; by El-Beshmo spring; s/d E£50/80, with air-con E£100/120; ✹) A study in curvaceous construction, this small but homely hotel has several teardrop-shaped rooms, some with balconies overlooking the expansive palm groves nearby.

Western Desert Hotel (☎ 012-433 6015, 012-301 2155; www.westerndeserthotel.com; off Sharia Misr; s/d E£110/160; ✹ 💻) The clean, tiled rooms are good value – the ones in back have views of the gardens and desert in the distance – and the staff is a good bunch who aren't pushy about their safaris.

Old Oasis Hotel (☎ 012 232 4425; www.oldoasissafari. com; by El-Beshmo spring; s/d/tr E£90/120/180, with air-con E£120/180/220; ✹ 🍴) The Old Oasis Hotel sits above a pretty, shaded garden of palm and

olive trees, and has a dozen or so simple but impeccable fan rooms, as well as a few fancier stone-wall air-con rooms.

Food options are limited to the hotels, a basic cafeteria near the petrol station or the town's **Popular Restaurant** (☎ 847 2239; set meals E£20; ☺ 5am-midnight), which lives up to its name and offers good set meals.

Getting There & Away

Buses run to Cairo (E£30, four to five hours) at 6.30am, 10am and 3pm from the kiosk near the post office. These are often full, so it's strongly advised to buy tickets the day before travelling.

There are two more Cairo-bound buses that originate in Dakhla and pass through Bawiti around noon and midnight, stopping at the Hilal Coffeehouse at the western end of town. For those, buy your ticket on the bus, and hope there are seats!

If you're heading to Farafra (E£20, two hours) or Dakhla (E£40, four to five hours), you can hop on one of the buses headed that way from Cairo. They leave Bahariya around noon and 11.30pm from the Upper Egypt kiosk and Hilal Coffeehouse.

FARAFRA OASIS

☎ 092

The smallest of the oases, Farafra is the best place from which to visit the spectacular **White Desert** – an outstanding area of windblown rock formations. The only tourist attraction in town is **Badr's Museum** (☎ 751 0091; admission E£5; ☺ 8.30am-sunset), a gallery run by enthusiastic local artist Badr Moghny.

Al-Waha Hotel (☎ 016 209 3224, 012 720 0387; wahafarafra@yahoo.com; d without bathroom E£30, r E£50) is a small, spartan hotel opposite Badr's Museum, and the only real budget choice in town.

Al-Badawiya Safari & Hotel (☎ 751 0060, 012-214 8343; www.badawiya.com; s/d €25/35, villas with air-con €35/55; ✹ 💻 🍴) has a wide choice of stylishly designed and traditionally themed rooms and is dotted with cushioned sitting areas, has a refreshing pool, and boasts more than its fair share of arches and domes.

Buses travel to Cairo (E£45, eight to 10 hours) via Bahariya (E£20, two hours) daily at 10.30am and 10.30pm. Buses coming from Cairo go on to Dakhla (E£20, four to five hours) and leave from outside the shops at the Dakhla end of the main street.

DAKHLA OASIS
☎ 092

With more than a dozen fertile hamlets sprinkled along the Western Desert circuit road, Dakhla lives up to most visitors' romantic expectations of oasis life. Lush palm groves and orchards support traditional villages, where imposing, ancient mudbrick forts still stand guard over the townships and allude to their less tranquil past.

The oasis of Dakhla contains two small towns, **Mut** and **Al-Qasr**. Mut is the larger, with most of the hotels.

The **tourist office** (☎ 782 1685/6; Sharia as-Sawra al-Khadra; ☺ 8am-3pm) is on Mut's main road. The Abu Mohamed Restaurant, opposite the tourist office, offers **internet access** (per hr E£5; ☺ 7am-midnight). In Mut, **Bank Misr** (Sharia Al-Wadi) changes cash and travellers cheques, and has an ATM.

There are 600 **hot springs** in the vicinity and an atmospheric mudbrick citadel at Al-Qasr with a small **Ethnographic Museum** (admission E£5; ☺ 8am-2pm Sat-Thu). In exchange for baksheesh, aged local guides escort you through the citadel's narrow alleyways, unlock *madrassas*, houses and mosques, and show you working forges.

Sleeping & Eating

El-Kasr Hotel (☎ 787 6013; r E£30) Conveniently located on the main road near the old town, El-Kasr is the best backpacker option in town.

Bedouin Oasis Village (☎ 782 0070, 012-669 4893; s/d E£70/150, incl full board E£100/200) This attractive mudbrick building with outdoor terrace and fort-style annexe is good value.

Desert Lodge (☎ 772 7061/2, in Cairo 02-690 5240; www.desertlodge.net; s/d/tr incl half board US$80/120; ❌ 💻 ☎) Perched on a hill near the escarpment overlooking Al-Qasr, this fort-style ecolodge has added some desert whimsy to the landscape. With a billiard room, giant outdoor chess set, licensed restaurant, and Bedouin tent for evening sheeshas, it's hard to find the motivation for the desert safaris on offer.

A couple of good restaurants are recommended in town, including the long-established **Abu Mohamed Restaurant** (☎ 782 1431; Sharia as-Sawra al-Khadra; dishes E£8-10) and **Ahmed Hamdy's Restaurant** (☎ 782 0767; Sharia as-Sawra al-Khadra; dishes E£16).

Getting There & Around

Buses leave from the main square in Mut at 6am and 6pm travelling to Farafra (E£20, four to five hours), Bahariya (E£40, four to five hours) and Cairo (E£55, eight to 10 hours). Buses to Al-Kharga (E£16, three hours) leave at 5am, 11am, 2pm, 11pm, 1am and 3.30am.

Local pick-ups depart from near the police station in Mut and travel to Al-Qasr for 75pt. Abu Mohamed Restaurant hires out bikes for E£10 per day.

AL-KHARGA OASIS
☎ 092

Except for the impressive **Antiquities Museum** (Sharia Gamal Abdel Nasser; adult/student E£30/15; ☺ 9am-4pm), which houses mummies and gilded masks, embalmed birds and rams, the town of Al-Kharga is of little interest. You are likely to be escorted by police from your arrival in town.

There's a helpful **tourist office** (☎ 792 1206; Midan Nasser; ☺ 8am-3pm, variable evening hr Sat-Thu), and **Banque du Caire** (off Sharia Gamal Abdel Nasser) has an ATM and changes cash and travellers cheques.

North of town is the well-preserved **Temple of Hibis** (adult/student E£30/15; ☺ 8am-5pm), built by the Persian emperor Darius I. To the east you'll find the remains of the **Temple of An-Nadura**, built by the Romans, and the nearby 4th-century Coptic **Necropolis of Al-Bagawat**. South of town are the fortified Roman temples of **Qasr al-Ghueita** and **Qasr az-Zayyan**.

You can camp in the palm-filled garden of the affable **Kharga Oasis Hotel** (☎ 792 4940; Midan Nasser; s/d E£175/260; ❌) for E£7.50 per person and use the shared bathrooms for a few piastres more. Behind the museum is clean and comfortable **El-Radwan Hotel** (☎ 792 1716, 012-747 2087; off Sharia Gamal Abdel Nasser; s/d E£45/65; ❌ 💻). Four-star pink confection **Pioneers Hotel** (☎ 792 9751-3; www.solymar.com; Sharia Gamal Abdel Nasser; s/d incl half board from €66/84; ❌ 💻 ☎) is a favourite with Egyptian businessmen.

Restaurants are scarce in Kharga. Eat in the hotels or try Al-Ahram, at the front of the Waha Hotel on Sharia an-Nabawi, which sells cheap roast chicken and salads.

Buses leave from the bus station behind Midan Basateen. Daily services include Cairo (E£60, eight to 10 hours) and Dakhla (E£16, three hours).

EGYPT

NILE VALLEY

Measuring 6680km in length, the Nile is the world's longest river. It brought the nation of Egypt into being and its banks are clustered with the temples and tombs of the country's illustrious past. Luxor and Aswan are the jewels in the crown and few can resist time spent on the water itself.

LUXOR

☎ 095 / pop 451,300

Built around the 4000-year-old site of Thebes, the ancient capital of the New Kingdom, contemporary Luxor is an eccentric combination of provincial town and staggering ancient splendour. The concentration of monuments is extraordinary: they tower incongruously above the buzz of everyday life and make this a most compelling destination.

There is simply nothing in the world that comes close to the grandeur of ancient Thebes. The mid-19th-century traveller Florence Nightingale described it as 'the deathbed of the world' and likened it to the writings of Shakespeare, somewhere one learned the origin and meaning of many things one took for granted.

Although the modern east-bank city has grown rapidly in recent years, the setting is still breathtakingly beautiful, the Nile flowing between the modern town and the west-bank necropolis, backed by the enigmatic Theban escarpment. Scattered across the landscape is an embarrassment of riches, from the temples of Karnak and Luxor on its East Bank to the temples of Deir al-Bahri and Medinat Habu, the Colossi of Memnon and the Valley of the Kings on the West Bank.

Orientation

Luxor comprises the town of Luxor on the East Bank of the Nile; the village of Karnak, 2km to the northeast; and the villages and ancient monuments on the West Bank of the Nile.

In town, there are three main thoroughfares: Sharia al-Mahatta (running from the station to Luxor Temple), Sharia al-Karnak (Luxor Temple to the Temples of Karnak) and the corniche. Most budget hotels are located between the train station and Sharia Televizyon. Banks, the main tourist office and other services are clustered around the Old Winter Palace Hotel on the corniche.

Information

There are ATMs at Banque du Caire and National Bank of Egypt on the corniche.

Aboudi (☎ 237 2390; Corniche el-Nil; per hr E£10; 🕒 9am-10pm) Internet access.

American Express (☎ 237 8333; Old Winter Palace Hotel, Corniche el-Nil; 🕒 9am-4.30pm)

Main post office (Sharia al-Mahatta)

Main tourist office (☎/fax 237 2215; Corniche el-Nil; 🕒 8am-8pm) This helpful place is in the tourist bazaar.

Passport office (☎ 238 0885; 🕒 8am-2pm Sat-Thu) For visa extensions; opposite the Isis Pyramisa Hotel.

Rainbow Net (☎ 238 7938; Sharia Yousef Hassan; per hr E£6; 🕒 9am-midnight) Internet access.

Telephone centrale (🕒 8am-10pm) By the Old Winter Palace Hotel.

Thomas Cook (☎ 237 2196; Old Winter Palace Hotel, Corniche el-Nil; 🕒 8am-2pm & 3-8pm)

Sights

EAST BANK

The **Luxor Museum** (Corniche el-Nil; adult/student E£80/40; 🕒 9am-2pm & 4-9pm) has a select collection of Theban relics and an informative video presentation. To learn more about the ancient journey into the afterlife, visit the **Mummification Museum** (Corniche el-Nil; adult/student E£50/25; 🕒 9am-1pm & 4-9pm).

The town centre spills around magnificent **Luxor Temple** (☎ 237 2408; adult/student E£50/30; 🕒 6am-9pm). Largely built by the New Kingdom Pharaoh Amenhotep III, it was continually added to over the centuries. In the 13th century, the Arabs built a mosque in an interior court.

Of the more than 700 human-headed, lion-bodied statues that once lined the **Avenue of Sphinxes** between the temples of Luxor and Karnak, around 60 still remain.

Much more than a temple, **Karnak** (☎ 238 0270; adult/student E£65/40; 🕒 6am-5.30pm) is a spectacular complex of sanctuaries, pylons and obelisks. Its crowning glory is the **Great Hippostyle Hall**, constructed around 134 lotus-blossom pillars. Begun in the Middle Kingdom, the complex was added to, dismantled, restored, enlarged and decorated over 1500 years.

If you can tolerate the crowds and the kitsch, the **sound and light show** (☎ 238 6000/2777; www.soundandlight.com.eg; adult/student E£100/60, video camera E£35; 🕒 6.30pm, 7.45pm & 9pm winter, 8pm, 9.15pm & 10.30pm summer) offers a nonetheless

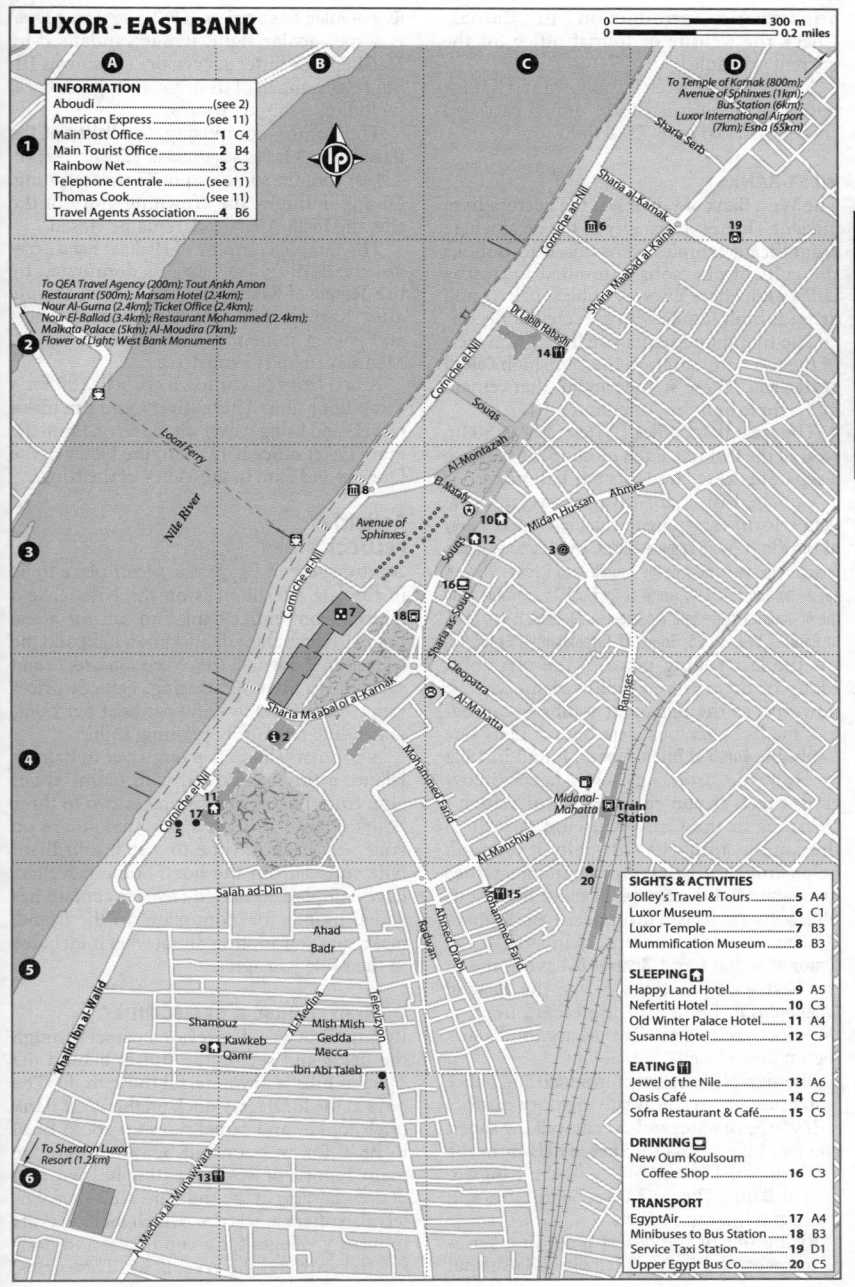

LUXOR - EAST BANK

0 — 300 m
0 — 0.2 miles

INFORMATION
Aboudi...........................(see 2)
American Express.............(see 11)
Main Post Office...............**1** C4
Main Tourist Office...........**2** B4
Rainbow Net...................**3** C3
Telephone Centrale..........(see 11)
Thomas Cook..................(see 11)
Travel Agents Association....**4** B6

To QEA Travel Agency (200m); Tout Ankh Amon
Restaurant (500m); Marsam Hotel (2.4km);
Nour Al-Gurna (2.4km); Ticket Office (2.4km);
Nour El-Ballad (3.4km); Restaurant Mohammed (2.4km);
Malkata Palace (5km); Al-Moudira (7km);
Flower of Light; West Bank Monuments

To Temple of Karnak (800m);
Avenue of Sphinxes (1km);
Bus Station (6km);
Luxor International Airport
(7km); Esna (55km)

Nile River

Sharia Serb

Corniche an-Nil

Sharia al-Karnak

Sharia Maabad al-Karnak

Dr Labib Habashi

Souqs

Al-Montazah

El-Matafi

Souqs

Midan Hussan Ahmes

Avenue of Sphinxes

Sharia as-Souq

Cleopatra

Al-Mahatta

Mohammed Farid

Sharia Maabad al-Karnak

Local Ferry

Corniche el-Nil

Corniche el-Nil

Ramses

Midanal-Mahatta Train Station

Salah ad-Din

Al-Manshiya

Mohammed Farid

Ahmed Orabi

Ahad Badr

Shamouz

Kawkeb Qamr

Mish Mish Gedda Mecca

Ibn Abi Taleb

Al-Medina

Televizyon

Radwan

Khalid Ibn al-Walid

To Sheraton Luxor Resort (1.2km)

Al-Medina al-Munawwara

SIGHTS & ACTIVITIES
Jolley's Travel & Tours.......**5** A4
Luxor Museum.................**6** C1
Luxor Temple..................**7** B3
Mummification Museum....**8** B3

SLEEPING
Happy Land Hotel.............**9** A5
Nefertiti Hotel.................**10** C3
Old Winter Palace Hotel.....**11** A4
Susanna Hotel.................**12** C3

EATING
Jewel of the Nile..............**13** A6
Oasis Café.....................**14** C2
Sofra Restaurant & Café....**15** C5

DRINKING
New Oum Koulsoum
Coffee Shop................**16** C3

TRANSPORT
EgyptAir.......................**17** A4
Minibuses to Bus Station....**18** B3
Service Taxi Station...........**19** D1
Upper Egypt Bus Co..........**20** C5

EGYPT

atmospheric introduction to Karnak. Check the website or tourist office for the current schedule.

Microbuses between Luxor town and Karnak cost 50pt. A *calèche* (horse-drawn carriage) costs E£7; a taxi costs E£10 to E£15.

WEST BANK

The West Bank of Luxor was the necropolis of ancient Thebes, a vast city of the dead where magnificent temples were raised to honour the cults of pharaohs entombed in nearby cliffs, and where queens, nobles, priests and artisans built tombs with spectacular decor.

The first monuments you'll see, 3km west of the ferry crossing, are the 18m-high **Colossi of Memnon**. These statues are all that remain of a temple built by Amenhotep III.

The **main ticket office** (6am-4pm) is 500m west of the Colossi. Each monument requires a separate ticket. Students pay half price.

Couched in a sun-ravaged ravine of **Al-Qurn** (Horn) escarpment, the celebrated **Valley of the Kings** (Wadi Biban al-Muluk; www.thebanmapping project.com; adult/student for 3 tombs excl Ramses VI, Ay & Tutankhamun E£80/40, Tomb of Ay E£25/15 available from the Antiquities Inspectorate office near Medinat Habu, Tomb of Ramses VI E£50/25, Tomb of Tutankhamun E£100/60;) is the last resting place of the pharaohs. Many of them weren't allowed much rest, however, as the pillage of tombs began before the last pharaohs were buried. Only one tomb, the **tomb of Tutankhamen**, found in 1922 by Howard Carter, has so far been discovered intact. If you've seen Tutankhamen's treasures in the Cairo Museum, a visit to the simple tomb of this minor pharaoh helps indicate what unimaginable riches once attended the tombs of more illustrious pharaohs such as Tuthmosis I or Ramses II. The corridors and antechambers of the **tombs of Sethos I** and **Ramses IX** have some of the best wall paintings, while the **tomb of Amenophis II**, hidden in the escarpment, is the most exciting to visit. Many tombs are, regrettably, closed.

Photography is strictly forbidden and police won't hesitate to confiscate memory cards.

If you have water and decent walking shoes, you can hike across the **Theban Hills** from the tomb of Seti I in the Valley of the Kings to Deir al-Bahri. The walk takes 50 minutes and is extremely steep in parts.

Rising out of the desert plain in a series of terraces, the **Funerary Temple of Hatshepsut**

(Deir al-Bahri; adult/student E£30/15; 6am-4.30pm) is a spectacular sight. It was vandalised by Hatshepsut's bitter successor, Tuthmosis III, but retains much of its original magnificence, including elaborate friezes.

The tombs composing the **Valley of the Queens** (for 3 tombs adult/student E£35/20; 6am-4.30pm) contain some exquisite wall painting. Disappointingly, the crowning glory of the site, the **Tomb of Nefertari**, remains closed.

The temple complex of **Medinat Habu** (adult/student E£30/15; 6am-4.30pm) is dominated by the **Temple of Ramses III**. The largest temple after Karnak, with many colourful reliefs and golden stone that catches fire at sunset, Medinat Habu is a must-see.

A taxi from Luxor town costs E£100 for a three-hour tour. Alternatively, you can hire a bicycle and bring it over on the ferry. From the main ticket office it's 1km to the Valley of the Queens and 5km to the Valley of the Kings.

Activities
FELUCCA RIDES

As elsewhere in Egypt, the nicest place to be in the late afternoon is on the Nile. Take a felucca from either bank and sail for a few hours to catch the soft afternoon light and the sunset; cool down in the afternoon breeze and calm down after sightseeing. Felucca prices range from E£30 to E£50 per boat per hour, depending on your bargaining skills.

A popular felucca trip is upriver to Banana Island, a tiny isle dotted with palms about 5km from Luxor. The trip takes two to three hours. Plan it in such a way that you're on your way back in time to watch a brilliant Nile sunset from the boat. Some travellers have complained that the felucca captain has added money for 'admission' to the island; make sure you are clear about what is included in the price you agree.

DONKEY, HORSE & CAMEL RIDES

Riding a horse, a donkey or a camel through the fields and seeing the sunset behind the Theban hills is a wonderful thing to do. The boys at the local ferry dock on the West Bank offer donkey and camel rides for about E£30 to E£40 for an hour, but beware. There are many reports of women getting hassled, and of overcharging at the end. The West Bank hotels also offer camel trips, which include visits to nearby villages for a cup of tea, and donkey treks around the West Bank. These trips, which start at around 7am (sometimes 5am) and finish near lunchtime, cost a minimum of about E£50 per person.

Tours

Jolleys Travel & Tours (☎ 237 2262; www.jolleys. com; Corniche el-Nil; ☼ 9am-10pm) This reputable company, located next to the Old Winter Palace, also runs day trips to the main sites.

QEA Travel Agency (☎ 231 1667; Al-Gezira) A different approach from this British-run agency that runs tailor-made tours in and around Luxor, as well as further afield to the Red Sea or in the Western Desert.

Sleeping

Many Luxor hotels charge 50% less in summer. For a more tranquil experience, try West Bank hotels.

EAST BANK

Happy Land Hotel (☎ 227 1828; www.luxorhappyland. com; Sharia Qamr; s/d without bathroom E£30/45, s/d/tr with bathroom, fridge & air-con E£70/80/110; ☒ ▣) A back-packers' favourite, Happy Land offers clean rooms and spotless bathrooms, as well as very friendly service, a copious breakfast with fruit and cereal and a rooftop terrace.

our pick **Nefertiti Hotel** (☎ 237 2386; www.nefertitihotel.com; Sharia as-Sahabi, btwn Sharia al-Karnak & Sharia as-Souq; s/d/tr US$9/13/16; ☒ ▣) The energetic Aladin as-Sahabi runs his family's hotel with great care, offering recently renovated, midrange facilities at budget prices. No wonder this hotel is popular with our readers: the rooms are simple but cosy, the small private bathrooms are spotless and the staff is super friendly.

Susanna Hotel (☎ 236 9915; www.susannahotelluxor. com; 52 Sharia Mabad al-Karnak; city view s/d/tr US$30/35/50, Nile view s/d/tr US$40/45/60; ☒ ▣) Set between the Luxor temple and the souq, this new modern hotel has comfortable beds and great views, as well as a good rooftop terrace restaurant with views over Luxor temple and the Nile.

Sheraton Luxor Resort (☎ 237 4544; www.starwoodhotels.com/sheraton; Sharia Khaled ibn al-Walid; s/d from US$75/90; ☒ ☒ ▣) This secluded three-storey building is set amid lush gardens at the far southern end of Sharia Khaled ibn al-Walid – close enough to walk to some restaurants but far enough away to avoid any street noise.

Old Winter Palace Hotel (☎ 237 1197; www.sofitel. com; Corniche el-Nil; old wing r €180-350, ste €420-890, new wing pavilion r €108-120, ste €325; ☒ ☒ ▣) A wonderfully atmospheric Victorian pile, this place has high ceilings, lots of gorgeous textiles, fabulous views over the Nile, an enormous garden with exotic trees and shrubs, a huge great swimming pool, table-tennis tables and a tennis court.

WEST BANK

Marsam Hotel (☎ 237 2403, 231 1603; www.luxor-westbank.com/marsam_e_az.htm; Gurna; s/d without bathroom E£50/100, s/d E£75/150) Built for American archaeologists in the 1920s, the Marsam, formerly the Sheikh Ali Hotel, is the oldest on the West Bank. The hotel is charming, with 30 simple rooms set around a lovely courtyard, with ceiling fans and traditional palm-reed beds.

Flower of Light (☎ 231 4043, 010-232 4475; www.floweroflight.com; al Gourna; d E£200-205; ☒ ▣ ☒) Small new ecolodge with mudbrick bungalows set in a shady and tranquil garden, with a lovely swimming pool and Bedouin-style tent where drinks are served.

Malkata Palace (☎ 012-773 4312, 010-116 8531; www.hughsowdenegypt.com; Malqatta; per person E£300, meals E£100; ☒) Built right on the edge of the desert, on the site of the palace of Amenhotep III (1.5km south of Medinat Habu temple), this wonderful domed mudbrick house in traditional Egyptian style, offers a unique stay on the West Bank.

our pick **Al-Moudira** (☎ 012-325 1307; www.moudira.com; Daba'iyya; r €220, ste €270; ☒ ☒ ▣ ☒) The Al-Moudira is a Moorish fantasy of soaring vaults, pointed arches and enormous domes. Each room is different in shape, size (all are very large, though) and colour, each with its own hand-painted theme and with antiques found throughout Egypt. Cushioned benches and comfortable antique chairs invite pashalike lounging and the enormous vaulted bathrooms have the feel of a private *hammam* (bathhouse).

Eating & Drinking

EAST BANK

our pick **Sofra Restaurant & Café** (☎ 235 9752; www.sofra.co.eg; 90 Sharia Mohamed Farid; mains E£20-55; ☼ 11am-midnight) Sofra remains our favourite restaurant in Luxor. Located in a 1930s house, away from all the tourist tat, it is as Egyptian as can be, both in menu and decor – and even in price.

Oasis Café (☎ 012-336 7121; Sharia Dr Labib Habashi; mains E£15-60; ☼ 10am-10pm; ☒) Set in a renovated 1930s building right in the centre of town, this bistro has dining rooms with high ceilings and

---

NO MORE POLICE CONVOY AROUND LUXOR

Until early 2009, getting out of Luxor by road involved travelling in an armed police convoy. But now most restrictions have been lifted. With the exception of the roads from Aswan to Abu Simbel, and Asyut to Cairo, it is now once again possible to travel by private taxi or car to Denderah and Abydos. You can also make the trip from Luxor to Aswan and stop for as long as you like at the temples along the way. But there are still security checks and if you do take a private car south to Aswan, or to Qena or Abydos, bear in mind that, in the morning, the driver will need to take your passport to the **Travel Agents Association** (cnr Sharia Televizyon & Sharia Ibn Abu Taleb) for a *tasrih* (permission), which is fortunately easy to get and surprisingly free of charge.

---

old tiled floors, painted in soft colours with local artwork on the walls, and furnished with traditional-style furniture.

Jewel of the Nile (☎ 016-252 2394; mains E£25-35, set menu E£50-60; ☻ 10am-midnight winter, 1pm-midnight summer; ☒ ☐) Laura and Mahmud offer traditional Egyptian food using organic vegetables from their own farm.

New Oum Koulsoum Coffee Shop (Sharia as-Souq; ☻ 24hr) Pleasant *ahwa* right at the heart of the souq, on a large terrace with welcome mist machines, where you can recover from shopping and haggling in the souq and watch the crowds without any hassle.

WEST BANK

Restaurant Mohammed (☎ 231 1014; Gurna; set meals E£20-40; ☻ 24hr) This eccentric but recommended restaurant is set in the peaceful courtyard of Mohammed Abdel Lahi's mudbrick house, near the ticket office. Mohammed's mother cooks delicious *kofta tagen* (spiced mince meat served in an earthenware pot; E£20), served with home-grown salad leaves.

Tout Ankh Amon Restaurant (☎ 231 0918, 016-461 6598; Al-Geziră; mains E£30-50; ☻ 11am-10pm) Hagg Mahmoud was a cook at one of the French archaeological missions and he and his sons are still cooking his excellent *tagens*, *duck à l'orange*, chicken with rosemary and other dishes.

Getting There & Away
AIR
EgyptAir (☎ 238 0581; Corniche an-Nil; ☻ 8am-8pm) operates several daily flights between Cairo, Luxor and Aswan.

BOAT
During the high season (October to May), an armada of cruise boats travels the Nile between Esna (for Luxor) and Aswan, stopping at Edfu and Kom Ombo en route. They vary wildly in cost from US$50 to US$200 per night for full board, and reservations can be made through any travel agent or even your accommodation.

BUS
The bus station is out of town, located approximately 1km from the airport, but tickets for **Upper Egypt Bus Co** (☎ 232 3218, 237 2118; ticket office, Midan al-Mahatta) buses can be bought at its office in town, south of the train station. A taxi from the town to the bus station will cost around E£25 to E£35, but check because some buses leave from the office near the train station.

Buses heading to Cairo leave at 6.30pm from the office near the railway station and 7pm from the bus station (E£100, 10 to 11 hours), but booking ahead is essential as the bus fills up quickly. Six daily buses head to Hurghada (E£30 to E£35, five hours) from 6.30am to 8pm.

TRAIN
Luxor Station (☎ 237 2018; www.egyptrail.gov.eg; Midan al-Mahatta) has left-luggage facilities, plenty of cardphones and a post office.

The **Abela Egypt Sleeping Train** (☎ 237 2015, 02-2574 9474; www.sleepingtrains.com) goes daily to Cairo at 9.40pm and 12.50am (single/double including dinner and breakfast US$80/120, children four to 19 years US$45, nine hours). There are no student discounts; tickets must be paid for in US dollars or euros.

The only other trains to Cairo permitted for foreigners are the air-conditioned 85 leaving at 8.15pm and arriving in Cairo at 7.15am (E£165), and the 981 (adult 1st/2nd class E£79/41, student 1st/2nd class E£45/30, 10 hours).

There are several trains to Aswan (adult 1st/2nd class E£41/25, student 1st/2nd class

E£32/20, three hours) a day: the 996 at 7.30am, the 1902 at 9.30am and the 980 at 5.45pm.

Getting Around
A taxi from **Luxor International Airport** (☎ 237 4655), 7km east of town, costs around E£25 to East Bank destinations and E£50 to West Bank destinations. There are no buses between the airport and town.

For about E£20 per hour you can get around town by *calèche*, but be sure to bargain hard.

SOUTH OF LUXOR
Edfu
The attraction in this town is the **Temple of Horus** (adult/student E£50/25; ⏰ 6am-4pm), the most completely preserved temple in Egypt. Built by the Ptolemies over a period of 200 years, it was dedicated to the falcon-headed son of Osiris.

Trains running between Luxor and Aswan stop here; the station is approximately 4km from the temple and taxis to the site cost E£10. Most cruise boats stop here and a *calèche* from the waterfront costs around E£20.

Kom Ombo
Spectacularly perched on the Nile near the village of Kom Ombo, the **Temple of Sobek & Haroeris** (adult/student E£30/20; ⏰ 6am-4pm) is dedicated to the crocodile god and falcon-headed sky god. In ancient times sacred crocodiles basked in the sun along the river bank here; these days, crocodiles are unable to swim past the High Dam at Aswan.

If you're travelling from Luxor you can stop here on the train and take a taxi to the site (E£10). A return taxi from Luxor to Edfu and Kom Ombo costs E£250 to E£300. Cruise boats moor alongside the temple steps.

ASWAN
☎ 097 / pop 241,000
Egypt's southernmost city sits on the banks of a particularly beautiful stretch of the Nile, decorated with palm-fringed islands and flotillas of white-sailed feluccas. Associated with the Nubian people, a distinct ethnic group with their own language and customs, the town is more African in character than the cities of the north.

Orientation
The bus and train stations are at the northern end of town. The lively souq (Sharia as-Souq) runs parallel to the corniche. Banks, restaurants and shops are located on the corniche, which ends at the imposing Coptic cathedral, the Nubia Museum and the city's better hotels.

Information
The main banks have branches on the corniche; there are ATMs at Banque Misr, Banque du Caire and the National Bank of Egypt.
American Express (☎ 230 6983; Corniche an-Nil; ⏰ 9am-5pm) Cashes travellers cheques.
Aswan Internet Café (☎ 231 4472; Corniche an-Nil; per hr E£10; ⏰ 9am-midnight)
Aswanet (☎ 231 7332; Kelany Hotel, Sharia Keylany; per hr E£10; ⏰ 9am-1am) Internet access.
Main post office (Corniche an-Nil; ⏰ 8am-2pm Sat-Thu) Next to the rowing club.
Main tourist office (☎ 231 2811; Midan al-Mahatta; ⏰ 8am-3pm & 6-8pm) Next to the train station.
Passport office (1st fl, Police Bldg, Corniche an-Nil; ⏰ 8.30am-1pm Sat-Thu) Visa extensions are available here.
Telephone centrale (Corniche an-Nil; ⏰ 24hr) Just past the EgyptAir office.
Thomas Cook (☎ 230 4011; Corniche an-Nil; ⏰ 8am-2pm & 5-9pm) Cashes travellers cheques.

Sights
You don't have to be in Aswan long to recognise local ethnic pride. Justice is given to the history, art and culture of the local people in the excellent **Nubia Museum** (Sharia Abtal at-Tahrir; adult/student E£50/25; ⏰ 9am-1pm & 5-9pm). The 'Nubia Submerged' exhibition, which includes photographs of Philae and Abu Simbel before they were re-sited, tells the story of how the Nubian homeland was submerged by the building of Lake Nasser. The entrance is opposite the Basma Hotel, a 15-minute walk from the town centre.

The **unfinished obelisk** (adult/student E£30/20; ⏰ 7am-5pm) lies in the granite quarries that supplied the stone for pyramids and temples. Three sides of the shaft, which is nearly 42m long, were excavated before it was discarded due to a flaw in the granite. Taxis charge E£5 from the centre of town.

From Aswan, felucca trips (from E£25 per hour) can be organised to Kitchener's Island's verdant **botanical garden** (admission E£15; ⏰ 8am-5pm) and the 6th-century Coptic **Monastery of St Simeon** (adult/student E£20/10; ⏰ 7am-4pm winter). To reach the monastery, take a camel from the dock (from E£50). You can also get a boat to Old and Middle Kingdom **tombs** (adult/student

EGYPT

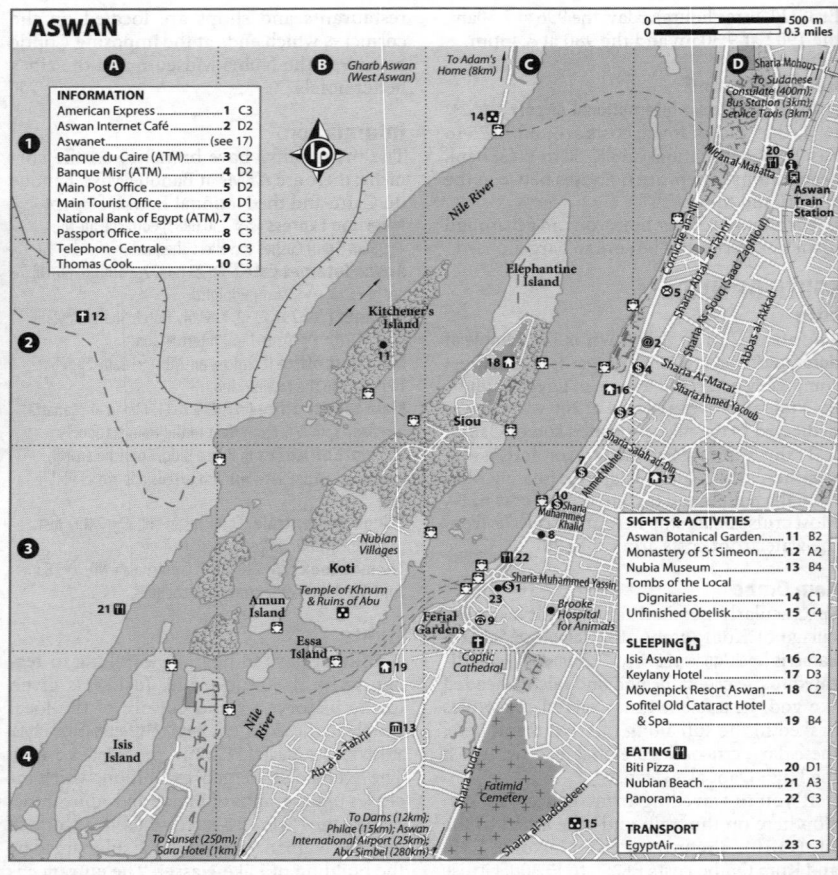

ASWAN

INFORMATION
American Express.....................1 C3
Aswan Internet Café..................2 D2
Aswanet...............................(see 17)
Banque du Caire (ATM)..............3 C2
Banque Misr (ATM)..................4 D2
Main Post Office......................5 D2
Main Tourist Office...................6 D1
National Bank of Egypt (ATM).7 C3
Passport Office.......................8 C3
Telephone Centrale..................9 C3
Thomas Cook.........................10 C3

SIGHTS & ACTIVITIES
Aswan Botanical Garden......11 B2
Monastery of St Simeon......12 A2
Nubia Museum.................13 B4
Tombs of the Local
   Dignitaries.................14 C1
Unfinished Obelisk............15 C4

SLEEPING
Isis Aswan....................16 C2
Keylany Hotel................17 D3
Mövenpick Resort Aswan..18 C2
Sofitel Old Cataract Hotel
   & Spa.......................19 B4

EATING
Biti Pizza.....................20 D1
Nubian Beach................21 A3
Panorama....................22 C3

TRANSPORT
EgyptAir.....................23 C3

E£20/10; 8am-4pm) of local dignitaries on the West Bank.

Tours

Small hotels and travel agencies arrange day tours of the area's major sights. Half-day guided tours usually include the Temple of Isis at Philae, the Unfinished Obelisk and the High Dam, and start at E£300 (per person with three to five people). Travel agencies will also arrange felucca trips to Elephantine and Kitchener's Islands for about E£75 to E£100 per person, based on a group of three to five people, but it is cheaper to deal directly with the boatmen.

All travel agencies and most hotels in Aswan offer trips to Abu Simbel, but watch out for huge price differences, and check that the bus is comfortable and has air-con. Thomas Cook charges about E£1000 per person, including a seat in an air-con minibus, admission fees and guide, and E£1400 by air, including transfers, fees and guide. By contrast, budget hotels offer tours for about E£200 to E£300 in a smaller bus, often not including the entrance fee or guide.

Sleeping

Adam's Home (010-640 4302; www.adamsnubyana. com; Sheikh Mohammed, Gharb Aswan; r E£50) A different experience awaits you at this beautiful Nubian house in the village of Sheikh Mohammed on the West Bank, 7km north of Aswan, and about 2.5km south of the bridge. Overlanders have long known of this place, which provides camping facilities as well as little mudbrick rooms – bring your sleeping bag.

Keylany Hotel (☎ 231 7332; www.keylanyhotel. com; 25 Sharia Keylany; s/d/tr US$16.50/24/32; ❄ ☐) Aswan's best budget hotel has simple but comfortable rooms, furnished with pine furniture and with spotless bathrooms with proper showers and hot water.

Sara Hotel (☎ 232 7234; www.sarahotel-aswan. com; s/d US$50/80; ❄ ♨) Built on a clifftop overlooking the Nile about 2km beyond the Nubia Museum, the Sara is isolated but has fantastic views over the First Cataract and the Western Desert.

Isis Aswan (☎ 231 5100; www.pyramisaegypt.com; Corniche an-Nil; s/d US$100/120; ❄ ♨) Built right on the riverbank, the Isis has a prime location in the centre of town, and is popular with budget tour groups

Mövenpick Resort Aswan (☎ 230 3455; www.mo evenpick-aswan.com; Elephantine Island; s/d from US$160/190; ❄ ♨) Hidden in a large garden, and characterised by an ugly tower, for many years now rumoured to be demolished soon, the Mövenpick recently had a total makeover and has simple but very comfortable rooms, decorated in Nubian style and colours.

Sofitel Old Cataract Hotel & Spa (☎ 231 6000; www.sofitel.com; Sharia Abtal at-Tahrir; ❄ ♨) The grande dame of hotels on the Nile, the Old Cataract brings you back to the days of Agatha Christie, who is said to have written part of her novel *Death on the Nile* here. Following decades of neglect, President Mubarak saved the hotel from total demolition because he wanted to preserve the place where he spent his honeymoon. At the time of writing, it was scheduled to reopen in 2010 following extensive renovations.

Eating & Drinking

Panorama (☎ 231 6169; Corniche an-Nil; dishes E£8-20) With its pleasant Nileside terrace, this is a great place to chill and sip a herbal tea or fresh juice.

Biti Pizza (Midan al-Mahatta; ❂ 10am-midnight; dishes E£15-22; ❄) Biti is a popular air-conditioned restaurant that serves good Western-style pizzas, but more recommended are the delicious sweet and savoury *fiteer* (flaky Egyptian pizzas).

Sunset (☎ 233 0601, 012-166 1480; Sharia Abtal at-Tahrir in Nasr City; set menu E£45-60; ❂ 9am-3am) This great cafe terrace and restaurant is the place to be at sunset, with spectacular views over the First Cataract.

Nubian Beach (West Bank, past the Aga Khan Mausoleum; set menu per person E£45) Wonderful Nubian cafe-restaurant set in a quiet garden on the west bank of the Nile, against the backdrop of a towering sand dune.

Getting There & Away
AIR
Daily flights are available with **EgyptAir** (☎ 231 5000; Corniche an-Nil; ❂ 8am-8pm) from Cairo to Aswan.

BOAT
See p123 for details of the weekly ferry to Sudan via Wadi Halfa.

Aswan is the best place to arrange overnight felucca trips, because even if the winds fail, the Nile's strong currents propel boats north. The most popular trips are to Kom Ombo and Edfu. Prices are negotiable depending on the season and the size of your party, but you can expect to pay around E£50 per person plus the cost of food and drink supplies.

You could also try a three-night cruise on one of the superbly luxurious boats that slide along the Nile towards Luxor. They vary in cost from US$50 to US$200 per night for full board, and reservations can be made through any travel agent or even your accommodation.

BUS
The bus station is 3.5km north of the train station. There are no buses to Luxor at the time of writing, and travelling by bus to Abu Simbel is restricted to four foreigners per bus. Upper Egypt Bus Co has two daily buses to Abu Simbel (E£25, four hours, departing 8am and 5pm). A direct bus to Cairo (E£100, 14 hours) leaves at 6am and 3pm daily.

TRAIN
From the **Aswan Train Station** (☎ 231 4754) a number of daily trains run north to Cairo, but officially foreigners can only buy tickets in the station for one 1st-class-only train (E£165, 14 hours, 6.45pm). No-one will stop you boarding other trains if you buy the ticket on the train and pay E£6 extra. All trains heading north stop at Daraw (1st/2nd class

---

FEAST, FAMINE OR WAR

Egypt's fate has always been closely intertwined with the amount of water in the Nile, and although the river flows through many countries, it is Egypt that has gained the most from its beneficence. Ancient Egyptians called their country Kemet (Black Land), after the fertile silt that the Nile's receding waters left in their wake. This annual dumping of a thick layer of dark, wet topsoil allowed ancient Egypt's agricultural system to develop and thrive, leading in turn to an accumulation of wealth and the flourishing of a sophisticated society and culture. When the floods failed and hunger turned to famine, the entire system broke down: consecutive years of inadequate flooding often coincided with the collapse of central authority or invasion by a foreign power.

Because of this dependence on the Nile, the Egyptians developed a highly organised irrigation system to help them deal with its unpredictability. Nilometers, a series of steps against which the rising water would be gauged, were used to measure the level of the flood, which was crucial for predicting soil fertility and crop yields. Authorities also used the level of the flood to predict the size of the harvest and therefore fix the level of taxes farmers should pay.

E£20/13, 45 minutes), Kom Ombo (E£22/15, one hour), Edfu (E£25/17, two hours), Esna (E£35/20, 2½ hours) and Luxor (E£40/24, three hours). Student discounts are available on all of these trains.

Abela Egypt Sleeping Train (☎ 230 2124; www.sleep ingtrains.com) has two daily services to Cairo at 5pm and 7pm (single/double cabin per person US$60/120, children aged four to nine years US$45 including dinner and breakfast, 14 hours). Note that there is no student discount, and tickets must be paid for in US dollars.

Getting Around

Service taxis from the **Aswan International Airport** (☎ 248 0333) to the town centre cost E£1. A private taxi should be no more than E£25.

You can get around Aswan by *calèche* (E£10 per hour). A 3½-hour taxi tour to the Temple of Philae, High Dam and Unfinished Obelisk costs around E£30. A taxi anywhere within town (including from the town centre to the bus station) costs E£5.

AROUND ASWAN
High Dam

The original dam across the Nile was built by the British at the beginning of the 20th century; however, it was insufficient to keep the Nile in check during the annual spate. The Egyptian government was assisted by various nations in building a new dam in the 1960s. It was opened with due pomp and ceremony in 1971 and came to be seen as a symbol of Egypt's independence in the modern world. As the full environmental impact of the dam began to be understood, however, it became

source of controversy, not least on account of the disruption it caused to the Nubian communities swallowed up by the creation of Lake Nasser.

To reach the High Dam, taxis cost E£40 to E£50 (round trip).

Philae (Aglikia Island)

Built by the Ptolemies and Romans and relo- cated to a different island after the building of the High Dam in the 1960s, the **Temple of Philae** (adult/student E£50/25; ⏰ 7am-4pm) is a ro- mantic sight. It was dedicated to Isis, who found the heart of her slain brother, Osiris, on Philae Island. Early Christians later turned the hypostyle hall into a chapel.

A nightly **sound-and-light show** (☎ 230 5376; admission E£70), lasting 1½ hours, is held at the temple.

To reach Philae, taxis cost E£40 for the round trip and the boat costs E£35.

Abu Simbel
☎ 097

Perhaps the most striking temple in Egypt, the magnificent **Great Temple of Ramses II** (adult/student E£90/45; ⏰ 5am-5pm) was cut from the hillside to honour the gods Ra-Harakhty, Amun, Ptah and the deified Pharaoh Ramses II. Discovered by Burkhart in 1813, pro- truding from the interring desert sands, the four famous colossal statues of Ramses II sit majestically facing east. Each statue is over 20m tall and flanked by smaller stat- ues of the Pharaoh's mother and his beloved wife, Nefertari.

The neighbouring **Temple of Hathor** is guarded by six further standing statues of Ramses and Nefertari. In the 1960s both temples were winched to higher ground to avoid the rising waters of Lake Nasser in an ingenious feat of engineering.

Don't miss the spectacular **sound-and-light show** (www.soundandlight.com.eg; adult/child E£80/45); with a succinct script and inventive imagery, it's the best in Egypt. With the waters of Lake Nasser quietly lapping the shore behind, a canopy of stars presiding overhead, and the repeated forms of Ramses teased into life by the caresses of superimposed images in front, this is one show that could best be described as 'in the round'.

ourpick Eskaleh (Beit an-Nubi; ☎ 340 1288, 012-368 0521; d €50-70; ✖ 💻) is part Nubian cultural centre with a library dedicated to Nubian history and culture, part small ecolodge in a traditional Nubian mudbrick house, and something of a destination in its own right. Comfortable rooms are simply furnished with local furniture, and have fans, air-con and good private bathrooms. Nubian women prepare home-cooked meals (three-course lunch or dinner E£60) with organic produce from Fikry's garden and fish from the lake.

Getting There & Away

Foreigners travelling from Aswan to Abu Simbel by road must travel in police convoy. The police have deemed taxis off limits to foreigners, so luxury coach or minibus are your only options. Most people opt for a tour and get the admission and guide included.

You can avoid the convoy by taking a bus. Buses from Abu Simbel to Aswan leave at 6am, 9.30am, 1pm and 4pm from the Wadi el-Nil Restaurant on the main road. There are no advance booking sand tickets (E£21) are purchased on board. Note that the official limit is four foreign passengers per bus, although they will generally turn a blind eye to one or two extra.

EGYPT DIRECTORY

ACCOMMODATION

Egypt offers visitors the full spectrum of accommodation: hotels, flotels (Nile cruisers), resorts, pensions, bed and breakfasts, youth hostels, camping grounds and ecolodges.

PRACTICALITIES

- Local news/information in English: *Egyptian Gazette; Al-Ahram Weekly* (www.ahram.org.eg/weekly) appears every Thursday with good what's-on listings

- English broadcasts: BBC World Service (www.bbc.co.uk/worldservice), FM95 (557kHz) and Nile FM (104.2kHz)

- TV News: CNN and BBC World in hotels

- Electrical current: 220V AC, 50Hz (except Alexandria and parts of Cairo: 110V AC, 50Hz)

- Sockets: round, two-pin, European-type

- Measurements: metric

Prices cited in this book are for rooms available in the high season and include taxes. Breakfast is included in the room price unless indicated otherwise in the review. We have roughly defined budget hotels as any that charge up to E£120 for a room, midrange as any that charge between E£120 and E£600 and top end as those that charge E£600 or more for a room. However, there is some variation in pricing brackets throughout the chapter, as certain destinations are pricier than others.

ACTIVITIES

For those with monument fatigue, non-archaeological pursuits include desert safaris in the Sinai and Western Desert. as well as world-class diving and snorkelling in the Sinai and Red Sea area.

BUSINESS HOURS

The official weekend is Friday and Saturday. Note that during Ramadan, all banks, offices, shops, museums and tourist sites keep shorter hours. Note also that all tourist sites are officially open an hour later in summer months: in reality, it's rather more ad hoc.

Banks and government offices 8.30am to 1.30pm Sunday to Thursday.

Post offices 8.30am to 2pm Saturday to Thursday.

Private offices 10am to 2pm and 4pm to 9pm, except Friday.

Restaurants and cafes Noon to midnight daily.

Shops 9am to 2pm and 5pm to 10pm summer, 10am to 7pm winter; some close on Sundays.

CUSTOMS

Visitors may import duty-free 1L of alcohol and 400 cigarettes. Currency, cameras, sports equipment, electronic devices and jewellery are meant to be declared on entry. Note that you can't take Egyptian pounds out of the country.

DANGERS & ANNOYANCES

The incidence of crime, violent or otherwise, in Egypt is negligible compared with most Western countries. Most visitors and residents would agree that Egyptian towns and cities are safe to walk around in during the day or night. Unfortunately, the hassle factor often means that this isn't quite the case for an unaccompanied foreign woman.

Lack of crime aside, terrorist acts against foreign tourists between 1997 and 2009 resulted in a great many deaths, and have led to the government giving security the highest possible priority. That said, we can't blame the government for doing its utmost to convince tourists that their security is of paramount importance to Egypt. After all, the income derived from tourism constitutes an extraordinary 20% or so of the country's GDP.

DISCOUNT CARDS

Discounts to museums and sites are available for students with an International Student Identity Card (ISIC). With proof of status, you can obtain one of these in Cairo from **ESTS** (Map pp88-9; ☎ 02-531 0330; www.estsegypt.com; 23 Sharia Manial, Midan el-Mammalek, El-Roda). Avoid buying bogus cards, or discounts for bona-fide students may be jeopardised.

EMBASSIES & CONSULATES

Most foreign embassies and consulates open from 8am to 2pm Sunday to Thursday.

Australia (Map pp88-9; ☎ 02-2575 0444; 11th fl, World Trade Centre, 1191 Corniche el-Nil, Cairo)

Canada (Map pp88-9; ☎ 02-2791 8700; 26 Sharia Kamal el-Shenawy, Cairo)

Eritrea (Map pp88-9; ☎ 02-3303 3503; eritembe@ yahoo.com; 6 El Fallah St, Mohandessine)

Ethiopia (Map pp88-9; ☎ 02-3335 3696; 3 Sharia al-Missaha, Doqqi)

France Cairo (Map pp94-5; ☎ 02-2394 7150; www. ambafrance-eg.org; 29 Sharia el-Fadl); Alexandria (Map p104; ☎ 03-487 5615; 2 Midan Orabi, Mansheyya)

Germany Cairo (Map pp88-9; ☎ 02-2728 2000; www. kairo.diplo.de; 8 Hassan Sabry, Zamalek); Alexandria (☎ 03-4867 503; 9 Sharia el-Fawateem, Azarita)

Ireland (Map pp88-9; ☎ 02-2735 8264; www.embassy ofireland.org.eg; 22 Hassan Assem, Zamalek)

Israel Cairo (Map pp88-9; ☎ 02-3332 1500; 8 Sharia Ibn Malek, Giza); Alexandria (☎ 03-544 9501; 15 Rue Mina Kafr Abdou, Rushdy)

Jordan (Map pp88-9; ☎ 02-3748 5566; 6 Sharia Gohainy, Cairo)

Libya Cairo (Map pp88-9; ☎ 02-735 1269; fax 735 0072; 7 Sharia el-Saleh Ayoub, Zamalek); Alexandria (☎ 03-494 0877; fax 494 0297; 4 Sharia Batris Lumomba, Bab Shark)

Netherlands (Map pp88-9; ☎ 02-2739 5500; http:// egypt.nlembassy.org; 18 Sharia Hassan Sabry, Zamalek)

New Zealand (Map pp88-9; ☎ 02-2461 6000; www. nzembassy.com; level 8, North Tower, Nile City Towers, 2005C Corniche el-Nil)

Sudan Cairo (Map pp88-9; ☎ 02-2794 9661; 3 Sharia al-Ibrahimy, Garden City); Aswan (Map p116; ☎ 097-230 7231; Bldg 20, Atlas; ⏱ 9am-3pm)

UK Cairo (Map pp88-9; ☎ 02-2791 6000; 7 Sharia Ahmed Ragheb, Garden City); Alexandria (☎ 03-546 7001/2; Sharia Mena, Rushdy)

USA (Map pp94-5; ☎ 02-2797 3300; http://cairo.us embassy.gov; 8 Sharia Kamal el-Din Salah, Garden City)

FESTIVALS & EVENTS

January

Book Fair Held at the Cairo Exhibition Grounds over two weeks, this is one of the major cultural events in the city.

February

Ascension of Ramses II 22 February – one of the two dates each year when the sun penetrates the inner sanctuary of the temple at Abu Simbel, illuminating the statues of the gods within.

April/May

South Sinai Camel Festival Camel races that prove these animals have fire in their bellies.

August

Tourism and Shopping Festival A countrywide promotion of Egyptian products. Participating shops offer discounted prices.

September

Experimental Theatre Festival Held over 10 days, this theatre festival brings to Egypt a vast selection (40 at the last outing) of international theatre troupes and represents almost the only time each year when it's worth turning out for the theatre in Cairo.

October

Alexandrias of the World Festival A four-day celebration attended by delegations from all the cities bearing the name Alexandria (there are over 40 in the world).

November
Arabic Music Festival A 10-day festival of classical, traditional and orchestral Arabic music held at the Cairo Opera House early in the month. Programs are usually in Arabic only, but the tourist office should have details.

December
Cairo International Film Festival (www.cairofilm festival.com) This 14-day festival, held early in the month, gives Cairenes the chance to watch a vast range of recent films from all over the world.

INTERNET ACCESS
Access to the internet is widely available throughout Egypt. In this chapter, selected internet cafes are listed in each town.

MAPS
Excellent site maps of all the major monument areas are provided in Alberto Siliotti's informative booklets in the *Egypt Pocket Guide* series (E£30 each), published by the American University in Cairo Press. The *Bartholomew World Educational Map of Egypt* (E£60) is user-friendly. See p87 for recommended maps of Cairo.

MONEY
The official currency is the Egyptian pound (E£; in Arabic, a *guinay*). One pound consists of 100 piastres (pt). Collect plenty of E£1 and E£5 notes for baksheesh.

Money can be changed at commercial banks, foreign exchange bureaus and some hotels. Rates don't vary much. Travellers cheques can be cashed at banks, Amex and Thomas Cook offices.

ATMs are found in major towns throughout Egypt, though they are less common in the Western Desert. In general, those belonging to Banque Misr, Banque du Caire, the National Bank of Egypt and HSBC accept Visa and MasterCard for cash advances.

Although now widely accepted throughout Egypt, credit cards still aren't accepted in budget hotels and restaurants, nor in remote areas such as the Western Oases.

Bargaining, for everything from hotel rooms to clothes, is part of life in Egypt. Tipping, called baksheesh, is indispensable and is relied upon to supplement low salaries. In hotels and restaurants, taxes of up to 25% are added to the bill and a further 15% should be given to the waiter. A guard who shows you something at an archaeological site expects a pound or two. Asking for directions is about the only service that is baksheesh-exempt.

POST
Postcards cost less than a US dollar, and take four or five days to get to Europe, and a week to 10 days to the USA and Australia. Sending a letter is also less than a US dollar, and stamps are usually available at post offices, and some souvenir kiosks, shops, newsstands and the reception desks of major hotels. Sending mail from the post boxes at major hotels instead of from post offices seems to be quicker. If you use the post boxes, blue is for international airmail, red is for internal mail and green is for internal express mail.

SHOPPING
Egypt has a long lineage in arts and crafts, as a glimpse of Tutankhamen's treasure amply shows. Handmade beadwork from Sinai, basketry from the Western Oases, glass from Alexandria and alabaster pots from Luxor form part of that ancient tradition.

TELEPHONE
The country code for Egypt is ☎ 20, followed by the local area code (minus the zero), then the number. Local area codes are given at the start of each city or town section. The international access code (to call abroad from Egypt) is ☎ 00. For directory assistance call ☎ 140 or ☎ 141. The most common mobile phone prefixes in Egypt are ☎ 010 and ☎ 012.

Two companies sell phonecards in Egypt. Menatel has yellow-and-green booths, while Nile Tel's are red and blue. Cards are sold at shops and kiosks and come in units of E£10, E£15, E£20 and E£30. Once you insert the card into the telephone, press the flag in the top left corner to get instructions in English.

TIME
Egyptian time is two hours ahead of GMT.

TOURIST INFORMATION
The Egyptian government has tourist information offices throughout the country, some of which are better than others. The usefulness of the offices depends largely on the staff. The Aswan, Luxor, Dakhla, Siwa, Alexandria and Suez offices are staffed by people who have wide-ranging local knowledge and who will go out of their way to help you. Government-

EGYPT

produced reference materials, such as maps and brochures, tend to be out of date and too general.

VISAS

Most foreigners entering Egypt must obtain a visa. The only exceptions are citizens of Guinea, Hong Kong and Macau. There are three ways of doing this: in advance from the Egyptian embassy or consulate in your home country, at an Egyptian embassy abroad or, for certain nationalities, on arrival at the airport. This last option is the cheapest and easiest of the three.

Visas are available on arrival for nationals of all Western European countries, the UK, the USA, Australia, all Arab countries, New Zealand, Japan and Korea. At the Cairo airport, the entire process takes only 20 minutes or so, and costs US$15. No photo is required.

Nationals from other countries must obtain visas in their countries of residence. Processing times and costs for visa applications vary according to your nationality and the country in which you apply.

A single-entry visa is valid for three months and entitles the holder to stay in Egypt for 40 days. Multiple-entry visas (for three visits) are also available, but although good for presentation for six months, they still only entitle the bearer to a total of one month in the country.

Visa Extensions & Re-Entry Visas

Six-month and one-year extensions of your visa for tourist purposes can easily be obtained at passport offices, and only cost a few dollars. You'll need one photograph and photocopies of the photo and visa pages of your passport. You have a short period of grace (usually 14 days) to apply for an extension after your visa has expired. If you neglect to do this there's a fine of approximately E£100, and you'll require a letter of apology from your embassy.

In Cairo, all visa business is carried out at the monolithic, Egypto-Stalinist **Mogamma** (Map pp94-5; Midan Tahrir, Downtown; 8am-1.30pm Sat-Wed). Collect and submit a form (window 12 on the 1st floor) with stamps (from window 43), one photograph and photocopies (both available on the ground floor) of the photo and visa pages of your passport. The visa extension is processed overnight and available for collection from 9am the next day.

In other cities, extensions of tourist visas (from E£11) are easily obtained at passport offices.

If you don't have a multiple-entry visa, it's also possible to get a re-entry visa that is valid to the combined expiry dates of your visa and any extensions. A re-entry visa for one to several entries costs less than US$5.

Visas for Onward Travel

See the Embassies & Consulates section (p120) for contact details.

Eritrea Visas between US$50 and US$60 and are usually issued the same day.

Ethiopia Bring two photos and a return air ticket. One-month visas cost US$70, and are usually issued within 24 hours. Visas are also issued on arrival at Bole International Airport.

Libya Visas for independent travel to Libya are not being granted at present.

Sudan Both consulates can issue same-day visas to Sudan. You need your passport, four passport photos, a letter from your embassy and US$100.

WOMEN TRAVELLERS

Hassling is more or less constant in Egypt, though assault is rare. To avoid problems, dress conservatively (ie no shorts or bare shoulders, except in beach resorts).

A couple of useful Arabic phrases are: *la tilmasni* (don't touch me) and *ihtirim nafsak* (behave yourself). Swearing at would-be Romeos only makes matters worse.

TRANSPORT IN EGYPT

GETTING THERE & AWAY

Air

Most air travellers enter Egypt through Cairo, Alexandria or Sharm el-Sheikh.

Egypt's international and national carrier is **EgyptAir** (MS; national call centre 0900 70000; www.egyptair.com.eg; 8am-8pm), which has its hub at Cairo International Airport. Humorously (or perhaps terrifyingly) dubbed 'Egypt Scare' by jaded travellers the world over, EgyptAir's service isn't particularly good. If you're looking for an international flight to Egypt, you'd do better flying with a different airline – anyone will do.

Land

Egypt has land borders with Israel and the Palestinian Territories, Libya and Sudan.

The land border with Sudan, however, is closed, and the only way to travel between both countries is to fly or take the Wadi Halfa ferry (p211).

It's worth noting that almost all international bus and ferry tickets must be paid for in US dollars.

ISRAEL & THE PALESTINIAN TERRITORIES

The Taba border with Israel is open 24 hours. Taxis or buses to Eilat (4km from the border) are available on the Israeli side, with frequent connections to Jerusalem and Tel Aviv. The Rafah border was closed at the time of research due to instability in the Gaza Strip.

Coming from Israel to Egypt, you must have a visa in advance unless your visit is limited to Sinai, or you have prearranged your entry with an Egyptian tour operator.

Vehicles can be brought into Egypt from Eilat; the amount of entry duty depends on the type of vehicle, but averages about E£100.

JORDAN

From Cairo, there's a twice-weekly **Superjet** (☎ 02-2290 9017) service to Amman (US$85) leaving from Al-Mazah Garage on Sunday and Thursday at 5am. There is also a daily **East Delta Bus Co** (☎ 02-2574 2814) service from Cairo to Aqaba (US$45) at 8pm. Both of these bus services use the ferry between Nuweiba and Aqaba, so you will be liable for the port tax and the cost of a ferry ticket (see Sea & Lake).

LIBYA

Superjet has buses to Benghazi leaving on Tuesday, Thursday and Saturday at 11am (E£150, 17 hours), as well as buses to Tripoli leaving on Tuesday, Friday and Sunday at 10am (E£275, 24 hours). East Delta Bus Co also has buses to Benghazi, which leave at noon on Tuesday, Thursday and Saturday, and buses to Tripoli on Tuesday and Friday at 11am.

Sea & Lake

JORDAN

There's a so-called 'fast-ferry' service between Nuweiba in Egypt and Aqaba in Jordan, leaving Nuweiba at 3.30pm and in theory taking between one and two hours assuming normal sea conditions (though delays are common). Heading back to Nuweiba, fast ferries depart from Aqaba at noon. One-way tickets cost US$70 for economy and US$90 for 1st class,

---

PORT TAX

Egyptian international ferries charge E£50 port tax per person on top of the ticket price.

---

while round trip tickets cost US$120 and US$155, respectively.

Free Jordanian visas can be obtained on the ferry if you have an EU, US, Canadian, Australian or New Zealand passport.

SUDAN

The **Nile River Valley Transport Corporation** Aswan (☎ 097-303 348; in the shopping arcade behind the tourist police office; ☼ 8am-2pm Sat-Thu) Cairo (☎ 02-2575 9258; next to the 3rd-class ticket window at Ramses station) runs one passenger ferry per week from Aswan to Wadi Halfa. One-way tickets cost E£385 for 1st class with a bed in a cabin, E£240 for an airline seat and E£165 for deck class.

Tours

Literally thousands of companies offer tours to Egypt. For one of the most famous, try **Thomas Cook** (www.thomascook.com), which has been showing people the pyramids for over a century.

GETTING AROUND
Air

EgyptAir is the main domestic carrier, and flights – however dodgy they may be – are a surprisingly cheap and convenient means of bypassing countless hours on buses or trains. Fares vary considerably depending on season and availability, but sometimes it's possible to snag domestic one-way fares for less than US$100.

Bicycle

While you'd have to have a death wish to contemplate cycling in Cairo, it's a great way of getting round the sights of the delta and the flat Nile Valley. Cycling is a particular pleasure in Luxor, where hiring a bicycle is cheap and easy. Bringing your own is another matter: police restrictions in Upper Egypt mean that you'll have to take the bike on the train between most points of interest on the Nile.

Boat

From liners plying the Suez Canal to ferries crossing the Nile, transport in Egypt has traditionally taken place on the water,

EGYPT

EGYPT

and some form of boat ride is an experience you shouldn't miss. Options include taking a glass-bottom boat in Sharm el-Sheikh, crossing the Red Sea to Hurghada, cruising from Luxor to Aswan in luxury, and sailing around the islands near Aswan in a traditional white-sailed felucca. For more information, see the respective sections of this chapter.

Bus

Bus services cover almost every destination in Egypt. Deluxe buses, with decent seats, air-con and loud Arabic videos, travel between main cities. Keep your ticket until you disembark, as inspectors board the bus to check fares. There are no student discounts on bus fares.

Car & Motorcycle

Driving in Cairo is a crazy affair, so think seriously before you decide to hire a car there. Driving in other parts of the country, at least in daylight, isn't so bad, though you should avoid intercity driving at night. And having a car – or better still a 4WD – opens up entire areas of the country where public transport is nonexistent.

At the time of research, it was no longer necessary to travel by police-escorted convoys, which opens large swathes of the Nile Valley and Red Sea Coast that were previously difficult to access. While tourist infrastructure is limited outside of major destinations, we have received numerous reports from intrepid readers that self-driving is a wonderful way to leave the tour buses behind in the dust.

If you choose to hire a car, rates are around US$50 to US$100 a day for a small Toyota to US$100 to US$200 a day for a 4WD. Foreign drivers will need an International Driver's Licence.

Fill up when you can – many stations run out of petrol.

The official speed limit is 100km/h on motorways. For those caught speeding, driving licences are confiscated and fines are payable at the police station.

Hitching

With police checkpoints throughout Egypt, hitching is not recommended.

Local Transport

Travelling by *servees* (usually microbuses or Peugeot 504 cars) is a quick way of travelling between cities. A driver won't leave until all the seats are paid for.

Calèche (horse-drawn carriages) are a popular way to get around many towns.

Train

Although trains travel along more than 5000km of track to almost every major city and town in Egypt, the system is badly in need of modernisation (it's a relic of the British occupation). Most services are grimy and battered and are a poor alternative to the deluxe bus. The exceptions are the *turbini* and *espani* services from Cairo to Alexandria and the tourist and sleeping trains from Cairo down to Luxor and Aswan – on these routes the train is the preferred option over the bus.

If you have an ISIC, discounts are granted on all fares, except those for the sleeping-car services.

Libya

Libya has it all – ancient Roman and Greek cities of rare splendour, the Sahara that you thought existed only in your imagination and an unmistakeable cachet that comes from having been ruled for almost four decades by one of the iconic figures of the 20th century.

Libya was one of the great crossroads of civilisations and within striking distance of Tripoli, Libya's ancient and cosmopolitan capital, Leptis Magna is the extravagant jewel in Libya's crown and sufficient reason on its own to come. Sabratha, too, is splendid, while more ancient cities await in Libya's northeast; for many travellers, Cyrene is Leptis' equal.

If it's the solitude and otherworldly beauty of the world's largest desert that you crave then Libya has few peers. The great sand seas of the Sahara are home to palm-encircled lakes surrounded by soaring dunes, and desert massifs such as Jebel Acacus with its stunning land formations and superbly rendered prehistoric rock art. Amid scenes such as these, Waw al-Namus feels like an unimaginable bonus. And there's no finer caravan town in the Sahara than Ghadames.

But there's more. While Egypt, Tunisia and Morocco were selling their souls to the god of tourism, Libya was holding fast to its traditions and here you'll find one of the most hassle-free destinations on earth. Libyans have an old saying that you should enter the country with its people and it's true that the only way to visit is as part of an escorted tour. Visa arrangements can be a hassle, but by the time you leave Libya you'll have seen the country through Libyan eyes.

LIBYA

FAST FACTS

- **Area** 1.8 million sq km
- **ATMs** Widespread
- **Borders** Tunisia (Ras al-Jedir) and Egypt (Amsaad) open; Chad, Sudan and (usually) Niger and Algeria closed to non-Libyans
- **Budget** US$75 to US$100 per day
- **Capital** Tripoli
- **Languages** Arabic, Berber
- **Money** Libyan dinar (LD); US$1 = 1.23LD, €1 = 1.78LD
- **Population** 6.3 million
- **Seasons** Hot (June to August), wet (March and October), dry (rest of the year)
- **Telephone** Country code ☎ 218; international access code ☎ 00
- **Time** GMT/UTC +1
- **Visa** Arranged as part of organised tour; can be picked up on arrival

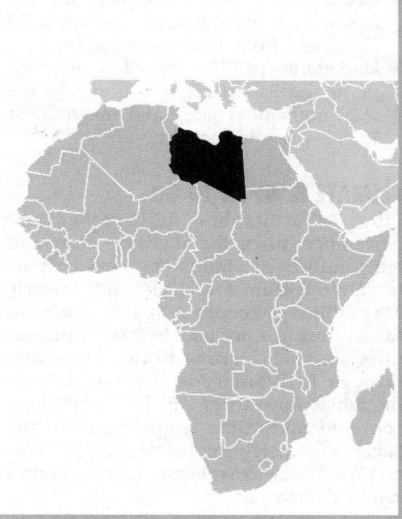

HIGHLIGHTS

■ **Leptis Magna** (p133) One of the world's best-preserved Roman cities, with bath complexes, theatres and forums by the Mediterranean.

■ **Tripoli** (p130) An atmospheric white-washed medina replete with Ottoman mosques and houses, and the world-class Jamahiriya Museum.

■ **Ghadames** (p135) A labyrinthine, palm-fringed old city and possibly the Sahara's most enchanting oasis town.

■ **Cyrene** (p134) An extraordinary ancient city with a fine location and splendid Greek and Roman monuments.

■ **Jebel Acacus** (p137) A jagged desert massif in the Sahara's heart, home to the semi-nomadic Tuareg and magnificent 12,000-year-old rock art.

CLIMATE & WHEN TO GO

Libya is at its best in October and November, when the skies are clear and temperatures are mild. The next best alternative is from March through to early May, although there's a higher chance of sandstorms in April and, by May, temperatures are really starting to rise. December through to February is also popular, although temperatures can be surprisingly cool and night-time temperatures in the Sahara routinely drop below zero. In summer (mid-May to September), temperatures can be fiercely hot.

ITINERARIES

■ **One Week** Tripoli (p130) deserves at least two days, with a further day each for Leptis Magna (p133) and Sabratha (p133). For the rest of the time, it's a two-day round-trip to Ghadames (p135), visiting the Jebel Nafusa (p135) en route, for an unforgettable taste of the desert. An alternative is to fly to Benghazi (p134) and spend two days visiting the ancient cities of Cyrene (p134) and Apollonia (p135).

■ **Two Weeks** Depending on what you've covered from the one-week itinerary, devote the rest of your time in Libya to the Sahara. Fly to Sebha and then spend a couple of days exploring the Ubari Lakes and Idehan Ubari (Ubari Sand Sea; p136). An extra two days will allow you to make it to Waw al-Namus (p137) and back, while you'll need at least three days for Jebel Acacus (p137).

HISTORY

Throughout history Libya has been blighted by its geography, lying in the path of invading empires and the wars of other nations.

The Great Civilisations of Antiquity

From 700 BC, Lebdah (Leptis Magna), Oea (Tripoli) and Sabratha formed some of the links in a chain of safe Phoenician (Punic) ports stretching from the Levant around to Spain. Traces of the Phoenician presence in Libya remain at Sabratha (p133) and Leptis Magna (p133).

On the advice of the Oracle of Delphi, in 631 BC Greek settlers established the city of Cyrene (p134) in the east of Libya. Within 200 years the Greeks had built four more cities of splendour as part of the Pentapolis (Five Cities), which included Apollonia (p135). But with Greek influence on the wane, the last Greek ruler, Ptolemy Apion, finally bequeathed the region of Cyrenaica to Rome in 75 BC.

Meanwhile, the fall of the Punic capital at Carthage (in Tunisia) prompted Julius Caesar to formally annex Tripolitania in 46 BC. The Pax Romana saw Tripolitania and Cyrenaica become prosperous Roman provinces. Such was Libya's importance that a Libyan, Septimius Severus, became Rome's emperor (r AD 193–211).

VISITING LIBYA

Since late 2000, visits to Libya have only been possible as part of organised tours and visas are only issued to those with an invitation from a Libyan tour operator. The official reason for this restriction is that European tourists were caught red-handed trying to take priceless antiquities and prehistoric rock art out of the country.

You will at all times be accompanied by a guide from your Libyan tour operator and they will be responsible for you throughout your stay. Discuss your itinerary with them in advance, although most likely you will have little choice when it comes to hotels and restaurants. All your transport while in Libya will be similarly organised for you and, apart from domestic air travel, it is highly unlikely that you will travel by public transport. For this reason, we have covered sleeping, eating and transport options only in brief throughout this chapter.

For a full list of Libyan tour operators, see p141. Information on obtaining visas can be found on p139.

Islamic Libya

By AD 643, Tripoli and Cyrenaica had fallen to the armies of Islam. From 800, the Abbasid-appointed emirs of the Aghlabid dynasty repaired Roman irrigation systems, restoring order and bringing a measure of prosperity to the region, while the mass migration of two tribes – the Bani Salim and Bani Hilal – from the Arabian Peninsula forever changed Libya's demographics. The Berber tribespeople were displaced from their traditional lands and the new settlers cemented the cultural and linguistic Arabisation of the region.

The Ottomans occupied Tripoli in 1551. The soldiers sent by the sultan to support the Ottoman pasha (governor) grew powerful and cavalry officer Ahmed Karamanli seized power in 1711. His Karamanli dynasty would last 124 years. The Ottoman Turks finally reined in their erstwhile protégés in 1835 and resumed direct control over much of Libya.

On 3 October 1911, the Italians attacked Tripoli claiming to be liberating Libya from Ottoman rule. During almost three decades of brutal Italian rule, a quarter of Libya's population died as a result of the occupation, whether from direct military attacks, starvation or forced migration.

With the onset of WWII, devastating fighting broke out in the area around Tobruk. By January 1943, Tripoli was in British hands and by February the last German and Italian soldiers were driven from Libya.

Qaddafi's Libya

Desperately poor Libya became independent in 1951, but the country's fortunes were transformed by the discovery of oil in 1959 at Zelten in Cyrenaica. Over the decade that followed, Libya was transformed from an economic backwater into one of the world's fastest-growing economies.

With the region in turmoil, it came as no surprise when a Revolutionary Command Council, led by a little-known but charismatic 27-year-old Muammar Qaddafi, seized power in Libya on 1 September 1969. Riding on a wave of anti-imperialist anger, the new leader closed British and American military bases, expanded the armed forces and closed all newspapers, churches and political parties. Some 30,000 Italian settlers were deported.

As the colonel balanced his political theories of participation for all Libyans with the revolutionary committees that became renowned for assassinating political opponents, the US accused Libya of involvement in a string of terrorist attacks across Europe. On 15 April 1986, the US Navy fired missiles into Tripoli and Benghazi.

After Libyan agents were charged with the 1988 bombing of Pan Am flight 103 (aka the Lockerbie disaster) and the 1989 explosion of a French UTA airliner over the Sahara, UN sanctions came into effect. Finally, in early 1999, a deal was brokered and the suspects were handed over for trial by Scottish judges in The Hague. The sanctions, which had cost Libya over US$30 billion in lost revenues and production capacities, were immediately lifted.

Libya Today

Libya today is like a country awakening from a nightmare. Libya's payment of compensation to victims of the Lockerbie disaster and its announcement on 19 December 2003 that it would abandon its chemical and nuclear

LIBYA

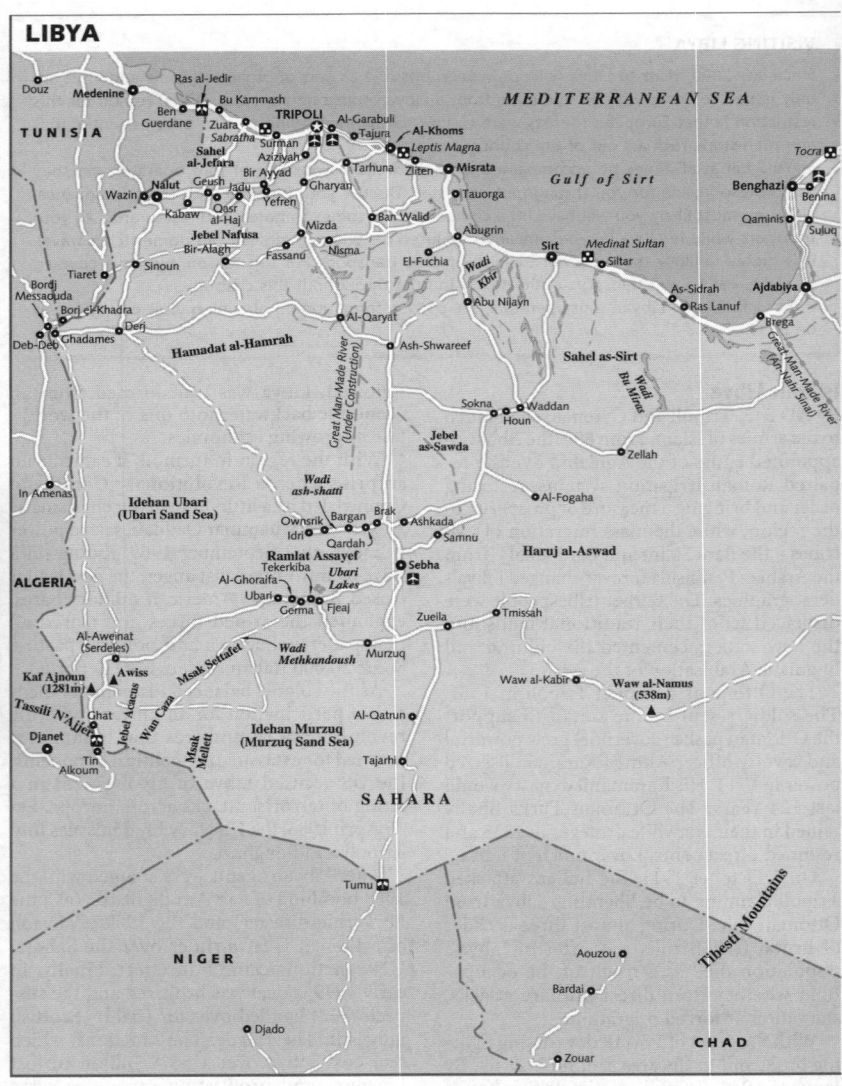

LIBYA

weapons programs, finally ended its international isolation. Suddenly, Libya was the West's best friend, held up as an example to so-called rogue states across the region.

World leaders have since flocked to Libya, the US reopened its embassy in Tripoli in 2006, and Western businesspeople are clamouring for lucrative oil contracts. In late 2008,

Italy's government officially apologised to Libya for its occupation of the country and its treatment of Libyan civilians during the colonial period. In doing so, it also pledged billions of dollars in compensation, primarily for developing Libya's infrastructure. For its part, the Libyan government has promised far-reaching economic reforms as part of its plans

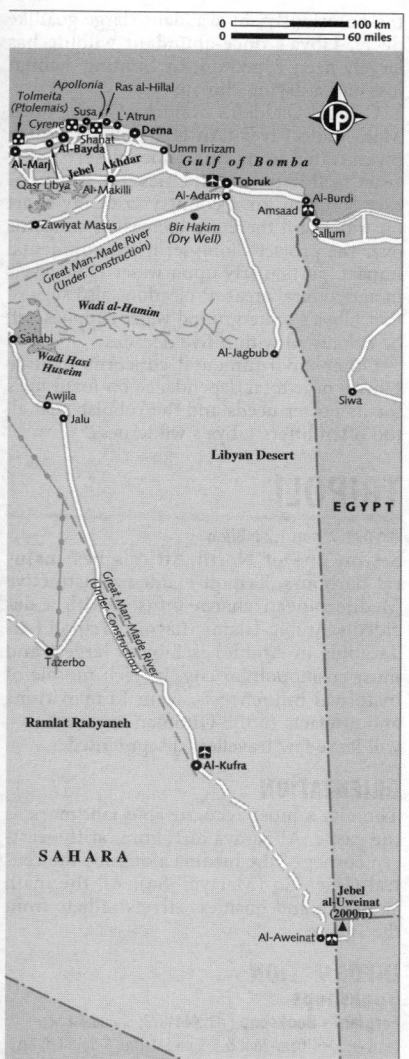

fostered during the long years of sanctions. Libyans are also deeply attached to their land, proud of it and even loath to leave it, especially at such an exciting time in their history. Libyans never forget where they came from, whether it be their home village or the dark years of isolation. Surprisingly knowledgeable about the world, they remain refreshingly untouched by it. Above all, for the first time in decades, Libyans are optimistic, convinced that the future is theirs.

Life revolves around the family, a bond that took on added significance during the years of international isolation, when Libyan society turned inwards in search of company and support. Grafted onto the immediate family are multiple layers of identity, among them extended family, tribe and village, with an overarching national component of which every Libyan is proud.

Libyan women nominally have equal status with men, from marriage and divorce laws to rights of equal pay in the workplace. The reality is somewhat different, with men still the predominant players in public life and few women reaching the summit of any industry.

Libya's population density (fewer than three per square kilometre) is one of the lowest in the world. Up to 90% of people live in urban centres, in stark contrast to Libya's pre-oil days, when less than 25% lived in cities. Libya also has an overwhelmingly youthful population, with more than a third under 15 years of age.

Libya's demographic mix is remarkably homogenous – 97% are of Arab or Berber origin. Other groups include the Tuareg and Toubou, who both inhabit Libya's southern desert regions.

More than 95% of Libya's population is Sunni Muslim, with most following the Maliki school of Quranic interpretation, which preaches the primacy of the Quran (as opposed to later teachings) and tolerance.

In Libya's arts scene there is a handful of celebrated figures. The country's best-known writer is Ibrahim al-Koni, whose works reveal a fascination with the desert. He has published eight volumes of short stories and a number of novels, including *The Bleeding of the Stone* and *Anubis: A Desert Novel*, which have both been translated into English. Another writer of note is Hisham Matar, a young novelist from an exiled Libyan family whose *In the*

to overhaul the country's moribund economy, although progress thus far has been slow.

CULTURE

In some ways, Libyans are everything that Colonel Qaddafi isn't known for – reserved, tolerant and discreet. They are self-sufficient and wonderful improvisers, characteristics

Country of Men took the literary world by
storm in 2006.

One of the most famous traditional music
forms in Libya is the celebratory *mriskaawi,*
which came from Murzuq and forms the basis
for the lyrics of many Libyan songs. *Malouf,*
with its origins in Andalucía, involves a large
group of seated revellers singing and reciting
poetry of a religious nature or about love.

Important popular singers to watch out
for include Mohammed Hassan, Salmin al-
Zarouk and Mohammed Sanini.

FOOD & DRINK

The staple tourist diet consists of couscous
and chicken in Tripolitania and the Fezzan,
with rice replacing couscous in Cyrenaica.
For a little variety, try the macaroni-based
dishes inspired by the Italians; you might
come across vegetable stews and potatoes if
you're lucky. *Shwarma* (strips of sliced meat
in a pocket of bread) is also widely available
as a street snack.

Tripoli, Benghazi and a few other cities have
some wonderful restaurants serving dishes
of great variety. Particular highlights are the
seafood dishes at specialist fish restaurants
in Tripoli.

Many restaurants will assume that you will
have a banquet-style meal, which consists
of soup, salad, a selection of meat (or fish)
dishes, rice or couscous, a few vegetables and
tea or coffee. Prices in this chapter are given
for banquet-style meals where appropriate, or
in some cases for single, main dishes.

Vegetarians should always specify their
requirements as soon as they arrive in the
restaurant. Vegetarianism is rare in Libya,
but most restaurants are obliging and keen
to make sure you don't leave hungry.

For drinks, soft drinks and bottled mineral water will be your staples, along with
coffee or tea. Nonalcoholic beer is also
widely available.

ENVIRONMENT

Libya is the fourth-largest country in Africa
and twice the size of neighbouring Egypt.
Despite the fertile coastal plain of Sahel al-
Jefara, and the mountains of Jebel Nafusa
and Jebel al-Akhdar in northern Libya,
95% of the country is swallowed up by the
Sahara Desert.

Apart from desert species such as gazelles,
fennec foxes, wolves, snakes, scorpions and
the notoriously shy waddans (large goatlike
deer), Libya's once-abundant wildlife has
largely been wiped out by hunting, habitat
loss and a drying climate.

Colonel Qaddafi's brainchild – the Great
Man-Made River (An-Nahr Sinai), which
pipes water from vast under-desert reser-
voirs to thirsty coastal cities – is a temporary solution for a country critically short
on water and there are increasing concerns
over the project's long-term environmental
impact, particularly upon water table levels
in agricultural areas. Projections also suggest
that Libya's underground water supplies will
be exhausted within five decades.

Other environmental concerns include
Libya's near-total dependence on fossil fuels
for its power needs and the rubbish that all
too often litters Libya's wilderness.

TRIPOLI

☎ 021 / pop 1.2 million

Set on one of North Africa's best natural harbours, Tripoli exudes a distinctive
Mediterranean charm infused with a decidedly Arabic-Islamic flavour. Tripoli (Al-
Tarablus in Arabic) is Libya's largest and
most cosmopolitan city. Its rich mosaic of
historical influences – from Roman ruins
and artefacts to the Ottoman-era medina –
will leave few travellers disappointed.

ORIENTATION

The city's most recognisable landmark is
the castle, Al-Saraya al-Hamra, at the eastern corner of the medina alongside the central Green Sq (Martyrs' Sq). All the main
shopping and business streets radiate from
the square.

INFORMATION
Bookshops

Fergiani's Bookshop (☎ 4444873; Sharia 1st September; 🕑 10am-2pm & 5-9pm Sat-Thu, 5-9pm Fri) An
excellent selection of hard-to-find English-language books
on Libya.

Emergency

Emergency Hospital (☎ 121) Five kilometres south
of the centre.

Internet Access

Bakka Net (cnr Sharias Mizran & Haity; per hr 1LD;
🕑 8.30am-midnight Sat-Thu, 5pm-midnight Fri)

LIBYA

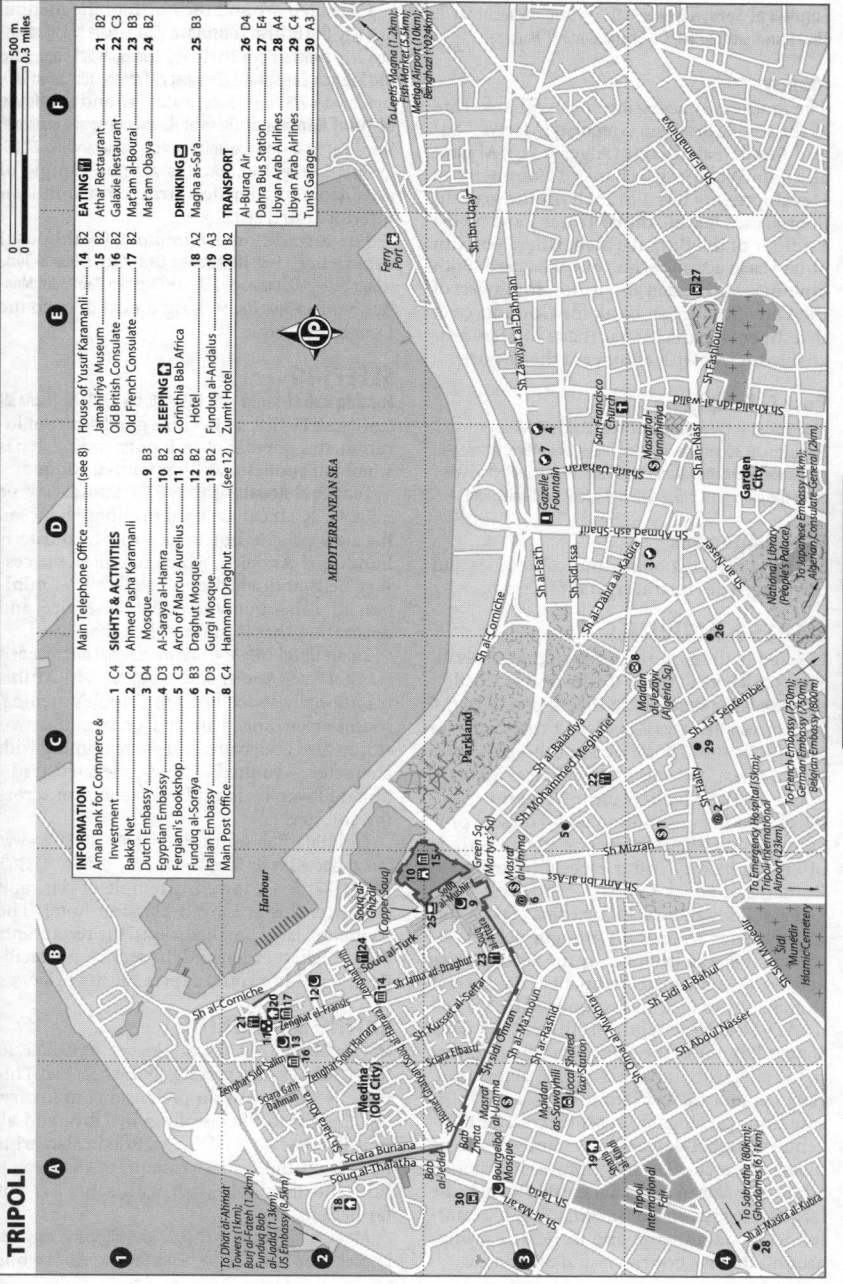

TRIPOLI

INFORMATION
Aman Bank for Commerce &
Investment................................**1** C4
Bakka Net.....................................**2** C4
Dutch Embassy.............................**3** D4
Egyptian Embassy.........................**4** D3
Fergiani's Bookshop.....................**5** C3
Funduq al-Soraya.........................**6** B3
Italian Embassy.............................**7** D3
Main Post Office..........................**8** C4
Main Telephone Office...............(see 8)

SIGHTS & ACTIVITIES
Ahmed Pasha Karamanli
Mosque....................................**9** B3
Al-Saraya al-Hamra.....................**10** B2
Arch of Marcus Aurelius.............**11** B2
Draghut Mosque.........................**12** B2
Gurgi Mosque.............................**13** B2
Hammam Draghut......................(see 12)

House of Yusuf Karamanli..........**14** B2
Jamahiriya Museum....................**15** B2
Old British Consulate..................**16** C3
Old French Consulate.................**17** B2

EATING
Athar Restaurant........................**21** B2
Galaxie Restaurant.....................**22** C3
Mat'am al-Bourai.......................**23** B3
Mat'am Obaya...........................**24** B2

SLEEPING
Corinthia Bab Africa
Hotel..**18** A2
Funduq al-Andalus.....................**19** A3
Zumit Hotel................................**20** B2

DRINKING
Magha as-Sa'a...........................**25** B3

TRANSPORT
Al-Buraq Air...............................**26** D4
Dahra Bus Station.......................**27** E4
Libyan Arab Airlines...................**28** A4
Libyan Arab Airlines...................**29** C4
Tunis Garage..............................**30** A3

500 m
0.3 miles

MEDITERRANEAN SEA

Funduq al-Soraya (per hr 1LD; 🕙 9am-midnight Sat-Thu, 5pm-midnight Fri) Off Sharia Omar al-Mukhtar.

Money

The most easily accessible *masraf* (banks) are in the streets between Green Sq (Martyrs' Sq) and Maidan al-Jezayir (Algeria Sq). Masraf al-Tijara Watanmiya (Bank of Commerce & Development) has a branch on the ground floor of the Dhat al-Ahmat Tower 1 and on the 1st floor of the Burj al-Fateh, where you can obtain cash advances on your Visa card. Both buildings are located about 1km southwest of the Old City. Aman Bank for Commerce & Investment (Sharia Mizran) has a MasterCard-enabled ATM, with another at the airport.

Post & Telephone

Main post & telephone office (Maidan al-Jezayir; 🕙 8am-10.30pm Sat-Thu) The telephone office, where you can make international and local calls, is on your left as you enter the main post office hall and opens until midnight.

Travel Agencies

See p141 for a list of the tour companies and travel agencies operating out of Tripoli.

SIGHTS & ACTIVITIES

Housed in the eastern corner of the sturdy **Al-Saraya al-Hamra** (Tripoli Castle or Red Castle), the **Jamahiriya Museum** (☎ 3330292; Green Sq (Martyrs' Sq); admission 3LD, camera/video 5/10LD, compulsory guide 50LD; 🕙 9am-1pm & 2-5pm Tue-Sun) is home to one of the finest collections of classical art anywhere in the Mediterranean. The museum, developed in consultation with Unesco, provides a comprehensive overview of all periods of Libyan history and is especially strong on Roman and Greek Libya.

Tripoli's whitewashed **medina** (Old City) mostly dates from the Ottoman period, although it is watched over by the **Arch of Marcus Aurelius**, the only intact remnant of the ancient Roman city of Oea and completed in AD 163 to AD 164. Nearby, the 19th-century **Gurgi Mosque** has one of the most beautiful interiors in the city, with imported marble pillars from Italy, ceramic tilework from Tunisia and intricate stone carvings from Morocco. The 16th-century **Draghut Mosque** has elegantly rendered pillars and arches (15 in the prayer hall alone), while the **Ahmed Pasha Karamanli Mosque**, the largest mosque in the medina, has a beautiful octagonal minaret and intricate carvings around the five doorways and 30 domes.

Clustered around the north of the medina are the **Old British Consulate** (Sharia Hara Kbira; admission 2LD, camera/video 2/5LD; 🕙 9am-5pm Sat-Thu), the **Old French Consulate** (Zenghat el-Fransis; admission 2LD, camera/video 2/5LD; 🕙 9am-5pm Sat-Thu) and the **House of Yusuf Karamanli** (Hosn al-Harem or Dar al-Karamanli; Sharia Homet Gharyan; admission 2LD, camera/video 2/5LD; 🕙 9am-5pm Sat-Thu); each is a fine example of an Ottoman mansion arrayed around an interior courtyard.

For a traditional *hammam* (bathhouse) experience, try **Hammam Draghut** (Souq al-Turk; steam bath 2LD, massage 5LD; 🕙 women 8am-3pm Mon-Wed, men 8am-3pm Thu-Sun), right next door to the Draghut Mosque.

SLEEPING

Funduq Bab al-Jadid (☎ 3350670; fax 3350670; Sharia al-Corniche; s/d 25/35LD; 🏠) With a good seafront location, this popular place is outstanding. It has small but spotless, well-appointed rooms.

Funduq al-Andalus (☎ 3343777; Sharia al-Kindi; s/d US$39/48; 🏠) It can be hard to choose between the new private hotels, but our favourite is Funduq al-Andalus, which has all the necessary bells and whistles – satellite TV, minibar, air-con – but with attentive service, and decoration that is more stylish than most.

Zumit Hotel (☎ 3342915; www.zumithotel.com; next to Arch of Marcus Aurelius; d/ste 150/200LD; 🏠) At this traditionally styled hotel in Tripoli's medina, rooms are arranged around a charming, two-storey tiled courtyard and are brimming with character – vaulted ceilings, elevated traditional Libyan beds, and artefacts from across the country.

Corinthia Bab Africa Hotel (☎ 3351990; www.corinthiahotels.com; Souq al-Thalatha; d from US$300; 🅿 🏠 🖥 🛗) A towering temple of glass and elegance, this is Libya's classiest hotel. The rooms are large and luxurious, the restaurants of the highest order, and the service and facilities everything you'd expect for the price.

EATING & DRINKING

Mat'am Obaya (Obaya Seafood Restaurant; ☎ 0925010736; Souq al-Turk 114; mains from 5LD; 🕙 lunch Sat-Thu) This place is small with no pretensions to luxury, but there's no finer seafood in Libya and all of it is home cooked. The stuffed calamari is just about the tastiest restaurant dish you'll find and the *shola* (fish with sauce) is not far behind.

Mat'am al-Bourai (☎ 0927166560; Sharia Jama ad-Draghut; meals from 10LD; 🕙 lunch Sat-Thu) Above one of the liveliest thoroughfares in the medina, this bright, busy restaurant has excellent food. Its speciality is the delicious *rishda* (noodles with chickpeas and onions).

Athar Restaurant (☎ 4447001; starters around 3LD; mains mostly 10-15LD; ☽ lunch & dinner) This excellent place, next to the Arch of Marcus Aurelius, has a wonderful location and the outdoor table is among the most pleasant in Tripoli. The high-quality food ranges from more traditional couscous or tajine (a lightly spiced lamb dish with a tomato-and-paprika-based sauce) to mixed grills and fish. Visa cards are accepted.

Galaxie Restaurant (☎ 4448764; Sharia 1st September; meals 14-18LD; ☽ lunch & dinner) One of the best restaurants in the area, Galaxie is tastefully decorated and does the usual dishes with a touch more imagination than similar places elsewhere. The *jara* (meat stew) is excellent but needs to be ordered three hours in advance.

Magha as-Sa'a (☎ 0925032511; Maidan al-Sa'a; ☽ 7am-2am) Opposite the Ottoman clock tower in the medina, this is Tripoli's outstanding traditional teahouse.

For a totally different eating experience, head 5.5km east of the port along the road to Tajura, where there's a ramshackle **fish market**. Buy the fish or other seafood that you want, then take it to one of the restaurants, where they'll grill it for you for a small fee (around 1.5LD).

GETTING THERE & AWAY

Libyan Arab Airlines Sharia Haity (☎ 3331143; Sharia Haity); Sharia Omar al-Mokhtar (☎ 3616738; Sharia Omar al-Mokhtar) flies from Tripoli International Airport, 25km south of the city, and **Al-Buraq Air** (☎ 4444811; www.buraqair.com; Sharia Mohammed Megharief) flies from Metiga Airport, 10km east of Tripoli. They both operate domestic flights to Benghazi (from 37.50LD) and Sebha (37.50LD, daily).

Long-distance buses and shared taxis for most cities around Libya depart from the area near Tunis Garage at the western end of Sharia al-Rashid, or from Dahra Bus Station; the latter is 1.5km east of the centre.

GETTING AROUND

A private taxi to/from Tripoli International Airport costs 10LD. Elsewhere in the city, a trip rarely costs more than 2LD.

NORTHERN LIBYA

SABRATHA

The expansive and well-preserved ruins of ancient **Sabratha** (☎ 622214; adult/child 3/1LD, camera/video 5/10LD, compulsory guide 50LD; ☽ 8am-6pm), 80km west of Tripoli, include one of the finest theatres of antiquity.

Settled by the Phoenicians in the 4th century BC, Sabratha was resettled by the Greeks in the 2nd century BC. In the 1st century AD, the Romans made the city their own.

Highlights of Sabratha include the mosaics and frescos of the **Roman Museum** (adult/child 3/1LD, camera/video 5/10LD; ☽ 8am-6pm Tue-Sun) as well as the elevated **Antonine Temple**, **Judicial Basilica**, **Roman forum**, the **Capitoleum** and the **Temple of Liber Pater**, which dominate the monumental heart of Sabratha. The 6th-century **Basilica of Justinian** is the finest remnant of Byzantine Sabratha, but it is the magnificent 2nd-century **Roman theatre**, the largest in Africa, that will live longest in the memory. Its three-tiered facade with 108 fluted Corinthian columns is adorned with exquisite carvings of Roman divinities.

Most travellers visit Sabratha on a day trip from Tripoli.

LEPTIS MAGNA

Leptis Magna (Lebdah; ☎ 624256, 627641; adult/child 3/1LD, camera/video 5/10LD; ☽ 8am-6pm) is one of the best-preserved, most evocative Roman cities in the Mediterranean. It's a testament to extravagance, with examples of lavish decoration, grand buildings of monumental stature, indulgent bath complexes and forums for entertainment.

First settled in the 7th century BC, Leptis Magna became Africa's premier Roman city during the reign of Leptis' favourite son, Septimius Severus (r AD 193–211).

The ornately carved **Arch of Septimius Severus** is a grand introduction to the architectural opulence of Leptis, but its grandeur is rivalled by the superb **Hadrianic Baths**, one of the social hubs of the ancient city. Equally splendid are the **Severan Forum**, **Severan Basilica**, the octagonal halls of the **market** and Leptis' **theatre**, one of the oldest stone theatres anywhere in the Roman world. Around 1km east of the city is the evocative **amphitheatre** (adult/child 3/1LD, camera/video 5/10LD; ☽ 8am-6pm), which once held 16,000 people and overlooks the Roman **circus**, where chariot races were held. Close to the site entrance, the **museum** (adult/child 3/1LD, camera/video 5/10LD; ��� 8am-6pm Tue-Sun) is outstanding.

Although most people visit Leptis on a day trip from Tripoli, it's possible to camp (5LD) in car park No 1 under the pine and eucalyptus trees. The neighbouring town of Al-Khoms has a number of hotel options.

Inside Leptis, between the ticket office and the museum, is atmospheric **Mat'am Addiyafa** (☎ 621210; meals 15LD; ☺ lunch).

BENGHAZI
☎ 061 / pop 670,000

Libya's second-largest city makes a comfortable base for exploring the ancient cities of eastern Libya. While it may lack the cosmopolitan charm of Tripoli and has few monuments to its ancient past, Benghazi is known for its pleasant climate and friendly people.

Benghazi's **Old Town Hall** runs along the western side of **Freedom Sq**. It's largely derelict, but strong traces of its former elegance remain in its whitewashed Italianate facade. The covered **Souq al-Jreed** stretches for more than a kilometre and, like any African market worth its salt, offers just about anything you could want and plenty that you don't.

If you end up staying at any of the following places, you'll be well pleased.

Funduq al-Fadheel (Funduq el-Fadeel; ☎ 9099795; elfadeelhotel@hotmail.com; Sharia el-Shatt; s/d/ste from 40/50/70LD; ☒ ☐ ☒) is one of the best hotels in Libya. The pleasant rooms are spacious and well appointed, and come with laundry service. There are two restaurants, a swimming pool, large-screen TVs in the rooms and an internet cafe on-site.

The rooms at **Funduq al-Nouran** (☎ 3372091; www.alnoranhotel.com; Sharia al-Jezayir; s 50-60LD, d 60-75LD; ☒) are large and tasteful, with clean lines and an almost European sense of style and balconies. It is only a few years old, so let's hope this fine place stands the test of time.

One of Benghazi's top hotels, **Funduq Uzu** (☎ 9095160; Sharia al-Jezayir; s/d without lake view 50/65LD, with lake view 60/75LD, ste 100-220LD; ☒ ☐) has superbly appointed rooms with all the facilities you'd expect. The buffet breakfasts are among the best in town.

On the northern side of the harbour, **Funduq Tibesti** (☎ 9090017; fax 9098029; Sharia Jamal Abdul Nasser; s/d without lake view from 75/100LD, with lake view from 80/115LD, ste from 150LD; ☒) is another classy hotel with a luxurious ambience. Facilities include a patisserie, a health club, three coffee shops and four restaurants.

For a bite to eat you can't go past **Mat'am al-'Arabi** (☎ 9094468; Sharia Gulf of Sirt; meals US$13; ☺ lunch & dinner Sat-Thu, dinner Fri), one of Benghazi's finest restaurants. It has a delightful ambience, with a mosaic floor, a tented roof, soft lighting and an eminently reasonable price tag. Another good option is the Turkish restaurant **Mat'am Turki** (☎ 9091331; Sharia 23 July; sandwiches from 1LD, pizza 2-6LD, meals 12LD; ☺ 10am-1am).

Benghazi's Benina Airport handles both international and domestic flights. **Libyan Arab Airlines** (☎ 9092064; Sharia al-Jezayir) and **Al-Buraq Air** (☎ 2234469; www.buraqair.com; Benina Airport) share four daily flights to Tripoli (from 37.50LD).

There are daily buses and shared taxis to Tripoli, Sirt, Al-Bayda, Sebha and Tobruk from Al-Funduq market.

CYRENE
☎ 084

Looking out towards the Mediterranean from its hilltop perch, **Cyrene** (admission 3LD, camera/video 5/10LD, compulsory guide 50LD; ☺ 7.30am-6pm May-Sep, 8am-5pm Oct-Apr) rivals Leptis Magna for the title of Libya's most captivating ancient city.

Founded by Greek settlers from the island of Thera (modern Santorini) in 631 BC, Cyrene was the pre-eminent city of the Greek world in the 4th century BC, renowned for its philosophers and scholars. After the change from Greek to Roman administration in 75 BC, it became an important Roman capital.

The large, open **gymnasium**, originally built by the Greeks in the 2nd century BC and later converted by the Romans into a forum, is most people's introduction to the city. Nearby, the mosaics of the **House of Hesychius** are remarkable, while the agora – the heart of ancient Cyrene – is littered with stunning monuments such as the **Temple of the Octagonal Bases**, the **Naval Monument**, the unusual **Sanctuary of Demeter & Kore** and the **Capitoleum**. Down the hill from the agora, the **Sanctuary of Apollo** includes the 6th-century-BC **Temple of Apollo** and the adjacent **Temple of Artemis**, which may predate the Apollo temple. The spectacularly situated **theatre** is also fascinating, while the 5th-century-BC **Temple of Zeus**, up the hill from the rest of Cyrene, was once larger than the Parthenon in Athens. Cyrene's **museum** (admission US$2.40, camera/video US$4/8; ☺ 8am-6.30pm Tue-Sun), southeast of the Temple of Zeus, has wonderful statues, sculptures and other artefacts that once adorned this extraordinary Graeco-Roman city.

Although many tour groups stay in the nearby town of Al-Bayda, the hills around Cyrene are home to the **Cyrene Resort** (☎ /fax 0851-64391; s/d 35/45LD; ✗), which has pleasant rooms and an excellent cafe and restaurant cut into one of the caves.

Also in the hills around Cyrene, **Cave Restaurant** (☎ 635206; meals from 15LD; ☯ lunch), living up to its name, is a friendly, atmospheric place offering tasty food and good views down towards the coast.

APOLLONIA
☎ 084

Another wonderful ancient Greek city, **Apollonia** (admission 3LD, camera/video 5/10LD; ☯ 7.30am-7pm May-Sep, 8am-5pm Oct-Apr) was the port of Cyrene and came to rival its mother city in significance in the late Roman period. Most of what remains today dates from the Byzantine era, when Apollonia was known as the 'city of churches'.

The Apollonia ruins are strung out along a narrow strip of coastline and include the **Western Church**, with its mixture of Roman and Byzantine columns; the 2nd-century **Roman baths** and **gymnasium**; and the **Byzantine Duke's Palace**, once one of the biggest palaces in Cyrenaica. Some mosaics remain in the **Eastern Church**, while the plunging and picturesque **Greek theatre** stands at the eastern reaches of the site.

In a prime location 50m from the site entrance, **Al-Manara Hotel** (☎ 5153001; fax 5152188; s/d/ste 45/60/95LD; ✗ 💻) is a lovely private hotel with outstanding rooms and a good restaurant (meals 15LD).

TOBRUK
☎ 087 / pop 130,000

Tobruk was the scene of some of the most important WWII battles. Its main (and only) attraction is the **war cemeteries** (admission free; ☯ 9am-5pm Sat-Thu, 2-5pm Fri).

The **Knightsbridge (Acroma) Cemetery**, 20km west of town, is the largest in Tobruk, with 3649 graves of Allied soldiers. Between the Knightsbridge Cemetery and Tobruk is the former battlefield dressing station known as the **Australian (Fig Tree) Hospital**. The **Tobruk (Commonwealth) War Cemetery**, 6km south of the harbour, has an air of simplicity and dignity and contains 2479 graves. More than 300

soldiers are buried in the **French Cemetery**, 8km south of the harbour, while the names of 6026 German soldiers are inscribed in mosaic slabs lining the inside walls of the **German Cemetery**, a forbidding sandstone fort 3.2km south of the harbour.

Funduq el-Jaghbub (☎ 628260; hot-jag@yahoo.com; Sharia al-Jamahiriya; d with/without bathroom 35/25LD, with bathroom & balcony 40LD) is the newest of Tobruk's hotels. This would probably be our pick as the best place to stay. The rooms are fine and you'll be in the centre of town.

If you spend any time in Tobruk, you'll likely end up eating at **Mat'am al-Khalij** (☎ 0925785344; Sharia al-Jamahiriya; meals 10-12LD; ☯ lunch & dinner) every night as it's easily the best place in town. Take a table on the upstairs terrace with views over the harbour and order from a range of pizzas, grilled meats and fish dishes.

NORTHWEST LIBYA

JEBEL NAFUSA

The barren Jebel Nafusa (Western Mountains) protect Libya's northwestern coast from the Sahara, which stretches away deep into the heart of Africa from the mountains' southern slopes. It's a land of rocky escarpments and stone villages clinging to outcrops high above the plains. It's worth exploring as you make your way to Ghadames.

Gharyan sprawls across the top of a plateau and has a number of unusual underground Berber houses. It's famous for its pottery.

Further west, **Qasr al-Haj** is home to a stunning *qasr* (fortified granary) that has stored the local harvests since the 12th century. The main courtyard is breathtaking, with the walls completely surrounded by 114 cavelike rooms. Other stunning *qasrs* are to be found in **Kabaw**, which hosts the **Qasr Festival** in April, and **Nalut**.

GHADAMES
☎ 0484 / pop 20,000

The Unesco World Heritage–listed old city of Ghadames has everything that you imagine a desert oasis to have – abundant palm groves, a wonderfully preserved, labyrinthine old town, and a pace of life largely unchanged for centuries. It's an extraordinary place.

The old city was founded around 800 years ago and was occupied by both the Ottomans and the Italians. In recent decades, Libya's old cities, including that of Ghadames, have fallen victim to the revolutionary government's push towards modernisation. In 1982–83 the Libyan government began building a new town beyond the walls and new houses were given to Ghadamsis to encourage them to leave the homes of their ancestors. In 1984 there were 6666 people living in the old town; four years later there was just one family left.

Old Ghadames (adult/child 5/1LD, camera/video 5/10LD; compulsory guide half/full day 40/60LD) is another world of covered alleyways, whitewashed houses and extensive palm gardens irrigated by wells. The old city comprised loosely configured concentric areas containing residential and commercial districts and covering around 10 hectares. The city was divided into seven 'streets', each the domain of a different subsection of the Bani Walid and Bani Wazid tribes. Each 'street' was essentially a self-contained town, with a mosque, houses, schools, markets and a small communal square for public events.

The designers of the **traditional houses** of Ghadames made maximum use of vertical space and visiting one is a must while in Libya. Eye-catching, with whitewashed walls and brightly painted interiors, all of the houses were connected. The rooftops were the domain of women in the same way that the public laneways below belonged to men. At least three of the old houses have been stunningly restored and are now open to the public.

In the new part of town, **Ghadames Museum** (☎ 62225; adult/child 3/1LD, camera/video 5/10LD; ☒ 9am-1.30pm) is a worthwhile window on old Ghadames.

In October, the annual three-day **Ghadames Festival** brings the old city alive in a riot of colour and activity.

Ghadames has a shortage of good accommodation but there are villas (private homes) that open their doors to travellers all across town (B&B 20LD). Otherwise, try one of the following hotels:

Bab al-Fatah Hotel (Funduq Bab al-Fatah; ☎ 63356; fax 021-3615262; s/d/tr 35/50/75LD; ☒)

Ben Yedder Hotel (Funduq Ben Yeddar; ☎ 63410; yeddar@hotmail.com; s/d 35/50LD; ☒)

Dar Ghadames Hotel (Funduq Dar Ghadames; ☎ 021-3621414; fax 63408; www.darsahara.com; s/d/ste 100/110/150LD; ☒ ☒)

Winzrik Hotel (Funduq Winzrik; ☎ /fax 62485; campsites per person 5LD; s/d 30/40LD; ☒)

The only problem with **Restaurant Awwal** (☎ 62429; meals 12-15LD; ☒ lunch & dinner) is that it's so good most of the other restaurants in town have closed. Its chicken and lamb dishes, especially the tajine, are great.

The ultimate eating experience in Ghadames is, however, lunch in one of the traditional houses of the old town. The most frequently prepared meal is the delicious *fitaat* (lentils, mutton and buckwheat pancakes cooked together in a tasty sauce in a low oven and eaten with the hands from a communal bowl). **Dan Do Omer** (☎ 62300; dandoomer731@yahoo.com) does this to perfection; ask for the owner of the house, At-Tayeb Mohamed Hiba.

SOUTHERN LIBYA

IDEHAN UBARI & THE UBARI LAKES

The Idehan Ubari (Ubari Sand Sea) is a dramatic sea of towering sand dunes. There are at least 11 lakes in the area. Although many have dried up and most require longer expeditions, three – pretty **Mavo**, dramatic **Gebraoun** and enchanting **Umm al-Maa** (Mother of Water) – are easily accessible and majestically beautiful at sunset. Swimming in the buoyant waters surrounded by sand dunes and palm trees is one of *the* great desert experiences. The only drawback of the lakes is that this is one of the busiest corners of the Libyan Sahara.

GERMA & WADI METHKANDOUSH

South of the Idehan Ubari, the town of Germa was once the seat of the ancient Garamantian Empire, a sophisticated desert empire that made the Sahara bloom from 900 BC to AD 500. The mud ruins of their capital **Garama** (adult/child 3/1LD, camera/video 5/10LD; ☒ 8am-7pm May-Sep, 9am-5pm Oct-Apr) is well worth a visit. Germa has numerous camp grounds and a handful of hotels.

A two-hour drive by 4WD southwest of Germa, **Wadi Methkandoush** (adult/child 3/1LD, camera/video 5/10LD; ☒ 8am-5pm daily) has one of the richest concentrations of prehistoric rock carvings in the world, with most dating back 12,000 years. This open-air gallery contains hundreds of wonderful carvings of giraffe (including a bullet-scarred engraving of a giraffe herd), hippopotamus, elephant, crocodile, ostrich and rhinoceros. The carving of two catlike figures sparring on their hind legs alongside four ostriches is the single most spectacular rock carving in Libya.

IDEHAN MURZUQ

The Idehan Murzuq (Murzuq Sand Sea) is an incomprehensibly vast mountain range (over 35,000 sq km and not much smaller than Switzerland) made entirely of sand – dunes rise hundreds of metres high and myriad wave-like ridges, sculpted by the wind, ascend to razor-sharp summits. The Idehan Murzuq is far less frequented than the Idehan Ubari further north. Indeed, if you venture deeper into the Idehan Murzuq beyond the northern reaches of the sand sea, you'll likely travel for days without seeing another vehicle.

WAN CAZA

The golden sand dunes of Wan Caza form a narrow, roughly north–south chain that separates the Idehan Murzuq from the Jebel Acacus. Wan Caza may lack the epic scope of the sand seas elsewhere (it's all relative), but the dunes are as beautiful as any in Libya. The valley at the main crossing point is famous for its multicoloured sand beneath the surface.

GHAT & THE JEBEL ACACUS

☎ 0724 / pop 27,000

The ancient trading centre of Ghat is one of the most attractive of the Libyan oasis towns. There's an evocative mudbrick **medina** in the heart of town and a superb setting: a backdrop of stunning sand dunes, the dark ridges of Jebel Acacus to the east and the distant peaks of the Tassili N'Ajjer (in Algeria) to the west.

The Jebel Acacus is an otherworldly landscape of dark basalt stone monoliths rising up from the sands of the central Sahara. This Unesco World Heritage–listed area is home to some wonderful scenery, featuring a number of unique natural rock formations enhanced by the ever-shifting sands of the desert. There are also prehistoric rock paintings and carvings including elephants, giraffes, wedding ceremonies and dancing human figures. The most spectacular scenery and rock-art sites are close to Wadi Tashwinat, with its 101 tributary valleys. The next best area is the Awiss region in the north.

The **Acacus Festival** (December to January) features a spectacular sunset concert amid the cathedral-like Jebel Acacus, with Tuareg dancing and re-enactments of traditional ceremonies in the medina to bring in the New Year.

WAW AL-NAMUS

The extraordinary volcanic crater of Waw al-Namus is a weird and wonderful place, and one of the most remote destinations in the world, 300km southeast of where the paved road ends at Tmissah. The black-and-white volcanic sand is stunning, as are the three palm-fringed lakes with red, green and blue waters. The crater is 7km in circumference and the summit of the rocky mountain in the centre affords stunning views. Be sure to use the existing tracks down into the crater to avoid scarring the landscape. Visiting here is a major undertaking and involves a two-day round trip in reliable, well-equipped vehicles. A permit is officially needed to visit Waw al-Namus, but this should be handled by your tour company and the price included in the overall cost of your tour.

LIBYA DIRECTORY

ACCOMMODATION

Libya has an extensive network of *buyut ash-shabaab* (youth hostels), which are pretty basic but dirt cheap and fine for a night. As for camping, sleeping on the desert sand under a canopy of stars is free and unrivalled in beauty. The government-run hotels are often well situated and possess rooms of a reasonable standard, but service is often dysfunctional.

PRACTICALITIES

- A handful of international newspapers are available in Tripoli. The *Tripoli Post* (www.tripolipost.com) is Libya's government-run English-language newspaper.

- Radio coverage in Libya includes the BBC World Service (15.070MHz and 12.095MHz) and other European radio on short wave.

- Libya's electricity system caters for 220V to 240V AC, 50Hz; plugs are mostly of the mainland-European two-pin type, although the three-pin UK plugs are also common.

- Libya uses the metric system.

LIBYA

The crop of new private hotels is cheaper, friendlier and much better maintained.

Note that while you can discuss accommodation with your tour operator, in reality you may not be given much control in choosing your hotels.

ACTIVITIES

Desert safaris by 4WD (and occasionally camel) enable you to experience some of the finest scenery the Sahara has to offer. All Libyan tour companies (p141) can arrange such expeditions, lasting from two days up to deep desert expeditions of two weeks.

BUSINESS HOURS

Banks 9am to 1pm Sunday to Tuesday and Thursday, 8am to 12.30pm and 3.30pm to 4.30pm (or 4.30pm to 5.30pm) Wednesday and Saturday.
Government offices 7am to 2pm Saturday to Thursday April to September, 8am to 3pm Saturday to Thursday October to March.
Internet cafes 9am to 1am Saturday to Thursday and 5pm to midnight Friday.
Restaurants Lunch from 12.30pm to 3pm, dinner from 6.30pm to 10pm Saturday to Thursday and 6.30pm to 10pm Friday.
Shops 10am to 2pm and 5pm to 8pm Saturday to Thursday; some shops also open Friday evening.

CUSTOMS

Libyan customs checks on arrival are pretty cursory, although bags are X-rayed. Don't even think of trying to bring alcohol into the country. If you're bringing your own car (see p140), expect an hour or two of inspections at the border. Customs inspections upon departure tend to be slightly more rigorous; they're especially concerned about antiquities.

DANGERS & ANNOYANCES

Libya is a very safe country in which to travel and Libyans are generally a hospitable and friendly bunch. Police checkpoints can be tiresome and slow your journey, but you'll rarely be asked to show identification. Don't point your camera at restricted sites (ie government buildings or police stations). Driving in Libya can be hazardous, with the major danger being people driving at high speed.

Another frustration for those who don't read it is that most road (and many other) signs are written in Arabic.

EMBASSIES & CONSULATES

Algeria (☎ 021-3610877; off Sharia Jama'a as-Saqa'a, Tripoli) Consulate-General.
Australia (☎ 021-3351468; Office 203, 20th fl, Tower 1, Burj al-Fateh, Tripoli) Consulate-General run by Austrade.
Belgium (☎ 021-4782044; www.diplomatie.be/tripoli; Jasmin St, Hay Andalus, Area 2, Tripoli)
Chad (☎ 021-4443955; 25 Sharia Mohammed Mossadeq, Tripoli)
Egypt Tripoli (☎ 021-4448909; egyemblib@hotmail.com; Sharia al-Fat'h, Tripoli) Benghazi (☎ 061-2223099, Sharia el-Awarsi)
France (☎ 021-4774891; www.ambafrance-ly.org; Sharia Beni al-Amar, Hay Andalus, Tripoli)
Germany (☎ 021-4448552; www.tripolis.diplo.de; Sharia Hassan al-Mashai, Tripoli)
Italy (☎ 021-3333630; www.ambtripoli.esteri.it; 1 Sharia Uaharan, Tripoli)
Japan (☎ 021-4781041; Sharia Jamal al-Din al-Waeli, Hay Andalus, Area 1, Tripoli)
Netherlands (☎ 021-4440216; www.mfa.nl/tri-uk/; 20 Sharia Galal Bayar, Tripoli)
Sudan (☎ 021-4778052; sudtripoli@hotmail.com; Sharia Mohammed Mossadeq, Tripoli)
UK (☎ 021-3351084; http://ukinlibya.fco.gov.uk; 24th fl, Burj al-Fateh, Tripoli)
USA (☎ 091-2203239; http://libya.usembassy.gov; Serraj Area, Tripoli)

EMERGENCIES

Ambulance, Fire & Police ☎ 121

FESTIVALS & EVENTS

Qasr Festival Honours the Berber traditions of the Jebel Nafusa and centres on Kabaw's evocative qasr. Held in April.
Ghadames Festival Held each October in the old city, with celebrations of traditional culture and weddings.
Acacus Festival Held in Ghat during December and January, this festival celebrates the town's Tuareg heritage and includes concerts in the mountains.

HOLIDAYS

For a full list of religious holidays celebrated in Libya, see p1140. The main national holidays include the following:
Declaration of the People's Authority Day 2 March
British Evacuation Day 28 March
US Evacuation Day 11 June
Revolution Day 1 September
Day of Mourning 26 October

INTERNET ACCESS

Libya has joined the internet revolution and internet cafes are present in almost every small town – look for the blue Internet Explorer sign

LIBYA

on the window. Connections can be slow, and costs start from 1LD per hour in Tripoli. You may find wi-fi in some of the better hotels, but don't count on it.

MAPS

For desert expeditions in remote areas, the most reliable map is Michelin's Map No 953, *Africa North and West* (1:4,000,000). The best map available in Libya is probably Malt International's *Map of the Socialist People's Libyan Arab Jamahiriya* (1:3,500,000), although its southern borders are not to be trusted as they're extremely generous in Libya's favour.

MONEY

The unit of currency is the Libyan dinar (LD). The dinar is divided into 100 piastres, or 1000 dirhams (also known as *mileem*). For changing money, the bank and black-market exchange rates are almost identical. Large-denomination euros, US dollars or British pounds are preferred. No banks change travellers cheques – cash is king in Libya. Unless you've already paid for your hotel as part of your tour, payment will be required in Libyan dinars, except for a handful of five-star hotels where payment is sometimes requested in euros or US dollars.

It's now possible to obtain a cash advance on your Visa card at the Masraf al-Tijara Watanmiya (Bank of Commerce & Development) branches in Tripoli (p132) and Benghazi. MasterCard holders will need to rely on the far less widespread branches of the Aman Bank for Commerce & Investment.

Payment by credit card is rarely accepted, but an increasing number of hotels, restaurants and shops allow it.

POST

Almost every town has a post office; they're easily recognisable by the tall telecommunications mast rising above the centre of town. It costs 0.3/1LD to send a postcard/letter to most places, including Europe and Australia.

TELEPHONE

Libya's telephone country code, if you're dialling from outside Libya, is 218. To make an international call from inside Libya, dial 00 and then the number. Area codes (listed beneath each destination heading) are required as a prefix to numbers listed throughout this chapter if you're calling long distance.

NO ANSWER? TRY AGAIN

Libya has numerous professionally run tour companies, although all of them suffer from an occasional inability to answer emails promptly. In fact, many don't answer at all. The actual visa process takes only a couple of weeks, but you're advised to start contacting tour companies long before that to take into account the incomprehensible periods of silence from Tripoli. This problem particularly afflicts lone travellers but is something of an established Libyan business practice in all fields. Be persistent by following up with phone calls and, as a last resort, you could always threaten to write to us if visa deadlines are approaching.

Numbers beginning with 091 or 092 are mobile numbers.

Calls within Libya invariably receive instant connections and are quite cheap (around 0.25LD). The cheapest international phone calls are internet-connected calls made in internet cafes; most cafes sell 8LD cards and can help you connect.

There's a fair chance your mobile will work in Libya, although using it for anything more than sending and receiving SMS can be prohibitively expensive. **Libyana** (www.libyana.ly), which has the most extensive network, and **Al-Madar** (www.almadar.ly) sell 5LD and 10LD SIM cards.

TOURIST INFORMATION

Libya's tourism ministry operates as an overseer of the tourism industry and tour companies, rather than a source of practical information. Your tour company should be able to provide you with all the information you need.

VISAS

To obtain a Libyan visa you'll need an invitation from a Libyan tour company. The tour company will then send you a visa number. Make sure you have an Arabic-language confirmation to smooth the process with airlines, the embassy or immigration officials. You can collect your visa either from the Libyan embassy in your home country or at your entry point to Libya, but specify which you prefer when making contact with the tour company. The process generally takes two weeks but allowing for a month is safer (see also boxed text, above). Visas are valid for 30 days from the date of entry. For a list of Libyan tour operators, see opposite.

Visas for Onward Travel

Visas to Tunisia and Egypt are available at the border crossings. Visas to Chad, Sudan, Niger and Algeria are not available from the embassies of these countries in Tripoli.

WOMEN TRAVELLERS

In general, Libya is one of the easiest countries in North Africa for women to travel in, largely because of Libyan government policies that have contributed to a more rounded view of Western women than in some other countries of the region. As a result, most female travellers have reported being treated with respect, with few incidents of unpleasant behaviour.

TRANSPORT IN LIBYA

GETTING THERE & AWAY

Air

Most international flights into Libya arrive at **Tripoli International Airport** (TIP) and Benghazi's **Benina Airport** (BEN). A small number of flights also use Tripoli's **Metiga Airport** (MJI) and **Sebha Airport** (SEB).

Many airlines serve Tripoli, including the following:

Afriqiyah Airways (8U; ☎ 021-3333647; www.afriqiyah99.eu)

Air Malta (KM; ☎ 021-3350579; www.airmalta.com)

Al-Buraq Air (UZ; ☎ 021-4444811; www.buraqair.com)

Alitalia (AZ; ☎ 021-3350298; www.alitalia.com)

Austrian Airlines (OS; ☎ 021-3350242; www.aua.com)

British Airways (BA; ☎ 021-3351281; www.britishairways.com)

EgyptAir (MS; ☎ 021-3335781; www.egyptair.com)

Emirates (EK; ☎ 021-3350597; www.emirates.com)

KLM Royal Dutch Airlines (KL; ☎ 021-3350018; www.klm.com)

Lufthansa (LH; ☎ 021-3350375; www.lufthansa.com)

Qatar Airways (QR; ☎ 3351818; www.qatarairways.com)

Royal Air Maroc (AT; ☎ 021-3350111; www.royalairmaroc.com)

Royal Jordanian (RJ; ☎ 021-4442453; www.rj.com)

Sudan Airways (SD; ☎ 021-3351330; www.sudanair.com)

Syrian Arab Airlines (RB; ☎ 021-4446716; www.syriaair.com)

Tunis Air (TU; ☎ 021-3336303; www.tunisair.com)

Turkish Airlines (TK; ☎ 021-3351252; www.turkishairlines.com)

Land

Libya's borders with Algeria, Chad, Niger and Sudan were not open to travellers at the time of writing. Niger's (and Algeria's) border does open from time to time depending on the political winds; check the situation in Tripoli before setting out as it's a long road back to anywhere if it's closed.

EGYPT

The Libya–Egypt border, 139km east of Tobruk at Amsaad and 12km west of Sallum in Egypt, is remote, chaotic and, in summer, perishingly hot; bring your own water.

Long-distance buses run from Benghazi to Cairo (24 hours). On the Egyptian side of the border, shared taxis go from Sallum and service taxis travel from Marsa Matruh to the Libyan border, where your Libyan tour operator will meet you by prior arrangement.

TUNISIA

To get to Libya many travellers fly to Tunisia (for which there are numerous cheap flights) and then cross the Tunisia–Libya border by land at Ras al-Jedir. There are numerous buses between Tripoli and Tunis (10 to 20 hours), although most travellers take a Tunisian shared taxi from Sfax or Ben Guerdane as far as the border, where their Libyan tour company will meet them and arrange onward travel.

GETTING AROUND

In this era of organised tours, getting around Libya couldn't be easier because all transport within the country will be taken care of by your tour company.

Air

Libya's domestic airline network is restricted to flights between Tripoli, Benghazi and Sebha, although there are always plans to extend the network (and flights sometimes appear on the schedule) to Ghat, Houn, Ghadames and Lebreq (near Al-Bayda). On the schedule) to Ghat, Houn, Ghadames and Lebreq (near Al-Bayda).

The two airlines that fly domestically in Libya are **Al-Buraq Air** (☎ 021-4444811; www.buraqair.com) and **Libyan Arab Airlines** (☎ 021-3616738, 021-3331143).

Car & Motorcycle

If you have your own vehicle, especially a 4WD, there are few limits on where you can go – the Tibesti region in the far southeast of the country is one area that's off limits to travellers. You must be accompanied by at least one representative of the Libyan tour company that arranged your visa and remains responsible for you for the duration of your stay. For information on customs inspections when bringing your own car into the country, see p138.

Driving is on the right-hand side of the road, and Libyans generally drive as fast as they think they can get away with. For the record, all cars (including 4WDs) must stay on or below 100km/h on highways and 50km/h inside towns.

Libyan roads are maintained in excellent condition and petrol is cheap; you'll fill your tank for around 5LD to 10LD. No matter how many times you've been waved through a checkpoint, never assume that you will be. Always slow down or stop until you get the wave from your friendly machine-gun-toting soldier.

Tours

The following companies are among those that we either recommend or have had recommended to us by travellers. All are based in Tripoli unless stated otherwise.

Ocean Travel & Tours Services (☎ in Benghazi 061-9082084; www.almuheettours.net)

Robban Tourism Services (☎ 021-4441530; www.robban-tourism.com)

Sabri Tours & Travel (☎ 021-7264452; www.sabritours.com)

Sahara Friends Tours (☎ in Sebha 071-633354; www.saharafriendstours.com)

Sea & Desert Tours (☎ 021-7265971; www.sea-desert.net)

Sukra Travel & Tourism (☎ 021-3340604; www.sukra-travel.com)

Taknes Co (☎ 021-3343761; www.taknes.com)

Tilwan Tourism Services (☎ 021-4836243; www.tilwan.com)

Winzrik Tourism Services (☎ 021-3611123; www.winzrik.com)

LIBYA

Morocco

For many travellers Morocco might be just a short hop by ferry from Spain or by one of the myriad budget airlines but, culturally, it's a much further distance to travel. The regular certainties of Europe are suddenly swept away by the full technicolour arrival of Africa and Islam. It's a complete sensory overload.

Tangier – that faded libertine on the coast – has traditionally been a first port of call, but the winds quickly blow you along the Atlantic coast to the cosmopolitan, movie-star famous Casablanca and the whitewashed fishing-port gems of Asilah and Essaouira. Inland the great imperial cities of Marrakesh and Fez attract visitors in droves, as they have done for centuries. The winding streets of their ancient medinas hold enough surprises to fill a dozen repeat trips. Away from the urban beat, you'll find Roman ruins and craggily dramatic valleys to distract you.

If you really want to escape from everything, Morocco still has a couple of trump cards. The High Atlas mountains seem custom-made for hiking, with endless trails between Berber villages, and North Africa's highest peak to conquer. Or, if you prefer someone else to do the walking, simply saddle up your camel and ride straight into the Sahara, to watch the sun set over an ocean of sand.

Morocco can feel like another world, but you don't need a magic carpet to get there.

FAST FACTS

- **Area** 446,550 sq km (710,000 sq km if you include Western Sahara)
- **ATMs** Throughout the country except in small villages
- **Borders** Algeria closed; Mauritania open, but no public transport
- **Budget** US$25 to US$60 per day
- **Capital** Rabat
- **Languages** Moroccan Arabic (Darija), French, Berber
- **Money** Dirham (Dh); US$1 = Dh7.83, €1 = Dh11.33
- **Population** 33.2 million
- **Seasons** Hot (June to August), cold (November to February)
- **Telephone** Country code ☎ 212; international access code ☎ 00
- **Time** GMT/UTC
- **Visas** 90-day visas issued on entry for most nationalities

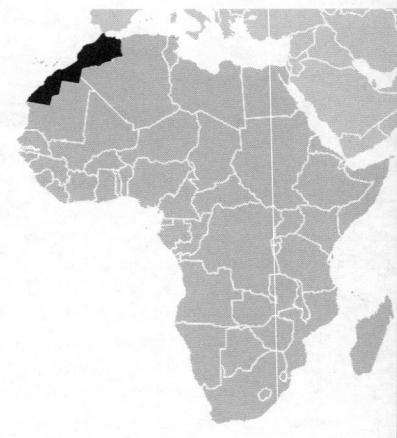

HOW MUCH?

- Pot of mint tea US$1
- Local hammam US$1.30
- Petit-taxi ride US$0.65 to US$1.30
- City bus ride US$0.25 to US$0.40
- Local SIM card US$3.85

LONELY PLANET INDEX

- 1L bottled water US$0.75
- Bottle of Flag Beer US$1
- Souvenir T-shirt US$1
- Grilled brochette US$2.55 to US$3.85

HIGHLIGHTS

- **Marrakesh** (p177) Dive into the clamour and endless spectacle that is Morocco's most dynamic city.
- **Fez** (p169) Lose yourself in the exotic charms of a medieval city replete with sights, sounds and smells.
- **Essaouira** (p165) Laze by the sea in Morocco's coolest and most evocative resort.
- **High Atlas** (p182) Trek deep into a world of stunning scenery and isolated Berber villages.
- **Drâa Valley** (p185) Explore Morocco's richest collection of kasbahs and then soak up the solitude of the Sahara.

CLIMATE & WHEN TO GO

Morocco is at its best in spring (mid-March to May), when the country is lush and green, followed by autumn (September to November), when the heat of summer has eased. At other times, don't underestimate the extremes of summer heat and winter – particularly in the High Atlas, where snowcapped peaks persist from November to July. If you are travelling in winter, head for the south – but be prepared for bitterly cold nights. The north coast and the Rif Mountains are frequently wet and cloudy in winter and early spring.

Apart from the weather, the timing of Ramadan (the traditional Muslim month of fasting and purification, which will occur during August or July during the life of this edition of this guidebook) is another important consideration, as some restaurants and cafes close during the day and general business hours are reduced.

ITINERARIES

- **Two Weeks** From Tangier (p147), head to Tetouan (p152) or the mountains around chilled-out Chefchaouen (p153), where you'll end up staying longer than you planned. Then make a beeline for Fez (p169) and Marrakesh (p177), imperial cities in the Moroccan interior that deserve as much time as you can spare. If you've time, a detour to artsy Essaouira (p165) is a wonderful way to step down a gear after the onslaught of Morocco's most clamorous cities.
- **One Month** Follow the itinerary above, but on your way south check out cosmopolitan Casablanca (p161), imperial Rabat (p157) or laid-back Asilah (p156), depending on your inclination. Save time also for a detour to Meknès (p175) while you're in Fez. Count on a three-day round trip from Marrakesh to trek up Jebel Toubkal (p183), and four or five days to explore Aït Benhaddou (p185), Todra Gorge (p187), Dadès Gorge (p186), the Drâa Valley (p185), and the sand dunes around either Merzouga (p188) or M'hamid (p186).

HISTORY
The Berbers and Romans

Morocco's first-known inhabitants were Near Eastern nomads who may have been distant cousins of the ancient Egyptians. Phoenicians appear to have arrived around 800 BC. When the Romans arrived in the 4th century BC, they called the expanse of Morocco and western Algeria 'Mauretania' and the indigenous people 'Berbers', meaning 'barbarians'.

In the 1st century AD, the Romans built up Volubilis (p177) into a city of 20,000 (mostly Berber) people but, fed up with the persistently unruly locals, the Roman emperor Caligula declared the end of Berber autonomy in North Africa in AD 40. But, whereas the Vandals and Byzantines failed to oust the Romans from their home turf, Berbers in the Rif and the Atlas ultimately succeeded through a campaign of near-constant harassment – a tactic that would later also put the squeeze on many an unpopular Moroccan sultan.

As Rome slipped into decline, the Berbers harried and hassled any army that dared to invade, to the point where the Berbers were free to do as they pleased.

MOROCCO

MOROCCO

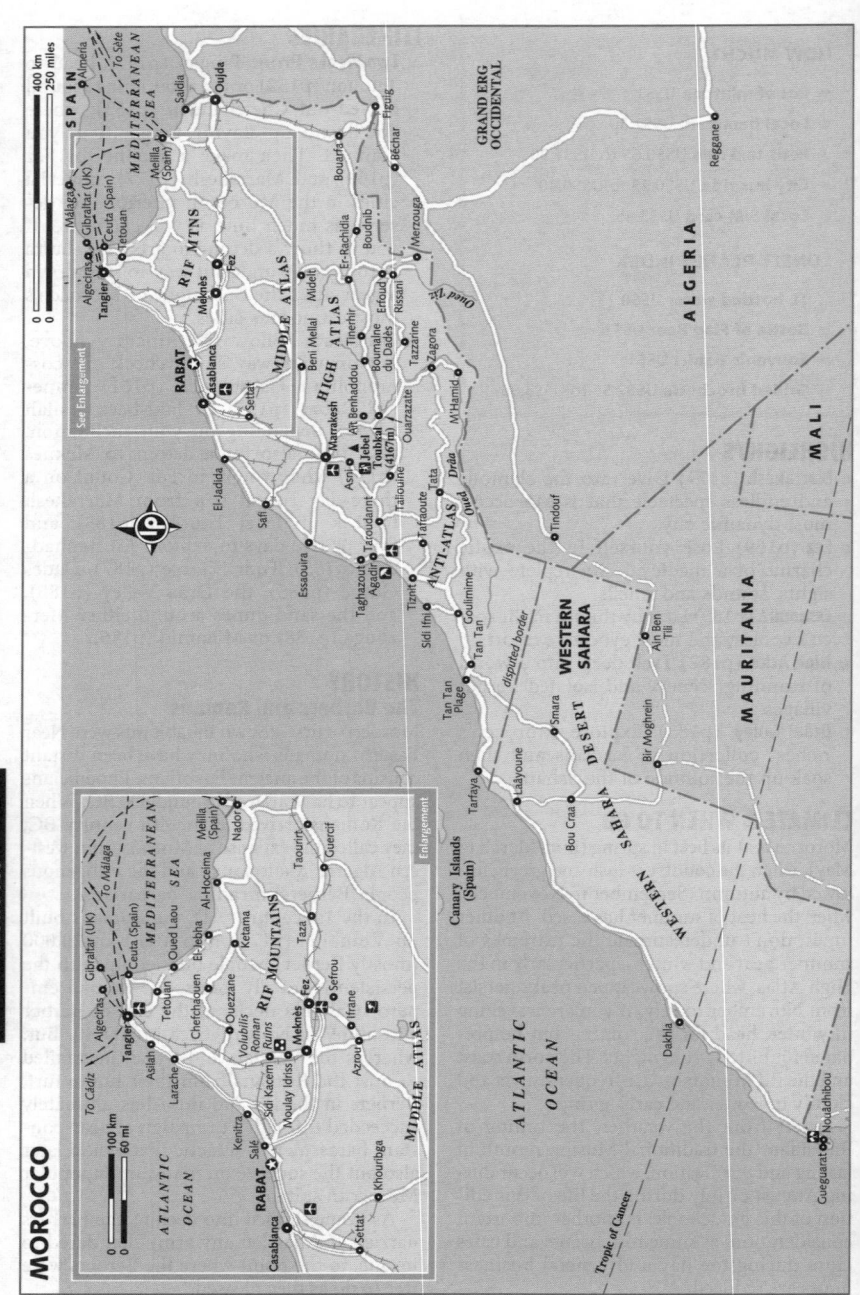

The Islamic Dynasties

In the second half of the 7th century, the soldiers of the Prophet Mohammed set forth from the Arabian Peninsula and overwhelmed the peoples of North Africa. Within a century, nearly all Berber tribes had embraced Islam, although, true to form, local tribes developed their own brand of Islamic Shi'ism, which sparked rebellion against the eastern Arabs.

By 829, local elites had established an Idrissid state, with its capital at Fez, dominating all of Morocco. Thus commenced a cycle of rising and falling Islamic dynasties, which included the Almoravids (1062–1147), who built their capital at Marrakesh; the Almohads (1147–1269), famous for building the Koutoubia Mosque (p178); the Merenids (1269–1465), known for their exquisite mosques and *madrassas* (Quranic schools), especially in Fez; the Saadians (1524–1659), responsible for the Palais el-Badi (p178) in Marrakesh; and the Alawites (1659–present), who left their greatest monuments in Meknès.

France took control in 1912, making its capital at Rabat and handing Spain a token zone in the north. Opposition from Berber mountain tribes was officially crushed, but continued to simmer away and moved into political channels with the development of the Istiqlal (independence) party. Sultan Mohammed V proved vocally supportive of movements opposing colonial rule, and the French eventually packed him off to exile in Madagascar.

Morocco Since Independence

Under increasing pressure from Moroccans and the Allies, France allowed Mohammed V to return from exile in 1955, and Morocco successfully negotiated its independence from France and Spain in 1956.

When Mohammed V died suddenly of heart failure in 1961, King Hassan II became the leader of the new nation. Hassan II consolidated power by cracking down on dissent and suspending parliament for a decade. With heavy borrowing and an ever-expanding bureaucracy, Morocco was deeply in debt by the 1970s.

In 1973 the phosphate industry in the Spanish Sahara started to boom. Morocco staked its claim to the area and its lucrative phosphate reserves with the 350,000-strong Green March into Western Sahara in 1975. It settled the area with Moroccans while greatly unsettling indigenous Sahrawi people agitating for self-determination. The UN brokered a cease-fire in 1991, but the promised referendum, in which the Sahrawis could choose between independence and integration with Morocco, has yet to materialise, and Western Sahara's status remains undecided in international law.

Such grand and patriotic flourishes notwithstanding, the growing gap between the rich and the poor ensured that dissent remained widespread across a broad cross-section of Moroccan society. Protests against price rises in 1981 prompted a brutal government crackdown, but sustained pressure from human rights activists achieved unprecedented results in 1991, when Hassan II founded the Truth & Reconciliation Commission to investigate human rights abuses that occurred during his own reign – a first for a king.

Morocco Today

Hassan II died in 1999 and Morocco held its breath. In his first public statement as king, Mohammed VI vowed to right the wrongs of the era known to Moroccans as 'the Black Years'. Today Morocco's human rights record is arguably the cleanest in Africa and the Middle East, though still not exactly spotless – repressive measures were revived after 9/11 and the 2003 Casablanca bombings. But the Commission has nonetheless helped cement human rights advances by awarding reparations to over 9000 victims of the Black Years.

Mohammed VI has overseen small but real reformist steps, including elections, the introduction of Berber languages in some state schools, and the much-anticipated Mudawanna, a legal code protecting women's rights to divorce and custody. The king has also forged closer ties with Europe and overseen a tourism boom with a much-vaunted plan to attract 10 million visitors to Morocco by the year 2010 (a number likely to be hit within a year or so of its target).

CULTURE

Culturally, Moroccans cast their eyes in many directions – to Europe, the economically dominant neighbour; to the east and the lands of Islam; and to its traditional Berber heartland. The result is an intoxicating blend of the modern and the traditional, the liberal and the conservative, hospitality and the

MOROCCO

need to make a dirham. Away from the tourist scrum, a Moroccan proverb tells the story – 'A guest is a gift from Allah'. The public domain may belong to men, but they're just as likely to invite you home to meet the family. If this happens, consider yourself truly privileged but remember: keep your left hand firmly out of the communal dish! Feel free to slurp your tea and belch your appreciation loudly.

In present-day Morocco, *jellabas* (flowing cloaks) cover Western suits, turbans jostle with baseball caps, European dance music competes with sinuous Algerian rai and mobile (cell) phones ring in the midst of perhaps the greatest of all Moroccan pastimes – the serious and exuberant art of conversation. An inherently social people, Moroccans have a heightened sense of mischief, love a good laugh and will take your decision to visit their country as an invitation to talk…and drink tea and perhaps buy a carpet, a very beautiful carpet, just for the pleasure of your eyes…

People

Morocco's population is of mixed Arab-Berber descent. The population is young, growing and increasingly urbanised. Nearly 60% of Moroccans live in cities and the median age is just 25 years and decreasing – two trends that present the country with clear social and economic challenges. Ninety-nine percent of Moroccans are Muslim. Muslims share their roots with the Jewish and Christians and respect these groups as Ahl al-Kteb (People of the Book). Fundamentalism is mostly discouraged, but remains a presence – especially among the urban poor who have enjoyed none of the benefits of economic growth. That said, the majority of Muslims do not favour such developments and the popularity of fundamentalism is not as great as Westerners imagine.

Emigration to France, Israel and the US has reduced Morocco's once-robust Jewish community to approximately 7000 from a high of around 300,000 in 1948. The Jewish communities that once inhabited the historic *mellahs* (Jewish quarters) of Fez, Marrakesh, Safi, Essaouira and Meknès have largely relocated to Casablanca.

Arts & Crafts

ARCHITECTURE

Moroccan religious buildings are adorned with hand-carved detailing, gilded accents, chiselled mosaics and an array of other decorative flourishes. A mosque consists of a courtyard, an arcaded portico and a main prayer hall facing Mecca. Great examples include the 9th-century Kairaouine Mosque (p170) in Fez and the colossal Hassan II Mosque (p162) in Casablanca. While all but the latter are closed to non-Muslims, the *madrassas* that bejewel major Moroccan cities are open for visits.

Although religious architecture dominates, Casablanca in particular boasts local architectural features grafted onto whitewashed European edifices in a distinctive crossroads style that might be described as Islamic geometry meets art deco.

The street facades of the Moroccan riads (traditional courtyard houses; also called *dars*) usually conceal an inner courtyard that allows light to penetrate during the day and cool air to settle at night. Many classy guesthouses occupy beautifully renovated traditional riads.

MUSIC

The most renowned Berber folk group is the Master Musicians of Jajouka, who famously inspired the Rolling Stones and collaborated with them on some truly experimental fusion. Lately the big names are women's, namely the all-female group B'net Marrakech and the bold Najat Aatabou, who sings protest songs in Berber against restrictive traditional roles. Joyously bluesy with a rhythm you can't refuse, Gnaoua music, which began among freed slaves in Marrakesh and Essaouira, may send you into a trance – and that's just what it's meant to do. To sample the best in Gnaoua, head to Essaouira on the third weekend in June for the **Gnaoua & World Music Festival** (www.festival-gnaoua.co.ma).

Rai, originally from Algeria, is one of the strongest influences on Moroccan contemporary music, incorporating elements of jazz, hip-hop and rap. A popular artist is Cheb Mami, famous for vocals on Sting's 'Desert Rose'.

FOOD & DRINK

Influenced by Berber, Arabic and Mediterranean traditions, Moroccan cuisine features a sublime use of spices and fresh produce.

It would be a culinary crime to skip breakfast in Morocco. Sidewalk cafes and kiosks put a local twist on a Continental breakfast, with Moroccan pancakes and doughnuts, French pastries, coffee and mint tea. Follow your nose into the souqs, where you'll find tangy olives and local *jiben* (fresh goat's or cow's milk cheeses) to be devoured with fresh *khoobz* (Moroccan-style pita bread baked in a wood-fired oven).

Lunch is traditionally the biggest meal of the day in Morocco. The most typical Moroccan dish is tajine, a meat-and-vegetable stew cooked slowly in an earthenware dish. Couscous, fluffy steamed semolina served with tender meat and vegetables, is another staple. Fish dishes also make an excellent choice in coastal areas, while *harira* is a thick soup made from lamb stock, lentils, chickpeas, onions, tomatoes, fresh herbs and spices. *Bastilla*, a speciality of Fez, includes poultry (chicken or pigeon), almonds, cinnamon, saffron and sugar, encased in layer upon layer of very fine pastry.

Vegetarians shouldn't have any problems – fresh fruit and vegetables are widely available, as are lentils and chickpeas. Salads are ubiquitous in Morocco, particularly the traditional *salade marocaine* made from diced green peppers, tomatoes and red onion. Ask for your couscous or tajine *sans viande* (without meat), or go for beans (*loubiya*) or pea-and-garlic soup (*bsara*).

For dessert, Moroccan patisseries concoct excellent French and Moroccan sweets. Local sweets include flaky pastries rich with nuts and aromatic traces of orange-flower water. Another variation is a *bastilla* (multilayer pastry) with toasted almonds, cinnamon and cream.

Cafe culture is alive and well in Morocco, and mint tea – the legendary 'Moroccan whisky' – is made with Chinese gunpowder tea, fresh mint and copious amounts of sugar. Fruit juices, especially freshly squeezed orange juice, are the country's greatest bargain. It's not advisable to drink tap water in Morocco. Beer's easy to find in the Villes Nouvelles – local brands include Casblanca and Flag. Morocco also produces some surprisingly good wines from the Meknès area: try President Cabernet and Medallion Cabernet for reds, or the whites Coquillages and Sémillant Blanc.

ENVIRONMENT

Morocco's three ecological zones – coast, mountain and desert – host more than 40 different ecosystems and provide habitat for many endemic species, including the iconic and sociable Barbary macaque (also known as the Barbary ape). Unfortunately the pressure upon these ecosystems from ever-more-sprawling urban areas and the encroachment of industrialisation in Morocco's wilderness has ensured that 18 mammal (a staggering 15% of the total) and 11 bird species are considered endangered.

Pollution, desertification, overgrazing and deforestation are the major environmental issues (among many) facing the Moroccan government. Despite plantation programs and the development of new national parks, less than 0.05% of Moroccan territory is protected, one-third of Morocco's ecosystems are disappearing, 10% of vertebrates are endangered and 25,000 hectares of forest are lost every year.

MEDITERRANEAN COAST & THE RIF

Bounded by the red crags of the Rif Mountains and the crashing waves of the Mediterranean Sea, northern Morocco's wildly beautiful coastline conceals attractions as diverse as the cosmopolitan hustle of Tangier, the Spanish enclaves of Ceuta and Melilla, the old colonial capital of Tetouan and the superbly relaxing town of Chefchaouen.

TANGIER
pop 650,000

Like the dynamic strait upon which it sits, Tangier is the product of 1001 currents, including Islam, Berber tribes, colonial masters, a highly strategic location, a vibrant port, the Western counterculture and the international jetset. It has been Morocco's face to the world for longer than anyone cares to remember, and has regularly passed between Moroccan and Western control – for half of the 20th century it was under the dubious control of an international council, making it a byword for licentious behaviour and dodgy dealings.

Some of the hustlers remain, notably looking out for tourists fresh off the ferry from Spain, although the ministrations of the tourist police have greatly reduced these stresses. Many travellers simply pass through, but if you take it head on and learn to handle the

MOROCCO

hustlers, you'll find it a lively, cosmopolitan place with an energetic nightlife.

Orientation

Tangier's small medina climbs up the hill to the northeast of the city, while the Ville Nouvelle surrounds it to the west, south and southeast. The large, central square known as the Grand Socco (officially called Place du 9 Avril 1947) provides the link between the two.

Information

Blvd Pasteur and Ave Mohammed V are lined with numerous banks with ATMs and bureau de change counters. Blvd Pasteur also has plenty of internet places.

Clinique du Croissant Rouge (Red Cross Clinic; ☎ 0539 946976; 6 Rue al-Mansour Dahabi)

Espace Net (16 Ave Mexique; per hr Dh5; ⏱ 9.30am-1am)

Main post office (Blvd Mohammed V)

ONMT (Délégation Régionale du Tourisme; ☎ 0539 948050; 29 Blvd Pasteur; ⏱ 8.30am-4.30pm Mon-Fri) Little tourist literature, but staff attempt to be helpful.

Sights

The Kasbah sits on the highest point of Tangier, behind stout walls. Coming from the medina, you enter through Bab el-Aassa, the southeastern gate, to find the **Kasbah Museum** (☎ 0539 932097; admission Dh10; ⏱ 9am-12.30pm & 3-5.30pm Wed, Thu & Sat-Mon, 9am-12.30pm Fri). Housed in the 17th-century palace of Dar el-Makhzen, this is now a worthwhile museum devoted to Moroccan arts. Before leaving, take a stroll around the Andalucían-style **Sultan's Gardens**.

In the southwest corner of the medina, the **Old American Legation Museum** (☎ 0539 935317; www.legation.org; 8 Rue d'Amerique; donations appreciated; ⏱ 10am-1pm & 3-5pm Mon-Fri) is an intriguing relic of the international zone, with a fascinating collection of memorabilia from the international writers and artists who passed through Tangier.

Housed in a former synagogue, the **Musée de la Fondation Lorin** (☎ 0539 930306; lorin@wanadoo.net.ma; 44 Rue Touahine; admission free, donations appreciated; ⏱ 11am-1pm & 3.30-7.30pm Sun-Fri) has an engaging collection of photographs, posters and prints of Tangier from 1890 to 1960.

Sleeping

Hôtel Mamora (☎ 0539 934105; www.hotelmamora.site.voila.fr; 19 Rue des Postes; low season s/d with sink Dh60/120, with toilet Dh100/150, with shower Dh200/230) With a variety of rooms at different rates, this is a good bet. It's a bit institutional, like an old school, but clean, well run and strong value for the money. The rooms overlooking the green-tiled roof of the Grande Mosquée are the most picturesque, if you don't mind the muezzin's call.

Hôtel El-Muniria (☎ 0539 935337; 1 Rue Magellan; s/d Dh150/200) This is your best low-end option in the Ville Nouvelle, and an important cut above the gloomy and often dirty competition. French windows and bright, flowery fabrics set it apart, revealing the careful touch of a hands-on family operation. Room 4 is a great hideaway, a quiet corner double with lots of light, as is Room 8, which is a quiet single room with a harbour view. Potential noise from the bar below is the only drawback.

La Tangerina (☎ 0539 947733; www.latangerina.com; Rue Riad Sultan, Kasbah; d incl breakfast Dh400-1000) This is easily the best midrange choice in Tangier. A perfectly renovated riad at the very top of the Kasbah, it has 10 rooms of different personality, fairly priced and with highly attentive hosts. Bathed in light and lined with rope banisters, it feels like an elegant, Berber-carpeted steamship cresting the medina, with the roof terrace overlooking the ancient crenellated walls of the Kasbah. Dinner is also available on request.

Marco Polo (☎ 0539 941124; www.marco-polo.ma; 2 Rue al-Antaki; s/d from Dh420/560, breakfast Dh35) This newly renovated hotel is the perfect choice if you aren't looking for local atmosphere. Lots of light, sparkling marble floors, and pastel walls make this a bright and welcoming, though generic, space. An excellent, central location across from the beach provides easy access to both the Ville Nouvelle and the medina.

El-Minzah (☎ 0539 935885; www.elminzah.com; 85 Rue de la Liberté; s/d incl breakfast from Dh1700/2100; ☒ ☒) El-Minzah is the classiest five-star hotel in Tangier proper, and a local landmark. This beautifully maintained 1930s period piece offers three excellent restaurants, three equally good bars, a fitness centre, a spa, pleasant gardens and even a babysitting service. Shaped like an enormous hollow square, complete with a tremendous Spanish-Moorish courtyard, it has history oozing from its walls. Portside rooms offer beautiful views.

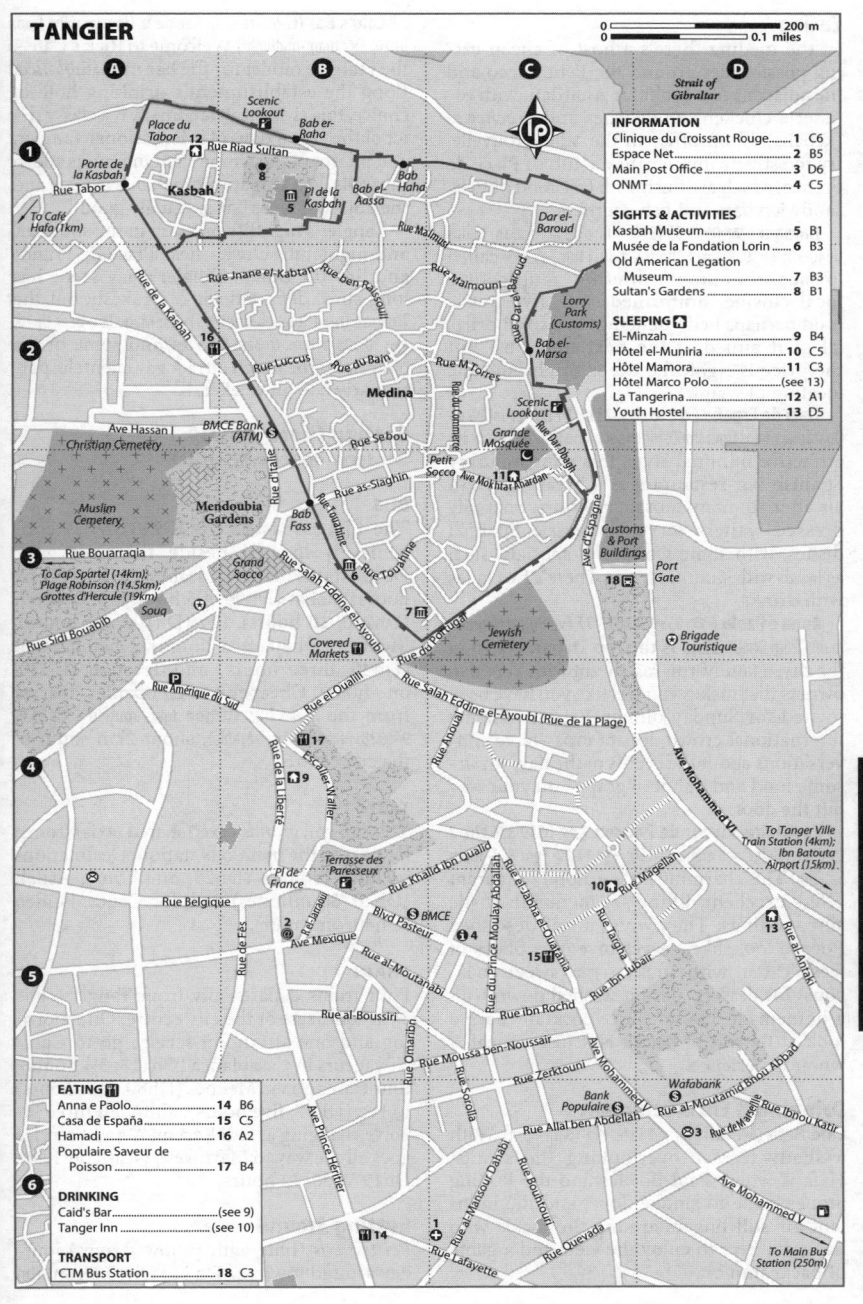

TANGIER

0 — 200 m
0 — 0.1 miles

MOROCCO

Eating

In the medina there's a host of cheap eating possibilities around the Petit Socco and the adjacent Ave Mokhtar Ahardan, with rotisserie chicken, sandwiches and *brochettes* (kebabs) all on offer. In the Ville Nouvelle, try the streets immediately south of Place de France, which are flush with fast-food outlets, sandwich bars and fish counters.

Hamadi (☎ 0539 934514; 2 Rue de la Kasbah; mains Dh40-70; ✆ 9.30am-3.30pm & 7.30-11pm) A so-called 'palace restaurant' offering multicourse local cuisine, uniformed staff, live music (and perhaps belly-dancing) at a fixed price, all of it aimed at the next tour bus. But the price is right, the decor bright and the location pleasant.

Casa de España (☎ 0539 947359; 11 Rue el-Jabha el-Ouatania; mains from Dh60, lunch set menu Dh60) With its attractive minimal style, this contemporary Spanish bar-restaurant is a breath of fresh air after so many mosaic interiors. Snappily dressed waiters serve up classic Spanish dishes, with some wonderful specials, such as lamb with summer fruits. There's free tapas with drinks.

Anna e Paolo (☎ 0539 944617; 77 Ave Prince Héretier; mains from Dh60) This is the top Italian bistro in the city: a family-run restaurant with Venetian owners that makes you feel like you have been invited for Sunday dinner. Expect a highly international crowd, lots of cross-table conversations about the events of the day, wholesome food and a shot of grappa on your way out the door.

Populaire Saveur de Poisson (☎ 0539 336326; 2 Escalier Waller; set menu Dh150; ✆ 12.30-4pm & 7-10pm Sat-Thu) This charming little seafood restaurant offers excellent, filling set menus in rustic surroundings. The owner, a self-described Popeye lookalike, serves inventive plates of fresh catch, with sticky *seffa* (sweet couscous) for dessert, all of it washed down with a homemade 15-fruit juice cocktail (have a look at the vat in back). Not just a meal, a whole experience.

Drinking & Entertainment

Café Hafa (Ave Mohammed Tazi; ✆ 10am-8pm) With a shady terrace overlooking the straits, Hafa is where Paul Bowles and the Rolling Stones came to smoke dope, and the indolent air still lingers among the locals who hang out here to enjoy the view and a game of backgammon.

Caid's Bar (El-Minzah, 85 Rue de la Liberté; wine from Dh20; ✆ 10am-midnight) Welcome to Rick's Café – the real-life model for the bar in *Casablanca*. Long the establishment's drinking hole of choice, this el-Minzah landmark is a classy relict of the grand days of international Tangier, and photos of the famous and infamous adorn the walls. Women are more than welcome and the adjacent wine bar is equally good.

Tangier's nightlife picks up in the summer, and nightclubs cluster near Place de France and line the beach. Tangier's gay scene has long since departed for Marrakesh, but the **Tanger Inn** (Hotel el-Muniria, 1 Rue Magellan; beer Dh10; ✆ 10.30pm-1am, to 3am Fri & Sat) and some of the bars along the beach attract gay clientele, particularly late on weekends.

Getting There & Away

For ferry options, see p193.

BUS

The **CTM bus station** (☎ 0539 931172) is conveniently located beside the port gate. Destinations include Casablanca (Dh120, six hours), Rabat (Dh90, 4½ hours), Marrakesh (Dh210, 10 hours), Fez (Dh100, six hours), Meknès (Dh80, five hours), Chefchaouen (Dh40, three hours) and Tetouan (Dh20, one hour). Cheaper bus companies operate from the **main bus station** (gare routière; ☎ 0539 946928; Place Jamia el-Arabia), about 2km south of the city centre.

TAXI

You can hail *grands taxis* (shared taxis) from a lot next to the main bus station. Destinations include Tetouan (Dh25, one hour), Asilah (Dh20, 30 minutes) and, for Ceuta, Fnideq (Dh40, one hour).

TRAIN

Four trains depart daily from Tanger Ville, 3km southeast of the city centre. One morning and one afternoon service go to Casa-Voyageurs in Casablanca (Dh118, 5½ hours); four trains go via Meknès (Dh80, four hours) to Fez (Dh97, five hours), although three involve changing at Sidi Kacem. A night service goes all the way to Marrakesh (seat/couchette Dh197/350, 12 hours).

Getting Around

Petits taxis (blue with yellow stripes) journey around town for Dh7 to Dh10. From **Ibn**

Batouta airport (☎ 0539 393720), 15km southeast of the city, take a cream-coloured *grand taxi* (Dh150).

AROUND TANGIER

Just 14km west of Tangier lies the dramatic **Cap Spartel**, the northwestern extremity of Africa's Atlantic coast. Below Cap Spartel, the lovely beach **Plage Robinson** stretches to the south. Five kilometres further along here you reach the **Grottes d'Hercule** (admission Dh5), next to Le Mirage hotel. Mythically, these caves were the dwelling place of Hercules when he mightily separated Europe from Africa.

CEUTA

pop 76,000

Jutting out east into the Mediterranean, this 20-sq-km peninsula has been a Spanish enclave since 1640. Its relaxed, well-kept city centre, with bars, cafes and Andalucían atmosphere, provides a sharp contrast to the other side of the border. Nonetheless, Ceuta is still recognisably African. Between a quarter and a third of the population are of Rif Berber origin, giving the enclave a fascinating Iberian-African mix.

Orientation & Information

Most of the hotels, restaurants and offices of interest are on the narrow spit of land linking the peninsula to the mainland. The Plaza de Africa, unmistakable for its giant cathedral, dominates the city centre. The port and ferry terminal are a short walk to the northwest. The border is 2km to the south along the Avenida Martinez Catena.

To phone Ceuta from outside Spain, dial ☎ 0034 before the nine-digit phone number. Also remember that Ceuta is on Spanish time and uses the euro.

Banks with ATMs are plentiful around the pedestrianised Paseo de Revellin, and Plaza Ruiz.

Cyber Ceuta (☎ 956 512303; Paseo Colón; per hr €2.40; ⏰ 11am-2pm & 5-10pm Mon-Sat, 5-10pm Sun)

Main Tourist Office (☎ 956 200560; Baluarte de los Mallorquines; ⏰ 8.30am-8.30pm Mon-Fri, 9am-8pm Sat & Sun) Friendly and efficient, with good maps and brochures.

Post Office (59 Calle Real; ⏰ 8.30am-8.30pm Mon-Fri, 9.30am-2pm Sat)

Sights

Ceuta's history is marked by the **Ruta Monumenta**, a series of excellent information boards in English and Spanish outside key buildings and monuments around the city.

The impressively restored **Royal city walls** (☎ 956 511770; Ave González Tablas; admission free; ⏰ 10am-2pm & 5-8pm) are worth a visit, and contain the striking **Museo de los Muralles Reales** art gallery tucked inside.

The most intriguing museum is the underground **Museo de la Basilica Tardorromana** (Calle Queipo de Llano; ⏰ 10am-1.30pm & 5-7.30pm Mon-Sat, 10am-1.30pm Sun). Integrated into the architectural remains of an ancient basilica discovered during street work in the '80s, it includes a bridge over open tombs – skeletons included.

Sleeping

Pensión La Bohemia (☎ 956 510615; 16 Paseo de Revellín; s/d €25/35) This well-run operation, one flight above a shopping arcade, offers a bright and spotless set of rooms arranged around a central courtyard. Bathrooms are shared, with plenty of hot water and communal showers. Rooms have small TVs and fans.

Hostal Central (☎ 956 516716; www.hostalesceuta. com; Paseo del Revellín; s/d/tr €34/44/54; 🖳) This good-value, centrally located two-star hotel is the next step up from a *pension* (guesthouse), but has the same cosy charm. Bright rooms are small but spotless, and all come with bathroom and fridge. Low-season discounts can tip this place into the budget bracket.

Hostal Plaza Ruiz (☎ 956 516733; www.hostalesceuta. com; 3 Plaza Ruiz; s/d/tr from €45/60/76; 🖳) Sister hotel to the Central, this place has a similar, welcoming style and a charming location. Rooms are airy, with nice pine furniture; the best have wrought-iron balconies overlooking the cafes of the plaza.

Parador Hotel La Muralla (☎ 956 514940; ceuta@ parador.es; 15 Plaza de Africa; s/d from €65/90; 🖳 🖳) Ceuta's top address is this spacious four-star hotel perfectly situated on the Plaza de Africa. Rooms are comfortable, but not luxurious, with balconies overlooking a palm-filled garden – all for a bargain price.

Eating

In addition to the places listed here, the Pablado Marinero (Seamen's Village) beside the yacht harbour is home to a variety of decent restaurants. The best place to look for tapas bars is in the streets around Millán Astray to the north of Calle Camoens.

Cala Carlota (☎ 956 525061; Calle Edrisis; set menu from €7) This simple restaurant has a prime location overlooking the yacht harbour. The daily set menu is a popular choice, while the fish dishes will set you back the same amount on their own.

La Marina (☎ 956 514007; 1 Alférez Bayton; mains from €12, set menu €8; ☺ closed Sun & Feb) This smart, friendly restaurant specialises in fish, but also does a great-value three-course set menu.

El Angulo (☎ 956 514810; 1 Muralles Reales; mains from €15; ☺ noon-4pm & 8.30pm-midnight Mon-Sat) Here's your chance to eat inside the Royal Walls. The local meats and seafood are as good as the unique atmosphere under the stone fortifications.

Getting There & Away

Bus 7 runs up to the Moroccan border (*frontera*) every 10 minutes from Plaza de la Constitución (€0.60). The large *grands taxis* lot next to the Moroccan border control has departures to Tetouan (Dh30, 40 minutes). For Tangier, take a *grand taxi* to Fnideq (Dh5, 10 minutes), just south of the border, and change there.

The **estación marítima** (ferry terminal; Calle Muelle Cañonero Dato) is west of the town centre, and from here there are several daily high-speed ferries to Algeciras (see p193).

TETOUAN
pop 320,000

Tetouan is unlike anywhere else in the Rif, or even Morocco. For more than 40 years, from 1912 to 1956, it was the capital of the Spanish Protectorate, bequeathing it a unique Hispano-Moorish atmosphere. The neat medina – a Unesco World Heritage Site – sits hard against the modern Spanish part of town, with its whitewashed buildings, high shuttered windows and a spectacular backdrop of the Rif Mountains.

About 8km northeast of Tetouan is the beach town of **Martil**. Once Tetouan's port and home to pirates, it's altogether quieter now, especially out of season. The pleasant beach lined with waterfront cafes comes to life in July and August.

Information

There are plenty of banks with ATMs along Ave Mohammed V.

BMCE foreign exchange office (Place Moulay el-Mehdi; ☺ 10am-2pm & 4-8pm) Change cash and travellers cheques outside regular banking hours.

Main hospital (☎ 0539 972430; Martil Rd) About 2km out of town.

ONMT (Délégation Régionale du Tourisme; ☎ 0539 961915; 30 Ave Mohammed V; ☺ 8.30am-12.30pm & 1.30-4.30pm Mon-Fri) Poor service.

Post office (Place Moulay el-Mehdi; ☺ 8am-4.30pm Mon-Fri)

Remote Studios (13 Ave Mohammed V; per hr Dh9; ☺ 9am-midnight) Internet access.

Sights

The whitewashed medina (home to some 40 mosques, of which the **Grande Mosquée** and **Saidi Mosque** are the most impressive) opens through its main gate, Bab er-Rouah, onto Place Hassan II, Tetouan's grand main square. At the opposite end of the medina, the **Musée Marocaine** (Musée Ethnographique; admission Dh10; ☺ 9.30am-noon & 3.30-6.30pm Mon-Fri) is housed inside the bastion in the town wall.

Opposite Bab el-Okla, the medina's oldest gate, students learn traditional arts and crafts at the **artisanal school** (☎ 0539 972721; admission Dh10; ☺ 8am-noon & 2.30-5.30pm Mon-Fri).

Sleeping

Pension Iberia (☎ 0539 963679; 5 Place Moulay el-Mehdi; s/d/tr Dh50/80/120) This is the best budget option in town, with classic high-ceilinged rooms and shuttered balconies that open out on the Place Moulay el-Mehdi. Bathrooms are shared, and hot showers an extra Dh10.

Riad Dalia (☎ 018 025049; www.riad-dalia.com; 25 Rue Ouessaa; s without bathroom/small ste/master ste Dh150/400/600) This family-run option is an eclectic adventure. A 300-year-old former Dutch consul's house has been transformed into a hotel, and it feels like the consul may turn up at any moment. The master suite is fit for royalty, but mixed pricing allows a room for every budget.

El Reducto (☎ 0539 968120; www.riadtetouan.com; Zanqat Zawya 38; s/d incl breakfast Dh425/550, half board Dh500/700) This is the premier place to stay in Tetouan if you want an upscale medina experience at a very reasonable price. The spotless, palatial rooms are truly fantastic, with big baths, the highest-quality antique furniture and beautiful silk bedspreads.

Eating

Jenin (☎ 0539 962246; 8 Rue al-Ouahda; coffee Dh8; ☺ 6am-9.30pm winter, to 11pm summer, closed Fri afternoon) This sparkling, modern cafe is the trendiest in town and popular with courting couples. The 10 blends of different fruit juices are the highlight.

Snack Yousfi (Rue Youseff ben Tachfine; sandwiches from Dh15; ☺ until midnight) Fill up on a sandwich here for lunch and you might not be hungry again until breakfast. Baguettes are stuffed to overflowing with various fillings, topped out with salad and a handful of chips. Great value.

Restaurant Restinga (21 Ave Mohammed V; fish dishes from Dh50, beer Dh18; ☺ noon-9pm) The open-air courtyard covered by a canopy of eucalyptus is this charming restaurant's primary attraction – along with the rare alcohol licence. It's a great place to duck out of the crowded boulevard for a rest and a beer, as well as some seafood from the coast.

Palace Bouhlal (☎ 0539 998797; 48 Jamaa Kebir; set menu Dh100; ☺ 10am-4pm) A sumptuous palace option, with plush couches, wall rugs, intimate dining spaces (especially upstairs), gurgling fountains and a grand Moorish arch complementing the usual four-course meal. Follow the lane north around the Grande Mosquée and look for signs directing you down a tiny alley.

Getting There & Away

Several bus companies operate from the **bus station** (cnr Rue Sidi Mandri & Rue Moulay Abbas). **CTM** (☎ 0539 961688) has buses running to the usual array, including Tangier (Dh20, 1¼ hours, daily), Casablanca (Dh125, six to seven hours, twice daily) via Rabat (Dh10, 4½ hours), and Chefchaouen (Dh25, 1½ hours, three daily), Fez (Dh 93, four hours), Marrakesh (Dh235, 11 hours) and many more.

Grands taxis to Fnideq (for Ceuta; Dh30, 30 minutes) and Martil (Dh5, 15 minutes) leave from Ave Hassan II, southeast of the bus station.

CHEFCHAOUEN
pop 50,000

Set beneath the striking peaks of the Rif Mountains, Chefchaouen has long been charming travellers. One of the prettiest towns in Morocco, its old medina is a delight of Moroccan and Andalucían influence, with red-tiled roofs, bright-blue buildings and narrow lanes converging on a delightful square.

Orientation & Information

Chefchaouen is split into the eastern medina and the western *ciudad nueva* (new city). The heart of the medina is Plaza Uta el-Hammam,

with its unmistakable kasbah. The principal route of the *ciudad nueva* is Ave Hassan II, which stretches into the medina by Place el-Majzen. The bus station is a 1km hike southwest of the town centre.

Banque Populaire (Plaza Uta el-Hammam; ☺ 9.30am-1pm & 3.30-9pm Mon-Fri) Has an ATM.

Hospital Mohammed V (☎ 0539 986228; Ave al-Massira al-Khadra)

Post office (Ave Hassan II; ☺ 8am-4.30pm Mon-Fri, to noon Sat & Sun)

Saadoune.net (Plaza Uta el-Hammam; per hr Dh10; ☺ 9am-2pm & 3pm-midnight)

Sights

Chefchaouen's medina is one of the loveliest in Morocco, with blinding blue-white hues and a strong Andalucían flavour. The heart of the medina is the shady, cobbled **Plaza Uta el-Hammam**, which is dominated by the red-hued walls of the **kasbah** (☎ 039 986343; admission incl museum & gallery Dh10; ☺ 9am-1pm & 3-6.30pm Wed-Mon, 9-11.30am & 3-4.30pm Fri) and the striking **Grande Mosquée**, which is noteworthy for its unusual octagonal tower. Inside the kasbah's gardens is a modest **ethnographic museum**, where the photos of old Chefchaouen are the highlights.

Sleeping

Hotel Mauritania (☎ 0539 986184; 15 Rue Qadi Alami; s/d Dh45/80) Rooms are basic here, but staff are helpful, there's a comfy courtyard lounge ideal for meeting other travellers and the breakfasts (Dh20) are great.

Hostal Yasmina (☎ 0539 883118; yasmina45@hotmail.com; 12 Calle Lalla Horra; r per person Dh70) For the price bracket, this place sparkles. Rooms are bright and clean, the location is a stone's throw from Plaza Uta el-Hammam and the roof terrace is very welcoming. This bargain doesn't have many rooms, though, so it can fill up quickly.

Hostal Guernika (☎ 0539 987434; 49 Onssar; r Dh200) This is a warm and charming place, not too far from Plaza Uta el-Hammam. There are several great, streetside rooms – large and bright, facing the mountains – but others are dark. All have showers.

Dar Terrae (☎ 0539 987598; darterrae@hotmail.com; Ave Hassan I; s/d/tr incl breakfast Dh250/350/450) These funky, cheerfully painted rooms are individually decorated, have their own bathroom and fireplace, and are hidden up, down and around a tumble of stairs and odd corners. The Italian

MOROCCO

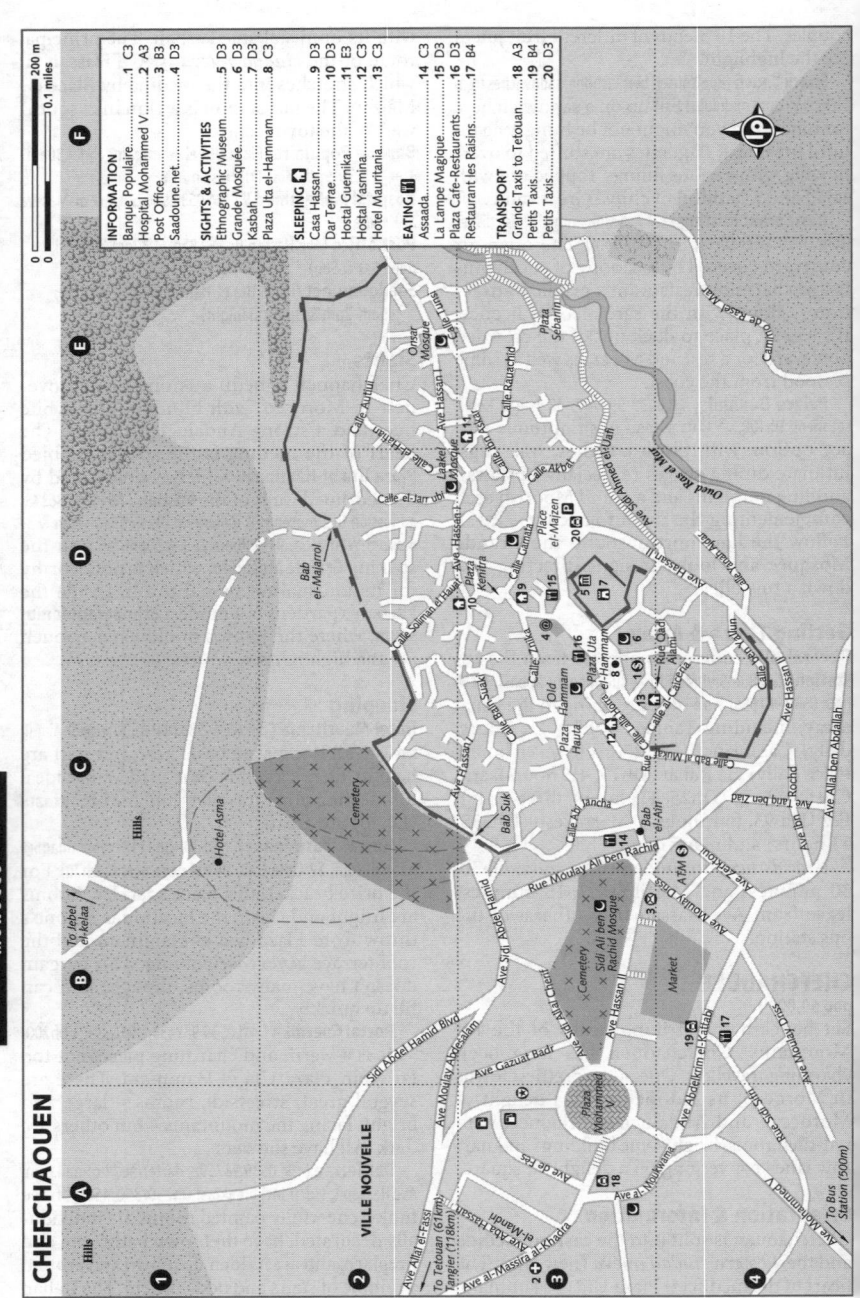

CHEFCHAOUEN

VILLE NOUVELLE

Hills

0 — 200 m
0 — 0.1 miles

JEBEL EL-KELAÂ

Looming over Chefchaouen at 1616m, Jebel el-Kelaâ might initially appear a daunting peak, but with an early start and a packed lunch it can easily be climbed in a day if you're in reasonably good shape.

The hike starts from behind the old Hôtel Asma road, following the 4WD track that takes you to the hamlet of Aïn Tissimlane. Rocks painted with a yellow-and-white stripe indicate that you're on the right path. The initial hour is relatively steep, as you climb above the trees to get your first views over Chefchaouen before cutting into the mountains along the steady *piste*. You should reach Aïn Tissemlane within a couple of hours of setting out, after which the path climbs and zigzags steeply through great boulders for nearly an hour to a pass. Turn west along the track that leads to the saddle of the mountain, from where you can make the final push to the summit. There's a rough path, although you'll need to scramble in places. The peak is attained relatively quickly, and your exertions are rewarded with the most sublime views over this part of the Rif.

It's straightforward and quick to descend by the same route. Alternatively, you can head north from the saddle on a path that takes you to a cluster of villages on the other side of the mountain. El-Kelaâ, one of these villages, has 16th-century grain stores and a mosque with a leaning minaret. From here, a number of simple tracks will take you back to Chefchaouen in a couple of hours.

owners prepare a fantastic breakfast spread every day, and other meals on request.

Casa Hassan (☎ 0539 986153; www.casahassan.com; 22 Rue Targui; s/d/tr incl half board from Dh500/650/800; ✹) A large hotel with a boutique-hotel feel, this long-established upmarket choice has sizable rooms with creative layouts, and an in-house *hammam*. The terrace provides an elegant lounge, and the cosy Restaurant Tissemlal a warm hearth.

Eating

A popular eating option in Chefchaouen is to choose one of about a dozen **plaza cafe-restaurants** (Plaza Uta el-Hamman; breakfast from Dh15, mains from Dh25; ✹ 8am-11pm) on the main square. Menus are virtually identical – Continental breakfasts, soups and salads, tajines and seafood – but the food is generally pretty good and the ambience lively.

Assaada (☎ 0666 317316; Bab el-Ain; set menu Dh40) This reliable cheapie tries hard to please. Located on both sides of the alley just prior to Bab el-Ain, it offers the usual *menu complet*, but also great fruit shakes and a funky graffiti rooftop terrace that exudes an urban charm. The staircase is not for the faint-hearted.

Restaurant Les Raisins (☎ 0667 982878; 7 Rue Sidi Sifri; tajines Dh20, set menu from Dh40; ✹ 7am-9pm) A bit out of the way, this family-run place is a perennial favourite with locals and tourists alike, and known for its couscous royal. Late, lazy lunches are the best, with the front terrace catching the afternoon sun.

La Lampe Magique (☎ 065 406464; Rue Targui; mains from Dh45, set menu Dh75) This magical place overlooking Plaza Uta el-Hammam serves delicious Moroccan staples in a grand setting. Three bright-blue floors include a laid-back lounge, a more formal dining area and a rooftop terrace. The menu – featuring favourites like lamb tajine with prunes and some great cooked salads – is better than average, but this place is really about atmosphere.

Getting There & Away

Many bus services from Chefchaouen originate elsewhere, so buy your ticket a day in advance if possible to avoid missing out. **CTM** (☎ 039 987669) serves Casablanca (Dh120, eight hours), Rabat (Dh90, six hours), Fez (Dh70, four hours), Tangier (Dh40, three hours) and further destinations.

Grands taxis heading to Tetouan (Dh30, one hour) leave from just below Plaza Mohammed V – change there for Tangier or Ceuta.

MELILLA
pop 65,000

Occupied by the Spanish since 1496, Melilla is the smaller and less affluent of the two enclaves that mark the last vestiges of Spain's African empire. With nearly half of its inhabitants being of Rif Berber origin, it has an atmosphere all of its own – neither quite Europe nor Africa. The centre of Melilla is a delight of modernist architecture and quiet gardens.

MOROCCO

Information

The Ville Nouvelle is centred on Place Moulay el-Mehdi and the pedestrian stretch of Ave Mohammed V, which runs west to the vast Place Hassan II. Around here you'll find the hotels, banks, most of the restaurants and cafes, and the bus station.

As with Ceuta, to phone Melilla from outside Spain, dial ☎ 0034 before the nine-digit phone number; and also remember that Melilla is on Spanish time and uses the euro.

Sights

The main entrance to the fortress of Melilla la Vieja (Old Melilla), which perches over the Mediterranean, is **Puerta de la Marina** (Calle General Macías), where you'll find a pair of 15th-century water cisterns, **Aljibes de las Peñuelas** (admission free; ☾ 10am-2pm & 5-9.30pm Tue-Sat, 10am-2pm Sun Apr-Sep, 10am-2pm & 4.30-8.30pm Tue-Sat, 10am-2pm Sun Oct-Mar). The terrace of the small **Museo de Arqueología e Historia de Melilla** (☎ 952 681339; Plaza Pedro de Estopiñán; admission free; ☾ 10am-1.30pm & 4-8.30pm Tue-Sat, 10am-2pm Sun) has fantastic views overlooking the city.

The new part of town, west of the fortress, is considered by some to be Spain's 'second modernist city', after Barcelona. The highlight is Plaza de España, with the lovely facade of the **Palacia de la Asamblea**.

Sleeping & Eating

Hostal La Rosa Blanca (☎ 952 682738; 7 Calle Gran Capitán; s/d €20/32) A very basic option, the rooms are clean but vary in quality, so make sure to look before you buy. Rooms have sinks and shared bathrooms.

Hostal Residencia Cazaza (☎ 956 684648; 6 Calle Primo de Rivera; s/d €26/36) While the rooms here are beat up, this old building with its high ceilings and small balconies manages to be charming and has a central location in the Golden Triangle.

Parador de Melilla (☎ 956 684940; Avenida Cándido Lobera; s/d €94/118; ☒ ☒) A classy choice with large, grand rooms, warm use of wood throughout, a high level of quality furnishings and balconies with great views to sea.

Parnaso (☎ 952 684184; 30 Avenida Duquesa de la Victoria; sandwiches from €2.50; ☾ 7am-1am Mon-Sat) This bistro with outdoor seating offers tasty sandwiches and tapas. Popular during lunch and with the after-work crowd.

La Pérgola (Calle General Marcías; ☾ noon-midnight) A waterfront terrace, white tablecloths and cafe music make this a pleasant place for a meal or late-afternoon drink. The speciality is seafood, and at €10 the fixed-price menu cannot be beaten.

Los Salazones (☎ 952 673652; Calle Conde de Alcaudete 15; mains from €12; ☾ 1.30-4.30pm & 9pm-close) Another local favourite, a block from the beach – the perfect place to end a day in the sun. Sit at the marble-topped barrels and enjoy the grilled fish.

Getting There & Away

To get to the border you'll need to catch local bus 2 (marked 'Aforos'), which runs between Plaza de España and the Beni Enzar border post (€0.60) every 30 minutes from 7.30am to 11pm. On the Moroccan side of the border, jump into a *grand taxi* to Nador (Dh5, 15 minutes) for onward transport.

There are daily ferries to Málaga and Almería. Tickets are available for purchase at the **estación marítima** (☎ 956 681633).

THE ATLANTIC COAST

Morocco's Atlantic shoreline is surprisingly varied, with sweeping beaches and lagoons, the economic motor of the urban sprawl around the political and economic capitals of Rabat and Casablanca, respectively, and the pretty fishing ports/tourist drawcards of Essaouira and Asilah.

ASILAH

pop 30,000

A strategic port since the days of Carthage and Rome, the gorgeous, whitewashed, resort town of Asilah feels as much like somewhere on a Greek island as North Africa. It's an intimate, sophisticated introduction to Morocco, with galleries lining the narrow streets, swarms of holidaying Moroccans in summer and foreigners trying to find property bargains. Given its increasing popularity, consider visiting out of season to appreciate the old-world charm of this lovely town at its best.

Sights

Asilah's **medina** is surrounded by sturdy stone fortifications built by the Portuguese in the 15th century. It is these walls, flanked by palms, that have become the town's landmark. The medina and ramparts have been largely restored and the tranquil narrow streets lined with whitewashed houses are well worth a wander. Craftsmen and artists have opened workshops along the main streets and invite passers-by in to see them work. The southwestern bastion of the ramparts is the best for views over the ocean.

Paradise Beach, Asilah's best beach, is 3km south of town and is a gorgeous, pristine spot that really does live up to its name.

Sleeping

Hôtel Sahara (☎ 0539 417185; 9 rue de Tarfaya; s/d/tr Dh98/136/204, hot showers Dh5) This small, immaculately kept hotel offers simple rooms set around an open courtyard. The compact rooms are comfortable and well maintained. The sparkling shared toilets and showers are all new and scrubbed till they gleam.

Hôtel Patio de la Luna (☎ 0539 416074; 12 Place Zellaka; s/d Dh300/450) This intimate, Spanish-run place is secluded behind an unassuming door on the main drag. The simple, rustic rooms have wooden furniture, woven blankets and tiled bathrooms, and are set around a lovely leafy patio. It's very popular, so book ahead.

Hôtel Azayla (☎ 0539 416717; e-elhaddad@menara. ma; 20 Rue ibn Rochd; s/d Dh390/480) Big, bright, comfy and well equipped, the rooms here are a really good deal. The bathrooms are new, the decor is tasteful – with great photographs (by the owner) of Morocco – and the giant windows bathe the rooms in light. The place may lack local character, but the staff are very friendly and helpful.

Eating

Asilah has a string of restaurants clustered around Bab Kasaba and along the medina walls on Ave Hassan II. There are a few other cheap options on Rue Ahmed M'dem near the banks on Place Mohammed V.

Restaurant Yali (☎ 071 043277; Ave Hassan II; mains Dh25-50) Although there's little to choose between them, this is one of the most popular of the string of restaurants along the medina walls. It serves up a good selection of fish, seafood and traditional Moroccan staples.

Restaurant de la Place (☎ 0539 417326; 7 Ave Moulay Hassan ben el-Mehdi; mains Dh40-80) Friendly, less formal and more varied than its neighbours, this restaurant offers a choice of traditional Moroccan dishes as well as the ubiquitous fish and seafood. The delicious fish tajine provides the best of both worlds.

Casa García (☎ 0539 417465; 51 Rue Moulay Hassan ben el-Mehdi; mains Dh55-80) Spanish-style fish dishes and fishy tapas are the specialities at this small restaurant opposite the beach. Go for succulent, grilled fresh fish or octopus, eels, prawns and barnacles, served with a glass of crisp Moroccan rosé wine on the large and breezy terrace.

Getting There & Away

The tiny bus station is on the corner of Ave Moulay Ismail and the Tangier–Rabat road. CTM doesn't really serve Asilah, but several private bus companies offer services, including Rabat (Dh60, 3½ hours), Marrakesh (Dh 130, nine hours), Tangier (Dh10, one hour) and Fez (Dh60, 4½ hours). Buses to Tangier and Casablanca leave roughly every half-hour.

Three trains run daily to Rabat (Dh77, 3½ hours) and Casablanca (Dh101, 4½ hours), one to Meknès (Dh66, three hours) and Fez (Dh81, four hours), and six daily to Tangier (Dh14, 45 minutes). One overnight train goes direct to Marrakesh (Dh174, nine hours), but this train originates (and fills up) in Tangier, so buy your ticket in advance.

Grands taxis to Tangier (Dh20) depart when full from Ave Moulay Ismail, across from the mosque.

RABAT

pop 1.7 million

Relaxed, well kept and very European, flag-waving capital Rabat is just as cosmopolitan as Casablanca down the coast, but lacks the frantic pace and grimy feel of its economic big brother. Its elegant, tree-lined boulevards and imposing administrative buildings exude an unhurried, diplomatic and hassle-free charm that many travellers grow to like.

Orientation

Ave Hassan II divides the medina from the Ville Nouvelle and follows the line of the medina walls to the Oued Bou Regreg, the river that separates the twin cities of Rabat and Salé. The city's main thoroughfare – the wide, palm-lined Ave Mohammed V – is home to many hotels, while most embassies cluster around Place Abraham Lincoln and Ave Fès east of the city centre.

Information

Numerous banks (with ATMs) are concentrated along Ave Mohammed V.

MOROCCO

RABAT

INFORMATION

BMCE (ATM)	**1** B7
Dutch Embassy	**2** E8
French Consulate-General	**3** C8
German Embassy	**4** C7
Italian Embassy	**5** F7
Librairie Livre Service	**6** B7
Main Post Office	**7** B7
Spanish Consulate	**8** E8
UK Embassy	**9** F6

SIGHTS & ACTIVITIES

Andalucian Gardens	**10** B3
Le Tour Hassan	(see 11)
Mausoleum of Mohammed V	**11** F6
Mosque	**12** B3

Musée des Oudaïa	**13** B7
Souq el-Ghezel	**14** E8
Souq el-Merzouk	**15** C8

SLEEPING

Hôtel Balima	**16** F7
Hôtel Dorhmi	**17** B7
Hôtel Splendid	**18** B7
Le Pietri Urban Hotel	**19** C8
Riad Oudaya	**20** A5

EATING

Café Maure	**21** B3
Restaurant de la Libération	**22** E1
Restaurant Dinarjat	**23** A4
Restaurant el-Bahia	**24** B6

TRANSPORT

Grands Taxis for Fez, Meknès & Salé	**25** D5
Petits Taxi Stand	**26** B6

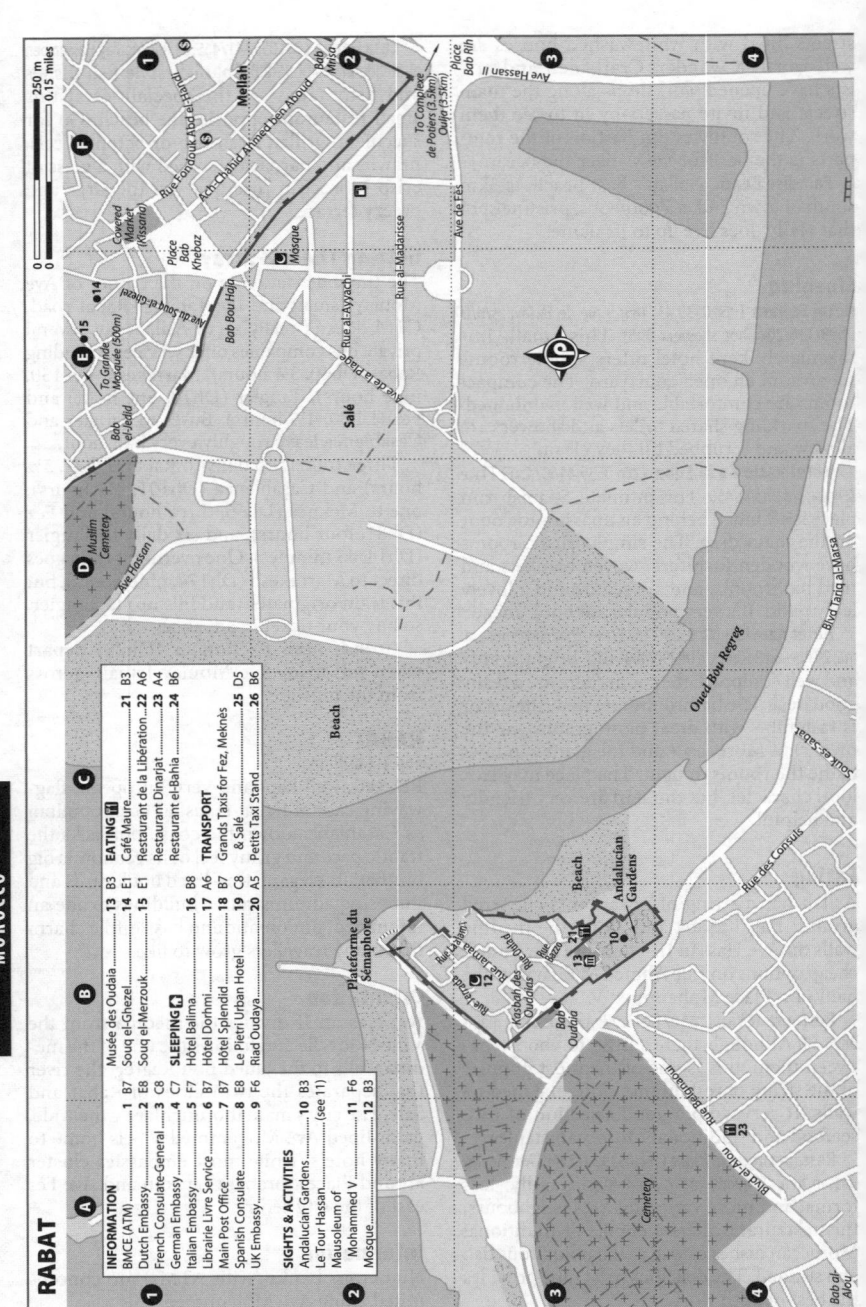

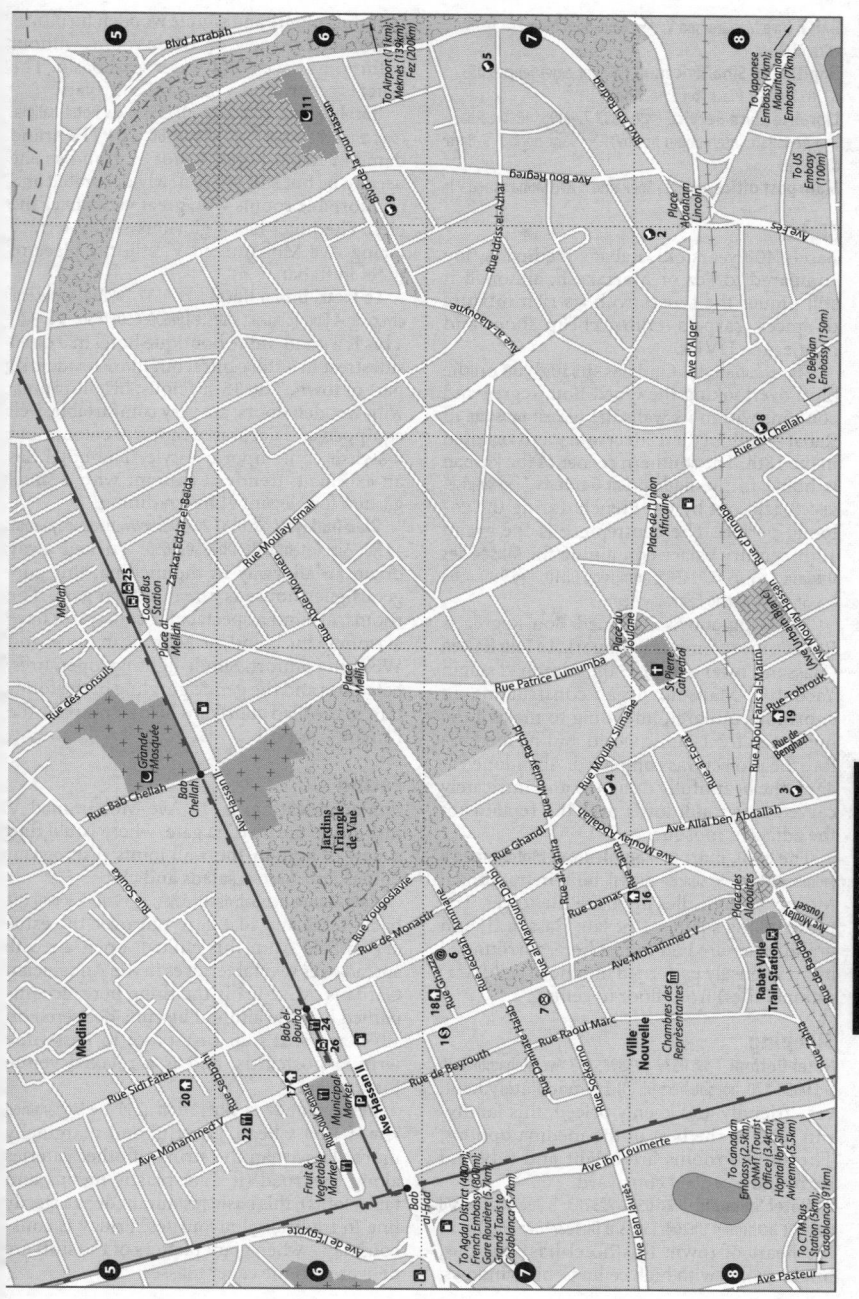

BMCE (Ave Mohammed V; ☾ 8am-8pm Mon-Fri) Bank with ATM.

Hopital Ibn Sina/Avicenna (☎ for emergencies 0537 672871/4450; Place Ibn Sina, Agdal)

Librairie Livre Service (☎ 0537 724495; 46 Ave Allal ben Abdallah; internet per hr Dh7; ☾ 9am-noon & 3-8pm Mon-Sat)

Main post office (cnr Rue Soékarno & Ave Mohammed V)

Sights

Barely 400 years old, Rabat's medina is tiny compared to Fez or Marrakesh, although it still piques the senses with its rich mixture of spices, carpets, crafts, cheap shoes and bootlegged DVDs.

The Kasbah des Oudaias sits high up on the bluff overlooking the Oued Bou Regreg and contains within its walls the oldest **mosque** in Rabat – built in the 12th century and restored in the 18th. The southern corner of the kasbah is home to the **Andalucían Gardens** (☾ sunrise-sunset), laid out by the French during the colonial period. The centrepiece is the grand 17th-century palace containing the **Musée des Oudaia** (☎ 0537 731537; admission Dh10; ☾ 9am-noon & 3-5pm Oct-Apr, to 6pm May-Sep).

Towering above the Oued Bou Regreg is Rabat's most famous landmark, **Le Tour Hassan** (Hassan Tower). In 1195 the Almohad sultan Yacoub al-Mansour began constructing an enormous minaret, intending to make it the highest in the Islamic world, but he died before the project was completed. Abandoned at 44m, the beautifully designed and intricately carved tower still lords over the remains of the adjacent mosque.

The cool, marble **Mausoleum of Mohammed V** (admission free; ☾ sunrise-sunset), built in traditional Moroccan style, lies opposite the tower. The present king's father (the late Hassan II) and grandfather are laid to rest here, surrounded by an intensely patterned mosaic of *zellij* (traditional tiles) from floor to ceiling.

Sleeping

Hôtel Dorhmi (☎ 0537 723898; 313 Ave Mohammed V; s/d Dh80/120, hot showers Dh10) Immaculately kept, very friendly and keenly priced, this family-run hotel is the best of the medina options. The simple rooms are bright and tidy and surround a central courtyard.

Hôtel Splendid (☎ 0537 723283; 8 Rue Ghazza; s/d without bathroom Dh104/159, s/d Dh128/187) Right in the heart of town, this hotel has spacious, bright rooms with high ceilings, big windows,

cheerful colours and simple wooden furniture. Bathrooms are new, and even rooms without bathrooms have a hot-water washbasin. The hotel is set around a pleasant courtyard.

Hôtel Balima (☎ 0537 707755; www.hotel-balima. com; Ave Mohammed V; s/d Dh450/580; ☒) The grand dame of Rabat hotels is not as grand as she used to be but still offers newly decorated and comfortable rooms with great views over the city. The hotel has a glorious shady terrace facing Ave Mohammed V, still the place to meet in Rabat.

Le Pietri Urban Hotel (☎ 0537 707820; www.lepi etri.com; 4 Rue Tobrouk; s/d/ste Dh600/650/1050; ☒ ▯) This is a good-value boutique hotel in a quiet sidestreet in a still central but more residential part of town. The 36 spacious, bright rooms, with wooden floors, are very comfortable, well equipped and decorated in warm colours and a stylish contemporary style. The hotel has an excellent, trendy restaurant with a small garden for elegant al fresco dining.

Riad Oudaya (☎ 0537 702392; www.riadoudaya.com; 46 Rue Sidi Fateh; r/ste Dh1350/1650) Tucked away down an alleyway in the medina, this gorgeous guesthouse is a real hidden gem. The rooms, around a spectacular courtyard, have a wonderful blend of Moroccan style and Western comfort. Subtle lighting, open fires, balconies and the gentle gurgling of the fountain in the tiled courtyard below complete the romantic appeal.

Eating

For quick eating, go to Ave Mohammed V just inside the medina gate, where you'll find a slew of hole-in-the-wall joints dishing out tajines, *brochettes*, salads and chips.

Café Maure (Kasbah des Oudaias; ☾ 9am-5.30pm) Sit back, relax and just gaze out over the estuary to Salé from this chilled, open-air cafe spread over several terraces in the Andalucían Gardens. Mint tea is the thing here, accompanied by little almond biscuits delivered on silver trays. It's an easy place to pass time writing postcards, and is a relaxed venue for women.

Restaurant de la Libération (256 Ave Mohammed V; mains Dh30) Cheap, cheerful and marginally more classy than the string of other eateries along this road (it's got plastic menus and tablecloths), this basic restaurant draws a steady line in traditional favourites. Friday is couscous day – when giant platters of the stuff are delivered to the eager masses.

MOROCCO

Restaurant el-Bahia (☎ 0537 734504; Ave Hassan II; mains Dh50; ⊙ 6am-midnight, closes at 10.30pm in winter) Built into the outside of the medina walls, and a good spot for people-watching, this laid-back restaurant has the locals lapping up hearty Moroccan fare. Choose to sit on the pavement terrace, in the shaded courtyard or upstairs in the traditional salon.

Restaurant Dinarjat (☎ 0537 724239; 6 Rue Belgnaoui; gourmet menu Dh450, bottle wine Dh80) Very stylish and the most elegant of medina restaurants, Dinarjat is a favourite with well-heeled locals and visitors alike. Set in a superb 17th-century Andalucían-style house at the heart of the medina, carefully restored and decorated in a contemporary style but in keeping with tradition, the tajines and couscous as well as the salads are prepared with the freshest ingredients. Book in advance.

Getting There & Away

Rabat Ville train station (☎ 0537 736060) is in the centre of the city. Trains run every 30 minutes until 10.30pm to Casa-Port train station in Casablanca (Dh36, one hour), with services to Fez (Dh70, 3½ hours, eight daily) via Meknès (Dh55, 2½ hours), Tangier (Dh91, 4½ hours, seven daily) and Marrakesh (Dh112, 4½ hours, eight daily).

Rabat has two bus stations: the main **gare routière** (☎ 0537 795816) where most buses depart and arrive, and the less-chaotic **CTM station** (☎ 0537 281488). Both are about 5km southwest of the city centre on the road to Casablanca. CTM has eight daily services to Casablanca (Dh35, 1½ hours), three to Essaouira (Dh115, three hours), seven to Fez (Dh68, 3½ hours), three to Marrakesh (Dh120, five hours), five to Tangier (Dh90, 4½ hours) and one to Tetouan (Dh88, five hours). Arriving by bus from the north, you may pass through central Rabat, so it's worth asking if you can be dropped off in the city.

Grands taxis leave for Casablanca (Dh35) from just outside the intercity bus station. Other *grands taxis* leave for Fez (Dh65), Meknès (Dh50) and Salé (Dh4) from a lot off Ave Hassan II behind the Hôtel Bouregreg.

Getting Around

Rabat's blue *petits taxis* are plentiful, cheap and quick. A ride around the centre of the city will cost about Dh10.

AROUND RABAT
Salé
pop 400,000
A few hundred metres and half a world away, Salé is a walled city and a strongly traditional backwater on the far side of the Oued Bou Regreg estuary. But change is coming, and by the time you read this the Amwaj mega project will link Rabat and Salé by developing the waterfront on both sides of the river.

Salé is best seen on a half-day trip from Rabat. The main entrance to the medina is Bab Bou Haja, on the southwestern wall, which opens onto Place Bab Khebaz. The **Grande Mosquée** (off Map pp158–9) is 500m further northwest along Rue Ras ash-Shajara; it's closed to non-Muslims, but the **medersa** (admission Dh10; ⊙ 9am-noon & 2.30-6pm) is open as a museum.

Shaded by trees and unchanged for centuries, the **Souq el-Ghezel** (Wool Market; Map pp158–9) makes an interesting stop. In the nearby **Souq el-Merzouk** (Map pp158–9), textiles, basketwork and jewellery are crafted and sold.

The most atmospheric way to reach Salé is to take one of the small **rowboats** (per person Dh1) that cross the Oued Bou Regreg from just below the *mellah*. Alternatively, take bus 12, 13, 14 or 16 (Dh4) and get off after passing under the railway bridge.

In the village of **Oulja**, 3km southeast of Salé, the **Complexe de Potiers** (Potters' Cooperative; ⊙ sunrise-sunset) is a top spot for the souvenir hunter. A huge selection of ceramics is produced and sold here, including tajine dishes of every size and colour.

CASABLANCA
pop 4 million
Many travellers stay in 'Casa', as Casablanca is popularly known, just long enough to change planes or catch a train, but Morocco's economic heart offers a unique insight into the country. This sprawling, European-style city is home to racing traffic, simmering social problems, wide boulevards and parks. The facades of imposing Hispano-Moorish and art deco buildings stand in sharp contrast to Casablanca's modernist landmark: the enormous, incredibly ornate Hassan II mosque.

Orientation
The medina – the oldest part of town – is relatively small and sits in the north of the city close to the port. To the south of the medina

is Place des Nations Unies, a large traffic junction that marks the heart of the city. The CTM bus station and Casa-Port train station are in the centre of the city. Casa-Voyageurs train station is 2km east of the city centre and Mohammed V international airport is 30km southeast of town.

Information

There are banks – most with ATMS and bureaux de change – on almost every street corner in the centre of Casablanca.

Central Market post office (cnr Blvd Mohammed V & Rue Chaouia)

Crédit du Maroc (☎ 0522 477255; 48 Blvd Mohammed V) Central bureau de change.

Gig@net (☎ 0522 484810; 140 Blvd Mohammed Zerktouni; per hr Dh10; ☼ 24hr)

LGnet (☎ 0522 274613; 81 Blvd Mohammed V; per hr Dh6; ☼ 9am-midnight)

Main post office (cnr Blvd de Paris & Ave Hassan II)

Service d'Aide Médicale Urgente (SAMU; ☎ 0522 252525; ☼ 24hr) Private ambulance service.

Sights

Rising above the Atlantic, northwest of the medina, the **Hassan II Mosque** is the world's third-largest mosque, built to commemorate the former king's 60th birthday. The mosque rises above the ocean on a rocky outcrop reclaimed from the sea, a vast building that holds 25,000 worshippers and can accommodate a further 80,000 in the courtyards and squares around it. To see the interior of the mosque you must take a **guided tour** (☎ 0522 482886; adult/child/student Dh120/30/60; ☼ 9am, 10am, 11am & 2pm Sat-Thu).

Central Casablanca is full of great **art deco and Hispano-Moorish buildings**. The best way to take them all in is by strolling in the area around the Marché Central and Place Mohammed V. This grand square is surrounded by public buildings that were later copied throughout Morocco, including the law courts, the splendid Wilaya, the Bank al-Maghrib and the main post office. After that, explore the slightly dilapidated 19th-century medina near the port.

Set in a beautiful villa surrounded by lush gardens, the **Jewish Museum of Casablanca** (☎ 0522 994940; 81 Rue Chasseur Jules Gros, Oasis; admission Dh20, with guide Dh30; ☼ 10am-5pm Mon-Fri) is the only Jewish museum in the Islamic world.

Sleeping

Hôtel Galia (☎ 0522 481694; 19 Rue Ibn Batouta; s/d/tr Dh170/250/330, without bathroom Dh150/220/300) With tiled floors; plastic flowers; gold, tasselled curtains and matching bedspreads, Galia is a top-notch budget option with excellent-value rooms and rather dubious taste in decor. Management is friendly and helpful.

Hôtel Astrid (☎ 0522 277803; hotelastrid@hotmail.com; 12 Rue 6 Novembre; s/d/tr Dh256/309/405) Tucked away on a quiet street south of the city centre, the Astrid offers the most-elusive element of Casa's budget hotels: a good night's sleep. There's little traffic noise here and the spacious, well-kept rooms with frilly decor all have bathrooms.

Hôtel Guynemer (☎ 0522 275764; www.guynemerhotel.com; 2 Rue Mohammed Belloul; s/d/tr incl breakfast Dh398/538/676; ✖ ▯ ▨) The 29 well-appointed and regularly updated rooms here are tastefully decked out in cheerful colours. Fresh flowers, plasma TVs, wi-fi access, new bathroom fittings and firm, comfortable beds make rooms a steal at these rates, and the service is way above average.

Hôtel Transatlantique (☎ 0522 294551; www.transatcasa.com; 79 Rue Chaouia; s/d/tr Dh600/750/950; ✖ ▯) Set in one of Casa's art deco gems, this 1922 hotel – shaped like a boat – has buckets of neo-Moorish character. The grand scale, decorative plaster, spidery wrought iron and eclectic mix of knick-knacks, pictures and lamps at the front of the house give the Transatlantique a whiff of colonial-era decadence crossed with '70s retro. It has a lovely outdoor seating area, but the rooms themselves are a little plain, although comfortable.

Eating

Rue Chaouia, opposite the central market, is the best place for a quick eat, with a line of rotisseries, stalls and restaurants serving roast chicken, *brochettes* and sandwiches

Taverne du Dauphin (☎ 0522 221200; 115 Blvd Houphouët Boigny; mains Dh70-90, set menu Dh110; ☼ Mon-Sat) A Casablanca institution, this traditional Provençal restaurant and bar has been serving up *fruits de mer* (seafood) since it opened in 1958. On first glance it's a humble, family-run place, but one taste of the succulent grilled fish, fried calamari and *crevettes royales* (king prawns) will leave you smitten.

Sqala Café Maure and Restaurant (☎ 0522 260960; Blvd des Almohades; mains Dh70-160; ☼ 8am-10.30pm

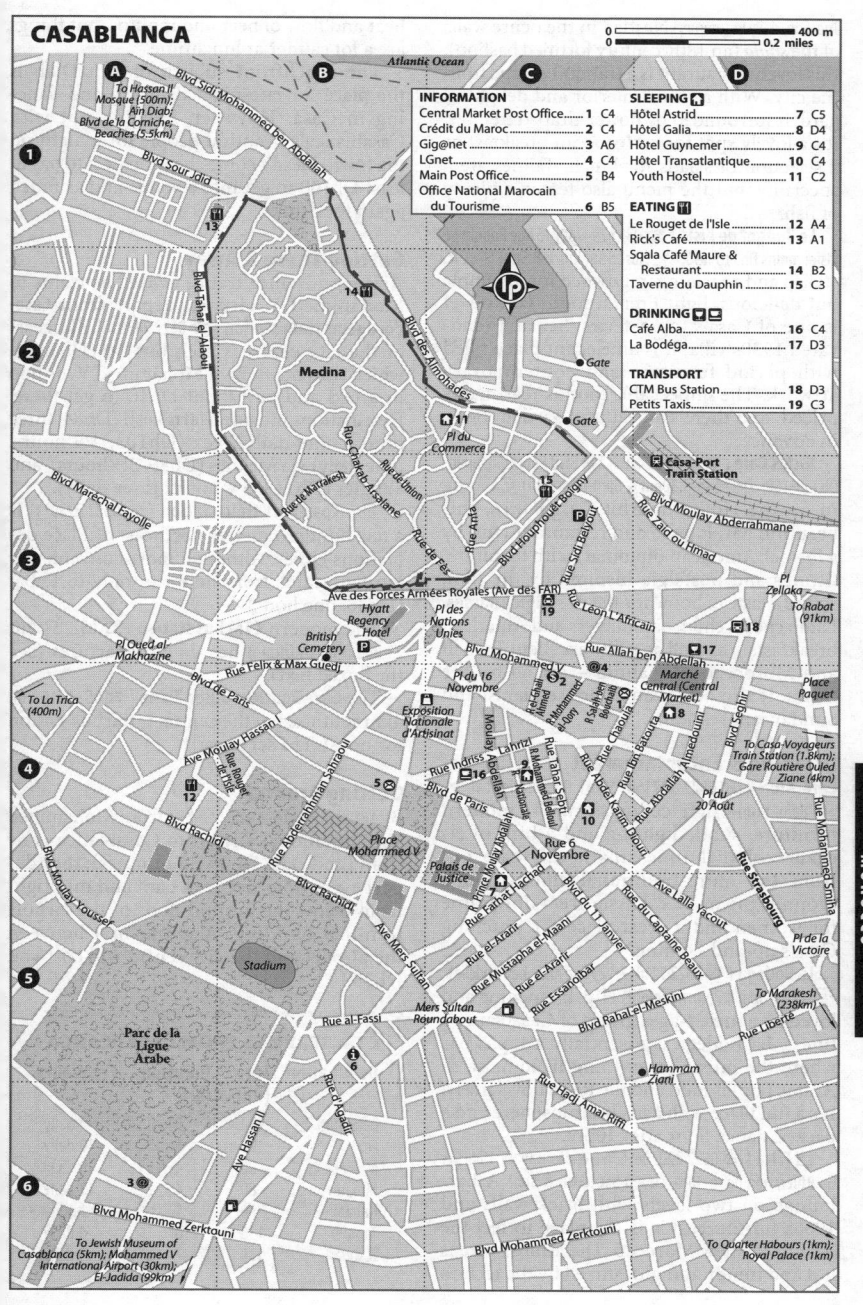

CASABLANCA

INFORMATION	
Central Market Post Office	**1** C4
Crédit du Maroc	**2** C4
Gig@net	**3** A6
LGnet	**4** C4
Main Post Office	**5** B4
Office National Marocain du Tourisme	**6** B5

SLEEPING	
Hôtel Astrid	**7** C5
Hôtel Galia	**8** D4
Hôtel Guynemer	**9** C4
Hôtel Transatlantique	**10** C4
Youth Hostel	**11** C2

EATING	
Le Rouget de l'Isle	**12** A4
Rick's Café	**13** A1
Sqala Café Maure & Restaurant	**14** B2
Taverne du Dauphin	**15** C3

DRINKING	
Café Alba	**16** C4
La Bodéga	**17** D3

TRANSPORT	
CTM Bus Station	**18** D3
Petits Taxis	**19** C3

MOROCCO

Tue-Sun, daily in summer) Nestled in the ochre walls of the *sqala* (an 18th-century fortified bastion), this lovely restaurant is a tranquil escape from the city. With a rustic interior and delightful garden surrounded by flower-draped trellises, it's a lovely spot for a Moroccan breakfast or a selection of salads for lunch. Tajines are a speciality, but the menu also features plenty of fish.

Le Rouget de l'Isle (☎ 0522 294740; 16 Rue Rouget de l'Isle; mains Dh110-130; ☻ closed Sat lunch & Sun) Sleek, stylish and charming, renowned for its simple but delicious, light French food, Le Rouget is one of Casa's top eateries. Set in a renovated 1930s villa, it is an elegant place filled with period furniture and contemporary artwork. The impeccable food is reasonably priced, and there's a beautiful garden. Book in advance.

Rick's Café (☎ 0522 274207; 248 Blvd Sour Jdid; mains Dh130-160; ☻ noon-3.30pm & 6pm-midnight) Cashing in on the Hollywood hit *Casablanca*, this beautiful bar, lounge and restaurant (run by a former American diplomat) with furniture, fittings and nostalgia inspired by the film, serves a taste of home for the nostalgic masses. Lamb chops, chilli, hamburgers and American breakfasts – as well as a few excellent French and Moroccan specialities – are all on the menu. It also boasts an in-house pianist and Sunday jazz session.

Drinking & Entertainment

Café Alba (☎ 0522 227154; 59-61 Rue Indriss Lahrizi; ☻ 8am-1am) High ceilings; swish, modern furniture; subtle lighting and a hint of elegant colonial times mark this cafe out from the more-traditional smoky joints around town. It's hassle-free downtime for women and a great place for watching Casa's up-and-coming.

La Bodéga (☎ 0522 541842; 129 Rue Allah ben Abdellah; ☻ 12.30-3pm & 7pm-midnight) Hip, happening and loved by a mixed-ages group of Casablanca's finest, La Bodega is essentially a tapas bar where the music (everything from Salsa to Arabic pop) is loud and the Rioja flows freely. It's a fun place with a lively atmosphere and a packed dance floor after 10pm.

La Trica (☎ 0522 220706; 5 Rue el-Moutanabi, Quartier Gauthier; ☻ noon-1am, closed Sat lunch & Sun) A bar-lounge on two levels with brick walls and 1960s furniture, this is the place to feel the beat of the new Morocco. The atmosphere is hot and trendy at night, stirred by the techno beat and flow of beer and mojitos, but things are a lot calmer at lunchtime.

The beachfront suburb of Aïn Diab is the place for late-night drinking and dancing in Casa. However, hanging out with Casablanca's beautiful people for a night on the town doesn't come cheap: expect to pay at least Dh100 to get into a venue and as much again for drinks.

Getting There & Away

All long-distance trains, as well as trains to Mohammed V airport, depart from **Casa-Voyageurs train station** (☎ 0522 243818), 4km east of the city centre. Catch bus 30 (Dh3.50), which runs down Blvd Mohammed V, or hop in a taxi and pay about Dh10 to get there. Destinations include Marrakesh (Dh84, three hours, nine daily), Fez (Dh103, 4½ hours, nine daily) via Meknès (Dh86, 3½ hours), and Tangier (Dh118, 5¾ hours, three daily).

The **Casa-Port train station** (☎ 0522 223011) is a few hundred metres northeast of Place des Nations Unies. Although more conveniently located, trains from here run only to Rabat (Dh36, one hour).

The modern **CTM bus station** (☎ 0522 541010; 23 Rue Léon L'Africain) has daily departures (see the boxed text).

The **Gare Routière Ouled Ziane** (☎ 0522 444470), 4km southeast of the centre, is the bus station for non-CTM services.

Getting Around

By far the easiest way to get from Mohammed V international airport to Casablanca is by train (2nd class Dh30, 35 minutes); they depart every hour between 6am and midnight from below the ground floor of the airport terminal building. A *grand taxi* between the airport and the city centre will cost you Dh250.

CTM SERVICES FROM CASABLANCA			
Destination	**Fare (Dh)**	**Duration (hr)**	**Frequency**
Essaouira	130	7	2 daily
Fez	100	5	10 daily
Marrakesh	80	4	9 daily
Meknès	80	4	11 daily
Rabat	30	1	hourly
Tangier	130	6	6 daily
Tetouan	130	7	3 daily

MOROCCO

Expect to pay Dh10 in or near the city centre for a trip in one of the red *petits taxis*.

ESSAOUIRA
pop 70,000

Essaouira has long been a favourite of the travellers' trail: laid-back and artsy, with sea breezes and picture-postcard ramparts that all conspire to make a short visit from Marrakesh turn into a stay of several nights. Although it can appear swamped with visitors in the height of summer, once the day trippers get back on the buses there's more than enough space to sigh deeply and just soak up the atmosphere.

Information

There are several banks with ATMs around Place Moulay Hassan. There are also plentiful internet cafes, most opening from 9am to 11pm and charging Dh8 to Dh10 per hour.

Délégation du Tourisme (☎ 0524 783532; www.essaouira.com; 10 Rue du Caire; ⊗ 9am-noon & 3-6.30pm Mon-Fri) Very helpful staff.

Hôpital Sidi Mohammed ben Abdallah (☎ 0524 475716; Blvd de l'Hôpital) For emergencies.

Main post office (Ave el-Mouqawama)

Sights & Activities

Essaouira's walled medina was added to Unesco's World Heritage list in 2001 – its well-preserved, late-18th-century, fortified layout is a prime example of European military architecture in North Africa. The mellow atmosphere, narrow winding streets lined with colourful shops, whitewashed houses and heavy old wooden doors make the medina a wonderful place to stroll. The easiest place from which visitors can access the ramparts is at **Skala de la Ville**, the impressive sea bastion built along the cliffs. Down by the harbour, the **Skala du Port** (adult/child Dh10/3; ⊗ 8.30am-noon & 2.30-6pm) offers picturesque views over both the fishing port and the **Île de Mogador**.

A number of outlets rent water-sports equipment and offer instruction along Essaouira's wide sandy beach. **Océan Vagabond** (☎ 0524 783934; www.oceanvagabond.com, in French; ⊗ 8am-8pm daily) rents surfboards (Dh500 for three days) and gives two-hour surfing lessons (Dh350). It also offers kitesurfing lessons (six hours, Dh1950) and rental (Dh1200 for three days), and windsurfing lessons (one hour/six hours Dh500/1200)

and rental (per hour Dh60). Be aware of the strong Atlantic currents.

The **Gnaoua & World Music Festival** (held on the third weekend in June) is a four-day musical extravaganza with concerts on Place Moulay Hassan.

Sleeping

Dar Afram (☎ 0524 785657; www.dar-afram.com; 10 Rue Sidi Magdoul; s Dh250, d Dh400-450) This extremely friendly guesthouse has simple, spotless rooms with shared bathrooms and a funky vibe. The Aussie-Moroccan owners are musicians, and impromptu sessions often follow the evening meal shared around a communal table.

Riad Nakhla (☎ /fax 0524 474940; www.essaouiranet.com/riad-nakhla; 2 Rue Agadir; s/d Dh225/325, ste Dh400-500) Riad Nakhla looks like any other budget place from the outside, but inside the weary traveller is met with a friendly reception in a beautiful courtyard with elegant stone columns and a trickling fountain. The well-appointed bedrooms are simple but comfortable and immaculately kept. Breakfast on the stunning roof terrace with views over the ocean and town is another treat.

Hotel Beau Rivage (☎ 0524 475925; beaurivage@menara.ma; 14 Place Moulay Hassan; s/d/tr Dh250/350/450, d without bathroom Dh200, breakfast Dh20) A long-time backpackers' favourite, this cheery hotel on the central square could hardly be better located. Rooms are clean, comfortable and airy.

Lalla Mira (☎ 0524 475046; 14 Rue d'Algerie; www.lallamira.net; s/d/ste Dh436/692/920; ⌨) This gorgeous little place has simple rooms with ochre *tadelakt* (polished plaster) walls, wrought-iron furniture, natural fabrics and solar-powered underfloor heating. The hotel also has a great *hammam* and a good restaurant (mains Dh90 to Dh120) serving a decent selection of vegetarian food.

La Casa del Mar (☎ 0524 475091; www.lacasa-delmar.com; 35 Rue D'Oujda; s/d incl breakfast Dh825/990) A delightful guesthouse blending contemporary design with traditional style. Retire to your room, join the other guests for a communal Moroccan meal or Spanish paella (Dh180), arrange a home visit from a masseur or henna-artist, or just watch the sunset from the seafront terrace.

Eating

The unpretentious **outdoor fish grill** (port end of Place Moulay Hassan; around Dh40) stands offer one

MOROCCO

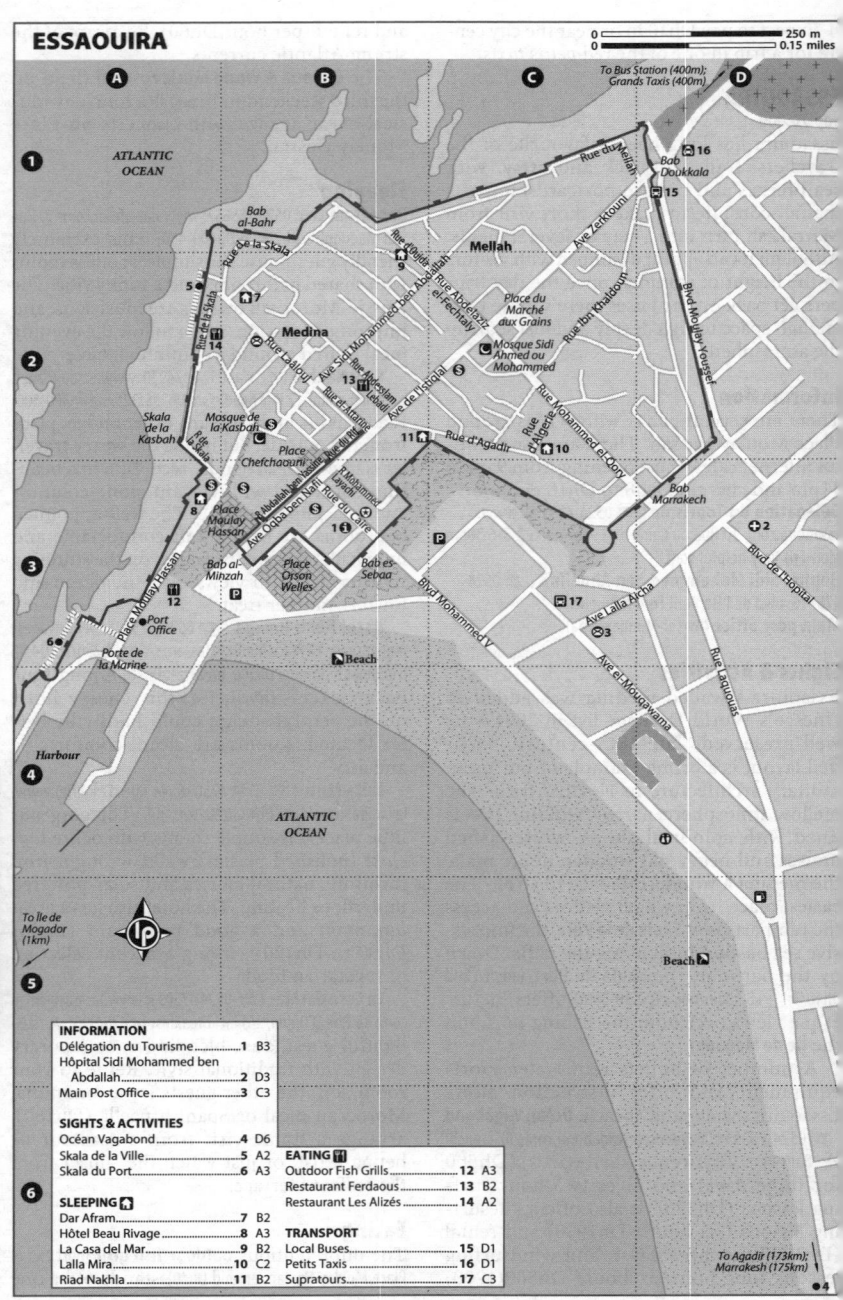

ESSAOUIRA

0 ———— 250 m
0 ———— 0.15 miles

of the definitive Essaouira experiences. Just choose what you want to eat from the colourful displays of freshly caught fish and shellfish at each grill, and wait for it to be cooked on the spot and served with a pile of bread and salad.

Restaurant Ferdaous (☎ 0524 473655; 27 Rue Abdesslam Lebadi; mains Dh60-80, set menu Dh105; ⏰ closed Mon) Delightful Moroccan restaurant, and one of the few places in town that serves real (like homecooked) traditional Moroccan food. The seasonal menu offers an innovative take on traditional recipes, the service is very friendly, and the low tables and padded seating make it feel like the real McCoy.

Restaurante Les Alizés (☎ 0524 476819; 26 Rue de la Skala; mains Dh75-90) This popular place run by a charming Moroccan couple in a 19th-century house (above Pension Smara) has delicious Moroccan dishes. The couscous with fish and the tajine of *boulettes de sardines* (sardine balls) are particularly good. Book well ahead as it fills up every night, with both Moroccans and visitors.

Getting There & Away

The **bus station** (☎ 0524 785241) is about 400m northeast of the medina, an easy walk during the day but better in a *petits taxi* (Dh10) if you're arriving/leaving late at night. **CTM** (☎ 0524 784764) has several buses daily for Casablanca (Dh125, six hours), and one apiece to Marrakesh (Dh75, 2½ hours) and Agadir (Dh70, three hours). Other companies run cheaper and more-frequent buses to the same destinations, as well as to Taroudannt (Dh70, six hours).

Supratours (☎ 0524 475317) runs buses to Marrakesh train station (Dh65, 2½ hours, four daily) to connect with trains to Casablanca. You should book several days in advance for this service, particularly in summer.

AGADIR

pop 680,000

Devastated by a terrible earthquake in 1960, Agadir has managed to rise from its ruins as Morocco's main beach resort. Rebuilt into a neat grid of residential suburbs and wide boulevards, the town feels strangely bereft of the sort of bustling life often associated with Moroccan cities. Its lure, however, lies in its huge sandy bay, which is more sheltered than many other Atlantic beaches.

Orientation

Agadir's bus stations and most of the budget hotels are in Nouveau Talborjt, in the northeast of the town. From here it's about a 15-minute walk down to Blvd du 20 Août, the main strip, which is lined with cafes, restaurants and big hotels.

Information

Banks with ATMs proliferate along Blvd Hassan II; those listed here also have bureaux de change.

Banque Populaire (Blvd Hassan II)

Délégation Régionale du Tourisme (ONMT; ☎ 0528 846377; Immeuble Ignouan, Ave Mohammed V; ⏰ 8.30am-noon & 2.30-6.30pm Mon-Thu, 8.30-11.30am & 3-6.30pm Fri) The best place for local and regional information.

Internet Swiss (Blvd Hassan II; per hr Dh10; ⏰ 9am-11pm) The busiest, most conveniently located cybercafe.

Main post office (Ave Sidi Mohammed; ⏰ 8.30am-6.30pm Mon-Fri, to noon Sat)

Wafa Bank (Blvd Hassan II)

Sleeping

Hôtel Canaria (☎ 0528 846727; Place Lahcen Tamri; s/d Dh80/100) One of the better budget options, Canaria is near the bus offices. The hotel overlooks a pleasant square, although the rooms – with pine furniture and potted plants – all face into the internal upper courtyard. Rooms without bathroom are Dh10 cheaper.

Hôtel Tiznine (☎ 0528 843925; 3 Rue Drarga; s/d Dh100/150, with shower Dh120/150) One of Agadir's best budget places, with a dozen good-sized rooms around a green-and-white tiled flowering courtyard. Some rooms have bathroom, but even the communal facilities are spotless.

Hôtel Kamal (☎ 0528 842817; fax 0528 843940; Ave Hassan II; s/d Dh405/462) An extremely popular and well-run central hotel in a modernist white block near the town hall, the Kamal manages to appeal to a wide range of clients, including package-tour groups and travelling Moroccans. Rooms are bright and clean, the staff are helpful and there's a pool large enough to swim laps in.

Eating

The cheap snack bars in Nouveau Talborjt and around the bus stations are open after hours. For ultrafresh, no-nonsense fish, try one of the many **fish stalls** (meals around Dh50) at the entrance to the commercial port. There

MOROCCO

WESTERN SAHARA'S DISPUTED STATUS

In the 19th century, Spain increased its colonial holdings in Africa by claiming the Western Sahara and renaming it Rio de Oro (River of Gold; it had neither water nor gold, but proved rich in phosphate deposits). An uneasy colonial peace prevailed until Moroccan independence in 1957, when new nationalist fervour contributed to the establishment of the Polisario Front and the guerrilla war against the Spanish.

When the region was abandoned by Spain in 1975, Morocco and Mauritania both raised claims to it, but Mauritania soon bailed out. In November 1975 Morocco's King Hassan II orchestrated the Green March – 350,000 Moroccans marched south to stake Morocco's historical claims to the Western Sahara.

In the following years 100,000 Moroccan troops were poured in to stamp out resistance. When the Polisario lost the support of Algeria and Libya, it soon became clear that Rabat had the upper hand. The UN brokered a ceasefire in 1991, but the promised referendum, in which the Saharawi people could choose between independence and integration with Morocco, has yet to materialise.

Ever since, Morocco has strengthened its hold on the territory, pouring money into infrastructure projects, particularly offshore oil exploration, and attracting Moroccans from the north to live here tax-free. The debate is still open but despite the large UN presence in Western Sahara, to all intents and purposes, Morocco seems to have succeeded in its claim to the territory.

---

are plenty of places along the beach to chill at midday or toast the sunset. Some of the places along Palm Beach stay open till 1am in summer.

Bab Marrakesh (☎ 0528 826144; Rue de Massa; sandwiches Dh25-35, couscous Dh70, tajine for 2 Dh100) Near Souq al-Had, this is the real thing – far removed from the tourist traps near the beach. Highly regarded by locals, it serves authentic Moroccan food at authentic prices.

La Scala (☎ 0528 846773; Rue du Oued Souss; meal with wine Dh350) An excellent Moroccan restaurant popular with wealthy Moroccans, Arab tourists and Westerners, La Scala has a pleasantly cosmopolitan atmosphere. The food is elegant and fresh, and beautifully presented.

Getting There & Away

Although a good number of buses serve Agadir, it is quite possible you'll end up in the regional transport hub of Inezgane, 13km south – check before you buy your ticket. Plenty of *grands taxis* (Dh8) and local buses shuttle between there and Agadir.

The bus station is on Rue Chair al-Hamra Mohammed ben Brahim, past the Souq el-Had. CTM has buses to Casablanca (Dh180, eight hours, six daily); the 10.30pm service continues to Rabat (Dh195, 10 hours). There are also departures for Marrakesh (Dh80, four hours, seven daily) and Essaouira (Dh60, two hours, one daily). **Supratours** (☎ 0528 224010) has fast services to Marrakesh train station (Dh90,

four hours, several daily) and Essaouira (Dh60, three hours, several daily).

The main *grand taxi* rank is located at the south end of Rue de Fès. Destinations include Taroudannt (Dh35), Essaouira (Dh70) and Marrakesh (Dh120). A *grand taxi* to the airport will cost you Dh150 by day, Dh200 at night.

Orange *petits taxis* run around town.

WESTERN SAHARA

Ask any Moroccan about the status of the Western Sahara and they will insist it belongs to them, yet the UN is clear that this is still under dispute. Moroccan maps may show this region as part of the country but few outside Morocco will agree.

For visitors, it's mainly an empty windswept stretch of country; most people who visit will be passing through to or from Mauritania.

There is no officially designated border between Morocco and the Western Sahara. In both Laâyoune and Dakhla you will be more aware of the military and police, both of whom remain sensitive to photography around military installations.

LAÂYOUNE
pop 200,000

The former Spanish phosphate-mining outpost of Laâyoune has been turned (through massive Moroccan investment) into the principal city of the Western Sahara. Now neither Sahrawi nor Spanish, its population is mostly Moroccan, lured from the north by the promise of healthy wages and tax-free goods. It's not much of a destination, but whether you're heading north or south, distances here are so great that you may have to stop.

The town's showpiece is the vast Place du Méchouar (where bored youths hang about at night), but there is no obvious centre. The post office, banks and most hotels are along either Blvd Hassan II or Blvd de Mekka.

Sleeping & Eating

Hôtel Jodesa (☎ 0528 992064; fax 0548 893784; 223 Blvd de Mekka; s/d Dh100/144, with shower Dh144/155) North of Place Dchira – so, centrally located – this modern hotel is a good budget option. Rooms are basic but reasonably spacious, and some have bathroom.

Hôtel Parador (☎ 0528 892814; fax 0528 890962; Ave de l'Islam; s/d Dh1100/1400; ⓧ ⓡ) A survivor from Spanish days, built in hacienda style around gardens, the Parador has a faintly colonial bar and a good, if expensive, restaurant (set menu Dh200). The rooms are equipped with all the creature comforts you'd expect and have small terraces.

Restaurant el-Bahja (Blvd Mohammed V; set menu Dh20) Simple grilled meat – lamb, certainly, camel perhaps – is served without ceremony here, but with plenty of grease and frites. For when you've had enough of fresh fish.

Le Poissonier (☎ 0528 993262, 0661 235795; 183 Blvd de Mekka; meals Dh60-90) Apart from the restaurants at the top-end hotels, this is the best dining in town; if you have to be in Laâyoune, there are worse ways to spend your time than over a fish soup or lobster in this friendly place.

There are many cafes and simple restaurants around Place Dchira, where Dh20 should get you a filling meal. More-lively food stalls can be found at the Souq Djemal.

Getting There & Away

CTM (Blvd de Mekka) has a morning bus to Dakhla (Dh140, seven hours, one daily) and services to Agadir (Dh190, 10½ hours, three daily). **Supratours** (Place Oum Essad) has two daily buses to Marrakesh (Dh270, 16 hours).

Grands taxis heading south to Dakhla (Dh170) leave from Place Boujdour.

DAKHLA
pop 40,000

The last stop before the Mauritanian border, Dakhla feels a long way from anywhere. Its whitewashed, arcaded streets are rather soulless, but it is a pleasant enough place and the government continues to pour money into the town.

Dakhla is reasonably easy to get around, with the bus offices, central post office, and most hotels and cafes situated around the old central market. A corniche lines the seafront.

Hôtel Sahara (☎ 0528 897773; Ave Sidi Ahmed Laaroussi; s/d Dh60/80) is a reliable budget option, with friendly staff who are used to overlanders passing through on their way to or from Mauritania.

Grands taxis to the border cost between Dh250 and Dh400. Ask the driver to ferry you across the 3km no-man's-land direct to the Mauritanian border post. If you're driving south, fill your tank before crossing – petrol is a lot cheaper in Western Sahara (the last petrol station is 80km before the border).

IMPERIAL CITIES & THE MIDDLE ATLAS

The rolling plains that sweep across the north, along the base of the Middle Atlas, is Morocco's most fertile agricultural region, dotted with olive groves and wheat fields. Several of Morocco's most-important cities have also taken root here, including ancient Fez with its teeming medina, imperial Meknès and the Roman city of Volubilis, now Morocco's most interesting archaeological site.

FEZ
pop 1 million

Marrakesh might be modern Morocco's tourist capital, but 1400-year-old Fez is Morocco's spiritual beating heart. Its medina (Fès el-Bali) is the largest living medieval Islamic city in the world. A first visit can be overwhelming: an assault on the eyes, ears and nose through covered bazaars, winding alleys, mosques, workshops, people and pack animals that seem to take you out of the 21st century and back to imagined *Arabian Nights*.

Orientation

Fez can be neatly divided into three distinct parts: Fez el-Bali (the core of the medina; the main entrance is Bab Bou Jeloud) in the east; Fez el-Jdid (containing the *mellah* and Royal Palace) in the centre; and the Ville Nouvelle – the modern administrative area constructed by the French – to the southwest. It's a 45-minute walk between the Ville Nouvelle and the medina, or a short Dh10 hop in a *petit taxi*.

Information

INTERNET ACCESS

Cyber Batha (Map p171; Derb Douh; per hr Dh10; ⊙ 9am-10pm) Has English as well as French keyboards.
Cyber Club (Map p172; Blvd Mohammed V; per hr Dh6; ⊙ 9am-10pm)

MEDICAL SERVICES

Hôpital Ghassani (off Map p172; ☎ 0535 622777) One of the city's biggest hospitals; located east of the Ville Nouvelle in the Dhar Mehraz district.
Night Pharmacy (Map p172; ☎ 0535 623493; Ave Moulay Youssef; ⊙ 9pm-6am) Located in the north of the Ville Nouvelle; staffed by a doctor and a pharmacist.

MONEY

There are plenty of banks (with ATMs) in the Ville Nouvelle along Blvd Mohammed V. In the medina, **Société Générale** (Map p171; Ave des Français; ⊙ 8.45am-noon & 2.45-6pm Mon-Thu, 8.45-11am Fri, 8.45am-noon Sat) has an ATM and bureaux de change.

POST

Main post office (Map p172; cnr Ave Hassan II & Blvd Mohammed V)
Post office (Map p171; Place Batha) In the medina.

TOURIST INFORMATION

Tourist Information Office (Syndicat d'Initiative; ☎ 0535 623460; Place Mohammed V)

Dangers & Annoyances

Fez has long been notorious for its *faux guides* (false guides). The situation has improved with the introduction of a *brigade touristique*; still, high unemployment forces many to persist – most hang out around Bab Bou Jeloud, the main western entrance to the medina.

Sights

THE MEDINA (FEZ EL-BALI)

Within the old walls of Fez el-Bali lies an incredible maze of twisting alleys, blind turns and hidden souqs. Navigation can be confusing and getting lost at some stage is a certainty, but this is part of the medina's charm: you never quite know what discovery lies around the next corner.

If Fez is the spiritual capital of Morocco, the **Kairaouine Mosque** (Map p171) is its true heart. Built in 859 by refugees from Tunisia, and rebuilt in the 12th century, it can accommodate up to 20,000 people at prayer. Non-Muslims are forbidden to enter and will have to suffice with glimpses of its seemingly endless columns from the gates on Talaa Kebira and Place as-Seffarine.

Located 150m east of Bab Bou Jeloud, the 14th-century **Medersa Bou Inania** (Map p171; admission Dh10; ⊙ 9am-6pm, closed during prayers) is the finest of Fez's theological colleges constructed by the Merenids. The *zellij* (tiling), *muqarna* (plasterwork) and woodcarving are amazingly elaborate, and views from the roof are also impressive.

Founded by Abu Said in 1325 in the heart of the medina, the **Medersa el-Attarine** (Map p171; admission Dh10; ⊙ 9am-6pm, closed during prayers) displays the traditional patterns of Merenid artisanship. The *zellij* base, stucco work and cedar wood at the top of the walls and the ceiling is every bit as elegant as the artistry of the Medersa Bou Inania.

The **Nejjarine Museum of Wooden Arts & Crafts** (Map p171; ☎ 0535 740580; Place an-Nejjarine; admission Dh20; ⊙ 10am-7pm) is located in a wonderfully restored *funduq* (which is a caravanserai for travelling merchants), with a host of fascinating exhibits. Photography is forbidden. The rooftop cafe has great views over the medina.

Housed in a wonderful 19th-century palace, the **Batha Museum** (Map p171; ☎ 0535 634116; Rue de la Musée, Batha; admission Dh10; ⊙ 8.30am-noon & 2.30-6pm Wed-Mon) houses an excellent collection of traditional Moroccan arts and crafts.

The **tanneries** (Map p171) are one of the city's most iconic sights (and smells). Head northeast of Place as-Seffarine and take the left fork after about 50m; you'll soon pick up the unmistakeable waft of skin and dye that will guide you into the heart of the leather district.

FEZ

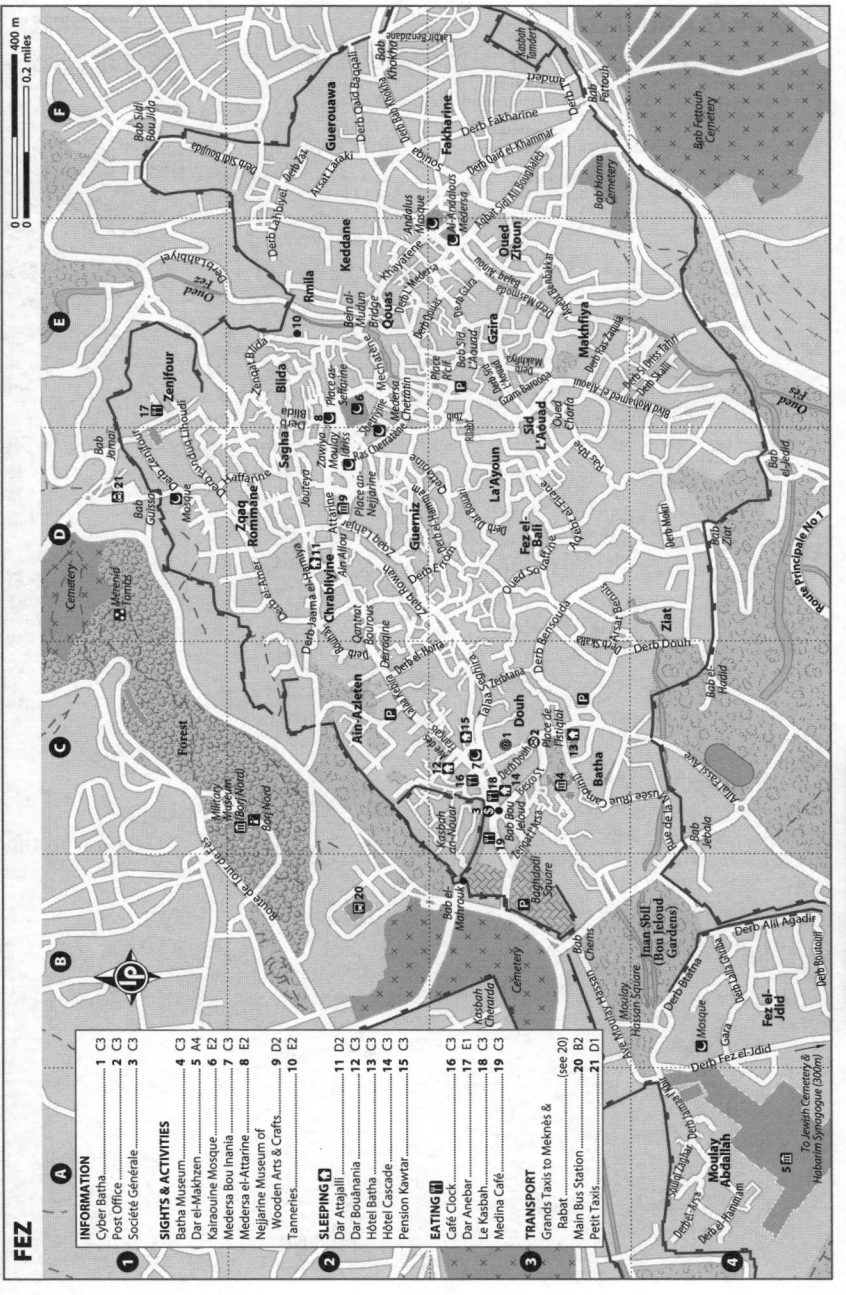

INFORMATION	
Cyber Batha.....................	1 C3
Post Office......................	2 C3
Société Générale.............	3 C3

SIGHTS & ACTIVITIES	
Batha Museum.................	4 C3
Dar el-Makhzen..............	5 A4
Kairaouine Mosque.........	6 E2
Medersa Bou Inania........	7 C3
Medersa el-Attarine........	8 E2
Nejjarine Museum of	
Wooden Arts & Crafts.....	9 D2
Tanneries......................	10 E2

SLEEPING	
Dar Attajalli..................	11 D2
Dar Bouânania..............	12 C3
Hôtel Batha..................	13 C3
Hôtel Cascade..............	14 C3
Pension Kawtar............	15 C3

EATING	
Café Clock...................	16 C3
Dar Anebar..................	17 E1
Le Kasbah...................	18 C3
Medina Café................	19 C3

TRANSPORT	
Grands Taxis to Meknès &	
Rabat.......................	(see 20)
Main Bus Station..........	20 B2
Petit Taxis..................	21 D1

MOROCCO

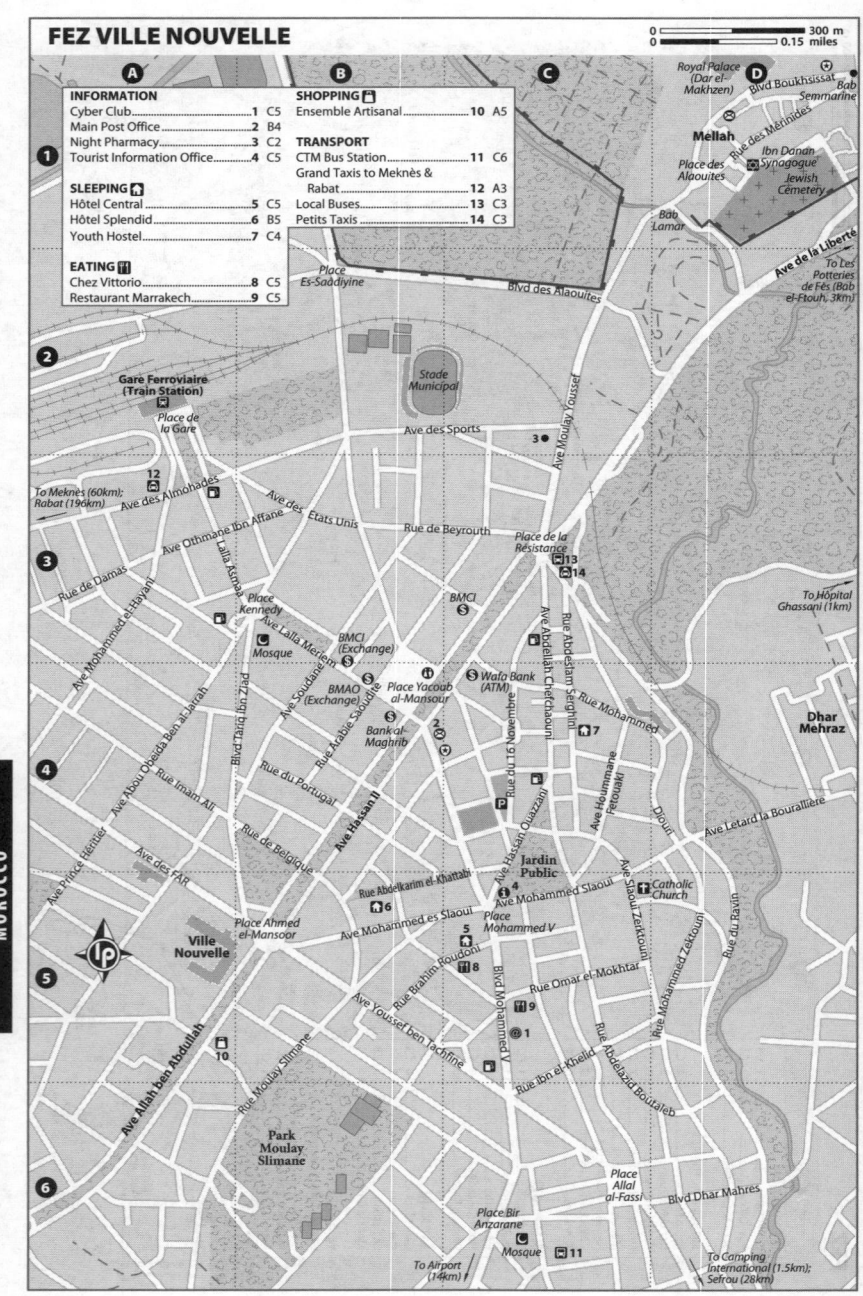

FEZ VILLE NOUVELLE

| | | | 0 | 300 m |
| | | | 0 | 0.15 miles |

INFORMATION
Cyber Club...................................**1** C5
Main Post Office.........................**2** B4
Night Pharmacy..........................**3** C2
Tourist Information Office.........**4** C5

SLEEPING 🏠
Hôtel Central.............................**5** C5
Hôtel Splendid..........................**6** B5
Youth Hostel..............................**7** C4

EATING 🍴
Chez Vittorio.............................**8** C5
Restaurant Marrakech..............**9** C5

SHOPPING 🛍
Ensemble Artisanal...................**10** A5

TRANSPORT
CTM Bus Station........................**11** C6
Grand Taxis to Meknès &
   Rabat......................................**12** A3
Local Buses................................**13** C3
Petits Taxis................................**14** C3

FEZ EL-JDID (NEW FEZ)

Only in a city as old as Fez could you find a district dubbed 'new' because it's only 700 years old. It's home to the Royal Palace, whose entrance at **Dar el-Makhzen** (Royal Palace; Map p171; Place des Alaouites) is a stunning example of modern restoration, but the 80 hectares of palace grounds are not open to the public.

In the 14th century, Fez el-Jdid became a refuge for Jews, thus creating a *mellah*. The *mellah's* southwest corner is home to the fascinating **Jewish Cemetery & Habarim Synagogue** (off Map p171; donations appreciated; ☺ 7am-7pm).

Festivals & Events

Every June the **Fez Festival of World Sacred Music** (☎ 0535 740691; www.fesfestival.com) brings together music groups and artists from all corners of the globe. It's become an established favourite on the 'world music' festival circuit.

Sleeping

MEDINA

Pension Kawtar (Map p171; ☎ 0535 740172; pension _kaw@yahoo.fr; Derb Taryana, Talaa Seghira; dm/s/d without bathroom Dh60/200/300, d with bathroom Dh350, breakfast Dh25) Well signposted in an alley off Talaa Seghira, the Kawtar is a friendly, Moroccan, family-run concern. There are 10 rooms tucked into the place – those on the ground floor are a bit gloomy, but they get better the closer you get to the roof terrace.

Hôtel Cascade (Map p171; ☎ 0535 638442; 26 Rue Serrajine, Bab Bou Jeloud; dm/r Dh80/160, breakfast Dh20) One of the grand-daddies of the Morocco budget-hotel scene, the Cascade still keeps drawing them in. You shouldn't expect much for the price – it's all pretty basic – but if you're up for stretching your wallet and meeting plenty of like-minded travellers, then this might be the place for you.

Dar Bouânania (Map p171; ☎ 0535 637282; 21 Derb be Salem, Talaa Kebira; s from Dh200, s/d with shower 300/600, q Dh400, breakfast Dh30) A popular choice with backpackers, this is as close as tight budgets will get to a riad. A traditional house with courtyard, *zellij* and painted woodwork, there are several well-sized rooms on several levels. Shared bathrooms are clean, and there's a roof terrace. There's a high-season supplement of Dh100 per person.

Hôtel Batha (Map p171; ☎ 0535 741077; fax 0535 741078; Place Batha; s/d Dh395/520; ✉ ▣) The great location, room capacity and pool keeps the Batha perennially busy. It's a reasonably modern set-up, with fair rooms and cool quiet areas to retreat from the hustle of the medina. It's good value, although only providing hot water at particular (often inconvenient) hours has been a frustration for many years now.

Dar Attajalli (Map p171; ☎ 0535 637728; www. attajalli.com; Derb Qettana, Zqaq Rommane; r & ste from Dh1000-1500; ☏) Dar Attajalli is a magnificent testament to the art of patient and sympathetic restoration, maintaining the building's integrity while still managing to produce a supremely comfortable guesthouse. Decoration is set off with gently colour-themed Fassi fabrics – the colours are further reflected in the planting of the terrace roof garden – and all designed to get you instantly relaxing.

VILLE NOUVELLE

Hôtel Central (Map p172; ☎ 0535 622335; 50 Rue Brahim Roudani; s/d Dh130/160, with shower Dh150/180) A bright and airy budget option just off busy Blvd Mohammed V, all rooms have external toilets, but even those without a shower have their own sinks. It's good value and popular, so there's sometimes not enough rooms to go around.

Hôtel Splendid (Map p172; ☎ 0535 622148; splendid@ iam.net.ma; 9 Rue Abdelkarim el-Khattabi; s/d Dh318/412; ✉ ▣) For the price, this hotel makes a good claim for three stars. It's all modern and tidy, with good bathrooms and comfy beds, plus a pool for the heat and a bar for the evenings. There's a dining room, but breakfast isn't included in your room price.

Eating

MEDINA

In the medina, you won't have to walk far to find someone selling food – tiny cell-like places grilling *brochettes*, cooking up cauldrons of soup, sandwich shops or just a guy with a pushcart selling peanut cookies. Bab Bou Jeloud has quite a cluster of options, with streetside tables for people-watching.

Le Kasbah (Map p171; Rue Serrajine; mains Dh40, set menu Dh70; ☺ 8am-midnight) On several floors opposite the cheap hotels at Bab Bou Jeloud, this restaurant occupies a prime spot. The top floor looks out over the medina. The menu itself isn't overly exciting – tajines, couscous and meat from the grill – but is good value (though drinks are marked up if you're not eating).

MOROCCO

Café Clock (Map p171; ☎ 0535 637855; www.cafeclock. com; 7 Derb el-Mergana, Talaa Kebira; mains Dh55-80; ☺ 9am-10pm; ☞) In a restored townhouse, this funky place has a refreshing menu with offerings such as falafel, some interesting vegetarian options, a monstrously large camel burger and some delicious cakes. Better still, its 'Clock Culture' program includes sunset concerts every Sunday (cover charge around Dh20), attracting a good mix of locals, expats and curious tourists.

Médina Café (Map p171; ☎ 0535 633430; 6 Derb Mernissi, Bab Bou Jeloud; mains Dh70-100; ☺ 8am-10pm) Just outside Bab Bou Jeloud, this small restaurant is an oasis of serenity, decorated in a traditional yet restrained manner. During the day it's good for a quick bite or a fruit juice; in the evening better Moroccan fare is on offer – the lamb tajine with dried figs and apricots is a winner, while the plates of couscous are big enough for two.

Dar Anebar (Map p171; ☎ 0535 635787; 25 Derb el-Miter, Zqaq Rommane; mains from Dh120; ☺ from 7.30pm) Another good riad for dining – you'll eat in truly fine surroundings here, in the splendid courtyard or one of the cosy salons. The menu is strictly Moroccan – but of the highest standard – and you can accompany dinner with a bottle of wine.

VILLE NOUVELLE

Chez Vittorio (Map p172; ☎ 0535 624730; 21 Rue Brahim Roudani; salads/pizza & pasta/mains from Dh30/56/80) This dependable favourite covers the rustic Italian restaurant angle well, right down to the candles and checkered tablecloths. Food is good value and, while the initial service can be a bit creaky, your meal tends to arrive in a trice. Go for the pizzas or steak, as the pasta often disappoints. You can also enjoy a glass of wine with your meal.

Restaurant Marrakech (Map p172; ☎ 0535 930876; 11 Rue Omar el-Mokhtar; mains from Dh55; ☒) A charming restaurant that goes from strength to strength behind thick wooden doors. Red *tadelakt* walls and dark furniture, plus a cushion-strewn salon at the back, add ambience, while the menu's variety refreshes the palate, with dishes like chicken tajine with apple and olive, or lamb with aubergine and peppers (there's also a set three-course menu).

Shopping

Fez is and always has been the artisanal capital of Morocco. The choice of crafts is wide,

quality is high and prices are competitive. As usual, it's best to seek out the little shops off the main tourist routes.

Ensemble Artisanal (Map p172; Ave Allah ben Abdullah; ☺ 9am-noon & 2.30-6.30pm) Slightly out of the way in the Ville Nouvelle, the state-run Ensemble Artisanal is always a decent place to get a feel for quality and price.

Les Potteries de Fès (off Map p172; ☎ 0535 669166; www.artnaji.net; Ain Nokbi; ☺ 8am-6pm) An attraction in itself, this is the home of the famous Fassi pottery. You can see the entire production process, from pot throwing to the painstaking hand painting and laying out of *zellij* – it's a joy to behold.

Getting There & Away
BUS

The main station for **CTM buses** (☎ 0535 732992) is near Place Atlas in the southern Ville Nouvelle. See the boxed text (above) for services.

Non-CTM buses depart from the **main bus station** (Map p171; ☎ 0535 636032) outside Bab el-Mahrouk.

CTM SERVICES FROM FEZ			
Destination	**Fare (Dh)**	**Duration (hr)**	**Services per day**
Casablanca	105	5	7
Chefchaouen	45	4	3
Marrakesh	150	9	2
Meknès	25	1.5	6
Rabat	70	3.5	7
Tangier	115	6	3
Tetouan	100	5	2

TAXI

There are several *grand taxi* ranks dotted around town. Taxis for Meknès (Dh16) and Rabat (Dh59) leave from in front of the main bus station (outside Bab el-Mahrouk) and from near the train station.

TRAIN

The **train station** (Map p172; ☎ 0535 930333) is in the Ville Nouvelle, a 10-minute walk northwest of Place Florence. Trains depart every two hours between 7am and 5pm to Casablanca (Dh103, 4½ hours), via Rabat (Dh76, 3½ hours) and Meknès (Dh18, one hour), plus two overnight trains. Eight trains go to Marrakesh (Dh180, eight hours) and one to Tangier (Dh97, five hours).

MOROCCO

Getting Around

There is a regular bus service (bus 16) between the airport and the train station (Dh3, 25 minutes), with departures every half-hour or so. *Grands taxis* from any stand charge a set fare of Dh120.

Drivers of the red *petits taxis* generally use their meters without any fuss. Expect to pay about Dh9 from the train or CTM stations to Bab Bou Jeloud.

MEKNÈS

pop 690,000

Morocco's third imperial city is often overlooked by tourist itineraries, but Meknès is worth getting to know. Quieter and smaller than its neighbour, it's also more laid-back and less hassle, but still awash with the winding, narrow medina streets and grand buildings befitting a one-time capital of the sultanate.

Meknès is also the ideal base from which to explore the Roman ruins at Volubilis and the hilltop holy town of Moulay Idriss, two of the country's most significant historical sites.

Orientation

The valley of the (usually dry) Oued Bou Fekrane neatly divides the old medina in the west and the French-built Ville Nouvelle in the east. Ave Moulay Ismail connects them, then becomes the principal route of the Ville Nouvelle, where its name changes to Ave Hassan II.

Moulay Ismail's tomb and imperial city are south of the medina. Train and CTM bus stations are in the Ville Nouvelle, as are most offices and banks, as well as the more expensive hotels. It's a 20-minute walk from the medina to the Ville Nouvelle, or blue *petits taxis* and urban *grands taxis* shuttle between the two.

Information

There are plenty of banks with ATMs in both the Ville Nouvelle (mainly on Ave Hassan II and Ave Mohammed V) and the medina (Rue Sekkakine).

Cyber Bab Mansour (Zankat Accra; per hr Dh6; ☺ 9am-midnight)

Délégation Régionale du Tourisme (☎ 0535 524426; fax 0535 516046; Place de l'Istiqlal; ☺ 8.30am-noon & 2.30-6.30pm Mon-Thu, 8-11.30am & 3-6.30pm Fri)

Hôpital Moulay Ismail (☎ 0535 522805) Off Ave des FAR.

Main post office (Place de l'Istiqlal)

Quick Net (28 Rue el-Emir Abdelkader; per hr Dh6; ☺ 9am-10pm)

Sights

The heart of Meknès' medina lies to the north of the main square, Place el-Hedim, with the *mellah* to the west. To the south, Moulay Ismail's imperial city opens up through one of the most impressive monumental gateways in all of Morocco, **Bab el-Mansour**. Following the road around to the right, you'll come across the grand **Mausoleum of Moulay Ismail** (donations appreciated; ☺ 8.30am-noon & 2-6pm Sat-Thu), named for the sultan who made Meknès his capital in the 17th century.

Overlooking Place el-Hedim on the north is the 1882 palace that houses the **Dar Jamaï museum** (☎ 0535 530863; Place el-Hedim; admission Dh20; ☺ 9am-noon & 3-6.30pm Wed-Mon). Deeper in the medina, opposite the Grand Mosquée, the **Medersa Bou Inania** (Rue Najjarine; admission Dh20; ☺ 9am-noon & 3-6pm) is typical of the exquisite interior design that distinguishes Merenid monuments.

Sleeping

Maroc Hôtel (☎ 0535 530075; 7 Rue Rouamzine; s/d Dh90/180) Perennially popular, the Maroc has kept its standards up over the many years we've been visiting. Friendly and quiet, rooms (with sinks) are freshly painted and the shared bathrooms are clean. The great terrace and courtyard filled with orange trees add to the ambience.

Hôtel Majestic (☎ 0535 522035; 19 Ave Mohammed V; s/d with shared bathroom Dh127/168, with shower Dh165/198, with bathroom Dh197/229, breakfast Dh22) Built in the 1930s, this grand old lady carries her age well. There's a good mix of rooms (all have sinks) and there's plenty of character to go around, plus a peaceful patio and panoramic roof terrace. Management is helpful.

Maison d'Hôtes Riad (☎ 0535 530542; www.riad meknes.com; 79 Ksar Chaacha, Dar el-Kbir; r incl breakfast Dh650-750; ☒ ▢) This riad is located amid the ruins of the Palais Ksar Chaacha. There are just six rooms, each one tastefully decorated in traditional-meets-modern style. It's also noted for its food, and there are a couple of different salons where you can eat or just relax by the chic plunge pool and cactus garden.

Ryad Bahia (☎ 0535 554541; www.ryad-bahia. com; Derb Sekkaya, Tiberbarine; r incl breakfast Dh670, ste

MOROCCO

MEKNÈS

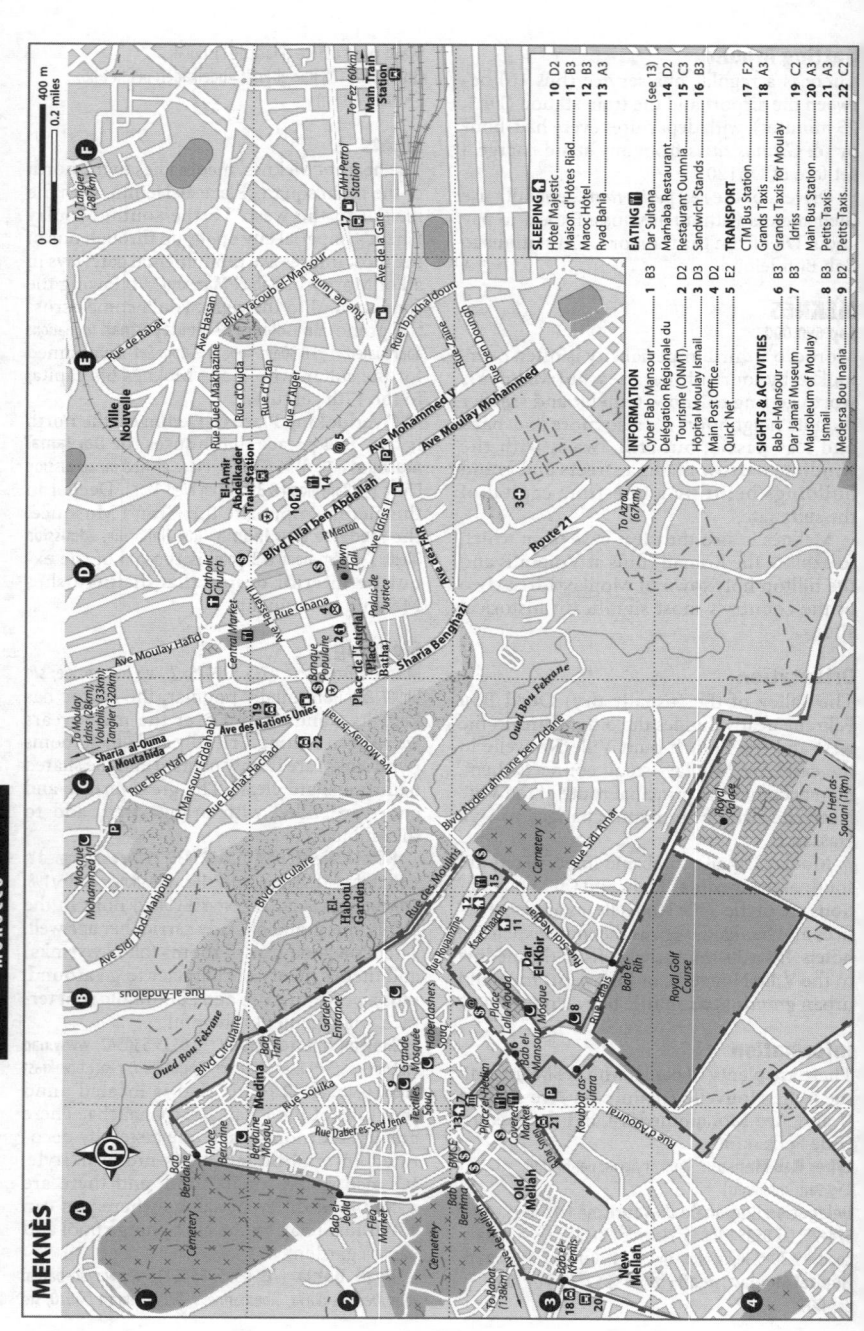

INFORMATION
Cyber Bab Mansour.......................1 B3
Délégation Régionale du
   Tourisme (ONMT)....................2 D2
Hôpital Moulay Ismail.................3 D3
Main Post Office..........................4 D2
Quick Net....................................5 E2

SIGHTS & ACTIVITIES
Bab el-Mansour...........................6 B3
Dar Jamaï Museum.......................7 B3
Mausoleum of Moulay
   Ismail......................................8 B3
Medersa Bou Inania.....................9 B2

SLEEPING 🛏
Hotel Majestic............................10 D2
Maison d'Hôtes Riad..................11 B3
Maroc Hôtel...............................12 B3
Ryad Bahia.................................13 A3

EATING 🍴
Dar Sultana..........................(see 13)
Marhaba Restaurant...................14 D2
Restaurant Oumnia......................15 C3
Sandwich Stands........................16 B3

TRANSPORT
CTM Bus Station.........................17 F2
Grands Taxis...............................18 A3
Grands Taxis for Moulay
   Idriss.....................................19 C2
Main Bus Station........................20 A3
Petits Taxis.................................21 A3
Petits Taxis.................................22 C2

Dh950-1200; 🔲 🛜) This charming guesthouse is a stone's throw from Place el-Hedim. The main entrance opens onto a courtyard and the whole place has an open, airy layout compared to many riads. Rooms are pretty and carefully restored, and the owners (keen travellers themselves) eager to swap travel stories as well as guide guests in the medina.

Eating

Take your pick of any one of the **sandwich stands** (Place el-Hedim; sandwiches around Dh30; ☯ 7am-10pm) lining Place el-Hedim, and sit at the canopied tables to watch the scene as you eat. There are larger meals like tajines, but the sandwiches are usually quick and excellent. A few places nearer the medina walls do a good line in sardines.

Marhaba Restaurant (23 Ave Mohammed V; tajines Dh25; ☯ noon-10pm) The essence of cheap and cheerful, we adore this basic, canteen-style place. While you can get tajines and the like, do as everyone else does and fill up on a bowl of *harira* or a plate of *makoda* (potato fritters) with bread and hard-boiled eggs – and walk out with change from Dh15. We defy you to eat better for cheaper.

Restaurant Oumnia (☎ 0535 533938; 8 Ain Fouki Rouamzine; set menu Dh80) Less a formal restaurant than a few rooms of a family home converted into dining salons, the emphasis at Restaurant Oumnia is on warm service and hearty Moroccan fare. There's just a three-course set menu, but it's a real winner, with delicious *harira*, salads and a choice of several tajines of the day.

Dar Sultana (☎ 0535 535720; Derb Sekkaya, Tiberbarine; mains from Dh70, 3-course set menu Dh150) A small restaurant in a converted medina house, the tent canopy over the courtyard gives an intimate atmosphere, set off by walls painted with henna designs and hung with bright fabrics. The spread of cooked Moroccan salads is a big highlight of the menu.

Getting There & Away

Although Meknès has two train stations, head for the more central **El-Amir Abdelkader** (☎ 0535 522763). There are plentiful trains to Fez (Dh18, one hour), and Casablanca (Dh86, 3½ hours) via Rabat (Dh59, 2¼ hours), five for Marrakesh (Dh162, seven hours) and one for Tangier (Dh80, four hours) – or take a westbound train and change at Sidi Kacem.

The **CTM bus station** (☎ 0535 522585; Ave des FAR) is about 300m east of the junction with Ave Mohammed V. The main bus station lies just outside Bab el-Khemis, west of the medina. CTM departures include Casablanca (Dh90, four hours, six daily), Rabat (Dh55, 2½ hours), Marrakesh (Dh160, eight hours, daily) and Tangier (Dh100, five hours, three daily).

The principal *grand taxi* rank is a dirt lot next to the main bus station at Bab el-Khemis. There are regular departures to Fez (Dh16, one hour) and Rabat (Dh44, 90 minutes). *Grands taxis* for Moulay Idriss (Dh12, 20 minutes) leave from opposite the Institut Français – this is also the place to organise round trips to Volubilis.

AROUND MEKNÈS

In the midst of a fertile plain about 33km north of Meknès, **Volubilis** (Ouailili; admission Dh20, parking Dh5, guide Dh140; ☯ 8am-sunset) are the largest and best-preserved Roman ruins in Morocco. One of the country's most important pilgrimage sites, the lovely whitewashed hill town **Moulay Idriss**, is only about 4.5km from Volubilis.

A half-day outing by *grand taxi* from Meknès will cost around Dh350, including a stop at Moulay Idriss.

CENTRAL MOROCCO & THE HIGH ATLAS

Marrakesh is the queen bee of Moroccan tourism, but look beyond it and you'll find great trekking in the dramatic High Atlas, and spectacular valleys and gorges that lead to the vast and empty sands of the Saharan dunes.

MARRAKESH

pop 2 million

Marrakesh grew rich on the camel caravans threading their way across the desert, but these days it's cheap flights from Europe bringing tourists to spend their money in the souqs that fatten the city's coffers. As many locals have taken the opportunity to move out of the medina into modern housing, foreigners have arrived to transform those houses into style magazine–friendly guesthouses.

MOROCCO

But Marrakesh's old heart still beats strongly enough, from the time-worn ramparts that ring the city to the nightly spectacle of the Djemaa el-Fna that leaps from the pages of the *1001 Nights* on the edge of the labyrinthine medina.

Orientation

Most budget hotels are clustered in the narrow streets and alleys south of Djemaa el-Fna, the main square in the heart of the old city. The souqs and principal religious buildings lie to the north and the palaces to the south. To the southwest rises the city's most prominent landmark, the minaret of the Koutoubia Mosque.

The Ville Nouvelle is home to the majority of midrange and luxury hotels. The train station lies southwest of the Guéliz district, following Ave Hassan II from the central Place du 16 Novembre.

It takes 30 minutes to walk along Ave Mohammed V from the centre of the Ville Nouvelle to Djemaa el-Fna.

Information

Cybercafes ringing the Djemaa el-Fna charge Dh8 to Dh12 per hour; just follow signs reading 'c@fe'. There are plenty of ATMs along Rue de Bab Agnaou off the Djemaa el-Fna.

Crédit du Maroc (☎ 8.45am-1pm & 3-6.45pm Mon-Sat) Medina (**Rue de Bab Agnaou**); Ville Nouvelle (**215 Ave Mohammed V**)

Hassan Internet (☎ 0524 441989; Immeuble Tazi, 12 Rue Riad el Moukha; per hr Dh8; ☽ 7am-1am)

Main post office (☎ 0524 431963; Place du 16 Novembre; ☽ 8.30am-2pm Mon-Sat) In the Ville Nouvelle.

Office National Marocain du Tourisme (ONMT; ☎ 0524 436179; Place Abdel Moumen ben Ali, Guéliz; ☽ 8.30am-noon & 2.30-6.30pm Mon-Fri, 9am-noon & 3-6pm Sat)

Polyclinique du Sud (☎ 0524 447999; cnr Rue de Yougoslavie & Rue Ibn Aicha, Guéliz; ☽ 24hr)

Post office (Rue Bab Agnaou; ☽ 8am-noon & 3-6pm Mon-Fri) A convenient branch office in the medina.

Sights

The focal point of Marrakesh is **Djemaa el-Fna**, a huge square in the medina and the backdrop for one of the world's greatest spectacles. Although it can be lively at any hour of the day, Djemaa el-Fna comes into its own at dusk, when the curtain goes up on rows of open-air food stalls smoking the immediate area with mouth-watering aromas. Jugglers,

storytellers, snake charmers, musicians, the occasional acrobat and benign lunatics consume the remaining space, each surrounded by jostling spectators.

Dominating the Marrakshi landscape, southwest of Djemaa el-Fna, is the 70m-tall minaret of Marrakesh's most famous and most venerated monument, the **Koutoubia Mosque**. Visible for miles in all directions, it's a classic example of Moroccan-Andalucían architecture.

The largest and oldest-surviving of the mosques inside the medina is the 12th-century **Ali ben Youssef Mosque** (closed to non-Muslims), which marks the intellectual and religious heart of the medina. Next to the mosque is the 14th-century **Ali ben Youssef Medersa** (☎ 0524 441893; Place ben Youssef; admission Dh40; ☽ 9am-6pm winter, to 7pm summer), a peaceful and meditative place with some stunning examples of stucco decoration.

Inaugurated in 1997, the **Musée de Marrakesh** (☎ 0524 390911; www.museedemarrakech.ma; Place ben Youssef; admission Dh30; ☽ 9am-7pm) is housed in a beautifully restored 19th-century palace Dar Mnebhi. A combined ticket that also covers Ali ben Youssef Medersa costs Dh60.

South of the main medina area is the Kasbah (Royal Quarter), which is home to the most famous of the city's palaces, the now-ruined **Palais el-Badi** (Place des Ferblantiers; admission Dh10; ☽ 8.30-noon & 2.30-6pm). All that remains of 'the Incomparable' (once reputed to be one of the most beautiful palaces in the world), to give an impression of its former splendour, are the towering pisé walls (now taken over by stork nests) and the staggering scale. The nearby **Palais de la Bahia** (☎ 0524 389564; Rue Riad Zitoun el-Jedid; admission Dh10; ☽ 8.30-11.45am & 2.30-5.45pm Sat-Thu, 8.30-11.30am & 3-5.45pm Fri), the 'Brilliant', is the perfect antidote to the simplicity of the el-Badi.

Long hidden from intrusive eyes, the area of the **Saadian Tombs** (Rue de la Kasbah; admission Dh10; ☽ 8.30-11.45am & 2.30-5.45pm), alongside the Kasbah Mosque, is home to ornate tombs that are the resting places of Saadian princes.

Marrakesh has more gardens than any other Moroccan city, offering the perfect escape from the hubbub of the souqs and the traffic. The rose gardens of Koutoubia Mosque, in particular, offer cool respite near Djemaa el-Fna. In the Ville Nouvelle, the **Jardin Majorelle** (☎ 0524 301852; www.jardinmajorelle.com; cnr Ave Yacoub el-Mansour & Ave Moulay Abdullah; garden Dh30, museum Dh15; ☽ 8am-6pm summer, to 5pm winter) is a sublime mix of art deco buildings and psychedelic desert mirage.

Sleeping

Hôtel Souria (☎ 0524 445970; 17 Rue de la Recette; s/d Dh130/170) 'How are you? Everything's good?' Even if it's been mere minutes since you last saw them, the staff – who run this place expertly – never fail to ask. The sentiment is straightforward and so are the rooms – 10 no-frills rooms with shared bathrooms around a garden courtyard, with a patchwork-tiled terrace. Book yesterday.

Hôtel Central Palace (☎ 0524 440235; hotelcentral palace@hotmail.com; 59 Derb Sidi Bouloukat; d with bathroom/ with shower/without bathroom Dh305/205/155) Sure it's central, but palatial? Actually, yes! With 40 clean rooms on four floors arranged around a burbling courtyard fountain, and a roof terrace lording it over the Djemaa el-Fna, this is a rare example of a stately budget hotel.

Jnane Mogador (☎ 0524 426323; www.jnane mogador.com; Derb Sidi Bouloukat, 116 Riad Zitoun el-Kedim; s/d/tr/q Dh360/480/580/660; 🖳) An authentic 19th-century riad with all the 21st-century-guesthouse fixings: prime location, in-house *hammam*, double-decker roof terraces and owner Mohammed's laid-back hospitality. Perennially popular, book in advance.

Riad Nejma Lounge (☎ 0524 382341; www.riad -nejmalounge.com; 45 Derb Sidi M'Hamed el-Haj, Bab Doukkala; d incl breakfast Dh495-795; 🆇 🖳 🗔) Lounge lizards chill on hot-pink cushions in the whitewashed courtyard, and graphic splashes of colour make wood-beamed guestrooms totally mod, though the rustic showers can be temperamental. Handy for Ville Nouvelle restaurants and shops.

Dar Soukaina (☎ 0661 245238; www.darsoukaina. com; 19 Derb el-Ferrane, Riad Laârouss; s/tr incl breakfast Dh790/1150, d incl breakfast Dh970-1400; 🆇 🗔) Sister riads: the original is all soaring ceilings, cosy nooks and graceful archways, while the newer extension across the street is about sprawling beds, the grand patio and handsome woodwork. A 20-minute walk from the Djemaa, but worth the discovery.

Riad el Borj (☎ 0524 391223; www.riadelborj; 63 Derb Moulay Adbelkader; d Dh935-1540 🆇 🖳 🗔) Once this was a grand vizier's lookout, and now you too can lord it over the neighbours in the suite with original *zellij*, double-height ceilings and skylit tub, or the tower hideaway with the rippled ceiling and book nook. Loaf by the pool in the 'Berber annex' or let off

steam in the *hammam*. Babysitting services are also available.

Eating

The cheapest and most exotic place in town to eat remains the food stalls on Djemaa el-Fna, piled high with fresh meats and salads, goats' heads and steaming snails.

Just before noon, the vendors at a row of stalls in **Mechoui Alley** (250g lamb with bread Dh30-50; ☯ 11am-2pm), on the east side of Souq Ablueh (Olive Souq), start carving up steaming sides of *mechoui* (slow-roasted lamb). Point to the best-looking cut of meat and ask for a '*nuss*' (half) or '*rubb*' (quarter) kilo. Some haggling might ensue, but will procure a baggie of falling-off-the-bone-delicious lamb with fresh-baked bread, cumin and olives.

Earth Café (2 Derb Zouak, Riad Zitoun el-Qedim; mains around Dh60; ☯ 9am-11pm; 🆅) Run by an enthusiastic Moroccan-Australian, Earth Café claims to be Morocco's first vegetarian/vegan restaurant. The atmosphere is laid-back hippy-chic, and the food fresh and fabulous (we fell in love with the ricotta-and-squash *bastilla*). Produce comes from the owner's nearby farm, to which visits can be arranged.

Narwama (☎ 0524 442510; 30 Rue el-Koutoubia; ☯ 8pm-1am) Opposites attract at Narwama – true to its name (fire and water) – with unconventional combinations: Thai green curries and almond-and-cream *bastilla*, a DJ spinning Brazilian/Italian/Arabic tunes, and the best Moroccan mint mojitos in town, all in a 19th-century riad with 21st-century Zen decor, near Djemma el-Fna.

Catanzaro (☎ 0524 433731; 42 Rue Tariq ibn Ziyad, Guéliz; pizzas & pasta Dh60-80, mains Dh80-120; ☯ noon-2.30pm & 7.30-11pm Mon-Sat; 🆇) Where are we, exactly? The thin-crust, wood-fired pizza says Italy, the wooden balcony and powerful air-con suggest the Alps, but the spicy condiments and spicier clientele are definitely mid-town Marrakesh. Grilled meat dishes are juicy and generous, however, the Neapolitan pizza with capers, local olives and Atlantic anchovies steals the show.

Beyrouth (☎ 0524 423525; 9 Rue Loubnane; mains Dh80-150) Bright, lemony, Lebanese flavours, with a mix-and-match mezze (appetisers) that's a feast for two, with tabouleh, spinach pies and felafel for Dh160. The smoky, silky *baba ghanoush* (eggplant dip) here gives Moroccan eggplant caviar serious competition for best Middle Eastern spread.

MARRAKESH

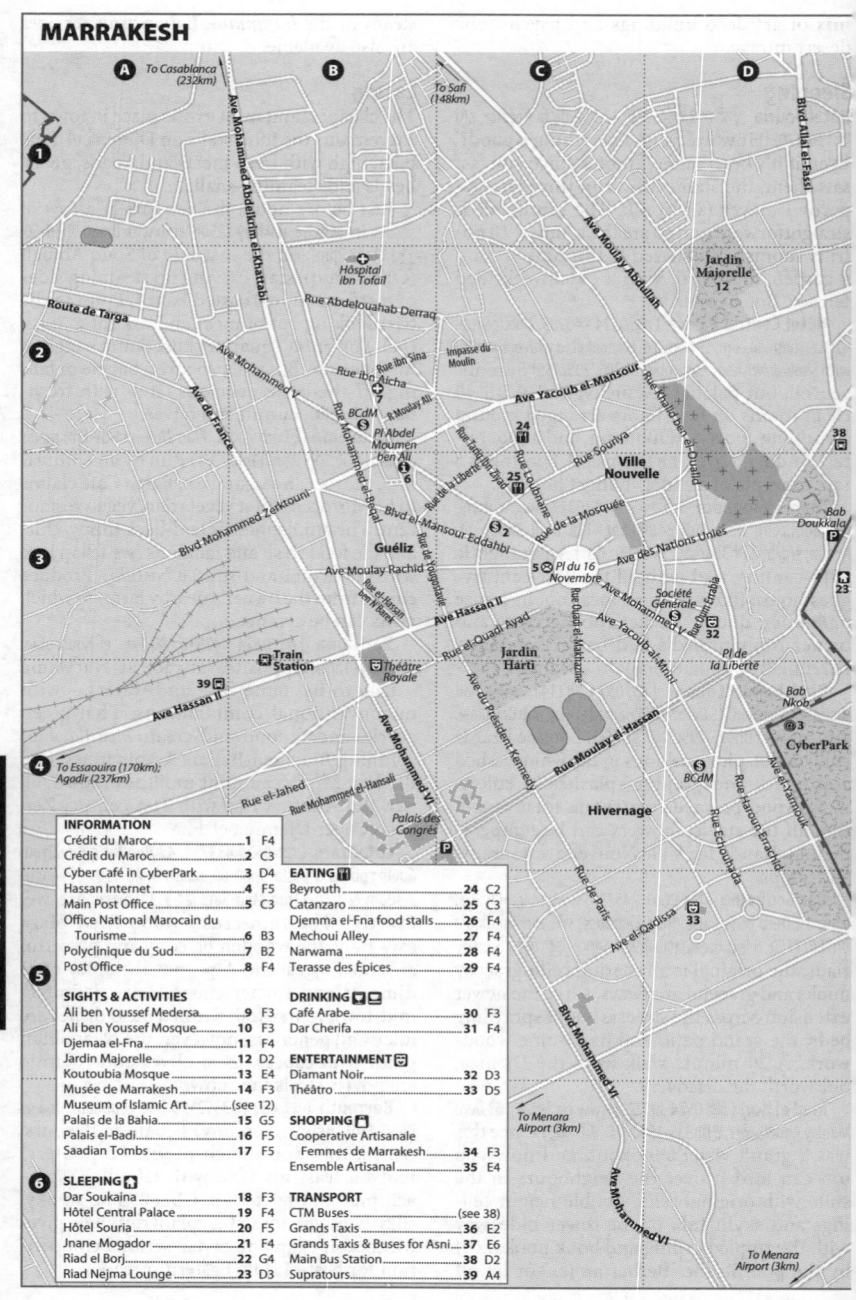

MOROCCO

INFORMATION
Crédit du Maroc..............................**1** F4
Crédit du Maroc..............................**2** C3
Cyber Café in CyberPark...............**3** D4
Hassan Internet...............................**4** F5
Main Post Office.............................**5** C3
Office National Marocain du
   Tourisme.....................................**6** B3
Polyclinique du Sud.......................**7** B2
Post Office......................................**8** F4

SIGHTS & ACTIVITIES
Ali ben Youssef Medersa................**9** F3
Ali ben Youssef Mosque...............**10** F3
Djemaa el-Fna................................**11** F4
Jardin Majorelle.............................**12** D2
Koutoubia Mosque........................**13** E4
Musée de Marrakesh.....................**14** F3
Museum of Islamic Art............(see 12)
Palais de la Bahia..........................**15** G5
Palais el-Badi.................................**16** F5
Saadian Tombs...............................**17** F5

SLEEPING
Dar Soukaina..................................**18** F3
Hôtel Central Palace......................**19** F4
Hôtel Souria...................................**20** F5
Jnane Mogador..............................**21** F4
Riad el Borj....................................**22** G4
Riad Nejma Lounge.......................**23** D3

EATING
Beyrouth...**24** C2
Catanzaro.......................................**25** C3
Djemaa el-Fna food stalls.............**26** F4
Mechoui Alley.................................**27** F4
Narwama..**28** F4
Terasse des Épices.........................**29** F4

DRINKING
Café Arabe......................................**30** F3
Dar Cherifa....................................**31** F4

ENTERTAINMENT
Diamant Noir..................................**32** D3
Théâtro...**33** D5

SHOPPING
Cooperative Artisanale
   Femmes de Marrakesh.............**34** F3
Ensemble Artisanal........................**35** E4

TRANSPORT
CTM Buses..................................(see 38)
Grands Taxis...................................**36** E2
Grands Taxis & Buses for Asni.......**37** E6
Main Bus Station............................**38** D2
Supratours.....................................**39** A4

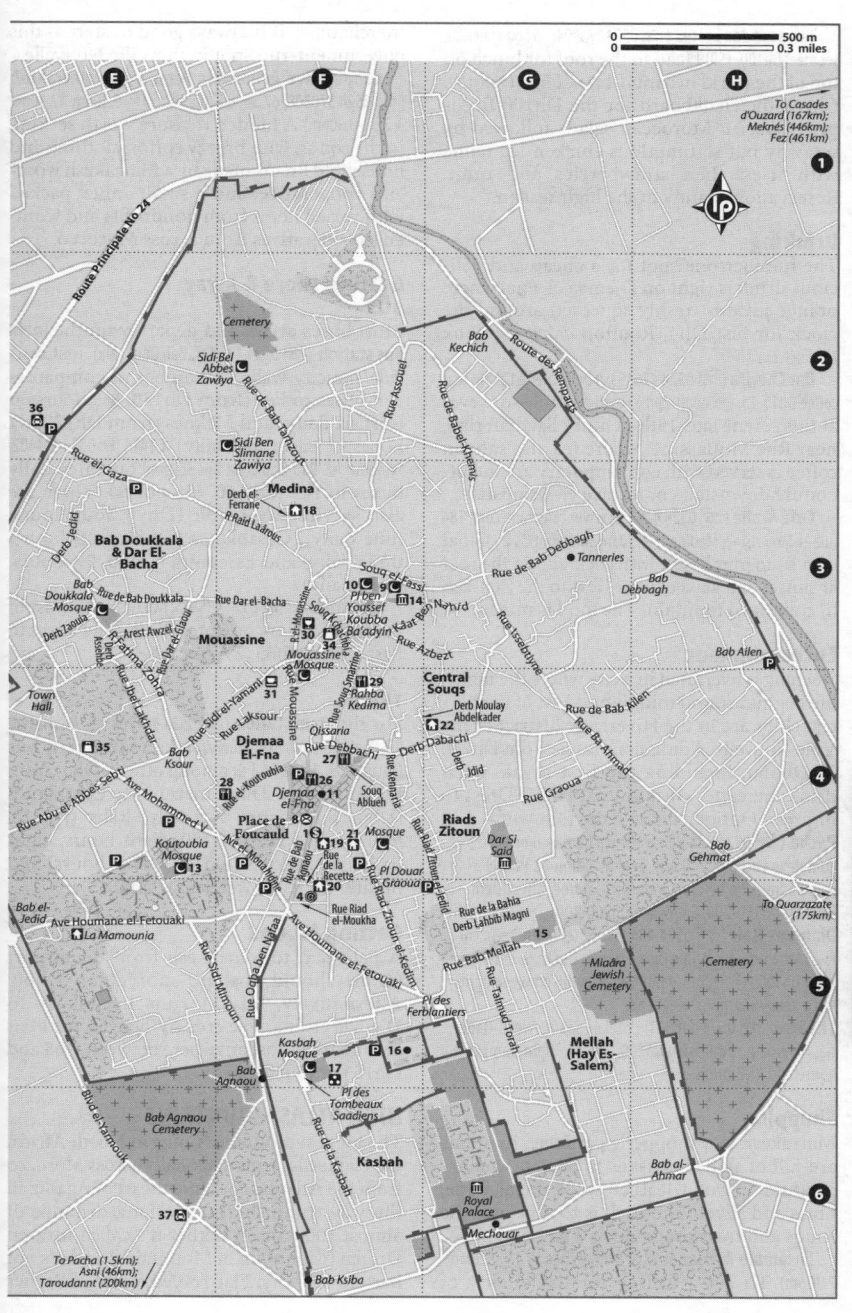

Terrasse des Èpices (☎ 0524 375904; 15 Souq Cherifia; set meal Dh100-150) Head to the roof for lunch on top of the world in a mud-brick *bhou* (booth). Check the chalkboard for the Dh100 fixed-price special: Moroccan salads followed by scrawny but scrumptious chicken-leg tajine with fries, then strawberries and mint. Reservations handy in the high season.

Drinking

The number one spot for a cheap and delicious drink is right on Djemaa el-Fna, where orange juice is freshly squeezed around the clock for just Dh4. Rooftop cafes overlook the square.

Dar Cherifa (☎ 0524 426463; 8 Derb Cherfa Lakbir; tea/coffee Dh15-25; ☿ noon-7pm) Revive souq-sore eyes at this serene late-15th-century Saadian riad, near Rue Mouassine, where tea and saffron coffee is served with contemporary art and literature downstairs or terrace views upstairs.

Café Arabe (☎ 0524 429728; www.cafearabe.com; 184 Rue el-Mouassine, Medina; ☿ 10am-midnight; ⊠) Gloat over souq purchases, with cocktails on the roof at sunset or a glass of wine next to the Zen-*zellij* courtyard fountain. The food is mixed.

Entertainment

Sleeping is overrated in a city where the nightlife begins around midnight. Most of the hottest clubs are in the Hivernage district of the Ville Nouvelle. Admissions range from Dh150 to Dh350, including the first drink. Each drink thereafter costs at least Dh50. Dress to impress. Options include the following:

Pacha (☎ 0524 388405; www.pachamarrakech.com; Complexe Pacha Marrakech, Blvd Mohammed VI, Hivernage; admission before 10pm Mon-Fri free, after 10pm Mon-Fri Dh150-200, Sat & Sun Dh200-300; ☿ 8pm-5am)

Diamant Noir (☎ 0524 434351; Hôtel Marrakech, cnr Ave Mohammed V & Rue Oum Errabia, Guéliz; admission from Dh100; ☿ 10pm-4am) Gay-friendly on weeknights; has a seedy charm on weekends.

Théâtro (☎ 0524 448811; Hôtel es Saadi, Ave el-Qadissia, Hivernage; admission Dh200; ☿ 11.30pm-5am) Lively house and R&B tunes.

Shopping

Marrakesh is a shopper's paradise: its souqs are full of skilled artisans producing quality products in wood, leather, wool, metal, bone, brass and silver. The trick is to dive into the souqs and treat shopping as a game.

Ensemble Artisanal (Ave Mohammed V; ☿ 8.30am-7.30pm) To get a feeling for the quality of merchandise it is always good to start at this government-run spot in the Ville Nouvelle.

Cooperative Artisanale Femmes de Marrakesh (☎ 0524 378308; 67 Souq Kchachbia; ☿ 9.30am-12.30pm & 2.30-6.30pm) A hidden treasure worth seeking in the souqs, with breezy cotton clothing and household linens made by a Marrakesh women's cooperative, and a small annex packed with varied items from nonprofits and women's cooperatives from across Morocco.

Getting There & Away

BUS

Most buses arrive and depart from the **main bus station** (☎ 0524 433933; Bab Doukkala), just outside the city walls. A number of companies run buses to Fez (from Dh130, 8½ hours, at least six daily) and Meknès (from Dh120, six hours, at least three daily). **CTM** (☎ 0524 434402; Window 10, Bab Doukkala bus station) operates daily buses to Fez (Dh160, 8½ hours). There are also services to Agadir (Dh90, four hours, nine daily), Casablanca (Dh85, four hours, three daily) and Essaouira (Dh80, 2½ hours, three daily).

Supratours (☎ 0524 435525; Ave Hassan II), west of the train station, operates three daily buses to Essaouira (Dh65, 2½ hours).

TRAIN

For the **train station** (☎ 0524 447768; cnr Ave Hassan II & Blvd Mohammed VI, Guéliz), take a taxi or city bus (Bus 3, 8, 10 and 14, among others; Dh3) from the city centre. There are trains to Casablanca (Dh84, three hours, nine daily), Rabat (Dh112, four hours), Fez (Dh180, eight hours, eight daily) via Meknès (Dh162, seven hours) and nightly trains to Tangier (Dh190).

Getting Around

A *petit taxi* to Marrakesh from the airport (6km) should cost no more than Dh60. Alternatively, bus 11 runs irregularly to Djemaa el-Fna. The creamy-beige *petits taxis* around town cost anywhere between Dh5 and Dh15 per journey.

HIGH ATLAS MOUNTAINS

The highest mountain range in North Africa, the High Atlas runs diagonally across Morocco from the Atlantic coast northeast of Agadir all the way to northern Algeria, a distance of almost 1000km. In Berber it's called Idraren Draren (Mountain of Mountains) and it's not hard to see why. Flat-roofed, earthen Berber villages cling tenaciously to the valley sides, while irrigated terraced gardens and walnut groves flourish below.

Hiking

The Moroccan tourist office, Office National Marocain du Tourisme (ONMT), publishes an extremely useful booklet called *Morocco: Mountain and Desert Tourism* (2005), with lists of *bureaux des guides* (guide offices), *gîtes d'étape* (hikers' hostels) and other useful information. Hikes of longer than a couple of days will almost certainly require a guide (Dh300 per day) and mule (Dh100; to carry kit and supplies). There are *bureaux des guides* in Imlil, Setti Fatma, Azilal, Tabant (Aït Bou Goumez Valley) and El-Kelaâ M'Gouna, where you should be able to pick up a trained, official guide. Official guides carry ID cards.

Club Alpin Français (CAF; ☎ 0522 270090; www.cafmaroc.co.ma, in French; 50 Blvd Moulay Abderrahman, Quartier Beauséjour, Casablanca) operates key refuges in the Toubkal area, particularly those in Imlil and Oukaïmeden and on Jebel Toubkal. The club website is a good source of trekking information and includes links to recommended guides.

JEBEL TOUBKAL HIKE

One of the most popular hiking routes in the High Atlas is the ascent of Jebel Toubkal (4167m), North Africa's highest peak. The Toubkal area is just two hours' drive south of Marrakesh and easily accessed by local transport.

You don't need mountaineering skills or a guide to reach the summit, provided you follow the standard two-day route and don't do it in winter. You will, however, need good boots, warm clothing, a sleeping bag, food and water, and you should be in good physical condition before you set out. It's not particularly steep, but it's a remorseless uphill trek all the way (an ascent of 1467m) and it can be very tiring if you haven't done any warm-up walks or spent time acclimatising.

The usual starting point is the picturesque village of **Imlil**, 17km from Asni off the Tizi n'Test road between Marrakesh and Agadir. Most trekkers stay overnight in Imlil.

The first day's walk (10km; about five hours) winds steeply through the villages of Aroumd and Sidi Chamharouch to the **Toubkal Refuge** (☎ 0664 071838; dm CAF members/HI members/nonmembers Dh46/69/92). The refuge sits

at an altitude of 2307m and sleeps more than 80 people.

The ascent from the hut to the summit on the second day should take about four hours and the descent about two hours. It can be bitterly cold at the summit, even in summer.

There is plenty of accommodation in Imlil. Try **Hôtel el-Aïne** (☎ 0524 485625; per person rooftop beds/r Dh30/45) or **Dar Adrar** (☎ 0670 726809; http://toubkl.guide.free.fr/gite; d incl breakfast/half board Dh220/330), at the top of the village. Imlil is also well stocked with shops with hiking supplies.

Frequent local buses (Dh15, 1½ hours) and *grands taxis* (Dh30, one hour) leave south of Bab er-Rob in Marrakesh to Asni, where you change for the final 17km to Imlil (Dh15 to Dh20, one hour).

OTHER HIKES

In summer, it's quite possible to do an easy one- or two-day trek from the ski resort of **Oukaïmeden**, which also has a CAF refuge, southwest to Imlil or vice versa. You can get here by *grand taxi* from Marrakesh.

From **Tacheddirt** (where the CAF refuge charges Dh60 for nonmembers) there are numerous hiking options. One of these is a pleasant two-day walk northeast to the village of **Setti Fatma** (also accessible from Marrakesh) via the village of **Timichi**, where there is a welcoming *gîte*. A longer circuit could take you south to **Amsouzerte** and back towards Imlil via **Lac d'Ifni**, Toubkal, **Tazaghart** (also with a refuge and rock climbing) and **Tizi Oussem**.

TAFRAOUTE

Nestled in the enchanting **Ameln Valley** is the village of Tafraoute. Surrounded on all sides by red granite mountains, it's a pleasant and relaxed base for exploring the region. In late February and early March the villages around Tafraoute celebrate the almond harvest with all-night singing and dancing.

There are two banks in Tafraoute – a BMCE behind the post office and **Banque Populaire** (Place Mohammed V; ☼ Wed).

Sights & Activities

The best way to get around the beautiful villages of the Ameln Valley is by walking or cycling. Bikes can be rented from **Artisanat du Coin** (per day Dh60). You can also rent mountain bikes or book a mountain-biking trip from **Tafraoute Aventure** (☎ 0661 387173) or **Au Coin des Nomades** (☎ 0661 627921), which offers

MOROCCO

mountain-biking and hiking trips either up Jebel Lekst (2359m) or along the palm-filled gorges of Aït Mansour, leading towards the bald expanses of the southern Anti-Atlas.

Sleeping & Eating

Hôtel Salama (☎ 0528 800026; s/d Dh199/298; ✖ ▢) Completely renovated, the long-established Salama mixes local materials with modern standards. The result is the best midrange hotel in town, with great views from the terrace, a restaurant serving full meals and a teahouse overlooking the market square.

Hôtel Les Amandiers (☎ 0528 800088; hotellesamandiers@menara.ma; s/d from Dh350/450; ✖ ▣) Sitting like a castle on the crest of the hill overlooking the town, Les Amandiers wants to be Tafraoute's top hotel, in every sense. The kasbah-style hotel has spacious, if unglamorous, rooms and a pool with spectacular views, as well as a bar and restaurant.

Restaurant Marrakech (☎ 0663 229250; Rue Annahda; set menu Dh55) A cheap, family-run restaurant on the road up from the bus station, with a small terrace and good, dependable food.

Restaurant L'Étoile d'Agadir (☎ 0528 800268; Place de la Marche Verte; meals around Dh75; ☉ 8am-6pm) Locals swear by this place for its succulent tajines, all beautifully presented. This is also the place to ease into the day over a coffee.

Getting There & Away

Buses depart from outside the various company offices on Sharia al-Jeish al-Malaki, including to Agadir (Dh40, six hours, daily), Casablanca (Dh100, 14 hours, five daily) and Marrakesh (Dh90, seven hours, four daily).

TAROUDANNT

Hidden behind magnificent red-mud walls and with the snow-capped peaks of the High Atlas beckoning beyond, Taroudannt appears a touch mysterious at first. It is, however, every inch a market town, with busy souqs where the produce of the rich and fertile Souss Valley is traded.

Information

There are three banks with ATMs on Place al-Alaouyine, and all have exchange facilities and accept travellers cheques. BMCE also does cash advances. The main **post office** (Rue du 20 Août) is off Ave Hassan II, to the east of the kasbah. Internet access is available at **Wafanet** (Ave Mohammed V; per hr Dh8).

Sights & Activities

The 5km of **ramparts** surrounding Taroudannt are the best preserved in Morocco, their colour changing from golden brown to the deepest red depending on the time of day. They can easily be explored on foot (1½ hours); preferably in the late afternoon.

Taroudannt is a great base for hiking in the western High Atlas region and the secluded **Tichka Plateau**, a delightful meadow of springtime flowers and hidden gorges. There are several agencies in town offering hikes, but beware as there are many stories of rip-offs and unqualified guides.

Sleeping

Hôtel Taroudant (☎ 0528 852416; Place al-Alaouyine; s/d/tr Dh140/160/200) The Taroudant is faded, the rooms, though clean, have seen better days and its bar can get rowdy. And yet its jungle-style courtyard and faintly colonial public areas have a unique atmosphere – and the bar closes early. There is a good restaurant, and the hotel can organise treks.

Naturally Morocco Guest House: Centre Culturel & Environmental (☎ 0528 551628, 0667 297438; www.naturallymorocco.co.uk; 422 Derb Afferdou; per person half board Dh410) If only there were more places like this: a medina house run by locals offering a rare glimpse into Moroccan life. Dedicated to sustainable tourism and cultural contact, they can arrange ecotours on botany, birdwatching, flora and fauna.

Kasabat Annour (☎ 0528 854576; www.kasabatannour.com; Kasbah; s/d incl breakfast Dh880/1320; ▣ ✖) This guesthouse is built around a former colonel's house in the medina and has six elegant and spacious rooms around a swimming pool. Meals, *hammam* and treatments are available on request.

Eating

The best place to look for cheap eateries is around Place an-Nasr and north along Ave Bir Zaran, where you find the usual tajines, *harira* and salads. Several places around Place al-Alaouyine serve sandwiches and simple grills.

Chez Nada (☎ 0528 851726; Ave Moulay Rachid; set menu Dh70; ✖) West of Bab al-Kasbah, this is a quiet, modern, family-run place, famous for its excellent and good-value tajines, including one of pigeons. There's a cafe downstairs and a dining room on the 1st-floor terrace with great views over the gardens. Food is home cooked and excellent. Pigeon *bastilla* and couscous should be ordered a couple of hours ahead.

Jnane Soussia (☎ 0528 854980; set menu Dh75; ☾ dinner; 🗙 🗷) Delightful restaurant, outside Bab Zorgane, with tented seating areas set around a large pool, in a garden adjacent to the ramparts. The house speciality is a mouthwatering *mechoui*, which must be ordered in advance.

Getting There & Away
All buses leave from the main bus station outside Bab Zorgane. CTM (with an office at Hotel Les Arcades, Place al-Alaouyine) has the most reliable buses, with one departure per day for Casablanca (Dh150, 10 hours) via Marrakesh (Dh90, six hours).

Other companies run services throughout the day to both these cities, as well as to Agadir (Dh30, 2½ hours) and Ouarzazate (Dh80, five hours).

AÏT BENHADDOU
Aït Benhaddou, 32km from Ouarzazate, is one of the most exotic and best-preserved kasbahs in the entire Atlas region. This is hardly surprising, since it has had money poured into it as a result of being used for scenes in many films, notably *Lawrence of Arabia, Jesus of Nazareth* (for which much of the village was rebuilt) and, more recently, *Gladiator*. The kasbah is now under Unesco protection. It's a very special place.

The best place to stay is **Dar Mouna** (☎ 0528 843054; www.darmouna.com; s/d incl breakfast Dh480/600, s/d half board Dh720/840, ste incl breakfast/half board Dh780/960; 🗙 🗷), an elegant pisé guesthouse that threatens to steal scenes from the movie star directly across the valley. Light, high-ceilinged rooms facing the valley are the ones to get. Amenities include great food, a bar, a *hammam*, and bike and camel rental.

To get here from Ouarzazate, take the main road towards Marrakesh as far as the signposted turn-off (22km); Aït Benhaddou is another 9km down a bitumen road. *Grands taxis* run from outside Ouarzazate bus station when full (Dh20 per person) or cost Dh250 to Dh350 per half-day with return.

DRÂA VALLEY
A ribbon of technicoloured palmeraies (palm groves), earth-red kasbahs and stunning Berber villages, the Drâa Valley is a very spe-

cial place. The valley eventually seeps out into the sands of the desert, and it played a key role in controlling the ancient trans-Saharan trade routes that Marrakesh's wealth was built on.

Zagora
The iconic 'Tombouktou, 52 jours' ('Timbuktu, 52 days') signpost was recently taken down in an inexplicable government beautification scheme, but Zagora's fame as a desert outpost is indelible. The Saadians launched their expedition to conquer Timbuktu from Zagora in 1591, and the many desert caravans that passed through this oasis have added to its character.

Zagora feels very much like a border town, fighting back the encroaching desert with its lush palmeraie. Though modern and largely unappealing, it does have its moments, particularly when a dust storm blows up out of the desert and the light becomes totally surreal. The spectacular **Jebel Zagora**, which rises up across the other side of the river Drâa, is worth climbing for the views.

INFORMATION
Banks, including Banque Populaire and BMCE, with ATMs and normal banking hours are on Blvd Mohammed V.

Placenet Cyber Center (95 Blvd Mohammed V; per hr Dh10) Internet access.

ACTIVITIES
Camel rides are not only possible in Zagora, but practically obligatory. Count on around Dh350 per day if you're camping, and ask about water, bedding, toilets and how many other people will be sharing your campsite. Decent agencies include the following:

Caravane Dèsert et Montagne (☎ 0524 846898, 0666 122312; www.caravanedesertetmontagne.com; 112 Blvd Mohammed V)

Caravane Hamada Drâa (☎ /fax 0524 846930; www.hamadadraa.com, in French; Blvd Mohammed V)

Découverte Sud Maroc (☎ 0524 846115; www.geocities.com/decousudma)

SLEEPING & EATING
Hôtel la Rose des Sables (☎ 0524 847274; Ave Allal Ben Abdallah; s/d without bathroom Dh50/60, with bathroom Dh60/90) Off-duty desert guides unwind in these basic, tidy rooms right off the main drag. You might be able to coax out stories of travellers gone wild, over tasty tajine meals at the outdoor cafe (set menu Dh40 to Dh50).

MOROCCO

Auberge Restaurant Chez Ali (☎ 0524 846258; www. chezali.prophp.org; Ave de l'Atlas Zaouiate El Baraka, Zagora; garden tents per person Dh40, r per person incl breakfast/full board Dh100/260, with terrace Dh200/360, showers Dh5) The peacocks stalking the garden can't be bothered, but otherwise the welcome here is very enthusiastic. The skylit rooms upstairs have new pine furnishings and tiled floors, though some mattresses are a tad lumpy. Meals are down-home Berber cooking.

Dar Raha (☎ 0524 846993; http://darraha.free.fr; Amezrou; s/d incl breakfast Dh220/410, half board Dh300/550) 'How thoughtful!' is the operative phrase here, with oasis-appropriate details such as local palm mats, recycled wire lamps and thick straw pisé walls eliminating the need for a pool or air-con. Enjoy homecooked meals and chats in the kitchen like family, and check out the exhibition of local paintings and crafts.

Villa Zagora (☎ 0524 846093; www.mavillaausahara. com; Amezrou; Berber tent Dh220, d without/with bathroom Dh286/365, ste Dh495, d without/with bathroom incl half board Dh 418/506, ste incl half board Dh638; ✗ ☲) Light, breezy and naturally charming, with staff that fuss over you like the Moroccan aunties and uncles you never knew you had. Forget the camels and read the day away on the verandah. All room rates include breakfast.

All hotels have their own restaurants and will provide set meals to nonguests by prior reservation for Dh100 to Dh150. Moroccan fare with less flair can be had at cheap, popular restaurants along Blvd Mohammed V.

GETTING THERE & AWAY

The **CTM bus station** (☎ 0524 847327) is at the southwestern end of Blvd Mohammed V, and the main bus and *grand taxi* lot is at the northern end. CTM has a daily service to Marrakesh (Dh100) and Casablanca (Dh175) via Ouarzazate. Other companies also operate buses to Boumalne du Dadès (Dh75) and Erfoud (Dh85). A bus passes through headed to M'Hamid (Dh20, two hours) in the morning; there are also minibuses (Dh25) and *grands taxis* (Dh30).

M'hamid

Once it was a lonesome oasis, but M'Hamid is a wallflower no more. Today the road is flanked by hotels to accommodate travellers lured here by the golden dunes of the Sahara. This one dot on a map actually covers two towns: M'hamid Jdid is a typical one-street administrative centre with a

mosque, a few restaurants, small hotels craft shops and a Monday market; M'Hamid Bali, the old town, is 3km away across the Oued Drâa. It has an impressive and well-preserved kasbah.

M'hamid's star attraction is **Erg Chigaga**, a mind-boggling 40km stretch of golden Saharan dunes that's the equal of Erg Chebbi near Merzouga (p188). It's 56km away – a couple of hours by 4WD or several days by camel. A closer alternative is **Erg Lehoudi**, but it's in bad need of rubbish collection. **Sahara Services** (☎ 0661 776766; www.saharaserv ices.info), located 300m down the road after the M'Hamid entry, and **Zbar Travel** (☎ 0668 517280; www.zbartravel.com) are both reliable agencies offering tours – an overnight camel trek should start at about Dh380.

If you're not sleeping with your camel in the desert, **Dar Azawad** (☎ 0524 848730; www. darazawad.com; Douar Ouled Driss, M'Hamid; tent/d/ste incl half board Dh500/700/900; ✗ ☲) is a deluxe hotel ideal for Armani-clad nomads, while **Camping Hammada du Drâa** (☎ 0524 848080; campsite/Berber tent per person Dh15/50, per car Dh20) offers simpler but still decent fare.

There's a daily CTM bus at 4.30pm to Zagora (Dh25, two hours), Ouarzazate (Dh70, seven hours), Marrakesh (Dh120, 11 to 13 hours) and Casablanca (Dh205, 15 hours), plus an assortment of private buses, minibuses and *grands taxis*.

DADÈS GORGE

Those art deco tourism posters you see all over southern Morocco showing a striking pink-and-white kasbah in a rocky oasis aren't exaggerating: the Dadès Gorge really is that impressive.

The main access to the gorge is from **Boumalne du Dadès**, a pleasant, laid-back place with a good Wednesday market. From there, a well-sealed road wriggles past 63km of palmeraies, fabulous rock formations, Berber villages and some beautiful ruined kasbahs to Msemrir, before continuing as dirt track to Imilchil in the heart of the High Atlas.

If you have plenty of time, you could easily spend several days pottering about in the gorge – watching nomads bring vast herds of goats down the cliffs to the river, fossicking for fossils and generally enjoying the natural splendour.

There are a number of places to stay; the kilometre markings given as addresses for the following places refer to the distance into the gorge from Boumalne du Dadès.

Auberge des Gorges du Dadès (☎ 0524 831719; www.aubergeaitoudinar.com; Km 25.5; campsite per person Dh15, r per person incl breakfast/half board Dh120/200) A bubbly personality overlooking the river, the Auberge has 12 rooms with splashy Amazigh motifs and big bathrooms, as well as a pleasantly shaded camping area.

Hôtel le Vieux Chateau du Dadès (☎ 0524 831261; fax 0524 830221; Km 27; r per person incl half board downstairs/upstairs Dh150/220) River views, good value and a terrace restaurant amid the chirping songbirds make this hotel worth going the extra mile to find. The tiled rooms upstairs have better views, but the snug pisé-walled downstairs guestrooms are equally charming.

Chez Pierre (☎ 0524 830267; http://chezpierre.ifrance.com; 27km; r per person incl half board Dh570; 🏊) This rock-climbing hotel has eight airy rooms and one apartment shimmying right up the gorge (there's a two-person minimum on the room price). Decor is kept simple to focus attention on what really matters: the view over the valley from flowering terraces and poolside sun decks. Picnics and hikes with official guides can be arranged.

Grands taxis and minibuses run up the gorge from Boumalne du Dadès and charge Dh15 per person to the cluster of hotels in the middle of the gorge and Dh30 to Msemrir – ask to be dropped at your chosen hotel. To return, simply wait by the road and flag down a passing vehicle. Boulmane du Dadès itself has good onward connections to major destinations, including Zagora (Dh65), Tinerhir (Dh25), Fez (Dh135), Casablanca (Dh150 to Dh190), Erfoud (Dh60) and Marrakesh (Dh70 to Dh90).

TODRA GORGE

The spectacular pink canyons of the Todra Gorge, 15km from Tinerhir, at the end of a lush valley thick with stunning palmeraies and Berber villages, are one of the highlights of the south. A massive fault in the plateau dividing the High Atlas from Jebel Sarhro, with a crystal-clear river emerging from it, the gorge rises to 300m at its narrowest point. It's best in the morning, when the sun penetrates to the bottom of the gorge, turning the rock from rose pink to a deep ochre. In the afternoon it can be very dark and, in winter, bitterly cold.

Sights & Activities

This is prime hiking and climbing country. About a 30-minute walk beyond the main gorge is the Petite Gorge. This is the starting point of many pleasant day hikes, including one starting by the Auberge-Camping Le Festival, 2km after the Petite Gorge. **Assettif Aventure** (☎ 0524 895090; www.assettif.org, in French), located 700m before the gorge, arranges hikes and horse riding (day trip Dh500) and hires out bikes (per day Dh100) and mountaineering equipment.

Sleeping & Eating

Auberge Etoile des Gorges (☎ 0524 895045; fax 0524 832151; s/d/tr without bathroom Dh50/70/100, r with bathroom 120) A plucky little budget hotel in the mouth of the mighty gorge, featuring six simple rooms with orthopaedically stiff beds, solar-heated showers and minor road noise easily ignored on a roof deck with a close-up view of the gorge and reasonable meals (three-course meals Dh60 to Dh70).

Dar Ayour (☎ 0524 895271; www.darayour.com; Km 13, Gorges du Todra, Tinghir; r with/without bathroom Dh150/100, r incl breakfast/half board Dh200/350) Riads have arrived in Todra with this warm, artsy, five-storey guesthouse. The 2nd floor is a three-room suite that can sleep a family of seven, the third storey has three guestrooms, and breakfast with a view is served up on the terrace (breakfast Dh35 or half board per person Dh250).

Auberge Le Festival (☎ 0661 267251; http://auberge lefestival.com; s/d main house incl half board Dh300/460, s/d tower room Dh400/700, d/tr cave room Dh700/900) Get in touch with your primal instincts in a cave guestroom dug right into the hillside, or do your best *Romeo and Juliet* impersonation on your private wrought-iron tower balcony.

Hôtel Amazir (☎ 0524 895109; d/tr incl breakfast Dh400/600, d/tr incl half board Dh600/800; 🏊) Don't be fooled by its stern, stony exterior: inside, this place is relaxed, with pretty, unfussy rooms, a pool terrace surrounded by palms, and the lulling sound of the rushing river below. It's on a bend in the road at the southern end of the gorge, 5km before you enter, away from gorge-gawking crowds.

If you need a bed for the night in Tinerhir, the **Hôtel de l'Avenir** (☎ 0524 834599; www.avenir. tineghir.net; 27 Rue Zaid Ouhmed; mattress on roof/d/tr Dh30/100/150) is a sociable spot, with cafes lining the plaza outside, bike hire and a steady stream of travellers.

MOROCCO

Getting There & Away

Buses from Tinerhir leave from the Place Principale to Marrakesh (Dh105, five daily) via Ouarzazate (Dh45), and to Casablanca (Dh165), Erfoud (Dh30, three daily), Meknès (Dh115, six daily) and Zagora (Dh80). Anything westbound will drop you in Boumalne du Dadès (Dh15). *Grands taxis* run throughout the day to Todra Gorge (Dh8).

MERZOUGA & THE DUNES

Erg Chebbi is Morocco's greatest Saharan *erg* (sand sea). It's an impressive, drifting chain of sand dunes that can reach 160m and seems to have escaped from the much larger dune field across the nearby border in Algeria. The *erg* is a magical landscape that deserves much more than the sunrise or sunset glimpse many visitors give it. The dunes are a scene of constant change and fascination as sunlight transforms them from pink to gold to red. The largest dunes are near the villages of Merzouga and Hassi Labied. At night, you only have to walk a little way into the sand, away from the light, to appreciate the immense clarity of the desert sky and the brilliance of its stars.

Merzouga, some 50km south of Erfoud, is a tiny village, but does have Téléboutiques, general stores, a mechanic and, of course, a couple of carpet shops. It also has an internet place, **CyberInternet** (per hr Dh5; ⊙ 9am-10pm), and is the focus of fast-expanding tourism in the area. As a result, it is acquiring a reputation for some of the worst hassle in Morocco.

Most hotels offer excursions into the dunes, which can range from Dh80 to Dh200 for a couple-of-hours' sunrise or sunset camel trek. Overnight trips usually include a bed in a Berber tent, dinner and breakfast, and range from Dh300 to Dh650 per person. Outings in a 4WD are more expensive – up to Dh1200 per day for a car taking up to five passengers.

Sleeping & Eating

Purists lament the encroachment, but a string of hotels now flank the western side of Erg Chebbi, from Merzouga north past Hassi Labied. On the upside, many of these places have spectacular dune views from rooms and terraces. Most offer half-board options, and often you can sleep on a terrace mattress or in a Berber tent for Dh30 to Dh50 per person.

HASSI LABIED

This tiny oasis village, 5km north of Merzouga and some way off the tarmac, has a good range of accommodation.

Auberge Camping Sahara (☎ 0535 577039; terrace camping per person Dh20, s half board without bathroom Dh110, d/tr/ste half board with bathroom Dh140/170/250) Basic but spotless rooms and Turkish toilets in a friendly place backing right onto the dunes at the southernmost end of the village.

Kasbah Sable d'Or (Chez Isabelle & Rachid; ☎ 0535 577859; http://kasbah-sable-dor.co; Bedouin tent Dh25, r per person incl half board with/without bathroom Dh170/140) When the goat bleats welcome, you know you've come to the right place. There are just four rooms in here, with hand-painted murals on the doors, fans instead of air-con and tasty homecooked dinners in the family salon.

Dar el Janoub (☎ /fax 0535 577852; www.dareljanoub. com; d standard/large/ste per person Dh500/600/700; ☒ ☒) An ode to local building tradition, the architect here stuck to elemental building shapes, because when you're facing the dunes, why compete? For the price, you get great rooms with a million-dirham view, half board, a pool and pure poetry.

MERZOUGA

Chez Julia (☎ 0535 573182; s/d/tr/q Dh160/180/200/230) Pure charm in the heart of Merzouga, Chez Julia offers nine simply furnished rooms in soft, sunwashed colours, with immaculate white-tiled shared bathrooms. The Moroccan ladies who run the place can cook up a storm of delicious meals.

Riad Totmaroc (☎ 0670 624136; www.totmaroc. com; Merzouga; r per person half board Dh350) A modern kasbah that provides instant relief from the white-hot desert, with five guestrooms in bold, eye-soothing shades of blue and green, shady patios looking right onto the dunes and an open kitchen turning out tasty meals.

Getting There & Away

Thankfully, the sealed road now continues all the way to Merzouga. Most hotels are located at least a kilometre off the road at the base of the dunes, but all are accessible by car. The *pistes* can be rough and there is a possibility, albeit remote, of getting stuck in sand, so make sure you have plenty of water for emergencies, and a mobile phone.

If you don't have your own transport you will have to rely on *grands taxis* or on the minivans that operate from Merzouga to the transport junction towns of Rissani and Erfoud and back.

MOROCCO DIRECTORY

ACCOMMODATION

Auberges de jeunesses (youth hostels) operate in Casablanca (Map p163), Chefchaouen, Fez (Map p172), Meknès, Rabat and Tangier (Map p149). Hotels vary dramatically, ranging from dingy dives to fancy five-star options (the latter mostly in larger cities). Cities that see many tourists also offer gorgeous guesthouses in the style of a riad (traditional courtyard house).

You might expect to pay up to Dh400 for budget-style accommodation, Dh400 to Dh800 for midrange and over Dh800 for top end. The exceptions to this are the pricier towns of Casablanca, Essaouira, Fez, Rabat and Tangier. For these towns, budget accomodation may cost up to Dh600, midrange Dh600 to Dh1200 and top end more than Dh1200. In this book, places are listed in order of price and include a private bathroom unless otherwise stated. Prices given are for high season and include tax; always check the price you are quoted is TTC (all taxes included).

Advance reservations are highly recommended for all places listed in this chapter, especially in summer.

ACTIVITIES
Camel Treks & Desert Safaris

Exploring the Moroccan Sahara by camel is one of the country's signature activities and one of the most rewarding wilderness experiences, whether done on an overnight excursion or a two-week trek. The most evocative stretches of Saharan sand include the Drâa Valley (p186), especially the Tinfou Dunes and Erg Chigaga, and the dunes of Erg Chebbi (opposite) near Merzouga.

Autumn (September to October) and winter (November to early March) are the only seasons worth considering. Prices hover around Dh350 to Dh450 per person per day, but vary depending on the number of people involved, the length of the trek and your negotiating skills.

Hammams

Visiting a *hammam* (traditional bathhouse) is a ritual at the centre of Moroccan society and a practical solution for those who don't have hot water at home (or in their hotel). Every town has at least one public *hammam,* and the big cities have fancy spas – both are deep cleaning and relaxing. A visit to a standard *hammam* usually costs Dh10, with a massage costing an extra Dh15 or so.

Surfing & Windsurfing

With thousands of kilometres of Atlantic coastline, Morocco has some great surfing spots. Highlights are the beaches in Essaouira (p165) for windsurfing and around Rabat (p160) for surfing.

Hiking

Morocco is a superb destination for mountain lovers, offering a variety of year-round hiking possibilities. It's relatively straightforward to arrange guides, porters and mules for a more independent adventure. Jebel Toubkal (4167m; p183), the highest peak in the High Atlas, attracts the lion's share of visitors, but great possibilities exist throughout the country, including

---

PRACTICALITIES

- For a full list of Moroccan newspapers online, go to onlinenewspapers.com (www.onlinenewspapers.com/morocco.htm).

- Radio Moroccan radio encompasses only a handful of local AM and FM stations, the bulk of which broadcast in either Arabic or French. Midi 1 at 97.5 FM covers northern Morocco, Algeria and Tunisia, and plays reasonable contemporary music.

- TV Satellite dishes are everywhere in Morocco and pick up dozens of foreign stations. There are two government-owned stations, TVM and 2M, which broadcast in Arabic and French.

- The electric current is 220V/50Hz but older buildings may still use 110V. Moroccan sockets accept the European round two-pin plugs.

- Morocco uses the metric system for weights and measures.

in the Rif Mountains around Chefchaouen (p153). The Dadès and Todra Gorges also offer good hiking opportunities (p186). Spring and autumn are the best seasons for trekking.

BUSINESS HOURS

Standard business hours:

Cafes ☯ 7am to 11pm
Restaurants ☯ noon to 3pm and 7 to 11pm
Shops ☯ 9am to 12.30pm and 2.30 to 8pm Monday to Saturday (often closed longer from noon on Friday).
Tourist offices ☯ 8.30am to 12.30pm and 2.30 to 6.30pm Monday to Thursday.

DANGERS & ANNOYANCES

Morocco's era as a hippy paradise is long past. Plenty of fine *kif* (dope) is grown in the Rif Mountains, but drug busts are common and Morocco isn't a good place to investigate prison conditions.

A few years ago the *brigade touristique* (tourist police) was set up in the principal tourist centres to clamp down on Morocco's notorious *faux guides* and hustlers. Anyone convicted of operating as an unofficial guide faces jail time and/or a huge fine. This has reduced but not eliminated the problem of *faux guides*. You'll still find plenty of these touts hanging around the entrances to medinas and train stations (and even on trains approaching Fez and Marrakesh), and at Tangier port. Remember that their main interest is the commission gained from certain hotels or on articles sold to you in the souqs.

If possible, avoid walking alone at night in the medinas of the big cities; knife-point muggings aren't unknown.

For women travellers see p193.

EMBASSIES & CONSULATES

For details of all Moroccan embassies abroad and foreign embassies in Morocco, go to www.maec.gov.ma.

The following embassies are in Rabat:

Belgium (off Map pp158–9; ☎ 0537 268060; info@ ambabel-rabat.org.ma; 6 Ave de Marrakesh)
Canada (off Map pp158–9; ☎ 0537 687400; fax 0537 687430; 13 Rue Jaafar as-Sadiq, Agdal)
France (off Map pp158–9; ☎ 0537 689700; www. ambafrance-ma.org; 3 Rue Sahnoun, Agdal)
Germany (Map pp158–9; ☎ 0537 709662; www.ambal lemagne-rabat.ma; 7 Rue Madnine)
Ireland No embassy. Some consular services provided by the Canadian embassy.
Italy (Map pp158–9; ☎ 0537 706598; ambaciata@iambitalia .ma; 2 Rue Idriss el-Azhar)

Japan (off Map pp158–9; ☎ 0537 631782; fax 0537 750078; 39 Ave Ahmed Balafrej, Souissi)
Mauritania (off Map pp158–9; ☎ 0537 656678; ambassa deur@mauritanie.org.ma; 7 Rue Thami Lamdaouar, Soussi)
Netherlands (Map pp158–9; ☎ 0537 219600; nlgov rab@mtds.com; 40 Rue de Tunis)
Spain (Map pp158–9; ☎ 0537 633900; emb.rabat@ mae.es; Rue Ain Khalouiya, Km 5.300, Route des Zaers, Souissi)
UK (Map pp158–9; ☎ 0537 238600; www.britain.org.ma; 17 Blvd de la Tour Hassan) Also provides consular support for New Zealand.
USA (off Map pp158–9; ☎ 0537 762265; www.us embassy.ma; 2 Ave de Marrakesh)

EMERGENCIES

Ambulance ☎ 15
Fire ☎ 16
Police ☎ 19

FESTIVALS & EVENTS

Religious festivals are significant for Moroccans. Local *moussems* (saints days) are held all over the country throughout the year and some draw big crowds.

Major festivals:

Festival of World Sacred Music (Fez; www.fesfestival. com) Every June.
Gnaoua & World Music Festival (Essaouira; www. festival-gnaoua.co.ma) Held in June.
International Cultural Festival (Asilah) July/August.
Marrakesh Popular Arts Festival (www.maghrebarts. ma, in French) Held in July.
Moussem of Moulay Idriss II (Fez) September/October.

GAY & LESBIAN TRAVELLERS

Homosexual acts (including kissing) are officially illegal in Morocco – in theory you can go to jail and/or be fined. In practice, although not openly admitted or shown, male homosexuality remains relatively common and platonic affection is freely shown, more so among men than women. In most places, discretion is the key and public displays of affection should be avoided (aggression towards gay male travellers is not unheard of) – this advice applies equally to homosexual and heterosexual couples as a means of showing sensitivity to local feelings.

Some towns are certainly more gay-friendly than others, with Marrakesh winning the prize, followed by Tangier. That said, gay travellers generally follow the same itineraries as everyone else and, although 'gay' bars can be found here and there, Moroccan nightlife tends to include something for everybody.

MOROCCO

Lesbians shouldn't encounter any problems; it's commonly believed by Moroccans that there are no lesbians in their country. Announcing that you're gay probably won't make would-be Romeos magically disappear. For Moroccan men it may simply confirm their belief that Western men don't measure up in the sexual department.

It is also worth bearing in mind that the pressures of poverty mean than many young men will consider having sex for money or gifts. Needless to say, exploitative relationships form an unpleasant but real dimension of the Moroccan gay scene.

HOLIDAYS

All banks, post offices and most shops are shut on the main public holidays:

New Year's Day 1 January
Independence Manifesto 11 January
Labour Day 1 May
Feast of the Throne 30 July
Allegiance of Oued-Eddahab 14 August
Anniversary of the King's and People's Revolution 20 August
Young People's Day 21 August
Anniversary of the Green March 6 November
Independence Day 18 November

In addition to secular holidays there are many national and local Islamic holidays and festivals, all tied to the lunar calendar, including:

Eid al-Adha Marks the end of the Islamic year. Most things shut down for four or five days.
Eid al-Fitr Held at the end of the month-long Ramadan fast, which is observed by most Muslims. The festivities last four or five days, during which Morocco grinds to a halt. Ramadan will fall in summer during the lifetime of this guide.
Mawlid an-Nabi (Mouloud) Celebrates the birthday of the Prophet Mohammed.

INTERNET RESOURCES

The Lonely Planet website (www.lonely planet.com) has up-to-date news and the Thorn Tree bulletin board, where you can post questions.

Al-Bab (www.al-bab.com/maroc) Also called The Moroccan Gateway, Al-Bab has excellent links, especially for current affairs, news and good books about Morocco.
Maghreb Arts (www.maghrebarts.ma, in French) Up-to-the-minute coverage of theatre, film, music, festivals and media events in Morocco.
Maroc Blogs (http://maroc-blogs.com) Useful blog aggregator pulling in feeds from the entire Moroccan blogging community.

Tourism in Morocco (www.tourism-in-morocco.com/index_en.php) Morocco's official tourist information website; user-friendly, with guided tours, links and news.

Internet Access

Internet access is widely available, efficient and cheap (Dh5 to Dh10 per hour) in internet cafes, usually with pretty impressive connections speeds. One irritant for travellers is the widespread use of French or Arabic (non-qwerty) keyboards, which will reduce most travellers to one-finger typing and fumbled searches for hidden punctuation marks.

Most top-end and many midrange hotels offer wi-fi, and it's more or less standard in most riads and *maisons d'hôtes*. If you're bringing your laptop, check the power supply voltage and bring a universal adaptor.

MONEY

The Moroccan currency is the dirham (Dh), which is divided into 100 centimes. There is no black market, although it's forbidden to take dirhams out of the country. The Spanish enclaves of Ceuta and Melilla use the euro.

ATMs *(guichets automatiques)* are widespread and generally accept Visa, MasterCard, Electron, Cirrus, Maestro and InterBank cards. Major credit cards are widely accepted in the main tourist centres, although their use often attracts a surcharge of around 5% from Moroccan businesses. Amex, Visa and Thomas Cook travellers cheques are also widely accepted for exchange by banks. Australian, Canadian and New Zealand dollars are not quoted in banks and are not usually accepted.

Tipping

Tipping and bargaining are integral parts of Moroccan life. Practically any service can warrant a tip, and a few dirham for a service willingly rendered can make your life a lot easier. Tipping between 5% and 10% of a restaurant bill is appropriate.

POST

Post offices are distinguished by the 'PTT' sign or the 'La Poste' logo. You can sometimes buy stamps at *tabacs*, the small tobacco and newspaper kiosks you see scattered about the main city centres.

The postal system is fairly reliable, but not terribly fast. It takes about a week for letters to get to their European destinations, and two weeks or so to get to Australia and

MOROCCO

North America. Sending post from Rabat or Casablanca is quicker.

The parcel office, indicated by the sign 'colis postaux', is generally in a separate part of the post office building. Take your parcel unwrapped for customs inspection. Some parcel offices sell boxes.

TELEPHONE

A few cities and towns still have public phone offices, often next to the post office, but more common are privately run Téléboutiques, which can be found in every town and village on almost every corner. Most public payphones are card operated, with télécartes (phonecards) sold in general stores and news kiosks.

All domestic phone calls in Morocco require a 10-digit number, which includes the four-digit area code (or GSM code). When calling overseas from Morocco, dial ☎ 00, the country code and then the city code and number. Morocco's country code is ☎ 212.

Morocco has three GSM mobile phone networks, Méditel, Maroc Telecom and Wana, which cover 90% of the population. A local SIM card costs around Dh30 and top-up scratch cards are sold everywhere.

TOURIST INFORMATION

The national tourism body, **Office National Marocain du Tourisme** (ONMT; www.visitmorocco.com), has offices in the main cities, with the head office in Rabat. These offices are often called Délégation Régionale du Tourisme. Regional offices, called Syndicat d'Initiative, are to be found in smaller towns. Although there are some notable exceptions, most tourist offices inside Morocco are of limited use, offering the standard ONMT brochures and the simplest of tourist maps, along with helpless smiles.

VISAS

Most visitors to Morocco do not require visas and are allowed to remain in the country for 90 days on entry. Exceptions to this include nationals of Israel, and most sub-Saharan African countries (including South Africa). Moroccan embassies have been known to insist that you get a visa from your country of origin. Should the standard 90-day stay be insufficient, it is possible (but difficult) to apply at the nearest police headquarters (Préfecture de Police) for an extension – it's simpler to leave (eg travel to the Spanish enclaves of Ceuta and Melilla) and come back a few days later. Your chances improve if you re-enter by a different route. The Spanish enclaves have the same visa requirements as mainland Spain.

Visas for Onward Travel

Algeria Although Algeria has now emerged from over a decade of civil war, the border with Morocco remains closed and visas are not being issued.

Mali Visas are required for everyone except French nationals and are valid for one month (Dh300), but are renewable inside Mali. Two photographs and a yellow-fever vaccination certificate are required and the visa is usually issued on the spot. Malian visas are available at Malian border posts, but by no means count on that if you're crossing at a remote desert border post.

Mauritania Everyone, except nationals of Arab League countries and some African countries, needs a visa, which is valid for a one-month stay. These are issued in 24 hours at the Mauritanian embassy in Rabat (apply before noon). Visas cost Dh340, with two photos and a passport photocopy. An onward air ticket to Nouakchott is no longer required. Visas (normally for shorter stays, according to the whim of the official) can also be obtained at the border for €25.

VOLUNTEERING

There are many international and local organisations that organise voluntary work on regional development projects in Morocco. They generally pay nothing, sometimes not even lodging, and are aimed at young people looking for something different to do for a few weeks over the summer period.

A good place to start looking is the Morocco page for **Volunteer Abroad** (www.volunteerabroad. com/Morocco.cfm), which provides links to NGOs with Morocco-specific programs. Also worth getting hold of is Lonely Planet's The Big Trip, which lists hundreds of NGOs that organise volunteer and other work and study programs around the world – although unless you have a working knowledge of Arabic or Berber, or have specific specialist skills, many organisations in Morocco will not be interested.

International or local NGOs that sometimes have Morocco placements or camps include the following:

Baraka Community Partnerships (www.barakacom munity.com) Near Telouet. Organises volunteers to build schools, plant trees, supply basic medical care and work on initiatives to improve local food security between partnerships.

Chantiers Sociaux Marocains (☎ 0537 262400; csm@wanadoo.net.ma; Rabat) Local NGO engaged in health, education and development projects, with international volunteers aged 18 to 30.

International Cultural Youth Exchange (www.icye.org) Allows you to search for upcoming Moroccan volunteer opportunities.

Jeunesse des Chantiers Marocains (http://perso.menara.ma/youthcamps) A nonprofit group open to 18 to 30 year olds, promoting cultural exchange through three- to four-week courses in Moroccan Arabic, during which you stay with local families and take part in cultural events.

WOMEN TRAVELLERS

Women can expect a certain level of sexual harassment when travelling in Morocco. It comes in the form of nonstop greetings, leering and other unwanted attention, but it is rarely dangerous. It is best to avoid overreacting and to ignore this attention. In the case where a would-be suitor is particularly persistent, threatening to go to the police or the *brigade touristique* is amazingly effective. Women will save themselves a great deal of grief by avoiding eye contact, dressing modestly (covering knees and shoulders) and refraining from walking around alone at night.

TRANSPORT IN MOROCCO

GETTING THERE & AWAY
Air
Morocco's two main international entry points are **Mohammed V international airport** (☎ 0522 539040), 30km southeast of Casablanca, and Marrakesh's **Ménara Airport** (☎ 0524 447865). Other international airports are in Fez, Tangier and Agadir. For comprehensive information on all of Morocco's airports, check the website of **Office National des Aéroports** (www.onda.org.ma, in French).

Direct flights are possible from cities across Europe, the Middle East, West Africa and North America, and they mostly arrive in Casablanca and Marrakesh. Morocco's national carrier, Royal Air Maroc, and Air France take the lion's share of flights, with increasing competition from the budget airlines (including RAM's own subsidiary, Atlas Blue).

INTERNATIONAL AIRLINES IN MOROCCO
Air Algérie (AH; ☎ 0522 314181; www.airalgerie.dz)
Air France (AF; ☎ 0522 294040; www.airfrance.com)
Alitalia (AZ; ☎ 0522 314181; www.alitalia.it)
Atlas Blue (BMM; ☎ 0582 009090; www.atlas-blue.com)

British Airways (BA; ☎ 0522 229464; www.ba.com)
EasyJet (EZY; www.easyjet.com)
EgyptAir (MS; ☎ 0522 315564; www.egyptair.com)
Gulf Air (GF; ☎ 0522 491212; www.gulfairco.com)
Iberia (IB; ☎ 0522 279600; www.iberia.com)
KLM-Royal Dutch Airlines (KL; ☎ 0522 203222; www.klm.com)
Lufthansa Airlines (LH; ☎ 0522 312371; www.lufthansa.com)
Regional Airlines (RGL; ☎ 0522 536940; www.regionalmaroc.com)
Royal Air Maroc (RAM; ☎ 0522 311122; www.royalairmaroc.com)
Ryanair (FR; www.ryanair.com)
Thomsonfly (BY; www.thomsonfly.com)
Tunis Air (TU; ☎ 0522 293452; www.tunisair.com.tn)

Sea
Regular ferries run to Europe from several ports along Morocco's Mediterranean coast. The most trafficked is Tangier, from where there are boats to Algeciras (€31, 60 to 70 minutes, every 90 minutes) and Tarifa, Spain (€40, 35 minutes, five daily) and Sete, France (€165, 36 hours, two weekly). Hourly ferries also run from Ceuta to Algeciras (€28, 35 minutes, hourly). Daily ferries go from Al-Hoceima (summer only), Melilla and Nador to Almería and Málaga in Spain. Bringing a bicycle costs €8 to €15 extra, while a car adds €60 to €80. Children travel for half price. Tickets are available at the port of departure or from any travel agent in town.

Land
The Moroccan bus company **CTM** (☎ in Casablanca 0522 458080; www.ctm.co.ma) operates buses from Casablanca and most other main cities to France, Belgium, Spain, Germany and Italy. Another Moroccan bus service with particularly good links to Spanish networks is **Tramesa** (☎ 0522 245274; http://perso.menara.ma/tramesa07, in French). **Eurolines** (www.eurolines.com) is a consortium of European bus companies that operates across Europe (including the UK) and to Morocco. It has offices in all major European cities.

ALGERIA
The border with Algeria has been closed for some time due to ongoing political disputes.

MAURITANIA
The trans-Saharan route via Mauritania is now the most popular route from North

MOROCCO

Africa into sub-Saharan Africa. This crosses the internationally disputed territory of Western Sahara, although the border itself is administered by Morocco.

The only border crossing between Morocco/Western Sahara and Mauritania is at Guegarat, north of Nouâdhibou. Crossing this border is straightforward and the road is entirely tarred to Nouakchott, except for the 3km no-man's-land that separates the two border posts. There are direct bush taxis heading north from Nouâdhibou to Dakhla (Western Sahara), but travelling in the opposite direction you'll need to change vehicles at the border. The 425km trip can easily be accomplished in a day.

GETTING AROUND
Air
Royal Air Maroc (RAM; ☎ 0890 000800; www.royalairmaroc.com) dominates the Moroccan airline industry, with paltry competition from one other domestic airline, **Regional Air Lines** (☎ 0522 538080). Both airlines use Casablanca as their hub, with internal flights routed through Mohammed V international airport. Student and under-26 youth discounts of 25% are available on all RAM domestic flights, but only if the ticket is bought in advance from one of its offices. For most routes, flying is an expensive and inconvenient option compared to road or rail.

Bus
A dense network of buses operates throughout Morocco, with many private companies competing for business alongside the comfortable and modern buses of the main national carrier, **CTM** (☎ in Casablanca 0522 45 80 80).

The **ONCF** (www.oncf.org.ma, in French) train company runs buses through Supratours to widen its train network; for example, running connections from Marrekesh to Essaouira. Morocco's other bus companies are all privately owned and only operate regionally. It's best to book ahead for CTM and Supratours buses, which are slightly more expensive than those of other companies.

Car & Motorcycle
Taking your own vehicle to Morocco is straightforward. In addition to a vehicle registration document and an International Driving Permit (although many foreign licences, including US and EU ones, are also acceptable), a Green Card is required from the car's insurer. Not all insurers cover Morocco.

Renting a car in Morocco isn't cheap, with prices starting at Dh3500 per week or Dh500 per day for a basic car with unlimited mileage. International rental companies are well represented, and booking in advance online secures the best deals. Most companies demand a returnable cash deposit (Dh3000 to Dh5000) unless you pay by credit card.

In Morocco you drive on the right-hand side. On a roundabout, give way to traffic entering from the right.

Local Transport
Cities and bigger towns have local *petits taxis,* which are a different colour in every city. They are not permitted to go beyond the city limits, are licensed to carry up to three passengers and are usually metered. Fares increase by 50% after 8pm.

The old Mercedes vehicles you'll see belting along roads and gathered in great flocks near bus stations are *grands taxis* (shared taxis). They link towns to their nearest neighbours. *Grands taxis* take six extremely cramped passengers and normally only leave when full.

Train
Morocco's train network is run by **ONCF** (www.oncf.org.ma, in French). There are two lines that carry passengers: from Tangier in the north down to Marrakesh; and from Oujda in the northeast, also to Marrakesh, joining with the Tangier line at Sidi Kacem.

Trains are comfortable, fast and generally preferable to buses. There are different 1st- and 2nd-class fares on all these trains, but 2nd-class is more than adequate on any journey. Couchettes are available on the overnight trains between Marrakesh and Tangier. Children aged under four travel free. Those aged between four and 12 years get a reduction of 10% to 50%, depending on the service.

Two types of rail discount cards are available in Morocco. The Carte Fidelité (Dh149) is for those aged over 26 and gives you 50% reductions on eight return or 16 one-way journeys in a 12-month period. If you're under 26, the Carte Jaune (Dh99) will give you the same discounts. To apply for the card you will need one passport-sized photo as well as a photocopy of your passport.

Sudan

Wake at the break of day under the golden pyramids of God-like kings of old; traverse a searing desert to the place where two Niles become one; walk through the green hills where Africa bumps into Arabia; watch a million blood-red fish swarm through gardens of coral or a million stampeding antelope splash through an unexplored swamp. Whichever way you look at it, there's just no denying that among Sudan's sweeping hills of sand lie treasures we are only just beginning to understand.

Sudan is the largest, yet one of the least visited and least understood, countries in Africa. Although various ongoing conflicts mean much of this vast nation remains off-limits, the northeast is one of the safest places in Africa. And the easing of travel restrictions is opening up new swathes of territory to explore in the lush south, where pale desert browns transition into a riot of tropical extravagance.

And while the solitude is a top draw, visitors invariably agree that the Sudanese are among the friendliest and most hospitable people on earth, with a natural generosity that belies their poverty, and this alone makes any trip worthwhile. Whether you rush through on a Cairo–to–Cape Town trip or spend a slow month soaking up the history and hospitality, visiting Sudan is such an eye-opening and rewarding experience that more than a few people come away saying that Sudan was their favourite country in the entire continent.

FAST FACTS

- **Area** 2.5 million sq km
- **ATMs** Only work with local accounts
- **Borders** Egypt and Ethiopia open; crossing to Central African Republic (CAR), Democratic Republic of Congo (DRC), Kenya, Libya and Uganda not recommended; Eritrea open but difficult for foreigners to cross; Chad closed
- **Budget** Khartoum from US$50 a day, elsewhere from US$25 a day
- **Capital** Khartoum
- **Languages** Arabic, English, over 100 regional languages
- **Money** Sudanese Pound; US$1 = S£2.2, €1 = S£3.2
- **Population** 41 million
- **Seasons** Rainy season in north (July to September), Red Sea coast (October to December) and south (April to November)
- **Telephone** Country code ☎ 249; international access code ☎ 00
- **Time** GMT/UTC +3
- **Visa** Best bought in Cairo or Aswan (Egypt), or with the help of a Khartoum travel agent

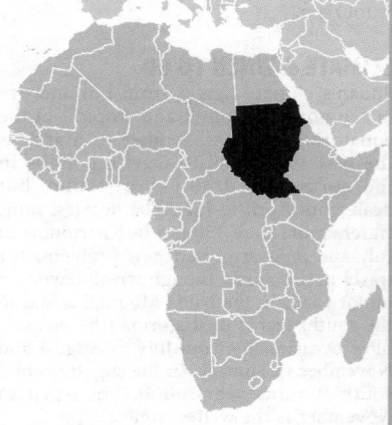

HOW MUCH?

- **Admission to historic sites** US$8.70
- **100km bus ride** US$0.50
- **Cup of tea** US$0.20
- **Internet per hour** US$0.90
- **Plate of fuul** US$0.50

LONELY PLANET INDEX

- **1L diesel** US$0.43
- **1.5L bottled water** US$0.90
- **Bottle of beer** Not available
- **Lokanda bed** US$3
- **Midrange hotel** US$45

HIGHLIGHTS

- **Begrawiya** (p204) Enveloped in sand dunes and just waiting for you to discover them, Begrawiya has Sudan's best-preserved pyramids.
- **Wadi Halfa to Dongola** (p205) Follow the sluggish Nile through searing desert past beautiful old ruins and remote sun-baked towns.
- **Kassala** (p206) Dive into exotic markets and scramble around the Taka Mountains.
- **Karima** (p205) Sweep away the sandy layers of time and discover a wealth of Pharaonic ruins, tombs and pyramids.
- **Nuba Mountains** (p208) Relish the lush greenery of the mountains where Africa meets Arabia in this new frontier for tourism.

CLIMATE & WHEN TO GO

Sudan's climate ranges from hot and dry in the north to humid and tropical in the equatorial south. November to March is the best time to visit. Daytime highs in the north exceed 40°C year-round, but peak from April to July. The heaviest rains (rarely more than 150mm in Khartoum) in July and August present few problems for travel in the north, though wreak havoc on minor roads in the Nuba Mountains and in the south. Fierce dust storms (the *haboob*) blow occasionally from July to August and November to January. In the slightly cooler south it rains year-round, but April to November is the wettest time.

ITINERARIES

- **Three Days** Three days is plenty of time to visit Khartoum (p200) and get out to the Meroe Sites (p204).
- **Two Weeks** After seeing Khartoum and the Meroe Sites, follow the Nile on its lethargic amble through history. Don't miss the pyramids and other ruins near Karima (p205), the lazy days of Dongola (p205) and the fascinating site of Soleb (p205). Then either head to the seaside for some Red Sea scuba-diving out of Port Sudan (p208) or head south to explore the gorgeous, green Nuba Mountains (p208), where few other tourists tread.

HISTORY

Modern Sudan is situated on the site of the ancient civilisation of Nubia, which predates Pharaonic Egypt. For centuries sovereignty was shuttled back and forth between the Egyptians, indigenous empires such as Kush, and a succession of independent Christian kingdoms.

After the 14th century AD the Mamelukes (Turkish rulers in Egypt) breached the formidable Nubian defences and established the dominance of Islam. By the 16th century the kingdom of Funj had become a powerful Muslim state and Sennar, 200km south of present-day Khartoum, was one of the great cultural centres of the Islamic world.

Colonialism & Revolt

In 1821 the viceroy of Egypt, Mohammed Ali, conquered northern Sudan and opened the south to trade. Within a few decades British interests were also directed towards Sudan, aiming to control the Nile, contain French expansion from the west and draw the south into a British–East African federation. The European intrusion, and in particular the Christian missionary zeal that accompanied it, was resented by many Muslim Sudanese.

The revolution came in 1881, when one Mohammed Ahmed proclaimed himself to be the Mahdi – the person who, according to Muslim tradition, would rid the world of evil. Four years later he rid Khartoum of General Gordon, the British-appointed governor, and the Mahdists ruled Sudan until 1898, when they were defeated outside Omdurman by Lord Kitchener and his

SUDAN

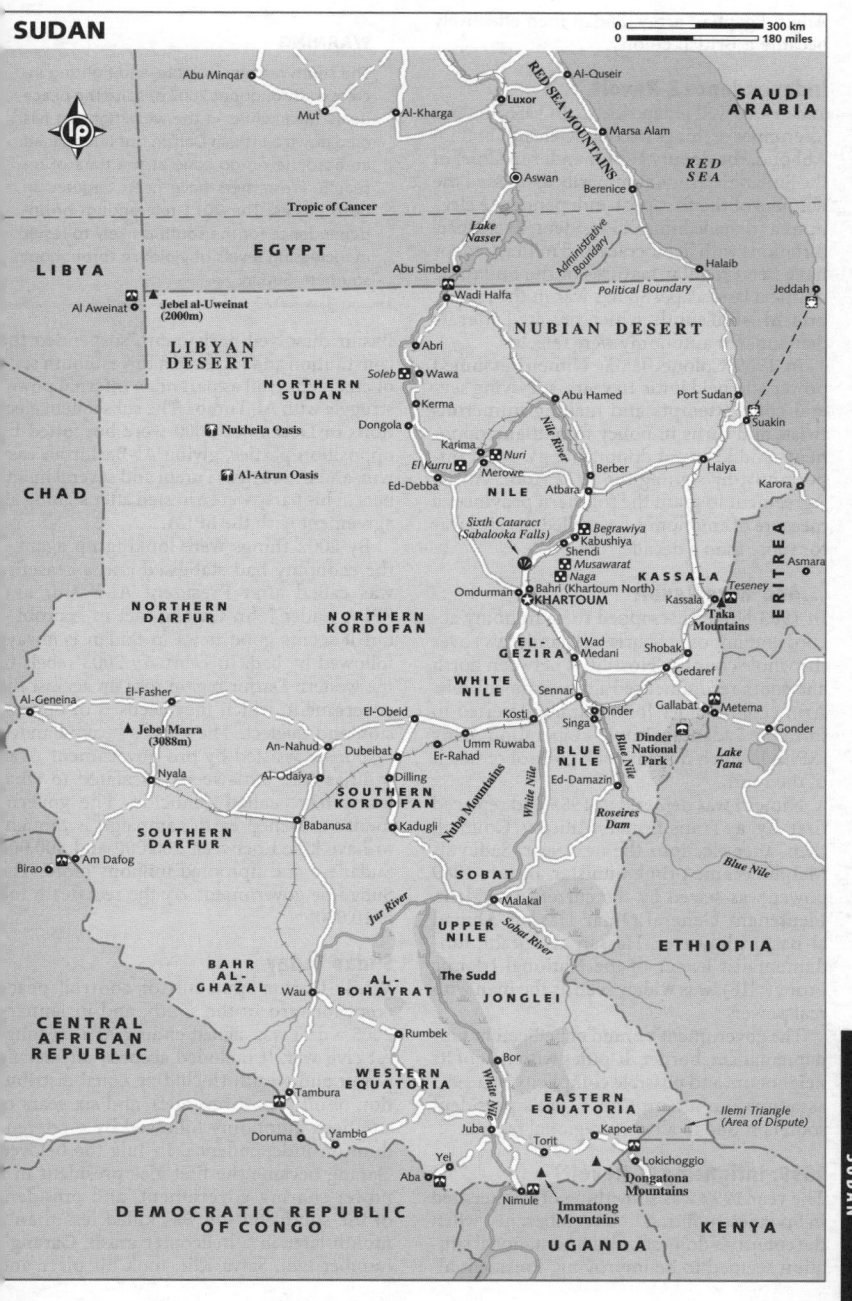

Anglo-Egyptian army. Sudan then effectively became a British colony.

Independence & Revolt

Sudan achieved independence in 1956, but in a forerunner of things to come, General Ibrahim Abboud, the deputy Commander in Chief of the Sudanese army, summarily dismissed the winners of the first post-independence elections and made himself President. Ever since, flirtations with democracy and military coups have been regular features of the Sudanese political landscape. So has war in the mostly non-Muslim south, which revolted after its demands for autonomy were rejected.

In 1969 Colonel Jaafar Nimeiri assumed power and held it for 16 years, surviving several coup attempts and making numerous twists and turns in policy to outflank opponents and keep aid donors happy. Most importantly, by signing the 1972 Addis Ababa Agreement to grant the southern provinces a measure of autonomy, he quelled the civil war for more than a decade.

...And More Revolt

In 1983 Nimeiri scrapped the autonomy accord and imposed Sharia'a (Islamic law) over the whole country. Hostilities between north and south recommenced almost immediately. Army commander John Garang deserted to form the Sudanese People's Liberation Army (SPLA), which quickly took control of much of the south.

Nimeiri was deposed in 1985 and replaced first by a Transitional Military Council, then, after elections the next year, Sadiq al-Mahdi became prime minister. In July 1989 power was seized by the current president, Lieutenant General Omar Hassan Ahmad al-Bashir; however, Hassan al-Turabi, fundamentalist leader of the National Islamic Front (NIF), was widely seen as the man with real power.

The government's brand of belligerent fundamentalism, border disputes with half of its neighbours and possible complicity in a 1995 assassination attempt on Egypt's president soon cost Sudan all of its regional friends.

1999: Infighting (& Revolt)

The year 1999 was something of a watershed in Sudanese politics: in December, just when the country's domestic and international situation seemed to be improving, President al-

---

WARNING

The south remains volatile, and fighting increased throughout 2009 despite the peace deals. Meanwhile, in the west, fighting has died down a little in Darfur, but it remained an absolute no-go zone at the time of research. Westerners have been targeted in both places. The 2011 referendum on independence for the south is likely to result in increasing levels of violence throughout southern Sudan.

Bashir dissolved parliament, suspended the constitution and imposed a three-month state of emergency; all as part of an internal power struggle with Al-Turabi. The subsequent elections in December 2000 were boycotted by opposition parties, giving Al-Bashir an easy win, and in 2001 Al-Turabi and several members of his party were arrested after signing an agreement with the SPLA.

By 2002 things were looking up again – the economy had stabilised and a ceasefire was called after President Al-Bashir and SPLA leader John Garang met in Nairobi – but it seems good news in Sudan is always followed by bad. In February 2003 rebels in the western Darfur region rose up against the government, which they accused of oppression and neglect. The army's heavy-handed response, assisted by pro-government Arab militias (the Janjaweed), escalated to what many have called genocide. The government's scorched-earth campaign is thought to have killed between 200,000 and 400,000 Sudanese and uprooted millions more. The Sudanese government say the real death toll is 10,000.

Sudan Today

While Darfur spun out of control, peace crept forward in the south, and in January 2005 a deal was signed ending Africa's longest civil war. It included accords on sharing power and wealth (including equal distribution of oil export revenue), and six years of southern autonomy followed by a referendum on independence. In July the beloved Garang became the first vice president in a power-sharing government, and president of the south, but he was killed less than a month later in a helicopter crash. Garang's number two, Salva Kiir, took his place and has earned international praise for his more diplomatic stance than his predecessor.

By 2009 more twists and turns had developed. In March of that year an international arrest warrant was issued for Al-Bashir after the International Criminal Court accused him of war crimes and crimes against humanity in Darfur. However, both the African Union and the Arab League have condemned the arrest warrant. Ironically the warrant was issued just as things were finally starting to calm down in Darfur, but equally ironically violence has now flared up again in the south. In the first eight months of 2009 more people are said to have been killed in fighting in southern Sudan than in Darfur and southern political and tribal leaders accuse the government in Khartoum of fuelling this violence. Whatever the truth of the matter, with national elections scheduled for April 2010 and a full referendum for the south on independence in January 2011, the potential for disaster remains very high.

CULTURE

Sudan's 41 million people are divided into hundreds of ethnic groups. Some 75% of Sudan's population, including around two million nomads, live in rural areas and agriculture still employs 80% of the workforce. About 70% of the population is Muslim (Sunnis, mostly), although the south is dominated by traditional animists (25%) and Christians (around 5%). Despite their differences, hospitality is a key concept for all Sudanese, and wherever you go you'll constantly find people paying for things for you, sharing meals or even inviting you to stay in their homes!

Although there are differing perspectives on the issue, the reunification of north and south is on everybody's mind. Northerners hope peace will bring back 'the old and nice days' when the economy was strong, while southerners talk of a 'new Sudan'. The more practical minded in both halves are dreaming of money: peace brings many new business opportunities.

Sharia'a is not as strictly enforced as it once was. Alcohol is pretty easy to find (foreigners are usually spared the 40 lashes Sudanese get when caught with it), and there is much more of a sense of ease in the air. As one Sudanese man put it, there are 'a lot more beautiful women on the streets of Khartoum these days'.

FOOD & DRINK

Sudanese food isn't particularly varied – the staples are *fuul* (stewed brown beans) and *ta'amiya,* known elsewhere as falafel. Outside the larger towns you'll find little else.

Meat dishes include *kibda* (liver), shish kebabs and *shwarma,* hunks of chicken or lamb sliced fresh from the classic roasting spit. Along the Nile you can find excellent fresh perch.

Tea is the favourite drink, served as *shai saada* (black, sometimes spiced), *shai bi-laban* (with milk) or *shai bi-nana* (with mint). Also common is *qahwa turkiya* (Turkish coffee) and *jebbana* (spiced coffee), served in distinctive clay or metal pots and spiked with cardamom, cinnamon or ginger. Local fruit juices are usually made with untreated water or ice.

THE GREATEST SHOW ON EARTH?

So you've heard all about the wildebeest migration in Kenya and Tanzania and how it's been described as the greatest wildlife show on earth. Well, have you heard about Sudan's own wildlife migration involving possibly even larger numbers of animals? When the Wildlife Conservation Society conducted aerial surveys of southern Sudan in 2007, the last thing they expected to find were migrating herds of over a million white-eared kob, tiang antelope and Mongalla gazelle, but that's exactly what they found. The Sudd, where the White Nile turns into a vast area of marshy grassland, has always been a barrier between north and south and is considered one of the largest and least known wildernesses in Africa. It was thought that 25 years of war would have destroyed animal populations in this region – but not so. In addition to the antelope and gazelle there are thought to be over 8000 elephants, 8900 buffalo and 2800 ostriches as well as lions, leopards, giraffe, hippos and numerous other species. Of course, it's not all good news – with development taking place all across the south, it's going to take a concerted effort from the Sudanese government and international conservation bodies to preserve what scientists are now describing as the 'Greatest wildlife show on earth'.

Sharia'a law means that alcohol is hard to come by in the north the country, but the opposite is true in the south. Non-Muslims are exempt from Sharia's law; however, we wouldn't recommend getting caught with alcohol in the north, where the penalty is 40 lashes.

ENVIRONMENT

Northern and western Sudan are vast, desolate areas of desert that support little life, and Nubia in the northeast is semidesert. Except for a few mountain ranges, the country is largely flat. The Nuba mountains are a surprising splash of green among the desert beiges while the far south positively glows in green. Sudan was once crawling with animals big and small, but years of hunting and war have obliterated Sudan's wildlife and wildlife conservation remains way down the government's list of priorities. It's not all bad news though, the swamps of the Sudd are rumoured to be home to hundreds of thousands of antelope (see the boxed text, p199), and Dinder National Park near the Ethiopian border is seeing a resurgence of governmental interest, which in turn is drawing back a few hardy tourists (and hopefully even animals!).

KHARTOUM

pop 8 million (Greater Khartoum)
Built where the two Niles meet, Khartoum defies expectations. Rather than the run-down, undeveloped city many people imagine, Khartoum is a boisterous, modern, flashy city with an ever-increasing number of glass tower blocks altering its skyline. As well as an excellent museum, some fascinating souqs and Nile-side views, Khartoum's good facilities, hospitable people and laid-back vibe mean that most people find it an agreeable place to come to terms with being in Sudan.

ORIENTATION

Three cities sit at the confluence of the White and Blue Niles: Khartoum, Bahri (Khartoum North) and Omdurman, each separated by an arm of the river. You'll find everything you need in central Khartoum; continuing south, the city gets more upscale and international.

INFORMATION

Al-Faisal Hospital (Map p202; ☎ 0183789555; al-Isbitalya St) Has a 24-hour casualty centre.

Central Bookshop (Map p202; al-Jamhurya St) Stocks English-language novels.
Main post office (Map p202; al-Khalifa St) The place to send parcels from.

Cultural Centres
British Council (Map p202; ☎ 0187028000; Abo Sin St)
French Cultural Centre (Map p202; ☎ 0183798035; Ali Dinar St)
Goethe-Institut Khartoum (Map p202; ☎ 0183777833; al-Mek Nimir St)

Internet Access
There are internet cafes everywhere in Khartoum and connections are usually good. Most midrange to top-end hotels also have internet access – often via wi-fi. The following two are conveniently close to the budget hotels.
Marfa Net (Map p202; al-Sharif al-Hindi St; per hr S£2)
Net Gate (Map p202; 2nd fl, al-Sharif al-Hindi St; per hr S£2; ☒ 8am-10pm) Located at the back of the building.

Money
The following all do foreign exchange.
Alamon Exchange Al-Baladyya St (Map p202); Sayyd Abd al-Rahman St (Map p202) Agents for Travelex money transfers. There are branches throughout the city but these are the two most convenient ones in the city centre.
Bank of Khartoum (Map p202; al-Barlman St)
Blue Nile Mashreg Bank (Map p202; al-Barlman St) Handles Western Union money transfers.
Sudanese-French Bank (Map p202; al-Quasar St)
UAExchange (Map p202; al-Jamhurya St) Agents for Travelex money transfers. There are also other branches throughout the city.

Travel Agents
There are a cluster of travel agencies selling plane tickets around the EgyptAir office on al-Barlman St; another option is **Air Handling** (Map p202; ☎ 0183780364; al-Jamhurya St).

DANGERS & ANNOYANCES
Khartoum has to be one of the safest cities in Africa. Petty crime is rare, although, as a 'rich' foreigner, care should be taken in crowded areas. Violent crime against foreigners is virtually unheard of.

There is a risk of terrorist acts and you should keep away from political gatherings and demonstrations.

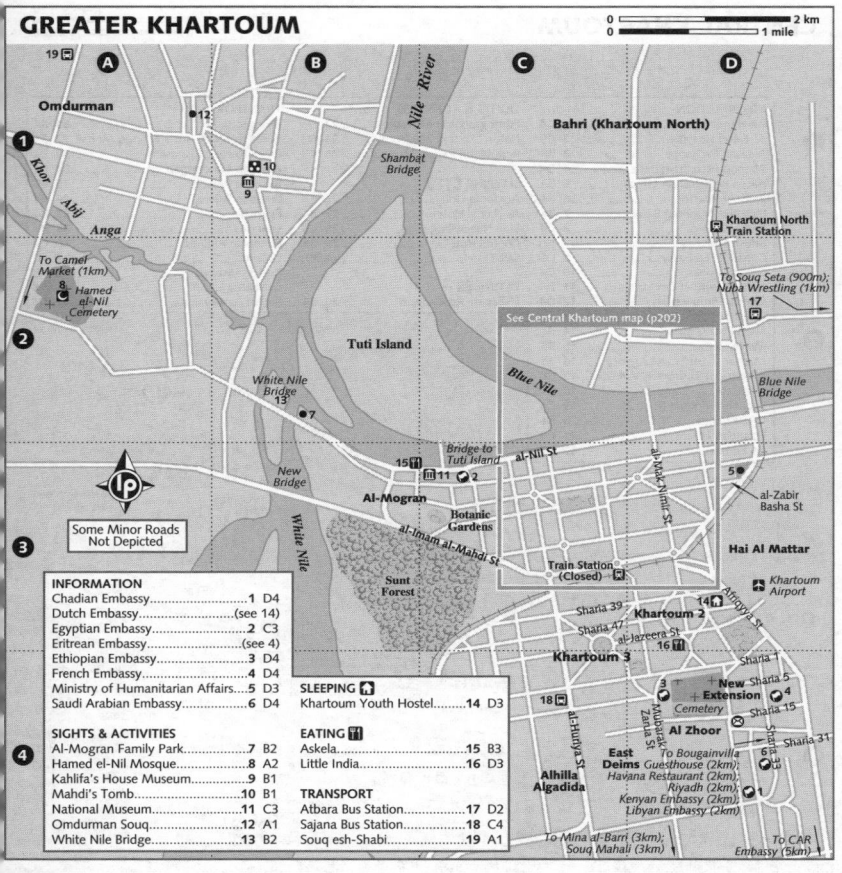

GREATER KHARTOUM

INFORMATION
Chadian Embassy	**1** D4
Dutch Embassy	(see 14)
Egyptian Embassy	**2** C3
Eritrean Embassy	(see 4)
Ethiopian Embassy	**3** D4
French Embassy	**4** D4
Ministry of Humanitarian Affairs	**5** D4
Saudi Arabian Embassy	**6** D4

SIGHTS & ACTIVITIES
Al-Mogran Family Park	**7** B2
Hamed el-Nil Mosque	**8** A2
Kahlifa's House Museum	**9** B1
Mahdi's Tomb	**10** B1
National Museum	**11** C3
Omdurman Souq	**12** A1
White Nile Bridge	**13** B2

SLEEPING
Khartoum Youth Hostel	**14** D3

EATING
Askela	**15** B3
Little India	**16** D3

TRANSPORT
Atbara Bus Station	**17** D2
Sajana Bus Station	**18** C4
Souq esh-Shabi	**19** A1

SIGHTS

The **National Museum** (Map p201; al-Nil St; admission S£1; ☼ 8.30am-6.30pm, closed noon-3pm Fri & Mon) has some fine exhibits, notably some Pharaonic stone carvings and stunning Christian frescoes. Outside are some temples rescued, Abu Simbel–style (see p118), from the rising waters of Lake Nasser. The previously superb **Ethnographical Museum** (Map p202; al-Jamia St) was closed for major renovations when we went past. There was no indication of when, or if, it will reopen. The mostly unlabelled taxidermied animals in the **Natural History Museum** (Map p202; al-Jamia St; admission free; ☼ 8.30am-6pm Tue-Sun, closed noon-3pm Fri) look happier than the handful of live ones in sorry cages outside. The **Republican Palace Museum** (Map p202; al-Jamia St; admission free; ☼ 9am-1pm & 4-8pm Wed & Fri-Sun) is a hall of heroes, of sorts, with mementos such as presidential limos and General Gordon's piano.

The confluence of the Blue and White Niles, best seen from the **White Nile Bridge** (Map p201), is a languid high point of the world's longest river. You can actually see the different colours of each Nile flowing side by side before blending further downstream – although neither are blue or white! Don't attempt to take a photograph of the Nile from this bridge; numerous foreigners have been arrested for doing so. For an original perspective, and a hassle-free photography one, try the fast-moving Ferris wheel in the **Al-Mogran Family Park** (Map p201; al-Nil St; admission S£3; ☼ 10am-11pm) or

SUDAN

CENTRAL KHARTOUM

0 — 400 m
0 — 0.2 miles

INFORMATION
Air Handling..........................1 C4
Al-Faisal Hospital.................2 C5
Alamon Exchange................3 B5
Alamon Exchange................4 D4
Aliens Registration Office....5 B3
Bank of Khartoum................6 B4
Blue Nile Mashreg Bank.......7 B4
British Council......................8 C4
British Embassy...............(see 12)
Canadian Embassy...............9 D5
Central Bookshop................10 C4
French Cultural Centre........11 D4
German Embassy.................12 D4
Goethe Institut Khartoum....13 D4
Main Post Office.................14 B3
Marfa Net...........................15 B4
Mashansharti Travel Agency..16 B5
Ministry of Tourism & Wildlife..17 C4
Net Gate............................18 B4
Sudanese-French Bank........19 C4
UAExchange.......................20 B4
Ugandan Embassy...............21 C4
US Embassy.......................22 A4

SIGHTS & ACTIVITIES
Ethnographical Museum........23 D3
Natural History Museum........24 D3
Republican Palace Museum....25 C3

SLEEPING 🏠 🏔
Acropole Hotel....................26 C4
Al-Nakhil Hotel....................27 B4
Blue Nile Sailing Club..........28 C3
Central Hotel......................29 B5
Salli Hotel......................(see 29)

EATING 🍴
El-Zaeam Restaurant...........30 B4

TRANSPORT
Buses to Bahri....................31 B4
Buses to Khartoum 2 & Souq Mahali..32 B4
Buses to New Extension........33 B4
Buses to Omdurman.............34 B4
Buses to Riyadh..................35 B5
Buses to Sajana..................36 B4
EgyptAir.............................37 B4
Emirates............................38 B4
Ethiopian Airlines................39 C4
Gulf Air........................(see 41)
Kenya Airways....................40 A5
Lufthansa..........................41 B4
Sudan Airways...................42 D4

rent a boat (from S£200 per hour) from the Blue Nile Sailing Club (opposite).

The traditional Muslim city of **Omdurman** (Map p201), founded by the Mahdi in the 1880s, is a big attraction; the famous **Omdurman souq** (Map p201) – the largest in the country – has an amazing variety of wares. The **camel market** (Souq Moowaileh; off Map p201) on the far west-

ern edge of the city is equally spectacular, especially on Saturday, but there is no public transport. The rocket-topped **Mahdi's Tomb** (Map p201; admission free; 🕒 8am-5pm Fri) is worth making the effort to see, though foreigners aren't always allowed inside. The original was destroyed on Kitchener's orders by General Gordon's nephew 'Monkey', who, somewhat unsportingly, threw the Mahdi's ashes into the Nile! The Mahdi's successor lived across the street, and the 1887 **Khalifa's House Museum** (Map p201; admission S£1; 8am-6pm Tue-Thu, Sat & Sun) showcases the history of the Mahdi era.

Every Friday afternoon you can see the **Halgt Zikr**, where a colourful local troupe of whirling dervishes stirs up the dust in worship of Allah at Omdurman's **Hamed el-Nil Mosque** (Map p201). Things start at 4pm, but don't really get going until about 5.30pm (5pm in winter) and they don't dance during Ramadan. If you're used to the dour colours of Arabian Islam, you'll find the circus-like atmosphere here refreshingly colourful and laid-back. Over in **Bahri** (Map p201; take a minibus from UN square to Omdurman getting off at Ghobba al-Hamed al-Nil), traditional **Nuba wrestlers** (Souq Seta; admission S£2) go through their paces at roughly the same time. They're both very friendly occasions.

SLEEPING

Blue Nile Sailing Club (Map p202; 0912350778; al-Nil St; campsite per person S£25) Most overlanders pitch their tents here, but few enjoy the experience. The place is very run-down and the manager is never around. We went past several times; the guard told us the above rates but we were unable to contact the manager or a receptionist to confirm.

Salli Hotel (Map p202; 0919214800; Abdul al-Munami Mhammad St; s/d S£25/45) A friendly place with colourful mosaics on the wall and basic but perfectly habitable rooms. It's perfect for someone with a cold – they won't be able to smell the stench emanating from the communal toilets.

Khartoum Youth Hostel (Map p201; 0912500322; info@sudaneseyha.net; Sharia 47; dm S£35;) This is a slick and clean budget option, and some rooms contain just two beds. There's a relaxing garden, spotless shared bathrooms and enthusiastic staff.

Al-Nakhil Hotel (Map p202; 0183786709; al-Sharif al-Hindi St; s with/without air-con S£40/25, d with/without air-con S£50/40;) Aside from some market noise that might make lie-ins a wistful dream, this is a decent cheapie with clean and spacious rooms. The ones with air-con are particularly good value.

Central Hotel (Map p202; 0918030986; Abdul al-Munami Mhammad St; s/d S£75/85;) Osman, the owner, runs a spiffy joint here and it's probably the best budget hotel in town. If

you're travelling alone it's worth splashing out on a double as you get a much bigger and brighter room.

Bougainvilla Guesthouse (off Map p201; 0183222104; www.bougainvillaguesthouse.com; Block 21; s with/without bathroom US$110/70, d with/without bathroom US$154/126;) This Norwegian-owned hotel, with its family atmosphere, in the upscale Riyadh neighbourhood has comfortable rooms, a rooftop restaurant and bar, and staff who are on the ball with tourist information. It's very popular so book ahead. Staff can also help organise visas and car hire.

Acropole Hotel (Map p202; 0183772860; www.acropolekhartoum.com; al-Ziber Basha St; d without bathroom incl breakfast/full board US$96/121, d with bathroom incl breakfast/full board US$116/141;) This hotel, the first choice of journalists, reeks of history and intrigue, and although its youthful days are long gone, its old-fashioned charm means it's still the most memorable place to stay.

EATING

The many informal, cheap joints south of Al-Kabir Mosque and around al-Tijani al Mahi St serve the staples for S£1 per plate, and plenty of larger restaurants throughout the city centre also serve kebabs, burgers and *shwarma* for around S£1 to S£3. As a rule they're all pretty much of a muchness.

El-Zaeam Restaurant (Map p202; UN Sq; mains S£2; breakfast, lunch & dinner) On the northern side of UN Sq, this place is popular with the city's youngsters. It's a fast food–style place where you select your preferred poison (chicken, falafel, *fuul* etc) from one of several booths.

Little India (Map p201; al-Jazeera St, Khartoum 2; mains S£10-25; lunch & dinner) Expensive but wonderful Indian, Thai and continental cuisine.

Askela (Map p201; al-Nil St; mains up to S£25; breakfast, lunch & dinner) A large riverside restaurant opposite the National Museum, with plenty of fish on the menu and wonderful views. It's also a great place for an evening drink.

Havana Restaurant (off Map p201; Airiyad Almashtal St; mains S£25; breakfast, lunch & dinner Sat-Thu, dinner Fri) Out in the Riyadh neighbourhood, this friendly and informal Lebanese restaurant serves up huge piles of decent nosh, including excellent fresh salads, mixed grills and hummus.

GETTING THERE & AWAY
Air
See p211 for flight information to destinations throughout Africa and the rest of the world.

SUDAN

A flash new international airport is due to open in 2010, 22km south of Khartoum. After this the old airport will be used for domestic flights only.

Bus

Most road transport departs from one of four bus stations. Almost everything rolling south, east and west – including for Gedaref, Kassala and Port Sudan – goes from the modern and chaotic Mina al-barri (off Map p201) near Souq Mahali in southern Khartoum. There's a S£1.50 entrance fee even if you're just reserving a ticket. The Sajana bus station (Map p201) serves Dongola and Wadi Halfa; Karima, Merowe, El-Obeid, Dilling and further Dongola buses use Omdurman's Souq esh-Shabi (Map p201); and the Atbara bus station (Map p201) is in Bahri.

GETTING AROUND

Buses (S£0.40 to S£0.80) and minibuses (S£0.80 to S£1.50) cover most points in Khartoum and run early to very late. See the Central Khartoum map (Map p202) for major departure points.

Taxi prices (if they have no passengers the minibuses work like taxis and often cost less) are negotiable: expect to pay around S£5 to S£10 for journeys within the city centre and S£20 to S£30 for destinations within greater Khartoum. For shorter trips (except in central Khartoum) there are also cheaper motorised rickshaws.

You have more chance of building a snowman in the Sahara than persuading a taxi driver to take you the short distance from the airport to downtown for anything less than S£35.

AROUND KHARTOUM

MEROE SITES

Seemingly lost under the folds of giant apricot-coloured dunes, the ancient royal cemetery of **Begrawiya** (admission S£20; ☺ 6am-6pm), with its clusters of narrow pyramids blanketing the sand-swept hills, is one of the most spectacular sights in Sudan – and the best thing is that you'll probably have the place largely to yourself. The Meroitic Pharaohs thrived from 592 BC until they were overrun by the Abyssinians in AD 350. Some

of the tombs' antechambers contain well-preserved hieroglyphics. You can also visit the remains of the **Royal City** across the highway, where the so-called Roman bath is the top attraction.

Two other Meroitic sites, **Naga** (admission S£20) and **Musawarat** (admission S£20), lie in an area of wild and remote desert 35km off the highway southeast of Shendi, and are about the same distance from each other. Naga's Lion Temple has wonderful exterior carvings, while the crumbling foundations in Musawarat's enormous Great Enclosure let you imagine how this former pilgrimage site once looked. Check out the former elephant stables and the marriage room with the engravings of newlyweds 'getting to know one and other'.

If you want to catch the sunset over the Begrawiya pyramids, you can camp in the desert (head towards the mountains) or splash out at the **Meroe Tented Camp** (☎ 0183487961; www.italtoursudan.com; s/d incl 2 meals S£450/500), close to the pyramids, which has 10 comfy walk-in safari-style tents with private bathrooms. Much cheaper *lokanda*-style accommodation can be found in Shendi.

These ruins are easily visited from Khartoum. If you hire a car and driver (starting at about S£265 plus fuel), you can visit the **Sixth Cataract (Sabalooka Falls)**, too. A pickup truck in Shendi should cost around half that. Begrawiya is just 700m off the highway and easily reached by public transport: take an Atbara bus (S£20) from Bahri and ask to be let out at Al-Ahram (Pyramids). Coming back, flag down vehicles heading south; you'll probably have to change in Shendi. Note that while most tourists refer to the pyramids at Begrawiya as Meroe, if you were to tell a Sudanese person that you want to go to Meroe, you'll probably end up by the dam near Karima!

NORTHERN SUDAN

WADI HALFA

pop 15,725

Founded by a handful of Nubian families from the original Halfa (now buried under Lake Nasser) who resisted the government's forced relocation, Wadi Halfa is where the ferry to Egypt docks. And that's really about all that can be said for the place!

The biggest difference between the half-dozen or so rough **lokandas** (dm S£7) is the names – snag the first bed you can find when the ferry is in town because they fill fast.

Most transport runs in line with the ferry, though the weekly plane from Khartoum (S£270, two hours) comes on Wednesday (if it comes at all). You can get off the boat and right onto a bus to Khartoum (S£85, 24 hours) or, better, make the journey in stages (Dongola S£50). Otherwise take the train (1st/2nd class S£80/70, 36 to 50 hours), which supposedly leaves on Wednesday, but the reality is often rather different.

WADI HALFA TO DONGOLA

Hundreds of historic sites and some striking desert and river scenery line this 400km stretch of the Nile, while the many villages offer a fascinating taste of Nubian life. Travel can be tough through here, but it's the highlight of Sudan for many visitors.

The first significant town is **Abri** (market day is Monday), the base for visiting **Sai Island** (admission S£20), 10km south. With a temple from Egypt's Middle Kingdom, a medieval church and an Ottoman fort among the many ruins, Sai Island is something of a synopsis of ancient Sudanese history. None of the sites are in good condition, but walking between them is fun. **El-Fager** (dm S£7), Abri's only *lokanda*, can't be described as the nicest hotel we've ever seen.

A little further south, easily reached by boat from Wawa, **Soleb** (admission S£20) is not only one of the few west-bank sites in good enough condition to warrant a visit, it is the only one easy to reach without your own transport. It was built in the 14th century BC by Amenhotep III, the same Pharaoh who gave us Luxor in Egypt, and the design and carvings are similar.

Kerma (market day Sunday) was an important trade centre during Egypt's Middle Kingdom and is presumed to have been the capital of the first Kingdom of Kush. Around 2400 BC Kerma's kings built two giant mud-brick temples, known as **deffufas** (admission S£20). The western *deffufa*, a 15-minute *boksi* (Toyota pick-up; plural *bokasi*) ride and 15-minute walk away from town, stood about 19m high and stretched 50m long. Today it has crumbled into an oddly appealing form and you can still climb to the top. There's a new **museum** (admission S£5; ☾ 4-7pm Tue-Sun) next door that contains interesting relics from the site. Few people visit the smaller, eastern *def-*

fufa, about 3km away; many locals don't even know that it exists, which makes finding it difficult. The **Kerma Hotel** (dm S£7) is a pretty grim *lokanda*, but the town's Nile-side restaurants sort of compensate. At the time of research a new hotel was being constructed next to the museum.

Buses and *bokasi* run fairly frequently between all these towns and Dongola and Wadi Halfa.

DONGOLA

Famous for its palm groves, the relaxed little town of Dongola is full of character and boasts good amenities. The east-bank ruins of the **Temple of Kawa**, which are almost totally buried under sand, are about 4km south of the bus station. Many people find the two-hour walk there along the banks of the Nile more of a highlight than the temple.

Most hotels and restaurants are clustered together on the main road, near the market. **Lord Hotel** (☎ 0915586888; dm/s/d S£10/15/20) stands head and shoulders above all the other *lokandas* in town. Rooms are well looked after, come in a range of styles and some have bathroom. The owner will do all he can to help passing tourists. The extension being tacked onto the top of the **Al-Muallem** (☎ 024724425; r S£55) was putting some rather scary cracks in the walls of this hotel but, assuming it hasn't collapsed in the meantime, you'll find the town's tidiest rooms here, as well as an excellent downstairs restaurant.

Buses run to Kerma (S£7, one hour), Karima (S£15, 2½ hours) and Khartoum (S£35, seven hours). The road to Karima might now be fast and smooth, but that doesn't take anything away from the feeling of utter awe felt while crossing the terrifyingly bleak desert between Dongola and Karima.

KARIMA

Karima itself is just a dusty Nile-side Nubian village. If it weren't for its extraordinary collection of ancient sites, which together have given the whole area Unesco World Heritage status, there would be little reason to stop here. As it is though, the majesty of Karima's past will probably remain with you for a long time. **Jebel Barkal**, the table-topped mountain hanging on the town's south side, was sacred ground for the Egyptians at the time of the 18th-dynasty Pharaohs and has some well-preserved **pyramids** and a **temple complex** around it. It costs S£20 to enter the fresco-decorated **Temple of Mut**, but otherwise the sites are free. Don't miss watching the pyramids turn to a rusty gold at sunset. The **museum** (admission S£5; ☾ 8am-3pm Sat-Thu) is also pretty good.

Across the river at **Nuri** (admission S£20; ☾ 6am-6pm), there are some delightfully dilapidated pyramids – among the largest in Sudan – lost among a stormy sea of orange sand. Take a minibus (S£2, 30 minutes) from Karima. **El Kurru** (admission S£20), 20km south of Karima, has twin tombs cut into the rock, with wonderful paintings. Again, take a minibus (S£20, 30 minutes) from Karima; buy the ticket from the museum in Karima in advance.

The lovely **Nubian Rest-House** (☎ 0231820368; www.italtoursudan.com; s/d incl 2 meals S£450/500) is a mud-brick Nubian-style structure built around lush, flowering gardens at the foot of Jebel Barkal. If you can't afford this, the best place to stay, although still a little overpriced, is **Ahmed Mousa Homestay** (☎ 0912585462; r S£75). Ahmed has a couple of clean rooms with fans set around a sandy, chicken-filled courtyard. The communal bathrooms are spotless. You can normally find him at the ticket office for the museum where he works. **Al Nasser** (dm/tw S£5/20) is a cleaner and greener *lokanda* than most. Many of Karima's restaurants fill a block on a nearby street. **Al-Taybat** (sign in Arabic only; mains S£3-7) is the best place to eat – as well as superb *fuul*, it has fruit salads with jelly!

There are frequent buses to Dongola (S£20, 2½ hours) and Atbara (S£30, four hours), as well as less-common ones to Khartoum (S£30, 16 to 20 hours) and Wadi Halfa (S£70, 16 to 20 hours).

ATBARA
pop 111,339

Hot, dusty, noisy – and did we mention hot? Atbara is not a place that many people would wish to linger in. Fortunately, with Sudan's ever-improving transport infrastructure you're unlikely to need to spend longer than a night here. The town makes a good base for the pyramids at Begrawiya.

Close to the Bank of Khartoum, **Nahar Atb Hotel** (r S£30) is your usual dusty *lokanda*. The bright and friendly **Nile Hotel** (☎ 0912994029; s/d S£42/70; ☒) is a bit of a hike north of the town centre, but it has smart, clean rooms, with hot water in the shared showers. There's a pretty garden to kick back in and meals can be prepared with notice. By far the best rooms can be found at the excellent **Al-Asfia A Hotel** (☎ 0912343910; r S£140; ☒ ▣ ☏), close to the railway lines on the southern edge of town. As well as spick-and-span rooms, they also throw in friendly banter with the manager, wi-fi and a decent restaurant into the bargain.

There are many buses to Khartoum (S£20, 4½ hours) and several through the desert to Port Sudan (S£40, six hours), plus *bokasi* to Karima (S£30, four hours).

EASTERN SUDAN

KASSALA
pop 420,000

Kassala, with its wonderful setting at the foot of the melting granite peaks of the Taka Mountains, is where half the tribes of northern Sudan seem to meet. Its huge souqs are an ethnic mosaic of colours, smells, noises and experiences. All this makes it one of the most exotic towns in Sudan. There are famous **camel races** annually in September or October. It's possible to scramble around the bizarre peaks of the **Taka Mountains** and rock climbers can have a field day on the sheer-sided peaks.

At the base of the mountains is the **Khatmiyah Mosque**, centre of the Khatmiyah Sufi sect. It's a lovely mud-brick building and non-Muslims are quite welcome to take a peek about.

The colourful **Toteel Hotel** (r S£25) is a good budget option. Nearby, **El-Nada Tourism Hotel** (☎ 041122280; r with/without bathroom S£65/50; ☒) has spacious rooms with paper-thin mattresses on the beds and cheerful Eritrean staff in reception. The **Hipton Hotel** (☎ 0411822357; r S£72; ☒) has the best-appointed rooms in town and there's a reasonable restaurant on the roof.

Cheap eats abound around town, but clued-up locals insist that the **Lulua Restaurant** (name in Arabic only; mains S£7-15) by the central *bokasi* stand is the bee's knees, and after tasting its delicious chicken tikka we'd be silly to argue. Don't miss the chance to try the brain-bending spicy Eritrean coffee, whose aroma wafts through the streets of Kassala.

Minibuses (S£0.50) and taxis (S£10) shuttle from town to Souq esh-Shabi (about 6km), where the buses to Port Sudan (S£47, six hours) and Khartoum (SD£49, seven hours) arrive and depart. For details on crossing to Eritrea, see p212.

PORT SUDAN
pop 489,275

Sudan's only major industrial port is the base for some of the world's most spectacular and undeveloped diving (see p208). Above the waves, watching ships unload in the port is about as exciting as it gets.

Sleeping & Eating

There are plenty of *lokandas* around the market, with facilities ranging from basic to bomb site.

Saba Hotel (☎ 0311822252; tw from S£20; ⊠) Probably the pick of the cheapies, it's pleased to accept foreign guests and has a range of rooms, from scrappy non-air-con twins up to comfortable triples with little kitchenettes.

Baashar Palace Hotel (☎ 0912334634; s/d from S£175/200; ⊠) This is a sweet deal with spotless, quiet rooms guaranteeing a decent night's sleep. There's a pleasant courtyard garden and a juice bar, and the restaurant conjures up such exotics as curry.

Mercure Hotel (☎ 0311839800; www.mercure.com; s/d from US$175/245; ⊠ ▢ ▨) This fancy-pants business hotel is the place to go to pretend you're not in Sudan anymore.

The area around the local bus station teems with brightly lit, cheap restaurants and juice bars, giving it a fairground atmosphere at night. For something swankier try the clutch of restaurants along the waterfront, which spring to life in the evening and do a good range of meat and fish dishes for a few bucks.

Getting There & Away

Minibuses (S£3, 45 minutes) for Suakin leave from the city centre. The major bus companies serving Kassala (S£47, six hours), Atbara (S£40, six hours) and Khartoum (S£64, 10 hours) have offices in the city centre and at the bus station (Souq esh-Shabi). There are daily flights to/from Khartoum with Sudan Airways and Nova Airlines.

SUAKIN

Suakin was Sudan's only port before the construction of Port Sudan, once handling the thousands of pilgrims bound for Mecca and slaves bound for Jeddah and Cairo. Abandoned in the 1930s, it's now a melancholy ghost town, full of crumbling **coral**

buildings, demonic cats said to be cursed, and circling kites and hawks with a devil's shrill call. The **ruins** (admission S£10; ☾ 6am-6pm), connected to the mainland by a short causeway, are fascinating to explore and the 'modern' town has a delightfully sleepy feel to it. Suakin is best visited as a day trip from Port Sudan.

It's still possible to set sail for Arabia from here; for details, see p211.

SOUTH OF KHARTOUM

WADI MEDANI
pop 315,105

Love is in the air! Wadi Medani, a couple of hours south of Khartoum, is every Sudanese newlywed's favourite honeymoon destination. Though you might not choose it for your honeymoon, it certainly makes a pleasant night stop if you're looping between Kassala and El-Obeid. Its location on the banks of the Blue Nile is romantic even for the single and cynical.

The **Continental Hotel** (☎ 0912362185; r S£85; ⊠) is in a gorgeous old colonial building overlooking the languid Nile. It has giant rooms and a foliage-filled garden.

Set beside the Nile, the excellent-value ourpick **Imperial Hotel** (☎ 09511841501; s/d S£120/105; ⊠ ▢ ⊚) has enormous, cool and clean rooms, very helpful staff, wi-fi and a good restaurant serving more than the staples.

Buses head to Khartoum (S£15), Kassala (S£37) and El-Obeid (S£44).

GEDAREF

The busy market and farming town of Gederef lies just a couple of hours from the main border crossing into Ethiopia and, if you're heading to or from Ethiopia, you stand a good chance of spending a night here. You wouldn't want to stay any longer!

All accommodation is overpriced. The **El-Hawwad Tourist** (☎ 0912215596; r with/without bathroom S£60/80; ⊠) has small and tatty rooms. The **Al-Motawakhil Hotel** (☎ 0441843232; s/d S£84/124; ⊠) is much plusher, but the manager has clearly modelled his customer-service style on Basil Fawlty and his extraordinary rudeness makes it hard to truly recommend.

SUDAN

Buses run along the smooth new road to Gallabat (the Sudanese border town with Ethiopia) for S£10; the journey takes two hours. Buses to Khartoum cost S£33, and take around 3½ hours.

EL-OBEID
pop 410,000

El-Obeid has long been a prosperous market centre and today over half the world's supply of gum arabic passes through here. The **Shikan Museum** (admission free; ☉ 8am-3pm) has some intriguing displays, including many ancient Nubian pieces. The nearby tan-and-red **El-Obeid Cathedral** is also worth a look.

our pick **Al-Madina Hotel** (☎ 0915181990; zainkoua@ yahoo.com; dm S£20, r without bathroom S£60, r with bathroom from S£130; ☒ 💻) has had a recent major makeover and is easily the smartest boy in town. The swimming pool–blue rooms at the **Kordofan Hotel** (☎ 0915485318; r S£100; ☒) are set around a peaceful garden on the edge of town. If you're looking for a *lokanda* (most priced around S£7 per bed), wander west of the souq until you find an acceptable one; this may take a while as they are all quite grim; the Hotel Lebanon is almost passable.

our pick **Gagdoura Restaurant** (mains S£1-4) is the best by a mile of the numerous basic eateries around the souq. The name is in Arabic only, but it's easy to spot – thanks to the queues of people waiting for a table and the gently cooking chickens, meat and pots full of divine *fuul* bubbling away outside.

Buses go to Khartoum (S£49, seven hours), Kadugli (S£20, four hours) and Dilling (S£11, two hours).

NUBA MOUNTAINS

Smack in the heart of the country, the beautifully green and, in places, forested Nuba Mountains are, in a sense, a gateway to sub-Saharan Africa. This Scotland-sized slab of fertile land is inhabited by the Nuba people, 60-some related tribes and subtribes with as many differences as similarities. During the autumn harvest, generally November to February, you might get to see some of the Nuba's famous festivals (called Sebir), which usually include wrestling and dancing.

The whole region feels like another country altogether from the sandy wastes of northern Sudan. That, of course, is the problem – the Nuba people long fought on the side of the SPLA against the government. With the signing of the peace agreement, parts of the area have recently opened up to intrepid travellers. But there are still several difficulties and dangers, particularly the unexploded ordinance and landmines left behind after the war – get local advice (or find a guide) before leaving any road, and don't climb to the tops of hills. Most villages do not welcome visitors, so you will probably not be allowed to spend the night if you just show up. *Bokasi* connect towns along the highway to some nearby villages, but beyond this you'll need to rely on the occasional truck or walk and bike, as most locals do.

Dilling, at the northern foot of the hills, is a good base and has several interesting villages nearby. For accommodation try the ultrabasic **Wadi Salaam** (☎ 0918116806; dm S£10). Buses run to El-Obeid (S£11, two hours) and Kadugli (S£11, two hours). **Kadugli**, capital of the region and home to UN peacekeepers and a who's who of NGOs, is another good base. The simple **Joes Guest House** (☎ 0924918314; s S£40) is easily the best-value place to stay. Buses go to El-Obeid (S£22, four hours) via Dilling.

SUDAN DIRECTORY

ACCOMMODATION

Due to the influx of oil and aid workers, prices in Sudan have risen sharply over the past few years and you rarely get good value for your money.

The most basic places to stay are called *lokandas,* with beds in shared rooms or courtyards, though you can take all of the beds in a room if you want privacy. It's best to pack a sleep sheet if you will be using them. Women are often not welcome in *lokandas.*

In many cheap and midrange places you'll be asked to register with the police before checking in – whatever time you arrive!

ACTIVITIES

With many sharks, manta rays and incredibly good visibility, Sudan's Red Sea dive sites are as good as Egypt's, but without the crowds. Most people use live-aboard operations based outside the country, but there are some captains in Port Sudan. One recommended operator is **Regal Dive** (☎ 0044 1353 659999; www.regal-diving.co.uk). For local operators try **Sudan Red Sea Resort** (☎ 0912465650; www.sudan

redsearesort.com) and **Arous Resort** (☎ 0912398919; www.arousresort.com).

BUSINESS HOURS

Banking hours are 9am to 12.30pm, while most government, airline and similar offices are usually open until 3pm. Most local shops stay open late, but might close briefly between 1pm and 5pm. Few places open on Friday. Breakfast, which most people take between 9am and 10am, is a Sudanese institution – don't be surprised if that vital functionary isn't at his desk.

DANGERS & ANNOYANCES

While there are still many no-go areas (see the boxed text, p198), the rest of Sudan is a very safe place – one of the safest in Africa, in fact. Crime is almost unheard of – almost: watch your wallet among crowds and lock your luggage in hotels.

EMBASSIES & CONSULATES

The following embassies and consulates can be found in Khartoum.

Canada (Map p202; ☎ 0156550500; Africa Rd)
Central African Republic (CAR; off Map p201; ☎ 0922815860; off Medani Rd, El-Maamoura)
Chad (Map p201; St 57) The embassy was closed at the time of research.
Egypt (Map p201; ☎ 0183777646; al-Nil St)
Eritrea (Map p201; ☎ 0183483834; off Sharia 15, New Extension)
Ethiopia (Map p201; ☎ 0183471379; Khartoum 3)
France (Map p201; ☎ 0183471082; off Sharia 15, New Extension)
Germany (Map p202; ☎ 0183777990; al-Baladyya St)
Kenya (off Map p201; ☎ 0155772801; Riyadh)
Libya (off Map p201; ☎ 0183222457; Mashtel St, Riyadh)
Netherlands (Map p201; ☎ 0183471012; Sharia 47, Khartoum 2)
Saudi Arabia (Map p201; ☎ 0183472583; Sharia 33, New Extension)
Uganda (Map p202; ☎ 0183797869; Abu Qarga St)
UK (Map p202; ☎ 0183777105; al-Baladyya St)
USA (Map p202; ☎ 0187016000; Ali Abdul al-Latif St)

HOLIDAYS

As well as religious holidays in the Africa Directory chapter (p1140), the following are the principal public holidays in Sudan:
Independence Day 1 January
Revolution Day 30 June

PRACTICALITIES

- Sudan uses mostly imperial weights and measures, but distances are measured in kilometres.

- Electricity is 230V/50Hz and plugs usually have two round pins.

- There are several private, English-language daily newspapers, such as *Khartoum Monitor* and *Citizen*, but press freedom is limited.

- Satellite TV is so common that few people watch the three government-owned stations.

- Both the government-owned Omdur-man Radio (95FM) and the BBC World Service (95FM) occasionally broadcast news in English.

INTERNET ACCESS

Internet access is generally very good in Sudan – even in small towns connection speeds are decent and prices low.

MONEY

The official currency is the newly introduced Sudanese Pound (S£/SDG), which is divided into 100 piastres.

Private exchange offices have the same rates as banks, but longer hours. Euros and US dollars are the easiest to change (outside Khartoum you'll be hard pressed to change anything else), though British pounds and most Middle Eastern currencies are widely accepted in Khartoum and Port Sudan. The only way to change Egyptian pounds and Ethiopian Birr is on the black market, which is easy at the borders.

Money can be wired to Khartoum and Port Sudan (even from the US and UK, though this could always change because of sanctions) with Western Union and Travelex. Credit cards and travellers cheques are useless and there are no ATMs accepting foreign cards; bring all the money you might need in cash.

PHOTOGRAPHY

Photo permits are obligatory for foreigners. Get one from Khartoum's **Ministry of Tourism & Wildlife** (Map p202; ☎ 83773711; Abu Sinn St). It's free, but you need a passport photo and copies of your passport and visa.

SUDAN

POST

Mail in and out of Sudan, like the poste restante services throughout the country, is unreliable.

TELEPHONE

Private telephone centres are found all over the country and many in big cities offer Net2phone service for international calls. Mobile phone reception is excellent throughout the country.

TOURS

There are very few local tour operators and of those that exist all are overpriced, disorganised and unreliable and cannot be recommended wholeheartedly. However, in order to obtain a visa you will probably have to deal with one of them. The best of a bad bunch:

Italian Tourism Company (☎ 0183487961; www.italtoursudan.com)

Mashansharti Travel Agency (Map p202; ☎ 0912253484; www.tour-sudan.com; Sati Bldg, cnr Sayyd Abd al-Rahman St and al-Tayyar Izz al-Din St) Note that this agency goes under several names, including Glob Tours and the name of the owner, Midhat Mahir.

VISAS & DOCUMENTS

Everyone, except Egyptians, needs a visa (most people pay US$160; if there is evidence of travel to Israel, you will be denied) and getting one could be the worst part of your trip. Some embassies are easier to deal with than others and in all cases a transit visa (which gives you up to a fortnight to transit the country) is easier to get than a month-long tourist visa. Currently Cairo and Aswan (Egypt) remain the easiest places to get a visa, where they are normally issued in a couple of days. A tourist visa is very hard to get in Addis Ababa (Ethiopia), but transit visas are possible. Recently the embassy in Uganda has been issuing visas on the same day for overland entry through northern Uganda to Juba (and onward to the rest of Sudan – see the boxed text, opposite). In Europe the embassy in London is barely worth bothering with, but the embassy in Paris was issuing tourist visas within 48 hours; in the US it's a slow old process to say the least! Expect all the above information to change constantly. The Thorn Tree forum on Lonely Planet's website (www.lonelyplanet.com/thorntree) is the best place to keep abreast of developments.

If you need a tourist visa rather than a transit visa, it helps to let an agent (see Tours, left, for recommendations) arrange it. Most of the time they will get you a counter visa: they arrange everything at the Ministry of Interior in Khartoum and you pick it up at the airport. This service is likely to cost around US$150 and, if you are lucky, can take as little as two days. The other option, used primarily by those crossing overland – since it costs more is an invitation visa, in which you are sent a number that you give the embassy or consulate that *should* speed up the normal process. With either option, there is a good chance something will go wrong along the way, so get started as early as possible.

If the listed tour companies give you the run around, it's also worth trying some of the hotels in Khartoum. The Bougainvilla Guesthouse (p203) is very helpful in this regard.

Registration

You have to register within three days of arrival in Khartoum, Port Sudan, Gallabat or Wadi Halfa. In Khartoum, go to the **Aliens Registration Office** (Map p202; al-Tayyar Murad St; ☽ 8am-2.15pm); the process costs S£100 and you need one photo and photocopies of your passport and visa (there's a photocopier in the building). If you registered on entry at a land border, you need to do it again in Khartoum, but you don't have to pay again. In many towns you will need to register with the police – this is free.

Travel Permits

A travel permit is required for most journeys outside Khartoum, excepting northern destinations. Take one photo and a copy of your passport and visa to the **Ministry of Humanitarian Affairs** (Map p201; al-Ziber Basha St) and expect to wait 24 hours. Carry photocopies of this permit along with copies of your passport and visa to give to police. Note that a recent ruling says that you must obtain a new travel permit each and every time you re-enter Khartoum, although how anyone knows that you've done this isn't clear.

Visa Extensions

Visa extensions are issued at the Aliens Registration Office (above) in Khartoum. You need one photo and varying amounts of money and patience to get your extra 30 days.

Visas for Onward Travel

Visas for the following neighbouring countries are available from embassies in Khartoum (see p209).

Central African Republic A one-month visa costs US$100; you'll need two photos and it takes two days.

Chad The embassy was closed at the time of research.

Egypt This consulate is not the most organised place – arrive early to beat the worst queues. For most people visas are free but you'll need two photos and staff sometimes ask for a letter of introduction. The visa is ready the same day. It's easier to get a tourist visa on arrival (which most but not all nationalities can do), especially if you're flying.

Eritrea One-month visas cost US$40 and are ready in three days, or pay an extra US$10 for same-day service. You need two photos and a copy of your passport.

Ethiopia Three-month visas cost US$30 and require two photos. You can pick your visa up the same day.

Kenya A single-entry visa valid for three months costs US$50 and is issued the same day. You need one photo and staff sometimes ask for a letter of introduction.

Libya Applications must go through a Libyan travel agent, but you can pick up the visa here.

Saudi Arabia Visa applications are handled by travel agents (many of which surround the embassy), which can get you a transit visa in two days (perhaps one day if you go very early). You need a visa to a neighbouring country (normally Jordan), two photos, a letter of introduction from your embassy and US$100. Visas are not issued during the haj and nor are they issued to unmarried women under 40 unless they are accompanied by their husband or brother (and can prove it).

Uganda Single-entry visas valid for up to three months cost US$30 and are ready in two days. You need two photos.

VOLUNTEERING

The London-based **Sudan Volunteer Programme** (SVP; ☎ 020-7485 8619; www.svp-uk.com) sends people to Sudan to teach English.

TRANSPORT IN SUDAN

GETTING THERE & AWAY

Air

Khartoum is well connected to Africa and the world.

EgyptAir (Map p202; ☎ 0183780064; New Abuella Bldg) Connections to Cairo.

Emirates (Map p202; ☎ 0183799899) Has flights worldwide via the Middle East.

Ethiopian Airlines (Map p202; ☎ 0183762088) Connections to Addis Ababa.

Gulf Air (Map p202; ☎ 0183778503; al-Tayaar Murad St) Flights worldwide via the Middle East.

Kenya Airways (Map p202; ☎ 0183782579; Ali Abdel al-Latif St) Services to Nairobi.

Lufthansa (☎ 0183771322; El Tayar Murad St) Flies to North America via Europe.

Sudan Airways (Map p202; ☎ 0183787544; al-Baladaya St; ⊗ 8am-6pm Sat-Thu, 9-11am Fri) Has frequent flights to north and east Africa and the Middle East, though its competitors usually have similar prices and better service.

Land & Sea

Sudan shares borders with many countries, but there are few crossing options. The south is slowly opening up, but overland travel to the Central African Republic, Kenya and Democratic Republic of Congo remains dangerous and/or difficult. Libya is also risky and, because of that country's travel regulations, would be impractical anyway. The Chadian border is officially closed.

EGYPT

The roads between Sudan and Egypt are for cargo traffic only, but you can take the weekly passenger ferry on Lake Nasser from Wadi Halfa to the port near Aswan in Egypt. It heads north at about 5pm on

---

TRAVEL IN THE SOUTH

Ever so slowly, southern Sudan is opening up to adventurous travellers. It's now possible to travel overland between Uganda and Juba. Direct buses (USh80,000) leave Kampala every day and take 10 hours. Accommodation in Juba is generally very expensive (US$200 to US$300 for a bed in a tent!), but there are a couple of cheaper alternatives opening up, including the **Juba Tourist Motel** (d S£40) near the university. Although buses do now run from Juba to Khartoum (S£200 to S£250, three to four days), the insecurity on this route means that it cannot yet be recommended. Another option is to find a place on a cargo ship sailing up the Nile to Kosti, although as this can take two to three weeks and security is poor, it too is not yet recommended. Flying to Khartoum (around S£450) remains the only realistic (and safe) way of moving on from Juba.

Wednesday (though if the train is delayed, the ferry waits), returning on Monday. The journey takes around 16 hours plus immigration time, and costs S£141/88 in 1st/2nd class. First-class passengers share two-bunk cabins, whereas in 2nd class you fight for seats with hundreds of others. You can buy tickets in Wadi Halfa at the port and from Mashansharti Travel Agency (see p210) in Khartoum.

Vehicles go on the barge attached to the rear of the ferry, but you should arrive in Wadi Halfa several days in advance if you want to do this. **Midhat Mahir** (☎ 0122380740), which is the same company as Mashansharti, has a good reputation for speeding people through the paperwork.

ERITREA

The crossing between Kassala and Teseney is open, but don't start celebrating just yet. Although you can cross the border, actually getting any further into Eritrea remains very difficult as you need a travel permit, which is issued only in Asmara, to travel anywhere else around the country. In effect this ruling makes it impossible for travellers to cross this border!

ETHIOPIA

From Gedaref take a pick-up to the border town of Gallabat (S£10, two hours) and walk over the bridge to Metema, where buses go direct to Gonder (Birr31, seven hours) or, if you miss the bus, you can reach Gonder by changing vehicles in Shihedi.

SAUDI ARABIA

Regular ferry services run between Suakin and Jeddah (1st/2nd class S£215/118, 13 hours). Tickets are available through travel agents in Khartoum and Port Sudan.

GETTING AROUND

Air

Half a dozen airlines connect Khartoum to all large Sudanese cities.

Sudan Airways (Map p202; ☎ 0183787544; al-Baladaya St; ◷ 8am-6pm Sat-Thu, 9-11am Fri) has the most flights and, along with **Marsland** (www.marsland -avi.com), the fewest problems with cancellations and overbookings; though neither company will win a reliability award. There's a domestic airport tax of S£15.

Local Transport

Sudan is undergoing a road-building frenzy and all significant towns northeast of El-Obeid (except Wadi Halfa, although the road between there and Dongola should be completed by the time this book hits the shelves) are now linked by excellent paved roads. Fast comfortable buses have almost totally replaced most of the *bokasi* that formerly bounced over the desert between big northern towns. It's best to buy bus tickets a day in advance.

Train

The only remaining practical passenger service by train is the Khartoum to Wadi Halfa run, though there is also a monthly train from Atbara to Port Sudan and a western line to Nyala. Sleepers and 1st-class seats are expensive but comfortable; 2nd class is bearable; in 3rd class you really get what you paid for!

Tunisia

Tunisia is one of Africa's easiest destinations. Most visitors come here for the long, golden beaches, nonstop summer sunshine and Maghrebi exoticism on tap (package holidaymakers almost outnumber the locals in high summer), but, outside the high season and off the well-trodden routes, it's a surprisingly underrated and often tourist-free destination.

Once-gritty Tunis has refashioned itself as an ambitiously modern capital, though its traditional-Arab and French-colonial pasts still have a powerful, palpable presence. In the north, lakes teem with pink flamingos, surprising deep green forests rise up from a spectacularly beautiful coastline and gentle rolling plains are dotted with olive and citrus trees. On the island of Jerba, sun-bleached roundhouses, soft sand beaches and one of North Africa's last Jewish communities make a fascinating mix. In the south, the traditions of the indigenous Berbers persevere, and the ever-enchanting sands of the Sahara stretch deep into Africa.

Tunisia also has some interesting places to stay: luxury desert digs, revamped ancient inns on the island of Jerba and a growing number of fabulously restored medina town houses.

Economic and political prudence, as well as a commitment to education, has ensured relative prosperity in most parts of the country and, despite a government that keeps firm tabs on its citizens, the much-touted spirit of tolerance and traditional Arab hospitality are ever present. Make the most of it, and discover wonderfully distinct cultures and incredible extremes of landscape, even in just a few short days.

FAST FACTS

- **Area** 164,000 sq km
- **ATMs** In all large towns
- **Borders** Algeria, Libya
- **Budget** TD60 per day
- **Capital** Tunis
- **Languages** Arabic, French
- **Money** Tunisian dinar; US$1 = TD1.3, €1 = TD1.9
- **Population** 10.3 million
- **Seasons** Cool (November to April), warm (May to October)
- **Telephone** Country code ☎ 216; international access code ☎ 00
- **Time** GMT/UTC +1 hour
- **Visa** Unnecessary for most EU, American, Canadian and Japanese citizens; TD40 for Australians and South Africans, available at airport; others need to apply in advance

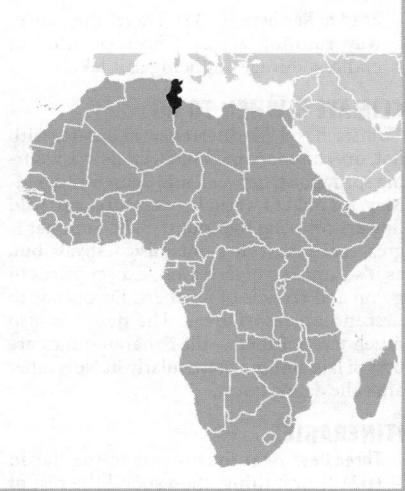

TUNISIA

HIGHLIGHTS

- **Sidi Bou Saïd** (p222) Explore this gorgeous bougainvillea-clad Mediterranean town with views of the intensly blue Gulf of Tunis.
- **Bardo Museum** (p218) Be overwhelmed by the splendour of Roman Africa, and the gorgeous Islamic decoration of the palace in which it's contained.
- **Jerba** (p235) Experience fascinating architecture, great beaches and unusual ethnic diversity.
- **Grand Erg Oriental** (p235) Melt in a Sahara sunset amid dreamy postcard-perfect dunes.
- **Road to Nowhere** (p233) Travel the causeway running across Chott el-Jerid, an endless, mirage-inducing salt lake.

CLIMATE & WHEN TO GO

Tunisia has a Mediterranean climate, with hot, dry summers and mild winters. Visit during springtime, between mid-March and mid-May, for mild to warm temperatures and wild flowers covering the countryside. Summer is great for beach frolics and music festivals, but, as it's Tunisia's high season, expect prices to go up and crowds of northern Europeans to descend on resort areas. The desert is also much too hot then – the Saharan dunes are best in late autumn, particularly in November after the date harvest.

ITINERARIES

- **Three Days** Beat the crowds to the Bardo (p218) first thing, then spend the rest of

the day in the beautiful Tunis suburb of Sidi Bou Saïd (p222), returning to Tunis for dinner in a grand medina restaurant (p221). Next day, head out along the northern coast towards Tabarka (p223). Explore the deep green forests around Ain Draham (p223) and the magnificent underground villas of Bulla Regia (p224) before sunbathing and scuba-diving your way along the coast to Tunis.
- **One Week** Enjoy a few days on Jerba (p235), spending mornings on the beach, middays snoozing and late afternoons exploring the interior. Then head inland to the extraordinary underground Berber houses at Matmata (p235), before heading back along the coast to Tunis, not missing the untouristed medina at Sfax (p231).
- **Two Weeks** Two weeks is a perfect amount of time for incorporating a bit of the north and a lot of the south. Start with Tunis and the north as described above, then drive to the Islamic holy city of Kairouan (p228). From there, head to Mahdia (p230) and enjoy its gorgeous harbour or to El-Jem (p230) for the Roman Empire's third-largest colosseum. Drive down to Jerba (p235) to relax on the island for a few days. Then head to the Sahara, taking in Tataouine and the picturesque *ksour* (castles) district (p238), continuing on to the laid-back Douz (p234). From there, join a tour to the sand sea of the Grand Erg Oriental (p235), or drive through the Chott el-Jerid (p233) to the enormous palmeraie of the oasis town of Tozeur (p233).

HISTORY

Tunisia's long history is a rich and storied one. Nature, luck and canny political stewardship have produced a calm, safe country, despite being the subject of a tug of war between successive great civilisations over the millennia.

Empires Strike Back

The Phoenicians set their sights on Tunisia around 800 BC, and their capital Carthage – today a suburb of Tunis – was the main power in the western Mediterranean by the 6th century BC. The burgeoning Roman Empire became uneasy with a nation of mercantile genius and mercenary strength on its doorstep and 128 years of conflict – including the three

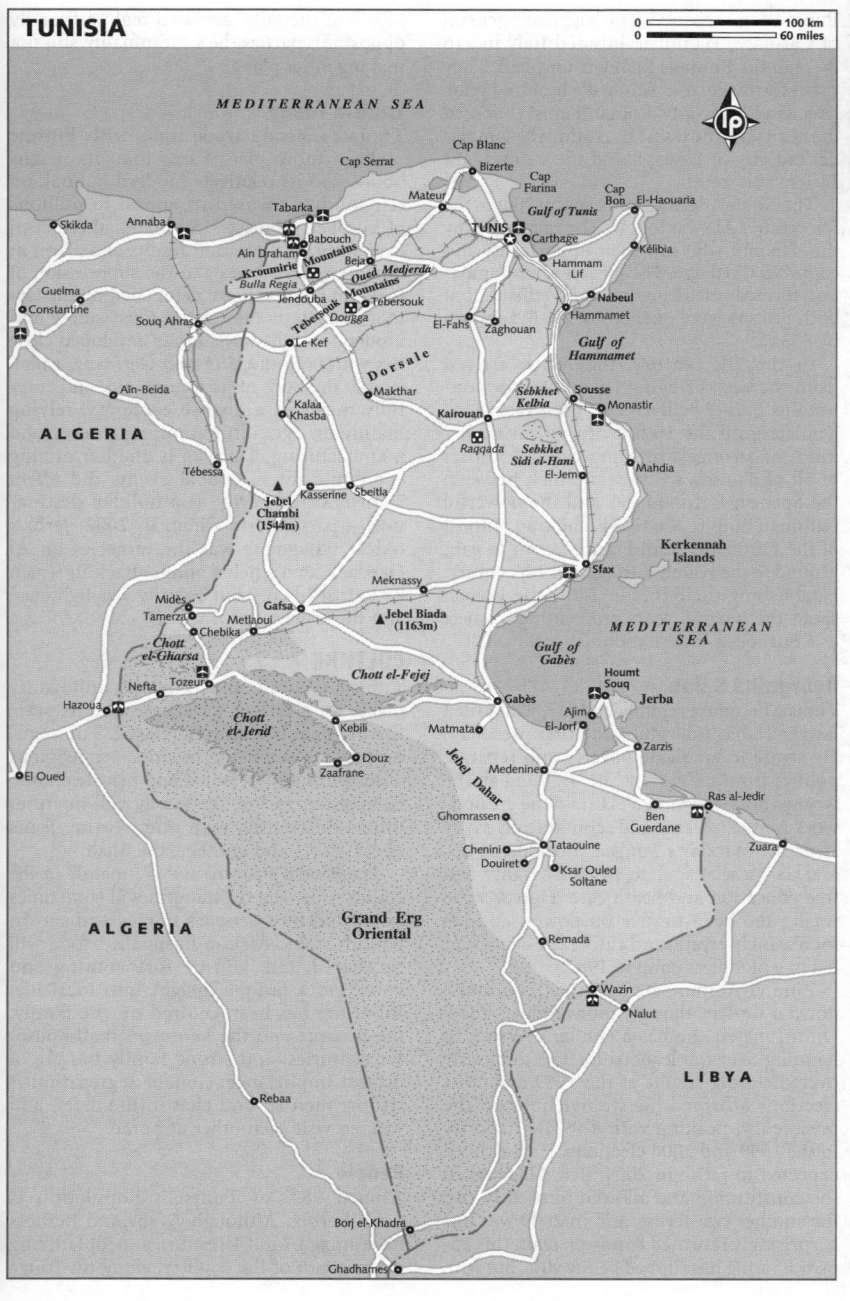

Punic Wars – ensued. The legendary general of Carthage, Hannibal, invaded Italy in 216 BC, but the Romans finally triumphed. They razed Carthage, re-creating it a hundred years later as a Roman city. Roman Tunisia boomed in the first centuries AD, creating the temple-decked city of Dougga and the extravagant El-Jem colosseum.

The Roman decline and eventual fall in the 5th century AD was followed by rampaging by the Vandals, who saw their opportunity and captured Carthage. The local Berber population formed small kingdoms and rebelled, but both groups were quelled by the Byzantines by 533.

In the 7th century, the Arabs arrived from the east, bringing Islam. Despite continuous Berber belligerence, the Arabs ruled Tunisia until the 16th century, leaving behind the strongest ongoing cultural impact of all of Tunisia's invaders. Stuck between the Spanish Reconquistas and the powerful Ottoman Empire, Tunisia became an outpost of the Ottomans until France began to gain ground in the region during the 19th century. Establishing their rule in 1881, the French spent the next 50 years reinventing Tunisia as a European-style nation.

Bourguiba & Ben

Tunisia became a republic in 1957, with exiled lawyer Habib Bourguiba the first president. He swore to eradicate poverty and separate politics from religion, while 'righting all the wrongs done to women'. He laid the groundwork for the tolerant and economically savvy structure of today's Tunisia, introducing liberal laws, a secular state, women's rights, and free education and heath care. However, he wasn't too keen to give up power, and his increasingly erratic and autocratic behaviour led to a bloodless coup in 1987.

Zine el-Abidine Ben Ali has continued down a similar, though not as radical, road. Unfortunately, he has a similar aversion to handing over the leadership. The dubiously overwhelming results at the 1989 and 1994 elections affirmed his stranglehold on the presidency, peaking with a 99.4% majority in the 1999 and 2004 elections. Having been expected to retire in 2004, Ben Ali tweaked the constitution and allowed himself to run for another two terms, and in 2009 was unsurprisingly returned to power again (his approval rating has slipped below 90%, but with

89.6% of the vote, and two regime-friendly opposition parties, he's presumably still not making other plans).

Tunisia Today

Tunisia's strong trade links with Europe make it more prosperous than its neighbours, and its relatively modern outlook on religion has ensured its appeal to millions of European tourists. International criticism over suspicious election results and alarm at human rights abuses and the suppression of freedom of speech are dampened by the fact that Tunisia is one of the most stable and moderate Arab states. It has developed close ties with both the USA and Germany, which supply the bulk of its foreign aid, and carefully nurtured a diverse economy, relying mainly on agriculture, mining, energy and manufacturing. Tourism is another driving economic force. Global events did affect Tunisia's popularity as a holiday destination – particularly when, in 2002, Jerba's oldest synagogue was the target of an Al Qaeda–linked suicide bomb attack in which 21 tourists died – but security was tightened and the tourists returned.

CULTURE

Tunisia's ethnic and religious uniformity makes for a certain social ease, and its practice of Islam is relatively relaxed. Tunisians, especially those living in cities, see religious observance as a personal and private choice. Even sisters in the one family will interpret things differently, with one wearing jeans and T-shirts and another, the hijab.

Traditional customs survive mainly in the countryside, where strangers will sometimes be invited into people's homes and shown typical Arabic-African hospitality: food will be shared, talk will be forthcoming and you'll get a unique insight into local life. Rural life has been centred on the family, the mosque and the *hammam* (bathhouse) for centuries, and strong family ties are of utmost importance. Gender segregation is strong: men sit and chat in the cafes, and women visit each other at home.

People

Almost 98% of Tunisia's population is Arab-Berber. Although Arabs and Berbers have mixed for 14 centuries, people living in the south of the country, along the fringe of the Sahara desert, claim a purely Berber heritage. Europeans and Jews make up the remaining 2% of the population.

Islam is the official religion in Tunisia, and over 98% of the population are Sunni Muslims. Jews and Christians make up the remaining 2% of the population.

Arts

Tunisia's national poet is Abu el-Kacem el-Chabbi, whose poem *Will to Live* is taught to every school child. It's hard to find English translations of Tunisian writing, with notable exceptions being Mustapha Tlili's *Lion Mountain*, a novel about the impact of tourism on a remote village, and the highly influential nonfiction work *The Colonizer and the Colonized* by Parisian-based Albert Memmi. Memmi has also written several novels that explore issues of Jewish–North African immigrant identity.

During the colonial period, European artists were drawn to Tunisia, attracted by its beautiful light and distinct architecture. The country's influence was particularly notable on the painter Paul Klee, who visited only briefly in 1914 but whose work was forever transformed. Yahia Turki is considered the father of the nation-building figurative painting school, producing work that exalts Tunisian daily life. After independence, artists such as Hédi Turki and Nja Mahdaoui began to explore and deconstruct the Islamic traditions of geometric decoration and calligraphy.

Tunisia's film industry is not particularly prolific, but has turned out a number of acclaimed arthouse flicks over the years. Directors include Férid Boughedir (*Halfaouine*, 1990; *A Summer in La Goulette*, 1996), Moufida Tlatli (*The Silences of the Palace*, 1997; *Keswa: Le Fil Perdu*, 1997) and Nouri Bouzid (*Bezness*, 1992; *Tunisiennes*, 1997). The Tunisian diaspora also produces some excellent films – César Award–winning *The Secret of the Grain* (2007), directed by Abdel Kechiche, and Karin Albou's *The Wedding Song* (2008) are recent examples.

FOOD & DRINK

Tunisians love spicy food, and it's almost impossible to encounter a meal that doesn't involve harissa, a fiery chilli paste. Fresh produce is plentiful and salads feature heavily on most menus. The most popular are *salade tunisienne*, a mix of tomato, onions and cucumber with lemon and olive-oil dressing and the ever-present topping of tuna, and *salade mechuoia*, a smoky capsicum stew.

Couscous is ubiquitous. It's generally served with lamb, legumes and vegetables, but Tunisians – unlike their Maghreb neighbours – serve theirs with fish, too. Fabulous French bread is also to be found everywhere, along with *tabouna*, the traditional flat Berber bread strewn with dark seeds. Traditional pastries (a wonderful combination of the Ottoman and Sicilian bakers' arts) will compete for your affection with perfectly made French legacies, such as *pain au chocolate* and *gateaux*.

Street food here is an absolute treat. At any time of the day, tuck into *briq* – this deep-fried, crispy pastry pocket is filled with egg and meat, prawns or tuna. *Lablabi* – chickpea soup – and huge sandwiches or rolls filled with tuna, egg and harissa are other all-day hunger busters.

ENVIRONMENT

It may be small, but Tunisia packs in a range of landscapes worthy of a continent, from its thickly forested northern mountains to crystallised salt lakes and endless dunes in the south.

The Kroumirie and Tebersouk Mountains in the north are the easternmost extent of the High Atlas Mountains, and are covered with dense forests where there's a chance of glimpsing wild boars, jackals, mongooses and genets. Their foothills dive down to the lavish, northern coastal plain. Further south, the country's main mountain range is the rugged, dry central Dorsale, which runs from Kasserine in the west and peters out into Cap Bon in the east. Between these ranges lies the lush Medjerda Valley, once the Roman larder, watered by the country's only permanent river, Oued Medjerda. Olive trees cover the east coast, particularly around Sfax. South of the Dorsale, a high plain falls away to a series of huge, glittering *chotts* (salt lakes) and the silent *erg* (sand sea).

Tunisia's environmental headaches include a millennium of deforestation, regional desertification and various forms of pollution: industrial pollution, sewage disposal and litter. Its trawler fleet has been accused of serious overfishing in the Gulf of Gabès. In the south, especially Jerba, the huge water requirements of the tourist industry have depleted artesian water levels and dried up springs.

TUNIS

pop 992,900

Tunis is a good introduction to the wildly divergent layers that make up modern Tunisia. The medina's organic tangle of souqs, squares, mosques and shuttered town houses is surrounded by the straight, colonial lines of the Ville Nouvelle. French Tunis centres on Ave Habib Bourguiba, a wide, tree-lined street where locals stroll in the evenings and cafes dot the sidewalks. Tunis' main attractions, however, are outside of town: the wonderful Bardo Museum and the mysterious ruins of ancient Carthage are Tunisia's archaeological and cultural trump cards. The young and hip head north to the gorgeous Mediterranean suburbs for beach outings and night-time fun.

ORIENTATION

The city's main thoroughfare, Ave Habib Bourguiba, runs west–east from Place de l'Indépendance to Lake Tunis. It is lined with cafes, banks, cinemas and restaurants, and hums day and night. The main north–south thoroughfare of the Ville Nouvelle is Ave de Carthage to the south of Ave Habib Bourguiba and Ave de Paris to the north. Ave de Carthage runs south to Place Barcelone, hub of the *métro léger* (tram) network, with the train station on its southern side.

The western extension of Ave Habib Bourguiba is Ave de France, which terminates in front of Bab Bhar (Porte de France), a huge arch, beyond which is the medina. The medina's two main streets lead off the western side of Bab Bhar: Rue de la Kasbah, which leads to Place du Gouvernement at the other side of the medina; and Rue Jemaa Zaytouna, which leads to the Zaytouna Mosque (Grande Mosquée) at its heart. At the eastern end of Ave Habib Bourguiba, a causeway carries road and rail traffic across to La Goulette, the charming old port, and then north along the coast to the upmarket suburbs of Carthage, Sidi Bou Saïd and La Marsa.

INFORMATION

Bookshops

Bohemian-feeling **Al-Kitab** (Map p220; 43 Ave Habib Bourguiba; 8am-9pm Mon-Fri, 8am-11pm Sat) has French-language maps, travel guides and cookery books, as well as a variety of English-language titles.

Internet Access

Publinet (per hr TD0.8); 28 Ave Habib Bourguiba (**Map p220**); Rue de Grèce (**Map p220**)

Money

There are lots of banks with ATMs, mostly along Ave Habib Bourguiba. Branches of Amex can be found in a few UIBC bank offices in the city centre.

Post & Telephone

The **main post office** (Map p220; Rue Charles de Gaulle) is open daily and has a poste-restante service.

Taxiphone offices (Map p220) dot the city centre. Two of the most convenient are on Rue Jamel Abdelnasser and Ave de Carthage.

Tourist Offices

The **tourist office** (Map p220; ☎ 71 341 077; 1 Ave Mohammed V; 8am-6pm Mon-Sat, 9am-noon Sun) has a free map of Tunis, a road map of Tunisia and brochures on Carthage and the medina. There's another branch at the train station, open the same hours. You'll be able to find someone who speaks English (but probably won't be much help besides).

SIGHTS & ACTIVITIES

The **medina** is a sprawling maze of tiny streets, alleyways, tunnel-like coves and tiny shops selling anything from shoes to *shisha* pipes. There are busy souqs, gorgeous, ancient doorways and tiled cafes. An atmospheric time to explore is the early morning, before the stalls are set up and people cluster around the coffee shops. The main drag at any other time is often unbearably hot, crowded and noisy, but the bustle soon dissipates a few streets either side of the main drag. At the medina's heart lies the beautiful **Zaytouna Mosque** (Grande Mosquée; Map p219; admission TD2; non-Muslims 8-11.30am Thu-Tue), its forest of columns scrounged from Roman Carthage. There are also a number of steam-filled, ancient **hammams** (ask your hotel for a recommendation).

The country's top museum is the **Bardo Museum** (☎ 71 513 650; admission TD7, camera TD1; 9.30am-4.30pm Tue-Sun mid-Sep–Mar, 9am-5pm Tue-Sun Apr & Jun–mid-Sep, closes early during Ramadan). This magnificent, must-see collection provides a taste of ancient life, and is housed in a glorious Husseinite palace. The many, incredibly well-preserved mosaics are stunning, and are some of Africa's oldest. It's 4km northwest of the city centre. The best way to get there is by

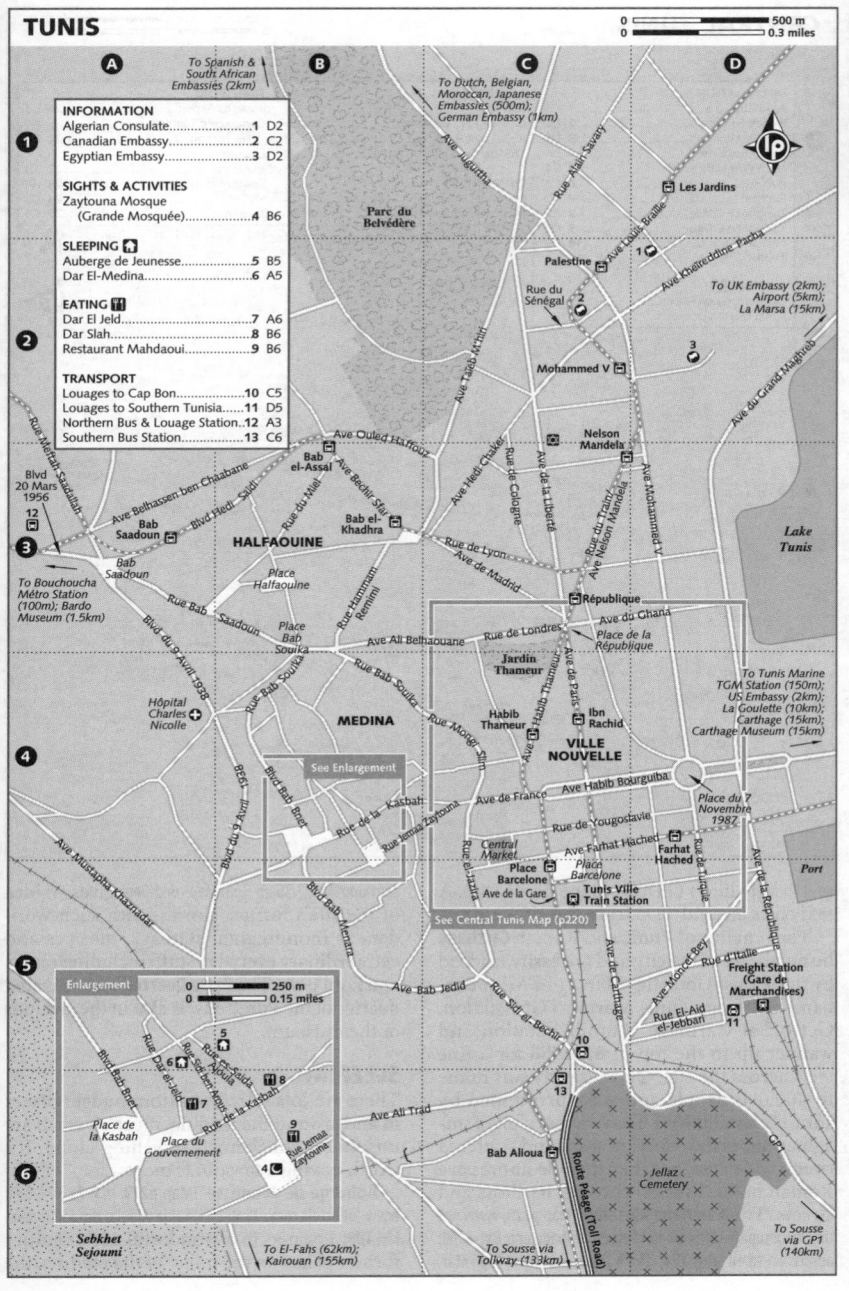

TUNIS

0 —————— 500 m
0 —————— 0.3 miles

INFORMATION
Algerian Consulate.....................1 D2
Canadian Embassy.....................2 C2
Egyptian Embassy......................3 D2

SIGHTS & ACTIVITIES
Zaytouna Mosque
(Grande Mosquée)..................4 B6

SLEEPING
Auberge de Jeunesse..................5 B5
Dar El-Medina............................6 A5

EATING
Dar El Jeld.................................7 A6
Dar Slah....................................8 B6
Restaurant Mahdaoui..................9 B6

TRANSPORT
Louages to Cap Bon...................10 C5
Louages to Southern Tunisia......11 D5
Northern Bus & Louage Station...12 A3
Southern Bus Station.................13 C6

TUNISIA

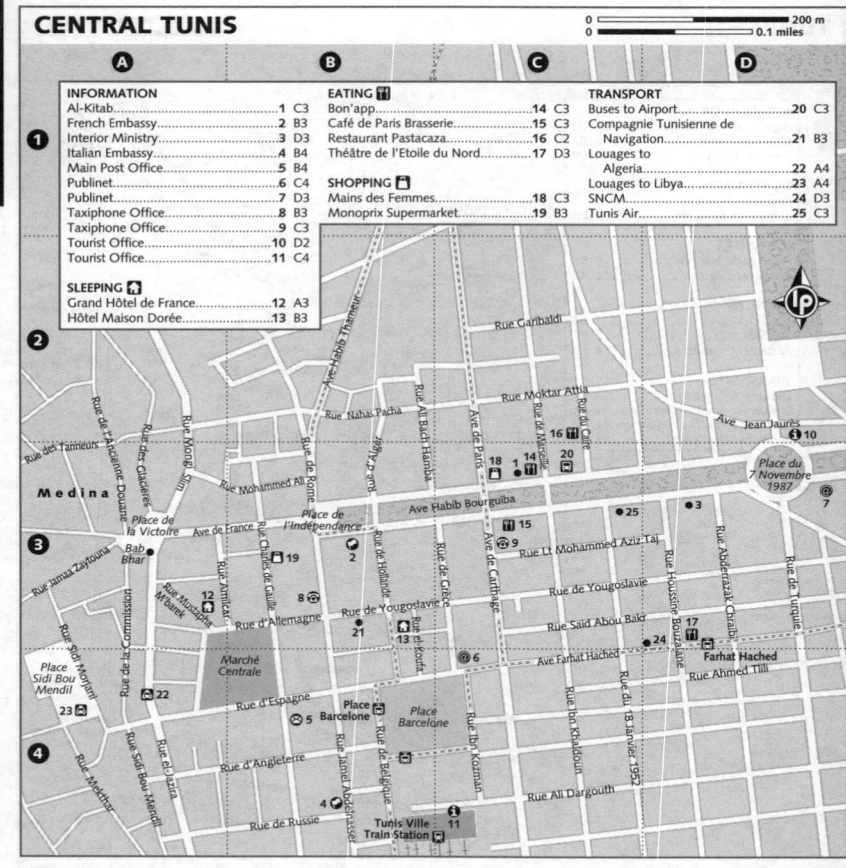

CENTRAL TUNIS

INFORMATION	
Al-Kitab	1 C3
French Embassy	2 B3
Interior Ministry	3 D3
Italian Embassy	4 B4
Main Post Office	5 B4
Publinet	6 C4
Publinet	7 D3
Taxiphone Office	8 B3
Taxiphone Office	9 C3
Tourist Office	10 D2
Tourist Office	11 C4

SLEEPING	
Grand Hôtel de France	12 A3
Hôtel Maison Dorée	13 B3

EATING	
Bon'app	14 C3
Café de Paris Brasserie	15 C3
Restaurant Pastacaza	16 C2
Théâtre de l'Etoile du Nord	17 D3

SHOPPING	
Mains des Femmes	18 C3
Monoprix Supermarket	19 B3

TRANSPORT	
Buses to Airport	20 C3
Compagnie Tunisienne de Navigation	21 B3
Louages to Algeria	22 A4
Louages to Libya	23 A4
SNCM	24 D3
Tunis Air	25 C3

métro léger line 4 (TD0.5) to the Bardo stop. A taxi costs around TD5 from the city centre.

The remains of Punic and Roman **Carthage** lie northeast of the city and are easily reached by the Tunis–Goulette–Marsa (TGM) suburban train from Tunis Marine TGM station. Get off at Carthage Hannibal station and wander up to the top of **Byrsa Hill** for a fine view across the site. Once the city was home to 400,000 people and was surrounded by 13m-high walls. You'll have to use a bit of imagination, as the ruins are scant and scattered over a wide area, but they include impressive Roman baths, houses, cisterns, basilicas and streets. The **Carthage Museum** (Map p220; www.patrimoinedetunisie.com.tn/eng/musees/carthage.php; Byrsa Hill; admission to all sites TD8; 8.30am-5pm mid-Sep–Mar,

8am-6pm Apr, 7.30am-7pm May–mid-Sep) gives an idea of the site's former glories, with such wonders as monumental statuary, mosaics and extraordinary everyday stuff, including razors and kohl pots. The **Byrsa Quarter**, an excavated quarter of the Punic city, is also in the grounds of the museum.

SLEEPING

There are lots of rock-bottom budget places in and around the medina, most of which are unsuitable for women travelling alone. It's worth paying a few dinar more.

Auberge de Jeunesse (Map p219; ☎ 71 574 884; www.hihostels.com; 25 Rue Es-Saida Ajoula; dm incl breakfast TD8) Located in a wonderful 18th-century former palace in the midst of the medina, the rooms here are basic: white walls and bunk beds upstairs; comfortable but stuffy doubles downstairs. There's a pretty, tiled courtyard, the welcome is friendly and the position is priceless.

Grand Hôtel de France (Map p220; ☎ 71 326 244; hotelfrancetunis@yahoo.fr; 8 Rue Mustapha M'barek; s TD12, d with/without bathroom TD27/24, with air-con TD39, tr TD54; 🅿) This colonial-era hotel is in a bustling location and has welcoming, English-speaking staff. It's airy, high ceilinged and light, with a faded 1930s elegance. Rooms have marble fireplaces and balconies. Ask for one overlooking the leafy inner courtyard.

our pick Hôtel Maison Dorée (Map p220; ☎ 71 240 632; 3 Rue el-Koufa; d with/without bathroom TD42/TD32, with air-con TD45; 🅿) Maison Dorée is charming: simple and spotless with an old-fashioned formality, shuttered balconies and comforting 1950s fittings. There's an attached restaurant downstairs.

Dar El-Medina (Map p219; ☎ 71 563 022; www.darelm edina.com; 64 Rue Sidi ben Arous; s/d €130/140; 🅿 🖵) This glamorous 19th-century courtyard mansion has been decorated in a simple, stylish mix of the traditional and the contemporary. All rooms are individually furnished and there's an ornate courtyard sitting room and a roof terrace where you can sip mint tea while the evening call to prayer echoes across the city.

EATING

You can buy slightly addictive spicy tuna-filled *chapattis* (a mixture of egg and spicy harissa paste stuffed inside a wonderful, hot bread parcel, tuna optional) in the medina for around TD1.5, or dine like a king in one of the grand medina restaurants.

Théâtre de l'Etoile du Nord (Map p220; ☎ 71 254 066; www.etoiledunord.org; 41 Ave Farhat Hached; sandwiches from TD3; 🕒 10am-8pm; 🖵) This spacious theatre-cafe-bar is the city's sole 'alternative hang-out' frequented by both men and women. It's a refreshing place with good music and theatrical events, though no alcohol.

Bon'app (Map p220; 37 Ave Habib Bourgiba; pasta mains TD3.6-5; 🕒 7.30am-midnight) Take away pastas and French desserts, or eat in at the smartly decorated, secluded back bar.

Restaurant Pastacaza (Map p220; ☎ 71 996 341; 4 Rue du Caire; dishes TD4-7.5; 🕒 noon-10pm) Bright (perhaps too bright) Sfax-style place that pulls the Tunisian families with friendly

service, simple standards and regional specialties, such as *riz au lapin* (rabbit rice).

Café de Paris Brasserie (Map p220; ☎ 71 240 583; Ave Habib Bourguiba; mains TD4-12; 🕒 11.30am-10pm; 🅿) This handy little place has a nice, neat interior and a few outside tables. Pizzas, pastas, couscous and French, Italian and Tunisian salads come in gargantuan serves. It also serves alcohol.

Restaurant Mahdaoui (Map p219; 2 Rue Jemaa Zaytouna; mains TD4.5-9; 🕒 noon-3.30pm Mon-Sat) Central and cheap, the tables fill a narrow alley by the Zaytouna Mosque. The simple daily menu offers couscous, fish, chicken, half a head of lamb and so on.

our pick Dar Slah (Map p219; 145 Rue de la Kasbah; set menu TD17-19; 🕒 noon-3.30pm Mon-Sat; 🅿) Dar Slah is calm and clean lined despite its location on the medina's busiest thoroughfare. A daily changing menu is built around fresh seasonal ingredients and is a feast of traditional flavours.

Dar El Jeld (Map p219; ☎ 71 560 916; 5-10 Rue Dar el-Jeld; mains TD25-35) A special experience from the moment you knock on the grand bee-yellow arched doorway, the magnificent dining room is in the covered central courtyard of an elaborate 18th-century mansion. Try dishes such as *lahma m'jamra* (stuffed lamb shoulder) or lighter options, like a generous seafood salad. If you're dining *au deux*, ask for one of the secluded balcony tables.

SHOPPING

Mains des Femmes (Map p220; 1st fl, 47 Ave Habib Bourguiba; 🕒 9am-6.30pm Mon-Fri, 9am-5pm Sat) A women's co-operative that sells quality handicrafts, including rugs, jewellery and clothing, at fixed prices. The profits are ploughed back into the rural communities that make them.

For perfume, tiles, *chechias* (traditional red felt hats), cheap clothes, accessories and tonnes of glorious tat, head to the medina. In and around the **marché centrale** (central market; Map p220; Rue Charles de Gaulle; 🕒 6am-3pm), you can buy olives, differing date varieties, harissa and cheeses. There's also a **Monoprix supermarket** (Rue Charles de Gaulle; 🕒 8.30am-9pm Mon-Sat, 8.30am-3pm Sun) that stocks local wine.

GETTING THERE & AWAY
Air

The airport is 8km northeast of the city centre: a taxi costs around TD10; bus 35 (half-hourly 6.30am to 5.30pm) heads to Ave Habib Bourguiba.

Sevenair (Map p219; ☎ 71 942 626, www.sevenair. tn), the domestic arm of **Tunis Air** (☎ 71 330 100; www.tunisair.com; 48 Ave Habib Bourguiba), flies direct to Jerba, Tozeur and Tabarka, with tickets starting at around TD100. Getting a booking to coastal towns in the middle of summer can be hard.

Boat

Ferries from Europe arrive at La Goulette. The cheapest way to reach the city from there is by TGM suburban train or by taxi, which will cost around TD5.

The **Compagnie Tunisienne de Navigation** (CTN; Map p220; ☎ 71 322 802; www.ctn.com.tn; 122 Rue de Yougoslavie) handles tickets for ferries to Genoa and Marseilles, as does its French partner **SNCM** (Société Nationale Maritime Corse Méditerranée; Map p220; ☎ 71 338 222; www.sncm.fr; 47 Ave Farhat Hached). **Grandi Navi Veloci** (☎ in Italy 01 0209 4591; www.gnv. it) sails to Genoa, Civitavecchia (Rome) and Palermo. **Tirrenia Navigazione** (☎ in Italy 02 2630 2803; www.tirrenia.it) handles tickets to and from Genoa from within Italy.

Bus

Tunis has two intercity bus stations: the **southern bus station** (Gare Routière Sud de Bab el-Fellah; Map p219; ☎ 71 399 391, 71 399 440), for international buses, buses to the south and *louages* (shared taxis) for Cap Bon, is opposite the huge Jellaz Cemetery on *métro léger* line 1 to Bab Alioua station; and the **northern bus station** (Gare Routière Nord de Bab Saadoun; Map p219; ☎ 71 562 299, 71 563 653; Gare Routière Nord de Bab Saadoun), for buses heading north, is reached by *métro léger* line 4 to Bouchoucha station. *Louages* from the north also arrive and leave from the northern bus station. **SNTRI** (www.sntri.com.tn) has timetables and prices online.

Local Transport

Tunis has a number of main *louage* stations. Cap Bon *louages* leave from opposite the southern bus station, and services to other southern destinations leave from the station at the eastern end of Rue El-Aid el-Jebbari, off Ave Moncef Bey. *Louages* to the north leave from the northern bus station. The station on Place Sidi Bou Mendil in the medina serves Libya (Tripoli; around TD40, 20 hours); services to Algeria leave from nearby. Prices are usually equivalent to bus fares.

Train

The **Tunis Ville train station** (Map p219; ☎ 71 345 511; www.sncft.com.tn; Place Barcelone) is centrally located.

GETTING AROUND
Taxi

Private taxis are cheap. It's hard to run up a fare of more than TD15, even out to the northern beach suburb of La Marsa. A short hop will cost less than TD2; a longer one, such as to the Bardo Museum, around TD5.

Train

The TGM rail system connects central Tunis with the northern beachside suburbs of La Goulette, Carthage, Sidi Bou Saïd and La Marsa. Fares cost between TD0.5 and TD1.2; services run from 5am to midnight.

Tram

The modern *métro léger* system has six routes running to various parts of the city. The useful lines are 1 for the southern bus and *louage* stations, 2 for the consulates on and around Ave de la Liberté, and 3 and 4 for the northern bus and *louage* station. Line 4 also has a stop for the Bardo Museum. The main stations are Place Barcelone and Place de la République. The basic fare costs around TD0.5.

AROUND TUNIS

Carthage, Sidi Bou Saïd and La Marsa were once distinct villages and towns, and although they are now part of Tunis' suburban sprawl, they have each retained an individual atmosphere. **Sidi Bou Saïd**, 30 minutes up the TGM line, has to be one of the prettiest spots in Tunisia. With cascading bougainvilleas, bright-blue window grills, narrow, steep cobbled streets and jaw-dropping glimpses of azure coast, it's a tour-bus favourite, but wears its popularity surprisingly well.

Eat at **Au Bon Vieux Temps** (☎ 71 744 733; 56 Rue Hedi Zarrouk; mains TD18-24; ☼ noon-midnight; ⊠), known for its excellent seafood, the ridiculously romantic terrace centred around a trickling fountain, and amazing big blue views. Or for budget dining, try **Le Chargui** (☎ 71 740 987; 39 Rue Habib Thameur; mains TD5-12; ☼ noon-midnight Apr-Oct, noon-8pm Nov-Mar), with its big open-air courtyard and simple, fresh traditional favourites.

There are also some particularly lovely places to stay. Exclusive **Hôtel Dar Saïd** (☎ 71 729 666; www.darsaid.com.tn; Rue Toumi; r from TD285, with view TD350; 🅿 🖵 🖳) is housed in a converted villa and features sweeping views of the sea from its shady, flower-scented garden and pool. **Hôtel Sidi Bou Fares** (☎ 71 740 091; 15 Rue Sidi Bou Fares; s/d/t TD68/104/144; 🅿) has small, prettily tiled, barrel-vaulted rooms with Goldilocks-style wooden beds and crisp white linen, surrounded by a fig-shaded courtyard.

NORTHERN TUNISIA

Northern Tunisia is a rolling, green, magnificently lush region, little explored by foreign visitors. Trump the tour buses and have your fill of hazy valleys, quiet beach towns and the wonderfully preserved Roman cities of Dougga and Bulla Regia.

TABARKA
pop 15,600

Tabarka, a quiet coastal town with a tough old Genoese **fort** watching over a long curve of white sand, is locally known as 'music town', thanks to the music festivals that take place here. In July, the renowned jazz festival (p240) segues into the sounds of rai, Latin and world beats (p240), both definitely dance-all-day affairs. This midsummer action and excellent scuba-diving aside, Tabarka is a Tunisians' resort, with a mellow, old-fashioned feel.

The small town has a grid layout, bisected by the main street, Ave Habib Bourguiba. There are banks and ATMs along here, and the **post office** (Rue Hedi Chaker) and **Publinet** (Ave 7 Novembre 1987; per hr TD2) are nearby.

Sleeping & Eating

Tabarka has a reasonable range of accommodation, though none of it particularly remarkable. Prices drop by over half in the low season.

Hôtel La Plage (☎ 78 670 039; 11 Ave 7 Novembre 1987; s/d without air-con TD25/40, with air-con TD35/50; 🅿) Clean, small, central and great value, the nicest rooms here have balconies overlooking the street.

Hôtel Novelty (☎ 78 670 176; fax 78 673 008; 68 Ave Habib Bourguiba; s/d TD65/90; 🅿) This centrally located establishment has 26 bright and airy rooms, all of them simply furnished but neat and clean.

Hôtel Les Mimosas (☎ 78 673 018; www.hotel-les-mimosas.com; Ave Habib Bourguiba; s/d TD78/107; 🅿 🖳)

The interior here is more stylish than the exterior suggests, and there's a good pool that also happens to be the top spot for sundowners. Perched on a hill, there are sweeping views.

Dar Ismail (☎ 78 670 188; www.darismailhotels.com; Zone Touristique; d incl half board TD240; 🅿 🖳) Situated 1.5km east of the marina, this five-star place has comfortable rooms and a sensational pool with canals, bridges and large swimming basins. There is also a fine stretch of beach and a beautifully maintained garden.

Restaurant Khemir (11 Ave Habib Bourguiba; mains TD8-15) Were it located on the marina, the Khemir would be the best address in town. As it is, you get excellent value, uberfresh and wonderfully tasty seafood.

Getting There & Away

The office of **Société Régionale de Transport de Jendouba** (SRTJ; 84 Ave Habib Bourguiba, cnr Rue Mohammed Ali) is the main bus stop in town. It runs buses to Ain Draham (TD1.2, 45 minutes, about 15 daily), Jendouba (TD3.3, 1¾ hours, 10 daily) and Le Kef (TD6.1, 3½ hours, twice daily). SNTRI buses to Tunis (TD9.8, 3¼ hours, five daily) depart from the SRTJ stop. *Louages* leave from Ave Habib Bourguiba for Ain Draham (TD1.4), Jendouba (TD4.9) and Tunis (TD9.4).

AIN DRAHAM
pop 8900

In the middle of the cork forest of the Kroumirie Mountains, you'll find the alpine village of Ain Draham, whose primary appeal lies in the hunting, hiking and horse riding opportunities it affords and the welcome respite offered by the cooler temperatures during summer. Situated at an altitude of around 900m, Ain Draham usually has snow during winter. The road between here and Tabarka is one of Tunisia's most beautiful.

Paragliding wild boar welcome you into the **Hôtel Beau Séjour** (☎ 78 656 112; hotelbeausejour@ live.fr; s/d TD35/50) hunting lodge. Sipping a beer under the shady fig tree on the verandah is a delight. **Résidence Le Pins** (☎ 78 656 200; Ave Habib Bourguiba; s/d TD35/60) has a friendly owner and a place to shoot some pool, as well as sweeping views from the back rooms' balconies and roof terrace. The 74 rooms at **Royal Rihana Hôtel** (☎ 78 655 391; www.royalrihana-hotel.com; s/d TD85/120; 🅿 🖳) are spotless and unpretentious, with wonderful forest views; amenities include a barside fireplace and indoor pool. One of the most professional outfits in the region, and the only place to do organised excursions in the Kroumirie Mountains, it's 2km south of the fountain roundabout along Ave Habib Bourguiba.

There are regular buses to Jendouba (TD2.1, one hour, hourly), Tabarka (TD1.2, 45 minutes, half-hourly), Le Kef (TD5.5, two hours, twice daily) and Tunis (TD10.8, four hours, four daily). Regular *louages* go to/from Tabarka and Jendouba. You can also get public transport to the Algerian border. A taxi to Babouch and the border post costs TD1. You'll have to cross the border on foot and find transport on the other side.

BULLA REGIA

Famed for its extraordinary underground villas, the Roman city of **Bulla Regia** (admission TD4, camera TD1; ☾ 8am-7pm Apr–mid-Sep, 8.30am-5.30pm mid-Sep–Mar), 7km northwest of Jendouba, offers a rare opportunity to walk into complete, superbly preserved Roman rooms; there's no need to extrapolate how things once looked from waist-high walls. To escape the summer heat, the ever-inventive Romans retreated below the surface, building elegant homes – complete with colonnaded courtyards – that echo the troglodytic Berber homes at Matmata. The name each villa is known by reflects the theme of the mosaics found inside. Some (but not all) of the best are now in the Bardo Museum (p218). Especially lovely examples can be seen at the oldest though simplest structure, the House of Fishing, which dates from the 2nd century. The newer villas become increasingly more elaborate. The star attraction is the House of Amphitrite: nude Venus and centaurs, with attendant cherubs riding dolphins (what's not to like?).

For an informative guided tour, call **Amel Ayadi** (☎ 96 014 141) or ask for her at the entrance. Tours cost around TD30 for a couple of hours.

Bulla Regia is approximately 160km west of Tunis and may be easily visited on a day trip from Tunis, Le Kef or Tabarka. Trains or buses to Jendouba are your best bet to/from Tunis, and there are also regular buses and *louages* to/from Le Kef and Tabarka. A taxi from Jendouba costs around TD4. Any bus travelling between Jendouba and Ain Draham can drop you off at the Bulla Regia turn-off, from where it's a 3km walk.

LE KEF
pop 45,200

High in the hills, Le Kef (El Kef in Arabic, meaning 'rock') is topped by a storybook Byzantine kasbah. On the slope below is the medina, a maze of narrow cobbled streets and blue-shuttered low-rise buildings, whose highlights include a fine museum that focuses on Berber culture, and Muslim, Christian and Jewish places of worship. The city centre, around Place de l'Indépendance, is a 10-minute walk uphill from the bus and *louage* station, or a TD0.70 ride in a shared taxi.

There are several banks scattered throughout Place de l'Indépendance, and a busy **post office** (Rue Hedi Chaker) is located nearby. For internet access, head to **Publinet** (Place de l'Indépendance; per hour TD2).

Sights

Many of Le Kef's sights are free but their custodians will generally expect a tip, particularly if they show you around. The **kasbah** (☾ 8am-1pm & 2-7pm), frequently used as a film location, dominates the city from a spur running off Jebel Dyr. From here, there are great views looking out across the rolling blue-green landscape dotted with Tuscan trees. A stronghold of some sort has occupied this site since the 5th century BC. To get to the kasbah, follow the stone steps leading uphill through the old **medina** from Place de l'Indépendance. The road that flanks the kasbah leads to the well-laid-out **Musée des Arts et Traditions Populaires** (admission TD3, camera TD1; ☾ 9.30am-4.30pm Tue-Sun mid-Sep–Mar, 9am-1pm & 4-7pm Tue-Sun Apr–mid-Sep), housed in a sprawling, ornate Sufi complex founded in 1784. The museum concentrates on the culture of the region's Berber nomads, and exhibits include Berber tents and silver jewellery. Below the kasbah sits the enchanting 17th-century **Zaouia of Sidi Boumakhlouf** (☾ 10am-noon & 3-6pm Thu & Sat-Tue, 10am-6pm Wed & Fri), with its white cupolas and a brilliantly tiled interior. Just outside is a bewitchingly pretty, tree-shaded square with a particularly atmospheric cafe.

The **Al Ghriba Synagogue** (Rue Farhat Hached; ☾ 7am-7pm), in the heart of the former Jewish quarter, the Hara, pays tribute to that now-vanished part of local culture. As well as the restored interior, there are a collection of touching objects and documents.

Sleeping & Eating

Le Kef has a good selection of clean, comfortable accommodation options.

Hôtel Ramzi (☎ 78 203 079; Rue Hedi Chaker; s/d with bathroom TD25/50, without bathroom TD20/40) This is a central and very welcoming hotel, with 14 rooms that are clean and decorated by lots of colourful wall tiles. It has a restaurant.

ourpick Hôtel-Résidence Vénus (☎ 78 204 695; www.hotel-lespins.com, in French; Rue Mouldi Khamessi; s/d TD28/40) Nestled beneath the outer walls of the old kasbah, this especially pleasant *pension* has twittering canaries in the courtyard, great views from the rooftop and 20 rooms that are simple and clean. It's under the same management as Hôtel Les Pins and, if you ask nicely, they will let you use the pool there.

Restaurant Boumakhlouf (☎ 98 285 211; Rue Hedi Chaker; mains TD3.5-7) This good-value cheapie is very popular for lunch, and specialities include couscous, *lablabi* (soup), and the town's best chicken and chips.

Restaurant Vénus (Rue Farhat Hached; mains TD8-14) Under the same management as Hôtel-Résidence Vénus, this is the only 'proper' restaurant in town, and not a bad option. The dining room doubles as a bar.

Getting There & Away

There are SNTRI buses travelling to/from Tunis (TD8.3, 3¼ hours, hourly). To visit Dougga, take the Le Kef–Tunis bus and ask to be dropped off at the New Dougga turnoff (TD3.4, one hour).

DOUGGA

A Roman city with a view, **Dougga** (☎ 78 466 636; admission TD4, camera TD1; ☼ 8am-7pm Apr–mid-Sep, 8.30am-5.30pm mid-Sep–Mar) is set on a hillside surrounded by olive groves and overlooking fields of grain, with forested hills beyond. Built of tan stone, its mellow tones meld harmoniously with the landscape of the Kalled Valley and Tebersouk Mountains.

One of the most magnificent Roman monuments in Africa, Dougga's ancient remains are startlingly complete, giving a beguiling glimpse of how well-heeled Romans lived, flitting between the baths (including the fine **Thermes de Caracalla**), the imposing **Capitole** (the 3500-seat theatre) and various temples (21 have been identified). The city was built on the site of ancient Thugga, a Numidian settlement, which explains why the streets are so uncharacteristically tangled. The 2nd-century-BC Libyo-Punic **mausoleum** is the country's finest pre-Roman monument.

The site is located 110km southwest of Tunis and can easily be visited on a day trip from there or Le Kef – or en route between the two cities. Buses and *louages* stop at Tebersouk, about 8km northeast of Dougga. From Tebersouk's *louage* station, hiring an entire yellow-striped *louage* or a taxi to Dougga should cost about TD10 one way and TD15 return (the driver will return to pick you up at a pre-arranged time), though iffy operators may demand a lot more or set an exorbitant per-person rate. If you're driving from Le Kef, turn at Nouvelle Dougga. The best time to visit is early in the morning or late in the day; allow at least three hours and don't forget to pack a picnic.

CENTRAL TUNISIA

Home to Kairouan, one of Islam's most holy cities, several of Tunisia's largest beach resorts and El-Jem, its most impressive Roman monument, this region is hardly lacking in superlatives. Despite its great diversity – from fortified ancient medinas and an Islamic heartland of quiet, timeless villages to the sparkling Mediterranean and the hedonism of exclusive modern hotels – it's a short commute to get from one site to the other.

SOUSSE
pop 173,000

Sousse is Tunisia's third-biggest city and its enduring popularity as a tourist destination is somewhat baffling: it's loud, brash and sports an odd mix of traditional architecture and the dubious fruits of '80s mass tourism. Sousse is at least as popular with Tunisians as it is with foreigners: witness summer evenings on Boujaffar Beach, when everyone turns out for a stroll on the seafront. The central fortified medina hasn't escaped the tourist circus completely, but you're guaranteed some history and culture once you've made it past the umpteen stalls.

Orientation & Information

Ave Habib Bourguiba connects the medina and Place Farhat Hached in the south to Boujaffar Beach and Place Sidi Boujaffar in the north. North of the city centre, Blvd de la Corniche is behind Ave Hedi Chaker, where many hotels, restaurants, banks and shops are found.

The staff at the **tourist office** (☎ 73 225 157; 1 Ave Habib Bourguiba; ⏰ 7am-7pm Mon-Sat, 9am-noon Sun Jun-Sep, 8.30am-1pm & 3-5.45pm Mon-Thu, 8.30am-1.30pm Fri & Sat Oct-May) can be rude but has timetables for buses and trains. The post office and **Publinet** (per hr TD2; ⏰ 8am-10pm Mon-Sat, 9.30-8pm Sun) are just up from Place Farhat Hached on Ave Mohamed Maarouf, and Taxiphone offices are scattered about. Banks with ATMs can be found along Ave Habib Bourguiba.

Sights

The medina's pride and joy is the 8th-century **ribat** (admission TD4, camera TD1; ⏰ 8am-7.30pm Jun-Sep, 8am-5.30pm Oct-May), once garrisoned by devout Islamic warriors who would divide their time between fighting and silent study of the Quran. Nearby is the wide, sunny courtyard of the **Grande Mosquée**. Both are in the northeast corner, near Place Farhat Hached.

The **kasbah** on top of the hill contains the **Musée de Source** (☎ 73 219 011; Ave du Maréchal Tito), with a collection of mosaics second only to the Bardo Museum in Tunis. It was closed for renovations at the time of writing but is due to open in 2011.

Sousse's **Boujaffar Beach**, with its multi-kilometre stretch of high-rise hotels, cafes and restaurants, is the city's landmark. Named somewhat incongruously after a local Muslim holy man, the soft, sandy strip is a playground where families picnic, children frolic and foreigners sunbathe.

Sleeping

The hotels vary from medina fleapits to seaside medium comfort, though none are outstanding.

Hôtel de Paris (☎ 73 220 564; 15 Rue du Rempart Nord; s/d TD15/26) The Paris has small but impeccable rooms with shared facilities, and a huge rooftop terrace, perfect for enjoying the evening breeze. The Restaurant du Peuple (right) next door is great value.

Hôtel Emira (☎ 73 226 325; 52 Rue de France; s/d TD22/30) Brightly painted, with gleaming colourful tiles, rooms here are like a modest version of a *bey*'s (king's) palace. The rooftop terrace is also excellent (if only the owner were less grumpy...).

Hôtel Medina (☎ 73 221 722; www.hotel-medina.com; 15 Rue Othman Osman; s/d incl breakfast TD44/68; ✹) On a shady corner opposite the Grande Mosquée, this attractive hotel has large, bright rooms, with good bathrooms (including hot water); a number of rooms have balconies.

Eating

For quick snacks go to Rue Remada, between the train station and Ave Habib Bourguiba, or the medina, particularly along Rue de Paris. Coffee houses and restaurants with outdoor streetside seating are chock-a-block along Ave Habib Bourguiba, and many restaurants here serve alcohol.

Café Presse (Ave Habib Bourguiba; ⏰ 7am-2am) Young Tunisians come here for milkshakes, *citronade* (Tunisian lemon drink) and ice creams.

Restaurant du Peuple (Rue du Rempart Nord; 3-course meal TD6) Hearty meat and couscous dishes are served at this pleasant little establishment, just inside the medina walls next to Hôtel de Paris (left). The bargain *menu complet* (set menu) includes starters, a dessert of fresh seasonal fruit and mint tea.

Restaurant-Café Seles (☎ 97 286 862; Rue Abou Nawas; mains TD5-10) By far the most attractive establishment in the medina, with a cosy curtained room full of cushions and a handful of alfresco tables beneath the ramparts.

L'Escargot (☎ 73 224 779; 87 Route de la Corniche; mains TD13-20) The interior is reminiscent of a 19th-century French auberge (inn), which, although slightly out of place, is not unpleasant. There is a lovely terrace and the French cuisine is excellent.

Getting There & Away

The train stations are conveniently central. There are a dozen trains a day north to Tunis (TD7.7, 2¼ hours). There are only four trains to Sfax (TD7, 1¾ hours), including two late-night services, one train to Gabès (TD12.5, 3¾ hours) and one to Gafsa (TD13.2, 5¾ hours). The *métro*, essentially decommissioned train cars, connects Sousse to the airport (TD0.9, 30 minutes). These depart from the Bab el-Jedid station near the southeastern corner of the medina every 45 minutes or so from 6am to 8pm.

Long-distance buses depart from the new **bus station** (Souq el-Ahad), 800m southwest of the medina, with destinations including Douz, (TD20.6, 6½ hours, one daily), El-Jem (TD2.7, 1¼ hours, five daily), Tozeur (TD19.2, 5¾ hours, one daily) and Tunis (TD8.1, 2½ hours,

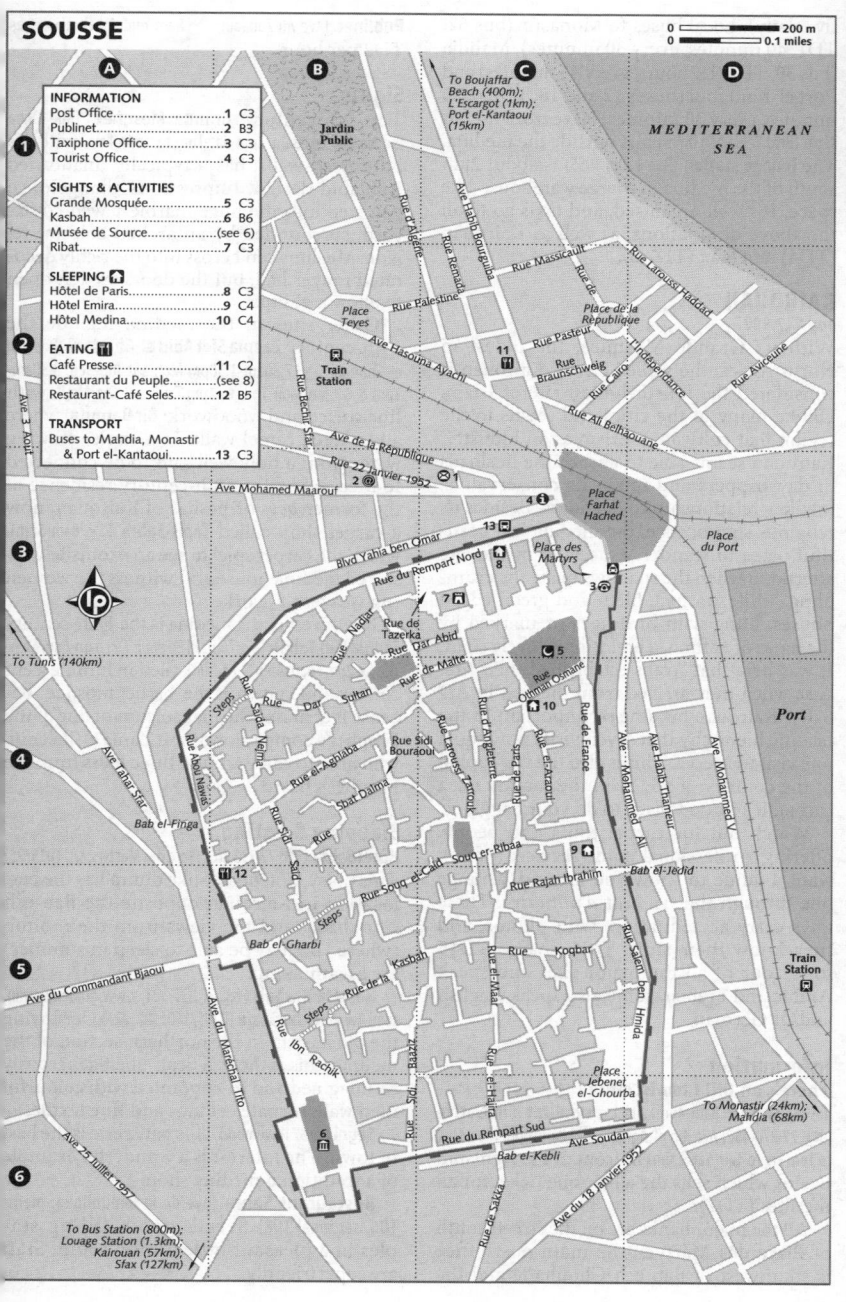

SOUSSE

five daily). Local buses to Monastir (bus 52; TD1, 40 minutes, every 30 minutes), Mahdia (bus 30; TD2, 1½ hours, every 45 minutes) and Port el-Kantaoui (buses 12 and 18; TD0.6, 20 minutes, every 30 minutes) leave from the **bus stop** (Blvd Yahia ben Omar) just outside the medina. The **louage station** (Rue 1 Juin 1955) is about 2km south of the medina in a large warehouse-like space. It's well organised, and taxis go to all the above destinations, as well as Kairouan (TD4) and Sfax (TD7.6).

KAIROUAN
pop 117,900

With its Grande Mosquée, the oldest in North Africa, the walled city of Kairouan is considered the fourth-holiest site of Islam. Unlike many of the cities and towns in the region that cultivate tourism as an industry, Kairouan seems able to absorb the busloads of day trippers and retain its conservative, low-key relationship to outsiders. Besides its religious significance, the medina is a beautiful place to wander, especially in the late afternoon when the shadows make the crumbling, white-washed, blue- and green-edged houses, hung with birdcages or marked by the hand of Fatima, a hauntingly lovely sight. It was here that Arabs established their first base when they arrived from the east in AD 670 – Kairouan became so important in the Islamic hierarchy that seven visits now equal one visit to Mecca. This is also the rug capital of the country: if you're in the market for a carpet, it's a good place to do your haggling.

Watch out for carpet touts and people offering 'professional guide services'; if you want a guide to show you around, arrange one through the *syndicat d'initiative*. These guys carry accreditation, with photos, and they know their stuff. They charge TD15 for a tour of all the major sites and speak Arabic and French, some also speak English and/or German.

Information

There's an **ONTT tourist office** (☎ 77 231 897; Place des Martyrs; ☉ 8am-4pm) and a **syndicat d'initiative** (☎ 77 270 452; Ave Ibn el-Aghlab; ☉ 8am-6pm Mon-Thu, to 1pm Fri, to 4pm Sat & Sun) in front of the Aghlabid Basins which sells the all-in-one ticket for all the sites (TD7).

All the major banks are on the streets south of Place des Martyrs, the main post office is southwest of Bab ech Chouhada and the

Publinet (Ave Ali Zouaoui; ☉ 8am-midnight) charges TD2 per hour.

Sights

The 9th-century **Grande Mosquée** (Rue Okba ibn Nafâa; ☉ 8am-2pm Sat-Thu, to noon Fri), with its buttressed walls, has a typically unadorned Aghlabid design. Impressions change once you step into the huge marble-paved courtyard, surrounded by an arched colonnade. Non-Muslims can't cross into the richly decorated prayer hall, but the doors are left open to allow a glimpse.

Other sites in the medina include the 14th-century **Zaouia Sidi Abid el-Ghariani** (Rue Sidi el-Ghariani; ☉ 7.30am-1.30pm Mon-Sat Jun-Sep, 8.30am-1pm & 3-6pm Mon-Thu, to 1pm Fri & Sat Oct-May), with fine stucco and woodwork; **Bir Barouta**, where a blinkered camel walks in a circle, drawing water from a holy well said to be connected to Mecca; and the 18th-century residence of the former *beys* or pashas of Kairouan, now a carpet shop called **Tapis-Sabra** (☉ 8am-5pm), worth the carpet spiel to see an exquisitely restored medina house and witness the women rug weavers at work.

Northwest of the medina is the 17th-century **Zaouia Sidi Sahab** (Ave Zama el Belaoui; ☉ 8am-6pm Mon-Thu, to 2pm Fri, to 4pm Sat & Sun), tiled in luminescent colours and known as the 'barber mosque', because it contains the mausoleum of one of the Prophet's companions, Abu Zama el-Belaoui, who used to carry around three hairs from the Prophet's beard.

Sleeping & Eating

Hôtel Sabra (☎ 77 230 263; Place des Martyrs; s/d TD15/25) This noisy, hot, hostel-like dump has the best location in Kairouan opposite the Bab ech Chouhada, and the views from the rooftop (where you may be able to sleep in summer) are breathtaking.

Hôtel la Kasbah (☎ 77 237 301; www.goldenyasmin. com; Ave Ibn el-Jazzar; s/d TD105/160; ⌧ ⌨) Occupying the old kasbah in the northern section of the medina, this is the real deal, albeit generously re-imagined and re-appointed with colourful tiled walls, ornate ceilings and fine textiles.

Segni (Ave 7 Novembre) This patisserie is the best in town. The interior is a wonderful example of a traditional medina shop.

Restaurant Sabra (Ave de la République; mains TD6, set meal TD8) Serves good, filling staples in a pleasant little dining room. Staff are superfriendly.

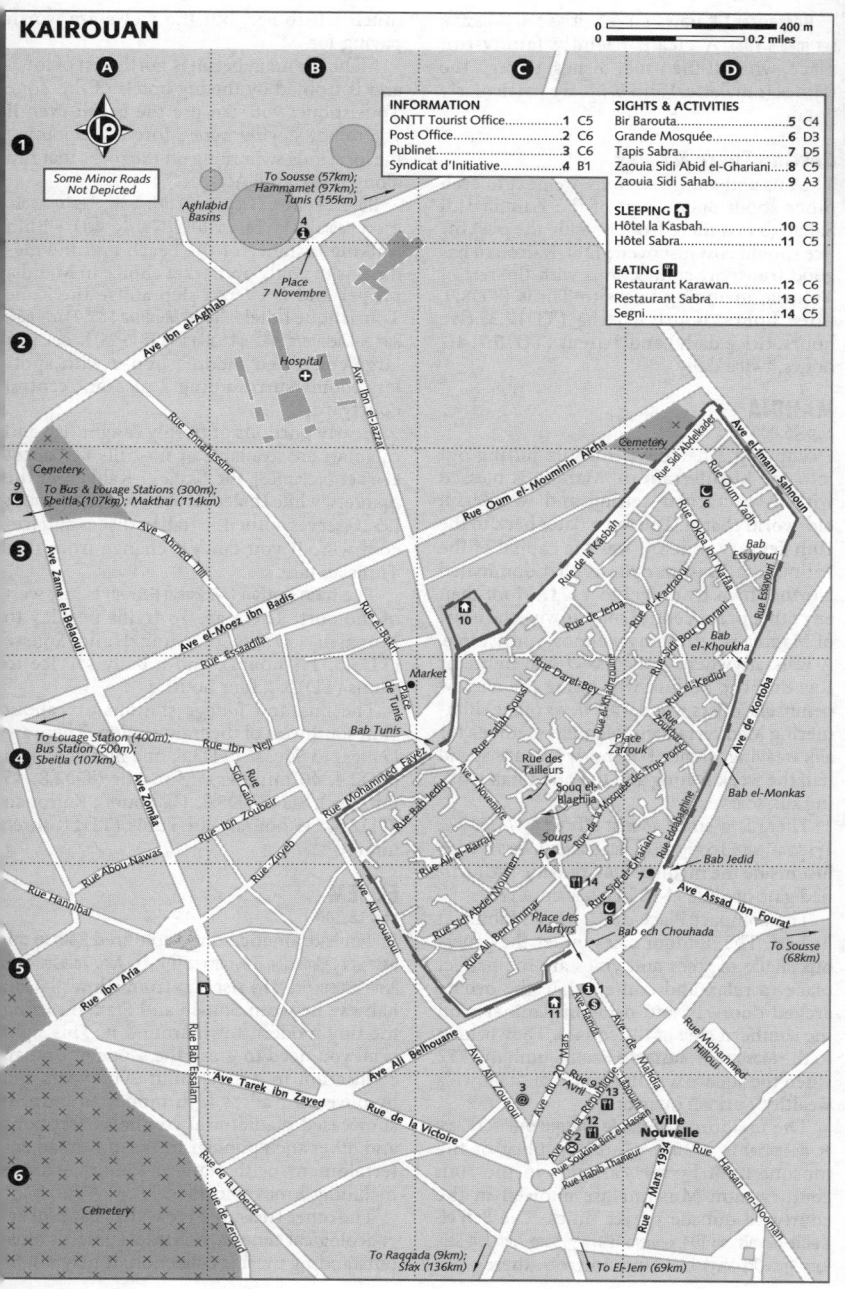

KAIROUAN

0 ———————— 400 m
0 ———————— 0.2 miles

INFORMATION
ONTT Tourist Office...............1 C5
Post Office...............2 C6
Publinet...............3 C6
Syndicat d'Initiative...............4 B1

SIGHTS & ACTIVITIES
Bir Barouta...............5 C4
Grande Mosquée...............6 D3
Tapis Sabra...............7 D5
Zaouia Sidi Abid el-Ghariani....8 C5
Zaouia Sidi Sahab...............9 A3

SLEEPING
Hôtel la Kasbah...............10 C3
Hôtel Sabra...............11 C5

EATING
Restaurant Karawan...............12 C6
Restaurant Sabra...............13 C6
Segni...............14 C5

Some Minor Roads Not Depicted

Aghlabid Basins

To Sousse (57km);
Hammamet (97km);
Tunis (155km)

Place 7 Novembre

Hospital

Ave Ibn el-Aghlab

Ave Ibn el-Jazzar

Rue Emnkassine

Cemetery

To Bus & Louage Stations (300m);
Sbeitla (107km); Makthar (114km)

Ave Ahmed Tlili

Ave Zama el-Belaoui

Ave el-Moez Ibn Badis

Rue Essaadla

Rue el-Rkim

Market

Place de Tunis

Bab Tunis

To Louage Station (400m);
Bus Station (500m);
Sbeitla (107km)

Rue Ibn Neji

Rue Sidi Cald Zouber

Ave Zomlia

Rue Ibn Zouber

Rue Abou Nawas

Rue Zineb

Rue Hannibal

Rue Ibn Aria

Rue Bab Essalam

Rue Mohammed Fayez

Rue Bab Jedid

Rue Ali el-Barrak

Rue Ali Zouaoui

Rue Sidi Abdel Noumen

Rue Ali Ben Ammar

Ave Ali Belhouane

Ave Tarek ibn Zayed

Rue de la Victoire

Rue de la Liberté

Rue de la Zeqid

Cemetery

Rue de la Kasbah

Cemetery

Rue Sidi Abdelkader

Rue Oum el-Moumimin Aicha

Ave el-Imam Sahnoun

Rue Oum Yadh

Rue Okba Ibn Nafda

Bab Essayouri

Rue el-Kachoui

Rue de Jerba

Rue Sidi Bou Otman

Bab el-Khoukha

Rue el-Khaldoune

Rue el-Kedjoi

Rue Dar-el-Bey

Ave de Kortoba

Rue Sabat-Soualt

Place Zarrouk

Rue Zorbouk

Bab el-Monkas

Rue des Tailleurs

Souq el-Blaghija

Ave de la Mosqué des Trois Portes

Souqs

Rue Sidi el-Chairani

Rue el-Djebaliya

Bab Jedid

Ave Assad ibn Fourat

Bab el-Monkas

Place des Martyrs

Bab ech Chouhada

To Sousse (68km)

Ville Nouvelle

Rue Mohammed Hilloul

Rue de Matida

Rue Okba Ibn el-Nafda

Ave du 20 Avril

Ave de la Republique

Ave Zama el-Belaoui

Rue Habib Thameur

Rue Soukina bint el-Hassan

Rue 2 Mars 1934

Rue Hassan en-Nooman

To Raqqada (9km);
Sfax (136km)

To El-Jem (69km)

Restaurant Karawan (Rue Soukina bint el-Hassan; set meals TD8) A clean, friendly family-run place, with all the usual dishes, though the tajines (omelettes) and *briqs* are particularly good.

Getting There & Away

The bus and *louage* stations are next to each other about 300m west of the Zaouia Sidi Sahab (a taxi there from outside the post office should cost just over TD1). Kairouan has good transport connections with the rest of Tunisia, including buses to Tunis (TD8.9, three hours, hourly), Jerba (TD17.3, five hours, twice daily) and Tozeur (TD15.7, 4½ hours, twice daily).

MAHDIA
pop 46,000

Occupying a narrow peninsula jutting out into the Mediterranean, Mahdia is blessed with a spectacular setting and wonderful old-world charm. The town dates back to the 10th century, when it was the capital of the Fatimids, a Muslim dynasty that dominated North Africa from 909 to 1171. More than any other of the central coast towns, the heart of Mahdia is refreshingly almost tourist free. A walk anywhere along Ave 7 Novembre or Rue du Borj, both of which hug the narrow peninsula, offers wonderful views of the shimmering Mediterranean. Mahdia is famous for silk weaving (some of the burly artisans spend half the week fishing and the other half making silk scarves).

There is a small **tourist office** (☎ 73 681 098; 8am-1pm & 3-5.45pm Mon-Thu, 8.30am-1.30pm Fri & Sat) just inside the medina. **BIAT**, outside the fortified gate of Skifa el-Kahla, has an ATM.

The compact Place du Caire is Mahdia at its best. The outdoor cafes under the generous shade of trees and vines are the perfect place to relax and contemplate the ornate arched doorway and octagonal minaret on the southern side of the square. They belong to the **Mosque of Mustapha Hamza**, built in 1772 when the square was the centre of the town's wealthy Turkish quarter.

The unadorned **Grande Mosquée** (Place Khadi en-Noamine) is a 20th-century replica of the mosque built by the Fatimids in the 10th century; non-Muslims are allowed in the courtyard outside prayer times. The **Borj el-Kebir** (admission TD4, camera TD1; 9am-7pm Jun-Sep, 9am-4pm Oct-May) is a large fortress; there's not

much left to see, but the views are worth paying for.

Mahdia's main beach is northwest of town and is fronted by the big hotels of the Zone Touristique; you can use the beach even if you're not staying here. More fun is joining the local kids swimming off the rocks that run along Rue Cap d'Afrique.

Hôtel Le Phenix (☎ 73 690 101; www.phenixmahdia.tk; Ave Habib Bourguiba, s/d TD100/170;), within walking distance of the beach and the medina, is the only upmarket choice in Mahdia proper and is even a step above the Zone Touristique hotels. **Hôtel Médina** (☎ 73 694 664; Rue el-Kaem; s/d without bathroom TD15/25) is set in a large converted medina house with spotless rooms surrounding a pleasant central courtyard.

Hearty portions of freshly caught fish and calamari are available at no-frills **Restaurant el-Moez** (mains TD5), the Skifa el-Kahla and the markets, while **Le Meriem** (Route de la Corniche; mains TD5-15) serves authentic Italian dishes and ice-cold wine if you fancy a change from trad Tunisian fare.

The **train station** (Ave Farhat Hached) is just west of the port. There are 16 trains per day to Monastir (TD1.8, one hour) and Sousse (TD3.5, 1¾ hours), and a daily service to Tunis (TD10.4, four hours).

The bus and *louage* stations are about 1km southwest of the train station. There are *louages* to Sousse (TD3.6, one hour), El-Jem (TD2.4, 40 minutes), Monastir (TD2.8, 45 minutes), Sfax (TD5.8, 1½ hours), Kairouan (TD7.5, 1½ hours) and Tunis (TD11, three hours).

EL-JEM
pop 18,300

El-Jem's dramatic honey-coloured **Roman colosseum** (admission TD7, camera TD1; 7am-7pm Jun-Sep, 8am-5.30pm Oct-May) rises up from a low plateau halfway between Sousse and Sfax, dwarfing the tiny modern town around it. This sight is all you need to grasp the scope of Roman civilisation in Africa. Built 2000 years ago by olive-oil traders with money to burn, it showcased gladiatorial combat, executions and other such popular forms of Roman entertainment, with state-of-the-art features including a movable floor.

The other treasure here is the beautiful archaeological **museum**, home to Tunisia's most outstanding mosaic collection. It may not be as big as that in the Bardo, but the mosaics' vividness and pristine condition definitely outdo those in the capital, plus some of them are in situ, in a street of excavated villas alongside the museum proper. There's nowhere to stay, but you can eat at **Restaurant Le Bonheur** (☎ 73 632 384; mains TD6; ⚒), just across the road from the train station.

The *louage* station is 300m west of the train station along Ave Hedi Chaker. There are frequent departures to Mahdia (TD2.4, 35 minutes), Sousse (TD4, 40 minutes) and Sfax (TD4, 40 minutes). For Kairouan and Tunis, you'll need to change at Sousse. The last *louage* has usually left the station by 7pm and often well before. There are trains north to Sousse (TD4.5, one hour) and Tunis (TD10.4, three hours), and south to Sfax (TD4.5, one hour), but only a couple are at times that are of any use to colosseum visitors.

SFAX
pop 265,000

Locals from Sfax (see Map p232) have the reputation of being hard-working, dull and thrifty, which, in Tunisia, doesn't do them any favours (everyone will advise you to skip Sfax and carry on down to Jerba). But the country's second-largest city is worth a look, if only to have a lunch of delicious *ojja* (prawn stew with eggs and tomatoes), a Sfax speciality, and to check out the town medina. Surrounded by crenulated walls that could have been filched from a child's toy castle, this tourist-tat-free medina hasn't been prettified for visitors and bustles with everyday life. Female travellers might find the atmosphere somewhat oppressive, as local men are not so used to seeing foreign women.

The **tourist office** (☎ 74 211 040; Ave Mohammed Hedi Khefecha; ☑ 8.15am-1pm & 2.30-5pm Mon-Thu, 8.30am-1.30pm Fri & Sat) is by the port. There are lots of banks, several with ATMs, around Ave Habib Bourguiba, where you'll also find a **Publinet** (2nd fl, Ave Habib Bourguiba; per hr TD2; ☑ 8am-midnight). Highlights of the Sfax medina include the atmospheric covered **souqs**, which were filmed as Cairo in the film *The English Patient*; the 9th-century **Grande Mosquée** (closed to non-Muslims); and the **Dar Jellouli Museum of Popular Traditions** (admission TD3, camera TD1; ☑ 9.30am-4.30pm Tue-Sun), housed in a stunning 17th-century courtyard mansion with carved wooden panelling and ornate

stucco, displaying jewellery, costumes and painted glass.

On the northern edge of the medina, the white and blue **Hôtel Ennacer** (☎ 74 211 037; 100 Rue des Notaires; s/d TD15/25; ⚒) is spotless and air-con can be had for TD5 more; there are great views from the rooftop. **Hôtel Thyna** (☎ 74 225 317; www.hotel-thyna.com; 37 Rue Habib Maazoun; s/d TD35/55; ⚒) is well located and good value (though more Ikea than the high-end boutique hotel the lobby suggests), plus the *pains au chocolat* served for breakfast are fabulous.

Le Bagdad (☎ 74 223 856; 63 Ave Farhat Hached; mains TD9-15) comes across as slightly formal at first, but the service is friendly and the menu gives pride of place to traditional dishes such as *kamounia* (cumin-flavoured stew) and *koucha* (melt-in-your mouth lamb and potatoes stewed in tomato sauce), as well as seasonal fish. **Restaurant au Bec Fin** (Place du 2 Mars; mains TD7-12) serves decent Tunisian fare: pan-fried dogfish, squid kebab and prawn or merguez *ojja*. **Café Maure Diwan** (off Rue de la Kasbah; ☑ 6am-midnight), cut into the medina wall between Bab Diwan and Bab el-Kasbah, is a refuge from the heat and a great spot to kill a few hours with a mint tea with pine nuts (TD1).

The train station is at the eastern end of Ave Habib Bourguiba. There's three trains per day south to Gabès (2½ hours), and two services to Gafsa (three hours), Metlaoui (four hours) and Tozeur (4½ hours). Heading north, there are five trains daily to El-Jem (one hour), four to Sousse (two hours) and seven to Tunis (3½ hours).

SNTRI buses leave from the gare routière du port, southwest of the port, with regular buses to Tunis (TD14.2, four hours, eight daily), Sousse (TD7.3, two hours, 10 daily), Douz (TD14.7, four hours, two daily), El-Jem (TD3.6, one hour, 10 daily) and Tripoli (TD18.3, eight hours).

The *louage* station is 300m west of the **southern bus station** (Soretras) on Rue Commandant Bejaoui. *Louages* run to all of the above destinations for around the same price, as well as to El-Jem (TD4, one hour) and Tripoli (TD36, eight hours). Kairouan, Medenine and Jerba are serviced by Soretras.

Ferries to the Kerkennah Islands (TD0.7, 11 daily) leave from the docks on Ave Mohammed Hedi Khefecha.

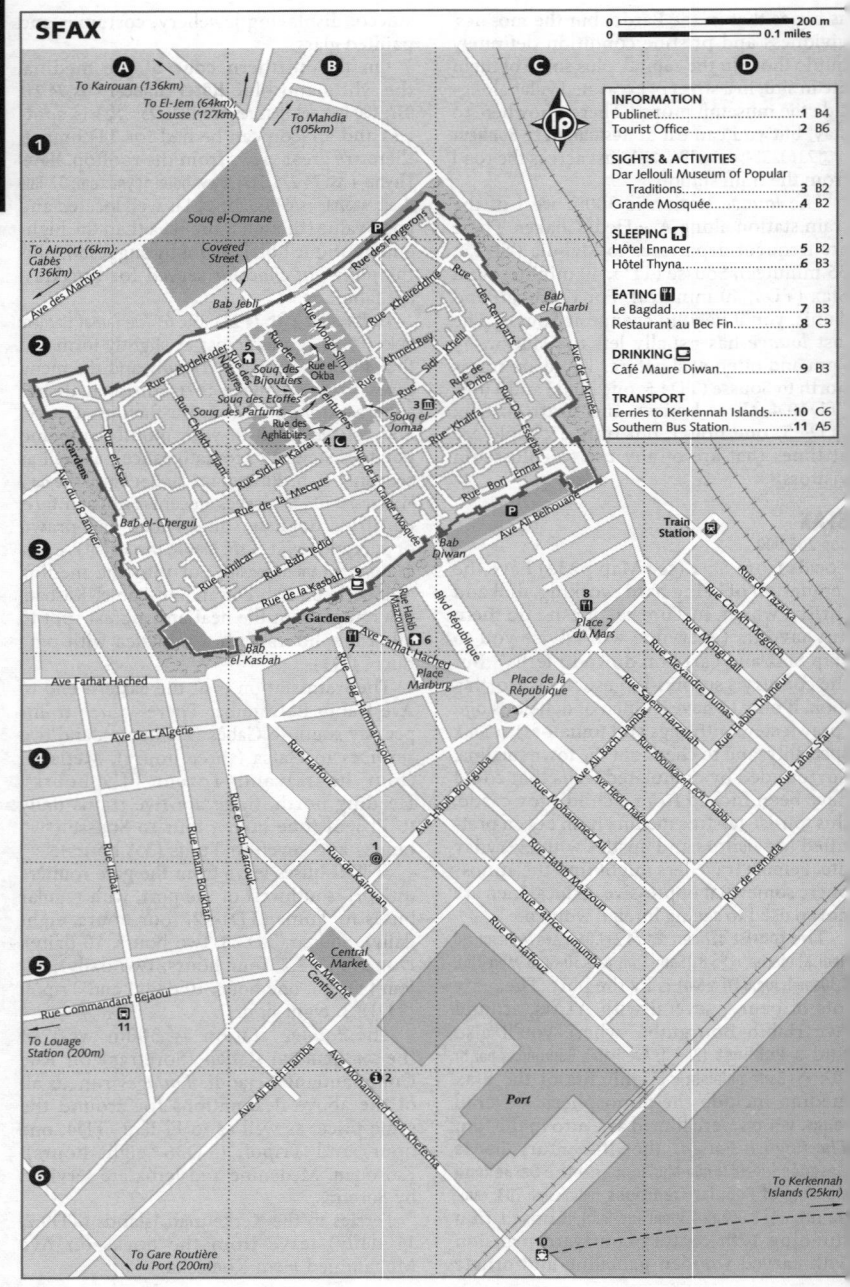

SFAX

0	200 m
0	0.1 miles

INFORMATION
Publinet................................**1** B4
Tourist Office.......................**2** B6

SIGHTS & ACTIVITIES
Dar Jellouli Museum of Popular
    Traditions.......................**3** B2
Grande Mosquée..................**4** B2

SLEEPING
Hôtel Ennacer.....................**5** B2
Hôtel Thyna........................**6** B3

EATING
Le Bagdad...........................**7** B3
Restaurant au Bec Fin.........**8** C3

DRINKING
Café Maure Diwan...............**9** B3

TRANSPORT
Ferries to Kerkennah Islands...**10** C6
Southern Bus Station..........**11** A5

SOUTHERN TUNISIA

In the south you'll find the desert landscapes that have enchanted travellers for centuries, their seeming emptiness the stuff of both dreams, nightmares and much colonial musing. Life-giving palmeraies grow like tufts of hair mid-desert and promise autumn harvests of the world's best dates. Salt lakes shimmer in the sun like mirages. Fortified Berber towns stare from barren hilltops over scarred scrubland. Hot springs offer pampering dips deep in desert towns, while back on the coast, the island of Jerba is a fascinating destination in its own right.

TOZEUR
pop 35,500

Tozeur, boasting a wide range of hotels and restaurants, makes an excellent base for longer forays into the surrounding area, including the mesmerising Chott el-Jerid, Tunisia's largest salt lake. Bounded on one side by an enormous palmeraie and then the desolate snow-white expanse of salt on the other, the town itself feels simultaneously far-flung and welcoming. It's easy to spend a few days here occupied by the labyrinthine old quarter, Ouled el-Hadef, with its distinctive traditional brickwork, and some interesting museums located in the town itself.

There's an **ONTT tourist office** (☎ 76 454 503; ☼ 7.30am-1.30pm & 5-8pm Jul-Aug, 8.30am-1pm & 3.30-6pm Sun-Thu, 8.30am-1.30pm Fri & Sat Sep-Jun) located on Ave Abdulkacem Chebbi. Another tourist office is the **syndicat d'initiative** (☎ 76 462 034; Place Bab el-Hawa). There are several banks with ATMs around the northern end of Ave Habib Bourguiba.

The **Publinet** (11 Ave du 7 Novembre; per hr TD2; ☼ 24hr) has surprisingly good internet connections.

Sights & Activities

The 14th-century **Ouled el-Hadef** has a unique, striking architecture of patterned, relief brickwork; the easiest way in is from Ave de Kairouan. The families living in the quarter come outside at dusk – strolling at this time is lovely.

The enormous **palmeraie**, with over 200,000 palms, as well as fig and pomegranate trees, is best explored by foot (or bicycle when it's too hot). There's **bicycle hire** on Ave

Abdulkacem Chebbi for between TD2 and TD5 per hour. There's **calèche hire** (horse-drawn-carriage hire) from opposite the Hôtel Residence Karim for TD10 per hour.

The **Dar Charaït Museum** (Ave Abdulkacem Chebbi; admission TD3.4, camera TD1.7; ☼ 8am-midnight) has displays of pottery, jewellery and textiles, as well as gloriously tacky tableaux of Ottoman and Bedouin history. It's beautifully lit and more atmospheric at night. A sandy track running south of the museum leads to the **Belvedere Rocks**. Steps have been cut into the highest, giving access to a spectacular sunset view over the oasis and the *chott*.

Excursions that can be made from Tozeur include a half-day trip via 4WD to **Ong Jemal**, a dramatic location used in both *Star Wars* and *The English Patient*, **Nefta** (see the Top Ten *Star Wars* Locations boxed text, p238), or the beautiful **Berber villages** of Midès, Chebika and Tamerza. Half-day trips cost from TD30 upwards. Wherever you go, be prepared for the 4WD scrum once you get there.

Sleeping & Eating

Camping Les Beaux Rêves (☎ 76 453 331; http://beaux reves.koi29.com; Ave Abdulkacem Chebbi; tent/bungalow per person TD5/8, car TD4, showers TD1.5) This is one of the more enchanting campsites in the south. The whole area is shaded by trees – you can even set up a hammock to sleep on – and there's a stream running alongside the palmeraie.

Hôtel Residence Karim (☎ 76 454 574; 150 Ave Abdulkacem Chebbi; s/d TD17.5/25; ✄) Offering excellent value, the Karim has bright and cheerful tiled rooms, shady courtyards and a rooftop terrace.

Residence el-Amen (☎ 76 473 322; amentozeur@ yahoo.fr; 10 Ave Taoufik el-Hakim; s/d TD25/32; ✄) The friendly el-Amen, on a side street off Ave Abdulkacem Chebbi, has tiny, cute rooms. Rooftop rooms have excellent views.

Dar Charait Hôtel (☎ 76 452 100; www.darcherait. com; Route Zone Touristique; s/d TD203/310; ✄ ☀) The five-star Dar Charait is one of the few places where the opulent interior fulfils the promise of its palatial facade, with fabulously designed decor placing you firmly in the Maghreb.

Patisserie el Qods (Ave Habib Bourguiba) A handy place to drop into for a quick sandwich, or something sweet and sticky, washed down with some freshly squeezed juice.

Restaurant Capitole (☎ 76 462 631; 152 Ave Abdulkacem Chebbi; mains from TD3) This small place is popular with Tunisian families. Preorder

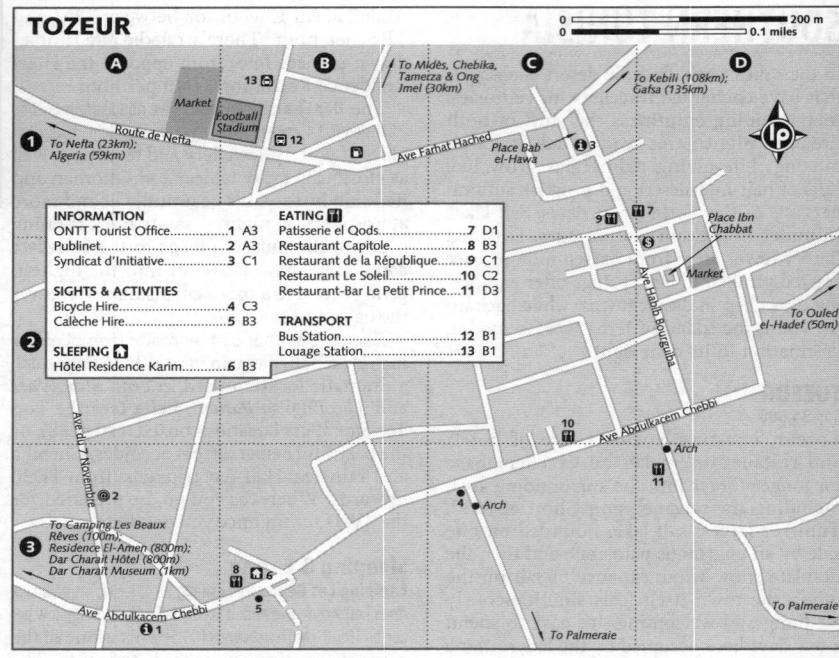

TOZEUR

INFORMATION
ONTT Tourist Office..............1 A3
Publinet...............................2 A3
Syndicat d'Initiative............3 C1

SIGHTS & ACTIVITIES
Bicycle Hire..........................4 C3
Calèche Hire.........................5 B3

SLEEPING
Hôtel Residence Karim..........6 B3

EATING
Patisserie el Qods.................7 D1
Restaurant Capitole..............8 B3
Restaurant de la République...9 C1
Restaurant Le Soleil............10 C2
Restaurant-Bar Le Petit Prince....11 D3

TRANSPORT
Bus Station..........................12 B1
Louage Station.....................13 B1

the *metabgha* (Berber pizza; TD3) or stick to camel steak.

Restaurant Le Soleil (☎ 76 454 220; 58 Ave Abdulkacem Chebbi; mains from TD4) Try the camel if it's available, or enjoy the decor of plaster palm trees and the vegetarian dishes if it's not.

Restaurant de la République (☎ 76 452 354; 108 Ave Habib Bourguiba; mains from TD4) In an arcade next to the Mosque el-Ferdous, this is a good place for a simple couscous and salad.

Restaurant-Bar Le Petit Prince (☎ 76 452 518; off Ave Abdulkacem Chebbi; mains TD8-17) Lingering over French and Tunisian dishes and wine in the palm-shaded courtyard here is a memorable experience.

Getting There & Away

The bus and *louage* stations are near each other just north of the road to Nefta. There are five buses travelling daily to/from Tunis (TD22.1, seven hours), via Kairouan (TD15.2, 4½ hours) and Gafsa (TD7.1, 1½ hours), and one daily to Nefta (TD1.3, 30 minutes), Douz (TD6.6, three hours) and Gabès (TD12, 4½ hours). SNTRI also does runs to Sousse (TD14.6, 5¾ hours) in the morning. There

are *louages* travelling to/from Nefta, Tunis and Gabès for the same prices, and to/from Kebili (TD5.7, 1½ hours).

DOUZ
pop 28,000

Douz, a strictly modern and functional oasis, is but a curtain to the wonders just to the south, especially the Grand Erg Oriental (one of the Sahara's most expansive sand seas). The sleepy town comes alive after dark – people are open and friendly, accustomed to the fact that the local economy is largely dependent on groups of foreigners turning giddy at the prospect of riding a camel. In addition to the Zone Touristique hotels, whose inflated prices are mostly justified by their desertside locations, there are several hotels in the town centre that cater to independent travellers. Every Thursday, the souq is home to a colourful weekly market, where the last of Tunisia's nomadic camel herders come to trade. It's worth arranging to be here just to see it. The **palmeraie**, at the town's edge, is the largest in the country: more than 400,000 trees slice into the fierce sunlight.

Information

The **ONTT tourist office** (☎ 75 470 351; Place des Martyrs; ⏰ 8am-1pm & 3-5.45pm Sun-Thu, 8.30am-1.30pm Fri & Sat) can give recommended prices for camel expeditions. There's an **STB** (Ave Taieb Mehiri) and **Banque de Sud** (Route de Kebili), or the post office has an exchange counter. **Publinet** (cnr Rue 20 Mars & Rue el-Hounine; per hr TD2; ⏰ 8am-10pm) has good internet connections.

Sights & Activities

Douz is the most convenient place to get a taste for the Sahara, though it's really only a taste. The Sahara desert proper starts 50km south of the Zone Touristique. Unless you're planning a longer excursion, you'll end up at the **great dune**. It can't compare with the sand seas of the **Grand Erg Oriental**, 50km to the south, but it's a gentle introduction for those with limited time. **Pegase** (Café de Dunes; ☎ 75 470 793) is a one-stop shop that seems to have a monopoly on the great dune. Part of the fun of a camel trip (if alone, you should be able to negotiate a ride for around TD15 per hour) is being outfitted in a long Berber-style tunic.

Overnight treks are equally easy to organise; longer treks generally require 24 hours' notice. It's possible to even arrange trips of two to three weeks during the winter months. The biggest challenge is choosing between the treks on offer. The tourist office advises travellers to stay clear of the town's many unlicensed guides, pointing out that they are uninsured and unaccountable if problems arise, though in reality many travellers use them. Officially recognised agencies include **Espace Libre** (☎ 75 470 620; www.libre-espace-voyages.com; cnr Ave Taieb Mehiri & Ave du 7 Novembre) and **Ghilane Travel Services** (☎ 75 470 692; gts@planet.tn; 38 Ave Taieb Mehiri).

The **Sahara Festival** usually takes place in November. This is very popular with Tunisians as well as foreign tourists, and has displays of traditional desert sports, colourful parades and music.

Sleeping & Eating

Camping Desert Club (☎ /fax 75 470 575; brahim2020@yahoo.fr; off ave du 7 Novembre 1987; per person TD5, plus motorbike/car/campervan TD3/4/5) One of the better campsites in the country, not only because of its setting among palm trees, but also because it has excellent modern facilities. Tentless? Sleep on a mattress inside a Berber tent.

Hôtel 20 Mars (☎ 75 470 269; hotel20mars@planet.tn; Rue 20 Mars; s/d with bathroom TD15/20, without bathroom TD13/18; ☒) A popular traveller's option, with its helpful staff and the interior courtyard, this feels more like a guesthouse.

Hôtel Medina (☎ 75 470 010; Rue el-Hounine; r per person with/without bathroom & air-con TD40/20; ☒) Another excellent choice with a flowering courtyard and spacious, modern rooms. The in-house restaurant does decent pizzas, too.

Restaurant Chez Magic (Ave des Martyrs; mains TD3-4) A lunchtime favourite, usually busy with a mix of locals, guides and tourists, all tucking into to speedily served dishes of couscous, soups, salads and grills.

Tej el-Khayem (☎ 75 472 446; Zone Touristique; mains TD10; ☒) Whether you eat indoors, in a Berber-style tent or out on the sand, Tej el-Khayem serves up some of the best meals in Douz.

Getting There & Away

There are regular local buses and *louages* running to Kebili (TD1.8, 30 minutes), Tozeur (TD7.5, two hours), Gabès (TD6, three hours) and Zaafrane (TD0.5, 20 minutes). SNTRI has two air-con services per day to Tunis, direct at 6am (TD27, eight hours) and via Gabès (TD12, two hours) and Sfax (TD17, four hours) at 10am.

MATMATA
pop 1500

From above, the troglodytic pit homes that have made Matmata famous look like bomb craters. Home to around 500 people, the ingenious dwellings only come into focus up close and are a testament to humankind's urge to domesticate, even somewhere as inhospitable as here. More recently, the town has drawn its fame from playing the home planet of Luke Skywalker in *Star Wars*. It's not often you get the locals offering to show you outer space, but this little village brims with such delights.

The best place to stay is **Hôtel Marhala** (☎ 75 240 015; s/d incl breakfast TD14/22, incl half board TD18/30), run by the Touring Club de Tunisie. It's everything you might hope a troglodytic hotel to be (there's even a dining-room cave).

There are regular buses and *louages* to/from Gabès (TD1.8, 45 minutes) and one SNTRI bus to/from Tunis (TD19.4, eight hours).

JERBA & HOUMT SOUQ

Jerba is an island with an intoxicating mixture of sandy beaches, desert heat and beautiful (and wonderfully peculiar) architecture.

Berber culture is dominant (watch for local women wrapped in cream-striped textiles, topped with straw hats), while a Jewish community, once integral to the island's ethnic make-up, still retains a small presence. To the classically inclined, the name Jerba conjures up images of Homer's Land of the Lotus Eaters, an island so seductive that it's impossible to leave ('drugged by the legendary honeyed fruit', poor Ulysses had a lot of trouble prising his crew away). The many visitors voluntarily sequestering themselves at the chain hotels along beautiful Sidi Mahres beach tend to agree. While the appeal of a luxury beach resort speaks for itself, the rest of fascinating Jerba shouldn't be missed.

The island is linked to the mainland by a causeway built in Roman times. In addition, convenient 24-hour car ferries ply between Ajim (where Obi-Wan Kenobi had his house; see the Top Ten *Star Wars* Locations boxed text, p238) and El-Jorf.

Houmt Souq is the island's 'capital', standing in the middle of the north coast. It's a polished, charming small town, chock-a-block with outdoor cafes, craft and carpet sellers, and a handful of ancient *funduqs* (inns), the town's architectural trademark. There's a **syndicat d'initiative** (☎ 75 650 915; Ave Habib Bourguiba; 🕙 8am-2pm Nov-Mar, 8am-3pm Mon-Sat Apr-Oct) in the centre and an **ONTT tourist office** (☎ 75 650 016; Blvd de l'Environnement; 🕙 8.30am-1pm & 3-5.45pm Mon-Thu, 8.30am-1.30pm Fri & Sat) out on the beach road. There are also banks with ATMs, a **post office** (ave Habib Bourguiba) and a Taxiphone office, all on Ave Habib Bourguiba. **Djerba Cyber Espace** (per hr TD2; 🕙 9am-midnight) is upstairs from the courtyard of Restaurant el-Foundouk.

Sights & Activities

The **old town** is filled with some fine examples of Jerba's traditional architecture, including white walls enclosing living quarters and domes dotting the skyline. Virtually every nook and cranny is given over to tantalising wares, from striking carpets to jewellery, ceramics and miniature birdcages, the colours creating a beautiful contrast to the whitewashed buildings lining the maze of alleyways.

The fairy-tale fort **Borj Ghazi Mustapha**, on the beach 500m north of town, was first built in the 13th-century by the Aragonese. When the Ottomoans captured the fort in 1560, they stacked the skulls of their Spanish victims into a tower, although this grim monument was dismantled last century.

The most important synagogue on Jerba and the oldest in North Africa is **El-Ghriba** (admission TD1; 🕙 7.30am-6pm Sun-Fri), 7km south of Houmt Souq and signposted 1km south of the town of Erriadh, also called Hara Seghira (Small Ghetto). The synagogue is a major place of pilgrimage in May. As part of the festivities, local Jews and pilgrims carry the community's holy books through the town. The interior of the synagogue is an attractive combination of blue tilework and sombre wooden furniture. The inner sanctuary, with its elevated pulpit, is said to contain one of the oldest Torahs in the world. Bring ID for the security checks outside.

Sleeping & Eating

Houmt Souq has some wonderful places to stay, many converted from *funduqs*, lodging houses for the camel caravans that stopped here in Ottoman times; the merchants stayed on the top floor, while their animals were housed below.

Hôtel Marhala (☎ 75 650 146; Rue Moncef Bey; s/d TD14/28) A converted *funduq* with barrel-vaulted rooms that are very simple indeed, but it's great fun and has bags of character.

Hôtel Erriadh (☎ 75 650 756; mounirherbegue@gnet.tn; Rue Mohammed Ferjani; s/d TD19/30; 🏊) Comfortable and charmingly decorated, this architecturally delightful hotel is again housed in one of the old *funduqs*.

Hôtel du Lotos (☎ 75 650 026; hoteldulotos@topnet. tn; Blvd de l'Environnement; s/d TD35/60; 🏊) Most of the spartanly furnished rooms in this attractive and airy whitewashed complex get good sunlight.

Dar Dhiafa (☎ 75 671 166; www.hoteldardhiafa.com; d TD180, ste TD220-260; 🏊 📖 🛁) Built in local architectural style, Jerba's loveliest hotel is a small warren of rooms with decor straight out of an interiors magazine. Plus it has its own *hammam*.

Restaurant du Sportif (Ave Habib Bourguiba; mains TD3) Frequented by locals rather than tourists, Restaurant du Sportif is friendly and no-nonsense.

Restaurant de l'Ile (Rue de Bizerte; mains TD8-14) Noted for its seafood, including overflowing plates of fresh clams and squid, the *briq au fruits de mer* is almost big enough for a meal in and of itself. Alcohol is available.

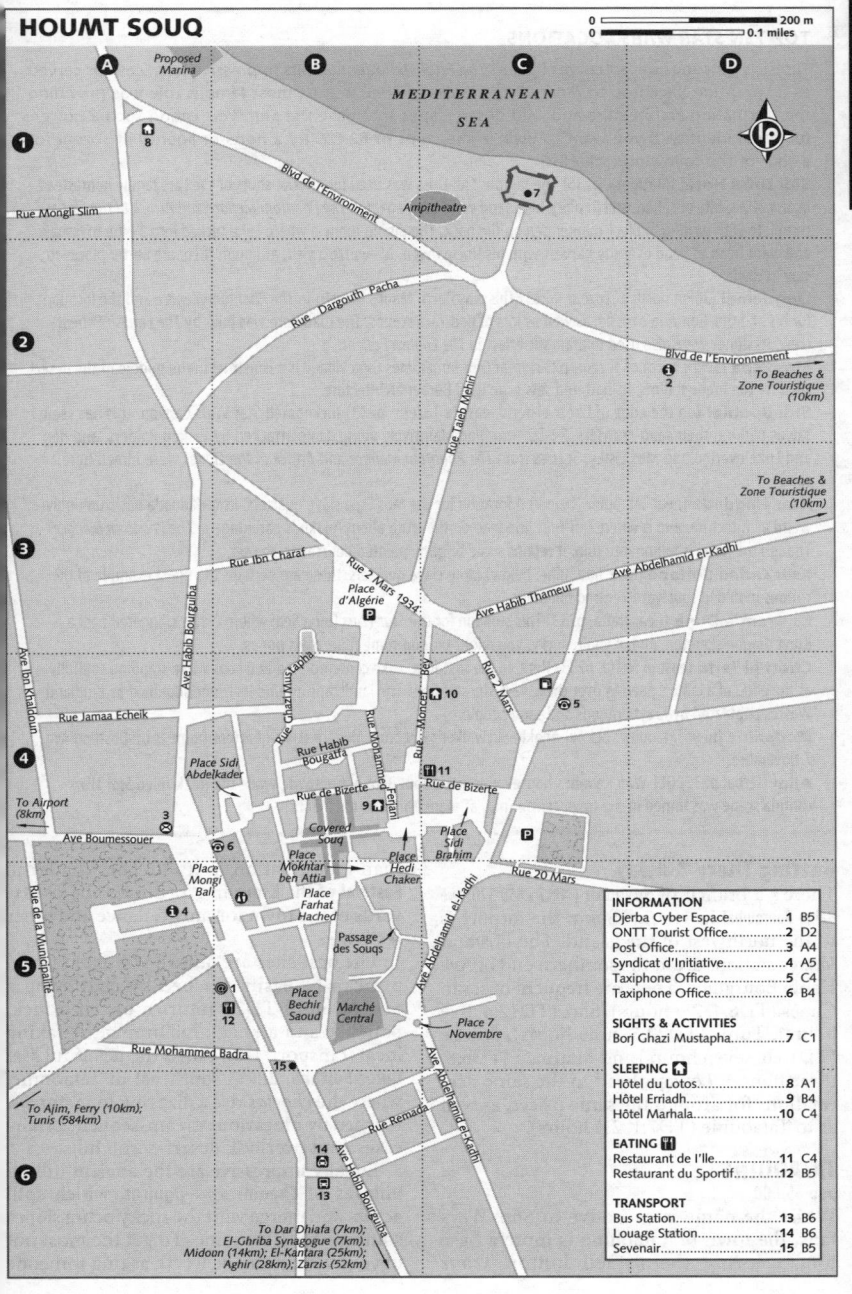

HOUMT SOUQ

0 ———————— 200 m
0 ———————— 0.1 miles

Proposed Marina

MEDITERRANEAN SEA

Blvd de l'Environment

Ampitheatre

Rue Mongli Slim

Rue Dargouth Pacha

Blvd de l'Environnement

To Beaches & Zone Touristique (10km)

To Beaches & Zone Touristique (10km)

Rue Ibn Charaf

Rue 2 Mars 1934

Place d'Algérie

Ave Abdelhamid el-Kadhi

Ave Habib Thameur

Rue Taieb Mehiri

Ave Habib Bourguiba

Rue Ibn Khaldoun

Rue Jamaa Echeik

Rue Ghazi Mustapha

Rue Mohammed Ferjani

Rue Moncef Bey

Rue 2 Mars

Place Sidi Abdelkader

Rue Habib Bougatfa

Rue de Bizerte

Rue de Bizerte

To Airport (8km)

Ave Boumessouer

Covered Souq

Place Mokhtar ben Attia

Place Sidi Brahim

Place Hedi Chaker

Rue 20 Mars

Rue de la Municipalité

Place Mongi Bali

Place Farhat Hached

Passage des Souqs

Place Bechir Saoud

Marché Central

Place 7 Novembre

Rue Mohammed Badra

Ave Abdelhamid el-Kadhi

To Ajim, Ferry (10km); Tunis (584km)

Rue Remada

Ave Habib Bourguiba

To Dar Dhiafa (7km); El-Ghriba Synagogue (7km); Midoun (14km); El-Kantara (25km); Aghir (28km); Zarzis (52km)

INFORMATION
Djerba Cyber Espace..............1 B5
ONTT Tourist Office...............2 D2
Post Office...............................3 A4
Syndicat d'Initiative..............4 A5
Taxiphone Office...................5 C4
Taxiphone Office...................6 B4

SIGHTS & ACTIVITIES
Borj Ghazi Mustapha.............7 C1

SLEEPING ⌂
Hôtel du Lotos......................8 A1
Hôtel Erriadh........................9 B4
Hôtel Marhala.....................10 C4

EATING ⌘
Restaurant de l'Ile...............11 C4
Restaurant du Sportif..........12 B5

TRANSPORT
Bus Station.........................13 B6
Louage Station....................14 B6
Sevenair.............................15 B5

TOP TEN *STAR WARS* LOCATIONS

Tunisia's sensuous desert curves hosted *The English Patient* and its impressive fortifications served as a Levantine backdrop to *Monty Python's Life of Brian,* but its most famous role was providing the fascinating architecture and wild desertscapes that gave the *Star Wars* canon such a powerful visual identity. If you want to walk in the steps of R2-D2, try a hotel or agency in Tozeur for a tour of the following locations:

Sidi Driss Hotel (Matmata, p235) The famous Sidi Driss was used for interior shots of the Lars family homestead in *Star Wars*. Bits of set are still in place here (and were used again in *The Phantom Menace* and *Attack of the Clones*), complete with writing in black marker pen on the back. The dining room is where Luke tucked into a blue milkshake and went head to head over the harvest with his Uncle Owen. It's worth a visit, although there are better places to stay in town.

Ong Jemal (30km north of Tozeur, p233) This was Darth Maul's lookout in *The Phantom Menace* and the location for his and Qui-Gon Jinn's tussle, as well as lots of pod-race scenes. The road here was built by *The English Patient* crew. Its dunes were also used to dramatic effect in *The English Patient*.

Mos Espa (30km north of Tozeur, p233) Near Ong Jemel, Mos Espa village is a construct in the middle of the desert used for the prequel films; its battered sets echo local Berber architecture.

Sidi Bouhlel (on the edge of Chott el-Jerid, east of Tozeur, p233) Nicknamed Star Wars Canyon, this has seen Jawas parking their sand-crawlers, R2-D2 trundling plaintively along, Luke attacked by Tusken Raiders, and Ben and Luke overlooking Mos Eisley. Scenes from *The Phantom Menace* and *Attack of the Clones* were filmed here, too.

Ksar Haddada (near Tataouine, below) A location for the Mos Espa slave quarters, Ksar Haddada has stunningly weird architecture, and is where Qui-Gon Jinn learned the truth about Anakin's parentage in *The Phantom Menace*. Though the hotel is falling into ruin, it retains some brightly painted doors from the set.

Ksar Ouled Soltane (near Tataouine, below) More slave quarters, these are perhaps the finest example of the curious moulded courtyard-centred buildings.

La Grande Dune (near Nefta, p233) This stood in for the *Star Wars* Dune Sea, where C-3PO staggered past a Krayt dragon skeleton, and, if you're lucky, you might pick up some fibre-glass bones.

Chott el-Jerid (east of Nefta, p233) Here, in the first film, Luke contemplated two suns while standing soulfully at the edge of a crater, peering over these vast, dry salt flats. The landscape around its fringes doubled as Jundland Wastes populated by Krayt dragons and sand people.

Medenine (near Tataouine, below) Anakin Skywalker's *Phantom Menace* slave-quarters' home is off bustling Ave 7 Novembre.

Ajim (Jerba, p235) Obi-Wan Kenobi's house exterior is about 3km out of town, while the freak-filled *Star Wars* cantina scene was filmed in the town centre (not, as many think, at the Sidi Driss).

Getting There & Away

There's a branch of **Sevenair** (☎ 75 650 320; Ave Habib Bourguiba) in Houmt Souq; the airport is to the northwest of the island. The bus and *louage* stations are at the southern end of Ave Habib Bourguiba. There are frequent buses to Gabès (TD6.4, 2½ hours), Sfax (TD12.4, five hours), Tunis (TD22.5, nine hours), Sousse (TD18.6, seven hours) and Matmata (TD6.8, three hours). *Louages* head to the same destinations for around the same prices, as well as to Tataouine (TD7.1, 2½ hours).

TATAOUINE

pop 65,000

While the name is evocative to *Star Wars* fans, the town of Tataouine is more a base for exploring the ruined hilltop *ksour* than a destination in itself. The wonderful **Festival of the Ksour** in April uses the courtyards of the town for music, dance and other festivities.

The best sites are quite a way from town, but can be easily reached by chartering a taxi (around TD20 return), or, with luck, patience and a knack for timing, by taking local transport. Don't miss the beautiful **Ksar Ouled Soltane**, 22km southeast of Tataouine, where the *ghorfas* rise a dizzying four storeys, reached by precarious dream-sequence staircases, and overlook desert-scrub hills.

Equally impressive are the ancient hilltop villages of **Chenini** and **Douiret**, which spill across and merge with the rocky ochre slopes southwest of Tataouine. To get the most out of your visit, it can be worth asking someone to show you around, as some of the features can be hard to find.

Hôtel Résidence Hamza (☎ 75 863 506; Ave Hedi Chaker; s/d incl breakfast TD18/28; ✖) has four simple, bright and clean rooms and tidy common areas, plus there's a friendly welcome. Stylish **Hôtel Sangho Tataouine** (☎ 75 860 124; www.sangho-tataouine.com; off Route de Chenini; s/d TD77/114; ✖ 🛜 🌐 🏊) has large, low-slung bungalows, designed to match the local architecture, plus resort-style facilities.

For dinner, **Hôtel La Gazelle** (starters from TD2.5, mains TD6; ✖ lunch & dinner) is one of the more upmarket places (alcohol is served); **Restaurant el-Baraka** (Ave Ahmed Tili) does Tunisian standards for around TD2. Don't neglect to visit one of the many **patisseries** selling the local speciality, *corne de gazelle* (TD0.4) – a pastry case, shaped like a gazelle's horn, filled with chopped nuts and soaked in honey.

Buses and *louages* leave from the centre of town. SNTRI runs three daily air-con buses to Tunis (TD25, eight hours) that travel via Gabès (TD6.5, two hours), Sfax (TD12.6, four hours) and Sousse. Regular *louages* run to Tunis (TD23.5, eight hours) and Gabès (TD7, two hours).

You can reach Chenini, Douiret and sometimes Ksar Ouled Soltane via *camionnette* (pick-up; US$2). These leave from near the Banque du Sud on Rue 2 Mars, though they serve the destinations only in the mornings, so, unless you start out early, you could get stuck there.

TUNISIA DIRECTORY

ACCOMMODATION

Tunisia has few campsites with good facilities, but you can often pitch a tent if you have the landowner's permission. In many Tunisian towns, there is a *zone touristique*, bland and overrun by large package operators, though it leaves Tunisia's historic centres free of major tourist developments.

Women are likely to feel uncomfortable in bottom-end budget places. Tunisia's *auberges de jeunesse* (youth hostels) are often excellent and can be fine for women travelling alone, and cheap hotels *outside* the medina are mostly a better bet. Midrange options are usually decent, with air conditioning, some with swimming pools. Top-end hotels don't usually compare to four- or five-star hotels elsewhere, but are cheap by European standards. There are an increasing number of boutique places that offer a lot in the way of atmosphere but charge in euros.

DANGERS & ANNOYANCES

Tunisia is generally a safe place to travel, and the 2002 suicide bomber attack (see p216) seems to have been an isolated incident. Most travellers' complaints are about sexual harassment (see Women Travellers, p241) and touts – you're well advised to keep an eye on your bag in crowded medinas.

PRACTICALITIES

- Daily newspapers include the French-language *La Presse* (www.lapresse.tn) and *Le Temps* (www.letemps.com.tn), and Arabic-language *Assabah* (www.assabah.com.tn) and *Al-Hourriah* (www.alhourriah.org). In English, *Tunisia News* (www.tunisiaonlinenews.com) is available weekly, and the website has a weather feed, plus you can usually find (two-day-old) major European and US papers, and (week-old) *Time* and *Newsweek*. *Jeune Afrique* (www.jeuneafrique.com) is a pan-African newsmagazine, founded in Tunisia but now based in Paris; *iD déco Tunisie* is a new interiors glossy for the country's style set (both are in French).

- Tune in to local French-language Radio Tunis (98FM; www.radiotunis.com), BBC World Service on short wave (15.070MHz and 12.095MHz) or Mosaïque FM (94.9FM; www.mosaiquefm.net).

- The French-language TV station (www.tunisiatv.com) includes 30 minutes of news at 8pm daily; satellite TV can be found in top-end hotels.

- Electricity is 220V, and almost universal and reliable; wall plugs have two round pins (as in Europe).

- Tunisia uses the metric system (weight in kilograms, distance in metres); conversion charts are on the inside front cover of this book.

EMBASSIES & CONSULATES

The following embassies and consulates are in Tunis. The Canadian embassy handles consular affairs for the Australian government.

Algeria (Map p219; ☎ 71 908 588; fax 71 908 780; www.consalg.com.tn, in French; 18 Rue de Niger)

Belgium (☎ 71 781 655; 47 Rue du 1 Juin)

Canada (Map p219; ☎ 71 104 000; 3 Rue du Sénégal)

Egypt (Map p219; ☎ 71 800 447; off Ave Mohammed V)

France (Map p220; ☎ 71 245 700; 1 Place de l'Indépendance)

Germany (off Map p219; ☎ 71 786 455; 1 Rue el-Hamra)

Italy (Map p220; ☎ 71 321 811; 37 Rue Jamel Abdelnasser)

Japan (off Map p219; ☎ 71 791 251; 9 Rue Apollo 11)

Morocco (off Map p219; ☎ 71 782 775; 39 Rue du 1 Juin)

Netherlands (off Map p219; ☎ 71 797 724; 6-8 Rue de Meycen)

South Africa (off Map p219; ☎ 71 801 918; 7 Rue Achtart)

Spain (off Map p219; ☎ 71 782 217; 22 Rue Dr Ernest Conseil)

UK (off Map p219; ☎ 71 108 700; Rue du Lac Windermere, Berges du Lac)

USA (off Map p219; ☎ 71 107 000; 1053 Berges du Lac)

Tunisia has embassies in Libya, Algeria, Egypt and Morocco.

FESTIVALS & EVENTS

Tabarka International Jazz Festival (www.tabark ajazz.com; ☉ Jul) Outdoor festival with international headliners.

Carthage International Festival (www.festival-carth age.com; ☉ Jul & Aug) Big names in the Roman theatre.

Festival des Variétés de Tabarka (www.tabarkajazz. com; ☉ Aug) Dancefest with rai, world music and Latin acts.

Carthage International Film Festival (www.jccarth age.org; ☉ Oct, biennially) Cinema with an Arabian and African focus.

Sahara Festival (☉ Nov) Camel racing, as well as music, parades and poetry.

HOLIDAYS

As well as the religious holidays listed in the Africa Directory chapter (p1140), the principal public holidays in Tunisia are as follows:

New Year's Day 1 January
Independence Day 20 March
Youth Day 21 March
Martyrs' Day 9 April
Labour Day 1 May
Republic Day 25 July
Women's Day 13 August
Evacuation Day 15 October
Anniversary of Ben Ali's Accession 7 November

INTERNET ACCESS

Publinet has offices in all the main towns. Most charge around TD2 per hour for access. Some, but not all, social media is restricted and connections can be sluggish. Wi-fi is available in some top-end hotels.

MEDIA

Freedom of speech is guaranteed under the Constitution, but not so in practice. Print, broadcasting and the internet are all heavily censored, whether directly or via self-imposed restrictions.

MONEY

The unit of currency is the Tunisian dinar (TD), which is divided into 1000 millimes (mills). It's illegal to import or export dinars and they are not accepted in the duty-free shops at Tunis Airport.

You can re-exchange up to 30% of the amount you changed into dinar, up to a certain limit. You need bank receipts to prove you changed the money in the first place.

Major credit cards, such as Visa, American Express and MasterCard, are widely accepted at big shops, tourist hotels, car-rental agencies and banks. ATMs are found in major towns and resort areas. Cash advances are given in local currency only.

POST & TELEPHONE

The Tunisian postal service is slow but reliable: allow a week to Europe and at least 10 days to North America, Asia and Oceania.

The telephone system is fairly modern and easy to operate. Few people have a phone at home, so there are lots of public telephones, known as Taxiphones. They accept 100-mill, 500-mill and one-dinar coins. All public telephones can be used for international direct dialling.

Mobile phones are ubiquitous and you can buy a local SIM card at the airport. Top up cards are also widely available.

TOURIST INFORMATION

To get tourist information before you leave home, contact the government-run **Office National du Tourisme Tunisien** (ONTT; www.tourism tunisia.com). Inside Tunisia, most tourist offices are friendly and offer glossy brochures and basic local information, but don't expect much more.

VISAS

Nationals of most Western European countries and Canada can stay up to three months without a visa – just collect a stamp in your passport at the point of entry. Those from the US can stay for up to four months. Australians and South Africans can get a three-month visa at the airport for TD40. Other nationalities, including Israelis, can apply before they arrive. It should take 14 to 21 days in person or via post, and the length of stay is up to the embassy.

Visa Extensions

Applications can be made only at the **Interior Ministry** (Map p220; Ave Habib Bourguiba) in Tunis. They cost around TD10 (payable only in *timbres fiscales* – revenue stamps available from post offices) and take up to 10 days to issue. You'll need two photos, and may need bank receipts and a *facture* (receipt) from your hotel, for starters. It's a process to be avoided – far easier to leave the country and return instead.

Visas for Onward Travel

The Algerian and Libyan embassies in Tunis do not issue visas. If you want to visit either country from Tunisia, you should apply to the Algerian or Libyan representatives in your home country. Australians and New Zealanders can apply in London. It can be a lengthy process and you usually need an invitation, obtained from a citizen or through a travel agency.

WOMEN TRAVELLERS

Tunisian women enjoy freedoms that women in most Muslim societies don't, but that doesn't mean that sexual mores aren't still extremely conservative in all but the most privileged cosmopolitan circles. Foreign women, especially those travelling alone or without male companions, are seen as existing outside the protective family structure and this freedom is usually equated with promiscuity. Compounding the notion that all foreign women are up for it is the thriving beach gigolo scene (known as *beezness*).

All these factors mean that unwanted attention, from constant stares to actual sexual harassment, is par for the course for women travelling without male companions, and especially for those travelling solo. It's tiring at best, and can become very intimidating. Physical assault is rare, but does happen.

You will reduce your hassle quota if you completely ignore sexist remarks and come-ons, as passivity is equated with modesty. Any engagement, even an angry one, will be seen as an opportunity. Sunglasses are a good way of avoiding eye contact, and affecting a demure, downcast gaze will sometimes discourage men from taking the next step. Dressing modestly – covering at least your shoulders, upper arms and legs – can make a difference, especially in rural areas. If someone does touch you, '*Harem alek*' (Arabic for 'Shame on you') is a useful phrase.

TRANSPORT IN TUNISIA

GETTING THERE & AWAY

Air

There are regular flights, both scheduled and chartered, from Tunisia to destinations all over Europe, but no direct flights to the Americas, Asia or Oceania. **Tunis Air** (Map p220; ☎ 71 330 100; www.tunisair.com; 48 Ave Habib Bourguiba, Tunis) flies to most European destinations.

Other airlines flying to and from Tunisia:
Air France (☎ 71 105 324; www.airfrance.com; 1 Rue d'Athènes, Tunis)
Alitalia (☎ 71 767 722; www.alitalia.com; Tunis-Carthage Airport)
British Airways (☎ 71 963 120; www.british-airways.com; Residence Nour el Bouhaira, Rue du Lac Turkana, Berges du Lac, Tunis)
Lufthansa (☎ 71 751 096; www.lufthansa.com; Tunis-Carthage Airport)

Boat

Boats run from Tunis to Genoa, Naples, Civitavecchia (Rome), Palermo, Salerno and Trapani in Italy. There are also frequent crossings to Marseilles. See Tunis' Getting There and Away section (p222) for more details.

Land

ALGERIA

All bus and train services between the two countries have been cancelled since the start of the Algerian civil war in 1993. *Louages* are the only form of public transport still operating. They leave from Place Sidi Bou Mendil in the Tunis medina to Annaba and Constantine, or you can walk across the border at Babouch, a taxi ride away from Ain Draham.

LIBYA
The only crossing point open to foreigners is at Ras al-Jedir, 33km east of Ben Guerdane. The main obstacle is obtaining a visa, which is difficult; you have to arrange a tour to Libya with an agency that will arrange your visa (see p127). There are daily buses to Tripoli from the southern bus station in Tunis. The trip costs TD30 and takes up to 16 hours. *Louages* (yellow with a white stripe) are faster, with regular services to Tripoli via Ras al-Jedir from many Tunisian towns.

GETTING AROUND
Air
Domestic flights to Jerba, Tozeur, Sfax, Gafsa and Tabarka are operated by Tunisair subsidiary **Sevenair** (www.sevenair.com.tn, in French), formerly Tuninter.

Boat
There is a 24-hour car ferry that plies the short hop between El-Jorf and Ajim on the island of Jerba. There are ferries from Sfax to the sleepy Kerkennah Islands.

Buses & Louages
The national bus company, **Société Nationale du Transport Rural et Interurbain** (SNTRI; www.sntri.com.tn), operates daily air-conditioned buses from Tunis to just about every town in the country. Frequency for large towns can be up to half-hourly. The buses run pretty much to schedule, and they're fast, usually comfortable and inexpensive. Local buses – creaky and never air-conditioned – go to all but the most remote villages.

Louages (long-distance shared taxis) are colour-coded: a red stripe signifies long-distance, a blue stripe regional, and a yellow-stripe local or rural. In most towns, the *louage* station is close to, or combined with, the bus station, enabling you to choose between them. Fares cost around the same as those for the equivalent bus service (working out at around TD5 per 100km), but *louages* depart when full rather than following a timetable. Don't leave catching your *louage* too late – most stop running by 7pm.

All towns have metered private yellow taxis. These can either be hired privately or operate on a collective basis – they collect four passengers for different destinations. You will sometimes need to insist the meter is used.

Hitching
Many local people hitch as a matter of course. Because of the risks, we can't recommend sticking your own thumb out, but in remote areas almost anything that passes is sure to stop for you (though you may be expected to pay something). Women should never, ever attempt to hitch (or pick up male passengers) without a male companion.

Train
The rail network isn't extensive. The best-serviced route is the north–south line from Tunis to Sousse and Sfax.

West Africa

West Africa has cachet and soul in equal measure. Home to signature African landscapes and inhabited by an astonishing diversity of peoples who still hold fast to their traditions, this is Africa as it used to be.

Magic and music are the life forces of this land. See the masks and stilt dancing of the Dans in Côte d'Ivoire and, if you dare, go to Lake Togo – headquarters of the cult of voodoo. Elsewhere, extraordinarily rich musical traditions animate an already epic landscape, from the live music scene in Bamako and Dakar or Mali's world-renowned music festivals, to the melancholy soundtrack of Cape Verde beneath its austerely beautiful volcanoes.

For magic of a different kind, West Africa's allure will take hold amid the verdant rainforests of Cameroon (a country that is home to 280 distinct cultural groups); while contemplating an Atlantic sunset alongside swaying palm trees; or with the red Sahel dust beneath your feet.

West Africa is in-your-face, full-volume Lagos, or the silent steps of a camel caravan silhouetted against a blood-red Saharan sunset. It's the colourful markets that bring together a melting pot of peoples from across the region. And it's a beat, a rhythm, an idea of Africa that has somehow survived the considerable ravages of time.

Another big part of West Africa's appeal resides in its isolation as one of the least-known corners of the continent. Emerging destinations such as Sierra Leone, Benin and the Tamberma Compounds of northern Togo sit easily alongside the better-known attractions of Timbuktu, the Dogon Country, and a slow boat up the Niger River.

But West Africa's biggest asset is its people, and even in the most desolate and inhospitable of places, you will be welcomed by your West African hosts and come to know their strength, grace and endurance.

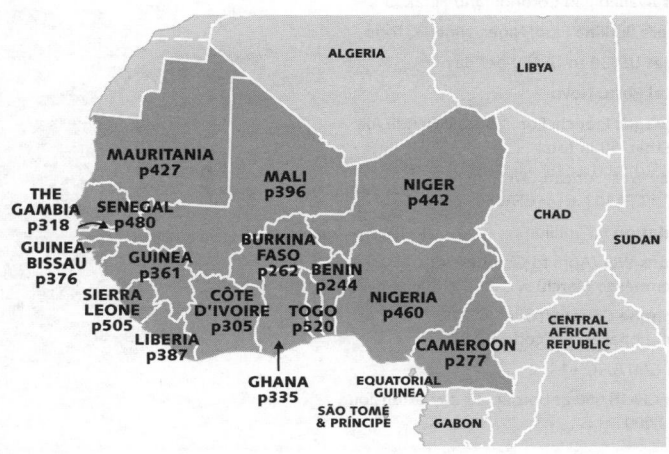

Benin

It's surprising that Benin rings so few bells in people's geographical awareness when its role in history is so significant. The birthplace of voodoo and a pivotal platform of the slave trade for nearly three centuries, Benin is steeped in a rich and complex history still very much in evidence across the country.

A visit to this small, club-shaped nation could therefore not be complete without exploring the Afro-Brazilian heritage of Ouidah and Porto Novo, shivering at the litany of massacres of the kings of Dahomey or learning about spirits and fetishes in Ouidah and Lake Ahémé.

But Benin will also wow visitors with its natural beauty, from the palm-fringed beach idyll of the Atlantic coast to the rugged scenery of the north. The Parc National de la Pendjari is one of the best wildlife parks in West Africa. Lions, cheetahs, leopards, elephants and hundreds of other species thrive here, and the infrastructure to see them is remarkably good.

In fact, Benin is wonderfully tourist friendly compared to most of its neighbours. There are good roads, reliable intercity bus services, professional guides to tour the country with and ecotourism initiatives that offer travellers the chance to delve deeper into Beninese life: how does learning traditional fishing techniques or sleeping in a *tata somba* house sound?

Finally, Benin's economic capital Cotonou may not be a love-at-first-sight sort of place, but spend a Sunday afternoon chilling out in Fidjrossé, hanging out at the daring Fondation Zinsou or bargaining hard at the Dantokpa market and you'll soon find the big smoke has its perks, too.

FAST FACTS

- **Area** 112,622 sq km
- **ATMs** Available in Cotonou and Parakou
- **Borders** Burkina Faso, Niger, Nigeria, Togo
- **Budget** US$30 to US$50 per day
- **Capital** Porto Novo
- **Languages** French, Fon, Yoruba, Dendi, Aja; more than 50 in total
- **Money** West African CFA franc; US$1 = CFA463, €1 = CFA656
- **Population** 6.7 million
- **Seasons** Wet (April to October), dry (November to March)
- **Telephone** Country code ☎ 229; international access code ☎ 00
- **Time** GMT/UTC +1
- **Visas** CFA10,000 at border, 30-day extension CFA12,000

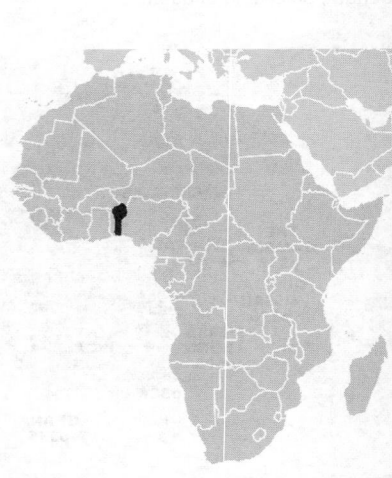

BENIN

HOW MUCH?

- **Guided ecowalk** US$6.50
- **Mashed yam** US$0.40
- **Appliqué hat** US$3.20
- **Zemi-john** US$0.40
- **National park entry** US$21.50

LONELY PLANET INDEX

- **1L petrol** US$0.65 to US$1.30
- **1.5L bottled water** US$1
- **Bottle of La Béninoise beer** US$0.55
- **Souvenir T-shirt** $4.30
- **Aloko** US$0.20

HIGHLIGHTS

- **The Atakora Region** (p257) Explore the rugged landscapes of northern Benin.
- **Lake Ahémé** (p254) Learn traditional fishing techniques and get up close and personal with voodoo traditions.
- **Parc National de la Pendjari** (p257) Spot lions, cheetahs, elephants and more in West Africa's best wildlife park.
- **Porto Novo** (p252) Discover Benin's mellow capital, with its Afro-Brazilian heritage and visionary sustainable farming centre.
- **Grand Popo** (p254) Relax on Benin's beautiful, palm-fringed coast

CLIMATE & WHEN TO GO

In southern Benin, there are two rainy seasons: April to mid-July, and mid-September to late October. The rains in the north fall from June to early October. Harmattan winds billow out of the Sahara between December and March, and the hottest time of the year is from February to April. The coolest, driest time to visit is between November and February.

Smaller roads throughout Benin may be impassable during the rainy seasons; notably those in the wildlife parks.

ITINERARIES

- **One Week** Start off in busy Cotonou (p247), where good food, cold beers, great markets and insane traffic give you a taste of things to come. Porto Novo (p252), the tranquil capital, and Ganvié (p252), the lacustrine stilt village, are both within two hours' taxi journey of Cotonou. A little further along the country's main roads are two historical highlights: Abomey (p255), home to the ruined palaces of the kings of Dahomey, and Ouidah (p253), once a capital of the slave trade and now the centre of voodoo worship.
- **Two Weeks** After a few days in Cotonou, put your bags down at lovely Grand Popo (p254) for a couple of idle days, before heading north via the stunning shores of Lake Ahémé (p254). Then head to Abomey via Lokossa, and on to Natitingou (p256), gateway to the beautiful Atakora region (p257) and the Parc National de la Pendjari (p257).

HISTORY

More than 350 years ago the area now known as Benin was split into numerous principalities. Akaba of Abomey conquered his neighbouring ruler Dan and called the new kingdom Dan-Homey, later shortened to Danhomey by French colonisers. By 1727, Dahomey spread from Abomey down to Ouidah and Cotonou and into parts of modern Togo. The kingdoms of Nikki, Djougou and Parakou were still powerful in the north as was the Kingdom of Toffa in Porto-Novo.

Each king pledged to leave his successor more land than he inherited, achieved by waging war with his neighbours. They grew rich by selling slaves to the European traders, notably the Portuguese, who established trading posts in Porto Novo, Ouidah and along the coast. For more than a century, an average of 10,000 slaves per year were shipped to the Americas. Southern Dahomey was dubbed the Slave Coast.

Following colonisation by the French, great progress was made in education, and many Dahomeyans were employed as government advisers throughout French West Africa.

Independence & Le Folklore

When Dahomey became independent in 1960, other former French colonies started deporting their Dahomeyan populations. Back home without work, they were the root of a highly unstable political situation. Three years after independence, following the example of

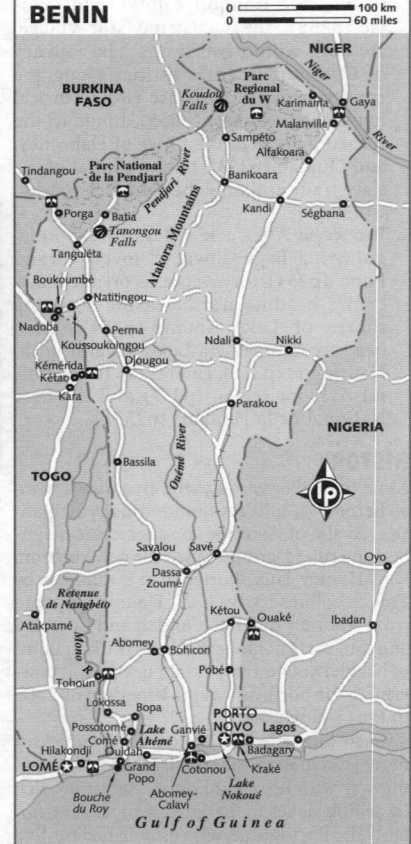

neighbouring Togo, the Dahomeyan military staged a coup.

During the next decade Dahomey saw four military coups, nine changes of government and five changes of constitution: what the Dahomeyans called in jest *le folklore*.

Revolution

In 1972 a group of officers led by Lieutenant Colonel Mathieu Kérékou seized power in a coup, then embraced Marxist-Leninist ideology and aligned the country with superpowers such as China. To emphasise the break from the past, Kérékou changed the flag and renamed the country Benin. He informed his people of the chance by radio on 13 November 1975.

The government established Marxist infrastructure, which included implementing collective farms. However, the economy became a shambles, and there were ethnic tensions between the president, a Natitingou-born northerner, and the Yoruba population in the south. There were six attempted coups in one year alone.

In December 1989, as a condition of French financial support, Kérékou ditched Marxism and held a conference to draft a new constitution. The delegates engineered a coup, forming a new cabinet under Nicéphore Soglo.

Soglo won the first free multiparty elections, held in March 1991, but his autocracy, nepotism and austere economic measures – following the devaluation of the CFA franc – came under fire. Kérékou was voted back into power in March 1996.

Benin Today

Kérékou's second and final five-year term in office finished with the presidential elections in March 2006, bringing an end to his 33 years at the top. The current president, Yayi Boni, former head of the West African Development Bank, beat Adrien Houngbédji in a run-off. In his campaign, which he based around the slogan of 'change', Kérékou pledged to fight corruption and revive the country's economy.

It hasn't, however, been plain sailing: despite winning a majority of seats in the parliamentary elections of 2007 and a number of local seats in the 2008 municipal elections, reforms have come about more slowly than hoped. With the next presidential election in March 2011, the pressure will be on President Boni to demonstrate he can be entrusted with a second mandate.

CULTURE

Benin's economy is primarily dependent on subsistence farming, which accounts for 38% of its gross domestic product. Yams, maize, cassava and corn are the principal food crops. The country's main exports are cotton, palm oil, cashew and cocoa beans, with cotton accounting for more than 75% of Benin's export earnings.

There is an array of different ethnic groups within Benin's narrow borders, although three of them account for nearly 60% of the population: Fon, Adja and Yoruba.

Average life expectancy is 56, with an HIV/AIDS infection rate of about 2.1%. Literacy is still low, with just 40% of the population aged over 15 able to read and write, but improving thanks to Benin's young population: 45% are aged 14 or under.

Beninese women may be a formidable presence on the streets, but Benin has a firmly patriarchal society and women still suffer inequalities.

Some 40% of the population is Christian and 25% Muslim, but most people practice voodoo, whatever their religion. The practice mixed with Catholicism in the Americas, where the Dahomeyan slaves took it and their Afro-Brazilian descendants brought it back. Christian missionaries also won over Dahomeyans by fusing their creed with voodoo.

Under the Dahomeyan kings, distinctive appliqué banners were used to depict the rulers' past and present glories. With their bright, cloth-cut figures, the banners are still being made, particularly in Abomey. The *cire perdue* (lost wax) method used to make the famous Benin bronzes originates from Benin City, which lies in present-day Nigeria. However, the method spread west and the figures can be bought throughout Benin itself.

Angélique Kidjo, a major international star, is Benin's most famous recording artist. Other well-known Beninese artists include Gnonnes Pedro, Nel Olivier and Yelouassi Adolphe, and the bands Orchestre Poly-Rythmo and Disc Afrique.

Benin has a substantial Afro-Brazilian architectural heritage, best preserved in Porto Novo. The Lake Nokoué stilt villages and the *tata somba* houses around Natitingou are remarkable examples of traditional architecture.

The Viceroy of Ouidah, by Bruce Chatwin, is a biographical sketch of the notorious Brazilian slave trader Francisco da Silva, who formed the trade with the kings of Dahomey.

FOOD & DRINK

Beninese grub is unquestionably among the best in West Africa and is very similar to Togolese food (p523), the main differences being the names: *fufu* is generally called *igname pilé* and *djenkoumé* is called *pâte rouge,*

for instance. But whatever the name, you're bound to eat well in Benin.

The local beer, La Béninoise, is a passable drop. The adventurous could try the millet-based brew *tchoukoutou* or *sodabe* (moonshine).

ENVIRONMENT

Sandwiched between Nigeria and Togo, Benin is 700km long and 120km across in the south, widening to about 300km in the north. Most of the coastal plain is a sand bar that blocks the seaward flow of several rivers. As a result, there are lagoons a few kilometres inland all along the coast, which is being eroded by the strong ocean currents. Inland is a densely forested plateau and, in the far northwest, the Atakora Mountains.

Wildlife thrives in Parc National de la Pendjari (p257), with elephants and several feline species.

Deforestation and desertification are major issues because of the logging of valuable wood, such as teak.

COTONOU

pop 761,900

Cotonou is Benin's capital in everything but name: a vibrant, bustling, full-on city, and very much the economic engine of Benin. As a first port of call, it can be a little overwhelming, but life can be sweet in Cotonou, with good nightlife, great restaurants and excellent shopping (ideal for end-of-trip souvenirs).

ORIENTATION

The heart of town is around the intersection of Ave Clozel and Blvd Steinmetz. The area was undergoing significant works at the time of writing, with the construction of a flyover underway. Heading north, Blvd Steinmetz runs perpendicular into Blvd St Michel, which becomes Ave du Nouveau Pont as you head east; Ave Clozel becomes the Ancien Pont. Both bridges head in the direction of Porto-Novo and Lagos. At the western end of town, following Ave Jean-Paul II, is the popular Haie Vive area, as well as the airport.

Only major roads have names – small, unsealed alleyways are called *von* and directions given with reference to another main street or a landmark.

BENIN

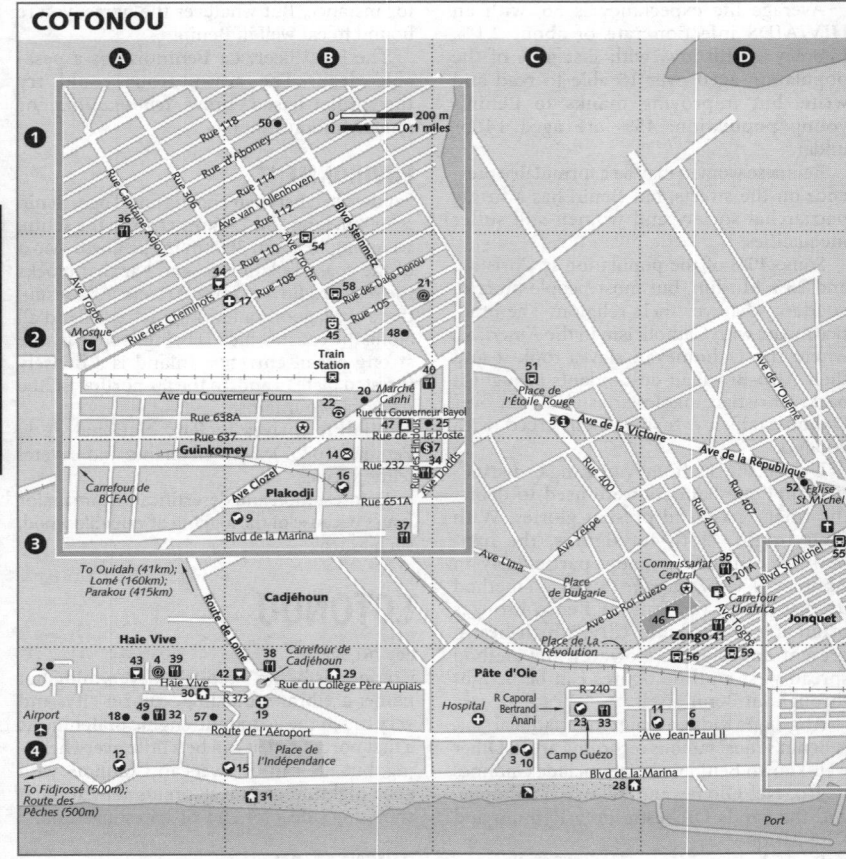

Maps

The 1:15,000 IGN *Cotonou* map, which lists the city's hotels, cinemas, banks and markets, is available at bookshops.

INFORMATION
Bookshops

Librairie Notre-Dame (☎ 21 31 40 94; Ave Clozel; 9am-12.30pm & 4-7pm Tue-Sat, 4-7pm Mon) This bookshop is next to the cathedral, and has an excellent selection of books on Benin (in French) and maps of Cotonou and Benin.

Sonaec (☎ 21 31 22 42; Ave Clozel; 8.30am-12.30pm & 3.30-7pm Mon-Fri, 9.30am-12.30pm & 4-6.30pm Sat) A smart bookshop which stocks the latest periodicals, maps and some photography books on West Africa.

Cultural Centres

Centre Culturel Français (☎ 21 30 08 56; www.ccfcotonou.net; Ave Jean-Paul II; 9.30am-12pm & 3-7pm Tue-Sat, closed morning Thu) This busy centre has a gallery, outdoor theatre, library and cinema.

Internet Access

Ave Clozel, Blvd Steinmetz and Rue des Cheminots have the most internet cafes.

Cyber Océane (☎ 21 30 69 41; Haie Vive; per hr CFA400; 9am-11pm)

Star Navigation (☎ 21 31 81 28; off Blvd Steinmetz; per hr CFA500; 8am-10pm)

Medical Services

Pharmacie Jonquet (☎ 21 31 20 80; Rue des Cheminots) Open 24 hours a day, seven days a week.

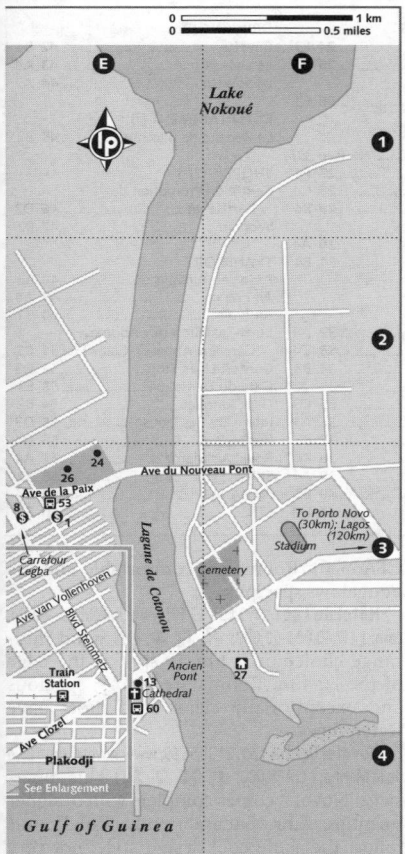

Polyclinique les Cocotiers (☎ 21 30 14 20; Rue 373) A private clinic at Carrefour de Cadjéhoun; also has a dentist.

Money

All banks change cash; Ecobank changes travellers cheques. There are plenty of ATMs in Cotonou, most of which accept Visa. There's a thriving black market for currencies, including the Nigerian naira, around the Jonquet district and Gare du Dantokpa. The airport's *bureau de change* doesn't change travellers cheques but there is a Visa-enabled ATM.

Banque Atlantique (Blvd St Michel; ⊙ 8am-5pm Mon-Fri, 9am-12.30pm Sat) Has a MasterCard and Visa ATM.

Ecobank (⊙ 8am-5pm Mon-Fri, 9am-1pm Sat) There are branches on Blvd St Michel and Rue de la Poste, close to Marché Ganhi.

Post

Main post office (off Ave Clozel; ⊙ 7am-7pm Mon-Fri, 8am-11.30am Sat)

Telephone

Telecom (OPT) building (Ave Clozel; ⊙ 7.30am-7pm Mon-Sat, 9am-1pm Sun) You can make overseas telephone calls and send faxes.

Tourist Information

Direction du Tourisme et de l'Hôtellerie (☎ 21 32 68 24; Place de l'Étoile Rouge; ⊙ 8am-12.30pm & 3-6.30pm Mon-Fri) Inconveniently located out of the city centre, behind Pharmacie de l'Étoile Rouge; of limited use.

Visa Extensions

Direction Emigration Immigration (☎ 21 31 42 13; Ave Jean-Paul II; ⊙ 8am-12.30pm & 3-6.30pm Mon-Fri) Issues 30-day visas.

DANGERS & ANNOYANCES

The biggest danger in Cotonou is the traffic, the 80,000 reckless *zemi-johns* (taxi-motos) in particular. They're unavoidable, however, so always make sure that the driver agrees to drive slowly *(aller doucement)* before hopping on.

The Jonquet, the beach and the port area all have their fair share of undesirables: don't walk alone at night and watch your bag at traffic lights if you're on a *zem*.

SIGHTS

The seemingly endless **Grand Marché du Dantokpa** is Cotonou's throbbing heart. Everything under the sun can be purchased in its labyrinthine lanes, from fish to soap, plastic sandals to goats, pirated DVDs to spare car parts. More traditional fare, such as batiks and Dutch wax cloth, can be found in the market building. The **fetish market** section is at the northern end of the larger market.

For a different kind of culture shock, head to the amazing **Fondation Zinsou** (☎ 21 31 50 51; www.fondationzinsou.org; Rue du Gouverneur Bayol; free admission; ⊙ 10am-7pm, closed public holidays). This fantastic exhibition space seeks to promote contemporary African art among Beninese people.

COURSES

For Fon-language classes, call **Vinawamon** (☎ 97 87 37 72), also contactable via the Centre Culturel Français (opposite).

BENIN

SLEEPING

Maison de Passage des Allemands (☎ 21 30 45 76; Haie Vive; r with air-con CFA7000) This discreet villa next to Bar Le Lambi's is a bargain if you manage to get a room: it was set up to accommodate German aid workers and, since there are only seven rooms and lots of aid workers, it's often full. Bathrooms and toilets are shared but clean.

Le Chant d'Oiseau (☎ 21 30 57 51; www.chant doiseau.net; Rue du Collège Père Aupiais; s/d/tr with fan CFA9000/13,500/17,500, with air-con CFA16,500/22,000/27,500; ☒ ▢) A safe, excellent budget option run by a catholic community and within walking distance of the lively Haie Vive area. The building looks a little austere but the rooms are quiet and spacious.

our pick **Chez Clarisse** (☎ 21 30 60 14; Camp Guézo; s/d incl breakfast CFA25,000/30,000; ☒ ▣) The closest thing to a guesthouse you'll find in Cotonou, this is a charming place, with seven immaculate rooms in a villa at the back of the popular Chez Clarisse restaurant.

Hôtel du Port (☎ 21 31 44 44; www.hotelduport-co tonou.com; Blvd de la Marina; s/d from CFA38,600/44,200, s/d bungalow CFA46,600/54,200; ▣ ☒ ▢ ▣) The surrounding towers of containers from the next-door port are slightly surreal and in sharp contrast to the oasis-like pool (non-guest CFA2500), garden and *paillote* (straw hut) restaurant-bar (meals CFA3800 to CFA6500). Rooms are comfortable and the bungalows spacious.

Hôtel du Lac (☎ 21 33 19 19; www.hoteldulac-benin. com; r CFA40,000-60,000; ☒ ▢ ▣) A good mid-range choice on a breezy spot at the edge of the lagoon. Rooms are sunny, spacious and exceptionally clean, and most have water views.

Novotel Orisha (☎ 21 30 56 69; www.novotel.com; Blvd de la Marina; r CFA85,000; ▣ ☒ ▢ ▣) This super-swish Novotel comes complete with designer furniture, funky bar and trendy pool. Rooms follow the same cool design style: not very African, but definitely comfortable.

EATING

Boulangerie-Pâtisserie (Route de l'Aéroport; ⏲ 7am-8pm) The bread, croissants, éclairs and cakes from this little bakery next to the Air France office can rival those of any French bakery.

Chez Maman Bénin (☎ 21 32 33 38; Rue 201A; meals CFA500-3000) This long-standing no-frills canteen off Blvd St Michel has a large selection of West African dishes scooped from steaming pots. There's no decor but a couple of blaring TVs showing the latest football action.

Chez Léa (off Rue des Hindous; meal CFA1500) Fill up on *poulet moyo* at this crazily popular lunch joint set up under an awning and corrugated iron roof. Plates are piled high with chicken, *aloko* (fried plantain), fries, rice, peas and salad. Perfect for taking in the vibe from Cotonou's working crowd.

ourpick Pili Pili (☎ 21 31 29 32; Zongo; meals CFA2500-3800) This slightly upmarket *maquis* (open-air restaurant) rates equally highly with Beninese and expats for its amazing West African food. Prices are very reasonable and the jugs of freshly squeezed pineapple juice at lunch time are a refreshing godsend.

Fleur de Sel (☎ 97 59 19 59; off rue 651A; mains CFA3500) Savour Lebanese specialities with a side of ocean breeze and great port views at this beachside restaurant. As well as succulent kebabs and oily hummus, the house also serves fab seafood, with lobster, crayfish and whole fish big enough to feed a party of 10.

Chez Clarisse (☎ 21 30 60 14; Camp Guézo; mains CFA3500) This small French restaurant, in a pretty residential area next to the US embassy, is a perennial favourite that churns out excellent European and African specialities.

Hai King (☎ 21 30 60 08; Carrefour de Cadjéhoun; mains CFA4000; ☉ 10am-2.30pm & 6-11.30pm) Close to Haie Vive, Hai Kind is popular with expats and serves great Chinese food on an atmospheric covered roof terrace overlooking the bustling Carrefour de Cadjéhoun.

Chez Mimi (☎ 21 31 49 07; Rue d'Abomey; mains from CFA5000) Run by the savvy Mireille, this *'maquis de luxe'* is Afro-European fusion cuisine at its best: homemade fresh fruit punch, divine monkfish gratin and delicious desserts, all served in a lovely alfresco setting.

In the city centre, around Marché Ganhi, are a number of good supermarkets, including **La Pointe** (☎ 21 31 69 45; off Ave Clozel; ☉ 9am-8pm) and **La Championne** (☎ 21 30 69 43; Haie Vive; ☉ 9am-10pm).

DRINKING & ENTERTAINMENT

Haie Vive is a good, safe area by night, with many of the city's best bars and restaurants.

ourpick The buvette (Carrefour de Cadjéhoun) with no name at is brilliant for sundowners. Tables spill out of nowhere as soon as darkness falls and there is often live music.

Le Livingstone (☎ 21 30 27 58; livin@leland.bj; Haie Vive; meals CFA3500-4500; ☉ 11am-late) is popular with expats who come here to chill out to the tune of Western pop and sport channels.

The Jonquet strip is bristling with pumping music and wild and wicked bars, such

as **Le Soweto** (☎ 97 44 17 49; Rue des Cheminots; ☉ 7am-4am).

Le Repaire de Bacchus (☎ 21 31 75 81; Ave Proche; ☉ 11am-midnight Sun-Wed, to 2am Thu, to 4am Fri & Sat) has live jazz on Thursday from 10.30pm, and music such as rumba and Ivorian sounds on Friday and Saturday.

SHOPPING

At **Centre de Promotion de l'Artisanat** (Blvd St Michel; ☉ 9am-7pm) you'll find woodcarvings, bronzes, batiks, leather goods, jewellery and appliqué banners. For quality Dutch wax fabric, head to **Woodin** (Rue des Hindous; ☉ 8.30am-1pm & 4-7pm Tue-Fri, 9am-1pm Sat, 3.30-7pm Mon), where *demi-pièces* (6m of material) start at CFA14,000.

GETTING THERE & AWAY
Air

The international airport is on the western fringe of town. For information on airlines flying to Cotonou, see p259.

Bush Taxi, Minibus & Bus

Cotonou has a confusingly large number of stations for minibuses, buses and bush taxis. It's easiest to ask a taxi or a *zemi-john* to take you to the right one.

Gare Jonquet (Rue des Cheminots), just west of Blvd Steinmetz, services western destinations such as Ouidah (CFA700, one hour), Grand Popo (CFA1500, two hours) and Lomé (CFA3500, three hours).

Bush taxis for Porto Novo (CFA500 to CFA700, 45 minutes) and Lagos (CFA3000, three hours) leave from **Gare du Dantokpa** (Ave de la Paix) at the new bridge; those to Abomey-Calavi (for Ganvié; CFA400, 25 minutes) and Abomey (CFA2200, two hours) leave just north of Rond-Point de l'Étoile Rouge.

For more-distant destinations, such as Parakou, Malanville or Natitingou, take the bus (above).

For information on international buses to/from Cotonou, see above.

GETTING AROUND
To/From the Airport

A private taxi from the city centre to the airport costs around CFA2000, although drivers will demand double this amount *from* the airport. *Zemi-johns* will be happy to load you and your luggage for much less.

BENIN

Taxi
A *zemi-john* will whiz you around town for CFA100 to CFA300, depending on the distance.

Fares in shared taxis are CFA150 to CFA400. Otherwise, taxis can be hired for CFA2000 per hour; rates increase from early evening on. Gare du Dantokpa is a good place to find taxis.

AROUND COTONOU

GANVIÉ
The main attraction near Cotonou is Ganvié, where 30,000 Tofinu people live in bamboo huts on stilts several kilometres out on Lake Nokoué. In the 17th century, the Tofinu fled to this swampy region from the Dahomey slave hunters, who were banned by a religious custom from venturing into the water.

The town has become a tourist magnet but is a victim of its own success: pollution of the lagoon is a chronic problem and guides seem more interested in making a quick buck than providing informative commentary.

To get there, get a taxi from Place de l'Étoile Rouge to Abomey-Calavi (CFA400, 25 minutes), not to be confused with Abomey. The embarkation point is 800m downhill. At the **official counter** (☎ 95 05 27 01; ⏰ 9am-6pm), return fares to Ganvié in a regular/motorised *pirogue* are CFA6050/7050 per person, CFA4050/5050 each for two to four people.

Prices include a circuit of the village with stop-offs. The trip takes about 2½ hours.

THE SOUTH

PORTO NOVO
pop 223,168

Nestling on the shores of Lake Nokoué, Porto Novo is Benin's unlikely capital. Its leafy streets, wonderful colonial architecture and interesting museums are in striking contrast with full-on Cotonou.

Information
Bank of Africa (Ave Liotard) Changes money.

Sights & Activities
The **Centre Songhai** (☎ 20 24 68 81; www.songhai. org; Route de Pobè) is a major research, teaching and production centre in sustainable farming. There are one-hour **guided tours** (CFA500; ⏰ 8.30am, 10.30am, noon, 3.30pm & 5pm Mon-Sat) to visit the plantations and workshops. You can also buy the centre's products, anything from fresh quail eggs to biscuits and preserves. Songhai is about 1km north of town. Every *zem* knows where it is.

Porto Novo has a couple of museums, which will fill you in on Benin's history and culture. The wonderfully eccentric and eclectic **Musée da Silva** (☎ 20 21 50 71; Ave Liotard; admission CFA2000; ⏰ 9am-6pm) is housed in a beautiful 1870 Afro-Brazilian house. **Musée Éthnographique de Porto Novo** (☎ 20 21 25 54; Ave 6; admission CFA1000; ⏰ 8am-6pm Mon-Fri, from 9am Sat,

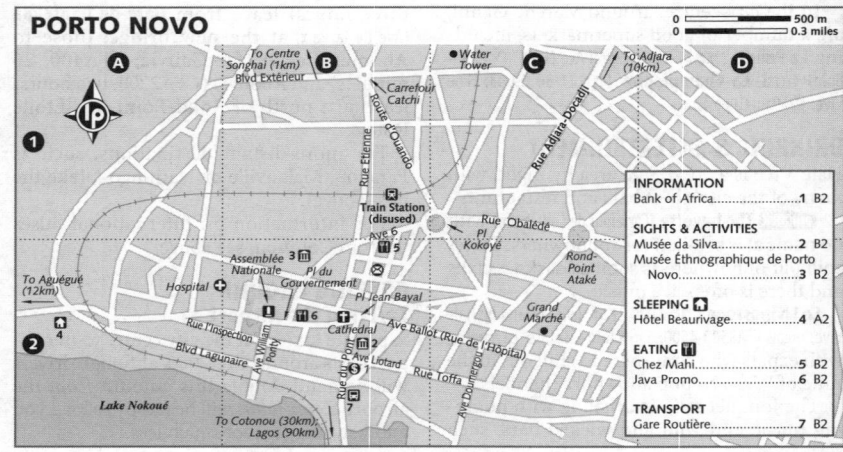

PORTO NOVO

INFORMATION	
Bank of Africa	.............1 B2
SIGHTS & ACTIVITIES	
Musée da Silva	...............2 B2
Musée Éthnographique de Porto Novo	.....3 B2
SLEEPING	
Hôtel Beaurivage	...........4 A2
EATING	
Chez Mahi	..................5 B2
Java Promo	.................6 B2
TRANSPORT	
Gare Routière	...............7 B2

Map labels: To Centre Songhai (1km); Blvd Extérieur; Carrefour Catchi; Water Tower; To Adjara (10km); Rue Etienne; Route d'Ouando; Rue Adjara-Dacadji; Train Station (disused); Ave 6; Rue Obalédé; Pl Kokoyé; Assemblée Nationale; Pl du Gouvernement; Rond-Point Ataké; Hospital; To Aguégué (12km); Rue l'Inspection; Rue William Ponty; Pl Jean Bayal; Ave Ballot (Rue de l'Hôpital); Cathedral; Ave Liotard; Rue Toffa; Grand Marché; Blvd Lagunaire; Rue Peinture; Rue Dombocoun; Lake Nokoué; To Cotonou (30km); Lagos (90km)

0 — 500 m / 0 — 0.3 miles

Sun & holidays, closed 1 May & 1 Jan) is where you can learn about voodoo mores.

Iroko Tours (☎ 97 17 59 82, 93 80 60 59; iroko1992@yahoo.fr) organise themed walking tours of Porto Novo as well as *pirogue* trips to the stilt village of Aguégué (half-day trips CFA15,000 for two people, and CFA7000 per extra person).

Sleeping & Eating

ourpick **Centre Songhai** (☎ 20 22 50 92; Route de Pobè; r with fan CFA4000, with air-con CFA12,500-15,500; P ❷ ☒ 🖵) Built to accommodate its numerous visitors, the 70 rooms at Centre Songhai (see opposite) are basic but clean. Fan rooms have a shower cubicle but shared toilets; the more-expensive air-con rooms have a private bathroom but are still very good value. The centre has two good restaurants: a cheap African *maquis* (mains CFA1200) and a more upmarket restaurant (set menu CFA5000). There's also an internet cafe (CFA250 per hour).

Hôtel Beaurivage (☎ 20 21 23 99; Blvd Lagunaire; r CFA15,500-25,500; ❷) Tired but spacious rooms (and new beds, finally!) with the town's best lagoon views and a wonderful terrace bar and restaurant. Even if you don't sleep there, you should definitely come for sundowners.

Chez Mahi (Ave 6; meals CFA500-1000; ☾ lunch only, closed Sun) Locals swear by this restaurant, just south of Place Kokoyé. It's not an attractive place (bare concrete walls), but the mashed yam is excellent and the atmosphere jovial.

Java Promo (☎ 20 21 20 54; Place du Gouvernement; meals CFA1500-3000) Hidden behind the aquamarine shutters of a crumbling colonial building and shielded from the sun by a big *paillote*, this is a popular haunt for an omelette at brekkie or meat and pâté for lunch.

Getting There & Away

Plenty of minibuses and bush taxis leave for Cotonou (minibus/bush taxi CFA500/700, 45 minutes) from the *gare routière* (bus station) and Carrefour Catchi. To Abomey from Porto Novo is CFA2700.

For Nigeria, you can get a taxi to the border point in Kraké (CFA700, 30 minutes), but you'll have to change there to go on to Lagos.

OUIDAH

pop 87,200

Ouidah is a must-see for anyone interested in voodoo or Benin's history of slavery. Until a wharf was built at Cotonou in 1908, Ouidah had the only port in Benin. Its heyday was 1800

to 1900, when slaves from across West Africa left from Ouidah for the Americas. The annual **Voodoo Festival** is celebrated here in January.

Information

There are several internet cafes on Rue Olivier de Montaguere, including **FIC** (per hr CFA350; ☾ 8.30am-11pm). **Continental Bank Bénin** (☎ 21 34 14 32; Place du Marché; ☾ 8.30am-noon & 3-6pm Mon-Fri) changes cash.

Sights & Activities

Ouidah's main site is its **Musée d'Histoire de Ouidah** (☎ 21 34 10 21; www.museeouidah.org; Rue van Vollenhoven; admission CFA1000; ☾ 8am-12.30pm & 3-6pm Mon-Fri, 9am-6pm Sat & Sun), housed in the beautiful Fortaleza São João Batista, a Portuguese fort built in 1721. It retraces the town's slave-trading history and explores the links between Benin, Brazil and the Caribbean.

Slaves were taken from the fort to the beach down the 4km **Route des Esclaves**. Lining the sandy track now are fetishes and monuments, such as the Monument of Repentance and the Tree of Forgetfulness. There is a poignant memorial on the beach, the **Point of No Return**.

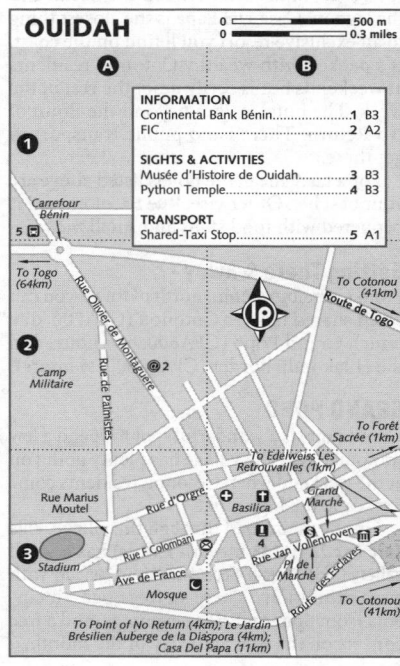

Those interested in voodoo could visit the **python temple** (☎ 95 40 08 90; off Rue F Colombani; admission CFA1000, photos CFA5000; ◷ 8am-7pm), home to 40 sleepy pythons, and the **forêt sacrée** (☎ 97 68 89 22; admission incl guide CFA1000; ◷ 8am-6pm), once off-limits to the uninitiated and harbouring important fetishes.

Sleeping & Eating

Edelweiss Les Retrouvailles (☎ 21 10 10 86; Rue du Général Dodd; r with fan/air-con CFA6500/15,500; P ☒) About 1km east of the Musée d'Histoire de Ouidah, this excellent budget choice is set in leafy grounds with a *paillote* restaurant (meals CFA2000 to CFA3500). The name of the hotel will draw a blank with most *zems* so try asking for 'Les Paillotes'.

Le Jardin Brésilien Auberge de la Diaspora (☎ 21 34 11 10; r CFA10,000-25,000; P ☒ ☛) On the beach near the Point of No Return. Go for a category B room with air-con and fab views and avoid the fan rooms – overpriced and furnace-like. The restaurant (meals CFA3000 to CFA9000) is pricey but is in a beautiful setting.

Casa Del Papa (☎ 95 95 39 04; www.casadelpapa. com; Ouidah Plage; d incl breakfast CFA47,000-68,000; P ☒ ☛) Squeezed between the ocean and the lagoon, Casa Del Papa is the closest thing to an exclusive resort you'll find on the coast. It's packed with wealthy Cotonou residents at weekends but is eerily quiet the rest of the week. The hotel is 7km beyond the Point of No Return. There is no public transport to get there.

For a tasty meal, the hotels listed above are your best bet. Otherwise, Rue F Colombani is peppered with food stalls and small *maquis*.

Getting There & Away

From Carrefour Bénin, north of town, you can catch shared taxis to Cotonou (CFA700, one hour), Grand Popo (CFA600, one hour) and the Hilakondji border (CFA1000, 1½ hours).

GRAND POPO

Grand Popo is a wonderful spot to spend a few tranquil days. The village has plenty going on at the weekend when Cotonou residents come to escape the big smoke.

On the main road through the village, **Villa Karo** (☎ 22 43 03 58; www.villa-karo.org) has a small **gallery** (◷ 8-11am & 4-6pm Mon-Fri, 8-11am Sat) with great exhibitions. There's a free open-air cinema from 8pm on Friday evenings, and a free concert on the first Saturday of the month.

Local guide **Gaston** (☎ 95 85 74 40) organises excursions on the **Mono River** or to the **Bouche du Roy**, where the river meets the ocean. Trips on the river last about two hours and cost CFA5000 per person. Trips to the Bouche du Roy cost CFA45,000 as you need a motorised boat; boats fit up to eight people and the trip lasts about six hours.

The hideout of choice for Cotonou's expat beatniks is **Lion Bar** (☎ 95 42 05 17; kabla_gildas@ yahoo.fr; r CFA5000). Drinks flow at all hours of the day and night, parties are a staple, rooms are super funky and the shared facilities surprisingly clean. Meals cost CFA1500. It's right on the beach and you can pitch your tent for CFA2500.

More comfortable is the resort-like **Awalé Plage** (☎ 22 43 01 17; www.hotel-benin-awaleplage.com; Route de Togo; d bungalow with fan/air-con CFA14,000/22,000, f bungalow with fan/air-con CFA20,000/28,000; P ☒). On the main highway to Togo, it has a good restaurant (meals CFA2500 to CFA6000) and throws monthly full-moon parties with poolside live music.

our pick **Auberge de Grand Popo** (☎ 22 43 00 47; www.hotels-benin.com; campsite per person CFA1500, d CFA17,000-25,000; P), right by the beach, oozes colonial charm and serves divine cuisine in its attractive terrace restaurant (meals CFA3800 to CFA9000).

From Cotonou, take a bush taxi from Gare Jonquet (CFA1500, two hours) and have it drop you off at the Grand Popo junction on the main coastal highway, 20km east of the Togo border crossing at Hilakondji. The beach and village are 3.5km off the main road and are easily accessible via *zemi-john* (CFA250).

POSSOTOMÉ & LAKE AHÉMÉ

The fertile shores of Lake Ahémé are voodoo strongholds and even nonbelievers will admit there is something very spiritual and peaceful about this area.

Lake Ahémé features **trips and excursions** (www.lacaheme.com) designed and run by ecotourism NGO **Eco-Bénin** (www.ecobenin.org). Learn traditional fishing techniques or go on a fascinating two-hour botanic journey to hear about local plants and their medicinal properties. There are half a dozen thematic circuits to choose from (from two hours to day trips, CFA3500 to CFA12,000), all run by delightful local guides.

Camp at the atmospheric but basic **Camping de Possotomé** (☎ 90 11 53 35; campsite CFA2500) on the

---

GÉNÉRATION GOGOHOUN

They're aged 11 to 17, they live in two rural villages in southern Benin (Hlodo and Sagon), and they dream of being school teachers, doctors, custom officials, diplomats and artists. They could be your average Benin schoolchildren, but **Génération Gogohoun** (www.gogohoun.com) is instead embracing an all-singing-and-dancing future, literally.

Gogohoun is a group of 30 schoolchildren who sing and dance about issues they encounter in everyday life, such as emigration, HIV/AIDS, child labour and unemployment. If it doesn't sound all that upbeat, wait till you hear them sing.

Their songs are all based on Adja rhythms – ancestral, rhythmic beats used in traditional ceremonies in the Zou and Mono areas. Originally called Agbahoun and characterised by its jerky buttock moves, it was adapted as a slightly less raunchy dance and renamed Gogohoun – although women in the villages will be keen to show you how it's *really* done!

Génération Gogohoun is the product of not-for-profit Franco-Beninese artists' group Cacy-Albatros-Tingo Gars, whose aim is to promote a better and fairer society through art. In 2008, Génération Gogohoun did their first tour of Benin and played their show, Fiers d'Être Villageois (Proud To Be Villagers), in Boukoumbé, Parakou, Lokossa and the Centre Culturel Français in Cotonou. More tours and shows are planned, funding permitting. Check their website for updates.

---

lakeshore. At **Hôtel Chez Théo** (☎ 22 43 08 06; www.chez-theo.com; r CFA15,000-20,000; P), 600m north of the village, rooms are impeccable, and the bar-restaurant (mains CFA3000) sits on a stilt platform with wondrous views.

To get there, take the turn-off north to Lokossa and Comé from the coastal highway. Taxis that ply the Hilakondji–Cotonou route will generally drop you off at the Comé turn-off, from where the only option to Possotomé is a *zemi-john* (CFA1000).

ABOMEY
pop 114,600

Its winding lanes dotted with Dahomeyan palaces and temples, Abomey is a remarkable town. The main attraction is a tour of these ruins. The newly opened **tourist office** (Office du Tourisme d'Abomey; ☎ 22 50 15 77; Place Goho; 2hr tour for 1/2 people CFA3000/CFA4000; 9am-1pm & 3-6pm Mon-Fri, 9am-4pm Sat) runs guided tours.

The kings of Dahomey were a bloody lot, and their litany of slave trading, human sacrifice and war is illustrated by the appliqué banners and bas-reliefs in the **Musée Historique d'Abomey** (☎ 21 50 03 14; www.epa-prema.net/abomey; admission CFA1500; 9am-6pm). The sprawling museum and its gory exhibits are housed in two palaces – all that remains of what was once one of the most impressive structures in West Africa.

our pick Chez Monique (☎ 22 50 01 68; north of Rond-Point de la Préfecture; r CFA7500-12,000; P), one of the two best hotels in town, both close to

the Préfecture, has an exotic pleasure garden, breezy rooms and friendly staff. The other, **Auberge d'Abomey** (☎ 97 89 87 25; Rond-Point de la Préfecture; s/d with fan CFA11,500/12,500, with air-con CFA15,500/18,500;), is the latest addition to the reliable 'Auberge de' chain, with signature understated decor and a colonial feel.

our pick Chez Delphano (☎ 93 64 02 40; meals CFA1600) is the place for sustenance. Pierre and Marguerite prepare exquisite Beninese cuisine in a jovial atmosphere. Marguerite also prepares crêpes in the morning, with fresh ground coffee and a mountain of fruit. Find Chez Delphano north of Rond-Point de la Préfecture, on the way to Chez Monique.

Plenty of bush taxis depart from Cotonou (CFA2400, three hours), sometimes with a connection at Bohicon (9km east of Abomey). Bush taxis (CFA300) and *zemi-johns* (CFA500) frequently run between Abomey and Bohicon. Vehicles going to Parakou leave frequently from the *gare routière* in Bohicon.

Inter City Lines (☎ 21 00 85 54; www.intercity-lines.com) and **Confort Lines** (☎ 21 32 58 15) buses (between Cotonou and Parakou, Malanville and Natitingou) stop in Bohicon on the way.

THE NORTH

PARAKOU
pop 198,000

There's not much to keep you in Parakou, but it makes a relaxing stopover en route to the northern wildlife parks.

The Bank of Africa has a 24-hour ATM and there is internet access at **Parak Cyber Café** (per hr CFA400; 9am-midnight).

Hôtel les Canaris (☎ 23 61 11 69; Route de l'Hôtel Canaries; r with fan/air-con CFA6500/9500) Rooms at this budget establishment are nothing to write home about, but the management is friendly.

our pick **Auberge de Parakou** (☎ 23 61 03 05; www.hotels-benin.com; Route de l'Hôtel Canaris; s/d with fan CFA10,000/12,000, with air-con CFA14,000/16,000; P) This delightful auberge (inn) is great value for money, with large, spotless rooms. The lounge area, with its pool table and patio, is perfect to chill out in and the French restaurant serves delicious food (meals cost CFA4500).

There are some great *maquis* in Parakou: **Le Secret de la Vieille Marmite** (☎ 90 94 24 37; off Carrefour de l'Aviation; meals CFA1000), with its lively ambience and bright-blue cladding, does some of the best Beninese grub around.

From the *gare routière*, north of the Grand Marché, bush taxis and minibuses regularly go to Cotonou (CFA7100, eight hours) and Malanville (CFA4500, five hours).

Inter City Lines (☎ 23 10 04 75; www.intercity-lines.com) has two daily services to Cotonou (CFA7500, 7½ hours) and one to Malanville.

Aïr Transport (☎ 93 96 00 63) and **Maïssadjé** (☎ 90 03 38 04) run buses between Niamey and Parakou (see p260). The depots are about 1.5km north of town on the road to Niger. Ask a *zem*.

NATITINGOU

pop 75,600

Affectionately known as Nati, Natitingou is the most vibrant town in northern Benin and is a fabulous base for excursions to the nearby Atakora Mountains and the Parc National de la Pendjari (opposite).

Information

Internet access is available at **Cyber Centre** (☎ 98 77 29 37; per hr CFA400; 8.30am-11pm Mon-Sat, from 10am Sun) in the town centre.

Ecobank (8am-6pm Mon-Fri, 9am-3pm Sat) and **Financial Bank** (8am-noon & 3-5pm Mon-Fri) both change cash and travellers cheques, but neither accepts credit cards.

The **Pharmacie Tissanta** (☎ 23 82 10 13), at the southern end of town, is open 24 hours, seven days a week.

Sights & Activities

The **Musée d'Arts et de Traditions Populaires** (☎ 23 02 00 53; admission CFA1000; 8am-12.30pm & 3.30-6.30pm Mon-Fri, 9am-noon & 4-6.30pm Sat & Sun) gives an overview of life in Somba communities (opposite).

The **Kota Falls** (CFA400), 15km southeast of Natitingou, off the main highway, is a great spot for a picnic and is an easy day excursion from town.

Sleeping & Eating

Auberge Le Vieux Cavalier (☎ 23 82 13 24; r with fan/air-con CFA6500/9000;) Water sometimes struggles to make it all the way to your bathroom at the top of the hill, but that's our only quibble about this otherwise great budget option.

our pick **Hôtel de Bourgogne** (☎/fax 23 82 22 40; www.natitingou.org/bourgogne; s/d with fan CFA10,000/13,000, with air-con from CFA15,000/18,000; P) This delightful hotel will feel like a home away from home. Thérèse Oudot, the owner, is a mine of information and is wonderfully welcoming. Rooms were being repainted in warm colours at the time of writing and the restaurant is hands-down the best in town.

Hôtel Bellevue (☎ 23 82 13 36; www.hotel-bellevue-benin.com; s/d with fan CFA8000/9000, with air-con CFA12,000/14,000; P) Perched at the top of a hill, in a rambling garden, the Bellevue is a charming collection of sweet bungalows and *paillotes*. Myriam, the formidable owner, runs a tight ship and rooms are spotless.

Natitingou has a fine array of places to grab a beer and a bite. Among the great *maquis* is **Le Karité** (mains from CFA500; lunch only), world champion of *igname pilé* (pounded yam) and lost in a maze of alleyways on the eastern side of town (ask a *zem* to take you there).

The nameless **restaurant grill** (☎ 95 28 37 58; mains CFA2000-4500) opposite the Pharmacie Tissanta has good music and better food, such as grilled *capitaine* (Nile perch) with yam fries.

Very popular and highly original is **La Brèche** (☎ 90 92 43 20; menu du jour CFA4000), a *tata somba* house with views of the Atakora Mountains.

There is a supermarket, **Quidata** (8.30am-1pm & 3.30-8pm Mon-Sat, 9am-2pm Sun), opposite Financial Bank.

Getting There & Away

From the *gare routière* on the main road, bush taxis and minibuses go to Parakou (CFA3500, five hours) and Porga (CFA3000, 2½ hours), on the border with Burkina Faso, via Tanguiéta (CFA1500, one hour).

Bus services linking Nati and Cotonou (CFA8500, eight hours) include **Inter City Lines** (☎ 23 03 01 06; www.intercity-lines.com; Rue du Marché, opposite Pharmacie Tissanta) and **Confort Lines** (☎ 95 86 67 02; off Rue du Marché). All buses arriving from Cotonou drop passengers off outside the post office. Cotonou-bound services pick passengers up at their respective offices. Services leave at 7am; book ahead or arrive early on the day.

THE ATAKORA REGION
About 30km west of Nati is the mountain village of **Koussoukoingou** (also known as Koussou-Kovangou), famous for its stunning location and breathtaking views of the Atakora range.

Ecotourism association **Perle de l'Atakora** (Pearl of the Atakora; ☎ 97 44 28 61; www.ecobenin.org/koussoukoingou) offers guided walks in the area (CFA2000 to CFA4000 for 2½ to 3½ hours) taking in local sights such as the famous *tata* houses (see the boxed text, right). You can arrange to spend the night at a *tata* (CFA4500 per person including an evening meal).

It's best to get to the Atakora with your own transport, but bush taxis do ply the dusty trail between Nati and Boukoumbé (CFA2000, two hours), where you can cross into Togo (if you do, make sure you get your passport stamped at the *commissariat* (police station) as there is no border check point). Otherwise, *zemi-johns* (CFA5000, three hours) will take you.

PARC NATIONAL DE LA PENDJARI
Amid the majestic landscape of the Atakora's rugged cliffs and wooded savannah live lions, cheetahs, leopards, elephants, baboons, hippos, myriad birds and countless antelopes. The 275,000-hectare **Parc National de la Pendjari** (Penjari National Park; www.pendjari.net; admission per person CFA10,000, per vehicle CFA3000), 100km north of Natitingou, is one of the best in West Africa. The best viewing time is near the end of the dry season, when animals start to hover around water holes.

To maximise your chances of seeing animals, go for an accredited guide (graded as 'A' or 'B' and listed on the park's website).

Many visitors stay in Natitingou and make excursions from there, but you'll have a better chance of seeing wildlife if you stay at the park itself. Camping is allowed at selected sites, otherwise **Hôtel de la Pendjari** (☎ 23 82 11 24; www.hoteltatasomba.com; r with fan/air-con CFA21,000/29,000; 🕙 15 Dec-31 Jul; 🅿 🖭), at the heart of the park, has simple but adequate rooms. There is an atmospheric bar-restaurant (meals CFA6000) under a huge central *paillote* and, amazingly, a swimming pool. You must book in advance.

THE SOMBA

Commonly referred to as the Somba, the Betamaribé people are concentrated to the south of Natitingou, in the plains of Boukoumbé and around Perma.

Their *tata somba* houses – fort-like huts with clay turrets and thatched spires – are a reflection of their fierce individuality, which has seen them resist both Dahomey slave hunters and Christianity and Islam.

Their principle religion is animism – as seen in the rags and bottles they hang from the trees. Once famous for their nudity, they began wearing clothes in the 1970s. See also the boxed text, p532.

The main entrances to Pendjari are roughly 100km north of Natitingou, in Porga (near the border with Burkina Faso) and Batia (41km northeast of Tanguiéta, on a good track).

Travellers without vehicles could try to team up with other parties at hotels in Natitingou. **Bénin Aventure** (☎ 23 02 00 17; www.beninaventure.com) rents out 4WD vehicles for CFA75,000 per day (for up to four people), including a chauffeur-guide (rated 'A' by the park) and fuel.

MALANVILLE
The only reason you would stop in this dusty border town is to break up the journey between Cotonou and Niamey. **La Sota** (☎ 97 64 97 48; s/d with fan CFA18,000/19,500, with air-con CFA22,000/25,000; 🅿 🖭 🖭) provides an unexpected overnight haven. Rooms are a little underwhelming for the price but the facilities are tops, with a good restaurant (meals CFA5000) and a pool. The hotel is 2km south of town.

Malanville is well connected with Parakou by bush taxi (CFA4500, five hours). Inter City Lines runs a daily service to Cotonou (CFA11,000, 12 hours). Niger buses Rimbo and SNTV travel between Cotonou and Niamey via Malanville (see p260), but they are often full. A *zemi-john* to Gaya in Niger, where you can get taxis to Niamey, is about CFA1200.

BENIN DIRECTORY
ACCOMMODATION
Basic rooms with fans cost as little as CFA5000, while comfortable air-conditioned midrange rooms hover around CFA20,000. Top-end

prices range from CFA35,000 outside Cotonou to CFA100,000 in the economic capital.

ACTIVITIES

The beaches along the coast are not safe for swimming because of strong currents. Stick to hotel swimming pools or the lagoon, where you can also canoe.

Guided walks are available through eco-tourism NGO Eco-Bénin in Possotomé (p254) and Perle de l'Atakora in Koussoukoingou (p257).

BUSINESS HOURS

Businesses Open 8am to 12.30pm and 3pm to 6.30pm Monday to Friday, plus 9am to 3pm Saturday. Some banks are open through lunch time.

Restaurants Lunch and dinner daily, unless specified.

Shops Open 8am to noon and 3pm to 7pm Monday to Saturday; sometimes open Sunday morning, too.

DANGERS & ANNOYANCES

Cotonou has its fair share of traffic accidents and muggings (see p249), so be careful. In Ouidah, avoid the roads to and along the coast at any time of day.

Children – and sometimes also adults – will shout 'Yovo! Yovo!' (meaning 'white person') ad nauseam. It's normally harmless but tiresome, although travellers have reported being intimidated by the sheer scale of the phenomenon. Abomey is particularly bad.

EMBASSIES & CONSULATES

France Consulate (Map pp248-9; ☎ 21 31 26 38; Rue 651A, Cotonou); Embassy (Map pp248-9; ☎ 21 30 02 25; Route de l'Aéroport, Cotonou)

Germany (Map pp248-9; ☎ 21 31 56 93; Ave Jean-Paul II, Cotonou; ☒ 9am-noon)

Ghana (Map pp248-9; ☎ 21 30 07 46; off Route de l'Aéroport, Cotonou; ☒ 8am-2pm)

Niger Consulate (☎ 23 61 28 27; Route de l'Hôpital, Parakou; ☒ 8am-1pm & 3.30-6.30pm Mon-Fri); Embassy (Map pp248-9; ☎ 21 31 56 65; Rue 651A, Cotonou; ☒ 8am-4pm Mon-Thu, to 1pm Fri)

Nigeria (Map pp248-9; ☎ 21 30 11 42; Blvd de la Marina, Cotonou; ☒ 10-11.30am)

UK (Map pp248-9; ☎ 21 30 12 74; Haie Vive, Cotonou) Officially, British Nationals must deal with the British Deputy High Commission in Lagos (Nigeria; p476). However, the Community Liaison Officer for the British community in Benin, Pauline Collins, based at the English International School, can be of some help.

USA (Map pp248-9; ☎ 21 30 06 50; http://cotonou.us embassy.gov; Rue Caporal Bernard Anani, Cotonou)

FESTIVALS & EVENTS

Apart from the colourful annual Muslim celebrations in the northern towns, the main event is the annual **Voodoo Festival**, held in Ouidah (p253) on 10 January.

HOLIDAYS

Benin celebrates Muslim holidays; see the Africa Directory, p1140, for details. Public holidays include the following:

New Year's Day 1 January
Vodoun 10 January
Easter Monday March/April
Labour Day 1 May
Ascension Thursday May
Pentecost Monday May
Independence Day 1 August
Assumption 15 August
Armed Forces Day 26 October
All Saints' Day 1 November
Christmas 25 December

MAPS

The best map by far is IGN's 1:600,000 *République du Bénin Carte Touristique*. With good country detail and inset city maps of Porto Novo and Cotonou, it costs about CFA7500 in Cotonou bookshops.

MONEY

The unit of currency in Benin is the West African CFA (Communauté Financière Africaine) franc. All banks in the country change cash, although outside of Cotonou banks will only change euros.

PRACTICALITIES

- Cotonou's daily newspapers include *La Nation* and *Le Matinal*.
- Foreign newspapers and magazines can occasionally be found at newspaper stands.
- The state-owned ORTB broadcasts on the radio in French and local languages.
- Cotonou has some 15 commercial radio stations, including Radio Afrique (101.7MHz).
- The electricity supply is temperamental and network cuts are frequent.
- Benin uses the metric system.

Benin's neighbours all use CFA francs apart from Nigeria, where the currency is the naira. There is no official way to get hold of naira in Benin, but Cotonou has a healthy black market around the Jonquet district and Gare du Dantokpa.

Travellers cheques can be changed in Cotonou and Natitingou. ATMs are available in Cotonou and Parakou.

PHOTOGRAPHY

Be careful when taking shots of cultural and religious buildings and ceremonies. Rules are not clear-cut, so it's best to ask first. For general information, see p1144.

TELEPHONE

International calls can be made at telecom offices and private telephone agencies throughout Benin. The cost per minute varies hugely but allow CFA400 per minute to Europe and North America, CFA600 to Asia.

Mobile phones are now a staple and the network coverage is surprisingly good. MTN is the main operator. A SIM card costs CFA2000, international SMS CFA75 and international calls CFA125 per minute. Top-up vouchers are readily available.

TOURIST INFORMATION

There is a lacklustre tourist office in Cotonou (p249).

VISAS

Visas are required for all travellers except nationals of the Ecowas (Economic Community of West African States). If flying into Cotonou you will need a visa before arrival. A 30-day, single-entry visa costs UK£55 from the Beninese consulate in the UK; the embassy in the USA charges $100.

If crossing overland, you can get a visa at the border, where the 24-hour posts issue 48-hour, single-entry transit visas (CFA10,000).

You can then obtain a 30-day, single- or multiple-entry visa (CFA12,000) at the Direction Emigration Immigration (p249) in Cotonou. Applications take two days. You need one photo.

Note that at the time of research the Visa des Pays de l'Entente (see p1147) was not available in Benin.

A yellow-fever vaccination certificate is required to enter Benin.

Visas for Onward Travel

For onward travel to Burkina Faso and Côte d'Ivoire, the French consulate issues three-month visas (CFA20,000) and transit visas (CFA6000) in 24 to 48 hours, with two photos required.

The Nigerian embassy only issues two-day transit visas to travellers with a Nigerian embassy in their home country (there is no need to contact the embassy in your home country beforehand). You need two photos, along with photocopies of your passport and, if you have one, your ticket for onward travel from Nigeria. Fees vary according to nationality (CFA30,000 for UK, CFA68,000 for US, CFA20,000 for Australia) and are issued on the same day. You cannot get visas at the border.

For Niger, you must obtain a visa before travelling, as border officials at the Malanville/Gaya crossing no longer issue visas. The embassy in Cotonou or the consulate in Parakou (opposite) both issue 30-day visas. They cost CFA22,500 and you'll need two photos. Allow three to four working days.

As for Togo, seven-day visas (CFA10,000) are issued at the border (see p535).

WOMEN TRAVELLERS

Beninese men can be sleazy and women travellers will get a lot of unwanted attention. Particularly unnerving are military and other officials using their power to get more of your company than is strictly necessary. Always stay polite but firm and make sure you have a good 'husband story'.

For more advice, see p1148.

TRANSPORT IN BENIN

GETTING THERE & AWAY
Air

The main airport is on the western fringe of Cotonou, in Cocotiers. Air France has the most reliable and frequent services between Benin and Europe. The following airlines have offices in Cotonou:

Afriqiyah Airways (8U; ☎ 21 31 76 51; Blvd Steinmetz)

Air France (AF; ☎ 21 30 18 15; www.airfrance.com/bj; Route de l'Aéroport)

Air Ivoire (VU; ☎ 21 31 86 14; www.airivoire.com; Blvd Steinmetz)

Point-Afrique (6V/DR; ☎ 21 30 98 62; www.point-afri que.com; Route de l'Aéroport) Flights only in summer, organised tours the rest of the year.

Royal Air Maroc (AT; ☎ 21 30 86 04; www.royalair maroc.com; Route de l'Aéroport)

Land

BURKINA FASO

There's at least one bush taxi per day along the 97km of tarred road from Natitingou to Porga (CFA1900, two hours), where you can cross to Tindangou in Burkina Faso. Monday, Porga market day, is a good day to find a ride.

SKV (☎ 98 59 88 00) runs buses between Cotonou and Bamako (CFA35,000, 48 hours) via Ouagadougou (CFA17,000, 18 hours) on Wednesdays and Fridays (departure is at 8pm).

NIGER

From Malanville, a *zemi-john* or shared taxi can take you across the Niger River to Gaya in Niger (*zemi-john*/shared taxi CFA1200/700). You cannot get a visa for Niger at the border – get one in Cotonou or Parakou (see p259).

From Gaya, it's easier to find a Peugeot bush taxi to Niamey (CFA4250, five hours) or a minibus (CFA4600, 5½ hours) than it is to squeeze onto one of the Cotonou–Niamey coaches, which are usually full. From Cotonou, try **Rimbo** (☎ 95 23 24 82), with daily services to Niamey (CFA19,700, 19 hours), or **SNTV** (☎ 93 91 40 42; www.sntv.biz) also with daily trips to Niamey (CFA17,500, 15 hours).

NIGERIA

In Cotonou, bush taxis and minibuses leave for Lagos throughout the day from Gare du Dantokpa (CFA4000, three hours excluding border crossing mayhem). There are no direct taxis to Lagos from Porto Novo, so you'll have to change at the Kraké/Seme border (CFA700, 30 minutes). Make sure you have some naira to pay for your journey on the other side. Another option is the Lagos–Accra bus service run by **ABC Transport** (☎ 21 33 33 77; www.abctransport.com), which stops in Cotonou (CFA4000, four hours).

There are countless police checkpoints between Seme and Lagos, so travellers with their own vehicle will be better off crossing further north at Kétou, and then travelling on to Ibadan.

You may have to grease a few palms at Kraké, although asking for a receipt is a good way to discourage corrupt officials. If hiring a taxi across the border, check whether the price includes bribes.

TOGO

Cotonou and Lomé are connected by frequent bush taxis (CFA3500, three hours), which regularly leave the Gare Jonquet in Cotonou for Lomé. Alternatively, pick up a taxi to the border point at Hilakondji and grab another taxi on the Togolese side of the border. **STIF** (☎ 97 98 11 80) buses also plough the Cotonou–Lomé route every other day (CFA4000, four hours).

Other crossings are at Kétao/Ouaké, on the Kara–Djougou road, and between Nadoba in Togo and Boukoumbé in Benin along a good track. The latter crossing takes you through spectacular countryside but has little public transport except on Wednesdays, Nadoba market day.

GETTING AROUND
Bush Taxi & Bus

Minibuses and bush taxis are the principal means of transport between towns. There is sometimes a surcharge for luggage.

Benin also has a range of excellent bus services. The best is **Inter City Lines** (☎ 21 00 85 54; www.intercity-lines.com), with comfortable seats, air-con and dreadful Ivorian soap videos that get the entire bus roaring with laughter. It runs daily services between Cotonou and Parakou (CFA7500, 7½ hours), Malanville (CFA11,000, 12 hours) and Natitingou (CFA8500, eight hours), stopping in all major towns en route. **Confort Lines** (☎ 21 32 58 15) also runs daily services between Cotonou and Natitingou (CFA8000, eight hours) and Parakou (CFA7000).

Car & Motorcycle

Petrol costs between CFA300 and CFA600 per litre. Petrol is cheaper in Nigeria, so much of it is carried illegally across the border and sold on the black market at prices slightly below the official rate. Just look for the guys along the roads with 1L to 5L bottles.

If you're driving, you need an International Driving Permit. Roads are in relatively good condition throughout Benin.

Local Transport

The omnipresence of *zems* (*zemi-johns*; motorbike taxis) has translated into the near disappearance of car taxis for short journeys. While they are by far the fastest and most convenient way of getting around, they are dangerous: most drive like lunatics and helmets are not available. Hail them just as you would a taxi, and be sure to agree on a price before the journey. The typical fare is CFA150 to CFA250 for trips within a town. They are also an easy way to get to remote destinations.

Tours

The excellent Bénin Aventure (see p257) organises guided, tailor-made trips around Benin in chauffeur-driven 4WDs. Allow CFA75,000 a day (for up to four people) for car rental, fuel and guiding fees, CFA15,000 to CFA40,000 per night for a double room, and about CFA50,000 in excursion fees (park entrance etc).

Burkina Faso

Forget about big-ticket attractions in Burkina Faso. Bar a scattering of dunes and colourful markets in the Sahel, a range of eerie rock formations around Banfora in the southwest and a couple of national parks (but none that can rival those in eastern or southern Africa), the country has few iconic calling cards. So why does it invariably win the hearts of travellers? The answer: the people. The Burkinabé (as people from Burkina Faso are called) are the country's greatest asset. They're disarmingly charming and easygoing. Wherever you go, you'll be greeted with a memorable *bonne arrivée* (welcome).

The country's other big draws include arts, craftwork and culture. There's a fantastic arts scene in Ouagadougou, the enjoyable and gloriously named capital, along with a famous musical tradition and beautiful handicrafts. Throw in Fespaco, Africa's premier film festival, and there's enough to engage your mind and senses for a couple of weeks or so. Burkina Faso is also alive with a vibrant cultural mix of peoples, from the proud Fulani people of the Sahel to the animist societies of the Senoufo or the Lobi.

Tourism infrastructure is fairly limited, but there is a handful of gems, especially in Bobo-Dioulasso and Ouagadougou, as well as family-run, ecofriendly *campements* in more remote areas.

FAST FACTS

- **Area** 274,122 sq km
- **ATMs** In all major towns (Visa only)
- **Borders** Benin, Côte d'Ivoire, Ghana, Mali, Niger and Togo; all borders open
- **Budget** US$20 to US$50 per day
- **Capital** Ouagadougou
- **Languages** French, More, Fulfulde and Lobi
- **Money** West African CFA franc; US$1 = CFA463, €1 = CFA656
- **Population** 14.9 million
- **Seasons** Wet (June to October), dry (November to February), hot (March to May)
- **Telephone** Country code ☎ 226; international access code ☎ 00
- **Time** GMT/UTC
- **Visa** Issued at Ouagadougou airport (CFA10,000), some border posts or Burkina Faso embassies (up to US$100); Burkina Faso is covered by the Visa des Pays de l'Entente, p1147

HOW MUCH?

- **Ouagadougou–Bobo-Dioulasso bus ride** US$13.50
- **Museum admission** US$2.25
- **Guide per day** US$22.50 to US$38
- **Internet connection (per hour)** US$1.10
- **4WD rental (per day)** US$125 plus petrol

LONELY PLANET INDEX

- **1L petrol** US$1.45
- **1.5L bottled water** US$1.10
- **Bottle of Brakina beer** US$1.80
- **Souvenir T-shirt** US$11.20
- **Serve of riz sauce** US$1.10

HIGHLIGHTS

- **The Sahel** (p273) Experience the magic of the Sahelian markets and landscapes.
- **Ouagadougou** (p266) Let the beat get under your skin in Burkina Faso's wonderfully named capital.
- **Bobo-Dioulasso** (p269) Wind down a few gears in Burkina's mellow second city.
- **Ranch de Nazinga** (p273) Come face to face with elephants in this wildlife sanctuary.
- **Sindou Peaks** (p272) Wander amid craggy rock formations and bizarrely shaped peaks.

CLIMATE & WHEN TO GO

The best time to visit is from mid-October to December. It can be downright wet between June and September, when the south can be uncomfortably humid and many roads throughout the country are impassable. From December to February the weather is marginally cooler, although dusty harmattan winds can produce hazy skies in January and February. The hot season is from March to early June, when the mercury can rise well above 40°C in the capital.

ITINERARIES

- **One Week** Plan on spending a couple of days in the capital Ouagadougou (p266), which has few sights as such but boasts steamy nightlife, a thriving arts scene and fine restaurants. Then bus it to Bobo-Dioulasso (p269) and soak up the mellow vibes of this charming city.
- **Two Weeks** You could add the Sahel to your trip and head up to Gorom-Gorom (p273) and the nearby Sahelian settlements, or consider further exploration of the southwest by renting a moped in Banfora (p271).

HISTORY
The Mossi & the French

By the 14th century, the territory of present-day Burkina Faso was occupied by the Bobo, Lobi, Gourounsi and the Mossi. The Mossi, who now make up almost half of Burkina Faso's population, founded their first kingdom more than 500 years ago in Ouagadougou. Three more Mossi states ruled over the remainder of the country, known for their devastating attacks against the Muslim empires in Mali.

During the Scramble for Africa in the second half of the 19th century, the French broke up the traditional Mossi states, but French rule in Upper Volta, as Burkina Faso was then known, saw money and resources go elsewhere – mostly Côte d'Ivoire. By the time that independence came in 1960, Upper Volta had become little more than a repository for forced labour.

Thomas Sankara

Between 1966 and 1982 Upper Volta suffered a cycle of coups and countercoups and the country stagnated. In November 1982 Captain Thomas Sankara, an ambitious young left-wing military star, seized power.

Over the next four years 'Thom Sank' (as he was popularly known) recast the country. He changed its name to Burkina Faso (meaning 'Land of the Incorruptible'), restructured the economy to promote self-reliance in rural areas and tackled corruption with rare zeal. The economy improved, financial books were kept in good order and people developed a genuine pride in their country.

Despite his popularity, in late 1987 a group of junior officers seized power; Sankara was taken outside Ouagadougou and shot.

The Compaoré Years

The new junta was headed by Captain Blaise Compaoré, Sankara's former friend and

BURKINA FASO

lonelyplanet.co

BURKINA FASO

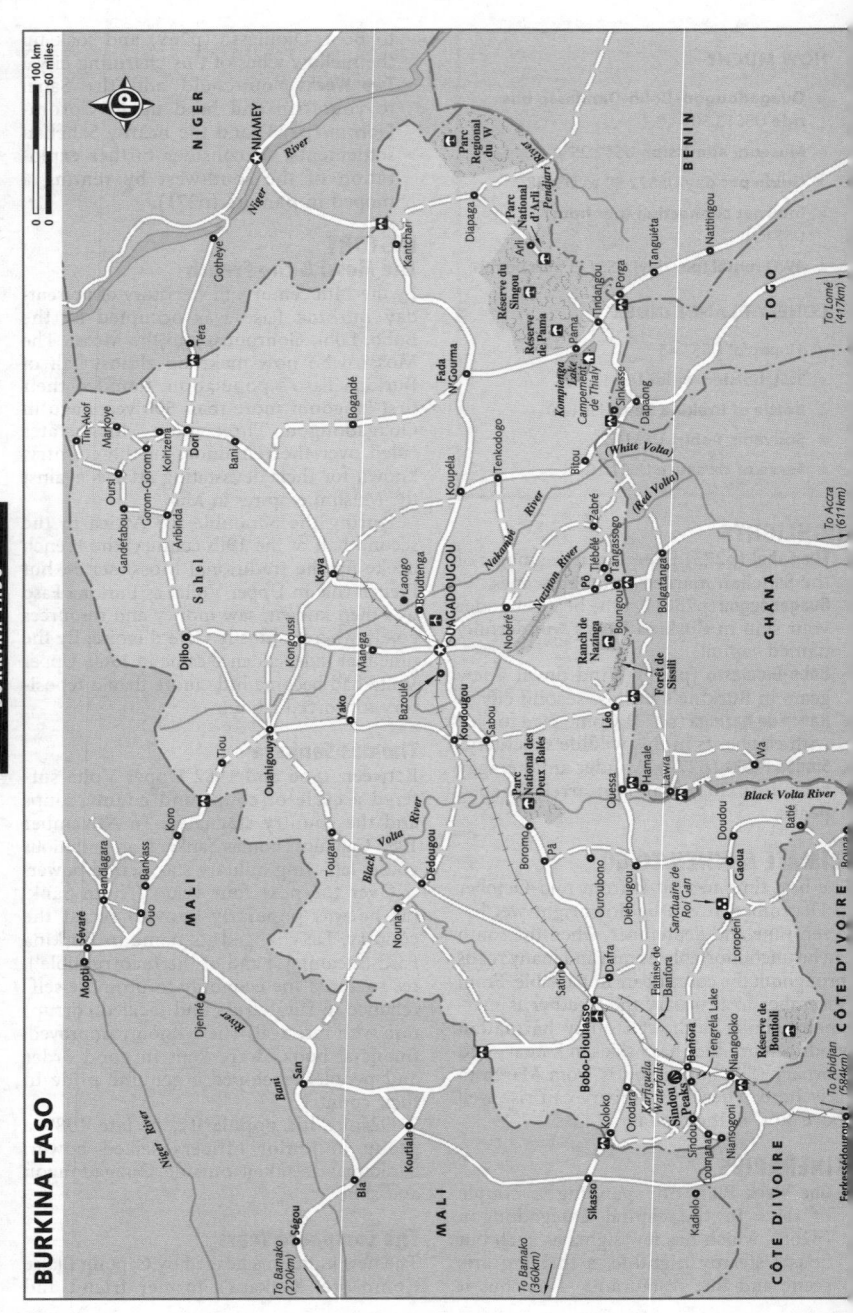

co-revolutionary, and son-in-law of Côte d'Ivoire's long-standing leader, the late Houphouët-Boigny. In late 1991 Compaoré achieved a modicum of legitimacy when, as sole candidate and on a low turnout, he was elected president. However, Clément Ouédraogo, the leading opposition figure, was assassinated a couple of weeks later.

In legislative and presidential elections in 1997 and 1998, the president and his supporters won more than 85% of the vote.

Burkina Faso Today
The country remains one of the more stable in the region, although rumblings of discontent continue. Street demonstrations in April 2000 forced the government to draft a constitutional amendment that limits presidents to two terms in office. Arguing that this two-term limit did not apply to terms served before the amendment was passed, and with the opposition divided, President Compaoré won re-election for a third term on 13 November 2005 with 80% of the vote. President Compaoré intends to run for another term in 2010.

CULTURE
Burkinabés are a laid-back lot and have a genuine pride in their country. Although ethnicity (along with religion) is the bedrock of identity, you'll see little if any antagonism between members of different ethnic groups. People are also proud that, in a troublesome region riven with conflict, they have become known as a beacon of stability.

For all of their friendliness and relaxed nature, life for the Burkinabé is as tough as it gets. In 2008 the UN ranked Burkina Faso 173rd out of 179 countries across a number of quality-of-life indicators.

People
Burkina Faso, which occupies an area about half the size of France, is extremely diverse, with its almost 15 million people scattered among some 60 ethnic groups. The largest of these is the Mossi (48%), who are primarily concentrated in the central plateau area. Important groups in the south include the Bobo (7%), Senoufo (5%), Lobi (7%) and Gourounsi (5%). In the Sahel areas of the north are the Hausa, Fulani (8%), Bella and Tuareg. Around 80% of Burkinabés live in rural areas.

FESPACO
From humble origins in 1969, **Fespaco** (Festival Pan-Africain du Cinema; Map p267; ☎ 50 39 87 01; www.fespaco.bf; Ave Kadiogo, Ouagadougou) has become Africa's most prestigious film festival. Fespaco, held in Ouagadougou every odd year in February/March, sees 20 African films selected to compete for the prestigious Étalon d'Or de Yennenga – Fespaco's equivalent of the Oscar.

Ouagadougou is invariably spruced up for the occasion. Tickets and hotel rooms can be hard to find at this time, so book ahead. The next Fespaco will be held in 2011.

Religion
Around 90% of Burkina Faso's population observe either Islam (about 50%) or traditional animist beliefs based mainly on the worship of ancestors and spirits (40%) – although there is often considerable overlap.

Arts
Burkina Faso has a vibrant contemporary arts scene (painting, sculpture, wood carving, bronze- and brass-work, and textiles). Artists' works are exhibited in Ouagadougou's galleries, cultural centres and collective workshops. Craftwork is also well developed, and there's no shortage of artisans' stalls and craft shops, selling masks and leatherwork, in Ouagadougou and Bobo-Dioulasso.

Burkina Faso has a thriving film industry, which receives considerable biennial stimulation from the Fespaco film festival held in Ouagadougou (see the boxed text, above).

Burkina Faso's modern musicians draw on influences from across the continent (especially Mali, Congo and Côte d'Ivoire), Jamaican reggae and Europe.

FOOD & DRINK
Burkinabé food is largely influenced by Senegalese and Côte d'Ivoire cuisines. Sauces, especially *arachide* (groundnut) or *graine* (a hot sauce made with oil palm nuts), are the mainstay and are always served with a starch – usually rice (it's called *riz sauce* or *riz gras*) or the Burkinabé staple, *tô*, a millet- or sorghum-based *pâte* (a pounded dough-like substance). The Ivorian *attiéké* (grated cassava), *alloco* (ripe bananas fried with chilli in palm oil) and *kedjenou*

(simmered chicken or fish with vegetables) are also commonly found.

Grilled dishes of chicken, mutton, beef, guinea fowl, fish (especially Nile perch, known locally as *capitaine*) and *agouti* (a large rodent) also feature on the menu.

In the Sahel, couscous (semolina grains) is widely available.

Castel, Flag, Brakina, Beaufort and So.b.bra are popular and palatable lagers. Locally produced juices include the hibiscus drink *bissap, gingembre* (ginger) and mango.

ENVIRONMENT

Landlocked Burkina Faso's terrain ranges from the harsh desert and semidesert of the north, to the woodland and savannah of the green southwest. The country's dominant feature, however, is the vast central laterite plateau of the Sahel, where hardy trees and bushes thrive.

Burkina Faso's two main protected areas – Parc National d'Arli, close to the border with Benin, and Ranch de Nazinga – are in the southeast of the country. Parc National d'Arli hosts elephants, hippos, warthogs, antelopes and monkeys, while Ranch de Nazinga is famous for its elephants. Parc Regional du W straddles Burkina Faso, Niger and Benin, but the best sections are across the border. Unfortunately, hunting (including by tourists) is still a problem around the parks' perimeters.

Burkina Faso suffers acutely from deforestation and soil erosion, not to mention drought.

OUAGADOUGOU

pop 1.4 million

Ouaga, as it's affectionately dubbed, lacks standout sights and its architecture doesn't have much to turn your head, but stick around this bustling city long enough and you might fall prey to its unexpected charms.

The capital thrives as an eclectic arts hub, with dance and concert venues, live bands, theatre companies and beautiful handicrafts. If your visit is in late February, try to make it coincide with Fespaco, Africa's major film festival, which attracts film buffs from all over the world.

If every town had a symbol, Ouagadougou's would surely be the *mobylette* (moped) –

masses of them swarm down the boulevards like frantic bumblebees. At night, you'll see hundreds of them parked in front of the innumerable *maquis* (open-air restaurants) that are dotted around the city, where the beat is alive and pumping.

ORIENTATION

It's easy to get disoriented in Ouagadougou as there are no obvious landmarks. Large buildings and roundabouts serve as de facto points of reference.

Some 5km south of the city centre, the 'Ouaga 2000' development is part of an ambitious town-planning project.

INFORMATION

Internet Access

Cybercentres (internet cafes) are easy to find in the city centre. Most upmarket hotels and guesthouses provide wi-fi access.

Medical Services

There are numerous well-stocked pharmacies in the city centre. For medical treatment or a consultation, expats recommend **Clinique Philadelphie** (☎ 50 33 28 71; Ave du Maurice Yaméogo; ☾ 24hr).

Money

There are bureaux de change on Ave Kwame N'Krumah. Banks, such as **Biciab** (☾ 7-11am & 3.30-5pm Mon-Fri) and **Ecobank** (☾ 7-11am & 3.30-5pm), are also an option. A quicker alternative is to change your euros at **Marina Market** (Ave Yennenga; ☾ 8am-9pm Mon-Sat, 9am-9pm Sun) – head to the manager's office.

You'll have no trouble finding banks with ATMs (Visa only) in the city centre.

Post

Main post office (off Ave de la Nation; ☾ 7.30am-12.30pm & 3.30-5.30pm Mon-Fri)

Telephone & Fax

For international and local calls, head to any *télécentre* booth – they are ubiquitous in Ouagadougou and stay open late.

Tourist Information

Travel agencies (see p268) and guesthouse owners are the best source of information.

OUAGADOUGOU

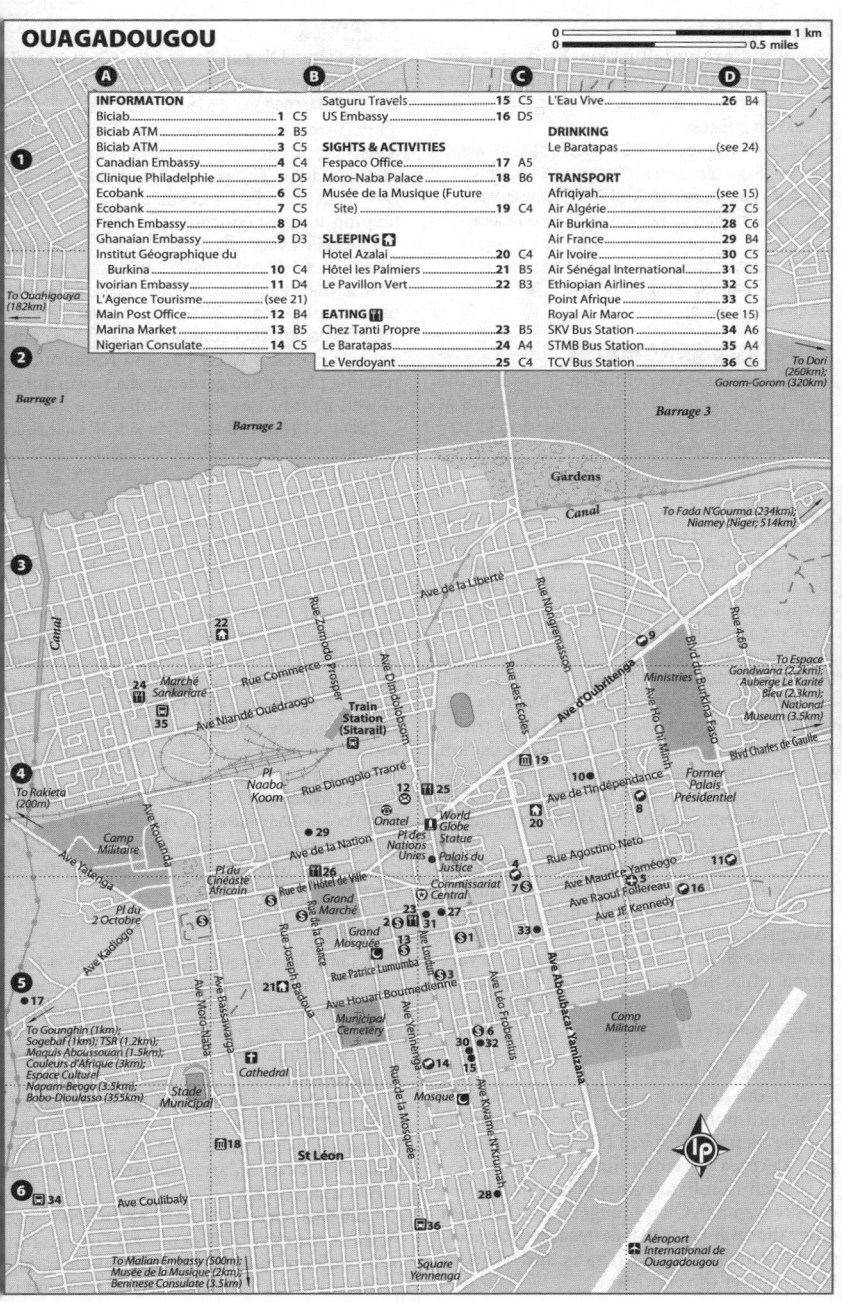

0 — 1 km
0 — 0.5 miles

INFORMATION		
Biciab	1	C5
Biciab ATM	2	B5
Biciab ATM	3	C5
Canadian Embassy	4	C4
Clinique Philadelphie	5	D5
Ecobank	6	C5
Ecobank	7	C5
French Embassy	8	D4
Ghanaian Embassy	9	D3
Institut Géographique du Burkina	10	C4
Ivoirian Embassy	11	D4
L'Agence Tourisme	(see 21)	
Main Post Office	12	B4
Marina Market	13	B5
Nigerian Consulate	14	C5
Satguru Travels	15	C5
US Embassy	16	D5

SIGHTS & ACTIVITIES		
Fespaco Office	17	A5
Moro-Naba Palace	18	B6
Musée de la Musique (Future Site)	19	C4

SLEEPING		
Hotel Azalai	20	C4
Hôtel les Palmiers	21	B5
Le Pavillon Vert	22	B3

EATING		
Chez Tanti Propre	23	B5
Le Baratapas	24	A4
Le Verdoyant	25	C4

L'Eau Vive	26	B4

DRINKING		
Le Baratapas	(see 24)	

TRANSPORT		
Afriqiyah	(see 15)	
Air Algérie	27	C5
Air Burkina	28	C6
Air France	29	B4
Air Ivoire	30	C5
Air Sénégal International	31	C5
Ethiopian Airlines	32	C5
Point Afrique	33	C5
Royal Air Maroc	(see 15)	
SKV Bus Station	34	A6
STMB Bus Station	35	A4
TCV Bus Station	36	C6

BURKINA FASO

To Ouahigouya (182km)

Barrage 1

Barrage 2

Barrage 3

To Dori (260km);
Gorom-Gorom (320km)

Gardens

Canal

To Fada N'Gourma (234km);
Niamey (Niger) (514km)

Ave de la Liberté

Rue Nongremasson

Rue Nongremasson

Rue 4.69

To Espace
Gondwana (2.2km);
Auberge Le Karité
Bleu (2.3km);
National
Museum (3.5km)

Canal

Marché
Sankariaré

Rue Commerce

Rue Zoniodo Prosper

Ave Dimdolobsom

Ave Niandé Ouédraogo

Train
Station
(Sitarail)

Rue Diongolo Traoré

Rue des Écoles

Ave d'Oubritenga

Rue Ho Chi Minh

Ministries

Blvd du Burkina Faso

Blvd Charles de Gaulle

To Rakieta
(200m)

Pl
Naaba-
Koom

Onatel
Pl des
Nations
Unies

World
Globe
Statue

Palais du
Justice

Ave de l'Indépendance

Former
Palais
Présidentiel

Camp
Militaire

Ave Kouanda

Ave de la Nation

Rue Agostino Neto

Ave Valenga

Pl du
Cinéaste
Africain

Rue de l'Hôtel de Ville

Grand
Marché

Commissariat
Central

Rue Maurice Yaméogo

Ave Raoul Follereau

Ave JF Kennedy

Pl du
2 Octobre

Ave Kadiogo

Grand
Mosquée

Rue Léon

Rue Patrice Lumumba

Ave Léo Frobenius

Ave Abouakar Yamizana

To Gounghin (1km);
Sogebaf (1km); TSR (1.2km);
Maquis Aboussouan (1.5km);
Couleurs d'Afrique (3km);
Espace Culturel
Napam-Beogo (3.5km);
Bobo-Dioulasso (355km)

Ave Moro-Naba

Ave Raswewga

Ave Joseph Badoua

Rue de la Chance

Ave Houari Boumedienne

Municipal
Cemetery

Ave Yennenga

Rue de la Mosquée

Ave Kwame N'Kuruma

Camp
Militaire

Cathedral

Stade
Municipal

Mosque

St Léon

Square
Yennenga

Ave Coullibaly

To Malian Embassy (500m);
Sogebaf (1km); Musée de la Musique (2km);
Beninese Consulate (3.5km)

Aéroport
International de
Ouagadougou

Travel Agencies

For tours around Burkina Faso and further afield, the following companies are recommended, and can arrange English-speaking guides:

Couleurs d'Afrique (☎ 50 34 19 56, 78 81 11 48; www.couleurs-afrique.com; Ave de l'Olympisme, Gounghin)

L'Agence Tourisme (☎ 50 31 84 43; www.agence-tourisme.com; Hôtel les Palmiers, Rue Joseph Badoua)

To purchase domestic or international air tickets, head to **Satguru Travels** (☎ 50 30 16 52; Ave Kwame N'Krumah).

DANGERS & ANNOYANCES

Ouagadougou is one of the safer cities in the region, but avoid walking around alone at night. Bag snatching is a problem: don't carry valuables with you.

SIGHTS & ACTIVITIES

The **national museum** (☎ 50 39 19 34; Blvd Charles de Gaulle; admission CFA1000; ⊗ 9am-12.30pm & 3-5.30pm Tue-Sat), almost 4km east of the city centre, has displays of the various masks, ancestral statues and traditional costumes of Burkina Faso's major ethnic groups.

It's worth popping your head into the **Musée de la Musique** (off Map p267; ☎ 50 32 40 60; Blvd Tengsoba; admission CFA1000; ⊗ 9am-noon & 3-6pm Tue-Sat) if you have an interest in traditional music. At press time, the museum was on Blvd Tengsoba (also known as Blvd Circulaire) but should be relocated to its original premises on Ave d'Oubritenga by the time you read this.

On Fridays at 7am the Moro-Naba of Ouagadougou, emperor of the Mossi and the most powerful traditional chief in Burkina Faso, presides over the Moro-Naba ceremony at the **Moro-Naba Palace** (Ave Moro-Naba). It's a very formal ritual that lasts only about 15 minutes. Travellers are welcome to attend but photos are not permitted.

FESTIVALS & EVENTS

Apart from its lively nightlife, Ouagadougou is the undisputed capital of African film, hosting the biennial Fespaco (see the boxed text, p265), Africa's premier film festival.

In even-numbered years in late October or early November, Ouagadougou hosts the **Salon International de l'Artisanat de Ouagadougou** (www.siao.bf), which attracts artisans and vendors from all over the continent.

SLEEPING

Espace Culturel Napam-Beogo (☎ 50 35 35 14; www.napam-beogo.org; Gounghin; dm CFA4000, s/d without bathroom CFA6000/8500, d with bathroom CFA10,000; ▢) This 16-room guesthouse also operates as an artists' residence and a crafts centre (based on fair trade). The rooms are utterly without frills, but the vibe is casual, with your rent helping support educational programs.

Le Pavillon Vert (☎ 50 31 06 11; hotelpavillonvert@yahoo.fr; Ave de la Liberté; r with fan & with/without bathroom CFA12,500/7500, with air-con CFA17,000; ▨) Under new management since 2009, the stalwart 'PV' is the best backpacker spot in Ouaga. It has competitive prices, a lively bar and restaurant, a relaxing plant-filled garden and an assortment of well-kept rooms for all budgets.

Auberge Le Karité Bleu (☎ 50 36 90 46; karite.bleu@yahoo.fr; Zone du Bois, 214 Blvd de l'Onatel; s incl breakfast CFA25,000-35,000, d incl breakfast 28,000-38,000; ▨ ☎) Hidden behind ochre walls in a residential neighbourhood, this adorable B&B offers five spiffy rooms and two quirky huts, all adorned with masks and paintings. It's about 2km west of the city centre.

Hôtel les Palmiers (☎ 50 33 33 30, 78 81 30 96; www.hotellespalmiers.net; Rue Joseph Badoua; d CFA32,000-41,000; ▨ ▢ ▨) This hotel is something special, an oasis blending African touches with European levels of comfort. The rooms are arranged around a leafy compound and embellished with local decorations. The garden is easily one of the nicest in Ouaga.

Hotel Azalai (☎ 50 30 60 60; www.azalaihotels.com; Ave de l'Indépendance; d from CFA60,000; ▣ ▨ ▢ ▩ ▨) One of Ouaga's swankiest hotels, the Azalai has 176 rooms that are outfitted with all the trimmings.

EATING

Chez Tanti Propre (Ave Loudun; mains CFA500-1000; ⊗ lunch & dinner Mon-Sat) You'll find no cheaper place for a sit-down meal in the city centre. Order a *riz gras*, a *tô* or an *alloco* prepared grandma style. Perfect for a quick bite at lunchtime.

Le Baratapas (☎ 78 85 24 80; Rue Commerce; CFA1200-4500; ⊗ 9am-11pm Tue-Sun) Just around the corner from the STMB bus station, this snazzy spot has an arty vibe and the food is varied and creative.

L'Eau Vive (Rue de l'Hôtel de Ville; mains CFA2000-7000; ⊗ lunch & dinner Mon-Sat) This peaceful oasis is run by an order of nuns and features a welcoming garden dining area out the back. The menu is

BURKINA FASO

mainly French but has the occasional nod to African flavours.

Maquis Aboussouan (☎ 50 34 27 20; Rue Simon Compaoré; mains CFA2500-4500; ☺ lunch & dinner Tue-Sun) This reassuring *maquis* is the place that you should reserve to sample your first *kedjenou poulet* (slowly simmered chicken with peppers and tomatoes) or *attiéké*.

Le Verdoyant (☎ 50 31 54 07; Ave Dimdolobsom; mains CFA3000-6000; ☺ lunch & dinner Thu-Tue) A favourite haunt of expats, the ultracentral Le Verdoyant is famous for its pasta and wood-fired pizzas.

Espace Gondwana (☎ 50 36 11 24; Rue 13.14, Zone du Bois; mains CFA4000-9000; ☺ lunch Mon-Sat, dinner daily) Tucked away in eastern Ouaga, Espace Gondwana sports sensational decor, with four dining rooms richly adorned with masks and traditional furniture. The food impresses, too, with an imaginative menu that runs the gamut from frogs' legs and fish dishes to grilled meats and salads.

DRINKING & ENTERTAINMENT

Maquis dancing (simple open-air eatery-bars that feature live dance bands or sound-system jams in the evenings) are scattered all around Ouaga, but the most happening area is Gounghin, west of the centre. Another G-spot of the city's bar scene is the area around Ave de la Liberté, north of the centre. Nightclubs abound along Ave Kwame N'Krumah.

One of our favourite places is **Le Baratapas** (☎ 78 85 24 80; Rue Commerce; admission CFA1200-4500; ☺ 9am-11pm Tue-Sun). It has a cool atmosphere, a variety of rums and you might hear some quality live music on Friday nights.

GETTING THERE & AWAY

Leaving Ouagadougou can be confusing, as most buses leave from the bus companies' depots rather than from the *gare routière* (bus station). **STMB** (off Rue Commerce) has the most extensive network of routes throughout Burkina Faso, but the most comfortable buses are those of **TCV** (Rue de la Mosquée) and **SKV** (Ave Coulibaly), which both run services between Ouaga and Bobo-Dioulasso (CFA6000, five daily). **TSR** (Ave Kadiogo) has services to Dori (CFA4000, two daily) and Bobo-Dioulasso (CFA6000, six daily).

For Gorom-Gorom (CFA6000, six to seven hours), try STMB or the old clunkers of **Sogebaf** (Ave Kadiogo), although it's easier to travel to Dori and arrange transport from there.

GETTING AROUND

The 2km taxi journey from the Aéroport International de Ouagadougou to the city centre costs about CFA3000.

Shared taxis, mostly beaten-up old green Renaults, cost CFA300 for a short ride within town. The basic rate for a private taxi, which you commission just for yourself, is CFA500 – more for longer journeys. Rates double after 10pm.

THE SOUTHWEST

BOBO-DIOULASSO

pop 459,261

Bobo, as it's widely known, may be Burkina Faso's second-largest city, but it has a small-town charm and its quiet tree-lined streets exude a languid, semi-tropical atmosphere that makes it a favourite rest stop for travellers – one of West Africa's most enjoyable. It has a thriving market, a couple of interesting museums, a smattering of welcoming B&Bs and hotels, good restaurants and numerous craft workshops. The spectacular mosque adds yet another dollop of character to the city.

Information

INTERNET ACCESS

You'll find a few internet cafes in the centre.

MONEY

Biciab, Ecobank and BIB have offices in the centre and are equipped with Visa-friendly ATMs. You'll also find several bureaux de change, but a quicker alternative is to change your euros at **Marina Market** (Ave de la République; ☺ 8am-1pm & 4-8pm Mon-Sat, 9am-1pm Sun) – this Lebanese-run supermarket offers the best rates and stays open late.

Sights

Bobo's **Grande Mosquée** (admission to grounds CFA1000), built in 1893, is an outstanding example of Sahel-style mud architecture and is easily Bobo's standout sight. Although entry is forbidden for non-Muslims, it's the exterior that is so captivating, especially at sunset when the facade turns golden.

Just across the street to the east of the mosque is **Kibidwé**, the oldest part of town. Unaccompanied travellers will be hassled if they try to get around on their own, so make

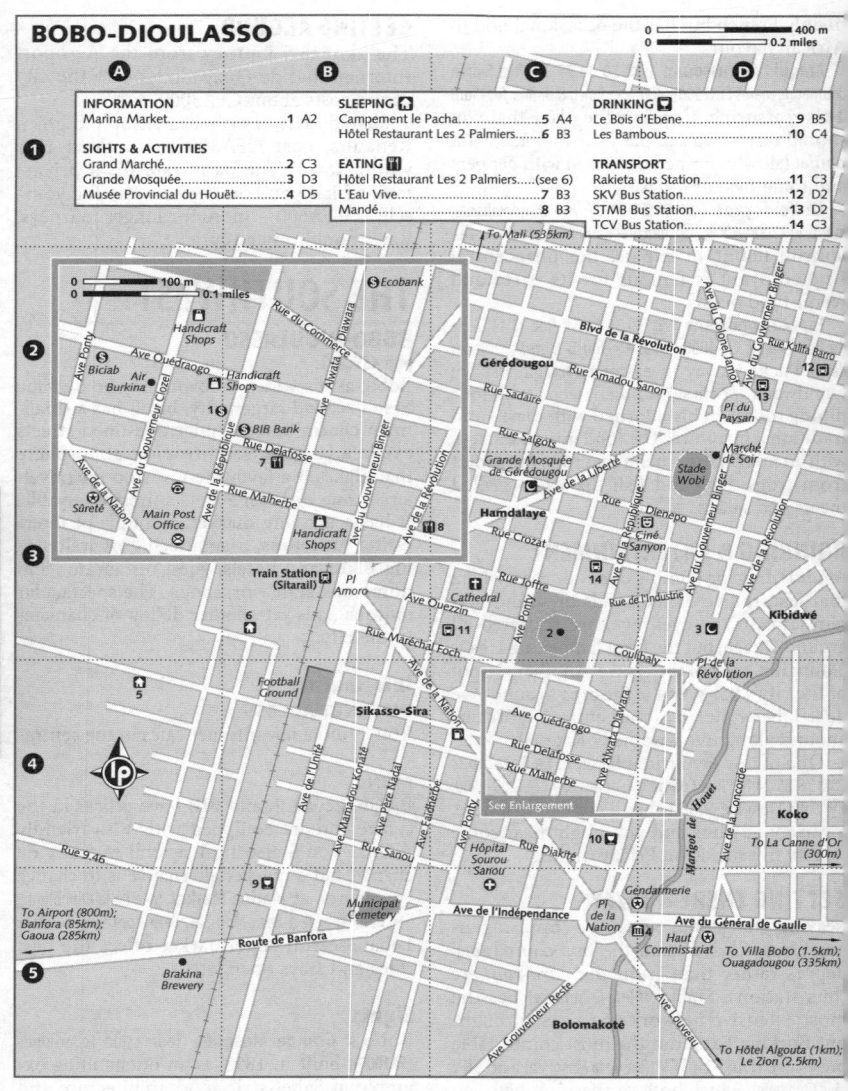

BOBO-DIOULASSO

INFORMATION	
Marina Market................................**1** A2	

SIGHTS & ACTIVITIES	
Grand Marché...............................**2** C3	
Grande Mosquée...........................**3** D3	
Musée Provincial du Houët............**4** D5	

SLEEPING ⌂	
Campement le Pacha.....................**5** A4	
Hôtel Restaurant Les 2 Palmiers......**6** B3	

EATING ⏍	
Hôtel Restaurant Les 2 Palmiers.....(see 6)	
L'Eau Vive....................................**7** B3	
Mandé...**8** B3	

DRINKING ⊡	
Le Bois d'Ebene............................**9** B5	
Les Bambous................................**10** C4	

TRANSPORT	
Rakieta Bus Station.......................**11** C3	
SKV Bus Station............................**12** D2	
STMB Bus Station..........................**13** D2	
TCV Bus Station............................**14** C3	

a contribution 'for the elders', and let yourself be guided.

Bobo-Dioulasso's centrepiece, the expansive **Grand Marché**, is a wonderful (and largely hassle-free) place to experience a typical African city market.

The small but interesting **Musée Provincial du Houët** (Place de la Nation; admission CFA1000; ☉ 9am-12.30pm & 3-5.30pm Tue-Sat) showcases masks, statues and ceremonial dress from all over Burkina Faso, and there are full-scale examples of traditional buildings in the grounds.

Sleeping

Le Zion (☎ 78 86 27 25, 78 83 75 30; http://le.zion.free.fr; Kuinima; rooftop mattress CFA2000, d with fan & with/without bathroom CFA7500/5000) On the outskirts of town and very much a part of the local community, Le Zion offers unflashy yet acceptable rooms, live music most weekends, home-cooked meals, *mobylette* rental and loads of advice on the surrounding area.

Campement le Pacha (☎ 20 98 09 54, 76 61 16 01; lepachabo@yahoo.fr; Rue Malherbe; campsite per person/car CFA2500/3000; d with fan & without bathroom CFA10,500-11,500, with air-con CFA18,500-19,500; P ☒) For a Franco Swiss venture, the unadorned rooms are a tad disappointing, but there's an attractive courtyard and a great garden restaurant. Location is ace, too.

our pick Villa Bobo (☎ 20 98 20 03, 70 53 78 17; www.villabobo.com; Koko; s/d with fan CFA9000/13,000, with air-con CFA13,000/18,000; P ☒ ☐ ☎ ☒) This charming B&B comprises three zealously maintained rooms (two of which share a bathroom), prim bathrooms, a communal kitchen and a colourful garden with a pool. Xavier, the French owner, speaks English and can arrange excursions in the area.

our pick Hôtel Algouta (☎ 20 98 07 92, 78 85 84 42; www.hotel-algouta.com; Bolomakoté; d with fan/air-con CFA9000/17,000; P ☒ ☐) The well-kept Algouta features a range of tidy rooms at remarkably reasonable prices, and the public spaces are enlivened with African handicrafts. Best of all, it's in a tranquil neighbourhood and the on-site restaurant serves up excellent African food.

Hôtel Restaurant Les 2 Palmiers (☎ 20 97 27 59; hotel les2palmiers@fasonet.bf; off Rue Malherbe; d CFA37,000-42,000; P ☒ ☎) In a nice quiet street, this excellent option gets an A+ for its spotless rooms embellished with African knick-knacks. The on-site restaurant is hailed as one of the best in Bobo.

Eating

As well as restaurants, there are lots of *maquis* in the centre that serve inexpensive food.

our pick Hôtel Restaurant Les 2 Palmiers (☎ 20 97 27 59; off Rue Malherbe; mains CFA1000-4000; ☽ lunch & dinner) This upmarket venture is famous for its faultlessly cooked meat and fish dishes. Try the *filet mignon de porc* (a choice piece of pork) or the *darne de thon rouge* (red tuna steak).

our pick Mandé (Ave de la Révolution; mains CFA1000-4000; ☽ lunch & dinner) With an open-air terrace, very reasonable prices and a wide-ranging menu specialising in African dishes, Mandé is an excellent deal. If you just eat *riz sauce* or couscous and drink tamarind juice, you'll be well fed for around CFA1500.

La Canne d'Or (☎ 20 97 15 96; Koko; mains CFA2000-5000; ☽ lunch & dinner) This villa-style eatery in a serene neighbourhood serves French fare with an African twist. House faves include marbled frogs' legs, homemade spring rolls and antelope steak.

L'Eau Vive (Rue Delafosse; mains CFA2500-5000; ☽ lunch & dinner Mon-Sat) The sister venue to the restaurant of the same name in Ouagadougou, and also run by nuns, L'Eau Vive offers imaginative French cooking and a varied menu.

You can also enjoy well-prepared meals at Les Bambous, Le Zion and Le Bois d'Ebene (see Drinking & Entertainment, below).

Drinking & Entertainment

The bars are all pretty similar, with outdoor tables under straw *paillotes* (awnings). Just follow your nose to find one you like. If you like live music with your beer, try the following places:

Le Bois d'Ebene (Ave de l'Unité; admission CFA500; ☽ noon-late) The best venue in town for live music.

Le Zion (☎ 78 86 27 25, 78 83 75 30; http://le.zion.free.fr; Kuinima; ☽ Fri & Sat) Another lively, but more intimate, place for live music.

Les Bambous (Ave du Gouverneur Binger; admission CFA500; ☽ 6am-2.30pm & 6pm-midnight Mon-Sat, 6pm-midnight Sun) A popular outdoor venue.

Getting There & Away
BUS

STMB (Blvd de la Révolution), **TCV** (Rue Crozat) and **SKV** (Blvd de la Révolution) have the best buses to Ouagadougou (CFA6000, five hours), with five daily departures each.

For getting around the southwest, **Rakieta** (Ave Père Nadal) is a reliable company that has regular departures for Banfora (CFA1500, 1½ hours, six daily). Another option is TCV, with six daily services to Banfora (same price).

Getting Around

To hire a bicycle for the day (CFA2000), ask at your hotel or guesthouse. For a moped, expect to pay at least CFA4000 per day, and up to CFA7000 for a motorbike.

Taxis are plentiful and most trips within town cost from CFA300.

BANFORA
pop 76,000

Banfora is a sleepy little town in one of the more beautiful areas in Burkina Faso. As such,

BURKINA FASO

it serves as a good base for exploring the lush green surrounding countryside.

Banfora has several banks that have ATMs; it also has a Cyberposte and innumerable *télécentres*.

Budget travellers will head to **Camping Siakadougou** (☎ 76 43 30 89; off the road to Karfiguéla Waterfalls; campsite per person CFA2000, d CFA3500–4500), with five traditional huts arranged around a courtyard. It's in a quiet neighbourhood, 10- to 15-minutes' walk to the centre. If you're after more creature comforts, look no further than **Le Calypso** (☎ 20 91 02 29, 70 74 14 83; famille_houitte@yahoo.fr; Route de Bobo-Dioulasso; dm CFA2500, d with fan & with/without bathroom from CFA9000/7000, with air-con CFA16,000; ✖ ▢), which has a neat dorm, fan-cooled units and rooms with air-con. Another safe bet is **Hôtel la Canne à Sucre** (☎ 20 91 01 07; www.banfora.com; off Rue de la Poste; d with fan CFA9000, with air-con CFA21,000-31,000, 4-bed apt CFA50,000; ✖ ✖), which is Banfora's most complete atmospheric hotel.

You'll find a few good restaurants in or near the centre, including **McDonald** (off Rue de la Préfecture; mains CFA1000-3000; ☺ lunch & dinner Thu-Tue) and **Le Calypso** (☎ 20 91 02 29; off Rue de la Poste; mains CFA1000-3500; ☺ breakfast, lunch & dinner) – Le Calypso is under the same ownership as the eponymous hotel but in a different location. Hôtel la Canne à Sucre has an excellent on-site restaurant.

Drinking & Entertainment

You'll find a gaggle of *buvettes* (refreshment stalls) in Banfora, but the most atmospheric venue at the time of writing was, by far, **Nabissa** (☎ 76 25 33 36, 75 27 68 86; ☺ 8am-late). It features traditional live music from 9pm.

Getting There & Away

Rakieta (Rue de la Poste) has regular departures for Bobo-Dioulasso (CFA1300, 1½ hours, six daily). **TCV** (Rue de la Poste) also has six daily services for Bobo-Dioulasso, while **STMB** (Rue de la Poste) leaves three times a day.

AROUND BANFORA

Just 7km west of Banfora, **Tengréla Lake** (admission CFA2000) is home to a variety of bird life and, if you're lucky, you'll see hippos (especially from January to April). The admission price includes a *pirogue* (traditional canoe) trip. Want to laze a few days away in the area? Park your backpack at **Campement Kenignigohi – Chez Seydou** (☎ 70 24 68 93, 70 29 34 61; Tengréla; d/tw

without bathroom CFA3000/6000), a five-minute walk from the lake.

Some 11km northwest of Banfora, **Karfiguéla Waterfalls** (Cascades de Karfiguéla; admission CFA1000) are reached through a magnificent avenue of mango trees. You can take a dip in the lovely natural pools on the upper part of the waterfalls.

From Karfiguéla Waterfalls, you can walk (about 3km) to the awesome **Dômes de Fabedougou** (admission CFA1000), huge limestone formations that have been sculpted over millennia by water and erosion into quirky, dome-like shapes.

SINDOU PEAKS

One of Burkina Faso's most spectacular landscapes, the **Sindou Peaks** (Pics de Sindou; admission CFA1000) are a narrow, craggy chain featuring a fantastic array of tortuous cones that were sculpted and blasted by the elements.

This fantasyland is ideal for a one-hour stroll amid the cones, a day hike, or even a couple of days' hiking. Coming from Banfora, the main gateway is about one kilometre before the entrance to Sindou town. There's a little booth staffed by guides. They belong to **Association Soutrala Tyera** (☎ 76 08 46 60; mokopic@yahoo.fr), which is active in promoting responsible travel in the Senoufo country through cultural exchanges and community tourism, including tailor-made courses in African percussion, village stays, guided hikes and cooking courses.

In Sindou, you can stay at the humble **Campement Djatiguiya** (☎ 76 24 71 61, 70 71 57 28; r CFA4000). A more atmospheric option is

Campement Soutrala (☎ 76 08 46 60; r per person CFA2500), operated by Association Soutrala Tyera, near the guides' booth.

Coming from the village of Loumana, about 23km further west, a few minibuses stop in Sindou on their way to Banfora's *gare routière* (CFA1250). The last one leaves Sindou at around 11am.

THE SAHEL

Northern Burkina Faso is dominated by the desolate confines of the Sahel. It's certainly inhospitable at most times of the year, but it also features stupendously colourful markets, fascinating local cultures and traditions, and landscapes that are much less monotonous than you'd think.

Dori, 261km northeast of Ouagadougou, is a mere overnight stop before heading further north to the 'real Sahel', including **Gorom-Gorom** (which takes two hours). Gorom-Gorom's Thursday market ranks as one of the most colourful in the country. You'll see a variety of Sahel and Sahara ethnic groups, including Tuaregs, Bellas, Songhaï farmers and Fulani herders (who wear conical straw hats).

For the true Sahelian experience, save a couple of days for the small settlements around Gorom-Gorom. **Oursi**, some 35km northeast of Gorom-Gorom, features some spectacular sand dunes and a colourful Sunday market, while **Gandefabou**, 30km northwest of Gorom-Gorom, reached via a sandy track, boasts an atmospheric *campement* (guesthouse). **Markoye**, 45km northeast of Gorom-Gorom, in the heart of Fulani country, has a vibrant camel and cattle market every Monday.

All *campements* can arrange **camel trips** into the surrounding desert (about CFA25,000 per person per day).

There's only one bank, in Oursi, so bring plenty of cash.

Sleeping & Eating
If you're looking for ecofriendly accommodation options and cultural immersion, the rustic (read: no electricity and showers with a bucket) Sahelian *campements* will fulfil your expectations. They can organise camel or 4WD trips.

One of the Sahel's best organised *campements*, the Tuareg-run **Campement Edjef** (☎ 40 46 68 54, 70 61 21 30; www.gandefabou.org; Gandefabou; r per person CFA4500) is positioned in an idyllic spot on a sand dune, with sweeping views over a valley. The same family also owns **Relais du Campement Edjef – Chez Rissa** (☎ 40 46 93 96; Gorom-Gorom; r without bathroom per person CFA4500) in Gorom-Gorom. Beds are in mud huts or under the stars. In Oursi, bookmark **Gîte Aounaf** (☎ 40 46 70 12, 70 25 62 15; Oursi; r per person CFA5000), in a scenic location, with soft sand and a clutch of attractive mud huts and traditional thatch-and-straw Fula tents.

Getting There & Away
Independent travel is a bit tricky to organise, as only Dori is served by regular buses. STMB and TSR operate daily services between Ouagadougou and Dori (CFA4000, four to six hours), from where you can find bush taxis (CFA2000, two hours) for Gorom-Gorom. They are plentiful on market day; otherwise, they leave when they are full, so nothing's guaranteed. It's much more

BURKINA FASO

ELEPHANT SPOTTING

According to the wildlife specialists and tour operators we met, there are two great spots in Burkina Faso where you can see elephants:

■ **Parc National des Deux Balés** (park fee per person CFA3000; ☸ Oct-Jun) Halfway between Ouaga and Bobo, the best time to visit the park is during March and April. Accommodation is available at the well-run **Campement Le Kaïcedra** (☎ 76 62 65 40; http://kaicedra.waika9.com/camp.htm; campsite CFA3000 per person, 2-/4-bed bungalow CFA18,000/22,000, meals CFA5500; ☸ Oct-Jun).

■ **Ranch de Nazinga** (☎ 50 41 36 17; admission per vehicle CFA1000, per person CFA8500, dm CFA5000, 2-bed apt CFA10,000, bungalows CFA12,500; ☸ 6am-6pm) This 97,000-hectare ranch near Pô and the Ghanaian border shelters a variety of species, but elephants are the stars of the show. According to tour operators, the best times to spot elephants are January and March, when they can regularly be seen roaming the ranch, very close to the sleeping quarters. Accommodation is in basic dorm-style rooms or in bungalows.

convenient to arrange transfers from Dori or Gorom-Gorom with the *campements* (give them a call the day before).

You can also hire a 4WD with a driver (at least CFA40,000 per day, plus petrol) in Gorom-Gorom (or in Ouagadougou).

BURKINA FASO DIRECTORY

ACCOMMODATION

Ouagadougou, Bobo-Dioulasso and, to a lesser extent, Banfora have a good range of accommodation, including charming B&Bs. Elsewhere, choice is limited.

A single/double in a decent budget hotel costs anything from CFA6000/8000 to CFA12,000/16,000. Midrange hotels cost from CFA12,000/16,000 to CFA32,000/41,000, and top-end from CFA32,000/41,000 and up.

The Sahel doesn't have hotels, only rustic *campements*.

BUSINESS HOURS

Banks Typically open between 7am and 11am, and from 3.30pm to 5pm Monday to Friday.

Bars Normally serve from noon until late, and nightclubs generally go from 9pm into the wee hours.

Restaurants Usually serve food between 11.30am and 3pm, then open again from 6.30pm to 10.30pm.

Shops and businesses Operate 7.30am to noon and 3pm to 5.30pm Monday to Friday, and 9am to 1pm Saturday.

DANGERS & ANNOYANCES

Burkina Faso is one of the safest countries in West Africa. Crime isn't unknown, particularly around big markets, cinemas and

---

PRACTICALITIES

- Electricity supply is 220V and plugs are of the European two-round-pin variety.

- International versions of French- and (a few) English-language publications are available in Ouagadougou and Bobo-Dioulasso.

- BBC World Service (www.bbc.co.uk/worldservice) is on 99.2FM in Ouagadougou. For a French-language services, tune in to RFI, 94FM.

- Burkina Faso uses the metric system.

---

gares routières, but it's usually confined to petty theft and pickpocketing.

EMBASSIES & CONSULATES

Embassies and consulates in Ouagadougou include the following:

Benin (☎ 50 38 49 96; 401 Rue Bagen Nini)

Canada (☎ 50 31 18 94; ouaga@dfait-maeci.gc.ca; 586 Rue Agostino Neto) Also represents Australia in consular matters.

Côte d'Ivoire (☎ 50 31 82 28; cnr Ave Raoul Follereau & Blvd du Burkina Faso)

France (☎ 50 49 66 66; www.ambafrance-bf.org; Ave de l'Indépendance)

Ghana (☎ 50 30 76 35; Ave d'Oubritenga)

Mali (☎ 50 38 19 22; 2569 Ave Bassawarga) Just south of Ave de la Résistance.

Niger (☎ 50 30 53 59; Ave Yennenga)

USA (☎ 50 30 67 23; http://ouagadougou.usembassy.gov; 622 Ave Raoul Follereau)

HOLIDAYS

New Year's Day 1 January
Women's Day 8 March
Good Friday & Easter Monday March/April
Labour Day 1 May
Ascension Day 4 to 5 August
Anniversary of Sankara's Overthrow 15 October
All Saints' Day 1 November
Christmas Day 25 December

Burkina Faso also celebrates Islamic holidays, which change dates each year. See p1140 for details of Islamic holidays.

INTERNET ACCESS

You'll find internet cafes in larger cities, but your best bet is to head to Cyberposte outlets, which are within (or next door to) the post office, keep longer hours and have the best connections (per hour CFA500).

Wi-fi access is increasingly available in Ouagadougou and Bobo-Dioulasso.

MAPS

Burkina Faso (1:1,000,000), a map published by the French-based Institut Géographique National (IGN), is available at the **Institut Géographique du Burkina** (IGB; Map p267; ☎ 50 32 48 23; Ave de l'Indépendance) in Ouagadougou, and in many European bookshops.

MONEY

The unit of currency in Burkina Faso is the West African CFA franc. The best foreign currency to carry is euros. Travellers cheques are not useful; euros in cash and an ATM card (Visa only) are the way to go.

Most banks have an exchange counter. Quicker alternatives are the bureaux de change and the Lebanese supermarkets in Ouagadougou and Bobo-Dioulasso, which keep longer hours.

ATMs are available in larger cities, including Ouagadougou, Bobo-Dioulasso and Banfora, but they only issue cash advances for Visa (not MasterCard) and transaction fees are prohibitive; take out as much as the machine lets you each time.

TELEPHONE & FAX
You can make international phone calls at any *télécentre* (phone booth equipped with metered telephone). International calls cost from CFA500 per minute.

Mobile phone coverage is excellent across all of Burkina Faso. Local mobile phone companies include Telmob, Zain or Telecel. If you have a GSM phone and it has been 'unlocked', it's possible to buy a local SIM card (from CFA2000).

VISAS
Everyone except Economic Community of West African States (Ecowas) nationals needs a visa. You can buy a tourist visa at Ouagadougou airport for CFA10,000 (paid in local currency; head to any bank or bureau de change in the centre and come back with the requisite amount). Travellers also report that visas are issued at Burkina Faso's land borders for the same price, although they're invariably issued on the spot.

Burkina Faso embassies require two photos, may ask for proof of yellow fever vaccination and charge from €20 in Europe to US$100 in the USA. In countries where there is no Burkina Faso embassy, French embassies sometimes issue 10-day visas.

Note that you can obtain the Visa des Pays de l'Entente (p1147) in Ouagadougou.

Visas for Onward Travel
Visas for the following neighbouring countries can be obtained in Burkina Faso. See opposite for embassy information.
Benin Visas are issued the same day (CFA15,000). You need two photos and photocopies of your passport. If you just want to slip over the border to Benin, you can get a 48-hour visa at the border post.

Côte d'Ivoire A one-month single-entry visa costs CFA20,000 (CFA10,000 for French citizens) and requires one photo.
Ghana Two-month visas are issued within 24 hours for CFA15,000 and require four photos.
Mali One-month visas cost CFA20,000, are issued the same day and require two photos.
Niger A one-month single-entry visa costs CFA20,000, requires one photo and is issued in 72 hours.

TRANSPORT IN BURKINA FASO

GETTING THERE & AWAY
Air
Burkina Faso's two international airports are Aéroport International de Ouagadougou and Aéroport International Borgo (Bobo-Dioulasso). Airlines connect Ouagadougou with Addis Ababa (Ethiopia), Accra (Ghana), Algiers (Algeria), Abidjan (Côte d'Ivoire), Bamako (Mali), Casablanca (Morocco), Cotonou (Benin), Dakar (Senegal), Douala (Cameroon), Libreville (Gabon), Lomé (Togo), Paris (France) and Tripoli (Libya).

The following airlines have offices in Ouagadougou:
Afriqiyah (Map p267; 8U; ☎ 50 30 16 52; www.afriqiyah.aero; Ave Kwame N'Krumah) Represented by Satguru Travels.
Air Algérie (Map p267AH; ☎ 50 31 23 01; www.airalgerie.dz; Ave Kwame N'Krumah)
Air Burkina (2J; ☎ 50 49 23 43; www.air-burkina.com; Ave Kwame N'Krumah)
Air France (Map p267; AF; ☎ 50 30 63 65; www.airfrance.com; Ave de la Nation)
Air Ivoire (Map p267; VU; ☎ 50 30 04 50; www.airivoire.com; Ave Kwame N'Krumah)
Air Sénégal International (Map p267; V7; ☎ 50 31 39 05; www.air-senegal-international.com; Ave Loudun)
Ethiopian Airlines (Map p267; ET; ☎ 50 30 10 24; www.ethiopianairlines.com; Ave Kwame N'Krumah)
Point-Afrique (Map p267; ☎ 50 33 16 20; www.point-afrique.com; Ave Aboubacar Yamizana)
Royal Air Maroc (Map p267; AT; ☎ 50 30 50 81; www.royalairmaroc.com; Ave Kwame N'Krumah)

Land
The main border crossings are at Niangoloko for Côte d'Ivoire; Tanguiéta for Benin; 15km south of Pô, or Hamale for Ghana; Sinkasse for Togo; east of Kantchari for Niger; and Koloko or west of Tiou for Mali. Borders tend

BURKINA FASO

to be closed by 5.30pm or 6.30pm at the latest. Remember that there is a time change of one hour going from Burkina Faso into Benin or Niger (both ahead of Burkina Faso).

BENIN

SKV and TSR have a twice weekly bus service from Ouagadougou to Cotonou (CFA20,000, 20 hours), while TCV has a weekly departure (on Sunday).

The alternative is to take a bus (eg STMB) to Fada N'Gourma (CFA4000, five hours, 225km), from where bush taxis and minibuses lie in wait (sometimes all day because transport to the border – CFA4000 – is scarce and fills up slowly).

CÔTE D'IVOIRE

Passenger train services between Burkina Faso and Côte d'Ivoire (three weekly) have resumed, but it's a long, tiring journey to Abidjan (at least 36 hours!). Get an update while in Bobo before setting off.

TCV has a daily bus service to Bouaké from Bobo-Dioulasso (CFA12,000, 22 hours). You could also take one of Rakieta's two daily buses from Banfora (CFA800, one hour) to Niangoloko, from where onward transport may be possible.

GHANA

SKV and STMB have two buses per week from Ouagadougou to Kumasi (CFA10,000, 720km), while TCV has a weekly service (on Sunday).

The other frequently used border crossing is at Hamale in the southwest of Burkina Faso. Coming from Ghana, you may have to stay at Hamale's cheap hotel and catch a bus to Bobo-Dioulasso the next morning. From Bobo-Dioulasso, Rakieta has two buses per day (at 8am and 2.30pm) to Hamale (CFA4500) that pass through Banfora en route.

MALI

Almost every bus company in Bobo-Dioulasso offers a daily service to Bamako (CFA11,000, 14 hours).

If you're heading from Bobo-Dioulasso to Mopti, your best bet is to change in Bla (Mali; CFA9000), where you'll easily find onward transport.

If you're heading for Dogon country, bush taxis depart from Ouahigouya for Koro (CFA3000, three to four hours). From Koro you'll need to connect by bush taxi to Bankass and then Mopti.

NIGER

SKV and STMB each operate daily bus services between Ouagadougou and Niamey, via Fada N'Gourma (CFA10,000, duration eight to 10 hours).

TOGO

SKV and TSR have twice-weekly bus services to Lomé (CFA15,000 to CFA17,500, 21 hours), while STMB and TCV have weekly departures.

If you want to break up your journey, you can take an STMB bus to Sinkasse (CFA5000, twice daily), which straddles the border, and find onward transport to Dapaong in Togo. The border is open from 6am to 6pm.

GETTING AROUND
Air

Air Burkina has two flights per week between Ouagadougou and Bobo-Dioulasso (CFA46,000).

Bus

Buses are the most reliable and comfortable way to get around. There are a multitude of companies from which to choose, although STMB, TCV, TSR, SKV and Rakieta buses are better maintained and more reliable than those of other companies. STMB has the most extensive network in Burkina Faso. Buses invariably leave from their own stations, rather than the *gares routières*.

Buses almost always operate with guaranteed seating and fixed departure times.

Bush Taxi & Minibus

Minibuses and bush taxis, mostly ageing Peugeot 504s, cover outlying communities that large buses don't serve. Most leave from the *gares routières,* and morning is the best time to find them.

Car & Motorcycle

Burkina Faso's road network is excellent, with the sealed roads connecting major cities driveable year-round. Travel agencies in Ouagadougou (p268) can organise 4WD rental for about CFA55,000 per day (with driver).

Cameroon

For many, the word 'Africa' conjures a certain image: dense jungle of deep green, women balancing baskets on their bright headwraps, men strolling down rust-red roads made of earth that looks like Mars, whip-thin herders driving cows and goats across dry yellow grasslands, pygmies whispering through the forest, and masked dancers jumping in rhythm in front of mud and thatched-roof huts, their carved face masks fascinating.

This, then, is Cameroon, a country that markets itself, with some justification, as all of Africa in one. The description is apt, even eerie: geographically, from the southern rainforests to the lazy beaches, from the Mountain of Thunder, an active volcano, to the brown hills of the Sahel and across to the wild eastern frontier that tempts the adventurous; culturally, in its blend of religions and ancient tribal traditions; linguistically, as one of the few Anglophone and Francophone nations on the continent. Even politically – Cameroon is both blessed by the stability many African nations vie for and hamstrung by accusations of corruption.

This, too, is Cameroon. But that's the reward of travelling here: seeing Africa in all its diversity, warts and all. None of it stops us from loving this country and the continent it encompasses, an affection that's easy to feel as your first Cameroonian evening slips over you, and *makossa* music or a guitar made of gourds sets the rhythm, the street smells like roasting bananas and all that you need for African bliss is grilled fish and a sweaty beer.

FAST FACTS

- **Area** 469,440 sq km (a little smaller than Spain, a little bigger than California)
- **ATMs** At banks in large cities, linked to Visa
- **Borders** Chad, Central African Republic, Equatorial Guinea, Gabon, Nigeria all open; border with Congo sometime closed, check in advance
- **Budget** US$40 to US$60 per day
- **Capital** Yaoundé
- **Languages** French, English and many local languages
- **Money** Central African franc; US$1 = CFA463, €1 = CFA656
- **Population** 18.8 million
- **Seasons** Hot (year-round), wet (north, April to September), heavy rains (south, June to October)
- **Telephone** Country code ☎ 237; international access code ☎ 00
- **Time** GMT/UTC +1
- **Visa** Required by all, available in neighbouring countries for US$60

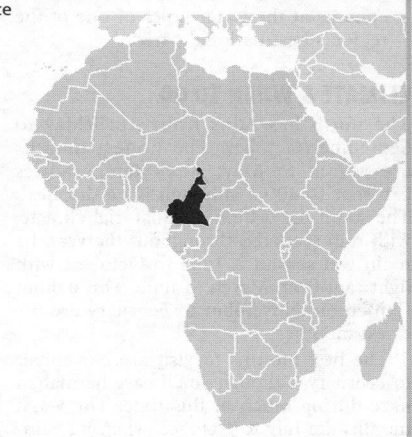

CAMEROON

HOW MUCH?

- Ingredients for juju fetish US$1.10
- 100km bus ride US$2.20
- Moto-taxi ride across town US$0.22 to US$0.33
- Bottle of palm wine US$1.77
- Carved mask US$45 to US$50

LONELY PLANET INDEX

- 1L petrol US$1.40
- 1.5L bottled water US$1
- Bottle of '33' beer US$1.50
- Souvenir football shirt US$10
- Stick of brochettes US$1.50 to US$2

HIGHLIGHTS

- **Mt Cameroon** (p289) Don your hiking boots to climb the mist-shrouded slopes of West Africa's highest peak.
- **Kribi** (p295) Chill on the white beaches and practise your French with the locals over grilled fish.
- **Ring Road** (p293) Explore the cool green scenery and rolling countryside near Bamenda.
- **Mandara Mountains** (p300) Head into the remote landscape and trek from village to village.
- **Parc National du Waza** (p300) Watch elephants at the water holes of one of the region's best national parks.

CLIMATE & WHEN TO GO

The north has rains from April/May to September/October. The hottest months are March to May, when temperatures can soar to 40°C, although it's a dry heat. The south has a humid, equatorial climate, with rain scattered throughout the year. Its main wet season is June to October, with light rain from March to June. Throughout Cameroon, November to February are the driest months.

The best months to visit are November to February, although you'll have harmattan haze during much of this time. The worst months are July to October, when it's raining, and many roads are impassable.

ITINERARIES

- **One Week** Starting from either Douala (p287) or Yaoundé (p282), go to Limbe (p289) for a night or two to get your bearings before climbing Mt Cameroon (p289). Alternatively, leave the cities for Foumban (p294) or Bamenda (p291) and then head to the open country of the Ring Road area (p293). Finish back in Douala or Yaoundé.
- **Two to Three Weeks** Spend the first week exploring the Ring Road area (p293) and visiting Foumban (p294). Then head to Yaoundé (p282), fly north to Maroua (p298) and venture into the Mandara Mountains (p300) for a few days of hiking. With more time, you could go from Yaoundé to N'Gaoundéré (p296) by train, and from there make your way north by road to Maroua.
- **One Month** Start with a night or two in Limbe (p289), followed by a climb of Mt Cameroon (p289) before making your way up to Bamenda (p291) and the Ring Road area (p293). Cross to Foumban (p294), and from here make your way to Yaoundé (p282) before taking the train to N'Gaoundéré (p296). Spend the remainder of your time exploring northern Cameroon (p296).

HISTORY

Cameroon is another example of colonial powers creating a country without regard for tribal boundaries or geography. The parts of what is now Cameroon were divided and ceded between European countries throughout the colonial era until the modern boundaries were established in 1961, creating

IDENTIFY YOURSELF

In Cameroon it's a legal requirement to carry identification with you at all times. If you're not happy with always carrying your passport, it's possible to get an official certified copy. Photocopy the title and visa pages and go to the main police office in any large town during office hours and ask to have it 'legalised'. The process is quick and easy, leaving you with a passport copy with enough official stamps to satisfy even the surliest of checkpoint police. The certification costs CFA1000.

a part-Anglophone, part-Francophone nation.

Prawns for Starters

Portuguese explorers first sailed up the Wouri River in 1472, and named it Rio dos Camarões (River of Prawns). Soon after the Portuguese arrived by sea, Fulani pastoral nomads from what is now Nigeria began to migrate overland from the north, forcing the indigenous forest peoples southwards. The Fulani migration took on added urgency in the early 17th century as they fled the increasingly predatory attentions of Dutch, Portuguese and British slave-traders.

British influence was curtailed in 1884 when Germany signed a treaty with the well-organised chiefdoms of Douala and central Bamiléké Plateau, although for the local inhabitants the agreement meant little more than a shift from one form of colonial exploitation to another. After WWI the German protectorate of Kamerun was carved up between France and Great Britain.

Local revolts in French-controlled Cameroon in the 1950s were brutally suppressed, but the momentum throughout Africa for throwing off the shackles of colonial rule soon took hold. Self-government was granted in French Cameroon in 1958, quickly followed by independence on 1 January 1960.

Wily Ahidjo

Ahmadou Ahidjo, leader of one of the independence parties, became president of the newly independent state, a position he was to hold until his resignation in 1982. Ahidjo, a man with a total lack of charisma, ensured his longevity through the cultivation of expedient alliances, brutal repression and wily if authoritarian regional favouritism.

In October 1961 a UN-sponsored referendum in British-mandated northwestern Cameroon split the country in two, with the area around Bamenda opting to join the federal state of Cameroon and the remainder joining Nigeria. In June 1972 the federal structure of two Cameroons was replaced by the centralised United Republic of Cameroon – a move that is bitterly resented to this day by Anglophone Cameroonians, who believe that instead of entering a true union they have become second-class citizens.

The Biya Era

In 1982 Ahidjo's hand-picked successor, Paul Biya, distanced himself from his former mentor, but adopted many of Ahidjo's repressive measures, clamping down hard on calls for multiparty democracy. Diversions such as the national football team's stunning performance in the 1990 World Cup bought him time. But the demands for freedom would not go away and Biya was forced to legalise 25 opposition parties. When it became apparent that plurality placed limitations upon the president, these parties were quickly, though temporarily, suspended, along with the constitution.

The first multiparty elections in 25 years were grudgingly held in 1992 and saw the Cameroonian Democratic People's Movement – led by Biya – hanging on to power with the support of minority parties. International observers alleged widespread vote-rigging and intimidation – allegations repeated in elections in 1999 and, most recently, in 2004.

Cameroon Today

The arrival of Chinese immigrants in great numbers – especially visible in Yaoundé and Douala – is changing the face of the country. Cheap Chinese motorbikes have made private transport a possibility for many Cameroonians and 'Medecine Chinois' shops can be found offering acupuncture in small villages. But corruption remains Cameroon's great bogeyman. The paperwork for opening a business takes a very long time to process compared with the rest of Africa, and, according to the Global Integrity 2008 report, more than 50% of Cameroonians have complained that they have had to pay bribes to get government services. The international anticorruption organisation, Transparency International, consistently ranks Cameroon among the world's most corrupt countries. Until this malaise is seriously addressed and genuine political openness is permitted, Cameroon will continue to limp along for the foreseeable future.

CULTURE

It's hard to pigeonhole more than 280 distinct ethnolinguistic groups divided by colonial languages, Christianity and Islam and the urban-rural split, among other factors, into one cut-out identity. The Cameroonian psyche is, ultimately, anything and everything African – like all else in this country, diversity is the key.

CAMEROON

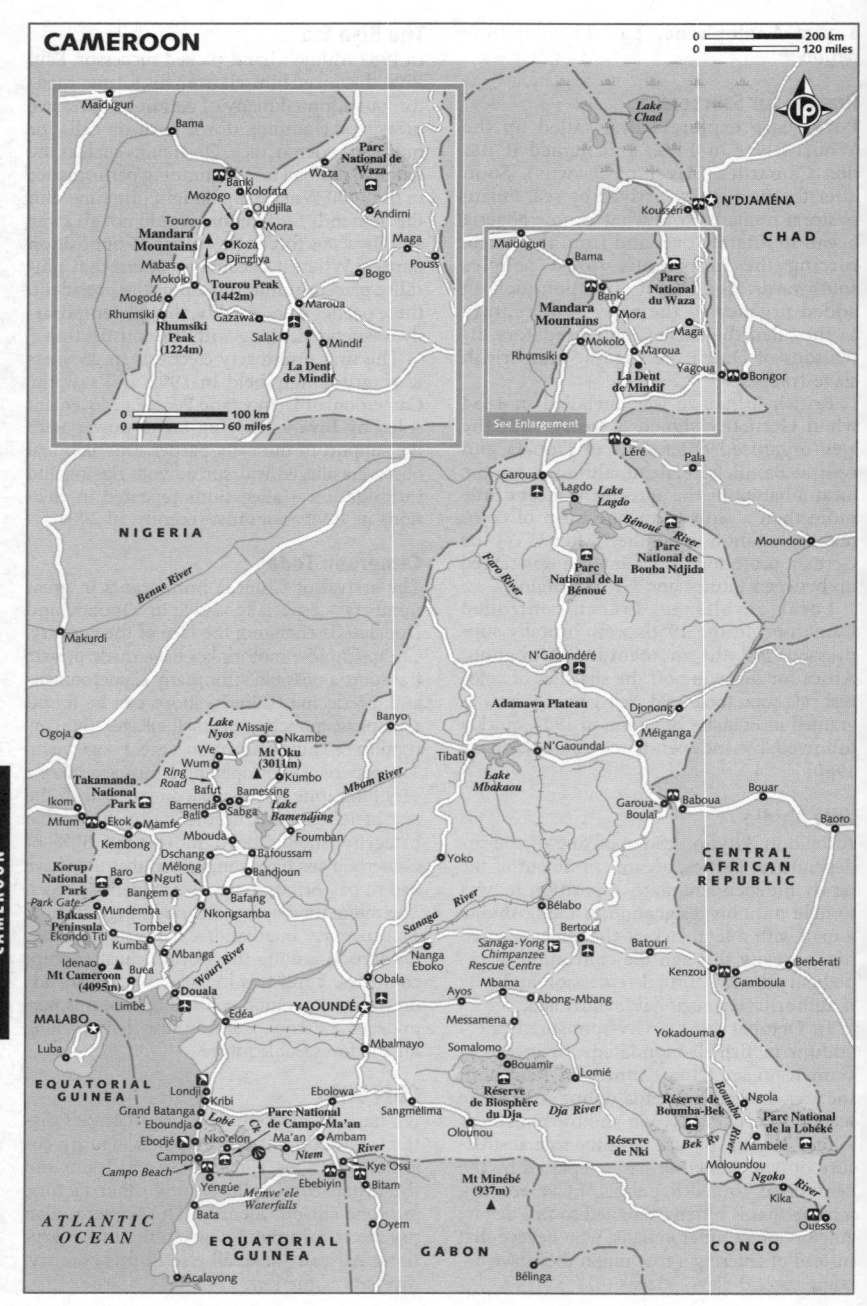

CAMEROON

0 — 200 km
0 — 120 miles

See Enlargement

There's a distinct cultural and political gap between the Francophone and Anglophone parts of Cameroon, albeit one felt predominantly by the Anglophone minority. The country is far from being truly bilingual, and Anglophones complain of discrimination in education (most universities lecture in French only) and in the workplace.

A few characteristics do seem shared across Cameroon's divides. Traditional social structures dominate life. Local chiefs (known as *fon* in the west or *lamido* in the north) still wield considerable influence, and when travelling in places that don't receive many tourists, it's polite to announce your presence.

Many Cameroonians possess a half-laconic, half-angry sense of frustration with the way their country is run. Most seem aware that while Cameroon does OK compared with its neighbours, it could be immeasurably better off if corruption didn't curtail so much potential. Mixed in with this frustration is a sort of resignation ('such is life'), an acceptance that comes off as serenity in good times, simmering rage in bad times.

Arts

Cameroon has produced a few of the region's most celebrated artists. In literature, Mongo Beti deals with the legacies of colonialism. Musically, Manu Dibango is the country's brightest star.

Woodcarving makes up a significant proportion of traditional arts and crafts. The northwestern highlands area is known for its carved masks. These are often representations of animals, and it's believed that the wearers of the masks can transform themselves and take on the animal's characteristics and powers. Cameroon also has some highly detailed bronze- and brasswork, particularly in Tikar areas north and east of Foumban. The areas around Bali and Bamessing (both near Bamenda), and Foumban, are rich in high-quality clay, and some of Cameroon's finest ceramic work originates here.

Sport

Cameroon exploded onto the world's sporting consciousness at the 1990 World Cup when the national football team, the Indomitable Lions, became the first African side to reach the quarterfinals. Football is truly the national obsession. Every other Cameroonian male seems to own a copy of the team's strip; go into any bar and there'll be a match playing on the TV. When Cameroon narrowly failed to qualify for the 2006 World Cup, the country's grief was almost tangible. In contrast, when Cameroon qualified for the 2010 World Cup, the nation exploded into wild celebration. This qualification marked the sixth time Cameroon entered the tournament, setting a record for any African nation. The Lions hold a proud record in the continent-wide Cup of Nations, winning four times – most recently in 2002.

FOOD & DRINK

Cameroonian cuisine is more functional than flavourful. The staple dish is some variety of peppery sauce served with starch – usually rice, pasta or *fufu* (mashed yam, corn, plantain or couscous). One of the most popular sauces is *ndole,* made with bitter leaves similar to spinach and flavoured with smoked fish.

Grilled meat and fish are eaten in huge quantities. Beer is incredibly popular and widely available, even in the Muslim north.

A street snack of fish or *brochettes* (kebabs) will rarely cost you more than CFA1500, and can come much cheaper depending on how much you order. In sit-down restaurants and business hotels outside of the major cities, expect to pay around CFA5000 to CFA7000 for a full meal; that price can climb to CFA10,000 and more in Yaoundé and Douala. Prices in this chapter are for a full meal, unless noted.

ENVIRONMENT

Cameroon is as diverse geographically as it is culturally. The south is a low-lying coastal plain covered by swathes of equatorial rainforest extending east towards the Congo Basin. Heading north, the sparsely populated Adamawa Plateau divides the country in two. To the plateau's north, the country begins to dry out into a rolling landscape dotted with rocky escarpments that are fringed to the west by the barren, beautiful Mandara Mountains. That range represents the northern extent of a volcanic chain that forms a natural border with Nigeria down to the Atlantic coast, often punctuated with stunning crater lakes. Most are now extinct, but one active volcano remains in Mt Cameroon – at 4095m the highest peak in West Africa.

There is a range of wildlife here, although more exotic species are in difficult to reach areas. Lions prowl in Parc National du Waza (p300) in the north, and elephants stomp through the southern and eastern jungles. Of note are several rare primate species, including the Cross River Gorilla, Mainland Drill, chimpanzees and Preuss' Red Colobus.

Bushmeat has traditionally been big business in Cameroon. While there have been crackdowns on the trade both here and abroad (African expats are some of the main consumers of bushmeat), it has not been entirely stamped out either, and is likely not to be given the prevalence of corruption.

YAOUNDÉ

pop 1.6 million

Let's be brutally honest: West Africa is famous for many things, but pleasant cities – especially capitals – are not one of them. Then Yaoundé comes along. Green, spread over seven hills, green again; it's not exactly a garden city, but the capital feels planned, thoughtfully laid out and self-contained. Plus, its hilly geography wards off the worst of the humidity of the plains, making this a fine stop before getting a visa and/or heading off into the rest of Cameroon.

ORIENTATION

Central Yaoundé is easy to navigate. The anchor is Place Ahmadou Ahidjo. From there, Ave Ahidjo runs northwest past the Marché Central and good hotels and restaurants (especially near Ave Kennedy); parallel, Blvd du 20 Mai leads past the landmark Hilton Hotel to the administrative district (Quartier du Lac). Here, the road winds uphill to Carrefour (Rond-Point) Nlongkak, a major roundabout. About 1.5km further up is Carrefour Bastos and the upscale Bastos residential quarter, where many embassies and restaurants are located. Overlooking town to the northwest, about 5km from the centre, is Mt Fébé.

INFORMATION

Cultural Centres

British Council (Map p283; ☎ 220 3172; Ave Charles de Gaulle)

Centre Culturel Français (Map p284; ☎ 222 0944; Ave Ahidjo)

Internet Access

Expect to pay around CFA500 per hour.

Cometé Internet (Map p284; Rue de Narvik) One of several near the US embassy.

Espresso House (Map p283; Carrefour Bastos; per 30min CFA1000) Offers broadband.

Medical Services

Pharmacie Bastos (Map p283; ☎ 220 6555; Carrefour Bastos) Well-stocked pharmacy.

Polyclinique André Fouda (off Map p283; ☎ 222 6612) For medical emergencies; in Elig-Essono, southeast of Carrefour Nlongkak.

Money

There are ATMs at most of the major banks; see the maps for locations. As always in Cameroon, travellers cheques are problematic to change in banks – try the following:

Bicec Bank (Map p284; Ave Ahidjo) Has an ATM.

Crédit Lyonnais (Map p284; near Place Ahmadou Ahidjo)

Express Exchange (Map p284; Ave Kennedy) Also accepts US dollars.

Post

Central post office (Map p284; Place Ahmadou Ahidjo; ⊗ 7.30am-3.30pm Mon-Fri, 7.30am-noon Sat)

DANGERS & ANNOYANCES

Yaoundé is more relaxed than Douala, but muggings happen. Daytime is generally fine, but take taxis at night and be particularly wary around the Marché Central (Map p284) and tourist hotels.

SIGHTS & ACTIVITIES

At the Benedictine monastery on Mt Fébé, north of the city centre, the **Musée d'Art Camerounais** (off Map p283; Quartier Fébé; donation requested; ⊗ 3-6pm Thu, Sat & Sun) has an impressive collection of masks, bronze- and woodwork and other examples of Cameroonian art. The chapel is also worth a look.

Mvog-Betsi Zoo (off Map p283; Mvog-Betsi; admission CFA2000, camera CFA5000; ⊗ 9am-6pm) is one of the better zoos in West Africa, co-run by the **Cameroon Wildlife Aid Fund** (www.cwaf.org), with a sizeable collection of native primates, rescued from poachers and the bushmeat trade.

SLEEPING

Foyer International de l'Église Presbytérienne (Map p283; ☎ 985 236; off Rue Joseph Essono Balla; tent/dm/tw CFA2000/3000/5000; ⓟ) Tucked behind the water towers looming over Nlongkak, rooms and (communal) facilities are simple and clean, and the grounds have enough trees to laze under.

Ideal Hotel (Map p283; ☎ 220 9852; Carrefour Nlongkak; r CFA8000; ⓟ) Recommended by

CAMEROON

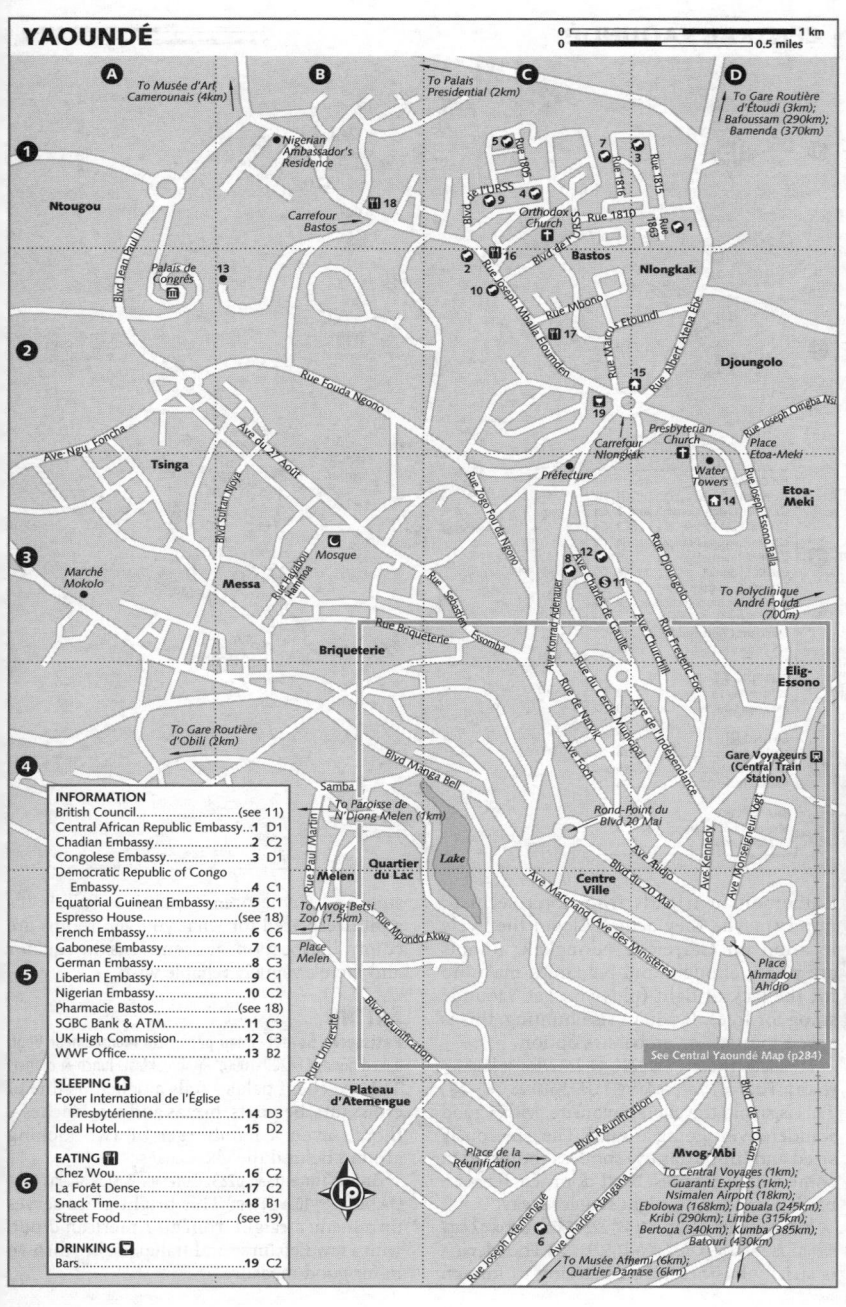

YAOUNDÉ

To Musée d'Art Camerounais (4km)

To Palais Presidential (2km)

To Gare Routière d'Étoudi (3km); Bafoussam (290km); Bamenda (370km)

Nigerian Ambassador's Residence

Ntougou

Carrefour Bastos

Palais de Congrès

Bastos

Nlongkak

Djoungolo

Rue Fouda Ngono

Orthodox Church

Presbyterian Church

Place Etoa-Meki

Carrefour Nlongkak

Etoa-Meki

Tsinga

Préfecture

Water Towers

Messa

Mosque

Marché Mokolo

To Polyclinique André Fouda (700m)

Rue Briqueterie

Briqueterie

Elig-Essono

To Gare Routière d'Obili (2km)

Blvd Manga Bell

Samba

To Paroisse de N'Djong Melen (1km)

Melen

Gare Voyageurs (Central Train Station)

Rond-Point du Blvd 20 Mai

Quartier du Lac

Lake

Centre Ville

To Mvog-Betsi Zoo (1.5km)

Place Melen

Place Ahmadou Ahidjo

See Central Yaoundé Map (p284)

Plateau d'Atemengue

Mvog-Mbi

Place de la Réunification

Blvd Réunification

To Central Voyages (1km); Guaranti Express (1km); Nsimalen Airport (18km); Ebolowa (168km); Douala (245km); Kribi (290km); Limbe (315km); Bertoua (340km); Kumba (385km); Batouri (430km)

To Musée Afhemi (6km); Quartier Damase (6km)

INFORMATION

British Council	(see 11)
Central African Republic Embassy	1 D1
Chadian Embassy	2 C2
Congolese Embassy	3 D1
Democratic Republic of Congo Embassy	4 C1
Equatorial Guinean Embassy	5 C1
Espresso House	(see 18)
French Embassy	6 C6
Gabonese Embassy	7 C1
German Embassy	8 C3
Liberian Embassy	9 C1
Nigerian Embassy	10 C2
Pharmacie Bastos	(see 18)
SGBC Bank & ATM	11 C3
UK High Commission	12 C3
WWF Office	13 B2

SLEEPING

Foyer International de l'Église Presbytérienne	14 D3
Ideal Hotel	15 D2

EATING

Chez Wou	16 C2
La Forêt Dense	17 C3
Snack Time	18 B1
Street Food	(see 19)

DRINKING

Bars	19 C2

CAMEROON

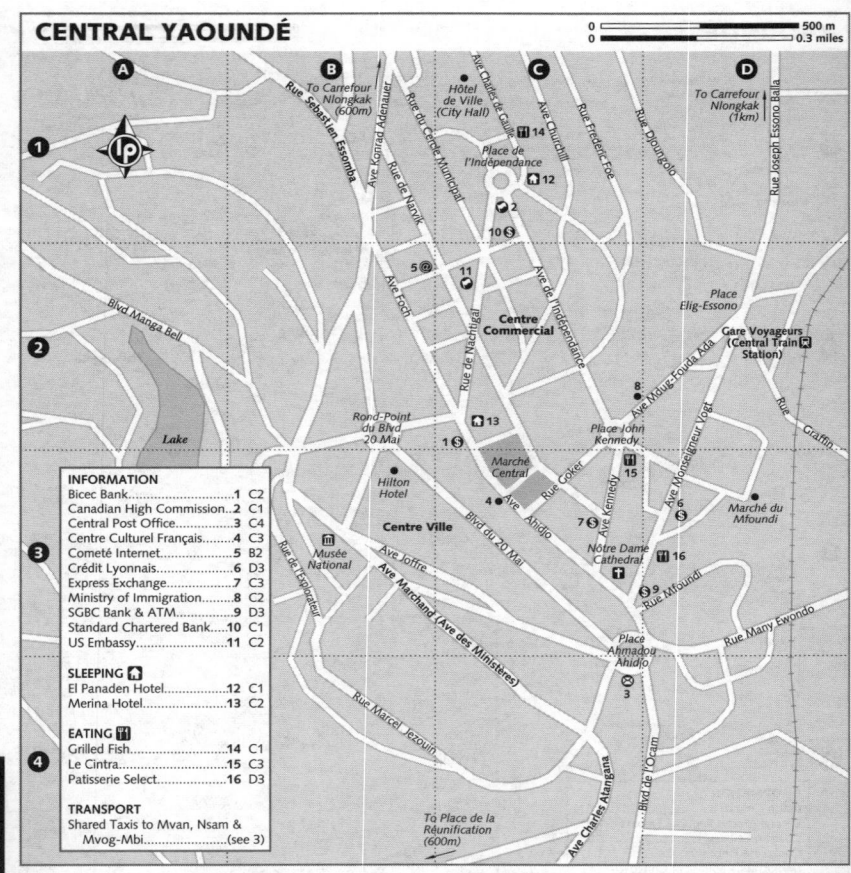

CENTRAL YAOUNDÉ

INFORMATION
Bicec Bank.................................1 C2
Canadian High Commission..2 C1
Central Post Office..................3 C4
Centre Culturel Français.........4 C3
Cometé Internet.......................5 B2
Crédit Lyonnais........................6 D3
Express Exchange....................7 C3
Ministry of Immigration...........8 C2
SGBC Bank & ATM..................9 D3
Standard Chartered Bank.....10 C1
US Embassy............................11 C2

SLEEPING
El Panaden Hotel....................12 C1
Merina Hotel..........................13 C2

EATING
Grilled Fish............................14 C1
Le Cintra...............................15 C3
Patisserie Select.....................16 D3

TRANSPORT
Shared Taxis to Mvan, Nsam &
   Mvog-Mbi........................(see 3)

Cameroonian friends who don't seem to mind (maybe they actually love) the lively location on Carrefour Nlongkak. Rooms are pretty enough, and balconies make up for the lack of light (plus you get Yaoundé smog for free). If you're visa hunting, this is a well-located-for-embassies option.

El Panaden Hotel (Map p284; ☎ 222 2765; elpanaden@ yahoo.fr; Place de l'Indépendance; r CFA15,500-28,000; ❄) This is an old travellers' favourite, with a good wanderer vibe going around. The generously sized and (importantly) spotless rooms often come with balconies. Next door, La Terrasse bar is a handy late-night stagger away.

Merina Hotel (Map p284; ☎ 222 2131; www.oog2.org/ merina; Ave Ahidjo; r CFA32,000-41,500; ❄) The Merina is strictly business class, catering to foreign

suits and Cameroonian politicos. While it's a bit overpriced for what you get, rooms are comfy, the location is as central as the equator and there's vaguely reliable wi-fi.

EATING

Patisserie Select (Map p284; Ave Monseigneur Vogt; baked goods CFA200-1000; ❄ breakfast, lunch & dinner) This excellent bakery sells a delicious line of croissants, beignets, pizzas and sandwiches – there's even a hamburger or two kicking around behind the glass cases.

Snack Time (Map p283; Carrefour Bastos; mains from CFA2700; ❄ 10am-11pm) This bright place serves up a menu straight from an American diner, with a few Lebanese and Italian dishes thrown in for good measure.

Chez Wou (Map p283; Rue Joseph Mballa Eloumden; mains from CFA4000; ⏰ noon-3.30pm & 6-11pm) One of Yaoundé's older Chinese restaurants, this one has nice tables set under a wide porch, and a comprehensive menu.

Le Cintra (Map p284; Ave Kennedy; dishes from CFA4000) This is as close as we got to finding the sort of Cameroonian French restaurant where we'd film a movie about the colonial period with an Edith Piaf soundtrack. It's unfortunately not quite that atmospheric, but it makes an effort, and the French mains (such as *steak au povre* – pepper steak) make up the extra mile.

La Forêt Dense (Map p283; Rue Joseph Mballa Eloumden; meals from CFA5500) Every African capital has a restaurant where you get the local traditional stuff done up sexy and overpriced; welcome to La Forêt. If you have ever wondered what crocodile *mbongo* (stew) tastes like, this is the place to find out.

Around Carrefours Bastos and Nlongkak you can find grills serving brochette (kebab) throughout the day. On Place de l'Indépendance, near El Panaden Hotel, there are women grilling delicious fish, served with chilli or peanut sauce from CFA1000.

DRINKING

The best bars are in Carrefours Bastos and Nlongkak, most with open-air seating facing the street – great for people-watching. Solo female travellers might find the atmosphere uneasy in some bars once the sun dips. Bars in upscale/business hotels become sex-worker central at night.

GETTING THERE & AWAY
Air

For internal flights, try **Elysian Airlines** (☎ 9909 8748; www.elysianairlines.com), which offers a spotty schedule that flies to Douala (CFA28,500, 45 minutes), Garoua (CFA96,400, three hours), N'Gaoundéré (CFA86,500, 2½ hours) and Maroua (CFA125,000, four hours). **Toumai Air Tchad** (☎ 7420 8734, 7711 0974; www.toumaiair.com) flies to Douala (CFA30,000).

Bus

There are buses between Yaoundé and all major cities in Cameroon. Buses leave from their companies' offices, spread out on the outskirts of town. For Douala (CFA3800, three hours), **Central Voyages** (Mvog-Mbi) and **Guaranti Express** (Quartier Nsam) are recommended. Guaranti Express is also recommended for Limbe

(CFA5000, five hours), Bamenda (CFA5000, six hours), Bafoussam (CFA2500, three hours) and Kumba (CFA4000, four hours).

Otherwise, all agency and nonagency buses for Kribi, Bertoua, Batouri, Ebolowa, Limbe and Douala depart from Blvd de l'Ocam, about 3km south of Place Ahmadou Ahidjo (direct taxi drivers to Agences de Mvan).

Transport to Bafoussam, Bamenda and points north departs from Gare Routière d'Etoudi, 5km north of Centre Ville.

Train

The most popular and convenient way to travel north from Yaoundé is by train, which runs all the way to N'Gaoundéré. Trains depart daily at 6pm, taking around 18 hours. Delays on the line are not uncommon.

For seating, there's a choice of comfortable 1st-class couchettes (sleeping compartments) for CFA25,000/28,000 per person in a four-/two-bed cabin, 1st-class airline-style seats (CFA17,000) and crowded 2nd-class benches (CFA10,000). Seats in 1st and 2nd class are in open wagons, with no way to secure your bag. Even in couchettes, be alert for thieves.

The train has a restaurant car where you can buy surprisingly good meals (CFA1000/2500 for breakfast/dinner). If you're in 1st class, someone will come and take your order and deliver it to you. At every station stop, people will offer street food at the windows.

There are also services between Yaoundé, Douala and Kumba, though these are used much less frequently, as buses are cheaper, faster and more convenient.

GETTING AROUND

Shared taxis are the only public-transport option. Fares are CFA200 for short- to medium-length rides. Flag them down on the street and shout out the name of your destination – the drivers will sound the horn if they're not going your way. A private taxi to Nsimalen airport from central Yaoundé should cost CFA4000 to CFA6000 (40 minutes).

WESTERN CAMEROON

Imagine Africa: wormy red tracks and vegetation so intensely green you can almost taste the colour. This image comes alive in Western Cameroon. The country's economic heart intermittently beats in Douala, and from

DOUALA

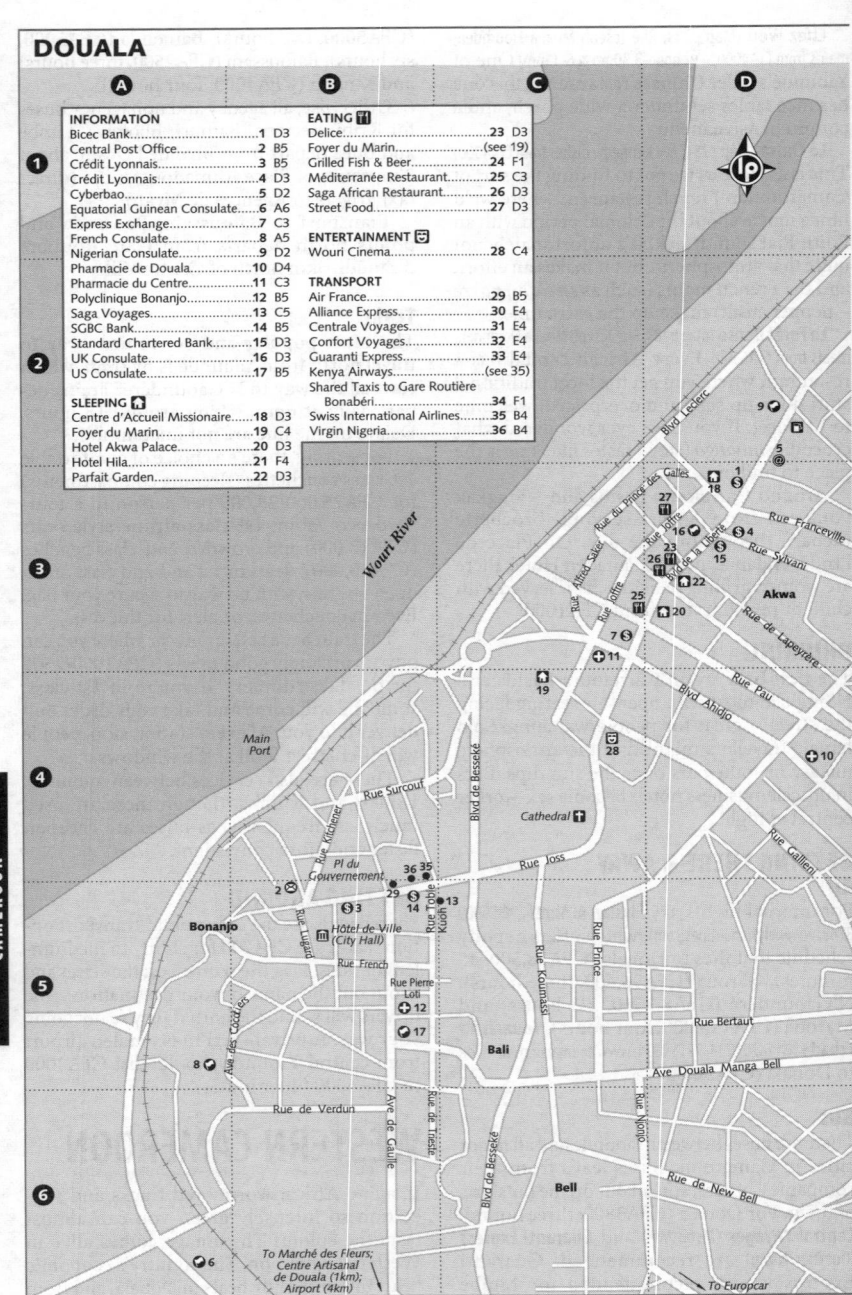

INFORMATION
Bicec Bank....................................1 D3
Central Post Office........................2 B5
Crédit Lyonnais.............................3 B5
Crédit Lyonnais.............................4 D3
Cyberbao......................................5 D2
Equatorial Guinean Consulate......6 A6
Express Exchange.........................7 C3
French Consulate..........................8 A5
Nigerian Consulate.......................9 D2
Pharmacie de Douala..................10 D4
Pharmacie du Centre...................11 C3
Polyclinique Bonanjo...................12 B5
Saga Voyages..............................13 C5
SGBC Bank..................................14 B5
Standard Chartered Bank............15 D3
UK Consulate...............................16 D3
US Consulate...............................17 B5

SLEEPING
Centre d'Accueil Missionaire.......18 D3
Foyer du Marin............................19 C4
Hotel Akwa Palace.......................20 D3
Hotel Hila...................................21 F4
Parfait Garden............................22 D3

EATING
Delice...23 D3
Foyer du Marin.......................(see 19)
Grilled Fish & Beer......................24 F1
Méditerranée Restaurant.............25 C3
Saga African Restaurant..............26 D3
Street Food.................................27 D3

ENTERTAINMENT
Wouri Cinema.............................28 C4

TRANSPORT
Air France...................................29 B5
Alliance Express..........................30 E4
Centrale Voyages........................31 E4
Confort Voyages.........................32 E4
Guaranti Express.........................33 E4
Kenya Airways.......................(see 35)
Shared Taxis to Gare Routière
  Bonabéri..................................34 F1
Swiss International Airlines...........35 B4
Virgin Nigeria.............................36 B4

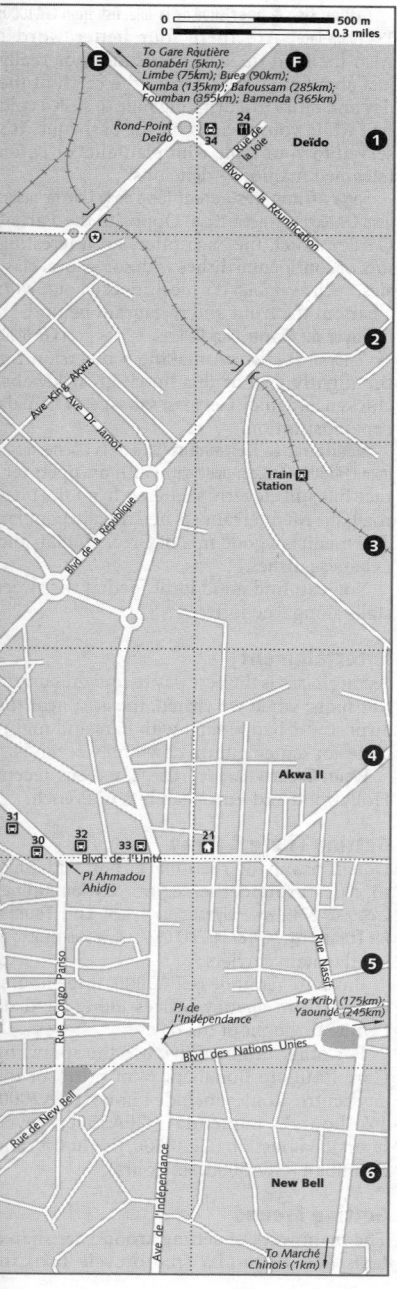

here it's a short hop to the haze and laze of beach towns like Limbe and the savannah-carpeted slopes of the Mountain of Thunder – Mt Cameroon. In the Anglophone north-west you can slip between sunburnt green hills while exploring a patchwork of secret societies, traditional chiefdoms and some of the country's best craftwork, particularly the wooden masks that are the aesthetic image we so often associate with Africa.

DOUALA
pop 2 million
Sticky, icky and frenetic, Douala isn't as bad as some say, but not likely to be your first choice for a honeymoon, either. By any measurement but political power this is Cameroon's main city: primary air hub, port, business centre and a bit chaotic. There are few charms, but as veins go this is the main one: set your finger here to gauge Cameroon's pulse.

Orientation
Akwa district is at the heart of Douala, bisected by Blvd de la Liberté, where you'll find many hotels, internet cafes, banks and restaurants. South of here, near Rue Joss in Bonanjo, is the administrative quarter, with airline offices and government buildings. The airport is 4km south of town.

Information
INTERNET ACCESS
Cyberbao (Blvd de la Liberté; per hr CFA400) Reliable, as are the connections in upscale hotels.

MEDICAL SERVICES
Pharmacie du Centre (Blvd de la Liberté)
Pharmacie de Douala (Blvd Ahidjo)
Polyclinique Bonanjo (☎ 342 7936, 342 9910, emergencies 342 180; www.clibo.com; Ave de Gaulle) For medical emergencies.

MONEY
For changing money, try the banks along Blvd de la Liberté or Rue Joss – most have ATMs. **Express Exchange** (Blvd de la Liberté) conveniently changes travellers cheques and US dollars. Hôtel Akwa Palace on Blvd de la Liberté has plenty of touts outside for changing cash after hours, but watch yourself.

POST
Central post office (Rue Joss)

TRAVEL AGENCIES
Saga Voyages (☎ 342 1203; Rue Joss) Well-organised travel agency.

Dangers & Annoyances

Muggings happen: if you'd rather be safe than sorry, it's recommended to take a taxi after dark. Leave valuables in a safe place, and be extra careful around nightspots.

Sleeping

Centre d'Accueil Missionaire (☎ 342 2797; progemis.douala@camnet.cm; Rue Franceville; r with/without shower CFA8000/7000; P ⓧ) Praise be to this Catholic mission, with its clean twin rooms, pleasant verandah and pool. Next to the pink Axa building.

Hotel Hila (☎ 342 1586; Blvd de l'Unité; s CFA10,000-12,000, d CFA15,000; ⓧ) Ideally located for the Yaoundé bus agencies, the Hila sits on a very busy road, so get a room at the back if you can. Rooms are threadbare, but fair value for the price.

our pick Foyer du Marin (☎ 342 2794; douala@seemannsmission.org; Rue Gallieni; s/d CFA15,000/28,000; P ⓧ ▣ ⓐ) Every developing-world city of a certain size gets one surreal hotel, and this is Douala's: a dark-wood verandah shading British overlanders, tattooed NGOers, dressed-to-impress locals and the odd journalist, plus a crystal pool and…German merchant marine regulations. This is the German Seaman's Mission, and tidy rooms are kept as such for tourists and sailors on shore leave. Fills fast – book early.

Parfait Garden (☎ 342 6357; hotel.parfait-garden@globalnet2.net; Blvd de la Liberté; r from CFA37,500; ⓧ) Rooms are spacious and plush. There's a nice bar and restaurant, and the liveried bellboys inject a little class.

Hotel Akwa Palace (☎ 342 2601/6; www.hotel-akwa-palace.com; Blvd de le Liberté; r CFA116,000-180,000; P ⓧ ▣ ⓐ) Very much the best hotel in town, the Akwa Palace is the sort of place where movies about the indolence of expat existence are filmed. Rooms are plush, staff obsequious and decor tasteful.

Eating & Drinking

There are plenty of good restaurants along Blvd de la Liberté.

Delice (Blvd de la Liberté; snacks from CFA500; ❍ 7am-9.30pm) A great early morning stop for pastries and a shot of coffee; there are also some good toasted sandwiches.

Grilled fish & beer (Rue de la Joie; fish from CFA1000; ❍ 10am-late) Are there four better words? Also try Blvd de la Réunification, or really just about anywhere. Order the catch of the day and retire to a drinking hole to sink a cold one while your meal is on the barbeque. It's served to your table with plantains or *baton* (steamed manioc) – delicious!

Saga African Restaurant (Blvd de la Liberté; mains from CFA2000; ❍ noon-10pm) Opposite the Parfait Garden hotel, the Saga offers an interesting mix of continental dishes with some local classics, such as *ndole*. It's nicely decked out, with a bar out the front and restaurant behind.

Foyer du Marin (Rue Gallieni; kebabs from CFA2000; ❍ 7-10pm) It's worth making a diversion for the nightly grill at this hotel; great kebabs, chicken and juicy German sausage. A Douala expat institution.

Méditerranée Restaurant (Blvd de la Liberté; mains from CFA2500; ❍ 8am-midnight) With an open terrace but still cleverly sheltered from the busy road, the Méditerranée is perennially popular. The menu is a good mix of Greek, Italian and Lebanese dishes.

You can find good local food at the street stalls along Rue Joffre.

Entertainment

Asking locals is the best way to find the current hot spots; when we visited, the area near the airport was happening, with bars and nightclubs for dancing until dawn on weekends.

Wouri Cinema (Blvd de la Liberté) screens recent Hollywood and European hits in French.

Getting There & Away

Douala has an international airport with links to cities around the region. **Elysian Airlines** (☎ 9909 8748; www.elysianairlines.com) and **Toumai Air Tchad** (☎ 7420 8734, 7711 0974; www.toumaiair.com) are the main carriers.

Buses to Yaoundé (CFA3800, three hours) depart from agency offices along Blvd de l'Unité throughout the day.

For other destinations, use the sprawling Gare Routière Bonabéri, 6km north of the city centre. Routes include Limbe (CFA2000, 1½ hours), Bamenda (CFA5000, seven hours), Bafoussam (CFA3500, five hours) and Foumban (CFA5000, six hours).

Getting Around

The main ways of getting around are shared taxis and *moto-taxi* (motorcycle taxi), or which there are thousands; they are cheaper than taxis (CFA100 to CFA150). Charter taxis from central Douala to Bonabéri generally charge CFA3000. A taxi to the airport costs CFA3000.

BUEA

Basically built into the side of Mt Cameroon, Buea (pronounced boy-ah) has a hill station's coolness, especially compared to sticky Limbe. If you're going up the mountain, you're inevitably coming here.

Conveniently, **Express Exchange** (Molyko Rd) will exchange euros, US dollars and travellers cheques.

At the **Presbyterian Church Synod Office** (☎ 332 2336; Market Rd; campsites CFA1000, s with/without bathroom CFA3000/2500, d with/without bathroom CFA5000/4000; **P**) rooms are comfy and spotless, and there's a tidy communal sitting room and cooking facilities. This church mission is a gem.

The **Paramount Hotel** (☎ 332 2074; Molyko Rd; s/d CFA6000/10,000, with hot water CFA14,000/17,000; **P** **🖳**) lives up to its name, a good-value place that brings a bit of flashness to otherwise middling Buea lodgings. The pretty rooms come with TV and are a nice respite from the mountain.

There are several cheap eating establishments on Molyko Rd around the Paramount Hotel.

HIKING MT CAMEROON

Most hikes to the summit of West Africa's highest peak take two or three days, but it's no stroll in the park. The difficulty stems not only from its height (4095m), but from the fact that you start from near sea level, making a big change in altitude in a relatively short distance. November to April is the main climbing season, and although it's possible to climb the mountain year-round, you won't get much in the way of views during the rainy season. Warm clothes and waterproofs are a must. A popular ascent is a two-night, three-day hike via the Mann Spring route and descending via the Guinness Route.

Hikes are arranged in Buea through the **Mt Cameroon Ecotourism Organisation** (☎ 332 2038; mountceo@yahoo.uk; Buea Market; ☷ 8am-5pm Mon-Fri, 7am-noon Sat & Sun). The organisation works closely with the 12 villages around the mountain, employing many villagers as guides and porters. All hikers pay a flat 'stakeholder fee' of CFA3000, which goes into a village development fund and is used for community projects, such as improving electricity and water supply. The organisation's office also has a small shop selling locally produced handicrafts.

Guides, well versed in the local flora and fauna, cost CFA6000 per day (maximum five hikers per guide); porters cost CFA5000. Establish a comfortable pace for yourself; some guides have a tendency – conscious or not – of rushing up the mountain. Equipment can be hired on a daily basis in Buea.

LIMBE

Pop an 'o' in place of the 'e' at the end of 'Limbe', add 'tropical' to the front and you've got a fair idea of what this town is all about – chilling out by the ocean with a beer and some fish. Popular with both foreign and Cameroonian tourists, the main hub of the Anglophone southwest is sultry, sweating and partying in the shade of Mt Cameroon and hills overgrown with banana plantations.

Information

The **Fako Tourist Board** (☎ 333 2861; Banley St; ☷ 7.30am-5pm Mon-Sat) can arrange local tours, hotels and bookings with the Mt Cameroon Ecotourism Organisation. Internet access is available at **Computer World** (Banley St; per hr CFA400; ☷ closed Sun). Ahidjo St has several ATMs.

Sights

Many zoos in Africa are depressing places, but the **Limbe Wildlife Centre** (www.limbewildlife.org; admission CFA3000; ☷ 9am-5pm) is a shining exception. Jointly run by the Ministry of the Environment and the primate charity Pandrillus, it contains rescued chimpanzees, gorillas, drills and other primates, all housed in large enclosures, with heaps of information about local conservation issues. Staff are well informed, and are heavily involved in community education.

The second-oldest and biggest **botanic gardens** (www.mcbcclimbe.org; admission CFA1000, camera CFA2000; ☷ 8am-6pm) in Africa are the home of, among others, cinnamon, nutmeg, mango, ancient cycads and an unnamed tree locals describe as 'African Viagra'. There's a small visitors centre and an area with Commonwealth War Graves. Guides (CFA1000) aren't required but are recommended.

About an hour south of Limbe is the **Bimbia rainforest and mangrove trail**, which runs through the only coastal lowland rainforest remaining between Douala and

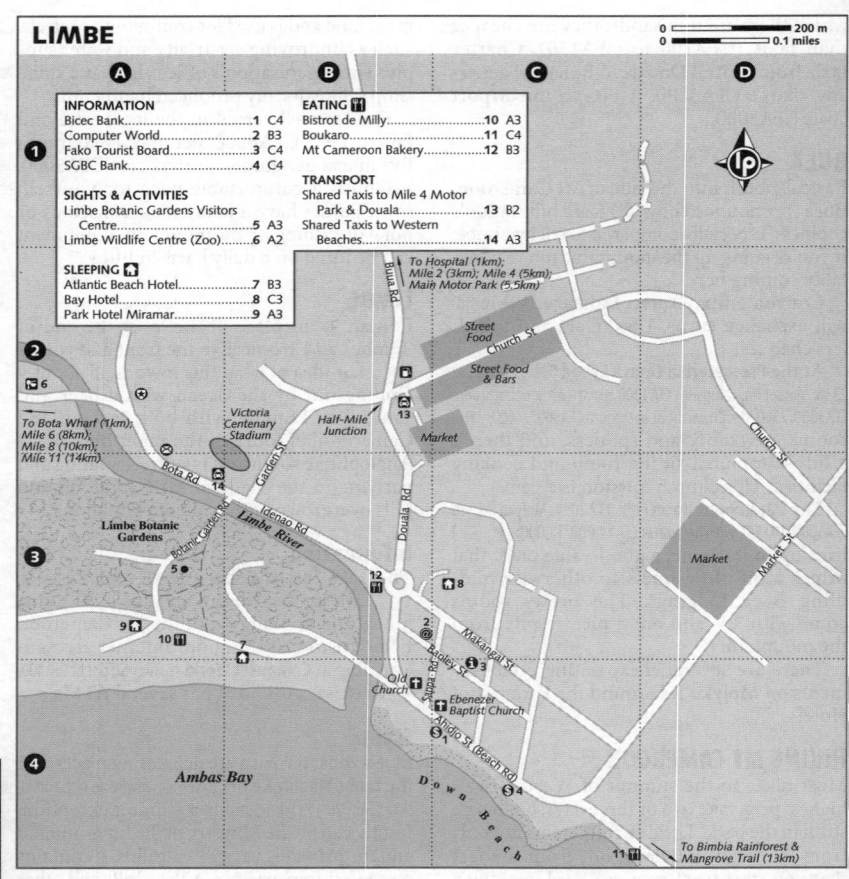

LIMBE

0 ————— 200 m
0 ————— 0.1 miles

INFORMATION
Bicec Bank.............................1 C4
Computer World.....................2 B3
Fako Tourist Board.................3 C4
SGBC Bank.............................4 C4

SIGHTS & ACTIVITIES
Limbe Botanic Gardens Visitors
  Centre...............................5 A3
Limbe Wildlife Centre (Zoo)....6 A2

SLEEPING
Atlantic Beach Hotel...............7 B3
Bay Hotel..............................8 C3
Park Hotel Miramar.................9 A3

EATING
Bistrot de Milly.....................10 A3
Boukaro...............................11 C4
Mt Cameroon Bakery.............12 B3

TRANSPORT
Shared Taxis to Mile 4 Motor
  Park & Douala....................13 B2
Shared Taxis to Western
  Beaches............................14 A3

Lime. An experienced guide will take you on day tours through some rather lovely submerged woods, birdwatching areas and old slave-trading sites. You'll have to pay CFA5000 for the local development fee, which goes towards the village of Bimbia and mangrove preservation, CFA3000 for a guide, and CFA15,000 for a *taxi brousse* (bush taxi) from Limbe (this is currently the only way to get here, although there is talk of arranging cheaper local transport), making this a trip best done in a group. To arrange tours talk to the guys who hang around the botanic gardens, arrange a trip through the Fako Tourist Board or contact **Bimbia Rainforest and Mangrove Trail** (☎ 333 3325; www.bbcforest.org/eco; bbcnaturetrail@yahoo.com).

The best of Limbe's **beaches** are north of town and known by their distance from Limbe. Mile 6 and Mile 11 beaches are popular, but our favourite is at the village of Batoké at Mile 8, from where the lava flows of one of Mt Cameroon's eruptions are still visible.

Sleeping

Bay Hotel (☎ 773 3609; off Makangal St; s/d/ste CFA5000/7000/10,000) The Bay is the best of a cluster of hotels in this corner of Limbe, with big rooms that, in some cases, come with wide verandahs – all good for catching the sea breeze. Unfortunately, they also tend to pick up the noise of the party people in the nearby bars.

Park Hotel Miramar (☎ 332 2332; Botanic Garden Rd; campsites CFA5000, s/d CFA13,650/18,400, all incl breakfast; ⓟ ⌧ ⓢ) These cute, stucco-and-blue cottages lip onto a wave-kissed cliff backed by screaming jungle – it's all very romantic. This is Limbe's most popular hotel, but don't worry; there's no sense of crowds, just quiet and escape.

Atlantic Beach Hotel (☎ 332 2689; near Limbe Bridge; r CFA16,500-23,500; ⓟ ⌧ ⓢ) There's a slightly romantic state of dishevelment to this hotel. The sea-view rooms indeed have nice vantages over the water, but the rooms with a garden (more like 'parking lot') view give more space for your franc.

Eating

Boukaro (Down Beach; dishes from CFA800) You'll find this cluster of open-air grills with attached seating where the fishing boats haul up on the beach. Soak up your beer with something from the sea that was probably happily unaware it would be your dinner a few minutes before you ordered it.

Bistrot de Milly (Botanic Garden Rd; mains from CFA2000) Peer hard onto Ambas Bay and you may be able to spot Equatorial Guinea as you polish off some excellent seafood and the cold drink of your choice.

Mt Cameroon Bakery (Idenao Rd; mains from CFA2500) Although this spot does nice beignets in the morning, in the evening it becomes a hopping resto-bar, serving French-ish standards and lots of loud music. The pork in mustard sauce is lovely, assuming it's on the somewhat changeable menu.

Getting There & Away

The main motor park is Mile 4, about 6km out of town. Minibuses and *taxis brousses* leave approximately hourly to Buea (CFA700, 25 minutes) and Douala (CFA1300, 70 minutes). From Mile 2, there are buses to Yaoundé (CFA5000, five hours).

Ferries travel every Monday and Thursday from Limbe to Calabar in Nigeria (CFA37,000, 10 hours), departing at around 11pm and returning on Tuesday and Friday at 6pm. Take your own food and water, and fight hard for a seat.

Ferries weren't going to Malabo in Equatorial Guinea at the time of research, although you could arrange a speedboat (popularly called 'stick-boats' – we like 'death trap') for around CFA65,000. The trip takes four hours, but the boats have poor safety records and cannot be recommended.

BAMENDA

The capital of Northwest Province is a dusty sprawl that tumbles down a hill at an altitude of more than 1000m. With a decent range of hotels and restaurants, it's a good jumping-off point for exploring the Ring Road circuit. Anglophone Bamenda is the centre of political opposition to President Biya.

Information

The **tourist office** (☎ 336 1395) can provide basic maps and dates of local festivals. You can access the internet at **Maryland Cybercafe** (Commercial Ave; per hr CFA300), which also has internet phone, and at **Horizon Internet** (Commercial Ave; per hr CFA300). **Express Exchange** (City Chemist's Roundabout) changes travellers cheques as well as US dollars cash. **SGBC Bank** (Commercial Ave) has an ATM.

Sleeping

Baptist Mission Resthouse (☎ 336 1285; Finance Junction; dm CFA2500; ⓟ) Drawbacks: it's a shared cab to the town centre and service can be absent-minded. Now the good news: it's cheap, secure and clean as all get out, three concepts that are a holy trinity indeed for tired travellers.

Ex-Serviceman's Rest House (☎ 7624 6185; Hotel Rd; r CFA5000) This compound is intended for ex-soldiers, but if rooms are available they'll be happily rented out. It's a decent deal, but solo female travellers may feel uncomfortable. There's a loud bar next door; boon or burden depending on your disposition.

Hotel Mondial (☎ 336 1832; off Hotel Rd; s/d CFA12,500/14,000; ⓟ) The Mondial feels a little more modern than its equivalents elsewhere in Bamenda. Comfortable rooms come with water heater and satellite TV, and there are a few decent cheaper options without them (CFA 7500), for those with slimmer budgets.

International Hotel (☎ 336 2527; off Commercial Ave; r CFA15,000-18,000) Very convenient for buses, and service is friendly enough. The interior is a bit drab and mildewed on the walls, but rooms are big and most come with balconies offering sweeping views over, er, 'scenic' Bamenda.

Eating

CTT Restaurant & Handicrafts Cooperative (near Finance Junction, Upstation; mains from CFA1000; ☺ 8am-9pm) The

CAMEROON

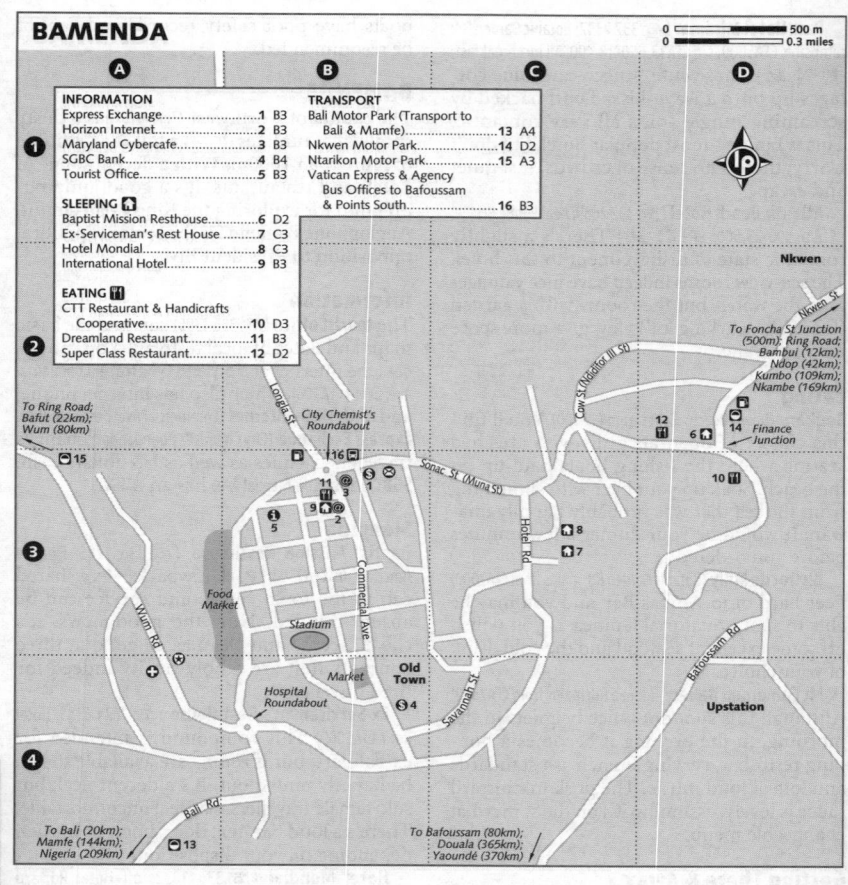

BAMENDA

0   500 m
0   0.3 miles

INFORMATION
Express Exchange....................1 B3
Horizon Internet.....................2 B3
Maryland Cybercafe................3 B3
SGBC Bank.............................4 B4
Tourist Office.........................5 B3

SLEEPING
Baptist Mission Resthouse.......6 D2
Ex-Serviceman's Rest House 7 C3
Hotel Mondial........................8 C3
International Hotel...................9 B3

EATING
CTT Restaurant & Handicrafts
  Cooperative.........................10 D3
Dreamland Restaurant...........11 B3
Super Class Restaurant..........12 D2

TRANSPORT
Bali Motor Park (Transport to
  Bali & Mamfe)....................13 A4
Nkwen Motor Park.................14 D2
Ntarikon Motor Park..............15 A3
Vatican Express & Agency
  Bus Offices to Bafoussam
  & Points South....................16 B3

Nkwen

To Foncha St Junction
(500m); Ring Road;
Bambui (12km);
Ndop (42km);
Kumbo (109km);
Nkambe (169km)

Finance
Junction

To Ring Road;
Bafut (22km);
Wum (80km)

City Chemist's
Roundabout

Food
Market

Stadium

Market

Old
Town

Hospital
Roundabout

Upstation

To Bali (20km);
Mamfe (144km);
Nigeria (209km)

To Bafoussam (80km);
Douala (365km);
Yaoundé (370km)

CAMEROON

food here is decent – OK Cameroonian and slightly better Western fare, but the real drawcard is the surrounds, specifically a workshop of regional handicrafts and great views of Bamenda below.

Dreamland Restaurant (Commercial Ave; mains from extra CFA1300; ☯ 7am-11pm) Dreamland is a bustling buffet, where you can catch some football at night and enjoy a very good execution of steak and chips and – really? in Cameroon? – a salad bar for those needing a graze.

Super Class Restaurant (near Finance Junction; meals CFA3000-7000) A Cameroonian friend of ours sagely informed us that 'many whites meet here'. 'Many' is a relative term, but there were a few missionary types around when

we visited, enjoying both African standards and decent (if expensive) pizzas.

Getting There & Away

Most agency offices for destinations to the south are on Sonac St. Destinations include Yaoundé (CFA5000, six hours), Douala (CFA5000, seven hours) and Bafoussam (CFA1500, 90 minutes). Nkwen Motor Park has transport to the east stretch of the Ring Road, including Ndop (CFA1200, 90 minutes) and Kumbo (CFA3000, five hours). The west Ring Road is served by Ntarikon Motor Park, which runs minibuses to Wum (CFA2000, two hours). Shared taxis to the further motor parks shouldn't cost you any more than CFA150.

THE RING ROAD

The northwest highlands bear the pretty name 'Grassfields', an appellation too pleasant to really capture the look of this landscape. These aren't gentle fields; they're green and yellow valleys, tall grass, red earth and sharp mountains. Clouds of mist rise with wood smoke and dung smoke that marks the location of villages speckled on this deceptively inviting – but hard and rugged – terrain.

The 367km Ring Road runs a circle around the Grassfields, and if it were in better shape, it'd be one of Cameroon's great scenic drives. In fairness, it still can't be missed – but get your butt ready for some bumpy, red-earth roads. The payoff? Mountains dolloped with lakes, cattle loping into the hills and one of the greatest concentrations of *fondoms* (traditional kingdoms) in Cameroon. Tourism is DIY here. At the time of research vehicles weren't going past Wum, and the trip from there to Bamenda was a painful three hours. Hiking, cycling and camping are all options, but always ask the permission of the local chief, and bring some gifts (whiskey always works).

Transport links are reasonable but not particularly frequent, with minibuses usually leaving very early in the morning. Roads are poor throughout. Kumbo is the Ring Road's largest town, but apart from here there's little infrastructure and nowhere to change money (stock up on CFA before leaving Bamenda). There are basic hotels in Ndop, Kumbo, Nkambe and Wum.

Starting from **Bamenda** and heading east, you pass **Sabga Hill**, which rises powerfully above **Ndop**, then **Bamessing**, with a handicraft centre and pottery workshop. After that you reach **Kumbo**, dominated by its Catholic cathedral and *fon's* (traditional chief's) palace. It's a good place to base yourself, with a nice market and the Ring Road's best hotels. From there you go north to Nkambe, then Missaje and the end of the road.

The road from Missaje to We is just a dirt track in places, and in the rainy season you won't find it. Some travellers continue on foot, sometimes with help from ~~~ Fulani herdsmen. It can take a co~~~ ~~~m couple of days to get to We, so brin~~~ ~~~ng supplies.

If you make the hike from Missaje to We, you'll pass **Lake Nyos**, a volcanic lake that was the site of a natural gas eruption in 1986, which resulted in around 1700 deaths. Continuing south you reach **Wum**, the biggest village on the west side of the Ring Road. South of Wum the road passes the **Metchum Falls**, where most shared-taxi drivers will stop to let you have a quick peek or photo.

The last town on the Ring Road (or the first, if you're heading clockwise) is **Bafut**, traditionally the strongest of the kingdoms in this region. The **fon's palace** (admission CFA1000, camera CFA1500, museum CFA2000) is a highlight of the Ring Road and includes a tour of the compound where the *fon's* large family lives.

BAFOUSSAM

There's initially little to love about Bafoussam. The Bamiléké stronghold seems haphazardly built on agriculture money and a refined sense of chaos. But it's friendly as hell and has one of the best traditional palaces in the country. Make sure you check out the huge **chefferie** (chief's compound; www.museumcam.org; admission CFA2000; ☺ 10am-5pm), about 15km south at Bandjoun.

Good value, with a decent bar to boot, the rooms at **Hotel Federal** (☎ 344 1309; Route de Foumban; r CFA6000-9000) are neat and tidy. Although located in a blocky bomb-shelter chic building, the rooms in **Hotel du Centre** (☎ 344 2079; Carrefour Total; s/d CFA12,000/20,000) are open and fresh, many come with a balcony, and the toilets – bless – have seats. It's well located (as the name suggests) and a useful landmark.

Boulangerie La Paix (Route de Foumban; pastries from CFA150; ☺ 8am-10pm) sells good bread and sticky sweet treats in the morning, and is a handy general food shop the rest of the day. **Supermarché le Point** (Ave de la République), at the opposite end of Rue de Marché, fulfils the same function. The usual fish and meat stalls come out at night.

Minibuses to Foumban (CFA800 to CFA1000, one hour) depart from near Carrefour Total, along with shared taxis. Agencies to Yaoundé (CFA2500 to CFA3000, three hours) and Douala (CFA4000, five hours) have offices along the main road south from the town centre. Transport to Bamenda (CFA1200, 1½ hours) leaves from the Bamenda road, north of the ~~~ (CFA150 i~~~ ~~~

CAMEROON

FOUMBAN

Foumban has a deep tradition of homegrown arts and the traditional monarchy centred around a sultan, who resides in a palace. The town is plopped architecturally and conceptually between West and North Africa, as if the Sahel and its sharp music, bright robes and Islam – this is the city with most Muslims in the south – was slowly creeping into the eastern corner of West Province.

The **Grand Marché** is a warren of narrow stalls and alleys, which are great fun to explore; the paths eventually lead to where the **Grande Mosquée** faces the palace. There's a slow internet cafe east of the market. CPAC bank (south of the market) may change euros if you're lucky, but it's best to change money in Bafoussam.

Sights

The must-see attraction of Foumban is the **Palais Royal** (Rue du Palais; admission CFA2000, camera CFA1500; 8.30am-6pm), the sultan's palace, currently home to the 19th sultan of the Bamoun dynasty. The palace has a fascinating and well-organised museum containing previous sultans' possessions and great historical insight on the region – assuming you know French.

South of town, the **Village des Artisans** (Rue des Artisans) seems to produce more handicrafts than the rest of Cameroon combined. Close by, the **Musée des Arts et Traditions Bamoun** (admission CFA1000; 9am-5pm) houses a private collection of art and historical artefacts.

Festivals & Events

Every year at **Tabaski** (the Islamic holiday of Eid al-Adha), Foumban attracts thousands of pilgrims for an extraordinary blend of Muslim and traditional Bamoun ceremonies.

It all starts before sunrise with the call to prayer blasting from loudspeakers at the mosque. Thousands of men and boys, dressed in their finest, climb the hill to the Sacred Mountain and kneel in prayer. Around dawn the imam arrives, followed by the sultan in his white Cadillac. There are sunrise prayers, a sermon from the imam and a blessing from the sultan (on Eid al-Adha this is when the sheep is sacrificed). The sultan then gets on his horse surrounded by warriors in full regalia, and everyone follows him in an enormous parade to the palace, while the women and girls, so far absent from the proceedings, line _____ ____ __ssed all in white and ululate as

After the parade there's a rest, and then horses race through town. Then another break until it gets dark, when the drumming and dancing start in front of the Palais Royal. Meanwhile (this is still Cameroon, after all) people pack the bars and clubs, and when these are full they set up speakers on the streets for heavy drinking and dancing until the sun comes up.

Sleeping & Eating

Hotel Beau Regarde (348 2183; Rue de l'Hotel Beau Regarde; r CFA6500-10,000) 'Shabby and big' about sums it up. The rooms are, well, roomy, and decently priced (a bed and worn bathroom), but the entire place could use a decent scrub and a bit more brightness beyond the Hannibal Lecter lighting scheme.

Hotel Complexe Adi (743 1181; Rue de l'Hotel Beau Regarde; r CFA8000-10,000) Look for the giant voodoo statue of a man studded by nails to find Adi's entrance – now that's better than a doorman. While the rooms here are clean, they're smallish, and the bar downstairs gets pretty loud.

Rifam Hotel (348 2878; Route de Bafoussam; s/d CFA15,000/25,000;) Near the bus agency offices, this hotel is easily Foumban's plushest. Doubles are huge and come with a balcony large enough to play football on.

Bars, beer and grilled meat are abundant. Happy days.

Getting There & Away

There are a few direct buses to Yaoundé (CFA3000, five hours) and Douala (CFA4500, six hours); otherwise head for Bafoussam (CFA800 to CFA1000, one hour) and change there. Bus agency offices are on the west side of town, about 3km from the Grande Marché (CFA150 in a shared taxi).

Transport between Foumban and Kumbo (CFA3000, around six hours) runs year-round, with times varying according to the rains. Although the road is very poor, it's easily one of the most beautiful in the country, skirting along the edge of the spectacular Mbam Massif.

SOUTHERN CAMEROON

A great jungle belt lays across Africa's belly, and Cameroon's South Province is the belt's buckle. You will see jungle here that redefines your concept of lush; you will not see, unless you're very lucky, the elephants and pygmies and plants of the deep jungle, which grasps towards the blue Atlantic, white waves and some of Cameroon's best beaches.

KRIBI

Very rarely does the vibe here feel like 'crowded beach resort', despite this being the country's exemplar of the genre. The sand is fine, the water cool and inviting (but prone to hard rips; be careful) and all of the above is kept refreshingly clean. Plus, the seafood is fresh, and when it's paired with a cold beer, a grilled banana and a starry sky…well, there are times when Africa hugs you.

Most of Kribi's hotels, usually with their own beachfronts, start at the southern end of town, but camping isn't advised. The **Chutes de la Lobé**, 8km south of town (*moto-taxi* CFA500), are an impressive set of water-falls that empty directly into the sea – it's a beautiful sight.

Stock up on CFA before coming to Kribi – the banks don't like changing money and there's no ATM, although this may change with the opening of a local **Bicec Bank** (Rue des Banques).

Sleeping

If you're visiting in the rainy season, ask for a discount.

Hotel Panoramique (☎ 346 1773, 9694 2575; hotel panoramique@yahoo.fr; Rue du Marché; r CFA6000-14,000; ☒) This semi-sprawling compound feels like a down-at-heels villa evolved into low-rent flophouse. Some rooms are good value, but at the cheapest end you're in an ugly annex with the dust and roaches.

New Hôtel Coco Beach (☎ 346 1584; off Route de Campo; s CFA15,000-28,000, d CFA25,000-32,000, tr CFA46,000; P ☒ ☒) If a little metropole bras-siere dropped onto the buttery sand of Kribi appeals, may we direct you to Coco Beach? There's an endearingly cluttered Gallic flair to this spot, and the sea pretty much laps up on your shoes.

Framotel (☎ 3461541,33461640,99948222;www.camer oun-evasion.com; r from CFA20,000; ☒ ☒) Framotel is a low-slung compound that may bring to mind the cheap and cheerful rentals your fam-ily used on holidays. It's located 150m up a side road a little north of Kribi; two nearby hotels offer identical accommodation.

Les Bougainvillers (☎ 9608 4745; off Route de Campo; r CFA25,000-35,000; P ☒) 'The Bougainvillers'

sounds like the name of a funk band, and if there was such a band they'd be likely to crash this plush hotel, with its frankly fantastic rooms – plush beds, sparkly clean everything and balconies that look out onto screaming jun-gle or palms blowing over whitecaps. Funk on, Bougainvillers.

Hotel Ilomba (☎ 346 1744; Route de Campo; s/d CFA25,000/30,000; P ☒ ☒ ☒) Some way out of Kribi, this is the loveliest hotel in the area. Rooms are in *boukarous* (open-sided circular mud huts), all well furnished and tastefully decorated. Just a short walk to the Chutes de la Lobé waterfalls.

Auberge du Phare (☎ 346 1106; off Route de Campo; r CFA28,000-40,000; P ☒) Blonde-wood accents, navy-blue sheets and nautical embellishments give rooms some character, while the peeling courtyard, crystal pool and thatched bar are tropically indulgent.

Eating

All of the beach hotels have restaurants, and these are the nicest dining options in Kribi. Expect to pay from CFA3000 per meal; sea-food obviously features heavily.

Fish Market (meals from CFA1000; ☒ 10am-5pm Wed & Sat) This market (supported by the Japanese government) at the marina grills the day's catch over coals. From crab and lobster to massive barracuda, you'd be hard-pressed to find a better and tastier selection of seafood anywhere in Cameroon.

Le Colisee (mains CFA3000-7000) Le Colisee offers air-con, pizza and a building that looks like a Colombian drug dealer's villa. Despite the look of the place there's no cocaine on the menu – just good Italian mains and some of the best pizza around.

On Carrefour Kingué you'll find plenty of **fish and meat stands** (meals from CFA1000; ☒ 10am-late) lined up in front of the bars.

Getting There & Away

Bus agencies have offices on Rue du Marché in the town centre. Nonagency transport leaves from the main *gare routière* (bus station). Buses for Douala (CFA1800 to CFA2000, three hours) leave throughout the day, along with transport to Campo (CFA2000, three hours) and Yaoundé (CFA3000, 3½ hours).

EBOLOWA

Ebolowa, capital of Ntem district, is a bustling place and a possible stopping point en route between Yaoundé and Equatorial Guinea or Gabon. Its main attraction is the artificial Municipal Lake in the centre of town.

The best accommodation is at **Hôtel Porte Jaune** (☎ 228 4339; Route de Yaoundé; r CFA10,000-12,000) in the town centre, with some cheaper auberges (hostels) near the main roundabout, including **Hôtel Âne Rouge** (Place Ans 2000; r CFA4000).

During the dry season there's at least one vehicle daily along the rough road between Ebolowa and Kribi. There are also many buses daily to Yaoundé (CFA3000, three hours). Several vehicles depart in the morning for Ambam (CFA1000, one hour), from where you can find transport towards Ebebiyin (Equatorial Guinea) or Bitam (Gabon).

CAMPO & EBODJÉ

Campo is the last town before the Equatorial Guinea border. Taking the road here is half the attraction – it's a hard but rewarding slog through immense rainforest past pygmy villages with views out to the ocean and fire-spouting petrol platforms shimmering in the west.

For travellers, Campo mainly serves as a jumping-off point for visiting Parc National de Campo Ma'an as well as the community tourism project in nearby Ebodjé. There's scruffy accommodation, simple meals and very friendly faces at **Auberge Bon Course** (☎ 7451 1883; r CFA5000) at Bon Course Supermarché at the main junction in Campo.

Parc National de Campo-Ma'an (2608 sq km) protects rainforest, many plants and various animals, including buffalo, elephants and mandrills. The park is being developed by WWF as an ecotourism destination, with plans for canopy walks and river trips on the drawing board. Before planning a trip, check with the **WWF office** (Map p283; ☎ 221 6267; www.wwfcameroon.org; Bastos) in Yaoundé to see what progress is being made.

Ebodjé, a small fishing village 25km north of Campo, is home to a **sea turtle conservation project** and ecotourism site run by **KUDU Cameroun** (☎ 348 1648, 9622 0829; bebeaclotilde@yahoo.fr). Visitors are taken out at night to spot egg-laying turtles, although there's no guarantee you'll see any – some tour groups encounter none, some as many as six. Even if you don't see any turtles, the beach is gorgeous, pristine and better than anything you'll see in Kribi.

The total cost of a turtle walk (around CFA10,500 per person) includes accom-

modation in a local home, village development fee, meal and tour. A proportion of fees helps locals, many of whom have been trained as guides, and for between CFA5000 and CFA10,000 you can arrange trips up local rivers or cultural nights with traditional dancing and singing. Remember to bring your own water or filter, mosquito net and sleeping sheets.

There are daily minibuses between Campo and Kribi (CFA1500), which also stop at Ebodjé. *Moto-taxis* to Campo Beach (for Equatorial Guinea) cost CFA500. Taxis to Ebodjé from Campo cost CFA500. *Moto-taxis* to Ebodjé cost around CFA2000.

NORTHERN CAMEROON

The north of Cameroon is the fringe of the world's greatest dry zone. This is the Sahel, a red and ochre and yellow and brown rolling sea of dust, dirt and strange, utterly beautiful hills and pinnacles of rock, crisscrossed by the dry wind, the thin strides of Fulani people and the broad steps of their long-horned cattle.

N'GAOUNDÉRÉ

N'Gaoundéré is the terminus of the railway line and beginning of the great bus and truck routes to the far north and Chad. The sense of adventure imparted upon reaching the Sahel is helped by the sight of government soldiers – there's a major training facility nearby – striding through the desert lanes with AK-47s strapped to their backs and extra banana claps taped to the stocks of their guns.

Some areas of N'Gaoundéré have bad reputations for safety at night, including the area around the stadium and north of the cathedral. If in doubt, take a *moto-taxi*.

To enter the **Palais du Lamido** (admission CFA2000, guide CFA1000, camera CFA1000; ⏳ 9am-5pm), you pass between three pillars stuffed with the remains of individuals who were buried alive to consecrate the site. Past this macabre foyer is a complex of low-slung, heavily thatched roundhouses. Come on Friday or Sunday, when nobles pay their respects, thin desert music settles over the nearby square dominated by the Grande Mosquée and there's a palpable sense of being…well, somewhere else.

Beware of black-painted areas within the compound – these sections are reserved for the *lamido* (local Muslim ruler).

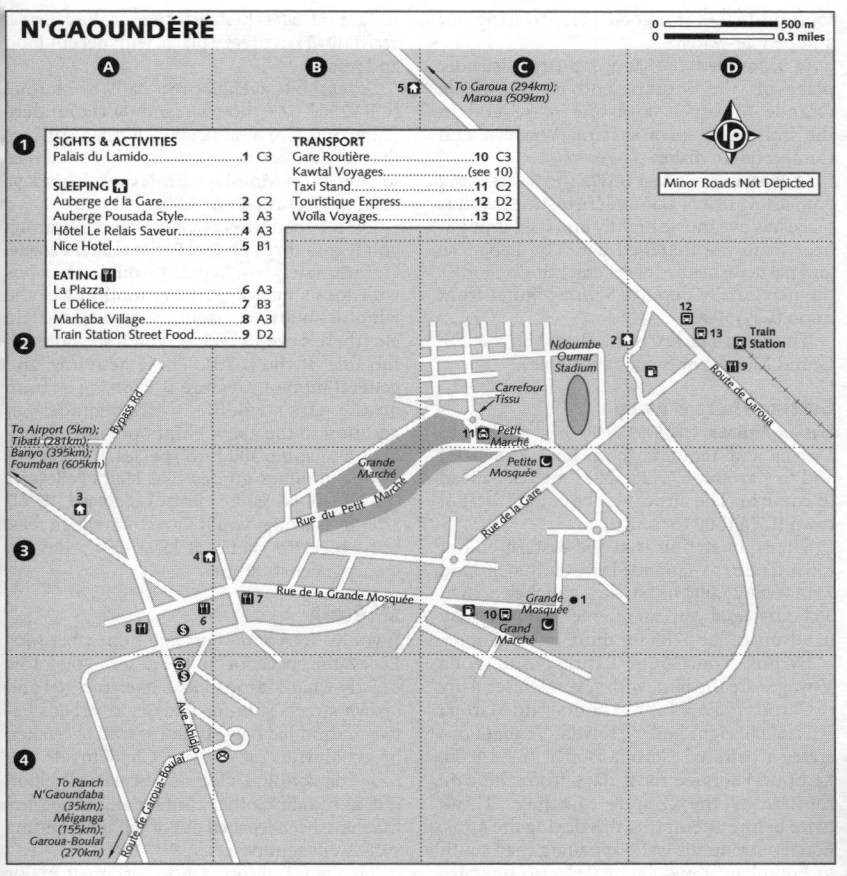

N'GAOUNDÉRÉ

SIGHTS & ACTIVITIES	
Palais du Lamido....................1 C3	
SLEEPING	
Auberge de la Gare.................2 C2	
Auberge Pousada Style...........3 A3	
Hôtel Le Relais Saveur............4 A3	
Nice Hotel..............................5 B1	
EATING	
La Plazza...............................6 A3	
Le Délice...............................7 B3	
Marhaba Village......................8 A3	
Train Station Street Food.........9 D2	

TRANSPORT	
Gare Routière...........................10 C3
Kawtal Voyages...................(see 10)
Taxi Stand................................11 C2
Touristique Express..................12 D2
Woïla Voyages.........................13 D2

Minor Roads Not Depicted

Sleeping

The cool air of N'Gaoundéré means there's no need for air conditioning.

Auberge Pousada Style (☎ 225 1703; r CFA5000–9000) A basic but friendly resthouse that's kept as clean as a barracks (it has about the same atmosphere as well). Take a *moto-taxi* late at night in this area.

Auberge de la Gare (☎ 225 2217; r CFA8500) This is probably N'Gaoundéré's best-located hotel, offering easy access to bus agencies and the train station. Rooms are tidy, if not much else.

Hôtel Le Relais Saveur (☎ 225 1141; r with/without TV CFA18,000/15,000) Well located, near the intersection of Rue du Petit Marché and Rue de la Grande Mosquée, rooms here are

scrubbed if a little musty. Try not to wrinkle your nose too much and enjoy a beer at the attached bar.

Nice Hotel (☎ 225 1013; Route de Garoua; r from CFA18,000) With spacious rooms, a peaceful, leafy setting, long cool corridors and TV in all rooms, the Nice is just that, and about as good as midrange options get in town.

Eating

The best street food is easily found at the row of shops, stalls and bars opposite the train station – worth the detour even if you don't have a train to catch.

Marhaba Village (mains from CFA1500; ⏰ 9am–11pm) An open-air restaurant, with a snack bar and a more formal eating area. Its central

CAMEROON

location makes it a good place to hang out and people-watch.

Le Délice (meals CFA1500; ⊗ 9am-11pm) Friendly place off the western end of Rue de la Grande Mosquée, and one of several in the immediate area serving Western and Cameroonian dishes.

La Plazza (meals from CFA3000; ⊗ 9am-midnight) Something of a N'Gaoundéré institution, this place has live music nightly and cold draught beer from the thatched bar. The Lebanese and pasta dishes are excellent, but don't miss the perennially popular Sunday buffet from noon (CFA5000).

The main market is the Petit Marché; the Grand Marché only sells vegetables.

Getting There & Away

Elysian Airlines (☎ 9909 8748) has flights to Douala and Yaoundé (both for CFA86,500) and to Garoua (CFA28,500) – but call ahead to confirm. The airport is about 5km west of town (CFA1500 for a taxi).

The train station is at the eastern end of town. Trains to Yaoundé leave daily at around 7pm (CFA25,000 in 1st-class couchette, 18 to 36 hours), and you can reserve your seat a day in advance. See p285 for more information.

By bus, Touristique Express and Woïla Voyages are the best, with several buses daily to Garoua (CFA3500, five hours) and Maroua (CFA6000, eight hours). Kawtal Voyages operates a battered Garoua-Boulaï (CFA4000, 12 hours) service most days from the *gare routière* by the Grande Mosquée. Think twice before attempting this during the rains. Equally strenuous is the appalling road south to Foumban. Kawtal Voyages also operates along this route, as far as Banyo (CFA5000, around 10 hours), from where you can change for Foumban.

GAROUA

Garoua is a pleasant enough spot to spend the night or wait for a vehicle transfer, which is the extent of most people's plans here. You may need to make a stopover if you're over-landing into Chad; pay a visit to the **Chadian consulate** (☎ 2227 3128) for visas (sometimes unavailable here, so check beforehand), or make friends with a member of Garoua's huge Chadian expat community.

Near the port, **Auberge Hiala Village** (☎ 227 2407; Rue Cicai; r CFA5000-7000; P ⊠) has decent self-contained rooms, with a good bar and

restaurant. **Super Restaurant** (Route de Maroua; mains from CFA1000) is a breezy place, with decent food and juices.

Several bus agencies run daily to Maroua (CFA2500, 2½ hours), and N'Gaoundéré (CFA3500, five hours), while Elysian Airlines flies to Yaoundé and Douala. Air Tchad flies to Douala on Mondays, Fridays and Sundays (one way/return CFA12,000/192,000).

On the road from N'Gaoundéré to Garoua you'll pass through **Parc National de la Bénoué**. Unfortunately, you'll pass through it in a bus with locals happily tossing food out of the window to attract baboons, elands, buffalo etc (there's even a chance you'll see lions off the side of the road). These activities and general human pressure is exerting a strain on the park's wildlife, which includes (in addition to the above) hippopotami, crocodiles and some 300 bird species. To arrange a tour, contact guides like **Janick Pelleteret** (☎ 227 2694, 342 5338) or **Borge Ladefoged** (☎ 227 2778) in Garoua; you'll have to arrange fees, but expect to spend at least €60 a day on transport costs alone.

MAROUA

If you've seen *Star Wars* and remember Mos Eisley, the spaceport in the desert, you know exactly what Maroua looks like: low, red and brown streets running like dry riverbeds between rounded beige buildings, all overtaken by a colourful cast – Fulani, Chadians etc – in robes of sky blue, electric purple and blood red, as if their clothes contain all the colours that have been leeched out of the surrounding sun-swept semidesert.

This is Cameroon's northernmost major town and its best base for exploring the extreme North Province, particularly the Mandara Mountains, as well as a good place to plan border crossings into Nigeria and Chad.

Information

Internet is slow; try **Braouz** (per hr CFA750), or **Marouanet** (per hr CFA400), which is a cheaper option.

For medical emergencies, try Meskine Hospital, southwest of town off Garoua road.

Maroua's banks can be reluctant to change even cash euros. If the main banks won't help, try CCA Bureau de Change next to SGBC Bank. The latter also has an ATM, as does **Bicec Bank** (Route de Maga).

CAMEROON

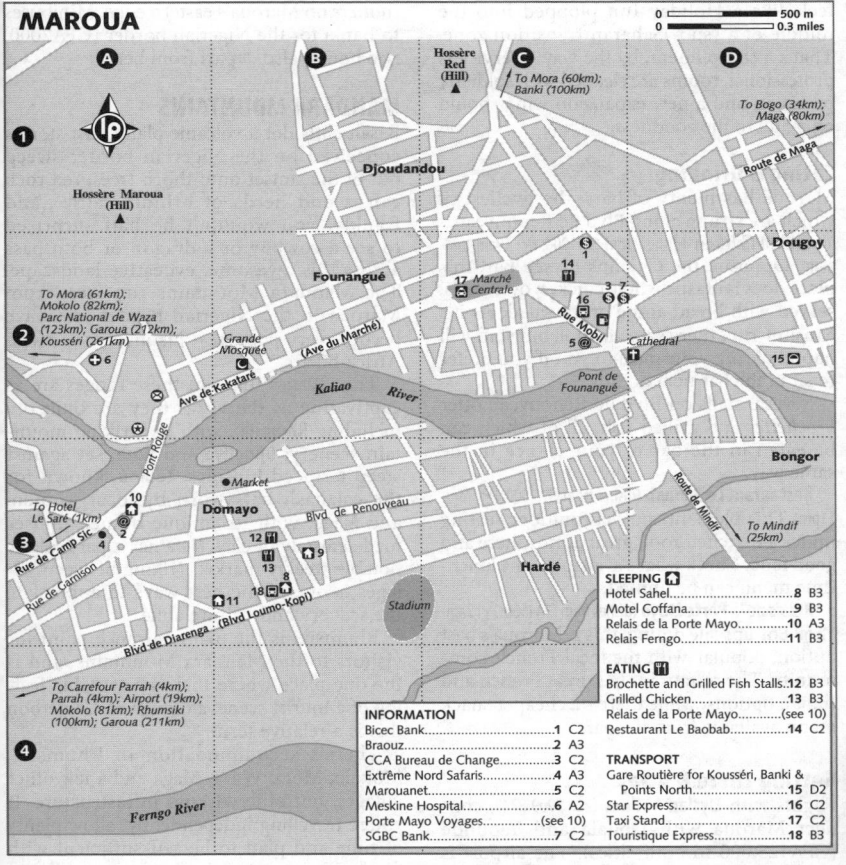

MAROUA

INFORMATION
Bicec Bank	1	C2
Braouz	2	A3
CCA Bureau de Change	3	C2
Extrême Nord Safaris	4	A3
Marouanet	5	C2
Meskine Hospital	6	A2
Porte Mayo Voyages	(see 10)	
SGBC Bank	7	C2

SLEEPING 🛏
Hotel Sahel	8	B3
Motel Coffana	9	B3
Relais de la Porte Mayo	10	A3
Relais Ferngo	11	B3

EATING 🍴
Brochette and Grilled Fish Stalls	12	B3
Grilled Chicken	13	B3
Relais de la Porte Mayo	(see 10)	
Restaurant Le Baobab	14	C2

TRANSPORT
Gare Routière for Kousséri, Banki & Points North	15	D2
Star Express	16	C2
Taxi Stand	17	C2
Touristique Express	18	B3

Maroua has numerous tour operators that can arrange hiking in the Mandara Mountains and visits to Parc National du Waza. Better ones include the following:

Extrême Nord Safaris (☎ 229 3356; deliteri@hotmail.com)

Fagus Voyages (☎ 9986 1871; www.fagusvoyages.com)

Porte Mayo Voyages (☎ 9984 1573) Through Relais de la Porte Mayo.

Sleeping

Relais Ferngo (☎ 229 2153; off Blvd de Diarenga; r CFA6000; 🅿 ❄) By far the best value in town: sleep in airy, whitewashed *boukarous* in the shade of willowy neem trees and…well, do whatever (how about taking a shower in the alfresco but walled-off bathrooms?).

Motel Coffana (☎ 970 9643; off Blvd de Diarenga; r CFA6000-10,000; 🅿) You'll find nicely turned-out *boukarous* here, freshly painted and welcoming. Cheaper rooms in the main block have fans only, but are airy enough with their high ceilings. Say Hi to the resident chickens and enormous turkey in the morning.

Relais de la Porte Mayo (☎ 229 2692; Pont Rouge; s/d/apt CFA13,900/16,900/18,500; ❄ 🖵) French-run and popular with tourists, this is as good as Maroua lodging gets. It is skilled at giving a relaxed, modern-amenities-but-you're-still-in-the-Sahel kinda vibe, with roomy *boukarous*, a good (if touristy) restaurant-bar and fancy souvenir-shop-cum-boutique.

Hotel Sahel (☎ 229 2960; Blvd de Diarenga; r CFA15,000-25,000; 🅿 ❄) Here's a high-end option that

CAMEROON

feels like a Holiday Inn plopped into the middle of a (sub-)Saharan transition zone. That's a compliment, by the way – service is professional, rooms are cleaned with soldierly precision and a new expansion wing should only add to the goodness.

Eating & Drinking

Maroua has plenty of bars, the liveliest of which are strung along Blvd de Renouveau.

Grilled Chicken (dishes from CFA1000; ☺ 10am-midnight) Opposite the Champs Elysée Bar, this place does fantastic whole chicken over coals, served with bread and a green salad. As it's Muslim-run, there's no alcohol, but staff will happily bring your meal to you if you prefer to sit in the bar next door.

Several stalls on Blvd de Renouveau offer *brochettes* and grilled fish, all of which can be eaten in the bar of your choice in the same way.

Restaurant Le Baobab (dishes from CFA2000; ☺ 7am-11pm) This pleasant spot has outdoor seating under a thatched roof, great atmosphere and good food. Check what's available – the lunchtime menu can be limited.

Relais de la Porte Mayo (dishes from CFA4500; ☺ 7am-11pm) For upscale dining, this is Maroua's best option, popular with the local French community. The restaurant has great French and Italian options, while there's a cheaper snack menu available from the bar.

Getting There & Away

Flights with **Elysian Airlines** (☎ 9909 8748) connect Maroua with Douala and Yaoundé (CFA125,000 to both cities). The airport is 20km south of town along the Garoua road (CFA3000 in a chartered taxi, if you can find one).

Touristique Express has several daily buses to Garoua (CFA2500, 2½ hours) and N'Gaoundéré (CFA6000, eight hours). You can book tickets for the N'Gaoundéré–Yaoundé train here at the same time. Several other bus agencies operate along the N'Gaoundéré route, with depots on the same road; Star Express in the town centre is also good.

Plentiful transport to Mokolo (CFA1000, 1½ hours) and less frequently to Rhumsiki (CFA2000, around three hours) departs from Carrefour Parrah in Djarangol at the southern end of town.

Transport to Kousséri for the Chad border (CFA3500, five hours) departs from the *gare routière* on Maroua's eastern edge. Minibuses to Banki for the Nigerian border (CFA2000, two hours) also depart from here.

MANDARA MOUNTAINS

Basalt cliffs dot a volcanic plain, dust storms conceived on the Nigerian border sweep out of the sunset onto thorn trees, red rock cairns and herds of brindle cattle...and frankly, you wouldn't be half surprised to see a cowboy or a dragon or both pass across this awesome, evocative landscape. The Mandara Mountains run west from Maroua to the Nigerian border and have become very popular – justifiably so – with Africa hikers.

The villages that dot these ranges are as captivating as the vistas they are built on, including **Rhumsiki**, with its striking mountain scenery; **Djingliya** and **Koza**, set against steep terraced hillsides; **Tourou**, known for the calabash hats worn by local women; and **Maga**, with its unique domed houses made entirely of clay. **Mora** has a particularly notable weekly market. Hiking between villages is one of the best ways to appreciate the scenery and culture alike.

Rhumsiki is the main entrance point for visitors to the Mandara Mountains, and is the one place where there's a tangible feeling of a tourist scene, although in Cameroon this is a relative term.

There's accommodation in Rhumsiki, Mokolo, Mora, Waza, Maga and a few other villages, but otherwise no infrastructure. If you're travelling independently, allow plenty of time and plan to be self-sufficient with food and water. Local minibuses usually set off around 6am. *Moto-taxis* are sometimes the only option for getting around.

For those with limited time, travel agencies in Maroua can organise visits, although it's just as easy to arrange things on the spot in Rhumsiki or Mokolo, which will ensure that more of the money you spend is pumped directly into the local economy. Expect to pay around CFA9000 per day, including guide, simple meals and accommodation.

PARC NATIONAL DU WAZA

The most accessible of Cameroon's national parks, **Waza** (admission CFA5000, vehicle CFA2000, camera CFA2000; ☺ 6am-6pm 15 November-15 May) is also the best for viewing wildlife. While it can't compare with East African parks, you're likely to see elephants, hippos, giraffes, antelopes and – with luck – lions. Late March to April is the best time for viewing, as the animals congregate at water holes before the rains. Waza is also notable for its particularly rich birdlife. The park is closed during the rainy season.

A guide (CFA3000) is obligatory in each vehicle. Walking isn't permitted.

The park entrance is signposted and about 100m off the main highway. Unless you have your own vehicle, the best way to visit is to hire a vehicle in Maroua (about CFA30,000 per day plus petrol). See p298 for listings of tour operators. A 4WD vehicle is recommended.

Accessing the park by public transport is difficult; any bus between Maroua and Kousséri should be able to drop you off at the park turn-off, but after that you'll be reliant on hitching a lift into the park itself, which is likely to involve a long wait.

Sleeping

Waza can easily be done as a day trip from Maroua if you start early (bring a packed lunch). Otherwise, there are three places to stay near the park entrance.

Centre d'Accueil de Waza (☎ 229 2207; campsite per person CFA2500, r CFA7000) This simple place at the park entrance has accommodation in no-frills two-person *boukarous* with shared bathroom facilities. Meals can be arranged (CFA2000) and there is a small kitchen.

Campement de Waza (☎ 229 1646, in Maroua 229 1646, in Waza 765 7717, 765 7558; r CFA16,000; ❄) Plucked onto a hill amid smooth boulders are these *boukarous*, with views that stretch out to the scrub plains and some lizards thrown in for gratis. The huts are comfy, staff obsequious and the on-site restaurant good for sinking a beer post lion-spotting.

There's (very) basic accommodation in Waza village, just north of the park entrance.

EASTERN CAMEROON

Cameroon's remote east is wild and untamed. Seldom visited by travellers, it's very much a destination for those with plenty of time and the stamina to back up an appetite for adventure. There's little infrastructure and travel throughout is slow and rugged, with dense green forest and red laterite earth roads. The rainforest national parks are the main attraction, along with routes into the Central African Republic and Congo.

BERTOUA

The capital of East Province, Bertoua is a genuine boomtown, born of logging and mining. Here you'll find all the facilities lacking elsewhere in the region, including banks and sealed roads.

Hôtel Mansa (☎ 224 1650; Mokolo II; r CFA25,000-35,000; ❄) is the town's best – it's worth a splurge if you've been lost in the forest. Hôtel Montagnia, near the *gare routière*, and Hôtel Mirage, near the post office, have basic rooms for around CFA6000. The usual spills and grills are located near the *gare routière*.

Buses to Yaoundé (CFA5000, seven hours), Bélabo (for the train; CFA1000, one hour) and Garoua-Boulaï, leave from the *gare routière* near the market.

GAROUA-BOULAÏ

If you're looking for a rough African frontier town, Garoua-Boulaï is it. On the Central African Republic border, it's a place of bars, trucks and prostitutes. The auberges aren't recommended, so try the **Mission Catholique** (dm for a donation, r about CFA5000) instead.

There's a bus to N'Gaoundéré (CFA4000, 12 hours, one daily) during the dry season and year-round service to Bertoua; both roads are just tolerable. The Central African Republic border crossing is on the edge of Garoua-Boulaï next to the motor park.

CAMEROON DIRECTORY

ACCOMMODATION

Cameroon has a decent range of accommodation options, from simple auberges (hostels) and dorm beds in religious missions to luxury hotels. Expect to pay around CFA15,000 for a decent single room with bathroom and a fan. Most hotels quote prices per room – genuine single and twin rooms are the exception rather than the norm.

Throughout this chapter, we've considered budget accommodation as costing up to CFA15,000, midrange from CFA15,000 to CFA40,000 and top end from CFA40,000 and up. Rather than seasonal rates, most hotels in Kribi and Limbe generally charge more during holidays and weekends.

ACTIVITIES

Hiking is a big drawcard in Cameroon. The two most popular hiking regions are Mt

CAMEROON

Cameroon (p289) near the coast and the Mandara Mountains (p300) in the north. The Ring Road (p293) near Bamenda also offers great hiking possibilities, but there's nothing organised so you'll need to be self-sufficient.

BUSINESS HOURS

Banks From 7.30am or 8am to 3.30pm Monday to Friday.
Businesses From 7.30am or 8am until 6pm or 6.30pm Monday to Friday, generally with a one- to two-hour break sometime between noon and 3pm. Most are also open from 8am to 1pm (sometimes later) on Saturday.
Government offices From 7.30am to 3.30pm Monday to Friday.

DANGERS & ANNOYANCES

The major cities, Douala and Yaoundé, both have reputations for petty crime, especially in the crowded central areas. The roads pose a greater risk, with plenty of badly maintained vehicles driven at punishing speeds.

Scams and official corruption are a way of life in Cameroon; keep your guard up and maintain a sense of humour.

EMBASSIES & CONSULATES

The following embassies and consulates are located in Yaoundé, except as noted. Australians and New Zealanders should contact the Canadian High Commission in case of an emergency. Opening hours listed are for visa applications.
Canada (Map p284; ☎ 223 2311; Immeuble Stamatiades, Ave de l'Indépendance, Centre Ville)
Central African Republic (Map p283; ☎ 220 5155; Rue 1863, Bastos; ☽ 8am-3pm Mon-Fri)
Chad Garoua (☎ 227 3128); Yaoundé (Map p283; ☎ 221 0624; Rue Joseph Mballa Eloumden, Bastos; ☽ 7.30am-noon & 1-3.30pm Mon-Fri)
Congo (Map p283; ☎ 223 2458; Rue 1815, Bastos; ☽ 8am-noon Mon-Fri)
Democratic Republic of Congo (Map p283; ☎ 220 5103; Blvd de l'URSS, Bastos; ☽ 9.30am-3.30pm Mon-Fri)
Equatorial Guinea Douala (Map pp286-7; ☎ 342 2729; Rue Koloko; ☽ 9am-3pm Mon-Fri); Yaoundé (Map p283; ☎ 342 2729; Rue 1805, Bastos; ☽ 9am-3pm Mon-Fri)
France Douala (Map pp286-7; ☎ 342 6250; Ave des Cocotiers, Bonanjo); Yaoundé (Map p283; ☎ 222 7900; Rue Joseph Atemengué, near Place de la Réunification)
Gabon (Map p283; ☎ 220 2966; Rue 1816, Bastos; ☽ 9.30am-3pm Mon-Fri)
Germany (Map p283; ☎ 221 0056; Ave Charles de Gaulle, Centre Ville)

PRACTICALITIES

■ The *Cameroon Tribune* is the government-owned bilingual daily. The thrice-weekly *Le Messager* (in French) is the main independent newspaper.

■ Most broadcast programming is government run and in French, through Cameroon Radio-TV Corporation (CRTV). TVs at top-end hotels often have CNN or French news stations.

■ Electricity supply is 220V and plugs are of the European two-round-pin variety.

■ Cameroon uses the metric system.

Liberia (Map p283; ☎ 223 0521, 221 1296; Blvd de l'URSS, Bastos)
Nigeria Buea (☎ 332 2528; Nigeria Consulate Rd; ☽ 8am-4pm Mon-Fri); Douala (Map pp286-7; ☎ 343 2168; Blvd de la Liberté); Yaoundé (Map p283; ☎ 223 4551; Rue Joseph Mballa Eloumden, Bastos; ☽ 9.30am-3.30pm Mon-Fri) Visas not issued in Douala.
UK Douala (Map pp286-7; ☎ 342 8896; Immeuble Standard Chartered, Blvd de la Liberté); Yaoundé (Map p283; ☎ 222 0545; Ave Churchill, Centre Ville)
USA Douala (Map pp286-7; ☎ 342 5331; Immeuble Flatters, off Ave de Gaulle, Bonanjo); Yaoundé (Map p284; ☎ 220 1500; Rue de Nachtigal, Centre Ville)

EMERGENCIES

☎ 112 is the number for all emergencies, but it really only applies in big cities.

FESTIVALS & EVENTS

Tabaski (p294) is the biggest festival celebrated in Cameroon, with the most festivities taking place in Foumban. Each February Cameroonian and international athletes gather for the **Race of Hope** to the summit of Mt Cameroon, attracting large crowds of spectators. Considerably faster than the leisurely hike most people opt for, winners usually finish in a staggering 4½ hours for men and 5½ hours for women. For more information contact **Fako Tourist Board** (p289) in Limbe or the **Fédération Camerounaise d'Athlétisme** (☎ 222 4744) in Yaoundé.

HOLIDAYS

Public holidays include the following:
New Year's Day 1 January
Youth Day 11 February
Easter March/April

Labour Day 1 May
National Day 20 May
Assumption Day 15 August
Christmas Day 25 December

Islamic holidays are also observed throughout Cameroon (see p1140).

INTERNET ACCESS

Internet access can be found in any town of a reasonable size. Connections range from decent to awful, and costs average CFA300 to CFA600 per hour.

MONEY

The unit of currency is the Central African Franc (CFA), which is pegged to the West African Franc. Cash is king in Cameroon, especially in remote regions where it's the only way to pay – bring plenty of euros. Banks regularly refuse to change travellers cheques, and charge around 5% commission when they do – try Bicec, SGBC, Crédit Lyonnais and Standard Chartered Bank.

Most towns now have at least one ATM, which is always tied to the Visa network. SGBC is usually the most reliable when using foreign cards. Banks won't generally offer cash advances on credit cards. If you get stuck, Western Union has branches throughout Cameroon for international money transfers.

Express Exchange moneychangers change travellers cheques and US dollars cash; there are branches in Yaoundé, Douala, Bamenda and Buea, with further plans for expansion.

POST

Yaoundé and Douala have reliable poste restante services at their central post offices, with letters held for about two weeks (CFA200 per letter collected). International post is fairly reliable for letters, but international couriers should be preferred for packages – there are branches in all large towns.

TELEPHONE

There are private Téléboutiques or streetside phone stands in all towns. International calls cost about CFA1000 per minute. Internet telephony is increasingly popular, costing around a quarter of normal rates. Mobile numbers begin with 7, 8 or 9. There are no city area codes in Cameroon – all landline numbers begin with a 2 or 3. The seven-digit numbers provided in this chapter work inside Cameroon, but if calling from outside the country, press the first digit twice, ie 345-6789 in Cameroon would be 3345-6789 outside of the country.

VISAS

Visas are required for all travellers and must be bought prior to arrival in the country. At Cameroonian embassies in neighbouring countries, visas are issued quickly for around US$60. Applications in Europe and the US will require a confirmed flight ticket, hotel reservation and proof of funds for the trip (a copy of a recent bank statement should suffice).

Visa Extensions

You can obtain visa extensions at the **Ministry of Immigration** (Map p284; ☎ 222 2413; Ave Mdug-Fouda Ada) in Yaoundé, where one photo plus CFA15,000 is required.

Visas for Onward Travel

Thirty-day visas for Central African Republic (CFA35,000), Chad (CFA30,000), Congo (CFA70,000), Equatorial Guinea (CFA37,000), Gabon (CFA37,000) and other nearby countries are available from embassies in Yaoundé; see opposite. For visas to Nigeria, see p478.

TRANSPORT IN CAMEROON

GETTING THERE & AWAY
Air

Both Yaoundé and Douala have international airports linking Cameroon to major cities in Africa and Europe. Cameroon Airlines went under in 2008, so Cameroon has no national carrier. The departure tax stands at CFA10,000, or US$20.

Land

Neighbouring countries' borders are open, but the border with Congo is sometime closed, so check in advance.

CENTRAL AFRICAN REPUBLIC

The standard, if rough, route is via Garoua-Boulaï (p301), which straddles the border, and on to Bangui (via Bouar). An alternative is to travel to Kenzou, south of Batouri.

CAMEROON

CHAD

Travellers head to Kousséri in the north for the border near N'Djaména. Minibuses go to Kousséri from Maroua; some of the border officials have been known to rip travellers off.

CONGO

This border is as remote as you can get, but possible to reach if it's the dry season. From Yokadouma, travel south to Sokamba, where you can catch a ferry (large enough for 4WDs) or *pirogue* (traditional canoe) across the Ngoko River to the Congolese port of Ouesso. From there, head for Pokola and the logging road to Brazzaville. If you come this way, you should visit Congo's Parc National Nouabalé-N'doki (see p571). It's one of the best parks in Central Africa, and is (relatively) convenient to access from here.

EQUATORIAL GUINEA & GABON

The main border crossings into Equatorial Guinea and Gabon are a few kilometres from each other, and are accessible from Ambam. The road splits here, with the easterly route heading for Bitam and Libreville (Gabon) and the westerly route heading for Ebebiyin and Bata (Equatorial Guinea).

The Cameroon–Equatorial Guinea border at Campo is normally closed.

NIGERIA

To and from Nigeria the main crossing points are Ekok, west of Mamfe, where you cross to Mfum for shared taxis to Calabar (treacherous in the rainy season), and at Banki in the extreme north for crossings to Maiduguri.

Sea
NIGERIA

A twice-weekly ferry sails from Limbe to Calabar on Monday and Thursday, and in the opposite direction every Tuesday and Friday – see p291. Boats are dangerous and not recommended.

GETTING AROUND
Air

For internal flights, try **Elysian Airlines** (☎ 9909 8748; www.elysianairlines.com) or **Toumai Air Tchad** (☎ 7420 8734, 7711 0974; www.toumaiair.com). Flights between Douala and Yaoundé cost around CFA30,000 one way; from Douala to Maroua they will cost around CFA125,000 one way.

Bus

Agences de voyages (agency buses) run along all major and many minor routes in Cameroon. Prices are low and fixed, and on some bus lines you can even reserve a seat. From Yaoundé to Douala it costs CFA3800 and from N'Gaoundéré to Maroua CFA6000. However, some drivers are extremely reckless, and bus accidents occur all too frequently. *Taxis brousses* (bush taxis) are also popular.

Train

Cameroon's rail system (Camrail) operates three main lines: Yaoundé to N'Gaoundéré; Yaoundé to Douala; and Douala to Kumba. In practice, only the first one is of interest to travellers, as it's the main way to get between the southern and northern halves of the country. For details, see p285.

CAMEROON

Côte d'Ivoire

Côte d'Ivoire offers a wealth of starfish-studded beaches and pockets of deep, green jungle – the domain of forest elephants, tangled lianas, savannah palms and fat mahogany trees.

However, CI lost its footing as a travel destination when a 2002 rebellion tore the country in half. From that moment on, travellers forgot about the beaches, hearing only the echoes of gunfire in their minds. Though political insecurity is still a possibility, the country is gradually embracing peace.

Head to Abidjan, where shimmering skyscrapers and cathedral spires pierce the heavens. When the daylight fades, sit back with a cocktail and watch the blue sky blush, making room for nightfall, warm laughter and the clever beats of *coupé-decalé* (see p309). Try *poisson braisé* and listen as musicians tease bass notes from banjos. Check out colonial architecture, spot monkeys between baobab trees, and make footprints on white-sand beaches embroidered with shells and sea urchins.

Though its beaches most certainly are perfect, Côte d'Ivoire is not. The skyscrapers of Abidjan stand tall, but forests have fallen. Yet these early days of peace taste as good as the chocolate produced from this soil, and that's something worth sharing.

FAST FACTS

- **Area** 322,465 sq km
- **ATMs** In Abidjan and Yamoussoukro
- **Borders** Liberia, Ghana, Mali, Burkina Faso, Guinea
- **Budget** US$70 to US$100 per day in Abidjan, US$30 to US$60 elsewhere
- **Capital** Yamoussoukro
- **Languages** French, Mande, Malinke, Dan, Senoufo, Baoulé, Agni, Dioula
- **Money** West African CFA franc; US$1 = CFA463, €1 = CFA656
- **Population** 18.4 million
- **Seasons** Wet (May to July and October to November), hot and humid (rest of the year)
- **Telephone** Country code ☎ 225; international acess code ☎ 00
- **Time** GMT/UTC
- **Visa** Required by almost everyone (Americans are no longer exempt) – arrange in advance; also covered by the Visa des Pays de l'Entente (see p1147)

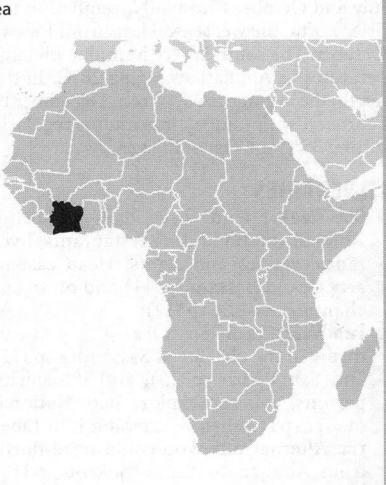

WARNING

Due to the risk of political insecurity in the north and west at the time of research, we were unable to travel to some areas outside of Abidjan. Instead, we relied on friends and journalists working in those places for our research. At the time of writing, the British Foreign and Commonwealth Office was advising against travel to areas north of Bouaké. See p315 for more information.

HIGHLIGHTS

- **Abidjan** (p309) Order Ivorian haute cuisine, then, as night falls, dance to *coupé-decalé* – never taking your eyes off the illuminated skyline.
- **Grand Bassam** (p311) Get some downtime, explore colonial streets and ride horses along white-sand beaches.
- **Man** (p314) Watch stilt dancers; hike to the summit of Mt Tonkoui and, breathless, take in the view of three West African countries.
- **Assinie** (p312) Take a lazy *pirogue* ride, watch surfers slide to shore and tuck into *poisson braisé* under the stars.
- **Yamoussoukro** (p313) Explore the quiet village that became a shiny capital.

CLIMATE & WHEN TO GO

The south has two wet seasons: May through July and October through November. In the drier north, the wet season lasts from June to October. The south is very humid, with temperatures in Abidjan averaging 28°C. In the north, the average is 26°C from December to February, with midday maximums regularly hitting 35°C the rest of the year.

ITINERARIES

- **One Week** Spend three days exploring Abidjan (p309) and its restaurants, live-music venues and sights. Head east to arty Grand Bassam (p311) and on to enchanting Assinie (p312).
- **Two Weeks** With an extra week you can throw in the charms of Sassandra (p312) and San Pédro (p313), and if security permits, you can explore Parc National du Taï (p313) before crossing into Liberia. Alternatively, you could head north from Abidjan to Yamassoukrou (p313) and on to Man (p314).

HISTORY

Until the 1840s, the indigenous people of Côte d'Ivoire were protected from European colonialism by the inhospitable coastline. In this relative isolation, kingdoms such as the Krou, Senoufo, Lubi, Malinke and Akan flourished. When the French began a big push towards colonising the region, they met fierce resistance, but eventually took control, trading for ivory and establishing coffee and cocoa plantations, which are still the backbone of the economy today.

When independence came in 1960, Félix Houphouët-Boigny was the obvious choice for president. Born in 1905, Houphouët-Boigny was a labour leader who turned his trade union into a pro-Independence political party. He was elected to the French parliament and eventually became the first African to be a minister in a European government. His policies were, for a long time, wildly successful – Côte d'Ivoire became the world's largest producer of cocoa and the economy maintained a 10% annual growth rate for 20 years. But it didn't last. World recession, drought, collapsing prices on agricultural products and over-logging all contributed to Côte d'Ivoire's economic troubles. Although Houphouët-Boigny initiated hardship measures, he was re-elected in the 1990 elections, which were open to other parties for the first time. He died in 1993 after 33 years as the country's president.

HOW MUCH?

- **Hand-spun Korhogo cloth** CFA10,000 to CFA30,000
- **Coupé-decalé album** CFA2000
- **Shared taxi across town** CFA200
- **Local celebrity magazine** CFA1700
- **Mobile phone top-up voucher** CFA1000

LONELY PLANET INDEX

- **1L petrol** CFA425
- **1.5L bottled water** CFA500
- **Bottle of Flag beer** CFA650
- **Souvenir football shirt** CFA3000
- **Plate of poisson braisé aloco** CFA800

CÔTE D'IVOIRE

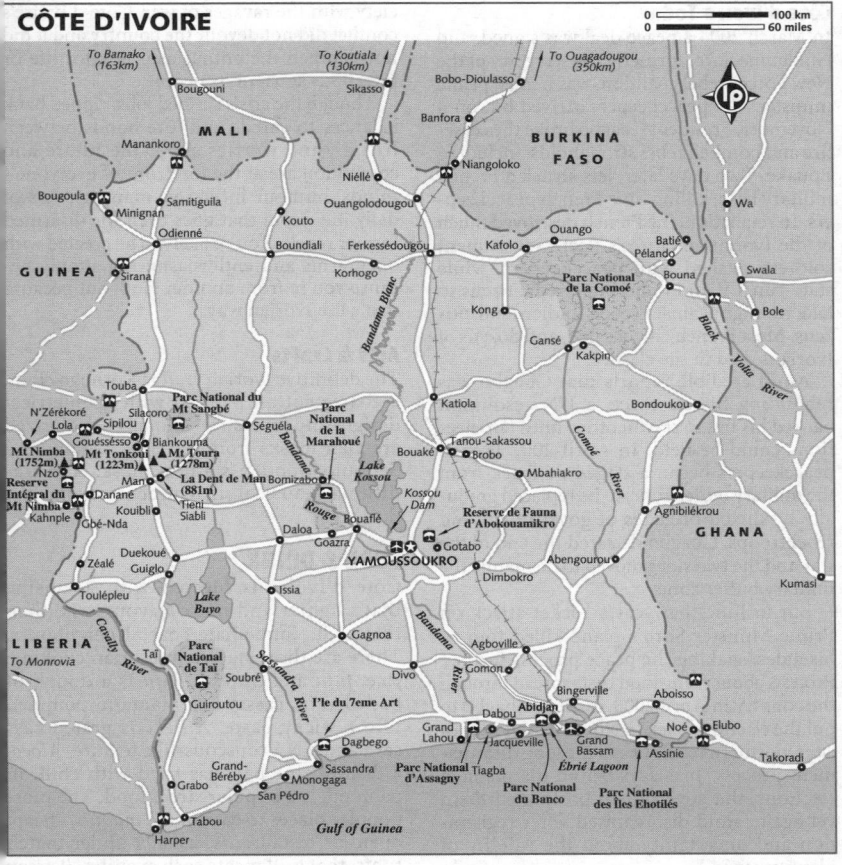

CÔTE D'IVOIRE

In December 1999, Côte d'Ivoire suffered its first coup. President Bédié, Houphouët-Boigny's handpicked successor, was overthrown by forces local to General Robert Guei. In the elections held in October 2000, Guéi declared himself the official winner, but was chased from power by massive popular uprisings. His successor, Laurence Gbagbo, faced a number of attempted coups and tensions in the first two years of his presidency.

On 19 September 2002, troops from the north gained control of much of the country. Initially, a ceasefire was agreed to between the government and the rebels, who had the full backing of the mostly Islamic northern populace, but the truce was short-lived

and fighting resumed, this time also over prime cocoa-growing areas. France sent in troops to maintain the ceasefire boundaries; meanwhile, Liberian tensions from that country's war began to spill over the border, which escalated the crisis in parts of western Côte d'Ivoire.

In January 2003, President Gbagbo and the leaders of the New Forces, a newly formed coalition of the rebel groups, signed accords creating a 'government of national unity', with representatives of the rebels taking up places in a new cabinet. Curfews that had been in place at the height of the conflict were lifted and French troops cleaned up the lawless western border, but the harmony was short-lived.

Côte d'Ivoire Today

In March 2004 a peace deal was signed, and Guillaume Soro, formerly the secretary of the New Forces rebel coalition, was named prime minister. UN peacekeepers arrived but on 4 November, President Gbagbo broke the cease-fire and bombed rebel strongholds, including Bouaké. Two days later, jets struck a French military base, killing nine French peacekeepers. In retaliation, the French destroyed much of the Ivorian air force's fleet. Government soldiers clashed with peacekeepers, while state-run TV and radio implored citizens to take revenge against French soldiers and citizens. Most French citizens fled, and dozens of Ivorians died in the clashes.

Amid credible reports that Gbagbo was rebuilding his air force, a UN resolution backed his bid to stay in office until fair elections could be held. In April 2007 French peacekeepers began a staged pullback from the military buffer zone, to be replaced gradually by mixed brigades of government and rebel troops. Gbagbo declared the end of the war and the two sides moved to dismantle the military buffer zone.

But in June that year a rocket attack on Prime Minister Soro's plane killed four of his aides, shaking the peace process further. Protests about rising food costs spread through the country in April 2008, causing Gbagbo to put the elections back to November. A month later, northern rebels began the long disarmament process. Just days before the planned elections, the government postponed them yet again, amid disorganised voter registration and uncertainty about the validity of identity cards.

Côte d'Ivoire began to embrace a wary peace and was looking to 2010 elections. In early 2010, however, President Laurent Gbagbo dissolved both the government and the electoral commission. Voter registration was suspended and Gbagbo declared that the peace process was under threat. At the time of research, the much-hyped election date was – yet again – up in the air.

CULTURE

Ivorians have become used to living on an emotional rollercoaster. But it's both ironic and testament to their spirit that, though the north and south could not get along for so long, Ivorians have been able to reconcile living in a modern, relatively progressive society with the ravages of war. Côte d'Ivoire's conflict did not devour the country and it did not dampen the enthusiasm, joy for life or infectious spirit of its people.

Though the crisis slashed jobs, ripped bank balances to shreds and tore bonds between friends, and worries about the future and corruption are at the forefront of everyone's minds, humour infiltrates many aspects of daily life – and that goes even for disarmed former rebels. You're likely to be greeted with open arms and enthusiasm, not simply because you're from another land, but because that's the Ivorian way.

Arts & Crafts

The definitive Ivorian craft is Korhogo cloth, a coarse cotton painted with geometrical designs and fantastical animals. Also prized are Dan masks from the Man region, and Senoufo wooden statues, masks and traditional musical instruments from the northeast.

FOOD & DRINK

Côte d'Ivoire is blessed with a cuisine that's lighter and more flavoursome than that of its immediate coastal neighbours. There are three staples in Ivorian cooking: rice, *fufu* and *attiéké*. *Fufu* is a dough of boiled yam, cassava or plantain, pounded into a sticky paste. *Attiéké* is grated cassava and has a couscous-like texture. *Aloco,* a dish of ripe bananas fried with chilli in palm oil, is a popular street food. The most popular places to eat out are *maquis,* cheap, open-air restaurants, usually under thatch roofs, that grill meats each evening. *Poisson braisé,* a delicate dish of grilled fish with tomatoes and onions cooked in ginger, is a must.

The standard beer is Flag, but if you're after a premium lager, call for a locally brewed Tuborg.

ENVIRONMENT

Côte d'Ivoire used to be covered in dense rainforest, but most of it was cleared during the agricultural boom, and what remains today is under attack from illegal logging. According to 2008 World Bank data, Côte d'Ivoire is still losing more than 3000 sq km of forested land per year.

Several peaks in the west rise more than 1000m, and a coastal lagoon with a unique

COUPÉ-DECALÉ: CUT AND RUN

Picture the scene: it's 2002 and you're at the swish l'Atlantic nightclub in Paris. Around you, tight-shirted Ivorian guys are living it up – knocking back champagne, throwing euros into the air and grinding their hips on the dance floor.

Coupé-decalé is one of the most important music movements to hit Côte d'Ivoire. From the French verb couper, meaning to cheat, and decaler, to run away, the term loosely translates as 'cut and run'. It evolved as a comment on the shrewd but stylish Ivorian and Burkinabé guys – modern-day Robin Hoods, if you like – who ran away to France at the height of the conflict in 2002, where they garnered big bucks and sent money home to their families.

Known as 'the jet set', they splashed the rest of their cash on the Paris club scene and it wasn't unusual for them to shower audiences with crisp notes. The late Douk Saga, one of the founders of the movement, was famous for wearing two designer suits to his shows. Halfway through, he'd strip provocatively and throw one into the crowd.

It wasn't long before this music genre took off in Côte d'Ivoire, becoming increasingly popular as the conflict raged on. With curfews in place and late-night venues closed, Ivorians started going dancing in the mornings. The more normal life was suppressed, the more they wanted to break free from the shackles of war. Coupé-decalé, the who-gives-a-damn dance, allowed them to do exactly that.

Early coupé-decalé was characterised by repetitive vocals set to fast, jerky beats. Lyrics were either superficial, facetious or flippant – 'we don't know where we're going, but we're going anyway', sang DJ Jacab – and for many Ivorians, listening to the music became a form of escapism. As the trend has matured, coupé-decalé lyrics have become smarter, more socially aware and dripping with double and triple entendres. Listening out for the puns and wordplays may not be quite as challenging as doing the New York Times crossword, but it's not a million miles off, either. The movement is now a national source of pride and, above all, a comment on Ivorian society. Despite years of conflict, misery and fear, Ivorians have never stopped dancing.

Today's coupé-decalé is cheeky, crazy and upbeat, and to fully appreciate it you should get yourself to an Abidjan dance floor. Tracks to seek out include Bablée's 'Sous Les Cocotiers', Kaysha's 'Faut Couper Decaler', 'Magic Ambiance' by Magic System, DJ Jacab's 'On Sait Pas Ou On Va', 'Guantanamo' by DJ Zidane and Douk Saga's 'Sagacité'. The latter spawned the Drogbacité dance craze, inspired by the footballer Didier Drogba. In 2006 DJ Lewis' hugely popular 'Grippe Aviaire' did for bird flu what early coupé-decalé did for the conflict – it replaced fear with joy.

ecosystem stretches 300km west from the Ghanaian border. The north is dry scrubland.

ABIDJAN

pop 5 million

Abidjan, Côte d'Ivoire's capital in all but name, looks like it could be a mirage. The city's interlinked peninsulas and lagoons look more like a hedonistic slice of Manhattan than the West African city that many travellers picture prior to their arrival. Restaurants dish up Ivorian haute cuisine, daring structures rub the clouds and hip boutiques welcome Ivorian fashionistas. As it rises curiously from the calm waters of a lagoon, Côte d'Ivoire's economic engine will surely show you a good time.

INFORMATION
Internet Access

Internet access is widely available in Abidjan and most large hotels offer wi-fi to their guests.

Inkoo (☎ 21-247065; Cap Sud Centre Commercial & Gallerie Sococé, Deux Plateaux; ☽ 9am-8pm) Speedy connections, a printing centre, phone booths, faxes and scanners.

Medical Services

The US embassy publishes a list of recommended practitioners on its website (http://abidjan.usembassy.gov).

Polyclinique des Deux Plateaux (☎ 22-413320; Deux Plateaux)

PISAM (Polyclinique Internationale St Anne-Marie; ☎ 22-445132; off Blvd de la Corniche, Cocody) Recommended by UN staff. Has a 24-hour intensive care unit.

CÔTE D'IVOIRE

Money

Euros and dollars can be changed at main branches of banks in Le Plateau. Most branches of SGBCI and Bicici have ATMs that accept Visa, MasterCard and Maestro.

Bicici Bank (www.bibici.org; Ave Delafosse) Has an ATM.

SGBCI Bank (www.sgbci.org; Ave Anoma) Good ATM option – accepts Visa, MasterCard and Maestro.

Post & Telephone

For postal services, head to **La Poste** (Place de la République; 🕒 7.30am-noon & 2.30-4pm Mon-Fri), which also has a Western Union and poste restante. Mobile phone SIM cards are sold on the roadside all around town (from CFA2000). Inkoo (see p309) has phone booths for local, national and international calls.

Tourist Information

Côte d'Ivoire Tourisme (🕿 20-251600/10; Place de la République, Le Plateau; 🕒 7.30am-noon & 2.30-4pm Mon-Fri) There's a good map on the wall and the helpful staff will happily shower you with brochures.

Travel Agencies

Agence Catran (🕿 21-759163; Blvd de Marseille, Zone 4)

Amak Agence (🕿 20-211755; www.amak-interna tional.com; Ground fl, Botreau Roussel Bldg, Le Plateau)

SIGHTS

Abidjan gets props for its breathtaking skyline. It all started with **La Pyramide** (cnr Ave Franchet d'Esperey & Rue Botreau-Roussel), by the Italian architect Olivieri. Designed by the Italian Aldo Spiritom, the **Cathedrale St Paul** (Blvd Angoulvant, Le Plateau; admission free; 🕒 8am-7pm) is a bold and innovative modern cathedral. The stained glasswork is as warm and rich as that inside the Yamassoukrou basilica. The **Musée National** (Blvd Nangul Abrogoua, Le Plateau; admission CFA2000; 🕒 9am-5pm Tue-Sat) houses a dusty but interesting collection of traditional art and craftwork, including wooden statues and masks, pottery, ivory and bronze. On the northwest edge of town is the cool and shaded **Parc du Banco** (Autoroute de Nord; admission CFA1000) rainforest reserve. It has pleasant walking trails, majestic trees and a lake, but you'll be lucky to see any wildlife. Though it's had some bad press in the past (escaped prisoners and ousted rebels hung out here during the crisis), if you pay CFA3000, the rangers will give you a guided tour.

SLEEPING

Hôtel le Marly (🕿 21-258552; Blvd de Marseille, Zone 4; s/d/ste CFA40,000/50,000/60,000; 🅿 🆇 🍴 🔊) Le Marly offers simple plantation-style huts in a pretty garden setting. At the end of a short track just off Blvd de Marseille.

Hostellerie de la Licorne (🕿 22-410730; www.licog riff.com; Rue des Jardins, Deux Plateaux Vallons; r CFA40,000-70,000; 🅿 🆇 🖥 🔊) Owned by a friendly, bilingual French couple, this is our favourite place to stay in Abidjan. Each room is clean, spacious and stylish. There's also a pool and restaurant.

Le Griffon (🕿 22-416622; www.licogriff.com; Rue des Jardins, Deux Plateaux Vallons; r CFA40,000-70,000; 🆇 🖥 🔊) This boutique hotel offers beautifully decorated rooms complete with Ivorian art and coffee-table books. With friendly staff, great food, wi-fi and a hot tub in the backyard, it's a gem.

Residence Eburnéa (🕿 22-527005; www.residence -eburnea.net; 7eme tranche, Deux Plateaux; r CFA40,000/60,000; 🅿 🆇 🖥 🔊) This place has several types of room, including charming duplexes and cute apartments with miniature kitchens and balconies. There's also a small pool and wi-fi access.

Le Wafou (🕿 21-256201/2; Blvd de Marseille, Zone 4; standard/ste bungalow CFA48,000/100,000; 🅿 🆇 🖥 🔊) If the Flintstones won the lottery and moved to Mali, they'd live somewhere like this. Le Wafou's gorgeous bungalows take cues from traditional Dogon villages. At night you can enjoy great food and wine beside the stylish pool-bar area. A hit with kids, too.

Le Pullman Abidjan (🕿 20-302020; www.sofitel. com; Rue Abdoulaye Fadiga, Le Plateau; r/ste US $206/209; 🅿 🆇 🖥 🔊 🔊) This is the best of the upmarket chain hotels. Loads of plush rooms equipped with wi-fi and everything you could possibly need.

EATING

For food on the run, Mille Maquis should be your first stop. This part of town (in the Marcory district north of Zone 4) is teeming with *maquis* – it's a sprawling, overgrown food market blaring *coupé-decalé* music.

Allocodrome (Rue Washington, Cocody; mains around CFA2000; 🕒 dinner) This fantastic outdoor spot, with dozens of vendors grilling meats, sizzles until late.

Le Nandjelet (opposite cemetery, Blockosso; mains from CFA2000; 🕒 dinner) Tucked away in Blockosso, this enchanting local spot offers good, basic fare.

Make a beeline for one of the outdoor tables on the edge of the lagoon – they offer a breathtaking panorama of the Abidjan skyline.

La Maison des Combattants (Ave Marchand, Le Plateau; mains from CFA5000; ☯ lunch & dinner) Next to the war memorial, this restaurant, housed in a renovated colonial building, has a great range of dishes, including escargot, *sauce feuille* (manioc-leaf sauce with beef tail, fish and crab) and other dishes not often found in sit-down restaurants.

Galerie Kajazoma (☎ 21-246416; Rue G177/Marconi, Zone 4; mains from CFA7000; ☯ noon-late Mon-Sat) Part art gallery, part restaurant, this is one of our favourite places to eat in Abidjan. Grab a table in the garden or head inside, where everything is for sale – from painted plates to sofas.

Le Grand Large (☎ 21-242113; 149 Blvd de Marseille; mains from CFA13,000; ☯ dinner) This French-run, upmarket dining room has a first-rate menu – everything from foie gras to crème brûlée, Irish coffees, and chocolate and caramel tart.

Chez Georges (☎ 20-321084; www.restaurantchez georges.com; Rue du Commerce, Le Plateau; ☯ lunch & dinner) The menu here is huge – everything from *salade Roquefort* to stuffed crab, duck and *steak-frites* – though not to the detriment of the food.

DRINKING

Expats and travellers congregate at **Le Bidule** (cnr Blvd du 7 Decembre & Rue Paul Langevin, Zone 4) on weekends, a drinking lounge with walls the colour of Ivorian soil. **Havana Café** (Rue Mercedes, Zone 4) is also a perennial favourite. There's a tiled counter bar, and the South American theme is reflected in the great mojitos. For a bit of Ivorian bling, head to **Place Vendôme** (Blvd de la Republique, Le Plateau), which is almost as fancy as its Paris namesake, or **Le Café Theatre** (Blvd du 7 Decembre, Zone 4).

If you're into reggae, **Parker Place** (www.parkerplaceabidjan.com; Rue Paul Langevin, Zone 4) is an Abidjan institution, not least because Alpha Blondy and Tiken Jah Fakoly played here before they were famous. On Friday and Saturday, **Rue Princesse** in the working-class district of Youpagon becomes a cross between London's Notting Hill Carnival and Bangkok's Khao San Rd. In 2008, President Gbago went dancing at **Le Queen** (Rue Princesse, Youpagon) – owned by the footballer Didier Drogba – to signify the end of the crisis.

GETTING THERE & AWAY

The shiny Félix Houphouët-Boigny International Airport takes all of the international air traffic. The main bus station is the chaotic Gare Routière d'Adjamé, some 4km north of Le Plateau. Most UTB and Sotra buses and bush taxis leave from here, and there's frequent transport to all major towns.

Bush taxis and minibuses for destinations east along the coast, such as Grand Bassam, Aboisso and Elubo at the Ghanaian border, leave primarily from the Gare de Bassam on the corner of Rue 38 and Blvd Valéry Giscard d'Estaing, south of Treichville.

GETTING AROUND

Woro-woro (shared taxis) cost between CFA250 and CFA700, depending on the length of the journey. They vary in colour according to their allocated area. Those between Plateau, Adjamé, Marcory and Treichville, for example, are red, while those in Les Deux Plateaux and Cocody are yellow, and Yopougon's are blue.

A short hop in a cab from Le Plateau to Zone 4 costs around CFA2000 at the time of research. If you want to hire a taxi driver for a day, bank on between CFA18,000 and CFA30,000.

THE EASTERN BEACHES

GRAND BASSAM
☎ 21

Hugged by a long, white, sandy beach, laid-back Grand Bassam feels a world away from gridlocked Abidjan. Arty and full of faded glory, it wasn't so long ago (1893) that Bassam, as it's known, was declared capital of the French colony. Six years later a major yellow-fever epidemic broke out, prompting the French to move their capital to Bingerville.

The city is laid out on a long spit of land with a quiet lagoon on one side and the turbulent Atlantic Ocean on the other. If you take a dip, watch the (strong) currents.

A walk through town will take you past the **colonial buildings** the city is known for, some being restored while others are slowly falling apart. The **Palais de Justice**, on Blvd Treich-Laplene, should be your first stop. Built in 1910, it was in this building that members of Côte d'Ivoire's PDCI-RDA political group –

that of Houphouët-Boigny – were arrested by the French authorities in 1949; a struggle that preceded independence. The **Musée National du Costume** (Blvd Treich-Laplene; admission by donation), in the former governor's palace, has a nice little exhibit showing housing styles of various ethnic groups.

If you're in the market for an Ivorian painting, head to **Nick Amon's art gallery** on Blvd Treich-Laplene. One of Côte d'Ivoire's most-respected contemporary artists, he'll greet you with paint-splattered clothing and a warm smile. His canvases start at around CFA50,000; profits go to an organisation that gives street kids art classes. Augustin Édou runs a **horse-riding school** on the same street (next to La Playa hotel). You can arrange riding trips (one-/two-hour for CFA13,000/20,000) along the coast at sunrise. Dugout-canoe trips to see traditional crab fishers, mangroves and birdlife can be arranged with local boatmen.

Sleeping & Eating

There are guesthouses spread all along Blvd Treich-Laplene, Bassam's main road.

Hôtel Boblin la Mer (☎ 21-301418; Blvd Treich-Laplene; r with air-con CFA15,000-20,000; P ✖) Easily the best value in Bassam, the rooms here are decorated with masks and woodcarvings, and breakfast is served on the beach.

Taverne la Bassamoise (☎ 21-301062; Blvd Treich-Laplene; r/bungalows incl breakfast CFA25,000/29,000; P ✖ ✖) It's worth a visit just to check out the courtyard – wooden monkeys and parrots hang from every branch of a colossal tree. Bungalows (a little shabby) are hidden underneath a canopy of bougainvillea.

Koral Beach Annexe (☎ 21-302589; r with fan from CFA25,000; P ✖) Koral Beach has a pool and a handful of bungalows, but it's better known for its restaurant. The menu includes French starters and the best pizzas (CFA8000) outside of Abidjan.

Étoile du Sud (☎ 21-302939; Blvd Treich-Laplene; standard/ste CFA45,000/60,000 P ✖ ▢ 🛜 ✖) Bassam's upmarket option, dressed with stylish woodcarvings and comfortable sofas. Outside, there's a large pool with its own (excellent) restaurant and bar. It has the fastest wi-fi in town.

Getting There & Away

Shared taxis (CFA500, 40 minutes) leave from Abidjan's Gare de Bassam. In Bassam, the

gare routière (bus station) is beside the Place de Paix roundabout, north of the lagoon.

ASSINIE

Quiet little Assinie tugs at the heartstrings of overlanders, washed-up surfers and rich weekenders from Abidjan who run their quad bikes up and down its peroxide-blonde beach. Perhaps because Assinie is split into several parts – Assinie village, Assinie Mafia and Assouindé – somehow they all coexist in relative harmony. If you're here to surf, watch the undertows; they can be strong.

Sleeping & Eating

The following options are in the Assouinde part of town. Assinie Mafia has a small selection of resort-style hotels and the eccentric Crocodile Dipi reptile farm. At the time of research there were plans to renovate the old Club Med resort on the beach.

L'Hotel de l'Amitié (☎ 07-135300; s/d CFA20,000/30,000) This great Burkinabé-run guesthouse tunes right into the Assinie vibe. The wooden dining area (mains from CFA2000) is so close to the sea that you can taste the sea spray. It's the kind of place where you can share overlanding stories by candlelight over a good bottle of red and a seafood salad.

ourpick Hôtel l'Océan (☎ 05-668189; r from CFA35,000) Run by Ivorian–North African friends, whitewashed l'Océ has clean, comfy rooms with sea views.

O Sole Mio (☎ 07-872771/05-964913; r/ste CFA38,000/48,000; ✖) Antonio's (you'll be on first-name terms before long) beachfront set-up gets props for its luxurious rooms and wooden-roofed Italian restaurant serving good salads and pastas.

Getting There & Around

Coming from Grand Bassam or Abidjan, take a shared taxi to Samo (CFA2000, 45 min). From here you can pick up another car to Assouinde, 15 minutes away. Once there, the rest of the area is accessible by *pirogue* (traditional canoe) or shared taxi.

THE WEST COAST

SASSANDRA & AROUND
☎ 34

Though it's looking a little dog-eared these days, there's something endearing about Sassandra, with its colourful Fanti fish-

NUT-CRACKING CHIMPS

The threatened chimps of Parc National de Taï have a special talent: they're one of the world's few documented groups of chimps to have mastered the knack of using fairly advanced tools. Animal-behaviour researchers and some anthropologists believe their techniques mirror those of early humans.

First the chimp selects its stone. The art of selection is believed to be passed down from generation to generation – because no carving is involved, each stone must already look like a perfect nutcracker. Next the chimp heads to a tree bearing nuts to its taste; it can't be any old tree, however – it must have a nook or tree stump nearby to serve as an anvil. With the golf-ball sized nut of choice in hand, it lifts the hammer and…wait! It takes at least seven years to master the art of nut cracking. The chimp's mother will have to give it a lesson first, and it will have to grow a little. It takes around 1000kg of force to break open the nut without bashing it to pieces.

Prime nut-cracking season runs from February to August. Each large nut contains around 30 calories so, on a good day, an expert nut cracker will break open around 100 of those to get their nutritional fill for the day. It's an exercise in precision, care and skill.

ing harbour and impressive ocean views. It's also the gateway to **Best of Africa** (☎ 34-720606; best@bestofafrica.org; bungalow CFA40,000-60,000; ⓟ 🕮 🖳), a gorgeous low-key resort, 35km east of Sassandra at **Dagbego**, offering wood-clad bungalows a few metres from the calm waters of Dagbego Beach.

In Sassandra itself, **Hôtel le Pollet** (☎ 34-720578; lepollet@hotmail.fr; Route du Palais de Justice; r/ste CFA17,000/CFA38,000; 🕮) overlooks the Sassandra river. Rooms are splashed with Ivorian art and some have sunken beds. Its open-air Le Phare Ouest restaurant whips up Ivorian and European dishes. A cheaper option is the **Hôtel Grau** (☎ 34-720521; r with fan/air-con CFA5000/CFA8000; 🕮) right in the centre of town, a short walk from the market. Near the post office, **La Route de la Cuisine** (meals from CFA1000) throws the day's catch on the grill, sometimes including swordfish and barracuda.

SAN PÉDRO
☎ 34

Closer to Liberia than Abidjan, San Pédro has a far-flung feel. It's also the jumping-off point for the **Parc National de Taï** (☎ 712353; www.parc-national-de-tai.org), one of the largest remaining virgin rainforests in West Africa. At the time of research, the park was still closed to visitors (rebels sheltered here during the conflict), but there are plans to run excursions to visit the park's population of tool-using chimpanzees (see above). Enquire at Hotel Sophia for more information.

In San Pédro itself, **Les Jardins d'Ivoire** (☎ 713186; Quartier Balmer; r CFA25,000; ⓟ 🕮 🖳)

has elegant rooms and good food. On the outskirts of town, **Hôtel Sophia** (☎ 713434; Rue a la Plage; s/d CFA40,000/50,000; ⓟ 🕮 🖳) is also pretty plush and has a saltwater pool overlooking the bay.

UTB buses link San Pédro with Abidjan once daily (CFA5000). Shared taxis go west to the balmy beaches of **Grand-Béréby** (CFA2500) and east to Sassandra (CFA3000). For Harper, just across the Liberian border, you can take a shared taxi to Tabou (about CFA4000), then continue on to by a combination of road and boat; it's not worth attempting in the rainy season.

THE CENTRE

YAMOUSSOUKRO
☎ 30

Six-lane highways leading nowhere, streetlights brighter than the stars and impressive monuments too hard to get to, to Yamkro (as it's affectionately dubbed) is known mainly for its basilica and other grandiose excesses – all pet projects of Félix Houphouët-Boigny, who was born here.

Sights

Yamassoukrou's spectacular **basilica** (route de Daloa; admission CFA2000; 🕑 8am-noon & 2-5.30pm Mon-Sat, 2-5pm Sun) will leave you wide eyed. It remains in tip-top shape, with English-speaking guides on duty. Don't forget to take your passport, which the guard holds until you leave. The **presidential palace**, where Houphouët-Boigny is now buried, can only be seen from afar. Sacred crocodiles live in the lake on its southern side and the keeper tosses them some meat around 5pm. The **tourist office** (☎ 30-640814; Ave Houphouët-Boigny; ⏱ 8am-noon & 3-6pm Mon-Fri) arranges Baoulé dancing performances in nearby villages.

Sleeping & Eating

Hôtel Akraya (☎ 30-641131; s/d CFA15,000/18,000) is one of the few budget options in town. It's a bit out of the way but rooms are pleasant enough.

Hôtel Président (☎ 30-641582; Route d'Abidjan; s/d/ste US$56/65/117; ⏸ ⏸), Yamoussoukro's signature hotel, is a little ostentatious. Rooms are as luxurious as you'd imagine and there is an 18-hole golf course, as well as three restaurants (including a panoramic eatery on the 14th floor), four bars and a nightclub.

There is cheap and abundant street food at the *gare routière* and many lakefront *maquis*. **Maquis le Jardin** (meals CFA3000-5000; ⏱ lunch & dinner), across from Habitat market, is more upmarket and expensive than the others, but the chef usually makes it worthwhile. French-owned **A la Bella Pizza** (Ave Houphouët-Boigny; meals CFA3500-5000; ⏱ lunch & dinner) serves pasta, crêpes and local fare.

Getting There & Away

MTT and UTB, whose bus stations are south of town, run buses frequently to Abidjan (CFA4500), with the latter also going frequently to Bouaké (CFA3800) and once daily to Man (CFA5000) and San Pédro (CFA6000).

THE NORTH

BOUAKÉ

The beating heart of former rebel territory, gritty Bouaké isn't exactly a dream holiday destination. When the New Forces took the country's second-largest city in 2002, thousands fled. Before the war it had around 500,000 inhabitants; there's probably less than half that today.

Hôtel Mon Afrik (☎ 06-349749; nlciabid@aviso.ci; Quartier Kennedy; s/d CFA20,000/30,000; ⏸ ⏸) is easily the best address in Bouaké. It's run by the enthusiastic Madame Delon, who can advise you on all the dos and don'ts of Bouaké.

For food, head to **Restaurant Black & White** (Ave Jacque Aka; meals CFA4000-6000; ⏱ lunch & dinner,

closed Mon), whose extensive menu is popular with former rebels. **Patisserie Boikoise** (☎ 31-631033) on the main drag does good croissants and pastries, or you can head to the *maquis* around the market.

Buses and shared taxis depart from Gare Routière du Grand Marché. UTB has several buses a day to/from Abidjan (CFA7000) and one to San Pédro (CFA8000) – both via Yamoussoukro – from its station south of the market.

MAN

Man is an absolute stunner: a succession of mountains rises out of the dusty earth like a many-humped camel carpeted in green and grey. It's a great base for exploring surrounding villages and going hiking. Some war damage is still visible.

The centrally located **Hôtel Leveneur** (☎ 33-791776; Rue de l'Hôtel Leveneur; r CFA12,000; ⏸) has the dishevelled backpacker thing down to a T, though we suspect it's not deliberate. **Hôtel Amointrin** (☎ 33-792670; Route du Lycé e Professionel; r standard/superior CFA14,000/16,000; ⏸) is the latest UN favourite and sometimes has hot water. Man is a host of decent *maquis* – Le Boss and **Maquis Jardin Bis** (Route du Lycée Professionnel) both do great *attiéke* (a light, slightly bitter couscous dish) and *brochettes* (kebabs). The **Pâtisserie la Brioche** (Rue du Commerce; croissants CFA240) is a great place for breakfast or morning coffee.

You can reach Abidjan by shared taxi (CFA7000) or UTB bus (CFA7000). Taxis for N'zérékoré in Guinea run via Sipilou.

Though Man is still getting back on its feet after the conflict, at the time of research it was safe to visit. Check before you travel.

AROUND MAN

If you're considering scaling Mt Tonkoui, give **La Dent de Man** (Man's Tooth) a shot first. Northeast of town, this steep, molar-shaped mountain hits a height of 881m. Allow at least four hours for the round trip and bring snacks. The hike starts in the village of **Zobale**, 4km from Man.

At 1223m, **Mt Tonkoui** is the second-highest peak in Côte d'Ivoire. The views from the summit are breathtaking and extend to Liberia and Guinea, even during the dusty harmattan winds. The route begins about 18km from Man.

The area around Man is also famous for **La Cascade** (admission CFA300), 5km from town, a crashing waterfall that hydrates a bamboo forest. You walk a pretty paved path to reach it.

One of Man's most celebrated neighbours is **Silacoro**, about 110km north, which is famous for its stilt dancing.

CÔTE D'IVOIRE DIRECTORY

ACCOMMODATION
Accommodation in Abidjan isn't particularly good value. Reliable cheapies are hard to come by, largely because the city is frequented by business travellers more often than backpackers. Elsewhere in the country, you'll find better value for money, especially if the peace holds and tourism begins to pick up.

ACTIVITIES
Several spots on the coast, most notably Assinie and Dagbego, have decent surfing. Côte d'Ivoire also has a lot to offer birdwatchers, particularly during the (European) winter migration season from December to March, although the country is still not really set up for it and most of the parks remain closed. This could change over the next few years, so you should consult with hotel staff for more information.

BOOKS
There is a wealth of books in French about the country's trials and tribulations. Guillaume Soro's autobiography, *Pourquoi Je Suis Devenu Rebelle* (Why I became a rebel), is a page-turner. *Le peuple n'aime pas le peuple* (The people don't like the people), by Kouakou-Gbahi Kouakou, describes the conflict as well in its content as it does in its title.

BUSINESS HOURS
Banks 8am to 11.30am and 2.30pm until 4.30pm Monday to Friday.
Government offices 7.30am to 5.30pm Monday to Friday, with breaks for lunch.
Shops 8am to 6pm.

DANGERS & ANNOYANCES
Any step in a peace process should be viewed with caution. That said, there's no real reason why you shouldn't visit Abidjan, Yamassoukrou and the country's coastline. These areas were largely unaffected by the conflict and remain friendly and welcoming. At the time of research there were still security checkpoints in Abidjan and along the coast. Make sure your documents are in order and comply with requests if you feel tension. Travelling to Bouaké and further north was not recommended at the time of research. Again, this will change, so check regularly for updates.

Finally, take care at the beach. The Atlantic has fierce currents and a ripping undertow and people drown every year – often strong, overly confident swimmers. Heed local advice.

EMERGENCIES
Fire ☎ 180
Medicins Urgence (private company) ☎ 07 08 26 26
SOS Medecins (private company) ☎ 185

EMBASSIES & CONSULATES
The following embassies are located in Abidjan.
Belgium (☎ 20-219434/0088; 4th fl, Immeuble Alliance, Ave Terrasson des Fougéres 01) Also assists Dutch nationals.
Burkina Faso (☎ 20-211501; Ave Terrasson de Fougères) There's also a consulate in Bouaké.
Canada (☎ 20-300700; www.dfait-maeci.gc.ca/abidjan; Immeuble Trade Centre, 23 Ave Noguès) Also assists Australian nationals.
France (☎ 20-200404; www.consulfrance-abidjan.org; 17 Rue Lecoeur)
Germany (☎ 22-442030; 39 Blvd Hassan II)
Ghana (☎ 22-410288; Rue des Jardins, Deux Plateaux)
Guinea (☎ 20-222520; 3rd fl, Immeuble Crosson Duplessis, Ave Crosson Duplessis)
Liberia (20-324636; Immeuble Taleb, Ave Delafosse)
Mali (☎ 20-311570; Maison du Mali, Rue du Commerce)
Senegal (☎ 20-332876; Immeuble Nabil, off Rue du Commerce)

PRACTICALITIES

- Côte d'Ivoire uses the metric system.
- Electricity voltage is 220V/50Hz and plugs have two round pins.
- Among the nearly 20 daily newspapers, all in French, *Soirinfo, 24 Heures* and *L'Intelligent d'Abidjan* steer independent courses. *Gbich!* is a satirical paper.
- Radio Jam (99.3FM) and Radio Nostalgie (101.1FM) play hit music. The BBC World Service broadcasts some programs in English on 94.3FM.

FESTIVALS & EVENTS

Fête du Dipri Held in Gomon, northwest of Abidjan, in March or April. An all-night and all-the-next-day religious ceremony where people go into trances.

Fête de l'Abissa Held in Grand Bassam in October or November. A week-long ceremony honouring the dead.

HEALTH

Whether you're travelling by air or by land, you'll need a yellow-fever certificate to enter Côte d'Ivoire. If you don't have one, you'll probably be ushered behind a curtain for an on-the-spot jab when you arrive.

HOLIDAYS

New Year's Day 1 January
Labour Day 1 May
Independence Day 7 August
Fête de la Paix 15 November
Christmas 25 December

MONEY

ATMs are widespread in Abidjan, Grand Bassam, Yamassoukrou and major towns. Most SGBCI branches have ATMs that accept Visa, MasterCard and sometimes Maestro. There are no banks in Assinie but there is a branch of SGBCI (with an ATM) in Grand Bassam.

TELEPHONE

If you have a GSM mobile (cell) phone, you can buy SIM cards from CFA2500. Street stalls also sell top-up vouchers from CFA550. Calls generally cost between CFA25 and CFA150 per minute. The Orange network is reliable and accessible in most parts of the country, even some rural areas.

VISAS

Until 2009, US citizens visiting Côte d'Ivoire didn't need visas. That's now changed and everyone except nationals of Economic Community of West African States (Ecowas) countries must apply for one. You'll need to arrange it in advance; visas are rarely issued at Côte d'Ivoire's air and land portals. For information on the multicountry Visa des Pays de l'Entente, see p1147.

Visas can be extended at **La Sureté Nationale** (Police de l'Air et des Frontieres, Blvd de la République, Immeuble Douane; ☑ 8am-noon & 3-5pm Mon-Fri) near the main post office in Le Plateau in Abidjan.

In Abidjan, you can get visas for onward travel to the following nearby countries:

Benin Visas cost CFA25,000 and you'll need four passport photos. Also issues the five-francophone-country Visa Touristique d'Entente.

Burkina Faso Three-month single-/multiple-entry visas cost CFA30,000 and require two photos.

Ghana At the time of writing, the Ghanaian embassy had made a temporary decision to only grant visas to Ivorian nationals, due to international security concerns. Check back to see if services resume. When they do, prices are single/multiple entry CFA25,000/40,000. Apply for visas before 11.30am. You'll need four passport photos, though there's usually an on-site camera person.

Guinea One-month single-entry visas cost CFA32,000 for most nationalities. Everyone pays CFA96,000 for a three-month multiple-entry visa.

Liberia One-month single-entry visas, issued the same day, cost CFA30,000 for most nationalities.

Mali For most nationalities, one-month single-entry visas cost CFA25,000 and three-month multiple-entry visas cost CFA40,000.

TRANSPORT IN CÔTE D'IVOIRE

GETTING THERE & AWAY
Air

Félix Houphouët-Boigny is Côte d'Ivoire's swish international airport, complete with wi-fi access. Airlines serving Côte d'Ivoire include the following:

Afriqiyah Airways (8U; ☎ 20-338785; www.afriqiyah. aero; Abidjan Universel Voyages, Crosson Duplessis, Le Plateau)

Air France (AF; ☎ 20-202424; www.airfrance.com; Immeuble Kharrat, Rue Noguès, Le Plateau)

Air Ivoire (VU; ☎ 20-251400/561; www.airivoire.com; Immeuble Le République, Place de la République)

Ethiopian Airlines (ET; ☎ 20-215284; www.flyethiopian .com; Ave Chardy, Le Plateau)

Kenya Airways (KQ; ☎ 20-320767; www.kenya-airways .com; Immeuble Jeceda, Blvd de la République, Le Plateau)

SN Brussels (SN; ☎ 27-232345; www.flysn.com) Behind Supermarché Cap Sud, off Blvd Valéry Giscard d'Estaing, Treichville. Offers short hops between Abidjan and Monrovia.

South African Airways (SA; ☎ 20-218280; www.flysaa. com; Immeuble Jeceda, Blvd de la République, Le Plateau)

Land

At the time of research all major border crossings were open, though they may close around election times.

Burkina Faso Passenger train services (36 hours, three times a week) run between Abidjan and Bobo-

Dioulasso in Burkina Faso. Romantic in a gritty way, the Abidjan–Ouagadougou sleeper (Sitarail ☎ 20-208000) takes two days.

Ghana It will take you about three hours to reach the crossing at Noé from Abidjan. Note that the border shuts at 6pm promptly, accompanied by a fancy flag ceremony.

Guinea The most frequently travelled route to Guinea is between Man and N'zérékoré, either through Danané and Nzo or Biankouma and Sipilou.

Liberia Minibuses and shared taxis make the quick hop from Danané to the border at Gbé-Nda. A bus takes this route from Abidjan to Monrovia (two days) several times a week.

Mali Buses and shared taxis run from Abidjan, Yamassoukrou and Bouaké to Bamako, usually via Ferkessédougou, and Sikasso in Mali.

GETTING AROUND
Air
Air Ivoire (opposite) can't seem to commit to internal flights, but the situation may change as the country stabilises further. **Sophia Airlines** (☎ 21-588043) has five flights from Abidjan to San Pédro per week (return CFA150,000).

Bus
The country's large, relatively modern buses are around the same price and are significantly more comfortable than bush taxis or minibuses.

Bush Taxi & Minibus
Shared taxis (ageing Peugeots or covered pick-ups, known as *bâchés*) and minibuses cover major towns and outlying communities not served by the large buses. They leave at all hours of the day, but only when full – so long waits may be required.

Train
The romantically named *Bélier* and *Gazelle* trains link Abidjan with Ferkessédougou (CFA12,000, daily).

The Gambia

The tiny sliver of the Gambia is wedged into surrounding Senegal, and is either seen as a splinter in its side, or the tongue that makes it speak, depending on who you talk to. For most travellers, it's an easily negotiated country with a sandy shoreline that invites visitors to laze and linger. But there's more to Africa's smallest country than sun and surf. Small fishing villages, nature reserves and historical slaving stations are all within easy reach of the clamorous resort zones on the Atlantic. Like a green belt around the coast, this area is dotted with inspired community projects, star-studded ecolodges and small wildlife parks that make this tiny nation a key player in responsible tourism.

Bird-lovers might be tempted to book an annual holiday here (and many do). On a leisurely river cruise, you'll easily spot more than 100 species, as your *pirogue* charts an unhurried course through mangrove-lined wetlands and lush gallery forests. Even if your ornithological skills don't go beyond identifying an inner-city pigeon, you'll be tempted to wield binoculars here, and can rely on an excellent network of trained guides to help you tell a pelican from a flamingo.

FAST FACTS

- **Area** 11,295 sq km
- **ATMs** At banks in Banjul, on the Atlantic Coast, in Serekunda and at the airport
- **Borders** Senegal
- **Budget** US$40 to US$80
- **Capital** Banjul
- **Languages** English, Mandinka, Wolof, Pulaar (Fula)
- **Money** Dalasi; US$1 = D26; €1 = D37
- **Population** 1.7 million
- **Seasons** Dry (November to May), wet (June to October)
- **Telephone** Country code ☎ 220; international access code ☎ 00
- **Time** GMT/UTC
- **Visa** One-month visas cost US$45 (purchase before travel) but are not needed for citizens of the British Commonwealth, Germany, Italy, Luxembourg, the Netherlands, Scandinavian or Ecowas (Economic Community of West African States) countries

HOW MUCH?

- **Soft drink** US$0.75
- **Newspaper** US$0.75
- **Sandwich** US$3
- **French bread** US$0.30
- **1hr internet** US$1

LONELY PLANET INDEX

- **1L of petrol** US$1
- **1L of bottled water** US$1
- **Bottle of JulBrew** US$0.75
- **Souvenir T-shirt** US$7 to US$10
- **Shwarma** US$2.20

HIGHLIGHTS

- **Atlantic Coast resorts** (p324) Indulge in fabulous food, then party the night away.
- **Abuko Nature Reserve** (p330) Look out for rare birds and giant crocodiles in one of Africa's smallest nature reserves.
- **Gambia River National Park** (p332) Chatter with chimps and cruise past tropical islands.
- **Kartong** (p330) Watch the sun slide into the Atlantic from your exclusive ecolodge.
- **Makasutu Culture Forest** (p330) Tour the whole country, squeezed into 1000 hectares of abundant nature.

CLIMATE & WHEN TO GO

Most tourists travel to the Gambia during the dry and relatively cool months from November to February (daytime maximums around 24°C). This is also the best time to watch wildlife and birds.

The rainy season starts around late June and lasts until late September, when 30°C feels even hotter due to humidity. Many hotels and restaurants close during the wet months.

ITINERARIES

- **One Week** Spend a good amount of time at the beaches of the Atlantic Coast (p324), and tie in the occasional day trip to the busy market of Serekunda (p329), sleepy Banjul (p321), the pretty museum of Tanji (p330), Makasutu Culture Forest (p330) and Abuko Nature Reserve (p330).
- **Two Weeks** Follow the one-week itinerary, then go on a *Roots* tour to Jufureh (p331) and travel upriver to Baobolong Wetland Reserve (p331), Gambia River National Park (p332), Janjangbureh (p331) and Basse Santa Su (p332).

HISTORY

The Empires of Ghana (5th to 11th centuries) and Mali (13th to 15th centuries) extended their influence over the region that is now the Gambia. By 1456 the first Portuguese navigators landed on James Island, turning the place into a strategic trading point.

Built in 1651 by Baltic Germans, the James Island fort was claimed by the British in 1661 but changed hands several times. It was an important collection point for slaves until the abolition of slavery in 1807. New forts were built at Barra and Bathurst (now Banjul), to enforce compliance with the Abolition Act.

The British continued to extend their influence further upstream until the 1820s, when the territory was declared a British protectorate ruled from Sierra Leone. In 1886 Gambia became a Crown colony.

Gambia became self-governing in 1963, although it took two more years until real independence was achieved. Gambia became the Gambia, Bathurst became Banjul, and David Jawara, leader of the People's Progressive Party, became Prime Minister Dawda Jawara and converted to Islam, while the queen remained head of state.

High groundnut prices and the advent of package tourism led to something of a boom in the 1960s. Jawara consolidated his power, and became president when the Gambia became a fully fledged republic in 1970. The economic slump of the 1980s provoked social unrest. Two coups were hatched – but thwarted with Senegalese assistance. This co-operation led to the 1982 confederation of the two countries under the name of Senegambia, but the union collapsed by 1989. Meanwhile, corruption increased, economic decline continued and popular discontent rose. In July 1994, Jawara was overthrown in a reportedly bloodless coup led by Lieutenant Yahya Jammeh. After a brief flirtation with military dictatorship, the 30-year-old Jammeh bowed to international pressure, inaugurated a second republic, turned civilian and won the 1996 election comfortably.

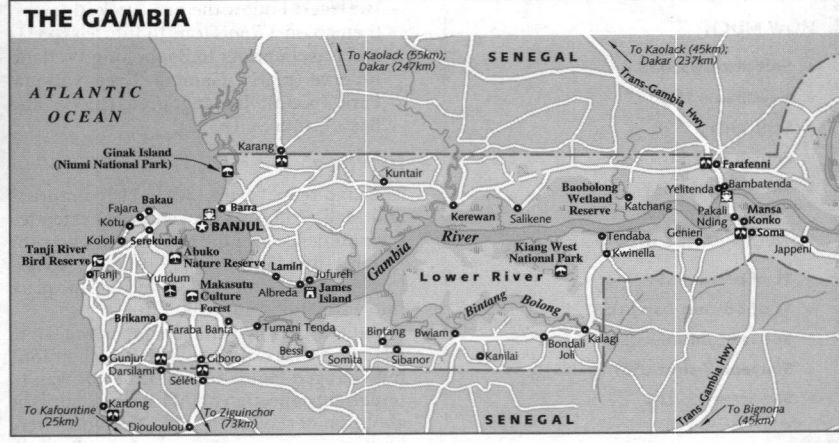

THE GAMBIA

The Gambia Today

Jammeh's leadership style has always been authoritarian, but he is clamping down even harder as he piles on the decades spent in power. Amnesty International, Reporters Without Borders and other human rights organisations denounce the climate of fear felt by opposition voices and journalists. Worrying are also Jammeh's witch-hunts, and his claim to have found cures for HIV/AIDS and asthma, which he administers in weekly TV shows. A 2009 televised declaration in which he threatened human rights activists with death heightened international concern about the direction the Gambia is taking.

CULTURE

Holiday brochures like to describe Gambia as the 'Smiling Coast'. Hospitality certainly is part of Gambian culture, but it's more easily found upcountry, away from the large tourist centres, where social relations have become somewhat distorted.

Years of authoritarian rule have also resulted in a climate of distrust. Conversations are often conducted with care, and few people will express their views on governmental politics openly – you never know who might be listening. Short-term travellers might not readily notice this. Yet being aware of the troubles that the population faces will help you to understand the country better and gradually grant you an insight into the real Gambia, the one that lies beyond the polished smiles and tourist hustling.

With around 115 people per sq km, the Gambia has one of the highest population densities in Africa. The strongest concentration of people is around the urbanised zones of the Atlantic Coast. Forty-five percent of the Gambia's population is under 14 years old.

The main ethnic groups are the Mandinka (comprising around 42%), the Wolof (about 16%) and the Fula (around 18%). Smaller groups include the Serer and Diola (also spelt Jola).

About 90% of the Gambia's population is Muslim. Christian faith is most widespread among the Diola.

The *kora*, Africa's most iconic instrument, was created in the region of Gambia and Guinea-Bissau after Malinké groups came here to settle from Mali. Famous *kora* players include Amadou Bansang Jobarteh, Jali Nyama Suso, Dembo Konte and Malamini Jobarteh.

In the 1960s the Gambia was hugely influential in the development of modern West African music. Groups like the Afrofunky Super Eagles and singer Labah Sosse had a huge impact in the Gambia, Senegal and beyond. Today, it's locally brewed reggae and hip hop that get people moving. Even the president has been seen rubbing shoulders with the world's reggae greats, proud to see his country nicknamed 'Little Jamaica'.

Banjul's national museum has a few good examples of traditional statues and

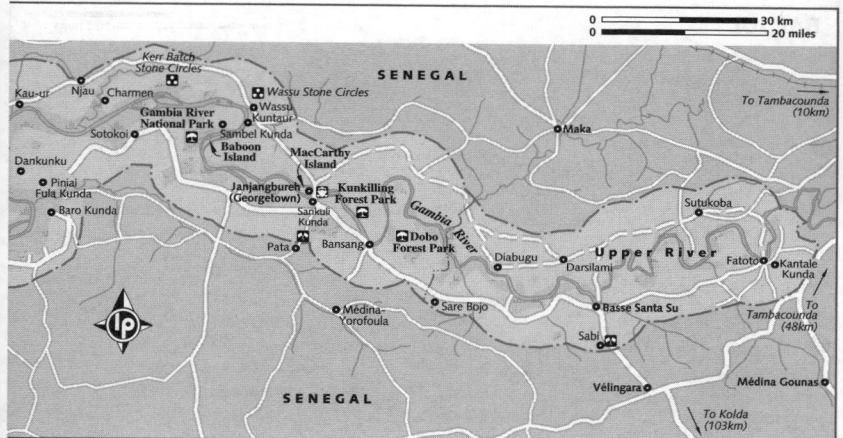

carved masks on display. Leading contemporary artists Njogu Touray and Etu produce colourful works from mixed materials. Fabric printers such as Baboucar Fall and Toimbo Laurens push the art of batik in new creative directions.

FOOD & DRINK

National dishes include *domodah* (rice with groundnut sauce) and *benachin* (rice cooked in tomato, fish and vegetable sauce). Vegetarians ought to try *niebbe*, spicy red beans that are served with bread on street corners.

The Gambia has great local juices, such as *bissap* (made from sorrel) and creamy *bouyi* (made from the fruits of the baobab tree). *Ataaya* (strong, syrupy green tea) is a great pick-me-up. For something more potent, try a cup of thick, yeasty palm wine or an ice-cold JulBrew beer.

In this chapter, budget prices are under US$6, midrange US$6 to US$12 and top end above US$12. Prices vary enormously - from around US$1 for a plate of local rice and sauce to US$15 for dinner in a classy restaurant.

ENVIRONMENT

At only 11,295 sq km, the Gambia is mainland Africa's smallest country. It's also the most absurdly shaped one. Its 300km-long territory is almost entirely surrounded by Senegal and dominated by the Gambia River that runs through it. The country is flat, and vegetation consists mainly of savannah woodlands, gallery forests and saline marshes. Six national parks and reserves protect 3.7% of the country's landmass. Some of the most interesting ones – Abuko, Kiang West and Gambia River – are mentioned in this chapter. The Gambia boasts a few large mammals, such as hippos and reintroduced chimps, but most animal lovers are attracted by the hundreds of spectacular bird species that make Gambia one of the best countries in West Africa for birdwatching.

Among the main environmental problems are deforestation, overfishing and coastal erosion, though this has partly been reversed through a sophisticated, US-sponsored sand-trapping program.

BANJUL

pop 35,000

It's hard to imagine a more unlikely, more consistently ignored capital city than the tiny seaport of Banjul. It sits on an island and sulks, crossed by sand-blown streets and dotted with fading colonial structures. And yet, it tempts with a sense of history the plush seaside resorts lack, and is home to a busy harbour and market that show urban Africa at its best.

ORIENTATION

The July 22 Sq is the centre of town. From here, several main streets run south, including Russell St, which leads past the bustling Albert Market into Liberation St. West of the October 17 Roundabout is the old part of

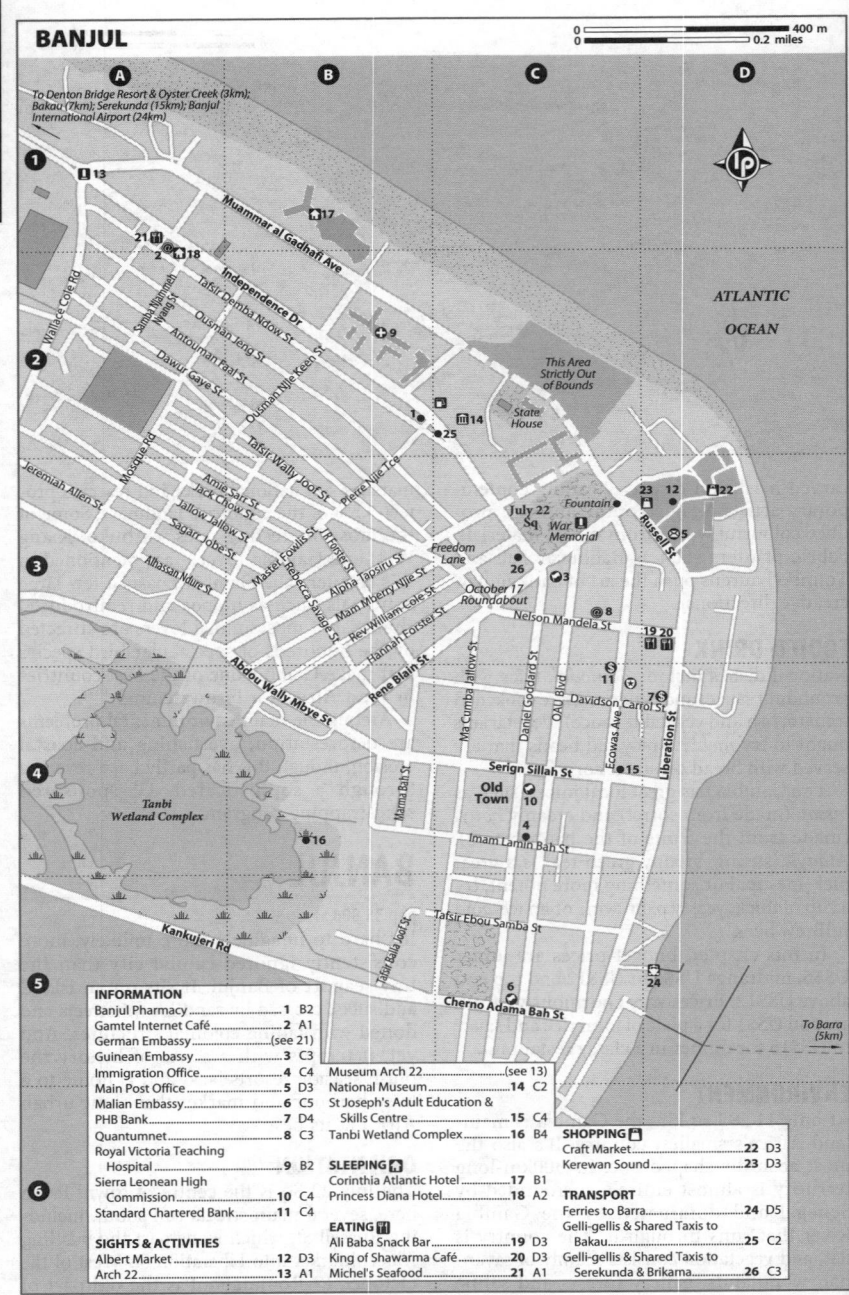

BANJUL

To Denton Bridge Resort & Oyster Creek (3km);
Bakau (7km); Serekunda (15km); Banjul
International Airport (24km)

ATLANTIC
OCEAN

This Area
Strictly Out
of Bounds

State
House

Tanbi
Wetland Complex

July 22 Sq.

War
Memorial

Fountain

Freedom
Lane

October 17
Roundabout

Nelson Mandela St

Old
Town

Imam Lamin Bah St

Kankujeri Rd

Cherno Adama Bah St

To Barra
(5km)

Banjul – a maze of narrow streets and ramshackle houses rarely visited by tourists.

INFORMATION

Banjul Pharmacy (☎ 4227470; ⊙ 9am-8.30pm) Across the road from the hospital.

Gamtel Internet Café (Independence Dr; per hr US$1; ⊙ 8am-midnight) Internet access and phone service.

Main post office (Russell St; ⊙ 8am-4pm Mon-Sat) Has telephone facilities next door.

PHB Bank (☎ 4428144; 11 Liberation St; ⊙ 8am-4pm Mon-Thu, to 1.30pm Fri) Has an ATM and changes money.

Quantumnet (Nelson Mandela St; per hr US$1; ⊙ 9am-10pm) Internet access.

Royal Victoria Teaching Hospital (☎ 4228223; Independence Dr) The Gambia's main hospital has an A&E department, but facilities aren't great.

Standard Chartered Bank (☎ 4222081; Ecowas Ave; ⊙ 8am-4pm Mon-Thu, to 1.30pm Fri) Withdraw at ATM or change money here.

DANGERS & ANNOYANCES

The Barra ferry is rife with pickpockets, and tourists are easy prey at the ferry terminals and at Albert Market.

SIGHTS & ACTIVITIES

Since its creation in the mid-19th century, **Albert Market** (Russell St), an area of frenzied buying, bartering and bargaining, has been Banjul's hub of activity. From shimmering fabrics and false plaits to tourist-tempting souvenirs, you can find almost anything here and then some.

Tucked away inside an ancient Portuguese building, the **St Joseph's Adult Education & Skills Centre** (☎ 4228836; stjskills@qanet.com; Ecowas Ave; ⊙ 9am-2pm Mon-Thu, to noon Fri) offers free tours and also sells beautiful craftwork at reasonable prices.

Arch 22 (Independence Dr; admission US$4; ⊙ 9am-11pm), a massive, 36m-high gateway built to celebrate the military coup of 22 July 1994, grants excellent views. There's also a cafe and a small **museum** (☎ 4226244) that enlightens visitors about the coup d'état and often houses good exhibitions. The **National Museum** (☎ 4226244; www.ncac.gm; Independence Dr; admission US$2; ⊙ 9am-4pm Mon-Thu, to 5pm Fri-Sun) has interesting, if slightly dusty exhibits about history and culture.

The 6300-hectare site of the **Tanbi Wetland Complex**, with its mangroves and creeks, is a great birdwatching area, with Caspian terns, gulls, egrets and several species of wader.

SLEEPING

Not many tourists stay in Banjul, and the best hotels are along the coast.

Princess Diana Hotel (☎ 4228715; 30 Independence Dr; r US$21) This is slightly better than most Banjul dosshouses, simply because it has doors that lock, occasional live music in the bar, and even a kind of breakfast in the morning.

our pick Denton Bridge Resort (☎ 7773777; s/d US$30/40; 🏊) Near Oyster Creek, this is a watersports centre, *pirogue* landing and excursion point, as well as a breezy, decent hotel with large rooms.

Corinthia Atlantic Hotel (☎ 4228601; www.corinthiahotels.com; Muammar al Gadhafi Ave; s/d incl breakfast US$60/100; P 🞐 🖳 🏊) This plush palace has all the makings of a classy hotel (good restaurants, massage centre, nightclub), though its most amazing feature is the birdwatchers' garden.

EATING

Banjul's restaurant scene is so calm that many eateries roll down the blinds before the evening has even started. Around Albert Market you can find several cheap chop shops where plates of rice and sauce start at about US$1. Denton Bridge Resort and Corinthia Atlantic Hotel also have good restaurants.

Ali Baba Snack Bar (☎ 4224055; Nelson Mandela St; dishes around US$4; ⊙ 9am-5pm) Banjul's main snack bar has a deserved reputation for tasty *shwarmas* (sliced, grilled meat and salad in pita bread) and felafel sandwiches.

King of Shawarma Café (☎ 4229799; Nelson Mandela St; dishes US$5-8; ⊙ 9am-5pm Mon-Sat) Friendly, fresh and happy to relax its opening hours, this place serves delicious meze and pressed fruit juice.

Michel's Seafood (☎ 4223108; 29 Independence Dr; dishes US$6-10; ⊙ 8am-11pm) Banjul's classiest restaurant is particularly renowned for its seafood menu. Outside the hotels, this is your only real dinner option.

SHOPPING

In Banjul, the best place to go shopping is the busy maze of stalls that is Albert Market, with souvenirs on offer at the Craft Market. Near the main entrance, you'll also find **Kerewan Sound** (Russell St), the Gambia's best place to buy CDs.

GETTING THERE & AWAY

For information on travelling to and from Banjul by air, see p334.

Ferries (☎ 4228205; Liberation St; passengers US$0.40, cars US$6-8) travel between Banjul and Barra, on the northern bank of the Gambia River. They are supposed to run every one to two hours from 7am to 9pm and take one hour, though delays and cancellations are frequent.

Gelli-gellis (minibuses) and shared taxis to Bakau (US$0.30) and Serekunda (US$0.40) leave from their respective taxi ranks near the National Museum. Note that you might have to pay a bit more for luggage. A private taxi to the coastal resorts will cost you around US$6.

GETTING AROUND
To/From the Airport
A green tourist taxi from Banjul International Airport to Banjul costs around US$12 to US$15. With yellow taxis, the price depends entirely on your haggling skills; expect to pay US$8 to Banjul. There is no airport bus.

Gelli-Gelli & Shared Taxi
A short ride across Banjul city centre (known as a 'town trip') in a private taxi costs about US$1 to US$2.

SEREKUNDA & THE ATLANTIC COAST

pop 323,000
Chaotic, splitting-at-the-seams Serekunda is the nation's largest urban centre, and appears to consist of one big, bustling market. The nearby Atlantic Coast resorts of Bakau, Fajara, Kotu Strand and Kololi are where the sun'n'sea tourists flock. If you can manage to dodge the persistent ganja peddlers and beach 'bumsters' (otherwise known as touts and hustlers), this is a great place to spend long days on the beach and late nights on the dance floor.

ORIENTATION
Running north–south, Bakau, Fajara, Kotu and Kololi are a string of former fishing villages that have merged into one big tourist centre. Serekunda, a couple of kilometres inland, is a real city, and Westfield Junction is the hub of its wheel.

INFORMATION
Bookshops
Timbooktoo (☎ 4494345; timbooktoo@qanet.gm; Garba Jahumpa Rd, Fajara; ☺ 10am-7pm Mon-Thu, 10am-1pm & 3-7pm Fri, 10am-8pm Sat) The best bookshop around. The Cultural Encounters offices upstairs provide information on sustainable tourism.

Cultural Centres
Alliance Franco-Gambienne (☎ 4375418; alliancefg@ hotmail.com; Kairaba Ave, Serekunda; ☺ 9.30am-5pm Mon-Fri) Has regular concerts, films, shows and exhibitions and a good, cheap garden restaurant.

Internet Access
Wi-fi connections are getting popular with restaurants and hotels, typically free for guests. Connections are usually slow. Most internet cafes charge US$1 per hour.
Gamtel (☎ 4229999; gen-info@gamtel.gm; Senegambia Strip; ☺ 8am-11pm)
Net Bar (☎ 44982128; Atlantic Rd, Bakau; ☺ 9am-midnight) Possibility to plug in a laptop and headsets. Small snack bar outside.
Quantumnet (☎ 4494514; Kairaba Ave, Fajara; ☺ 8.30am-10pm) Near Timbooktoo bookshop.

Medical Services
Medical Research Council (MRC; ☎ 4495446; Fajara) If you find yourself with a potentially serious illness, head for this British-run clinic.
Stop Steps Pharmacy (☎ 4371344; Serekunda; ☺ 9am-10pm Mon-Sat) Well stocked, has several branches.
Westfield Clinic (☎ 4398448; Westfield Junction, Serekunda)

Money
The main banks – Standard Chartered Bank, Trust Bank and PHB – have ATM-enhanced branches across the resort zone (see p332 for standard opening hours). You can also change money at hotels, or ask your reception to put you in touch with an informal changer.
PHB Bank (☎ 4497139; Atlantic Rd, Bakau)
Standard Chartered Bank Bakau (☎ 4495046; Atlantic Rd); Serekunda (☎ 4396102; Kairaba Ave)
Trust Bank Bakau (☎ 4495486; Atlantic Rd); Kololi (☎ 4465303; Wilmon Company Bldg, Badala Park Way)

Post
The main post office is off Kairaba Ave, about halfway between Fajara and Serekunda. The

smaller **Gampost Bakau** (☎ 8900587; Atlantic Rd, Bakau; ☙ 8.30am-4pm Mon-Thu, to noon Fri & Sat) has a telecentre and internet access.

Tourist Information

Cultural Encounters (☎ 4497675; www.asset-gambia.com; above Timbooktoo bookshop, Fajara) is perfect for finding out about sustainable tourism options.

Travel Agencies

Tour specialists are listed in the Transport chapter (p334). Most also do ticketing.

DANGERS & ANNOYANCES

Crime rates in Serekunda are low. However, tourists (and especially women) will have to deal with the constant hustling by 'bumsters'. Decline unwanted offers firmly – these guys are hard to shake off. Steer clear of the beaches after dark.

SIGHTS & ACTIVITIES

Bakau's **botanic gardens** (☎ 7774482; adult/child US$2/free; ☙ 8am-4pm) were established in 1924 and offer shade, peace and good bird-spotting chances.

You can get up close and personal with a croc at the nearby **Kachikally Crocodile Pool** (☎ 7782479; www.kachikally.com; admission US$2; ☙ 9am-6pm), a sacred site for the local people and perhaps for tourists, too, judging by their numbers. There's also a nature trail and a small museum.

Bijilo Forest Park (☎ 9996343; admission US$2; ☙ 8am-6pm) is a small wildlife reserve in Kololi. The 4.5km nature trail is great for spotting birds and being teased by the monkeys.

Art lovers should try Njogu Touray's **Sakura Arts Studio** (☎ 7017351; Latrikunda) for a private view of the acclaimed painter's colourful works. The **African Living Art Centre** (☎ 4495131; Garba Jahumpa Rd, Fajara) is a fairy-tale cross between an antique gallery, an orchid garden and an Eastern restaurant, where artists mingle and the cocktails taste great.

The **Sportsfishing Centre** (☎ 7765765; Denton Bridge) is the best place in Serekunda to arrange fishing and *pirogue* excursions. Various companies are based there, including **African Angler** (☎ 7721228; www.african-angling.co.uk; Denton Bridge), which runs fishing excursions, and the **Watersports Centre** (☎ 7773777; Denton Bridge), which

can organise your jet-skiing, parasailing, windsurfing or catamaran trips.

The nicest swimming beaches are in Kotu and Fajara. Note that currents can be strong.

SLEEPING
Budget

Sukuta Camping (☎ 9917786; www.campingsukuta.com; Sukuta; campsite per person US$4, per car/van US$0.80/1, s/d US$9.50/18) This well-organised campsite in Sukuta (southwest of Serekunda) also offers simple rooms for those that have temporarily tired of canvas. Facilities are great and there's an on-site mechanic.

Praia Hotel (☎ 4394887; Mame Jout St, Serekunda; r US$20; ☒) Right in fumes-filled Serekunda, this clean, spacious hostel comes as such a surprise you may feel like hugging Mr Ceesay, the friendly manager.

Jabo Guesthouse (☎ 4494906; 9 Old Cape Rd, Bakau; d US$22) This down-to-earth place surprises with large, clean rooms and a pretty courtyard. Some rooms have self-catering facilities.

Fajara Guesthouse (☎ 4496122; fax 4494365; Fajara; s/ d US$23/28; ☒ ☗) This cosy place exudes family vibes with its leafy courtyard and welcoming lounge. There's hot water and self-caterers can use the kitchen for a small extra charge.

Banana Ville (☎ 9906054; njieadama@hotmail.com; off Kololi Rd, Kololi; d US$30; ☒) Very tiny and very simple, this is a great budget bet. The furniture looks a bit wonky, but beds are comfortable enough for a good night's sleep.

Midrange

our pick **Luigi's** (☎ 4460280; www.luigis.gm; Palma Rima Rd, Kololi; s/d incl breakfast US$28/41, apt from US$75; ☒ ☐ ☒) This impressive complex has three restaurants and attractive lodgings set around the pool and jacuzzi. Despite this tropical growth rate, the place manages to keep its family feel.

Leybato (☎ 4390275; www.leybato.abc.gm; off Atlantic Rd, Fajara; d incl breakfast from US$30) This slightly worn guesthouse overlooks the ocean from a great location. Rooms vary in quality and size and, of course, cost (go for the pricier ones; they're much better).

African Heritage Centre (☎ 4496778; www.african heritagegambia.com; 16 Samba Breku Rd, Bakau; s/d incl breakfast US$34/38, apt US$47/56; ☒ ☒) This art-gallery-cum-restaurant has six clean, nicely furnished rooms and even apartments for families and self-caterers.

ATLANTIC COAST RESORTS & SEREKUNDA

INFORMATION
Alliance Franco-Gambienne	1 G5
Belgian Consul	(see 29)
Cultural Encounters	(see 14)
Danish Consul	2 G3
Gampost Bakau	3 G2
Gamtel	4 A5
Guinea-Bissau Embassy	5 G2
Main Post Office	6 G4
Mauritanian Consulate	7 B5
Medical Research Council	8 F3
Net Bar	9 G2
Norwegian Consul	(see 2)
PHB Bank	10 G2
Quantumnet	11 F3
Senegalese High Commission	12 F4
Standard Chartered Bank	13 H5
Standard Chartered Bank	(see 5)
Stop Steps Pharmacy	(see 43)
Swedish Consul	(see 2)
Timbooktoo	14 F3
Trust Bank	15 G2
Trust Bank	16 B5
UK High Commission	17 E3
US Embassy	18 F4
Westfield Clinic	19 H6

SIGHTS & ACTIVITIES
African Living Art Centre	20 F3
Bijilo Forest Park Headquarters	21 A6
Botanic Gardens	22 G2
Kachikally Crocodile Pool	23 G2
Sakura Arts Studio	24 F5

SLEEPING
African Heritage Centre	25 H2
Banana Ville	26 D5
Fajara Guesthouse	27 E3
Jabo Guesthouse	28 H2
Kairaba Hotel	29 A5
Leybato	30 E3
Luigi's	31 D4
Ngala Lodge	32 F2
Praia Hotel	33 G5
Roc Heights Lodge	34 H2
Safari Garden	35 E3

EATING
Ali Baba's	36 A5
Butcher's Shop	37 E3
Calypso	38 H2
Come Inn	39 F4
Gaya Art Café	40 A5
Green Mamba	41 A5
Jojo's	42 A5
Kairaba Supermarket	43 F4
La Pailotte	(see 1)
Luigi's Pizza & Pasta House	(see 31)
Paradiso Pizza	44 B5
Ritz	45 E3
Safe Way Afra King	46 F5
Solar Project	47 G5
Soul Food	48 F3

DRINKING
Blue Bar	49 F3
Chapman's	50 G2
Sinatra's	51 G2
Weezo's	52 E3

ENTERTAINMENT
Aquarius	53 A6
Destiny	54 D4
Jokor	55 H6

SHOPPING
African Heritage Centre	(see 25)
Bakau Market	56 G2
Equigambia	57 D5
Salam Batik	58 F6

TRANSPORT
AB Rent-A-Car	(see 29)
Brussels Airlines	59 B5
Gambia Experience	60 A5
Gambia River Excursions	61 F3
Hertz	(see 67)
Minibuses to Banjul	62 H6
Shared Taxis to Bakau and Serekunda	63 F3
Shared Taxis to Fajara & Bakau	64 H5
Shared Taxis to Kololi (Senegambia)	65 F4
Tilly's Tours	66 A6
Total Petrol Station	67 F6

Kotu Point

Palma Rima Rd

Kololi Rd

Kololi Point

Kololi

Senegambia Strip

See Senegambia Enlargement

0 — 500 m
0 — 0.3 miles

Senegambia Strip

Badala Park Way

Bertil Harding Hwy

Senegambia

Bijilo Forest Park

To Gambia Tours (1km);
Tanji (8km); Kartong (38km)

THE GAMBIA

THE GAMBIA

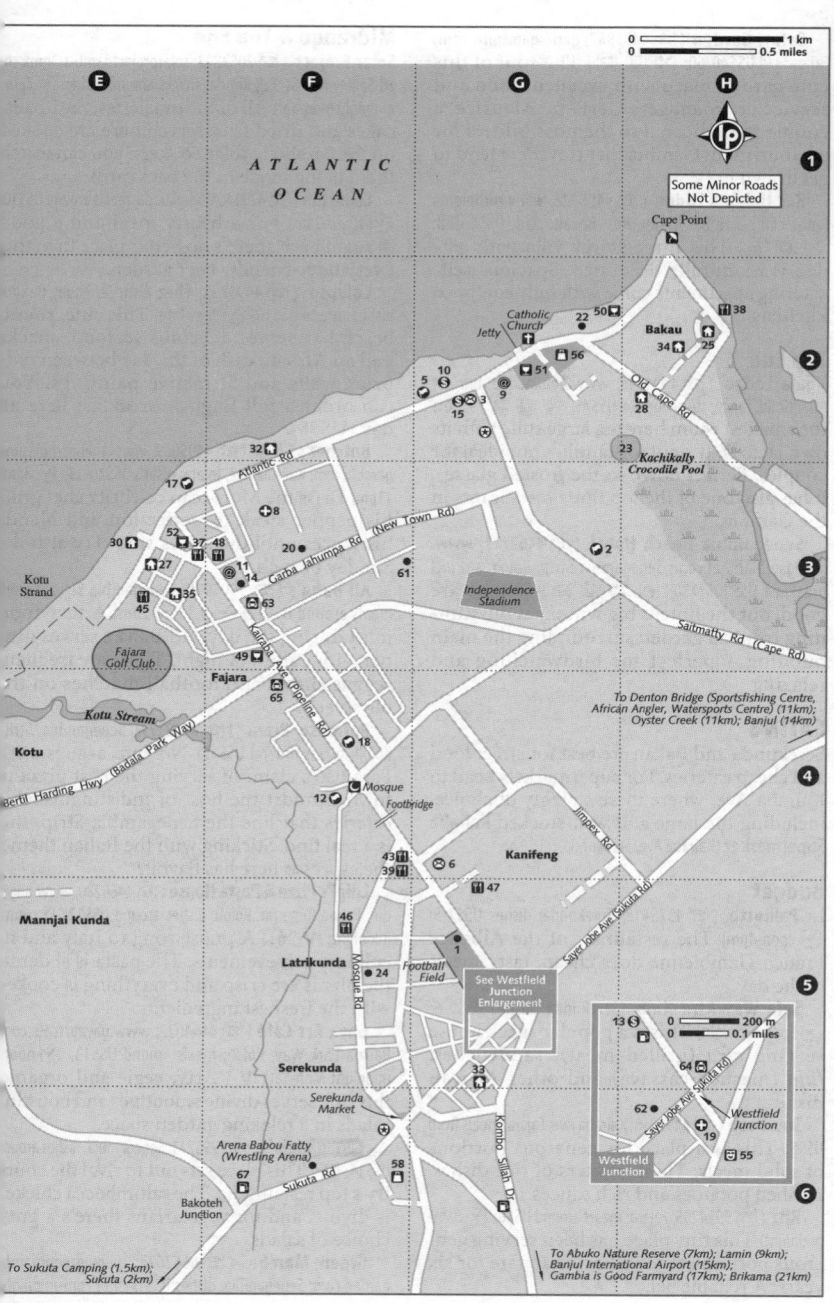

ATLANTIC OCEAN

Some Minor Roads Not Depicted

Cape Point

Bakau

Catholic Church

Jetty

Old Cape Rd

Kachikally Crocodile Pool

Atlantic Rd

(New Town Rd)

Garba Jahumpa Rd

Independence Stadium

Kotu Strand

Saitmatty Rd (Cape Rd)

Fajara Golf Club

Fajara

To Denton Bridge (Sportsfishing Centre, African Angler, Watersports Centre) (11km); Oyster Creek (11km); Banjul (14km)

Kotu Stream

Kotu

Bertil Harding Hwy (Badala Park Way)

Mannjai Kunda

Mosque Footbridge

Kanifeng

Jimpex Rd

Latrikunda

Football Field

See Westfield Junction Enlargement

Serekunda

Serekunda Market

Arena Babou Fatty (Wrestling Arena)

Bakoteh Junction

Sukuta Rd

Mosque Rd

Kombo Sillah Dr

Sayer Jobe Ave Sukuta Rd

To Sukuta Camping (1.5km); Sukuta (2km)

To Abuko Nature Reserve (7km); Lamin (9km); Banjul International Airport (15km); Gambia is Good Farmyard (17km); Brikama (21km)

Westfield Junction

Sayer Jobe Ave Sukuta Rd

Westfield Junction

THE GAMBIA

Safari Garden (☎ 4495887; geri@gamspirit.com; Fajara; s/d US$40/60; ✗ ▢ ⬛) The soul of this cute garden place with excellent food and service are managers Geri and Maurice, a couple so dedicated to the possibilities for ecotourism in Gambia that travellers tend to get drawn in.

Roc Heights Lodge (☎ 4495428; www.rocheights lodge.com; Samba Breku Rd, Bakau; s/d US$60/88; ✗ ▢ ⬛) This three-storey villa with garden is beautifully decorated. Spacious self-catering apartments come with fully equipped kitchens.

Top End

Ngala Lodge (☎ 4494045; www.ngalalodge.com; 64 Atlantic Rd, Fajara; ste per person US$75; ✗ ▢ ⬛) Even the smallest room here is a large suite with its own jacuzzi. It's not for families but ideal for couples. Perfect down to the frosted glasses, it has also one of the top three restaurants in the Gambia.

Senegambia Beach Hotel (☎ 4462717; www. senegambiahotel.com; Senegambia Strip, Kololi; s/d incl breakfast US$105/130; ℗ ✗ ▢ ⬛) Rooms are good, but the hotel's big winner is the stunning tropical garden surrounding the main building – perfect for birdwatching and relaxing.

EATING

Serekunda and Bakau are best for street food and cheap eateries. For supermarkets head to Kairaba Ave, where there's plenty of choice, including the large and well-stocked **Kairaba Supermarket** (Kairaba Ave, Serekunda).

Budget

La Paillotte (☎ 4375418; Serekunda; dishes US$2-5; ☾ noon-4pm) The restaurant of the Alliance Franco-Gambienne does cheap, tasty meals of the day.

Safe Way Afra King (Serekunda; dishes US$2-6; ☾ 5pm-midnight) This is a popular snack house serving *afra* (grilled meat), sandwiches, *fufu* (mashed cassava) and other African dishes.

Soul Food (☎ 4497858; Kairaba Ave, Fajara; meals from US$6) This is a place for generous portions of solid meals. Think platters of rice dishes, mashed potatoes and rich sauces.

Ritz (☎ 9924205; Fajara; meals around US$8; ☾ 8am-midnight) This tiny place has been serving generous portions of solid European fare for six years. A reliable bet.

Midrange & Top End

Solar Project (☎ 7053822; solarprojectgambia@gmx.ch; 18 Sainey Njie St, Faji Kunda; snacks around US$4; ☾ 7am-midnight Mon-Sat) All of the omelettes, meatballs, cakes and dried fruit served here are cooked on the parabolic solar cookers; you can watch them being made in the backyard.

Come Inn (☎ 4391464; Serekunda; meals around US$10; ☾ 10am-2am) For a hearty meal and a good draught beer, there's no better place than this overlander-friendly beer garden.

Calypso (☎ 4496292; Chez Anne & Fode, Bakau; dishes around US$10; ☾ 9am-late) This cute, round beach bar serves delicious seafood, snacks and an African dish of the day between red brick walls and attractive paintings. You can order a full English breakfast here all day (US$8).

Butcher's Shop (☎ 4495069; www.thebutchersshop gambia.com; Kairaba Ave, Fajara; dishes US$10-15; ☾ 8am-11pm) Driss the Moroccan celebrity chef grill his pepper steak to perfection and blend his sauces until the spices sing. Try also the Sunday brunch.

Ali Baba's (☎ 9905978; Senegambia Strip, Kololi; meals around US$12; ☾ 9.30am-2am) A fast-food joint during the day, Ali Baba's serves dinner with a show at night. There are frequent reggae shows and football matches on the big screen.

Paradiso Pizza (☎ 4462177; Senegambia Strip, Kololi; pizzas around US$12) No one argues with Paradiso's claim of serving the best pizza in town. Amidst the host of indistinguishable eateries that line the Senegambia Strip, this is a real find. Sticking with the Italian theme, the espresso here has flavour.

Luigi's Pizza & Pasta House (☎ 4460280; www.luigis. gm; Palma Rima Rd, Kololi; dishes around US$12; ☾ 6pm-midnight; Ⓥ ⬛) A praise song to Italy and it culinary achievements. The pasta is al dente, the pizzas are crisp and everything is cooked with the freshest ingredients.

Gaya Art Café (☎ 4464022; www.gayaartcafe.com; Badala Park Way, Kololi; meals around US$13; ☾ noon-midnight Mon-Sat; Ⓥ) Arty, vegie and organic, this cafe serves divine smoothies and boosting salads in a relaxing garden space.

our pick **Jojo's** (☎ 7295711; Senegambia; dishes around US$14; Ⓥ) This place sets out to rival the country's top restaurants. The saltimbocca chicken is divine, and for vegetarians there's a great choice of salads.

Green Mamba (☎ 6662622; www.greenmamba garden.com; Senegambia; dishes US$17; ☾ 7pm-midnight

THE GAMBIA

FRESH FOOD ON THE FARM

Near Yundum, the **Gambia is Good Farm Yard** (Alhagie Darboe; ☎ 4494473, 9891560; adult/child US$4/2) is the public face of a socially engaged marketing company that has, since 2004, helped over 1000 poor (and mostly female) farmers sell the produce of their small agricultural farms. On a visit, you can learn about the farmers' horticultural techniques, attend cookery classes (minimum of four people, per person US$19) and taste an organic Gambian stew in the restaurant (US$9 including tour). Do phone before setting out so that they can prepare for your visit. A return trip from the coastal resorts by taxi will cost you around US$15.

(Ⓥ) At this oriental grill, you get to pick the raw ingredients for your personalised stir-fry and watch it being cooked. Staff are attentive, the house cocktails great and the garden space beautiful.

DRINKING

Chapman's (☎ 4495252; Atlantic Rd, Bakau; ☾ 11am-10pm Thu-Tue) Very popular, this pub is usually packed with a mixed crowd. Good, varied meals are washed down with pints of draught beer and good conversations.

Sinatra's (☎ 7781727; Atlantic Rd, Bakau) With a different program every day (movies on Monday, live music on Friday and Saturday, grill party on Sunday afternoon) and the fixed point of cheap draught beer to guide you through it all, this is a place you're unlikely to visit only once.

Blue Bar (☎ 9991539; Kairaba Ave, Fajara; ☾ 11am-3am) This cheerful, dimly lit bar has an excellent selection of drinks to be sipped in the relaxed vibe and good company on the outdoor terrace.

Weezo's (☎ 4496918; Kairaba Ave, Fajara) After sunset, Fajara's favourite Mexican diner turns the lights down, the vibes up and brings the cocktail menu out.

ENTERTAINMENT

Aquarius (☎ 4460247; Bijilo Forest Park Rd, Senegambia Strip; ☾ 10am-3am) A smart cafe during the day, Aquarius turns into a glittering dance floor at night. The drinks are expensive and the atmosphere is strict party-vibe.

Destiny's (Kotu Beach) This sparkling place is where parties go on until late, clothes are tight and tiny and the beat is thumping. It's the nightlife version of a holiday beach club.

Jokor (☎ 4375690; 13 Kombo Sillah Dr, near Westfield Junction) This open-air club in Serekunda is a raucous local affair, and makes a convincing claim to be the most entertaining club of them all.

SHOPPING

For colourful, locally made and fairly traded fabrics, try **Equigambia** (☎ 7794374; www.equigambia.org; Kololi; ☾ 10am-6pm Mon-Sat) and **Salam Batik** (☎ 9820125; salam_batik_mp_art@yahoo.co.uk; London Corner, Serekunda). You might be able to arrange workshops at Salam Batik. To get here, turn left after Lana's bar in Serekunda. It's on the left-hand side, after the big mango tree. The **African Heritage Centre** (☎ 4496778; www.africanheritagegambia.com; 16 Samba Breku Rd, Bakau) and Bakau Market are good places to pick up sculptures, batiks and souvenirs.

GETTING THERE & AWAY

Bush taxis and *gelli-gellis* for most destinations in the Gambia leave from Westfield Junction and **Tippa petrol station** (Bakoteh Junction, Serekunda) in Serekunda. Destinations include Brikama (US$0.50, one hour), Soma (US$3, five hours) and Gunjur (US$0.70, 45 minutes). For journeys eastwards, you're better off going to Barra and using the northbank road.

GETTING AROUND
To/From the Airport

A green tourist taxi from Banjul International Airport to the coastal resorts costs around US$5. Yellow taxis cost about US$2.50, if you negotiate well.

Taxi

Shared taxis called *six-six* (a short hop costs D6, or US$0.25) operate on several routes around the coastal resorts. They connect Bakau to Westfield Junction and Serekunda, passing through Sabina Junction near the Timbooktoo bookshop at Fajara. You can also get *six-six* from the traffic-lights junction in Fajara to Senegambia Strip in Kololi and from there to Bakau. Simply flag a taxi down, pay your fare and get off where you want.

You can also hire yellow or green taxis (they're more expensive) for trips around town. Rates are negotiable.

WESTERN GAMBIA

ABUKO NATURE RESERVE

Abuko Nature Reserve (☎ 4375888; adult/child US$1.30/0.70; ☼ 8am-6pm) is one of Africa's tiniest wildlife reserves but boasts an amazing variety of vegetation and animals. With over 250 recorded bird species and well-placed hides, it is particularly of interest to birdwatchers.

To get here, take a private yellow taxi (US$15) or a minibus headed for Brikama from Banjul or Serekunda (US$0.40).

MAKASUTU CULTURE FOREST & BALLABU CONSERVATION PROJECT

Like a snapshot of the Gambia, **Makasutu Culture Forest** (☎ 9951547; www.makasutu.com; admission full/half day US$28/21, night extravaganza US$32) bundles the country's array of landscapes into a dazzling 1000-hectare package. The adjacent, 8500-hectare **Ballabu Conservation Project** (Makasutu Wildlife Trust; ☎ 7782633; m.wildlifetrust@yahoo. co.uk) is an ambitious community conservation project, supporting 14 villages within the zone and protecting animals.

If you have the budget and feel like having a treat, you can stay in the forest at the exclusive and very stunning ecotreat **Mandina River Lodge** (☎ 9951547; www.makasutu.com; s/d incl half board US$138/275; ☼ ☼). Bookings are made through the website.

Phone beforehand, and get picked up from Brikama at 9am and dropped off at 4.30pm with the park's bus (US$4 one way). A private taxi from Brikama costs around US$6.

TANJI & AROUND

pop 10,000

Located just to the south of the Atlantic Coast resorts, Brufut has rapidly changed from a tranquil fishing village to a built-up tourist centre. Small and attractive **Hibiscus House** (☎ 7982929; www.hibiscushousegambia.com; Brufut; r incl breakfast US$105; ☼ ☼) is tucked away at the end of a bougainvillea-lined road. A short drive southwards takes you to Tanji, with its charming **Tanji Village Museum** (☎ 9926618; tanje@ dds.nl; adult/child US$4/1; ☼ 9am-5pm) and the **Tanji River Bird Reserve** (☎ 9919219; admission US$1.50; ☼ 8am-6pm), an area of dunes, lagoons, woodland and Bijol Island, which is a protected breeding ground for the Caspian terns.

Tanji village, 3km south of the reserve office, has a couple of good lodgings. **Nyanya's**

Beach Lodge (☎ 9808678; s/d US$15/23) has bright bungalows in a leafy garden on the bank of Gambia River branch, while **Paradise Inn Lodge** (☎ 9810112; per person incl breakfast US$27) sits in a bird-attracting garden (mangroves close by) in the village.

A little further south in Tujering, put in a stop at the quirky and wonderful **Tunbung Arts Village** (☎ 9982102; etundow@yahoo.com; Tujering Village), where artist Etu runs sculpture workshops (enquire for rates).

The beautiful beaches of Sanyang, the next spot on the coast, are popular with tour groups from the Kombos. Have a drink at **Rainbow Beach Bar** (☎ 9726806; www.rainbow.gm; d US$20), which has clean, thatched-roof bungalows, a generator, a chef that knows how to grill prawns properly.

GUNJUR & KARTONG

pop 15,000

Ten kilometres south of Sanyang lies the tranquil fishing village of Gunjur, one of the Gambia's largest fishing centres. The place is all about fish, guts and nets, though the **Gunjur Environmental Protection and Development Group** (GEPADG; ☎ 8800986; gepadg@yahoo.com) can introduce you to the ecological side of town, notably its community reserve and lagoon. Stay ecofriendly at the excellent **Footsteps Eco Lodge** (☎ 7411609; www.footstepsgambia.com; bungalows incl breakfast US$93; ☼ ☼) and indulge in the great food. Five kilometres further south, **Balaba Nature Camp** (☎ 9919012; Medina Salaam; s/d US$20/27) is much more basic, but also environmentally committed.

On the Gambian border, Kartong is a tranquil village with fabulous beaches and tall palm trees. Reptile lovers will enjoy trips to the sacred **crocodile pool** of Mama Bambo Folonko and the **Reptile Farm** (admission US$4). The pretty **Lemon Fish Art Gallery** (☎ 9922884; www.lemonfish.gm; r US$27) has great exhibitions and can put you up. Bouba Jaiteh's **Halahin Lodge** (☎ 9933193; boubajaiteh@yahoo.co.uk; s/d incl breakfast US$23/30) is one of a few decent budget bets with some eco-pedigree. **Stala Adventures** (☎ 9915604; www.stala-adventures.com; campsites US$9, per person r incl full board US$56) is a tranquil spot for fishing and birding, right on the Hallahin River, and **Sandele Eco-Retreat** (☎ 4495887; www. sandele.com; per person r/lodge incl half board US$67/93) is a stunning eco-castle with magnificent domes made from compressed bricks and dead wood.

LOWER GAMBIA RIVER

GINAK ISLAND (NIUMI NATIONAL PARK)

Parts of **Niumi National Park** remain stunning mangroves, lagoons and woodlands, while others have been eroded and replaced with marijuana plantations. Foday's cute **Madiyana Safari Lodge** (☎ 9920201; www.paradise island-gambia.com; per person incl breakfast US$30) sits in a pretty spot on the western seafront and has thatched huts, kerosene lighting and fabulous food. It's tricky to reach by public transport – contact Foday to arrange pick-up.

JUFUREH & JAMES ISLAND

When Alex Haley, the American author of *Roots*, traced his origins to **Jufureh**, the tiny village quickly turned into a favourite tourist destination. Apart from the Kinte family, Haley's supposed relatives, there's little to see, though the small **slavery museum** (☎ 7710276; admission US$2; ☺ 10am-5pm Mon-Sat) is worth a visit. A *pirogue* trip to **James Island** with its crumbling foundations of a 1650s slave fort is worth doing.

In Albreda, right next to Jufureh, you can stay in the bungalows of the **Kunta Kinte Roots Camp** (☎ 9905322; baboucarrlo@hotmail.com; s/d US$20/38).

The easiest way to visit Jufureh is with an organised tour (see p334 for operators). Otherwise, take the ferry to Barra and find a shared (US$1) or hire taxi (return US$38).

BAOBOLONG WETLAND RESERVE & KIANG WEST NATIONAL PARK

A *pirogue* cruise through the *bolongs* (creeks) and thick mangroves of the **Baobolong Wetland Reserve** is great for bird-spotting. Nearby **Kiang West National Park** (admission US$1.30) has even more bird species, as well as bushbucks and sitatungas, but is less accessible. An easy-to-reach viewpoint is Toubab Kollon, from where an escarpment follows the river.

The easiest way of exploring both is by organised tour with **Tendaba Camp** (☎ 6401130, 9766588; tendaba@qanet.gm; bungalows per person US$11, VIP r US$38), a popular upriver stop and simple holiday camp. The scenic way of getting there is on a river tour (see p334 for operators).

UPPER GAMBIA RIVER

WASSU STONE CIRCLES

About 25km northwest of Janjangbureh, near Kuntaur, are the **Wassu Stone Circles** (admission US$1.30), a 1200-year-old megalith arrangement which archaeologists believe to have been used as burial grounds. There's a small historical museum.

Wassu lies off the northbank road. Take it in as a side trip while travelling up or on a day trip from Janjangbureh (the hotels there can arrange tours).

JANJANGBUREH

pop 107,000

Janjangbureh (Georgetown) is a sleepy, former colonial administrative centre. It is situated on the northern edge of MacCarthy Island in the Gambia River, and is reached via ferry links from either bank. There is little in terms of infrastructure – no banks and no hospital. A walk around town reveals a few historical buildings, including the old Commissioner's Quarter, a 200-year-old wooden house once inhabited by freed slaves, and the foundations of a colonial warehouse. The surroundings are great for birdwatching.

Sleeping & Eating

At the eastern end of town, **Baobolong Camp** (☎ 5676133; fax 5676120; Owen St; s/d US$13/26) has a lovely, riverine garden setting, though rooms aren't exactly spotless and plenty of young 'guides' haunt the place. Across the river, **Janjangbureh Camp** (☎ 9816944; www.gambia-river. com; s/d US$11/19) has quirky if dusty bungalows on a vast terrain between forest and water. It's a good base for river trips with Gambia River Excursions (see p334). Some 2.5km westwards, near a patch of woodland, **Bird Safari Camp** (☎ 7336570, Skype 01202884100; www.bsc.gm; per person incl breakfast US$34; 🖳 🖳) is the remotest of the lot – not a problem if you come with a Hidden Gambia boat excursion (see p334), and fantastic if you're here for birdwatching. Simple meals are served at **Talamanca Lodge** (☎ 9921100; talamancalodge@yahoo.com; Findlay St), and the courtyard of **Bendula Restaurant** (Owen St) is a good address for cold beer.

Getting There & Away

MacCarthy Island can be reached by ferry (passenger/car US$0.20/2) from either the southern or northern bank of the river. Most bush taxis turn off the main road between Soma and Basse Santa Su to drop off passengers at the southern ferry ramp; request this when entering the taxi.

GAMBIA RIVER NATIONAL PARK

South of Kuntaur, five islands in the Gambia River are protected as a national park. It's home to the **Chimpanzee Rehabilitation Trust** (CRA; www.chimprehab.com), which helps once-captured chimpanzees to live in the wild again. The only way to get more than just a chance sighting of the chimps is by spending a night in the luxury safari tents of **Badi Mayo Camp** (☎ 9947430; badimayo@yahoo.com; per person US$150). However, when this book went to press, the brilliant project was under threat of closure. Check the situation before setting out.

To travel here, call Badi Mayo to arrange pick-up by boat from Kuntaur, or even a private taxi all the way from the coast. If you can't stay at Badi Mayo, go to Kuntaur and contact **Faldeh** (☎ 9707770). He can take you on a boat tour around the park's navigable channel – a beautiful trip with good bird-spotting chances. You might even glimpse a chimp.

BASSE SANTA SU
pop 182,000

With its dusty roads and packed trading stalls, the Gambia's easternmost town almost spills into the scenic river bend that frames it.

Trust Bank (☎ 5668907) and **Standard Chartered Bank** (☎ 4668218) can change money (no ATMs). If you haven't found all the necessary immigration officials at the border, you can get your entry stamp from the immigration office in town.

The colonial warehouse **Traditions** (☎ 7335562; r US$10) is a simple, clean place to stay. It overlooks the waters and ferry crossing, and is a great birding spot. Across the river, **Fulladu Camp** (☎ 9906791; r per person US$13) is another option, with bungalows on a vast, leafy terrain.

There are plenty of street stalls and simple chop shops in town. Try Mike's Bar Peace & Love for cold beers.

Getting There & Away

Gelli-gellis go to the ferry ramp for Janjangbureh (US$2, one hour), Soma (US$4, four hours) and Serekunda (US$10, eight hours).

The ferry (passenger/car US$0.20/3) to the Gambia River's northern bank takes one car at a time. Small metal tubs can push you across for US$2.

Sept-place (seven-seat) taxis go to Vélingara in Senegal (US$1, one hour), from where you can carry on to Tambacounda. The border crossing is usually smooth just make sure you get all the correct stamps there or at the Basse immigration post.

THE GAMBIA DIRECTORY

ACCOMMODATION

At the Atlantic Coast resorts of Bakau, Fajara, Kotu Strand and Kololi the choice of accommodation ranges from simple hostels to five-star hotels. Upcountry, your options are normally limited to basic guesthouses and hotels. Budget prices in this chapter are under US$30, midrange US$30 to US$95 and top end above US$95. All prices quoted are high-season rates (applicable from October to April) in low season, they may be 25% or even 50% lower.

ACTIVITIES

Beach-related activities such as swimming, water sports and fishing are popular around the coast. Upcountry, it's all about birdwatching tours around the national parks and *pirogue* excursions.

BUSINESS HOURS

Banks From 1pm to 4pm Monday to Thursday, with lunch break from 1pm to 2.30pm on Friday.

Government offices From 8am to 3pm or 4pm Monday to Thursday, and from 8am to 12.30pm on Friday.

Restaurants Lunch from 11am to 2.30pm, dinner from 6pm onwards.

Shops and businesses From 8.30am to 1pm and from 2.30pm to 5.30pm Monday to Thursday; from 8am until noon on Friday and Saturday.

DANGERS & ANNOYANCES

Serious crime is fairly rare in the Gambia, though muggings and petty theft do occur, particularly around the tourist centres. Avoid walking around alone after dark. Women in particular should be careful at the beaches, where some readers have reported instances of sexual assault.

Many visitors to the Gambia complain about the beach boys (known as 'bumsters') who wait outside hotels and offer tourists anything from souvenirs to drugs and sex. It's best to ignore these guys completely.

They might respond with verbal abuse, but it's all hot air.

EMBASSIES & CONSULATES

Germany (Map p322; ☎ 4227783; 29 Independence Dr, Banjul; ☉ 8am-1pm, closed Tue)
Guinea (Map p322; ☎ 4226862, 909964; top fl, 78A Daniel Goddard St, Banjul; ☉ 9am-4pm Mon-Thu, 9am-1.30pm & 2.30-4pm Fri)
Guinea-Bissau (Map pp326-7; ☎ 4226862; Atlantic Rd, Bakau; ☉ 9am-2pm Mon-Fri, to 1pm Sat)
Mali (Map p322; 26 Cherno Adama Bah St, Banjul)
Mauritania (Map pp326-7; ☎ 4491153; Badala Park Way, Kololi; ☉ 8am-4pm Mon-Fri)
Senegal (Map pp326-7; ☎ 4373752; off Kairaba Ave, Fajara; ☉ 8am-2pm & 2.30-5pm Mon-Thu, to 4pm Fri)
Sierra Leone (Map p322; ☎ 4228206; 67 Daniel Goddard St, Banjul; ☉ 8.30am-4.30pm Mon-Thu, to 1.30pm Fri)
UK (Map pp326-7; ☎ 4495133/4; fax 4496134; http://uk ingambia.fco.gov.uk; 48 Atlantic Rd, Fajara; ☉ 8am-1pm Mon-Thu, to 12.30pm Fri)
USA (Map pp326-7; ☎ 4392856; http://banjul.usem bassy.gov; 92 Kairaba Ave, Fajara; ☉ 8.30am-12.30pm)

Several European countries have honorary consuls, including Belgium (at the Kairaba Hotel, Kololi; Map pp326–7), Denmark, Sweden and Norway (Saitmatty Rd, Bakau; Map pp326–7).

EMERGENCIES
Ambulance ☎ 16
Fire ☎ 18
Police ☎ 17

FESTIVALS & EVENTS
Held biannually in June, the one-week **Roots Homecoming Festival** features concerts by Gambian and diaspora artists, as well as seminars and lectures. The high point is the weekend in Jufureh, where local dance troupes and bands drown the village in music.

HOLIDAYS
As well as the religious holidays listed in the Africa Directory chapter (p1140), these are the public holidays observed in the Gambia:
1 January New Year's Day
18 February Independence Day

VACCINATION CERTIFICATES

A yellow-fever vaccination certificate is re-quired of travellers coming from an infected area.

PRACTICALITIES

- Despite the British legacy, Gambians drive on the right-hand side of the road.
- The electricity supply in the Gambia is 220V. Most plugs have three square pins, as used in Britain, though two round pins, as with those in continental Europe, are also in use.
- The Gambia uses the metric system.

---

1 May Workers' Day
15 August Assumption

INTERNET ACCESS
It's easy to find a sluggish internet cafe along the coast – Quantumnet is the main provider. Upcountry, access is harder to find.

MONEY
The local currency dalasi (D) fluctuates strongly. There aren't any official changing points at the border, just very persistent black-market changers. You'll be fine using CFA, though, until you get to the coast, where changing money is easier. Many hotels can recommend an informal changer, though the rates may be similar to those the banks propose.

There are no ATMs upcountry, and you're best off changing all you need at the coast.

TELEPHONE
The telephone system is handled by Gamtel, which has offices and telecentres in Banjul, Bakau, Serekunda and most upcountry towns. To connect to a local mobile network, buy a SIM card from one of the providers (Comium, Gamcel or Gamtel) and top up with cards available at shops and stalls.

TOURIST INFORMATION
The Association of Small Scale Enterprises in Tourism (ASSET) is a great source of information for those wanting to travel responsibly. Check its site or visit it at **Cultural Encounters** (Map pp326-7; ☎ 4497675; www.asset-gambia.com; above Timbooktoo bookshop, Fajara).

VISAS
Visas are not needed for nationals of Commonwealth countries, Germany, Italy, Australia, Luxembourg, the Netherlands,

Scandinavian and Ecowas countries for stays of up to 90 days. For those needing one, visas are normally valid for one month and cost around US$45; you'll need to provide two photos. The **Immigration Office** (Map p322; ☎ 4228611; OAU Blvd, Banjul; ☏ 8am-4pm) deals with visa extensions (US$10). For onward travel, get your visa from the relevant embassy. Most embassies will deal with requests within 48 hours. You cannot buy visas on the borders with Senegal.

TRANSPORT IN THE GAMBIA

GETTING THERE & AWAY
Air
Brussels Airlines is the only scheduled airline connecting Gambia and Europe. Most people get here on charter flights with **Gambia Experience** (in UK ☎ 0845 330 4567; www.gambia.co.uk). For inner-African flights, you'll usually have to go to Dakar first.

Brussels Airlines (Map pp326-7; ☎ 4466880; www.brusselsairlines.com; Badala Park Way, Kololi)

Land
Minibuses and bush taxis run regularly between Barra and the border at Karang (US$2), where Dakar-bound bush taxis and minibuses (US$12, six hours) are normally waiting.

To get to southern Senegal (Casamance), minibuses and bush taxis leave from Serekunda petrol station (US$6, five hours). Transport also goes from Brikama to Ziguinchor.

At the far-eastern tip of the Gambia, bush taxis run from Basse Santa Su to Vélingara (US$3, 45 minutes, 27km), and from there bush taxis go to Tambacounda (US$3, three hours).

GETTING AROUND
Boat
Two private operators offer excursions, including tailor-made trips upriver.

Gambia River Excursions (Map pp326-7; ☎ 4494360; www.gambia-river.com; Fajara) Also has a base at Janjangbureh Camp in Janjangbureh. Renowned for its bird-and-breakfast excursions.

Hidden Gambia (☎ Skype 01202884100; www.hiddengambia.com) Has a base at Bird Safari Camp in Janjangbureh and arranges trips from the coast. Great for tailor-made tours.

Car & Motorcycle
Reliable car-hire companies include the following:

AB Rent-a-Car (Map pp326-7; ☎ 4460926; abrentacar@gamtel.gm; Kairaba Hotel, Senegambia Strip, Kololi)

Hertz (Map pp326-7; ☎ 4390041; hertz@gamtel.gm; Total Petrol Station)

Local Transport
The southbank road from the coast eastwards was in a terrible state when we visited, though roadworks had been announced. Unless this has been fixed, the recently sealed northbank road is the better option for journeys upcountry. It's best to cross on the ferry from Banjul to Barra on foot and get a *sept-place* taxi (shared seven-seater) to Kerewan, from where you can change for transport heading further east. *Sept-place* taxis are by no means a comfy way of travelling – however, they are still infinitely better than the battered *gelli-gelli* minibuses. A few green, government-owned 'express' buses also ply the major roads. You can get on at Tippa petrol station in Serekunda – prepare for a slow, bouncy ride.

Tours
See left for agencies that organise boat tours.

Gambia Experience (Map pp326-7; ☎ 4461104; www.gambia.co.uk; Senegambia Beach Hotel, Kololi) Gambia's biggest tour operator.

Gambia Tours (off Map pp326-7; ☎ 4462601/2; www.gambiatours.gm) Efficient, family-run enterprise.

Tilly's Tours (Map pp326-7; ☎ 9800215; www.tillystours.com; Senegambia Strip, Kololi) Small company with responsible tourism products.

Ghana

Hailed as West Africa's golden child, Ghana deserves its place in the sun. Its beaches are buttered with thick white sand and its savannahs are blessed with the footprints of elephants – no wonder travellers can't get enough.

Often labelled Africa's greatest success story, Ghana's green-gold-and-red flag has been flying high since 1957. The country stands proudly as a beacon of hope on the rocky West African coastline. The wind of change that once swept through Ghana is now a soft, salty breeze; it cools the air and kisses the coastline, still haunted by the legacy of the slave trade.

Linking the dry, dusty north with the spectacular seascape of the south, Accra is where the music comes alive. Laced with laughter, hip-life music permeates cocktail bars, swish clubs and restaurants. Let the hot sun hug you and the beat get under your skin; follow it as it draws you into its relentless rhythm.

Travel to the crashing waterfalls of the east and the world-class waves of the west; past mud-and-stick mosques and crumbling colonial architecture. Don't miss Mole National Park, where sunburnt savannahs host populations of elephants, antelopes and monkeys. At the end of a long, hot day, slip into the night and take a peek at the inky sky: we bet you the stars will be out.

There's a good reason they call Ghana 'Africa for beginners': you'll never want your trip to end.

GHANA

FAST FACTS

- **Area** 231,000 sq km
- **ATMs** In Accra and large towns
- **Borders** Burkina Faso, Côte d'Ivoire, Togo
- **Budget** Accra US$50 to US$70, elsewhere US$30 to US$50
- **Capital** Accra
- **Languages** English, Akan, Dagbani
- **Money** Cedi; US$1 = C1.43, €1 = C2.05
- **Population** 23 million
- **Seasons** Hot and humid year-round with rains June to August and September to October
- **Telephone** Country code ☎ 233; international access code ☎ 00
- **Time** GMT/UTC
- **Visa** Arrange in advance; US$80

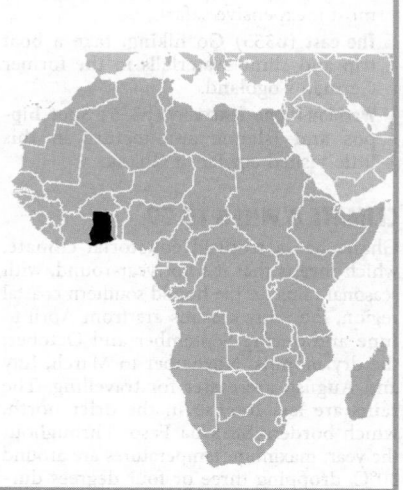

HOW MUCH?

- **Purse made from recycled water sachets** US$3.50
- **Elephant safari** US$0.50
- **Taxi ride across Accra** US$4
- **Hip-life album** US$4
- **Barbecued bat** US$0.70

LONELY PLANET INDEX

- **1L petrol** US$0.50
- **1.5L bottled water** US$1
- **Bottle of Star beer** US$1.40
- **Souvenir football shirt** US$5.60
- **Plate of jollof rice** US$1.40

HIGHLIGHTS

- **The coast** (p347) Dance and take drumming lessons on the beaches of Kokrobite and Anomabu. Then head out west in search of surf and sea turtles at Busua, Akwidaa Beach and Axim.
- **Ghosts of the slave trade** (p347 and p349) Tour the castles of Cape Coast and Elmina to learn about the history of slavery.
- **Mole National Park** (p355) Join the world's most inexpensive safari.
- **The east** (p355) Go hiking, take a boat trip and climb waterfalls in the former German Togoland.
- **Wechiau Hippo Sanctuary** (p355) Spot hippos and Islamic architecture in this little-visited corner of Ghana.

CLIMATE & WHEN TO GO

Ghana has a tropical equatorial climate, which means that it's hot year-round, with seasonal rains. In the humid southern coastal region, the rainy seasons are from April to June and during September and October; the dry months, November to March, July and August, are easier for travelling. The rains are less intense in the drier north, which borders Burkina Faso. Throughout the year, maximum temperatures are around 30°C, dropping three or four degrees during the brief respite between rainy seasons. Humidity is constantly high, at about 80%.

ITINERARIES

- **Two Weeks** Begin in Accra (p341; two nights), then fly up north (you could travel by road, but it will rob you of a night) to Tamale (p354; two nights), then on to Larabanga (p354; one night) and Mole (p355; two nights) to lock eyes with an elephant. Then head down south to Kumasi (p350; two nights) to pay a visit to the nearby Ashanti villages, before continuing back to Accra (one night). Then check out the beaches of Anomabu (p347; two nights) or Kokrobite (p347), before returning to the capital to catch your flight home. Alternatively, you could head straight to Kumasi (p350; two nights) from Accra, then travel to Cape Coast (p347; three nights) to explore Kakum and the surrounding area. You could then move further west to Busua (p349; two nights) and Akwidaa Beach (p349; three nights) before returning to Accra.
- **One Month** With a month to spare, you can do all of the above plus throw in visits to the east. If possible, fly from Accra to Tamale (p354) – if not, take your time bussing it to Kumasi (p350) and then further north – and then travel to Mole National Park (p355) and Larabanga (p354). Continue west to the Wechiau Hippo Sanctuary (p355).

HISTORY

Present-day Ghana has been inhabited since 4000 BC, filled by successive waves of migrants from the north and east. By the 13th century several kingdoms had developed, growing rich from the country's massive gold deposits and gradually expanding south along the Volta River to the coast.

Power & Conflict

By the 16th century one of the kingdoms, the Ashanti, emerged as the dominant power, conquering tribes left, right and centre and taking control of trade routes to the coast. Its capital, Kumasi, became a sophisticated urban centre, with facilities and services equal to those in Europe at the time. And it wasn't long until the Europeans discovered this African kingdom. First the Portuguese came sniffing around the coast, and then came the British, French, Dutch, Swedish and Danish. They all built forts by the sea

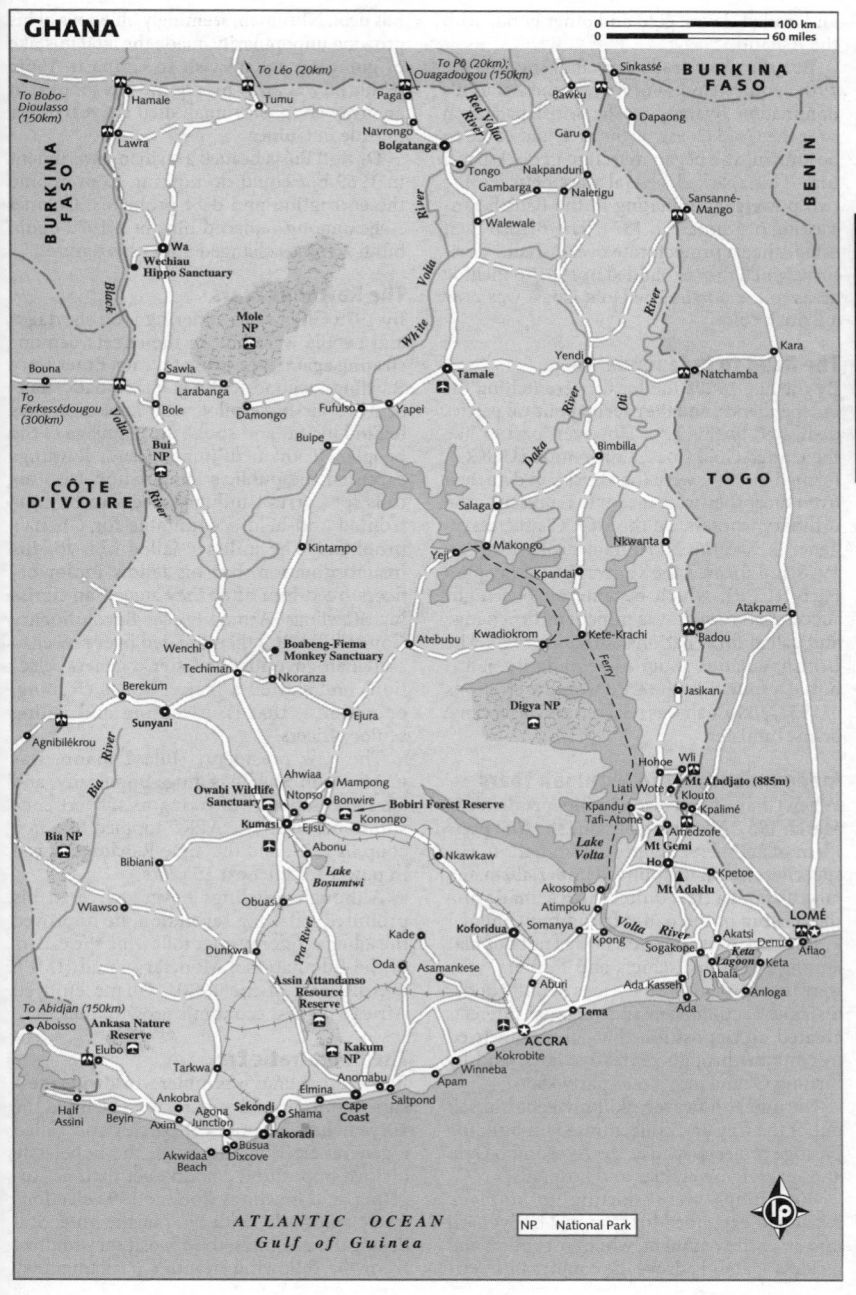

GHANA

GHANA

To Bobo-
Dioulasso
(150km)

To Léo (20km)

To Pô (20km);
Ouagadougou (150km)

To
Ferkessédougou
(300km)

To Abidjan (150km)

To Abidjàn (150km)

0   100 km
0   60 miles

**BURKINA
FASO**

BURKINA
FASO

CÔTE
D'IVOIRE

TOGO

BENIN

Hamale
Tumu
Paga
Sinkassé
Bawku
Dapaong
Lawra
Navrongo
Garu
Bolgatanga
Tongo
Nakpanduri
Sansanné-
Mango
Gambarga
Nalerigu
Wa
Wechiau
Hippo Sanctuary
Walewale
Kara
Mole
NP
Yendi
Natchamba
Bouna
Sawla
Tamale
Larabanga
Bole
Damongo
Fufulso
Yapei
Buipe
Bimbilla
Bui
NP
Kintampo
Salaga
Nkwanta
Yeji
Makongo
Atakpamé
Kpandai
Badou
Wenchi
**Boabeng-Fiema
Monkey Sanctuary**
Atebubu
Kwadiokrom
Kete-Krachi
Jasikan
Berekum
Techiman
Nkoranza
Agnibilékrou
Ejura
Digya NP
Hohoe
Wli
Mt Afadjato (885m)
**Owabi Wildlife
Sanctuary**
Ahwiaa
Mampong
Liati Wote
Klouto
Bia NP
Ntonso
Bonwire
Bobiri Forest Reserve
Kpandu
Tafi-Atomé
Kpalimé
Bibiani
Kumasi
Ejisu
Konongo
Amedzofe
Abonu
Mt Gemi
Wiawso
Obuasi
Lake
Bosumtwi
Nkawkaw
Akosombo
Ho
Kpetoe
Lake
Volta
Mt Adaklu
Atimpoku
LOMÉ
Dunkwa
Kade
Koforidua
Somanya
Akatsi
Denu
Aboisso
Oda
Asamankese
Kpong
Sogakope
Dabala
Keta
Aflao
**Ankasa Nature
Reserve**
Aburi
Ada Kasseh
Keta
Lagoon
Anloga
Elubo
**Assin Attandanso
Resource Reserve**
Tema
Ada
Half
Assini
Beyin
Tarkwa
**Kakum
NP**
ACCRA
Ankobra
Agona
Junction
Sekondi
Elmina
Anomabu
Kokrobite
Winneba
Axim
Shama
Saltpond
Apam
Akwidaa
Beach
Búsua
Dixcove
Takoradi
**Cape
Coast**

*Red Volta
River*

Black

Volta

White

Volta

River

*Daka
River*

*Oti
River*

*Bia
River*

Pra River

Volta River

ATLANTIC OCEAN
Gulf of Guinea

NP   National Park

and traded slaves, gold and other goods with the Ashanti.

But the slave trade was abolished in the 19th century, and with it went the Ashanti's domination. By that time the British had taken over the Gold Coast, as the area had come to be known, and began muscling in on Ashanti turf. This sparked several wars between the two powers, culminating in the British ransacking of Kumasi in 1874. The British then established a protectorate over Ashanti territory, which they expanded in 1901 to include areas to the north. The Gold Coast was now a British colony.

The Road to Independence

By the late 1920s the locals were itching for independence, and they set up political parties dedicated to this aim. However, parties like the United Gold Coast Convention (UGCC), formed in 1947, were too elitist and detached from those they were meant to represent – the ordinary workers. So the UGCC's secretary-general, Kwame Nkrumah, broke away in 1948 and formed the Conventional People's Party (CPP), which became an overnight success. Nkrumah was impatient for change and called for a national strike in 1949. The British, anxious about his popularity, jailed him. Despite this, the CPP won the elections of 1951, Nkrumah was released and he became prime minister.

Independence & the Nkrumah Years

When Ghana finally won its independence in March 1957, Nkrumah became the first president of an independent African nation. His speeches, which denounced imperialism and talked about a free, united Africa, made him the darling of the pan-African movement.

But back home Nkrumah was not popular among traditional chiefs and farmers, who were unimpressed with the idea of unity under his rule. Factionalism and regional interests created an opposition that Nkrumah tried to contain through repressive laws, and by turning Ghana into a one-party state.

Nkrumah, however, skilfully kept himself out of the fray and concentrated on building prestige projects, such as the Akosombo Dam and several universities and hospitals.

But things were starting to unravel. Nkrumah expanded his personal bodyguard into an entire regiment, while corruption and reckless spending drove the country into seri-

ous debt. Nkrumah, seemingly oblivious of his growing unpopularity, made the fatal mistake of going on a state visit to China in 1966. While he was away his regime was toppled in an army coup. Nkrumah died six years later in exile in Guinea.

Dr Kofi Busia headed a civilian government in 1969 but could do nothing to overcome the corruption and debt problems. Colonel Acheampong replaced him in a 1972 coup, but few things changed under his tenure.

The Rawlings Years

By 1979 Ghana was suffering food shortages and people were out on the streets demonstrating against the army fat cats. Enter Jerry Rawlings, a good-looking, charismatic, half-Scottish air-force pilot, who kept cigarettes behind his ear and spoke the language of the people. Nicknamed 'Junior Jesus', Rawlings captured the public's imagination with his calls for corrupt military rulers to be confronted and held accountable for Ghana's problems. The military jailed him for his insubordination, but his fellow junior officers freed him after they staged an uprising. Rawlings' Armed Forces Revolutionary Council (AFRC) then handed over power to a civilian government (after a general election) and started a major 'house cleaning' operation – that is, executing and jailing senior officers.

The new president, Hilla Limann, was uneasy with Rawlings' huge popularity, and later accused him of trying to subvert constitutional rule. The AFRC toppled him in a coup in 1981, and this time Rawlings stayed in power for the next 15 years.

Although Rawlings never delivered his promised left-wing revolution, he improved the ailing economy after following the orders of the International Monetary Fund (IMF). During part of the 1980s, Ghana enjoyed Africa's highest economic growth rates.

The Democratic Era

By 1992 Rawlings was under worldwide pressure to introduce democracy, so he lifted the 10-year ban on political parties and called a general election. However, the hopelessly divided opposition couldn't get their act together, and Rawlings won the 1992 elections freely and fairly, with 60% of the vote. Still licking their wounds, the opposition withdrew from the following month's parliamentary elections, giving Rawlings' newly formed National Democratic Congress (NDC) an easy victory. In 1996 he repeated this triumph in elections that were again considered free and fair. At much the same time, the appointment of Ghanaian Kofi Annan as UN secretary-general boosted national morale. In 1998 in an effort to improve tax collection and spread the burden more equitably, a VAT was successfully introduced. However, a drought in the late 1990s led to morale-sapping electricity and water rationing throughout the country, while a fall in the world prices of cocoa and gold diminished Ghana's foreign-exchange earnings.

After eight years of Rawlings and the NDC (the constitution barred Rawlings from standing for a third term in the 2000 presidential elections), his nominated successor and former vice-president, Professor John Atta Mills, lost to Dr John Kufuor, leader of the well-established New Patriotic Party (NPP). When Kufuor was elected in 2000, he vowed to help elevate Ghana to a middle-class country within 15 years. Some fun-loving members of Accra's growing middle class say his biggest legacy is the creation of the Accra Mall, a shiny shopping mall on the outskirts of town, complete with the country's first multiscreen cinema. Under the Kufuor administration, primary-school enrolment increased by 25% and many of Ghana's poor were granted access to free health care.

Ghana Today

The 2008 election was widely regarded as a test of Ghana's ability to become a modern democracy. Despite an anxious two-round vote and marked tension between John Atta Mills and his NPP competitor Nana Akufo-Addo, the election passed without serious violence. Akufo-Addo, darling of the West and a member of the Ashanti ethnic group, vowed to pour oil profits into free education, healthcare and the creation of jobs. Atta Mills, who won by a slim margin, campaigned on a platform of change, scoring points with minority groups, the poor and the disheartened.

Today Ghana is regarded by international analysts as West Africa's golden child: one of the continent's most stable and promising democracies. Indeed, it was picked by the US administration for President Barack Obama's first official visit to sub-Saharan Africa, ostensibly for that very reason.

CULTURE

When oil reserves were discovered off the coast in 2007, many Ghanaians felt like they'd won the lottery. Ghana has been on the cusp of change for some time and this, many felt, heralded a leap into the arms of the developed world. Others, jaded by the failings of long-gone leaders, didn't dare get their hopes up.

As you travel through Ghana, you'll see, hear, feel and smell every aspect of this country's struggle for place. Ghana can't be lumped in with the most underdeveloped parts of Africa. The broken roads of Guinea and Liberia are a world away from Ghana's smooth, sealed coastal highways. If you're a middle-class young professional living in the leafy 'burbs of Accra, life is good. Chances are you have running water, power, street lights and a fair wage. Your mobile phone never stops ringing, you go on dates to restaurants and the kids next door don't have to share a textbook in class.

But in Accra's poorest suburbs, places like Jamestown and Korle Gonno, streams of stagnant sewage mark the streets, babies are bathed in buckets and school-aged children sell water sachets in the street. Though education is supposed to be accessible to all, the reality is that uniforms and textbooks are too expensive for many. Look around, if you decide to visit these areas, and you'll notice details that hint at greater problems.

For years Ghana has had a reputation as Africa's friendliest, most welcoming country. That's not strictly true, as much of Africa welcomes travellers with open arms. What Ghana does possess is an amazing joy for life. Celebrations are a big part of Ghanaian culture, and the good times don't stop when the last drink is served. Here, singing is relied upon as a means of expression; melodic tones drift down rust-red alleys and children practice dance moves in the street. You'll rarely hear anyone swear in Ghana.

Whichever part of the country you visit, be it the gritty urban cities of Accra or Takoradi, the sun-drenched coast or soporific villages, Ghana's soundtrack will be a constant travel companion. From the age of three or four children are taught to dance, and we're not

GHANA

GHANA

HOME-GROWN BEATS

Until the early 1990s, Ghana's music scene was dominated by high-life, a mellow mix of big band jazz, Christian hymns and sailors' sonnets. High-life began in the 1920s, when the trend for fancy European-style nights out leaked into Ghana (hence the name).

The first hip-life tracks aired in 1992, a hybrid of rhythmic African lyrics poured over imported American hip-hop beats. Ghana has been dancing to it ever since, and you won't be able to get through a few days here (let alone an entire trip) without letting the sweet sounds of hip-life into your world. It's more than just a musical genre; it's an insight into Ghanaian society, steeped in its own traditions and languages, but increasingly influenced by the diaspora in America and Britain.

Reggie Rockstone, Ghana's 'godfather of hip-life' is the man to listen to. His early work, such as the 1998 classic 'Keep Your Eyes on the Road', is a happy marriage of high-life notes and 1990s lyrics. 'Eyes', a comment on Africa's relationship with the West, is another good bet. In 1999, Obrafuor exploded onto the hip-life scene with his track 'Kwame Nkrumah', a resounding tribute to the former leader and one that united the older generation with the experimental hip-life crowd. Obrafuor's *Pae Mu Ka* album is widely regarded as one of the most influential hip-life recordings ever made. Other artists to look out for include Obour, Castro, Tinny and Shoeshine Boy.

It follows that this genre, so strongly influenced by a sense of place in the world, has regional accents. Northern hip-life, produced predominately in the Muslim city of Tamale, is pretty different from the tracks produced down south. Up north, where the air is dustier and the land drier, hip-life takes cues from the haunting, melismatic style of music popular across the Sahel, with vocals sometimes in Dagbani. Arguably, nobody has had a greater impact on the northern hip-life scene than Big Adam. If you listen to only one album of his, make it *Asalamu-Alaakum*, acclaimed for its mesmerising Islamic praise vocals.

talking ballet. It's not unusual to see little kids copying the hip grinding and ass shaking that characterises the average Ghanaian party.

The Akan people of the southern and central regions of Ghana are famous for their goldwork, woodcarving and weird and wonderful chiefs' insignia such as swords and umbrella tops. The Ashanti, in particular, are famous for their gorgeous kente cloth, with its distinctive basketwork pattern. It was originally worn only by royalty, but you can now buy beautiful swathes from fabric markets.

FOOD & DRINK

Fiery sauces and oily soups are the mainstay of Ghanaian cuisine and are usually served with a starchy staple like rice, *fufu* (cooked and mashed cassava, plantain or yam) or *banku* (fermented maize meal). Groundnut stew is a warming, spicy dish cooked with liquefied groundnut paste (available at markets), ginger and either fish or meat. Palm-nut soup (fashioned from tomatoes, ginger, garlic and chilli pepper, as well as palm nut) is often served with oil floating on the top; it looks downright greasy, but it tastes good. You may wish to go easy on the *fufu* – some travellers say it makes them sweat like crazy.

ENVIRONMENT

Ghana is dominated by flat or gently undulating lowlands, with coastal plains punctuated by saline lagoons in the south, forested hill ranges in the centre and a low plateau in the northern two-thirds. All of the country lies below 1000m. Keta Lagoon, east of Accra, near the Togolese border, is Ghana's largest lagoon. Dominating the eastern flank of the country is Lake Volta, formed when the Volta River was dammed in the mid-1960s. It's the world's largest artificial lake.

The World Bank estimates that as much as 75% of Ghana's forest cover has been destroyed by logging, much of it illegal. Marine and coastal areas are threatened by high levels of erosion and dense population concentrations.

Ghana has five national parks and nine protected areas. Mole National Park (p355), in the northwest of the country, protects savannah woodland and is the best place to see wildlife, including elephants, baboons, warthogs and antelope species.

ACCRA

pop 2.9 million

Ghana's beating heart probably won't inspire love letters, but you might just grow to like it. The capital's hot, sticky streets are perfumed with sweat, fumes and yesterday's cooking oil. Like balloons waiting to be burst, clouds of dirty humidity linger above stalls selling mangoes, *banku* and rice. The city's tendrils reach out towards the beach, the centre and the west, each one a different Ghanaian experience.

INFORMATION
Bookshops

Bookshelf.net (Map p342; 17th Lane, Osu) Stocks a reasonable selection of new and secondhand material. Opposite Frankie's.

Vidya Books (Map p342; 18th Lane, Osu) Accra's most popular stop for new fiction and magazines.

Cultural Centres

Alliance Française (Map p342; ☎ 021-773134; www. alliancefrancaiseghana.com; Liberation Link, Airport Residential Area) Cultural events and lectures.

British Council (Map p344; ☎ 021-610090; www. britishcouncil.org/ghana; Liberia Rd) Air-con library with English newspapers and magazines. Organises cultural events and lectures.

Internet Access

There are hundreds of internet cafes dotted all over Accra. Wi-fi is available at many top-end and midrange hotels.

Busy Internet (Map p344; www.busyinternet.com; Ring Road Central, Asylum Down; ⏱ 24hr) Ghana's sleekest web cafe by far. Fast browsing, printing services and a laptop lounge. There is a second (much smaller) branch in the Accra Mall.

SharpNet (Map p342; Ring Road East) As popular as Busy Internet but not quite as high-tech.

Medical Services

Ask your embassy for a list of recommended doctors and specialists. The main public hospitals in Accra are included here. Pharmacies are everywhere.

Lister Hospital (off Map p342; ☎ 021-812325; www. listerhospital.com.gh; Airport Hills) Ultra-modern 25-bed hospital. Has lab, pharmacy and ER services. General consultations cost around C20 plus a registration fee longer stays can be pricey.

Nyaho Medical Centre (off Map p342; ☎ 021-775341; Airport Residential Area) Large, well-equipped facility.

Trust Hospital (Map p342; ☎ 021-776787; Cantonments Rd, Osu) A private, slightly shabby-looking hospital that nevertheless has decent general-practitioner and lab services.

Money

The main branches of Barclays and Standard Chartered banks are on High St; there are smaller branches around town, including a Barclays on Kwame Nkrumah Ave in Adabraka. Almost all of their branches have working ATMs. Foreign-exchange bureaux are easy to find – try Kojo Thompson Rd in Adabraka or the main shopping drags in Osu.

Post

Accra North post office (Map p344; Nsawam Rd) Just north of Nkrumah Circle.

IN GOD'S NAME

From sleepy coastal villages to edgy, urban parts of Accra, you'll spot curiously named shops, chop bars and businesses. Many of these take cues from religion, while others are influenced by family, friends and hopes for the future. Either way, they almost always rouse a smile in even the most travel weary. Here are a few to look out for:

- Covered in the Blood of Jesus Hair Salon, Takoradi
- If God Say Yes Snack Shop, Accra
- If You Can Read This, Give Thanks to the Teacher Provision Store, Axim
- Jesus Loves Fashion, Accra
- Meek and Mild Preparatory School, Axim
- You May Cry for Me Chop Bar, Accra

GHANA

GHANA

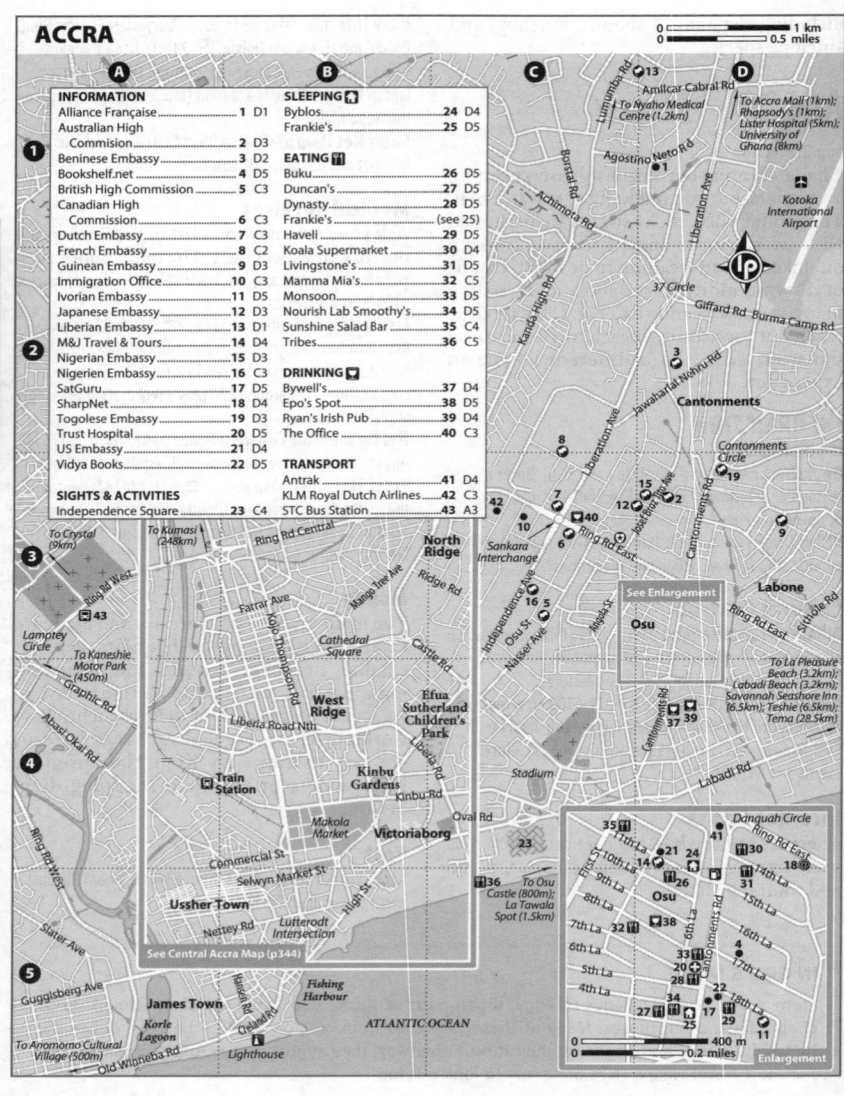

ACCRA

0 ——— 1 km
0 ——— 0.5 miles

INFORMATION	
Alliance Française	1 D1
Australian High Commision	2 D3
Beninese Embassy	3 D2
Bookshelf.net	4 D5
British High Commission	5 C3
Canadian High Commission	6 C3
Dutch Embassy	7 C3
French Embassy	8 C2
Guinean Embassy	9 D3
Immigration Office	10 C3
Ivorian Embassy	11 D5
Japanese Embassy	12 D3
Liberian Embassy	13 D1
M&J Travel & Tours	14 D4
Nigerian Embassy	15 D3
Nigerien Embassy	16 C3
SatGuru	17 D4
SharpNet	18 D4
Togolese Embassy	19 D3
Trust Hospital	20 D5
US Embassy	21 D4
Vidya Books	22 D5

SIGHTS & ACTIVITIES	
Independence Square	23 C4

SLEEPING	
Byblos	24 D4
Frankie's	25 D5

EATING	
Buku	26 D5
Duncan's	27 D5
Dynasty	28 D5
Frankie's	(see 25)
Haveli	29 D5
Koala Supermarket	30 D4
Livingstone's	31 D5
Mamma Mia's	32 C5
Monsoon	33 D5
Nourish Lab Smoothy's	34 D5
Sunshine Salad Bar	35 C4
Tribes	36 C5

DRINKING	
Bywell's	37 D4
Epo's Spot	38 D5
Ryan's Irish Pub	39 D5
The Office	40 C3

TRANSPORT	
Antrak	41 D4
KLM Royal Dutch Airlines	42 C3
STC Bus Station	43 A3

To Crystal (9km)

To Kumasi (248km)

North Ridge

Ring Rd Central

Ring Rd West

Lamptey Circle

To Kaneshie Motor Park (450m)

Graphic Rd

Abasi Okai Rd

Ring Rd West

Slater Ave

Gugglisberg Ave

To Anomomo Cultural Village (500m)

James Town

Korle Lagoon

Old Winneba Rd

Ring Rd West

Ratmal Ave

Fatrai Ave

Kojo Thompson Rd

Cathedral Square

West Ridge

Liberia Road Nth

Train Station

Makola Market

Commercial St

Selwyn Market St

Ussher Town

Nettey Rd

Lutterodt Intersection

See Central Accra Map (p344)

Fishing Harbour

Lighthouse

ATLANTIC OCEAN

Ridge Rd

Castle Rd

Efua Sutherland Children's Park

Kinbu Gardens

Kinbu Rd

Victoriaborg

Oval Rd

High St

Sankara Interchange

Independence Ave

Osu St

Naiser Ave

Nagela St

Stadium

To Osu Castle (800m); La Tawala Spot (1.5km)

Liberation Ave

Ako Adjei Interchange

Ring Rd East

Ring Rd East

See Enlargement

Osu

Labone

Ring Rd East

Cantonments Rd

To La Pleasure Beach (3.2km); Labadi Beach (3.2km); Savannah Seashore Inn (6.5km); Teshie (6.5km); Tema (28.5km)

Labadi Rd

Lumumba Rd

Amilcar Cabral Rd

To Nyaho Medical Centre (1.2km)

Agostino Neto Rd

Achimota Rd

Barkai Rd

Kanda High Rd

Liberation Ave

Jwaharlal Nehru Rd

Ring Rd East

Liberation Ave

Giffard Rd

Burma Camp Rd

To Accra Mail (1km); Rhapsody's (1km); Lister Hospital (5km); University of Ghana (8km)

Kotoka International Airport

37 Circle

Cantonments

Cantonments Circle

Sittelle Rd

Danquah Circle

Ring Rd East

0 ——— 400 m
0 ——— 0.2 miles

Enlargement

13th La
10th La
9th La
8th La
7th La
6th La
5th La
4th La

Osu

Cantonments Rd

14th La
15th La
7th La

Main post office (Map p344; Ussher Town; 🕑 8am-4.30pm Mon-Fri) Has a poste-restante service.

Telephone
Inexpensive mobile-phone SIM cards are available on almost every street corner throughout Accra; the MTN network is one of the most reliable.

Tourist Information
There's a small tourist-information counter located in the international arrivals hall at the airport.

Tourist office (Map p344; ☎ 021-231817, 021-2202153; 🕑 8am-4pm Mon-Fri) Located 50m down Education Close, off Barnes Rd. Some leaflets are free, others are for sale.

Travel Agencies

Travel agencies are dotted all over Accra, with plenty in Osu. **M&J Travel & Tours** (Map p342; ☎ 21 773 498; www.mandjtravelghana.com; 11th Lane, Osu) and **SatGuru** (Map p342; ☎ 021-227744; Cantonments Rd) are reputable agencies in Osu.

SIGHTS & ACTIVITIES

Set in pleasant grounds, the **national museum** (Map p344; ☎ 021-2021633; Barnes Rd; adult C4.50; ⏰ 9am-6pm Tue-Sun) features excellent displays on various aspects of Ghanaian culture and history. The displays on local crafts, ceremonial objects and the slave trade are excellent.

There is no front door or welcoming sign to the **Makola Market** (Map p344). It's a gradual transition from the usual pavements clogged with vendors hawking secondhand clothes and shoes to the market itself, which only becomes obvious once you can't take a step without tripping over a pile of Chinese-made locks or tube socks and you're sucked into the vortex of the swirling crowds.

Independence Square (Black Star Square; Map p342) is a vast, baking expanse of concrete dominated by an enormous McDonald's-like arch, beneath which the Eternal Flame of African Liberation, lit by Kwame Nkrumah, still flickers. From the square, looking east along the coast towards La Pleasure Beach, you can see **Osu Castle** (off Map p342). Built by the Danes around 1659 and originally called Christiansborg Castle, it's now the seat of government and is off limits to the public.

It's all bronze statues and choreographed fountains at the **Kwame Nkrumah park** (Map p344; High St; adult/child C6/1; ⏰ 10am-6pm), dedicated in the early 1990s to Ghana's first president. The park museum houses a curious collection of Nkrumah's personal belongings, including his presidential desk, bookcase, jacket and student sofa. A prolific writer and teacher, many of Nkrumah's book jackets are also on display.

Because they are fairly concentrated and walkable, James Town and Ussher Town, two of the oldest neighbourhoods in Accra, provide a chance to witness how ordinary Ghanaians go about their everyday lives. These aren't shanty towns like you'd find in Johannesburg or Nairobi, but the people are undoubtedly poor and you may feel uncomfortably voyeuristic just walking around on your own. Ask a local to take you around; negotiate a fee in advance.

SLEEPING

Accra has a good range of places to sleep, though prices are generally expensive. Osu is an excellent central base, but the location usually commands hiked-up hotel bills. Cheaper options can be found around Ring Road East and Asylum Down.

Asylum Down

New Haven (Map p344; ☎ 021-222053; off Ring Road Central; s/d C15/28) For those who don't want to shell out to stay at the fancier Paloma eat-drink-sleep complex, this is an excellent compromise. Tucked behind that hotel on a back street, the New Haven is a nice place in its own right. Rooms are spacious (some have enormous beds) and have private bathrooms, there's a decent courtyard restaurant and you can pop to the Paloma for a beer. Book ahead.

Lemon Lodge (Map p344; ☎ 021-227857; 2nd Mango Tree Ave; r C20) Korkdam's next-door neighbour offers seven rooms arranged around a dingy reception area. Recent renovations have spruced the place up a little and it's a reasonable budget option.

Korkdam Hotel (Map p344; ☎ 021-226797; 2nd Mango Tree Ave; s/d C27/45; 🖳 🛜) The Korkdam's biggest draw is that it's one of the few budget options with (unreliable) wi-fi access. Rooms are large but shabby, with running water, TVs, desks and paper-thin walls. Staff are friendly and there are usually charter taxis waiting nearby. A few steps from Burkina Faso's embassy.

Paloma (Map p344; ☎ 021-228700; Ring Road Central; r from C70; 🅿 🖂 🖳 🛜) Cool, comfortable rooms and bungalows with hot water, wi-fi and every comfort. The centrally located complex includes several restaurants with good food (including breakfast pancakes), a sports bar, a garden area and a courtyard bar. There's car parking and a taxi service.

Osu

Frankie's (Map p342; ☎ 021-773567; www.frankies-ghana.com; Cantonments Rd; s/d US$59/98; 🖂 🖳 🛜) Frankie's is an Osu institution and an Accra landmark. Rooms here are stylish and clean and come with wi-fi access and hot running water. Downstairs, there's an ice-cream parlour, a lounge bar and the famous fast-food joint of the same name.

Byblos (Map p342; ☎ 021-228200; 11th Lane; r from US$65; 🖂 🖳 🛜) Smack-bang in the middle

GHANA

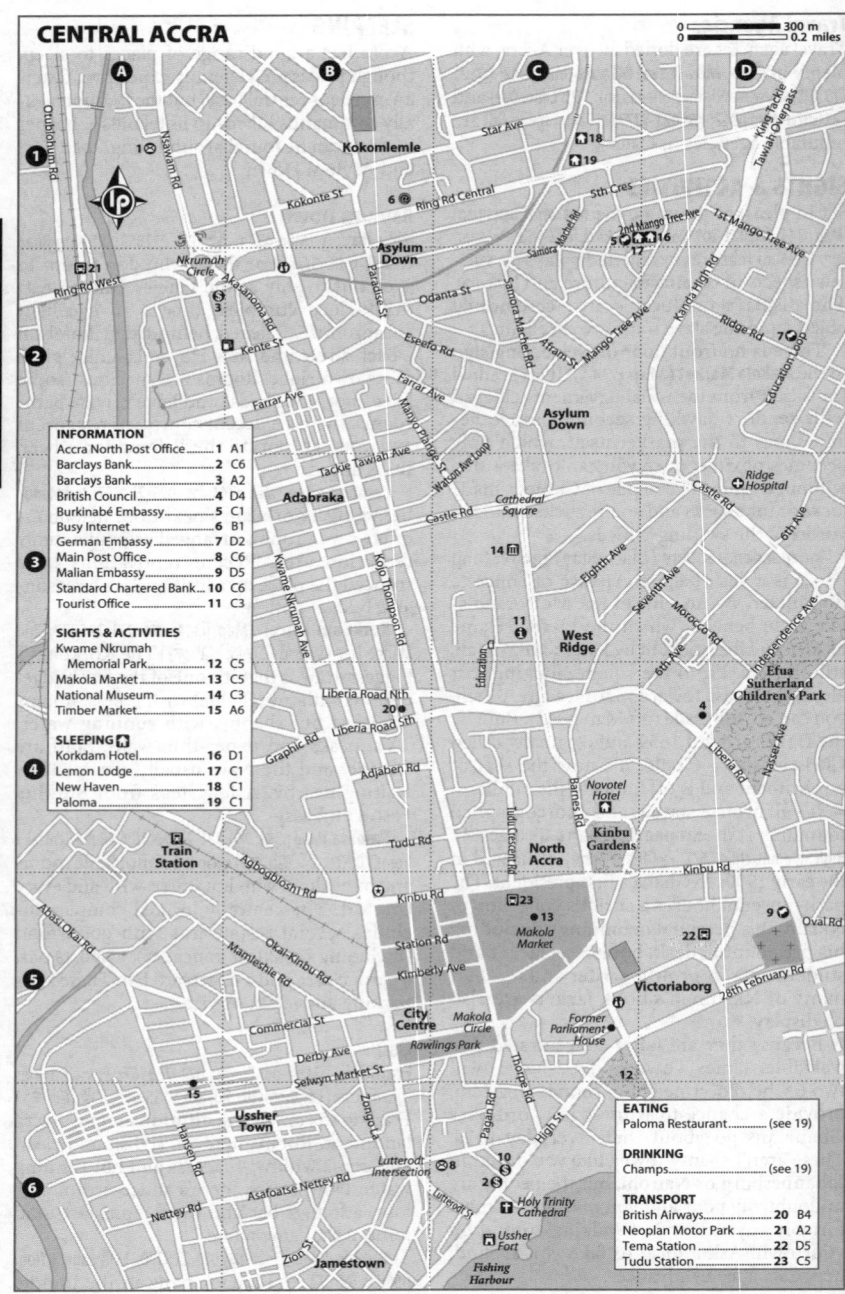

CENTRAL ACCRA

0 —————— 300 m
0 —————— 0.2 miles

INFORMATION
Accra North Post Office	**1** A1
Barclays Bank	**2** C6
Barclays Bank	**3** A2
British Council	**4** D4
Burkinabé Embassy	**5** C1
Busy Internet	**6** B1
German Embassy	**7** D2
Main Post Office	**8** C6
Malian Embassy	**9** D5
Standard Chartered Bank	**10** C6
Tourist Office	**11** C3

SIGHTS & ACTIVITIES
Kwame Nkrumah Memorial Park	**12** C5
Makola Market	**13** C5
National Museum	**14** C3
Timber Market	**15** A6

SLEEPING
Korkdam Hotel	**16** D1
Lemon Lodge	**17** C1
New Haven	**18** C1
Paloma	**19** C1

EATING
| Paloma Restaurant | (see 19) |

DRINKING
| Champs | (see 19) |

TRANSPORT
British Airways	**20** B4
Neoplan Motor Park	**21** A2
Tema Station	**22** D5
Tudu Station	**23** C5

f Osu, this is an excellent midrange option. There's a quiet courtyard set back from the main road and all 28 rooms are well kept nd air-conditioned, with hot water and vi-fi access. The adjacent Venus Cocktail 3ar serves as the hotel's restaurant and offers ood breakfasts.

Suburbs

avannah Seashore Inn (off Map p342; ☎ 024-3523363; vww.ghanaguesthouse.org; 35 Lagoon Rd, Teshie; d C10, ste 15-20) Owned by an American artist, this place makes simple sexy. Basic mud huts with great ocean views, plenty of shade and a vegetarian snack bar. In the suburb of Teshie, about 25 minutes from the city depending on traffic.

Anomomo Cultural Village (off Map p342; ☎ 024-648703; sharonswyer@hotmail.com; Korle Gonno; r C14) Everything is simple and ultra-laid-back at this low-key beachfront set-up, run by a young, welcoming Ghanaian-British family. The handful of rooms (shared bathroom with buckets) attached to the family's outdoor courtyard are basic and the decor is peeling. You'll sometimes hear reggae coming from the music room. Behind the Cambridge School in Korle Gonno.

Crystal (off Map p342; ☎ 021-304634; 27 Akorlu Close, Darkuman; dm/s/d US$10/15/20, camping US$15; 🖳 🛜) The hosts go out of their way to make travelers welcome at this lovely budget set-up in the quiet suburb of Darkuman. Rooms have private bathrooms, TV, and fridges. There's a leafy communal lawn area, a rooftop bar, wi-fi access and good Ghanaian food.

Labadi Beach (off Map p342; ☎ 021-772501; www.legacyhotels.co.za; Labadi Beach; s/d US$270/310; 🅿 🛏 🖳 🖨) Famous as much for its former guests – Tony Blair, Queen Elizabeth II – as for its comforts, the South African chain's offering is one of the most sumptuous in town. The stylish rooms, pool area and interior have a colonial twist. There's every style of room imaginable, including two specially adapted rooms for disabled guests. Rates include a lavish breakfast.

EATING

Accra has the best choice of restaurants in the country, and the food will seem like haute cuisine if you're returning to the city after time spent elsewhere in Ghana. Osu is China Town, Little Italy and your mall food court rolled into one long, clogged road. Some of the upmarket restaurants, where you'll spend

at least C30, are found off the main road, down one of the residential streets.

Most of the midrange and all of the top-end hotels have restaurants and are especially recommended for breakfast splurges. If you're self-catering, the supermarkets in Osu are good, especially **Koala Supermarket** (Map p342; Cantonments Rd), just off Danquah Circle at the top of Cantonments Rd. The **Accra Mall** (off Map p342; near Tetteh Quarshie Interchange) is home to South African supermarkets Game and Shoprite; these are shinier, sleeker and cheaper than Osu's equivalents.

African

La Tawala Spot (off Map p342; around C3) Big, tasty plates of *jollof rice*, the sounds of the ocean and banter with the locals. Simple pleasures.

Buku (Map p342; 10th Lane, Osu; mains from C5) Dig into Ghanaian, Nigerian, Togolese and Senegalese specials at hip Buku. The stylish 2nd-floor open-air dining room seals the deal.

Duncan's (Map p342; 3rd Lane, Osu; mains from C5) Duncan's is another one of those low-key, outdoor chop bars that manage to get it right. Fresh, grilled fish and simple Ghanaian dishes draw a mixed, appreciative crowd.

Tribes (Map p342; Afia African Village; mains from C7; 🕐 7am-10pm) While not quite haute cuisine, the excellent food and location make Tribes one of the best places to go for a relaxed supper. The decked outdoor dining area overlooks a lush garden. The vanilla ice cream with papaya and ginger sauce is recommended.

Livingstone's (Map p342; Osu; mains from C10) First-class West African and French food in an upmarket, atmospheric dining room. If you're facing the entrance to Koala Supermarket, it's the first right.

Rhapsody's (off Map p342; ☎ 024-3225181; www.rhapsodys.co.za; Accra Mall; mains from C10) There's a light, stylish dining room and an outdoor patio at this South African–owned chain. The line-up includes dishes like avocado-brie fillet steak, African-inspired curries and chocolate fudge cake.

Asian & Middle Eastern

Haveli (Map p342; 18th Lane; mains from C7; 🛜) Push back the mosaic door to find a plain but atmospheric dining room and friendly servers. Excellent Indian and Pakistani dishes – not just chicken tikka masala.

GHANA

Dynasty (Map p342; Cantonments Rd; mains from C8; ⊠) Accra's most central Chinese restaurant is also its plushest, with white tablecloths and a good dim sum night most Sundays.

Monsoon (Map p342; Cantonments Rd; mains around C10; ⊠) West Africa has a number of great sushi bars and dressy Monsoon ranks somewhere in the middle. Overpriced sashimi served in a stylish open-air dining room and terrace.

European & American

Nourish Lab Smoothy's (Map p342; 3rd Lane; smoothies from C3; ⊙ 8am-10pm; ⊚) Escape the heat at this air-conditioned smoothie bar. The staff will whip up anything you fancy while you sit back on the sofas, use the free wi-fi or watch MTV.

Paloma Restaurant (Map p342; Ring Road Central; mains from C5; ⊠ ▯) The line-up at the outdoor restaurant attached to the Paloma Hotel includes Ghanaian and Lebanese dishes, burgers and sandwiches.

Sunshine Salad Bar (Map p342; Osu; ☎ 024-4383064; meals C5-10; ⊙ 9am-5pm Mon-Sat) Plates brim high with wonderful big salads, wraps and brown-bread sarnies. There's a good range of fresh juices and vegetarian salads. Sit in the shaded, fan-cooled outdoor courtyard.

Mamma Mia's (Map p342; ☎ 021-264151; 7th Lane; pizzas from C7) Expats swear by the pizza here and the pretty outdoor garden dining area makes everything taste better. Spaghetti and kid-friendly chicken fingers are also served.

Frankie's (Map p342; Cantonments Rd; mains from C7; ⊙ 7am-midnight) Stainless-steel tables, big-screen sports and a vast menu covering everything from hot dogs to meze. Though it feels a bit like the kind of diner you might find at a bowling alley, Frankie's is a crowd-pleaser.

DRINKING

Epo's Spot (Map p342; Osu; ⊠) Climb to the rooftop terrace of this low-slung building for cold drinks and good conversation. Epo's Spot is popular with Ghanaian couples who order simple dishes from the chop bar next door.

The Office (Map p342; Osu Ave Extension, Osu; cover charge Fri & Sat; ⊠) Furnished with desks and ringbinders, this themed bar feels like a drunken office party. Thankfully there's no photocopier.

Ryan's Irish Pub (Map p342; behind Cantonments Rd, Osu; ⊠) This Osu gastro pub is homely and welcoming. Ever true to its roots, there's beer on tap, footy on TV and a stash of board games.

Bywell's (Map p342; Cantonments Rd, Osu) Live music on Thursday and Saturday nights transforms this otherwise laid-back hang-out at the southern end of Cantonments Rd into a fun party.

Champs (Map p344; Ring Road Central; ⊠) Part of the Paloma Hotel complex, this expat hang-out beams in sports from abroad. Thursday is quiz night; Friday, karaoke night; Saturday, live music night; and Sunday, movie night. One of the few places that serves Mexican food in Accra.

GETTING THERE & AWAY
Air

Kotoka international airport (Map p342) is served by major airlines, including British Airways, KLM Royal Dutch Airlines, Kenya Airways, Afriqiyah Airways, South African Airways and the flag-bearing Ghana International Airlines. For a list of other airlines that fly into Accra, see p358.

Bus & Tro-Tro

The main **STC bus station** (☎ 021-2021414) is on Ring Road West just east of Lamptey Circle. Buses leave hourly from early morning to early evening for Kumasi (C10, four to six hours) and Takoradi (four hours), and four times a day to Cape Coast (C6.50, three to four hours) and Tamale (C20, 12 to 13 hours). STC buses also serve Ho (four hours), Hohoe (3½ hours), Kpando and Aflao, near the border with Togo. All timetables and prices can change without warning; your best bet is to head to the station a day before departure to check and, ideally, to purchase tickets in advance. Other destinations include Wa, Bolgatanga and Bawku, with trips three days a week each. There are fewer trips on all routes on Sundays.

Private buses and tro-tros (minibuses or pick-ups) leave from four main motor parks. Those for Cape Coast, Takoradi and other destinations to the west leave from Kaneshie motor park (off Map p342), 500m northwest of Lamptey Circle. Neoplan motor park (Map p344), 250m west of Nkrumah Circle, has buses to north points such as Kumasi and Tamale. From Tema station (Map p344), east of Makola market, tro-tros leave for local destinations as well as Tema and Aburi. From the chaotic Tudu station (Map p344), at the northeast corner of Makola Market, tro-tros leave for destinations such as Aflao, Ada, Keta, Hohoe and Akosombo. In addition, there's a small station tucked in behind Tema station from which *tro-tros* go to Ho and Hohoe. Kingdom Transport Services (KTS) runs comfortable minivans with leather seats and air-con to Ho from here.

GETTING AROUND
Shared taxis and *tro-tros* travel on fixed runs from major landmarks or between major circles, such as Danquah Circle, 37 Circle and Nkrumah Circle (usually just called 'Circle'). Fares are usually very cheap. Major routes include Circle to Osu via Ring Road; Circle to the main post office via Kwame Nkrumah Ave; Tudu station to Kokomlemle; 37 Circle to Osu; Makola Market to Osu; and Circle to the airport. Any ride within the city shouldn't cost more than C6; short hops should be around a third of that price.

THE COAST

KOKROBITE
Endowed with a long stretch of white sand, Kokrobite has become something of an institution among backpackers and volunteers. All you'll need here is a pair of flip-flops, a beach towel and a book to read. Though small and sleepy, the town is charming in a laid-back, bohemian way.

Drumming lessons are the main draw here and are a big hit with tired volunteers who are feeling out of sync. The **Academy of African Music and Arts** (AAMAL), founded by top percussionist Mustapha Tettey Addy, runs courses.

Big Milly's Backyard (☎ 024-2206971, sms 028-7288889; www.bigmilly.com; camping with own/rented tent C3.5/6.5, dm/s/d with shared bathroom C4.5/10/20, r/ste C23/65; **P** 🍴 🖳) is one of the most famous beachfront set-ups in Ghana. Here, hammocks sway from skinny palm trees, backpackers peruse the cocktail list and volunteers grab bar meals, served with a healthy dollop of laid-back hedonism. At weekends, the place erupts into a party, with live bands, ice-cold beers, bonfires and barbecues.

Kokrobite Gardens (☎ sms 024-6785746; r C12, mains from C4; **P**) is a good spot for a beer or Italian food, served in a lush garden setting (behind Big Milly's).

Tro-tros (C0.50, 45 minutes) to Kokrobite go from the western end of Kaneshie motor park in Accra. Depending on your ability to negotiate, a taxi from Accra will cost from C8 to C20.

ANOMABU
Many travellers rate Anomabu's stunning beaches as second only to those further west, like Busua and Akwidaa. The sands and ribbons of low-key surf are certainly a big draw, but the village has its charms, too, among them seven *posubans* (shrines). The easiest to find is Company No 3's, which features a whale between two lions. It's about 50m from the main road, opposite the Ebeneezer Hotel.

Anomabu Beach Resort (☎ 042-291562; anomabu@ hotmail.com; camping with own/rented tent US$6/15, huts with/without bathroom US$38/27; **P**) is without a doubt the best place to stay here, and has attractive bungalows set within a sandy and shady grove of coconut palms.

CAPE COAST
Forever haunted by the ghosts of the past, Cape Coast is one of the most culturally significant spots in Africa. This former European colonial capital, originally named Cabo Corso by the Portuguese, was once the largest slave-trading centre in West Africa. At the height of the slave trade it received a workforce from locations as far away as Niger and Burkina Faso, and slaves were kept locked up in the bowels of Cape Coast's imposing castle. From the shores of this seaside town, slaves were herded onto vessels like cattle, irrevocably altering the lives of generations to come.

Today, Cape Coast is an easy-going fishing town with an arty vibe, fanned by salty sea breezes and kissed by peeling waves. Crumbling colonial buildings still line the streets, while seabirds prowl the beaches and fishermen cast nets where slave ships once sailed. There's a host of good restaurants and bars, making Cape Coast a logical base for Kakum National Park and the sandy beaches further downstream.

The centre of town is the **castle** (admission C5; 🕙 9am-5pm) which overlooks the sea.

Sleeping
Oasis Guest House (☎ 042-35958; ali_d@gmx.da; seafront, Cape Coast; hut with/without bathroom C25/C15; **P**) Like a hip party spot, a night at Oasis is loud, hot and sweaty. Backpackers, volunteers and Cape Coast's beautiful people gravitate towards the

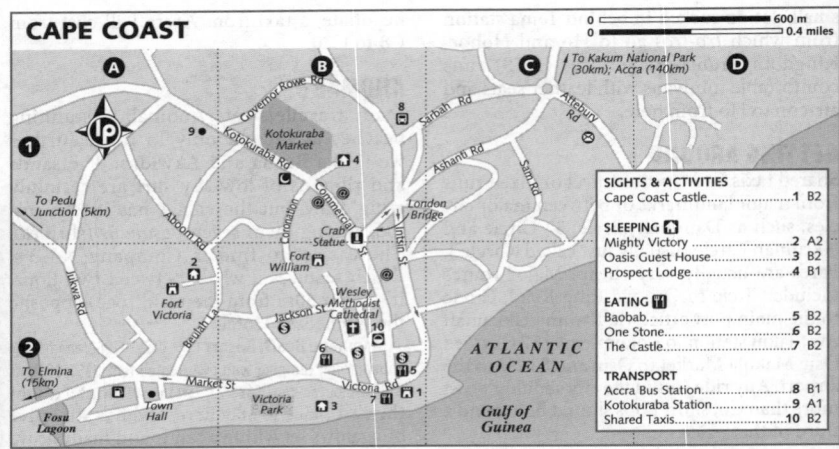

CAPE COAST

SIGHTS & ACTIVITIES
Cape Coast Castle......................1 B2

SLEEPING 🛏
Mighty Victory 2 A2
Oasis Guest House....................3 B2
Prospect Lodge........................4 B1

EATING 🍴
Baobab...................................5 B2
One Stone...............................6 B2
The Castle...............................7 B2

TRANSPORT
Accra Bus Station......................8 B1
Kotokuraba Station....................9 A1
Shared Taxis...........................10 B2

beachfront bar, which does a good line in sandwiches, salads and cocktails.

Mighty Victory (☎ 042-30135; r with fan/air-con C20/30; 🅿 ⊠ 🖥 🛜) Rooms are modern and cool, with crisp white sheets and hot running water. There's a good on-site restaurant, fast wi-fi (for a fee) and the American-Ghanaian owners are friendly and welcoming.

Prospect Lodge (☎ 042-31506; www.prospectlodge. com; s/d US$25/40; 🅿 ⊠ 🖥 🛜) Cape Coast's closest thing to a boutique hotel, Prospect Lodge, atop a steep hill, has fabulous views of the city, a terrace bar-resto and wi-fi. Rooms aren't particularly jazzy, but they are bright and spacious.

Hans Cottage Botel (☎ 042-91456; www.hans botel.com; camping US$5, s/d with fan US$31/45, with air-con US$54/72; 🅿 ⊠) An old traveller favourite, this curious place is suspended over an artificial crocodile swamp (hence 'botel' rather than 'hotel'). There's an internet cafe, a good restaurant and a pool. Though the enormous crocs are fed regularly, they technically roam free. It's located outside of town on the road to Kakum.

Eating
One Stone (meals from C2) This little place with a Rasta spin has backpacker breakfasts nailed. The menu includes fresh banana juice and chocolate pancakes (it's never too early for a chocolate fix). After dark, there are cocktails to be had.

Baobab (from C2; Commercial St; 🕒 9am-5pm) Tiny organic food bar with a wholesome touch.

Cecilia serves up great aubergine sarnies, soy lattes and refreshing *bissap* juice, a Senegalese staple made from hibiscus and ginger.

The Castle (mains from C3) Though not as impressive as its next-door neighbour (Cape Coast castle), this wooden bar-restaurant is a charmer. The fare (a mix of Ghanaian and international dishes) is good, though not sensational.

Getting There & Away
STC buses pull into the Goil petrol station at Pedu junction, about 5km northwest of the town centre. There are buses twice a day to and from Accra (C5, three hours) and Takoradi (C3, one hour) and once a day to and from Kumasi (C5, four hours). Shared taxis to Pedu junction leave from Commercial St.

There are two main motor parks in Cape Coast. The Accra bus station, at the junction of Sarbah and Residential Rds, serves long-distance routes, such as Accra and Kumasi. **Kotokuraba station** (Governor Rowe Rd), near the market, serves destinations around Cape Coast, such as Anomabu, Kakum National Park and Takoradi. Shared taxis to Elmina (C0.75, 15 minutes) leave from the station on Commercial St.

KAKUM NATIONAL PARK
An easy day trip from Cape Coast, **Kakum National Park** (admission C3) is home to over 300 species of bird, 600 species of butterfly and 40 mammal species, including forest elephants, antelopes, flying squirrels and colobus

monkeys. With the exception of monkeys, you're extremely unlikely to spot any of the larger creatures.

Kakum's biggest draw is its 30m-high **canopy walkway** (adult/student C9/5), which gives a monkey's-eye view of the forest below. It consists of seven wooden viewing platforms linked by a string of bouncy suspension bridges. It takes a minimum of 20 minutes to complete, longer if you linger and savour the view. The canopy walk is a 20-minute hike (partly on paved trails) from the visitor centre at the main park entrance, just off the Kakum Hwy. Wear hiking boots or sturdy shoes – the bite of a soldier ant can be painful.

Off-the-beaten-track enthusiasts can arrange overnighters to **Mesomagor tree platform** (admission C9) on the far-eastern outskirts of the park. This section of Kakum is beautiful and wild and is also the home of the famous **Kukyekukyeku Bamboo Orchestra**. The main visitor centre, adjacent to the park entrance, off the Kakum Hwy, has plenty of literature on Mesomagor and can help arrange a trip.

At the main entrance to the park, Kakum's **Rainforest Café** serves basic food, snacks and homemade ginger juice.

ELMINA
pop 20,000

Elmina lies on a narrow finger of land between the Atlantic Ocean and Benya Lagoon. Here, the air is salty and the architecture a charming mix of colonial remnants and elderly *posubans*.

At the end of a rocky peninsula, **St George's Castle** (adult/student C7/4; ☑ 9am-4.30pm) is one of the oldest European structures still standing in sub-Saharan Africa. A Unesco World Heritage Site, it was built by the Portuguese in 1482 and captured by the Dutch in 1637. The informative tour (included in the entry fee) takes you to the grim dungeons, punishment cells, Door of No Return and the turret room where the British imprisoned the Ashanti king, Prempeh I, for four years. Facing St George's Castle across the lagoon is the much smaller **Fort St Jago** (admission US$1.10; ☑ 9am-5pm), built by the Dutch between 1652 and 1662 to protect the castle.

Bridge House (www.coconutgrovehotels.com.gh; s/d from US$50/60; ☒) is the best place in Elmina to eat, drink and sleep. It occupies a fabulous brick building right on the harbour. Another

nice bet is the **Almond Tree Guesthouse** (☎ 024-4281098; www.almond3.com; r C32-63; ☒ ☒), a boutiquey hotel where rooms named after famous Jamaicans are spruced up with wicker furniture and yellow bed linen. Halfway between Elmina and Cape Coast, Mabel's Table serves excellent, simple Ghanaian fare in a pretty outdoor setting.

From the main taxi and *tro-tro* station (outside the Wesley Methodist Cathedral) you can get *tro-tros* to Takoradi (C10) or passenger taxis to Cape Coast. In Cape Coast, shared taxis to Elmina (C0.75, 15 minutes) leave from the station on Commercial St, a block north of Barclays Bank. A private taxi between Elmina and Cape Coast costs about C5.

SEKONDI-TAKORADI
pop 300,000

Although the conjoined sister cities of Sekondi and Tekoradi form the third-largest urban centre in Ghana, there is little reason to stick around here. Takoradi, the larger of the two, was just a fishing village until it was chosen as Ghana's first deep-water seaport; since then it has prospered. Now feeding on Ghana's oil boom, Takoradi (or Taadi, as it's known) is growing larger by the day. Sekondi, the older of the two settlements, is about 10km northeast of Takoradi.

Hotel de Mexico (☎ 031-23923; s/d/ste C30/35/40) is a good midrange option in Taadi's most attractive part of town. For a more upmarket option, try **Planter's Lodge** (☎ 031-22233; www. planters.com.gh; r/ste C150/220; ☒ ☒ ☒ ☒), originally built to accommodate British Royal Air Force flying officers and now a stylish hideaway popular with oil magnates and the Takoradi jet set. **Silver Pot Restaurant** (Liberation Rd; meals from C5) is a clean and calm oasis, good for a drink or a meal of Ghanaian or Continental cuisine. When the air-con is cranked up, **North Sea** (Axim Rd; meals from C5) can get as chilly as its namesake. It's right next to the STC station and serves pizza and Ghanaian food.

AKWIDAA BEACH, BUSUA & DIXCOVE

Some 30km west of Takoradi, these three settlements occupy a perfect stretch of Atlantic coastline, embroidered with sandbars, seashells and skinny palm trees. Busua, the largest of the three, reels in laid-back travellers and surfers chasing world-class waves.

You can hire boards at the **Black Star Surf Shop** (www.blackstarsurfshop.com; Busua beach; � 9am-7pm Mon-Sun). About 2km away is Dixcove, a lively fishing village. Akwidaa beach, a little slice of heaven 11km further west, is well worth the detour.

Sleeping & Eating

Green Turtle Lodge (☎ sms only 024-4893566; www.greenturtlelodge.com, Akwidaa Beach; campsite/dm C3/5, d with/without bathroom C30/15) One of two excellent reasons to come to Akwidaa beach. Built entirely from locally sourced, natural materials, the Green Turtle has cute bungalows dotted all over a private stretch of beach. The bar plays laid-back tunes, the restaurant churns out chocolate-covered bananas and there's a stack of board games. Turtle-spotting tours leave nightly. Magical.

Alaska Beach Club (Busua; hut with/without bathroom C20/15; P) Owned by an Alaskan with an eccentric sense of humour, this is the best value in Busua and is popular with the overlanding crowd.

Safari Beach Lodge (☎ sms only 024-6651329; www.safaribeachlodge.com; Akwidaa beach; d with/without bathroom C40/30) The Green Turtle's next-door neighbour offers rustic romance at its best. Huts are furnished in the style of a Kenyan safari lodge, complete with four-poster beds, desks and artwork. Everything is designed from locally sourced materials and the solar-heated showers are open to the sun and stars. The phenomenal food seals the deal.

Busua Inn (☎ 020-7373579; www.busuainn.com; Busua; tw with fan/air-con from US$23/45; P ✗) Busua's most charming midrange option. Owners Danielle and Olivier offer four clean, spacious and breezy rooms with sea views. There's a leafy terrace restaurant that backs onto the beach, serving excellent French and West African dishes against a fabulous wine list.

Okorye Tree (Busua; mains from C3.5; ☳ 9am-9pm) Attached to the Black Star Surf Shop in Busua, the Okorye Tree does a roaring trade in chicken sandwiches and big burritos. Grab a table on the wooden deck, order a frozen margarita and watch the waves break. If this place can get it so right, why do others still get it wrong?

Getting There & Away

Busua and Dixcove are each about 12km from the main coastal road. There's no direct transport to and from either Busua or Dixcove; you have to get to Agona junction on the main road and then take a *tro-tro* or shared taxi from there. From Takoradi, regular *tro-tros* (C2, 45 minutes) leave for Agona junction. From Agona junction there is frequent transport to Busua (C1) and Dixcove (C1). A private taxi between Busua and Takoradi will cost around C10. To get to Akwidaa beach from Agona Junction, any *tro-tro* heading to Akwidaa village can drop you at one of the two ecolodges.

AXIM

Located 70km from the border with Côte d'Ivoire, Axim is pronounced with a French accent (Akzeem or Azeem). As you near it, you'll notice the landscape changing, with patches of dry land replacing thick, jungly forest.

Axim is the site of the huge **Fort San Antonio** (admission C7, camera C5). From the top of the fort, there are spectacular views of the stunning coastline in both directions.

About 6km from Axim, near the village of Ankobra, is **Lou Moon Lodge** (☎ 031-021394; www.loumoon-lodge.com; d €50-105, f €75-120), which gets our vote for the most stylish place to stay in all of Ghana. Everything here is beautifully designed, from the light-filled bungalows to the executive suites, which come with floor-to-ceiling windows and your own private island. **Axim Beach Hotel** (☎ 031-22260; www.aximbeach.com; r $10, d with fan/air-con US$20/30, villa with air-con US$100-200) is also something special, even if you can only shell out for a budget room. Bungalows and villas spill onto hilly slopes overlooking the ocean. A five-minute drive from Axim town, along a rough track – charter a taxi to take you there for C3.

THE CENTRE

KUMASI
pop 1 million

Once the capital of the rich and powerful Ashanti kingdom, Ghana's second city is still dripping with Ashanti traditions. Its heart, the huge Kejetia market, throbs like a traditional talking drum and its wares spill into the city so that no matter where you are in Kumasi, it sometimes feels like one enormous marketplace. Among the urban sprawl are green spaces, remains of colonial architecture and a number of great sightseeing spots – three reasons why many travellers speak fondly of

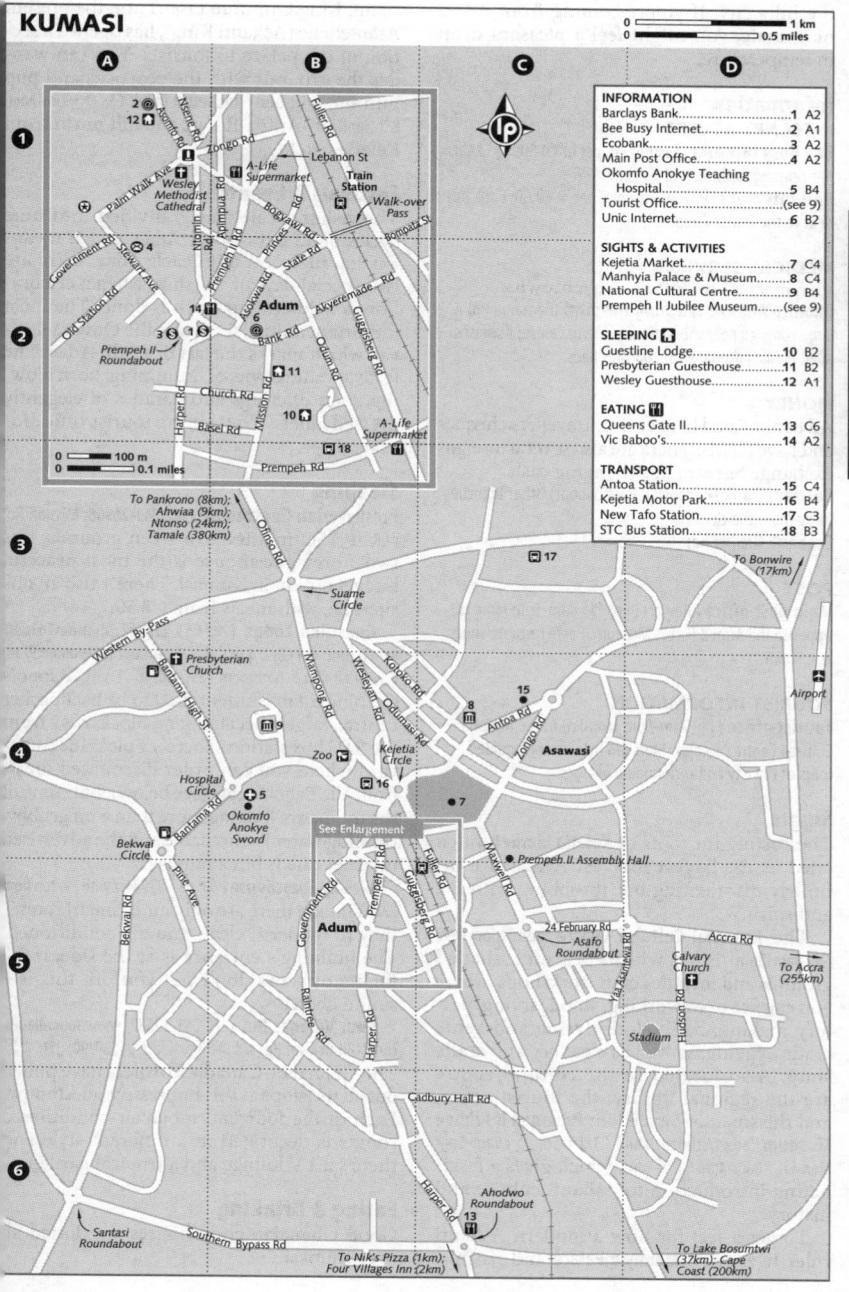

KUMASI

0	1 km
0	0.5 miles

INFORMATION
Barclays Bank..........................**1** A2
Bee Busy Internet...................**2** A1
Ecobank.................................**3** A2
Main Post Office....................**4** A2
Okomfo Anokye Teaching
Hospital..............................**5** B4
Tourist Office.......................(see 9)
Unic Internet........................**6** B2

SIGHTS & ACTIVITIES
Kejetia Market.......................**7** C4
Manhyia Palace & Museum....**8** C4
National Cultural Centre.........**9** B4
Prempeh II Jubilee Museum....(see 9)

SLEEPING
Guestline Lodge....................**10** B2
Presbyterian Guesthouse.......**11** B2
Wesley Guesthouse................**12** A1

EATING
Queens Gate II......................**13** C6
Vic Baboo's..........................**14** A2

TRANSPORT
Antoa Station.......................**15** C4
Kejetia Motor Park...............**16** B4
New Tafo Station..................**17** C3
STC Bus Station....................**18** B3

the hilly city. If you're coming from Accra or Tamale, you might feel a pleasant drop in temperature.

Information

INTERNET ACCESS
Bee Busy Internet (Asomfo Rd; per hr C0.80; ☼ 24hr) Has printing facilities and air-con.
Unic Internet (☼ 7.30am-8pm; per hr C0.60; Bank Rd) Next to the British Council.

MEDICAL SERVICES
Pharmacies are dotted all over town.
Okomfo Anokye Teaching Hospital (Bantama Rd) A large complex near the National Culture Centre; Kumasi's main public hospital with 700-plus beds.

MONEY
All banks listed here change travellers cheques and have ATMs. There are also several foreign-exchange bureaux for changing cash.
Barclays Bank (Prempeh II Roundabout) Other branches throughout the city.
Ecobank (Harper Rd)

POST
Main post office (Stewart Ave; ☼ 8am-5pm Mon-Fri) Opposite the Armed Forces Museum. Poste restante shuts at 4.30pm.

TOURIST INFORMATION
Tourist office (☼ 7am-5pm Mon-Fri) In the National Cultural Centre complex. Staff can help arrange guided tours of the city and surrounding villages.

Sights
The rusting tin roofs of **Kejetia Market**, often cited as the largest in West Africa, are infinitely disorienting but throbbing with life and spirit.

The **National Cultural Centre** (admission free; ☼ 8am-5pm) is set within peaceful, shaded grounds and includes craft workshops, where you can see brassworking, woodcarving, pottery making, batik cloth dyeing and kente cloth weaving, as well as a gallery and crafts shop. Also located in the cultural centre are the regional library, the tourist office, and the small but excellent **Prempeh II Jubilee Museum** (adult/student/child C3/2/0.50; ☼ 9am-5pm Mon-Fri, 10am-4pm Sat & Sun), which gives a fascinating introduction to Ashanti culture and history.

To get a feel for how a modern Ashanti ruler lives, visit **Manhyia Palace** and its museum. King Otumfuo Osei Tutu, the present Asantehene (Ashanti King), has opened a section of the palace to tourists. You can wander the grounds with the peacocks and pop into the adjacent **museum** (adult C5; ☼ 9am-noon & 1-5pm) off Antoa Rd, up the hill north from Kejetia Circle.

Festivals & Events
The Ashanti calendar is divided into nine cycles of 42 days called Adae, which means 'resting place'. Within each Adae, there are two special days of worship, when a celebration is held and no work is done. The most important annual festival is the Odwira festival, which marks the last or ninth Adae. The festival features lots of drumming, horn blowing, food offerings and parades of elegantly dressed chiefs. Contact the tourist office for exact dates.

Sleeping
Presbyterian Guesthouse (☎ 051-26966; Mission Rd, r C8; ℗) Set in attractive green grounds, this two-storey guesthouse is the most peaceful budget option in Kumasi. There's also an onsite cafe, with meals from C2.50.

Guestline Lodge (☎ 051-227657; mahesh161us@yahoo.com; dm C8; s/d with fan & without bathroom C9/14, d with air-con & bathroom C39; ✗ ▣) Vic Baboo's sleeping establishment used to be backpacker central, largely because it's a block away from the STC bus station. There's a pleasant courtyard where you can order discounted meals from Vic Baboo's cafe (see below), but some of the rooms are looking more than a bit grubby, running water is unreliable and the advertised internet cafe is but a fantasy.

Wesley Guesthouse (☎ 051-82984; r with air-con from C23) Though there are only nine (small) rooms they're modern, clean and air-conditioned. The building's entrance is at the side; if the flights of stairs don't put you off, this is a sound choice.

Four Villages Inn (☎ 051-22682; www.fourvillages.com; Old Bekwai Rd; s/d incl breakfast US$80/90; ℗ ✗) The Ghanaian-Canadian owners have pulled out all the stops at this impressive guesthouse. Each of the four enormous air-conditioned rooms is decorated in a different style and there's a TV lounge and a tropical garden.

Eating & Drinking
Good Ghanaian chop houses are dotted all over Kumasi.

Vic Baboo's (Prempeh II Rd; mains C3-10; ⊙ 11am-
30pm; ⊠) Vic Baboo's is an institution among
ravellers and expats. With the biggest menu
1 town, this place is whatever you want it to
e – Indian takeaway, decent burger joint,
ebanese deli or cocktail bar. It also has ice
ream, cashew nuts and popcorn. Last orders
re around 9pm.

Queens Gate II (Apino Plaza; mains from C5) Locals
till call this place 'Funkies', which, quite
rankly, feels much more apt. It serves good
izza and excellent kebabs in an outdoor gar-
len sprinkled with fairy lights. It manages to
e both laid-back and lively; there's often a
)J playing loud hip hop in what would oth-
rwise be a quiet courtyard setting. There's
 selection of beers and a good wine shop in
he adjacent plaza.

Nik's Pizza (off Old Bekwai Rd; pizzas C8-10) New
mage Kitchen, or Nik's as it's known, is a
<umasi gem. Friendly waiters serve excel-
ent pizza (and only pizza) in a quiet, leafy
;arden setting. It's worth the 15-minute walk
hrough Kumasi's fanciest neighbourhood.
From Apino Plaza on the Old Bekwai Rd, turn
eft: Nik's is signposted from there.

Getting There & Away
<umasi airport is on the northeastern out-
skirts of town, about 2km from the centre.
The most efficient airline is **Antrak** (www.an
rakair.com), which flies propeller planes between
<umasi and Accra twice a day (one-way costs
around US$90).

The **STC bus station** (www.intercitystc.com) is
on Prempeh Rd, a two-minute walk from
Guestline Lodge. Buses to Accra (C7, four
hours) leave regularly between 3.30am and
5pm. STC buses also stop at Cape Coast
(C4, four hours) on their way to Takoradi
(C7, five hours). There are two buses a day
to Tamale (C12, eight hours) and you can
also join the Accra–Ouagadougou bus from
here.

Non-STC buses to Tamale, Bolgatanga
and Bawku leave from New Tafo station
(Kurofurom station) in Dichemso, about 2km
north of Kejetia market.

AROUND KUMASI
Craft Villages
Because of their proximity to Kumasi, the
craft villages in the region offer a convenient,
if touristy, way to experience how some of
Ghana's traditional workshops operate.

There are two villages just on the outskirts
of Kumasi, on the Mampong road beyond
Suame Circle. Pankrono, located 8km away,
is a major pottery centre. One kilometre further is Ahwiaa, known for its woodcarving
and an aggressive sales approach. Ntonso,
15km further along, is the centre of *adinkra*
cloth printing. Bonwire, which is 18km
northeast of Kumasi, is the most famous
(and therefore the most touristy) of several
nearby villages that specialise in weaving
kente cloth.

The easiest way to visit the central region's
craft villages is to hire a private taxi (about
C30 for a full day). Less convenient, especially
if you want to make a number of stops in one
day, is a *tro-tro* from Kejetia motor park for
the villages on the Mampong road or from
Antoa station for Bonwire.

LAKE BOSUMTWI
With a depth of 86m, Lake Bosumtwi is a
crater lake that was formed from the impact
of a huge meteorite. The lake is hugged by
lush green hills in which you can hike, visiting some of the small villages around the
lake's perimeter. Located 38km southeast of
Kumasi, Lake Bosumtwi is a popular weekend holiday spot for Kumasi residents, who
come here to relax, swim (the water is said
to be bilharzia free) and jet ski. For those so
inclined, it's also possible to cycle the lake's
30km circumference.

Not only is Bosumtwi the country's largest
and deepest natural lake, it's also a sacred
site. The Ashanti people believe that their
souls come here after death to bid farewell
to the god Twi. Historically, dugout canoes
and boats were forbidden on the lake, but
the tide has turned and Bosumtwi becomes
a haven for water-sport enthusiasts on the
weekends.

If you want to bed down for a night or
two, try **Rainbow Garden Village** (☎ sms 024-
3230288; www.rainbowgardenvillage.com; campsite/dm
C6/9, d C24-29), 3.5km from Abono. This laid-
back German-Ghanaian-owned place is the
Big Milly's of Lake Bosumtwi. The dorms
and waterfront bungalows are popular with
a backpacker and volunteer crowd; there
are tours on offer and big, convivial camp-
fires every weekend. **Lake Point Guesthouse**
(☎ sms 024-3452922; www.ghana-hotel.com; dm/d/tw/tr
C8/26/26/30) is a good, quieter option not far
from the shore.

THE NORTH

TAMALE

If the northern region is Ghana's breadbasket, Tamale is its kitchen. If you can take the heat, you'll discover a town with some good food, charm and a whole lot of soul. (If you can't, don't panic: Mole National Park is generally cooler.)

In the heart of town is the sprawling central **market**, marked by the tall radio antenna near the STC bus station. You can buy pretty much anything here, including parasols and trekking boots (only in men's sizes) for Mole.

Tamale's population is largely Muslim and there are several interesting **mosques** around town, notably on Bolgatanga Rd. The **National Cultural Centre** (off Salaga Rd), has an echoing auditorium where music and dance performances are occasionally put on; there are **craft shops** around the back that rarely see visitors. There's also a **public library** with a nice collection of fiction and nonfiction books, located just south of Sparkles restaurant opposite the entrance to the football stadium.

Sleeping

Catholic Guesthouse (☎ 071-22265; Gumbihini Rd; r C14-25; P ☒) The most popular of the cheapies. Simple, air-conditioned rooms wrap around a pretty courtyard and there's an OK restaurant and outdoor bar.

King's Guesthouse (☎ 020-8380950; Kalpohin Estates; r from C15; P ☒) Another courtyard setup, King's has a range of rooms – some with satellite TV, fridge and air-con.

Relax Lodge (☎ 071-24981; gkc1955@yahoo.com; r from US$50; P ☒) Pretty in pink, this friendly Pakistani-run place has undergone renovation and is now a decent midrange option.

Gariba Lodge (☎ 071-23041; gariba@africaonline.com.gh; Bolgatanga Rd; d US$85-110; P ☒ 🛜) Clean, stylish rooms (with hot water) in a tranquil garden setting. For a fee, you can use the fastest wi-fi connection in Tamale. About 7km north of the town centre on Bolgatanga Rd.

Eating & Drinking

Sparkles (mains from C3; ☷ 8am-8pm Mon-Sat) A simple cafe serving good Ghanaian food alongside Western staples such as sandwiches.

Swad Fast Food (☎ 071-23588; near Catholic Guesthouse; mains C7; ☷ 11am-10pm) The name might not be a winner, but this is one of the best places to grab a bite in Tamale. The speciality is Indian, but there are also such delights as French onion soup, red red (a Ghanaian dish with beans), *banku* and fish-finger sandwiches.

Jungle Bar (TICCS Guesthouse, Gumbihini Link Rd) The Jungle Bar, on the grounds of the TICCS Guesthouse, is on a leafy balcony with an all-wood bar, cable TV and comfy benches and is probably the nicest spot for a drink in Tamale. Also serves food.

Giddipass (Crest Restaurant, Salaga Rd) Sit on the rooftop terrace and let an ice-cold beer and the sweet sounds of northern hip-life (see the boxed text, p340) into your world at this decent drinking spot.

Getting There & Away

The airport is about 20km north of town, on the road to Bolgatanga; a private taxi there costs about C10. Antrak flies between Tamale and Accra for US$175 one way.

The STC bus station is just north of the central market, behind the Mobil petrol station. There are four buses daily to Accra (12 hours) and two buses a day to Kumasi (four to seven hours). There's also a service to Cape Coast and Takoradi (12 hours). The daily Metro Mass bus to Mole National Park (C4, four to six hours) leaves in theory at 2.30pm but in practice a lot later. Buy a ticket in advance or arrive at the bus station well before the scheduled departure time to be sure of a seat.

LARABANGA

The tiny Muslim village of Larabanga is 4km from Mole and is most famous for its striking Sudanese-style mud-and-stick mosque, purported to be the oldest of its kind in Ghana. The town itself is hot, dusty and soporific; alleys wrap around traditional mud homes and bedraggled goats roam the streets.

Most travellers choose to stay with the **Salia brothers** (☎ 027-5544071) at one of their two guesthouses in the village. Good, basic meals are available on request. You can even sleep on the roof, under a mosquito net and the stars.

To Tamale, there's the daily bus from Mole and a daily bus from Wa, both of which pass through town early in the day; heading west, there are two daily buses to Bole in the early afternoon and a daily bus to Wa at around 9.30am. To get to Mole, you can hire a bicycle or a private taxi or motorbike; walking is

definitely not advisable in the heat of the day
or, for that matter, after dark.

MOLE NATIONAL PARK

With its swathes of saffron-coloured savan-
nah, **Mole National Park** (adult/student C4/2.50, camera
C5) offers what must surely be the cheapest
safaris in Africa. There are at least 300 species
of bird and 94 species of mammal, including
African elephants, kob antelopes, buffalos,
baboons and warthogs. There's one main
escarpment, on which the motel and park
headquarters are situated.

Mole Motel (☎ 027-7564444, 024-4316777; dm C8,
tr with/without air-con C45/35; ☒) is no stunner,
but frankly there are better things to look
at, not least the warthogs sniffing around
the breakfast tables and, if you're lucky, elephants thundering across the plains. There's
also a reasonable restaurant, serving a mix
of Ghanaian and international fare (mains
from C6).

From the motel, informative **walking safaris**
(2hr safari C0.70; ☯ 6.30am & 3.30pm) usually leave
twice daily, offering unrivalled opportunities to get up close to beautiful, bus-sized elephants. Sturdy, covered footwear is a must
for the two-hour walk through patches of
jungle and scrub; if you come without your
own boots, the rangers will insist on lending
you a pair of ill-fitting Wellington boots for
a fee of C2.

The daily Metro Mass bus from Tamale (see
opposite) arrives at the park motel around
7pm, if all goes well. The same bus overnights
at the park, returning to Tamale the next day,
leaving the park at around 4.30am.

WECHIAU HIPPO SANCTUARY

This remote hippo sanctuary along the Black
Volta River is one of Ghana's most under-
hyped ecotourism projects. Initiated by village chiefs in 1999, the 40-sq-km sanctuary
is a safe haven for female hippos, who give
birth in the flooded streams during the rainy
season. Hippos are among West Africa's most
threatened creatures; slash-and-burn farming
has already destroyed some habitats.

The C9 admission fee covers basic guesthouse accommodation (pit toilet and bucket
shower) and canoe trips to see the hippos;
November through June is the best time to see
these prehistoric-looking beasts. Meals can be
prepared, but you'll need to bring your own
provisions, too. Wechiau village is reached by
tro-tro (one hour, 46km) from the main lorry
park in Wa. The sanctuary is about 20km
from Wechiau.

If you find yourself in Wa at nightfall, you
can hit the hay at the **Hotel du Pond** (☎ 075-
620018), **Kunateh Lodge** (☎ 075-6202102) or the
Catholic Guesthouse (☎ 075-622375), all located
within a few minutes' walk of the motor
park, offering wallet-friendly, basic rooms.
It's also worth checking out the impressive
mud-and-stick mosque.

BOLGATANGA

Bolgatanga – 'call me Bolga' – was once the
southernmost point of the ancient trans-
Saharan trading route, running through
Burkina Faso to Mali. As well as serving as a
jumping-off point for travellers heading into
the dust, it's an interesting base for exploring
the surrounding villages.

Nsamini Guesthouse (☎ 072-23403; off Navrongo
Rd; r from C7) is one of Bolga's best budget buys,
up a lane leading off the Navrongo Rd. The
Sand Gardens (☎ 072-23464; r with fan/air-con C30/C35;
☒) has concrete bungalows and an on-site
restaurant. Head east down Zuarungu Rd
until you reach the fire station, then turn left
down the dirt road. The best upmarket option
is **Tienyine Hotel** (☎ 072-22355; r from C30), in the
same complex as the recommended Comme
Ci Comme Ça restaurant.

Tro-tros to Tamale (2½ hours) leave from
the motor park on Zuarungu Rd east of the
intersection with Navrongo and Tamale Rds.
Buses to Tamale, Kumasi and Accra leave
from the STC station on Tamale Rd. If you're
headed for Burkina Faso, take a tro-tro to the
border at Paga (40 minutes) or board the STC
direct service to Ouagadougou (three times
weekly, leaves around 6am).

THE EAST

AKOSOMBO

Built in the early 1960s to house construction
workers involved in the completion of the
hydroelectric dam, Akosombo is the site of
the world's largest artificial lake.

The **visitors centre** (☎ 0251-20550; tours C2; ☯ tours
9am-3pm Mon-Sun) arranges tours of the dam.
An alternative is the **Dodi Princess**, more like a
booze cruise than a love boat. It chugs out to
nearby Dodi Island on Saturday, Sunday and
holidays (adults C20).

One of the least expensive though comfortable options in town is the **Adomi Hotel & Restaurant** (☎ 0251-20095; r with fan/air-con C20/26), which has basic but comfortable rooms with excellent views of the traffic. A good midrange choice is **Aylos Bay** (☎ 0251-20901; r from US$30), set in lush green grounds with good-value bungalows. There's a garden bar and restaurant.

The main transport hub is at Kpong, on the Accra–Ho road 10km south of Atimpoku. Regular *tro-tros* travel between Kpong, Atimpoku and Akosombo. From Accra, *tro-tros* for Kpong/Akosombo (C4) leave from Tudu station. Alternatively, get any transport to Ho from Accra or to Accra or Kpong from Ho and get off at the suspension bridge at Atimpoku.

WLI FALLS

After a scenic, undemanding 40-minute walk along a bubbling stream, it's hard not to gawk at Wli's 40m-high cascade. Entering the Agumatsa Wildlife Sanctuary, which contains the falls, costs C7, payable at the wildlife office. You can reach the lower falls by yourself, but a hike to the upper falls (C2) is a demanding two-hour climb and a guide is necessary. The German-owned **Waterfall Lodge** (☎ 028-9547459; www.ghanacamping.com; from C10) is a few hundred metres from the wildlife office, and is a great place to sleep after a day at the falls. Tasty food is served indoors or in the palava hut (gazebo) on the lawn.

Regular *tro-tros* (40 minutes) and shared taxis make the scenic run between Wli and Hohoe throughout the day. If you're heading for Togo, the Ghanaian border post is on the eastern side of Wli (turn left at the junction as you enter the village). From there, it's a 10-minute walk to the Togolese side.

BIAKPA MOUNTAIN PARADISE

Mountain Paradise (☎ 024-4166226; www.mountainparadise-biakpa.com; campsite C5, r C8-12) is a former government rest home converted into a fabulous mountain hideaway. There's a book swap and a good restaurant, and staff can arrange hikes and canoe excursions along the Kulugu River. Shared transport between Ho and Hohoe stops at the village of Fume, 4km from Mountain Paradise – you might be able to persuade the driver to drop you at the lodge for an extra fee. Alternatively, it's a short drive from Amedzofe.

GHANA DIRECTORY

ACCOMMODATION

If you're looking for a bargain, Ghana probably isn't it. Though there is some decent budget accommodation to be had, Ghana will stretch your pockets more than you would like.

Off the tourist trail there are few hotels and guesthouses, but it's usually possible to arrange to sleep on a floor or roof somewhere. Most of the ecotourism projects offer overnight stays in simple guesthouses or homestays. Some of the smaller coastal forts might be prepared to put you up for a few cedis.

ACTIVITIES

With such a beautiful, long coastline, one of the best things to do in Ghana is head to the beach, where you can surf or simply do nothing, which should be considered an activity. However, ask before swimming since currents and undertow may be present, making conditions unsafe.

Good hiking can be found in the Volta region around the Tongo Hills near Bolgatanga (p355) in the north.

For drumming and dancing lessons, contact Big Milly's (p347) or the Academy of African Music and Arts (p347) in Kokrobite or the Oasis Guest House (p347) in Cape Coast.

BUSINESS HOURS

Administrative buildings From 8am until 1pm or so. Embassies tend to keep similar hours.
Banks Between 9am and 3pm Monday to Friday; some additionally run until noon on Saturdays.
Markets In predominately Muslim areas, markets are quiet on Friday, the day of rest, and busier on Sunday.
Shops From 9am until 5pm or 6pm every day except Sunday, when only large stores open.

CHILDREN

Ghana's a great place to take little ones and they'll receive a warm welcome from Ghanaians. While there aren't any theme parks or specifically child-oriented activities, Mole National Park (p355), the canopy walk at Kakum National Park (p348) and Cape Coast's castles (p347) make children wide-eyed. As far as beach resorts and restaurants go, most places welcome kids; the stylish Lou Moon Lodge (p350) in Axim is very child friendly.

ANGERS & ANNOYANCES

One of Ghana's competitive advantages, as far as tourism in West Africa goes, is that it's a stable and generally peaceful country. Having said that, ethnic violence continues to affect the very far northeast around Bawku; it generally has little effect on the rest of Ghana. Take care of your valuables on the beaches west of Accra and always try to be aware of your surroundings, especially if you're walking alone at night. Otherwise, reckless *tro-tro* drivers, dehydration and open sewers are as bad as it gets.

EMBASSIES & CONSULATES

All of the embassies and consulates listed below are located in the capital, Accra. Most are open between 8.30am and 3.30pm from Monday through Friday. Most West African embassies like visa applications before noon.

Australia (Map p342; ☎ 021-777080; www.ghana. embassy.gov.au; 2 Second Rangoon Close, Cantonments) Australian High Commission.

Benin (Map p342; ☎ 021-774860; Switchback Lane, Cantonments)

Burkina Faso (Map p344; ☎ 021-2021988; 2nd Mango Tree Ave, Asylum Down; ⊙ 8am-2pm Mon-Fri)

Canada (Map p342; ☎ 021-228555; 46 Independence Ave, Sankara Interchange)

Côte d'Ivoire (Map p342; ☎ 021-774611; 9 18th Lane, Osu; ⊙ 9am-2.30pm Mon-Thu)

Denmark (☎ 021-226972; 67 Isert Rd, 8th Ave Extension) Near World Bank office.

France (Map p342; ☎ 021-228571; 12th Rd, Kanda) Off Liberation Ave.

Germany (Map p344; ☎ 021-2021311; 6 Ridge Rd, North Ridge)

Guinea (☎ 021-7779021; 4th Norla St, Labone)

Ireland (☎ 021-772866; 5th Circular Extension)

Italy (☎ 021-7756021; Jawaharlal Nehru Rd)

Japan (Map p342; ☎ 021-775616, fax 021-775951; 8 Josef Broz Tito Ave, Cantonments)

Liberia (Map p342; ☎ 021-775641; off Lumumba Rd)

Mali (Map p344; ☎ 021-663276; Liberia Rd, West Ridge)

Netherlands (Map p342; ☎ 021-231991; nlgovacc@ncs. com.gh; 89 Liberation Ave, Sankara Circle)

Niger (Map p342; ☎ 021-224962; E104/3 Independence Ave, Ringway Estate)

Nigeria (Map p342; ☎ 021-776158, fax 021-774395; 5 Josef Broz Tito Ave, Cantonments)

Togo (Map p342; ☎ 021-777950; Togo House, Cantonments Circle, Cantonments)

UK (Map p342; ☎ 021-2021665, fax 021-2021745; 1 Osu Link, Ringway Estate) British High Commission.

USA (Map p342; ☎ 021-776601, 021-741150; http:// ghana.usembassy.gov; cnr 10th Lane & 3rd St, Osu)

EMERGENCY

Ambulance ☎ 193
Fire ☎ 192
Police ☎ 191

FESTIVALS & EVENTS

Ghana has many festivals and events, including the Fetu Afahye Festival (first Saturday of September) in Cape Coast (p347), the Bakatue Festival (first Tuesday in July) in Elmina (p349), the Fire Festival (dates vary according to the Muslim calendar) of the Dagomba people in Tamale (p354) and various year-round Akan celebrations in Kumasi (p352). Panafest, an arts festival, is celebrated most years in Cape Coast (p347).

HOLIDAYS

Public holidays include the following:
New Year's Day 1 January
Independence Day 6 March
Easter March/April
Labour Day 1 May
Africa Day 25 May
Republic Day 1 July
Farmers' Day 1st Friday in December
Christmas Day 25 December
Boxing Day 26 December

INTERNET ACCESS

You can get online in all major towns and some smaller ones. Finding a speedy connection, however, is a bit of a hit-and-miss game. Rates can be anywhere from C0.60 to C3 per hour.

MONEY

In 2007 four zeros were lopped off the value of the old Ghana cedi, making it the highest-value currency in West Africa. For the most part, Ghanaians have adjusted, but you'll occasionally hear people asking for C10,000 when they really want C1.

The best currencies to bring are US dollars, UK pounds and euros. Barclays and Standard Chartered Banks exchange cash and well-recognised brands of travellers cheques without a commission. Foreign-exchange bureaux are dotted around most major towns, though there are fewer in the north. Most Barclays and Standard Chartered Banks throughout the country have ATMs that accept Visa,

Mastercard and Maestro. Credit cards (generally only Visa and MasterCard) are accepted by major hotels and travel agencies.

STUDYING

Ghana is one of the more popular options for foreign students wishing to study in Africa, at least in part because courses are offered in English. Many universities in the US and Europe have collaborative programs with **University of Ghana** (off Map p342; www.ug.edu.gh) in Accra, the **University of Cape Coast** (www.ucc.edu.gh), and **University for Development Studies** (uds@ug.gn.apc.org) in Tamale. The University for Development Studies specialises in studying rural poverty and the environment, combining academic work with practical hands-on training in rural communities. The **Tamale Institute of Cross-Cultural Studies** (TICCS; www.ticcs.com/index.htm) offers two masters degree programs: Cross-Cultural Development and Cross-Cultural Ministry.

TELEPHONE

Mobile (cell) phones are ubiquitous in Ghana and you'll hear their dulcet tones everywhere, especially at around 5am when you're trying to sleep. SIM cards can be picked up in shopping centres, communication centres and, in fact, on most street corners. MTN and Vodafone are fairly reliable networks.

VISAS

Visas are required by everyone except Ecowas (Economic Community of West African States) nationals. Though it's technically possible to pick up a visa upon arrival at Accra's Kotoka International Airport, they only tend to be granted in rare cases. Flying into Ghana without a visa is not recommended. Land border officials might sometimes be a little more lenient, but procuring a visa in Côte d'Ivoire, Togo or Burkina Faso is highly advisable.

You can get a visa extension at the **immigration office** (Map p342; ☎ 021-2021667) in Accra near the Sankara Interchange. Applications are accepted between 8.30am and noon Monday to Friday. You need two photos, a letter stating why you need an extension, and an onward ticket out of Ghana. Your passport is retained for the two to three weeks (longer if you're unlucky) that it takes to process the application.

Visas for Onward Travel

Most nationalities need a visa for onward travel throughout West Africa. For embassy details, see p357.

BURKINA FASO

The embassy issues visas for three months on the same day if you get there early. You need three photos and rates fluctuate, but it should cost about C50.

CÔTE D'IVOIRE

The embassy issues visas in 48 hours and you need two photos. After years of free entry, Americans now need a visa to go to Côte d'Ivoire.

TOGO

The embassy issues visas for one month on the same day. Alternatively, you can get a visa at the border at Aflao, but it's only valid for seven days and you'll need to extend it in Lomé.

TRANSPORT IN GHANA

GETTING THERE & AWAY

You need a yellow fever vaccination certificate to enter Ghana. Though it's rarely checked at airports, border guards often ask to see it. Worst-case scenario: you'll be made to have a yellow-fever jab on the spot – don't risk it.

Air

Kotoka International Airport in Accra is Ghana's international hub, home to **Ghana International Airlines** (www.fly-ghana.com), owned by the Ghanaian government and a US consortium. Other international airlines flying in and out of Kotoka include the following:

Afriqiyah Airways (8U; www.afriqiyah.aero) Flights to Europe with stopover in Tripoli, Libya; office at Accra airport.

Air Ivoire (VU; www.airivoire.com) Office at Accra airport.

British Airways (www.ba.com)

Delta (☎ 21 213 111; www.delta.com)

Emirates (www.emirates.com; Meridian House, Ring Rd Central, Accra) Four flights a week connecting Accra and Dubai. Also offers short, surprisingly inexpensive hops to Abidjan.

Kenya Airways (www.kenya-airways.com; North Ridge Crescent, Ring Rd) Serves destinations in West and East Africa.

KLM Royal Dutch Airlines (www.klm.com; Ring Rd Central, Accra)

South African Airways (www.flysaa.com; Millennium Heights, Airport Residential)

Virgin Nigeria (www.virginnigeria.com; La Palm Royal Beach Hotel, Accra)

Land

Ghana has land borders with Côte d'Ivoire to the west, Burkina Faso to the north and west, and Togo to the east. The main border crossing into Côte d'Ivoire is at Elubo; there are less-travelled crossings between Sunyani and Agnibilékrou and between Bole and Ferkessédougou. Into Burkina Faso the main crossing is at Paga, with other crossings at Tumu, Hamale and Lawra. The main crossing into Togo is at Aflao, just outside Lomé. Note that Ghana's borders all close promptly – with a flag ceremony – at 6pm.

BURKINA FASO

Between Accra and Ouagadougou, the usual route is via Kumasi, Tamale, Bolgatanga, Paga and Pô. A direct STC bus runs to Ouagadougou from Accra and Kumasi three times a week, leaving Accra in the early morning and arriving in Ouagadougou the next afternoon. The bus makes a lengthy stop in Bolgatanga in the wee hours – you can (try to) get some shut-eye on the benches in the bus station. If you do brave the 26-hour ride, you might want to bring headphones: the TV usually plays all night long. From Bolgatanga, there are frequent *tro-tros* to the border at Paga (40 minutes), from where you can get onward transport to Pô and Ouagadougou.

You can also enter Burkina Faso from the northwest corner of Ghana, crossing between Tumu and Léo or from Hamale or Lawra on to Bobo-Dioulasso.

CÔTE D'IVOIRE

Crossing into Côte d'Ivoire at Elubo is relatively straightforward. You can make your way to the border post in stages, or take a *tro-tro* or air-conditioned van from Takoradi or an STC bus from Accra to Abidjan (around 13 hours). Once you reach Elubo, it's a 10-minute walk to the border itself and the same distance again to Noé on the Ivorian side. Other much more adventurous crossings are from Kumasi via Sunyani and Berekum to Agnibilékrou (you'll have

to do this in short stages as there are no direct buses) and between Bole and Bouna to Ferkessédougou.

TOGO

Tro-tros and share taxis run between Accra and Aflao (C5, three hours). Efficient, air-conditioned STC buses ply the route from Abidjan to Lomé via Accra (C8 from Accra, four times a day). The border at Aflao, just 2km from Lomé, is open from 6am to 10pm daily, but you should cross between 9am and 5pm if you need a Togolese visa (valid for seven days, extendable in Lomé). *Tro-tros* deposit you on the Ghanaian side of the border. Other crossings are at Wli near Hohoe and between Ho and Kpalimé.

GETTING AROUND
Air

Two domestic airlines, **Citylink** (☎ 021-785725; www.citylink.com.gh) and **Antrak** (☎ 021-777134; www.antrakair.com; Antrak House, Danquah Circle) operate in Ghana. Both have two to three flights daily between Accra and Kumasi (one way US$60 to US$80, 45 minutes) and three to four weekly flights to Tamale (around US$300 return).

Bus

The best bus service in the country is provided by STC. Compared to other transport in the region, it's fairly reliable and, despite the loud Nigerian movies, you travel in air-conditioned comfort. It's wise to book in advance; tickets get snapped up fast on the more popular routes. STC charges a little extra for hold luggage – you'll have it weighed and be charged by the kilogram. Sample fares and times are given below:

Route	Fare (C)	Duration (hr)
Accra to Cape Coast	6.50	3-4
Accra to Tamale	20	12-13
Accra to Kumasi	10	4-6
Kumasi to Takoradi	9	3-5
Kumasi to Aflao	14	3-5
Kumasi to Accra	10	3-5
Kumasi to Cape Coast	7.50	3-4
Tamale to Kumasi	13	6-8
Tamale to Bolgatanga	7	3

Other operators, which may have the only buses on some routes (such as between

Tamale and Mole National Park), include Metro Mass, Omnibus Service Authority (OSA), Kingdom Transport Services (KTS) and City Express. Fares are often much cheaper than those offered by STC, but you can't predict what kind of bus you'll end up on or how packed it will be.

Car & Motorcycle

Driving is on the right in Ghana. Most main roads in Ghana are now in pretty good condition, though almost all secondary roads are unsealed. Self-drive car rental is available in Accra but is not recommended unless you are used to all the quirks of driving in West Africa. An international driver's license and many foreign countries' licenses are recognised. Hiring a car with a driver is a good option if you're short on time. Depending on the distance, car and driver experience, factor in anything from US$40 to US$120 per day.

Taxis

Within towns and on some shorter routes between towns, shared taxis are the usual form of transport. They are cheap and run on fixed routes, along which they stop to pick up and drop off passengers. Private taxis don't have meters and rates are negotiable. It's best to ask a local in advance for the average cost between two points. You'll soon have a handle on what is fair. Taxis can be chartered for an agreed period of time, anything from one hour to a day, for a negotiable fee. Drivers will often try to renegotiate after a deal has been struck and you've started moving, saying things like 'it's really not enough'. Stick to your guns, within reason. Most taxis don't have air-con, which isn't a problem unless the back windows don't open, which is not unusual.

Train

Ghana's train service should be viewed as a supplemental, not alternative, form of internal travel. Kumasi and Takoradi have had an on-off relationship with a night train for many years. When it runs, it takes around 13 hours. There is also a commuter service between Accra and Tema.

Tro-Tros

Tro-tro is a catch-all category that embraces any form of transport that's not a bus or taxi. They cover all major and many minor routes and, without them, Ghana would come to a standstill. Except on real back-country routes *tro-tros* are minibuses of all shapes, sizes and degrees of roadworthiness. They don't work to a set timetable but leave when full, having squeezed in as many passengers as they can. You can get a rough idea of when the *tro-tro* you're sitting in will leave by counting the number of passengers on board (though others may have done the same thing and subsequently escaped for lunch). The average *tro-tro* carries 11 to 14 passengers; if there are only five on board, you're usually in for a long wait. Most fares are under a dollar or two but frequently change by small amounts, and, for that matter, the fares on many routes are not given. For long journeys, though, buses are safer and more comfortable. Many *tro-tro* drivers demand a negotiable luggage fee, though this seems to be applied fairly arbitrarily and is more commonly requested of foreigners than Ghanaians.

Most towns have an area where *tro-tros* and buses congregate, usually in or near the market. These are called lorry parks or motor parks (the terms are used interchangeably), or, quite often, stations. You may hear the term *tro-tro* used, but taxis and minibuses are often just called 'cars'.

Guinea

Imagine you're travelling on smooth highway, then get tempted by a tiny, dusty turn-off into rugged terrain, where surprising beauty and treacherous vistas define the route. Guinea is that turn-off. This is a country blessed with amazing landscapes, from the cragged mountain plateau Fouta Djalon to wide Sahelian lands and thick forests. Overland drivers are drawn here by rugged tracks, and the challenge of steering their vehicles over rocks, steep laterite and washed-out paths. Nature lovers can lose themselves on long hikes past the plunging waterfalls, proud hills and tiny villages of the Fouta. And for music fans, the country is something of a pilgrimage site – this is where West Africa's 1960s sounds were created.

There's virtually no tourist infrastructure and creature comforts are scarce. Instead, you get to explore paths that few tourists travel.

For most Guineans, life has been tough ever since the country defiantly broke from France and ventured out on a difficult post-independence journey. Despite the hard times, the country's diverse people have largely stood together through the decades, rather than turning on each other. In conversations and encounters you will catch glimpses of that strong stance and hear about the nation's troubles as well as its hopes.

GUINEA

FAST FACTS

- **Area** 245,855 sq km
- **ATMs** There's one in Conakry
- **Borders** Côte d'Ivoire, Guinea-Bissau, Liberia, Mali, Senegal, Sierra Leone
- **Budget** US$30 to US$60
- **Capital** Conakry
- **Languages** French, Malinke, Pulaar (Fula) and Susu
- **Money** Guinean franc (GFr); US$1 = GFr4950, €1 = GFr7083
- **Population** 9.8 million
- **Seasons** Dry season (November to April), rainy (May to October)
- **Telephone** Country code ☎ 224; international access code ☎ 00
- **Time** GMT/UTC (no daylight saving)
- **Visa** Required in advance

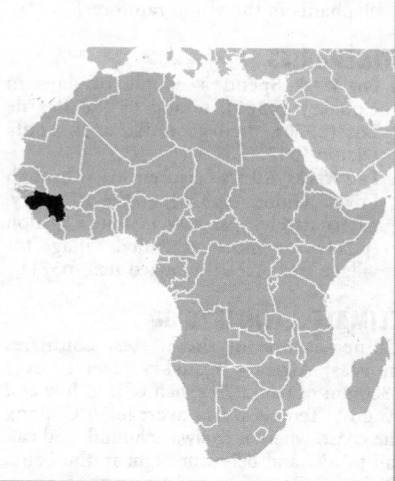

HOW MUCH?

- **Handmade leather sandals** US$8
- **100km bush taxi ride** US$5
- **4WD hire per day** US$120
- **Two metres of hand-woven indigo cloth** US$8
- **Music show** US$1

LONELY PLANET INDEX

- **1L petrol** US$1
- **1.5L bottled water** US$0.70
- **Bottle of Skol** US$0.80
- **Souvenir T-shirt** US$8
- **Plate of rice and sauce** US$1

HIGHLIGHTS

- **Îles de Los** (p370) Stretch out on palm-fringed strands, sipping fresh coconut juice.
- **Fouta Djalon** (p371) Ramble through the mountains and swim in the waterfalls of this majestic mountain plateau.
- **Bossou** (p373) Come face to face with chattering chimps.
- **Conakry** (p369) Hop through the capital's dubious dives, getting drunk on some of West Africa's best live music.
- **Forêt Classée de Ziama** (p372) Track elephants in the virgin rainforest.

ITINERARIES

- **One Week** Spend a couple of days in Conakry (p365), taking in the Îles de Los (p370), then go trekking in Fouta Djalon (p371).
- **Two Weeks** Add a leisurely trip through Lower Guinea (p370) to the itinerary. Alternatively, just stay in Fouta Djalon (p371) for more extended village-to-village treks (see the boxed text, p371).

CLIMATE & WHEN TO GO

Guinea is one of the wettest countries in West Africa – Conakry receives over 4300mm of rain a year, half of it in July and August. Temperatures average 30°C along the coast, where it is always humid, and can fall to 6°C and below at night in the Fouta Djalon in December and January.

The best time to visit is November and December, after the rains and before the dusty harmattan winds, though the Fouta Djalon is at its greenest and best during the rainy season.

HISTORY

Guinea was part of the Empire of Mali, which covered a large part of western Africa between the 13th and 15th centuries; the empire's capital Niani is situated in eastern Guinea. From the mid-1400s Portuguese and other European traders settled Guinea's coastal region, and the country eventually became a French colony in 1891.

The end of French West Africa began with Guinea. In 1958, Sekou Touré was the only West African leader to reject a French offer of membership in a commonwealth and demanded total independence. French reaction was swift: financial and technical aid was cut off, and there was a massive flight of capital.

Sekou Touré called his new form of state a 'communocracy', a blend of Africanist and communist models. It didn't work; the economy went into a downward spiral, and his growing paranoia triggered a reign of terror. 'Conspiracies' were being sensed everywhere; thousands of supposed dissidents were imprisoned and executed. By the end of the 1960s over 250,000 Guineans lived in exile.

Towards the end of his presidency Touré changed many of his policies and tried to liberalise the economy. He died in March 1984.

In the Grip of the Military

Days after Touré's death, a military coup was staged by a group of colonels, including the barely known, barely educated Lansana Conté, who became president. He introduced austerity measures, and in 1991 bowed to pressure to introduce a multiparty political system. Initial hopes for a new era of freedom and prosperity were quickly dashed. Conté claimed victory in three highly disputed elections, and there were incidents of obstruction and imprisonment of opposition leaders. In 2007 demonstrations were violently quashed, though a few concessions (such as the nomination of a prime minister) were made. Severely ill and barely able to govern, Conté stayed in power until his death in December 2008.

Guinea Today

The day following Conté's death, an army contingent under Captain Moussa Dadis Camara took power in a coup d'état. 'Dadis' promised that he'd quickly clean up the Guinean house, organise elections and return to the army barracks. His initial measures, such as cracking down on Guinean drug rings (Guinea is one of West Africa's hubs of the cocaine trade), announcing anti-corruption measures and new mining deals (Guinea is hugely rich in natural resources, owning 30% of the world's bauxite resources), gained him many followers. However, his announcement in 2009 that he considered standing in the upcoming elections and increasing violence committed by members of the army pro-

voked furious reactions. On 28 September 2009, army elements quashed a large demonstration with extreme violence. A UN commission denounced the events as a crime against humanity, and it is thought that over

WARNING

Since the attempted assassination of self-declared president Moussa Dadis Camara in December 2009, Guinea's future was more uncertain than ever. The military regime turned increasingly violent and oppressive, and chaos appeared to reign within military ranks. Check travel advice carefully before setting out.

150 people were killed. Two months later, 'Dadis' was shot following a dispute with his aide-de-camp Toumba Diakite, and was still receiving medical treatment at the time of writing. The shooting highlighted the anarchic conditions within the army currently ruling the nation. As this book went to press, Guinea's future was extremely precarious and uncertain.

CULTURE

The face of Guinean culture changes along with the natural zones you pass. Each of the country's main ethnic groups has its own, proud past, and yet there's an equally strong sense of national identity.

Today, Guinea is one of the world's poorest nations, despite sitting on some of its richest soils. That paradox sometimes puzzles people, yet for a long time, Guineans, who have only experienced autocratic rule, bore their conditions silently. In 2007, people finally rose up against corruption, economic mismanagement and poverty, an act they repeated in 2009. Tragic as the loss of lives has been, the fact that Guinea's youth has finally cried out may indicate an important cultural shift.

People

Guinea's main ethnic groups are the Fula (about 40% of the population), Malinke (about 30%) and Susu (about 20%). Fifteen other groups, living mostly in the forest region, constitute the rest of the population. Susu predominantly inhabit the coastal region; Fula, the Fouta Djalon; and Malinke, the north and centre. The total population is about 9.8 million. About 85% of the population is Muslim (the Fouta Jalon being a centre of Islam), 8% are Christian and the remainder follow traditional animist religions (especially in the forest region and the Basse Côte).

Arts & Crafts

Sekou Touré's form of communism was an economic disaster, but the government's emphasis on nationalist *authenticité* in the arts, and state patronage of artistic institutions was a boon. Great orchestras, such as Bembeya Jazz, were created during that time, and many of Guinea's greatest artists (including Sekouba Bambino Diabaté, the nation's biggest pop star) learned their craft in that era. The dance group Les Ballets Africains today remains the 'prototype' of West African ballet troupes while Circus Baobab mixes trapeze shows and acrobatics with their dance shows. To see bands such as Ba Cissoko or Espoirs de Coronthie live, head for Conakry's bars and clubs (p369).

Camara Laye, author of *L'Enfant Noir*, is the country's best-known writer.

To pick up some typical arts and crafts try the indigo and mud-cloth cooperatives in many towns.

FOOD & DRINK

Outside Conakry there are few proper restaurants, though most towns have a couple of basic eating houses serving *riz gras* (rice fried in oil and tomato paste and served with fried fish, meat or vegetables) or simple chicken and chips. In Fouta Djalon, creamy sauces made from meat and potato leaves (*haako putte*) or manioc leaves (*haako ban tara*) are common. The coast is fantastic for grilled fish.

Guinea has plenty of basic coffee bars where you can enjoy sweet, black coffee (*café noir*). The most common beers available are Skol, a light lager, the darker Guilux and Flag.

ENVIRONMENT

Guinea has four distinct zones, all stunningly beautiful: a narrow coastal plain, the Fouta Djalon plateau, northeastern dry lowland and the forest region (*Guinée forestière*) of the southeast. The Fouta Djalon plateau rising to over 1500m, is the source of the Gambia and Senegal Rivers (the source of the Niger River lies to the south, near the Sierra Leone border).

Guinea's environmental record is atrocious. Deforestation is rampant, none of the protected areas are well maintained and animals are often hunted. Parks and reserves include the seldom visited Parc Transfrontalier Niokolo-Badiar and Parc National du Haut Niger, as well as the Forêt Classée de Ziama, with its rainforest areas and nearby Mt Nimba Nature Reserve (an endangered Unesco World Heritage Site, spoilt by an iron mine). The Jane Goodall Institute has started work on a park straddling the border with Sierra Leone.

Find out more at the Direction Nationale des Forêts et de la Faune (opposite).

ONAKRY

op 2 million

Conakry doesn't try to please its guests, nd yet many fall in love with the city, like vomen going for the wrong guy. There ren't many sights in this dusty mess of rumbling buildings and traffic jams, and andom police checks make getting around n exercise in extreme patience. From the auseating fishing port of Boulbinet and he street kitchens of Coronthie to the ontainers-turned-shops of Taouyah, this ity goes about its business noisily and vith ingenuity, proud and unruffled by the isitor's gaze.

HISTORY

n 1887, the French officially founded Conakry on the island Tumbo (now the tip of the Kaloum peninsula), the site of several iny fishing villages.

Conakry grew rapidly throughout the late 9th and early 20th century, and was chosen as the capital of young, independent Guinea. Today, the city and its surrounding townships house almost a quarter of Guinea's population.

ORIENTATION

Conakry is a long, narrow city, built on the Kaloum Peninsula. In the city centre you'll find the banks, airline offices, several restaurants and the best internet cafe. About 2km east of the city centre, the peninsula narrows, and then at Pont du 8 Novembre the road divides into Route de Donka to the north, leading to the buzzing Camayenne neighbourhood; Corniche Sud to the south; and the Autoroute up the middle. About 10km north of the city centre are the lively Rogbané and Taouyah *quartiers* (neighbourhoods).

INFORMATION

Bookshops

La Maison du Livre (Map p366; ☎ 64 24 83 50; Carrefour Moussoudougou; ☑ 9am-1pm & 2-6pm Mon-Sat) Good for books, magazines, postcards and stationery.

Cultural Centres

American Cultural Center (off Map p366; ☎ 65 10 40 00; Transversale 2, Ratoma; ☑ 9am-3pm Mon-Thu, to noon Fri) Has American books and magazines, an internet cafe and occasional events.

Centre Culturel Franco-Guinéen (Map p366; ☎ 63 40 96 25; Corniche Nord, Tumbo) A hub of cultural activity, with regular concerts, films, exhibitions and a cafe.

Internet Access

MouNa (Map p368; Ave de la République, Kaloum; per hr US$1.20, wi-fi per hr US$2; ☑ 24hr) Guinea's best internet cafe on three floors; also has laptop points.

Medical Services

There are pharmacies along Ave de la République.

Clinique Pasteur (Map p368; ☎ 30 43 00 76; 5th Blvd, Kaloum) Fairly good for malaria tests and minor injuries.

Hôpital Ambrose Paré (Map p366; ☎ 63 35 10 10; Dixinn) Considered the best in Guinea, though still very basic.

Money

Street changers line Ave de la République, and a popular black market spot is the so-called 'Wall Street' in town.

Bicigui (Map p368; ☎ 30 41 45 15; Ave de la République) The main branch claims to change travellers cheques, but doesn't always do so. The 24-hour ATM takes Visa.

SGBG (Map p368; ☎ 30 45 60 00; Cité Chemin de Fer) Has a 24-hour ATM for Visa cards and changes cash.

Post

DHL (Map p368; ☎ 30 41 12 21; 4th Blvd, Almamy)

Main post office (Map p368; 4th Blvd, Almamya; ☑ 8am-5pm Mon-Fri, to noon Sat)

Telephone

MouNa Télécentre (Map p368; Ave de la République; ☑ 8am-10pm) Largest *télécentre* downtown.

Tourist Information

Direction Nationale des Forêts et de la Faune (Map p366; ☎ 30 46 81 23; Rte de Donka, Conakry) Gives information on Guinea's national parks.

Guinée Ecologie (Map p366; ☎ 60 28 79 94; madou salioupop@yahoo.com; Pharmaguinée Dixinn) Great on environmental information; can arrange birdwatching tours.

Jane Goodall Institute (Map p366; ☎ 60 21 68 88; mcgauthier@janegoodall.org; Blvd Bellevue, Dixinn Centre 1) Information on chimpanzee protection and chimp sites.

Travel Agencies

Ambassador Voyages (Map p368; ☎ 63 27 00 09; ambassadorvoyages@hotmail.com; 6 Ave de la République) Good ticketing service.

IPC Voyages (Map p368; ☎ 30 45 56 62; Imm Nafaya, Kaloum) Bookings and ticketing.

GUINEA

Mondial Tours (Map p368; ☎ 30 43 35 50; www.mondialtours.net; Imm Nafaya, Kaloum) The best for tours around the country.

DANGERS & ANNOYANCES

Incidents of military aggression and extortion are frequently reported. Always carry your passport and vaccination certificates with you, especially if you're out on the town after 11pm – *gendarmerie* (police) checkpoints are set up at Pont du 8 Novembre and near the UK embassy (Résidence 2000), and you will usually have to show your papers. If everything is in order, you shouldn't have to pay any 'fines', though you might have to discuss a little with the often-intimidating soldiers.

Plenty of pickpockets roam March
Madina and the Ave de la République.
there's any civil unrest, the youth areas
Kipé, Ratoma and Taouyah are usually th
first to rise up.

SIGHTS & ACTIVITIES

The **Musée National** (Map p368; ☎ 30 41 50 60; 7
Blvd, Sandervalia; admission GFr5000; ☺ 9am-5.30pm Tue
Sun) has a modest collection of masks an
musical instruments. For a real sense
history, visit the ancient, shaded **Cimetièr
de Boulbinet** (Map p368; near Port de Boulbinet
abandoned since 1946.

Nearby, the grand **Palais des Nations** (Ma
p368; Boulbinet) is being renovated, having bee
destroyed in 1996.

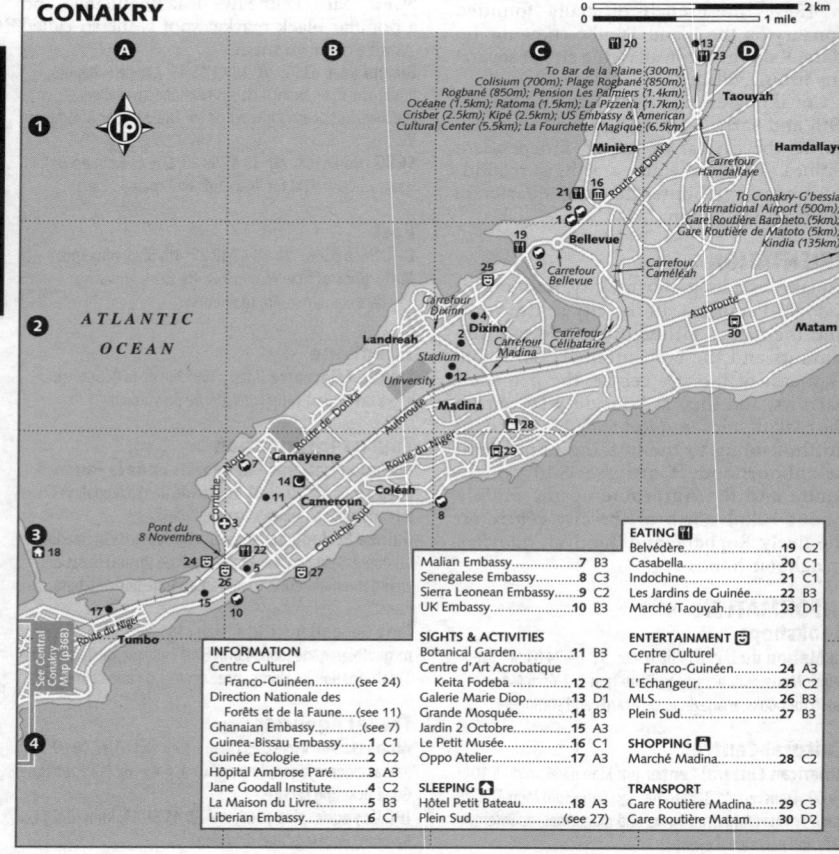

CONAKRY

0 —————— 2 km
0 —————— 1 mile

To Bar de la Plaine (300m);
Colisium (700m); Plage Rogbané (850m);
Rogbané (850m); Pension Les Palmiers (1.4km);
Océane (1.5km); Ratoma (1.5km); La Pizzeria (1.7km);
Crisber (2.5km); Kipé (2.5km); US Embassy & American
Cultural Center (5.5km); La Fourchette Magique (6.5km)

To Conakry-G'bessia
International Airport (500m);
Gare Routière Bambeto (5km);
Gare Routière de Matoto (5km);
Kindia (135km)

ATLANTIC OCEAN

CONAKRY ACROBATICS

Just behind the large Dixinn Stadium, in a tall building and outdoor terrain, one of Conakry's most amazing spots announces itself with drumbeats, *balafon* sounds and shouts of excitement. This is where the **Centre d'Art Acrobatique Keita Fodeba** (Map p366; Dixinn Stadium, Conakry) unites street kids and artists in focussed daily practice. Launched by the success of the Guinean troupe Circus Baobab, this magical place takes stage performance to a whole new level. The centre not only trains some of Africa's greatest acrobats, it provides youngsters with a whole range of skills. The discipline of practice for progress is one of them; practical expertise in crafts, literacy and much more are also part of the rigorous training. The centre's success has made waves across the world – young performers have been sought out to participate in circus performances from East Asia to the US. Seeing them rehearse is inspiring, shining a light on possibility in a country where most people preach despair. And if you've caught the bug, ask them to give you some classes – you might take trapeze or juggling skills, along with a whole new insight into the lives of Guinea's youngsters, back from your journey.

Seeing worshippers flock to Conakry's impressive **Grande Mosquée** (Map p366; Autoroute, amayenne) on a Friday is amazing.

Driving into town on the Corniche Nord, heck out the funky scrap-metal sculptures of **ippo Atelier** (Map p366; Corniche Nord, Tumbo) and have our custom statues made. Equally funky is Centre d'Art Acrobatique Keita Fodeba (see he boxed text, above), Conakry's brilliant acrobatics centre, providing street kids with new kills and a future. They can arrange courses.

The **Botanical Garden** (Map p366; Rte de Donka, amayenne) is great for relaxed walks under apok trees and **Jardin 2 Octobre** (Map p366; ☎ 66 36 38 85; Corniche Nord, Tumbo) is a vast, pretty hildren's playground and park.

Tucked away in Minière, **Le Petit Musée** (Map 366; ☎ 64 21 54 98; Minière; ⏰ 9am-7.30pm Mon-Sat), s a beautiful space with a small stage featuring theatre and music shows. Part of a cultural complex with cafe and cinema in Taouyah, he tiny **Galerie Marie Diop** (Map p366; ☎ 63 66 66 60; mariediop@hotmail.com; Espace Rogbane, Taouyah) is a cute art gallery exhibiting Marie's original works.

SLEEPING

Inexpensive lodging is scarce and rough, possibly without running water or electricity.

Maison d'Accueil (Map p368; ☎ 60 42 06 67; Rte du Niger, Kaloum; r with/without air-con US$45/15; P ❌ 💻) Conakry's Catholic Mission has clean, simple rooms in a peaceful setting. It's safer than most hotels, and is often fully booked.

Plein Sud (Map p366; ☎ 60 20 35 35; off Corniche Sud; r US$20-24; P ❌) Conakry's most relaxed open-air restaurant has three clean, simple rooms right next to its large, sea-view garden.

our pick **Pension Les Palmiers** (off Map p366; ☎ 60 59 38 03, 62 29 44 84; ighussein@yahoo.fr; Rte de Donka, Ratoma; s/d incl breakfast US$45/50; ❌ 💻) The doily-adorned couches, cute living room and caring owner will remind you of your visits to grandma's. There's a small garden with a teeny pool.

Océane (off Map p366; ☎ 67 90 90 90; Rte de Donka, Ratoma; r incl breakfast US$53; P ❌ 💻) The pool is popular with weekenders; rooms aren't particularly well maintained but have good views.

Hôtel Petit Bateau (Map p366; ☎ 63 40 61 06; www.hotelpetitbateau.net; Port de Plaisance; s/d US$50/60; P ❌ 💻 💻) Past the industrial zone sits this pretty sea-view place with impeccable rooms and a marina outside. It's only easily accessible if you have your own car.

Galaxie Hotel (Map p368; ☎ 62 08 90 26; 5th Ave, Kaloum; s/d US$90/100; ❌) The beds here are impressive enough to make a porn star blush. A decent inner-city choice.

Le Rocher (Map p368; ☎ 60 55 98 77; essiarnat oussi@yahoo.fr; Sandervalia; s/d incl breakfast US$120/140; P ❌ 💻 📶 💻) Service is personalised, rooms impeccable (with free wi-fi) and the food excellent at this small family hotel.

Novotel (Map p368; ☎ 30 41 50 22; h0509@accor.com; Kaloum; r with/without sea view US$170/160; P ❌ 💻 💻) This is Conakry's regular choice for anyone from airline staff to foreign consultants, providing good service, safety and noncommittal smiles to anyone who can afford it.

EATING

For good street food, try Marché du Niger (see p369) or Marché Taouyah (Map p366), where bowls of rice cost less than US$2.

GUINEA

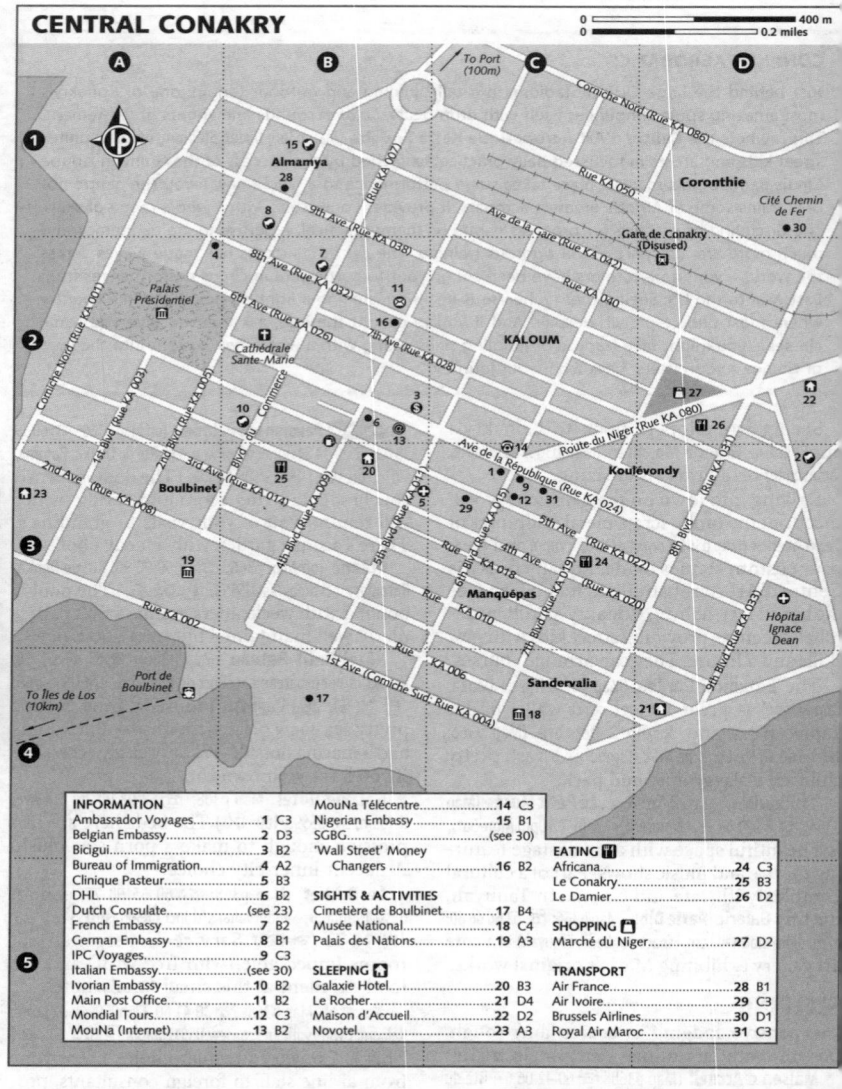

CENTRAL CONAKRY

Belvédère (Map p366; ☎ 60 43 25 26; Rte de Donka, Bellevue; meals US$5-12; 🕑 2pm-2am) The large garden is a favourite for family parties and live concerts. The menu is made of fast-food staples, but the garden space is pleasant.

La Pizzeria (off Map p366; Rte de Donka, Ratoma; meals US$6-10; 🕑 dinner Wed-Sun; Ⓥ) The Conakry grapevine has this humble house down as the nation's best pizza oven. Pizzas are large, with thin crusts and imaginative toppings; the vibe, family friendly.

Le Conakry (Map p368; ☎ 30 41 26 82; 4th Ave; meals US$7; 🕑 lunch & dinner Mon-Sat) Small and very French, this expat favourite has a great selection of simple dishes.

Africana (Map p368; ☎ 30 41 35 18; Manquépas; meals US$8) Located behind the Anglican church, the tables here heave with delicious Senegalese and Guinean meals and the place is always packed around lunchtime. There's usually live *kora* music.

Les Jardins de Guinée (Map p366; ☎ 64 21 89 38; Coléah; meals US$8-10; ☺ lunch & dinner) Once one of Conakry's great music venues, this garden place is today one of the city's favourite restaurants, all thanks to the excellent French food and pizza it serves. It's best to come for lunch, when it's less busy.

Le Damier (Map p368; ☎ 30 41 17 86; www.damier -conakry.com; Rte du Niger; meals US$8-14; ☺ breakfast & lunch Mon-Sat; Ⓥ) The downstairs patisserie sells the best bread and chocolates in town, but the soul of this place is the cosy upstairs restaurant. It's a favourite with Guinea's young, upwardly mobile classes.

Casabella (Map p366; ☎ 60 21 77 55; Taouyah; dishes US$10-16; ☺ noon-midnight Mon-Thu, 5pm-midnight Fri & Sat; ☒ ☒ Ⓥ) Between chubby baroque angels and faintly lit fountains, you get to enjoy spicy Mexican meals and good pizzas. The pool outside invites for sundowners.

Indochine (Map p366; Minière; meals US$12-18; ☺ lunch Tue-Sun, dinner daily; Ⓥ) Conakry's first address for Southeast Asian cuisine is pricier than most, but that's because the owners import all those rare spices. One of Conakry's classiest dining experiences.

DRINKING & ENTERTAINMENT

Conakry is riddled with conspicuous drinking holes and live music dives. The nightclubs are fun, too. **Bar de la Plaine** (off Map p366; Marché Taouyah) is a plain, streetside place; Ba Cissoko's musicians hang out here and can arrange *kora* and drumming classes. Nearby, **Plage Rogbané** (off Map p366; Taouyah; ☺ lunch & dinner) is a chilled-out spot, with tasty seafood, cold beers and neighbourhood vibes.

For live music, head first to the humble **L'Echangeur** (Map p366; Dixinn II), where many of Guinea's biggest stars play on Saturday. **La Fourchette Magique** (off Map p366; ☎ 60 36 86 50; Kaporo Port) is where Guinea's intellectuals debate the country's future over a few Skols and excellent live jazz. The palm-shaded garden of **Plein Sud** (Map p366; ☎ 60 20 35 35; off Corniche Sud) features live music every weekend. Bigger concerts usually take place at **Centre Culturel Franco-Guinéen** (Map p366; ☎ 63 40 96 25; Corniche Nord, Tumbo).

Good nightclubs include **Crisber** (off Map p366; Rte de Donka, Kipé) and **Colisium** (off Map p366; Carrefour Transit), though designer **MLS** (Map p366; ☎ 65 81 18 11; Place 8 Novembre; ☺ 5.50pm-5am; Mon-Thu free, Fri-Sun US$10-20) is the chicest party spot of all.

SHOPPING

The hectic, noisy sprawl of **Marché Madina** (p366; Madina) is where you get everything from Chinese house wares to indigo cloth, and sometimes a lost copy of Plato between faded women's magazines at one of the many street booksellers. Marché du Niger (Map p368) isn't quite as crazy, and has fewer pickpockets, too – it's a great place for buying fruit, veg and patchwork trousers.

GETTING THERE & AWAY

Conakry has a number of *gares routières:* Bambeto (off Map p366), Madina (Map p366) and Matam (Map p366). Bambeto is the main departure point for taxis to Fouta Djalon, while Matam is the departure spot for buses to Kankan, Kissidougou and N'zérékoré. From Madina, you find taxis to all destinations.

There are several taxis daily from each *gare routière* for Freetown (Sierra Leone; US$20, seven hours) and Diaoubé (Senegal; US$40, two days). For Bamako (Mali; US$40, 24 hours), cars use the *gare routière* Madina. The three-day marathon to Monrovia (US$45) begins at the *gare routière* Matoto (off Map p366). See also p374.

GETTING AROUND

To hail a shared taxi around town just stand at the side of the road and shout your destination as the taxi passes, or ask someone to show you the appropriate hand signal. Taxis cost US$0.20 per 3km zone. Minibuses (*magbanas*) are a bit cheaper but much slower. The two main destinations from Ratoma are Kaloum (*ville*) and Madina.

To charter a taxi (called *déplacement*), find an empty one and bargain hard: Kaloum to Taouyah should cost around US$4. Dixinn–Taouyah is around US$2.

WESTERN GUINEA

Most travellers leaving Conakry stay on the bus as it rumbles along the main highway through Kindia, and even fewer turn north along the coast, but both have worthy natural attractions.

ÎLES DE LOS

Off Conakry's shores, Îles de Los are palm-fringed islands that tempt with beaches the city lacks. On tiny **Île Room** you can stay right on the beach at the pricey **Le Sogué** (☎ 64 25 70 59; r incl breakfast US$100; ☷ Nov–mid-Jun; ☷); go for the guesthouse **Villa Elisa** (d US$30) or one of the rootsy drumming camps.

Île de Kassa is closer to Conakry and is more regularly served by *pirogues*. **Le Magellan** (☎ 64 39 54 20, 60 36 75 74; pascaldemattos@yahoo.fr; s/d from US$60/66; ☷ Oct–mid-Jun; ☷ ☷) is the place to stay.

For Île de Kassa, you can get on one of the overcrowded *pirogues* (around US$2) from Port de Boulbinet. To Roume, it's best to hire a *pirogue* (around US$40). Le Magellan arranges pick-up from Hôtel Petit Bateau (p367).

KINDIA
pop 100,000

Kindia is a spread-out town, located up the first mountain as you wind your way into the Fouta Djalon. **La Voile de la Mariée** (Bridal Veil Falls; admission US$1) is the town's most famous waterfall, although **Les Eaux de Kilissi** (☎ Aboubacar Keita 62 35 22 51; Foulayah; admission US$1) are much prettier and are perfect for picnics.

Le Masabi (☎ 64 72 65 69; s/d incl breakfast US$24/28; ☷ ☷) is a decent hotel with hot water, good rooms and moody staff. Tucked away up a hill, **Le Sooli** (☎ 60 49 09 33; Khaliakhori; s/d US$18/23; ☷ ☷ ☷) is large and friendly, though a tad rundown.

Daily taxi destinations include Mamou (US$4, three hours), Labé (US$7) and Conakry (US$3, three hours).

LOWER GUINEA
Dubréka

Between June and December, Dubréka's waterfalls **Cascades de la Soumba** (☎ 63 35 20 24; admission/r US$2/55; ☷ ☷) and the river spot **Merveilles de la Soumba** (☎ 64 60 96 20; r US$15) are worth a visit. Both have simple accommodation. Ask locals to guide you to **Tafory** (Khorira), where sculptor Nabisco puts you up in his community-supporting arts project (rates are reasonable, and depend on length and nature of stay).

Fria

In Fria, forthcoming staff at **Hôtel Yaskad** (☎ 63 85 65 44, 65 66 54 15; signposted off Rte Unite; with fan/air-con US$6/10; ☷ ☷) and guesthouse **La Mariame** (s/d US$12/17; ☷) can arrange guides to the caves and river spots in the surrounding hills. Fria is Guinea's oldest bauxite mining town and has a diverse population. There are several restaurants – the **Rose de Casablanca** (near the hospital; meals around US$6) is a solid, simple option – and nightclubs. A very rough route will take you from here to Télimélé.

Boffa

Nearby Boffa, an old colonial trading point, is famous for its May pilgrimage. Thousands of pilgrims march from Conakry to the town's **Catholic church** (1876, rebuilt in 1934) and mission.

Sobané

About 25km from the highway is **Village Touristique Sobané** (☎ 63 93 71 28; Sobané; bungalows with/without air-con US$40/36; ☷ ☷), with its large but run down bungalows on a wide beach (come at high tide). It's best reached by private taxi from Boffa or Boké (US$30 to US$60).

Boké

Boké was once a colonial trading centre. The 1878 **Fortin de Boké** (☎ 60 68 26 74; admission by donation; ☷ 8am-6pm) tells the town's historical story. Staff at the **Jane Goodall Institute** (☎ Mr Soumah 64 08 11 63, Bokar Sylla 65 46 50 76; near Stadium Boké) can indicate (and take you to) good chimp sites in the area. For bush taxis to Senegal and Guinea-Bissau, ask at the *gare routière*.

Kamsar

The better hotels in the area are in Kamsar, a soulless town that is rapidly growing around a huge bauxite plant. Two darkish rooms share a bathroom at hotel **RBQ** (☎ 30 32 65 01; r from US$25; ☷ ☷), but the pool is fabulous. **Hôtel le Kamsar** (☎ 63 35 52 62; kikeyambe.kamsar@gmail.com; r US$54; ☷ ☷ ☷) is one of the best places in the country.

Food is excellent at the **Auberge de Kamsar** (☎ 63 35 52 62, 63 35 11 07; dishes around US$10; ☷ 9am-3.30pm & 6.30-11pm Mon-Sat), and **Club Nautique** (dishes around US$8), behind the bauxite plant, is a popular outdoor restaurant on the river.

FOUTA DJALON

Fouta Djalon's green, rolling hills are more than a come-on for restless hiking boots – they're must-see Guinea. This undulant plateau is full of interesting villages and natural sites, and it's cooler than the lowlands.

DALABA

A former colonial spa, 1200m-high Dalaba is a great base for **hiking** tours. For an idea of routes, drop in at the **tourist office** (☎ 67 26 93 48; Quartier des Chargeurs; ⏰ 8.30am-6.30pm). **Case de Palabres**, decorated with Fula bas-relief designs, and the impressive **Chutes de Ditinn**, belong on any itinerary.

There are some good craft outlets in town, including the **Association des Couturières de Tangama** (☎ 64 36 82 75; ⏰ 9am-4pm Mon-Sat), great for fair-trade indigo fabrics, and the **Cooperative des Cordonniers** (☎ 62 52 96 64), which sells handmade leather goods.

Good places to stay include the rootsy **Auberge Seidy II** (☎ 60 57 53 70; r US$8), where Koffi serves grilled chicken; and **Le Bouchon Lyonnais** (☎ 60 34 61 76, 64 35 51 05; r incl breakfast from US$30), slightly more upmarket, with fresh food. **SIB Hôtel du Fouta** (☎ 60 27 61 71; s/d US$20/25; P) has rundown rooms but great views.

Bush taxis go to Pita (US$2, one hour), Labé (US$4, two hours), Mamou (US$2, one hour) and Conakry (US$7, seven hours).

DOUCKI

About 45km from Pita on the Télimélé road is the village of Doucki, where Hassan Bah runs a small **campement** (s US$5),with traditional Fula huts. The spot is perfect for hikes to the area's spectacular slot canyons. *Taxis brousses* (bush taxis) from Pita to Donghol-Touma drop you 2km from the village. Visits can be arranged through Fouta Trekking (see the boxed text, right).

LABÉ
pop 70,000

Guinea's third-largest town is not particularly attractive but is great for its busy market vibe and practical stuff, such as checking emails and catching your next *taxi brousse*. The **Petit Musée du Fouta Djallon** (☎ 30 52 00 10; admission by donation; ⏰ 8am-6pm) is a quiet spot, where you learn about the region's unique Fula culture. The **Maison des Artisans** (☎ 60 57 08 30; Quartier Kouroula;

> **FOUTA TREKKING AVENTURE**
>
> With over 10 years' experience in hiking and researching, the association **Fouta Trekking Aventure** (☎ 60 57 02 79; www.foutatrekking. org; Quartier N'Djoulou, Labé) has identified the best hikes, cliffs, mountains and waterfalls in Fouta Djalon and develops circuits to help the local communities. Tours can be tailored to individual wishes, and last anything from a day to over a week. The rate is US$36, including the guide, food and accommodation, but excluding transport. Try one of its exclusive circuits, taking you to rarely visited spots of the Fouta, with accommodation in *campements solidaires* (traditional-style lodgings run for community benefit) built by the association.

⏰ 8.30am-5pm Mon-Sat) is the best place to pick up locally made crafts. For your hikes through the Fouta, contact the friendly and competent Fouta Trekking Aventure (see the boxed text, above).

Travellers on a budget should seek out **Auberge la Calebasse** (☎ 60 41 08 51, 62 23 50 48; Quartier Ghadha Pounthioun; r US$10; P), the least rundown of the cheapos (hire a *moto-taxi* to get here). **Auberge la Campagne** (☎ 60 57 17 02; Quartier Pounthioun; camping US$6, r incl breakfast US$20; P) has large, clean rooms and offers camping on the 1st-floor terrace. The best place in town is the friendly **Hôtel Tata** (☎ 60 41 08 51; Quartier Pounthioun; r US$20; P 🖳 ♿), with cosy, natural-stone walls and great pizzas.

Try **Le Calebasse** (meals US$4; ⏰ lunch & dinner) for simple meals, or the market and *gare routière* for street food.

Most buses and *taxis brousses*, including to Mamou (US$5, three hours) and Conakry (US$11, eight hours), leave from the main *gare routière* in the town centre. Vehicles heading to Bissau in Guinea-Bissau and Diaoubé, Senegal (US$13, eight hours) go from *gare routière* Daka, 2km north of town.

MALI-YEMBEREM

Intrepid overlanders pass through Mali-Yemberem on the very rocky track from Kédougou (Senegal) into Guinea. At over 1400m, this is the highest town in the Fouta; it's also the coldest. Mali-Yemberem is famous for Mt Loura, known as **La Dame de Mali**, a mountainside resembling a woman's

GUINEA

profile. Hike up 7km for stunning views. Fouta Trekking Aventure (see the boxed text, p371) operates an ecocamp in town.

SOUTHERN GUINEA

Guinea's southern forest region is arguably the most stunning part of the country, but it's incredibly hard to reach. Just to the north, the towns of Upper Guinea are dry and dusty – the perfect introduction to neighbouring Mali.

KANKAN
pop 120,000

Kankan is a sand-blown university town and Guinea's second city, though it's shockingly neglected (there's no electricity). It's the heart of Guinea's Malinke population. You might hear some great Mande music being performed; as for actual sights, there aren't many.

Across the Milo River (a tributary of the Niger), you can walk up the small hill from which legendary Mande leader and anticolonial fighter Samory Touré staged his historical siege of Kankan in the late 19th century. In town, there's the **Grande Mosquée** and three busy markets. Sekou Touré's once-stately **Villa Syli** has been transformed into hotel **Bakonko** (☎ 64 71 21 87; r incl breakfast US$24/40), Kankan's most decent accommodation option. Most budget travellers prefer the clean and tidy **Centre d'Accueil Diocésain** (☎ 60 59 67 57; r with/without bathroom US$16/12; P), the Catholic mission guesthouse (phone in advance). **Le Calao** (☎ 63 19 78 36; r US$16; P), behind the fish market, has well-maintained rooms grouped around a calm yard.

Chez Isidor (Le Répère; ☎ 64 35 94 15; dishes around US$4; ☼ 7.30am-10pm), near the university, is a lively eatery serving spaghetti, salads and Guinean meals.

Taxis brousses for most destinations, including Conakry (US$20, 13 hours), Kissidougou (US$10, six hours), Siguiri (US$6, two hours) and N'zérékoré (US$20, 12 hours), leave from the twin *gares routières* near the bridge. Taxis to Dabola (US$10, four hours) leave from Rond-Point N'Balia.

KISSIDOUGOU

Kissidougou, the entry to *Guinée forestière* (forest region), sits where the main road from Conakry divides north to Kankan and south to N'zérékoré. The small **Musée Préfectoral** (admission US$0.20; ☼ 9am-5pm Mon-Sat) has some wonderful masks and objects deemed magical. The museum's staff are able to direct you to some fine vine bridges in surrounding villages.

Hôtel Mandela (☎ 60 39 25 42; r US$6) is an acceptable budget option. The nicest place for food and lodging is the flower-filled **Hôtel Savanah** (☎ 60 43 97 54; Quartier Sobèla; r with/without air-con US$16/12; P), on the highway.

Bush taxis go daily to Kankan (US$10, five hours), Macenta (US$5, five hours) and Conakry (US$17, 12 hours).

MACENTA & FORÊT CLASÉE DE ZIAMA

The forest region begins in Kissidougou, but the area's beauty (or what's left of it) really kicks in outside Macenta. The town itself doesn't have many charms, but is a jumping-off place for the 116,000-acre **Forêt Classée de Ziama** (admission US$20, mandatory guide US$5), a beautiful stretch of rainforest. Headquarters are in Sérédou, though it's best to call the **Centre Forestier** (☎ 33 91 03 89) in N'zérékoré first so that staff can prepare for your visit.

Macenta's hotels have never been great. Both **Hôtel Bamala** (☎ 60 58 52 27, 66 67 87 89; r US$6-8; P) and **Hôtel Palm** (☎ 60 52 61 13; r US$3-8; P) are very basic and hardly spotless.

Bush taxis head daily to Kissidougou (US$8, five hours) and to N'zérékoré (US$6, 2½ hours). If you're heading to Monrovia it's better to go from N'zérékoré.

N'ZÉRÉKORÉ
pop 110,000

N'zérékoré is the major city of the forest region, and is a smuggling base, transport hub, refugee centre and southern Guinea's NGO centre all in one.

The **Musée Ethnographique** (admission US$2; ☼ 8.30am-5pm Mon-Sat) is small but interesting. You can watch crafts being made and traditional dancing in the **artisan village** in the small 'sacred' forest at the northern entrance to town.

The **Catholic Mission** (Quartier Dorota; r US$6; P), on the road to the airport, has simple, mosquito-netted rooms with shared toilets. Rooms at **Hôtel Haida** (Gbama 1; r with fan/air-con US$7/8; P) are basic; the attached restaurant is one of the most popular in town. The big-spender option is **Hôtel Le Mont Nimba** (☎ 64 38 45 24; Quartier au Sud; r per person US$36-50; P). Nonguests can use the pool for a fee.

For plates of *riz gras*, try restaurant **Mouminatou Binta** (meals US$1.50-2; 🕙 lunch & dinner) or the street stalls near the *gare routière*.

BOSSOU

Researchers at the **Bossou Environmental Research Institute** (☎ 60 58 47 61; douakomakan@ yahoo.fr) track the chimpanzees living in the surrounding scenic hills, so your chances of finding them are excellent. A guide for a couple of hours in the forest costs US$15, with half the money going towards the village. The **guesthouse** (s/d US$3/4) at the base of Mt Gban has simple rooms with shared toilets.

From N'zérékoré, take a *taxi brousse* to Lola (US$4, 30 minutes) and then another to Bossou (US$4, 30 minutes).

GUINEA DIRECTORY

ACCOMMODATION

Conakry has a couple of upmarket hotels, lots of very dingy dives and a few, generally overpriced, basic lodgings. Up-country, most hotels are in a desolate state. Only in Conakry's pricier places can you expect 24-hour electricity.

A tourism tax of US$1.50 per person per night applies to most top-end and some midrange hotels.

BUSINESS HOURS

Most businesses are open from 8am to 6pm Monday to Saturday, except Friday, when many close at 1pm. Businesses also close for an hour or so at lunch.

Banks 8.30am to 12.30pm and 2.30pm to 4.30pm Monday to Thursday, and 8.30am to 12.30pm and 2.45pm to 4.30pm Friday.

Government offices 8am to 4.30pm Monday to Thursday and 8am to 1pm Friday.

DANGERS & ANNOYANCES

See the boxed text, p363, for a travel warning concerning general security issues.

Electricity, running water and phones (even mobiles) all have intermittent service.

EMBASSIES & CONSULATES

All of the following are in Conakry.
Belgium (Map p368; ☎ 30 41 21 82; Corniche Sud, Koulévondy; 🕙 9am-12.30pm Mon-Fri)

PRACTICALITIES

- Guinea uses the metric system.
- Electricity is 220V/50Hz and plugs are of the European two-round-pin variety.
- Guinea's best-selling newspaper is the satirical weekly *Le Lynx*.
- The only TV station is the government-owned RTG, which shows lots of music clips and speeches.
- The BBC World Service is broadcast in French on FM and English on short wave.

Côte d'Ivoire (Map p368; ☎ 30 45 10 82; Blvd du Commerce; 🕙 8.30am-2pm Mon-Fri)
France (Map p368; ☎ 30 41 16 55; Blvd du Commerce; 🕙 7-11am Mon-Fri)
Germany (Map p368; ☎ 30 41 15 06; www.conakry. diplo.de; 2nd Blvd; 🕙 8am-noon Mon-Fri)
Ghana (Map p366; ☎ 30 40 95 60; Corniche Nord, Camayenne; 🕙 9am-3pm Mon-Fri)
Guinea-Bissau (Map p366; ☎ 60 58 73 36; Rte de Donka, Bellevue; 🕙 8am-1pm Mon-Fri)
Italy (Map p368; ☎ 62 66 38 29; Cité Chemin de Fer; 🕙 8.30am-noon Mon-Fri)
Liberia (Map p366; ☎ 30 46 20 59; Rte de Donka, Bellevue; 🕙 9am-1pm Mon-Fri)
Mali (Map p366; ☎ 30 46 14 18; Corniche Nord, Camayenne; 🕙 7.30am-1pm Mon-Fri)
Netherlands (Map p368; ☎ 30 41 50 21; room 121, Novotel, Kaloum; 🕙 8-11am Mon-Fri)
Nigeria (Map p368; ☎ 30 43 11 31; Ave de la Gare; 🕙 11am-1pm Mon, Wed & Fri)
Senegal (Map p366; ☎ 63 40 90 35; Corniche Sud, Coléah; 🕙 8am-12.30pm Mon-Fri)
Sierra Leone (Map p366; ☎ 30 46 40 84; Carrefour Bellevue; 🕙 9am-1pm Mon-Fri)
UK (Map p366; ☎ 63 35 53 29; britembconakry@hotmail. com; Villa 1, Residence 2000, Corniche Sud; 🕙 8am-1pm Mon-Fri) Assists Australian and Canadian citizens.
USA (Off p366; ☎ 65 10 40 00; http://conakry.usemba ssy.gov; Transversale 2, Ratoma; 🕙 7.30am-noon Mon-Fri) The American Cultural Center (p365) is in the same building.

EMERGENCIES

Fire ☎ 30 45 41 14
Ambulance (☎ 30 41 15 00) At Ignace Deen hospital.

FESTIVALS & EVENTS

The festival **Kora & Cordes**, run by Wakili Guinée, regroups some of the leading acoustic groups from across West Africa. It's normally held in December. During the annual **Festagg** (www. festagg.com, in French) you get to enjoy live concerts by major bands from Guinea and beyond for a whole week. It's held around April/May. In Kankan, the **Fête des Mares** is held at the beginning of each rainy season, and is a great opportunity to see Mande music being performed.

HOLIDAYS

As well as religious holidays listed in the Africa Directory (p1140), Guinea celebrates the following national holidays:
New Year's Day 1 January
Declaration of the 2nd Republic 3 April
May Day 1 May
Market Women's Revolt 27 August
Referendum Day 28 September
Independence Day 2 October

INTERNET ACCESS

Internet (usually US$1 per hour) is usually slow. Outside Conakry, connections are rare.

MAPS

Institut Géographique National's (IGN) 2002 map of Guinea is outdated but still useful. It's sold on the street and is available from bookshops and stationery stores (US$10).

MONEY

US dollars, euros and West African CFA francs are easily changed; travellers cheques are not. Rates are always best in Conakry. Black-market dealers, widely used throughout Guinea, give better rates. They are your only option to convert francs back into hard currency. Bicigui bank branches in most cities advance cash from Visa cards; its central Conakry branch has an ATM that accepts Visa cards – maximum withdrawal is US$40.

POST

The postal service is unreliable.

TELEPHONE

All large- and medium-sized towns have government-owned Sotelgui offices, though most people purchase a SIM card on one of the many mobile networks. You can buy top-up cards anywhere in the street.

TOURIST INFORMATION

There isn't much in terms of tourist information. See p365 for useful Conakry-based

addresses and the boxed text, p371, for a good starting point in Fouta Djalon.

VISAS

All visitors, except nationals of Ecowas (Economic Community of West African States) countries, Morocco and Tunisia, need a visa. Visas, usually valid for three months, are not available at airports or land borders.

Visa Extensions

Visas can be extended for up to three months at the **Bureau of Immigration** (☎ 30 44 13 39; 8th Ave) in Conakry.

Visas for Onward Travel

Visa regulations, prices and the speed of processing are all subject to change. Contact the relevant embassy of your destination country to find out how to proceed (see p373). You normally need a photocopy of the first three pages of your passport, two passport photographs, the relevant amount of money and a completed application form.

TRANSPORT IN GUINEA

GETTING THERE & AWAY
Air

Conakry-G'bessia International Airport can be chaotic and exasperating. Expect your bags to be inspected by imposing customs ladies.

Direct flights from Europe are available with Air France (Paris) and Brussels Airlines. Direct African destinations include Dakar (Senegal), Bamako (Mali) and Abidjan (Côte d'Ivoire). For other inner-African flights, you connect either at Dakar or Abidjan.

The following airlines service Guinea and have offices in Conakry:
Air France (AF; ☎ 64 20 22 03; www.airfrance.fr; 9th Ave, Conakry)
Air Ivoire (VU; ☎ 64 20 20 96; www.airivoire.com; 5th Ave, Conakry)
Brussels Airlines (SN; ☎ 63 45 10 61; www.brussels airlines.com; Cité Chemin de Fer)
Royal Air Maroc (RAM; ☎ 63 27 11 11; Ave de la République, Conakry)

Land
CÔTE D'IVOIRE

The most frequently travelled route is between Lola and Man either via Nzo and Danané or via Sipilou and Biankouma. By public transport, the latter is the fastest choice. From Kankan it is easiest to go via Bamako as the road to Odienné via Mandiana is very rough. There's also a seldom-travelled route between Beyla and Odienné (via Sinko).

GUINEA-BISSAU

Most people travelling by taxi get to Bissau via Labé, Koundara and Gabú. You have to taxi hop beyond Koundara. Infrequent bush taxis go from Boké and Kamsar up the rough road to Québo. With your own vehicle you can shave some distance, though not necessarily time, off this journey by going directly from Koumbia to Pitche. The roads are in a terrible state.

LIBERIA

There is quite a lot of traffic to Liberia. The primary route is from N'zérékoré to Ganta via Diéké. Bush taxis go frequently from N'zérékoré to the border, where you can get a *moto-taxi* or walk the remaining 2km to Ganta for a Monrovia-bound taxi.

The Macenta–Zorzor, Macenta–Voinjama, Guéckédou–Foya and Lola–Yekepa routes are all passable, but are in a bad state. For all of these routes, you buy a single ticket but change cars at the border.

MALI

Taxis and buses travel directly to Bamako from Kankan, Siguiri, Labé and Conakry. The road is sealed and in good, sometimes excellent shape from Kankan to Bamako (except for a 50km-stretch in Mali), though you pass a terrible stretch of potholed tarmac between Dabola and Kouroussa. If you have your own, very sturdy 4WD, you can also go from Kankan via Mandiana to Bougouni; or Mali-Yemberem, via Kita.

SENEGAL

There are several *taxis brousses* daily for Diaoubé, via Koundara (US$40, two days) from both *gare routière* Bambeto and *gare routière* Matam in Conakry. The road is terrible, but not as bad as the one passing via Mali-Yemberem to Kédougou (Senegal).

SIERRA LEONE

When we visited, it had once again been promised that the infamous Conakry–Freetown Hwy would be sealed; check the latest situation in country. There are several *taxis brousses* daily to Freetown (US$25, seven hours) from both *gare routière* Bambeto and *gare routière* Matam in Conakry. A bus also goes to Freetown (US$20) from *gare routière* Matam.

From Kindia to Kamakwie there are regular taxis to the border at Medina-Oula, but little transport further south. The road on the Sierra Leone side is quite bad and, during the rainy season, the Little Scarcies River sometimes runs so high that the ferry shuts down. The road from Faranah to Kabala is also in bad shape and is sparsely travelled, but taxis do go a couple of times per week.

River

During the rainy season (July to November), barges run once a week or so from Siguiri to Bamako in Mali. It's a one-day journey downstream (Siguiri–Bamako) and at least two days coming back up (Bamako–Siguiri).

Sea

The ferry service to/from Conakry to Freetown is expected to begin again, so it's worth asking around at the port.

GETTING AROUND

Taxis brousses (bush taxis; usually Peugeot station wagons) are the main way of getting around Guinea, which means most travellers will have to contend with two major hassles: terrible roads and severe overcrowding (10 or 11 passengers in a car made for seven, plus luggage, bananas, live goats and poultry, and a few more people on the roof). Minibuses are a bit cheaper, but they're even more uncomfortable and take ages to fill up. Guinean drivers are reckless beyond belief, racing up serpentine roads and cutting blind corners – try to pick your taxi carefully. Guinean roads are terrible even by West African standards and, in remote locations, taxis might take days to fill up.

GUINEA

Guinea-Bissau

History hasn't been kind to Guinea-Bissau. Decades of Portuguese colonisation, a long, painful liberation struggle and cycles of civil war have locked this pretty nation in grinding poverty. And when peace finally seemed to last, the country plunged yet again into turmoil and gained an unwholesome reputation as West Africa's key entry port for hard drugs.

It's a pretty chaotic country, and yet you will still bring back holiday stories of endless white beaches, thick rainforest and, most of all, talk about the country's disarmingly friendly people.

Like a microcosm of Africa, this tiny nation hands you a spectacular variety of landscapes, cultures and small town scenes, all within easy reach of the capital, Bissau. The jewel in the nation's crown is the labyrinth of tropical islands that makes up the Arquipélago dos Bijagós. With its vast, deserted sand strands and clear waters quivering with fish, it's a dream destination for sports fishermen and sea-and-sun lovers. This protected ecosystem is home to turtles, hundreds of bird species and rare saltwater hippos. Similar preservation efforts have so far saved the last vestiges of rainforest and its thriving populations of monkeys, chimps and buffalos.

FAST FACTS

- **Area** 36,120 sq km
- **ATMs** There are none; come with cash
- **Borders** Guinea (Kandika); Senegal (São Domingos, Salikénié, Pirada)
- **Budget** From US$50 to US$80
- **Capital** Bissau
- **Languages** Portuguese, Crioulo
- **Money** West African CFA franc; US$1 = CFA463,€1 = CFA656
- **Population** 1.4 million
- **Seasons** Dry and mild (late November to February), hot and humid (March to May, November), hot and rainy (June to October)
- **Telephone** Country code ☎ 245; international access code ☎ 00
- **Time** GMT/UTC
- **Visa** All visitors except citizens of Ecowas (Economic Community of West African States) nations require a visa. Visas need to be arranged before arrival and cost US$60 for 45 days

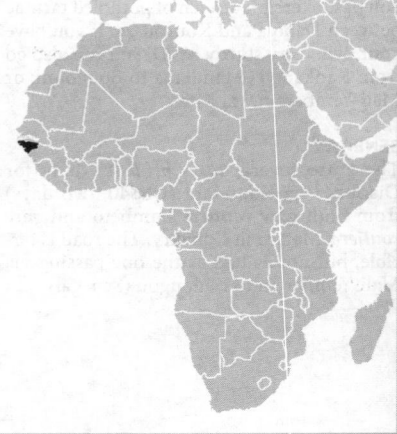

GUINEA-BISSAU

HOW MUCH?

- **Small souvenir mask** US$4.50
- **Taxi ride through Bissau** US$1.10
- **Wi-fi in Bissau's better restaurants** free
- **Woven indigo cotton cloth (40cm by 80cm)** US$13.20
- **Main course in Western-style restaurant** US$11

LONELY PLANET INDEX

- **1L petrol** US$1.20
- **1L bottled water** US$2.20
- **Bottle of Guinean Pampa beer** US$2.20
- **Souvenir T-shirt** US$5.50
- **Omelette sandwich from street vendor** US$1.30

HIGHLIGHTS

- **João Vieira** (p383) Sip fresh coconut juice on the island's endless, palm-fringed sand strands.
- **Orango Islands National Park** (p382) Stalk rare saltwater hippos after visiting the tombs of Bijagós' kings and queens.
- **Bissau** (p379) Squeeze through the narrow alleyways of Bissau Velho.
- **Varela** (p383) Bounce your car over mighty potholes to get to this beautiful, isolated beach.
- **Parque Nacional do Catanhez** (p384) Follow buffalo, chimp and elephant trails through dense rainforests.

CLIMATE & WHEN TO GO

The rainy season lasts from June to October. Conditions are especially humid in the months before the rains (April and May), when average maximum daytime temperatures rise to 34°C and rarely fall below 30°C.

The best time to visit is from late November to February, when conditions are dry and relatively cool.

ITINERARIES

- **One Week** Spend a day or two in the relaxing capital Bissau (p379), before heading to Ilha de Bubaque in the Arquipélago dos Bijagós (p382).

- **Two Weeks** During a second week, consider further explorations of the Bijagós, such as trips to hippo-inhabited Orango (p382) and paradisaical João Vieira (p383). Alternatively, head south, cruising the lagoons of Parque Natural da Lagoa de Cafatada (p384) and chimp spotting in the Cantanhez rainforest (p384).

HISTORY

In around 1200, when a group of Malinké was led to present-day Guinea-Bissau by a general of Sunjata Keita, the region became an outpost of the Empire of Mali. In 1537, it transformed into a state of its own right – the Kaabu Empire. Gabù became the capital of this small kingdom. See also p29.

European Arrival & Colonisation

Portuguese navigators first reached the area around 1450, and established lucrative routes for trading slaves and goods. With the abolition of the slave trade in the 19th century, the Portuguese extended their influence beyond the coast towards the interior in order to continue extracting wealth.

Portuguese Guinea descended into one of the most repressive and exploitative colonial regimes in Africa, particularly accentuated when right-wing dictator António Salazar came to power in Portugal in 1926.

War of Liberation

By the early 1960s African colonies were rapidly winning independence, but Salazar refused to relinquish those under his control. The result: one of Africa's longest, bloodiest wars of liberation.

The father of independence was Amílcar Cabral, who in 1956 helped found the Partido Africano da Independência da Guiné e Cabo Verde (PAIGC). In 1961 the PAIGC started arming and mobilising peasants, and controlled half of the country within five years. Cabral was assassinated in 1973, but independence had become inevitable. When Salazar's regime fell in 1974, the new Portuguese government quickly recognised the fledgling nation.

Independence

Once in power, the PAIGC government faced staggering problems of poverty, lack of education and economic decline. The socialist

GUINEA-BISSAU

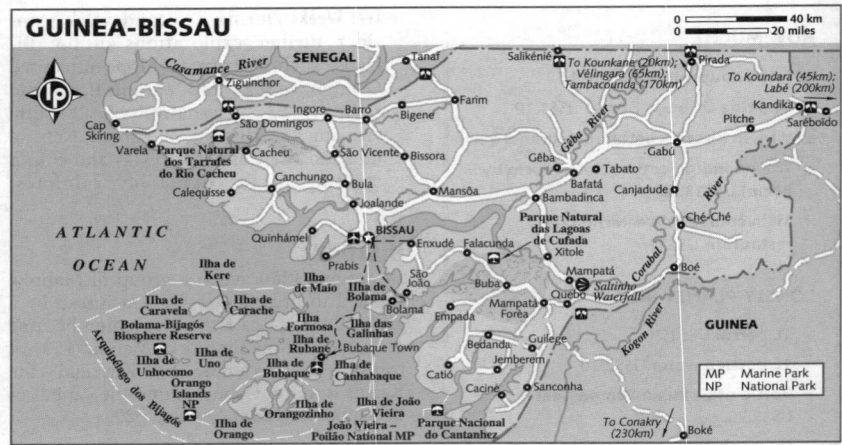

model didn't propose a way out of the crisis and a 1986 coup attempt forced President João Vieira to privatise state enterprises.

Intractable poverty and growing corruption under Vieira culminated in national strikes in 1997, which quickly spiralled into a bloody civil war. Vieira was ousted in a 1999 coup, and, though the military commanders handed power back to civilians, the country never found complete peace, and further coup attempts followed.

Guinea-Bissau Today

In 2005 deposed president João Vieira won the presidential elections. He ran the country against a background of feuding army factions, political rivalry and a cocaine trade seemingly bigger in size than the nation itself. In March 2009 Vieira was assassinated in what many believed to be a revenge act for the murder of his chief of staff the previous day. Following elections in June 2009, the little-known Malam Bacai Sanhá became Guinea-Bissau's new president and people were waiting to see what direction their tiny, impoverished nation was going to take.

CULTURE

Despite grinding poverty, a severely damaged infrastructure and wide religious and ethnic differences, Guineans are united by a remarkable neighbourly goodwill. Outside the political conspiracies and army intrigues, violence is rare – you don't even find the aggressive salesmanship of other West African capitals.

The mainland people share many cultural aspects with those of southern Senegal and western Guinea. However, the Bijagós people from the islands of the same name have very distinct and fascinating customs (see p382).

People

Guinea-Bissau's 1.4 million inhabitants are divided among some 23 ethnic groups. The two largest are the Balante (30%) in the coastal and central regions and the Fula (20%) in the east and south. Other groups include the Manjak, Papel, Fulup and the Mandinka. The offshore islands are mostly inhabited by the Bijagós people (see the boxed text, p382).

About 45% of the people are Muslims and 10% Christians. Animist beliefs remain strong along the coast and in the south.

Arts

The Bijagós people are famous for their traditions of mask making and sculpture – see them come out in carnival season.

WARNING

Peaceful presidential elections in 2009 have raised hopes of lasting stability following years of war and turmoil. However, underlying tensions remain, so be sure to check the latest situation before arrival. Note that the region around São Domingos and along the Senegalese border is particularly prone to instability.

Eastern Guinea-Bissau is a centre of *kora* playing, being the ancient seat of the Kaabu Empire, where the instrument was invented. The traditional Guinean beat is *gumbé*, though contemporary music is mainly influenced by zouk from Cape Verde. Guinea-Bissau's classic band is Super Mama Djombo; Manecas Costa and Justino Delgado are two contemporary stars.

FOOD & DRINK

Seafood is the highlight of Guinean cuisine, including shrimp, oysters and meaty *bica* (sea bream), best served sautéd with onion and lime. The national dish is *chabeu*: deep-fried fish served in a thick palm-oil sauce with rice. Vegetarian options are very limited.

Local brews include palm wine and the very potent liquors *caña* (rum) and *cajeu* (cashew liquor). The best beers are the imported Portuguese brands.

ENVIRONMENT

Guinea-Bissau has an area of just over 36,000 sq km (about the size of Switzerland). Coastal areas are flat, and feature estuaries, mangrove swamps and patches of forest. Up-country, it transitions into the Sahel. The natural savannah woodlands have largely been replaced by cashew plantations.

In the Bijagós archipelago you find rare saltwater hippos, aquatic turtles, dolphins and sharks. The rainforests of the southeast are the most westerly home of Africa's chimpanzee population. The coastal wetlands harbour a stunning variety of birds, including parrots, cranes and peregrine falcons.

Among the main environmental issues are mangrove destruction, deforestation, soil erosion and overfishing. A number of areas are protected, including the Bolama-Bijagós Biosphere Reserve, the mangroves of Parque Natural dos Tarrafes do Rio Cacheu (p383), the saltwater wetlands of Parque Natural de Lagoa de Cafatada (p384) and the rainforests and islands of Parque Nacional do Cantanhez (p384).

For more information, contact **IBAP** (☎ 3207106; Rua São Tomé), the institute that oversees all the parks from Bissau.

BISSAU

pop 385,000

In the early evening, the fading sunlight lends the crumbling colonial facades of Bissau Velho (Old Bissau) a touch of old-age glamour. Dozens of generators set the town trembling, and ignite the lights of stylish bars and restaurants that form something of a modern, indoor city in startling contrast with the worn exterior.

ORIENTATION

Bissau's main drag is the wide Ave Amílcar Cabral, running between the port and Praça dos Heróis Nacionais. On the northwestern edge of the centre is the Mercado de Bandim. From here, Ave de 14 Novembro leads northwest to the main *paragem* (bus and taxi park), the airport and all inland destinations.

INFORMATION
Cultural Centre

Centre Culturel Franco-Bissao-Guinéen (☎ 3206816; Praça Ché Guevera; ☽ 9am-10pm Mon-Sat) This bright, modern centre has a library, an art gallery, a performance space and a small cafe.

Internet Access

Restaurants with free wi-fi connections include Restaurant Tamar and Oporto (see Eating, p380).

Cybernet Café (Rua Vitorino Costa; per hr CFA1000; ☽ 9am-10pm) Slow but dependable connections.

Moby's Club (6685746; per hr CFA1500; ☽ to 10pm Mon-Sat, to 6pm Sun) Doubles as a cool cafe with live music.

Medical Services

Pharmacie Moçambique (☎ 3205513) Bissau's best-stocked pharmacy.

Policlinica (☎ 3207581; info@policlinica.bissau.com; Praça Ché Guevera) A better option for illnesses than a trip to the hospital.

Simão Mendes (☎ 3212861; Ave Pansau Na Isna) Bissau's main hospital, in a desolate state.

Money

Unless things have changed (and they might), you won't find an ATM accepting international cards. Bring sufficient cash. To change money, either ask your hotel for an informal moneychanger or try the following:

BAO (Banco da Africa Occidental; ☎ 3202418; Rua Gerra Mendes)

Ecobank (☎ 7253194; Ave Amílcar Cabral) Changes dollars and euros.

Supermercado Mavegro (☎ 3201224; Rua Eduardo Mondlane; ☽ 3.30-6pm Mon, 9am-12.30pm & 3-6pm Tue-Fri, 9am-12.30pm Sat)

Post

Main post office (Correio; Ave Amílcar Cabral)

GUINEA-BISSAU

THE WORLD ACCORDING TO NGALA

On the road to Bafatá, just after the Mansôa junction, Ngala (meaning God), an old, toothless Balante man, has built a bizarre and moving miniature universe from recycled materials. Christian crosses stand next to a toy-town mecca, peace doves fly over huge bazookas, policemen and soldiers. Ngala remembers the liberation struggle, and his world is marked by the many conflicts his home country has seen. He smiles when questioned, quietly stating that 'all of this is part of the same world: war, peace, struggle, love'. This improvised museum tells a better story about Guinea today than the news.

You pass the place on the main road from Bissau to Bafatá; pictures can be taken for a small donation, but the works can't be bought.

Travel Agencies

Weekend Loisirs Vacances (☎ 6830674; julienho@ hotmail.com) Arranges pick-ups and ferry tickets.

SIGHTS

Bissau Velho (Old Bissau), a stretch of narrow alleyways and derelict buildings, is 'guarded' by the **Fortaleza d'Amura**, an imposing fort that is unfortunately not accessible to visitors. With its bombed-out roof and shrapnel-riddled neoclassical facade, the former **presidential palace** on Praça dos Heróis Nacionais sends a powerful message about Guinea-Bissau's simmering conflicts. The rebuilt and brushed-up **Assembleia Ministério da Justiça**, by contrast, is an architectural expression of democratic hopes.

FESTIVALS & EVENTS

Bissau's **Carnival** is the country's biggest party. Carnival takes place every year in February or early March during the week leading up to Ash Wednesday and the beginning of Lent. Music, masks, drinking and dancing are the order of the day.

SLEEPING

Accommodation in Bissau is expensive and generally of poor value.

Pensão Creola (☎ 6633031; marcelkuehne@yahoo. com; Ave Domingos Ramos; s/d from CFA15,000/17,000) This family house with the toy-strewn lounge is also Bissau's best budget hotel. Electricity is limited to five hours of generator power at night.

Pensão Centrale (☎ 3213270; Ave Amílcar Cabral; r without bathroom CFA20,000) Dona Berta is the eccentric grandma to the whole city and has put up stranded travellers for decades in her historical, balcony-adorned building with dozens of basic rooms.

Aparthotel Jordani (☎ 3201719; Ave Pansau Na Isna; s/d CFA25,000/30,000; ⌘) Even though the water is only cold and the generator prone to breakdowns, this remains a decent budget choice. There's a noisy nightclub next door.

Hotel Kalliste (☎ 6064215; Ave Domingos Ramos; r from CFA35,000; ⌘) Rooms are thankfully better than the dark staircase and bored receptionist suggest, but are still overpriced. The terrace restaurant and casino are great for a taste of Bissau life.

Aparthotel Lobato (☎ 3201719; Ave Pansau Na Isna; s/d from CFA35,000/45,000; ⌘ ▣) The slightly pricier rooms in this maze-like hotel are the best deal – clean, comfy and with hot water. Its internet cafe is across the road.

ourpick **Residencial Coimbra** (☎ 6112122; www.residencialcoimbra.com; Ave Amílcar Cabral; s/d CFA85,500/101,000; ⌘ ▣ 🛜) This lovingly cared for family business has tall, spacious rooms in a charming old Bissau building. There's wi-fi throughout, a leafy terrace, and the breakfast buffet is the best in town.

EATING

Bissau's varied restaurant scene comes as a surprise. You can find anything here, from simple rice bars to atmospheric eateries, and even a couple of places serving truly refined cuisine. Unless otherwise indicated, the following restaurants are open for lunch (around noon to 3pm) and dinner (around 7pm to 10pm) daily.

Mana Mbutcha (☎ 6701947; Rua Justino Lopes; dishes around CFA2500) So what if the courtyard looks like a parking lot? You won't notice the lack of glamour once you've tasted the grilled *bica* or prawns.

Oporto (☎ 6622417; Rua Justina Lopes; ☽ 7am-11pm Tue-Sun; ▣ 🛜) What looks like a humble outdoor terrace on a mango-tree, shaded street is in fact a tiny world of small-town glitz with big screen, wi-fi and ice-cold beer.

Restaurant Samaritana (☎ 6131392; off Ave Pansau Na Isna; mains CFA2500) It's made from a cut-out container and buzzes with Guineans of all ranks and incomes eager to sample Mamadou's reliably delicious and solid Senegalese and Guinean meals.

Restaurant Tamar (☎ 6609349; Bissau Velho; mains CFA3500; 🖵) Try a palm-oil-bathed *chabeu* or Cape Verdean *cachoupa* (stew) at this under-stated eatery in Bissau's old town – until the live music kicks in and the tables get pushed out on a Friday night.

Bistro (☎ 3206000; Ruo Eduardo Mondlane; mains CFA4000; 🕑 noon-3pm & 7-10.30pm) This cute corner stop is run by a Frenchman and, clichés being what they are, this means very fine food indeed. Come here in the evenings, when the atmosphere is at its best.

A Padeira Africana (☎ 6131393; Rua Marien N'Gouabi; mains CFA4000; 🍴) This air-conditioned Portuguese restaurant is a favourite dinner address for affluent Guineans and expats. The adjacent Ponto de Encontro is one of Bissau's best coffee and croissant places.

Restaurant Coimbra (☎ 6112122; Ave Amílcar Cabral; buffet CFA7500; Ⓥ) Every night, Bissau's most stylish restaurant offers a huge, varied buffet, renowned for its quality, as well as for its excellent vegie choices (the owner is a vegetarian himself). Red wine and water are included in the rate.

DRINKING & ENTERTAINMENT

Moby's Club (☎ 6685746; Bissau Velho; 🕑 8am-8pm Mon-Wed, to 4am Thu-Sun; 🖵) Between painted palms, Bissau's party people sip on Pampa beer or push the wobbly rattan chairs to zouk away in rhythm with the live band.

X Club (☎ 3213467; Rua Osualdo Vieira) Join the odd assembly of hard-working UN staff, shady businessmen and sparkling party folk on their glitzy trip through the night.

Bambu 2000 (Ave de 14 Novembro) The ambience is relaxed and local at this bustling club out of town. Less dressed up than the X Club, it's the one with the more raucous party.

Mansaflema (near Ave Nações Unidas) The rootsiest party of all happens at Mansaflema. This is where you'll get to learn that *gumbé* hip swing, or sway across the dance floor to sensual zouk beats under the glitter ball, Guinean style.

SHOPPING

On the ground floor of the Pensão Centrale, **Artissal** (☎ 6604078; Ave Amílcar Cabral) is great for woven goods. Outside, traders sell wooden masks. **Centro Artistico Juvenil** (Ave de 14 Novembro) sells craftwork made by young trainees in a skills training and job creation project.

GETTING THERE & AWAY

There are daily flights to Bissau with TACV Cabo Verde Airlines and TAP Air Portugal. For more information, see p386.

You can get *sept-place* taxis and *transporte misto* buses to just about anywhere in the country, as well as to Senegal, at the *paragem* (stop), about 5km outside town. For more information, see p386.

To get to the *paragem*, take a *toca-toca* (minibus) from the Mercado de Bandim (CFA100) or a taxi (about CFA1000) from anywhere in town.

GETTING AROUND

The airport is 9km from the town centre. A taxi to town should be around CFA3000.

Shared taxis – generally blue, well-worn Mercedes – are plentiful and ply all the main routes. In the town centre, trips cost CFA500. Rates for longer routes vary and have to be negotiated.

Blue-yellow *toca-tocas* serve main city routes (for CFA100), including Ave de 14 Novembro towards the *paragem* and airport.

ARQUIPÉLAGO DOS BIJAGÓS

Imagine palm-fringed strands, endless, white-sand beaches and turquoise waters. The Bijagós islands look like your perfect postcard from paradise. Protected by swift tides and treacherous sandbanks, the Bijagós, a matriarchal people (see the boxed text, p382), eluded Portuguese control until the 1930s. Now the entire archipelago, including its rich marine life, has been declared a biosphere reserve, while two island groups form national parks.

You need to bring a bit of time and money – transport to and between the islands is difficult and pricey (see p382). Life swings to the rhythm of the tide; prepare to adjust to more

GUINEA-BISSAU

QUEENS OF THE BIJAGÓS

The peoples of the Arquipélago dos Bijagós have, over the centuries, developed a largely matriarchal culture, quite distinct from that of mainland Guinea. Islanders are ruled by a king and queen (they're neither married nor even related) who serve as co-regents – the king managing men's affairs and the queen managing women's affairs. Women often serve as chiefs of individual villages, and they're also the sole homeowners – only fair since they are entirely responsible for building homes, from making bricks to actual construction.

relaxed rhythms – and mind the stingrays lurking in the waters.

Getting There & Away

The ferry **Expresso dos Bijagós** (☎ 6538739; Bissau Velho; CFA7500-12,500) normally leaves Bissau port for Bubaque every Friday, returning from Bubaque Sunday. Exact departure times depend on the tide but are between midday and 3pm. The journey takes four to five hours. Any other day, your choice is between rough and risky *canoas* (per person CFA2500, six hours) or speed-boat (per four-seater boat CFA150,000 to CFA200,000, 1½ hours).

The 1950s cruise ship **Africa Queen** (www.africa-queen.com) can take you island hopping for a week (from CFA620,000).

Getting Around

The islands Rubane and Canhabaque are still fairly easily (and cheaply) reached from Bubaque. For more far-flung places, you're best off arranging a boat trip with your hotel (CFA100,000 to CFA200,000 per four-seater boat, depending on distance). Public *canoas* have unpredictable departure times, meaning you'll rarely know how many days you might have to spend on an island before the next pick-up turns up.

ILHA DE BUBAQUE

At the centre of the Bijagós, Bubaque is home to the archipelago's largest town, which serves as its major transport 'hub'. If you can't make it to more remote islands, Bubaque makes a comfortable place to unwind. Its best beach is Praia Bruce on the southern tip.

There's an internet cafe, the research and information centre **Casa do Ambiente** (☎ 3207106) and a small **museum** (☎ 6115107; admission CFA1000; ⊗ 10am-1pm & 4-7pm).

Sleeping & Eating

Most hotels serve meals if you order ahead. For cheap eats, head to the port area.

Le Cadjoco (☎ 5949012, 6161638; r CFA10,000) If you're in a small group, you can book the four rooms and make this village-set place your private home. There are fishing and boat excursions on offer and bikes available for hire (per day CFA5000).

Chez Dora (☎ 6928836; sosybubaque@gmail.com; s/d CFA10,000/15,000) The bungalows of this lovingly cared for hotel are large, adorned with pretty splashes of colour and swept clean every morning. In the garden restaurant, you get to dig into large platters of seafood in the shade of mango trees.

Le Calypso (☎ 5949207; calypsohotel@neuf.fr; s/d CFA20,000/22,000; ☒) Hard to decide where you relax better – in the lazy bar, the Mauritanian tent or the sunny poolside. Rooms are cute, with colourful decor and a fan to provide a breeze. They can arrange bivouac trips to Canhabaque.

Kasa Afrikana (☎ 7243305, 5949213; wwww.kasa-afrikana.com; per person incl breakfast CFA30,000; ☒ ▯ ⊗ ☒) Rooms at this welcoming hotel are cushy and well equipped – and that includes the large bathrooms. Wi-fi is CFA2000 per day, and there are tailor-made excursions and fishing trips on offer.

Getting There & Away

For travel to/from Bissau, see left.

ORANGO ISLANDS NATIONAL PARK

Home to rare saltwater hippos, Ilha de Orango is the heart of Orango Islands National Park. The island is also the burial site of the Bijagós kings and queens. Pretty **Orango Parque Hotel** (☎ 6615127; laurent.durris@cbd-habitat.com; r incl full board CFA30,000) is run in association with the local community, and village residents can take you hippo spotting. Use the local guides – hippos can be dangerous creatures.

From Orango, take a trip to beautiful **Kere** island, where the hotel owners operate a brilliant little hostel.

Phone the hotel in advance to arrange your transfer from Bissau to Orango (around CFA200,000).

JOÃO VIEIRA – POILÃO NATIONAL MARINE PARK

At the southeast end of the archipelago, the four islands and surrounding waters of João Vieira – Poilão National Marine Park are a key nesting area for endangered sea turtles. Idyllic Ilha João Vieira has stunning beaches and accommodation in simple huts at **Chez Claude** (☎ 6520374; www.bijagos-joaovieira.com; bungalow CFA35,000). Nearby **Mêio** island is the best place to watch sea turtles come ashore to lay their eggs in October (enquire at Casa do Ambiente, opposite).

Pick-up by Claude's speedboat is CFA200,000 per boatload.

OTHER ISLANDS

Close to Bubaque, the large island **Canhabaque** is a good place to experience village life in the Bijagós. On **Rubane**, you can enjoy delicious food and spend the night in the exquisite hotel **Ponta Acachana** (☎ in Senegal 33 993 5161, in Guinea-Bissau 7250714; s/d CFA65,000/100,000; 🗶 🖭). They've also got a great sports fishing centre and can take you on trips to other islands.

Both Rubane and Canhabaque are easily reached from Bubaque (hotels charge around CFA4000 per transfer).

THE NORTHWEST

QUINHÁMEL

Located about 30km west of Bissau, Quinhámel serves as the capital of the Biombo region, traditional home of the Papel people. The very inspiring community project **Artissal** (☎ 6604078; artissal@gmail.com; ⏲ 9am-5pm) introduces visitors to the Papel's unique weaving traditions. You can watch the craftsmen and purchase the goods. Try some oysters with the Portuguese lady (known all the way to Bissau) to complete a day trip from Bissau.

Transporte misto from Bissau is CFA500; a private taxi is around CFA15,000 return.

CANCHUNGO & CACHEU

The route to Cacheu passes through **Canchungo**, a lively small town with a busy market. Pick up some hand-woven baskets before moving on.

Sleepy **Cacheu** used to be a regional capital under Portuguese colonial rule and is worth the visit for the sense of history. Nearby **Parque Natural dos Tarrafes do Rio Cacheu**, for intrepid animal lovers, boasts gazelles, manatees, hippos and over 200 bird species; there's little in terms of infrastructure. Contact the **IBAP office** (☎ 3207106; Rua São Tomé) in Bissau before setting out.

Transporte misto from Bissau to Cacheu is CFA3000. The daily *canoa* between Cacheu and São Domingos also crosses the park (CFA2000).

SÃO DOMINGOS

On the border with Senegal, this busy junction town is where you do your immigration formalities – usually a swift process. There are small eateries, but for a bed you'll have to make your way to Ingore, on the way to Bissau.

All public transport from Bissau to Ziguinchor (CFA2500) and Varela (CFA3000) passes through here. The trip takes two to three hours.

VARELA

The ride from São Domingos is rough, even in a good 4WD – and that's why the beautiful beaches of Varela remain deserted. At the friendly guesthouse **Chez Fatima** (☎ 7270876; r CFA15,000) you can relax from the journey and enjoy the solitary surroundings.

Transporte misto from São Domingo (CFA3000) takes around four hours. You can also come in from Senegal: from Kabrousse near Cap Skiring (see p501), walk along the beach, then jump on a *pirogue*. You need an exit stamp from Senegal Fatima can deal with the Guinean formalities.

THE NORTHEAST

BAFATÁ

With its crumbling colonial centre on the Gêba River, the birthplace of Amílcar Cabral looks like a ghost town. To enjoy a day among Bafatá's eerily beautiful walls, pick a room at the fading **Hotel Maimuna Capé** (☎ 6648383; s/d CFA10,000/15,000; 🗶) or the modern monstrosity of **Aparthotel Triton** (☎ 6938100; r CFA25,000; 🗶 🖳 🖭). **Ponto de Encontro** (Chez Celia; ☎ 6921690; dishes around CFA3500) is the classic eatery in this town, and serves hearty Portuguese meals.

Transporte misto to Bissau (CFA3000), Gabú (CFA1500) or Buba (CFA3000) depart from the petrol station area.

GABÚ

Gabú used to be the capital of the eponymous 19th-century kingdom (also spelled Kaabu). Plenty of stories circulate about its former glory, but there are no sights. Today, Gabú is mainly a stopover on the way to Guinea, or a base for excursions to the rocky lands of **Boé** (which are 40km from Gabú).

There are a number of small restaurants in town, as well as a large market. If you wish to spend the night, head for the friendly **Hotel Visiom** (☎ 6866699; r with fan/air-con CFA8000/15,000; 🏊) or quirky **Residencial Djaraama** (☎ 6938442; r without bathroom CFA15,000). **Hotel HBC** (☎ 6444403; francois.margalef@wanadoo.fr; r CFA24,000; 🏊 🖵 🖳) at the entry to town is classy and features a good restaurant and pool.

Getting There & Away

Sept-places and *transporte misto* go to Bissau regularly (CFA4000, six hours). For details of travelling from Gabú to Guinea, see p386. You can easily change CFA into Guinean francs at the taxi park.

THE SOUTH

BUBA

Buba is a small, tranquil town (at least until the massive port that is currently in planning has been built), and is the perfect starting point for cruises through the bird-inhabited lagoons of **Parque Natural das Lagoas de Cufada**.

Gabi, the manager of **Pousada Bela Vista** (☎ 6647011, 6072244; r CFA13,000; 🏊) can put you up in pretty garden bungalows and help you organise your river tours.

Transporte misto run regularly along the asphalt road from Bissau to Buba (CFA3000).

JEMBEREM & PARQUE NACIONAL DO CANTANHEZ

The roads to Jemberem are rough – you'll need a 4WD – but the corner is too beautiful to miss. Jemberem hosts a fully fledged ecotourism project to support the adjacent **Parque Nacional do Cantanhez**, Guinea-Bissau's last remaining stretch of rainforest and home to chimps, elephants, buffalos and many other species. At the clean and simple **U'Anan Camp** (☎ 6060019, 6637263; d/q CFA15,000/25,000), you get to stay in double bungalows and organise your forest trails. The resident guides are excellent and track the chimps, so sightings are almost guaranteed.

Call the camp to arrange your transport before setting out. Hiring a 4WD from Bissau is around CFA60,000 per day.

GUINEA-BISSAU DIRECTORY

ACCOMMODATION

The lack of electricity and subsequent need for generator power pushes up prices for accommodation. Good budget places are rare and even midrange options (upwards of CFA35,000) aren't always great. If you want to travel with a certain amount of comfort, plan a generous accommodation budget, allowing a minimum of CFA35,000 on average per night.

TELLING TIME

There's nothing to suggest that Gabú was once the capital of the powerful kingdom of Kaabu (1537–1867). And yet, its story is being remembered. Kaabu's living memory sits 40km further southwest, in a tiny village called Tabato. This extraordinary community is home to El Hadj Mountarou Diabaté and his extended family of *griots* (praise singers and historians), who have told the story of Kaabu for generations.

Tabato is certainly not the only *griot* village around, but its family has chosen to open their world up to others. Busking in the streets of Bissau, they raised sufficient funds to build a little museum, where you can look at the *griots'* instruments and hear about the stories of the region's past. It's also the place to arrange *kora*, drumming, *balafon* or singing courses, or simply drop by to enjoy a full-blown *griot* party (for a donation).

Contact the Diabaté family on ☎ 6651847.

ACTIVITIES

The Arquipélago dos Bijagós (p381) and especially Varela (p383) have great sandy beaches, and the waters around the Bijagós are renowned for their deep-sea fishing spots. The national parks are fabulous for birdwatchers.

BUSINESS HOURS

Banks and government offices Usually open from 8am to noon and 2pm to 5pm Monday to Friday, although hours vary.

Post offices Generally open mornings only, apart from the main post office in Bissau (open to 6pm).

Shops From 8am or 9am until 6pm Monday to Friday and 8am until 1pm or 2pm Saturday. Some close for lunch.

EMBASSIES & CONSULATES

All embassies and consulates are in Bissau. The consul for the UK and the Netherlands is **Jan van Maanen** (☎ 6622772; Supermercardo Mavegro, Rua Eduardo Mondlane, Bissau).

France (☎ 3201312; cnr Ave de 14 Novembro & Ave do Brazil)

Gambia (☎ 3251099; Rua Vitorino Costa; ☺ 8.30am-3pm Sat-Thu, to 12.30pm Fri)

Germany (☎ 3255020; escritorio-bissau@web.de; SITEC Bldg; ☺ 9-11am Mon-Fri)

Guinea (☎ 3201231; Rua 12; ☺ 8.30am-3pm Sat-Thu, to 1pm Fri) East of the central stadium.

Portugal (☎ 3203379; Ave Cidade de Lisboa; ☺ 8am-noon)

Senegal (☎ 3212944; off Praça dos Heróis Nacionais; ☺ 8am-noon)

Spain (Praça dos Heróis Nacionais; ☺ 8am-noon)

EMERGENCY

Fire (☎ 118)
Police (☎ 117)

FESTIVALS & EVENTS

Guinea-Bissau's main event is Carnival (see p380). The biggest party happens in Bissau, but Bubaque's has the more interesting masks and costumes.

HEALTH

A certificate with proof of yellow-fever vaccination is required of all travellers.

HOLIDAYS

Islamic feasts, such as Eid al-Fitr (at the end of Ramadan) and Tabaski, are celebrated; for dates, see the Africa Directory (p1140).

PRACTICALITIES

- The national radio and TV stations broadcast in Portuguese. Most interesting for travellers is Radio Mavegro FM (100.0MHz), which combines music with hourly news bulletins in English from the BBC.

- Newspapers come and go quickly in Bissau. If you sit at one of the city's cafes or restaurants, a vendor will quickly offer you the latest options.

- Electricity supply is 220V and plugs are of the European two-round-pin variety.

- Guinea-Bissau uses the metric system.

Guinea-Bissau also celebrates the following public holidays:

New Year's Day 1 January
Anniversary of the Death of Amílcar Cabral 20 January
Women's Day 8 March
Easter March/April
Labour Day 1 May
Pidjiguiti Day 3 August
Independence Day 24 September
Christmas Day 25 December

INTERNET ACCESS

Bissau has several internet cafes (per hour CFA1000 to CFA1500) and wi-fi is increasingly common. Don't count on internet access outside the capital.

LANGUAGE

Portuguese is the official language, though the common tongue is Crioulo – a mix of Portuguese and local languages. Most ethnic groups also preserve their own language. As Guinea-Bissau is increasingly being drawn into the Afro-Francophone world, you can usually get by with French.

MONEY

At the time of writing, there were no ATMs accepting international cards in Guinea-Bissau, and credit cards were not accepted anywhere. Bring cash – euros are the easiest to exchange. It's harder to get CFA franc for your US dollars; outside Bissau it can be downright impossible. It's always best to change the cash you need in Bissau.

GUINEA-BISSAU

The unit of currency is the West African CFA franc.

POST

The postal service is slow – you're probably better off posting mail home from Senegal or Gambia.

TELEPHONE

In Bissau, you'll find public phones at corner stalls for local calls, and a call centre in the **main post office** (Ave Amílcar Cabral) for international calls. Alternatively, charge your mobile with an Orange or MTN SIM card and buy top-up credit on the street. Service can be unreliable in remote areas, including the Arquipélago dos Bijagós.

VISAS

All visitors, except nationals of Ecowas countries, need visas. These visas are normally valid for 45 days and are issued for around US$60 at embassies. They are not always issued at borders; get your visa before arrival.

Visa Extensions

Extensions are easy to obtain at **Serviço de Estrangeiros** (Praça dos Heróis Nacionais, Bissau). For virtually all nationalities, 45-day visa extensions cost around CFA4000 and are ready the same day if you apply early.

Visas for Onward Travel

Visas for the neighbouring countries to Guinea-Bissau can be obtained at their embassies in Bissau (see p385).

TRANSPORT IN GUINEA-BISSAU

GETTING THERE & AWAY
Air

Guinea-Bissau's only international airport is on the outskirts of Bissau. The main airlines flying to Guinea-Bissau are TAP Air Portugal (the only direct flight from Europe) and TACV Cabo Verde Airlines. To fly between Bissau and anywhere else in Africa, you have to pass through Dakar.

TACV Cabo Verde Airlines (VR; ☎ 3206087; www. tacv.com; Ave Amílcar Cabral)

TAP Air Portugal (TP; ☎ 3201359; www.flytap.com; Praça dos Heróis Nacionais)

Land
GUINEA

Bush taxis go to the border daily from Gabú, travelling through to Koundara (CFA5000). It can take all day to cover this 100km stretch, although the winding road through the Fouta Djalon foothills is beautiful. A less-travelled route, open only in the dry season, links southeastern Guinea-Bissau and western Guinea via Quebo and Boké.

SENEGAL

Most overland travel between Senegal and Guinea-Bissau passes through Ziguinchor (Senegal), via the Guinean border town of São Domingos. Check the security situation in Senegal's Casamance (see p497); if there's trouble, the border might be closed. Otherwise, the trip from Ziguinchor to Bissau is quick (two to three hours) and easy. It costs CFA5000 by *sept-place*.

GETTING AROUND
Boat

The Expresso dos Bijagós links Bissau with Ilha de Bubaque (see p382). It's a reliable, regular ferry service. Between individual islands, you also have regular *canoas*; the only stretch where the *canoa* trip is recommended, however, is on the relatively short distance from Bissau to Bolama. All hotels on the Bijagós hire boats for fishing trips, excursions or pick-up from Bubaque, but that's always expensive.

Car & Motorcycle

The main roads between Bissau and the towns of Bafatá, Gabú, São Domingos and Buba are relatively good asphalt. Most other routes, including the stretches from Buba to Jemberem and São Domingos to Varela, are unpaved, and often only manageable by 4WD.

Sept-Place & Transporte Misto

Sept-places are seven-seater Peugeots that link Guinea-Bissau's main towns. More common and far less comfortable are the large minibuses called *transporte misto*. In Bissau, short distances are covered by *toca-tocas*: smaller, blue-yellow minibuses.

Mornings (before 8am) are always the best time to get transport. For an idea of fares across the country, from Bissau to Gabú (around 200km) is CFA3500 by *sept-place*, and CFA2000 by *transporte misto*.

Liberia

Peace and a modicum of stability have finally come to Liberia, a country that for decades has been a festering sore on West Africa's benighted coastline, known only for child soldiers and warlords. Having elected Africa's first female president and being subject to an unprecedented effort by the international community to get it back on its feet, Liberia is now safe and open for visitors once again.

Liberia itself is a lush, beautiful land criss-crossed by rivers and largely made up of impenetrable rainforest. It again offers visitors a fascinating glimpse into one of West Africa's most hospitable and enigmatic societies. The country's artistic traditions – especially carved masks, dance and storytelling – rival those of anywhere on the continent, and traditional culture remains strong.

The country's natural attractions are equally impressive. In contrast with its ravaged infrastructure, Liberia's dense, humid rainforests – some of the most extensive in West Africa – are alive with the screeching and twittering of hundreds of birds, who are kept company by forest elephants, pygmy hippos and other wildlife padding around the forest floor.

FAST FACTS

- **Area** 111,370 sq km
- **ATMs** None
- **Borders** Côte d'Ivoire, Guinea and Sierra Leone
- **Budget** From US$50 per day
- **Capital** Monrovia
- **Languages** English and more than 20 indigenous languages
- **Money** Liberian dollar; US$1 = L$70, €1 = L$102
- **Population** 3.3 million
- **Seasons** Dry (November to April), wet (May to October)
- **Telephone** Country code ☎ 231; international access code ☎ 00
- **Time** GMT/UTC
- **Visa** Vary in cost and must be obtained in advance

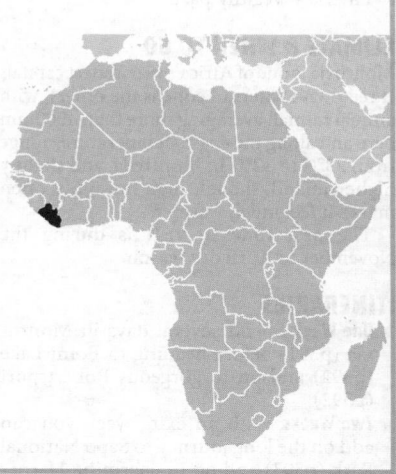

HOW MUCH?

- **Sachet of water** US$0.07
- **Kilo of bananas** US$0.40
- **Fufu and soup** US$0.75
- **Short taxi ride** US$1
- **Soda** US$0.30

LONELY PLANET INDEX

- **1L petrol** US$1.13
- **1L bottled water** US$0.15
- **Bottle of Club beer** US$1
- **Souvenir T-shirt** US$15
- **Cassava leaf** US$0.75

HIGHLIGHTS

- **Monrovia** (p391) Stroll through central Monrovia and absorb the chaos and drama of this great African city.
- **Robertsport** (p392) Join the surfers and sun-worshippers at this little slice of beach paradise and stay for a couple of days at Liberia's coolest hotel.
- **Sapo National Park** (boxed text, p393) Really get off the beaten track and wander under the lush, humid canopy of one of West Africa's last remaining rainforests.
- **Harper** (p392) Kick back in this out-of-the-way town, an elegant reminder of Liberia's wealthy past.

CLIMATE & WHEN TO GO

Monrovia is one of Africa's two wettest capitals (Freetown in Sierra Leone is the other), with annual rainfall averaging more than 4500mm here and along the coast. Temperatures range from 23°C to 32°C in Monrovia, and slightly higher inland, though high humidity often makes it feel much warmer.

The best time to visit is during the November to April dry season.

ITINERARIES

- **One Week** Spend several days in Monrovia (p391) before heading to Bomi Lake (p392) and on to gorgeous Robertsport (p392).
- **Two Weeks** With an extra week you can add on the long journey to Sapo National Park (p393) and on to charming Harper

(p392), before carrying on into Côte d'Ivoire.

HISTORY

After being populated for a mere few thousand years, Liberia struck American abolitionists as an ideal place to resettle freed slaves. In 1822, the first group stepped off the boat at Providence Island, Monrovia. They saw themselves as part of a mission to bring civilisation and Christianity to Africa, but their numbers were soon depleted by tropical diseases and hostile indigenous residents, who resented being dominated by the new arrivals.

The surviving settlers, known as Americo-Liberians, declared an independent republic in 1847. Yet, fatally for the new republic's future, citizenship excluded indigenous peoples, and every president until 1980 was of American freed-slave ancestry. For nearly a century, Liberia foundered economically and politically while the indigenous population suffered under a form of forced labour that would have been called slavery anywhere else.

During William Tubman's presidency (1944–71) the tides began to change. Thanks to the image of stability that Tubman was able to project, foreign investment flowed into the country, and for several decades Liberia sustained sub-Saharan Africa's highest growth rate. Firestone and other American companies made major investments, and Tubman earned praise as the 'maker of modern Liberia'.

Yet the influx of new money exacerbated existing social inequalities, and hostilities between Americo-Liberians and the indigenous population worsened. While indigenous Liberians were finally granted the right to vote in 1963, the concession was too little too late. The government continued to be controlled by about a dozen interrelated Americo-Liberian families, and corruption was rampant.

Coup d'Etat & Years of Darkness

Resentment began to simmer, and in April 1980 William Tolbert (who had succeeded Tubman as president) was overthrown and killed in a coup led by uneducated master-sergeant Samuel Doe. For the very first time, Liberia had a ruler who wasn't an Americo-Liberian, giving the indigenous population a taste of political power and an opportunity for vengeance. The 28-year-old Doe shocked the world by ordering 13 ex-ministers be publicly executed on a beach in Monrovia.

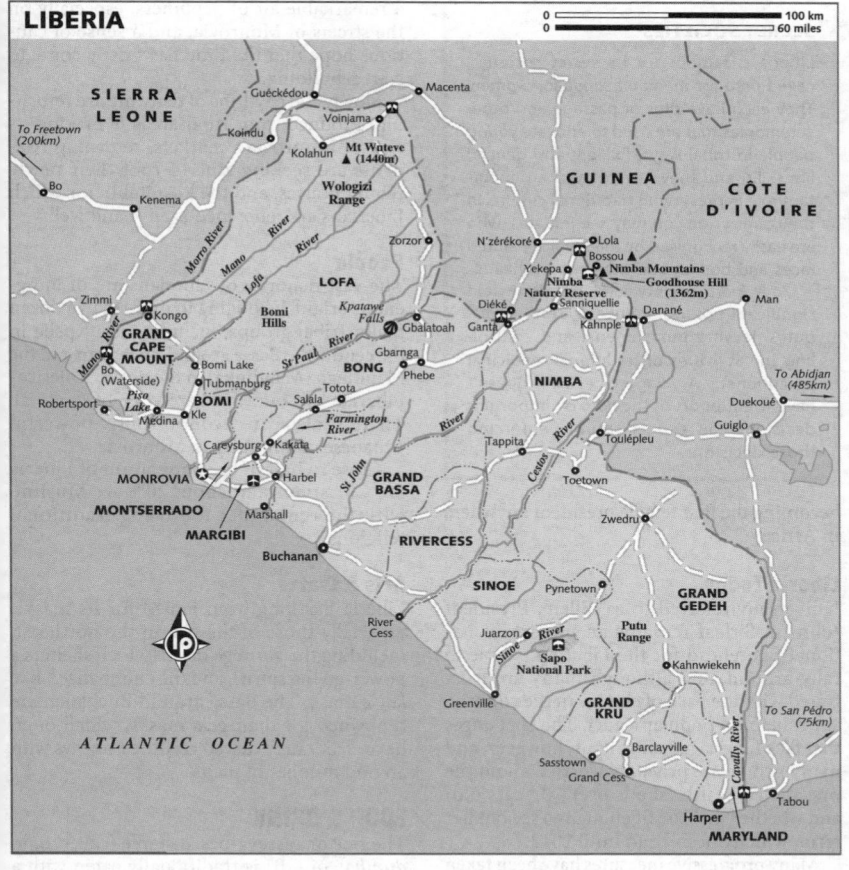

LIBERIA

While the coup gave power to the indigenous population, it was widely condemned regionally and internationally. Relations with neighbouring African states soon thawed. However, the post-coup flight of capital, coupled with ongoing corruption, caused Liberia's economy to plummet.

Doe struggled to maintain his grip on power, but to no avail. Opposition forces began to gain strength and intertribal fighting broke out. On Christmas Eve 1989, Charles Taylor (former head of the Doe government's procurement agency) launched an invasion from Côte d'Ivoire. Doe's troops arrived shortly thereafter, indiscriminately killing hundreds of unarmed civilians, raping women and burning villages. By mid-1990, Taylor's forces controlled most of the countryside.

Following a series of failed peace accords interspersed with factional fighting, 1996 elections brought Charles Taylor to the presidency with a big majority, in large because many feared the consequences if he lost.

Finally, in August 2003, with rebel groups controlling most of the country, and under heavy pressure from the international community, Charles Taylor went into exile in Nigeria. A transitional government was established, leading to elections in late 2005. In a hotly contested run-off vote between former World Bank economist Ellen Johnson-Sirleaf and international soccer star George Weah, Johnson-Sirleaf won the presidency,

LIBERIA

SECRET SOCIETIES

Liberia is famous for its secret societies, called *poro* for men and *sande* for women. They each have rites of passage and other ceremonies that are used to educate young people in tribal ways, folklore and general life skills, and they have played an important role in preserving traditional culture. In the countryside you may see initiates, who are easily recognised by their white-painted faces and bodies, and their shaved heads.

Zoes (*poro* society leaders) also wield significant political influence, settling disputes, levying punishments and controlling the activities of traditional medicinal practitioners. A village chief who doesn't have the support of the *poro* on important decisions can expect trouble enforcing those decisions.

becoming the first female president anywhere in Africa.

Liberia Today

Universally referred to as 'Ellen', President Johnson-Sirleaf remains an important national figurehead for the Liberian people to rally around, and although many are frustrated with the pace of change in the country, she remains a popular leader. The challenges that face Liberia are enormous, however, and many people are privately worried about the president's health (she is over 70 years old) and whether she'll be fit enough to see out her term, which doesn't end until 2012.

Many progressive measures have been taken in the past few years to overcome the wounds of the civil war, including the introduction of free elementary schooling throughout the country. Perhaps most significant is the establishment of the Truth and Reconciliation Commission of Liberia, which, on the South African model, seeks to honestly and openly come to terms with the crimes committed over two decades of war.

CULTURE

If there's any word that characterises Liberians, it's resilience. Here, in this war-ravaged land, almost half of the Liberians were displaced from their homes during the long years of conflict, and many witnessed unspeakable atrocities. Yet despite all the suffering, there's a remarkable air of peppiness, especially on the streets of Monrovia, and a sense of cautious hope that the time has finally come to start rebuilding.

Slowly the rhythms of daily life are returning. Produce from rural areas is making its way to Monrovia's markets, returning residents are seeking zinc to roof their newly rebuilt houses, and the hospitality for which Liberians are renowned is alive and well.

People

The vast majority of Liberians are of indigenous origin, belonging to more than a dozen major tribal groups, including the Kpelle in the centre, the Bassa around Buchanan and the Mandingo (Mandinka) in the north. Americo-Liberians account for barely 5% of the total. There's also an economically powerful Lebanese community in Monrovia.

Close to half of the population of Liberia are Christians and about 20% are Muslim, with the remainder following traditional religions.

Arts & Crafts

Liberia has long been famed for its masks, especially those of the Gio in the northeast, including the *gunyege* mask (which shelters a power-giving spirit), and the chimpanzee-like *kagle* mask. The Bassa around Buchanan are renowned for their *gela* masks, which often have elaborately carved coiffures, always with an odd number of plaits.

FOOD & DRINK

The rice or cassava-based staple (called *fufu, dumboy* or GB) is traditionally eaten with a soup or sauce made with greens and palm oil, and sometimes also meat or fish. Other popular dishes include *palava* sauce (made with plato leaf, dried fish or meat and palm oil), *jollof* rice and palm butter (a sauce made from palm nuts).

ENVIRONMENT

Liberia's low-lying coastal plain is intersected by marshes, creeks and tidal lagoons, and bisected by at least nine major rivers. Inland is a densely forested plateau rising to low mountains in the northeast. The highest point is Goodhouse Hill (1362m) in the Nimba range bordering Guinea and Côte d'Ivoire.

Liberia's rainforests, which now cover about 40% of the country, comprise a critical part of the Guinean Forests of West Africa Hotspot – an exceptionally biodiverse area stretching across 11 countries in the region. In 2003 the Nimba Nature Reserve was declared – contiguous with the Guinean–Côte d'Ivorian Mont Nimba Strict Nature Reserve (a Unesco World Heritage Site).

MONROVIA

pop 1 million

Home to one in three Liberians, Monrovia in many ways *is* Liberia, a huge collection of villages, towns and slums that has grown and grown during decades of war to the point where it's the country's only true city and centre of almost all its economic and cultural life.

The centre of Monrovia retains a few elegant buildings, as well as its fair share of burned-out shells and makeshift shops and housing. The overall impression is one of optimistic chaos, epitomised by the bustling Waterside Market, the city's mercantile heart. Only sights such as the iconic Broken Bridge or the ruin of the Ducor Palace Hotel remind you that until recently this was a war zone.

ORIENTATION

The heart of town is around Benson and Randall Sts, and along Broad St, where you'll find most shops and businesses. Southwest of here at Mamba Point is Monrovia's tiny diplomatic enclave. To the southeast is Sinkor, extending several kilometres until reaching Elwa junction and Red Light Motor Park.

INFORMATION

There are internet cafes, foreign-exchange bureaus and banks around Broad St.

Charif Pharmacy (☎ 06-519 999; Randall St; ⏲ 7.30am-7pm Mon-Sat) Has a good selection of European and US medicines.

JFK Hospital (Tubman Blvd, Sinkor) Monrovia's main hospital is for dire emergencies only.

Karou Voyages (☎ 06-515 439; karoumlwkl@yahoo.com; Mamba Point Hotel, UN Dr) Flight bookings.

Main post office (cnr Randall & Ashmun Sts; ⏲ 8am-4pm Mon-Fri, to noon Sat)

WOW Travel (☎ 06-841 582) Offers hiking expeditions to Mt Nimba, trips to the beach and to the Kpatawe Falls.

DANGERS & ANNOYANCES

Be careful around Waterside (especially near the Broken Bridge) and avoid West Point and any of the beaches in town. Always keep your wits about you and avoid displaying cash. After dark it's only safe to travel around Monrovia by car.

SIGHTS

The **National Museum** (☎ 06-498 488; Broad St; admission free, donation expected; ⏲ 8am-4pm Mon-Fri) is a steadily improving entity, having been rescued from decline during the years of war. The **Masonic Temple** (Benson St), now a ruin, was once Monrovia's major landmark.

Chaotic **Waterside Market** (Water St) offers almost everything for sale, including colourful textiles. Just opposite is Providence Island, where the first expedition of freed American slaves landed in 1822.

The beautiful beaches south of Monrovia fill up with locals on weekends. Before jumping in, get local advice, as currents can be dangerous. One of the most popular is **Silver Beach**, 15km southeast of town off the airport road, with a restaurant, craft vendors, showers, toilets, and umbrellas for hire.

SLEEPING

Sleeping in Monrovia is extremely expensive by African standards, but these are the best value for each budget.

St Theresa's Convent (☎ 06-784 276, 422 930; archdiocesanpastoralcenter@yahoo.com; Randall St; r with/without bathroom US$20/30, ste US$50) This is the only place in town that is both budget and safe. The sparse rooms are basic with just a bed in each, the very cheapest sharing toilets and showers.

Metropolitan Hotel (☎ 06-472 977; Broad St; r/tw incl breakfast US$75/90; ❄) This place has a rather sleazy feel overall, but its 33 rooms are fine and good value by local standards, although they can be rather dark. Wi-fi is planned.

Palm Hotel (☎ 06-535 177, 585 959; palmhotelmonrovia@yahoo.com; cnr Broad & Randall Sts; s/d incl breakfast US$91/139; ❄ 💻 📶) Located in the very heart of the city, the Palm is secure, clean and comfortable, with free in-room wi-fi and a great rooftop restaurant.

Cape Hotel (☎ 07-700 6633, 06-496 046; www.thecapehotel.com.lr; UN Dr, Mamba Point; s/d incl breakfast US$150/200, ste incl breakfast US$175-250; P ❄ 💻 📶) The city's best hotel overlooks the beach at Mamba Point and offers free wi-fi, good breakfast espresso and sparkling clean rooms, all with fridges, TVs, phones and safes.

EATING

Monrovia has a surprisingly vibrant eating scene due to the foreign presence in the city, which also means that eating out is not always very cheap.

Sweet Lips (Newport St; meals US$1.50-2.50; ☺ 11am-9pm Mon-Sat) This firm favourite is said to serve up the very best Liberian food in town – try the excellent *fufu* rice and palm butter.

Living Room (☎ 06-850 333; Royal Hotel, cnr Tubman Blvd & 14th St; sushi US$3-10; mains from US$15; ☺ lunch & dinner) Celebrated by expats for its transcendent tuna salad, Monrovia's top sushi bar feels very glamorous with smart leather chairs, sleek black tables and a gleaming sushi counter. Takeaway is available.

Sajj House (☎ 06-830 888; Tubman Blvd; mains US$5-10; ☺ 9am-10pm) Monrovia's most celebrated Lebanese restaurant is Sajj, where the *zatar* is famous but you can give the felafel a miss.

Evelyn's (☎ 06-710 104; Broad St; mains US$7-12; ☺ 7.30am-11pm Mon-Sat) This spotless oasis of air-conditioned calm is a great haven from the chaos of Broad St.

For self-catering, try **Abi Jaoudi** (Randall St; ☺ 8am-7pm Mon-Fri) or **Stop & Shop** (Randall St; ☺ 8am-6pm).

GETTING THERE & AROUND

Flights arrive at **Roberts International Airport** (ROB; Robertsfield), 60km southeast of Monrovia, from where a taxi into the city costs around US$40. There is also the smaller Spriggs Payne Airport (MLW) in Sinkor.

Bush taxis for Tubmanburg and the Sierra Leone border leave from Duala Motor Park, 9km northeast of the town centre. Transport for most other domestic destinations leaves from the Red Light Motor Park, Monrovia's main motor park, 15km northeast of the centre. Nearby Guinea Motor Park is where to head for buses heading to Guinea and Côte d'Ivoire.

THE COAST

If you only visit one other place outside Monrovia, make it lovely **Robertsport**, Liberia's closest thing to a beach resort. Fantastic ecofriendly **Nana Lodge** (☎ 06-668 332, 852 394; tent sleeping up to 4 incl breakfast US$100) is right on the beach and an excellent deal if you share your luxury tent with a friend or two.

About 125km southeast of Monrovia, **Buchanan** is Liberia's second port. The town boasts the unusually excellent **Sparks Hotel** (☎ 06-452 781, 523 732; cnr Church & Gardner Sts; r US$75-125; ☒) near the beach, boasting 15 large, well-equipped and clean rooms. Bush taxis run daily to/from Monrovia (US$6.50, three hours) and several times weekly in the dry season to/from River Cess.

Greenville (also known as Sinoe) is a logging centre, and the jumping-off point for excursions to Sapo National Park (see boxed text, opposite). The main route to/from Monrovia is via Buchanan along the coastal road.

Surrounded by beautiful countryside at Liberia's southeastern tip, **Harper** is the capital of Maryland (once a separate republic), and boasts the remains of some fine old houses, including former president William Tubman's mansion. **Adina's Guest House** (☎ 06-620 005; r US$20) is the town's best-established hotel, which has several basic rooms with fans. Elysian Airways flies twice a week between Monrovia and Harper (US$175/200 one way/return). Road access from Monrovia is via Tappita and Zwedru, then southeast to the coast. Under good conditions, it's a two-day journey in a 4WD; during the rainy season the road from Zwedru can become impassable.

THE INTERIOR

Tubmanburg (also called Bomi) is a pleasant place that was once an important iron ore– and diamond-mining centre. The town is recovering from war damage admirably but is really worth visiting for nearby **Bomi Lake**, an absolute stunner in the hills a well-signposted 4km beyond the town. The semi-crater lake has very clean and clear water and makes for a great picnic spot.

During the war years, **Gbarnga** (pronounced 'Banga') gained notoriety as Charles Taylor's centre of operations, and became virtually the second capital of Liberia. Today its prominence has faded, but it remains a major town, and is easily reached on tarmac from Monrovia.

There's no real reason to stop in the town itself, but the must-see here is the **Kpatawe Falls**, 18km off the main road from the town of Phebe, 10km southwest of Gbarnga. Take

> ### SAPO NATIONAL PARK
>
> Sapo, Liberia's only national park, is a lush 1808-sq-km tract containing some of West Africa's last remaining primary rainforest, as well as forest elephants, pygmy hippos, chimpanzees, antelopes and other wildlife. There are still war refugees living in Sapo despite a big drive in recent years to totally clear the park. Work is now getting started on rebuilding infrastructure, including park headquarters, and on enforcing its protected status.
>
> Currently, there are no commercial tours into Sapo, though it's still possible to visit. The best contact for updated information is the **Society for the Conservation of Nature of Liberia** (☎ 06-572 377; scnlib2001@yahoo.com; Monrovia Zoo, Larkpase). Allow a full day to reach Sapo from Monrovia by 4WD along the road paralleling the coast, and at least two days going via Zwedru. Once at the park, you can arrange guided hikes and canoe rides, but you'll have to bring all your own food and camping gear as there is nowhere on site to stay.

the dirt road opposite Phebe Hospital to get here, where you can swim or hike up through the forest to the waterfalls higher up. It's well worth the detour and is one of Liberia's most picturesque spots.

LIBERIA DIRECTORY

ACCOMMODATION
Monrovia has a decent selection of hotels, although most are expensive (from around US$50 for a 'budget' double, US$80 to US$100 for midrange and from US$150 for top end). Elsewhere, there's the occasional guesthouse.

BOOKS
Journey Without Maps is Graham Greene's classic tale of adventuring across Liberia on foot in the 1930s.

For a gripping take on the war, look for *The Final Days of Dr Doe* by Lynda Schuster (published in *Granta 48*, 1994).

BUSINESS HOURS
See also p1136 for standard business hours. Banks in Liberia are open from 9.30am to noon Monday to Thursday and until 12.30pm on Friday.

DANGERS & ANNOYANCES
The security situation in Liberia is fragile and can change quickly. Check the latest situation before setting off. At the time of writing travel was generally safe throughout the country, though it's recommended that you hire a private driver for travel outside Monrovia.

EMBASSIES & CONSULATES
Canadians and Australians should contact their high commissions in Abidjan, Côte d'Ivoire (see p315) and Accra, Ghana (see p357), respectively.

Côte d'Ivoire (☎ 06-519 138; Warner Ave btwn 17th & 18th Sts, Sinkor)
France (☎ 031-235 576; German Compound, Congo Town)
Germany (☎ 06-438 365; UNMIL Bldg, Tubman Blvd, Congo Town)
Ghana (☎ 07-701 6920; cnr 15th St & Cheesman Ave, Sinkor)
Guinea (☎ 06-573 049; Tubman Blvd btwn 23rd & 24th Sts, Sinkor)
Nigeria (☎ 06-261 148; Nigeria House, Tubman Blvd, Congo Town)
Sierra Leone (☎ 06-427 404; cnr 15th St & Coleman Ave, Sinkor)
UK (☎ 06-516 973; chalkleyroy@aol.com; Clara Town, UN Dr, Bushrod Island) Honorary consul, emergency assistance only; otherwise contact the British High Commission in Freetown, Sierra Leone (p516).
USA (☎ 07-705 4826; http://monrovia.usembassy.gov/; UN Dr, Mamba Point)

HEALTH
You will need a valid yellow-fever vaccination certificate in order to enter Liberia.

HOLIDAYS
New Year's Day 1 January
Armed Forces Day 11 February
Decoration Day Second Wednesday in March
JJ Roberts' Birthday 15 March
Fast & Prayer Day 11 April
National Unification Day 14 May
Independence Day 26 July
Flag Day 24 August
Thanksgiving Day First Thursday in November

LIBERIA

Tubman Day 29 November
Christmas Day 25 December

MONEY

The unit of currency is the Liberian 'unity' dollar (L$). US dollars are accepted everywhere at a standard exchange of US$1 to L$70. Outside Monrovia hotels you'll nearly always get change in L$, meaning that you don't really need to change your dollars to get local money.

Bringing US cash in a variety of denominations is the simplest way to travel. Euros are the only other easy-to-exchange currency, aside from neighbouring African currencies around border towns. There are no ATMs in Liberia at present, so you should bring all the cash you need for your stay. In an emergency, Western Union transfers are available in larger towns throughout the country.

TELEPHONE

The country code is ☎ 231 and the international access code is ☎ 00. There are no area codes. Rates for intercontinental calls start at US$3 per minute. The national telephone network is defunct, with mobile phones (prefixes 04, 05, 06 or 07) the main way to connect in Monrovia.

VISAS

Visas are required by all (except nationals of Ecowas countries), with costs varying depending on where they are procured. In the US a three-month single-entry visa for US citizens costs US$131, or US$70 for all other nationals.

Visa Extensions

Visas can be extended at the **Bureau of Immigration** (Broad St; ☽ 9am-5pm Mon-Fri, to 3pm Sat) in Monrovia.

Visas for Onward Travel

CÔTE D'IVOIRE

Bring one passport photo and leave your passport between 9am and 1pm or 2pm to 3pm Monday to Friday. A one-month single-entry visa costs US$75 for all nationals. Processing usually takes five working days but can be done faster at no extra cost if you're in a hurry.

GUINEA

Bring two passport photos and leave your passport between 9.30am and 4pm Monday

---

> **PRACTICALITIES**
>
> ■ Voltage is 110V, and most plugs are US-style (two flat pins).
>
> ■ There's little power outside the capital except through generators. Power cuts are common in Monrovia.
>
> ■ Local dailies include the *Inquirer* and the *Monrovia Guardian*.
>
> ■ Liberia uses the imperial system for weights and measures.

---

to Friday. One-month single-entry visas cost US$65 for citizens of the EU, Australia and New Zealand, or US$100 for US and Canadian nationals. Processing takes 24 hours.

SIERRA LEONE

You'll need two passport photos and a photocopy of your passport to get a visa. Applications are accepted only between 10am and 2pm on Monday, Wednesday and Friday, and single-entry visas valid for up to three months cost US$100 for citizens of the EU, Canada, Australia and New Zealand. US citizens are charged US$131.

TRANSPORT IN LIBERIA

GETTING THERE & AWAY
Air

Airlines serving Monrovia include the following.

Aero (AJ; ☎ 06-877 866, 511 895; www.flyaero.com; Randall St)

Brussels Airlines (SN; ☎ 06-520 777, 974 677; www.brusselsairlines.com; Randall St)

Delta Air Lines (DL; www.delta.com)

Elysian Airlines (E4; ☎ 06-444 747; www.elysianairlines.com)

Kenya Airways (KQ; ☎ 06-556 693, 511 522; www.kenya-airways.com; KLM Bldg, Broad St)

Royal Air Maroc (AT; ☎ 06-951 951, 956 956; www.royalairmaroc.com; Tubman Blvd)

Slok Air International (SO; ☎ 06-590 178; www.slok-air.com; KLM House, Broad St)

SN Bellview Airlines (B3; ☎ 07-727 3693, 06-463 409; www.flybellviewair.com)

Virgin Nigeria (VK; ☎ 06-511 197; www.virginnigeria.com)

Land
CÔTE D'IVOIRE
Border crossings with Côte d'Ivoire are just beyond Sanniquellie towards Danané, and east of Harper, towards Tabou.

There's a bus several times weekly from Monrovia to Abidjan and on to Accra via Sanniquellie (US$40 to Abidjan, US$60 to Accra, plus approximately US$20 for border fees).

Daily bush taxis go from Monrovia to Ganta and Sanniquellie, from where you can continue in stages to Danané and Man (12 to 15 hours).

In the south, a road connects Harper with Tabou, but you'll still need to cross the Cavally River in a ferry or canoe as there is no bridge. Once across, there are taxis to Tabou, from where there's transport to San Pédro and Abidjan.

GUINEA
For Guinea, the main crossing is just north of Ganta. From just north of Ganta's Public Market you can take a *moto-taxi* (US$0.50) the 2km to the border and walk across. Once in Guinea, there are frequent taxis to N'zérékoré. From Sanniquellie's bush-taxi rank known as the 'meat packing' there are irregular bush taxis via Yekepa to the Guinean town of Lola (US$6.50). A place in a shared taxi is the same price. A *moto-taxi* (if you can find one!) from Yekepa to the border should cost only US$0.50, after which there are Guinean vehicles to Lola. There is also a border crossing at Voinjama to Macenta via a bad road from Gbarnga (often impassable in the wet season).

The Monrovia–Conakry bush taxi (US$50) takes two days and leaves from Monrovia's Guinea Park near the Red Light Motor Park in Paynesville. A place in a shared taxi on the same route is US$60.

For information on boats between Conakry (Guinea) and Monrovia (at least 36 hours), enquire at Monrovia's Freeport. Fishing boats run sporadically between Harper and San Pédro (Côte d'Ivoire).

SIERRA LEONE
The main Sierra Leone crossing is at Bo (Waterside). There are frequent daily bush taxis between Monrovia and the Bo (Waterside) border (three hours), from where it's easy to find onward transport to Kenema (about eight very rough hours further), and then on to Freetown.

GETTING AROUND
Bush Taxi & Bus
Public transport is still not considered safe for foreigners in Liberia, meaning your choice is between taking risks with your security and paying for a driver. Bush taxis go daily from Monrovia to Buchanan, Gbarnga, Ganta, Sanniquellie and the Sierra Leone border. Several weekly bush taxis link Monrovia with almost everywhere else, although many routes (especially those connecting Zwedru with Greenville and Harper) are restricted during the rainy season. Minivans (called 'buses') also ply most major routes, although they're more crowded and dangerous than bush taxis.

Car & Motorcycle
Vehicle rental can be arranged through better hotels from about US$100 per day for a 4WD. Expect frequent stops at security checkpoints.

MALI

Mali

Mali is West Africa's heart and soul, a country as rich in historical significance as it is blessed by an extraordinary array of sights and cultures.

Mali's natural wonders range from the Sahara in the north to the fertile greenery of the south, with the Niger River cutting a swath through the centre. The Niger, one of the grand old rivers of Africa, still provides the country's lifeblood.

Not far from the riverbank, the extraordinary Falaise de Bandiagara shelters one of West Africa's most intriguing peoples, the Dogon, whose villages still cling to the rocky cliffs and whose complex cultural rituals are among Africa's most intriguing.

Some of Africa's greatest empires also bequeathed to Mali some of its most dramatic attractions: the legendary city of Timbuktu and the glorious mudbrick mosque at Djenné are two among many. Even in places where the landscape seems too barren to support life, you find Mali's famous elephants sharing the Sahel with Tuareg and Fulani nomads.

There's almost as much to hear in Mali as there is to see: Mali's two major music festivals – in the Sahara near Timbuktu and on the shores of the Niger in Ségou – are worth planning your trip around.

It all adds up to a simple equation – if you visit just one country in West Africa, make it Mali.

FAST FACTS

- **Area** 1,240,140 sq km
- **ATMs** Visa-enabled ATMs in most major towns
- **Borders** Algeria, Burkina Faso, Côte d'Ivoire, Guinea, Mauritania, Niger, Senegal
- **Budget** US$35 to US$50 per day
- **Capital** Bamako
- **Languages** French, Bambara, Fulfulde, Tamashek, Dogon and Songhai
- **Money** West African CFA franc; US$1 = CFA458.57, €1 = CFA656
- **Population** 13.1 million
- **Seasons** Hot (October to February), very hot (April to June), wet (July to August)
- **Telephone** Country code ☎ 223; international access code 00
- **Time** GMT/UTC
- **Visa** Renewable five-day visa available at border for CFA15,000; one-month visas, at any Malian embassy

HOW MUCH?

- **Bamako–Mopti bus ride** US$17
- **4WD rental with driver** US$102 to US$114 per day, plus petrol
- **Sunset camel ride into Sahara** From US$17
- **Internet access** US$1.40 to US$3.40 per hour
- **Guide in Dogon Country** US$28.40 to US$51 per day

LONELY PLANET INDEX

- **1L petrol** US$1.20
- **1.5L bottled water** US$1.15
- **Small bottle of Castel beer** US$1.15
- **Souvenir T-shirt** US$11.35 to US$13.60
- **Portion of riz arachide** US$1.15

HIGHLIGHTS

- **Dogon Country** (p412) West Africa as it used to be, with timeless villages clinging to the Falaise de Bandiagara.
- **Djenné** (p408) Stunning mudbrick town with a fairy-tale mosque overlooking a clamorous Monday market.
- **Niger River** (p412) One of Africa's epic rivers, lined with fascinating villages, picturesque mosques and Mali's culturally diverse ethnic groups.
- **Timbuktu** (p416) City of Saharan legend and the gateway to the desert.
- **Bamako** (p406) West Africa's live music capital, with weekend performances by Mali's musical superstars.

CLIMATE & WHEN TO GO

The best time to visit Mali is from November to January, with generally fine weather, moderate temperatures and sufficient water levels on the Niger River to allow boat trips. January is also when Mali's two world-famous music festivals – the Festival in the Desert (p418) and the Festival sur le Niger (p407) – take place. January is Mali's tourist high season, so accommodation can be at a premium. Mali is wettest between July and August, although the rainy season runs from June to September. It's hottest between April and June, when temperatures frequently exceed 40°C; September and

October are also hot. From January to June, the dusty harmattan is common, irritating throats and reducing visibility.

ITINERARIES

- **One Week** Stay Friday night in Bamako for a taste of Mali's live-music scene (p406) and spend Monday at Djenné's weekly market (p409). Otherwise, we recommend a three-day trek in Dogon Country (p412), with one night in the lively port town of Mopti (p409) en route.
- **Two Weeks** An extra week will allow you a night in languid Ségou (p407) and another in Teriya Bugu (p408). From Mopti, you could also take a three-day slow-boat journey (see the boxed text, p412) up the Niger River to Timbuktu (p416), from where short desert excursions are possible.

HISTORY
The Early Empires

Rock art in the Sahara suggests that northern Mali has been inhabited since 10,000 BC, when the Sahara was fertile and rich in wildlife. By 300 BC, large organised settlements had developed, most notably near Djenné (see p409), one of West Africa's oldest cities. By the 6th century AD, the lucrative transSaharan trade in gold, salt and slaves had begun, facilitating the rise of West Africa's great empires.

From the 8th to the 16th centuries, Mali formed the centrepiece of the great empires of West African antiquity, most notably the empires of Ghana, Mali and Songhaï. The arrival of European ships along the West African coast from the 15th century, however, broke the monopoly on power of the Sahel kingdoms.

Later the Bambara Empire of Ségou rose briefly to control huge swathes of Mali, before having its power usurped by two waves of Fula-led Islamic jihadists, the second originating from the Tukulor Empire of northern Senegal. The Tukulor were still around when the French arrived in Mali during the mid-19th century.

Throughout the French colonial era, Mali was the scene of a handful of major infrastructure projects, including the 1200km Dakar–Bamako train line, which was built with forced labour to enable the export of cheap cash crops, such as rice and cotton. But

MALI

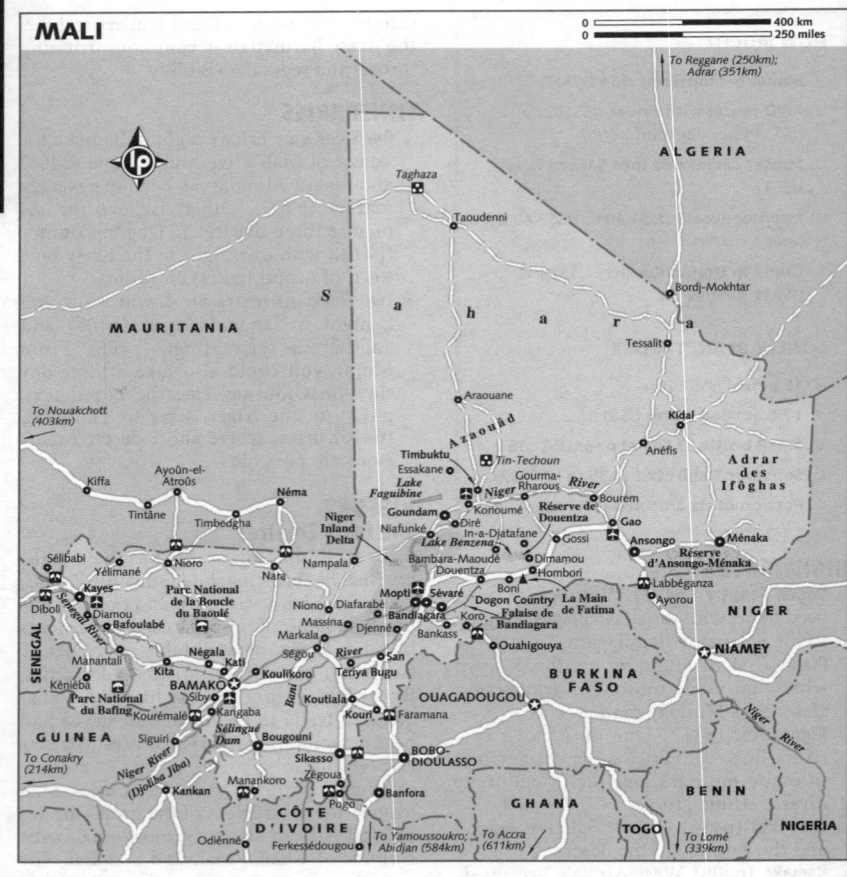

MALI

Mali remained the poor neighbour of Senegal and Côte d'Ivoire.

Independence

Mali became independent in 1960 (for a few months it was federated with Senegal). Under the one-party rule of Mali's first president, Modibo Keïta, newly formed state corporations controlled the economy, but all except the cotton enterprise lost money and the economy wilted. In 1968, Keïta was overthrown by army officers led by Moussa Traoré.

During the Cold War, Mali was firmly in the Soviet camp; food shortages were constant, especially during the devastating droughts of 1968–74 and 1980–85. Between 1970 and 1990 there were five coup attempts and the

early 1980s were characterised by strikes, often violently suppressed. One bright spot came in 1987 when Mali produced its first grain surplus.

The Tuareg rebellion began in 1990, and later that year a peaceful prodemocracy demonstration drew 30,000 people onto the streets of Bamako, followed by strikes and further demonstrations. On 17 March 1991, security forces met students and other demonstrators with machine-gun fire. Three days of rioting followed, during which 150 people were killed. The unrest finally provoked the army, led by General Amadou Toumani Touré (General ATT as he was known), to seize control.

Touré established an interim transitional government and gained considerable respect

MALIAN MUSIC

Mali's music may have taken the world by storm in recent decades, yet it's anything but a recent phenomenon. For centuries, Mali's *griots* (also called *jelis*), a hereditary caste of musicians, have served as the praise singers and storytellers of Malian society and continue to play an important role. Toumani Diabaté, the undisputed master of the 21-string *kora*, told us that 'each ethnic group in Mali has deep cultural roots and long musical traditions. Almost all of Mali's musicians come from *griot* families. As *griots* we learn the *kora*, the music in our families when we are growing up'. As if to prove the point, Diabaté is himself the 71st generation of *kora* players in his family. Other renowned Malian *kora* players, such as Ballaké Sissoko and Mamadou Diabaté, also come from *griot* families.

The blues are another Malian speciality – some scholars believe that the roots of American blues lie with the Malian slaves who worked on US plantations. The genius of Ali Farka Touré, who died in 2006, was largely responsible for Malian music's breakthrough beyond Africa's shores. Other much-loved blues performers include many from Ali Farka's stable, among them Afel Bocoum, Ali Farka's son Vieux Farka Touré, Baba Salah and Lobi Traoré.

A different take on the blues comes from Tinariwen, a beguiling Tuareg group of former rebels from Kidal. Terakaft and Toumast, whose members include former Tinariwen performers, are also gaining popularity for their desert-blues style. For more traditional Tuareg music, Tartit is the best-known group.

Another pillar of the Malian music scene is its wealth of talented female singers, among whom Oumou Sangaré is the most famous. Her songs deal with contemporary social issues, such as polygamy and arranged marriages; her music is influenced by the musical traditions of the Wassoulou region of southwestern Mali; and her repertoire features the *kamelen-ngoni*, a large six-stringed harp-lute. Other internationally renowned female singers to watch out for include Ami Koita and Kandia Kouyaté.

The breadth and depth of Mali's musical soundtrack is attributable not just to centuries of tradition but also to the policies of Mali's post-independence government. As elsewhere in West Africa, Mali's musicians were promoted as the cultural standard-bearers of the newly independent country and numerous state-sponsored 'orchestras' were founded. The legendary Rail Band de Bamako (actual employees of the Mali Railway Corporation) was one of the greatest, and one of its ex-members, the charismatic Salif Keita, has become a superstar in his own right.

Rounding out the pantheon of musical superstars are the female songstress Rokia Traoré, the dynamic duo of Amadou & Mariam and Ségou's *ngoni* master Bassekou Kouyate.

Many of Mali's best-loved performers can be found playing most Friday nights in Bamako (p406). Music lovers will also want to be near Timbuktu in early January for the Festival in the Desert (p418) or in Ségou in late January for the Festival sur le Niger (p407).

Music by Malian musicians can be surprisingly difficult to pick up within the country, other than from wandering sellers of bootlegged CDs. One exception is Mali K7 (p406) in Bamako.

---

when he resigned a year later, keeping his promise to hold multiparty elections. Alpha Oumar Konaré (a scientist and writer) was elected president in June 1992, and his party, the Alliance for Democracy in Mali (Adema), won a large majority of seats in the national assembly. Konaré oversaw considerable political and economic liberalisation, but had to deal with a 50% devaluation of the CFA in 1994 (which resulted in rioting and protests) and an attempted coup.

Konaré stood down in 2002, as the new constitution he'd helped draft dictated; he went on to become chairman of the African Union. The former general, Amadou Touré, was rewarded for his patience and elected president in April 2002.

Mali Today

On many fronts Mali is a model West African democracy, one in which the overall health of the system has proven more enduring than the ambitions of individual leaders. It has become Africa's third-largest gold producer and one of its largest cotton producers. At the same time, the Tuareg rebellion in the 1990s and again from 2006 continues to threaten the country's stability. Although widely liked, President ATT has seen a dip in his popularity due to his inability to end the rebellion and his perceived closeness to France and Libya's Colonel Qaddafi (whom many Malians accuse of also supporting the rebels). The next presidential and parliamentary elections are due in 2012.

Although there have been improvements in recent years, Mali remains one of the world's poorest countries: 72% of the population lives on less than US$2 a day, adult literacy is just 24%, one in every five Malian children dies before the age of five and life expectancy hovers around just 50 years.

CULTURE

For centuries the country's diverse peoples have shared a country that is not always bountiful, and they've learned to do it pretty well. Ethnic identity is still important, but, where once there was enmity, in most cases a *cousinage* ('joking cousins') relationship now exists. People from different groups commonly tease and poke fun at ethnic stereotypes and past deeds, to everyone's enjoyment. The only exceptions are the Tuareg, who remain a people apart.

For many Malians, life is a struggle and those Malians with a steady job must support a large network of family and friends. Urban Malian society is becoming increasingly sophisticated, although its enjoyment is limited to a privileged few: UN figures suggest that more than 90% of Mali's urban population lives in slums. In rural areas, it's not unusual to find Malians who have never left their village or who continue to eke out a semi-nomadic existence. These Malians hold fast to tradition, but their numbers are dwindling and their lives are made increasingly difficult by environmental degradation and a growing population competing for diminishing resources.

Greeting people in Mali is very important, and you'll often encounter highly formalised ritual greetings that last for minutes. People think it impolite to ask for directions before saying hello or enquiring about their health.

People

Mali's population is growing by almost 3% per year, which means that the number of Malians doubles every 20 years; 48% of Malians are under 15 years of age.

Concentrated in the centre and south of the country, the Bambara are Mali's largest ethnic group (33% of the population) and they hold much political power. Together with the Soninké and Malinké (who dominate western Mali) they make up 50% of Mali's population.

Fulani (17%) pastoralists are found wherever there is grazing land for their livestock, particularly in the Niger inland delta. The farmlands of the Songhaï (6%) are concentrated along the 'Niger Bend', while the Sénoufo (12%) live around Sikasso and Koutiala. The Dogon (7%) live on the Falaise de Bandiagara in central Mali. The lighter-skinned Tuareg (6%), traditionally nomadic pastoralists and traders, inhabit the fringes of the Sahara. Other groups include the Bozo fisher people of the Niger River and the Bobo (2.5%), who live close to the border with Burkina Faso.

Between 80% and 90% of Malians are Muslim, and 2% are Christian. The remainder retains animist beliefs, although these often overlap with Islamic and Christian practices, especially in rural areas.

Arts

The most famous exponents of Mali's famous sculptural and mask-making traditions are the Bambara and the Dogon. Bambara masks and statues are usually bold, solid and angular in form, with cowrie shells and human and animal features incorporated into the design. The best known is the *chiwara*, a headpiece carved in the form of an antelope, used in ritualistic dances.

The large Dogon mask and headdress called the *imina-tiou* (*imina-sirou* in Sanga) is in the form of a prostrate serpent and is sometimes almost 10m high. Other masks used by the Dogon include the birdlike *kanaga*, which protects against vengeance (of a killed animal), and the houselike *sirige*, which represents the house of the *hogon*, which takes responsibility for passing on traditions. Most ceremonies at which you may see masks take place between April and May.

The Bambara also produce striking *bogolan* (mud cloth). Djenné (p409) and Ségou (p407) are the best places to find quality *bogolan* pieces.

FOOD & DRINK

Food in Mali is similar to that found in Senegal, with *poulet yassa* (chicken in an onion and lemon sauce), *riz yollof* (rice with vegetables and/or meat) and *riz arachide* (rice with peanut sauce) on many menus. All along the Niger River, restaurants serve grilled or fried *capitaine* (Nile perch).

Street food is widely available and is usually excellent. Look out for beef brochettes, fried fish, fried bananas, omelette sandwiches, sweet-potato chips and plates of rice and sauce.

Soft drinks are omnipresent, but local drinks such as ginger juice, or red *bissap* or *djablani* juice (brewed from hibiscus petals) are sometimes also available (but not always sterile).

Although Mali is predominantly Muslim, most towns have at least one bar or hotel where you can buy Castel, a Malian lager. Flag, from Senegal, is also available.

ENVIRONMENT

Mali has four national parks and reserves, but its wildlife has been devastated by centuries of human encroachment and the parks are not easily accessible. Of most interest to visitors is the Réserve de Douentza (see the boxed text, p421), a vast area of semidesert north of the main road between Douentza and Gossi inhabited by Africa's northernmost elephants.

Mali's most urgent environmental issues are deforestation (just 10.3% of Mali is covered by forest), overgrazing and desertification (an estimated 98% of Mali is at risk from desertification). Pollution and dwindling water levels in the Niger River (1626km of its 4100km are within Mali) are also major concerns.

BAMAKO

pop 1.73 million

Mali's capital is sprawling and gritty, and can be a little overwhelming if you let the streets full of people, cars, buzzing flocks of *mobylettes* (mopeds) and clouds of pollution get to you. And yet, most expats love the place; they're drawn in by great restaurants, nightlife and the chance to see some of Africa's best music stars. Bamako's hotels are also excellent, while the National Museum is arguably the best in the region. If you're looking for a tranquil stay, however, head elsewhere. But if you like your markets colourful, clamorous and spilling into the surrounding streets and if you appreciate energy that illuminates the night, Bamako might just get under your skin.

ORIENTATION

Bamako's city centre is on the north bank of the Niger River, roughly focused on the triangle formed by Ave Kassa Keïta (and its continuation Ave de la République), Blvd du Peuple and Ave de l'Indépendance. The Quinzambougou and Hippodrome districts, northeast of the centre, are great places to find hotels, restaurants and nightclubs. South of the centre, Pont des Martyrs leads across the river to Rte de Ségou (also called Ave de l'Unité Africaine, OUA), the main road out of town; the Sogoniko *gare routière* is about 6km along this road.

INFORMATION
Cultural Centres

Centre Culturel Français (Map p404; ☎ 2022 4019; www.ccfbamako.org; Ave de l'Indépendance; ⏲ 9.30am-1pm & 2-5.30pm Tue, Wed, Fri & Sat, 1.30-5.30pm Thu) Pick up the bimonthly program of concerts and events.

GUIDES IN MALI

Everywhere in Mali, guides will sidle up and offer to guide you around the city or further afield. Guides are certainly not necessary (except in Dogon Country), but a knowledgeable local guide can greatly enhance your visit.

So, how to choose a guide? All guides who passed the government's accreditation exams must now carry cards indicating whether they are accredited to guide nationally (blue) or only in their local district (yellow). Not every guide who has passed the exam is necessarily good and some who began guiding after 2006 have yet to sit the exam. In general, however, the system works. To find a guide, ask at the local tourist office, guide association, hotel or tour operator, or ask other travellers for recommendations. For Dogon Country, see the boxed text, p415.

BAMAKO

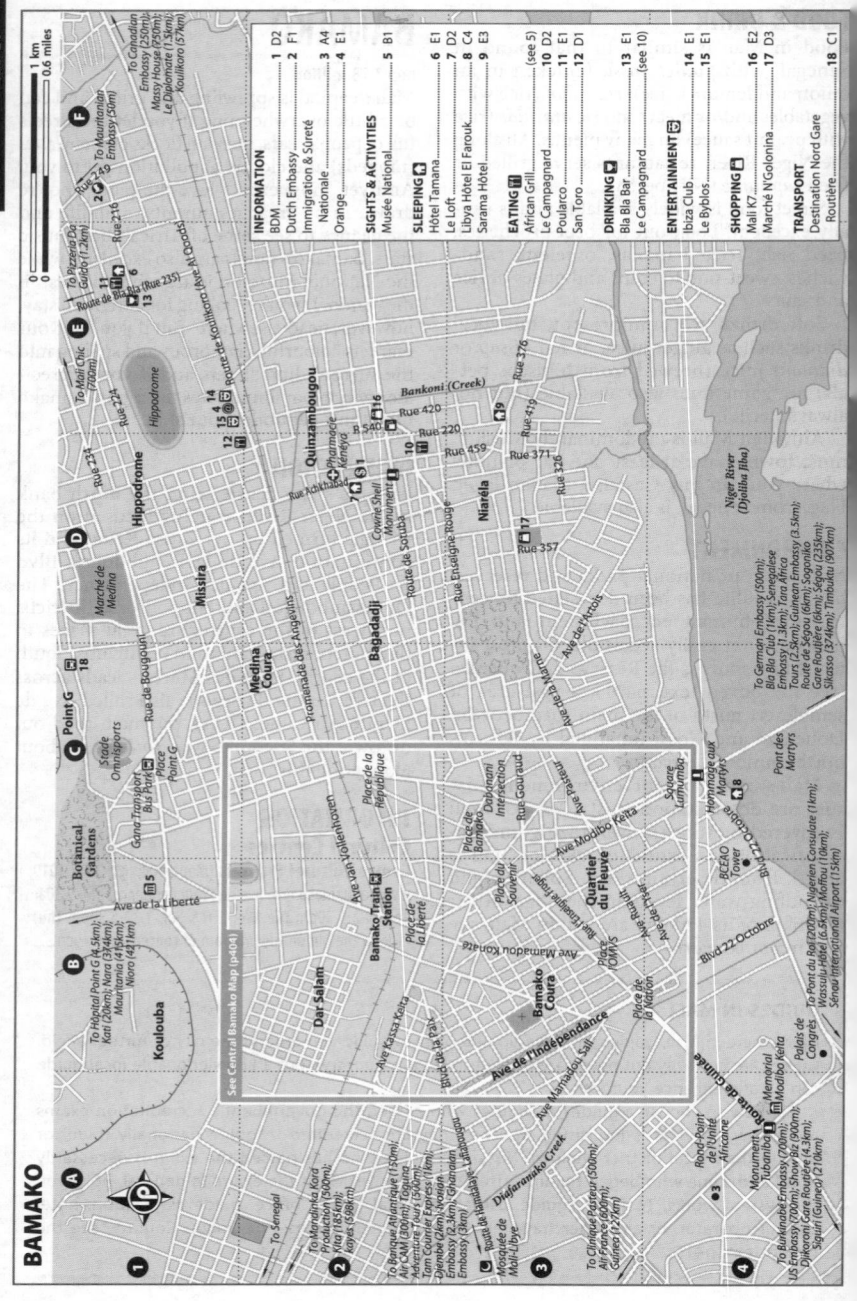

INFORMATION	
BDM	1 D2
Dutch Embassy	2 F1
Immigration & Sûreté	
Nationale	3 A4
Orange	4 E1

SIGHTS & ACTIVITIES	
Musée National	5 B1

SLEEPING	
Hôtel Tamana	6 E1
Le Loft	7 D2
Libya Hôtel El Farouk	8 C4
Sarama Hôtel	9 E3

EATING	
African Grill	(see 5)
Le Campagnard	10 D2
Poularco	11 E1
San Toro	12 D1

DRINKING	
Bla Bla Bar	13 E1
Le Campagnard	(see 10)

ENTERTAINMENT	
Ibiza Club	14 E1
Le Byblos	15 E1

SHOPPING	
Mali K7	16 E2
Marché N'Golonina	17 D3

TRANSPORT	
Destination Nord Gare	
Routière	18 C1

Internet Access

Cybercafé HTM (Map p404; Place l'OMVS; per hr CFA500; 7.30am-10.30pm)

Orange (Map p402; Rte de Koulikoro; per hr CFA1000; 8am-10pm Mon-Fri, 9am-10pm Sat)

Medical Services

Clinique Pasteur (off Map p402; 2029 1010; ACI2000; 24 hr) West of town, this is Mali's best hospital for African diseases, emergencies and other consultations; it has its own labs and handles insurance claims.

Money

Banque Atlantique (off Map p402; Rte de Hamdalaye-Lafiabougou) *May* do cash advances on MasterCard.

Banque de Développement du Mali (BDM) Ave Modibo Keïta (**Map p404**) Rue de la Cathédrale (**Map p404** Rue Achkhabad (**Map p402**) Exchanges cash and does cash advances on Visa card; most branches also have a Visa-enabled ATM.

Ecobank (Blvd 22 Octobre **Map p404**; cnr Blvd du Peuple & Rue Famolo Coulibaly **Map p404**) Changes travellers cheques and euros and US dollars in cash.

Post

Main post office (Map p404; Rue Karamoko Diaby)

Tam Courrier Express (off Map p402; 2029 9152; yvesbko@yahoo.fr; ACI2000 Hamdallaye) Local representatives for UPS.

Tourist Information

Office Malien du Tourisme et de l'Hôtellerie (Omatho; Map p404; 2023 6450; www.tourisme.gov.ml, www.officetourisme-mali.com; Rue Mohammed V)

Travel Agencies

AIR TICKETS

ESF (Map p404; 2022 5144; ankata@esftravel; Hôtel de l'Amitie, Ave de la Marne; 8am-12.30pm & 2-5pm Mon-Fri, 8am-noon Sat)

TOURS

Tara Africa Tours (off Map p402; 2028 7091; www.tara-africatours.com; Baco Djicoroni) Dutch-Dogon-run agency.

Toguna Adventure Tours (off Map p402; /fax 2029 5366; www.togunaadventuretours.com; ACI2000) American-Malian-run Toguna is extremely professional.

Visa Extensions

Visa extensions are processed in 24 hours at Immigration & Sûreté Nationale (Map p402), located 200m northwest of Rond-Point de l'Unité Africaine. For more information on visas, see p424.

DANGERS & ANNOYANCES

Bamako is largely safe, although, like any city, it has its share of pickpockets and bag snatchers, so take the normal security precautions and never carry valuables. Bamako train station, the trains themselves and Rue Baba Diarra are popular haunts for thieves, especially at night. The streets around Sq Lumumba (especially close to the river) should be avoided after dark.

SIGHTS

The **Musée National** (National Museum; Map p402; 2022 3486; Ave de la Liberté; admission CFA2500, guide CFA3000; 9am-6pm Tue-Sun), a 10-minute walk north of the centre, is outstanding. Its permanent collection includes stunning textiles, masks, statues and archaeological artefacts. The expansive grounds have scale models of Mali's major architectural landmarks. There's an excellent French-language bookshop and a good restaurant (African Grill; see p405).

The mother of all Bamako markets is the **Grand Marché** (Map p404), a warren of streets overtaken by traders of food, clothing and household goods. The **fetish stalls** (Map p404; Blvd du Peuple), near the Maison des Artisans, offer up a stomach-turning array of bones, skins, dried chameleons and rotting monkey heads.

COURSES

Want to learn how to play the *kora* from Toumani Diabaté, the world's undisputed king of the *kora*? His **Mandinka Kora Production** (off Map p402; dtoumani@hotmail.com; Rue 506, Porte 322, Badialam III) organises classes (€10 per hour) that run for just a few hours or a few weeks. If Toumani's in town and not on tour (which he often is), he may be your teacher. If he's not, one of his well-trained professionals will take over. This is also the premier *kora*-making workshop in Mali.

SLEEPING

L'Auberge Lafia (Map p404; 7636 6894; bocoume@yahoo.fr; Rue 367, Bamako Coura; dm CFA5000, d with fan from CFA10,000) As far as cheapies go, the simple, clean rooms here, with mosquito nets, are excellent. The sleeping quarters are arranged around a bare courtyard that has the feel of an African family compound.

Massy House (off Map p402; 6676 3155; www.malifantasytours.com, in French; Rue 434, Porte 144, off Rte de Koulikoro, Boulkassoumbougou; roof mattress CFA2500, s CFA5000-18,000, d CFA8000-24,000) Run by the super-friendly Massy, who is a mine of information

MALI

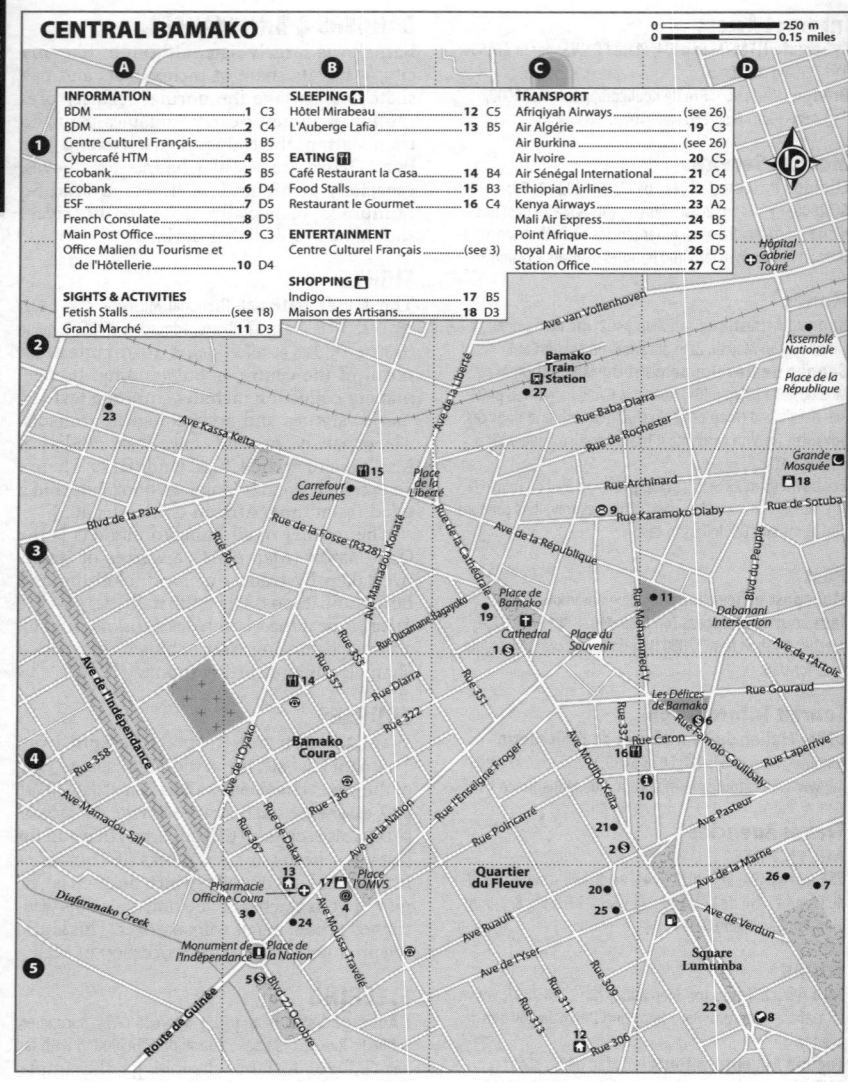

CENTRAL BAMAKO

0 ————— 250 m
0 ————— 0.15 miles

INFORMATION
BDM	1	C3
BDM	2	C4
Centre Culturel Français	3	B5
Cybercafé HTM	4	B5
Ecobank	5	B5
Ecobank	6	D4
ESF	7	D5
French Consulate	8	D5
Main Post Office	9	C3
Office Malien du Tourisme et de l'Hôtellerie	10	D4

SIGHTS & ACTIVITIES
Fetish Stalls	(see 18)	
Grand Marché	11	D3

SLEEPING
Hôtel Mirabeau	12	C5
L'Auberge Lafia	13	B5

EATING
Café Restaurant la Casa	14	B4
Food Stalls	15	B3
Restaurant le Gourmet	16	C4

ENTERTAINMENT
Centre Culturel Français	(see 3)	

SHOPPING
Indigo	17	B5
Maison des Artisans	18	D3

TRANSPORT
Afriqiyah Airways	(see 26)	
Air Algérie	19	C3
Air Burkina	(see 26)	
Air Ivoire	20	C5
Air Sénégal International	21	C4
Ethiopian Airlines	22	D5
Kenya Airways	23	A2
Mali Air Express	24	B5
Point Afrique	25	C5
Royal Air Maroc	26	D5
Station Office	27	C2

on all things Malian, this *maison d'hôte* is sparklingly clean, friendly and has a lovely African family atmosphere. Ring ahead for help in getting here.

Hôtel Tamana (Map p402; ☎ /fax 2021 3715; www.hoteltamana.com; Rue 216, Hippodrome; dm CFA8500, d incl breakfast with/without bathroom CFA26,000/24,000; ❄ 💻 🅿) This charming French-run hotel

out by the Hippodrome has rooms with understated character, the local staff are among Bamako's friendliest, the bathrooms are immaculate and the leafy garden is a wonderful retreat. There's also a swimming pool. The rooms in the annexe are quieter.

Sarama Hôtel (Map p402; ☎ 2021 0563; www.hotelsarama.com; Rue 220, Niaréla; s/d/ste CFA20,500/26,000/30,500;

⊠ ⊠) Tucked away in the quiet streets of Niaréla, the Sarama sees fewer tourists than it deserves. Rooms are spacious, quiet and attractively furnished. The only downside is the *tiny* swimming pool.

Le Loft (Map p402; ☎ 2021 6690; leloft@orangemali. net; Rue Achkhabad, Niaréla; s/d/ste CFA32,500/36,500/50,500; ⊠ ⊡) Rooms here are light, airy and spacious. Wrought-iron furnishings and European-standard bathrooms set the tone, with the occasional nod to African themes. Good service, satellite TV, double-glazed windows and an excellent restaurant are among the other highlights.

Hôtel Mirabeau (Map p404; ☎ 2023 5318; www. hotelmirabeaubko.net; Rue 311, Quartier du Fleuve; s/d/ste CFA44,000/48,500/60,000; ⊠ ⊡ ⊠) This place is terrific, with some of the most comfortable rooms in Bamako and a more intimate feel than the top-end places. Rooms are large and well appointed, with satellite TV, and there's a pleasant garden and pool. Prices are negotiable.

Libya Hôtel El Farouk (Map p402; ☎ 2023 1830; www. laicohotels.com; Blvd 22 Octobre; s/d/ste from CFA89,000 /99,000/139,000; ⊠ ⊡ ⊠) Opened in 2003, this is Bamako's most atmospheric top-end hotel. The public areas boast African art and the rooms are large, supremely comfortable and have all the bells and whistles, as well as river views.

EATING

Snacks like brochettes (grilled meat pieces on a stick) are cooked on small barbeques all around town. In the centre, try west of Pl de la Liberté, across from Carrefour des Jeunes, where food stalls (Map p404) serve cheap rice and sauce.

Restaurant le Gourmet (Map p404; Rue Caron; meals from CFA750; 🕒 7am-6pm Mon-Sat) This small, simple place, just east of Ave Modibo Keïta, offers only two or three dishes per day (often rice with a stew or sauce). But the atmosphere's pleasant and the clientele is predominantly African.

Café Restaurant la Casa (Map p404; Rue Ousmane Bagayoko; meals from CFA1000; 🕒 lunch & dinner) This chilled backpacker hang-out in the city centre dishes out spaghetti, couscous and ragout dishes with the freshest ingredients. If you want meat, you'll need to order in advance.

Poularco (Map p402; Rte de Bla Bla; panini CFA1500-2300, pizzas CFA3500-7000, mains CFA4500-7000; 🕒 lunch & dinner) Out by the Hippodrome, this Lebanese-run place is terrific for snacks such as panini (the *panini capt pané* for CFA2000 is delicious), sandwiches, salads, *shwarmas* and hamburgers, as well as more substantial grilled dishes.

African Grill (Map p402; Musée National, Ave de la Liberté; starters from CFA2000, mains from CFA4500; 🕒 lunch & dinner Tue-Sun) Located within the tranquil grounds of the Musée National, African Grill is a wonderful place to sample African specialities like *foutou* (sticky yam or plantain paste), *kedjenou* (slowly simmered chicken or fish with peppers and tomatoes) and *poulet yassa* (grilled chicken in onion and lemon sauce).

Pizzeria Da Guido (off Map p402; Rue 250, Porte 320, off Blvd Nelson Mandela, Hippodrome; starters CFA2000-3000, mains CFA4500-7500; 🕒 lunch & dinner Fri-Wed) The friendly Italian owners produce what expats claim to be Bamako's best pasta and pizza, the salads are a delicious meal in themselves and the tiramisu has no equal south of the Mediterranean.

San Toro (Map p402; ☎ 2021 3082; djeneart@afribone. net.ml; Rte de Koulikoro; starters CFA2500, mains CFA4500; 🕒 lunch & dinner) This original place has charmingly African decor and the specialities are quality Malian and regional West African dishes; there's no alcohol. In the evenings from around 8pm (and occasionally at lunch time), there's live *kora* music with *djembe* and *balafon* sometimes thrown in.

Le Campagnard (Map p402; off Rte de Sotuba, starters CFA3200-6000, mains CFA4200-6250; 🕒 6am-11.30pm) Top marks for this place. High-quality French cooking, French wines and a switched-on ambience ensure plenty of regular customers among the expat community. The salad bar (CFA3100) is a nice touch and the wood-fired pizzas are good.

DRINKING

Bla Bla Bar (Map p402; Rte de Bla Bla, Hippodrome; small beers CFA1500) Regulars here lament that it has lost something since being glassed in and blasted with air-con and that prices have soared, but it's still a Bamako institution.

Le Campagnard (Map p402; ☎ 2021 9296; off Rte de Sotuba; small beers CFA1000; 🕒 11am-late) This is the sort of place where South African gold miners rub shoulders with Peace Corps volunteers, which should give some idea of the breadth of its appeal, although it's mainly a foreign crowd. In 1995 *Newsweek* voted this one of the best bars in Africa – it's not *that* good, but it is terrific.

If Bla Bla Bar is too highbrow for you, there are plenty of earthy bars with an exclusively African clientele and outdoor tables between the Bla Bla and Rte de Koulikoro. In addition, some of the nicest places for a drink are Bamako's live music venues, even when no-one's playing; our favourite is Le Diplomate (see Entertainment, below).

ENTERTAINMENT
Live Music
Bamako has some of the best live music in the world. For more information on Mali's musicians, see the boxed text, p399.

Le Diplomate (off Map p402; ☎ 7678 1707; admission free; Rte de Koulikoro) Le Diplomate is one of the best venues in Bamako, with a classy crowd, a sophisticated set-up and great music. Toumani Diabaté and his Symmetric Orchestra play here many Friday nights. When Toumani's not in town, his band still takes the stage.

Wassulu Hôtel (off Map p402; ☎ 2028 7373; Route de l'Aéroport; admission CFA2500) Although she doesn't appear here as often as she used to, Oumou Sangaré sometimes takes to the stage at her hotel at 9pm on Saturday evenings.

Moffou (off Map p402) Located 10km southwest of Pont du Roi, this nightclub, owned by the legendary Salif Keita, is really only worth it (and boy, is it worth it!) on the rare Saturday nights when he's playing.

Centre Culturel Français (Map p404; ☎ 2022 4019; www.ccfbamako.org; Ave de l'Indépendance) The CCF's excellent regular program of events is always worth checking out because all the big names of the Malian music scene make an appearance here at some stage. Details are listed on the website.

Djembe (off Map p402; Lafiabougou; admission CFA2500) This earthy live venue west of the centre may have a seedy feel about it and the sound system is terrible, but it remains one of the best places in Bamako to see live music. It's mostly up-and-coming local bands with a few Guinean groups. This place really rocks on Friday and Saturday nights into the wee small hours.

Nightclubs
Bamako is a party town on the weekends. Clubs don't get going before midnight and close around 6am. Cover charges (CFA5000 to CFA7500) usually only apply on Friday and Saturday nights and include a drink; after that, small beers and soft drinks start at CFA2000

and you'll pay around CFA5000 for spirits. The most popular places are as follows:

Bla Bla Club (off Map p402; off Ave de l'OUA, Badalabougou Est)

Ibiza Club (Map p402; Rte de Koulikoro, Hippodrome)

Le Byblos (Map p402; Rte de Koulikoro, Hippodrome)

Show Biz (off Map p402; Rue 267, Porte 27, Djicoroni Para, ACI2000; ⏰ Tue-Sun)

SHOPPING
Mali Chic (off Map p402; ☎ 2021 2442; malichic06@yahoo.fr; Rue 234, Porte 1528; ⏰ 9am-5pm Mon-Sat) The most innovative and stylish boutique in Mali, Mali Chic has an array of items of the highest quality for sale, such as silver jewellery, masks, statues, textiles, artwork and home furnishings.

Mali K7 (Map p402; ☎ 2021 7508; www.mali-music.com; off Rue 540, Niaréla; ⏰ 7.30am-4.45pm Mon-Fri, 8am-noon Sat) Set up by Ali Farka Touré, this is Mali's most reliable place for original CDs/cassettes, which cost CFA1600/1000. Proceeds go to the artists; there's also a small outlet in the Centre Culturel Français (p401).

Other places selling locally made handicrafts (textiles, in particular) with fixed prices include **Indigo** (Map p404; ☎ 2022 0893; www.indigo.com.ml; Place l'OMVS; ⏰ 9am-6.30pm Mon-Sat), as well as the boutique attached to San Toro (p405).

Traders drive a hard bargain at the **Maison des Artisans** (Map p404; Blvd du Peuple), where you'll find leather goods, jewellery and woodcarvings, and at **Marché N'Golonina** (Map p404).

GETTING THERE & AWAY
Air
Bamako's **Sénou International Airport** (off Map p402; ☎ 6600 7071) serves a number of domestic routes. **Mali Air Express** (MAE; Map p404; ☎ 2023 1465; www.mae-mali.com; Ave de la Nation) flies to Mopti/Sévaré (CFA60,500, twice weekly), Timbuktu (CFA69,500, twice weekly) and Kayes (CFA69,000, three times weekly). **Air CAM** (off Map p402; ☎ 2022 2424; www.camaero.com; Ave Cheick Zayed, Hamdallaye) is generally less reliable but operates services between Bamako and Gao (CFA115,000, once weekly) in addition to serving Mopti, Timbuktu and Kayes.

For airlines operating international flights into Bamako, see p425.

Boat
The big boats depart from Koulikoro, which lies some 50km downstream of Bamako.

For details on the Niger River boat service, see p426.

Bus

Long-distance transport for destinations south of the Niger River leaves from the Sogoniko *gare routière*, 6km south of the city centre (CFA2000 by taxi, CFA150 by *sotrama*). This is home to **Bani** (☎ 2020 6081) and **Bittar** (☎ 2020 1205), among others, with dozens of services heading north along the Bamako–Gao road. Transport for destinations north of the Niger River leaves from the Destination Nord *gare routière* (Map p402; near Place Point G), although some Timbuktu services now leave from the Sogoniko *gare routière*. Sample fares and trip times from Bamaka to various destinations are given in the table below:

Destination	Fare (CFA)	Duration (hr)
Bandiagara	8000	9-11
Hombori	12,000	12-14
Gao	15,000	16-20
Mopti	7500	7-10
Ségou	3000	3
Sikasso	4500	3-4
Timbuktu	15,000	15

Train

Tickets can be bought from the **station office** (Map p404; ☎ 2022 8110) in Bamako's main train station. You should beware of thieves amid the crowds.

Express operates international services on Saturday and Wednesday to Dakar in Senegal (see p425), which also stop in Kayes (2nd-class seat/2nd-class couchette/1st-class seat/1st-class couchette CFA7300/11,500/16,190 /22,190, 12 to 20 hours).

GETTING AROUND

The official rate between the airport and the city centre via private taxi is CFA7500; it should cost you around CFA5000 going the other way.

Most taxis in Bamako are coloured yellow. Those with a 'taxi' sign on the roof are shared, while those without signs are for private hire *(déplacement)* only. The longest journey (such as heading from Sogoniko *gare routière* to Hippodrome) in a private taxi should never cost you more than CFA2000, and the majority of journeys should cost half that.

THE CENTRE

SÉGOU

pop 104,987

Strung out lazily along the riverbank 230km east of Bamako, Ségou carries a wealth of historical associations for the Bambara people (Ségou was the capital of an important Bambara kingdom until the early 19th century) and has enough sights to warrant staying at least a couple of nights.

Information

Association des Guides Segouvienne pour le Tourisme Solidaire (AGSTS; ☎ 7622 8609, 7302 4870; agstsmali@yahoo.fr; Rue 21) Local guides' association with fixed prices on the wall.
BDM (Blvd de l'Indépendance) Changes euros and has a Visa-enabled ATM.
Cybercafé Sotelma (Blvd de l'Indépendance; per hr CFA1000; ☺ 8am-9pm) Internet access.

Sights & Activities

On the riverbank southwest of the centre, a small but interesting **pottery market** is a worthwhile endpoint for a pleasant riverside stroll.

From the waterfront, *pirogues* can take you on river excursions to nearby villages. A good place to organise these trips is AGSTS (see above).

The historic and beautiful mud village of **Ségou Koro** lies 9km upstream, just off the main Ségou–Bamako road. In the 18th century it was the centre of Biton Mamary Coulibaly's Bambara empire; the great man's former palace is being restored. Introduce yourself to the chief, who collects the CFA2500 tourist tax. A guided tour costs CFA15,000 per person, including transport from Ségou.

Two *bogolan* (mud cloth) workshops – **Ndomo** (☎ 2132 2794; www.promali.org/ndomo; Rte de Mopti; guided tours CFA500; ☺ guided tours 8am-2pm daily, shop 8am-5pm daily), around 5km south of the centre on the road to Mopti, and **Galerie Soroble** (☎ 2132 1367; soroblecentre@yahoo.fr; off Blvd El Hadj Omar Tall; guided tours CFA500; ☺ guided tours 2-6pm daily, shop 8am-6pm daily) – run guided tours that take you through the *bogolan* story, design techniques and have good (fixed price) shops.

Festivals & Events

First held in 2005, Ségou's **Festival sur le Niger** (☎ 2132 1804; www.festivalsegou.org; 3-day festival pass €100), in late January or early February, has evolved into one of West Africa's premier music and cultural festivals.

Sleeping

Soleil de Minuit (☎ 2132 1505; soleildeminuitsegou@gmail.com; cnr Rue 21 & Blvd El Hadj Omar Tall; roof mattress CFA4000, s/d with fan from CFA12,500/15,000, d with air-con from CFA20,000; ❄) Simple rooms are the order of the day at this place, and they're the cheapest beds you'll find in the heart of town.

Hôtel le Djoliba (☎ /fax 2132 1572; www.segou-hotel-djoliba.com; cnr Rue 21 & Blvd El Hadj Omar Tall; s/d from CFA21,500/24,500; ❄) You can't get any more central than this well-run place not far from the riverbank. The rooms are large and attractive and the service is good.

Espace Bajidala (Chez Michel; ☎ 2132 3437; www.bajidala.com; Rue 529, Quartier Administratif; d with air-con CFA24,000, breakfast CFA4000; ❄) Located 3km southwest of the town centre, Espace Bajidala is wonderful. The rooms, arrayed around a verdant garden with contemporary art installations, are large and filled with character, and the riverside location is quiet and picturesque.

Eating & Drinking

Alphabet Restaurant (☎ 6676 2076; Place de Monzon; meals CFA1000-5000; ❧ 6pm-late) Alphabet gets rave reviews from travellers for its good food and friendly atmosphere. Dishes include some vegetarian choices and a host of river fish beyond the usual *capitaine*.

Espace Kora (☎ 2132 0950; Rue 21; mains CFA1500-5000; ❧ 7.30am-late) Although better known as a live music venue (see Entertainment, below), Espace Kora serves reasonable food in a lovely garden setting. The atmosphere is great in the evening.

Restaurant de l'Esplanade (☎ 2132 0127; Quai Ousmane Djiri; starters from CFA1800, pizza from CFA5000, pasta from CFA4800) An Italian host who knows his pizza plus an excellent location right by the water's edge make a fantastic combination. It's not cheap, but there's no better pizza in Mali.

Entertainment

For live music, **Espace Kora** (Rue 21; ❧ live music from 9pm Thu-Sun) is the best venue in town, with lively local bands and a terrific setting. Also good is **Alphabet Restaurant** (Place de Monzon; ❧ live music from 9pm) with live acts most nights. At both places, admission is free but you're expected to buy a drink.

Getting There & Away

The only reputable bus company with a handy central location is **Bittar** (☎ 7642 1673; off Blvd de l'Indépendance), which has services to Bamako (CFA3000, six to seven daily, three hours), Mopti (CFA5000, two daily, five to six hours), Sikasso (CFA4500, four hours) and to Bobo-Dioulasso (CFA8000) and Ouagadougou (CFA15,000) in Burkina Faso. Otherwise, most other companies leave from the *gare routière*, 3km south of town.

TERIYA BUGU

Ecotourism projects are few and far between in Mali, but **Teriya Bugu** (☎ 2133 1000; www.tb-mali.com; guided visit CFA2500, dm CFA5000, d with fan/air-con CFA17,500/25,000, meals from CFA3000; ❄), about 30km off the main highway, is a slice of Malian paradise. Teriya Bugu employs 60 locals and supports 7000 people in 30 surrounding villages. Self-sufficiency is the aim (Teriya Bugu produces 80% of its own food), with most power generated by solar energy and locally produced biofuels. There are also 250,000 eucalyptus trees and thousands of water pumps across the region, and the project supports schools, health clinics and microcredit schemes in nearby villages.

If you stay overnight, there are delightful, large rooms and a restaurant just back from the riverbank. It's worth taking the guided tour around the project; they also organise *pinasse*-and-picnic excursions (from CFA5000 per person).

You'll need your own vehicle to get to Teriya Bugu, with two unpaved roads signposted off the main Ségou–Sévaré highway.

DJENNÉ

pop 23,790

Djenné's Unesco World Heritage–listed old town, which sits on an island in the Bani River, is one of our favourite places in Mali, not to mention one of West Africa's oldest towns.

Information

Visitors to Djenné must pay a CFA1000 tourist tax per person; it's collected at the checkpoint at the Djenné turn-off, soon after leaving the Bamako–Mopti road.

BIM (opposite Restaurant Kita Kouraou) Changes euros only.
Bureau de Guides (☎ 7618 1698; next to Restaurant le Fleuve)
Omatho (Office Malien du Tourisme et de l'Hôtellerie; ☎ 2142 1429; ❧ 8am-4pm Mon-Fri) Helpful tourist

office with a good photocopied map (CFA100) and a list of guides.

Sights

Djenné's incomparable **Grande Mosquée** (Great Mosque) – the largest mud-built structure in the world – is like an apparition from a child's imagination and provides Djenné with a backdrop to its huge, lively and colourful **Monday market**. You will find some outstanding views of the mosque from the roofs of surrounding houses (CFA500) or the Petit Marché.

On a stroll through the dusty streets, you'll pass numerous signposts to sights from Djenné's days as a renowned centre of Islamic scholarship. With the help of a guide, you can also see the beautiful **house of the traditional chief**.

About 3km from Djenné, the low-slung ruin of **Jenné-Jeno** dates back to about 300 BC and is one of the oldest archaeological sites in West Africa.

Sleeping & Eating

Book ahead if you're coming on Sunday and Monday nights during the high season.

Le Campement (☎ 2142 0497; campdjenne@afribone. net.ml; roof mattress CFA4000; dm CFA5000; s CFA10,000-20,000, d CFA12,500-25,000, meals from CFA4000; 🍴) This handily located place has dozens of rooms across a wide price range and a large open-air restaurant. The generally clean and tidy rooms have the bare essentials and nothing more.

Djenné-Djenno (☎ 7933 1526; www.hoteldjenne djenno.com; d/ste with air-con CFA25,000/35,000, meals CFA6500; 🍴) Everything about this place carries a designer touch, from the beautifully decorated rooms to the traditional architectural features in the rooms and public areas. It's an oasis, just beyond the city but close enough to get there on foot.

Restaurant le Fleuve (dishes CFA1250-3000; 🕑 6am-10pm) For simple Malian dishes such as *riz sauce*, this place is good; it also serves *tion-tion* (dried onions, tomato and local spices served with rice and chicken or meat), *wig-ila* (sun-dried dumplings dipped in a meat sauce) and pigeon.

Shopping

Chez Tanti – Association des Femmes de Semani (☎ 7928 3650; 🕑 7am-10pm) On your left just after crossing the main bridge into Djenné,

Chez Tanti is run by 'Tanti Bogolan', who can arrange *bogolan* courses.

Pama Sinatoa (☎ 7614 3259; almamydiaka@yahoo. fr; 🕑 6am-9pm) The longest-established of the workshops and with perhaps the largest selection, Pama Sinatoa can arrange courses in *bogolan* design from a negotiable CFA12,500/40,000 per day/week.

Getting There & Away

When the Bani River is high enough (usually from July to December), it's possible to arrive by public *pinasse* (CFA4000) from Mopti.

There's usually one shared taxi (CFA2500) or minibus (CFA2250) per day from the Sévaré taxi park in Mopti; get there at 6am and be prepared to wait. Otherwise, you'll need to get transport to the Djenné–Mopti turn-off on the Bamako–Sévaré highway (ask for the Carrefour de Djenné), 30km from Djenné, from where a shared/private taxi will cost CFA1500/15,000.

The short ferry crossing just before Djenné costs from CFA500 to CFA2000, depending on the vehicle size and the hour.

MOPTI
pop 103,428

Boats from Mopti, one of West Africa's largest river ports, go to Timbuktu, and Mopti serves as a gateway for Dogon Country. As a result, the city swarms with guides and hangers-on and every conversation can seem to have an ulterior motive. But Mopti's port is Mali's most lively, its recently restored mosque is beautiful and there are a couple of terrific hotels here. If it all gets too much, stay in Sévaré, 12km away, and just come into Mopti when you have to.

Information

Association des Guides Dogon de Mopti (Dogon Vision; ☎ 7612 2387, 7622 5277; assodogonvision@yahoo.fr)

BDM (off Ave de l'Indépendance) A visa-enabled ATM.

Bureau de Change (off Ave de l'Indépendance) Opposite the entrance to BDM; changes euros and US dollars.

Bureau Régional du Tourisme (Omatho; ☎ 2143 0506; moptitourisme@hotmail.com; Blvd l'Indépendance) Located 200m north of Hôtel Kanaga.

Commissariat de Police & Sûreté (Rte de Sévaré; 🕑 7.30am-5pm Mon-Fri, to noon Sat & Sun) One-month visa extensions cost CFA5000; you'll need two photos and extensions take about 15 minutes. It's best to come in the morning.

MALI

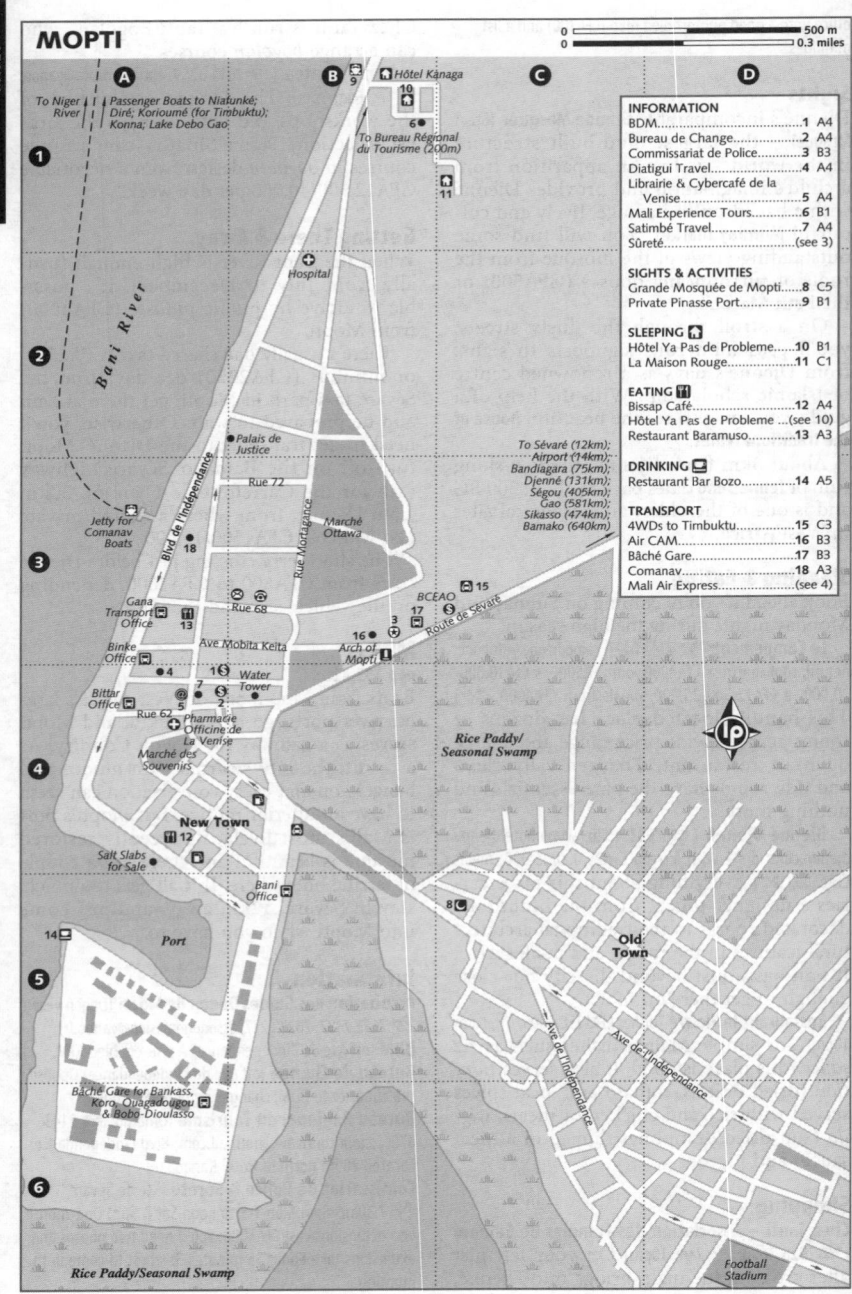

MOPTI

0 — 500 m
0 — 0.3 miles

INFORMATION

BDM	1 A4
Bureau de Change	2 A4
Commissariat de Police	3 B3
Diatigui Travel	4 A4
Librairie & Cybercafé de la Venise	5 A4
Mali Experience Tours	6 B1
Satimbé Travel	7 A4
Sûreté	(see 3)

SIGHTS & ACTIVITIES

Grande Mosquée de Mopti	8 C5
Private Pinasse Port	9 B1

SLEEPING

Hôtel Ya Pas de Probleme	10 B1
La Maison Rouge	11 C1

EATING

Bissap Café	12 A4
Hôtel Ya Pas de Probleme	(see 10)
Restaurant Baramuso	13 A3

DRINKING

Restaurant Bar Bozo	14 A5

TRANSPORT

4WDs to Timbuktu	15 C3
Air CAM	16 B3
Bâché Gare	17 B3
Comanav	18 A3
Mali Air Express	(see 4)

To Niger River
Passenger Boats to Niafunké; Diré; Korioumé (for Timbuktu); Konna; Lake Debo Gao

Hôtel Kanaga

To Bureau Régional du Tourisme (200m)

Bani River

Hospital

Jetty for Comanav Boats

Palais de Justice

Rue 72

Bivd de l'Indépendance

Rue Mortagnance

Marché Ottawa

To Sévaré (12km);
Airport (14km);
Bandiagara (75km);
Djenné (131km);
Ségou (405km);
Gao (581km);
Sikasso (474km);
Bamako (640km)

BCEAO

Gana Transport Office

Rue 68

Binke Office

Ave Mobita Keita

Bittar Office

Arch of Mopti

Rue 62

Water Tower

Pharmacie Officine de la Venise

Marché des Souvenirs

Route de Sévaré

Rice Paddy/Seasonal Swamp

New Town

Salt Slabs for Sale

Bani Office

Port

Old Town

Bâché Gare for Bankass, Koro, Ouagadougou & Bobo-Dioulasso

Ave de l'Indépendance

Ave de l'Indépendance

Rice Paddy/Seasonal Swamp

Football Stadium

Librairie & Cybercafé de la Venise (Ave de l'Indépendance; per hr CFA1000; ✆ 8am-1pm & 4-8pm Mon-Sat)

Sights & Activities

In Mopti's **port** you'll see slabs of salt from Timbuktu, dried fish, firewood, pottery, goats, chickens and a wonderful cast of characters. Boat building happens next to Restaurant Bar Bozo (right).

The classic Sahel-style **Grande Mosquée de Mopti** (Great Mosque of Mopti; Ave de l'Indépendance) was built in 1933 and beautifully restored in 2007 by the Aga Khan Development Network's Historic Cities Programme (www.akdn.org/aktc_hcp_mali.asp?type=p). The mosque is off-limits to non-Muslims, but CFA500 to CFA1000 can buy you a view from a nearby rooftop.

Sleeping

Hôtel Ya Pas de Probleme (✆ 2143 1041; www.yapasd eprobleme.com; off Blvd de l'Indépendance; roof mattress CFA4000, dm CFA5000, s CFA10,000-22,000, d CFA13,000-25,000; ✖ 🖳 🛋) A delightful French-Dogon-run place, Ya Pas de Probleme is one of Mopti's best places to stay, with tastefully decorated rooms, an intimate and homely atmosphere and something for everyone regardless of your budget. In addition to the spacious rooms, the swimming pool is one of Mali's best and the rooftop bar-restaurant is very, very cool.

La Maison Rouge (✆ 2143 1402; www.lesmaisons dumali.com; off Blvd de l'Indépendance; s/d/ste with aircon CFA30,000/35,000/60,000, dinner CFA9000; ✖ 🖳) Architecturally, this place is stunning and the rooms are some of the most beautiful in all of Mali. Our only complaint? Service could be friendlier and, as a result, the whole place lacks warmth.

Eating & Drinking

Restaurant Baramuso (Rue 68; meals from CFA500; ✆ lunch & dinner) This is the place for a hearty cheap meal (think rice in all its manifestations) in the town centre.

Bissap Café (✆ 2143 1353; www.bissapcafe.com; Blvd de l'Indépendance; mains CFA2800-5800; ✆ 7am-midnight) At last Mopti's port area has a place where you can eat great food, find a vantage point to watch all the comings and goings and enjoy a laid-back atmosphere. The food (a mix of African dishes, pizza and fusion fare) is terrific and the back garden and salon is as agreeable as the roof.

Hotel Ya Pas de Problem (✆ 2143 1041; www.ya pasdeprobleme.com; off Blvd de l'Indépendance; meals from CFA4000) The bar-restaurant atop the hotel of the same name serves terrific food and the chilled atmosphere is ideal for a drink.

Restaurant Bar Bozo (✆ 2143 0246; ✆ 6am-11pm) Bar Bozo, superbly located at the mouth of Mopti harbour, is *the* place to nurse whatever beverage they *do* have (supplies often run low) as the sun nears the horizon.

Getting There & Away
AIR

The airport is about 2km southeast of Sévaré and 14km from Mopti. **Mali Air Express** (MAE; ✆ 2143 0273; www.mae-mali.com; Diatigui Travel, Rue de la Pâtisserie Dogon) has two weekly flights to/from Bamako (CFA60,500) and Timbuktu (CFA69,500). Less reliably, **Air CAM** (✆ 7631 7401; www.camaero.com; Hôtel Campement Mopti, next to Arch of Mopti) has three weekly flights to Bamako (CFA65,500) and Timbuktu (CFA69,560).

A private taxi from Mopti to the airport costs at least CFA6000.

BOAT

Comanav (✆ 2143 0006; Blvd de l'Indépendance) ferries head for Korioumé (Timbuktu's port) by boat from July or August to December, although tickets are scarce as this is the busiest sector on the boat's itinerary. For details, see p426.

For details on travelling by *pirogue* or *pinasse*, see the boxed text, p412.

BUS & BUSH TAXI

Although some buses continue as far as (and originate in) Mopti, Sévaré is the main transport hub for the region (see p412).

To Timbuktu (CFA12,500 to CFA15,000, six to eight hours on a good day), 4WDs leave most mornings from 9am from behind the *bâché gare*. There are 11 or 12 people to a car.

SÉVARÉ

This bustling town along the main highway has not a single sight worth seeing, but it's more relaxed than its more famous neighbour, and has terrific places to stay and transport connections. Bandiagara and Dogon Country are just 63km away.

Maison des Arts (✆ 2142 0853; www.maisondesarts. co.uk; Rue 106, Porte 377, Banguetaba Sect III; dm CFA8000, s CFA12,000-20,000, d CFA16,000-25,000, meals CFA3000-4000; ✖) Arrayed around a traditional mud-walled compound, and watched over by delightful

MALI

BOAT TRIPS ON THE NIGER

Although many travellers opt for a sunset boat excursion (motorised *pinasse* CFA25,000, non-motorised *pirogue* CFA5000), the most rewarding boat trip is the memorable three-day journey downriver from Mopti to Korioumé (Timbuktu's port).

To charter a boat to Timbuktu that comfortably seats 10 people, expect to pay CFA375,000 to CFA400,000; petrol is included and food should be for a small group. Otherwise, count on CFA15,000 per person for food for three days. You could try negotiating with the wily boat owners, but you're likely to fare better if you make the arrangements through the Bureau Régional du Tourisme (p409) or through **Diatigui Travel** (☎ /fax 2143 0273; www.diatiguitravel.com, in French; Rue de la Pâtisserie Dogon), **Mali Experience Tours** (☎ 2143 1409; www.maliexperience.com; off Blvd de l'Indépendance), or **Satimbé Travel** (☎ 2143 0791; www.satimbetravel.com, in French; Ave de l'Indépendance).

Getting a ride on a *pinasse transporteur* (cargo *pinasse*) or smaller *pinasse publique* (public *pinasse*) is another option. Prices should be CFA5000 for a tiny corner of downstairs deck space, or CFA10,000 on the roof, but you'll need to bargain hard and bring your own food. These chartered *pinasses* leave from the private *pinasse* port.

Anglo-Dogon hosts, Maison des Arts is, quite simply, a lovely place. The spacious but un-elaborated rooms come with mosquito nets, comfy mattresses, occasional African handicrafts and cold showers.

Hôtel Ambedjele (☎ 2142 1031; www.ambedjele hotel.com; Rte de Mopti; d/ste CFA39,500/55,000, meals CFA7500; ❄ ▢ ▨) Styled like a Dogon village, just off the road between Mopti and Sévaré, this charming Spanish-run place has expansive gardens, a rock pool for swimming and bungalows shaped like Dogon granaries. The restaurant (Spanish flair wedded to African flavours) is one of Mali's best.

Getting There & Away

AIR

For details about flights between Sévaré/Mopti and other Malian towns, see p411.

BUS

Sévaré is on a busy transport route, with plenty of transport leaving from the **gare routière** (Rte de Bandiagara). Represented here are **Bani Transport** (☎ 6672 6663), **Sonef** (☎ 6669 1149) and **Gana Transport** (☎ 7629 5076). Major destinations include Bamako (CFA7500, eight to 10 hours), Ségou (CFA5000, five to six hours), Hombori (CFA5000, five to six hours) and Gao (CFA7500, nine to 12 hours).

Transport to Dogon Country leaves from outside the *gare routière* along the Rte de Bandiagara. Occasional minibuses go to Bandiagara (minibus/shared taxi CFA1500/1600, one hour), Bankass (minibus/shared taxi CFA3000/3500, two hours) and, even less frequently, Koro (minibus/shared taxi CFA3500/4000, three hours). There's more traffic on the market days in Bandiagara (Monday and Friday) and Bankass (Tuesday).

Bâchés (pick-up trucks) head to/from Mopti (CFA225) from close to the post office.

DOGON COUNTRY

Mali's Dogon Country (Pays Dogon in French) is a world apart. Here, unique houses and granaries cling to the massive escarpment known as the Falaise de Bandiagara, which extends some 150km to the east of Mopti and is 500m high around Tireli and Ireli. But more than this, a journey through Dogon Country takes you through a fascinating animist culture with traditions and cosmology as elaborate as any in Africa.

October or November to February is the best time to trek, with daytime temperatures close to 30°C. From March to May, it's fiercely hot, though early in the morning it's fine for walking. June to September is the rainy season, but downpours are short, the air is clear and the waterfalls and flowers are spectacular.

DOGON GATEWAYS
Bandiagara
pop 6853

This small, dusty town lies 63km east of Sévaré, and about 20km from the edge of the Falaise de Bandiagara. It's a place to arrange a guide – we recommend **Association Tamakadi** (☎ 2144 2053; http://tamakadi.wordpress.com; Rte de Sévaré, next to Palais Agibou Tall; ◷ 7.30am-1pm &

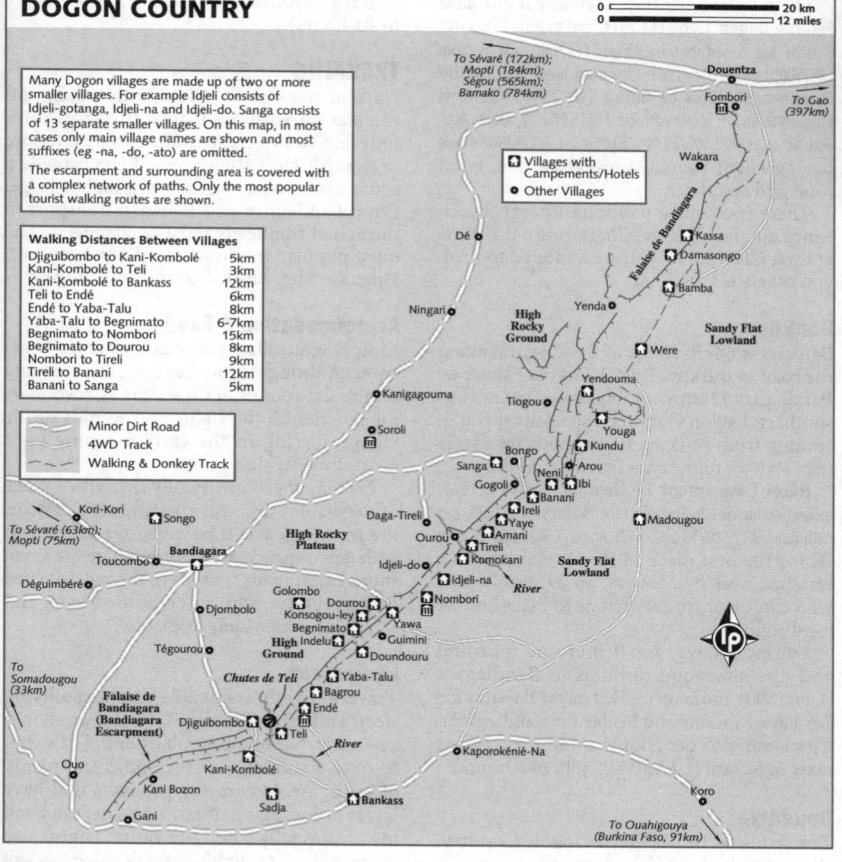

DOGON COUNTRY

Many Dogon villages are made up of two or more smaller villages. For example Idjeli consists of Idjeli-gotanga, Idjeli-na and Idjeli-do. Sanga consists of 13 separate smaller villages. On this map, in most cases only main village names are shown and most suffixes (eg -na, -do, -ato) are omitted.

The escarpment and surrounding area is covered with a complex network of paths. Only the most popular tourist walking routes are shown.

Villages with Campements/Hotels
Other Villages

Walking Distances Between Villages

Djiguibombo to Kani-Kombolé	5km
Kani-Kombolé to Teli	3km
Kani-Kombolé to Bankass	12km
Teli to Endé	6km
Endé to Yaba-Talu	8km
Yaba-Talu to Begnimato	6-7km
Begnimato to Nombori	15km
Begnimato to Dourou	8km
Nombori to Tireli	9km
Tireli to Banani	12km
Banani to Sanga	5km

Minor Dirt Road
4WD Track
Walking & Donkey Track

4-8pm) – and check your email at **Cybercafé Clic** (Rte de Djiguibombo; per hr CFA1000; 8.30am-1pm & 3-6pm Mon-Fri, 9am-3pm Sat).

Auberge Kansaye (7322 9992, 6684 2456; kansaye bouba@yahoo.fr; roof mattress & dm CFA3000, s/d with fan & without bathroom CFA5000/8000, meals from CFA1500) has a chilled ambience and basic rooms by the riverbank. **Le Kambary** (Cheval Blanc; /fax 2144 2388; www.kambary.com; s CFA5000-25,000, d CFA8000-28,000, meals CFA5000-8500;) and **Hôtel de la Falaise** (2144 2128; contact@hotel-lafalaise-mali. com; roof mattress CFA1500, dm CFA4000, s CFA14,000-22,500, d CFA16,000-25,000, meals CFA5500;) offer high levels of comfort and the best restaurants.

Of the cheap restaurants, **La Fraternité** (7601 0779; Rte de Sévaré; snacks CFA1200, mains CFA1700-2750; 7am-midnight) is probably the

pick, with a friendly Nigerian owner and a range of dishes.

Most transport leaves Bandiagara around 7am or 5pm. There are four daily departures to Sévaré/Mopti (minibus/shared taxi CFA1500/1600), and two to Bankass (CFA1500).

Sanga

Sanga (also written 'Sangha'), 44km east of Bandiagara and close to the top of the escarpment, is one of the largest Dogon villages in the region. Of particular interest is the Ogol Da section, which is full of temples, fetishes and shrines. However, it's a favourite of tour groups and has become quite touristy in recent years.

Of the places to stay, **Campement Gîte de la Femme Dogon** (☎ 2144 2013; roof mattress CFA2500, d with fan & without bathroom CFA7000, meals from CFA2500) is simple, friendly and well run, while **Campement-Hôtel La Guina** (☎ 2144 2028; hotel sangha@yahoo.fr; s/d/tr with fan CFA15,000/20,000/25,000, with air-con CFA22,500/25,000/30,000, meals CFA2500-4000) has excellent rooms, a lovely garden, good food and cold beer.

There's no regular public transport between Sanga and Bandiagara. Chartering a taxi costs at least CFA15,000; getting a moped to drop you off costs CFA7500.

Bankass

Bankass is 64km south of Bandiagara, along the road to Burkina Faso. With the Falaise de Bandiagara 12km away, it's a good gateway to southern Dogon Country, especially if you're coming from Burkina Faso. **Association Bandia** (☎ 7448 0965) represents Bankass' guides.

Hôtel Campement Le Nommo (☎ 7448 0965; moussaouedrago1@yahoo.fr; roof mattress CFA2500, s/d with fan CFA12,500/16,000, with air-con CFA22,500/25,000; 🐕) is the best place to stay in Bankass. It's watched over by Moussa, an agreeable host who can organise excursions to little-known local sights.

On most days, you'll find one morning and one afternoon minibus to Bandiagara (CFA1500), more on market days (Tuesday for Bankass, Monday and Friday for Bandiagara). There are also occasional minibuses/shared taxis to Sévaré (CFA3000/3500, two hours).

Douentza

The gateway to northern Dogon Country, Douentza, has good places to stay.

Auberge Gourma (☎ 2145 2054; roof mattress CFA2500, s/d with fan & without bathroom CFA4000/8000, meals CFA4500) has simple rooms and a reasonable restaurant, while its sister property next door, **Campement Dogon Adventures** (☎ 2145 2094; www.dogon-adventures-mali.com; roof mattress CFA3000, s/d from CFA8000/10,000; 🐕), is marginally better. **Campement Hogon** (☎ 7943 3104; hogondtza1@yahoo.fr; camping CFA2500, Fulani tent site CFA7500, d without bathroom & with fan/air-con CFA7500/15,000; 🐕) has a more intimate feel than many other places in Douentza, while **Campement Chez Jérôme** (☎ 2145 2052; half-board per person CFA15,000) has attractive, airy tents and wonderful food.

Buses pass through Douentza en route between Sévaré (CFA3000, three hours) and Gao (CFA6000, seven hours), with an occa-sional service to Timbuktu (CFA8000, five to six hours).

TREKKING

Ancient tracks link village with village and the plateau with the plains. In places carefully laid stones create staircases up a fissure in the cliff face; elsewhere ladders provide a route over a chasm or up to a higher ledge. From Bandiagara and Bankass, transport to the actual trailheads must be arranged. The most popular trailheads are Kani-Kombolé, Djiguibombo, Endé, Dourou and Sanga.

Accommodation & Food

Most Dogon villages have at least one *campement*. Although some have rooms, sleeping on the flat roof under the stars is a wonderful experience: the sights and sounds of the village stirring in the early-morning light are unforgettable.

Evening meals are usually rice with a sauce of vegetables or meat (usually chicken). In the morning, you'll be given tea and bread with jam or processed cheese. There are small shops catering for tourists in the most-visited Dogon villages, while beer, bottled water and soft drinks are widely available.

Equipment

Travel as lightly as possible because paths are steep and sandy in places. Footwear should be sturdy, but boots aren't essential. It's vital to have a sunhat, a water bottle and plenty of water. Avoid carrying products that have layers of packaging. A mosquito net is a good idea, especially after the rains. Nights are warm, although a lightweight sleeping bag will keep off the predawn chill from November to February. Dogon villages are dark at night, so a torch (flashlight) is useful, and you'll need toilet paper. Wearing shorts to below the knee for trekking is OK, although women will feel more comfortable wearing a skirt or long trousers when staying in a village. Women should not expose their shoulders.

Costs

We recommend negotiating an all-inclusive fee with your guide – such a fee will include everything except water, drinks, souvenirs and masked dance ceremonies. When agreeing the fee with your guide, make sure you discuss everything, from the above fees to who'll be paying for the guide's food and

---

FINDING A GOOD DOGON GUIDE

Finding a Dogon guide is easy, but finding a good one is more challenging. For a start, your guide to Dogon Country should be a Dogon – non-Dogon guides are unlikely to speak Dogon or know anything about the culture or local paths, which can lead to problems. Your guide should also be an accredited guide able to produce the official blue or yellow guiding card (see the boxed text, p401) and recommendations from other travellers. Places for finding a good Dogon guide include Bureau Régional du Tourisme (p409) and Association des Guides Dogon de Mopti (Dogon Vision; p409), both in Mopti, and Association Tamakadi (p412) in Bandiagara.

---

lodging (most get free food and lodging in the *campements*).

Standard costs include the following:

Item	Cost (CFA)
Breakfast	1000
Lunch or dinner with/without meat	3000/2000
Guide per day per person all inclusive (group of 1-3 people)	20,000-22,500
Guide per day per person all inclusive (group of 4 or more)	15,000-17,500
Porter per day	2500
Village tourist tax per person (not applicable if just passing through)	500-1000
Rooftop mattress in village *campement*	1500-2000
Room in village *campement*	4000
Masked dance ceremony (Nombori, Begnimato)	40,000
Masked dance ceremony (Tireli)	60,000
Masked dance ceremony (Sanga)	70,000
1.5L of bottled water	CFA1000-1500
Soft drink	CFA1000

The village tourist tax should allow you to take photos of houses and other buildings (but *not* people, unless you get their permission).

Your only other cost is reaching the escarpment, although some guides will include this in their price. From Bandiagara, a taxi to any of the local trailheads will cost CFA15,000 to CFA20,000 (one way). From Bankass to the escarpment at Endé or Kani-Kombolé (12km) by horse and cart costs around CFA5000.

Guides

Guides are essential in Dogon Country. Ideally a guide will be your translator, fixer (for accommodation and food) and verbal guidebook, not to mention a window onto the Dogon world. Without one you'll miss many points of interest, and could genuinely offend the Dogon villagers by unwittingly stumbling across a sacred site. All guides speak French and some speak English.

Dangers & Annoyances

We have received isolated reports of travellers having things stolen from their luggage when left on the roofs of *campements*. Stow your valuables away and securely lock your bag when you go off to explore the villages and carry money, all important documents and other valuables with you at all times.

Trekking Routes

For longer treks than those described below, any of the routes can be extended or combined.

DAY TREKS

If you are very short of time, there are three circular walks from Sanga, aimed at tour groups on tight schedules. The Petit Tour (7km) goes to Gogoli, the Moyen Tour (10km) goes to Gogoli and Banani, and the Grand Tour (15km) goes to Gogoli, Banani and Ireli.

Another option in southern Dogon Country is to trek Djiguibombo to Kani-Kombolé and on to Teli (8km), but you'll need transport from/to Bandiagara.

TWO DAYS

One 23km-trek begins with a lift from Bandiagara to Kani-Kombolé, then a trek to Teli, Endé (overnight), Yaba-Talu and Begnimato, before meeting a pre-arranged car at Dourou back to Bandiagara.

Another option (16km) is to start from Bankass, take a car or horse-cart to Kani-Kombolé, then walk to Teli and sleep in Endé. The next morning, walk to Bagrou, then to Yaba-Talu to meet your transport back to Bankass. Another possibility from Bankass is a short but rewarding circuit to Kani-Kombolé through Teli to Endé (spending the night at either) and then back (18km).

One final choice (23km) is to start in Sanga, climb down to Banani and continue through Ireli and Amani, and sleep in Tireli. The next morning, climb up to Daga-Tireli to get your car back to Sanga.

MALI

THREE TO FOUR DAYS
For a good three-day trek (33km) from Bandiagara, start with a lift to Djiguibombo, then continue by car to Kani-Kombolé to commence the trek. Continue on to Teli, then spend the night in Endé. The next day takes you to Yaba-Talu, then up to Indelu and on to sleep in Begnimato. On the third day, trek to Konsogou-ley for nice views of the plain, then on to Dourou to take a car back to Bandiagara.

In the less-touristed northern Dogon Country, walk from Sanga to Yendouma (a gentle, 18km downhill walk). The next morning, hike the three Youga villages, then sleep in Kundu. On your third day, hike up to the top of the escarpment, down through Arou and on to sleep in Ibi or Banani. On the fourth day, climb back up to Sanga (53km in total).

An excellent three- or four-day alternative (30km) is to start from Bandiagara, take transport to Dourou, then trek down the escarpment to Nombori (first night), head northeast to Tireli (second night), on to Ireli (third night), then up the escarpment to Sanga.

THE NORTH & EAST

TIMBUKTU
pop 35,638
Timbuktu (Tombouctou in French), that most rhythmical of African names, has for centuries been synonymous with Africa's mysterious inaccessibility, with an end-of-

the-earth allure. After it was 'discovered' by Western explorers, Timbuktu became a byword for the West's disappointment with Africa. Even today, Timbuktu is a shadow of its formerly grand self, existing as a sprawl of low, often shabby, flat-roofed buildings and streets filled with sand blown in from the desert. And yet, still the travellers come and you'll get the most from your visit here if you take time to understand Timbuktu's isolation and historical significance.

History
Timbuktu is said to have been founded around AD 1000 as a seasonal encampment for Tuareg nomads. In the 11th century, Timbuktu was developed as a trading centre: gold, slaves and ivory were sent north and salt (from the mines of Taghaza and Taoudenni) came south. Kankan Musa, the greatest king of the Empire of Mali, passed through in 1336 and commanded the construction of the Dyingerey Ber Mosque. Thereafter the city drew Islamic scholars, thus beginning a great tradition of Islamic education, which grew when Sonni Ali Ber and the Empire of Songhaï took the town in 1468.

In 1591 Moroccan armies sacked Timbuktu, killing many scholars and sending others to Fez (along with much of the city's riches), signalling the start of the city's decline. When the French explorer René Caillié became the first European to arrive in Timbuktu and live to tell the tale, he found 'a jumble of badly built mud houses, surrounded by arid plains of jaundiced white sand', and a city 'ruled over by a heavy silence'. The French marched in during 1894, and found the place pretty much how it looks today.

Information
BDM (Rte de Korioumé) Changes euros or US dollars and does Visa cash advances.
Bibliothèque Al-Imam Essayouti (next to Dyingerey Ber Mosque; per hr CFA1000; ☺ 8am-8pm) Internet access.
Bureau Régional du Tourisme (☎ 2192 1779; Blvd Askia Mohamed; ☺ 8am-4pm) The friendly staff can arrange an accredited guide or place a free 'Tombouctou' stamp in your passport.
Commissariat de Police (☎ 2192 1007; Pl de l'Indépendance) Will place a free 'Tombouctou' stamp in your passport.
Post office (Rte de Korioumé) For that all-important postmark.

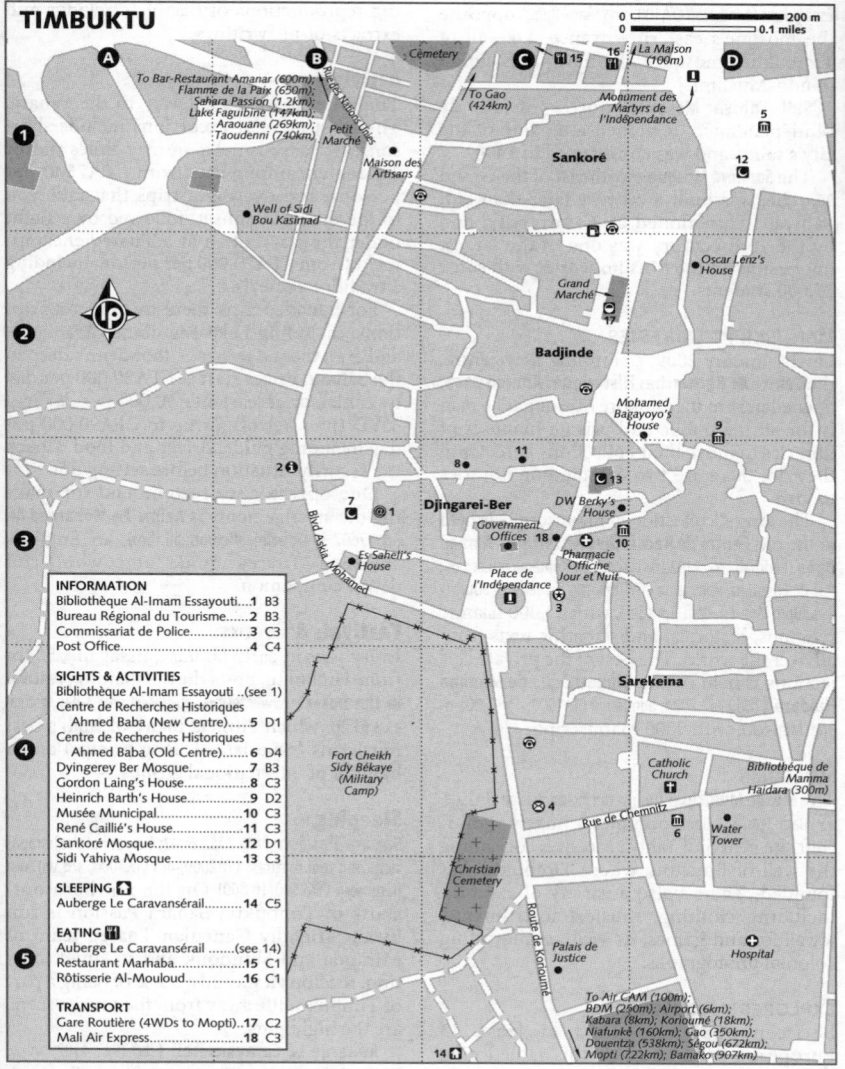

TIMBUKTU

INFORMATION
Bibliothèque Al-Imam Essayouti....**1** B3
Bureau Régional du Tourisme......**2** B3
Commissariat de Police.............**3** C3
Post Office..................................**4** C4

SIGHTS & ACTIVITIES
Bibliothèque Al-Imam Essayouti ..(see 1)
Centre de Recherches Historiques
Ahmed Baba (New Centre).....**5** D1
Centre de Recherches Historiques
Ahmed Baba (Old Centre)......**6** D4
Dyingerey Ber Mosque..............**7** B3
Gordon Laing's House................**8** C3
Heinrich Barth's House...............**9** D2
Musée Municipal........................**10** C3
René Caillié's House...................**11** C3
Sankoré Mosque........................**12** D1
Sidi Yahiya Mosque....................**13** C3

SLEEPING 🏠
Auberge Le Caravansérail...........**14** C5

EATING 🍴
Auberge Le Caravansérail ....(see 14)
Restaurant Marhaba...................**15** C1
Rôtisserie Al-Mouloud................**16** C1

TRANSPORT
Gare Routière (4WDs to Mopti)..**17** C2
Mali Air Express.........................**18** C3

Tourist tax Officially, every visitor to Timbuktu must pay a CFA2500 tourist tax; it's collected at the Musée Municipal (p418).

Sights
MOSQUES

The oldest of Timbuktu's mosques, dating from the early 14th century, is **Dyingerey Ber Mosque**. Its mud minaret with wooden struts is one of the city's most enduring images. At the time of writing, the mosque was undergoing painstaking restoration work under the auspices of the **Aga Khan Development Network's Historic Cities Programme** (www.akdn.org/aktc_hcp_mali.asp?type=p). For the best view of the mosque, climb to the roof of the **Bibliotheque Al-Imam**

MALI

Essayouti (admission CFA1000; ☎ 8am-8pm), opposite the mosque's eastern entrance. Like all of Timbuktu's mosques, the mosque is closed to non-Muslims.

Sidi Yahiya Mosque, north of Pl de l'Indépendance, is named after one of the city's saints and was constructed in 1400.

The **Sankoré Mosque**, northeast of the Grand Marché, was built a century later than Sidi Yahiya. It functioned as a university, and by the 16th century was one of the largest universities in the Muslim world, with some 25,000 students.

MANUSCRIPT LIBRARIES

On 24 January 2009, a stunning new centre, the **Centre de Recherches Historiques Ahmed Baba**, opened next to the Sankoré Mosque. The plan is for all the public and private manuscript libraries to move their collections here. Until they do, there are two outstanding libraries to visit.

The largest collection of manuscripts is held at the old **Centre de Recherches Historiques Ahmed Baba** (Cedrhab; ☎ 2192 1081; cedrhab@tombouctou.org.ml; Rue de Chemnitz; admission CFA1000; ☎ 7.30am-12.30pm & 2-4.30pm Mon-Fri, 8am-1pm Sat), with 23,000 Islamic religious, historical and scientific texts from all over the world. The best of the private collections is held by the **Bibliothèque de Mamma Haidara** (☎ 7942 7084; admission CFA1000; ☺ 7.30am-3pm Mon-Sat), with 9000 manuscripts.

MUSEUMS

The **Musée Municipal** (tourist tax incl admission CFA2500; ☺ 8am-1pm & 3-6pm) occupies a hugely significant site near Sidi Yahiya Mosque, containing the well of Bouctou, where Timbuktu was founded. There's also a variety of exhibits, including clothing, musical instruments, jewellery and games, as well as interesting colonial photographs.

EXPLORERS' HOUSES

Between 1588 and 1853 at least 43 Europeans tried to reach this fabled city; only four made it there and only three made it home. Only a couple of rooms of **Gordon Laing's house** (admission free; ☺ 8am-6pm) are open to the public; Gordon Laing was the first European to reach Timbuktu but was murdered shortly after leaving. **René Caillié's house** has been restored but remains closed to the public. **Heinrich Barth's house** (admission CFA1000; ☺ 8am-6pm) is now a tiny museum containing reproductions of Barth's drawings and extracts of his writings.

Activities

Timbuktu is Mali's gateway to the Sahara. The most popular excursions include short sunset trips by camel to nearby dunes and/or Tuareg encampments (from CFA7500 per person), and overnight trips that take you to the dunes at sunset, followed by a night under the stars, often at a Tuareg encampment (from CFA20,000 per person, including a traditional meal).

For extended trips, there are numerous options, including Lake Faguibine, Araouane, and even the salt mines at Taoudenni, deep in the Sahara. Prices start at CFA20,000 per day by camel, or at least CFA50,000 per day in a 4WD (plus petrol), or up to CFA90,000 per day including guide, driver and food. Check the security situation before setting out.

One operator we recommend for making the arrangements is **Azima Ag Mohamed Ali** (☎ 7602 3547; azimaali@hotmail.com), an English-speaking Tuareg guide and wonderful desert companion.

Festivals & Events

Every year in early January, Essakane, 50km from Timbuktu, hosts the outstanding **Festival in the Desert** (www.festival-au-desert.org; 3-day festival pass €139), which attracts many of Mali's best musicians (especially Tuareg groups) and a handful of international groups.

Sleeping

Sahara Passion (☎ 7942 6947; http://hotelsaharapassion.com; roof mattress CFA2000, dm CFA3000, s/d without bathroom CFA7500/10,000) On the northern outskirts of Timbuktu, Sahara Passion is run by the friendly Canadian-Tuareg team of Miranda and Shindouk and its quiet location, rooftop views and a sense of being a part of Timbuktu life away from the tourist scene are the highlights.

Auberge Le Caravansérail (☎ 7541 4302; www.tombouctoucaravanserail.com; off Rte de Korioumé; roof mattress CFA5000, roof tent CFA10,000, d with fan CFA10,000-25,000, ste with air-con CFA28,000; ☒) This French-run place has large, high-ceilinged rooms brimful of rustic charm and the public areas are among the most agreeable in Mali. The laid-back garden bar is chilled and the foot pool for dusty Timbuktu feet is a lovely touch.

La Maison (☎ 2192 2179; www.lesmaisonsdumali.com; s/d with air-con CFA30,000/35,000; ⊠) Timbuktu's best hotel, La Maison, is a stunning oasis that incorporates traditional Timbuktu architectural features and a subtle designer touch in each room. The roof terrace is superb and the meals here are exceptional (see below).

Eating
Our favourite place for a cheap meal is the unsigned place just west of the Monument des Martyrs de l'Indépendance. Known by every Timbuktu carnivore as **Rôtisserie Al-Mouloud** (meals from CFA1000; ☒ 9am-10pm), it serves up terrific grilled meats and *luttres* (sausages; CFA500 each) for lunch and after sunset.

Restaurant Marhaba (☎ 7887 4946; mains from CFA600; ☒ 6am-midnight) Restaurant Marhaba, just north of the centre, is a friendly place with hearty servings. Apart from spaghetti, couscous and rice, this is a good place to order (with five hours' notice) the local speciality of *toukassou* (CFA1250), a rather stodgy bread that you dip into a meat sauce.

Bar-Restaurant Amanar (mains CFA1250-2000; ☒ lunch & dinner) This mellow place opposite the Flamme de la Paix monument on Timbuktu's northwestern outskirts is decent for the traveller staples of soup, spaghetti, couscous, steak and chicken. The music is usually Malian blues, except on Saturday and Sunday night, when a DJ spins dance tracks until late.

La Maison (☎ 2192 2179; www.lesmaisonsdumali. com; breakfast/lunch/dinner CFA3500/5000/9000) The meals here are exquisite, if on the small side. The menu changes daily, but French cook Gaetane brings subtlety, colour and flair to traditional and modern French cuisine. Although the ingredients are local, you won't eat another meal like this in Mali.

Of the other hotel restaurants, the best choice is **Auberge Le Caravansérail** (☎ 7541 4302; www.tombouctoucaravanserail.com; off Rte de Korioumé; meals CFA5000).

Getting There & Away
AIR
Timbuktu's **airport** (☎ 2192 1320) is 6km south of town off Rte de Korioumé.

Mali Air Express (MAE; ☎ 7602 3929; www.mae-mali. com; Pl de l'Indépendance) has the most reliable flights to/from Bamako (CFA97,600, two weekly), Mopti (CFA69,500, three weekly) and Gao (CFA45,000, one weekly). The other option is **Air CAM** (☎ 7602 3548; www.camaero.com; Rte de Korioumé).

BOAT
Between late July and late November (sometimes into February or March for the stretch between Gao and Timbuktu), the large Comanav passenger boats stop at Kabara (Timbuktu's old port), 18km south of town. For details on prices, see p426. The **Comanav ticket office** (☎ 2192 1206) is in Kabara.

Alternatively, you can travel between Mopti and Korioumé (the official port for Timbuktu) by public or private *pinasse*; for details see the boxed text, p412. You may be able to negotiate a cheaper rate with a private *pinasse* returning empty to Mopti.

LAND
In the dry season, battered 4WDs carrying up to 12 passengers run most days between Timbuktu and Mopti (CFA12,500 in the back, CFA15,000 in the front, six to eight hours). They leave from the open area around the Grand Marché.

Getting Around
A private taxi/*bâché* to Kabara costs CFA9500/550 and to Korioumé CFA600/350, but you may be asked for up to five times as much. A taxi to the airport will cost at least CFA3000.

GAO
pop 46,608

Although Gao never had the cachet of Timbuktu, this one-time capital of the Empire of Songhaï was perhaps the greatest of Mali's illustrious centres of power. Apart from the delicious feeling of being 350km beyond Timbuktu in one of Africa's most forgotten corners, Gao's attractions include a Unesco World Heritage–listed mosque-tomb complex and a stunning riverside dune just across the river.

Information
BDM (Ave des Askia) Changes euros and has a Visa-enabled ATM.
Ecobank (Ave des Askia; ☎ 8am-4pm Mon-Fri, 9am-2pm Sat) Change euros, US dollars and travellers cheques.
Internet Café (Rte de l'Aéroport; per hr CFA500; ☒ 8am-2pm & 4-8pm Mon-Sat)
Omatho (Office Malien du Tourisme et de l'Hôtellerie; ☎ 2182 1182; Pl de l'Indépendance;

MALI

(🕙 7.30am-12.30pm & 2-4pm Mon-Fri) One of the best tourist offices in Mali.

Sights & Activities

The Unesco World Heritage–listed **Tomb of the Askia** (admission CFA1500; 🕙 daylight hr, closed during prayers Fri), north of the centre, was built in 1495 by Askia Muhammad Touré, one of the greatest rulers of the Empire of Songhaï. The tomb is an evocative combination of mudbrick, wooden struts and a tapering tower; local legend has it that the Askia was inspired by the Pyramids of Egypt during his pilgrimage to Mecca. The wooden struts are used by the Askia's surviving descendants, who replaster the mosque over two days every second April or May (usually in even years). You can climb the 10m-high minaret for good views of the city and river.

For many travellers, Gao's premier tourist attraction is a sunset trip to **La Dune Rose** (The Pink Dune; known locally as Koïma), a towering sand dune on the eastern bank of the Niger, visible from town 7km away. The views are exceptional. To get to La Dune Rose, you'll need to hire a motorised *pinasse* (the official price is CFA30,000, but we negotiated down to CFA22,500) or slower *pirogue* (CFA7500).

Sleeping

Auberge Tilafonso (🕾 7605 1350; Aljanabandia; roof mattress CFA2500, s/d with fan & half-board & without bathroom CFA11,750/17,500, lunch CFA2500) This place sparkles from its regularly whitewashed walls to the superclean shared bathrooms. The rooms are simple but cleanly swept and spread around two pretty courtyards.

Camping Euro (🕾 7608 7827; shaolumese@yahoo. com; Rue 527, Porte 570, Aljanabandia; roof mattress CFA3500, s/d with fan & shared bathroom CFA7500/10,500) Easily Gao's friendliest accommodation, Camping Euro is run by Shaka, a charming Nigerian who keeps his place spotless. The rooms are simple but tidy and there's an attractive rooftop terrace and a small courtyard. Meals are available.

Auberge Tizi-Mizi (🕾 2182 0194; camping & roof terrace CFA3500, d with fan CFA7500-12,500, with air-con CFA17,500; 🏊) Probably the best of the many *campements* surrounding Gao, Auberge Tizi-Mizi, 4km southeast of the centre along Rte de l'Aéroport, is a pleasant place to stay. The rooms are nicely kept and are extremely quiet.

Eating

Around the Grand Marché you can get coffee and bread in the mornings, and street food in the evenings (check out the excellent local sausages).

Pharmacie de la Sante (Belláh Rôtisserie; 🕾 7632 3513; Ave des Askias; meals CFA1500; 🕙 6am-midnight) Known by the name of its exuberant owner, Belláh, this place is terrific. He does little else but delicious, lightly spiced, grilled *mouton* (sheep or goat) and he claims to open around the clock – as he says, you won't want to sleep once you smell his meat.

Adama 'Le Petit Dogon' (🕾 7627 1416; Rte de Bac, 2km south of Pl de l'Indépendance; meals CFA2500-5000; 🕙 breakfast, lunch & dinner Mon-Sat, lunch & dinner Sun) Dogon-run and with the cleanest kitchen we inspected in Mali, Le Petit Dogon has excellent meals – which include couscous, pizza, pasta and *filet de chameau* (camel fillet; CFA2500) – and a delightful atmosphere to which the owner, Adama, contributes much warmth. Meals take a long time to prepare.

Getting There & Away

Air CAM (🕾 7605 2555) has one flight per week (Saturday) to Bamako (CFA115,000) via Mopti (CFA81,000) and Timbuktu (CFA45,000).

Bani (🕾 2182 0424; Pl de l'Indépendance), **Binke** (🕾 2182 0558; near Greenwich Monument) and **Sonef** (🕾 2182 0391; off Rte de Bac) have bus departures to Bamako (CFA15,000, 16 to 20 hours) via Hombori (CFA4000, three to four hours) and Sévaré (CFA7500, nine to 12 hours). For transport to Niamey in Niger, see p425.

HOMBORI

In the flatlands of the Sahel, the magnificent sandstone buttresses near Hombori can seem like an apparition: some people call the 80km stretch of road between Hombori and Douentza 'Mali's Monument Valley'. The stone-built village of **Old Hombori** overlooks the new town from the south.

Around 13km west of Hombori and visible from the main highway, the two narrow, finger-like towers of **La Main de Fatima** (The Hand of Fatima) soar 600m from the plains and provide world-class technical rock climbing – check out **Salvador Campillo** (http://avired.com/maindefatma, in French & Spanish) – from October to March. A spectacular three-hour walking trail climbs up from the village of Daari, and then down to the village of Garmi, where you can flag down buses and bush taxis. To climb or

DETOUR – RÉSERVE DE DOUENTZA

The last elephants in the Sahel (around 350) roam the vast area north of Hombori from January to June. The main access to the reserve is from Douentza, Hombori and Bambara-Maoudé; the best guides are those from In-a-Djatafane, Dimamou and Boni. You'll need to be self-sufficient in food and water, have a 4WD (around CFA50,000 per day, including driver but not petrol) and a guide (from CFA15,000 per day). There's also a tourist tax (CFA5000) in In-a-Djatafane.

trek, there's a CFA1000 tourist tax payable at Daari's Campement Bongujje.

In Hombori, **Campement de Mangou Bagni** (☎ 7543 0988; campsite with/without mattress CFA2500/2000, s/d without bathroom CFA4000/6000, meals CFA1000–3000) and **Le Tondanko Campement** (☎ 7515 6144; douncy@gmail.com; campsite or roof mattress CFA2000, s/d Fulani tent CFA3500/5000, s/d without bathroom CFA4000/7000, meals up to CFA3000) are simple and electricity is by generator.

Hombori lies along the main Sévaré–Gao road, and all transport between these two towns passes through Hombori.

THE SOUTH

SIKASSO
pop 192,400

Agreeable, if unexciting, Sikasso stands at the heart of a relatively lush region known as the 'market garden of Mali'. Although it has a handful of sights – such as the fascinating **Grottes de Missirikoro**, a lump of limestone roughly 12km southwest of Sikasso – its main attraction is the lack of tourists and it's useful as a quiet stopover if you're coming from Bobo-Dioulasso in Burkina Faso.

Of the places to stay, **Hôtel Lotio** (☎ 2162 1001; Blvd Coiffet; s/d with fan & without bathroom CFA7500/10,000) is basic but friendly, while **Hôtel Tata** (☎ 2162 0411; Rte de Bamako; d with fan/air-con CFA9000/15,000; ❄) has well-priced rooms that are better maintained than most in town. The attached restaurant, where they do all the usual traveller staples, is also reasonably priced.

Blvd Coiffet has several cheap eateries serving good, filling meals (heavy on the rice) for around CFA500 to CFA1500. **La Vieille Marmite** (Blvd Coiffet) and **Restaurant Kénédougou** (Blvd Coiffet) provide good Malian fare, and the enormous Sunday market is a real bonus for street-food fans.

The *gare routière* is a 15-minute walk (CFA225 in a shared taxi) from the centre. There are daily buses to Bamako (CFA4500, three to four hours), Mopti (CFA6000, six hours) and Ségou (CFA4500, four hours).

THE WEST

KAYES
pop 133,101

The principal settlement in western Mali, Kayes (pronounced Kai) is a convenient place to break up the long journey between Bamako and Dakar. Kayes is hot and dusty, and was the first place the French settled in Mali (several colonial buildings remain). There's a thriving, chaotic market, the town is largely hassle-free and a number of interesting excursions are possible.

Centre d'Accueil de Jeunesse (☎ 2152 1254; campsite or roof mattress CFA3000, s/d with fan & without bathroom CFA5000/7500) is one of the most basic places to sleep in Mali, while the crumbling, colonial-style **Hôtel du Rail** (☎ 2152 1233; d with air-con CFA18,000–28,000; ❄) is handy to the train station. But **Hôtel Le Khasso** (☎ 2153 1666; s/d with air-con from CFA17,500; ❄) is the best place in town, with simple but well-kept bungalows and a riverside location.

Cheap food stalls abound near the train station and in the market. **Restaurant Yankadi** (Rue 122; meals CFA500-1000), near the junction with Rue Magdeburg, serves filling meals, while **Poulet Doré** (Ave du Capitaine Mamadou Sissoko) does roast chicken (whole chicken CFA3000).

DETOUR – FORT DE MÉDINE

The recently renovated Fort de Médine, 15km upstream from Kayes, was part of a chain of defence posts built along the Senegal River in French colonial times. Although something has been lost by the overhaul, the buildings here still hold a real sense of history and you'll find the old train station to be particularly beautiful. *Pinasses* to Médine (which cost CFA1500) leave from opposite the Total petrol station in Kayes. A taxi there and back costs around CFA12,500.

MALI

Air CAM (☎ 7615 3600; www.camaero.com) and **Mali Air Express** (MAE; ☎ 7672 9396; www.mae-mali.com; Rue Soundiata Keita) each have three weekly flights between Kayes and Bamako (CFA69,000). There are also five weekly train services between Kayes and Bamako (2nd-class seat/2nd-class couchette/1st-class seat/1st-class couchette costs CFA7300/11,500/16,190/22,190).

For cross-border transport to Senegal and Mauritania, see p425 and p425.

MALI DIRECTORY

ACCOMMODATION

Mali has some outstanding hotels, although by West African standards you pay a lot more for quality. Everywhere, budget hotels (up to CFA10,000/12,500 for a single/double) vary from basic and depressing to simple and tidy. Sleeping on flat roofs (mattresses provided) is the cheapest accommodation in Mali; prices range from CFA1500 to CFA4000. The standard of midrange hotels (from CFA12,500/15,000 for a single/double up to CFA45,000/55,000) is generally quite high. There are excellent midrange hotels in Bamako, Ségou, Djenné, Mopti, Sévaré, Bandiagara and Timbuktu. In Bamako there are dozens of top-end hotels (above CFA46,000/60,000 for a single/double) to choose from, but elsewhere there's nothing to speak of.

ACTIVITIES

Possible activities include trekking in Dogon Country (p412), world-class rock climbing near Hombori (p420), and desert expeditions

---

---

by camel or 4WD into the Sahara around Timbuktu (p418).

BOOKS

Ségu, by Maryse Condé, is a beautifully written generational novel about a late-18th-century family living in the Niger River trading town of Ségou.

Dogon – Africa's People of the Cliffs, by Stephenie Hollyman and Walter van Beek, is a beautifully photographed study of the Dogon, with informative anthropological text.

There are a host of travel literature titles set in Mali. They include *The Cruelest Journey: Six Hundred Miles to Timbuktu*, by Kira Salak; *The Road to Timbuktu*, by Tom Fremantle; *To Timbuktu*, by Mark Jenkins; and *Frail Dream of Timbuktu*, by Bettina Selby.

For books about Timbuktu, see the boxed text, p416.

BUSINESS HOURS

Banks From 8am to noon and 3pm to 5pm Monday to Friday, plus 8am to noon Saturday.
Bars From noon to late.
Nightclubs From 10pm to late.
Restaurants From noon to 3pm and 6.30pm to 11pm.
Shops From 8am to noon and 3pm to 5pm Monday to Friday, plus 8am to noon Saturday.

COURSES

Mali's master *kora* player Toumani Diabaté runs Mandinka Kora Production (p403) in Bamako, where you can learn from the genius himself. If you'd like to try your hand at making *bogolan*, Mali's famous mud cloth, there are places to learn in Djenné (p409).

DANGERS & ANNOYANCES

Much of northern Mali is off limits due to rebellion and banditry, especially the area north and east of the Niger River between Timbuktu and the Niger border. Other areas of concern are the road between Gao and Niamey in Niger, where travel in private vehicles is not recommended.

Crime is not a big problem in Mali, although in Bamako you should be careful about walking around at night in some areas (see p403). People travelling by train should take extra care.

The main annoyance for visitors are the young would-be guides and salesmen who lurk outside hotels in any town where tourists congregate.

EMBASSIES & CONSULATES

The following embassies are located in Bamako:

Burkina Faso (off Map p402; ☎ 2029 3171; off Rte de Guinée; ⏰ 7.30am-noon & 2-4pm Mon-Thu, 7.30am-noon & 3.30-6pm Fri)

Canada (off Map p402; ☎ 2021 2236; www.bamako.gc.ca; Rte de Koulikoro) Assists Australian and UK nationals.

Côte d'Ivoire (off Map p402; ☎ 2021 2289; ACI2000 Hamdallaye; ⏰ 8am-12.30pm Mon-Fri)

France (Map p404; ☎ 2021 3141; Sq Lumumba) Consulate; assists Austrian, Belgian, Spanish, Greek, Italian and Portuguese nationals.

Germany (off Map p402; ☎ 2022 3715; Ave de l'OUA, Rue 14, Porte 334, Badalabougou Est)

Guinea (off Map p402; ☎ 2020 2036; Rue 37, off Ave de l'OUA, Faso-Kanu; ⏰ 9am-4.30pm Mon-Thu, to 1.30pm Fri)

Mauritania (off Map p402; ☎ 2021 4815; Rue 213, off Rte de Koulikoro, Hippodrome; ⏰ 8am-4pm Mon-Fri)

Netherlands (Map p402; ☎ 2021 5611; www.mfa.nl/bam; Rue 437, off Route de Koulikoro, Hippodrome)

Niger (off Map p402; ☎ 2023 8868; Rue 136, Porte 739, Badalabougou Sema II; ⏰ 8am-4.30pm Mon-Fri)

Senegal (off Map p402; ☎ 2023 8273; Rue 50, Badalabougou Sema; ⏰ 7.30am-1pm & 1.30-4pm Mon-Fri)

USA (off Map p402; ☎ 2070 2300; http://mali.usembassy.gov; Rue 243, Porte 297, ACI2000)

EMERGENCY

Ambulance (☎ 15)
Police (☎ 17)

FESTIVALS & EVENTS

In addition to mask ceremonies in Dogon villages (usually held in April or May), the following are worth checking out:

Bamako Jazz Festival (Bamako) Held in February.
Biennal (Bamako) Held in September in even years.
Festival in the Desert (p418)
Festival sur le Niger (p407)

HOLIDAYS

For Islamic holiday dates, see p1140. Public holidays:

New Year's Day 1 January
Army Day 20 January
For the Martyrs of the 1991 Revolution 26 March
Easter March/April
Labour Day 1 May
African Unity Day 25 May
Independence Day 22 September
Christmas Day 25 December

INTERNET ACCESS

Internet access is widely available throughout the country, although connections can be slow. Access usually costs CFA1000 per hour. Wi-fi access is almost universal in most midrange and top-end hotels in Bamako and Mopti.

MAPS

The French **IGN** (www.ign.fr) produces the excellent *Mali* (1:2,000,000), but it's not available in Mali itself. It also sells the Carte Internationale du Monde series (1:1,000,000), which is outdated for roads but good for physical geography. Michelin's 953 *Africa North and West* (1:4,000,000) is large scale, but shows Mali's minor roads accurately. For information on where to buy maps, see p1141.

MONEY

The unit of currency is the West African CFA franc.

Most of Mali's banks change foreign cash. Euros are the best to carry. US dollars are OK, but commissions are usually higher and exchange rates poor. Both BNDA and Ecobank will change travellers cheques, although commissions can be prohibitive.

Banque de Développement du Mali (BDM) has Visa-enabled ATMs. Take as much money out as you can in one hit, as some ATMs won't let you withdraw twice from the same bank in a week. Payment by Visa card is rarely possible.

For MasterCard, Banque Atlantique promises cash advances, but our advice is not to rely on these for all your money in Mali; its relationship with MasterCard was uncertain at the time of research. Payment by MasterCard is almost nonexistent.

POST

Letter and parcel post from Mali's cities is reasonably reliable, but letters can still take weeks to arrive. Parcels do go missing, but usually only items sent from overseas. Anything of real value should be sent by TAM Courrier Express (p403).

TELEPHONE

Most towns have privately owned *télécentres* or *cabines téléphoniques,* which allow easy telephone and fax communication.

Malitel (www.malitel.com.ml) and **Orange Mali** (www.orangemali.com) are the two mobile providers; coverage is expanding all the time, but generally works within 15km of any medium-sized town. Orange generally has the best coverage and a local pre-paid Orange SIM card costs CFA2000, including CFA1000 credit. Top-up cards are available from street vendors throughout the country.

You'll find that most GSM mobiles from European and other Western countries work in Mali.

TOURIST INFORMATION

Mali's **Office Malien du Tourisme et de l'Hôtellerie** (Omatho; www.tourisme.gov.ml) is improving. Some local offices (such as Gao) are outstanding, although in most places their primary purpose is to provide a list of accredited guides. Most towns also have a privately run guides' association, which is useful for finding an accredited local guide.

VISAS

Visas are required by everyone. If there's no Malian embassy in your home country (and, usually, even if there is), it's possible to get your visa upon your arrival in the country. It will cost you CFA15,000 (€23) and you'll need three passport photos. The visa is valid for an initial period of five days and must then be extended (see below), whereafter it will be valid for one month. Note that Air France won't let you on the plane to Bamako unless you have a valid visa in your passport.

At Malian embassies in West Africa, you'll usually pay CFA20,000 for a one-month single-entry visa.

Visa Extensions

One-month visa extensions cost CFA5000, require two photos and are only available at the Immigration & Sûreté Nationale building in Bamako (p403) or at the Comissariat de Police & Sûreté office in Mopti (p409). If you obtained your five-day visa at the border, the cost of a one-month extension is free in Bamako (where it usually takes 24 hours), but costs CFA5000 in Mopti (where they'll do it on the spot).

Visas for Onward Travel

For information on embassies in Mali, see p423.

BURKINA FASO

Single-/multiple-entry three-month visas cost CFA28,200/33,200 and require you to have three identical photos. Leave your passport in the morning and pick it up in the afternoon.

CÔTE D'IVOIRE

The embassy will issue visas (one-month single-/multiple-entry CFA30,000/60,000; two photos required) in three days. You'll require an invitation from a Côte d'Ivoire company or a confirmed hotel reservation.

GHANA

For Ghanaian visas you'll require four photos and they're usually issued the same day, although they can take up to 48 hours. Single-entry one-month/multiple-entry nine-month visas cost CFA12,000/30,000.

GUINEA

The Guinean embassy issues visas in 24 hours and requires two photos and a photocopy of your passport. For European nationals, it's CFA46,500/60,000 for single-entry one-month/two-month visas, while multiple-entry three-month visas cost CFA76,500. US, UK, Canadian and Australian citizens pay CFA60,000 for single-entry, one-month visas and CFA80,000 for multiple-entry, three-month visas.

MAURITANIA

At the time of writing, the embassy was issuing visas (free; three photos with an extension required once in Mauritania for stays of longer than 10 days). Expect that to change, however, and come with CFA16,000 just in case.

NIGER

The Nigerien consulate issues one-/two-/three-month multiple-entry visas for CFA30,000/45,000/60,000. You'll need to have two photos and the process takes three days.

SENEGAL

For those nationals requiring visas (including Australians and New Zealanders), one-month single-entry visas cost CFA5000, while three-month multiple-entry visas cost CFA10,000. You'll need two photos and visas are issued in 24 hours.

TRANSPORT IN MALI

GETTING THERE & AWAY
Air
Mali's main international airport is **Sénou International Airport** (☎ 2020 4626). Point-Afrique also flies into Mopti and Gao.

Numerous airlines fly into Bamako:

Afriqiyah Airways (Map p404; ☎ 2023 1497; www.afriqiyah.aero; Ave de la Marne)

Air Algérie (Map p404; ☎ 2022 3159; www.airalgerie.dz; Rue de la Cathédrale)

Air Burkina (Map p404; ☎ 2021 0178; www.air-burkina.com; Ave de la Marne)

Air CAM (off Map p402; ☎ 2022 2424; www.camaero.com; Ave Cheick Zayed, Hamdallaye)

Air France (off Map p402; ☎ 2070 0330; www.airfrance.com; ACI2000)

Air Ivoire (Map p404; ☎ 2023 9558; www.airivoire.com; off Ave de l'Yser)

Air Sénégal International (Map p404; ☎ 2023 9811; www.air-senegal-international.com; Ave Modibo Keïta)

Ethiopian Airlines (Map p404; ☎ 2022 2208; www.flyethiopian.com/et; Sq Lumumba)

Kenya Airways (Map p404; ☎ 2022 1235; www.kenya-airways.com; cnr Ave Kassa Keita & Ave de l'Indépendance)

Mali Air Express (MAE; Map p404; ☎ 2023 1465; www.mae-mali.com; Ave de la Nation)

Point Afrique (Map p404; ☎ 2023 5470; www.point-afrique.com; Ave de l'Yser)

Royal Air Maroc (Map p404; ☎ 2021 6703; www.royalairmaroc.com; Ave de la Marne)

Land
The Tanezrouft trans-Saharan route through Algeria is closed to travellers due to the Tuareg rebellion.

BURKINA FASO
Numerous buses leave Bamako's Sogoniko *gare routière* daily for Ouagadougou (CFA18,000, 20 hours) via Bobo-Dioulasso (CFA11,500, 15 hours). Three daily Sogebaf buses link Koro with Ouahigouya (CFA3000, up to four hours).

CÔTE D'IVOIRE
The main route into Côte d'Ivoire is along the bitumen road through Zégoua, to the south of Sikasso. Daily buses leave Bamako's Sogoniko *gare routière* for Abidjan (CFA24,000, 36 to 48 hours). Bush taxis for towns in northern Côte d'Ivoire also leave from Sikasso.

GUINEA
Peugeot taxis or minibuses run most days from Bamako's Djikoroni *gare routière* to the border at Kourémalé (CFA3500, three hours) and then on to Siguiri (CFA6500). A weekly bus continues all the way to Conakry (CFA25,000).

MAURITANIA
Battered 4WDs and trucks depart daily in the dry season from Kayes Ndi *gare routière* to Sélibabi (CFA11,500, eight hours) and from Nioro to Ayoûn el-Atroûs (CFA18,000). The latter option gets you onto the paved road to Nouakchott.

NIGER
Sonef departs Gao at 6am heading for Niamey (CFA8500, 16 to 30 hours) via Ayorou (CFA6000). The Nigerien company SNTV departs for Niamey (CFA7425) two times per week. All passport formalities must be completed at the main police station in Gao the day before departure or upon your arrival in the town.

SENEGAL
A new road planned between Kita and Saraya (via Kéniéba) will significantly cut travel time between the two countries. In the meantime, most travellers fly or take the train between Bamako and Dakar.

In theory the train departs Bamako for Dakar (2nd-class seat/1st-class seat/1st-class couchette CFA25,500/34,620/53,145) on Saturday and Wednesday. It could take forever but, if not, it should take around 50 hours.

There's also an overnight bus direct to Dakar from Kayes (CFA15,000, 24 hours) twice a week.

GETTING AROUND
Air
Two airlines fly domestically in Mali:

Air CAM (off Map p402; ☎ 2022 2424; www.camaero.com; Ave Cheick Zayed, Hamdallaye)

Mali Air Express (MAE; Map p404; ☎ 2023 1465; www.mae-mali.com; Ave de la Nation)

Both airlines fly the same routes: Bamako–Kayes and Bamako–Mopti–Timbuktu. Air CAM also flies to Gao from Bamako (via Mopti and Timbuktu). Mali Air Express is the more reliable.

MALI

SAMPLE PASSENGER BOAT FARES					
Route	Luxe (CFA)	1st (CFA)	2nd (CFA)	3rd (CFA)	4th (CFA)
Koulikoro–Ségou	46,500	27,500	18,000	11,000	2750
Koulikoro–Mopti	120,500	65,500	46,000	27,000	6150
Koulikoro–Korioumé	210,000	112,000	79,500	47,000	10,350
Koulikoro–Gao	302,500	160,500	114,500	67,500	14,550
Mopti–Korioumé	95,500	51,500	36,500	21,500	5050
Mopti–Gao	188,500	101,000	71,500	42,000	9350

Boat

Most boat journeys on the Niger River are only possible from August to December, when water levels are high. For information on travelling by public or private *pinasse*, see the boxed text, p412.

Large passenger boats operated by the Compagnie Malienne de Navigation (Comanav) ply the Niger River between Koulikoro (50km east of Bamako) and Gao from August to November or December, stopping at Mopti and Korioumé (for Timbuktu) en route. One boat heads downstream from Koulikoro at 10pm Tuesday, arrives in Mopti at 3pm Thursday, in Timbuktu at 7am Saturday and Gao at midnight Sunday. Another boat heads upstream from Gao at 8pm every Monday, reaching Timbuktu at 6pm on Wednesday, Mopti at 4pm Friday and Koulikoro at midnight Sunday. The boats are like floating villages – people and cargo are everywhere, the cabins are sweltering, the toilets frequently flood and the food, well it ain't cordon bleu. But it *is* a quintessentially African experience.

The *'luxe'* cabins have a bathroom and air-con, 1st-class cabins have two bunk beds, toilet and washbasin, and 2nd-class cabins have four berths, with a washbasin and shared toilets. Third class is an eight-berth cabin and in 4th class you get to fight for a space on deck.

Booze, food and water are all available (three meals per day are included in all except 4th class), but it's a good idea to take extra supplies as you may get stranded. For sample passenger boat fares for the various classes see the boxed text, above.

Bus

Sadly, no bus company consistently uses high-quality buses. In our experience, the better companies are **Bani** (☎ 2020 6081), **Bittar** (☎ 2020 1205) and **Gana Transport** (☎ 2021 0978), all of which run regular services between the main towns south of the Niger River.

Bush Taxi

Bush taxis and minibuses, which are slightly pricier than buses (you're likely to be charged a CFA500 luggage fee), are handy on shorter, less frequented routes, where they may be the only option. These are either Peugeot 504s, carrying nine people; *bâchés* (pick-ups), with about 16 passengers; or minibuses, with 25 to 30 passengers.

Train

The train between Bamako and Kayes is never on time and is not without security issues. For details, see the relevant section for Bamako (p407).

Second-class travel is cramped, chaotic and makes the journey seem eternal.

Mauritania

If West Africa is a playground for overlanders, then Mauritania often seems to be little more than a 'drive-through' country – less a destination in itself than somewhere to transit between the better-known attractions of Marrakesh, Dakar or Bamako. That's a shame because Mauritania has some tremendous secrets to reveal to those travellers prepared to stop and take a closer look.

Culturally, Mauritania is a place apart. The population is almost equally divided between Moors of Arab-Berber descent and black Africans. It's a Muslim country with a black African twist. It's a transition between the North African Arab world and black Africa, it doesn't really belong to either. This striking cultural combination is part of its appeal.

Just as striking is some of the grandest scenery the entire continent has to offer. The Adrar region offers up epic sand dunes, eye-popping plateaus, green oases and even the biggest monolith this side of central Australia. The Tagânt has similar charms, and both hide ancient (and World Heritage–listed) caravan towns – Chinguetti, Ouadâne and Oualâta. The World Heritage feast continues along the coast at Parc National du Banc d'Arguin, which attracts millions of migratory birds and is renowned as one of the best birdwatching sites on earth.

If you just breeze through and stop at the (admittedly, uninspiring) capital, Nouakchott, you'll miss out on a truly incredible country. No one in Mauritania is in a rush, and you shouldn't be either.

MAURITANIA

FAST FACTS

- **Area** 1,030,700 sq km
- **ATMs** None
- **Borders** Morocco, Mali, Senegal open; Algeria unadvisable
- **Budget** US$30 per day
- **Capital** Nouakchott
- **Languages** Arabic (Hassaniyya), French, Pulaar (Fula), Soninke and Wolof
- **Money** Ouguiya (UM); US$1 = UM260, €1 = UM378
- **Population** 3 million
- **Seasons** Very hot (April to October), hot (November to March)
- **Telephone** Country code ☎ 222; international access code ☎ 00
- **Time** GMT/UTC
- **Visa** In advance US$50 to US$65, at Moroccan border US$30

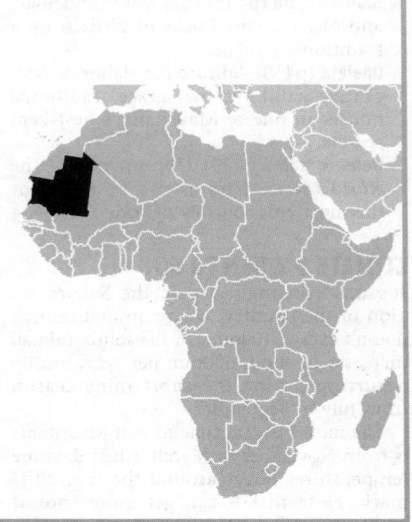

MAURITANIA

HOW MUCH?

- **Cup of tea in a nomad's tent** Free
- **Taxi ride in Nouakchott** US$0.76
- **Camel ride in the desert** About US$23 per day
- **Bush taxi fare (Nouakchott to Nouâdhibou)** US$17.15
- **Auberge room** US$7.60 per person

LONELY PLANET INDEX

- **1L of petrol** US$0.90
- **1L of bottled water** US$0.76
- **Bottled beer** US$3.80
- **Souvenir T-shirt** US$2.30
- **Plate of mafé (peanut-based stew with rice)** US$1.15

HIGHLIGHTS

- **Chinguetti** (p436) Wake up at the crack of dawn in order to catch a glorious sunrise from the labyrinthine lanes of the old city.
- **4WD tours or camel trips** (p435) Experience the magic of the Sahara and sleep beneath the star-studded skies at the saffron dunes in the Adrar region.
- **Banc d'Arguin** (p434) Pack your binoculars and observe vast flocks of birds from a traditional *pirogue*.
- **Oualâta** (p438) Admire the elaborate decorative paintings that grace traditional houses in one of Mauritania's best-kept secrets.
- **Iron-ore train** (p440) Hop on one of the world's longest trains and be ready for the most epic journey of your life!

CLIMATE & WHEN TO GO

It's unsurprisingly dry in the Sahara region of the country, where annual rainfall doesn't exceed 100mm. In the south, rainfall increases to about 600mm per year, mostly occurring during the short rainy season from July to September.

The most pleasant time to visit Mauritania is from November to March, when daytime temperatures hover around the mid-20°C mark. Note that it can get quite cool at night, especially in the desert.

ITINERARIES

- **One Week** Head straight to Nouakchott's fish market (p431) and spend a couple of days sampling the luscious cuisine of the capital. Then push on to Atâr (p435) and take either a 4WD tour or a camel trip to the grandiose dunefields around the city.
- **Two Weeks** Spend a couple of days trekking in the Adrar, explore the ancient desert towns of Chinguetti (p436) and Ouadâne (p437) and revitalise yourself in an idyllic palm-filled oasis. Then forge west to the Atlantic Coast and observe vast flocks of birds at Parc National du Banc d'Arguin (p434). Journey on to Nouakchott (p431) and its melange of chaotic markets and modern buildings.

HISTORY

From the 3rd century AD, the Berbers established trading routes all over the Western Sahara, including Mauritania. In the 11th century, the Marrakesh-based Islamic Almoravids pushed south and, with the assistance of Mauritanian Berber leaders, destroyed the Empire of Ghana, which covered much of present-day Mauritania. That victory led to the spread of Islam throughout Mauritania and the Western Sahara. The descendants of the Almoravids were finally subjugated by Arabs in 1674.

As colonialism spread throughout Africa in the 19th century, France stationed troops in Mauritania, but it was not until 1904 that, having played one Moorish faction off against another, the French finally managed to make Mauritania a colonial territory. Independence was fairly easily achieved in 1960 because the French wanted to prevent the country from being absorbed by newly independent Morocco. Mokhtar Ould Daddah became Mauritania's first president.

Ould Daddah took a hard line, especially against the (mainly black African) southerners, who were treated like second-class citizens and compelled to fit the Moors' mould. Any opposition was brutally suppressed.

The issue of Western Sahara (Spanish Sahara) finally toppled the government. In 1975 the very sandy Spanish Sahara (a Spanish colony) was divided between Morocco and Mauritania. But the Polisario Front launched a guerrilla war to oust both beneficiaries from the area. Mauritania was incapable, militarily

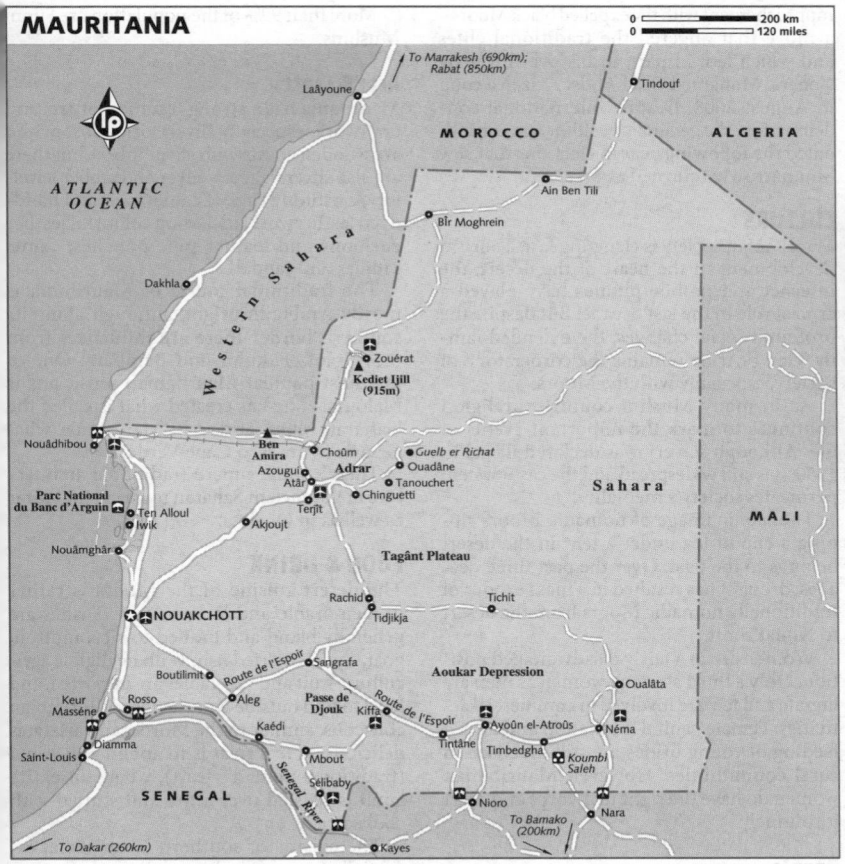

and economically, of fighting such a war. A bloodless coup took place in Mauritania in 1978, bringing in a new military government that renounced all territorial claims to the Western Sahara.

A series of coups ensued. Finally, Colonel Maaouya Sid' Ahmed Ould Taya came to power in 1984. For black Africans, this was even worse than under Ould Daddah. Ethnic tensions culminated in bloody riots between the Moors and black Africans in 1989. More than 70,000 black Africans were expelled to Senegal, a country most had never known.

In the 1990s the government became increasingly extremist. In 1991 Mauritania supported Iraq during the Gulf War, and aid dried up. To counter criticism, Taya intro-

duced multiparty elections in 1992, which were boycotted by the opposition. Riots over the price of bread in 1995 worsened the political situation. Cosmetic elections were held in 2001, with Taya still holding the whip hand.

Mauritania Today

Recent Mauritanian history has been marked by coups. In June 2005, Taya was toppled in a bloodless coup led by Colonel Ely Ould Mohamed Vall. Vall was largely popular and formulated a new constitution and voluntarily gave up power by holding elections in March 2007. Sidi Ould Cheikh Abdallahi was returned as Mauritania's first democratically elected president. He openly condemned the 'dark years' of the late 1980s, and sought rapprochement with the expelled black Moors – a move that angered the traditional elites and which led, in part, to his overthrow by General Mohamed Ould Abdel Aziz in a coup in August 2008. Despite international condemnation, the general's position was consolidated the following year in elections that saw him narrowly returned as president.

CULTURE

Mauritanian society is changing fast. Tourism development in the heart of the desert, the internet and mobile phones have played a crucial role in the last decade. But despite the profound social changes, the extended family, clan or tribe remains the cornerstone of society, especially with the Moors.

As in many Muslim countries, religion continues to mark the important events of life. Although slavery was declared illegal in 1980, it is still widespread and the caste system permeates society's mentality.

The iconic image of nomadic Moors sipping a cup of tea under a tent in the desert belongs to the past. Over the past three decades, drought has resulted in a mass exodus of traditionally nomadic Moors from the desert to Nouakchott.

Women are in a fairly disadvantaged position. Only a third as many women as men are literate and few are involved in commercial activities. Female genital mutilation and forced feeding of young brides are still practised in rural communities. However, Mauritanian women do have the right to divorce and exert it routinely.

People

Of Mauritania's estimated three million inhabitants, about 60% are Moors of Arab and Berber descent. The Moors of purely Arab descent, called 'Bidan', account for 40% of the population, and hold the levers of political power. The other major group is black Africans, ethnically split into two groups. The Haratin (black Moors), the descendants of people enslaved by the Moors, have assimilated the Moorish culture and speak Hassaniyya, an Arabic dialect. Black Mauritanians living in the south along the Senegal River constitute 40% of the total population and are mostly Fulani or the closely related Tukulor. These groups speak Pulaar (Fula). There are also Soninke and Wolof minorities.

More than 99% of the population are Sunni Muslims.

Arts & Crafts

Mauritania has a strong tradition of arts and craftwork, especially silverwork. Most prized are wooden chests with silver inlays, but there are also silver daggers, silver and amber jewellery, earthtone rugs of camel hair, and hand-dyed leatherwork, including colourful leather cushions and leather pipe pouches, camel saddles and sandals.

The traditional music of Mauritania is mostly Arabic in origin, although along its southern border there are influences from the Wolof, Tukulor and Bambara. One of the most popular Mauritanian musicians is Malouma. She has created what is called the 'Saharan blues' and is to Mauritania what Cesària Évora is to Cape Verde.

There's some superb traditional architecture in the ancient Saharan towns in the Adrar as well as in Oualâta.

FOOD & DRINK

The desert cuisine of the Moors is rather unmemorable and lacks variety. Dishes are generally bland and limited to rice, mutton, goat, camel or dried fish. With negligible agriculture, fruit and vegetables are imported, and hard to find outside Nouakchott. Mauritanian couscous, similar to the Moroccan variety, is delicious. A real treat is to attend a *méchoui* (traditional nomad's feast), where an entire lamb is roasted over a fire and stuffed with cooked rice.

The cuisine of southern Mauritania, essentially Senegalese, has more variety, spices and even a few vegetables. Look for rice with fish and *mafé* (a peanut-based stew).

Mauritanian tea is also ubiquitous, invariably strong and sweet and endlessly decanted between tiny glasses to produce a pleasing frothy head. It's polite to accept the first three glasses offered. *Zrig* (unsweetened curdled goat or camel milk) often accompanies meals served in private homes. Alcohol is technically forbidden but in practice is widely (and expensively) available in Nouakchott, usually in restaurants catering to foreigners.

ENVIRONMENT

Mauritania is about twice the size of France. About 75%, including Nouakchott, is desert, with huge expanses of flat plains broken by occasional ridges, sand dunes and rocky plateaus, including the Adrar (about 500m high).

The highest peak is Kediet Ijill (915m) near Zouérat. Mauritania has some 700km of shoreline, including the Parc National du Banc d'Arguin, one of the world's major bird-breeding grounds and a Unesco World Heritage Site. The south is mostly flat scrubland.

Major environmental issues are the usual suspects of desertification, overgrazing and pollution. Overfishing is another concern, with hundreds of tonnes of fish caught every day off the Mauritanian coastline.

NOUAKCHOTT

pop 1 million

Barely 50 years old, Nouakchott has to be simultaneously one of Africa's strangest and most unassuming capital cities. This is urban planning nomad style: a city simply plonked down 5km from the coast as if on an overnight caravan stop and left to grow by accident. Most travellers use it as a staging post before the Adrar, Banc d'Arguin or the next international border.

Although it's not a highlight of the country, Nouakchott is intriguingly idiosyncratic and you could do worse than spend an afternoon at the gloriously frantic fish market (one of the busiest in West Africa), treat yourself to a comfy guesthouse or feast in a hip restaurant. It's also laid-back and amazingly safe – bliss after the rigours of the desert.

ORIENTATION & INFORMATION

The main streets are Ave Abdel Nasser, running east to west, and the parallel streets Ave du Général de Gaulle and Ave Kennedy running north to south. The ocean is 5km west along Ave Abdel Nasser, while the airport is 3km northeast of the centre.

There's also a profusion of internet cafes in the centre. There are bureaux de change on Ave du Général de Gaulle (amid the telephone offices) and on Ave Abdel Nasser, as well as in the Marché Capitale. CFA and Moroccan dirham can be changed.

BNP Paribas (Rue Mamadou Konaté) Has a Visa ATM.

Cabinet Médical Fabienne Sharif (☎ 525 1571) English-speaking doctor, recommended by expats.

Cyber Neja (off Ave Kennedy; per hr UM200; ⏰ 8am-midnight)

Main post office (Ave Abdel Nasser; ⏰ 8am-3pm Mon-Thu, to noon Fri)

SIGHTS

An absolute must-see, the **fish market** (locally called Port de Pêche or Plage des Pêcheurs), is by far Nouakchott's star attraction. It's incredibly lively and extremely colourful. You'll see teams of men, mostly Wolof and Fula, dragging in heavy hand-knotted fishing nets. Small boys hurry back and forth with trays of fish, which they sort, gut, fillet and lay out on large trestles to dry. The best time to visit the market is between 4pm and 6pm, when the brightly painted fishing boats return and are hauled up through the surf onto the beach. A taxi is about UM500 from the centre.

Culture vultures will make a beeline for the **Musée National** (Rue Mohamed el Habib; admission UM300; ⏰ 8am-3.30pm Mon-Fri), which is an excellent introduction to Moorish civilisation.

Major landmarks in the centre include the **Grande Mosquée** (Rue Mamadou Konaté), also called the Mosquée Saoudienne, with its slender minarets, and the large **Mosquée Marocaine** (Rue de la Mosquée Marocaine), which towers over a bustling market area.

SLEEPING

Auberge du Sahara (☎ 670 4383; www.auberge-sahara. com, in French; tent per person UM1500, dm UM2500, d UM4000; P) Well-signed on the road to Nouâdhibou; your cordial hosts, Sidi, Hermann and Katia go the extra yards here. Dorms and rooms are plain but functional and shared bathrooms are kept in good nick. The other pluses are the outdoor areas, a kitchen for guests' use and a rooftop terrace. You'll need a taxi or your own vehicle to get to the centre.

Auberge Menata (☎ 636 9450; off Ave du Général de Gaulle; tent per person UM2000, dm UM2500, d UM5000, vehicle UM1500; P) A centrally located and perennially popular haunt for backpackers and overlanders, the laidback Menata is a decent option. Good meals are available upon request or you can use the kitchen. The only drawback? It can be noisy, and shared bathrooms could be a lot better kept.

Auberge La Bienvenue (☎ /fax 525 1421, 676 7871; Ave du Général de Gaulle; s UM10,000-12,000, d UM12,000-14,000; 🅿 💻) Although it's on the main drag, this auberge is surprisingly peaceful and

MAURITANIA

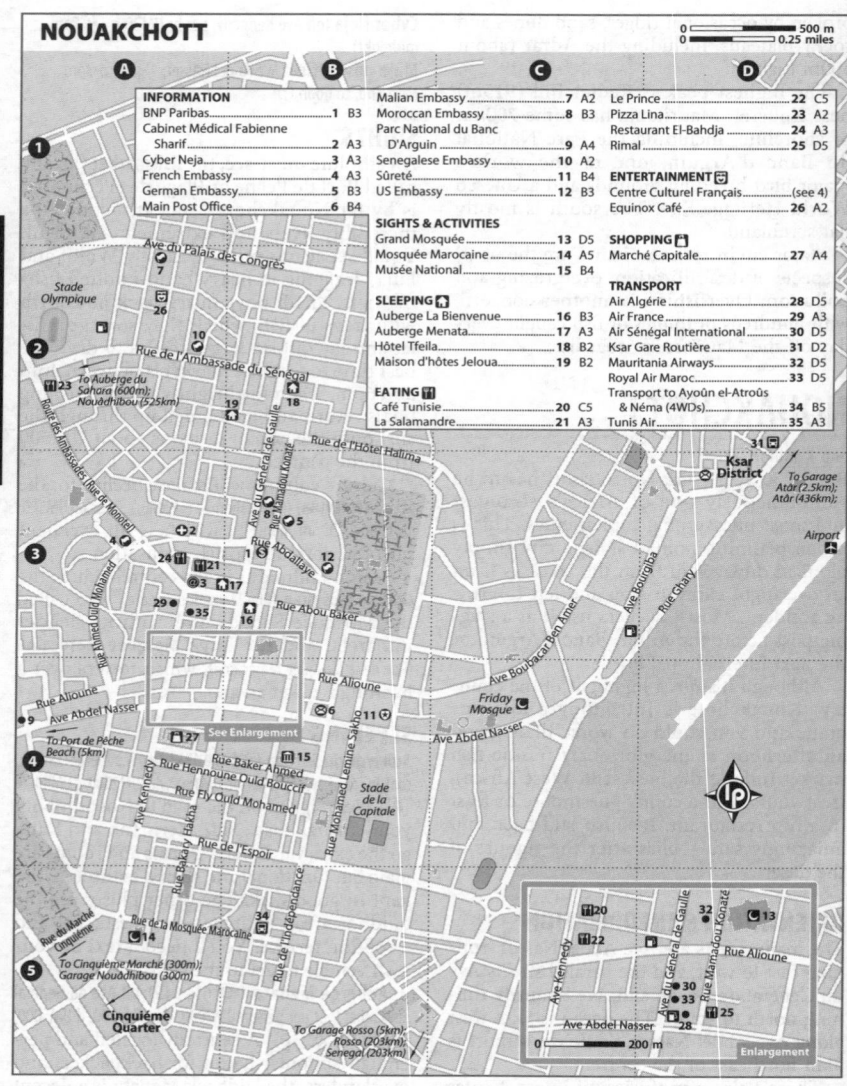

NOUAKCHOTT

0 ──── 500 m
0 ──── 0.25 miles

INFORMATION	
BNP Paribas	**1** B3
Cabinet Médical Fabienne	
Sharif	**2** A3
Cyber Neja	**3** A3
French Embassy	**4** A3
German Embassy	**5** B3
Main Post Office	**6** B4

Malian Embassy	**7** A2
Moroccan Embassy	**8** B3
Parc National du Banc	
D'Arguin	**9** A4
Senegalese Embassy	**10** A2
Sûreté	**11** B4
US Embassy	**12** B3

SIGHTS & ACTIVITIES
Grand Mosquée	**13** D5
Mosquée Marocaine	**14** A5
Musée National	**15** B4

SLEEPING 🏠
Auberge La Bienvenue	**16** B3
Auberge Menata	**17** A3
Hôtel Tfeila	**18** B2
Maison d'hôtes Jeloua	**19** B2

EATING 🍴
Café Tunisie	**20** C5
La Salamandre	**21** A3

Le Prince	**22** C5
Pizza Lina	**23** A2
Restaurant El-Bahdja	**24** A3
Rimal	**25** D5

ENTERTAINMENT 🎭
Centre Culturel Français	(see 4)
Equinox Café	**26** A2

SHOPPING 🛍
Marché Capitale	**27** A4

TRANSPORT
Air Algérie	**28** D5
Air France	**29** A3
Air Sénégal International	**30** D5
Ksar Gare Routière	**31** D2
Mauritania Airways	**32** D5
Royal Air Maroc	**33** D5
Transport to Ayoûn el-Atroûs	
& Néma (4WDs)	**34** B5
Tunis Air	**35** A3

there's a pleasant leafy garden at the front, ideal for breakfast. Rooms (all with bathrooms) are good value for the price tag.

Maison d'hôtes Jeloua (☎ 636 9450, 643 2730, 525 0914; maison.jeloua@voila.fr; r UM10,000-12,000, with shared bathroom UM5000; Ⓟ ⬡ 💻 📶) Run by the same people as the Auberge Menata, this is a lovely *maison d'hôtes* (B&B). It's charmingly

decorated and there's free wi-fi. Popular with business travellers.

Hôtel Tfeila (☎ 525 7400; www.hoteltfeila.com.com; Ave du Général de Gaulle; s from UM45,200, d UM47,200; Ⓟ ⬡ 💻 📶 🅿) Forget the blinding orange and yellow facade of this former Novotel, the interior shows money and a classy eye bonded with impeccable service. From swish rooms to free wi-fi, a good restaurant and a pool, this is by some degree Mauritania's best hotel.

EATING & DRINKING

Unless otherwise stated, all restaurants are open for lunch and dinner every day. In principle, alcohol is available at higher-end places.

Le Prince (Rue Alioune; mains UM500-1300) A bit grander than most fast food joints, Le Prince claims to be Nouakchott's oldest restaurant. Plonk yourself on a wobbly chair in the room at the back and tuck into a plate of well-prepared *shwarma*, sandwiches, salads and ice cream – all great value.

Café Tunisie (Ave Kennedy; set breakfast UM1000) On the corner next to Tunis Air, this cafe is fine for coffee and smoking a water pipe, but comes into its own with fantastic breakfasts – freshly squeezed orange juice, bread, jam, pastries, yoghurt, coffee and a bottle of mineral water. A fine way to start the day.

Rimal (☎ 525 4832; Ave Abdel Nasser; mains about UM1000; ✆ closed lunch Sun) This place thoroughly lacks any pretensions but is all the better for it. The surroundings might have seen better days, but the service is fast and the food piping hot. There are good salads, chicken dishes and a variety of tasty fish straight from the Port de Pêche.

Pizza Lina (☎ 525 8662; Rte des Ambassades; mains UM1500-3500) A long-established player on the Nouakchott dining scene, Pizza Lina now faces stiff competition from the many similar places along this stretch of Rte des Ambassades. Whichever you go for, though, you'll find decent crispy pizzas and a selection of pasta and meat dishes.

La Salamandre (☎ 524 2680; off Rte des Ambassades; mains UM2000-4000; ✆ Mon-Sat) La Salamandre enjoys a deserved reputation for lip-smacking French cooking, but throws in a little Mexican and even Japanese for variety. The sleek setting, with lashings of bright colours splashed all over the walls, is another draw.

Restaurant El-Bahdja (☎ 630 5383; off Rte des Ambassades; mains UM2500-3000) Mauritania imports plenty of produce from Morocco, so a restaurant serving tajine (Moroccan stew) and couscous should always do well. It doesn't disappoint – filling classics are served up in bright surroundings at very reasonable prices.

Rue Alioune between Ave Kennedy and Ave du Général de Gaulle is good for fast food, with most places open until 11pm or later – most have a Lebanese bent.

ENTERTAINMENT

Centre Culturel Français (☎ 529 9631; www.ccf-nkc.com; next to French Embassy) Pick up a program for the CCF from most hotels; it's a good place for concerts by popular local musicians, as well as films and art exhibitions.

Equinox Café (☎ 502 5238; www.equinoxcentre. com; btwn Ave du Palais des Congrés & Rue de l'Ambassade du Sénégal) Although mainly a cafe-restaurant, the Equinox has started inviting local musicians to play on Friday evening and has plans to expand into larger concerts.

SHOPPING

You'll find a bit of everything at Marché Capitale (also called Grand Marché) on Ave Kennedy, including brass teapots, silver jewellery, traditional wooden boxes and colourful fabrics.

GETTING THERE & AWAY
Air

Airlines with offices in Nouakchott:

Air Algérie (☎ 529 0992; www.airalgerie.dz; cnr Ave du Général de Gaulle & Ave Abdel Nasser)

Air France (☎ 525 1808, 525 1802; www.airfrance.com; Ave Kennedy)

Air Sénégal International (☎ 525 4852; www.air -senegal-international.com; Ave du Général de Gaulle)

Mauritania Airways (☎ 524 7474, www.fly-mauritania airways.com; Rue Mamadou Konaté)

Point Afrique (☎ in France 00 33 4 75 97 20 40; www. point-afrique.com)

Royal Air Maroc (☎ 525 3564, 525 3094; www. royalairmaroc.com; Ave Abdel Nasser)

Tunis Air (☎ 525 8762; www.tunisair.com.tr; Ave Kennedy)

For details of international and domestic flights to/from Nouakchott, see p440 and p441.

Bush Taxi

There are specific garages for Mauritania's different regions.

For Nouâdhibou (about UM4500, six hours), Garage Nouâdhibou is close to Cinquième Marché; for Rosso (about UM2000, 3½ hours), Garage Rosso is just over 5km south of the centre. For Atâr (UM3500, six hours), Garage Atâr is on the road to Atâr, about 3km north of the airport. Ksar Gare Routière (near the airport) serves destinations to the southeast: Kiffa (UM4500, 10 hours), Ayoûn el-Atroûs (UM6000, 14 hours) and

MAURITANIA

Néma (UM7500, 24 hours). You should also be able to find bush taxis to Tidjikja (UM5600, 10 hours) from here.

GETTING AROUND

A taxi ride within the centre costs around UM200. From the airport, the standard taxi fare to the centre is about UM1000, but it's cheaper to hail a taxi from the highway nearby (UM300).

THE ATLANTIC COAST

No tacky resorts. No pollution. This coastline is a rapturous place for tranquillity seekers and nature-lovers. It's mostly occupied by the Parc National du Banc d'Arguin, something of a pilgrimage site for birdwatchers.

NOUÂDHIBOU
pop 80,000

With the new tar road connecting the Moroccan border to Nouakchott, the fishing port of Nouâdhibou has lost much of its *raison d'être* for travellers, who prefer to dash to the capital or to the Adrar region. It's a good base, though, if you plan to visit Banc d'Arguin. The setting is also appealing: Nouâdhibou is on the Baie du Lévrier, in the middle of a narrow 35km-long peninsula.

There are several bureaux de change along the city's main drag, Blvd Médian, and most of the internet outlets along here also double as telephone offices. The 'station' is about 5km south of town.

Sleeping & Eating

Camping Chez Abba (☎ 574 9896; fax 574 9887; Blvd Médian; tent per person UM1500, s/d UM3200/4400; **P**) A good overlanders' haunt, this has plenty of space to park and pitch a tent, and a few decent rooms with their own bathrooms and hot water. Recommended.

Camping Baie du Lévrier (☎ 574 6536, mobile 650 4356; Blvd Médian; s/d UM3000/5000; **P**) Also known as Chez Ali, this auberge-style place has a good location and a welcoming and knowledgeable owner-manager. Rooms are a bit cell-like, and bathroom facilities are shared, but there is a tent to relax in and cooking facilities.

Hôtel Al Jezira (☎ 574 5317; Blvd Maritime; s/d incl breakfast UM13,000/15,000; **P** ✗) Nouâdhibou isn't overrun with top-class accommodation, but this midrange hotel slightly north of the centre just about works out. Rates

are slightly high for what's on offer, but the rooms are fair, and occasionally border on the comfy.

Restaurant-Pâtisserie Pleine Lune (☎ 574 9860; off Blvd Médian; mains UM1000-1500) We like this place for its breakfasts – decent coffee and a good selection of pastries, but it's good at any time of day, with pizzas and sandwiches as quick fillers, or grilled fish and *brochettes* for something more substantial.

Le Mérou (☎ 574 5980; Blvd Médian; mains UM1500-2500) This restaurant on the main drag is as upscale as Nouâdhibou's dining scene gets. Marine murals on the wall remind you that fish is always the dish of the day, from plates of tasty shrimp to some serious seafood steaks.

In the centre, you'll find a slew of cheap restaurants along Rue de la Galérie Mahfoud. They're nothing fancy, serving fish and *mafé* for around UM300 a plate.

Getting There & Away

Mauritania Airways flies four times a week to Nouakchott (UM20,000, one hour).

There are plenty of bush taxis from the *gare routière* to Nouakchott (UM4500, six hours). You can also get transport from here to Morocco (Western Sahara). Taxis go most days to Dakhla (UM11,500, eight hours). Arrive early – any later than 8am and you'll be facing a long wait for the vehicles to fill and go.

For more information on the train from Nouâdhibou to Choûm and Zouérat, see the boxed text, p440.

PARC NATIONAL DU BANC D'ARGUIN

This World Heritage–listed **park** (www.mauritania.mr/pnba, in French; per person per day UM1200) is an important stopover and breeding ground for multitudes of birds migrating between Europe and southern Africa, and as a result is one of the best birdwatching sites on the entire continent. It extends 200km north from Cape Timiris (155km north of Nouakchott) and 235km south of Nouâdhibou. The ideal way to approach the birds is by traditional fishing boat (UM15,000, plus UM3000 for the guide), best organised from the fishing village of **Iwik**.

Inside the park there are official campsites that are equipped with traditional tents (UM3000 to UM6000 per tent). Meals can also be ordered. There's no public transport, so you'll need to hire a 4WD with a knowledgeable driver, either in Nouakchott or in Nouâdhibou, allowing three days for the trip. Permits are issued either at the entrance gates or in Nouâdhibou at the **park office** (☎ 574 6744; Blvd Médian; ☺ 8am-4pm Mon-Thu, to noon Fri). Both this office and the park's Nouakchott **headquarters** (☎ 525 8514; Ave Abdel Nasser) sell a map and guide to the park, including GPS waypoints.

THE ADRAR

The Adrar is the undoubted jewel in Mauritania's crown. It's epic Saharan country, and shows the great desert in all its variety: the ancient Saharan towns of Chinguetti and Ouadâne, mighty sand dunes that look sculpted by an artist, vast rocky plateaus and mellow oases fringed with date palms. For desert lovers, the Adrar is a must.

ATÂR
pop 25,000

With the grandiose Adrar on your doorstep, this secluded town in the middle of the desert is an excellent place in which to organise camel or 4WD forays into the dunefields.

A large *rond-point* (roundabout) marks the centre of Atâr and the market is just north of it. You'll find several bureaux de change, telephone offices and internet cafes on or around the main drag.

Activities

There are over a dozen agencies in Atâr that can arrange **camel rides** or **4WD tours**, so shop around. The main costs are the vehicle and driver, so trips are a lot cheaper if you're in a group. Count on paying up to UM21,000 per day for a Toyota Hilux plus petrol. Add about UM2000 per day per person for food. Camel trips start at UM12,000 per day with food and lodging.

Sleeping & Eating

Auberge du Bonheur (☎ 546 4537; fax 546 4347; tent/hut per person UM1500, r UM4000; ☒ ▢) Those wanting a reliable base could do worse than this welcoming outfit, a five-minute stroll from the centre. It's nicely turned out, with simple but decent rooms, a large tent in the courtyard and everything kept scrubbed pretty clean.

our pick Auberge Bab Sahara (☎ 546 4573, 647 3966; justusbuma@yahoo.com; tent per person UM2000, stone hut/caravan UM8000/5000, parking motorbike/ car/truck UM200/400/1000; ℗ ☒) Off Rte de Azougui, Bab Sahara has been a little slice of overlanders' heaven for over a dozen years. There's a selection of *tikits* (stone huts, with AC), caravans and tents, plus a campsite in another compound and a mechanic's workshop. Meals are available on request. The Dutch-German couple who run it are great sources of local information and travel advice.

Auberge Tivoujar (☎ 678 1342, 625 5182; www. vuedenhaut.com; tikit/r per person incl half-board UM6000/10,000; ℗ ☒ ▢) About 4km from the centre on the road to Nouakchott, this hotel packs the tour groups in during the season. Rooms have bathrooms, amenities are good and services run to hot air balloon rides over the desert.

Hôtel Monod (☎ 546 4236; Rte de Chinguetti; r UM8000; ☒) One of the few proper hotels in Atâr, the Monod offers the novelty of rooms with bathrooms. It's all perfectly serviceable, although thoroughly lacking in personality.

Restaurant du Coin (market, off Rte de Chinguetti; meals UM300) From the *rond-point* head down the Chinguetti road for a block, then turn left. This place is on the right-hand corner, marked by a tiny sign. It's as down-at-heel as you can get, serving up great quantities of rice, fish and Senegalese *mafé*. It's always busy, and the food piping hot and delicious.

Restaurant Agadir (Rte de Chinguetti; mains UM500-700) Near the *rond-point*, this cheap and cheerful eatery rustles up some good couscous and tajines as well as sandwiches and lighter bites.

L'Assiette F (☎ 610 7150; Rte de Chinguetti; set menu UM2500; ☺ closed May-Aug) This French-run place brings a touch of culinary sophistication to rough and ready Atâr. It has good fish, potato omelettes, *crêpes* (pancakes) and the occasional salad, as well as good breakfasts. There's shady outdoor seating at the rear.

Getting There & Away

The main *gare routière*, in the heart of town, is where you can get vehicles for Nouakchott (UM3500, six hours) and Choûm (UM1500, three hours). Choûm transport is timed to meet the train heading to/from Nouâdhibou.

Vehicles for Chinguetti (car/4WD UM1500/2500, about two hours) leave once a day from near a shop located a block north of Hotel Monod. Most days there is also transport to Ouadâne (bush taxi/4WD UM3000/4000, about four hours), leaving from a street north

MAURITANIA

BEN AMIRA

Big rocks don't come much more awesome than Ben Amira. Rising 633m out of the desert, it's Africa's biggest monolith, and in size is second only to Australia's Ayers Rock (Uluru). It's clearly visible from the train between Nouâdhibou and Zouérat, but if you have a 4WD it makes a brilliant one-night camping trip from Atâr.

There are actually two granite monoliths. Ben Amira is the largest, with slightly smaller Aïsha to the west. While Ben Amira is more massively spectacular, Aïsha holds a delightful surprise of her own. In December 1999, a symposium of 16 international sculptors was held here to celebrate the millennium, turning many of the boulders at the base of Aïsha into art. The natural shapes of the rocks were reinterpreted as animals, birds, faces and abstract creations. It's a wonderful spot, all the more so for being completely unheralded by its surroundings.

The monoliths are 4km north of the train track between Nouâdhibou and Choûm, at Km 395 (Ben Amira village sits next to the tracks here). The route is sand rather than gravel *piste* (track). Aïsha is 5km west of Ben Amira. To find the sculptures, head for the eastern side of Aïsha, where it appears to join a lower mound made of giant 'melted' rocks: the sculptures are here.

of the roundabout (ask for *'gare de Ouadâne'*). For Azougui (UM500, 20 minutes) and Terjît (UM1000, one hour), infrequent 4WDs leave from near the roundabout.

TERJÎT

We've never visited an oasis quite like Terjît. About 40km south of Atâr, a streak of palm groves is hemmed in by great red cliffs. At its head, two springs tumble out of the rocks. One is hot, the other cold, and they mix to form a natural swimming pool the perfect temperature for a dip. It's simply bliss. You pay UM1000 to enter the site.

The main spring has been taken over by **Auberge Oasis de Terjît** (☎ 644 8967, in Atâr 546 5020; tents/huts per person UM1500), where a mattress in a tent by the trickling stream is on offer. A meal costs about UM1500. The only other place to stay is the **Auberge des Caravanes** (r/tikits per person UM1500; P), a traveller-friendly place at the entrance of the village.

To get here by private car, drive 40km south of Atâr on the road to Nouakchott, then turn left at the checkpoint and follow a sandy track for 11km. By public transport, take anything headed towards Nouakchott and hitch a ride from the checkpoint.

CHINGUETTI
pop 4000

One of the more attractive of the ancient caravan towns in the Sahara, Chinguetti is shrouded with a palpable historic aura. Once famous for its Islamic scholars, it was the ancient capital of the Moors, and some of the buildings date from the 13th century.

Chinguetti butts up against Erg Warane, Mauritania's biggest stretch of dunes, and more than enough to meet expectations of the great Saharan sand ocean.

The highlight of any visit is a wander through the labyrinthine lanes of **Le Ksar** (the Old Town). The principal attraction is the 16th-century stone mosque (no entry to non-Muslims). Also of great interest are the five old libraries, which house the fragile-as-dust ancient Islamic manuscripts of Chinguetti.

The best way to see the fascinating dunes around Chinguetti is by camel. Numerous *méharées* (camel trips) are available. Standard costs start from UM8000 per person per day for the camel, food and guide. Any reputable travel agency in Atâr or auberge owner can arrange **camel rides**. If you don't want to sweat it out, you can hire a 4WD and driver. They cost from UM17,000 per day, petrol not included.

Sleeping & Eating

All the places listed here have shared bathroom unless stated otherwise. Breakfast and meals are available on request (about UM2000 per meal).

Auberge La Rose des Sables (☎ 540 0148; New Town; stone hut/tent per person UM1500) Stumbling distance from Auberge Abweir, this auberge is run by the amiable Cheikh Ould Amar. It is a touch more rundown than its competitors but still fits the bill for shoestringers, with adequate stone huts arranged in a compact compound.

Auberge des Caravanes (☎ 540 0022; fax 546 4272; New Town; r per person UM2000) With its eye-catching, traditional architecture, it's hard to miss this place right in the centre of town. Rooms are pretty simple, and it can feel a bit impersonal, but it's adequate for the price.

Auberge Abweir (☎ 540 0124; abweirauberge@yahoo. fr; New Town; stone hut/tent per person UM2500) Next door to Auberge des Caravanes, this welcoming place will appeal to a more sedate crowd, with a bunch of simple yet well-organised stone huts and small tents set around a plant-filled courtyard. The well-scrubbed ablution block is an added bonus.

L'Eden de Chinguetti (☎ 540 0014; New Town; r UM6000-8000) This impressive auberge is a great place to stay. It's neat, well tended and embellished with well-chosen knick-knacks and a nice garden. The English-speaking owner is a mine of information. It's on the road to Atâr, not far from Auberge La Rose des Sables.

ourpick **Le Maure Bleu** (☎ 540 0154, 205 3819; www.maurebleu.com; Old Town; s with/without bathroom €30/24, d with/without bathroom €34/40) One of Adrar's most appealing places to stay. This peach of a place has oodles of rustic charm and features well-arranged rooms and is trying to be green with its composting toilets (rooms with private bathrooms only). Breakfast is included, while other meals are good enough to make a detour for.

Restaurant 7 Merveilles (☎ 609 7837; New Town; meals UM500-1500) Centrally located, with a pleasant roof terrace offering Saharan views. Meals range from simple sandwiches to pasta and couscous, plus it's a good place to nurse a cold drink or coffee.

Getting There & Away

There is at least one vehicle a day to/from Atâr (car/4WD UM1500/2500, two hours) They leave from just behind the market. There are no bush taxis between Chinguetti and Ouadâne; you'll have to go back to Atâr.

OUADÂNE

Sitting on the edge of the Adrar plateau, 120km northeast of Chinguetti, Ouadâne is one of the most enchanting semi-ghost towns of the Sahara. As you arrive across the sands or plateau from Atâr or Chinguetti, the stone houses of **Le Ksar al Kiali** (Old Quarter; admission UM1000) seem to tumble down the cliff. The top of the hill is dominated by the minaret of the new mosque, which is a mere 200 years old, while at the western end, at the base of the town, is the 14th-century **old mosque**. In

between, the crumbling structures seem to have been piled up higgledy-piggledy by some giant child playing with building blocks. Like Chinguetti, Ouadâne was a place of scholarship and is home to over 3000 manuscripts held in private libraries. Only 20 to 30 families still live in the old town.

All places to stay can prepare meals for their guests (about UM2000 for lunch or dinner) – try the *ksour*, a local thick pancake made of wheat. The places listed here are down on the plateau. Mellow **Auberge Vasque – Chez Zaida** (☎ 681 7669; tikits/tents per person UM1700) is run by Zaida, a congenial lady who goes out of her way to make your stay a happy one. There are five *tikits* and a couple of nomad's tents. Rooms at **Auberge Warane I** (☎ in Atâr 546 4604; r/tents per person UM1500) are a bit bunker-like but serviceable enough, although **Auberge Agoueidir – Chez Isselmou** (☎ 525 0791; agoueidir@yahoo.fr; tikits/ tents per person UM1200/2500, s/d UM5000/7000) is the best outfit, with orderly rooms (with proper beds), as well as a number of tents and *tikits*. The shared bathrooms won't make you squirm and the well-tended sand-floored courtyard is a good place to idle away some time.

Getting There & Away

Without your own vehicle, getting to Ouadâne isn't always straightforward. Atâr is the place to look for transport, and vehicles run between the two most days, usually in the morning (bush taxi/4WD UM3000/4000, about four hours). Direct transport between Ouadâne and Chinguetti runs next to never.

If driving you have two alternatives: the southerly Piste du Batha, which passes through sand dunes and requires a 4WD and guide, and the northerly Piste du Dhar Chinguetti along the plateau, which is in very good condition. The latter departs the Atâr–Chinguetti road 18km before Chinguetti.

THE ROAD TO MALI

The Rte de l'Espoir (Road to Hope) from Nouakchott to Néma (around 1100km) is now entirely tarred, giving a smooth (if still very long) trip to the border.

The first major town on the road to the Malian border is **Kiffa** (population 30,000), an important regional trading centre and

MAURITANIA

crossroads, where you can bunk down at **Auberge Le Phare du Désert** (☎ 644 2421; phare rim@yahoo.fr; tikits UM10,000; 🏶) on the outskirts of Kiffa.

You could also break up your journey at lively **Ayoûn el-Atroûs**, which is a good place to spend your last ouguiyas before crossing into Mali. For accommodation, try the unpretentious **Hôtel Ayoûn** (☎ 515 1462; s/d UM5000/8000; 🏶), which is in the centre, or **Auberge Saada Tenzah** (☎ 515 1337, 641 1052; r UM2500-6000), about 3km east of the centre on the road to Néma.

The tarred road ends at the town of **Néma**, the jumping-off point for Oualâta. You'll find several petrol pumps here, a couple of modest stores and a police station at which you can get your passport stamped. You can base yourself at **Complexe Touristique N'Gady** (☎ 513 0900; bungalows s/d UM7000/9000; r 12,000-15,000; Ⓟ 🏶), a few kilometres west of the centre.

For more details on reaching this area by public transport, see p433.

OUALÂTA

Possibly one of Mauritania's best-kept secrets, Oualâta is another ancient Saharan town high on atmosphere and personality. Dating from 1224, it used to be the last resting point for caravans heading for Timbuktu. It's about 100km north of Néma but is definitely worth the gruelling ride to get here.

Entering the town you'll be struck by the red **mudbrick houses** adorned with decorative paintings on the exterior and interior. There's also a small museum and a library, which houses ancient Islamic manuscripts. There are also several rock paintings and archaeological sites in the vicinity. Various camel trips can also be organised (ask your hosts).

Although you're miles from anywhere, you'll find about six guesthouses to rest your weary limbs, including **Auberge Tayib/Gamni - Auberge de l'Hotel de Ville** (r per person UM3000) and **Auberge de l'Amitié** (r per person UM1500). A notch up, **Auberge Ksar Walata** (r per person UM5000) features a lovely patio and attractive rooms. They all serve meals.

There are two dirt tracks between Néma and Oualâta (approximately 110km). Land Rovers ply the route between the two towns (UM2000, 2½ hours) on an infrequent basis. Ask around in Néma market.

MAURITANIA DIRECTORY

ACCOMMODATION

In general, you can expect to spend less than US$15 per person in places we list as budget options and up to US$50 for midrange. There's also a sprinkle of air-conditioned hotels meeting international standards in Nouakchott and, to a lesser extent, Nouâdhibou and Atâr. In the desert, you'll find numerous basic auberges or *campements*. They consist of a series of *tikits* (stone huts) or *khaimas* (tents) that come equipped with mattresses on the floor.

The last couple of years have seen a gradual improvement in the choice on offer, with a growing number of tasteful, midrange *maisons d'hôtes*.

ACTIVITIES

Camel rides and 4WD expeditions in the desert are the most popular activities. For birdwatching, nothing can beat the Parc National du Banc d'Arguin, one of the world's greatest birdlife-viewing venues.

BUSINESS HOURS

Although it's a Muslim country, for business purposes Mauritania adheres to the Monday to Friday working week. Friday is the main prayer day, so many businesses have an extended lunch break on Friday afternoon. Many shops are open every day.

Government offices, post offices and banks Usually open from 8am to 4pm Monday to Thursday and from 8am to 1pm on Friday.

CUSTOMS REGULATIONS

It is illegal to bring alcohol into the country.

DANGERS & ANNOYANCES

Mauritania is generally one of the safest countries in Africa, particularly the capital and the main tourist region of the Adrar.

In 2008, the Paris–Dakar Rally was cancelled due to threats against the Mauritanian leg by Islamist groups. Although there have subsequently been a small number of incidents, these have been restricted to remote areas unvisited by foreigners, such as around the Algerian border. In the southeast, however, security problems in Mali have threatened to spill across the border. Coupled with periodic reports of banditry on the roads, travellers should take trusted advice before planning to travel in this region.

EMBASSIES & CONSULATES
The following countries are represented in Nouakchott:

France (☎ 525 2337; Rue Ahmed Ould Mohamed)
Germany (☎ 525 1729; Rue Abdallaye)
Mali (☎ 525 4081, 525 4078; Tevragh Zeina)
Morocco (☎ 525 1411; Ave du Général de Gaulle)
Senegal (☎ 525 7290; Rue de l'Ambassade du Sénégal)
USA (☎ 525 2660; fax 525 1592; Rue Abdallaye)

HOLIDAYS
Public holidays include:
New Year's Day 1 January
National Reunification Day 26 February
Workers' Day 1 May
African Liberation Day 25 May
Army Day 10 July
Independence Day 28 November
Anniversary of the 1984 Coup 12 December

Mauritania also celebrates the usual Islamic holidays – see p1140.

INTERNET ACCESS
You can get online in any reasonably sized town, although outside Nouakchott connection speeds can often be wanting. Expect to pay around UM200 an hour.

MONEY
The unit of currency is the ouguiya (UM). Take wads of euros and US dollars; travellers cheques and credit cards are pretty useless. At the time of research only one ATM in the entire country (at BNP Paribas in Nouakchott) accepted international bank cards. Credit cards are accepted only at top-end hotels in Nouakchott.

TELEPHONE
You can make international calls and send faxes at post offices. The innumerable privately run phone shops in the major cities and towns cost about the same and are open late. A GSM SIM card for the Mauritel and Mattel networks costs around UM2000.

There are no telephone area codes.

VISAS
Visas are required for all except nationals of Arab League countries and some African countries. In countries where Mauritania has no diplomatic representation, including Australia, French embassies will issue visas for around US$30. For overlanders, Rabat (Morocco) is a good place for visas; they're also issued at the Moroccan border (€25).

One-month visa extensions can be obtained for UM5000 at the **Sûreté** (off Ave Abdel Nasser, Nouakchott; ⊙ 8am-3pm Mon-Thu).

Visas for Onward Travel
In Nouakchott you can get visas for the following neighbouring countries:

MALI
One-month visas are issued the same day (UM6500). You need two photos and a passport photocopy.

MOROCCO
Most nationalities do not require visas, and simply get an entry stamp valid for 90 days on arrival. Nationalities that do (mostly Africans, including Mauritanians) must pay UM8700 and provide two photos and passport photocopies and (according to whim) an air ticket.

SENEGAL
One-month visas (UM1500) are issued in 24 hours. You need to supply four photos plus passport photocopies.

WOMEN TRAVELLERS
Mauritania is a conservative Muslim country, but it is by no means the most extreme in this regard. Women might get the odd bit of sexual harassment, but it's nothing in comparison with some North African countries. It's wise to dress modestly, covering the upper legs and arms and avoiding shorts or skimpy T-shirts.

PRACTICALITIES

- Mauritania uses the metric system for weights and measures.
- Electrical current is 220V AC, 50Hz and most electrical plugs are of the European two-pin type.
- Mauritania's only TV station is TVM, with programs in Hassaniyya and French, but top-end hotels have satellite TV.
- For the news (in French), pick up *Le Calame* or *Horizons*.

TRANSPORT IN MAURITANIA

GETTING THERE & AWAY

Air

Nouakchott, Nouâdhibou and Atâr have international airports. Nouakchott's airport handles most traffic.

The only direct flights from Europe are through Paris, with Air France, Mauritania Airways and Point Afrique.

Mauritania Airways flies five times a week between Nouakchott and Dakar, twice weekly to Bamako and four times to Abidjan. Air Senegal flies every day except Sunday. For other Saharan or sub-Saharan countries, you'll have to change in Dakar or Abidjan.

Mauritania is well connected to North Africa. Royal Air Maroc operates between Casablanca and Nouakchott five times a week, while Tunis Air connects Tunis with Nouakchott (three times a week). Air Algérie flies to Algiers twice a week.

All airlines flying to/from Nouakchott have an office in the capital (see p433).

Land

MALI

At the time of research, the most straightforward route to Mali was from Ayoûn el-Atroûs to Nioro. You can also cross at Néma, Timbedgha (both connecting with Nara in Mali) and Kiffa (connecting with Nioro in Mali).

From Nouakchott, you can catch bush taxis to Néma and Ayoûn el-Atroûs. From these places you can catch a bush taxi to Nara or Nioro. It's also possible to travel from Sélibaby to Kayes.

If crossing into Mali, have your passport stamped by police at the first town you reach after crossing the border. You must also clear customs, which is done in Néma or Ayoûn el-Atroûs.

MOROCCO

The trans-Sahara route via Mauritania is now a very popular route from North Africa into sub-Saharan Africa. This crosses the internationally disputed territory of Western Sahara, although the border itself is administered by Morocco.

The only border crossing between Morocco/Western Sahara and Mauritania is north of Nouâdhibou. Crossing this border is straightforward and the road is entirely tarred to Nouakchott, except for the 3km no-man's land that separates the two border posts.

There are direct bush taxis heading north from Nouâdhibou to Dakhla (Western Sahara), but travelling in the opposite direction you'll need to change vehicles at the border. The 425km trip can easily be accomplished in a day.

SENEGAL

The main border crossing for Senegal is at Rosso (by ferry), but it's also possible to cross by bridge at Diamma (Keur Masséne), west of Rosso. The latter is a much calmer experience, as Rosso is notorious for its hassles, although road conditions make Diamma largely a dry-season option.

From Dakar to Nouakchott by public transport usually takes from 11 to 13 hours depend-

---

AN EPIC JOURNEY ON THE IRON-ORE TRAIN

Africa offers some pretty wild train trips, but the train ferrying iron ore from the mines at Zouérat to Nouâdhibou might just be the wildest. One of the longest trains in the world (typically a staggering 2.3km long), when it arrives at the 'station' in Nouâdhibou, a decrepit building in the open desert, a seemingly endless number of ore wagons pass before the passenger carriage at the rear finally appears. The lucky ones find a place on one of the two long benches (UM2500); the rest stand or sit on the floor. There are also a dozen 'berths' (3000) that are so worn out you can see the springs. It's brutally basic. It's also possible to clamber into the ore cars and travel for free. Impossibly dusty, it's only for the really hardcore. Plastic sheets are essential to wrap your bags (and person), plus plenty of warm clothes, as the desert gets fearsomely cold at night, as well as food and drink.

The train leaves Nouâdhibou at around 2pm to 3pm daily. Most travellers get off at Choûm, 12 hours later, where bush taxis wait to take passengers to Atâr, three hours away. In the other direction, the train leaves Zouérat around midday and passes through Atâr at about 5.30pm.

ing on the wait at the border. At Rosso, most travellers without vehicles cross by *pirogue* (UM200/CFA500, five minutes) as the ferry crosses only four times daily. Immigration is only open on the Mauritanian side from 9am to 11am and 3.30pm to 5pm.

Vehicles cost from UM2000/CFA5000. Customs fees are around UM1500 if you're entering Mauritania, CFA2000 for Senegal, but officials here are reported to be notoriously greedy, so keep your paperwork (and vehicle) in good order.

GETTING AROUND
Air
Mauritania Airways flies four times a week from Nouakchott to Nouâdhibou (UM20,000, one hour) and three times a week to Zouérate (UM39,000, three hours). There are plans to extend services to the south.

Bush Taxi
The bush taxi *(taxi brousse)* is the main form of public transport in Mauritania, primarily Mercedes 190s and Peugeot 504s in that order of expense, followed by the occasional Land Rover and battered minibus when tarmac roads are replaced by *piste*. Bush taxis go to all the major towns daily.

Car & Motorcycle
Mauritania's road network is mostly good, with tarred roads leading from the border with Western Sahara to Nouakchott, and on to the Senegalese and Malian borders at Rosso

and Nioro respectively. The roads from the capital to Atâr and Tidjikja are also tarred. Elsewhere, *piste* is the order of the day, although great swathes of the country are little more than sandy tracks (at best). Police checkpoints abound; make your own form *(fiche)* to hand over. List all the personal details from your passport (including visa number), home address, occupation and parents' names, plus your vehicle's make, colour and registration number. Make plenty of photocopies.

Consider renting a 4WD and driver if you want to reach more remote parts of the country. The standard Toyota Hilux usually costs around UM21,000 per day for the vehicle, plus petrol.

Tours
There are numerous travel agencies in Nouakchott that offer tours around the country, but it's not a bad idea to arrange a tour with a more regional-focused company – eg in Atâr for the Adrar or the Tagânt. If there are at least four travellers, prices should average around UM17,000 to UM21,000 per person per day.

Train
The Nouâdhibou–Zouérat train (see the boxed text, opposite) is certainly an epic adventure. It's an iron-ore train with no passenger terminals, but it's become a passenger train for lack of better alternatives. The trip takes 16 to 18 hours, but most travellers get off at Choûm (close to Atâr), 12 hours from Nouâdhibou.

MAURITANIA

Niger

Niger only seems to make the news for bad reasons: its recent coup, the Tuareg Rebellion, famine and – incredibly, as revealed in a trial in 2008 – its ongoing slavery problem. But if you make the effort to visit this desert republic, you'll find a warm and generous Muslim population and some superb tout-free West African travel through ancient caravan cities at the edge of the Sahara.

Sadly, at the time of writing the country's greatest attractions, the Ténéré Desert and the Aïr Mountains in the north remained closed to travellers due to the Tuareg Rebellion. However, Libyan-brokered ceasefire talks between the Niger Movement for Justice (MNJ) and the government brought an end to the conflict, on paper at least, in 2009. The situation on the ground remains unstable, however, and you should always check the latest information before heading to the country's north.

Despite the closure of much of the county's north, at the time of writing the fascinating trans-Saharan trade-route town of Agadez was still accessible, as well as a bevy of attractions in the peaceful south: the ancient sultanate of Zinder, the fantastic W National Park, West Africa's last herd of wild giraffe at Kouré and the impossibly romantic Sunday market of Ayorou. Add to this the laid-back but cosmopolitan capital of Niamey and a trip down the mighty Niger River in a dugout pirogue, and you've got yourself a West African adventure that can cheerfully rival any other in this book.

FAST FACTS

- **Area** 1,267,000 sq km
- **ATMs** Nonexistent
- **Borders** Algeria, Mali, Burkina Faso, Benin, Nigeria, Chad; the land border with Libya is currently closed
- **Budget** US$15 to US$70 a day
- **Capital** Niamey
- **Languages** French, Hausa, Djerma, Fulfulde, Tamashek
- **Money** West African CFA franc; US$1 = CFA463, €1 = CFA656
- **Population** 14.7 million
- **Seasons** Hot and dry (September to May), wet (June to August)
- **Telephone** Country code ☎ 227; international access code ☎ 00
- **Time** GMT/UTC + 1
- **Visa** Required by almost everyone except West African citizens. Obtained easily in Algeria, Benin, Chad, Mali and Nigeria. Niger is covered by the Visa des Pays de l'Entente.

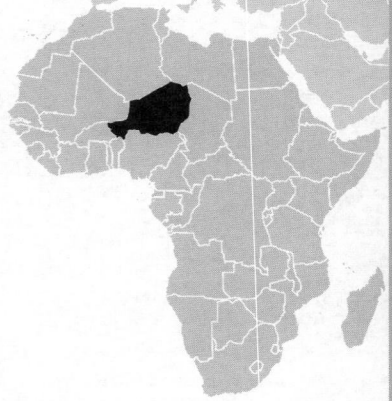

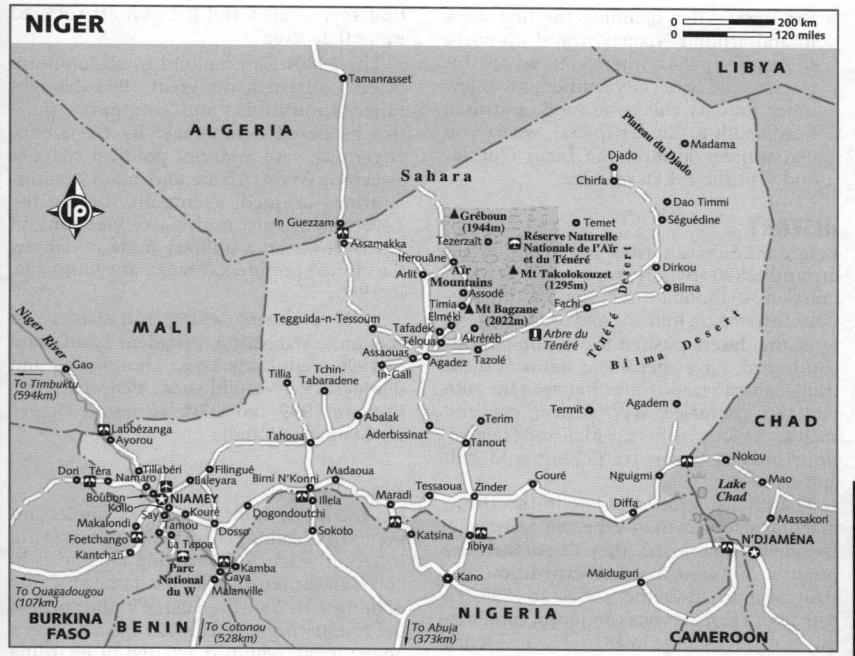

HIGHLIGHTS

- **Agadez** (p454) Spiral up to the spiky summit of the majestic mud mosque here for incredible views over the Sahara and beyond.

HOW MUCH?

- Sachet of purified water US$0.10
- Croix d'Agadez (historically stylised silver cross) US$3.30
- Simple Tuareg grigri (amulet) US$4.40
- Street snack (beignet) US$0.05
- Moto-taxi across any town US$0.50

LONELY PLANET INDEX

- 1L petrol US$1.50
- 1.5L bottled water US$1.10
- Bottle of Bière Niger US$1.10
- Souvenir T-shirt US$3.30
- Grilled beef brochettes US$0.20

- **Ayorou** (p450) Savour the aromas at the country's most exciting market.
- **Kouré** (p450) Wander in wonder with West Africa's last wild herd of giraffes.
- **Zinder** (p452) Explore the Birni Quartier and soak up the brutal history at the sultan's palace in this fascinating Hausa city.
- **Parc Regional du W** (p451) Come face to face with lions, crocodiles, monkeys and elephants in this incredibly diverse national park.

CLIMATE & WHEN TO GO

December to February, the coolest and driest period, is the best time to visit. Temperatures can soar beyond 45°C from March through to June, making desert travel unfeasible. Rains dampen the south from late May until September.

ITINERARIES

- **One Week** Base yourself in Niamey and make a series of day trips to Ayorou (p450), Filingué (p451) and to the giraffes near Kouré (p450), before spending two nights in the wonderful Parc Regional du W (p451) in the south.

■ **Two Weeks** After spending the first week in and around Niamey, travel up north to Agadez (p454), where you can see this glorious old Sahel city confident that few other tourists will be around, and then head south to Zinder (p452), where you can wander around the Birni Quarter and visit the sultan's palace.

HISTORY

Before the Sahara started swallowing Niger around 2500 BC, it supported verdant grasslands, abundant wildlife and populations thriving on hunting and herding. Long after the desert pushed those populations southward, Niger became a fixture on the trans-Saharan trade route. Between the 10th and 18th centuries, West African empires, such as the Kanem-Borno, Mali and Songhaï, flourished in Niger, trafficking gold, salt and slaves.

The French strolled in late in the 1800s, meeting stronger-than-expected resistance. Decidedly unamused, they dispatched the punitive Voulet-Chanoîne expedition, destroying much of southern Niger in 1898–99. Although Tuareg revolts continued, culminating in Agadez's siege in 1916–17, the French had control.

French rule wasn't kind. They cultivated traditional chiefs' power, whose abuses were encouraged as a means of control, and the enforced shift from subsistence farming to high-density cash crops compounded the Sahara's ongoing migration.

In 1958 France offered its West African colonies self-government in a French union or immediate independence. Countless votes disappeared, enabling France to claim that Niger wished to remain within its sphere of influence.

Maintaining close French ties, Niger's first president, Hamani Diori, ran a repressive one-party state. After surviving several coups, he was overthrown by Lieutenant Colonel Seyni Kountché after food stocks were discovered in ministerial homes during the Sahel drought of 1968–74. Kountché established a military ruling council.

Kountché hit the jackpot in 1968 when uranium was discovered near the town of Arlit. Mining incomes soon ballooned, leading to ambitious projects, including the 'uranium highway' between Agadez and Arlit. Yet not everyone was smiling: infla-

tion skyrocketed and the poorest suffered more than ever.

The 1980s were unkind to all: uranium prices collapsed, the great 1983 drought killed thousands, and one-party politics hindered democracy. By the 1990s, Nigeriens were aware of political changes sweeping West Africa and mass demonstrations erupted, eventually forcing the government into multiparty elections in 1993. However, a military junta overthrew the elected president, Mahamane Ousmane, in 1996.

In 1999, during widespread strikes and economic stagnation, president Mainassara (a 1996 coup leader) was assassinated and democracy re-established. Peaceful elections in 1999 and 2004 witnessed victory for Mamadou Tandja.

Niger Today

On the home front, a series of unpleasant events have defined Niger to the outside world in recent years. A devastating food crisis in 2005 saw the return of all-too-familiar scenes of hunger. In 2007 the Tuareg in the north of the country began a rebellion against Niger's government, whom it accused of hoarding proceeds from the region's enormous mineral wealth and failing to meet conditions of previous ceasefires, in a conflict that has reignited at regular intervals since the early 20th century.

A year later Niger again made headlines around the world for less-than-positive reasons when in a landmark case an Ecowas (West African regional trade group) court found Niger guilty of failing to protect a young woman from the continued practice of slavery in the country.

In 2009 Mamadou Tandja won a referendum allowing him to change the constitution to allow him to run for a third term. In the presidential elections that year Tandja won by a large magin, though Ecowas did not accept the result and suspended Niger's membership. The tables were turned on Tandja in February 2010 when a military coup in Niamey led to his arrest and more uncertainty about the country's future. Despite worldwide condemnation and Niger's suspension from the African Union, at the time of writing the coup was enjoying support and its leaders were promising democratic elections.

CULTURE

Niger boasts the highest birth rate in the world: women have a staggering average of eight children each. The population is predicted to reach 21.4 million by 2025.

More than 90% of Nigeriens live in the south, which is dominated by Hausa and Songhaï-Djerma, making up 56% and 23% of Niger's populace respectively. The next largest groups are nomadic Fulani (8.5%) and Tuareg (8%), both in Niger's north, and Kanuri (4.3%), located between Zinder and Chad.

Nigeriens are predominantly Muslim (over 90%), with small percentages of Christian urban dwellers. Several rural populations still practise traditional animist religions. Due to the strong influence of Nigeria's Islamic community, some Muslims around the border town of Maradi call for Sharia'a law.

Arguably the world's poorest people, Nigeriens are also proud and quick with welcoming smiles and occasional spontaneous acts of generosity. Similarly refreshing is their willingness to work to improve Niger.

Despite most Nigeriens being devoutly Muslim, the government is steadfastly secular and Islam adopts a more relaxed aura than in nations with similar demographics. Women don't cover their faces, alcohol is quietly consumed and some Tuareg, recognising the harshness of desert life, ignore Ramadan's fast.

While Islam plays the greatest role in daily life, shaping beliefs and thoughts, little is visible to visitors. The biggest exceptions are *salat* (prayer), when Niger grinds to a halt – buses even break journeys to partake.

Religion aside, survival occupies most people's days. Around 90% make their tenuous living from agriculture and livestock, many surviving on US$1 or less per day. Producing numerous children to help with burdening workloads is a necessity for many, a fact contributing to population growth. The fact of children being obliged to work has led to staggering adult illiteracy rates.

Niger's best-known artisans are Tuareg silversmiths, who produce necklaces, striking amulets, ornamental silver daggers and stylised silver crosses, each with intricate filigree designs representing areas boasting Tuareg populations. The most famous cross is the *croix d'Agadez*. To Tuareg, crosses are powerful talismans protecting against ill fortune.

SUPERSIZE ME!

During years of bountiful harvests, Niamey's Djerma population celebrate the festival of Hangandi. Although festivities are enjoyable, it's the beauty contest's reputation that keeps on growing and growing, much like its competitors. You see, in the eye of the Djerma, the larger the better. Prior to Hangandi, Djerma women who've been chosen to compete (some plucked off buses!) train by ingesting as much food as possible. Everything culminates with the most gorgeous (read massive) woman being crowned at the Palais du Congrès. Her reward? More food!

Leatherwork by *artisans du cuir* is well regarded, particularly in Zinder, where traditional items – such as saddlebags, cushions and tasselled pouches – rank alongside attractive modernities like sandals and briefcases.

Beautifully unique to Niger are vibrant *kountas* (Djerma blankets), produced from bright cotton strips.

FOOD & DRINK

Dates, yoghurt, rice and mutton are standard Tuareg fare, while *riz sauce* (rice with sauce) is omnipresent in Niger's south. Standard restaurant dishes include grilled fish (particularly capitaine, or Nile perch), chicken, and beef brochettes. Couscous and ragout are also popular. Outside Niamey vegetarian options diminish.

Sitting for a cup of Tuareg tea is rewarding and thirst-quenching. For a wobble in your step, try Bière Niger. For a serious stagger, down some palm wine.

ENVIRONMENT

Two-thirds of Niger is desert, with the remaining one-third being Sahel, the semidesert zone south of the Sahara. Notable features include the Niger River (Africa's third-longest), which flows 300km through Niger's southwest; the Aïr Mountains, the dark volcanic formations of which rise over 2000m; and the Ténéré Desert's spectacularly sweeping sand dunes.

Desertification, Niger's greatest environmental problem, is primarily caused by overgrazing and deforestation. Quartz-rich

NIGER

soil also prevents topsoil anchoring, causing erosion.

The southwest's dry savannah woodland hosts one of West Africa's better wildlife parks, Parc Regional du W.

NIAMEY

pop 795,000

Compared to many West African capitals, Niamey is a charmer, with the Niger River and its verdant banks providing a focal point to the city, more than its fair share of restaurants and far livelier nightlife than you'd expect in a devoutly Muslim country.

Managing to be both bustling seat of government and relaxed backwater, the Nigerien capital is the kind of place where locals are rarely too busy to greet you with a friendly 'bonjour' and pass the time of day with you in time-honoured West African fashion.

ORIENTATION

Niamey is fairly spread out, which means more walking than other Sahel capitals. The layout is rather confusing, but signs now aid navigation. Criss-crossing through the town's hub, like a wheel's spokes – hosting restaurants, bars and banking facilities – are Rue du Président Heinrich Lubké, Ave de la Mairie and Rue du Commerce.

INFORMATION

Cultural Centres

American Cultural Center (☎ 20 73 31 69; Rue de la Tapoa; ☺ 8am-4.30pm Mon-Fri) You can use the library here, which has a selection of English-language newspapers and magazines.

Centre Culturel Franco-Nigérien Jean Rouch (☎ 20 73 48 34; Rue du Musée; ☺ 9am-12.30pm & 3.30-6.30pm Tue-Sat, 9am-noon Sun) Hosts lectures, exhibits, dance and theatre as well as a lovely garden bar perfect for a sundowner.

Internet Access

Cyber@Bebto (Blvd de l'Indépendance; per hr CFA500; ☺ 7.30am-11pm) A handy option for west Niamey.

Cybercafe Terminus (Rue du Sahel; per hr CFA500; ☺ 9am-11pm) A well-located option with lots of terminals.

Cybernet (Rue du Grand Hôtel; per hr CFA600; ☺ 8am-11pm) The best place in town, this central internet cafe has speedy connections and air-con.

Medical Services

Clinique de Gamkalé (☎ 20 73 20 33; Corniche de Gamkalé; ☺ 8.30am-12.30pm & 3.30-6.30pm Mon-Fri, 8.30am-12.30pm Sat)

Nouvelle Poly-Clinic Pro-Santé (☎ 20 72 26 50, 20 72 50 50; Ave du Général de Gaulle; ☺ 24hr)

Tafadeck (☎ 20 73 20 34; Rue du Président Heinrich Lubké; ☺ 8.30am-12.30pm & 2.30-6.30pm Mon-Fri, 8.30am-12.30pm Sat) Niamey's best dentist.

Money

BIA-Niger (Rue du Commerce; ☺ 7.45am-12.30pm & 2.15-3.45pm Mon-Fri, 8-11.30am Sat) Credit-card cash advances cost CFA10,000 per transaction and are available upstairs.

Eco Bank (Blvd de la Liberté; ☺ 8.30am-3.30pm Mon-Fri, 9am-1pm Sat, 9am-3pm Sun) Changes cash for free.

Post & Telephone

Dozens of private telecentres now dot Niamey's streets. International calls cost CFA150 for each 10-second block. Some charge nothing for incoming calls. If your mobile is unlocked, consider buying a local SIM card and using that, as rates are low and competitive even for international calls.

Grande Poste (☎ 20 73 31 44; Rue de la Grande Poste; ☺ 7.30am-12.15pm & 3.30-6.30pm Mon-Fri, 8am-noon Sat)

Tourist Information

ONT (☎ 20 73 24 47; Rue de Président Heinrich Lübke; ☺ 7.30am-4.30pm Sat-Thu, 7.30am-12.30pm Fri) Though little English is spoken, the staff at this government agency mean well.

Travel Agencies

Agadez Tourisme (☎ 20 44 01 70; www.agadez -tourisme.com) Offers River Niger tours, trips to Parc W and vehicle hire.

Turbo Tours (☎ 96 96 09 92; wallymamoudou@yahoo. fr) Rents 4WDs and organises Parc W and Kouré tours.

Satguru Travel and Tours (☎ 20 73 69 31; Rue de la Copro) Satguru offers air tickets, excursions to Kouré and Parc W and car hire.

DANGERS & ANNOYANCES

While violent incidents are generally rare in Niamey, do exercise caution along the waterfront at Corniche de Yantala and Corniche de Gamkalé – always take a taxi after dark. The Grand and Petit Marchés are prime pickpocket grounds.

SIGHTS & ACTIVITIES

Wade through labyrinthine lanes shaded by kaleidoscopes of tattered sheets in the **Grand Marché** (Blvd de la Liberté; 8am-6pm), inhaling spices and heady aromas all the way. It's great for observing Nigeriens interacting – peace amid the pandemonium. At the **Petit Marché** (Ave de la Mairie; 8am-6pm), let your hands do the walking (squeeze fruit to your heart's content).

The sprawling **Musée National du Niger** (20 73 43 21; Rue du Musée; adult/student CFA1000/500, camera/video CFA1000/5000; 9am-noon & 3.30-5.30pm Tue-Sun) is one of West Africa's best national museums, where numerous themed pavilions delve into Niger's present and past. There's also a cramped **zoo** and **artisans' centre** (8am-6.30pm Tue-Sun) here.

There's no better way to experience the Niger River than from a peaceful **pirogue** skimming its surface at sunset. You can even take a day or two and explore villages upriver. Although 'guides' wandering around town offer these trips, go directly to the *piroguers* on the riverfront near La Flottile restaurant. Four-passenger *pirogues* should cost CFA2000 per person per hour – triple that for a motor. If negotiating isn't your bag, talk to one of the Niamey-based travel agencies, as they can all organise a trip (see opposite).

The best pool in town is the excellent **Piscine Olympique d'Etat** (Rue du Sahel; admission CFA1000; 10am-5pm Sat-Thu, 6-10.30pm Fri), a superb 50m public pool by the Niger River.

SLEEPING
Budget

Camping Touristique (20 75 44 89; Blvd des Sy et Mamar; campsite per person CFA2000, vehicle CFA1000;) This dusty site in western Niamey is the only option for campers. It's a long walk (or CFA200 in a shared taxi) to town.

Hôtel Moustache (96 59 66 65; Ave Soni Ali Ber; r with/without bathroom CFA5000/7500, r with bathroom & aircon CFA10,000;) Niamey's cheapest bed can be found at this memorable establishment, where stinky bathrooms and mosquito-infested rooms are only slightly more welcoming than the crowd of hookers hanging out in the courtyard.

Chez Tatayi (20 74 12 81; www.tatayi.com; Rue de Président Heinrich Lübke; dm CFA6000, s/d without bathroom from CFA12,000/14,000;) This charming hotel is stacked full of character and makes for the best budget option in Niamey. All rooms are spotless and share decent bathrooms, and there's a communal kitchen and social area including a good library. For aircon add CFA4000.

Midrange & Top End

Hôtel Terminus (20 73 26 92; hotermi@intnet.ne; Rue du Sahel; s CFA37,000-45,000, d CFA45,000-50,000, ste CFA60,000;) This large, centrally located complex is highly recommended for its friendly staff and pleasant atmosphere. Free wi-fi, a large pool and pleasant gardens sweeten the deal.

Résidences Croix du Sud (20 73 44 30; www.niger-croixdusud.com; Rue NB 29; s/d/ste CFA27,500/37,500/45,000;) A welcome addition to Niamey's midrange options is this professionally run guesthouse near the Petit Marché.

Hôtel Ténéré (20 73 20 20; www.hotel-tenere-niger.com; Blvd de la Liberté; s/d CFA44,500/51,000, ste CFA60,500-70,500;) Clean, comfy bungalows host large, sunny rooms with TVs and gargantuan bathrooms.

Grand Hôtel du Niger (20 73 26 41; www.grandhotelniger.com; Rond-point du Grand Hôtel; s/d from CFA49,500/59,500, ste CFA60,000-87,000;) Attentive service, value for money and top-notch rooms with satellite TVs and lovely river views.

EATING

Until 9am street stalls near Petit Marché serve fried-egg sandwiches. After that, it's *riz sauce*. Late-night *suya* stalls on Rue du Commerce hawk braised brochettes (CFA100; *suya* is Hausa for brochette).

Amandine (20 73 25 25; Ave de la Mairie; 5am-midnight) This invaluable addition to Niamey's eating scene is a great place for breakfast, with fresh croissants, good coffee and a host of other pastries.

Le Dragon d'Or (20 73 41 23; Rue du Grand Hôtel; mains CFA2500-7500; noon-2pm & 6.30-11.30pm) Slurp delicious Vietnamese soups, sharpen your teeth on frog legs, or work chopstick magic on tasty chicken with cashew nuts and fresh ginger.

Byblos (20 72 44 05; Blvd de l'Indépendance; mains CFA1000-2000; noon-11pm) This open-air Lebanese restaurant serves Niger's best tabouli and hummus.

Le Pilier (20 72 49 85; Rue de la Tapoa; mains CFA3000-6500; lunch & dinner Wed-Mon;) Hands down, *the* place for Italian. Enjoy plentiful pastas, from ravioli to gnocchi dripping in gorgonzola.

NIGER

NIAMEY

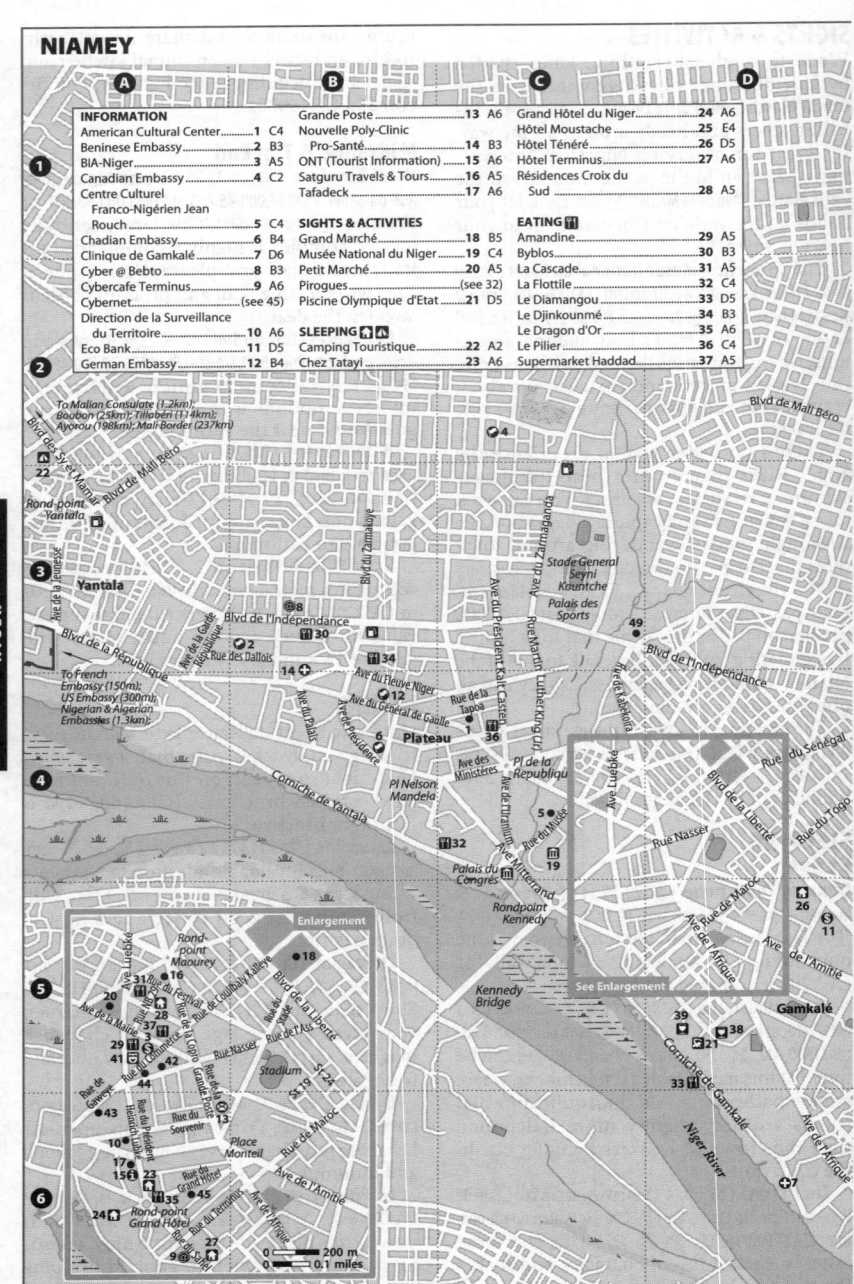

INFORMATION
American Cultural Center...........................1 C4
Beninese Embassy.....................................2 B3
BIA-Niger...3 A5
Canadian Embassy.....................................4 C2
Centre Culturel
    Franco-Nigérien Jean
    Rouch...5 C4
Chadian Embassy.......................................6 B4
Clinique de Gamkalé..................................7 D6
Cyber @ Bebto..8 B3
Cybercafe Terminus...................................9 A6
Cybernet..(see 45)
Direction de la Surveillance
    du Territoire..10 A6
Eco Bank...11 D5
German Embassy......................................12 B4

Grande Poste...13 A6
Nouvelle Poly-Clinic
    Pro-Santé..14 B3
ONT (Tourist Information)......................15 A6
Satguru Travels & Tours..........................16 A5
Tafadeck..17 A6

SIGHTS & ACTIVITIES
Grand Marché..18 B5
Musée National du Niger........................19 C4
Petit Marché...20 A5
Pirogues...(see 32)
Piscine Olympique d'Etat.......................21 D5

SLEEPING
Camping Touristique...............................22 A2
Chez Tatayi..23 A6

Grand Hôtel du Niger..............................24 A6
Hôtel Moustache......................................25 E4
Hôtel Ténéré..26 D5
Hôtel Terminus..27 A6
Résidences Croix du
    Sud...28 A5

EATING
Amandine...29 A5
Byblos...30 B3
La Cascade...31 A5
La Flottile...32 C4
Le Diamangou..33 D5
Le Djinkounmé...34 B3
Le Dragon d'Or..35 A6
Le Pilier..36 C4
Supermarket Haddad..............................37 A5

To Malian Consulate (1.2km);
Bouboin (25km); Tillabéri (114km);
Ayorou (198km); Mali Bordet (237km)

Blvd de Mali Béro

Blvd de Syd Maimal

Blvd de Mali Béro

Rond-point
Yantala

Yantala

Ave de la Jeunesse

Ave de la Garde
Nationale

Blvd de l'Indépendance

Blvd du Zarmakoye

Ave du Zarmaganda Zip Road

Ave du Président Kait Castel

Blvd de la République

Rue des Dallois

To French
Embassy (150m);
US Embassy (300m);
Nigerian & Algerian
Embassies (1.3km)

Ave du Palais

Ave de Residence

Ave du Fleuve Niger

Ave du Général de Gaulle

Rue de la Tapoa

Ave Martin Luther King Chr.

Stade General
Seyni
Kountche
Palais des
Sports

Blvd de l'Indépendance

Ave de l'Islande

Plateau

Corniche de Yantala

Pl Nelson
Mandela

Ave des
Ministères

Ave de Tiramana

Ave Mitterand

Pl de la
Républiqu

Ave Luebke

Rue du Niller

Rue Nasser

Blvd de la Liberté

Rue du Togo

Rue du Sénégal

Rue de Maroc

Palais du
Congrès

Rondpoint
Kennedy

Ave de l'Afrique

Ave de l'Amitié

Kennedy
Bridge

See Enlargement

Gamkalé

Enlargement

Rond-
point
Maourey

Ave Luebke

Rue du Festival de Coulboly Kalley

Blvd de la Liberté

Rue de l'Ass

Ave de la Marie

Rue de la Copro

Rue Nasser

Rue Heinrich Lübke

Stadium

S 24

Ave de l'Commerce

Ave de Gaweye

Rue du Souvenir

Rue du Président Heinrich Lübke

Place
Monteil

Rue de Maroc

Ave de l'Amitié

Rue du
Grand Hôtel

Ave de l'Afrique

Rond-point
Grand Hôtel

Rue du Terminus

Corniche de Gamkalé

Niger River

Ave de l'Afrique

0   200 m
0   0.1 miles

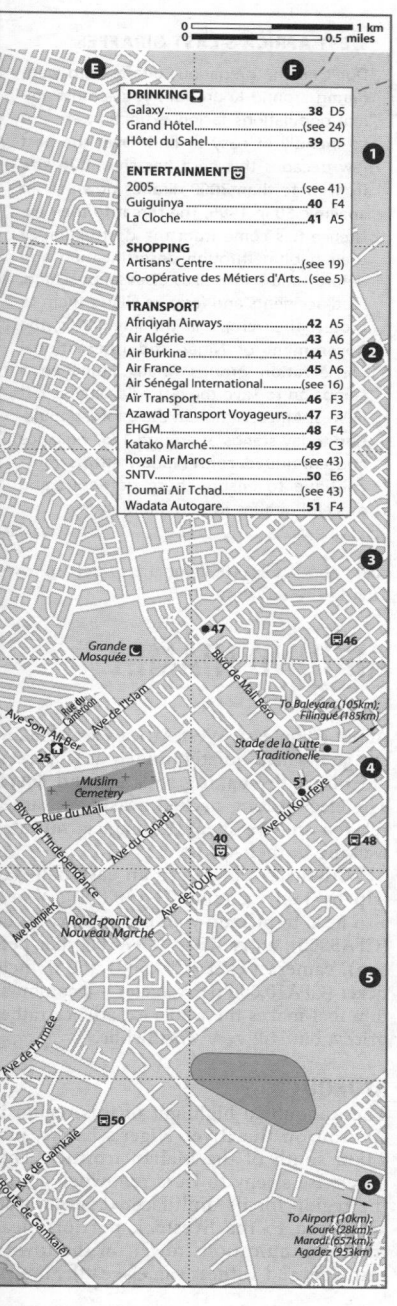

Le Diamangou (☎ 96 29 14 17; Corniche de Gamkalé; meals CFA2000-4000; 🕙 9am-11pm) Housed on a creaky boat moored on the river (smother yourself in insect repellent) from where the views are gorgeous. The fresh *capitaine* is divine. Arrange a taxi after sunset.

La Flottile (☎ 21 76 58 55; Corniche de Yantala; mains CFA3000-8500; 🕙 10am-2pm & 5-11pm Wed-Mon) Indulge in fresh fish in this shady garden restaurant. The *capitaine* is excellent. For safety, organise a taxi after sunset.

Other enticing options include the following:

La Cascade (☎ 20 73 28 32; Rue NB 29; mains CFA2500-6000; 🕙 lunch Tue-Sun, dinner daily; 🈂)

Le Djinkounmé (☎ 20 72 21 81; Ave du Fleuve Niger; meals CFA3000-7000; 🕙 lunch & dinner Mon-Sat)

Supermarket Haddad (Rue du Commerce) Niamey's best-known supermarket.

DRINKING

Grand Hôtel du Niger (Rond-point du Grand Hôtel) Few places in town can beat the Grand Hôtel's poolside terrace for a sunset beer – the river views are tremendous.

Hôtel du Sahel (Rue du Sahel) While lacking the posh feel of the Grand Hôtel, this hotel's riverside terrace is another great spot for a beer.

Galaxy (Rue du Sahel) For a more African experience, head to this bar perched on the river behind the Piscine Olympique D'Etat (Olympic swimming pool).

ENTERTAINMENT

Reverberating with Western and African tunes, the lively **2005** (Ave Luebké; admission CFA2500) club remains the city's most popular. The streets nearby are filled with busy bars and restaurants, including **La Cloche** (Ave Luebké; admission free). Further east **Guiguinya** (Ave de l'Entente; admission free) is another solid option.

SHOPPING

Peruse the nether regions of the Grand Marché for leatherwork, silver jewellery and *les couvertures Djerma* (also known locally as *kountas*). *Kountas* are large, bright strips of cotton sewn together into a large blanket, which are truly spectacular and unique to Niger. The museum's **artisans' centre** (Rue du Musée; 🕙 closed Mon) and **Co-opérative des Métiers d'Arts** (Rue du Musée) are also good.

You'll find local music CDs at stalls on Ave Luebké, near the Petit Marché.

NIGER

GETTING THERE & AWAY
Air
For airlines operating from Niamey, see p458.

Bus
The main bus companies are **SNTV** (☎ 20 73 30 20; Ave de Gamkalé), **EHGM** (☎ 20 74 37 16; Blvd de Mali Béro), **Rimbo Transport Voyageurs** (RTV; ☎ 20 74 14 13; Blvd de Mali Béro), **Azawad Transport Voyageurs** (ATV; ☎ 20 73 93 57; Blvd de Mali Béro) and **Aïr Transport** (☎ 20 74 36 50; off Ave de l'Aïr). They all serve similar routes and charge similar prices, with buses leaving Niamey between 4am and 6am.

Destination	Fare (CFA)	Duration (hr)	Frequency
Agadez	14,000	14	daily except Mon & Wed
Arlit	17,500	16	daily except Mon & Wed
Maradi	9300	11	daily
Zinder	12,400	15	daily

Bush Taxi
The following is a list of one-way fares for Peugeots from **Wadata Autogare** (Ave du Kourfeye), their estimated durations and level of patience required.

Destination	Fare (CFA)	Duration (hr)
Agadez	11,250	16½
Birni N'Konni	4650	7½
Filingué	3000	2
Maradi	8250	11
Zinder	11,250	14

GETTING AROUND
To/From the Airport
The airport is about 13km southeast of the city. A taxi from the airport costs CFA5000 to CFA10,000; coming from town costs about CFA2500. During daylight hours you could also walk from the terminal to the nearby highway and catch a shared taxi to town (CFA200).

Taxi
Shared taxis simply head in the direction requested by the first passenger and troll for subsequent passengers en route. To catch one, simply hold out your arm or shout 'taximan!' and say your destination when the taxi slows. If it's going your way, you get the nod and you're only out CFA250. A taxi to yourself (*déplacement* or *location*)

WEST AFRICA'S LAST GIRAFFES
Don't let the gregarious giraffe herd wandering around Kouré fool you – most animal populations facing extinction are not so friendly or easy to find. Over the past few decades this herd has shrunk in size from more than 3000 giraffes down to an anaemic 50 in 1996. The threat to their existence has come from the destruction of their habitat through desertification and deforestation, as well as disease, poaching, road accidents and farmers killing them to protect their crops. In the late 1990s, the government of Niger and international conservation groups finally launched a campaign to save the last wild giraffes left in West Africa. Although the giraffe population today stands at around 175, vigilance and continued conservation efforts must continue to ensure these gorgeous and graceful giraffes live on another day.

---

costs about CFA1000 for a trip across town during the daytime.

AROUND NIAMEY

KOURÉ
About 60km east, West Africa's last remaining **giraffe herd** quietly munch acacia trees, patrolling the baking soils around **Kouré**. The elegant long-necked beasts are rather relaxed and we spent 30 magical minutes walking in their midst.

Without a vehicle, it's an easy half-day trip by taxi (around CFA30,000). You'll also need to pick up your compulsory guide (CFA5000), entry ticket (CFA4000 per person), camera ticket (CFA500) and vehicle ticket (CFA10,000 per vehicle) – a combination that makes the whole experience rather pricey, but still very worthwhile.

AYOROU
The undoubted highlight of this region is Ayorou on the River Niger's banks, just 24km south of the Malian frontier. This otherwise sleepy town is renowned across the region for its multifaceted **Sunday market**. Head to the livestock portion, near the communications tower on the town's east side, and witness camels, cattle, mules,

sheep and goats overrunning the place, along with their fascinating nomadic Bella, Fulani and Tuareg owners. The market's western section near the river is more subdued, but just as intoxicating. The market warms up around noon, so if you arrive early, watch cattle swimming across the Niger or enjoy a *pirogue* trip on the Niger River (CFA5000 for two hours) to see the local hippos. Although guides and *piroguers* can be persistent around town, it's not a bad idea to hire a guide (CFA5000 per day) as they'll help arrange photo permissions in the market.

Sleeping & Eating

The choice here is between the neglected **Hôtel Amenokal** (☎ 20 71 14 24; abdoulkatia@yahoo.fr; s/tw from CFA10,000/12,000; P ⊠), which has old rooms with cement floors and sporadic running water in the bathrooms, and the far better value **Île aux Mangues** (☎ 96 11 21 98; bed per person 12,500), a charming campsite 3km south of the town where five well-appointed tents await you, each sleeping up to three. The price includes a *pirogue* transfer from Ayorou, dinner and breakfast, and there are toilets and showers for guests, not to mention a dreamy setting on the river.

Getting There & Away

There are several daily bush taxis between Niamey's Katako Marché and Ayorou (CFA3500, five hours). Boats run north to Gao, Mali (CFA50,000 per seat, two days) on Monday.

FILINGUÉ
pop 12,100

Filingué offers up a surprisingly dynamic **Sunday market** where you can wander around looking at traditional architecture, or head up the small hill for a bird's-eye view of the action.

If you come on a Sunday, don't fail to stop in **Baleyara** (meaning 'where the Bella meet'), halfway between Niamey and Filingué. Baleyara's **Sunday market**, shaded by a heavenly canopy of trees, is equally pleasing – the animal bartering, which takes place on the town side of the market, is particularly worth seeing.

Regular bush taxis run to Niamey's Wadata Autogare (CFA3000, two hours) along good tarmac roads.

SOUTHWEST NIGER

PARC REGIONAL DU W

This excellent **national park** (www.parc-w.net; admission CFA6000) is named rather charmingly for the double bend in the Niger River at the park's northern border. Shared between Niger, Benin and Burkina Faso, the Parc Regional du W offers some of the most diverse wildlife-spotting opportunities in West Africa. Antelopes, buffalos, elephants, hippos, lions, leopards, cheetahs, baboons, crocodiles, hyenas and over 300 species of migratory bird all call this unique environment home.

The best wildlife viewing is March to May, when migratory birds arrive and animals congregate around shrinking water supplies. The park's entrance at La Tapoa has park maps guidebooks (CFA5000) and is where you pick up your obligatory guide (CFA10,000 per day).

The budget accommodation is the Niger Car Voyages **campsite** (campsites CFA4000, in set-up tents bed only/half board CFA6000/13,500), located right on the riverside with great views.

The comfortable 28-room riverside **Hotel de la Tapoa** (☎ 96 87 46 05, 96 28 81 83; www.hoteltapoa.com; s/d CFA15,000/20,000, with air-con CFA29,500/34,500; ☾ mid-Oct–mid-Jun; P ⊠ ⊠) in Tapoa village is the midrange option.

There is no point reaching the park independently without a vehicle. The journey from Niamey to Tapoa is about three hours by 4WD. Get a quote from a number of travel agencies for this trip (they usually include hotel, meals, guide and park fees, petrol and road tolls in the cost) as they vary hugely.

BIRNI N'KONNI
pop 50,000

About 420km east of Niamey, Birni N'Konni (or 'Konni') sits at the junction for Zinder and Agadez. It's also an important border town with Nigeria. There's little to see, but it's a convenient place to break your journey.

Hôtel Nevada (☎ 20 64 04 34; off Rte de Niamey; s/d without bathroom CFA11,300/14,600 s/d CFA12,300/15,600; ⊠) is great value. Rooms are well kept and all have TV and air-con. The hotel is signposted from the crossroads in the centre of town – walk down to the small thatched village and turn left.

East of town and the cream of Konni's crop, the bright rooms at **Le Motel** (☎ 20 64 06 50; Rte de Niamey; r CFA22,500-37,500; P ⊠)

sport TVs, modern bathrooms and comfortable beds. Its restaurant is also the best in town.

SNTV, EHGM, RTV and Aïr Transport (all on Rte de Niamey) serve the same main routes from Konni. Daily buses go to Zinder (CFA6300 to CFA6600, six hours), Niamey (CFA6250 to CFA6800, six hours) and Maradi (CFA3500, three hours), while buses to Agadez (CFA7750, 5½ hours) only run Tuesday and Thursday to Sunday. Most northbound and eastbound buses arrive around 11am. Westbound buses pull in around 1pm.

Bush taxis regularly leave the **autogare** (Rte de Nigeria) for Dogondoutchi (CFA1800, two hours), Maradi (CFA2800, four hours) and Tahoua (CFA1400, 1½ hours).

SOUTHEAST NIGER

MARADI
pop 179,000

Maradi, the country's third-largest city, remains the administrative capital and commercial centre for agriculture. Its proximity to northern Nigeria has fostered staunchly conservative Islamic views. Although not the most engaging place, it's fine for an overnight stop.

As you might imagine, sinking into Maradi's **Grande Marché** (BRJ Rue 1; ☾ sunrise-sunset) on market days (Monday and Friday) is a pleasurable assault on the senses. Vending of an entirely different variety goes on at the **Centre Artisanal de Maradi** (BRJ Rue 1; ☾ 8am-10pm), 2km north of town. It's worth a stop – wander the workshops, witness the workmanship and wonder where to start the negotiations.

Sleeping & Eating

Hôtel Larewa (☎ 96 87 01 44; d with fan/air-con from CFA6500/12,500; **P** **❄**) Maradi's budget offering is located north of town, east of the EHGM bus station. The western side's rooms, with clean showers and shared toilets, are brighter and slightly less expensive than the eastern side's rooms, which have private bathrooms.

Restaurant Marthaba (43 SGI Rue 10; meals CFA500-1000; ☾ breakfast, lunch & dinner) is a sleepy outdoor place that's not bad for local dishes like *riz sauce* (rice with meat or chicken).

Getting There & Around

All the main bus companies serve Maradi on the Niamey–Zinder 'axis'. Buses usually depart Niamey around 6am heading east (CFA9000, nine hours). Bush taxis regularly depart the *gare routière* for Zinder (CFA3000, four hours) and Konni (CFA3500, five hours).

ZINDER
pop 205,500

Zinder feels like the last stopover before the middle of nowhere, yet it wasn't always so – this was once the capital of the mighty Damagaram state, which thrived on the trans-Saharan trade in ivory, salt, slaves and gold. Today the Sultan of Zinder still rules from his fascinating palace, complete with colourfully attired attendants. With its celebrated traditional Hausa houses, the labyrinthine alleys of the old quarters and the classic French fort, Zinder is by far the most interesting town in southern Niger and well worth a day or two of your time.

Information

BIA-Niger (Ave des Banques) Changes travellers cheques, euros and US dollars.
Centre Culturel Franco-Nigérien (☎ 20 51 05 35; Rue du Marché) French-language library and art gallery.
Cybercafé Kandarga (Rue du Marché; per hr CFA500; ☾ 8am-11pm)

Sights

Few things beat losing your bearings (and a few hours) within the Birni Quartier's innumerable crooked alleys. The old *banco* (mudbrick) houses actually represent some of Africa's best Hausa architecture. Linger outside the 19th-century **Palais du Sultan** (Place de la Grande Mosquée, Birni Quartier) to score a guided tour to the area; ask about the infamous *chambre des scorpions* (a tip of CFA2000 should suffice).

The jaded **Musée Régional de Zinder** (☎ 60 59 61 35; Ave de la République; admission CFA500; ☾ 8am-noon & 3-6pm) has a few dusty exhibits you can peruse.

The **Grand Marché** (Blvd de l'Hippodrome; ☾ dawn-dusk), one of Niger's liveliest, warrants a walkabout (especially on Thursday) through the leathers of Niger's best *artisans du cuir*. More leatherwork resides at **Cooperative du Village Artisanal** (Ave de Maradi; ☾ 8am-6.30pm), 2km west of town.

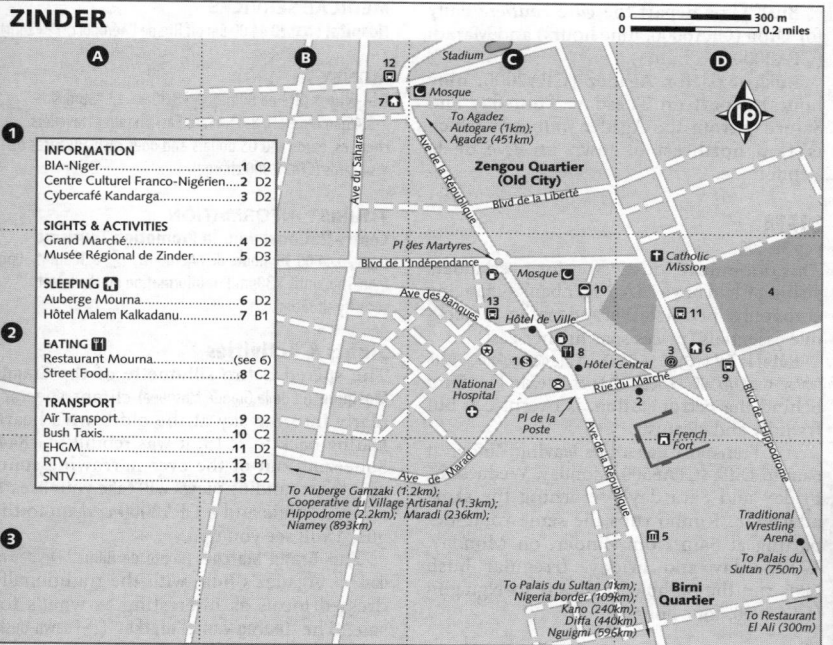

ZINDER

INFORMATION
BIA-Niger...................................1 C2
Centre Culturel Franco-Nigérien...2 D2
Cybercafé Kandarga......................3 D2

SIGHTS & ACTIVITIES
Grand Marché..............................4 D2
Musée Régional de Zinder.............5 D3

SLEEPING
Auberge Mourna...........................6 D2
Hôtel Malem Kalkadanu................7 B1

EATING
Restaurant Mourna.....................(see 6)
Street Food..................................8 C2

TRANSPORT
Aïr Transport...............................9 D2
Bush Taxis..................................10 D2
EHGM..11 D2
RTV...12 B1
SNTV...13 C2

There's also a charming and stereotypical **French fort** that you'll see rising from a pile of massive rounded boulders just south of the town centre.

Sleeping

Hôtel Malem Kalkadanu (☎ 96 66 66 53; Ave de la République; r CFA3400-6400; P) West of the Zengou Quartier, this rambling budget place has the cheapest rooms in town. Though it's a lot prettier inside the courtyard than you'd expect from the grotty exterior, the rooms are basic and cell-like.

Auberge Mourna (☎ 20 51 22 80, 96 95 03 06; off Rue du Marché; s/tw/d from CFA20,00/30,000/35,000; P) Right in the heart of town, the Mourna has eight large, clean rooms, all in a safe courtyard setting with a restaurant attached. Reservations are usually essential.

Auberge Gamzaki (☎ 20 51 02 80, 96 98 83 31; www.gamzaki-voyages.com; r CFA30,000-33,000; P) This new venture is a real treat. There are currently four rooms (although six more are planned), all furnished in Hausa style with pebble floors, stylish bathrooms and even a minibar.

Eating & Drinking

Restaurant El Ali (meals CFA500-2000; ☽ breakfast, lunch & dinner) Devour African favourites beneath the *paillotes* (thatched shelters). It's east of Birni Quartier and lacks signs; ask for directions.

Restaurant Mourna (off Rue du Marché; mains CFA1000-4500; ☽ breakfast, lunch & dinner) The best choice in town is this Chinese-influenced establishment. Try the excellent *salade de maïs* (sweetcorn salad), or the Cantonese rice.

The best **street food** (Ave de la République; brochettes CFA100, roast pigeons/chickens CFA900/1500; ☽ dinner) is in front of Hôtel Central.

Getting There & Away

SNTV (☎ 20 51 04 68; Ave des Banques) buses run to Niamey (CFA12,400, 14 hours, daily) and Agadez (CFA7600, eight hours, Tuesday and Saturday). **Aïr Transport** (☎ 51 02 47; Blvd de l'Hippodrome) and **RTV** (☎ 51 04 16; off Ave de la République) have similar services, including a bus to Diffa (CFA6500, seven hours, 5am Monday, Wednesday and Friday) from where it's possible to connect to Nguigmi and on into Chad. There are currently no direct services to Nguigmi from Zinder.

NIGER

Bush taxis depart the *gare routière* daily for Diffa (CFA6000, nine hours) and Maradi (CFA3000, 4½ hours).

Bush taxis for Agadez (CFA7000, nine hours) depart on Tuesday, Thursday and Saturday from the Agadez *autogare*, which is 1km northeast of town on Ave de la République.

DIFFA
pop 30,600

This diminutive, dusty stop for overlanders visiting Chad has a BIA-Niger bank (changing euros only), petrol station and market to stockpile essentials (prices soar further east).

Hôtel le Tal (☎ 20 56 03 32; off Rte de Nguigmi; d with fan/air-con CFA7500/13,500; ☒) off Rte de Nguigmi behind the petrol station, is overpriced but friendly and cleanish.

Aïr Transport has a bus leaving Zinder at 6am to Diffa (CFA6500, Monday, Wednesday, Friday and Saturday), returning the same afternoon. Rimbo runs the same route departing at 5am from Zinder, on Monday, Wednesday and Friday. Irregular bush taxis run the potholed highway to Nguigmi (CFA3000, four hours).

NORTHERN NIGER

AGADEZ
pop 88,569

Once Niger's tourism capital, Agadez has fallen on decidedly hard times since the Tuareg Rebellion reignited in 2007. Yet after a few years of being a ghost town, since the Tuareg Rebellion ended travellers have gradually begun to return to this most enchanting of Saharan cities, and while visitor numbers remain low, this is a great chance to see an ancient caravan town without the tour groups. When you're standing in the porcupine shadow of the famous Grand Mosquée, or weaving through the sandy streets with their distinctive mudbrick architecture, it's not hard to imagine what it was like at its zenith some four centuries ago.

Information
INTERNET ACCESS

Cybercafe le Dounya (off Pl de la République; per hr CFA600; ☒ 8am-10pm) A central option handy for the bus stations.

MEDICAL SERVICES
Hospital (☎ 20 44 00 84; off Rte de l'Aéroport; ☒ 24hr)

MONEY
BIA-Niger (Rte de Bilma; ☒ 8.30am-12.45pm & 2-3.45pm Mon-Fri, 8-11.45am Sat) Changes travellers cheques, euros and US dollars and does cash advances on Visa cards (CFA10,000 charge).

TOURIST INFORMATION
Centre National pour la Promotion Tourisme (☎ 20 44 00 36; Route de l'Aéroport; ☒ 8.30am-4.30pm Mon-Thu, until 1.30pm Fri) Information on the latest security situation.

Sights & Activities

The spiked ochre silhouette of the **Grande Mosquée** (Pl de la Grande Mosquée) climbs spectacularly into the sky at the old town's heart. Dating back to 1515, it was rebuilt in 1844. Squeezing out of the ever-narrowing staircase to astounding views will take your breath away. A smile and a CFA2000 *cadeau* to the guard will see you up.

The **Grand Marché** (Route de Bilma; ☒ dawn-dusk) is Agadez's hub, with the traditionally dressed locals as interesting as what's for sale. The **Tuareg camel market** (☒ dawn-dusk) on Agadez's western outskirts is equally colourful, if more odoriferous. Visit at sunrise or sunset.

The enchanting maze of small, crooked alleys and fascinating mudbrick architecture of Tuareg and Hausa inspiration in the **Vieux Quartier** is a bona-fide time machine.

Sleeping

At the time of writing many of Agadez's hotels were shut due to lack of travellers. The following were open in early 2009.

BUDGET

Hôtel Agreboun (☎ 20 44 05 75, 96 98 63 32; s/tw/ tr with shared toilet CFA4000/8000/12,000; ℗) The Agreboun is on the western edge of Agadez, a short walk from the bus stations. Rooms are rather rudimentary and bunker-like, but they're cheap and clean.

MIDRANGE & TOP END

Hôtel de l'Aïr (☎ 96 55 67 44; Pl de la Grande Mosquée; CFA10,000-15,000; ℗ ☒) This nine-room former sultan's palace makes up in atmosphere what it may lack in terms of service. Rooms can be dark and rather hit-and-miss, but with

NIGER

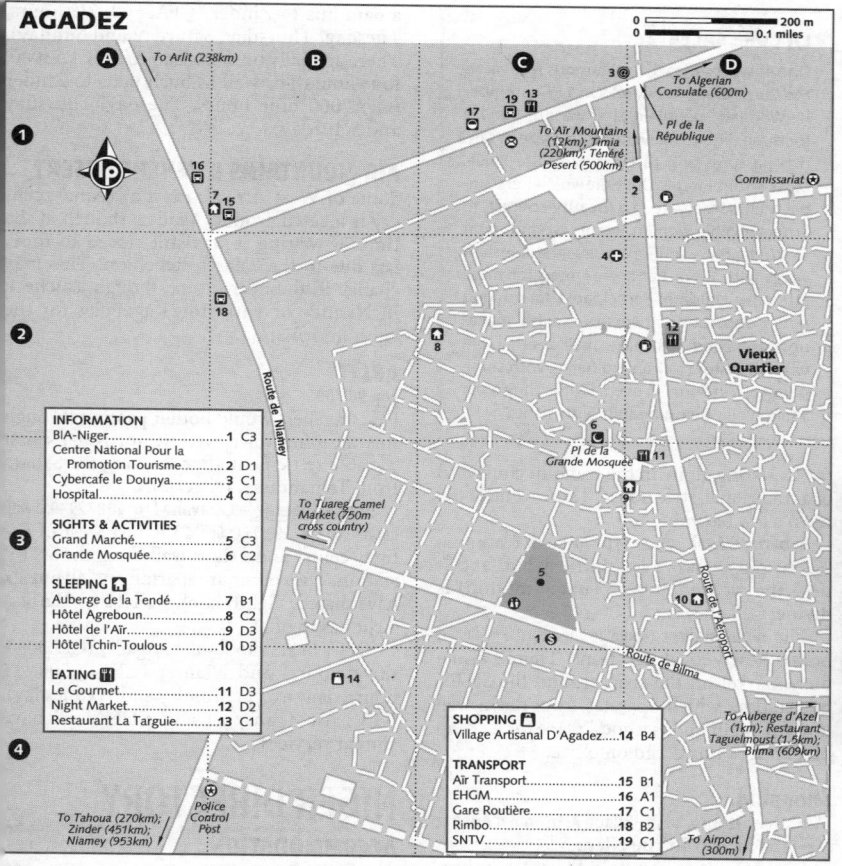

AGADEZ

To Arlit (238km)

To Algerian Consulate (600km)

To Aïr Mountains (12km); Timia (220km); Ténéré Desert (500km)

Pl de la République

Commissariat

Route de Niamey

To Tuareg Camel Market (750m cross country)

Vieux Quartier

Pl de la Grande Mosquée

Route de l'Aéropot

Route de Bilma

To Auberge d'Azel (1km); Restaurant Taguelmoust (1.5km); Bilma (609km)

To Tahoua (270km); Zinder (451km); Niamey (953km)

Police Control Post

To Airport (300m)

INFORMATION
BIA-Niger.................................**1** C3
Centre National Pour la
  Promotion Tourisme...........**2** D1
Cybercafe le Dounya.............**3** C1
Hospital..................................**4** C2

SIGHTS & ACTIVITIES
Grand Marché........................**5** C3
Grande Mosquée....................**6** C2

SLEEPING
Auberge de la Tendé.............**7** B1
Hôtel Agreboun.....................**8** C2
Hôtel de l'Aïr.........................**9** D3
Hôtel Tchin-Toulous.............**10** D3

EATING
Le Gourmet............................**11** D3
Night Market.........................**12** D2
Restaurant La Targuie...........**13** C1

SHOPPING
Village Artisanal D'Agadez.....**14** B4

TRANSPORT
Air Transport.........................**15** B1
EHGM....................................**16** A1
Gare Routière........................**17** C1
Rimbo....................................**18** B2
SNTV.....................................**19** C1

NIGER

his courtyard space, history and location,
who cares?

Hôtel Tchin-Toulous (☎ 96 49 85 79; caravanevoy
ages@hotmail.com; Rte de l'Aéroport; r with/without bathroom
FA15,000/10,000; ❄) Reopening when we visited,
he charming Tchin-Toulous wins points for
ts quirky Tuareg style.

Auberge de la Tendé (☎ 96 98 18 83; Route de
Niamey; s/tw from CFA11,000/14,000; ❄) Slightly
overpriced it may be, but this friendly hos-
elry is excellently located for those arriving
ate at night by bus. Rooms are charming
and equipped with mosquito nets.

Auberge d'Azel (☎ 20 44 01 70; www.agadez-tour
isme.com; Rte de Bilma; twd CFA30,000/40,000; ❄ ℗)
Without doubt the most charming hotel in

Agadez, the Auberge d'Azel is a boutique-
style oasis of calm.

Eating & Drinking
Le Gourmet (Pl de la Grande Mosquée; meals CFA500-1500;
❄ breakfast, lunch & dinner) This local haunt lies
almost in the shadow of the Grande Mosquée
and serves simple but decent dishes, from
omelettes to couscous.

Restaurant La Targuie (meals CFA800-1500; ❄ breakfast, lunch & dinner) Of all the restaurants in town,
La Targuie has the most buzz and the biggest
local clientele. Well located for the buses,
you're guaranteed a decent meal here.

Restaurant Taguelmoust (☎ 20 44 04 50; off Rte de
Bilma; mains CFA3000-4000; ❄ breakfast, lunch & dinner) It
may be a hotel restaurant, but it's worth a visit

LA CURE SALÉE

One of West Africa's most famous festivals is the Cure Salée (Salt Cure). On 11 September he Wodaabé people gather west of Agadez for three days to allow herds to graze in salt-rich pastures and to celebrate Cure Salée. Most enthralling is the Gerewol, where single men participate in a 'beauty contest' to attract eligible women. Beauty is paramount to Wodaabé – some men even share their wives with more handsome men for more attractive children! Participants spend long hours decorating themselves with make-up (blackened lips make their teeth seem whiter). Suitor rivalries are fierce, with some partaking in Soro, an event where they must smile while being beaten with sticks.

for its setting alone in the tranquil courtyard of a traditional-style house. There's one of the town's few bars here too.

Auberge d'Azel (☎ 20 44 01 70; Rte de Bilma; meals CFA3500-5500; ☾ lunch & dinner) Pricey but fantastic – the *mouton targui* (Tuareg mutton) is divine. Call ahead.

The **night market** (Route de l'Aéroport; ☾ dinner) boasts hearty local selections. There's also a busy market on the strip around the SNTV bus station, which operates from dawn well into the night and is a good place for a cheap breakfast of bread and omelette.

Shopping

For silver items, visit **Village Artisanal d'Agadez** (☾ 8am-6pm), off Rte de Niamey.

Vieux Quartier houses leatherworkers producing Tuareg *samaras* (sandals), *coussins* (cushions) and magnificent *selles de chameau* (camel saddles).

Want a turban? Expect to pay CFA500 per metre in the market (indigo costs more); 3m should suffice.

Getting There & Away

All road travel to Agadez needs to be in a military convoy to protect travellers, so timetables are restrictive, with convoys travelling once a day to/from Niamey (except Monday and Wednesday) and just three times a week to/from Zinder (Tuesday, Thursday and Saturday). SNTV, EHGM and RTV all run 6am buses to Niamey (CFA14,000, 12 hours, except Monday and Wednesday) and

a 6am bus to Zinder (CFA7500, 7½ hours, Tuesday, Thursday, Saturday and Sunday). There are daily bush taxis to Arlit (CFA3000, four hours), as well as bush taxis to Zinder (CFA7000 nine hours, Tuesday, Thursday and Saturday).

AÏR MOUNTAINS & TÉNÉRÉ DESERT

Some of West Africa's most awesome scenery is located around Agadez, though at the time of writing it was still closed to tourists due to the Tuareg Rebellion. This may change in the near future, though, so check in Niamey or with travel agencies for the latest information.

ARLIT

pop 90,700

Few travellers would bother passing through this uranium town were it not Niger's first sizeable settlement after crossing the Sahara from Tamanrasset (Algeria).

Hôtel l'Auberge la Caravane (☎ 20 89 29 49; d with fan/air-con CFA6000/14,000; ☒) is just west of the town centre and a short walk from the SNTV station. The rooms are spartan and all but six have shared, slightly stinky toilets. It's the best Arlit has to offer.

SNTV buses run south to Agadez (CFA3000, three hours) and Niamey (CFA17,500, 15 hours, daily except Monday and Wednesday). RTV, Aïr Transport and EHGM all have similar services.

NIGER DIRECTORY

ACCOMMODATION

Cheap single rooms range from CFA3000 (cockroach sighting: unsurprising) to CFA8000 (cockroach sighting: mildly surprising). Camping (typically CFA2000 per person) is possible in Niamey, Birni N'Konni and Parc Regional du W.

Midrange hotels generally offer more cleanliness and private bathrooms. Prices start at CFA11,000 with fan (air-con adds CFA5000), though prices double in Agadez and Niamey.

Upmarket hotels in Niamey and Agadez cost CFA30,000 to CFA85,000.

ACTIVITIES

Coasting in a *pirogue* through hippos and the Niger River's moist environments, and watching the animal and birdlife in the Parc Regional du W are the most obvious activities on offer in Niger. Sadly, due to the recent Tuareg Rebellion, travelling with a camel train through the Sahara is not presently an option.

BUSINESS HOURS

Typical business hours are 8am to noon and 3pm to 6pm weekdays, and 8am to noon Saturday.

Banking hours 8am to 11.30am and 3.45pm to 5pm weekdays, and 8.30am to noon Saturday.

Government offices 8.30am to 12.15pm and 3.30pm to 6pm weekdays.

Restaurants Simple local eateries open around 6am and don't shut the doors until 10pm, while fancier options serve breakfast from 7am to 10am, lunch from noon to 2pm and dinner between 6pm and 11pm.

CUSTOMS

The thoroughness of customs officials' searches varies, though travellers rarely receive painstaking searches. Ignore requests for 'special taxes'. There's no limit on movement of foreign currencies.

DANGERS & ANNOYANCES

Due to the recent Tuareg Rebellion, the north of Niger is under military control, with foreigners restricted to visiting Agadez and Arlit. Travel to and from these cities from the south is only possible within military convoys. If you do visit the north, follow the rules and do not attempt to leave the towns.

EMBASSIES & CONSULATES

There's no UK diplomatic representation in Niger – British citizens should contact their embassy in Accra, Ghana (see p357). In emergency situations Australians should contact the Canadian representative office in Niamey.

All embassies and consulates listed below are in Niamey unless otherwise stated.

Algeria Agadez (☎ 20 44 01 17; ☻ 8am-2.30pm Mon-Fri, to noon Sat); Niamey (☎ 20 72 35 83; Blvd des Ambassades; ☻ 9-11.30am Tue-Fri)

Benin (☎ 20 72 28 60; Rue des Dallois; ☻ 9am-4pm Mon-Fri) A new embassy out by Blvd des Ambassades was being constructed at the time of writing.

Canada (☎ 20 75 36 86; off Blvd de Mali Béro)

Chad (☎ 20 75 34 64; Ave de Presidence; ☻ 8.30am-3.30pm Mon-Thu, 8am-noon Fri)

France (☎ 20 72 24 31/32/33; Blvd des Ambassades; ☻ 8am-12.30pm Mon-Fri)

Germany (☎ 20 72 35 10; Ave du Général de Gaulle; ☻ 9am-noon Mon-Fri)

Mali (☎ 20 75 42 90; off Blvd des Ambassades; ☻ 8am-noon Mon-Fri)

Nigeria (☎ 20 73 24 10; Blvd des Ambassades; ☻ 10am-1pm Mon-Fri).

USA (☎ 20 73 31 69, 20 72 39 41; www.niamey.usembassy .gov; Rue des Ambassades; ☻ 8am-5.30pm Mon-Thu, to 1pm Fri)

FESTIVALS & EVENTS

Niger's largest festival is the annual Cure Salée (see opposite). July and August abound with Saharan festivities, with different villages holding a feast almost weekly.

HOLIDAYS

Islamic holidays dominate (see p1140 for dates and details). Other public holidays:

New Year's Day 1 January
Easter March/April
Labour Day 1 May
Independence Day 3 August
Settlers' Day 5 September
Republic Day 18 December
Christmas Day 25 December

INTERNET ACCESS

Internet access is readily available in all large towns via web cafes. A few hotels in Niamey have wireless. Prices for web-cafe access range from CFA500 to CFA1000 per hour.

MONEY

The unit of currency is the West African CFA franc. Carrying cash in euros is best, though US dollar equivalents suffice. The best bank for transactions is BIA-Niger.

NIGER

There are no ATMs in Niger and credit-card advances are only a (costly) possibility in Niamey and Agadez.

POST

Postal services outside Niamey are unreliable, so send everything from the capital. Postcards to Europe/North America cost CFA525/550.

TELEPHONE

Private telecentres abound, offering international calls for CFA900 per minute. Post offices offer better quality, with three-minute (the minimum) calls costing CFA5000. Subsequent minutes cost CFA1600.

Niger's mobile-phone network covers most major cities, and anyone with an unlocked handset can buy a local SIM card and make cheap local calls.

VISAS

Visas are required by non–West African citizens. Acquiring visas outside Africa is generally straightforward, although you'll need three photos, proof of yellow-fever vaccination, recent bank statements and proof of onward travel. Passports must be valid for six months after your Niger exit date. You can find up-to-date information and printable visa application forms from the websites of Niger's embassies in Paris (www.ambassadeniger.org) and Washington DC (www.nigerembassyusa.org).

There's less hassle obtaining visas at the Nigerian consulate of a neighbouring African country. Note that Niger is one of the five countries covered by the Visa Entente scheme that covers Benin, Burkina Faso, Côte d'Ivoire and Togo as well (see p1147).

Visa Extensions

For a one- to three-month visa extension, take two photos, your passport and CFA20,000 to the **Direction de la Surveillance du Territoire** (☎ 20 73 37 43, ext 249; Rue du Président Heinrich Lübké, Niamey; ☺ 8am-12.30pm & 3.30-6.30pm Mon-Fri). Extensions are typically processed the same day.

Visas for Onward Travel
ALGERIA

Two passport photos, a photocopy of your passport and CFA22,500 gets you an Algerian visa. Lodge the documents any time between 9am and 11.30am Tuesday to Friday and collect at 11.30am on the dot on Friday. You can also get an Algerian visa from the consulate in Agadez if you have a letter from an Algerian travel agency (stating your plans with the agency), a photocopy of your vehicle's *carte grise* and three colour photos.

BENIN

Transit visas cost CFA10,000, three-month single-entry tourist visas are CFA12,000 and three-month multiple-entry visas go for CFA25,000. You'll need to bring two photos and your passport between 9am and 4pm Monday to Friday. Visas are issued within 48 hours.

CHAD

For a single-entry one-month visa you'll need two photos, CFA15,000 and a pleasant demeanour. Visas are usually ready the same day.

MALI

A one- or two-month single-entry visa costs CFA20,000, and requires one photo and leaving your passport at the embassy for 24 hours. Unluckily for them, US citizens are singled out to pay an extraordinary US$131 for their visas.

NIGERIA

Two passport photos and a photocopy of your passport are required to get a visa here. Prices vary according to your nationality. Handily no other documents are required, and contrary to what the ancient sign at the entrance gate says, passports are taken daily between 10am and 1pm and visas issued within 48 hours.

TRANSPORT IN NIGER

GETTING THERE & AWAY

Despite needing to provide a yellow-fever vaccination certificate to obtain a visa, you'll still need to show it when entering the country.

Air

Airlines flying to/from Niamey include the following.

Afriqiyah Airways (8U; ☎ 20 73 65 68, 20 73 65 72; www.flyafriqiyah.eu; Rue Nasser) Flies between Tripoli and Niamey twice a week.

Air Algérie (AH; ☎ 20 73 38 99; www.airalgerie.dz; Rue du Gaweye) Links Niamey to Algiers Mondays and Fridays.

Air Burkina (2J; ☎ 20 73 90 55; www.air-burkina.com; Rue du Commerce) Flies to Ouagadougou.

Air France (AF; ☎ 20 73 31 21, 20 73 31 22; www. airfrance.com; Rue du Grand Hôtel) Flies four times a week to Paris Charles de Gaulle, continuing to Amsterdam.

Air Sénégal International (V7; www.air-senegal -international.com). Flies to/from Dakar. Satguru Travel is the local representative. See p446.

Royal Air Maroc (AT; ☎ 20 73 28 85; www.royalair maroc.com; Rue du Gaweye) Flies to/from Casablanca five times a week.

Toumaï Air Tchad (☎ 20 73 04 05; Rue du Gaweye) Flies between Niamey and N'Djaména on Thursday.

Land
ALGERIA
The crossing between Arlit and Tamanrasset at Assamakka/In Guezzam is open, though you must travel with licensed travel agencies on both sides (even with private 4WDs).

BENIN
Bush taxis don't cross the border, so you'll have to use a *moto* (CFA500) to link Gaya and Malanville.

Easier still, SNTV connects Niamey and Cotonou (CFA17,500, 13 to 15 hours), continuing to Lomé (CFA18,500). EHGM runs a similar daily service to Cotonou for CFA18,700, as does Rimbo.

BURKINA FASO
The main crossing is Foetchango, south-west of Niamey. Minibuses (CFA8500, 10 to 12 hours) leave Niamey's *gare routière*, and SNTV and Rimbo buses cover the 500km between Niamey and Ouagadougou (CFA10,000, nine to 11 hours, daily). Those with vehicles can also cross via Téra, northwest of Niamey.

CHAD
Banditry is rife around the Niger–Chad border, so take this route only in daylight. There's no scheduled public transport travelling across the border, but there are a couple of 4WDs that make the dusty day-long journey from Nguigmi to Mao in Chad (CFA20,000) each week.

LIBYA
At present the border with Libya is closed to all travellers.

MALI
Buses make the journey to Gao from Niamey every day. SNTV (CFA7225 daily except Sunday) and Rimbo (CFA8500, daily) leave at 6am from the capital, and the journey can take between 24 and 30 hours.

It's also possible to take a slow boat from Ayorou to Gao (CFA50,000, two days) on Monday. There's no shade, so a hat or an umbrella is as crucial as a large supply of water.

NIGERIA
The quickest option from Niamey is the Gaya/Kamba crossing. Several buses/bush taxis make daily runs from Niamey to Gaya (CFA5500/4250, five hours), from where you can hop on a *moto* or grab a shared taxi to the Nigerian border (CFA100). From there you can get another *moto* to Kamba.

Crossing at Birni N'Konni/Illela is also straightforward. Take a *moto* from Birni N'Konni to the border (CFA150), where you'll find minibuses/Peugeots running to/from Sokoto (1½ hours).

Peugeots link Maradi with the Nigerian towns of Katsina (CFA1200, 1½ hours) and Kano (CFA3000, four hours).

Zinder is also connected to Kano via the Jibya crossing. Several Peugeots (CFA3000, 3½ hours) ply this route each day.

GETTING AROUND
Bus
With decent sealed roads stretching the breadth of the country, bus transport is comprehensive, reliable and efficient. Seating is reserved, so book early. Buses depart their company offices, not from *autogares*.

Bush Taxi
Bush taxis (Peugeot 504s and minibuses) are cheaper and more frequent than buses, though they're crowded and take much longer.

Car & Motorcycle
Car and 4WD hire can be organised in Niamey, though in general it's expensive. Shop around for the best deals. It's usually only possible to hire a car or 4WD with a driver, although some agencies may be flexible about this.

NIGER

Nigeria

It's safe to say that Nigeria's reputation precedes it. Everyone seems to know the 'facts': it's big, crazy and dangerous, with email scams its most famous export. Enough to make you draw a big detour line on your travel map through West Africa? Think again, because we'd like to change your mind. Simply put: we love Nigeria.

It's a superlative country in every sense. It's the most populous nation on the continent – every fifth African is a Nigerian – it dominates the region economically, and its cultural output ranges from literary masterpieces such as *Things Fall Apart* and *Purple Hibiscus* to the infectious grooves of Fela Kuti's Afrobeat.

Contrasts abound. The sprawling megalopolis of Lagos contrasts sharply with the ancient Muslim cities of the north and the river deltas and lush forests of the south and east. There's wildlife too, from pioneering conservation organisations in Calabar to Gashaka-Gumti National Park, recently reorganised to accept visitors.

Nigeria can feel like more than the sum of its parts – a collection of regions and ethnicities pulling against each other with a force that occasionally bursts into chaos. But against this, the hard work and proud smiles of Nigerians offer the perfect corrective for visitors.

We can't lie: getting around can sometimes be exhausting, and it's not a destination for first-timers to Africa. But put the scare stories to one side and you might be in for a pleasant surprise. If you don't visit Nigeria you can barely say that you've been to West Africa.

FAST FACTS

- **Area** 924,000 sq km
- **ATMs** In major cities only, though not all accept international bank cards
- **Borders** Benin, Niger, Chad, Cameroon
- **Budget** US$40 to US$70 per day
- **Capital** Abuja
- **Languages** English, Hausa, Yoruba, Igbo, Edo, Efik
- **Money** Naira (N); US$1 = N150, €1 = N212
- **Population** 146 million
- **Seasons** Wet (April to October in north; March to November in south); dry (November to March in north; December to February in south)
- **Telephone** Country code ☎ 234; international access code ☎ 00
- **Time** GMT/UTC +1
- **Visa** US$70 to US$150 for one month; best obtained in country of residence, letter of invitation usually required

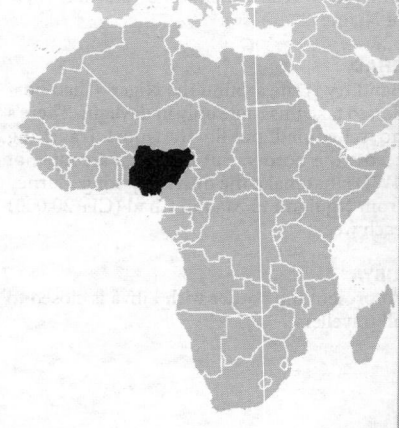

NIGERIA

HOW MUCH?

- Okada ride across town US$0.25
- Replica Benin brass sculpture US$80
- Afrobeat CD US$2.70
- Bribe at police roadblock US$0.15
- One-minute local phone call US$0.15

LONELY PLANET INDEX

- 1L of petrol US$0.45
- 1L of bottled water US$0.65
- Bottle of Star beer US$1.35
- Souvenir football shirt US$6.00
- Stick of suya (Nigerian kebab) US$0.65

HIGHLIGHTS

- **Lagos** (p464) Plunge in and sample the adrenalin charge and social scene of Nigeria's wild beating heart.
- **Calabar** (p471) Take in colonial history and cutting-edge conservation in this easygoing old river port.
- **Kano** (p473) Find a trace of the old Saharan trade routes in the old city and the indigo dye pits.
- **Gashaka-Gumti National Park** (p475) Head into the real wilds to explore this newly reorganised mountain-meets-savannah national park.

CLIMATE & WHEN TO GO

If you're travelling to the south of Nigeria, March to August are the wettest months to visit Nigeria, and best avoided if possible. Temperatures are hot year-round, peaking in the spring; the humidity is constant. Late spring to summer is the hottest part of the year in the north, with the mercury dropping slightly between October and January at the beginning of the dusty harmattan winds.

As well as the weather, take note of political developments when planning your trip. Although Nigeria is generally calm, local trouble flare up pretty quickly, so once you're in the country keep an eye on the news for developments and be prepared to change your plans at short notice if necessary.

ITINERARIES

- **One to Two Weeks** No one should visit Nigeria without at least a few days in Lagos (p464), trying to navigate the city's mindset and traffic jams, and spending late nights in the bars and clubs. When Lagos gets too much, head east to Benin City (p470) to see the ancient craft of brass sculpture, before carrying on to the old port city of Calabar (p471), where you can also check out pioneering primate conservation work in the lush forests of the Afi Mountain Drill Ranch (p471).
- **One Month** A longer trip allows you to further explore the south, but also to take in northern Nigeria. From Lagos, fly to Abuja (p471), and then continue by road to the old trading city of Kano (p473). An interesting detour would be via the cool plateau city of Jos (p472), with a side-trip to the remote Gashaka-Gumti National Park (p475).

HISTORY
Early Nigeria

Northern and southern Nigeria are essentially two different countries, and their histories reflect this disparity. The first recorded empire to flourish in this part of West Africa was Kanem-Borno around Lake Chad, which grew rich from the trans-Saharan trade routes. Islamic states based in the Hausa cities of Kano, Zaria and Nupe also flourished at this time.

Meanwhile, the southwest developed into a patchwork of small states, often dominated by the Yoruba. The Ijebu kingdom rose in the 10th century and constructed the mysterious earthworks at Sungbo's Eredo. Most famously the Benin kingdom became an important centre of trade and produced some of the finest metal artwork in Africa. In the southeast, the Igbo and other agrarian peoples never developed any centralised empires, instead forming loose confederations.

Colonial Era

The first contact between the Yoruba empires and the Europeans was made in the 15th century, when the Portuguese began trading in pepper, and later, slaves. In contrast, the northern Islamic states remained untouched by European influence until well into the 19th century.

NIGERIA

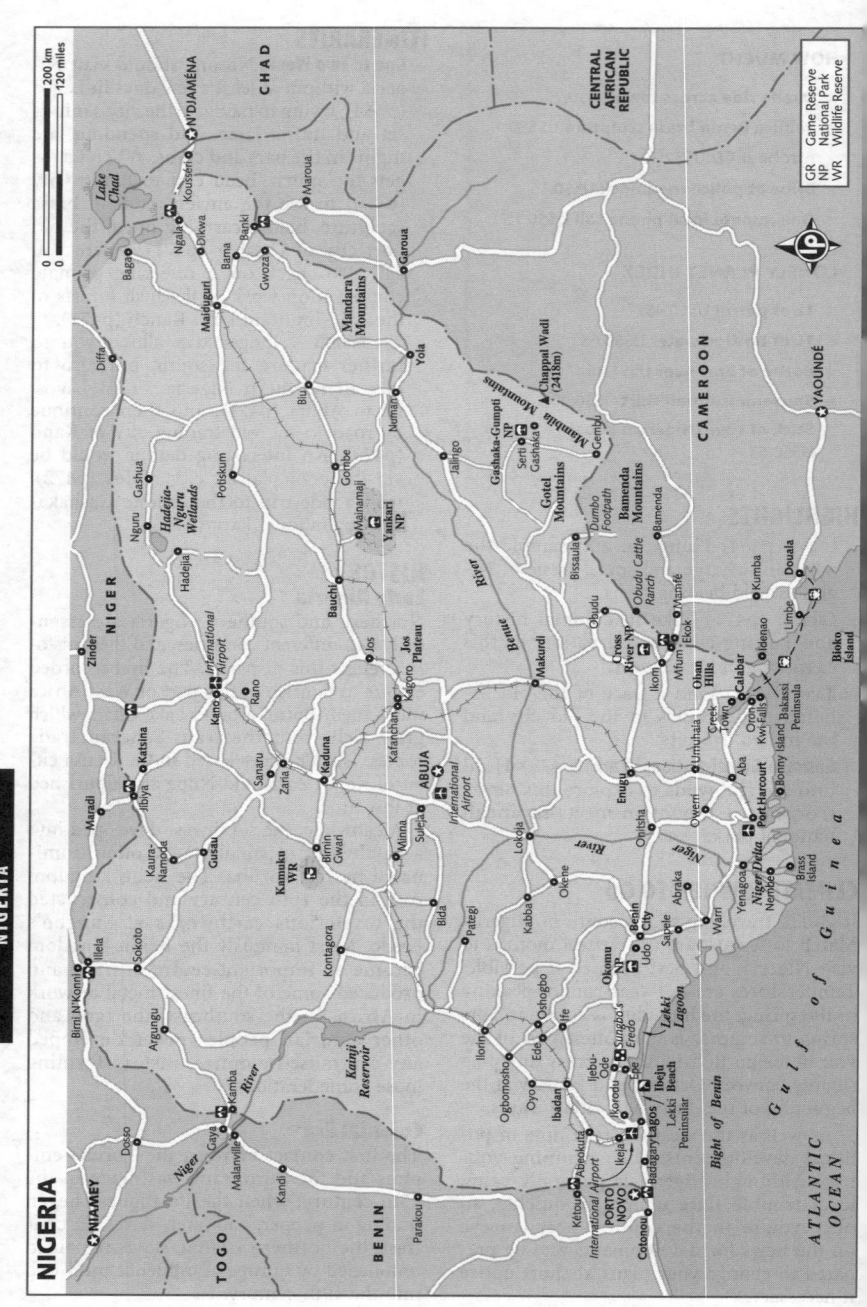

In the early 19th century, the British took a lead in suppressing slavery along the Niger delta, leading to the annexation of Lagos port – a first colonial toehold. This led to further annexation to thwart the French, who were advancing their territory along the Niger River. By the beginning of the 20th century, British soldiers had advanced as far north as the cities of Kano and Sokoto, where Islamic revivalism had created a rapidly expanding caliphate.

Nigeria was divided in two – the southern, mainly Christian, colony and the northern Islamic protectorate. The British chose to rule indirectly through local kings and chiefs, exacerbating ethnic divisions for political expediency.

Military Misrule

These divisions came back to haunt Nigeria when independence came in October 1960. Politics split along ethnic lines, and in 1966 a group of Igbo army officers staged a coup. General Johnson Ironsi took over as head of state. Another coup quickly followed on its heels, along with massacres of Igbos, which in 1967 provoked civil war by secessionist Igbos.

The war dragged on for three years. Biafra was blockaded, and by the time its forces capitulated in 1970, up to a million Igbos had died, mainly from starvation.

An oil boom smoothed Nigeria's path to national reconciliation, but as the army jockeyed for political control, the next two decades were marked by a series of military coups, with only a brief democratic interlude in the early 1980s. When General Ibrahim Babangida offered elections in 1993, he annulled them when the result appeared to go against him, only to be toppled in a coup soon after by General Sani Abacha.

Abacha was ruthless, purging the army and locking up intellectuals, unionists, and pro-democracy activists. His rule reached a nadir in 1995 with the judicial murder of the Ogoni activist Ken Saro-Wiwa, an act that led to Nigeria's expulsion from the Commonwealth.

Salvation finally came in June 1998, in what Nigerians called the 'coup from heaven'. Aged 54, and worth somewhere between US$2 billion and US$5 billion in stolen government money, Abacha died of a heart attack while in the company of two prostitutes. His successor immediately announced elections and in February 1999, Olusegun Obasanjo, a former military leader, was returned as president.

Nigeria Today

Obasanjo inherited a country in tatters. Freed from the military yoke, the deep political and cultural differences between the north and south of the country began to play themselves out violently. A major test came in 2000 when several northern states introduced Sharia'a (Islamic law). Tensions between communities became inflamed, resulting in mass riots and bloodshed. During Obasanjo's first term as president, over 10,000 people were killed in communal violence.

Nigeria's economy didn't prosper. Corruption was still rife, and the oil industry neglected. In recent years, the oil-producing delta has been aflame with violence and kidnapping, with local militia groups like MEND (Movement for the Emancipation of the Niger Delta) leading attacks against foreign oil installations, and demanding economic and political power for the region.

In 2007, elections marred by violence and described as 'deeply flawed' by international observers saw northerner Umaru Yar'Adua returned as president. His quiet and deliberative style has earned him the nickname 'Baba Go-Slow', but governing as complicated a country as Nigeria is a balancing act that would tax the keenest of minds, and slow but steady progress is perhaps the best that the immediate future can offer.

CULTURE

With nearly 150 million people, Nigeria has a huge and expanding population. By the middle of the 21st century it's thought that as many as one in three people on the African continent will be a Nigerian. The main ethnic groups are the Yoruba (in the southwest), Hausa (north) and Igbo (southeast), each making up around a fifth of the population, followed by the northern Fulani (around 10%). It's thought that up to 250 languages are spoken in Nigeria. Ordinary Nigerians struggle against systematic corruption through the natural entrepreneurship of one of Africa's better-educated populations.

Chinua Achebe (*Things Fall Apart*) is probably Nigeria's (and Africa's) most famous author; equally acclaimed writers from Nigeria include the Nobel laureate Wole Soyinka, Booker Prize–winner Ben Okri (author of *The Famished Road*) and Chimamanda Ngozi Adichie (author of *Purple Hibiscus* and *Half a Yellow Sun*).

Some of Africa's best-known musicians have been Nigerian. Two styles have traditionally been dominant, Afrobeat and *juju*, with their respective masters being the late Fela Kuti and King Sunny Ade.

Nigerian sculpture is also renowned, from the 2000-year-old Nok terracottas (the oldest known sub-Saharan Africa sculptures), to the brass statuary of Benin City.

FOOD & DRINK

Nigerians like their food ('chop') hot and starchy. The classic dish is a fiery pepper stew ('soup') with a little meat or fish and accompanied by starch – usually pounded yam or cassava (*garri, eba*, or the slightly sour *fufu*). Another popular dish is *jollof* – peppery rice cooked with palm oil and tomato. Cutlery isn't generally used – the yam or cassava is used to soak up the juices of the stew. As in most of Africa, you only eat with your right hand.

Look for signs saying 'food is ready' when you're hungry. Vegetarians will have a hard time in Nigeria. Drinking water is sold on the streets in plastic bags as 'pure water'. Star is the most popular local beer.

ENVIRONMENT

Nigeria's topography is relatively unvaried. The north touches on the Sahel and is mostly savannah with low hills. Mountains are found only along the Cameroon border in the east, although there is a 1500m-high plateau around Jos in the centre of the country. The coast is an almost unbroken line of sandy beaches and lagoons running back to creeks and mangrove swamps and is very humid most of the year.

An underfunded national parks service does exist, but in practice very little land in Nigeria is effectively protected. The expanding population has contributed to widespread deforestation – 95% of the original forests have been logged. However, the oil industry has caused the greatest number of environmental problems: oil spills and gas flaring have damaged the fishing industry, with little of the industry's wealth trickling down to the local level.

LAGOS

☎ 01 / pop 14 million

Lagos is chaos theory made flesh and concrete. It's the largest city in Africa, with wall-to-wall people, bumper-to-bumper cars, noise and pollution beyond belief, a crime rate out of control, and public utilities that are simply incapable of coping with the demands of the huge population. Elevated motorways ring the city, jammed with speed freaks and traffic jams ('go-slows') on top, and tin-and-cardboard shacks underneath.

The city takes its name from the Portuguese for lagoon and has been a Yoruba port, a British political centre and, until 1991, Nigeria's capital. It remains the economic and cultural powerhouse of the country, and has a superb live music scene and West Africa's most inimitable street life. It won't be to everyone's taste, but if you're up for an urban adventure then you might find Lagos truly compelling. A true megacity and the face of modern Africa as much as any picture-postcard national park – jump right in.

ORIENTATION

For the traveller, there are four main areas of Lagos: Yaba on the mainland, south of the international and domestic airports; Lagos Island, the heart of the city; Ikoyi, a smart suburb with some embassies and top-end hotels; and Victoria Island (VI), an even smarter suburb facing the Atlantic Ocean with the bulk of the embassies and a number of top-end hotels. The islands are connected by elevated expressways and bridges.

INFORMATION

Internet Access

Expect to pay around N100 per hour.

Cool Café (Map p466; Cool FM Bldg, Etim Inyang Cres; per hr N300) Expensive but fast.

Mega Plaza Internet (Map p466; Mega Plaza, Idowu Martin St) On the top floor.

Medical Services

Chyzob Pharmacy (Map p466; ☎ 269 4545; Awolowo Rd; ⏱ 8am-8pm Mon-Sat)

St Nicholas Hospital (Map p468; ☎ 260 0070; 57 Campbell St) Has a 24-hour emergency clinic.

Money

There are exchange bureaux at Lagos airport, while on VI, ATMs are everywhere.

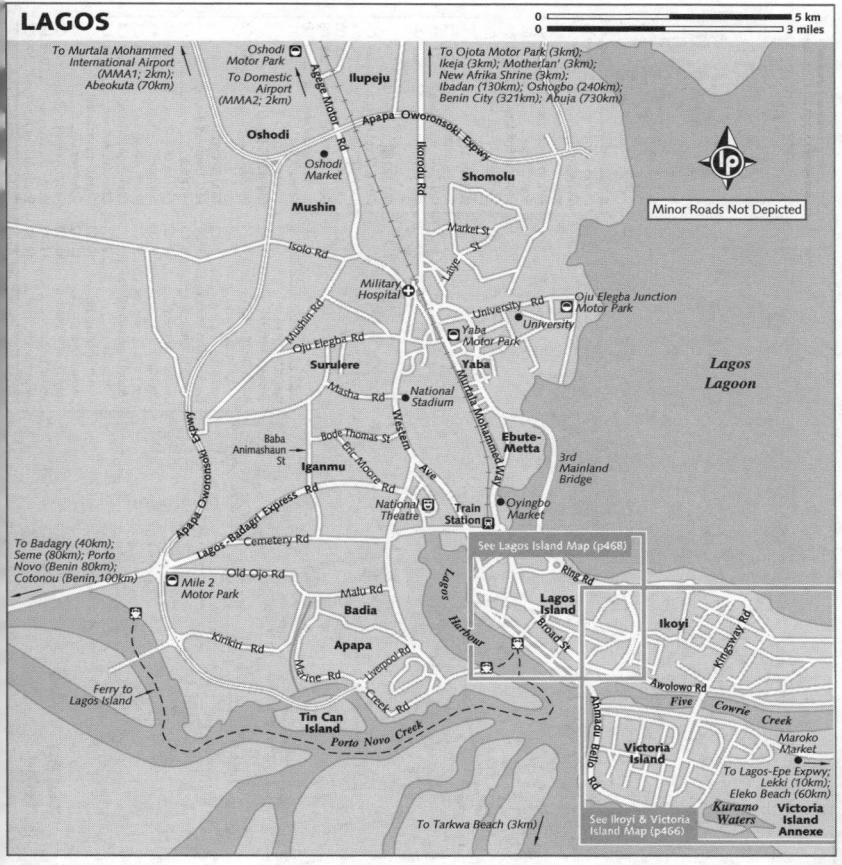

LAGOS

Eko Hotel (Map p466; Adetokumbo Ademola St) Find Hausa moneychangers at the craft shops by the gatehouse.
Ikoyi Hotel (Map p466; Kingsway Rd) There's a bureau de change office and Hausa moneychangers outside the (closed) hotel.

Post

Main post office (Map p468; Marina St; ☻ Mon-Fri)
Post office (Map p466; Adeola Odeku St, VI)

DANGERS & ANNOYANCES

Contrary to popular perception, violent crime has decreased in Lagos in recent years. Most crime against foreigners targets expats in expensive cars, and travellers are unlikely to encounter any serious problems. That said, never carry any more money than is necessary and avoid flaunting valuables. Avoid walking at night where possible, particularly around hotels and restaurants frequented by foreigners, including on Victoria Island.

SIGHTS & ACTIVITIES

Lagos doesn't have sights *per se* – the life of the city is the experience itself.

On Lagos Island, head for the many markets. They're safe enough to get lost in during the day, but photography isn't usually appreciated. **Jankara Market** (Map p468; off Adeyinka Oyekan Ave) sells fabric and a witches' brew of juju ingredients. **Balogun Market** (Map p468; off Breadfruit St) sells fabric from across West Africa. Finally, **Sandgrouse Market** (Map p468; off

IKOYI & VICTORIA ISLAND

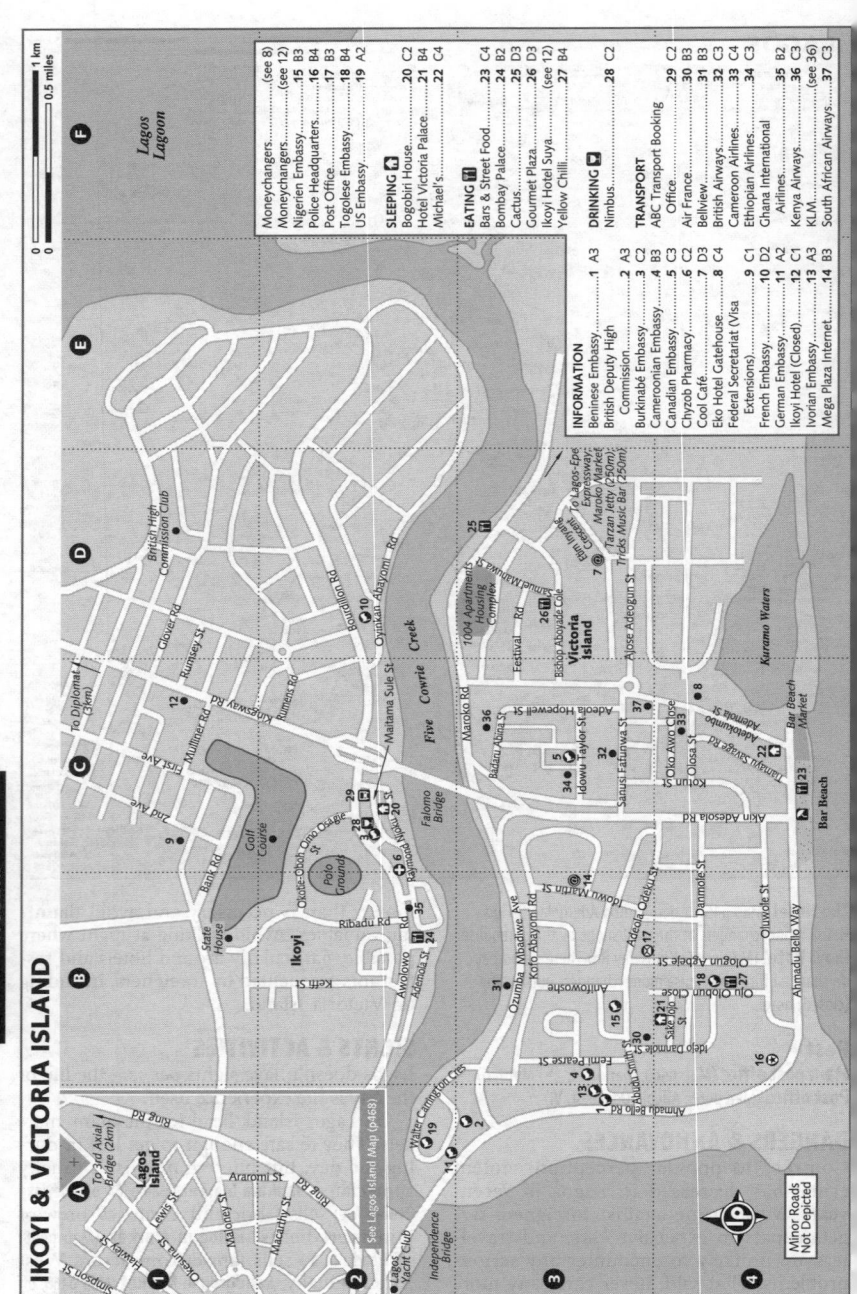

NIGERIA

419

Ever received an email offering you a share of untold riches in exchange for help repatriating a hidden fortune, quite possibly from the widow of an African dictator? Chances are it came from Lagos, spiritual home of the internet scam. Known locally as a 419 (from its classification in the Nigerian criminal code), so-called 'advance fee fraud' is rife in Nigeria. Successful scammers ('yahoo yahoos') can make thousands of dollars a month from 419. In Nigeria, there's often little sympathy for the *maghas* (Yoruba slang for fool) who lose their shirts – they're as often seen as victims of their own greed and gullibility, yet more foreigners hoping to make a cynical fortune out of Africa. Scams provide rich inspiration for local musicians, with songs like '419 State of Mind' by rapper Modenine and Osuofia's 'I Go Chop Your Dollar' both celebrating and satirising the hustle.

But foreigners aren't the only victims of fraud. Inside Nigeria, a popular scam is to break into an empty property and then sell it on to an unsuspecting buyer – watch out for painted signs everywhere announcing 'This house is not for sale: beware 419'.

Lewis St) slightly further east is the place for interesting food, as much of it is sold live.

On Lagos Island also look out for examples of old Brazilian architecture in the distinctive houses built by former slaves and their descendants who returned from Brazil.

The **National Museum** (Awolowo Rd; admission N100; 9am-5pm) has some interesting displays and exhibits, including many fine works of ancient sculpture. It also has a nonprofit craft centre. No cameras allowed.

SLEEPING

Lagos has both some of the best hotels in Nigeria and some of the worst, with very little in the midrange bracket.

Ritz Hotel (Map p468; 263 0481; King George V Rd; r with fan & without bathroom N2000, with ac N2900-4000;) The name's a bit of a misnomer, but this hotel is a reasonably decent budget option. Rooms are fine in a grubby 'by the hour' sort of way, but they're secure and management is friendly.

Famoss Guesthouse (Map p468; 0802 322 9172; 59 Lawson St, Lagos Island; r N3000-4000;) Another fairly basic outfit, with rooms priced according to size. All have bathrooms, none are spectacular, but it's secure and the management seem used to backpackers.

Hotel Victoria Palace (Map p466; 262 5901; victoriapalace@gmail.com; 1623 Sake Jojo St; s/d N12,500-14,000;) The closest thing that VI gets to budget accommodation, the Victoria Palace is a good option down a reasonably quiet street. Rooms are fitted out well, and there's an Indian restaurant on the top floor.

Michael's (Map p466; 461 6802; michael@hyperia.com; Plot 411, Adetokumbo Ademola St; r incl breakfast from

N19000;) This hotel has two blocks – one overlooking a small pool (rooms are rather less generously proportioned than the mermaids on the pool mural), and slightly plusher rooms in the block with the hotel reception. With good and friendly service, it's a neat little choice.

Bogobiri House (Map p466; 270 7406; www.bogobirilagos.com; 9 Maitama Sule St, Ikoyi; r incl breakfast from N25,000;) A charming boutique hotel. Beautifully decorated with paintings and sculptures by local artists, its side-street location provides a calm escape from the Lagos buzz. There are just 10 rooms, each exceedingly comfortable and as much salon as sleeping place.

EATING

Broad St and Campbell St in Lagos Island are good for chophouses and *suya*; the better restaurants are in Ikoyi and VI.

Ikoyi Hotel Suya (Map p466; Ikoyi Hotel, Kingsway Rd, Ikoyi; suya from N100; 10am-10pm) Lagosians claim the best *suya* in town can be found at the stall outside the Ikoyi Hotel. Not just beef and goat, but chicken, liver and kidney, plus some great fiery *pepe* (pepper) to spice it all up.

Gourmet Plaza (Map p466; 879 Samuel Manuwa St, VI; meals around N800; 8am-10pm) One serving fits all at this place, and you can have it any way you like – lip-smacking noodles, stuffed tortillas, sandwiches and burgers. Quick, cheap and filling.

Bombay Palace (Map p466; Awolowo Rd; mains from N1200; noon-3pm & 6-10pm) Vegetarians suffer in Nigeria, but this Indian restaurant comes to the rescue. With tasty and filling portions at

NIGERIA

LAGOS ISLAND

INFORMATION
Ghanaian High Commission..**1** D4
Main Post Office..................**2** B3
St Nicholas Hospital............**3** C3

SIGHTS & ACTIVITIES
Balogun Market..................**4** A2
Jankara Market..................**5** B2
National Museum................**6** C4
Sandgrouse Market............**7** C3

SLEEPING
Famoss Guesthouse............**8** D4
Ritz Hotel..........................**9** D4

TRANSPORT
Lufthansa..........................**10** A2
Obalende Motor Park.......**11** D4

good prices, this is a great option. It's on the top floor of the Victoria Palace Hotel.

Cactus (Map p466; Maroko Rd; mains from N1200; 8am-10pm) This place labels itself primarily as a patisserie, but it also serves up proper meals throughout the day. Breakfasts of pancakes or bacon are good, as are the pizzas, and the club sandwiches with salad and chips are simply huge – excellent value at N1800.

Yellow Chilli (Map p466; 27 Ojo Olubun Close, VI; mains N1500-2500; 11am-10pm) The concept here is well-presented Nigerian dishes in swish surroundings. It's carried off well, with tasty dishes in reasonable portions and good service – a great way to eat your way around the country without leaving your table.

DRINKING

Nimbus (Map p466; Maitama Sule St; 8am-11pm) Part of the Nimbus art gallery, this is a lovely place for a drink – mellow in the day and happening at night. At weekends there's usually live music, so there's often a cover charge to get in.

Tricks Music Bar (off Map p466; Tarzan Jetty, VI; 24hr) Right next to the ferry jetty, Tricks is a laid-back open-air bar that's a good place to unwind and sink a couple of cold ones with a plate of *suya*, although male patrons might get some attention from the bar girls.

ENTERTAINMENT

Lagos' nightlife is legendary, with the happening nightclubs in Ikeja (13km north of Lagos

Island) and Yaba. Don't even think of turning up before 11pm.

New Afrika Shrine (Pepple St, Ikeja; cover charge N500; ⌚ Thu-Sun) Fela Kuti's original Shrine was burnt down, but this replacement is run by his son Femi, who plays on Friday and Sunday when he's in town. It's a huge shed, but the music blows the roof off.

Motherlan' (Opebi Rd, Ikeja; cover charge N1000; ⌚ Thu-Sun) Owned by musician Lagbaja, who mixes groovy jazz with African drums while always remaining hidden under a traditional Yoruba mask (his name simultaneously means anybody and nobody).

GETTING THERE & AWAY
Murtala Mohammed International Airport (MMA1) is the main gateway to Nigeria and is roughly 10km north of Lagos Island. The domestic terminal (MMA2) is 4km away, and tickets are bought on departure.

Airline offices based in Lagos include the following:

Aero Contractors (☎ 764 7571; www.acn.aero; Airport desk)

Air France (Map p466; ☎ 461 0461; www.airfrance.com; Idejo Danmole St)

Bellview (Map p466; ☎ 791 9215; www.flybellviewair.com; Ozumba Mbadiwe Ave)

British Airways (Map p466; ☎ 262 1225; www.britishairways.com; 1st fl, C&C Tower, Sanusi Fafunwa St)

Cameroon Airlines (Map p466; ☎ 261 6270; Oko Awo Close)

Chanchangi Airlines (☎ 493 9744; www.chanchangi-airlines.com; airport desk)

Ethiopian Airlines (Map p466; ☎ 263 1125; www.flyethiopian.com; Idowu Tayor St)

Ghana International Airlines (Map p466; ☎ 266 1808; www.fly-ghana.com; 130 Awolowo Rd, Ikoyi)

Kenya Airways (Map p466; ☎ 461 2501; www.kenya-airways.com; Churchgate Tower, Badaru Abina St)

KLM (Map p466; ☎ 461 2501; www.klm.com; Churchgate Tower, Badaru Abina St)

Lufthansa (Map p468; ☎ 266 4227, www.lufthansa.com; Broad St, Lagos Island)

South African Airlines (Map p466; ☎ 262 0607; www.flysaa.com; Adetokumbo Ademola St)

Sosoliso (☎ 497 1492; www.sosoliso.airline.com; airport desk)

Virgin Nigeria (☎ 461 2747; www.virginnigeria.com; Sheraton Hotel, Ikeja)

Lagos' motor parks are pictures of anarchy. Ojota Motor Park (with Ojota New Motor Park next door), 13km north of Lagos Island, is the city's main transport hub. Minibuses and bush taxis leave to just about everywhere in the country from here. Sample fares are Benin City (N1600, four hours), Ibadan (N500, 90 minutes), Oshogbo (N450, three hours) and Abuja (N2600, 10 hours).

Mile-2 Motor Park serves destinations east of Lagos, including the Benin border at Seme (N400, 90 minutes). You'll also find a few minibuses going as far north as Ibadan from here.

ABC Transport (www.abctransport.com) is a good intercity 'luxury' bus company, serving many major cities, as well as destinations in Benin, Ghana and Togo. The depot is at Jibowu motor park (Map p465), but there's a useful **booking office** (Map p466; ☎ 740 1010; Block D, Falomo Shopping Centre, Awolowo Rd) inside a shoe shop in Ikoyi.

GETTING AROUND
Always allow more time than you think to get to the airport when catching a flight. There are no airport buses. A licensed airport taxi costs from N2500 to reach Lagos Island.

Arriving in Lagos can be complicated and you may be dropped at one of several motor parks – Oshodi, Yaba and Oju Elegba Junction are the likeliest candidates. Minibuses run from these to more central points, such as Obalende Motor Park on Lagos Island.

Minibuses (*danfos*; fares N30 to N200 according to distance) serve points all over Lagos – prices increase when you cross a bridge from one part of Lagos to another. Yellow private taxis start at N200. For short distances, *okadas* (motorcycle taxis) are a better bet; a medium-length trip shouldn't top N100. If you're in a go-slow, an *okada* may be the only way out.

SOUTHERN NIGERIA

IBADAN
☎ 02 / pop 1.4 million
The word sprawling could have been invented to describe Ibadan. You're likely to pass through this major transport junction, but there's little to amuse yourself with here before pushing on to more exciting destinations.

If you're looking for a bed, try **Hotel Influential** (☎ 751 3588; Premier Hill, Mokola; r N5000-7000; P 🔲), opposite the plush Premier Hotel. Rooms aren't elaborate, but they're clean and

NIGERIA

comfortable enough, with fridge and satellite TV. If possible get a room with a view over Ibadan's hills.

A cheaper option is **Motel Liberty** (☎ 200 3418; Liberty Rd; r N3200-3800; P ⊠), budget Nigeria at its most stripped down – an adequate but basic hotel without a restaurant. There are plenty of chophouses in the area for eating, but also many prostitutes.

There are plenty of 'food-is-ready' places around Dugbe Market. For something different, go for **Pancho Vino** (off Town Planning, Oluyole; pizzas around N1400; ⊗ noon-3pm & 6-11pm). Formerly 'All-in-One', it's a great option for pizzas and Lebanese food in clean, modern surroundings.

Iwo Rd is Ibadan's major motor park; minibuses run to all points from here, including Lagos (N500, 90 minutes), Abuja (N2000, eight hours) and points north. For Oshogbo (N300, 90 minutes), go to Gate Motor Park in the east of the city.

OSHOGBO

This quiet Yoruba city has been a centre for contemporary Nigerian art since the 1950s. It's worth a visit to see the Osun Sacred Forest, a shrine to Yoruba religion that's a real Nigerian highlight. While here, also wander through the Oja Oba Market across from the Oba's Palace – it's packed with stalls selling juju material.

The delightful **Osun Sacred Forest** (Osun Shrine Rd; admission N200, camera N500; ⊗ 10am-6pm) is a cool, green oasis. An ancient centre for Yoruba goddess Osun, its groves are filled with sculptures and shrines revering the traditional deities. The forest is a lovely place to walk in, and was declared a Unesco World Heritage Site in 2006.

Several contemporary art galleries are also worth checking out, including the **Nike Centre for Arts & Culture** (Old Ede Rd), **Jimoh Buraimoh's African Heritage Gallery** (1 Buraimoh St) and the **New Sacred Art Shop** (41A Ibokun Rd).

Rooms at the **Heritage Hotel** (☎ 241881; www.buraimoh.com; Gbongan Rd; r N2875-5100; P ⊠ 🖳) are fair-sized with huge beds, although the mustard walls make them seem gloomier than they should be. But electricity is open 24 hours, and there's a decent restaurant-bar.

Once Oshogbo's grand old lady, the **Osun Presidential Hotel** (☎ 232299; Old Ikurin Rd; r from N9800; P ⊠) is adequate but, to be honest, is almost ready to be pensioned off. Rooms

are average for the price, which also sums up the restaurant.

Old Ede Rd is the main drag for chophouses serving 'food-is-ready'.

Okefia Rd is the main motor park. Minibuses leave pretty regularly for Ibadan (N300, 90 minutes) and Lagos (N600, three hours).

BENIN CITY
☎ 052
Benin City is one of the old Yoruba capitals. The kingdom, which flourished here in the medieval period, gave rise to one of the first African art forms to be accepted internationally – the 15th-century Benin brasses. The art of brass statuary has recently been revived, and you can see craftsmen at work near the museum.

The **National Museum** (King's Sq; admission N100; ⊗ 9am-6pm) is primarily dedicated to the Benin kingdom, with a display of beautiful brasses. The upstairs galleries are more ethnological in nature, providing a survey of traditional cultures from across Nigeria.

Brass Casters St nearby has been given over to reviving the 'lost-wax' sculpture technique. The brassmakers are happy to show you their works in progress, usually copies of the most famous Benin sculptures, and sell you one of your own.

For a budget sleeping option, try **Edo Delta Hotel** (☎ 252722; Akpakpava Rd; s N2000-3000, d from N3500; ⊠). It has a jumble of chalets and a hotel block proper. The cheapest rooms feel a little cramped and have fans only; other rooms are better value.

Formerly the Genesis Hotel, the **Lixborr Hotel** (☎ 256699; Sakowpba Rd; s/d N3000/3250-5000; ⊠) is a well-run place with comfortable rooms. Look for the giant statue of the Benin woman outside; it's opposite the brass caster's street.

Aside from hotel-restaurant options, **Mr Biggs** (Akpakpava Rd; ⊗ 8am-10pm) and **Sizzlers** (Sakopba Rd; ⊗ 8am-10pm) both offer Nigerian fast food with bright lights and clean toilets. Mr Biggs has a 'Village Garden' counter with traditional Nigerian fare, while Sizzlers offers similar with its 'Foodies' counter. The southern end of Akpakpava Rd has plenty of chophouses serving 'food-is-ready' fare.

Aero Contractors (☎ 271 1512) has a daily flight to Lagos (N8000, 40 minutes). Iyaro motor park is the main place for Lagos transport, with minibuses leaving throughout the day

(N1600, six hours), with more minibuses to Calabar (N1900, eight hours). Also try Edo-Delta depot, next to the Edo-Delta hotel on Akpakpava Rd, which serves most destinations useful for travellers.

CALABAR

☎ 087 / pop 500,000

Tucked into Nigeria's southeastern corner, the capital of Cross River state is one of the most likeable cities in Nigeria for visitors. Its port has historically made the town a prosperous place – Calabar was once one of Nigeria's biggest slave ports and later a major exporter of palm oil. A popular stopover for travellers heading to Cameroon, Calabar has a great museum and two excellent primate-conservation centres.

Sights

Calabar Museum (Court Rd; admission N100; ⏰ 9am-6pm) is housed in the beautiful old British governor's building overlooking the river. It has a fascinating collection covering Calabar's days as the Efik kingdom, the slave and palm-oil trade, and the colonial period.

Home to a colony of rescued drill monkeys and chimpanzees, the **Drill Ranch** (☎ 234310; www.pandrillus.org; Nsefik Eyo Layout, off Atekong Rd; donations appreciated; ⏰ 9am-5pm) is home to Pandrillus, one of Africa's most progressive primate-conservation bodies. Placing great emphasis on local education to combat poaching and the bushmeat trade, it can arrange trips to its excellent **Afi Mountain Drill Ranch** (community charge N250; guide N1000; car/motorbike N500/250; campsite N2000, huts N6000) near Cross River National Park. This is one of Nigeria's highlights, with a rainforest-canopy walk and close primate encounters.

On the other side of town in the Botanic Gardens, **Cercopan** (www.cercopan.org; Mary Slessor Ave; donations appreciated; ⏰ 9am-5pm) works with smaller monkeys such as guenons and mangabeys. The **gardens** (www.irokofoundation.org) are worth visiting to learn about the amazing biodiversity of the area.

Sleeping & Eating

Nelbee Executive Guesthouse (☎ 232684; Dan Achibong St; s/d N3600-4650; P ✗) Close to Watt Market is this handy budget option. Rooms are comfortable, the management friendly, and there's a terrifically formal dining room.

Jahas Guesthouse (Marian Rd; r N3500; ✗) This clean and tidy budget choice has a warm welcome, and is a pleasantly quiet option, off the main road.

Marian Hotel (☎ 220233; Old Ikong Rd; r N7000-8000; P ✗) Well located, the Marian has had a lick of paint and A tidy-up since our last visit, and is all the better for it. Rooms are spacious, tidy and comfortable.

Cosy Garden Restaurant (Nsefik Eyo Layout, off Atekong Rd; mains from N300; ⏰ 9am-8pm) If your mama was Nigerian, she'd cook like this. Choose hot and tasty pepper soup or delicately flavoured *egusi* with a mountain of pounded yam. It's poorly signed: look for the lime-green building near the Drill Ranch.

K's Court (74 Ndidan Usang Iso Rd; dishes from N300; ⏰ 11am-late) An open-air chophouse and bar, this place gets going better the later the day gets. It serves up fiery bowls of cow-leg soup with plantain, and once that's gone, pushes back the tables and cranks up the music to dance the weekend nights away.

For filling sit-down fast food from pies to *shwarmas*, try **Crunchies** (74 Ndidan Usang Iso Rd) or **Mr Fans** (30 Ndidan Usang Iso Rd).

Getting There & Away

Virgin Nigeria (www.virginnigeria.com), **Aero Contractors** (www.acn.aero) and **Bellview** (www.flybellviewair.com) all fly daily to Lagos and Abuja (both around N16,000).

Destiny (☎ 085-514475; Calabar dock) sails every Tuesday and Friday to Limbe in Cameroon (N6000, 10 to-12 hours). For more information, see p479.

The main motor park is tucked between Mary Slessor Ave and Goldie St. Sample minibus fares include Lagos (N3200, 10 hours) and Ikom (for Afi Mountain Drill Ranch; N700, three hours).

NORTHERN NIGERIA

ABUJA

pop 1.3 million

Nigeria's made-to-measure capital, Abuja was founded during the boom years of the 1970s. After the divisive Biafran war the decision was made to move the capital from Lagos to the ethnically neutral centre of the country. Clean, quiet and with a good electricity supply, sometimes Abuja hardly feels like Nigeria at all. There's not much to do, but it's a good place to catch your breath and do some visa shopping.

Abuja tends to empty at weekends, with people leaving for more exciting destinations, so many hotels offer discounts for Friday and Saturday nights.

For a nice quiet budget option, try **African Safari Hotel** (☎ 234 1881; Plot 11, Benue Cres; r from N3000-7000; ✴ ▢). It has a range of rooms increasing in size and price. Nearby, Area 1 Shopping Centre is good for street food.

Pridemark Hotel (☎ 870 3405; Plot 1373, Borno St; r N5500-9100; ✴) Formerly the Valley Pride, this hotel has cosy rooms and friendly management, and it's close to restaurants on Moshood Abiola.

The main draw at **Smi Msira Restaurant** (Moshood Abiola Way; dishes from N700) is being able to sit out in the pleasant leafy surroundings – something of a genuine beer garden. Claims to never close are exaggerated, but the Nigerian food is still good.

Mama Cass (Aminu Kano Cres; dishes from N650; ☯ 9am-10pm) This popular chain restaurant is a few doors up from Salamander Café, and serves up big and healthy portions of Nigerian classics in pleasing surroundings, washed down with fresh juices.

For a splurge, hit the restaurants at the Hilton and Sheraton hotels.

The airport is 40km west of Abuja – N3500 in a taxi. Flights depart hourly for Lagos with several airlines (N14,000, one hour). There are also daily flights to Kano and Port Harcourt, as well as flights several times a week to Ibadan, Calabar and Maiduguri.

Jabi Motor Park (also called Utoka) is the main terminus for Abuja. Transport goes to all points from here; sample minibus fares include Kano (N1000, four hours), Jos (N800, three hours), Ibadan (N1500, eight hours) and Lagos (N2600, 10 hours).

Okadas have been banned in Abuja. Instead, there are plentiful green taxis (around N200 a drop).

JOS
☎ 073

The temperate climes of the Jos plateau are one of the older inhabited parts of Nigeria; the ancient Nok terracottas originated in the area. At 1200m above sea level, it's noticeably cooler than most other parts of the country. Although Jos seems an outwardly relaxed city to the visitor, it sits astride one of Nigeria's major Christian–Muslim fault lines. With communal violence not unknown, it's es-

sential to keep your ear to the ground before planning a visit.

The **Jos National Museum** (admission N50; ☯ 8.30am-5.30pm) has a superb collection of pottery, including several Nok terracotta sculptures – at over 2500 years old they're Africa's oldest figurative sculptures. On the same site, the **Museum of Traditional Nigerian Architecture** (admission free; ☯ 8.30am-5.30pm) has full-scale reproductions of buildings from each of Nigeria's major regions. You can see a reconstruction of the Kano wall, traditional mosques and village architecture. The museum also has an excellent restaurant.

Cocin Guesthouse (☎ 452286; 6 Noad A St; dm N350, r N800-1000; Ⓟ) One of two church missions on this street. Accommodations are clean but spartan and bathroom facilities are shared, but it's hard to beat the price. Next door, **Tekan Guesthouse** (☎ 453036; 5 Noad St; dm 350, r N1000) has more of the same.

Les Rosiers (☎ 0803 357 5233; 1 Rest House Rd; r from N6000; Ⓟ ✴) This bungalow B&B is a delightfully unexpected find. There are a couple of chalets amid pleasant gardens, and the French-Nigerian hosts are a good source of information. It lacks a proper sign, though – the entrance is opposite the Plateau Hotel.

Elysur (☎ 455 300; Hill Station Hotel, Tudun Wada Rd; mains N950-1050; ☯ noon-3pm & 7-10pm) A decent restaurant for a splurge, offering a good but unorthodox mix of Chinese and Lebanese dishes.

AfriOne Net Café (24 Ahmadu Bello Way; dishes from N400; ☯ 9am-10pm) This reliable cafe-diner is popular as a meeting place, with a kitchen quickly serving up generous plates of chicken, pasta, burgers and sandwiches, with cake and coffee for afters.

There is a daily flight between Jos and Lagos with **Arik Air** (☎ reservations 01-279 9999; www.arikair.com). The airport is 30km south of Jos – N1800 by taxi.

Head for Bauchi Motor Park if you're going north or east. Minibuses run to Bauchi (N300, two hours) and Kano (N900, five hours). From Plateau Express Motor Park, minibuses leave for Abuja (N800, three hours) and points further south.

YANKARI NATIONAL PARK

Yankari, 225km east of Jos, is Nigeria's best-known **national park** (admission N300, car N500, photo permit N1250) for observing wildlife. The park still holds reasonable numbers of buffaloes, waterbucks, bushbucks and plenty of baboons.

The biggest draw is the 500-strong population of elephants and it's possible that lions may also survive. The birdwatching is excellent.

The best time to see animals is from late December to late April, before the rains, when the thirsty animals congregate at the Gaji River. You're permitted to drive your own vehicle if you take a guide; otherwise, the park has a safari truck that takes two-hour tours (N300) at 7.30am and 3.30pm daily.

Yankari's other attraction is the **Wikki Warm Spring** (admission N200), near the park campsite. The crystal-clear water is a constant 31°C, forming a lake 200m long and 10m wide. Bring your swimming gear – the spring is a real highlight and shouldn't be missed.

The **Wikki Warm Springs Hotel** (☎ 077-542174; campsite per person N600, bungalows 4200; ❄) is set high above the spring and has a serene view over the lush area. There's a decent restaurant and bar.

You can get to the park gate at Mainamaji by minibus from Bauchi (N600, five hours). After paying the entrance fee, you'll need to arrange transport to the camp – around N3000 in a taxi or N1000 by *okada*.

KANO

☎ 064 / pop 4 million

Kano is the oldest city in West Africa (it was founded around 1400 years ago) and Nigeria's third largest. It was a major crossroads in the trans-Saharan trade routes and, from the Middle Ages, an important centre for Islamic scholarship. A favoured traveller destination, Kano has terrible air pollution, with traffic fumes mixed with the dusty harmattan wind.

Kano is also at the forefront of the imposition of Sharia'a law, with issues such as alcohol and segregation of public transport cutting across community fault lines, and although these are unlikely to impact on foreign visitors, it's important to be aware of the issues.

Information

Try the moneychangers at the craft stalls outside the Central Hotel; they'll also exchange West African CFA francs. The tourist office has a bureau de change.

Friends Internet (Murtala Mohammed Way; per hr N200) Also serves coffee, cakes and sandwiches.

Kano State Tourist Board (☎ 646309; Tourist Camp, Bompai Rd) A rarity in Nigeria – a working tourist office.

Has pamphlets and can arrange guides to the Old City (per hour N1500).

See & Sweet Bakery Cybercafé (Bompai Rd; per hr N200) Also a good place for a quick bite.

Sights

With thousands of stalls in a 16-hectare area, **Kurmi Market** is one of the largest markets in Africa and is the city's main attraction. It's a centre for African crafts, including gold, bronze and silver work, and all types of fabric. Away from the throng are the **Kofar Dye Pits** (Kofar Mata Gate; ☯ 7am-7pm), where indigo cloth has been dyed for hundreds of years. Finished cloth is for sale, starting from around N1500 according to the design. A dash of around N100 is appropriate for a guided tour.

The **Gidan Makama Museum** (Emirs Palace Rd; admission N100; ☯ 8am-6pm) stands on the site of the original emir's palace (the modern one sits opposite) and is a wonderful example of traditional Hausa architecture. The museum has a fascinating photographic history of Kano, and displays on Nigerian Islam and traditional culture. The **Gidan Dan Hausa** (Dan Hausa Rd; admission N50; ☯ 8am-4pm Mon-Thu, to 1pm Fri) is another museum in a beautifully restored traditional house showcasing regional crafts and ceremonial costumes.

Festivals & Events

The **Kano Durbar**, the biggest festival of its kind in Nigeria, is held annually just after the end of Ramadan. Exact dates are variable, so check in advance if possible (see also Holidays, p1140). There is a cavalry procession featuring ornately dressed men mounted on colourfully bedecked horses, finishing outside the emir's palace, where there is drumming, singing, and massed cavalry charges.

Sleeping

Ecwa Guesthouse (☎ 631410; 1 Mission Rd; r N1500-3500; ❄) This Christian mission guesthouse is a great budget option. The cheapest rooms are in the old block and have fan only, and some have shared facilities; the more expensive rooms in the new block have bathrooms, TV and air-con. Alcohol is forbidden on site.

Ocean Palace Hotel (☎ 941568; 35 Warri Rd; r N3500-4800; ❄) For the price, this Sabon Gari hotel is an absolute bargain. Some rooms are pretty compact, but you get satellite TV, a fridge and a 24-hour generator. Staff are

NIGERIA

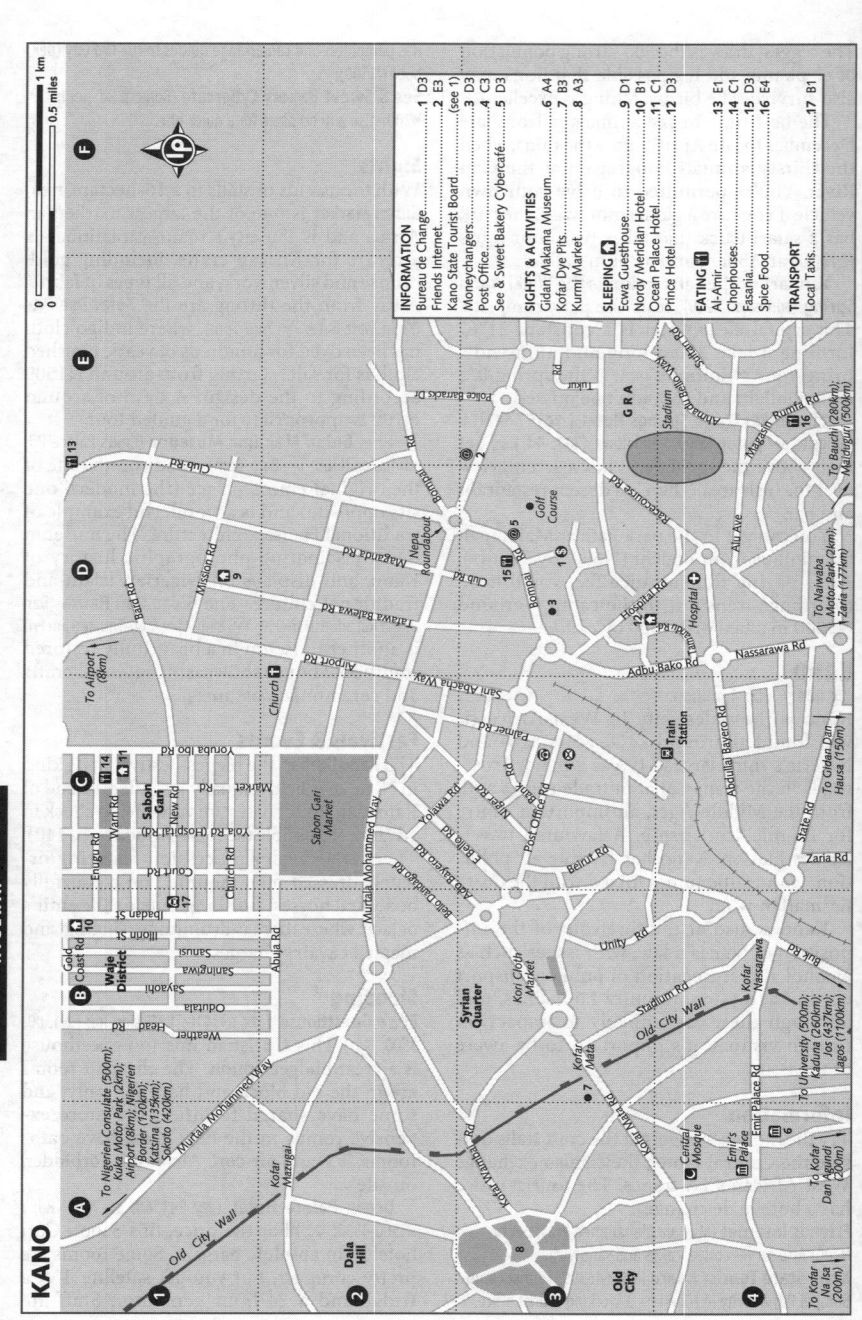

KANO

INFORMATION	
Bureau de Change	1 D3
Friends Internet	2 E3
Kano State Tourist Board	(see 1)
Moneychangers	3 D3
Post Office	4 C3
See & Sweet Bakery Cybercafé	5 D3

SIGHTS & ACTIVITIES	
Gidan Makama Museum	6 A4
Kofar Dye Pits	7 B3
Kurmi Market	8 A3

SLEEPING	
Ecwa Guesthouse	9 D1
Nordy Meridian Hotel	10 B1
Ocean Palace Hotel	11 C1
Prince Hotel	12 D3

EATING	
Al-Amir	13 E1
Chophouses	14 C1
Fasania	15 D3
Spice Food	16 E4

TRANSPORT	
Local Taxis	17 B1

friendly, food is available, and there's a good bar attached too.

Nordy Meridian Hotel (☎ 939468; 26 Gold Coast Rd; r N3500-3700; 🛋) Another good Sabon Gari deal, rooms here aren't quite as nicely finished as at the Ocean Palace, but the facilities easily match up – including a decent bar (with live music) and the all-important round-the-clock electricity.

Prince Hotel (☎ 639402; Tamandu Rd; r N16,200-21,000; P 🛋 🛜) Professionally understated, the Prince is a classy operation in a quiet part of town. Rooms are modern and exceedingly comfortable. It's a very popular place; even nonguests should enjoy visiting the posh restaurant and bar.

Eating & Drinking

Kano is the home of *suya,* so if you're looking for a quick 'meat-on-a-stick' eat, you'll be in heaven here.

Al-Amir (12B Club Rd; dishes N250-400; 🕙 11am-10pm) If you want to eat as a local, head here. Food is cheap and filling, and it's always full of happy diners. The 'special plate' has a bit of everything in a serving, but we'd also recommend northern specialities like the fragrant *miyan taushe* (pumpkin-seed soup) and *tuwo shunkafa* (pounded rice), washed down with a glass of *zobo* (hibiscus tea).

Spice Food (Magasin Rumfa Rd; dishes from N550; 🕙 noon-3.30pm & 6-11pm) If you've been craving some vegetarian food in Nigeria, this fantastic Indian restaurant will answer your prayers (meat dishes are also served). The spices range from delicate to lively, and the owner loves talking to backpackers. The N750 buffet every Sunday at 7.30pm is absolutely not to be missed.

Fasania (Ahmadu Bello Way; mains N680-1100; 🕙 noon-11pm) This Chinese restaurant has a better-than-average selection of dishes, all cooked and served confidently and efficiently. Alcohol is served. Dishes are priced according to size, with medium or large servings.

The best 'food-is-ready' fare is found in Sabon Gari, with plenty of pepper soup and the like on offer. Enugu Rd has plenty of **chophouses** (dishes from N250; 🕙 8am-late), most also doubling as bars.

Getting There & Away

The airport is 8km northwest of Sabon Gari – N150 by *okada,* three times that in a taxi.

There are daily flights to Lagos (N20,000, 90 minutes) and Abuja (N15,000, one hour). Kano also has a few international connections to Niamey (Niger), Cairo (Egypt), Tripoli (Libya) and N'djamena (Chad).

Kuka Motor Park is the motor park for the north and the Niger–Nigerian border. Naiwaba Motor Park serves points south and west. Sample fares and times: Zaria (N500, 90 minutes), Kaduna (N700, three hours), Maiduguri (N1300, six hours), Sokoto (N900, six hours) and Jos (N700, four hours).

GASHAKA-GUMTI NATIONAL PARK

Nigeria's largest national park, **Gashaka-Gumti** (admission N1000, vehicle N500), is also the remotest and least-explored part of the country. Its 6700-sq-km area contains rolling hills, savannah, montane forest – as wild and spectacular a corner of Africa as you could wish for. It also holds incredible diversity and is one of West Africa's most important primate habitats, as well as supporting lions, elephants, hippos and buffaloes.

Recently, the UK-based **Gashaka Primate Project** (www.ucl.ac.uk/gashaka) has been working with authorities to radically improve access and infrastructure within the park boundaries. Get in touch beforehand for advice on logistics – accessing the park is not a casual affair.

The park entrance is at Serti, 10 hours from Jos (double by public transport). There is a small **tourist camp** (r N750-2875) here, from where you can also hire excellent local guides (N500 per day). There are also 4WDs to rent (N3000 per day), although the real attractions of Gashaka-Gumti are the myriad walking trails. From Serti, you can head to the riverside park headquarters at **Gashaka** (campsite N200, chalets N300), or take an *okada* to Kwano (a further 12km), where the primate researchers are mainly based. All accommodation is self-catering, so bring supplies. Exploring with a guide, you can go chimp tracking by foot (there are plentiful other monkeys to see too), or do a great two- or three-day hike to the mountains, via several Fulani villages. It's a truly magical place.

The park is open year-round, although access is easiest during the dry season (December to March).

NIGERIA DIRECTORY

ACCOMMODATION

Hotels are of a fair standard throughout Nigeria, although they're poor value compared to neighbouring countries. Most towns and cities have something to suit all pockets; the big exception to this is Lagos, where rooms are either very cheap and not particularly wonderful or very expensive – there's not much middle ground.

Rooms come with air conditioning and attached bathroom as standard, but take promises of hot water with a pinch of salt. Watch and listen for the ubiquitous power cuts and sound of generators striking up (bring a torch, too). You'll also be asked to pay a deposit, which is usually somewhere between one and two nights' room rate. This is refundable against your final bill.

BUSINESS HOURS

General business hours are from 8.30am to 5pm Monday to Friday. Sanitation days are held on the last Saturday of the month – traffic isn't allowed before 10.30am to allow the streets to be cleaned.
Banks 8am to 3pm Monday to Thursday and 8.30am to 1pm Friday.
Government offices 7.30am to 3.30pm Monday to Friday and 7.30am to 1pm Saturday.

DANGERS & ANNOYANCES

Nigeria has a poor reputation for safety and civil unrest and yet, for the traveller, it can seem like the friendliest and most welcoming country in western Africa. Navigating these apparently contradictory states is the key to getting the most out of your visit.

PRACTICALITIES

- Privately owned English-language daily newspapers include the *Guardian, This Day,* the *Punch* and *Vanguard.*

- There are over 30 national and state TV stations, broadcasting in English and all major local languages. South African satellite DSTV is hugely popular.

- Electricity supply is 220V. Plugs are square British three pin, but most hotels have European two-pin adaptors.

Consistently the most troubled region of the country is the Niger delta, due to the long-running grievances between the local population and the big oil companies, where the kidnapping of Western employees is a continued threat. In the north, communal disturbances between Muslims and Christians periodically spill over into bloody violence. Stay clear of demonstrations and areas where you suddenly see large numbers of police or army troops. Lagos has a reputation for violent crime, not always undeserved.

As a traveller you're unlikely to have trouble with corruption and bribery. Police roadblocks are common, but fines and bribes are paid by the driver. Some caution should be exercised on the major highways into Lagos, where armed robbery is a problem, although almost always at night.

EMBASSIES & CONSULATES

Some embassies have yet to relocate from Lagos to Abuja. Opening hours listed are for visa applications.
Australia (☎ 09-461 2780; www.nigeria.embassy.gov.au; 5th fl, Oakland Centre, 48 Aguyi Ironsi St, Maitama, Abuja)
Benin Abuja (☎ 09-413 8424; Yedseram St; ☽ 9am-4.30pm Mon-Fri); Lagos (Map p466; ☎ 01-261 4411; 4 Abudu Smith St VI; ☽ 9am-11am Mon-Fri)
Burkina Faso (Map p466; ☎ 01-268 1001; 15 Norman Williams St, Ikoyi, Lagos)
Cameroon Calabar (☎ 087-222782; 21 Ndidan Usang Iso Rd; ☽ 9am-3.30pm Mon-Fri); Lagos (Map p466; ☎ 261 2226; 5 Femi Pearse St, VI; ☽ 8am-11am Mon-Fri)
Canada Abuja (☎ 09-413 9910; 15 Bobo St, Maitama); Lagos (Map p466; ☎ 01-262 2616; 4 Anifowoshe St, VI, Lagos)
Chad (☎ 09-413 0751; 53 Mississippi St, Abuja; ☽ 9am-3pm Mon-Fri)
Côte d'Ivoire (Map p466; ☎ 01-261 0963; 5 Abudu Smith St, VI, Lagos)
France (Map p466; ☎ 01-260 3430; 1 Oyinkan Abayomi Rd, Ikoyi, Lagos)
Germany (Map p466; ☎ 01-261 1011; 15 Walter Carrington Cres, VI, Lagos)
Ghana (Map p468; ☎ 01-263 0015; 23 King George V Rd, Lagos Island, Lagos)
Ireland (☎ 09-413 1751; Plot 415 Negro Cres, off Aminu Kano, Maitama, Abuja)
Netherlands (☎ 01-261 3005; 24 Ozumba Mbadiwe Ave, VI, Lagos)
Niger Abuja (☎ 01-413 6206; Pope John Paul II St; ☽ 9am-3pm Mon-Fri); Kano (☎ 0806 548 1152; Airport Roundabout; ☽ 9am-3pm Mon-Fri); Lagos (Map p466;

☎ 01-261 2300; 15 Adeola Odeku St, VI; ⏲ 9am-
2.30pm Mon-Fri)
Spain (☎ 01-261 5215; 21c Kofo Abayomi St, VI, Lagos)
Togo (Map p466; ☎ 261 1762; Plot 976, Oju Olobun Cl,
VI, Lagos)
UK Abuja (☎ 09-413 4559; www.ukinnigeria.fco.gov.
uk; Dangote House, Aguyi Ironsi St, Maitama); Lagos (Map
p466; ☎ 01-261 9541; 11 Walter Carrington Cres, VI)
USA Abuja (☎ 09-461 4000; http://nigeria.usembassy.
gov/; Plot 1075, Diplomatic Dr, Central Business District);
Lagos (Map p466; ☎ 01-261 0050; 2 Walter Carrington
Cres, VI)

FESTIVALS & EVENTS
The most elaborate festivals are the celebra-
tions in northern Nigeria (particularly in
Kano, Zaria and Katsina) for two important
Islamic holidays: the end of Ramadan, and
Tabaski, 69 days later, which feature colour-
ful processions of cavalry. Ramadan can be a
tiring time to travel in the north – head for the
Sabon Gari (foreigners' quarter) in each town,
where food is served throughout the day.

Around mid-February, the spectacular three-
day Argungu Fishing and Cultural Festival
takes place on the banks of the Sokoto River
in Argungu, 100km southwest of Sokoto.

On the last Friday in August, the Osun
Festival takes place in Oshogbo. It has music,
dancing and sacrifices and is a centrepiece of
the Yoruba cultural and spiritual year.

The Igue (Ewere) Festival, held in Benin
City, usually in the first half of December,
has traditional dances, a mock battle and a
procession to the palace to reaffirm loyalty to
the *oba*. It marks the harvest of the first new
yams of the season.

HOLIDAYS
Public holidays include the following:
New Year's Day 1 January
Easter March or April
May Day 1 May
National Day 1 October
Christmas 25 December
Boxing Day 26 December

Islamic holidays are observed in northern
Nigeria; see p1140.

INTERNET ACCESS
Good, cheap connections are widespread
in major towns, for around N100 to N150
per hour. Never use internet banking in a
Nigerian cybercafe.

DASH

Used freely as both a noun and a verb, dash
is a word you'll hear a lot in Nigeria. It can
mean either a bribe or a tip. The most frequent form of dash you're likely to encounter is at roadblocks, where the driver pays.
In large-scale corruption, money is referred
to as 'chopped' (literally 'eaten'). Although
you're actually unlikely to be asked for dash
as a bribe, dashing someone who performs
a service for you, such as a guide, is often
appropriate.

MONEY
The unit of currency is the naira. Bring only
cash (US dollars) to Nigeria – travellers
cheques are useless. ATMs are increasingly
widespread, although many are not tied to
international systems like Mastercard or Visa,
and some expats we spoke to registered concerns about the security of using international
bank cards at Nigerian ATMs. Avoid using a
credit card in Nigeria because of fraud.

There are banks aplenty, but virtually
none offer currency exchange – you'll have
to change on the street. Moneychangers are
almost always Hausa, so it's usually a safe bet
to ask around at the town's mosque. In our
experience, the moneychangers are among
the most honest in Africa. Western Union
branches are everywhere if you need to get
money wired to you.

POST
Mail sent to or from Nigeria is notoriously
slow. Worldwide postcards cost about N80.
For parcels, use an international courier
like DHL or FedEx, which have offices in
most towns.

TELEPHONE
Nigeria is in love with the mobile phone,
and networks are more reliable than the
creaky Nitel fixed-line company. Calls at
roadside phone stands are quick and easy to
make, costing around N20 per minute inside
Nigeria, and around N60 for an international
call. Most mobile numbers start with 080.

Local GSM SIM cards cost from N300.
Operators MTN and Glo are the market
leaders and have the best coverage. You'll
find that street vendors everywhere sell top-
up scratch cards.

VISAS

Everyone needs a visa to visit Nigeria, and applications can be quite a process. Many Nigerian embassies issue visas only to residents and nationals of the country in which the embassy is located, so it's essential to put things in motion well before your trip. Exact requirements vary, but as a rule of thumb, forms are required in triplicate, along with proof of funds to cover your stay, a round-trip air ticket, and possibly confirmed hotel reservations. You also need a letter of invitation from a resident of Nigeria or a business in the country. The cost of a 30-day visa is from US$70 to US$100 according to nationality.

If you're travelling overland to Nigeria, the embassy in Accra (Ghana) is consistently rated as the best place in West Africa to apply for a visa, as no letter of introduction is required. The embassy in Niamey (Niger) also claims to issue visas the same way.

Visa Extensions

Visas can reportedly be extended at the **Federal Secretariat** (Map p466; Alagbon Close, Ikoyi) in Lagos, but it's a byzantine process of endless forms, frustration and dash, with no clear sense of success.

Visas for Onward Travel

BENIN

One-month visas cost CFA15,000 (CFA, not naira), with one photo, and take 24 hours to issue. The embassy in Lagos carries an uninviting reputation, and unexpected extra fees are not unknown.

CAMEROON

A one-month single-entry visa costs CFA50,000 (CFA, not naira), with one photo, and is issued in a day. As well as Lagos and Abuja, there's a useful consulate in Calabar.

CHAD

Two photos and N5500 will get you a one-month single-entry visa, which you can pick up the next day.

NIGER

Best obtained in Abuja, a one-month single-entry visa costs N5300 with two photos, and is issued in 48 hours. The consulate in Kano (where the fee can also be paid in CFA) is also an excellent and speedy place to apply – take three photos.

TRANSPORT IN NIGERIA

GETTING THERE & AWAY
Air

The vast majority of flights to Nigeria arrive in Lagos, although there are also international airports in Abuja, Port Harcourt and Kano. Horror stories of arriving at Murtala Mohammed International Airport in Lagos are a thing of the past. Nigerian airports have official porters, and notices urge passengers to ignore the services of touts. The three leading Nigerian carriers are Virgin Nigeria, Bellview and Aero Contractors, all of which have regional as well as domestic connections.

Land

BENIN

The main border crossing is on the Lagos to Cotonou (Benin) highway. Expect requests for bribes. There's a good direct Cotonou–Lagos bus service run by Nigerian bus company **ABC Transport** (☎ in Cotonou 21 33 33 77, ☎ in Lagos 740 1010; www.abctransport.com). An alternative border crossing is further north at Kétou, but there's not so much public transport that way.

CAMEROON

There are two main border crossings. The northern border post is at Bama, 2½ hours from Maiduguri, across to Banki in Cameroon. A remote alternative crossing is at Ngala (Nigeria), which is used mainly for transiting to Chad.

The southern border crossing is at Mfum (Nigeria), near Ikom. The road infrastructure collapses pretty much as soon as you cross to Ekok (Cameroon), making this border problematic during the rainy season, so consider taking the Calabar–Limbe ferry instead during the wettest months (see opposite).

CHAD

Although there are no official border crossings between the two countries, it's possible to make a quick transit across Cameroon. In Nigeria, the border crossing into Cameroon is at Ngala. On the Cameroon side ask for a *laissez-passer* to allow you to make the two-hour traverse to the Chad border point at Kousséri.

NIGER

There are four main entry points into Niger. The busiest is the Sokoto route, which crosses at Ilela (Nigeria). Minibuses and bush taxis run daily to the border, just past Ilela. Crossing to Birni N'Konni, you can get on a bus straight for Niamey. Travelling between Kano (Nigeria) and Zinder (Niger) is equally straightforward. The final option is between Katsina and Maradi.

From Niger, it's easiest to cross at Gaya. You'll probably have to hire a bush taxi to take you from the Nigerian side at Kamba on to Sokoto. Beware the potholes.

Sea

A ferry operated by **Destiny** (☎ 085 514475; Calabar dock) sails from Calabar to Limbe every Tuesday and Friday evening (N6000, 10 hours), returning on Monday and Thursday. It's an overnight trip in each direction. Your passport is collected on boarding and returned at immigration. Try to keep hold of your luggage – if it gets stowed in the hold you'll be waiting hours to get it back.

GETTING AROUND
Air

Internal flights are a quick and cheapish way of getting around Nigeria. Flights start at around N15,000. Most cities are linked by air to Lagos; you'll usually have to change planes here (or possibly Abuja) if you want to fly between two smaller cities.

The most reliable domestic airlines with the best connections are **Virgin Nigeria** (☎ 460 0505; www.virginnigeria.com), **Bellview** (☎ 270 2700; www. flybellviewair.com) and **Aero Contractors** (☎ 764 7571; www.acn.aero). Smaller alternatives include **Sosoliso** (☎ 497 1492; www.sosoliso.airline.com) and **Chanchangi Airlines** (☎ 493 9744; www.chanchangi-airlines.com).

Car & Motorcycle

Nigeria's road system is good, although for drivers this can bring problems in itself, as the smooth, sealed roads allow Nigerians to exercise their latent talents as rally drivers. The accident rate is frighteningly high, and the only real road rule is survival of the fittest. Avoid driving at night at all costs.

Foreigners driving in Nigeria shouldn't get much hassle at roadblocks, particularly if your vehicle has foreign plates. If you get asked for dash, a smile and some patience will often defuse the request. Note, however, that it's a legal requirement to wear a seatbelt; not doing so leaves you open to both official and 'unofficial' fines. Petrol stations are everywhere, but keep your ear to the ground for strikes than can cause fuel shortages. Diesel can sometimes be hard to come by, so keep your tank topped up.

Local Transport

Each town has at least one motor park full of minibuses and bush taxis that serves as the main transport depot. They're Nigeria in microcosm – sprawling, chaotic and noisy. Vehicles have wooden signs on their roofs showing their destination, while touts shout out those that need filling. Minibuses don't run to any schedule but depart when full.

Bush taxis – big old Peugeots – cost about 25% more. All travel at horrendous speeds, slowing only for potholes and to pay bribes at police checkpoints.

Motorcycle-Taxi

The quickest way to get around town is on the back of a motorcycle-taxi called an *okada* (*achaba* in the north), although many drivers seem to have a fatalist's view of their own mortality. Fares shouldn't top N50 for a short trip; sling your backpack over the handlebars.

Train

Maps show a Nigerian train line, but barely any services run these days. The main lines are Lagos–Kano (via Ibadan and Kaduna) and Port Harcourt–Maiduguri (via Jos).

NIGERIA

Senegal

Couched between the arid desert lands of the north and lush tropical forests in the south, Senegal boasts a vast array of sights, sounds and flavours. The capital, Dakar, is a dizzying introduction to the country. Perched on the tip of a peninsula, this city is composed elegance and street hustler rolled into one. Its busy streets, vibrant markets and glittering nightlife sit next to tranquil Île de Gorée and the beaches of Yoff and N'Gor. In the north of Senegal, the historical capital of Saint-Louis, the first French settlement in West Africa, tempts with historical architecture and proximity to two beautiful national parks.

Most visitors head to Senegal for its beaches, and for good reason. Along the Petite Côte and Cap Skiring, wide strips of sand greet the Atlantic. At the wide deltas of the Casamance and Saloum Rivers, the straight coastline is broken up into a maze of thick mangroves, tiny creeks, wide lagoons and shimmering plains. A *pirogue* trip through these striking zones reveals hundreds of bird species, from the gleaming wings of tiny kingfishers to the proud poise of pink flamingos.

Whether you want to mingle with the trendsetters of urban Africa or be alone with your thoughts and the sounds of nature, you'll find your place in Senegal.

FAST FACTS

- **Area** 197,000 sq km
- **ATMs** In all major towns
- **Borders** The Gambia, Guinea, Guinea-Bissau, Mali and Mauritania; all borders open from dawn to dusk
- **Budget** US$60 to US$80 per day
- **Capital** Dakar
- **Languages** French, Wolof, Malinke, Pulaar (Fulfulde), Diola
- **Money** West African CFA franc; US$1 = CFA463, €1 = CFA656
- **Population** 12.9 million
- **Seasons** Dry (November to May), wet (June to October)
- **Telephone** Country code ☎ 221; international access code ☎ 00
- **Time** GMT/UTC
- **Visa** Required by all except nationals of Canada, the EU, Ecowas (Economic Community of West African States), Israel, Japan, Norway, South Africa and the USA

HIGHLIGHTS

- **Casamance** (p497) Weave your way via tiny villages to Senegal's best beaches on Cap Skiring.
- **Saint-Louis** (p493) Follow in the footsteps of history in West Africa's first French settlement.
- **Dakar** (p484) Spend sleepless nights touring the capital's vibrant nightclubs, bars and concerts.
- **Siné-Saloum** (p492) Wind through the mangroves of the Siné-Saloum Delta in a *pirogue*.
- **Île de Gorée** (p491) Contemplate history and breathe in the atmosphere of this ancient slaving station and peaceful island.

CLIMATE & WHEN TO GO

Senegal's main tourist season lasts from November to February, the dry, cool season, when Dakar's average daytime maximums are around 24°C (75°F). Most music festivals take place in December and between March and June.

July to late September is hot and humid. Some national parks are inaccessible or even closed during the wet season, but it's also the time everything is lush and green, and many hotels reduce their prices by up to 50%.

ITINERARIES

- **One Week** Spend a couple of days tasting the urban life of Dakar (p484) and the calm of Île de Gorée (p491). Head north to Saint-Louis (p493), the Parc National des Oiseaux du Djoudj (p496) and Parc National de la Langue de Barbarie (p496).
- **Two Weeks** Start as above, then head from Dakar south to the Petite Côte. Enjoy the beaches of Saly (p492) and surrounding villages, then check out the fish market of Mbour (p492) and the seashell town Joal-Fadiout (p492). Palmarin (p492) is the stunning entry port to the Siné-Saloum Delta. Discover also Ndangane (p492), Mar Lodj (p492) and Toubakouta (p493) – other beautiful delta spots.

HISTORY

Senegal was part of several West African empires, including the Empire of Ghana (8th century), and the Djolof kingdom, in the area between the Senegal River and Dakar (13th and 14th centuries). In the early 16th century, Portuguese traders made contact with coastal kingdoms, and became the first in a long line of 'interested' foreigners: soon the British, French and Dutch jostled for control of strategic points for the trade in slaves and goods. In 1659, the French built a trading station at Saint-Louis; the town later became the capital of French West Africa.

Dakar, home to tiny fishing villages, was chosen as capital of the Senegalese territory, and as early as 1848 Senegal had a deputy in the French parliament.

Independence

In the run-up to independence in 1960, Senegal joined French Sudan (present-day Mali) to form the Mali Federation. It lasted all of two months, and in August 1960, Senegal became a republic. Its first president, Léopold Sédar Senghor, a socialist and poet of international stature, commanded respect in Senegal and abroad. His economic management, however, didn't match his way with words. At the end of 1980, he voluntarily stepped down and was replaced by Abdou Diouf, who soon faced a string of mounting crises.

The early 1980s saw the start of an ongoing separatist rebellion in the southern region of Casamance. Seven years later a minor incident on the Mauritanian border led to riots and deportations in both countries, as well as a three-year suspension of diplomatic relations and hundreds of casualties. Tensions mounted in

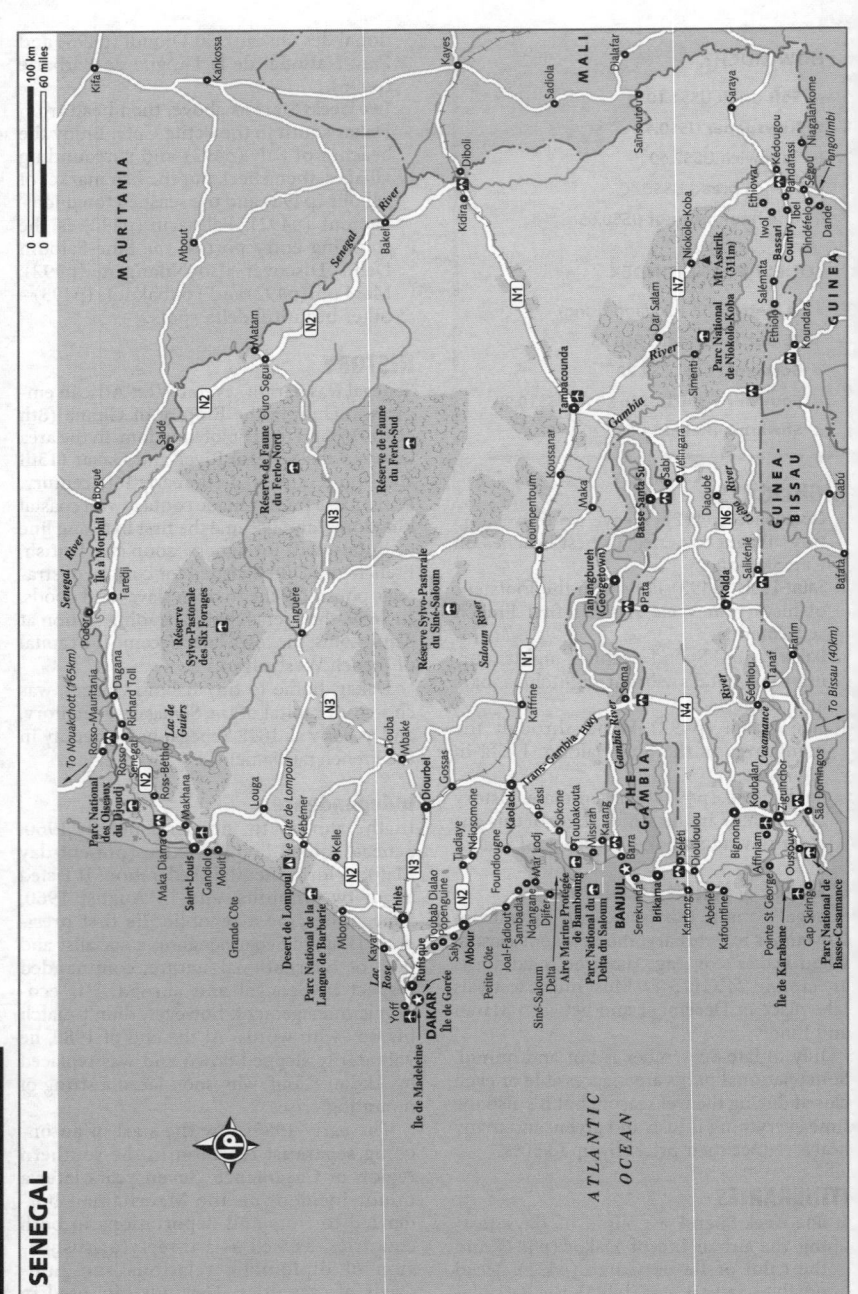

SENEGAL

other parts of the country as a result of austerity measures.

The arrest of opposition leader Abdoulaye Wade in February 1994 only increased his huge popularity. In March 2000, Wade won in a free and fair presidential election, thanks to his hope-giving *sopi* (change) campaign. Diouf peacefully relinquished power. The following year, a new constitution was approved, allowing the formation of opposition parties and consolidating the prime minister's role.

In 2002 the country was shaken by a huge tragedy when the MS *Joola,* the ferry connecting Dakar and the Casamance capital, Ziguinchor, capsized due to dangerous overloading, leaving almost 2000 people dead.

Senegal Today

In 2009 Wade declared in a very early announcement that he intended to stand as candidate at the 2012 elections. There wasn't much cheering; after promising initial measures, Wade's government has not been able to lead the country out of crisis. The steadily rising cost of living, increasing power cuts and widening gap between rich and poor provoke anger and despair among the population. The images of young Senegalese emigrants crossing to the Canary Islands in tiny boats have been beamed around the world. In 2009, conflicts flared up again in Casamance, which had been calm since the peace deal in 2004.

Compared to those of other West African countries, Senegal's democratic system functions fairly well, though the strategic positioning of the president's son is interpreted by many as an attempt to form a 'Wade dynasty'.

CULTURE

'A man with a mouth is never lost' goes a popular Wolof saying, and indeed, conversation is the key to local culture, and the key to conversation is a great sense of humour. The Senegalese love talking and teasing, and the better you slide into the conversational game, the easier you'll get around.

Personal life stories in Senegal tend to be brewed from a mix of traditional values, global influences, Muslim faith and family integration. More than 90% of the population is Muslim, and many of them belong to one of the Sufi brotherhoods that dominate religious life in Senegal. The most important brotherhood is that of the Mourides, founded by Cheikh Amadou Bamba. The *marabouts*

who lead these brotherhoods play a central role in social life and wield enormous political and economic power (possibly the power to make or break the country's leaders).

The dominant ethnic group is the Wolof (43% of the population), whose language is the country's lingua franca. Smaller groups include the Fula (around 24%); the Tukulor, a sub-branch of the Fula (10%); the Serer (14%); and the Diola (5%). Senegal's population is young: around 42% are under 14 years old. The greatest population density is found in the urban areas of Dakar.

Senegal has a vast music scene; names such as Youssou N'Dour and Baaba Maal are famous worldwide. The beat that moves the nation is *mbalax*. Created from a mixture of Cuban music (hugely popular in Senegal in the 1960s) and traditional, fiery *sabar* drumming, *mbalax* was made famous by Youssou N'Dour in the 1980s.

Hip hop is also an exciting scene in Senegal, with leading names including Didier Awadi and Daara J. 'Urban folk', led by Carlou D, is on the rise.

Visual arts are also huge (and celebrated every two years during the Dak'Art Biennale). Leading artists include Soly Cissé, Souleymane Keita and Ndaary Lô. Moussa Sakho, Babacar Lô and Gora Mbengue are famous artists practising *sous-verre* (reverse-glass painting).

The doyen of Senegalese cinema is the late Ousmane Sembène, and there's a new generation producing exciting work.

FOOD & DRINK

Senegal's national dish is *thiéboudieune* (rice cooked in a thick tomato sauce and served with fried fish and vegetables). Also typical are *yassa poulet* or *poisson yassa* (marinated and grilled chicken or fish) and *mafé* (peanut-based stew).

Local drinks include *bissap,* made from sorrel flowers, and *bouyi,* made from the fruits of the baobab. The best local beer is Flag.

ENVIRONMENT

Senegal consists mainly of flat plains, cut by three major rivers: the Senegal River in the north, which forms the border with Mauritania; the Gambia River; and the Casamance River in the south, watering the lush green lands of Casamance.

The national parks of the coastal regions, including the Siné-Saloum Delta, the Parc

National de la Langue de Barbarie and the Parc National des Oiseaux du Djoudj, are noted for their spectacular birdlife. Parc National de Niokolo-Koba has some large mammals, though they're hard to spot.

Overfishing, deforestation, desertification, and coastal erosion, largely caused by uncontrolled illegal sand mining, are the main environmental issues the country faces. The dwindling of fish stocks also threatens the economy.

DAKAR

pop 2.6 million

Once a tiny settlement in the south of the Cap Vert peninsula, Dakar now spreads almost across its entire triangle, and keeps growing. This is a city of contrasts, where horse-cart drivers chug over swish highways and gleaming SUVs squeeze through tiny sand roads; where elegant ladies dig skinny heels into dusty walkways and suit-clad businessmen kneel down for prayer in the middle of the street. A fascinating place – once you've learned how to beat its scamsters, hustlers and traders at their own game.

ORIENTATION

The expansive Pl de l'Indépendance is the city's heart. From here, major streets lead in all directions, including Ave Léopold Senghor and Ave Pompidou, which leads west to Marché Sandaga. From here, Ave du Président Lamine Guèye goes north to Gare Routière Pompiers. The quickest route out of the centre is the coastal Rte de la Corniche-Ouest. To the north of the city centre lie the suburbs Point E, Fann, Mermoz and Ouakam, all of which have good bars and restaurants. The airport is 19km north of the town centre, and north of there are Les Almadies, Yoff and N'Gor, with Dakar's best beaches.

Maps

The best city map is the colourful, detailed one by **Editions Laure Kane** (www.editionslaurekane.com; CFA4000), available in most souvenir shops and hotels.

INFORMATION
Bookshops

Librairie 4 Vents (Map p488; ☎ 33 821 8083; 55 Rue Félix Faure; ☟ 9am-1pm & 3-7pm Mon-Sat)

Librairie Clairafrique (Map p485; ☎ 33 864 4429; University Grounds, Ave Cheikh Anta Diop; ☟ 8.30am-6.30pm Mon-Sat)

Cultural Centres

British Council (Map p485; ☎ 33 869 2700; Rue AAB-68, Amitié Zone A&B) Has English magazines and occasional events.

Goethe Institut (Map p485; ☎ 33 869 8880; www.goethe.de/ins/sn/dak; cnr Rue de Diourbel & Piscine Olympique) The German cultural centre frequently hosts exhibitions and shows films. The terrace cafe, VoundaBar, has excellent Sunday brunches and tasty meals.

Institut Français Léopold Sédar Senghor (Map p488; ☎ 33 823 0320; www.institutfr-dakar.org; 89 Rue Joseph Gomis) A hub of arts activity with a great cafe.

Internet Access

There are a few internet cafes and wi-fi is spreading fast; it's offered for free in dozens of hotels and restaurants.

Espacetel Plus (Map p488; ☎ 33 822 9062; Blvd de la République; ☟ 8am-midnight)

Media

The cultural magazine *221* (CFA500) has the best entertainment listings and information on music, sports and other events around the country.

Medical Services

Pharmacies are plentiful in Dakar; 24-hour shifts rotate.

Clinique de la Madeleine (Map p487; ☎ 33 821 9470; 18 Ave des Jambaars) General service and maternity department.

Hôpital Principal (Map p487; ☎ 33 839 5050; Ave Léopold Senghor) Main hospital and emergency department.

Pharmacie Guigon (Map p488; ☎ 33 823 0333; 1 Ave du Président Lamine Guèye; ☟ 8am-11pm Mon-Sat) Pharmacy.

SOS Médecin (Map p485; ☎ 33 889 1515; cnr Rue 62 & Rue 64, Baie de Soumbédioune) Emergency service.

Money

ATM-equipped banks are never too far away in Dakar. Main branches are at Pl de l'Indépendance:

BICIS (Map p488; ☎ 33 839 0390)

CBAO (Map p488; ☎ 33 849 9300)

SGBS (Map p488; ☎ 33 842 5039)

Post & Telephone

There are many small *télécentres* (call centres); post offices also have telephone facilities.

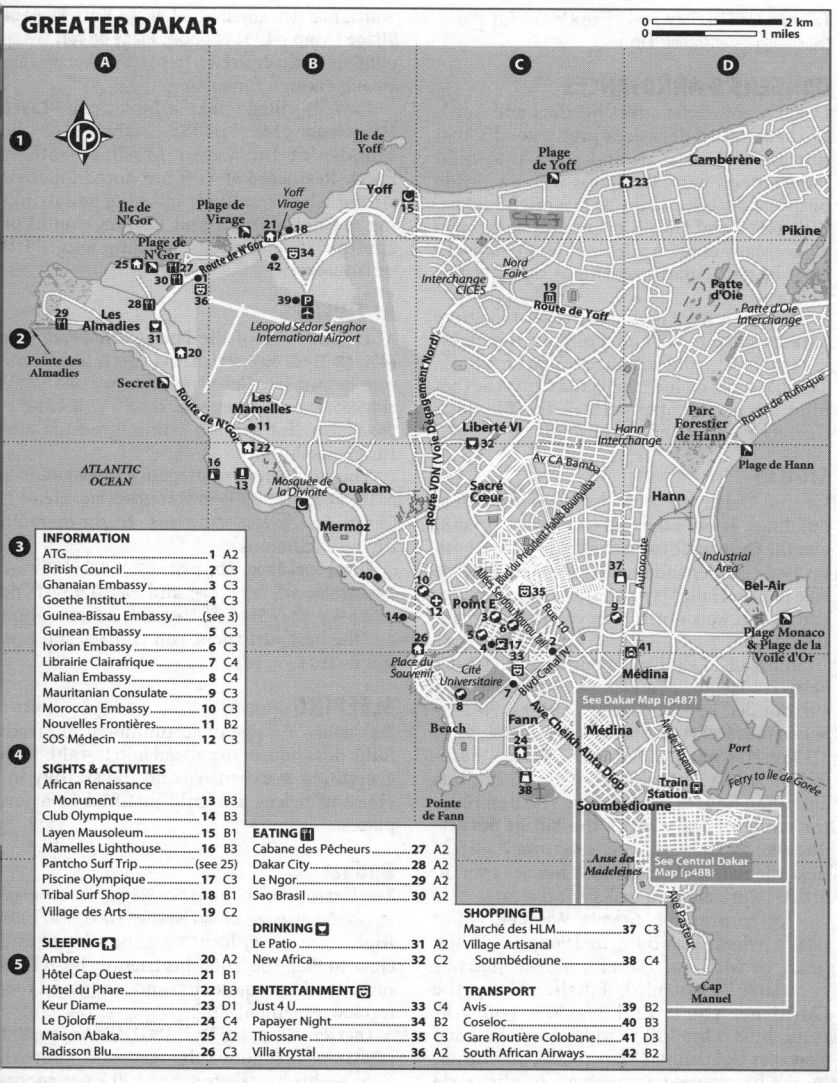

GREATER DAKAR

INFORMATION	
ATG	1 A2
British Council	2 C3
Ghanaian Embassy	3 C3
Goethe Institut	4 C3
Guinea-Bissau Embassy	(see 3)
Guinean Embassy	5 C3
Ivorian Embassy	6 C3
Librairie Clairafrique	7 C4
Malian Embassy	8 C4
Mauritanian Consulate	9 C3
Moroccan Embassy	10 C3
Nouvelles Frontières	11 B2
SOS Médecin	12 C3

SIGHTS & ACTIVITIES	
African Renaissance Monument	13 B3
Club Olympique	14 B3
Layen Mausoleum	15 B1
Mamelles Lighthouse	16 B3
Pantcho Surf Trip	(see 25)
Piscine Olympique	17 C3
Tribal Surf Shop	18 B1
Village des Arts	19 C2

SLEEPING	
Ambre	20 A2
Hôtel Cap Ouest	21 B1
Hôtel du Phare	22 B3
Keur Diame	23 D1
Le Djoloff	24 C4
Maison Abaka	25 A2
Radisson Blu	26 C3

EATING	
Cabane des Pêcheurs	27 A2
Dakar City	28 A2
Le Ngor	29 A2
Sao Brasil	30 A2

DRINKING	
Le Patio	31 A2
New Africa	32 C2

ENTERTAINMENT	
Just 4 U	33 C4
Papayer Night	34 B2
Thiossane	35 C3
Villa Krystal	36 A2

SHOPPING	
Marché des HLM	37 C3
Village Artisanal Soumbédioune	38 C4

TRANSPORT	
Avis	39 B2
Coseloc	40 B3
Gare Routière Colobane	41 D3
South African Airways	42 B2

Main post office (Map p488; ☎ 33 839 3400; Blvd el Haji Djily Mbaye; ☒ 7am-7pm Mon-Fri, 8am-5pm Sat)
Post office (Map p488; ☎ 33 839 3400; Ave Pompidou) Has a small *télécentre*.

Travel Agencies
Try the following for ticketing and charter flights:

ATG (Map p485; ☎ 33 869 7900; www.africatravel -group.com; Rte de N'Gor) Great for tours.
Nouvelles Frontières (Map p485; ☎ 33 859 4447; www.nfsenegal.com; Rte des Almadies, Lot 1 Mamelles Aviation; ☒ 8.30am-6pm Mon-Fri, 9am-12.30pm Sat)
Senegal Tours (Map p488; ☎ 33 839 9900; 5 Pl de l'Indépendance) Large tour operator that does ticketing and tours.

TPA (☎ 33 957 1256; www.lesenegal.info) Offers unique tours along lesser-travelled routes.

DANGERS & ANNOYANCES

Dakar's notorious street hustlers and hard-to-shake-off traders do a pretty good job at turning any walk around town into mild punishment, particularly for women. Stride purposefully on, and throw in a brief 'bakhna' ('it's OK') and they'll eventually leave you alone. Many of them also double as pickpockets – be particularly vigilant at markets and in town.

Muggings were on the increase at the time of research, often at knifepoint or from passing scooters. Avoid walking around after dark. Trouble spots include the Petite Corniche (behind the presidential palace), the Rte de la Corniche-Ouest and the beaches.

SIGHTS

Central Dakar has a few impressive colonial buildings. There's the **Gouvernance** (Map p488) and the **Chambre de Commerce** (Map p488), both on Pl de l'Indépendance. The stately **Hôtel de Ville** (Town Hall; Map p488) sits right behind, and a short walk north takes you to the elegant **train station**.

South of Pl de l'Indépendance, the 1907 **Palais Présidentiel** (Map p488; Ave Léopold Senghor) is surrounded by sumptuous gardens. Nearby **Musée Théodore Monod** (Musée IFAN; Map p488; ☎ 33 823 9268; Pl de Soweto; adult/child CFA2200/200; ⊙ 9am-6pm Tue-Sun) has interesting historical exhibits and often houses exhibitions. The best place for contemporary art is the **Village des Arts** (Map p485; ☎ 33 835 7160; www.vdesarts.com; Rte de Yoff) near the national stadium. It houses over 30 artists' workshops, a gallery and a cafe.

The impressive **Grande Mosquée** (Map p487), which was built in 1964, sits in the heart of Médina, Dakar's oldest *quartier populaire* (township). Further along the Corniche, you'll find Dakar's two volcanic hills. One hill is topped by the 1864 **Mamelles Lighthouse** (Map p485); the other, by the brand-new, imposing, socialist-style **African Renaissance Monument** (Map p485). Measuring a height of 50m, the controversial bronze beast is taller than the Statue of Liberty.

Dakar's best beaches are found in the north of the peninsula. **Plage de N'Gor** (Map p485; admission CFA500) is often crowded. There are regular *pirogues* (CFA500) to **Île de N'Gor** (Map p485), which has two small beaches. In Yoff, **Plage de Virage** (Map p485) is good; **Plage de Yoff** (Map p485) is rubbish strewn in parts and waves are strong enough for surfing.

In Yoff village, take a look at the **Layen Mausoleum** (Map p485), a shrine to the founder of the Layen Muslim brotherhood. Residents of Yoff are noted for their strong Islamic culture; smoking and drinking are not allowed and visitors should be appropriately dressed (meaning long skirts or trousers).

ACTIVITIES

The 50m pool of the **Piscine Olympique** (Map p485; ☎ 33 869 0606; Tour de l'Œuf, Point E) is for serious swimmers. **Club Olympique** (Map p485; ☎ 33 864 5655; www.olympique-club.com; Rte de la Corniche-Ouest) also has a pool, tennis grounds and fitness facilities.

The environmental agency **Océanium** (Map p487; ☎ 33 822 2441; www.oceanium.org; Rte de la Corniche-Est; ⊙ Mon-Sat) runs recommended diving excursions.

Tribal Surf Shop (Map p485; ☎ 33 820 5400; www.tribalsurfshop.net; Yoff Virage) and **Pantcho Surf Trip** (Map p485; ☎ 77 534 6232; Plage de N'Gor) can point out the best surf spots, run courses and hire out boards.

SLEEPING

Dakar has a range of accommodation, from filthy doss houses to palatial hotels – although everything is expensive and the steadily increasing prices are only justified in a few places.

Budget

Keur Diame (Map p485; ☎ 33 855 8908; keurdiame@orange.sn; Parcelles Assainies; s/d incl breakfast CFA13,000/21,300) Right in a busy, local neighbourhood and close to Plage de Yoff, this friendly hostel has rooms with mosquito nets and fans, and a roof terrace for sunbathing.

Chez Nizar (Map p488; ☎ 77 319 1224; 25 Ave Pompidou; r CFA15,000) Just above the fast-food joint Ali Baba's, this hostel stretches 100 basic rooms into the Dakar skies. It's got all the charm of social housing.

Hôtel du Phare (Map p485; ☎ 33 860 3000; info@lesmamelles.com; Les Mamelles; s with/without bathroom CFA22,000/15,000, d with/without bathroom CFA28,000/20,000; ❄ 🖳) This family-friendly, patio-adorned guesthouse has a handful of rooms with simple charm and a homely ambience.

SENEGAL

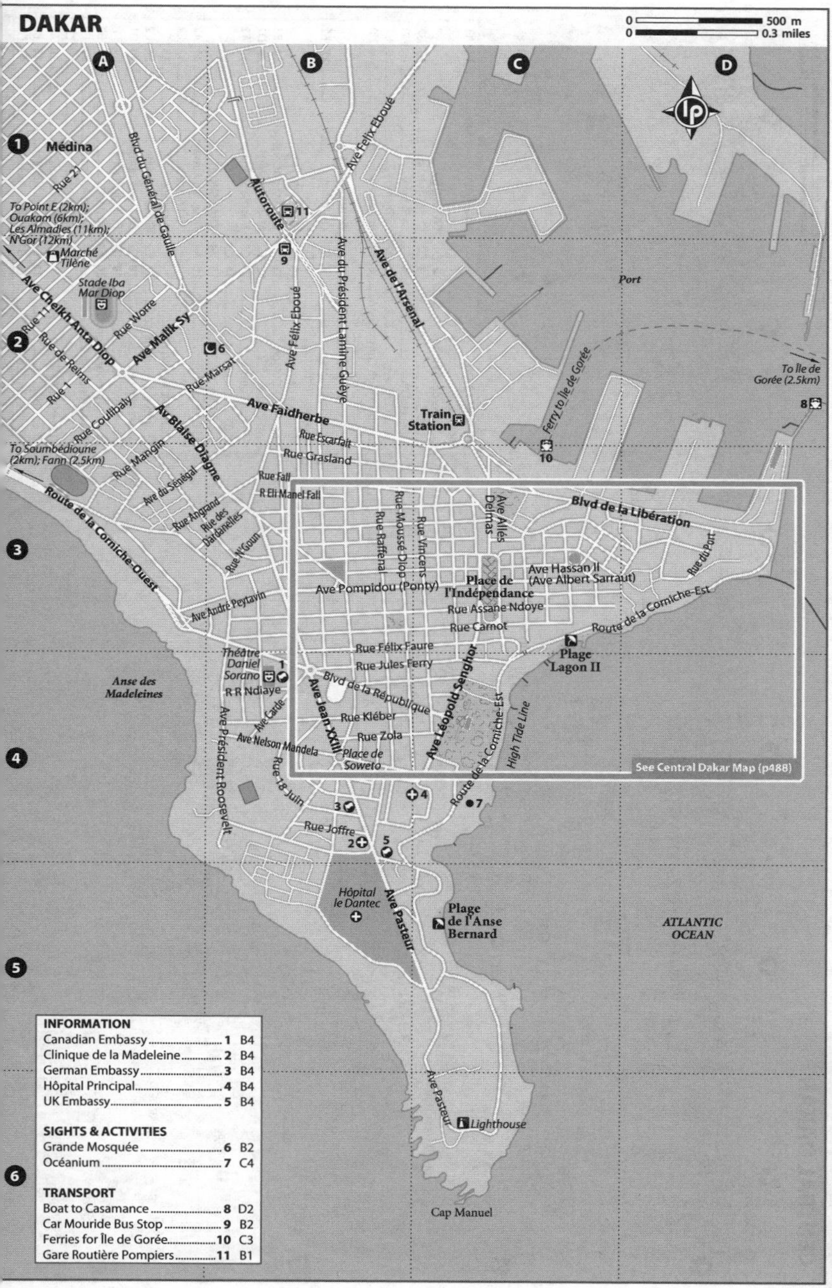
DAKAR
0 500 m
0 0.3 miles
A
B
C
D
1
2
3
4
5
6
Médina
Rue 21
To Point E (2km); Ouakam (6km); Les Almadies (11km); N'Gor (12km)
Marché Tilène
Blvd du Général de Gaulle
Autoroute
11
9
Ave Félix Eboué
Ave du Président Lamine Guèye
Ave de l'Arsenal
Port
Stade Iba Mar Diop
Ave Cheikh Anta Diop
Rue 11
Rue Wore
Ave Malik Sy
6
Rue de Reims
Rue 1
Rue Marsat
Ave Faidherbe
Rue Coulibaly
Av Blaise Diagne
Rue Escarfait
Rue Grasland
Train Station
Ferry to Île de Gorée
To Île de Gorée (2.5km)
8
10
To Soumbédioune (2km); Fann (2.5km)
Rue Mangin
Ave du Sénégal
Rue Fall
R Eli Manel Fall
Route de la Corniche-Ouest
Rue Angrand
Rue des Dardanelles
Rue N'Goun
Rue Mousse Diop
Rue Raffenel
Rue Vincens
Ave Allés Delmas
Blvd de la Libération
Rue du Port
Ave Pompidou (Ponty)
Place de l'Indépendance
Ave Hassan II (Ave Albert Sarraut)
Rue Assane Ndoye
Rue Carnot
Route de la Corniche-Est
Ave André Peytavin
Rue Félix Faure
Rue Jules Ferry
Plage Lagon II
Théâtre Daniel Sorano
1
R R Ndiaye
Anse des Madeleines
Blvd de la République
Ave Jean XXIII
Ave Léopold Senghor
Ave Carde
Rue Kléber
Rue Zola
High Tide Line
Ave Nelson Mandela
Place de Soweto
See Central Dakar Map (p488)
Ave Président Roosevelt
Rue 18 Juin
3
4
7
Rue Joffre
2
5
Hôpital le Dantec
Ave Pasteur
Plage de l'Anse Bernard
ATLANTIC OCEAN
Lighthouse
Cap Manuel
INFORMATION
Canadian Embassy 1 B4
Clinique de la Madeleine 2 B4
German Embassy 3 B4
Hôpital Principal 4 B4
UK Embassy 5 B4
SIGHTS & ACTIVITIES
Grande Mosquée 6 B2
Océanium 7 C4
TRANSPORT
Boat to Casamance 8 D2
Car Mouride Bus Stop 9 B2
Ferries for Île de Gorée 10 C3
Gare Routière Pompiers 11 B1

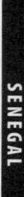

CENTRAL DAKAR

SENEGAL

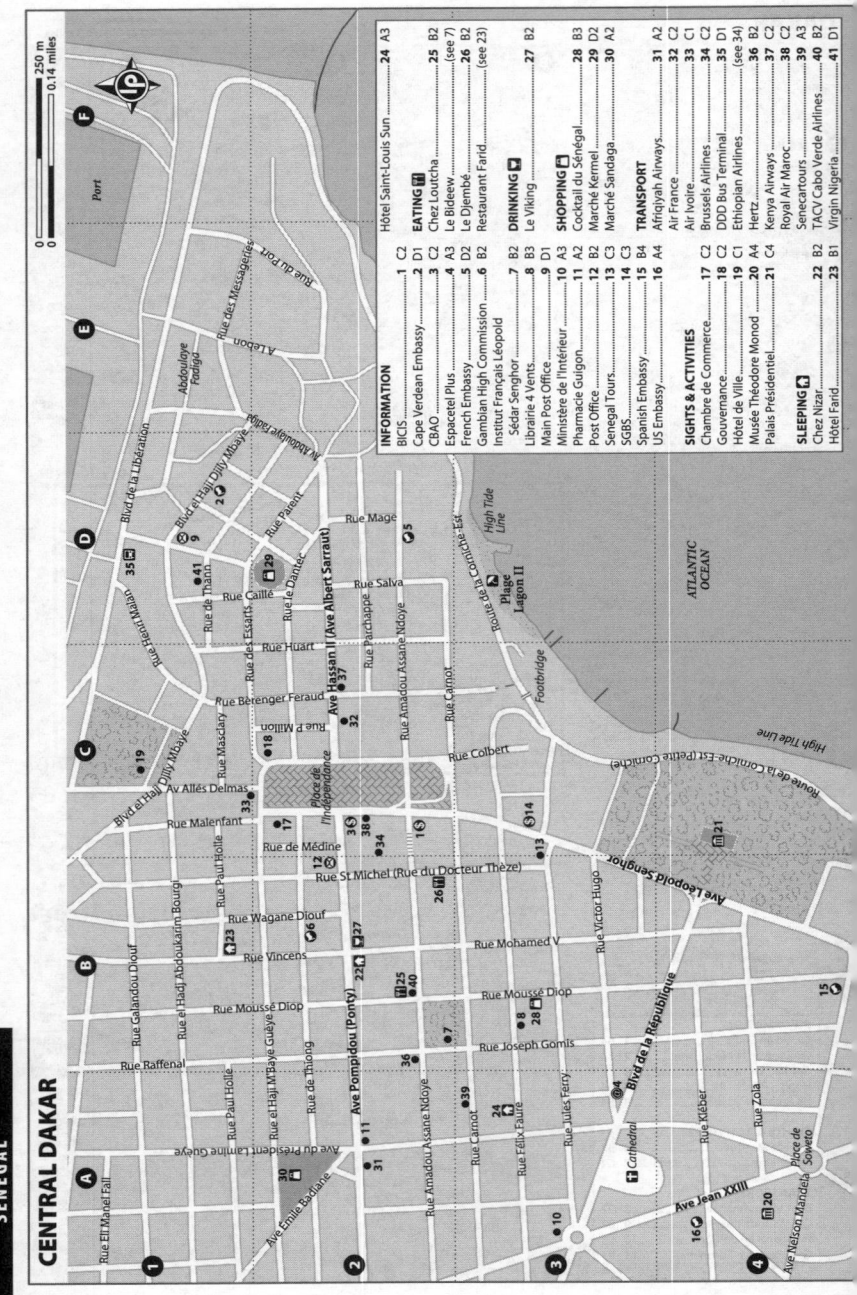

INFORMATION		
BICIS...........................	1	C2
Cape Verdean Embassy............	2	D1
CBAO...........................	3	C2
Espacetel Plus.................	4	A3
French Embassy.................	5	D2
Gambian High Commission........	6	B2
Institut Français Léopold		
Sédar Senghor...............	7	B2
Librairie 4 Vents..............	8	B3
Main Post Office...............	9	D1
Ministère de l'Intérieur.......	10	A3
Pharmacie Guigon...............	11	A2
Post Office....................	12	B2
Senegal Tours.................	13	C3
SGBS..........................	14	C3
Spanish Embassy................	15	B4
US Embassy.....................	16	A4

SIGHTS & ACTIVITIES		
Chambre de Commerce............	17	C2
Gouvernance....................	18	C2
Hôtel de Ville.................	19	C1
Musée Théodore Monod...........	20	A4
Palais Présidentiel............	21	C4

SLEEPING		
Chez Nizar.....................	22	B2
Hôtel Farid....................	23	B1

Hôtel Saint-Louis Sun..........	24	A3

EATING		
Chez Loutcha..................	25	B2
Le Bideew.....................	(see 7)
Le Djembé.....................	26	B2
Restaurant Farid..............	(see 23)

DRINKING		
Le Viking.....................	27	B2

SHOPPING		
Cocktail du Sénégal...........	28	B3
Marché Kermel.................	29	D2
Marché Sandaga................	30	A2

TRANSPORT		
Afriqiyah Airways.............	31	A2
Air France...................	32	C2
Air Ivoire...................	33	C1
Brussels Airlines............	34	C2
DDD Bus Terminal..............	35	D1
Ethiopian Airlines...........	(see 34)
Hertz........................	36	A4
Kenya Airways.................	37	C2
Royal Air Maroc...............	38	C2
Senecartours.................	39	A3
TACV Cabo Verde Airlines......	40	B2
Virgin Nigeria................	41	D1

GETTING UNDER DAKAR'S SKIN

A brilliant way of getting to know this city, its changeable moods and early-morning faces is by staying with a local family, sharing their lives for a few days and finding out what their Dakar looks like. There are now a couple of excellent organisations that can put you in touch with recommended families, and help you out should things go wrong. **Senegal Chez l'Habitant** (☎ 77 517 2666; www.senegalchezlhabitant.com) maintains a regularly updated register of families across the country who would like to open their houses to foreigners. **Océanium** (Map p487; ☎ 33 822 2441; www.oceanium.org) has built an excellent database of private stays on Île de N'Gor. Both organisations have checked the places they recommend, and can connect you with a home that fits your profile, from the most basic to a more luxurious stay.

Hôtel Cap Ouest (Map p485; ☎ 33 820 2469; capouest@arc.sn; Yoff Virage; s/d from CFA19,500/23,000) Good ocean-view value. Make sure you get one of the newly decorated 1st-floor rooms – they're much, much better.

Hôtel Saint-Louis Sun (Map p488; ☎ 33 822 2570, fax 33 822 4651; Rue Félix Faure; s/d CFA23,500/29,500; 🆒 🖳) Rooms are pretty basic, but the central courtyard with huge palm trees turns the space into a calm oasis in the heart of Dakar.

Midrange

Maison Abaka (Map p485; ☎ 33 820 6486; www.maison-abaka.com; Plage de N'Gor; r from CFA30,000; 🆒 🖳 🖭) This surfers' favourite has airy and lovingly decorated rooms located right behind the beach.

Hôtel Farid (Map p488; ☎ 33 821 6127; www.hotelfarid.com; 51 Rue Vincens; s/d from CFA36,100/41,200; 🆒 🖳) This small place with a fabulous Lebanese restaurant, Restaurant Farid (right), is by no means luxurious but is a safe and comfortable option in the city centre.

Ambre (Map p485; ☎ 33 820 6338; www.ambre.sn; Rte des Almadies; r from CFA42,000; 🆒 🖳 🖭) Green, art-adorned and beautifully designed, this small guesthouse is as friendly as a smile. A unique gem close to the city's best hotels and bars.

Le Djoloff (Map p485; ☎ 33 889 3630; www.hoteldjoloff.com; Fann Hock; s/d CFA50,000/60,000; 🆒 🖳) Designed to make you feel like Malian royalty, this place comes with a wide, wonderful roof terrace and a good restaurant. Rooms are a little dark.

Top End

Radisson Blu (Map p485; ☎ 33 869 3333; www.radissonblu.com; Rte de la Corniche-Ouest; d from CFA165,000) In 2009 this was Dakar's newest and most luxurious hotel. One for a weekend of reckless spending and guilty indulgence.

EATING

Dakar's restaurant scene unites the scents and flavours of the world, though you need a healthy budget to eat out. If you're getting by on a few crumpled CFA notes a day, stop at the makeshift street stalls selling rice and sauce or one of the many *shwarma* places. The best-stocked supermarket is Casino, whose largest branch is at the **Dakar City** (Map p485; Rte de N'Gor) mall.

Chez Loutcha (Map p488; ☎ 33 821 0302; 101 Rue Moussé Diop; dishes CFA2500-4000; 🕑 noon-3pm & 7-11pm Mon-Sat) A restaurant like a bus stop, this always overflowing place serves huge portions of Cape Verdean and Senegalese cuisine. It gets busy during lunch hours.

Le Djembé (Map p488; ☎ 33 821 0666; 56 Rue St Michel; dishes CFA3000-5000; 🕑 11am-5pm Mon-Sat) Behind Pl de l'Indépendance, this humble eatery is the whispered insider-tip for anyone in search of a filling platter of *thiéboudieune*.

Restaurant Farid (Map p488; ☎ 33 823 6123; 51 Rue Vincens; dishes CFA3500-6000; 🕑 6am-midnight; 🖳 🅥) Squeezed between grey inner-city walls, this little oasis serves the best Lebanese meze in town. Try the grilled prawns.

Le Ngor (Map p485; ☎ 77 504 3006; Rte du Méridien Président; dishes CFA4000; 🕑 Tue-Sat) At this quirky, seashell-adorned place, waves lap at your feet while you enjoy a perfectly grilled fish. The next-door bar is good, too.

Le Bideew (Map p488; ☎ 33 823 1909; 89 Rue Joseph Gomis; dishes around CFA5000; 🕑 9am-11pm; 🅥) In the cool shade of the Institut Français' garden, this colourful arts cafe is perfect for a break from the city. Little touches, like the drizzle of honey on the chicken, make all the difference.

Sao Brasil (Map p485; ☎ 33 820 0941; Station Shell, Rte de N'Gor; pizzas CFA5000; 🕑 noon-4pm & 6.30pm-midnight; 🛃) Very confusingly named, this is one of Dakar's best Italian addresses, where pizzas

SENEGAL

come with a huge diameter, a thin base and a large range of toppings.

Cabane des Pêcheurs (Map p485; ☎ 33 820 7675; Plage de N'Gor; meals CFA6000-9000; ⏱ 11am-3pm & 7-11pm) Dakar's best fish restaurant serves you absolutely fresh treats, like amberjack and dolphinfish, that you'll find hardly anywhere else in the city. It's right behind Plage de N'Gor.

DRINKING

Le Viking (Map p488; ☎ 77 244 8056; 21 Ave Pompidou) At this old-style, beer-scented pub, the pints spill over and the guests are red-faced. Women will feel safer if they've come with a few friends.

Le Patio (Map p485; ☎ 33 820 5823; Rte de N'Gor) Past the broad-shouldered bouncers and across the red carpet, this large outdoor place serves excellent cocktails within stumbling distance to the nightclubs.

New Africa (Map p485; ☎ 33 827 5371; 9794 Sacré Cœur III) This may be the only bar where there's no pressure to dress up and sparkle. The Friday salsa nights are fantastic.

ENTERTAINMENT

Live-music places spring up almost daily in Dakar, and acoustic sounds are the latest trend on Dakar's restaurant scene. Nights on the dance floor start late – don't even get your kit on before 1am. And always, always overdress.

Just 4 U (Map p485; ☎ 33 824 3250; www.just4udakar.com; Ave Cheikh Anta Diop; ⏱ 11am-3am) The small stage of this outdoor restaurant has been graced by the greatest Senegalese and international stars. There's a concert on every day, and you often get to catch the big names.

Villa Krystal (Map p485; ☎ 76 877 7777; Rte de N'Gor) This bar sparkles with atmosphere, has a good crowd, and treats you to a quality gig every night.

Papayer Night (Map p485; ☎ 77 513 1841; Rte de l'Aéroport) Some of Dakar's best parties happen here, at this nightclub with live music. Upstairs, it's whispering folk guitars; downstairs, raunchy *mbalax*.

Thiossane (Map p485; Rue 10) Youssou N'Dour's legendary nightclub was about to reopen in a new sparkling guise when we passed. Check whether the party has started.

SHOPPING

You need plenty of energy and a safe place to hide your purse for a Dakar market tour.

Marché Sandaga (Map p488; cnr Ave Pompidou & Ave du Président Lamine Guèye) in the centre is the largest market, with rickety stalls that claim most of the area around Ave Pompidou. Marché des HLM (Map p485) is stacked with dazzling African fabrics. The Village Artisanal Soumbédioune (Map p485) is a popular place for buying wood carvings, metal work and batiks, and there are a couple of souvenir shops across from it on the Rte de la Corniche-Ouest. In the town centre, the historical Marché Kermel (Map p488) and the shop **Cocktail du Sénégal** (Map p488; ☎ 33 823 5315; 108 Rue Moussé Diop) are good for picking up souvenirs.

GETTING THERE & AWAY
Air

See p503 for details on airlines serving Dakar.

Boat

The *Aline Sitoé Diatta* travels between Dakar and Ziguinchor twice weekly in each direction. See p500.

Local Transport

Road transport for long-distance destinations leaves from Gare Routière Pompiers (Map p487) off Ave Malik Sy (a taxi from Place de l'Indépendance should cost around CFA1500). Rates are fixed, but change frequently with fluctuations in the cost of petrol. Main destinations include Mbour (CFA2500), Kaolack (CFA3600), Saint-Louis (CFA4500), Karang at the Gambian border (CFA5000), Tambacounda (CFA9000) Ziguinchor (CFA10,000).

Train

Dakar's train station is 500m north of Pl de l'Indépendance. For more information on the connection between Dakar and Bamako (Mali), see the Transport in Senegal section, p504.

GETTING AROUND
Bus

Dakar Dem Dikk (DDD; www.dakardemdikk.com) buses are a pretty good way of travelling cheaply. There are several connections to the town centre. Fares cost around CFA150. They're quite reliable and only crammed full during rush hour. Check the website for a detailed list of DDD routes.

More frequent but less user-friendly are the white Ndiaga Ndiaye minivans and the blue-yellow *cars rapides*, Dakar's battered, crammed and dangerously driven symbols of identity. Unless you know your way around, it's hard to find out where they are going. They stop randomly and suddenly – tap a coin on the roof to signal that you're getting off.

Car

Car-hire agencies in Dakar include (among many, many others):

Avis (Map p485; ☎ 33 849 7757; www.cfaogroup.com) At the airport.

Coseloc (Map p485; ☎ 33 869 2525; www.coseloc.sn; Km 5.5, Ave Cheikh Anta Diop, Fann) Tends to give good deals.

Hertz (Map p488; ☎ 33 822 2016; www.hertz.sn; 64 Rue Joseph Gomis) In the centre; also has a branch at the airport.

Senecartours (Map p488; ☎ 33 889 7777; www.senecartours.sn; 64 Rue Carnot) One of Senegal's biggest operators; also has branches in Almadies.

Taxi

Taxis are the easiest way of getting around town. Rates are entirely negotiable. A short hop costs from CFA500 upwards. Dakar centre to Point E is around CFA1500; it's up to CFA2500 from the centre to N'Gor and Yoff.

The official taxi rates for trips from Léopold Sédar Senghor International Airport are put up outside the airport. Don't pay more.

AROUND DAKAR

ÎLE DE GORÉE

The historical Île de Gorée is enveloped by an almost eerie calm. There are no sealed roads and no cars on this island, just narrow alleyways with trailing bougainvilleas and colonial brick buildings with wrought-iron balconies. But Gorée's calm is not so much romantic as meditative, as the ancient buildings bear witness to the island's role in the Atlantic slave trade.

You pay a tourist tax of CFA500 at the booth to the left of the ferry landing. If you need a guide, you can arrange it there, but the island is easily explored independently.

Sights & Activities

Gorée is an internationally famous symbol for the tragedy of the Atlantic slave trade. Though relatively few slaves were actually shipped from here, the island was a place where much

of the trade was orchestrated. The **Maison des Esclaves** (admission CFA500; ☒ 10.30am-noon & 2.30-6pm Tue-Sun), with its famous doorway, is an important monument to the inhumanity of the slave trade. The **IFAN Historical Museum** (☎ 33 822 2003; admission CFA500; ☒ 10am-1pm & 2.30-6pm Tue-Sat) and the Fort d'Estrées that houses it are worth seeing, as is the **Musée de la Femme** (admission CFA500; ☒ 10am-5pm Tue-Sun). Climb to the top of the **Castel** for great views and seek out tiny arts workshops across the island.

Sleeping & Eating

Many Gorée residents keep a spare room for unexpected (and paying) visitors. One of the prettiest private options is **Chez Valerie** (☎ 33 821 8195; 7 Rue St Joseph; csaodakar@orange.sn; r from CFA15,000), an old Goréen house. Gorée's classic **Hostellerie du Chevalier de Boufflers** (☎ 33 822 5364; www.boufflers.com; r from CFA18,000-23,000, meals CFA5000-7000) is mainly famous for its garden restaurant, but also has good rooms.

For cheaper food options than the Hostellerie, check out any of the many eateries opposite the jetty.

Getting There & Away

A **ferry** (☎ 33 849 7961, 24hr info line 77 628 1111) runs regularly from the wharf in Dakar to Gorée (CFA5000 return for nonresidents, 20 minutes).

LAC ROSE

This lake on the Cap Vert peninsula owes its name to its pink colouring, caused by high mineral and salt content. It's popular with tour groups, their faithful souvenir sellers and Dakarois weekenders.

Most hotels here are clustered near the Village Artisanal, a spot that's plagued by touts and hustlers. The cheapest of those is **Ker Djinné** (☎ 77 634 0468; r with/without air-con CFA19,000/14,000; ☒ ☒), with accommodation in well-maintained round huts. The best place is **Chevaux du Lac** (☎ 77 630 0241; www.leschevauxdulac.com; half/full board CFA14,000/19,000) on the other end of the lake. It's friendly and welcoming and offers tours around the lake on horseback (1½/three hours costs CFA10,000/20,000).

Trying to get here by public transport involves a journey by minibus, *car rapide* (CFA500) or DDD bus 11 to Keur Massar; from there it's a 5km walk to the lake. It's much easier to hire a private taxi (round trip with some waiting time costs around CFA15,000).

PETITE CÔTE & SINÉ-SALOUM DELTA

The 150km Petite Côte stretches south from Dakar and is one of Senegal's best beach areas. Where the Siné and Saloum Rivers meet the tidal waters of the Atlantic Ocean, the coast is broken into a stunning area of mangrove swamps, lagoons, forests and sand islands. It forms part of the magnificent 180-sq-km Siné-Saloum Delta.

MBOUR & SALY

Eighty kilometres south of Dakar, Mbour is the main town on the Petite Côte, though the nearby Saly, a strip of big ocean-front hotels, is the heavier weight when it comes to tourism.

Mbour has a vibrant fishing industry, and the busy, slightly nauseating fish market on the beach is a sight to behold. **Ndaali** (☎ 33 957 4724; www.ndaali.com; Zone Résidentielle; r CFA15,000; ✗ ▢) is a cosy, impeccable and friendly *campement* (guesthouse) with good food. Next door, **Tama Lodge** (☎/fax 33 957 0040; www.tamalodge.com; s/d from CFA33,000/46,000) has exquisitely designed bungalows and a great restaurant, while the simple **New Blue Africa** (☎ 33 957 0993; Rte de Niakhniakhal; s/d CFA23,000/28,000) sits on Mbour's finest dune.

If it's a beach holiday you're after, then Saly is the perfect corner for soaking up the sun and sipping cocktails. **our pick** **Ferme de Saly & Les Amazones** (☎ 77 638 4790; www.farmsaly.com; d incl half board Ferme/Amazones CFA16,500/30,200) is a classic with overlanders, a place of sound sleep, good food and the generous company of host Jean-Paul. Nearer Saly village, **La Medina** (☎ 33 957 4993; Terrain de Football, Saly village; s/d 15,000/20,000; ✗ ▢ ⍅) has good, clean rooms surrounding a leafy patio. To spend big, head for **Lamantin Beach Hotel** (☎ 33 957 0777; www.lelamantin.com; s/d incl breakfast from CFA85,000/130,000; ✗ ▢ ⍅), where the service is as fabulous as the massages and the food.

JOAL-FADIOUT

The twin villages of Joal and Fadiout are located south of Mbour at the end of the tar road. Joal sits on the mainland, while Fadiout is on a small island made of clam and oyster shells, reached by an impressive wooden bridge.

The tiny auberge (hostel) **Le Thiouraye** (☎ 77 515 6064; s/d incl breakfast CFA10,000/12,000; ✗) has basic, riverside rooms and a menu composed by one of Senegal's top chefs. **Keur Seynabou** (☎ 33 957 6744; www.keurseynabou.com; r CFA35,000; ✗ ▢ ⍅) sparkles with magazine-perfect lodgings overlooking a pool.

A minibus to/from Mbour is CFA700; to/from Palmarin, CFA1300. A *sept-place* taxi goes directly to Dakar most mornings (without changing at Mbour) for CFA2000.

PALMARIN & DJIFER

Palmarin, with its soft lagoons, tall palm groves and labyrinthine creeks, is one of Senegal's secretly most beautiful spots.

There's a seductively good choice of *campements*. The straw huts of **Yokam** (☎ 77 567 0113; www.au-senegal.com/pages/yokam; Palmarin Facao; per person incl breakfast CFA8000) are cheap and lightweight, but the company is good. The red-mud structure of **Lodge de Diakhamor** (☎ 33 957 1256; www.lesenegal.info; s/d incl half board CFA23,000/41,000) is a stylish redbrick place where *pirogue* excursions, horse riding, and bicycle and fishing trips are all included in the price. **Lodge des Collines de Niassam** (☎ 77 639 0639; www.niassam.com; per person incl half board CFA52,000; ✗ ⍅) is one of Senegal's most original *campements*. You can sleep in classy tree houses that cling to the mighty branches of baobabs, or sit on stilts in the river.

On a nearby island, hidden in the mangroves, **M'boss-Dor** (☎ Nov-Jun 77 541 9683, Jul-Oct in France 05 58 77 91 89; www.mboss-dor.com; per person incl full board CFA53,800) houses you in lovingly decorated log cabins, and offers ultralight-aircraft tours (20 minutes costs CFA25,000). You won't find this place on your own - arrange pick-up either from Dakar (CFA40,000 to CFA50,000) or the mosque at Palmarin Ngallou.

Palmarin is most easily reached from Mbour, via Joal-Fadiout and Sambadia (where you may have to change). The fare from Joal to Sambadia is CFA500 in a Ndiaga Ndiaye, and from Sambadia to Palmarin it's CFA400.

NDANGANE & MAR LODJ

Ndangane is a thriving traveller centre from where you can take a *pirogue* to almost any point in the delta.

SENEGAL

Ndangane's cheapie is the lively **Le Barracuda** (Chez Mbacke; ☎ 33 949 9815; r per person CFA6000), with great views from the restaurant terrace. Brightly coloured **Auberge Bouffe** (☎ 33 949 9313; info@aubergebouffe.com; s/d incl breakfast CFA16,000/24,000; 🍷) has well-maintained rooms and plenty of character. Opposite, **Les Cordons Bleus** (☎ 33 949 9312; www.lescordonsbleus.com; s/d/tr CFA34,000/46,000/58,000; P 🍴 💻 🍷) has the best rooms in town.

On Mar Lodj, **Le Bazouk** (☎ 77 633 4894; www.bazoukdusaloum.com; per person incl half board CFA18,000) has spacious bungalows scattered over a vast, sand-covered garden where bougainvilleas lend shade and palm trees carry hammocks. **Essamaye** (☎ 77 555 3667; www.senegalia.com; Marfafako; per person incl full board CFA17,500) on the other side of the island is a place like a hug from a loved one – highly recommended for family vibes and its impressive Casamance-style *case à l'impluvium* (large, round traditional house).

Take any bus between Kaolack and Mbour, and get off at Ndiosomone, from where bush taxis shuttle back and forth to Ndangane. For Mar Lodj, contact your *campement* for *pirogue* pick-up or hire a boat at the **GIE des Piroguiers** (☎ 77 213 7497, 77 226 6168), the boat's owners association at the jetty in Ndangane. Prices are fixed.

TOUBAKOUTA & MISSIRAH

Toubakouta is a fantastically calm and pretty spot in the south of the Siné-Saloum Delta, and is one of the country's best places for birdwatching. In town, **Keur Youssou** (☎ 33 948 7728; s/d CFA6250/12,500; 🍴) has beautifully furnished rooms and a relaxed ambience. **Keur Thierry** (☎ 77 439 8605; d incl breakfast CFA12,500; 🍴) has the better kitchen and cold Belgian beers. **Hôtel Keur Saloum** (☎ 33 948 7715; www.keursaloum.com; s/d incl breakfast CFA34,200/55,000; P 🍴 💻 🍷 ♿) is the classiest place in town. A *pirogue* and donkey-cart ride away, **Keur Bamboung** (☎ 77 510 8013; www.oceanium.org; bungalow, incl half/full board CFA17,000/22,000) is the hub of the Marine Protected Area surrounding it. Things are simple and green, and the location is stunning. Phone to arrange pickup from Toubakouta.

South of Toubakouta, Missirah is the point of entry to the **Parc National du Delta du Saloum**, which encompasses the Forêt de Fathala woodlands, mangrove swamps and a large marine section. The peaceful **Gîte de Bandiala** (☎ 33 948 7735; www.gite-bandiala.com; per person incl half/full board CFA16,300/22,600) sits right on its edge, has a water hole on site and organises tours through the Forêt de Fathala.

Kaolack to Toubakouta is CFA3000 by *sept-place* taxi. A private taxi from Toubakouta to Missirah is around CFA5000.

NORTHERN SENEGAL

SAINT-LOUIS
pop 171,300

With its crumbling colonial architecture, horse-drawn carts and peaceful ambience, West Africa's first French settlement has a unique historical charm. The old town centre sits on an island in the Senegal River, but the city sprawls into Sor on the mainland, and onto the Langue de Barbarie, where you'll find the lively fishing community of Guet N'Dar.

The island is reached via the 500m-long Pont Faidherbe, a feat of 19th-century engineering.

Information

BICIS (☎ 33 961 1053; Rue de France; 🕐 7.45am-12.15pm & 1.40-3.45pm Mon-Thu, 7.45am-1pm & 2.40-3.45pm Fri)

CBAO (☎ 33 938 2552; Rue Khalifa Ababacar Sy; 🕐 8.15am-5.15pm Mon-Fri) Also has a Western Union office.

Internet cafe (Ave de Gaulle; per hr CFA500; 🕐 8am-11pm) Decent terminals and several phone booths.

Sahel Découverte (☎ 33 961 4263; www.sahel decouverte.com; Rue Blaise Diagne) Quite simply the best address for exploring the northern region.

Syndicat d'Initiative (☎ 33 961 2455; sltourisme@ orange.sn; Gouvernance; 🕐 9am-noon & 2.30-5pm) A haven of regional information with excellent tours.

Sights & Activities

In the centre of the Saint-Louis island is **Place Faidherbe** and the **Governor's Palace**. It's flanked north and south by the 1837 **Rognât Casernes**, as well as by other 19th-century houses.

At the southern tip of the island is the **Musée de CRDS** (☎ 33 961 1050; Quai Henri Jay; adult/child CFA500/250; 🕐 9am-noon & 3-6pm), with yellowing photos, dusty artefacts and informative displays (in French). **Galerie Mame Thiouth** (☎ 33 961 3611; Rue Blaise Diagne; 🕐 8am-7pm) sometimes has good arts exhibitions, and **Les Ateliers Tësss** (☎ 33 961 6860; Rue Khalifa Ababacar Sy)

SAINT-LOUIS

0		300 m
0		0.2 miles

To Mauritanian
Border (Restricted
Area; 2.5km)

Place
de
Liège

Stadium
Route des Conducteurs

14

20

23

8

Lodo

Rue Bouet

Grand
Mosquée

Rue Brue

Pont Geole

18

Rue Pierre Loti

Rue AC Diaw

Rue Lt PM Diop

Rue D Seck Bou el Mogdad

19

Watertowers

Rue Aynima Fall

6

Rue Paul Holle

13

Hôtel de Ville

Rue Potin

15

4

Rue El Hadj Seydou Nourou Tall

1

Rue André Guillabert

12

Rue Augustin HL Guillabert
3

21

Ave de Gaulle

Market

Pont Mustapha
Malick Gaye

Place
Faidherbe

11

5

Pont Faidherbe

To Airport (7km); Bango (8km);
Podor (220km)

Train
Station

Old Gare
Routière

Sor

Pointe à Pitre

22

Cathedral
Rue Schocker
Rue Lanneau

17

Rue Duret

Sindoné
Rue Chassanlet

Saint-Louis
Hospital

Rue A Ndiaye Sarr

Rue Ibrahima Tall

Guet
N'Dar

Rue Ribet

Île de N'Dar

Rue A Fall

Muslim
Cemetery

To Hôtel Cap Saint-Louis (4km);
Hôtel Dior & Camping Océan (4km);
Hydrobase (4km);
Le Papayer (4km);
Parc National de la
Langue de Barbarie (18km)

10

To Gare Routière (3.5km);
Gandiol (18km); Mouit
(20km); Dakar (260km)

ATLANTIC OCEAN

Langue de Barbarie Peninsula

N'Dar
Tout

Senegal River

Senegal River

Ave Dodds

Quai Giraud

R Adanson

R de France

Khalifa Ababacar Sy

Rue Abdoulaye Seck

Av Jean Mermoz

R Blaise Diagne

Quai Bacre Waly Gueye

16

9

2

1

Rue Millis Lacroix

Quai Henri Jay

Blvd Abdoulaye Mar Diop

Rue Ibrahim Sarr

Rue Blaise Dumont

Rue Babacar Seye

Route de la Corniche

INFORMATION
BICIS...............................1 B4
CBAO..............................2 B3
Internet Cafe....................3 B4
Sahel Découverte..............4 C3
Syndicat d'Initiative..........5 C4

SIGHTS & ACTIVITIES
Galerie Mame Thiouth.......6 C3
Governor's Palace.............7 C4
Institut Jean Mermoz........8 C2
Les Ateliers Tèss..............9 B3
Musée de CRDS................10 B6
Rognât Casernes..............11 B4

SLEEPING
Auberge l'Harmattan.........12 B4
Jamm.............................13 B3
La Louisiane.....................14 B1
La Résidence....................15 C3
Sunu Keur.......................16 B2

EATING
Chez Agnes.....................17 B5
La Signare.......................18 C3
Le Casino........................19 C3
Pointe Nord.....................20 C1

DRINKING
Flamingo.........................21 C4
La Chaumière...................22 A4

ENTERTAINMENT
Quai des Arts...................23 C1

SENEGAL

displays beautiful woven products (you can see the artisans at work).

Guet N'Dar on the Langue de Barbarie is a fantastically busy fishing town, where you can watch dozens of *pirogues* being launched, and fish being brought in, gutted and smoked on the shore.

Festivals & Events

The famous **Saint-Louis Jazz Festival** (www.saintlouisjazz.com) happens in May. **Les Fanals**, a historic lantern procession, is celebrated around Christmas. For other events, check the **Institut Jean Mermoz** (☎ 33 938 2626; www.ccfsl.net; Ave Jean Mermoz).

Sleeping

Hotel Dior & Camping Océan (☎ 33 961 3118; www.hotel-dior.com; Hydrobase; campsite CFA3500, s CFA24,100-32,000, d CFA31,200-40,000) With Mauritanian tents tucked away behind sand dunes, this overlander favourite feels like a desert home. For more comfort, rent a bungalow with hot water, wi-fi and minibar.

La Louisiane (☎ 33 961 4221; www.aubergelalouisiane.com; Pointe Nord; r from CFA14,500; ☒ ☐) Its enviable location on the river, a great restaurant and the engaging company of Marcel the owner make this an enduring travellers' favourite.

Auberge l'Harmattan (☎ 33 961 8253; mimi-saint louis@hotmail.com; Rue Abdoulaye Seck; d/tr CFA15,000/20,000; ☒) With huge rooms packed with trinkets, paintings of topless beauties and odd bits of old furniture, this looks like the illegal sublet of a naughty grandmother.

Sunu Keur (☎ 33 961 8800; www.sunu-keur.com; Quai Giraud; s/d from CFA18,000/23,000; ☒ ☐) Based in a completely rebuilt historical house, this is a place for good food, a homely atmosphere and a magnificent view across town from the terrace.

Hôtel Cap Saint-Louis (☎ 33 961 3939; www.hotelcapsaintlouis.com; Hydrobase; s/d CFA28,000/35,000; ℗ ☒ ☐ ☒ ⅙) This child-friendly, family-run place has a fantastic sea-view restaurant, vast sand beaches and one of the best swimming pools around.

La Résidence (☎ 33 961 1260; www.hoteldelaresidence.com; Ave Blaise Diagne; s/d/ste CFA30,000/36,000/40,000; ☒ ☐ ⅙) The Bancals, the old Saint-Louisian family that owns this classic place, have done a great job of evoking history. The restaurant is one of the town's very best.

Jamm (Chez Yves Lamour; ☎ 77 443 4765; http://jamm-saintlouis.com; Rue Paul Holle; s/d incl breakfast CFA50,000/55,000; ☒ ☐) You purchase the privilege of staying in Saint-Louis' most beautifully restored house.

Eating

Chez Agnes (Complexe Aldiana; ☎ 33 961 4044; Rue Duret; meals around CFA2000) In this pretty, tree-lined patio-restaurant, lovely Agnes serves portions of Senegalese rice and sauce that are so generous the word generosity itself ought to be redefined.

Pointe Nord (☎ 33 961 8716; Ave Jean Mermoz; dishes around CFA3000; ⊗ 11am-4pm & 7pm-midnight Mon-Sat) This laughter-filled greasy spoon is Saint-Louis' best place for grilled fish served Ivory Coast–style, with *athieke* (cassava couscous) and *aloko* (fried plantains).

Le Casino (La Terrasse; ☎ 33 961 5398; Quai Bacre Waly Guèye; mains CFA5000; ⊗ 7pm-midnight Wed-Mon) This gambling den serves the best pizzas in town, and also offers gems such as goat's-cheese salad with local honey and homemade bread.

La Signare (☎ 33 961 1932; www.lasignare.com; Rue Blaise Diagne; mains CFA5000) Management may have changed, but not the list of refined dishes (try the hot goat's-cheese salad or squid in garlic butter) that made this diner one of Saint-Louis' most popular addresses.

Drinking & Entertainment

Any night out here starts at the pool-adorned riverside bar **Flamingo** (☎ 33 961 1118; Quai Bacre Waly Guèye; ⊗ 11am-2am). Always packed, it's Saint-Louis' best place for live music. Smart and glittering, **La Chaumière** (☎ 77 495 6086; Pointe à Pitre; admission from CFA2000; ⊗ from 10pm) is the best and closest to the town centre. Pick the right night: it's Senegalese soirée on Wednesday and Friday, global beats on weekends. On Hydrobase, **Le Papayer** (☎ 77 566 8382; Carrefour de l'Hydrobase; ⊗ 10am-5am) is the party place of choice. The biggest concerts in town (including the main acts of the jazz festival), happen at the vast **Quai des Arts** (☎ 33 961 5656; Ave Jean Mermoz).

Getting There & Away

There are frequent *sept-place* taxis between Dakar and Saint-Louis (CFA4500, five hours, 264km). You'll be dropped off at the *gare routière* (bus station), 3.5km south of Saint-Louis. A taxi to the island costs CFA500.

PARC NATIONAL DE LA LANGUE DE BARBARIE

This **national park** (admission CFA2000, pirogue 1 or 2 people/extra person CFA9000/2500; ☻ 7am-7pm), 18km south of Saint-Louis, covers the southern tip of the Langue de Barbarie Peninsula and a section of the mainland on the other side of the river's mouth. It's a great place for *pirogue* tours, relaxing and birdwatching.

There are several *campements* that provide meals and transfers, and offer a range of activities, including kayaking and birdwatching. On the mainland, *campement* **Zebrabar** (Mouit; ☎ 77 638 1862, 33 962 0019; www.zebrabar.net; campsite per person CFA2500, s CFA4000-20,000, d CFA7000-25,000) has simple huts and spacious bungalows spread over a huge terrain. Close by, the family-run **Auberge Teranga** (☎ 33 962 5853; www.gandiole-teranga. com; Gandiol; r CFA17,000; ☻) is a homely place between lagoon and lush garden; the coco punch here is delicious and the massages come with river views. At the ultra-relaxed **Campement Océan et Savane** (☎ 77 637 4790; www.oceanetsavane. com; tent per person CFA10,000, bungalow from CFA30,000), you can stay in Mauritanian-style tents, rustic log cabins or stylish bungalows on the river.

Private taxis to Zebrabar and Auberge Teranga cost around CFA5000 from Saint-Louis; call the hotels and they can organise a taxi for you. For Campement Océan et Savane, take a taxi to Gandiol lighthouse (around CFA4000), from where *piroguer* **Jules** (☎ 77 656 4633) takes you across (CFA2500). Otherwise, contact La Résidence (see p495) to organise your trip.

PARC NATIONAL DES OISEAUX DU DJOUDJ

With almost 300 species of bird, this 16,000-hectare **park** (☎ 33 968 8708; admission CFA2000, pirogue CFA3500, car CFA5000; ☻ 7am-dusk Nov-Apr) is one of the most important bird sanctuaries in the world. Flamingos, pelicans and waders are most plentiful, and large numbers of migrating birds travel here in November. The park is best explored by *pirogue*. Boats trips can be arranged at the park entrance or at the hotels.

The main hotel is the large **Hôtel du Djoudj** (☎ 33 963 8702; www.hotel-djoudj.com; r CFA27,000; ☻ Nov-May; ☻) near the park headquarters. They arrange *pirogue* rides around the park, and hire bicycles (half/full day CFA3000/6000). The **Station Biologique** (☎ Ibrahima Camara 77 524 0105, Ibrahima Diop 77 656 7038; per person incl full board CFA16,000) at the park headquarters is really intended for

researchers but sometimes puts up budget-bound travellers. You can camp here.

The park is 25km off the main road, and there's no public transport. You can either negotiate a private taxi from Saint-Louis (around CFA25,000) or join an organised tour.

CENTRAL SENEGAL

KAOLACK

pop 186,000

A dusty, polluted sprawl of a town, this is where every vehicle from Gambia or Tambacounda to Dakar stops for food and, more commonly, repairs. You can do your banking at **CBAO** (Rue de la Gare) and **SGBS** (Rue de la Gare). Apart from its round, covered **market** (one of the biggest in Africa) and the Moroccan-style **Grande Mosquée** of the Baye Niass brotherhood, there's little to see. The **Alliance Franco-Senegalaise** (☎ 33 941 1061; www. kaolack.af-senegal.org; Rue Galliene) frequently hosts concerts and other events.

The best cheap accommodation is the hostel **Arc en Ciel** (☎ 33 941 1212; Ave Valdiodio Ndiaye; s/d CFA18,000/21,000; ☻ ☻), which is friendly and great value with air-con rooms and free wi-fi. Run by the same management, **Le Relais** (☎ 33 941 1000; Plage de Kundam; s/d CFA25,000/30,000; ☻ ☻ ☻), is Kaolack's most sparkling choice, with all the amenities of a quality hotel.

There are plenty of tiny eateries. Laid-back **Le Brasero Chez Anouar** (☎ 33 941 1608; Ave Valdiodio Ndiaye; meals about CFA3000; ☻ 7am-11pm) is a classic stop for travellers; great for food and local information. The busiest bar in town is the indefatigable **Etoile du Siné** (Ave Cheikh Ibra Fall).

Transport for Dakar (CFA3600, three hours, 192km) and other western and northern destinations leaves from the Gare Routière de Dakar on the northwestern end of town. *Sept-place* taxis to Tambacounda (CFA6000, five hours), Karang (CFA2500, two hours) and other southern destinations depart Garage Nioro (Sud), to the southeast of town.

TAMBACOUNDA

The junction town Tambacounda is all about dust, sizzling temperatures and lines of traffic heading in all directions. It's a jumping-off point for Mali, Guinea, Gambia and, closer to home, the Parc National de Niokolo-Koba.

Bloc Gadec (☎ 77 531 8931; dm/r CFA3000/8000) is a friendly hostel in the centre of town with clean rooms and shared toilets. **Hôtel Niji** (☎ 33 981 1250; www.hotelniji.com; s/d CFA18,500/22,000; Ⓟ Ⓧ Ⓛ Ⓡ) has everything from simple bungalows to lush (but soulless) quarters. Try **Oasis Oriental Club** (☎ 33 981 1824; www.oasisoriental. com; Rte de Kaolack; s/d incl breakfast CFA27,500/34,500; Ⓟ Ⓧ Ⓛ Ⓡ) for some comfort and service.

Restaurant Rose (☎ 77 554 6542; dishes from CFA1000; ◷ noon-2.30pm & 6-11pm) and **Relais du Rais** (☎ 77 552 7096; dishes from CFA2000; ◷ noon-2.30pm & 6-11pm) are two small, decent eateries. A bit further out, **Saveur Orientale** (☎ 77 322 5619; Garage Kothiary; meals CFA2500; ◷ 11am-1am) does good pizzas and snacks. **Chez Nanette** (meals about CFA1500; ◷ 8am-midnight), right outside Bloc Gadec, is a busy, rootsy drinking hole.

If you're travelling on to Mali, you get your *sept-place* taxi to Kidira (CFA5000, three hours) at Garage Kothiary on the eastern side of town. Vehicles to other destinations go from the larger *gare routière* near the market. The Dakar–Bamako train stops here, but it's often full; the fare to Dakar is 1st/2nd class CFA15,000/10,000.

PARC NATIONAL DE NIOKOLO-KOBA

Niokolo-Koba, at 900 sq km, is Senegal's largest national park. It's listed as a World Heritage Site in danger, as park resources barely suffice to adequately protect the remaining animals (including elephants, lions, warthogs, and various monkey and antelope species).

You can explore the park by 4WD, though sightings of the rare mammals are far from guaranteed. The best option is a river tour (CFA6500), where you'll most certainly spot hippos and crocodiles, combined with an exploration of Simenti, the centre of the park. The waterhole nearby is a good viewing spot.

The park is officially open from 15 December to 30 April, as most areas are inaccessible during the wet months. The entrance fee (adults/children under 10 CFA2000/free, vehicles CFA5000) gives you access for 24 hours. You get your obligatory guide (CFA8000) at the entrance gate.

To spend a night in the park, you can either stay simply in the thatched huts of **Camp du Lion** (☎ park headquarters 33 981 2454; campsite CFA4000, s/d CFA8000/12,000) or a bit more comfortably at the concrete monstrosity that is **Simenti Hotel** (☎ 33 982 3650; Simenti; s/d CFA15,000/25,000; Ⓟ Ⓧ Ⓡ), situated at a stunning river bend.

You will need a vehicle to enter the park. It's best to hire a 4WD (CFA80,000 to CFA110,000) in Tambacounda. Enquire at the *gare routière*, at the hotels or at the **National Park Office** (☎ 33 981 2454; Tambacounda; ◷ 7.30am-5pm). You won't save any money using public transport, as pick-up and drop-off from the park entrance and the tours will also add up to around CFA80,000.

CASAMANCE

With its lush tropical landscapes, watered by the graceful, winding Casamance River, and the unique culture of the Diola, this area seems far from Dakar and its surroundings, in every sense. That's what many locals feel as well, so strongly that separatist rebellions have troubled the region for years. Things have largely calmed down, but they've left a destabilising legacy of banditry that flared up again in 2009.

If the area is safe enough for visits, you'll discover a fascinating place. Between the sleepy capital, Ziguinchor, and the wide,

---

BASSARI COUNTRY

You cross the entire country to get there, but the natural beauty of the southeastern Bassari country makes it all worth it. This is the only area in Senegal where you'll find hills, and you can go on some fabulous trekking tours through remote regions. It's easy to think that you've left Senegal altogether; the traditions of the local Bassari and Bédik people differ widely from the Senegalese cultures you'll have encountered in other places. Many people hold animist faiths; the region is renowned for its mask dances and initiation rites.

Get a good guide to explore this zone; they'll know how to show people proper respect and can indicate rarely walked routes. Recommended guides include **Alpha Diallo** (☎ 77 652 6450; http://alphaguia.blogspot.com) and **Doba Diallo** (☎ 77 360 6401; http://dobadiallo.mi-website.es), who can pick you up from hotel **Le Bédik** (☎ 33 985 1000) in Kédougou and take you on tours (from day trips to extended one-week hikes) around Iwol, Ibel, Ethiolo, Salémata, Dindéfelo, Dande and other even more rarely visited places.

WARNING

Since the 1980s, conflicts in Casamance have flared up regularly. The latest peace deal between the Movement of Democratic Forces in Casamance (MFDC) rebels and the Senegalese government was signed in 2004 and was largely adhered to. Still, there were occasional incidents of road blocks and armed street robberies, and in 2009 reports of violence, gun fire and attacks of military posts became more frequent. Whether the work of common criminals or rebels with a cause, it can render trips to Casamance dangerous. Check the situation carefully before setting out, never travel after dark and don't venture off into the bush without a guide.

---

sandy beaches of Cap Skiring, the banks of the Casamance River are dotted with tiny, community *campements* that nestle between mangroves and lagoons.

ZIGUINCHOR
pop 158,400

Ziguinchor is the largest town in southern Senegal, and the main access point for travel in the Casamance region. With its old houses, tree-lined streets and busy markets, this former colonial centre exudes real atmosphere.

Information
CBAO (Rue de France; ◷ 7.45am-noon & 1.15-2.30pm Mon-Thu, 7.45am-1pm & 2.45-3.45pm Fri)
Diambone Voyages (☎ 77 641 5132; www.diambonevoyages.com; Rue de France) Flight bookings, tours, car hire and more.
Hospital (☎ 33 991 1154) Has an emergency department.
SGBS (Rue du Général de Gaulle) Change or withdraw money here.

Sights
Ziguinchor has some colourful historical buildings, including the central **post office** and the **Conseil Régional**. The huge *case à impluvium* of the **Alliance Franco-Sénégalaise** (☎ 33 991 2823; ◷ 9.15am-noon & 3-7.15pm Mon-Sat), with its stunning South African–Casamançais decor, is a beauty worth admiring. At **Africa Batik** (☎ 77 653 4936), you can try your hand at making batiks.

For *pirogue* excursions, ask your hotel or speak to the boat owners at the *pirogue* jetty near Le Perroquet.

Sleeping
Auberge Aw-Bay (☎ 33 936 8096; Kolobane; per person CFA3600) Clean and friendly, this *auberge* has a hammock-adorned garden and spotless shared toilets.
Le Perroquet (☎ 33 991 2329; perroquet@orange.sn; Rue du Commerce; s/d CFA11,000/13,000) Dozens of yellow-billed storks attract you with their noisy chatter to Zig's favourite budget place. Invest in a 1st-floor room for the river views.
Ferme de Djibelor (☎ 33 991 1701; s/d CFA15,000/22,000) The three log cabins on this croc farm are cosy, and strangely reminiscent of ski chalets, until the lush gardens remind you where you are.
Le Flamboyant (☎ 33 991 2223; www.casamance.info; Rue de France; s/d CFA16,000/18,000; ☒ ▢ ▨) Rooms here offer comfort way above the price you pay. The setting is pretty and the service friendly. Add CFA4000 for air-con.

Eating & Drinking
There are lots of small eateries, though they're hardly spectacular.
Le Tamarinier (☎ 33 992 0022; Ave Carvalho; meals CFA2000-4000) Manager Marie-Agnès infuses this lively bar-cum-restaurant with her energy. The grilled prawns here taste even better to the live music on weekends.
Le Kassa (☎ 33 991 1311; Rond-Point Jean-Paul II; mains around CFA2500-4000; ◷ 8am-2am) It's proven itself for years, this patio-pretty place on the Ziguinchor roundabout. The kitchen stays open late and there's live music on weekends.
Walkunda Bar (☎ 33 991 1845; Rond-Point Jean-Paul II; mains CFA3000-5000; ◷ 9am-1am) A popular haunt for affluent locals and localised expats, the Walkunda has a good kitchen and a relaxed atmosphere.
Hôtel Tourisme (☎ 33 991 2223; Rue de France; mains CFA4000; ◷ noon-2.30pm & 7-10pm) Small and simple, this is a great place to wind down over a plate of seafood or excellent Senegalese *plats du jour*.

Self-caterers can buy all the fresh fruit, vegetables and fresh prawns they can carry at **Marché Escale** (Rue Javelier), right in the heart of town. There's also a small **Superette** (Rue Lemoine), as well as a good **pâtisserie** (Rue Javelier) in the centre of town.

Entertainment
Le Rubis (Rue de Santhiaba; admission CFA1000-2000) is the trendy choice, while **Le Bombolong** (☎ 33 938 8001; Rue du Commerce; admission CFA1500-3000) has the most raucous party.

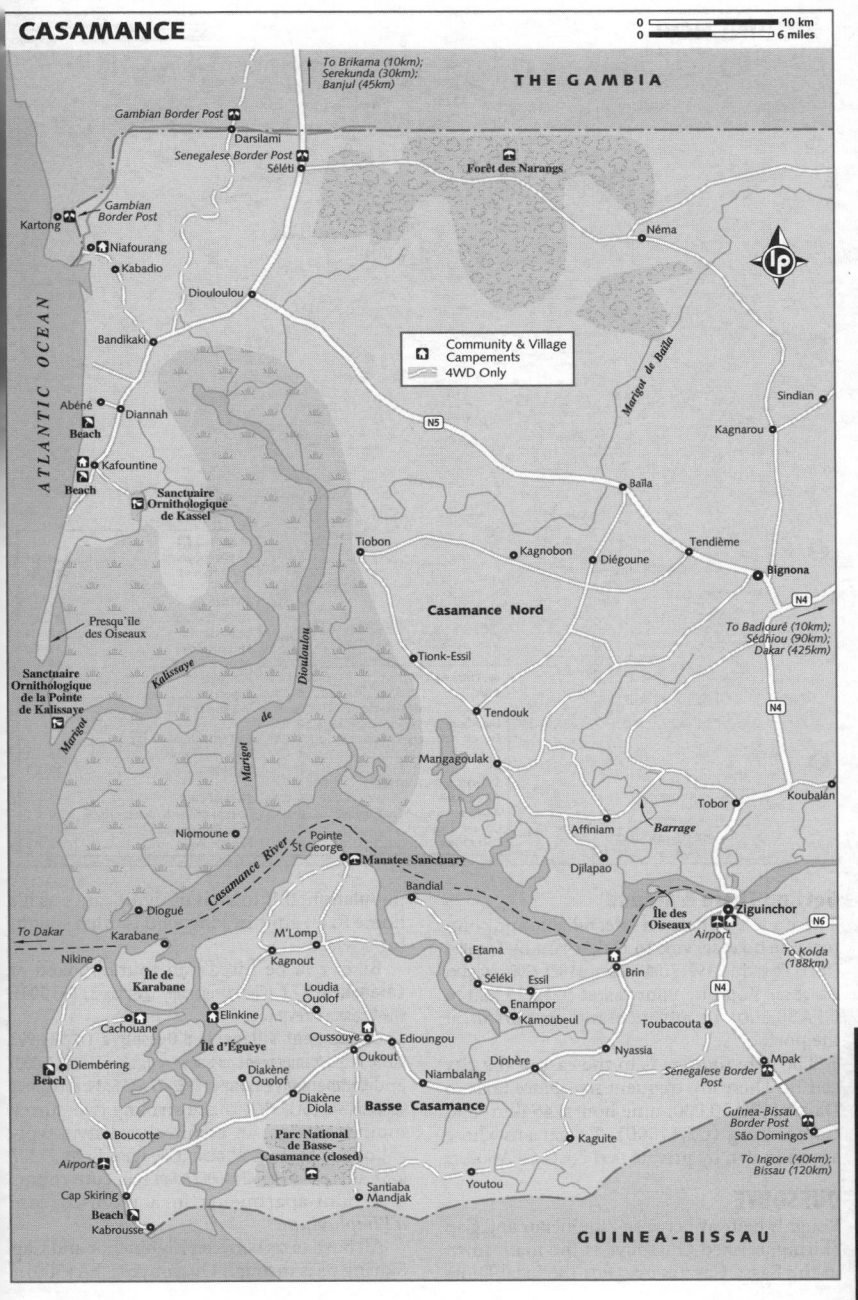

CASAMANCE

0 — 10 km
0 — 6 miles

To Brikama (10km);
Serekunda (30km);
Banjul (45km)

THE GAMBIA

Gambian Border Post
Darsilami
Senegalese Border Post
Séléti

Forêt des Narangs

Kartong
Gambian
Border Post

Niafourang
Kabadio

Néma

Diouloulou

Bandikaki

Sindian

Abéné
Beach
Diannah

Kagnarou

N5

Kafountine
Beach

Baïla

Tendième

BIGNONA

**Sanctuaire
Ornithologique
de Kassel**

Tiobon

Kagnobon
Diégoune

N4

To Badioure (10km);
Sédhiou (90km);
Dakar (425km)

Casamance Nord

Presqu'île
des Oiseaux

N4

**Sanctuaire
Ornithologique
de la Pointe
de Kalissaye**

Tionk-Essil

Tendouk

Mangagoulak

Tobor
Koubalan

Niomoune

Affiniam
Barrage

Pointe
St George
Manatee Sanctuary

Djilapao

Ziguinchor

N6

Diogué

Bandial

**Île des
Oiseaux**
Airport

To Kolda
(188km)

To Dakar
Karabane

M'Lomp

Etama

Brin

N4

Nikine

Kagnout

Séléki
Essil

Enampor

**Île de
Karabane**

Loudia
Ouolof

Kamoubeul

Toubacouta

Cachouane
Elinkine

Oussouye
Ediougou

Diohère

Nyassia

Île d'Éguèye

Oukout

Niambalang

Senegalese Border
Post

Mpak

Diembéring
Beach

Diakène
Ouolof
Diakène
Diola

Basse Casamance

Guinea-Bissau
Border Post
São Domingos

Boucotte

**Parc National
de Basse-
Casamance (closed)**

Kaguite

To Ingore (40km);
Bissau (120km)

Airport

Cap Skiring
Beach
Kabrousse

Santiaba
Mandjak

Youtou

GUINEA-BISSAU

Marigot de Baïla

Marigot de Dioulou

Kalissaye

Marigot de

Casamance River

ATLANTIC OCEAN

Community & Village
Campements
4WD Only

SENEGAL

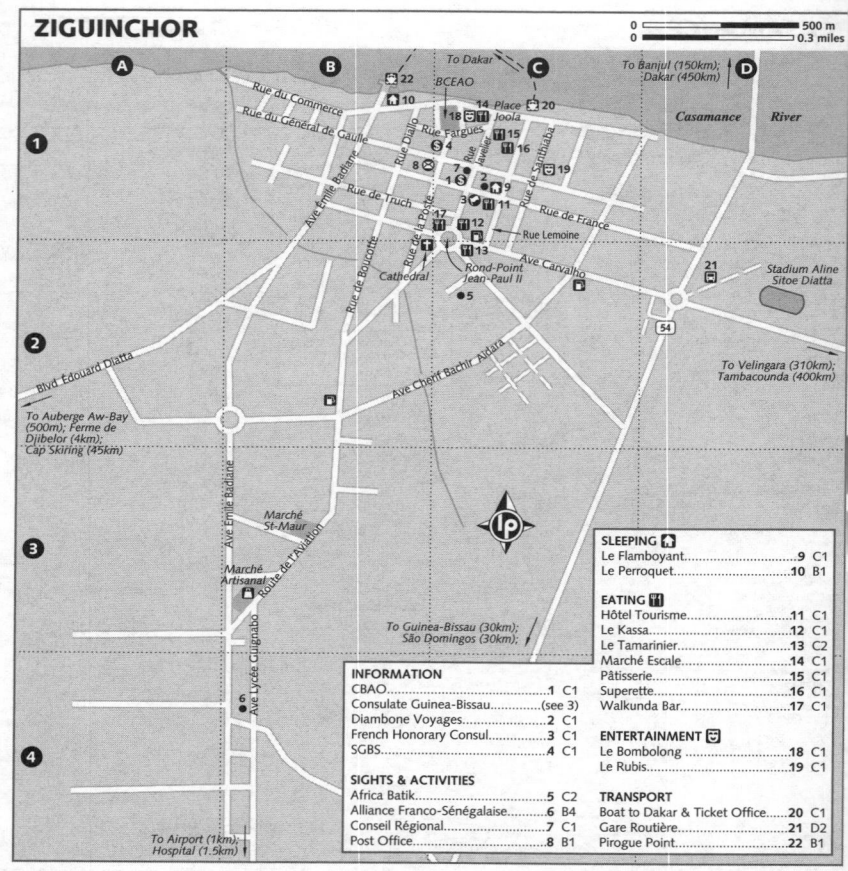

ZIGUINCHOR

INFORMATION
CBAO	**1** C1
Consulate Guinea-Bissau	(see 3)
Diambone Voyages	**2** C1
French Honorary Consul	**3** C1
SGBS	**4** C1

SIGHTS & ACTIVITIES
Africa Batik	**5** C2
Alliance Franco-Sénégalaise	**6** B4
Conseil Régional	**7** C1
Post Office	**8** B1

SLEEPING
Le Flamboyant	**9** C1
Le Perroquet	**10** B1

EATING
Hôtel Tourisme	**11** C1
Le Kassa	**12** C1
Le Tamarinier	**13** C2
Marché Escale	**14** C1
Pâtisserie	**15** C1
Superette	**16** C1
Walkunda Bar	**17** C1

ENTERTAINMENT
Le Bombolong	**18** C1
Le Rubis	**19** C1

TRANSPORT
Boat to Dakar & Ticket Office	**20** C1
Gare Routière	**21** D2
Pirogue Point	**22** B1

Getting There & Around

Twice a week, there's a safe, reliable and comfortable boat service to Dakar run by **Cosama** (in Ziguinchor 33 991 7200, in Dakar 33 821 2900; cosama@orange.sn). You buy your ticket (CFA15,500 to CFA30,500) in advance and in person at the port.

The *gare routière* is to the east of the city centre. There are frequent *sept-place* taxis to Dakar (CFA10,000, nine hours, 454km) and Cap Skiring (CFA1500). To get anywhere around town by private taxi costs CFA500.

OUSSOUYE

Roughly halfway between Ziguinchor and Cap Skiring, relaxed Oussouye is the main town in the Basse Casamance. For the local Diola

population, this town is of significance as it's home to an animist king who is often sought for advice.

Bikes can be hired and tours booked at **Casamance VTT** (Chez Benjamin; /fax 33 993 1004; www.casamancevtt.com).

Campement Villageois d'Oussouye (33 993 0015; http://campement.oussouye.org; s/d CFA4500/6000) and **Campement Emanaye** (77 573 6334; emanaye@yahoo.fr; s/d CFA4500/7000) are striking two-storey mud dwellings, an architectural style typical of the region. **Aljowe** (Chez François; 77 517 0267; s/apt per person CFA4000/7000) has cute rooms and mini-apartments in a redbrick *case à l'impluvium*.

All bush taxis between Ziguinchor and Cap Skiring pass through Oussouye (CFA1500).

POINTE ST GEORGE

Pointe St George is a stunning spot, couched between rice fields, forest and the Casamance River. It's also a Marine Protected Area and manatee sanctuary – one of the very few places in West Africa where you reliably get to see manatees. It's a rich birdwatching area to boot. The protection project is partly financed through the small village *campement*.

Contact **Océanium** (Map p487; ☎ 33 822 2441; www. oceanium.org; Rte de la Corniche-Est, Dakar; ☺ Mon-Sat) to arrange your stay.

ELINKINE & ÎLE DE KARABANE

Elinkine is a busy fishing village and jumping-off point for the peaceful Île de Karabane, a former French trading station (1836–1900). On the island, you can still see the Breton-style church, with dusty pews and crumbling statues.

In Elinkine, the simple but charming **Campement Villageois d'Elinkine** (☎ 77 376 9659; campementelinkine@free.fr; per person CFA8000) was newly restored and looked great when we passed.

On Karabane, **Campement Le Barracuda** (☎ 77 659 6001; r incl half/full board CFA7300/9800) has a recommended fishing and excursions centre, and helpful management. **Hôtel Carabane** (☎ 77 569 0284; hotelcarabane@yahoo.fr; r incl half/full board CFA16,500/25,000), in the former Catholic mission, is the most upmarket option on the isle.

For drinks and good food, try **Africando** (☎ 77 533 3842), nestled among the giant roots of a kapok tree.

Elinkine can be reached by minibus from Ziguinchor (CFA2000, two hours) or Oussouye (CFA600, one hour). For Karabane, take the public *pirogue* from Elinkine (CFA1500, five minutes, twice daily). Hiring a private *pirogue* costs around CFA15,000 one way.

CAP SKIRING

The beaches at Cap Skiring are some of the finest in West Africa and, better still, they are usually empty. Most *campements* and hotels are on the beach, 1km from the village, at the end of a dirt track off the Ziguinchor road.

Le Paradise (☎ 33 993 5303; r CFA14,000; ☒) is the best of a row of cheap *campements*. Opposite Club Med in Cap Skiring village, the small **Auberge Le Palmier** (☎ 33 993 5109; d from CFA10,000; ☒) is a decent budget bet, while the riverside **Kaloa les Palétuviers** (☎ 33 993 5210; www.hotel-kaloa.com; s/d incl breakfast CFA15,000/26,000; ☒ ☒) is more upmarket. Excellent options on the beach include **Villa des Pêcheurs** (☎ 33 993 5253; www.villadespecheurs.com;

s/d incl breakfast CFA19,000/23,500; ☒), which also has a brilliant restaurant, and tiny **Mansa Lodge** (☎ 33 993 5147; www.capsafari.com; s/d CFA30,000/44,000; ☒ ☒), where family vibes reign.

Cap Skiring has plenty of restaurants. Try **Chez Les Copains** (☎ 77 548 1593; Allée du Palétuvier; dishes around CFA2000) for Senegalese food, **Bar de la Mer** (☎ 33 993 5280; Kabrousse; d from CFA30,000) for seafood on the beach and **Le Djembé** (☎ 77 533 7692) for tasty French cuisine and live jazz.

Case Bambou (☎ 33 993 5178) is the flashest nightclub, and **Bakine** (☎ 33 641 5124; Croisement du Cap; ☺ 10pm-3am) hosts rootsy drumming jam sessions.

Cap Skiring's airport is served by a number of charter airlines. Otherwise it's a *sept-place* taxi (CFA1500) from Ziguinchor.

BOUCOTTE

A brief and bumpy taxi ride from Cap Skiring, Boucotte sits on a seemingly endless stretch of white beach, and offers excellent accommodation in the pretty bungalows of **Hôtel Maya** (☎ 77 575 6177; www.hotel-maya.com; s/d incl breakfast 23,000/36,000; ☒ ☒ ☒ ☒), right behind the beach.

Hiring a taxi from Cap Skiring to Boucotte should cost you around CFA3000, though the hotel can arrange pick-up.

DIEMBÉRING & CACHOUANE

A tiny village surrounded by kapok trees, Diembéring is becoming more popular with tourists. Stay at **Campement Asseb** (☎ 77 541 3472; sembesene@yahoo.fr; per person incl breakfast CFA5500) to support the local community. A stunning 4km hike from there (or a *pirogue* ride from Île de Karabane) takes you to Cachouane, where Papis, the friendly manager of **Campement Sounka** (☎ 77 645 3707; per person incl half board CFA 8500), can take you dolphin spotting.

KAFOUNTINE & ABÉNÉ

The engine of these villages is fuelled by marijuana, grown illegally on neighbouring islands. They are favourites with dreadlock-sporting *djembe* players and birdwatchers, and attract plenty of tourist hustlers.

Most of Kafountine's places are a couple of kilometres from the village, near the beach. A recommended cheapo is **Le Bolonga** (☎ 33 994 8515; per person incl breakfast CFA7500), with clean rooms in a redbrick building behind the beach.

our pick **Esperanto Lodge** (Chez Eric; ☎ 33 936 9519; www.esperantolodge.com; per person incl breakfast CFA13,500;

⊠ ▣) is beautifully located between the beach and a creek, and is highly recommended. Next door, **Le Fouta Djalon** (☎ 77 503 9922; lefoutadjalon@ yahoo.fr; r CFA15,000; ⊠) nestles behind some beautiful dunes and has a clean stretch of beach. For food, head to **Mama Africa** (dishes CFA1500) in the village for generous portions of rice.

In Abéné village **Maison Sunjata** (☎ /fax 33 994 8610; info@senegambia.de; s/d CFA10,000/16,000) has large, whitewashed rooms, while **Le Kossey** (☎ 77 223 8052; r per person CFA6000) puts you up in simple huts spread across a vast tropical garden. The main restaurant in town is the lively **Chez Vero** (☎ 77 617 1714; meals CFA3000; ⏰ 10am-10pm).

From Ziguinchor, *sept-place* taxis (CFA2200) run directly to Kafountine. Abéné can be reached by any transport going to Kafountine, although the village is 2km off the main road, and the beach a further 2km walk.

NIAFOURANG

Between the river and sea, **Tilibo Horizons** (☎ 77 501 3879; bungalow incl half board CFA11,000) is a small *campement villageois*. It's simple, but run with a rare passion by the very available Ousmane Sané. If you're interested in hidden Casamance corners, ask him to arrange a tour.

Phone Tilibo Horizons to pick you up from Ziguinchor or Bandikaki, where the *sept-place* from Ziguinchor to Kafountine can drop you off.

SENEGAL DIRECTORY

ACCOMMODATION

Senegal has a very wide range of places to stay, from top-class hotels to dirty dosshouses. Dakar has the biggest choice, though you're

---

PRACTICALITIES

■ *Focus on Africa* (BBC) often has excellent news stories on Senegal, and is sold in the country.

■ If you read French, *Jeune Afrique* and *L'Intelligent* are good sources of political and cultural news.

■ The electricity supply in Senegal is 220V. Plugs have two round pins, as in France and elsewhere in continental Europe.

■ Senegal uses the metric system.

---

hard-pushed to find a budget place there. Many rural areas, particularly the Casamance, have pleasant *campements*. All hotels and *campements* charge a tourist tax of CFA600 per person per night.

BUSINESS HOURS

Banks Usually close around 4pm; only a few open Saturday morning.
Business and government offices Open 8.30am to 1pm and 2.30pm to 5pm Monday to Friday.
Restaurants Offer lunch from noon to 2.30pm and dinner from 7pm onwards; many are closed on Sunday.

DANGERS & ANNOYANCES

There are two main dangers you may encounter in Senegal: civil unrest in Casamance (see the boxed text, p498) and street crime in Dakar (see p486).

EMBASSIES & CONSULATES

If you need to find an embassy that is not listed here, check www.ausenegal.com/prac tique_en/ambassad.htm. Most embassies close late morning or early afternoon Monday to Friday, so set off early.
Canada (Map p487; ☎ 33 889 4700; Immeuble Sorano, 3rd fl, 45-47 Blvd de la République, Plateau)
Cape Verde (Map p488; ☎ 33 821 3936; 3 Blvd el Haji Djily Mbaye, Plateau)
Côte d'Ivoire (Map p485; ☎ 33 869 0270; www. ambaci-dakar.org; Allées Seydou Nourou Tall, Point E)
France (Map p488; ☎ 33 839 5100; www.ambafrance -sn.org; 1 Rue Amadou Assane Ndoye, Dakar) There's also an honorary consul in Ziguinchor (Map p500).
Gambia (Map p488; ☎ 33 821 7230; 11 Rue de Thiong)
Germany (Map p487; ☎ 33 889 4884; www.dakar.diplo. de; 20 Ave Pasteur)
Ghana (Map p485; ☎ 33 869 4053; Rue 6, Point E)
Guinea (Map p485; ☎ 33 824 8606; Rue 7, Point E)
Guinea-Bissau Dakar (Map p485; ☎ 33 824 5922; Rue 6, Point E; ⏰ 8am-12.30pm Mon-Fri); Ziguinchor (Map p500; ☎ 33 991 1046; ⏰ 8am-2pm Mon-Fri)
Mali (Map p485; ☎ 33 824 6252; 23 Rte de la Corniche-Ouest; ⏰ 9am-1pm Mon-Fri)
Mauritania (Map p485; ☎ 33 823 5344; Fann Mermoz; ⏰ 8am-2pm Mon-Fri)
Morocco (Map p485; ☎ 33 824 3836; Ave Cheikh Anta Diop, Mermoz)
Spain (Map p488; ☎ 33 821 3081; 18-20 Ave Nelson Mandela)
UK (Map p487; ☎ 33 823 7392; 20 Rue du Dr Guillet) One block north of Hôpital le Dantec.
USA (Map p488; ☎ 33 823 4296; Ave Jean XXIII)

EMERGENCIES
Fire ☎ 18
Police ☎ 17
SOS Medecin ☎ 33 889 1515
SUMA Urgences ☎ 33 824 2418

FESTIVALS & EVENTS
December, May and June are the best times for music and arts festivals, including the **Saint-Louis Jazz Festival** (☎ 33 9612455; www.saintlouisjazz.com, in French), the **Dak'Art Biennale** (☎ 33 823 0918; www.dakart.org, in French) and **Kay Fecc** (☎ 33 824 5154; www.kaayfecc.com, in French).

The **Grand Magal** pilgrimage and festival is held annually 48 days after the Islamic New Year in Touba to celebrate the return from exile of the founder of the Mouride Islamic brotherhood.

HOLIDAYS
As well as the Islamic religious holidays listed in the Africa Directory chapter (p1140), the principal public holidays in Senegal are the following:
New Year's Day 1 January
Independence Day 4 April
Workers Day 1 May
Assumption 15 August

INTERNET ACCESS
Internet cafes are plentiful, and the numbers of wi-fi spaces is increasing almost daily (particularly in Dakar). Surfing costs about CFA300 per hour; wi-fi in hotel lobbies and bars is usually free with a purchase.

MAPS
The **DTGC** (Direction des Travaux Géographiques et Cartographiques; www.dtgc.au-senegal.com) produces detailed regional maps that are on sale in Dakar bookstores. On www.au-senegal.com you will find an excellent interactive map, listing major sites, hotels, restaurants and more.

MONEY
The unit of currency is the West African CFA franc. Banks with ATMs are found in all larger towns across the country. Banks and exchange bureaux tend to offer similar rates; the currency most easily changed is the euro.

POST
Senegal's postal service is inexpensive though not entirely reliable.

TELEPHONE
Good mobile phone coverage means that many of the public *télécentres* have now closed. You'll still find them, but it's much easier to buy an Orange, Tigo or Expresso SIM card. Top-up credit is available absolutely anywhere. Network coverage (especially for Orange) is excellent across the country.

The country code is ☎ 221. For directory assistance dial ☎ 1212.

TIME
Senegal is at GMT/UTC, which for most European visitors means there is no or very little time difference. There is no daylight saving time.

VISAS
Visas are not needed by citizens of the EU, Ecowas, Canada, Norway, South Africa, Japan, Israel, USA and some other (mainly African) countries. Tourist visas for one to three months cost about US$20 to US$40.

Visa Extensions
If you don't need a visa, just hop across the Gambian border and earn another three months on re-entry to Senegal. Otherwise, submit a request to the **Ministère de l'Intérieur** (Map p487; Ave Jean Jaurès, Dakar).

Visas for Onward Travel
You can get visas for other African countries in Dakar, often within 24 hours. Each requires two photos. For embassy contact details, see opposite.

TRANSPORT IN SENEGAL

GETTING THERE & AWAY
Air
Dakar is one of Africa's transport hubs, with links across Africa, Europe and America. Senegal's main airport is **Léopold Sédar Senghor International Airport** (DKR; ☎ 24hr info line 77 628 1010; www.aeroportdakar.com).

Airlines servicing Senegal with offices in Dakar include the following (see www.ausenegal.com for a full listing):
Afriqiyah Airways (8U; Map p488; ☎ 33 849 4930; www.afriqiyah.be)
Air France (AF; Map p488; ☎ 33 839 7777; www.airfrance.fr)
Air Ivoire (VU; Map p488; ☎ 33 889 0280; www.airivoire.com)

SENEGAL

Brussels Airlines (SN; Map p488; ☎ 33 823 0460; www.brusselsairlines.com)
Ethiopian Airlines (ET; Map p488; ☎ 33 823 5552; www.flyethiopian.com; 16 Ave Léopold Sédar Senghor)
Kenya Airways (KQ; Map p488; ☎ 33 823 0070; www.kenya-airways.com)
Royal Air Maroc (AT; Map p488; ☎ 33 849 4748; www.royalairmaroc.com)
South African Airways (SA; Map p485; ☎ 33 869 4000; www.flysaa.com)
TACV Cabo Verde Airlines (VR; Map p488; ☎ 33 821 3968; www.flytacv.com)
Virgin Nigeria (VK; Map p488; ☎ 33 889 9010; www.virginnigeria.com)

Land
THE GAMBIA
From Dakar there are *sept-place* taxis south to Karang (CFA6000, six hours) at the Gambian border, where you connect to Barra and then via ferry to Banjul (see p323).

From southern Senegal, *sept-place* taxis run regularly between Ziguinchor and Serekunda (CFA4500, five hours), and between Kafountine and Brikama (CFA3000, two hours).

In eastern Senegal, *sept-place* taxis go from Tambacounda to Vélingara (CFA1500, three hours), and from there to Basse Santa Su (CFA1000, 45 minutes, 27km).

GUINEA
Most traffic is by *sept-place* from Diaoubé (Senegal), via Koundara (Guinea), where you may have to change, and some goes via Kédougou (Senegal). The very rough ride costs CFA20,000 and takes up to 48 hours.

GUINEA-BISSAU
Sept-place taxis leave every morning from Ziguinchor for Bissau (CFA6000, 147km, four hours), via the main border post at São Domingos, and Ingore. The road is sealed and in good condition. Fights flared up around the border crossing in 2009; always check the latest situation before setting out.

MALI
A popular, though tedious way to travel from Senegal to Mali is on the Dakar–Bamako 'express' train. There's no longer a regular schedule; you need to check at the train station in Dakar (see p486). The ride can take anything from 48 hours up to a week.

Sept-place taxis leave regularly from Tambacounda to Kidira (CFA5000, three hours), where you cross the border to Diboli in Mali, from where long-distance buses run to Kayes and Bamako. If you're brave, you can do Dakar–Bamako by long-distance bus (CFA22,000); buses leave from Gare Routière Pompiers (Map p487) in Dakar.

Roadworks have started between Saraya (Senegal) and Kita (Mali). Once completed (expected in late 2010), this will be an attractive option for entering Mali from the Bassari country.

MAURITANIA
Sept-place taxis run regularly from Dakar to the main border point at Rosso (CFA6000, six hours, 384km), a crowded, hasslesome place, where four daily ferries (CFA2000/3000 per passenger/car) cross to Rosso-Mauritania.

If you have your own wheels, you can cross at the Maka Diama dam, 97km southwest of Rosso and just north of Saint-Louis, where the border crossing is swift.

GETTING AROUND
Air
As Air Sénégal International went bankrupt in 2009, there were no internal flights at the time of writing. Check whether a new carrier has taken on the routes.

Local Transport
The quickest (though still uncomfortable) way of getting around the country is by *sept-place* taxi – battered Peugeots that negotiate even the most ragged routes. Slightly cheaper, but infinitely less reliable are the minibuses (Ndiaga Ndiaye or *grand car*), carrying around 40 people. Vehicles leave from the *gare routière* when they're full, and they fill up quickest in the morning, before 8am.

Taxi prices are theoretically fixed, though they're steadily increasing as petrol prices rise. There's an extra, negotiable charge for luggage (10% to 20% of the bill).

Cars mourides (large buses, financed by the Mouride brotherhood) connect major towns in Senegal. Book ahead of travel. In Dakar, go to **Gare Routière Pompiers** (Map p487; ☎ 33 821 8585; off cnr Ave Malick Sy), where most *sept-places* also go from. Arriving in Dakar, *sept-places* stop at Gare Routière Colobane (Map p485).

SENEGAL

Sierra Leone

Sierra Leone has largely stayed out of the news lately, which, considering how it earned most of its press in the 1990s, is a good thing. The decade-long civil war garnered regular headlines thanks to widespread atrocities committed by rebel soldiers, many of them not yet in their teens.

But oh how things have changed. Peace was declared in 2002 and it has blossomed. Life has largely returned to normal and today Sierra Leone is one of West Africa's safest destinations. Reconstruction continues apace, investors are arriving in droves and travellers are trickling in. The one recent event that did make headlines was a free and fair election.

With some of the most perfect palm-lined sands on the continent, it won't be long before Sierra Leone takes its place in Europe's packaged-beach-holiday scene, but for now visitors can have the surf outside the capital pretty much to themselves. Travel to the provinces, where roads are often abysmal and facilities usually basic (but getting better), remains in the realm of the adventurous, but with cheerful people and wonderful parks, the rewards are many.

To be sure, Sierra Leone still has problems. It ranks third from last (after many years at the very bottom) in the UN's Human Development Index, unemployment remains high and corruption seems to be getting worse. But most locals hang on to their optimism and most visitors come away enchanted.

FAST FACTS

- **Area** 72,325 sq km
- **ATMs** Available in Freetown
- **Borders** Guinea and Liberia
- **Budget** from US$15 per day
- **Capital** Freetown
- **Languages** English, Krio, Mende, Temne
- **Money** Leone; US$1 = Le3825, €1 = Le5540
- **Population** 6.4 million
- **Seasons** Dry (mid-November to mid-May), wet (mid-May to mid-November)
- **Telephone** Country code ☎ 232; international access code ☎ 00
- **Time** GMT/UTC
- **Visas** Required by everyone except most West African citizens. Should be arranged before arrival.

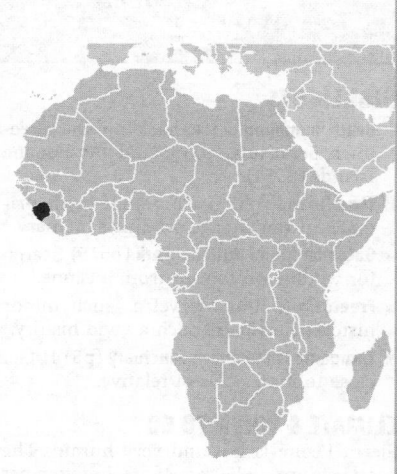

SIERRA LEONE

SIERRA LEONE

NP	National Park
WS	Wildlife Sanctuary
FR	Forest Reserve

HIGHLIGHTS

- **Beach bumming** Kick back on the Freetown peninsula (p513) and the Banana Islands (p514).
- **Tiwai Island** (p515) Commune with primates at the famous wildlife sanctuary.
- **Outamba-Kilimi National Park** (p515) Search for wildlife on foot or from a canoe.
- **Freetown** (p509) Marvel as such minor historic sites paint such a vivid history.
- **Tacugama Chimpanzee Sanctuary** (p514) Get close to man's closest relative.

CLIMATE & WHEN TO GO

Sierra Leone is hot and very humid. The coast gets up to 3250mm of precipitation per year during the mid-May to mid-November wet season. July and August are the wettest months, except in the far south, which gets a bit of a break then.

The best time to visit is November, after the rains and before the dusty harmattan winds blow in. During the rainy season, washed out roads make travel to some destinations difficult or impossible.

ITINERARIES

- **One Week** Many people spend their whole week at the beach, though it's worth taking a few days upcountry to visit Tiwai Island Wildlife Sanctuary (p515) and a town or two. If you're here for the wildlife you can get to both Tiwai and

Outamba-Kilimi National Park (p515) and still have a day on the sands.

- **Two Weeks** You can see most of the country without travelling too fast.

HISTORY

The North American slave trade was effectively launched from Freetown in 1560, and by the 18th century Portuguese and British trading settlements lined the coast. In the late 1700s, freed slaves from places such as Jamaica and Nova Scotia were brought to the new settlement of Freetown. Soon after, Britain abolished slavery and Sierra Leone became a British colony. Many subsequent settlers were liberated from slaving ships intercepted by the British navy and brought here. These people became known as Krios and assumed an English lifestyle together with an air of superiority.

But things didn't all run smoothly in this brave new world. Black and white settlers dabbling in the slave trade, disease, rebellion and attacks by the French were all characteristics of 19th-century Sierra Leone. Most importantly, indigenous people were discriminated against by the British and Krios and in 1898 a ferocious uprising by the Mende began, ostensibly in opposition to a hut tax.

Diamonds Are Forever

Independence came in 1961, but the 1960s and 1970s were characterised by coups (once there were three in one year, an all-African record), a shift of power to the indigenous Mende and Temne peoples, and the establishment of a one-party state (which lasted into the 1980s). By the early 1990s the country was saddled with a shambolic economy and rampant corruption. Then the civil war began.

It's entirely possible that buried in the depths of Foday Sankoh's Revolutionary United Front (RUF) was a desire to end the corruption and abuses of power committed by the ruling military-backed elites in Freetown, who had turned the country into a basket case. But any high ideals were quickly forgotten, replaced by a ferocious desire for Sierra Leone's diamond and goldfields, with looting, robbery, rape, mutilation and summary execution all tools of the RUF's trade. While their troops plundered to make ends meet, Charles Taylor in Liberia and the RUF's leaders enriched themselves from diamonds smuggled south.

The Sierra Leone government was pretty ineffective and tried using South African mercenaries against the RUF who, bolstered by disaffected army elements and Liberian irregulars, were making gains across the country. In 1996, elections were held and Ahmad Tejan Kabbah was declared president, but a year later, after peace talks had brought some hope, the Armed Forces Revolutionary Council (AFRC) grabbed control of government and decided to share power with the RUF. By this time fractionalisation and desertion on both sides had led to an utter free-for-all, with the civilian population suffering atrocities at every turn.

Hopes & Fears

In March 1998 Ecomog, a Nigerian-led peacekeeping force, retook Freetown and reinstated Kabbah. Some sort of peace held until January 1999, when the RUF and AFRC launched 'Operation No Living Thing'. The ensuing carnage in and around Freetown killed 6000 people, mutilated many more (lopping a limb off was an RUF calling card) and prompted the government to sign the Lomé Peace Agreement. A massive UN peacekeeping mission (Unamsil) was deployed, but 10 months later it came under attack from the RUF. Three hundred UN troops were abducted, but as the RUF closed in on Freetown in mid-2000 the British government deployed 1000 paratroopers and an aircraft carrier to prevent a massacre and shift the balance of power back to Kabbah's government and UN forces. By February 2002 the RUF was disarmed and its leaders captured. Elections were held a few months later; Kabbah was re-elected and the RUF's political wing soundly defeated.

Unamsil became the largest and most expensive peacekeeping mission in UN history to that time, and also one of its most effective. The last of the 17,500 soldiers departed in 2005. Peace had won.

Sierra Leone Today

September 2007 brought about a peaceful change of government via the ballot box. With President Kabbah stepping aside after serving his constitutionally permitted second term, Sierra Leoneans gave power to insurance broker Ernest Bai Koroma of the opposition All People's Congress (APC) party, which also netted a parliamentary majority. There was sporadic violence before and after the voting, but both candidates denounced it and international observers declared the vote 'free, fair and credible'. Sierra Leoneans are already gripped by party posturing in the lead-up to the 2012 elections.

CULTURE

The two largest of the 18 tribal groups, the Temnes of the north and Mendes of the south, each make up about one-third of the population. Krios, mostly living in Freetown, constitute about 1.5% of the population but a large percentage of the professional class.

About 75% of Sierra Leoneans are Muslim; most of the 30% who are Christian live in the south. Sierra Leoneans are very tolerant, and mixed marriages are common.

The Mendes and Temnes operate a system of secret societies responsible for maintaining culture and tradition. For example, if you see young girls with their faces painted white, you'll know that they're in the process of being initiated. They wear coloured beads when finished.

When Sierra Leoneans get together, talk always seems to turn to politics, development and corruption. The war did much to foster nationalism (everyone suffered together), but the elections showed that a significant north–south/Temne–Mende divide remains and it has become natural for the political parties to exploit it. Some people worry about how this will play out in coming years.

Sierra Leone is known for its fabrics, especially country cloth, a coarse, naturally dyed cotton material, and *gara,* a thin tie-dyed or batik-printed sheet. Distinctive Temne basketry also makes good souvenirs.

Sierra Leone's principal contribution to the world of music is *maringa* (AKA palm-wine music), but it's been on the decline since its best-known exponent, SE Rogie, passed away in 1994. Sierra Leone's traditional dances are some of the most animated in West Africa.

The war spawned many harrowing books, fiction and nonfiction, and Graham Greene's colonial-era classic *The Heart of the Matter* is set in Freetown. Dozens of poets share their work online at www.sierra-leone .org/poetry.html.

FOOD & DRINK

Sierra Leone is known for its cuisine, and every town has at least one *cookery* (basic eating house) serving *chop* (meals). Rice is the staple and *plasas* (pounded potato or cassava leaves, cooked with palm oil and often fish or beef) is the most common sauce. Other typical dishes include okra sauce, groundnut stew and pepper soup. Street food, such as fried chicken, roasted corn, chicken kebabs, and *fry fry* (simple sandwiches), is easy to find.

The top-selling beer, Star, is reasonable. *Poyo* (palm wine) is light and fruity, but getting used to the smell and the wildlife floating in your cup takes a while.

ENVIRONMENT

Sierra Leone's coast is lined with cracking beaches, mangrove swamps and many islands. The Freetown peninsula is one of the few places in West Africa where mountains rise near the sea. Inland are sweeping plains punctuated by random mountains, including Mt Bintumani (1945m), one of West Africa's highest peaks. About 30% of the country is forested and significant patches of primary rainforest remain in the south and east.

Outamba-Kilimi National Park (which still has elephants) in the north, and Tiwai Island Wildlife Sanctuary (incredible for primates) in the south are worth a visit, but don't expect East African–style wildlife encounters.

FREETOWN

☎ 022 / pop 1 million

Reminders of the recent violence have largely disappeared in the capital, but evidence of the nation's growing pains is never far away. Freetown is still crammed with war victims who've chosen not to return to their upcountry homes, traffic jams last from morning until night and there hasn't been reliable electricity since the 1980s.

But, despite the difficulties, Freetown feels more relaxed than other large West African cities, and the beautiful setting compensates for the chaos. Besides, if you spend all your time in the tourist-focused Lumley and Aberdeen areas you'll rarely encounter these problems. But when you do head into the heart of town to explore the historical sights and markets, you'll soon find there's more to the city than initially meets the eye. Freetown is filthy and frantic, but you can't help loving it.

ORIENTATION

Central Freetown, where most services are still found, is set out on a grid pattern with Siaka Stevens St as the main thoroughfare. Budget hotels are clustered near PZ Turntable, which stays busy (and thus generally safe) late into the night. Aberdeen and Lumley, where most visitors spend their time, lie 30 minutes to an hour west, depending on traffic.

INFORMATION
Cultural Centres

British Council (Map p512; ☎ 224683; www.british council.org; Tower Hill; ☼ 8.30am-4.30pm Mon-Thu, 8.30am-2pm Fri)

Emergency

☎ 999

Internet Access

Lumley Beach Dot Com (off Map pp510-11; Lumley Turntable; per hr US$1.30; ☼ 24hr)
Sylvia Blyden Dot Com (Map p512; 24 Garrison St; per hr US$1; ☼ 24hr)

Medical Services

Central Pharmacy (Map p512; ☎ 076-615503; 30 Wallace Johnson St)
Choitram Memorial Hospital (off Map pp510-11; ☎ 232598; Hill Station) Freetown's best hospital.

Money

Forex bureaus are found throughout the city. Rates at the airport's exchange bureau aren't horrible, but you'll do better in town. **ProCredit** Central (Map p512; 11 Rawdon St) Lumley (Off Map pp510-11; 157 Wilkinson Rd) bank has Visa card–linked ATMs.

Post

DHL Central (Map p512; ☎ 033-315299; 15 Rawdon St) Greater (Map pp510-11; ☎ 236156; 30 Main Motor Rd)
Post office (Map p512; 27 Siaka Stevens St)

Tourist Information

Conservation Society of Sierra Leone (Map pp510-11; ☎ 033-470043; cssl_03@yahoo.com; 2 Pike St; ☼ 9am-5pm Mon-Fri) Very helpful for travellers to Sierra Leone's natural reserves, including the Turtle Islands.
Tourist Information Office (Map pp510-11; ☎ 236620; Lumley Beach Rd; ☼ 8am-6.30pm) Has little to offer other than postcards.

Travel Agencies

IPC Travel Central (Map p512; ☎ 221481; info@ ipctravel.com; 22 Siaka Stevens St) Greater (Map pp510-11; ☎ 231543; 10 Sir Samuel Lewis Rd)
Visit Sierra Leone (Map pp510-11; ☎ 076-877618; www.visitsierraleone.org; 28 Main Motor Rd) Doesn't sell flights out of Freetown but handles everything else visitors might need, including transport, guides and landing visas.

DANGERS & ANNOYANCES

Freetown has less of a crime problem than most other African capitals, but petty thieves work the markets, the Tagrin ferry and Lumley Beach. Don't walk on the beach alone, even in the daytime. The East End is rough as a badger, so watch your back in the light and stay out at night.

Beach boys and would-be gigolos are becoming more common on Lumley Beach, but they're tame compared to those in the Gambia.

SIGHTS & ACTIVITIES

The city's historic sites are modest but interesting. The 500-year-old **Cotton Tree** (Map p512), Freetown's principal landmark and most beloved resident, casts its shadow on the **Sierra Leone National Museum** (Map p512; ☎ 223555; Siaka Stevens St; admission free; ☼ 10.30am-4pm Mon-Fri), which has a small collection of juju trinkets and historical artefacts, and the ornate **Law Courts** (Map p512; Siaka

SIERRA LEONE

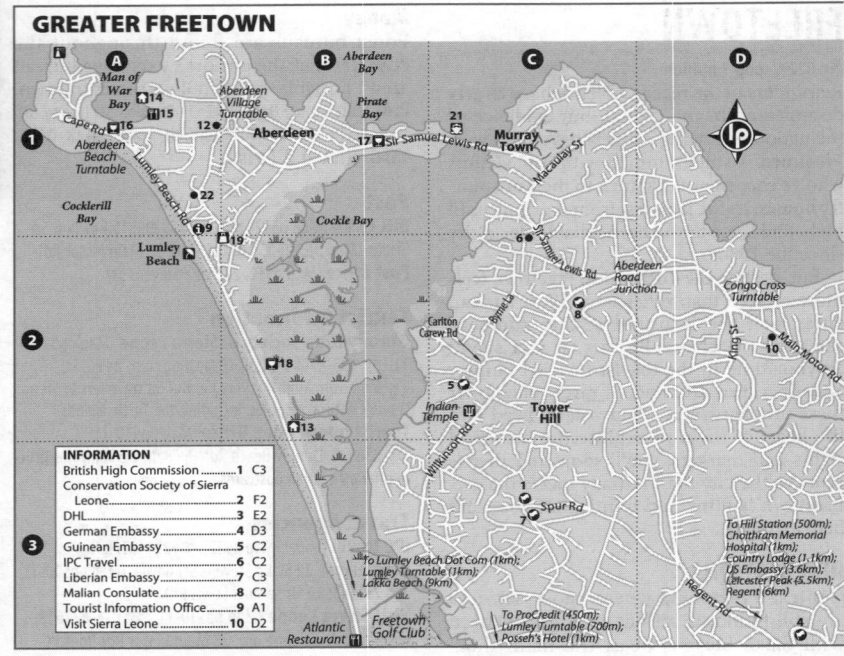

GREATER FREETOWN

INFORMATION		
British High Commission	1	C3
Conservation Society of Sierra		
Leone	2	F2
DHL	3	E2
German Embassy	4	D3
Guinean Embassy	5	C2
IPC Travel	6	C2
Liberian Embassy	7	C2
Malian Consulate	8	C2
Tourist Information Office	9	A1
Visit Sierra Leone	10	D2

Stevens St). The **State House** (Map p512; Independence Ave), incorporating the bastions and lion gate from Fort Thornton (built at the turn of the 19th century), is just up the hill, and the 1820 **St John's Maroon Church** (Map p512; Siaka Stevens St) is two blocks southwest.

The ancestors of nearly all present-day Krios passed through **King's Yard Gate** (Map p512; Wallace Johnson St) to await resettlement by the British. Many of these new arrivals climbed the nearby **Old Wharf Steps** (Map p512), sometimes erroneously called the Portuguese Steps. The area west of Tower Hill is a good place to gawp at interesting 19th-century, wood-framed **Krio houses**.

You need not be a rail fan to enjoy the **National Railway Museum** (Map pp510–11; Cline St; admission free; ☽ 9.30am-5pm Mon-Sat) in Clinetown, but it helps.

Freetown's beauty and potential show clearly when seen from above. The views are especially good from **Leicester Peak** (off Map pp510–11), the big hill with the transmission towers. It's 1.7km to the top up a good paved road starting opposite the US embassy.

Lumley Beach (Map pp510–11) is the busiest beach on the peninsula but not the best.

Development is coming fast, but for now it still makes for a low-key afternoon.

Visitors are welcome to stop by the wishfully named Freetown Cultural Village to watch the **Sierra Leone National Dance Troupe** (Map pp510–11; Cape Rd) practise; usually on weekday mornings around 8.30am to 10.30am.

SLEEPING

Quality hotels tend to fill up fast, so reservations are a good idea.

Place Guest House (Map p512; ☎ 076-662358; 42 Rawdon St; s without bathroom US$12; r US$14-20) The best budget hotel in Freetown, the Place is simple but clean.

YMCA (Map p512; ☎ 223608; www.ymca-sl.org; 32 Fort St; s without bathroom US$13, d & tr with/without bathroom US$48/25; P ⊒) Rooms at the revamped Y are now pretty decent, though ambitiously priced. The views over the city are a nice bonus, however.

China Town Guest House (Map pp510–11; ☎ 076-625239; 84 Lumley Beach Rd; r US$75-85; P ⊗) The priced-right rooms at this Oriental-themed complex lie just across the road from a quiet stretch of Lumley Beach.

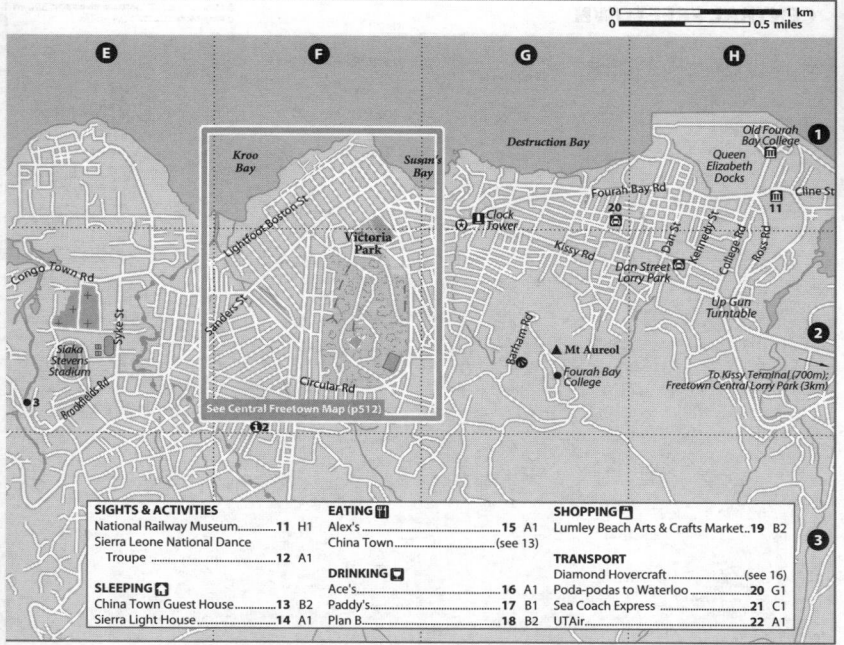

SIGHTS & ACTIVITIES		EATING		SHOPPING	
National Railway Museum	**11** H1	Alex's	**15** A1	Lumley Beach Arts & Crafts Market	**19** B2
Sierra Leone National Dance		China Town	(see 13)		
Troupe	**12** A1			TRANSPORT	
		DRINKING		Diamond Hovercraft	(see 16)
SLEEPING		Ace's	**16** A1	Poda-podas to Waterloo	**20** G1
China Town Guest House	**13** B2	Paddy's	**17** B1	Sea Coach Express	**21** C1
Sierra Light House	**14** A1	Plan B	**18** B2	UTAir	**22** A1

Sierra Light House (Map pp510–11; ☎ 076-706036; 5 Man of War Bay; s/d US$95/105; 🅿 ❌ 🖳 🛜) Though the building is profoundly ugly from the out-side, all 38 of the large rooms have a balcony sticking right out over the bay.

Country Lodge (off Map pp510–11; ☎ 076-691000; www.countrylodgesl.com; Hill Station; r US$150-195, ste US$250-300; 🅿 ❌ 🖳 🛜 🏊) The first choice for Freetown's most discerning visitors, Country Lodge has lovely rooms, most with big views. All rooms have the expected mod cons and the complex features a tennis court, a gym and a pool large enough for a real swim.

EATING

ourpick **Diaspora Café** (Map p512; ☎ 076-411144; 2 Priscilla St; meals US$2.50-10; 🕑 lunch daily, dinner Mon-Sat; ❌ 🛜 🔢) This wonderful little oasis is a sliver of sophistication. The food, a mix of local and beyond, is excellent, and although it encompasses only a few shelves, this is also Sierra Leone's best bookstore.

China Town (Map pp510–11; ☎ 076-625239; 84 Lumley Beach Rd; meals US$3-26.50; 🕑 lunch & dinner; ❌) Arguably Freetown's best Chinese food; served with views of the beach or actually right on it.

Café de la Rose (Map p512; ☎ 076-772919; 2 Howe St; meals US$3.50-8.50; 🕑 lunch & dinner Mon-Sat; ❌) Popular with bankers and businesspeople, Rose serves tasty local dishes indoors and on a breezy 1st-floor patio.

Alex's (Map pp510–11; ☎ 076-679272; off Cape Rd; meals US$5-23; 🕑 lunch Sat & Sun, dinner Tue-Sun) Freetown's loveliest dining spot looks west over Man of War Bay from under the palm trees. Seafood is the speciality, but the large menu is global. The adjacent sports bar has projection TVs and a pool table.

Delicious (Map p512; ☎ 076-610797; 67 Siaka Stevens St; meals US$8.50-17; 🕑 lunch & dinner Mon-Sat; ❌ ❌ 🔢) Freetown's first Indian restaurant, which also serves European food, is one of the most pleasant sitting spots downtown.

Most downtown restaurants close by 7pm, though street-food vendors work their can-dlelit stalls around PZ Turntable late into the night.

DRINKING & ENTERTAINMENT

Paddy's (Map pp510–11; 63 Sir Samuel Lewis Rd) Long Freetown's most famous bar, Paddy's is the one place where everyone, no matter what

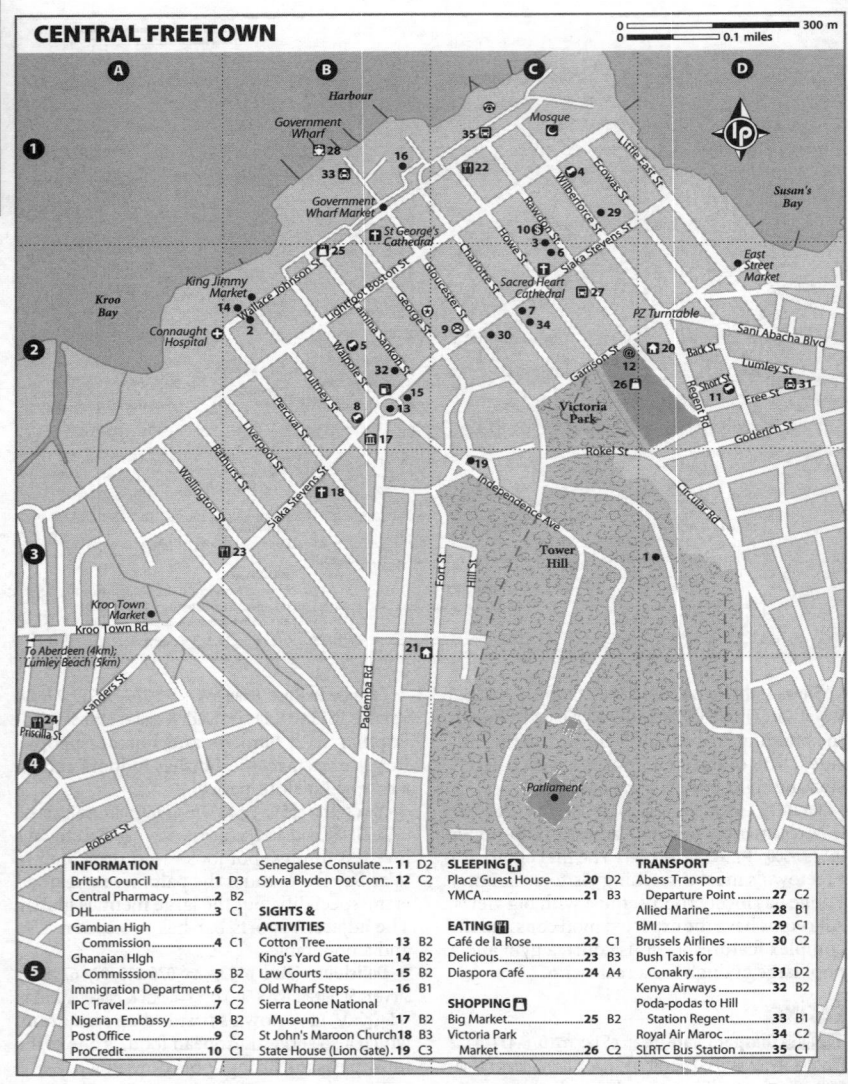

CENTRAL FREETOWN

INFORMATION			SIGHTS &		
British Council	1	D3	Senegalese Consulate	11	D2
Central Pharmacy	2	B2	Sylvia Blyden Dot Com	12	C2
DHL	3	C1	SIGHTS & ACTIVITIES		
Gambian High Commission	4	C1	Cotton Tree	13	B2
Ghanaian High Commisssion	5	B2	King's Yard Gate	14	B2
Immigration Department	6	C2	Law Courts	15	B2
IPC Travel	7	C2	Old Wharf Steps	16	B1
Nigerian Embassy	8	B2	Sierra Leone National Museum	17	B2
Post Office	9	C2	St John's Maroon Church	18	B3
ProCredit	10	C1	State House (Lion Gate)	19	C3

SLEEPING			TRANSPORT		
Place Guest House	20	D2	Abess Transport Departure Point	27	C2
YMCA	21	B3	Allied Marine	28	B1
EATING			BMI	29	C1
Café de la Rose	22	C1	Brussels Airlines	30	C2
Delicious	23	B3	Bush Taxis for Conakry	31	D2
Diaspora Café	24	A4	Kenya Airways	32	B2
SHOPPING			Poda-podas to Hill Station Regent	33	B1
Big Market	25	B2	Royal Air Maroc	34	C2
Victoria Park Market	26	C2	SLRTC Bus Station	35	C1

their stripe, can really let their hair down, at the bar or on the dance floor.

Ace's (Map pp510–11; 74 Cape Rd; ☻7pm–late) The internationally renowned Refugee All Stars play this large, multifaceted venue on Thursday nights.

Plan B (Map pp510–11; Lumley Beach Rd) A jazz-infused wine bar.

SHOPPING

Most people do their souvenir shopping at the **Lumley Beach Arts & Crafts Market** (Map pp510–11), but the **Big Market** (Basket Market; Map p512; Wallace Johnson St) downtown is better – besides the usual textiles and woodcarvings, it also offers many traditional household goods. **Victoria Park Market** (Map p512; Garrison St),

---

TO/FROM THE AIRPORT

Lungi International Airport is inconveniently located across the Sierra Leone River from Freetown. The fastest ways to town are **UTAir** (Map pp510-11; ☎ 033-807420; one way US$80) helicopters, followed by **Diamond** (Map pp510-11; ☎ 076-614888; one way/round trip US$30/50) hovercraft. Both drop and depart at Aberdeen, but they don't meet every flight. **Sea Coach Express** (Map pp510-11; ☎ 033-111118; one way US$40) runs slower, smaller boats to Aberdeen Bridge for every flight. **Allied Marine** (Map p512; ☎ 033-664545; one way US$40) uses buses and ferries to take you to Government Wharf in the city centre. Other companies also plan to enter the airport transport game.

The slowest, cheapest option is the **ferry** (passengers 2nd-class/1st-class/VIP US$0.65/1.65/10, car/4WD US$8.50/10) that crosses from Tagrin to Kissy Terminal (some services may shift during the life of this book to the more convenient Government Wharf) five times a day between 8am and 9pm. **Abess Transport** (☎ 033-350003; one way US$25) uses the ferry for its door-to-door shuttle. You can speed things up on the ferry route by taking a shared taxi (US$0.65) to Tagrin and then either one of the *pam-pahs* (large cargo passenger boats) for US$0.65 or the less overcrowded speedboats for US$1.65 (plus extra if you have lots of luggage). These are wet landings, but men wait to carry passengers to the boats for a small tip.

Taxis stake out all the landing sites.

---

where locals shop, is the best place for county cloth and *gara*.

GETTING THERE & AWAY

SLRTC buses leave from the downtown **bus station** (Map p512; Wallace Johnson St), though not every day to every town. The queue starts around 5am, the ticket office opens at 6am and the buses leave by 7.30am. Cities served include Bo, Kabala, Kenema, Kono, Makeni and Conakry (Guinea). An air-conditioned express service to Bo (US$6.50, four hours) and Kenema (US$7.25, six hours) leaves at 6am and tickets are sold 24 hours in advance. **Abess Transport** (Map p512; ☎ 033-350003) buses to Bo, Kenema and Kono park on Rawdon St and begin departing around 6am. Prices are a bit higher, but competition for tickets isn't fierce as for SLRTC.

Most bush taxis leave from **Freetown Central Lorry Park** (off Map pp510-11; Bai Bureh Rd), AKA Clay Factory, at Texaco Junction on the far east side of town. Taxis to Conakry park along Free St near Victoria Park Market.

GETTING AROUND

Shared taxis and *poda-podas* (minibuses) cost US$0.25. Taxis generally make short hops, while *poda-podas* run long distance, including downtown (Regent Rd at Circular Rd) to Lumley and Aberdeen. Taxis don't use meters, so for private hire, bargain hard. A trip from downtown to Aberdeen during bad traffic will cost about US$5, while a short hop won't be less than US$1. *Okada* (motorcycle

taxis) can wind through the traffic jams, but drivers can be astoundingly reckless: don't hesitate to tell them to slow down. Short rides (up to about 2km) cost US$0.35.

AROUND FREETOWN

BEACHES

Some of Africa's best beaches lie south of Freetown, and on weekdays you can have many of them to yourself. Fishing and, between September and January, whale-watching, trips are available.

It's infrequent, but transport runs down the coast from Freetown to Tokeh (US1.20, 1½ hours). Take a *poda-poda* from Lumley Bridge, 250m south of Lumley Turntable, to Funkia (US0.25, 20 minutes) and change vehicles there. Transport is better the other way around, with taxis running from Waterloo to Tokeh (US$1, one hour). Get to Waterloo (US$0.40, 30 to 60 minutes) by *poda-poda* from Bombay St in the East End.

Six kilometres after **Goderich** and its animated afternoon fish market is **Lakka Beach**, the first good beach out of Freetown, and thus a popular place on weekends. The best of several places to sleep, eat and drink is **ourpick** **Hard Rock** (☎ 033-464908; r US$43.50), with three rooms on a lovely little peninsula.

About halfway down the peninsula is gorgeous **Sussex Beach**, where you'll find **Franco Diving Centre** (☎ 076-744406; r US$66; P), with cosy rooms and good Italian and seafood meals (US$5 to US$10). **Julcy's** (☎ 033-871649; julcyholidayresort@yahoo.com; s/d US$40/45; **P**), in a colourful compound on a rocky point, is a cheaper alternative.

Many people rank **River No 2** as the choicest beach in the country, and scenery-wise it's a clearly a contender, but it's also one of the busiest. Community-run **Sankofa Entertainment Complex** (☎ 033-457012; campsites US$20, r US$50, day entry US$1.65; **P**) offers overpriced rooms right on the beach and arranges excellent canoe trips up to the waterfall on River No 2, passing monkeys and crocodiles on the way.

Around the bend is **Tokeh Beach** (you can walk here from River No 2, using a boat over the river at high tide) where the guys running **Africana Tokeh Beach** (☎ 077-934243) set up mattresses and mozzie nets under thatched roofs for US$10, or let you pitch a tent for less. They'll also build bonfires and cook dinner.

Ask someone in **York**, an interesting Krio village, to show you the caves on York Beach where slaves supposedly stayed before being loaded onto ships. From here you can look across Whale Bay to deserted and tough-to-reach **Black Johnson Beach**. It may be possible to walk here in the dry season; otherwise get a boat in York or follow the unmarked mile-long dirt road (veer right at the first junction) that begins just after the Whale River Bridge.

Next up is stunning **John Obey Beach** where **our pick John Obey Beach Boys** (☎ 076-896669; s/d US$13.50/20) has a similar but superior sleeping set-up to what's available at Tokeh, though bring your own drinks.

At **Bureh Beach**, arguably the loveliest stretch of sand in West Africa and the best surfing in Sierra Leone, there's one simple room available through **Bureh Beach Boys** (☎ 077-721899), which also have tents for hire. All prices are negotiable. A hotel is under construction, but it won't ruin the views.

At the tip of the peninsula is **Kent**, with its ruined fort and yet another beach.

BANANA ISLANDS

Dangling off the southern tip of the peninsula like an emerald pendant, the Banana Islands provide an easy journey to a world seemingly far away. Dublin (*doo*-blin) on the northern tip of the main island has several minor historic sites like the jungle-encased remains of St Luke's Church (1881), and further afield

there's a bat cave and decent snorkelling. A boat ride around the island is lovely, but it's best to stop at Ricketts Island and walk back to Dublin, crossing the rock bridge between the two isles.

There are now several good places to spend the night. Friendly, family-run **our pick Dalton's Banana Guest House** (☎ 076-570208; r with/without bathroom US$17/13.50) faces the loveliest (though not the cleanest) beach. It has the best budget rooms (cheaper ones are planned) on any beach in Sierra Leone. Community-run **our pick Banana Island Guest House** (☎ 076-989906; www.bananaislandguesthouse-biya.org; r US$65-115) is pricier and correspondingly better in quality. Solar cells provide the power and the fairly large menu (meals US$8 to US$14.25) even has wine.

Dalton charges US$30 for the round-trip ride to the island, while the Banana Island Guest House charges US$40. Or just wait around Kent until a boat is going: locals pay US$0.65 for this option, but travellers pay US$1.65.

BUNCE ISLAND

An intriguing ruined fort built in 1794 lies some 30km up the Sierra Leone River from the ocean. Slave traders began operations here around 1670, and before the British outlawed the industry in 1807 some 30,000 men, women and children were shipped off into exile, including the Gullah people of South Carolina.

Any travel agency in town can take you there. Doing it yourself is cheapest from Kissy Terminal (off Map pp510–11), where a *pam-pah* will cost US$67 (plus 12 gallons of fuel and one gallon of oil) and take two hours to reach Bunce. A speedboat (about US$200 all inclusive) can do it in under an hour from Man of War Bay.

TACUGAMA CHIMPANZEE RESERVE

Up beyond the Sugar Loaf Mountain you can watch rescued chimps in this great little **reserve** (☎ 076-611211; www.tacugama.com; adult/child US$10/3.50; ☼ tours by appointment 10.30am & 4pm). It can also provide you with a walking map to nearby **waterfalls**.

Shared taxis (US$0.35) run from Government Wharf in Freetown to **Regent**, an interesting little village with many old Krio houses, and from there it's a 3km uphill walk to Tacugama. Chartering a car round trip from Regent can cost US$1.65.

Tacugama has three excellent, solar-powered **our pick** **cottages** (incl breakfast & tour US$80-120; P). For the time being, you'll need to cook your own lunch and dinner.

THE NORTH

MAKENI
pop 82,000

Makeni, the quiet capital of Northern Province and birthplace of President Koroma, is a market town. Climbing **Wusum and Mena hills** on the edge of town is quite fun. Other peaks along the road to Kabala are just begging for rock-climbing hounds to break out the ropes.

Thinka Hotel (☎ 076-805542; 24 Loya St; s/d without bathroom, US$6.50/10, r US$13.50; P) is the city's best budget lodge, while **Wusum Hotel** (☎ 076-341079; wusum.hotel@yahoo.co.uk; 65 Teko Rd; s/d US$88/110, chalet US$117; P 🕸 📃 🍴) is as good as similarly (over)priced places in Freetown. The aging **MJ Motel** (☎ 076-713945; 14 Azzolini Hwy; s/d US$33.50/43.50; P 🕸) serves as middle ground, though the AC only runs from 9pm to 2am.

Bush taxis and *poda-podas* run to many destinations including Freetown (US$4, three hours), Kamakwie (US$4, four hours) and Bo (US$5, four hours), plus the SLRTC buses from Freetown to Kono and Kabala will drop passengers here.

OUTAMBA-KILIMI NATIONAL PARK

This remote **national park** (admission US$4), known locally as the Wilderness Camp, is a beautiful, peaceful place with rolling hills, rainforest, savannah and rivers, which you explore by canoe and foot as there are no roads. You can look for elephants on the hiking trails and paddle past hippos (sightings almost guaranteed in the dry season), and no matter where you go you'll see many of the 260 bird species. These excursions cost US$3.50 per person, plus US$1.65 for the guide.

Cosy thatched **huts** (per person US$3.50) sit right on the riverbank, and someone will cook food if you bring it. If you have your own tent you can camp in the bush. Without your own transport you'll need to hire a motorcycle (try for US$10) or 4WD (much more) in Kamakwie, the nearest sizeable town, for the 26km trip. Alternatively, you can try to catch a northbound vehicle (but they're rare) and walk the 6km from the main road.

THE SOUTH

BO
pop 149,000

Sierra Leone's second-largest city, Bo is a lively town in the heart of Mende country, but there's little to see or do. Crime is on the rise, so be careful at night.

If you're pinching pennies you may like **Hotel Demby** (☎ 076-379503; 3 Tikonko Rd; r without bathroom US$3.50-8.50), but there's no generator and all rooms share bucket-shower bathrooms. Centrally located **Hotel Sir Milton** (☎ 076-921774; 6 Kissy Town Rd; s/d US$17/18.50, r with air-con US$23-37; P 🕸) is friendly and fair for the price.

Bush taxis to Freetown (US$6, four hours) depart frequently each morning from Maxwell Khobe Park near the centre, as do SLRTC buses (regular/express US$5.25/ US$6.50). This is also the spot for buses to Matrru Jong (US$4.25, three hours) and the Liberian border (see p518 for full details). To reach Freetown after 7.30am, head to the New London Park on the highway. Abess buses (US$6) leave from Tikonko Rd around midnight.

Kenema (US$1.35, 1½ hours), Potoru (US$3.50, two hours) and Makeni (US$5, four hours) vehicles park at the market. The quickest way to Kenema is usually to go out to Shell-Mingo on the highway and jump in a taxi there.

TIWAI ISLAND WILDLIFE SANCTUARY

Set on a small island in the Moa River, **Tiwai Island** (www.tiwaiisland.org; day-trip/overnight US$10/20) Freetown (☎ 076-755146) Potoru (☎ 076-748542) has one of the highest concentrations of primates on the continent and they're easily seen on the trails. Many other animals that are rare elsewhere also thrive here, including pygmy hippopotamuses, river otters and white-breasted guinea fowl. Guided excursions on the island and nearby villages cost US$6.50 to US$10. Overnight visitors sleep in tents perched on covered platforms (bedding provided), and local meals (US$2 to US$3.50) are available.

Generally three taxis make the trip to Potoru daily from Bo (US$3.50, two hours) and one from Kenema (US$5, three hours). *Okada* drivers in Potoru hold out for US$5 for the final 16km to Kambama village, where you take a boat to the island. Visitors are requested to call before arrival.

SIERRA LEONE

BONTHE

Bonthe, the only notable town on Sherbro Island, was used by the British as an anti-slaving post from 1861; later it grew into a prosperous port. Old colonial buildings, including several large churches, still dot the sandy streets, and despite a pervasive decrepitude, the car-free town has genuine charm. You can trek across the island or hire boats to explore the surrounding mangrove forests, outlying beaches and the rarely visited **Turtle Islands**.

Homely **John Cole Guest House** (☎ 076-441653; r without bathroom US$10), on the clock tower road, is the best of the three simple guesthouses. Primarily the domain of fanatical fishermen, **Bonthe Holiday Village** (☎ 076-532544; www.bonthe holidayvillage.com; r incl meals US$235; ☐ ☒) is a very utilitarian place, but on the comfort scale, it's as good as anything Freetown has, minus in-room TVs and air conditioners. Locals call it 'Complex'.

Bush taxis go from Bo to Matrru Jong (US$4.25, 2½ hours) early in the morning, and from there you catch the 1pm boat (US$4, four to five hours) for a beautiful ride down the Jong River to Bonthe. The return boat leaves Bonthe at 8am. On Sunday, boats only connect Bonthe with Yagoi, but there are usually enough passengers travelling that you can reach Yagoi by taxi from Mattru Jong (US$2.25, one hour) in time for the afternoon boat.

KENEMA

pop 127,000

The provinces' most prosperous town is a busy trade centre for coffee, cacao, timber and, most visibly, diamonds. The main artery, Hangha Rd, is a crush of Lebanese diamond merchants. Mines around town can be visited, but don't show up alone; find a friend in town to take you.

It's overpriced, but the **Capitol Hotel** (☎ 033-161616; 51 Hangha Rd; s/d US$52/85, ste US$138; P ☒ ☒) has the best rooms in town. The well-located **Makasa Guest House** (☎ 088-947199; 27 Humonya Ave; r with bathroom US$8.50-15/without bathroom US$20; ☒) is simple but clean. The **Capitol Restaurant** (51 Hangha Rd; sandwiches US$2-3.50, meals US$3.50-10; ☺ lunch & dinner) has good local and Lebanese food.

Bush taxis to Bo (US$1.35, 1½ hours), Potoru (US$5, three hours), Freetown (US$7.75, five hours) and the Liberian border (see p518 for full details) depart from the new bus station in the centre of town.

SLRTC (regular/express US$6.50/7.25) buses to Freetown run mornings, while Abess (US$7.75) buses depart around midnight.

SIERRA LEONE DIRECTORY

ACCOMMODATION

Freetown is full of classy, comfortable and costly hotels, and new ones are slowly opening on the peninsular beaches. There are also many budget choices in the capital, but few good ones. Upcountry, most large towns have several hotels, though few that will satisfy those needing plenty of creature comforts.

Always request discounts for stays of more than one night, as you'll often get them. Also note that two people of the same sex, regardless of whether they're actually a couple, usually cannot share a room. Westerners are sometimes exempt from this rule, but don't count on it.

BUSINESS HOURS

Banks Usually Monday to Friday 8.30am to 3.30pm, with a select few also open Saturday 9am to 1pm.

General shops and offices 9am to 5.30pm Monday to Saturday, though some places close at 1pm on Saturday.

DANGERS & ANNOYANCES

Sierra Leone is one of the safest destinations in West Africa, though it pays to remain vigilant with your valuables.

Except in Bo and Kenema, which have reliable power during the rainy season, electricity is either sporadic or nonexistent, though the new Bumbuna hydroelectric dam should improve things. Just about all hotels have generators, though most budget places only run them from around 7pm to midnight.

EMBASSIES & CONSULATES

The following embassies are in Freetown:

Gambia (Map p512; ☎ 225191; 6 Wilberforce St)

Germany (Map pp510-11; ☎ 231350; 3 Middle Hill Station)

Ghana (Map p512; ☎ 223461; 13 Walpole St)

Guinea (Map pp510-11; ☎ 232496; 6 Carlton Carew Rd)

Liberia (Map pp510-11; ☎ 230991; 2 Spur Rd)

Mali (Map pp510-11; ☎ 033-422994; 40 Wilkinson Rd)

Nigeria (Map p512; ☎ 224229; 37 Siaka Stevens St)

Senegal (Map p512; ☎ 030-230666; 2nd fl, 7 Short St)

UK (Map pp510-11; ☎ 232961; http://ukinsierraleone. fco.gov.uk; 6 Spur Rd) Assists French nationals.

USA (☎ off Map pp510-11; 076-515000; http://freetown. usembassy.gov; Leicester Rd)

FESTIVALS & EVENTS
Freetown's recently revived **Lantern Parade** is a procession of illuminated floats on April 26, the night before Independence Day.

HOLIDAYS
Besides the Islamic and Christian holidays listed on p1140, Sierra Leone celebrates New Year's Day (January 1) and Independence Day (27 April).

INTERNET ACCESS
Freetown has plenty of internet cafes with good high-speed connections; most charge US$1 per hour. Access in the provinces is rare and painfully slow.

MONEY
The most easily exchangeable currencies in Sierra Leone are US dollars, UK pounds and euros, in that order. Large denominations get the best rates. Forex bureaus (and street traders, though avoid them unless somebody you trust makes the introduction) invariably offer better rates than banks.

You can rarely pay with a credit card in Sierra Leone, but some Rokel Commercial Bank branches give cash advances (up to US$2000) on Visa cards, and ProCredit Bank has ATMs in Freetown that spit out up to US$100 per day for those with Visa credit and debit cards, but don't rely on them too heavily, as they sometimes don't work.

POST & TELEPHONE
Mobile phone service is good and so popular that landlines are disappearing. SIM cards cost around US$1.65. If you don't have a mobile, countless small telecentres generally charge US$0.17 to US$0.35 per minute for domestic calls and US$0.35 to US$0.70 to the USA/UK/Australia.

Sierra Leone's regular post is generally reliable if you send something from Freetown.

TOURIST INFORMATION
The **National Tourist Board** (www.welcometosierraleone. org) might be helpful, but the best source of pre-departure information is **Visit Sierra Leone** (www.visitsier raleone.org).

VISAS
Everyone from outside Ecowas (Economic Community of West African States) countries needs a visa. Prices and rules vary widely by nationality of applicant and embassy of issuance, but generally you need a plane ticket and a letter of invitation (a hotel reservation should suffice), and your passport needs one year of validity, rather than the typical six months.

Travel agents in Freetown can arrange 30-day, single-entry landing visas, which you present at immigration. Australians, New Zealanders and most EU residents pay US$79; Canadians US$82; British US$92; and Americans get socked for US$210 (much more than what one-year multiple-entry visas from the embassy in Washington DC cost). Visit Sierra Leone (p509) charges US$40 for this service, and everything can be done online in a couple of days with payment through PayPal.

Some people manage to get visas on arrival for an extra fee, but this is unofficial and you risk being turned away.

Visa Extensions
Visas can be easily extended for 30 days at the **Immigration Department** (Map p512; ☎ 223220; Rawdon St; ☾ 10am-3.30pm Mon-Fri) in Freetown.

Visas for Onward Travel
Three-month, multiple-entry visas for Guinea cost US$50 for most Westerners and US$100

PRACTICALITIES

- Sierra Leone uses British weights and measures.

- Electricity is 230V/50Hz and plugs have three large pins, like the UK.

- *Awoko* and *Concord Times* are the most respected newspapers, though the satirical *Peep* is more popular.

- Magazines like *Newsweek* and *BBC Focus On Africa* are sold at supermarkets.

- Sierra Leone's two TV stations are the government-owned SLBS and the private ABC, both of whose most popular programming is Nigerian soap operas.

- The BBC World Service is heard on 94.3FM and Voice of America on 102.4FM. SKYY (106.6FM) plays the most local music.

SIERRA LEONE

for Americans. Bring two photos and a photocopy of your passport. Two-month, single-entry visas to Liberia cost US$75 and require one photo plus a passport photocopy. Both embassies issue them on the spot.

TRANSPORT IN SIERRA LEONE

GETTING THERE & AWAY

Air

BMI (Map p512; ☎ 076-541230; www.flybmi.com; 14 Wilberforce St) is currently the only carrier to London (though others likely will start) and it charges around £800 return, while **Brussels Airlines** (Map p512; ☎ 076-333777; www.brusselsairlines.com; 30 Siaka Stevens St) charges more for better service from Brussels.

Kenya Airways (Map p512; ☎ 076-536899; www.kenya-airways.com; 13 Lamina Sankoh St) flies from Nairobi for around US$1300 return and **Royal Air Maroc** (Map p512; ☎ 076-221015; www.royalairmaroc.com; 19 Charlotte St) flies from Casablanca for US$1000. Various regional airlines can get you here from most large West African capitals. These flights are usually expensive.

Land

GUINEA

The main route to Guinea is via Pamelap. Bush taxis from Freetown to Conakry (US$16) run regularly, and there's an SLRTC bus (US$13.50) on Monday and Thursday. The Sierra Leonean side of the highway is a mess (though it's supposed to get paved soon) and the journey usually takes eight to 10 hours. You can also get to Conakry from other large towns.

From Kamakwie to Kindia (Guinea) there's little transport on the Sierra Leone side, where the road is quite bad. 4WDs usually leave Kamakwie every two or three days; the trip takes eight to 10 hours and costs US$10. Alternatively, hire an *okada* to the border (they'll ask for US$20), where it's about a

1.5km walk to Medina-Oula in Guinea, which has plenty of transport.

The road from Kabala to Faranah (Guinea), is also in bad shape and only has 4WDs (US$13.50, four to eight hours, twice weekly). *Okada* drivers will take you to Faranah for US$50 in four hours or you could stop in Hérémakono to get a taxi.

In the far east, the most common crossing is between Koindu and Guéckédou (Guinea). First get a taxi from Kailahun to Koindu (US$5, three hours) and then an *okada* (US$1.65) to the border, where a dugout canoe will probably be your transport over the Moa River. Then at Nongowa you can get a taxi or motorcycle taxi the rest of the way.

LIBERIA

The only practical route to Liberia is over the Mano River Bridge by Bo (Waterside). Taxis (US$13.50) and sometimes *poda-podas* (US$12) depart from Bo and Kenema to the border post at Gendema (taking six to eight hours in the dry season and 10 to 12 in the wet), where you walk over to Liberia and continue in one of the frequent taxis to Monrovia. Check the security situation before attempting any other crossing.

GETTING AROUND

Boat

Pam-pahs operate to several towns, most notably between Mattru Jong and Bonthe (p516).

Speedboat hire costs from US$285 per day plus fuel and oil (and boats burn plenty of both), while slower *pam-pahs* (that can hold 20 people) cost around US$165. In Freetown, enquire at Man of War Bay, Government Wharf, Kissy Terminal and the Conservation Society (p509).

Car

Car hire is expensive (starting at around US$80 in Freetown, much more to head up-country), but don't choose a company only on the price; ask about the terms too. Kilometres will always be unlimited and a driver included, but fuel costs and after-hours charges vary. The travel agencies listed with Freetown (p509) have good cars and service.

You could also just charter ('chatah') a taxi. By the hour in Freetown you can usually negotiate to US$5 for one and US$4 per hour for several.

Local Transport

Bush taxis and *poda-podas* (minibuses) link most towns; however, except for departures to and from Freetown and between Bo and Kenema, you'll find that traffic is usually pretty sparse, especially on Sunday. Buses will usually cost a little less, but they are slower.

Okada

Okada rule the roads in many towns. Outside Freetown a ride costs US$0.35 no matter how far you're going. It's sometimes convenient to hire *okada* for long journeys because on really bad roads they travel faster than shared taxis and *poda-podas,* plus they depart on demand.

TOGO

Togo

Once regarded as the pearl of West Africa for its scenic landscapes, elegant capital and affluent markets, Togo fell by the tourism wayside following the political turmoil of the 1990s and mid-2000s. Two decades of visitors' neglect have taken their toll: national parks have been reclaimed by desperate farmers, information for travellers is virtually nonexistent, roads are in appalling condition, and getting around without your own transport requires the patience of a saint and the determination of a fighter.

But for those fond of travelling off the beaten track, Togo will prove a rewarding destination. It is as beautiful as ever, with a great diversity of landscapes and wildlife. Elephants, crocs, monkeys and antelopes can be found in Parc National De Fazao-Malfakassa, and the coast remains a favourite mating area for whales and nesting ground for marine turtles.

The end of mass tourism has also given the chance for independent outfits to make their mark: great little guesthouses are stealing the show from the once-grand hotels of the 1970s, passionate guides are working the ecotourism trend and an outstanding West African art collection has opened its doors in Lomé.

Culturally, Togo is a melting pot. The fortified compounds of Koutammakou and the vertigo-inducing caves of Nano are a reminder that the country's ethnically diverse population didn't always get along. Nowadays, however, voodoo, Muslim, Christian and traditional festivals crowd the calendar and are often colourful celebrations for all. And if one thing can definitely bring all six million Togolese together, it is their conquering football (soccer) team, Les Éperviers.

FAST FACTS

- **Area** 56,790 sq km
- **ATMs** In Lomé and Kara
- **Borders** Benin, Burkina Faso, Ghana
- **Budget** US$30 to US$50 a day
- **Capital** Lomé
- **Language** French (official), Ewe, Mina, Kabye
- **Money** West African CFA franc; US$1 = CFA457, €1 = CFA656
- **Population** 6.6 million
- **Seasons** Wet (May to October), dry (November to February)
- **Telephone** County code ☎ 228; international access code ☎ 00
- **Time** GMT/UTC
- **Visa** CFA10,000 seven-day visa at border; 30-day extension of seven-day visa free

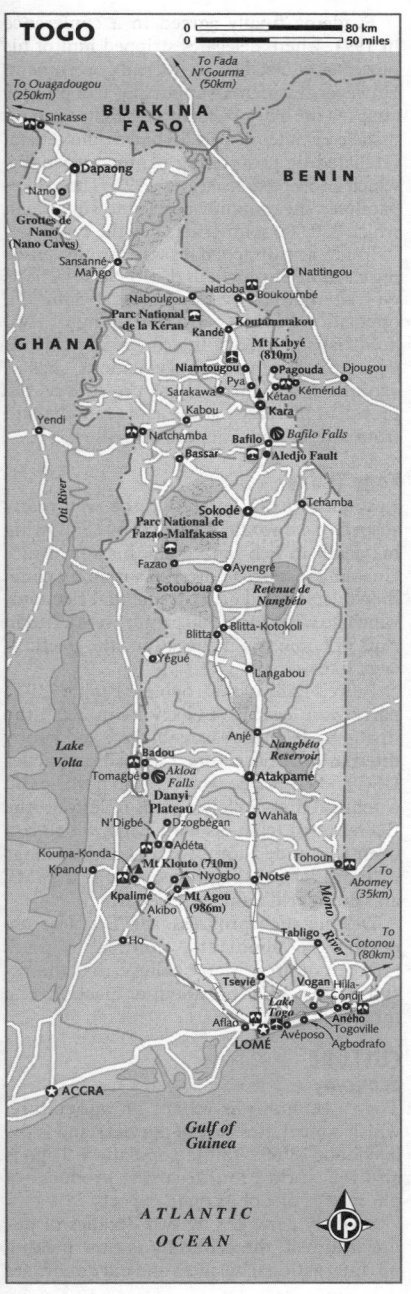

TOGO

0 _____ 80 km
0 _____ 50 miles

HIGHLIGHTS

- **Lomé** (p524) Hit the bars and restaurants to see the coastal capital in all its decaying glory.
- **Musée International du Golfe de Guinée** (p526) Marvel at the exquisite West African art displayed at this unique gallery.
- **Kpalimé** (p529) Hike in lush forested hills and take in the chilled vibe of coffee country.
- **Togolese gastronomy** (p523) Tuck into *fufu sauce arachide* (a yam paste served with a peanut and ground-nut sauce), *aloko* (fried plantain), *koliko* (yam chips) or grilled Nile perch and wash it down with a shot of *sodabe* (firewater distilled from palm wine).
- **Koutammakou** (p532) Seek out northern Togo's remote clay-and-straw fortresses, the *tata* compounds, amid stunning scenery.

CLIMATE & WHEN TO GO

Togo's climate ranges from tropical in the south to savannah in the north. Rain falls from May to October, with a dry spell in the south from mid-July to mid-September. Mid-February (after the harmattan lifts) to mid-April is the hottest period throughout the country, while November to February is the driest and best time to visit. Unsealed roads can be unpassable during the rains. Parc National Fazao-Malfakassa is usually open from December to May (depending on the rains).

ITINERARIES

- **One Week** Spend a couple of days in Lomé (p524) checking out the sights. Make a day trip to the Friday market in Vogan (p528) or Lake Togo (p528) for a spot of relaxation before heading to the hills of Kpalimé (p529).
- **Two Weeks** Start off with week one in Lomé (p524) and Kpalimé (p529), then make your way to the vibrant Kabye town of Kara (p531) and make a day trip to the beautiful and intriguing Koutammakou country (p532).

HISTORY

Togo's name comes from *togodo*, which means 'behind the lake' in Ewe – a reference to Lake Togo. The country was once on the fringes of several great empires and, when the

HOW MUCH?

- **Pagne Ewe kente cloth** CFA8000
- **Butterfly walk** CFA5000
- **Koutammakou access** CFA1500
- **Taxi-moto** CFA200
- **National park entry** CFA13,000

LONELY PLANET INDEX

- **1L petrol** CFA550
- **1.5L bottled water** CFA500
- **Bottle of Flag beer** CFA350
- **Souvenir T-shirt** CFA2500
- **Small bunch of bananas** CFA100

Europeans arrived in the 16th century, this power vacuum allowed the slave-traders to use Togo as a conduit.

Following the abolition of slavery, Germany signed a treaty in Togoville with local king Mlapa. Togoland, as the Germans called their colony, underwent considerable economic development, but the Togolese didn't appreciate the Germans' brutal 'pacification' campaigns. When the Germans surrendered at Kamina – the Allies' first victory in WWI – the Togolese welcomed the British forces.

However, the League of Nations split Togoland between France and Britain – a controversial move that divided the populous Ewe. Following a 1956 plebiscite, British Togoland was incorporated into the Gold Coast (now Ghana). French Togoland gained full independence in 1960 under the country's first president, Sylvanus Olympio. But his presidency was short-lived. Olympio, an Ewe from the south who appeared to disregard the interests of northerners, was killed by Kabye soldiers in 1963. His replacement was then deposed by Kabye sergeant Gnassingbé Eyadéma. The new leader established a cult personality and became increasingly irrational following a 1974 assassination attempt.

In 1990, France began pressuring Eyadéma to adopt a multiparty system, but he resisted. The following year, after riots, strikes and the deaths of pro-democracy protestors, 28 bodies were dragged from a lagoon and dumped in front of the US embassy, drawing attention to the repression in Togo.

Eyadéma finally agreed to a conference in 1991, where delegates stripped him of his powers and installed an interim government. However, Eyadéma-supporting troops later attacked the new president's residence and re-installed Eyadéma. Back in power, the general retaliated by postponing planned elections, which prompted strikes in 1992. The strikes paralysed the economy and led to violence in which 250,000 southerners fled the country.

Eyadéma triumphed his way through ensuing elections throughout the 1990s – elections typically marred by international criticism, opposition boycotts and the killing of rival politicians. Amnesty International made allegations of human rights violations, such as executions and torture, and pressure on the president increased at the same rate that aid from international donors decreased.

Togo Today

Eyadéma finally left office the way many suspected he would – in a coffin. Following his death in February 2005, his son, Faure Gnassingbé, seized power in a military coup, then relented and held presidential elections, which he won. Some 500 people were killed in riots in Lomé, amid allegations the elections were fixed.

Faure's Rally of the Togolese People (RPT) party won legislative elections in 2007, the first to be deemed reasonably free and fair by international observers. Opposition parties UFC and CAR also won seats in parliament, a political first. Following this milestone, the EU resumed relations with Togo, which had been suspended for 14 years, and dealings with international agencies such as the IMF and the World Bank have restarted.

Despite such progress, the Togolese are pessimistic about the political outlook for the country. Many believe that the result of the 2010 presidential election is a foregone conclusion.

CULTURE
Economy

Togo's economy is reliant on agriculture, which contributes 40% of the GDP and is the livelihood of 65% of the population. Togo is also the world's fourth-largest producer of phosphate, one of its main exports.

Severely damaged by two decades of political unrest, the economy is now picking up. International business and aid donors are returning to Togo and Lomé's port infrastructure is expanding.

Population

With about 40 ethnic groups in a population of over six million people, Togo has one of Africa's more heterogeneous populations. The three largest groups are the southern Ewe and Mina, and the northern Kabye; the latter counts President Gnassingbé among its population and are concentrated around Kara.

Polygamy is still common – the president himself has numerous wives – and the bulk of daily domestic tasks remain the responsibility of women.

Overall, the country is young, with more than 40% of the population under the age of 14; and life expectancy is 58. Literacy is better than in many neighbouring countries, with more than half the population able to read and write. Officially, HIV's prevalence is 3.2%, although the actual figure is thought to be much higher.

Sport

Togo's football team, Les Éperviers (the Sparrow Hawks), has been successful given Togo's tiny size, having qualified for the 2006 World Cup. Togo failed to qualify for the 2010 World Cup but had gone through the 2010 African Cup of Nations. Tragically, however, the Togolese team pulled out after it was attacked by militants in northern Angola. Three people died in the attack and nine were injured. Striker Emmanuel Adebayor (who currently plays for the English team Manchester City) is a national icon.

Religion

Christianity and Islam are the main religions in Togo – in the south and north respectively. However, a majority of the population have voodoo beliefs, which are strongest in the southeast.

Arts

Batik and wax printing is popular throughout Togo, but the most well-known textile is the Ewe kente cloth, which is less brilliantly coloured than the Ashanti version.

Music and dance play an important part in Togolese daily life. Today, traditional music has fused with contemporary West African, Caribbean and South American sounds, creating a hybrid that includes highlife, reggae and soukous. Togo's most famous singing export was Bella Bellow, who, before her death in 1973, ruled the local music scene, toured internationally and released an album, *Album Souvenir*. Nowadays, King Mensah is Togo's best-known artist, at home and abroad.

The country's best-known author is Tété-Michel Kpomassie. His unlikely sounding autobiography, *An African in Greenland*, contains his unique perspective on life in the land. *The Village of Waiting*, by George Packer, is an interesting observation on life in Togo. It covers a Peace Corp's two years in Lavié, and is quite candid about the country's autocratic politics.

The fortified Tamberma compounds in Koutammakou are some of the most striking structures in West Africa.

FOOD & DRINK

Togolese dishes, some of the best in West Africa, are typically based, as in much of the region, on a starch staple such as *pâte* (a dough-like substance made of corn, manioc or yam) accompanied by sauce. Some Togolese specialities are *fufu* (cooked and puréed yam served with vegetables and meat), *djenk-oumé* (a *pâte* made with cornflour cooked with spices and served with fried chicken) and *pintade* (guinea fowl).

Common snacks include: *aloko* (fried plantain), *koliko* (yam chips), *gaou* (bean-flour fritters) and *wagasi* (a mild cheese fried in hot spice). You'll also find fresh fruit everywhere you go.

Togo has its fair share of generic (Flag, Castel, Lager) and local brews. *Tchoukoutou* (fermented millet) is the preferred tipple in the north. Elsewhere, beware of *sodabe*, a terrifyingly potent moonshine distilled from palm wine.

ENVIRONMENT

Togo's coastline measures only 56km, but the country stretches inland for over 600km. The coast is tropical; further inland are rolling hills covered with forest, yielding to savannah plains in the north.

Wildlife is disappointing because larger mammals have largely been killed or scared off. The country's remaining mammals (monkeys, buffaloes and antelopes) are limited to the north; crocodiles and hippos are found in some rivers. Swiss nonprofit organisation **Fondation Franz Weber** (www.ffw.ch, in German

& French) manages the Parc National Fazao-Malfakassa and has been working with local populations to protect the last few remaining elephants from poaching and promote sustainable income-generating activities such as bee-keeping.

The coastline faces serious erosion and pollution problems.

LOMÉ

pop 675,000

Togo's capital may be a shadow of its former self, but it retains a charm and nonchalance that is unique among West African capitals. The people are friendly and welcoming, the markets colourful and easy to navigate, and the palm-fringed boulevards retain a certain elegance.

ORIENTATION

The centre of town nestles in the D-shaped area shaped by the coastal highway and the semicircular Blvd du 13 Janvier (often called Blvd Circulaire). The heart of town is around the intersection of Rue de la Gare and Rue du Commerce,

INFORMATION
Bookshops

Librairie Bon Pasteur (☎ 221 36 28; cnr Rue du Commerce & Ave de la Libération; ☯ 8am-12.15pm & 3-6pm Mon-Fri, 9am-1pm Sat) Sells maps and, occasionally, English publications, such as the *International Herald Tribune* and *Time*.

Cultural Centres

Centre Culturel Français (☎ 223 07 60; www.ccf-lome.org, in French; 19 Ave du 24 Janvier; ☯ 10am-8pm Tue-Sat, 5-8pm Sun) Offers regular films, concerts and exhibitions, and has a good selection of books and up-to-date newspapers.

Espace Culturel Africain Le 54 (☎ 220 62 20; Blvd du 13 Janvier; ☯ 10am-midnight Tue-Sun) A nice blend of exhibition space, affordable craft and jewellery, and a vibrant restaurant-bar.

Emergency

Centre Hospitalier Universitaire de Tokoin (☎ 221 25 01; Route de Kpalimé) The main hospital, 1.5km northwest of the city.

Internet Access

There are numerous internet cafes in Lomé. Expect to pay CFA300 to CFA500 per hour.

Cybercafé MZ (☎ 236 90 08; Ave du 24 Janvier; per hr CFA350; ☯ 7am-10pm Mon-Sat, 1-10pm Sun) A little cramped but friendly and open on Sunday.

Cyber Poste (Rue Kponvene; per hr CFA400; ☯ 7am-9pm Mon-Fri, 8am-6pm Sat) Reliable connection.

Media

Newspaper racks at major road intersections stock newspapers.

Medical Services

If you need a doctor or a dentist, contact your embassy for a list of recommended practitioners. Out of hours, ring ☎ 242 (these are usually French-speaking services) to find out which pharmacy is on call.

Dr Noël Akouvi (☎ 221 32 46; Cabinet Dentaire NIFA 10, Rue Amouzou) For dental emergencies.

Pharmacie Bel Air (☎ 221 03 21; Rue du Commerce; ☯ 8am-7pm Mon-Fri, 8am-1pm Sat)

Money

Banks listed here all change cash; Ecobank changes travellers cheques. All are open without a lunch break and on Saturday, too, albeit for shorter hours (see p533). Moneychangers congregate on Rue du Commerce, but there is a good chance you'll pay over the odds.

Banque Atlantique (☎ 220 88 92; Place du Petit Marché; ☯ 8am-4pm Mon-Fri, 9am-2pm Sat) This is the only place that accepts MasterCard in Togo; also accepts Visa and has an ATM.

Ecobank (☯ 7.45am-5pm Mon-Fri & 8am-4pm Sat) Rue de Chemin de Fer (☎ 222 65 74; 1 rue de Chemin de Fer); Rue du Commerce (☎ 221 71 14; 20 rue du Commerce) Both branches are equipped with Visa cash machines.

Post

Post office (☎ 221 31 95; Ave de la Libération; ☯ 7.30am-5pm Mon-Fri, 7.30am-12.30pm Sat) Has an efficient poste-restante service.

Telephone

Local and international calls can be made from any of the multitude of private telephone agencies around the city.

Cyber Poste (Rue Kponvene; ☯ 7am-6pm Mon-Fri, 8am-noon Sat) Just behind the post office, offers private phone booths, fax services and sells mobile-phone SIM cards and top-up vouchers.

Tourist Information

Direction de la Promotion Touristique (☎ 221 43 13; www.togo-tourisme.com; Rue du Lac Togo) Located in a run-down building near Marox Supermarché. Staff

TOGO

TOGO

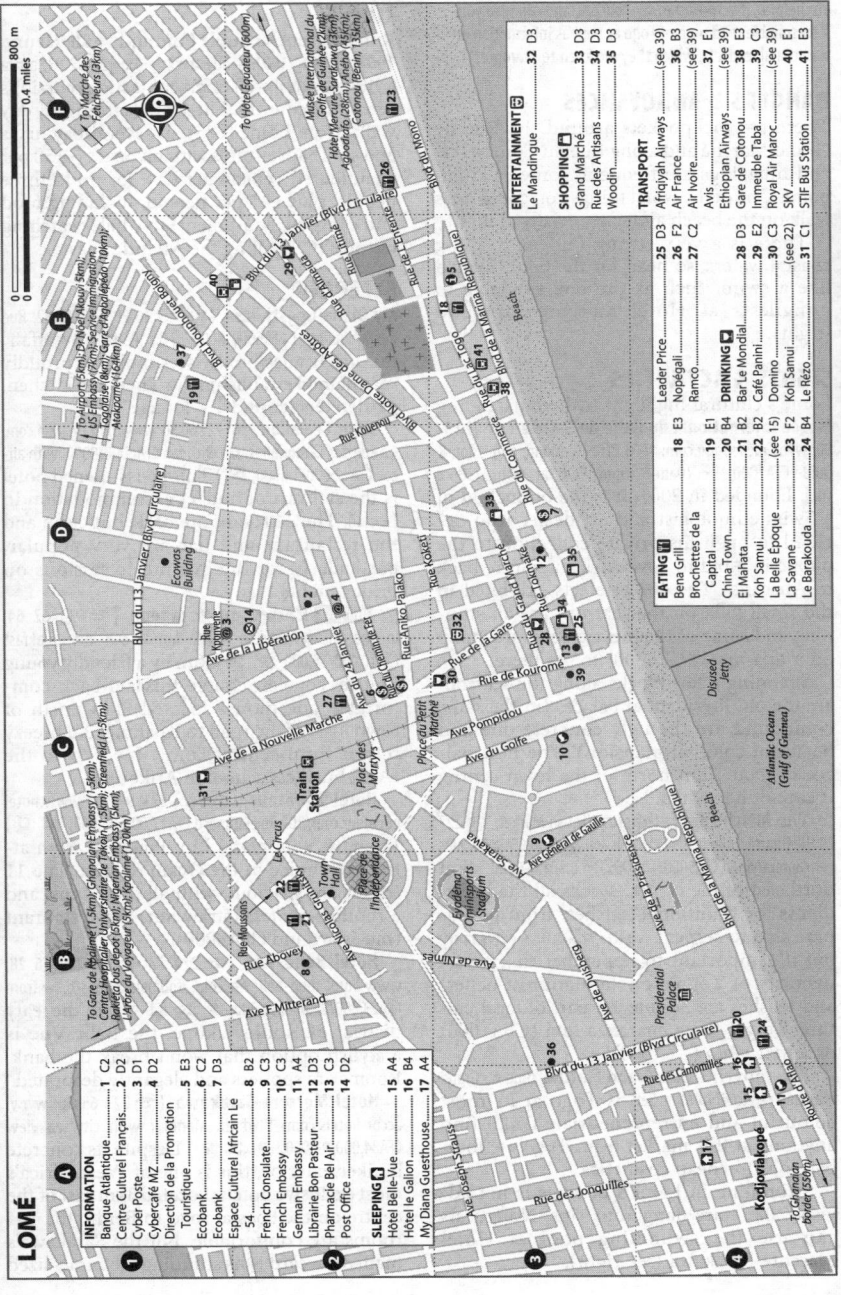

LOMÉ

are helpful, if surprised to see tourists, and can give you a reasonable road map of Togo as well as information on traditional festivals, which they are keen to promote.

DANGERS & ANNOYANCES

There are pickpockets around the Rue de Grand Marché and along Rue du Commerce, and muggings are frequent, some at knifepoint. One of the worst things you could do is walk on the beach alone, especially at night.

There is a very strong undertow along coastal waters, so head for the pool if you'd like a swim, such as the one available to nonguests at Hôtel Mercure-Sarakawa (right).

SIGHTS & ACTIVITIES

Lomé's cultural highlight is the outstanding **Musée International du Golfe de Guinée** (☎ 220 57 90; www.musee-igg.com; 1603 Blvd du Mono; admission & guide CFA1000; ☼ 10am-5.30pm Wed-Sat, from 2.30pm Tue). Founded in 2007, is the brainchild of a Swiss ethnologist and art dealer who decided to open his private collection to the public in a bid to 'give African culture back to Africans'. The 400 artefacts exhibited in the small villa on the seafront are all stunning and some of them extremely rare. Jump on a *taxi-moto* (CFA300) to get there.

Spanning a few blocks along the seafront are the old Presidential Palaces (in the same compound are the ugly concrete one and beautiful colonial mansion). The new palace is about 7km north of the town centre; it cannot be visited.

The **Marché des Féticheurs** (Fetish Market; ☎ 227 20 96; Quartier Akodessewa; admission & guide CFA3000, plus per camera/video CFA5000/10,000; ☼ 8.30am-6pm), 4km northeast of the centre, stocks all the ingredients for traditional fetishes, from porcupine skin to serpent head. It's all a bit grisly but it's important to remember that a vast majority of Togolese retain animist beliefs and fetishes are an integral part of local culture. To get there charter a taxi (CFA1000) or a *taxi-moto* (CFA500).

The labyrinthine **Grand Marché** (Rue du Grand Marché; ☼ to 4pm Mon-Sat) is Togo at its most colourful and entrepreneurial. You'll find anything at this market from Togolese football tops to cheap cosmetics.

Swimming in Lomé's beaches is not advised; there are dangerous rips. Nonguests can use the swimming pool at Hôtel Mercure-Sarakawa (see right).

TOURS

Run by French couple Loïc and Paule Henry, **1001 Pistes** (1001 'sandy tracks'; ☎ 927 52 03; africa toy1001pistes@yahoo.fr) offers fantastic excursions across the country. These range from easy day walks from Lomé (€75), to several-day hikes and 4WD adventures with bivouacs (€150 per chauffeured vehicle per day, for up to three people, plus €45 per person, including food and camping equipment) to whale-watching outings (€75) along the Atlantic coast.

SLEEPING

My Diana Guesthouse (☎ 995 46 20, 983 45 82; Rue des Jonquilles; r CFA6000-8000; ☒) A family affair, this lovely guesthouse is a simple but proudly maintained establishment. There is a kitchen, garden terrace and TV lounge.

Hôtel Le Galion (☎ 222 00 30; www.hotel-galion.com; 12 Rue des Camomilles; s/d with fan CFA6000/8000, with aircon CFA12,000/14,000; ☒) This Swiss-owned hotel is the stalwart of budget accommodation in Lomé. The 24 rooms are basic but clean and the restaurant and bar are very popular, particularly for the live-music sessions on Friday nights.

[our pick] L'Arbre du Voyageur (☎ 933 62 64; lpennaneach@yahoo.fr; r with fan/air-con incl breakfast CFA10,000/15,000; P ☒) Run by a friendly young French-Togolese couple, this laid-back, comfortable guesthouse located 5km north of town just off the road to Kpalimé, is a breezy retreat from central Lomé. It's next to the IAEC business school in Atikoumé.

Hôtel Équateur (☎/fax 221 99 92; www.hotel equateur.com; 102 Rue Litimé; d CFA17,000-25,000; ☒ ▦) Friendly, young and hip, Équateur is an attractive choice in the Ocam district. The 11 rooms are spacious, with all mod-cons, and a rooftop-*paillote* (straw hut) bar-restaurant (meals around CFA4000).

Hôtel Belle-Vue (☎ 220 22 40; fax 220 76 28; www.hotel-togo-bellevue.com; Kodjoviakopé; s/d/tw from CFA23,000/27,000/32,000; P ☒ ▦ ☞) In the leafy district of Kodjoviakopé, the Belle-Vue is a stylish option that won't break the bank. Rooms are spotless and elegantly decorated.

Hôtel Mercure-Sarakawa (☎ 227 65 90; www. accor-hotels.com; Blvd du Mono; r with city/sea view CFA84,000/94,000; P ☒ ▩) Despite its concrete bunker exterior, this is one of West Africa's most exclusive hotels. Located 3km east of the centre on the coastal road to Benin, the 164 rooms are comfortable, but the Sarakawa's main drawcard is its stunning Olympic-sized swimming pool (nonguests aged over/under 13 years CFA6000/3000) set in acres of coconut grove.

EATING

Brochettes de la Capitale (Blvd du 13 Janvier; kebabs CFA200; ☿ 5pm-1am) This Lomé institution is somewhat suffering from its popularity and location on the increasingly polluted Blvd Circulaire, but it's still a cool place to devour lip-smacking kebabs with a CFA300 beer.

Bena Grill (☎ 222 41 38; Rue du Lac Togo; meals CFA2000-4700) Under two huge *paillotes* and a battery of fans, this informal joint serves inexpensive grilled meats and salads.

Greenfield (☎ 222 21 55; Rue Akati; pizza & tortillas from CFA2000, mains CFA2500-4500; ☿ 6pm-midnight) Near Centre Hospitalier Universitaire de Tokoin, this great French-owned garden bar-restaurant has a super original decor. It is family-friendly, with films screened for youngsters at 4pm on Saturdays, in addition to the adult films at 8.30pm on Tuesdays (in French with English subtitles).

Nopégali (☎ 222 80 62; Blvd du 13 Janvier; meals around CFA2500) Another classic Lomé establishment, hugely popular, particularly for lunch. It's very much a canteen, but a good one, with friendly service and an outdoor terrace.

El Mahata (Blvd du 13 Janvier; meals CFA3000) This great Lebanese establishment makes a brisk trade with its flame-grilled chicken, flatbread and mounds of hummus.

our pick **La Savane** (☎ 906 17 48; Blvd du Mono; mains CFA3000-4500; ☿ lunch Mon-Fri & dinner Mon-Sat) This Swiss-owned haunt is hugely popular with expats and well-off Togolese. Regulars prop the bar for an aperitif before settling down for delicious French staples, such as *blanquette de veau* (creamy veal stew with mushrooms and rice) or its African counterparts such as *poulet Yassa*.

Koh Samui (☎ 336 64 11; Rue Moussons; mains from CFA6000; ☿ dinner Mon-Sat) This upmarket Japanese and Thai restaurant has raised the bar of Asian cuisine in Lomé. The food is excellent, if pricey, and the decor infused with southeast Asian influences.

Le Barakouda (☎ 220 17 54; Blvd de la Marina, Kodjoviakopé; mains CFA6000-10,000; ☿ lunch & dinner Tue-Sat, dinner Sun) The name gives it away: this is a fantastic seafood place where you'll enjoy succulent lemon sole, gambas *à la plancha* (cooked on a griddle) and red mullet fillets.

Portions are generous and the atmosphere is jovial.

La Belle Époque (☎ 220 22 40; Kodjoviakopé; menu du jour CFA6500, mains CFA6000-12,000) Lomé's finest table, La Belle Époque, all crisp white table cloths and dimmed lighting, serves a refined cuisine, such as grilled sole with spiced red wine or turbot in vanilla butter. There are also some 50-odd wines on offer.

China Town (☎ 222 30 06; 67 Blvd du 13 Janvier; meals around CFA8000; ☿ lunch & dinner Wed-Mon) Welcoming, reliable and in a good location at the Kodjoviakopé end of the Blvd Circulaire, you'll find a great selection of steamed dumplings and meat dishes.

You'll find fruit and vegetable stalls at every street corner. For groceries, there are good supermarkets, such as the following:

Leader Price (Rue du Commerce; ☿ 8.30am-1pm & 3-6.30pm Mon-Sat, 9am-1pm Sun)

Ramco (☎ 221 46 10; Rue de Kouromé; ☿ 8.30am-12.30pm & 2.30-7.30pm Mon-Sat, 9am-1pm Sun)

DRINKING

our pick **Bar Le Mondial** (Rue Tokmaké; ☿ 11am-1am) With African football shirts decorating the walls, Le Mondial has a great international chilled-out vibe and conversations tend to flow as fast as the beer.

Domino (665 Rue de la Gare; ☿ from 6pm) Den-like but cool and very popular, Domino houses Lomé's biggest selection of beers (50 or so) as well as a dozen whiskies.

Koh Samui (☎ 336 64 11; Rue Moussons; ☿ from 7pm Mon-Sat) The rooftop bar of this restaurant is simply stunning and a fabulous place for sundowners. You'll find all the usual beers as well as elaborate cocktails.

Le Rézo (☎ 338 21 38; 21 Ave de la Nouvelle Marche; ☿ 10am-1am) Inside, it's like a 1980s disco, but Le Rézo is more contemporary than it looks: giant screens showing European football games, karaoke nights and live jazz on Thursdays.

Café Panini (☎ 904 00 56; Blvd du 13 Janvier; ☿ from 5pm) Heaving, loud and seedy – the gloriously sleazy epicentre of Lomé's nightlife. Avoid if you object to being hustled by multilingual prostitutes.

ENTERTAINMENT

Lomé has great live-music venues.

our pick **Le Mandingue** (Rue Koketi; ☿ from 9pm Tue-Sat) Le Mandingue is a top piano bar with a good mix of jazz, Latin vibes and blues.

Hôtel Le Galion (p526) and Le Rézo (p527) both feature regular live music, too.

SHOPPING

The Grand Marché (see p526) is perfect for bric-à-brac. If you can't face haggling over cloth, **Woodin** (☎ 221 28 00; 16 rue du Commerce; ⏰ 10.30am-6pm Tue-Fri, 9am-noon Sat, 12.30-6pm Mon]) has air-con and fixed (but reasonable) prices.

Rue des Artisans (Rue des Artisans; ⏰ 7.30am-6.30pm Mon-Sat) is where to buy woodcarvings, leather bags and sandals as well as jewellery from across West Africa. Come with your haggling cap firmly on.

GETTING THERE & AWAY

Air

The international airport is 5km northeast of central Lomé. For details on airlines to and from Lomé, see p535.

Bus & Bush Taxi

Rakiéta (☎ 923 25 38) runs a daily bus service between Lomé and Kara (CFA6000, 6½ hours). It leaves at 7.30am from its depot in Atikoumé and stops in Sokodé (CFA5200, five hours) on the way. Bag surcharge is CFA500. Book ahead or arrive early (6am) on the day.

There are also a number of bus services between Lomé and many other major West African cities – see p535.

Bush taxis and minibuses travelling east to Lake Togo/Agbodrafo (CFA600, 45 minutes) and to Cotonou (in Benin; CFA3500, three hours) leave from **Gare de Cotonou** (Blvd de la Marina), just west of the STIF bus station.

If you're going to Ghana, it's best to catch a taxi (shared/chartered CFA500/1500) or taxi-moto (CFA500) to the border and cross on foot. Buses for Accra leave from just across the Ghanaian border in Aflao. See p535 for more details.

Gare d'Agbalépédo (Quartier Agbalépédo), 10km north of central Lomé, serves all northern destinations. Services include Atakpamé (CFA2700, two hours), Dapaong (CFA8800, 10 hours), Kara (CFA6000, five hours) and Sokodé (CFA5200, four hours).

Minibuses to Kpalimé (CFA1900, two hours) leave from **Gare de Kpalimé** (Rue Moyana), 1.5km north of the centre on Route de Kpalimé.

GETTING AROUND

To the airport the taxi fare is about CFA1500 (but count on CFA2000 from the airport into the city).

Taxis are abundant and have no meters. Fares are CFA250 for a shared taxi (CFA350 after 6pm, more to the outlying areas) and CFA1000 nonshared. A taxi by the hour should cost CFA2500 if you bargain well.

Zippy little taxi-motos are also popular, if rather dangerous. You should be able to go anywhere in the centre for CFA200 to CFA300.

You can rent a car from **Avis** (☎ 221 05 82; avis_togo@yahoo.fr; 252 Blvd du 13 Janvier; ⏰ 7.30am-12.30pm & 2.30-7pm Mon-Sat).

AROUND LOMÉ

AGBODRAFO & TOGOVILLE

On the southern shores of **Lake Togo** – part of the inland lagoon that stretches all the way from Lomé to Aného – Agbodrafo is a popular weekend getaway for frazzled Lomé residents. It is also a good place to find a pirogue (traditional canoe; CFA2000 per person) to **Togoville**, which was the former seat of the Mlapa dynasty and Togo's historical centre of voodoo.

East of Agbodrafo is **Hôtel Le Lac** (☎ 320 65 79; www.hotellelactogo.com, in French; r/ste CFA44,000/68,000; 🅿 🍴), a breezy retreat on the shores of Lake Togo. The recently renovated rooms are spacious, with private patios and sweeping lake views. Meals are generally available from CFA4200; the popular Sunday buffet (adult/child CFA10,000/5000) is an all-you-can-eat African and European cuisine extravaganza. The price includes use of the swimming pool. There is also a small beach from where you can swim in the lake.

From the Gare de Cotonou in Lomé, bush taxis frequently travel along the coastal road to Aného (CFA600), via Agbodrafo.

THE SOUTH

ANÉHO

pop 28,100

All that remains of Aného's days as colonial capital in the late 19th century are crumbling pastel buildings. Voodoo is strong here and most obvious at **Vogan's Friday market**, one of the biggest and most colourful in Togo. The

---

HIKING IN THE KPALIMÉ AREA

The heartiest walk is up Togo's highest peak, **Mt Agou** (986m), 20km southeast of Kpalimé. The path climbs between backyards, through cocoa and coffee plantations and luxuriant forests bristling with life. Small terraced mountain villages pepper the slopes and provide fabulous views of the area. On a clear day, you can see Lake Volta in Ghana.

To get to Mt Agou, catch a taxi from Kpalimé to the village of Nyogbo. The track can be hard to find so it's best to take a guide. The walk takes four hours' return. Alternatively, there is a road to the top so you could walk one way and arrange a taxi for your walk back.

The area around **Mt Klouto** (741m), 12km northwest of Kpalimé, is another walking heaven, with forested hills, waterfalls and a myriad butterflies.

The following local guides are recommended: **Adetop** (☎ 441 08 17; www.adetop-togo.org, in French; Route de Klouto; ☷ 7.30am-noon & 3-5pm Mon-Fri) and **ARPV** (☎ 989 20 27; afelete2002@yahoo.fr); Guillaume, one of the founders of ARPV, is particularly recommended, although all guides at Adetop and ARPV have excellent knowledge of the local flora and fauna, but speak little English.

TOGO

fetish market is the largest in the country. The market is 20km northwest of Aného; taxis from Aného (CFA600, 30 minutes) leave from the junction on route to Lomé.

La Becca Hôtel (☎ 331 05 13; Route de Lomé-Cotonou; r with fan/air-con CFA8800/12,800; ✷), southwest of the market, is a good budget establishment. More upmarket and with fabulous lagoon views is **Hôtel Oasis** (☎ 331 01 25; oasisaneh@hotmail.com; Route de Lomé-Cotonou; d with fan/air-con CFA1000/14,000; ✷). The restaurant serves fine cuisine (mains around CFA5000).

From the *gare routière* (bus station), bush taxis and minibuses head to Lomé (CFA900, one hour), as well as to the Beninese border and Cotonou (CFA2500, 2½ hours).

KPALIMÉ
pop 48,300

Kpalimé is only 120km from Lomé, but feels like another world. Hidden among the forested hills of the cocoa and coffee region, it offers some of Togo's best scenery and hiking (above). It's also a busy place thanks to its proximity to the Ghanaian border and important market (Tuesdays and Saturdays), where local farmers sell their products along with the usual bric-a-brac of plastic ware and clothes.

Information

If you want to buy or sell Ghanaian Cedis, moneychangers can be found at the *gare routière*.

Cifaid (☎ 441 07 38; Rue Kuma; per hr CFA350; ☷ 8am-8pm Mon-Sat) For internet, head here. It's southwest of the church.

Ecobank (☎ 441 03 29; Rue du Marché; ☷ 7.45am-5pm Mon-Fri, 8am-4pm Sat) Opposite the Total petrol station; changes money.

Sleeping & Eating

Hôtel Bafana Bafana (Rue de l'Hôpital; r with/without bathroom CFA5000/4000; ✷) Budget travellers can opt for this place. It has stuffy rooms with fan but it's a good central location near the church.

our pick **Chez Fanny** (☎ /fax 441 00 99; hotelchezfanny@yahoo.fr; Route de Lomé; r CFA15,000; ✷ P) Much nicer but a little more expensive is Chez Fanny. Run by a delightful French-Togolese couple, this charming guesthouse 2km south of town is a homey retreat. The six rooms are huge and the patio is a lovely spot to relax. The restaurant (mains CFA3000 to CFA5000) is the best in town, and Fanny and Jean-René can offer invaluable advice on the area.

Le Fermier (☎ 902 98 30; meals CFA3000-4000; ☷ Tue-Sun) Also good for sustenance is Le Fermier, on the northwestern outskirts of town, with great African dishes and a nostalgic 1970s rock soundtrack.

Drinking & Entertainment

For a late-night drink and to catch up on African and European football, the cheerful and easy-going bar **Chez Fomen** (☎ 916 10 17; Rue de Bakula) is the place to go.

Getting There & Away

The *gare routière* is in the heart of town, two blocks east of the Shell petrol station. North-bound bush taxis leave from Rond-point Texaco. The road between Kpalimé and Atakpamé is the worst in the country, which means few taxis from Kpalimé travel further north than Atakpamé (CFA1700, two hours) and you'll have to change there for services to Sokodé or Kara.

You can get minibuses direct to Lomé (CFA1900, two hours), to the Ghanaian border (CFA1000, 30 minutes) and to Ho in Ghana (CFA1500, 1½ hours).

ATAKPAMÉ
pop 41,300

Once the favourite residence of the German colonial administrators, Atakpamé today is a commercial centre. There are no sights, but it makes a pleasant enough stopover on long journeys.

Information

Banks close on Sunday and Monday and only change cash.

BIA-Togo (☎ 440 01 92; Rue du Commerce)

BTCI (☎ 440 01 74; Rue du Commerce)

Cib-Inta (per hr CFA300) Ave de la Libération (☎ 440 03 07; ☼ 7.30am-12.30pm & 2.30-7pm Mon-Fri, 7.30am-12.30pm Sat, 9am-8pm Sun); Rue de la Station de Lomé (☼ 7.30am-8pm Mon-Fri) There is slow web access at both branches.

Sleeping & Eating

Hôtel de l'Amitié (☎ 440 06 25; Agbonou, off Route Internationale; r with fan/air-con CFA4000/7800; ❄) Here you'll find colourful rooms, good views and atmosphere, but it's in a bad location up a dirt track from the Route Internationale, with no street lighting. Meals are available for CFA2000 to CFA3000.

our pick **Hôtel California** (☎ 335 85 44; resto_cali fornia@yahoo.fr; Route Internationale; r with fan & without bathroom CFA2500, r with air-con & bathroom CFA8000; ❄) Run by the inimitable Jeanne, this lovely hotel-restaurant is a gem: the rooms are spotless, the food is delicious and the welcome is superfriendly. It's at the back of the Total petrol station.

Le Sahélien (☎ 440 12 44; Route Internationale; meals CFA2800-5000) The downstairs *maquis* (an informal, street-side eatery) with its enormous grill and informal atmosphere does a brisk trade with the town's *taxi-motos*. Upstairs is more upmarket, and the roof terrace is a nice spot to catch the evening breeze.

There are plenty of cheap food stalls lining Route Internationale.

Drinking

Saint-Louis (Rue du Grand Marché; ☼ 8am-11pm) The music is quite loud at this roof-top *paillote* bar, but it's the perfect place to sink a beer

and watch the clouds of bats spanning the sky at sunset.

Getting There & Away

The T-junction between Route de Lomé and Route Internationale serves as the unofficial terminal for most public transport. Wait south of the junction for taxis to Lomé (CFA2700, two hours); and east of the junction on Route Internationale for taxis to Sokodé (CFA3050, four hours), Kara (CFA4200, five hours) and Dapaong (CFA8500, eight hours).

Taxis to Kpalimé (CFA1700, two hours) leave from next to the market in the centre of town.

PARC NATIONAL DE FAZAO-MALFAKASSA

This 192,000-hectare **national park** (admission per person/private vehicle CFA3000/10,000; ☼ Dec-May) is one of the most diverse West African parks in terms of landscape – with forest, savannah, rocky cliffs and waterfalls. The park boasts 203 species of bird and many species of mammal – including monkeys, antelopes and 60 elusive elephants.

The park is run by Swiss **Fondation Franz Weber** (☎ 550 02 96; www.ffw.ch; Route de Kara; ☼ 7.30am-noon & 2.30-5.30pm Mon-Fri, 7.30am-noon Sat), which has an office in Sokodé.

The foundation organises **guided trips** (1 person CFA18,000, 2-3 people per person CFA13,000, 4-6 people per person CFA9000), which leave Sokodé (below) at 4.30am – contact the office 24 hours in advance.

THE NORTH

SOKODÉ
pop 120,400

Sokodé is Togo's second-biggest city but it doesn't feel like it, with no major sites beyond the odd colonial building. It is the best base for trips to the Parc National Fazao-Malfakassa. Head to Fondation Franz Weber's office (above) for more information.

There are two branches of the cybercafé **CIB-Inta** (per hr CFA300); Route de Bassar ☼ 7am-9pm); Route de Kara ☼ 7am-8pm Mon-Fri). **UTB** (☎ 550 01 62) and **BTCI** (☎ 550 01 07) change money.

Hôtel Essofa (☎ 550 09 89; off Route de Bassar; r with fan/air-con CFA4800/8800, r with air-con & TV CFA10,800; ❄) is one of the better options in Sokodé, with a nice garden and clean rooms (the bathrooms could do better, though). Main meals cost CFA1600.

The fan rooms are not such good value at the **Hôtel Ave Kedia** (☎ 550 05 34; off Route de Kara; r with fan/air-con CFA13,000-24,000, ste CFA28,000; 🔀), but the air-con rooms are very clean and guaranteed to stay cool as it's the only hotel in town with a generator (power cuts are all-too-frequent). Meals here cost around CFA1900 to CFA3000.

If you're not eating at your hotel, try the tee-total (BYO beer) **Cafeteria 2000** (off Route de Kara; mains from CFA1000; 🕑 open 24 hr), whose menu spells out every possible combination of meat and side dish. **Bar Temps en Temps** (Route de Kara; kebabs from CFA200; 🕑 dinner only), with its massive BBQ and candle-lit tables, is a nice joint, as is the friendly **Bar Bon Compte** (Route de Lomé; mains from CFA1000; 🕑 7am-11pm), which also serves beer.

You can catch taxis from the *gare routière* – one block west of the market, behind the Shell petrol station on Route de Bassar – or on the main square between the market and the mosque. Minibuses go regularly to Kara (CFA1600, two hours), Atakpamé (CFA3050, four hours) and Lomé (CFA5200, six hours).

KARA
pop 34,900

Laid out by the Germans on a spacious scale, Kara is the relaxed capital of northern Togo and a good base for trips to Koutammakou (p532). Because Eyadéma was from Pya, a Kabye village about 20km to the north, he pumped a lot of money into Kara and the region has remained a political stronghold of the Eyadéma clan.

The area is famous for the **Evala** coming-of-age festival in July. The main event is *la lutte* (wrestling), in which greased-up young men try to topple each other in a series of bouts.

Information

BTCI (Ave Eyadéma; 🕑 7.30-noon & 2.30-4.30pm Mon-Fri, 9am-3pm Sat) Changes cash.

CIB-Inta (per hr CFA200) Rue de Chaminade (🕑 7am-11pm Mon-Sat); Route Maman N'Danida (🕑 7am-11pm Mon-Sat) Internet access is available at both branches.

Cyber Kara-OK (Ave du 13 Janvier; per hr CFA300; 🕑 8am-7.30pm Mon-Sat, 3-6pm Sun) Offers internet access.

Ecobank (Ave Eyadéma; 🕑 7.45am-5pm Mon-Fri, 8am-4pm Sat) Changes cash and travellers cheques.

Hospital (Ave Eyadéma) The hospital is north of the centre, just past the BTCI and UTB banks.

Sleeping & Eating

Kara has some of the best accommodation for independent travellers in Togo.

our pick **La Douceur** (☎ 660 11 64; douceurkara@yahoo.fr; off Rue de Chaminade; r with fan/air-con CFA5000/8000, ste CFA12,000; 🔀) Down a dirt track in the stadium's neighbourhood, this is a hidden gem. Rooms are spotless and the compound is lovingly maintained. The bar serves the coldest beer in town and the *paillote* restaurant (mains CFA1500 to CFA4000) does great food.

Marie-Antoinette (☎ 660 15 04; http://ma.kara-tg.com; Route Internationale; s/d with fan CFA7500/8500, s/d with air-con from CFA9500/12,500; 🅿 🔀) In a pretty house 2km south of Kara, Marie-Antoinette is a little oasis. Rooms have access to a pleasant patio or small balcony. The restaurant cooks up decent meals for CFA2500 and you can camp in the annex (per car/person CFA1000/1500).

Hôtel Le Jardin (☎ 660 01 34; r CFA8500; 🔀) This delightful hotel, off Rue de l'Hôtel Kara, is aptly named: it's all about the beautifully tended garden. Rooms are small but attractive; toilets are outside (each room has its own).

Hôtel Kara (☎ 660 05 16; fax 660 62 42; Rue de l'Hôtel Kara; s/d from CFA18,500/21,500, s/d bungalow CFA25,000/28,500; 🖭 🔀 🅿) Kara's only top-end hotel has seen better days but its claims to fame include the only swimming pool north of Kpalimé (nonguests CFA1000). The stone bungalows are the most appealing with TV and a little patio. Meals cost CFA6000.

Chez Navi (☎ 660 19 02; Ave Eyadéma; meals CFA500) This is a traditional Togolese eatery where you'll get a blob of *pâte* and ladle of sauce for next to nothin'.

our pick **Centre Grill** (cnr Route de Prison & Ave Eyadéma; meals CFA4000) An attractive place with its straw roof, wicker light shades and blackboard menus, Centre Grill (also known as Marox) serves divine Togolese food and good Western dishes. Try its *fufu sauce arachide* with grilled fish, or guinea fowl with *koliko*.

In addition to the large Tuesday produce market, there is the well-stocked **Supermarché Arc-en-Ciel** (Ave du 13 Janvier; 🕑 8am-8pm Mon-Sat).

Drinking

For drinks, **Le Château** (☎ 660 60 27; Ave du 13 Janvier) is a great bar, popular with the Peace Corps. For more *maquis*-like atmosphere, try the

TOGO

mellow **Bar Le Citoyen** (Rue de Chaminade), perfect to sit under the trees or watch the stars with a (cheap) beer.

Shopping

For great souvenirs, head to **Afasa** (Rue Batascon; ⏰ 8am-12.30pm & 2.30-5pm Mon-Fri), south of town. This women's group sells fabulous bags (CFA1200 to CFA2000), blankets (CFA20,000) and batiks (CFA3000 to CFA20,000). The money finances literacy classes and income-generating activities' training for local women.

Getting There & Away

From the main *gare routière*, about 2km south of the town centre, minibuses regularly head south to Sokodé (CFA1200 1½ hours), Atakpamé (CFA4200, four hours) and Lomé (CFA4600, seven hours). Taxis heading north to Dapaong (CFA3800, four hours) are scarce and it's not unusual to have to wait half a day for one to fill up.

For buses heading to Lomé, **Rakiéta** (Rue du 23 Septembre) has a daily departure at 7.30am (CFA6000, six hours) from its depot.

To get to the border with Benin via Kétao (CFA600, 30 minutes), get a minibus or bush taxi from **Station du Grand Marché** (Ave Eyadéma), next to the market.

KOUTAMMAKOU

Also known as Tamberma Valley after the people who live here, Koutammakou has a unique collection of fortress-like mud houses, founded in the 17th century by people fleeing the slave-grabbing forays of Benin's Dahomeyan kings (see the boxed text, below). The site was listed as World Heritage by Unesco in 2004, and the area is one of the most scenic in the country, with stunning mountain landscapes and intense light.

You can visit Koutammakou as a day trip from Kara. To get there, turn eastward off the Kara–Dapaong highway in Kandé and follow the track in the direction of Nadoba, the area's main village. About 2km down the road, you'll have to pay CFA1500 at the **police post** (☎ 909 08 14; ⏰ 7am-7pm) to enter the site.

The *piste* is in good condition and crosses the valley all the way to Boukoumbé and Natitingou in Benin (see also p535). If you don't have your own transport, chartering a taxi for the day will cost around CFA20,000.

The best guide in the valley is the articulate and super-friendly **Jacques** (☎ 996 20 29). He runs the small souvenir shop in Nadoba and organises walking and cycling tours. Expect to pay about CFA5000, including all *tata* entrance fees.

DAPAONG
pop 31,800

This lively little town is a West African melting pot, with the Burkinabé and Ghanaian borders both within 30km. It sits in the middle of Togo's most arid landscape and gets the full force of the harmattan between November and February.

Information

CIB-Inta (Route de Nasablé; per hr CFA300; ⏰ 7.30am-8pm Mon-Fri, from 8am Sat & 9am Sun) Internet access is available.
Ecobank (Route de Nasablé; ⏰ 7.45am-5pm Mon-Fri, 8am-4pm Sat) Changes travellers cheques, but only in the morning and not on Saturdays.

Sleeping & Eating

Hôtel Le Campement (☎ 770 80 55; Route de la Station de Lomé; r with fan/air-con CFA9800/14,800; 🏊) Dapaong's only midrange hotel, but overpriced. However, rooms are pleasant and spacious, and the overgrown garden that is filled with oversized sculptures is a cool place to laze around. The

---

TAMBERMA COMPOUNDS

A typical Tamberma compound, called a *tata*, consists of a series of towers connected by a thick wall with a single entrance chamber, used to trap an enemy so he can be showered with arrows. The castlelike nature of these extraordinary structures helped ward off invasions by neighbouring tribes and, in the late 19th century, the Germans. As in the *tata somba* in nearby Benin (see the boxed text, p257), life in a *tata* revolves around an elevated terrace of clay-covered logs, where the inhabitants cook, dry their millet and corn, and spend most of their leisure time.

Skilled builders (that's what Tamberma means), the Tamberma only use clay, wood and straw – and no tools. There may be a fetish shrine in front of the compound.

CAVE WITH A VIEW

During the 19th century the Chokossi established a feudal empire over much of northern Togo. The Moba people, who lived on and around the plateau, built cliffside stores in caves on Mt Semoo to protect themselves from Chokossi soldiers and tax collectors. The site is dramatic (not good for people scared of heights) and proffers miles of breathtaking views.

To reach the escarpment, which is known locally as **Grottes de Nano** (Nano Caves; admission CFA2000), head to the village of Nano, 25km southwest of Dapaong. From Nano, ask for directions to the village of Kpierik, another 5km southwest, from where the walk to the cliff and back will take about three hours. The local village chief will ask for a baksheesh.

You should be able to get a guide (CFA1500 to CFA2000 will be adequate) in Nano or Kpierik.

If you don't have your own vehicle, you'll need to charter a taxi (CFA12,000). Otherwise, you'll find shared taxis (CFA700, 30 minutes) on Thursdays, Nano's market day.

French bar-restaurant is expensive (mains CFA4000), but the food is very tasty and the desserts are amazing.

Auberge Idriss (☎ 770 83 49; off Route Internationale; r with fan/air-con & without bathroom CFA4000/6500, r with air-con & bathroom CFA11,000-13,000; ☒) A tidy little guesthouse in a quiet neighbourhood 2km north of town. Rooms in the main building are spacious; those in the annex have shared facilities but are cosier.

Bethel Maquis (☎ 770 88 38; meals from CFA2000) Behind Auberge Idriss north of the centre, this place serves delicious African and Western food in a tranquil garden.

Bar Kadu (Route de Nasablé) Pick and choose your meal from the cauldrons in the kitchen and tuck in while watching Ivorian soap operas. Good fun.

Getting There & Away

Taxis leave the station on Route de Nasablé for Sinkasse on the Burkinabé border (CFA1000), from where transport heads to Ouagadougou.

From Station de Lomé on Route Internationale, 2km south of the centre, bush taxis head to Kara (CFA3800, four hours) and Lomé (CFA8000, 12 hours).

TOGO DIRECTORY

ACCOMMODATION

Togolese accommodation is generally cheap. Expect to pay less than CFA8000 for budget rooms, CFA8000 to CFA15,000 for midrange and CFA15,000 to CFA25,000 for top end. In Lomé, prices are higher, with budget rooms costing up to CFA12,000 and top-end hotels upwards of CFA35,000.

ACTIVITIES

There are plenty of hiking opportunities in Togo, particularly in the Kpalimé region (see p529).

For swimming, head for hotel pools or swim in Lake Togo (p528).

BUSINESS HOURS

Administrative offices Open 7am to noon and 2.30pm to 5.30pm Monday to Friday.

Banks Open 7.45am to 4pm or 5pm Monday to Friday. Most banks are now open through lunch time and on Saturdays, too.

Restaurants Open for lunch and dinner daily, unless otherwise specified.

PRACTICALITIES

■ The government daily is *Togo Presse*. Opposition weeklies include *Le Combat du Peuple* and *Liberté*.

■ Radio remains the main mass media. Radio Lomé and Radio Kara are the state stations. Commercial stations include Radio Zephyr. For the best international news coverage, tune in to RFI on 91.5FM.

■ The state channel is TV Togolaise (TVT). Private satellite provider Media Plus has foreign channels, such as CNN and TV5 (French public TV).

■ The electricity supply is temperamental everywhere.

TOGO

Shops Operate 7.30am to 12.30pm and 2.30pm to 6pm Monday to Saturday.

DANGERS & ANNOYANCES

Petty theft and muggings are common in Lomé, especially on the beach and near the Grand Marché (see p526). *Taxi-motos* in the city may be convenient, but they are dangerous.

People will endlessly try to attract your attention, either by making a 'psssst' or kissing sound. It's tiresome, irritating at worst, but harmless.

Driving in Togo is, to say the least, hair-raising: take care on the roads, particularly at night.

EMBASSIES & CONSULATES

Angola, the Democratic Republic of Congo (DRC, formerly Zaïre), Egypt, Gabon, Libya and Senegal have representation in Lomé. For more details, check out www.republicoftogo.com (in French).

France Consulate (☎ 223 46 40; www.ambafrance-tg.org; Ave Général de Gaulle, Lomé; ☉ 8am-noon); Embassy (☎ 223 46 00; www.ambafrance-tg.org; 13 Ave du Golfe, Lomé)

Germany (Map p525; ☎ 221 23 38; fax 222 18 88; Blvd de la Marina, Lomé)

Ghana (off Map p525; ☎ 221 31 94; 8 Rue Paulin Eklou, Tokoin, Lomé; ☉ 8am-2pm Mon-Fri)

Nigeria (off Map p525; ☎ 221 34 55; Atikoumé, Lomé)

UK British Nationals should contact the British high commission in Accra (p357).

USA (Map p525; ☎ 261 54 70; http://togo.usembassy.gov; Blvd Eyadéma, Lomé; ☉ 8am-5pm Mon-Thu, 8am-12.30pm Fri)

FESTIVALS & EVENTS

Special events include **Evala** in July, the coming-of-age and wrestling festival in the Kabye region around Kara (see p531). There are many others; contact the tourist office in Lomé (p524) for details.

HOLIDAYS

Public holidays include the following:
New Year's Day 1 January
Meditation Day 13 January
Easter March/April
National Day 27 April
Labour Day 1 May
Ascension Day May
Pentecost May/June
Day of the Martyrs 21 June

Assumption Day 15 August
All Saints' Day 1 November
Christmas Day 25 December
See p1140 for details of Islamic holidays.

INTERNET RESOURCES

Republic of Togo (www.republicoftogo.com, in French) The best website, with plenty of country information.
Togo Globe (www.togodaily.com) A useful English-language newspaper online.

MAPS

The 1:500,000 *Carte Touristique du Togo* (Institut Géographique National) is the best country map but can't always be found in Lomé's bookshops. Its 1977 predecessor, the *Carte Routière et Touristique du Togo* can, however, for about CFA3000. The Direction de la Promotion Touristique (p524) in Lomé also gives out dated but free road maps.

MONEY

The unit of currency is the West African CFA franc. Travellers cheques can be exchanged in Lomé, Kara and Dapaong, but you'll pay a commission. Make sure to bring your receipt (*preuve d'achat*) as well as your passport. You'll find Visa cash machines in Lomé and Kara. Only Banque Atlantique in Lomé accepts MasterCard.

Moneychangers can be found in most border towns.

PHOTOGRAPHY & VIDEO

Do not photograph or film government buildings. See also p1144.

POST

Postcards and letters cost CFA550 to Europe, and CFA650 to Australasia and North America. The poste-restante service at the main post office in Lomé is efficient and reliable.

TELEPHONE

Make international calls at Telecom offices, or the private telephone agencies in every town. The latter charge from CFA200 per minute to North America and Europe, and CFA300 to Australasia.

The Togocel and Telecel networks cover 80% of Togo. It costs CFA3000 to get a pay-as-you-go SIM card; top-up vouchers range from CFA450 to CFA45,000. It costs CFA20 to send a local SMS, CFA90 for an international SMS and CFA300 per minute for international calls.

VISAS

Visas are required for everyone except nationals of the Economic Community of West African States (Ecowas) countries. One-week extendable visas (CFA10,000) are issued at major border crossings with Ghana (Aflao/Lomé), Benin (Hilakondji) and Burkina Faso (Sinkasse) and at the airport.

The **Service Immigration Togolaise** (off Map p525; ☎ 250 78 56; Route d'Atakpamé, Lomé; ☒ 7.30am-noon & 2.30-6pm), near the GTA building 8km north of central Lomé, issues 30-day visa extensions in two days. They're normally free when you extend the seven-day visa, or cost CFA10,000 if you're extending a one-month visa. Four photos are required.

The French consulate in Lomé (see opposite) issues visas for Burkina Faso.

You can get a 48-hour transit visa (CFA10,000) for Benin at the Hilakondji border and extend it in Cotonou.

The Ghanaian embassy (see opposite) issues one-month visas within three days for CFA12,000; four photos are needed.

The Visa des Pays de l'Entente (see p1147) is not available in Togo but you should be able to enter the country with it.

WOMEN TRAVELLERS

The Togolese are rather conservative when it comes to marriage: it is therefore incomprehensible to them that women past their 20s might not be married. This will lead to many questions, but it is generally harmless. To avoid attracting any more attention, dress conservatively (legs in particular). For more information and advice, see p1148.

TRANSPORT IN TOGO

GETTING THERE & AWAY
Air

Togo's international airport is 5km northeast of the centre of Lomé. The following airlines operate in Togo and have offices in Lomé.

Afriqiyah Airways (8U; Map p525; ☎ 220 88 51; www.afriqiyah99.eu; Immeuble Taba, Lomé)

Air France (AF; Map p525; ☎ 223 23 23; www.airfrance.com/tg; Immeuble UAT, Lomé) Has the most frequent and reliable services between Togo and Europe.

Air Ivoire (VU; Map p525; ☎ 221 67 13; Immeuble Taba, Lomé)

Ethiopian Airlines (ET; Map p525; ☎ 221 70 74; Immeuble Taba, Lomé)

Royal Air Maroc (AT; Map p525; ☎ 223 48 48; www.royalairmaroc.com; Immeuble Taba, Lomé)

Land
BENIN

Bush taxis regularly ply the road between Gare de Cotonou in Lomé and Cotonou (Benin; CFA3500, three hours) via Hilakondji (CFA800, one hour), while **STIF** (☎ 221 38 48; Gare de STIF) in Lomé has buses to Cotonou (CFA3000, three hours) every other day.

The main northern crossing is at Kétao (northeast of Kara). You can also cross at Tohoun (east of Notsé) or Nadoba (in Koutammakou country), arriving in Boukoumbé, but public transport is infrequent and Beninese visas are not readily available.

BURKINA FASO

The best way to get to Ouagadougou from Lomé is by bus (CFA15,000, 22 hours), via Dapaong. **SKV** (Map p525; ☎ 220 03 01; Blvd du 13 Janvier, Lomé) has two weekly departures, on Tuesday and Friday at 5pm, and is reliable. The service goes on to Bamako (CFA33,000, 48 hours).

Minibuses to Ouagadougou go daily from Gare d'Agbalépédo in northern Lomé (CFA12,000, 24 hours). From Dapaong, you'll easily find a taxi to Sinkasse (CFA1000, 45 minutes), which straddles the border. From there it's CFA5000 to Ouagadougou by bus. The border is open from 6am to 6pm.

GHANA

From central Lomé it is only 2km – CFA500/1500 in a shared/chartered taxi or *taxi-moto* (CFA500) – to the chaotic border crossing (open 6am to 10pm) with Aflao in Ghana. From there, you can cross on foot to pick up minibuses to Accra. The Lomé–Abidjan buses leave from the **STIF bus station** (☎ 221 38 48; Gare de STIF) in Lomé, and go via Accra (CFA6000, four hours).

There are quieter crossings from Kpalimé to Ho and Klouto to Kpandu, but you'll need to have visas and currency sorted out beforehand.

GETTING AROUND
Bush Taxi

Togo has an extensive network of dilapidated bush taxis, which can be anything from an old pick-up truck to a normal sedan car or nine- or 15- seat people carriers. Travel is often agonisingly slow; unfortunately, these bush taxis are generally the only way to get around. Fares are fixed-ish. There is occasionally a surcharge for luggage, generally about CFA500.

Car

Parts of the sealed Route Internationale are still in good condition, but they're few and far between.

Cars can be rented from **Avis** (Map p525; ☎ 221 05 82; avis_togo@yahoo.fr; 252 Blvd du 13 Janvier; ☽ 7.30am-12.30pm & 2.30-7pm Mon-Sat)) in Lomé. If you're driving, you will need an International Driving Permit (IDP). Police checkpoints are common throughout the country but rarely nasty or obstructive.

Petrol stations are plentiful in major towns and you'll find numerous clandestine roadside stalls everywhere selling smuggled Nigerian fuel.

Local Transport

You'll find taxis in most cities. *Taxi-motos*, also called *zemi-johns*, are everywhere. A journey across town costs about CFA200 – more in Lomé. They are also a handy way to get to remote locations in the bush, but tell your driver to go slowly.

Chartering a taxi will generally cost CFA2000 to CFA3000 per hour.

Tours

The tour operator 1001 Pistes (p526) organises excellent trips across the country.

Central Africa

Central Africa is a hot, steamy and precarious place. Travelling here is deep African immersion, in a land rich in dense virgin jungles, fabled rivers, pygmy tribes, hallucinogenic rituals, surfing hippos and soulful gorillas. It has also been off limits for more than a decade.

Gabon and São Tomé & Príncipe aside, until recently instability and appalling infrastructure across a swathe of Central Africa ensured that visiting the region was only for seriously hard-core adventurers. While it would be wrong to paint a picture of Central Africa as an oasis of peace, much of the region can now be visited.

Wildlife wedded to this extraordinary natural beauty is a major drawcard. Gabon's decision to lock away 10% of its territory in national parks has made it an ecotourism destination *par excellence*. Habituated gorillas live in the national parks of the Central African Republic, Congo and the Democratic Republic of Congo's far east, and these reserves combine deliciously remote locations with so many iconic moments of the African wild. Off the coast, São Tomé & Príncipe offers the chance to watch whales, snorkel with dolphins, dive in azure waters, laze on unspoiled beaches and soak up the languid equatorial air.

Yes, Central Africa can be hard-core, but if you're looking for the road less travelled, you've found it. The rewards are worth it.

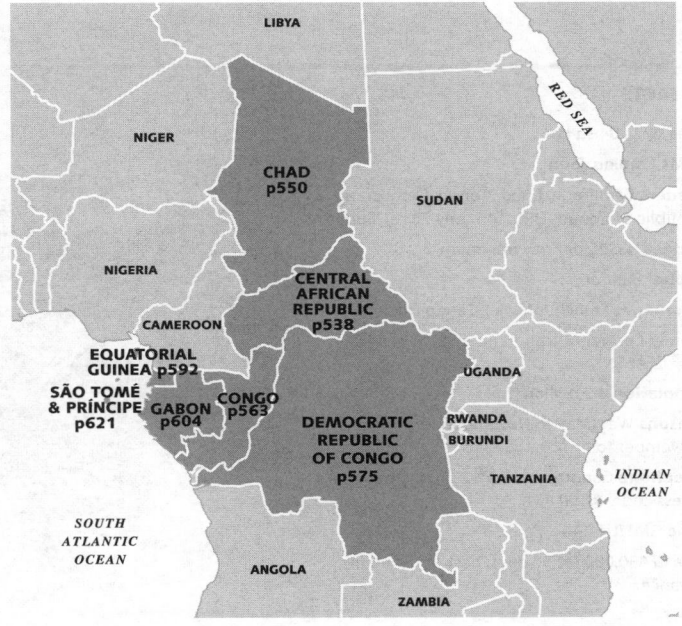

Central African Republic

If you're looking for the 'real' Africa, Central African Republic (CAR) may be it. It's a country with some stunning landscapes and amazing wildlife in the Dzanga-Sangha Reserve, though it's also one of the most impoverished and least developed countries on the continent. It's that pesky 'government-that-doesn't-care-about-its-people' factor keeping it down. For centuries CAR has endured rapacity from invaders and then its own leaders. So, why would the people of such a historically plundered nation be so open and friendly? And why will their conversations with you be far more full of hope than despair? As we said, that's the real Africa for you.

Travelling here is a backpacking bungee jump. Only a handful of independent visitors get CAR bragging rights each year, and they have to earn them. Although CAR is landlocked, difficult and dangerous border crossings make it something of an island, and flights are expensive and rare. And if you do come here, you won't get to visit very much of the country due to long-standing insecurity. But you're sure to love what you can see, so the effort is more than rewarded for those intrepid souls who take the challenge.

FAST FACTS

- **Area** 622,984 sq km
- **ATMs** Coming soon
- **Borders** Cameroon, Chad, Congo, Democratic Republic of Congo (DRC, formerly Zaïre), Sudan
- **Budget** US$25 per day minimum
- **Capital** Bangui
- **Languages** French (official), Sango (national)
- **Money** Central African franc; US$1 = CFA463, €1 = CFA656
- **Population** 4.5 million
- **Seasons** Wet (May to November), dry (November to April)
- **Telephone** Country code ☎ 236; international access code ☎ 00
- **Time** GMT/UTC +1
- **Visa** CFA30,000 for 30 days; best obtained in advance

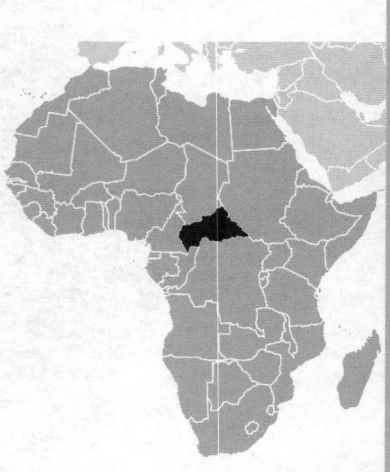

HOW MUCH?

■ **Internet per hour** US$1.65

■ **Cup of coffee** US$1 to US$2

■ **4WD hire per day** US$210

■ **Small malachite necklace** US$5.50

■ **Plate of fish and cassava** US$3.25

LONELY PLANET INDEX

■ **1L petrol** US$1.65

■ **1.5L bottled water** US$1

■ **500mL bottle of '33' beer** US$1

■ **Souvenir T-shirt** US$8

■ **Grand Café baguette** US$0.20

CLIMATE & WHEN TO GO

The rainy season runs from May to October in the south (it's shorter by a month on each end in the north), with July to September the wettest months. Roads get bad at this time, but the waterfalls are at their scenic peaks. Temperatures change little over the year, though December to March, with many days over 30°C, is the hottest time.

HISTORY

Although stone tools provide evidence of inhabitancy from 6000 BC, the most notable ancients resided around present-day Bouar some 2500 years ago. Little is known about them, though it must have been a highly organised civilisation because it left behind about 70 groups of megaliths, some weighing three or four tonnes. The present cultures most likely arrived in the 15th century, probably fleeing Arab slave traders, but by the 18th century they, too, were sending their captives across the Sahara to markets in Egypt or down the Congo River to the Atlantic Ocean. This

---

WARNING

While southwestern CAR is generally secure, the rest of the country remains largely lawless and potentially very dangerous since fighting continues between the government and various rebels. Highway robbery is common. Check the situation before travelling here.

---

industry, which didn't completely end until 1912, decimated entire cultures and largely depopulated the eastern half of the country.

Colonial Days

France launched into CAR in 1885, finding a shattered society rich in agricultural potential and under the rule of Sudanese-born Sultan Rabah. France killed Rabah in 1900 and soon after consolidated its control of the country, which it divided into 17 parts and offered them to European companies in exchange for a fixed annual payment plus 15% of agricultural profits. Vast cotton, coffee and tobacco plantations were established and worked by an often brutally conscripted local population. They resisted for decades, but opposition was eventually broken through a combination of French military action, famine and severe smallpox epidemics.

The first signs of nationalism sprang up after WWII via Barthélemy Boganda's Mouvement d'Evolution Sociale de l'Afrique Noire. In 1960, a year after Boganda was killed in a suspicious plane crash, his party forced the French to grant independence.

Forty Years of Chaos

The leadership was taken over by David Dacko, who became the country's first president. Dacko's rule quickly became repressive and dictatorial and in 1966 he was overthrown by an army commander and close relative, Jean-Bédel Bokassa, kicking off 13 years of one of the most brutal regimes Africa has ever experienced. In one instance Bokassa reportedly ordered the killing (some claim he participated) of schoolchildren who protested against expensive mandatory school uniforms made by a company owned by his wife.

France, coveting the uranium deposits at Bakouma and the abundant big-game hunting grounds near the Sudan border (personally sponsored by the former French president, Valéry Giscard d'Estaing), supported Bokassa and bailed out his floundering economy. Using the country's mineral resources as carrots, Bokassa also negotiated loans from South Africa and private US banks. He then squandered virtually all this money. His final fantasy was to have himself crowned 'emperor' of a renamed Central African Empire in 1977. Despite the worldwide derision, France helped to fund much of his coronation's price tag of more than US$20 million.

CENTRAL AFRICAN REPUBLIC

Such excess, together with the out-of-control violence, made Bokassa an embarrassment to his backers. In 1979, France abruptly cut off aid to the 'empire' and, while Bokassa was in Libya seeking still more funds, flew in former president David Dacko together with loads of French paratroopers. Dacko did no better this time around and was overthrown again in 1981 and replaced by André Kolingba, who in 1986 created a one-party state that was also widely seen as corrupt. At this point Bokassa popped up again but was promptly convicted of treason, murder and, for good measure, cannibalism, and sentenced to death. This was changed to life imprisonment and he was confined to the palace he'd constructed at Berengo.

Kolingba's 12 years of absolute rule ended when he was defeated in presidential elections in 1993, held at the insistence of the US and France, and Ange-Félix Patassé became the leader of CAR's first real civilian government. Patassé immediately stacked the government with fellow ethnic group members, which prompted a 1996 army mutiny, led by officers from a southern ethnic group. The capital became a war zone, although a peace deal signed the next year was backed up by an 800-strong African peacekeeping mission, later replaced by UN forces. Patassé's 1999 re-election was followed by riots over government mismanagement and corruption in 2000 and attempted coups in 2001 and 2002.

Former army chief of staff General François Bozizé, who led the 2002 coup attempt, didn't stop fighting after Libyan forces sent to protect the regime thwarted his initial bid on Bangui, and the next year, when Patassé made the familiar African mistake of popping out of the shop (for a state visit to Niger), Bozizé marched into the capital and made himself president. Patassé scooted off to exile in Togo. The euphoria was short-lived, however, as little changed under the Bozizé regime. He made the usual promise to hold elections, but abandoned the second part of the promise, not to stand himself. Bozizé won the election in 2005, though Patassé was not allowed to run.

CAR Today

After Bozizé came to power the safety situation in Bangui improved dramatically, as did the economy, but not much changed elsewhere. Fighting continued upcountry, and by the end of 2006 rebel attacks in the northeast and northwest forced some 300,000 people to flee their villages. The start of 2007 saw Libyan-backed peace talks begin and crawl along until June 2008 when most rebel groups signed a peace agreement with the government. Fighting didn't stop, though it did slow considerably. A unity government, including leaders of the main rebel groups, kicked off 2009; just a few months later rebel attacks were back on the increase. Today the government still controls less than half the country.

CULTURE

Religion is paramount here; more so than in most of Africa. Fifty percent of Central Africans are Christian, 15% are Muslim and 35% have stuck wholly with traditional animistic convictions; these ancient customs still strongly influence most people's lives, regardless of their principal faith.

CAR encompasses over 80 ethnic groups, which can basically be grouped into riverine, grassland and forest cultures; the latter include the Aka people (pygmies – though they don't like that term; singular is MoAka, plural is BaAka). The Baya-Mandjia and Banda, originating in the western and central savannas respectively, compose 75% of the population.

Some 70% of the population lives a rural existence and subsistence agriculture remains the backbone of the economy. The same percentage lives on less than a dollar a day.

FOOD & DRINK

While rice and yam are sometimes available, Central Africans love their cassava, eating it at virtually every meal with a meat, fish or vegetable sauce. Koko, which is a little like eating grass only it's pretty tasty, is another popular sauce ingredient. Bushmeat, particularly monkey, boa and antelope, is also common in markets and even on menus. Forest caterpillars are a popular treat during June. A dash of *piment* (hot sauce) is put on almost everything.

Palm wine is the most popular firewater in the south, while *bili-bili,* a sorghum-based alcohol, predominates in the north. Both are available in Bangui, but here beer is king.

ENVIRONMENT

CAR, just a tad smaller than France, is landlocked smack bang in the middle of the continent. The country is one immense plateau varying in height mostly between 600m and 700m, tapering down to 350m in

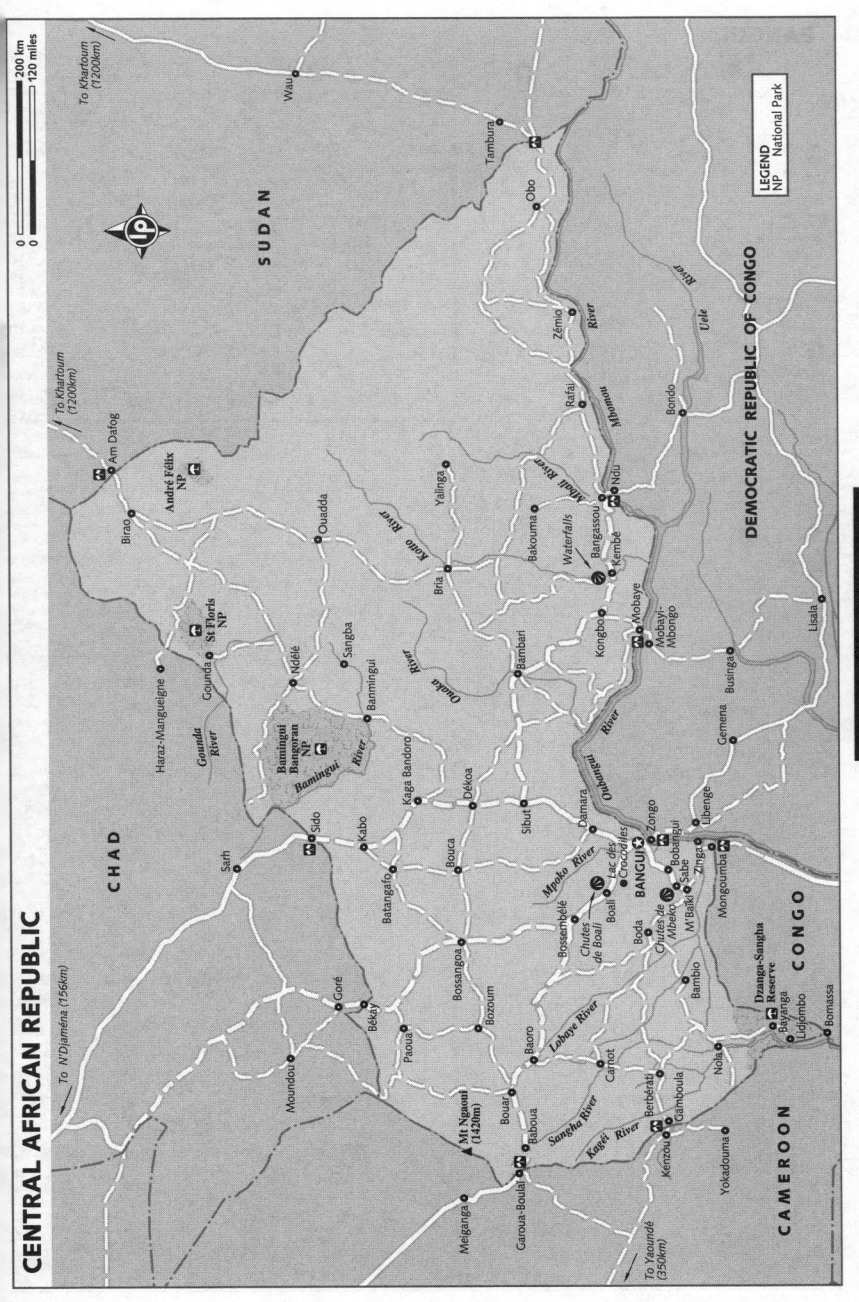

CENTRAL AFRICAN REPUBLIC

LEGEND
NP National Park

200 km
120 miles

SUDAN

To Khartoum
(1200km)

To Khartoum
(1200km)

To N'Djaména (156km)

To N'Djaména

CHAD

DEMOCRATIC REPUBLIC OF CONGO

CAMEROON

CONGO

To Yaoundé
(350km)

Wau

Tambura

Obo

Aïn Dafog

André Félix
NP

Birao

Ouadda

Yalinga

Zémio

Rafaï

Ndu

Bondo

Lisala

Uele
River

Mbomou

Mbari River

Bangassou

Kembé

Waterfalls

Bakouma

Bria

Kongbo

Mobaye

Mobayi-
Mbongo

Bambari

Bustinga

Gemena

Libenge

Zongo

Bangui

Bossembélé

Bocaranga

Sibut

Dékoa

Kaga Bandoro

Kabo

Sido

Sarh

Batangafo

Bouca

Damara

Bangui

Lac des
Crocodiles

Mpoko River

Boali

Chutes de
M'Baéli

Boda

Bambio

Dzanga-Sangha
Reserve

Bayanga

Lidjombo

Bomassa

Nola

Gamboula

Berbérati

Carnot

Baoro

Bossangoa

Bozoum

Paoua

Béká

Goré

Moundou

Melganga

Garoua-Boulaï

Bouar

Baboua

Mt Ngaoui
(1420m)

Yokadouma

Kenzou

Kaga River

Sangha River

Labaye River

Lobaye River

Sangha
River

Ouaka River

Kotto River

Kotto River

Gribingui

Bamingui
River

Bamingui

Bamingui Bangoran
NP

Sangha

Adélé

Goundi

Haraz-Mangueigne

Gounda
River

St Floris NP

M'Baïki

Mongoumba

Bimbo

Bocaranga

Zinga

Mbaïki

Chutes de
Boali

Bossemptélé

Kaga Bandoro

Ndélé

Bangui

CENTRAL AFRICAN REPUBLIC

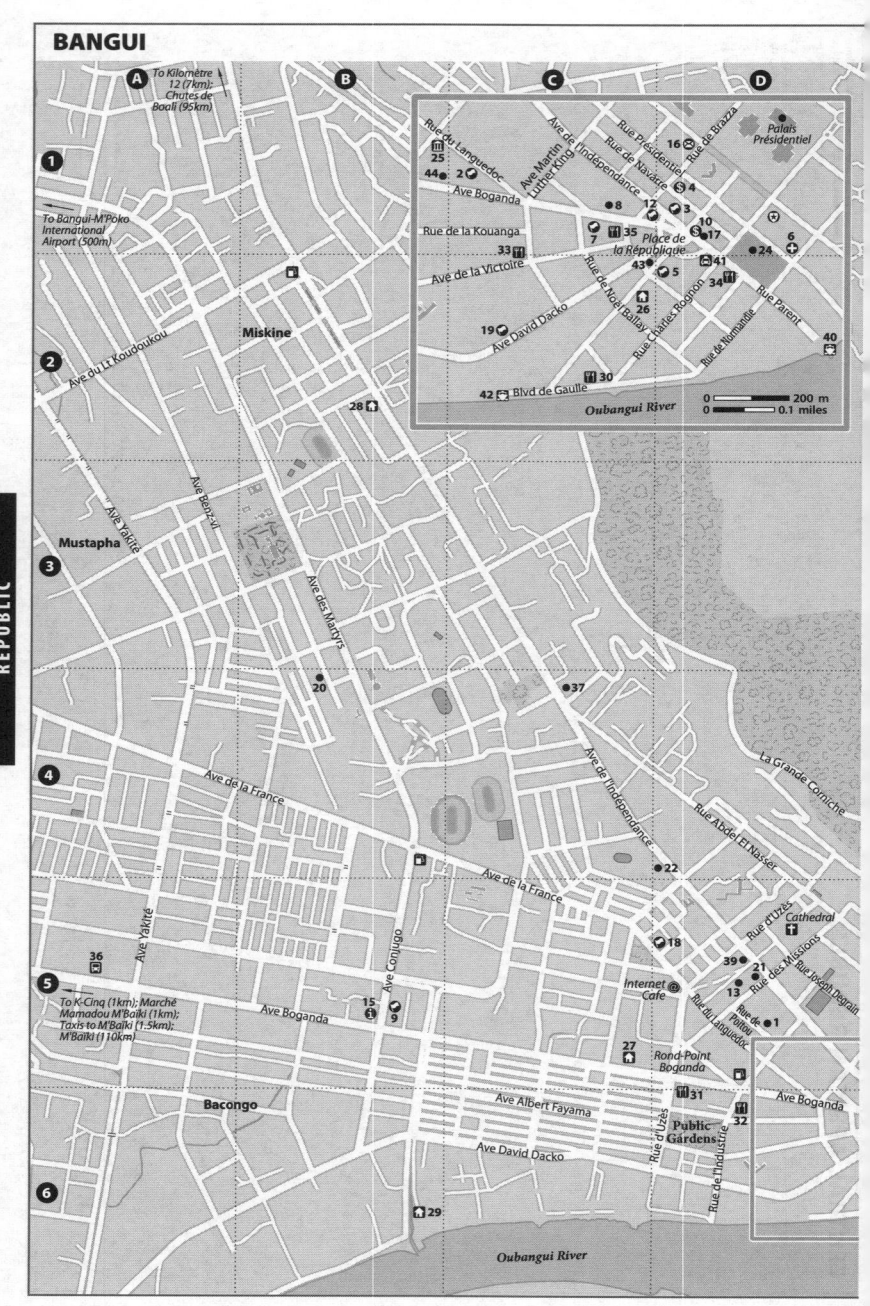

BANGUI

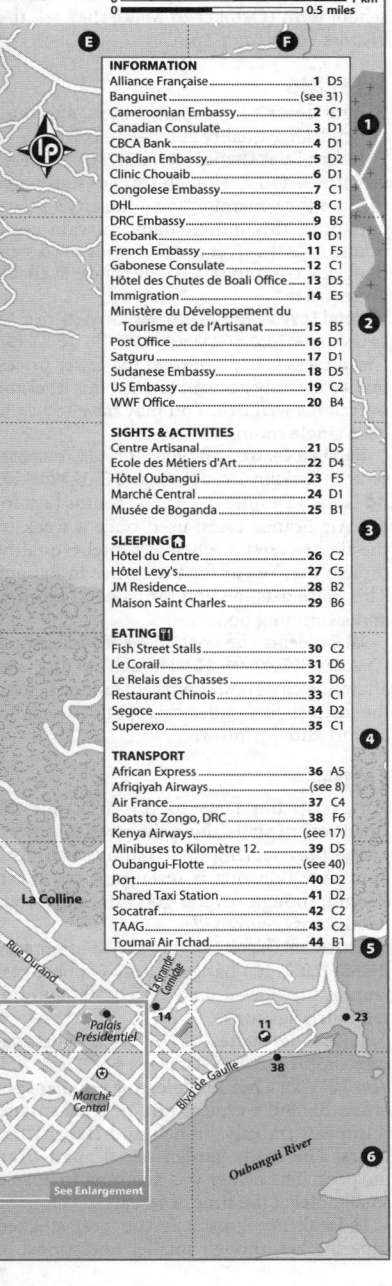

| 0 | 1 km |
| 0 | 0.5 miles |

INFORMATION
Alliance Française..................................1 D5
Banguinet...(see 31)
Cameroonian Embassy..........................2 C1
Canadian Consulate...............................3 D1
CBCA Bank...4 D1
Chadian Embassy...................................5 D2
Clinic Chouaib.......................................6 D1
Congolese Embassy................................7 C1
DHL..8 C1
DRC Embassy..9 B5
Ecobank..10 D1
French Embassy.....................................11 F5
Gabonese Consulate............................12 C1
Hôtel des Chutes de Boali Office.......13 D5
Immigration..14 E5
Ministère du Développement du
    Tourisme et de l'Artisanat...............15 B5
Post Office...16 D1
Satguru...17 D1
Sudanese Embassy................................18 D5
US Embassy...19 C2
WWF Office...20 B4

SIGHTS & ACTIVITIES
Centre Artisanal...................................21 D5
Ecole des Métiers d'Art.......................22 D4
Hôtel Oubangui...................................23 F5
Marché Central.....................................24 D1
Musée de Boganda...............................25 B1

SLEEPING
Hôtel du Centre...................................26 C2
Hôtel Levy's..27 C5
JM Residence..28 B2
Maison Saint Charles...........................29 B6

EATING
Fish Street Stalls...................................30 C2
Le Corail..31 D6
Le Relais des Chasses..........................32 D6
Restaurant Chinois...............................33 C1
Segoce..34 D2
Superexo...35 C1

TRANSPORT
African Express.....................................36 A5
Afriqiyah Airways..............................(see 8)
Air France..37 C4
Boats to Zongo, DRC...........................38 F6
Kenya Airways...................................(see 17)
Minibuses to Kilomètre 12..................39 D5
Oubangui-Flotte..............................(see 40)
Port...40 D2
Shared Taxi Station..............................41 D2
Socatraf...42 C2
TAAG..43 C2
Toumaï Air Tchad................................44 B1

La Colline
Rue Durand
Palais Présidentiel
Marché Central
Bld de Gaulle
La Grande Corniche
Oubangui River
See Enlargement

the far southwest. The closest thing to a real mountain is Mt Ngaoui, which at 1420m is the highest point in the country.

Though CAR is mostly associated with its tropical rainforest, these are found only in the southwest; sweeping savannas, interspersed with many rivers, cover most of the country. Poaching is a huge problem, and logging is on the increase which threatens CAR's standing as one of the last great wildlife refuges.

BANGUI

pop 690,000

Bangui (rhymes with 'on key'), CAR's capital and only significant city, stretches along the Oubangui River with a row of lush green hills behind it. The French founded it in 1889 to stake their claim to the region, and by the 1970s it was known as La Coquette (The Beautiful). The moniker, still featured prominently around town, is a little ironic these days, though finally signs of rebirth are far more common than remnants of war.

ORIENTATION

All major avenues radiate from the Place de la République, and nearly everything of interest or importance is within walking distance from here. The heart of the African quarter is the lively K-Cinq junction (Kilomètre 5) west of town, which is known variously as Kilo 5, Kam Cinq or PK5 (pronounced 'peeka sink'). It has the largest market, many bars and plenty of thieves.

INFORMATION

Alliance Française (☎ 72701148; Rue de Poitou; ⏲ 7.30am-12.30pm & 3-8pm Mon-Fri, 7.30am-12.30pm Sat) Features a very active cultural calendar and an art gallery.

Banguinet (Ave Boganda; per hr CFA800; ⏲ 7.30am-9pm) Speedy connections, most of the time.

Clinic Chouaib (☎ 21612162; Rue de Normandie) This hospital can handle simple emergencies.

DHL (☎ 21619393; Ave Boganda)

Ministère du Développement du Tourisme et de l'Artisanat (☎ 75055310; Ave Boganda; ⏲ 9am-4pm Mon-Fri)

Pharmacie Sambo (☎ 21610343; Ave Koudoukou; ⏲ 8am-8pm Mon-Fri, 8am-12.30pm Sat) Bangui's best pharmacy.

Post office (Rue Joseph Degrain; ⏲ 7.30am-2.30pm Mon-Fri) Poste restante has been discontinued.

CENTRAL AFRICAN REPUBLIC

Satguru (☎ 70102814; Place de la République; ⏰ 8am-6pm Mon-Sat) Reliable place to buy plane tickets.

DANGERS & ANNOYANCES

Overall, Bangui is quite hassle-free these days. At K-Cinq, criminals (often drunk and stoned) come out even before the sun goes down, so plan to leave about 5pm. Downtown isn't nearly as rough, but still take a taxi after dark. The police and military set up checkpoints to demand bribes from drivers: you may be able to talk your way through if your papers are in order, otherwise CFA1000 should do the trick. Electricity remains unreliable, and while most hotels have generators they usually don't power the air conditioners.

SIGHTS & ACTIVITIES

The small **Musée de Boganda** (Rue du Languedoc; ⏰ 8.30am-3.30pm Mon-Fri), in the leader's former home, isn't well tended, but the collection, from bark-cloth clothing to 'Emperor' Bokassa's bed, is quite interesting. French-speaking guides will explain it all. Admission price is negotiable.

Probably the most entertaining thing to do in Bangui is to take a stroll and sip a beer along the Oubangui River east of downtown. The Hôtel Oubangui (ex-Sofitel) has seating out on a rocky peninsula, but you pay dearly for the views. There are plenty of *pirogues* (traditional canoes) down here, and a ride on the river is fun. Bargain hard.

La Grande Corniche, a dirt road winding through the forest reserve on the hills behind town, is a cool, quiet escape. Looking down from above will confirm the feeling you had that Bangui is as much a big village as a big city. It starts behind the Palais Présidentiel. Plan on a couple of hours to walk it, and don't go alone.

Bangui has many markets. **Marché Central** (Rue Parent), filled mostly with food and clothes, is stroll worthy. **Marché Mamadou M'Baïki** (Ave Boganda) at K-Cinq is more interesting for the madness than the merchandise. For artisan goods, head to Bangui's top attraction for the few thousand visitors who arrive each year: the **Centre Artisanal** (Ave de l'Indépendance; ⏰ 8am-6pm). It has masks, malachite, batiks and all the other crafts common to the whole Congo basin. You can see many of these items being made by the students and their teachers at **Ecole des Métiers d'Art** (Artisan Training School; Ave de l'Indépendance). During the school term (October to May), they ask that visitors come after 1pm.

SLEEPING

Bangui doesn't have many hotels, and most are midrange quality at top-end prices.

Maison Saint Charles (☎ 72259237; off Ave David Dacko; r CFA4000; P) Though simple (staff *might* turn on the generator when the city's power cuts out), this quiet, shady mission compound near the river provides the only decent budget accommodation. Meals are available on request.

Hôtel Levy's (☎ 75553802; www.levyhotel.com; Ave Boganda; s CFA12,300, d CFA18,300-30,500; P ✂ 🖳 ☎) Cleanliness is haphazard at the lower prices, but it's the only game in town at this level and overall it's well run. You may have to beg to get a single room.

Hôtel du Centre (☎ 21610279; hotelducentre@banguinet.net; Ave Valéry Giscard d'Estaing; s/d CFA39,140/41,200; ✂ 🖳 ☎) Despite the prices, rooms (ask for the Air France ones, used once a week by the flight crew) are below Motel 6 quality, though they're par for the course in Bangui. This place gets the nod for its good location and swimming pool.

JM Residence (☎ 75577767; Ave de l'Indépendance; r CFA45,000-100,000; P ✂) Though no four-star affair, the city's best rooms are hidden behind the fortress-like wall at this spot between the airport and downtown.

EATING

For cheap but tasty food, check out the small row of stalls along the river southwest of the port serving their famous fish until 5pm. Ave Boganda is restaurant central in Bangui, though several good ones are scattered across *centre-ville*.

Restaurant Chinois (☎ 21617240; Rue Grandin; mains CFA2600-12,000; ✂) Bangui's only Chinese restaurant provides a little variety, though not too much flavour.

Le Relais des Chasses (☎ 77771515; Rue de l'Industrie; mains CFA3800-16,000; ⏰ 11am-3pm & 6-10.30pm Wed-Mon; ✂) Aka Chez Freddie, this popular spot offers Bangui's typical mix of African and European (mostly French and Italian) flavours. The shady garden sets it apart from the pack. The owner was planning to open a small hotel at the time of research.

Le Corail (Ave Boganda) is the best-stocked supermarket, though smaller ones (most of which have no signs) like **Superexo** (Rue de la Résistance) and **Segoce** (Rue Parent) are cheaper.

DRINKING & ENTERTAINMENT
The top restaurants are also the most popular watering holes for expats, aid workers and French soldiers. For bars with local flavour, try the Miskine quartier, with many to choose from along Ave du Lt Koudoukou west of Ave des Martyrs, though absolutely take a taxi or go with a local friend at night.

Rue de la Kouanga is Bangui's nightclub hub, and Hôtel Levy's hosts a soukous band every Sunday from 8pm to 11pm; admission is CFA1000.

GETTING THERE & AWAY
Bangui-M'Poko International Airport is located 7km northeast of downtown. See p548 for flight information. A private taxi should cost CFA2000 to CFA2500. For a shared taxi walk straight out the front for 750m or so, but don't try this at night.

With the exception of the comfy, air-con buses run by **African Express** (☎ 21610278; Ave Boganda), which go to Bossangoa via Boali (CFA2000, two hours) every other day at 7.30am, transport to all points north departs from Kilomètre 12. Catch rides to M'Baïki from the junction just west of Kilomètre 5.

GETTING AROUND
Shared taxis (CFA150) and minibuses (CFA125) zip along all main arteries: the former depart from Marché Central and Place de la République, while the latter have stations further out, most notably by the cathedral, and this is where you need to go to get to Kilomètre 12. Chartering a taxi costs CFA1000 (daytime) and CFA1500 (night-time) for short hops, and CFA3500 per hour.

AROUND BANGUI

CHUTES DE BOALI
This **waterfall** (admission CFA1000; ☙ 6.30am-5pm), 95km northwest of Bangui, tumbles 50m down and stretches 250m wide. It's spectacular in the rainy season, but no more than a trickle when it's dry due to water being diverted for a dam. Just upstream is a pseudo *pont de lianes* (vine bridge), and on the way to Boali is **Lac des Crocodiles** (admission CFA1000; ☙ daylight hr), where

villagers lure the lake's residents onto shore with a chicken, which costs CFA1500 if the chicken gets to survive; more if it doesn't. It's 10km south of the highway.

Hôtel des Chutes de Boali (☎ 75048830; r CFA12,000-20,000; ✸) has very simple rooms (shared bathroom and fan in the cheapest; concrete floors in all) and a **restaurant** (mains CFA2500-6000; ☙ 6.30am-10pm) above the falls.

Bush taxis (CFA1500 to sit inside, 1½ hours) are frequent from Kilomètre 12 to the turn-off, just before Boali village. From here it's a 5km walk or *moto-taxi* ride (CFA500) to the chutes. On Friday, Saturday and Sunday the hotel has a van departing from its office in Bangui at 9am and returning at 4pm. It's CFA6000 per seat, but only goes if all six seats are paid for. For a little extra, it will take you to the crocs, too.

THE ROAD TO M'BAÏKI
There are some interesting diversions along National Hwy 6 as it heads out of Bangui. At the 80km mark, you'll reach **Berengo**, the site of one of Bokassa's retreats. It's now an army base, but if you ask the soldiers (and give them a few thousand CFA), they'll let you peek briefly at his grave, oversized statue and ruined palace.

Both Bokassa and independence hero Barthélemy Boganda were born just up the road in **Bobangui**, where an attractive memorial rings the latter's grave. His family's house (the old one with the metal roof) is across the street, and some personal effects are stored in a small building behind the ornamental gate, though the key is kept in Bangui so it's rarely possible to see them.

Next up is **Sabe**, known for its ebony carvings, and 1km further, just at the head of the next village, is the start of the 3.5km track to **Chutes de Mbeko** (admission per person CFA500). It's often overgrown, but a saloon car can handle it in the dry season. Just as tall as Boali, but narrow, Mbeko falls have a lovely jungle setting, making this a nice destination even at low flow. You can swim at the base.

The paved road ends at **M'Baïki**, a former colonial centre that used to be a jumping-off point for visiting nearby pygmy encampments. These days, settled pygmies, living in mudbrick villages indistinguishable from those of their taller neighbours, are found in several places along the highway around here, but those who remain genuine forest dwellers live far from town. There's a little cultural centre on the highway by the large church where tour groups sometimes come to see song and dance shows. Paradise it's not, but should you wish to stay the night, the very basic **Hôtel Paradis Palace de la Lobaye** (☎ 72799482; r CFA3000) has the best rooms available.

Minibuses and trucks to M'Baïki, costing CFA1500 to CFA2000 and taking three to four hours, run all day but most frequently in the morning. Hiring a taxi in Bangui to check out all of the above should cost no more than CFA30,000.

DZANGA-SANGHA RESERVE

A visit to this 4379-sq-km **national park** (www.dzanga-sangha.org; admission per person/vehicle CFA15,000/10,000) is mainly about gorillas and elephants, and a day out with both can be magical.

More than a hundred elephants at a time often congregate at **Bai Dzanga** (per person CFA30,000), a natural forest clearing where they dig deep holes to eat the mineral-rich mud. It also attracts buffalo, bongo antelope, giant forest hogs and more. After an easy but wet trail (thigh-high water at times), you'll reach a large viewing platform with great views. It's best visited in the afternoon. Nearby are two sites where people (12 per day) can visit habituated western lowland gorillas (per person CFA100,000). The trackers find them nearly every time. Truck hire to the sites is CFA100,000 per day, though if you take a guard, you're allowed to walk to Bai Dzanga, 14km away. Nobody under the age of 16 can visit the gorillas.

This corner of CAR is the domain of the BaAka, who lead all forest trips, but you can also join them in cultural activities (from CFA5000 per person; national park fees don't apply), such as net hunting and gathering medicinal plants. For a more intensive immersion in BaAka life, join a trip deep into the forest with **Louis Sarno** (akkaman11@yahoo.co.uk), an American and author of *Song from the Forest: My Life Among the Ba-Benjelle Pygmies*, who came to the area in the 1980s to study the music and stayed. His tours are expensive but genuine, and some of the money goes back into the community. The local Bantu residents take visitors out in *pirogues* to collect raffia palm wine.

Arrangements can be made at 'The Project' offices above the village of Bayanga or at the **WWF office** (☎ 21614299; Ave des Martyrs; ☽ 10.30am-3pm Mon-Fri) in Bangui. Reservations (highly advisable) can also be made on the national park website.

SLEEPING & EATING

our pick **Doli Lodge** (r without bathroom CFA10,000, s/d/ CFA45,000/65,000/85,000; ⓟ) The park-affiliated place along the Sangha River is where most visitors bunk down. It has comfortable stilted rooms with river-view decks, plus simpler huts. A

DZANGA-SANGHA UNDER THREAT

We had one of our best-ever days in Africa visiting Dzanga-Sangha, but unfortunately we must add a footnote to our glowing review. Talking to both locals and resident foreigners we heard alarming stories of mismanagement and indifference by park management and staff; and we experienced some examples of this personally. It's an ill-timed malaise as the park is at a serious crossroads.

There are questions about sustainable levels of logging around national park lands, and the population living on the edge of the park is growing fast, but the gravest threat is rampant poaching, often with the complicity of government officials and even park employees. Although it's not sold openly in the market, elephant and gorilla meat is available in Bayanga and Bangui for locals on the grapevine. Talk to people who were here just a decade ago and they'll tell you stories of vast herds of animals, of regularly encountering gorillas in the forest and of seeing hippos on the river, which clearly shows the wasted potential.

These issues haven't reached a critical level for the park yet, but if people don't step up soon, they probably will. We're not suggesting people stay away. Just the opposite…we're begging you to go. More visitors (only about 700 people come annually) is probably the best way to turn the tide.

filling dinner, served on a riverside terrace with intoxicating sunset views, costs CFA7000.

A new choice is the similarly rustic-but-comfortable **Sangha Lodge** (www.sanghalodge.com; s/d/f CFA45,000/65,000/155,000; (P)) with seven bungalows on the river 10km north of town, well away from the bustle of the village. It leads some of its own forest activities, including night-time spotlighting trips on the river and camping with the BaAka, and can arrange transport from Bangui.

Bayanga has some rough guesthouses, the best of which is **Auberge Zo-Kwe-Zo** (r CFA2000; (P)), near the entrance to town. It also has several small restaurants and one shop stocking expensive imported goods.

GETTING THERE & AWAY

Dzanga-Sangha is 500km southwest from Bangui. Unless you're lucky enough to score a free or cheap ride with someone driving there, getting to the park is either difficult or expensive. In the dry season a 4WD can reach Bayanga in 10 hours. Police checkpoints are frequent but not overly onerous. Charter flights cost CFA1,800,000.

If you're patient and not too concerned about comfort, the journey can be made in a series of truck trips through Boda, Berbérati and Nola. The route is shorter and the road better via Bambio, which is how people with their own cars go, but there's much less traffic. If all goes well, expect to travel for three days and to pay around CFA20,000.

No matter how you travel, enquire with the WWF about the current situation.

CAR DIRECTORY

BUSINESS HOURS

Office hours are 8am to 5pm weekdays with one- or two-hour rest for lunch.
Banks From 7.30am to 2pm Monday to Friday and from 8.30am to noon on Saturday.
Restaurants From 7am to midnight, except the Western ones, which open at 11am and break between 3pm and 6pm.
Shops Typically close at 7pm Monday to Saturday.

DANGERS & ANNOYANCES

In most of the country, aggressive rebels, unruly soldiers, heavily armed poachers and highway bandits are sinister enough to their own people, but particularly target foreigners: even NGOs have been attacked. Outside

PRACTICALITIES

- CAR uses the metric system.
- Electricity is 220V/50Hz. Plugs have two round pins, as in continental Europe.
- Except for BBC World Service, heard in Bangui on 90.2FM, all press is in French or Sango. If you understand these languages, UN-run Radio Ndeke Luka (100.8FM) is reliable for local news.

Bangui, drive only at night, and fuel up often as petrol shortages are common.

EMBASSIES & CONSULATES

All embassies and consulates listed here are located in Bangui (Map pp542–3).
Cameroon (☎ 21611687; Rue du Languedoc)
Canada (☎ 21613039; Ave de l'Indépendance)
Chad (☎ 21614677; Ave Valéry Giscard d'Estaing)
Congo (☎ 21614390; Ave Boganda)
Democratic Republic of Congo (☎ 21618240; Ave Conjugo)
France (☎ 21613000; Blvd de Gaulle) Assists British citizens with emergencies.
Gabon (☎ 75558989; Ave de l'Indépendance)
Sudan (☎ 21613821; Ave de la France)
USA (☎ 21610200; http://bangui.usembassy.gov; Ave David Dacko)

HOLIDAYS

New Year's Day 1 January
Boganda Day 29 March
Easter March/April
Labour Day 1 May
Mother's Day June
Independence Day 13 August
Assumption Day 15 August
All Saints' Day 1 November
Proclamation Day 1 December
Christmas Day 25 December

MAPS

The *IGN République Centraficaine* (1:1,500,000) map is very old, but still the best available. Buy it before you come.

MONEY

Central African Republic uses the Central African franc (CFA). US dollars are easy to change, but rates are usually poor, so bring euros. Official exchange facilities are only available in Bangui: **Ecobank** (Place de la République; 🕑 7.30am-4pm Mon-Fri, 8-11am Sat), which accepts

CENTRAL AFRICAN REPUBLIC

US dollars, euros and rand, is the handiest. **CBCA Bank** (Rue de Brazza; ☺ 7.30am-2pm Mon-Fri, 7.30am-noon Sat) will change American Express travellers cheques issued in euros.

During our visit, banks were negotiating to bring internationally linked ATM service for Visa cards (and perhaps MasterCard) to Bangui, and Ecobank had already installed some machines. Credit cards are rarely accepted.

TELEPHONE

Land lines, which are unreliable, start with 21, while mobile codes begin with 7. There are no area codes.

SIM cards cost CFA500. At research time, Nationlink had by far the lowest international rates: CFA180 per minute to France or the US versus CFA300 per minute for the other companies, though calls to some countries can be as high as CFA350 per minute regardless of which company you use. Local calls cost CFA100 to CFA150 per minute depending on the network.

VISAS

Visas are required by most visitors and cost around CFA30,000 for one-month single entry. Where there's no CAR embassy, French embassies can issue CAR visas. If you know someone in Bangui, they can make arrangements for a visa on arrival at the airport for you, but it's a hassle. Unofficially, visas may be issued at land borders, but you risk being turned away or paying through your teeth.

Rather than granting extensions, **immigration** (Ave Mobutu, Bangui; ☺ 7am-1pm Mon-Sat) issues new visas. You'll pay a CFA200,000 penalty if you apply after your current visa has expired. The office is just inside the army base gate.

Visas for Onward Travel

Cameroon One-month visas cost CFA50,000 and take two days to issue. Bring two photocopies of your passport (including the page with your CAR visa) and two photos.
Chad Cost for 30-day visas is CFA36,000 for most nationalities and they're issued the next day. Bring two photos and a photocopy of your passport.
Congo A one-month visa, ready the next day, costs CFA30,000 (double for same-day service) for most nationalities. You need a photocopy of your passport and two photos.
DRC Thirty-day single-/multiple-entry visas cost CFA44,000/64,000. You need one passport photocopy and two photos. Depending on who is in the office when you apply, it can be ready the same day or the next.
Sudan See p210 for details.

TRANSPORT IN CAR

GETTING THERE & AWAY
Air

There are only about a dozen flights to Bangui per week, and they're not cheap. Both **TAAG** (☎ 21617378; www.taag.aero; Ave Valéry Giscard d'Estaing Bangui) and the less reliable **Toumaï Air Tchad** (☎ 21611408; www.toumaiair.com; Ave Boganda, Bangui) connect Bangui to Douala (Cameroon). TAAG also flies to Luanda (Angola), Pointe-Noire and Brazzaville (Congo), and Toumaï also does N'Djaména (Chad). **Kenya Airways** (☎ 70102814; www.kenya-airways.com; Place de la République, Bangui) comes twice a week from Nairobi. **Afriqiyah Airways** (☎ 75052118; www.afriqiyah.aero; Ave Boganda Bangui) comes twice a week from Tripoli and **Air France** (☎ 21614900; www.airfrance.com; Ave de l'Indépendance, Bangui) has a weekly Paris flight.

Land & River

All border crossings to CAR are difficult, and most are dangerous. At the time of research the only really safe crossings were south to Congo and DRC. These things change rapidly however, so it's vital to check the security status with reliable sources before trying any land crossing.

CAMEROON

Most truck traffic uses the rough road through Garoua-Boulaï. Trucks and bush taxis run from Bangui to Garoua-Boulaï, overnighting in Bouar. The price is CFA4000 for each leg of the trip. Expect to pay more than US$100 in bribes along the way to some of Africa's surliest soldiers. Transport on the Cameroonian side is more comfortable and more frequent. Perhaps more convenient, to the Dzanga Sangha Reserve, is the less trafficked Gamboula crossing between Berbérati and Kenzou.

CHAD

Most trucks travel between Bangui and Sarh crossing at Sido. It's also possible to head further west through Bossangoa to Goré or Moundou, crossing at Békay. Transport to N'Djamena is easy from all three places. Even in the best of times these are difficult voyages and bad roads are the least of your concerns.

DEPARTURE TAX
Airport departure tax is CFA10,000.

BOATS ON THE OUBANGUI

Riverboats still sail the Oubangui River between Bangui and Brazzaville every two or three weeks when water levels are high enough; generally July to December. If all goes well, the trip takes seven to 10 days downstream and twice as long going up. Boats don't travel to a schedule, but leave when they're fully loaded. Just show up at the port and ask around, though take stated departure dates with a whole sack of salt. In Brazzaville, start your search at the Di.Ge.Na.F. office (the third building), which keeps a blackboard list of boats that may be leaving soon. You can also inquire at Socatraf (in Bangui it's based 1.2km west of the port), though officially the company only carries passengers who are accompanying cargo.

Most of the time you'll need to sleep out on the deck of the barge (about CFA20,000) with hundreds of other passengers, but one company **Oubangui-Flotte** (☎ 21614680; Bangui port) offers passenger cabins ranging from CFA25,000 in a six-bed room to CFA70,000 for a private room. You can also usually arrange to rent a cabin from the crew. Food can be bought on board (sometimes) and from locals in *pirogues* along the way.

If you don't want to make the whole journey by boat, there's a new road running south to Impfondo in Congo (where there are more boats than at Bangui), though traffic is largely limited to logging trucks and hitching a ride here could be difficult.

---

both rebels and government soldiers often run some pretty serious shakedowns.

CONGO

An interesting way to travel to Congo is down the Sangha River, which connects the two countries' premier national parks. A proper motor boat from Bayanga to Bomassa will cost around CFA350,000, while a *pirogue* with a motor should be about half that. Someone will paddle you down to Bomassa for CFA50,000 to CFA60,000, while the upriver rate is higher. Paddling takes more than a day from Bayanga, though you could send the boat down to Lidjombo the first day and take a *moto-taxi* to meet it the next morning.

See the boxed text, above, for information about travel between Bangui and Brazzaville.

DEMOCRATIC REPUBLIC OF CONGO

The only practical border crossing between CAR and DRC is across the Oubangui River from Bangui to Zongo, where after an awful road to Lisala you'll have to wait (perhaps a week or two) for a boat. Expect four days upstream to Kisangani and 10 to 12 days downstream to Kinshasa.

Pirogues (CFA500 per person) go back and forth between Bangui and Zongo all day, and though there's no regularly scheduled car ferry, arrangements can be made to get a vehicle across if you're overlanding it. At the little unmarked immigration stand in Bangui, expect to pay CFA8400 port taxes per person (but don't expect a receipt) and plan to keep doling out cash along the entire route.

SUDAN

Don't even think about it.

GETTING AROUND

Some of the most decrepit and overcrowded bush taxis and minibuses on the continent connect Bangui with surrounding towns. Trucks and pick-ups are also a popular way to travel; if you ride in the cab, prices are similar to minibus fares.

The only paved highways connect Bangui to Bossembélé, Sibut and M'Baïki, and though they're in pretty good shape, they're degrading fast. When the rains begin, other roads become very muddy and can be closed for days.

Chad

Wave goodbye to your comfort zone and say hello to Chad. Put simply, Chad is a place and an experience that you'll never forget! If Ghana and Gambia are Africa for beginners, Chad is Africa for the hardcore.

To say that travel here can be tough is a major understatement. In much of the country the roads are utterly diabolical, the tourist infrastructure somewhere below zero, the paperwork overwhelming, the corruption wallet draining, the summer heat mind melting, the costs astronomical and the security situation highly unstable.

So why bother you may ask? Well, we could list the sublime oases lost in the northern deserts, tell you about the stampeding herds of wildlife in the national parks or the deep blue lure of a boat trip on Lake Chad. But let's be honest about it, these things alone aren't why people come to Chad. People come here because Chad promises them an opportunity to fall completely off the edge of the known world and into a place that promises experiences, good and bad, that you'll be recalling forever.

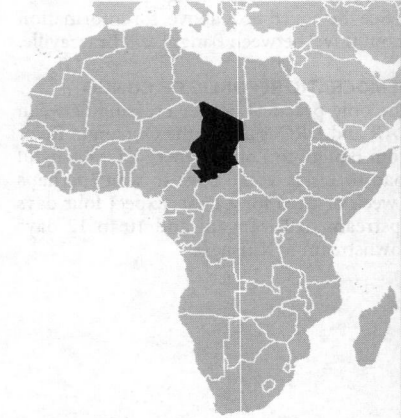

FAST FACTS

- **Area** 1,284,000 sq km
- **ATMs** N'Djaména
- **Borders** Cameroon, Libya, Niger and Nigeria open; Sudan closed; Central African Republic (CAR) often closed; Libya and CAR not recommended
- **Budget** From US$50 per day in N'Djaména, US$25 to US$50 per day in other towns
- **Capital** N'Djaména
- **Languages** French, Arabic and more than 120 local languages
- **Money** Central African CFA; US$1 = CFA463, €1 = CFA656
- **Population** 10 million
- **Seasons** Dry (October to May), wet (June to September)
- **Telephone** Country code ☎ 235; international access code ☎ 00
- **Time** GMT/UTC +1
- **Visa** Must be obtained before arrival

HIGHLIGHTS

- **Zakouma National Park** (p559) Track herds of elephants and ogle dazzling birds in the Zakouma National Park
- **Gaoui** (p558) Sigh over the beautiful painted houses of Gaoui, a fascinating village just minutes from N'Djaména.
- **Sarh** (p559) See the green and pleasant side of sandy Chad and chill out along the Chari River.
- **Guetè** (p558) Scan the horizon for egrets and hippos on Lake Chad, Africa's most mysterious lake.
- **Ennedi** (p560) Marvel at dramatic desert scenery and rock formations.

CLIMATE & WHEN TO GO

Chad has three distinct climatic zones: in the tropical south, temperatures usually range from 20°C to 25°C, but can rise to 40°C before the rains; the centre, where N'Djaména and Lake Chad are located, often exceeds 45°C before the rains; and temperatures can get even higher in the north.

November to January is the coolest and thus best time for general travel, unless you are here for Zakouma National Park – then it's March and April (the hottest months). It is fascinating to see the Sahel turn green in July, but travel in the rainy season is not pleasant. You can't believe how water-logged the capital becomes during July and August and road travel elsewhere slows dramatically.

ITINERARIES

- **Three Days** Visit N'Djaména (p554), Gaoui (p558) and Guetè (p558).
- **One Week** Visit N'Djaména, Gaoui and Guetè while you get your permits in order, then head north to Mao (p559) and Bol (p559) or south to Moundou (p558) and Sarh (p559).
- **Two Weeks** Sign up for a two-week organised tour of the spectacular Ennedi desert (p560).

HISTORY

Dominated historically by slave-trading Arab Muslims from the northern regions, Chad is primarily an agricultural nation with over 80% of the population living at subsistence level. Its recent history was shaped when the French began taking an interest in central and western Africa in the 1900s. By 1913 the

> **WARNING**
>
> Make no mistake, travelling in Chad is no walk in the park. There is intense rebel activity all across the south and southeast and the chances of further rebel attacks on N'Djaména are high. All Western governments advise against travel to Chad. Check the situation very carefully before travelling here (see p1139 for details of government travel advisory services).

country was fully colonised: sadly the new rulers didn't really know what to do with their conquest, and investment all but dried up after a few years, leaving much of the territory almost entirely undeveloped.

When independence was granted in 1960, a southerner became Chad's first head of state. Unfortunately, President François Tombalbaye was not the best choice. By arresting opposition leaders and banning political parties, he provoked a series of conspiracies in the Muslim north – the violent repression of which quickly escalated into full-blown guerrilla war. For the next quarter of a century, Chadian politics was defined by armed struggles, shifting alliances, coups and private armies, overseen and often exacerbated by France and Libya, who took a keen interest in the area. In addition, the Sahel drought of the 1970s and early 1980s destroyed centuries-old patterns of existence and cultivation, causing large-scale migration to urban centres.

In 1975 Tombalbaye was assassinated, and succeeded by General Félix Malloum, a fellow southerner. Over US$1 million in cash was found in Tombalbaye's residence, along with plans to proclaim himself emperor.

Modern Politics

The Government of National Unity was then formed by Malloum and Hissène Habré (a former northern rebel commander); it was a tenuous alliance between two men who shared little more than mutual distrust. The resulting internal power struggle in 1979 pitted north against south, and Muslim against Christian or animist, all colliding with destructive force in the capital, where thousands of civilians were massacred. Eventually Malloum fled the country, and Goukouni Oueddei – the son of a tribal chieftain from

CHAD

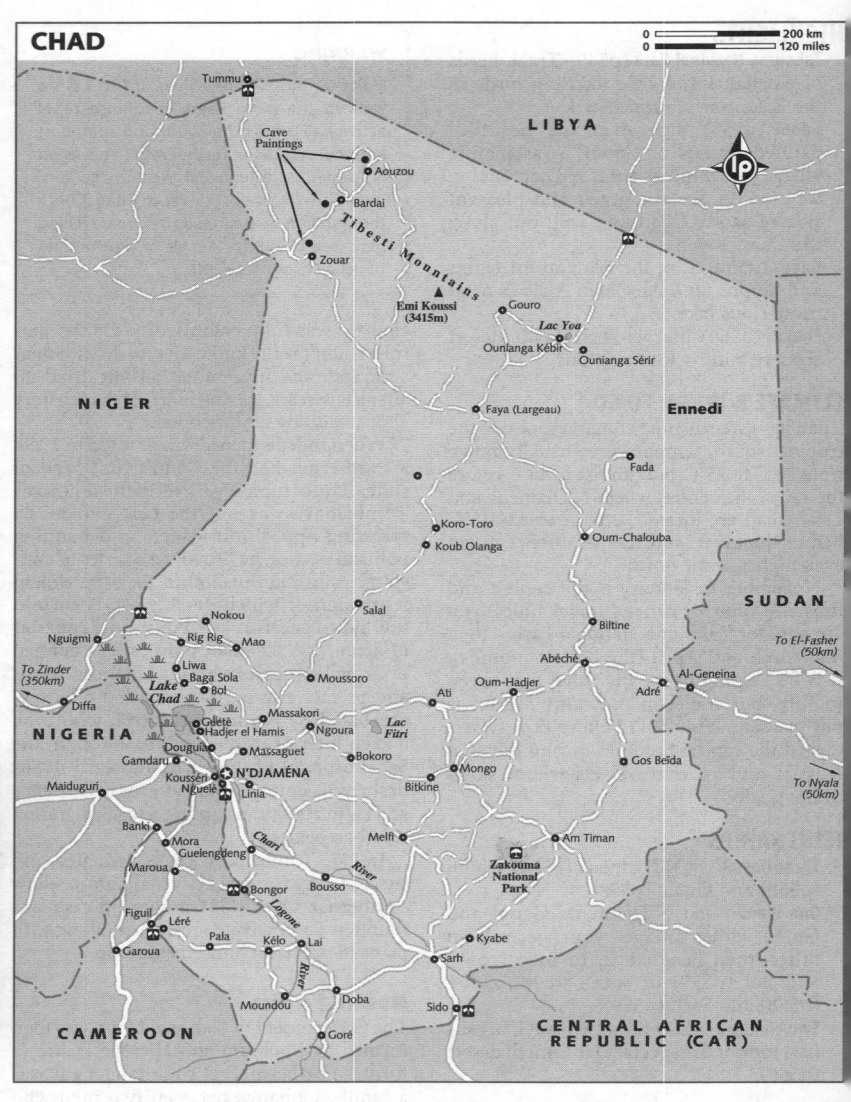

CHAD

LIBYA

NIGER

Tummu

Cave Paintings

Aouzou

Bardai

Zouar

Tibesti Mountains

Emi Koussi (3415m)

Gouro

Lac Yoa

Ounianga Kébir

Ounianga Sérir

Faya (Largeau)

Ennedi

Fada

Koro-Toro

Koub Olanga

Oum-Chalouba

Salal

SUDAN

To El-Fasher (50km)

Nokou

Nguigmi

Rig Rig

Mao

Liwa

Baga Sola

Bol

Moussoro

Biltine

Abéché

Adré

Al-Geneina

To Zinder (350km)

Diffa

Lake Chad

Galeté

Massakori

Hadjer el Hamis

Ngoura

Ati

Oum-Hadjer

NIGERIA

Douguia

Gamdaru

Kousséri

Massaguet

Bokoro

Lac Fitri

Mongo

Gos Beida

To Nyala (50km)

Maiduguri

N'Guelé

N'DJAMÉNA

Linia

Bitkine

Banki

Mora

Guelengdeng

Melfi

Am Timan

Zakouma National Park

Maroua

Chari

Bousso

River

Figuil

Léré

Bongor

Logone

Pala

Kélo

Lai

Sarh

Kyabe

Garoua

River

Moundou

Doba

Sido

CAMEROON

Goré

CENTRAL AFRICAN REPUBLIC (CAR)

0 — 200 km
0 — 120 miles

northwestern Chad and an arch-enemy of Habré – took over.

In 1980 Libyan forces supporting Oueddei briefly occupied N'Djaména. The French army drove them northwards, leaving Habré as the nominal ruler of Chad.

In 1990 Idriss Déby, a northern Muslim warlord in self-imposed exile in Sudan, swept back into Chad with a private army of 2000 soldiers and Libyan backing. Habré fled to Senegal leaving Déby with a clear run to N'Djaména and the presidency of his war-ravaged country, which Déby consolidated by winning the first-ever presidential elections in 1996. While this ballot was widely regarded as rigged, the parliamentary elections a year later were considered much fairer. In 1998 a new rebellion broke out in the north, led by the Movement for Democracy and Justice (MDJT) under Déby's former minister Youssouf Togoimï.

Although Chad has enjoyed relative peace and close relations with Libya over the past few years (despite regular guerrilla raids in the Tibesti region of northern Chad), politically, little has changed. To nobody's surprise, Déby won the May 2001 presidential elections by a comfortable margin, although results from a quarter of the polling stations had to be cancelled because of irregularities.

Chad Today

In 2004 Chad became an oil exporter. The World Bank helped fund the 1000km-long pipeline crossing Cameroon to the coast only after Chad agreed to dedicate 80% of oil income to reducing poverty. Even before Déby broke this agreement at the start of 2006, there was virtually no change for average citizens in what Transparency International ranks as the third most corrupt country in Africa.

But the World Bank is not Déby's biggest worry. Several rebel groups based in Sudan, and some led by members of Déby's family and former senior army officers, have their eyes on N'Djaména. They almost got it in April 2006 and again in February 2008 after launching unsuccessful attacks on the capital. In 2006 the government was helped by the incompetence of the rebels, who had to ask directions when they arrived and ended up at the empty Palais du Peuple (the parliament) instead of the Palais du President; in 2008 it was the French military who bailed out Déby. Three weeks after the failed 2006 coup and one year after the constitutional two-term presidential limit was overturned, Déby won a presidential election boycotted by the opposition and most citizens. Power in Chad has always changed hands by the bullet, not the ballot, and most observers expect that, sooner or later, this will happen again – something most Chadians would welcome.

The fact that Déby's government has not already fallen is probably more to do with the presence of the French than anything else. The French maintain a huge military base on the edge of N'Djaména and, while the French have never admitted to actual involvement in repelling the rebel attacks of 2006 and 2008, it

HOW MUCH?

- **Cheapest N'Djaména hotel** US$40
- **Seven-hour bus ride** US$15
- **Coke** US$0.50
- **Thirty minutes of internet use** US$2
- **Handmade leather sandals** US$6

LONELY PLANET INDEX

- **1L petrol** US$1.50
- **1L bottled water** US$1
- **Bottle of Gala beer** US$2
- **Paris–N'Djaména flight** from US$1600
- **Small bag of peanuts** US$0.05

was reported in the French media that in the 2008 attack France provided logistical support to the government, funnelled weapons to the government via Libya, offered to evacuate Déby to France and sent special forces in to fight the rebels.

By 2009 the capital and environs were calm, but in the east the situation was highly volatile. Rebel groups (possibly supported by the Sudanese government) were slipping in and out of Sudan's Darfur region and essentially extending that war into Chad. Fighting once again broke out between government forces and rebel groups in the east in May 2009. This chaos has created some 170,000 internal refugees as well as thousands of refugees fleeing into Chad from fighting in Sudan and the Central African Republic (CAR).

Whatever way you look at it, the situation for Chad looks extremely grim.

CULTURE

Chad's history of war, corruption and oppression is appalling, even by African standards, and it has drained most people of hope. Even those who, a few years back, believed the flow of oil would bring change have humbly accepted their friends' and families' 'I-told-you-so's.

The population of Chad is around 10 million with a growth rate of 3%. Around 64% of people live below the poverty line and the country is rated 175 out of 182 on the UNDP Human Development Index. The north is populated by people of Arab descent, as well as nomadic Peul-Fulani and Toubou people. The black Africans are in the majority in the south – the Sara are by far the biggest ethnic group (25% of the population) and have traditionally dominated business and the civil service. The difference between these two broad groups is profound – the Christian (35% of the population) or animist southerners are mostly peasant farmers, tilling fertile land, while the northern Muslims (54%) are desert-dwelling pastoralists.

Surprisingly, for such a subsistence economy, education is looked upon favourably and literacy stands at 48%. Freedom of speech is also fiercely, if somewhat vainly, defended – but as the security situation continues to deteriorate, so too does the media's room to move.

Most of the crafts you'll see in Chad are imported from Nigeria and Cameroon, though the leatherwork and pottery is usually made locally and many of the large wool rugs come from Abéché and other desert towns.

FOOD & DRINK

The food in Chad is typical of the region: tiny street stalls dish up meals of rice, beans and soup or stew, while indoor restaurants offer omelettes, liver, salads, *brochettes* (kebabs), fish and *nachif* (minced meat in sauce). To drink you have the usual range of *sucreries* (soft drinks), including the local Top brand, and fresh *jus*, fruit concoctions with more resemblance to smoothies than normal juice – bear in mind they're usually made with local water and ice. Beer is the favoured poison in bars, with a choice of local brews, Gala and Chari, or Cameroonian Castel. Also popular is *bili-bili*, a millet beer; *cochette* is a low-alcohol version.

ENVIRONMENT

Physically you couldn't mistake landlocked Chad for anything except a Sahel country, though the far south turns a little tropical. The northern deserts include the Tibesti Mountains, which rise to the peak of Emi Koussi (3415m), the highest point in the Sahara.

N'DJAMÉNA

pop 721,000

If you're flying straight in from Europe, or many other parts of Africa, first impressions of N'Djaména are normally ones of shock. The capital appears to be little more than a beaten up, broken down village with mud buildings hugely outnumbering brick buildings, electricity and running water a mere dream for many neighbourhoods, and even a smooth tarmac road a fairly rare sight. You feel immediately like you've arrived in a city on edge and in many ways N'Djaména simply doesn't function like most other cities. But take a deep breath, dive into the markets and kick back in the numerous bars and you'll soon come to appreciate the capital's brighter side.

ORIENTATION

The airport is less than 1km from downtown; despite the small distance involved, you'll have to bargain hard to get a taxi there or back for less than CFA5000, particularly at night. There are no airport buses.

The city's two distinct sectors highlight its colonial roots. To the west of the Marché Central is the commercial district, sheltering well-to-do Chadians and a small expat community. Its wide, leafy streets must once have been very pleasant; today the area looks as if it's been hit by a hurricane. The western end of Ave Charles de Gaulle is a 1km strip boasting banks, airline offices, restaurants and similar services – it's not as glamorous as it sounds. On the other side of the Marché Central, the main residential areas consist mostly of mudbrick houses with little in the way of modern amenities but plenty of character.

INFORMATION
Internet Access

Internet access is widely available, with most places charging CFA2000 per hour. **PC Zone** (Ave Charles de Gaulle; per hr CFA 2000; ⊗ 8am-6.30pm Mon-Sat) is reliably fast. Many of the better hotels also have decent internet connections.

Medical Services

The French embassy–affiliated **Centre Médico Social** (☎ 2522837; Rue de la Gendarmerie) is the best place to go if you're sick. For anything serious, you'll need to be evacuated. The pharmacies on Ave Charles de Gaulle are generally reliable.

Money

The best bank for travellers is the Société Générale Tchadienne de Banque (SGTB), with its main branch just off Ave Charles de Gaulle, which changes cash and travellers cheques and doles out cash to those with Visa cards.

CHAD

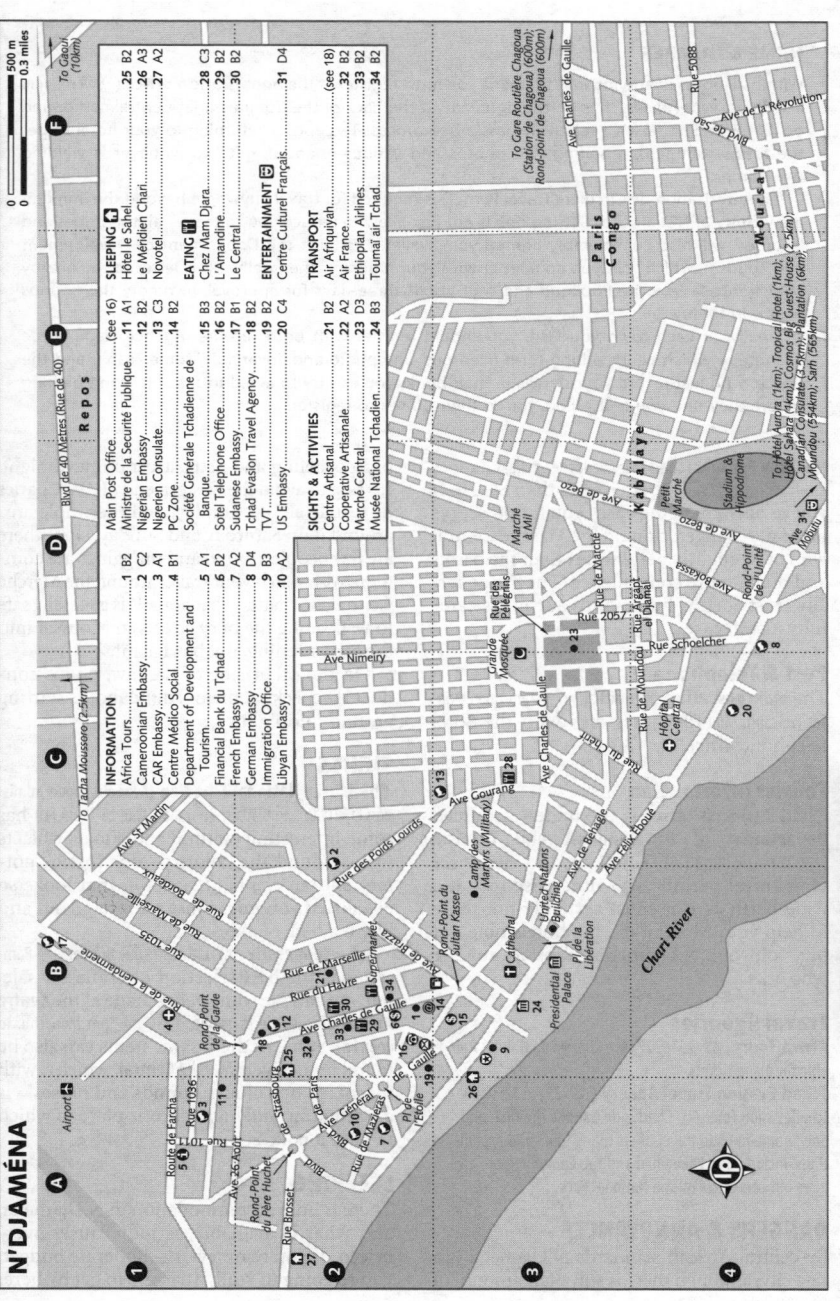

N'DJAMÉNA

0   500 m
0   0.3 miles

INFORMATION

Africa Tours..........................1 B2
Cameroonian Embassy...........2 C2
CAR Embassy.........................3 A1
Centre Médico Social.............4 B1
Department of Development and
  Tourism.............................5 A1
Financial Bank du Tchad.........6 B2
French Embassy.....................7 A2
German Embassy....................8 D4
Immigration Office.................9 B3
Libyan Embassy....................10 A2

Main Post Office...................11 B2
Ministre de la Sécurité Publique...12 C2
Nigerian Embassy..................13 C3
Nigerien Consulate................14 B2
PC Zone..............................(see 16)
Société Générale Tchadienne de
  Banque............................15 B3
Sotel Telephone Office..........16 B2
Sudanese Embassy................17 B1
Chad Evasion Travel Agency...18 B2
TVT....................................19 B2
US Embassy.........................20 C4

SIGHTS & ACTIVITIES

Centre Artisanal....................21 B2
Cooperative Artisanale...........22 A2
Marché Central.....................23 D3
Musée National Tchadien........24 B3

SLEEPING

Hôtel le Sahel......................25 B2
Le Méridien Chari..................26 A3
Novotel...............................27 A2

EATING

Chez Mam Diara....................28 C3
L'Amandine..........................29 B2
Le Central............................30 B2

ENTERTAINMENT

Centre Culturel Français..........31 D4

TRANSPORT

Air Afriquiyah.......................(see 18)
Air France............................32 B2
Ethiopian Airlines..................33 B2
Toumaï air Tchad..................34 B2

CHAD

NAME & NUMBER

Within 72 hours of arriving in N'Djaména you must register at the **immigration office** (🕙 7am-3pm Mon-Thu, to noon Fri), which is on the right side at the back of the Commissariat Central compound on Ave Félix Éboué. It's a relatively hassle-free process (except for returning to your hotel to get the forms stamped), requiring two photos and various financial 'gifts' to whoever is yielding the stamps.

An Autorisation de Circuler (Travel Permit) is required for travel anywhere beyond the immediate vicinity of N'Djaména. Getting one is not just likely to reduce you to tears – all the bribes and 'charges' will also considerably lighten your wallet. First visit the Department of Development and Tourism, which will type up a letter with your itinerary. Then deliver this letter to the nearby Ministre de la Securité Publique and wait about three days for approval. In theory this sounds easy – in theory…

Finally, in each town you visit, you should register with both *securité* (Agence National de Securité) – which needs a long form filled out, one photo and, invariably, some cash – and the police, who just record your details in their book. You can try to avoid this, but it won't be long before they find you and escort you to their offices to register.

Financial Bank du Tchad (Ave Charles de Gaulle) changes cash at marginally better rates than SGTB. If you're only changing cash, you'll find scores of moneychangers around the Marché Central who offer slightly better rates than the banks and much more convenience. They're generally trustworthy, but count your notes carefully just in case.

Post & Telephone

The **main post office** (Blvd de Paris; 🕙 7am-noon Mon-Sat & 3-5pm Mon-Fri) shares digs with the Sotel telephone office.

Tourist Information

Chad's tourist office is the under-resourced **Department of Development and Tourism** (☎ 2524416; Rue 1011). You'll need to visit it for your travel permits, but otherwise give it a wide berth as it is most certainly not there to help you! Most of the big hotels dole out big, fold-out N'Djaména maps to anyone who asks.

Travel Agencies

Africa Tours (☎ 2518727; Ave Charles de Gaulle) Reliable for plane tickets.
Tchad Evasion Travel Agency (☎ 2526532; www.tchadevasion.com; Ave Charles de Gaulle) The first, and only, name in Chad travel offers many tours and expeditions, including to Lake Chad and the Ennedi region, and hires out cars for Zakouma National Park.

DANGERS & ANNOYANCES

By central African standards N'Djaména is a safe city; although there is still a fair amount of

pickpocketing and petty street crime at night. It's best to avoid the western end of Ave Charles de Gaulle all day Sunday, and the whole area around it on Saturday and Sunday, since there are few people around and muggings are common. Also watch your wallet around the Marché Central, no matter what hour. It is generally safe to walk along the busy streets in Moursal into the early evening, but be vigilant.

On the other side of the law, police conduct ID checks at major roundabouts starting around midnight.

SIGHTS

The **Musée National Tchadien** (Ave Félix Éboué; admission CFA1000; 🕙 8.30am-2pm Mon-Thu, to 11am Fri) has some interesting cultural and tribal artefacts from around the country, plus fossils, pottery and an elephant skeleton that looks so exhausted you might just want to go out and buy it a bed.

The **Cooperative Artisanale** (Rue Brosset; 🕙 8am-6pm) has the best selection of crafts for sale, but you can see some being made at the **Centre Artisanal** (Rue de Marseille; 🕙 7am-3pm Mon-Thu, to noon Fri). Some of these same items can also be found in the lively **Marché Central**, which – with it's mixed up colours, sounds and noises – is a fascinating and highly exotic place in which to have a poke about.

SLEEPING

There is little accommodation in N'Djaména, and what is available, is ludicrously over-priced. If you're on even a moderate budget, you're going to really struggle to get by here.

In order to obtain a visa you normally have to prove that you have a hotel booked in N'Djaména. This is only really possible through the Méridien or Novotel hotels, both of which offer such poor value for money that in normal circumstances we wouldn't recommend them at all.

Hôtel Aurora (☎ 6497705; Ave Mobutu; r CFA18,000) This is the cheapest place that we can recommend (though really, we don't). The dark and skanky rooms play host to lots of 'by the hour' customers.

Hôtel Sahara (☎ 2517171; off Ave Bealoum Kondol; r from CFA25,000; ☒) The sweetest budget deal in town, the rooms here are immaculate, the bed sheets are stain free, the plumbing works and there's even 24-hour electricity.

Cosmos Big Guest-House (☎ 6643260; Ave Bealoum Kondol; r from CFA30,000; ☒) On a busy street in Moursal, the clean and orderly rooms come with oh-so-pleasant wafts of air-con cooled air as well as satellite TV. It surrounds a popular restaurant.

our pick Tropical Hotel (☎ 2534301/3546; www.tropicalhoteltchad.com; off Ave Bealoum Kondol; r from CFA40,000; P ☒ ☐) With comfortable and spotless rooms and friendly staff, staying at this new venture feels more like kipping at a friend's house. A gently humming generator provides around-the-clock electricity and all rooms have hot-water showers or baths and satellite TV. Breakfast is included and there's an excellent internet cafe on site.

Hôtel le Sahel (☎ 2520333; tv2000@internet.td; Blvd de Strasbourg; s/d CFA55,000/65,000; ☒ ☐) Set in shady gardens, this old colonial building is loaded with character. The rooms are cool and clean, and bright African art adorns the walls.

Le Méridien Chari (☎ 2525350; www.starwood hotels.com; s/d CFA120,000/130,000) This is where most foreign visitors end up staying and for good reason. The security is good, the welcome warm and the riverside setting pleasant, but the rooms are fading fast. By booking online you can often get weekend bargains of around €100 per night – which at such times makes it the best deal in the city.

Novotel N'Djamena (☎ 2523311; www.accor.com; r CFA133,000; ☐ ☒) Even for N'Djaména, this place is mega overpriced and it should be considered only if the Meridien is full.

EATING

At lunchtime there's plenty of basic street food around the Marché Central. At night you'll find many similarly cheap unlit stalls in Moursal and Paris Congo. Formal, sit-down restaurants are a little harder to track down.

L'Amandine (Ave Charles de Gaulle; croissants CFA500; ☽ 7am-7pm) A proper French patisserie that's as Gallic as a shrug. It's packed with well-to-do locals and expats gorging on its wonderful croissants and coffee.

Chez Mam Djara (off Ave Gourang; plat du jour CFA1500; ☽ lunch) A little hard to find (just ask around; everybody knows it) but worth it for the fantastic plates of Senegalese rice.

Cosmos Big Guest-House (Ave Bealoum Kondol; mains CFA4000-5000; ☽ lunch & dinner) Part of the hotel of the same name, the busy courtyard restaurant here has a great atmosphere day and night. It serves a tummy-satisfying range of meaty meals, including a good mutton *brochette* with rice and sauce. It's an equally popular place to knock back a beer or three.

Le Central (☎ 6150471; Ave Charles de Gaulle; mains CFA7000-8000; ☽ lunch & dinner Mon-Sat) If you're out to impress, then this refined French-run restaurant is the place to do it. The food is truly excellent and features such delights as *salade landaise* (CFA8000) and beef bourguignon (CFA7500).

ENTERTAINMENT

Moursal has many simple bars and nightclubs that are popular with locals, but are also welcoming of outsiders; though get local advice before you head out as a few are pretty rough. Those downtown on Ave Charles de Gaulle are more exclusive, but have just as many prostitutes. One out-of-the-ordinary club experience can be found on a Sunday afternoon (don't get stuck out in this part of town in the evening) at Plantation. It's a relaxed place across the river (about a CFA5000 taxi ride), playing a good mix of African and Western music for a throng of middle-class Chadians and a few expats.

As is normally the case with French cultural centres, the **Centre Culturel Français** (☎ 2519156; Ave Mobutu) has an energetic and lively program of cultural events and exhibitions (CFA3000 to CFA4000), as well as regular screenings of African and French films (CFA1000).

GETTING THERE & AWAY

All of the following have offices on the west end of Ave Charles de Gaulle:
Air Afriquiyah (☎ 2526532)
Air France (☎ 2524981)

Ethiopian Airlines (☎ 2523143)
Toumaï air Tchad (☎ 2524107)

Land transport for southern destinations departs the chaotic Gare Routière Chagoua, east of the centre. For points north, head to Tacha Moussoro.

GETTING AROUND
Shared taxis and minibuses around town should cost about CFA150 per seat: the price depends on how far the vehicle, not you, is going. They run all night, but start getting scarce after 10pm. To get to downtown from Moursal, first get a taxi to the Marché Central and then hop in one heading *'en ville'*. A taxi course (private hire) is negotiable, but the minimum is CFA1000.

AROUND N'DJAMÉNA

GAOUI
In a landscape of dusky browns, the brightly painted mud houses of the village of Gaoui, just 10km from N'Djaména, bring colour to this otherwise drab world. The former sultan's palace has been turned into a small **museum** (admission CFA2000, guide CFA2000; ☺ by request) that discusses the culture of the local Sao people. The building itself is an impressive mud castle and would be worth seeing even if it weren't for the museum. In the mornings women can often be found making clay pots in the museum grounds. Minibuses (CFA250) from Char Gaoui (Gaoui Rd), by the Kempinski Hotel, will drop you nearby; either walk the last 2km or hop on a motorcycle.

DOUGUIA & LAKE CHAD
A fantastic day trip from the capital (travel permits not required) is to head up to the village of Douguia, 70km north and set on the banks of the Chari River, and then on to the remote village of Guetè on the southern fringes of Lake Chad. The two places couldn't be more different from one another.

Douguia is the home of the **Station Touristique de Douguia** (☎ 6288030; www.douguia.com; bungalows from CFA25,000, meals CFA7000), a popular weekend retreat for expats. There's a swimming pool full of French military in tiny speedos, a decent French restaurant and

some reasonably priced but basic bungalows. It's a good place for twitchers to set up camp as the relatively fertile surrounding countryside is crammed with squawking birds. Boats can also be hired (CFA25,000 per hour) from the hotel to cruise up and down the river in search of the not-so-elusive hippo population.

Guetè, a further 50km north, is the African chalk next to Douguia's French cheese. Although this miniscule village is the easiest place to get to grips with Lake Chad, foreign visitors are utterly unheard of. The centre of the village is a couple of very pleasant kilometres' walk from the lake itself. Down on the surprisingly green lake shore (it's actually only a small branch of the lake that reaches the village) you'll discover enormously elongated and garishly coloured motorised *pirogues* (traditional canoes) and many fishermen.

There are no facilities of any sort in Guetè – even buses are as rare as a cold day. The easiest way to get here is to hire a taxi in N'Djaména for the day (4WD not needed) for around CFA30,000.

SOUTH OF N'DJAMÉNA

Think Chad is all sand? Think again. In the deep south the soils turn red and the vegetation becomes riotous. It is a much more developed area than the north, but the soldiers are even more of a pain.

MOUNDOU
Set on the north bank of the Logone River, Chad's second-largest town doesn't have a huge amount to detain you, but the atmosphere is relaxed and it's a pleasant place in which to stroll around. Don't miss catching the wood-carvers and painters at work at the **Centre Artisanal.**

Right by the *gare routière* (bus station), **Residence de Palmiers** (r from CFA25,000; ☒) is a fairly new construction so the rooms, which come with TV, are in good shape.

A crush of women serving street food line Moundou's main road in Quartier Geuldjeme near the centre, as do many bars and a nightclub. Further south you'll find many open-air restaurants.

Frequent transport leaves for N'Djaména (CFA9000, seven hours) and Sarh (CFA7000, six hours) from scattered locations around the *gare routiére*. Many pick-ups to Sarh also depart from across the river. Minibuses go to Léré (CFA6000, four hours) on the Cameroon border, but it's usually quicker to go to Kélo and change there.

SARH

An agreeably sleepy town shaded by enormous trees, Sarh – the cotton capital of Chad – is little more than a provincial backwater.

The **Museé Regional de Sarh** (admission CFA2000; ☻8am-3pm Mon-Fri) has old weapons, musical instruments and masks. Most nights at dusk, **hippos** feed on the banks of the Chari River below the Hôtel de Chasses.

With its fading glory, **Hôtel de Chasses** (☎ 6429575; r CFA25,000-30,000; ❄) is a whimsical throwback to times past. A plant-filled, screened dining room overlooks the river, and all rooms have balconies.

For cheap food, head over to the Grand Marché or Ave Cascani near the central truck park.

Most vehicles depart for Moundou (CFA7000, six hours) and N'Djaména (CFA15,000, 12 hours) from near the market, but pick-ups have their own park north of town.

ZAKOUMA NATIONAL PARK

A few years ago the 305,000-hectare Zakouma National Park, 800km southeast of N'Djaména, was touted as a kind of Garden of Eden with herds of elephants hundreds strong. Unfortunately, almost as soon as these words were uttered, the slaughter began (actually it had been going on for years but nobody had really noticed before). By early 2010 it was estimated that only 550 elephants remained from a 2005 population of 4000. At one point in 2006 it was estimated that around three elephants a day were being poached but, incredibly, 1kg of ivory sells for just US$42 in Chad. And it's not just the elephants that have suffered – numbers of all large mammals are thought to have dropped in the last few years thanks to poaching and hunting.

Nevertheless, Zakouma is still one of the best places in Central Africa to see large mammals – you stand a good chance of seeing elephants, giraffes, wildebeests, lions and a wide variety of antelope, primates and birdlife. The best time to come is March or April when the animals congregate around watering holes. It is not possible to visit from June to October because of the rains.

Visiting the park costs CFA7500 per person, plus CFA10,000 per vehicle. A guide costs CFA5000. Public transport to the park is practically nonexistent, so the most realistic option is to organise a trip through one of N'Djaména's travel agencies. Tchad Evasion (p556) is the most reliable and charges CFA75,000 per day for a 4WD and driver. You'll need to allow a minimum of six days to make this trip, since it takes two just to reach the park (you'll overnight in Mongo).

Inside Zakouma, **Le Campement Hôtelier Tinga** (☎ 2524412; www.zakouma.com; r CFA30,000, meals CFA10,000; ❄) has comfortable rooms and a good restaurant.

NORTH OF N'DJAMÉNA

A land of sand-blown horizons and vast voids, central and northern Chad consists of classic Sahel and Saharan landscapes that culminate in the beauty of the Ennedi desert. (Sadly, the even more spectacular Tibesti Mountains in the far north remain very much off-limits).

BOL

Lake Chad was once one of the largest freshwater lakes in the world. Its dry-season area of less than 10,000 sq km can increase to 25,000 sq km at the height of the rains; however, it is slowly drying up and even vanished during the worst of the Sahel drought in 1984. Its slow disappearance is creating problems for, and conflicts between, fishermen and farmers.

A finger of the lake reaches Bol year-round, and trade with Nigeria has made this small town relatively prosperous.

The **Société de Développement du Lac** (Sodelac; villa CFA25,000; ❄) has large villas. Cleaning, maintenance and the water supply are spotty, but there's usually air-con until around midnight.

MAO

Perched high above a long oasis, Mao is the capital of the once-powerful Kanem Empire. The sultan still lives here, and if you so much as ask about him someone will probably offer to arrange a meeting. A few of his effects, along with regional crafts, are on display in the tiny **Museé du Kanem** (admission free; ☾ Mon-Sat), which the caretaker will open by request – if he can find the key. Wednesday is market day, and the thriving traditional **donkey and camel market** draws people from far and wide.

There's no official accommodation, but the **Maison de Culture**, home of the museum, has dusty, cell-like rooms (per person CFA5000) with no electricity and plenty of roaches for company.

ENNEDI

The Ennedi desert is the Sahara at its best – an endless tract of sand and rock blasted by the centuries into grotesque and bizarre formations.

It is just about possible to get to Faya Oases, on the fringes of the Ennedi, by public transport, but we cannot overestimate how tough this trip is (and occasionally dangerous). To get to Faya firstly take a 'bus' to Abeche from N'djaména (CFA20,000, 18 hours). In Abeche you can overnight at the **Pension Cesar** (from CFA25,000). Then take a land-cruiser north to Biltine (two hours) and negotiate a place on top of the load of a truck heading to Faya (CFA15,000 to CFA25,000, two to five days; you'll be sharing your transport with lots of would-be immigrants to Europe). Note that there's nowhere to stay in Faya so you'll need to rely on other peoples' hospitality. Needless to say it's probably the biggest adventure you'll ever have.

Alternatively, Tchad Evasion (p556) leads 14-day trips for €1400 per person (six-person minimum). Or, better still, try Italian-based tour company **Spazid'Avventura** (☎ +39 2 70637138; www.spazidavventura.com), which runs regular two-week winter tours to the Ennedi (from €3450 per person including flights from Italy). Those who've taken one of Spazid'Avventura's tours come back with huge smiles plastered across their faces. The company also organises equally excellent tours to the Zakouma National Park and elsewhere in the Chadian Sahara.

CHAD DIRECTORY

ACCOMMODATION

Outside the capital, most hotels are very basic and overpriced. In N'Djaména all hotels are grossly overpriced, but there are

---

some good ones. Singles can usually be shared by two people for no extra cost.

DANGERS & ANNOYANCES

Where to begin? While the situation is better than it was in 2008, when every man and his machine gun predicted all-out civil war, Chad is still teetering on a knife's edge. Simmering rebel activity and unexploded mines mean that travel to far northern Chad, including the Tibesti region, is impossible. The growing rebellion rules out most of the east, and the border regions with the Central African Republic remain very dangerous. Most Western governments advise against all but essential travel to N'Djaména and all travel to the rest of the country.

Corruption is endemic in Chad and, according to Transparency International, Chad is tied with Sudan and Guinea as the third most corrupt country in Africa after Somalia and Sudan. While in Sudan the corruption doesn't really affect travellers too much, in Chad it does and almost every official you meet will expect a healthy sum of cash from you before even considering signing that all-important form.

The police and the army can be a real pain. This is mainly because they're not used to seeing travellers and so are unsure how to ensure your papers are in order. Expect lots of questions and to give a fair few 'cadeaux' (presents).

Even in N'Djaména electricity and running water are only intermittently available, and many towns are completely off the grid.

CHAD

All but the cheapest hotels have generators, but low-end places usually turn them off by midnight.

EMBASSIES & CONSULATES

The following are in N'Djaména (Map p555).
Cameroon (☎ 2522894; Rue des Poids Lourds)
Canada (☎ 2534280; signposted 1km from Rond-point de Chagua)
Central African Republic (☎ 2523206; Rue 1036)
France (☎ 2522576; off Ave Félix Éboué)
Germany (☎ 2515647; Ave Félix Éboué)
Libya (☎ 2519289; Rue de Mazieras)
Niger (☎ 2518813; off Ave Gourang)
Nigeria (☎ 2522498; Ave Charles de Gaulle)
Sudan (☎ 2525010; off Rue de la Gendarmerie) If closed, try the Libyan embassy.
USA (☎ 2516211; Ave Félix Éboué)

HOLIDAYS

As well as religious holidays in the Africa Directory (p1140), these are the principal public holidays in Chad:
New Year's Day 1 January
Labour Day 1 May
Africa Freedom Day 25 May
Independence Day 11 August
All Saints' Day 1 November
Republic Day 28 November
Day of Liberty and Democracy 1 December

INTERNET ACCESS

Reliable and pretty-fast connections are widely available in N'Djaména. You'll find cybercafes in Moundou, Sarh and other southern towns, but good luck actually getting online.

MAPS

The outdated country map published by IGN is the best available: buy it before you come.

MONEY

SGTB's ATMs in N'Djaména work with Visa cards, although they should not be relied on. The main bank in N'Djaména will give you a cash advance against your card for a fee of US$20. Most people bring cash (euros get a better return than US dollars, but both are widely accepted) and, despite the obvious security issues, this is still the best way to go. Travellers cheques can be changed in N'Djaména, but remember to take some patience to the bank!

PHOTOGRAPHY

Cameras and Chad don't go together and, while it's normally OK to take pictures out in the countryside (as long as there are no officials around) trying to do the same in N'djaména is asking for trouble.

You should apply for a photo permit in N'djaména; bring a letter requesting permission to take tourism photos, US$40 and two passport photos to the Service de Controle de Films at **TVT** (Ave Général de Gaulle). Then you'll fill out a three-page form and all this will be taken to the police for approval, which takes several days. If you decide to skip it, as most people do, be very discreet: the police do check, particularly in N'Djaména.

POST

The postal service is reliable, but can be slow outside N'Djaména.

TELEPHONE

Sotel, the national telecom company, has phone offices in most towns, charging US$1.65 per minute for calls to Europe and about US$0.50 for local calls. Private telephone offices, usually just a guy with a mobile and a sign, are common everywhere and charge the same, though late-night rates on international calls drop. There are no local telephone area codes in Chad.

VISAS

Everybody except nationals of some Central and West African countries needs a visa to visit Chad. As visas are not available at the airport or borders, travellers should obtain one before they arrive or in their home country. Costs for 30-day visas can be as high as US$100 for some nationalities.

Visa Extensions

The **Immigration office** (Map p555; Ave Félix Éboué) in N'Djaména issues visa extensions, usually on the same day. Generally it just reissues a visa at the same price as the first one.

Visas for Onward Travel

Cameroon Three month-tourist visas cost CFA50,000, require one photo and take two days to process. Transit visas are free and valid for 72 hours. They also take two days to issue.
CAR A three-month tourist visa costs CFA30,000 and requires two photos. It takes two days to issue. A 10-day transit visa costs CFA20,000.
Libya The friendly staff will give you visa advice, but all requests must go through a Libyan travel agency, which

arranges your invitation. This might take two weeks, but plan on several more.

Niger Costs CFA20,000; you'll need two photos and it will take 24 hours.

Nigeria One month costs between CFA30,000 (French) and CFA52,000 (USA) and requires two photos and a letter of invitation. Takes 24 hours.

Sudan The embassy was closed at the time of research. Chad used to be an easy place to get a Sudanese visa, but that has probably changed.

TRANSPORT IN CHAD

GETTING THERE & AWAY
Air
Air connections between N'Djaména, Europe and other African cities are limited and universally expensive. The following airlines all have offices located on Ave Charles de Gaulle in N'Djaména:

Air Afriquiyah (☎ 2526532) Links N'Djaména with various west African cities as well as Europe. The booking agent for Afriqiyah is Tchad Evasion (see p556).

Air France (☎ 2524981) Flies direct to Paris several times a week for around €1100 return.

Ethiopian Airlines (☎ 2523143) Connects Chad to Addis Ababa (around US$900 return) and onward to the reminder of the continent and Europe.

Toumaï air Tchad (☎ 2524107) Flies to various West and Central African nations but good luck trying to actually book a flight and we wish you even more luck once onboard.

Land
Chad's borders with Libya and CAR are not currently safe for travellers, and Sudan is closed (the CAR border also frequently closes).

CAMEROON
Minibuses (US$0.50, 15 minutes) and *clandos* (motorbike taxis; US$2) run from Rond-point de Chagoua in N'Djaména out to the border town of Nguelé. From there you can catch a motorcycle taxi over the bridge into Kousséri, where there are regular minibuses to Maroua. You may have to pay 'taxes' on both sides of the border. You can also enter Cameroon further south, via Léré or Bongor.

NIGER
The main route between Chad and Niger is a sandy track looping round to the north of Lake Chad from N'Djaména to Nguigmi, via Mao. There are Land Cruisers daily to Mao and then occasional ones onto to Nguigmi. Pick-ups and big lorries also cover this route, but you'll probably have to do the journey in stages via Massakori and Nokou, which can take several days. Get your passport stamped in Mao and Nguigmi.

NIGERIA
The easiest way to Nigeria is through Cameroon. Follow the directions above to reach Maroua, from where you can take a bush taxi straight to Maiduguri or a minibus to the border at Banki. You could also hop on a boat across Lake Chad from Bol, though seek local advice first.

GETTING AROUND
In Chad, Land Cruisers, pick-ups and minibuses are your main choices for cross-Chad travel. Buses, which depart at set times, are rare except to Moundou. Land Cruisers are the fastest choice because, unlike the others, they rarely stop to drop off or pick up passengers en route.

Toumaï Air Tchad may (or more likely may not) have very erratic flights to Abéché.

Outside N'Djaména you'll find fleets of *clandos* charging a fixed fee (unless you are going very far) of about CFA300 to CFA500 per trip. A 4WD rental (driver included, but not petrol) can be as high as €150 per day.

CHAD

Congo

Not to be confused with the Democratic Republic of Congo (DRC, formerly Zaïre) across the Congo River, Congo (officially known as the Republic of Congo and also sometimes called Congo-Brazzaville) offers a friendlier and less-threatening version of its sprawling neighbour, though the crumbling infrastructure makes travel here just as tough.

Congo remains an unknown quantity to most outsiders, but you're probably aware of its vast rainforests; home to at least half the world's lowland gorillas. Parc National Nouabalé-Ndoki is one of the most pristine preserves in Africa and a highlight of the whole of Central Africa, not just Congo. The vast tropical plains of the north are juxtaposed against a 169km-long coastal strip that plays host to a nascent oil industry, but also has a wild side of its own at Parc National Conkouati-Douli. And then there are the French-flavoured cities of Brazzaville and Pointe-Noire, which are both low on excitement, but high on allure.

Congo has much to offer those who make the effort to explore it, and now that the civil war is largely over, expect a growing number of people to take up the challenge.

FAST FACTS

- **Area** 342,000 sq km
- **ATMs** Available in Brazzaville and Pointe-Noire
- **Borders** Angola (Cabinda), Cameroon, Central African Republic (CAR), Democratic Republic of Congo (DRC) and Gabon
- **Budget** A minimum of US$20 per day; far more if you visit national parks
- **Capital** Brazzaville
- **Languages** French (official), Lingala (north), Munukutuba (south)
- **Money** Central African CFA franc (CFA); US$1 = CFA463, €1 = CFA656
- **Seasons** Wet seasons are October to May (south) and June to September (north)
- **Telephone** Country code ☎ 242; international access code ☎ 00
- **Time** GMT/UTC +1
- **Visa** Available on arrival, but to avoid hassles, get it from an embassy beforehand if possible

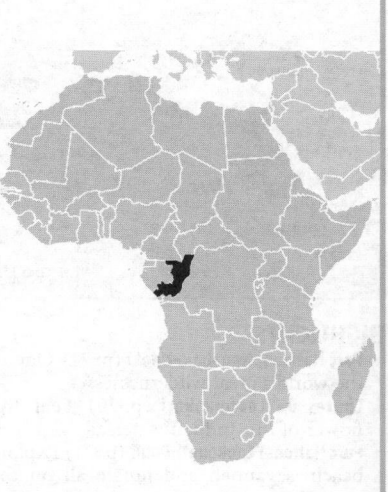

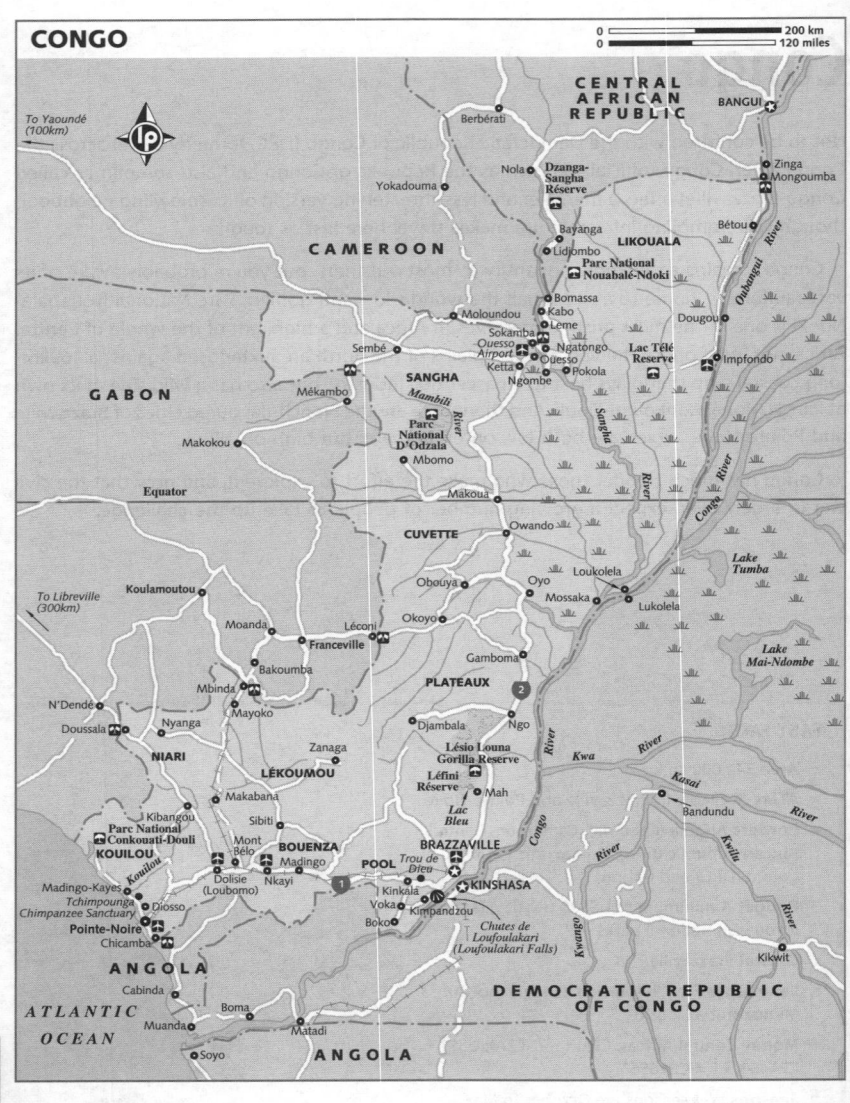

HIGHLIGHTS

- **Parc National Nouabalé-Ndoki** (p571) One of the world's great wildernesses.
- **Chutes De Loufoulakari** (p570) Feel the power of this hidden waterfall.
- **Parc National Conkouati-Douli** (p571) Explore beach, savannah and jungle all on the same day.

- **Barge travel** (p574) Journey for the sake of the journey.
- **Brazzaville** (p566) Relax in this big city's small-town feel.

CLIMATE & WHEN TO GO

It gets hot, often over 30°C, during the rainy months (October to May in the south) but

HOW MUCH?

- **Internet per hour** slow/fast US$1/2
- **Cup of coffee from street vendor** US$0.20
- **4WD hire per day** US$300
- **Brazzaville to Pointe-Noire flight** US$74 to US$90
- **Fish platter from street vendor** US$2

LONELY PLANET INDEX

- **1L petrol** US$0.75
- **1.5L bottled water** US$1
- **500ml bottle of Ngok beer** US$1
- **Souvenir T-shirt** Don't exist
- **Baguette sandwich** US$0.35

night-time temperatures can drop to half that during the dry season (June to September). In the north, the seasons are reversed with the wettest months falling between June and November, and this is the best time to travel in Congo: in the south because it's dry and cool and in the north because it's the best time to spot wildlife at Parc National Nouabalé-Ndoki.

HISTORY

Pygmies, arriving from the east, were most likely Congo's first inhabitants. Later several kingdoms of Bantu origin (the Kongo, Loango and Teke among them) arrived and opened trade links across the Congo River basin.

The Portuguese were the first Europeans to arrive on the banks of the Congo River, quickly establishing a slave-trade system with partnering coastal tribes. The French had an early presence here, too, and it was Franco-Italian empire builder Pierre Savorgnan de Brazza who led a major expedition inland in 1875, and then five years later charmed local rulers into putting their land on the river's west bank under French control.

French Rule

Predictably, the French government made quick work of acquiring Congo's considerable natural resources such as ivory, tropical hardwoods and rubber, as well as raising hell with the local population who were used as forced labour. Because of human rights scandals perpetrated by the companies running the region, the French were forced to take a greater role in overseeing things and by 1910, Congo (called Middle Congo) had been formally streamlined into French Equatorial Africa along with Chad, Gabon and the Central African Republic. Brazzaville was the capital.

Except for initiating construction of the Congo-Ocean Railway (1924–34) the French made few significant changes and locals revolted in protest in 1928.

Brazzaville had its moment in the sun during 1940–43 when it served as the symbolic capital of Free France. In 1944, genuine reforms such as the abolition of forced labour and the election of local councils were enacted, but ethnic integration was never a colonial priority. Tribal differences continued to fester, and with independence in 1960 the bubbling pot finally boiled over.

Africa's First Marxist State

Congo's first president, Fulbert Youlou, lasted just three tumultuous years before being deposed in a popular uprising that put Alphonse Massamba-Débat in power. Introducing a one-party state and treading a socialist path, he proved to be equally unpopular and was ousted in a 1968 military coup by Captain Marien Ngouabi. The next year Ngouabi formed the Congolese Worker's Party (PCT) and inaugurated the People's Republic of Congo, ushering in Africa's first Marxist-Leninist state. After Ngouabi was assassinated in 1977, the PCT appointed Joachim Yhombi-Opango as successor but, charged with 'deviation from party directives' and corruption, he was replaced in 1979 by vice president and defence minister Denis Sassou-Nguesso. Sassou-Nguesso's political survivalism proved to be superior to his predecessors (he's still in power today) and his pragmatism got results. Congo forged ties with both capitalist and communist countries and gradually moderated its political course. Following the downfall of the economy and the subsequent collapse of the Soviet Union, Sassou agreed to allow multiparty elections in 1992.

Civil War

Sassou lost the election to former prime minister Pascal Lissouba, who had been exiled for complicity in the assassination of Ngouabi. Accusations that he rigged 1993's

WARNING

Most of Congo is quite safe these days, though not the Pool region west of Brazzaville where Ninja rebels continue to occasionally terrorise civilians. Get current, on-the-ground advice before travelling there.

parliamentary elections sparked violent unrest between pro-government and opposition militias (both tribally based) until a 1994 ceasefire. Congo fell under full-scale civil war in 1997. Brazzaville was devastated (most of its citizens were forced to flee to the bush for many months) and Sassou's 'Cobra' militia, with the help of Angolan troops, put him back into power.

The coming years saw sporadic fighting, including more attacks on the capital; peace-agreement signings with some rebels groups; the approval of a new constitution in a national referendum; and Sassou winning another election (in which his main rivals, including Lissouba, were barred) in 2002. In 2003 the main rebel group, the 'Ninjas', finally agreed to a peace accord, but there was no follow through on disarmament and even after another peace deal in 2007 the Ninjas have continued their low-level insurgency in the Pool region. These days, however, they're more interested in banditry than politics.

Congo Today

The economy's heavy reliance on oil revenues is said to substantially contribute to Sassou's ability to maintain tight control over the country. (He is currently under investigation in France for using millions of dollars of embezzled public funds to buy luxury homes and cars there.) This is despite the resentment of southerners of Sassou's northern bias, and dissatisfaction by most Congolese over the slow pace of development (74% of the population lives on less than US$2 a day).

Sassou's allies won a strong majority in the 2007 parliamentary elections, which were boycotted by the opposition. Sassou took 79% of the presidential vote in July 2009. Both elections were widely criticised as illegitimate. These days you'll be hard pressed to meet any Congolese who has positive opinions about Sassou or optimism about the future.

CULTURE

Congolese are formal and reserved, often downright shy, but if you offer a handshake they'll open up quickly. There's definitely truth in the adage that the average Congolese would rather dress well than eat well. You *will* be judged on what you wear, so try to dress as smart as you can.

Of Congo's 16 ethnic groups, the Kongo people predominate, making up nearly half the population. Other key groups include the Sangha (20%), Teke (17%), M'Bochi (12%) and pygmies (2%). Seventy percent of the population lives in Brazzaville, Pointe-Noire and along the railroad in between these two cities. In terms of faith, Congo is divided about half and half between Christian and animist, with a tiny Muslim minority.

FOOD & DRINK

Northern Congolese are meat eaters (very often bush meat) while southern Congolese love their fish. Both eat their protein almost exclusively with cassava, though you will sometimes find yams or rice in restaurants.

ENVIRONMENT

The north and southwest regions of Congo are blanketed by the dense tropical rainforest the country is famous for, but the central plateau, between Brazzaville and Oyo, is an unexpected swathe of savannah where trees are rare. The Atlantic Ocean crashes onto some respectable pale-yellow beaches – and those aren't bright stars hovering low over the horizon, rather the lights of offshore oil rigs.

BRAZZAVILLE

pop 800,000

Founded in 1880 on the Stanley Pool (called Malebo Pool in the DRC) area of the Congo River, 'Brazza' has always been the junior partner economically with Kinshasa (DRC), which tempts and taunts from the other shore; though for travellers it's the more pleasant and interesting town.

Low-key and unassuming, with most evidence of the war years washed away, Brazzaville retains a French air, which gives the town some of its charm. Many people end up sticking around longer than planned, even though there's not a whole lot to do.

ORIENTATION

The city centre, home to most banks, airline offices and chichi restaurants, stretches from around the landmark Tour Nabemba building in the east to Ave Foch, home to many outdoor cafes. But the beating heart of Brazzaville lies in the neighbourhoods that splay beyond the centre, such as Poto-Poto to the north and Bacongo to the west.

INFORMATION

Camal Voyages (☎ 2810175; Rue du Village Chrétien) Sells plane tickets and organises tours around the country.

Centre Culturel Français (☎ 2811900; Rond-Point CCF; ☼ 9am-7pm Mon-Sat, 2-7pm Sun) Hosts a busy cultural calendar. Also has fast internet (per hour CFA1000).

Clinique Netcare (☎ 5470911; Blvd du Maréchal) Brazzaville's top hospital.

Crédit du Congo (Ave Cabral) Has Brazzaville's only ATMs.

Cyber-Gni (Pl de la Plaine; per hr CFA1000; ☼ 7.30am-10pm Mon-Sat, 7.30am-7.30pm Sun) One of Congo's few fast internet connections.

DHL (☎ 2810103; Ave Foch; ☼ 8am-6pm Mon-Fri, 8am-1pm Sat) Reliable postal services.

Pharmacie Mavre (☎ 2811839; Rond-Point City Centre; ☼ 8am-7pm Mon-Sat) Brazzaville's best pharmacy.

Post office (Rond-Point de la Poste; ☼ 7.30am-5pm Mon-Fri, 7.30am-1pm Sat) No longer offers poste-restante services.

Wildlife Conservation Society (☎ 2810346; www.wcs-congo.org; Ave de Gaulle; ☼ 8am-4pm Mon-Fri) For information about the national parks.

SIGHTS

The body of Pierre Savorgnan de Brazza, who founded the city, was returned to Congo in 2006 and interred in the gleaming **Brazza Memorial** (Ave Cabral; admission free; ☼ 10.30am-10.30pm).

The modernist 1949 **Basilique Sainte-Anne** (Ave Orsii) was the crowning achievement of French architect Roger Erell, who was known for fusing Western architectural ideas with local building techniques. It's as striking inside as out.

Marché Total (Ave Matsoua), Brazza's biggest market, in Bacongo, sells everything from caterpillars and monkeys to Congolese fabrics and aphrodisiac charms. Sift through all the schlock at the **Marché Touristique** (Marché Plateau Ex-Trésor; Ave de Gaulle; ☼ 8am-5pm Mon-Sat, 8am-1pm Sun) and you'll find some decent weavings and woodcarvings, though perhaps the best place to pickup a souvenir is **Ecole de Peinture de Poto-Poto** (☎ 5567961; Ave de la Paix; ☼ 9am-6pm), association of painters; many of its members have exhibited in Europe and the USA.

Les Rapides, wide and powerful rapids on the Congo River at the outskirts of the city, are an impressive site. Take a minibus to Pont Djoué from next to Centre Culturel Français. Most people observe the rapids from the nearby bar **Site Touristique Les Rapides** (☼ 7am-11pm), but the best viewing is at the other end, down the sandy track after the bridge.

SLEEPING

Good budget and genuine luxury accommodation are still rare in Brazzaville, though there are many nice midrange hotels.

Armée du Salut (☎ 5580968; off Ave des Trois Martyrs; r with/without bathroom CFA7000/5000; P) The spic-and-span Salvation Army has the cheapest beds in Brazza, in part because the mattresses are exceptionally thin.

SIL Congo (☎ 5218054; Ave Foch; r with/without bathroom CFA8500/6500) Rooms at this Christian missionary centre are less basic than those at Armée du Salut, and far closer to downtown. Check-in is between 9am and 3pm and curfew is at 10pm.

Hôtel M Domingo (☎ 5213308; Ave de la Paix; r with fan CFA10,000, with air-con CFA15,000-20,000; ✲) This aging, no-nonsense place in Poto-Poto is popular due to its low prices and location, though electricity and water often cut out.

Hôtel Siringo 1 (☎ 5898797; Ave de la Paix; r with fan CFA15,000, with air-con CFA20,000-25,000; ✲) Just south of the Domingo, this similar but better place is worth the extra CFA5000.

Hôtel Hippocampe (☎ 6686068; www.hippocampe.asia, in French; Rue Behangle; r CFA26,000-36,000; P ✲ ☐ ☎) A clean, comfortable, well-maintained French-owned hotel offering very good value. Overlanders often camp in the parking lot and many expats converge on the restaurant (mains CFA2500 to CFA6900) for the Vietnamese food.

Hôtel de la Paix (☎ 6797580; Ave de la Paix; r CFA35,000-75,000; ✲ ☎) The little industrial-chic touches at this shiny new place almost earn it a boutique hotel label. Rooms are comfortable and well equipped.

Olympic Palace Hôtel (☎ 2813436; Ave de l'Amitié; r CFA100,000-150,000, ste CFA180,000; P ✲ ✲ ☎ ⊠) The Olympic Palace is in the hills above town. The old wing is dated, but rooms have the the attention to detail you deserve at these prices.

EATING

La Plaine (Rue de Reims; dishes CFA1000-1500; ☼ 7am-5pm Mon-Sat) Cheap eats are very rare downtown,

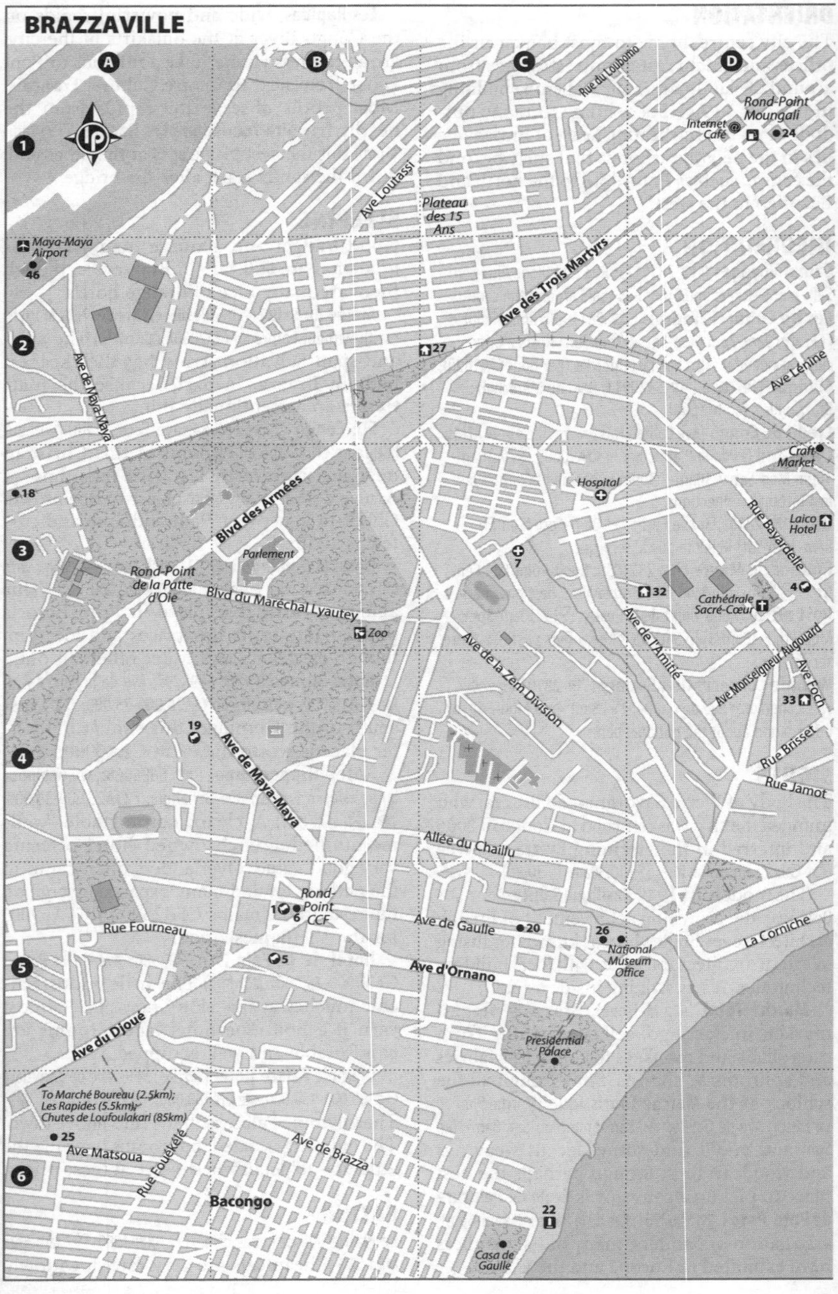

BRAZZAVILLE

Ⓐ **Ⓑ** **Ⓒ** **Ⓓ**

1

Rue du Loubomo

Rond-Point Moungali
Internet Café @ ● 24

Ave Loutassi

Plateau des 15 Ans

Maya-Maya Airport
● 46

Ave de Maya-Maya

Ave des Trois Martyrs

2
☐ 27

Ave Lénine

● 18

Blvd des Armées

Craft Market

Hospital ✚
Rue Bayardelle

Laico Hotel

3
Rond-Point de la Patte d'Oie
Parlement
Blvd du Maréchal Lyautey
☐ 7
☐ 32
Cathédrale Sacré-Cœur
● 4

Ave de l'Amitié
Ave Monseigneur Augouard
Ave Foch

Zoo
33 ☐

Ave de la Zem Division
Rue Brisset

4
● 19
Ave de Maya-Maya
Rue Jamot

Allée du Chaillu

5
1 ● 6 Rond-Point CCF
Ave de Gaulle ● 20
● 26 National Museum Office
La Corniche

Rue Fourneau
● 5
Ave d'Ornano

Ave du Djoué
Presidential Palace

6
To Marché Boureau (2.5km);
Les Rapides (5.5km);
Chutes de Loufoulakari (85km)
● 25
Ave Matsoua
Rue Fouékélé
Ave de Brazza

Bacongo
22 ☐
Casa de Gaulle

CONGO

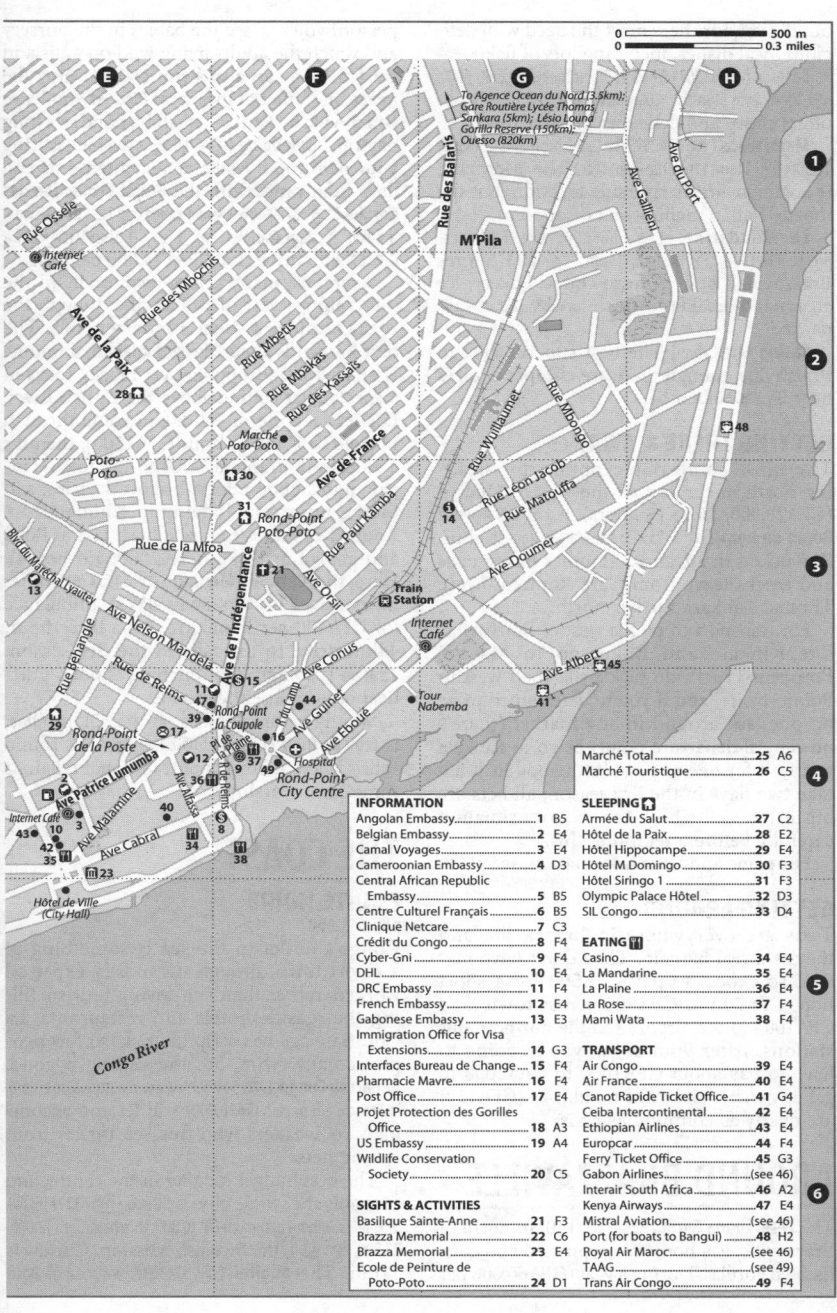

but the vendors here meet the need with delicious local dishes, including lots of fish.

La Rose (☎ 5386713; Pl de la Plaine mains CFA2300-6000; ☻ 10am-2am Mon-Sat, 10am-8pm Sun; ☒) La Rose offers cheap and delicious Chinese food.

Mami Wata (☎ 5342879; La Corniche; mains CFA6500-11,500; ☻ 11am-11pm Tue-Sun; ☒) The 'Mermaid' is a winner for its riverside location, but the mostly Italian menu won't disappoint.

La Mandarine (☎ 6666600; Ave Foch; espresso CFA1000; ☻ 6.30am-11pm; ☒ ☒) Serves Brazzaville's best espresso coffee, bakery, ice cream and breakfast; which is why it's always packed.

Casino (Ave Cabral) The best supermarket in Brazzaville, though there are cheaper choices near Tour Nabemba.

GETTING THERE & AWAY

The most comfortable option for heading north, including all the way to Ouesso (CFA28,000, 16 to 18 hours), is on an **Agence Ocean du Nord** (☎ 5321523; Ave Marien Ngouabi) bus. Buy tickets in advance. All other buses, taxis and trucks leave from Gare Routière Lycée Thomas Sankara further north.

For transport to points west of Brazzaville, like Kinkala and Boko, go to Marché Boureau. Trucks do tackle the road west to Pointe-Noire, and if you're determined to be on one, ask around in any market (there's no central departure point) or go to Kinkala and wait for one to pass. With good luck it'll take two days in the dry season; all bets are off in the wet. Check the security situation carefully before attempting this.

For plane and train information, see p573.

GETTING AROUND

Taxis are everywhere in Brazzaville and they're a real bargain. They don't have meters, so expect to pay CFA500 for a short hop, CFA700 to CFA800 across town, and CFA1000 to the airport and the northern bus stations. After 9pm or so, you're going to have to pay about CFA1000 to CFA2000 to get anywhere. Crowded minibuses (CFA150) are nearly as common as taxis.

AROUND BRAZZAVILLE

The **Lésio Louna Gorilla Reserve**, 140km north of Brazzaville, is a home for orphaned and confiscated gorillas. During a visit (CFA60,000 per person) you can see the babies in the nursery and watch the adults living wild on an island get fed. You can also swim or just enjoy the peace and quiet at lovely **Lac Bleu**. If you leave Brazzaville by 5am it can all be done as a long daytrip, but lodging (r CFA30,000) is available; bring your own food. Make arrangements several days in advance with the **Projet Protection des Gorilles** (☎ 5879999; www.ppg-congo.org; 125 Rue Matsiona-Nzoulou; ☻ 8am-4pm Mon-Fri). They'll also hire you a 4WD with driver for CFA144,000 per day.

There are many remote waterfalls in the hill country west of Brazzaville, though the roads leading to them are horrendous. The best known is **Chutes de Loufoulakari**, a unique U-shaped falls dropping over blocky rocks in a spectacular setting above the Congo River. Lorries take the direct, 80km route through Linzolo to Kimpandzou (CFA1500), then it's a 7km walk to the falls. Until the road is repaired this option doesn't allow daytrips, and there's no formal lodging in Kimpandzou. Another option is to take a bush taxi to Boko and get off at Voka (CFA2000, 1½ hours). Here the **Catholic Mission** (☎ 6455326) sometimes drives visitors in its 4WD ambulance for CFA400 per kilometre. It's a three-hour, 44km drive to the falls in the dry season. Traffic is so light that hitching is not a practical option on either route.

Shortly before Kinkala, at the 55km pillar, is **Trou de Dieu** (God's Hole), a curious round valley where followers of traditional religions sometimes worship.

THE COAST

POINTE-NOIRE

pop 663,000

Congo's outlet to the sea is something of a resort town, though it's mostly expat oil workers rather than sun-loving tourists filling the seaside hotels and restaurants. La Côte Sauvage has a riptide risk, so few people actually swim, but the surfing is good. **Rénatura Congo** (☎ 5449999; www.renatura.asso.eu.org, in French; per person CFA10,000) will let you accompany its workers who free sea turtles from fishing nets.

The best budget lodging in the centre, and probably the whole city, is **Sueco** (☎ 6321716; Ave Moe Teli; r without bathroom CFA10,000, with bathroom 12,000-22,000; ☒ ☒), the Swedish Mission. Curfew is 11pm. The **Migitel** (☎ 5743636; www.congo-hotel

-migitel.com; Blvd de Gaulle; s/d/ste US$45,000/50,000/60,000;
☒ ☒ ▣ ☎) has plain but comfortable rooms
at half the price you'd pay on the beach or
elsewhere on Ave de Gaulle. With attractive
thatched-roof cottages overlooking a little lagoon and a private beach **Malonda Lodge**
(☎ 5575151; www.malondalodge.com; s/d CFA88,000/95,000
incl breakfast; ▣ ☒ ☒), 18km south of town, is
the loveliest hotel in Congo. The restaurant
(CFA6500 to CFA9500) is open to all. Truly
excellent Congolese cuisine, like smoked gazelle
with palm oil soup, makes **Restaurant Gaspard**
(Blvd Moe Mokasso; dishes CFA2500; ☽ 9am-10.30pm) a
must-do. The full roster isn't ready until 1pm.

Because travel by road and rail from
Brazzaville is both dangerous and difficult,
most people fly here: see p574 for details.
Most taxi trips cost CFA700, though a very
short one is CFA500 and it's CFA1000 to
the airport.

DIOSSO & AROUND

On the edge of the village of Diosso, 25km north
of Pointe-Noire, runaway erosion has created
the colourful **Diosso Gorge**, which looks like a
mini Badlands. Also in town, the **Musée Ma-
Loango** (☎ 5336816; CFA2000; ☽ 10am-5pm Sat & Sun, by
appointment Mon-Fri) has good displays on Congolese
culture, the Loango kingdom and slavery: the
town of Loango on the coast here was a major
slaving port, though there's nothing to see now
except a toppled monument. Bush taxis run
from Grande Marché in Pointe-Noire (CFA600,
45 minutes). Both the gorge and the museum
are then a couple of kilometres walk (in opposite directions) from the village centre.

Twenty-five kilometres north of Diosso
is the Jane Goodall Institute's **Tchimpounga
Chimpanzee Sanctuary** (☎ 5105792), a home for
orphaned chimps. It was recently closed to
visitors, but should reopen someday.

PARC NATIONAL CONKOUATI-DOULI

Congo's most diverse **national park** (☎ 5440034;
www.wcs-congo.org) stretches from the Atlantic
Ocean though a band of coastal savannah up
into jungle-clad mountains. Poaching problems (fed by demand for bushmeat in Pointe-
Noire) mean the wildlife-watching is limited,
but the scenery is superb. The main activities
are boat rides (CFA25,000 per person) up the
Ngongo River, which is frequently crossed
by elephants; feeding the island-dwelling
chimpanzees (CFA50,000) being prepared
for reintroduction to the forest; and, between

November and February, watching sea turtles
lay their eggs on the beach (CFA20,000).

The only lodging is a nice **house** (1-2 people/6-8
people CFA90,000/160,000) with full kitchen overlooking Conkouati Lagoon, though there
should soon be camping facilities and some
cheaper bungalows on the beach. You must
bring all your own food.

Traffic is so sparse that hitching isn't an option. Either hire a 4WD (around CFA200,000
per day) in Pointe-Noire or wait for the **Wildlife
Conservation Society** (☎ 5249676) to have space in
its vehicles coming from Pointe-Noire. No
matter how you travel, you must call the park
before visiting.

THE NORTH

OUESSO
pop 25,000
Some 800km from Brazzaville, Ouesso
('*way*-so') is the last city of the north. It's a
rather lifeless town, but if you're heading to
Nouabalé-Ndoki National Park you'll probably spend some time here. There's internet
access at **Caritas** (Ave Marien Ngouabi; per hr CFA800;
☽ 9am-2pm Mon-Sat), behind the cathedral.
Ouesso's one bank doesn't change money.

Auberge Le Kassou (☎ 5341930; off Ave Marien Ngouabi;
r without bathroom CFA4000) has simple, clean rooms
around a little garden. The cottages at **Nianina
Auberge** (☎ 5871906; Rue Ile Elapas; r CFA20,000; ▣ ☒)
are surprisingly colourful and cozy considering the brick exteriors. It's not the best hotel in
town, but arguably the best value.

PARC NATIONAL NOUABALÉ-NDOKI

The **Nouabalé-Ndoki National Park** (www.wcs-congo.
org; park entry per day CFA15,000) has been called the
world's 'last Eden'. In all likelihood humans
have never inhabited this swampy forest and
populations of elephants, gorillas, chimpanzees, leopards and other large mammals
remain healthy. The main activities are visiting a habituated gorilla family at Mondika
(CFA262,500 per person per day) and watching a variety of wildlife from an elevated mira-
dor at Mbeli Bai (CFA97,500), a natural forest
clearing. Prices include transport by truck and
boat from the headquarters at Bomassa, rustic
lodging (tents at Mondika and stilted cottages
at Mbeli), meals and French-speaking guides.
Wali Bai (CFA5000 per person, plus CFA3000
for the guide), just a 4km walk from Bomassa,
is good for elephant- and buffalo-sightings.

CONGO

Bookings should be made with the **Wildlife Conservation Society** (WCS; ☎ 5230059; ☼ 7am-3pm Mon-Fri, 7am-noon Sat) office in Ouesso as far in advance as possible. Children under 14 cannot visit the gorillas and those under 16 are not allowed at Mbeli Bai or Wali Bai.

Very simple rooms sleeping up to six people at the park headquarters cost an indefensible CFA65,000 per person, but the only other choice is far more basic rooms or camping (price negotiable; ask for the chief) at the market in town.

The easiest way to reach Bomassa is to charter a boat. The park charges CFA195,000 from Ouesso or Bayanga (Central African Republic) and CFA120,000 from Libongo (Cameroon) for one to three people. You can also negotiate with private boat owners, though prices won't be much lower unless they paddle you rather than use a motor. If you're lucky, the WCS will be sending a supply boat from Ouesso to Bomassa or Kabo and you can catch a ride, but they're often full. Public boats fan out from Ouesso to most river towns, though not every day, and then you can try to hitch a ride (not easy because traffic is very rare) or pay to have the park send a vehicle to get you. They charge CFA12,000 from Kabo to Bomassa.

CONGO DIRECTORY

ACCOMMODATION
Outside Brazzaville and Pointe-Noire, accommodation options remain limited, but the situation is improving and new hotels are popping up in towns across the country. Prices are usually high regardless of whether you prefer budget, midrange or top-end accommodation.

BUSINESS HOURS
Banks Open around 8am and typically close at 2pm.
Offices Open 8am to 5pm weekdays and until noon on Saturdays. Many close for an hour or two over lunch.

PRACTICALITIES

- Congo uses the metric system.
- Electricity is 230V/50Hz. The plugs are two-pin Continental Europe style.
- For English-language news tune into the BBC World Service on 92.6FM. All other print and broadcast media is in French.

DANGERS & ANNOYANCES
Except for the Pool region west of Brazzaville, travel in Congo is quite safe these days. Brazzaville and Pointe-Noire are typical African cities: trouble-free by day, but best traversed by taxi at night. Power cuts and fuel shortages are common. Be very discreet taking photos or the police are likely to hassle you; you could easily end up in jail for several days.

Congo has an annoying number of beggars. Not the disabled and destitute, of which there are very few, but gainfully employed people like hotel staff, security guards and government workers.

Don't give at roadblocks just because you're asked. Most soldiers are just trying it on when they ask for *un jus* (a juice), though some absolutely won't let you leave until you've handed over money. The best you can do is try to negotiate a lower bribe.

EMBASSIES & CONSULATES
The following countries have diplomatic representation in Brazzaville. France, Belgium and Angola also have consulates in Pointe-Noire.
Angola (Map pp568-9; ☎ 2814721; Ave de Gaulle)
Belgium (Map pp568-9; ☎ 2813712; brazzaville@diplobel.org; Ave Patrice Lumumba)
Cameroon (Map pp568-9; ☎ 6755726; Rue Bayardelle)
Central African Republic (Map pp568-9; ☎ 7343296; Rue Fourneau)
DRC (Map pp568-9; ☎ 2813052; Ave de l'Indépendance)
France (Map pp568-9; ☎ 2815541; www.ambfrance-cg.org; Rue Alfassa)
Gabon (☎ 5514651; Blvd du Maréchal Lyautey)
USA (Map pp568-9; ☎ 6122000; http://brazzaville.usembassy.gov; Ave de Maya-Maya)

HOLIDAYS
Public holidays in Congo:
New Year's Day 1 January
Easter March/April
Labour Day 1 May
Reconciliation Day 10 June
Independence Day 15 August
All Saints' Day 1 November
Christmas Day 25 December

MONEY
Euros are the best currency to bring, though you can change US dollars and British pounds in Brazzaville and Pointe-Noire. Banks are rare outside these cities, but Lebanese- and West African–owned businesses usually change

money: rates vary widely so shop around. Make sure the bills are in pristine condition.

Crédit du Congo bank has ATMs in Brazzaville and Pointe-Noire that accept Visa, MasterCard and Plus cards, and Ecobank ATMs will be linked for international Visa cards soon. Interfaces Bureau de Change changes travellers cheques and has branches in Brazzaville (Map pp568–9) and Pointe-Noire.

POST & TELEPHONE

Landlines (starting with ☎ 281 – there are no proper area codes throughout the country) are appalling in Congo and you'll be lucky if they work. Most businesses use mobile phones (numbers listed in this chapter are mobile numbers). SIM cards cost around CFA500 and international calls are usually CFA100 per minute.

The postal system is thoroughly unreliable.

VISAS

All visitors to Congo need a visa. You can buy a 15-day, single-entry visa (CFA20,000) on arrival at most borders, if you have a letter of introduction (a hotel reservation *should* suffice), but there will likely be hassles and additional 'fees' if you take this route. Visas from embassies in neighbouring nations are around CFA30,000 for one month.

If you want to extend your stay, you can get a three-month visa (CFA31,000) from the Immigration office (Map p568-69; ⏰ 9am-3pm Mon-Fri) in Brazzaville and Pointe-Noire. In the capital, apply for visas at the unmarked office building on an unnamed street behind the Toyota dealership near the train station.. You'll be grilled as to your plan, but detailing a long itinerary with visits to national parks should be enough.

Visas for Onward Travel

Angola Generally only gives visas (CFA47,000 for 15-day tourist visa, CFA15,000 five-day transit) to Congolese residents. Others can apply and then wait 15 days to see if they get approved. Your chances of success are higher in Pointe-Noire than Brazzaville, but still low. The long list of requirements includes a letter of invitation and a photocopy of the identity card of the person who invited you.

Cameroon One-month, single-entry visas cost CFA51,000, and require two photos, a photocopy of your passport and a hotel reservation. They're usually issued in 48 hours.

Central African Republic One-month, single-entry visas require two photos, a photocopy of your passport and CFA40,000. It'll be ready the next day, or maybe the same day if you apply early.

Democratic Republic of Congo One-month single-entry/two-month multiple-entry visas cost CFA35,000/60,000 and you need two photos and a photocopy of your passport. Apply in the morning and it'll be ready in the afternoon.

Gabon Single-/multiple-entry visas valid for three months cost CFA35,000/70,000. Bring a letter of invitation, a hotel reservation, a photocopy of your passport and two photos.

TRANSPORT IN CONGO

GETTING THERE & AWAY
Air

All airlines have offices at the airports, but it's easier to use their offices in town (if they have one) or a travel agency. Many airlines connect Brazzaville with their busy African hubs.

Air France (Map pp568-9; ☎ 5312151; www.airfrance. com; Ave Cabral, Brazzaville) Flies direct to/from Europe (nonstop four days weekly to Brazzaville and three times weekly to Pointe-Noire).

Ceiba Intercontinental (Map pp568-9; ☎ 5517344; Ave Foch, Brazzaville) A smaller airline that connects Brazzaville and Pointe-Noire to most nearby nations and many in West Africa.

Ethiopian Airlines (Map pp568-9; ☎ 6885012; www. ethiopianairlines.com; Ave Foch, Brazzaville)

Gabon Airlines (Map pp568-9; ☎ 7088676; www. gabonairlines.com) This smaller operator connects Brazzaville and Pointe-Noire to most nearby nations and many in West Africa. Has an office at Maya-Maya Airport.

Interair South Africa (Map pp568-9; ☎ 6656937; www.interair.co.za) Has an office at Maya-Maya Airport.

Kenya Airways (Map pp568-9; ☎ 7073659; www. kenya-airways.com; 2nd fl, Rue de Reims, Brazzaville)

Royal Air Maroc (Map pp568-9; ☎ 6282828; www.royal airmaroc.com) This airline's office is at Maya-Maya Airport.

TAAG (Map pp568-9; ☎ 6768990; www.taag.aero; Ave Cabral, Brazzaville) Another smaller airline that links Brazzaville and Pointe-Noire with most nearby nations and many in West Africa.

Land & River
ANGOLA

Crossing to Cabinda is possible on good roads, but check the situation carefully before trying

---

DEPARTURE TAX

You must pay CFA1000 at the airport for domestic flights if you have a paper ticket. For electronic tickets and all international flights, the tax is paid when you buy the ticket.

it, especially if you are driving your own vehicle, as attacks by separatists are on the rise.

CAMEROON

Travel to Cameroon is slow-going, but possible in the dry season. The best way is to take a boat from Ouesso to Sokamba (CFA5000, two hours) and continue through remote southwest Cameroon to Moloundou and Yokadouma. If you're driving, first head southeast of Ouesso to Ngombe, where there's a car ferry over the Sangha River, and then drive to Ngatongo, where another ferry will get you to Sokamba.

CENTRAL AFRICAN REPUBLIC & DEMOCRATIC REPUBLIC OF CONGO

For the scoop on how to get to/from the Central African Republic, see Boats on the Oubangui (p549). For information on crossing to/from the DRC, see Going To Le Beach (p590).

GABON

Although it's possible to cross the border at Doussala or Mbinda north of Dolisie, most people heading to Gabon travel between Oyo and Franceville via Léconi (Gabon; it's not on the border, but take care of Gabonese immigration formalities here). There's no public transport along most of this route and few lorries, so it can take several days. Be ready for a lot of payouts to police along the way.

GETTING AROUND
Air

Trans Air Congo and Air Congo are the two most reliable airlines in Congo. There are flights with the airlines listed here, but there are also a few fly-by-night airlines flying to Dolisie, Impfondo, Nkayi and other remote towns. Flight schedules are rarely followed; cancellations are common. Travel agencies can often get seats when airlines say their planes are full.

Trans Air Congo (Map pp568-9; ☎ 6262605; Ave Cabral, Brazzaville) Flies frequently between Brazzaville and Pointe-Noire (one way CFA33,000 to CFA40,000).

Air Congo (Map pp568-9; ☎ 6710071; Ave Conus, Brazzaville) Flies frequently between Brazzaville and Pointe-Noire (one way CFA33,000 to CFA40,000) and from Brazzaville to Ouesso three times a week for CFA53,000.

Mistral Aviation (☎ 6200042) Also flies from Brazzaville to Ouesso three times a week for CFA53,000.

Land

Hwy 1 to Pointe-Noire, paved only to Kinkala, is appalling and traffic is rare. It'll be many

years before this changes. Hwy 2 north to Ouesso, however, is paved and in mostly good condition to Owando. North of Makoua there are still some horribly rough spots, but reconstruction work was underway and a floating bridge was being installed on the Mambili River when we were there, so travel times (and probably prices) should decline dramatically.

A few proper buses now run to the north, but it's still mostly bush taxis and lorries. **Europcar** (www.europcar.com; Brazzaville Map pp568-9; ☎ 6662020; Pointe-Noire ☎ 6662626) offers car hire from CFA57,000 (40km free) per day, but it's easier and about half the price to just charter a taxi with driver. Europcar also has outrageously expensive 4WD hire, or you can go to Brazzaville's Marché Total (p567) to haggle with truck drivers parked on Ave Matsoua; the best price we found was CFA100,000 per day.

River

Between June and December, when river levels are high enough, barges run up the Oubangui River from Brazzaville. Some go to Bangui (Central African Republic; see Boats On The Oubangui, p549). and others veer left at Mossaka taking the even wilder Sangha River to Ouesso. There are more or less weekly departures (CFA13,000 to CFA15,000), though no schedule; boats go when they're ready. Ideally the journey between Ouesso and Bangui can be done in five days downstream and eight upstream, but it's likely to take many more. Heading downstream you might need to go to nearby Pokola or Ngombe to catch a boat since many start their journeys there.

Train

Trains still run twice a week between Brazzaville and Pointe-Noire, though check on safety before taking this option. Over the past few years there's been an ebb and flow with the aggressiveness of the Ninja rebels, who provide on-board security (an element of the peace agreement) for part of the trip. They have big guns and if they want something of yours, there's no stopping them. Should you determine that it's safe, purchase tickets (1st-/2nd-class CFA20,000/11,705, 12 to 24 hours) the day before. First class gets you a seat, 2nd class is standing in the aisles.

CONGO

Democratic Republic of Congo

As much a geographical concept as a fully fledged nation, the Democratic Republic of Congo (DRC, formerly Zaïre) has written one of the saddest chapters in modern history: from the brazen political folly of King Leopold of Belgium to the hideously corrupt kleptocracy of maverick leader Mobutu Sese Seko, and the blood-stained battlegrounds of Africa's first 'world war'. All of which make the inevitable *Heart of Darkness* references painfully apt.

But, after a decades-long decline in which much of the country descended into anarchy, Africa's third-largest nation is now squarely headed in the right direction. It still has a long way to go (militias continue to brutalise civilians in many areas), but new roads, enormous untapped mineral wealth, the world's largest UN peacekeeping force and fair elections have bred optimism among its tormented but resilient population.

Carpeted by huge swathes of rainforest and punctuated by gushing rivers and smoking volcanoes, DRC is an ecodestination just waiting to happen. Travel here remains difficult and frustrating, but the door is definitely open again.

FAST FACTS

- **Area** 2,345,410 sq km
- **ATMs** Available in large cities
- **Borders** Angola, Congo, Central African Republic, Uganda, Rwanda, Burundi, Tanzania and Zambia open. Sudan closed.
- **Budget** US$30 to US$40 per day minimum
- **Capital** Kinshasa
- **Languages** French (official), Lingala, Swahili, Tshiluba
- **Money** Congolese franc; US$1 = CDF890, €1 = CDF1288
- **Population** 68.7 million
- **Seasons** The rainy season lasts April to November north of the equator, and October to May south of the equator
- **Telephone** Country code ☎ 243; international access code ☎ 00
- **Time** GMT/UTC + 1 (west); GMT/UTC + 2 (east)
- **Visa** One-month single-entry visas cost US$75 to US$100 and around US$135 for a two-month, multiple-entry tourist visa

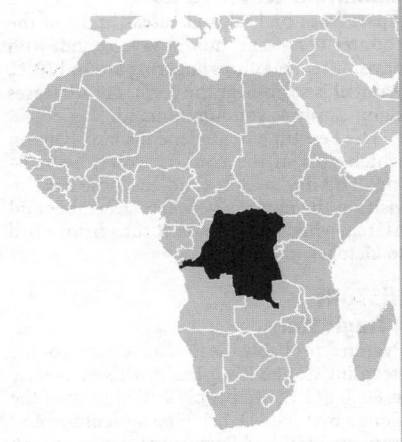

HOW MUCH?

- **Internet per hour** US$1.20 to US$2.50
- **Cup of coffee** US$2
- **4WD hire** US$135 per day
- **Small malachite bracelet** US$1
- **Dinner at a fancy restaurant** US$20 to US$50

LONELY PLANET INDEX

- **1L petrol** US$1.05
- **1L bottled water** US$1
- **500ml bottle of Primus beer** US$1.10
- **Souvenir T-shirt** Don't exist
- **Bag of spaghetti** US$0.50

HIGHLIGHTS

- **Nyiragongo** (p585) Gaze into a volcano's liquid eye.
- **Parc National des Virunga** (p585) and **Parc National de Kahuzi-Biéga** (p586) Get up close and personal with gorillas.
- **Lola Ya Bonobo Sanctuary** (p584) Meet the bonobo, a rare, peace-loving relative of chimpanzees.
- **Congo River** (p586) Take the legendary boat trip down this still-wild river.
- **Museé National** (p582) Be amazed by this enormous archive.

CLIMATE & WHEN TO GO

Apart from high-altitude areas, most of the country is hot and humid year-round, with daytime temperatures lingering around 30°C. Rainfall is scant near the coast, but increases significantly as you move inland.

The best time to go depends largely upon which area of the country you'll be visiting. The dry season (and the best time to visit) in the north is between December and March, while in the south it runs from April to October.

HISTORY
A Tragic Story

Pygmies, probably the first inhabitants of the steaming Congo River Basin, arrived as early as 8000 BC. Bantu people settled most of the Congo by 1000AD, bringing agriculture and iron-smelting, and Portuguese explorers took home the first stories from the region 500 years later. Trading goods such as ivory, cloth, pottery ironware and slaves, the Portuguese made contact with a highly developed kingdom known as the Kongo that was ruled over by a patriarchal monarch and stretched as far south as the Kwanza River in Angola. Kongo royalty became enthusiastic allies, adopting Portuguese names, clothes and customs and converting to Christianity.

In the mid-19th century, Arab traders crossed East Africa to eastern Congo, taking back slaves and ivory. Some, most famously Muhammad bin Hamad (AKA Tippu Tib), ran their own powerful fiefdoms. During the same era, Dr David Livingstone opened up the African interior to European exploration.

In 1874 the *New York Herald* and the British *Daily Telegraph* newspapers sent Henry Morton Stanley (the man who had found Dr Livingstone in 1871) across Africa to trace the course of the Congo River. His epic 999-day journey cemented the Welsh-American explorer's place in history and piqued the interest of King Leopold II of Belgium. Devious, greedy and wholly ignorant of African affairs, Leopold had been eyeing the unclaimed African gateau for some time, but he was unable to convince the Belgian government to go along. To solve the problem he decided to acquire a colony of his own.

In 1878 Leopold commissioned Stanley to return to the Congo under the smokescreen of the International African Society; a supposed philanthropic organisation. Over the ensuing five years Stanley signed treaties with chiefs on Leopold's behalf, tricking them to hand over their land rights in return for paltry gifts. At the Berlin Conference called by Bismarck in 1884 to carve up Africa, Leopold, aware of a German desire to offset French and British colonial interests, managed to convince the famous Iron Chancellor to declare the Congo a free-trade area and cede it to him.

Philanthropy was the last thing on Leopold's mind as he set about fleecing his Congo Free State of its ivory, copper and rubber. Hideous crimes were committed against the Congolese by Leopold's rubber traders. These included raiding villages and taking women and children captive as an incentive for the men to bring back ever-greater supplies of rubber from the forest. Those who did not return their quota had their hands chopped off. And all the while,

DEMOCRATIC REPUBLIC OF CONGO

n one of the earliest examples of cynical political spin-doctoring, Leopold passed off his Congo venture as a shining example of fine governorship and benevolence.

WARNING

Although rebel armies continue marauding around parts of the east, these days most places in DRC are safe most of time. But this is a country where anything can happen, from rebellion to riots to volcanic eruptions. It's imperative to get up-to-the-minute information before travelling here. For more details, see the Dangers & Annoyances section, p588.

Independence

As Leopold's crimes gradually became public knowledge, the Belgian government realised enough was enough and took over in 1908. Thereafter, things improved. The new Belgians ended forced labour, built schools and roads, and nearly eradicated sleeping sickness. By the 1940s mining had made this Africa's richest country, though even up to the end of their reign, the Belgians largely excluded Congolese from roles in the government or economy and very few Congolese had college educations.

Gathering pace in the 1950s under charismatic revolutionary Patrice Lumumba, the independence movement finally wrested control from the colonisers on 30 June 1960. Lumumba became prime minister of the new

Republic of Congo, but tribalism and personal quests for power came to the front, and just a week later the army mutinied. By the end of the year, army chief Joseph Mobutu had seized power, Lumumba had been arrested (and would soon be assassinated) and Congo had split into four quasi-independent states. An aggressive intervention by UN and Belgian troops plus several mercenary armies put the country together again by 1965, though there were further small-scale rebellions in the following years.

Renaming himself Mobutu Sese Seko, and the country Zaïre, the new leader embarked on a campaign of 'Africanisation', with colonial city names changing and suits giving way to the *abacost* (a Congolese version of the Mao jacket); though Mobutu himself was no communist, allying the country firmly in the US camp.

He'd brought stability to Congo, but also ruled with an iron fist, quashed opposition, and turned corruption and the squandering of state resources into an art form later named kleptocracy. His extravagance became legendary: for example, it is claimed that he hired Concorde to take him on Parisian shopping trips. It's estimated he pocketed US$5 billion during his rule.

Civil War

Throughout the 1970s and '80s Mobutu survived several coup attempts and repelled armed insurrections in various parts of the country. By the early 1990s he'd driven an economic collapse so epic in scale that most of the country had degenerated to, in the words of Tim Butcher (from his book *Blood River*), 'a feral state of lawlessness and brutality'. Not only did schools and hospitals cease to function, but highways were reclaimed by the jungle.

Backing the Hutu perpetuators of the 1994 Rwandan genocide who escaped into Zaïre, Mobutu enraged local Tutsis, who, supported enthusiastically by Rwandan and Ugandan troops, started a march across the country in 1996 and easily took Kinshasa in 1997. Mobutu died four months later of cancer in Morocco.

Soon after renaming the country the Democratic Republic of Congo, the new leader, Laurent Kabila, a one-time protégé of Che Guevara, dashed any hopes of change by outlawing political opposition. Proving himself every bit as corrupt and repressive as Mobutu, he lost support at home and abroad, including the same governments who propelled him to power.

The DRC's second war (aka 'Africa's World War') started in 1998 when Rwandan and Ugandan troops again entered the country. Kabila was saved by troops from Angola, Zimbabwe, Namibia and other countries, but much of DRC was now under the control of Rwanda and Uganda, and even they clashed at times, leading to the destruction of the DRC town of Kisangani.

Laurent Kabila was shot by one of his bodyguards in January 2001, though the details of and motivations behind the assassination remain mysteries. He was succeeded by his 29-year-old son Joseph, largely raised in Tanzania, who, to the surprise of nearly everyone, proved a competent leader. Kabila the younger welcomed UN troops and presided over a peace agreement that in 2002 paved the way for a transitional government. He also oversaw a new constitution and heeded the advice of the World Bank and IMF, setting the economy back on course. In 2006 Kabila won DRC's first legitimate elections in over 40 years. Though marred by incidents of violence, outside observers pronounced them free and fair.

DRC Today

DRC has turned a corner, but the challenges facing it remain huge. The war ended in 2003, but in the volatile east, the fighting didn't stop. Despite the presence of 19,000 UN blue-helmets (the world's largest peacekeeping mission), ill-disciplined government soldiers and a plethora of militias continue to terrorise the population, particularly in North and South Kivu provinces. Due to conflict, and the hunger, disease and disruption of health services it has caused, most reports say that some three million people have died since 2004, nearly as many as perished during the official five-year war, and millions more remain displaced.

And things still aren't easy in the rest of the nation. Life expectancy is just 46 years and 90% of the population lives on less than US$2 per day.

CULTURE

Though DRC plays host to more than 250 ethnic groups (and over 700 different languages and dialects), four tribes dominate. The Kongo, Luba, Mongo and Mangbetu-Azande groupings collectively make up 45% of the population.

Half the population practises Roman Catholicism, while 20% are Protestant and 10% Muslim. The remaining 20% follow traditional beliefs or a religion that merges Christianity with indigenous ideas, such as Kimbanguism. Founded by faith-healer Simon Kimbangu in 1921 (that same year Belgian authorities, fearing his popularity, sentenced him to life in prison) it now has three million adherents.

Congolese wood carvings are world-famous: and if the vendors in DRC are to be believed, they're all 'antiques'. Less common beyond its borders is the fantastic raffia cloth of the Kuba Kingdom in what are now Kasai and Bandundu provinces. Also popular in craft markets and stores is the banded green mineral malachite, made into jewellery and ashtrays.

ENVIRONMENT

Encompassing 18 different ecoregions and blanketing the greater part of the Congo River basin, DRC is Africa's most biologically rich country. Savannas cover much of the south and there's 37km of coast on the Atlantic, but tropical rainforests, home to all manner of creatures found nowhere else in the world, including bonobo and okapi, dominate the ecological scene.

The eastern border runs through a cornucopia of geological wonders, including Lake Tanganyika, the second-deepest lake in the world, and several other Great Rift Valley waters; the Rwenzori Mountains, which exceed 5000m; and several active volcanoes.

KINSHASA

pop 8 million

Once touted as Kin la Belle (beautiful Kinshasa), locals have long since redubbed their chaotic capital 'Kin la Poubelle' (Kinshasa the trashcan). Sprawling seemingly forever from the banks of the Congo River, 'Kin' has the same maniacal drivers, dismaying poverty, mounds of trash, belching black tailpipes and persistent street hawkers that you've seen in many other African cities, but here it's all bigger, faster and louder than you've probably experienced before.

Romantics, however, describe the capital as musical, and not just the swinging sound of soukous (African rumba) but also the rhythm of daily life, such as the click-clack of the shoeshine boys and the spontaneous song-and-dance of its citizens. It's also a city with great food and nightlife.

Regardless of their opinions of the town, few travellers end up staying long due to the high prices and lack of attractions.

ORIENTATION

Getting your head around Kinshasa can be tough, but the city centre, laid out sort of on a grid running west from the train station and Beach Ngobila, is easy enough. Blvd du 30 Juin, a six-lane (eight if you're a taxi driver) behemoth runs through the heart of it and continues west through the diplomatic district (this, together with downtown, is Cummune Gombé) and beyond. To the south are earthier neighbourhoods like Matonge, a major transport hub where most budget travellers stay, and the less convenient but generally more relaxed Bandalungwa (usually just called Bandal). Both are flush with cheap food and beer and stay lively deep into the night. N'Djili International Airport is 20km southeast of the centre.

INFORMATION

Numerous BCIA, Ecobank, Procredit and Rawbank bank branches with ATMs are shown on the map, pp580–1.

CMK (☎ 08950300; Ave Wagenia; ☒ 24hr) The best-equipped hospital in Kinshasa.

Excel Voyage (☎ 0817152744; excelvoyagekin@yahoo.fr; Blvd 30 du Juin) Reliable for buying plane tickets.

Fastnet (Ave de la Presse; per hr CDF1400; ☒ 8.30am-6pm Mon-Sat) One of Kinshasa's best internet cafes.

Post Office (Blvd du 30 Juin; ☒ 7.30am-4pm Mon-Fri, 8am-noon Sat) Poste restante costs CDF1700 per letter.

Pharmacie Apothéek (☎ 098222221; Blvd du 30 Juin; ☒ 24hr)

DANGERS & ANNOYANCES

Kinshasa has a crime problem, so always remain vigilant. Never walk where there aren't many other people around, and don't walk anywhere in the city centre after dark. In Gombé and Ngaliema hold-ups and kidnappings (sometimes by people posing as police) are genuine concerns, though shegue (aggressive street kids who work in gangs) are

KINSHASA

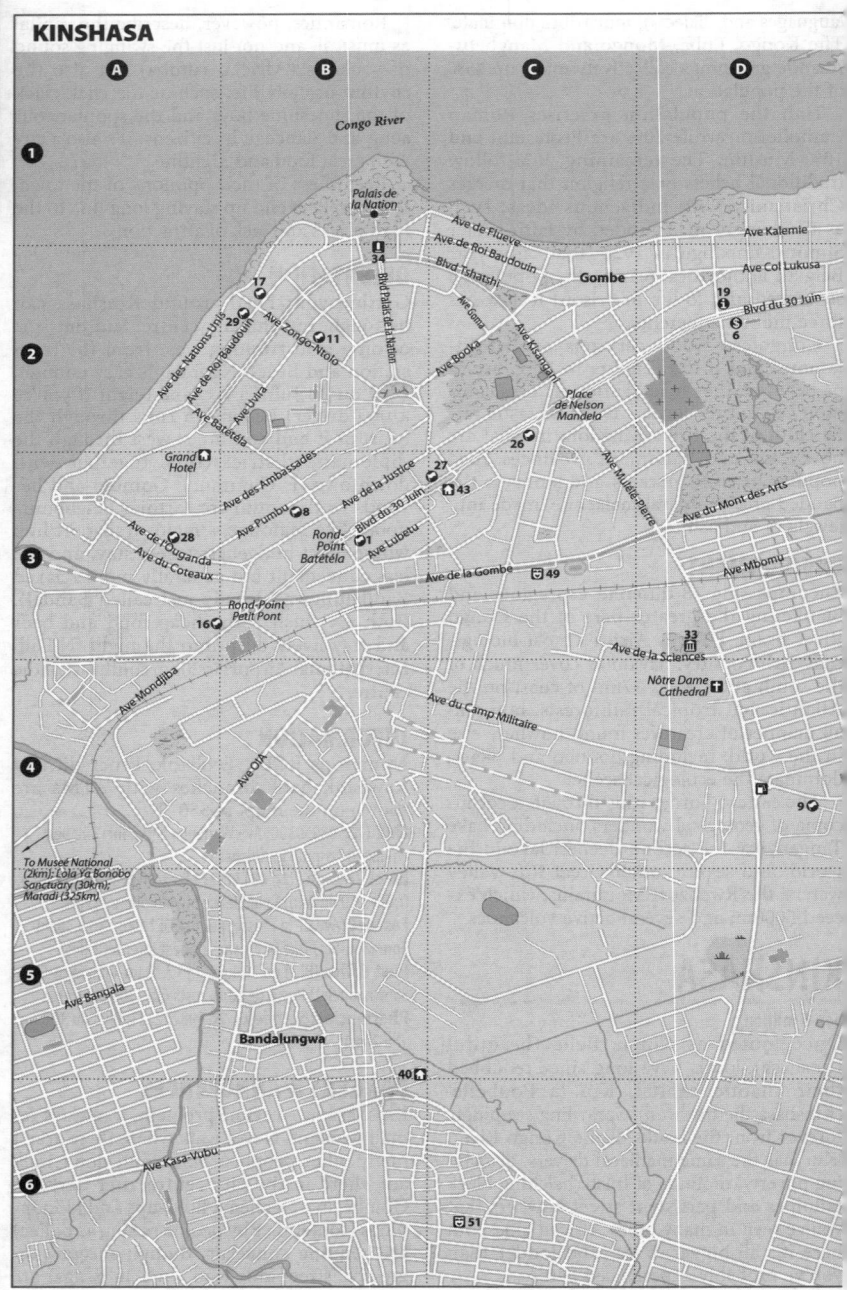

INFORMATION

Angolan Embassy	**1**	B3
BCIA Bank	**2**	F1
BCIA Bank	**3**	E2
Belgian Embassy	**4**	F1
BIAC Bank	**5**	H3
BIAC Bank	**6**	D2
BIAC Bank	**7**	F5
Canadian Embassy	**8**	B3
Central African Republic Embassy	**9**	D4
CMK	**10**	F1
Congolese Embassy	(see 1)	
Dutch Embassy	**11**	B2
Ecobank	**12**	E2
Excel Voyage	**13**	E1
Fastnet	**14**	F2
French Embassy	**15**	F1
French Embassy (future site)	**16**	A3
German Embassy	**17**	B2
Immigration (DGM)	**18**	E2
Office National du Tourisme (ONT)	**19**	D2
Pharmacie Apothéek	**20**	F1
Post Office	**21**	E2
Procredit	**22**	F1
Rawbank	**23**	E1
Rawbank	**24**	E2
Rawbank	**25**	E1

Sudanese Embassy	**26**	C2
Tanzanian Embassy	**27**	C3
Ugandan Embassy	**28**	A3
UK Embassy	**29**	B2
US Embassy	**30**	F1
Wildlife Conservation Society Office	**31**	G2
Zambian Embassy	**32**	F2

SIGHTS & ACTIVITIES

Académie des Beaux-Arts	**33**	D3
Laurent Kabila's Tomb	**34**	B2
Marché Central	**35**	F2
Marché du Art	**36**	F1
Museé National de Kinshasa	(see 33)	

SLEEPING

Hôtel Ave-Maria	**37**	F2
Hôtel Estoril	**38**	G2
Hôtel La Crèche	**39**	F6
Hôtel Lita	**40**	B5
Hôtel Pacha 786	**41**	F2
Procure Ste Anne	**42**	F1
Residence 165	**43**	C3

EATING

Chez Molifa	**44**	F1
Extrême	**45**	F1

New Relais	**46**	F1
Super Aubaine	**47**	F2

ENTERTAINMENT

Black & White	**48**	F1
Centre Culturel Français	**49**	C3
Centre Wallonie-Bruxelles	**50**	F1
Espace Mutombo Buitshi	**51**	C6
Hôtel La Crèche	(see 39)	
Ibizabar	(see 44)	
Zamba Playa	**52**	F5
Zoo	**53**	E2

TRANSPORT

Air France	(see 61)	
Beach Ngobila	**54**	G1
Beach Rafi	**55**	E1
Brussels Airlines	**56**	E2
Buses to Luanda	**57**	F6
CAA	**58**	F1
Ethiopian Airlines	**59**	E2
Gare Fluvial	**60**	E1
Hertz	**61**	F2
Hewa Bora	**62**	F2
Kenya Airways	**63**	F2
Port Public	**64**	E1
Royal Air Maroc	**65**	E2
South African Airways	**66**	E2
TAAG	**67**	E1

a more common threat. Keep doors locked and windows rolled up when riding in cars. In Matonge and, to a lesser extent, Bandal, pick-pocketing is rife, but, as one Congolese friend told us, these areas are safer than Gombé 'because someone might rob you, but they won't shoot you'.

SIGHTS

While the amazing ethnographic archive of the **Museé National** (☎ 0815110311; Ave de la Montagne, Mont Ngaliema; admission US$10; ☒ 7.30am-3pm Mon-Fri) awaits a proper home, staff will gladly show you around the warehouses.

The **Académie des Beaux-Arts** (Ave Mulélé-Pierre) has loads of sculpture around the grounds, and you can often see students and professors at work. The so-called **Museé National de Kinshasa** (admission US$5; ☒ 8am-2pm Mon-Wed & Thu-Fri, 8am-noon Sat), at the back of the school, holds just a few dozen masks.

It's worth losing yourself in the massive **Marché Central**, though for crafts and souvenirs the most convenient shopping is **Marché du Art** (Pl de la Gare; ☒ 7am-6pm) by the train station.

Also worth seeing is **Laurent Kabila's tomb**. Visiting **Les Rapides** (p567), large rapids on the Congo River, is easier done on the Brazzaville side of the river.

SLEEPING

Hôtel Lita (☎ 0899480625; r CDF4000-12,500; ℗ ☒) Though it's one of Kinshasa's cheapest hotels, rooms (some with shared bathrooms) are cleaner than many higher-priced places. It's down an unnamed dirt road just off Ave Kasa-Vubu in the fun and safe Quartier Bakayao, Bandalungwa Commune, but don't tramp all the way out here without reservations; it's usually full.

Hôtel La Crèche (☎ 0991597592; Ave Badjoko; r CDF10,000-US$20; ☐) Matonge's best-known hotel is rather rough, very noisy (especially on weekends) and even the three deluxe rooms have the same odd odours as the others.

Procure Ste Anne (☎ 0810755604; propas-kin@ micronet.cd; Ave Dumi; s/d with shared toilets US$40/50 incl breakfast; ℗ ☒ ☐ ☎) This quiet colonial-era compound offers the city-centre's best value. Rooms are historic and immaculate.

Hôtel Ave-Maria (☎ 015164710; hotel.avemaria@ gmail.com; Ave Col Ebeya; r US$65-95; ☒ ☒ ☎) Formerly the Fontana Inn, this simple city-centre spot exudes a hint of Miami Beach, but it's the prices that make it a popular midrange option.

Hôtel Pacha 786 (☎ 0991088786; www.hotel pacha786.com; Ave du Tchad; r US$80-100; ☒ ☎) Across the street from the landmark Hôtel Memling (where nothing-special rooms start at US$335!) the rooms, set around a triangular terrace, are large and have bold furnishings that distinguish them from the normally staid competition at this price.

Hôtel Estoril (☎ 0810206209; Ave Kabasele; r US$90-140 incl breakfast; P ✕ 🖳 🛜) This green-themed place on the edge of downtown sometimes shows its age, but it's one of the few hotels in Kinshasa with genuine character and style. You can lounge and dine (Congolese, French and Portuguese cuisine) on the streetside terrace or in the shady backyard.

Residence 165 (☎ 0818512345; Blvd du 30 Juin; r US$130-150, ste US$185 incl breakfast; P ✕ 🖳 🛜) Outside – but convenient to – the city centre, this small compound has comfortable, well-appointed rooms and a nice restaurant.

EATING
Outside Gombé, most neighbourhoods have plenty of streetside vendors working deep into the night.

our pick Chez Molifa (☎ 0990141491; Ave de la Nation; mains CDF1000-6000; ✆ 8.30am-10pm Mon-Sat; Ⓥ) Offers Congolese home-cooking like *pondu* (cassava leaves) and stewed goat, which are rarely served in sit-down restaurants.

Extrême (☎ 0999925126; Ave de l'Equateur; mains US$12-35; ✆ 12.30-10.30pm Tue-Sun; ✕) A trendy Italian restaurant that also makes a good drinking destination. The pizzas are wood-fired beauties.

New Relais (☎ 0998129243; Blvd du 30 Juin; mains US$13-28; ✆ noon-11pm; ✕ Ⓥ) We can only vouch for the Indian food (a very nice paneer tikka masala in particular) but if your dining party has mixed desires, there's also Chinese, French and Italian.

Super Aubaine (☎ 0815085586; Ave du Haut Congo; mains US$20-30, all-day buffet US$30; ✆ noon-10pm; ✕) Takes Congolese cooking to the gourmet level with choices like grilled pigeon and crocodile in tomato sauce.

Downtown Kinshasa is flush with supermarkets selling expensive imported goods.

ENTERTAINMENT
Werrason, one of Congo's biggest stars, holds court at **Zamba Playa** (Ave de l'Enseignement; admission US$2.50-$10) several nights a week. As in many music clubs, the band is as likely to play in the afternoon as in the evening. Live bands rock the rooftop of **Hôtel La Crèche** (Ave Badjoko) weekend nights. Trust us, you don't want to visit Kinshasa's **zoo** (Ave du Commerce) for the animals,

but Staff Benda Belili, a group of homeless paraplegic musicians now making waves on the world music scene, often perform here.

During our visit, **Black & White** (Ave Bousin), which spins music from all corners of the globe Wednesday to Saturday, had Kinshasa's favourite dance floor. Upstairs is a bar with a pool table. **Ibizabar** (Ave de la Nation) is a relaxing lounge with live jazz on weekends.

The **Centre Culturel Français** (☎ 0810581512; www.ccf-kinshasa.org; Ave de la Gombé) is Kinshasa's premier arts venue. It has a good restaurant-bar, too. There are also sometimes music and other performances at **Centre Wallonie-Bruxelles** (☎ 0998010800; Ave de la Paix). For a deeply local experience, check out a Friday night (starting 7pm) theatre, music or dance performance at **Espace Mutombo Buitshi** (☎ 089687268; Ave Lubumbashi; foreigners US$5) way out in Bandal.

GETTING THERE & AWAY
Buses to Matadi (CDF10,000, seven to eight hours) leave every morning between 7am and 8am from Place Commercial de Limete, south of N'Dolo Airport. If you want to go to Matadi later in the day, or just to nearer points like Kisantu, you need to take a taxi from Rond-Point Nganba, much further south.

If you're heading overland you'll begin the journey at Marché de la Liberté, well east of town, where jeeps to Kikwit (US$50, 13 to 15 hours) leave around 5pm; reservations are recommended. On Saturdays, rickety buses to Luanda (Angola; US$150, two to three days) leave from 'Force', south of Place Victoire.

Flights shorter than Kisangani use the convenient N'Dolo Airport (all airlines have ticket offices here), while for anything longer, you must head out to N'Djili International Airport.

GETTING AROUND
Few taxis wear the official blue-and-yellow paint job, but it's easy to tell which vehicles are taking passengers. Drivers charge from CDF300 to CDF500 depending on the length of the trip and they rarely take more than four passengers, so your ride will be comfortable. To charter a taxi, ask for 'express' and negotiate the price. Minibuses cost CDF250 and are always crowded. A few big buses (CDF400 for a guaranteed seat) run along Blvd du 30 Juin.

Several international car-hire firms, including **Hertz** (☎ 0817005733; www.hertz.com; Hôtel Memling, Ave du Tchad), have cars from US$85 a day, but it's cheaper and easier to just charter a taxi for about US$50 a day.

A taxi from the city centre to N'Djili airport will take over an hour and cost US$20 for 'express'. Heading the other direction, if you walk out to the highway, you might get a taxi into town for US$10. Shared taxis charge CDF1000 to/from centre-ville or Matonge.

AROUND KINSHASA

Ninety minutes west of Kinshasa, just beyond the city's sprawl, **Lola Ya Bonobo Sanctuary** (Paradise for Bonobos; ☎ 0813330234; www.friendsofbonobos.org; foreigners US$5; ◷ 9.30am-4pm Tue-Sun) provides a home for orphaned members of the bonobo species, one of the world's most fascinating primates. Trails lead around the large, forested enclosures, but the playful bonobos often hang out right at the front, especially in the morning. The sanctuary is 8km off the Matadi road: follow the signs for Chutes de Lakaya, which has a little beach and weekend-only restaurant. If you're patient, you can hitch the last 8km off the highway.

Nearby, forest-rimmed **Lac de ma Vallee** (weekdays/weekends US$6/11) is principally a weekend retreat, but the lakeside restaurants serve food and hire paddleboats daily.

On Sundays and holidays Kinshasa's jetsetters descend on **Kinkole**, well east of Kinshasa, to drink beer, eat the country's best *liboké de poisson* (fish cooked in banana leaves) and listen to live music. The action starts around midday, but peaks after dark. The market at **Libongo ya ba Pêcheurs** (Fisherman's Beach), served by villagers living upriver, is also worth a look. Talk to boatmen here if you'd like a ride on the river. Taxis (CDF500, one hour) run from Marché de la Liberté; the last ones return around 10.30pm on Sunday.

BAS-CONGO

DRC's far-western finger feels quite different from the rest of the country, and while there's little excitement here, it's the easiest place to travel.

CHUTES DU ZONGO

A popular trip for those who can afford 4WD hire, gorgeous **Zongo Falls** is about 100km out of Kinshasa, the last half signed off the highway at Sona-Bata. There's a simple **hotel** (☎ 0998580636; campsites/r US$30/60 ⊠). Reservations must be made three days in advance.

KISANTU

Kisantu, 100km out of Kinshasa, has many colonial-era relics, including the incongruously large **Cathèdrale Notre Dame de Sept Douleurs** and the 222-sq-km **Jardin Botanique de Kisantu** (admission CDF500; ◷ 8am-5pm), with trees from around the world. A big restoration is underway here, and there's now a small natural history museum, a cactus garden and a pleasant restaurant.

MATADI

pop 246,000

Located at the furthest navigable point up the Congo River from the ocean, Bas-Congo's prosperous capital, founded in 1879 by Henry Morton Stanley, hosts DRC's principal port. Matadi's main landmark is the **OEBK Bridge** (aka Pont Maréchal) over the Congo River, though it's hardly another Golden Gate. There are some nice views (and cold beers) atop **Point Belvédère**, the tallest point inside the city. If you want to explore further, you could continue uphill to **Peak Cambier**, which has far better vistas, or go upriver towards **Yelala Falls** and the **Rock of Diego Caõ**, where the Portuguese explorer marked the extent of his travels in 1485; it's a beautiful area.

The simple but friendly **Hôtel l'Embouchure** (☎ 0997865302; Ave Kinshasa; r CDF10,000) is near downtown, but the streets here aren't completely dead at night. **New Air Brousse Hôtel** (☎ 0855118470; Ave Luthelo; r US$25-30; ℗ ⊠) has by far the best rooms at this price, plus river views.

It's no longer the best address in Matadi, but if you can overlook the need for some TLC and just soak up the historic character, you'll love **Hôtel Metropole** (☎ 0855137800; Ave Kinkanda; r US$60-100 incl breakfast; ⊠), a solid stone landmark in the heart of downtown. It has a 5th-floor restaurant.

Taxis to Boma (CDF7000, two hours) are frequent, but it's best to reserve a seat for buses to Kinshasa (CDF10,000, seven to eight hours) a day in advance.

BOMA

pop 172,000

Another large port town, Boma was the Congolese capital before power shifted to

Kinshasa. Stanley finished his cross-continent trek here in 1877, and local tourism authorities want you to believe that he slept in an enormous, hollow baobab tree. The story is rubbish (he was feasted for several days by the European traders living there) but the **Baobab de Stanley** (Ave du Commerce; foreigners CDF3000; ☺ 8am-5pm Mon-Sat) is still pretty cool. Also not to be missed is **Congo's first cathedral**, an all-metal, prefab affair shipped in from Belgium in 1890.

Centrally located **Hôtel Excelsior** (☎ 0990296360; Ave Makhuku; r CDF15,000-40,000; **P** 🏊) offers four classes of rooms. The road to Muanda (CDF10,000, four hours) is in poor shape, but it's due for paving soon. There are also occasionally boats between Boma and Muanda.

MUANDA
pop 75,000

Beyond Boma, National Hwy 1 becomes beautiful, and after 110km it deposits you in this growing but still sleepy oil town. It was once something of a resort destination and **Tonde Beach** (admission CDF1000), on the north edge of the city, is quite beautiful. **Nsiamfumu Beach**, 15km north of town just past the namesake village (full of colonial-era homes), is also attractive and popular on weekends. Get local advice before actually stepping in the water, as currents can be deadly strong.

If you're not going to sit on the sands, about the only thing to do is take a gander at the mouth of the Congo River, 8km south of Muanda in the hamlet of **Banana**, once a slaving centre To see it, you'll either need to get official permission from the port authority or befriend the soldiers guarding the entrance to the naval base – the latter is the easiest option.

Le Relais (☎ 0997857532; Ave du Commerce; r US$15-20; **P**) is quiet and good for the price.

EASTERN DRC

GOMA
pop 450,000

This dusty border town, home to a massive UN presence, hosts more travellers than any other place in DRC, though still very few. Mostly they pop over briefly to track mountain gorillas and climb Nyiragongo Volcano in **Parc National des Virunga** (ICCN office; ☎ 0995693627; http://gorillacd.org; Ave Pelican, ☺ 8am-4pm Mon-Fri), one of Africa's most diverse parks, but also one of its most threatened. Most visitors let a guide

from Goma, Kisoro (Uganda) or Gisenyi (Rwanda) arrange everything, but you can do it yourself at the park office.

The nearest habituated gorilla families are at Bukima, about 40km north of Goma. Permits are US$400, and there's rarely a long wait to get one. Transport to the site costs around US$120 in a 4WD or US$35 on a motorcycle. The volcano's appeal is the incredible lava lake nested in the crater. It can be seen on a day trip, but overnight trips are best, and the park intends to start hiring tents and sleeping bags (it gets very cold). Permits cost US$200, and guides are mandatory.

The city itself has no proper attractions, but you can witness the destruction caused by Nyiragongo's 2002 eruption at the **ruined cathedral** and **Hôtel Volcano**, where the basement used to be the ground floor before three meters of lava engulfed the building. Northeast of the airport is a moonscape with several **lava vents** that sent the stream of lava straight through the city centre. **Lac Vert**, a US$4, 90-minute roundtrip *taxi-moto* ride west of town, is a much older crater now filled with a greenish-tinged lake. Also, check out what's happening at **Yole! Africa** (☎ 0997123055; www.yoleafrica.org; Ave Butembo), an inspiring arts centre.

If price is your primary concern, head to **Lotus Hotel** (☎ 0896963386; Ave Touriste; r without bathroom US$10, with bathroom US$15-25), a reasonably clean place attached to a bar. A little rough, but still a big step up is the MC Escher-esque **Victoria Hotel** (☎ 0993693064; Ave Touriste; r without US$15, with toilet US$20-50; **P**), where rooms at the cheaper end of the range are good value and there's a rooftop terrace. **Stella Matutina Lodge** (☎ 0811510760; lodgestellamatutina@yahoo.fr; r US$55-85, ste US$100-130 incl breakfast; **P** 🛜) is better than anything in the town centre, plus it has great gardens and sweeping lake views. **Salt and Pepper** (☎ 0899275588; Ave du Rond-Point; mains US$4-7; ☺ 8am-10pm; **V**), a friendly hole-in-the-wall opposite Monuc Hospital, has good food (mostly Indian) and great prices. Nearby, **Soleil Place** (☎ 0991351060; Ave du Rond-Point; mains US$3-20; ☺ noon-late) serves a US$5 Congolese buffet plus Chinese and continental cuisine under a big thatched roof. It's a popular bar at night.

Road travel out of Goma to the rest of DRC is generally unsafe, but taking the boat to Bukavu (p586) is rarely a problem.

See p590 for border-crossing information. Also, a couple of airlines serve Goma from Uganda and Kenya.

CROSSING CONGO

It would still be foolish to retrace Stanley's legendary cross-Congo trail (as Tim Butcher did for his excellent book *Blood River*), but there are other reasonably safe routes across the country.

The classic path crosses east to west and requires a 1730km boat ride down the Congo River to Kinshasa through still-untamed jungle, which is precisely why it was once so popular. These days the trip must begin at Kasindi on the Ugandan border, near Beni (below), since this road, passing through the heart of pygmy country, is the only safe route (there are still some bandits, so it's best not to drive your own vehicle). This route will take you to Kisangani (opposite), where you catch the boat. You'll probably spend a lot of time in this legendary town; not because it's so appealing but because boats are still quite infrequent. There's usually one or two departures a month and the trip (costing around US$25, though prices aren't fixed) typically takes two weeks. Bear in mind that, unlike the old days, there are no longer steamers with passenger cabins, although you can try to rent one from a crew member. You'll be living out on the deck of the barges (go early to find a space under a roof) with hundreds of other people, plus all their cargo and livestock. Villagers sell food from *pirogues* (traditional canoes) along the way, but this trip still requires careful preparation for cooking, water and shelter.

Travelling in reverse, the trip will last three weeks if you're lucky. Normally it takes four, and you should be prepared for five or six. The price is about double. The best places to seek boats in Kinshasa are Gare Fluvial and Beach Rafi; boats docked at Port Public rarely take passengers, but it can't hurt to ask there, too.

A typically quicker, but more hassle-filled, journey substitutes a train for a barge. From Kinshasa there are jeeps to Kikwit, where you take another jeep to Kananga (US$100, 24 hours), the journey's midpoint and the place to catch the bimonthly train to Lubumbashi in DRC's far southwest. There's no fixed departure day, though you can enquire when – and, more importantly, if – trains are running by calling ☎ 0092484937. When the train does go, it's a fairly comfortable (if you get a sleeper; US$107) three- or four-day trip to Lubumbashi, DRC's second-largest city and, thanks to mining, one of its most prosperous. From here it's just a short hop to Kasumbalesa and the Zambian border.

BUKAVU
pop 472,000

DRC's most attractive city, which crawls along a contorted shoreline at the southern tip of Lake Kivu, is a good gateway to the country and the base for visiting **Parc National de Kahuzi-Biéga** (ICCN office; ☎ 0814876354; Ave Lumumba; ☽ 7.30am-4pm Mon-Fri), Virunga's little-known neighbour, where you can track habituated eastern lowland gorillas. Due to the scarcity of visitors, permits (US$400 per person) are often available for same-day hiking. The starting point is at Tshivanga, 30km northwest of town. *Taxi-motos* there and back cost about US$20 to US$30, while return taxis cost US$60 to US$70. The park also has a chimpanzee orphanage and some worthy hikes up the mountains.

Hôtel Lolango (☎ 0813177348; Ave Lumumba; r without bathroom US$15), right by the cathedral, has some of the best lake views in town, but the rooms are *very* rough. The plant-filled **Hôtel de Goma** (☎ 0997004429; Ave Kalene, r US$30) is a better budget choice. The sort-of-fancy **Hôtel la Roche** (☎ 0810696262; r US$45-100 incl breakfast; P ⊡) sits right on the lake.

Several boats depart daily to Goma. Choices range from US$8 on the shadeless, grossly overcrowded deck of a ferry (six to seven hours) to US$50 for a *canot rapide* (speedboat; two to three hours). The road to Kisangani is so devastated that only motorcycles can manage it.

BENI
pop 82,000

If you're crossing DRC by land, ho-hum Beni, sitting in the shadow of the Rwenzori Mountains, is likely to be your gateway or goodbye. If you need to stick around, **Hôtel Panasonic** (☎ 0994043370; Blvd Rwenzori; r with shared/private toilets US$7/10 P), near Parking TCB (departure point for taxis to Uganda), is a good, though not spotless, cheapie, while manicured gardens and tiled roofs make **Hôtel Beni** (☎ 0997705249; Blvd Nyamuvisi; r US$30-60; P) one of DRC's most attractive hotels.

Several companies have transport to Kisangani (US$45 to US$60, jeeps 12 to 15 hours, buses 16 to 20 hours) from offices near Rond-Point Beni; cheaper lorries load at Parking Publique.

OKAPI WILDLIFE RESERVE

Created to protect prime habitat of its bizarre namesake mammal (which can be seen up close at the breeding centre for US$5), this is one of the biggest (1,372,625 hectares) and best protected nature reserves in DRC. Its 17 resident primate species is the highest total for any African forest and the elephant population remains healthy. Hikes (US$18 per group per day), ranging from a few hours to days, lead to some lovely spots, and overnight cultural trips (US$20 per person) are possible.

The gorgeous riverside setting of the **lodging** (rosmarieruf@hotmail.com; campsites per person US$5, s/d US$20/30; ⊠), which has a kitchen, at Epulu might suck you into a few days R&R. There's also the clean **Hôtel Okapi** (r without bathroom US$5) and several simple shops and restaurants in the village.

Any vehicle running between Kisangani (jeeps/buses US$25/20, jeeps six to eight hours, buses eight to 10 hours) and Bunia, Butembo or Beni (jeeps/buses US$30/25, jeeps six to eight hours, buses eight to 10 hours) can drop you here, though you may have to wait a while to catch a ride out.

KISANGANI

pop 683,000

Kisangani was known in colonial times as Stanleyville and was immortalised as the unnamed city in VS Naipaul's classic novel *A Bend in the River*. Once a pleasant place and a major hub for travellers, Kisangani suffered as much as any town during the war years. It's lively with commerce once again, but the scars remain deep. The city was founded by its original namesake in 1883 because it's the last point ships can travel upriver from Kinshasa before being blocked by **Boyoma Falls**, a 100km stretch with seven major waterfalls. The final drop, just east of town, is a gorgeous spot, with a rocky stage and a jungle-clad backdrop, though the **Wagenia Fishermen** (best seen on the south bank) are pushing it in their demands for US$20 to look at their famous scaffolds and conical fish traps. **Tshopo Falls**, 3km north of town by the dam and the old Skol Brewery, is far smaller, but still nice. There are sandy beaches and a bar-restaurant (popular at night) nearby.

The cheapest place to sleep is the **Sun City** (Blvd du 30 Juin; r without bathroom US$10) nightclub, where the cell-like rooms (rarely used for an entire night) have fans, but there's no proper shower. Rooms are small, but copious plants and other quaint touches make **Les Chalets** (no sign; ☎ 085714295; bego_bergesio@hotmail.com; Ave de l'Industrie; r US$58 incl breakfast; P ❄ 💻 🍽) Kisangani's best address. **Guest House Saint Charles** (☎ 0998539701; Ave de l'Eglise; r US$30-50; ❄ P 💻) offers solid middle ground. **Riviera Restaurant** (☎ 0854002075; Ave Bondekwe; mains US$5-20; 🕑 6am-late; ❄ 📶), fronted by a terrace, trees and colonial homes, is the most pleasant place to dine.

Almost everyone arrives from Kinshasa by air, but riverboats (see the boxed text, opposite) are sailing once again. Land transport departs from northeast of the central market. There are several jeeps and buses to Beni (US$45 to US$60, jeeps 12 to 15 hours, buses 16 to 20 hours) daily; most travelling overnight to avoid hassles with the police.

DRC DIRECTORY

ACCOMMODATION

Real budget accommodation is hard to come by, and where it does exist it's often grotty. At the US$20 to US$30 level you might get a fan or TV, but running water is still unlikely. Move into the US$50 to US$80 range and rooms will be much more comfortable, but no matter what you pay, your hotel will usually be much simpler than similarly priced properties back home.

BUSINESS HOURS

Banks and offices are usually open 8.30am to 3pm Monday to Friday and 8.30am to noon

PRACTICALITIES

- DRC uses the metric system.
- Electricity is 220V/50Hz. The European two-pin plug is the most common.
- UN-funded Radio Okapi (103.5FM) is the best source of local news and culture. You can sometimes catch English-language programming on BBC World Service (92.6FM).

on Saturday. It's common to close for an hour around lunchtime.

DANGERS & ANNOYANCES

There are still rebel armies and bandits (plus, government soldiers are often just as dangerous) terrorising people around (but not in) the cities of Goma, Bukavu and Bunia and across Northern Katanga province. They, and military offensives against them, cause frequent closures of the Virunga and Kahuzi-Biéga National Parks. Also in recent years the Lord's Resistance Army has based itself inside Garamba National Park.

Though the situation is improving, police and other officials, particularly those working for immigration (you're supposed to register with them every time you arrive or depart from a town), frequently request money, though they rarely demand it. Learning to say 'I'm hungry' in English seems to be part of their job training. In all cases, calm and confident is your best play. Do all you can to avoid handing over your passport (present copies instead) since it might cost you to get it back.

DRC is one country where it's best to leave your camera behind. Taking photos in public places isn't always illegal (as long as there's nothing official or strategic like a government building, soldier or bridge in the frame) but you're just asking for heaps of hassles if anyone sees you.

Finally, if everyone around you comes to a halt, follow suit. It's required by law during the raising and lowering of the national flag, which occurs daily around 7.30am and 6pm.

EMBASSIES & CONSULATES

A great many countries have diplomatic representation in Kinshasa.

Angola (Blvd du 30 Juin)
Belgium (☎ 0898924233; www.diplobel.org/congo; Pl du 27 Octobre)
Canada (☎ 08950310; www.congo.gc.ca; Ave Pumbu)
Central African Republic (☎ 0813569255; Rue de TV) Just east of Radio and TV tower.
Congo (☎ 0999909544; Blvd du 30 Juin)
France (☎ 0815559999; www.ambafrance-cd.org; Ave du Tchad) Will soon be moving to Ave Mondjiba, west of Ave de la Gombe.
Germany (☎ 08948201; www.kinshasa.diplo.de; Ave de Roi Baudouin)
Netherlands (☎ 0998001140; Ave Zongo-Ntolo)
Sudan (☎ 0999937396; Blvd du 30 Juin)
Tanzania (☎ 0815565850; Blvd du 30 Juin)

Uganda (☎ 0810519260; Ave de l'Ouganda)
UK (☎ 0817150761; http://ukindrc.fco.gov.uk; Ave de Roi Baudouin)
USA (☎ 0812255872; http://kinshasa.usembassy.gov; Ave Dumi)
Zambia (☎ 0815565995; Ave de l'Ecole)

HOLIDAYS

Public holidays are as follows:
New Year's Day 1 January
Martyrs of Independence Day 4 January
Heroes' Day 16-17 January
Easter March/April
Labour Day 1 May
Liberation Day 17 May
Independence Day 30 June
Parents' Day 1 August
Christmas Day 25 December

INTERNET ACCESS

The internet isn't everywhere in DRC yet but it has reached most middle-sized towns. Connection speeds are a crapshoot: sometimes you'll fly, sometimes you'll crawl.

MONEY

The local currency, the Congolese franc (CDF), is worthless beyond the borders. CDF500 is currently the biggest bill available, which results in a massive bundle of banknotes when you change money; but DRC is unofficially undergoing dollarisation and US dollars are widely accepted for purchases of US$10 and up. In Goma, US dollars can be used for everything. It used to be that dollar bills needed to be pristine. That's no longer the case, but many merchants still won't accept dirty bills and nobody will take one with even a tiny tear. Learn to spot counterfeits, as there are many.

Moneychangers (the same people selling phonecards) work on nearly every block of every city. They all change US dollars, plus sometimes euros and local currency from nearby neighbours. Rates are invariably better than the banks.

Internationally linked ATMs are now common in Kinshasa (Look for the prominent Visa and MasterCard signs; though note that the signs go up long before the service is actually available) and are also available (or a machine at the counter that works like an ATM) in several other major towns, including Goma, Matadi and Boma. Kisangani was still off the grid, but banks have big expansion plans in DRC and so many more cities should get service in the lifetime of this book.

Credit cards (usually Visa *or* MasterCard) are accepted in many hotels, restaurants and upper-end shops, but fraud is a problem so cash is still best. In Kinshasa, **Rawbank** (Blvd 30 du Juin) cashes American Express travellers cheques in US dollars and euros with a 5% (minimum charge US$100) commission.

POST & TELEPHONE

Landlines are virtually extinct in DRC. In any town that has mobile-phone service, there are plenty of street hawkers who let people use their mobile phones: fees are about CDF150 per minute within Congo and CDF250 per minute international. If calling from outside DRC, drop the zero at the front of the number. SIM cards cost just US$1.

The postal system remains unreliable.

TOURIST INFORMATION

There are **Office National du Tourisme** (ONT; ont_rd congo@yahoo.fr) offices in most towns, though you'll rarely find anybody who knows anything about tourism working in them.

VISAS

All visitors need a visa, and they're not available on arrival. In the east, crossing to Beni, Goma, Bukavu or Lubumbashi, it used to be that you could just roll up to the border and get an eight-day visa, valid only for the province where it was issued, for US$35. These days, officially, you must have somebody in the country apply for you at the immigration office three days before you arrive, but realistically it depends who you meet at the border. Some travellers still get visas at the border with no hassles, most others get it by paying a small (around US$10) bribe, while a few are simply denied entry. Presenting a letter of invitation or a hotel reservation can help matters.

You can get new visas (one-month single-entry cost US$125 to US$155, depending on where you apply) at any immigration (DGM) office.

Visas for Onward Travel

Rwanda and Burundi do not have embassies in Kinshasa, but visas are available at the border.

Angola Tourist visas are only issued to residents of DRC. Travellers can get five-day transit visas, which are best obtained at the consulates in Matadi or Muanda. Bring two photos, a photocopy of your passport, including the DRC visa, and US$30/80 in Matadi/Muanda. You'll then need to wait about five days.

Central African Republic A one-month, multiple-entry visa costs US$150 and requires two photos and a photocopy of your passport and DRC visa. You can wait three days or pay US$20 for same-day service.

Congo Bring a photo and US$80/120 for a 15-day/three-month visa. They're typically ready in two days, but you can pay an extra US$90/120 for same-day service.

Sudan Does not issue tourist visas.

Tanzania A US$50, 30-day single-entry visa requires two photos and two days' waiting.

Uganda Same as Tanzania.

Zambia If you bring a letter of invitation or hotel reservation, a copy of a return plane ticket (from any city in Africa), proof of sufficient funds for travelling and two photos, you can get a three-month single-/multiple-entry visa for US$50/80 in two days.

WOMEN TRAVELLERS

Female travellers need to exercise extra caution, especially in the northeast where rape is used extensively as a weapon of war. In Kinshasa, never drive alone after dark.

TRANSPORT IN DRC

GETTING THERE & AWAY
Air

Few airlines fly to Kinshasa due to the massive mismanagement and corruption at the airport, so despite the hassles, some people use Brazzaville (Congo) as their gateway to DRC. The only two options direct from Europe are nonstop from Paris with **Air France** (☎ 0998001014; www.airfrance.com; Hôtel Memling, Ave du Tchad) and from Brussels via Cameroon with **Brussels Airlines** (☎ 0996017000; http://congo. brusselsairlines.com;.Blvd du 30 Juin). **Ethiopian Airlines** (☎ 0817006585; www.ethiopianairlines.com; Blvd du 30 Juin), **Kenya Airways** (☎ 0999911239; www. kenya-airways.com; Blvd du 30 Juin), **Royal Air Maroc** (☎ 0817252526; www.royalairmaroc.com; Blvd du 30 Juin), **South African Airways** (☎ 0999925121; www. flysaa.com; Blvd du 30 Juin) and **TAAG** (☎ 081426385; www.taag.com.br; Blvd du 30 Juin) all link their respective capital cities to Kinshasa. South African Airways and Kenya Airways fly to Lubumbashi and the latter also serves Kisangani. **Jetlink** (☎ 0997696358; www.jetlink. co.ke) connects Goma and Nairobi, while **TMK Air Commuter** (☎ 0994337156; www.tmkcongo.com)

DEMOCRATIC REPUBLIC OF CONGO

GOING TO LE BEACH

Travel between Kinshasa (the port is called Beach Ngobila, or just 'Beach') and Brazzaville ('Le Beach') can be a real headache. It helps to travel in the afternoon and on weekends when the crowds are thinner. The easiest way across is a *canot rapide* (speedboat), which takes five minutes and costs US$25/CFA11,000. The overcrowded passenger ferries charge CDF10,000/CFA6500 and take 45 minutes. Boats sail 8.30am to 4pm Monday to Saturday, and there's also speedboat service until noon on Sunday. Boats usually don't run on holidays.

On the Brazzaville side, various departure taxes (payable behind the *canot rapide* ticket office) total CFA4400; plus it costs CFA150 just to enter the grounds. There's no need to pay extra money on the DRC side, though you'll be asked to. Because of the lack of signs and the abundance of hustlers many people pay a fixer to get them through the process, but it's not really necessary; and some of these guys have their own cons going on, so be careful.

If you're driving, there are two car ferries daily, and you'll have to shell out about US$150 to various officials before boarding.

---

flies between Goma and Entebbe (Uganda) stopping in Butembo, Beni and Bunia on the way.

Land & River

Whether you're heading to Goma or Bukavu, crossing from Rwanda couldn't be any easier. Transport from Kigali to the respective border towns of Gisenyi and Cyangugu is frequent, and from there you just walk into DRC and hire a *taxi-moto* to take you to your destination in town.

Various bus companies running from Bukavu to Bujumbura, Burundi, via the border at Gatumba, charge US$9 to US$10 and take about four hours in the dry season. In the rainy season, it could be quicker to travel through Rwanda where the roads are better.

The principal route to Uganda is from Beni to Kasindi (US$10, two hours), where you walk over the border and get another taxi to Kasese (USh 4000, 1½ hours). Tour guides in Kisoro sometimes take clients across at Bunagana to see Parc National des Virunga's gorillas at Djomba, but it's not safe to travel further.

If you're driving to Angola, the easiest route is via Luvo where the road is better than that from Matadi (technically this border is at Ango-Ango, 3km from Matadi), but there's little traffic through either of these borders

---

DEPARTURE TAX

The 'Go-Pass' departure tax is US$10/50 for domestic/international flights.

---

except for Luvo on Saturdays, so the best bet for those without wheels is Soyo, at the mouth of the Congo River, from where buses head to Luanda, though these are in short supply. Boats (US$20) head there daily from Boma; however, once the road to Muanda is paved the service might shift there. For Cabinda take a taxi from Muanda to the border (CDF1000, 45 minutes) and then another to Cabinda city (400Kz, 30 minutes). Transport is frequent.

Few travellers cross to/from Central African Republic (see p549), Tanzania (there are twice-weekly Kigoma–Kalemie ferries, US$20, seven hours) or Zambia (the crossing is at Kasumbalesa, south of Lubumbashi) because of the difficulties of moving on to other places in DRC. The border with Sudan remains extremely dangerous.

GETTING AROUND
Air

The combination of long distances and terrible roads means flying is often the best (and sometimes the only practical) way to reach many towns, and airlines, usually flying small prop planes, reach every sizable town from Muanda to Beni. DRC is not known for effective safety regulations. Hewa Bora, CAA, Kin-Avia, Filair and TMK Air Commuter are considered the most reliable airlines. In most cases you can buy tickets a day or two before departure, and often even the same day. For most cities you can only buy tickets at N'Dolo Airport since travel agencies don't do business with the smaller airlines. Typical one-way fares from Kinshasa are US$260 to Kisangani and US$290 to Goma.

Boat

River traffic on the Congo has restarted. See Crossing Congo, p586, for details.

Road

Although there's still much work to be done, DRC is on a road-repair binge, which is making getting around the country easier for those who don't want to fly. Most roads remain dirt; however, so rainy season travel is slow and difficult. Buses are available where the roads are good enough, but the fastest way to travel is in 4WDs, which are called jeeps.

Train

During our visit, trains from Kinshasa to Matadi (US$10, six to seven hours) weren't running since the workers stopped working after the government stopped paying them. The lines from Kamina to Kalemie and Kindu were also down. For details on the Lubumbashi–Kananga line, see Crossing Congo, p586.

EQUATORIAL GUINEA

Equatorial Guinea

Failed coups, danger money, bushmeat and buckets of oil – you could say Equatorial Guinea has something of a reputation. But mercenaries and crime writers aren't the only ones attracted to the country's beautiful black-and-white shores. This is the land of primates with painted faces, soft clouds of butterflies and insects so colourful they belong in the realm of fiction.

If the excited beats of Equatorial-Guinean hip hop don't get you dancing, the architecture will – Gothic cathedrals, ancient wooden churches and butter-coloured homes. Though the country is dripping in oil wealth, many people's taps run dry. Poverty deeply permeates ordinary life, making a trip to Malabo – alive with the flames of oil rigs and the buzz of rapid construction – at once hedonistic and heartbreaking. You'll spot glass-fronted buildings, fountains high as waterfalls and mini skyscrapers that rub clouds as swollen as ripe mangoes.

On the mainland, white beaches, forest paths and junglescapes await, while Bioko Island is home to mellow fishing villages and ethnicities found nowhere else in the world. We wouldn't be surprised to find – way above the mahogany trees and the rain-soaked hills – a cloak of mystery spread over this country like cling film, keeping its heat, humidity and secrets locked inside.

FAST FACTS

- **Area** 28,050 sq km
- **ATMs** None at the time of research
- **Borders** Cameroon and Gabon
- **Budget** US$90 per day in Malabo, US$30 to US$60 per day elsewhere
- **Capital** Malabo
- **Languages** Spanish, French, Fang, Creole English (Pidginglis)
- **Money** Central African CFA; US$1 = CFA463, €1 = CFA656
- **Population** 659,200
- **Seasons** Bioko Island is dry December to February and rainy the rest of the year; Rio Muni is dry from June to August, with high humidity and sporadic-to-frequent rainfall the rest of the year
- **Telephone** Country code ☎ 240; international access code ☎ 00
- **Time** GMT/UTC +1; no daylight saving
- **Visa** Required by all except Americans; must be acquired before arrival

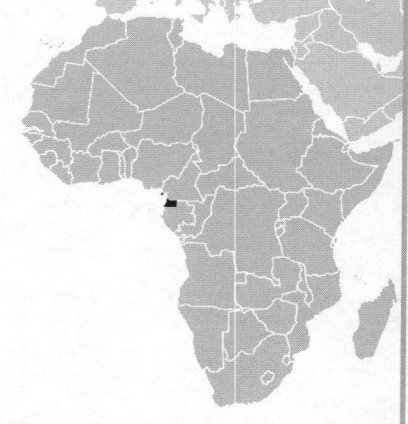

HOW MUCH?

- **Tailor-made dress** US$14
- **Short taxi ride in Malabo** US$1.10
- **Guided jungle hike** US$26
- **Fried plantain snack** US$2.15
- **President Obiang's California mansion** US$32 million

LONELY PLANET INDEX

- **1L petrol** US$0.80
- **1L bottled water** US$1.10
- **Cold beer** US$1.75
- **Souvenir mini xylophone** US$8.65
- **Plate of rice and fish** US$6.50

HIGHLIGHTS

- **Malabo** (p595) Explore the architecture and nightlife of this bizarre oil town.
- **Bioko Island** (p599) Go wide-eyed over the strange combination of dense rainforest, rare wildlife and oil platforms.
- **Monte Alen National Park** (p601) Whisper during forest walks in search of gorillas, elephants and chimps.
- **Isla Corisco** (p601) Tread softly on the squeaky-clean sand of this undiscovered paradise isle.
- **Bata** (p599) Watch the city grow vertically with oil money.

CLIMATE & WHEN TO GO

Equatorial Guinea is hot, humid and tropical. The mainland, Rio Muni, has a dry season from June to August while Bioko Island is dry from December to February. Rainfall is likely in both places outside of those months, though Bioko generally receives much more rain than the mainland. Depending on your tolerance of heat and humidity, the dry season is probably the best time to travel; temperatures fall during the wet season but roads are less easily navigated.

ITINERARIES

- **One Week** Kick off your visit in Malabo (p595), working in a day trip to Moka (p599), then get yourself on a plane to the mainland, pausing in Bata (p599) before an overnight trip to Monte Alen National Park (p601).
- **Two Weeks** Using Gabon's Libreville (p608) as a cheap entry point, make your way down south to Cogo (p600) and catch the boat to Isla Corisco (p601) to kick off your shoes on the gorgeous beach. Then head up to Monte Alen National Park (p601) to hike through the forest, winding up in Bata (p599). From there, fly to Malabo (p595) for a few days in the city and exploring Bioko Island (p599). Fly back to Bata to leave via Libreville, or if money permits, exit from Malabo.

HISTORY
The Early Days

Bantu tribes, including the Bubi, came to the mainland in the 12th century from other parts of West and Central Africa. The Bubi are said to have fled to Bioko to escape the Fang, who are believed to have become the dominant ethnic group in the 1600s. Europeans made their first contact on the distant island of Anobón, which was visited by the Portuguese in 1470. In the 18th century, Bioko, Anobón and parts of the mainland were traded to Spain in exchange for regions in Latin America. Bioko subsequently became an important base for slave-trading in the early 19th century and later a naval base for England, which by then was trying to stop the slave trade. Cocoa plantations were started on the island in the late 19th century, making Malabo Spain's most important possession in equatorial Africa.

Independence & Coup Attempts

Equatorial Guinea attained independence in October 1968 under the presidency of Macias Nguema. Months later, relations with Spain deteriorated rapidly and Nguema's 10-year dictatorship began. Thousands of people were tortured and publicly executed or beaten to death in the forced-labour camps of the mainland. Much of the violence was tribally motivated – the Bubis were particularly sought. By the time Nguema's regime was finally toppled in 1979, only a third of the 300,000 Guineans who lived there at the time of independence remained. In August 1979, Nguema was overthrown by his nephew Teodoro Obiang Nguema, who then ordered his uncle's execution. A coup attempt was made on Obiang in 2004; see the boxed text, p596.

EQUATORIAL GUINEA

Equatorial Guinea Today

The US imports up to 100,000 barrels of oil every day from Equatorial Guinea's shores and there's even a direct flight from Houston, Texas, to Malabo. But though the country has a per-capita income of about US$50,000, profits have not trickled down to most of the population, who linger in appalling poverty while the government generates an oil revenue of about US$3 billion a year. According to the anti-corruption watchdog Transparency International, Equatorial Guinea is the 12th most corrupt country in the world. The group accuses President Obiang of using public money on fancy cars, sleek jets and luxury homes in Los Angeles, where his neighbours include Britney Spears. Obiang is believed to

be suffering from prostate cancer but shows no sign of releasing his grip; in 2009 he was voted in for another presidential term, in an election that banned EU monitors and some foreign media. Obiang won, as he predicted, 97% of the vote.

CULTURE

There's no absence of joy in Equatorial Guinea – like everywhere else in the world, there's work, laughter, religion and passions – fear is the thread running through daily life. Though some of the oil money has gone towards brand-spanking-new hospitals, most of the population won't be able to afford to go to them. Daily life revolves around the oil industry in Bata and Malabo. Otherwise peo-

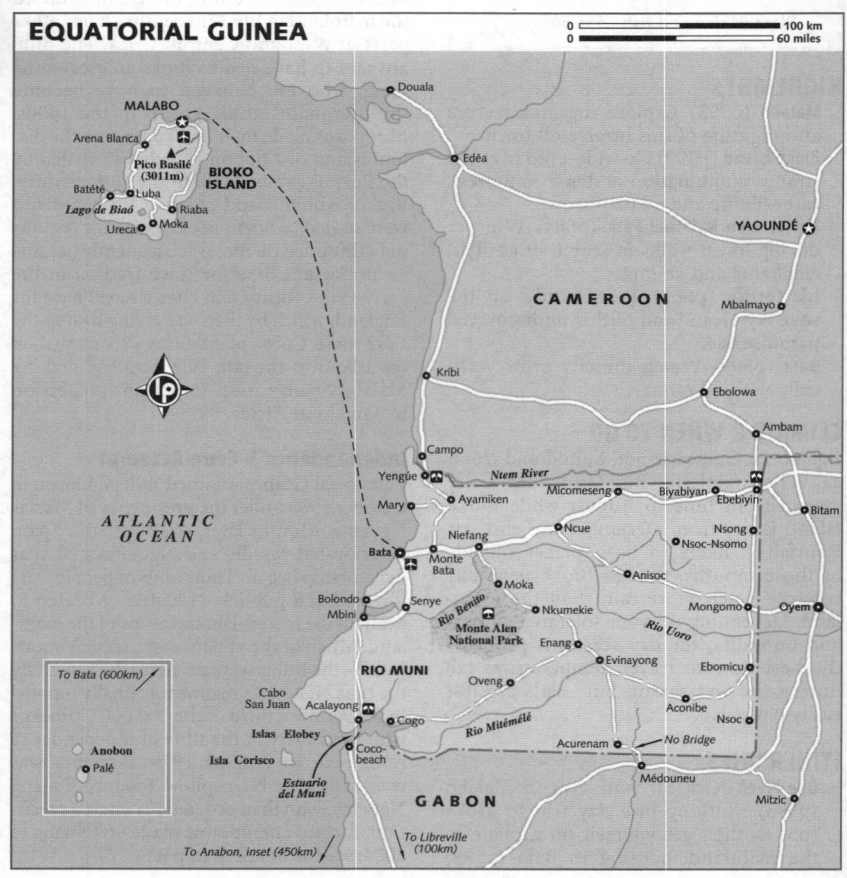

INVISIBLE INK

Most countries with a GDP as high as Equatorial Guinea's have flourishing literary scenes. But, deterred by a press so tightly regulated that it can be hard to breathe, the vast majority of Equatorial-Guinean writers live in exile in Spain. Among the diaspora are brave souls like Donato Ndongo, the highly acclaimed author of *Shadows of Your Black Memory*, a magical page-turner laced with reflections on the country's troubles. Only a handful of Equatorial-Guinean writers remain in the country, including Juan Tomás Avila Laurel, the Malabo-based author of *The Burden*, a 1999 novel that criticises Spain's colonial policy, and *Nadie Tiene Buena Fame en Este Pais* (Nobody Has a Good Reputation in This Country). English novelist Frederick Forsyth, the author of *The Dogs of War*, lived in Equatorial Guinea in the early 1970s, supposedly to research the impact of a fictional coup on a small tropical country. Decades later he admitted – in a *Times* article – to 'chewing the fat' in a real coup attempt in 1973.

---

ple live a very traditional African lifestyle, in small villages of mud-wattle houses, with agriculture the main occupation. People work sunrise to sunset, drinking starts early, and talking continues until sleep comes. In many rural villages there's a noticeable absence of boys aged 12 to 30, who go to the city for school and work.

People

On the mainland 80% of the population is Fang, while on Bioko Island the Bubis are the most numerous group, making up about 15% of the total population. Smaller ethnicities, including the Benga, inhabit the other islands. Oil has brought many Americans, and a lot of Chinese have started to set up shop in Bata and Malabo.

The majority of the population is Roman Catholic, owing to 400 years of Spanish occupation, but traditional animist beliefs are strong and are often practised concurrently.

Arts & Crafts

Traditional rituals and arts including dance are still performed, including mask arts and the balélé, which is accompanied by drums, wooden xylophones, sanzas and bow harps. There's a strong oral tradition, with stories passed down through the generations, often involving the same cast of famous characters such as the grumpy tortoise and the wily monkey.

ENVIRONMENT

Both Bioko Island and the mainland hide a wealth of wildlife, some of which is endangered. Rio Muni is home to a hefty wedge of Central African rainforest with gorillas, chimpanzees and forest elephants. It is unknown exactly how many large mammals remain. Large sections of the interior have been set aside as protected areas, including Monte Alen National Park (p601), which covers much of the centre of Rio Muni and offers some amazing hikes. Logging is being more carefully controlled than in the past, but deforestation and the bushmeat trade are still big problems. Over the past decade, conservation staff have recorded the number of monkeys in meat markets; the tally had reached more than 20,000 by the end of March 2008, according to the Bioko Biodiversity Protection Program.

MALABO

pop 130,000

If you've got this far, you've likely also typed 'Malabo' into a flight booker or search engine only to be greeted with the words 'Did you mean Malibu?'. Equatorial Guinea's steamy little island capital is hardly the stuff of California dreams but it does have its charms – colonial architecture, stretches of black beaches and its centrepiece, a cloud-topped volcano. While the ocean burns with the flames of oil rigs, the broken dreams of much of the population are reflected in the skyscrapers of Malabo Two, the capital's new clone city – hailed as Africa's answer to Dubai.

ORIENTATION

The airport is 6km west of the city, which hugs the northern shore of Bioko Island. Ave de la Independencia is the main drag, flanked by the stunning Cathedral de Santa Isabel and its square. On the northeast tip

LIFE AT BLACK BEACH

Though it's not far from the warm waters of the Atlantic, the whitewashed prison at Playa Negra (Black Beach) is one of Africa's most notorious hellholes. It's here that South African mercenary Nick du Toit and fellow coup plotter Simon Mann were locked up for their roles in a 2004 attempted coup, an operation that aimed to overthrow President Obiang and install exiled opposition leader Severo Moto in his place. Oil rights were promised to the coup's financiers and plotters, among them Sir Mark Thatcher, the son of former British prime minister Margaret Thatcher. But the coup attempt failed spectacularly: in March 2004 Mann, du Toit and 60 others were arrested when their Boeing jet landed in Harare, Zimbabwe, on a weapons-gathering stop. While du Toit was sent to Black Beach immediately, Mann served four years in jail in Zimbabwe before being extradited to Malabo in 2007, where he was handed a 34-year sentence. The same year, Amnesty International called a Black Beach term a 'slow, lingering death sentence'. President Obiang released Mann, du Toit and other accused prisoners early in 2009, citing good behaviour.

of Bioko, oil rigs burst forth from the port, and in the shadow of the old town, construction of Malabo Two – the sequel, the stuff of fantasies, with smart government offices, landscaped parks and shiny shopping centres – is almost complete.

INFORMATION

French Cultural Centre (☎ 594544; Calle de Acacio Muñe) Also organises excellent festivals and arts events. Has a good library (open Monday to Friday, 2pm to 8pm) with a handful of publications in English.

Ministry of Culture, Tourism & Information (Ave 3 de Agosto) Mandatory stop for tourist and photo permits, which you'll need unless you're in Malabo on an official business trip. This should be your first port of call before you do anything else, other than check into your hotel.

Proser Internet Cafe (☎ 093163; Ave de la Libertad)

Santa Isabel Clinic (Carretera de Luba) The best medical facility, with an on-site lab and pharmacy. There's a sister clinic on Ave Parques de Africa.

SGBGE Bank (Ave de la Independencia) Has a Western Union booth. You can exchange US dollars and sometimes euros here. Travellers cheques can't be cashed anywhere in town.

Spanish Cultural Centre (☎ 092186; Carretera del Aeropuerto) Stop here for a cold drink and a peek at the cultural calendar of shows, concerts and films.

DANGERS & ANNOYANCES

Malabo is safer than many people will have you think, but as in any city, carry more common sense with you than cash. The capital is a hybrid of the new and the old; Hummers and 4WDs whiz by cabs without seatbelts. Remember that whipping out your camera near government buildings is likely to get you in as much trouble as unzipping your trousers.

SIGHTS AND ACTIVITIES

Lovers of colonial architecture go gaga over Malabo. The Gothic **Cathedral de Santa Isabel** (Ave de la Independencia) is the country's largest catholic seat, impressive in pale yellow and duck-egg blue. Its facade is flanked by two 40m-high towers, the work of Spanish architect Llairadó Luis Segarra Llairadó. It was completed in 1916. The pretty **Plaza de España** (Calle de 12 Octubre) is a great place for a stroll. The blood-orange **Seat of Government** and the **Sofitel Malabo** on Plaza de España (also known as Plaza de la Independencia) are also beautiful throwbacks to Spanish rule. When it's finished, the Jetsonsesque mini-city **Malabo Two** will include revamped government buildings replete with glass-domed roofs and a park intended to rival New York's Central Park – with dancing fountains and woodland trails.

If you're yearning for the great outdoors, check out the website of the **Bioko Biodiversity Protection Program** (☎ 267876, 267112; www.bioko.org). They can point you in the direction of good guided hikes to other parts of the island including the steamy waterfalls of Moka, Crater Lake, Pico Malabo and the Caldera de Luba, which has the highest concentration of primates in the area, including many endangered species.

SLEEPING

Though many visitors are sleeping on oil money, there are some budget beds to be found. Try **Hostel Nely** (☎ 092090; Ave de las Naciónes Unidas). At the time of research the Hilton Malabo (with everything you would expect from the US hotel chain) was scheduled to open in 2010. Credit cards were not,

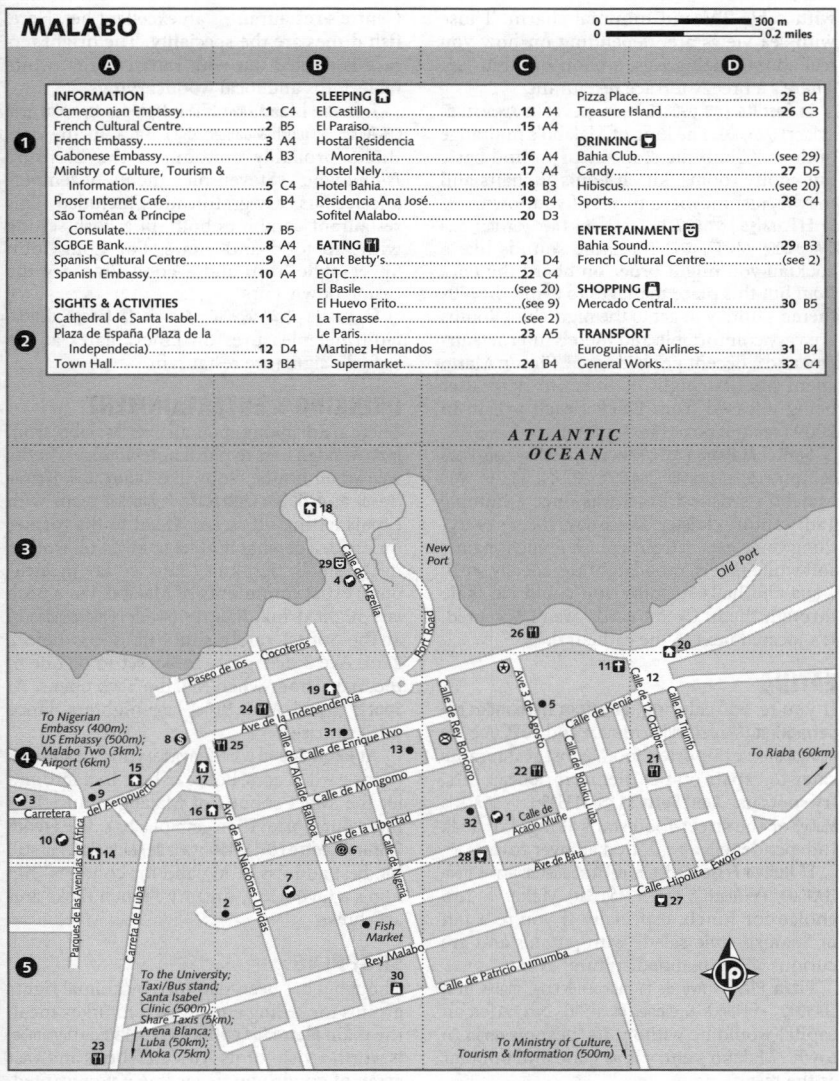

MALABO

0 — 300 m
0 — 0.2 miles

INFORMATION
Cameroonian Embassy.................1 C4
French Cultural Centre.................2 B5
French Embassy............................3 A4
Gabonese Embassy.......................4 B3
Ministry of Culture, Tourism &
  Information...............................5 C4
Proser Internet Cafe......................6 B4
São Toméan & Príncipe
  Consulate..................................7 B5
SGBGE Bank.................................8 A4
Spanish Cultural Centre................9 A4
Spanish Embassy........................10 A4

SIGHTS & ACTIVITIES
Cathedral de Santa Isabel............11 C4
Plaza de España (Plaza de la
  Independencia)........................12 D4
Town Hall...................................13 B4

SLEEPING 🏠
El Castillo..................................14 A4
El Paraíso..................................15 A4
Hostal Residencia
  Morenita................................16 A4
Hostel Nely................................17 A4
Hotel Bahia................................18 B3
Residencia Ana José....................19 B4
Sofitel Malabo............................20 D3

EATING 🍴
Aunt Betty's...............................21 D4
EGTC...22 C4
El Basile................................(see 20)
El Huevo Frito.........................(see 9)
La Terrasse.............................(see 2)
Le Paris.....................................23 A5
Martinez Hernandos
  Supermarket...........................24 B4

Pizza Place................................25 B4
Treasure Island..........................26 C3

DRINKING 🍸
Bahia Club..............................(see 29)
Candy..27 D5
Hibiscus................................(see 20)
Sports.......................................28 C4

ENTERTAINMENT 🎭
Bahia Sound..............................29 B3
French Cultural Centre.............(see 2)

SHOPPING 🛍
Mercado Central........................30 B5

TRANSPORT
Euroguineana Airlines.................31 B4
General Works............................32 C4

EQUATORIAL GUINEA

ATLANTIC OCEAN

New Port

Old Port

To Nigerian
Embassy (400m);
US Embassy (500m);
Malabo Two (3km);
Airport (6km)

To Riaba (60km)

Carretera

To the University;
Taxi/Bus stand;
Santa Isabel
Clinic (500m);
Share Taxis (5km);
Arena Blanca;
Luba (50km);
Moka (75km)

Fish
Market

To Ministry of Culture,
Tourism & Information (500m)

at the time of research, accepted at any of the following hotels.

Residencia Ana José (☎ 092786; Ave de la Independencia; r from CFA30,000) There are two types of comfort: the kind you find in a swish hotel, and the kind you find sitting and chatting with guests at places like Ana José's. Call ahead for a warm welcome that doesn't tug on the purse strings.

Hostal Residencia Morenita (☎ 091026; Calle de Mongomo; r CFA40,000; ❄) Better than your average hostel, with basic but cared-for rooms, a bit of art on the walls and toothpaste-coloured bedspreads. There's a communal lounge.

Hotel Bahia (☎ 090649; Calle de Argelia; r from CFA56,000) A decent bet if you're not dripping in oil money. Rooms are comfortable enough, with cable TV and minimal charm. Those with sea views are, depending on how you feel about blazing rigs, a boon or a burden. There's a breezy terrace restaurant.

El Castillo (☎ 090835/36; Parques de las Avenidas de Africa; r CFA65,000) The king of Malabo's midrange options. Climb the stone steps to find basic but comfy rooms, kitsch Louis V chairs and maybe, just maybe, a turret of your own.

El Paraiso (☎ 099336; Carretera del Aeropuerto; r from CFA80,000; ✖ ⬛ ⬛) Its name sounds like a cocktail you might order on board the *Love Boat* but this place manages to avoid the '70s theme – until you get to the nightclub. Rooms are very comfortable and there's internet, air-con and a decent poolside area. Simon Mann spent his first night of freedom here after being released from Black Beach prison in 2009 (see the boxed text, p596).

Sofitel Malabo (☎ 099940; www.sofitel.com; Plaza de España; d CFA205,000-284,000; ℗ ✖ ⬛ 🛜 ⬛) Malabo's swishest hotel was once a humble 18th-century cloister. These days there's everything you'd expect from a plush French chain – soft white sheets, mood lighting, speedy wi-fi, a spa and halls so shiny you could ice skate through them. Credit cards aren't accepted. It's located next to the cathedral.

EATING

If you're self-catering, **Martinez Hernandos supermarket** (Ave de la Independencia) and **EGTC** (Ave 3 de Agosto) stock imported food. Most restaurants cater to expats on per diems; for cheap eats, try spots like **Aunt Betty's** (☎ 511519; Calle de Acacio Muñe) or the street-food stalls along Ave de la Independencia and dotted all over town.

El Huevo Frito (Carretera del Aeropuerto; mains from CFA4000; ☽ lunch & dinner Mon-Sat) Makes a top choice for lunch, especially if you're a fan of Spanish-style salads with *patatas* and are curious about planned cultural events.

Pizza Place (Ave de la Independencia; mains from CFA5000; ☽ lunch & dinner Mon-Sat) No African capital would be without its 'best pizzeria in town'. Malabo's entry is as good and popular as the rest.

Le Paris (Carretera de Luba; mains from CFA5000; ☽ lunch & dinner) This air-con happy French place does Malabo's best tapas, believe it or not, and it has a good cocktail list. Located inside Hotel Tropicana.

La Terrasse (☎ 594544; Calle de Acacio Muñe; mains from CFA6000; ☽ lunch & dinner Mon-Sat) Like most of its eateries in Africa, the French Cultural Centre's restaurant is an excellent bet. Here, fish dishes are the speciality. The bright terrace is decked out with rattan chairs, white tablecloths and local woodcarvings.

Treasure Island (Ave de la Independencia; mains from CFA7000; ☽ lunch & dinner; ✖) Back in the day, Bioko probably epitomised the *Treasure Island* vibe – Stevenson's theme of temperance versus easy gratification included. This restaurant combines both, in a posh setting with fab food and views. For Long John Silver–style 'rum and a good fling' try the casino downstairs.

El Basile (☎ 099005; Ave de la Independencia) Gourmet pleasures on fancy plates at the Sofitel's signature restaurant.

DRINKING & ENTERTAINMENT

There are drinking spots all over Malabo, from lazy wooden bars to plush hotel lounges. In the wee small hours, clubs like **Candy** (Calle Hipolita Eworo) and **Bahia Club** (Calle de Argelia) teem with expats letting off steam. Head to the former for an idea of what it's like to be an oil worker in the small, tightknit (dare we say incestuous?) expat community of Malabo. For a posh late-night drink, **Hibiscus** (Ave de la Independencia) at the Sofitel rarely shuts its doors before 2am. Ave 3 de Agosto looks set to be one of the main drags when Malabo Two opens. At **Sports** (Calle de Acacio Muñe) late-nighters dance until sunrise.

At **Bahia Sound** (Calle de Argelia) you can sit back in the garden area, bottle of beer in hand, and let the sweet sounds of Malabo's musicians into your world. It's a gem of a bar. The **French Cultural Centre** (☎ 594544; Calle de Acacio Muñe) is still the best address in Malabo for concerts (hip hop's a favourite), dreamy French flicks and art shows.

SHOPPING

Though it has been slammed by animal rights groups for selling endangered monkey meat, the main **Mercado Central** (Calle de Patricio Lumumba) is worth a visit for its African fabrics and vast array of goods you never knew you wanted. For clothes in locally produced fabrics, ask among expats for the tailor of the moment – they can usually whip up a design quickly and cheaply.

GETTING THERE & AROUND

Malabo is increasingly well served by Euro and African airlines and there's even a regular charter flight direct from Houston, Texas. Bata and the mainland are a half-hour hop on **Euroguineana Airlines** (☎ 090836; Calle de Nigeria 14) or the aptly named **General Works** (☎ 099890; Calle de Rey Boncoro). See p603 for more information.

CFA3000 should get you from the airport into town and a short cab ride in Malabo itself is CFA500 to CFA700, double at night. Depending on your bargaining skills, you can hire a taxi for around CFA3500 per hour. Shared taxis leave from a small market about 4km past the university where you can get rides to Luba (one hour) and Moka (two hours).

BIOKO ISLAND

LUBA
pop 8000

A few years ago, Luba was a soporific fishing town remarkable for nothing more than its butter-coloured buildings and beaches shingled with seashells and volcanic rocks. Now it's on its way to becoming one of the most significant oil ports in Africa, with a helipad, duty-free shopping and a micro-community. Development has arguably been a good thing, bringing jobs to the town, but the beaches aren't so great for swimming these days – nor for casting nets.

The two-storey **Hotel Jones** (☎ 094591; r from CFA50,000), on the main road, is the best place to lay your head; it has an outdoor bar and an attractive corner balcony lined with blue-shuttered windows. Next door is the good restaurant **Cuatro Ases de Luba** (meals from CFA8000). Nearby is **Isla Mujeres** (mains from CFA4000), with an outdoor terrace, and **El Bar Miramar** (mains from CFA6000), which has a nightclub. There's a sailing club next to the port. Not to be outdone by Malabo, Luba Two is under construction, with residential estates and new schools springing up. Jump in a shared taxi from Malabo for the one-hour trip here.

An hour south of the capital on the road to Luba is **Arena Blanca**, Bioko's only white-sand beach. In the dry season, clouds of butterflies look like confetti raining down on the expats who head here. Half an hour's drive from Luba is pretty **Batété**, famous for its glorious wooden church, believed to be the oldest in the country.

MOKA
elev 1300m

Wedged between charcoal peaks, mahogany giants and glossy lakes, this little highland town is a breath of fresh air if you're coming from Malabo. Thanks to the altitude, you might even want to bring a thin jumper to throw on after dark. But you don't come to Moka for after-dark pleasures; rise with the sun and ask your hosts to help you arrange a (low-grade, usually) hike, cutting through slices of evergreen forest. Moka is the kind of place that makes you understand why fans of the TV series *Lost* reckon Bioko served as inspiration for the fictional island.

Accommodation up here is in the house provided by the Bioko Biodiversity Protection Program (see p596) or the nearby South African House, both of which can sort you out for food and beer. Though Moka feels remote, there's usually good access to the mobile phone networks, largely because the Obiang family owns property here. Plan on paying no more than CFA15,000 for the two-hour taxi ride from Malabo.

RIO MUNI

BATA
pop 70,000

Though a trip to Rio Muni is all about the rich red soil and the return – if you're coming from Bioko – to Mama Africa, Bata is the exception. It's undergoing the kind of makeover that would make for good reality TV. Until recently, the largest town on the mainland was a pleasant enough stop that didn't really warrant a raised eyebrow. Now it's positively gleaming, with wide California boulevards like the Avenida Juan Pablo II. There are further plans for swish condos, convention centres, a ferris wheel, an enormous sperm-shaped lake, a glass-fronted shopping centre and an eternal flame. You can almost picture it running its fingers through its peroxide-blonde beaches, showing off its new look.

As in Malabo, you'll need a tourist permit if you're not here on business. Head to the inefficient Ministro de Turismo with around US$50 to get one.

Orientation & Information
The new, curved-roof airport is a few kilometres north of the main town. Bar Centrale is a good, central place to get your bearings. Proser has the best internet in town. Both BGFI and CCEI banks are just up the road from Bar Centrale on Calle Patricio Lumumba. You can usually change US currency

at BGFI bank, though at the time of research neither had a functional ATM.

Sleeping

Auberge Finistère (Avenida Patricio Lumumba; r from CFA20,000) Cheap, cheerful and friendly, it's not the cleanest place in town (at least when we were there) but it'll do if you're pinching pennies. No reliable phone number.

Hostal Ayuntamiento (Ayuntamiento Sq; r from CFA30,000) Another budget bet. This hostel is officially nameless but everyone refers to it as the Ayuntamiento – it's on the square of the same name. The host sometimes serves up big bowls of paella.

Bar Centrale (r from CFA30,000) A mainstay on Bata's midrange scene, this place does what it says on the tin. If you're after a good location (it's between Avenidas Patricio Lumumba and Mbogo Nsogo), a beer, a bite to eat and a clean bed you're all set. There's a Lebanese bakery next door.

Les Pagaies (☎ 545032; Playa de Utonde; r with air-con CFA50,000; ☒ ☎) On the gorgeous white sands of Playa de Utonde on the edge of town, we vote Les Pagaies is the best address in Bata. Four villas, a couple of suites, a pool and hearty Spanish fare. Hop in a cab from the airport if you're heading here; it's a five-minute ride.

Aparthotel Plaza (☎ 080253/54; Plaza del Reloj; r from CFA60,000; ☒ ☐) It's Bata suit heaven at this Lebanese-owned hotel, with conference rooms, plush suites, king-size beds and funky rugs under the roof of a mini (OK, six-storey) skyscraper.

Eating

Bambu (Avenida Juan Pablo II; mains from CFA3000) is a great spot for simple Equatorial-Guinean fare. **La Armistad** (mains around CFA4000) is a Senegalese chop bar opposite the main market at the crossroads with Avenida Jésus Bacale. **Akena** (mains from CFA5000; ☺ dinner Mon-Sat) is a steady bet for a pizza fix, next door to the ultra-modern **Spanish Cultural Centre** (☎ 084940; Calle Lumu Matindi; ☺ Mon-Sat), which shows flicks, tunes and art. The **French Institute** (☎ 082070; Avenida Naciones Unidas; ☺ Mon-Sat) has similar offerings in, of course, French. The fish restaurant **Miramar** (mains from CFA5000; ☺ lunch & dinner Mon-Sat) has taken over a gorgeous colonial building overlooking the sea. A great lobster supper costs around CFA10,000. Alternatively, buy fresh lobster

or shrimp from local fishermen and take it to one of the nameless old-fashioned chop bars in the old town for preparation.

Drinking & Entertainment

If all you want is a simple cold beer, nobody does it better than **La Salsa** (Paseo Marítimo; ☺ most evenings). Though the indoor dance floor can feel a little sleazy, **Drink Cool** (Plaza del Reloj) has a nice terrace where you can grab a late-night beer. Run away with the night at **Tabu** (Avenida Mboso Nsogoon), a dance club with traditional instruments strung up on the walls. For a cheekier night out, head to **Discoteca Panafrica** (Calle ONU).

Getting There & Away

Bata is a 45-minute flight from Malabo with either **General Works** (☎ 099890) or **Euroguineana** (☎ 090836); tickets can be bought at the airport or in town at the offices near the radio station.

Catch shared taxis (which either drop you at the Bolondo ferry or cross with you) to Mbini (CFA2000, one hour) and areas south at the Mercado Grande. For Rio Campo, Monte Alen National Park (CFA3000, 1½ hours) and Ebebeyin (CFA5000, four hours) catch a taxi to Ngolo and ask the driver to point you in the right direction of the proper taxi to your destination. A short taxi ride around town should be CFA500.

MBINI

Mbini, 85km from Bata, is a good base for *pirogue* (traditional canoe) rides up the eponymous river towards Gabon or for hikes out to the waterfalls at Wele. The town itself isn't spectacular, but there's a colourful old round market in the centre of town, and a few other architectural gems including the Ayuntamiento building. There are a few basic hotels in town that cost around CFA15,000 a room. **Hotel Pastura** (r from CFA12,000) is near the ferry, and **El Parador** (mains from CFA1500) has cheap food. Minibuses from Bata to Mbini (one hour, CFA2000, including a ferry from Bolondo to Mbini), and areas south, run from the Mercado Grande in the mornings.

COGO

Cogo is one of those hot, heavy equatorial towns that people fall in love with for no real reason. Cogo's most famous *amant* is the American writer Robin Cook, who set his genetic thriller *Chromosone 6* in the town. Dripping with sleepy charm, Cogo is the equivalent of an old man with a glint in his eye – if you stick around long enough, who knows what stories you'll hear? It's also the jumping-off point for the dreamy Isla Corisco.

The basic but charming **Hotel Estuario** (r with toilet & bucket CFA15,000-20,000) has electricity at night; look for the bright blue doors. There are a few eateries and bars that do food and drink, and some beautiful colonial churches and homes. Check in with the Commissar (and pay the requisite fee) before poking around town.

A *pirogue* across the estuary to much smaller Acalayong runs all day (CFA1500), from where you can get a car or truck to Mbini and Bata. **Hotel Acalayong** (s/d CFA5000/8000) is right next to the estuary if you get stuck overnight. Overloaded *pirogues* leave for Isla Corisco from Cogo once or twice a week for around CFA5000. You can also cross to Gabon by *pirogue* for the same price. Ask at the port for daily departures.

MONTE ALEN NATIONAL PARK

Gorillas? In Equatorial Guinea? Damn right there are. Monte Alen is one of the least known national parks in Africa and therefore one of the cheapest places to see a gorilla family picnic – though sightings are by no means guaranteed. Covering 2000 sq km, the park's lush velvety jungle is also home to chimpanzees, forest elephants, mandrills (plus 13 more species of primate), crocs and burping frogs the size of footballs.

Base camp is the **Hotel Monte Alen** (s/d/weekend double CFA18,000/30,000/50,000), perched on a jungle ridge with a sweeping view of the valley below. There are also a couple of campsites deeper into the park, including one at **Esamalen**, where most gorilla treks begin. Guided treks in small groups are led by park rangers and start at around CFA25,000, depending on the weather, length of trek and your specifications.

To get here, take a route taxi in Bata headed for Evinayong (CFA5000, two to three hours in the dry season). It'll drop you at the entrance labelled 'Ecofac' after the body that runs the park.

ISLA CORISCO

With lashings of powdery white sand, a long limb of a sandbar, gentle waves to send you to sleep and seashell trails to your front door, Isla Corsico – Manji Benga to locals – is honeymoon perfect. Located 20 miles off the coast of Gabon, Corisco has both Spanish and French colonial influences and fabulous seafood. An airport and fancy resort are planned.

Hostal Corisco (☎ 212630; d CFA30,000) is a lovely house on the water, run by Pa Santiago Hinestrosa and his family. You can dive, hike, spy tiger fish, swim among battered yellow fishing vessels, fish for giant crabs by candlelight or flag down a fisherman with a boat to get a cheap tour.

Grab a table at **Mondi** (on the beach; mains from CFA4000) for giant plates of stuffed crab, cassava leaves and even crocodile steak. A village *pirogue* leaves for Corisco from Cogo a few times a week but it's not the safest trip in the world; if you have the cash, we recommend shelling out for a private hire. Ask in Cogo for a reputable *pirogue* owner. It is necessary to declare yourself to the commandante of the island soon after arrival.

EQUATORIAL GUINEA DIRECTORY

ACCOMMODATION

A bed doesn't come cheap in Equatorial Guinea. Expect to pay at least CFA15,000 for budget zzzs in most towns; much more in the capital, Malabo.

BOOKS

The Wonga Coup: Guns, Thugs and a Ruthless Determination to Create Mayhem in an Oil-Rich Corner of Africa by Adam Roberts will give you a rich history of the failed coup plot and the politics of oil in the Gulf of Guinea.

Tropical Gangsters: One Man's Experience With Development and Decadence in Deepest Africa by Robert Klitgaard is a highly entertaining account of the World Bank's attempt at developing Equatorial Guinea before the oil boom. See the boxed text, p595, for more on Equatorial-Guinean writing.

BUSINESS HOURS

Business hours are Monday to Saturday 8am to 1pm and 4pm to 7pm. There's generally a three-hour siesta in the middle of the day. Many shops don't adhere to business hours at all, especially in rural areas.

DANGERS & ANNOYANCES

Life is much more dangerous and annoying for Equatorial-Guineans than it is for you. While violence is unlikely, bribery is commonplace. Speaking out against the leadership can lead straight to jail. Be careful with your camera: a permit is necessary for taking photos. Wherever you are in Equatorial Guinea, someone will ask you to prove why you're there. In Malabo and Bata, you must pick up mandatory tourist permits from the respective ministries of tourism. Elsewhere (especially in small towns and villages) it makes sense to present yourself to the community leader upon arrival, before local people start asking questions. They do so not to annoy you, but because there is a very real threat of them being detained for spending time with unknown visitors. Though it can be a pain, following the rules will usually spare you (and the locals you encounter) further grief.

EMBASSIES & CONSULATES

The following embassies are in Malabo, though their ambassadors are often based in neighbouring countries. Canadian, British and German representatives can be found in Yaoundé, Cameroon.

Cameroon (Map p597; ☎ 092263; Calle de Rey Boncoro)
France (Map p597; ☎ 092005; Carretera del Aeropuerto; ☺ 9am-1pm Mon-Fri)
Gabon (Map p597; ☎ 093180; Calle de Argelia; ☺ 8am-1pm & 3pm-5pm Mon-Fri)
Nigeria (off Map p597; ☎ 092487; Paseo de los Cocoteros; ☺ 8am-1pm & 3pm-5pm Mon-Fri)
São Tomé & Príncipe (Map p597; Calle de Acacio Muñe)
Spain (Map p597; ☎ 092020; embespgq@correo.mae.es; Parque de las Avdas de África; ☺ 8am-3pm Mon-Fri)
USA (off Map p597; ☎ 098895; http://malabo.usembassy.gov; Carretera del Aeropuerto; ☺ citizen services 10am-3pm Mon-Thu, 8am-12noon Fri)

HOLIDAYS

New Year's Day 1 January
Labour Day 1 May
Organization of African Unity (OAU) Day 25 May
President's Birthday 5 June
Liberation Day 3 August
Independence Day 12 October
Human Rights Day 10 December
Christmas Day 25 December

INTERNET ACCESS

Connections can be slow at web cafes in Malabo and other towns, but you'll usually

find speedy wi-fi in the lobbies of the best hotels. Access costs vary greatly; expect to pay anything from CFA2000 per hour to four times that, depending on where (and, for that matter, who) you are.

MONEY

ATMs are planned in Malabo and Bata but credit cards were not accepted anywhere at the time of research. Travellers cheques tend to generate a lot of hassle; bring cash or rely on Western Union transfers from elsewhere if you're planning a lengthy stay.

VISAS

Unless you're American, securing a visa for Equatorial Guinea is no easy feat. (Visas are required for all but Americans, though some embassies outside the country are not always aware of this exemption.) Information, prices and the formalities required vary wildly. Some embassies require letters of invitation for a tourist visa; others do not and there is no hard-and-fast rule to help you out. Some travellers find that applying for a visa in a neighbouring country such as Gabon or Cameroon is easier than doing so from home; others report being asked only to apply in their country of residence. We recommend trying the latter first. If you're coming to work on a project of some kind, you'll likely have a (slightly) easier ride.

Visas for Onward Travel

Visas for Cameroon and Gabon are available from embassies in Malabo (see left for addresses). Equatorial Guinea is one of the best places to get a Gabonese visa: 30-day visas take three days to process. Visas for Cameroon are available at all border crossings.

WOMEN TRAVELLERS

Travellers of any kind are rare here and women travellers in particular will attract a lot of attention in Malabo, which is teeming with (male) oil workers. Elsewhere, single women will receive a warm welcome, like most travellers, though may be subject to the usual 'Are you married? Why not?' exchange. Don't take comments, or indeed proposals, too seriously but do keep your wits about you.

TRANSPORT IN EQUATORIAL GUINEA

GETTING THERE & AWAY
Air

Air France (www.airfrance.com) Paris to Malabo three times a week.

Ethiopian Airlines (www.ethiopianairlines.com) Via Addis Ababa.

Iberia Airlines (www.iberia.com) Madrid to Malabo three times weekly.

KLM (www.klm.com) Amsterdam to Malabo a few times a week.

Kenya Airways (www.kenya-airways.com) Nairobi to Malabo.

Lufthansa (www.lufthansa.com) Flies via Frankfurt.

Royal Air Maroc (www.royalairmaroc.com) Serves Malabo via Casablanca.

World Airways (www.worldairways.com) Charter flights from Houston, Texas.

Land
GABON

You can cross from Cogo/Acalayong to Cocobeach by *pirogue* (see p600) without too much hassle (at least when we tried) but do bring sunblock and make sure you have your yellow-fever certificate with you. Some travellers have had success crossing via Mongomo to Oyem and Bitam.

CAMEROON

Travellers can always cross to Cameroon at Ebebiyin; the border at Rio Campo (two to three hours from Bata) isn't always open, so check before you head there. The rules change all the time so you need to be careful.

GETTING AROUND

General Works (☎ 099890) and **Euroguineana** (☎ 090836) both fly between Bata and Malabo. It's possible to get a *pirogue* to some of the smaller islands, including Corisco. Ships occasionally go from Malabo to Douala (Cameroon), but there's certainly no fixed schedule and you'd have to get lucky. Shared taxis, private hires and over-packed minibuses are the way to get around outside of Bata and Malabo.

EQUATORIAL GUINEA

Gabon

What do you want to do most on this earth? Lock eyes with a gorilla in the jungle? Drink margaritas on sands so white they flash silver in the sun? Watch ribbons of surf wash hippos to shore, while at the same time softening the beach footprints of elephants? Dance until your feet fall off, fuelled by cold beer and the promise of tomorrow by the sea?

You could make an appointment with a 'have it all' travel agency – those VIP one-stop shops promising experiences you thought you could only dream of – or you could go to Gabon, where – if your wallet can take it – you can do all of those things and more. From the showy bars of Libreville to the unbeatable feeling of hitting a stretch of good road after hours on a bad one, from unfathomably loud cities to picnics in the jungle, Gabon will take you from one extreme to the next.

From the air, this land is a mass of velvety jungle, a *perroquet*'s view of nothing but trees, leaves and humid bushland. The domain of gorillas, it looks impenetrable: as if you could never make your way through all that foliage. But once your feet touch that ubiquitous soft red soil, you'll realise that Gabon is ripe for exploring. The late president Omar Bongo turned 10% of the country into national parks, and you can fly right in.

GABON

FAST FACTS

- **Area** 267,670 sq km
- **ATMs** In Libreville
- **Borders** Equatorial Guinea, Cameroon and Congo
- **Budget** US$100 per day in Libreville; US$50 to US$200 per day in the interior
- **Capital** Libreville
- **Languages** French, Fang
- **Money** Central African CFA; US$1 = CFA463, €1 = CFA656
- **Population** 1.45 million
- **Seasons** Wet (September to November and February to May), dry (May to September and December to January)
- **Telephone** Country code ☎ 241; international access code ☎ 00
- **Time** GMT/UTC +1; no daylight saving
- **Visa** Required by all; must be acquired before arrival

HOW MUCH?

- **Fancy grilled fish supper** US$13
- **Concert ticket** US$4
- **Cocktail in a Libreville bar** US$6.50
- **Forest walk among mandrills** US$75
- **Weekend for two with the gorillas** US$800

LONELY PLANET INDEX

- **1L petrol** US$1.10
- **1L bottled water** US$1.30
- **Bottle of Régab beer** US$1.10
- **Souvenir football shirt** US$17.50
- **Plate of manioc leaves with fish** US$4.30

HIGHLIGHTS

- **Loango National Park** (p615) Gape at beaches full of elephants, buffalo and surfing hippos.
- **Réserve de la Lopé** (p617) Track vibrant mandrill troupes.
- **Lambaréné** (p614) Explore the town made famous by the Nobel-winning doctor Albert Schweitzer.
- **Mayumba National Park** (p616) Body-surf the waves while watching humpback whales breach in the distance.
- **Kongou** (p617) Head to the falls before the developers do.

CLIMATE & WHEN TO GO

There's no escaping it: Gabon is one hot slice of Africa. The rainy season runs from September to May, broken up by a short dry period from December to January, and a longer dry season from May to September. The temperature is 25°C on average, but with about 80% humidity – so it feels much hotter.

Whale season is from July to September, and turtles come ashore to lay eggs from November to January. Mammals wander from forest to savannah depending on the temperatures – check with the national parks for seasonal wildlife migration.

ITINERARIES

- **Ten Days** Kick off the adventure in Libreville (p608), but don't stick around too

long or you'll have fewer pennies for the charms of Lambaréné (p614), Loango National Park (p615) and the surrounding towns. You can then fly back to Libreville and spend a couple of days exploring the city.
- **Three Weeks** Fly into Libreville (p608) and take the train down to Réserve de la Lopé (p617). After a couple of nights there, explore Mikongo (p617) and Ivindo National Park (p617), before moseying down to Franceville (p617) for a night. Fly west to Gamba (p616) via Libreville, then head onto magical Mayumba (p616) where you can enjoy the beaches, the whales (in season) and some forest walks. Then fly back up to Libreville and spend some time exploring the city.

HISTORY

When the late President Omar Bongo died in 2009, he was Africa's longest-serving ruler, presiding over an economy so rich in oil income that it had ducked and dived its way out of the crises that brought nearby nations to their knees. Strong relations with Paris have helped keep Gabon on the straight and narrow, and though the country's corruption record is appalling and the oil is running dry, the late president's son, and successor, Ali Ben Bongo is growing in popularity.

Of Petroglyphs & Pygmies

Gabon has been inhabited for at least 400,000 years. Some 1200 rock paintings made by iron-working cultures that razed the forest for agriculture, creating today's savannah, have been found in the area around Réserve de la Lopé. The earliest modern society, the Pygmies, was displaced between the 16th and 18th centuries by migrating peoples from the north, principally the Fang, who came after settling in what is now Cameroon and Equatorial Guinea.

Contact with Europeans, starting with the arrival of the Portuguese in 1472, had a profound effect on tribal structures. British, Dutch and French ships traded for slaves, ivory and tropical woods. The coastal tribes established strong ties with these colonial powers, but the interior tribes defended their lands against European encroachment. To this day, animosity still lingers between the coastal tribes and the rest of the country.

GABON

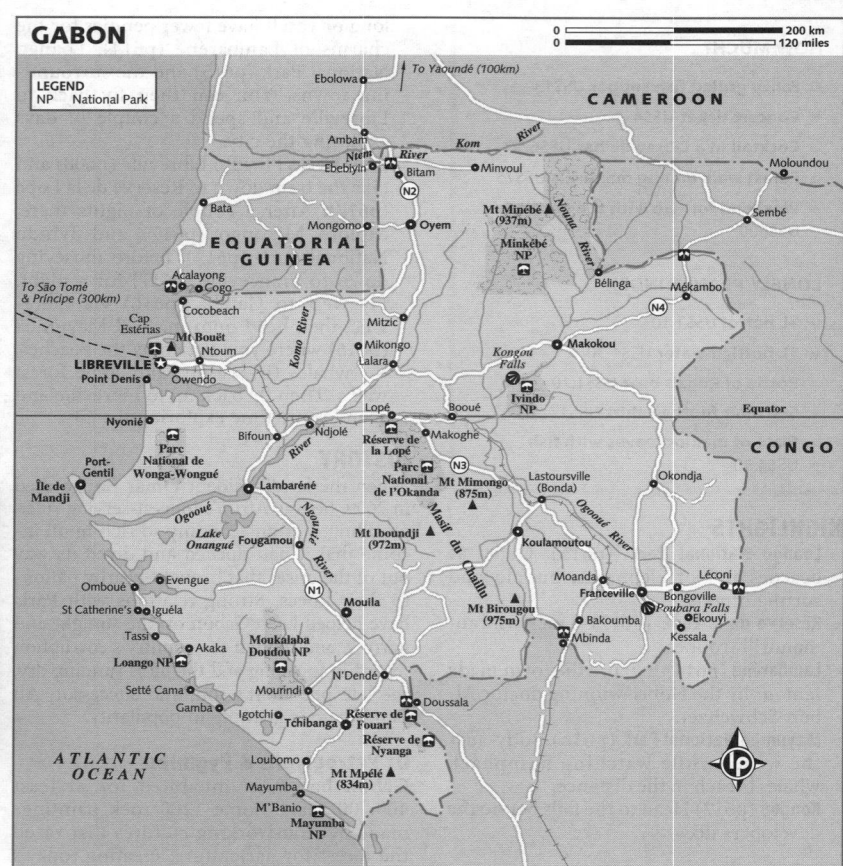

GABON

LEGEND
NP   National Park

The capital, Libreville, was established in 1849 for freed slaves, on an estuary popular with traders. In 1885 the Berlin Conference of European powers recognised French rights in Gabon, which became part of the French Congo and later French Equatorial Africa. The country became self-governing in 1958, and won independence in 1960 under President Léon M'Ba. After M'Ba died in a French hospital in 1967, his vice president, Albert Bernard Bongo, took power of the nation (changing his name to Omar when he adopted Islam in 1974).

The Omar Bongo Years

The newly independent nation got off to an extravagant start. As money rolled in from the sale of timber, manganese ore, iron ore, chrome, gold, diamonds and, finally, oil, Gabon's per-capita income soared higher than South Africa's. Relations with France remained tight throughout Bongo's rule – 'Gabon without France is like a car with no driver. France without Gabon is like a car with no fuel,' he said of the relationship with the former colonial power.

In 1976 Bongo's government announced a four-year, US$32 billion plan to create a modern transport system, encourage local industry and develop mineral deposits. Few of these projects ever took shape. The government did, however, spend vast sums hosting a summit of the Organization of African Unity in 1977 and (conservative estimates say) US$250 million on the presidential palace.

In 1990, after the country's first real political unrest, Bongo ended more than two decades of one-party rule by legalising the opposition (though subsequent elections were marred by fraud). He died, at the age of 73, in a Spanish hospital in 2009, officially of a heart attack though it's widely believed that he was suffering from cancer. Gabon initially denied the death of the man it couldn't bear to see gone, but two days after the news leaked from Paris, it was confirmed by Libreville. At the funeral in Libreville, France's President Sarkozy was jeered at – many Gabonese felt the relationship with Paris had gone too far.

Gabon Today

After the death of his father, Ali Ben Bongo (at the age of 50) won the 2009 presidential election with just 42% of the vote. The former foreign affairs minister was born in neighbouring Republic of Congo and doesn't speak local languages – something that has alienated him from his people. In the wake of the election, riots spread through Port Gentil as rumours flew that France had helped propel Bongo to power.

One of Ali Ben Bongo's first decisions as president was to downsize the government, reducing the ministerial count to 30. Though opinion was divided over the president when he first stepped into his father's shoes, he is becoming increasingly popular. The boulevards of Libreville are lined with life-size posters of the president – during campaigning his slogan was the ultra-laid-back, hip 'Ali '09'. Though he has slashed the lunch breaks of civil servants, he has pledged to double the minimum wage, build new social housing and back changes to the justice system. As the oil runs dry and Gabon invests more heavily in ecotourism and the maritime industry, the younger Bongo's presidency will be the one to watch.

CULTURE

In the early oil days, Gabon knocked back more Champagne than anywhere else on earth. Though there's still a hefty gap between the country's rich and poor, even in remote villages you won't find the kind of poverty seen in parts of Congo and Equatorial Guinea, Gabon's poorer neighbours. In the clubs of Libreville, you'll see Gabonese hot shots splashing the cash and acting – as someone once said – more French than the French themselves. Oil wealth has brought a fairly good education system to Gabon; the World Bank estimates that 95% of young women can read and write – a rarity in Central Africa. Still, infant disease and human trafficking are issues, especially in rural areas.

People

Of the people living in Gabon today, the original forest-dwelling tribes (often referred to as Pygmies) survive only in the remote north of the country, barely keeping their fascinating culture intact. Most other people are descendants of the Bantu peoples, and the Fang are still the most numerous. There is also a sizeable French expat community.

Missionary influence is palpable; over 50% of the country counts itself as Christian, though traditional animist beliefs are still strong and beliefs in superstition and witchcraft hold great power over much of the Gabonese population. Stay in the country long enough and you'll notice yourself referring to the 'spirits' and 'ancestors'.

Arts & Crafts

Traditional masks, carvings and bieri (ancestral sculpture) using natural materials such as

---

BACH IN GABON

What does Johann Sebastian Bach c 1724 have in common with Gabon's Bantu drummers? Until the 1990s, not a lot. But that was before Pierre Akendengué, one of Africa's most celebrated composers, holed up for one hundred days in a Paris studio and recorded 'Lambarena', a fabulously energetic track that sets traditional Gabonese drumming and singing to the pure notes of Bach's 'St John Passion'. Akendengué – who has worn the hats of 1970s protest singer and cultural advisor to the late Omar Bongo since his first foray into music in the 1940s – recorded the track as a tribute to Dr Albert Schweitzer, founder of the eponymous, world-renowned hospital at Lambaréné. The result is a beautiful, unlikely marriage, like coming across a violin concerto in the middle of the Réserve de la Lopé.

GABON

THE 'CONSERVATION COUP'

In the late 1990s Mike Fay, of National Geographic and the Wildlife Conservation Society, walked more than 3200km through Central Africa, documenting the stunning natural environment he passed through. The late President Omar Bongo, after seeing the photos of what became known as the 'Megatransect', did the unthinkable: in 2002 he created a 13-park network of protected lands that covers 10% of the country. Overnight Gabon leapt from last to first in land conservation. Hailed as a 'conservation coup', it was a wise move for Bongo, who was looking for new sources of revenue. Wildlife organisations and ecotourist outfits subsequently rushed in to set up camps in the parks to support the fledgling conservation economy. It's just one of the measures lined up by the late president to ease the impact of rapidly decreasing oil supplies.

---

wood, raffia and feathers are found throughout Gabon. However, they're rarely sold in the markets as they are still used in religious ceremonies and activities. (Though you will find these kinds of items from neighbouring countries in the markets.) Fang masks are prized throughout the world and sold for big bucks at art auctions.

Dancing is a national pastime, and recent dance crazes include the Ivorian *coupé-decalé*, and the L'Oriengo, which originated as a dance for people handicapped by polio. Traditional tribal dance is still widely practised and can be seen at cultural villages.

Hip hop is big in Gabon, and there are plenty of home-grown groups playing on the radios. You'll also find recordings of the sacred music of the Bwiti, which uses, among other extraordinary instruments, harps played with the mouth, as well as brilliant, inspiring Pygmy group recordings.

FOOD & DRINK

If you don't like *fufu*, don't sweat. The heat-inducing cassava staple is a long-time favourite in Gabon, but the cuisine is just as heavy in other Central and West African staples, such as fried plantains and rice and fish dishes. Okra, spinach and palm oil are widely eaten here, and in a country coated with such thick forest, the lure of bushmeat – notably bush hogs, antelopes, primates (including chimpanzees and to a lesser extent gorillas) and crocodiles – has been hard to shake. The local beer is Régab and you'll see the orange signs for it everywhere.

ENVIRONMENT

Gabon is a country of astonishing landscapes and almost insane biodiversity, much of which is still undiscovered and unexploited. Though almost 75% of the country is covered in dense tropical rainforest, this equatorial country is also full of endless white-sand beaches, savannahs, rushing rivers, hidden lagoons, rocky plateaus and canyons, cloud-tipped mountains and *inselbergs* (isolated rock domes overlooking the surrounding forest canopy), all of which are home to an amazing array of flora and fauna.

You're likely to come across gorillas, chimpanzees, mandrills, forest elephants, buffalo, crocodiles, antelopes, hippos, humpback and killer whales, monkeys of all shapes and sizes, leopards, red river hogs, sea turtles and a rainbow of rare birds – to name just a few. New conservation efforts to save endangered species are now underway (see the boxed text, above).

LIBREVILLE

pop 557,000

The muscular heart of Gabon, Libreville has a bit of a glint in its eye. At once charming and ostentatious, it's the gent eyeing you up from the bar, too busy knocking back the juice to sweep you into his arms. It's the guy lounging on the beach come Sunday, secretly eager to get back to work and make some more money. But between the flashy hotels and the expensive boutiques, it's also got a softer side, a love of good food, music and art and, some say, the future of the country. While you might not want to shack up with him, he'll show you a good time, though he certainly won't split the bill. Enjoy it for a few days, then move on, we say.

ORIENTATION

The airport is 11km north of town. Travelling south, all *quartiers* (suburbs) shoot off the corniche, simply known as Au Bord de Mer.

Street names are never used; landmarks are. Some useful ones are M'bolo, the Intercontinental, Le Meridien, the main post office (La Grand Poste), Port Môle, the casino, Mont Bouet and the major embassies.

Distant areas are referred to in kilometres from a specific point in the city centre on Blvd Bessieux (called PK), so PK8, for example, designates the transport hub that is 8km from PK.

INFORMATION
Bookshops
Maison De La Presse (☎ 772695) Libreville's best selection of French-language novels, magazines and the like.

Internet Access
Centre Culturel Français (CCF; ☎ 761120, 726198; per hr CFA1000; ⏰ internet 10am-9pm Mon-Sat) This air-conditioned centre has internet access as well as cultural events, films, concerts and helpful staff.

Medical Services
Fondation Jeanne Ebori (☎ 732012) Across from Port Môle in Quartier Louis. One of Libreville's biggest hospitals, with modern lab facilities and 300 beds.
Polyclinique El Rapha (☎ 447000) The best hospital in Libreville.
SOS Medecins (☎ 747474) Offers a home/hotel emergency service.

Money
Banks in Libreville will change cash and travellers cheques. Hotels also change at good rates, as do local merchants. There are ATMs (accepting Visa cards only) in town at some banks, M'bolo and top-end hotels.

Post
Main post office (La Grand Poste; Au Bord de Mer) Located in the heart of the city. Western Union is directly behind it.

Tourist Information
Ebando (☎ 06250917; www.ebando.org; Rte des Pecheurs) Organises quirky ecotourism ventures. Located north of Libreville in the neighbourhood of La Sablière.
Gabon Tourist Office (☎ 728504; www.gabontour.ga) Has official info and some glossy brochures to hand.

Travel Agents
Eurafrique Voyages (☎ 762787; www.eurafrique voyages.c.la) A family-run agency that organises reputable trips to Loango.
Mistral Voyages (☎ 760421; www.ecotourisme -gabon.com) Of the many travel agencies, this is the most utilised. Owner Patrice knows everything about the country (though front-office staff can be cranky) and most tour packages can be booked here.

DANGERS & ANNOYANCES
Libreville is not a particularly safe city and theft is on the rise. Be careful in the back of shared taxis and getting out of taxis at night. Don't wander onto the beach after dark. Take all the precautions you would in any big city and carry a copy of your passport with you at all times.

SIGHTS & ACTIVITIES
The **Musée des Arts et Traditions** (☎ 761456; musee gabon@numibia.net; Au Bord de Mer; admission by donation of around CFA5000; ⏰ 8am-6pm Mon-Fri, 10am-6pm Sat) has exhibitions on tribal crafts and culture, and a great collection of masks. Just as interesting are the **folk-art sculptures** on the waterfront across from the Intercontinental and, a nice walk south along the water, across from the casino.

The row of **ministry buildings** with Soviet-inspired architecture on Blvd Triomphal is worth a drive-by, as is the northern suburb of **Sabliére**, the pillow of ministers and ambassadors. The city's most interesting market is at **Mont Bouet**.

On weekends most of Libreville heads to the beach; young people congregate in front of the Tropicana. You can use the pools at the Meridien and Intercontinental for a fee.

There are two cultural associations that organise traditional dance performances and ceremonies. **Ebando** (left) is headed up by the wacky, wonderful shaman Tatayo, a Frenchman who has lived in Gabon forever. Costs are variable (if you want to do an initiation, for example), but if you want to go and hang out with Tatayo and chat about Bwiti culture it's free.

SLEEPING
Maison Liebermann (☎ 761955; r with fan/air-con CFA10,000/15,000; ❄) Cleanliness is next to Godliness at this Catholic guesthouse, Libreville's best budget digs.

Somotel (☎ 765846; r with fan/air-con CFA16, 000/21,000; ❄) From the French *sommeil* (to sleep), Somotel is just that – a clean, cheap place to crash. It won't inspire romance but the location is perfect if you're in nocturnal mode.

Tropicana (☎ 731531; tropicana@inet.ga; s/d CFA16,000/25,000; ❄) Just across from the airport, all of Libreville is likely to pass through the Tropicana while you eat *brochettes* (kebabs) and sip sundown drinks. The manager, Eric,

GABON

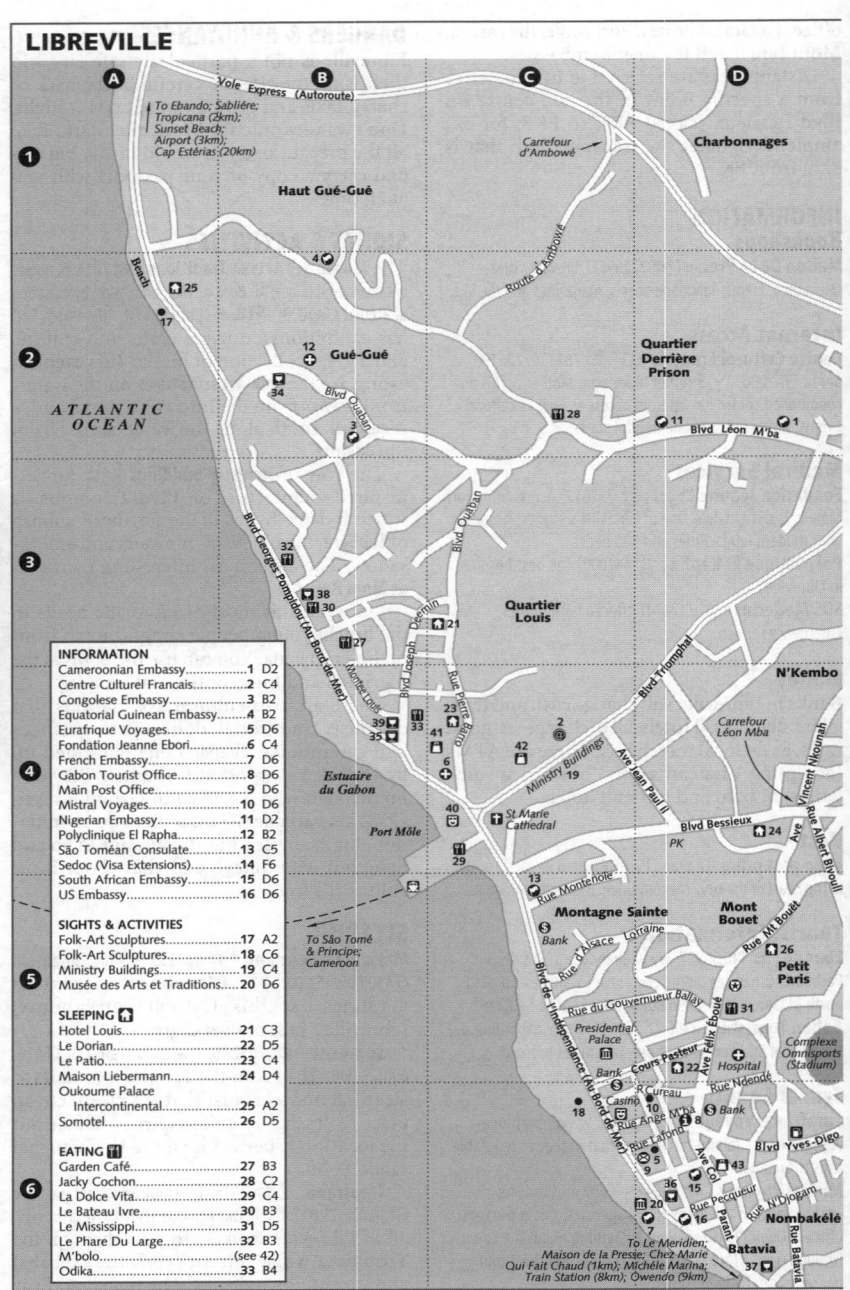

LIBREVILLE

INFORMATION

Cameroonian Embassy	1 D2
Centre Culturel Francais	2 C4
Congolese Embassy	3 B2
Equatorial Guinean Embassy	4 B2
Eurafrique Voyages	5 D6
Fondation Jeanne Ebori	6 C4
French Embassy	7 D6
Gabon Tourist Office	8 D6
Main Post Office	9 D6
Mistral Voyages	10 D6
Nigerian Embassy	11 D2
Polyclinique El Rapha	12 B2
São Toméan Consulate	13 C5
Sedoc (Visa Extensions)	14 F6
South African Embassy	15 D6
US Embassy	16 D6

SIGHTS & ACTIVITIES

Folk-Art Sculptures	17 A2
Folk-Art Sculptures	18 C6
Ministry Buildings	19 C4
Musée des Arts et Traditions	20 D6

SLEEPING

Hotel Louis	21 C3
Le Dorian	22 D5
Le Patio	23 C4
Maison Liebermann	24 D4
Oukoume Palace Intercontinental	25 A2
Somotel	26 D5

EATING

Garden Café	27 B3
Jacky Cochon	28 C2
La Dolce Vita	29 C4
Le Bateau Ivre	30 B3
Le Mississippi	31 D5
Le Phare Du Large	32 B3
M'bolo	(see 42)
Odika	33 B4

Map labels:

Voie Express (Autoroute)

To Ebando; Sablière; Tropicana (2km); Sunset Beach; Airport (3km); Cap Estérias (20km)

Carrefour d'Ambowé

Charbonnages

Haut Gué-Gué

Quartier Derrière Prison

Gué-Gué

Blvd Quaban

Blvd Léon M'ba

ATLANTIC OCEAN

Blvd Georges Pompidou (Au Bord de Mer)

Quartier Louis

Blvd Triomphal

N'Kembo

Carrefour Léon Mba

Rue Joseph Deemin

Montée Louis

Estuaire du Gabon

Ministry Buildings

Ave Jean Paul II

Blvd Bessieux

Port Môle

St Marie Cathedral

PK

To São Tomé & Principe; Cameroon

Rue Montenote

Bank

Montagne Sainte

Mont Bouet

Rue d'Alsace-Lorraine

Petit Paris

Rue Mt Bouet

Blvd de l'Indépendance (Au Bord de Mer)

Rue du Gouverneur Ballay

Presidential Palace

Complexe Omnisports (Stadium)

Bank

Cours Pasteur

Hospital

Rue Ndende

Ave Félix Éboué

Casino

R Gureau

Bank

Rue Ange M'ba

Rue Laford

Ave Col

Blvd Yves-Digo

Rue Pecqueur

Nombakélé

Rue N'Diogam

Batavia

Rue Batavia

To Le Meridien; Maison de la Presse; Chez Marie Qui Fait Chaud (1km); Michéle Marina; Train Station (8km); Owendo (9km)

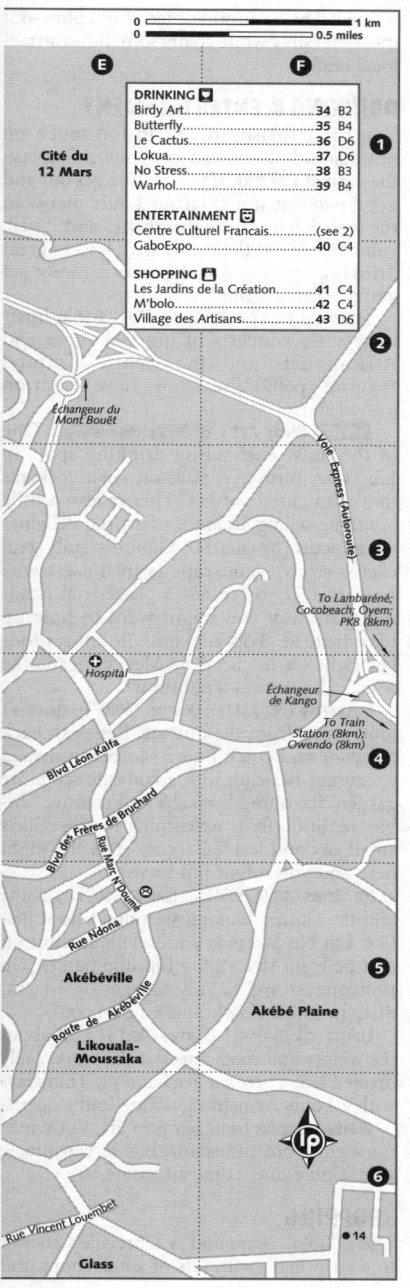

DRINKING 🍸
Birdy Art.................................34 B2
Butterfly.................................35 B4
Le Cactus...............................36 D6
Lokua....................................37 D6
No Stress...............................38 B3
Warhol..................................39 B4

ENTERTAINMENT 📽
Centre Culturel Francais............(see 2)
GaboExpo..............................40 C4

SHOPPING 🛍
Les Jardins de la Création...........41 C4
M'bolo..................................42 C4
Village des Artisans..................43 D6

is constantly aflutter but he knows everyone and everything. On Sundays the beach gets slamming; be careful on the road outside after dark as there have been some thefts. Book ahead and opt for a double if you can.

Hotel Louis (☎ 730400; r with air-con from CFA20,000; ⊠) This shabby-chic hotel is an old favourite in the Quartier Louis – it's no oil painting, but there's decent food on offer. Some of the rooms have fridges.

Le Patio (☎ 734716; s/d CFA30,000/40,000; ⊠) It's tapas before bed at this Spanish-owned hotel in the heart of the action. There's a pool table and a blossoming little patio garden that's all the more welcome after a day inhaling taxi fumes. Rooms are clean and well maintained.

Sunset Beach (☎ 06715890; s/d with air-con CFA30,000/50,000; ⊠) Libreville's most low-key midrange option overlooks the beautiful briny, away from all the action. With a Djino in hand in Sunset's sandblown garden, we couldn't be happier. A great place to lay your head after a mad day in town.

Le Lotus Bleu (☎ 778185; s/d CFA35,000/40,000; 🛜) Step into the wood-panelled lobby and you could be anywhere, from Bangkok to Birmingham; but there's a well-stocked bar, comfy (though basic) rooms, friendly service and wi-fi.

our pick **Le Dorian** (☎ 725546; r from CFA48,000; ⊠ 💻 🛜) If, on the other hand, you're travelling to remember, Dorian's your girl. Gorgeous, ultra-design-conscious rooms with Gabonese art on the walls, wi-fi access (at nearby sister hotel Le Leet), filling breakfasts and DVD rentals.

Le Meridien (☎ 766161; www.lemeridien-rendama. com; d from CFA95,000; ⊠ 💻 🏊) A full-service hotel with health club; further downtown than the Intercontinental, it has a beautiful pool area with an ocean view.

Oukoume Palace Intercontinental (☎ 732619; www. intercontinental.com; d from CFA110,000; ⊠ 💻 🛜 🏊) Everything you expect from the swish hotel chain, including a gym, wi-fi and beds comfy as clouds.

EATING
There are clusters of street food stands – among them beignet sellers known as *les bédoumeuses* – around Blvd Bessieux and on Ave John Paul II. Chez Ali (between the market and Gros Bouquet traffic light in Quarter Louis) is a backpacker favourite.

Port Môle also makes for an unlikely lunch spot during the week – there are some surprisingly good places to grab a drink or some seafood and watch the port grow.

For self-caterers, M'bolo is the (overpriced) French-style supermarket.

Le Mississippi (mains from CFA3500) *Brochettes, brochettes, brochettes.* And plenty of fresh fish too. Le Miss' is a great relaxed lunchtime spot.

Chez Marie Qui Fait Chaud (mains from CFA5000) Libreville is hot enough, but for those times when you need a home-cooked meal and a warm welcome, Marie's outdoor *maquis* (open-air restaurants) is where it's at. The *poisson braisé* (a dish of grilled fish served with vinegary onions and tomatoes) does the trick.

Odika (☎ 737313; mains from CFA6000) If you need further proof that there's more to Central African cuisine than steaming platefuls of rice and fish, eat at Odika. Unusual dishes are the speciality here, be it carpaccio, colourful vegie combinations, snake or in-house smoked fish, all served in a dining room adorned with Gabonese art.

La Dolce Vita (☎ 724238; mains from CFA6000) Ocean views and fabulous seafood make this a Libreville favourite. Great specials, even if the dishes were too big for us to finish. Sweet indeed.

Garden Café (☎ 738989; mains from CFA7000) African dishes in a buzzing garden bar with its own crazy-golf course. Beware, the Senegalese *poulet yassa* (chicken with onions and light spices) is so good you might find yourself contemplating a detour to Dakar.

our pick Jacky Cochon (☎ 731848; jackycochon@hotmail.com; mains from CFA7000) It's beside a prison, the decor is rasta chic and your food is fixed by a charmer of a long-dredded musician who's been rearing pigs for years. Pork heaven, even more so if you've flown in from a Muslim country (we had). The terrines and smoked hams are good and the wine flows.

Le Phare Du Large (☎ 730273; Au Bord de Mer; mains from CFA15,000) If you want to eat like a king – or maybe a president (the late Omar Bongo was a frequent client) – this restaurant is the epitome of fine dining. Though the plush boat-and-sea decor is a little much, the food is top-notch. The proprietor himself catches fish daily, often serving rare varieties.

Le Bateau Ivre (☎ 443487; mains from CFA16,000) The Bateau isn't drunken at all, in fact it's rather refined. This is another place for a blow-out meal – its silky white chairs sometimes attract local celebs.

DRINKING & ENTERTAINMENT

You can't splash around in too much oil nowadays, but you can certainly still splash the cash at the bar. If you wanna get out and get down, hit the Quartier Louis. Between the *trois b* bars (*biére, brochettes* and…well, you'll figure out the third) are a host of great drinking spots and clubs, which rarely get going before midnight.

The GaboExpo next to Port Môle hosts large-scale concerts of big Gabonese and African acts and the Centre Culturel Français (p609) also knows how to put on a good show.

our pick Birdy Art (☎ 06224108; Gué-Gué) One of the most enchanting drinking spots in Libreville, Birdy Art pulls off great cocktails in a manicured garden. There's also a little boutique selling all kinds of artistic delights.

Le Cactus (☎ 06251347) Gabon's only real cactus-strewn landscape is in the extreme northeast; if you're not a brave soul heading that-away you might want to hole up here instead. Top cocktails in an outdoor bar right on Au Bord de Mer, opposite the Musée des Arts et Traditions.

Butterfly (☎ 734125; Quartier Louis) It doesn't look much from the outside, but push back the door and you'll find a Moroccan-owned restaurant-bar-club with a fantastic sculpture garden, flavoured hookahs and creative ambience. Butterfly is welcoming to Libreville's small gay and lesbian scene. Start the night here and you might not leave.

No Stress (☎ 06253811; Au Bord de Mer) The name and the Gothic-looking sign don't do it justice, but No Stress is a Libreville institution that pulls in Africa's top hip-hop names. On nonconcert nights you can get down and dirty to *coupé-decalé* and a bit of soul.

Lokua (☎ 05436425; Quartier Glass) It's all about the whisky and roots music at this impeccably dressed bar. There's a live band on Thursdays with a Louis Armstrong–esque lead singer.

Warhol (Quartier Louis) No pop-art, but winking lights, fun tunes and big-screen music vids. Come one, come all, come late.

SHOPPING

The M'bolo compound is Libreville's answer to a strip mall, with lots of small shops and one Walmart-esque hypermarket (M'bolo itself) selling food and just about anything else you might need. Next door, M'bolo Disco sells local tunes. You'll also find the French supermarket Géant.

At the **Village des Artisans** (Ave Col Parant) most of the goods (and the merchants) are imports. Try **Les Jardins de la Création** (Quartier Louis) for (expensive) Gabonese art.

GETTING THERE & AWAY
Air
Air Service (☎ 747118, 747119), **SCD** (☎ 07949495) and the less reliable **La Nationale** (☎ 06669077/88) fly to Port-Gentil, Koulamoutou, Franceville, Mouila, Oyem, Gamba and Makokou. Flights to cities in nearby countries include Douala (Cameroon), Pointe-Noire and Brazzaville (Congo), and São Tomé (São Tomé & Príncipe). See p619 for more.

Local Transport
All *taxis-brousses* (bush taxis) leave from PK8 (pronounced peek-a-weet), 8km out of Libreville. Overpacked minibuses, 4WDs, pick-ups and *clandos* (cars that act as long-distance taxis) can be found daily for most destinations; early morning is the best time to show up. You can pay double to secure yourself a seat in the front alone (otherwise two share it). From Libreville, you can catch local transport to Lambaréné (CFA5000, four hours), Cocobeach (CFA4000, two to three hours) and Oyem (CFA20,000, 11 hours).

Train
Many eastern destinations are best reached by the Transgabonaise train that leaves 8km south of the city, in Owendo. It's a comfortable ride, but expect delays and breakdowns; overpriced food is available. Trains run to Lopé (the town at the entrance to the reserve; 1st/2nd class CFA22,500/16,000, six to eight hours) and Franceville (1st/2nd CFA50,000/33,000, 11 hours).

GETTING AROUND
If you pick up a cab at the airport, be prepared to pay at least CFA2000, even if your hotel is just across the road.

The fancier hotels have airport shuttle buses. Shared taxis on predetermined routes cost CFA200. *Une course* in a private hire should be CFA1000 for a short hop, though rates differ depending on the mood of the driver and your bargaining skills. You'll pay more at night.

AROUND LIBREVILLE

POINT DENIS
Like Kokrobite to Accra, in Ghana, and Saly to Dakar, in Senegal, Point Denis is Libreville's easy weekender. A shuttle boat from Port Môle (CFA8000) and Michéle Marina (CFA10,000) deposits visitors on the pretty peninsula every weekend morning. Stick to the beaten track and you'll find boutique hotels, lazy restaurants and (noisy) watersports; walk to the Atlantic side of the point and you'll chance upon miles of empty white sand, the nesting ground of sea turtles from November to January.

A wise old elephant (OK, not a real one) will greet you at **Assala Lodge** (☎ 07376969, assalalodge@inet.ga; r from CFA45,000), the doyenne of Point Denis. The Kenyan-safari-lodge theme continues inside the hotel, decked out with canopy beds and colourful art. Down the road, **La Maringa** (☎ 732677) has cute villas from CFA35,000. Further down the coast is the beautiful, isolated **Phare de Ngombé** (☎ 06629999), a lodge situated at the old lighthouse in front of Pongara forest. A Saturday to Sunday visit, including forest excursions, turtle watching and fishing, costs around CFA170,000 per person.

COCOBEACH
Though it sounds like the stuff of honeymoon fantasies, Cocobeach won't have you getting down on one knee in a hurry. But if it's adventure you're after, this dusty little seaside town is a *pirogue* (traditional canoe; CFA5000) trip away from Equatorial Guinea's Cogo, the gateway to handsome Isla Corisco (p601; now we're talking). You can bed down for the night at the basic **Motel Esperance** (r from CFA11,000) down the road from the local Sedoc branch, which will grant you an exit stamp in your passport. Get a visa beforehand or be prepared for all hell to break loose at the border. There's a shady terrace at Chez Tante Mado on the main street if you want to fill up on reasonably priced food before leaving the country.

Shared taxis leave from PK8 in Libreville and cost CFA4000 for a space in a packed vehicle.

GABON

NORTHERN GABON

The rough and rugged north, with its big blue skies (you won't find any 'scrapers here) and rainforests so dense and humid that they glisten like sparkling emerald velvet, is the last word in off-the-beaten-trackness.

OYEM

pop 30,000

Oyem, Oyem, the town of fat tree trunks, apricot-coloured lanes and all manner of secrets. Though it's the hearth of Fang culture, few travellers make it here, largely because it's suffered from bad publicity – a rabies outbreak in 2004 and the unsolved murder of a peace corps volunteer in the 1990s. But if you do take the road less travelled you'll find a pleasant little lakeside town surrounded by forest villages. It's also a good spot to cross into Equatorial Guinea and Cameroon.

The best place to stay is undoubtedly the **Hotel Mvet Palace** (☎ 986172; r from CFA12,000; ❄).

There are buses from Libreville (in addition to the *taxis-brousses*) that leave from PK8 (CFA10,000, around 11 hours) with a stop at Ndjolé. By plane from Libreville to Oyem costs around CFA40,000 one way and takes just under an hour.

Taxis-brousses leave from Oyem to Mongomo in Equatorial Guinea daily; you must already have a visa. It takes about 30 minutes to the border, where you can switch cabs on the EG side.

MINKÉBÉ NATIONAL PARK

Shingled with cacti and rock-dome *inselbergs*, Minkébé is one of Gabon's most inaccessible parks, the home of forest elephants and isolated ethnic groups. Conservation programs are in place through the **WWF** (☎ 730028), which is trying to boost the income of villagers through artistic endeavours. Though travel here is tricky, it's not an impossibility. You can contact the WWF or head to **Bitam**, a little rubber town not far from the park. There, bed down at **Hotel des Voyageurs** (☎ 968020; r from CFA6000), where staff can help you get deeper into the region. From Bitam you can also find shared-taxi rides to the Cameroon border (CFA2500 to river border, CFA2500 for the *pirogue* across). Don't forget to stop at immigration and get an exit stamp or you'll be turned back at the border checkpoint.

SOUTHERN GABON

PORT-GENTIL

pop 80,000

Your first thought after stepping off the boat in Port-Gentil is that it doesn't feel very welcoming or kind. But then, some who know Libreville will tell you that Gabonese cities don't always live up to their French names. Most travellers don't make it to Gabon's second city, named for former French administrator Émile Gentil, but if you do swing by you'll gain an insight into Gabon's economy and its driving force. The centre of the petroleum industry is swiftly becoming the centre of the country's nascent shipping industry.

The centre of town is of course the port, and Gentil stretches northeastwards from there. There's a shortage of good budget accommodation; a midrange bet is the **Hirondelle** (☎ 551782; r from CFA28,000), off Ave Savorgnan. It has bungalows and a tidy garden area. For a taste of Port-Gentil's high life, the **Hotel du Parc** (☎ 552528; r from 50,000; ☎) is down by the new port. There's every comfort, including wi-fi and even a mini zoo.

Á Table and the busier Chez Fatou, opposite the Toyota building downtown, serve platefuls of good-value Gabonese food. For a fancier dinner, try Amiral, a short walk from the Hirondelle. In the Cap Lopez area of town, Le Petrolier is Port-Gentil's best seafood spot. After midnight, the clubs Safari and Pacha (yes, really) are awash with industrial types.

Sonaga (☎ 564334) runs boats from Libreville to Gentil three times a week. A one-way trip in 2nd-class is CFA19,000. You can also fly with the major air carriers (see p620).

LAMBARÉNÉ

pop 20,000

'Everyone has his Lambaréné', Nobel winner Albert Schweitzer said. This, then, is his, with its glossy lakes and foliage and ingrained sweetness. The town is somehow kinder and gentler than the rest of Gabon, as if the profound humanitarian efforts of Schweitzer ('the greatest man in the world' said *Life* magazine in 1947) changed the character of the land. And his legacy is indeed felt everywhere, from the wonderful, still-operational hospital (founded in 1924 to treat lepers) to the volunteer-staffed lab that researches malaria and other tropical diseases. At the **hospital museum** (admission CFA5000) you can see photos, paintings and the impeccably arranged house and artefacts of Schweitzer and his wife.

The town is divided into three areas spanning the river, quite close to each other. The near bank has the **Schweitzer hospital** grounds; across the bridge is the island with the main **markets** and town; across another bridge is the far bank of **Quartier Isaac**, where you'll find nightlife and action. Short taxi rides around town vary from CFA300 to CFA800 depending on how many bridge crossings you make.

Explore the many **lakes** by *pirogue*, arranged at the port in town, through the Ogooué Palace. A long boat trip will cost around CFA40,000 but can be split with many people.

Sleeping & Eating

Mission Soeurs de l'Immaculée Conception (☎ 581073; d CFA6000-10,000) This place won't, in the words of Schweitzer, 'let your soul have no Sunday'. It's staffed by adorable nuns who make you feel as if you've been spirited into *The Sound of Music*. The grounds are gorgeous, there's a kitchen available for use, and the fan-cooled rooms are clean and have mozzie nets.

Banana's (☎ 581228; r with fan/air-con CFA10,000/ 13,000) If you're looking for a simple place in the Quartier Isaac to lay your head and fill your belly, Banana's might be your Lambaréné. It's diagonally opposite the main supermarket.

Hotel Schweitzer (☎ 581033, 581145; r CFA18,000) It's eccentric in every way, but has spacious rooms and plenty of old-school style. 'There are two means of refuge from the miseries of life – music and cats', Schweitzer said. If you're going to find those anywhere in Lambaréné, it's here.

Hotel Ogooué Palace (☎ 581864; www.actionweb -gabon.com; r CFA30,000-60,000) Lambaréné's fancy-pants option, the gardens here are manicured and there are pretty bungalows, a tennis court and a mini zoo. Though it can feel a bit like a holiday camp, it's a popular choice.

At night fish and *brochette* stands line the streets, or try the low-key La Pleide, which does a good *soupe de poissons*. If you're looking for something more tantalising try the French cuisine of Petit Detour or cross the bridge to Les Délices du Lac, which has its own vegie garden outside town. The Ogooué Patisserie churns out some mighty fine *pains au chocolat*.

And what might Schweitzer make of Lambaréné's nightlife? 'Happiness' he said (yes, one last quote, indulge us) 'is nothing more than good health and poor memory'. Quartier Issac's Padouk (*coupé-decalé* and *zouk* beats with a CFA3000 cover charge) and its neighbour Soweto will speed one of the two.

Getting There & Away

If you beat the Libreville traffic, you can be in Lambaréné in four hours in a shared taxi (around CFA5000).

LOANGO NATIONAL PARK

The conservationist Mike Fay called Loango 'Africa's last eden'. Here, warm streams crisscross pockets of thick forest and salty savannah. Established by the late Omar Bongo in 2002, Loango is that rare thing, a national park that has swallowed a lagoon (the Iguéla), and it's teeming with animal action. Perhaps best known for its mythically surfing hippos (see the boxed text, p616), you'll also find the largest concentration and variety of whales and dolphins, elephants wandering white-sand beaches and an assortment of rare land mammals cavorting in the savannah. If your pockets can take it, Loango is one of the best wildlife-watching destinations on the planet.

Africa's Eden (☎ 07127152; www.africas-eden.com), formerly Operation Loango, is the only show in town to visit the northern end of the park. Gabon's premier high-end ecotourist destination uses tourist dollars to support conservation efforts. Whale, crocodile and turtle studies and a gorilla habituation project are in progress, while the luxury ecolodge and satellite camps host tourists. At Iguéla, the base camp, everything is regally appointed and finely delivered, with a grand price tag to match (prices start at US$400 per person without drinks). There are several equally stunning satellite camps in the varied environments: St Catherine's, on the beach; Akaka, where animals roam; Evengue ('gorilla island'), where gorilla rehabilitation is underway; and Tassi, in the savannah and coastal grasslands. Activities include whale-watching trips, savannah and lagoon tours, 13-day gorilla odysseys and visits to Mission Sainte Anne, where Gustave Eiffel's prefab iron church is still in use.

All logistics and travel arrangements are made through **SCD Aviation** (☎ 564100, 885666; scd-aviation@inet.ga, reservation-iguela@inet.ga) in Libreville.

GABON

SURFING HIPPOS

Though it hardly seems credible – a fantasy that belongs in the realm of children's novels, unicorns and flying carpets – Gabon's surfing hippos have been making waves around the world since their hobby was outed by conservationist Mike Fay in the 1990s. Unlike human surfers, the two-ton creatures are hardly a picture of grace as they frolic among the waves, but surf they do: wading into the ocean and opening their legs to catch the swell. It's thought that the pastime is a relatively new adrenalin fix in hippo circles; their name, after all, comes from the Greek for 'river horse' and many zoologists believe they prefer freshwater to seawater. Still, who can blame them for seeking a bit of extra excitement? Watch the action at Loango National Park (p615).

GAMBA & SETTÉ CAMA

Though it hurts to be this close to Loango and not have the cash to fully explore it, Gamba and its head-turning neighbour Setté are still sweet commiseration prizes for those who don't. The former is a simple fishing town with cheap accommodation; the latter an enchanting traveller respite not far from sandy beaches decorated with the footprints of elephants.

If you choose to sleep in cheaper Gamba, try the pleasant **Hotel Guiema** (☎ 07941674; r from CFA15,000), affiliated with the Auberge Missala restaurant-cybercafe in town. Exploring Loango is possible from here if you have a little time to play with and are willing to take the initiative. Otherwise, Setté Cama is a better base. There, **Case Abietu** (☎ 07737576, 07141718; gambareservations@yahoo.fr) offers six fan-cooled bedrooms, a lounge, a small library, and a delightful terrace overlooking the lagoon. Villagers prepare traditional meals and act as ecoguides. The profits of the all-inclusive (minus drinks) tariff (from CFA60,000 per person per night) go to set up community projects. The price does not include travel to Loango but a visit can easily be set up from here.

A picture in wood and tumbling bougainvillea, **Setté Cama Safaris** (☎ 262309; r incl park entry & dinner from CFA90,000) has pricier villas and a great little restaurant that does top-notch fish. Nearby, **Missala Lodge** (☎ 500454; missalalodge@ yahoo.fr; d from CFA35,000, daily excursions from CFA100,000) is a magical spot, with mahogany bungalows, that specialises in more original excursions, including fishing for what looked, to us, like the biggest tarpon in the world.

Setté is accessible from Gamba, which, in turn, is a long, bumpy haul in a pick-up from the capital. The trip can often be broken into two days, with a stay in forest-hugging Tchibanga at the welcoming **Hotel Modibotie** (☎ 06042049; r from

CFA25,000). In total, the trip by *taxi-brousse* will cost you about CFA35,000 (total driving time is 10 to 16 hours depending on road conditions and waiting around for transport). You'll need to change cars at Gamba, a couple of hours from Setté Cama on a good day.

Air Service (☎ 747118, 747119) flies from Libreville to Gamba six times a week, and clients of Case Abietu get a 15% discount, making the cost around CFA130,000 return.

MAYUMBA NATIONAL PARK

Closer to the Republic of Congo than to Libreville, Mayumba feels like the edge of the earth. No wonder expats whisper about it – the **national park** (www.mayumbanationalpark.com) is the domain of barnacled whales and shy sea turtles, and the land, if you listen to the locals, is hushed by the spirits of ancestors.

Safari Club (☎ 07426355; r from CFA15,000) is part fishing club, part hotel; it's dressed like a Kenyan beach lodge – all wood and grassy slopes. The new kid in town, **Mbidia Koukou** (07488276; r CFA15,000) looks a bit like a surf camp. A cheaper, though less charming, bet is the central **Motel Mayeye Foutou** (☎ 07283358; r around CFA12,000), which is owned by the mayor. Chez Mamissa is the hottest place in town to eat, run by the fabulous Mamissa herself, who is as good in the kitchen as she is at championing the education of local girls.

If you're not coming from Gamba, fly here if you can (the road takes forever – bank on at least a day and a half from Libreville). **La Nationale** (☎ 06669077, 031903) offers one-way trips from Libreville from CFA70,000. From Gamba, there are direct *taxis-brousses* on Saturdays (CFA15,000); otherwise you'll have to negotiate two ferry crossings. Flights from Gamba to Mayumba start at CFA60,000 with La Nationale.

People travelling by *taxi-brousse* from Libreville often break up the long travel with a stopover in Tchibanga. There are also flights to Tchibanga and Gamba where you can then hop on a *taxi-brousse* to Mayumba. The park's excellent website has many details to navigate the long journey there.

EASTERN GABON

RÉSERVE DE LA LOPÉ

Smack bang on the equator, Gabon's calling card doesn't disappoint. Undulating hills meet scrubby patches of savannah and enclaves of rainforest so thick and so lush that all you see is leaves, leaves, leaves, even when you shut your eyes in bed at night. Rest well and the next morning your peepers can feast on elephants, buffalo, gorillas and some of the biggest mandrill troupes in the world. There are vehicle and foot safaris (from CFA5000) on offer and there's an eco-museum near the park entrance.

Lopé Hotel (☎ 778561; r from CFA30,000; 🏊) runs the show here. Bungalows of varying sizes offer astounding views of the surrounding hills and savannah. You'll often have the grounds – including the bar, restaurant and pool – to yourself. Budget travellers can skip out on high costs by staying at **Case de Passage** (☎ 07696596; r around CFA15,000) on the edge of the park, run by a ranger. There's also **Chez Jules** (☎ 07871827; r from CFA5000) in the village. Rooms are basic, but waking up in the centre of rural daily life is well worth it. *Brochettes* and beer are found across the road at the Cameroonian hangout of El Dorado. Don't walk around at night though; you might get charged by a herd of buffalo. Both Case and Jules' place can sort you out for cheaper ecotreks.

The train from Libreville takes about four hours. Lopé Hotel vehicles meet the train. Otherwise, walk to Chez Jules down the road or charter a cab to Case de Passage.

MIKONGO

Mikongo (☎ 07358023) is a forest camp set up by the Zoological Society of London. Conditions are simple and there's no hot water, but the likelihood of a gorilla sighting more than makes up for it. Accommodation in huts costs CFA25,000, with hikes starting at around the same price. The adjacent conservation centre works purely on gorilla projects, largely with local guides and workforce.

IVINDO NATIONAL PARK

Langoué Bai, in the dense, tropical Ivindo National Park (3000 sq km), is perhaps the *pièce de résistance* of all the Gabonese eco-destinations, presenting the rare opportunity to view forest animals undisturbed in their own environment. The Bai, a Pygmy word for a marshy clearing in the forest, serves as a source of minerals for the animals and acts as a magnet for large numbers of forest elephants, western lowland gorillas, sitatungas, buffalo, monkeys and rare bird species. A Wildlife Conservation Society–built research station and ecocamp near the clearing allow visitors to easily view the wildlife.

All-inclusive stays at the stunning, ecologically friendly base camp, designed to reduce human impact on the environment (composting toilets, solar energy, no chemicals), are pricey – US$315 per night – but worth it.

Arrangements to get to the Bai must be made well in advance through travel agents in Libreville (p609).

MAKOKOU & KONGOU FALLS

Gabon's answer to Niagara is the gushing falls at Kongou, and Makokou – the small capital of the Ogooué-Ivindo region – is their gateway. But there's been trouble in paradise: a deal with Chinese investors to turn the falls into a hydro dam and milk the iron-ore mines at nearby Bélinga has angered conservationists and locals, who say wildlife and the Congo basin would be seriously threatened. At the time of research, the deal was on hold and you could still visit the falls, but check before you visit, with Joseph at the excellent **Fondation Internationale Gabon Eco-tourisme** (FIGET; ☎ 07905513, 06068247; www.trusttheforest.org). FIGET organises camping trips into the rainforest and to the falls, *pirogue* excursions and a long list of other activities, all at fairly reasonable prices. You can also negotiate a bed for the night.

From Libreville, take the train to Booué and then a *taxi-brousse* to Makokou. Flights to Makokou's small airport go a few times a week. It's possible to then go on to the Republic of Congo via Mékambo, but the road is terrible. Ask around for a *taxi-brousse*.

FRANCEVILLE & AROUND
pop 41,000

Birthplace of the late Omar Bongo – check out the statue of him in town – Gabon's third city, Franceville, is a provincial stop that makes a nice change if you need a break from jungles and beaches (as if you do...). It's well worth a couple of days of your time, especially as the jumping-off point for the amazing sights around the stunning Batéké Plateau.

On the Poto-Poto roundabout, **Bien et Bien** (☎ 06216572; r CFA12,000) is, well, *bien*. If luxury's calling you, the top-notch **Poubara Hotel** (☎ 671374, 07849172; hotel_poubara@hotmail.com; r US$50-200; 🏊) has more amenities than anyone would ever need, including a beautiful pool and a popular Sunday brunch. Also along the main drag are some great places to eat, namely 5éme Dimension, Bord de Mer and the curiously named Les Braises du Couloir de la Mort.

Off the main drag is Afrikando, with occasional live music, and down by the river is Buké-Buké, a favourite with young researchers from the primate research station of Centre International de Recherches Medicales de Franceville (CIRMF). Shake it at the Cristal or the upscale disco at the Poubara.

On the road to Kessala you can stop at the tiny town of **Ossele** to trek for animals with Hilaire, who is often referred to as a forest magician – an ex-hunter with astounding knowledge of plants and animals. To arrange a meeting with him, find his sister Romaine in Franceville at the Musuku Hotel. East of Franceville the savannah rises up into the **Batéké Plateau**, a dry, cool and flat stretch of land that extends south and east into Congo, encompassing the spectacular **Cirque de Léconi**, a deep, circular, red-rock canyon of loose sand. Locals say spirits lie within. Also in the area (but harder to find) are some spectacular green-and-white canyons.

After trips into the canyons, you can bathe in the endlessly clear L'Eau Claire at **Abouyi** village, just five minutes from Léconi towards Franceville. Infrequent *taxis-brousses* go to Léconi from Franceville, but a 4WD is necessary to get to the cirque. It's possible to camp overnight if you have your own equipment.

GABON DIRECTORY

ACCOMMODATION

Gabon's no bargain destination, and hotels will take the biggest bite out of your budget. Most towns have cheap and basic convent hotels – they're generally your best bet if you're pinching pennies. In remote villages, if you greet the chief and bring a small gift you'll likely be welcome to stay in a hut.

ACTIVITIES

This country isn't really set up for the independent traveller and you'll have an easier time if you book tours through the travel agents in Libreville (p609). Waiting can be involved, so start early in making plans for forest hikes or trips out to the national parks.

BUSINESS HOURS

Shops and businesses open early and close for siesta between noon and 1pm and 3pm. Most shops are closed on Sundays, with some banks opening Saturday mornings but not afternoons.

DANGERS & ANNOYANCES

Treat Libreville like any big city with its fair share of crime. Police will hassle you, so always carry your passport or a copy (and a copy of your visa).

The dreaded *fourous* (tiny insects) will leave red splotches, but won't hurt until a few days into the forest when infernal itchiness ensues. Insect repellent is a must, and calamine lotion will ease the itchiness. The terrible roads, crazy drunk drivers and huge trucks carrying unsecured loads of old-growth forest are probably the biggest dangers in the country.

EMBASSIES & CONSULATES

Most embassies are open from 8am to noon and 2.30pm to 5pm, but call before showing up as some are often unstaffed. Countries with diplomatic representation in Libreville include the following:

Cameroon (Map pp610-11; ☎ 732800; Face Université)
Congo (Map pp610-11; ☎ 730062; Batterie IV)
Equatorial Guinea (Map pp610-11; ☎ 732523; Haut Gué-Gué)
France (Map pp610-11; ☎ 761056; Au Bord de Mer)
Germany (☎ 760188; Immeuble 'Les Frangipaniers')
Nigeria (Map pp610-11; ☎ 732203; Blvd Léon M'ba)
São Tomé & Príncipe (Map pp610-11; ☎ 721527; Au Bord de Mer)
South Africa (Map pp610-11; ☎ 774530; Immeuble des Arcades)
USA (Map pp610-11; ☎ 762003; Au Bord de Mer)

EMERGENCIES

Ambulance ☎ 1300 (from landline only, goes direct to Libreville's Polyclinique El Rapha, who can send transport within the capital)
Fire ☎ 18
Police ☎ 177

HOLIDAYS

As well as religious holidays listed in the Africa Directory (p1140), the following are the principal public holidays in Gabon:

New Year's Day 1 January
Renovation Day 12 March
Labour Day 1 May
Independence Day 17 August
All Saints' Day 1 November

MAPS

There is an old but detailed road map of Gabon available at **Maison de la Presse** (off Map pp610-11; ☎ 772695), in Libreville, for an astonishing sum. Better to buy in Europe or the US, in good travel bookstores.

MONEY

A word of warning – money seems to fall out of your pockets in Gabon: to get anywhere or do pretty much anything you'll be spending it like nobody's business.

ATMs in Libreville will only work with Visa cards, and credit cards are only accepted at top-end hotels. There is a national change shortage so ask for small notes wherever possible.

TELEPHONE

Mobile phones are used more widely than landlines, although they can be unreliable outside of Libreville. You can buy a CST-Mobicell SIM card cheaply and quickly in most places, including small towns, and recharge cards are available pretty much everywhere.

TOURIST INFORMATION

Major travel agents and conservation organisations will have information on the various sights in country. See p609 for contact details of some organisations in Libreville.

VISAS

Visas are required by all travellers and must be obtained before arrival; they are not available at the airport or at border crossings. Getting a visa for Gabon is notoriously difficult and expensive. From countries outside Africa it can cost more than US$100. Unless you're flying straight to Libreville from Europe, it is best to apply for one at the Gabonese embassy in a nearby African country, where it only takes a couple of days and costs around US$50.

Gabon is one of the few countries that may insist on seeing an outgoing plane ticket or other proof of onward travel before issuing a visa, as well as an invitation from a hotel or company in Gabon.

At the **Directeur Genérale de la Documentation** (Map pp610-11; ☎ 762424; PK5, Libreville; ☼ 8am-3pm Mon-Fri), formerly known as Sedoc, you can obtain visa extensions.

Visas for Onward Travel

Thirty-day visas for Cameroon (48 hours, US$60), the Republic of Congo (48 hours, US$120), Equatorial Guinea (three days, US$80) and São Tomé & Príncipe (48 hours, US$45) can be picked up in Libreville. See opposite for embassy information.

WOMEN TRAVELLERS

Equality is on the up in Gabon, but in rural areas a woman without a man is still generally viewed as a let-down to her family – either that or a strange curiosity. Though passive in many areas of life, the Gabonese are generally much more active about seeking couple-dom than most Europeans and Americans. Bring a photo of a fictitious husband (Johnny Depp will do) if you're concerned about unwelcome advances.

TRANSPORT IN GABON

GETTING THERE & AWAY
Air

Royal Air Maroc (www.royalairmaroc.com) flies from Paris (France) to Libreville with a stop in Casablanca (Morocco) and sometimes a change in Douala (Cameroon). **Air France** (www.airfrance.com) flies straight from Paris to Libreville. Libreville is also linked to most major cities in West and Central Africa by a rotating cast of regional airlines. Libreville's Léon M'Ba Airport has flights to and from Abidjan (Côte d'Ivoire), Brazzaville (Congo), Douala (Cameroon), Lagos (Nigeria),

---

PRACTICALITIES

- Electricity is 220v AC, 50Hz (European-style two-round-pin plugs).
- Weights, measures and road distances use the metric system.
- *L'Union* is one of the biggest national papers. Radio France International broadcasts at 104FM.

GABON

São Tomé town (São Tomé & Príncipe), Johannesburg (South Africa) and sometimes Malabo (Equatorial Guinea), among others.

Land
CAMEROON
Travellers to and from Cameroon cross at the Ntem River between Bitam (Gabon) and Ambam (Cameroon). From the town of Ebolowa in Cameroon there's a regular bus service to Yaoundé and Douala. Visas can be purchased at the border.

EQUATORIAL GUINEA
Crossings can be made at Cocobeach (Gabon) by *pirogue* to Cogo and Acalayong (Equatorial Guinea), and via Oyem and Bitam (Gabon) to either Mongomo or Ebebiyin (Equatorial Guinea). Taxis leave daily from all towns and the ride to Bata is around four hours with the new roads. You must have a visa before travelling.

REPUBLIC OF CONGO
The main crossing to Congo is between Leconi (the official, but not geographical border – don't leave here without getting your exit stamp) and Oyo. There's no public transport along most of this route and few cargo trucks, so it can take several days and involve more than a few police checkpoints. There's another crossing at N'Dendé (Gabon) and Doussala (Congo), from where you head to Loubomo to connect with the Pointe-Noire–Brazzaville railway. The border with Congo in eastern Gabon is easily crossable; you can sometimes cross without having papers checked. That, though it sounds Africa romantic, is almost always a bad thing – someone will spot your stampless passport and you'll pay heavily.

Sea
SEM (☎ 773141) plies the seas between Port Môle and São Tomé (one way from CFA60,000, two days). There are occasional cargo ships to and from Cotonou (Benin), São Tomé & Príncipe and Cameroon. Expect long, uncomfortable journeys and schedules that shift without warning. Ask for details at the Maritime Express office at Port Môle in Libreville.

GETTING AROUND
Air
Gabon's flying machines include:
Air Service (☎ 747118, 747119)
La Nationale (☎ 06669077, 031903)
SCD Aviation (☎ 07949495, 564100; scd-aviation@inet.ga)

Boat
There are **Sonaga** (☎ 05938361) passenger boats between Lambaréné and Port-Gentil (about five hours) and between Port-Gentil and Libreville (CFA19,000, about three hours). Inquire at the Maritime Express office on Port Môle.

Car & Motorcycle
Car hire is always more expensive than renting a vehicle with a driver, but **Europcar** (☎ 745845), **Hertz** (☎ 732011) and **Avis** (☎ 724251) have offices at the airport.

Local Transport
Comically overpacked *taxis-brousses*, minibuses and pick-up trucks are options for travelling outside Libreville.

Train
Taking the Transgabonaise train line that crosses the country is a cheaper, faster and far more comfortable option than taking a *taxi-brousse*.

São Tomé & Príncipe

If you adore quietude, take a trip to São Tomé & Príncipe, Africa's second-smallest country. These two tiny volcanic bumps anchored off the Gabonese coast easily win the hearts of foreigners with their Portuguese-Creole flavour and relaxed vibes, and it won't take too long before you're infected with the pervasive *leve leve* (which loosely means 'take it easy') mood.

The sublime laid-back tempo is enhanced by a wealth of natural attractions. These green specks offer all that an island getaway should: miles of heartbreakingly perfect palm-fringed beaches, huge swathes of emerald rainforest, soaring volcanic peaks, lush valleys suspended in time, and cute-as-can-be fishing villages. The birdlife is excellent, and endemic plants (especially orchids) plentiful. In season, turtle- and whale-watching opportunities abound.

But it's not all about nature and cool vibes. This two-island nation has its cultural gems as well, with a surprising number of heritage buildings dating back to the colonial era, including impressive *roças* (plantation estates) that can be visited. And bons viveurs can sip some of the world's best coffee, feast on fresh fruits and seafood, and delight in gourmet chocolate.

Tourism is still low-key and is being developed in a carefully controlled, ecologically minded way. There are no tacky resorts, just a number of locally run, enticing, nature-oriented lodges and hotels – no wonder that some have already dubbed São Tomé & Príncipe the 'Galápagos of Africa'.

FAST FACTS

- **Area** 1000 sq km
- **ATMs** There are no ATMs; come with cash
- **Borders** Gabon lies 300km to the east
- **Budget** €70 per day
- **Capital** São Tomé
- **Languages** Portuguese, Portuguese-based Creole
- **Money** Dobra; US$1 = 16,624Db, €1 = 24,356Db
- **Population** 200,000
- **Seasons** Dry (January to February and June to September), wet (October to December and March to May)
- **Telephone** Country code ☎ 239; international access code ☎ 00
- **Time** GMT/UTC
- **Visa** Required by all; costs €40 to €50

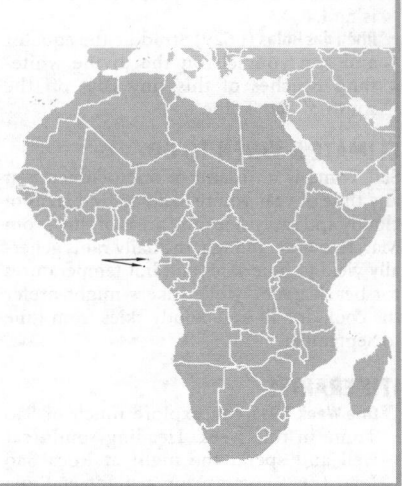

HOW MUCH?

- **A day's jungle trek** US$44
- **Cup of good coffee** US$0.60
- **One night in a plantation estate** US$44
- **Mangrove tour** US$14.50
- **Fresh grilled con-con fish** US$5.80

LP INDEX

- **1L petrol** US$1.50
- **1.5L bottled water** US$1.20
- **Bottle of Creoula beer** US$0.90
- **Souvenir T-shirt** US$14.50
- **Grilled corn** US$0.70

HIGHLIGHTS

- **São Tomé town** (p624) Wander amid the faded colonial buildings of this charming capital town.
- **Roça São João** (p629) Feast on gourmet eats and stay the night in this ethereal, rejuvenated plantation estate.
- **Banana Beach** (p630) Dive into the crystal-clear waters of this deserted beach, one of many ringing the island of Príncipe.
- **Praia Jalé** (p629) Witness the nesting sea turtles in this ecotourism haven, located at the southernmost point of São Tomé island.
- **Ilhéu das Rolas** (p629) Straddle the equator and sun yourself on the divine white-sand beaches of this tiny islet off the south of São Tomé.

CLIMATE & WHEN TO GO

São Tomé is an island of microclimates; at any time of year you're likely to find areas of cloudy and rainy skies and areas of sun. From March to May, though, the daily rains generally yield to blue skies and hot temperatures for beach goers, while hikers might prefer the cool, dry air and cloudy skies from June to September.

ITINERARIES

- **One Week** You can explore much of São Tomé in one week. Heading south, eat well and spend the night at Roça São João (p629), camp for a night at Praia Jalé (p629), take in a mangrove tour and then jump on the boat to Ilhéu das Rolas (p629) for a night or two. Head back to São Tomé town and day hike in the forest, stay the night at Roça Bombaim (p629), and then head north to hit Neves (p628) for crabs and a night at Roça Monteforte (p628).
- **Two Weeks** Follow the above itinerary and then fly on to Príncipe (p630) and chill out for at least a week in a deserted island paradise.

HISTORY

Before being 'discovered' and colonised by the Portuguese during the late 15th century, the islands of São Tomé & Príncipe were comprised of rainforests dense with vegetation and birdlife, but, most likely, no people (though there is a legend that present-day Angolares were really the first inhabitants of the land). The islands' volcanic soil proved good for cultivation, and, under Portuguese rule, by the mid-16th century the islands were the foremost exporter of sugar, though the labour-intensive process required increasing numbers of slaves from Africa. When the price of sugar fell and slave labour proved difficult to control, the islands increasingly looked towards the slave trade to bolster the economy, becoming an important weigh station for slave ships heading from Africa to Brazil. In the 19th century two new cash crops, coffee and cocoa, overtook the old sugar plantations. By the early 20th century São Tomé was one of the world's largest producers of cocoa.

In 1876 slavery was outlawed, but was simply replaced with a similar system of forced labour for low wages. Contract workers came in from Mozambique, Cape Verde and other parts of the Portuguese empire. During these times there were frequent uprisings and revolts, often brutally ended by the Portuguese. In 1953 the Massacre of Batepá, in which many Africans were killed by Portuguese troops, sparked a fully fledged independence movement in the country. Portugal held on, however, until the fall of its fascist government in 1974, after which it got out of its colonies in a hurry. São Tomé & Príncipe achieved its independence on 12 July 1975.

The Portuguese exodus left the country with virtually no skilled labour, an illiteracy

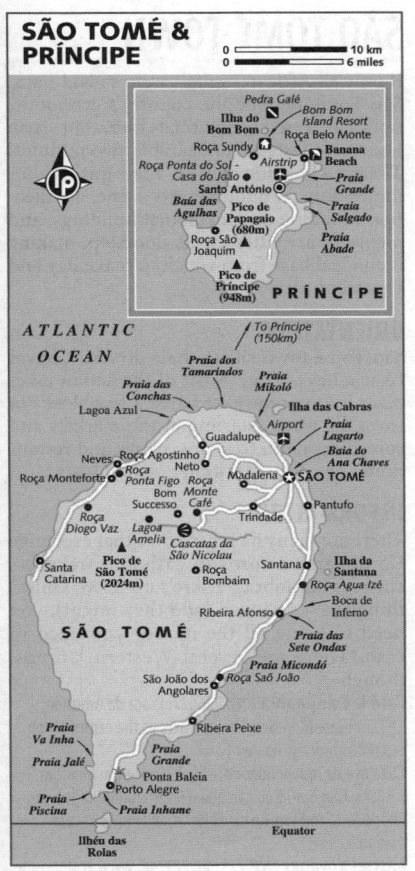

rate of 90%, only one doctor and many abandoned cocoa plantations. The majority of the plantations were nationalised four months after independence.

The country remained closely aligned with Angola, Cuba and communist Eastern Europe until the demise of the Soviet Union, when São Toméans began to demand multiparty democracy. The first multiparty elections were held in early 1991, and led to the inauguration of the previously exiled Miguel Trovoada as the new president in April of that year.

São Tomé & Príncipe Today

Elections in 2001 brought Fradique de Menezes to power. De Menezes pledged to use revenues from increased tourism and exploitation of the country's newly discovered offshore oilfields to improve the standard of living and modernise the islands' infrastructure. Grand changes seemed imminent. But complications with extracting the oil, in addition to possible overestimations of the oil deposits, have delayed economic progress, and there is a palpable growing restlessness in the deeply indebted nation. A brief and bloodless coup attempt was peacefully resolved in 2003 while the president was out of the country. De Menezes was re-elected in 2006 in internationally observed, peaceful elections.

CULTURE

Leve leve (taking it easy) is the name of the game in São Tomé. Island life is slow and there's no use in getting all fussed up about anything. This is as evident in daily life as it is in the islands' politics. During the 2006 elections, disruptions were rare. The very few villages that protested did so by politely turning vote staff away from their polling stations, saying essentially 'no water, no electricity, no votes, thank you'.

A recent influx of young repatriates from Portugal determined to make something good happen here has brought a new energy to the islands.

Outside the capital most São Toméans still live very simple island lives, with agriculture and fishing being the main occupations. In the morning the boats come in and fish are distributed, the market bustles late morning, a siesta is taken to avoid the afternoon heat and then it's time to drink some imported boxes of *vinho*. In the evening, people gather wherever there's a TV set and a generator, or a full deck of cards.

São Toméans are a mixed bunch, consisting of Mestiços, mixed-blood descendants of Portuguese colonists and African slaves; Angolares, reputedly descendants of Angolan slaves who survived a 1540 shipwreck and now earn their livelihood fishing; Forros, descendants of freed slaves; Tongas, the children of Serviçais (contract labourers from Angola, Mozambique and Cape Verde when slavery was 'abolished'); and Europeans, primarily Portuguese.

About 80% of São Toméans belong to the Roman Catholic Church, though traditional animist beliefs are still strong.

In addition to the traditional crafts of the island (including intricately carved wooden boxes, masks, and seed and shell jewellery), there is a budding arts scene drawing international attention revolving around the Teia D'Arte gallery (opposite), which has held several biennales and holds arts workshops for the local population. Famed São Tomé artist (and gourmet chef/TV host) João Carlos Silva, who runs the Roça São João (p629), heads up the gallery.

Auto de Floripes (performed once a year, by the entire population of Príncipe) and Tchiloli are famous day-long pieces of musical theatre that have been performed since the 16th century, and can now be seen as distinctly anticolonial stories.

Much of the music and dance of São Tomé is shared or influenced by other Portuguese-speaking nations, including Cape Verde, Brazil and Angola.

FOOD & DRINK
Don't miss out on the *con-con,* an ugly, prehistoric-looking fish grilled and served with baked breadfruit. Traditional stews, such as *calulu,* are made with more than 20 different plants and can take hours to prepare. Other traditional dishes include fish or meat with beans, rice or plantains, and omelettes cooked with endemic spices, some said to be aphrodisiacs. Palm wine, freshly gathered from the trees, is a local favourite.

ENVIRONMENT
The islands are of volcanic origin and almost 30% of the land is covered by high-altitude, virgin rainforest, referred to as the Obo, and filled with over 700 species of flora and a stunning array of bird species, some of which exist nowhere else in the world. In the interior are lakes, waterfalls and volcanic craters. Since São Tomé's forests were classified as the second-most important in Africa in biological terms, they have received much attention, and conservation groups have started to set up protection programs and ecotourism outfits.

Outside the jungle the island is comprised of varying beaches, some of which are grounds for nesting sea turtles from October to December. Whales and dolphins can be observed from July to September.

SÃO TOMÉ TOWN
If only all African capitals were so laid-back. São Tomé may be the country's economic, political and commercial hub, but rush hour here lasts an unbearable five minutes! There's a bustling market, a few quality dining options, a budding arts scene, a collection of fading pastel colonial buildings, and plenty of activities on its doorstep, making it an ideal base from which to make day and overnight trips.

ORIENTATION
São Tomé town sits on Baia do Ana Chaves (Ana Chaves Bay). Most of the action takes place in one centralised area a few blocks in from the water, starting at the markets and spreading south to shops, banks and restaurants. The airport is 4km north of town.

INFORMATION
There are many banks in town that exchange US dollars or euros in cash and travellers cheques for dobras. There's no ATM. Unless things have changed (and they might), you need to bring all the money you need in cash. There are several Western Unions, though.

Café & Companhia (☎ 226622; Praça da Amizade; ⊙ 8am-late Mon-Sat) The cafe acts as the centre of the expat community. Has wi-fi.

CST (Ave da Independência; ⊙ 7.30am-9pm Mon-Sat, 7.30am-7pm Sun) You can make international calls here. Phonecards and top-up cards (for mobile phones) are available.

Mistral Voyages (☎ 223344, 221246; www.ecotourisme-gabon.com; Ave Marginal 12 Julho) Can arrange car rentals and tours, including flights to Príncipe, and visa applications.

Navetur-Equatour (☎ 222122; www.navetur-equatour.st; Rua Viriato da Cruz) Locally owned outfit that has a comprehensive list of services (flights, cars, tours, hotels), with an emphasis on ecotourism. Staff speak English.

DANGERS & ANNOYANCES
Beware of the usual petty crimes, though the town is pretty safe.

SIGHTS
A good place to start discovering the capital is the **National Museum** (Ave Marginal 12 Julho; admission €3), in the old **Fort São Sebastião**. It has artefacts from all stages of the islands' colonial history.

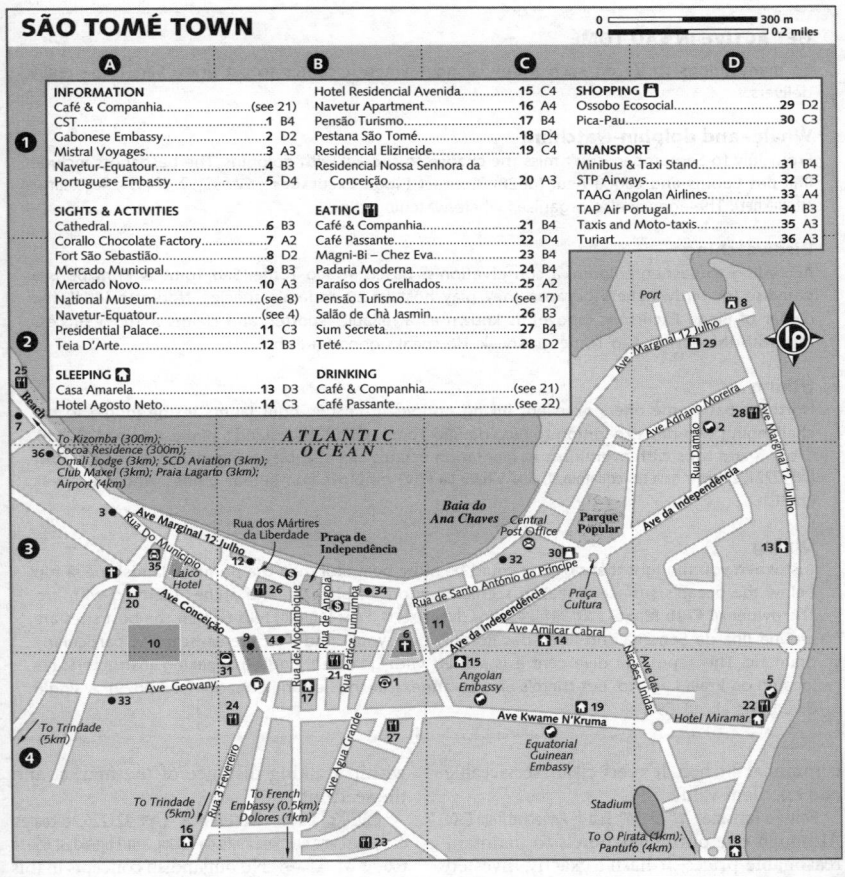

SÃO TOMÉ TOWN

INFORMATION
Café & Companhia.....................(see 21)
CST...**1** B4
Gabonese Embassy.........................**2** D2
Mistral Voyages................................**3** A3
Navetur-Equateur............................**4** B3
Portuguese Embassy.......................**5** D4

SIGHTS & ACTIVITIES
Cathedral..**6** B3
Corallo Chocolate Factory..............**7** A2
Fort São Sebastião...........................**8** D2
Mercado Municipal..........................**9** B3
Mercado Novo................................**10** A3
National Museum.........................(see 8)
Navetur-Equateur.......................(see 4)
Presidential Palace........................**11** C3
Teia D'Arte.....................................**12** B3

SLEEPING
Casa Amarela.................................**13** D3
Hotel Agosto Neto.........................**14** C3

Hotel Residencial Avenida.............**15** C4
Navetur Apartment........................**16** A4
Pensão Turismo..............................**17** B4
Pestana São Tomé..........................**18** D4
Residencial Elizineide.....................**19** C4
Residencial Nossa Senhora da
   Conceição...................................**20** A3

EATING
Café & Companhia..........................**21** B4
Café Passante.................................**22** D4
Magni-Bi – Chez Eva......................**23** B4
Padaria Moderna............................**24** B4
Paraíso dos Grelhados....................**25** A2
Pensão Turismo..........................(see 17)
Salão de Chà Jasmin......................**26** B3
Sum Secreta...................................**27** B4
Teté..**28** D2

DRINKING
Café & Companhia.....................(see 21)
Café Passante............................(see 22)

SHOPPING
Ossobo Ecosocial...........................**29** D2
Pica-Pau..**30** C3

TRANSPORT
Minibus & Taxi Stand.....................**31** B4
STP Airways...................................**32** C3
TAAG Angolan Airlines...................**33** A4
TAP Air Portugal............................**34** B3
Taxis and Moto-taxis.....................**35** A3
Turiart...**36** A3

It's well worth the admission price just to walk on the ramparts of the old fort (1576) and catch views of the town.

Keep striding down the main avenue along the seafront, and the massive **cathedral** (Ave Agua Grande) soon comes into view. Across the road you can't miss the pinkish facade of the **Presidential Palace** (Ave da Independência).

An area of frenzied buying, bartering and bargaining, the **Mercado Municipal** and the nearby **Mercado Novo** form the city's hub of activity.

Teia D'Arte (Rua dos Mártires da Liberdade), a gallery of contemporary painting and sculpture, is in the centre of town.

Those with a sweet tooth shouldn't miss the family-run **Corallo Chocolate Factory** (☎ 222236;

www.claudiocorallo.st) to taste test what are possibly the finest chocolate and coffee beans in the world. The factory is open by appointment; there's no sign on the outside.

There are beautiful beaches within a short walk of town but none that offer particularly good swimming. The best swimming beach near town is **Praia Lagarto**, about 3km to the north.

SLEEPING

Cheap lodging is getting increasingly harder to come by in town.

Navetur Apartment (☎ 222122; Rua 3 Fevereiro; s/d without bathroom €25/30; ☒) The Navetur-Equatour travel agency (see opposite) offers a house for rent with three bedrooms and a

---

GET ACTIVE IN SÃO TOMÉ

So many things to do on such a tiny island – when it comes to activities, São Tomé really delivers.

Whale- and dolphin-watching

From July to September, don't miss the chance to snorkel with dolphins. The best spots include Ilha das Cabras and Lagoa Azul (p628). Contact **Floga Excursões** (☎ 909199, 224394; flogatours@ cstome.net). The agency also organises whale-watching trips.

Birdwatching

According to Bastien Loloum, a conservationist based in São Tomé, São Tomé & Príncipe is a paradise for birdwatchers because they play host to 29 endemic species. Norberto Vidal, the owner of Floga Excursões (above), is known as a reliable 'spotter' and claims a 100% success rate with the elusive São Tomé grosbeak. He speaks good English.

Hiking

Northern São Tomé offers excellent hiking options, from two-hour jaunts in the jungle to the challenging two-day expedition to Pico de São Tomé (p629), the island's highest point (2024m). Cross-island trips with overnights in plantation estates can also be arranged. **Navetur-Equatour** (☎ 222122; www.navetur-equatour.st; Rua Viriato da Cruz) employs competent guides who can speak English.

Diving

Just when you thought that nothing could be more beautiful than the primeval landscape, a trip below the ocean's surface reveals a scenic kingdom of plateaus and arches teeming with life. The owner of **Club Maxel** (☎ 904424; www.clubmaxel.st; Praia Lagarto) tells us that the best sites are around Ilha da Santana and Ilhéu das Rolas, where you'll find that the seascape is particularly dramatic. This reputable dive centre is staffed with qualified, English-speaking instructors. It's located on Praia Lagarto, but there's also an annexe at the Pestana Equador (see p629). A single dive costs about €50.

---

communal kitchen. It's very clean, serviceable and excellent value.

Pensão Turismo (☎ 222340; Rua de Angola; d from €30) Although one of the few hotels to maintain reasonable prices, it hasn't exactly invested in its rooms. Its greatest attributes are the central location, the family atmosphere and the on-site restaurant.

Residencial Nossa Senhora da Conceição (☎ 224648; rnsc@cstome.net; Ave Conceição; d €35-45; ✕ 🖳 🛜) Behind the tiny reception some stairs lead to three floors of clean and well-maintained rooms. It's by no means luxurious, but the ultracentral location is ideal if you want to feel the heartbeat of the capital from your room.

Residencial Elizineide (☎ 224711; Ave Kwame N'Kruma; d €40; ✕ 🛜) Behind the gates hides a good surprise, with nicely furnished and spacious rooms (the ones upstairs are better). The courtyard offers chill-out space in the shade of a tree. The location is ace – you're within walking distance of the market and the seafront.

ourpick Cocoa Residence (☎ 227226; cocoaresi dence@cstome.net; Rua Pinto da Rocha; s incl breakfast €50, d €60-70; ✕ 🖳 🛜) No outlandish concepts in this discreet number that features only nine rooms. Just good-quality, practical and welcoming accommodation, as well as attentive staff. It's in a tranquil street, not far from the seafront.

Hotel Residencial Avenida (☎ 241700; ravenida@ cstome.net; Ave da Independência; s/d €55/65; ✕ 🖳 🛜) Near the Presidential Palace, this feels more personable than other midrange places, thanks to the friendly and professional service you get. Rooms are well appointed and there's a well-tended garden.

Casa Amarela (☎ 222573; www.casaamarelacasaver melha.blogspot.com; Ave Marginal 12 Julho; d incl breakfast €65, q €80; 🛜) Nora Rizzo, a local architect, rents out this villa overlooking the seafront. It has two bedrooms with shared bathrooms, and a kitchen for guests' use.

Hotel Agosto Neto (☎ 226728; www.hotelagostoneto.com; Ave Amilcar Cabral; s incl breakfast €65-75, d €100; ☒ ▣ ☜) Comfortable, neat as a pin, convenient and as smooth as a boardroom table, the Agosto Neto is aimed at business travellers or tourists in search of a reassuring port of call. With only 18 rooms, it doesn't feel too impersonal.

Pestana São Tomé (☎ 244500; Ave Marginal 12 Julho; d incl breakfast from €160; ☒ ▣ ☜ ▣) With more than 100 rooms, this is a giant on the local scene. This hotel's best features include the infinity pool and the prolific list of amenities, including a disco, a restaurant and a gym.

Omali Lodge (☎ 222350; www.africas-eden.com; Praia Lagarto; d incl breakfast from €175; ☒ ▣ ☜ ▣) A bit north of town towards the airport and right across from the ocean, the Omali boasts a gorgeous pool and a stunning tropical garden. With only 30 bungalows, it feels more intimate than the Pestana.

EATING

Unless otherwise stated, places are open for lunch and dinner from Monday to Saturday.

Pensão Turismo (☎ 222340; Rua de Angola; mains €2-5) No culinary acrobatics in this family-run affair: just well-executed classics such as soup, fish or chicken that you'll enjoy in an atmospheric stained-glass dining area.

Salão de Chà Jasmin (☎ 227130; Rua do Municipio; mains €2-6; ☽ breakfast, lunch & dinner Mon-Fri) Don't miss this upmarket cafeteria-style eatery set in a heritage building near the market. Both the clean-cut indoor dining room and the agreeable terrace provide the perfect setting in which to nosh on a pizza, a *shawarma* (kebab) or simply a pastry.

ourpick **Paraíso dos Grelhados** (The Blue Container; Ave Marginal 12 Julho; fish dishes €3-5) Yes, it's the blue ship container right on the seafront. It offers superb locally caught fish – cooked simply and with care, and served with baked *frutapão* (breadfruit).

Café & Companhia (☎ 226622; Praça da Amizade; mains €3-6; ☜) Set in a handsomely restored warehouse, this congenial joint is something of a social focal point for expats and well-heeled São Toméans. It does a sturdy line in snacks, salads, omelettes and desserts, and the open-plan kitchen inspires confidence.

Sum Secreta (☎ 224604; Ave Kwame N'Kruma; mains €3-6) This well-established venture with a large covered terrace is popular with flirting couples (it's not called 'Mr Secret' for nothing). The menu sticks to classics such as fish dishes with fries, chicken and salads.

ourpick **Teté** (☎ 222355; Ave Marginal 12 Julho; mains €3-6) Locals and expats rave about this family-run eatery specialising in flavoursome fish dishes. There's no shop sign. Note that the owner had plans to move into a new house in a different neighbourhood at the time of research.

O Pirata (☎ 907400; Estrada do Pantufo; mains €3-7) The stage is set: a terrace overlooking the beach (with a rusting wreck in the distance) and paintings by local artists covering the walls. Grilled fish takes centre stage, with a support cast of crunchy salads. Guest stars include beef fillet and chicken.

Magni-Bi – Chez Eva (☎ 227562; near Ave Agua Grande; mains €6-10; ☽ lunch & dinner daily) This is the place towards which all heads turn when it comes to feasting on Cameroonian classics, especially *ndole* (beef or fish cooked with vegetables and peanuts).

Other temptations:

Café Passante (Ave Marginal 12 Julho; ☽ 7am-7pm daily) Has dangerously addictive fruit tarts and pastries.

ourpick **Padaria Moderna** (Rua 3 Fevereiro) Irresistible chocolate cakes. And croissants. And buns. You can see the problem.

At the top end of the spectrum you'll find the hotel restaurants, which serve good international cuisine.

DRINKING & ENTERTAINMENT

Parque Popular has a bevy of pleasant *quiosques* (kiosks) that serve cheap food and good drinks. **Café & Companhia** (☎ 226622; Praça da Amizade) has happy hours on Thursday at 7pm. If all you want is an energy bolt, **Café Passante** (Ave Marginal 12 Julho) has the best espresso in town.

If you want to tear it up on the dance floor, try **Dolores** (Bairro Dolores) or **Kizomba** (Rua Pinto da Rocha). The posh disco at the Pestana São Tomé is popular with expats and the elite crowds.

SHOPPING

Ossobo Ecosocial (☎ 227933; ossoboecosocial@cstome.net; Ave 12 Marginal Julho), run by a local NGO, is a great place to get ecofriendly handicrafts, arts and local food products. **Pica-Pau** (Praça Cultura) is a good place to stock up on woodcarvings.

GETTING THERE & AWAY

See p632 for details on flights to/from São Tomé.

GETTING AROUND

The airport is 4km north of the town centre; a taxi costs about €6. For vehicle rentals, contact one of the travel agencies (see p624) or **Turiart** (☎ 223748; Ave Marginal 12 Julho).

Minibuses can be found near the Mercado Municipal in town. They leave for destinations north and south several times daily (from €2).

Taxis around town cost €2 to €6. They can also be chartered to most destinations around the island.

AROUND SÃO TOMÉ

NORTH & WEST OF SÃO TOMÉ

The 50km road that leads north from São Tomé town is a dramatic, beautiful drive ending just past Santa Catarina on the northwest coast. There are deserted beaches all along the route, best found by 4WD, though it's possible to take public transport and hike in. Minibuses from São Tomé town will cost you from €2.

Travelling north, the old **Roça Agostinho Neto** has sprawling grounds and stunning colonial architecture.

Further north, down a dirt road, is **Praia Micoló**, where barbecues abound on weekends.

Past the small town of Guadalupe and a short walk off the road, **Praia das Conchas** and **Praia dos Tamarindos** are both considered the nicest beaches in the north. Nearby is **Lagoa Azul**, where there is excellent snorkelling in azure waters but only a rocky beach.

With its great lines of wooden *pirogues* (traditional canoes) on the rocky beach, the fishing village of **Neves** is adorable. After treating yourself to seafood at Petisqueira Santola (right), head to the large **Roça Ponta Figo**.

Continue on to the old crumbling **Roça Monteforte**, which has gorgeous views of the mountains and sea. It's still a working farm on which guava, oranges and cacao are grown by the descendants of the old contract workers. A few kilometres to the south, the secluded **Roça Diogo Vaz** (www.natcultura.org) is another working plantation. It welcomes volunteers, especially teachers.

Sleeping & Eating

Roça Monte Forte (☎ 911362; d incl breakfast €25) This colonial-era building has seven simple rooms, one of which has a sea view (ask for the *quarto da ponta*, at the corner). Bathrooms are shared. Meals are available on request (€10).

Petisqueira Santola (☎ 936845; Neves; mains €2-4; ☖ lunch & dinner daily) This very simple affair is famous for one thing and one thing only: seafood. Feast on red crab, sea snails or grilled fish served with baked banana or breadfruit.

EAST & SOUTH OF SÃO TOMÉ

As you head south away from the capital, the unhurried pace of life is complemented by the splendid scenery of fertile volcanic slopes and secluded beaches, with a sprinkling of coastal villages thrown in for good measure. The entire southern route takes about four hours to drive.

Heading south of São Tomé town you'll first hit the attractive fishing village of **Pantufo**. A few kilometres to the south, **Santana** village is known mostly for Club Santana, a resorty venture with a lovely, calm beach; nonguests are allowed and pay only for the deckchairs (€3). Boat trips for the tiny **Ilha da Santana**, which has great waters for snorkelling, can be arranged from the resort (€5).

Carry on to **Roça Agua Izé**, one of the biggest plantations in the country. The foreman will show you around the workshops inside the bright yellow buildings. For wraparound views of the estate, walk up through the plantation to the top of the hill, where the crumbling hospital lies.

Further south off the main road you can spend a few minutes tripping out on the mesmerising aqua blowhole of **Boca de Inferno**.

In this area, almost any side road towards the ocean will bring you to a scenic and secluded beach, including **Praia das Sete Ondas** and **Praia Micondó**.

If you're hungry (and tired) by the time you reach **São João dos Angolares**, check into Roça São João (opposite), a working plantation and a gem of a B&B.

Past São João dos Angolares is where the real wilderness of São Tomé begins to unfold. Among the charming treasures you'll come across are lovely deserted beaches shaded by palm and coconut trees and a couple of sleepy villages. You eventually hit **Porto Alegre**, a fishing community where the paved road ends.

Though the village itself is pleasant, it's the surrounding area that will take your breath away, with a string of idyllic beaches. Many people rank **Praia Piscina**, just past the village, as the choicest beach on the island, but we found the nearby **Praia Jalé**, **Praia Inhame** and **Praia Va Inha** no less impressive, with sweeping expanses of golden sand framed by black volcanic boulders. From November to March, these beaches are great for watching female turtles nesting.

The area also hosts the island's largest mangrove. Two-hour **mangrove tours** (€10) in a traditional dugout canoe can easily be organised through Jalé Ecolodge (below).

And there's **Ilhéu das Rolas**, which is about 20 minutes by boat off the coast of Porto Alegre. In addition to having lovely beaches, this islet is cut in two by the equator line, which you can literally stand on. If you can't afford to stay at the posh Pestana Equador Island Resort, you can spend the day here (see below).

Sleeping & Eating

Jalé Ecolodge (☎ 222792; http://praiajale.free.fr; Praia Jalé; bungalows €25) A fair walk from Porto Alegre (or a short 4WD drive), this beachfront place feels like a Robinson Crusoe–inspired adventure playground, with three lovely coco-palm huts and communal dining, all managed by the villagers. It sits on a lovely beach, Praia Jalé, where sea turtles nest during the season. It's the perfect place to do very little at all, but if your energy flows over you can tour the mangroves nearby, take locally guided hikes into the forest, learn to fish traditionally or wander the beach trails. Proceeds support a local NGO and the nearby villages.

Roça São João (☎ 261140, 225135; www.rocasaojoao.com; São João; s/d incl breakfast €28/35) Expats and tourists get a misty look in their eyes when they talk about this colonial-era plantation building that has been turned into a cultural and ecotourism centre and guesthouse. The eight bedrooms are attractively furnished with objects recovered from the destroyed estate and are candlelit at night. Another highlight is the food; master chef and artist João Carlos Silva concocts delicious meals (from €10). Profits are reinvested in local development projects. In line with that ethos, it also sets up biking and hiking trips from the *roça* as well as various workshops.

Pestana Equador Island Resort (☎ 261106; www.pestana.com; Ilhéu das Rolas; d from €190; ✂ 🖳 🛜 🖳)

São Tomé's most sought-after resort boasts an unbeatable location on peaceful Ilhéu das Rolas. Digs are in spacious bungalows, but the cheaper ones don't have sea views and are in need of a touch-up. Activities include diving and deep-sea fishing. It's possible to arrange a day trip for €20. Boats leave from Ponta Baleia, a point a bit north of Porto Alegre.

THE INTERIOR

The dramatic interior is prime hiking and birdwatching territory.

From São Tomé town, a short drive into the mountains leads to **Roça Monte Café**, where you can observe the traditional coffee-producing process at what was once the biggest coffee plantation on the island, and which still makes some of the best coffee in the world.

Deeper in the interior is **Bom Successo**, an ecotourism camp and a botanic garden. Many hikes start here. One of the most popular routes is the four-hour hike to **Lagoa Amelia**, from where you can overlook swampy mangroves replete with bird and plant life.

If you're up for a challenge, the two-day trip up and down the highest point on the island, **Pico de São Tomé** (2024m), will take you through four different forest belts. Pico de São Tomé can also be tackled from Neves (see opposite).

A short detour from Bom Successo is the gorgeous waterfall known as **Cascatas da São Nicolau**.

To the south, the crumbling **Roça Bombaim** is an old cacao plantation. You can see the decrepit hospital and the old plantation slaves' quarters. There are some excellent hikes in the area, as well as scenic waterfalls – ask for a guide at Hotel Bombaim (below).

Sleeping & Eating

Bungalows Bom Successo (☎ 223284 in São Tomé town; Bom Successo; r €20-40) Three bungalows are available at the botanic garden. They're unspectacular but serviceable.

Hotel Bombaim (☎ 227988, 903240; Roça Bombaim; s/d incl breakfast €30/35) As far away from the rest of the island as it's possible to get, this hotel – set in a historic colonial plantation house at Roça Bombaim – is a great base if you want to see the interior and tropical forests. The 10 rooms are not fancy but they are well kept; the rooms downstairs share bathrooms (cold water).

SÃO TOMÉ & PRÍNCIPE

PRÍNCIPE

Close your eyes. Just imagine: a dramatic landscape of jutting volcanic mountains covered mostly by dense, virgin forest; perfect beaches with astonishingly clear water; old plantation estates from colonial times; and warm greetings from friendly locals at every turn.

Príncipe is the perfect place to shift into low gear, but action-seekers won't get bored, as the island also offers excellent hiking and diving options.

Allow at least three days (more if you plan to dive or hike) to get the most out of this island.

INFORMATION

In Santo António, you'll find two banks where you can change money (cash only) as well as a CST branch where you can make phone calls.

The owner of **Principe Tours** (☎ 916024, 251058; agenciaprincipetour@hotmail.com, pinheiro_2000@hotmail.com; Santo António), Carlos Pinheiro, is well clued up and speaks English. He can organise any kind of tour on the island, and also handles plane ticketing.

SIGHTS & ACTIVITIES

The island's sole town is **Santo António**, where nothing happens fast. It has a few faded, cracked, pastel colonial buildings and charming gardens. The Catholic church and the government buildings are also worth a peek.

The island is home to a few lovely *roças*. Don't miss **Roça Sundy**, the biggest on the island, **Roça Belo Monte**, which boasts a quirky crenellated entrance gate, and the smaller **Roça São Joaquim**, which offers stupendous views of Baía das Agulhas, with the spiky peaks of the south forming an awesome backdrop.

In the beach department, Príncipe is no small player either. The picture-perfect **Banana Beach**, made famous by a Bacardi ad, really is as spectacular as the photos look. Closer to Santo António, it's hard not to resist a snooze under the swaying palms at **Praia Salgado**. Nearby **Praia Abade** is occupied by a picturesque fishing community.

The island features superb **hiking** potential amid splendid scenery, but you'll need a guide – contact Principe Tours (above).

Serious hikers can scale **Pico de Papagaio**, the island's second-highest peak (680m).

Príncipe is blessed with a host of absolutely pristine **dive sites**, where fish action is guaranteed (we were thrilled by Pedra Galé, an offshore rocky plateau to the north of the island). There's a state-of-the-art dive centre at Bom Bom Island Resort (below).

Praia Grande offers excellent **turtle-watching** opportunities from November to March. Between August and December, humpback whales can be seen frolicking around the island.

SLEEPING & EATING

The closest thing Santo António has to a restaurant is **Palhota** (meals €10), in the garden next to the eponymous *pensão* (pension). You'll also find a number of *quiosques* in town, including **Pasteleria** (mains €3-5), near the church, and the little shacklike **Quiosque Beira Mar** (mains €2-4), where you can chow down on 'cracks' (local crabs, considered a delicacy).

Pensão Arca de Noé (☎ 251054; Santo António; d with shared bathroom €25) Of the few very basic *pensãos* in town, this one was the best at the time of research, with bare but clean rooms, all the way to the sheets. Avoid nearby Residencial Palhota, which is overpriced.

Roça Ponta do Sol – Casa do João (☎ 925105, 925114; brankinho_STP@hotmail.com; Ponta do Sol; s/d incl half board €30/45) Your Belgian host Jean-Claude goes out of his way to make travellers welcome at his beautifully restored *roça*. The four rooms are simple and share bathrooms, but have bags of character. The dinner terrace alone – with views of the sea and the forest – is worth the stay. Jean-Claude is an adept chef too. Various tours can be organised.

Residencial Roça Abade (☎ 916024, 251058; pinheiro_2000@hotmail.com; Abade; s/d incl breakfast €35/70) You'll be impressed by this converted *roça*, the pride and joy of the owner of Principe Tours. Much of the heritage structure of its former life remains, but the rooms have been extensively renovated and are comfortable, and the wraparound views are unforgettable.

Bom Bom Island Resort (☎ 251141, 251114; www.africas-eden.com; r incl full board per person €200; ❄ ☐ ☎ ☑) Walk into a picture-postcard at this low-key resort lying on the northern shore of Príncipe. It's surrounded by lush vegetation and emerald waters, and features two sunbather-friendly strips of beach. Activities include hikes, plantation tours, snorkelling, kayaking, turtle-watching, diving and deep-sea fishing. It prides itself on its ecocredentials, heavily supporting environmental-development projects. Nonguests can spend the day here (€20). One downside: we found the food a bit disappointing.

GETTING THERE & AROUND

See p632 for information on connections with São Tomé.

Moto-taxis near the market can take you virtually anywhere on the island. As an indication of price, a ride from Santo António to Bom Bom Island costs €3.

SÃO TOMÉ & PRÍNCIPE DIRECTORY

ACCOMMODATION

Prices for *pensãos* and hotels in São Tomé start around €35 and go up to more than €200. *Roças* outside of town are cheaper and are great places to meet locals and get an authentic cultural experience.

ACTIVITIES

The islands have great snorkelling and diving and some of the best deep-sea fishing in the world. Interior hikes in the forest can be arranged through local travel agencies. Birdwatching, dolphin-, turtle- and whale-watching also feature prominently.

BUSINESS HOURS

Businesses and small shops generally close around 12.30pm for long siestas and reopen around 3pm.

DANGERS & ANNOYANCES

São Tomé is for the most part an exceedingly safe country, but on deserted beaches, keep an eye on your bags.

EMBASSIES & CONSULATES

The following countries have embassies or consulates in São Tomé town:

France (☎ 222266; Bairro de Santo António)
Gabon (☎ 224434; Rua Damão)
Portugal (☎ 221130; Ave Marginal 12 de Julho)

Angola and Equatorial Guinea both have diplomatic representation in São Tomé

PRACTICALITIES

■ Weights, measures and road distances use the metric system.

■ Electricity supply is 220-240V AC (50Hz) and plugs are of the European two-round-pin variety.

---

but didn't issue tourist visas at the time of research.

FESTIVALS & EVENTS

Independence Day is celebrated across the islands on 12 July. **Mardi Gras**, held on the Tuesday before Lent, is also a big party. On Príncipe, the biggest event is **Auto de Floripes** (aka São Laurenço), which is held in mid-August.

At several times during the year various saints are honoured in **Saint Festivals**, which are held in different villages around the island. For a complete listing of these festival days, check out **Navetur-Equatour** (www.navetur-equatour.st).

HOLIDAYS

The following public holidays are observed in São Tomé & Príncipe:

New Year's Day 1 January
Good Friday March/April
Holy Saturday March/April
Easter Monday March/April
International Workers' Day 1 May
Independence Day 12 July
Christmas Day 25 December

INTERNET ACCESS

You'll find that internet access is available in São Tomé town and, to a lesser extent, on Príncipe.

MONEY

All purchases can be made in dobras, the local currency, but often you can also pay in euros or US dollars or both, especially at tourist outlets and for big purchases. Prices in this chapter are quoted in more stable euros.

There are no ATMs on the islands. Credit cards (MasterCard and Visa) are accepted only at the top-end hotels. Euros and US dollars can be changed at banks and at moneychangers in São Tomé town and in Santo António on Príncipe.

SÃO TOMÉ & PRÍNCIPE

POST & TELEPHONE

The central post office in São Tomé town is open during business hours.

Public telephones are available at the telecommunications centre in São Tomé and in some larger towns.

TOURIST INFORMATION

Travel agencies in São Tomé town are the best resource for information.

VISAS

Visas are required by everyone, and can no longer be purchased on arrival at the airport (although we saw a tourist getting one for €80). Visas cost €40 to €50. Proof of yellow fever vaccination is mandatory.

Visas for Onward Travel

Visas for Gabon can be purchased at its embassy in São Tomé town (see p631) and cost around €40.

TRANSPORT IN SÃO TOMÉ & PRÍNCIPE

GETTING THERE & AWAY

Air

Almost all travellers arrive by air via Gabon or Portugal. Flights leave several times weekly

---

> **DEPARTURE TAX**
>
> Departure tax hovers around US$21, and is payable in euros, US dollars or dobras.

from Libreville (Gabon) with **Air Service Gabon** (☎ 241-747118/119 in Gabon; www.airservice.aero), costing around €250 return.

Direct flights from Lisbon (Portugal) leave once or twice weekly with either **TAP Air Portugal** (☎ 222307; www.flytap.com; Ave Marginal 12 Julho, São Tomé town) or **STP Airways** (☎ 221160; www.stpairways.st; Ave Marginal 12 Julho, São Tomé town). Prices start at €800.

There are also direct twice-weekly flights to Angola and Cape Verde with **TAAG Angolan Airlines** (☎ 241150; Ave Geovany, São Tomé town). STP Airways also operates a direct flight to Angola. Prices start at €320.

GETTING AROUND

STP Airways (☎ 221160) and **SCD Aviation** (☎ 222350; Omali Lodge) have flights from São Tomé to Príncipe two to three times weekly (from €170).

A ferry service to Príncipe was launched in late 2009. It operates on a twice-weekly basis between the two islands. It costs €10 per passenger and the duration of the trip is about four hours in the Sao Tomé to Príncipe direction (about two hours more in the reverse direction). Tickets can be bought at the harbour.

East Africa

From Addis Ababa to Dar es Salaam, and Mogadishu to Kigali, East Africa plays host to profound cultural riches, overwhelming natural splendour, and the daily trials and tribulations of the human condition. Once upon a time, humankind's earliest ancestors loped over prehistoric plains and valleys, eventually coalescing to form civilisations that stretched along the coastline and deep into the interior. On the islands of Zanzibar and Lamu, cities of hewn coral pay tribute to these once vast trading empires. Further inland, Ethiopia's rock churches and ruined palaces serve as poignant reminders of treasures won and subsequently lost.

Time has passed, but the East African landscape is as devastatingly beautiful now as it was back then. The region is home to the nine highest mountains on the continent, Africa's largest lake, swathes of primate-rich equatorial rainforest and some of the world's greatest wildlife parks. The word safari, meaning simply 'journey' in the Swahili language, was born from the same land that now fosters the annual wildebeest migration between the Serengeti and Masai Mara. Higher up in the heavens, the summits of Mt Kilimanjaro and Mt Kenya beckon to be conquered by hardened shoe leather.

East Africa seduces the spirit, but it also throws up some mighty challenges that test the limits of even the most seasoned of travellers. Much of the region has suffered from – or is currently embroiled in – tragic conflict that has claimed the lives of so many innocents. While countries like Rwanda have begun to heal their scars, others like Somalia continue to throw salt in their wounds. However, from this chaos emerges an incredible resilience that characterises the East African people. This is Africa at its most intriguing and beautiful, and any time spent here among its people and places will surely inspire.

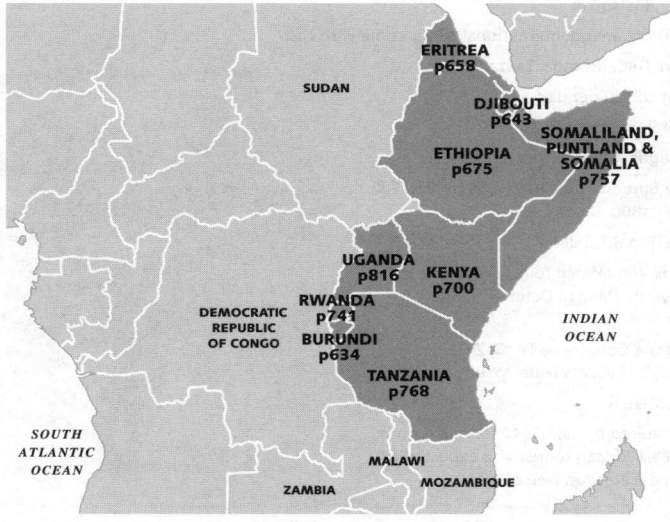

Burundi

A tiny nation sandwiched between the giants of the Democratic Republic of Congo (DRC) and Tanzania, Burundi is defined by a mix of soaring mountains, languid lakeside communities and ongoing ethnic conflict. Burundi has been devastated by intertribal tensions since independence, and, despite recent peace accords, violence could flare up at any time. Simply, Burundi remains a potentially unstable country in a potentially unstable region of Africa.

The tourist industry died a quick death with the outbreak of civil war in 1993. Since then, many of the upcountry attractions have been off limits, including the southernmost source of the Nile, the ancient forest of Parc National de la Kibira, and the legendary spot where Stanley was reputed to have uttered the timeless words 'Dr Livingstone, I presume?'

However, the steamy capital Bujumbura has a lovely location on the shores of Lake Tanganyika, and just outside the city are some of the best inland beaches on the continent. Burundians themselves also have an irrepressible *joie de vivre*.

At the time of research, travel to the capital Bujumbura was reasonably safe, as was the main road north to Rwanda, though greater caution needs to be exerted while travelling in the countryside. If the peace process holds and the situation stabilises, Burundi may once again find itself on the overland map of Africa. In the meantime, however, check, double-check and triple-check on the latest security situation before heading into the country or travelling anywhere beyond Bujumbura.

FAST FACTS

- **Area** 27,835 sq km
- **ATMs** There are no international ATMs; come with cash
- **Borders** DRC, Rwanda, Tanzania
- **Budget** US$20 per day
- **Capital** Bujumbura
- **Languages** Kirundi, French, Swahili
- **Money** Burundi franc (BFr); US$1 = BFr1200, €1 = BFr 1800
- **Population** 8.7 million
- **Seasons** Wet (March to May, October to January) dry (May to October, January to March)
- **Telephone** Country code ☎ 257; international access code ☎ 00
- **Time** GMT/UTC +2
- **Visa** Required by all; US$40 for one month; single East African tourist visa expected to be introduced soon (see p737)

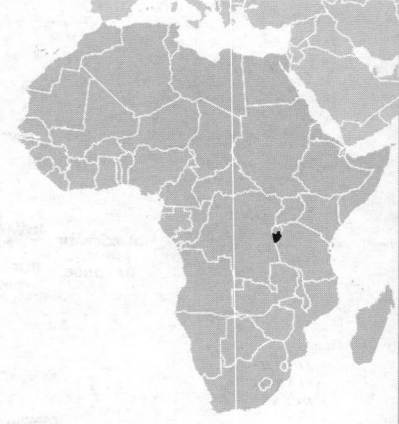

BURUNDI

HOW MUCH?

- **Hotel** US$50 to US$100
- **Plate of garnished brochettes** US$2 to US$3
- **Internet access per hour** US$1 to US$2
- **Local newspaper** US$0.50
- **100km bus ride** US$2

LONELY PLANET INDEX

- **1L petrol** US$1 to US$2
- **1L bottled water** US$0.50
- **Primus beer** US$1 to US$2
- **Souvenir T-shirt** There aren't any…
- **Street snack (grilled goat)** US$1

HIGHLIGHTS

- **Bujumbura** (p637) Dine out in style before dancing the night away in this city where people love to live it up.
- **Beaches** (p639) Hit the best inland beaches in East Africa for some fun in the sun.
- **Source du Nil** (p640) Journey to the southernmost source of the Nile at Mt Kikizi.
- **La Pierre de Livingstone et Stanley** (p639) Visit the rock where those fateful words 'Dr Livingstone, I presume?' were uttered.
- **Being in Burundi** Enjoy the novelty of being pretty much the only tourist in the entire country.

CLIMATE & WHEN TO GO

The climate in Burundi varies widely depending on whether you are in the hot and steamy lowlands around Lake Tanganyika, where temperatures average 30°C, or the more mountainous north, where the usual temperature is a much milder 20°C.

ITINERARIES

It is hard to talk of itineraries in such a small country with a long history of civil war. Most people do a hit and run on Bujumbura, entering via Rwanda, and spending a few days exploring the capital and surrounding environs. Assuming peace holds, it is likely travellers will continue south along the shores of Lake Tanganyika to link up with Gombe Stream National Park (p803) in western Tanzania. However, the security situation in the countryside must be sized up on the ground before considering any overland travel in Burundi.

HISTORY

The original Burundians were the Twa Pygmies, but they were soon squeezed out by bigger groups. First came the Hutu, mostly farmers of Bantu stock, from about AD 1000. Later, in the 16th and 17th centuries, the tall, pastoral Tutsi from Ethiopia and Uganda arrived. Relations were cordial, but the Tutsi gradually subjugated the Hutu in a feudal system similar to that of medieval Europe.

At the end of the 19th century, Burundi and Rwanda were colonised by Germany, but after WWI the League of Nations mandated Rwanda-Urundi to Belgium. Taking advantage of the status quo, the Belgians ruled through the Tutsi chiefs and princes. The establishment of coffee plantations and the resulting concentration of wealth in the hands of the Tutsi elite provoked tensions between the two tribal groups.

Independence Days

In the 1950s a nationalist organisation based on unity between the tribes was founded under the leadership of the king's eldest son, Prince Rwagasore. But, in the lead-up to independence, he was assassinated with the connivance of the colonial authorities, who feared their commercial interests would be threatened if he took power.

Despite this setback, it appeared that Burundi was headed for a majority Hutu government following independence in 1962. But in the 1964 elections, Mwami Mwambutsa refused to appoint a Hutu prime minister, even though Hutu candidates were the clear winners. Hutu frustration boiled over, and Hutu military officers and political figures staged an attempted coup. A wholesale purge of Hutu from the army and bureaucracy followed.

In 1972 another large-scale revolt resulted in more than 1000 Tutsi killed. The Tutsi military junta responded with selective genocide: any Hutu with wealth, a formal education or a government job was rooted out and murdered, often in the most horrifying way. After three months, 200,000 Hutu had been killed and another 100,000 had fled the country.

Stalemate

In 1976 Jean-Baptiste Bagaza came to power in a bloodless coup. During the Bagaza years,

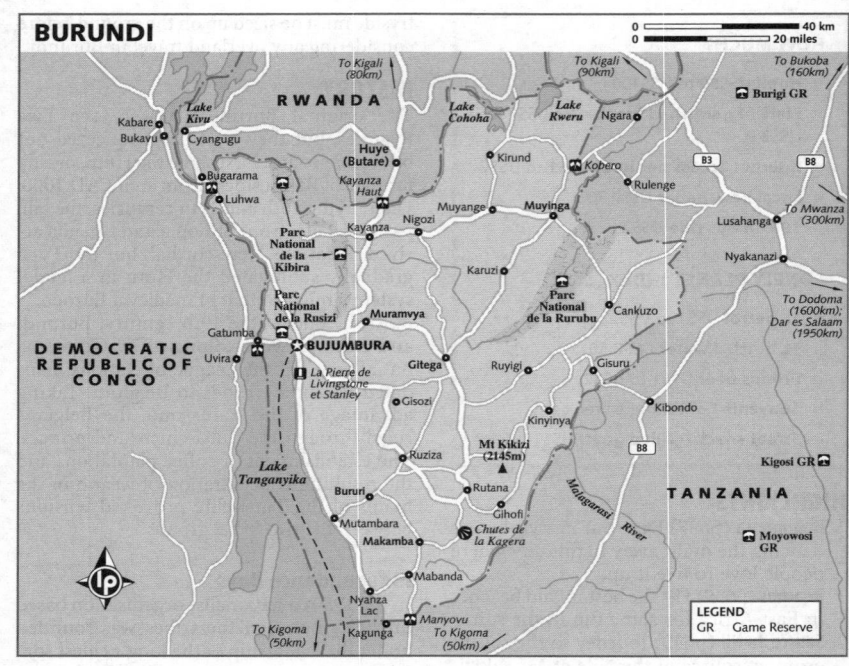

there were some half-hearted attempts by the Tutsi government to remove some of the main causes of intertribal conflict, but these were mostly cosmetic.

Bagaza was toppled in September 1987 in a coup led by his cousin Major Pierre Buyoya. The new regime attempted to address the causes of intertribal tensions yet again by gradually bringing Hutu representatives back into positions of power in the government.

Civil War Breaks Out

Buyoya eventually bowed to international pressure and allowed multiparty elections in June 1993. These brought a Hutu-dominated government to power, led by Melchior Ndadaye. But he was assassinated by a dissident army faction in October. The coup failed, but, in the chaos that followed the assassination, thousands were massacred in intertribal fighting.

In April 1994 the new president, Cyprien Ntaryamira (a Hutu), died in the infamous plane crash that killed Rwanda's President Habyarimana and sparked the planned genocide there. Back in Burundi, both Hutu militias and the Tutsi-dominated army went on the offensive. No war was actually declared, but at least 100,000 people were killed in clashes between mid-1994 and mid-1996. In July 1996 the former president, Pierre Buyoya, again carried out a successful coup and took over as the country's president with the support of the army.

Peace talks staggered on during the conflict, mediated first by former Tanzanian president Julius Nyerere and later by the revered Nelson Mandela. A breakthrough came in April 2003, when President Buyoya handed over power to Hutu leader Domitien Ndayizeye and both sides promised to work towards elections. Tragically, the conflict had already claimed the lives of about 300,000 Burundians.

Burundi Today

In 2004 the UN began operations in Burundi, sending more than 5000 troops to enforce the peace. Parliamentary elections were successfully held in June 2005, and the former rebels, the Forces for the Defence of Democracy (FDD), emerged victorious. Pierre Nkurunziza, leader of the FDD, was sworn in as president in August that year.

As of 2009, the Hutu-led Forces for National Liberation (FNL), the country's last active rebel group, was in the process of being disarmed by forces deployed from the African Union (AU). Ex–rebel fighters will either be integrated into the national army, or return to civilian life with a small compensation cheque to help them start life anew. The FNL is also slated to become an officially recognised political party.

At long last, the country is on the road to stability, though both Hutu and Tutsi need to embrace the spirit of national unity to bring Burundi back from the brink.

CULTURE

Like Rwanda to the north, Burundi has been torn apart by tribal animosities. However, like most conflicts, it is more about politics than people, and it is the people that end up the victims of political manipulation. The Belgians mastered the art of divide and rule, using the minority Tutsis to control the majority Hutus. The population was forced into choosing sides, Hutu or Tutsi.

Unlike Rwanda, Burundi debates its divisions. In Rwanda, there are only Rwandans, and their history is being reinterpreted in the spirit of unity. In Burundi, there are Hutus and Tutsis, and they work together in political parties and drink together in bars and discuss their differences. With two very different approaches to the same problem of ethnic division, both countries could learn a little from each other.

Burundi is more Francophone than any other country in the region, and city dwellers take their siestas seriously. Shops and businesses shut down from noon to 3pm. Do as the locals do and save some energy for the evening.

Out in the countryside, most of the people are engaged in farming, at least when they have not been fleeing the civil war as refugees in neighbouring countries. Coffee and tea are the main export crops.

Burundi's population comprises 84% Hutu, 15% Tutsi and 1% Twa Pygmies. Although the stormy relations between Hutu and Tutsi dominate the headlines, it is the Twa who have had the roughest deal, their forests stripped by successive outsiders.

Burundi is famous for its athletic and acrobatic dances. Les Tambourinaires is the country's most famous troupe and they perform all over the world. Their performances are a high-adrenaline mix of drumming and dancing that drowns the audience in a wave of sound and movement.

FOOD & DRINK

Brochettes (kebabs) and *frites* (fries) are a legacy of the Belgian colonial period, but there is also succulent fish from Lake Tanganyika and serious steaks. When it comes to drink, Burundi is blessed with a national brewery churning out huge bottles of Primus.

ENVIRONMENT

Rwanda may be the 'land of a thousand hills', but Burundi isn't far behind. The north is a stunning landscape of dramatic peaks and deep valleys, best experienced on the bus between Bujumbura and Kigali (Rwanda). Many of the mountains are carved with gravity-defying terraces that plunge into deep valleys below, where farmers somehow eke out a living from the land. To the southwest, it levels out along the shores of lovely Lake Tanganyika. The capital, Bujumbura, is on the northern tip of this vast lake. Sadly, however, Burundi's tourist infrastructure is in tatters after the long war, and most of the national parks have been closed for more than a decade.

BUJUMBURA

Frozen in time thanks to more than a decade of conflict, there has been almost no development in Burundi's capital since the 1980s, a stark contrast to the changes in Kigali and Kampala (Uganda) to the north. Bujumbura retains much of its grandiose colonial town planning, with its wide boulevards and imposing public buildings, and continues to function as one of the most important ports on Lake Tanganyika.

'Buj' has earned a free-wheelin' reputation for its dining, drinking and dancing scene, especially given the recent influx of international peacekeepers, aid workers and foreign officials. But the capital isn't exactly the safest city in the region, so keep your wits about you, especially once the sun goes down.

ORIENTATION

Bujumbura has a striking location on the shores of Lake Tanganyika, and many of its suburbs sprawl up the looming mountains that ring the city to the north and east. Most of

BUJUMBURA

INFORMATION	SIGHTS & ACTIVITIES	DRINKING
Banque du Crédit	Musée Vivant..................10 A4	Havana Club.....................16 C3
de Bujumbura..................1 C3		
Belgian Embassy.................2 C3	SLEEPING	SHOPPING
DRC Embassy.....................3 D3	Hotel Botanika.................11 C2	Craft Market....................17 C3
Interbank Burundi..............4 C3	Novotel Bujumbura...........12 C2	
Main Post Office................5 C3	Saga Residence Hotel.........13 C3	TRANSPORT
Office National du		Gaso Bus........................18 D3
Tourisme.....................6 C4	EATING	Minibuses.......................19 C3
Rwandan Embassy..............7 D3	Boulangerie-Pâtisserie	New Yahoo Express...........20 C3
Tanzanian Embassy.............8 D3	Trianon.......................14 C3	Taxis.............................21 C2
US Embassy......................9 D3	Le Kasuku.....................15 C3	Venus Travel..................(see 20)
		Yahoo Car.....................(see 13)

To Bujumbura
International Airport (12km)

Rue du Marais

Rue des Usines

Blvd du 1er Novembre

To Plage des Cocotiers
(Coconut Beach; 5km);
Park National de la
Rusizi (11km); Uvira (25km)

Lake Tanganyika

Ave de la Plage

Stadium

Ave de l'Université

To Butare (133km);
Kigali (266km)

Chaussée du Peuple Burundi

Ave du Stade

To Immigration
Office (500m);
French Embassy (500m)

Blvd de l'Uprona

Rue des Pêcheurs

Rue de l'Imbo

Mosque

Place de
l'Indépendance

Rue des Swahilis

Ave de Tanganika

Avenue des Paysans

Rue de l'Industrie

Ave du Commerce

Rue Science

Ave Victoire

Ave France

Ave United Nations Rd

Ave de l'Amitié

Ave du RD Congo

Chaussée Prince Rwagasore

Market

Ave de l'Enseignement

To Chez
André (500m)

Ave du 13 Octobre

Blvd du Septembre

Blvd de la Liberté

Ave du Revolution

Rue Gouvernement

Rue Eucalypt

Ave des Euphorbes

Ave Pierre Ngendandumwe

Some Minor Roads
Not Depicted

To La Pierre de
Livingstone et
Stanley (10km)

Cathedral

the action, however, takes place on Chaussée Prince Rwagasore and the streets nearby.

INFORMATION
Emergency
The official emergency number for police is ☎ 17, though it's best to make contact with your embassy in the event of an emergency.

Internet Access
There are various internet cafes throughout the city centre.

Medical Services
In the event of a medical emergency, it is best to get out of the country to somewhere with first-class medical facilities, like Nairobi.

Money
Banque du Crédit de Bujumbura (Rue Science) and **Interbank Burundi** (Blvd de la Liberté) both offer credit-card cash advances and change travellers cheques.

Post
Main post office (cnr Blvd Lumumba & Ave du Commerce; ☽ 8am-noon & 2-4pm Mon-Fri, 8-11am Sat)

Tourist Information
Office National du Tourisme (☎ 222202; Ave des Euphorbes; ☽ 7.30am-noon & 2-4.30pm Mon-Fri)

DANGERS & ANNOYANCES
It is generally safe to wander about on foot during the day, though the streets empty at

BURUNDI

night – take a taxi once the sun goes down. The character of the city changes around 8pm, as *'les petits bandits'* move in. Take particular care near popular nightspots, as you never know who is lurking in the dark.

SIGHTS & ACTIVITIES

The **Musée Vivant** (Ave du 13 Octobre; admission BFr2000) is a reconstructed traditional Burundian village with some exhibits about baskets, pottery and drums. Unfortunately, this museum has suffered from decades of neglect, and is now rough around the edges in parts and ageing less than gracefully.

Bujumbura's beaches are some of the best to be found in any landlocked country in Africa. The sand is white and powdery, and the waves should keep the bilharzia at bay. The stretch of beach that lies about 5km northwest of the capital is the most beautiful and is commonly known as **Plage des Cocotiers** (Coconut Beach).

'Dr Livingstone, I presume?' The Burundians presume so. The Tanzanians presume not. **La Pierre de Livingstone et Stanley**, a large rock at Mugere, about 10km south of the capital, is alleged to mark the spot where the encounter between Livingstone and Stanley took place. Some graffiti marks the date as 25 November 1871. Ujiji in Tanzania is the other contender.

SLEEPING

Hotel prices in Bujumbura shot up when the UN came to town, though this is definitely the kind of city where you should consider indulging in something a bit nicer (and ultimately much safer).

Saga Residence Hotel (☎ 242225; Chaussée Prince Rwagasore; r from US$45) One of the more atmospheric hotels in this price range, the Saga is safe, secure and affordable.

Hotel Botanika (☎ 226792; hotelbotanika@hotmail. com; Blvd de l'Uprona; r from US$85; 🗷) Bujumbura's very own boutique hotel, the seven-room Botanika is a charming retreat from the rigours of life in Burundi.

Novotel Bujumbura (☎ 222600; novobuja@cbinf.com; Chaussée du Peuple Burundi; s/d US$120/135; 🗷 🖳 🖲) The preferred spot for visiting dignitaries, the Novotel is the only hotel in town that meets international four-star standards.

EATING & DRINKING

One of the best things about Bujumbura is the food. There are great bakeries, lively cafes and some of the finest restaurants in the region.

Boulangerie-Pâtisserie Trianon (Ave du Commerce; dishes BFr1000-4000) This place is packed out for breakfast thanks to a great combination of fresh croissants, healthy omelettes and local coffee.

Le Kasuku (☎ 243575; Rue de l'Industrie; mains BFr5000-12,000) A little garden oasis in the heart of the city, Kasuku has a hearty range of European dishes.

Chez André (Chaussée Prince Rwagasore; mains BFr7500-20,000) Housed in a huge villa on the eastern extreme of Chaussée Prince Rwagasore, this French- and Belgian-inspired institution is one of the best restaurants in the city.

Havana Club (Blvd de l'Uprona) One of the city's most popular nightspots, Havana Club draws a mixed crowd of locals and internationals most nights of the week.

SHOPPING

Burundi is hardly famous for its handicrafts, but a lot of excellent work makes its way across the border from DRC. The best place to browse is the small **craft market** (Ave du Stade). Haggle hard to get a good price.

GETTING THERE & AWAY

Minibuses ply the major routes around the country, and leave from the minibus station near the market area.

For more information on getting to and from Burundi, see p641.

GETTING AROUND

The centre of Bujumbura is small and negotiable on foot by day. After 8pm, always take a taxi in the city, no matter how short the distance, as robberies are common. Taxi fares range from BFr1000 for short hops in the centre to BFr5000 out to the beaches and to Mugere. *Moto-taxis* (motorcycle taxis) are another good option if you're not scared of Bujumbura's racing traffic.

AROUND BUJUMBURA

For a tiny landlocked country, Burundi has a surprising diversity of sights, though your ability to access them is entirely dependent on the security situation. At the time of research, there were still reports of splinter groups from the FNL causing disturbances in the countryside. However, as the AU-led disarmament continues, it is highly possible that routine

BURUNDI

travel across Burundi will once again become a possibility for locals and foreigners alike.

The information in this section is intended to serve as a brief outline of possible tourist destinations around the country, though you should seek out local advice before leaving Bujumbura. It has been quite some time since there was any tourist infrastructure firmly in place, though Burundi has a lot of potential as a travel destination, despite its present short-comings. If you happen to visit any of the sights listed below, we welcome your letters, and join you in hoping that the peace will hold long enough for us to expand our coverage of Burundi in future editions.

GITEGA

Gitega, the second-largest town in Burundi, is home to the **National Museum** (☎ 402359; admission BFr2000), which is locally famous for its collection of traditional Burundian musical instruments. There is also a limited number of accommodation and restaurant options.

A good day trip from Gitega is to the **Chutes de la Kagera**, near Rutana. These waterfalls are spectacular in the wet season (October to January), but there's no public transport there, so you will need to either charter a taxi or have your own vehicle.

Double-check the latest security situation before undertaking a road trip from Bujumbura to Gitega. Minibuses run throughout the day, making the trip in about one hour.

SOURCE DU NIL

This insignificant-looking little spring, south-east of Bujumbura, high up on the slopes of Mt Kikizi (2145m), is supposedly the south-ernmost source of the Nile. Naturally, the Ugandans dispute this, claiming the source as Jinja – where the Nile flows out of Lake Victoria. In Burundi 'le source' is no more than a trickle – not exactly a riveting sight – and access is impossible without a private or chartered vehicle. Ask around at hotels in Bujumbura about vehicle rental, road condi-tions and the latest security situation.

NATIONAL PARKS

The long civil war essentially wiped the na-tional parks off the map, and it's question-able whether or not wildlife can ever return to previous concentrations without the im-plementation of sweeping environmental policy reform. While it remains to be seen whether or not the government will seek to capitalise on the ecotourism movement that has very recently rejuvenated neighbouring Rwanda (see p741), Burundi is – at least on paper – home to three national parks that once protected a wide range of East African wildlife and habitats.

Parc National de la Kibira, the largest rainforest in Burundi, is contiguous with Parc National de Nyungwe (p752) in Rwanda, and is be-lieved to still be home to hundreds of colobus monkeys, and very possibly chimpanzees.

Parc National de la Rurubu is the largest park in the country, and was once famous for its wonderful hiking and expansive views.

The most accessible national park is **Parc National de la Rusizi**, 15km from Bujumbura. It's a wetland environment, and provides a habitat for hippos, sitatungas (aquatic antelopes) and a wide variety of birds.

BURUNDI DIRECTORY

ACCOMMODATION

The choice of accommodation is reasonable in Bujumbura, but tends to be skewed upmarket due to the large foreign presence. Elsewhere in the country, accommodation is fairly limited, though this may change during the shelf life of this book.

BUSINESS HOURS

Businesses tend to close for a couple of hours at lunch. Most eateries are open from 7am to about 9pm.

DANGERS & ANNOYANCES

At long last, Burundi's civil war has ended, though the country is still far from stable. Travel overland as little as possible, and consider restricting your visit to the capital. Bujumbura is safe by day due to a massive military presence, though the streets are best avoided at night.

Kigali (Rwanda) and Kigoma (Tanzania) are probably the best places to pick up reliable in-formation about current events in Burundi.

EMBASSIES & CONSULATES

Foreign embassies in Bujumbura include the following:
Belgium (☎ 233641; Blvd de la Liberté)
DRC (Ave du RD Congo)
France (☎ 251484; 60 Blvd de l'Uprona)

Rwanda (☎ 226865; Ave du RD Congo)
Tanzania (☎ 248636; 4 United Nations Rd)
USA (☎ 223454; Chaussée Prince Rwagasore)

HOLIDAYS
Unity Day 5 February
Labour Day 1 May
Independence Day 1 July
Assumption 15 August
Victory of Uprona Day 18 September
Anniversary of Rwagasore's Assassination 13 October
Anniversary of Ndadaye's Assassination 21 October
All Saints' Day 1 November

INTERNET ACCESS
Internet access is widespread and inexpensive in Bujumbura.

INTERNET RESOURCES
The official UN website covering the Burundi mission is www.un.org/depts/dpko/missions/onub.

MAPS
Rwanda Burundi – International Travel Map, published by ITMB Publishing at a scale of 1:400,000, is a good choice.

MONEY
The unit of currency is the Burundi franc (BFr). This is a cash economy and the US dollar is king. There were no ATMs on the international network in Burundi at the time of writing, though cash advances on credit cards are possible at major banks. There's an open black market in Bujumbura for changing money.

POST
The postal service is reasonably efficient and items take about one week to get to Europe or North America.

TELEPHONE
There are no telephone area codes within the country. The country code for Burundi is ☎ 257.

VISAS
Visas are required by all, and are best obtained from a Burundian embassy before arrival. Two photographs are required and visas are often available in the afternoon if you apply early in the morning. One-month tourist visas cost US$40.

> **PRACTICALITIES**
>
> - Burundi uses the metric system and distances are in kilometres.
> - Electricity in Burundi is 240V, 50 cycles, and plugs are mainly of the European two-round-pin variety.
> - The local press includes French-language *Le Renouveau*.
> - Government-controlled Radio Burundi broadcasts in Kirundi, French, Swahili and English.

See the boxed text, p737, for information about the forthcoming East African tourist visa.

Visas for Onward Travel
Visas for DRC, Rwanda and Tanzania are available from their respective embassies in Bujumbura (see opposite for contact details).

TRANSPORT IN BURUNDI
GETTING THERE & AWAY
Air
Bujumbura International Airport (BJM) is located about 12km north of the city centre. There are very few international airlines still serving Burundi as flights were severely disrupted during the long civil war. However, the following carriers occasionally offer air connections to Bujumbura:
Kenya Airways (KQ; www.kenya-airways.com)
Rwandair Express (WB; www.rwandair.com)

Lake
TO/FROM TANZANIA
Regular passenger ferry service between Bujumbura and Kigoma is currently suspended.

Land
Burundi shares land borders with DRC, Rwanda and Tanzania. Due to the long-running civil war, however, very few travellers have crossed this way in the last decade or more.

TO/FROM DRC
The main crossing between Burundi and DRC is at Gatumba on the road between Bujumbura and Uvira, about 15km west of the capital.

BURUNDI

TO/FROM RWANDA

The main crossing point is between Kayanza (Burundi) and Butare (Rwanda) on the main road linking Bujumbura and Kigali. The safest and quickest option for travel between Bujumbura and Kigali is to use one of the scheduled bus services that depart daily. Yahoo Car, New Yahoo Express, Venus Travel and Gaso Bus all run buses in both directions (BFr9000 to BFr12,000).

TO/FROM TANZANIA

For Kobero: there are several direct buses weekly between Mwanza and the border.

For the Manyovu crossing: *dalla-dalla* (pick-up trucks or minibuses) leave Kigoma from behind Bero petrol station. Once through the Tanzanian side of the border, you'll need to take one of the many waiting vehicles on to Makamba, where the Burundian immigration post is located. From there get another vehicle on to Bujumbura.

GETTING AROUND

Air

There are no internal domestic flights in Burundi.

Road

Travelling around the countryside is not as dangerous as it once was, though things change quickly in this part of the world. Ask around before heading out of Bujumbura, even to the second city of Gitega.

Most major roads in Burundi are sealed and public transport is mainly by minibus. Destinations are displayed in the front window of minibuses, which depart when full. They depart throughout the day from the *gare routière* (bus station) in any town.

Djibouti

Never heard of Djibouti? Don't feel bad – at the crossroads of two continents, it's more famous for its military bases and busy port than for its tourist attractions. It's a shame because this tiny speck of a country packs a big punch; what it lacks in size, it more than makes up for in beauty, especially if you're a fan of geological oddities. Hiking on the salt crust of Lac Assal, the third-lowest point on earth, or wandering amid hundreds of spikelike limestone chimneys belching out puffs of steam around Lac Abbé are just a couple of the many fascinating experiences on offer.

When the awesome landscapes have finished working their magic on you, there's a good mix of land and water activities to keep you buzzing. Diving fiends rave about Les Sept Frères Archipelago, while kitesurfers are thrilled by the optimal year-round conditions in the Gulf of Tadjoura. When it comes to snorkelling alongside whale sharks, the Bay of Ghoubbet is unsurpassable. For those who prefer to keep their feet dry, hiking opportunities abound – from guided walks in the Forêt du Day to memorable multiday hikes led by Afar nomads along ancient salt routes.

Barring Djibouti City, the country is refreshingly void of large-scale development. It's all about ecotravel, with some great sustainable *campements touristiques* in the hinterland – the perfect way to immerse yourself in local culture.

Sure, Djibouti is pricey, but it's worth the splurge.

FAST FACTS

- **Area** 23,000 sq km
- **ATMs** A few in Djibouti City (most Visa only)
- **Borders** Eritrea closed; Ethiopia and Somaliland open
- **Budget** US$50 to US$120 per day
- **Capital** Djibouti City
- **Languages** Arabic, French, Afar, Somali
- **Money** Djibouti Franc (DFr); US$1 = DFr163, €1 = DFr238
- **Population** Approximately 900,000
- **Seasons** Hot (May to September), cool (mid-October to mid-April), wet (October to April)
- **Telephone** Country code ☎ 253; international access code ☎ 00
- **Time** GMT/UTC +3
- **Visa** US$30 to US$60 for 30 days; obtainable at the airport for most Western nationals

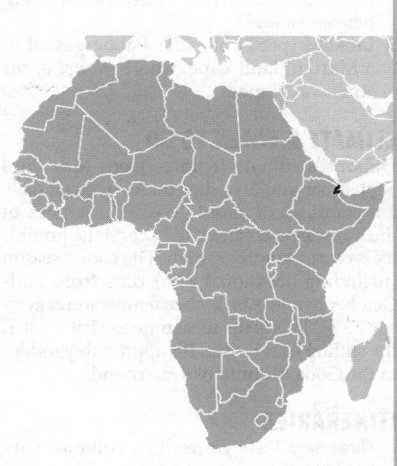

DJIBOUTI

HOW MUCH?

- **Internet** US$2.50 per hour
- **One night all-inclusive in a campement** US$50
- **Day trip to Lake Assal** US$90
- **Single dive in the Gulf of Tadjoura** US$43
- **Bunch of qat** Depends on quality!

LONELY PLANET INDEX

- **1L petrol** US$2
- **1.5L bottled water** US$1.20
- **Bottle of Heineken** US$4.30
- **Souvenir T-shirt** US$12
- **Fruit juice** US$2.50

HIGHLIGHTS

- **Djibouti City** (p647) Explore the alleyways of the Marché Central – full of pungent odours and bright colours – and test-drive the dance floors.
- **Moucha Island** (p652) Forget the hardships and take some time out on a white-sand beach.
- **Bay of Ghoubbet** (p649) Experience the thrills of snorkelling alongside (harmless) whale sharks.
- **Lac Assal** (p652) Descend to the lowest point on the African continent at 150m below sea level.
- **Lac Abbé** (p652) Wander flabbergasted in a Martian landscape, where *Planet of the Apes* was filmed.

CLIMATE & WHEN TO GO

Djibouti's climate is hot – from May until September you'll swelter under average daily temperatures of about 40°C. At the peak of the hot season it can hit 45°C, and the humidity is correspondingly high. The cooler season (including occasional rain) runs from mid-October to mid-April, when temperatures average 25°C. This is the ideal time to visit – when the stifling heat is over. It's appreciably milder in the Goda Mountains year-round.

ITINERARIES

- **Three days** Base yourself in Djibouti City (p647) and take a tour to explore Lac

Assal (p652) and Lac Abbé (p652). Back in the capital, enjoy its culinary delights and spend your last night in the bars and clubs.

- **One week** Recharge on a porcelain-sand beach on Moucha Island (p652) or explore the little-known Goda Mountains (p652). In season, be sure to take a whale-watching tour to the Bay of Ghoubbet (p649) or a diving trip to the Gulf of Tadjoura (p649).

HISTORY

From Aksum to Islam

Around the 1st century AD, Djibouti made up part of the powerful Ethiopian kingdom of Aksum, which included modern-day Eritrea and even stretched across the Red Sea to parts of southern Arabia. It was during the Aksumite era, in the 4th century AD, that Christianity first appeared in the region.

As the empire of Aksum gradually fell into decline, a new influence arose that superseded the Christian religion in Djibouti: Islam. It was introduced to the region around AD 825 by Arab traders from southern Arabia.

European Ambitions

In the second half of the 19th century, European powers competed to grab new colonies in Africa. The French, seeking to counter the British presence in Yemen on the other side of the Bab al-Mandab Strait, made agreements with the Afar sultans of Obock and Tadjoura that gave them the right to settle in these areas. In 1888 construction of Djibouti City began on the southern shore of the Gulf of Tadjoura. French Somaliland (present-day Djibouti) began to take shape.

France and the emperor of landlocked Ethiopia then signed a pact designating Djibouti as the 'official outlet of Ethiopian commerce'. This led to the construction of the Addis Ababa–Djibouti City railway, which was of vital commercial importance until recently. Before the independence of Eritrea, Ethiopia also used the ports of Assab and Massawa.

Throwing Off the French Yoke

As early as 1949 there were a number of anticolonial demonstrations led by the Issa Somalis, who were in favour of the reunification of the territories of Italian, British and

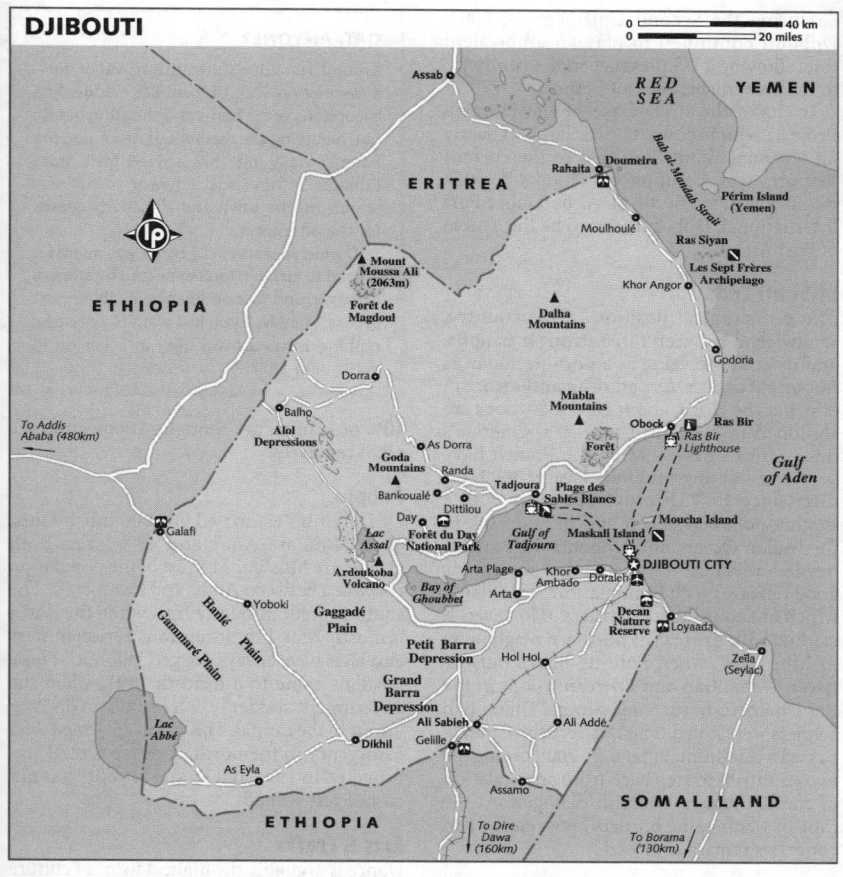

DJIBOUTI

French Somaliland. Meanwhile, the Afars were in favour of continued French rule.

Major riots ensued, especially after the 1967 referendum, which produced a vote in favour of continued French rule. This vote took place after the arrest of opposition leaders and the massive expulsion of ethnic Somalis. After the referendum, the colony's name was changed from French Somaliland to the French Territory of the Afars and Issas.

In June 1977, the colony finally won its sovereignty from France. The country became the Republic of Djibouti.

Small Country, Adroit Leaders

Despite continuous clan rivalries between the two main ethnic groups, the Afars and Issas,

who have been jostling for power since the 1970s, Djibouti has managed to exploit its strategic position.

When the Gulf War broke out in 1990, the country's president, Hassan Gouled Aptidon, while claiming to oppose the military build-up in the Gulf, simultaneously allowed France to increase its military presence in the country, as well as granting the Americans and Italians access to the naval port. And he skilfully managed to retain the support of Saudi Arabia and Kuwait for the modernisation of Djibouti port. During the war between Eritrea and Ethiopia in the 1990s, Ethiopia stopped using the ports of Massawa and Assab and diverted all its foreign trade through Djibouti.

During the Second Gulf War, in 2003, Djibouti continued to play an ambivalent role, allowing a US presence in the country – to the great displeasure of France.

In 2006, the first phase of the Doraleh Project, which consists of a large-capacity oil terminal about 8km east of the current seaport, was completed. Thanks to this megaproject, partly financed by Dubai Port International, Djibouti aims to be the 'Dubai of East Africa'.

Djibouti Today

The geographical position of the country, sandwiched between three stronger nations, and its strategic value as a port are today as important as ever. As part of an antiterrorism effort in the Horn, about 1000 US troops are stationed in Djibouti City – it's America's only African base – while the French have been maintaining a military base of 3000 soldiers since 1977. It provides France with a staging post between it and its outposts in the Indian Ocean, and Djibouti with much-needed revenue. Djibouti also maintains good relations with Ethiopia and Somaliland, which are considered 'partners'. However, it clashed with Eritrea (its northern neighbour) in June 2008, when fighting broke out between Djiboutian and Eritrean troops in the Ras Doumeira border area. Several Djiboutian soldiers were killed. The UN Security Council passed a resolution in January 2009 urging the two countries to step back from an escalation of conflict and re-establish dialogue. At the time of writing, the borders between the two countries remained closed.

CULTURE

Djiboutians are charming, respectful and very hospitable people. This attitude has its origins in the traditionally nomadic culture of the two main ethnic groups, the Afars and Issas. Despite an increasing tendency towards a more sedentary lifestyle, most Djiboutians living in towns retain strong links with their nomadic past.

Something that will immediately strike you in Djibouti is the overwhelming presence of qat. The life of most Djiboutian males seems to revolve entirely around the consumption of this mild narcotic. Every day, qat consumers meet their circle of friends in the mabraz (qat den) to brouter (graze). Qat is said to be the reason behind numerous divorces. Only

---

QAT, ANYONE?

Around 1pm, don't miss the arrival of qat – a fascinating slice of local life. Suddenly a cacophony of car horns and shouting breaks out, heralding the marvellous news: qat, the nation's daily 'hit', has arrived fresh from Ethiopia. Afterwards a heavy torpor descends on the town and all activity ceases for the afternoon.

During your stay in Djibouti, you might be invited to 'graze'. Don't expect to be stoned, however, and take antidiarrheal tablets, just in case. Frankly, if you just want to get tipsy, nothing beats a fresh beer in a bar on Pl du 27 Juin 1977.

10% of women are thought to consume the plant regularly.

People

Of Djibouti's estimated 900,000 inhabitants, about 46% are Afars and 45% Issas. Both groups are Muslim. The rest of the population is divided between Arabs and Europeans. The south is predominantly Issa, while the north is mostly Afar. Ethnic tensions between Afars and Issas have always dogged Djibouti. These tensions came to a head in 1991, when the government suddenly cracked down on Afar unrest in the capital. This led to an armed Afar insurgency in the north. A peace accord was brokered in 1994, but ethnic hostility has not completely waned.

Arts & Crafts

Dance is arguably the highest form of culture in Djibouti, along with oral literature and poetry. Some dances celebrate major life events, such as birth, marriage or circumcision.

If you are looking for handicrafts, the traditional Afar and Somali knives and the very attractive Afar woven straw mats (known in Afar as fiddima) are among the finest products.

FOOD & DRINK

Djibouti City is endowed with a plethora of tasty restaurants that will please most palates – a testimony to French presence. You'll find excellent seafood, rice, pasta, local meat dishes, such as stuffed kid or lamb, and other treats imported from France. In the countryside, choice is obviously more limited, with goat meat and rice as the main staples. Alcohol is widely available.

ENVIRONMENT

Djibouti's 23,000 sq km can be divided into three geographic regions: the coastal plains, which feature white, sandy beaches; the volcanic plateaus in the southern and central parts of the country; and the mountain ranges in the north, where the altitude reaches more than 2000m above sea level. Essentially the country is a vast wasteland, with the exception of pockets of forest and dense vegetation to the north.

Livestock rearing is the most important type of agriculture. As demand for scarce grazing land mounts, the forests of the north are increasingly coming under threat, including the country's only national park, the fragile Forêt du Day.

DJIBOUTI CITY

pop 600,000

After a long-haul or regional flight, what a surprise to be greeted in French and to dine on *steak de boeuf sauce Roquefort* and baguettes. Due to its colonial past, and the current heavy French military presence, Djibouti City is like a Gallic outpost in the Horn. Truth is, it's a strange African anomaly, with jarring cultural and social combinations and surprisingly cosmopolitan vibes: traditionally robed Afars, stalwart French legionnaires (and the odd GI), Somali ladies wearing colourful garments and frazzled businessmen with the latest mobile phones stuck to their ears all jostle side by side.

Djibouti City is mostly an air hub (mainly for military purposes) and a busy port. Sights are scarce, but it's the obvious place to organise forays into the fantastic hinterland or boat excursions. It boasts good infrastructure – including hotels, bars, clubs and restaurants – but it doesn't come cheap. If you come via neighbouring countries, be prepared for a financial shock.

ORIENTATION

Djibouti City is small enough to explore on foot. The centre comprises the European Quarter to the north and the African Quarter to the south. There are no street numbers and not all streets have names.

Northwest of the town centre, a causeway known as L'Escale leads to a small marina. Northeast are the Plateau du Serpent and Ilot du Heron, where many of the foreign embassies can be found.

The train station is about 1km north of the centre, while Djibouti-Ambouli Airport is 5km south of town.

INFORMATION

Internet Access

There's a slew of internet outlets in the town centre. They all offer fast connections; expect to pay around DFr400 per hour.

Medical Services

Pôle Médical (☎ 352724; off Pl du 27 Juin 1977; ☺ 8am-noon & 4-7pm Sat-Thu) A well-equipped clinic.

Money

There are banks and two bureaux de change in the town centre, as well as a few Visa-friendly ATMs (but only one ATM that accepts MasterCard).

Banque Indosuez Mer Rouge (Pl Lagarde; ☺ 7.30am-noon & 4-7pm) Changes cash and has two ATMs.

BCIMR Pl Lagarde (☺ 7.30-11.45am Sun-Thu); Plateau du Serpent (Ave F d'Esperey; ☺ 7.45am-noon & 4-5.15pm Sun-Thu) The branch on Pl Lagarde has two ATMs, but only one was functioning at the time of writing.

Dilip Corporation (Pl du 27 Juin 1977; ☺ 8am-noon & 4-7.30pm Sat-Thu) Authorised bureau de change. Changes cash (no commission) and does cash advances on Visa and MasterCard. It also accepts travellers cheques.

Mehta (☎ 353719; Pl du 27 Juin 1977; ☺ 7.30am-noon & 4-7.30pm Sun-Thu) Authorised bureau de change. Next door to Dilip, Mehta also changes cash (no commission) and usually accepts travellers cheques but charges a 2% commission.

Saba Islamic Bank (off Pl du 27 Juin 1977) Has one ATM, which accepts both Visa and MasterCard.

There's also a small bureau de change in the departure hall at the airport, but it closes around 6pm.

Post

Main post office (Blvd de la République; ☺ 7am-1pm Sat-Thu) North of the town centre.

Telephone

The most convenient places to make international or local calls are the various telephone outlets scattered around the city centre.

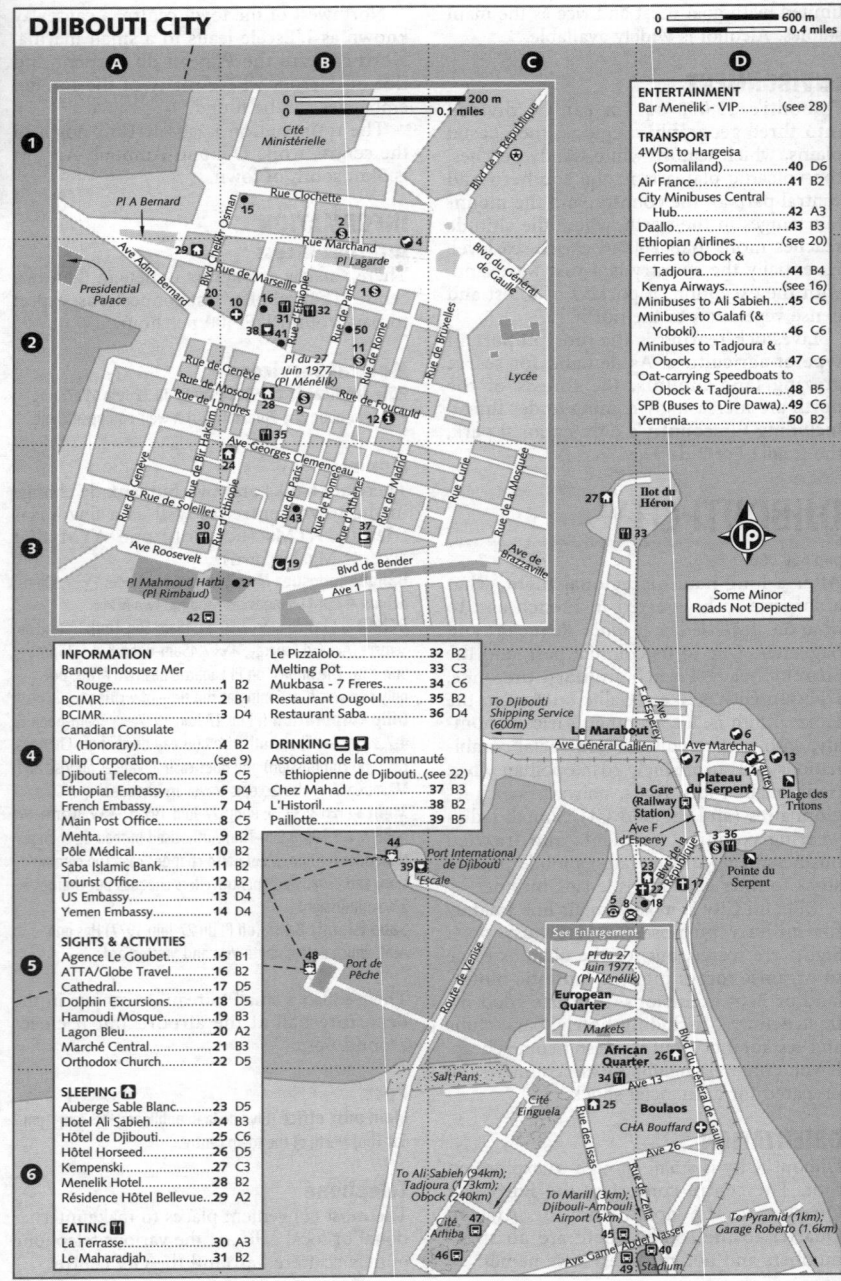

DJIBOUTI CITY

0 — 600 m
0 — 0.4 miles

0 — 200 m
0 — 0.1 miles

Cité
Ministérielle

Pl A Bernard

Cité
Ministérielle

Rue Clochette

Rue Marchand

Pl Lagarde

Presidential
Palace

Pl du 27
Juin 1977
(Pl Ménélik)

Rue de Genève

Rue de Moscou

Rue de Londres

Ave Georges Clemenceau

Ave Roosevelt

Blvd de Bender

Pl Mahmoud Harbi
(Pl Rimbaud)

Ave 1

Ilot du
Héron

Some Minor
Roads Not Depicted

INFORMATION

Banque Indosuez Mer Rouge.......................1	B2
BCIMR.......................2	B1
BCIMR.......................3	D4
Canadian Consulate (Honorary).......................4	B2
Dilip Corporation.......................(see 9)	
Djibouti Telecom.......................5	C5
Ethiopian Embassy.......................6	D4
French Embassy.......................7	D4
Main Post Office.......................8	C5
Mehta.......................9	B2
Pôle Médical.......................10	B2
Saba Islamic Bank.......................11	B2
Tourist Office.......................12	B2
US Embassy.......................13	D4
Yemen Embassy.......................14	D4

SIGHTS & ACTIVITIES

Agence Le Goubet.......................15	B1
ATTA/Globe Travel.......................16	B2
Cathedral.......................17	D5
Dolphin Excursions.......................18	D5
Hamoudi Mosque.......................19	B3
Lagon Bleu.......................20	A2
Marché Central.......................21	B3
Orthodox Church.......................22	D5

SLEEPING

Auberge Sable Blanc.......................23	D5
Hotel Ali Sabieh.......................24	B3
Hôtel de Djibouti.......................25	C6
Hôtel Horseed.......................26	D5
Kempenski.......................27	C3
Menelik Hotel.......................28	B2
Résidence Hôtel Bellevue..29	A2

EATING

La Terrasse.......................30	A3
Le Maharadjah.......................31	B2

Le Pizzaiolo.......................32	B2
Melting Pot.......................33	C3
Mukbasa - 7 Freres.......................34	C6
Restaurant Ougoul.......................35	B2
Restaurant Saba.......................36	D4

DRINKING

Association de la Communauté Ethiopienne de Djibouti..(see 22)	
Chez Mahad.......................37	B3
L'Historil.......................38	B2
Paillotte.......................39	B5

ENTERTAINMENT

Bar Menelik - VIP............(see 28)	

TRANSPORT

4WDs to Hargeisa (Somaliland).................40	D6
Air France.......................41	B2
City Minibuses Central Hub.......................42	A3
Daallo.......................43	B3
Ethiopian Airlines.......................(see 20)	
Ferries to Obock & Tadjoura.......................44	B4
Kenya Airways.................(see 16)	
Minibuses to Ali Sabieh.......45	C6
Minibuses to Galafi (& Yoboki).......................46	C6
Minibuses to Tadjoura & Obock.......................47	C6
Oat-carrying Speedboats to Obock & Tadjoura.......48	B5
SPB (Buses to Dire Dawa).....49	C6
Yemenia.......................50	B2

To Djibouti
Shipping Service
(600m)

Le Marabout

Ave El Espero

Ave Général Galliéni

Ave Maréchal

Plateau
du Serpent

La Gare
(Railway
Station)

Plage des
Tritons

Ave F
d'Esperey

Pointe du
Serpent

Port International
de Djibouti

L'Escale

Port de
Pêche

See Enlargement

Pl du 27
Juin 1977
(Pl Ménélik)

European
Quarter

Markets

Route de Venise

Salt Pans

African
Quarter

Boulaos

CHA Bouffard

Cité
Einguela

Ave 13

Ave 26

Salt Pans

Cité
Arhiba

To Ali-Sabieh (94km);
Tadjoura (173km);
Obock (240km)

To Marill (3km);
Djibouli-Ambouli
Airport (5km)

To Pyramid (1km);
Garage Roberto (1.6km)

Ave Gamel Abdel Nasser

Stadium

NOSE TO NOSE WITH THE LEVIATHAN OF THE SEA

The Bay of Ghoubbet is one of most dependable locations in the world for close encounters with whale sharks, the world's largest fish. During the peak season (October to January) the question isn't whether you will see a shark, but how many you will see. 'If you come in the right period of the year and stay a few days in Djibouti, sightings of whale sharks are guaranteed; there are up to 15 individuals, close to the shore, and it's very easy to snorkel with these graceful creatures', one operator told us.

This activity has exploded in recent years. However, the way it is conducted often leaves something to be desired. Stick to Dolphin Excursions or Lagon Bleu (below); at least these two operators are more ecologically sensitive and follow protocols. Give the sharks a berth of at least 4m; touching them is an absolute no-no.

Tourist Information

Tourist office (☎ 352800; www.office-tourisme.dj; Rue de Foucauld; ☽ 7am-1pm & 4-6pm Sat, Mon & Wed, 7am-1pm Sun, Tue & Thu) Mildly helpful.

SIGHTS

Djibouti City is big on atmosphere but short on sights. The European Quarter, with its whitewashed houses and Moorish arcades, is a strange mix of Arab and European. To the south lies the shambolic Pl Mahmoud Harbi (Place Rimbaud), dominated by the minaret of the great **Hamoudi mosque**. Nearby, the chaotic **Marché Central** (Central Market) is a criss-cross of alleyways flanked by loads of stalls and shops.

The **cathedral** (Blvd de la République) and the diminutive **Orthodox Church** (west of Blvd de la République) are also well worth a look.

The only decent beach is at the Kempinski (p650), but there's an entrance fee of DFr3000 for nonguests.

ACTIVITIES

Diving, kitesurfing, whale-shark spotting and hiking can all be organised from Djibouti City.

Diving

Most diving takes place off the islands of Maskali and Moucha (see p652) in the Gulf of Tadjoura, which rewards divers with a host of scenic sites for all levels. Wreck enthusiasts should make a beeline for the monster-sized *Faon*, a 120m-long cargo ship that lies in 27m of water on a sandy floor; it's also heavily overgrown with marine life. Other shipwrecks worthy of exploration include *L'Arthur Rimbaud*, a tugboat that was scuttled in 2005, and the nearby *Nagfa*, a small Ethiopian boat, each of which lies in about 25m of water. Some

excellent reef dives also beckon, including Le Tombant Nord (The Northern Drop-Off), blessed with healthy corals and prolific marine life, and Les Patates Air France (Air France Bommies), where you'll see a smorgasbord of reef fish, including shoals of groupers, especially in March and April when they mate.

The weak point is the low visibility, which seldom exceeds 10m to 15m.

You'll find two professional dive centres in Djibouti City staffed with qualified instructors who speak English. A single dive costs about DFr7000.

Dolphin Excursions (☎ 350313, 812300; www.dolphin-excursions.com; Blvd de la République)

Lagon Bleu (☎ 250296, 825733; http://bluelagon.net; off Pl du 27 Juin 1977) Operates out of Lagon Bleu Village (p652) on Moucha Island; transfers can be organised from this office in Djibouti City.

Kitesurfing

The combination of constant strong breezes, protected areas with calm water conditions and a lack of obstacles makes Djibouti a world-class destination for kitesurfers. In the Bay of Ghoubbet, winds can reach 35 knots and blow about 300 days a year. For beginners, Île de la Tortue, near the international airport, is a hot favourite, with shallow waters and more manageable breezes (about 15 knots). 'And there's the added thrill of fantastic mountainous backdrops', says Dante Kourallos, who runs **Djibouti Kitesurf** (☎ 828614, 357233; www.djiboutikitesurf.com). Tuition and courses for all levels can be arranged, as well as a half-day 'discovery' session (€70).

Hiking

In the cooler months, various hikes led by Afar nomads can be arranged along ancient salt routes in western Djibouti. It's the best

DETOUR TO DECAN

Weary of the hustle and bustle of Djibouti City? Have a soft spot for endangered species? Wanna support a local conservation initiative? Make a beeline for **Decan** (☎ 340119; http://decan.djibouti. googlepages.com; admission DFr1500; ☷ 3.30-6.30pm Mon, Wed & Sat). This small wildlife refuge about 15km south of Djibouti City (on the road to Somaliland) makes for an easy two- to three-hour excursion from the capital.

Decan was set up as a rehabilitation centre for various species that have been orphaned or illegally caged for trafficking purposes. You'll see six endlessly appealing cheetahs (don't forget your camera for that fantastic close-up!), and two striped hyenas, as well as ostriches, turtles, Somali donkeys, caracals, squirrels and a variety of birds. 'Make no mistake', says Bertrand Lafrance, the French vet who runs Decan, 'it's not a zoo, but a small nature reserve, with its own ecosystem. We have plans to extend it from 30 acres to 500 acres, down to the coastline, which would encompass a mangrove area.' Decan also runs education programs for customs officers, the police and school kids. Watching the big cats being fed is just one of the many exhilarating moments at Decan. Want to help? Volunteers are welcome.

The only practical option for getting here from Djibouti City is by taxi (DFr3000).

way to immerse yourself in traditional nomadic culture. Duration varies from two-day hikes near Lac Assal to 10-day expeditions as far as Ethiopia.

The following operators are based in Djibouti City and have good credentials:

Dolphin Excursions (see p649)

La Caravane de Sel (☎ 810488; caravanedusel@ hotmail.com) Ask for Said Baragoita.

SLEEPING

If you're coming from, say, Ethiopia or Eritrea, be prepared to grit your teeth – prices are shockingly expensive for what you get.

Budget

Hôtel Horseed (☎ 352316; Blvd du Général de Gaulle; s/d with shared bathroom DFr5000/7500; ☒) Despite being raggedy, the Horseed has presentable rooms. However, cleanliness is only just OK in the shared bathrooms – wear flip-flops and pray you're not the last in line to shower.

Hôtel de Djibouti (☎ 356415; Ave 13; s/d DFr6500/8800; ☒) This place is located in the heart of the African Quarter and is appropriately colourful. Fight tooth and nail to get a room at the back of the hotel, otherwise the crazy road noise will make sleep a wishful dream. Keep your expectations in check, especially regarding the quality of the plumbing.

Auberge Sable Blanc (☎ 351163; west of Blvd de la République; d with/without bathroom DFr8000/6900; ☒) A short stagger from Blvd de la République, this little modern construction is a discreet place with clean, if rather unloved, rooms and salubrious bathrooms.

Midrange

Hotel Ali Sabieh (☎ 353264; alsabhot@intnet.dj; Ave Georges Clemenceau; s DFr10,800-11,800, d DFr14,500; ☒) While most units at the Ali Sabieh are petite and charmless, the attentive staff, well-sprung mattresses and rooms that are scrubbed by a team of cleaning addicts make this a sure-fire bet. It's right in the thick of things, too.

Menelik Hotel (☎ 351177; menelikhotel@intnet. dj; Pl du 27 Juin 1977; s/d incl breakfast DFr15,900/20,500; ☒ ▯ ☎) It's hard to top the Menelik's location, smack dab in the centre of town. The modernish rooms provide excellent levels of comfort and hygiene but, to be honest, you pay for the location. Visa credit cards are accepted, but you'll also pay 5% commission.

Residence Hôtel Bellevue (☎ 358088; bellevue@ intnet.dj; Blvd Cheikh Osman; s DFr17,500-19,500, d DFr19,500-21,500; ☒) The Bellevue gets by on its handy location, a waddle away from the restaurants, bars and clubs. The well-equipped rooms are decent enough but they lack any real sparkle.

Top End

Kempinski (☎ 325555; www.kempinski.com; Ilot du Héron; s DFr85,000-90,000, d DFr90,000-97,000; ☒ ▯ ☒) You know exactly what you'll get at the swanky Kempinski: shiny-clean rooms and a host of top-notch facilities. What you won't get is any indication that you are in Djibouti; but, as you flake out on the beach or do laps in the gleaming pool, you probably won't be that bothered.

EATING

The city is endowed with a smattering of restaurants that will please most palates. If you're on a budget, you'll also find inexpensive snack stands in the town centre.

our pick La Terrasse (☎ 350227; Rue d'Ethiopie; mains DFr400-700; ☺ dinner) Bargain! This place has plenty of mood and serves up 'good Ethiopian food at good prices in a good atmosphere', as one regular patron put it. It occupies a rooftop, with a moodily lit dining area and an open kitchen – not to mention the heady scents of incense. If only it was licensed!

Restaurant Saba (☎ 354244; Ave Maréchal Lyautey; mains DFr1200-2500; ☺ lunch Sat-Thu, dinner daily) Close to the railway station, this unpretentious joint serves well-prepared fish and meat dishes without fuss. Some reliable choices are skewered fish, fillet of barracuda, and *poisson yemenite* (oven-baked fish). There are some good pastas and salads (from DFr700), too, as well as superb fruit juices.

Le Pizzaiolo (☎ 354439; Rue d'Ethiopie; mains DFr1300-3000) Perfect crusts and well-chosen ingredients are two of the components that make Le Pizzaiolo the best pizza place in town. Pasta and meat dishes are also available.

Restaurant Ougoul (☎ 353652; Ave Georges Clemenceau; mains DFr1600-4400; ☺ lunch & dinner) Ougoul is *the* place towards which all heads turn when it comes to tasting a range of bounteous marine offerings. Push the boat out with, say, lobster (grilled, stuffed, flambéed or thermidor), prawns, barracuda, wahoo or grouper.

Mukbasa - 7 Freres (☎ 351188; Ave 13; fish dishes DFr2000; ☺ lunch & dinner) This straightforward eatery specialises in *poisson yemenite*. It's served with a chapatti-like bread and a devilish *mokbasa* (purée of honey and either dates or banana). It's so finger-licking good that you'll quickly forget about the dull decor.

our pick Melting Pot (☎ 350399; Ilot du Héron; mains DFr2000-7000; ☺ lunch & dinner) Cute and cosy, Melting Pot is a lovely spot for supper or a relaxed, drawn-out meal. As the name suggests, the menu is eclectic, with a wide range of Japanese dishes, Greek specialities (their tarama is divine) and French classics (mmmm, the *andouillette dijonnaise* – cooked sausage with mustard sauce). The atmosphere is sophisticated but relaxed.

Le Maharadjah (☎ 356616; Rue d'Ethiopie; mains DFr2600-3700; ☺ dinner) Elegant Maharadjah takes its inspiration from the Middle East, with an ample selection of tastebud-titillating specialities. Among the many winners are *shish tawooq* (chicken grilled on skewers), *kofta* (meatballs) and *shanklish* (goat's cheese served with onions, oil and tomatoes).

DRINKING

There's no shortage of watering holes in Djibouti City, especially around Pl du 27 Juin 1977. **L'Historil** (Pl du 27 Juin 1977) has an appealing terrace, which offers excellent people-watching opportunities. Other G-spots of the city's bar scene include **Paillotte** (Port de Pêche), easily the hippest place when we visited, and the down-to-earth **Association de la Communauté Ethiopienne de Djibouti** (west of Blvd de la République), also known as 'Club Ethiopien', where a bottle of St George costs only DFr400. Club Ethiopien also serves good Ethiopian fare at puny prices.

Our favourite juice bar is **Chez Mahad** (off Rue de Madrid; juices DFr200-400; ☺ 7.30am-noon & 4-8.30pm Sat-Thu, 4-9pm Fri), which has a dizzying array of fruity concoctions.

Plenty of teahouses are scattered around the town centre.

ENTERTAINMENT

Most clubs are on or around Rue d'Ethiopie, in the European Quarter. Expect the company of stalwart legionnaires and Ethiopian working girls. They are at their liveliest on Thursday and Friday nights. Entrance is free, but a beer costs from DFr1000. The **Bar Menelik – VIP** (Pl du 27 Juin 1977), in the basement of Menelik Hotel, was the 'most happening' (make it 'least sleazy') place at the time of research.

GETTING THERE & AWAY
Air

For details of international flights to and from Djibouti City, see p656.

Boat

There are talks of opening a ferry route between Djibouti City, Tadjoura and Obock. Check while in Djibouti City. Meanwhile, you can rely on the speedboats that carry the precious *qat* to Tadjoura and Obock.

Car

For 4WD rental (from DFr25,000 per day, with driver), contact the following outfits:

Garage Roberto (☎ 352029; Route de Boulaos)
Marill (☎ 327433; Route de l'Aéroport)
Pyramid (☎ 358203; Route de Boulaos)

Local Transport

Minibuses leave from various departure points south of town. They connect Djibouti City to Ali Sabieh, Tadjoura, Galafi (at the Ethiopian border) and Obock. Most minibuses leave early in the morning and only when they are full. Most journeys cost from DFr500 to DFr2000, depending on distance.

Train

The Djibouti–Ethiopia train departs three times a week and runs as far as Dire Dawa (DFr4200 in 1st class). You can take it and get off at Ali Sabieh (about DFr1500). You're well advised to buy your ticket one day in advance at the **railway station** (Ave F d'Esperey; 7am-noon Tue, Thu & Sat).

GETTING AROUND

The central hub for city minibuses (DFr50) is on Pl Mahmoud Harbi. A taxi ride within the centre costs about DFr500 (DFr1000 to/ from the airport).

AROUND DJIBOUTI

MOUCHA ISLAND

It ain't Bora Bora, but this island, easily accessible from Djibouti City, is a welcome respite from the hustle and bustle of the capital, with uncrowded beaches and warm waters. The **Lagon Bleu Village** (250296, 847247; http://bluelagon.net; Moucha Island; s incl full board from DFr17,000;) is a good place to take up a Robinson Crusoe lifestyle without sacrificing comfort, with 19 well-equipped bungalows, a good restaurant and a reputable **diving** centre (see p649). As an indication of prices, a two-day/one-night full-board package including transfers to/from Djibouti City costs from DFr18,500/10,500 per adult/child. Day trips are also possible (from DFr8500/5500, including lunch). For bookings contact ATTA/ Globe Travel (see p656).

LAC ASSAL

Just over 100km west of the capital lies one of the most spectacular natural phenomena in Africa: Lac Assal. Situated 150m below sea level, this crater lake is encircled by dark, dormant volcanoes. It represents the lowest point on the African continent. The aquamarine water is ringed by a huge salt field,

60m in depth. The salt field has been mined by the Afar nomads for centuries, and they can still be seen loading up their camels for the long trek south to Ethiopia.

There's no public transport to Lac Assal. Most visitors come with tours (see p656) or hire their own vehicles from the capital. A tour should set you back about DFr15,000.

LAC ABBÉ

You'll never forget your first glimpse of Lac Abbé. The scenery is sensational: the plain is dotted with hundreds of limestone chimneys, some standing as high as 50m, belching out puffs of steam. It is often described as 'a slice of moon on the crust of earth'. *Planet of the Apes* was filmed here, and it's no wonder.

Though desolate, it is not uninhabited. Numerous mineral-rich hot springs feed the farms of local nomads who graze their camels and goats here. The banks of the lake are also where flamingos gather at dawn.

There are three *campements touristiques* near Lac Abbé. The best organised is **Campement Touristique d'Asbole** (822291; full board DFr8000), which lies on a plateau that proffers stupendous views of the big chimneys. As in all *campements*, accommodation is rudimentary, but who cares? You'll be hypnotised by the scenery anyway. Prices include a guided walk to the chimneys.

To get there, you'll need to rent a 4WD with driver or take a tour from the capital (see p656). The *campement touristique* can organise transfers if you have (or can find) a group of people.

GODA MOUNTAINS

If you want to get away from it all, look no further. Northwest of the Gulf of Tadjoura, the Goda Mountains rise to a height of 1750m and are a spectacular natural oddity. This area shelters one of the rare speckles of green on Djibouti's parched map, like a giant oasis – a real relief after the scorched desert landscapes. It's a real shock for some visitors, who find it inconceivable that the tiny settlements of **Dittilou**, **Day**, **Bankoualé** and **Randa** belong to the same country as the one they left on the burning plain just an hour before.

The Goda Mountains also boast Djibouti's only national park, **Forêt du Day National Park**, which offers ample **hiking** opportunities. Owners of *campements touristiques* will be happy to suggest guided walks suited to your level of ability.

Sleeping & Eating

This area is favoured by expats in search of cool air, and there's a smattering of traditional, ecofriendly *campements touristiques*. Showers and toilets are communal; the prices quoted include guided walks.

our pick **Campement Touristique de la Forêt du Day** (☎ 354520; Day; full board DFr8000) If you like peace, quiet and sigh-inducing views, you'll have few quibbles with this atmospheric *campement* in the Forêt du Day National Park, at an altitude of 1400m. The traditional huts are welcoming, the ablution block is in good nick and electricity is solar-generated. Other draws include the host of walking options available and the healthy food.

Campement Touristique de Dittilou (☎ 810488; Dittilou; full board DFr8000) The traditional huts *(das)* here are set against a lush and totally peaceful landscape, at the edge of Forêt du Day National Park. It's a good base for hiking – don't miss the waterfall of Toha (a three- to four-hour return visit).

Campement Touristique de Bankoualé (☎ 814115; Bankoualé; full board DFr8000) This is another ecofriendly camp (electricity is solar powered) in a scenic location – it overlooks a lush valley and there's an Afar village nearby, where you can stock up on local handicrafts. Huts 5 and 6 boast the best views. The ablution block is well scrubbed and the food gets good reports. Houmed, the owner, is a beekeeper, and the home-grown honey is delicious. There are excellent hiking possibilities, too.

Getting There & Away

The most convenient way to visit the Goda Mountains area is on a tour (see p656) or with a rental 4WD. Transport can also be organised by the *campements* if there's a group (usually a minimum of four people).

TADJOURA
pop 25,000

Originally a small Afar village trading in slaves, this whitewashed town is now a quiet backwater. Poor and run-down, its setting is nevertheless attractive, nestled in the shadow of the green Goda Mountains with the bright blue sea lapping at its doorstep.

If you're after sustainably produced local handicrafts, the women-run **Association des**

Femmes de Tadjoura (☺ 7.30am-12.30pm & 4-6pm Sat-Thu) sells colourful Afar basketware.

Plage des Sables Blancs, 7km east of Tadjoura, is tranquillity incarnate and a lovely place to sun yourself, with a good string of white sand.

Sleeping & Eating

Hôtel-Restaurant Le Golfe (☎ 424091/153; hot_rest _legolfe@hotmail.com; bungalows DFr11,000; ❄ ❑) Under French-Ethiopian management, this low-key but well-kept resort is popular with French soldiers and their families. It's situated in a relaxing waterfront setting about 1.5km from the town centre. The 14 units are not fancy but are functional, and there's a good on-site restaurant (seafood!). There's no beach to speak of, but the owners can organise transfers to Plage des Sables Blancs.

Plage des Sables Blancs Campement (☎ 354520; Plage des Sables Blancs; full board DFr13,000) Right on the beach, this is a good place to chill out for a couple of days. Accommodation is simple (beds and mattresses only). Transfers can be organised from Djibouti City at weekends (DFr17,500 flat rate including full board). Contact Agence Le Goubet (see p656).

There's a smattering of cheap and cheerful eateries right by the seafront.

Getting There & Away

There is a good sealed road from the capital to Tadjoura; regular morning buses ply this route (about DFr1500, three hours).

You can also take one of the *qat*-laden dhows or speedboats that leave every day sometime between noon and 2pm from Port de Pêche in Djibouti City (DFr600 to DFr1000 one way).

There's a ferry service between Djibouti City and Tadjoura (DFr700 one way, three times weekly).

OBOCK & LES SEPT FRÈRES ARCHIPELAGO

The last significant town before the border with Eritrea, Obock exudes a kind of 'last frontier' feel – light years away from the hullabaloo of Djibouti City. With the completion of the sealed road from Tadjoura in 2008, tourism is slowly, slowly taking off in this area.

It has a couple of sights, including **Ras Bir lighthouse**, about 6km east of the town centre, and the eerily quiet **Cimetière Marin** (Marine Cemetery), on the western outskirts of town.

You can lay your head at the welcoming **Village Mer Rouge** (☎ 810799, 862812; www.villamer rouge.dj; d DFr8000-10,000; ✗), about 2km west of the centre. Choose between the six rustically cosy bungalows on the beach, the 'hill bungalows' (with air-con but no views) or the stylish 'luxury bungalows' with all mod cons and splendid seaviews. Expect some water shortages, though. Staff are young locals who were trained in Djibouti City – a nice initiative. The on-site restaurant serves up toothsome local dishes. Various tours in the area can be organised. A cheaper option is the basic **Campement de Ras Bir - Ougef** (☎ 822446; huts incl full board DFr8000), about 5km east of the centre. Location is top-notch – it's right on the beach. Accommodation is in traditional huts and the shared bathrooms are rudimentary.

Just off the coast, at **Les Sept Frères Archipelago**, the Bab al-Mandab Strait separates two worlds: the Red Sea and the Gulf of Aden. The archipelago offers fantastic **diving**. Here, divers are awed by frequent pelagic encounters, including giant trevallies, barracudas and huge shoals of wrasses. Trips to Les Sept Frères Archipelago are expensive due to the distance and are usually organised as liveaboards departing from Djibouti City, usually with week-long (sometimes three- or five-daylong) itineraries. Contact the dive operators based in Djibouti City (p649) for bookings.

Getting There & Away

The road is entirely sealed from the capital to Obock. A regular morning minibus service operates between Djibouti City and Obock (about DFr2000, about 4½ hours).

You can also take one of the *qat*-laden speedboats that leave every day sometime between noon and 2pm from Port de Pêche in Djibouti City (around DFr1500 one way, about 1½ hours).

There's a twice-weekly ferry service between Djibouti City and Obock (DFr700 one way).

ALI SABIEH

Bar a distinct Somali flavour, Ali Sabieh doesn't have much to detain you, but you might want to explore it on your way to (or from) Ethiopia.

By far the best place to stay is **La Palmeraie d'Ali Sabieh** (☎ 426198; r DFr8000-10,000; ✗), on the outskirts of town. It has 10 well-appointed rooms, clean bathrooms and a leaf-dappled courtyard, as well as a decent on-site restaurant (mains from DFr800).

If you're watching the pennies, try **Hotel Iljano** (☎ 325308; s with shared bathroom DFr1500), just off the main square. Rooms are shoe-boxsized and cleanliness is only just OK in the bathrooms (wear flip-flops) but it's tolerable for a night's kip. For a cheap and tasty meal, the nearby **Restaurant Arrey** (☎ 426191; mains DFr1000-2000; ⊙ lunch & dinner) is acceptable.

There are daily bus services (DFr600) to Djibouti City, mostly in the morning. You can also hop on the train (DFr1500) that runs three times a week from Dire Dawa to Djibouti City via Ali Sabieh.

For Dire Dawa in Ethiopia, you can also take a bus to Gelille at the Ethiopian border (DFr400) then change to another bus heading to Dire Dawa. For more information on transport to Ethiopia, see p656.

DJIBOUTI DIRECTORY

ACCOMMODATION

Djibouti's accommodation is limited. Most hotels are in the capital, with few options outside. Hotel categories are limited in range; most of them fit into the upper echelon and are expensive. Prices for budget accommodation average DFr6000 to DFr10,000 for doubles. For midrange hotels you'll pay about DFr10,500 to DFr22,000. A top-end option will set you back up to DFr100,000.

A rather popular option that is developing around the major attractions in the hinterland is the *campements touristiques*. These are traditional huts with shared showers and toilets. These low-key establishments are great places to meet locals and get an authentic cultural experience. They're family-run, which ensures your money goes straight into local pockets. They're also a good budget option, but there's no public transport to get to them.

ACTIVITIES

Djibouti is a great destination for divers. Most diving takes place in the Gulf of Tadjoura. If you want to see a dazzling aggregation of pelagics, Les Sept Frères Archipelago can't be beaten. However, this is not for the faint-hearted because of the rough seas and strong currents.

Winds are strong and steady throughout the year in the Gulf of Tadjoura, and there are no obstacles, which makes Djibouti a prime destination for kitesurfing. It's also an ideal place to learn the sport.

Hiking is popular in the Goda Mountains. From canyons and valleys to waterfalls and peaks, the mountainscape is fantastic. Most *campements touristiques* can organise guided nature walks, from one-hour jaunts to more-challenging day hikes.

Snorkelling with whale sharks is possible in the Bay of Ghoubbet from October to January. This spot is one of only a few places in the world where these giant yet gentle creatures appear regularly in near-shore waters, easily accessible to observers.

BUSINESS HOURS

Friday is the weekly holiday for offices and most shops, and Saturday and Sunday are normal working days.

Government offices, shops and institutions Open from 7.30am to 1.30pm Sunday to Thursday.

Private businesses Open from 7.30am to 1.30pm Sunday to Thursday; reopen from 4pm to 6pm.

DANGERS & ANNOYANCES

Djibouti is a relatively safe country, and serious crime or hostility aimed specifically at travellers is very rare. However, the usual big-city precautions apply.

Djibouti's security services are known for being sensitive and active. There is no reason why travellers should attract the attention of the police, but if it happens, remain polite and calm – it's usually pretty harmless.

EMBASSIES & CONSULATES
Djiboutian Embassies & Consulates

Djiboutian diplomatic representation abroad is scarce. In countries without representation, travellers should head for the French embassy, which acts for Djibouti in the issuing of visas. Elsewhere, Djiboutian embassies and consulates include the following:

Egypt (☎ 333 6435; 15 Dr Muhammad Abdou As-Said St, Dokki, Cairo)

Eritrea (☎ 125990; Saro St, Asmara)

Ethiopia (☎ 0116-613200; PO Box 1022) Off Bole Rd.

France (☎ 01 47 27 49 22; rue Emile Menier, 75116 Paris)

USA (☎ 202-331 0270; Ste 515, 1156 15th St NW, Washington DC, 2005)

Yemen (☎ 445 236; 6th Amman St, Sana'a)

PRACTICALITIES

■ Djibouti uses the metric system.

■ Djibouti uses the 220V system, with two-round-pin plugs.

■ The most widely read newspaper is *La Nation* (www.lanation.dj), published weekly in French.

Embassies & Consulates in Djibouti

All embassies are closed on Friday.

Canada (☎ /fax 355950; Pl Lagarde)

Ethiopia (☎ 350718; fax 354803; Ave Maréchal Lyautey)

France (☎ 350963; www.ambafrance-dj.org; Ave F d'Esperey)

USA (☎ 353995; www.djibouti.usembassy.gov; Plateau du Serpent)

Yemen (☎ 352975; Plateau du Serpent)

EMERGENCIES

Fire and ambulance services ☎ 18

Police ☎ 17

HOLIDAYS

As well as religious holidays listed in the Africa Directory (p1140), these are the principal public holidays in Djibouti:

New Year's Day 1 January

Labour Day 1 May

Independence Day 27 June

Christmas Day 25 December

MAPS

The best map of the country is the 1:200,000 map published in 1992 by the French Institut Géographique National (IGN).

MONEY

There are several banks and a couple of authorised bureaux de change in the capital. Outside the capital, banking facilities are almost nonexistent. The euro and the US dollar are the favoured hard currencies.

Djibouti City has a few Visa-friendly ATMs. At the time of research, only one ATM accepted MasterCard.

TELEPHONE

There are no area codes in Djibouti. International and local calls are best made from the post office or from one of the numerous phone shops (look for the *cabine telephonique* signs). Mobile (cell) phones are also widespread. Depending on which mobile network you use at home, your phone may or may not work while in Djibouti – ask your mobile network provider. You can also bring your phone and buy a local SIM card from **Djibouti Telecom** (off Blvd de la République, Djibouti City; 7.30am-noon Sat-Thu).

TOURIST INFORMATION

The only tourist office in the country is in Djibouti City. Travel agencies are also reliable sources of travel information (see Tours following).

Information for travellers is hard to come by outside the country. In Europe, the most knowledgable organisation is the **Association Djibouti Espace Nomade** (ADEN; ☎ 01 48 51 71 56; aden@club-internet.fr; 64 Rue des Meuniers, 93100 Montreuil-sous-Bois, France).

TOURS

Because of the lack of public transport, Djibouti is not properly geared up for DIY tourism. The only way of getting to some of the country's principal attractions is by joining an excursion. They're expensive (from DFr15,000 per person), but the price includes food and accommodation. Try to join an existing group – the more people, the less you pay. The chances of joining an existing group are greater at weekends (Thursday and Friday).

Agence Le Goubet (☎ 354520; valerie@riesgroup.dj; Blvd Cheik Osman) Can organise trips to Plage des Sables Blancs and make bookings in the *campements touristiques*. Also sells flight tickets. Ask for Valerie, who can get by in English.

ATTA/Globe Travel (☎ 353036, 250297; atta@intnet.dj; off Pl du 27 Juin 1977) A long-standing operator with good credentials. Can organise tours. Also sells flight tickets.

Dolphin Excursions (☎ 350313, 812300; www.dolphin -excursions.com; Blvd de la République) Run by Bruno Pardigon, this well-established operator can organise all kinds of tours throughout the country, on land and at sea, including multiday guided hikes, excursions to Lac Abbé and Lac Assal, as well as live-aboard dive boats to Les Sept Frères Archipelago. Bruno speaks English well.

VISAS

All visitors, including French nationals, need visas. Tourist visas cost from US$30 to US$60 depending on where you apply, and are valid for one month. Visas can be obtained at the nearest Djibouti embassy (including Addis Ababa and Asmara if you're in the Horn) or, where there

is none, from the French embassy. Note that travellers from most Western countries can also obtain a tourist visa on arrival at the airport; it's issued on the spot. It costs DFr5000 for three days and DFr10,000 for one month. Payment can be made in US dollars or in euros.

Visas for Onward Travel

For information on embassies, see p655.
Ethiopia A one-month single-entry visa costs DFr3600 (DFr12,600 for US nationals). You need to supply two photos. It takes 24 hours to process. Visas are also easily obtained at Bole International Airport in Addis Ababa; from 8am to 1pm Sunday to Thursday and 9am to 1pm Saturday.
Yemen Visas are valid for one month and cost DFr7000. You need one photo and a copy of your passport. It takes 24 hours to process. Visas are also easily obtained at Sana'a International Airport.

TRANSPORT IN DJIBOUTI

GETTING THERE & AWAY
Air

Djibouti has one international gateway for arrival by air, **Djibouti-Ambouli Airport** (☎ 341646), about 5km south of Djibouti City. Airlines connect Djibouti with Addis Ababa (Ethiopia), Dubai (UAE), Hargeisa (Somaliland) and on to other destinations in Somalia), Nairobi (Kenya), Sana'a (Yemen) and Paris. For Eritrea, you'll have to travel via Sana'a (Yemen).

The following airlines fly to and from Djibouti, with offices in Djibouti City:
Air France (☎ 351010; www.airfrance.com; Pl du 27 Juin 1977)
Daallo (☎ 353401; www.daallo.com; Rue de Paris)
Ethiopian Airlines (☎ 351007; www.ethiopianairlines. com) Off Blvd Cheikh Osman.
Kenya Airways (☎ 353036; off Pl du 27 Juin 1977) Same office as ATTA/Globe Travel.
Yemenia (☎ 355427; www.yemenia.com; Rue de Paris)

Land
ERITREA

Travel overland to Eritrea is no longer possible. When the border was open, shared taxis (usually Land Cruisers) travelled from Obock to Moulhoulé (with no fixed schedule), the last town before the border. Then other taxis plied the route from Moulhoulé to Assab in Eritrea.

ETHIOPIA
Bus

There is a daily service between Djibouti City and Dire Dawa – a strenuous 10- to 12-hour

---

DEPARTURE TAX

The airport departure tax is DFr3000 for neighbouring countries and DFr5000 for further-flung destinations. In some cases it's included in the cost of your ticket; check with your airline while in Djibouti.

---

ride on a gravel road. You'll take your first bus to the border town of Gelille, then another bus to Djibouti City; see p698.

From Djibouti City, **SPB** (☎ 812445) buses leave at dawn from Ave Gamel Abdel Nasser. Buy your ticket (DFr2500) at least a day in advance to be sure of getting a seat.

Hitching

Hitching is never entirely safe in any country, and we don't recommend it. Still, if you want to enter Djibouti from Ethiopia via the border town of Galafi, you can hitch a lift (front seats only) with one of the legions of trucks that ply the route between Addis Ababa and Djibouti City via Awash, Gewane, Logiya and Dikhil. This option is best avoided by women.

Train

Passengers can take the old Djibouti City–Addis Ababa train as far as Dire Dawa in Ethiopia (minimum duration 13 hours). The train leaves three times a week.

See p652 and p698 for more information.

SOMALILAND

Four-wheel drives depart daily to Hargeisa from Ave Gamel Abdel Nasser. They usually leave around 3pm (it's wise to buy your ticket in the morning). The border crossing is at Loyaada; it costs DFr5000. Be warned: it's a taxing journey. Bring plenty of mineral water.

Sea

It's possible to board a freight boat to Aden or Mukha (Yemen) from Djibouti port. It costs DFr8000. Inquire at **Djibouti Shipping Service** (☎ 870274; ✆ 7.30am-noon Sat-Thu) at the entrance of the port, just before the gate, to the left. Ask for 'Okar Transit'.

GETTING AROUND

The road network links all major villages in the country with the capital. The Route de l'Unité, a good sealed road, covers the 240km from the capital around the Gulf de Tadjoura, as far as Obock. From Obock to Moulhoulé at the Eritrean border, there's a gravel road only passable by 4WDs.

There is public transport, but it's pretty limited. By bus you can go to Ali Sabieh and Dikhil in the south, to Tadjoura and Obock in the north, and to Galafi at the Ethiopian border.

Obock and Tadjoura are accessible by speedboat or dhow from Djibouti City. The train linking Djibouti City to Addis Ababa in Ethiopia makes several stops en route; Ali Sabieh is of most interest to travellers.

Eritrea

Let's start with the bad news. In just 10 years, Eritrea has gone from being a success story and a model state for the whole of Africa – egalitarian, well governed, optimistic – to being one of the most isolated nations in the world. The once progressive government has slipped to become a repressive regime. The economy is in a shambles and Eritreans are doing it tough.

But there's a brighter side. Being locked in a time capsule and almost completely unexploited by commercial tourism, Eritrea offers excitement for travellers who have a hankering for secretive places. Though some parts of the country are off limits to foreigners (especially Dankalia and western Eritrea), the sense of discovery is overwhelming. Southern Eritrea combines quintessentially Abyssinian landscapes – escarpments, plateaus and soaring peaks – with a couple of archaeological sites. Heading north, the market town of Keren offers a fascinating glimpse into Eritrea's diverse cultural fabric. On the Red Sea coast, Massawa, a Zanzibar-esque town redolent with Islamic influence, is the starting point for trips to the Dahlak Islands, a bijou archipelago with peroxide-blonde beaches and thriving reefs.

The cherry on top is Asmara, Eritrea's utterly adorable capital. This whimsical art-deco city boasts the most dazzling collection of colonial architectural wonders in Africa, as well as the frothiest macchiatos this side of the Colosseum.

Here's the paradox: despite the tough political and economic landscape and the odd travel restriction, Eritrea remains one of the most inspiring destinations in Africa, with a unique blend of Abyssinian, Arabic and Mediterranean influences – which makes it all the more tempting to peek into.

FAST FACTS

- **Area** 124,320 sq km
- **ATMs** None
- **Borders** Djibouti, Sudan, Ethiopia; all land border crossings are currently closed
- **Budget** US$20 to US$35 per day
- **Capital** Asmara
- **Languages** Tigrinya, Arabic and other regional languages
- **Money** Nakfa; US$1 = Nfa15, €1 = Nfa21.9
- **Population** 5.7 million
- **Seasons** Cool (October to May), hot (June to September), wet (July to September)
- **Telephone** Country code ☎ 291-1; international access code ☎ 00
- **Time** GMT/UTC +3
- **Visa** From US$50 to US$60 for 30 days

HOW MUCH?

- **Internet connection** US$0.70 per hour
- **Asmara–Massawa bus ride** US$2
- **One night in a guesthouse in the capital** US$13
- **Travel permit** US$1.30
- **4WD hire** US$135 per day

LONELY PLANET INDEX

- **1L petrol** US$2.50
- **1.5L bottled water** US$1
- **Bottle of Asmara beer** US$0.85
- **Souvenir T-shirt** US$6 to US$7
- **Pastry** US$0.30

HIGHLIGHTS

- **Asmara** (p663) Discover the capital's fantastic Italian colonial architecture and its lively cafe culture.
- **Massawa** (p669) Get lost in Massawa Island's maze of narrow streets and feast on Yemeni fish.
- **Dahlak Islands** (p670) Relish the pristine beauty of this wild archipelago, then comb the beach of Dissei Island.
- **Qohaito** (p669) Conjure up a vanished civilisation at this archaeological site shrouded in peaceful solitude.
- **Keren** (p668) Soak up the languid atmosphere of Eritrea's beguiling second city.

CLIMATE & WHEN TO GO

In the eastern lowlands, temperatures range from a torrid 30°C to 39°C during the hot season (June to September) and from 25°C to 32°C during the cooler season (October to May). In the Dankalia region, temperatures can reach 50°C in the shade and rainfall is practically zero.

In the highland zone, the average annual temperature is 18°C. May is the hottest month, when daily temperatures can reach around 30°C. The coldest months are from December to February, when lows can approach freezing point.

Although it's possible to visit Eritrea any time of year, the ideal time climatewise is September to October and January to April. Avoid travelling during June to August, when it's the rainy season in the highlands and hot and torrid in the eastern lowlands.

ITINERARIES

- **One Week** Spend two full days in Asmara (p663), visiting its gob-smacking portfolio of architectural wonders, lapping up squidgy cakes and sipping frothy macchiatos. Push onto Keren (p668), which deserves a day or two for its attractive architecture and active markets. Back to Asmara, then it's time to roll down to Massawa (p669) on the Red Sea coast.
- **Two Weeks** Follow the one-week agenda then explore the pristine Dahlak Islands (p670), which are blessed with good diving and snorkelling opportunities. Head back through Asmara, then forge south to explore the poignant ruins of Qohaito (p669) and Metera (p669).

HISTORY

During the 1st millennium BC, tribes from present-day Yemen migrated to the southern highlands of Eritrea, settling on both sides of today's Eritrea–Ethiopia border. The contemporary Tigrinya and Amharic languages derive from their language, Ge'ez.

The powerful Aksumite kingdom flourished in Eritrea from the 4th century BC to the 9th century AD. While the kingdom's capital city, Aksum, was in today's Ethiopia, important Aksumite towns were built in Eritrea. Much foreign trade – on which Aksum's prosperity depended – was seaborne, and came to be handled by the ancient port of Adulis, to the south of today's Massawa.

Christianity is supposed to have been brought here by Christian Syrian merchants who were shipwrecked on the Red Sea coast. By the 4th century AD, Christianity had become the Aksumite state religion.

Islam, the arrival of which coincided with Christian Aksum's decline in the 7th century, was the other great influence on the region. For centuries the dividing line between the Muslim Red Sea coast and the Christian Ethiopian highlands moved back and forth over what is now Eritrea.

From the early-16th century to the late-19th century, the Ottoman Turks and the Egyptians fought each other for control of the Eritrean coast and its ports, but they left few imprints – unlike the European colonising powers of the 19th century. The Italians managed to grab

ERITREA

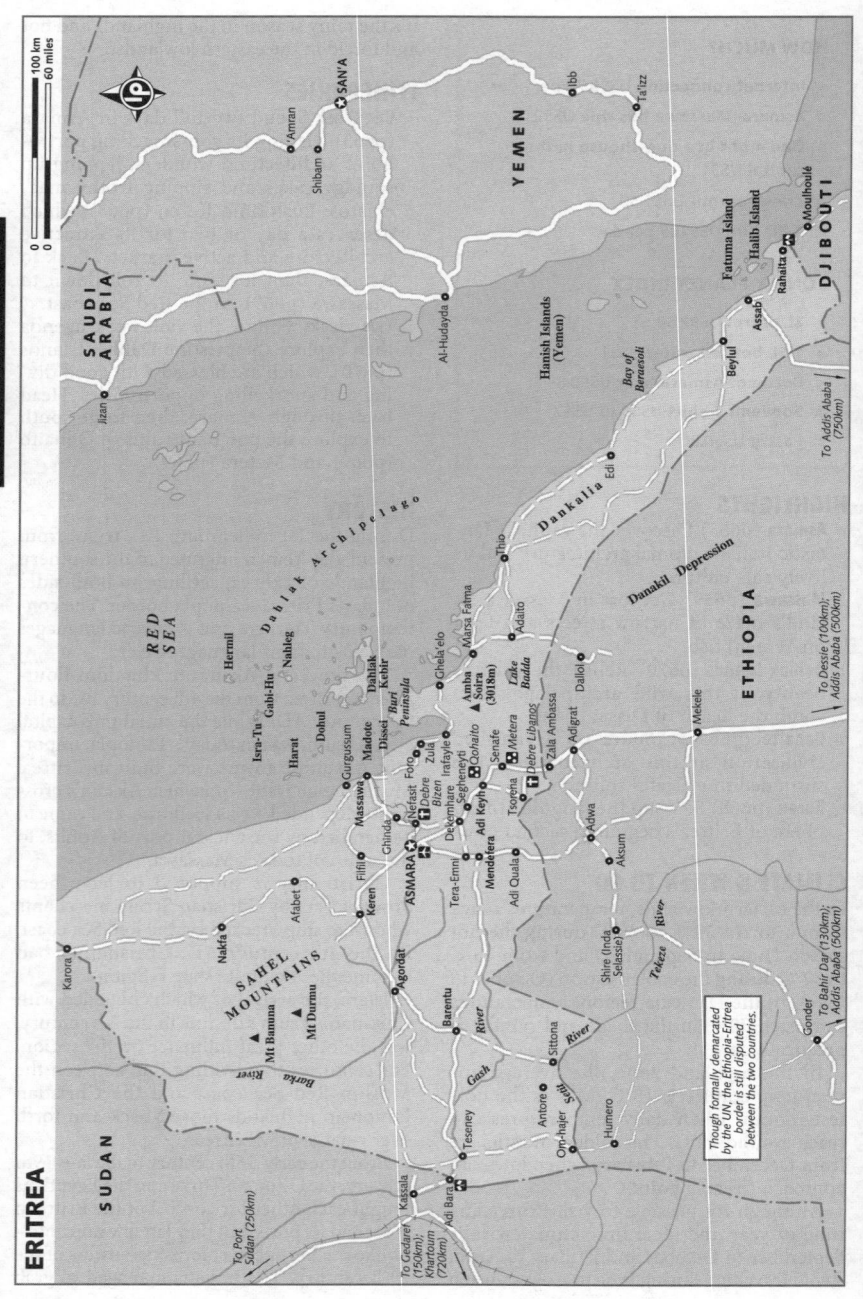

ERITREA

Though formally demarcated by the UN, the Ethiopia-Eritrea border is still disputed between the two countries.

a slice of North and East Africa, and Eritrea became a full-blown Italian colony in 1896. By the end of the 1930s, Eritrea was one of the most highly industrialised colonies in Africa. All the architectural treasures in Asmara date from this period.

The Italians' golden era ceased in 1941, when the Allied forces defeated the Italian army in Europe. Italy was forced to give up its African possessions, including Eritrea. The colony became an administration of the British until 1950, when a contentious UN resolution granted Eritrea self-government within a federal union with Ethiopia. Eritrea disappeared from the map of Africa.

Little by little, Ethiopia began to exert an ever-tighter hold over Eritrea and formally annexed it in violation of international law in the early 1960s. This was unbearable for the Eritrean people, who started their struggle for independence in 1961. This was the beginning of Africa's longest conflict of the 20th century. After numerous harsh guerrilla attacks, fierce fights and major offensives, the Eritrean People's Liberation Forces (EPLF) finally won the war in 1991 and the Ethiopian troops left the country. Following a referendum, independence was declared on 24 May 1993. Eritrea was back on the African map.

Alas, after only five years of peaceful relations between Eritrea and Ethiopia, another conflict, known as the 'border dispute', reared its head in 1998. What followed were two bitter years of conflict that saw tens of thousands killed. After tortuous negotiations, a ceasefire was signed on 18 June 2000. According to the peace deal that was brokered, a UN peacekeeping force was deployed in Eritrean territory pending a final demarcation of the disputed border. In April 2002 the UN Boundary Commission announced its decision on the demarcation of the border. Surveying of boundary posts began in May 2003, but Ethiopia soon began to contest the demarcation and the two countries were on the brink of war in 2005 – again.

Eritrea Today

The current situation can be summed up as 'neither peace nor war'. The border dispute between Eritrea and Ethiopia rumbles on. In May 2008, the UN peacekeeping mission had withdrawn completely from Eritrea (some observers say the Eritrean authorities forced it to leave), and there was no solution in sight

to reach terms on the border issue. Ethiopian troops still occupy the border town of Badme, which was 'awarded' to Eritrea by the UN Boundary Commission.

In June 2008, Eritrea clashed with Djibouti, its southern neighbour, over the Ras Doumeira border area. The UN Security Council passed a resolution in January 2009 urging the two countries to step back from an escalation of conflict and re-establish dialogue.

Eritrea is also accused by the American government of aiding the Islamic Court forces that took power in Somalia in 2009 after defeating the Ethiopian-backed Somalia Transitional Federal Government.

Eritrea's isolation is mounting, as is internal resentment against its intransigent government. Freedom of press and speech is nonexistent. The state has taken control of all private companies, and the country has one of the most restrictive economies on the planet. Mass conscription has deprived many industries of manpower. For young Eritreans, the only way to escape indefinite military conscription is to attempt to flee the country. Remittances from diaspora Eritreans are virtually the only source of income.

CULTURE

Eritreans are different in temperament from Ethiopians (which partly explains the bitter relations between the two countries). Years of invasion have created a siege mentality and a sense of isolation. Though impoverished, the nation has from the outset shown self-reliance, vigour and independence.

Initially indifferent to strangers (at least by comparison with other African nations), Eritreans may appear somewhat taciturn at first meeting, but once the ice has been broken you will find intense friendships.

The contrast in lifestyle between Asmara and elsewhere is stark. No matter the state of the economy and rationing, Asmarans still take the *passeggiata* (a daily social ritual; see the boxed text, p667) very seriously – a legacy of the Italian era. Then there is the rest of Eritrea, where poverty is about the only prevalent excess.

In a country where people have lost faith in their government, the family remains one pillar of society on which Eritreans continue to depend. Religious occasions and public holidays are vigorously celebrated, as are more personal, family events, such as weddings.

People

With only 5.7 million inhabitants, Eritrea might be a tiddler of a country by Africa's standards, but it hosts a kaleidoscopic range of tribes. There are nine ethnic groups, each with their own language and customs, as well as a handful of Italians who live in Asmara. The most important ethnic group is the Tigrinya, who make up approximately 50% of the population, followed by the Tigré (30%), the Saho (5%) and the Afar (5%).

Approximately 35% of the population are nomadic or seminomadic. About one million Eritreans live abroad, mostly in Europe and the USA.

Women enjoy far greater equality in Eritrea than in most other African countries. Eritrea's women themselves contributed more than one-third of troops in both the recent wars against Ethiopia.

Religion

The population of Eritrea is almost equally divided between Christians and Muslims. Christians are primarily Orthodox; the Eritrean Orthodox church has its roots in the Ethiopian one. There are also small numbers of Roman Catholics and Protestants. The Muslims are primarily Sunnis.

Roughly speaking, the agriculturalist Orthodox Christians inhabit the highland region and the Muslims are concentrated in the lowlands, the coastal areas and towards the Sudanese border.

Arts & Crafts

From dance to music and theatre, Eritrean arts reflect the diversity of the country's many people. Dance plays a very important social role in Eritrea. It marks the major events of life, such as births and marriages, and is used in celebrating special occasions and religious festivals. *Iskista* (traditional dancing) features a lot of shaking of body parts (some of which is hard to imagine, until you see it). It's certainly unique in style.

Traditional musical instruments of Eritrea have their roots in Ethiopia. They include the *krar* and *wata*, both string instruments; the *shambko*, a type of flute; and the *embilta*, a wind instrument.

Established local stars, both traditional and modern, include Faytinga, Helen Meles, Samuel Berhane, Vittorio Bossi, Tesfay Mehari and Abraham Afewerki.

Faytinga is the most famous Eritrean singer internationally.

In Asmara and many of the larger towns such as Keren, Massawa and Dekemhare, the colonial heritage can be seen in the Italian-style buildings. Many of them are remarkable historical and artistic pieces.

Asmara has a small but dynamic contemporary plastic arts scene and the country's sole gallery.

FOOD & DRINK

Italian dishes, including pasta, pizza and pastries, are available in most restaurants throughout Eritrea. Outside the capital, these may be limited to just one dish: lasagne or spaghetti bolognese. Traditional Eritrean cuisine is almost the same as in Ethiopia; expect *injera* (large Ethiopian pancake-style bread), *tibsi* (sliced lamb, pan fried in butter, garlic, onion and sometimes tomato) and *zigni* (lamb, goat or beef cooked in a hot sauce). There are regional variations, though. In Massawa, the Arabic influence is evident, with kebabs and Yemeni-style charcoal-baked fish on offer.

In Asmara and, to a lesser degree, the larger towns, innumerable little cafes and bars dot the centre. They serve macchiato (an espresso with a dash of milk), espresso and fragrant cappuccino, along with a selection of pastries and cakes. Tea is also widely available, as is bottled water. If you want to put some wobble in your steps, all the usual favourites are available, including whisky, gin, *araki* (a distilled aniseed drink) and vodka, as well as local beer and wine.

ENVIRONMENT

Eritrea has three main geographical zones: the eastern escarpment and coastal plains, the central highland region, and the western lowlands.

The eastern zone consists of desert or semi-desert, with little arable land. The northern end of the East African Rift Valley opens into the infamous Dankalia region in the east, one of the hottest places on earth.

The central highland region is more fertile, and it is intensively cultivated by farming communities.

The western lowlands, lying between Keren and the Sudanese border, are watered by the Gash and Barka Rivers.

Several mountains exceed 2500m, with the highest peak, Amba Soira, reaching 3018m. The are 350 islands offshore, including the Dahlak Archipelago, the largest in the Red Sea.

Eritrea's birdlife is very rich. According to Solomon Abraha, who is a regular contributor to the **African Bird Image Database** (www.birdquest. net/afbid), 'of the 2600 species of birds in Africa, Eritrea hosts 560 to 660 species, including 18 endemic ones – a fact that's sure to raise the pulse of twitchers everywhere'.

The main environmental issue is deforestation. Less than 1% of the country is covered by woodland, compared to 30% a century ago – this says it all.

ASMARA

pop 1 million

Asmara is a pleasant surprise. Arrive here on a clear day, and you'll feel like you've been transported to a southern Italian town. Peaceful neighbourhoods, pavement cafes with vintage Italian coffee machines, tantalising pastry shops, a relaxed pace of life. Then there's the fabulous architecture, with a melee of architectural wonders from the Italian era. The balmy climate is another draw: Asmara is bathed in sunshine eight months of the year.

Alas, the battered economy and the clampdown on civil liberties have taken their toll over past years, and it shows. Gone is the *dolce vita* (life of luxury) – belt-tightening is now the order of the day, with queues in front of petrol stations, slack business, and deserted streets at night. Despite all this, Asmara's ability to dazzle hasn't vanished.

ORIENTATION

The centre encompasses the area on, and just north of, Harnet Ave (the main artery). To the south of Harnet Ave was once the Italian residential quarter.

To the southwest, Sematat Ave leads to the airport, about 6km from the centre. The railway station is about 1.5km east of the centre.

INFORMATION

Internet Access

Internet services have sprung up all over town in recent years, but connections can be exasperatingly slow. It costs about Nfa10 per hour.

Medical Services

There's a profusion of pharmacies around town.

Sembel Hospital (☎ 150175; HDAY St) The most reputable hospital in town, on the road to the airport.

Money

Changing money won't cause any headaches: rates are fixed daily by the government and are the same everywhere in the country, whether for cash or travellers cheques, and there's only one government-run exchange bureau (Himbol). All transactions must be registered on your currency declaration form. There's a black market, but it's illegal and the penalties incurred are huge (see p672).

There are currently no ATMs in Asmara.

Commercial Bank of Eritrea (☎ 122425; Harnet Ave; 8-11am & 2-4pm Mon-Fri, 8-11am Sat) Changes cash and travellers cheques.

Himbol Bahti Meskerem Sq (☎ 120735; Bahti Meskerem Sq; 8am-8pm); Harnet Ave (☎ 115962; Harnet Ave; 8am-8pm Mon-Fri, 8am-noon & 2-7pm Sat & Sun) Changes cash and travellers cheques, and can do cash advances on your credit card for a commission of 7%. Also acts as an agent for Western Union.

There's also a Himbol booth at the airport; it's open to meet all arriving flights and changes cash only.

Post

Main post office (8am-noon & 2-6pm Mon-Fri, 8am-12.30pm Sat) Just north of the western end of Harnet Ave.

Telephone & Fax

Eritel (Harnet Ave; 8am-8pm)

Tourist Information

In addition to the tourist office, the most reliable sources of information are the travel agencies (see following).

Tourist Information Centre (☎ 124871; Harnet Ave; 7am-noon & 2-6pm Mon-Fri, 7am-noon Sat) Has some brochures and issues the compulsory travel permit.

Travel Agencies

Both agencies employ English-speaking staff.

Explore Eritrea Travel & Tours (☎ 125555, 120259; explore@tse.com.er; Adi Hawesha St; 8.30am-noon & 2-6pm Mon-Sat)

Travel House International (☎ 201881, 201882; www.travelhouseeritrea.com; 175-15 St; 8am-noon & 2-6pm Mon-Fri, 8.30am-noon & 3.30-6pm Sat)

ERITREA

ERITREA

ASMARA

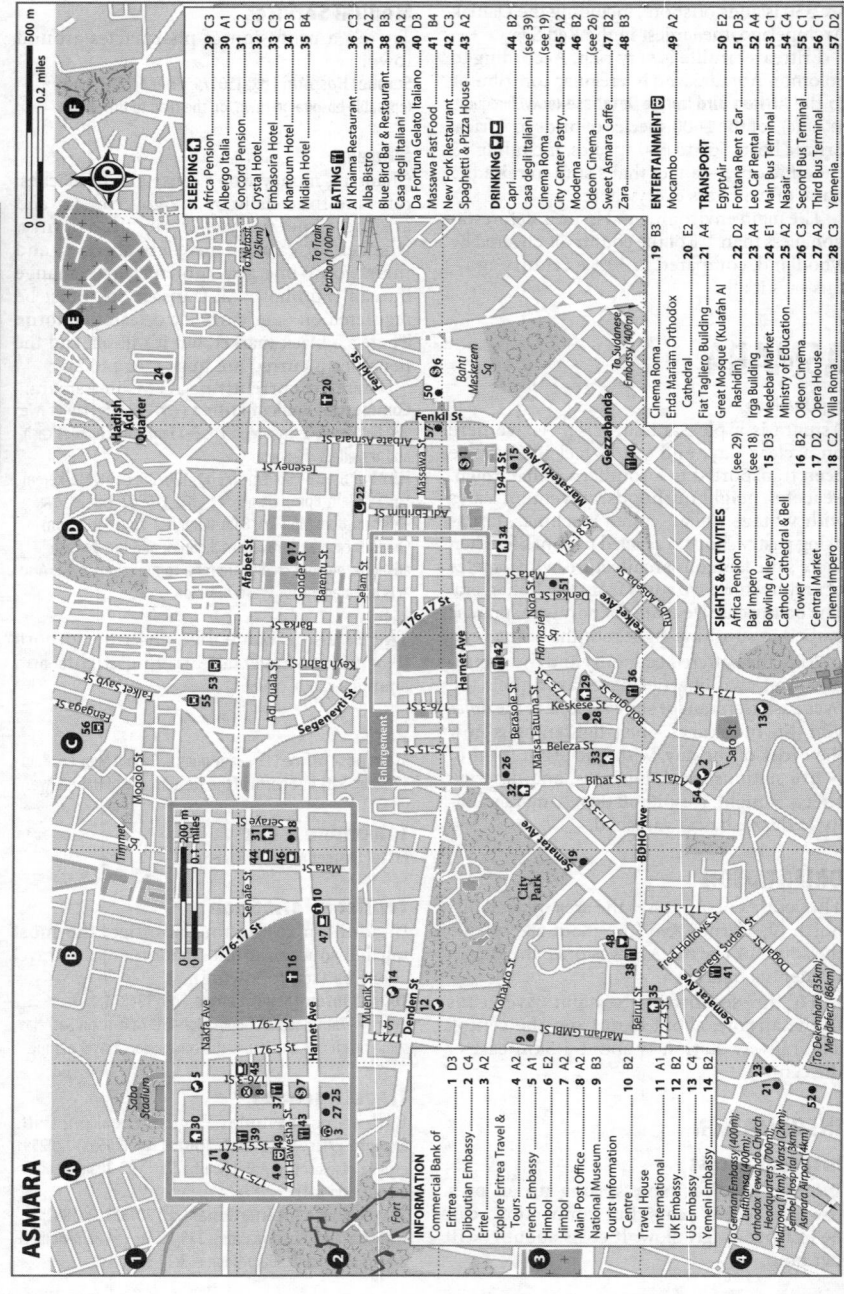

Travel Permits

To travel outside Asmara you'll need a travel permit, obtainable at the Tourist Information Centre. The permit is usually issued the same day, provided you come early in the morning. Don't forget your passport.

A permit is also necessary to visit the monasteries. For more details on permits, see p672.

SIGHTS

Asmara is one of the most entrancing cities in Africa, with a host of splendiferous buildings harking back to the city's heyday as the 'Piccolo Roma' (little Rome) in the 1920s and 1930s. Most sights are clustered in the centre or within easy walking distance from it.

Harnet Avenue

The best place to start exploring is the **Opera House** (Harnet Ave), at the western end of Harnet Ave. Completed around 1920, it's one of Asmara's most elegant early-20th-century buildings. By contrast, the adjacent **Ministry of Education** (Harnet Ave), with its massive stepped tower, looks strikingly austere. Just off Harnet Ave, near the telecommunications building, the quirky **Odeon Cinema** (Bihat St), with its authentic art-deco interior, is attractive.

As you amble down Harnet Ave you'll soon come across Asmara's most iconic monument, the elaborate, brick-walled **Catholic cathedral** (Harnet Ave). Consecrated in 1923, it is thought to be one of the finest Lombard-Romanesque–style churches outside of Italy. The tallest structure in Asmara, the narrow, Gothic **bell tower** (🕑 8-11am & 2-5pm) offers unrivalled views over the town.

Another eye-catching building, the nearby **Cinema Impero** (Harnet Ave) is made up of three massive windows that combine strong vertical and horizontal elements with 45 porthole lamps. Next door, the **Bar Impero** (Harnet Ave) is original with its 'zinc' bar, dark wood panels and old cash register.

Other Sights

A block south of the Municipality building, the **bowling alley** (194-4 St; 🕑 8am-8pm) is one of the few genuine 1950s alleys left in the world. It was probably built for US servicemen when they were manning military bases in the region.

Tucked away in a residential district further west, the **Africa Pension** (Keskese St) is a gem of place. This huge cubist villa was built in the 1920s by an Italian millionaire. The villa is now a very affordable hotel (see below). Opposite the Africa Pension, the gleaming **Villa Roma** (173-3 St) is reminiscent of a Roman villa with its marble staircases, louvred shutters, curving balustrades and shady portico.

North of Harnet Ave, the sprawling **central market** (🕑 Mon-Sat morning) is one of Asmara's major attractions. The best time to visit is early on Saturday (from 7am), when people come in from all over the country.

Duck up northeast to soak up the atmosphere of the **Medebar Market** (Qelhamet St). This mind-boggling place is like an open-air workshop where absolutely everything is recycled: old tyres are made into sandals, corrugated iron is flattened and made into metal buckets, and olive tins from Italy are made into coffee pots and tiny scoopers.

Thread your way back to the south until you reach the **Great Mosque** (Kulafah Al Rashidin; Selam St). Completed in 1938, this grand complex combines rationalist, classical and Islamic styles.

Another outstanding monument, the **Enda Mariam Orthodox Cathedral** (Arbate Asmara St), to the east, was built in 1938 and is a curious blend of Italian and Eritrean architecture. Its central block is flanked by large square towers.

Back on the main thoroughfare, walk to the west until you see the **Cinema Roma** (Sematat Ave). Another fine example of Italian architecture, the appealing exterior of this building features four entrances with double doors and a magnificent marble-coated facade.

At the southern end of Sematat Ave, the quirky **Fiat Tagliero Building** (Sematat Ave) ranks among the most outstanding in Asmara. Built in 1938, it is designed to look like a plane (or a spaceship, or a bat). A sandal's throw from the Fiat Tagliero Building, the harmonious **Irga Building** (Sematat Ave) is both neoclassical in its proportions and very modern.

SLEEPING
Budget

our pick **Africa Pension** (☎ 121436; Keskese St; d without bathroom Nfa180-230) This pension is for shoestringers who want to surround themselves with character. Housed in a cubist villa dating from the 1920s, it features a marble staircase, generous-sized rooms with tiled floors and a serene garden. Although the rooms show their

ERITREA

age a bit, Africa Pension is a safe bet, and its location is ace.

Khartoum Hotel (☎ 128008; 176-13 St; s without bathroom Nfa200-250, d without bathroom Nfa250-300, s/d with bathroom Nfa300/380) If you want a comfy sleep without blowing big bucks, you can't go wrong at the super-central Khartoum. One grumble: avoid the teensy singles, such as room 5; a bit more dosh simply gets you a more spacious 'suite' (especially rooms 14 and 19).

Midrange & Top End

Most hotels in this price bracket quote their prices in US dollars but accept local currency, provided you have your currency declaration form. If you pay in hard currency, the transaction must be registered on your form.

Concord Pension (☎ 110073; fax 110186; Seraye St; s/d Nfa300/400) Tucked back slightly from the road, Concord has the feel of a friendly B&B, features an agreeable plant-filled courtyard and is ultracentral. The rooms are on the cramped side, though.

Embasoira Hotel (☎ 123222; www.embasoirahotel. com; Beleza St; s incl breakfast US$40-48, d incl breakfast US$57-68; 🛜) A favoured haunt of European tour groups, with practical rooms and salubrious bathrooms. The real steal is the lovely gardens at the back. There's also a bar and restaurant. Credit cards are accepted, but with an 8% commission.

Crystal Hotel (☎ 120944; www.crystalhoteleritrea.com; Bihat St; s incl breakfast US$45-58, d incl breakfast US$58-77; 🛜) In a quiet street near Harnet Ave, this tightly managed outfit sports appealing rooms with modern furnishings, spanking-clean bathrooms, satellite TV and decent breakfast. An added bonus is the restaurant. Payment with credit cards incurs 5% commission.

Midian Hotel (☎ 126232; www.midianhotel.com; 172-4 St; d with breakfast US$50; 🖥 🛜) Sterile bathrooms, bright rooms, modern furnishings and competent staff make for an excellent stay, and there's a restaurant. It's in a peaceful area and is sensibly set a little way back from the main avenue, but is close enough to the centre to be worthwhile.

Albergo Italia (☎ 120740; www.albergoitaliaasmara. com; Nakfa Ave; s incl breakfast US$90-135, d incl breakfast US$135-165, ste s/d US$165/190) The most stylish accommodation in Asmara, the Albergo Italia features well-appointed rooms decorated with period furniture and communal areas awash with heritage aesthetics. There's a cafeteria and restaurant.

EATING

Unless otherwise specified, most eateries are open every day for lunch and dinner.

Da Fortuna Gelato Italiano (173-18 St; 🕑 8.30am-10pm) This friendly place will tempt the devil in you with its creamy concoctions. A *cono* (scoop) is Nfa15.

Alba Bistro (☎ 202421; Adi Hawesha St; mains Nfa45-100) Brimming with good cheer, this place is an ideal refuelling stop after a walking tour in the area. Its energetic staff serve up pasta, meat and fish dishes, as well as tempting ice creams.

our pick Massawa Fast Food (☎ 114503; Geregr Sudan St; mains Nfa45-110) This attractive restaurant has received high marks from expats for its quality fare – try *shiro* (chickpea purée), *kitfo* (spiced raw beef) and *tibsi* (beef). Salads also feature on the menu. The outdoor dining area is ideal for an alfresco meal.

New Fork Restaurant (☎ 116571; 173-5 St; mains Nfa45-110) New Fork buzzes all day long with folks munching on hearty salads, zesty pastas and savoury meat and fish dishes.

Casa degli Italiani (☎ 120791; 175-15 St; mains Nfa50-140) Recipe for a perfect morning: grab an outdoor table at this courtyard restaurant and order up a frittata. Italian ingredients pervade the lunch and dinner menu; try the well-presented *piatto del giorno* (dish of the day: osso bucco, lasagne, cannelloni...). Closed on Sunday nights.

Al Khaima Restaurant (☎ 116469; 173-1 St; mains Nfa50-165) *The* spot for a restorative morning fry-up. We're talking about *ful* (based on chickpea purée) and omelettes, all served with a chapatti-like bread. Lunch (and dinner) moves into Yemeni-influenced dishes, such as *mendi* fish (oven-baked). No alcohol is served.

Spaghetti & Pizza House (☎ 122112; Harnet Ave; mains Nfa50-180; 🕑 Tue-Sun) This trattoria-like venue has a loyal cult following among Italian expats, and it's no surprise – it cooks up scrumptious Italian fare. Fish dishes also grace the menu.

Blue Bird Bar & Restaurant (☎ 117965; Sematat Ave; mains Nfa80-150) You wouldn't know it from the street, but the Blue Bird is one of the most atmospheric places in town for great Eritrean food. Western dishes are also available.

Hidmona (☎ 182979; Expo Park; mains Nfa85-130) Hidmona is an eclectic mix of restaurant, cafe, bar and disco. Bookmark it if you're after a traditional experience: traditional food in traditional surroundings with traditional music in the evening.

DRINKING

Asmara boasts a superb selection of atmospheric bars and cafes. Sometimes it's hard to distinguish between a cafe and a bar, as you can drink just about anywhere, any time.

Sweet Asmara Caffe (Harnet Ave) This sleek pastry shop is a treasure trove for the sweet tooth, with a tempting array of diet-busting treats.

City Center Pastry (176-3 St) Has an appetising selection of croissants and other girth-expanding delicacies.

Capri (Mata St; juices Nfa10-20) Capri is famous for its oh-so-smooth, oh-so-thick fruit juices.

Moderna (Harnet Ave) This humming venue on the main drag concocts melt-in-the-mouth croissants and cakes. The pavement terrace is packed elbow-to-elbow during *passeggiata*.

Odeon Cinema (Bihat St) An inspiring place, with one of Asmara's finest historic interiors – see the art-deco bar on the south side of the lobby.

Cinema Roma (Sematat Ave) The cafeteria in the lobby area is a killer. It's high on personality, with dark wood fixtures and an impressive old projection camera.

Casa degli Italiani (175-15 St) With its wonderfully laid-back palm-shaded courtyard, it's the perfect salve after (or before) a day spent exploring the city.

Zara (Sematat Ave) This snazzy lounge bar is a popular hang-out for well-heeled diaspora Eritreans on holiday, as well as foreigners. It's a good place to warm up before hitting the clubs.

ENTERTAINMENT

Most of the country's facilities for leisure and entertainment are in Asmara. Most clubs open only on Friday and Saturday (from around midnight to 5am). Entrance costs between Nfa50 and Nfa100.

Mocambo (Adi Hawesha St) One of the most hip nightclubs, Mocambo doesn't pick up until after midnight, but once it does, it rocks.

Hidmona (Expo Park, Warsay St) The most authentic place in town. It gets frantic at weekends, with a live band knocking out Eritrean tunes and plenty of drinks flowing.

Warsa (Tiravolo District) Everybody seems to have a good time at this Asmara institution. It's very much a local nightclub, but it's fine for adventurous foreigners too.

> **PASSEGGIATA**
>
> For a typical Asmarean experience, be sure to join the evening *passeggiata* between 5pm and 6.30pm, when the whole town emerges from its torpor and promenades up and down Harnet Ave. All terraces and cafes fill up with chattering locals sampling macchiatos.

GETTING THERE & AWAY

Air

For details of international flights to/from Asmara airport, see p673.

Bus

The long-distance bus station is about 10 minutes' walk due north of Harnet Ave, and is split into three different terminals.

Buses to Massawa (Nfa30, 3½ hours), Assab (Nfa201, two days) and Barentu (Nfa62, six hours) depart from Asmara's **main bus terminal** (off Afabet St). There are a number of buses to Massawa until late in the afternoon.

Buses to Keren (Nfa33, three hours) leave every half hour from the **second bus terminal** (Falket Sayb St).

Southbound buses to Dekemhare (Nfa12, one hour), Mendefera (Nfa16, two hours), Adi Keyh (Nfa32, four hours) and Senafe (Nfa35, four hours) leave from the **third bus terminal** (Fengaga St).

Most buses leave early in the morning and when they are full.

Train

An old train trundles along a remarkable railway line constructed during the Italian era. The line runs between Asmara and Nefasit. It leaves every Sunday from the **train station** (☎ 123365) at 8am and arrives in Nefasit at 9.45am, before returning to Asmara at 10am (arrival time: noon). It costs US$50 or Nfa750. Seats must be booked in advance, as a minimum of 10 passengers is needed for the train to run.

GETTING AROUND

Eritrea's one international airport lies 6km from the capital (around Nfa200 during the day in a taxi).

A taxi ride in the centre will set you back about Nfa60.

ERITREA

THE REBIRTH OF THE OLD RAILWAY

The old Italian railway, which once climbed 2128m from Massawa up the escarpment to Asmara, passing through three climate zones, 30 tunnels and 65 bridges, is a masterpiece of civil engineering. At independence, Eritrea appealed for help to rehabilitate the old line. 'Impossible', said most. 'Too expensive', said some; 'It depends', said others. Undeterred, the Eritreans pulled the old railway workers, metal forgers and blacksmiths out of retirement, called for volunteers and set to work. The great line reopened in 2003 and ranks among the world's great scenic railways. Each year it attracts its fair share of train buffs from all over the world. See p667 for booking details.

Asmara is the obvious base from where to rent a car or 4WD. Reliable outfits include **Fontana Rent a Car** (☎ 120052; fax 127905; Mata St) and **Leo Car Rental** (☎ 125859, 202306; Sematat Ave).

NORTHERN ERITREA

Bar the well-known town of Keren, northern Eritrea still remains *terra incognita* for foreigners.

KEREN
pop 75,000

Easily accessible from Asmara, Keren is perhaps the most remarkable of all of Eritrea's provincial towns. Hemmed in by a range of rugged, good-looking mountains, it boasts an attractive setting, as well as an appealing melange of architectural styles. It's also an active market town with an agreeable multiethnic

buzz – the Tigré, the Tigrinya and the Bilen have all made Keren home.

If you're in town on a Monday between 9am and 2pm, don't miss the clamour of the picturesque **camel market**, 2km out of town on the road to Nakfa. It's a fascinating place to wander, with dozens of camels and busy traders.

Several Italian Roman Catholic churches are dotted around the town, including **St Antonio** and **St Michael**. The old Italian **railway station** (now a bus station) also testifies to Keren's Italian heritage.

Albergo Sicilia (☎ 401059; Agordat Rd; r without bathroom Nfa75-90, r with bathroom Nfa135) occupies a time-warped colonial house right in the centre but its facilities are rudimentary. A more comfortable option is **Sarina Hotel** (☎ 400230; fax 402685; Asmara Rd; s incl breakfast Nfa225-390, d incl breakfast Nfa340-520; 🖵), about 2km from the centre on the road to Asmara. It sports spruce rooms and prim bathrooms and there's a good restaurant (mains from Nfa50).

You'll also find acceptable, cheap eateries in the heart of town.

Nearly 30 buses depart daily to Asmara (Nfa33, three hours).

SOUTHERN ERITREA

Eritrea's south remains open to travellers and is the easiest part of the country in which to travel. All the better, because this is the most scenic part of the country, with a mix of jagged peaks, bulky rocky outcrops, vast plateaus and awesome escarpments.

For history buffs, southern Eritrea offers an unparalleled chance to step back in time. Though much less spectacular than the more famous ruins found to the south in Ethiopia,

EXCURSION TO DEBRE BIZEN MONASTERY

From Asmara, a visit to the Debre Bizen monastery makes for an excellent day trip, if only for the breathtaking views and the prolific birdlife. The monastery lies 2400m above sea level, near Nefasit (east of Asmara).

As with all Orthodox monasteries, Debre Bizen is not open to women. But even if you can't enter the monastery, the journey still makes a great hike (it's a 1½- to two-hour steep walk from Nefasit). Men need to obtain a permit (see p672).

You will be welcomed with *sewa* (home-brewed beer) and bread when you arrive. It's normal to make a contribution to the upkeep of the monastery.

To get to Debre Bizen (and return to Asmara), your best bet is to hire a taxi for the day from Asmara (around Nfa1500).

many of southern Eritrea's ruins are no less important.

QOHAITO

Shrouded in peaceful solitude amid a vast, barren plateau, the archaeological site of Qohaito is recommended for anyone with an interest in Eritrea's ancient past. Don't expect colossal monuments, though: the scant finds of this site are spread over a large area measuring 2.5km wide and include a temple, a dam, an Egyptian tomb and rock art sites – not to mention fantastic views from the edge of a vast canyon. Admission is free but you'll need a permit from the National Museum office in Asmara (see p672).

Qohaito lies some 121km south of Asmara. Public transport being almost nonexistent, your best bets are to book a tour with one of the travel agencies in Asmara or to hire a 4WD with driver.

METERA & SENAFE

Although it's visually underwhelming, the site of Metera is another worthwhile site to visit, if only for its magnificent setting and eerie atmosphere late afternoon. Like Qohaito, Metera flourished around the time of the ancient civilisation of Aksum. The scattered ruins, including a stele and various excavations, testify to the existence of a once large and prosperous town.

The site lies about 2km south of the town of Senafe and is easily reached on foot. Admission is free but you'll need a permit from the National Museum office in Asmara (p673). In Senafe, you'll also need to obtain a permit from the military, which is issued on the spot.

Three or four buses ply the route every morning between Asmara and Senafe (Nfa35, four hours). If you're stuck, Senafe has a couple of accommodation options.

RED SEA COAST

A mere three-hour bus or car ride from Asmara (and a whopping loss of 2500m in altitude) will transport you to yet another world. With its distinct atmosphere and refreshingly humble scale, Massawa is a great place to kick back for a few days. Then there are the mysterious Dahlak Islands, which are haphazardly scattered off the coast. This ar-

chipelago is the kind of place you go to just drop off the planet for a while.

MASSAWA

pop 35,000

Though only about 100km to the northeast of Asmara, Massawa could not be more different from the capital. Entering the old town, you could be forgiven for thinking you're in Zanzibar or Yemen.

Sadly, Massawa was all but flattened during the struggle for independence, and many visitors are shocked by the derelict state of a number of historical buildings. Like Asmara, Massawa has been severely hit by the battered economy. During the day, business is slack, and you won't see more than a couple of cargo ships in the international harbour. Lots of bars and clubs have closed down. Despite all this, Massawa is still a fascinating place to explore because of its exotic (and melancholic) character.

Massawa is the obvious launching pad for exploring the Dahlak Islands.

Sights & Activities

The most interesting part of the city is **Massawa Island**, where the port and old town lie. It's a fascinating blend of Egyptian, Turkish and Italo-Moorish architecture, and it's pure joy to explore the alleyways and streets flanked by low whitewashed buildings, porticoes and arcades.

Massawa Island is connected to **Taulud Island** by a causeway. From Taulud Island, a second causeway leads to the mainland.

Take note that Massawa doesn't have a proper beach. If you really fancy a dip, head to **Green Island** (p670).

Sleeping

All reliable options are on Taulud Island. Though not in the old town, they offer higher standards. Sadly, there's no beach where you can cool off.

Corallo Hotel (☎ 07113852; Taulud Island; r Nfa160-270; ❄) It's good budget-hotel fodder here, with simple yet well-scrubbed rooms in a colonial building. The more expensive ones have (noisy) air-con and balconies with sea views.

Central Hotel (☎ 552002; Taulud Island; s/d Nfa275/410, ste Nfa495; ❄) Soothingly positioned by the shore, the well-managed Central Hotel offers neat and serviceable rooms. Some have (oblique) sea views. The on-site restaurant

ERITREA

gets an A+ for its eclectic menu (mains from Nfa60).

Red Sea Hotel (☎ 552839; fax 552544; Taulud Island; s/d Nfa420/480; ✺) Although it's beginning to age, this Italian-designed hotel features 50 well-equipped rooms with air-con and satellite TV. Facilities include a restaurant and gardens at the back.

Eating & Drinking

You'll find a handful of cheap eateries and supermarkets on and around the main street on Massawa Island. Most hotels on Taulud Island also have a restaurant and welcome nonguests.

Beaches Bar & Restaurant (Taulud Island; mains Nfa60-110) Found at the back of the rather incongruous 'Twin Towers' building, this independent restaurant serves up tasty Eritrean staples as well as spaghetti.

Sallam Restaurant (Massawa Island; fish dishes from Nfa150; ☾ dinner) Though it doesn't look like much from the outside (plastic chairs and dim lighting), this Massawa institution is famous for its Yemeni speciality of fresh fish sprinkled with hot pepper and baked in a tandoori oven. No alcohol.

There's a host of lively little bars on Massawa Island.

Getting There & Around

There are frequent buses leaving from the bus station on the mainland for Asmara (Nfa30, 3½ to four hours).

Shared taxis and town minibuses are convenient for short hops around town (Nfa3).

DAHLAK ISLANDS

Some 350 islands lie off the Eritrean coast, the majority (209) of which make up the Dahlak Archipelago. Largely arid, barren and flat, the islands are austere and desolate. Fresh water is very scarce, and very few of the islands are inhabited (only three within the Dahlak Archipelago).

Tourist infrastructure is almost nonexistent, but camping on one of these islands (we suggest Dissei or Madote) certainly makes for a memorable Robinson Crusoe experience. Nature lovers looking to splash about in sparkling sapphire waters will love it here. There's also a good selection of unspoiled diving and snorkelling sites that are accessible to all levels.

HOT TIP: ACCESSING THE DAHLAK

As there aren't any regular boat services to the Dahlak Archipelago, organising a trip there has always been problematic, especially if you're travelling solo. Your best bet is to team up with a group of tourists or expats. You stand the best chance at weekends, when expats from Asmara (mostly Italian teachers) rent boats to relax on the islands. If there's space available, they'll be happy to have you on board provided you share the expenses. Contact the operators in Massawa or the travel agencies in Asmara (p663) well in advance – they'll let you know when there's a group departing.

This untouched world is not within everyone's reach. Independent travel is not really possible, and there aren't any regular boat services to the islands. You'll have to go through a travel agent in Asmara (p663) or a boat rental operation in Massawa. In Massawa, you can contact the **Eritrea Diving Centre** (☎ 552688, 552198; fax 551287; Taulud Island, Massawa) or **Dahlak Sea Touring** (☎ 07123126; Massawa Island). The journey from Massawa to most of the islands takes between 45 minutes and two hours by motorboat. Rates are roughly Nfa240 per nautical mile, which makes about Nfa10,000 for Dissei, Madote or Dur Gaam (the most popular islands). There's an overnight charge of Nfa4000.

Green Island is only 10 to 20 minutes from Massawa and is the most accessible place for decent snorkelling and tolerable beaches.

The Eritrea Diving Centre can organise diving trips to the islands. Including all gear, the cost of a single dive is Nfa600.

You need a permit to visit any of the Dahlak Islands (US$20), except Green Island. If you're joining a tour or hiring a boat, the permit should be organised for you.

DANKALIA

Frustrating news: most of Dankalia is out of bounds (foreigners are allowed to go as far as Buri Peninsula, but no further south). Imagine a narrow strip of land about 50km wide that stretches south of Massawa down to Djibouti (about 600km), along the coastline. It's a volcanic desert blessed with otherworldly, lunar landscapes, with a strong appeal. This secretive world is known as one of the hottest and most inhospitable places on Earth: there's little to see, nothing to do, and no great destination awaiting you at the other end, but the sense of exploration is real.

Between Massawa and Assab (the only significant town), there's only a smattering of little fishing villages.

If, by chance, Dankalia is again open to travellers during the lifetime of this book, don't miss the opportunity to get there. The best time to go is from November to March.

WESTERN ERITREA

It's so sad that this region is now closed to foreigners, because it has a truly peculiar appeal. Time seems to have stood still in these often forgotten lowlands, which lack the development and bustle of the densely populated south or east. A bit like the Australian outback, western Eritrea seduces with wild expanses and empty spaces – not to mention its fascinating inhabitants. In climate, geography, religion, industry, people and way of life, Eritrea's Muslim lowlands could not be more different from the Christian highlands. The more you forge west, the more you feel a Sudanese flavour.

The most significant town in Western Eritrea is Barentu, which is the heartland of the Kunama people.

ERITREA DIRECTORY

ACCOMMODATION

Only Asmara and, to a lesser extent, Massawa, offer a good range of hotels. Elsewhere the hotel scene is very modest. All the small towns have hotels, but they're often pretty basic affairs and many lack running water (you get a bucket shower instead).

Prices for budget accommodation in the capital average US$8 to US$12 for singles and US$10 to US$15 for doubles. For midrange hotels, you'll pay about US$15 to US$30 for singles and US$20 to US$60 for doubles. In the rest of the country, rates are usually cheaper.

Few hotels accept credit cards.

ACTIVITIES

Eritrea has great potential for outdoor pursuits but there are few well-organised facilities. Eritrea's best-known activity is diving in the Red Sea. The Dahlak Archipelago is cur-

rently the only place where organised diving and snorkelling takes place.

Eritrea offers excellent opportunities for birdwatching, especially around Filfil and Dekemhare, but there's no infrastructure in place yet.

BUSINESS HOURS

See p1136 for standard business hours.
Banks Open 8am to 11am and 2pm to 4pm Monday to Friday, and from 8am to 11.30am on Saturday.
Government offices and private businesses Usually closed between noon and 4pm (in eastern Eritrea only).

CUSTOMS REGULATIONS

Any person entering the country must fill in a foreign currency declaration form. The declaration form is mandatory for changing money, so don't lose it. You'll have to hand it in upon departure and an official will check your statement.

DANGERS & ANNOYANCES

Eritrea is a very safe country in which to travel. The biggest threat outside of the capital is the risk of land mines and unexploded munitions. Make sure you never stray off the road.

There are army checkpoints at the entrance and exit of each major town. They are pretty straightforward and foreigners never get hassled or asked for bribes; just show your passport and your travel permit (see p672).

PRACTICALITIES

- Eritrea uses the metric system for weights, measures and road distances.

- Eritrea predominantly uses the 220V system, with two-round-pin plugs.

- The only local publication in English is the twice-weekly *Eritrea Profile*.

- Eritrean national radio broadcasts three times a day in the nine Eritrean national languages.

- BBC World, Euronews, France 24, Al Jazeera and CNN can be received on satellite TVs.

- The government-controlled EriTV has two national TV channels.

EMBASSIES & CONSULATES

All embassies and consulates are based in Asmara. They are open from Monday to Friday and keep regular business hours.

Djibouti (☎ 125990; Saro St)
France (☎ 126599; Nakfa Ave)
Germany (☎ 186670; Saba Bldg, Warsay St)
Sudan (☎ 115546; Gezzabanda District)
UK (☎ 120145; Mariam GMBI St)
USA (☎ 120004; http://eritrea.usembassy.org; 173-1 St)
Yemen (☎ 123910; off Denden St)

HOLIDAYS

As well as the religious holidays listed in the Africa Directory (p1140), these are the principal public holidays in Eritrea:

New Year's Day 1 January
Leddet (Christmas) 7 January
Timkat (Epiphany) 19 January
International Women's Day 8 March
Tensae (Easter) March/April (variable)
Workers' Day 1 May
Liberation Day 24 May
Martyrs' Day 20 June
Start of the Armed Struggle 1 September
Kiddus Yohannes (Orthodox New Year) 11 September
Meskel (Finding of the True Cross) 27 September

MAPS

The best map currently available is the one produced by ITMB Publishing in Canada (1:9,000,000). At the time of writing, no maps of the country were available in Eritrea.

MONEY

The unit of currency is the Nakfa (Nfa). There are currently no ATMs in Eritrea. US dollars (cash or travellers cheques) and euros are the best currencies to carry. You can change cash with a minimum of hassle at the Commercial Bank of Eritrea in all cities and major towns. Himbol exchange offices in Asmara also change money. Each transaction must be registered on your currency declaration form, which is handed out at your arrival at the airport. Changing money on the black market still exists but is no longer widespread due to the heavy penalties and the introduction of a currency declaration form, which makes the business more complicated and risky to handle.

Travellers cheques are best carried in US dollars or euros. Don't forget to list your travellers cheques on your currency declaration form upon arrival, otherwise you won't be able to cash them.

The larger hotels in the capital, some airlines and some travel agents accept credit cards but they usually charge an additional 5% to 10% commission; check in advance.

Himbol in Asmara can do cash advances on your credit card, but the commission exacted is a ludicrous 7%.

TELEPHONE

To call Eritrea from abroad, dial your international access code, then ☎ 291 (the country code for Eritrea), then 1 (the area code) and the local number. International calls can be made from telecommunications offices (called 'Eritel') found in all the main towns.

Mobile phones are widespread. Mobile-phone numbers use eight digits: a two-digit number starting with 0, followed by six digits. To reach a mobile phone from outside Eritrea, dial the country code, then the mobile number without the initial 0.

TOURIST INFORMATION

Eritrea's tourist facilities are fairly woeful, with little literature and only one tourist office, in Asmara. But you could try one of the privately run travel agencies in Asmara (see p663).

VISAS

All foreign nationals require visas for entry to Eritrea. Tourist visas are single entry only, and are valid for 30 days from the date of arrival in Eritrea. They cost between US$50 and US$60.

Visas should be obtained from the Eritrean embassy or consulate before you leave your home country.

Travel Permits

Due to the ongoing tension with Ethiopia (and, to a lesser extent, Djibouti), travelling in Eritrea has become pretty bureaucratic and there are increasing travel restrictions (see the boxed text, opposite).

To travel outside Asmara, you'll need travel permits, obtainable at the Tourist Information Centre in Asmara. You'll need a permit for every place you intend to visit in the country (eg Massawa, Keren, Qohaito), and you'll be granted a number of days for each destination. Permits are not issued all at once; after having visited one place, you'll have to go through the Tourist Information Centre in Asmara to get your next permit for your next destination.

Permits are usually processed the same day. If you rent a car or a 4WD, you'll have to mention the model of the car and the registration number. Keep this travel permit at all times outside Asmara, as you'll be asked to show it at checkpoints, along with your passport.

To visit any of the archaeological sites of Eritrea, you'll need to get a special permit from the **National Museum office** (☎ 122389; Mariam GMBI St, Asmara; ⏲ 8.30-11.30am & 2.30-5.30pm Mon-Fri). You'll need your passport and Nfa150 per site (or US$10).

You'll also need a permit to visit the Dahlak Islands, but this should be handled by the travel agency or the owner of the boat that takes you there. It costs US$20.

To visit any Orthodox monastery, you'll need a permit from the **Orthodox Tewahdo Church Headquarters** (☎ 182098; Warsay St; ⏲ 8am-noon & 2-4.30pm Mon-Fri) in Asmara. It's about 300m past the Lufthansa office, across the street. It costs Nfa150 per monastery.

Visas for Onward Travel

For contact details of embassies and consulates in Eritrea, see opposite.

Djibouti Visas are available at Djibouti-Ambouli Airport in Djibouti City.

Sudan Obtaining a visa can take ages (or simply prove impossible). You'll need two photos, a letter of invitation from a sponsor in Sudan, a copy of your passport pages and a medical examination.

Yemen Most Western nationals can get a visa on arrival at Sana'a international airport.

TRANSPORT IN ERITREA

GETTING THERE & AWAY

Flying is the only way to enter the country; as all land borders are closed, it's no longer possible to travel overland. There are only a few airlines that serve the country.

Air

Eritrea's one international airport lies 6km from the capital. The privately run Nasair is the national carrier. Airlines connect Asmara with Cairo (Egypt), Dubai (UAE), Frankfurt

TRAVEL RESTRICTIONS

At the time of writing, most of Dankalia (south of Ghela'elo), Nakfa, Adi Quala and western Eritrea were off limits to travellers. Only Asmara, Filfil, Massawa, the Dahlak Islands, Keren, Dekemhare, Mendefera, Adi Keyh, Qohaito, Senafe (but not Debre Libanos) and Metera were accessible to foreigners. A travel permit is needed for all these places, except Asmara.

(Germany), Khartoum (Sudan), Nairobi (Kenya) and Sana'a (Yemen).

The following are airlines flying to and from Eritrea, with offices in Asmara:

EgyptAir (MS; ☎ 127034; www.egyptair.com; Bahti Meskerem Sq)

Lufthansa (LH; ☎ 186904; www.lufthansa.com; Warsay St)

Nasair (UE; ☎ 200700; www.nasair.aero; off Adal St)

Yemenia (IY; ☎ 121035; www.yemenia.com; Harnet Ave)

Land

DJIBOUTI

There's only one border crossing, at Rahaita/Moulhoulé, about 110km south of Assab, but it's not open because of the tension between Eritrea and Djibouti.

When the border was open, shared taxis (usually 4WDs) travelled from Assab to the border (with no fixed schedule), from where it was possible to find onward transport to Obock.

ETHIOPIA

As long as the conflict with Ethiopia remains unresolved, the borders between the two countries will remain closed. The most convenient way to get to Ethiopia is to fly through Sana'a (Yemen) or Cairo (Egypt).

SUDAN

At the time of writing, it was not possible to cross the border from Eritrea to Sudan. Check the current situation when you get there.

The road is sealed from Asmara to Teseney, near the border.

GETTING AROUND

Travel around Eritrea is restricted. A travel permit (see opposite) is necessary to travel outside Asmara, and a number of areas are off limits to foreigners (see above). Check the situation when you get to Asmara.

Bus

The bus service in Eritrea is reasonably efficient and extensive, but few would call it comfortable – expect something resembling a battered school bus. Coverage of Keren, Massawa, Mendefera and Dekemhare is excellent. Services thin out the further away from the capital you get. There are usually at least 10 a day between the larger towns (Asmara, Massawa and Keren), and in principle one bus a day between the smaller ones.

Car & Motorcycle

Vehicle hire is expensive in Eritrea. If you're just planning on travelling on the main routes between towns, a 2WD vehicle is sufficient. But some sights, including Qohaito, are only accessible by 4WD. A driver is usually provided for your 4WD.

Cars cost Nfa400 to Nfa700 per day; a 4WD costs around Nfa2000 per day, including third-party insurance. The first 50km to 90km are free, and each additional kilometre costs between Nfa2 and Nfa3. Note that payment is by cash only. See p667 for car rental agencies in Asmara.

Train

The old Italian railway that stretched between Massawa, Asmara, Keren and Agordat has been repaired and there's now a regular service on Sunday morning between Asmara and Nefasit, provided there's a minimum of 10 people. See p667 for more details.

Ethiopia

Remember when you were a child tucked up in bed and your parents, opening a book, read aloud the words 'Once upon a time'? Within moments you were transported to a magical world where castles were made of crystal, monks from Syria climbed serpents' tails to build invisible monasteries, deserts were made of gold, women wore plates for jewellery, emperors turned solid rock into beautiful churches, wild and dangerous hyenas begged for titbits from the hands of men, a queen known only as Sheba seduced a king named Solomon and the words of God were hidden in a secret ark for the world to ponder. Well, that fairy tale has a name – its name is Ethiopia and it's every bit as fantastical as the wildest bedtime story.

Of course, as for any brave knight heading forth into a fairy tale, there is a certain amount of challenge involved in a journey through Ethiopia. Though the nation is anything but the desert wasteland of perpetual famine and war that the media likes to portray, Ethiopia is monetarily poor – making travel here testing, awe-inspiring and heartbreaking. You don't explore Ethiopia for a relaxing getaway; you venture here to be moved. And moved you shall be.

ETHIOPIA

FAST FACTS

- **Area** 1,098,000 sq km
- **ATMs** Addis Ababa and large towns in the north; Visa cards only
- **Borders** Kenya, Sudan, Djibouti, Somaliland, Eritrea (closed)
- **Budget** US$10 to US$30 per day
- **Capital** Addis Ababa
- **Languages** Amharic, Tigrinya, Oromo
- **Money** Birr; US$1 = Birr12.62, €1 = Birr18.02
- **Population** 85 million
- **Seasons** Wet (mid-March to early October), hot in lowlands (June to September)
- **Telephone** Country code ☎ 251; international access code ☎ 00
- **Time** GMT/UTC +3
- **Visa** One-month visa US$20 at airport; Ethiopian embassies charge more

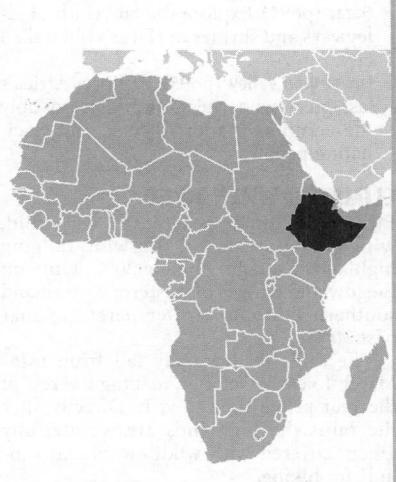

HOW MUCH?

- **Steaming macchiato** US$0.20
- **100km by bus** US$1.50 to US$3
- **Minibus across town** US$0.20
- **Internet per hour** US$1 to US$2
- **Tip for helpful priest** US$0.75 to $US1

LONELY PLANET INDEX

- **1L petrol** US$0.55
- **1.5L bottled water** US$0.45
- **Bottle of Bedele beer** US$0.45
- **Souvenir T-Shirt** US$3 to US$6
- **Roasted barley** US$0.15

HIGHLIGHTS

- **Lalibela** (p692) Immerse yourself in Christianity in its most raw and powerful form in this mind-blowing maze of rock-hewn churches.
- **Aksum** (p690) Search for hidden treasure in the dank gloom of ancient tombs and ponder the mysteries of the stelae of Aksum.
- **Simien Mountains** (p690) Lace up your boots and hike through this sublime national park, home to magnificent wildlife and unparalleled panoramas of endless Abyssinian abysses.
- **Harar** (p694) Explore the labyrinth of alleyways and shrines in Harar's old walled city.
- **Lower Omo Valley** (p695) Explore 'Africa's last great wilderness' and visit possibly the continent's most diverse and fascinating peoples.

CLIMATE & WHEN TO GO

Ethiopia's climate is typically very mild, with temperatures on the wide-ranging highlands averaging below 20°C. Only on the lowland fringes of western, eastern and southern Ethiopia can temperatures soar past 30°C.

The rains traditionally fall from mid-March to early October, making the rest of the year prime time to visit. Directly after the rains the highlands are wonderfully green, covered with wildflowers and sublime for hiking.

ITINERARIES

- **Two Weeks** Those simply filling the gap between Sudan and Kenya could blaze through in two weeks, though you'd be missing the opportunity of a lifetime. Africa's real-life Camelot, Gonder (p688), is first, before Bahir Dar (p687) and the island monasteries of Lake Tana (p687). Next is Addis Ababa (p681) for splendid dining and museum action. Break the long haul south to Kenya at Awasa (p695).
- **One Month** Complete the north's historical circuit: after Addis Ababa (p681), loop north through Bahir Dar (p687), Lake Tana (p687) and Gonder (p688) before hiking the glorious Simien Mountains (p690). The tombs and stelae of Aksum (p690) are next before the mesmerising rock-hewn churches of Lalibela (p692).
- **Two Months** Mix Harar (p694) in eastern Ethiopia and the wildlife and tribes of the Lower Omo Valley (p695) with the one-month itinerary above.

HISTORY

Ethiopia's human history dates back at least 4.4 million years, landing it squarely in East Africa's heralded cradle of humanity. Recorded history dates to 1500 BC, when a civilisation with Sabaean influences briefly blossomed at Yeha.

Kingdom of Aksum

This kingdom, ranking among the ancient world's most powerful, rose shortly after 400 BC. Its capital, Aksum, sat in a fertile area lying at an important commercial crossroads between Egypt, Sudan's gold fields and the Red Sea. At its height the kingdom extended well into Arabia.

Aksum flourished on trade, exporting frankincense, grain, skins, apes and, particularly, ivory. In turn, exotic imports returned from Egypt, Arabia and India. Aksumite architecture was incredible, and Aksum's impressive monuments still stand today (see p690).

The 4th century AD brought Christianity, which enveloped Aksum and shaped Ethiopia's future spiritual, cultural and intellectual life.

Aksum flourished until the 7th century, when its trading empire was fatally isolated by

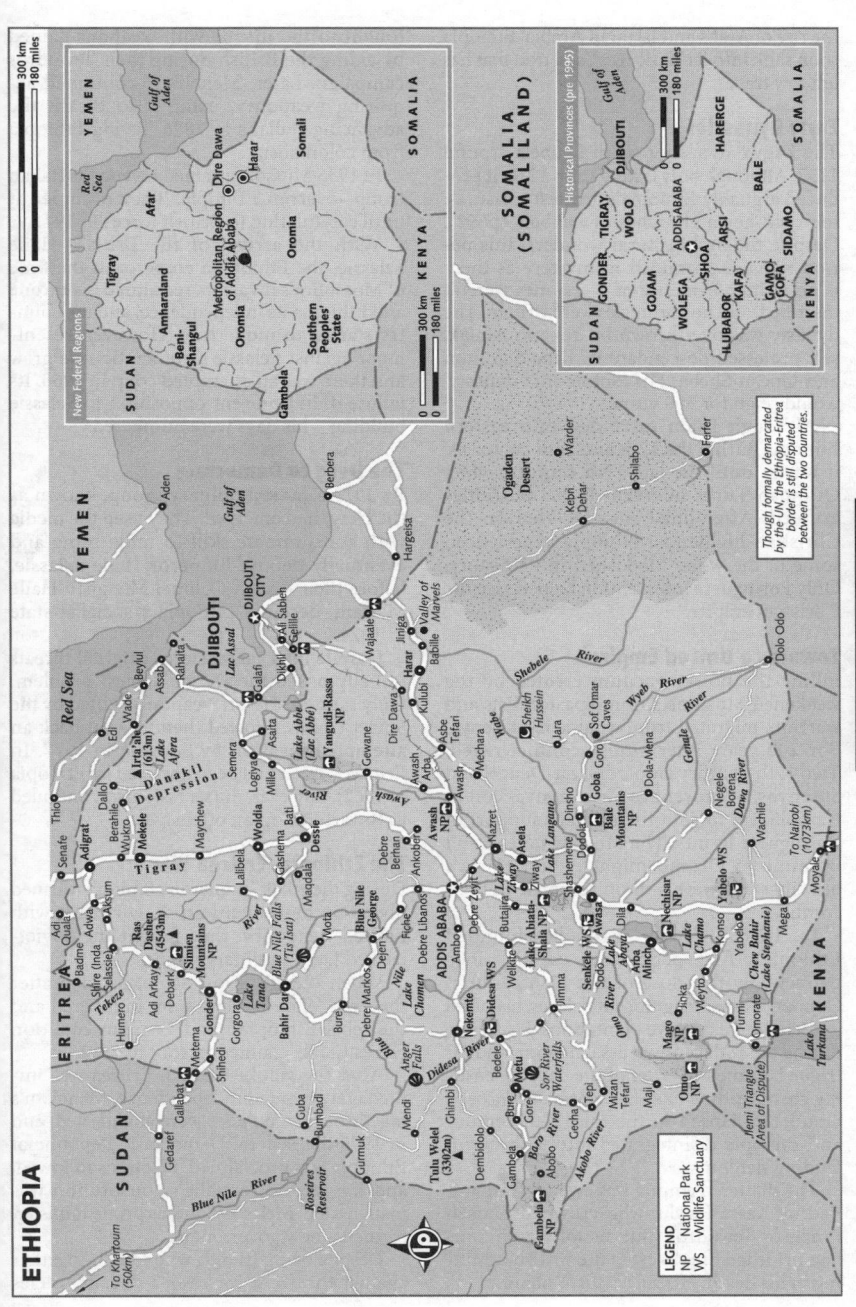

ETHIOPIA

LEGEND
NP   National Park
WS   Wildlife Sanctuary

Though formally demarcated by the UN, the Ethiopia-Eritrea border is still disputed between the two countries.

the rise of Arabs and Islam in Arabia. Ethiopia soon sank into its 'dark ages', a period that has left few traces.

Early Dynasties

The Zagwe dynasty rose in Lalibela around 1137. Although only lasting until 1270, it produced arguably Ethiopia's greatest treasures: the rock-hewn churches of Lalibela (p692). Despite the architectural wonders, this period remains shrouded in mystery as there is no written evidence of it – stones weren't inscribed, and no chronicles were written. The dynasty was overthrown by Yekuno Amlak, self-professed descendant of King Solomon and Queen Sheba. His 'Solomonic dynasty' would reign for 500 years.

Although Islam expanded into eastern Ethiopia during the 12th and 14th centuries, it wasn't until the late 15th century, when Ottoman Turks intervened, that hostilities erupted. After jihad was declared on the Christian highlands, Ethiopia experienced some of the worst bloodshed in its history. Only Portuguese intervention helped save the Christian empire.

Towards a United Empire

Filling the power vacuum created by the weakened Muslims, Oromo pastoralists and warriors migrated from what is now Kenya. For 200 years intermittent conflict raged. Two 17th-century emperors, Za-Dengel and Susenyos, even went as far as conversion to Catholicism to gain the military support of Portuguese Jesuits. The Muslim state wasn't immune to Oromo might either; Harar's old city walls were built in response to their conflicts.

In 1636 Emperor Fasiladas founded Ethiopia's first permanent capital since Lalibela. By the close of the 17th century, Gonder boasted magnificent palaces, beautiful gardens and extensive plantations. However, during the 18th century, assassination and intrigue became the order of the day, the ensuing chaos reading like Shakespeare's *Macbeth*. Gonder collapsed in the mid-19th century and Ethiopia disintegrated into a cluster of feuding fiefdoms.

The shattered empire was eventually reunified by Kassa Haylu, who crowned himself Emperor Tewodros. But his lofty ambitions and pride led him to cross the British, resulting in his death. His successor, Yohannes IV, fought to the throne with weapons gained by aiding the British during their Tewodros campaign. Later, Menelik II continued acquiring weaponry, using it to thrash the advancing Italians in 1896, saving Ethiopia from colonialism.

In 1936 Mussolini gained revenge as Italian troops overran Ethiopia. They occupied it until capitulating to British forces in 1941.

With the arrival of the British, Haile Selassie, the Ethiopian emperor at the time of Mussolini's invasion, reclaimed his throne and Ethiopia its independence, and the country started to modernise. However, resentment against Selassie's autocratic rule grew and there was an attempted coup in 1960. Its failure didn't prevent opposition to Selassie building – his days were numbered.

The Derg to Democracy

By 1973 a radical military group, known as the Derg, had emerged. They used the media with consummate skill to undermine and eventually depose Emperor Haile Selassie, before their leader, Colonel Mengistu Haile Mariam, declared Ethiopia a socialist state in 1974.

Despite internal tensions, external threats initially posed the Derg's biggest problem. Only state-of-the-art weaponry, gifted by the Soviet Union, allowed them to beat back an attempted invasion by Somalia in 1977. In Eritrea (which had been annexed by Ethiopia in 1962), however, the secessionists continued to thwart Ethiopian offensives.

The Ethiopia–Eritrea War

During the 1980s, numerous Ethiopian armed liberation movements arose. For years, with limited weaponry, they fought the Soviet-backed Derg's military might.

When Mengistu lost Soviet backing after the Cold War, his days were numbered and the rebel Ethiopian and Eritrean coalition forces finally claimed victory in 1991.

After the smoke cleared, Eritrea was immediately granted independence, Mengistu's failed socialist policies were abandoned, and in 1995 the Federal Democratic Republic of Ethiopia was proclaimed. Elections followed, and the second republic's constitution was inaugurated. Meles Zenawi, as prime minister, formed a new government.

Despite being friends who fought together against the Derg for over a decade, Meles

Zenawi and Eritrea's President Isaias soon clashed. Bickering over Eritrea's exchange-rate system for its new currency led to Eritrea occupying the border town of Badme in 1998. Soon full-scale military conflict broke out, leaving tens of thousands dead on both sides before ceasing in mid-2000. The settlement included the installation of an OAU (Organization for African Unity)–UN buffer zone on Eritrean soil.

Ethiopia Today

Ethiopia is again at a poignant period in its history. Controversial 2005 elections and the government's heavy-handed reprisals have cast doubts on democracy, and everyone's hoping another democratic freedom fighter hasn't turned dictator.

Despite many opposition members being unjustly jailed, their parties continue to rally, and in mid-2006 Ethiopia's largest opposition party formed a new political alliance with Ethiopia's four largest rebel groups.

As if internal political turmoil wasn't enough, tensions with Eritrea continue to bubble and boil and the two neighbours almost came to blows again in 2005. With the UN – citing impossible travel and supply restrictions – pulling out of Eritrea in 2008, the possibility of events spiralling out of control very quickly remains high.

The southern front took an interesting turn in August 2006, when Ethiopian troops entered Somalia in support of the Somali government's fight against the Islamic militia who control Mogadishu. Things escalated in December 2006, when Ethiopia officially declared war against the Somali Islamic militia and launched air attacks on several Somalian border towns. Officially Ethiopia withdrew its troops from Somalia in early 2009, but by the middle of that year Ethiopia admitted that some of its forces had returned to Somalia.

CULTURE

The Ethiopians are nothing if not proud – and for good reason. To them, Ethiopia has stood out from all African nations and proved itself to be a unique world of its own – home to its own culture, language, script, calendar and history. Ethiopian Orthodox Christians and Muslims alike revel in the fact that Ethiopia was the only nation on the continent to successfully fight off colonisation.

The highlands have been dominated by a distinctive form of Christianity since the 4th century. Although undeniably devout and keen to dispense centuries worth of Orthodox legends and tales dating back to Aksum and the Ark of the Covenant, Christians, like all Ethiopians, nonetheless still cling to a surprising amount of belief in magic and superstition.

Other than religion, it's agriculture and pastoralism that fill the days of over 80% of Ethiopians. Everyone is involved, right down to stick- and stone-wielding four-year-old children, who are handed the responsibility of herding their families' livestock.

With most people toiling in the fields, it's not surprising that only 42.7% of Ethiopians are literate. Only 66% of children attend primary school; a mere 31% attend secondary school. If all children under 16 attended school, Ethiopia's workforce would be ravaged, as almost half of Ethiopia's population would be attending classes.

Families are incredibly close, and most children live with their parents until marriage. After marriage, couples usually join the husband's parents' household. Eventually, they'll request land for a house.

Music and dance is an extremely important part of most Ethiopians' lives, playing parts in religious festivities and social occasions, such as weddings and funerals.

People

Ethiopia's population has just squeezed past 85 million, which is astounding considering 1935's population was just 15 million. Ethiopia's annual population growth rate of 3.2% is one of the highest in the world and this high rate promises to be one of the biggest problems that Ethiopian governments of the future will face. Though a trend of urbanisation is emerging, 83% of people live in rural areas.

Although 84 languages and 200 dialects are spoken, the population can be divided into eight broad groups, Oromo, Amhara and Tigrayan being the main three. Under the new republic's policy of 'ethnic federalism', the modern federal regions are demarcated largely along ethnic-linguistic lines.

Faith is paramount to most Ethiopians. Although Christians only slightly outnumber Muslims (50% to 32%), Christianity has dominated history. Most highlanders are Orthodox, and Christianity heavily influences the highlands' political, social and cultural scene. Most

WHO DOES SHE THINK SHE IS?

Ethiopia has long been a source of legend and mystery. The Danakil desert was said to have once been made not of salt like today, but of gold. Medieval Europe considered Ethiopia the home of Prester John, a legendary Christian king who lived in a palace of crystal; and the Rastafarians of today believe that the last emperor, Haile Selassie, was a living god. But there is a woman whose name has resonated through time and multiple cultures. She is, of course, the Queen of Sheba.

Though she appears in the writings of all three monotheistic religions, it is in Ethiopia (where she is known as Makeda) where the story of her life has become the cornerstone of culture, history and lifestyle. According to the *Kebra Negast* (Ethiopia's national epic), the Queen of Sheba's first public appearance was when she paid a visit to the court of King Solomon in Jerusalem, in the 10th century BC. Solomon became enraptured with her beauty and devised a plan to have his wicked way with her. He agreed to let her stay in his palace, on the condition that she touched nothing of his. Shocked that he would consider her capable of such a thing, she agreed. That evening Solomon laid on a feast of spicy and salty foods. After the meal, Sheba and Solomon retired to separate beds in his sleeping quarters. During the night Sheba awoke, thirsty from all the salty food she had consumed, and reached across for a glass of water. The moment she put the glass to her lips Solomon awoke and triumphantly claimed that she had broken her vow. 'But it's only water', she cried, to which Solomon replied, 'And nothing on earth is more precious than water'.

Ethiopian tradition holds that the child that resulted from the deceitful night of passion that followed was to become Menelik I, from whom the entire royal line of Ethiopia claims direct descent (in truth the line, if it ever existed, has been broken a number of times).

But there's more to this tale than just the birth of the Ethiopian royal line. This is also the story of the arrival of the Ark of the Covenant in Ethiopia. It's said that the centrepiece of Solomon's famous temple was the Ark of the Covenant, and that as long as the Jews had the Ark, nothing bad could come of them. However, when Menelik came of age he journeyed to Jerusalem in order to meet his father. When he returned home his luggage was a little heavier than before – secreted away among his dirty laundry was the Ark of the Covenant, which every Ethiopian will tell you is, to this very day, hidden inside a small chapel in Aksum.

Muslims inhabit the lowlands, but significant populations live in Ethiopia's predominantly Christian highland cities.

Numerous traditional African beliefs are still practised by 11% of Ethiopians, particularly in the southern and western lowlands.

The church, traditionally enjoying almost as much authority as the state, is responsible for both inspiring Ethiopia's art forms and stifling them with its great conservatism.

FOOD & DRINK

Ethiopia's food is much like Ethiopia, completely different from the rest of Africa. Plates, bowls and utensils are replaced by *injera*, a unique pancake of countrywide proportions. Atop its rubbery confines sits anything from *kai wat* (spicy meat stew) to colourful dollops of *gomen* (minced spinach) and *tere sega* (cubes of raw beef).

Whether it's *berbere* (a famous Ethiopian spice) joyfully bringing tears to your eyes, or an *injera*'s slightly sour taste sending your tongue into convulsions, one thing's certain: Ethiopian fare provokes strong reactions and though you might not always enjoy it, you won't forget it!

Ethiopia is the original home of coffee, which is still ubiquitous throughout the country. Sip a macchiato made from a vintage Italian espresso machine, or sit down for a traditional coffee ceremony. Another beverage you must savour is *tej* (honey wine).

ENVIRONMENT

Ethiopia's topography is remarkably diverse, ranging from the vast central plateau (Ethiopian highlands), with elevations between 1800m and 4543m, to one of the earth's lowest points: the infamous Danakil Depression, sinking 120m below sea level. The highlands supply four large river systems, the most famous being the Blue Nile.

Southern Ethiopia is bisected by the Rift Valley. The valley hosts several lakes, and most are havens for birdlife. The Rift Valley's northern end opens into the Danakil Depression.

Ethiopia's flora and fauna reflect its diverse topography, and the nation plays host to numerous species seen nowhere else on earth. Unfortunately, demographic pressures are putting the environment under extreme pressure, and 95% of Ethiopia's original forest has been lost.

There are three wildlife sanctuaries and 15 national parks, including the justifiably honoured Simien and Bale Mountains National Parks.

ADDIS ABABA

pop 2.8 million

Since its formation in the 19th century, Addis Ababa has always acted like a magical portal and a gateway to another world. For the rural masses of Ethiopia it was, and is, a city whose streets are paved in gold – at least for some. For foreign visitors Addis stands on the verge of an ancient and mystical world.

Yet for both of these groups, Addis, Africa's fourth-largest city and diplomatic capital, is often considered a place to traverse as quickly as possible. But by doing so, travellers skip the key that links these two worlds. Put simply, if you bypass the contrasts and contradictions of Addis – the shepherd from the countryside bringing his flock to a city market, the city priest with the business investments, the glossy nightclubs with the country-girl prostitutes – then you risk failing to understand Ethiopia altogether.

ORIENTATION

Massive and incoherent, Addis can be broken down into distinct districts. The city centre is found at Churchill Ave's southern end, Gambia St. Here you'll find government and commercial buildings.

Piazza, a district atop the hill at Churchill Ave's northern end, whose legacy is owed to Italian occupation, houses budget hotels, cafes and bars, as well as more than its fair share of characters up to no good.

East of Piazza are Addis Ababa University, several museums and the landmark roundabouts of Arat Kilo and Siddist Kilo. South from there is Menelik II Ave, which boasts the UN's Africa Hall as well as the ugly Meskal Sq.

Thanks to the new Chinese-built ring road, Addis' southeast, around Bole Rd, is thriving with exciting new developments. An increasing number of travellers are opting to wave goodbye to the Piazza area and base themselves out here.

INFORMATION

Bookshops

Africans Bookshop (Hailesilase St; ☽ 9am–1pm & 2.30–7pm Mon–Sat) Secondhand books on Ethiopia.
Bookworld Friendship City Center (Bole Rd; ☽ 9am–9pm Mon–Sat, 11am–8pm Sun); Haile Gebreselassie Rd (**Haile Gebreselassie Rd**; ☽ 8am–9pm)

Emergency

Emergency 24-hour numbers:
Fire brigade (☎ 912)
Police (☎ 991)
Red Cross ambulance service (☎ 917)

Internet Access

Although the internet is widely accessible, fast connections are still as rare as a cheetah on Bole Rd. Some convenient outlets are listed here.
Compunet (Gambia St; per hr Birr15; ☽ 8.30am–9pm)
Fiber Computer Engineering (Dejazmach Jote St; per hr Birr15)
Maam Internet Café (Bole Rd; per hr Birr15; ☽ 7.30am–9pm)
Nina Internet Service (Mundy St; per hr Birr15; ☽ 8am–10pm)
TAD Business Centre (Off Haile Gebreselassie Rd; per hr Birr12; ☽ 9am–9pm)

Internet Resources

Addis All Around (www.addisallaround.com) This excellent website previews forthcoming cultural events, as well as listing general city information.

Media

Look out for the monthly *What's Up!*, listing restaurants, shopping venues, nightclubs and events.

Medical Services

Bethzatha Hospital (☎ 0115-514470; ☽ 24hr) This quality private hospital, off Ras Mekonen Ave, is recommended by most embassies.
Ghion Pharmacy (☎ 0115-518606; Ras Desta Damtew St)
Hayat Hospital (☎ 0116-624488; Ring Rd; ☽ 24hr)
St Gabriel Hospital (☎ 0116-613622; Djibouti St; ☽ 24hr)

ETHIOPIA

ADDIS ABABA

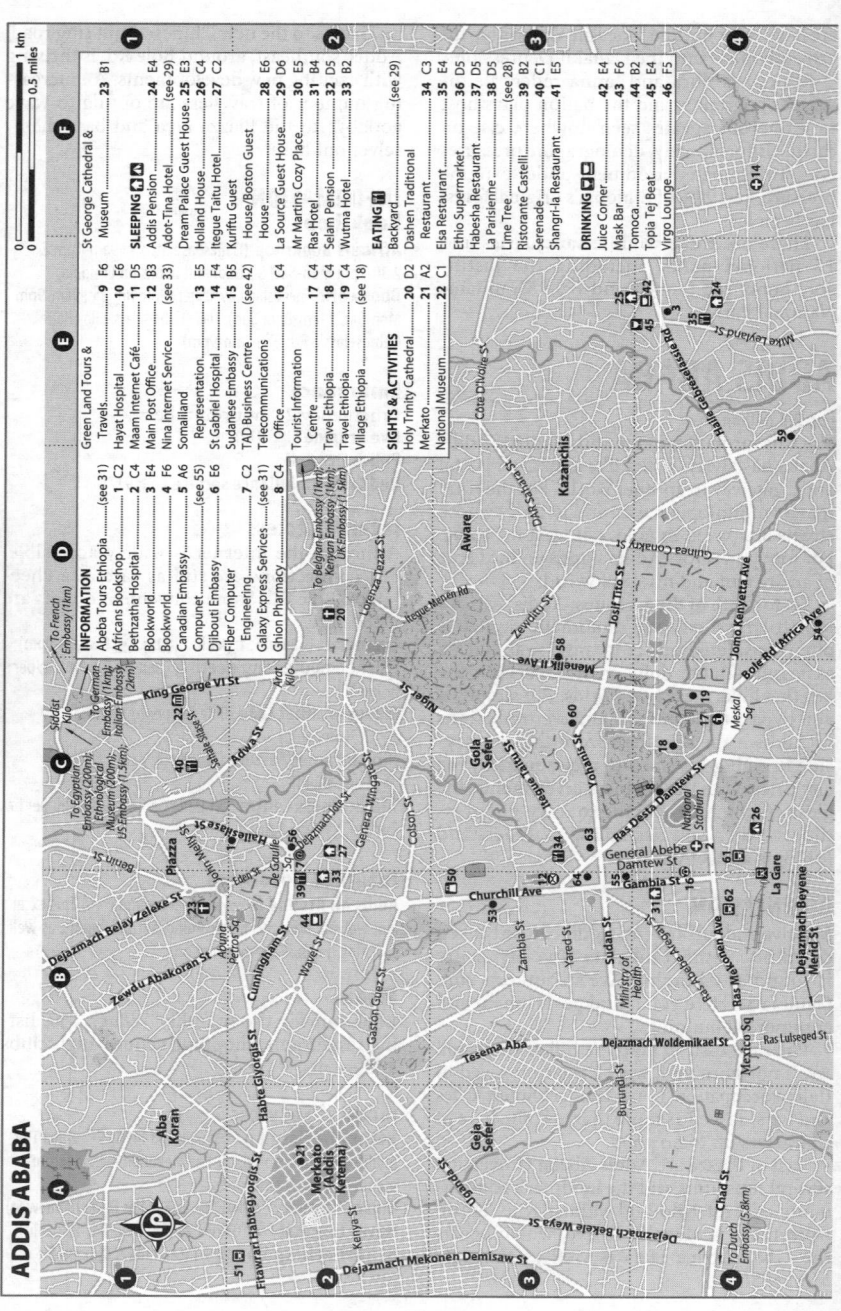

0   1 km
0   0.5 miles

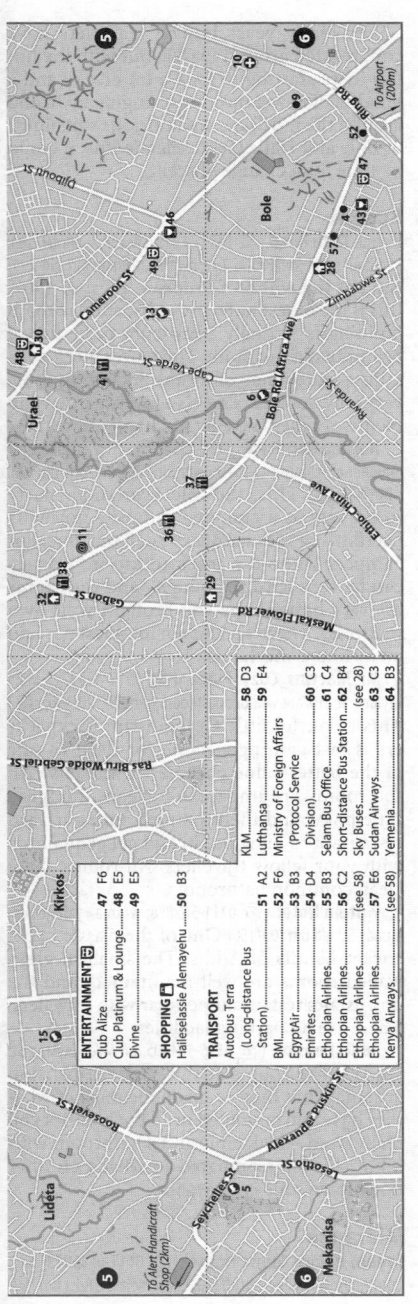

Money

You'll have no trouble at all finding a bank to change cash or travellers cheques, and most larger Dashen Bank branches have ATMs that accept foreign Visa cards (but not MasterCard, Plus or Cirrus cards).

Post

Main post office (Ras Desta Damtew St) Poste-restante and international-parcel services.

Telephone & Fax

Trying to use the public phones on the street will result in nothing but a few new additions to your growing collection of grey hairs.

Telecommunications office (☎ 0115-514977; Gambia St)

Tourist Information

Tourist Information Centre (☎ 0115-512310; Meskal Sq; ⏰ 8.30am-12.30pm & 1.30-5.30pm Mon-Thu, 8.30-11.30am & 1.30-5.30pm Fri) This helpful office does its best to provide information about the city and itineraries elsewhere.

Travel Agencies

Some recommended agencies in Addis include the following:

Abeba Tours Ethiopia (☎ 0115-159530; www. abebatoursethiopia.com; Ras Hotel, Gambia St)

Galaxy Express Services (☎ 0115-510355; www. galaxyexpressethiopia.com; Gambia St).

Green Land Tours & Travels (☎ 0116-299252; www. greenlandethiopia.com; Cameroon St)

Travel Ethiopia (www.travelethiopia.com) Ghion Hotel (☎ 0115-525479); National Hotel (☎ 0115-525478; Menelik II Ave)

Village Ethiopia (☎ 0115-523497; www.village-ethiopia. net; National Hotel, Menelik II Ave)

DANGERS & ANNOYANCES

Violent crime is rare in Addis, particularly where visitors are concerned. However, petty theft and confidence tricks are problematic.

The Merkato is the worst, as pickpockets abound, targeting *faranjis* (foreigners) and Ethiopians. Other spots requiring vigilance include Piazza, Meskal Sq, minibus stands and Churchill Ave.

Beware of distraction tactics (some involving someone enthusiastically grabbing your ankles, while others pilfer your pockets!).

ETHIOPIA

SIGHTS

Set within Haile Selassie's former palace and surrounded by Addis Ababa University's beautiful gardens and fountains is the enthralling **Ethnological Museum** (Algeria St; adult/student Birr20/10; ☺ 8am-5pm Mon-Fri, 9am-5pm Sat & Sun). One of the finest museums in Africa, the vibrant exhibitions inside are well laid out and give a great insight into Ethiopia's rich cultures.

Although less visually stimulating than the Ethnological Museum, the **National Museum** (☎ 0111-117150; King George VI St; admission Birr10; ☺ 8.30am-5pm) is no less thought-provoking. Its collection ranks among sub-Saharan Africa's most important. The palaeontology exhibit contains two remarkable casts of your 3.2-million-year-old great, great something-or-other grandmother, 'Lucy', a famously fossilised upright hominid discovered in 1974.

Off Niger St, the massive, ornate **Holy Trinity cathedral** (admission Birr30; ☺ 7am-6pm Mon-Fri, 9am-6pm Sat & Sun) is Ethiopia's second-most important place of worship. It's also the final resting place of Emperor Haile Selassie and his wife.

Commissioned by Emperor Menelik to commemorate his stunning 1896 defeat of the Italians in Adwa, Piazza's **St George Cathedral** (Fitawrari Gebeyehu St) was completed in 1911.

Just outside the cathedral is the **museum** (admission Birr20; ☺ 9am-noon & 2-5pm Tue-Sun), which contains one of Ethiopia's best collections of ecclesiastical paraphernalia.

Wading into the market chaos known as **Merkato** (☺ 6am-7pm Mon-Sat), west of the centre, can be as rewarding as it is exasperating. Some people say it's the largest market in Africa, but as its exact boundaries are as shady as some of its characters, this is a little hard to verify. If you're going to be robbed in Ethiopia it will be here.

FESTIVALS & EVENTS

Although Addis doesn't boast any major festivals of its own, it's a great place to catch the national festivals of Leddet, Timkat and Meskel. For festival dates see p697.

SLEEPING

Accommodation runs the gamut in Addis – you can snuggle up in bed next to giant insects or sink into a sumptuous suite. It's all up to you, your budget, and your choice in bed partners.

For many years budget travellers have congregated around Piazza, but with the hotels there starting to look a bit creaky and a handful of newer options springing up in and around the much more salubrious surrounds of Bole and Haile Gebreselassie Rds, it could be time for a change of scene.

Budget

Itegue Taitu Hotel (☎ 0111-560787; www.taituhotel.com; r without bathroom Birr66-191, r with bathroom Birr154-299) Built at the whim of Empress Taitu in 1907, this is the oldest hotel in Addis, and the main building is virtually a museum piece full of beautiful old furniture. The newer block contains a wide range of rooms, including some very jolly doubles. There's a lovely garden and plenty of other travellers to hang out with.

Holland House (☎ 0115-155279; wims_hollanhouse@ethionet.et; campsite Birr70, jeep Birr70, truck/bus Birr100, r Birr70; 🖵) This, the sole overlander party in the city, is a cramped campsite normally overflowing with hardened road warriors. For campers without a truck to kip in, privacy can be very hard to come by and the rooms are very basic (hope you brought your own mattress). There's a kitchen for guest use and an in-house mechanic.

Mr Martins Cozy Place (☎ 0911-423972; Mike Leyland St; s/d/apt without bathroom Birr100/120/180; 🖵) This colourful little German-run backpackers is fast gaining a name for itself as one of the better-value cheapies in the city. All the rooms are impeccably clean, though a little poky, and there's a pleasant courtyard restaurant to hang out in and get acquainted with your fellow travellers. All rooms share clean common bathrooms.

Wutma Hotel (☎ 0111-562878; wutma@yahoo.com; Mundy St; s/d Birr100/150) One of the classic backpacker haunts of Addis. The smallish grey-walled rooms are well maintained, and the downstairs restaurant popular with travellers. There are no parking facilities.

Addis Pension (☎ 0116-184495; off Mike Leyland St; r Birr150) The rooms at this modern pension are small, but they've made the most of what they have and crammed in all the luxuries you really need – bed, table and a bathroom with a hot shower. Compared to what's on offer downtown, this is a bargain.

Midrange

Dream Palace Guest House (☎ 0111-6635972; wub guesthouse@ethionet.et; off Haile Gebreselassie Rd; r Birr150-

500; 🖳) This superb option has something for all purse strings. There are a handful of simple cubicle rooms with hot-water showers; next up come the spacious, well-planned mid-range rooms (Birr300); and finally you get the magnificent Queen of Sheba–wannabe rooms, which have two-person Jacuzzis among other creature comforts. It's in a quiet location behind the run-down Axum Hotel.

Ras Hotel (☎ 0115-517060; fax 0115-517327; Gambia St; s/d incl breakfast from Birr151/202) Set squarely in the town centre, this government-run hotel might be frazzled around the edges and feel a bit like a sanatorium, but it's a real institution with a constant buzz of people coming and going. The large rooms are a fair deal and some have views over the slums – so that's nice.

our pick La Source Guest House (☎ 0114-665510; Meskal Flower Rd; s/d incl breakfast Birr220/288) Finally, Addis has produced a guesthouse that truly feels like it offers value for money. It's sparkling-clean, with constant hot water, and it even has that rare thing – character – in abundance. All the rooms have loud and lovely African art and masks adorning the walls, rainbow-tainted bedspreads and furnishings made of bendy, twisted tree branches.

Selam Pension (☎ 0101-18200159; selampension2@ yahoo.com; Gabon St; d/tw incl breakfast Birr230/450) An excellent deal. This brand-new and sparkling clean guesthouse is well run and far enough from the road to mean honking horns won't interrupt your sleep – too much! The sign is in Amharic only so ask someone to point it out.

Top End

Adot-Tina Hotel (☎ 0114-673939; www.adottina.com; Meskal Flower Rd; s/d incl breakfast US$87-100; 🖳) The small and plush rooms of this intimate business-class hotel, which come with either a deep relaxing bath or a space-age shower far to complicated for us to work out, are really good value. However, the seal on the deal might be the free sauna and the best internet we found anywhere in Ethiopia.

Kuriftu Guest House/Boston Guest House (☎ 0116-623809; thekuriftuguesthouse@yahoo.com; 6th Fl, Boston Partners Bldg, Bole Rd; r incl breakfast US$125; 🖳 🛜) It's not cheap, but if you're after class with a homely tint then this intimate hotel has the goods. The colours are sunburst Mediterranean and the furnishings a stylised orange and white, the beds are enormous and the showers like waterfalls. Other perks include free massages and a sauna.

EATING

Many of the more tourist-orientated Ethiopian restaurants offer a 'traditional experience': traditional food (called 'national food') in traditional surroundings with traditional music in the evening.

Many of the smarter restaurants add 15% tax and a 10% service charge to their bills; check before you order.

La Parisienne (Gabon St; pastries Birr2-5; ⏲ 6am-8pm) If you're staying in the Bole Rd area then don't miss the superb macchiato, croissants and freshly squeezed orange juice breakfasts of this terrace cafe.

Dashen Traditional Restaurant (☎ 0115-529746; mains Birr15-40; ⏲ 10am-10pm) This lovely low-key dining area, with stone walls, local art and bamboo furniture, is perfect for your first awkward attempts at *injera*. The fasting food is particularly good (it's also available with fish).

Lime Tree (Bole Rd; mains Birr17-34; ⏲ 7am-11pm) One of the hippest places in Addis to have a light lunch. The menu includes such delights as pita stuffed with tabouleh or falafel, and chicken coconut curry. There's an in-house bookshop, gallery and notice board.

Backyard (☎ 0114-673501; Meskal Flower Rd; mains Birr20-40; ⏲ 11am-midnight Mon-Fri, 9am-midnight Sat & Sun) This pastel cool restaurant has a tasty range of light pastas and salads, but it's the drool-inducing steaks that it's most renowned for.

Elsa Restaurant (Mike Leyland St; meals Birr25-35; ⏲ noon-10pm) This simple outdoor restaurant serves quality *yetsom beyaynetu* (variety of fasting foods), which is perfect for vegetarians, while *yedoro arosto* (roasted chicken) and *gored gored* (raw beef cubes with *awazi*, a kind of mustard and chilli sauce) assuage carnivorous cravings. Half the neighbourhood like to come here for an afternoon drink.

Shangri-la Restaurant (Cape Verde St; mains Birr30-60; ⏲ lunch & dinner) This is an atmospheric place to head for *tere sega*, which is available on Thursday, Saturday and Sunday. There's an outdoor dining area and a cosy bar serving quality *tej*.

Habesha Restaurant (Bole Rd; mains Birr60-80; ⏲ lunch & dinner) For an Ethiopian meal that looks as good as it tastes, come to this fashionable Bole eatery where serving is an art form. There's also live music and traditional dancing every night at 8pm.

ETHIOPIA

ourpick Serenade (☎ 0911-200072; mains Birr60-80; ☽ 7pm-midnight Wed-Sat, 10am-3pm Sun) This magnificent Mediterranean eatery, with a menu that fuses Beirut with Milan, will leave your stomach in a heavenly daze. Reserve in advance.

Ristorante Castelli (☎ 0111-571757; Mahatma-Gandhi St; mains Birr60-90; ☽ noon-2.30pm & 7-10.30pm Mon-Sat) The legendary home of Addis' best Italian food. The pasta is homemade and all the ingredients are as fresh and natural as an olive in a Sicilian garden. Reservations are wise.

DRINKING
Cafes

Cafes and pastry shops are omnipresent and they are perfect for early-morning and afternoon pick-me-ups.

ourpick Tomoca (Wavel St; coffee Birr3) Coffee is serious business at this great old Italian cafe in Piazza. The beans are roasted on site, and turned into what's likely the capital's best coffee.

Juice Corner (off Haile Gebreselassie Rd; juices Birr8-12) Bored of avocado and mango juices? Then you'll think this place, with such exotics as Energiser (banana, strawberry and yoghurt), rocks.

Pubs & Bars

With the recent addition of several chic bars in the Bole area, Addis' bar scene is more diverse than ever. Piazza continues to ooze with smaller unnamed places catering to locals wanting to let loose.

Virgo Lounge (Cameroon St; ☽ Tue-Sun) This hip drinking den sits above Kaldi's Coffee in southeastern Addis. It's an ideal place to kick back and chill out.

Mask Bar (off Bole Rd) This tiny bar is as gaudy as it is cool. The crowd ranges from expats to well-heeled locals. It's well signposted off Bole Rd.

Tej Beats

If authentic experiences are what you're after, then there's no better place than a *tej beat* (pronounced 'tedj bet') to down the famed golden honey wine.

Topia Tej Beat (☽ 10am-10pm) Off Haile Gebreselassie Rd, tucked up an alley behind the Axum Hotel, this is Addis' top *tej beat* and the only one to serve pure honey *tej*.

ENTERTAINMENT
Nightclubs

Addis' nightlife is slowly maturing, with modern clubs joining the circuit, and music almost gaining prominence over prostitution. Cover charges vary between Birr25 and Birr50 at most venues.

Divine (2nd fl, Sheger Bldg, Cameroon St) Slip into a sleek leather lounger, sip a cocktail and groove to heavy hip hop and rap in this slick nightclub.

Club Platinum & Lounge (Mike Leyland St; ☽ Thu-Sat) Currently the flavour of the month, and packed every weekend with teenagers and 20-somethings.

ourpick Club Àlize (off Bole Rd; entry Birr25) Thursday is Ethio-jazz night extraordinaire at this ubercool new bar-club, where a mixed expat and local crowd knocks back cocktails and beers to the unique tunes.

SHOPPING

Most cheap souvenir stalls sit around Churchill Ave and Piazza – haggling is always the way of the day!

Haileselassie Alemayehu (Churchill Ave) This shop sells a wide array of items, like paintings, baskets, icons, woodcarvings and traditional clothing. Thanks to fixed (and fair) prices, there's no hassle here.

Alert handicraft shop (☎ 0113-211518) Here, the Berhan Taye Leprosy Disabled Persons Work Group produces and sells beautiful handbags, pillow covers and wall hangings, each emblazoned with vibrant embroidery. The shop is off Ring Rd, southwest of the city centre in the Alert Hospital compound; follow the signs to the canteen.

GETTING THERE & AWAY
Air

Ethiopian Airlines (www.flyethiopian.com; Bole Rd ☎ 0116-633163; Bole Rd; Gambia St ☎ 0115-517000; off Gambia St; Hilton Hotel ☎ 0115-511540; Menelik II Ave; ☽ 7am-8.30pm Mon-Sat, 8am-noon Sun; Piazza ☎ 0111-569247; Hailesilase St) is the only domestic carrier, regularly serving almost a dozen Ethiopian destinations.

For information regarding international carriers serving Addis, see p698.

Bus

Journeys of less than 150km are served from the central **short-distance bus station** (Ras Mekonen Ave), while longer journeys depart from **Autobus Terra** (Central African Republic St), northwest of Merkato. Buses for the following destinations leave officially at 6.30am:

Destination	Fare (Birr)	Duration
Aksum	160	2 days
Arba Minch	64	12 hours
Awasa	37	6 hours
Bahir Dar via Dangala	71	1½ days
Bahir Dar via Mota	65	12 hours
Dire Dawa	68	11 hours
Gonder	92	2 days
Jinka	100	2 days
Lalibela	95	2 days
Moyale	99	1½ days

A couple of slick new 'luxury buses' now fly down the country's highways. These puppies have reclining seats, air-con, on-board toilets and even free snacks and drinks! The best established is **Selam Buses** (☎ 0115-544831, 0911-403978), whose station and ticket office is close to the railway station. Selam has daily services (all departing at 5.30am) to Bahir Dar (Birr130), Gonder (Birr170), Mekele (Birr200), Dessie (Birr102), Harar (Birr122), Dire Dawa (Birr120) and Jimma (Birr90). Possibly even slicker are **Sky Buses** (☎ 0116-630574; room 404, 4th fl, Friendship Bldg, Bole Rd), who have buses to Bahir Dar (Birr182.05, 12 hours, 6am Wednesday), Gonder (Birr203.95, one day, 5.30am Wednesday and Friday) and Dire Dawa (Birr175.05, one day, 6am Sunday).

Minibus
As well as the normal buses, speedy (not always a good thing!) minibuses serve Bahir Dar and Gonder. There's no station per se, but commission agents patrol for customers near the Wutma Hotel in Piazza. Prices are negotiable, but you'll probably pay around Birr180 for Bahir Dar and Birr210 for Gonder.

GETTING AROUND
There's an extensive network of minibuses servicing Addis that is efficient and cheap. Journeys cost around Birr1.30.

Taxis are everywhere. Journeys to 3km cost Birr30 to Birr40 (more at night), while medium/long journeys cost Birr40 to Birr50.

Bole International Airport, located 5km southeast of the city centre, is regularly served by both taxis (Birr30 to Birr60; more at night) and minibuses. There's a prepay taxi booth at the airport that charges a fixed rate of US$10. Taxi drivers who are a part of this scheme have yellow taxis.

NORTHERN ETHIOPIA

BAHIR DAR
pop 180,000

Ethiopians like to describe Bahir Dar as being their Riviera and, with its wide streets shielded by palm trees and sweeping views across shimmering blue waters, it would be hard to argue.

It's a great place to spend a few days. Besides sights around town, you're on the doorstep of Lake Tana's mystical monasteries.

Information
There are several banks and internet cafes, a small **tourist office** (☎ 0582-201686; 8.30am-12.30pm & 1.30-5.30pm Mon-Fri) and a telecommunications building. **Gamby Higher Clinic & Pharmacy** (☎ 0582-202017; 24hr), on the main drag, is the best medical facility.

Sights & Activities
Though lounging lakeside and watching pelicans skirting the surface might be a relaxing pastime, you absolutely shouldn't miss a day spent exploring Lake Tana's treasure-filled **monasteries** (admission to each Birr30, personal video cameras Birr50) lurking on 20 of its islands. Many date from the late 16th or early 17th centuries, though some may have been the site of pre-Christian shrines.

Boat operators abound and shifty commission agents lurk everywhere. Negotiated prices (for one to five people) range from Birr400 for a half-day trip to Birr1300 for 11 hours in a 40HP speedboat. Ensure your boat has life jackets and spare fuel.

The Blue Nile snakes out of Lake Tana's southern end, plummeting 30km later over the **Blue Nile Falls** (admission Birr15, personal video cameras Birr100; 7am-5.30pm). Named by locals Tis Isat (Water that Smokes), the once-mighty falls have now withered like an aged chain smoker, thanks to a hydroelectric project. Still, it's a pretty picnic spot with parrots, turacos, white-throated seedeaters and vervet monkeys. Buses (Birr5, one bumpy hour) access Tis Abay, a nearby village. The Ghion Hotel (p688) arranges tours.

Other interests include Bahir Dar's **market** and a massive new **war memorial**, near the Blue Nile bridge (a few kilometres northeast of town), dedicated to those who died fighting the Derg.

ETHIOPIA

Dangers & Annoyances

Women, accompanied by male companions or not, should not walk along the waterfront path that runs from the Ghion Hotel into town. We have received a large number of complaints regarding serious hassle from the slimy men hanging out here.

Sleeping

Walia Hotel (☎ 0582-200151; r Birr30) The tiny, but immaculately presented rooms here get fresh coats of paint on a regular basis, which leaves them looking like the smartest boy at the party. Hell, even the communal toilets don't smell too bad!

Bahir Dar Hotel (☎ 0582-200788; s with/without bathroom Birr60/50, d with/without bathroom Birr70/60) Even with its pongy toilets, this cheerful place, with simple rooms huddled around a popular courtyard restaurant (noise from diners can be a problem at times), is a good deal.

Ghion Hotel (☎ 0582-200363; ghionbd@telecom.net.et; campsite Birr50, r Birr177.60; P ▣) Although the rooms here are as tired and worn as your favourite pair of travel socks, there's no denying Ghion's beautiful lakeside setting. The gardens, full of flowers and paradise fly-catchers, are gorgeous. It's easily the most popular place for *faranjis* to rest their heads.

Kuriftu Resort & Spa (☎ 0582-2264868; www.kuriftu resortspa.com; r from US$168; ▣ ▣ P) At the time of research, this flash new lodge was about to open for business. The huge, luxurious stone cottages peer out across the lake waters and a soon-to-be completed pool.

Eating & Drinking

Bahir Dar Hotel (mains Birr9-15) For local atmosphere and great Ethiopian fare, nowhere beats this hotel's courtyard. Sit under the stars, enjoy the music (and bonfires at weekends) and dine for pennies.

Wude Coffee (mains Birr12-20; ☾ 6am-10pm) For high-class Ethiopian fare in a chic city-style cafe, come to this popular new restaurant where you can munch away inside or on an outdoor table.

Friendship Restaurant (mains Birr12-29; ☾ 8am-10pm) Make friends with a pizza or re-acquaint yourself with some great *injera* and *wat* at this 1st-floor restaurant.

Mango Park (beers Birr6-7) One of several lakeside places; this one is perfect for a chilled afternoon drink. It's usually packed with local students, families and the odd pelican (watch out, the pelicans never pay for their round).

Getting There & Around

Ethiopian Airlines (☎ 0582-200020) has two or three flights daily to Addis Ababa (US$113, one hour), and one or two to Gonder (US$74, 20 minutes), Lalibela (US$98, 1¼ hours) and Aksum (US$130, two to three hours).

There are two 'standard' buses a day to Addis, one via Debre Markos (Birr92, one day) and another via the Mota route (Birr80, two days). Minibuses take seven hours to Addis (Birr180) or you can cruise in style on the air-con Solomon Bus (Birr130, 10 hours, 6am). Note that touts will try to steer you onto a minibus. Other buses go to Gonder (Birr50, four hours), Tis Isat (Birr5, 45 minutes) for the Blue Nile Falls and a service to Lalibela (Birr90, 10 hours, 6am daily). All buses leave from the main station.

A ferry sails on Sundays for Gorgora (Birr157.20, 1½ days), on Lake Tana's northern shore. The **Marine Authority** (☎ 0582-200730; ☾ closed Sun) sells tickets.

Bikes are perfect for exploring; hire one just down the road from the Friendship Restaurant (Birr5 per hour). An airport taxi costs Birr60.

GONDER

pop 207,000

It's not what Gonder is, but what Gonder was, that is so enthralling. The city lies in a bowl of hills filled with eucalyptus trees and tin-roofed houses, but rising above these and standing proud through the centuries are the walls of castles bathed in blood and painted in the pomp of royalty. Often called the Camelot of Africa, this description does the Royal City a disservice, for whereas Camelot is legend, Gonder is reality.

It's a great place to spend a few days, and makes a convenient base from which to leap into the Simien Mountains.

Information

Piazza marks the town centre and it hosts banks, internet cafes, the post office and **Birhan Tesfa Clinic** (☎ 0581-115943; ☾ 24hr), Gonder's best medical facility. Just east of Piazza is the **tourist information centre** (☎ 0581-110022; amhtour@ethionet.et; ☾ 8.30am-12.30pm & 1.30-5.30pm Mon-Fri, 8.30am-12.30pm Sat), with information and city guides (Birr150 per day).

Sights & Activities

The Gonder of yesteryear was a city of extreme brutality and immense wealth. Today the wealth and brutality are gone but the memories linger in the form of the impressive **Royal Enclosure** (admission Birr50, personal video cameras Birr75, guides Birr50; ⊗ 8.30am-12.30pm & 1.30-6pm), with its castles and high stone walls. Constructed piecemeal by successive emperors between the mid-17th and mid-18th centuries, Unesco declared the entire 70,000-sq-metre site a World Heritage Site in 1979.

Around 2km northwest lies **Fasiladas' Bath** (admission incl in Royal Enclosure ticket; ⊗ 8.30am-12.30pm & 1.30-5.30pm), a shady, beautiful and historic spot attributed to Emperors Fasiladas (r 1632–67) and Iyasu I (r 1682–1706).

Melancholic, silent and little-visited, the **Kuskuam Complex** (admission Birr25, personal video cameras Birr75; ⊗ 8am-6.30pm), 3.5km northwest of the centre, was built in 1730 for the redoubtable Empress Mentewab upon her husband's death. Although less preserved than the Royal Enclosure, the complex offers an impressive mix of countryside views, each dramatically framed by its crumbling remnants.

Another great sight is the church of **Debre Berhan Selassie** (admission Birr25; ⊗ 6am-12.30pm & 1.30-6pm), an easy stroll 2km northeast of town. Despite its walls hosting the nation's most vibrant ecclesiastical artwork, it's the ceiling that captures most visitors' imaginations – rows and rows of winged cherubs smiling sweetly down at you.

Yenege Tesfa (☎ 0918-774745; www.yenegetesfa.org) is a local NGO working with street kids in Gonder. It has an orphanage and also provides educational programs for the town's children as well as medical facilities. Following the success of Hope Enterprises in Addis, Yenege Tesfa also sells meal tickets that you can distribute to the town's street children. Tickets are available from most of the bigger hotels for Birr0.50 per ticket. They also actively encourage tourists to visit some of their project sites. Contact them in advance if you're interested in doing this.

Link Ethiopia (☎ 0911-748055; www.linkethiopia.org) is a UK-based education charity providing materials and volunteer teachers to schools in the Gonder region. Each volunteer is given predeparture training.

Sleeping

Yimam Hotel (☎ 0581-110470; r without bathroom Birr60) The rooms here, which are set around a large courtyard, are cramped and not very inviting, but they get the job done.

Belegez Pension (☎ 0918-772997; d with/without bathroom Birr120/80) The small and simple rooms here are spick and span and the showers gush forth steamy hot H2O. The sunny courtyard provides safe parking and is a good place to make new friends. The staff are very traveller-aware. Reservations are wise.

our pick **Genetics Guesthouse** (☎ 0918-049191; d/tw Birr150/250) The stylish and bright rooms of this new guesthouse are huge and immaculate, and have that rare thing in Ethiopian hotels – character. It's easily the most exciting hotel in town.

Hotel Lammergeyer (☎ 0581-122993; r US$25-35) Very close to Fasiladas' Bath, this clean place, which has received lots of positive feedback from readers, has a warm, family vibe and sunny rooms. There's a small cafe/restaurant.

Goha Hotel (☎ 0581-110634; ghion@ethionet.et; s/d US$38/51; 🖳) Perched on a high natural balcony providing a vantage point that would make a soaring vulture sick with envy, this is easily the best top-end hotel in town. The rooms have stone walls and embroidered bedding, but the water and electricity are as erratic as everywhere else in Gonder.

Eating

Habesha Kitfo (mains Birr20-35) Lovingly decked out with a woven mat floor, cow-hide stools and the odd live duck, this place drips with character and is the ideal spot in which to indulge in great Ethiopian food.

Quara Hotel (mains Birr28-32) Most of the food at the restaurant of this central hotel is designed to suit the bellies of *faranjis*, and includes such items as steak and chips and pizza.

There are plenty of cafes for quick eats, and the **Ras Dashen Supermarket** (⊗ 8am-9pm) is perfect for stocking up on supplies if you're planning a trip to the Simien Mountains.

Getting There & Away

Ethiopian Airlines (☎ 0581-110129) flies once or twice daily to Addis Ababa (US$158, 1½ to two hours), Bahir Dar (US$74, 20 minutes), Lalibela (US$98, 30 minutes) and Aksum (US$110, 1¾ hours). Taxis to/from the airport cost between Birr50 and Birr60.

ETHIOPIA

Buses serve Addis Ababa (Birr94, two days) and Bahir Dar (bus/minibus Birr23/35, four hours, three buses daily, many minibuses); for Aksum, go to Shire first (Birr57, 11 hours) on the 6am bus. Salem Buses (Birr170, 11 to 12 hours, 5am) and Sky Buses (Birr204, 11hrs, 5am Thursday and Saturday) run luxury air-con buses to Addis.

SIMIEN MOUNTAINS NATIONAL PARK

No matter how you experience them, the Simien Mountains will leave you speechless. This massive table of rock, up to 4500m high and riven with gullies, offers easy but immensely rewarding hiking along the edge of a plateau that falls sheer to the plains far below. It's not just the scenery (and altitude) that will leave you speechless, but also the excitement of sitting among a group of 100 gelada baboons or watching magnificent walia ibex joust on the rock ledges.

Camping equipment, guides, mandatory scouts, cooks, mules and mule-handlers are all easily arranged at **park headquarters** (☎ 0581-113482, 0581-170407; admission per 12hr Birr90, 5-seat vehicle Birr20; ☽ 8.30am-12.30pm & 1.30-5.30pm Mon-Fri, 8.30am-noon & 2-5pm Sat & Sun) in Debark. Note that park entrance fees include camping charges.

While in Debark, sleep and eat at the **Simien Park Hotel** (☎ 0581-17005; s with/without bathroom Birr120/50, d with/without bathroom Birr180/70) or the slightly more classy **Giant Lobelia Hotel** (☎ 0581-170566; globeliahotel@yahoo.com; s/d Birr110/200).

If camping on a mountain just ain't your thing, then treat yourself to the **Simien Park Lodge** (☎ 0582-310741; www.simiens.com; dm US$31, r from US$135). At 3260m, Africa's highest hotel offers a polished service and comfortable rooms in *tukul* huts, which have underfloor heating and solar-powered hot showers. The dorm consists of bare bones, two bunks per room, and common showers. Local projects receive 2.5% of profits, which makes it about as close as north Ethiopia gets to an ecolodge.

Two morning buses run between Debark and Gonder (Birr21, 3½ hours). The only bus running north to Shire (for Aksum) is the Gonder service that passes through Debark between 9am and 10am, but it is almost always full. If you want to get a seat on it, then the park headquarters can reserve a place for you. They charge Birr200 for this service, and you need to arrange it at least a day in advance. Failing this, an uncomfortable seat in a goods truck can be all yours for around Birr150.

AKSUM
pop 45,000

Aksum is a riddle waiting to be solved. Did the Queen of Sheba really call the town's dusty streets home? Does the very same Ark of the Covenant that Moses carried down from Mt Sinai reside in that small chapel? Are there actually secret hordes of treasure hidden inside undiscovered tombs? And just what exactly do those famous stelae signify?

But Aksum is more than just a collection of lifeless ruins. The town, though rural at heart, has a vibrancy, life and continuing national importance very rarely found at ancient sites. Pilgrims still journey here in their thousands to pay homage at its great churches, and all Ethiopians believe passionately that the Ark of the Covenant resides here.

This Unesco World Heritage Site is undoubtedly one of the most important and spectacular ancient sites in sub-Saharan Africa. Don't miss it.

Information

Along the two main streets you'll find several banks, health clinics and internet cafes, along with a post office, a telecommunications office and the very helpful **Tigrai Tourism Commission** (☎ 0347-753924; ☽ 7am-6pm), which can provide informative official guides for Birr150.

Sights

One admission ticket (adult/student Birr50/25) covers all sights within the immediate vicinity of Aksum, except the St Mary of Zion church compound and the monasteries of Abba Pentalewon and Abba Liqanos. The ticket is good for the duration of your stay and is sold at the Tigrai Tourism Commission. All sights are open between 8am and 5pm unless stated otherwise.

Ancient Aksum obelisks (stelae) pepper the area, and looking down on a small specimen or staring up at a grand tower, you'll be bowled over. The Northern stelae field is the grandest, with over 120 stelae ranging from 1m to 33m. Beneath the rising monoliths are a series of tombs; 98% remain undiscovered, but the fantastic new museum reveals a little of Aksum's glory.

Immediately southwest are the **St Mary of Zion churches** (admission Birr120, personal video cameras Birr100; ☽ 7.30am-12.30pm & 2.30-5.30pm Mon-Fri, 9am-noon & 2.30-5.30pm Sat & Sun), Ethiopia's holiest shrine. The rectangular old church was built on the site of a 4th-century Aksumite church by Emperor Fasiladas, Gonder's founder, in 1665. Nearby is a little museum containing a breathtaking haul of treasure, including an unsurpassed collection of former Ethiopian rulers' crowns and a dazzling display of gold and precious stones. The real reason for most people's visit, though, is to sneak a peek at the carefully guarded chapel said to contain the original Ark of the Covenant. Nobody is allowed to enter the chapel or see the Ark and foreigners are not even allowed to approach the fence surrounding the chapel.

On a small hill 1.8km northeast of the Northern stelae field, offering views of Adwa's distant jagged mountains, are the monumental 6th-century **tombs** of Kings Kaleb and Gebre Meskel. En route, you will pass by **King Ezana's Inscription**, hiding in a timber shack. Dating back to the 4th century, it's the Ethiopian equivalent of the Rosetta Stone, a pillar inscribed in Sabaean, Greek and Ge'ez (the ancestor of Amharic).

Other important sites roundabout include **King Bazen's tomb** and the remains of a 6th- or 7th-century palace, wrongly attributed to Queen Sheba. Rewarding excursions outside of Aksum can be made to **Yeha** (admission Birr50, personal video cameras Birr100), considered to be the birthplace of Ethiopian civilisation. The site, 58km from Aksum, comprises of a set of well-preserved ruins dating from the 8th to the 5th century BC.

If you've got your own wheels, then it's easy enough to push on after Yeha to the fantastical **Debre Damo monastery** (admission Birr100, men only). Atop its sheer-sided *amba* (flat-topped mountain), this is one of the most fascinating, and least accessible, monasteries in the country. You might wonder how anybody first managed to climb the mountain walls in order to establish the monastery. The answer is that Abuna Aregawi, one of the Nine Saints (the group of wandering Syrian monks who helped establish Christianity in Ethiopia) and founder of the monastery, had a little helping hand in the form of a giant serpent that lowered its tail off the mountain and allowed Abuna Aregawi to clamber up. Fortunately you don't have to be a herpetologist to get there today; although you do have to like hauling yourself 20m up a very weathered-looking **leather rope** (Birr20; men only).

Festivals & Events

On 30 November thousands of pilgrims flood into Aksum to celebrate Mary during the **Festival of Maryam Zion**. Expect a cornucopia of music and dance.

Sleeping

Lalibela Hotel (☎ 0347-753541; d without bathroom Birr30) Plain, simple and to the point, the rooms here consist of a small bed plonked in the middle of a bare room.

Tropicana Hotel (☎ 0911-420374; tropicanayahoo. com; d without bathroom Birr60, d/tw with bathroom Birr80/160) With bubbly staff and clean-as-a-pin rooms with superb hot showers (at least when the water and electricity are both running!), this new hotel is vying for the top spot with the nearby Africa Hotel.

Africa Hotel (☎ 0347-753700; africaho@ethionet.et; d/tw Birr70/90; 🖳) With an eager and omnipresent owner, this place offers a smooth stay and is easily the most popular budget guesthouse in town. The rooms are bright and the bathrooms very clean. Call for a free airport transfer.

Remhai Hotel (☎ 0347-752168; campsites Birr150-200, s/d/ste Birr230/315/600; 🖳 🖳) The rooms here are as tired as a sprinter running a marathon, but otherwise the hotel is comfortable enough to ensure that it's often full.

Eating

Ask locals for the best place to eat, and they'll say the **Remhai Hotel** (mains Birr30; ☾ breakfast, lunch & dinner). Ask them where they like to eat, and they'll say the **Abinet Hotel** (mains Birr15-20; ☾ breakfast, lunch & dinner). Both do decent *faranji* and Ethiopian fare.

Getting There & Away

Ethiopian Airlines (☎ 0347-752300) flies to Addis Ababa (US$200, two to 3½ hours, daily) via Lalibela (US$112, 40 minutes) and Gonder (US$110, two hours) or via Mekele (US$78, one hour, Saturday). Airport taxis cost Birr50 to Birr60; Birr10 if 'shared'.

Go to Shire (bus Birr15 to Birr20, minibus Birr25, 1½ hours), for buses to Gonder and Debark (Simien Mountains). Regular buses cover Adwa (Birr6, 45 minutes), Adigrat (Birr30, five hours) and Mekele (Birr35, 8½ hours). To get to Yeha first take a bus to Adwa and change for Yeha (Birr8, 50 minutes). Unless you like very long, sweaty walks, then the only way to get to Debre Damo is by hiring a car for the day (you can also check

ETHIOPIA

out Yeha on the way) through one of the hotels (Birr700).

ROCK-HEWN CHURCHES OF TIGRAY

Perched precariously atop huge rock needles among the sandy, semidesert wasteland of northern Tigray is a little-known stash of ancient monasteries. Some of the 120-odd churches (plus a few invisible ones) found here may even predate those at Lalibela. It's one of the most other-worldly places in Ethiopia.

Orientation & Information

Most churches are located in groups or clusters. The Gheralta cluster, with the highest number of churches, located in the most mind-bending of settings, is considered the most important, while the Takatisfi cluster, only 3km east of the Mekele–Adigrat road, is the most accessible. Churches are supposed to charge Birr50 for admission. If you're asked for more, simply hand over Birr50 firmly but politely. Be aware that priests at the most popular churches aren't exactly welcoming to tourists, and you can expect all kinds of extra charges to be added onto your entrance fee.

Sights

Between Adigrat and Mekele there's a plethora of churches. Many are pretty inaccessible, meaning visiting some churches involves steep climbs or scrambling up almost sheer rockfaces using toeholds.

All this somehow adds to the churches' attraction. To come across an absolute jewel hidden for centuries in the mountains makes for a very rewarding excursion.

Of those in the Gheralta cluster, don't miss easily accessible **Abraha Atsbeha**, **Abuna Gebre Mikael** with its beautiful scenery, and the most spectacularly sited of all the churches, **Abuna Yemata Guh**, which involves a heart-in-the-mouth climb up a sheer mountainside.

In the Takatisfi cluster, gorge your eyes on **Medhane Alem Kesho** and meet the friendly monk at **Petros and Paulos**.

Sleeping & Eating

The sandy village of Hawsien, where the following are located, is probably the best base.

Tourist Hotel (☎ 0346-670238; s/d Birr80/100) Rooms here are set around a large courtyard and look and feel brand new – they even come with rare luxuries like hot-water showers and toilets with toilet seats.

ourpick Gheralta Lodge (☎ 0346-670344, Addis office 0111-5545489; www.gheraltalodgetigrai.com; s/d/tr from Birr230/460/700) Put simply, for the price this might well be the best quality, best value and most perfect accommodation this author has ever seen anywhere in Africa! They can also organise tours of the churches (Birr700; four people). A percentage of profits are used in community development projects.

Getting There & Around

Many of the churches are in remote places, some 20km to 30km off the main road. A private 4WD is the easiest way of reaching them. Jeeps can be hired in Aksum (Birr900 to Birr1200) or **G.K. Ahadu Tours & Travel Agency** (☎ 0344-406466; gkahadu@telecm.net.eto) or **Danakil Tour and Travel Agency** (☎ 0914-702648) in nearby Mekele.

LALIBELA

pop 15,000

With its buildings frozen in stone and its soul alive with the rites and awe of Christianity at its most ancient and unbending, stepping into Lalibela is like stepping into another time and another place. No matter what you've heard about Lalibela and its marvellous rock-hewn churches, nothing on earth can prepare you for the reality of seeing it for yourself.

Information

Facilities include a bank, post office, telecommunications office, **health centre** (☎ 0333-360416; 🕑 8.30am-noon & 1.30-5.30pm), helpful **tourism office** (☎ 0333-360167; 🕑 8am-noon & 1.30-5.30pm Mon-Fri) and a few internet cafes.

Sights

Lalibela's **rock-hewn churches** (admission Birr200, personal video cameras Birr100; 🕑 6am-6pm) are remarkable for three main reasons: because many are not carved into the rock, but freed entirely from it; because the buildings are so refined; and because there are so many within such a small area. Descend into tunnels and pass priests and monks floating through the confines like clouds of incense, smell beeswax candles and hear chanting within the deep, cool recesses, only to find yourself standing in the sunlight, slack-jawed, staring up at a structure that defies reason.

Although visiting without a guide is possible – getting lost in the warren of tunnels is quite memorable and usually not permanent – you'll miss many of the amazing subtleties each church has to offer. The tourism office has licensed guides (Birr150 per day).

Peel your eyes away from the churches and you won't be able to avoid noticing the spectacular mountain scenery around you. **Tourism in Ethiopia for Sustainable Future Alternatives** (TESFA; ☎ 0111-225024; www.community -tourism-ethiopia.com) runs rewarding multiday hikes in the nearby hills that combine scenery, culture and adventure into one neat package that many travellers rate as a highlight of Ethiopia.

Sleeping

Alif Paradise Hotel (☎ 0911-556211; alparahotel@ yahoo.com; s/tw in old block Birr80/120, s/tw in new block Birr150/200) Rooms in the new block are bright and clean, with bathtubs and views. The older rooms, though tatty, are still decent value. A new restaurant should be completed by the time you read this.

Asheton Hotel (☎ 0333-360030; r Birr100) This classic budget-traveller haunt offers genuine bang for your buck with cosy whitewashed rooms, hot showers and a relaxing garden courtyard.

Selam Guest House (☎ 0333-3600374; d/tw Birr100/200) This very friendly guesthouse has plain and simple rooms with bedspreads made from traditional Ethiopian textiles.

Seven Olives Hotel (☎ 0333-360020; s/d/tw US$15/27/27; 🖳) The oldest hotel in Lalibela continues to receive many positive recommendations. It has comfortable rooms that look across lovely gardens full of hundreds of unfeasibly colourful birds.

Yemereha Hotel (☎ 0333-360862; www.yemereha hotel.com; s/d/tw US$35/45/45) Spacious and beautifully furnished rooms make this new hotel an excellent choice.

Eating

Kedemt Cafe (mains Birr10-20) One of several identikit, and equally good, restaurants that locals flock to for a good *injera* stuffing.

Blue Lal Hotel (mains Birr12-20) This carefully groomed restaurant has a traditional grass-covered floor and big bright *injera* baskets on every table. The Ethiopian food is superb, and the *faranji* dishes aren't far behind.

Seven Olives Hotel (mains Birr15-35) An Ethiopian chef with experience in America has trained the staff here to make more than the usual *faranji* fare, and the result is the nicest eating experience for miles around.

Getting There & Away

Ethiopian Airlines (☎ 0333-360046) flies at least once daily to Addis Ababa (US$136, 1½ to two hours), Gonder (US$98, 30 minutes) and Aksum (US$112, 40 minutes). It's not currently possible to fly from Lalibela to Bahir Dar (though you can do it in the opposite direction).

Overland, the best approach is currently from Woldia via Gashema. Two buses depart Lalibela daily at 6am, heading for Woldia (Birr36, five to seven hours), with one continuing to Addis Ababa (Birr95, two days). The bus station is an inconvenient couple of kilometres out of town, and with no transport it's a long, hot and very sweaty walk. Call ahead and most hotels will collect you.

EASTERN ETHIOPIA

DIRE DAWA
pop 343,000

Ethiopia's second-most populous town, Dire Dawa always elicits strong reactions. Some travellers rave about its remarkably spacious and orderly layout (a rarity in Ethiopia), its tree-lined streets, neat squares and colonial buildings, while others think it's utilitarian and self-contained.

With Babel-like ambience, the enormous Kafira Market, in Megala, is the town's most striking sight. It attracts Afar herders, Somali pastoralists, Oromo farmers and, sometimes around dawn, large camel caravans from the Somali desert.

If you're staying on, the **Mekonen Hotel** (☎ 0251-113348; Kezira; r without bathroom Birr35), housed in an old Italian colonial building opposite the train station, is the best-value cheapie, with spacious rooms and plumbing in the shared bathrooms that's very much on its last legs. A minor hike from the town centre, **Tsehay Hotel & Restaurant** (☎ 0251-110023; Kezira; d/tw without bathroom Birr35/35, d Birr50) features clean, but frugal, rooms around pleasant, hedged gardens. Its best asset is the on-site restaurant. At the other end of the scale is the swanky new **Samrat** (☎ 0251-121400; Kezira; d/tw Birr357/423, ste Birr504-796; 🖳 🖳).

Paradiso Restaurant (☎ 0251-113780; Kezira; mains Birr20-50; ⊗ breakfast, lunch & dinner) is the town's most respected restaurant. Its menu roves from palatable Italian to traditional gut-busters, such as *kitfo* (uncooked

ETHIOPIA

minced beef or lamb in butter, *berbere* and sometimes thyme).

Getting There & Away

Ethiopian Airlines (☎ 0251-113069) flies to Addis Ababa at least once daily (Birr1684, one hour). It also operates five weekly flights to Jijiga (Birr1178, 20 minutes).

Daily buses serve Addis Ababa (Birr66, 12 hours) via Awash (Birr54, nine hours), while copious minibuses go to Harar (Birr10, one hour).

HARAR

pop 122,000

Harar is a place apart. With 368 alleyways, countless mosques and shrines, coffee-scented streets, animated markets, crumbling walls and charming people all squished into just 1 sq km, it will make you feel like you've floated right out of the 21st century. It is the east's most memorable sight and shouldn't be missed. And, as if that wasn't enough, an other-worldly ritual takes place every night when men feed wild hyenas scraps of meat from their hands.

Information

There are several internet cafes and a bank near Harar Gate. The **tourist office** (☎ 0256-669300; 1st fl, Ras Makonnen's Palace; ☯ 8-11.30am & 2-5.30pm Mon-Fri) is mildly useful. It's located inside Ras Makonnen's Palace in the old town.

Sights

INSIDE THE WALLED CITY

Harar's old walled town is a fascinating place that begs exploration. Within the walls the city is a maze of narrow, twisting alleys and lanes, replete with historic buildings, including 82 small mosques, numerous shrines and tombs, as well as traditional Harari houses. Specific buildings to keep your eyes peeled for include the four main **gates**, Harar, Shoa, Buda and Fallana; Arthur Rimbaud's house, which houses a **museum** (admission Birr10; ☯ 8am-noon & 2-5pm Mon-Thu & Sat & Sun, 8-11am & 2-5pm Fri) dedicated to the poet; and **Ras Tafari's house**, which contains the **Sherif Harar City Museum** (admission Birr20; ☯ 8am-noon & 2-5pm).

HYENA FEEDING

As night falls (from around 7pm), two sets of hyena men set themselves up just outside the city walls.

The easiest way to see the show is to let your guide know so that he can forewarn the hyena men. Be sure to establish the fee in advance; in principle, you'll be charged about Birr50 for the 'show', more if you have a video camera (usually Birr100).

Sleeping

Most commendable places are outside the walled old town.

Tana Hotel (☎ 0256-668482; new town; r Birr50) This outfit west of the new town is our favourite cheapie. The odd cockroach or two aside, the rooms are essentially clean, the staff friendly and the showers hot.

Tewodros Hotel (☎ 0256-660217; new town; d Birr60-80, tw without bathroom Birr70) Room with a hyena view…no joke! At night, from rooms 15, 16, 117 and 18, you'll watch hyenas rummaging behind the hotel. Unfortunately, the rooms aren't too clean, but they'll do you for a night.

our pick **Rewda Guesthouse** (☎ 0256-662211; old town; r without bathroom incl breakfast Birr250) From the rolled mat above the door (that indicates an eligible daughter resides within) to the raised seating platforms in the cocoonlike lounge, this Adare house percolates tradition and history into a comfy brew of warm welcome amid exotic decorations.

Eating

our pick **Fresh Touch Restaurant** (☎ 0915-740109; new town; mains Birr15-40) Reasonable prices, a tasty selection of national and international dishes, a leafy courtyard and a dedicated pizza oven mean that you will be hard-pressed to find better food in Harar.

Hirut Restaurant (☎ 0256-660419; new town; mains Birr15-40; ☯ 11am-9pm) Decorated with traditional woven baskets and specialising in authentic local cuisine, this is the most atmospheric place in Harar to sink your teeth into a super-filling *kwanta firfir* (dried strips of beef rubbed in chilli, butter, salt and *berbere*).

Getting There & Around

All transport leaves from the bus station near Harar Gate. Bountiful minibuses link to Dire Dawa (Birr10, one hour). Seven daily buses serve Jijiga (Birr20, 2½ to three hours) via Babille (Birr10, 45 minutes), while two access Addis Ababa (Birr68, one day). Buy tickets a day early. Several minibuses also serve Addis Ababa (Birr120, nine to 10 hours) – ask at your hotel.

Shared/contract taxis cost Birr1/5 for short hops.

SOUTHERN ETHIOPIA

RIFT VALLEY LAKES

Africa's renowned Rift Valley cuts through the south, and hosts lakes, astounding birdlife and national parks.

Less than 180km from Addis Ababa is a cluster of four Rift Valley lakes: **Lake Ziway, Lake Abiata, Lake Shala** and **Lake Langano**. While they're all known as havens for birdwatching, only Lake Langano has the double benefit of being safe for swimming (bilharzia- and crocodile-free). Lake Ziway sends twitchers into a twizzle of excitement – the place is crawling with feathered friends. There are also a couple of island monasteries here. The volcanic Lake Shala, part of **Lake Abiata-Shala National Park** (admission per 48hr Birr50), is easily the most attractive, with trails leading to lookouts.

Awasa, southern Ethiopia's largest city, is 100km further south and sits on the shores of attractive **Lake Awasa**. With plenty of facilities, a great fish market and row boats to boot, Awasa is a great place to stop.

The wildest and most attractive of southern Ethiopia's lakes must be **Lake Abaya** and **Lake Chamo**. They are ringed by savannah plains, loaded with crocodiles and divided by the 'Bridge of God', which hosts Ethiopia's best safari opportunity, **Nechisar National Park** (admission Birr100, vehicle Birr30, mandatory guide Birr200), as well as the infamous **crocodile market** (boat hire for 5 people Birr500, mandatory guide Birr80). Scruffy Arba Minch is the best base for Lakes Abaya and Chamo and the Nechisar National Park.

Sleeping & Eating

LAKE LANGANO

Lake Langano is a popular weekend escape. The prices below are for Sunday to Thursday. Add 50% at weekends.

Karkaro Cottages (☎ 0461-190543; willywarthog@msm.com; campsite Birr50) This is the place to drop a tent under the shade of a tree.

Bishangari Lodge (☎ 0115-517533, 0911-201317; www.bishangari.com; s/tw without bathroom incl breakfast US$30/54, s/tw with bathroom incl breakfast US$57/101) Hyped as Ethiopia's first ecolodge when it opened in 1997, Bishangari has nine beautiful *godjos* (bungalows), nestled privately along the lake's southeastern shore, and a monkey-friendly bar wrapped around a tree!

AWASA

Beshu Hotel (☎ 0462-206957; d without bathroom Birr40, d Birr70-80) The rooms here are small and functional. It's 100m west of the bus station.

Gebrekiristos Hotel (☎ 0462-202780; s/d/tw Birr75/115/115) This oldie-but-goodie is decent value, but it's wise to check a few rooms first, as bed size, room size and amenities vary widely.

Atnet Pension (☎ 0462-201686; d Birr100-125, tw Birr225) New, central and clean – if it weren't for the church next door, which occasionally broadcasts prayers at volumes that make you curse God, then it would be perfect.

ARBA MINCH

Rift Valley Pension (☎ 0468-812531; d/tw Birr130/130) The rooms here are clean, spacious and comfortable with tiled floors, satellite TVs and newish mosquito nets. It isn't the flashest hotel in town but it is the best value.

Swayne's Hotel (☎ 0468-811895; www.swayneshotel.com; campsite Birr75, s/tw incl breakfast Birr304/386) The colourful bungalows have hand-carved wooden furniture and a quirky, yet traditional feel.

Soma Restaurant (mains Birr25) This unassuming restaurant offers a small variety of mouthwatering fresh fish dishes.

Getting There & Away

Ethiopian Airlines flies between Addis Ababa and Arba Minch (US$153, 2½ hours).

Buses connect Addis Ababa with Lake Ziway (Birr23, three hours), Awasa (Birr35, 5½ hours) and Arba Minch (Birr67, 12 hours).

LOWER OMO VALLEY

If there's anything in southern Ethiopia that can rival the majesty of the north's historical circuit, it's the people of the Lower Omo Valley. Whether it's wandering through traditional Konso villages, watching Hamer people performing a Jumping of the Bulls ceremony or witnessing the Mursi's mystical stick fights and mind-blowing lip plates, your visit to the Omo will stick with you for a lifetime.

ETHIOPIA

Most people make a beeline straight for the **Mago National Park** (admission per person Birr100, per vehicle Birr80, mandatory scout per day Birr65), where the animals now play second fiddle to the people. This is the traditional stomping ground of the Mursi people, and though a visit to their villages is mind-blowing, it doesn't come without a catch. Firstly, the whole thing can feel rather like a zoo, with masses of tourists pouring into the Mursi villages every morning demanding photos while the Mursi demand ever larger sums of money. Secondly, a visit here cannot be described as cheap. Besides the various park admission fees, you are required to pay a village entrance fee of Birr100 per person (payable at the Mursi Indigenous Community Association in Jinka), hire a local guide for another Birr150 (from the Pioneers Guiding Association in Jinka) and pay individuals for any photos you take.

Jinka has decent facilities and most villages have some basic accommodation.

Most people visit this area as part of a tour from Addis, but it is possible to take a bus from Addis to Jinka (Birr100, two days) and hire transport (US$150 per day including driver) once there from the **Pioneers Guiding Association** (☎ 0467-751728; andualemgebre@yahoo.com).

BALE MOUNTAINS NATIONAL PARK

The beautiful **Bale Mountains National Park** (admission Birr50, vehicles Birr15) is renowned for wildlife. Over 60 mammal species and 260 bird species have been recorded here, including dozens of endemic species.

Within the park, rivers cut deep gorges, alpine lakes feed streams, and water accepts gravity's fate at several waterfalls. In the lower hills, highlanders canter along centuries-old paths on their richly caparisoned horses, and the noise of shepherds cracking their whips echoes around the valley.

You can arrange one- to six-day hikes at park headquarters in Dinsho, though you'll need your own equipment.

ETHIOPIA DIRECTORY

ACCOMMODATION

Accommodation in Ethiopia continues to improve and most towns now have at least one hotel that won't make your toes curl in fear.

Budget options (Birr30 to Birr150 per night), with spartan rooms and shared toilets, dominate. Only larger centres provide midrange options (Birr150 to Birr400), which are usually clean and quiet, but run down. True top-end picks (Birr400 and up) are limited to Addis Ababa and a few major tourist towns. Ethiopians call rooms with a double bed 'singles' and rooms with twin beds 'doubles'. We use typical Western interpretations in our reviews.

Outside of national parks there are few campsites. Some hotels allow camping, though it's not much cheaper than decent rooms.

ACTIVITIES

With two gorgeous 4000m mountain ranges and countless other peaks hosting unique wildlife, it's little wonder that hiking is a major activity. There's also plenty of rock-climbing potential. The waterways churning through Ethiopia's topographic delights host fine rafting and fishing. Lastly, Ethiopia's plethora of endemic and migratory birds makes it a world-class birding destination.

BUSINESS HOURS

Banks, post offices and telecommunications offices Open at least 8.30am to 11am and 1.30pm to 3.30pm weekdays and 8.30am to 11am Saturdays.
Government offices Open 8.30am to 12.30pm (to 11.30am Friday) and 1.30pm to 5.30pm weekdays.
Shops Open 8.30am to 1.30pm and 2.30pm to 5.30pm weekdays.

CUSTOMS REGULATIONS

There's no limit on foreign currency entering Ethiopia, but no more than Birr100 can be exported and imported. If you're bringing valuable items, like video cameras or laptop computers, you may have to register them on your passport at immigration.

Leaving with anything deemed historical is illegal.

DANGERS & ANNOYANCES

Compared with many African countries, violent crime is rare; against travellers it's extremely rare. Petty theft is common in Addis Ababa, but is less common elsewhere.

At the time of writing the Ogaden region, as well as the areas around Moyale in the south, were experiencing a mix of rebel activity or tribal violence. Though you're highly unlikely to get caught up in it, do keep your ear to the ground for developments.

In the annoyances department, Ethiopia has oodles of beggars, and travellers often resent being 'targeted'. Never give to children, whether it be money, sweets, pens, empty water bottles or food.

Self-appointed guides can be annoying. Be polite but firm.

EMBASSIES & CONSULATES

Embassies and consulates in Addis Ababa include the following:

Belgium (☎ 0116-621291; addisababa@diplobel.org; Fikremaryam Abatechan St)
Canada (☎ 0113-713022; addis@dfait-maeci.gc.ca; Seychelles St) Also represents Australia.
Djibouti (☎ 0116-613200) Off Bole Rd.
Egypt (☎ 0111-550021; egyptian.emb@ethionet.et; Madagascar St)
France (☎ 0111-550066; amba.france@telcom.net.et)
Germany (☎ 0111-235139; www.addis-abeba.diplo.de)
Italy (☎ 0111-235717; ambasciata.addisabeba@esteri.it)
Kenya (☎ 0116-610033; kenigad@telecom.net.et; Fikremaryam Abatechan St)
Netherlands (☎ 0113-711100; www.netherlands embassyethiopia.org) Off Ring Rd.
Somaliland (☎ 0116-635921; btwn Bole Rd & Cameroon St)
Sudan (☎ 0115-516477; sudan.embassy@ethionet.et; Ras Lulseged St)
UK (☎ 0116-612354; http://ukinethiopia.fco.gov.uk; cnr Fikremaryam Abatechan St & Comoros St)
USA (☎ 0115-174000; http://ethiopia.usembassy.gov; Algeria St)

FESTIVALS & EVENTS

Religious festivals, particularly Orthodox ones, are colourful events with pageantry, music and dancing. The most outstanding include the following:

Leddet (also known as Genna or Christmas) 6-7 January
Timkat (Epiphany, celebrating Christ's baptism) 19 January
Kiddus Yohannes (New Year's Day) 11 September
Meskel (Finding of the True Cross) 27 September

HOLIDAYS

Public holidays can be divided into three categories: national secular holidays, Christian Orthodox festivals and Islamic holidays.

National secular holidays include:

Victory of Adwa Commemoration Day 2 March
International Labour Day 1 May
Ethiopian Patriots' Victory Day (also known as 'Liberation Day') 5 May
Downfall of the Derg 28 May

INTERNET ACCESS

Internet is everywhere in Addis and is pretty easy to spot in major towns, but is nonexistent in places that see few tourists. However, just because internet cafes exist, that doesn't mean that the internet exists – connections in Ethiopia are among the worst on the continent. It can easily take an hour to download one simple, two-line email. And that's in Addis!

MAPS

The most up-to-date Ethiopia map is produced by International Travel Maps (1998; 1:2,000,000).

MONEY

Ethiopia's currency is the birr. US dollars are the best currency to carry, both in cash and travellers cheques, though euros are gaining popularity. You'll have no trouble exchanging cash in most cities, but travellers cheques are more of a headache. Dashen Banks in Addis Ababa, Bahir Dar, Gonder and Mekele now have ATMs that accept international Visa cards.

Converting birr to US dollars or euros can only be done for people holding exchange receipts and onward air tickets from Ethiopia – overlanders need to budget accordingly.

PHOTOGRAPHY & VIDEO

In general most Ethiopians love having their photos taken, though in remote areas people are still suspicious of cameras. In places like the Lower Omo Valley, you'll be chased by people demanding to have their photo taken! However, this eagerness relates to the fee they'll claim for each photo. Always agree to an amount first.

POST & TELEPHONE

Ethiopia's postal system is reliable and reasonably efficient. Airmail costs Birr2 for postcards. It's Birr2 for a letter up to 20g to Africa, Birr2.45 to Europe and the Middle East, and Birr3.45 to the Americas, Australia and Asia.

Government telecommunications offices are located in almost every town. Countless shops also operate as 'telecentres', connecting you anywhere worldwide for Birr15 to Birr25 per minute.

Ethiopia's telecommunications industry is entirely government run – and it shows. The industry is in desperate need of privatisation as currently making a phone call is certain to turn you grey. As with the internet (run by the same company), it's best to assume that you won't be calling home very much.

TIME

Time is expressed so sanely in Ethiopia that it blows travellers' minds! At sunrise it's 12 o'clock (6am our time) and after one hour of sunshine it's 1 o'clock. After two hours of sunshine? Yes, 2 o'clock. The sun sets at 12 o'clock (6pm our time) and after one hour of darkness it's…1 o'clock! When being quoted a time, always ask, '*Be habesha/faranji akotater no?*' – Is that Ethiopian/foreigners' time?

TOURIST INFORMATION

There's a helpful government tourist information office in Addis Ababa. Independent offices can be found in regional capitals. No national tourist office exists abroad.

VISAS

Nationals of most Western countries can obtain tourist visas on arrival at Bole International Airport. The process is painless and the one-month tourist visa costs only US$20, substantially less than that charged at some Ethiopian embassies abroad.

Visas for Onward Travel

DJIBOUTI

The embassy (p697) requires US$30 and two photos. It's usually a same-day service.

KENYA

Three-month visas cost US$20 (or Birr249) and require one photo. Apply in the morning and pick up the following afternoon. Visas are also easily obtained at the Moyale crossing and Nairobi's airport.

SOMALILAND

Visas require US$40 and one passport photo. It's issued while you wait.

SUDAN

All we can say is good luck! Basically, unless you are using the services of a Sudanese tour company you've got no chance of getting a tourist visa. However, don't go changing those plans just yet, as there is one way in. Transit visas, allowing up to a fortnight in Sudan, are issued fairly easily. For this you require a letter of introduction from your own embassy, an onward visa for Egypt, a couple of photos and, for most nationalities, US$100 cash. Americans, you get to pay US$200. It normally takes two days to issue.

TRANSPORT IN ETHIOPIA

GETTING THERE & AWAY

Air

Addis Ababa's Bole International Airport is the only international airport in Ethiopia. Airline offices in Addis Ababa include the following:

BMI (BD; ☎ 0116-620815; www.flybmi.com; Bole Rd)

EgyptAir (MS; ☎ 0111-564493; www.egyptair.com; Churchill Ave)

Emirates (EK; ☎ 0115-181818; www.emirates.com; Dembel City Centre)

KLM (KL; ☎ 0115-525495; www.klm.com; Menelik II Ave)

Kenya Airways (KQ; ☎ 0115-525548; www.kenya-airways.com; Menelik II Ave)

Lufthansa (LH; ☎ 0111-551666; www.lufthansa.com; Cameroon St)

Sudan Airways (SD; ☎ 0115-504724; www.sudanair.com; Ras Desta Damtew St)

Yemenia (IY; ☎ 0115-526440; www.yememia.com; Ras Desta Damtew St)

Land

DJIBOUTI

There are two current land routes: one via Dire Dawa and Gelille, and one via Awash and Galafi.

The tongue-twisting **Shirkada Gaadidka Daddweynaha Ee Yaryar Dhexe Iyo Xamuulkaa** (☎ 0251-118455) buses depart Dire Dawa daily at 2am (!) for Djibouti City (Birr130, 11 hours). An unreliable, dilapidated old train is supposed to run this route every second day (1st/2nd class Birr93/76).

Although further, the Awash/Galafi crossing is best for those driving, as it's entirely sealed.

ERITREA
The Eritrea–Ethiopia border remains closed.

KENYA
The most-used crossing is at Moyale, 772km south of Addis Ababa. Daily Ethiopian buses link Addis and Moyale (Birr99, 1½ days), while Kenyan versions connect the border to Marsabit (KSh600, 8½ hours) and Isiolo (KSh1500, 20 hours) along a bone-jarring dirt road. Trucks also serve the Kenyan side. Banditry has been reduced significantly in northern Kenya, though always check the latest updates.

With a serious 4WD and Kenyan visas acquired in Addis, there's an adventurous crossing accessing Lake Turkana via the Lower Omo Valley. Get stamped out in Omorate, before attempting the day-long drive to Koobi Fora research base at Kenya's Sibiloi National Park. There's no Kenyan border post, so you must wait to get stamped in at Nairobi. Since getting stamped out of Kenya isn't an option here, this route is only for those travelling south.

SOMALILAND
Daily buses run between Jijiga and Wajaale at the border (Birr20, 1½ to two hours). After immigration procedures, you'll find minibuses (Birr30 to Birr50) to Hargeisa, Somaliland's capital.

SUDAN
The only open Sudan crossing is Metema/Gallabat, 180km west of Gonder. Direct buses (Birr31, seven hours) run daily to Metema from Gonder. Cross the border on foot before hopping on a truck in Gallabat to Gedaref.

GETTING AROUND
Air
Ethiopian Airlines (www.flyethiopian.com) is the domestic carrier, regularly serving all major cit-ies (see relevant cities for details). Flight prices have risen but as they can save days of bumpy bus travel they're worth considering.

In Ethiopia standard rates always apply, whether buying tickets months or hours in advance.

Bus
A good network of buses slowly connects most towns. Unlike in most African countries, seated passengers in the aisles of long-distance buses are illegal, making them more comfortable (we said more comfortable, not comfortable!) and safer. They're also cheap, 100km costing Birr12 to Birr25.

Distances are the biggest problem. Northern Ethiopia's historical circuit requires around 10 days of bus time to cover the 2500km. Long-distance buses typically leave at 6am or earlier.

Car & Motorcycle
If you're bringing a 4WD or motorcycle, you'll need a *carnet de passage,* the vehicle's registration papers and proof of third-party insurance covering Ethiopia.

Ethiopia doesn't recognise international driving licences for more than seven days, so you're supposed to acquire an Ethiopian-endorsed licence at the Ministry of Foreign Affairs (Yohanis St) in Addis Ababa. However, this law is rarely enforced and most travellers take the chance.

Hiring 4WDs (with mandatory driver) is costly (US$120 to US$180 per day) and primarily done through travel agencies (p683).

Tours
For independent travellers, organising a private tour is useful for four things: specialised activities like white-water rafting; access to remote regions like the Lower Omo Valley or the Danakil Depression; 'themed trips' (eg birdwatching) with expert guides; and to help those with more money than time.

See p683 for a list of recommended agencies based in Addis Ababa.

Trucks
In remote regions trucks running between villages are the only way to travel. Seats in the cabin cost twice as much as riding in the back (always negotiate). Petrol stations and markets are typical collection points.

ETHIOPIA

Kenya

Few destinations the world over can evoke such powerful and visceral images as Kenya, one of East Africa's premier safari destinations. Here, the acacia-dotted savannahs are inhabited by classic African animals, from towering elephants and prancing gazelles to prides of lions and stalking leopards. The country also plays host to the annual wildebeest migration, which is the largest single movement of herd animals on the entire planet.

However, what makes Kenya truly stand out as a traveller's destination is the vast palette of landscapes that comprise this visually stunning country. While the flaunted image of the savannahs of Masai Mara is perhaps the single key selling point for Kenya's tourist industry, intrepid travellers can also explore the barren expanses of the Rift Valley, the glacial ridges of Mt Kenya and the beaches of the Swahili Coast. This rich diversity of quintessential African environments presents opportunities for walking, hiking, diving, ballooning and so much more.

But, to simply focus on Kenya's wildlife and nature is to ignore the very people that make this country so dynamic. Kenya is a thriving multicultural country that presents a wide cross-section of everything that is classic and contemporary Africa. Everyday life brings together traditional tribes and urban families, ancient customs and modern sensibilities. While internal political life is at times tumultuous, it seems that Kenyans retain an innate self-confidence, a belief that things are improving, and a desire to see their homeland take a prominent place on the world stage.

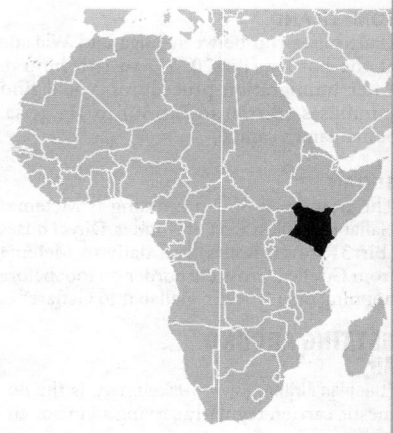

FAST FACTS

- **Area** 583,000 sq km
- **ATMs** Widely available in cities and large towns
- **Borders** Ethiopia, Somalia, Sudan, Tanzania, Uganda
- **Budget** Varies; camping safaris will set you back less than US$50 per day, while luxury tented camps can run hundreds of dollars a night
- **Capital** Nairobi
- **Languages** Swahili, English, tribal languages
- **Money** Kenyan shilling (KSh); US$1 = KSh75, €1 = KSh108
- **Population** 38.5 million
- **Seasons** Wet (March to May, October to December), dry (January and February, June to September)
- **Telephone** Country code ☎ 254; international access code ☎ 00
- **Time** GMT/UTC +3
- **Visa** Most visitors need a visa; the single East African tourist visa is expected to be introduced soon (see p737

KENYA

HIGHLIGHTS

- **Masai Mara National Reserve** (p719) Expansive savannah, unmatched wildlife and the world's most fascinating traffic jam – the annual wildebeest migration.
- **Mt Kenya** (p715) Tremendous hikes and jagged peaks await on this sacred mountain, Kenya's tallest and Africa's second tallest.
- **Lamu** (p727) The ultimate Swahili cultural immersion experience that makes Tanzania's Zanzibar blush with envy.
- **Amboseli National Park** (p730) Elephants and Kilimanjaro, two big bulks combined in Kenya's most famous picture-postcard views.
- **Loyangalani** (p718) Home to harsh conditions, unforgettable tribes and the sublime Lake Turkana, the jade jewel at the end of a long quest.

CLIMATE & WHEN TO GO

The weather is generally considered to be best in January and February, when it's hot and dry, with high concentrations of wildlife. However, the parks get crowded and rates for accommodation go through the roof. Avoid Christmas and Easter (high season) unless you want to pay a fortune.

June to September (also considered high season) is generally still dry and during this period the annual wildebeest migration takes place.

During the long rains (from March to the end of May, the low season) things are much quieter, and you can get some good deals; this is also true during the short rains from October to December.

ITINERARIES

- **One Week** Arrange things in advance so you can head out on safari straight after landing in Nairobi (p707). Take in the Masai Mara National Reserve (p719) for at least three days; most trips also include Lake Nakuru National Park (p715) en route. Spend half a day back in Nairobi then fly down to the coast. Spend the rest of the week soaking up the atmosphere in the crumbling Swahili ruins of Mombasa (p721), lying on tropical beaches and/or snorkelling at Watamu (p726) or Malindi (p725).
- **Two Weeks** To make the most of the beach and the bush, extend your stay in Masai Mara National Reserve (p719), then spend a few days hiking on mighty Mt Kenya (p715). Spend the remainder of your time working your way up the coast from Mombasa (p721) to Lamu (p727). Alternatively, spend the second week heading overland to the searing desert and colourful tribespeople at Lake Turkana (p718).
- **One Month** Any or all of the above trips can be combined in a month, allowing a bit of time to linger among, say, the Turkana people around Loyangalani (p718), the Samburu at Isiolo (p717) and, of course, the Maasai at Masai Mara. Other possibilities include Kakamega (p719) for a taste of Kenya's rainforests as they once were; Tsavo National Park (p731) for a real off-the-beaten-track safari; and scenic Amboseli National Park (p730) for dreamy sundowners under Mt Kilimanjaro.

HISTORY

The patchwork of ethnic groups, each with their own culture and language, which today exist side by side in modern Kenya are the result of the waves of migration, some from as early as 2000 BC, from every corner of Africa – Turkanas from Ethiopia; Kikuyu, Akamba and Meru from West Africa; and the Maasai, Luo and Samburu from the southern part of Sudan. Kenya, however, was occupied long before this: archaeological excavations around Lake Turkana in the 1970s revealed skulls thought to be around two million years

KENYA

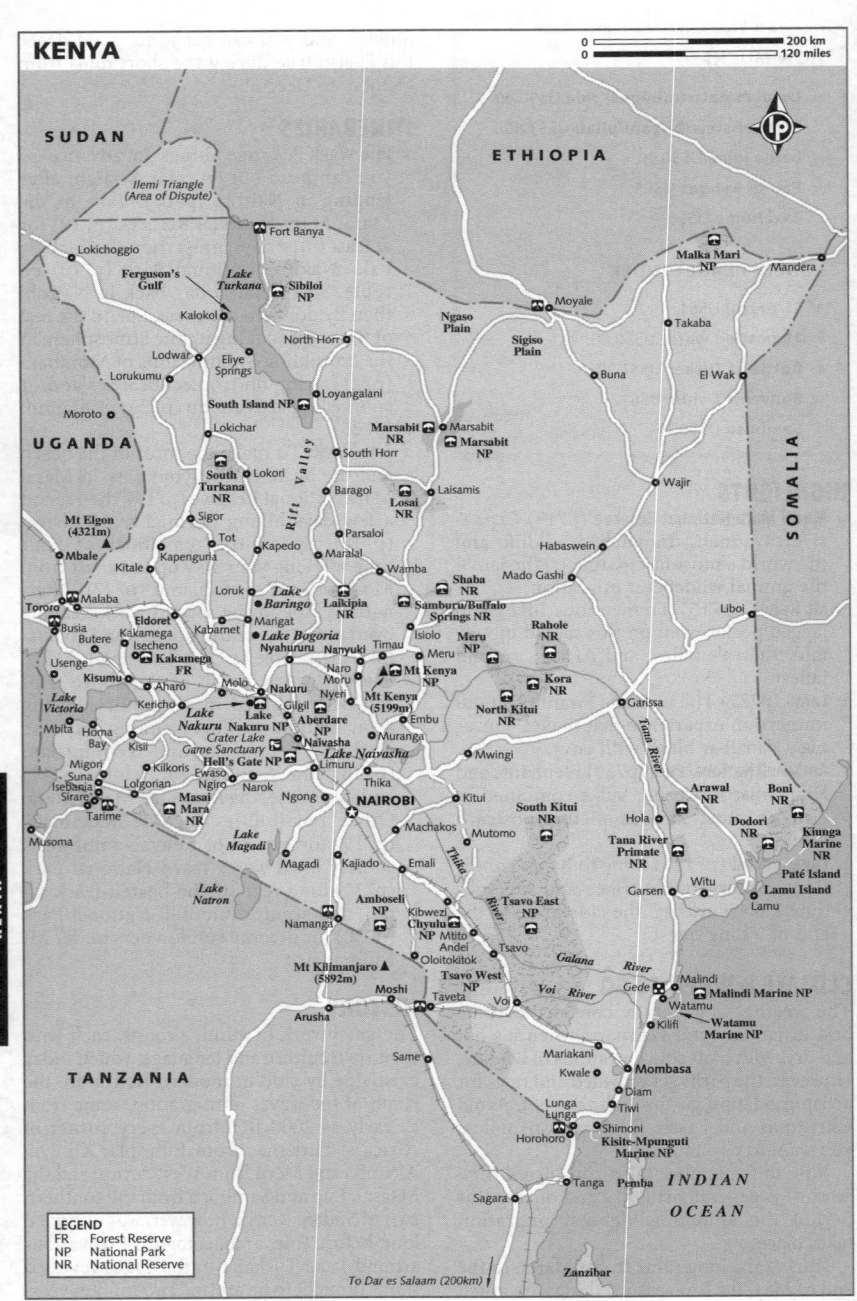

KENYA

| 0 | 200 km |
| 0 | 120 miles |

SUDAN

ETHIOPIA

Ilemi Triangle
(Area of Dispute)

Lokichoggio

Fort Banya

Malka Mari
NP

Mandera

Ferguson's
Gulf

*Lake
Turkana*

Sibiloi
NP

Moyale

Takaba

Kalokol

Ngaso
Plain

Sigiso
Plain

Buna

El Wak

Lodwar

Eliye
Springs

North Horr

Loyangalani

Moroto

Lokichar

UGANDA

South Island NP

Marsabit

Marsabit
NP

Wajir

SOMALIA

South Horr

Lokori

Baragoi

South
Turkana
NR

Losai
NR

Laisamis

Sigor

Tot

Kapedo

Parsaloi

Habaswein

Mado Gashi

Liboi

Mt Elgon
(4321m)

Mbale

Kitale

Kapenguria

Maralal

Wamba

Shaba
NR

Tororo

Malaba

Loruk

Marigat

*Lake
Baringo*

Laikipia
NR

Samburu/Buffalo
Springs NR

Rahole
NR

Busia

Butere

Eldoret

Kabarnet

Lake Bogoria

Nyahururu

Nanyuki

Timau

Isiolo

Meru

Meru
NP

Usenge

Isecheno

Kakamega

Kakamega
FR

Kisumu

Molo

Naro
Meru

Nyeri

Mt Kenya
(5199m)

Meru

Kora
NR

*Lake
Victoria*

Kencho

*Lake
Nakuru*

Nakuru

Gilgil

Mt Kenya
NP

North Kitui
NR

Garissa

Mbita

Homa
Bay

Kisii

Lake
Nakuru NP

Aberdare
NP

Embu

Tana River

Migori

Kilkoris

Ewaso

Crater Lake
Game Sanctuary

Naivasha

Lake Naivasha

Muranga

Suna

Isebania

Lolgorian

Ngiro

Hell's Gate NP

Limuru

Mwingi

Sirare

Tarime

Narok

Thika

NAIROBI

Kitui

South Kitui
NR

Arawal
NR

Boni
NR

Musoma

*Masai
Mara
NR*

Ngong

Machakos

Mutomo

Hola

Dodori
NR

*Lake
Magadi*

Magadi

Kajiado

Emali

Tana River
Primate
NR

Garsen

Witu

Kiunga
Marine
NR

Paté Island
Lamu Island

*Lake
Natron*

Amboseli
NP

Kibwezi

Chyulu
NP

Mtito
Andei

*Tsavo East
NP*

Lamu

Namanga

Oloitokitok

Tsavo

Galana

River

Malindi

Gede

Malindi Marine NP

Mt Kilimanjaro
(5892m)

Moshi

Tsavo West
NP

Taveta

Voi

Voi River

Watamu

Kilifi

Watamu
Marine NP

Arusha

Same

Mariakani

Kwale

Mombasa

TANZANIA

Diani

Tiwi

Lunga
Lunga

Shimoni

Horohoro

Kisite-Mpunguti
Marine NP

Sagara

Tanga

Pemba

**INDIAN
OCEAN**

Zanzibar

To Dar es Salaam (200km)

LEGEND
FR Forest Reserve
NP National Park
NR National Reserve

KENYA

old and those of the earliest human beings ever discovered.

By around the 8th century Arabic, Indian, Persian and even Chinese merchants were arriving on the Kenyan coast, intent on trading skins, ivory, gold and spices. These new arrivals helped set up a string of commercial cities along the whole of the East African coast, intermarrying with local dynasties to found a prosperous new civilisation, part African, part Arabic, known as the Swahili.

By the 16th century, Europeans too had cottoned on to the potential of the East African coast, and most of the Swahili trading towns, including Mombasa and Lamu, were either sacked or occupied by the Portuguese. Two centuries of harsh military rule followed, punctuated by regular battles for control of the former Swahili empire. The Omani Arabs finally ousted the Portuguese in 1720, but it wasn't long before the coast came into the control of more European colonisers – the British, who used their battleships to protect their lucrative route to India and to suppress the hated slave trade.

Mau Mau Rebellion

Despite plenty of overt pressure on Kenya's colonial authorities, the real independence movement was underground. Groups from the Kikuyu, Maasai and Luo tribes vowed to kill Europeans and their African collaborators. The most famous of these movements was Mau Mau, formed in 1952 by the Kikuyu people, which aimed to drive the white settlers from Kenya forever. In true African fashion, the Mau Mau rebellion was a brutal war of attrition on white people, property and 'collaborators'. The various Mau Mau sects came together under the umbrella of the Kenya Land Freedom Army, led by Dedan Kimathi, and staged frequent attacks against white farms and government outposts. By the time the rebels were defeated in 1956, the death toll stood at over 13,500 Africans (guerrillas, civilians and troops) and just over 100 Europeans.

In 1960 the British government officially announced its plan to transfer power to a democratically elected African government. Independence was scheduled for December 1963, accompanied by grants and loans of US$100 million to enable the Kenyan assembly to buy out European farmers in the highlands and restore the land to the tribes.

The run-up to independence was surprisingly smooth, although the redistribution of land wasn't a great success. The immediate effect was to cause a significant decline in agricultural production, from which Kenya has never quite recovered.

Jomo Kenyatta became Kenya's first president on 12 December, ruling until his death in 1978. Under Kenyatta's presidency, Kenya developed into one of Africa's most stable and prosperous nations. But while Kenyatta is still seen as a success story, he was excessively biased in favour of his own tribe and became paranoid about dissent. Opponents of his regime who became too vocal for comfort frequently 'disappeared', and corruption soon became endemic at all levels of the power structure.

The 1980s & '90s

Kenyatta was succeeded in 1978 by his vice president, Daniel arap Moi, a Kalenjin who became one of the most enduring 'Big Men' in Africa, ruling in virtual autocracy for nearly 25 years. In the process, he accrued an incredible personal fortune; today many believe him to be the richest man in Africa. Moi's regime was also characterised by nepotism, corruption, arrests of dissidents, censorship, the disbanding of tribal societies and the closure of universities.

Faced with a foreign debt of nearly US$9 billion and blanket suspension of foreign aid, Moi was pressured into holding multiparty elections in early 1992. Independent observers reported a litany of electoral inconsistencies, and about 2000 people were killed during ethnic clashes, widely believed to have been triggered by KANU agitation. Nonetheless, Moi was overwhelmingly re-elected.

Preoccupied with internal problems, Kenya was quite unprepared for the events of 7 August 1998. Early in the morning massive blasts simultaneously ripped apart the American embassies in Nairobi and Dar es Salaam in Tanzania, killing more than 200 people. The effect on Kenyan tourism, and the economy as a whole, was devastating.

Further terrorist activity shook the country on 28 November 2002, when suicide bombers slammed an explosives-laden car into the lobby of the Paradise Hotel at Kikambala, near Mombasa. Moments before, missiles were fired at an Israeli passenger plane taking off from Mombasa's airport. Al-Qaeda subsequently claimed responsibility for both the 1998 and 2002 acts.

Kenya Today

On 27 December 2007, Kenya held presidential, parliamentary and local elections. While the parliamentary and local government elections were largely credible, the presidential elections were marred by serious irregularities. Nonetheless, the Electoral Commission declared Mwai Kibaki the winner, triggering a wave of violence across the country.

The Rift Valley, Western Highlands, Nyanza Province and Mombasa – areas afflicted by years of political machination, previous election violence and large-scale displacement – exploded in ugly ethnic confrontations. The violence left more than 1000 people dead and over 600,000 people homeless. No longer would Kenyans stand by and be robbed by a cabal of discredited politicians.

Fearing the stability of the most stable linchpin of East Africa, UN Secretary Kofi Annan and a panel of 'Eminent African Persons' flew to Kenya to mediate talks. After protracted negotiations a power-sharing agreement was signed on 28 February 2008 between President Kibaki and Raila Odinga, the leader of the Orange Democratic Movement (ODM) opposition. The coalition provided for the establishment of a prime ministerial position (to be filled by Raila Odinga) as well as a division of cabinet posts according to the parties' representation in parliament. Key to the negotiations was the amendment of the constitution stating that the prime minister can only be sacked by parliament and not by the president.

Sworn in on 17 April 2008, the fragile coalition government has now started the complex task of long-term reform. If they are to succeed in any measure they have to address the key issues of land tenure reform, judicial reform and, more importantly, the poverty and inequality that plagues the country. Analysts stress that personal politics must be institutionalised and an effective system of checks and balances put in place to curb corruption and injustice. Local economists also estimate that Kenya needs to achieve growth of at least 12% if the country is to achieve any trickle-down effect, although election violence has caused an estimated US$1 billion loss in the tourism industry alone.

CULTURE

Many residents of Kenya are more aware of their tribal affiliation than of being 'Kenyan'; this lack of national cohesion undoubtedly presents the nation with some challenges, but is generally accompanied by an admirable live-and-let-live attitude. In fact, Kenyans generally approach life with great exuberance: on a crowded *matatu* (minibus); in a buzzing marketplace; or enjoying a drink in a bar. They are quick to laugh and are never reluctant to offer a smile.

Education is of primary concern to Kenyans. Literacy rates are around 85% and are considerably higher than in any of the neighbouring countries. Although education isn't compulsory, the motivation to learn is huge, particularly now that it's free, and you'll see children in school uniform everywhere in Kenya, even in the most impoverished rural communities.

Tribe may be important in Kenya, but family is paramount. Particularly as the pace and demands of modern life grow, the role of the extended family has become even more important. It is not unusual to encounter Kenyan children who are living with aunts, uncles or grandparents in a regional town, while their parents are working in Nairobi or at a resort in Watamu. The separation that brings about such circumstances in the first place is, without exception, a result of parents' desires to further opportunities for their families and their children.

For all this, as Kenya gains a foothold in the 21st century it is grappling with ever-increasing poverty. Once categorised as a middle-income country, Kenya has fallen to a low-income country, with the standard of living dropping drastically since the start of the new millennium.

People

Kenya's population in 2008 was estimated at 38.5 million. The population growth rate, currently at around 2.75%, has slowed in the last few years due to the prevalence of HIV/AIDS, which affects 7% to 8% of adults according to the UN (with life expectancy at 57 years). However, this still represents a significant growth rate and one that brings with it worrying concerns.

Most Kenyans outside the coastal and eastern provinces are Christians of one sort or another, while most of those on the coast and in the eastern part of the country are Muslim. Muslims make up some 30% of the population. In the more remote tribal areas you'll find a mixture of Muslims, Christians and those who follow their ancestral tribal beliefs, such as animism, though this last group is in the minority.

Arts

Benga is the country's contemporary dance music, characterised by electric-guitar licks and bounding bass rhythms. Well-known exponents include DO Misiani and his group Shirati Jazz, and you should also look out for Globestyle, Victoria Kings and Ambira Boys.

Popular bands today are heavily influenced by *benga,* soukous (African rumba) and Western music, with lyrics often in Swahili. These include bands such as Them Mushrooms (now reinvented as Uyoya) and Safari Sound. For upbeat dance tunes, Nameless, Ogopa DJs and Deux Vultures are recommended acts.

Local stars of American-influenced hip hop include Necessary Noize, Nonini, Emmanuel Jal, the Homeboyz DJs and the Nairobi Yetu collective.

Two of Kenya's best authors are Ngugi wa Thiong'o and Meja Mwangi. Ngugi's harrowing criticism of the Kenyan establishment landed him in jail for a year (described in his *Detained: A Prison Writer's Diary*). Meja Mwangi sticks more to social issues, but has a brilliant sense of humour that threads its way right through his books, including *The Mzungu Boy* and *The Boy Gift.*

Kenya's rising star is Binyavanga Wainaina, currently a writer for the South African *Sunday Times* newspaper, who won the Caine Prize for African Writing in July 2002. Marjorie Oludhe Magoye's *The Present Moment* follows the life stories of a group of elderly women in a Christian refuge. (For more writing by women in Africa, try *Unwinding Threads,* a collection of short stories by many authors from all over the continent.)

FOOD & DRINK

Food isn't one of Kenya's highlights, and the best dining is usually in upmarket hotels or safari lodges. The one local speciality is *nyama choma* (barbecued or roast meat). You buy the meat (usually goat) by the kilogram; it's cooked over a charcoal pit and served in bite-sized pieces with a vegetable side dish.

Kenya grows some of the finest tea (chai) and coffee in the world, but getting a decent cup of either can be difficult. Chai is drunk in large quantities, but the tea, milk and sugar are usually boiled together and stewed for ages. In Nairobi there are a handful of excellent coffeehouses, and you can usually get good filter coffee at any of the big hotels. Soft drinks are available everywhere under the generic term of 'soda'.

The local beers are Tusker, White Cap and Pilsner (all manufactured by Kenya Breweries). Castle (a South African beer) is also made under license by Kenya Breweries. Beers are cheapest from supermarkets (KSh45 for 500mL); bars charge KSh80 to KSh200. Imported wines are available in Nairobi restaurants and in big supermarkets. *Pombe* is the local beer, usually a fermented brew made with bananas or millet and sugar. It shouldn't do you any harm. Beware, however, of *chang'a*: in 2005, 48 people died from the effects of this dangerous brew; in some regions the drink is fermented with marijuana twigs, cactus mash, battery alkaline and formalin. Needless to say, we don't recommend you partake unless you're really looking to lose your mind, your eyesight and possibly your life.

ENVIRONMENT

Kenya straddles the equator and covers an area of some 583,000 sq km, including around 13,600 sq km of Lake Victoria. The modern landscape was shaped by the Rift Valley, a gigantic crack in the earth's crust that runs from Lake Turkana to the Tanzania border, and the activity of titanic (but now extinct) volcanoes such as Mts Kenya, Elgon and Kilimanjaro (across the border in Tanzania). The Rift Valley floor features numerous 'soda' lakes, rich in sodium bicarbonate, created by the filtering of water through mineral-rich volcanic rock and subsequent evaporation.

Around 10% of Kenya's land area is protected by law, and the national parks and reserves here rate among the best in Africa. No trip to Kenya would be complete without going on safari. Kenya is a virtual microcosm of African environments and its biodiversity is extraordinary for the country's size. Iconic species such as lions, elephants, leopards and buffalo are generally easy to see, but the biggest spectacle is the annual wildebeest migration that spills over from Tanzania's

KENYA

NATIONAL PARK ENTRY FEES

Kenyan Wildlife Service (KWS; www.kws.org) is a government-run body that actively conserves and manages the country's parks, protected spaces and wildlife.

Admission to national parks in Kenya is gradually being converted to a 'smartcard' system, for payment of entry and camping fees. The cards must be charged with credit in advance and can only be topped up at certain locations. Any credit left on the card once you finish your trip cannot be refunded.

There are four categories of parks in Kenya:

Category	Park
A	Aberdare, Amboseli, Lake Nakuru, Meru, Tsavo East, Tsavo West and Nairobi
B	Shimba Hills, Arabuko Sokoke, Ndere Island, Tana Primate, Kakamega and all other national parks and reserves
C	All marine parks and reserves
D	Nairobi Safari Walk, Animal Orphanage and Impala Sanctuary

The Masai Mara, Samburu, Buffalo Springs and Shaba National Reserves have the same entry fees as category A national parks; entry to Mt Kenya National Park is US$20/10 per adult/child. Entry and camping fees to the parks per person per day are as follows (unless otherwise specified):

Category	Entry adult/child (US$)	Camping adult (US$)
A	40/20	10
B	20/10	5
C	10/5	5
D	10/5	5

The land-based parks and reserves charge KSh300 for vehicles with fewer than six seats and KSh800 for vehicles seating six to 12. In addition to the public camping areas, special campsites cost US$25 per adult nonresident, plus a KSh7500 weekly reservation fee. Guides are available in most parks for US$30/KSh2500 per nonresident/resident per day.

All fees cover visitors for a 24-hour period, but you cannot leave and re-enter without paying twice. There are rumours that park fees will rise again shortly – the exact fee is not known, but expected to be in the region of US$60 for category A parks.

Serengeti Plains each year. Rhinos are very rare in Kenya, owing to a massive poaching problem. Lake Nakuru National Park almost guarantees sightings.

The variety of birds is extraordinary – some 1200 species – and a trip to Kenya has turned many a casual observer into a dedicated birder. Major reserves often support hundreds of bird species; interesting species include ostriches, vultures, colourful starlings and marabou storks. Wetlands support abundant flamingos, herons and pelicans, while the forests are home to hornbills, touracos, sunbirds, weavers and a host more.

Forest destruction continues on a large scale in Kenya – less than 3% of the country's original forest remains. Land grabbing, illegal logging, charcoal burning and agricultural encroachment all take their toll. The degazetting of protected forests is another contentious issue, sparking widespread protests and preservation campaigns. The main cause of this is untrammelled population growth; Kenya's population has doubled in the past 20 years and, not surprisingly, the land area hasn't. The not unexpected corollary is are a vicious cycle of deforestation, land degradation and erosion, causing people to open up and destroy still more land.

Renewed poaching raids on elephants and rhinos have led to talk of abandoning some of the more remote parks and concentrating resources where they can achieve the best results. At the same time, community conservation projects are being encouraged, and many community-owned ranches are now being opened up as private wildlife reserves.

An increasing number of important wildlife conservation areas now exist on private land. Supporting these projects is a great way for travellers to directly contribute to local communities as well as assist Kenyan wildlife preservation.

NAIROBI

☎ 020 / pop 3 million

One of the most vilified cities in Africa, Nairobi has a reputation among foreign tourists as being an incredibly dangerous place racked by violent crime and extreme poverty. The city has garnered the unfortunate nickname of 'Nai-robbery', and most first-timers are keen on holing up in their hotel rooms and counting down the minutes until their safari departure. While the crime statistics are unsettling, it's easy enough to sidestep the worst dangers here, and although you might not believe us at first glance, Nairobi is actually an extremely dynamic and cosmopolitan city.

HISTORY

When the East Africa railway arrived in the 1890s, a depot was established on the edge of a small stream known to the Maasai as *uaso nairobi* (cold water). Nairobi quickly developed into the administrative nerve centre of the Uganda Railway, and in 1901 the capital of the British Protectorate was moved here from Mombasa. Sadly, almost all of the colonial-era buildings were replaced by bland, modern office buildings following *uhuru* (independence) in 1963.

ORIENTATION

The compact city centre is in the area bounded by Uhuru Hwy, Haile Selassie Ave, Moi Ave and University Way. Kenyatta Ave divides this area in two; most of the important offices lie to the south, while hotels, the market and more offices are to the north.

North of the city centre are Nairobi University, the National Museum and the expat-dominated suburb of Westlands. Jomo Kenyatta International Airport is southeast of central Nairobi; also south are Langata and Karen suburbs and Wilson Airport.

INFORMATION
Bookshops
Book Villa (Map pp710-11; ☎ 337890; Standard St)
Bookpoint (Map pp710-11; ☎ 211156; Moi Ave)

Emergency
AAR Health Services (Map pp708-9; ☎ 717376; Williamson House, Fourth Ngong Ave)
Aga Khan Hospital (Map pp708-9; ☎ 3662000; Third Parklands Ave; ☺ 24hr)

Ambulance & fire (☎ 999) Emergency response.
Amref flying-doctor service (☎ 502699)
Police (☎ emergency services 999, 240000) Also for less urgent police business.

Internet Access

There are hundreds of internet cafes in central Nairobi, most of them tucked away in anonymous office buildings. Connection speed is usually pretty good and rates are around KSh1 per minute.
AGX (Map pp708-9; Barclays Plaza, Loita St; ☺ 8am-8pm Mon-Sat)
Avant Garde e-centre (Map pp710-11; Fedha Towers, Kaunda St; ☺ 7.30am-9pm Mon-Sat, 11am-6pm Sun)

Medical Services

Try to avoid the Kenyatta National Hospital.
AAR Health Services (Map pp708-9; ☎ 715319; Williamson House, Fourth Ngong Ave)
Acacia Medical Centre (Map pp710-11; ☎ 212200; info@acaciamed.co.ke; ICEA Bldg, Kenyatta Ave; ☺ 7am-7pm Mon-Fri, 7am-2pm Sat)
Aga Khan Hospital (Map pp708-9; ☎ 740000; Third Parklands Ave; ☺ 24hr)
KAM Pharmacy (Map pp710-11; ☎ 251700; Executive Tower, IPS Bldg, Kimathi St) Pharmacy, doctor's surgery and laboratory.
Medical Services Surgery (Map pp710-11; ☎ 317625; Bruce House, Standard St; ☺ 8.30am-4.30pm Mon-Fri)
Nairobi Hospital (Map pp708-9; ☎ 722160, Ngong Rd)

Money

In the centre of Nairobi, Barclays branches with guarded ATMs include those located on Muindi Mbingu St (Map pp710-11), Mama Ngina St (Map pp710-11), and on the corner of Kenyatta and Moi Aves (Map pp710-11).

Post
Post office (Map pp710-11; ☎ 243434; Kenyatta Ave; ☺ 8am-6pm Mon-Fri, 9am-noon Sat)

Telephone
Telkom Kenya (Map pp710-11; ☎ 232000; Haile Selassie Ave; ☺ 8am-6pm Mon-Fri, 9am-noon Sat)

Travel Agencies
Bunson Travel (Map pp710-11; ☎ 221992; www.bunsonkenya.com; Pan-African Insurance Bldg, Standard St)
Flight Centres (Map pp710-11; ☎ 210024; Lakhamshi House, Biashara St)
Let's Go Travel (Map pp710-11; ☎ 340331; www.lets-go-travel.net; Caxton House, Standard St)

KENYA

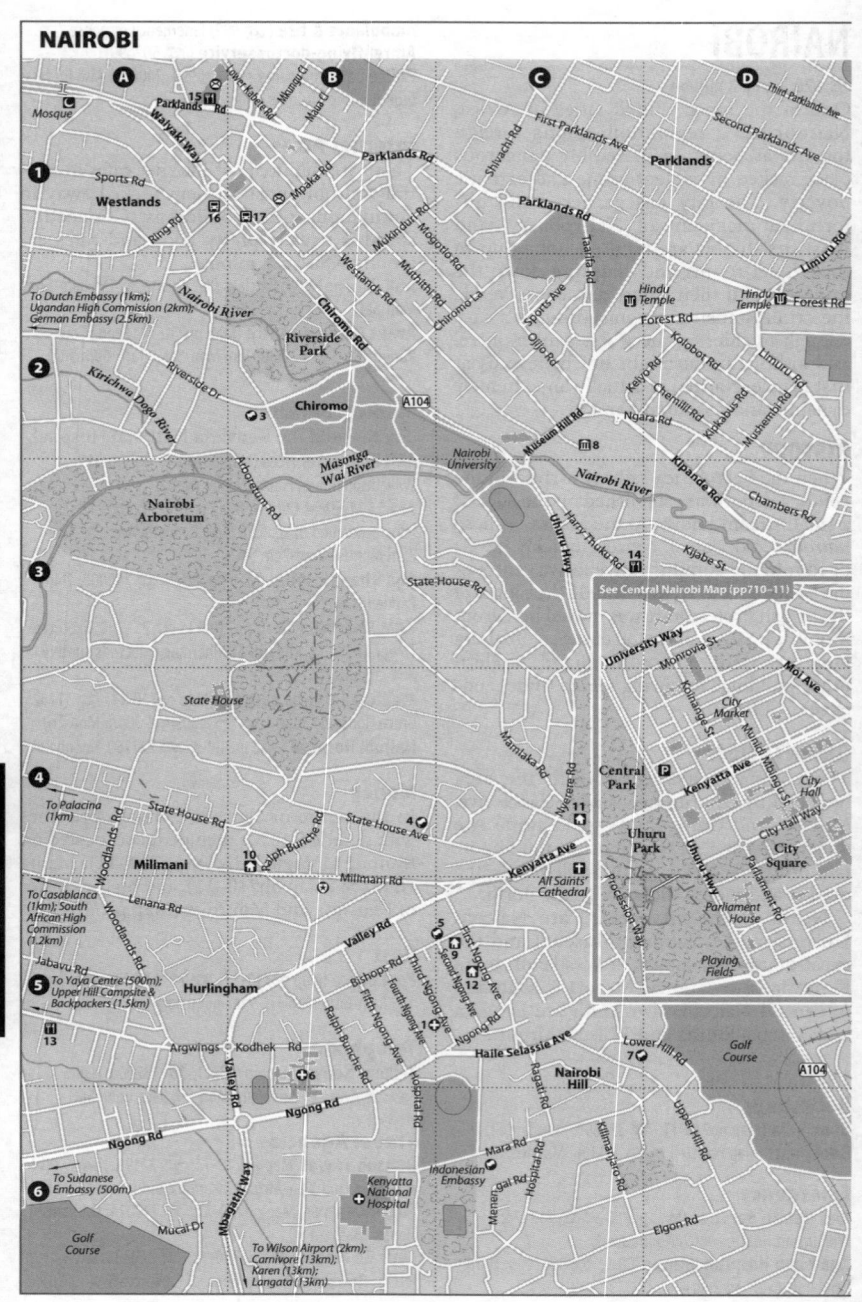

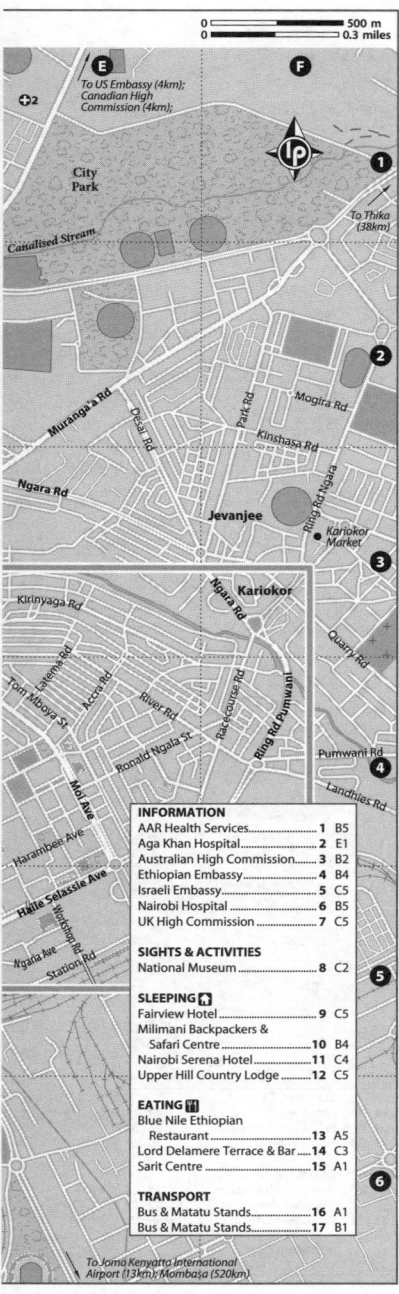

INFORMATION		
AAR Health Services	1	B5
Aga Khan Hospital	2	E1
Australian High Commission	3	B2
Ethiopian Embassy	4	B4
Israeli Embassy	5	C5
Nairobi Hospital	6	B5
UK High Commission	7	C5

SIGHTS & ACTIVITIES		
National Museum	8	C2

SLEEPING 🏠		
Fairview Hotel	9	C5
Milimani Backpackers &		
Safari Centre	10	B4
Nairobi Serena Hotel	11	C4
Upper Hill Country Lodge	12	C5

EATING 🍴		
Blue Nile Ethiopian		
Restaurant	13	A5
Lord Delamere Terrace & Bar	14	C3
Sarit Centre	15	A1

TRANSPORT		
Bus & Matatu Stands	16	A1
Bus & Matatu Stands	17	B1

Tropical Winds (Map p710-11; ☎ 341939; www.tropi cal-winds.com; Barclays Plaza, Loita St) STA representative.

DANGERS & ANNOYANCES

Prospective visitors to Nairobi are usually understandably daunted by the city's unenviable reputation. Carjacking, robbery and violence are daily occurrences, and the underlying social ills behind them are unlikely to disappear in the near future.

However, the majority of problems happen in the slums, far from the main tourist zones. The central Nairobi area bound by Kenyatta Ave, Moi Ave, Haile Selassie Ave and Uhuru Hwy is comparatively trouble-free as long as you use a bit of common sense, and there are plenty of *askaris* (security guards) around at night. Stay alert and you should encounter nothing worse than a few persistent safari touts and the odd con artist.

However, around the city centre there are places to watch out for: danger zones include the area around Latema and River Rds, a hotspot for petty theft, and Uhuru Park, which tends to attract all kinds of dodgy characters.

Once the shops have shut, the streets empty rapidly and the whole city takes on a slightly sinister air – mugging is a risk anywhere after dark. Take a taxi, even if you're only going a few blocks. This will also keep you safe from the attentions of Nairobi's street prostitutes, who flood into town in force after sunset.

SIGHTS

Kenya's grand **National Museum** (Map pp708-9; Museum Hill Rd; adult/child/student KSh200/20/100; ⊙ 8.15am-4.45pm) has a good range of cultural, geological and natural-history exhibits. Volunteer guides offer tours in English, Dutch and French; a donation is appropriate. The 1st floor also hosts the excellent Gallery of Contemporary East African Art.

The ground-floor atrium and gallery of the **National Archives** (Map pp710-11; ☎ 749341; Moi Ave; admission free; ⊙ 8.30am-5pm Mon-Fri, 8.30am-1pm Sat) display an eclectic selection of contemporary art, historical photos of Nairobi, cultural artefacts, furniture and tribal objects.

SLEEPING

Milimani Backpackers & Safari Centre (Map pp708-9; ☎ 2343920; www.milimanibackpackers.com; Milimani Rd, Milimani; campsites KSh350, dm KSh600, permanent tent KSh450, s/d cabin KSh1300/1500; 💻) Whether you camp out back, cosy up in the dorms

CENTRAL NAIROBI

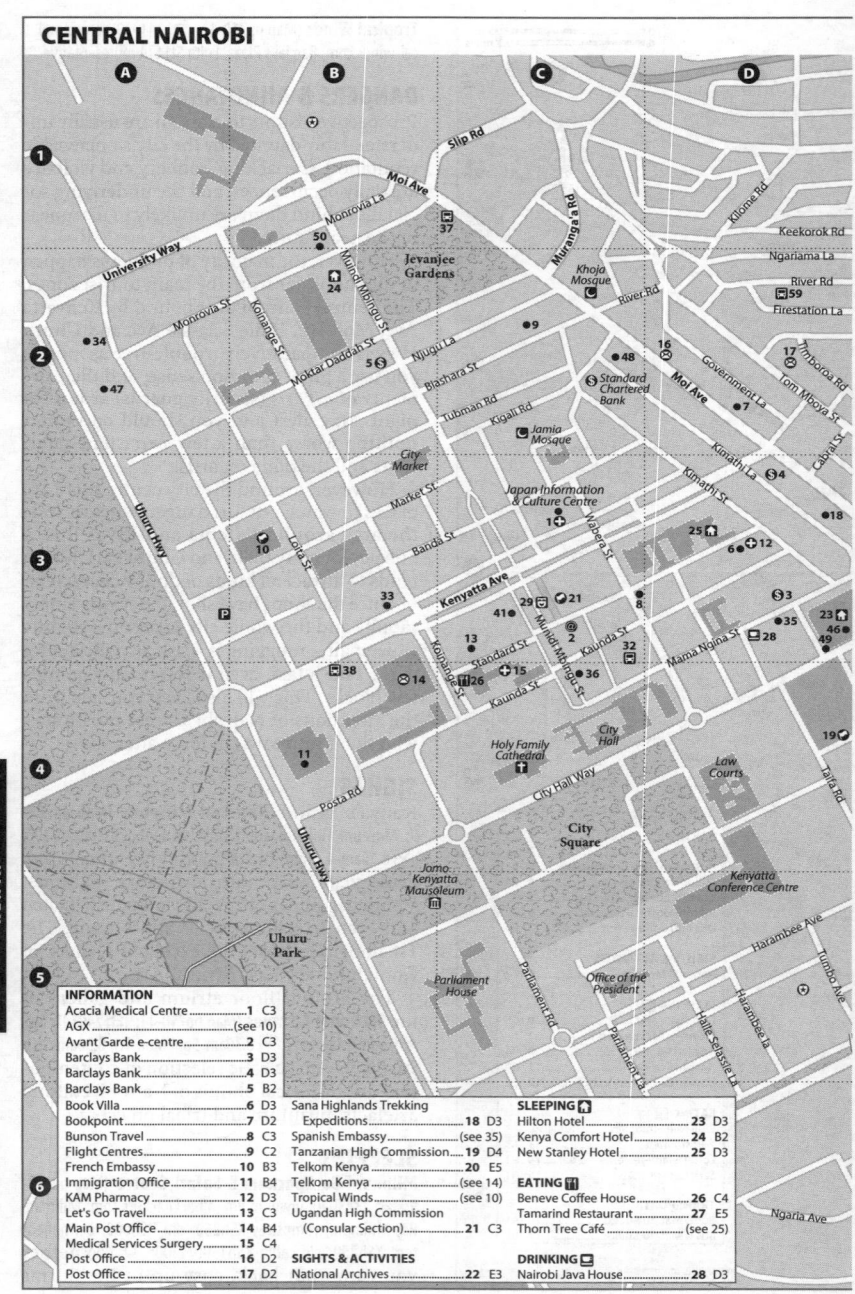

KENYA

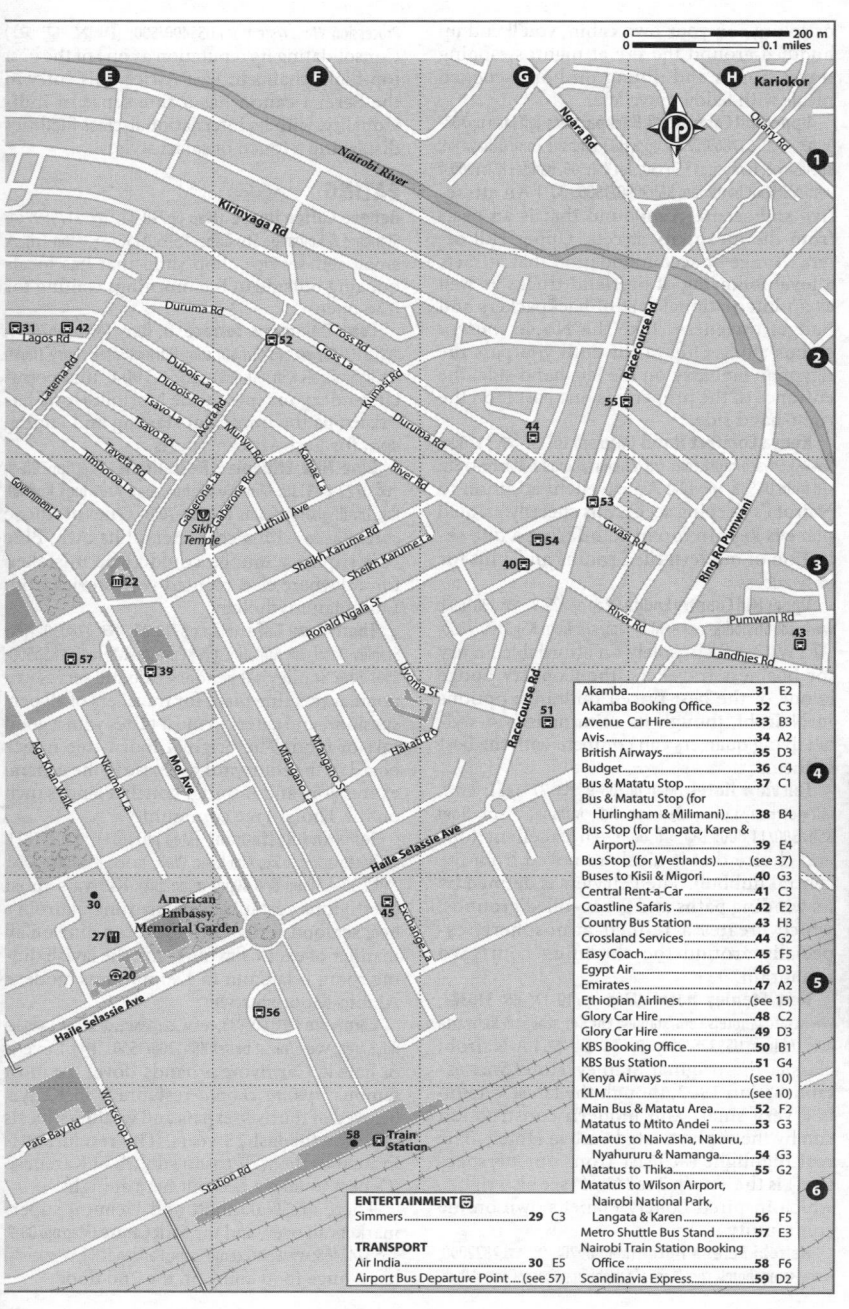

KENYA

Akamba..................................**31** E2
Akamba Booking Office...........**32** C3
Avenue Car Hire......................**33** B3
Avis...**34** A2
British Airways........................**35** D3
Budget.....................................**36** C4
Bus & Matatu Stop..................**37** C1
Bus & Matatu Stop (for
  Hurlingham & Milimani)........**38** B4
Bus Stop (for Langata, Karen &
  Airport).................................**39** E4
Bus Stop (for Westlands).....(see 37)
Buses to Kisii & Migori............**40** G3
Central Rent-a-Car..................**41** C3
Coastline Safaris.....................**42** E2
Country Bus Station................**43** H3
Crossland Services...................**44** G2
Easy Coach..............................**45** F5
Egypt Air.................................**46** D3
Emirates..................................**47** A2
Ethiopian Airlines................(see 15)
Glory Car Hire.........................**48** C2
Glory Car Hire.........................**49** D3
KBS Booking Office..................**50** B1
KBS Bus Station.......................**51** G4
Kenya Airways.....................(see 10)
KLM.....................................(see 10)
Main Bus & Matatu Area..........**52** F2
Matatus to Mtito Andei............**53** G3
Matatus to Naivasha, Nakuru,
  Nyahururu & Namanga...........**54** G3
Matatus to Thika......................**55** G2
Matatus to Wilson Airport,
  Nairobi National Park,
  Langata & Karen....................**56** F5
Metro Shuttle Bus Stand...........**57** E3
Nairobi Train Station Booking
  Office...................................**58** F6
Scandinavia Express.................**59** D2

ENTERTAINMENT
Simmers...................................**29** C3

TRANSPORT
Air India...................................**30** E5
Airport Bus Departure Point ....(see 57)

or splurge on your own cabin, you'll end up huddled around the fire at night, swapping travel stories and dining on home-cooked meals with fellow travellers.

Upper Hill Campsite & Backpackers (off Map pp708-9; ☎ 0721-517869; www.upperhillcampsite.com; Othaya Rd, Kileleshwa; campsites KSh350, dm KSh500, bandas KSh1200, r with/without bathroom KSh2000/1500; 🖳) An attractive and secure compound that is an oasis from the mean city streets, Upper Hill offers a range of accommodation that attracts a loyal following of overland trucks as well as an international mix of backpackers and budget travellers. Take the No 46 *matatu* or bus along Othaya Rd until you pass the Egyptian embassy on the left-hand side; the entrance to the property is just past it on the right-hand side.

Kenya Comfort Hotel (Map pp710-11; ☎ 317606; www.kenyacomfort.com; cnr Muindi Mbingu & Monrovia Sts; s/d from US$38/56; 🖳) An excellent addition to Nairobi's sleeping scene, this cheerily painted place is kept in top nick, offering a fine selection of modern tiled rooms and a lift for easy access.

Upper Hill Country Lodge (Map pp708-9; ☎ 2881600; www.countrylodge.co.ke; Milimani; s/d from KSh5100/7800; 🖳) With a focus solely on affordable luxury for business travellers, the Country Lodge is one of the best-priced midrange options in Nairobi, though its minimalist yet stylish living quarters can compete with the best of them.

Fairview Hotel (Map pp708-9; ☎ 2711321; www.fairviewkenya.com; Bishops Rd, Milimani; s/d from KSh7500/11,000; 🟩 🖳 🖳) An excellent top-end choice that is nicely removed from the central hubbub. The Fairview is defined by its winding paths and green-filled grounds, which creates a refined atmosphere, especially around the charming courtyard restaurant.

New Stanley Hotel (Map pp710-11; ☎ 316377; www.sarovahotels.com/stanley; cnr Kimathi St & Kenyatta Ave; s/d from US$225/250; 🅿 🟩 🖳 🖳) A Nairobi classic: the original Stanley Hotel was established in 1902, though the latest version is a very smart and modern construction run by the sophisticated Sarova Hotels. The real highlight (at least from our perspective!) is the Thorn Tree Café (see also right), which inspired Lonely Planet's own online community.

Nairobi Serena Hotel (Map pp708-9; ☎ 2822000; www.serenahotels.com/kenya/nairobi/home.asp; Central Park, Procession Way; r/ste from US$400/500; 🅿 🟩 🖳 🖳) Consolidating its reputation as one of the best top-flight chains in East Africa, this entry in the Serena canon has a fine sense of individuality, with its international-class facilities displaying a touch of safari style.

EATING

Beneve Coffee House (Map pp710-11; ☎ 217959; cnr Standard & Koinange Sts; dishes KSh50-150; 🕐 Mon-Fri) A small self-service chop shop that has locals queuing outside in the mornings waiting for it to open.

Lord Delamere Terrace & Bar (Map pp708-9; ☎ 216940; www.fairmont.com/NorfolkHotel; Harry Thuku Rd; light meals KSh300-600) Since 1904, this popular rendezvous spot at the Norfolk Hotel has existed as the unofficial starting and ending spot for East African safaris.

Blue Nile Ethiopian Restaurant (Map pp708-9; ☎ 0722-898138; bluenile@yahoo.com; Argwings Kodhek Rd, Hurlingham; mains KSh500-700) One of those rare places with a character all its own, Blue Nile's quirky lounge couldn't be mistaken for anywhere else, painted with stories from Ethiopian mythology.

Thorn Tree Café (Map pp710-11; ☎ 228030; New Stanley Hotel, cnr Kimathi St & Kenyatta Ave; mains KSh300-850) The Stanley's legendary cafe still serves as a popular meeting place for travellers of all persuasions, and caters to most tastes with a good mix of food. The original thorn-tree notice board in the courtyard gave rise to the general expression, and inspired Lonely Planet's own online Thorn Tree community.

Tamarind Restaurant (Map pp710-11; ☎ 251811; www.tamarind.co.ke; Aga Khan Walk; mains KSh1000-2000; 🕐 2.30-4.30pm & 8.30pm-midnight) Kenya's most prestigious restaurant chain runs Nairobi's best seafood restaurant – you can dine on all manner of exotic flavours, and the lavish dining room is laid out in a sumptuous modern Arabic-Moorish style.

Carnivore (☎ 605933; www.carnivore.co.ke; off Langata Rd, Karen; vegie/meat buffet KSh1200/1550; 🅿) Love it or hate it, Carnivore is hands-down the most famous *nyama choma* restaurant in Kenya, beloved of tourists, expats and wealthier locals alike for the last 25 years. The restaurant is located in the well-to-do suburb of Karen, so it's best to take a taxi out here at night.

There are Nakumatt and Uchumi supermarkets all over, and the **Sarit Centre** (Map pp708-9; ☎ 3747408; www.saritcentre.com; Parklands Rd, Westlands) has a huge food court on the 2nd floor.

DRINKING & ENTERTAINMENT

Nairobi Java House (Map pp710-11; ☎ 313565; www.nairobi java.com; Mama Ngina St; ⏰ 7am-8.30pm Mon-Sat) This fantastic coffeehouse is rapidly turning itself into a major brand, and aficionados say the coffee is some of the best in Kenya.

Casablanca (off Map pp708-9; ☎ 2723173; Lenana Rd, Hurlingham; ⏰ from 6pm) This Moroccan-style lounge bar has been an instant hit with Nairobi's fastidious expat community, and you don't have to spend much time here to become a convert.

Simmers (Map pp710-11; ☎ 217659; cnr Kenyatta Ave & Muindi Mbingu St; admission free) The atmosphere at this open-air nightclub is almost invariably amazing, with the ever-enthusiastic crowds turning out to wind and grind the night away.

GETTING THERE & AWAY
Air
Kenya Airways (Map pp710-11; ☎ 32074100; www.kenya-airways.com; Barclays Plaza, Loita St), the country's principal international and domestic carrier, has a booking office in the city centre, though its website is efficient and reliable.

Bus
Most long-distance bus-company offices in Nairobi are in the River Rd area. Numerous companies do the run to Mombasa, leaving in the early morning or late in the evening; the trip takes eight to 10 hours. Buses leave from outside each company's office, and fares cost KSh400 to KSh700. **Coastline Safaris** (Map pp710-11; ☎ 217592; cnr Latema & Lagos Rds) buses are the most comfortable.

Akamba (Map pp710-11; ☎ 340430; akamba_prs@sky web.co.ke; Lagos Rd) is the biggest private bus company in the country, with an extensive and reliable network. Buses serve Kakamega, Kisumu, Mombasa, Uganda and Tanzania, departing from Lagos Rd; there's a **booking office** (Map pp710-11; ☎ 222027; Wabera St) near City Hall.

The government-owned **KBS** (Kenya Bus Service; ☎ 229707) is another large operator. It's cheaper than Akamba, but the buses are much slower. The main depot is on Uyoma St, and there's a **booking office** (Map pp710-11; ☎ 341250; cnr Muindi Mbingu & Monrovia Sts) in the city centre.

Easy Coach (Map pp710-11; ☎ 210711; easycoach@wa nanchi.com; Haile Selassie Ave) is a reliable new company serving western Kenya destinations on the Kisumu/Kakamega route.

The **Country Bus Station** (Map pp710-11; Landhies Rd) is a disorganised place with buses running to Kakamega, Kisumu, Naivasha, Nanyuki, Nakuru and other destinations.

Typical fares and durations:

Destination	Fare (KSh)	Duration (hr)
Kakamega	1250	8
Kisumu	1350	7
Malindi	1100	12
Mombasa	800-1300	6-10
Naivasha	150	1½
Nakuru	250	3
Nanyuki	400	3

Matatu
Most *matatus* leave from Latema, Accra, River and Cross Rds, and fares are similar to the buses. The biggest operator here is **Crossland Services** (Map pp710-11; ☎ 245377; Cross Rd).

There are loads of *matatus* to Naivasha (KSh150, 1½ hours) and the Tanzanian border at Namanga (KSh250, three hours) from the corner of Ronald Ngala St and River Rd (Map pp710–11).

Train
Nairobi train station has a small **booking office** (Map pp710-11; Station Rd; ⏰ 9am-noon & 2-6.30pm), though don't bother trying to get in touch with it – you need to stop in person to book tickets a few days in advance of your intended departure. For Mombasa (1st/2nd class US$65/43, 14 to 16 hours), trains leave Nairobi at 7pm on Monday, Wednesday and Friday; arrive early.

GETTING AROUND
To/From Jomo Kenyatta International Airport
Kenya's main **international airport** (off Map pp708-9; ☎ 827638) is 15km out of town, off the road to Mombasa. There's now a dedicated airport bus (US$5, 40 minutes) run by Metro Shuttle (part of KBS), which runs every half-hour from 8am to 8.30pm, and can drop you off at hotels in the city centre. Going the other way, the main departure point is across from the Hilton Hotel.

To/From Wilson Airport
To get to **Wilson Airport** (off Map pp708-9; ☎ 501941), for Airkenya services or charter flights, the cheapest option is bus or *matatu* 15, 31, 34, 125 or 126 from Moi Ave (KSh20). A taxi to the centre of town will cost you KSh600 to KSh1000 depending on the driver.

Bus

The ordinary city buses are run by **KBS** (☎ 229707) but hopefully you won't need to use them much. Forget about them if you're carrying luggage – you'll never get on, and even if you do, you'll never get off! Most buses pass through the city centre, but the main KBS terminus is on Uyoma St, east of the centre.

Matatu

Nairobi's horde of *matatus* follow the same routes as buses and display the same route numbers. For Westlands, you can pick up No 23 on Moi Ave or Latema Rd. No 46 to the Yaya Centre stops in front of the main post office, and Nos 125 and 126 to Langata leave from in front of the train station. As usual, you should keep an eye on your valuables on all *matatus*.

Taxi

Fares around town are negotiable but end up pretty standard. Any journey within the city centre area costs KSh300, from the city centre to Milimani Rd costs KSh400, and for longer journeys such as Westlands or the Yaya Centre, fares range from KSh500 to KS650. From the city centre to Karen and Langata it is around KSh850 (one way).

THE RIFT VALLEY

LAKE NAIVASHA
☎ 0311

The area around Naivasha was one of the first settled by *wazungu* (whites), and is now one of the largest remaining expat communities in Kenya. The freshwater lake itself is home to an incredible variety of birds, including the African fish eagle. The surrounding countryside is a major agricultural area.

Sights & Activities

On the western side of Lake Naivasha, north of the village of Kongoni, is the **Crater Lake Game Sanctuary** (admission KSh700), a small park set around a beautiful volcanic crater. On the eastern side of the lake is **Crescent Island** (adult/child US$20/10), a protruding rim of a collapsed volcanic crater that can be explored by boat.

Elsamere Conservation Centre (☎ 2021055; www.elsamere.com; admission KSh600; ☼ 8am-6.30pm) is the former home of the late Joy Adamson of *Born Free* fame. Now a conservation centre focused on lake ecology and environmental awareness programs, the site is open to the public and entry includes afternoon tea complete with a mountain of biscuits on the hippo-manicured lawns. The centre is located on the southern rim of the lake.

Sleeping

Fisherman's Camp (☎ 05050462, 0726-870590; fishermanscampkenya@msn.com; campsites KSh300, tent hire from KSh400, bandas per person Sun-Thu KSh1000, per banda Fri & Sat KSh4000) Spread along the grassy tree-laden southern shore and full of hungry hippos, this is a perennial favourite of campers, overland companies and backpackers. While hippo movements have been restricted by electric fences for safety reasons, you still stand a real chance of seeing one of these great beasts grazing at night.

Following Fisherman's lead, the **Crayfish Camp** (☎ 2020239; www.crayfishcamp.com; campsites KSh500, s without bathroom KSh1000, s/d incl breakfast KSh2500/3200; ▣) can seem more like a beer garden than a campsite, but it's not a bad option.

The luxury tented **Crater Lake Camp** (☎ 2020613; crater@africaonline.co.ke; campsites KSh500, s/d incl full board US$187/280) is nestled among trees and overlooks the tiny jade-green crater lake dotted with blushing pink flamingos.

Getting There & Away

Matatus (KSh80, one hour) run along Moi South Lake Rd between Naivasha town and Kongoni on the lake's western side, passing the turn-offs to Hell's Gate National Park and Fisherman's Camp.

HELL'S GATE NATIONAL PARK

Hell's Gate (☎ 050-2020284; adult/child US$20/10, bicycle KSh50, guide KSh500) is unique among Kenya's parks, as you are encouraged to walk or cycle unguided across its breadth. There's dramatic scenery, with looming cliffs, gorges and basalt columns. Lurking lions and leopards add to the excitement! Marking the eastern entrance to Hell's Gate Gorge is **Fischer's Tower**, one of the park's many popular rock-climbing sites.

Lake Naivasha (see left) makes a convenient base for exploring the park, but camping here is recommended, and Ol Dubai and Naiberta campsites are probably the best. Access is by private car or even by bicycle.

NAKURU

☎ 051 / pop 163,000

Kenya's fourth-largest centre doesn't feel like anything more than an overgrown country town, and has a relaxed atmosphere and makes a pleasant base for a few days. It also sits on the doorstep of the delightful Lake Nakuru National Park (below).

Carnation Hotel (☎ 2215360; Mosque Rd; s/tw KSh750/1300) is the town's prettiest budget rose, featuring rooms with multicoloured tiled floors and kitsch bed sheets.

A contemporary tower, **Merica Hotel** (☎ 2216013; merica@kenyaweb.com; Kenyatta Ave; s/d incl half board US$65/110; ✗ ♨) hosts Nakuru's only top-end rooms. Ride the glass elevators up through the sunlit atrium to well-appointed rooms large enough to host a wildebeest migration.

Buses, *matatus* and occasional Peugeots leave for Naivasha (KSh120, 1¼ hours), Nairobi (KSh200, three hours), Kitale (KSh350, 3½ hours) and Kisumu (KSh350, 3½ hours).

LAKE NAKURU NATIONAL PARK

This **national park** (☎ 051-2217151; adult/child US$40/20, smartcard required) rivals Amboseli as Kenya's second most-visited park. This is one of the best places in Kenya to see leopards, and white rhinos are commonly seen at the lake's southern end. But the park's most famous attraction is the colony of pelicans and (occasionally) flamingos that ring the lake in thousands.

The main gate is 2km south of the centre of Nakuru. KWS smartcards are available here. The **Backpackers' Campsite** (adult/child US$10/5) is a large public campsite located just inside the main gate, and has the park's best camping facilities.

Wildlife Club of Kenya Guesthouse (☎ 051-851559; Nakuru town centre; per person without bathroom KSh1000) is great: facilities include hot showers, TV lounge, and use of a fridge, gas cooker and microwave. Rooms are clean and comfortable.

Sarova Lion Hill Lodge (☎ 051-850235; www.sarova hotels.com; s/d incl full board US$310/410; ♨) is an upmarket lodge that offers 1st-class service and comfort from high up the lake's eastern slopes. There are fantastic views from the

restaurant-bar as well as from the majority of rooms in the lodge.

In order to visit the national park, a taxi from Nakuru for a few hours should cost you around KSh2500, although note that you will most likely have to bargain hard for it.

CENTRAL KENYA

MT KENYA NATIONAL PARK

Africa's second-highest mountain, Mt Kenya, attracts spry hikers, long, dramatic cloud cover and all the eccentricities of its mother continent in equal measure. Here, mere minutes from the equator, glaciers carve out the throne of Ngai, the old high god of the Kikuyu. Mt Kenya's highest peaks, Batian (5199m) and Nelion (5188m), can only be reached by mountaineers with technical skills. However, Point Lenana (4985m), which is the park's third-highest peak, can be reached by hikers and is the usual goal for most mere mortals. The mountain offers hikers a fantastic experience as well as superb views out over the surrounding countryside.

Information

The daily fees for the **national park** (☎ 061-55645; adult/child US$55/20 plus additional KSh200 per day for each guide & porter) are charged upon entry, so you must estimate the length of your stay.

You can **camp** (adult/child US$10/5) anywhere on the mountain – the nightly fee is payable to KWS at any gate. Most people camp near the huts or bunkhouses, as there are often toilets and water nearby. KWS operates two more upscale lodges on the mountain: **Batian Guest House** (US$180), a plush, four-bedroom cottage located 1km from Naro Moru gate; and the surprisingly comfy stone **Sirimon Bandas** (US$80), which are located 9km from the Sirimon gates. Reservations for both lodgings must be made through KWS on ☎ 020-600800 or reservations@kws.org. You can also contact the warden of the national park on ☎ 061-55645/55201.

GUIDES, COOKS & PORTERS

KWS issues vouchers to all registered guides and porters, who should also hold identity

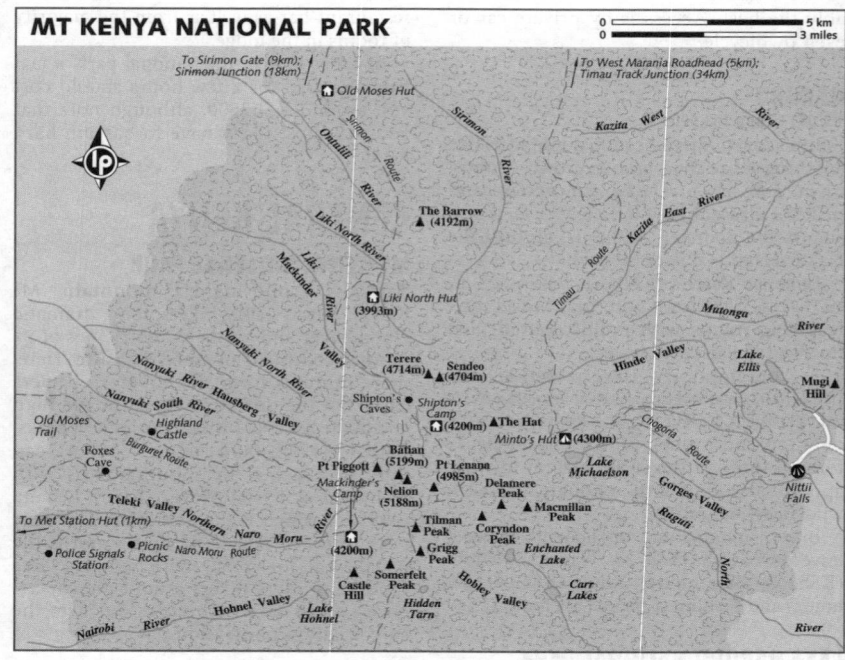

MT KENYA NATIONAL PARK

cards; they won't be allowed into the park without them.

The cost of guides varies depending on their qualifications, whatever the last party paid and your own negotiating skills. You should expect to pay a minimum of US$20 per day for a basic guide, while technical climbing guides can cost as much as US$50 per day. Cooks and porters cost US$15 to US$20 per day. Agree on all costs before you depart.

These fees don't include park entry fees and tips, and the latter should only be paid for good service.

ORGANISED HIKES

If you negotiate aggressively, a package hike may end up costing only a little more than organising each logistical element of the trip separately. As always, you need to watch out for sharks. Picking the right company is even more important here than on regular safari, as an unqualified or inexperienced guide could put you in real danger.

KG Mountain Expeditions (☎ 062-62403; www. kenyaexpeditions.com; Naro Moru)

Mountain Rock Safaris Resorts & Trekking Services (☎ 020-242133, 0722-511752; www.mountainrock kenya.com; Nairobi)

Naro Moru River Lodge (☎ 062-31047; www.alliance hotels.com; Naro Moru)

Sana Highlands Trekking Expeditions (Map pp710-11; ☎ 020-227820; www.sanatrekkingkenya.com; Contrust House, Moi Ave, Nairobi)

Hike Routes

NARO MORU ROUTE

Although the least scenic, this is the most straightforward, popular route, and still a spectacular and very enjoyable trail. Allow a minimum of four days for the hike; it's possible in three if you arrange transport between Naro Moru and the Met Station Hut, but doing it this quickly risks serious altitude sickness.

SIRIMON ROUTE

A popular alternative to Naro Moru, this route has more spectacular scenery, greater flexibility and a gentler rate of ascent, although it is still easy to climb too fast, so allow at least five days for the hike. It's well worth considering combining it with the Chogoria route for a six- to seven-day traverse that will really bring out the best of Mt Kenya.

CHOGORIA ROUTE

This route is justly famous for crossing some of the most spectacular and varied scenery on Mt Kenya, and is often combined with the Sirimon route (usually as the descent). The only disadvantage is the long distance between Chogoria village and the park gate. Allow at least five days for a hike here.

Getting There & Away

The traditional jumping-off point for Mt Kenya is the town of Naro Moru (below).

NARO MORU

☎ 062

Naro Moru is little more than a string of shops and houses, with a couple of very basic hotels and a market, but it's the most popular starting point for hikes up Mt Kenya.

The best accommodation options are a few kilometres out of town, and both have great campsites. **Mountain Rock Lodge** (☎ 62625, Nairobi 020-242133, 0722-511752; www.mountainrockkenya. com; campsites US$5, standard s/tw KSh3000/4000, superior s/tw KSh3500/5200) is 6km north of Naro Moru, tucked away in the woods less than 1km from the Nanyuki road. It is friendly and reliable, with a spacious dining room, two bars and a lounge.

Naro Moru River Lodge (☎ 31047, Nairobi 020-4443357, 0724-082754; www.alliancehotels.com; campsites US$10, s/tw incl half board from US$61/90; 🏊) is a relaxing lodge about 1.5km north of town with beautifully landscaped gardens. There's a well-equipped campsite and a dormitory block, and campers can use all the hotel facilities.

There are plenty of buses and *matatus* heading to Nanyuki (KSh80, 30 minutes) and Nairobi (KSh350, three hours).

NANYUKI

☎ 062

This small but bustling mountain town makes a living off sales, be it of hikes to climbers, curios to soldiers of the British Army (which has a training facility nearby) or drinks to pilots of the Kenyan Air Force (this is the site of their main air base). For all that mercantilism, it's laid-back for a market town.

The most innovative sleep in town (well, 4km outside of it) is the **Nanyuki River Camel Camp** (☎ 0722-361642; camellot@wananchi.com; off C76 Hwy; campsites US$6, huts without bathroom & incl half board low/high season KSh1500/2500) ecocamp, set off in a dry swab of scrub. Inhabited by 200 camels (available for hire) and a pack of friendly dogs, the camp offers lodging in genuine Somali grass huts imported from Mandera.

Equator Chalet (☎ 31480; theequatorchalet@yahoo. com; Kenyatta Ave; s/tw/d incl breakfast KSh1300/1700/2000) is as plush as it gets if you opt to stay inside the Nanyuki town limits. While it's no four-star hotel, the Equator is welcoming and comfortable.

There are daily buses and *matatus* to Nairobi (KSh400, three hours).

ABERDARE NATIONAL PARK

This **park** (☎ 061-2055024; adult/child US$40/20, smartcard required) protects a striking stretch of moorland, peaks and forest atop the western Kinangop Plateau, and the eastern outcrop of dense rainforest, known as the Salient. Wildlife sightings are dominated by elephants and buffaloes, but black rhinos, giant forest hogs, black servals and rare black leopards are also sometimes seen.

One of the most famous hotels in Kenya, **Treetops** (☎ Nairobi 020-3242425; www.aberdaresafari hotels.com; mid-Apr–mid-Jun s/tw without bathroom & incl full board US$168/225, mid-Jun–Nov & late Dec–early Jan US$277/348, rest of year US$247/312) has long been trading on its reputation, although its weathered exterior belies a certain charm.

Ark (☎ Nairobi 020-216940, 0724-478058; www.choices wild.com; s/tw incl full board low season US$150/210, high season US$180/250) is a modern, upscale version of Treetops, with a fantastic floodlit waterhole that attracts a wider array of animals.

With your own vehicle, you can take the B5 Hwy to the Wanderis, Ark, Treetops or Ruhuruini Gates.

NORTHERN KENYA

ISIOLO

☎ 064

Isiolo is the gateway to northeastern Kenya and a vital pit stop on the long road north. The region is populated by Samburu, Rendille, Boran and Turkana people.

NGO workers' favourite home, the **Bomen Hotel** (☎ 52389; s/tw/ste KSh900/1500/2500) has the town's brightest (ask for one facing outward) and most comfortable rooms.

Around 3km northeast of town is the Dutch-run **Gaddisa Lodge** (☎ 0724-201115; www. gaddisa.com; s/tw KSh3000/4000), where peaceful cottages overlook the fringes of the northern savannah country.

Lots of bus companies serve Nairobi (KSh500, 4½ hours) with most buses leaving between 6am and 6.30am from the main road through town and also stopping at the *matatu* and bus stand just south of the market. Nightly buses creep north to Marsabit (KSh800, nine hours) and Moyale (KSh1500, 20 hours).

MARSABIT
☎ 069

The area surrounding Marsabit is actually a giant shield volcano, whose surface is peppered with hundreds of cinder cones and volcanic craters, many flooded. Mt Marsabit's highest peak, Karantin (1707m), is a rewarding 5km hike from town through lush vegetation and moss-covered trees. The town has an interesting mixture of local tribespeople.

JeyJey Centre (☎ 2296; A2 Hwy; s KSh400, s/tw/tr without bathroom KSh250/400/600) is the best lodge in town. Clean rooms around a colourful courtyard have mosquito nets, and bathrooms have reliable hot water. There's also a TV room, a decent restaurant and an unattractive campsite (per person KSh150).

A bus now connects Marsabit to Moyale (KSh600, 8½ hours). There's no designated stop – simply flag it down on the A2 Hwy as it comes through town around 5pm each day (en route from Nairobi!). The same service heads south to Isiolo (KSh800, 8½ hours) at 9am.

LOYANGALANI

An oasis of palms and natural springs populated by vivid Turkana tribespeople, Loyangalani is one of northern Kenya's most fascinating places. It overlooks Lake Turkana and is surrounded by small ridges of pillow-lava dotted with traditional Turkana stick and palm dwellings. There's little in the way of services.

At the **Palm Shade Camp** (☎ 0726-714768; campsites KSh450, s/tw rondavel without bathroom KSh750/1500), drop your tent on some grass beneath acacias and palms or crash in its tidy domed *rondavels* (round huts). The huts have simple wood beds with foam mattresses and

---

> **DID YOU KNOW?**
>
> ■ Lake Turkana's shoreline is longer than Kenya's entire Indian Ocean coast.
>
> ■ The lake's water level was over 100m higher some 10,000 years ago and used to feed the mighty Nile.
>
> ■ The first Europeans to reach the lake were Austrian explorers Teleki and von Höhnel in 1888. They proudly named it Lake Rudolf, after the Austrian Crown Prince at the time. It wasn't until the 1970s that the Swahili name Turkana was adopted.

---

unique walls with meshed cut-outs that let light and heavenly evening breezes in.

Public transport in these parts is rare, which necessitates having your own private vehicle, preferably one with 4WD and high clearance.

LAKE TURKANA

If you go to Loyangalani you can't help but visit Lake Turkana. Formerly known as Lake Rudolf, and nowadays often evocatively called the 'Jade Sea', vast Lake Turkana stretches all the way to Ethiopia. High salt levels render the sandy, volcanic area around the lake almost entirely barren, but its desolation and stark, surreal beauty contrast with the colourful tribespeople who inhabit the lake's shore.

Made a Unesco World Heritage Site in 1997, **South Island National Park** (adult/child US$20/10) is uninhabited apart from a large croc population, poisonous snakes and feral goats. To get there, you can hire a boat (per hour KSh2500) from Palm Shade Camp (left).

WESTERN KENYA

KISUMU
☎ 057

Set on the sloping shore of Lake Victoria's Winam Gulf, the town of Kisumu is the third-largest in Kenya. Declared a city during its centenary celebrations in 2001, it still doesn't feel like one; its relaxed atmosphere is a world away from the likes of Nairobi and Mombasa.

KENYA

Orientation

Kisumu is a fairly sprawling town, but everything you will need is within walking distance. Most shops, banks, cheap hotels and other facilities can be found around Oginga Odinga Rd, while the train station and ferry jetty are short walks from the end of New Station Rd.

Information

Abacus Cyber Cafe (Al-Imran Plaza, Oginga Odinga Rd; per hr KSh60; ⊙ 8am-8pm) Internet access.
Barclays Bank (Kampala St)
Police station (Uhuru Rd)
Post office (Oginga Odinga Rd)

Sights & Activities

Unlike many local museums, **Kisumu Museum** (Nairobi Rd; admission KSh500; ⊙ 6am-6pm) is an interesting delve through the historical and natural delights of the Lake Victoria region.

Kisumu's **main market** (off Jomo Kenyatta Hwy) is one of Kenya's most animated, and certainly one of its largest, now spilling out onto the surrounding roads. If you're curious or just looking for essentials like suits or wigs, it's worth a stroll around.

Sleeping

Sooper Guest House (☎ 0725-281733; kayamchatur@yahoo.com; Oginga Odinga Rd; s/d/tr KSh800/1000/1500) This spotless ice-cube-white hotel boasts 18 highly sought-after rooms that really are 'sooper'.

Joy Guest House (☎ 0725-074837; Dunga; r with/without bathroom KSh1000/800) Think of a small-town Portuguese pension with a tropical African soundtrack and that's exactly what you get at this charmer, located 3km south of town near Hippo Point's turn-off.

Nyanza Club (☎ 2022433; off Jomo Kenyatta Hwy; s/tw incl breakfast KSh4000/4500; ⊠ ⊠) This recently renovated hotel might feel a little like a Western chain hotel, but after a while in the Kenyan back blocks, that might be no bad thing.

Eating

The fact that Kisumu sits on Lake Victoria isn't lost on restaurants here and fish is abundant. If you want an authentic local fish fry, there is no better place than the dozens of smoky tin-shack restaurants sitting on the lake's shore at Railway Beach at the end of Oginga Odinga Rd. Dive in between 7am and 6pm; a mid-sized fish served with *ugali* (stiff and doughy maize) or rice

is sufficient for two people and will set you back KSh400.

Getting There & Away

Akamba (off New Station Rd) has its own depot in the town's centre. Besides four daily buses to Nairobi (KSh1100 to KSh1350, seven hours) via Nakuru (KSh800, 4½ hours), Akamba also has daily services to Kampala (KSh1350, seven hours). **Easy Coach** (off Mosque Rd) serves similar destinations, as well as Kakamega (KSh250, one hour), with some added comfort and cost.

Matatus offer the only direct services to Kakamega (KSh200, 1½ hours).

KAKAMEGA FOREST RESERVE
☎ 056

This small slab of virgin tropical rainforest is all that's left in Kenya of the once-mighty Guineo-Congolian rainforest. It boasts an extraordinary biodiversity, including 330 species of bird, seven different primate species and around 400 species of butterfly. Excellent official **guides** (per person for short/long walk KSh300/600), trained by the Kakamega Biodiversity Conservation and Tour Operators Association, can help you find birds and monkeys.

Udo's Bandas & Campsite (☎ 30603, 0727-415828; campsites US$5, bandas per person US$10) is a tidy, well-maintained KWS-run campsite with simple *bandas* (thatched-roof huts). Mosquito nets are provided, but bring your own sleeping bag and supplies.

Rondo Retreat (☎ 30268; www.rondoretreat.com; adult/child incl full board KSh7400/5400) has an idyllic setting in a former 1920s saw-miller's residence, about 3km east of Isecheno. Seven cottages, each with striking traditional fittings and large verandahs, sit in gorgeous gardens through which plenty of wildlife passes.

Kakamega is best accessed via Kisumu (see opposite).

MASAI MARA NATIONAL RESERVE

The world-renowned Masai Mara is backed by the spectacular Siria Escarpment, watered by the Mara River and littered with an astonishing amount of wildlife. Its 1510 sq km of open rolling grasslands, the northern extension of the equally famous Serengeti Plains, is breathtaking at any time of year. However, the Mara reaches its pinnacle during the annual wildebeest migration in July and August, when

KENYA

literally millions of these ungainly beasts move north from the Serengeti seeking lusher grass before turning south again around October.

Information

Because most of the gates are located inside the **reserve** (adult/child US$40/20) boundary it is easy to enter the Masai Mara unknowingly. Wherever you enter, make sure you ask for a receipt: it is crucial for passage between the reserve's Narok and Transmara sections and your eventual exit.

Sights & Activities

WILDLIFE DRIVES & WALKS

Whether you're bouncing over the plains in pursuit of elusive elephant silhouettes or parked next to a pride of lions and listening to their bellowed breaths, wildlife drives are *the* highlight of a trip to the Mara.

BALLOONING

If you can afford US$530 (and yes, that is per person), then balloon safaris are superb and worlds away from the minibus circuit. Trips can be arranged through top-end lodges.

MAASAI VILLAGE

The Maasai village between Oloolaimutiek and Sekenani gates welcomes tourists, though negotiating admission can be fraught – prices start as high as KSh1500 per person, but you should be able to wrangle it down to KSh1000 or even a little less. If you're willing to drop this kind of cash for free rein with the camera, go ahead, but don't expect a genuine cultural experience.

Sleeping

OLOOLAIMUTIEK & SEKENANI GATES

Mountain Rock Camp (☎ 0736-149041, 0722-511252; www.mountainrockkenya.com; campsites per tent KSh500, safari tent per person KSh1500, s/d incl full board US$95/165) The simple safari tents here have cloth wardrobes and firm beds and sit in pretty, individual gardens. The camping area is pleasant and you can use the kitchen to prepare your own food or pay for full board.

Kimana Mara (☎ Nairobi 020-217335, 0723-052867; www.kimanamara.com; campsites KSh500, safari tent per person incl half/full board KSh3500/5000) This camp is entirely owned, managed and run by the local community with profits returning to the community as a whole. The camp has several large, clean tents that are nestled under the trees.

Keekorok Lodge (☎ Nairobi 020-532329; s/d incl full board US$350/440; 🏊) The oldest lodge in the Mara has over a hundred rooms and chalets kitted out in a modern tribal style, and despite its size it still manages to retain a personal service.

TALEK GATE

Chake (r per person KSh300) Chake is on the edge of Talek village and is very different to all the other accommodation in and around the reserve. It's a local hotel with tin-roofed cubicles, comfy beds, clean sheets and friendly management.

Aruba Mara Camp (☎ 0723-997524; info@aruba-safaris.com; campsites KSh450, safari tents accommodation only/full board per person KSh4200/6000) The tents are luxuriously appointed, but not overpowering, and have lots of privacy as well as memorable views over the Talek River.

Basecamp Masai Mara (☎ Nairobi 020-577490; www.basecampexplorer.com; s/d incl full board US$155/310) Everything has been thought through in the finest detail in order to reduce its environmental impact. If all this green scheming makes you worry that the accommodation might be rustic, fear not. The safari tents here fall squarely into the divine luxury bracket, and just wait till you get a load of the bathrooms.

Fig Tree Camp (☎ Nairobi 020-605328; www.mada hotels.com; s/d incl full board US$300/400; 🏊) Vegetate on your tent's verandah, watching the Talek's waters gently flow by in this sumptuous camp with its colonial feel.

MUSIARA & OLOOLOLO GATES

Kichwa Tembo Camp (☎ Nairobi 020-3740920; www.kichwatembo.com; campsites incl full board per person US$475; 🏊) Just outside the northern boundary, Kichwa has permanent tents with grass-mat floors, stone bathrooms and tasteful furnishings. Hop in a hammock and take in spectacular savannah views. The food has an excellent reputation.

Governors' Camp (☎ Nairobi 020-2734000; www.governorscamp.com; s/d incl full board US$596/890; 🏊) This camp and Little Governors' Camp (singles/doubles including full board US$652/972, with a swimming pool) are widely regarded as the most magisterial camps in the Mara and offer great service, pleasing riverside locations and activities a-plenty.

KENYA

Getting There & Away

AIR

Airkenya (☎ 020-605745; www.airkenya.com) and **Safarilink** (☎ 020-600777; www.safarilink-kenya.com) each have daily flights to Masai Mara. Return flights on Airkenya are US$237, while Safarilink will get you there and back for US$279.

MATATU, CAR & 4WD

Although it's possible to arrange wildlife drives independently, bear in mind that there are few savings in coming here without transport. That said, it is possible to access Talek and Sekenani Gates from Narok by *matatu*. From Kisii, a *matatu* will get you as far as Kilkoris or Suna on the main A1 Hwy, but you will have problems after this.

For those who drive, the first 52km west of Narok on the B3 and C12 are smooth enough, but after the bitumen runs out you'll find that it gets pretty bumpy. The C13, which connects Oloololo Gate with Lolgorian out in the west, is very rough and rocky, and it's poorly signposted – a highway it's not.

Petrol is available (although expensive) at Mara Sarova, Mara Serena and Keekorok Lodges as well as in Talek village.

THE COAST

MOMBASA

☎ 041 / pop 655,000

If your idea of Africa is roast meat, toasted maize, beer and cattle and farms and friendliness, those things are here. But it's all interwoven into the humid peel of plaster from Hindu warehouses, filigreed porches that lost their way in a Moroccan *riad* (traditional town house), spice markets that escaped India's Keralan coast, sailors chewing *miraa* (shoots chewed as a stimulant) next to boats bound for the Yemeni Hadramat and a giant coral castle built by invading Portuguese sailors. Thus, while this city sits perfectly at home in Africa, it could be plopped anywhere on the coast of the Indian Ocean without too many moving pains. Therein lies Mombasa's considerable charm.

Orientation

The main thoroughfare, Digo Rd and its southern extension Nyerere Ave, runs north–south through the city. The Likoni ferry leaves from the southern end of Nyerere Ave.

Running west from the junction between Nyerere Ave and Digo Rd is Moi Ave, where you'll find the tourist office and a useful landmark – huge aluminium elephant tusks forming an 'M' over the road. Heading east from the junction, Nkrumah Rd provides the easiest access to the Old Town and Fort Jesus.

North of the city centre, Digo Rd becomes Abdel Nasser Rd, where you'll find many of the bus stands for Nairobi and destinations north along the coast. There's another big group of bus offices west of here at the intersection of Jomo Kenyatta Ave and Mwembe Tayari Rd. The train station is at the intersection of Mwembe Tayari and Haile Selassie Rds.

Information

BOOKSHOPS

Bahati Book Centre (Map p724; ☎ 225010; Moi Ave)
Books First (Map p722; ☎ 313482; Nakumatt, Nyerere Ave; 🖳)

EMERGENCY

AAR Health Services (☎ 312409; ⏰ 24hr)
Police (☎ 222121, 999)

INTERNET ACCESS

Blue Room Cyber Café (Map p724; ☎ 224021; www.blueroomonline.com; Haile Selassie Rd; per min KSh2; ⏰ 9am-10pm)

KENYA WILDLIFE SERVICE

KWS office (Map p722; ☎ 312744/5; Nguua Court, Mama Ngina Dr; ⏰ 6am-6pm) Sells and charges smartcards.

MEDICAL SERVICES

Aga Khan Hospital (Map p722; ☎ 312953; akhm@mba.akhmkenya.org; Vanga Rd)
Pandya Memorial Hospital (Map p722; ☎ 229252; Dedan Kimathi Ave)

MONEY

Barclays Bank Nkrumah Rd (Map p724; ☎ 224573); Digo Rd (Map p724; ☎ 311660)
Fort Jesus Forex Bureau (Map p722; ☎ 316717; Ndia Kuu Rd)
Kenya Commercial Bank Moi Ave (Map p724; ☎ 220978); Nkrumah Rd (Map p722; ☎ 312523)

KENYA

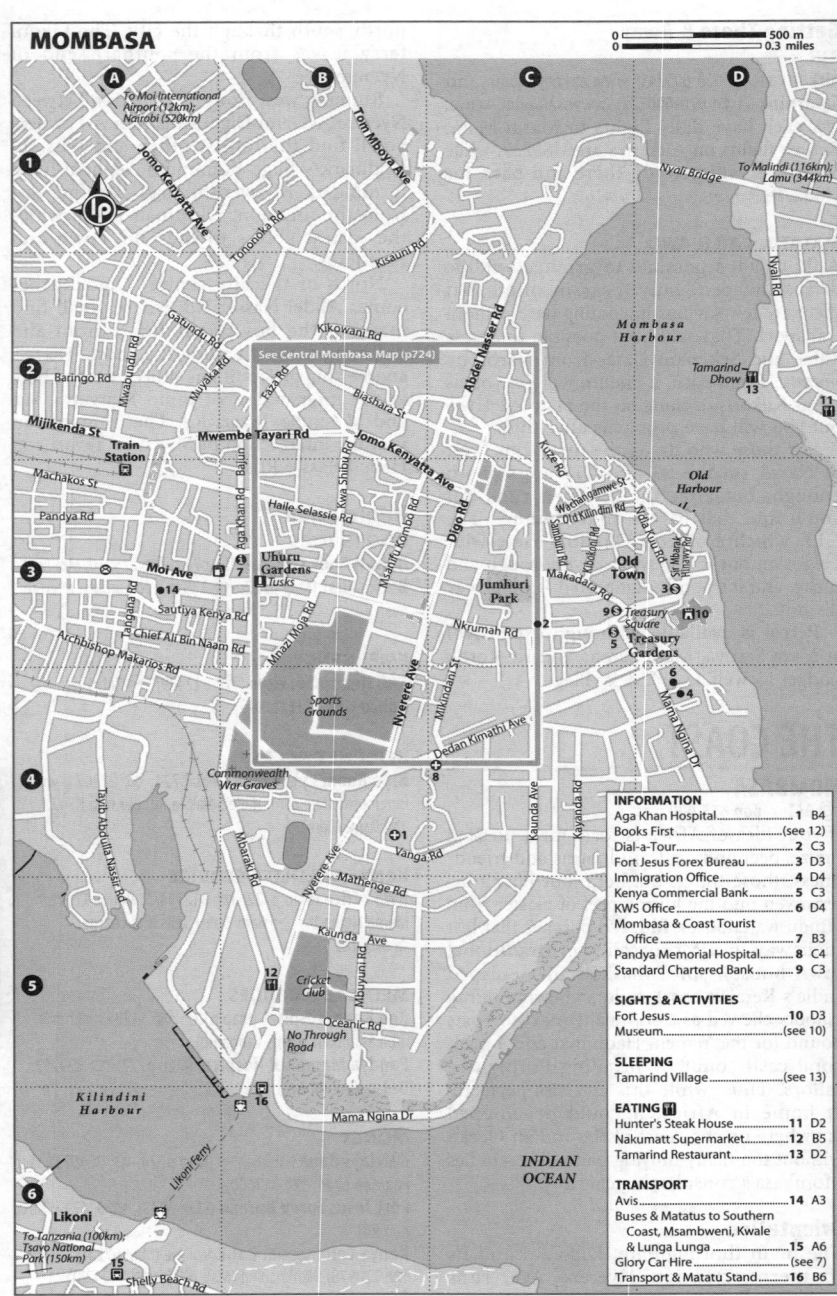

MOMBASA

INFORMATION
Aga Khan Hospital	**1** B4
Books First	(see 12)
Dial-a-Tour	**2** C3
Fort Jesus Forex Bureau	**3** D3
Immigration Office	**4** D4
Kenya Commercial Bank	**5** C3
KWS Office	**6** D4
Mombasa & Coast Tourist Office	**7** B3
Pandya Memorial Hospital	**8** C4
Standard Chartered Bank	**9** C3

SIGHTS & ACTIVITIES
Fort Jesus	**10** D3
Museum	(see 10)

SLEEPING
Tamarind Village	(see 13)

EATING
Hunter's Steak House	**11** D2
Nakumatt Supermarket	**12** B5
Tamarind Restaurant	**13** D2

TRANSPORT
Avis	**14** A3
Buses & Matatus to Southern Coast, Msambweni, Kwale & Lunga Lunga	**15** A6
Glory Car Hire	(see 7)
Transport & Matatu Stand	**16** B6

Pwani Forex Bureau (Map p724; ☎ 221727; Digo Rd)
Standard Chartered Bank (Map p722; ☎ 224614; Treasury Sq, Nkrumah Rd)

POST
Post office (Map p724; ☎ 227705; Digo Rd)

TELEPHONE
Post Global Services (Map p724; ☎ 230581; inglobal@africaonline.co.ke; Maungano Rd; 🕑 7.30am-8pm; 🖳)
Telkom Kenya (Map p724; ☎ 312811) Locations on Nkrumah Rd and Moi Ave.

TOURIST INFORMATION
Mombasa & Coast Tourist Office (Map p722; ☎ 225428; mcta@ikenya.com; Moi Ave; 🕑 8am-4.30pm)

TRAVEL AGENCIES
Dial-A-Tour (Map p722; ☎ 221411; dialatour@ikenya.com; Oriental Bldg, Nkrumah Rd)
Fourways Travel (Map p724; ☎ 223344; Moi Ave)

VISA EXTENSIONS
Immigration office (Map p722; ☎ 311745; Uhuru ni Kari Bldg, Mama Ngina Dr)

Dangers & Annoyances

Mombasa is relatively safe compared to Nairobi, but the streets still clear pretty rapidly after dark so it's a good idea to take taxis rather than walk around alone at night. You need to be more careful on the beaches north and south of town. The Likoni ferry is a bag-snatching hot spot.

Sights

Mombasa's biggest tourist attraction is partially ruined **Fort Jesus** (Map p722), which was built by the Portuguese in 1593 and dominates the harbour entrance. These days it houses a **museum** (☎ 222425; adult/child KSh200/100; 🕑 8am-6pm), which exhibits mostly ceramics, but also finds from the Portuguese frigate *Santo António de Tanná*, and the fascinating culture and traditions of the nine coastal Mijikenda tribes.

Mombasa's **Old Town** (Map p722) doesn't have the medieval charm of Lamu or Zanzibar, but it's still an interesting area to wander around. The houses here are characteristic of coastal East African architecture, with ornately carved doors and window frames and fretwork balconies.

Sleeping

Tana Guest House (Map p724; ☎ 490550; cnr Mwembe Tayari & Gatundu Rds; s/d/tr KSh400/500/600) A simple but friendly place. Rooms are small, tidy and pretty much what you'd expect for the price.

Beracha Guest House (Map p724; ☎ 0725-006228; Haile Selassie Rd; s/d KSh800/1300) This popular central choice is located in the heart of Mombasa's best eat-streets and has variable but clean rooms in a range of unusual shapes.

New Palm Tree Hotel (Map p724; ☎ 311758; Nkrumah Rd; s/d KSh1600/2200) This sociable option has rooms set off a main building that has a terraced roof, and while the amenities (like hot water) aren't always reliable, service is fine and there's a good vibe about the place.

Castle Royal Hotel (Map p724; ☎ 220373, 2222682; www.castlemsa.com; Moi Ave; s/d/tr KSh3500/4500/6000; 🕱 🖳) This slightly boutique place equals the best hotel deal in town (see Tamarind Village, below). Electronic door locks, TVs, air-con, balconies and rooms that actually have a decent design aesthetic all equals joy.

Tamarind Village (Map p722; ☎ 474600; www.tamarind.co.ke; Silos Rd, Nyali; apt KSh9500-20,000; 🕱 🖳 🕿) Located in a modern (and quite elegantly executed) take on a Swahili castle overlooking the blue waters of the harbour, the Tamarind offers crisp, fully serviced apartments with satellite TV, palm-lined balconies and a general sense of whitewashed, sun-lathered luxury.

Eating

Blue Room Restaurant (Map p724; ☎ 224021; www.blueroomonline.com; Haile Selassie Rd; mains KSh200-450; 🖳) Between the steaks, pizzas, curries and... internet access (really!), the Blue Room has basically been constructed to serve the needs of every traveller anywhere.

Shehnai Restaurant (Map p724; ☎ 222847; Fatemi House, Maungano Rd; mains from KSh300; 🕑 noon-2pm & 7.30-10.30pm Tue-Sun) Mombasa's classiest curry house specialises in tandoori and rich *mughlai* (North Indian) cuisine complemented by nice decor.

Hunter's Steak House (Map p722; 'Königsallee', Mkomani Rd, Nyali; mains KSh450-2000; 🕑 Wed-Mon) Where's *'die'* beef? Here, *meine freunde*, at this German-run steakhouse, generally regarded (by tourists and expats) as the best purveyor of cooked cow in town.

Tamarind Restaurant (Map p722; ☎ 474600; Silos Rd, Nyali; mains KSh1100-1800) Big Moorish palace exterior, big jewellery box dining room and a

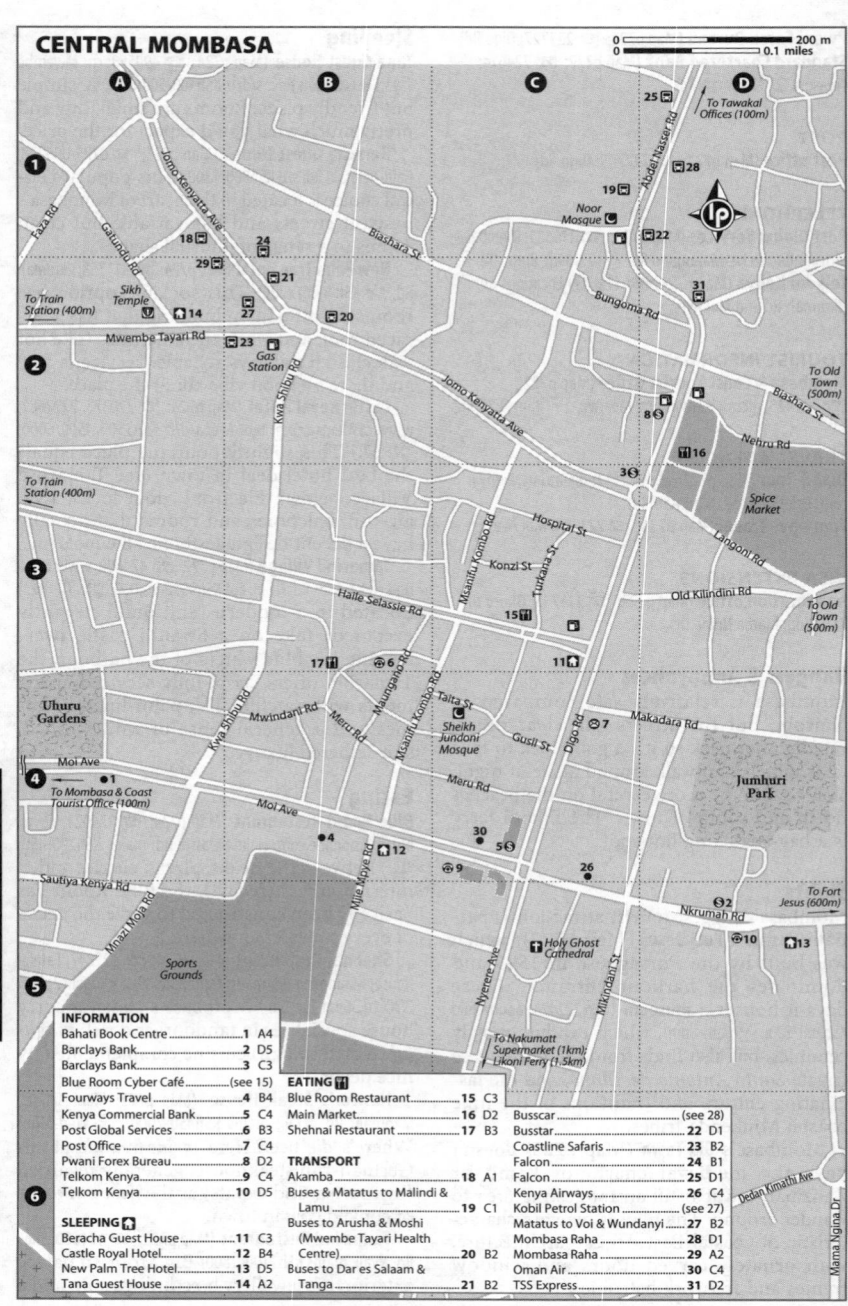

CENTRAL MOMBASA

KENYA

big menu that concentrates on seafood equals big satisfaction (and yeah, a big bill).

There are a couple of self-catering options:

Main market (Map p724; Digo Rd) Mombasa's dilapi-dated 'covered' market is packed with stalls selling fresh fruit and vegetables.

Nakumatt supermarket (Map p722; ☎ 228945; Nyerere Ave) Close to the Likoni ferry, with a good selection of provisions, drinks and hardware items.

Getting There & Away

AIR

Daily flights are available with **Kenya Airways** (Map p724; ☎ 221251; www.kenya-airways.com; TSS Towers, Nkrumah Rd) between Nairobi and Mombasa's **Moi International Airport** (off Map p722; ☎ 433211).

Airkenya (☎ Nairobi 020-605745; www.airkenya.com) doesn't have a ticket office in Mombasa (you can book online), but it also flies between Nairobi and Mombasa once a day.

BUS & MATATU

Daytime services to Nairobi take at least six hours; overnight trips take eight to 10 hours and include a meal/smoking break about halfway. Fares vary from KSh800 to KSh1300. Most companies have at least four departures daily.

There are numerous daily *matatus* and small lorry-buses up the coast to Malindi, leaving from in front of the Noor Mosque on Abdel Nasser Rd. Buses take up to 2½ hours (KSh100), *matatus* about two hours (KSh120). You can also catch an 'express' *matatu* to Malindi (KSh150), which takes longer to fill up but is then supposedly non-stop all the way.

Tawakal, Falcon, Mombasa Raha and TSS Express have buses to Lamu, most leaving at around 7am (report 30 minutes early) from their offices on Abdel Nasser Rd. Buses take around seven hours to reach the Lamu ferry at Mokoke (KSh650 to KSh800), stopping in Malindi (KSh200 to KSh300).

Getting Around

The two Likoni ferries (per pedestrian/car free/KSh35) connect Mombasa Island with the southern mainland, running at frequent intervals throughout the day and night. To get to the jetty from the city centre, take a Likoni *matatu* from Digo Rd (KSh10).

There is currently no public transport to/from the airport, so you're best taking off a taxi; the fare to central Mombasa is around KSh650.

MALINDI
☎ 042

Malindi is lot nicer than its haters realise, and probably not quite as nice as its lovers insist. It's easy to bash the place as an Italian beach resort – which it has undeniably become. But you can't deny it's got a *bella spiaggia* (beautiful beach), and, excuse the stereotype, all those Italians have brought some high gastronomic standards with them.

Orientation

It's no Lamu, but Old Town, which runs from the bus stands to the oceanfront curio market, is filled with narrow streets and medieval Swahili ambience. It also serves as the closest thing to Malindi's 'city centre'. Tourist services, restaurants and bars run from Uhuru Park up Lamu Rd. To the north and south of town and along the water are high-end resorts and expat palaces.

Information

Barclays Bank (☎ 20036; Lamu Rd)
Bling Net (☎ 30041; Lamu Rd; internet per min KSh2)
Dollar Forex Bureau (☎ 30602; Lamu Rd)
KWS office (☎ 20845; malindimnp@kws.org, malindi mnp@swiftmalindi.com) On the coast road south of town.
Post office (Kenyatta Rd)
Standard Chartered Bank (☎ 20130; Stanchart Arcade, Lamu Rd)
Tourist office (☎ 20689; Malindi Complex, Lamu Rd; ⏰ 8am-12.30pm & 2-4.30pm Mon-Fri)

Sights & Activities

The **Malindi Marine National Park** (adult/child US$10/5; ⏰ 7am-7pm) in Kenya covers 213 sq km of rainbow clouds of powder blue fish, organ pipe coral, green sea turtles and beds of Thalassian sea grass.

You'll likely come here on a snorkelling or glass-bottom **boat tour** (around KSh4000 per boat, 5 to 10 people; 2-hour trip), which can be arranged at the KWS office (above). Boats only go out at low tide, so it's a good idea to call in advance to check times (your hotel can help). Most hotels offer diving excursions. Or try:
Aqua Ventures (☎ 32420; www.diveinkenya.com; Driftwood Beach Club)
Blue Fin (☎ 0722-261242; www.bluefindiving.com) Operates out of several Malindi resorts.

KENYA

Sleeping

Ozi's Guest House (☎ 20218; ozi@swiftmalindi.com; Mama Ngina Rd; r KSh1500) Ozi's has long been popular with backpackers, likely because it perches on the attractive edge of Old Town (and next to a mosque – its call to prayer will help you keep time).

Jardin Lorna (☎ 30658; harry@swiftmalindi.com; Mtangani Rd; r KSh2500-3500; 🞩 🖭) Rooms are endearingly quirky, zebra-striped rugs and local art punctuate the interior, and the large family room even has a panic button!

Driftwood Beach Club (☎ 20155; www.driftwood club.com; Mama Ngina Rd; s/d/tr KSh8750/12,500/18,750, cottages KSh35,600; 🞩 🖭) One of the best-known resorts in Malindi, Driftwood prides itself on an informal atmosphere and attracts a more independent clientele than many of its peers.

Kilili Baharini Resort (☎ 20169; www.kililibaha rini.com; Casuarina Rd; s/d incl half board from US$153/182; 🞩 🖭) Italian-run and gorgeous, Kilili's options run between breeze-catching Swahili-inspired suites and a new wing influenced by a lush (but elegantly executed) Arabian nights theme.

Eating

I Love Pizza (☎ 20672; nwright@africaonline.co.ke; Mama Ngina Rd; pizzas KSh250-750, mains from KSh600) We do, too, and the pizza is done really, really well here. Waaay better than you might expect this far from New York or Naples.

Old Man & the Sea (☎ 31106; Mama Ngina Rd; mains KSh400-750, seafood KSh550-1100) The old man of Malindi's dining scene, this Old Man has been serving elegant, excellent cuisine using a combination of local ingredients and fresh recipes for years.

Baby Marrow (☎ 0733-542584; Mama Ngina Rd; mains KSh500-2000) Everything about this place is quirkily stylish, from the thatched verandah and plant-horse to the Italian-based menu and tasty seafood.

Getting There & Away

AIR

There are daily flights with **Airkenya** (☎ 30646; Malindi Airport) to Nairobi. **Kenya Airways** (☎ 20237; Lamu Rd) flies the same route at least once a day. **Mombasa Air Safari** (☎ 041-433061) has daily flights to Mombasa and Lamu (US$62, 30 minutes) in the high season.

BUS & MATATU

There are numerous daily buses to Mombasa (KSh150, two hours). Companies such as Busstar, Busscar, TSS Express and Falcon have offices opposite the old market in the centre of Malindi. All have daily departures to Nairobi (KSh850 to KSh1100, 10 to 12 hours) at around 7am and/or 7pm, via Mombasa. *Matatus* to Watamu (KSh50, one hour) leave from the old market in town.

There are usually at least six buses a day to Lamu. Tawakal buses leave at 8.30am, Falcon at 8.45am and Zam Zam at 10.30am; the fare runs from KSh400 to KSh600. The journey takes at least four hours between Malindi and the jetty at Mokowe (on the mainland, near Lamu). The ferry to Lamu from the mainland costs KSh50 (20 minutes); it's KSh100 for a speedboat.

WATAMU
☎ 042

This small fishing village has evolved into a small expat colony, a string of high-end resorts and a good base for exploring a glut of ruins, national parks and ecosites that are within an easily accessible radius. The main attraction is 7km of pristine beach and a cosy scene that caters to peace, quiet and/or big-game fishing.

Information

There are no banks here, but you can change money at foreign-exchange bureaus at the big hotels and **Tunda Tours** (☎ 32079; Beach Way Rd), which also has internet connection (KSh5 per minute).

Sights & Activities

WATAMU MARINE NATIONAL PARK

The southern part of Malindi Marine National Park, this **marine park** (adult/child US$5/2) includes some magnificent coral reefs and abundant fish life. It lies around 2km offshore from Watamu. To get to the park you'll need to hire a glass-bottomed boat, which is easy enough at the **KWS office** (☎ 32393), at the end of the coast road, where you pay the park fees. For marine park trips, boat operators ask anything from KSh1800 to KSh3500 per person, excluding park fees; it's all negotiable. All the big hotels offer 'goggling' (snorkelling) trips to nonguests for around KSh1500.

GEDE RUINS

Some 4km from Watamu, just off the main Malindi–Mombasa road, are the famous **Gede ruins** (adult/child KSh200/100; 🕒 7am-6pm), one of the principal historical monuments on the coast. Hidden away in the forest is a vast complex of derelict houses, palaces and mosques, made all the more mysterious by the fact that there seem to be no records of Gede's existence in any historical texts.

Sleeping & Eating

Malob Guest House (☎ 32260; Beach Way Rd; s KSh800) This is a cute option: a series of simple rooms set around an open courtyard, comfy and friendly and, for this area, incredibly cheap.

Marijani Holiday Resort (☎ 32448; www.marijani -holiday-resort.com; s/d KSh1950/2500, cottages €38.50-52) Best described as a coral villa, Marijani is a friendly, German-owned place that's probably the best sleep in Watamu village.

Turtle Bay Beach Club (☎ 32003; www.turtlebay. co.ke; s/d/tr KSh5500/6400/7000; ✷ 🖳 🖳) This is easily our favourite top-end resort in Watamu, if not the coast. It's an eco-minded hotel that uses managed tree-cover to hide its environmental imprint, runs enough ecotourism ventures to fill a book (including birdwatching safaris and turtle protection programs), contributes to local charities and all sorts of other do-gooder stuff.

Scary McNasty's (☎ 32500; dishes KSh350-700) With a name like that, how could we not include this place? For the record it's owned by an expat Brit, serves genuine black pudding (not McNasty, if scary) and does a very good line in all the other UK pub greats you may be missing.

Getting There & Around

There are *matatus* between Malindi and Watamu throughout the day (KSh50, one hour). All *matatus* pass the turn-off to the Gede ruins (KSh10). For Mombasa, the easiest option is to take a *matatu* to the highway (KSh10) and flag down a bus or *matatu*. A handful of motorised rickshaws ply the village and beach road; a ride to the KWS office should cost around KSh250.

LAMU

☎ 042

Few would dispute that the Lamu archipelago forms the most evocative destination on the Kenyan coast. Lamu town itself has that excel-lent destination quality of immediately standing out as you approach it from the water. The shopfronts and mosques, faded under the relentless kiss of the salt wind, creep out from behind a forest of dhow masts. Then you take to the streets, or more accurately, the labyrinth: donkey-wide alleyways; robed children grinning from the alleys; women whispering by in full length *bui-bui* (black cover-all garment worn by Islamic women outside the home); cats casually ruling the rooftops; blue smoke from meat grilling over open fires; and the organic, biting scent of cured wood affixed to a town house made of stone and coral. Many visitors call this town, the oldest living one in East Africa, the highlight of their trip to Kenya. Residents call it Kiwa Ndeo – the Vain Island – and, to be fair, there's plenty for them to be vain about.

Orientation

Although there are several restaurants and places to stay along the waterfront (Harambee Ave), most of the guesthouses are tucked away in the maze of alleys behind. Lamu's main thoroughfare is Kenyatta Rd, a long winding alley known popularly as 'Main St', which runs from the northern end of town, past the fort, and then south to the Muslim cemetery and the inland track to Shela village. If you walk west the town peters out in a series of row houses, then fields, then nothing.

Information

Immigration office (☎ 633032) There's an office off Kenyatta Rd near the fort where you should be able to get visa extensions, although travellers are sometimes referred to Mombasa (p723).

Kenya Commercial Bank (☎ 633327; Harambee Ave) The only bank on Lamu that has an ATM.

King Fadh Lamu District Hospital (☎ 633012) One of the most modern and well-equipped hospitals on the coast. It's south of the town centre.

Lamu Medical Clinic (☎ 633438; Kenyatta Rd; 🕒 8am-9pm)

Lynx Infosystems (internet per min KSh2; 🕒 8am-10pm) Inside Lamu Fort.

Post office (Harambee Ave) Postal services and cardphones.

Tourist information office (☎ 633132; Kenyatta Rd; 🕒 9am-1pm & 2-4pm)

Sights & Activities

All of Lamu's museums are open from 8am to 6pm daily. Admission to each is KSh500/250

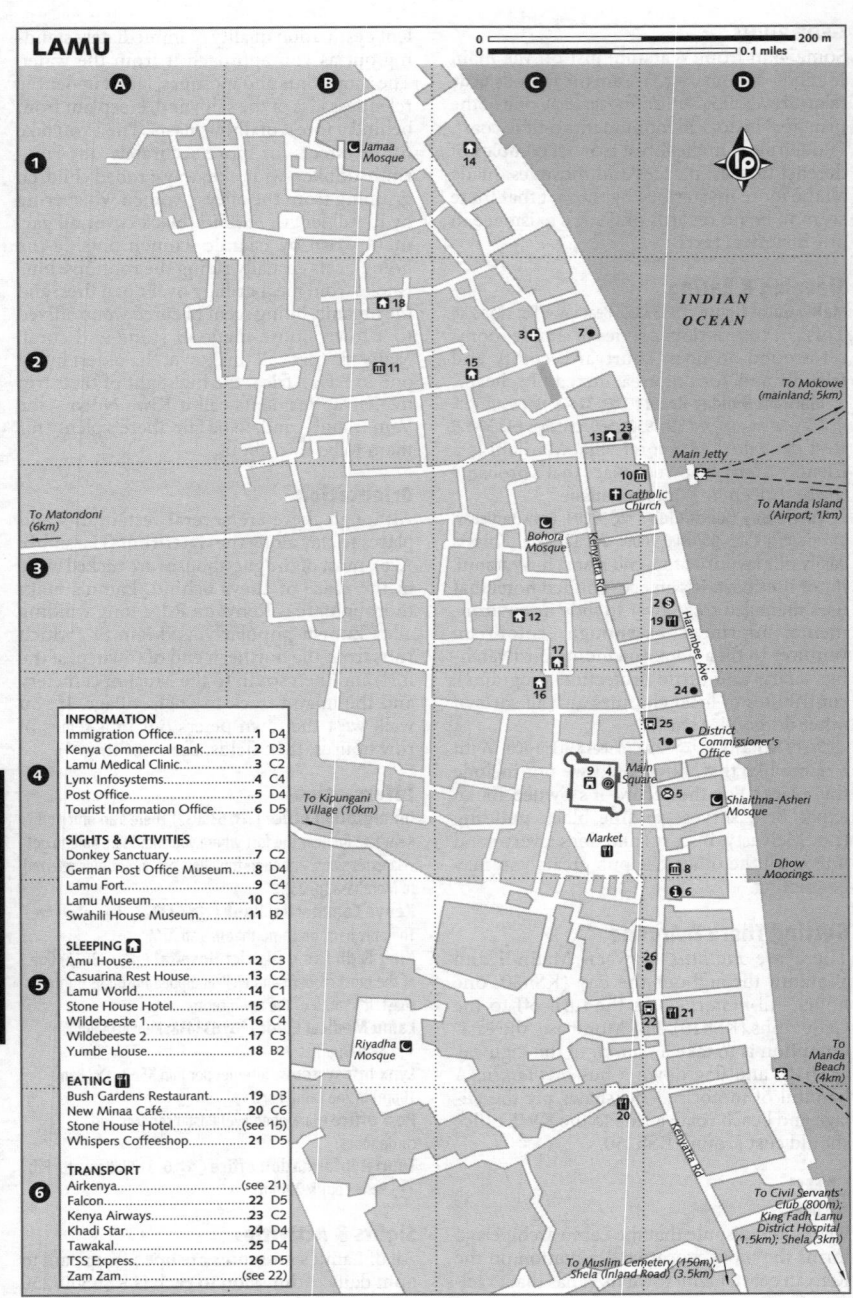

LAMU

0 ——————— 200 m
0 ——————— 0.1 miles

INDIAN OCEAN

To Mokowe
(mainland; 5km)

Main Jetty

To Manda Island
(Airport; 1km)

To Matondoni
(6km)

Catholic Church

Bohora Mosque

Jamaa Mosque

Swahili House Museum

To Kipungani
Village (10km)

Main Square

District Commissioner's Office

Shiaithna-Asheri Mosque

Market

Dhow Moorings

Riyadha Mosque

To Manda Beach
(4km)

To Civil Servants'
Club (800m);
King Fadh Lamu
District Hospital
(1.5km); Shela (3km)

To Muslim Cemetery (150m);
Shela (Inland Road) (3.5km)

INFORMATION
Immigration Office....................1 D4
Kenya Commercial Bank..........2 D3
Lamu Medical Clinic..................3 C2
Lynx Infosystems.......................4 C4
Post Office..................................5 D4
Tourist Information Office.........6 D5

SIGHTS & ACTIVITIES
Donkey Sanctuary......................7 C2
German Post Office Museum......8 D4
Lamu Fort...................................9 C4
Lamu Museum...........................10 C3
Swahili House Museum.............11 B2

SLEEPING 🏠
Amu House................................12 C3
Casuarina Rest House................13 C2
Lamu World...............................14 C1
Stone House Hotel....................15 C2
Wildebeeste 1...........................16 C4
Wildebeeste 2...........................17 C3
Yumbe House............................18 B2

EATING 🍴
Bush Gardens Restaurant.........19 D3
New Minaa Café.......................20 C6
Stone House Hotel...............(see 15)
Whispers Coffeeshop................21 D5

TRANSPORT
Airkenya...............................(see 21)
Falcon.......................................22 D5
Kenya Airways..........................23 C2
Khadi Star.................................24 D4
Tawakal....................................25 D4
TSS Express...............................26 D5
Zam Zam.............................(see 22)

KENYA

per (nonresident) adult/child, which is frankly extortionate.

The best museum in town is housed in a grand Swahili warehouse on the waterfront. The **Lamu Museum** is as good a gateway as you'll get into Swahili culture in general, and that of the archipelago in particular.

The preserved **Swahili house museum**, tucked away to the side of Yumbe House hotel, is beautiful, and a great site for those who love Swahili architecture.

Some say the squat castle of **Lamu fort** lords it over other structures on the island, but we think its distinctive muscularity sets it off from Lamu's elegant Swahili aesthetic.

In the late 1800s, the German East Africa Company set up a post office, and the old building is now the **German post office museum** (Kenyatta Ave), exhibiting photographs and memorabilia.

With around 3000 donkeys active on Lamu, *Equus asinus* is still the main form of transport here, and the **donkey sanctuary** (☎ 633303; Harambee Ave; admission free; ⏰ 9am-1pm Mon-Fri) was established by the International Donkey Protection Trust of Sidmouth, UK, to improve the lot of the island's hard-working beasts of burden.

Taking a **dhow trip** is almost obligatory and drifting through the mangroves is a wonderful way to experience the islands. Prices vary depending on where you want to go and how long you go for; with a bit of bargaining you should pay around KSh500 per person.

Sleeping

Casuarina Rest House (☎ 633123; s/d KSh400/800, s/d/tr without bathroom KSh300/500/700) This is a budget bargain: an Escher-esque tilted palace with a social lounge rooftop, fun staff and a general sense of that feel-good backpacker-y camaraderie you'd have to be an ogre not to love.

Yumbe House (☎ 633101; lamuoldtown@africaonline. co.ke; s/d/tr low season KSh1000/2100/2900, high season KSh1290/2700/3860) This coral castle – yup, you read that right! – has impressive carved-out rooms decorated with pleasant Swahili accents, open-air verandahs that are open to the stars and the breeze, and a ridiculously romantic top-floor suite.

Wildebeeste 1&2 (☎ 32261, 0723-6874008; www. wildebeeste.com; apt KSh1500-6000) A combination art gallery/hotel, the Wildebeeste buildings are stuffed with all manner of generally eccentric stuff, and the Swahili aesthetic is realised

in a classy but playful manner. The staff is fantastically friendly and in touch with many local artists.

Amu House (☎ 633420; www.amuhouse.com; s/d/tr KSh2200/2800/3500) This restored 16th-century Swahili 'house' feels more like an urban medieval Sultan's retreat, set with fine wooden doors, a spacious, red-tiled courtyard and wonderfully carved out rows of *vidakah* (wall niches).

Stone House Hotel (☎ 633544; s incl half board US$55-70, d incl half board US$90-110) This Swahili mansion is set into a Fez-like alleyway and is notable for its fine, whitewashed walls and fantastic rooftop, which includes a superb restaurant with excellent views over the town and waterfront.

Lamu World (☎ 633491; www.lamuworld.com; Harambee Ave; s/d €175/225; 🖳 🖳) A thoroughly modern but absolutely luxurious hotel. It looks like an old Swahili villa, but it feels like a contemporarily decked out four-star resort where they've blended the pale, breezy romance of the Greek islands into an African palace.

Eating

New Minaa Café (meals KSh120-200; ⏰ 6.30am-midnight) This is the place to eat Swahili food with Swahilis. Its version of fish (grilled or fried) and chips is pretty decent, as is the atmosphere of rowdy locals yelling at the nightly news.

Bush Gardens Restaurant (☎ 633285; Harambee Ave; mains KSh180-800) Bush Gardens is the template for a whole set of restaurants along the waterfront, offering breakfasts and seafood – excellent fish, top-value 'monster crab' and the inevitable lobster in Swahili sauce.

Whispers Coffeeshop (Kenyatta Rd; mains KSh240-750; ⏰ 9am-9pm) For a fresh pizza, real cup of cappuccino or the best desserts in town, we highly recommend this garden cafe, set in the same building as the Baraka House gallery.

Stone House Hotel (☎ 633544; mains KSh250-750; ⏰ noon-2pm & 7-9pm) This is a fine rooftop restaurant that really catches the breeze. The wonderful panorama of the town and seafront is matched by the quality of the food. There are usually several choices for lunch or dinner, and menus often feature crab and grilled barracuda.

Drinking & Entertainment

Along the waterfront towards Shela village, the Civil Servants' Club is virtually the only reliable spot for a drink and a dance at weekends.

KENYA

It's small, loud, rowdy and great fun, though women travelling alone should run for cover.

Getting There & Away

AIR

Airkenya (☎ 633445; Baraka House, Kenyatta Rd) offers daily afternoon flights between Lamu and Wilson Airport in Nairobi.

Kenya Airways (☎ 633155; Casuarina House, Harambee Ave) has daily afternoon flights between Lamu and the domestic terminal at Nairobi's Jomo Kenyatta International Airport.

The airport servicing Lamu is on Manda Island and the ferry across the channel to Lamu costs KSh100. You will be met by 'guides' at the airport who will offer to carry your bags to the hotel of your choice for a small consideration (about KSh200).

BUS

There are booking offices for several bus companies on Kenyatta Rd (including Falcon, Khadi Star, Tawakal, TSS Express and Zam Zam). The going rate for a trip to Mombasa is KSh600 to KSh700; most buses leave between 7am and 8am, so you'll need to be at the jetty at 6.30am to catch the boat to the mainland. Tawakal also has 10am and 1pm bus services. It takes at least four hours to get from Lamu to Malindi, plus another two hours to Mombasa. Book early.

Getting Around

There are ferries (KSh50) between Lamu and the bus station on the mainland (near Mokowe). Boats leave when the buses arrive at Mokowe; in the reverse direction, they leave at around 6.30am to meet the departing buses. Ferries between the airstrip on Manda Island and Lamu cost KSh100 and leave about half an hour before the flights leave. Expect to pay KSh200 for a custom trip if you miss either of these boats.

Between Lamu and Shela village there are plenty of motorised dhows in either direction throughout the day until around sunset; these cost about KSh150 per person and leave when full.

SHELA

Shela is sort of like Lamu put through a high-end wringer. It's cleaner and more medievally 'authentic' in spots, mainly because a lot of the houses have been lovingly done up by expats, who make up a sizeable chunk

of the population. As a result, Shela feels somewhere between the East African coast and a swish Greek island, which you'll find either off-putting or appealing based on your travelling tastes.

Most people are here for the **beach** – a 12km-long sweep of sand where you're guaranteed an isolated spot to pitch your kit and catch some rays. But as locals say, 'Yana vuta kwa kasi' – 'There is a violent current there'. And no lifeguards. Tourists drown every year, so don't swim out too far. Some backpackers camp in the long dunes behind the beach, but you risk a mugging if you do so.

Dodo Villas/Talking Trees Campsite (☎ 633500; campsites per tent KSh400, r KSh600-1200, apt per person KSh200) is Lamu's main budget beach option. Its nominal identity crisis reflects the varied nature of the accommodation: the main building has large, unfussy rooms, and several concrete blocks hold apartments for up to 10 people, with more being built.

Shella Pwani Guest House (☎ 633540; d KSh3000-3500) is a lovely Swahili house is all decked out with carved plasterwork and pastel accents. Some rooms have fine sea views, as does the airy roof terrace, and the bathrooms are the best in Shela – they're modelled to look like kiblahs (mosque niches).

If there were a capital of Shela it would be located at the **Peponi Hotel** (☎ 633421; www.peponi-lamu.com; r high season from US$230; ☒ closed May & Jun; ☒): this top-end resort has a grip on everything in this village, from tours to watersports to whatever the hell else you can imagine.

There are waterfront restaurants all over, but the **Stopover Restaurant** (☎ 633459; mains KSh250-800) has friendly staff and excellent grub (of the spicy Swahili seafood sort), which make it the clear cut above the competition.

To get to Shela, you can take a motorised dhow from the moorings at Lamu for KSh150 per person (or KSh250 to KSh300 for a solo ride). Alternatively, you can walk it in about 40 minutes.

SOUTHERN KENYA

AMBOSELI NATIONAL PARK

While it may lack the profusion of wildlife found at Masai Mara and Lake Nakuru, Kenya's third-most popular park boasts one of the country's most spectacular backdrops, namely Mt Kilimanjaro. Africa's highest peak broods over the southern boundary of the park, and while cloud cover can render the mountain's massive bulk invisible for much of the day, you'll be rewarded with some stunning vistas when the weather clears. Amboseli is also prime elephant country, so add this park to your safari itinerary if you want to shoot some pics of these monolithic beasts.

Information

At 392 sq km, Amboseli is a small **national park** (☎ 045-622251; www.kws.org/amboseli.html; adult/child US$40/20, smartcard required), though the landscape provides limited cover for wildlife. The vegetation here used to be much denser, but rising salinity, damage by elephants and irresponsible behaviour by safari vehicles has caused terrible erosion.

Sights & Activities

Amboseli's permanent swamps of Enkongo Narok and Olokenya create a marshy belt across the middle of the park. These spots are the centre of activity for elephants, hippos, buffalo and water birds, while the surrounding grasslands are home to grazing antelopes. Spotted hyenas are plentiful, and jackals, waterhogs, olive baboons and vervet monkeys all occur. Lions can still be found in Amboseli, although the once famous black-maned lions are no longer here. Black rhinos are also absent – the few that survived a sustained period of poaching were moved to Tsavo West National Park in 1995.

Sleeping & Eating

KWS campsite (campsites per adult/child US$10/2) Just inside the southern boundary of the park, with toilets, an unreliable water supply (bring your own) and a small bar selling warm beer and soft drinks.

Amboseli Sopa Lodge (☎ Nairobi 020-3750460; www.sopalodges.com/amboseli/home.html; s/d low season US$71/142, high season US$142/198; ☒) Located just outside the park boundaries on the road to Tsavo National Park, the Sopa Lodge offers a clutch of clay huts that are decked out in lavish safari spreads and a healthy smattering of Kenyan curios.

Ol Tukai Lodge (☎ Nairobi 020-4445514; www.ol tukailodge.com; s/d low season US$150/180, high season US$210/255; ☒) Lying at the heart of Amboseli on the edge of a dense acacia forest, Ol Tukai is a splendidly refined lodge with soaring *makuti* (thatched palm-leaved) roofs and tranquil gardens defined by towering trees.

Amboseli Serena Lodge (☎ Nairobi 020-2710511; www.serenahotels.com/kenya/amboseli/home.asp; s/d low season US$155/255, high season US$285/385; ☒) The poshest property in Amboseli, the Serena is comprised of fiery-red adobe cottages that overlook the wildlife-rich Enkongo Narok swamp, and are fringed by lush tropical gardens of blooming flowers and manicured shrubs.

Getting There & Away

AIR
Airkenya (www.airkenya.com) has daily flights (around US$175) between Wilson Airport in Nairobi and Amboseli. You'll need to arrange with one of the lodges or a safari company for a vehicle to meet you at the airstrip.

CAR & 4WD
The usual approach to Amboseli is via Namanga. The road is sealed and in surprisingly good condition from Nairobi to Namanga. If you're heading to Tsavo, convoys leave from the turn-off near the Sopa Lodge at scheduled times – enquire at your lodge as they change frequently.

TSAVO NATIONAL PARK

At nearly 21,000 sq km, Tsavo National Park is by far the largest national park in Kenya. For administrative and practical purposes, it has been split into Tsavo West National Park (9000 sq km; see below) and Tsavo East National Park (11,747 sq km; see p732), divided by the Nairobi–Mombasa road (A109). For information on how to explore the park, see the boxed text, p732.

Tsavo West National Park

Tsavo West covers a huge variety of landscapes, from swamps, natural springs and rocky peaks to extinct volcanic cones, rolling plains and sharp outcrops dusted with greenery. But for all of its diversity, Tsavo West is not a park where you will see animals constantly (although there are still some black rhinos here). Indeed, much of its appeal lies in its dramatic scenery and sense of space. If possible, come here with some time to spare,

EXPLORING TSAVO NATIONAL PARK

Both the Tsavo West and Tsavo East National Parks feature some excellent scenery, but the undergrowth here is considerably higher than in Amboseli or Masai Mara, so it takes a little more effort to spot the wildlife, particularly the big predators. The compensation for this is that the landscapes are some of the most dramatic in Kenya, the animals are that little bit wilder, and the parks receive few visitors compared to the hordes who descend on Amboseli and the Mara.

The northern half of Tsavo West is the most developed, with a number of excellent lodges, as well as several places where you can get out of your vehicle and walk. The landscape is also striking, and is largely comprised of volcanic hills and sweeping expanses of savannah. The southern part of the park, on the far side of the dirt road between Voi and Taveta on the Tanzanian border, is rarely visited.

Tsavo East is more remote, though most of the action here is concentrated along the Galana River – the north part of the park isn't truly secure due to the threat of banditry. The landscape here is drier, with rolling plains hugging the edge of the Yatta Escarpment, a vast prehistoric lava flow.

Entry is US$40/20 per adult/child per day, and camping at KWS campsites is US$10/5 per adult/child; as the two parks are administered separately you have to pay separate entrance fees for each. Both use the smartcard system – you'll need enough credit for your entry fee and any camping charges for as long as you're staying. Smartcards can be bought and recharged at the Voi Gate to Tsavo East.

There's a small **visitor centre** (admission free; ☼ 8am-5pm) near the Mtito Andei Gate to Tsavo West, with interesting displays on conservation issues and some of the animals and birds in the park.

rather than a need to dash about and tick off animals – if you get off the beaten path here, you could have it all to yourself.

SLEEPING

KWS campsites (per adult/child US$10/5) The public sites are at Komboyo, near the Mtito Andei Gate, and at Chyulu, just outside the Chyulu Gate. Facilities are basic, so make sure you're prepared to be self-sufficient. There are also some small independently run campsites along the shores of Lake Jipa.

Ngulia Bandas (☎ Voi 043-30050; bandas from US$55) This hillside camp is Tsavo's best luxury bargain, offering thatched tent-fronted stone cottages on the edge of the escarpment overlooking a stream where leopards are known to hide out. Meals cost from US$10 to US$15.

Severin Safari Camp (☎ Mombasa 041-5485001; www.severin-kenya.com; s/d low season US$78/156, high season US$159/224) Severin Safari Camp is a fantastic complex of thatched luxury tents with affable staff, Kilimanjaro views from the communal lounge area and nightly hippo visitations.

Kilaguni Serena Lodge (☎ 045-340000; www.serena hotels.com; s/d/ste low season US$115/225/575, high season US$320/435/700; 🖳 🕭) The centrepiece here is a splendid bar and restaurant overlooking a busy illuminated waterhole, though the extravagant suites are practically cottages in their own right, boasting chintzy living rooms and epic balconies.

GETTING THERE & AWAY

The main access to Tsavo West is through the Mtito Andei Gate on the Mombasa–Nairobi road in the north of the park, where you'll find the park headquarters and visitor centre. The main track cuts straight across to Kilaguni Serena Lodge and Chyulu Gate. Security is a problem here, so vehicles for Amboseli travel in armed convoys, leaving Kilaguni Serena Lodge at 8am and 10am.

Tsavo East National Park

Despite the fact that one of Kenya's largest rivers flows through the middle of the park, the landscape in Tsavo East is markedly flatter and drier than in Tsavo West. However, the contrast between the permanent greenery of the river and the endless grasses and thorn trees that characterise much of the park is visually arresting. In comparison to its more developed brother, Tsavo East doesn't see as many visitors, though it has an undeniable wild and primordial charm.

SLEEPING & EATING

Ndololo Camp (adult/child US$10/5) There's a single public camping area with basic facilities near Kanderi Swamp.

Tarhi Camp (☎ Mombasa 041-5486378; www.camp -tarhi.de; s/d incl half board US$65/120) This German-run campsite, located on the edge of the Voi River about 14km east of Voi Gate, is a good compromise between bare-bones camping and over-the-top luxury.

Voi Safari Lodge (☎ Mombasa 041-471861; s/d low season US$88/115, high season US$118/165; 🏊) Just 4km from Voi Gate, Voi Safari is a long, low complex perched on the edge of an escarpment overlooking an incredible sweep of savannah.

Kilalinda (☎ Nairobi 020-882598; www.privatewilder ness.com; s/d low season US$350/550, high season US$400/650; 🏊) This very fine ecolodge was built without felling a single tree, and the owners are spearheading a campaign to reintroduce wildlife to areas that were depleted by poachers in previous decades.

GETTING THERE & AWAY

The main track through the park follows the Galana River from the Tsavo Gate to the Sala Gate. Most tourist safaris enter Tsavo East via the Sala Gate, where a good dirt road runs east for 110km to the coast. If you're coming from Nairobi, the Voi Gate (near the town of the same name) and the Manyani Gate (on the Nairobi–Mombasa road) are just as accessible.

KENYA DIRECTORY

ACCOMMODATION

Kenya has a good range of accommodation options, from basic cubicle hotels overlooking city bus stands to luxury tented camps hidden away in the national parks. There are also all kinds of campsites, budget tented camps, simple *bandas* (often thatched-roof wooden huts) and cottages scattered around the parks and rural areas.

In this chapter we have classed budget accommodation listings as those under KSh1000, midrange between KSh1000 and KSh3500, and top-end over KSh3500. You will find rates quoted in shillings, US dollars or euros.

ACTIVITIES
Ballooning

It's definitely worth saving up your shillings for the incomparable experience of watching wildlife while floating silently above the savannah plains in a hot-air balloon. Flights are currently available in the Masai Mara (see p720).

Diving & Snorkelling

The Malindi Marine National Park (p725) offers opportunities for snorkelling and scuba diving. October to March is the best time; silt affects visibility during June, July and August.

Hiking & Climbing

For proper mountain hiking, look no further than Mt Kenya (p715), the country's greatest high-altitude challenge.

KENYA

PRACTICALITIES

- Major newspapers and magazines in Kenya include the *Daily Nation*, the *East African Standard*, the *East African*, the *Weekly Review* and the *New African*.

- KBC Radio broadcasts throughout the country on various FM frequencies. Most major towns also have their own local music and talkback stations, and the BBC World Service is easily accessible.

- KBC and NTV are the main national TV stations; the CNN, Sky and BBC networks are also widely available on satellite or cable (DSTV).

- Kenyan televisual equipment uses the standard European NSTC video system.

- Kenya uses the 240V system, with square three-pin sockets as used in the UK. Bring a universal adaptor if you need to charge your phone or run other appliances.

- Kenya uses the metric system; distances are in kilometres and most weights are in kilograms.

Wildlife Safaris

Kenya is one of the greatest wildlife-watching destinations on earth and virtually every visitor to Kenya goes on safari at least once. There are seemingly endless safari operators to choose from, and it's worth spending some time to select a reliable one that matches your budget and itinerary. It's worth checking with the **Kenyan Association of Tour Operators** (KATO; ☎ 020-713348; www.katokenya. org) in Nairobi before making a booking.

BUSINESS HOURS

Banks Banking hours are from 9am to 3pm Monday to Friday and from 9am to 11am on Saturday.
Government offices Open from 8am or 8.30am to 1pm and from 2pm to 5pm Monday to Friday.
Internet cafes Generally keep longer evening hours and may open on Sunday.
Post offices, shops and services Open roughly from 8am to 5pm Monday to Friday and 9am to noon on Saturday.
Restaurants As a rule cafes open at around 6am or 7am and close in the early evening, while more expensive ethnic restaurants will be open from 11am to 10pm daily, sometimes with a break between lunch and dinner.

CUSTOMS REGULATIONS

There are strict laws about taking wildlife products out of Kenya. The export of products made from elephant, rhino and sea turtle is prohibited. The collection of coral is also not allowed. Ostrich eggs will be confiscated unless you can prove you bought them from a certified ostrich farm. Always check to see what permits are required, especially for the export of any plants, insects and shells.

The usual regulations apply to items you can bring into the country: 50 cigars, 200 cigarettes, 250g of pipe tobacco, 1L of alcohol and 250mL of perfume. Obscene publications are banned, which may extend to some lads' magazines.

DANGERS & ANNOYANCES

A little street sense goes a long way here, and getting the latest local information is essential wherever you intend to travel throughout Kenya.

Banditry

Wars in Somalia, Sudan and Ethiopia have all affected stability and safety in northern and northeastern Kenya. However, tourists are rarely targeted and security has also improved considerably in previously high-risk areas, such as the Isiolo–Marsabit, Marsabit–Moyale and Malindi–Lamu routes. You should always check the situation locally before taking these roads, or travelling between Garsen and Garissa or Thika.

Crime

The country's biggest problem is crime, ranging from petty snatch theft and mugging to violent armed robbery, carjacking and corruption. As a visitor you needn't feel paranoid, but you should always keep your wits about you, particularly at night.

Perhaps the best advice for when you're walking around cities and towns is not to carry anything valuable with you. Most hotels provide a safe or secure place for valuables, although you should be cautious of the security at some budget places.

Always take taxis after dark or along lonely dirt roads. In the event of a crime, you'll need to get a police report if you intend to make an insurance claim.

Scams

At some point in Kenya you'll almost certainly come across people who play on the emotions and gullibility of foreigners. Nairobi is a particular hot spot, with 'friendly' approaches a daily, if not hourly, occurrence. You should always ignore any requests for money. Be sceptical of strangers who claim to recognise you in the street, and anyone who makes a big show of inviting you into the hospitality of their home probably has ulterior motives. The usual trick is to bestow some kind of gift upon the delighted traveller, who then becomes emotionally blackmailed into reciprocating to the order of several hundred shillings.

EMBASSIES & CONSULATES

A selection of countries that maintain diplomatic missions in Kenya are listed here. Missions are located in Nairobi unless otherwise stated.
Australia (Map pp708-9; ☎ 020-445034; www.embassy.gov.au/ke.html; ICIPE House, Riverside Dr, Nairobi)
Canada (off Map pp708-9; ☎ 020-3663000; www.nairobi.gc.ca; Limuru Rd, Nairobi)
Ethiopia (Map pp708-9; ☎ 020-2732050; State House Ave, Nairobi)
France (Map pp710-11; ☎ 020-316363; www.ambafrance-ke.org; Barclays Plaza, Loita St, Nairobi)

Germany (off Map pp708-9; ☎ 020-4262100; www.nairobi.diplo.de; 113 Riverside Dr, Nairobi)

Israel (Map pp708-9; ☎ 020-2722182; http://nairobi.mfa.gov.il; Bishops Rd, Nairobi)

Netherlands (off Map pp708-9; ☎ 020-4447412; Riverside Lane, Nairobi)

South Africa (off Map pp708-9; ☎ 020-2827100; Roshanmaer Pl, Lenana Rd, Nairobi)

Spain (Map pp710-11; ☎ 020-26568; International House, Mama Ngina St, Nairobi)

Sudan (off Map pp708-9; ☎ 020-575159; www.sudanembassynrb.org; Kabernet Rd, off Ngong Rd, Nairobi)

Tanzania (Map pp710-11; ☎ 020-311948; Reinsurance Plaza, Aga Khan Walk, Nairobi)

Uganda High Commission (off Map pp708-9; ☎ 020-4445420; www.uganda highcommission.co.ke; Riverside Paddocks, Nairobi); Consular section (Map pp710-11; ☎ 020-311814; Uganda House, Kenyatta Ave, Nairobi)

UK (Map pp708-9; ☎ 020-2844000; www.britishhighcommission.gov.uk/kenya; Upper Hill Rd, Nairobi)

USA (off Map pp708-9; ☎ 020-3636000; http://nairobi.usembassy.gov; United Nations Ave, Nairobi)

EMERGENCIES

The countrywide emergency number for ambulance, fire and police services is ☎ 999.

FESTIVALS & EVENTS

The major events around Kenya include the following:

Maulid Festival Falling in March or April for the next few years, this annual celebration of the prophet Mohammed's birthday is a huge event in Lamu town.

Tusker Safari Sevens (www.safarisevens.com) International rugby tournament held every June near Nairobi.

Kenya Music Festival (☎ 020-2712964) The country's longest-running music festival, held over 10 days in August in Nairobi.

Mombasa Carnival (zainab@africaonline.co.ke) November street festival, with music, dance and other events.

East African Safari Rally (www.eastafricansafarirally.com) Classic car rally now more than 50 years old, covering Kenya, Tanzania and Uganda using only pre-1971 vehicles. Held in December.

HOLIDAYS

Muslim festivals are significant events along the coast. Many eateries in the region close until after sundown during the Muslim fasting month of Ramadan.

Other public holidays in Kenya include the following:

New Year's Day 1 January
Good Friday and Easter Monday March/April
Labour Day 1 May

Mataranka (Self-Rule) Day 1 June
Moi Day 10 October
Kenyatta Day 20 October
Independence Day 12 December
Christmas Day 25 December
Boxing Day 26 December

INTERNET ACCESS

Most towns have at least one internet cafe (and Nairobi has lots) where you can surf and access webmail accounts or instant-messenger programs and Skype. Rates are cheapest in Nairobi and Mombasa (as little as KSh1 per minute), rising to up to KSh20 per minute in rural areas and top-end hotels.

MAPS

Bookshops, especially the larger ones in Nairobi, are the best places to look for maps in Kenya. The *Tourist Map of Kenya* gives good detail, as does the *Kenya Route Map*; both cost around KSh250.

The most detailed and thorough maps are published by the Survey of Kenya; many are out of print, but the better bookshops in Nairobi usually have copies of *Amboseli National Park* (SK 87), *Masai Mara Game Reserve* (SK 86), *Tsavo East National Park* (SK 82) and *Tsavo West National Park* (SK 78).

MONEY

The unit of currency is the Kenyan shilling (KSh), which is made up of 100 cents. Notes in circulation are KSh1000, 500, 200, 100, 50 and 20, and there are also new coins of KSh40, 20, 10, 5 and 1 in circulation.

The euro, US dollar and British pound are all easy to change throughout the country. Cash is easy and quick to exchange at banks and foreign-exchange bureaus; travellers cheques are not as widely accepted and often carry high commission charges.

Virtually all banks in Kenya have ATMs at most branches. Barclays Bank has the most reliable ATMs for international withdrawals, with ATMs in most major Kenyan towns supporting MasterCard, Visa, Plus and Cirrus international networks.

Credit cards are becoming increasingly popular, although connections fail with tedious regularity. Visa and MasterCard are now widely accepted, but it would be prudent to stick to upmarket hotels, restaurants and shopping centres to use them.

KENYA

Tipping is not common practice among Kenyans, but most tourist guides and all safari drivers and cooks will expect some kind of gratuity at the end of your tour or trip.

POST

The Kenyan postal system is run by the government Postal Corporation of Kenya, now rebranded as the dynamic-sounding **Posta** (www.posta.co.ke). Letters sent from Kenya rarely go astray, but can take up to two weeks to reach Australia or the USA. Incoming letters to Kenya can be sent care of poste restante to any town. Make sure your correspondents write your name in block capitals and also underline the surname. They take anywhere from four days to a week to reach the poste-restante service in Nairobi.

TELEPHONE

The Kenyan fixed-line phone system, run by **Telkom Kenya** (www.telkom.co.ke), is more or less functional. International call rates from Kenya are relatively expensive, though you can save serious cash by using voice-over-IP programs like Skype. Operator-assisted calls are charged at the standard peak rate, but are subject to a three-minute minimum. You can always dial direct using a phonecard. All phones should be able to receive incoming calls (the number is usually scrawled in the booth somewhere). The international dialling code for Kenya is ☎ 254. Kenyan phone numbers have an area code followed by a four- to seven-digit number.

More than two-thirds of all calls in Kenya are now made on mobile phones, and coverage is good in all but the furthest rural areas. Kenya uses the GSM 900 system, which is compatible with Europe and Australia but not with the North American GSM 1900 system. If you have a GSM phone, check with your service provider about using it in Kenya, and beware of high roaming charges. Remember that you will generally be charged for receiving calls abroad as well as for making them.

Alternatively, if your phone isn't locked into a network, you can pick up a prepaid starter pack from one of the Kenyan mobile-phone companies – the main players are **Safaricom** (www.safaricom.co.ke) and **Celtel** (www.ke.celtel.com). A SIM card costs about KSh100, and you can then buy top-up 'scratchcards' from shops and booths across the country. Cards come in denominations of KSh100 to

KSh2000; an international SMS costs around KSh10, and voice charges vary according to tariff, time and destination of call.

With the new Telkom Kenya phonecards, any phone can now be used for prepaid calls – you just have to dial the **access number** (☎ 0844) and enter in the number and passcode on the card. There are booths selling the cards all over the country. Cards come in denominations of KSh200, KSh500, KSh1000 and KSh2000, and call charges are slightly more expensive than for standard lines.

TIME

Time in Kenya is GMT/UTC plus three hours year-round. You should also be aware of the concept of 'Swahili time', which perversely is six hours out of kilter with the rest of the world. Noon and midnight are 6 o'clock (*saa sitta*) Swahili time, and 7am and 7pm are 1 o'clock (*saa moa*). Just add or subtract six hours from whatever time you are told; Swahili doesn't distinguish between am and pm.

VISAS

Visas are now required by almost all visitors to Kenya, including Europeans, Australians, New Zealanders, Americans and Canadians, although citizens from a few smaller Commonwealth countries are exempt. Visas (US$50/€40/£30) are valid for three months from the date of entry and can be obtained on arrival at Jomo Kenyatta International Airport in Nairobi. Tourist visas can be extended for a further three-month period – see below.

Under the East African partnership system (see also the boxed text, opposite), visiting Tanzania or Uganda and returning to Kenya does not invalidate a single-entry Kenyan visa, so there's no need to get a multiple-entry visa unless you plan to go further afield. The same applies to single-entry Tanzanian and Ugandan visas, though you do still need a separate visa for each country you plan to visit. Always check the latest entry requirements with embassies before travel.

Visa Extensions

Visas can be renewed at immigration offices during normal office hours, and extensions are usually issued on a same-day basis. Staff at the immigration offices are generally friendly

---

NEWS FLASH

In a July 2009 meeting of the East African Community (EAC), tourism and immigration officials from Tanzania, Kenya, Uganda, Rwanda and Burundi approved the long-discussed single tourist visa. Once implemented, the single visa will allow travellers to visit all five countries in the region. The target date for introduction of the visa has been set for June 2010, which might be rather optimistic, but it's well worth checking for an update with the relevant embassies when setting your plans.

---

and helpful, but the process takes a while. You'll need two passport photos and KSh2200 for a three-month extension. You also need to fill out a form registering as an alien if you're going to be staying more than 90 days. Immigration offices are only open Monday to Friday; note that the smaller offices may sometimes refer travellers back to Nairobi or Mombasa for visa extensions.

Local immigration offices:

Kisumu (1st fl, Reinsurance Plaza, cnr Jomo Kenyatta Hwy & Oginga Odinga Rd)

Lamu (Map p728; ☎ 042-633032) Off Kenyatta Rd.

Malindi (☎ 042-30876; Mama Ngina Rd)

Mombasa (Map p722; ☎ 041-311745; Uhuru ni Kari Bldg, Mama Ngina Dr)

Nairobi (Map pp710-11; ☎ 020-222022; Nyayo House, cnr Kenyatta Ave & Uhuru Hwy)

Visas for Onward Travel

Since Nairobi is a common gateway city to East Africa and the city centre is easy to get around, many travellers spend some time here picking up visas for other countries that they intend to visit. If you are going to do this, you need to plan ahead and call the embassy to confirm the hours that visa applications are received (these change frequently in Nairobi). Most embassies will want you to pay visa fees in US dollars (see p734 for contact details).

Just because a country has an embassy or consulate here, it doesn't necessarily mean you can get that country's visa. The borders with Somalia and Sudan are both closed, so you'll have to go to Addis Ababa in Ethiopia if you want a Sudanese visa, and Somali visas are unlikely to be available for the foreseeable future.

For Ethiopia, Tanzania and Uganda, three-month visas are readily available in Nairobi and cost US$50 for most nationalities. Two passport photos are required for applications and visas can usually be issued the same day.

TRANSPORT IN KENYA

GETTING THERE & AWAY

Air

Most international flights to and from Nairobi are handled by **Jomo Kenyatta International Airport** (NBO; off Map pp708-9; ☎ 020-825400; www.kenyaairports.co.ke), 15km southeast of the city. Some flights between Nairobi and Kilimanjaro International Airport or Mwanza in Tanzania, as well as many domestic flights, use **Wilson Airport** (WIL; off Map pp708-9; ☎ 020-501941), which is 6km south of the city centre on Langata Rd. The other arrival point in the country is **Moi International Airport** (MBA; off Map p722; ☎ 041-433211) in Mombasa, 12km west of the city centre, but apart from flights to Zanzibar this is mainly used by charter airlines and domestic flights.

Kenya Airways is the main national carrier, and has a generally good safety record, having had just one fatal incident since 1977.

The following are airlines flying to and from Kenya, with offices in Nairobi except where otherwise indicated:

African Express Airways (3P; ☎ 020-824333; Wilson Airport)

Air India (AI; Map pp710-11; ☎ 020-340925; www.airindia.com)

Air Madagascar (MD; ☎ 020-225286; www.airmadagascar.mg)

Air Malawi (QM; ☎ 020-240965; www.airmalawi.net)

Air Mauritius (MK; ☎ 020-229166; www.airmauritius.com)

Air Zimbabwe (UM; ☎ 020-339522; www.airzim.co.zw)

Airkenya (QP; ☎ 020-605745; www.airkenya.com)

British Airways (BA; Map pp710-11; ☎ 020-244430; www.british-airways.com)

Daallo Airlines (D3; ☎ 020-317318; www.daallo.com)

Egypt Air (MS; Map pp710-11; ☎ 020-226821; www.egyptair.com.eg)

Emirates (EK; Map pp710-11; ☎ 020-211187; www.emirates.com)

Ethiopian Airlines (ET; Map pp710-11; ☎ 020-330837; www.ethiopianairlines.com)

KENYA

Gulf Air (GF; ☎ 020-241123; www.gulfairco.com)
Jetlink Express (J0; ☎ 020-244285; www.jetlink.co.ke)
Kenya Airways (KQ; Map pp710-11; ☎ 020-3274100; www.kenya-airways.com)
KLM (KL; Map pp710-11; ☎ 020-3274747; www.klm.com)
Oman Air (WY; Map p724; ☎ 041-221444; www.oman-air.com)
Precision Air (PW; ☎ 020-602561; www.precisionairtz.com)
Qatar Airways (QR; www.qatarairways.com)
Rwandair (WB; ☎ 0733-740703; www.rwandair.com)
Safarilink (☎ 020-600777; www.safarilink-kenya.com) Kilimanjaro only.
SN Brussels Airlines (SN; ☎ 020-4443070; www.flysn.com)
South African Airways (SA; ☎ 020-229663; www.saakenya.com)
Swiss International Airlines (SR; ☎ 020-3744045; www.swiss.com)

Land
ETHIOPIA
With the ongoing problems in Sudan and Somalia, Ethiopia offers the only viable overland route into Kenya from the north. The security situation around the main entry point at Moyale (Ethiopia) is changeable, and although the border is usually open, security problems have forced its closure several times. Cattle- and goat-rustling are rife in the area, triggering frequent cross-border tribal wars, so make sure you check the security situation carefully before attempting this crossing.

TANZANIA
The main land borders between Kenya and Tanzania are at Namanga, Taveta, Isebania and Lunga Lunga, and can be reached by public transport. There is also a crossing from the Serengeti (Tanzania) to the Masai Mara, which can only be undertaken with your own vehicle and if you are an East African resident or citizen, and one at Oloitokitok, which is closed to tourists.

Main bus companies serving Tanzania include the following:
Akamba (☎ 020-340430; akamba_prs@skyweb.co.ke; Nairobi) Daily buses between Mwanza and Nairobi (12 to 14 hours).
Davanu Shuttle (☎ 057-8142; Arusha) Arusha/Moshi shuttle buses.
Easy Coach (☎ 020-210711; easycoach@wananchi.com; Nairobi)

Impala Arusha (☎ 027-250 7197/8448/8451; Impala Hotel, cnr Moshi & Old Moshi Rds, Arusha); Nairobi (☎ 020-2730953; Silver Springs Hotel)
Riverside Shuttle Arusha (☎ 027-250 2639/3916; riverside_shuttle@hotmail.com; booking office Sokoine Rd, departure point Bella Luna, Moshi Rd) Nairobi (☎ 020-229618, 020-241032; Pan African Insurance House, 3rd fl, Room 1, Kenyatta Ave, departure point Parkside Hotel, Monrovia St) Arusha/Moshi shuttle buses.
Scandinavia Express (Map pp710-11; ☎ 020-247131; Nairobi) Daily buses between Dar es Salaam and Mombasa (10 hours), between Dar es Salaam and Nairobi via Arusha (13 hours), between Mwanza and Nairobi (12 to 14 hours) and between Tanga and Mombasa (four to five hours).

UGANDA
Numerous bus companies run between Nairobi and Kampala, or you can do the journey in stages via Malabar (Kenya), or Busia if you are travelling via Kisumu.

Main bus companies serving Uganda include the following:
Akamba (Map pp710-11; ☎ 020-340430; akamba_prs@skyweb.co.ke)
Falcon (☎ 020-229692)
Scandinavia Express (Map pp710-11; ☎ 020-247131)

GETTING AROUND
Air
Four domestic operators, including the national carrier Kenya Airways, run scheduled flights within Kenya. Destinations served are predominantly around the coast and the popular southern national parks.

Book well in advance (essential during the tourist high season) with all these airlines. You should also remember to reconfirm return flights 72 hours before departure, especially when connecting with an international flight.

Airlines flying domestically:
Airkenya (☎ 020-605745; www.airkenya.com) Amboseli, Lamu, Masai Mara, Malindi, Nanyuki.
Kenya Airways (☎ 020-3274100; www.kenya-airways.com) Kisumu, Lamu, Malindi, Mombasa.
Mombasa Air Safari (☎ 041-433061; www.mombasaairsafari.com) Amboseli, Lamu, Malindi, Masai Mara, Mombasa, Tsavo.
Safarilink (☎ 020-600777; www.safarilink-kenya.com) Amboseli, Lamu, Masai Mara, Naivasha, Nanyuki, Tsavo West.

Bus
Kenya has an extensive network of long- and short-haul bus routes, with good coverage of

the areas around Nairobi, the coast and the western regions. Buses offer varying levels of comfort, convenience and roadworthiness, but as a rule services are frequent, fast and often quite comfortable. The downside is the often diabolical condition of Kenya's roads.

Car & Motorcycle

There are numerous car-hire companies who can hire you anything from a small hatchback to Toyota Land Cruiser 4WDs, although hire rates are some of the highest in the world.

An International Driving Permit (IDP) is not necessary in Kenya, but can be useful.

HIRE

Hiring a vehicle to tour Kenya (or at least the national parks) is an expensive way of seeing the country, but it does give you freedom of movement and is sometimes the only way of getting to remote areas.

A minimum age of between 23 and 25 years usually applies for hirers. Some companies prefer a licence with no endorsements or criminal convictions, and most require you to have been driving for at least two years. You will also need acceptable ID, such as a passport.

All the international companies have airport and/or town offices in Nairobi and Mombasa. Most safari companies will also hire out their vehicles, though you have few of the guarantees that you would with the companies listed here. **Let's Go Travel** (☎ 020-340331; www.letsgosafari.com) organises reliable car hire at favourable rates through partner firms.

Local and international hire companies:

Avenue Car Hire (Map pp710–11; ☎ 020-313207; www.avenuecarhire.com; Nairobi)

Avis (Map pp710–11; ☎ 020-316061; www.avis.co.ke; Nairobi) Also in Mombasa (Map p722).

Budget (Map pp710–11; ☎ 020-223581; www.budget -kenya.com; Nairobi)

Central Rent-a-Car (Map pp710–11; ☎ 020-222888; www.carhirekenya.com; Nairobi)

Glory Car Hire (Map pp710–11; ☎ 020-225024; www. glorycarhire.com; Nairobi) Also in Mombasa (Map p722).

ROAD HAZARDS

Driving practices in Kenya are some of the worst in the world and all are carried out at break-neck speed. Kenyans habitually drive on the wrong side of the road in order to avoid potholes or animals – flashing your lights at these vehicles should be enough to persuade

the driver to get back into their own lane. Never drive at night unless you absolutely have to, as very few cars have adequate headlights and the roads are full of pedestrians and cyclists.

Hitching

Hitching is never entirely safe in any country in the world, and we don't recommend it. Travellers who decide to hitchhike should understand that they are taking a small but potentially serious risk; it's safer to travel in pairs and let someone know where you are planning to go.

Local Transport

MATATU

Local *matatus* are the main means of getting around for local people, and any reasonably sized city or town will have plenty of services covering every major road and suburb. Fares start at KSh10 and may reach KSh40 for longer routes in Nairobi.

Matatus now comply with new safety laws, and must be fitted with seatbelts and 80km/h speed governors; conductors and drivers must wear clearly identifiable red shirts, route numbers must be displayed and a 14-person capacity applies to vehicles that used to cram in as many as 30 people. Frequent police checks have also been brought in to enforce the rules.

Matatus leave when full and the fares are fixed. Wherever you're going, remember that most *matatu* crashes are head-on collisions – under no circumstances should you sit in the 'death seat' next to the *matatu* driver. Play it safe and sit in the middle seats away from the window.

SHARED TAXI (PEUGEOT)

Shared Peugeot taxis make a good alternative to *matatus*, though they're not subject to the same regulations. Peugeots are quicker than *matatus* and so are slightly more expensive, but they also are commonly involved in horrific smashes. Many companies have offices around the Accra, Cross and River Rds area in Nairobi.

TAXI

You'll find taxis on virtually every corner in the larger cities, especially in Nairobi and Mombasa, where taking a taxi at night is virtually mandatory. Fares are invariably

KENYA

negotiable and start at around KSh200 for short journeys.

Train

The Uganda Railway was once the main trade artery in East Africa, but these days the network has dwindled to two main routes, Nairobi–Kisumu and Nairobi–Mombasa. At the time of research however, only the Nairobi–Mombasa train was running, and there remain a few question marks over the comfort and reliability of this route. Indeed, with a night service of around 13 hours, the Nairobi–Mombasa train is much slower and less frequent than going by air or road.

There are three classes on Kenyan trains, but only 1st and 2nd class can be recommended. Fares are US$65 in 1st class, US$54 in 2nd class, including bed and breakfast. Note that passengers are divided by gender.

First class consists of two-berth compartments with a washbasin, wardrobe, drinking water and a drinks service. Second class consists of plainer, four-berth compartments with a washbasin and drinking water. No compartment can be locked from the outside, so remember not to leave any valuables lying

around if you leave it for any reason. You might want to padlock your rucksack to something during dinner and breakfast. Always lock your compartment from the inside before you go to sleep. Third class is seats only and security can be a real problem.

Passengers in 1st class on the Mombasa line are treated to a meal that typically consist of stews, curries or roast chicken served with rice and vegetables. Tea and coffee are included; sodas (soft drinks), bottled water and alcoholic drinks are not, so ask the price before accepting that KSh1500 bottle of wine. Cold beer is available at all times in the dining car and can be delivered to your compartment.

There are booking offices in Nairobi and Mombasa, and it's recommended that you show up in person rather than trying to call. You must book in advance for 1st and 2nd class; otherwise there'll probably be no berths available. Two to three days is usually sufficient, but remember that these services run just three times weekly in either direction. Note that compartment and berth numbers are posted up about 30 minutes prior to departure.

Rwanda

Mention Rwanda to just about anyone with the smallest measure of geopolitical conscious and they'll no doubt recall images of the horrific genocide that brutalised this tiny country in 1994. In the span of just three months, an estimated 800,000 Tutsis and moderate Hutus were systematically butchered by the Interahamwe in one of the most savage genocides recorded in modern history.

Rwanda has done a remarkable job of healing its wounds and turning towards the future with a surprising measure of optimism. The government has taken measures to eliminate the labels associated with a tribal identity and successfully rallied the country under the unifying Rwandan banner.

Forming a natural frontier with the Democratic Republic of Congo (DRC, formerly Zaïre) and Uganda, the Virunga volcanoes are home to some of the world's last remaining mountain gorillas. Tracking these primate relatives through bamboo forests and equatorial jungles is for many the highlight of their African travels.

Travellers in East Africa are often unsure about crossing the border into Rwanda, given the country's grim history. However, the country remains stable and peaceful, and its attempts to build a sustainable ecotourism industry are certainly worth your support.

FAST FACTS

- **Area** 26,338 sq km
- **ATMs** None that accepts international cards
- **Borders** Burundi, Democratic Republic of Congo (DRC, formerly Zaïre), Tanzania, Uganda
- **Budget** US$50 to US$75 per day, but tracking gorillas will cost some serious cash
- **Capital** Kigali
- **Languages** Kinyarwanda, French and English
- **Money** Rwandan franc (RFr); US$1 = RFr571, €1 = RFr828
- **Population** 10.2 million
- **Seasons** Wet (mid-March to mid-May, mid-October to mid-December), dry (mid-May to mid-October, mid-December to mid-March)
- **Telephone** Country code ☎ 250; international access code ☎ 00
- **Time** GMT/UTC +2
- **Visa** US$60 for three months; available on arrival; single East African tourist visa expected to be introduced soon (see p737)

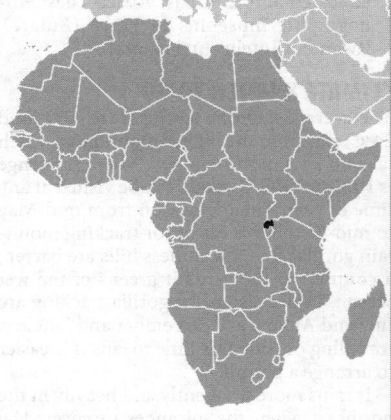

RWANDA

HOW MUCH?

- **Tracking the mountain gorillas** US$500

- **Fresh fish at a decent restaurant** US$5 to US$10

- **Internet access per hour** US$1 to US$2

- **New Times newspaper** US$0.50

- **100km bus ride** US$2

LONELY PLANET INDEX

- **1L petrol** US$1 to US$2

- **1L bottled water** US$0.75

- **Bottle of Primus beer 720ml** US$2

- **Souvenir T-shirt** US$10

- **Beef brochettes** US$1

HIGHLIGHTS

- **Parc National des Volcans** (p750) Hike along the forested-slopes of the Virungas in search of silverback gorillas.
- **Parc National de Nyungwe** (p752) Hike through steamy rainforests in search of colobus monkeys and chimpanzees.
- **Gisenyi** (p751) Kick back with a passion-fruit cocktail on the sandy shores of Lake Kivu.
- **Kigali Memorial Centre** (p747) Confront the horrors of the genocide at this haunting memorial on the outskirts of the capital.
- **National Museum of Rwanda** (p752) Get educated at one of East Africa's best ethnographic museums in Huye (Butare), Rwanda's intellectual capital.

CLIMATE & WHEN TO GO

The average daytime temperature is around 24°C, except in the higher mountains, which take up a lot of the country, where the range is 10°C to 15°C. Rwanda can be visited at any time of year. The dry season from mid-May to mid-October is easier for tracking mountain gorillas, but the endless hills are barren, a contrast to the verdant greens of the wet season. Peak seasons for gorilla tracking are July and August and December and January; travelling outside this time means it is easier to arrange a permit.

It rains more frequently and heavily in the northeast, where the volcanoes are covered by rainforest. The summit of Karisimbi (4507m), the highest peak in Rwanda, is often covered with sleet or snow.

ITINERARIES

- **One Week** Concentrate on the north of the country. Pay your respects at the Kigali Memorial Centre (p747) before heading for the brooding volcanoes that form the border between Rwanda, Uganda and the DRC. Track the gorillas at Parc National des Volcans (p750), one of life's ultimate experiences. Head west to Gisenyi (p751), the coastal riviera town on Lake Kivu, and chill out on the sands.
- **Two Weeks** Kick off from the capital Kigali, and head south to the intellectual heartland of Huye (Butare; p752) and its magnificent national museum. Spend a few days at Parc National de Nyungwe (p752) to see the huge troupes of chimps and Angolan colobus monkeys. Continue up the shores of Lake Kivu to Gisenyi (p751) before heading east to Parc National des Volcans (p750) to meet the majestic mountain gorillas.

HISTORY
Early Days

The original Rwandans, the Twa pygmies, were gradually displaced by bigger groups of migrating Hutu tribespeople from AD 1000. Later came the Tutsi from the north, arriving from the 16th century onwards. The authority of the Rwandan *mwami* (king) was far greater than that of his opposite number in Burundi, and the system of feudalism that developed here was unsurpassed in Africa outside Ethiopia. Tutsi overlordship was reinforced by ceremonial and religious observance.

European Meddling

The Germans took the country in 1890 and held it until 1916, when their garrisons surrendered to Belgian forces during WWI. During Belgian rule, the power and privileges of the Tutsi increased, as the new masters found it convenient to rule indirectly through the *mwami* and his princes.

However, in 1956 Mwami Rudahigwa called for independence from Belgium and the Belgians began to switch allegiance to the Hutu majority. The Tutsi favoured fast-track independence, while the Hutus wanted the introduction of democracy first.

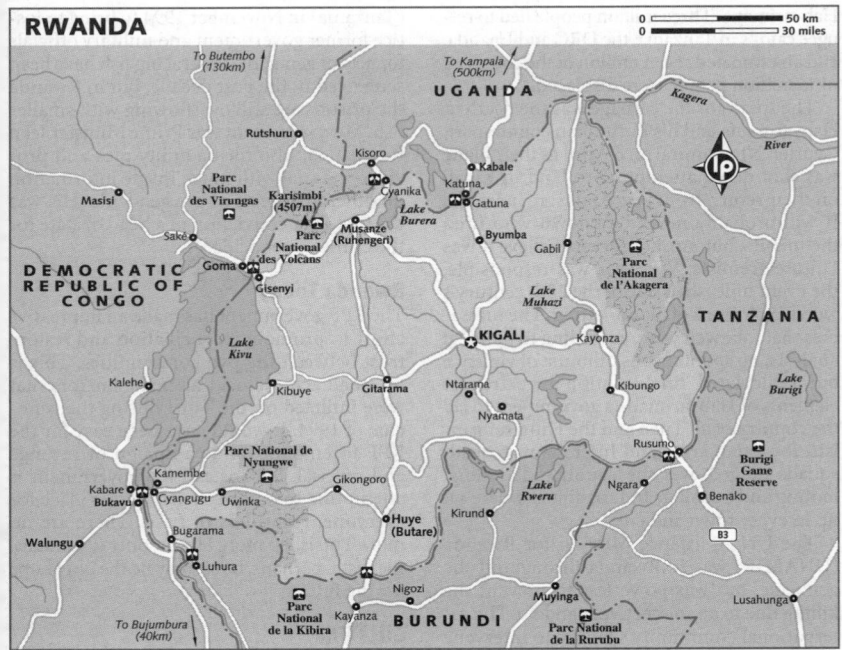

Following the death of the *mwami* in 1959, armed clashes began between the two tribes, marking the start of an ethnic conflict that was to culminate in the 1994 genocide (see right). Tutsi fled the country in numbers, resettling in neighbouring Uganda, Kenya and Tanzania.

Following independence in 1962, the Hutu majority came to power under Prime Minister Gregoire Kayibanda. The new government introduced quotas for Tutsis, limiting opportunities for education and work, and small groups of Tutsi exiles began to launch guerrilla raids from neighbouring Uganda. In the round of bloodshed that followed, thousands more Tutsis were killed by Hutus and Hutu-sympathisers and tens of thousands fled to neighbouring countries.

A Simmering Conflict

The massacre of Hutus in Burundi in 1972 (see p635) reignited the old hatreds in Rwanda and prompted the army commander, Major General Juvenal Habyarimana, to oust Kayibanda in 1973. Habyarimana made some progress towards healing the ethnic divisions

during the early years of his regime, but before long it was business as usual.

In October 1990, the entire intertribal issue was savagely reopened when 5000 well-armed rebels of the Rwandan Patriotic Front (RPF), a Tutsi military front, invaded Rwanda from their bases in western Uganda. Two days later, at Habyarimana's request, France, Belgium and Zaïre (as the DRC was then known) flew in troops to assist the Rwandan army to repulse the rebels.

The RPF invaded again in 1991, this time better armed and prepared. By early 1992 the RPF was within 25km of Kigali. A cease-fire was cobbled together and the warring parties brought to the negotiating table. A peace accord between the government and the RPF was finally signed in August 1993.

The Genocide

In 1994, the conflict erupted again on an incomprehensible scale. An estimated 800,000 Rwandans were killed in just three months, mostly by Interahamwe militias – gangs of youths armed with machetes, guns and other weapons supplied by officials close to

RWANDA

Habyarimana. Three million people fled to refugee camps in Tanzania, the DRC and Uganda, and an estimated seven million of the country's nine million people were displaced.

The spark for the carnage was the death of Habyarimana and his Burundian counterpart, Cyprien Ntaryamira, on 6 April as their plane was shot down attempting to land in Kigali on their return from peace talks in Tanzania. It will probably never be known who fired the missile, but most observers believe it was Hutu extremists. Whoever was responsible, the event unleashed one of the 20th century's worst explosions of blood-letting. The massacres that followed were, according to political analysts, no spontaneous outburst of violence but a calculated 'final solution' by extremist elements of Habyarimana's government to rid the country of all Tutsi and the Hutu reformists. Rwandan army and Interahamwe death squads ranged over the countryside killing, looting and burning, and roadblocks were set up in every town and city.

The UN Assistance Mission for Rwanda (UNAMIR) was in Rwanda throughout the genocide, but was powerless to prevent the killing due to an ineffective mandate. The international community's failure to intervene effectively to help the local population left Rwanda to face its fate. By the time UNAMIR was finally reinforced in July, it was too late. The genocide was already over and the RPF had taken power in Kigali.

The Aftermath

Hutu extremists and their allies fled into eastern DRC to regroup and launched cross-border raids into both Rwanda and Burundi from the refugee camps in the Goma and Uvira regions. Rwanda responded with raids into eastern DRC and support for Tutsi rebels north of Goma.

The Hutu fought alongside the Congolese army, and the entire situation turned ugly, as one million or so refugees were caught in the middle. But the RPF and their allies soon swept across the DRC, installing Laurent Kabila in power and breaking the grip of the extremists on the camps. However, they soon decided Kabila was not such a reliable ally and became embroiled in Africa's biggest war to date, fighting over the DRC's mineral wealth with nine other African states.

The **International Criminal Tribunal for Rwanda** (www.ictr.org) was established in Arusha (Tanzania) in November 1994 to bring to justice former government and military officials for acts of genocide. Several big fish have been sentenced in the past decade, but in Rwanda the prisons are still overflowing with smaller fish. Most important was Prime Minister Jean Kambanda, who filed a guilty plea and provided the trial with much inside information on other architects of the genocide. His was the first-ever conviction of a head of state for the crime of genocide.

Rwanda Today

The RPF government has made an impressive effort to promote reconciliation and restore trust between the two communities. This is no small achievement after the horrors that were inflicted on the Tutsi during the genocide of 1994. It would have been easy for the RPF to embark on a campaign of revenge and reprisal, but instead the government is attempting to build a society with a place for everyone, regardless of tribe. There are no more Tutsis, no more Hutus, only Rwandans. Idealistic perhaps, but it may be the only hope for the future.

CULTURE

Tribal conflict has torn Rwanda apart during much of the independence period, culminating in the horrific genocide that unfolded in 1994. There are two schools of thought when it comes to looking at Rwandan identity.

The colonial approach employed by the Belgians was to divide and conquer, issuing ID cards that divided the population along strict ethnic lines. They tapped up the Tutsis as leaders to help control the Hutu majority. Later, as independence approached, they switched sides, pitting Hutu against Tutsi in a new conflict, which crackled away until the 1990s when it exploded onto the world stage.

In the new Rwanda, the opposite is true. Ethnic identities are out, everyone is Rwandan. The government is at pains to present a Rwandan identity and blames the Belgians for categorising the country along tribal lines that set the stage for the savagery that followed. Rwanda was a peaceful place before: Hutu and Tutsi lived side by side for generations and intermarriage was common, or so the story goes.

The truth, as always, is probably somewhere in between. President Paul Kagame is trying to put the past behind and create a new Rwanda. It will take time, maybe a generation or more, but what has been achieved in just over a decade is astonishing. However, to avoid the divisions of the past once again surfacing in the new Rwanda, democratic development is required that favours all – urban and rural, rich and poor – and is blind to tribe.

People
The population is moving towards 11 million, which gives Rwanda one of the highest population densities of any country in Africa. While ethnic identities are very much a taboo subject in Rwanda, the population is believed to be about 85% Hutu, 14% Tutsi and 1% Twa pygmy.

About 65% of the population are Christians of various sects (Catholicism is predominant), a further 25% follow tribal religions, often with a dash of Christianity, and the remaining 10% are Muslim.

Arts & Crafts
Rwanda's most famous dancers are the Intore troupe. Their warrior-like displays are accompanied by a trancelike drumbeat similar to that of the famous Les Tambourinaires in Burundi.

Hotel Rwanda has put Rwanda back on the map for many moviegoers. Although it was shot in South Africa, it tells the story of Hotel des Milles Collines manager Paul Rusesabagina, played by Don Cheadle, turning his luxury hotel into a temporary haven for thousands fleeing the erupting genocide.

Gorillas in the Mist, starring Sigourney Weaver, is based on the autobiography of Dian Fossey and her work with the rare mountain gorillas in Parc National des Volcans. It's essential viewing for anyone wishing to track the gorillas.

FOOD & DRINK
In the rural areas of Rwanda, food is very similar to that in other East African countries. Popular meats include *tilapia* (Nile perch), goat, chicken and beef *brochettes* (kebabs), though the bulk of most meals are based on *ugali* (maize meal), *matoke* (mashed plantains) and so-called 'Irish potatoes'. In the cities, however, Rwanda's francophone roots are evident in the *plat du jour* (plate of the day), which is usually excellently prepared and presented Continental Europe–inspired cuisine.

LEAVE YOUR PLASTIC BAGS AT HOME

In an effort to preserve the natural beauty of Rwanda, the government enforces a strict ban on plastic bags throughout the country. Police are particularly vigilant at border crossings, and you will be searched and possibly fined if contraband is found. So please – help support this worthwhile initiative and leave your plastic bags at home.

ENVIRONMENT
Rwanda is not known as the 'land of a thousand hills' for nothing. The hills stretch into the horizon in every direction, making bus travel akin to a dose of the bends. To the west is the stunning shoreline of Lake Kivu, with its hidden bays, plunging cliffs and secret beaches.

Like Uganda, Rwanda is primate-tastic. Wildlife in Rwanda for most visitors is the mountain gorillas, the residents of Parc National des Volcans in the northwest, but there are also monkeys in Parc National de Nyungwe and chimp tracking is possible.

KIGALI

pop 850,000

Spanning several ridges and valleys, the Rwandan capital of Kigali is an attractive city of lush hillsides, flowering trees, winding boulevards and bustling streets. Kigali exists as a testament to the peace and order that has defined Rwanda's trajectory for more than a decade, though it bore the brunt of the genocide in 1994. After 100 days of systematic slaughter, dead and decaying bodies littered the streets. Dogs were shot en masse as they had developed a taste for human flesh. In recent years, a massive amount of rehabilitation work has restored the city to its former graces, while increasing waves of foreign investment have sparked a number of ambitious building projects.

ORIENTATION
The commercial centre of Kigali is located on a hill to the southwest of Place de l'Unité Nationale and is focused on Ave du Commerce and the network of streets that bisect it. To the south there are several *grandes artères* (major roads) leading into the diplomatic quarter where embassies and expensive restaurants are

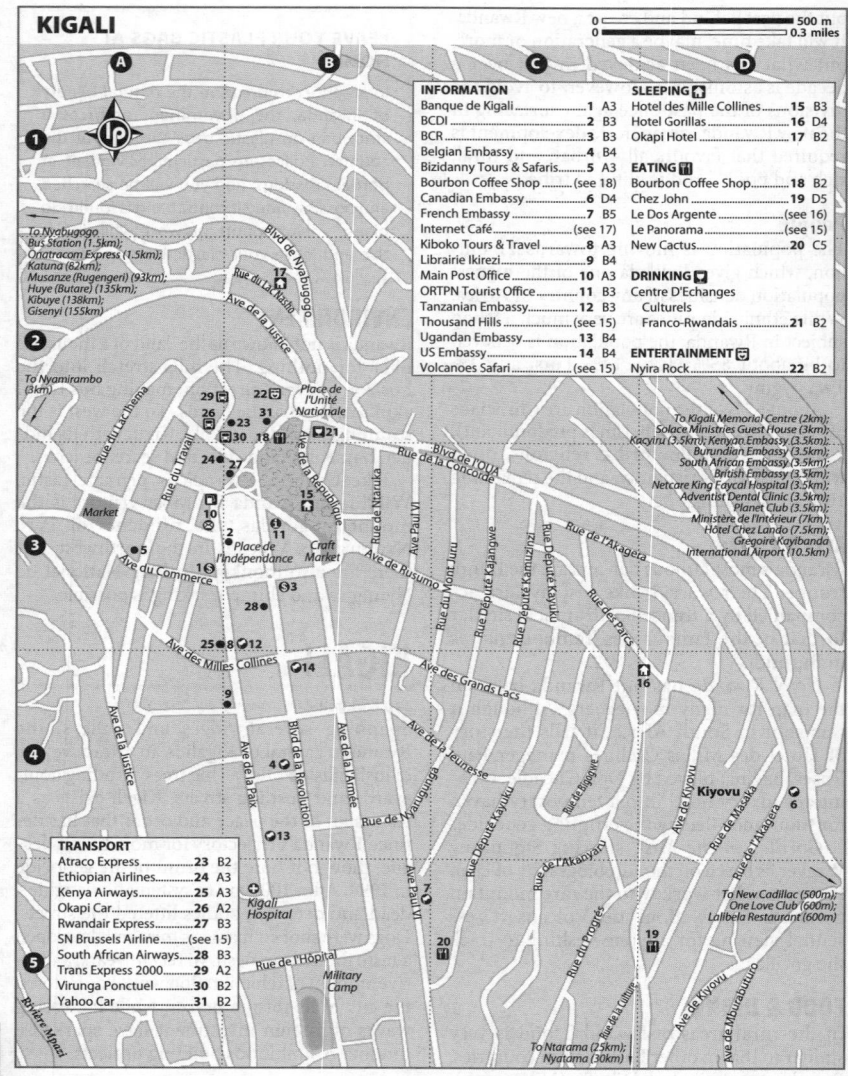

KIGALI

0 — 500 m
0 — 0.3 miles

INFORMATION
Banque de Kigali	1 A3
BCDI	2 B3
BCR	3 B3
Belgian Embassy	4 B4
Bizidanny Tours & Safaris	5 A3
Bourbon Coffee Shop	(see 18)
Canadian Embassy	6 D4
French Embassy	7 B5
Internet Café	(see 17)
Kiboko Tours & Travel	8 A3
Librairie Ikirezi	9 B4
Main Post Office	10 A3
ORTPN Tourist Office	11 B3
Tanzanian Embassy	12 B3
Thousand Hills	(see 15)
Ugandan Embassy	13 B4
US Embassy	14 B4
Volcanoes Safari	(see 15)

SLEEPING
Hotel des Mille Collines	15 B3
Hotel Gorillas	16 D4
Okapi Hotel	17 B2

EATING
Bourbon Coffee Shop	18 B2
Chez John	19 B3
Le Dos Argente	(see 16)
Le Panorama	(see 15)
New Cactus	20 C5

DRINKING
Centre D'Echanges Culturels Franco-Rwandais	21 B2

ENTERTAINMENT
Nyira Rock	22 B2

To Nyabugogo
Bus Station (1.5km);
Onatracom Express (1.5km);
Katuna (82km);
Musanze (Rugengeri) (93km);
Huye (Butare) (135km);
Kibuye (138km);
Gisenyi (155km)

To Nyamirambo
(3km)

Place de
l'Unité
Nationale

Market

Place de
l'Indépendance

Craft
Market

To Kigali Memorial Centre (2km);
Solace Ministries Guest House (3km);
Kacyiru (3.5km); Kenyan Embassy (3.5km);
Burundian Embassy (3.5km);
South African Embassy (3.5km);
British Embassy (3.5km);
Netcare King Faycal Hospital (3.5km);
Adventint Dental Clinic (3.5km);
Planet Club (3.5km);
Ministère de l'Intérieur (7km);
Hôtel Chez Lando (7.5km);
Grégoire Kayibanda
International Airport (10.5km)

Kiyovu

To New Cadillac (500m);
One Love Club (600m);
Lalibela Restaurant (600m)

TRANSPORT
Atraco Express	23 B2
Ethiopian Airlines	24 A3
Kenya Airways	25 A3
Okapi Car	26 A2
Rwandair Express	27 B3
SN Brussels Airline	(see 15)
South African Airways	28 B3
Trans Express 2000	29 A2
Virunga Ponctuel	30 B2
Yahoo Car	31 B2

Kigali
Hospital

Military
Camp

To Ntarama (25km);
Nyatama (30km)

---

located. Quite a lot of night-time action can be found east of the city centre in Kacyiru.

INFORMATION
Bookshops

Librairie Ikirezi (☎ 571314; Ave de la Paix; ✆ 9am-12.30pm & 2-6pm Mon-Fri, 9am-12.30pm Sat & Sun) French- and English-language books and magazines.

Emergency
Police (☎ 083 11170) A 24-hour emergency number.

Internet Access
Bourbon Coffee Shop (Union Trade Centre; free with purchase of item) The most popular cafe in town has a great wi-fi spot if you're travelling with your laptop (see also p748).

RWANDA

Main post office (Ave de la Paix; ⏰ 8am-5pm Mon-Fri, to noon Sat) Has an attached internet cafe.

Medical Services
Adventist Dental Clinic (☎ 582431)
Netcare King Faycal Hospital (☎ 582421)

Money
For cash advances on your credit or ATM card, the following banks can help you, though be prepared for long lines, loads of forms and a hefty charge.
Banque Commerciale de Rwanda (BCR; Blvd de la Revolution)
Banque de Kigali (Ave du Commerce)
Banque de Commerce, de Developement et de l'Industriel (BCDI; Ave de la Paix)

Post
Main post office (Ave de la Paix; ⏰ 8am-5pm Mon-Fri, to noon Sat)

Tourist Information
ORTPN (Office Rwandais du Tourisme et des Parcs Nationaux; ☎ 576514; ☎ /fax 576515; www.rwandatourism. com; 1 Blvd de la Revolution, BP 905; ⏰ 7am-5pm Mon-Fri, 7am-noon Sat & Sun) Known locally as 'Or-ti-pen,' Rwanda's national tourism office is located in the centre of town behind the Hotel des Mille Collines. ORTPN is also where independent travellers can make reservations to track the mountain gorillas in Parc National des Volcans, though it's recommended that you contact the office several months in advance as permits are extremely difficult to come by during the high season. If you've arrived in Kigali without a permit and are hoping that one will materialise in light of a last-minute cancellation, the staff at ORTPN can phone around to different operators for you. While there are no guarantees, you might get lucky if you're flexible and are prepared to wait a few days.

Travel Agencies
If you want some help in securing a gorilla-tracking permit, or in arranging transport to/from any of the national parks, the following travel agencies/tour operators are recommended as the first port of call:
Bizidanny Tours & Safaris (☎ 55102004; www. bizidanny.com; Rue Commerciale) A small start-up operator running individually customised tours.
Kiboko Tours & Travel (☎ 501741; www.kibokotravels .org.rw; Rue de la Paix) Another small operator that is a good starting point for securing permits.

Thousand Hills (☎ 501151; www.thousandhills.rw; Hotel des Mille Colines) One of the more well-established tour operators, Thousand Hills is an excellent choice.
Volcanoes Safaris (☎ 502452; www.volcanoessafaris. com; Hotel des Mille Collines) One of the most professional operators in Rwanda.

SIGHTS
Don't leave Kigali without a visit to the **Kigali Memorial Centre** – a sombre memorial to the 1994 Rwandan genocide. See also p748.

A visit to the luxury **Hotel des Mille Collines** (☎ 576530; www.millecollines.net; Ave de la République), the inspiration for the film *Hotel Rwanda*, can be an incredibly surreal experience, especially knowing full well the tragic events that once played out here.

Around Kigali
NYAMATA & NTARAMA GENOCIDE MEMORIALS
Two of the most powerful genocide memorials are churches located on the outskirts of Kigali. **Nyatama**, about 30km south of Kigali, is a deeply disturbing memorial where skulls and bones of the many victims are on display. While the visual remains of the deceased are a visceral sight, their inclusion here is to provide firm evidence of would-be genocide deniers.

The church at **Ntarama**, about 25km south of Kigali, is more understated but no less powerful. The church has not been touched since the bodies were removed more than a decade ago, and there are many bits of clothing scraps still on the floor.

Both of these memorials can be visited on a day trip, though you will need to either have your own transport or arrange for a taxi to bring you there and back.

SLEEPING
One Love Club (☎ 575412; www.oneloveproject.org; Ave des Poids Lourds; campsites US$10, r US$20-30; 🖵) Since 1997, profits from this small guesthouse have been ploughed back into a local non-governmental organisation (NGO) to help the disabled community in Rwanda. You can support this cause, which has so far supplied artificial limbs to more than 5000 Rwandans at no cost, by either pitching a tent in its shady campsite or bedding down in its simple but cosy rooms.

Solace Ministries Guest House (☎ 588005; www.sola cem.org; Kacyiru; r per person with/without meals US$25/14)

RWANDA

THE GENOCIDE REMEMBERED

More than a memorial for Kigali, more than a memorial for Rwanda and its tragedy, this is a memorial for all of us, marking the Rwandan genocide and many more around the world that never should have come to pass. The **Kigali Memorial Centre** (www.kigalimemorialcentre.org; admission free, donations welcome; ⊙ 10am-5pm, closed public holidays) is a must for all visitors in Rwanda wanting to learn more about how it was that the world watched as a genocide unfolded in this tiny landlocked country.

Why did Rwanda descend into 100 days of madness? The Kigali Memorial Centre explains it as best it can. The centre is a fitting memorial to the 1994 genocide, especially since the memorial gardens here hold the remains of more than 250,000 victims of the genocide.

The Kigali Memorial Centre was set up with assistance from the **Aegis Trust** (www.aegistrust. org), which was established in 2000 at the Holocaust Centre in the UK. The organisation, which is dedicated to understanding and preventing genocide, is involved in a number of activities including academic research, policy advocacy, education, public awareness and humanitarian support for victims of genocide.

The Kigali Memorial Centre is located in the northern Kisozi district of the capital, which is a short taxi ride (RFr2000) from the centre.

Solace Ministries is dedicated to providing antiretroviral drugs (ARVs) to women who were raped by the Interahamwe during the 1994 genocide. Funding for this vitally important project is partially obtained by opening the doors of the church to foreign tourists. Rooms are bright, airy and have proper bathtubs, though the highlight is the traditional Rwandan cooking provided with gusto to hungry guests.

Okapi Hotel (☎ 576765; www.okapi.co.rw; Blvd de Nyabugogo; s/d from US$35/46; 🖳) This well-established midrange hotel attracts a loyal following. The Okapi benefits from a decent location that's within easy walking distance of the city centre. The rooms themselves benefit from modern amenities, so you can watch satellite TV and take a steaming hot bath, or just relax on the balcony and watch the city go by.

Hôtel Chez Lando (☎ 584328; www.hotelchezlando. com; s/d from US$60/70) A long-standing Kigali institution located out in the suburb of Remera, the rooms at Chez Lando are single-storey units set around a lush garden. While it's a long way out of town for those without transport, the peace and quiet on offer here are big drawcards, assuming you either have your own wheels or don't mind relying on taxis.

Hotel Gorillas (☎ 501717; www.hotelgorillas.com; Rue des Parcs; s/d standard US$85/105, deluxe US$95/115; 🖳) A slick little hotel in the upmarket Kiyovu area of the city, this place is winning over a lot of customers thanks to its spacious rooms with touches of decorative flair. The highlight of the property is Le Dos Argente

(opposite) or Silverback Restaurant, which is an open-air bistro in the French tradition that has an eclectic offering of Rwandan and Continental classics.

Hotel des Mille Collines (☎ 576530; www.millecol lines.net; Ave de la République; s/d US$135/155; 🖳 🌊) Welcome to the *Hotel Rwanda*. With the international success of the movie, the 'Hotel of a Thousand Hills' looks set to see a surge in bookings, which is probably why it was in the midst of a major renovation at the time of research. The hotel used in the movie was actually in South Africa, though the original hotel where horror and hope collided was right here.

EATING

Bourbon Coffee Shop (☎ 505307; Union Trade Centre; coffee & pastry RFr1500-3000) If you don't like your morning blend served in a packet, head to this popular spot where locals and expats alike queue up for the real stuff. Assorted pastries and croissants are also available for a quick energy boost, and here's the best part – you get an hour of free wi-fi access with your purchase, so bring along your laptop if you need a quick internet fix.

Chez John (Rue de Masaka; meals RFr2000-4000) A popular local haunt with more than its fare share of foreign patrons, Chez John serves up true Rwandan standards, namely meat and maize.

Lalibela Restaurant (☎ 575412; Ave des Poids Lourds; mains RFr3000-4000) Kigali's premiere Ethiopian restaurant is set in the grounds of the One

Love Club, so you can dine comfortably knowing that part of the proceeds of your meal are going to charity (for more information, see One Love Club, p747).

New Cactus (☎ 572572; Rue Député Kayuku; mains RFr3000-5000) Outrageously popular with expats and well-to-do Rwandans alike, the New Cactus is set on a commanding ridge up in Kiyovu where you can soak up the sparkling lights of Kigali by night. Boasting a broad menu of French favourites, gourmet pizzas, rich fondues and a well-rounded wine list, spend a bit liberally here if you really want to live well.

Le Dos Argente (☎ 501717; Rue des Parcs; mains RFr5000-7000) Also known as the Silverback Restaurant, this is one of the best restaurants in Kigali, set in an open-air garden that has an extremely attentive wait staff. The accent here is most definitely French – foie gras, duck à l'orange and even frogs' legs and rabbit are available for the discerning diner.

Le Panorama (☎ 576530; www.millecollines.net; Ave de la République; mains RFr5000-10,000) Proudly perched on the top floor of the Hotel des Mille Collines, Kigali's most famous restaurant attracts its fare share of international scenesters, who flock here for formal banquets and panoramic views.

DRINKING & ENTERTAINMENT

Centre D'Echanges Culturels Franco-Rwandais (Ave de la République; admission from RFr2000, drinks RFr 500-1000) On Fridays and Saturdays, the Centre D'Echanges Culturels Franco-Rwandais plays host to leading local bands.

New Cadillac (admission from RFr2500, drinks from RFr1500; ☽ Wed-Sun) This long-running club remains the most popular place in town.

Nyira Rock (Ave du Commerce; admission from RFr1000, drinks from RFr500) A local nightclub in the city centre that boasts DJs, cheap beers and plenty of action towards the weekend.

Planet Club (Kigali Business Centre, Ave du Lac Muhazi; admission from RFr3500, drinks from RFr2000) This weekend spot draws in the beautiful people. While you really need to pay to play, you'll most likely be glad you did.

GETTING THERE & AWAY
Air

Gregoire Kayibanda International Airport (KGL) is located at Kanombe, which is 10km east of Kigali centre. For contact details of the international airlines serving Rwanda, see p755.

Bus & Minibus

Several bus companies operate services to major towns, which are less crowded and safer than local minibuses. Okapi Car travels to Huye, Gisenyi and Musanze; Atraco Express to Huye, Musanze and Gisenyi; Trans Express 2000 to Huye; and Virunga Ponctuel to Musanze (Ruhengeri). See the individual town entries for more details on journey times and road conditions.

All buses depart from company bus offices in the city centre. Onatracom Express has larger 45-seat buses (which could be considered safer) which run to Musanze and Gisenyi, plus Huye. These services depart from the Nyabugogo bus terminal.

Local minibuses depart from the Nyabugogo bus terminal for towns all around Rwanda, including Huye (RFr1400, two hours) and Gisenyi (RFr1800, four hours). These minibuses leave when full throughout the day, except on weekends when they tend to dry up after 3pm. Just turn up and tell someone where you're going. See the respective town entries for further details.

GETTING AROUND

A taxi from the airport to the city centre costs about RFr7500; a direct minibus from the city centre is (RFr400).

There are no metered taxis, but a fare within the city centre costs, on average, RFr1500 to RFr2000, double that out to the suburbs or later at night. *Taxi-motor*, which are informal moped taxis, can whisk you around the city for a negotiable price (usually less than RFr1000).

NORTHWESTERN RWANDA

The northwest of Rwanda is where the country really earns its nickname as the 'land of a thousand hills'. It's a beautiful region and the peaks culminate in the stunning Virunga volcanoes, forming a formidable natural border between Rwanda, Uganda and the DRC, and home to their share of the last mountain gorillas on the planet.

MUSANZE (RUHENGERI)

For most travellers, Musanze is the preferred staging post on their way to the magnificent

Parc National des Volcans, one of the best places in East Africa to track the rare mountain gorilla. Since permit holders are required to check in at the park headquarters in nearby Kinigi at 7am on the day of the tracking, staying in Musanze is a much safer option than leaving from Kigali at the crack of dawn.

Sleeping

Hotel Urumuri (☎ 546820; r RFr3500) Tucked away on a side street off Rue du Marché, this is a friendly-enough spot assuming you're not too fussy about the lack of hot water and the somewhat dilapidated rooms.

Tourist Rest House (☎ 546635; Rue Muhabura; s/tw RFr4000/6000) Rooms are slightly on the smallish side, but they're of good value considering their relative cleanliness and the generally reliable hot water.

Centre d'Accueil d'Eglise Episcopale (☎ 546857; cnr Rue du Pyrethre & Ave du 5 Juillet; r RFr5000-40,000) Cheap rooms at this church-run spot are in a small block with shared bathrooms, but as you start spending more, the facilities improve dramatically.

Centre Pastoral Notre Dame de Fatima (☎ 546780; Rue Virunga; s/d from RFr10,000/20,000; apt RFr30,000; 🖳) Another church-run spot, the modern rooms and one family-sized apartment are simple yet functional.

Hotel Muhabura (☎ 546296; Ave du 5 Juillet; r/apt RFr15000/20,000; 🖳) The town's leading hotel, the Muhabura offers spacious rooms that catch plenty a mountain breeze, which is fine as you can always warm up with a steamy shower in the bathrooms.

Virunga Lodge (☎ 502452; www.volcanoessafaris.com; s/d from US$465/700 incl all meals & activities) Widely regarded as one of the finest accommodation options in all of Rwanda, this lodge is nestled on a ridge above Lake Burera and offers incredible views across to the Virunga volcanoes. Guests stay in individual stone chalets that are decorated with local crafts and hardwood furnishings.

Getting There & Away

Numerous bus companies offer scheduled hourly services between Musanze and Kigali, including **Okapi Car** (Ave du 5 Juillet), **Virunga Express** (Ave du 5 Juillet) and **Atraco Express** (Ave du 5 Juillet), all charging around RFr1500 (two hours). These buses are less crowded than normal minibuses. **Onatracom Express** (Ave du 5 Juillet) has three large buses per day passing through,

connecting Kigali and Gisenyi (three hours) – tickets are available at the petrol station.

There are normal minibuses from Musanze to Kigali (RFr1300, two hours), on a breathtaking mountain road, and to Gisenyi (RFr1000, 1½ hours).

Note that there is no public transport between Musanze and Kinigi, where the park headquarters for Parc National des Volcans are located. For more information on accessing the national park, see below.

PARC NATIONAL DES VOLCANS

Volcanoes National Park, which runs along the border with DRC and Uganda, is home to the Rwandan section of the Virungas. Comprised of five volcanoes – the highest is Karisimbi (4507m) – the Virungas are one of the most beautiful sights in both Rwanda and the whole of Africa. As if this wasn't enough of a drawcard, the bamboo- and rainforest-covered slopes of these volcanoes are also home to some of the last remaining sanctuaries of the endangered eastern mountain gorilla (*Gorilla beringei beringei*).

Sights & Activities

GORILLA TRACKING

An encounter with these charismatic creatures is the highlight of a trip to Africa for many visitors. However, make no mistake about it – gorilla tracking is no joy ride. The guides can generally find the gorillas within one to four hours of starting out, but this often involves a lot of strenuous effort scrambling through dense vegetation up steep, muddy hillsides, sometimes to more than 3000m.

There are seven habituated gorilla groups in Parc National des Volcans, including the Susa group, which has more than 35 members. Visits to the gorillas are restricted to one hour, and flash photography is banned. While you are visiting the gorillas, do not eat, drink, smoke or go to the bathroom in their presence. If you have any potential airborne illness, do not go tracking as gorillas are extremely susceptible to human diseases.

Reservations

Fees are now a hefty US$500 per person for a gorilla visit, which includes park entry, compulsory guides and guards. This is a single-entry permit, but it's not a day-long permit as you're only allowed to visit for one hour during the scheduled window. Numbers of people allowed to visit each of the group are limited to a maximum of eight people per day, limiting the total number of daily permits to an absolute maximum of 56. Children under 15 are not allowed to visit the gorillas.

Bookings for gorilla permits can be made through the ORTPN tourist office in Kigali (see p747) or a Rwandan tour company (see p747). With tourism in Rwanda now on the up and up, it is getting more difficult to secure permits during the peak seasons of December/January and July/August, so book well in advance if you want to be assured of a spot.

Independent travellers who have only decided to visit the gorillas in Rwanda once in the East Africa region can turn up at the ORTPN office in Kigali and try to secure a booking at the earliest available date. During the high season, waits of several days to a week are not uncommon, though you might get lucky and snatch up a permit as cancellations do occur.

Having made a booking and paid the fees, head to the park headquarters of Parc National des Volcans in Kinigi and get ready for the experience of a lifetime. Ideally, you should spend the night before your track in either Kinigi or Musanze as you need to check in at 7am on the day that your permit is valid. If you are late, your designated slot will be forfeited and your money will not be refunded.

At 7.30am, gorilla groups are assigned, and around 8am trackers are requested to start making their way to their respective trailhead. By 8.30am the tracking has already commenced.

Sleeping

For more options, see opposite.

Kinigi Guesthouse (☎ 54698; s/d from US$40/50) Located very close to park headquarters in Kinigi village, all profits from this local lodge are ploughed back into the Association de Solidarité des Femmes Rwandaises, which assists vulnerable Rwandan women of all backgrounds and ages. Accommodation is in a small clutch of wooden bungalows that are set in lush gardens with views of the towering Virungas.

Gorilla's Nest Camp (☎ 546331; s/d from US$80/120) This upmarket option is situated near the park headquarters, so you don't have to worry about getting up early and making the drive from Musanze to arrive before registration. The rooms themselves are very

smart, with swish new amenities that complement the verdant views of the neighbouring forested slopes.

Getting There & Away

The main access point for Parc National des Volcans is the nearby town of Musanze. The park headquarters for Parc National Volcans is located in the village of Kinigi, approximately 12km north of Musanze along rough dirt roads. Assuming the rains haven't been too heavy and the road is in decent shape, you can make the trip from Musanze in about 30 to 45 minutes.

Note that there is no public transport from Musanze to Kinigi, though you can arrange to hire a vehicle and driver for the day through the ORTPN office or any of the travel agencies in Musanze (around US$100). However, considering that most people in Musanze need to be in Kinigi the next morning at 7am, it really isn't too hard to hitch a ride with fellow trackers, especially during the high season and on weekends.

One option worth considering if you have a few friends is to hire a car and a driver in Kigali. Prices are around US$150 per day, though you'll reliably have transport to/from Musanze, the park headquarters in Kinigi and the trailhead for the gorilla tracking. Any of the travel agencies in Kigali (p747) can make all of the necessary arrangements.

GISENYI

Land-locked Rwanda may be a long way from the ocean, but that doesn't mean that you can't have a beach holiday here. On the contrary, if you take another look at the map, you'll quickly realise that Rwanda's eastern border with DRC runs along the entire length of Lake Kivu. One of the Great Lakes in the Albertine Rift Valley, Lake Kivu has a maximum depth of nearly 500m, and is one of the 20 deepest and most voluminous lakes in the whole world. Even if you're not a devoted sun worshipper, Gisenyi is an incredibly scenic and picturesque spot to relax after a few days of rough tracking and hiking in Parc National des Volcans.

Gisenyi is roughly divided into upper and lower towns, though most tourist services cluster around the lower end along the shores of Lake Kivu.

Sleeping

Centre d'Accueil de l'Église Presbytérienne (☎ 540397; Ave du Marché; dm/d from RFr1500/6000) This church-run spot has the cheapest beds in town – dorms come with varying numbers of beds, while the double rooms are spic and span with bathroom facilities.

Auberge de Gisenyi (☎ 540385; Ave de l'Umuganda; s/d RFr5000/6000) The pick of the pack among the cheaper guesthouses in the upper part of town, this has rooms facing an attractive courtyard garden of tropical blooms.

Stipp Hotel (☎ 540540; www.stippag.co.rw; Ave de la Révolution; s/d from US$125/150; ✖ 🖳 🖳) Gisenyi's first true boutique hotel, the Stipp is one of the classiest places to bed down along the shores of Lake Kivu.

Lake Kivu Serena Hotel (☎ 541111; www.serenahotels.com/rwanda/lake_kivu/home.asp; Ave de la Coopération; s/d from US$135/165; ✖ 🖳 🖳) Regarded as the finest property in all of Gisenyi, this option brims with refined luxury from the grand colonial dining rooms to the manicured grounds.

Getting There & Away

Okapi Car (Ave du Marché) and **Atraco Express** (Ave du Marché) operate minibuses between Gisenyi and Kigali (RFr2500, three hours). There are also regular minibuses to Kigali (RFr1800, four hours) and Musanze (RFr1000, two hours).

Onatracom Express (Ave de l'Umuganda) runs big buses and has three services daily to Kigali (RFr2000) passing through Musanze (RFr1200). All the buses terminate on Ave de l'Umuganda.

SOUTHWESTERN RWANDA

The endless mountains don't stop as you head south towards Burundi. Highlights here include the intellectual capital of Huye (Butare) and the magnificent primate-filled forest of Parc National de Nyungwe.

HUYE (BUTARE)

Huye (Butare) is one of the most distinguished towns in Rwanda, having served as the country's most prominent intellectual centre since the colonial era. Home to the National University of Rwanda, the National Institute of Scientific Research and the excellent National Museum of Rwanda, Huye may be a step down in size after the capital, but it is certainly no lightweight on the Rwandan stage.

There are branches of BCR, BCDI and Banque de Kigali on the main Rue de Kigali, but they can only deal with cash. **Computer Link@Butare** (Rue de Kigali; per hr RFr500) is the best place for internet access.

The excellent **National Museum of Rwanda** (☎ 530586; Rue de Kigali; admission RFr1000; ⏱ 7am-5pm), one of the most beautiful structures in the city, wins top marks for having one of the best ethnological and archaeological collections in the entire region.

Strolling through the campus of the **National University of Rwanda** is a pleasant diversion, especially if you find yourself at the peaceful arboretum, a great place to learn about African flora while indulging in a bit of leafy shade.

Hôtel des Beaux-Arts (☎ 530032; Ave du Commerce; r RFr4000-6000) is attractively decorated with local products, and there's a handicraft shop selling a selection of what is displayed on the walls. **Expo Vente** (Rue de Kigali) is also a handicrafts shop exhibiting local products and is a great-value place to buy some Rwandan work.

A modern hotel on the road to the university, **Hotel Credo** (☎ 530505; Ave de l'Université; s RFr10,000-25,000, d RFr15,000-30,000; 🖳 ✖) draws well-to-do Rwandans visiting their kids at college, as well as business folk travelling between Rwanda and Burundi.

The **Hôtel Ibis** (☎ 530335; Rue de Kigali; s RFr10,000-25,000, d RFr15,000-30,000; 🖳 ✖) is a classic hotel that is positively brimming with personality and sophistication.

There are several bus companies operating between Huye and Kigali (around RFr2000, two hours) found on Rue de Kigali: Atraco Express, Okapi Car, Trans Express 2000 and Volcano Express have almost hourly services in both directions. The minibus stand is just a patch of dirt about 1km north of the town centre, by the stadium.

PARC NATIONAL DE NYUNGWE

Nyungwe Forest is Rwanda's most important area of biodiversity, and has been rated the highest priority for forest conservation in Africa. Nyungwe's strongest drawcard is the chance to track chimpanzees, which have been habituated over the years to human visits. While chimps tend to garner most of the spotlight in Nyungwe, the park's second billing is a semihabituated troop of around 400 Angolan colobus monkeys, the largest group of arboreal primates in all of Africa.

Information

The park headquarters is at the Uwinka Reception Centre on the Huye-Cyangugu road. Here is where you must pay your visitor fees: it costs US$20 per day to enter Nyungwe, chimpanzee tracking costs an additional US$50 per person, while all other guided walks cost an additional US$30 per person. It is also standard practice (and good manners) to tip your guides, especially if they do a good job tracking the primates. Note that unguided walks are not permitted in the park.

Sights & Activities

CHIMPANZEE TRACKING

Chimpanzee habitation in Nyungwe forest is still very much a work in progress, and there are no guarantees that you'll come face-to-face with one in the wild. If you are lucky and happen to come across a group of chimps on the move, you need to be quick with your camera. Chimps have a tendency to quickly disappear in the underbrush, or climb up into the canopy and out of sight. On the other hand, consider leaving your camera in your backpack for a few extra moments, and enjoy the privilege of being able to encounter humankind's closest living evolutionary link.

COLOBUS MONKEY TRACKING

A subspecies of the widespread black-and-white colobus, the Angolan colobus is an arboreal Old World monkey that is distinguished by its black fur and long, silky white locks of hair. While they may not be as charismatic as chimps, colobi are extremely social primates that form enormous group sizes – the semi-habituated troop in the Nyungwe forest numbers no less than 400 individuals and is by far the largest primate aggregation on the continent.

Sleeping & Eating

There is a **campsite** (per person US$20) at the Uwinka headquarters, occupying a ridge (2500m) overlooking the forest that offers impressive views in all directions.

A more sophisticated option for those without a tent is the **ORTPN Resthouse** (r per person $15-20, meals US$5-10), which offers accommodation in simple but functional rooms that share communal showers and toilets.

Note that advance bookings are recommended, and can be made through the ORTPN office in Kigali – see p747.

Getting There & Away

While public transport does pass along this route, your ability to access the park will be greatly restricted without access to a private vehicle. If you'd like to hire a rental car, it is recommended that you consult with any of the tour companies in Kigali (p747).

RWANDA DIRECTORY

ACCOMMODATION

Dorm accommodation at the mission hostels costs about RFr2000 per night. Compared with mission hostels, hotels are generally a bit more expensive, though you can usually expect satellite TV, hot showers and occasionally internet access. High-season prices, which come into effect from May to mid-October, have been used throughout this chapter.

In Rwanda, you can expect to find hotel prices listed in either US dollars or RFr (and sometimes both). Generally speaking, up-market hotels prefer payment to be made in US dollars.

ACTIVITIES

It's all about the gorillas here in Rwanda, and the tracking at Parc National des Volcans (p750) ranks up there with any activity on earth – just don't forget US$500 cash for the permit, however. Other monkey business includes primate tracking at Parc National de Nyungwe (left). For a change of scenery, there are water sports at Gisenyi (p751).

BUSINESS HOURS

Banks Open between 8.30am and 4.30pm or 5.30pm (with no break for lunch); closed Saturday afternoons; some banks close early at 3.30pm.

Government offices & businesses Generally open between 8.30am and 4.30pm or 5.30pm, with a short break for lunch sometime between noon and 2pm.

Restaurants Local restaurant hours are 7am to 9pm, and international-type restaurants are open 11.30am to 2.30pm and 5.30pm to 10.30pm.

Shops Open between 8.30am to 4.30pm or 5.30pm; most shops do not break for lunch.

DANGERS & ANNOYANCES

It is always worth checking on current security conditions before entering Rwanda. At the time of research, the country was very safe, but there is always the outside chance of problems spilling over from the DRC or Burundi. Urban

RWANDA

PRACTICALITIES

- Rwanda uses the metric system and distances are in kilometres.

- Electricity in Rwanda is 240V, 50 cycles, and plugs are mainly two-pin.

- The English-language *New Times* is published several times a week, plus the *New Vision* and *Monitor* are available from Uganda. French magazines and international titles are available in Kigali.

- Radio Rwanda, a government-controlled station, broadcasts in Kinyarwanda, French, Swahili and English.

- TV Rwandaise (TVR) is the state-owned broadcaster.

Rwanda is now one of the safer places to be in Africa, but in Kigali, like any capital, take care at night.

Out in the countryside, do not walk along anything other than a well-used track; there might still be landmines around. The potential risk is highest anywhere near the borders with the DRC and Burundi.

There are a number of roadblocks along all main roads to ensure security, but foreigners are never hassled.

EMBASSIES & CONSULATES

Quite a number of embassies are now located on Blvd de l'Umuganda, across the valley in the Kacyiru suburb of Kigali.

Belgium (Map p746; ☎ 575551; Rue de Nyarugenge)
Burundi (off Map p746; ☎ 517529; Kacyiru)
Canada (Map p746; ☎ 571762; Rue de l'Akagera)
France (Map p746; ☎ 575206; 40 Ave Paul VI)
Kenya (off Map p746; ☎ 583332; Blvd de l'Umuganda)
South Africa (off Map p746; ☎ 583185; Blvd de l'Umuganda)
Tanzania (Map p746; ☎ 505400; Ave de la Paix)
Uganda (Map p746; ☎ 572117; Ave de la Paix)
UK (off Map p746; ☎ 585280; Blvd de l'Umuganda)
USA (Map p746; ☎ 505601; Blvd de la Revolution)

HOLIDAYS

New Year's Day 1 January
Democracy Day 8 January
Easter (Good Friday, Holy Saturday and Easter Monday) March/April
Labour Day 1 May
Ascension Thursday May

Whit Monday May
National Day 1 July
Peace & National Unity Day 5 July
Harvest Festival 1 August
Assumption 15 August
Culture Day 8 September
Kamarampaka Day 25 September
Armed Forces Day 26 October
All Saints' Day 1 November
Christmas Day 25 December

INTERNET ACCESS

Email and internet access in Rwanda has fast improved and is now widely available in Kigali, as well as on a more limited basis in smaller towns.

MAPS

At the time of research the best map of Rwanda was *Rwanda Burundi: International Travel Map* published by ITMB Publishing at a scale of 1:400,000.

MONEY

Rwanda's unit of currency is the Rwandan franc (RFr), which is sometimes also abbreviated to 'Frw'. It's best to come to Rwanda with US dollars or euros in cash. US bank notes pre-2004 are not always accepted in Rwanda given counterfeit concerns and, as such, it's recommended that you exchange older bills at banks prior to arriving in Rwanda.

The only useful bank branch in the country is Banque de Kigali in the capital, which offers cash advances on credit cards and can change travellers cheques, neither of which is possible in the provinces. There are ATMs in Kigali, but they are not yet wired to an international network. Credit cards can be used in some upmarket hotels and restaurants in Kigali.

Bureaux de change – which are mostly in Kigali – offer slightly better exchange rates than banks. Moneychangers hang around central Kigali and usually give a slightly better rate, but count your money carefully. All banks, as well as the majority of bureaux de change, are closed on Saturday afternoon and Sunday.

PHOTOGRAPHY

Be extremely careful wherever taking photos in Rwanda, as the authorities are very sensitive. Always ask before you take a photograph of anybody or anything other than landscapes.

POST

Postal services from Rwanda are reasonably reliable. The main post office in Kigali has a poste-restante service and an attached internet cafe.

TELEPHONE

Telephone calls can be made at the post offices (abbreviated to PTT) or any of the private MTN or Rwandatel card phones or booths found in major towns.

There are no area codes in Rwanda. Mobile telephone numbers start with the prefixes ☎ 085, ☎ 086 and ☎ 083. Visit www.rwanda phonebook.com when looking for telephone numbers in Rwanda.

VISAS

Visas are required by everyone except nationals of Canada, Germany, South Africa, Sweden, the UK, the USA and other East African countries. For most other passport holders, visas cost US$60 and are issued instantly upon arrival at either the border or the airport.

See the boxed text, p737, for information about the forthcoming East African single tourist visa.

Visa Extensions

Both tourist and transit visas can be extended in Kigali at **Ministère de l'Intérieur** (MININTER; ☎ 585856) in the Kacyiru district, about 7km northeast of the city centre. Extensions take a week or more to issue and cost RFr15,000 per month.

Visas for Onward Travel

Visas for Burundi, the DRC, Tanzania and Uganda are available from embassies in Kigali (see opposite for contact details).

Burundi Visas cost US$40 for one-month single entry, although check on the security situation very carefully before visiting. Also available on the border.

Democratic Republic of Congo (DRC) For land crossings to eastern DRC eight-day visas (US$35) are available at Bukavu or Goma.

Kenya Visas cost US$50 or the equivalent in local currency, require two photographs and are issued the same day if you apply before 11.30am. However, visas are also available on arrival.

Tanzania Visas require two photos and generally take 24 hours to issue. The cost depends on nationality.

Uganda Visas cost US$30, require two photos and are issued in 24 hours. However, it is far easier to get them at the border on arrival.

TRANSPORT IN RWANDA

GETTING THERE & AWAY
Air

Gregoire Kayibanda International Airport is located at Kanombe, 10km east of Kigali centre. Airlines connect Kigali with Addis Ababa (Ethiopia), Bujumbura (Burundi), Entebbe (Uganda), Nairobi (Kenya), Johannesburg (South Africa) and Brussels (Belgium).

The following airlines have offices in Kigali:

Ethiopian Airlines (airline code ET; Map p746; ☎ 575045; www.flyethiopian.com)

Kenya Airways (airline code KQ; Map p746; ☎ 577972; www.kenya-airways.com; Ave des Mille Collines)

Rwandair Express (airline code WB; Map p746; ☎ 503687; www.rwandair.com)

SN Brussels Airline (airline code SN; Map p746; ☎ 575290; www.brusselsairlines.com)

South African Airways (airline code SA; Map p746; ☎ 577777; www.flysaa.com; Blvd de la Revolution)

Land
BURUNDI

The main border crossing between Rwanda and Burundi is via Huye and Kayanza (Burundi), on the Kigali to Bujumbura road, which is sealed pretty much all the way. The border post is called Kayanza Haut and Burundian visas are available on arrival for US$40. Bus companies Yahoo Car (Map p746), New Yahoo Coach and Gaso Bus all run daily buses between Kigali and Bujumbura (RFr5000 to RFr6000, about six hours), departing at about 7am. There is also a direct road from Bujumbura (Burundi) to Cyangugu, but this is not in such good condition and should be considered comparatively unsafe.

DEMOCRATIC REPUBLIC OF CONGO (DRC)

There are two main crossings between Rwanda and DRC, both on the shores of Lake Kivu. To the north is the crossing between Gisenyi and Goma, and this is considered safe to cross at the time of writing, though only for short trips to Goma, climbing Nyiragongo volcano or visiting the mountain gorillas. Longer trips into DRC or overland trips through the country were inadvisable at the time of writing. The southern border between Cyangugu and Bukavu (DRC) is also open for crossing, but the security situation around Bukavu is more volatile than Goma. Check carefully in Cyangugu before venturing across, and be

---

DEPARTURE TAX

International departure tax is US$20, but is included in the ticket price at the time of purchase.

---

very wary of visiting Parc National Kahuzi-Biega (DRC) as there have been security problems there.

TANZANIA

Daily minibuses go from Kigali to Rusumu (US$6.50, three hours), where you'll need to walk across the Kagera River bridge. Once across, there are pick-up taxis to the tiny town (and former refugee camp) of Benako (Tanzania; marked as Kasulo on some maps; Tsh2500, 25 minutes), about 20km southeast. Daily buses go from Benako to Mwanza (Tsh17,000, eight hours), though it's often easier to go in stages via Kahama and Shinyanga along the tarmac road. There are also daily connections from Benako to Nyakanazi junction, where you can try hitching a lift or squeezing into a bus on to Kibondo, Kasulu and Kigoma (Tsh4500, two hours from Benako to Nyakanazi plus Tsh9000 and about seven hours from there to Kigoma).

UGANDA

There are two main crossing points for foreigners: between Kigali and Kabale (Uganda) via Gatuna (Katuna on the Ugandan side), and between Musanze and Kisoro (Uganda) via Cyanika.

There are lots of minibuses between Kigali and the border at Gatuna (RFr2000, 1½ hours) throughout the day. There are also plenty of minibuses (USh1000) and special hire taxis (USh15,000 for the whole car) travelling back and forth between Katuna and Kabale.

From Musanze to Kisoro via Cyanika the road is in excellent shape on the Rwandan side and in poor condition on the Ugandan side. With Parc National des Volcans increasingly popular, the Rwandan military

have prioritised security on this stretch. Minibuses link either side of the border with Musanze (RFr1000, 25km) and Kisoro (USh1000, 12km).

Those travelling direct between Kigali and Kampala can travel with **Jaguar Executive Coaches** (☎ 086 14838), which offers buses (RFr5000 to RFr7000) departing in the morning from Nyabugogo bus station, and taking eight to nine hours, including a long border crossing. **Regional Coach** (☎ 575963) also offers morning bus services to Kampala), which continues to Nairobi (RFr16,000).

GETTING AROUND
Bus

Rwanda has a reasonable road system, for the most part due to its small size and a large dose of foreign assistance. The only major unsealed roads are those running alongside the shore of Lake Kivu and some smaller stretches around the country.

The best buses are privately run, scheduled services operated by Okapi Car, Trans Express 2000, Atraco Express and Virunga Ponctuel. Destinations covered include Huye, Gisenyi and Musanze, and departures are guaranteed to leave, hourly in many cases. They are less crowded and drive more carefully than the normal minibuses, but cost a little more.

Car & Motorcycle

Cars are suitable for most of the country's main roads, but those planning to follow the shores of Lake Kivu might be better off with a 4WD.

Car hire isn't well established in Rwanda, but most travel agents and tour operators in Kigali can organise something for RFr25,000 to RFr50,000 per day for a small car and up.

Local Transport

Taxis are necessary only in Kigali, but it is possible to find the occasional sole-occupancy taxi in most other major towns. In Kigali and other larger towns, you can use a *taxi-motor* – a motorcycle that doubles as a two-wheeled taxi.

Somaliland, Puntland & Somalia

Since 1991 the country that is still known among the diplomatic community as 'Somalia' has effectively been a patchwork state, with three countries stitched into one: Somalia in the south, Somaliland in the northwest on the Gulf of Aden, and Puntland perched in the northeast corner. The internal situation in each zone is radically different. Put simply: there's one success story – Somaliland – and two horror stories – Puntland and Somalia, where the law of the gun, kidnapping of foreigners, piracy, banditry, food shortages, fighting among rival factions and a host of humanitarian crises have created a post-apocalyptic feel.

While Puntland and Somalia have been sliding towards the abyss and are absolute no-go zones for all Westerners (and it's unlikely to change anytime soon), the self-proclaimed Republic of Somaliland has, like a phoenix, risen from the ashes by restoring law and order within its boundaries. Discreetly. So discreetly that nobody knows that it has a representative government, a capital, a flag, a currency, an army and a functioning administration! But it has yet to gain international recognition as an independent nation, with very few diplomatic supporters and little media coverage to voice its progress. It's slowly emerging as the ultimate destination for adventurous travellers. Its tourist infrastructure is still embryonic but it's this sense of pushing Africa's secret door ajar that makes Somaliland one of the most weirdly fascinating countries you could hope to visit right now. Even if you can't get a cold beer.

FAST FACTS

- **Area** 637,657 sq km
- **ATMs** None
- **Borders** Kenya, Ethiopia and Djibouti (only the Djiboutian and Ethiopian borders with Somaliland are open to travellers)
- **Budget** US$25 to US$100 per day
- **Capital** Mogadishu (Somalia), Hargeisa (Somaliland), Bosasso (Puntland)
- **Languages** Somali
- **Money** Somaliland shilling; US$1 = SISh1405, €1= SISh2059
- **Population** 10 million (3.5 million in Somaliland)
- **Seasons** Wet (April to June and October to November), dry (July to September, December to March)
- **Telephone** Country code ☎ 252-2; international access code ☎ 16
- **Time** GMT/UTC + 3
- **Visa** Somaliland US$30 to US$50

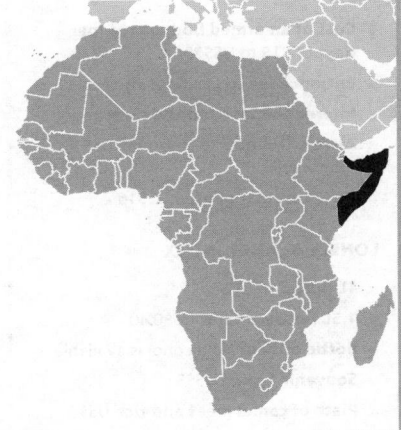

HIGHLIGHTS

- **Berbera** Nurse a soft drink, feast on fresh fish and relax on porcelain-sand beaches (p764).
- **Diving** Be a pioneer and take the plunge in the waters of the bay of Berbera (p764).
- **Hargeisa** Purchase your own ship of the desert at the camel market (p762).
- **Las Geel** One of the world's finest open-air galleries of prehistoric rock art (p763).
- **Sheekh** Feel the pulse of this laid-back, provincial town (p765).

CLIMATE & WHEN TO GO

There are regional variations but generally it goes like this: Somalia has two rainy seasons (April to June and October to November) and two dry seasons (July to September and December to March). From July to September temperatures are unbearable, reaching 40°C. In the south, near the border with Kenya, the climate is tropical.

Travel is much easier during the winter dry season, from December to March, when daily temperatures do not exceed 30°C.

HISTORY

Originally, Somalis probably hail from the southern Ethiopian highlands, and have been subject to a strong Arabic influence ever since the 7th century, when the Somali coast formed part of the extensive Arab-controlled trans-Indian Ocean trading network.

HOW MUCH?

- **Cost of an armed bodyguard (per day)** US$15 to US$20
- **Entrance fee to Las Geel site** US$20
- **Internet connection** US$1 per hour
- **Airfare Djibouti to Hargeisa** US$130 (one way)
- **1g (21 carats) of gold** US$16

LONELY PLANET INDEX

- **1L petrol** US$1.50
- **1.5L bottled water** US$0.40
- **Bottle of beer** No alcohol is available
- **Souvenir T-shirt** US$3
- **Plate of camel meat and rice** US$3

In the 19th century, much of the Ogaden Desert – ethnically a part of Somalia – was annexed by Ethiopia (an invasion that has been a source of bad blood ever since), and then in 1888 the country was divided by European powers. The French got the area around Djibouti and Britain much of the north, while Italy got Puntland and the south. It wasn't until 1960 that Somaliland, Puntland and southern Somalia were united.

Sadly, interclan tensions, radical socialism, rearmament by the USSR and the occasional (often disastrous) war with Ethiopia helped tear the country apart. Mohammed Siad Barre, Somalia's last recognised leader, fled to Nigeria in 1991. At the same time the Somali National Movement (SNM) moved quickly and declared independence for Somaliland. Puntland also broke away and declared itself an autonomous state in 1998.

Restoration of Hope?

Fierce battles between warring factions throughout southern Somalia took place throughout the 1990s, but in 1992 the US led a UN mission (Operation Restore Hope) to distribute food aid to the southern population. Without much ado a nasty little conflict between the US–UN and warlord General Aideed began, during which it's estimated that thousands of Somalis died. The last UN troops pulled out in 1995, having alleviated the famine to some extent, but the nation was still a disaster area.

Utter Failure

Designed to establish control across the whole of the country, Somalia's lame-duck Transitional National Government (TNG) was set up in 2000. Alas, it didn't manage to gain recognition from its own people in Somalia, who continue to regard it as a creature in the hands of international interests. Although it's the only internationally recognised body, it has proved too weak to impose its rule and has failed in curbing the power of militias. It has had to cower in the west in the town of Baidoa, its redoubt, leaving the rest of the country in the hands of feuding warlords.

The Case of Somaliland

The self-proclaimed Republic of Somaliland was formed in 1991 after the collapse of unitary Somalia. Thanks mainly to the pre-dominance of a single clan (the Isaq), it has remained largely peaceful since 1991. It voted for complete independence in 1997, before holding its first free presidential elections in 2003 (although opposition parties don't recognise the victory of President Dahir Riyale Kahin). Although its leaders are fighting to gain formal international recognition, Somaliland is not recognised as a separate state by the outside world. The main reason why the world is reluctant to accept Somaliland's independence is that the UN still hopes for a peace agreement covering all of Somalia, and its other neighbours are wary of an independent Somaliland, fearing a potential 'Balkanisation' of the Horn. To Somalilanders, this sounds profoundly unfair. Unlike the rest of Somalia, they have managed to establish law and order in their own country. Expat Somalilanders have kept doing their best to influence diplomatic corps in Europe, East Africa and North America – in vain, so far. However, Somaliland's leaders have nurtured good relations with Kenya, Ethiopia, France, the UK, Germany and Norway, and seem to be backed by the African Union.

In 2003 their efforts were partly ruined by the fact that 'terrorists' from Mogadishu illegally entered Somaliland and shot dead several aid workers with the aim of destabilising the fledgling country and causing it to lose its credibility on the international scene. This explains why local authorities tend to be overprotective of foreigners once they venture outside the capital. In October 2008 another group of terrorists from Mogadishu carried out suicide bombings in Hargeisa. The targets included the presidency, the Ethiopian Liaison Office and one UN office.

The second presidential elections are scheduled for early 2010, after having been delayed several times.

The Case of Puntland

Puntland is a different kettle of fish. It, too, did reasonably well up until 2001, when President Colonel Yusuf refused to stand down after losing an election, a point he reinforced by waging a little war. But the central government was too weak and Puntland started to descend into violence and anarchy.

Puntland is at odds with neighbouring Somaliland: there are territorial disputes over several border provinces, which translate into sporadic fighting. The biggest issue is piracy; over the last few years, piracy has exploded

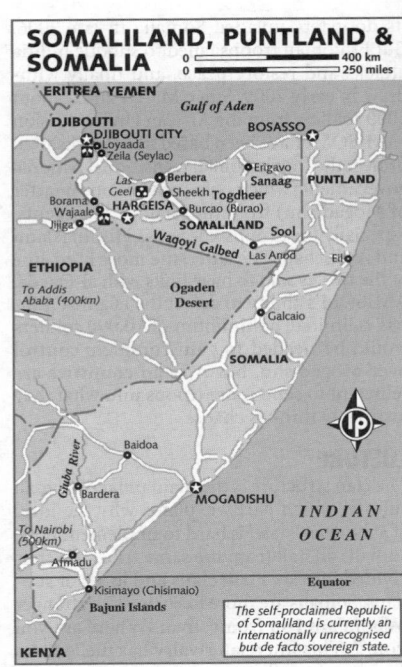

SOMALILAND, PUNTLAND & SOMALIA

0 _____ 400 km
0 _____ 250 miles

ERITREA YEMEN
        Gulf of Aden
DJIBOUTI
  DJIBOUTI CITY   BOSASSO
  Loyaada
  Zeila (Seylac)
                  Erigavo
              Las   Sheekh   Sanaag   PUNTLAND
  Borama Geel   Berbera Togdheer
  Wajaale HARGEISA
  Jijiga   SOMALILAND   Sool
              Wagoyi Galbed   Las Anod   Eil
ETHIOPIA
To Addis   Ogaden
Ababa (400km)   Desert
                          Galcaio
                      SOMALIA

                      Baidoa
  Bardera   MOGADISHU   INDIAN
To Nairobi   OCEAN
(500km)
      Afmadu
                              Equator
  Kisimayo (Chisimaio)
  Bajuni Islands   The self-proclaimed Republic
                       of Somaliland is currently an
KENYA   internationally unrecognised
                       but de facto sovereign state.

in the waters off the coast of Puntland, and it's now the region's most profitable industry. Despite the presence of US and French warships in the area, dozens of vessels are hijacked each year by pirates operating from Puntland.

Somalia Today

June and July 2006 marked an important turning point: Islamist militias ousted US-backed, secular warlords from Mogadishu and took control of the ravaged capital. Then they took swathes of southern Somalia. They restored a semblance of unity and order, but the US feared that Somalia could become a terrorist safe haven and a Talibanesque state under these new rulers. US-backed Ethiopia, fiercely opposed to any kind of Islamist ideology on

WARNING

All parts of Somalia and Puntland were an absolute no-go zone at the time of writing. We were unable to do on-the-ground research in Somalia and Puntland.

its doorstep, invaded Somalia in late 2006. But Ethiopian troops failed to subdue militia attacks and restore peace, and finally withdrew in early 2009. Since March 2007, about 5000 soldiers from the African Union mission (AMISOM) have been based in Mogadishu to protect the fragile Somali transitional national government (which only controls one quarter of Mogadishu) from the Islamist insurgents, especially the groups known as Hisbul Islami and Al Shebab. The latter, the more hard-line of the two, is said to have links with al-Qaeda. AMISOM's ability to defeat the Islamist militias is limited; a minimum of 10,000 soldiers would be needed to gain complete control over Mogadishu, but African countries are reluctant to send more troops into what they justifiably think is chaos.

CULTURE

The clan structure is the main pillar of Somali culture, which partly explains why the ideal of a modern 'state' is hard to implement here. Somalis all hail from the same tribe, which is divided into six main clans and loads of subclans. Somalis are more likely to ask a stranger 'Whom are you from?' than 'Where are you from?'. This interclan rivalry has fuelled two decades of conflict.

The nomadic lifestyle also exerts a major influence on Somali culture.

People

Somalis can be quiet and dignified, with a tendency to ignore strangers, but have a tremendous oral (often poetic) tradition. Written Somali is a very young language (the Somali Latin script was established in 1973) and spelling variations, especially place names, is very common. English is widely used in the north, but Italian dominates in the south.

Well over a million Somalis are scattered across Europe, North America and the Middle East; together they send hundreds of millions of dollars back to Somalia each year.

All Somalis are Sunni Muslims and Islam is extremely important to the Somali sense of national identity. Most women wear headscarves, and arranged marriage is still the norm in rural areas.

ENVIRONMENT

Characterised by desert or semidesert terrain, Somalia is distinguished by three main topographical features: the Oogo, a mountainous highland region in the north dominated by the Gollis Mountains; the Guban, a relatively barren, hot and humid coastal region (dominating southern Somalia); and the Hawd, a sweeping area of rich, rainy-season pasture prone to overgrazing and desertification. Serious drought continues to plague the south of the country.

Unsurprisingly, Somalia has some of the longest beaches in the world. Coral reefs and the relatively pristine Seylac Islands lie in the Red Sea off the coast of Somaliland.

FOOD & DRINK

Goat and camel meat are popular dishes in Somalia. The standard breakfast throughout Somalia is fried liver with onions and *anjeero,* a flat bread similar to the Ethiopian *injera.* Rice and noodles are also common staples. Camel is the preferred source of meat.

Tea is the favourite drink. Sheep, goat or camel's milk are also widespread. Alcohol is strictly prohibited and not available.

SOMALILAND

For seasoned (and well-prepared) travellers in search of a totally unusual travel experience, Somaliland is a goldmine. Las Geel shelters some of the best-preserved rock paintings in Africa; the port town of Berbera boasts too-perfect-to-be-real beaches on its doorstep; Hargeisa, the capital, has a fascinating camel market; and there's also the chance to – wait for it – go diving off the coast of Berbera and Zeila. Opening the door to a country that doesn't officially exist adds to the thrill. Travel logistics are easier than you'd think – access from Djibouti and Ethiopia is a doddle.

That said, Somaliland is *not* a regular holiday destination. It's economically crippled, tourism infrastructure is limited and it desperately lacks foreign investment to rebuild the economy. And despite what officials claim, there's still an element of uncertainty regarding the security situation. Get an update before setting off. One thing is sure: you'll feel like you're on another planet.

HARGEISA

pop 1.2 million

You'll never forget your first impression of Hargeisa. We're not talking of roadblocks and militiamen wielding machine guns (you're not in Mogadishu), but of an intriguing and

---

READ THIS FIRST

Somaliland was safe at the time of writing, and our on-the-ground research included Hargeisa, Las Geel, Berbera, Sheekh and Burcao. That said, foreigners must be accompanied by an armed soldier when outside Hargeisa. If you don't have a soldier with you, you'll be turned back at checkpoints.

Since the murder of three aid workers by Somali terrorists from Mogadishu in 2003 and three suicide bombings in Hargeisa in October 2008, local authorities have taken the safety of Westerners very seriously, to the point of being overprotective. This restrictive rule will be lifted, it is said, when the situation is considered perfectly safe for foreigners.

Keep in mind that Somaliland is still not a conventional country, and that its borders are not 100% terrorist-proof. The Somalilanders have established law and order in their own territory, but as long as their unruly brothers from Puntland and southern Somalia don't settle for peace, there will be an element of risk.

Seek local advice before setting off.

Organising a police escort

Most hotels can arrange a police escort. It costs about US$15 to US$20 per day for a soldier, plus food. Don't take this measure too harshly; it can even be fun. By 2pm, your guardian angel will have started chewing qat (a leaf used as a stimulant) and will probably be completely stoned until 7pm at least. The good thing is that he can also act as an interpreter and a de facto guide.

There is a way to (partly) escape the rule. The people at the Oriental Hotel will tell you how to get a special permit that allows you to travel to Berbera without the mandatory escort; they have good relations with a chief police officer, who will issue a kind of *laissez passer* with your name on it. This should be enough to let you through – but do so at your own risk!

---

energising city. Sure, the capital of Somaliland still bears the scars of the civil war that destroyed the country in the past decades, but it's a city in transition. The streets are alive, the roads are busy, and the air thick with a very bearable cacophony of vehicle horns and calls to prayer. And it's surprising to see that Hargeisa has all the conveniences a traveller could hope for: good-value hotels with English-speaking staff, a couple of tasty restaurants, internet cafes, electronics stores, tea shops, markets, bus stations, taxis...but no alcohol, and absolutely no nightlife (it would be too good to be true!).

Hargeisa lacks standout sights but if you like your markets colourful, clamorous and spilling into the surrounding streets, and enjoy the feeling of being the only tourist wandering its streets, you might just find it appealing.

Orientation

No city map is available, barring the one in this book. Most places of interest to travellers, as well as shops, businesses and hotels, are on or around the main thoroughfare, Independence Rd. Most streets don't have names; use the MiG jet, the Oriental Hotel and mosques as landmarks. The airport is about 5km from the city centre.

Information

INTERNET ACCESS

There's a profusion of internet cafes in the city centre (about US$1 per hour).

MEDICAL SERVICES

For medical treatment, **Edna Adan Hospital** (☎ 4426922; www.ednahospital.org) offers excellent facilities. It's staffed by English-speaking doctors.

MONEY

Somaliland is a strictly cash economy – forget about travellers cheques, credit cards and ATMs. Most transactions can be conducted using US dollars, but if you want to change money, head to one of the **Dahabshiil** (www.dahabshiil.com; Independence Rd; 7am-noon & 1-5.30pm Sat-Thu) branches. You can also find moneychangers near the Oriental Hotel. Most hotels also change money and don't take commission.

POST & TELEPHONE

There's no post office in Hargeisa. You'll have to use courier services, such as DHL. Ask at your hotel.

Making phone calls is easy and cheap. You can also bring your mobile phone and

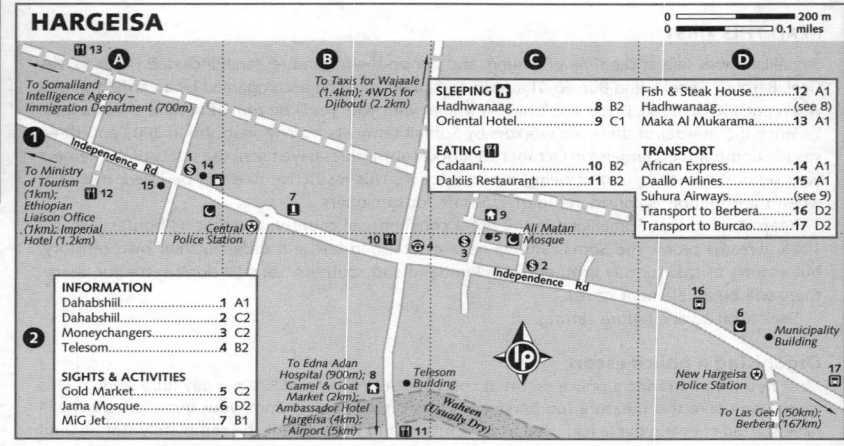

HARGEISA

INFORMATION		
Dahabshiil	1	A1
Dahabshiil	2	C2
Moneychangers	3	C2
Telesom	4	B2

SIGHTS & ACTIVITIES		
Gold Market	5	C2
Jama Mosque	6	D2
MiG Jet	7	B1

SLEEPING		
Hadhwanaag	8	B2
Oriental Hotel	9	C1

EATING		
Cadaani	10	B2
Dalxiis Restaurant	11	B2

Fish & Steak House	12	A1
Hadhwanaag	(see 8)	
Maka Al Mukarama	13	A1

TRANSPORT		
African Express	14	A1
Daallo Airlines	15	A1
Suhura Airways	(see 9)	
Transport to Berbera	16	D2
Transport to Burcao	17	D2

buy a local SIM card from **Telesom** (Independence Rd) or any other mobile phone company.

TOURIST INFORMATION
Hotel owners (especially at the Ambassador Hotel Hargeisa and the Oriental Hotel), are the best sources for travel information and can also help with visa matters and escort and car rentals. You can also contact the **Director of Tourism** (☎ 2-4424561; shabeelle7@yahoo.com; ⏱ 8am-1pm Sat-Thu) at the Ministry of Tourism.

Dangers & Annoyances
Law and order reign in Hargeisa. You can explore the city on your own; an escort is not mandatory in the capital. That said, the usual precautions apply. Avoid walking alone at night, don't be ostentatious with valuables and beware of pickpockets in crowded areas.

Always ask permission before taking photographs.

Sights
Let's be frank: it's the ambience and the sense of exploration that are the pull here. Visually, Hargeisa is fairly underwhelming, with nothing much of interest except perhaps the city's war memorial – a Somali Air Force **MiG jet** – and the imposing **Jama Mosque**.

An essential part of the Hargeisa experience is the **camel and goat market**, which lies on the outskirts of town. It's a fascinating place to wander. Always ask permission before taking photographs.

The **gold market**, a short stagger from the Oriental Hotel, is another wonderful place. There's a flurry of goldsmiths on the main street, too.

Sleeping
The following options come recommended as they're used to dealing with foreigners. As there are no street signs, most hotels do not have addresses. Prices include breakfast.

Hadhwanaag (☎ 521820, 300851; hhbulbul@hotmail.com; s US$8-10, d US$12-15; ⏅) As far as Hargeisa prices go, the Hadhwanaag is good value. The low-slung building occupies a leafy compound, a five-minute walk away from the main drag. The attention to detail could be sharper (you'll have to ask for a fan) but the rooms are acceptable. Oh, and you can eat well here, too. Hassan, the English-speaking owner, can help you with logistics.

our pick Oriental Hotel (☎ 514999; www.orientalhotelhargeisa.com; s/d US$15/30; 💻) The closest Hargeisa comes to a travellers' hang-out, the Oriental can't be beaten for convenience. It's ultracentral, there's a restaurant and it's nicely laid out, with the reception area opening onto the pleasant sun-filled patio. Rooms are kept clean and functional. Ask for Abdi Abdi, the owner, or Said, Abdi Abdi's relative; both speak excellent English and will go the extra mile to help you with logistics.

Imperial Hotel (☎ 515000, 520524; imperialhotel101@hotmail.com; Independence Rd; s/d US$20/30; 💻) The modernish Imperial Hotel is in a calm neighbourhood, but within walking distance of the centre. Expect well-appointed rooms, working fans, salubrious bathrooms and a restaurant in a shady courtyard at the back.

Ambassador Hotel Hargeisa (☎ 526666; www.ambassadorhotelhargeisa.com; Airport Rd; s/d US$45/80; P ✖ 🖳 🛜) Drop anchor here for a night or two if you need to reassure your family. The squeaky-clean rooms are equipped with everything to ensure a comfortable stay, including satellite TV, glittering bathrooms, a restaurant and a bar (not licensed). Staff speak excellent English and do an excellent job with car rental, tour guides, police escort and visa matters. Its single drawback is its location away from the central buzz, about 4km from the centre, near the airport.

Eating & Drinking

All places listed open for breakfast, lunch and dinner. No alcohol is served, but you'll enjoy superb Somali tea and fresh fruit juices.

Maka Al Mukarama (fruit juices US$2.50; ☽ 7am-8pm) Put some bounce in your step with a glass of mango juice at this juice haven. Cakes are also available.

Cadaani (Independence Rd; mains US$1-3) You can't miss this bustling cafeteria – look for the red-and-white building beside Telesom. It rustles up simple dishes, such as spaghetti and sandwiches.

our pick **Dalxiis Restaurant** (mains US$2-5) The Dalxiis is an enticing 'park restaurant', with a garden-like setting. Get your fingers dirty experimenting with the wide range of Somali dishes, including *geel hanid* (roast camel), basmati rice, mutton and grilled fish. Order *loxox* (if you can pronounce it: lo-cho-ch) at breakfast; it mixes *injera*-like bread with butter, eggs and honey.

Hadhwanaag (mains US$2-5) Near the Dalxiis, Hadhwanaag is another wonderful place to sample Somali specialities like *loxox*, fish dishes, mutton ('divine', according to our Somali friends), chicken and roast beef. Leave room for the Yemeni desserts – the *fata mus* (a concoction with banana) and the *fata timir* (a concoction with dates) are truly finger-licking good.

Fish & Steak House (Independence Rd; mains US$2-5) At this peaceful oasis set back from the main drag, the menu is more eclectic than anywhere else in Hargeisa, and no wonder; the cooks have worked in Djibouti. From lasagne and prawns to chicken curry and beef with pepper sauce, everything that emerges from the kitchen is produced with plenty of *savoir faire*.

Getting There & Away

AIR

Airlines with offices in Hargeisa:

African Express (☎ 523646; www.africanexpress.co.ke; Independence Rd)

Daallo Airlines (☎ 523003; www.daallo.com; Independence Rd)

Suhura Airways (☎ 524411) In the same building as the Oriental Hotel.

The Ethiopian Airlines office was closed at the time of research but should have reopened by the time you read this.

See p766 for details on flights to/from Somaliland.

LAND

Regular shared taxis travel between Hargeisa, Berbera, Sheekh, Burcao, and Wajaale at the Ethiopian border. They leave from various departure points (north of town for Wajaale and Djibouti; two blocks east from the Oriental Hotel for Berbera; and beside the Municipality building for Sheekh and Burcao). They cost from US$5 to US$12 depending on the destination. There are also daily services to Djibouti (see p766).

Getting Around

A taxi ride in the centre should cost no more than US$3, and about US$10 to the airport.

AROUND SOMALILAND

LAS GEEL

Las Geel is indisputably Somaliland's *pièce de résistance*. Were it not in Somaliland, this fantastic **archaeological site** (admission US$20) would immediately be declared a World Heritage Site. Sadly (well, not quite, if you like having the place to yourself), as long as Somaliland is not recognised by the international community, it will remain a hidden gem.

Hundreds of magnificent neolithic rock art paintings in perfect condition, representing humans and animals, adorn the walls of several interconnected caves and shelters. Some paintings exceed 1m in length and their state of preservation is exceptional. There are even some very risqué scenes! This

---

PIONEER DIVING IN SOMALILAND

'I saw a TV program on the BBC about Somaliland, and this sparked my curiosity,' says Steve Atkinson, the British dive instructor who runs Somaliland's sole diving centre, at the Maan-Soor Hotel in Berbera. 'After meeting the owner of the Maan-Soor Hotel, we decided to set up a diving base in 2008.' How is the diving near Berbera? 'There are no sprawling coral reefs and the visibility is usually low because the shores near Berbera are sandy, but there's the novelty factor!' Are there other areas that are worth diving? 'The islands off Zeila (Seylac) are fantastic. We're still in the exploratory phase, but we plan to organise dive expeditions out there. The waters are clear and there's fish in abundance. Plus you really feel you've reached the end of the earth; it's like Southern Egypt 20 years ago.'

---

archaeological wonder was only brought to light in 2003, following research conducted by a team of French archaeologists. There's a small museum at the entrance of the site with panels in English.

It's about 50km from Hargeisa, around 6km off the road to Berbera (the turn-off is at Dhubato village). You'll also need a guide (or a permit, obtainable at the Ministry of Tourism, see p762) and a private vehicle to get there, both easily arranged in Hargeisa. Hotels charge from US$60 to US$100 per vehicle.

BERBERA

The name alone sounds impossibly exotic, conjuring up images of tropical ports, spices and palm oil. The reality is a little more prosaic; today this shady town consists mostly of crumbling buildings and mud-and-thatch houses. There's great potential, though, with superb beaches and a relaxed atmosphere. If, one day, Somaliland appears on tourist brochures, Berbera will probably top the bill. Meanwhile, it's a great place to chill out for a few days.

Sights & Activities

In the centre, there's an **old mosque** that's worth a peek. You can also delve into the small **market** area and soak up the atmosphere. Not far from Al Xayaat Restaurant, the tiny **fishing harbour** deserves a few photo snaps (but ask permission first).

Berbera is also bound by blissful beaches, about 3km from the centre, including **Baathela Beach**, just in front of Maan-Soor Hotel. At dawn, dolphins can be seen frolicking in the bay – memorable.

Let's see; have we missed anything? Oh right. **Diving** is available in Berbera! There's a small, English-run **diving centre** (☎ 4138607, 4247030; steve_atk@hotmail.co.uk) based at the Maan-

Soor Hotel. A single dive costs US$40 (equipment included). See above for more info.

Sleeping & Eating

Al Madiina Hotel (☎ 740254; r without bathroom US$3, r US$5-30; ✗) Right in the centre, this venture doesn't feel the need for fancy touches and what you see is what you get, which in this case is a bed plonked in a threadbare room.

Esco Hotel (☎ 740767; r with fan & without bathroom US$6, r with bathroom & air-con US$25; ✗) A coin's toss from Al Xayaat Restaurant, the Esco has a mixed bag of rooms to suit all budgets. The better rooms have air-con. Plumbing could do with a bit of maintenance, but the sheets get a regular spin in the washing machine and fans are working.

Maan-Soor Hotel (☎ 4244240; http://maan-soor.com; s/d US$40/60; ✗) A resort-style hotel in such a remote place? Yes, it's possible. The owner, Abdulkader, is eager to promote Berbera as a beach-holiday destination, and this hotel is a first step. It consists of 16 clean-as-a-pin 'cottages' scattered around a large property just spitting distance from Baathela beach (but no direct seaviews). Amenities include an attached restaurant, satellite TV and a dive centre.

Al Xayaat Restaurant & Fish House (☎ 740224; mains US$3; ✗ lunch & dinner) Lap up a reviving fruit juice and scoff a piece of grilled fish at this colourful eatery overlooking the bay and you'll leave with a smile on your face. While eating you'll be surrounded by a menagerie of cats, crows and seagulls expecting a titbit. Ali, the amiable owner, speaks good English.

Getting There & Away

Regular shared taxis travel between Hargeisa and Berbera (US$5, 150km).

SHEEKH

From Berbera and the coastal plain, you can make a beautiful journey along the switchback ascent to the central plateau on the Berbera–Burcao road and stop at the hill town of Sheekh, which is a welcome refuge from the heat of the lowland areas. This is one of the main educational centres in the country, with a well-established veterinary school and various colleges.

Sheekh boasts a small **necropolis**, called Ferdusa, which dates from the 13th century. There's not much to be seen, as the site has not been excavated yet.

Sheekh is approximately halfway between Berbera and Burcao. You can break up your Somaliland odyssey at the no-frills **Mashaallah Hotel** (☎ 730167; r incl breakfast US$7-12).

BURCAO (BURAO)

The capital of Todgheer province and the second largest city in the country, Burcao feels a bit rougher around the edges than Berbera or Hargeisa, but that's part of the adventure. There's nothing of interest here, but you can soak up the atmosphere at the livestock market (and enjoy being the focus of attention).

By far the best place to stay is the ultra-central **Barwaaqo Hotel & Restaurant** (☎ 715800; barwaaqohotelburco@hotmail.com; s/d US$10/15), which features spotless rooms and an excellent rooftop restaurant. We saw a number of (veiled) female guests, too, so it's a sensible choice for women travellers.

Shamaxle Restaurant (mains US$4-7; ☯ lunch & dinner) The location, in a leafy compound right by the Todgheer River, at the foot of a bridge, is relaxing. And the juicy *hanid* (roast lamb) will have your tastebuds leaping around for joy. Zahra, the female owner, has lived in the USA and speaks very good English.

Getting There & Away

Shared taxis leave for Hargeisa (US$5 to US$10) via Berbera.

SOMALILAND DIRECTORY

ACCOMMODATION

Surprise: there's a fairly good range of options in Hargeisa and Berbera, at affordable prices (a cheapie doesn't cost more than US$5).

What's more, staff usually speak very good English.

BUSINESS HOURS

All shops, offices and businesses are closed on Friday, but most restaurants are open every day.

DANGERS & ANNOYANCES

Follow what hotel staff tell you – an armed soldier (at your own expense) and a tour guide might be compulsory outside Hargeisa. Check the situation while in Hargeisa. All travel in the Sool region to the southeast is currently unsafe due to conflict in Puntland.

EMBASSIES & CONSULATES

The only official foreign representation in Somaliland is the **Ethiopian Liaison Office** (Hargeisa; ☯ 8.30am-noon Sat-Thu), which acts as a de facto embassy.

Somaliland Liaison Offices abroad include:

Ethiopia (Map pp682–3; ☎ 11-635921; fax 11-627847; Bole Rd District, Addis Ababa)

France (☎ 09 50 81 50 94, 06 17 67 70 75; wakiil_sl_fr@hotmail.fr; 19 rue Augustin Thierry, 75019 Paris)

UK (☎ 020-7961 9098; 102 Cavel St; London E1 2JA)

USA (☎ 202-467 0602; 3705 South George Mansion, Falls Church, VA 22041)

MONEY

There are no ATMs anywhere in Somaliland, so carry considerable amounts of US dollars (vastly preferable to euros) that can be exchanged for shillings in hotels, shops and bureaux de change. Most hotels and shops also accept payment in US dollars. There's no chance of changing your travellers cheques. If you need to wire money, **Dahabshiil** (www.dahabshiil.com) transfers can be made at the various Dahabshiil offices in Hargeisa.

TELEPHONE

There are several private telephone companies in Somaliland, such as Telesom and Telecom. International telephone calls made from Somaliland are the cheapest in Africa (less than US$0.30 per minute).

VISAS

You will need a visa to enter Somaliland. Visas are *not* issued at the airport. The most convenient place to get a visa is Addis Ababa, Ethiopia. They are issued while you wait through the Somaliland Liaison Office (see p765) and cost US$40.

In the UK, the USA and France, you can contact the Somaliland Liaison Office. Another option is to go through a local sponsor, such as the Oriental Hotel, the Ambassador Hotel Hargeisa (see p762) or the Director of Tourism (see p761). Email them the (scanned) ID pages of your passport and give them at least three days to organise the visa. They will email a visa certificate back to you as an attached document. Print it and present it upon arrival at the airport (or at any land border). Note that this is a certificate; the original visa should have been deposited at the immigration office at the airport (or at the border post, if you arrive by land) by your sponsor. In practice, your sponsor will be waiting for you at the airport with the original visa. Hotels charge US$20 to US$50 for the service.

Visas for Onward Travel

The Ethiopian Liaison Office (see p765) can issue Ethiopian visas. You'll need two photos, US$20 and a letter from the Somaliland Intelligence Agency – Immigration Department.

SOMALILAND TRANSPORT

GETTING THERE & AWAY
Air

Somaliland has two international gateways for arrival by air: Hargeisa and Berbera. Hargeisa is the busiest. Daallo Airlines, the national carrier, as well as Ethiopian Airlines and Suhura Airways, use Hargeisa, while African Express uses Berbera.

The most common routes are from Djibouti or Addis Ababa, Ethiopia.

From Djibouti, Daallo Airlines has four weekly flights to Hargeisa (US$130, 40 minutes). For Addis Ababa, Daallo Airlines flies from Hargeisa twice a week (one way/return US$200/325), while Suhura Airways has a weekly flight (one way/return US$200/230). Ethiopian Airlines had suspended its flights to Hargeisa at the time of writing but should have resumed them by the time you read this.

Other destinations served by Daallo Airlines include Bosasso (Puntland), Mogadishu

---

DEPARTURE AND ARRIVAL TAX

International departure tax is US$32, payable in cash. Arrival tax is US$22. You'll also have to change US$50 at the airport at a ludicrously unfavourable exchange rate (half the normal exchange rate). If you arrive by land, you'll be exempt from paying taxes.

(southern Somalia) and Nairobi (Kenya; via Mogadishu).

From Berbera, African Express operates flights to Dubai (UAE; one way/return, US$330/430, twice weekly), Nairobi (Kenya; US$420/770, twice weekly) and Aden (Yemen; US$210/280, once weekly).

If you're coming from Australasia, your best bet is to fly to Dubai and find an onward connection to Djibouti (and on to Hargeisa) or to Berbera.

Land
DJIBOUTI

The land border between Somaliland and Djibouti is open. Shared taxis (usually Land Cruisers) ply the route on a daily basis from Hargeisa to Djibouti City – a strenuous 20-hour journey on a gravel road (about US$30). Taxis usually leave Hargeisa around 4pm so as to travel by night and avoid the scorching heat. Bring food and plenty of water. The border crossing is at Loyaada.

ETHIOPIA

From Jijiga in eastern Ethiopia there's regular bus traffic to the border town of Wajaale (see p699). In Wajaale, take a contract taxi (about US$50) or a minibus (about US$5) to Hargeisa, about 90km to the southeast. Ask the driver to drop you off in front of your hotel. Expect a couple of checkpoints, but no hassle.

Sea

It's possible to cross the Red Sea to either Aden or Mokha (Yemen). Yemeni boats carrying livestock leave from Berbera but there's no fixed schedule – they usually run on a twice-weekly basis. It costs about US$30 to US$50 and the crossing takes about 30 hours. Contact one of the shipping agencies in Berbera. They'll handle immigration formalities for you. You'll have to pay 'passport fees' (US$30).

SOMALIA AND PUNTLAND: NO FUTURE?

This French journalist based in Africa has done several trips to Somalia and Puntland over the last few years.

What does present-day Mogadishu look like?

Everything is decrepit, crumbling or riddled with bullets. After 18 years of war, the heritage buildings dating back to the Italian era, including the cathedral and the old harbour, have been almost completely destroyed. The only thing that's still standing is the statue of Ahmed the Left-Hander, who led the war against the kingdom of Ethiopia in the 16th century.

And what about security?

It's a no-go zone. All foreigners run the risk of being kidnapped, and there are no longer any expats based permanently in Mogadishu. The only ones who dare to come are journalists or aid workers on a quick trip, but they run a big, big risk.

Do you think the situation could improve during the lifetime of this book?

I don't think so. The transitional government controls only a handful of neighbourhoods, and there are daily battles between the forces of the African Union (who support the transitional government) and the Islamist militias. Nobody is in a position to control effectively or rule over the country. And the international community is reluctant to send more troops in what they consider a quagmire.

And Puntland?

Until 2007, it was relatively OK to go to Puntland, but the situation has worsened since. There's no war such as the one in Somalia, but the region is in the hands of pirates. That said, I've noticed that there's potential for tourism, with barrier reefs, clear waters and endless beaches. Hopefully this will be developed one day.

Stéphanie Braquehais is a French journalist based in Nairobi, from where she covers East Africa for Radio France Internationale and the daily newspaper Libération.

GETTING AROUND

Somaliland has a few sealed roads (like from Hargeisa to Berbera and from Berbera to Burcao). Medium-sized buses and crowded 4WDs service routes between major Somaliland settlements.

You can also hire a taxi for about US$70 per day (fuel and escort are extra) or a 4WD with driver for about US$140.

PUNTLAND

Forming the tip of the Horn of Africa, Puntland is the easternmost region of the continent. The peninsula of Raas Xaafuun should occupy a top spot in travellers' itineraries but, alas, is fraught with danger. Not only is the political situation pretty turbulent, the coast is renowned for piracy and kidnappings. Though slightly less anarchic than Somalia, the situation in Puntland has worsened over the last few years, mainly due to piracy.

There are also flashpoints in the Sool, southern and eastern Sanaag regions, all of which currently lie in Somaliland, but are claimed by Puntland. The 'capital' is Bosasso.

SOMALIA

If you're looking for good news, you've opened this guide on the wrong page. At the time of writing, Somalia was considered as possibly the most dangerous place in the world and one of the most lawless areas on earth. With such credentials, it is hardly likely to be on travellers' itineraries any time soon. See also above and p759.

At the time of writing, the ravaged capital of **Mogadishu** was possibly the most perilous city in the world and a definite no-go zone for foreigners.

What's left of this city that was founded in the 10th century AD by Arab merchants and ruled by sultans until the 20th century? It's probably now about as far from the glories of its 13th-century heyday as it's possible to get. Before the war, a number of isolated coves along the coast and pristine beaches were popular with expats. The **Bakara Market** is the infamous location where US Rangers and special forces units were pinned down for over 15 hours (as documented in the Hollywood kill-fest *Black Hawk Down*).

Tanzania

It is in Tanzania that some of Africa's most vivid images come to life: snow-capped Kilimanjaro, rhinos silhouetted against the backdrop of Ngorongoro Crater, wildebeests thundering over the Serengeti Plains, and white sands caressed by Indian Ocean breezes.

While most visitors head straight for the famed northern wildlife-watching circuit, followed by time relaxing on Zanzibar's beaches, Tanzania has much more to offer. Follow the coastline south into a Swahili culture where the rhythms have changed little over the centuries; journey through rolling hill country along the Tanzania–Zambia highway, detouring to Ruaha National Park; or explore Lake Tanganyika, with its remote fishing villages and chimpanzees.

The most popular areas have sealed main roads, and hotels and restaurants to suit every budget. Elsewhere, and especially in the south and west, you'll soon find yourself well off the beaten path, surrounded by a Tanzania that's far removed from Western development.

Wherever you go, take advantage of opportunities to get to know Tanzanians, as it is they who will inevitably wind up being the highlight of any visit. Chances are that you'll want to come back for more, to which most Tanzanians will say *Karibu tena* (Welcome again).

FAST FACTS

- **Area** 943,000 sq km
- **ATMs** All major towns (mostly Visa only)
- **Borders** Kenya, Uganda, Rwanda, Zambia, Malawi, Mozambique and Democratic Republic of Congo (DRC)
- **Budget** US$60 to US$100 per day
- **Capital** Dodoma
- **Languages** English, Swahili and many other African languages
- **Money** Tanzanian shilling (Tsh); US$1 = Tsh1340, €1 = Tsh1992
- **Population** 37.6 million
- **Seasons** Dry (June to August), wet (mid-March to May & November to December)
- **Telephone** Country code ☎ 255; international access code ☎ 000
- **Time** GMT/UTC + 3
- **Visa** US$50 for three months, available at most border crossings (single East African tourist visa expected to be introduced soon)

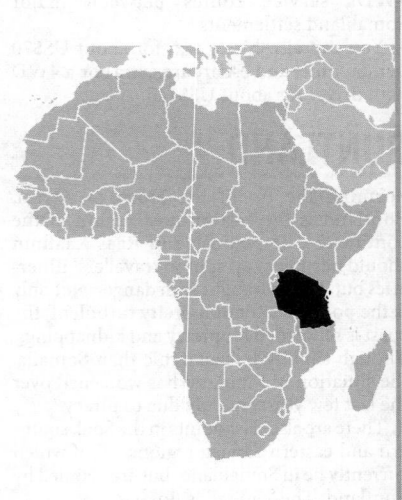

HOW MUCH?

- **Midrange safari** From US$200 per person per day
- **Plate of ugali** US$0.50
- **Serengeti National Park entry** US$50 per person per day
- **Papaya** US$0.25
- **Short taxi ride** US$2

LONELY PLANET INDEX

- **1L petrol** US$1.50
- **1.5L bottled water** US$0.50
- **Bottle of Safari Lager** US$1
- **Souvenir T-shirt** US$15
- **Mishikaki** US$0.20

HIGHLIGHTS

- **Serengeti National Park** (p798) Immerse yourself in the sounds and sights of the world's greatest wildlife spectacle.
- **Zanzibar Archipelago** (p778) Follow the lure of the Spice Islands back through the centuries on Zanzibar and little-visited Pemba.
- **Mount Kilimanjaro** (p789) Admire it from afar or climb its mighty shoulders, but do it before its icecap melts.
- **Picture-perfect beaches** (p784) Take your pick of the beaches, from idyllic offshore islands to the palm-fringed mainland coast or serene inland lakes.
- **Mahale Mountains National Park** (p802) Spend time with our closest relatives – wild chimpanzees – in one of the country's most remote corners.

CLIMATE & WHEN TO GO

The coolest months are from June to October and the warmest from December to March. Along the coast, there's high humidity and temperatures averaging between 25°C and 29°C. On the central plateau, temperatures range from 20°C to 27°C between June and August. Between December and March they can soar above 30°C.

There are two rainy seasons, with the *masika* (long rains) from mid-March to May, and the *mvuli* (short rains) during November, December and into January. The best time to travel is between late June and October, when the rains have finished and the air is coolest. However, this is also when hotels and park lodges are full and airfares most expensive. During the March to May rainy season, you can often save substantially on accommodation costs and have things to yourself.

ITINERARIES

- **One Week** Arriving in Dar es Salaam (p773), spend a day getting oriented, travel to Selous Game Reserve (p805) for a few nights and spend the remainder of the week on Zanzibar (p779).
- **Two Weeks** For the classic bush-and-beach itinerary, spend a week on the northern safari circuit or climbing Kilimanjaro (p789), followed by a week chilling out on Zanzibar.
- **One Month** With a month, combine any of the earlier itineraries; travel between Lake Victoria (p799) and northern or northeastern Tanzania via the western Serengeti (p798); make your way southwest via Mbeya (p804), with stops en route at Mikumi (p803) and Ruaha (p804) National parks; or follow the coast south to Mtwara (p805).

HISTORY

Tanzania's history begins with the dawn of humanity. Hominid (humanlike) footprints unearthed near Olduvai Gorge show that our earliest ancestors were roaming the Tanzanian plains and surrounding areas over three million years ago.

Seafaring merchants, who came from the Mediterranean and Asia, came looking for gold, spices and ivory, and intermarried with the families of their local trading contacts. They formed a civilisation known as the Swahili, with a common language (also Swahili) and a chain of prosperous cities stretching from Mozambique to Somalia. The Arabic kingdom of Oman eventually gained control of the Swahili coast, installing its sultan on Zanzibar and growing rich on the profits of the slaving expeditions that penetrated far into the country's interior.

Dr Livingstone, I Presume?

The first Europeans to arrive in East Africa were the Portuguese, who clashed with the Omanis for control of the lucrative trade routes to India. Later came British, Dutch

TANZANIA

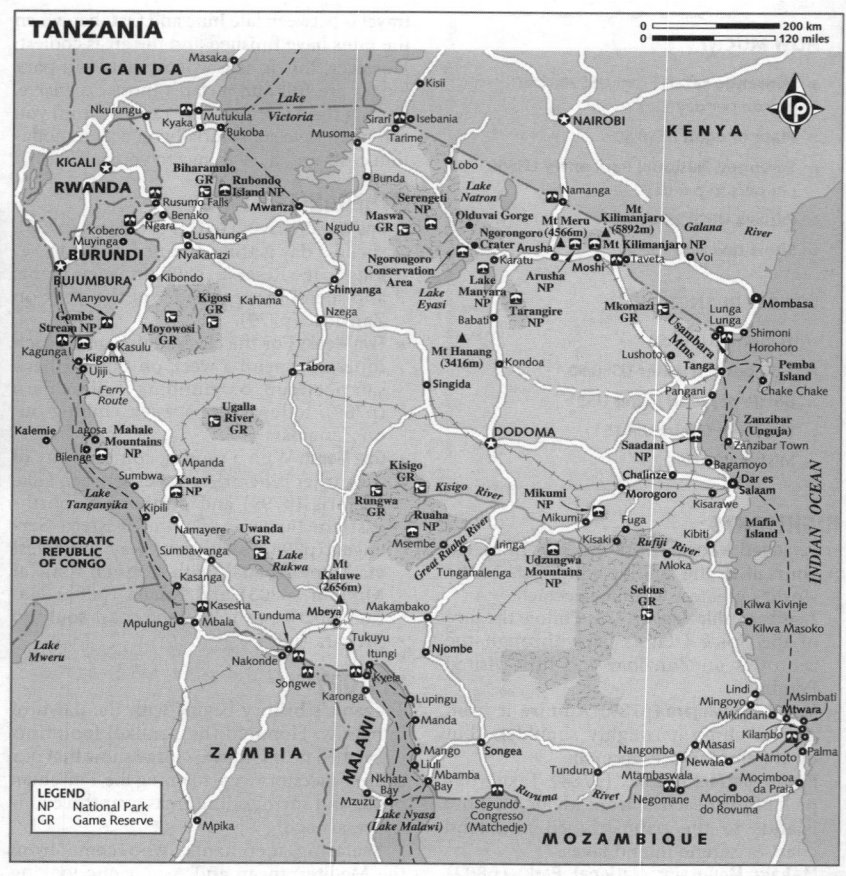

TANZANIA

and American merchant adventurers. By the 19th century, European explorers were setting out from Zanzibar into the unknown African interior. While searching for the source of the Nile, Dr David Livingstone became so famously lost that a special expedition headed by Henry Stanley was sent out to find him. Stanley caught up with Livingstone near modern-day Kigoma after a journey of more than a year, whereupon he uttered the famous words: 'Dr Livingstone, I presume?'

British efforts to suppress the slave trade ultimately led to the downfall of the Omani Empire. But it was Germany that first colonised what was then known as Tanganyika. Following WWI, the League of Nations mandated Tanganyika to Britain.

Independence

In 1959 Britain agreed to growing demands for the establishment of internal self-government. On 9 December 1961 Tanganyika became independent and on 9 December 1962 it was established as a republic, with Julius Nyerere as president.

On the Zanzibar Archipelago, which had been a British protectorate since 1890, the main push for independence came from the radical Afro-Shirazi Party (ASP), but when independence was granted in December 1963, two British-favoured minority parties formed the first government. Within a month, a Ugandan immigrant named John Okello initiated a violent revolution that toppled the government and the sultan, and led to the massacre or expulsion of most of the islands' Arab population. The sultan was replaced by the Zanzibar Revolutionary Council headed by Abeid Karume.

On 26 April 1964 Nyerere signed an act of union with Karume, creating the United Republic of Tanganyika (renamed the United Republic of Tanzania the following October). The union was resented by many Zanzibaris from the outset. In 1972 Karume was assassinated. Shortly thereafter, in an effort to subdue the ongoing unrest, Nyerere authorised the formation of a one-party state and combined his ruling Tanganyika African National Union (TANU) party and the ASP into Chama Cha Mapinduzi (CCM; Party of the Revolution). CCM's dominance of Tanzanian politics endures to this day.

The Socialist Experiment

The Arusha Declaration of 1967 committed Tanzania to a policy of socialism and self-reliance. The policy's cornerstone was the *ujamaa* (familyhood) village: an agricultural collective run along traditional African lines, whereby basic goods and tools were held in common and shared among members, while each individual was obliged to work on the land.

After an initial period of euphoric idealism, resentment at forced resettlement programs and other harsh measures grew, and the economy rapidly declined – precipitated in part by steeply rising oil prices and sharp drops in the value of coffee and sisal exports.

Democracy at Last

In 1985 Nyerere resigned, handing over power to Zanzibari Ali Hassan Mwinyi. Mwinyi tried to distance himself from Nyerere and his policies, and instituted an economic recovery program. The fall of European communism in the early 1990s and pressure from Western donor nations accelerated the move towards multiparty politics, and in 1992 the constitution was amended to legalise opposition parties.

The first elections were held in 1995 in an atmosphere of chaos, and the voting for the Zanzibari presidency was denounced for its dishonesty. In the ensuing uproar, foreign development assistance was suspended and most expatriates working on the islands left.

Similar problems have plagued successive elections, and tensions continue to simmer.

Tanzania Today

The 2005 presidential elections were won in a landslide by CCM's Jakaya Kikwete, Tanzania's charismatic former foreign minister. The next elections are scheduled for late 2010.

Perhaps more significant is the future of multiparty politics in Tanzania. If anything, this seems to have taken several steps backwards in recent years with the entrenchment of the CCM and splintering of the opposition. However, despite this – and the Zanzibar tensions notwithstanding – Tanzania as a whole remains reasonably well integrated, with comparatively high levels of religious and ethnic tolerance, particularly on the mainland. Tanzanians have earned a name for themselves in the region for their moderation and balance, and most observers consider it highly unlikely that the country would disintegrate into the tribal conflicts that have plagued some of its neighbours.

CULTURE

Tanzania is notable for its relatively harmonious and understated demeanour. In contrast to Kenya and other neighbours, tribal rivalries are almost nonexistent and the *ujamaa* ideals of Julius Nyerere still permeate society. Religious frictions are also minimal, with Christians and Muslims living side by side in a relatively easy coexistence. Although political differences flare up, especially on the Zanzibar Archipelago, they rarely come to the forefront in interpersonal dealings.

Tanzanians place a premium on politeness and courtesy. Greetings are essential, and you'll probably be given a gentle reminder should you forget this and launch straight into a question without first enquiring as to the wellbeing of your listener and his or her family. Children are trained to greet their elders with a respectful *shikamoo* (literally, 'I hold your feet'), often accompanied in rural areas by a slight curtsey, and strangers are frequently addressed as *dada* (sister), *mama* (for an older woman), *kaka* (brother) or *ndugu* (relative or comrade).

People

Most Tanzanians are of Bantu origin, with the largest groups including the Sukuma (who live around Mwanza and southern Lake Victoria), the Makonde (southeastern Tanzania), the Haya (around Bukoba) and the Chagga

TANZANIA

TANZANIA'S UNESCO WORLD HERITAGE SITES

Tanzania has a formidable collection of Unesco World Heritage Sites, and it's worth trying to visit at least a few during your travels. Those not included in this chapter are covered in Lonely Planet's *Tanzania* guide.

- Kilimanjaro National Park (p789)
- Kilwa Kisiwani & Songo Mnara ruins
- Kolo-Kondoa Rock Art Sites
- Ngorongoro Conservation Area (p798)
- Serengeti National Park (p798)
- Selous Game Reserve (p805)
- Zanzibar's Stone Town (p779)

(around Mt Kilimanjaro). The Maasai are of Nilo-Hamitic or Nilotic origin.

Just about 3% of Tanzania's total population (about one million people) live on the Zanzibar Archipelago, with about one-third of these on Pemba. Small but economically significant Asian (primarily from the subcontinent) and Arabic populations are concentrated in major cities and along the coast.

About 35% to 40% of Tanzanians are Muslim and between 40% and 45% are Christian. The remainder follow traditional religions, and there are small communities of Hindus, Sikhs and Ismailis.

Arts & Crafts

Shaaban Robert (1909–62) is considered to be the country's national poet, and was almost single-handedly responsible for the development of a modern Swahili prose style. Zanzibari Muhammed Said Abdulla, who gained fame with his *Mzimu wa watu wa kale* (Graveyard of the Ancestors), is considered the founder of Swahili popular literature.

A widely acclaimed contemporary writer is Zanzibari Abdulrazak Gurnah, whose *Desertion* was short-listed for the Commonwealth Writers' Prize in 2006.

May Balisidya, who authored the novel *Shida* (Hardships), is one of the few first-generation women writers of Swahili literature.

The single greatest influence on Tanzania's modern music scene has been the Congolese bands that began playing in Dar es Salaam in the early 1960s. Among the best known is Orchestra Super Matimila, which was pro-

pelled to fame by Congolese-born and Dar es Salaam–based Remmy Ongala.

Tanzania's best-known school of painting is Tingatinga, which takes its name from the self-taught artist Edward Saidi Tingatinga who developed it in the 1960s. Tingatinga paintings are traditionally composed in a square format, and feature brightly coloured animal motifs set against a monochrome background.

Tanzania's Makonde are known throughout East Africa for their beautiful and highly stylised ebony woodcarvings.

FOOD & DRINK

Tanzania's unofficial national dish is *ugali*. Another favourite is *mishikaki* (marinated meat kebabs). On Zanzibar look for the thick, soft, pancake-like bread called *mkate wa ufuta* (sesame bread).

In major towns there's a good selection of places to eat, ranging from local food stalls to Western-style restaurants. In smaller towns you're likely to just find *hoteli* (small, informal restaurants) and *mama lishe* (informal food stands where the resident 'mama' does the cooking) serving chicken, beef or fish with rice or another staple. The main meal is at noon.

Bottled water and soft drinks are widely sold; tap water should be avoided. Tanzania's beers include the local Safari and Kilimanjaro labels. Finding one cold can be a challenge.

ENVIRONMENT

Tanzania (943,000 sq km) is bordered to the east by the Indian Ocean and to the west by the deep lakes of the Western Rift Valley. Much of the mainland consists of a central highland plateau nestled between the eastern and western branches of the geological fault known as

---

GREAT CUPS OF COFFEE

Despite Tanzania's many coffee plantations, it can be difficult to find a cup of the real stuff. Here are a few suggestions to get you started – let us know if you find others.

- Stone Town Café, Zanzibar Town (p782)
- Utengule Country Hotel, Mbeya (p804)
- Zanzibar Coffee House (p782)
- Coffee Shop, Moshi (p789)
- Tanzania Coffee Lounge, Moshi (p789)

the Great Rift Valley. In the northwest is the enormous, shallow Lake Victoria basin. Off the coast is the Zanzibar Archipelago.

Tanzania's wild animal population includes all the 'classic' African mammals. Particularly notable are the country's large elephant populations, its big cats – especially lions, which are routinely seen in Serengeti National Park and Ngorongoro Crater – and its large herds of wildebeests, buffalos and zebras. Tanzania also is home to over 1000 bird species, including many endemics.

Although Tanzania has one of the highest proportions of protected land of any African country (about 39% is protected in some form), limited resources hamper conservation efforts, while erosion, soil degradation, desertification, deforestation and corruption continue to whittle away at the natural wealth. On the positive side, great progress has been made in recent years to involve communities directly in conservation, and local communities are now stakeholders in numerous lodges and other tourist developments.

A good local contact on environmental issues is the **Wildlife Conservation Society of Tanzania** (www.wcstonline.org; Garden Ave, Dar es Salaam).

National Parks & Reserves

Tanzania's unrivalled collection of protected areas includes 14 national parks, 14 wildlife reserves, the Ngorongoro Conservation Area (NCA), two marine parks and several protected marine reserves.

The 'northern circuit' (Serengeti, Lake Manyara, Tarangire, Arusha and Kilimanjaro National Parks, plus the NCA) is easily accessible and known for its high concentration, diversity and accessibility of its wildlife.

In the relatively less-developed 'southern circuit' – including Ruaha and Mikumi National Parks and the Selous Game Reserve – the wildlife is just as impressive, although it's often spread over larger areas.

All parks are managed by the **Tanzania National Parks Authority** (Tanapa; www.tanzaniaparks. com). For the northern parks, an electronic payment system is being introduced, but the situation was in flux at the time of research. If you will be visiting parks independently (ie not through a tour operator), our advice is to travel with Visa, MasterCard and enough cash to cover park fees until the

system is sorted out. For the southern and western parks, entry fees are payable only in hard currency, preferably US dollars cash, though this is also scheduled to change to an electronic system. Travellers cheques are not accepted in any parks.

Wildlife reserves (with Selous Game Reserve the main one) are administered by the **Wildlife Division of the Ministry of Natural Resources & Tourism** (☎ 022-286 6064, 022-286 6376; scp@africaonline.co.tz; cnr Nyerere & Changombe Rds, Dar es Salaam). Fees must be paid in US dollars cash.

DAR ES SALAAM

☎ 022 / pop 2.5 million

Dar es Salaam is Tanzania's major city and its capital in everything but name. Yet, despite its size, 'Dar' is a down-to-earth place, with a picturesque seaport, an intriguing mix of Africa, Arabic and Indian influences, and enough historical buildings, shops and restaurants to keep you busy for a few days.

HISTORY

In the 1860s Sultan Sayyid Majid of Zanzibar developed a humble East African fishing village into a port and trading centre, and named the site Dar es Salaam (Haven of Peace). When the sultan died the town sank again into anonymity until the 1880s, when Dar es Salaam resurfaced as a way station for Christian missionaries and as a seat for the German colonial government. Since then the city has remained Tanzania's undisputed political and economic capital, although the legislature was transferred to Dodoma in 1973.

ORIENTATION

The congested centre – with banks, bureaux de change, shops and street vendors – runs along Samora Ave from the clock tower to the Askari monument. Northwest of here, around India and Jamhuri Sts, it's chock-a-block with Indian traders. Northeast of the Askari monument there are shady tree-lined streets with the National Museum, Botanical Gardens and State House. Moving north along the coast you first reach the upper-middle-class section of Upanga, and then,

TANZANIA

CENTRAL DAR ES SALAAM

0 ———— 500 m
0 ———— 0.3 miles

INDIAN OCEAN

INFORMATION	
A Novel Idea	**1** C4
Barclays Bank ATM	**2** B3
British Council	**3** C4
British High Commission	**4** C3
Burundian Embassy	**5** A1
Canadian High Commission	**6** C3
Central Police Station	**7** B5
Coastal Travels	**8** B3
DRC Embassy	**9** B2
Kearsley Travel	**10** C3
Main Post Office	**11** B4
Malawian High Commission	(see 24)
Mövenpick Royal Palm Forex Bureau	**12** B3
Mozambique High Commission	**13** C3
NBC	**14** C4
Nyumba ya Sanaa	**15** B3
Post Office Internet Café	(see 11)
Rwandan Embassy	**16** B1
Southern Sun Business Centre	(see 10)
Stanbic Bank	**17** C4
Standard Chartered Bank	**18** C4
Tanzania Tourist Board Information Centre	**19** B4
Telecom Office	**20** B4
Traffic Police Headquarters	**21** B5
Wildlife Conservation Society of Tanzania	**22** C3
Wizara ya mambo ya ndani	**23** B3
YMCA Internet Café	(see 32)
Zambian High Commission	**24** C4

SIGHTS & ACTIVITIES	
Fish Market	**25** D4
National Museum	**26** C3

SLEEPING	
Econolodge	**27** A4
Harbour View Suites	**28** B4
Jambo Inn	**29** A4
Kilimanjaro Kempinski	**30** C4
Palm Beach Hotel	**31** A1
Safari Inn	(see 29)
YMCA	**32** B3
YWCA	**33** B3

EATING	
Chef's Pride	**34** A4
Holiday Out	**35** C3
Kibo Bar	(see 12)
YMCA	(see 32)

DRINKING	
Level 8	(see 30)

SHOPPING	
JM Mall	(see 28)
Mawazo Gallery & Art Café	(see 32)

TRANSPORT	
Air India	**36** B3
Air Tanzania	**37** C3
Avis	(see 2)
British Airways	(see 12)
Coastal Aviation	(see 8)
Emirates Airlines	**38** B3
Ethiopian Airlines	(see 2)
Ferries to Zanzibar Archipelago	**39** B4
Ferry to Kigamboni & Southern Beaches	**40** D4
Green Car Rentals	**41** A5
Kenya Airways	(see 42)
KLM	**42** B3
Linhas Aéreas de Moçambique	(see 28)
New Posta Transport Stand	**43** B4
Old Posta Transport Stand	**44** B4
Precision Air	**45** C4
Royal Coach	**46** A4
South African Airways	**47** B3
Stesheni Transport Stand	**48** B5
Swiss International Airlines	**49** C4
Taxi Stand	(see 2)
Taxi Stand	**50** C4
Zambian Airways	(see 38)

To Alliance Française (1km); Kenyan High Commission (3km); Ugandan High Commission (3km); US Embassy (3.5km); Travel Mate (4km); Garden Bistro (6km); Seacliff Village (7km); Village Museum (6km); Mwenge Carvers' Market (9km); Bagamoyo (70km)

To Swiss Garden Hotel (1km)

Upanga

Golf Course

Mövenpick Royal Palm Hotel

Southern Sun Hotel

Botanic Gardens

Kisutu

To Ubungo Bus Station (10km)

St Alban's Anglican Church

Haidery Plaza

Askari Monument

Kivukoni

State House

Azania Front Lutheran Church

Kivukoni Front

Mchafukoge

St Joseph's Cathedral

Mnanzi Mmoja Park

Clock Tower

Central Line Train Station

To Scandinavian Express (700m); Tazara Train Station (6km); Wildlife Division of the Ministry of Natural Resources & Tourism (6km); Julius Nyerere International Airport (12km)

To Zanzibar; Pemba

To Kigamboni

---

after crossing Selander Bridge, the diplomatic and upmarket residential areas of Oyster Bay and Msasani.

INFORMATION
Bookshops
A Novel Idea (☎ 022-260 1088) Msasani Slipway (Msasani Slipway, Msasani Peninsula); Steers (cnr Ohio St &

Samora Ave) Classics, modern fiction, travel guides, Africa titles, maps and more.

Cultural Centres
Alliance Française (☎ 022-213 1406/2; afdar@ africaonline.co.tz; Ali Hassan Mwinyi Rd)
British Council (☎ 022-211 6574/5/6; info@british council.or.tz; cnr Ohio St & Samora Ave)

Nyumba ya Sanaa (Mwalimu Julius K Nyerere Cultural Centre; Ohio St)

Emergency

Central police station (☎ 022-211 5507; Sokoine Dr) Near the Central Line Train Station.

IST Clinic (☎ 022-260 1307/8, 0784-783393, 24hr emergency line 0754-783393; www.istclinic.com; Ruvu Rd, off Chole Rd; ☺ 8am-6pm Mon-Fri, 8am-noon Sat) Western-run clinic with a doctor always on call.

Traffic police headquarters (☎ 022-211 1747; Sokoine Dr) Near the Central Line Train Station.

Immigration Office

Wizara ya mambo ya ndani (☎ 022-211 8640/3; cnr Ghana Ave & Ohio St; ☺ 8am-noon Mon-Fri for visa applications, until 2pm for visa collection)

Internet Access

Post Office Internet Café (Maktaba St; per hr Tsh1200; ☺ 8am-7pm Mon-Fri, 9am-2pm Sat)

Southern Sun Business Centre (Southern Sun Hotel, Garden Ave; per hr Tsh6000; ☺ 7am-10pm)

YMCA Internet Café (Upanga Rd; per hr Tsh1000; ☺ 8am-7.30pm Mon-Fri, 8am-2pm Sat)

Medical Services

For medical treatment, including medical emergencies, your best bet is to head to the IST Clinic, above.

Money

Bureaux de change give the fastest service and marginally better exchange rates. Most are in the city centre on or near Samora Ave, or try the following:

Mövenpick Royal Palm Forex Bureau (Mövenpick Royal Palm Hotel, Ohio St; ☺ 8am-8pm Mon-Sat, 10am-1pm Sun & public holidays) Cash and travellers cheques (receipts required).

NBC (cnr Azikiwe St & Sokoine Dr) Cash and travellers cheques, and has an ATM (Visa).

ATMS

Barclay's Bank (Ohio St) Located opposite the Mövenpick Royal Palm Hotel. Also at the Msasani Slipway. Visa and MasterCard.

Stanbic Bank (Sukari House, cnr Ohio St & Sokoine Dr) Visa, MasterCard, Cirrus and Maestro.

Standard Chartered Bank (NIC Life House, cnr Ohio St & Sokoine Dr) Also next to Southern Sun Hotel. Visa.

Post

Main post office (Maktaba St; ☺ 8am-4.30pm Mon-Fri, 9am-noon Sat)

Telephone

The **Telecom Office** (Bridge St & Samora Ave; ☺ 7.30am to 6pm Mon-Fri, 9am-3pm Sat) behind the Extelecoms House sells phonecards for Tsh1000 that you can top up and use at any Tanzania Telecom (TTCL; landline) phone for international calls. Starter packs and top-up cards for mobile operators are sold in shops all around the city.

Tourist Information

Tanzania Tourist Board Information Centre (TTB; ☎ 022-212 0373, 022-213 1555; www.tanzaniatourist board.com; Samora Ave; ☺ 8am-4pm Mon-Fri, 8.30am-12.30pm Sat) Just west of Zanaki St, with free tourist maps, brochures and city information.

Travel Agencies & Tour Operators

Afri-Roots (www.afriroots.co.tz) Budget cycling, hiking and camping in and around Dar es Salaam.

Authentic Tanzania (☎ 022-276 2093; www.authentic tanzania.com) Good-value southern circuit and southern coast itineraries.

Coastal Travels (☎ 022-211 7959/60; www.coastal. cc; Upanga Rd) Flights around the country, especially recommended for travel to Zanzibar, and to northern and southern safari circuit destinations. Also city tours, day trips to Zanzibar and Mikumi National Park excursions.

Kearsley Travel (☎ 022-213 1652/3; www.kearsleys. com; Southern Sun Hotel, Garden Ave)

DANGERS & ANNOYANCES

Dar es Salaam is considered to be safer than many other big cities in the region, though it has its share of muggings and thefts. During the day, watch out for pickpocketing, particularly at crowded markets and bus and train stations, and for bag snatching through vehicle windows. At night take a taxi – from a rank at an established hotel – rather than taking a *dalla-dalla* (minibus) or walking.

SIGHTS & ACTIVITIES

Central Dar es Salaam is full of historical buildings, colonial-era architecture and atmosphere.

The **National Museum** (☎ 022-211 7508; www. houseofculture.or.tz; Shaaban Robert St; adult/student US$5/2; ☺ 9.30am-6pm) houses the famous fossil discoveries from Olduvai Gorge (closed for renovations at the time of research), a small collection of vintage cars, and displays on the precolonial and colonial periods.

The open-air **Village Museum** (☎ 022-270 0437; www.museum.or.tz; cnr New Bagamoyo Rd & Makaburi St; adult/student US$5/2, ☺ 9.30am-6pm) features authentic

TANZANIA

dwellings showing traditional life in various parts of Tanzania and traditional dance performances on some afternoons. It's 10km north of the city centre – catch a Mwenge *dalla-dalla* from New Posta transport stand.

For a gentle initiation into Dar es Salaam's markets, head to the **fish market** (Ocean Rd), near Kivukoni Front.

SLEEPING

It's cheaper to stay in the city centre and more convenient if you're relying on public transport. There's a range of pricier hotels on Msasani Peninsula.

Budget

YWCA (☎ 0713-622707; ywca.tanzania@africaonline.co.tz; Maktaba St; s/d without bathroom Tsh10,000/15,000, d Tsh25,000) Central but faded, it has noisy rooms with net, fan and sink, clean-ish shared bathrooms and a cheap restaurant. Both women and men are accepted.

YMCA (☎ 022-213 5457; Upanga Rd; s/d without bathroom US$10/13) Around the corner from the YWCA, it's cleaner and quieter. The well-kept rooms have mosquito nets, and there's a canteen. Both men and women are accepted.

Safari Inn (☎ 022-213 8101; www.darsafariinn.com; Band St; s/d US$10/20, d with air-con US$25; ✷ 🖳) A popular travellers' haunt in Kisutu, on the western edge of the city centre. Rooms have fans and hot water but no nets.

Econolodge (☎ 022-211-6048/9; econolodge@raha.com; Libya St; s/d/tr US$18/24/30, s/d/tr with air-con US$30/35/40; ✷) Clean and good albeit faded no-frills rooms with hot water. It's hidden away in an aesthetically unappealing highrise around the corner from Safari Inn and Jambo Inn. Continental breakfast is included; otherwise there's no food.

Jambo Inn (☎ 022-211 4293; jamboinnhotel@yahoo.com; Libya St; s/d US$20/25) Around the corner from Safari Inn, and also popular, rooms have fans and flyscreens, but unreliable hot water. Downstairs is a good, cheap restaurant.

Midrange & Top End

Swiss Garden Hotel (☎ 022-215 3219; www.swisshostel.net; Mindu St; s/d from US$75/95; ✷ 🖳) A cosy B&B in a quiet, leafy neighbourhood, with small, spotless rooms. It's in Upanga, just off United Nations Rd.

Palm Beach Hotel (☎ 022-212 2931, 022-213 0985; www.pbhtz.com; Ali Hassan Mwinyi Rd; s/d/tr US$85/110/120; ✷ 🖳 🛜) Just north of the city centre (but close enough to walk), it has spartan but spacious and good-value rooms with TV and a restaurant.

Harbour View Suites (☎ 022-212 4040; www.harbourview-suite.com; Harbour View Towers, cnr Samora Ave & Mission St; s/d from US$150/170, breakfast US$10; ✷ 🖳 🛜) Well-equipped, centrally located business travellers' studio apartments with views over the city or the harbour.

Kilimanjaro Kempinski (☎ 022-213 1111; www.kempinski-daressalaam.com; Kivukoni Front; r from US$250; ✷ 🖳 🛜) This once-classic waterfront hotel has been completely refurbished and its ultramodern rooms are arguably the best in the city.

EATING

There's an array of eateries at both Msasani Slipway and Seacliff village, both north on the Msasani Peninsula. In town, try the following:

Holiday Out (Garden Ave; meals Tsh2500; 7.30am-4pm Mon-Fri) Great-value local food in an unsignposted lot diagonally opposite Southern Sun Hotel.

YMCA (☎ 022-213 5457; Upanga Rd; meals Tsh2500; lunch & dinner) Another spot for filling, inexpensive local food.

Chef's Pride (Chagga St; meals from Tsh2500; lunch & dinner, closed during Ramadan) A popular local eatery within easy walking distance of the Kisutu area budget hotels. The large menu features standard fare, plus pizzas, Indian and vegie with dishes.

Kibo Bar (☎ 022-211 2416; Mövenpick Royal Palm Hotel, Ohio St; meals Tsh10,000-15,000; lunch-11.30pm) Design-your-own pasta, sandwich, omelette and salad stations at lunchtime on weekdays, and pub fare at all hours.

For self-catering, try Shoprite in Msasani Slipway.

DRINKING

Slipway Pub (☎ 022-260 0893; Msasani Slipway; noon-11pm) A cosy British pub near the water, with drinks, meals and sports TV.

Garden Bistro (☎ 022-260 0800; Haile Selassie Rd; meals from Tsh5000) A relaxed restaurant-nightclub with a sheesha lounge, sports bar, happy hours Sunday to Thursday and live music on weekends.

Level 8 (8th fl, Kilimanjaro Kempinski hotel; Kivukoni Front) A rooftop bar with views over the harbour, lounge seating and live music some evenings.

SHOPPING

Shopping venues include **Msasani Slipway Weekend Craft Market** (Msasani Slipway; ☉ Sat & Sun), with a wide range of textiles, carvings and more; and **Mawazo Gallery & Art Café** (☎ 0784-782770; Upanga Rd; ☉ 10am-5.30pm Mon-Fri, 10am-2pm Sat), with paintings, woodcarvings and crafts. **Mwenge Carvers' Market** (Sam Nujoma Rd; ☉ 8am-6pm), opposite the Village Museum and just off New Bagamoyo Rd, is packed with woodcarvers and woodcarvings.

GETTING THERE & AWAY

Air

Julius Nyerere International Airport is Tanzania's domestic and international hub. Most regularly scheduled domestic flights and all international flights depart from Terminal Two ('new' terminal). Many flights on small planes (including most Zanzibar flights) depart from Terminal One ('old' terminal), 700m further down the road.

For a list of airline offices in Dar es Salaam, see p809.

Boat

The main passenger routes are between Dar es Salaam, Zanzibar and Pemba.

ZANZIBAR

There are several 'fast' ferry trips (on *Sea Star*, *Sea Express* or *Seabus*) daily between Dar es Salaam and Zanzibar, departing at 7am, 10am, 1pm and 4pm. All take 1½ hours and cost US$35/40 regular/VIP (VIP gets you a seat in the air-con hold).

There are also several slow ferries, including *Flying Horse,* which departs daily at 12.30pm (one way US$25, 3½ to four hours). Departures from Zanzibar are daily at 7am, 11am, 1pm, 4pm and 10pm (arriving before dawn the next day). Only buy your tickets at the ticket windows – all opposite St Joseph's Cathedral

Bus

Except as noted, all buses depart from and arrive at the main bus station at Ubungo, 8km west of town on Morogoro Rd (Tsh400 in a *dalla-dalla* from New Posta or Old Posta transport stands, or from Tsh10,000 in a taxi). It's a sprawling place with the usual bus-station hustle, so keep an eye on your luggage and your wallet, and try to avoid arriving at night. Buses to Mtwara and other points south leave from Ubungo, but it's better to catch them at the Sudan Market area of Temeke, about 5km southwest of the city centre, off Nelson Mandela Rd.

Dar Express Daily buses to Arusha (Tsh20,000 to Tsh25,000) departing at 6am, 7am, 8am, 9am and 10am.

Royal Coach (☎ 022-212 4073; Libya St, Kisutu) Daily departures to Arusha (Tsh22,000) at 9am. Tickets can be purchased at Ubungo, or at its Libya St office.

Scandinavian Express (☎ 022-218 4833/4; cnr Msimbazi St & Nyerere Rd) Has its own terminal for arrivals and departures (which is also where you book tickets), though all Scandinavian buses also pass by Ubungo. Daily buses to Iringa (Tsh17,000), Mbeya (Tsh26,000), Dodoma (Tsh12,000 to Tsh15,000) and Arusha (Tsh20,000 to Tsh25,0000).

Train

Tazara Train Station (☎ 022-286 5187, 0713-225292; www.tazara.co.tz; cnr Nyerere & Nelson Mandela Rds; ☉ ticket office 7.30am-12.30pm & 2-4.30pm Mon-Fri, 9am-12.30pm Sat), for trains to Mbeya and Kapiri Mposhi (Zambia), is 6km southwest from the city centre (Tsh8000 in a taxi). *Dalla-dallas* depart from the New and Old Posta transport stands, and are marked Vigunguti, U/Ndege or Buguruni.

Central Line train station (Tanzanian Railways Corporation station; ☎ 022-211 7833; www.trctz.com; cnr Railway St & Sokoine Dr), for trains to Kigoma and Mwanza from Dodoma (the Dar-Dodoma section is closed), is just southwest of the ferry terminal.

For more on train routes, see p815.

GETTING AROUND

Julius Nyerere International Airport is 12km from the city centre. *Dalla-dallas* (marked U/Ndege) go to the airport from New Posta transport stand. Taxis to central Dar cost from Tsh15,000 (Tsh25,000 to Msasani Peninsula).

Dalla-dallas are invariably packed to overflowing and difficult to board with luggage. First and last stops are shown in the front window, but routes vary, so confirm that the driver is really going to your destination. Rides cost Tsh300 to Tsh600. Terminals include the following:

New Posta (Maktaba St) In front of the main post office.

Old Posta (Sokoine Dr) Just down from Azania Front Lutheran Church.

Stesheni (Algeria St) Off Samora Ave near the Central Line train station. *Dalla-dallas* to Temeke bus stand also leave from here; ask for 'Temeke *mwisho*'.

Taxis charge from Tsh2500 per short trip within the centre. Fares to Msasani Peninsula start at Tsh8000. There are taxi stands near NBC bank and next to Barclay's Bank, opposite the Mövenpick Royal Palm Hotel.

AROUND DAR ES SALAAM

Bagamoyo (p786) and Saadani National Park (p786) also make good excursions from Dar es Salaam.

DAR BEACHES

The coastline south of Dar es Salaam gets more attractive the further south you go, and makes for an easy getaway. The budget places begin just south of **Kigamboni**, which is opposite Kivukoni Front and reached in a few minutes by ferry.

Kipepeo Beach & Village (☎ 0754-276178; www.kipepeovillage.com; campsites US$5, s/d/tr beach bandas US$15/25/35, s/d/tr cottage US$55/75/105), 8km south of the ferry dock at the centre of 'South Beach', has camping, basic *bandas* (thatched-roof huts), nicer raised cottages (back from the beach) and a beachside restaurant-bar.

Amani Beach Hotel (☎ 0754-410033; www.amanibeach.com; s/d incl full board US$270/480; ☒ 🖵 🏊), 25km further south, has large gardens, spacious cottages overlooking the beach and a restaurant.

The Kigamboni ferry (Tsh100/800 per person/vehicle, five minutes) runs throughout the day. Once there, *dalla-dallas* and taxis head south from Kigamboni to Kipepeo (Tsh200/5000 in a *dalla-dalla*/taxi).

ZANZIBAR ARCHIPELAGO

The 'spice islands' of Zanzibar (Unguja) and Pemba have an almost legendary allure and offer a complete change of pace from the Tanzanian mainland. Zanzibar gets most of the attention, with its historic Stone Town and its beautiful palm-fringed beaches. Pemba, by contrast, is seldom visited and laid-back, and offers a largely undiscovered culture and challenging diving.

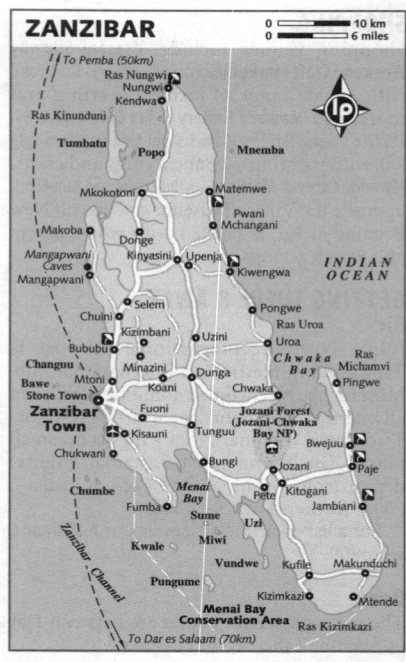

History

From around the 8th century, Shirazi traders from Persia established settlements in the archipelago. Then between the 12th and 15th centuries, Zanzibar became a powerful city-state, exporting slaves, gold, ivory and wood, and importing spices, glassware and textiles. In the early 16th century Zanzibar came under Portuguese control. Omani Arabs in the mid-16th century routed the Portuguese and by the 19th century had become so prosperous that in the 1840s the Sultan of Oman relocated his court from the Persian Gulf.

In 1862 Zanzibar became independent from Oman, although Omani sultans continued to rule under a British protectorate. On 10 December 1963 Zanzibar gained independence and in 1964 Abeid Karume signed a declaration of unity with Tanganyika (as mainland Tanzania was then known), forming a fragile union that soon became known as the United Republic of Tanzania.

Dangers & Annoyances

Zanzibar remains a relatively safe place, although there are occasional robberies and muggings in Zanzibar Town and along the beaches. *Papasi* (street touts) are persistent and can be irksome. Avoid isolated areas, especially stretches of beach, and keep your valuables out of view – it's generally better to leave them in your hotel safe, preferably sealed and locked. If you go out at night in Zanzibar Town, take a taxi or walk in a group. Also avoid walking alone in Stone Town during the predawn hours.

ZANZIBAR
☎ 024

Zanzibar's main attraction is Stone Town, where ancient Persia mixes with the old Omani sultanate and India's Goan coast, and quaint shops and bazaars line the winding, cobbled streets. Another of the island's drawcards is its spectacular sea, edged by fine, white-sand beaches, whitewashed coral-rag houses and waving palms. Although many places have become very developed, there are still some quiet spots left.

Zanzibar Town
ORIENTATION

Zanzibar Town, on the western side of the island, is the heart of the archipelago, and the first stop for most travellers. The best-known section is the old Stone Town, surrounded on three sides by the sea and bordered to the east by Creek Rd.

INFORMATION
Bookshops

Gallery Bookshop (☎ 024-223 2721; 48 Gizenga St; ☯ 9am-6pm Mon-Sat, 9am-2pm Sun) Travel guides, Africa titles, historical reprint editions, maps and more.

Internet Access

Shangani post office internet café (Kenyatta Rd; per hr Tsh2000; ☯ 8am-9pm Mon-Fri, 8.30am-7pm Sat & Sun)

Medical Services

Shamshuddin Pharmacy (☎ 024-231262, 024-223 3814; Market St; ☯ 9am-8.30pm Mon-Thu & Sat, 9am-noon & 3-8.30pm Fri, 9am-1.30pm Sun) Just behind (west of) the Darajani market.

Money

There are many bureaux de change (most open until about 8pm Monday through Saturday, and often also on Sunday) where you can change cash and travellers cheques. Rates vary so shop around, but they are better in Stone Town than elsewhere on the island.

Barclay's Bank (Kenyatta Rd) ATM: Visa, MasterCard, Cirrus and Maestro.

Maka T-Shirt Shop (Kenyatta Rd) Changes travellers cheques and cash.

NBC Bank (Shangani St) Changes cash and has an ATM: Visa only.

Speed Cash/TanPay (Kenyatta Rd) ATM: Visa, Master-Card, Cirrus and Maestro.

Post & Telephone

Shangani post office (Kenyatta Rd; ☯ 8am-4.30pm Mon-Fri, 8am-12.30pm Sat) Operator-assisted calls from Tsh1300 per minute.

Tourist Information

Tourist Information Office (☎ 0777-482356; Creek Rd; ☯ 8am-5pm) Near Darajani market, with tourist information, ferry bookings and standard tours at reasonable prices.

Travel Agencies

Try any of the following for help with island excursions, and plane and ferry tickets:

Eco + Culture Tours (☎ 024-223 0366; www.ecoculture-zanzibar.org; Hurumzi St)

Gallery Tours & Safaris (☎ 024-223 2088; www.gallery tours.net) Upmarket tours.

Madeira Tours & Safaris (☎ 024-223 0406; madeira@zanlink.com; just off Kenyatta Rd, Shangani) All price ranges.

THINGS TO DO IN STONE TOWN

■ Enjoy a cup of spiced coffee while watching the passing scene on the street (p782).

■ Watch sunset from the Forodhani Gardens promenade (p782).

■ Walk through Darajani market (p781) in the morning, when everything is still fresh.

■ Visit the old slave market (p781) near the Anglican cathedral.

■ Buy a *kanga* (printed cotton wraparound worn by Tanzanian women) or *kikoi* (printed cotton wraparound traditionally worn by men in coastal areas; p783).

■ Go diving or snorkelling (p781).

■ Indulge yourself with a traditional beauty treatment at **Mrembo** (www.mtoni.com/mrembo) or one of Stone Town's other spas..

TANZANIA

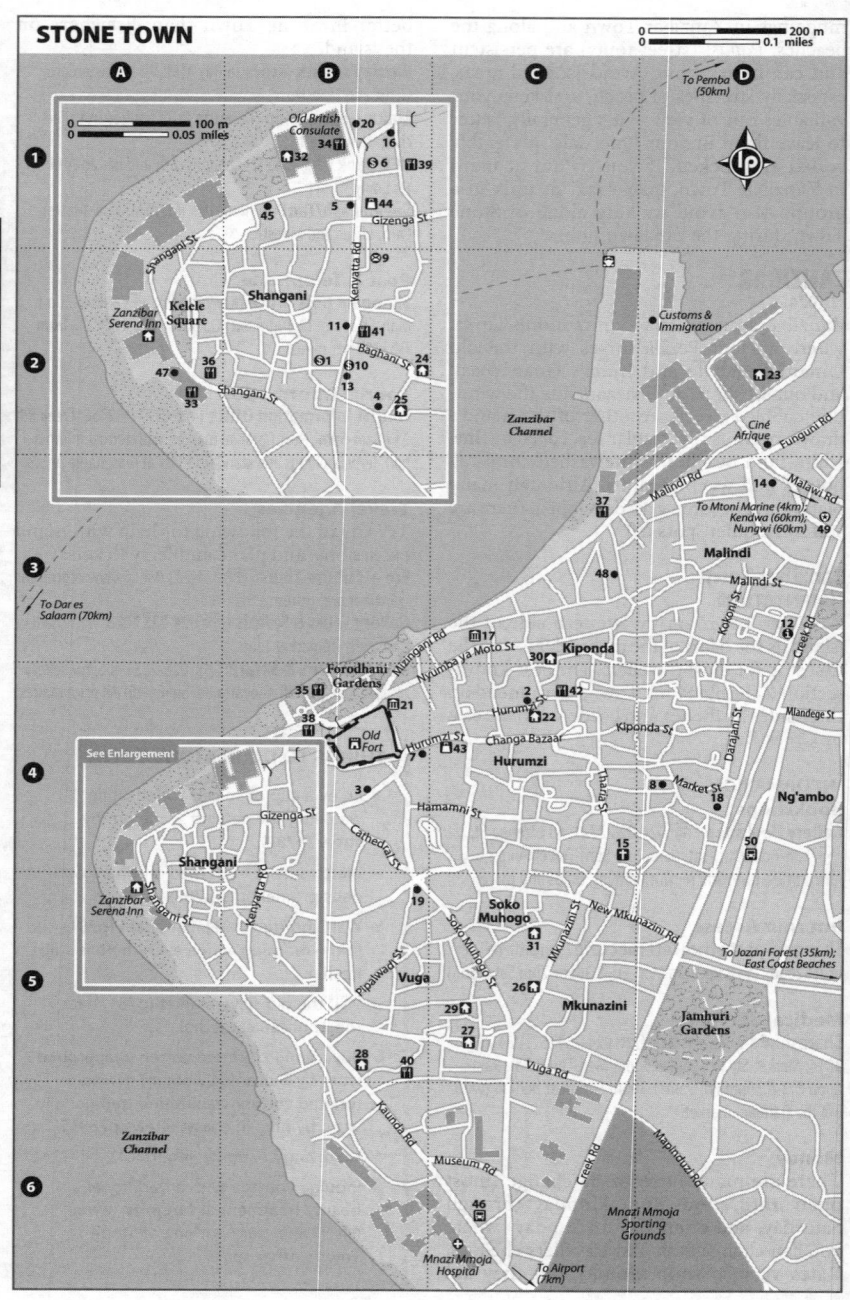

Sama Tours (☎ 024-223 3543; www.samatours.com; Hurumzi St) Budget tours.

Tabasam (☎ 024-223 0322; www.tabasamzanzibar. com; Kenyatta Rd) Opposite Stone Town Café; midrange and upmarket tours.

Tropical Tours (☎ 024-223 3695, 0777-413454; http:// tropicaltours.villa69.org; Kenyatta Rd) Budget tours.

Zan Tours (☎ 024-223 3042/3116; www.zantours.com; Malawi Rd) Upmarket tours.

SIGHTS
If Zanzibar Town is the archipelago's heart, **Stone Town** is its soul, and a historical wonder in itself, with a magical jumble of cobbled alleyways where it's easy to spend days wandering around. Each twist and turn of the narrow streets brings something new. Arabic-style houses with their recessed inner courtyards rub shoulders with Indian-influenced buildings designed with ornate balconies and latticework, and bustling oriental bazaars alternate with lively street-side vending stalls.

Zanzibar National Museum of History & Culture (www.zanzibarheritage.go.tz; Mizingani Rd; adult/child US$3/1; 🕙 9am-6pm), in the Beit el-Ajaib (House of Wonders), has exhibits on Swahili civilisation, the history of Stone Town and a *mtepe* (a traditional Swahili sailing vessel made without nails).

Beit el-Sahel (www.zanzibarheritage.go.tz; Mizingani Rd; adult/child US$3/1; 🕙 9am-6pm), a former sultan's palace, is now a museum devoted to the era of the Zanzibar sultanate. Outside is the Makusurani graveyard, where some of the sultans are buried.

Constructed in the 1870s, Stone Town's **Anglican cathedral** (Mkunazini St; admission Tsh1000; 🕙 8am-6pm Mon-Sat) was built on the site of an old slave market. Today only some holding cells remain.

The chaotic **Darajani market** (Creek Rd; 🕙 predawn–mid-afternoon) is at its best in the morning, before the heat and the crowds.

DIVING & SNORKELLING
Zanzibar offers fine diving and snorkelling. Trips average US$30 to US$50 per half day, often including lunch. Recommended operators include **Bahari Divers** (☎ 0777-415011, 0784-254786; www.zanzibar-diving.com; Shangani St) and **One Ocean/The Zanzibar Dive Centre** (☎ 024-223 8374; www.zanzibaroneocean.com; off Shangani St), a Professional Association of Diving Instructors (PADI) five-star centre.

FESTIVALS & EVENTS
Muslim holidays are celebrated in a big way on Zanzibar. Other festivals include **Mwaka Kogwa**, the **Zanzibar International Film Festival** and **Sauti za Busara** (see p807).

SLEEPING
Budget
Flamingo Guest House (☎ 024-223 2850; flamingoguesthouse@hotmail.com; Mkunazini St; s/d with bathroom US$15/30, without bathroom US$12/24) Straightforward but perfectly acceptable rooms with nets, fans and a rooftop breakfast area.

Bandari Lodge (☎ 024-223 7969; bandarilodge@hotmail.com; Malindi; s/d/tw/tr US$15/25/30/35) Clean rooms with high ceilings, nets and fan, plus a common kitchen and a fridge. Turn left as you exit the port – it's just two minutes' walk ahead on the right-hand side.

Haven Guest House (☎ 024-223 5677/8; Mkunazini; s/d US$15/30) A backpacker-friendly place with clean, no-frills rooms, a travellers' bulletin board, free coffee and tea, and a small kitchenette.

Jambo Guest House (☎ 024-223 3779; jamboguest@hotmail.com; Mkunazini; s/d/tr without bathroom US$20/30/45; ✷) Just around the corner from Flamingo Guest House, Jambo has free tea and coffee, clean rooms, including some with air-con, decent breakfasts and an internet cafe opposite.

Florida Guest House (☎ 0777-421421; floridaznz@yahoo.com; Vuga Rd; s/d/tr US$25/40/60; ✷) Small, clean rooms with hot water and minifridge (check out a few as they're all different). It's next to Culture Musical Club.

Hotel Kiponda (☎ 024-223 3052; www.kiponda.com; Nyumba ya Moto St; s/d/tr US$25/45/60) This hotel is slightly pricier than others in this category, but rooms are spotless and good value, and the location – tucked away in a small lane near the waterfront – is convenient. Most rooms have their own bathroom, and there a rooftop restaurant.

Garden Lodge (☎ 024-223 3298; Kaunda Rd; s/d/tr US$30/40/60) Diagonally opposite the High Court, with bright and spacious rooms upstairs with hot water, nets and ceiling fans. There's a rooftop breakfast terrace.

Midrange & Top End

Abuso Inn (☎ 024-223 5886; inafaa@hotmail.com; Shangani St; s/d/tr US$50/65/75) A family-run place with no-frills but spotless and mostly spacious rooms with large windows, wooden floors, hot water and fan or air-con. Some rooms have glimpses of the water.

Dhow Palace (☎ 024-223 3012; www.dhowpalace-hotel.com; Shangani; s/d from US$75/100; ☉ Jun-Mar; ▣) Old Zanzibari decor, a fountain in the lobby and well-appointed rooms. It's just off Kenyatta Rd, and under the same management as Tembo House Hotel.

Mtoni Marine (☎ 024-225 0140; www.mtoni.com; Bububu Rd; s/d from US$75/100; ✷ ▢ ▣) A long-standing family-friendly establishment with a mix of rooms in expansive gardens, a small beach, a restaurant and a sports bar. It's about 4km north of town along the Bububu road.

Chavda Hotel (☎ 024-223 2115; chavdahotel@zanlink.com; Baghani St; s/d from US$90/110; ✷) A quiet, reliable hotel with some period decor and a range of bland, carpeted rooms with TV, telephone and minibar. The rooftop bar and restaurant are open during the high season only.

Tembo House Hotel (☎ 024-223 3005; www.tembohotel.com; Shangani St; s/d US$95/110; ✷ ▢ ▣) A prime waterfront location including a small patch of beach (no swimming) and good-value rooms – some with sea views and many with Zanzibari beds – in new and old wings, plus a buffet breakfast and a restaurant.

236 Hurumzi (☎ 0777-423266; www.236hurumzi.com; Hurumzi St; r US$185-225, apt US$90) Formerly Emerson & Green, this Zanzibar institution is in two adjacent historic buildings that have been completely restored along the lines of an *Arabian Nights* fantasy. Each room is unique, and all are decadently decorated to give you an idea of what Zanzibar must have been like in its heyday.

EATING

During the low season and Ramadan many restaurants close or operate on reduced hours.

Forodhani Gardens (Mizingani Rd; meals from Tsh2000) Comes alive in the evening with dozens of vendors serving up grilled *pweza* (octopus), Zanzibari pizza (omelette or other filling cooked in a rolled-up circle of dough) and other delicacies.

Zanzibar Coffee House (coffeehouse@zanlink.com; Hurumzi St; snacks from Tsh4000) Coffees, milkshakes, cakes and more.

Stone Town Café (Kenyatta Rd; breakfast Tsh5000, meals Tsh4000-10,000; ☉ 8am-8pm Mon-Sat) All-day breakfasts, milkshakes, cakes, salads, quiche, vegie wraps and good coffee.

Archipelago Café-Restaurant (☎ 024-223 5668; Shangani St; mains Tsh5000-11,000; ☉ lunch & dinner) Breezes, sea views and meals, including vegetable coconut curry, chicken pilau and homemade cakes, near the Shangani tunnel.

Amore Mio (Shangani St; pastas/pizzas Tsh6000/7500; ☉ high season) Ice cream, cappuccino and sea views.

Mercury's (☎ 024-223 3076; Mizingani Rd; meals Tsh8000-16,000; ☉ 10am-midnight) A popular waterside hang-out with seafood grills, pasta and pizzas, a well-stocked bar and a sundowners terrace.

Radha Food House (☎ 024-223 4808; near NBC Bank in Shangani; thalis Tsh10,000) Strictly vegetarian, with thalis, lassis, homemade yogurt and other dishes from the subcontinent.

Monsoon Restaurant (Mizingani Rd; meals from Tsh10,000; ☺ lunch & dinner) Traditional dining on floor cushions, and Swahili cuisine served to a backdrop of *taarab* or *kidumbak* music on Wednesday and Saturday evenings.

La Fenice (☎ 0777-411868; Shangani St; meals from Tsh10,000; ☺ lunch & dinner) A breezy Italian place on the waterfront, with outdoor tables, thin-crust pizzas and well-prepared pastas.

Sambusa Two Tables Restaurant (☎ 024-223 1979; off Kaunda Rd; meals Tsh15,000; ☺ dinner) A small restaurant inside the family home, where the proprietors bring out course after course of the local delicacies. Reservations are required.

SHOPPING
Gizenga St is lined with small shops and craft dealers, and makes a good place to start.

Zanzibar Gallery (☎ 024-223 2721; gallery@swahili coast.com; cnr Kenyatta Rd & Gizenga St; ☺ 9am-6.30pm Mon-Sat, 9am-1pm Sun) Has a large collection of souvenirs, textiles, woodcarvings, antiques and more.

Memories of Zanzibar (Kenyatta Rd) has jewellery, textiles and curios, while **Moto Handicrafts** (www.solarafrica.net/moto; Hurumzi St) sells baskets, mats and other woven products made by local women's cooperatives using environmentally sustainable technologies

GETTING THERE & AWAY
Air
Daily flights with Coastal Aviation and ZanAir connect Zanzibar with Dar es Salaam (US$65), Arusha (US$170 to US$220), Pemba (US$90), Selous Game Reserve and the northern parks.

Airline offices in Zanzibar Town include the following:

Air Tanzania (☎ 023-223 0213; airtanzania@zanlink. com; Shangani St)

Coastal Aviation (☎ 024-223 3489, 024-223 3112; www.coastal.cc; Kelele Sq) Next to Zanzibar Serena Inn; also at the airport.

Kenya Airways (☎ 024-223 4520/1; www.kenya-air ways.com; Mizingani Rd)

Precision Air (☎ 024-223 4520/1; www.precisionairtz. com; Mizingani Rd) Together with Kenya Airways.

ZanAir (☎ 024-223 3670/2993, 0777-421300; www. zanair.com; Malindi) Opposite Ciné Afrique.

Boat
For ferry connections between Zanzibar and Dar es Salaam, see p777. For ferry connections between Zanzibar and Pemba, see p786. At the time of research, tickets for most Dar es Salaam ferries were being sold southwest of the port on Malindi Rd, while Pemba ferry offices were still at the port. The best thing to do is to ask your hotel, or to book through any of the listings under Travel Agencies (p779) or through the Tourist Information Office (p779).

Foreigners are not permitted on dhows between Dar es Salaam and Zanzibar.

GETTING AROUND
To/from the Airport
The airport is 7km southeast of Zanzibar Town and costs Tsh10,000 to Tsh15,000 in a taxi. The 505 bus line also does this route, departing from the corner opposite Mnazi Mmoja hospital.

Car & Motorcycle
To arrange car, moped or motorcycle hire, you'll need an International Driving Permit, a licence from Kenya, Uganda or South Africa, or a Zanzibar permit. Zanzibar permits can be obtained on the spot at the **traffic police office** (cnr Malawi & Creek Rds) or through any tour company.

Daily hire rates average from US$35 for a moped or motorcycle, and from US$60 for a Suzuki 4WD. Hires can be arranged through tour companies. Full payment is usually required at the time of delivery, but don't pay any advance deposits.

Dalla-Dallas
Open-sided pick-ups (known as *dalla-dallas*) link all major towns on the island, leaving early from Creek Rd opposite Darajani market. None of the routes costs more than Tsh1500, and all take plenty of time (eg about three hours from Zanzibar Town to Jambiani). Useful route numbers include the following:

Route No	Destination
116	Nungwi
309	Jambiani
324	Bwejuu (via Paje)
505	Airport (marked 'U/Ndege')

To Kendwa, have the No 116 Nungwi *dalla-dalla* drop you at the sign for Kendwa Rocks (a few kilometres south of Nungwi), from where it's a 2km walk to the beach.

Private Minivan

Private minivans run daily to Nungwi and to Paje, Bwejuu and Jambiani on the east coast. Book through any travel agency the day before you want to travel, and the vans will pick you up at your hotel in Stone Town between 8am and 9am. Travel takes 1½ to two hours to any of the destinations, and costs a negotiable Tsh6000 per person. Don't pay for the return trip in advance. Most drivers only go to hotels where they'll get a commission.

Taxi

Taxis don't have meters, so agree on a price with the driver before getting into the car. Town trips cost from Tsh2500.

Beaches

Zanzibar has superb beaches, with the best along the island's east coast and to the north. The east-coast beaches are protected by coral reefs offshore and have fine, white coral sand, although at low tide the sea recedes a long way and swimming isn't possible.

NUNGWI

The traditional and modern collide at Nungwi, a large dhow-building centre that has also become one of Zanzibar's major tourist destinations.

There's an internet cafe and bureaux de change at Amaan Bungalows.

Sleeping & Eating

Jambo Brothers Beach Bungalows (jambobungalows@yahoo.com; central Nungwi; s/d without bathroom US$20/30) Basic rooms on the sand.

Union Beach Bungalows (central Nungwi; s/d without bathroom US$20/30) Next door to Jambo Brothers and a step up, although nothing special, with small, two-room cottages near the beach.

Nungwi Guest House (☎ 0777-494899, 0784-234980; http://nungwiguesthouse.tripod.com; Nungwi village; d/tr US$25/30) In the village centre, with simple, clean rooms around a small garden courtyard, all with bathroom, nets and fans, plus meals on request.

Amaan Bungalows (☎ 024-224 0024/6; www.amaanbungalows.com; central Nungwi; tw from US$60, with seaview US$120; ☒ ☐) Various levels of accommodation, with some rooms offering garden or sea-view rooms, and all with fan or air-con and nets. There's also a restaurant and a bar.

Mnarani Beach Cottages (☎ 024-224 0494; www.lighthousezanzibar.com; east Nungwi; d/q family cottage US$140/249, deluxe d US$170, all incl half board; ☐ ☒) A recommended place on a small rise overlooking the sea with small, pleasant cottages with Swahili decor, plus deluxe rooms nearby, all with nets and some with sea views. Also a restaurant.

Flame Tree Cottages (☎ 024-224 0100; www.flametreecottages.com; east-central Nungwi; s/d US$105/130; ☒) Another good, quiet choice, with sparkling white, comfortable bungalows, all with nets, small porch and kitchenette use for self-catering (US$10 per day extra). It's on the eastern edge of central Nungwi.

KENDWA

Southwest of Nungwi is Kendwa, with a long, wide stretch of sand known for its laid-back atmosphere and its full-moon parties, and swimming at all hours. **Scuba Do** (www.scuba-do-zanzibar.com; Sunset Bungalows) offers dive courses and certification.

Kendwa Rocks (☎ 0777-415475; www.kendwarocks.com; s/d bandas without bathroom US$15/30, s/d wooden bandas from US$50/65, s/d stone bungalows from US$55/78) has straightforward wooden bungalows on the sand, cooler stone and thatch versions nearby, simple *bandas* sharing bathroom up on a small cliff away from the water, and the biggest full-moon parties.

At **Sunset Bungalows** (☎ 0777-414647; www.sunsetkendwa.com; s/d US$70/95, with air-con from US$60/75) there are rooms and cottages on a small cliff overlooking the beach, plus better ones on the sand, and a beachside restaurant-bar with evening bonfires.

PAJE

Paje, on the southeastern coast, is a wide, white beach with a cluster of places to stay and a party atmosphere, though it's quieter than Nungwi. For diving there's the **Paje Dive Centre** (☎ 024-224 0191; www.pajedivecentre.com; Arabian Nights Hotel).

Paje by Night (☎ 0777-460710; www.pajebynight.net; s/d from US$70/80, d jungle bungalow US$95) is a chilled place known for its bar and its vibe, with a mix of standard and more spacious king rooms, plus double-storey four-person thatched jungle suites. There's a restaurant with a pizza oven.

Hakuna Majiwe (☎ 0777-454505; www.hakunama jiwe.net; s/d US$180/235; ☒) Has nicely decorated cottages with shady porches and Zanzibari beds, and Zanzibari-Italian fusion decor. It's at the southernmost end of Paje, away from the main cluster.

BWEJUU

The large village of Bwejuu lies about 3km north of Paje on a long, palm-shaded beach. It's very spread out, and quieter than both Paje and Nungwi.

Simple, appealing rooms, some with their own bathroom and all with their own theme, make **Mustapha's Nest** (☎ 0776-718999; www.musta phasplace.com; r per person US$15-40) a great choice. The airy, raised 'Treetop Room' and the spacious 'Africa House' are just a couple of the possibilities. Meals are taken family style, and there's plenty to do (or, if you prefer, plenty of time to do nothing at all). It's just south of Bwejuu village, and across the road from the beach.

Robinson's Place (☎ 0777-413479; www.robinsons place.net; per person US$20-35) is a small getaway at the northern end of the village, with a handful of simple, spotless rooms (one in a treehouse) directly on the beach, plus good meals.

JAMBIANI

You could do worse than spend a few days at Jambiani Beach, gazing out at turquoise seas, and there's a good selection of budget accommodation.

Dhow Beach Village (☎ 0777-417763; www.dhow beachvillage.com; s/d/tw US$35/50/55, s/d without bathroom US$20/30) is a vibey place with a restaurant, a handful of straightforward rooms with bathroom, and three simpler, noisier rooms with fans and shared bathroom. Also beach volleyball and full-moon parties.

Kimte Beach Inn (☎ 024-224 0212, 0777-430992; www.kimte.com; dm US$15, d with/without bathroom US$45/40), at the southern end of Jambiani, is a friendly and laid-back place where rooms all have fans, nets and hot water. There's a restaurant, bar and evening beach bonfires.

Blue Oyster Hotel (☎ 024-224 0163; www.zanzibar. de; s/d US$63/69, with seaview US$78/85, without bathroom US$40/46) This German-run place on the beach at the northern end of Jambiani has pleasant, spotless and good-value rooms and a terrace restaurant.

Casa Del Mar Hotel Jambiani (☎ 024-224 0401, 0777-455446, www.casa-delmar-zanzibar.com; d downstairs/

upstairs US$80/100) has two double-storey blocks of six pleasant rooms each (the upper-storey rooms have lofts) set around a small, well-vegetated garden in a small, enclosed beach area. There's also a restaurant.

Jozani Forest

Now protected as part of the **Jozani-Chwaka Bay National Park** (adult/child incl guide US$8/4; ☒ 7.30am-5.30pm), Jozani is the largest area of mature forest left on Zanzibar, and is known in particular for its population of the rare red colobus monkey. There's a short nature trail and a tiny cafe. The best times to see the colobuses are in the early morning and late evening.

Jozani can be reached via bus 309 or 310, or with an organised tour from Zanzibar Town.

PEMBA
☎ 024

About 50km north of Unguja lies hilly, verdant Pemba – Zanzibar's 'other' island, which is seldom visited by tourists but has some idyllic offshore islets and an intriguing culture.

Information

There's a Speed Cash ATM (Visa only) at the old People's Bank of Zanzibar building on the main road. At the time research, this was the only place on the island to access cash, so carry some extra in case it's out of service.

Adult Computer Centre Internet Café (Main Rd; per hr Tsh1500; ☒ 8am-8pm)

Baacha (☎ 0777-423429, 0787-423429; samhamx@ yahoo.com; Main Rd) Ferry ticket bookings and excursions.

Sleeping & Eating

Jondeni Guest House (☎ 024-245 6042; jondeniguest@ hotmail.com; Mkoani; dm/s/d US$10/20/30, s/d with hot water US$25/35, meals Tsh7000) Offers no-frills rooms with nets and meals, and help organising excursions. It's near the ferry port in Mkoani: head left when exiting the port and walk about 700m up to the top of the hill.

Sharook Guest House (☎ 024-245 4386; sharook guest@yahoo.com; Wete; r with/without bathroom US$20/15) A small budget guesthouse just off the main road at the western end of Wete. Rooms are basic but clean, all with net and fan, there are meals available for order and the owner is helpful with organising excursions.

Pemba Island Hotel (☎ 024-245 2215; Wesha road, Chake Chake; s/d/tw US$35/45/55; ☒) Clean, quiet rooms with nets, TV, minifridge and hot water, plus a rooftop restaurant. It's about 100m downhill from the main junction.

Manta Resort (www.themantaresort.com; Kigomasha Peninsula; s/d all-inclusive from US$211/364) On an escarpment at the northernmost tip of Pemba, with views over the open ocean, it has several types of rooms, plus a spa, restaurant and PADI five-star dive operator.

Getting There & Away

AIR

ZanAir (☎ 024-245 2990, 0777-431143; Main Rd) and **Coastal Aviation** (☎ 024-245 2162, 0777-418343) fly daily between Chake Chake and Zanzibar (US$90), with connections to Dar es Salaam (US$110). Coastal also goes daily between Pemba and Tanga (US$70).

BOAT

Sea Express does the Pemba (Mkoani)–Zanzibar–Dar route on Monday, Thursday and Saturday, departing Dar at 7am, Zanzibar at 9.30am and Pemba at 12.30pm. It costs US$45 in economy class between Pemba and Zanzibar and US$60 between Pemba and Dar es Salaam, including port tax.

There are also slow ferries departing Zanzibar at 10pm on Monday, Tuesday, Thursday, Friday and Saturday, arriving in Pemba at about 6am. Departures from Mkoani are at 12.30pm, reaching Zanzibar about 4pm (US$25). Once in Mkoani, there are buses to Chake Chake and on to Wete.

NORTHEASTERN TANZANIA

BAGAMOYO
☎ 023

Bagamoyo was the capital of German East Africa from 1887 to 1891, when the capital was transferred to Dar es Salaam. Since then, Bagamoyo has been in a long decline, although its history, sleepy charm and nearby beaches make it an agreeable day excursion from Dar es Salaam. Don't miss strolling through central Bagamoyo, with its crumbling colonial-era buildings, and the **museum** (☎ 023-244 0010; adults/students Tsh1500/500; ☒ 10am-5pm) at Holy Ghost Catholic Mission, 2km north of town. About 5km south along the beach are the overgrown **Kaole ruins** (per adult/student Tsh1500/500; ☒ 8am-4pm Mon-Fri, 8am-5pm Sat & Sun), with the

remains of a 13th-century mosque and some 15th-century gravestones.

Travellers Lodge (☎ 023-244 0077; www.travellers-lodge.com; campsites with shower US$11, s/d from US$55/76; ☒) has pleasant cottages set around expansive grounds bordering the beach, a restaurant and a children's play area. It's on the road running parallel to the beach, just south of the entrance to the Catholic mission.

Dalla-dallas run throughout the day from Mwenge (north of Dar es Salaam along New Bagamoyo Rd, and accessed via *dalla-dalla* from New Posta) to Bagamoyo (Tsh1800, two hours), dropping you about 700m from the town centre.

SAADANI NATIONAL PARK

About 70km up the coast from Bagamoyo is tiny **Saadani National Park** (www.saadanipark.org; adult/child per day US$20/5), which makes a good excursion from Dar es Salaam if you don't have time to explore further afield. Wildlife can't compare with that in the better-known national parks, but hippos and crocs are likely, giraffes and elephants are a possibility and the long, lovely beach (with Zanzibar on the distant horizon) is a certainty.

Saadani Safari Lodge (☎ 022-277 3294; www.saadanilodge.com; s/d incl full board & 1 activity per day US$285/480; ☒) and **Tent With A View Safari Lodge** (☎ 022-211 0507; www.saadani.com; s/d incl full board US$275/390, s/d all inclusive US$385/590) are both on the beach, and both lovely. Both also offer road transport to/from Dar es Salaam (one way about US$250 per vehicle, five hours), and can help with travel arrangements – pickups or via public transport – from Tanga and with dhow charters to Zanzibar.

TANGA
☎ 027

The sleepy seaport of Tanga has little to attract the visitor, although it makes a convenient stop en route to/from Mombasa in Kenya.

Information

Kaributanga.com (Sokoine St; per hr Tsh1000; ☒ 9am-8pm Mon-Thu, 9am-noon & 2-7pm Fri, 9am-2pm & 4-7pm Sat & Sun) Internet access.

NBC Bank (cnr Bank & Sokoine Sts) Changes cash; has ATM.

Tayodea Tourist Information Centre (☎ 027-264 4350; www.tayodea.org; cnr Independence Ave & Usambara St; ☒ 8.30am-5pm) Information and guides for local excursions.

Sleeping & Eating

Kiboko Restaurant, Bar & Campsite (☎ 027-264 4929, 0784-469292; jda-kiboko@bluemail.ch; Amboni Rd; campsites US$4) Good, secure camping in large, green grounds (including tents for rent) with a well-stocked bar and a garden restaurant.

Ocean Breeze Hotel (cnr Tower & Sokoine Sts; r with fan/air-con Tsh10,000/20,000) Just east of the market, this is one of the better budget choices in the town centre. Tired but OK rooms, some with nets.

Panori Hotel (☎ 027-264 6044; panori@africaonline. co.tz; Ras Kazone; s/d Tsh31,000/42,000; ☒) A decent midrange choice 3km from the centre, with clean rooms and a restaurant.

Peponi Holiday Resort (☎ 0784-202962, 0713-540139; www.peponiresort.com; campsites US$4, s/d bandas US$50/55; ☒) Camping, *bandas* and a restaurant are all in expansive gardens bordering the beach 30km south of Tanga. Discounted family and backpacker rates. Take a Pangani bus to the turn-off, from where it's a short walk.

Patwas Restaurant (Mkwakwani Rd; meals from Tsh1500; ☺ 8am-8pm Mon-Sat) Fresh juices and local-style meals just south of the market.

Getting There & Away

New Spice Islander sails weekly between Tanga and Wete (on Pemba) for US$25 one way.

Buses go daily to Dar es Salaam (Tsh11,000, five hours), Arusha (Tsh15,000, seven hours), Lushoto (Tsh6000, three to four hours) and Pangani (Tsh2500, 1½ hours).

USAMBARA MOUNTAINS

With their wide vistas, cool climate, winding paths and picturesque villages, the Usambaras are one of northeastern Tanzania's highlights. It's easily possible to spend at least a week here hiking from village to village, or relaxing in one spot and exploring with day walks.

Lushoto

☎ 027

Lushoto is a leafy highland town nestled in a fertile valley at about 1200m. It's the centre of the western Usambaras and makes a fine base for hikes into the surrounding hills. **Friends of Lushoto Tourism Centre** (☎ 027-264 0132), diagonally behind the bank, and **Tayodea** (youthall2000@ yahoo.com), on the small hill behind the bus stand, can help with arranging guides and hikes (from Tsh15,000 per person per half-day up to a steep Tsh70,000 per person per day on multiday hikes). There's no ATM.

White House Annex (s/d Tsh9000/15,000), behind the bus stand, is cramped and noisy but one of the cheapest bets, with hot water, and meals available to order.

At **Lawns Hotel** (☎ 027-264 0005, 0784-420252; www.lawnshotel.com; campsites with hot shower US$6, s/d US$40/45; ▣) vine-covered buildings are surrounded by extensive gardens, spacious, musty rooms, a fireplace and a bar-restaurant, and large lawns (plus hot showers) for campers.

Tumaini Hostel (☎ 027-264 0094; tumaini@elct-ned. org; s/d US$10/17) has twin-bed rooms with nets and hot-water showers in a two-storey compound overlooking small gardens.

Daily buses travel between Lushoto and Tanga (Tsh6000, three to four hours), Dar es Salaam (Tsh10,000, seven to nine hours) and Arusha (Tsh11,000, six hours).

NORTHERN TANZANIA

MOSHI

☎ 027 / pop 144,300

Moshi, a bustling town at the foot of Mt Kilimanjaro, is home of the Chagga people and the centre of one of Tanzania's major coffee-growing regions. Most visitors use the town as a starting point for climbing Mt Kilimanjaro and it's generally a less expensive place to stay than Arusha.

Information

Easy.com (Ground fl, Kahawa House, Clock Tower Roundabout; per hr Tsh1500; ☺ 7.30am-8.30pm) Internet access.

Executive Bureau de Change (Boma Rd; ☺ 8.30am-6pm Mon-Fri, 9am-5pm Sat) Changes cash and travellers cheques.

Exim Bank (Boma Rd) ATM: Visa, MasterCard, Maestro and Cirrus.

Immigration office (Boma Rd; ☺ 7.30am-3.30pm Mon-Fri)

Stanbic Bank (Boma Rd) ATM: Visa, MasterCard, Maestro and Cirrus.

Standard Chartered Bank (Rindi Lane) ATM: Visa.

Sleeping

Kilimanjaro Backpackers Hotel (☎ 027-275 5159; www.kilimanjarobackpackers.com; Mawenzi Rd; s/tw without bathroom US$4/8) Formerly Da Costa Hotel, this place has tiny, clean rooms with fan, a bar and a restaurant

Buffalo Hotel (☎ 027-275 0270; New St; r without bathroom Tsh12,000, s/d from Tsh20,000/25,000) Straightforward rooms with fan and net, and

TANZANIA

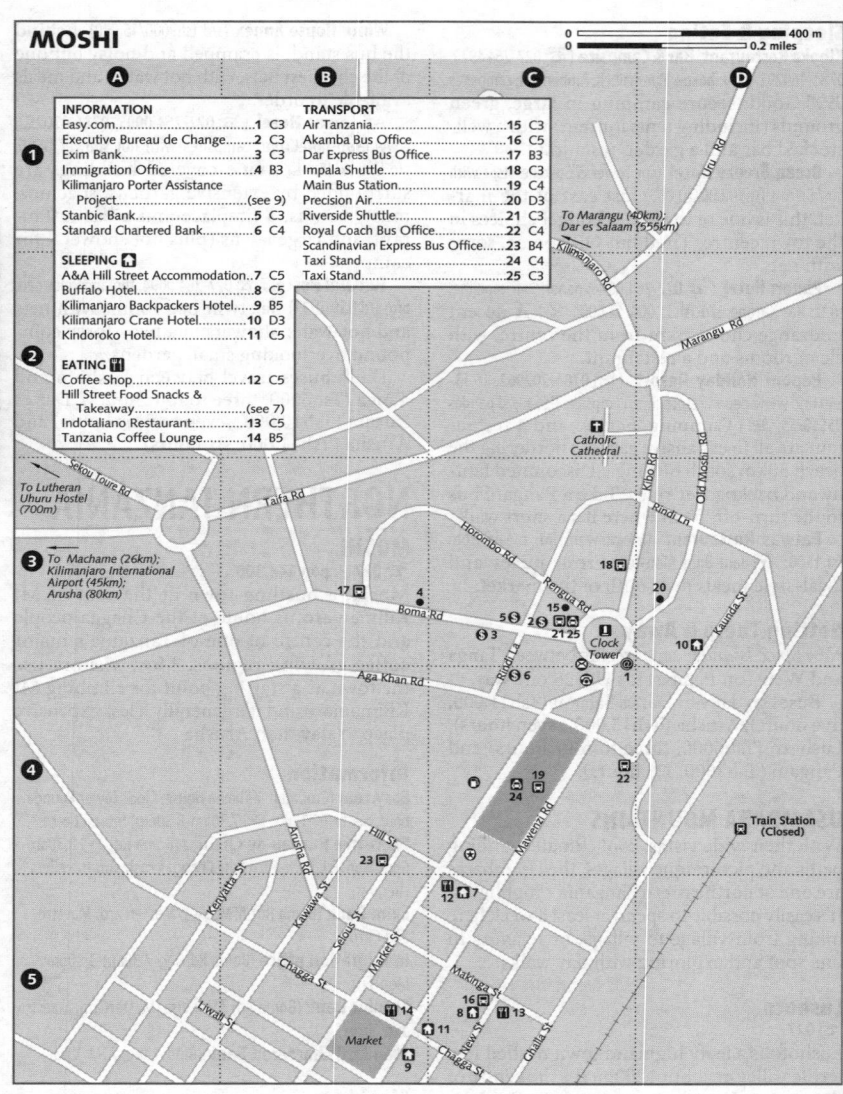

MOSHI

0 — 400 m
0 — 0.2 miles

INFORMATION
Easy.com..........................1 C3
Executive Bureau de Change......2 C3
Exim Bank........................3 C3
Immigration Office................4 B3
Kilimanjaro Porter Assistance
Project.........................(see 9)
Stanbic Bank.....................5 C3
Standard Chartered Bank..........6 C4

SLEEPING
A&A Hill Street Accommodation....7 C5
Buffalo Hotel....................8 C5
Kilimanjaro Backpackers Hotel....9 B5
Kilimanjaro Crane Hotel..........10 D3
Kindoroko Hotel..................11 C5

EATING
Coffee Shop......................12 C5
Hill Street Food Snacks &
Takeaway........................(see 7)
Indotaliano Restaurant...........13 C5
Tanzania Coffee Lounge...........14 B5

TRANSPORT
Air Tanzania.....................15 C3
Akamba Bus Office................16 C5
Dar Express Bus Office...........17 B3
Impala Shuttle...................18 C3
Main Bus Station.................19 C4
Precision Air....................20 D3
Riverside Shuttle................21 C3
Royal Coach Bus Office...........22 C4
Scandinavian Express Bus Office..23 B4
Taxi Stand.......................24 C4
Taxi Stand.......................25 C3

a restaurant. The entrance is on a small street off Mawenzi Rd.

A&A Hill St Accommodation (☎ 027-275 3455; sajjad_omar@hotmail.com; Hill St; s/d/tr Tsh15,000/20,000/30,000) Clean, quiet rooms with fans just one block from the bus stand, with an internet cafe and inexpensive restaurant just below. There's no breakfast.

Kindoroko Hotel (☎ 027-275 4054; www.kindoroko hotels.com; Mawenzi Rd; s/d US$25/35, d/tr without bathroom US$15/45; 🖳) Popular and an easy walk from the bus stand, with small but clean rooms, a rooftop bar, a bureau de change and a restaurant.

Lutheran Uhuru Hostel (☎ 027-275 4512; www. uhuruhotel.org; Sekou Toure Rd; s/d from US$40/50; 🖳)

Good-value rooms, some with balconies, in leafy grounds, and a restaurant. It's 3km northwest of the town centre on the Arusha road (Tsh2000 in a taxi).

Kilimanjaro Crane Hotel (☎ 027-275 1114; www. kilimanjarocranehotels.com; Kaunda St; s/d US$40/50; ❂ ▢ ▣) Good-value rooms with fans, nets, TV and large beds backing a small garden. Downstairs is a restaurant and upstairs is a rooftop terrace-bar. It's on a small side street running parallel to and just east of Old Moshi Rd.

Eating & Drinking

Coffee Shop (☎ 027-275 2707; Hill St; light meals from Tsh1000; ❂ 8am-5pm Mon, 8am-8pm Tue-Fri, 8am-6pm Sat) A laid-back vibe, garden seating, good coffee, and an assortment of homemade breads, cakes, yoghurt, breakfast and light meals. Proceeds go to a church project.

Hill Street Food Snacks & Take Away (Hill St; meals Tsh1500) Cheap plates of local fast food below A&A Hill Street Accommodation.

Tanzania Coffee Lounge (☎ 027-275 1006; Chagga St; snacks from Tsh2500; ❂ 8am-7pm Mon-Sat, noon-4pm Sun; ▣) Milkshakes, bagels, great coffee, waffles and an internet connection.

Indotaliano Restaurant (☎ 027-275 2195; New St; meals about Tsh5000; ❂ 10am-11pm) The Indo portion of the menu – a range of standards, including some vegie dishes – at this small, dark sidewalk restaurant is better than the Italian part (mediocre pizzas). It's opposite Buffalo Hotel.

Getting There & Away

AIR

Most flights to Moshi land at Kilimanjaro International Airport (KIA), 50km west of town. There are daily flights connecting KIA with Dar es Salaam (Tsh170,000), Zanzibar (from Tsh185,000) and Entebbe (Uganda) on **Air Tanzania** (☎ 027-275 5205; Rengua Rd). **Precision Air** (☎ 027-275 3495; Old Moshi Rd) has daily flights connecting KIA with Dar es Salaam, Mwanza (from about Tsh250,000) and Nairobi (US$250).

BUS

Buses and minibuses run throughout the day to Arusha (Tsh2000, one to 1½ hours) and Marangu (Tsh1500, one hour). To Dar es Salaam (Tsh25,000), lines include **Dar Express** (Boma Rd), with Moshi departures (all originating in Arusha) at 6.30am, 7.15am, 8.30am,

9.30am and 10.30am, and **Royal Coach** (Aga Khan Rd), opposite the bus stand and near the mosque, departing Moshi at 10.15am. The 6.30am Dar Express usually arrives in time for the afternoon ferry to Zanzibar.

To Nairobi, **Akamba** (☎ 027-275 3908; cnr New & Makinga Sts), around the corner from Buffalo Hotel, goes daily en route from Dar es Salaam. Alternatively take the **Riverside** (1st fl, THB Bldg, Boma Rd), just off Clock Tower Roundabout, or **Impala** (☎ 027-275 3444; Kibo Rd) shuttle, departing Moshi at 6.30am and 11.30am, though you'll need to wait an hour in Arusha in transit.

There are taxi stands at the bus station and Clock Tower Roundabout.

MARANGU
☎ 027

This small town on the slopes of Kilimanjaro makes a convenient overnight stop if you're trekking the Marangu route. It's also a pleasant place in its own right, with an agreeable highland atmosphere, and cool, leafy surroundings.

Most Marangu hotels organise Kilimanjaro treks.

At the main junction, behind the post office, is the **Marangu Computer Centre** (per hr Tsh2000; ❂ 8am-6pm), with internet access.

Prices are high for camping, but the grounds at **Coffee Tree Campsite** (☎ 0754-691433; www.coffeetreecampsite.com; campsites US$8, rondavel/chalet per person US$12/15) are green and well maintained, and there are hot-water showers, tents for hire (Tsh10,000 per day) and chalets.

The rustic **Kibo Hotel** (☎ 027-275 1308; www. kibohotel.com; s/d US$48/72) has wooden flooring, large old-fashioned windows, spacious rooms and a restaurant.

Minibuses run throughout the day between Marangu and Moshi (Tsh1500).

MT KILIMANJARO

At 5896m, Mt Kilimanjaro is the highest peak in Africa and one of the continent's most magnificent sights. From cultivated farmlands on the lower levels, the mountain rises through lush rainforest, alpine meadows and a barren lunar landscape to the twin summits of Kibo and Mawenzi.

A hike up 'Kili' lures hundreds of hikers each year. It's even more attractive, because with the right preparation you can walk all the way to the summit without ropes or technical

TANZANIA

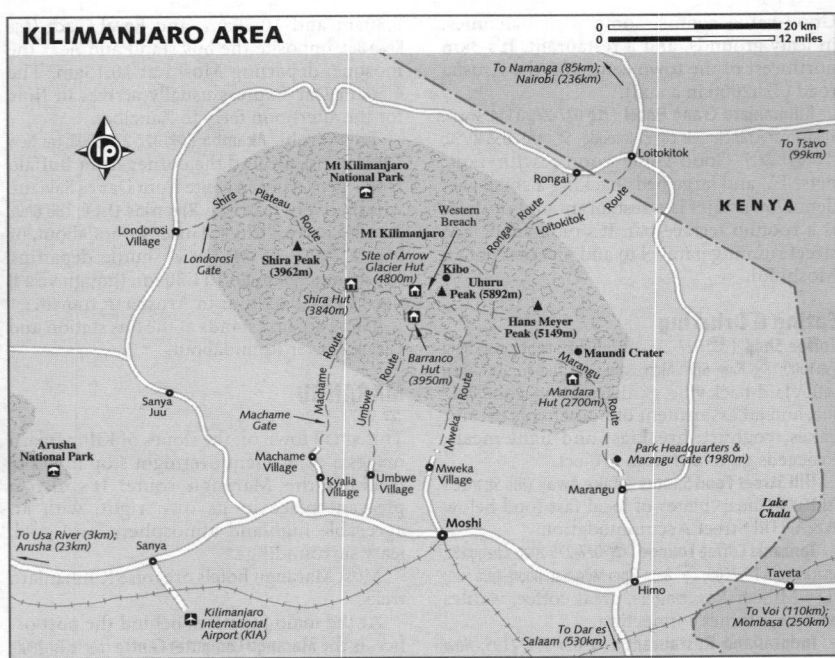

climbing experience. However, the climb is a serious undertaking and should only be undertaken with the right preparation.

Information

Entry fees for **Mt Kilimanjaro National Park** (☎ 027-275 6605/2; kinapa@iwayafrica.com) are US$60/10 per adult/child per day (not per 24-hour period). Huts (Marangu route) cost US$50 per person per night, as does camping on all routes, and there's a US$20 rescue fee per person per trip for hikes on the mountain. Kilimanjaro can only be climbed with a licensed guide. Unless you are a Tanzania resident and well versed in the logistics of Kili climbs, the only realistic way to organise things is through a tour company. Following are a few suggestions. Also see the listings on p794.

Key's Hotel (☎ 027-275 2250; www.keys-hotel-tours.com; Uru Rd, Moshi) Midrange.

Shah Tours (☎ 027-275 2370, 027-275 2998; www.kilimanjaro-shah.com; Sekou Toure Rd, Moshi) Midrange.

Tropical Trails (☎ 027-250 0358, 027-250 5578; www.tropical trails.com; Masai Camp, Old Moshi Rd, Arusha) Midrange.

Weather conditions on the mountain are frequently very cold and wet, no matter the time of year, so bring a full range of waterproof cold-weather clothing and gear. While you can hire sleeping bags and some cold-weather gear at the Marangu park gate, quality and availability can't be counted on.

Routes

There are at least 10 hiking routes that begin on the lower slopes, but only three continue to the summit. You'll need to camp on all except the Marangu route, which has a series of three 'huts' (bunkhouses) spaced a day's walk apart.

The **Marangu route**, which is the most popular, is usually sold as a five-day, four-night return package, although at least one extra night is highly recommended to help acclimatisation. Other routes usually take six or seven days. The increasingly popular **Machame route** has a gradual ascent before approaching the summit via the top section of the Mweka route. Beware of operators who try to sell an 'economy' version of the Machame route, which switches near the top to another route,

FAIR PLAY

Kilimanjaro's porters depend on tourism on the mountain for their livelihood, but as a hiker you can help ensure that they aren't exploited and that working conditions are fair. Before hiking, get in touch with the UK-based **Tourism Concern** (www.tourism concern.org.uk), which has mounted a world-wide campaign to improve conditions for porters. A local contact is the **Kilimanjaro Porter Assistance Project** (KPAP; www.kili porters.org; Kilimanjaro Backpackers Hotel, Mawenzi Rd, Moshi), which lobbies local tour operators to establish a code of conduct on porter pay and conditions. Both KPAP and Tourism Concern keep lists of trek operators who promote fair treatment of their staff.

and summits via the Western Breach. The **Rongai Route** starts near the Kenyan border and goes up the northern side of the mountain. It's possible to do this in five days, but it's better done in six.

Costs

Standard five-day four-night hikes up the Marangu route start at about US$900 including park fees (from about US$1000 for a six- to seven-day Machame route budget hike). Whatever you pay, remember that at least US$520 goes to park fees for a five-day Marangu route climb, and more for longer hikes. If you cut things too close, expect barely adequate meals, mediocre guides, and problems with hut bookings and park fees.

Guides & Porters

Guides and at least one porter (for the guide) are compulsory and are provided by the hiking company. Guides are required to be registered with the national park authorities, and should have permits showing this, though 'sharing' of permits among guides working for some of the less-reputable companies is fairly common. Porters will carry bags weighing up to 15kg (not including their own food and clothing); your bags will be weighed before you set off.

Most guides and porters receive only minimal wages from the trekking companies, and depend on tips as their major source of income. As a guideline, plan on tipping about 10% of the total amount you've paid for the

hike, divided among the guides and porters. For the Marangu route, tips are commonly from US$50 to US$60 for the guide, and US$20 each for the porters. Plan on more for the longer routes, or if the guide and porters have been particularly good.

ARUSHA
☎ 027

The fast-growing town of Arusha is the gateway to Tanzania's northern safari circuit. Towering Mt Meru forms an impressive backdrop. The surrounding lush countryside is dotted with coffee, wheat and maize estates tended by the Arusha and Meru people.

Orientation

Arusha is divided into two sections by the Naura River valley. The bus stations, market and many budget hotels are to the west, and upmarket hotels, the post office, immigration, government buildings, safari companies, airline offices, craft shops and the Arusha International Conference Centre (AICC) to the east. The heart of Arusha, and about a 10- to 15-minute walk from the bus stand, is the clock tower roundabout at the junction of Sokoine Rd (which turns into Dodoma Rd) and Old Moshi Rd.

Information
IMMIGRATION OFFICE
Immigration office (Simeon Rd; ☼ 7.30am-3.30pm Mon-Fri)

INTERNET ACCESS
Cybernet Café (India St; per hr Tsh1500; ☼ 9.30am-5pm Mon-Fri, 9.30am-1pm Sat)
New Safari Hotel (Boma Rd; per hr Tsh1000; ☼ 24hr)
Patisserie (Sokoine Rd; per hr Tsh1500; ☼ 7am-6.30pm Mon-Sat, 8.30am-2.30pm Sun) Also has wi-fi.

MEDICAL SERVICES
Arusha Medical Centre (☎ 027-250 8020; Plot 54, Haile Selassie Rd) Off Old Moshi Rd; lab tests and a doctor on call 24 hours.
Moona's Pharmacy (☎ 027-250 9800, 0713-510590; Sokoine Rd; ☼ 8.45am-5.30pm Mon-Fri, 8.45am-2pm Sat) Well-stocked pharmacy, west of NBC Bank.

MONEY
For changing cash, there are many bureaux de change clustered around the northern end of Boma Rd, and along Joel Maeda St near the clock tower.

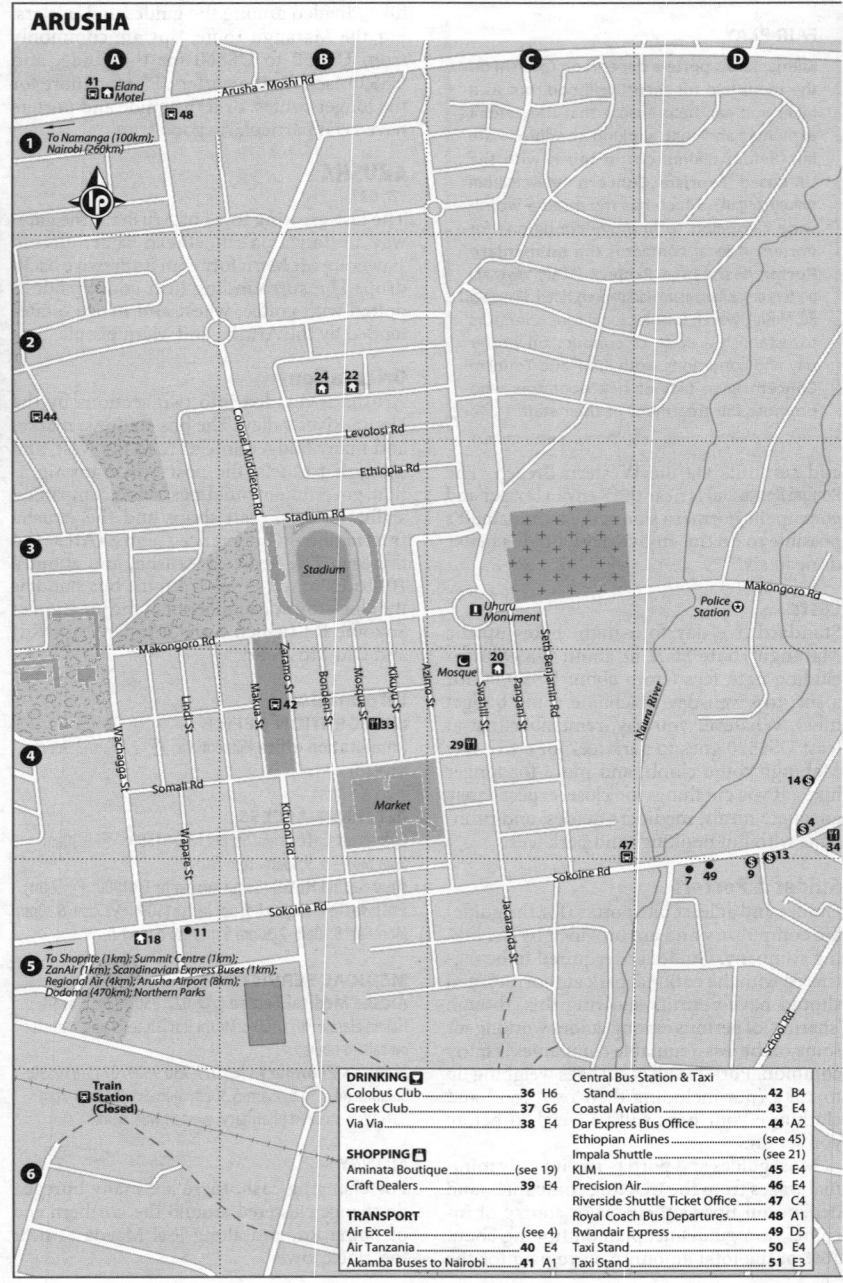

ARUSHA

TANZANIA

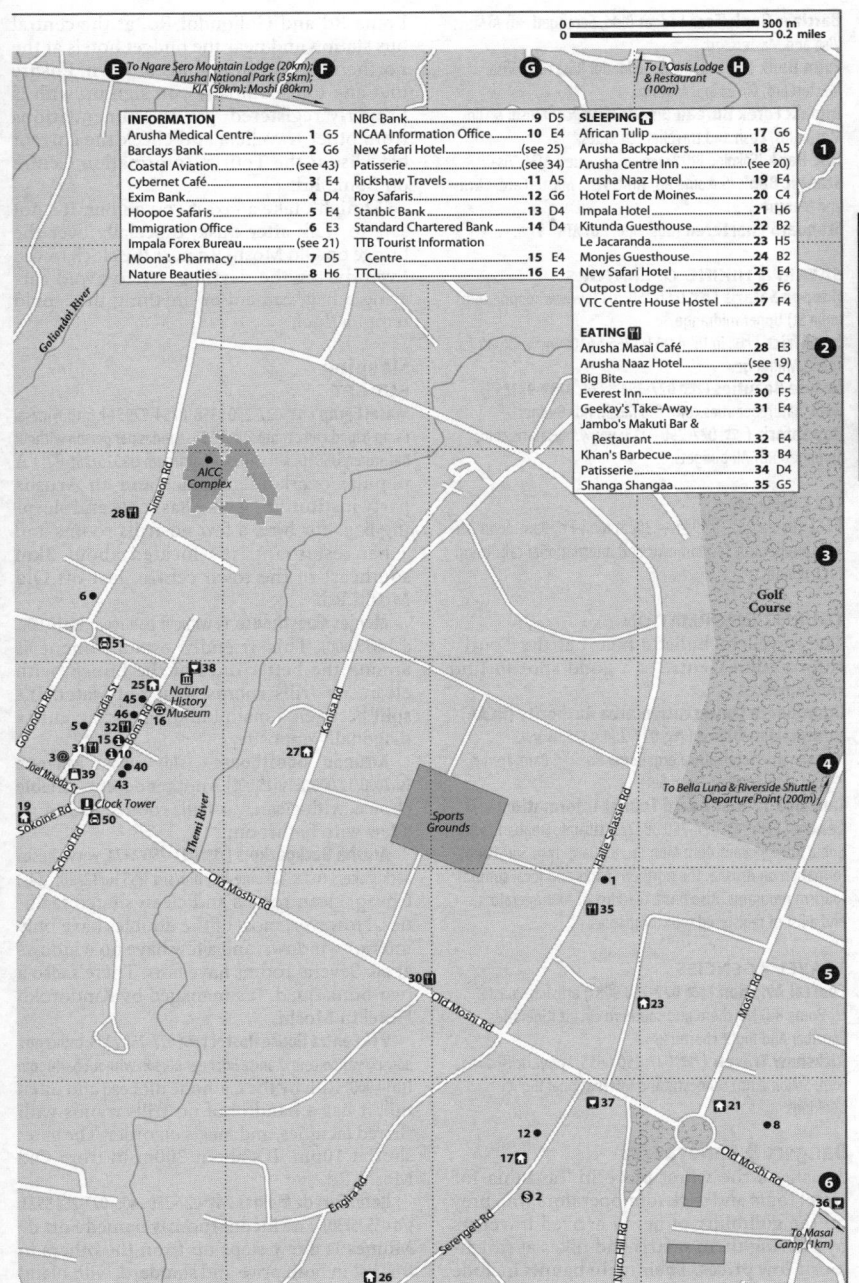

0   300 m
0   0.2 miles

To Ngare Sero Mountain Lodge (20km);
Arusha National Park (35km);
KIA (50km); Moshi (80km)

To L'Oasis Lodge
& Restaurant
(100km)

INFORMATION
Arusha Medical Centre...............1 G5
Barclays Bank............................2 G6
Coastal Aviation....................(see 43)
Cybernet Café...........................3 E4
Exim Bank.................................4 D4
Hoopoe Safaris..........................5 E4
Immigration Office.....................6 E3
Impala Forex Bureau..............(see 21)
Moona's Pharmacy.....................7 D5
Nature Beauties.........................8 H6

NBC Bank..................................9 D5
NCAA Information Office.............10 E4
New Safari Hotel...................(see 25)
Patisserie..............................(see 34)
Rickshaw Travels.......................11 A5
Roy Safaris..............................12 G6
Stanbic Bank............................13 D4
Standard Chartered Bank...........14 D4
TTB Tourist Information
  Centre..................................15 E4
TTCL.......................................16 E4

SLEEPING
African Tulip.............................17 G6
Arusha Backpackers...................18 A5
Arusha Centre Inn.................(see 20)
Arusha Naaz Hotel.....................19 E4
Hotel Fort de Moines.................20 C4
Impala Hotel............................21 H6
Kitunda Guesthouse..................22 B2
Le Jacaranda............................23 H5
Monjes Guesthouse...................24 B2
New Safari Hotel.......................25 E4
Outpost Lodge.........................26 F6
VTC Centre House Hostel...........27 F4

EATING
Arusha Masai Café.....................28 E3
Arusha Naaz Hotel.................(see 19)
Big Bite...................................29 C4
Everest Inn..............................30 F5
Geekay's Take-Away..................31 E4
Jambo's Makuti Bar &
  Restaurant............................32 E4
Khan's Barbecue.......................33 B4
Patisserie................................34 D4
Shanga Shangaa.......................35 G5

TANZANIA

Gollandeti River

Simeon Rd

AICC
Complex

28

Golf
Course

6

51

Gollandeti Rd

25
45
46
32
15
16
5
3
31
10
39
40
43

38
Natural
History
Museum

India St

Boma Rd

Kanisa Rd

27

Joel Maeda St

19
Sokoine Rd

School Rd

Clock Tower

50

Themi River

Old Moshi Rd

Sports
Grounds

Haile Selassie Rd

To Bella Luna & Riverside Shuttle
Departure Point (200m)

1
35

30
Old Moshi Rd

23

Moshi Rd

37

12

17

21

8

Old Moshi Rd

36

To Masai
Camp (1km)

Engira Rd

2

Serengeti Rd

Njiro Hill Rd

26

Barclays Bank (Sopa Lodges Bldg, Serengeti Rd) ATM: Visa and MasterCard.

Exim Bank (cnr Sokoine & Goliondoi Rds) ATM: Visa, MasterCard, Cirrus and Maestro.

Impala Forex Bureau (Impala Hotel, cnr Moshi & Old Moshi Rds) Cash and travellers cheques.

NBC Bank (Sokoine Rd) Travellers cheques; ATM: Visa.

Stanbic Bank (Sokoine Rd) ATM: Visa, MasterCard, Cirrus and Maestro.

Standard Chartered (Goliondoi Rd) ATM: Visa.

SAFARI & HIKING OPERATORS

Hoopoe Safaris (☎ 027-250 7011; www.hoopoe.com; India St) Upper midrange.

IntoAfrica (☎ in UK 44-114-255 5610; www.intoafrica. co.uk) Midrange.

Nature Beauties (☎ 027-254 8224, 0732-971859; www.naturebeauties.com; Old Moshi Rd) Budget

Roy Safaris (☎ 027-250 2115; www.roysafaris.com; Serengeti Rd) All budgets.

TELEPHONE

TTCL (Boma Rd; ☾ 9am-4.30pm Mon-Fri, 9am-noon Sat) Sells phonecards for domestic and international calls using TTCL phones.

TOURIST INFORMATION

The travellers' bulletin board at the Tourist Information Centre is a good spot to find safari mates.

Ngorongoro Conservation Area Authority (NCAA) Information Office (☎ 027-254 4625; www. ngorongoro-crater-africa.org; Boma Rd; ☾ 8am-1pm & 2-5pm Mon-Fri, 8am-1pm Sat)

Tanzania Tourist Board Tourist Information Centre (TTB; ☎ 027-250 3842/3; ttb-info@habari.co.tz; Boma Rd; ☾ 8am-4pm Mon-Fri, 8.30am-1pm Sat) For information on Arusha, the northern parks and local cultural tourism programs. Also has a blacklist of tour operators and a list of registered tour companies.

TRAVEL AGENCIES

Coastal Aviation (☎ 027-250 0087; arusha@coastal. cc; Boma Rd) Northern and southern circuit itineraries, Zanzibar and flight charters.

Rickshaw Travels (☎ 027-250 6655; www.rickshawtz. com; Sokoine Rd) Domestic and international flight bookings.

Dangers & Annoyances

Arusha is the worst place in Tanzania for street touts and slick tour operators who prey on the gullibility of newly arrived travellers by offering them safaris and hikes at ridiculously low prices. Their main haunts include

Boma Rd and Goliondoi Rd, at the central bus station and near the budget hotels at the northern and western ends of town. Ensure that any tour company you sign up with is properly registered; get recommendations from other travellers and check the current blacklist at the Tourist Information Centre on Boma Rd.

At night, take a taxi if you go out. It's not safe to walk after dusk, especially over the bridge on Old Moshi Rd near the clock tower. Even during the daytime, try to avoid carrying a bag, camera or anything that could tempt a thief.

Sleeping
BUDGET

Masai Camp (☎ 027-250 0358, 0754-829514; http://masai camp.tripod.com; campsites US$5, bandas per person without bathroom US$10, s/d without bathroom US$15/25; ▯) A popular overlanders' place and an Arusha party institution, it also has tents and sleeping bags for hire, a few no-frills rooms and a bar-restaurant. It's located about 3km southeast of the town centre, just off Old Moshi Rd.

Monjes Guesthouse (s without bathroom Tsh10,000, d Tsh15,000) This friendly establishment is among the better ones of the bunch, with clean, no-frills rooms with hot water. It's split between a main building and an annex diagonally opposite.

Kitundu Guesthouse (s/d without bathroom Tsh7000/12,000, d Tsh15,000) Another decent, reliable choice, with clean, no-frills rooms, including a few with bathroom.

Arusha Backpackers (☎ 027-250 4474; www.arusha backpackers.co.tz; Sokoine Rd; dm/s/d US$10/12/20; ▯) Cheap, clean rooms and clean shared facilities. However, most of the doubles have only interior windows, and a few have no windows at all. Several rooms have fans. There's also a two-bunk quad. It's managed by Kindoroko Hotel in Moshi.

VTC Centre House Hostel (☎ 027-250 2313; cathcenter house@yahoo.com; Kanisa Rd; r per person without bathroom Tsh14,000) Run by the Catholic diocese and often full, it has a handful of no-frills rooms with shared facilities, and meals on order. The gates shut at 10pm. It's about 300m in from Old Moshi Rd.

Hotel Fort de Moines (☎ 027-250 7406, 027-254 8523; s/d US$25/30) The incongruously named Fort de Moines is a few steps up from the others in this list in both price and standard, with bland straightforward rooms with fans but no nets. They're good value if you're looking for a 'proper' hotel at budget prices.

Arusha Centre Inn (☎ 027-250 0421; s/d US$25/37) Next door to Hotel Fort de Moines, and nicer, it has spotless rooms that are good value for the price, a restaurant and a location within easy walking distance of the bus stand.

Outpost Lodge (☎ 027-254 8405; www.outposttanzania.com; Serengeti Rd; 6-bed dm US$25, s/d/tr US$48/66/78; 🖳 🍴) On a leafy side street about 1km southeast of the clock tower roundabout, it has a few dorm-style rooms in an old two-storey house, plus garden bungalows and a restaurant.

Arusha Naaz Hotel (☎ 027-257 2087; www.arushanaaz.net; Sokoine Rd; s/d/tr US$45/60/75; 🍴 🖳) A convenient location just down from the clock tower with spotless rooms, all with TV, fan and hot water. Downstairs is restaurant with inexpensive breakfasts, a good-value daily (except Sunday) lunch buffet and a car-rental office.

MIDRANGE & TOP END

Le Jacaranda (☎ 027-254 4624; www.chez.com/jacaranda; s/d/tr US$45/50/70) Features spacious, pleasantly faded rooms in a large house set in small gardens, and a restaurant. It's on a quiet side street about 100m north of Old Moshi Rd at the eastern end of town.

L'Oasis Lodge & Restaurant (☎ 027-250 7089; www.loasislodge.com; s/d/tr US$79/97/127, backpackers r per person without bathroom US$20; 🖳 🍴) African-style *rondavels* and stilt houses are set around large gardens, and there's clean, twin-bedded backpacker rooms sharing hot-water bathrooms, a restaurant and a sports bar, plus full breakfast is included in the price. It's 2km northwest of the clock tower, about 1km off the Moshi–Nairobi road and signposted.

Impala Hotel (☎ 027-250 8448/51, 027-250 2362; www.impalahotel.com; cnr Moshi & Old Moshi Rds; s/d US$80/100; 🍴 🖳 🍴) A long-standing, reliable and centrally located place with a bureau de change, several restaurants and a small garden area. The showers are hot, breakfasts good, staff efficient and credit cards are accepted.

New Safari Hotel (☎ 027-250 3261; www.thenewsafarihotel.com; Boma Rd; s/d/tr US$85/105/135; 🍴 🖳) Good-value rooms catering to business travellers in a centrally located high-rise, plus a restaurant, secure parking and 24-hour internet access.

Ngare Sero Mountain Lodge (☎ 027-255 3638; www.ngare-sero-lodge.com; per person incl full board garden cottages/main house US$150/200) A former colonial-era farming estate set in lush, flowering gardens, with cosy accommodation, walking, canoeing, cultural tours and yoga.

African Tulip (☎ 027-254 3004/5; www.theafricantulip.com; Serengeti Rd; s/d from US$155/200; 🍴 🖳 🛜 🍴) Spacious, well-appointed rooms and a restaurant on a quiet side street off Old Moshi Rd. The hotel is run by Roy Safaris, and favourably priced safari-accommodation packages are offered.

Eating

Geekay's Take-Away (India St; meals from Tsh1000; 🕑 7.30am-6pm Mon-Sat) Inexpensive plates of rice, *ugali* and sauce.

Patisserie (Sokoine Rd; light meals from Tsh1500; 🕑 7.30am-6.30pm Mon-Sat, 8.30am-2pm Sun) Inexpensive burgers, pizza, sandwiches and light meals, located near the clock tower roundabout.

Arusha Naaz Hotel (☎ 027-257 2087; www.arushanaaz.net; Sokoine Rd; lunch buffet US$5; 🕑 lunch Mon-Sat) Great-value lunch buffet with mostly Indian and Tanzanian cuisine.

Jambo's Makuti Bar & Restaurant (Boma Rd; meals from Tsh6000; 🕑 to 10pm) European cafe vibes in a Tanzanian setting. There's an à la carte menu with a mix of Tanzanian and local dishes, and a plate of the day for about Tsh5500.

Khan's Barbecue (Mosque St; mixed grill from Tsh6000; 🕑 from 6.30pm) 'Chicken on the Bonnet' is an auto-spares shop by day and a popular barbecue by night, with a heaped spread of grilled, skewered meat and salads.

Arusha Masai Café (☎ 0755-765640; info@warmheartart.com; Simeon Rd; meals from Tsh6500; 🕑 10am-10pm Mon-Sat, noon-10pm Sun) Pastas, pizzas and culture opposite the AICC complex and near the Immigration office.

Everest Inn (☎ 027-250 8419; everesttzus@yahoo.com; Old Moshi Rd; meals from Tsh7000; 🕑 breakfast, lunch & dinner) Tasty Chinese food served in an outdoor garden, or indoors in an old, atmospheric house.

Big Bite (cnr Somali Rd & Swahili St; meals from Tsh8000; 🕑 closed Tue) A long-running favourite for delicious Indian food, including numerous vegetarian dishes, in a no-frills setting.

Self-caterers should head to **Shoprite** (TFA Centre, Dodoma Rd; 🕑 9am-7pm Mon-Fri, 8am-5pm Sat, 9am-1pm Sun), 2km west of town.

Drinking

Via Via (off Boma Rd) A good spot for a drink (it has food, too) and also for finding out about upcoming music and traditional dance events. Thursday is live music night. It's on the grounds of the Natural History Museum.

Greek Club (cnr Old Moshi & Serengeti Rds; closed Mon & Thu) A popular expat hang-out and sports bar, especially on weekend evenings.

Colobus Club (Old Moshi Rd; admission Tsh5000; 9pm-dawn Fri & Sat) Arusha's loudest and brashest nightclub.

Shopping

The small alley just off Joel Maeda St is full of craft dealers. Hard bargaining is required. **Aminata Boutique** (Sokoine Rd), in the entryway to Arusha Naaz Hotel, has textiles. **Shanga Shangaa** (www.shanga.org) – a cooperative for disabled artists – markets their lovely beaded necklaces at various spots around town, including the craft shop at Blue Heron restaurant on Haile Selassie Rd.

Getting There & Away

AIR

There are daily flights to Dar es Salaam and Zanzibar (ZanAir, Coastal Aviation, Precision Air and Air Tanzania); Nairobi (Precision Air); Seronera and other airstrips in Serengeti National Park (Coastal Aviation, Air Excel, Regional Air); Mwanza (Precision Air, via Shinyanga); and Lake Manyara and Tarangire National Parks (Coastal Aviation, Air Excel, Regional Air). Verify whether departure is from Kilimanjaro International Airport (KIA; about 50km east of town and about Tsh50,000 in a taxi) or Arusha airport (about 8km west of town and about Tsh8000 in a taxi) when buying your ticket. International airlines flying into KIA include KLM and Ethiopian Air.

Airline offices:

Air Excel (027-254 8429, 027-250 1597; reservations @airexcelonline.com; 2nd fl, Subzali (Exim Bank) Bldg, Goliondoi Rd)

Air Tanzania (027-250 3201/3; www.airtanzania. com; Boma Rd)

Coastal Aviation (027-250 0087; 0754-317808; arusha@coastal.cc; Boma Rd)

Ethiopian Airlines (027-250 6167/4231; www. ethiopianairlines.com; Boma Rd)

KLM (027-250 8062/3; reservations.arusha@klm.com; Boma Rd)

Precision Air (027-250 2818/36; www.precisionairtz. com; Boma Rd; 8am-5pm Mon-Fri, 8am-2pm Sat & Sun). Also handles Kenya Airways bookings.

Regional Air (027-250 4477, 027-250 4164; www. regionaltanzania.com; Nairobi Rd)

Rwandair Express (0732-978558; www.rwandair.com; Sokoine Rd)

ZanAir (027-254 8877; www.zanair.com; Ground fl, Summit Centre, Dodoma Rd)

BUS

Arusha's central bus station is near the market, although several of the major lines – Dar Express, Royal Coach, Scandinavian Express and Akamba – have their own booking offices and departure points (see below). It's chaotic and a haunt for safari touts. Watch your luggage and don't negotiate any safari deals at the stations.

Dar es Salaam

Main lines to Dar es Salaam (about Tsh25,000, nine hours) include the following:

Dar Express (Wachagga St) Departures at 5.15am, 6am, 7am, 8am, 9am and 9.30am. It's located several blocks north of Meru St post office and Arusha Backpackers, on the left.

Royal Coach (cnr Nairobi & Colonel Middleton Rds) Departures at 9am from Bamprass petrol station on the Nairobi road in Mianzini.

Scandinavian Express Departures at 8.30am and 11.30am from small side street branching off Sokoine Rd opposite Shoprite/TFA Centre.

Other Destinations

There are other lines serving Lushoto (Fasaha; Tsh11,000, six hours, daily at 6.30am), Tanga (Tashriff and Ngoryka; Tsh15,000, seven hours, daily at 8.30 and 11.30am).

Buses and minibuses run throughout the day between Arusha and Moshi (Tsh2000, one hour), or take one of the Arusha–Nairobi shuttles (p810; Tsh5000 between Moshi and Arusha).

Akamba buses to Nairobi en route from Dar es Salaam depart from next to Eland Motel along the Nairobi road.

ARUSHA NATIONAL PARK
027

Although it's one of Tanzania's smallest national parks, Arusha is one of its most beautiful and topographically varied. Its main features are Ngurdoto Crater, the Momela Lakes and towering Mt Meru.

Information

Entry fees are US$35/10 per adult/child per day. Armed rangers (required for all walks) cost US$15 per day and the huts on Mt Meru cost US$20.

The main park entrance is at Ngongongare Gate, about 10km from the main road. **Park headquarters** (☎ 027-255 3995, 0732-971303; ☒ 6.30am-6.30pm) – the main contact for making campsite or rest-house reservations, and for arranging guides and porters to climb Mt Meru – is about 14km further in near Momela Gate.

Sleeping

The park has four **public campsites** (per adult/child US$30/5).

Meru View Lodge (☎ 0784-419232; www.meru-view-lodge.de; s/d US$90/130; ☐ ☒) An unassuming place with cottages set in pleasant grounds along the main park road and vehicle rental.

Momella Wildlife Lodge (☎ 027-250 6423/6; www.lions-safari-intl.com/momella.html; d incl half board US$150) Near Momela Gate, it has small, serviceable cottages set around modest gardens and vehicle rental (US$175/250 per half-/full day).

Hatari Lodge (☎ 027-255 3456/7; www.hatarilodge.com; r per person incl full board US$280) The upmarket Hatari has a prime location on large lawns frequented by giraffes, and views to both Meru and Kilimanjaro on clear days.

Getting There & Away

Transfers from Arusha cost about US$100; arrange through your lodge. There's a daily bus between Arusha and Ngare Nanyuki (10km north of Momela Gate) that can drop you at the park gate (Tsh2000, 1½ hours from Arusha to Ngongongare Gate), but there's no onward transport from there to Momela Gate, 14km further on, where you need to arrange your guide and pay your mountain-climbing fees, and the park doesn't rent vehicles.

LAKE MANYARA NATIONAL PARK
☎ 027

Among the attractions of the often under-rated Lake Manyara National Park are superb birdlife, elusive tree-climbing lions and abundant hippos.

Entry fees are US$35/10 per adult/child per day. The park gate and **park headquarters** (☎ 027-253 9112/45; manyara@tanapa.org, manyarapark@africaonline.co.tz) are at the northern tip of the park near Mto Wa Mbu village.

The park has two **public campsites** (per adult/child US$30/5) and about 10 double **bandas** (per adult/child US$20/10) with hot water, bedding and a cooking area.

Kirurumu Luxury Tented Camp (☎ 027-250 7011/7541; www.kirurumu.com; s/d incl full board US$238/386) is a highly regarded camp that offers good food and a mix of spacious tents and chalets, all nestled in the vegetation, well spaced for privacy and most with views over the escarpment.

Lake Manyara Serena Lodge (☎ 027-253 9160/1; www.serenahotels.com; s/d incl full board US$375/550; ☒), a large complex on the escarpment overlooking the Rift Valley, has two-storey conical thatched bungalows, buffet-style dining and wonderful views from its pool-bar area. It's about 2km from the main road and signposted.

Most people visit Lake Manyara as part of a longer safari and independent travellers will need private transport inside the park. Via public transport, there are several buses daily between Mto Wa Mbu village, just before the Manyara park entrance, and Arusha (Tsh4500). Once in Mto Wa Mbu, arrange vehicle rental (about US$150 per day) for a Manyara safari with Jambo Campsite & Lodge or Twiga Campsite & Lodge – both next to each other along the main road.

Hoopoe Safaris (p794) offers upmarket cycling and cycling-safari combination trips in the Lake Manyara area. Budget cultural walks and cycling outside the park can be organised through the Mto Wa Mbu Cultural Tourism Program along the main road in Mto Wa Mbu.

TARANGIRE NATIONAL PARK
☎ 027

Between August and October, the baobab-studded Tarangire National Park has one of the highest concentrations of wildlife of any Tanzanian park.

Entry fees are US$35/10 per adult/child per day. There is a **public campsite** (per adult/child US$30/5) near park headquarters at the northwestern tip of the park. Bring supplies from Arusha.

Tarangire Safari Lodge (☎ 027-254 4752; www.tarangiresafarilodge.com; s/d from US$89/128; ☒) is a large lodge notable for its prime location on a bluff overlooking the Tarangire River, about 10km inside the park gate. Accommodation is in closely spaced tents or thatched bungalows.

TANZANIA

Tarangire is an easy two-hour drive from Arusha, and is often included as part of multi-night packages continuing on to the Serengeti or Ngorongoro Crater.

SERENGETI NATIONAL PARK

Serengeti, which covers 14,763 sq km and is contiguous with Masai Mara National Reserve in Kenya, is easily Tanzania's most famous national park. Among its most famous residents are the wildebeest, of which there are over one million, and their annual migration is the Serengeti's biggest drawcard.

Information

Park entry fees are US$50/10 per adult/child per day. Bookings for campsites, rest houses and the hostel should be made through the **Tourism Warden** (☎ 028-262 0091/1515/1504; www.serengeti.org). There's an excellent Visitors Information Centre at Seronera.

Wildlife concentrations are greatest between about December and June, although the Serengeti is a rewarding visit at any time of year. For the wildebeest migration, it's best to be based near Seronera or in the southeastern part of the park from about December to April. The famous crossing of the Grumeti River, in the park's Western Corridor, usually takes place between May and July. The northern Serengeti is a good base between about August and October.

Sleeping

There are nine **public campsites** (per adult/child US$30/5) in the park. The main lodge area is at Seronera, in the centre of the park, where there are also several rest houses with running water, blankets and cooking facilities. Bring your own food.

Serengeti Stop-Over (☎ 028-262 2273; www.serengetistopover.com; campsites US$10, s/d US$30/60) Two hours northeast of Mwanza and just 1km from the Serengeti's Ndabaka Gate, this place has camping with hot showers, *rondavel*-style rooms and a restaurant. Safari vehicle rental is sometimes possible (with advance notice only). Buses along the Mwanza–Musoma road can drop you at the entrance.

Robanda Safari Camp (☎ 0754-282251; www.robanda-safari-camp.com; s/d incl full board US$145/200) A small semipermanent camp just outside Ikoma Gate, it's rather spartan but nevertheless a good option between camping safaris and something more luxurious. There's no

vehicle rental at the moment, although it's planned – which means you could arrive here by public transport and do a safari.

Serengeti Tented Camp (☎ 027-255 3242; www.moivaro.com; s/d incl full board US$160/213) A small camp 3km from Ikoma Gate and just outside the park boundary, it has 12 no-frills tents with bathrooms and hot water, plus the chance for night drives and guided walks in the border area.

Ndutu Safari Lodge (☎ 027-250 6702/2829; www.ndutu.com; s/d incl full board US$249/385) Just outside the southeastern Serengeti in the far western part of NCA, this is an ideal base for observing the enormous herds of wildebeests during the wet season. In addition to NCA fees, you'll need to pay Serengeti fees any time that you cross into the park.

Seronera Wildlife Lodge (☎ 027-254 4595/4795; www.hotelsandlodges-tanzania.com; r per person incl full board US$400) A prime location in the heart of the Serengeti, well situated for wildlife drives, it has modest but pleasant rooms and a convivial end-of-the-day safari atmosphere at the evening buffet.

Lobo Wildlife Lodge (☎ 027-254 4595/4795; www.hotelsandlodges-tanzania.com; r per person incl full board US$440) Well located for the August to October migration, it's similar in standard to the Seronera Wildlife Lodge and overall good value.

Getting There & Away

Coastal Aviation, Air Excel and Regional Air fly daily to/from Arusha (one way US$175). Coastal's flight continues to Mwanza.

Most travellers visit the Serengeti with an organised safari or with their own vehicle. Access from Arusha is via **Naabi Hill Gate** (☉ 6am-6pm) at the southeastern edge of the park, from where it's 75km further to Seronera. **Ndabaka Gate** (☉ 6am-4pm), for the western corridor, is about 140km northeast of Mwanza along the Mwanza–Musoma road. Driving in the park isn't permitted after 7pm.

NGORONGORO CONSERVATION AREA
☎ 027

The world-renowned Ngorongoro Crater is just one part of a much larger area of interrelated ecosystems, including Olduvai (Oldupai) Gorge, alkaline lakes and the Crater Highlands – a string of volcanoes and collapsed volcanoes (calderas).

Information

The **Ngorongoro Conservation Area Authority** (NCAA; ☎ 027-253 7006/7019/9108; www.ngorongoro-crater-africa.org) has its headquarters at Park Village at Ngorongoro Crater, and there's a tourist information office in Arusha.

Entry fees (payable for all activities within the NCA) are US$50/10 per adult/child per 24-hour period. Guides, including for walking safaris, cost US$20 per day per group. There is a vehicle fee of US$40/Tsh10,000 per foreign-/Tanzanian-registered vehicle per entry and an additional crater-service fee of US$200 per vehicle per entry (valid for up to six hours) to drive down into Ngorongoro Crater.

Ngorongoro Crater

With high concentrations of wildlife offering close-range viewing opportunities, Ngorongoro is one of East Africa's most visited destinations. At about 20km wide it's also one of the largest calderas in the world. Within its walls you are likely to see lions, elephants, buffaloes and flamingos, and there's also a chance of seeing black rhinos. Local Maasai have grazing rights and you may come across them tending their cattle.

The gates down to the crater floor open at 7am, and close (for descent) at 4pm; all vehicles must be out of the crater area before 6pm.

Sleeping

Simba A, Ngorongoro's sole **public campsite** (per adult/child US$30/10), has crater views if there's no cloud cover. It's along the road from Lodoare gate.

Rhino Lodge (☎ 0762-359055; www.ngorongoro.cc; s/d incl full board US$125/220) Just 500m back from the crater rim (though there's no crater view), it's good value and can be reached by public bus from Arusha. Once at the lodge, vehicle rental can be arranged (for about the same price as in Karatu), as can walks with Maasai guides in the NCA.

Ngorongoro Wildlife Lodge (☎ 027-254 4595/4795, direct 027-253 7058/7073; www.hotelsandlodges-tanzania.com; r per person incl full board US$420) This former government hotel has a prime setting on the southern crater rim and reasonable rooms.

It's also possible to stay in or near Karatu village, 20km before Ngorongoro's **Lodoare Gate** (☎ 027-253 7031; ◷ 6am-6pm). Other options:

ELCT Karatu Lutheran Hostel (☎ 027-253 4230; s/d/tr Tsh22,000/30,000/40,000; meals Tsh6000) Simple, clean rooms with hot water, plus meals. It's on the main road at the western end of town.

Bougainvillea Safari Lodge (☎ 027-253 4083; www.bougainvillealodge.net; s/d/tr US$70/125/150) Just off the main road west of Karatu, it has two dozen spacious stone bungalows – all with fireplaces and verandas – plus a restaurant. Cultural activities can be arranged.

Getting There & Around

There are several buses daily between Arusha and Karatu (about Tsh6000, three hours), departing Arusha from the main bus station, with at least one daily (look for Ditto KK and Kulinge lines – both departing about 10am) continuing on to Lodoare gate (about four hours) and NCAA Park Village – and passing Rhino Lodge en route.

Vehicle hire and guides can be arranged at Lodoare Gate. Car hire (which is done informally with private cars belonging to staff, as the NCAA no longer rents vehicles) costs about US$150 per day plus crater and NCA fees. It's more reliable, and about the same price, to rent vehicles in Karatu or through Rhino Lodge inside the NCA.

CENTRAL TANZANIA & LAKE VICTORIA

DODOMA

Since 1973, Dodoma has been Tanzania's official capital and headquarters of the ruling CCM party, although Dar es Salaam remains the unrivalled economic and political centre of the country. **NBC Bank** (Kuu St) has an ATM (Visa card only) and **RAL Internet Café** (Kuu St; per hr Tsh1000; ◷ 8am-9pm Mon-Sat), just north of the main roundabout, has an internet connection.

Christian Council of Tanzania (CCT; s/tw/ste Tsh6000/10,000/12,000), at the main roundabout next to the Anglican church (and an easy walk from the bus stand), has no-frills rooms with mosquito nets, and buckets of hot water for bathing on request. Breakfast costs extra.

Cana Lodge (☎ 026-232 1199; Ninth St; s/d from Tsh15,000/22,000, ste Tsh25,000) is a few steps up, with small, spotless rooms and a restaurant.

New Dodoma Hotel (Dodoma Rock Hotel; ☎ 026-232 1641; reservation_newdodomahotel@yahoo.com; Railway St; s/d with fan Tsh45,000/60,000, s/d with air-con from Tsh65,000/80,000; 🔲 🔲 🔲), the former Railway Hotel, is Dodoma's most upmarket option, with straightforward rooms and a Chinese restaurant.

For milkshakes and soft-serve ice cream, head to **Aladdin's Cave** (snacks Tsh500-1500; ⏰ 9.30am-1pm Mon, 9.30am-1pm & 3.30-8.30pm Tue-Sun), just off Kuu St and north of the Ismaili mosque.

Scandinavian Express goes daily to/from Dar es Salaam from its terminal about 1km east of town along the Dar es Salaam road. There are daily buses to Iringa (Tsh12,000, nine to 10 hours) and to Arusha (done in stages via Kondoa and Babati) from the main bus station, diagonally opposite Scandinavian.

MWANZA
☎ 028

Mwanza is the economic centre of the Lake Victoria region and a jumping-off point for the western Serengeti. The surrounding area is the heartland of the Sukuma, Tanzania's largest tribe.

Orientation

To the west of the town centre, just a short walk from the clock tower, are the passenger-ferry docks and several banks and shops. East of the clock tower area are more shops, guesthouses and mosques; further east are the market and bus stand. The train station is about five minutes' walk southwest of the clock tower. Just beyond here is Capri Point.

Information

Organise visits to Rubondo Island National Park with the **Saa Nane/Tanapa office** (☎ 028-254 1819; ⏰ 8am-5pm Mon-Fri) about 200m north of Hotel Tilapia on Capri Point.

DBK Bureau de Change (Post St) At Serengeti Services & Tours, it's the easiest place to change cash and travellers cheques.

Exim Bank (Kenyatta Rd) ATM: MasterCard.

Karibu Corner Internet Café (cnr Post St & Kenyatta Rd; per hr Tsh1000; ⏰ 8am-8.30pm Mon-Fri, 8am-7pm Sat, 9am-7pm Sun)

Masumin Tours & Safaris (☎ 028-254 1127, 028-250 0233/0192/3295; www.masumintours.com; Kenyatta Rd)

NBC Bank (Liberty St) Travellers cheques; ATM: Visa.

Serengeti Services & Tours (☎ 028-250 0061/0754; www.serengetiservices.com; Post St)

Standard Chartered (Makongoro Rd) Near the clock tower; ATM: Visa.

Sleeping

St Dominic's Pastoral Centre (Nyakahoja Hostel) (☎ 028-250 0830; off Balewa Rd; s/d Tsh18,000/25,000, without bathroom Tsh10,000/15,000) A centrally located church-run hostel with spartan rooms sharing cold-water bathroom, and nicer ones with hot-water bathrooms. It's five minutes' walk north of the clock tower roundabout.

Lake Hotel (☎ 028-250 0658; Ground fl, Station Rd; s/d Tsh15,000/20,000, upstairs d Tsh30,000) Ageing and tatty, it's still a convenient place to sleep if you've just disembarked from a 24-hour-plus haul on the Central Line train. Upstairs rooms – with trickling hot-water shower, fan and net – are better.

Treehouse (☎ 028-254 1160; treehouse@streetwise-africa.org; s/d from US$45/55; 🔲) A B&B-style place with a range of clean rooms plus lake views in the distance, it's 2km northeast of town in Isamilo (Tsh2000 in a taxi). Volunteer discounts apply.

Hotel Tilapia (☎ 028-250 0517/0617; www.hoteltilapia.com; Capri Point; r US$90-130; 🔲 🔲 🔲) This business travellers' hotel has a breezy setting overlooking the water on Capri Point and a restaurant.

Eating

Kuleana Pizzeria (☎ 028-256 0566; Post St; meals from Tsh2500; ⏰ 7am-9pm) Simple good meals – pizzas, omelettes, sandwiches, fruit and freshly squeezed juices.

Binti Maringo (Balewa Rd; meals Tsh3000-Tsh7000; ⏰ 9am-10pm Mon-Sat) An open-air seating and local food, including a Saturday breakfast buffet, plus textiles and crafts for sale.

Getting There & Away
AIR

There are daily flights to/from Dar es Salaam (Tsh210,000) on **Air Tanzania** (☎ 028-250 0046; Kenyatta Rd) and **Precision Air** (☎ 028-250 0819; pwmwz@africaonline.co.tz; Kenyatta Rd). **Coastal Aviation** (☎ 028-256 0441; mwanza@coastal.cc; Airport) flies daily between Mwanza and Arusha (one way US$260) via the Serengeti. The airport is 10km north of town. A taxi will cost Tsh8000.

BUS

The main departure point for southern destinations is Nyegezi bus stand, 10km south of town along the Shinyanga road. Buses for Nairobi and other points north depart from Nyakato, 6km north of town along the Musoma road.

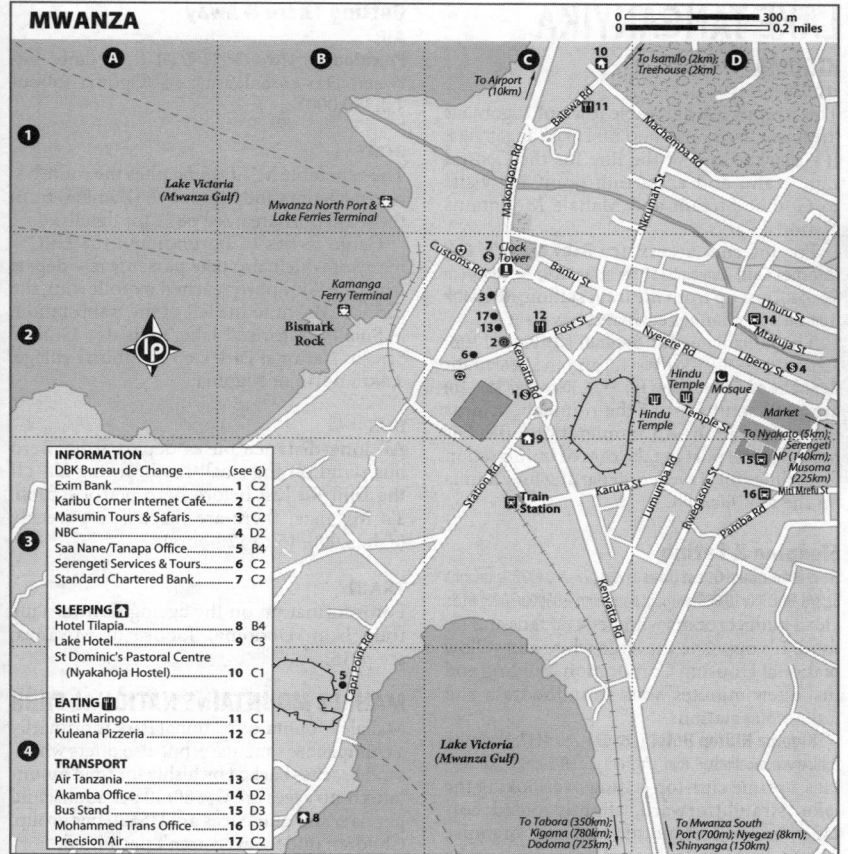

MWANZA

| 0 | 300 m |
| 0 | 0.2 miles |

TANZANIA

INFORMATION
DBK Bureau de Change	(see 6)
Exim Bank	**1** C2
Karibu Corner Internet Café	**2** C2
Masumin Tours & Safaris	**3** C2
NBC	**4** D2
Saa Nane/Tanapa Office	**5** B4
Serengeti Services & Tours	**6** C2
Standard Chartered Bank	**7** C2

SLEEPING 🛏
Hotel Tilapia	**8** B4
Lake Hotel	**9** C3
St Dominic's Pastoral Centre	
(Nyakahoja Hostel)	**10** C1

EATING 🍴
| Binti Maringo | **11** C1 |
| Kuleana Pizzeria | **12** C2 |

TRANSPORT
Air Tanzania	**13** C2
Akamba Office	**14** D2
Bus Stand	**15** D3
Mohammed Trans Office	**16** D3
Precision Air	**17** C2

Akamba buses start from the **Akamba office** (☎ 028-250 0272; off Mtakuja St), just north of the small footbridge near Majukano Hotel. Mohammed Trans buses depart from the **Mohammed Trans office** (off Miti Mrefu St) diagonally up from the town bus stand.

Akamba goes daily to Arusha/Moshi (Tsh47,000) and Dar es Salaam (Tsh71,000 plus US$20 for a Kenyan transit visa, about 30 hours) via Nairobi (Tsh28,000 plus visa costs, about 15 hours), changing buses in Nairobi. Better is Mohammed Trans via Singida (Tsh45,000, about 12 hours to Arusha).

It's also possible to go to Arusha via the Serengeti on the Coast Line bus, but in addition to the fare (Tsh30,000, 14 hours) you'll need to pay entry fees for both Serengeti ($50) and Ngorongoro Conservation Area ($50), and the bus goes too fast for any serious wildlife-watching.

To Kigoma (Tsh25,000, 15 to 17 hours), there are several buses weekly, going via Biharamulo and Lusahunga, and departing from Mwanza by 5am. At the time of research it left from the central bus station, though this may change.

See p810 and p811 for buses to Kenya and Uganda, respectively.

TRAIN

Mwanza is the terminus of a branch of the Central Line from Dar es Salaam. See p815.

LAKE TANGANYIKA

KIGOMA
☎ 028

The scrappy but agreeable town of Kigoma is the major Tanzanian port on Lake Tanganyika. It's also the end of the line for the Central Line train, and a starting point for visits to Gombe Stream and Mahale Mountains National Parks.

For internet access, try **Baby Come 'n' Call Internet Café** (Lumumba St; per hr Tsh2000; ☒ 8am-7pm Mon-Sat), just up from the train station. **NBC Bank** (Lumumba St) changes cash and has an ATM.

The consulates for **Burundi** (☎ 028-280 2865; Kakolwa St; ☒ 10am-3pm Mon-Fri) and the **Democratic Republic of Congo** (Kaya Rd; ☒ 8.30am-4pm Mon-Fri) are both southwest of the roundabout near the train station. An immigration officer is posted at the port to take care of immigration formalities for travellers departing for Zambia on the MV *Liemba*.

Sleeping & Eating
New Mapinduzi Guest House (☎ 028-280 4978; Lumumba St; s/d Tsh8000/10,000, without bathroom Tsh5000/7000) Has clean budget rooms with nets, no fans and no food. It's opposite the large white and yellow National Housing Corporation building and just a few minutes' walk from the train and *dalla-dalla* stations.

Kigoma Hilltop Hotel (☎ 028-280 4437; kht@raha. com; www.mbalimbali.com; s/d from US$60/80; ☒ 🖳 🖳) Has a prime cliff-top setting overlooking the lake, straightforward, slightly faded cottages and a restaurant, and can organise safaris to Mahale Mountains and Gombe Stream Parks.

Sun City (Lumumba St; meals Tsh1500-Tsh3000) Has inexpensive meals.

Getting There & Away
AIR
Precision Air (☎ 028-280 4720) flies daily between Dar es Salaam and Kigoma (about Tsh350,000).

BOAT
The venerable MV *Liemba* plies the route between Kigoma and Mpulungu (Zambia) from the main port area; see p812 for details.

Cargo ferries to Burundi and the DRC – many of which also take passengers – depart from the Ami port, reached by following the dirt lane down to the left of the train station.

Small, motorised lake 'taxis' for Gombe Stream National Park stop at Kibirizi village, 2.5km north of Kigoma.

BUS
All long-distance buses depart from Bero bus stand on the small road turning left off the Ujiji Rd just before Bero petrol station. To Mwanza, there are three buses weekly (Tsh25,000, 15 to 17 hours).

TRAIN
For information on the ageing Central Line train from Dodoma, Tabora or Mwanza, see p815.

MAHALE MOUNTAINS NATIONAL PARK

Mahale Mountains National Park is primarily a chimpanzee sanctuary, but also offers white-sand beaches backed by lushly forested mountains. Entry fees are US$80/30 per adult/child per day, and guide fees are US$20 per group. Children under seven aren't permitted.

Book self-catering **park bandas** (per person US$30) through **park headquarters** (sokwe@mahale. org; www.mahalepark.org) and bring all food and drink with you!

LAKE TANGANYIKA

Lake Tanganyika is the world's longest (670km) and second-deepest (over 1400m) freshwater lake, and makes an excellent adventure destination for anyone travelling in western Tanzania. Well down the lake shore from Mahale Mountains National Park is tiny Kipili village – an old mission station on a large bay – and the nearby and highly recommended **Lake Shore Lodge & Campsite** (☎ 0763-993166, 0752-540792; www.laketanganyikaadventuresafaris.com; campsites US$12, s/d bandas US$45/70, d/q chalet US$315/585; breakfast/lunch/dinner US$7/10/15; 🖳). It has camping, stone *bandas* with views over the lake and lovely four-person chalets directly on the lakeshore. Sunset on the beach in front of the lodge, with the Congo mountains in the distance, is magical. With advance notice, staff can organise combination itineraries with Katavi and Mahale Mountains Parks (including a vehicle for a safari to Katavi, about a four-hour drive away).

Kungwe Beach Lodge (☎ 027-254 7007; www.mbalimbali.com; per person all-inclusive US$465; ☯ May-Feb) has a lovely beachside setting, spacious double tents and a delicious restaurant – a recommended splurge.

Zantas Air (www.zantasair.com) flies twice weekly between Arusha and Mahale via Katavi National Park (about US$1500 return). **Safari Airlink** (www.safariaviation.info) offers a similarly priced service between Ruaha and Mahale via Katavi.

The MV *Liemba* stops at Lagosa (also called Mugambo) to the north of the park (US$25/20/15 in 1st/2nd/3rd class, about 10 hours from Kigoma). Email park headquarters in advance to arrange a pick-up from there to Bilenge (US$50 per boat, about two hours, plus US$50 per boat from Bilenge to the park *bandas*).

GOMBE STREAM NATIONAL PARK
☎ 028

In 1960 British researcher Jane Goodall arrived at Gombe Stream to begin a study of wild chimpanzees, which is still ongoing – making it the longest-ever study of a wild animal population. Gombe's approximately 150 chimps are well habituated and, with a few days' visit, sightings are highly likely.

Entry fees are US$100/20 per adult/child per 24 hours (children aged under seven are not permitted in the park). Guides cost US$20 per group per day.

There are basic rooms in the park **hostel** (per person US$20) and a restaurant is planned to open soon. Meanwhile, bring food and drink from Kigoma. Camping is not permitted. Make hostel bookings at the park office at the far end of the beach in Kibirizi village near Kigoma or directly through **park headquarters** (☎ 028-280 2586; gonapachimps@yahoo.com).

The only way to reach Gombe is by boat. Lake taxis depart from Kibirizi village between about noon and 2pm Monday to Saturday (Tsh2500, three to four hours), or charter a boat with local fishermen (about Tsh100,000 return).

SOUTHERN HIGHLANDS

MIKUMI NATIONAL PARK
☎ 023

Mikumi National Park is easily accessible from Dar es Salaam and a good destination if you don't have much time but want to see wildlife.

Entry fees are US$20/5 per adult/child, and there's a US$30 per person per day concession fee for all those staying at camps/lodges inside the park boundaries.

There are four **public campsites** (per adult/child US$30/5) and spotless **park bandas** (s/d US$50/60) just behind the park office complex with communal hot-water bathrooms, nets and a shared kitchen.

Vuma Hills Tented Camp (☎ 0754-237422; www.tanzaniasafaris.info; s/d incl full board plus wildlife drives US$335/510; ☒), 7km south of the main road, has 16 spacious tented cottages, and is a recommended family choice. The turn-off is diagonally opposite the park entry gate.

The best budget way to visit Mikumi is on one of the frequent special deals offered by Coastal Travels (p775) and other Dar es Salaam-based tour operators. Alternatively, take the bus to Mikumi town (about four hours from Dar es Salaam) and organise a safari through Genesis or Tan-Swiss hotels, both along the main highway.

IRINGA
☎ 026

With its bluff-top setting, jacaranda-lined streets and highland feel, Iringa makes an agreeable stop if you're travelling along the Dar es Salaam–Mbeya highway.

Iringa Info (☎ 026-270 1988; riversidecampsitetz@hotmail.com; Uhuru Ave; ☯ 9am-5pm Mon-Fri, 9am-3pm Sat) can help organise Ruaha safaris and car rentals. Next door is **Skynet** (Uhuru Ave; per hr Tsh1000; ☯ 8am-8pm Mon-Fri, 8.30am-3pm Sat & Sun), with internet access.

Campers, budget travellers and families should head to **Riverside Campsite** (☎ 0755-033024, 0787-111663; www.riversidecampsite-tanzania.com; campsites US$6, tented/stone bandas per person US$15/20), 13km northeast of Iringa along the main road on the banks of the Little Ruaha River. It also has a restaurant.

The small **Annex of Staff Inn** (Uhuru Ave; r Tsh10,000-25,000), five minutes' walk from the bus station, has no-frills rooms with hot water and a restaurant.

Central Lodge (Uhuru Ave; d Tsh15,000-20,000, tr Tsh30,000), behind Iringa Info, is quieter, with straightforward rooms with bathrooms.

Kisolanza – The Old Farm House (www.kisolanza.com; campsites with hot showers US$4, tw in stables US$22, tw chalets US$25, d/family cottages US$45/55, luxury cottage per person incl half board US$75, breakfast/dinner US$7/12) is a 1930s farm homestead fringed by stands of pine and rolling hill country about 50km southwest of Iringa and 1km off the highway. It comes highly recommended both for its accommodation (catering to all budgets) and for its cuisine.

For breakfast, yoghurt, milkshakes and reasonably priced main dishes, plus picnic sandwiches to take away, head to **Hasty Tasty Too** (☎ 026-270 2061; Uhuru Ave; snacks & meals from Tsh500; ☼ 7.30am-8pm Mon-Sat, 10am-2pm Sun).

Also well worth a stop is **Neema Crafts** (off Uhuru Ave at Kawawa Rd; ☼ 9am-5.30pm Mon-Fri, 9am-4.30pm Sat), a vocational training centre for Iringa's young deaf and disabled people, with crafts and light meals.

Getting There & Away

Scandinavian Express and Sumry head daily between Iringa and Dar es Salaam (Tsh17,000 to Tsh20,000, 7½ hours). Scandinavian's office is opposite the bus station in town; Sumry's is at the town bus station.

To Mbeya, Chaula Trans departs daily by 8am (Tsh13,000, four to five hours) or book a seat on Scandinavian from Dar es Salaam.

Arriving in Iringa, you'll likely be dropped at the main bus station at Ipogoro, about 3km southeast of town below the escarpment (about Tsh2500 in a taxi from town).

RUAHA NATIONAL PARK

Lovely, baobab-studded, elephant-packed Ruaha is Tanzania's largest national park, and the core of an extended ecosystem covering about 40,000 sq km. At its heart is the Great Ruaha River and a network of 'sand rivers'. Entry fees are US$20/5 per adult/child per day.

There are two **public campsites** (per adult/child US$30/5) with minimal facilities, plus basic **park bandas** (per person US$20).

Chogela Camp (campsites US$5), about 35km from the park gate near Tungamalenga village, has shaded camping grounds, a cooking-dining area and hot-water showers. Come with your own transport, food and drink, and bring your own tent or hire one through Riverside Campsite in Iringa.

Inside the park, the unpretentious and ideally situated **Ruaha River Lodge** (☎ 0754-237422; www.tanzaniasafaris.info; s/d incl full board & wildlife drives US$375/590) has spacious stone chalets, a restaurant and a raised bar, all directly on the river.

Iringa Info (p803) offers overnight safaris for US$200 per day. Organise fly-in safaris

from Dar es Salaam or Zanzibar with Coastal Travels (p775).

MBEYA
☎ 025

The bustling regional capital of Mbeya is the major town in southwestern Tanzania and an important transit point en route to/from Zambia and Malawi. There's not much to the town itself, but the surrounding area offers some hiking possibilities.

Information

Gazelle Safaris (☎ 025-250 2482, 0713-069179; www.gazellesafaris.com; Jacaranda Rd) Vehicle rental and excursions.

Nane Information Centre (per hr Tsh1000; ☼ 8am-6.30pm Mon-Sat) Internet access at the western side of Market Sq.

Stanbic Bank (Karume Ave) ATM: Visa, MasterCard, Maestro and Cirrus.

Sleeping & Eating

Karibuni Centre (☎ 025-250 3035/4178; mec@maf.or.tz; campsites Tsh4000, d/tr Tsh20,000/25,000) This clean, mission-run place has a small space to pitch a tent, straightforward rooms and a restaurant. It's 3km southwest of the town centre – take a taxi from the bus station (Tsh3000).

New Millennium Inn (☎ 025-250 0599; Mbalizi Rd; s Tsh14,000-20,000, without bathroom Tsh12,000) Directly opposite the bus station, it's noisy but convenient if you have an early bus. If it's full, there are several similarly priced places next door.

Utengule Country Hotel (☎ 025-256 0100; www.riftvalley-zanzibar.com; campsites US$10; r US$55-140; ⚑) Set on a working coffee plantation in the hills 20km west of Mbeya, it has camping and a mix of very pleasant rooms. Follow the Tunduma road 12km to Mbalizi and the signposted right-hand turn-off, from where it's 8.5km further.

Getting There & Away

Scandinavian Express departs daily to Dar es Salaam at 7am (Tsh30,000, 12 hours) from its office on Jacaranda St. Sumry departs daily at 6.30am from the main bus station.

Book train tickets at least several days in advance at the **Tazara station** (Tunduma Rd; ☼ 8am-noon & 2-5pm Mon-Fri, 10am-1pm Sat), 4km west of town. See Tazara (p815) for schedules and fares between Mbeya and Dar es Salaam, and connections with Zambia.

TUKUYU

☎ 025

This small town is set amid the hills and orchards north of Lake Nyasa, and makes a fine base for hiking en route to/from Malawi. Arrange guides through **Rungwe Tea & Tours** (www.rungweteatours.com), next to the post office.

Camp at **Bongo Camping** (☎ 0784-823610; www.bongocamping.com; campsites with your/its tent Tsh4000/6000), just off the main road just north of Tukuyu, or stay in more comfort at **Landmark Hotel** (☎ 025-255 2400; landmahotel@yahoo.co.uk; s/d/tw from Tsh20,000/25,000/30,000) at Tukuyu's main junction.

Minibuses run several times daily between Tukuyu and both Mbeya (Tsh1500, one to 1½ hours) and Kyela (Tsh1500, one hour).

SOUTHEASTERN TANZANIA

SELOUS GAME RESERVE

With an area of approximately 45,000 sq km, the Selous is one of Africa's largest wildlife reserves, although only the northernmost section is open for tourism. Entry fees are US$50/30 per adult/child, plus US$30 per vehicle per day. There's also a US$15 per person per day conservation fee payable by all those staying at camps inside the reserve boundaries.

There are two **public campsites** (per adult/child US$20/5).

Selous Mbega Camp (☎ 022-265 0250; www.selous-mbega-camp.com; campsites US$10, s/d incl full board US$135/190, excursions extra) is a laid-back budget choice with a small camping ground for which you'll need to be self-sufficient with food. It has a 'backpackers' special (s/d US$85/120) for those arriving by public bus at Mloka.

Sable Mountain Lodge (☎ 022-211 0507; www.selouslodge.com; s/d incl full board from US$200/290, all-inclusive from US$330/550; ☒) is friendly, relaxed and ideally positioned for independent travellers arriving at Selous with the Tazara train line (get off at Kisaki station, and arrange a pick-up in advance).

The long-standing **Rufiji River Camp** (☎ 0754-237422; www.rufijirivercamp.com; s/d incl full board & wildlife drives US$375/590; ☒) has a fine location on a wide bend in the Rufiji River

that is frequented by hippos. All tents have river views.

Akida bus goes daily between Dar es Salaam's Temeke bus stand (Sudan Market area) and Mloka village, about 10km east of Mtemere Gate (Tsh10,000, seven to nine hours) at 5am. From there you can arrange an advance pick-up with park lodges.

MTWARA & MIKINDANI

☎ 023

The sprawling town of Mtwara, a laid-back, likable place, is a good staging point on the overland journey to Mozambique. About 11km away is the tiny Swahili town of Mikindani, with a long history, coconut groves and a picturesque bay.

For internet access there's **Makonde Net** (per hr Tsh1000; ☒ 8.30am-6pm Mon-Sat, 9am-2pm Sun) in Mtwara centre. **NBC Bank** (Uhuru Rd, Mtwara) changes cash and travellers cheques, and has an ATM.

Mtwara Lutheran Centre (☎ 023-233 3294; Mikindani Rd, Mtwara; dm/s/d Tsh3000/12,000/15,000), at the southern edge of town, has no-frills rooms with nets. If arriving by bus, ask the driver to drop you at the roundabout.

Ten Degrees South Lodge (☎ 0784-855833; www.eco2tz.com; Mikindani; r with/without bathroom US$80/20), overlooking Mikindani Bay, has pleasant rooms, a restaurant and a small dive centre.

There are daily flights between Mtwara and Dar es Salaam (Tsh150,000 one way) on **Air Tanzania** (☎ 023-233 3147, 023-233 3147; Bodi ya Korosho Bldg, Tanu Rd; ☒ closed during flight arrivals & departures) and **Precision Air** (☎ 023-233 4116; Tanu Rd), next to CRDB bank.

Daily buses go to/from Dar es Salaam from about 6am (Tsh22,000, 10 to 12 hours). To Mozambique (arrange your visa in advance as they are not available at the border), there are several pick-ups each morning to the Tanzanian immigration post at Kilambo (Tsh3500), and then a dugout canoe crossing of the Rovuma River.

TANZANIA DIRECTORY

ACCOMMODATION

Carrying a tent can save you some money in and around the northern parks, although camping in the parks themselves will cost at least $30 per person per night. Camping isn't permitted on Zanzibar.

All of the national parks have 'public' or 'ordinary' campsites with basic facilities – generally pit toilets and sometimes a water source. Most parks also have simple huts or *bandas* and several have basic rest houses.

In Tanzanian Swahili, *hotel* (or *hoteli*) refers to food and drink, rather than accommodation. The better term if you're looking for somewhere to sleep is *nyumba ya kulala wageni* – or, less formally, *pa kulala*. Rooms (with private bathroom) are widely referred to as 'self-contained' or 'self-container' rooms.

Many lodges and luxury camps in or near national parks quote all-inclusive prices, which generally means accommodation plus excursions such as wildlife drives, short guided walks or boat safaris, and sometimes also park entry fees and airport transfers.

ACTIVITIES

The Zanzibar Archipelago offers fine diving and snorkelling, and an array of operators offering courses and certification.

The main hiking destinations are Mt Kilimanjaro (p789) and Mt Meru in Arusha National Park (p796). All hiking requires local guides and (usually) porters. Be aware of the dangers of Acute Mountain Sickness (AMS), especially on Kilimanjaro. In extreme cases it can be fatal.

Wildlife-watching is one of the country's top attractions and Tanzania delivers in spades, from the world-famous wildlife spectacles of Serengeti (p798) and Ngorongoro Crater (p798) to safaris in Selous Game Reserve (p805) and chimpanzee-tracking in Mahale Mountains (p802) and Gombe Stream (p803) National Parks.

BUSINESS HOURS

See p1136 for general Africa-wide business hours of restaurants, bars and clubs.

Currency exchange Many bureaux de change are open until 5pm Monday to Friday, and until noon on Saturday.

Shops and offices These often close for one to two hours between noon and 2pm, and on Friday afternoons for mosque services (especially in coastal areas).

CHILDREN

Parks and reserves are free for children under five years of age, and entry and camping fees are discounted for those under 16 years of age. Some wildlife lodges, especially those in the national parks, are restricted for children,

---

> ### PRACTICALITIES
>
> - Tanzania uses the metric system for weights and measures.
> - Electricity is 220-250V AC, 50Hz (use British-style three-square-pin or two-round-pin plug adaptors).
> - English-language newspapers include *Guardian* and *Daily News* (dailies), and *Business Times, Financial Times* and *East African* (weeklies).
> - The government-aligned Radio Tanzania broadcasts in English and Swahili.

so enquire when booking. Always specifically ask for children's discounts if booking a safari through a tour operator. Mosquito nets are best brought from home.

CUSTOMS

Exporting seashells, coral, ivory and turtle shell is illegal. You can export up to Tsh2000 without declaration. There's no limit on importation of foreign currency, but amounts over US$10,000 must be declared.

DANGERS & ANNOYANCES

Tanzania is in general a safe, hassle-free country, but you do need to take the usual precautions. Avoid isolated areas, especially isolated stretches of beach, and in cities and tourist areas take a taxi at night. When using public transport, don't accept drinks or food from someone you don't know, and be sceptical of anyone who comes up to you on the street asking you whether you remember them from the airport, your hotel or wherever.

In tourist areas – especially Arusha, Moshi and Zanzibar – touts and flycatchers can be extremely persistent, especially around bus stations and budget tourist hotels. Be very wary of anyone who approaches you on the street, at the bus station or in your hotel offering safari deals, and never pay any money for a safari or trek in advance until you've thoroughly checked out the company.

EMBASSIES & CONSULATES

All the following are in Dar es Salaam, and are open from 8.30am till at least noon. Visa applications should be made in the morning. Australians should contact the Canadian high commission.

Burundi (☎ 022-212 7008; Lugalo St, Upanga; 🕑 8am-3.30pm) Three-month single-entry visas cost US$50 plus two photos, and are issued in 24 hours. The consulate in Kigoma (p802) issues one-month single entry visas for US$40 plus two photos within 24 hours.

Canada (☎ 022-216 3300; www.dfait-maeci.gc.ca/tanzania; 38 Mirambo St)

Democratic Republic of Congo (435 Maliki Rd, Upanga; 🕑 10am-1pm & 2pm-3.30pm) Three-month single-entry visas cost US$150 plus two photos and a letter of invitation from someone in the DRC. Allow plenty of time for issuing. The consulate in Kigoma (p802) is much easier, issuing single-entry visas for US$50 (US$30 for Tanzania residents) plus two photos within two days or less.

Kenya (☎ 022-266 8285; www.kenyahighcomtz.org; 127 Mafinga St, Kinondoni)

Malawi (☎ 022-213 6951; 1st fl, Zambia House, cnr Ohio St & Sokoine Dr; 🕑 8am-3pm) Many nationalities, including USA, UK and various European countries, do not require visas.

Mozambique (☎ 022-211 6502; 25 Garden Ave; 🕑 8.30am-3pm) One-month single-entry visas cost US$40 (US$55 for express service) plus two photos and are issued within three days.

Rwanda (☎ 022-211 5889, 022-213 0119; 32 Ali Hassan Mwinyi Rd, Upanga; 🕑 8am-noon & 2-4pm) Three-month single-entry visas cost US$60 plus two photos, and are issued within 48 hours. Citizens of the USA, Germany, South Africa, Canada and various other countries do not require visas.

Uganda (☎ 022-266 7009; 25 Msasani Rd; 🕑 8.30am-3pm) Three-month single-entry visas cost US$30 plus two photos and are issued the same day.

UK (☎ 022-211 0101; www.britishhighcommission.gov.uk/tanzania; Umoja House, cnr Mirambo St & Garden Ave)

USA (☎ 022-266 8001; http://usembassy.state.gov/tanzania; Old Bagamoyo & Kawawa Rds, Msasani)

Zambia (☎ 022-212 5529; Ground fl, Zambia House, cnr Ohio St & Sokoine Dr; 🕑 9am-2pm Mon, Wed & Fri for visa applications, 2-3.30pm Tue, Thu & Mon for pick-up) One-month single-entry visas cost from Tsh25,000 to Tsh125,000 depending on nationality, plus two photos, and are issued the next day.

EMERGENCIES

There are no nationwide emergency numbers. If you are in trouble, try seeking help from your hotel or embassy. Medical evacuation coverage should be arranged in advance of your travels with **AAR** (www.aarhealth.com) or with the **Flying Doctors Society of Africa** (www.amref.org/flying-doctors). For Dar es Salaam–based emergency medical treatment, see p775.

FESTIVALS & EVENTS

Sauti za Busara (www.busaramusic.org) A Swahili music and dance festival held in February on Zanzibar.

Kilimanjaro Marathon (www.kilimanjaromarathon.com) In the foothills around Moshi; held in February or March.

Festival of the Dhow Countries (www.ziff.or.tz) Two weeks of dance, music, film and literature in early July, with the Zanzibar International Film Festival as its centrepiece.

Mwaka Kogwa A four-day festival held in late July to mark Nairuzim (the Shirazi New Year).

HEALTH

Tanzania (including Zanzibar) no longer requires you to carry a certificate of yellow-fever vaccination unless you're arriving from an infected area (which includes Kenya, although arrivals aren't always checked). However, it is a requirement in some neighbouring countries, including Rwanda, and is still sometimes requested – and thus is a good idea to carry. For more, see p1172.

HOLIDAYS

New Year's Day 1 January
Zanzibar Revolution Day 12 January
Easter (Good Friday, Holy Saturday and Easter Monday) March/April
Union Day 26 April
Labour Day 1 May
Saba Saba (Peasants' Day) 7 July
Nane Nane (Farmers' Day) 8 August
Nyerere Day 14 October
Independence Day 9 December
Christmas Day 25 December
Boxing Day 26 December

Major Islamic holidays are also celebrated as public holidays; see p1140.

INTERNET RESOURCES

Eco-Tanzania (www.ecotz.com) Tanzania's eco-portal; check out the link to Carbon Tanzania.

Tanzania National Parks (www.tanzaniaparks.com) Tanapa's official website, with general information and photos of the parks.

Tanzania Natural Resources Forum (www.tnrf.org) An overview of natural resource management, community-based tourism and more.

Tanzania On-line (www.tzonline.org) An intro to all things official, with links to the government website (www.tanzania.go.tz) and more.

Tanzania Page (www.sas.upenn.edu/African_Studies/Country_Specific/Tanzania.html) Heaps of links.

Tanzania Tourist Board (www.tanzaniatouristboard.com) The TTB's official site.

MAPS

Good country maps include those published by Nelles (1:1,500,000) and Harms-ic, both available in Tanzania. Harms-ic also publishes maps for Lake Manyara National Park, the Ngorongoro Conservation Area and Zanzibar. Colourful hand-drawn maps, marketed under the name **MaCo** (www.gtmaps.com) and covering Zanzibar, Arusha and many northern Tanzania parks, are widely available in major centres.

MONEY

Tanzania's currency is the Tanzanian shilling (Tsh). There are bills of Tsh10,000, Tsh5000, Tsh1000 and Tsh500, and coins of Tsh200, Tsh100, Tsh50, Tsh20, Tsh10, Tsh5 and Tsh1.

The easiest places to reconvert currency are at the airports in Dar es Salaam and Kilimanjaro, but save your exchange receipts in case they are checked. The most useful bank for changing money is National Bank of Commerce (NBC), which has branches throughout the country. (Note that US$50 and US$100 bills get better rates of exchange than smaller denominations.) Old-style US bills (ie pre-2004) are not accepted anywhere.

ATMs are widespread in major towns, with Standard Chartered, Barclay's, NBC, Stanbic, CRDB and TanPay/SpeedCash the major operators. All allow you to withdraw shillings to a maximum of Tsh300,000 to Tsh400,000 per transaction. Visa is by far the most useful card for ATM cash withdrawals (and often the only one possible in many towns – NBC and CRDB machines take only Visa). Barclays and Stanbic ATMs also accept MasterCard and cards tied in with the Cirrus/Maestro network, and there are a few machines that only work with MasterCard.

The best currency to bring is US dollars in a mixture of large and small denominations, plus a Visa card for withdrawing money from ATMs and some travellers cheques as an emergency standby (although these are changeable in major cities only). Credit cards are frequently not accepted, including by many upmarket hotels. If they are accepted, it's often only with a minimum 5% commission.

On hikes and safaris in Tanzania, it's common practice to tip drivers, guides, porters and other staff if the service has been good (see Guides & Porters, p791).

> **SWAHILI TIME**
>
> The Swahili clock begins at sunrise (6am) rather than midnight, so 7am becomes 1 o'clock, 8am becomes 2 o'clock and so on. Many Swahili speakers translate their time directly when speaking English, so always double-check when you're ienquiring about boat or train schedules etc.

TELEPHONE

Tanzania's country code is ☎ 255. To make an international call, first dial ☎ 000. Area codes (given with each number) must be used whenever you dial long distance or from a mobile phone.

There are few public phones, and Tanzania Telecom (TTCL) no longer provides call-and-pay service. Instead it sells dialling cards for Tsh1000, which you can then top up at any TTCL office and use at any landline (TTCL) phone for domestic and international calls. Budget on about US$2 per minute for international calls. Domestic long-distance rates average about Tsh1000 for the first three minutes. Calls to mobile phones cost about Tsh500 per minute.

The mobile network covers major towns throughout the country, plus most of the north and northeast. In the south, west and centre, coverage is more spotty. Major companies include Celtel, Vodacom, Tigo and Zantel. All sell prepaid starter packages for about US$2, and top-up cards are on sale at shops throughout the country. Watch for frequent specials, such as SIM card giveaways. Dialling internationally from the mobile network is generally cheaper than using TTCL.

TOURIST INFORMATION

The **Tanzania Tourist Board** (TTB; www.tanzaniatouristboard.com) has offices in Dar es Salaam (p775) and Arusha (p794). In the UK, the Tanzania Tourist Board is represented by the **Tanzania Trade Centre** (www.tanzatrade.co.uk).

VISAS

Almost everyone needs a visa, which costs between US$20 and US$50, depending on nationality, for a single-entry visa valid for up to three months. It's best to get the visa in advance (and necessary if you want a multiple entry visa), although at the time research single-entry visas were being readily issued at Dar es Salaam and Kilimanjaro airports, and at most land border crossings (all nationalities US$50, US dollars cash only, single entry only).

One month is the normal visa validity, and three months the maximum. For extensions within the three-month limit, there are immigration offices in all major towns; the process is free and straightforward. Extensions after three months are difficult – you'll usually need to leave the country and apply for a new visa.

Note that under the East Africa partnership system, single-entry visitors to Tanzania can enter Kenya or Uganda without invalidating their Tanzania visa; ie you won't need to pay for another visa to re-enter Tanzania from those countries.

See the boxed text, p737, for information about the forthcoming East African single tourist visa.

TRANSPORT IN TANZANIA

GETTING THERE & AWAY
Visas are available at all major points of entry, and must be paid for in US dollars cash. You'll need proof of yellow-fever vaccination only if you're coming from a yellow-fever infected area (including Kenya), though it often isn't checked. See p1172.

Air
Tanzania's air hub is **Julius Nyerere International Airport** (DAR; ☎ 022-284 2461/2402; www.tanzaniairports.com) in Dar es Salaam. **Kilimanjaro International Airport** (JRO; ☎ 027-255 4252/4707; www.kilimanjaroairport.co.tz) is the best option if you'll be concentrating on Arusha and the northern safari circuit. There are also international flights to/from **Zanzibar International Airport** (ZNZ). **Mwanza Airport** (MWZ) and **Mtwara Airport** (MYW) handle some regional flights.

Air Tanzania (TC; 022-211 8411, 022-284 4239; www.airtanzania.com; Ohio St, Dar es Salaam) is the national airline, with a limited but generally reliable network. Regional destinations include Moroni (Comoros), Entebbe (Uganda) and Johannesburg (South Africa).

Other regional and international carriers include the following (with useful flights between Tanzania and elsewhere in East

Africa highlighted). All airlines service Dar es Salaam, except as noted.

Air India (AI; ☎ 022-215 2642; cnr Ali Hassan Mwinyi & Bibi Titi Mohamed Rds, Dar es Salaam)

Air Kenya (REG; ☎ 027-250 2541; www.airkenya.com) Nairobi to Kilimanjaro.

Air Uganda (U7; www.air-uganda.com) Entebbe to Kilimanjaro, Dar es Salaam and Zanzibar; bookings at Air Tanzania offices or through travel agents.

British Airways (BA; ☎ 022-211 3820; www.britishairways.com; Mövenpick Royal Palm Hotel, Ohio St, Dar es Salaam)

Emirates Airlines (EK; ☎ 022-211 6100; www.emirates.com; Haidery Plaza, cnr Kisutu & India Sts, Dar es Salaam)

Ethiopian Airlines (ET; ☎ 022-211 7063; www.ethiopianairlines.com; Ohio St, Dar es Salaam) Also serves Kilimanjaro and Zanzibar international airports.

Kenya Airways (KQ; ☎ 022-211 9376/7; www.kenya-airways.com; Upanga Rd, Dar es Salaam) Nairobi and Mombasa to Dar es Salaam and Zanzibar in partnership with Precision Air.

KLM (KL; ☎ 022-213 9790/1; www.klm.com; Upanga Rd, Dar es Salaam) Also serves Kilimanjaro International Airport.

Linhas Aéreas de Moçambique (TM; ☎ 022-213 4600; www.lam.co.mz; 1st fl, JM Mall, Samora Ave, Dar es Salaam) At Fast-Track Travel (www.fasttracktanzania.com).

Precision Air (PW; ☎ 022-216 8000; www.precisionairtz.com; cnr Samora Ave & Pamba Rd, Dar es Salaam) In partnership with Kenya Airways; connections between Nairobi, Mombasa, Entebbe and various cities in Tanzania.

Rwandair Express (WB; ☎ 0732-978558; www.rwandair.com) Kigali to Kilimanjaro International Airport.

South African Airways (SA; ☎ 022-211 7044; www.flysaa.com; Raha Towers, cnr Bibi Titi Mohamed & Ali Hassan Mwinyi Rds, Dar es Salaam)

Swiss International Airlines (LX; ☎ 022-211 8870; www.swiss.com; Luther House, Sokoine Dr, Dar es Salaam)

Zambian Airways (Q3; ☎ 022-212 8885/6; www.zambianairways.com; Ground fl, Haidery Plaza, cnr Kisutu & India Sts, Dar es Salaam)

Land
Buses cross the borders between Tanzania and Kenya, Malawi, Uganda and Zambia. Apart from sometimes lengthy waits at the border

for passport checks, there are usually no hassles. At the border you'll need to disembark on each side to take care of visa formalities, then reboard your bus and continue on. Visa fees are not included in bus-ticket prices for transborder routes. Most main routes go direct, but sometimes you'll need to walk across the border and change vehicles on the other side.

If you're arriving by car or motorcycle, you'll need the vehicle's registration papers and your licence (p814), plus pay for a temporary import permit at the border (Tsh20,000 for one month), third-party insurance (Tsh50,000 for one year) and a one-time fuel levy (Tsh5000). You'll also need a *carnet de passage en douane*; see Carnets, p1158.

Most hire companies don't permit their vehicles to cross international borders.

BURUNDI
There are crossings at Kobero Bridge, between Ngara and Muyinga (Burundi); at Manyovu, north of Kigoma; and at Kagunga (south of Nyanza-Lac).

Kobero Bridge
This trip is done in stages via Nyakanazi and Lusahunga (from where there's regular transport north towards Lake Victoria and southeast via Kahama towards Nzega and Shinyanga).

Manyovu
Dalla-dallas leave Kigoma from behind Bero petrol station (about Tsh5000, three hours). Once through the Tanzanian side of the border, you can sometimes find cars going to Bujumbura (about Tsh5000, three to four hours). Otherwise, take one of the many waiting vehicles across the border and on to Makamba (about 70km from Manyovu) and the Burundian immigration post, and from there get another vehicle on to Bujumbura.

For the route via Kagunga and Nyanza-Lac, see p812.

KENYA
Border Crossings
The main route to/from Kenya is the sealed road connecting Arusha and Nairobi via the heavily travelled Namanga border post (open 24 hours). Other border crossings include Horohoro, north of Tanga (and called Lunga Lunga on the Kenyan side), and at Holili (Taveta on the Kenyan side), east of Moshi.

Only East African residents and citizens can cross between the northern Serengeti and Kenya's Masai Mara Game Reserve; there is no public transport.

Mombasa
Scandinavian Express and other lines between Tanga and Mombasa depart daily in the morning in each direction (Tsh8000, four to five hours). There's nowhere official to change money at the border. Touts here charge extortionate rates, and it's difficult to get rid of Kenyan shillings once in Tanga, so plan accordingly.

Nairobi
Akamba and Scandinavian Express go daily between Dar es Salaam and Nairobi via Arusha (Tsh40,000, 14 hours from Dar; Tsh18,000 from Arusha). Scandinavian continues on to Kampala. Akamba also has a daily bus between Mwanza and Nairobi (Tsh28,000, 15 hours).

Between Arusha and Nairobi, there are several buses daily (Tsh15,000, six hours) in each direction departing between 6.30am and 8am. Departures in Arusha are from the bus station; in Nairobi most leave from Accra Rd. More popular and more comfortable are the daily shuttle buses, departing daily at 8am and 2pm in each direction (five hours). Main companies:

Impala Arusha (☎ 027-250 7197/8448/8451; Impala Hotel, cnr Moshi & Old Moshi Rds, Arusha); Nairobi (☎ 020-273 0953; Silver Springs Hotel, Nairobi)

Riverside Arusha (☎ 027-250 2639/3916; riverside _shuttle@hotmail.com; booking office Sokoine Rd, departure point Bella Luna, Moshi Rd); Nairobi (☎ 020-229618, 020-241032; Pan African Insurance House, 3rd fl, Room 1, Kenyatta Ave, departure point Parkside Hotel, Monrovia St, Nairobi)

Both charge about US$25 one way between Nairobi and Arusha, and with a little prodding it's easy enough to get the residents' price (Tsh20,000). In Arusha departure and drop-off points are at Bella Luna. In Nairobi, the departure point is Parkside Hotel – from where several other Arusha-bound shuttles also depart – and from Jomo Kenyatta International Airport, if you've made an advance booking (they'll meet your flight). Drop-offs are at centrally located hotels and at Jomo Kenyatta International Airport. Confirm the drop-off point when booking, and insist on being dropped off as agreed.

MALAWI

The only crossing is at **Songwe River bridge** (⏰ 7am-7pm Tanzanian time, 6am-6pm Malawi time), southeast of Mbeya.

Buses go several times weekly between Dar es Salaam and Lilongwe (27 hours), though they are overcrowded (even if you have a ticket, it's often not possible to board midroute in Mbeya), often delayed and not recommended. It's better to travel from Dar es Salaam to Mbeya via bus or train, and then continue in stages from there: take one of the daily 'Coastals' (30-seater buses) going from Mbeya to Kyela (most of these detour to Songwe). It's about a seven-minute walk from the Songwe transport stand to the actual border. Once across, and through the approximately 500m of no-man's-land, catch an onward minibus to Karonga.

Coming from Malawi, the best option is to take a minibus from the border to Mbeya and then get an express bus from there towards Dar es Salaam. This entails overnighting in Mbeya, as buses to Dar es Salaam depart Mbeya between 6am and 7am.

MOZAMBIQUE

The main crossing is at Kilambo (south of Mtwara), with other crossings further west at Mtambaswala and south of Songea, the latter crossing to Segundo Congresso (Matchedje) in Mozambique. Travelling by boat, there are immigration officials at Msimbati (Tanzania) and at Palma and Moçimboa da Praia (Mozambique).

Pick-ups depart Mtwara daily between 6am and 9am to the Kilambo border post (about Tsh3000, one hour) and on to the Ruvuma, which is crossed adventurously or dangerously – depending on your perspective and water levels – via dugout canoe. There is no longer a ferry. Once across, there are two pick-ups daily to the Mozambique border post (4km further) and on to Moçimboa da Praia (US$12, four hours), with the last one departing by about noon.

Further west, the Unity Bridge (at Negomane) should be finished within the lifetime of this book, and possibly also some of the road work planned to link this with Mtwara and Mueda (Mozambique).

Still further west, there's a vehicle bridge and passport/customs posts at Segundo Congresso (Matchedje), with road links (and daily public transport) north to Songea and

south to Lichinga. Mozambique visas are not issued anywhere along the Tanzania border, so arrange one in advance.

RWANDA

The main crossing is at Rusumu Falls, southwest of Bukoba.

Daily minibuses go from Kigali to Rusumu (Rwanda), where you'll need to walk across the Kagera river bridge. Once across, there are vehicles to Benako (marked as Kasulo on some maps), about 20km southeast. From Benako, daily buses go to Mwanza, departing by about 7am (which means you'll need to overnight in Benako). Alternatively, go in stages via Kahama, Nzega and Shinyanga along the tarmac road (eight hours between Benako and Kahama). There are also daily connections from Benako to Nyakanazi junction, where you can try squeezing into a bus heading towards Kigoma (two hours from Benako to Nyakanazi, and about seven hours from there to Kigoma).

UGANDA

The main post is at Mutukula, northwest of Bukoba (although you actually get stamped in and out of Tanzania at Kyaka, about 30km south of the Mutukula border).

From Mwanza, Akamba buses go Wednesday, Friday and Sunday to/from Kampala (Tsh31,000, 19 hours), departing from Mwanza at 2pm. Another option is taking the ferry across Lake Victoria to Bukoba (see p813). Once in Bukoba, Dolphin (also called Gateway) and Ariazi Tours lines run daily between Bukoba and Kampala (Tsh13,000, six hours).

ZAMBIA

The main border crossing is at **Tunduma** (⏰ 7.30am-6pm Tanzania time, 6.30am-5pm Zambia time), southwest of Mbeya. There's also a crossing at Kasesha, between Sumbawanga and Mbala (Zambia).

At the time of research, there was no direct bus service to Lusaka from either Dar es Salaam or Mbeya, although there's talk of it resuming. (If this happens, plan on about Tsh75,000 and 30 hours from Dar es Salaam.) Meanwhile, minibuses ply the route between Mbeya and Tunduma (Tsh3000, two hours), where you walk across the border for Zambian transport to Lusaka (about US$20,

18 hours). Be prepared for more than the normal share of touts and chaos.

For the Kasesha crossing, there are pick-ups from Sumbawanga to the border, where you'll need to change to Zambian transport.

The Tanzania–Zambia (Tazara) train line links Dar es Salaam with Kapiri Mposhi in Zambia (Tsh55,000/40,000/33,000 in 1st/2nd/economy class, about 40 hours) twice weekly via Mbeya and Tunduma. From Kapiri Mposhi to Lusaka, you'll need to continue by bus.

Sea & Lake

There's a US$5 port tax for all boats and ferries from Tanzanian ports.

BURUNDI

Regular passenger-ferry services between Kigoma and Bujumbura were suspended at the time of research. However, it's possible to take a lake taxi from Kibirizi (just north of Kigoma) or from Gombe Stream National Park to Kagunga (the Tanzanian border post). Once there, look for passage in one of the frequent small cargo boats going on to Nyanza-Lac, from where there is regular transport on to Bujumbura.

DEMOCRATIC REPUBLIC OF CONGO

Cargo boats go two to three times weekly from Kigoma's Ami port, departing Kigoma about 5pm and reaching Kalemie (DRC) before dawn (US$20 in deck class only, seven hours). Check with the Congolese embassy in Kigoma (p802) about sailing days and times. Bring food and drink with you, and something to spread on the deck for sleeping.

KENYA

Dhows sail sporadically between Pemba, Tanga and Shimoni (Kenya), but the journey can be long, rough and risky and is not recommended.

There's no passenger ferry service on Lake Victoria between Tanzania and Kenya.

MALAWI

The MV *Songea* sails between Mbamba Bay and Nkhata Bay (Malawi), in theory departing Mbamba Bay on Friday morning and Nkhata Bay on Friday evening (US$10/4 in 1st/economy class, four to five hours). The schedule is highly variable and sometimes cancelled.

MOZAMBIQUE

The official route between southwestern Tanzania and Mozambique is via Malawi on the MV *Songea* between Mbamba Bay and Nkhata Bay, and then from Nkhata Bay on to Likoma island (Malawi) and Metangula (Mozambique) on the **MV Ilala** (☎ in Malawi 01-587311; ilala@malawi.net) Note that the *Ilala* no longer stops at Cóbuè (Mozambique).

There's an immigration officer at Mbamba Bay, Mozambique immigration posts in Metangula (and in Cóbuè, should you want to take a local boat there from Likoma island), and immigration officers on Likoma Island and in Nkhata Bay, for Malawi. You can get a Mozambique visa at Cóbuè, but not at Metangula.

UGANDA

There's no passenger-ferry service, but it's possible – although officially not permitted – to arrange passage between Mwanza's South Port and Kampala's Port Bell on cargo ships (about 17 hours). Check in at the immigration office at South Port to have your passport stamped. Expect to pay about US$20, plus Tsh5000 port tax, and bring some water and food along for the journey. Crew members are sometimes willing to rent out their cabins for a negotiable extra fee.

ZAMBIA

The venerable MV *Liemba*, which has been plying the waters of Lake Tanganyika for the better part of a century, connects Kigoma (departing at 4pm on Wednesday) with Mpulungu in Zambia weekly (US$60/45/40 in 1st/2nd/economy class, US dollars cash only, at least 40 hours). Stops include Lagosa (for Mahale Mountains National Park) and Kipili. Food is available on board, but it's best to bring some supplements and drinking water. Book early if you want a cabin. There's a dock at Kigoma, but at many smaller stops you'll need to disembark in the middle of the lake, exiting from a door in the side of the *Liemba* into small boats that take you to shore.

Tours

For tour operators covering Tanzania and elsewhere in East Africa, see p1162. For safari and trekking operators, see p794, p790 and p775.

DEPARTURE TAX

Airport departure tax for domestic flights is Tsh5000. It's sometimes included in the ticket price on the mainland. On Zanzibar, it's payable separately at the airport.

GETTING AROUND
Air

The national airline, **Air Tanzania** (☎ in Dar es Salaam 022-211 8411, 022-284 4293; www.airtanzania.com) has flights connecting Dar es Salaam with Mwanza, Mtwara and Kilimanjaro. Other airlines flying domestically:

Air Excel (☎ 027-254 8429, 027-250 1597; reservation@ airexcelonline.com) Arusha, Serengeti National Park, Lake Manyara, Dar es Salaam and Zanzibar.

Coastal Aviation (☎ 022-284 3293, 022-211 7959; www.coastal.cc; Upanga Rd, Dar es Salaam) Flights to many parks and major towns, including Arusha, Dar es Salaam, Dodoma, Lake Manyara National Park, Mwanza, Pemba, Ruaha National Park, Selous Game Reserve, Serengeti National Park, Tanga, Tarangire National Park and Zanzibar.

Precision Air (☎ 022-216 8000; www.precisionairtz. com) Services to most major destinations, including Dar es Salaam, Kigoma, Kilimanjaro, Mtwara, Mwanza and Zanzibar.

Regional Air Services (☎ 027-250 4477/2541; www. regionaltanzania.com) Arusha, Dar es Salaam, Kilimanjaro, Lake Manyara National Park, Serengeti National Park and Zanzibar.

Safari Airlink (☎ 0773-723274; www.safariaviation. info) Dar es Salaam, Katavi National Park, Mahale Mountains National Park, Ruaha National Park and Zanzibar.

ZanAir (☎ 024-223 3670/8; www.zanair.com) Arusha, Dar es Salaam, Lake Manyara National Park, Pemba, Selous Game Reserve, Serengeti National Park, Tarangire National Park, Zanzibar and other destinations.

Zantas Air (☎ 022-213 0553; www.mbalimbali.com) Twice-weekly scheduled charter between Arusha, Katavi and Mahale Mountains National Parks.

Boat

Ferries operate on Lake Victoria, Lake Tanganyika and Lake Nyasa (Malawi), and between Dar es Salaam, Zanzibar and Pemba. There's a US$5 port tax per trip on all routes. For details of ferries between Dar es Salaam, Zanzibar and Pemba, see p777 and p786.

LAKE NYASA

In theory, the MV *Songea* departs Itungi port at about noon on Thursday and makes its way down the coast via Lupingu, Manda, Lundu, Mango and Liuli (but not Matema) to Mbamba Bay (Tsh12,500/7500 for 1st/ economy class, 18 to 24 hours) and Nkhata Bay (Malawi) before returning.

The smaller MV *Iringa* services lakeside villages between Itungi and Manda, departing Itungi by about noon on Monday and stopping at Matema and several other ports before turning back again on Tuesday. Schedules for both boats are highly unreliable and change frequently.

LAKE TANGANYIKA

For the MV *Liemba* schedule between Kigoma and Mpulungu (Zambia), see opposite. See opposite for boat travel between Kigoma and Burundi.

LAKE VICTORIA

The MV *Victoria* departs Mwanza for Bukoba at 9pm on Tuesday, Thursday and Sunday (Tsh30,500/20,500/17,000/15,500 for 1st class/ 2nd-class sleeping/2nd-class sitting/3rd class, plus port tax, nine hours). Food is available on board.

Bus

Major long-distance routes are serviced by express and ordinary buses. Express buses make fewer stops, are less crowded than ordinary buses and depart on schedule. Some have air-con and toilets, and the nicest ones are called 'luxury' buses. On secondary routes, the only option is ordinary buses, which are often packed to overflowing, make many stops and run to a less rigorous schedule.

For popular routes, book your seat in advance, although you can sometimes get a place by arriving at the bus station an hour prior to departure. Scandinavian Express and Royal Coach buses fill up quickly on all routes, and should be booked at least one day in advance. Each bus line has its own booking office, usually at or near the bus station.

Prices are basically fixed, although overcharging isn't unheard of. Most bus stations are chaotic, and at the ones in Arusha and other tourist areas you'll be incessantly hounded by touts. Buy your tickets at the office, and not from the touts, and don't believe anyone who tries to tell you there's a luggage fee.

Major lines along the Dar–Arusha route include Dar Express, Royal Coach and Scandinavian Express. Scandinavian Express is also considered one of the better lines for destinations between Dar and Mbeya, although its fleet is ageing and service is often very mediocre these days. You'll generally need to pay for its luxury buses to enjoy a reasonably comfortable ride.

MINIBUS & SHARED TAXI

For shorter trips away from the main routes, the choice is often between 30-seater buses ('Coasters' or *thelathini*) and *dalla-dallas*. Both options come complete with chickens on the roof, bags of produce wedged under the seats and no leg room. Shared taxis are relatively rare, except in northern Tanzania near Arusha. Like ordinary buses, minibuses and shared taxis leave when full; they're probably the least safe of the various transport options.

Car & Motorcycle

If you are familiar with driving in East Africa and have a group to split the costs, touring mainland Tanzania by car poses no particular problems, although most rental companies require you to take a driver along. However, it's more common to focus on one part of the country and then arrange local transport through a tour or safari operator. On Zanzibar it's easy and economical to hire a car or motorcycle for touring, and self-drive is permitted.

DRIVING LICENCE

On the mainland you'll need your home driving licence or (preferably) an International Driving Permit. On Zanzibar you'll need an International Driving Permit, or a permit from Zanzibar (see p783), Kenya, Uganda or South Africa.

HIRE

In Dar es Salaam, daily rates for 2WD start about US$55, excluding fuel, plus US$20 to US$40 for insurance, plus tax (20%). Daily rates for 4WD range from US$80 to US$200 plus insurance (US$30 to US$40 per day), tax, fuel and driver (US$15 to US$35 per day). Outside the city most companies require you to hire a 4WD. Also most don't permit self-drive outside of Dar es Salaam, and none offers unlimited kilometres. Per-kilometre charges range from US$0.50 to US$2. Clarify what the company's policy is in the event of a breakdown.

Recommended car-rental companies:

Avis (☎ 022-211 5381, 022-212 1061/2; www.avisworld. com; Skylink Travel & Tours, Ohio St & Ali Hassan Mwinyi Rd, opposite Mövenpick Royal Palm Hotel, Dar es Salaam) Also at the Kilimanjaro Kempinski Hotel.

Green Car Rentals (☎ 022-218 2022, 022-218 2107; www.greencars.co.tz; Nyerere Rd, Dar es Salaam) A recommended place, with competitive rates. It's near MD Motors in the Gerezani area.

Travel Mate (☎ 022-260 0573; www.travelmate.co.tz; Chole Rd, Dar es Salaam, near the Slipway turnoff)

Elsewhere, you can rent 4WD vehicles in Arusha, Karatu, Mwanza, Mbeya, Zanzibar Town and other centres through travel agencies, tour operators, hotels and businesspeople. Except on Zanzibar, most come with driver.

ROAD CONDITIONS & HAZARDS

Around 25% of Tanzania's road network is sealed, with roadworks underway at an impressive pace. Secondary roads range from good to impassable, depending on the season. For most trips outside major towns you'll need 4WD with high clearance.

Hazards include vehicles overtaking on blind curves, pedestrians and animals in the road, and children running onto the road.

ROAD RULES

In theory, driving is on the left, and traffic already in roundabouts has the right of way. Unless otherwise posted, the speed limit is 80km/h; on major routes, police use radar. Tanzania has a seatbelt law for drivers and front-seat passengers. The official traffic fine is Tsh20,000.

Motorcycles aren't permitted in national parks, except for the section of the Dar es Salaam to Mbeya highway passing through Mikumi National Park.

Hitching

Hitching is generally slow going and is prohibited inside national parks. However, in remote areas, hitching a lift with truck drivers may be your only transport option, for which you'll need to pay. See p1161.

Local Transport
DALLA-DALLA

Local routes are serviced by *dalla-dallas* and, in rural areas, pick-up trucks or old 4WDs. Prices range from Tsh300 to Tsh600. The vehicles make many stops and are crowded.

Accidents are frequent, particularly in minibuses. Destinations are either posted in the front window, or called out by the driver's assistant, who also collects fares.

TAXI

Taxis can be hired in all major towns. None have meters; the base rate for town trips is Tsh2500.

Train

Tanzania has two rail lines: **Tazara** (☎ 022-286 5137/0340/0344, 0713-225292; www.tazara.co.tz; cnr Nyerere & Nelson Mandela Rds, Dar es Salaam), linking Dar es Salaam with Kapiri Mposhi in Zambia via Mbeya, and the Tanzanian Railway Corporation's **Central Line** (☎ 022-211 7833; www.trctz.com; cnr Railway St & Sokoine Dr, Dar es Salaam), linking Dodoma with Kigoma and Mwanza via Tabora (service between Dodoma and Dar es Salaam is suspended); and Central Line branches link Tabora with Mpanda, and Dodoma with Singida.

Tazara is more comfortable and efficient, but on both lines breakdowns and long delays – up to 12 hours or more – are common.

CLASSES

There are three classes of train travel: 1st class (two- or four-bed compartments), 2nd-class sleeping (six-bed compartments) and economy class (benches, usually very crowded). Some trains also have a '2nd-class sitting section', with one seat per person. Men and women can only travel together in the sleeping sections by booking the entire compartment.

RESERVATIONS

Tickets for 1st and 2nd class should be reserved at least several days in advance, although occasionally you'll be able to get a seat on the day of travel. Economy-class tickets can be bought on the spot.

SCHEDULES & COSTS

Both lines are undergoing renovations and management changes, so expect schedule and price changes.

Central Line

Trains depart from Dodoma four evenings weekly for both Kigoma and Mwanza (splitting at Tabora). Both journeys cost about Tsh40,000/28,000/13,000 in 1st/2nd-class sitting/economy class and take about 24 hours, though it's often much longer. Trains from both Mwanza and Kigoma eastwards depart in the mornings. Travelling between Mwanza and Kigoma, you'll need to overnight in Tabora.

Trains between Tabora and Mpanda (about 14 hours) run three times weekly, departing Tabora in the evening and Mpanda around midday.

Tazara

Tazara runs three trains weekly: two 'express' trains between Dar es Salaam and Kapiri Mposhi in Zambia via Mbeya; and an 'ordinary' train between Dar es Salaam and Mbeya.

For express train information, see Zambia, p811. Ordinary trains depart Dar es Salaam on Monday evening and Mbeya at midday on Tuesday (Tsh20,700/14,500/12,000 in 1st/2nd/economy class, 24 hours).

Uganda

Uganda is Africa condensed, with a bit of everything the continent has to offer packed into one small, stunning destination. It's home to the tallest mountain range in Africa, the glacier-capped Rwenzoris. The mighty Nile River, the world's longest, surges out of Lake Victoria, the continent's largest lake. One of the highest concentrations of primates in the world, including more than half of all remaining mountain gorillas, roams its forests. And the merging of habitats from eastern, western and northern Africa produces some of the world's best birdwatching.

On top of all this, a growing variety of activities has made Uganda the adrenalin centre of East Africa. There's no such thing as a crowd in even the most popular national parks, and the capital Kampala is safer and friendlier than most in Africa. Winston Churchill called it the 'Pearl of Africa'. He was right.

And now is an ideal time to visit because Uganda sits on the cusp of discovery. It's already popular enough that facilities are well developed in the places where most visitors go, but there's a genuine sense of adventure for those who get off the tiny tourist trail.

FAST FACTS

- **Area** 241,038 sq km
- **ATMs** Widely available
- **Borders** Democratic Republic of Congo (DRC; formerly Zaïre), Kenya, Rwanda, Sudan and Tanzania
- **Budget** US$20 a day in towns, US$50 in parks
- **Capital** Kampala
- **Languages** English, Luganda
- **Money** Ugandan shilling; US$1 = USh1934, €1 = USh2784
- **Population** 31.4 million
- **Seasons** Rainy seasons in the south are March to May and October to November; in the north it rains April to October
- **Telephone** Country code ☎ 256; international access code ☎ 00
- **Time** GMT/UTC + 3
- **Visa** US$50 for up to three months, issued at most borders; single East African tourist visa expected to be introduced soon (see p737)

HOW MUCH?

- **Tracking mountain gorillas** US$500
- **Meal at a decent restaurant** US$5 to US$15
- **National park entry** US$25 to US$30
- **Daily Monitor newspaper** US$0.60
- **White-water rafting** US$125

LONELY PLANET INDEX

- **1L petrol** US$1.65
- **1.5L bottled water** US$1
- **500mL Bell beer** US$0.75 to US$1.25
- **Souvenir T-shirt** US$7
- **Plate of matoke (mashed plantains) and beans** US$0.90

HIGHLIGHTS

- **Bwindi Impenetrable National Park** (p836) Jaunt through the jungle to marvel at mountain gorillas.
- **White-water rafting and kayaking** (p828) Take on the wild waters of the Nile River.
- **Murchison Falls** (p841) Check out the world's most powerful waterfall on a wildlife-watching bonanza of a boat ride up the Victoria Nile.
- **Lake Bunyonyi** (p838) Chill out at the most beautiful lake in Uganda.
- **Travelling overland to Kidepo Valley National Park** (p843) Cross unvarnished Africa at its wild and colourful best.

CLIMATE & WHEN TO GO

Uganda can be visited at any time of year. Most of Uganda enjoys the perfect tropical climate. Temperatures average 26°C during the day and 15°C at night. The hottest months are January and February, when temperatures can reach 32°C in the north. The rainy seasons in the south are March to May and October to November, the wettest month being April. In the north the wet season is from April to October.

ITINERARIES

- **One Week** Kick off in Kampala (p821) and then head south to track the gorillas in Bwindi Impenetrable (p836) or Mgahinga Gorilla (p840) National Parks. After some

hard hiking, chill out at Lake Bunyonyi (p838) for a few days.

- **Two Weeks** Take some wild rides in Jinja (p828), East Africa's adrenalin capital, and then wind down in Kampala (p821) before heading north to Murchison Falls National Park (p841), Uganda's best all-rounder. Pick some places to explore around Fort Portal (p833) and finish off with a visit to the gorillas in Bwindi Impenetrable (p836) or Mgahinga Gorilla (p840) National Parks.

HISTORY

Uganda experienced two great waves of migration. The first brought the Bantu-speaking peoples from further west in Africa, and the second, the Nilotic people from Sudan and Ethiopia. These broad families are still geographically split today; the Bantu in the centre and south of the country and the Nilotic peoples in the north.

Until the 19th century, landlocked Uganda saw few outsiders compared with its neighbours. Despite fertile lands and surplus harvests, trading links with the great Indian Ocean ports were limited. Firm contacts were finally made with Arab traders and early European explorers in the mid-19th century.

The British Arrive

After the Treaty of Berlin in 1890, when Europeans carved up Africa, Uganda, Kenya and Zanzibar were declared British Protectorates. The Brits ruled indirectly, giving the traditional kingdoms a considerable degree of autonomy, but favoured the Baganda (the name of the people of the Baganda kingdom) people for their civil service.

Other tribal groups, unable to make inroads into the Baganda-dominated colonial administration or commercial sector, were forced to seek other avenues for advancement. The Acholi and Lango people from the north soon became dominant in the military. Thus were planted the seeds for the intertribal conflicts that were to tear Uganda apart following independence.

Independence Time

By the mid-1950s a Lango schoolteacher Dr Milton Obote had cobbled together a loose coalition that led Uganda to independence in 1962, on the promise that the Baganda would have autonomy. The kabaka (king),

UGANDA

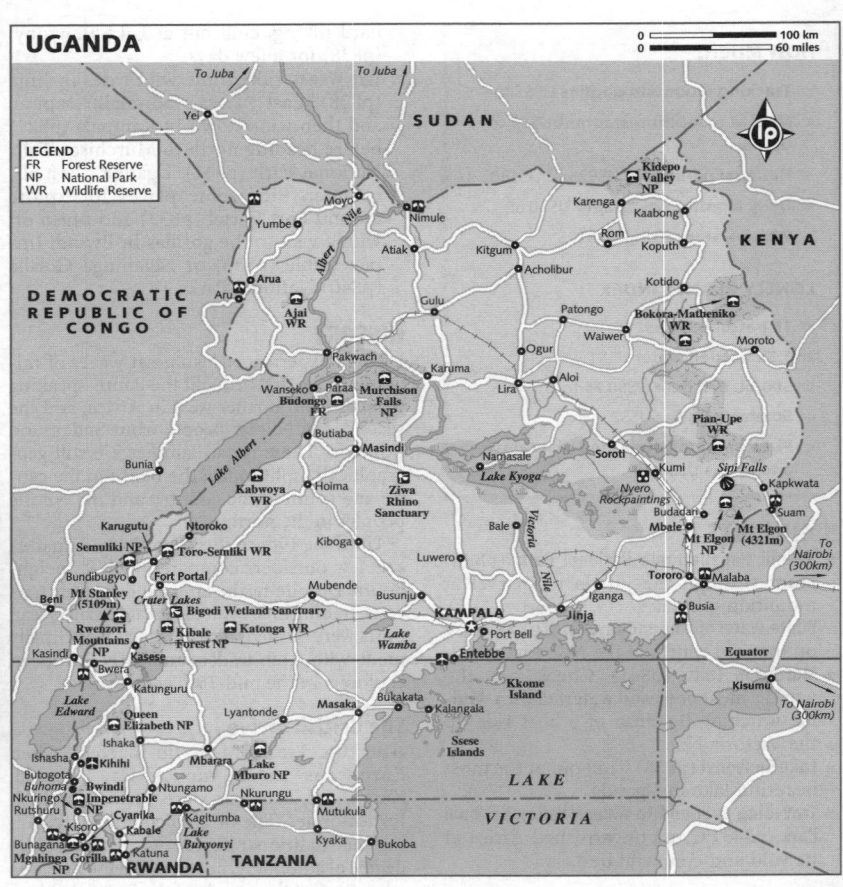

Edward Mutesa II, became the new nation's president, and Milton Obote became prime minister.

It wasn't the ideal time for Uganda to get to grips with independence. Civil wars were raging in neighbouring Sudan, Zaïre and Rwanda, and refugees poured into the country. And it soon became obvious that Obote had no intention of sharing power. A confrontation loomed.

Obote moved in 1966, arresting several cabinet ministers and ordering his army chief of staff, Idi Amin, to storm the kabaka's palace. Obote became president, the Bagandan monarchy (and all others) was abolished and Idi Amin's star was on the rise.

Enter Idi Amin

Amin staged a coup in January 1971, and so began Uganda's first reign of terror. All political activities were suspended and the army was empowered to shoot on sight anyone suspected of opposition to the regime.

Over the next eight years an estimated 300,000 Ugandans lost their lives, often in horrifying ways. Amin's main targets were the educated classes; the Acholi and Lango people of Obote; and the 70,000-strong Asian community, which in 1972 was given 90 days to leave the country.

Meanwhile, the economy collapsed, infrastructure crumbled, prolific wildlife was slaughtered by soldiers and the tourism industry evaporated. The stream of refugees across the border became a flood, inflation hit 1000% and the treasury ran out of money to pay the soldiers.

Amin's desperation became so great by the end of 1978 that he invaded Tanzania, ostensibly to teach that country a lesson for supporting anti-Amin dissidents as a diversion from the problems at home. It was his last major act of insanity, and in it lay his downfall. The Tanzanians, with the help of exiled Ugandans, soundly defeated Amin and pushed on into the heart of Uganda in early 1979. Amin eventually ended up in Saudi Arabia where he died in 2003, never having faced justice.

Obote Rides Again

The rejoicing in Uganda after Amin's downfall was short-lived. The 12,000 Tanzanian soldiers who remained in Uganda, supposedly to assist with the country's reconstruction and to maintain law and order, turned on the Ugandans as soon as their pay dried up. Once again the country slid into chaos and gangs of armed bandits roamed the cities, killing and looting.

Yusufu Lule and Godfrey Binaisa came and went as leaders before Obote returned from exile in Tanzania. He swept to victory in an election that was widely reported to be rigged. The honeymoon for Obote proved to be short. He continued a policy of tribal favouritism, replacing many southerners in military and civil-service positions with his northern Lango and Acholi supporters, and the prisons began to fill again.

Obote was about to complete the destruction that Amin had begun. Reports of atrocities leaked out of the country and several mass graves were discovered. In mid-1985 Obote was overthrown in a coup staged by the army under the leadership of Tito Okello.

A New Beginning

Okello, who turned out not to be much different from his predecessors, had many enemies, including Yoweri Museveni, who built a guerrilla army in western Uganda. Museveni's National Resistance Army (NRA) was different to the armies of Amin and Obote. New recruits, many of them orphans, were taught to be servants of the people, not oppressors, and discipline was tough. By January 1986 it was clear that Okello's days were numbered. The NRA launched an all-out offensive and easily took Kampala since most of Okello's troops chose to loot the capital rather than fight.

Museveni proved to be a pragmatic leader, appointing a number of arch-conservatives to his cabinet, and making an effort to avoid the tribal nepotism that had divided the country. The economy took a turn for the better, and aid and investment returned. Political parties were banned to avoid a polarisation along tribal lines. Prosperity followed stability, and this was helped by Museveni's bold decision to invite the Asians back. He also restored the monarchies. In 1996 he agreed to elections, which he won overwhelmingly. He was easily re-elected in 2001.

The darkness didn't end for northern Uganda, however, due to the Lord's Resistance Army (LRA). Its leader, Joseph Kony, grew increasingly delusional and paranoid during the 1990s and shifted his focus from attacking soldiers to attacking civilians in his bizarre attempt to found a government based on the biblical Ten Commandments. His tactics included torture, mutilation (slicing off lips, noses and ears), rape, and abducting children to use as soldiers and sex slaves. Eventually more than one million northerners fled their homes to refugee camps and tens of thousands of children became 'night commuters', walking from their villages each evening to sleep in schools and churches or on the streets of large and thus safer towns. According to a 2007 UN report, government forces committed their own atrocities, too, during their half-hearted fight against the LRA.

Uganda Today

Eventually Museveni shifted his position on political parties, but this shift was of much less concern to the average Ugandan than his successful push for a constitutional amendment scrapping presidential-term limits. International criticism was strong and even many Ugandans who back Museveni remain angry at his U-turn.

Despite all this, Museveni won his third election in 2006 with 59% of the vote, albeit not without some controversies along the way, such as imprisoning the main opposition leader, Kizza Besigye of the Forum for Democratic Change (FDC), for three months. Besigye had also been the runner-up in 2001 and spent most of the subsequent years in self-imposed exile due to previous harassment by the government. There's little doubt

Museveni will run again in 2011, and though he continues to lose popularity, no credible opposition has arisen.

The LRA's campaign of terror continued until 2005 when Kony fled to Garamba National Park in Democratic Republic of Congo (DRC; formerly Zaïre). The following year the Juba Peace Talks commenced, and though things progressed slowly they showed genuine promise. Museveni even guaranteed Kony amnesty, a move supported in Uganda as distasteful but practical. After on-again, off-again talks a peace deal was reached in February 2008; then Kony broke his promise to sign it. The LRA began abducting more child soldiers and started making its way across Sudan, Central African Republic and DRC. Although the LRA hasn't threatened Uganda for several years, many northern Ugandans remain too terrified to return to their homes.

Though Uganda only ranked 157 out of 182 nations on the UN's Human Development Index, it's a country with much promise. But, it can't fulfil its potential until it addresses the rampant corruption that continues to plague the government. Secondly, as political pluralism returns to Uganda, it's to be hoped that a new generation of politicians brought up on the no-party system will form their parties based on policy not pedigree, although this doesn't appear to be happening. Tribalism is worsening rapidly, especially amongst the Baganda, many of whom hold separatist aspirations.

CULTURE

Despite the years of terror and bloodshed, Ugandans are a remarkably positive and spirited people, and no one comes away from the country without a measure of admiration and affection. Ugandans are very polite and friendly, and will often greet strangers. Not just with a simple 'hello' but also an enquiry into how they and their family are doing; and the interest is sincere. They probably won't show it, but you genuinely risk offending someone if you don't at least ask 'How are you?' before asking a question or beginning a conversation. In fact, if you just say 'Hello', you'll often get a response of 'I'm fine' simply out of habit of hearing more personal greetings.

Despite the evident progress in Uganda, a serious north–south divide remains. Kampala and the south experienced peace and prosperity for two decades while Gulu and points north were mired in an intractable cycle of violence. Without Joseph Kony around to blame any more, northerners seem to be turning their resentment for the lack of prosperity and educational opportunity towards the south; and not without some justification. During the war, many military officers used their power to swipe land, and today many of the new businesses are owned and new jobs taken by carpetbaggers.

Agriculture remains the single most important component of the Ugandan economy, and it employs 75% of the workforce. Coffee, sugar, cotton, tea and fish are the main export crops. Crops grown for local consumption include maize, millet, rice, cassava, potatoes and beans.

Uganda has been heavily affected by HIV/AIDS. One of the first countries to be struck by an outbreak of epidemic proportions, Uganda acted swiftly in promoting AIDS awareness and safe sex. This was very effective in radically reducing the crisis throughout the country, and Uganda went from experiencing an infection rate of around 25% in the late 1980s to one that dropped as low as 4% in 2003. But things have changed. Due in large part to pressure from the country's growing evangelical Christian population, led on this issue by Museveni's outspoken wife (though the president himself has taken her lead), Uganda has reversed policy on promoting condoms and made abstinence the focus in fighting the disease. The infection rate has since risen to 6.7%.

People

Uganda is made up of a complex and diverse range of people. Lake Kyoga forms the northern boundary for the Bantu-speaking tribes, such as the Baganda (17%), Banyankole (9.5%), Basoga (8.5%) and Bagisu (4.6%). In the north are the Lango (6%) near Lake Kyoga and the Acholi (4.7%) towards the Sudanese border, who speak Nilotic languages. To the east are the cattle-herding Iteso (6.4%) and Karamojong (2%), both related to the Maasai and also speaking Nilotic languages. About 4000 Batwa pygmies live in the forests of the southwest. Non-Africans, including a sizeable community of Asians, compose about 1% of the population.

Eighty-five percent of the population is Christian, split about evenly between

Catholics and Protestants. Muslims, mostly northerners, compose about 12%. The Abayudaya are a small but devout group of native Ugandans living around Mbale who practise Judaism.

FOOD & DRINK

Local food is much the same as elsewhere in the region, except in Uganda *ugali* (a food staple usually made from maize flour) is called *posho*, and is far less popular than *matoke* (mashed plantains). Rice, cassava and potatoes are also common starches and vegetarians travelling beyond the main tourist destinations will end up eating these with beans quite often, though Indian food is usually available. One uniquely Ugandan food is the *rolex*, a chapatti rolled around an omelette.

Popular local beers include the light Bell and stronger Nile Special, plus locally brewed Tusker and Castle are available. Waragi is the local hard stuff, a little like gin, so it's best with a splash of tonic.

ENVIRONMENT

Uganda is small by African standards but of a similar area to Great Britain and it packs in everything from semidesert in the north to the snow-covered Rwenzori Mountains, the highest mountain range in Africa, in the southwest. Mt Stanley, its highest peak, tops out at 5109m. The southern half of the country is very lush. The tropical heat is tempered by the altitude, which averages more than 1000m in much of the country; even higher in the cooler southwest.

Uganda can't compete with Kenya or Tanzania for sheer density of wildlife, but with 500-plus species of mammal and 1041 species of bird, it has amazing diversity. Mountain gorillas (almost half the world's remaining population lives in Uganda) are the stars of Uganda's national parks, but big-game viewing can also be very good. Uganda's parks get far fewer visitors than the famous ones in Kenya and Tanzania, making them more enjoyable places to be. The downside of this is that accommodation is more limited, and, for budget travellers, getting around is more difficult, though budget safaris are available to the best parks. Some national parks charge US$25, although most charge US$30 (US$15 for children aged five to 15) per 24-hour entry and there's a 25% discount for International Student Identity Card (ISIC) holders.

Of course, Uganda has environmental problems, too; most ominously rampant population growth. The current 3.2% growth rate, one of the highest in the world, means that by 2050 Uganda's population could skyrocket from the current 31.4 million to 130 million, potentially wreaking havoc on the environment and society. Also, although it's early days, oil drilling and exploration along Lake Albert have the potential to threaten Queen Elizabeth and Murchison Falls National Parks.

KAMPALA

pop 1.5 million

Unlike what Nairobi does for Kenya, Kampala makes a good introduction to Uganda. It's a dynamic city with few of the hassles of its eastern neighbour and some worthy attractions to keep you occupied. It's safe to walk around virtually everywhere in the daytime, and downtown doesn't shut down until well into the evening. Mix in the excellent international restaurants and a thumping nightlife and there's enough going on to stop you from just touching down and rushing off.

ORIENTATION

Like Rome, Kampala is known as a city of seven hills, although it's since engulfed many more. The city centre is on Nakasero Hill, and it's almost a tale of two cities. Towards the bottom is a chaotic mix of shops, markets, budget hotels, Hindu temples, bus stations, taxi parks and out-of-control traffic. The upper end, on the other hand, has many office blocks and good restaurants, and is far more orderly. The dividing line, for the most part, is Kampala Rd (which turns into Jinja Rd to the east and Bombo Rd to the west). This artery stays busy (and safe) well into the night.

Old Kampala lies just west of the centre, around the namesake Kampala Hill, now topped by the immense National Mosque. Further out are Namirembe and Rubaga Hills, topped by the Protestant and Catholic cathedrals respectively; Mengo Hill, heart of the Baganda nation; and Kasubi Hill, topped by the Kasubi Tombs. Directly north of Old Kampala is Makerere Hill, home to the well-regarded Makerere University.

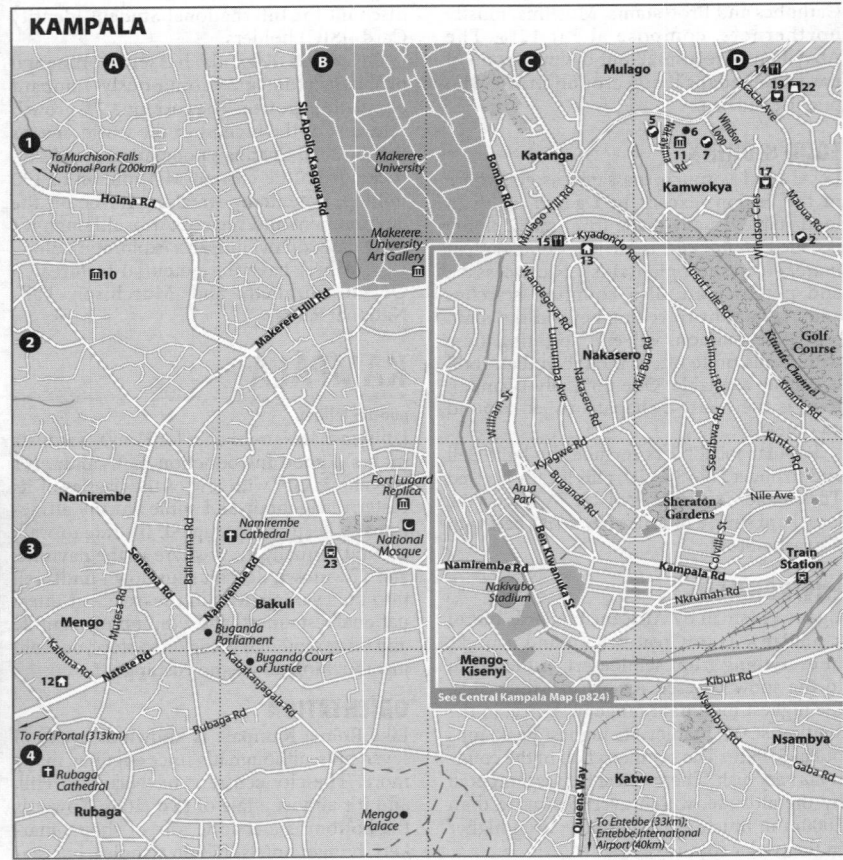

KAMPALA

To the east is the exclusive Kololo area, home to the popular Cooper Rd area (called Kisimenti), with its international roster of restaurants and bars, and the side-by-side Uganda Wildlife Authority and Uganda Museum. South of the city centre lies Kabalagala, home to some of the city's wildest bars.

INFORMATION
Bookshops

Aristoc (Map p824; 23 Kampala Rd) Overflowing with books and maps about Uganda, East Africa and beyond. Also has a branch in Garden City.

Emergency

Police and ambulance (☎ 999) You can also dial ☎ 112 from mobile phones.

Internet Access

Panorama Coffee Shop (Map p824; 9th fl, Worker's House, Portal Ave; ☺ 8.45am-10.15pm) Nice little coffee shop with big views and free wi-fi.

Web City Café (Map p824; Kimathi Ave; per hr USh3000; ☺ 8am-10pm Mon-Sat, 9am-8pm Sun) Has internet access.

Medical Services

International Hospital Kampala (Map pp822-3; ☎ 0772-200400; St Barnabus Rd; ☺ 24hr) This should be your destination if you're suffering from serious trauma.

The Surgery (Map p824; ☎ 0752-756003; www.the surgeryuganda.org; 2 Acacia Ave; ☺ 8am-6pm Mon-Sat, 9am-6pm Sun, emergency 24hr) A highly respected clinic.

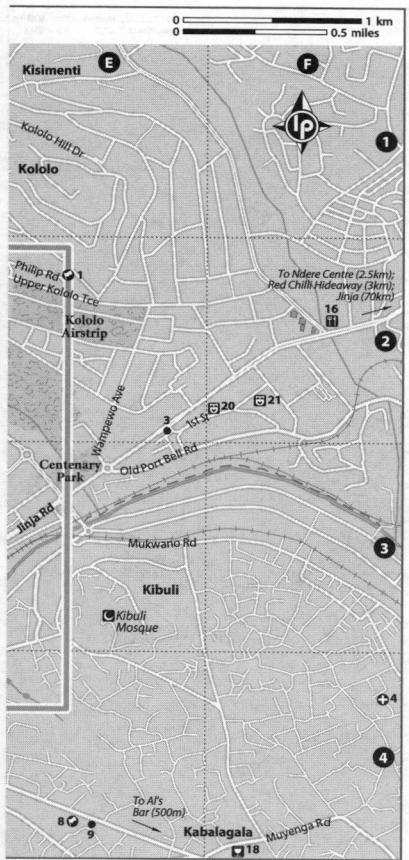

UGANDA

co.ug; Natete Rd, Lunguja) and **Red Chilli Hideaway** (off
Map pp822-3; ☎ 0414-223903; www.redchillihideaway.com),
where staff know what's going on in most of the
country. The free listings magazine the *Eye* is
available from selected hotels and restaurants.
Tourism Uganda (Map p824; ☎ 0414-342196; www.
visituganda.com; 15 Kimathi Ave) Staff will try to answer
your questions, but are frequently unable to.
Uganda Wildlife Authority (UWA; Map pp822-3;
☎ 0414-355000; www.ugandawildlife.org; 7 Kira Rd) For
national-park reservations and information.

Money

Most main bank branches and bureaux de
change sit on near Kampala Rd.
Barclays Bank (Map p824; Kampala Rd) The most
useful bank in Kampala converts Amex, Thomas Cook and
Visa travellers cheques and give cash advances on Visa,
MasterCard and JCB credit cards.
Speke Hotel (Map p824; Nile Ave) Changes money 24
hours a day at reasonable rates.

Post & Telephone

Main post office (Map p824; Kampala Rd) Offers postal
and telecom services. Poste restante service is at counter 14.

Tourist Information

The best sources of information are **Backpackers
Hostel** (Map pp822-3; ☎ 0772-430587; www.backpackers.

Travel Agencies

The following are reliable places to buy plane
tickets. For safari companies, see p848.
Global Interlink (Map p824; ☎ 0414-235233; www.
global-interlink.org; Grand Imperial Hotel) Hidden away in
the mall behind the hotel.
Let's Go Travel (Map p824; ☎ 0414-346667; www.
ugandaletsgotravel.com; Garden City, Kitante Rd) Part of the
Uniglobe empire and also a representative for STA Travel.

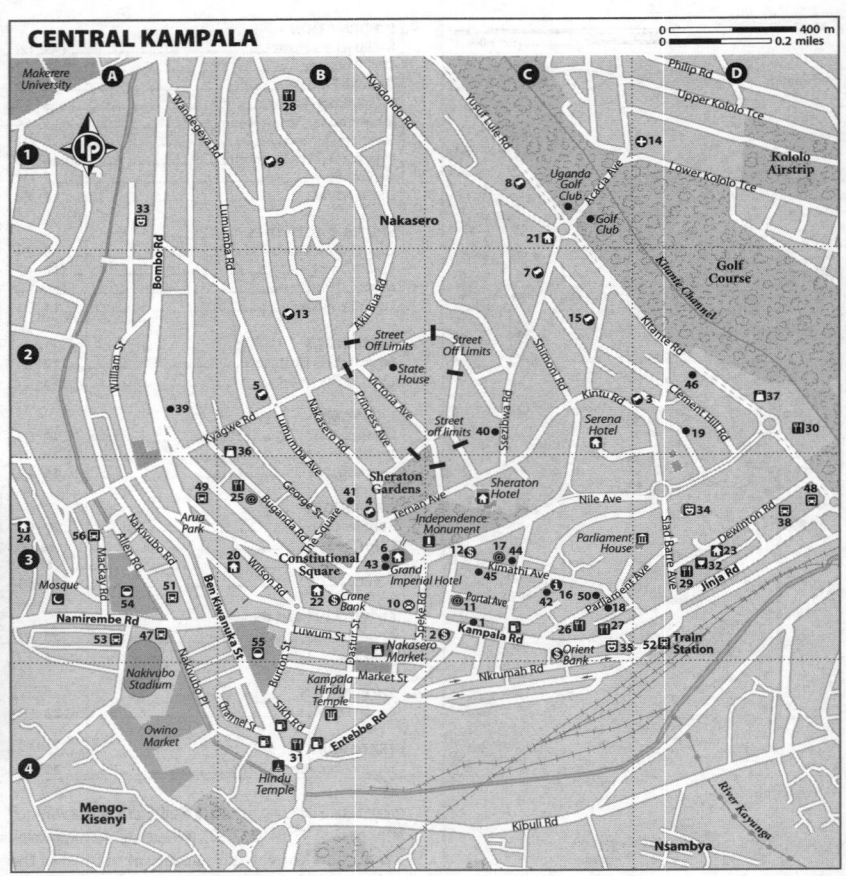

CENTRAL KAMPALA

DANGERS & ANNOYANCES

Kampala is a pretty safe city as far as African capitals go. See p1138 for the basics on staying safe in Africa's large cities. There are many beggars on Kampala Rd. Some of these are genuine hard-luck cases, but others are exploited children so it's best not to give. Nobody, especially women, should ride *boda-bodas* (motorcycle taxis) after dark: besides the obvious traffic hazards, there have been robberies and sexual assaults of passengers.

SIGHTS & ACTIVITIES

The Unesco World Heritage–listed **Kasubi Tombs** (Map pp822-3; admission incl guide USh10,000; ☒ 8am-6pm), a huge reed and bark cloth mausoleum for the previous four kings of the Baganda people,

was an amazing site until it burned down in March 2010. If it's rebuilt, definitely check it out. Take a minibus to Kasubi Trading Centre; from there it's 500m uphill.

Despite their neglect, the ethnographic exhibits (get the lowdown on banana beer here) at the **Uganda Museum** (Map pp822-3; Kira Rd; admission USh3000; ☒ 10am-6pm Mon-Sat, noon-6pm Sun) will hold your interest.

The best place for an art fix is the private **Tulifanya Gallery** (Map p824; ☎ 0782-327131; 28 Hannington Rd; ☒ 9.30am-5pm Tue-Fri, 9.30am-4pm Sat), which supports most of Uganda's serious artists.

You can trace back your coffee from the cup to the farm with the **Coffee Safari** (Map p824; ☎ 0775-667858; safari per person US$85; ☒ 7.30am

UGANDA

Fri) run by 1000 Cups Coffee House (p826).
Book before noon on Thursday.

SLEEPING

Budget lodging fills up fast, so reservations are
advised if you're arriving late in the day.

Backpackers Hostel (Map pp822–3; ☎ 0772-430587;
www.backpackers.co.ug; Natete Rd, Lunguja; campsites per
person USh7000, dm USh10,000–15,000, s without bathroom
USh20,000, d with/without bathroom USh50,000/40,000;
P 🖥 🛜) Set in lush gardens, Kampala's
original budget hostel is still going strong.
The facilities are quite good and become
almost sophisticated at the top of the price
range, while the bar draws a mix of travellers
and expats. Take a Natete/Wakaliga minibus
(USh1000 uphill, but only USh500 return!)
from the new taxi park (Map p824).

Red Chilli Hideaway (off Map pp822–3; ☎ 0414-
223903; www.redchillihideaway.com; campsites per person
USh7000, dm USh12,000–14,000, s/d/tr without bathroom
USh25,000/35,000–40,000/50,000, d with bathroom USh50,000,
cottages USh120,000; P 🖥 🛜 🍴) Similar to
Backpackers, Red Chilli is also very popular. It
gets most of the overland-truck business, but
also has quaint and quiet two-bedroom cottages with lounge and kitchen facilities. Take

a minibus from the eastern end of Kampala
Rd to Bugolobi for USh800, get off at the Shell
petrol station and walk up the hill, following
signs from there.

New City Annex Hotel (Map p824; ☎ 0414-254132; 7
Dewinton Rd; s without bathroom USh12,000–20,000, d without bathroom USh30,000, r USh40,000–70,000) A great
city-centre location with a variety of rooms.
Walls in the cheapest rooms are thin, but the
tiled floors give it a hint of distinction and the
restaurant downstairs is excellent.

Tuhende Safari Lodge (Map p824; ☎ 0772-468360;
tuhendesafarilodge@yahoo.com; 8 Martin Rd, Old Kampala;
dm/r USh10,000/60,000) Not many travellers stay
in Old Kampala, but this place has become
a favourite with aid workers on break
from upcountry due to its large comfortable rooms (no bunk beds here) and great
little cafe.

Hotel City Square (Map p824; ☎ 0414-256257; hotel
citysquare@yahoo.com; 42 Kampala Rd; s/d USh35,000/45,000;
🖥) Sitting in a strategic position on Kampala
Rd, the hotel looks pretty drab from the exterior, but the freshly painted rooms with TV
aren't bad.

Aponye Hotel (Map p824; ☎ 0414-349239; www.
aponyehotel.com; 17 William St; s USh50,000–70,000, d

USh60,000-85,000; (P) (X) (Q) (❂)) One of the best-value places in Kampala, this shiny glass tower offers high standards at midrange prices.

Fairway Hotel (Map p824; ☎ 0414-257171; www.fairwayhotel.co.ug; Kafu Rd; s/d/tr US$76/96/120; (P) (X) (Q) (❂)) Overlooking the golf course, this older property has a few quirks and is fast approaching the classic category, but for central Kampala it offers good value – especially considering the garden setting and free airport transfers.

Emin Pasha Hotel (Map pp822-3; ☎ 0414-236977; www.eminpasha.com; 27 Akii Bua Rd; s/d incl breakfast from US$307/342; (P) (X) (Q) (❂) (❂)) This beautiful boutique hotel fills an old colonial property. The 20 rooms are the best in the city, blending atmosphere and luxury.

EATING

1000 Cups Coffee House (Map p824; ☎ 0775-667858; 18 Buganda Rd; spiced coffee USh3000; ❂ 8am-6pm Mon-Sat, 9am-6pm Sun) For a coffee kick from Kentucky to Vietnam and everywhere in between, caffeine cravers should head here.

our pick **New City Annex Hotel** (Map p824; 7 Dewinton Rd; mains USh3500-12,000; (V)) Excellent local flavours, and more vegie choices than usual for Ugandan restaurants.

Masala Chaat House (Map p824; ☎ 0414-236487; 3 Dewinton Rd; mains USh4000-12,000; ❂ 9.30am-10pm; (V)) Good food and better prices have long made this a travellers' favourite.

Iguana (Map pp822-3; ☎ 0777-020658; 8 Bukoto St; lunch USh9000-11,000, dinner USh15,000-17,000; ❂ 12.30-3pm & 6pm-late Tue-Sun) Let Iguana's comfy couches and jazz music pull you in. The food, mostly French, is simple fare done well, plus there is a Ugandan lunch buffet. DJs spin on Friday and Saturday nights.

Café Pap (Map p824; ☎ 0414-254570; 13 Parliament Ave; mains USh10,000-20,000; ❂ 7.30am-11pm Mon-Sat, 9.30am-11pm Sun) This stylish cafe, popular with hip Kampalans, has great breakfasts, sandwiches and salads. The house coffee comes from the slopes of Mt Elgon, and many will tell you it's the best in town.

our pick **Haandi** (Map p824; ☎ 0414-346283; 7 Kampala Rd; mains USh10,000-41,700; ❂ noon-2.30pm & 7-10.30pm; (X) (V)) The gold standard in Indian cuisine, Haandi is worth a splurge even if you're travelling on a budget. It has a fast-food outlet at Garden City.

Mamba Point Pizzeria (Map pp822-3; ☎ 0772-743227; 62 Lumumba Ave; large pizza USh16,000-23,000; ❂ noon-2.30pm & 6-10pm Tue-Sat, noon-10pm Sun); Restaurant (Map p824; ☎ 0772-243225; 22 Akii Bua Rd; mains USh17,900-76,000; ❂ noon-2.30pm & 7-10.30pm Mon-Fri, 7-10.30pm Sat) For the best in Italian dining, make for Mamba Point, where the pasta is homemade and many ingredients imported.

For really cheap meals, the ubiquitous takeaways, which usually have seating too, offer greasy quick-serve dishes like chicken, sausages, fish and chips, and samosas for USh1500 to USh3500. At the other end of the fast-food spectrum, the **Garden City Food Court** (Map p824; Kitante Rd; ❂ 10am-10pm) has several appealing international options, including Cuban, Thai, Indian and Italian.

Shoprite (clock tower roundabout Map p824; Ben Kiwanuka St; Lugogo Mall Map pp822-3; Jinja Rd), **Nakumatt** (Map p824; ❂ 24hr) and **Uchumi** (Map p824; Garden City) are large supermarkets, while **Ranchers** (Map p824; Garden City) is a great little deli. Ideal stops for stocking up before heading upcountry.

DRINKING

Nightlife in Kampala is something to relish these days, with a host of decent bars and clubs throughout the city. Be prepared, though: almost all fill up with prostitutes as the night gets going.

Bubbles O'Learys (Map pp822-3; ☎ 0312-263815; 19 Acacia Ave) Kampala's obligatory Irish pub. Mind the cheeky USh5000 cover charge on big nights.

Fat Boyz (Map pp822-3; ☎ 0782-416900; 7 Cooper Rd; ❂ 11am-late Mon-Sat) This fun place is the closest Uganda has to a cantina. The menu has some vaguely Tex-Mex food.

Rock Garden (Map p824; Speke Hotel, Nile Ave) One of the definitive stops on the Kampala nightshift, this cool place has a covered bar and a huge outdoor area. Be careful here; pickpocketing is often part of the experience.

The Pub (Map p824; Dewinton Rd) A low-key 100%-local place in the city centre.

Kabalagala, southeast of the centre, has the wildest late-night scene with the legendary (notorious might be the better word) **Al's Bar** (off Map pp822-3; Gaba Rd) rocking through to the morning light. **Capital Pub** (Map pp822-3; Muyenga Rd) has more pool tables and gets going earlier in the evening than Al's, while **Café Cheri** (Map pp822-3; Muyenga Rd) is less raucous.

ENTERTAINMENT

The best entertainment in Kampala is at the **National Theatre** (Map p824; ☎ 0414-254567; Siad

Barre Ave). Monday is the **Musicians Club** (admission free; ☾ 8pm-midnight) open jam; Tuesday features **Percussion Discussion Africa** (admission USh3000; ☾ 8-9.30pm), which is an African fusion band; while Thursday's **Comedy Night** (admission USh5000; ☾ 8.30-10pm) attracts the biggest crowds.

The **Ndere Centre** (off Map pp822-3; ☎ 0414-288123; www.ndere.com; adult/child USh10,000/5000; ☾ 7-9.30pm Wed, 6-9pm Sun), way out in Ntinda, showcases traditional music and dance from several Ugandan ethnic groups.

Kampala's live-music scene is nearly dead, but the ever-popular Congolese soukous (African rumba) band Afrigo Band holds court on weekends at **Little Flowers** (Map p824; Bombo Rd), and Maurice Kirya, who offers a poetic, soulful take on R&B, plays the last Tuesday of the month at uberhip lounge club **Rouge** (Map p824; Kampala Rd).

The long-time leading discos are **Ange Noir** (Map pp822-3; 1st St; ☾ Thu-Sun) and **Club Silk** (Map pp822-3; 1st St; ☾ Thu-Sat).

Weekend cover charges in Kampala are typically USh10,000.

SHOPPING

The city's craft 'villages' all stock the same woodcarvings, batiks, basketry and '*muzungu*' T-shirts. With over 50 vendors, **Exposure Africa** (Map p824; 13 Buganda Rd) is the largest, though the **National Arts & Crafts Village** (Map p824; Dewinton Rd) has the best selection. For high-quality items try **Banana Boat** (Garden City Map p824; Kitante Rd; Kisimenti Map pp822-3; Cooper Rd).

GETTING THERE & AWAY

Most bus companies use the main bus park (Map p824), AKA old bus park, but there are also many departures from the more pleasant new bus park (Map p824), both just off Namirembe Rd near Nakivubo Stadium.

Kampala has two chaotic parks for minibuses, and both serve destinations inside and outside the city. The old taxi park (Map p824) is the busier of the two and serves towns in eastern Uganda; the nearby new taxi park (Map p824) services western and northern destinations.

Post Buses depart at 8am Monday to Saturday from Kampala's **main post office** (Map p824; Kampala Rd). Make reservations at counter 11.

For details about buses, boats and flights to neighbouring nations, see p846.

GETTING AROUND

The international airport is at Entebbe, 40km from Kampala. A private taxi (called a 'special-hire taxi') there costs about USh50,000. Or take a minibus between Kampala (from either taxi park) and Entebbe (USh2500, 45 minutes), and a shared taxi (USh1500 per person) to the airport, if you can find one. But, since these are rare, you'll probably end up needing a special-hire, which should be around USh6000.

The ubiquitous white and blue minibuses fan out from the city centre to virtually every point in Kampala. You just have to ask around to find the right one. Most pass down Kampala Rd.

Special-hire taxis are unmetered, and most are unmarked to avoid licensing and taxes: parked cars with open doors or a driver sitting behind the wheel are probably special-hires. Fares start from USh3000 to USh5000 for trips in the centre, more at night and during rush hour.

Boda-bodas (motorcycle taxis), by far the fastest but definitely not the safest way to get around, charge USh1000 around the city centre and USh2000 from the centre to the UWA compound.

AROUND KAMPALA

ENTEBBE
pop 70,000

Located on the shores of Lake Victoria, Entebbe is an attractive, verdant town that served duty as the capital city during the early years of the British Protectorate. But it's the relaxed pace of life and natural attractions rather than any notable colonial relics that provide its charm.

Most of the animals at the **Uganda Wildlife Education Centre** (☎ 0414-320520; www.uweczoo.org; Lugard Ave; adult/child USh20,000/5000; ☾ 9am-6.30pm), including rhinos, chimps and shoebill storks, were once injured or recovered from poachers and traffickers. Nearby, **Entebbe Botanical Gardens** (adult/child USh2000/1000; ☾ 9am-7pm) has some interesting and unusual trees. There's a little restaurant and picnic area down by the lake.

Day trips (from US$50 per person) to see the residents of **Ngamba Island Chimpanzee Sanctuary** (☎ bookings 0772-502155; www.wildfrontiers. co.ug) in Lake Victoria are popular. Plan ahead and you can join the **overnight experience** (per person incl full board US$395) and a **forest-walk** (per person US$400) with the chimps, who'll climb all over you.

The beaches around town get very crowded on weekends.

Sleeping

Entebbe has a very good selection of accommodation.

Entebbe Backpackers (☎ 0414-320432; www.en tebbebackpackers.com; 33/35 Church Rd; campsites per person with own/hired tent USh6000/9000, dm USh12,000, s/d without bathroom USh15,000/20,000, d USh25,000-45,000, tr USh35,000; P ☎) This crashpad is cosier than the similar spots in Kampala and Jinja. Book ahead.

Uganda Wildlife Education Centre (☎ 0414-322169; campsites US$5, dm US$10, bandas US$30, apt with kitchens US$40; P) The choices here are very smart for the price, and the nightly lions' roars and hyenas' howls are free.

Boma (☎ 0772-467929; Gomers Rd; s/d/tr incl breakfast US$90/115/150; P ☎ ☎) Entebbe's answer to the upmarket B&B, this luxurious guesthouse has grown to 12 rooms, but hasn't lost its intimate atmosphere.

Getting There & Away

Minibuses come from both taxi parks in Kampala (USh2500, 45 minutes) throughout the day. For details on the Ssese Island ferry, which leaves from near Entebbe, see p840.

EASTERN UGANDA

JINJA & AROUND
pop 83,000

Jinja, the largest city in the east, has some of the world's best white-water rafting on its doorstep, and has become the adrenalin centre of East Africa. Plus many expats use it as a weekend retreat, resulting in unexpected pockets of sophistication.

Jinja is also the **source of the Nile River**, though most people who visit it come away underwhelmed. The water spills out of Lake Victoria on its journey to the Mediterranean near two small islands. Most people take a peek from the garish **Ripon Falls Leisure Centre** (☎ 0782-026060; admission per person/car/motorcycle USh10,000/2000/500). It's more pleasant to look from the other side at **Source of the Nile Gardens** or hire a boat. This is cheapest from the Ripon Landing, next to the defunct Jinja Sailing

Club; a half-hour ride to the source and back costs about USh20,000.

Many people bypass Jinja proper altogether and spend their time at **Bujagali Falls**, 7km north, where most rafting trips start and a small backpacker community thrives. Construction of the Bujagali Dam will change the scenery, but not for several years.

Sleeping & Eating
JINJA

Explorers Backpackers (☎ 0434-120236; www.raftafrica. com; 41 Wilson Ave; campsites per person US$5, dm US$7 d US$25; P ☎ ☎) Jinja's original backpacker pad is a mellower alternative to the party scene at Bujagali Falls.

Bellevue Hotel (☎ 0434-120328; 4 Kutch Rd W; s without bathroom USh21,000, s/d USh31,000/41,000, all incl breakfast; ☎) This simple downtown hotel offers cleanliness, good value and a genuine African experience.

Gately on Nile (☎ 0434-122400; www.gately-on-nile. com; 34 Kisinja Rd; s/d annex US$50/70, s/d house US$80/110, s/d cottages US$95/130, all incl breakfast; P ☎ ☎) Set in a grand old colonial house with sumptuous grounds, this is the leading choice if you want a little pampering. The restaurant (mains USh8000 to USh15,000) is one of Jinja's best.

Indulge (☎ 0782-648544; Iganga Rd; smoothies USh4000-5000, sandwiches USh6500; ☁ 9am-5pm Mon & Wed-Sat, 10am-4pm Sun, weekend dinner by reservation; ☎) An upscale deli with sandwiches, salads and drinks.

Leoz (☎ 0434-120298; 11 Main St; mains USh5000-10,000; ☁ 9am-10.30pm Wed-Mon) This unassuming place is the first word in Indian, plus it also serves Chinese and Ugandan food, as well as pizza.

2 Friends (☎ 0772-984821; 6 Jackson Cres; mains USh10,500-16,500) Excellent Italian.

DOWNSTREAM

Explorers Campsite (☎ 0782-320552; www.raftafrica.com; campsites per person US$5, dm US$7, d/tr bandas US$25/30; P ☎) Nile River Explorers runs this rocking cliffside place at Bujagali, always full with overland trucks and backpackers. Sign up here for some day-long volunteer projects.

ourpick Hairy Lemon (☎ 0772-828338; www.hairy lemonuganda.com; campsites per person USh30,000, 10-bed dm USh40,000, s/d/q bandas USh70,000/110,000/180,000, all incl full board) Seemingly in the middle of nowhere, on a small island 30km out of Jinja, the Hairy Lemon is a peaceful and beautiful getaway. Take a minibus from Jinja to Nazigo

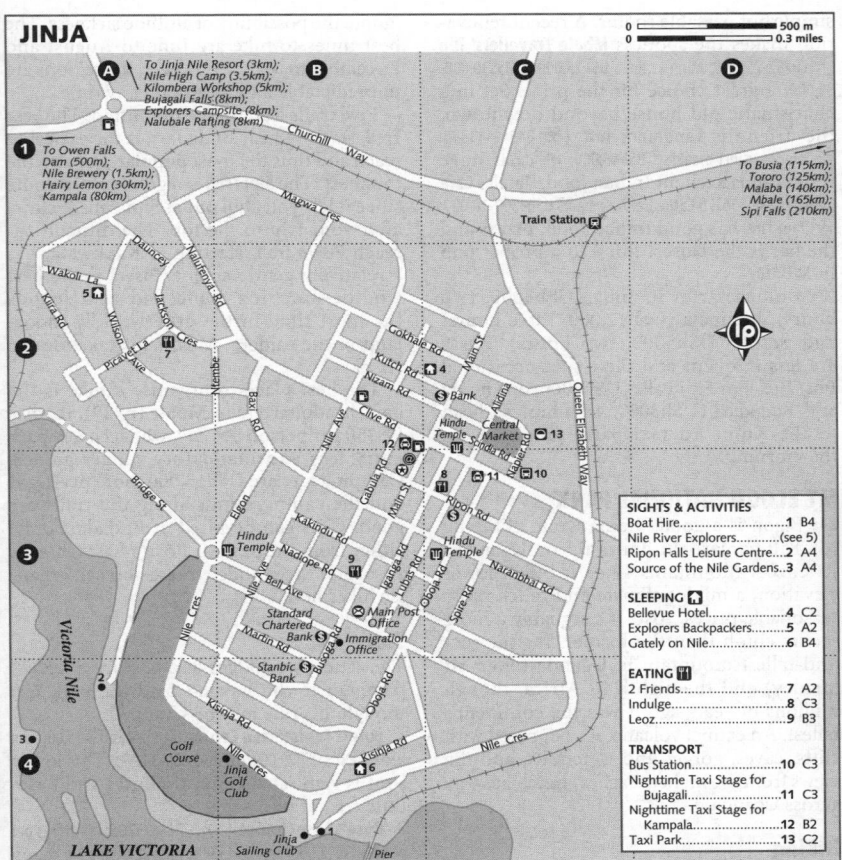

JINJA

SIGHTS & ACTIVITIES
Boat Hire.................................1 B4
Nile River Explorers............(see 5)
Ripon Falls Leisure Centre....2 A4
Source of the Nile Gardens....3 A4

SLEEPING
Bellevue Hotel........................4 C2
Explorers Backpackers..........5 A2
Gately on Nile........................6 B4

EATING
2 Friends.................................7 A2
Indulge....................................8 C3
Leoz..9 B3

TRANSPORT
Bus Station............................10 C3
Nighttime Taxi Stage for
Bujagali.................................11 C3
Nighttime Taxi Stage for
Kampala................................12 B2
Taxi Park...............................13 C2

UGANDA

(USh3000, one hour) and then a *boda-boda* (USh2000) the last 9km. Reservations are essential; so is arriving before 6pm.

Nile Porch (☎ 0782-321541; www.nileporch.com; s/d/tr US$75/95/120, f US$120-160, all incl breakfast; **P ☐ ☎ ☒**) Comfortable tents are superbly set high above the river while family units (minus the views) are also available. The **Black Lantern restaurant** (mains USh10,000-22,000) is Bujagali's fine-dining destination.

Getting There & Away
Buses and minibuses frequently travel to Kampala (USh4000, 1½ hours), Mbale (USh8000, two hours) and Busia (USh8000, 1½ hours) on the Kenyan border. Taxis also head towards Bujagali and Kampala. Minibuses to

Budondo pass near Bujagali (USh500, 30 minutes), but can take a while to fill up. *Boda-boda* rides to/from Jinja should cost about USh3000 and special-hires USh10,000; though prices go up late at night. Because the road is really rough *boda-bodas* are dangerous at night.

MBALE
pop 84,000
If you're charitable in your evaluation you might say Mbale has some charm, though about the only reason to come here is to organise a Mt Elgon expedition at the **national park headquarters** (☎ 0454-433170; 19 Masaba Rd; ☿ 8am-5pm Mon-Fri, 8am-3pm Sat & Sun).

Apule Safari Lodge (☎ 0454-433323; 5 Naboa Rd; s without bathroom USh10,000, s/d USh12,000/16,000) has simple but passable rooms. A recent renovation makes the spotless **Mbale Travellers' Inn** (☎ 0782-257999; Mumias Rd; s USh25,000, d US$30,000-35,000) a great choice for the price. Set in a charismatic old house beyond downtown, the friendly **Landmark Inn** (☎ 0454-443380; Wanale Rd; r incl breakfast USh46,000; P) has huge rooms and excellent Indian food. **Nurali's Café** (☎ 0772-445562; 5 Cathedral Ave; mains USh4500-10,000; ☻ 7am-late) has good Indian food, pizzas and the bar is the closest thing to a proper pub in Mbale.

Minibuses run to Jinja (USh8000, two hours), Kampala (USh12,000, three hours) and Soroti (USh5000, two hours). Buses are less frequent and there's an occasional Post Bus. For Sipi Falls (USh5000, one hour) and Budadari (USh3000, 45 minutes), head to the Kumi Rd taxi park, preferably in the morning.

MT ELGON NATIONAL PARK

Mt Elgon is a good alternative to climbing Mt Kilimanjaro in Tanzania or Uganda's Rwenzori Mountains since it offers lower elevation, a milder climate and much more reasonable prices. Also, it's arguably a more scenic climb than the former. It's the second-tallest mountain in Uganda (after Mt Stanley) and the eighth in Africa, though millions of years ago it was the continent's tallest. An extinct volcano, it's peppered with cliffs, caves, gorges and waterfalls, and the views from the higher reaches stretch halfway across Uganda.

Hiking

Visitors to Mt Elgon are on the rise, but it's possible to hike for days without seeing another climber; an impossible dream on Kilimanjaro. Climbing the highest peak, **Wagagai** (4321m), is nontechnical and relatively easy if you're in good shape, but don't ignore the possibility of altitude sickness. The best times to hike are June to August and December to March; however, the seasons are unpredictable and it can rain any time.

Five trails lead up the mountain. The **Sasa Trail**, starting near Budadari, is the easiest to reach and thus the most popular, but also the toughest. The **Sipi Trail** is a good return route since it lets you chill out at Sipi Falls (below) after your trip to the top. The difficult-to-reach **Piswa Trail**, starting at Kapkwata, has a relatively gentle ascent. Piswa is the best wildlife-watching route and also spends the most time in the otherworldly moorland in the caldera. Most trips take four to six days.

The best place to organise a hike is the park headquarters in Mbale (p829). It costs US$50 per person per day, which covers park entry fees and mandatory ranger-guides. Camping fees are USh15,000 more per night and the campgrounds along the trails are good. Gear can be hired at Budadari only; either from the park or Rose's Last Chance. Also, Sipi River Lodge (opposite) can organise hikes here.

Sleeping

The latter two lodges also require a US$20 payment if you haven't paid the park fee; though this rule may be scrapped.

Forest Exploration Centre (campsites USh15,000, dm USh10,000, s USh20,000, d USh30,000-50,000) This lovely spot is right at the Sipi trailhead and has a little restaurant.

Rose's Last Chance (☎ 0772-623206; campsites per person USh12,000, dm USh15,000, r USh22,000) For many people, a night at Rose's Last Chance, near the trailhead in Budadari, is part of the Mt Elgon experience. Prices include a local dinner and breakfast.

Kapkwata Guesthouse (per tent or bed USh15,000) This simple place serves the Piswa trailhead. Bring your own food.

SIPI FALLS

Sensational Sipi Falls has three tiers, but the iconic 95m main one drops straight over a sheer cliff and most lodging overlooks it. It's best to take a guide for walks along area trails. Figure on about USh5000 to get to the bottom of the main drop and USh10,000 to USh12,000 for the four-hour, 8km walk to all three. **Rob's Rolling Rock** (☎ 0752-369536) offers climbing and abseiling.

WARNING: HIKING MT ELGON

Hiking Mt Elgon can't really be classified as dangerous, but a Belgian climber was shot dead in February 2008. It's unknown who shot into the camp, and it's unlikely she was the intended target, but it highlights the fact that armed smugglers, cattle rustlers and Kenyan rebels work in the area, which is why armed escorts join all climbs.

ADRENALIN CAPITAL OF EAST AFRICA

The upper stretch of the Nile is a long, rollicking string of class 4 and 5 rapids, and for many travellers a river trip is the highlight of their visit to Uganda. Talk to people on the ground about safety records before choosing a company since not all have the same standards, but three trustworthy choices are **Adrift** (☎ 0312-237438; www.adrift.ug), based at the Uganda Wildlife Authority compound (p823) in Kampala and at Nile High Camp near Jinja; **Nile River Explorers** (☎ 0434-120236; www.raftafrica.com), with offices at Explorers Backpackers (p828) in Jinja and Explorers Campsite (p828) at Bujagali; and **Nalubale Rafting** (☎ 0782-638938; www.nalubalerafting.com), under the same ownership as Nile River Explorers. There are many options, but the typical half-/full-/two-day trips cost US$115/125/250. Adrift has jet-boat rides (US$75 for 30 minutes) and **Kayak the Nile** (☎ 0772-880322; www.kayakthenile.com), based at Explorers Campsite at Bujagali, offers lessons and tandem trips. All provide free transport from Kampala and often a night of free lodging.

Exhilarating choices on terra firma include a 44m plunge with **Nile High Bungee** (☎ 0772-286433; US$65; www.adrift.ug), a variety of rides with **Explorers Mountain Biking** (☎ 0772-422373; www.raftafrica.com; from US$30), a slow look at the countryside with **Nile Horseback Safaris** (☎ 0774-101196; www.nilehorsebacksafaris.com; from USh90,000) and a circuit on a quad-bike with **All Terrain Adventures** (☎ 0772-377185; www.atadventures.com; from USh85,000).

Moses' Campsite (☎ 0752-208302; campsites/bandas per person USh5000/10,000), a small, laid-back operation, is arguably Sipi's best-situated accommodation offering a good look at the falls (available from hammocks on the terrace) and unhindered views of the plains below. **Crow's Nest** (☎ 0752-286225; campsites per person USh6000, dm USh12,000, cabins USh30,000) has Scandinavian-style cabins and expansive waterfall views. Overland trucks sometimes stop here and the well-stocked bar can get happening. Gorgeous, colourful **Sipi River Lodge** (☎ 0751-796109; www.sipiriverlodge.com; dm US$35, s/d bandas US$75/95, d/q cottages US$155/260, all incl full board; 💻), founded by three river guides from Jinja, has the second waterfall in its backyard. The lodge grows much of its own food and meals are served around a fireplace.

Minibuses from Mbale to Kapchorwa will drop you right at your lodge of choice in Sipi (USh5000, one hour).

SOUTHWESTERN UGANDA

FORT PORTAL
pop 45,000

There may be no fort, but this city on the edge of the Rwenzori Mountains is definitely a portal to places with sublime scenery, abundant nature and genuine adventure. With a whole holiday's worth of spots to explore around town and all the services travellers need available downtown, many travellers spend some time here.

Sights & Activities

Fort Portal's attractions are pretty minor. Looking down on the city from its highest hill, **Tooro Palace** is the someday-to-be home of King Oyo, who ascended the throne in 1995 at age three. You can't go inside, but there's usually someone around who, for USh5000, will explain the ceremonies that take place here. Eventually King Oyo will join the previous three kings at the modest, brick **Karambi Royal Tombs** (Kasese Rd; admission USh5000; 🕑 8am-6pm). Learn all about local flora and organic farming techniques at **Tooro Botanical Garden** (☎ 0752-500630; www.toorobotanicalgardens.org; Km2 Kampala Rd; tours USh5000; 🕑 8am-5pm).

Kabarole Tours (☎ 0483-422183; www.kabaroletours.com; Moledina St; 🕑 8am-6pm Mon-Sat, 10am-4pm Sun) can take you anywhere in Uganda but focuses on its little corner of the country. And whether you book a tour or not, the staff is keen to answer questions about the area.

Sleeping
IN TOWN

Exotic Lodge (☎ 0774-771829; Moledina St; s/d without bathroom USh5500/7500) Downtown Fort Portal is flush with flophouses, but this one is cleaner and, dare we say it, cosier than the competition.

Continental Hotel (☎ 0752-514696; Lugard Rd; s/d without bathroom USh13,000/16,000, r incl breakfast

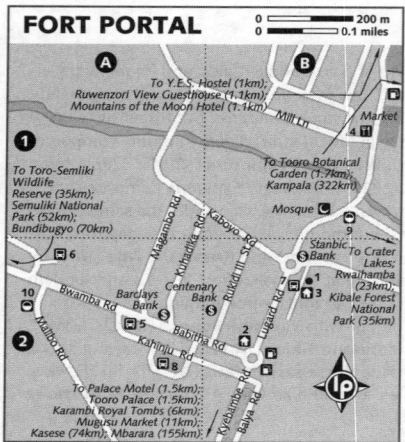

FORT PORTAL

0 ——————— 200 m
0 ——————— 0.1 miles

USh26,000) A good next-level choice after the Exotic.

Palace Motel (☎ 0772-837226; 33 Muzosi Rd; s USh30,000, d USh35,000-45,000, incl breakfast & car wash) Newer, cleaner, quieter, more comfortable and just plain better than even some more popular and expensive places. It's just south of the centre.

BOMA

This leafy, peaceful suburb, 3km north of town, has good mountain views and Fort Portal's best lodging.

Y.E.S. Hostel (☎ 0772-780350; yesuganda@gmail.com; Lower Kakiiza Rd; campsites per person USh5000, dm USh10,000, s USh15,000; P 🖳) Rooms at this Christian charity, which supports orphans, are simple but remarkably tidy. There's a large kitchen and solar hot-water showers.

ourpick Ruwenzori View Guesthouse (☎ 0483-422102; ruwview@africaonline.co.ug; Lower Kakiiza Rd; s/d without bathroom USh40,000/60,000, s/d USh72,000/95,000, all incl breakfast; P 🖳) This blissful little guesthouse run by an Anglo-Dutch couple is as homey as it gets in Uganda. The self-contained rooms have their own patios overlooking the garden.

Mountains of the Moon Hotel (☎ 0483-423200; www.mountainsofthemoon.co.ug; Nyaika Ave; r USh170,000-205,000, ste USh300,000, all incl breakfast; P 🖳 🛜 🖳) This colonial-era gem reopened in 2007 following an extensive makeover. Prices are high, but so are standards.

Eating

The best dining options are the home-cooked dinners served around the family table at

Ruwenzori View Guesthouse (per person USh22,000; 🕓 8pm) and the small but wide-ranging international menu at the **Mountains of the Moon Hotel** (mains USh8000-20,000; 🕓 12.30-3pm & 7-10.30pm). Most safari traffic passing through town dines at the **Gardens** (☎ 0772-694482; Lugard Rd; mains USh2700-8800), where the large lunch buffet (USh5500) is a great chance to sample some new foods.

Getting There & Away

Kalita Transport has the most daily buses to Kampala (USh10,000, four hours), but you can also get there with Link Coaches, whose buses tend to be more comfortable. There's also a Post Bus, which departs from the post office.

Both companies also go to Kasese (USh4000, one hour); catch the Kalita bus at its office downtown, not at its bus park as you do for Kampala. Kalita also has two early-morning buses to Kabale (USh20,000, eight hours), via Katunguru (USh8000, 1½ hours), the entrance to Queen Elizabeth National Park.

The easiest way to Hoima (USh25,000, six hours), from where connections are frequent to Masindi, is the 7am coaster that goes every other day from in front of the Bata shoe store, but you can also do the trip by minibus (USh20,000, seven hours) from the taxi park in two stages: first to Kagadi and then to Hoima.

There are also regular-ish departures from the taxi park to Ntoroko (USh5000, three hours) and Bundibugyo (USh7000, three hours); often in the backs of pick-up trucks.

Minibuses and shared taxis to Kamwenge (for Kibale Forest National Park; USh5000, 45 minutes) and Rwaihamba (for Lake Nkuruba; USh4000, 45 minutes) leave from the intersection near where the main road crosses the river.

AROUND FORT PORTAL
The Crater Lakes

The picturesque Crater Lakes south of Fort Portal are great places to settle in for a few days to explore the footpaths or cycle the seldom-used roads. The common wisdom is that the lakes are bilharzia-free, but some locals suggest otherwise.

LAKE NKURUBA

Arguably the most beautiful crater lake, Nkuruba, 25km south of Fort Portal, is one of the few still surrounded entirely by forest. Many monkeys, including black-and-white colobuses, frolic here.

our pick **Lake Nkuruba Nature Reserve Community Campsite** (☎ 0773-266067; www.lakenkuruba.com; campsites per person USh7000, tent hire USh5000, dm USh16,000, lakeside cottages USh36,000, bandas USh50,000, day visit USh5000; **P**), as the blue and yellow sign at the entrance gate says, is Nkuruba's original. It has great views and easy access to the lake, plus all funds go towards health and education programs. Be sure you're at the right place as the unrecommendable camp next door may try to entice you into walking up their drive instead.

Minibuses and shared taxis from Fort Portal to Rwaihamba pass Nkuruba (USh4000, 45 minutes).

LAKE NYINABULITWA

The midsized 'Mother of Lakes' is home to the attractive **Nyinabulitwa Country Resort** (☎ 0712-984929; www.nyinabulitwaresort.com; campsites per person US$10, s US$60-70, d US$110-120, tr US$150-160, all incl breakfast; **P**), an intimate place on the lake's south shore. It does boat trips around the lake and can deliver you to a treehouse for primate- and birdwatching. It's 20km from Fort Portal, 1.5km off the road to Kibale Forest National Park, just before Rweetera Trading Centre.

LAKE NYABIKERE

The lovely 'Lake of Frogs' lies along the road to Kibale (12km northwest of Kanyanchu visitor centre) and is a great lake to explore. **CVK Resort** (☎ 0772-906549; campsite per tent USh10,000, s bandas USh12,000-15,000, d bandas USh24,000-30,000, s USh25,000, d USh50,000-60,000; **P**) is fairly basic, but the prices are fair. Take any minibus (USh3000) heading south from Fort Portal.

LAKE KASENDA

Want to really get away from it all? Get to **Ruigo Beach Lodge** (☎ 0752-391826; campsites per person USh8000, s/d/tr USh20,000/30,000/45,000, day-visit USh2000), where visitors are very rare due to its isolation. Rooms are decent, but there's no actual beach. It's 35km south of Fort Portal and overloaded trucks trundle to Kesenda trading centre (USh4000, two to three hours), 2km before the lodge.

Kibale Forest National Park

This **national park** (☎ 0483-422202; admission per 24hr US$30; ☽ 8am-5pm) is believed to have the highest density of primates in Africa, but the chimpanzees are the stars. Three groups have been habituated to human contact, and despite being the most expensive place in Uganda for **chimp tracking** (per person US$90; ☽ 8am & 2pm), it's also the most popular (mostly because the walking is relatively easy), so reservations are recommended. Children 12 and under aren't permitted. Regular trackers get just one hour with the playful primates, but those on the **Chimpanzee Habituation Experience** (1/2/3 days US$220/400/550; ☽ Feb-Jun & Sep-Nov) can spend the whole day with them. To do this you must spend the night before at Kanyanchu. With frequent sightings of civets and the 12cm-long Demidoff's dwarf galago, **night walks** (per person US$25; ☽ 7.30pm) can be rewarding.

SLEEPING & EATING

It's easy to visit Kibale from Fort Portal or the Crater Lakes, but there're also good options in and near the forest.

Primate Lodge (☎ 0414-267153; www.primatelodge.com; campsites per person US$10, treehouses USh50,000, cottages incl breakfast US$70, safari tents s/d incl full board US$170/290; **P**) In the park at Kanyanchu (so you must pay park entrance), Primate Lodge has good fair-priced accommodation. The simple treehouse, 800m from the lodge, overlooks an elephant wallow.

our pick **Chimps' Nest** (☎ 0774-669107; www.chimpsnest.com; campsites per person US$5, dm US$8, s/d cottages US$59/76, treehouse s US$108, d & tr US$135; s/q family cottages US$130/189, cottages & treehouses incl breakfast half-/full-board per person USh25,000/50,000; **P** 🖳) This stunning place borders Kibale Forest and Magombe Swamp, so there's lots of wildlife around. All the choices are wonderful, but especially the amazing treehouse. It's 4km off the highway from Nkingo.

UGANDA

GETTING THERE & AWAY

Minibuses from Fort Portal to Kamwenge pass the Kanyanchu visitor centre (USh5000, 45 minutes), 35km southeast of Fort Portal.

Bigodi Wetland Sanctuary

Community-run **Bigodi Wetland Sanctuary** (☎ 0772-886865; www.bigodi-tourism.org; ☺ 8am-5pm) was established to protect important bird habitat on the edge of the forest. Three-hour swamp walks cost USh30,000 per person, including binoculars and gumboots.

But the cultural activities like **village walks** (per person USh20,000) and **interpretive meals** (per person USh10,000, book in advance), where your hosts share the stories behind the local food they serve you, are the real draw for many travellers. **Tinka's Homestay** (☎ 0772-468113; per person incl full board USh30,000) by the visitor centre lets you continue your cultural immersion.

Bigodi is 6km south of Kibale's Kanyanchu visitor centre. Take a Kamwenge-bound minibus (USh5000, 45 minutes) from Fort Portal.

Toro-Semliki Wildlife Reserve

Sightings of lions, leopards, elephants and buffaloes are all possible on a **game drive** (ranger-guide US$20) through the savannah at this lovely but seldom-visited **reserve** (☎ 0382-276424; admission US$25, saloon cars local/foreign registered USh20,000/US$50, trucks & 4WDs, local/foreign registered USh30,000/US$50). You're less likely to have success **chimp tracking** (per person US$30) here than at Kibale Forest National Park, but when you do find them the thinner forest means the views are superior. Rangers also lead **nature walks** (per person US$10) to scenic spots, and a **Lake Albert boat trip** (the lodge charges US$180 for a half-day; fishermen charge about US$90) will usually reveal hippos, crocodiles and shoebill storks.

There's a simple **UWA Camp** (campsites USh15,000, bandas without bathroom, s/d USh10,000/15,000) on Lake Albert at Ntoroko (this village has simple restaurants) and also camping at the headquarters near Karugutu. **Semliki Safari Lodge** (☎ 0414-251182; www.wildplacesafrica.com; s/d incl full board & game drives US$410/720; P ⛴) provides luxury tents, but you have to choose sunrise or sunset views.

The headquarters is 30km from Fort Portal. Minibuses and pick-ups from Fort Portal to Ntoroko (USh5000, three hours) pass by.

Semuliki National Park

The Semliki Valley is a little corner of DRC poking into Uganda. Here the steaming jungle of the Ituri Forest collides with the higher plateau that crosses East Africa. Most people visit the **national park** (☎ 0382-276424; admission US$25) for the beautiful and bizarre **hot springs** (guided walk per person US$10) near Sempaya Gate, but the two trails cutting through the forest to the border-forming Semliki River are fun and also very rewarding for birders. Outside the park is the **Batwa pygmy village** of Bundimusoli. Village visits (USh15,000 per person), which include singing and dancing, are arranged at the **'Office of the King of Batwa'** (☎ 0382-277215) in Ntandi, 5km past the hot springs.

The simple **Bumaga Campsite** (campsites USh15,000, r USh20,000) is 2km past the springs. There's a lovely elevated dining area, but you should bring your own food.

The park is just 52km from Fort Portal, but plan on two hours to reach it by car in the dry season. Minibuses and pick-ups between Fort Portal and Bundibugyo pass the park (USh6000, 2½ hours) and if you leave early you should be able to make it a day trip.

KASESE

pop 67,000

Kasese is the uninspiring base for climbing the Rwenzoris, otherwise there's no reason to stop here. But, if you must, nearby Kilembe is an interesting town to walk through with all the old mining equipment and company housing.

Mt Rwenzori Lodge (☎ 0772-930265; Alexander St; r without bathroom USh5000-10,000) is better than the budget average for Kasese, while the **White House Hotel** (☎ 0782-536263; whitehse_hotel@ yahoo.co.uk; Henry Bwambale Rd; s/d without bathroom USh15,000/23,000, r USh30,000; 🖳) is the pick of the pack in the midrange. Three kilometres outside town, **Hotel Margherita** (☎ 0483-444015; s/d US$70/95, ste US$139-189, all incl breakfast; P 🖳) is Kasese's best hotel due to lack of competition.

The quickest connection to Kampala (USh15,000, five hours) is via Fort Portal (USh4000, one hour). Buses and minibuses also run to Mbarara (USh10,000, three hours). For Kabale (USh18,000, seven hours) two buses pass the roundabout on the highway around 8am.

RWENZORI MOUNTAINS NATIONAL PARK

The fabled, mist-covered Mountains of the Moon, the Rwenzoris feature many peaks permanently covered by snow and glaciers. Hiking here is tough, and the mountains have a well-deserved reputation for being very wet, but unlike Kili or Kenya, you're likely to have the trails all to yourself. Mt Stanley (5109m) is Africa's third-highest mountain.

Hiking

There are two choices for hiking. The classic six-day Central Circuit starts at Nyakalengija and is controlled by **Rwenzori Mountaineering Services** (RMS; Kampala ☎ 0414-237497; UWA compound) Kasese (☎ 0483-444936; Rwenzori Rd; ☼ 8am-7pm) Nyakalengija (☎ 0782-586304), which doesn't have a stellar reputation. Check all the gear carefully before setting out and don't let your guide pressure you to move faster than you are comfortable with. The US$780 cost (US$990 if you want to summit Margherita Peak, the highest peak on Mt Stanley) covers everything, including porters.

An alternative is **Rwenzori Trekking Services** (☎ 0774-114499; www.backpackers.co.ug), part of Backpackers Hostel in Kampala. This company has just begun operating on a different route out of Kilembe. While it is new, reports indicate high standards. Three-/five-day hikes cost US$220/400 per person with a group of three or more, while 10-day summits of Margherita and Alexandra Peaks start at US$1270.

The driest times to hike are from late December to mid-March and from mid-June to mid-August, though you may get the enjoyment of snow in the wet seasons. Both companies hire climbing and cold-weather gear. Serious peak-baggers can talk to Adrift (p831) about hiring experienced and certified guides to join the trip.

If you just want a sample of the terrain, the lodges following offer day trips on the edge of the park.

Sleeping

ourpick **Ruboni Community Campsite** (☎ 0414-501866; www.rainforestuganda.org; campsites USh3000, safari tents USh15,000, bandas USh25,000, all prices per person) Two kilometres from Nyakalengija, this campsite has an attractive setting and comfortable lodging: all profits go towards a health centre, tree-planting projects and more.

Rwenzori Backpackers (☎ 0774-199022; www.backpackers.co.ug; campsites per person USh8000, dm USh15,000, s/d USh20,000/35,000; P) A scenic and peaceful place filling restored miners' housing, located in Kilembe. It's run by Backpackers Hostel in Kampala.

Getting There & Away

Minibuses run from Kasese to Ibanda (USh2000, one hour); from there take a *boda-boda* to Nyakalengija (USh2000). For Kilembe (USh2000, 20 minutes) go to the Shell petrol station on Kilembe Rd.

QUEEN ELIZABETH NATIONAL PARK

The 1978-sq-km **Queen Elizabeth National Park** (☎ 0483-444266; admission per 24hr US$30, saloon cars US$50, trucks & 4WDs US$50; ☼ booking office 6.30am-7pm, park gates 7am-7pm) is one of the most popular in Uganda. Though the wildlife populations remain lower than the top Tanzanian and Kenyan parks, few reserves in the world can boast such a high biodiversity rating, as exemplified by the amazing 610 bird species (more than found in all of Great Britain).

Besides **wildlife drives** (ranger-guides US$20), the park is well worth a visit for a **Kazinga Channel boat trip** (per person US$15; ☼ 9am, 11am, 11.30am, 3pm, 4pm & 5pm) to see the thousands of hippos plus other animals, and a walk through beautiful **Kyambura (Chambura) Gorge** (per person US$50; ☼ 8am & 2pm), a little Eden brimming with primates, including one difficult-to-find habituated troop of chimpanzees. The remote **Ishasha** sector, in the far south of the park, is famous for its tree-climbing lions.

Sleeping & Eating

MWEYA PENINSULA

Mweya is a great base because many animals roam through here (be careful at night) and you can also watch wildlife along the river down below.

Wildlife Education Centre (dm USh10,000) Known to everyone as the Students' Camp, the park's cheapest beds are here, but it's very basic and usually full.

Mweya Campgrounds (campsites per person USh15,000) Rustic facilities, but superb settings.

Mweya Hostel (☎ 0414-373050; s/d without bathroom USh57,000/84,000, q USh168,000, 3-bedroom cottages USh252,000, all incl breakfast) Still basic, but not with a capital B like the Students' Camp, and shockingly overpriced.

UGANDA

Mweya Safari Lodge (☎ 0312-260260; www.mweya lodge.com; s US$125, d US$220-260, ste US$285, cottages US$500-750, all incl breakfast; P ⊠ ⊡ ⊠) This large outfit has excellent views and is good value by national-park-lodge standards. Sitting on the terrace with dinner (buffet USh30,000 to USh35,000) or a cold beer at sunset is perfect.

Tembo Canteen (meals USh4000-8000; ⊙ 7.30am-10.30pm) Safari drivers hang out here during the day and park staff kick back at night. There's a pool table and satellite TV.

ELSEWHERE

Ishasha Camp (☎ 0782-308808; campsites per person USh15,000, dm USh10,000, s/d bandas USh15,000/20,000) This basic and blissfully remote set-up is small, so beds fill fast. Local meals are sometimes available for USh7000 to USh10,000.

Kingfisher Lodge Kichwamba (☎ 0774-159579; www.kingfishersafaris.net; s/d/tr US$75/154/185; P ⊡ ⊠) This little compound of whitewashed and thatched-roof towers is as lovely as it is unique. It's perched on the edge of the Kichwamba Escarpment (along the Kasese–Mbarara highway, fifteen minutes' drive south of Kyambura Gorge) and has some of Uganda's best vistas. Rooms are smallish but still good and most come with their own porches.

Getting There & Away

The main entrance is Katunguru Gate on the Kasese–Mbarara highway, very near the small village of Katunguru, where the bridge crosses the Kazinga Channel. From here it's 21km to Mweya where the visitor centre is found and the Kazinga Channel boat trips start (though Adrift, p831, plans to offer channel trips from Katunguru). Minibuses between Kasese (USh3000, one hour) and Mbarara (USh9000, three hours) stop at Katunguru and hitching to/from Mweya isn't too tough. If traffic is thin, chartering a vehicle costs USh25,000 to USh30,000.

Kyambura Gorge is 8km south of Katunguru on the highway, then 2km west down a dirt road. Ishasha is 100km from Mweya down a pretty good road in the far south of the park, but you can't realistically hitch here. From Ishasha, you can drive south for Butogota and Bwindi Impenetrable National Park in about two hours in the dry season.

Every safari company comes here. Backpackers Hostel (p825), Red Chilli

Hideaway (p825) and Great Lakes Safaris (p848) are the best budget providers.

BWINDI IMPENETRABLE NATIONAL PARK

Home to almost half the world's remaining mountain gorillas (about 340), **Bwindi** (☎ 0486-424121; admission per 24hr US$30; ⊙ park office 7.45am-5pm) is one of Africa's most famous national parks. Penetrating the 'Impenetrable Forest' is no picnic, as the terrain is improbably steep and the foliage unforgiving, but what a reward. All hardships are forgotten in an instant with the first glimpse of gorillas in their mountain kingdom.

Bwindi is more than just gorillas, however: both the scenery and the biodiversity are incredible. The 120 species of mammals is more than any of Uganda's other national parks, though sightings are less common because of the dense rainforest. And we do mean rainforest; up to 2.5m of rain falls here annually.

The headquarters is at Buhoma on the northern edge of the park; most of the gorilla visits start from here and most of the accommodation is here, too. Another good base camp is Nkuringo in the south, a *very* long way by road from Buhoma.

Activities

Bwindi has six habituated gorilla groups: four at and near Buhoma and two at Nkuringo. Demand for **gorilla-tracking permits** (per person incl park entry US$500) far exceeds supply, so book through the UWA office (p823) in Kampala or a reputable tour operator as far in advance as possible. For last-minute permits, check at the backpacker places in Kampala and Jinja, where safari companies sell excess permits. Cancellations and no-shows are rare, but you can get on the waitlist at the park office.

Other options are **forest walks** (per person US$10) in the park and a variety of **community walks** (per person USh15,000-30,000) in the surrounding villages and farms.

Sleeping & Eating

Bwindi has more beds than gorilla permits, but prices are higher than elsewhere in Uganda.

BUHOMA

Buhoma Community Rest Camp (☎ 0772-384965; buhomacommunity@yahoo.com; campsites per person US$5, dm US$13, s/d without bathroom US$35/70, s/d US$47/94) Enjoying a beautiful setting near the park headquarters, this community-run lodge remains popular even though its prices have shot up in recent years. *Bandas* (thatched-roof huts) and safari tents are spread out on a hill heading down the valley, and the best are at the bottom, right near the jungle. Breakfast is US$5 and a set four-course dinner is US$10.

Jungle View Lodge (☎ 0782-494823; r without bathroom USh20,000) Many safari drivers stay here. Rooms are simple, but cleanliness comes standard. There's a 1st-floor bar serving local meals (USh4000 to USh5000).

Silverback Lodge (☎ 0414-258273; www.geolodges africa.com; s/d incl full board US$250/380; **P**) The isolated location earns you Buhoma's best Bwindi views. The seven rooms are small but stylish and service is superb. Set-menu four-course meals cost USh30,000.

NKURINGO

our pick **Nkuringo Gorilla Campsite** (☎ 0754-805580; www.nkuringocampsite.com; campsites per person USh8000, s/d without bathroom USh22,000/35,000) Facilities are fairly basic, but the staff makes you feel like guests instead of customers, and the views are amazing. They're especially evocative with clouds floating between the peaks: that whole *Gorillas in the Mist* thing. Choose a hotel-style room, safari tent or traditionally built *banda*.

Getting There & Away
BUHOMA

Getting to Buhoma can be complicated. The first step is Butogota. There are trucks between Kabale and Butogota (USh20,000, four hours) on Tuesday, Friday and occasionally other days. Otherwise, take a Kihihi-bound vehicle as far as Kanyantorogo (USh15,000, three hours) and catch another vehicle to Butogota (USh3000, 30 minutes). The fastest way from Kampala is by bus to Kihihi (USh16,000, eight hours) and then a pick-up or shared taxi (USh4000, 1½ hours) to Buhoma.

Taxis from Butogota and Buhoma (USh2000, one hour) are infrequent, except on Thursday and Saturday. Special-hires will be USh30,000 and *boda-bodas* half that.

NKURINGO

Trucks travel between Kisoro and Nkuringo (USh4000, three to four hours) on Monday and Thursday, leaving Nkuringo around 8am and returning about 3pm. Other times you can try to hitch, but there's not much traffic. Special-hires costs USh60,000, or USh100,000

if you want the driver to wait and take you back in the afternoon. *Boda-boda* drivers charge USh25,000, but it's a long, arse-rattling ride. You can also just walk. **Nkuringo Walking Safaris** (☎ 0774-805580; www.nkuringowalkingsafaris.com; per 2 people from US$70) will lead you there with a three-hour paddle across Lake Mutanda and a 19km hike through the countryside.

Walking is the best way to get between Nkuringo and Buhoma, and it's mostly downhill in this direction. It's 6km along the road and then 14km on an easy trail through the jungle. As this is through the park, you need to pay the park fee and US$10 for a ranger-guide just as if this were a regular forest walk.

KABALE
pop 44,000

While Uganda's highest (2000m) town is nothing to write home about, it's the gateway to Lake Bunyonyi, the top spot for serious rest and relaxation in Uganda, and a good staging post for trips to Bwindi Impenetrable National Park.

Information

It can't actually book gorilla permits, but UWA's **Gorilla Parks Information Office** (☎ 0486-424121; Kisoro Rd; ☉ 8am-5pm) can help with transport and anything else relating to Bwindi Impenetrable or Mgahinga Gorilla National Parks.

Sights & Activities

Even if you're just planning on passing through town, make some time to visit the **Home of Edirisa** (☎ 0752-558222; www.edirisa.org; Muhumuza Rd; admission USh4000; ☉ 9am-11pm), a little museum with a replica traditional homestead, built of sticks and papyrus, showing how the local Bakiga people lived a century ago. Also while here, you can enquire about volunteer opportunities and grab the free *Lake Bunyonyi & Kabale In Your Pocket* guide.

Sleeping & Eating

With beautiful Lake Bunyonyi just a short hop away, few travellers stay in Kabale very long.

Home of Edirisa (☎ 0752-558222; www.edirisa.org; Muhumuza Rd; dm USh5000, s without bathroom USh8000, d with/without bathroom USh20,000/15,000; ☐ ☎) It's a hostel, museum, restaurant, cultural centre, fair-trade craft shop and a great place to hang out no matter which of these components tickles your fancy.

UGANDA

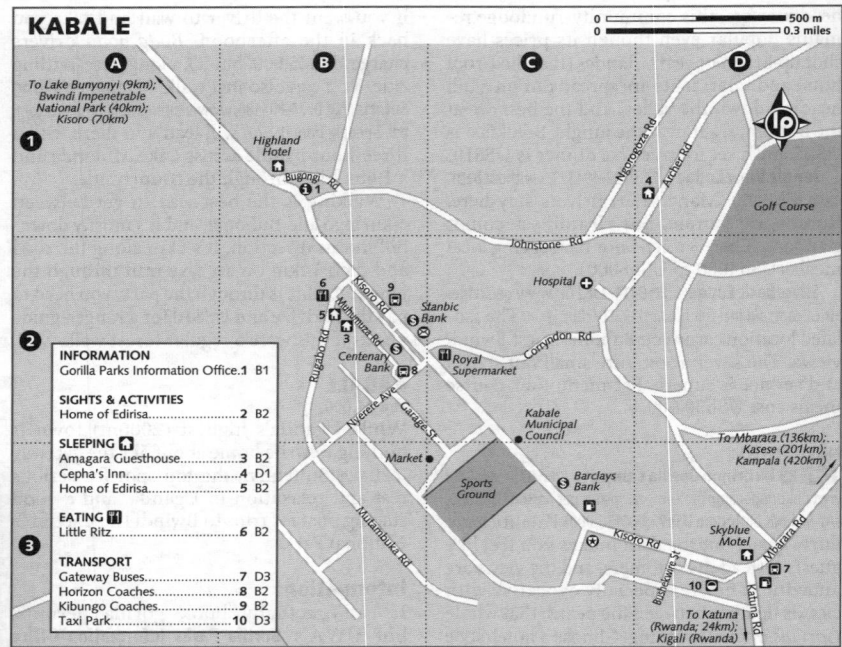

KABALE

INFORMATION
Gorilla Parks Information Office.**1** B1

SIGHTS & ACTIVITIES
Home of Edirisa........................**2** B2

SLEEPING
Amagara Guesthouse................**3** B2
Cepha's Inn.............................**4** D1
Home of Edirisa......................**5** B2

EATING
Little Ritz..............................**6** B2

TRANSPORT
Gateway Buses.......................**7** D3
Horizon Coaches.....................**8** B2
Kibungo Coaches.....................**9** B2
Taxi Park...............................**10** D3

Amagara Guesthouse (☎ 0772-959667; Muhumuza Rd; s USh17,000, d USh22,000-32,000; 🖳 🛜) The people behind Byoona Amagara on Lake Bunyonyi also run this little spot with simple, meticulously clean rooms.

Cepha's Inn (☎ 0486-422097; birungicephas@ yahoo.com; Archer Rd; s USh40,000, d USh60,000-80,000, ste USh120,000; 🅿 🛢) Fills two colourful buildings on the hill above town and offers good value.

You can eat well at Home of Edirisa and Amagara Guesthouse, which have a mix of local and international favourites in the USh3000 to USh10,000 range. Same for the more atmospheric **Little Ritz** (Rugabo Rd; mains USh2000-6000; ⏱ 7.30am-midnight) where you can sit beside the fireplace or on the balcony.

Getting There & Away

There are frequent buses to Kampala (USh20,000, eight hours), most picking up passengers by the Skyblue Motel at the main junction. The Post Bus departs around 7am.

It's easiest to find rides to Kisoro (USh10,000, two hours) in front of the

Highland Hotel on the northwest side of town. Horizon and Gateway buses depart for Fort Portal (USh20,000, eight hours), via Queen Elizabeth National Park (USh16,000, six hours), at 2am and 3am respectively.

For all the difficult details on getting from Kabale to Bwindi Impenetrable National Park, see p837. Transport to the Rwandan border at Katuna is frequent: see p847.

LAKE BUNYONYI

Lake Bunyonyi (Place of Many Little Birds) is undoubtedly the loveliest lake in Uganda. Its contorted shore encircles 29 islands, and the steep surrounding hillsides are intensively terraced.

The guesthouses offer a variety of walking and boat trips, the most intriguing being Home of Edirisa's (p837) three-day **canoe trekking** (per person for a group of 4 USh250,000). If you hire a dugout canoe on your own, practise before paddling off on an ambitious trip since many travellers end up going round in circles, doing what's known locally as the *muzungu* (foreigner) corkscrew.

Sleeping & Eating

our pick **Byoona Amagara** (☎ 0752-652788; www.lakebunyonyi.net; campsites USh6000, dm USh11,000-13,500, geodomes USh19,000-26,000, cabins USh27,000, cottages USh130,000, all rates per person; P 🖳) This island-set, community-project funded and totally solar-powered place offers a unique choice of rooms, most built of natural materials. A motorboat to the island costs USh15,000 one way and the dugout is free *to* the island but USh3000 per person heading back. There's secure parking in Rutinda. Private rooms have a two-person minimum June to September, Christmas and Easter, plus a 50% single supplement other times.

Kalebas Camp (☎ 0312-294894; campsites per person USh10,000, s/d safari tents USh25,000/35,000, s/d USh35,000/45,000; P) A pleasant place with good-value accommodation and tasty wood-fired pizzas. It's very near the road, but there's not much traffic at night.

Bunyonyi Overland Resort (☎ 0486-426016; www.bunyonyioverland.com; campsites/tent hire per person US$6/10, s/d safari tents US$20/30, s/d without bathroom US$23/30, s/d cottages US$20/40, f cottages with kitchen US$100; P 🖳) Sculpted gardens make this more attractive than most backpacker pads, but the vibe (and surfeit of overland trucks) is the same. Ride the shuttle (USh5000) from Kabale's Highland Hotel at 9.30am and 4.30pm and maybe for free around noon.

Arcadia Cottages (☎ 0486-423400; arcadiacottages@yahoo.com; campsite USh20,000 per tent, bandas s/d USh80,000/120,000; P 🖳) Set high above the lake, Arcadia has some intoxicating views over dozens of islands *way* down below and of the Virunga volcanoes in the distance.

Getting There & Away

Many pick-ups (USh1500) and shared taxis (USh2000) travel the 9km to the lake from Kabale's main market on Monday and Friday. Transport is rare on other days, so you'll probably have to choose between a special-hire (USh13,000) and a *boda-boda* (USh4000).

KISORO

pop 13,000

Kisoro is a one-horse town at the south-western tip of Uganda and the base for trips to Mgahinga Gorilla National Park to the south and Parc National des Virunga at Djomba just over the border in DRC. You won't be here long before would-be guides will approach you about **snake safaris** on Lake Mutanda (don't believe their hype, but on sunny days you might meet a 2m-to-3m python) and visits to **Batwa pygmy villages**. Not all guides are reliable, so get recommendations from fellow travellers or the **Mgahinga Gorilla National Park Office** (☎ 0486-430098; Main St; ☽ 8am-5pm).

Sleeping & Eating

Shobore Rutare Site Lodge (☎ 0782-414000; Bunagana Rd; s/d without bathroom USh6000/10,000) If price is all that matters, this pretty clean place is a good choice.

Lake Mutanda Eco-Camp (☎ 0774-519086; mecc_kisoro@yahoo.com; campsite per person USh6000, safari tents USh30,000, log cabins USh40,000) Also known as Sheba's, this is an extremely peaceful, community-run spot next to a papyrus swamp on Lake Mutanda, 4km north of town. *Boda-bodas* cost about USh3000.

Countryside Guesthouse (☎ 0782-412741; countrysideguesthouse@yahoo.com; Bunagana Rd; campsite US$6, s/d without bathroom USh10,000/20,000, r USh25,000, s/d/tw USh25,000/35,000/40,000 incl breakfast; P) A simple, friendly place with high standards for budget lodging, this is the Kisoro contact for Nkuringo Walking Safaris (p837) and it has reasonably priced car hire, too.

Travellers Rest Hotel (☎ 0772-533029; www.gorillatours.com; Mahuabura Rd; s/d/tr incl breakfast US$60/70; P) Through various little touches, this otherwise simple hotel, which Dian Fossey called her 'second home', has become a lovely little oasis. Reserve a seat for the buffet dinner (USh24,000) before 3pm.

Coffee Matters (Bunagana Rd; cappuccinos USh2000, mains USh3000-5000) Locally grown coffees, fruit smoothies and simple meals.

Getting There & Away

Several bus companies make the long run to Kampala (USh20,000 to USh25,000, eight to 11 hours), the fastest of which is Chuho Coaches Express (it has its own bus station in Kampala near the National Mosque), which makes the trip nonstop. Minibuses to Kabale (USh10,000, two hours) are frequent. See p847 for details about crossing to Rwanda at the nearby Cyanika border.

MGAHINGA GORILLA NATIONAL PARK

Although it's the smallest of Uganda's national parks at just 34 sq km, with the towering Virunga volcanoes providing a dramatic backdrop, **Mgahinga Gorilla National Park**

(☎ 0486-430098; admission per 24hr US$30) punches above its weight.

Activities

As in Bwindi Impenetrable National Park, there's **gorilla tracking** (incl park entrance fee US$500) here, though not all the time because the habituated family sometimes ducks over the mountains into Rwanda or DRC. Make your reservations by calling the park office in Kisoro no more than two weeks in advance and then pay at the park on the day of your trip. Permits for one or two people are often available with just a few days' wait.

Mgahinga also serves up some challenging but rewarding **hikes** (per person US$20) through the otherworldly afro-alpine moorland atop its three volcanoes, and tours of **Garama Cave** (per person US$10), which was once a haven for Batwa pygmies. Plus **golden-monkey tracking** (per person US$20) is almost as fun as hanging out with the big boys.

Sleeping & Eating

Amajambere Iwacu Community Campground (☎ 0382-278464; www.amajamberecamp.org; campsites per person USh6000, dm USh10,000, bandas with/without bathroom USh45,000/30,000) A friendly place with a variety of rooms and a nice verandah for soaking up choice views of the Virungas. It's just outside the park gate and the peace and quiet here is a bonus. Proceeds fund school projects in the area.

Getting There & Away

There's no public transport along the rough 14km track between Kisoro and the park; and traffic is too light to rely on hitching if you must get there early in the morning. Taking a *boda-boda*/special-hire costs about USh10,000/25,000.

SSESE ISLANDS

While hardly the Bahamas of Lake Victoria, this group of 84 islands along the northwestern shore does boast the best beaches in Uganda. A popular destination into the 1990s, these days most travellers chill out at Lake Bunyonyi instead. Rampant deforestation is hurting the scenery, but it's still a beautiful area.

The only full-on town is Kalangala, on Buggala Island, above Lutoboka Bay where the ferry lands and most of the resorts sit. There's a post office, internet cafe and a Stanbic Bank, which changes cash, but has no ATM.

Sleeping & Eating

Panorama Cottages (☎ 0772-406371; campsites per person USh5000, tent hire USh10,000, s bandas USh30,000-50,000, d bandas USh35,000-55,000; **P**) These large, clean *bandas* on Buggala Island are a five-minute walk from the beach.

Mirembe Resort (☎ 0392-772703; www.mirembe resort.com; campsites per person USh15,000, safari tent per person USh25,000, s/d/tr USh60,000/100,000/130,000, s/d/tr cottages USh80,000/120,000/150,000, all incl breakfast; **P** 🖳) The last resort on Lutoboka Bay is more peaceful than its neighbours.

our pick **Banda Island Resort** (☎ 0772-222777; banda.island@gmail.com; campsites per person USh30,000, dm USh40,000, d with/without bathroom USh120,000/100,000, all incl 'very full board') This ever-evolving *Gilligan's Island*–like place on Banda Island sits on a big beach. The accommodation is comfortable, the food is good and Dom is full of entertaining stories. Text messages work better than phone calls.

Getting There & Away

The MV *Kalangala* ferry (2nd-/1st-class seats USh10,000/USh14,000, vehicles USh50,000) from Nakiwogo, near Entebbe, departs from the mainland at 2pm daily and leaves the island at 8am.

For Banda Island, Dom from Banda Island Resort can send his boat to meet the ferry for USh50,000. You could also take the almost-daily small rickety wooden boats (USh10,000 per person, three to four hours) direct to the island from Kasenyi (near Entebbe, a 30-minute minibus ride from Kampala's old taxi park; USh3000). Schedules are fickle, so check with the resort for the latest.

From the west, minibuses connect Nyendo (3km east of Masaka) to Kalangala (USh9000, time varies according to the wait for the ferry) several times a day via the ferry at Bukakata.

NORTHERN UGANDA

ZIWA RHINO SANCTUARY

The Big Five is back. This private **reserve** (☎ 0772-713410; www.rhinofund.org; adult/child US$20/10, guide US$15; ⏱ 8am-5pm, last tracking starts 3pm), halfway between Kampala and Murchison Falls National Park, holds half a dozen southern white rhinos and after a drive into the bush (vehicle hire US$20 if needed), guides will walk you near them.

Book **accommodation** (campsites per person US$12, s/d without bathroom US$15/20, s/d with bathroom US$40/20; ⓟ) in advance. All buses from Kampala heading to Gulu or Masindi pass nearby. Get off at Nakitoma (USh9000, three hours) and take a *boda-boda* for USh1500.

MURCHISON FALLS NATIONAL PARK

Uganda's largest (at 3893 sq km; 5081 sq km with the adjoining Bugungu and Karuma reserves) and most popular **national park** (☎ 0772-746287; admission per 24hr US$30, saloon cars US$50, trucks & 4WDs US$50; ☉ booking office 7am-7pm, park gates 7am-6pm) is the best all-rounder in Uganda, with animals in plentiful supply and the raging Murchison Falls a sight to behold. Once described as the most spectacular thing to happen to the Nile along its 6700km length, the 50m-wide river is squeezed through a 6m gap and it shoots through this narrow gorge with explosive force.

During the 1960s, Murchison was one of Africa's best wildlife parks, full of animals and safari trucks. It suffered drastic poaching during Uganda's dark years, but its recovery has been successful. Unfortunately Murchison

is now under threat from an aggressive push for oil exploration.

Activities

A must at Murchison is the **launch trip** (per person US$15-20) to the base of the falls. The three-hour ride from Paraa goes mornings and afternoons and passes hippos, crocodiles, buffaloes and birds galore, plus usually elephants, too. It's possible to be dropped at the base of the falls for a spectacular **hike to the top** (per person US$10), which must be arranged the day before. If you take the morning launch, you can ride back in the afternoon; or camp and come back another day. It also costs US$10 if you drive to the top and just stay five minutes.

Also fruitful for wildlife and scenery are **delta cruises** (per person US$40, minimum 7) down to where the Nile empties into Lake Albert, **sunset cruises** (per person US$10, minimum 4) and **game drives** (ranger-guides US$20, vehicle hire US$160-300) north of the river where lions, leopards, spotted hyenas, elephants and giraffes all come out to play.

There's also **chimpanzee tracking** (per person US$40, ages 15yr & over only) of a habituated community at **Kaniyo Pabidi** on the main park road,

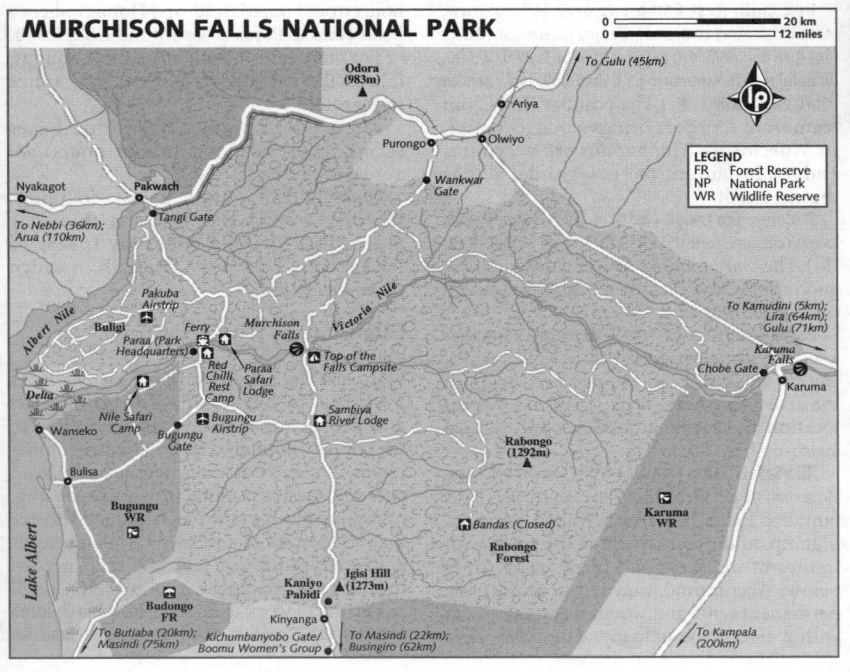

MURCHISON FALLS NATIONAL PARK

0 — 20 km
0 — 12 miles

LEGEND
FR Forest Reserve
NP National Park
WR Wildlife Reserve

To Gulu (45km)
Odora (983m)
Ariya
Purongo
Olwiyo
Wankwar Gate
Nyakagot
Pakwach
Tangi Gate
To Nebbi (36km); Arua (110km)
Pakuba Airstrip
Albert Nile
Buligi
Ferry
Murchison Falls
Victoria Nile
Paraa (Park Headquarters)
Top of the Falls Campsite
Red Chilli Rest Camp
Paraa Safari Lodge
Sambiya River Lodge
Delta
Nile Safari Camp
Bugungu Airstrip
Wanseko
Bugungu Gate
Bulisa
Rabongo (1292m)
To Kamudini (5km); Lira (64km); Gulu (71km)
Karuma Falls
Chobe Gate
Karuma
Bugungu WR
Bandas (Closed)
Rabongo Forest
Karuma WR
Budongo FR
Kaniyo Pabidi
Igisi Hill (1273m)
Kinyanga
Lake Albert
To Butiaba (20km); Masindi (75km)
Kichumbanyobo Gate/ Boomu Women's Group
To Masindi (22km); Busingiro (62km)
To Kampala (200km)

UGANDA

29km north of Masindi. Two lucky visitors are allowed to spend a whole day for US$100 per person. Also worthwhile here are the **forest walks** (1½/4hr US$10/15), which pass through East Africa's last remaining mahogany forest. Book through Great Lakes Safaris (p848).

With gargantuan Nile perch in the river, **sport fishing** (permits for 1/2/3 days US$70/120/150) is also popular.

Sleeping & Eating

our pick **Boomu Women's Group** (☎ 0772-448950; www.boomuwomensgroup.org; campsites per person USh4000, s/d bandas without bathroom USh10,000/20,000) Just outside the Kichumbanyobo Gate, this small set-up with simple thatched-room *bandas* (some with traditional mud walls) offers a chance to learn how rural Ugandans live, and your money funds a preschool. The fascinating cooking tour (USh8000 per person) lets you follow the making of your meal starting in the farm field. Call or send a text message and a *boda-boda* will be sent to pick you up in Masindi for USh5000.

Top of the Falls Campsite (per person USh15,000) On the river near the falls, it has pit toilets and nothing else.

Red Chilli Rest Camp (☎ 0772-509150; www. redchillihideaway.com; campsites per person USh10,000, tent hire USh5000, d/q safari tents USh35,000/70,000, tw bandas without bathroom USh45,000, tw/q bandas USh70,000/120,000; ℗) The popular Red Chilli team from Kampala brings a budget option to Murchison. The *bandas* are very nice, and the restaurant-bar is set under a huge thatched roof.

Budongo Eco Lodge (☎ 0414-267153; www.uganda lodges.com; dm/s/d/tr US$15/50/85/100, all incl breakfast; ℗) The only lodging at Kaniyo Pabidi has good cabins and dorms. A luxury lodge will open next door.

Paraa Safari Lodge (☎ 0312-260260; www.paraa lodge.com; s/d/ste/cottages incl full board US$140/220/280/509; ℗ 🖳 🖾) On the northern bank of the river, this hotel-style lodge has a great location and excellent facilities, including a swim-up bar.

Nile Safari Camp (☎ 0414-258273; www.geolodges africa.com; s/d incl full board US$165/280; ℗ 🖾) This fantastic lodge has an unrivalled position, high up on the south bank of the river, with tonnes of monkeys and birds in the trees below. Accommodation is in comfortable permanent tents and wooden cottages, each with a river-view balcony. The roads here are rough, but the lodge can pick you up in Paraa by boat.

Book ahead and you can **camp** (per person US$45) at Delta Point overlooking Lake Albert.

Getting There & Away

The park headquarters is at Paraa, on the southern bank of the Victoria Nile. By car from Masindi there's the choice of the direct route through the Kichumbanyobo Gate or the longer but more scenic route heading west to Lake Albert and then entering via the western Bugungu Gate. With security now restored to northern Uganda, the northern gates are viable options again.

There's no public transport, but hitching is possible. It's easiest if you ask other tourists in Masindi the night before. Park vehicles travel from Masindi several times a week, but they're often full. With a bit of bargaining you can charter a special-hire taxi for around USh120,000 including fuel and the driver's park fees. Rounding out the day with a wildlife drive will bump the price up to at least USh180,000.

Besides hitching, the cheapest way into the park is to get to Bulisa (USh10,000, 2½ to three hours from both Masindi and Hoima) where a *boda-boda* to Paraa costs around USh35,000.

For more information on all these options, talk to the friendly staff at the park office in Masindi.

Kampala–Masindi buses/minibuses (USh12,000/13,000, 3½ to four hours) are available all day.

Most budget travellers just do things the easy way and come on a three-day tour with Red Chilli Hideaway (p825) or Backpackers Hostel (p825), both of which earn rave reviews.

GULU

pop 142,000

Northern Uganda has suffered many attacks from the LRA, but these days it's growing fast and people are arriving from elsewhere in the country hoping to cash in on the coming boom. But even as the internally displaced persons' camps around town are closing, many people remain too frightened to return to their land; and many orphans never got an education and lack any skills needed to land a job. An alphabet soup of NGOs still has plenty of work to do here. **Invisible Children** (☎ 0471-432583; www.invisiblechildren.com; 101 Acholi Rd) can recommend short- and long-term volunteer opportunities in the area and will take you to visit the schools they work with.

According to locals, the cheap hotels inside the bus park cannot be considered secure. The charity **HEALS** (☎ 0774-099919; dm USh10,000) on the city's outskirts has two simple dorm rooms. **Hotel Binen** (☎ 0772-405038; Coronation Rd; r without bathroom USh16,000), near the bus station, is far less tatty than most of the competition at this price range. Bright, spotless and friendly, **JoJo's Palace** (☎ 0471-435770; Market St; s/d without bathroom USh25,000/35,000, s/d USh35,000/50,000) is the best-value option in town. All proceeds from the **Kope Café** (☎ 0777-649558; Olya Rd; mains USh4000-6000; ⏰ 7.30am-late), a Western-style coffeehouse south of the market, go to charity.

Frequent buses and minibuses run to Kampala (USh20,000, five hours) all day long. There's also a Gulu–Kampala Post Bus. Minibuses to Masindi (USh15,000, four hours) are rare, so it's usually quicker to go to Kafu Junction on the main highway and catch a connection there.

OVERLAND TO KIDEPO VALLEY NATIONAL PARK

For those hardy souls heading to Kidepo Valley National Park without using an airport, there are two possible routes. Both routes are long and at times difficult journeys, but this is one place where travel is its own reward.

All roads past the gateway towns of Mbale and Gulu are dirt, and require 4WD. There are simple hotels along the way and Stanbic Bank has ATMs in Kotido and Kitgum, but they're often offline.

Eastern Route

This journey takes you though the wilds of Karamojaland where many of the cattle-herding Karamojong people still wear traditional dress (similar to the Maasai) and AK-47s are as common as walking sticks. They're viewed with fear and disdain (because of their clothing) by most Ugandans, but their pride is unmistakable.

Begin by heading to Kotido where Omara Faustine at the **Uganda Wildlife Authority Information Office** (☎ 0774-209002; ⏰ 7am-8pm Mon-Fri & most weekends) can give you onward travel advice. Gateway has daily buses to Kotido (USh30,000, 15 hours), departing from Kampala's new bus park at 5.30am and passing through Mbale (USh20,000) at about 9am. From Kotido there are frequent trucks and pick-ups to Kaabong (USh5000, two to three hours). Then jump on the less frequent trucks to Karenga (USh7000, two to three hours) and get off at what locals call 'Tsetse Control', just 2km from Nataba Gate. If you've made arrangements with Omara back in Kotido, a vehicle will be waiting to ferry you the final 14km to the park headquarters. Or, continue to Karenga (an extra USh3000 and 30 minutes) and get a special-hire (USh40,000) to the park from there.

Northern Route

The shortest and easiest route, and currently the only one to consider if you're driving, runs through Gulu. The first leg is on one of the frequent buses to Kitgum (from Gulu/Kampala USh10,000/25,000, three/eight hours), where UWA recently opened a small office. Up until around midday, trucks head east from Kitgum to Karenga (USh20,000, five to seven hours), 24km from the park's headquarters and lodging area. In Karenga you might get lucky and be able to hitch a ride, but you'll probably need a special-hire (USh40,000).

KIDEPO VALLEY NATIONAL PARK

This lost valley in the extreme northeast has the most stunning scenery in Uganda. The rolling, short-grass savannah of the 1442-sq-km **Kidepo Valley National Park** (admission per 24hr US$30) is ringed by mountains and cut by rocky ridges. Kidepo also harbours many animals found in no other Ugandan national park, including cheetahs, aardwolves, caracals, Rothschild's giraffes, ostriches and Abyssinian ground hornbills, not to mention the copious elephants, zebras (these

> **WARNING: SECURITY IN KARAMOJALAND**
>
> Whether to travel in Uganda's far northeast is not a decision to be made lightly. Groups of Karamojong still sometimes ambush vehicles, and there have even been sniper attacks on the Gateway bus. Incidents, however, are pretty rare and the situation seems to be improving so travelling by public means is possible. Still, it's of paramount importance to enquire about security before setting out and again at every stop. Things can change very fast out here.

lack manes), buffaloes and lions. And many of these, including even the occasional lion, graze and lounge right near the park's accommodation, so you can see a whole lot without going very far: it's a safari from a lounge chair. A top target of **game drives** (per km USh3000-4000, plus guide fee US$20) is Narus Valley where the lions began climbing trees around 2005. **Nature walks** cost US$10 per person and staff can arrange **traditional dance performances**.

UWA's **Apoka Hostel** (campsites per person USh15,000, s/d USh30,000/50,000) offers good *bandas*. Bring your own food. If you want something really special, stay at **Apoka Safari Lodge** (☎ 0414-251182; www.wildplacesafrica.com; s/d incl full board & game drives US$450/810; P ⌷). You must book in advance.

Currently most park visitors fly with **Eagle Air** (☎ 0414-344292; www.flyeagleuganda.com; per group US$2050, plus per person US$270), which only comes on diversion status, arriving on Friday and returning on Monday. See p843 for details on travelling by land.

UGANDA DIRECTORY

ACCOMMODATION

Outside Kampala, single/double rooms without bathroom are available from around USh5000/9000, while rooms with bathroom usually start at USh12,000/16,000. For another USh5000 to USh10,000, breakfast will be included. Modern, more comfortable rooms can be found from USh40,000–50,000. Top-end hotels and lodges start at around US$150 and can go much higher.

Almost every popular destination in Uganda has campsites available, so it's worth carrying a tent if you're on a budget. There are luxury lodges and tented camps with outlandish prices in most of the national parks, and simple campsites and basic *bandas* in all. Hotels range from fleapit to five star, and even in many small towns there's plenty of choice. In and around national parks, book as far in advance as possible during the July to August and December to January high seasons. Keep in mind that in most of Uganda if you ask for a hotel you'll be directed to a restaurant, so if you want a place to sleep enquire about accommodation or lodging.

ACTIVITIES

The white-water rafting at Jinja is world class and other fun activities, such as bungee jump-

ing and horseback riding, have emerged in the area. See p831 for more info.

Hiking Uganda's mountains is another pull. The hard-core head for the Rwenzoris, one of the toughest climbs in Africa, but for something less taxing (on the wallet and legs) try Mt Elgon. Both are gorgeous and lack the crowds of Mts Kilimanjaro and Kenya.

On the wildlife side, gorilla tracking is one of the major drawcards in Uganda and most people consider the US$500 price tag worth it for a once-in-a-lifetime experience, but cheaper chimpanzee tracking is also awe-inspiring. Walking safaris, available in most national parks, can be a bug rush when you get real big wildlife. And, with 1041 species recorded (almost half the total in Africa), Uganda is an amazing birding destinations.

Finally, many popular towns and parks have community projects, such as village walks and cooking tours, available. These can be fascinating insights into the culture around you and also provide important funding for schools and health clinics.

BUSINESS HOURS

Banks Most close at 3pm and don't do business on Saturdays.

Businesses and government offices Generally open between 8.30am and 5pm, often with a short lunchbreak. Saturday hours, usually closing around 1pm, are increasingly common.

Restaurants Local restaurant hours are 7am to 9pm or 10pm, while international-type restaurants are likely to be open from 11.30am to 2.30pm and 5.30pm to 10.30pm.

DANGERS & ANNOYANCES

Except for the far northeast (see p843), and the border areas of the northwest, Uganda is a very safe destination; and even these areas see only sporadic confrontations. Also, although the ongoing conflict in eastern DRC rarely affects Uganda, cross-border incidents have happened in the past, so keep an ear to the ground for information.

EMBASSIES & CONSULATES

Unless otherwise indicated, the following embassies are located in Kampala:

Belgium (Map p824; ☎ 0414-349559; www.diplomatie. be/kampala; Rwenzori House, Lumumba Ave)

Burundi (Map p824; ☎ 0414-235850; Kintu Rd)

Canada (Map p824; ☎ 0414-258141; kampala@canada consulate.ca; Parliament Ave)

DRC (Map pp822-3; ☎ 0414-250099; 20 Philip Rd, Kololo)

France (Map p824; ☎ 0414-304500; 16 Lumumba Ave)

Germany (Map pp822-3; ☎ 0414-501111; www. kampala.diplo.de; 15 Philip Rd, Kololo)

Ireland (Map p824; ☎ 0414-344344; 25 Yusuf Lule Rd, Nakasero)

Kenya (Map p824; ☎ 0414-258235; 41 Nakasero Rd, Nakasero)

Netherlands (Map p824; ☎ 0414-346000; Rwenzori Courts, Lumumba Ave)

Rwanda (Map pp822-3; ☎ 0414-344045; 2 Nakayima Rd, Kamwokya; ⏰ 9.30am-noon Mon-Fri)

Southern Sudan (Map p824; ☎ 0414-271625; 2 Ssezibwa Rd)

Sudan (Map p824; ☎ 0414-230001; 21 Nakasero Rd)

Tanzania (Map p824; ☎ 0414-256272; 6 Kagera Rd)

UK (Map pp822-3; ☎ 0312-312000; http://ukinuganda. fco.gov.uk; Windsor Loop, Kamwokya)

USA (Map pp822-3; ☎ 0414-259791; http://kampala. usembassy.gov; Gaba Rd, Nsambya)

EMERGENCIES

In addition to the following number, you can also dial ☎ 112 from mobile phones.

Police or ambulance ☎ 999

HOLIDAYS

As well as religious holidays on p1140, the principal public holidays in Uganda are :

New Year's Day 1 January
Liberation Day 26 January
International Women's Day 8 March
Labour Day 1 May
Martyrs' Day 3 June
Heroes' Day 9 June
Independence Day 9 October

INTERNET ACCESS

Internet cafes, charging around USh3000 per hour, are ubiquitous in Kampala, and wi-fi hotspots are getting more common. Elsewhere, even most small towns have access for about the same price, although it's usually pretty slow.

MAPS

The Uganda maps by ITMB (1:800,000) and Nelles (1:700,000) will get you where you need to go. Only the latter is available in Uganda.

Being both beautiful and useful, Uganda Maps' national park maps, available in Kampala, are a great buy if you're headed to any of the popular parks.

MONEY

The Ugandan shilling (USh) is a relatively stable currency, though expect the prices given in this chapter to rise since inflation is high. Most tour operators and many hotels quote in US dollars (we quote prices using whichever currency the businesses do), but you can always pay with shillings.

Most banks, even in small remote towns, now have ATMs that accept international credit and debit cards. But, try not to let your cash run low in the assumption that you can easily get more since the system sometimes goes down and machines sometimes run dry. Credit cards (mostly Visa) are fairly widely accepted by businesses that deal with tourists, though commissions can be as high as 10%. And, as elsewhere in Africa, fraud is a concern.

US dollars are the most useful hard currency, though euros and UK pounds sterling are also widely accepted. Bureaux de change offer slightly better rates than banks plus much faster service and longer hours; however, they're rare outside Kampala. For dollars, bills printed before 2000 usually attract a lower rate (often dramatically so) of exchange than newer bills, but the big banks in Kampala don't play this game. Small denominations, however, *always* get a much lower rate than US$50 and US$100 notes. Few places outside Kampala change travellers cheques, but most Stanbic Bank branches handle Amex cheques at a rate less than cash.

Note that UWA accepts US dollars, UK pounds and euros (at fair rates) in either cash or travellers cheques (1% commission).

POST

Kampala's **post office** (Map p824; Kampala Rd) is slow but reliable, while there's a chance things will go missing at provincial branches.

TELEPHONE

Telephone connections, both domestic and international, are pretty good. SIM cards for mobile phones cost around USh2000.

Without your own mobile phone, the cheapest and easiest way to make a local call is from a payphone, which in Uganda is a person with a phone sitting at a little table along the street. Prices are almost always USh200 per unit, but units can range from 30 to 59 seconds, so always ask. For international calls, some internet cafes offer rates ranging from USh200 to USh450 per minute, which is cheaper than using a mobile or a payphone.

If you're calling Uganda from outside the country, drop the '0' at the start of the phone number.

VISAS

Most non-African passport holders require visas. Single-entry tourist visas valid for up to 90 days (but unless you ask for 90, you'll probably be given 30 or 60) cost US$50. It's easiest just to rock up at the airport or border and get one there; no photos needed.

See the boxed text, p737, for information about the forthcoming East African single-tourist visa.

Visa Extensions

Two-month extensions are free at immigration offices in large towns. Bring a copy of your passport and plane ticket, plus a letter explaining why you want to stay and when you'll be leaving.

Visas for Onward Travel

Burundi One-month single-entry visas cost US$40, require two passport photos and are ready the next day.
DRC One-month single-entry visas, costing US$55 and requiring two passport photos, are ready the next day.
Kenya Three-month visas costs US$50 and one passport photo is required. Ready the next day.
Rwanda Visas cost USh110,000, require two passport photos and can be picked up the next day.
Southern Sudan The Government of Southern Sudan issues its own travel permits for people only visiting the bottom half of the country, and they're much easier to come by than a proper Sudanese visa. Bring US$35 and one passport photo in the morning and pick up a one-month single-entry visa in the afternoon.
Sudan A single-entry visa costs USh55,000 (USh270,000 for Americans), but the embassy makes you jump through hoops to get one.
Tanzania Visas are valid for three months, require two passport photos and take 24 hours to issue. Costs vary according to your country of origin.

TRANSPORT IN UGANDA

GETTING THERE & AWAY

Air

Entebbe International Airport (off Map pp822–3), 40km south of the capital, is Uganda's only aerial gateway. It's well connected to Uganda's near neighbours, but usually the rest of the world uses Nairobi as the gateway to East Africa and flights are almost always cheaper and more frequent there.

The main airlines serving Uganda (all with offices in central Kampala):

Air Uganda (Map p824; ☎ 0414-258262; www.air-uganda.com; Parliament Ave)
British Airways (Map p824; ☎ 0414-257414; www.britishairways.com; Ssezibwa Rd)
Brussels Airlines (Map p824; ☎ 0414-234201; www.brusselsairlines.com; Lumumba Ave)
EgyptAir (Map p824; ☎ 0414-341276; www.egyptair.com.eg; Buganda Rd)
Emirates (Map p824; ☎ 0414-770444; www.emirates.com; Kimathi Ave)
Ethiopian Airlines (Map p824; ☎ 0414-345577; www.flyethiopian.com; Kimathi Ave)
Fly540 (Map p824; ☎ 0414-346915; www.fly540.com; Kitante Rd)
Kenya Airways (Map p824; ☎ 0312-360121; www.kenya-airways.com; Parliament Ave)
KLM (Map p824; ☎ 0414-338000; www.klm.com; Parliament Ave)
Rwandair Express (Map p824; ☎ 0414-344851; www.rwandair.com; Garden City, Kitante Rd)
South African Airways (Map p824; ☎ 0414-345772; www.flysaa.com; Portal Ave)

Land

DEMOCRATIC REPUBLIC OF CONGO

Because of the various rebels wreaking havoc just over Uganda's border, don't cross to DRC without checking the security situation very carefully. Except for quick hits from Kisoro to see mountain gorillas in Parc National des Virunga at Djomba, the only

> **DEPARTURE TAX**
>
> The US$40 departure tax on international flights is always included in the ticket price.

safe crossing at the time of research was the well-travelled border at Kasindi between Kasese and Beni, from where it's easy to carry on to Kisangani.

KENYA

There are many direct Nairobi–Kampala buses, most stopping in Jinja, and the journey takes about 12 hours. In recent years, some night buses have been robbed, so it's best to travel during the day. The two best companies, with good air-con buses and reliable service, are **Kampala Coach** (Map p824; ☎ 0711-553377; www.kampalacoach.com; Jinja Rd, Kampala; USh45,000) and **Akamba** (Map p824; ☎ 0414-250412; www.akambabus.com; 28 Dewinton Rd , Kampala; executive/royal USh46,000/64,000). Other companies like **Kalita** (Map p824; ☎ 0312-286137; Namirembe Rd , Kampala) use older, rattle-trap buses but charge as little as USh40,000.

Most buses use the busy crossing at Busia, though a few go the longer route through Malaba. To do the journey in stages, frequent minibuses link Jinja to Busia (USh7000, 2½ hours), and again from Busia to Kisumu.

Hikers in either the Ugandan or Kenyan national parks on Mt Elgon have the option of walking over the border.

RWANDA

The busiest crossing is between Kabale and Kigali via Katuna (Gatuna on the Rwandan side), and it can take over an hour to get through immigration. From Kabale there are shared taxis (USh3000, 30 minutes) to the border and a few minibuses each morning (except Sunday) direct to Kigali. On the Rwandan side, minibuses travel to Kigali (RFr1300, two hours) all day.

Another seldom-used but very convenient border is Cyanika, between Kisoro and Musanze; travel time is 1½ hours. The road on the Ugandan side is very rough and there's no public transport, so take a special-hire (USh20,000) or *boda-boda* (USh5000). Transport on the Rwandan side, however, is frequent and the road is excellent.

There are also many companies with direct Kampala–Kigali buses, a seven- to eight-hour journey. **Jaguar Executive Coaches** (Map pp822-3; ☎ 0414-251855; Namirembe Rd, Kampala; economy/standard/VIP USh20,000/25,000/30,000) is the most comfortable option. **Onatracom** (Map p824; ☎ 0782-867991; Mackay Rd, Kampala; USh18,000) uses older buses but also has morning departures.

SUDAN

Most Kampala–Juba buses travel via Gulu (where they pick up more passengers), crossing at Nimule. All leave in the wee morning hours from Arua Park in Kampala, and most charge about USh80,000, though the big, modern AC buses of **Kampala Coach** (Map p824; ☎ 0711-553377; www.kampalacoach.com; USh100,000) are definitely worth the extra cash on this rough 15-to-20-hour journey.

Government of Southern Sudan travel permits should be available at the border, but it's best to play it safe and get one in Kampala (opposite). Arranging permission to travel by land between northern and southern Sudan is nearly impossible, so Juba is effectively a dead end.

TANZANIA

The principal direct route into Tanzania follows the western side of Lake Victoria from Masaka to Bukoba via Mutukula. It's about six hours by bus from Kampala. Several companies, departing from both of Kampala's bus parks (Map p824), travel this route and charge USH15,000 to USh20,000. Very little transport uses the Nkurungu border due to bad roads.

Intrepid travellers can book overnight passage (USh30,000 paid to the captain, plus USh5000 port fee) on the MV *Umoja* cargo ferry that goes from Kampala's Port Bell to Mwanza about twice a week. Check the schedule at the Marine Services offices (Map p824) on the 2nd floor of the train station in central Kampala.

GETTING AROUND

Air

Eagle Air (Map p824; ☎ 0414-344292; www.flyeagleuganda.com; 11 Portal Ave, Kampala) has scheduled flights to some northern towns and also Kihihi, convenient for Bwindi Impenetrable National Park.

Bus

Uganda is the land of shared minibuses (called taxis or occasionally *matatus*), and except for long distances, these are the most

UGANDA

common vehicles between towns. They're usually jam-packed and the drivers are often maniacs, so crash stories are regular features in the newspapers. Out-of-the-way destinations use saloon-car shared taxis rather than minibuses, and when the roads are really bad pretty much your only choice is sitting atop the assorted cargo in the backs of cargo trucks.

Except for very short distances, you're better off in a standard bus or half-sized 'coaster'. Fares are similar to minibuses (usually a little less), they're safer in a crash and they travel faster due to less-frequent stops.

In addition to the normal private buses, there are Post Buses (Map p824) delivering mail and people between Uganda's main post offices and most large towns. They're slower but safer and sometimes cheaper. They depart from Kampala at 8am and provincial towns as early as 6am.

Car

Roads are good between most major centres in the southern part of the country, but the north lags behind in this regard and here you'll almost always need a 4WD once you get off the sealed roads. With a good driver, saloon cars can handle many of the south's dirt roads.

Due to high taxes and bad roads, car-rental prices are high. Add fuel costs and there'll be some real sticker shock. **Alpha Car Rentals** (Map p824; ☎ 0772-411232; www.alpharentals.co.ug; EMKA House, 3/5 Bombo Rd, Kampala) is a low-priced local outfit, or you could just negotiate with special-hire taxi drivers, though get a recommendation from your hotel to ensure you get a good driver.

Local Transport

Kampala has a local minibus network, as well as 'special-hire' taxis for private trips. Elsewhere you'll have to rely solely on two-wheel taxis, known as *boda-bodas*. Most are still bicycles, though motorcycles are now common. Never hesitate to tell a *boda* driver to slow down if you feel uncomfortable with his driving skills. Outside Kampala, there are few trips within any town that should cost more than USh500.

Tours

Uganda's safari industry is small scale compared with its neighbours, but the companies listed below are excellent for budget and mid-range trips.

Backpackers Hostel (Map pp822-3; ☎ 0772-430587; www.backpackers.co.ug; Natete Rd, Lunguja)

Great Lakes Safaris (Map pp822-3; ☎ 0414-267153; www.safari-uganda.com; Suzie House, Gaba Rd, Kampala) Mixes cultural encounters with wildlife-watching.

Magic Safaris (Map p824; ☎ 0414-342926; www.magic-safaris.com; 3 Parliament Ave, Raja Chambers, Kampala) Offers 'luxury camping' safaris at midrange prices.

Matoke Tours Kampala (Map pp822-3; ☎ 0782-374667; www.travel-uganda.net; 8 Bukoto St); Netherlands (☎ 31-736123364) One of the few quality companies going to Kidepo Valley National Park.

Red Chilli Hideaway (off Map pp822-3; ☎ 0414-223903; www.redchillihideaway.com) in Kampala also offer good budget safaris.

Train

There's always talk about reviving rail travel from Kampala to Jinja and eventually onto and through Kenya, and some day it will probably happen. So, if you're a fan of rail travel, it's worth enquiring about it when you get to Uganda.

Southern Africa

Southern Africa's ambient rhythm swoons visitors into a blissful stupor – change down a gear and immerse yourself in the region's enchanting offerings. This corner of the continent has some of Africa's most accessible wilderness – whether it's the astonishing variety and density of wildlife, dreamy landscapes, or world-class natural features like thundering Victoria Falls, a visit to southern Africa will sear itself into your mind. Enmeshed in this wilderness is a multitude of ethnic groups, many known for their hospitality, and some with direct links to our Stone Age ancestors. If you're serious about the family tree, this is where it all began.

You could spend a lifetime exploring southern Africa. Tour Botswana's wildlife-rich, water-soaked Okavango Delta; hike Namibia's quintessential African landscapes; put a toenail back into Zimbabwe, one of the region's most beautiful and untouristed countries; swim along the uncrowded beaches and romantic offshore islands of Mozambique; romp around some of the most majestic national parks on the continent in Zambia; or just revel in the multitude of pleasures and treasures at your fingertips in South Africa.

Wherever you decide to go, this is home for adventure seekers. Adventure comes in many forms. Want to bungee jump? Sure, no problem. Fly over mighty Victoria Falls? Absolutely. White-water raft raging rapids? Of course. Southern Africa will fill that part of your heart that yearns for adventure. But do you really want a rush? Then step onto the streets, catch a local bus, duck into a village, have a drink at a *shebeen* (an informal drinking establishment), or track lions in the African wilderness. This is where humanity kicked off – it's about time you came home.

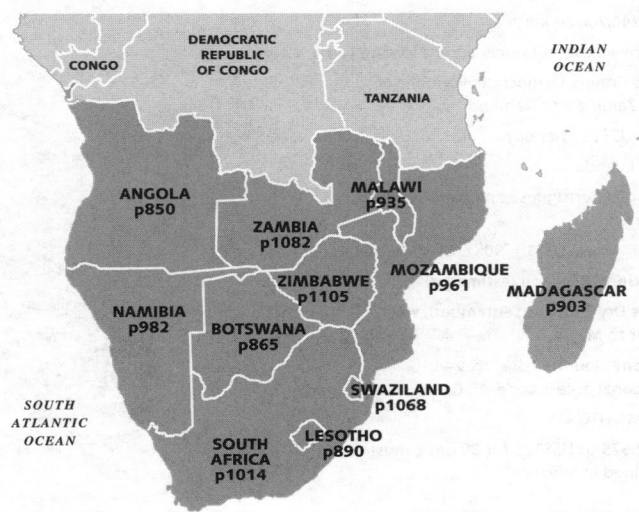

Angola

Angola is an eye-opener – in more ways than one. Scarred painfully by years of debilitating warfare and untouched by foreign visitors since the early 1970s, the country remains remote and undiscovered, with few observers privy to the geographic highlights and vast cultural riches that lie hidden behind an ostensibly violent veneer.

But, with the cessation of a 40-year civil conflict ushering in a prolonged period of peace and stability, opportunities for exploration are quietly opening up. For outsiders, the attractions are manifold. Despite widespread poverty, inbred corruption and an infrastructure devastated by decades of indiscriminate fighting, Angola holds a lure that few other countries can match. Here in the heady heat of equatorial Africa you'll encounter some of the continent's most gracious people and discover many of its most closely guarded secrets.

Chill out on expansive beaches, sample the solitude in virgin wildlife parks or sift through the ruins of Portuguese colonialism. From Luanda to Lubango the nuances are startling.

Despite advancements in infrastructure and a dramatically improved security situation, travel in Angola remains the preserve of adventurers, diehards or those on flexible budgets. But with the transport network gradually recovering and wildlife being shipped in to repopulate decimated national parks, the signs of recovery are more than just a mirage.

Angola is halfway along the road to political and economic atonement and it would be a shame to miss out on its dramatic rebirth.

FAST FACTS

- **Area** 1,246,700 sq km
- **ATMs** They exist, but rarely accept foreign cards
- **Borders** Congo, Democratic Republic of Congo, Zambia and Namibia
- **Budget** US$150 per day
- **Capital** Luanda
- **Languages** Portuguese and various Bantu languages
- **Money** Kwanza; US$1 = 90Kz, €1 = 128Kz
- **Population** 18 million (estimated)
- **Seasons** Dry (June to September), wet (October to May)
- **Telephone** Country code ☎ 244; international access code ☎ 00
- **Time** GMT/UTC + 1
- **Visas** US$75 to US$125 for 30 days; must be obtained in advance

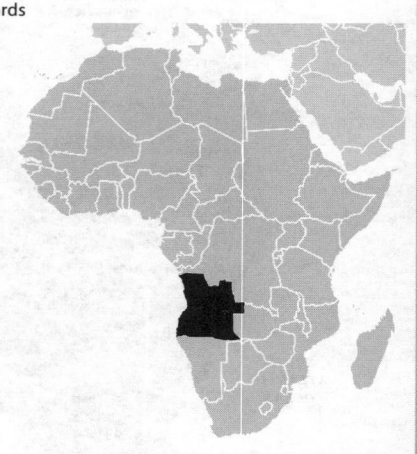

HOW MUCH?

- **Internet per hour** US$3
- **Cup of coffee** US$1.50
- **Car rental per day** US$100
- **Bottle of wine** US$20
- **Average meal** US$20

LONELY PLANET INDEX

- **1L petrol** US$0.50
- **1.5L bottled water** US$2
- **Bottle of beer** US$2
- **Souvenir T-shirt** US$10
- **Baguette** US$1

HIGHLIGHTS

- **Luanda** (p854) Expansive beaches, expensive bars and tatty overcrowded townships, Luanda is a kaleidoscopic vision of Angola at the sharp end.
- **Parque Nacional da Kissama** (p858) One of Africa's largest, emptiest and most surreal wildlife parks.
- **Benguela** (p859) Chill out on the blissfully empty beaches of Angola's most laid-back town.
- **Lubango** (p861) Almost untouched by the war, breezy Lubango offers cascading waterfalls, spectacular volcanic fissures and a vibrant small-city ambiance.
- **Miradouro de Lua** (p859) A spectacular lookout over a canyon of moonlike cliffs that cascade dramatically into the Atlantic Ocean.

CLIMATE & WHEN TO GO

Situated on the Atlantic littoral in a balmy subtropical setting, Angola's climate is heavily influenced by three local peculiarities; the cool Benguela sea current, the rugged interior mountains and the presence of the Namib Desert in the southeast. As a result, the country boasts a number of distinct climatic regions, including a wet, tropical northern jungle, a drier and cooler central plateau, and an arid southern belt influenced by its proximity to the Kalahari Desert.

Although different regions vary significantly, the best time to visit Angola is during the cooler, drier months of June to September.

ITINERARIES

- **One Week** Visit Luanda's Fortaleza de São Miguel (p857), along with the city's selection of churches and museums before heading south to Benfica market (p858) for a spot of bargaining. Continue along the coast road to the Miradouro de Lua (p859) and the Kwanza River (p859), and round off the proceedings with a quick tour of Parque Nacional da Kissama (p858).
- **Two Weeks to One Month** Follow the Luanda itinerary before catching a bus south for the spectacular journey to Benguela (p859) and Lobito (p859). A train ride on the famous Benguela railway (p859) is a must, though at present you can only sample a tiny section of the track. Head for Lubango (p861) to soak up the fresh mountain air and make a nifty side trip to unhurried Namibe (p861). Backtrack to battle-scarred Huambo (p860) for a few days before enjoying one of Angola's most scenic bus rides on your return to the capital.

HISTORY

Angola's often violent and bloody history has left a country endowed with a vast expanse of natural resources and development possibilities perennially trying to stave off starvation. A terrain rich in oil, diamonds, iron ore and copper, plus a measurable hydroelectric capacity, has the potential to be one of Africa's richest states. Instead, the more common reality is that of a nation of shattered infrastructure and devastated towns struggling to feed a desperately poor and eternally uprooted population.

Another Lost Empire

In 1483 Vasco da Gama first dropped anchor in Luanda Bay and unwittingly pre-empted the start of a conflict that, save for a few intermittent lulls in the fighting, continued for over half a millennium. The land now known as Angola was, at the time, inhabited by a number of small tribes living in loosely defined kingdoms that lacked the organisation and administrative cohesiveness of 15th-century Europe. But despite a natural curiosity borne out of years of seafaring exploration, the Portuguese had no real desire to settle on this malaria-ridden African shoreline. Post-1500, the more fertile and less-threatening

ANGOLA

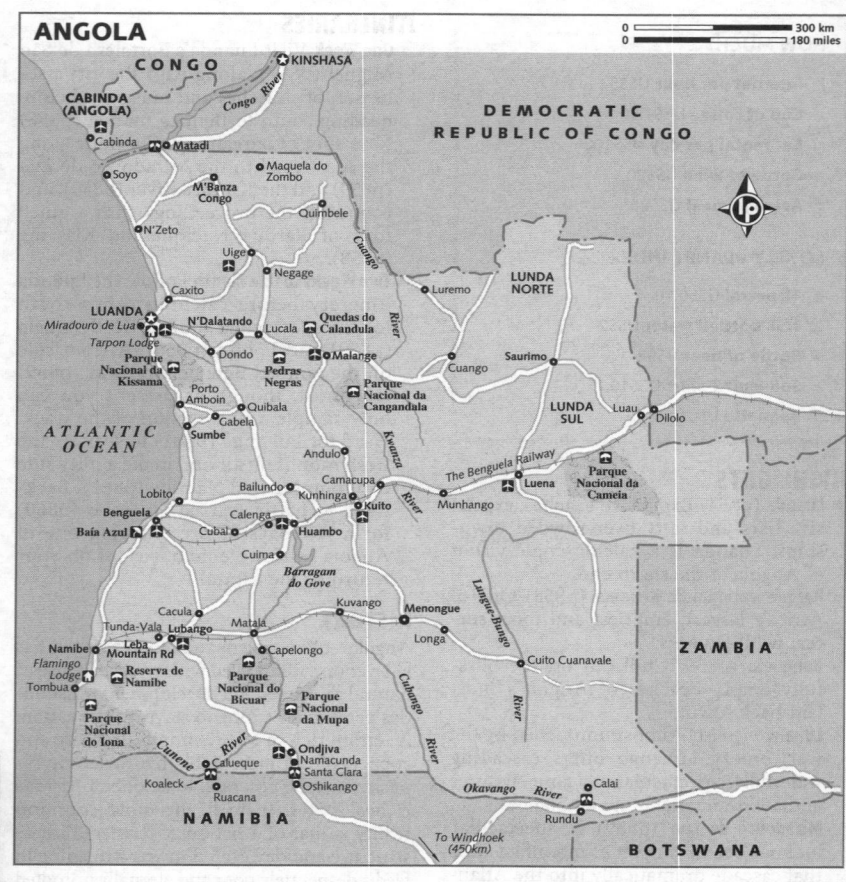

ANGOLA

lands of Brazil held a far greater attraction for colonial farmers and businessmen. For the next 300 years Portugal's African colonies had only two real functions: a strategic base on the route around the Cape of Good Hope, and a collecting centre for one of the largest forced human migrations in history.

Not surprisingly, slavery did little to endear the colonials to the Angolan people. Clashes first began after WWII and were inflamed in 1961 when colonial authorities began to crush increasingly zealous uprisings from dissidents.

The initial independence movement split into three main groups in line with the various tribal affiliations (and international interests) they claimed to represent. The National Front for the Liberation of Angola

(FNLA) was supported by northern tribes, Democratic Republic of Congo (DRC) and anti-communist Western countries; the Popular Movement for the Liberation of Angola (MPLA) began with Marxist sensibilities and was supported by southern tribes, the USSR, Cuba and other Soviet allies; and the National Union for Total Independence of Angola (Unita) originally had the support of the Ovimbundu people, but later formed alliances with the Portuguese right wing, the USA and apartheid South Africa.

In 1975 the Portuguese finally granted independence to Angola, following the overthrow of the fascist Salazar government at home. But the colonial withdrawal – a mad scramble involving one of the biggest airlifts in history –

was legendary in its ineptitude, converting central Luanda into a ghost town and robbing the country of its qualified human resources and administrative structure.

Not surprisingly, Angola in 1975 possessed all the essential ingredients for an impending civil war: a weak, uneven infrastructure, low levels of health and education, two feuding sets of tribally based elites and the inviting prospect of a large slice of unused government-oil revenue up for grabs. As the Moscow-backed MPLA party stepped into a dangerous power vacuum, a combination of new outside factors were dutifully thrown into an already crowded arena: US communist paranoia, Cuba's ambiguous aim to promote 'world revolution', South African security obsessions and the woefully inadequate process of decolonisation. The stage was set.

Angola's second major war was a long, protracted affair dominated by foreign intervention. Indeed, for the next 15 years the wishes and desires of the Angolan people were consistently undermined as foreign governments and Western business interests continued to fight greedily among themselves over a damaged and increasingly beleaguered country.

War & Peace
In 1991, prompted by the end of the Cold War, a ceasefire agreement was set in place by Cuba, the USA and Angola. But the accord broke down the following year after Unita, having lost a general election (seen by the UN as largely free and fair), returned to war with a newfound ferocity, claiming the poll was rigged. Almost 200,000 people died between May and October 1993 as Unita took war to the provincial cities, destroying most of the road, rail and communications network.

A revamped 'Lusaka Accord' signed in 1994 was consistently violated by both the governing MPLA and Unita, and the discovery of new diamond areas and oilfields allowed both sides to re-arm. UN sanctions against Unita diamonds caused Unita's cash supply to shrivel, and its control of the countryside gradually crumbled. Increasing military defeats drove a desperate Unita deeper into the hinterland and – hunted and on the run – its leader Jonas Savimbi was finally killed in a government operation on 22 February 2002.

A new peace accord was signed on 4 April 2002.

Angola Today
Since 2002 Angola has entered a period of peace and regeneration unprecedented in its history. With the 85,000-strong Unita army reintegrated into the national forces and old animosities ceremoniously brushed underneath the carpet, the biggest obstacles to war and instability have been temporarily neutralised.

But the country still faces massive challenges before it can right four decades of economic and political disarray. Corruption is the most pressing problem. In 2004 Human Rights Watch, an independent lobby group, estimated that US$4 billion of Angola's undeclared oil revenue had gone missing since the late 1990s. Voices inside the IMF (International Monetary Fund) were raised and supervisors were sent to investigate. Their conclusion: either the ever-elusive President Eduardo dos Santos was employing a very creative team of accountants or something, somewhere, was clearly not adding up.

It is these financial anomalies that have prevented the lion's share of Angola's new peacetime economy from trickling down to the majority of the poorest classes. While skyscrapers reach new heights in Luanda and oil-obsessed government ministries forge investment deals with China and India, poverty in the countryside remains rampant and widespread.

Economically speaking, Angola's future is brighter than it has been for decades. The country boasts the fastest-growing economy in Africa, undoubtedly boosted by Angola's admittance to the Organization of Petroleum Exporting Countries (OPEC) in 2007. Add to that a US$2 billion loan from China to rebuild the country's infrastructure and it's clear that Angola is rapidly rising from its ashes.

CULTURE
Angola's cornucopia of ethnic groups is dominated by the Ovimbundu, Kimbundu and Bakongo. Local tribal traditions remain strong, though Portuguese has evolved as the national language of choice, particularly among the young. Due in part to its volatile history, much of Angola's cultural legacy has been exported abroad through slavery and emigration, where it has re-emerged in elements of modern Brazilian culture, such as the samba, carnival, Afro-American religion and the combative martial art, capoeira.

ANTÓNIO AGOSTINHO NETO

Immortalised in street names and bespectacled busts across the country, you'd be forgiven for wondering who is António Agostinho Neto? A much-loved figure in Angolan history, Neto was a founding member of the MPLA and the country's first president, leading Angola towards independence in 1975. Despite the ensuing civil war, Neto is fondly remembered by most, and his birthday is marked with a national holiday, labelled National Heroes' Day (17 September).

Born in 1922, Neto moved to Portugal to practise medicine but spent much of his time avoiding (or sometimes succumbing to) arrest for revolutionary acts. During his 15-year exile he forged lasting ties with Che Guevara and Fidel Castro and gained huge support from an array of high-profile intellectuals.

Although largely remembered for his politics, Neto was also an accomplished poet and many statues depict him as an academic, holding a pen and paper in one hand while gripping his Kalashnikov in the other.

Neto never saw his country at peace, dying in 1979 in the USSR.

Angolans are Africa's perennial survivors, an open and gregarious populace whose spirit, once garnered, is highly infectious and whose fortitude is nothing short of remarkable. Badly damaged by the longstanding tribal conflicts that set neighbour against neighbour throughout the 1980s and '90s, Angolan culture has remained defiantly intact in a country divided by complex ethnic loyalties and 42 different indigenous languages. At the forefront of this colourful artistic patchwork is Angolan music, a rich and varied collection of offshoots and subgenres, with styles such as *kizombe,* samba, *zouk* and *rebita* manifesting themselves in countless dances and romantic songs.

Life in Angola is extremely hard. Many curable diseases are rife, infant mortality rates are the highest in the world and life expectancy is a mere 47 years. But for guarded optimists, hope springs eternal. Since 2002 many émigrés have returned to reclaim their businesses and farms, and economic activity throughout the country has been kick-started. Angola's participation in the 2006 World Cup was like a lightning bolt that reawakened a tired yet ever-hopeful population, and the 2010 Africa Cup of Nations being held in the country further bolstered national pride.

ENVIRONMENT

Angola's 1650km of Atlantic coastline hosts a plethora of unspoiled beaches, and the sedimentary deposits of numerous full-flowing rivers have led to the formation of a handful of distinctive coastal sandbars, such as Mussulo and La Ilha in Luanda and Restinga in Lobito.

The country's grassy savannah provides the setting for six national parks, namely: Iona, Bicuar, Mupa, Kissama, Cameia and Cangandala. Due to the devastation wreaked by decades of civil war, the wildlife in these parks has been almost completely eradicated.

LUANDA

☎ 222 / pop 4 million

Hot, heaving, oil rich and cash poor, Luanda is a city of unfathomable contrasts and vividly shocking extremes. Perched tantalisingly on the Atlantic coastline overlooking a narrow pine-fringed sandbar known colloquially as the Ilha, the balmy oceanside setting is as spectacular as it is exotic. The sweeping vistas would be even more stunning if it weren't for the teeming *bairros* (townships) and ramshackle makeshift dwellings that have taken root around Angola's rapidly expanding capital in the 30 years since independence.

Built for a healthy half million, Luanda now bursts with four million beleaguered inhabitants and the evidence of this rampant overpopulation resonates everywhere. Whiff the stench of fetid water that intoxicates early-morning joggers on the picturesque Marginal promenade, dodge the manic lines of traffic that make hot afternoons in gridlocked central Luanda even more cauldron-like, and contemplate how running water and electricity are still comparative luxuries for all but a highly privileged (and often foreign) minority. But despite such calamitous problems, Luanda still manages to retain a dash of panache in the face of all this adversity.

HISTORY
Founded as São Paulo de Loanda on the Ilha de Cabo by 400 Portuguese soldiers and 100 families in 1575, the settlement was moved to the mainland one year later. In 1605 Luanda became a city, and two centuries later its resplendent buildings and flourishing trade earned it the title of the 'Paris of Africa'. But the Napoleonic comparisons didn't last. Despite sitting out the worst of the civil war, Luanda quickly became a refugee camp for millions of desperate internally displaced people fleeing the fighting. Packed to the rafters, it's still getting over the shock.

ORIENTATION
The airport is 4km south of Luanda. The city itself is set along a harbour overlooking the 7km-long Ilha de Luanda ('the Ilha'). The 2km promenade along the harbour, Av 4 de Fevereiro, is known as the Marginal and is the heart of the city. It hosts the reserve bank, head offices and international airlines. South along the Marginal is Mutamba, where you are most likely to stay, play and get away – second only to the Ilha (1km away), with its endless beaches, bars and restaurants. North of the city and up the hill from the Marginal is Miramar, home to the president, most of the embassies, rich oil expats and poor Angolans.

INFORMATION
Internet Access
Internet access costs around US$3 per hour. The top hotels have free wi-fi.

Correios Commcenter (Av 1° Congresso MPLA; 8am-5pm Mon-Fri) In the post office building.

Havana Cyber Café (Rua Rainha Ginga, 8am-10pm Mon-Sat) The fastest option for internet access outside the upmarket hotels.

Medical Services
There are many 24-hour *farmacias* (pharmacies) in the capital. Luanda's best clinics are the following:

Clinica da Mutamba (39 37 83, emergency 912-85 80 28; Rua Pedro Felix Machado, 10/12) A one-stop medical facility that includes a pharmacy.

Clinica Sagrada Esperança (30 90 34; Av Murtala Mohamed; 24hr) Near the end of the Ilha.

Money
You can change money in banks and bureaux de change without a passport. There are plenty of options for changing money on the street (where you'll get a better rate). The kwanza is relatively stable.

Post & Telephone
The **post office** (Av 1° Congresso MPLA), just off the Marginal, is in a large building dating from 1850. Unfortunately, the postal system is similarly antiquated. In case of urgency, **DHL** (39 03 76; Rua da Missão) is a faster and more expensive option.

There are temperamental public telephones at the post office, but mobile phones are the most reliable way to make calls. SIM cards are available for purchase at the post office for 900Kz.

DANGERS & ANNOYANCES
Although Luanda isn't, on first impressions, as dangerous as many other African cities, it is important for visitors to keep their wits about them and abide by a few basic safety precautions. Being robbed is one of the biggest dangers you'll encounter, although strolling around the central areas during the daytime is relatively low risk. Don't walk anywhere at night. Don't wear gold or silver jewellery (even imitation), or an eye-catching watch. Keep money in a hidden money belt, and don't use a mobile phone on the street (phone robbery is one of Luanda's most common crimes). See also Dangers & Annoyances, p862.

SIGHTS & ACTIVITIES
The curvaceous sweep of the harbourside **Marginal** (Av 4 de Fevereiro) makes an interesting stroll at any time of day. Look out for the striking domed pink facade of the **Banco Nacional de Angola** (Av 4 de Fevereiro, 151) designed by architect Vasco Regaleira and inaugurated in 1956. Architectural buffs will also want to check the **Palácio de Ferro** (Rua Major Kanyangulo), designed by Gustave Eiffel in the 1890s for the Paris Universal Exhibition. The construction was dismantled and brought to Luanda in 1902. At the time of writing the **Palácio** was being revamped ready to reopen in 2010 as a museum showcasing Angola's diamond industry.

Luanda has a smattering of old colonial churches hidden among the skyscrapers. Sitting in a square just off the Marginal is the **Igreja de Nossa Senhora de Nazaré** (Praça do Ambiente), dating from 1664, and further west lies the

ANGOLA

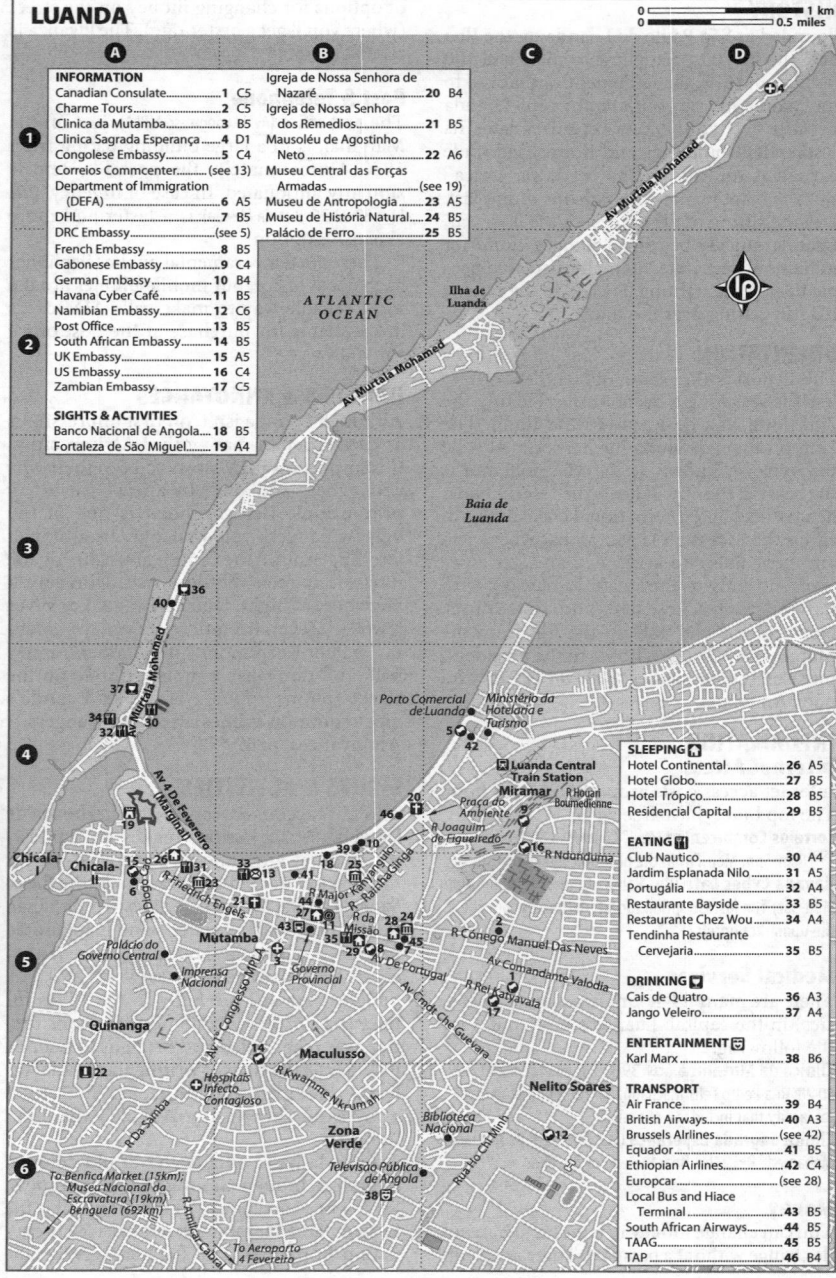

LUANDA

0 _____ 1 km
0 _____ 0.5 miles

INFORMATION
Canadian Consulate...............1 C5
Charme Tours.........................2 C5
Clinica da Mutamba................3 B5
Clinica Sagrada Esperança.......4 D1
Congolese Embassy.................5 C4
Correios Commcenter........(see 13)
Department of Immigration
  (DEFA)...............................6 A5
DHL.......................................7 B5
DRC Embassy....................(see 5)
French Embassy......................8 B5
Gabonese Embassy.................9 C4
German Embassy...................10 B4
Havana Cyber Café................11 B5
Namibian Embassy................12 C6
Post Office...........................13 B5
South African Embassy..........14 B5
UK Embassy.........................15 A5
US Embassy.........................16 C4
Zambian Embassy.................17 C5

SIGHTS & ACTIVITIES
Banco Nacional de Angola.....18 B5
Fortaleza de São Miguel........19 A4

Igreja de Nossa Senhora de
  Nazaré..............................20 B4
Igreja de Nossa Senhora
  dos Remedios.....................21 B5
Mausoléu de Agostinho
  Neto.................................22 A6
Museu Central das Forças
  Armadas.......................(see 19)
Museu de Antropologia.........23 A5
Museu de História Natural.....24 B5
Palácio de Ferro...................25 B5

ATLANTIC OCEAN

Ilha de Luanda

Baia de Luanda

Av Murtala Mohamed

Av 4 De Fevereiro (Marginal)

Porto Comercial de Luanda

Ministério da Hotelaria e Turismo

Luanda Central Train Station
Miramar

R Houari Boumedienne

Praça do Ambiente

R Joaquim de Figueiredo

R Ndanduma

R Cónego Manuel Das Neves

Chicala-I

Chicala-II

R Friedrich Engels

R Major Kanhangulo

R Rainha Ginga

R da Missão

R Comandante Valódia

Mutamba

Governo Provincial

Av De Portugal

Av Rei Katyavala

Palácio do Governo Central

Imprensa Nacional

Quinanga

Av Congresso MPLA

Maculusso

R Kwanme Nkrumah

Av Cmdt Che Guevara

Hospital Infecto Contagioso

Nelito Soares

Zona Verde

Biblioteca Nacional

Rua Ho Chi Minh

Televisão Pública de Angola

R Da Samba

R Amilcar Cabral

To Benfica Market (15km);
Museu Nacional da
Escravatura (19km);
Benguela (692km)

To Aeroporto
4 Fevereiro

SLEEPING
Hotel Continental................26 A5
Hotel Globo.........................27 B5
Hotel Trópico......................28 B5
Residencial Capital...............29 B5

EATING
Club Nautico.......................30 A4
Jardim Esplanada Nilo..........31 A5
Portugália...........................32 A4
Restaurante Bayside............33 B5
Restaurante Chez Wou.........34 A4
Tendinha Restaurante
  Cervejaria.........................35 B5

DRINKING
Cais de Quatro....................36 A3
Jango Veleiro......................37 A4

ENTERTAINMENT
Karl Marx...........................38 B6

TRANSPORT
Air France...........................39 B4
British Airways....................40 A3
Brussels Airlines.............(see 42)
Equador..............................41 B5
Ethiopian Airlines................42 C4
Europcar........................(see 28)
Local Bus and Hiace
  Terminal...........................43 B5
South African Airways..........44 D1
TAAG................................45 B5
TAP...................................46 B4

ANGOLA

impressive double-domed facade of the **Igreja de Nossa Senhora dos Remedios** (Rua Rainha Ginga), built in 1655 and restored in 1995.

The **Fortaleza de São Miguel** guarding the entrance to the bay was constructed by the Portuguese in 1576 and is Luanda's oldest surviving building. Altered in 1664, whereupon it took its present star shape, the fort today houses the **Museu Central das Forças Armadas** (admission 200Kz; 🕙 9am-6pm) and offers sweeping views of the city below. Other museums worth seeing are the **Museu de Antropologia** (Rua Friedrich Engels, 61; donation accepted; 🕙 9am-6pm Mon-Fri), with its African masks, musical instruments and indigenous hunting artefacts housed in an old colonial building, and the **Museu de História Natural** (Rua Nossa Senhora da Múxima, 47; adult/child 100/50Kz; 🕙 9am-1pm & 2.30-5pm Mon-Fri, 10am-5pm Sat & Sun), whose dimly lit halls house permanent exhibitions on mammals and marine creatures.

Unmistakable on the Luanda skyline is the thin needle-like structure of the **Mausoléu de Agostinho Neto**, Angola's first president. At the time of writing it was still unfinished and, as yet, is not open to the public.

A little further out but worth the detour is the **Museu Nacional da Escravatura** (admission 500Kz; 🕙 8.30am-3.30pm Mon-Fri, 9am-1.30pm Sat & Sun). The building alone merits a visit – a whitewashed 16th-century church perched over the ocean. Inside, a modest collection of paintings, photos and artefacts explores Angola's link to the slave trade. It's approximately 20km south of the city.

FESTIVALS & EVENTS

The **Carnival** is held in February and is set along the Marginal. It's a jovial and open affair, most notable for its ubiquitous half-dead cats (of which Angolans are very superstitious) tied to costumes and crucifixes.

Independence Day is held on 11 November and is also celebrated on the streets, with the added bonus of a public address and a few words from the president himself.

SLEEPING

There are a handful of classy hotels in Luanda, but most rooms are grossly overpriced. Expect to pay US$120 upwards for anything half decent.

Hotel Globo (☎ 33 32 44; Rua Rainha Ginga, 100; s/d 4900/5800Kz) Rock bottom, Luanda style, with cleanish, moth-eaten rooms in a centrally lo-

cated position. Consider bringing your own bedding.

Residencial Capital (☎ 914-36 11 59; Rua da Missão, 38; s/d US$120/150; 🏊) Based in a run-down apartment block, it doesn't look much from the outside, but rooms are bright, clean and offer excellent value for Luanda. A decent breakfast compensates for the grotty bathrooms.

Hotel Continental (☎ 33 42 41; Rua Rainha Ginga, 18; s/d 29,000/34,000Kz; 🏊 P 🛜) Stylish rooms near the Ilha, some with ocean views. Free airport transfers sweeten the deal.

Hotel Trópico (☎ 37 00 70; Rua da Missão, 103; s/d US$420/480; 🏊 P 🛜 🏋) An international-class hotel with rooms and facilities (including a top-notch gym and free internet) almost deserving of its astronomic price tag.

EATING

After a few days in Angola, restaurant menus become a familiar blur, but that doesn't mean that the fresh fish, fried chicken and steak sandwiches aren't worth shelling out US$15 per meal for. Thanks to the legacy of the Portuguese, *pastelerias* (pastry and coffee shops) have a distinctly European flavour.

Street food is easy to procure from the *bairro* women who sell fruit and baguette-like sandwiches from washing bowls across the city centre. More established street vendors sell beer and barbecued chicken.

Jardim Esplanada Nilo (Rua Rainha Ginga; 🕙 9am-6pm, closed Sun) A salubrious tree-covered patio offering drinks and sweet-tasting snacks.

Club Nautico (☎ 30 92 38; Av Murtala Mohamed; mains 1500-2500Kz; 🕙 noon-11pm, closed Mon) A bustling restaurant in Luanda's yacht club serving everything from tasty chicken to bog-standard *funje* (ground maize).

Tendinha Restaurante Cervejaria (☎ 923-54 28 68; Rua da Missão, 16; mains 2000Kz; 🕙 8am-10pm Mon-Fri) A perpetually busy bar with funky African decor, ice cold beers and good-value Portuguese cuisine.

Portugália (☎ 26 06 19; Av Murtala Mohamed; mains 2000-3000Kz; 🕙 noon-1am) Reasonable Portuguese fare in a fine location on the Ilha, with good service and pleasant surroundings.

Restaurante Bayside (☎ 921-66 76 25; Av 4 de Fevereiro, 185; mains 2000-4000Kz; 🕙 noon-3pm & 7-10pm) A stylish complex linked to Luanda's snazziest spa. Bayside offers salads, while Portofino, upstairs, is an upmarket Italian joint (with upmarket prices). The Emporium Café, also in the same complex, is a cheaper option.

ANGOLA

Restaurante Chez Wou (☎ 30 93 94; Av Murtala Mohamed; mains 2500Kz; ☻ closed Sat lunch) Angola's Chinese presence can be experienced (and tasted) at this ever-popular establishment at the entrance to the Ilha.

DRINKING & ENTERTAINMENT

Many flock to the Ilha in the evenings to enjoy sundowners by the ocean. **Cais de Quatro** (☎ 924-57 06 20; Av Murtala Mohamed; ☻ noon–1am) has an excellent menu and serves cocktails on the deck. Nearby **Jango Veleiro** (☎ 30 90 71; Av Murtala Mohamed; ☻ 24hr) is perfect for late drinks on the sand.

Karl Marx (Rua de Oliveira Martins, 19) This poignantly named, semi-outdoor bar-cinema screens Hollywood flicks with Portuguese subtitles. It occasionally hosts performance groups from Lisbon or Brazil.

SHOPPING

The best place to shop is at Benfica market, 16km south of Luanda on the Kissama road. The atmosphere is relatively hassle-free, and the handicrafts deftly sculpted and authentic. Don't buy the ivory.

GETTING THERE & AWAY

You can fly daily between Luanda and almost every major Angolan city with one of six different airlines (see p863). All flights depart from the domestic terminal at Aeroporto 4 de Fevereiro.

You can rent cars from **Avis** (☎ 32 15 51), which has offices at the airport, **Europcar** (☎ 64 15 80), in the Hotel Trópico, and **Equador** (☎ 33 07 46; Largo Tristão da Cunha, 11). Rental prices start per day at US$80 for a sedan or US$180 for 4WD; or car and driver from US$45 per day plus rental cost. The chaotic nature of Luanda traffic makes hiring a driver highly recommended.

There is a daily bus service running along the coast between Benguela and Luanda (2500Kz, seven hours). A similarly scenic trip connects Luanda with Huambo (3500Kz, eight hours). Two companies offer services from Luanda. Macon has slightly spiffier buses, but SGO is marginally cheaper. Buses to Benguela leave from Rocha Pinto; those to Huambo leave from Viana, both a trek south of the city but accessible by Hiace.

GETTING AROUND

Luanda's airport, Aeroporto 4 de Fevereiro, is 4km south of Luanda. Note that the domestic and international terminals aren't linked and to hop from one to the other you have to grab a shared taxi (50Kz) from the main road in front of the airport.

For getting around Luanda, buses and the ubiquitous Hiaces (blue-and-white Toyota Hiaces) start from a terminus in Mutamba, in front of the pink Governo Provincial building. They go to most places within Luanda and nearby (50Kz to 100Kz). Private taxis are in scarce supply and can be prohibitively expensive. Hotels can hook you up with reputable operators.

COASTAL ANGOLA

Travelling overland outside the capital is increasingly popular, and the overall security situation has improved immeasurably since lasting peace broke out in 2002. The best road link is between Luanda and Benguela via Sumbe and Lobito, closely followed by the spectacular drive in the southwest from Lubango to Namibe. The road from Luanda to Huambo is now in excellent condition and the Benguela–Huambo and Benguela–Lubango routes are mostly paved. Other passable routes (with a 4WD) include Luanda–Malange, Lubango–Santa Clara (Namibian border) and Lubango–Huambo. Decent bus services now connect most major towns, meaning Angola is finally accessible to independent travellers without their own wheels.

PARQUE NACIONAL DA KISSAMA & AROUND

Kissama (also spelt Quiçama), situated 70km south of Luanda, is Angola's most accessible and well-stocked wildlife park. Inaugurated as a nature reserve in 1938 and upgraded to a national park in 1957, this 990,000-hectare swath of coastal savannah punctuated by gnarly baobab trees is home to elephants, water buffaloes, indigenous *palanca* antelopes and a precarious population of nesting sea turtles. Despite years of poaching and neglect during the civil war, Kissama remains at the forefront of Angola's wildlife regeneration efforts, thanks largely to a pioneering relief project known as Operation Noah's Ark. Launched in 1996, the project's aim is to restock the park with animals imported from surrounding countries' reserves, as well as training locals to work as wardens.

ANGOLA

Visitors to Kissama can stay in **bungalows** (r US$180) or **tents** (US$100), though bookings must be made in advance (☎ 925-31 49 49). There is also a restaurant serving meals for US$15 to US$20. Wildlife viewing costs US$25 per person for two hours.

Other natural attractions in the area include the **Miradouro de Lua**, a veritable moonscape of rust- and silver-coloured rock formations that cascade like a mini Grand Canyon into the Atlantic just off the Luanda–Benguela coast road, approximately 30km south of the capital. Boat trips (US$125 for five people) on the nearby **Kwanza River** reveal copious amounts of birdlife, and can also be organised through the park or at the nearby **Tarpon Lodge** (☎ 912-82 50 45).

The park can sometimes arrange return transfers from Luanda, but realistically the only practical way of getting there is with an organised group (see p864).

BENGUELA

☎ 2722 / pop 300,000

Coastal Benguela is Angola's second-most important city and the self-proclaimed cultural capital. Nestled on the shores of the Atlantic approximately 30km south of the port of Lobito, the city is surrounded by fine beaches and bisected by the lush and agriculturally important Cavaco River valley; a veritable oasis of green in an otherwise dry and arid desert. Founded by the Portuguese in 1617, Benguela was once an important slave port and the embarkation point for shiploads of human cargo bound for Brazil. With the onset of the 20th century, it became the terminus for the Benguela railway, though its position as an Atlantic port was rapidly upsurged by neighbouring Lobito. Spared a direct hit in the bloody 40-year civil war, Benguela retains a laid-back ambience in a big-city setting. You'll encounter little hassle here and make plenty of spontaneous friends.

Benguela's yellow-sand beaches are rightly famous, with the centrally located **Praia Morena** acting as one of the city's unofficial meeting points. Watch out for svelte-looking athletes practising their capoeira here early in the morning. The most popular out-of-town beach is **Baía Azul**, situated 20km to the south on the road to Baía Farta (accessible by Hiace).

The town's only museum is the tiny **Museu de Arqueológica**, occupying a seafront warehouse that was once a holding shed for captured slaves. The church of **Nossa Senhora do Pópulo** (Av Combatentes da Grande Guerra) was built in 1748 from stone carried in ships from Brazil as ballast and is Benguela's most beguiling building. Other gems include the **Palácio das Bolas** (Av Agostinho Neto), used as a headquarters by the provincial MPLA party, and the **Palácio do Governo** facing the beach.

At the time of writing, the train line from Benguela was under construction, but a 5km section between Cubal and Lobito gives a brief feel for the once-glorious **Benguela railway** (20Kz, 20 min, two daily); see the boxed text, p860. Once in **Lobito**, it's a five-minute stroll to the magnificent **Hotel Terminus** (☎ 25 781; s/d US$240/270), whose beach bar merits a visit. From here you can wander to the sandy tip of **Restinga**, stopping to grab a beer and a seafood lunch with 180-degree ocean views.

Benguela's list of decent hostels and hotels is constantly growing.

Budget travellers will enjoy the facilities and atmosphere at **Nancy's English School e Hospedería** (☎ 923-59 40 93; Largo de Pioneiros, 16; s/d US$80/90; ✗ P 🖥). Run by a friendly American expat, it's a great place to stock up on country-wide information.

A little further from the beach, **Hotel Praia Morena** (☎ 37 125; Rua José Estevan, 25; s/d 13,000/15,000Kz) has stylish rooms, a good restaurant and a large rooftop terrace perfect for a scenic sundowner.

Pricey but offering good value for Angola, the **Hotel Luso** (☎ 31 292; Av Aires de Almeida Santos; s/d US$140/230; ✗ 🖥 🛍) is Benguela's most upmarket option, with elegant rooms and an exquisite pool area.

A hotel that doubles as one of Benguela's best-value eating joints, **Pensão Contente** (☎ 33 637; Rua Bernardino Correia, 81; s/d 7590/9000Kz; ✗) serves burgers, prawns and excellent desserts.

Benguela is emerging as the capital of Angola's gastronomy scene, with a wealth of delectable restaurants opening in recent years. An old favourite is **Restaurante Escondidinho** (☎ 33 206; Rua Cândido dos Reis, 7-9; mains 2500-5000Kz; ☯ 7am-midnight), known for its superb seafood dishes and late-night party atmosphere. The bar is open until 5am.

Restaurante Porta Avioes (☎ 36 479; Rua da Praia Morena; ☯ noon-12am) takes the title of best location, sitting just metres behind the beach. Inside it serves seafood specialities, while those on a budget can opt for snacks and beer on the terrace.

THE BENGUELA RAILWAY

Commissioned by the Portuguese in 1899 and built by the British over the ensuing 30 years, the Benguela railway comprised a feat of engineering unmatched in Africa. During its heyday the track stretched 1370km (850 miles) from coastal Lobito to Luau on the DRC border, but the civil war quickly put an end to the railway's glory days. By the early 1990s this once great link in southwest Africa's burgeoning oil, diamond and copper-based economy had – by a combination of ambush, sabotage and serial mine-laying – been reduced to a 30km spur between Benguela and Lobito.

Successive renovation schemes came up against crushing problems until 2006, when negotiations clawed their way back to the table. The Chinese were the successful bidders, fighting their way through an obstacle course of disincentives – minefields, blown-up bridges and collapsed ravines to name three – that stand in the way of making the reconstruction dream a reality. Even today the Benguela line is closed, leaving just a short stretch from Lobito to Cubal. But massive construction is evident along the track and it's only a matter of time before the railway is restored to its former glory.

Benguela is easily accessed by daily planes from Luanda (US$115). The city has two airports, one 3km south of the city centre and the other in Catumbela, 15km to the north. Regular planes also link Benguela with Lubango (US$90), Huambo (US$90) and other major cities.

Daily buses to Luanda (2500Kz, seven hours) leave from outside the train station; those to Lubango (2500Kz, six hours) and Huambo (2500Kz, seven hours) leave from the Navigantes *bairro*, 3km south of town. Trains run between Catumbela and Lobito twice daily and between Lobito and Cubal three times a week (500Kz, five hours).

SOUTHERN ANGOLA

HUAMBO
☎ 2412 / pop 400,000

Known formerly as Nova Lisboa (New Lisbon), Huambo was once renowned for its expansive parks and attractive colonial buildings. Indeed, in 1928 it was briefly touted by former Angolan high commissioner António Vicente Ferreira as the country's capital-in-waiting. But then came the war and, in 1993, a gruesome 52-day siege reduced the city to little more than a pile of pock-marked rubble. Demonstrating true Angolan resiliency, Huambo is now racing along the road to recovery and set to reclaim its crown as one of Angola's prettiest towns.

While true sights are few and far between, Huambo's latent beauty can be glimpsed in among the bullet-strafed buildings that make up the Cidade Alta (Upper City) and the Cidade Baixa (Lower City). Most hotels, restaurants and attractions are in Cidade Alta. The city's centrepiece is the charming **Jardim da Cultura**, a tree-lined square surrounded by pavement cafes and elegant buildings. It's overtaken the somewhat dishevelled **Parque Almirante Américo Tomás**, known as the *estufa*, as the top spot to enjoy Huambo's tropical heat. Worth a brief stop is the **Museu Regional do Huambo** (⏲ 8am-3.30pm Mon-Fri) on the south side of the Jardim. The collection of tools, weapons and carvings isn't the most impressive, but the curator's enthusiastic optimism makes it worth a stop.

A short walk west is the elegant **Praça Manuel de Ariaga**, watched over by a striking statue of Agostinho Neto and skirted with pink colonial buildings, including the **Palácio do Governo**. From here it's a 1km-walk west to the **Granja Por do Sol** (adult/child 500/250Kz, prices double on weekends; ⏲ 8am-10pm), a pleasantly landscaped tourist complex with caged birds, a boating lake and a swimming pool. Follow Av Vinte e Oito from the Praça or jump on a motorbike taxi (100Kz).

Huambo has some surprisingly good accommodation options.

Huambo's best *pensão* (pension), **Pensão Gigi** (☎ 23 491; Rua Dr Lacerda, Cidade Alta; s/d 6500/7800Kz), has clean rooms with a shared bathroom. Downstairs is a decent buffet restaurant.

Centrally located and with a range of room types, the **Hotel Nova Estrela** (☎ 22 689; Rua Eduardo Costa, Cidade Alta; s/d 7500/9800Kz; ⏲ P) offers superb value. If you fancy splurging, its ostentatious suites come with whirlpool baths, treadmills and enormous beds. The rooftop bar is perfect for watching the sun set over the **Praça**. Next door, a raucous place serves tasty, well-priced chicken.

Close to the train station in Cidade Baixa, the **Hotel Nino** (☎ 22 786; Rua 5 de Outubro, Cidade Baixa; s/d 10,500/14,000Kz; ✷ 🖳) is a cosy option, with friendly English-speaking staff and an adjoining internet cafe.

The Parisian-style **Novo Império** (☎ 23 176; Rua Dr Lacerda, Cidade Alta; mains 1000-2000Kz) overlooks the Jardim and has a choice of traditional dishes, as well as great burgers, pastries and coffee.

Doubling as a nightspot with live music and regular DJs, **Restaurante Jango Central** (☎ 927-82 14 20; Av da Imaculada Conceicão; mains 2000-2500Kz) is Huambo's coolest late-night hang-out.

There are daily flights to Luanda and connections to Benguela and Lubango three times a week. Daily buses connect Huambo to Benguela and Luanda via excellent roads. The road to Lubango is open but in a pretty poor condition. The bus station is 9km north of Huambo and is accessible only by motorbike taxi (300Kz).

LUBANGO
☎ 2612 / pop 200,000

Cool and picturesque, Lubango defies popular images of Angola's war-ravaged past and impoverished present. Relatively unscathed by the 40-year conflict that tore the heart of communities elsewhere, the order and tranquillity of Lubango's central core has more in common with Namibia than Huambo or Kuito. You'll encounter a handful of adventurous overlanders here, some quirky cafes and some of Angola's most charming hotels.

Surrounded by mountains and nestled in a cool central valley, one of the best ways to get a bird's-eye view of Lubango is to rent a taxi and motor up to the **Cristo Rei**, a statue of Jesus (a mini version of Rio's *Corcovado*) that overlooks the city (return taxi 3000Kz). Alternatively, you could hike the 5km trail from **Nossa Señora do Monte**. Other excursions include the **Tunda-Vala volcanic fissure**, 20km outside town, where you can climb to 2600m above sea level for stellar views, and the famous **Leba Mountain Rd** on the way to Namibe that drops 1000m via a succession of precipitous switchbacks.

An excellent and viable side trip from Lubango is to the fishing town of **Namibe** on the Atlantic coast. Aside from a blissfully under-visited beach and some well-priced seafood restaurants, Namibe also provides

easy access to **Flamingo Lodge**, a choice fishing spot 70km south of the town run by **Angolan Adventure Safaris** (☎ 912-82 50 45; www.aasafaris.com). Prebooking is essential and you need a 4WD to reach the lodge.

Lubango has a fine selection of hotels and restaurants.

The city's cheapest *pensão*, **Pensão Diocema** (☎ 21 788; Rua Deolinda Rodríguez, 98A; r 5800Kz), is scruffy, but friendly.

Situated on the edge of town, the burgeoning tourist park Complexo Turistico Nuestra Señora do Monte is home to a casino and half a dozen accommodation options, including the excellent-value **Somitour Lodge** (☎ 922-34 63 73; s/d 7500/8300Kz; ✷), with slightly worn yet clean and comfy thatched cottages. Next door is the delightful **Casper Lodge** (☎ 45 015; s/d 12,200/14,000Kz; ✷ Ⓟ), whose plush suites are kitted out in tasteful African decor.

Right in the town centre, the **Grande Hotel da Huíla** (☎ 20 910; Av Dr Agostinho Neto; s/d Kz12,000/13,500; ✷ Ⓟ 🏊) has helpful staff and a huge swimming pool (the only one in town actually boasting water).

Lubango's most popular daytime hang-out is the funky **Huíla Café** (☎ 24 582; Rua 10 de Dezembro; ☽ 7am-late), which does delicious burgers and top-notch *galãos* (Portuguese latte). Equally hip is **Mania Bar** (Rua Hoji ya Henda, 20; ☽ 8am-1am), which has an internet cafe upstairs and a couple of billiard tables out the back.

There are daily flights from Lubango to Luanda and regular connections to Huambo and Benguela. TAAG flies three times a week between Lubango and Windhoek in Namibia. The road between Lubango and the town of Namibe is one of the best in the country and regular buses (three hours) ply this route. There are also daily buses to Benguela (six hours). The bus station is 2km out of town en route to the airport.

ANGOLA DIRECTORY

ACCOMMODATION

Tourist accommodation has traditionally been scant in Angola, but the situation is changing and new hotels are shooting up across the country. Rooms, however, are not cheap. Expect to pay upwards of US$60 for the most basic (bathroomless) room in the countryside and at least US$100 in the cities. Advance booking is recommended in Luanda.

ANGOLA

PRACTICALITIES

■ Tipping is not expected but leaving small change is welcomed.

■ Electricity in Angola is 220/240 V, 50 Hz.

■ Plugs are European style, with two round pins.

■ Angola uses the metric system.

BUSINESS HOURS

Most businesses are open 8.30am to 12.30pm and 2pm to 6pm Monday to Friday, and 8.30am to 12.30pm Saturday.

DANGERS & ANNOYANCES

Contrary to popular belief, travelling in Angola is far safer than outsiders might first imagine – as long as you abide by a few basic ground rules. Crime against foreigners is low outside the capital and armed banditry in the provinces has diminished considerably since 2002, though visitors should exercise caution if visiting Cabinda or the diamond-producing provinces of Lunda Norte and Lunda Sul. Furthermore, Angolan police, while certainly not incorruptible, are generally friendlier than many of their African counterparts. Nevertheless, ask permission before taking photos in public areas, always carry a photocopy of your passport and make sure you don't wander off the road in rural areas – the threat of unexploded landmines is still a huge problem.

Luanda's street crime aside, your biggest danger is probably health, with malaria a particular worry in the coastal areas. Consult your doctor before you leave and don't cut corners when it comes to medication, mosquito nets and other preventative measures; for more details, see Health (p1168).

EMBASSIES & CONSULATES

The following countries have diplomatic representation in Luanda:

Canada (☎ 222-44 83 71; Rua Rei Katyavala, 113)
Congo (☎ 222-31 02 93; Av 4 de Fevereiro, 3)
Democratic Republic of Congo (☎ 222-31 02 93; Av 4 de Fevereiro, 3)
France (☎ 222-33 00 65; Rua Rev Agostinho Pedro Neto, 31)
Gabon (☎ 222-44 92 89; Rua Eng Armindo Adrade, 149)
Germany (☎ 222-33 45 16; Av 4 Fevereiro, 120)
Namibia (☎ 222-32 87 72; Rua da Liberdade, 20, Vila Alice)
South Africa (☎ 222-33 91 26; Rua Kwamme Nkrumah, 31)

UK (☎ 222-33 45 82; http://ukinangola.fco.gov.uk; Rua Diogo Cão, 4)
USA (☎ 222-64 10 00; http://angola.usembassy.gov; Av Houari Boumedienne, 32)
Zambia (☎ 222-33 11 45; Rua Rei Katyavala, 106)

HOLIDAYS

As well as religious holidays noted in the Africa Directory (p1140), these are the principal public holidays in Angola:

New Year's Day 1 January
Martyrs' Day 4 January
Liberation Day 4 February
Peace Day 4 April
Workers' Day 1 May
International Children's Day 1 June
National Heroes' Day 17 September
Independence Day 11 November

MONEY

Angola's currency is the kwanza (Kz). It is not convertible and cannot be taken out of the country. As with many developing economies, the US dollar is also widely accepted.

You can exchange money in banks, at bureaux de change or on the street, where rates are considerably better.

Angola is a cash economy and local ATMs rarely accept foreign bank cards. Credit cards are accepted by major hotels and airline companies, but the bulk of business is done in cash. Come prepared with plenty of hard cash and invest in a decent money belt.

Bargaining is possible when buying from markets or on the street. You can generally expect to haggle down to one-half to two-thirds of the initial asking price.

POST & TELEPHONE

The postal system is unreliable throughout the country. Angola Telecom often requires several attempts, but works in the main cities. Most Angolans rely on their mobile phones and if you're staying a while, it's wise to invest in a SIM card (900Kz).

VISAS

Costs for 30-day tourist visas vary depending on your country of origin (US$75 to US$125). Visa applications from embassies abroad are referred to Luanda, and while processing theoretically takes two to three weeks, you should allow up to six weeks. If travelling independently, you will require a letter of invitation from a person or organisation in Angola, but don't book a flight until you have your visa – a flight itinerary is sufficient.

Visa Extensions

Visas can be renewed for 30 days in Luanda at the Department of Immigration (DEFA; Map p856), adjacent to the British embassy, for US$50.

Visas for Onward Travel

Visas for the following countries can be obtained in Angola. See left for embassy and consulate information.

Congo All visitors need a visa. Visas can be issued on the same or next day and cost US$120.

Democratic Republic of Congo All visitors need a visa, which must be obtained before arrival. A one-month, single-entry visa costs US$180.

Gabon Visas cost US$120 for 30 days. Applications can be lodged 9am to 12.30pm Monday to Friday (air ticket and one photo required).

Namibia Many nationalities (including Australia, New Zealand, South Africa, UK, USA and most western European countries) don't need a visa to enter Namibia.

Zambia Visas cost US$50 for 30 days and applications can be lodged 9am to noon Monday to Friday. Visas can also be obtained at the border.

TRANSPORT IN ANGOLA

GETTING THERE & AWAY
Air

Direct flights from Europe are possible from Paris (Air France), London (British Airways), Brussels (SN Brussels Airlines) and Lisbon (TAP). Prices start around US$1800 return.

International flights fly into Luanda's Aeroporto 4 de Fevereiro.

Your best bet for a cheaper deal is with Ethiopian Airlines, which flies to Luanda from Europe via its hub of Addis Ababa twice weekly. Deals can be had for as little as US$900.

From inside Africa you can fly to Luanda from Brazzaville (Congo), Harare (Zimbabwe), Johannesburg (South Africa), Kinshasa (Democratic Republic of Congo) and Windhoek (Namibia). There are also regular flights from Windhoek to Lubango.

The following international airlines are based in Luanda and fly to/from Angola:

Air France (☎ 222-33 54 16; Av 4 de Fevereiro,123)
Air Namibia (☎ 222-33 67 26; Aeroporto 4 de Fevereiro)
British Airways (☎ 222-30 92 51; Av Murtala Mohamed)
Brussels Airlines (☎ 222-31 14 47; Largo 4 de Fevereiro, 9)

Ethiopian Airlines (☎ 222-31 06 15; Largo 4 de Fevereiro,10)
South African Airways (☎ 222-39 58 45; Rua Major Kanyangulo, 32)
TAAG (☎ 222-39 25 41; Rua Missão,123)
TAP (☎ 222-33 16 97; Av 4 de Fevereiro, 80)

Land

According to the Angolan tourist ministry, all of the country's land borders are now open. Thankfully, levels of bureaucracy have reduced considerably in recent years and border crossings are relatively straightforward, provided you have a visa and a legion of passport photos. Once you cross from the DRC or Zambia, transport is in short supply, though a little hunting will lead to a jeep or minibus that's Luanda bound. The terrible condition of the Matadi–Luanda road makes flying a tempting option, but at least the border procedures to cross into the DRC are simple, provided you obtained a visa in advance. The border with Namibia is a relative formality and transport from Lubango is easy to find, though the road is not in great condition. At the time of writing you could enter at either Santa Clara (Angola) from Oshikango (Namibia) or at Calai (Angola) from Rundu (Namibia).

GETTING AROUND
Air

Air travel is easy within Angola and flights can often be booked the same day. The national carrier is **TAAG** (☎ 222-35 25 86), but there are a number of equally good internal options, including **SAL Airlines** (☎ 222-35 08 69), **Sonair** (☎ 222-35 09 93), **Air 26** (☎ 222-39 53 95), **Air Gemini** (☎ 222-35 12 49) and **Diexim Expresso** (☎ 222-44 29 10). Flights between Luanda and major cities run daily and interprovincial flights are also possible.

Destinations include Benguela (US$115), Cabinda (US$100), Huambo (US$130), Malange (US$100), Namibe (US$140), Ondjiva (US$140) and Lubango (US$130). Flights depart from Aeroporto 4 de Fevereiro.

Bus

Public transportation is improving at a rapid rate and many of the main cities are now linked by uncrowded, efficient buses. See p858 for further information.

Car

Aided by Chinese and Portuguese investment, roads are slowly opening up in Angola, though

ANGOLA

you'll still need a 4WD if you want to wander away from the main cities. There are plenty of car-rental companies, though all with the same frustration – you can't take a rental car outside the province where it was hired.

Taxi

Every city is packed to the rafters with Hiaces – shared taxis that follow set routes for 50Kz to 100Kz a trip. A new addition to Angola's already congested city streets are the legions of motorbike taxis that offer a door-to-door service for 100Kz to 300Kz.

Tours

At the forefront of Angola's tourist renaissance, **Charme Tours** (☎ 912-20 33 24; www.charmetours.com; Rua Cónego Manuel das Neves, 101) organises flight book-

ings and tailored tours. **Ecotur** (☎ 923-50 13 87; www.eco-tur.com) is an equally professional outfit, co-run by a British expat, that specialises in adventure trips, such as big game fishing, bird-watching and Kissama trips. **Angolan Adventure Safaris** (☎ 912-82 50 45; www.aasafaris.com), which runs the Tarpon Lodge on the Kwanza River and the Flamingo Lodge south of Namibe, can organise visas and put together tailored trips.

Train

A one-time pioneer of 20th-century rail transport, Angola's war-damaged railways are currently getting a long-awaited Chinese makeover (see the boxed text, p860). Limited services are available between Luanda and Dondo (twice weekly); Lobito and Cubal (three per week) and Lubango and Namibe (twice weekly).

Botswana

The chorus of the African bush is a palette of distinctive earmarks: saw-throated leopard barks, elephant hoots, fish eagle screams and the crazy whoop of a running hyena. It's a soundtrack sourced from ruggedness, and as such, we often miss out on gentle music, like a *mokoro* (dugout canoe) slipping over papyrus, or the wind breezing through the thornveld.

And we often expect the African wilderness to be dry and harsh, all hills and bush and soul-spanning sky; so we can be surprised by the subtle, less-dramatic – but equally arresting – beauty of silent reed beds, and the casual incongruity of tufts of palm growing out of a carpet of marsh and slow streams.

Contrasts of image and sound – rock outcroppings uplifted from the moon, red deserts blown out of a surrealist's fantasy and the wet prairie of the largest inland river delta in the world – are commonplace in Botswana, one of the great wild wonderlands of southern Africa. Extending 1100km from north to south and 960km from east to west, 'Bots' is about the same size as Kenya, or France. By and large it is a land of wild border spaces: small towns and cattle posts separated by stretches of yellow grass and bleached thornbush, and some of best safari camps in the continent.

You know what's *not* here? No 1 Lady Detectives. Seriously – get that cliché out of your head. Instead, embrace the genial pride and laid-back friendliness of the Batswana people, gas up your 4WD and get ready to ride into sunsets that set the thornbush on fire – just watch out for all the cattle on the road when you do.

FAST FACTS

- **Area** 582,000 sq km
- **ATMs** Found in large towns
- **Borders** South Africa, Namibia, Zambia, Zimbabwe
- **Budget** US$50 to US$150 a day
- **Capital** Gaborone
- **Languages** English, Setswana
- **Money** Pula (P); US$1 = P6.85, €1 = P9.76
- **Population** 1.8 million
- **Seasons** Wet (November to March), dry (May to October)
- **Telephone** Country code ☎ 267; international access code ☎ 00
- **Time** GMT/UTC +2
- **Visa** None required for citizens of Australia, New Zealand, France, Germany, the UK, Ireland, Canada or the USA

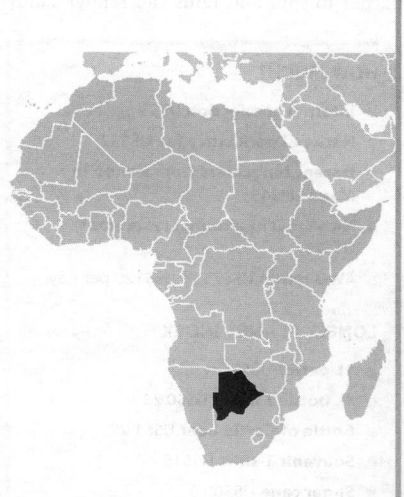

HIGHLIGHTS

- **Okavango Delta** (p875) Glide through watery expanses in a *mokoro,* a traditional dugout canoe.
- **Chobe National Park** (p883) Spot the Big Five (elephant, lion, rhino, leopard and buffalo) at Botswana's premier wildlife park.
- **Makgadikgadi & Nxai Pans National Park** (p884) Follow herds of migrating zebra and wildebeest in this baobab-dotted salt-pan complex.
- **Tsodilo Hills** (p881) Wander through the 'Wilderness Louvre' of ancient San rock paintings.
- **Savuti** (p884) Test the limits of your survival instincts on an intrepid 4WD camping expedition.

CLIMATE & WHEN TO GO

Although it straddles the Tropic of Capricorn, Botswana experiences extremes in both temperature and weather. In the winter (late May through August), days are normally clear, warm and sunny, and nights are cool to cold. Wildlife never wanders far from water sources, so sightings are more predictable than in the wetter summer season. This is also the time of European, North American and – most importantly – South African school holidays, so some areas can be busy, especially between mid-July and mid-September.

In summer (October to April), wildlife is harder to spot and rains can render sandy roads impassable. This is also the time of the highest humidity and the most stifling heat; daytime temperatures of over 40°C are common.

ITINERARIES

- **Three Days** Botswana's tourist highlight is the Okavango Delta (p875), and if you have only a few days, this is where you'll want to focus. Choose Maun (p879) or the Okavango Panhandle (p878) as your base and organise a *mokoro* trip through the wetlands, followed by a wildlife-viewing trip at Moremi Wildlife Reserve (p878).
- **One Week** Combine your visit to the delta with a safari through Chobe National Park (p883), one of the world's top safari experiences. Either go overland through the rugged interior or cruise along the wildlife-rich waterfront.
- **One Month** With a full month (and lots of money), you can hire a 4WD or use a reputable safari company and see the best of the country: do a *mokoro* trip through the Okavango Delta (p875), safari in Moremi Wildlife Reserve (p878) and Chobe National Park (p883), camp and hike in the Tsodilo Hills (p881), cruise along the Okavango Panhandle (p878) and explore the very furthest reaches of the Savuti (p884).

HISTORY
Pre-Colonial History

Archaeological evidence and rock art found in the Tsodilo Hills (see p881) suggests the San took shelter in caves throughout the region from around 17,000 BC. The tempera paintings representing the natural world in which they lived attest to increasing levels of mental and spiritual sophistication. On the physical side, clumsy stone tools gave way to bone, wood and, eventually, iron implements. Better tools meant more efficient hunting, which allowed time for further innovation, personal adornment and artistic pursuits such as the emerging craft of pottery.

Such progress prompted many of these hunter-gatherers to adopt a pastoral lifestyle – sowing crops and grazing livestock on the exposed pastures of the Okavango and the Makgadikgadi lakes. Some migrated west into central Namibia, and by 70 BC some had reached the Cape of Good Hope. Around AD 200–500, Bantu-speaking farmers started

---

HOW MUCH?

- **Internet connection** US$3 per hour
- **National park entry fee** US$22
- **Decent binoculars from a shop in Maun** US$45
- **Nice meal in a tourist restaurant** US$20
- **4WD rental** US$75 to US$120 per day

LONELY PLANET INDEX

- **1L petrol** US$1
- **1L bottled water** US$0.25
- **Bottle of Castle beer** US$1.25
- **Souvenir T-shirt** US$15
- **Sugar cane** US$0.10

BOTSWANA

to appear on the southern landscape from the north and east.

Perhaps the most significant development in Botswana's history was the evolution of the three main branches of the Tswana tribe during the 14th century. It's a King Lear–ish tale of family discord, where three brothers – Kwena, Ngwaketse and Ngwato – broke away from their father, Chief Malope, to establish their own followings in Molepolole, Kanye and Serowe, respectively. These fractures probably occurred in response to drought and expanding populations eager to strike out in search of new pastures and arable land.

Colonial History

From the 1820s the Boers began their Great Trek across the Vaal River; 20,000 Boers crossed into Tswana and Zulu territory and established themselves as though the lands were unclaimed and uninhabited. At the Sand River Convention of 1852, Britain recognised the Transvaal's independence. The Boers informed the undoubtedly surprised Batswana (people of Botswana) that they were now subjects of the South African Republic.

Prominent Tswana leaders Sechele I and Mosielele refused to accept white rule and incurred the wrath of the Boers. After heavy losses of life and land, the Tswana sent their leaders to petition the British for protection. By 1877 the British annexed the Transvaal and launched the first Boer War.

In 1882, Boers again moved into Tswana lands and subdued the town of Mafikeng, threatening the British route between the Cape and suspected mineral wealth in Zimbabwe. Again the Tswana lobbied for British protection and in 1885, thanks to petitions from John Mackenzie (a friend of the Christian Chief Khama III of Shoshong), lands north of the Molopo River became the British Crown Colony of Bechuanaland, attached to the Cape Colony. The area north became the British Protectorate of Bechuanaland.

A new threat to the Tswana chiefs' power base came in the form of Cecil Rhodes and his British South Africa Company (BSAC). By 1894, the British had all but agreed to allow him to control the country. An unhappy delegation of Tswana chiefs – Bathoen, Khama III and Sebele – accompanied by a sympathetic missionary, WC Willoughby, sailed to England to appeal for continued govern-

ment control (far less intrusive than Rhodes' proposed rule). Eventually, they turned to the London Missionary Society (LMS), which took the matter to the British public. Fearing the BSAC would allow alcohol in Bechuanaland, the LMS and other Christian groups backed Chief Khama III. Public pressure mounted and the British government was forced to concede.

In 1923, Chief Khama III died and was succeeded by his son Sekgoma, who died only two years later. The heir to the throne, four-year-old Seretse Khama, wasn't ready for the job of ruling the largest Tswana chiefdom, so his 21-year-old uncle, Tshekedi Khama, became clan regent.

After WWII, Seretse Khama went to study in England where he met and married an Englishwoman. Tshekedi Khama was furious at this breach of tribal custom, and apartheid-era South African authorities were none too happy either. The British government blocked Seretse's chieftaincy and he was exiled to England. Bitterness continued until 1956 when Seretse Khama renounced his right to power and returned with his wife to Botswana to serve as a minor official.

Nationalism & Independence

The first signs of nationalist thinking among the Tswana occurred in the late 1940s, and in 1955 it had become apparent that Britain was preparing to release its grip on Bechuanaland.

Following the Sharpeville massacre in 1960, when 69 people were killed by African police after protesting the apartheid pass laws system, South African refugees Motsamai Mpho of the African National Congress (ANC), Philip Matante, a preacher affiliated with the Pan-Africanist Congress, and KT Motsete, from Malawi, formed the Bechuanaland People's Party. Its immediate goal was independence for the protectorate. In 1962, Seretse Khama and Kanye farmer Quett Masire formed the more moderate Bechuanaland Democratic Party (BDP).

The BDP formulated a schedule for independence, drawing on support from local chiefs and traditional Batswana. They promoted the transfer of the capital into the country (from Mafikeng to Gaborone), drafted a new nonracial constitution and set up a countdown to independence to allow a peaceful transfer of power. General elections

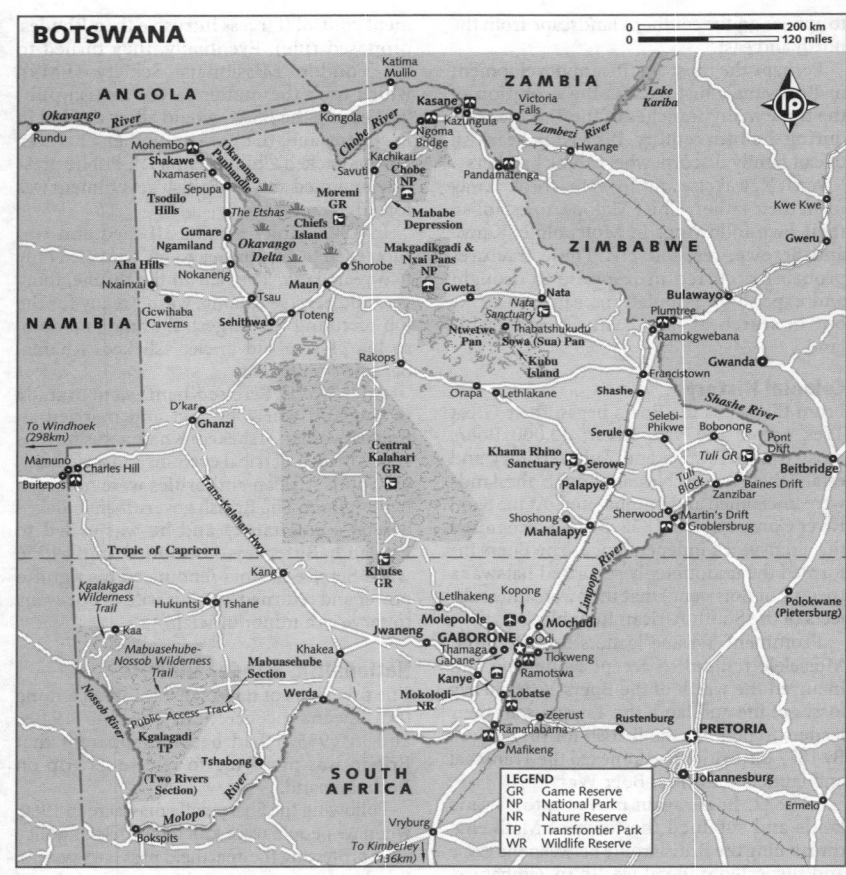

BOTSWANA

LEGEND
GR   Game Reserve
NP   National Park
NR   Nature Reserve
TP   Transfrontier Park
WR   Wildlife Reserve

were held in 1965 and Seretse Khama was elected president. On 30 September 1966, the Republic of Botswana gained independence.

Sir Seretse Khama – he was knighted shortly after independence – adopted a neutral stance (until near the end of his presidency) towards South Africa and Rhodesia (on each of which Botswana was economically dependent). Nevertheless, Khama refused to exchange ambassadors with South Africa and, in international circles, officially disapproved of apartheid.

Botswana was transformed by the discovery of diamonds near Orapa in 1967. The mining concession was given to De Beers, with Botswana taking 75% of the profits. For 40 years the BDP managed the country's diamond windfall relatively wisely. Diamond dollars were ploughed into infrastructure, education and health. Private businesses were allowed to grow and foreign investment was welcomed. From 1966 to 2005, Botswana's economy grew faster than any other in the world.

After the death of Khama in 1980, Dr Ketumile Masire took the helm. His popular presidency ended in March 1998, when president Festus Mogae assumed control of Botswana.

Botswana Today

Mogae handed over the presidency to Vice President Ian Khama (son of Sir Seretse Khama) on 1 April 2008; in the October 2009

AIDS IN BOTSWANA

According to UNAIDS and the World Health Organization, nearly 24% of all Batswana are HIV positive, and women represent over half of those cases. More than 11,000 people die of AIDS-related complications every year. In 2001, former president Festus Mogae lamented that unless the epidemic was reversed, his country faced 'blank extinction'. AIDS is also making Botswana poorer by the day, as the virus tends to hit people in their most productive years.

That said, Botswana has taken some of the most admirable steps of any sub-Sahara African nation in combating the virus. In 2001, it was the first African country to trial antiretroviral (ARV) drug therapy on a national scale. And Botswana is one of just a handful of countries worldwide that has committed to providing ARV treatment free to all of its affected citizens.

These policies are already bearing some fruit: life expectancy, which was once 33 years, is up to almost 62. In a 2008 report UNAIDS estimated that Botswana's public ARV treatment program was covering 91,780 people and natal transmission of the disease from mother to child was down from 20% to 40% to 4% to 6%.

But issues remain. Workers in medical NGOs in Gaborone told us the prevalence of ARVs has made some people less liable to practise safe sex. Traditional male circumcision, an integral part of black southern African culture, is also responsible for spreading the disease.

---

elections, Khama and the BDP garnered more than 45 seats in the 57-seat Parliament.

With an ever-diminishing source of diamonds, Botswana is now economically vulnerable. Local media buzzes with articles that worry the economy has not yet diversified enough into other industries. Unemployment has been curbed and stands at a respectable 7.5% (down from perhaps 40% in 2004), but 30% of the population still lives below the poverty line. And the economy is in a precarious position; in 2009 Reuters reported the country's GDP shrank by 20.3% in the first quarter of the year. A young generation of educated Batswana, lured by the malls of Gaborone, are demanding greater opportunities away from traditional rural life, and the government has some huge responsibilities to live up to. The greatest threat to Botswana's stability remains the deadly AIDS virus (see boxed text, above).

CULTURE
Proud, conservative, resourceful and respectful, the Batswana have an ingrained feeling of national identity and an impressive belief in their government and country.

Traditional culture acts as a sort of societal glue. Respect for one's elders, firmly held religious beliefs, traditional gender roles and the tradition of the *kgotla* (a specially designated meeting place in each village where grievances can be aired in an atmosphere of mutual respect) create a well-defined social structure with some stiff mores at its core. But despite some heavyweight social responsibilities, the Batswana have an easygoing and unhurried approach to life, and the emotional framework of the extended family generally makes for an inclusive network.

Arts & Crafts
The original Batswana artists managed to convey individuality, aesthetics and aspects of Batswana life in their utilitarian implements. Baskets, pottery, fabrics and tools were decorated with meaningful designs derived from tradition. Europeans introduced a new form of art, some of which was integrated and adapted to local interpretation, particularly in weavings and tapestries. The result is some of the finest and most meticulously executed work in southern Africa.

Botswana's most famous modern literary figure is South African–born Bessie Head (who died in 1988). Her works reflect the harshness and beauty of African village life and the Botswanan landscape. Her most widely read works include *Serowe: Village of the Rain Wind, When Rain Clouds Gather, Maru, The Cardinals, A Bewitched Crossroad* and *The Collector of Treasures* (the last is an anthology of short stories). Welcome recent additions to Botswana's national literature are the works of Norman Rush, which include the novel *Mating*, set in a remote village, and *Whites*, which deals with the country's growing number of expats and apologists from South Africa and elsewhere.

Unity Dow, Botswana's first female High Court judge, has also authored four books to date, all of them dealing with contemporary

---

NATIONAL PARK FEES PER DAY

These are the admission and camping rates for all Department of Wildlife and National Parks (DWNP) sites listed in this chapter. Infants and children up to the age of seven years are entitled to free admission into all national parks.

	Citizens (P)	Residents (P)	Foreigners (P)	Safari Participants (P)
adult	10	30	120	70
child (8-17 years)	5	15	60	35
campsites	5	20	30	
vehicles <3500kg	10	10	50	

---

social issues in the country; we recommend *Far and Beyon'* (2002).

FOOD & DRINK

The usual southern African fast food – Spar snack shops, meat-pie stands, and chicken and chips – are ubiquitous in tourist towns and Gaborone. In rural areas, *mabele* (sorghum) or *bogobe* (porridge made from sorghum) and, increasingly, maize mealies (pap) are staples. All of the above provide the base for an array of meat and vegetable sauces.

For breakfast, you might be able to try *pathata* (sort of like an English muffin) or *megunya,* also known as fat cakes. These are little balls of fried dough that are kind of like doughnuts minus the hole and, depending on your taste, the flavour.

The challenging environment of the Kalahari grows *morama, marula* fruit (of Amarula liqueur fame), wild plums, berries, *tsama* melons, wild cucumbers, honey and *grewia flava,* which is related to the European truffle but now known to marketing people as the 'Kalahari truffle'.

Don't forget mopane worms. These fat suckers are pulled off mopane trees and fried into little delicacies – they're tasty and a good source of protein. You might be able to buy some from ladies selling them by the bag in the Main Mall in Gaborone; otherwise, they're pretty common up in Francistown.

Decent locally made brews include Castle Lager (made under licence from the South African brewery), St Louis Special Light and Lion Lager; also available are the excellent Windhoek Lager (from Namibia) and Zambezi Lager (from Zimbabwe).

Legal home brews include *bojalwa,* an inexpensive, sprouted-sorghum beer which is brewed commercially as Chibuku. Light and nonintoxicating *mageu* is made from mealies or sorghum mash. Another is *madila,* a thick-ened sour milk used as a relish or drunk ('eaten' would be a more appropriate term) plain.

Mosukujane tea and *lengane* tea are used to treat headaches/nausea and arthritis, respectively. They're a bit strong in flavour, but locals faithfully tout their remedial properties.

ENVIRONMENT

With an area of 582,000 sq km, landlocked Botswana extends more than 1100km from north to south and 960km from east to west. The Kalahari (Kgalagadi) Desert covers 85% of the country, in the central and southwestern areas – but despite the name, it's semidesert and can be surprisingly lush in places. The best season for wildlife viewing takes place during the dry winter months (late May to August), when animals stay close to water sources.

Because the Okavango Delta and the Chobe River provide an incongruous water supply, nearly all southern African mammal species, including such rarities as pukus, red lechwe, sitatungas and wild dogs, are present in Moremi Wildlife Reserve, parts of Chobe National Park and the Linyanti Marshes (at the northwestern corner of Chobe). In the Makgadikgadi & Nxai Pan National Park, herds of wildebeest, zebra and other hoofed mammals migrate between their winter range on the Makgadikgadi plains and the summer lushness of the Nxai Pan region.

GABORONE

pop 186,000

A relatively large expat scene, the upper crust of Batswana society and a surprisingly diverse population of black, white, Indian and mixed-race African – plus, increasingly, Chinese – peoples makes Gaborone a spicier demographic stew than you might initially expect. Plus, its malls, movies and restaurants are a good distraction from the dust and the delta. And most importantly, this is the place to gauge the pulse of this rapidly changing nation.

ORIENTATION

'Gabs' lacks a definitive city centre, so many shops, restaurants and offices are located in or near suburban malls and shopping centres, which form their own pulsing nodes throughout the city. The Mall – also called the Main Mall – is the business heart of Gaborone and has a handful of shops, restaurants, banks and internet centres. Almost all government offices, and several embassies, are situated to the west of the Mall, in and around State and Embassy Drs. There are also a number of shopping malls that are located outside the city centre, which are easily accessible by combi (minibus).

INFORMATION

Bookshops

Botshalo Books (Game City Mall) Comes recommended by local expats for its good range of titles, focusing on both Africana and outside material.

Exclusive Books (Riverwalk Mall) This reader-recommended bookshop has a wide range of literature, nonfiction and travel books.

Kingston's Bookshop (Broadhurst Mall) A huge array of novels, postcards, books and maps about the region.

Emergency

Ambulance (☎ 997)

Central police station (☎ 355 1161; Botswana Rd) Opposite the Cresta President Hotel.

Fire (☎ 998)

Police (☎ 999)

Internet Access

Many hotels are increasingly offering internet access, via either wi-fi or network cables.

Aim Internet (Botswana Rd; per hr US$3) Next to the Cresta President Hotel.

Sakeng Internet Access Point (The Mall; per hr P20) In the Gaborone Hardware Building.

Medical Services

Gaborone Hospital Dental Clinic (☎ 395 3777; Segoditshane Way) Part of the Gaborone Private Hospital.

Gaborone Private Hospital (☎ 300 1999; Segoditshane Way) For anything serious, head to this reasonably modern but expensive hospital, opposite Broadhurst Mall. The best facility in town.

Princess Marina Hospital (☎ 355 3221; Notwane Rd) Equipped to handle standard medical treatments and emergencies, but shouldn't be your first choice.

Money

The following locations change travellers cheques and foreign currencies.

Barclays Bank (☎ 355 3411; Khama Cres) Head office. Has an ATM.

Edcom Bureau de Change (☎ 361 1123) Near the train station.

Post

Central post office (The Mall)

Tourist Information

Department of Tourism (☎ 391 3111; www.botswanatourism.co.bw; Ground Fl, Block B, Fairgrounds Office Park) There is also a tourism board kiosk in the lobby of the Cresta President Hotel (see p873).

Department of Wildlife & National Parks (DWNP; ☎ 318 0774; dwnp@gov.bw; Government Enclave, Khama Cres; ⊗ reservations 7.30am-12.45pm & 1.45-4.30pm Mon-Fri) One of the two accommodation booking offices for all national parks and reserves run by the DWNP. The other office is in Maun; see p879.

Garcin Safaris (☎ 393 8190; www.garcinsafaris.com) If you've got a day or two to kill in Gabs, contact local Marilyn Garcin. She does great tours of the city, including a No 1 Ladies Detective Agency–focused jaunt, and is a good contact for arranging onward travel into the rest of the country.

SIGHTS & ACTIVITIES

If you come with expectations reasonably lowered, you may enjoy the small but diverse **National Museum & Art Gallery** (☎ 397 4616; 331 Independence Ave; admission free; ⊗ 9am-6pm Tue-Fri, to 5pm Sat & Sun). It's a good way to kill an afternoon, especially if you're into taxidermy. The ethnographic displays are useful for anyone wanting to learn more about the demographic makeup of the country.

The **Gaborone Game Reserve** (☎ 318 4492; per person US$0.25, per vehicle US$0.50; ⊗ 6.30am-6.30pm), 1km east of Broadhurst, is accessible only by private vehicle (no bikes or motorcycles), and is home to a variety of grazers and browsers.

In the **Diamond Trading Company** (☎ 364 9000; Diamond Park; tours free) you can learn all about diamond mining if you have time and aren't put off by red tape; you'll have to muster a group and arrange a tour.

With a little love and a lot of work, the **Botanical Gardens** (☎ 397 3860; 17991 Okwa Rd; admission free; ⊗ 7.30am-6pm) could be a great spot to visit in the future, but right now they're just cordoned-off scrub inhabited by some, admittedly, cute monkeys. On site is the colonial hotel building (pretty much empty inside)

BOTSWANA

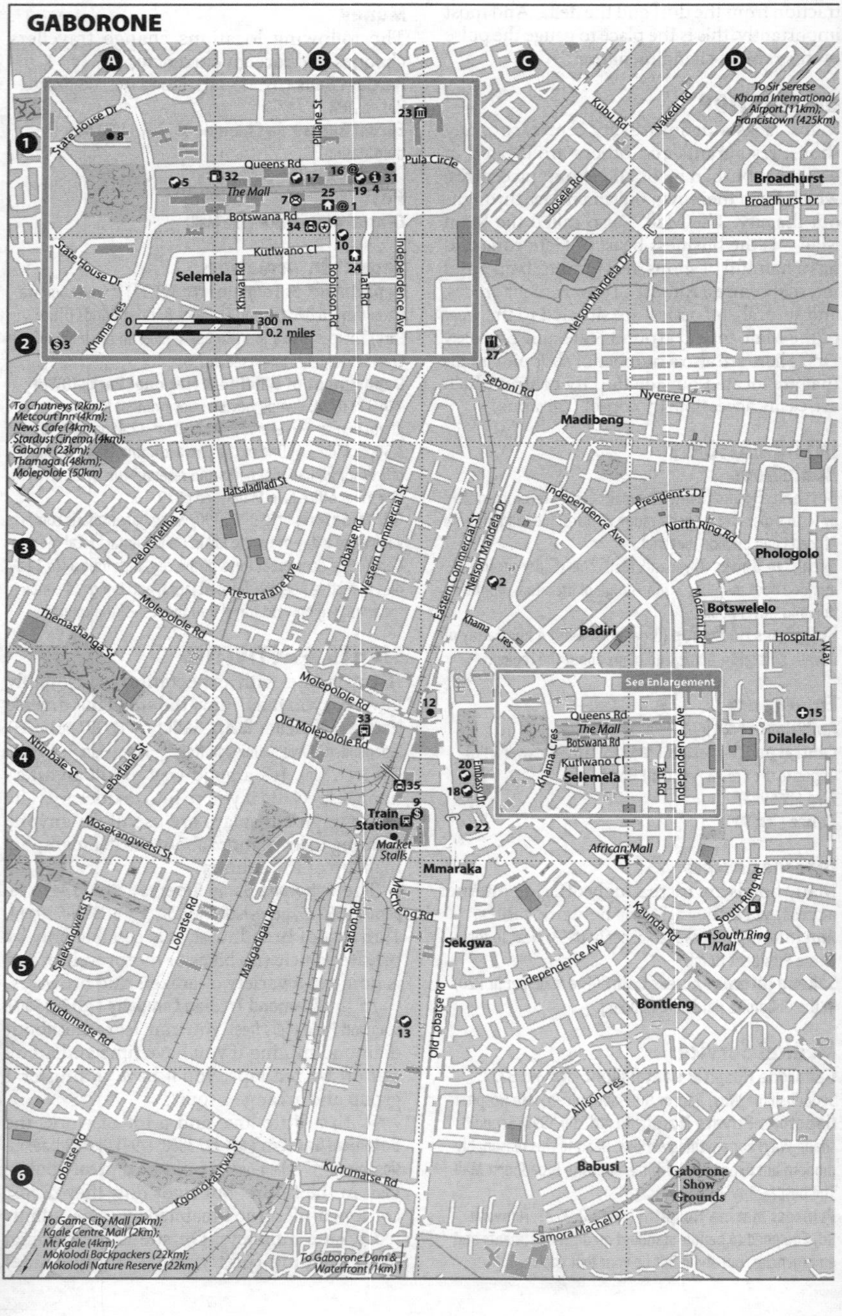

GABORONE

To Sir Seretse
Khama International
Airport (11km);
Francistown (425km)

State House Dr

Broadhurst

Broadhurst Dr

Kubu Rd

Bosele Rd

Naledi Rd

Pitlane St

23

Queens Rd

The Mall

Botswana Rd

Kutlwano Cl

Selemela

Khama Cres

Independence Ave

Robinson Rd

Tati Rd

State House Dr

0   300 m
0   0.2 miles

Pula Circle

16

17

25

34

32

5

8

3

7

6

10

24

1

19 4

31

Nelson Mandela Dr

Nyerere Dr

Madibeng

Seboni Rd

27

To Chutneys (2km);
Metcourt Inn (4km);
News Café (4km);
Stardust Cinema (4km);
Gabane (23km);
Thamaga (48km);
Molepolole (50km)

President's Dr

North Ring Rd

Phologralo

Botswelelo

Hospital Way

Independence Ave

Kgale Rd

Badiri

Dilalelo

See Enlargement

Queens Rd
The Mall
Botswana Rd
Kutlwano Cl
Selemela

Khama Cres

Tati Rd

Independence Ave

15

Hatsalatladi St

Lobatse Rd

Western Commercial St

Eastern Commercial St

Nelson Mandela Dr

Peloshatiha St

Aresutalane Ave

Molepolole Rd

Themashanga St

Ntlhole St

Kgale Rd

Molepolole Rd

Old Molepolole Rd

2

12

33

20

18

35

22

African Mall

Train
Station

Market
Stalls

Mmaraka

Kudumatse Rd

Mosekangwetsi St

Selakangwetsi St

Lobatse Rd

Station Rd

Nakgadingau Rd

Macheng Rd

Old Lobatse Rd

Sekgwa

Independence Ave

Raundo Rd

South Ring Rd

South Ring
Mall

Bontleng

Babusi

Gaborone
Show
Grounds

13

Allison Cres

Kudumatse Rd

Kgomokapitwe St

Samora Machel Dr

To Game City Mall (2km);
Kgale Centre Mall (2km);
Mt Kgale (4km);
Mokolodi Backpackers (22km);
Mokolodi Nature Reserve (22km)

To Gaborone Dam &
Waterfront (1km)

BOTSWANA

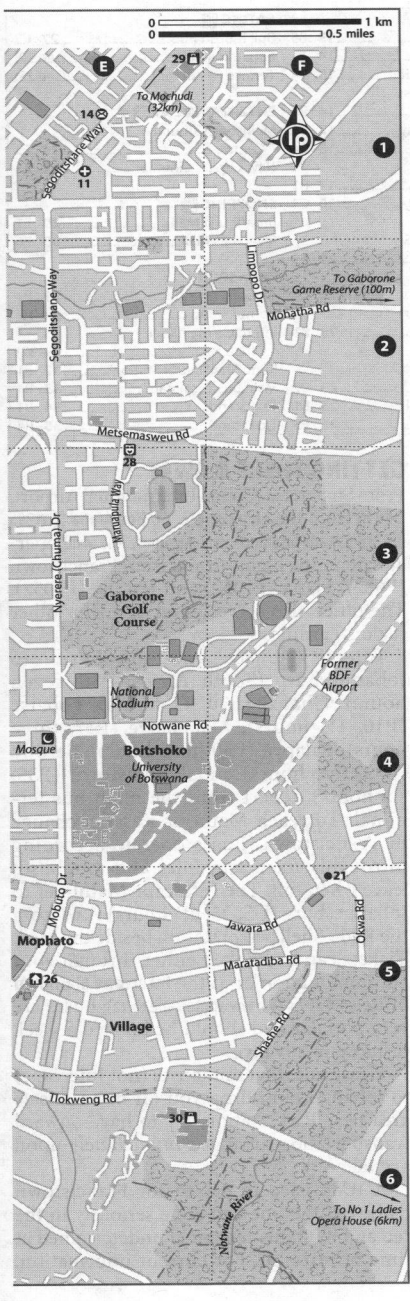

where, in 1895, Cecil John Rhodes helped plan the failed Jameson Raid – one of the causes of the Second Boer War, the conclusion of which put South Africa under British control.

SLEEPING

Mokolodi Backpackers (☎ 7411 1165; www.backpackers. co.bw; campsites/dm/chalets P75/120/325; 🖳) If you're doing the budget, self-drive or overland thing, this is a good option, and with the only real backpacker vibe around Gaborone. About 22km from the Mall and 10km from Game City Mall, there are chalets, good campsites and dorms.

Brackendene Lodge (☎ 391 2886; Tati Rd; r from P290; 🍴 🖳) The Brackendene is one of the better-value hotels in town. Rooms are simple but large and kitted out with TV and air-con. There's reliable internet in the lobby (supposedly also moving into the rooms, fingers crossed) and you're within easy walking distance of the Mall.

Metcourt Inn (☎ 391 2999, 363 7777; www.metcourt. com; s/d P465/535; 🍴) Located within the Grand Palm Hotel complex, this is a lovely little three-star option that is likely to remind you of every businessman's hotel you've ever stayed in, which can be a good thing after the bush.

Cresta President Hotel (☎ 395 3631; www.cresta -hospitality.co.bw; The Mall; r from P908; 🍴 🖳 🛎) The first luxury hotel in the city is smack dab in the middle of the Mall. It's modern, service is helpful and bows to your whims, and there are no surprises – a pleasant surprise itself!

Mondior Summit (☎ 319 0600; www.mondior.com; Cnr Mobuto & Maratadiba Rds; s/d from P1312/1922; 🍴 🖳 🛎) Probably the best hotel in town, the Mondior is chock-a-block with all the mod-cons you need plus African chic – think big, plush rooms in warm monochrome colours.

EATING

Equatorial Café (Riverwalk Mall; mains from US$2) The best espressos in town, along with fruit smoothies, felafel and gourmet sandwiches, and even bagels.

News Cafe (☎ 319 0600; Mondrian Hotel; mains P40-130) As trendy as Gabs gets, the News Cafe has a continental European menu and a modernist vibe about it. The swish decor and design are all the rage with Gaborone's young and moneyed and expats longing for urban cool.

Bull & Bush Pub (☎ 397 5070; off Francistown Rd; mains P45-80) A long-standing Gaborone institution renowned for its thick steaks and cold

BOTSWANA

beers. On any given night, the outdoor beer garden is buzzing.

Chutneys (☎ 319 0545; mains P50-90; West Ring Rd) This gorgeous spot serves the best Indian food in Botswana, a good and varied collection of curries that are a brilliant break from pap and meat and more pap.

Terrace Restaurant (☎ 395 3631; The Mall; mains from P85) On the terrace of the Cresta President Hotel, this eatery does very good chops and such off its grills, or you can enjoy some tea and watch life amble by.

ENTERTAINMENT

Stardust Cinema (☎ 395 9271; Grand Palm Hotel Casino Resort, Molepolole Rd) and **New Capitol Cinema** (☎ 370-0111; Riverwalk & Game City Malls) offer recent escapist Hollywood entertainment about every two hours between noon and 10.30pm daily.

Maitisong Cultural Centre (☎ 397 1809; http://maiti song.org; Maruapula Way; ☽ ticket office 8am-6pm Mon-Fri) Maitisong (Place of Entertainment) puts on incredible shows in its large theatre, with events ranging from Shakespearean plays to Batswana music most weeks. You'd be remiss not to check this spot out if you're in Gabs for longer than a few days. Part of the Maitisong Festival (see the boxed text, opposite) is held here.

No 1 Ladies Opera House (☎ 316 5459) Located a few kilometres south of Gaborone, this collaboration between author Alexander McCall Smith and the local arts scene showcases Setswana singing, community theatre performances and, hopefully by the time you read this, full-scale opera shows. There's a cute cafe on site.

GETTING THERE & AWAY

From Sir Seretse Khama International Airport, 14km from the city centre, **Air Botswana** (☎ 395 2812; Botswana Insurance Company House, the Mall) operates domestic flights to and from Francistown (P682), Maun (P1057) and Kasane (P1057). The office also serves as an agent for other regional airlines.

Intercity buses and minibuses to Johannesburg (South Africa; P80, seven hours), Ghanzi (P70, 11 hours), Lobatse (P10, 1½ hours), Mahalapye (P17, three hours), Palapye (P30, four hours), Serowe (P32, five hours) and Francistown (P35, six hours) depart from the main bus terminal. To reach Maun or Kasane, change in Francistown. Buses operate according to roughly fixed schedules and minibuses leave when full. The Intercape Mainliner to Johannesburg (US$25, 6½ hours) runs from the Kadu Shell petrol station beside the Mall. Tickets can be booked either through your accommodation or at the **Intercape Mainliner Office** (☎ 397 4294; www.intercape.co.za); buses are very popular and should be booked a week or more in advance.

Please note that minibuses (not Intercape) to Johannesburg drop you off in an unsafe area near Park Station; try to have onward transportation arranged *immediately* upon arrival.

A train used to depart for Francistown daily, but the line had gone seriously in the red and its status remained undetermined at time of research. For current information,

BOTSWANA

THE MAITISONG FESTIVAL

Established in 1987, the **Maitisong Festival** is the largest performing-arts festival in Botswana, and is held annually for seven days during mid-March or early April. The festival features an outdoor program of music, theatre, film and dance that takes place on several stages throughout the capital. There is also an indoor program that takes place in the Maitisong Cultural Centre.

Programs to events are usually available in shopping malls and centres during the month leading up to the festival. Outdoor events are free, while indoor events are priced from P25 to P150. For P400 you can buy a ticket that provides access to everything on offer during the event.

---

contact **Botswana Railways** (☎ 471 1375; www.botswanarailways.co.bw).

GETTING AROUND

White combis circulate according to set routes and cost P2.70. They pick up and drop off only at designated lay-bys marked 'bus/taxi stop'. The main city loop passes all the main shopping centres except the new Riverwalk Mall and the Kgale Centre Mall, which are on the Tlokweng and Kgale routes, respectively.

Taxis are surprisingly difficult to come by; if you manage to get hold of one, fares (negotiable) are generally P25 to P40 per trip around the city.

If you want to book a taxi:
Final Bravo Cabs (☎ 312 1785)
Speedy Cabs (☎ 390 0070)

AROUND GABORONE

MOCHUDI

This charming village was first settled in the 1500s by the Kwena, one of the three most prominent lineage groups of the Batswana. In 1871, the Kgatla moved in after being forced from their lands by northwards-trekking Boers. The Cape Dutch–style **Phuthadikobo Museum** (☎ 577 7238; www.phuthadikobomuseum.com; admission free, donations suggested; ☑ 8am-5pm Mon-Fri, from 2pm Sat & Sun) details the history of the area with colourful displays. After visiting the museum, it's worth spending some time appreciating the traditional Batswana designs in the town's mud-walled architecture. If you'd like to linger in Mochudi for a night, the easy-to-spot (it's bright pink) **Sedibelo Motel** (☎ 572 9327; Pilane-Mochudi Rd; d incl breakfast P150) has reasonably clean and comfortable rooms.

Buses to Mochudi (P8, one hour) depart from Gaborone when full. By car, head to Pilane and turn east. After 6km, turn left at the T-junction and then right just before the hospital to reach the historic village centre.

MOKOLODI NATURE RESERVE

This 3000-hectare private **reserve** (☎ 316 1955; www.mokolodi.com; ☑ 7.30am-6pm), home to giraffes, elephants, zebras, baboons and warthogs, is a good escape from Gaborone. It often closes during the rainy season (December to March) – phone ahead before you visit at this time. Visitors are permitted to drive their own vehicles around the reserve (you will need a 4WD in the rainy season), though guided tours by 4WD or on foot are also available.

Park entry fees cost P65 per person per day. If you're not self-driving, two-hour day or night wildlife drives cost P120 per person. There are a number of other activities on offer, such as cheetah petting (P290), rhino tracking (P485) and horse safaris (P145).

Though pricey, the **campsites** (per person P80) at Mokolodi are secluded and well maintained. If you want to safari in style, there are also **chalets** (3 person/6-8 person per weekday P420/560, per weekend day P560/765) situated in the middle of the reserve. Advance bookings are necessary. At the time of research, the Alexander McCall Smith Traditional Rest Camp, a cluster of African huts supported by the author of the same name, had just opened in the reserve, but prices were not yet available and the camp had not begun accepting visitors.

The entrance to the reserve is 12km south of Gaborone.

NORTHERN BOTSWANA

OKAVANGO DELTA

The Okavango Delta, the 16,000-sq-km expansion and expiration of the Okavango River, is this continent's realisation of a different kind of scenery: the bright tinkle of water versus the thorny forest and the slow drift of flood tides versus the Kalahari sun. Indeed, the jarring contrast the Okavango presents, compared with the rest of Botswana,

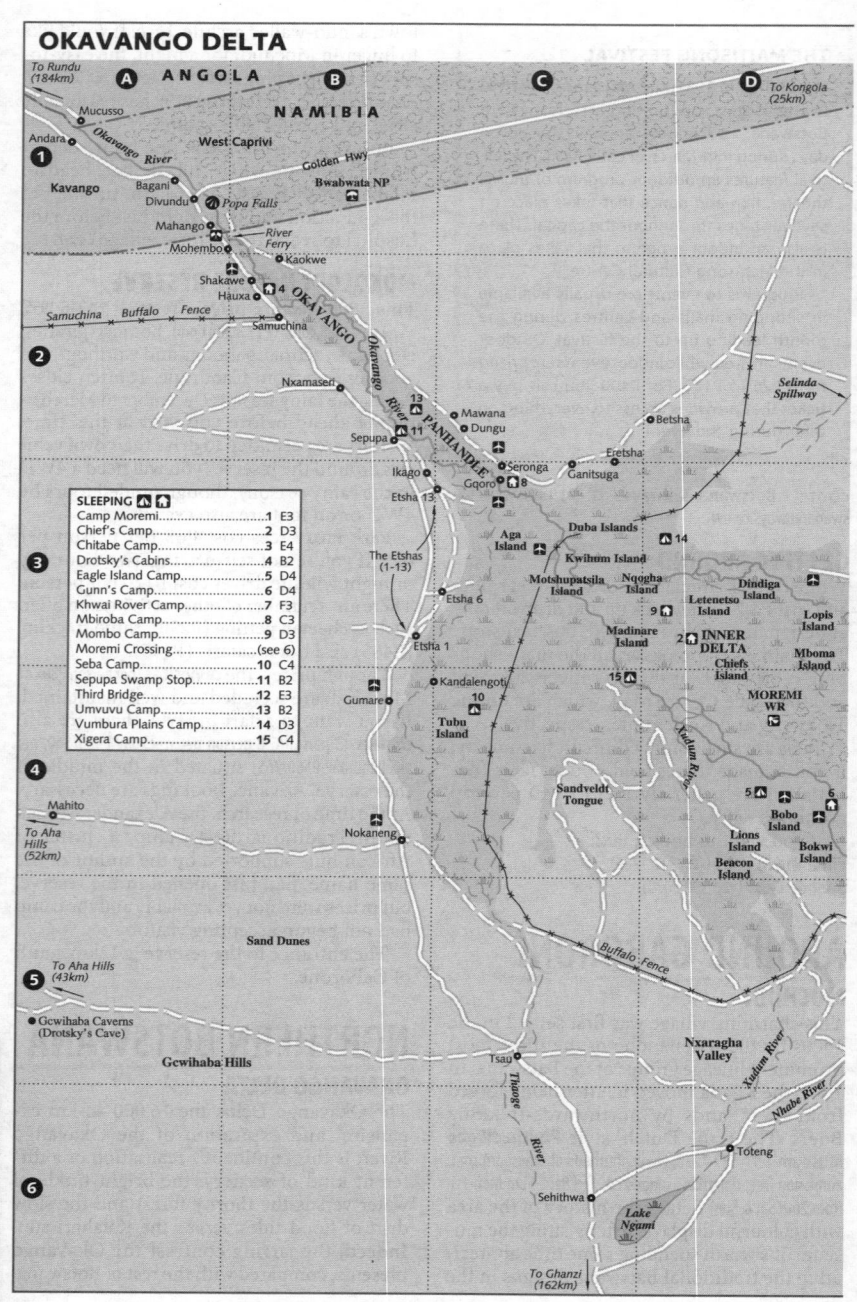

OKAVANGO DELTA

SLEEPING 🏕 🏠		
Camp Moremi	1	E3
Chief's Camp	2	D3
Chitabe Camp	3	E4
Drotsky's Cabins	4	B2
Eagle Island Camp	5	D4
Gunn's Camp	6	D4
Khwai River Camp	7	F3
Mbiroba Camp	8	C3
Mombo Camp	9	D3
Moremi Crossing	(see 6)	
Seba Camp	10	C4
Sepupa Swamp Stop	11	B2
Third Bridge	12	E3
Umvuvu Camp	13	B2
Vumbura Plains Camp	14	D3
Xigera Camp	15	C4

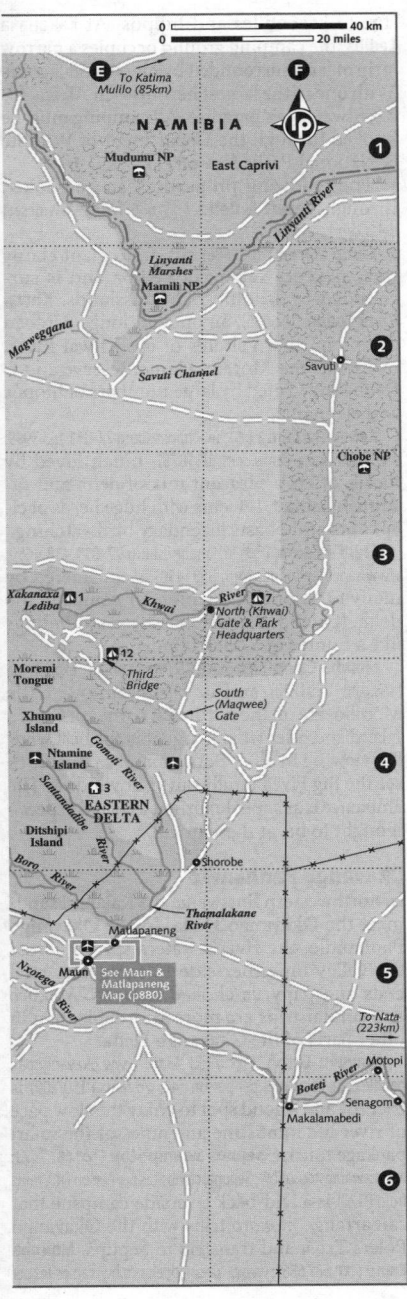

is one of her most memorable aspects. Here, in the heart of the thirstlands, is the world's largest inland river delta, an unceasing web of water – rushing, standing and flooding. These waters never make it to the sea, soaking into the salt pans of central Botswana; but before they do, they sustain vast quantities of wildlife and a similarly large tourist industry.

Generally, the best months to visit the delta are July to September, when the weather is dry and the water levels are high – unfortunately, along with the prices. Because most people visit at that time, the prices quoted here are for that period. Decent deals for delta lodges can be found during the low season (December to March), but be aware that *mokoro* trips out of Maun may be impossible at this time due to low water levels.

The Okavango Delta is usually subdivided into four areas: Eastern Delta, Inner Delta, Moremi Wilderness Reserve and Okavango Panhandle. The following rates include lodging, meals and activities.

Eastern Delta

The Eastern Delta includes the wetlands between the southern boundary of Moremi Wildlife Reserve and the buffalo fence that crosses the Boro and Santandadibe Rivers, north of Matlapaneng. If you're short of time and/or money, this part of the delta remains an affordable and accessible option. *Mokoro* trips in the Eastern Delta are mainly organised by Maun lodges and tour companies (see p889).

Situated near the Santandadibe River along the southern edges of the Moremi Wildlife Reserve, **Chitabe Camp** (per person low/high season US$365/700) is an island oasis renowned for the presence of Cape hunting dogs and other less-common wildlife. Book with **Wilderness Safaris** (☎ in Johannesburg 011-807 1800; www.wilderness-safaris.com).

Inner Delta

Roughly defined, the Inner Delta occupies the areas west of Chiefs Island and between Chiefs Island and the base of the Okavango Panhandle. *Mokoro* trips through the Inner Delta are almost invariably arranged with licensed polers affiliated with specific lodges, and operate roughly between June and December, depending on the water level.

Gunn's Camp (☎ 686 0023; www.gunnscamp.com; s/d US$375/470) combines great meals, attentive service and wonderful views over its island

BOTSWANA

location with a rugged sense of place; hippos, warthogs and elephants occasionally wander through the grounds. It's affiliated with nearby **Moremi Crossing** (☎ 686 0023; www.gunns-camp.com/moremi_crossing.php; s/d US$425/650), a collection of lovely chalets that is commended for pioneering a water/plumbing system that minimises environmental impact (it's also quite a feat of engineering – ask to see how it all works).

The following properties can be booked through **Wilderness Safaris** (☎ 686 0086, in Johannesburg 27-011 807 1800; www.wilderness-safaris.com). Regal **Vumbura Plains Camp** (low/high season US$1035/1455) is at the transition zone between the savannahs and swamps north of the delta, and is famous for attracting large buffalo herds. Accommodation is in either the six-tent Vumbura Plains Camp or the slightly smaller five-tent **Little Vumbura** (low/high season US$610/910). Pronounced 'kee-*jera*', **Xigera Camp** (low/high season US$610/910) is in an isolated spot deep in the heart of the Inner Delta and is renowned for its rich birdlife. **Seba Camp** (low/high season US$610/910) is set in an equally lovely riverine forest. What sets it apart is the emphasis on family service; unlike other properties, this one welcomes children.

Eagle Island Camp (☎ 686 0302; www.orient_express_safaris.com; per person low/shoulder/high season $805/100/1245) is widely considered one of the most beautiful camps in the delta, and occupies a fairly stunning concession deep in the waters. You'll be shacked up in silk-soft luxury tents, and helicopter safaris are part of your stay.

The only way in and out of the Inner Delta for most visitors is by air. Flights are typically arranged by lodges through local air charter companies.

Moremi Wildlife Reserve

The 3000-sq-km Moremi Wildlife Reserve is the part of the Okavango Delta officially designated for wildlife protection. The park has a distinctly dual personality, with two large areas of dry land – Chiefs Island and the Moremi Tongue – rising between vast wetlands. Habitats range from mopane woodland and thorn scrub to dry savannah, riparian woodlands, grasslands, flood plains, marshes, waterways, lagoons and islands.

The North (Khwai) and South (Maqwee) Gate entrances have both developed camping grounds. **Third Bridge**, 48km northwest of South Gate, is literally the third log bridge on the road and has a lovely camping ground. Be aware that swimming is extremely dangerous

due to crocodiles and hippos. At **Xakanaxa Lediba**, the camping ground occupies a narrow strip of land surrounded by marsh and lagoon. With one of the largest heronries in Africa, it's a birdwatcher's paradise. All camping must be booked through the Department of Wildlife & National Parks (see p871).

The following properties can be booked through **Desert & Delta** (☎ 686 1244; www.desert delta.com).

Camp Moremi (US$686) sits amid giant ebony trees next to Xakanaxa Lediba and is surrounded by wildlife-rich grasslands. **Khwai River Lodge** (US$686), an opulent lodge perched on the northern shores of the Khwai River, overlooks the Moremi Game Reserve and is frequently visited by large numbers of hippos and elephants.

Xakanaxa Camp (☎ in Johannesburg 27-011 463 3999; www.xakanaxa-camp.com; US$875), much loved by locals, offers a pleasant mix of delta and savannah habitat. It teems with huge herds of elephants and boasts legendary birdwatching.

Chief's Camp (☎ in Johannesburg 27-011 438 4650; www.sanctuarylodges.com; US$1450) is considered by many to be one of the premier camps in the delta. It blends into its marshy surroundings like a hunter in a duck blind.

Mombo Camp (☎ 686 0302; www.orient_express_sa faris.com; US$1770), and its sister camp – Little Mombo, are on the northwest corner of Chief's Island and offer what is arguably the best wildlife viewing in all of Botswana. It's possible to see the Big Five literally out your window. The ambience is as super luxurious as you'd expect – it ought to be, at these prices.

Okavango Panhandle

In northwestern Botswana, the Kalahari sands meet the Okavango Delta. In the Okavango Panhandle, the river's waters spread across the valley on either side to form vast reed beds and papyrus-choked lagoons. *Mokoro* and similar trips are more affordable than in other parts of the Okavango Delta.

Umvuvu Camp (☎ 7153 4340; www.okavangopan handle.com; campsites per person P40, s/d tents P150/200) is friendly and a good spot to enjoy the slow pace of river life minus the amenities of the safari package tourist. **Sepupa Swamp Stop** (☎ 687 7073; www.swampstop.co.bw; Sepupa; campsites per person P40, tents from P120) is a laid-back riverside campsite that can arrange *mokoro* trips with the Okavango Polers Trust and transfers to Sepupa. **Mbiroba Camp** (☎ 687 6861; www.okavangodelta.co.bw; campsites per

---

MAKING MOKORO TRIPS SUSTAINABLE

Mokoro trips from Maun are conducted through the Okavango Kopano Mokoro Community Trust (OKMCT), which sets rates for per person per day fees for clients and different grades of polers. Fees are then invested into community development programs.

Also, established in 1998 by the people of Seronga, the **Okavango Polers Trust** (☎ 687 6861; www.okavangodelta.co.bw) provides cheaper and more accessible *mokoro* trips and accommodation. As the collective is run entirely by the village, all profits are shared by the workers, invested into the trust and used to provide the community with better facilities. Although it's not uncommon to pay upwards of US$200 per day for a *mokoro* trip out of Maun, the trust charges around P500 per day for two people. Keep in mind, however, that you must self-cater (ie bring your own food, water and, if necessary, camping and cooking equipment).

There's no longer a daily bus from Mohembo to Seronga, but it's almost always possible to hitch from the free Okavango River ferry in Mohembo. Plan on paying about P5 for a lift. When they're operating, water taxis run along the Okavango between Sepupa Swamp Stop (opposite) and Seronga (P30, two hours).

---

person P55, rondavels P110, chalets from P250) is run by the Okavango Polers Trust and is the usual launch point for *mokoro* trips into the delta. **Drotsky's Cabins** (☎ 687 5035; drotskys@info.bw; campsites/5-person chalets P120/950, A-frames from P400) is a welcoming lodge set amid a thick riverine forest, with fabulous birdwatching and fine views across the reeds and papyrus.

MAUN
pop 35,000

Maun (pronounced 'mau-*uunn*') is Botswana's primary tourism hub and the self-proclaimed gateway to the Okavango Delta. Essentially consisting of a few intersections surrounded by long stretches of block housing, Maun attracts a reliably mad crew of bush pilots, tourists, campers, volunteers and luxury-safari heads. It's a decent enough base for a day or two; plus, Maun serves as a centre point between Kasane, the Makgadikgadi and the Kalahari.

Information

The Mall has branches of Barclays Bank and Standard Chartered Bank, which both have currency-exchange facilities and offer better rates than the bureaux de change.

Afro-Trek I-Café (Sedia Hotel, Shorobe Rd, Matlapaneng; internet per hr P50)

Avis (☎ 686 0039; Mathiba I St) Has a good selection of both 2WD and 4WD vehicles, but recommended you book ahead, especially during the dry season.

Department of Wildlife & National Parks (DWNP; ☎ 686 1265; Kudu St; ☒ 7.30am-12.30pm & 1.45-4.30pm Mon-Sat, to noon Sun) To book national parks' campsites, go to the reservations office, which is housed in a caravan behind the main building.

Post office (☒ 8.15am-1pm & 2.15-4pm Mon-Fri, 8.30-11.30am Sat) Near the Mall.

Tourist office (☎ 686 0492; Tsheke Tsheko Rd; ☒ 7.30am-12.30pm & 1.45-4.30pm Mon-Fri) Provides information on the town's many tour companies and lodges.

Sights

The **Maun Environmental Education Centre** (☎ 686 1390; admission free; ☒ 7.30am-12.30pm & 1.45-4.40pm), on the eastern bank of the Thamalakane River, aims to provide school children with an appreciation of nature.

The **Nhabe Museum** (☎ 686 1346; Sir Seretse Khama Rd; admission free, donations appreciated; ☒ 9am-5pm Mon-Fri, to 4pm Sat), housed in a historic building, has art exhibitions and outlines the natural history and cultures of the Okavango.

A visit to the community-run **Crocodile Farm** (admission P15; ☒ 9am-4.30pm Mon-Sat) is basically all the encouragement you need to keep your body inside the *mokoro* while cruising the delta. Under construction at the time of writing, a Moroccan-style **Cultural Centre** is set to open in 2010 in Matlapaneng, across from Audi Camp (p881). Owners say they want to have a marketplace and cafe on the bottom floor, and studios for arts, dance and music training.

Tours

Most delta lodges are affiliated with specific tour agencies and lots of safari companies run *mokoro* trips and 4WD safaris, so check around before choosing one (see p889).

Sleeping

Okavango River Lodge (☎ 686 3707/0298; www.okavango-river-lodge.com; Matlapaneng; campsites per person US$3,

BOTSWANA

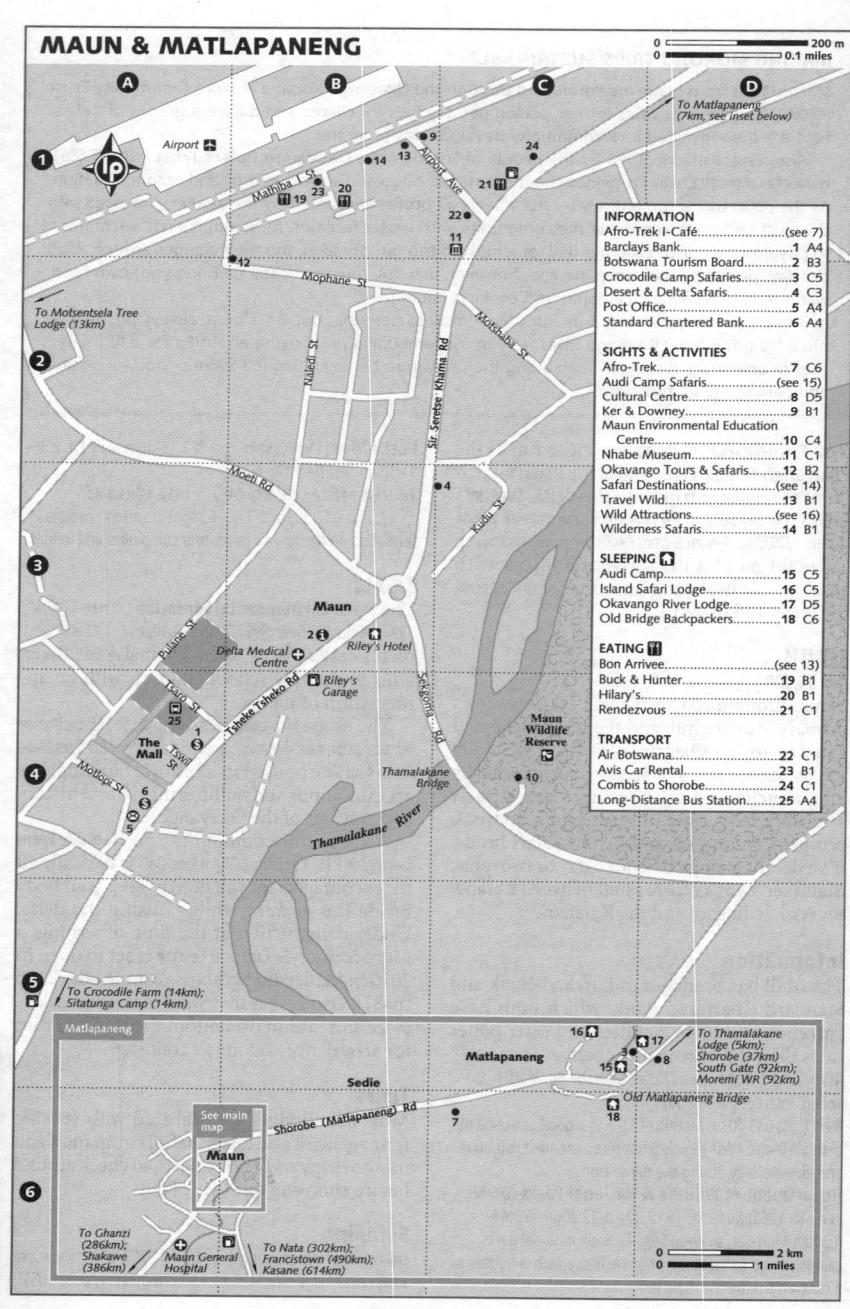

MAUN & MATLAPANENG

INFORMATION	
Afro-Trek I-Café.....................(see 7)	
Barclays Bank.....................**1** A4	
Botswana Tourism Board.....................**2** B3	
Crocodile Camp Safaries.....................**3** C5	
Desert & Delta Safaris.....................**4** C3	
Post Office.....................**5** A4	
Standard Chartered Bank.....................**6** A4	

SIGHTS & ACTIVITIES	
Afro-Trek.....................**7** C6	
Audi Camp Safaris.....................(see 15)	
Cultural Centre.....................**8** D5	
Ker & Downey.....................**9** B1	
Maun Environmental Education	
Centre.....................**10** C4	
Nhabe Museum.....................**11** C1	
Okavango Tours & Safaris.....................**12** B2	
Safari Destinations.....................(see 14)	
Travel Wild.....................**13** B1	
Wild Attractions.....................(see 16)	
Wilderness Safaris.....................**14** B1	

SLEEPING	
Audi Camp.....................**15** C5	
Island Safari Lodge.....................**16** C5	
Okavango River Lodge.....................**17** D5	
Old Bridge Backpackers.....................**18** C6	

EATING	
Bon Arrivee.....................(see 13)	
Buck & Hunter.....................**19** B1	
Hilary's.....................**20** B1	
Rendezvous.....................**21** C1	

TRANSPORT	
Air Botswana.....................**22** C1	
Avis Car Rental.....................**23** B1	
Combis to Shorobe.....................**24** C1	
Long-Distance Bus Station.....................**25** A4	

BOTSWANA

s/d chalets US$35/40) This down-to-earth spot off Shorobe Rd prides itself on giving travellers useful (and independent) information on trips through the delta. Between this spot and the Bridge Backpackers, you'll find most of Maun's tourist and expat-oriented nightlife. On that note, we've got to give it credit for the excellent name of its boat: Sir Rosis of the River.

The Old Bridge Backpackers (☎ 686 2406; www .maun-backpackers.com; Hippo Pools, Old Matlapaneng Bridge; campsites per person P30, s/d tents per person P120/90, s P80; ☐ ☎) 'The Bridge,' as it's known, has a great bar-at-the-end-of-the-world kind of vibe. Bush pilots and backpackers chat each other up, dogs play with kids and a regular cast of drunks keep the bar propped up (or is that the other way 'round?).

Island Safari Lodge (☎ 686 0300; www.africanse crets.net; Matlapaneng; campsites per person P40, s/d chalets P350/500) One of the original lodges in Maun, Island Safari Lodge is also still one of its best. The African-style *rondavel* housing is charming and comfy, and the verandah is a great spot for watching the river flow by.

Audi Camp (☎ 686 0599; www.okavangocamp.com; Matlapaneng; campsites per person from P45, s/d tents from P240/300; ☐ ☎) Off Shorobe Rd, Audi Camp is a fantastic campsite that's become increasingly popular with families, although independent overlanders will feel utterly welcome as well. Management is friendly and very helpful, and there is a wide range of safari activities to book.

Thamalakane Lodge (☎ 686 4313, 7250 6184; thamalakanelodge@ngami.net; Shorobe Rd; chalets P950; ☒ ☐ ☎) With a beautiful setting on a sun-drenched curve of the Thamalakane River, overlooking wading hippos and waving reeds, Thamalakne has beautiful chalets stuffed with modern amenities and a kitchen cranking out arguably the best food in Maun.

Motsentsela Tree Lodge (☎ 680 0757; treelodge@ netspread.co.bw; r from US$220; ☒ ☐ ☎) This private farm/reserve, about 13km west of the airport, is a lovely luxury option that maintains a good crew of regular visitors and wandering giraffe, kudu and ostrich. Contact the lodge to book ahead and arrange transfers or get directions.

Eating & Drinking

Rendezvous (☎ 7287 6183; Engen Complex; dishes cafe P35-65, restaurant P50-100) Rendezvous does pretty good pizzas, sandwiches and more upmarket fare and, thank the tech Gods, has reliable wi-fi internet.

Bon Arrivee (☎ 680 0330; Mathiba I St; meals P35-80) They lay on the pilot puns and flight-deck jokes thick at this airport-themed place, which sits, of course, right across from the airport itself. The food is good – loads of pasta, steak and seafood – but make sure you don't come here an hour before your flight expecting quick turnaround.

Hilary's (☎ 686 1610; meals from P40; ☽ 8am-4pm Mon-Fri, 8.30am-noon Sat) Just off Mathiba I St, this homey place offers homemade bread, baked potatoes, soups and sandwiches. It's ideal for vegetarians and anyone sick of greasy sausages and soggy chips.

Buck & Hunter (☎ 680 1001; Mathiba I St; meals P40-80) This used to be a pretty wild pub, the northern outpost of Gaborone's own Bull & Bush. Today, thanks to stricter alcohol enforcement, the Buck is a bit more sedate.

Getting There & Away

Air Botswana (www.airbotswana.co.bw; Airport Ave) has flights between Maun and Gaborone (US$155) and Kasane (US$100). Flights into the delta are typically arranged by lodges through local air-charter companies.

One bus leaves at least every hour between 6.30am and 4.30pm for Francistown (P55 to P60, five hours), via Gweta (P35, four hours) and Nata (P45, five hours). Combis also leave for Kasane (P60, six hours) when full. For Gaborone, you will have to change in either Ghanzi or Francistown.

To Ghanzi (P35 to P40, five hours), via D'kar (P28 to P32, 3½ hours), buses leave at about 7.30am and 10.30am, but it is best to check at the station or tourist office for current schedules. To Shakawe (P70, seven hours), five or six buses leave between 7.30am and 3.30pm, and stop at Gumare and Etsha 6. Combis to Shorobe (P3, one hour) leave when full from a spot just up from the bus station.

Getting Around

Local minibuses between town and Matlapaneng (P2.70) run when full from the bus terminal and airport; taxis cost around P30.

TSODILO HILLS

The four Tsodilo Hills (Male, Female, Child and North Hill) rise abruptly from a rippled, oceanlike expanse of desert. They are threaded with myth, legend and spiritual significance for the San people, who believe this was the site of Creation. More than 2750 ancient rock paintings have been discovered at well over 200 sites. And as in most of southern Africa, the majority of these are attributed to ancestors of today's San people.

There's a **museum** near Main Camp, extolling the undeniably spiritual nature of the hills, as well as several unmarked tracks that pass the main paintings and sacred sites. Normally, local San people will guide groups for around P100 per day.

Visitors can camp at either the Main (Rhino), Malatso or Makoba Woods **camping grounds** (campsites per person P40), but there are no shops or services.

You need a 4WD to explore the hills area, though tour operators in Maun (see p889) can help arrange private tours to the area.

KASANE & KAZUNGULA

Kasane sits in a riverine woodland at the meeting of four countries – Botswana, Zambia, Namibia and Zimbabwe – and the confluence of the Chobe and Zambezi Rivers. It's also the gateway to Chobe National Park. As such, this town of just a few thousand people is a focus of activity in northern Botswana. Immediately to the east, the tiny settlement of Kazungula serves as the border crossing between Botswana and Zimbabwe, and the landing for the Kazungula ferry, which connects Botswana with Zambia.

Information

Barclays Bank (President Ave) Generally offers better exchange rates than the bureaux de change. Be sure to

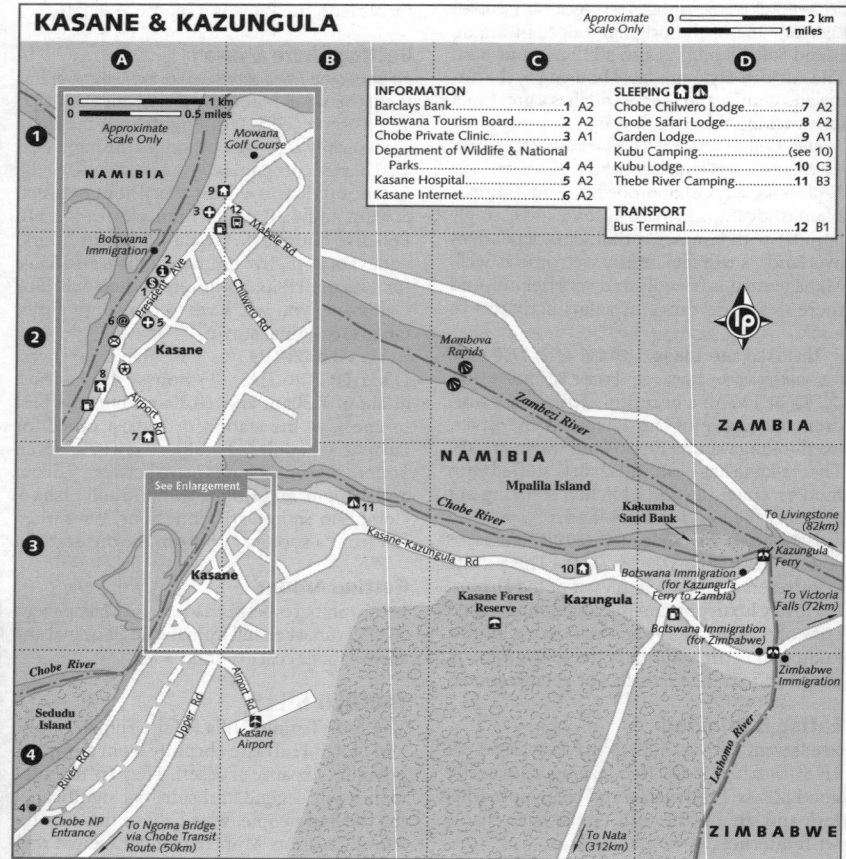

KASANE & KAZUNGULA

Approximate Scale Only	0 ————— 2 km
	0 ————— 1 miles

INFORMATION	
Barclays Bank	1 A2
Botswana Tourism Board	2 A2
Chobe Private Clinic	3 A1
Department of Wildlife & National Parks	4 A4
Kasane Hospital	5 A2
Kasane Internet	6 A2

SLEEPING	
Chobe Chilwero Lodge	7 A2
Chobe Safari Lodge	8 A2
Garden Lodge	9 A1
Kubu Camping	(see 10)
Kubu Lodge	10 C3
Thebe River Camping	11 B3

TRANSPORT	
Bus Terminal	12 B1

stock up on US dollars (post-1996) if you're heading to Zimbabwe.

Botswana Tourism Board (☎ 625 0357)

Chobe Private Clinic (☎ 625 1555; President Ave) 24-hour emergency service.

Department of Wildlife & National Parks (DWNP; ☎ 625 0235; Sedudu Gate) The booking office for campsites within Chobe National Park.

Kasane Hospital (☎ 625 0333; President Ave) Public hospital on the main road.

Kasane Internet (☎ 625 0736; Audi Centre; per hr P40; ☉ 8am-5pm Mon-Fri, to 1pm Sat) Internet in Kasane is dead slow and unreliable.

Sleeping & Eating

Thebe River Camping (☎ 625 0314; thebe@info.bw; Kasane-Kazungula Rd; campsites per person P60; ☒) Provides a green riverside setting, along with a bar, meals and Chobe wildlife drives and cruises.

Kubu Camping (☎ 625 0312; www.kubulodge. net; Kasane-Kazungula Rd; campsites per person P60; ☒) Adjacent to Kubu Lodge, this popular alternative to Thebe River Camping is a good option if you're looking for a more relaxed and independent scene.

Chobe Safari Lodge (☎ 625 0336; www.chobesafari lodge.com; President Ave; campsites US$14, r from US$134; ☒ ☒) One of the more affordable upmarket lodges in Kasane, Chobe Safari is excellent value, especially if you're travelling with little ones. Understated but comfortable rooms are priced according to size and location, though all feature attractive mosquito-netted beds and modern furnishings.

Garden Lodge (☎ 625 0051; www.thegardenlodge. com; President Ave; r incl breakfast & dinner from $US180; ☒) Built around a tropical garden, this place has a homey atmosphere. It's more quirky than the average lodge in these parts, with hints of eccentricity that put it above the pack.

Kubu Lodge (☎ 625 0312; www.kubulodge.net; Kasane-Kazungula Rd; s/d/tr US$290/345/300; ☒ ☒) Located 9km east of Kasane, this riverside lodge lacks the stuffiness and formality found in most other top-end lodges. Rustic wooden chalets are lovingly adorned with thick rugs and wicker furniture, and are scattered around an impeccably manicured lawn dotted with fig trees.

Chobe Chilwero Lodge (☎ 625 1362; Airport Rd; www. sanctuarylodges.com; low/high season per person US$590/900; ☒ ☒) Chilwero means 'place of high view' in Setswana, and indeed this exclusive, upmarket lodge boasts some fantastic panoramic views across the Chobe River.

Getting There & Away

Air Botswana connects Kasane's airport to Maun (US$100) and Gaborone (US$155). Combis heading to Francistown (P65, seven hours), Maun (P60, six hours), Nata (P55, five hours) and Gweta (P45, four hours) run when full from the Shell petrol station bus terminal on Mabele Rd. Thebe River Camping and Chobe Safari Lodge also run private shuttle buses to Livingstone/Victoria Falls (US$45, two hours).

CHOBE NATIONAL PARK

Chobe National Park, which encompasses 11,000 sq km, is home to Botswana's most varied assortment of wildlife. The riverfront strip along the northern tier, with its perennial water supply, supports the greatest wildlife concentrations. But when they contain water, the lovely Savuti Marshes of the Mababe Depression in western Chobe also provide prime wildlife habitat and attract myriad water birds. Rarely visited Ngwezumba, with its pans and mopane forests, is the park's third major region, and Chobe's northwestern corner just touches the beautiful Linyanti Marshes.

The northern park entrance lies 5km west of Kasane and is accessible to conventional vehicles. However, some Chobe riverfront drives require 4WD and to proceed through the park to places such as Savuti, or to approach from Maun, you'll need a high-clearance 4WD.

To transit between Kasane and the Namibian border at Ngoma Bridge is free of charge.

Chobe Riverfront

The Chobe riverfront is packed with wildlife. The most obvious feature of the landscape is the damage done by the area's massive elephant herds, but virtually every southern-African mammal species, except the rhino, is represented here.

A great way to enjoy Chobe is by taking a river trip or wildlife drive. The best time to cruise is late afternoon, when hippos amble onto dry land and the riverfront fills with elephants heading down for a drink and a romp in the water. All hotels and lodges arrange 2½- to three-hour wildlife drives and cruises in the morning and afternoon for between US$14 and US$22 (plus safari-discounted park fees). Note that if you take a morning wildlife drive you can also do an

BOTSWANA

afternoon 'booze cruise' and pay park fees for only one day.

The closest DWNP campsite to Kasane is Ihaha Camp Site. It's located along the riverfront about 27km from the Sedudu Gate.

Buffalo Ridge Camping (☎ 625 0430; campsites per person US$5.50; ℗) is a basic camping area located immediately uphill from the Ngoma Bridge border crossing near the western end of the Chobe transit route. Unlike Ihaha, Buffalo Ridge is privately owned, so you do not need a reservation with the DWNP to camp here.

One of Botswana's luxury pinnacles, **Chobe Game Lodge** (☎ 625 0340/1761; www.chobegamelodge. com; River Rd; low/high season per person US$500/720; ⊠) is a highly praised safari lodge. Individually decorated rooms are elegant and soothing, and some have views of the Chobe River and Namibian flood plains.

SAVUTI

Savuti's flat expanses are an obligatory stop for safaris and overland trips between Kasane and Maun. Gobabis Hill, south of the Savuti gate near the Savuti Channel, bears several sets of 4000-year-old rock art, which are thought to be of San origin. The wildlife populations, particularly the number of elephants and antelope, can seem overwhelming – especially after heavy rains. Due to potential high water, Savuti is normally closed (and inaccessible) between January and March.

There are a number of camping grounds in Savuti. Savuti Camp Site is a DWNP campsite with sit-down flush toilets, *braai* (barbecue) pits, (hot!) showers and plenty of shade.

Beside the former site of legendary Lloyd's Camp, **Savute Safari Lodge** (low/high season per person US$476/686) is an awesome upmarket retreat. It consists of 12 contemporary thatched chalets that are simple yet functional in their design. For booking information, contact **Desert & Delta Safaris** (☎ 686 1243; www.desertdelta.com; Maun).

Savute Elephant Camp (low/high season per person US$615/1205; ⊠) is the premier camp in Savuti, made up of 12 lavishly appointed East African–style linen tents complete with antique-replica furniture. The main tent houses a dining room, lounge and bar, and is next to a swimming pool that overlooks a water hole. For booking information, contact **Orient-Express Safaris** (☎ 686 0302; www.orient-express.com; Maun).

Under optimum conditions, it's a four- to six-hour drive from Kasane to Savuti. The road is passable by 2WD as far as Kachikau,

but after it turns south into the Chobe Forest Reserve the road deteriorates into parallel sand ruts that require high-clearance 4WD. Coming from Maun, you'll need 4WD to proceed north of Shorobe.

MAKGADIKGADI & NXAI PANS NATIONAL PARK

Comprising a landscape like no other on earth, the expansive Makgadikgadi & Nxai Pans National Park hosts Botswana's great salt pans – Sowa (Sua), Ntwetwe and Nxai.

Yellow lions, honey-coloured impala and dusty elephants blend into the scrub and thornbush. But even this sparse flora eventually disappears into a vast, unbroken sheet of shimmer – a space that encompasses a nothingness the size of Switzerland. The great salt pans are long, low and white, pulsing with an unstoppable glare under an electric-blue-sky ceiling.

The **Nata Sanctuary** (☎ 7154 4342; admission P25; ⏰ 7am-7pm), at Sua Pan, 15km southeast of Nata, is a beautiful, 230-sq-km wildlife refuge with a range of birdlife, as well as antelope and other grassland animals. In the dry season, you don't need a 4WD, but high clearance is advisable. The admission fee includes camping. During the wet season the sanctuary may be impossible to reach depending on the water levels, but in any case, you'll definitely need a 4WD.

Kubu Island, near the southwestern corner of Sua Pan, is surrounded by salt and covered with ghostly baobab trees and Iron Age ruins. You can camp on the salt or at the otherworldly campsite on the island, but there's no water. Campers must register with the Game Scouts, located at the camping ground, who expect 'donations' of US$6 per group; get a receipt. You need a 4WD to get here; the route is signposted 'Lekhubu' from the Nata–Maun road, 24km west of Nata. After 65km, you'll reach Thabatshukudu village, on a low ridge. South of here, the route skirts a salt pan and after 15km passes a veterinary checkpoint; 1.5km south of this barrier is the signposted left turn toward the island, which is about 20km away.

To explore the pans properly, or at all in the wet season, you need a 4WD and a good map and GPS system, as well as common sense and confidence in your driving and directional skills. Drive only in the tracks of other vehicles, and keep to the edges of the pan.

GWETA

Gweta, a dusty crossroads on the edge of the pans framed by bushveld and big skies, is an obligatory fuel stop if you're heading to either Kasane or Maun. The name of the village is derived from the croaking sound made by large bullfrogs, which, incredibly, bury themselves in the sand until the rains provide sufficient water for them to emerge and mate.

About 4km east of Gweta, you'll see a huge concrete aardvark (no, you're not hallucinating) that marks the turn-off for **Planet Baobab** (☎ 7283 8334, in Johannesburg +27-011-447 1605; www. unchartedafrica.com; campsite per person US$13, 2-person huts from US$139, 4-person US$227; ☒). This is one of the most inventive lodges in the country, and can we just say: thank God there's an African resort out there that's not full of masks and wildlife pix. Instead, you get a great open-air bar filled with vintage travel posters, metal seats covered in cow hide, beer-bottle chandeliers and the like. Campers can pitch a tent beneath the shade of a baobab tree while others can choose between Bakalanga-style 'mud huts' or San-style 'grass huts' (both are much plusher than they sound).

Hourly combis travelling between Kasane (P35, four hours) and Francistown (P30, three hours), and Maun (P25, four hours) and Francistown (US$3, three hours) pass by the Maano Restaurant.

EASTERN BOTSWANA

FRANCISTOWN
pop 115,000

Although the second-largest city in Botswana, Francistown is known primarily as a useful (and often necessary) stopover on the way to/from Kasane, Nata, Maun or Victoria Falls. You'll find most of the banks, the post office, the laundrette and several shopping centres along Blue Jacket St.

The only site of interest to travellers is the **Supa-Ngwao Cultural & Historical museum** (☎ /fax 240 3088; snm@info.bw; off New Maun Rd; admission free; ☯ 8am-5pm Mon-Fri, from 9am Sat), which displays local and regional culture and history, as well as visiting art exhibitions.

Tati River Lodge (☎ 240 6000; www.trl.co.bw; campsite per person P40, s/d from P540/629; ☒ ☒), located on the other side of the Tati River from the Marang Hotel, is a pleasant midrange option that feels like an old-school country motel. It's popular

with locals and strikes a decent balance between rustic retreat and roadside stopover.

Air Botswana (☎ 241 2393; www.airbotswana. co.bw; Francis Ave) flies between Francistown and Gaborone (US$100) at least once daily, except Sunday.

From the main bus terminal, located between the train line and Blue Jacket Plaza, buses and combis connect Francistown with Gaborone (P40, six hours), Maun (P60, five hours), Kasane (P65, seven hours), Nata (P25, two hours), Serowe (P23, 2½ hours), Selebi-Phikwe (P15, two hours) and Bulawayo (Zimbabwe; P30, two hours). Buses operate according to roughly fixed schedules and combis leave when full.

If the train from Gaborone is back up and running by the time you read this, you can also access Francistown by rail.

KHAMA RHINO SANCTUARY

In response to declining rhinoceros populations in Botswana, the residents of **Serowe**, which is the birthplace of Seretse Khama and the spiritual capital of the Batswana, banded together in 1989 to establish the 4300-hectare **Khama Rhino Sanctuary** (☎ 463 0713; www.khamarhino-sanctuary.com; per person/vehicle under 5 tonnes/vehicle over 5 tonnes P33/41/133; ☯ 8am-7pm). Today the sanctuary protects the country's last remaining rhino population – 34 white and two black rhinos currently reside in Khama (with a baby black on the way at the time of writing). The sanctuary is also home to wildebeests, ostriches, hyenas, leopards and over 230 species of bird.

The main roads within the sanctuary are normally accessible by 2WD in the dry season, though 4WD vehicles are necessary in the rainy season. However, all vehicles can reach the campsite and accommodation areas in any weather. The office at the entrance sells useful maps of the sanctuary as well as basic nonperishable foods, cold drinks and firewood.

No vehicle? Two-hour day/night wildlife drives cost P333 and can take up to four people. Nature walks (P133) and rhino-tracking excursions (P200), both one to two hours' long, can also be arranged. You can also hire a guide to accompany your vehicle for P115.

Shady campsites (P53 per person) with *braai* pits are adjacent to clean toilets and (steaming hot) showers, while six-person dorms go for P293. If you're looking to splurge for a night or two, rustic four-person chalets (P366 to P399) and six-person A-frames (P512 to P800) have basic kitchen facilities and private bathrooms. If you don't have a vehicle, staff can drive you to the campsite and accommodation areas for a nominal charge.

The entrance gate to the sanctuary is located about 26km from Serowe along the road to Orapa (turn left at the unsignposted T-junction about 5km northwest of Serowe). Khama is accessible by any bus or combi heading towards Orapa, and is not hard to reach by hitching.

TULI BLOCK

Tucked into the nation's right-side pocket, the Tuli Block is a swath of freehold farmland that encompasses the Tuli Game Reserve (also known as the North-East Tuli Game Reserve) and the Mashatu Game Reserve, a vast moonscape of muddy oranges and browns overlooked by deep-blue sky. It's the sort of Dali-esque desert that puts one in mind of Arizona or Australia, yet the barren beauty belies a land rich in wildlife.

Entrance to the Tuli Game Reserve is free. Night drives (not permitted in government-controlled parks and reserves) are allowed, so visitors can often see nocturnal creatures such as aardwolves, aardvarks and leopards. Unfortunately, exploring this region without a private vehicle is virtually impossible.

The most famous feature is **Solomon's Wall**, a 30m-high dolerite dyke cut naturally through the landscape on either side of the riverbed. Nearby are the **Motloutse Ruins**, a Great Zimbabwe–era stone village that belonged to the kingdom of Mwene Mutapa. Both sights can be explored on foot and are accessible from the road between Zanzibar and Pont Drift.

Set deep inside the block, **Kwa-Tuli Game Reserve** (☎ 27-015-964 3895; www.kwatuli.co.za; safari tents per person R395) consists of two camps of luxury safari tents (for a middle income price) perched on an island in the midst of the Limpopo River. Prices for tents include linen, bedding, soap and toilet paper, and you should bring food, drink and a torch with you.

Mashatu Game Reserve (☎ 27-011-442 2267; www.mashatu.com; luxury tents/chalets incl full board & wildlife drives per person US$250/375; ☒ ☒) is one of the largest private wildlife reserves in southern Africa, renowned for its big cats and frighteningly large elephant population (current estimates are well over 1000). Only prebooked guests are allowed on the reserve. Rates include transfer from the Limpopo Valley Airfield or the Pont Drift border post. The game reserve is also just beyond the Pont Drift border post.

Getting There & Away

Mashatu and Tuli support a scheduled flight between Johannesburg (South Africa), Kasane and the Limpopo Valley Airport that is usually booked as part of a package with either of the reserves. Most roads in the Tuli Block are negotiable by 2WD, though it can get rough in places over creek beds. If you're coming from South Africa, note that the border crossing at Pont Drift usually requires a 4WD, and can be closed when the river is too high. If you've prebooked your accommodation, you can leave your vehicle with the border police and get a transfer by vehicle (if dry) or by cableway (if the river is flooded) to your lodge.

BOTSWANA DIRECTORY

ACCOMMODATION

Botswana has a number of comfortable campsites and an array of upper-midrange hotels and top-end lodges – but there is little in between. Budget travellers may have to camp, so taking a tent is recommended.

Upmarket places tend to price in US dollars rather than pula; we have listed prices in the currency used by the relevant establishment. Note that there's a real dearth of midrange places in the Okavango Delta, which is largely given over to luxury camps and top-end lodges that can set you back around US$500 per night, although this can rise to around US$1000. Discounted rates for children are rare, although a number of lodges do offer special family rooms.

While most budget and lower-midrange options tend to have a standard room price, many top-end places change their prices according to low/shoulder/high season. High season is from June to November, low season corresponds to the rains (December to March or April) and the shoulder is a short April and May window. In this chapter, where seasonal prices haven't been included, we have listed high-season prices. A 10% government tax is levied on hotels and lodges (but not all campsites) and is included in prices listed in this book.

ACTIVITIES

Things to do in Botswana are centred on wildlife viewing, either by 4WD safari vehicle, boat

---

PRACTICALITIES

- Weights, measures and road distances use the metric system.

- Electricity is 220-240V AC, 50Hz (use South African–style two- or three-round-pin plugs).

- For English-language news see www.gazettebw.com or www.mmegi.bw.

- Radio Botswana broadcasts in both English and Setswana, while Botswana TV (BTV) broadcasts local, African and international news.

---

or *mokoro*. There are inexpensive opportunities for quad-biking at Planet Baobab (see p885) on the Makgadikgadi Pans. Expect to pay around US$30 to US$50 per day for quad-bike rental. There are hiking opportunities near Gaborone and the Tsodilo Hills in the northwest and several small ranges in the eastern and southeastern parts of the country.

DANGERS & ANNOYANCES

The greatest dangers in Botswana are posed by natural elements, combined with a lack of preparedness. Although Botswana enjoys a very low crime rate compared to other African (and many Western) countries, muggings do occur in Gaborone – don't walk around alone at night.

EMBASSIES & CONSULATES

All the diplomatic missions listed following are located in Gaborone (see Map pp872–3). Many more countries have embassies or consulates in South Africa (see p1062).

Angola (☎ 390 0204; fax 397 5089; cnr Khama Cres & Nelson Mandela Dr, PO Box 111)

France (☎ 397 3863; www.ambafrance-bw.org; 761 Robinson Rd, PO Box 1424; ☯ 8am-4pm Mon-Fri)

Germany (☎ 395 3143; www.gaborone.diplo.de; 3rd fl, Professional House, Broadhurst Mall, Segoditshane Way)

Namibia (☎ 390 2181; fax 390 2248; 2nd fl, Government Enclave, PO Box 987; ☯ 7.30am-1pm & 2-4.30pm Mon-Fri)

South Africa (☎ 390 4800/1/2/3; sahcgabs@botsnet.bw; 29 Queens Rd, Main Mall, PO Box 00402; ☯ 8am-12.45pm & 1.30-4.30pm Mon-Fri)

UK (☎ 395 2841; www.britishhighcommission.gov.uk/botswana; Plot 1079-1084 Queens Rd, Main Mall, PO Box 0023; ☯ 8am-12.30pm & 1.30-4.30pm Mon-Thu, to 1pm Fri)

USA (☎ 395 3982; http://gaborone.usembassy.gov/; Embassy Dr, PO Box 90; ☯ 9am-4pm Mon-Fri)

Zambia (☎ 395 1951; fax 395 3952; Plot No 1118 Queens Rd, Main Mall, PO Box 362; ☯ 8.30am-12.30pm & 2-4.30pm Mon-Fri)

Zimbabwe (☎ 391 4495; fax 390 5863; Government Enclave, Plot 8850, PO Box 1232; ☯ 8am-1pm & 2-4.30pm Mon-Fri)

EMERGENCIES

See p871 for Gaborone emergency numbers. In the event of an emergency outside of Gaborone, you should contact your hotel or safari operator.

HOLIDAYS

As well as religious holidays listed in the Africa Directory (p1140), the principal public holidays in Botswana are:

New Year's Day 1 January
Day after New Year's Day 2 January
Labour Day 1 May
Ascension Day April or May (40 days after Easter)
Sir Seretse Khama Day 1 July
President's Day 3rd Friday of July
Botswana/Independence Day 30 September
Day after Independence Day 1 October

MAPS

The most accurate country map is the *Shell Tourist Map of Botswana* (P50), which shows major roads and includes insets of tourist areas and central Gaborone. It's sold in a packet with a small tourist guide in bookshops all over the region.

MONEY

Botswana's unit of currency is the pula (P), which is divided into 100 thebe. 'Pula' means 'rain' – a valuable commodity in this desert land.

Full banking services are available only in major towns, although ATMs are sprouting up all over the country. Most credit cards are accepted at hotels and restaurants and cash advances are available at major banks (but not through ATMs).

TELEPHONE

Botswana's country code is ☎ 267; there are no internal area codes, so when you're phoning from outside Botswana, dial ☎ 267 followed by the phone number. Calling from Botswana, the international access code is ☎ 00, which should be followed by the country code, area code (if applicable) and telephone number.

BOTSWANA

TOURIST INFORMATION

The continually improving **Botswana Tourism Board** (☎ 391 3111; www.botswanatourism.co.bw; Ground Fl, Block B, Fairgrounds Office Park) is located in the Fairgrounds Office Park, a little way south of the Main Mall. It dispenses tourist information and distributes brochures, maps, and the annual *Botswana Focus* and *Discover Botswana* magazines. There is also a tourism board kiosk in the lobby of the Cresta President Hotel (see p873). The offices in **Kasane** (☎ 625 0357) and Maun (p879) are also becoming more useful.

VISAS

All visitors to Botswana need a valid passport, but no visas are required by citizens of most Commonwealth countries, EU countries (except Spain and Portugal), Israel, Norway, South Africa, Switzerland and the USA. On arrival you'll get a 30-day entrance stamp.

Extensions are available for up to three months. You may be asked to show an onward air ticket or proof of sufficient funds for your intended stay. For more than a three-month extension, apply to the **Immigration & Passport Control Office** (☎ 361 1300; fax 355 2996; cnr Molepole Rd & Nelson Mandela Dr, PO Box 942, Gaborone) before your trip.

TRANSPORT IN BOTSWANA

GETTING THERE & AWAY
Air

Botswana's main airport is **Sir Seretse Khama International Airport** (GBE; ☎ 391 4401), located 11km north of the capital, Gaborone. Although this is well served with flights from Jo'burg (South Africa) and Harare (Zimbabwe), it is seldom used by tourists as an entry point into the country. Far more popular are **Maun Airport** (MUB; ☎ 686 1589) and **Kasane Airport** (BBK; ☎ 625 0133). There is also an airstrip near Pont Drift (in the Tuli Block) for chartered flights from South Africa.

The national carrier is **Air Botswana** (www.airbotswana.co.bw), which flies routes within southern Africa. Air Botswana has offices in Gaborone, Francistown, Maun, Kasane and Victoria Falls (Zimbabwe). At present, you cannot reserve tickets via theitsir website.

Land

Overland travel to or from Botswana is usually straightforward as most travellers either arrive by private vehicle or by **Intercape Mainliner** (www.intercape.co.za) from South Africa. You can also try **Tenna Express Shuttle Tours and Safaria** (☎ 264-6126 2296; tennaexp@iway.na) from Namibia. At border crossings, arriving travellers are often requested to clean their shoes – even those packed away in their luggage – in a disinfectant dip to prevent them carrying foot-and-mouth disease into the country. Vehicles must also pass through a pit filled with the same disinfectant.

Border opening hours change all the time, but major crossings between Botswana and Namibia or South Africa generally open sometime between 6am and 8am and close sometime between 6pm and 10pm. The main crossings between Botswana and Zimbabwe are open from 6am to 8pm, and the Kazungula ferry to Zambia runs from 6am to 6pm.

The main border crossings into Botswana are as follows:

From South Africa – Martin's Drift (from Northern Transvaal), Tlokweng

(From Jo'burg) Ramatlabama (from Mafikeng)

From Namibia – Mamuno, Mohembo and Ngoma Bridge

From Zimbabwe – Kazungula, Ramokgweban/Plumtree and Pandamatenga

From Zambia – Kazungula Ferry

GETTING AROUND
Air

Air Botswana operates scheduled domestic flights between Gaborone, Francistown, Maun and Kasane.

Car & Motorcycle

The best way to travel around Botswana is to rent a vehicle. With your own car, you can avoid public transport (which is limited to routes between major towns) and organised tours. The downside is that distances are long and the cost of renting a vehicle is high: anywhere from US$50 to US$150 per day. Long-term rentals in South Africa can bring this figure down substantially.

When driving anywhere, look out for donkeys and cattle. Main highways are thick with livestock, plus other (larger) animals like elephants and kudu (if you hit one of these you're really screwed). Drive slowly, keep calm and remember that the extra amount of time it will take you to get from point A to B is just part of the journey.

If you're determined to rent a vehicle in Botswana, the following are some reputable companies:

Avis (www.avis.com) Offices in Gaborone, Francistown, Maun (p879), Kasane and all over southern Africa.

Budget (www.budget.co.za) Offices in Gaborone, as well as in South Africa, Zimbabwe and Namibia.

Europcar (www.europcar.co.za) Offices in Gaborone and in the major cities of South Africa, Namibia and Zambia.

Tempest (www.tempestcarhire.co.za) This large South Africa–based company has offices in Gaborone, throughout South Africa and in Namibia.

Hitching

Because public transport is somewhat erratic, hitching is relatively safe and fairly common, although it is still always a risk (see p1161). On main routes there should be no major problems, but ascertain a price before climbing aboard. Most drivers expect the equivalent of a bus fare.

Hitching the back roads isn't as straightforward. If you're hitching along the Trans-Kalahari Hwy, through the Tuli Block or from Maun to Kasane through Chobe National Park, carry camping gear and enough food and water for several days of waiting.

Local Transport

Public transport in Botswana is confined to main roads between major population centres. Although cheap and reliable, it is of little use to the traveller as most of Botswana's tourist attractions are off the beaten track.

Tours

A good place to start looking at tours is at **Travel Wild** (Map p880; ☎ 686 0822; www.travelwildbotswana.com; Mathiba I St, Maun), opposite Maun Airport, which serves as a central booking and information office for lodges, safaris and other adventures. **Safari Destinations** (Map p880; ☎ 686 0822/3; travelwild@dynabyte.bw; Mathiba I St, Maun) serves as a good clearing house for information on booking agencies. Staff can't provide you with direct bookings themselves, but they've got great contacts with all local safari providers.

The following tour operators are recommended (all have offices in Maun):

African Animal Adventures (☎ 7230 1054; www.africananimaladventures.com) A highly recommended outfit that does horse safaris into the delta and the salt pans of the northeast. Can be contacted by phone, email or through Back to the Bridge Backpackers (p881).

African Excursions (africanexcursions@botsnet.bw) Independent tour operator that does good cultural tours of Maun that include dancing, a handicrafts market and a traditional meal, all for P300.

Afro-Trek (Map p880; ☎ 686 2574; www.afrotrek.com; Shorobe Rd, Matlapaneng) Specialises in midrange safaris.

Audi Camp Safaris (Map p880; ☎ 686 0599; www.okavangocamp.com; Mathiba I St) Run out of the popular Audi Camp.

Back to the Bridge Backpackers (Map p880; ☎ 686 2406; www.maun-backpackers.com; Shorobe Rd, Matlapaneng) A budget operation.

Ker & Downey (Map p880; ☎ 686 0570; www.kerdowney.com; Mathiba I St) One of Botswana's most exclusive tour operators.

Okavango Tours & Safaris (Map p880; ☎ 686 0220; www.okavango.bw; Mophane St) This well-established operator specialises in upmarket lodge-based tours.

Wild Attractions (Map p880; ☎ 686 0300; www.africansecrets.net/wa_home.html; Mathiba I St) This excellent operation is run out of the Island Safari Lodge.

Wild Lands Safaris (☎ 686 1008; www.wildlandsafaris.com) A reliable operator with a good customer service record.

Wilderness Safaris (Map p880; ☎ 686 0086, in Johannesburg 27-011-807 1800; www.wilderness-safaris.com; Mathiba I St) Near the airport, this operator specialises in upmarket safaris.

Lesotho

Lesotho (le-*soo*-too) is called southern Africa's 'kingdom in the sky' for good reason. This small but stunningly beautiful, mountainous nation is nestled island-like in the middle of South Africa. It's an intriguing anomaly in a region of modernity, and makes a fascinating travel detour from its larger neighbour.

The country offers superb mountain scenery, a proud traditional people, endless hiking trails and the chance to explore remote areas on Basotho ponies.

The 'lowland' areas (all of which are still above 1000m) have craft shopping and dinosaur footsteps, while the highlands in the northeast and centre feature towering peaks (over 3000m) and verdant valleys.

Lesotho came into being during the early 19th century, when both the *difaqane* (forced migration) and Boer incursions into the hinterlands were at their height. Under the leadership of the legendary king, Moshoeshoe the Great, the Basotho people sought sanctuary and strategic advantage amid the forbidding terrain of the Drakensberg and Maluti Ranges.

Getting around is reasonably easy – ordinary rental cars will get you to most places; public transport is extensive, albeit slow. Hiking or pony trekking from village to village is the best way of exploring.

FAST FACTS

- **Area** 30,350 sq km
- **ATMs** Only in Maseru
- **Borders** South Africa (Lesotho is surrounded by South Africa)
- **Budget** US$30 to US$50 per day
- **Capital** Maseru
- **Languages** Southern Sotho (Sesotho), English
- **Money** loti (plural: maloti); US$1 = M7.40, €1 = M10.62
- **Population** 1.8 million
- **Seasons** summer (late November to March), winter (June to September)
- **Telephone** Country code ☎ 266; international access code ☎ 00
- **Time** GMT/UTC +2
- **Visa** Free two-week entry permit on arrival for most nationalities (but confirm on arrival)

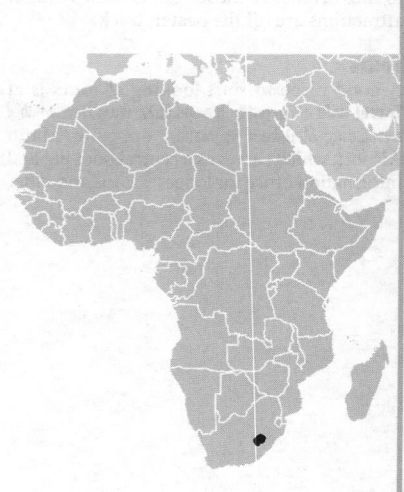

HOW MUCH?

- **Traditional dance/cultural group** US$4 to US$8
- **Internet** US$1.35 per hour
- **Coffee** US$1.35
- **Banana** US$0.40
- **Genuine (wool) Basotho blanket** US$90

LONELY PLANET INDEX

- **1L petrol** US$0.90 (but fluctuates)
- **1L bottled water** US$1 to US$1.35
- **Bottle of beer** US$1.35
- **Souvenir T-shirt** US$13.50 to US$20
- **Bag of fat cakes (fried savoury donuts)** US$0.15 to US$0.40

HIGHLIGHTS

- **Sani Top** (p899) Enjoy high and stunning vistas from atop Sani Pass.
- **National Parks** (p899) Revel in the splendid isolation and nature of the country's national parks.
- **Semonkong** (p897) Enjoy locally run tours of this isolated village, abseil from great heights or trot to the local race day, where Basotho ponies show what they're made of.
- **Malealea** (p898) Explore rugged, mountainous regions with breathtaking scenery and traditional Basotho villages.
- **Thaba-Bosiu** (p897) Discover the mountain stronghold of King Moshoeshoe the Great, where the struggle for Lesotho was won.

CLIMATE & WHEN TO GO

Clear, cold winters, with frosts and snow (and unpredictable changes) in the highlands, await you in Lesotho, so pack warm clothing. During summer, dramatic thunderstorms are common, as are all-enveloping clouds of thick mist. Temperatures at this time can rise to over 30°C in the valleys, though it's usually much cooler in the mountains, even dropping below freezing. Most of Lesotho's rain falls between October and April. Throughout the year, the weather is notoriously changeable. You can visit Lesotho any time; each season

has attractions. Many believe the best time to visit is in April to May, when visibility is high after the rains. September and October is another good time.

ITINERARIES

- **One Week** From Maseru (p894), head south to Morija (p898), where you'll find Morija Museum & Archives, a great museum with displays on Basotho culture. Continue to Malealea (p898) or Semonkong (p897) – the 'gems' of Lesotho – to go pony trekking and hiking. If you have time, head to Quthing (p898) to check out the 180-million-year-old dinosaur footprints.
- **Two Weeks** Visit Teyateyaneng (p900), the craft centre of Lesotho or, slightly further north, Bokong Nature Reserve (p899). Get a taste of the mountainous 'lowlands' by heading to Morija (p898), Semonkong (p897), Malealea (p898) and Quthing (p898), and continue northeast to the remote Sehlabathebe National Park (p899).
- **One month** Take in some of the country's most impressive scenery on a clockwise circuit to Mokhotlong (p900) and up to the magnificent Sani Top (p899), visiting Leribe (p900) and other towns and sights along the way. Return to Maseru (p894) via Likalaneng and Roma (p897), before heading south to Morija (p898) and following the two-week itinerary. Note: the road between Sehlabathebe in the east and Sehonghong in the northeast requires a 4WD.

HISTORY

Neighbouring South Africa has always cast a long shadow over Lesotho, fuelling a perpetual struggle for a separate identity on an ever-diminishing patch of territory.

The first inhabitants of the mountainous region that makes up present-day Lesotho were the hunter-gatherer people known as the Khoisan. They have left many examples of their rock art in the river valleys. Lesotho was settled by the Sotho peoples in the 16th century.

Moshoeshoe the Great

King Moshoeshoe (pronounced 'mo-shwe-shwe' or 'mo-shesh') is the father figure of Lesotho's history. Around 1820, while a local chief of a small village, he led his villagers

to Butha-Buthe, a mountain stronghold, where they survived the first battles of the *difaqane* (forced migration), caused by the violent expansion of the nearby Zulu state. The loosely organised southern Sotho society managed to survive due largely to the adept political and diplomatic abilities of the king. In 1824 Moshoeshoe moved his people to Thaba-Bosiu, a mountaintop that was even easier to defend.

From Thaba-Bosiu, Moshoeshoe played a patient game of placating the stronger local rulers and granting protection, as well as land and cattle, to refugees. These people were to form Basutholand; at the time of Moshoeshoe's death in 1870, Basutholand had a population of more than 150,000.

As the *difaqane* receded a new threat arose. The Voortrekkers (Boer pioneers) had crossed the Senqu (Orange) River in the 1830s and established the Orange Free State. By 1843 Moshoeshoe was sufficiently concerned by their numbers to ally himself with the British Cape Colony government. The British Resident in Basutholand decided that Moshoeshoe was becoming too powerful and engineered an unsuccessful attack on his kingdom.

Treaties with the British helped define the borders of Basutholand but the Boers pressed their claims on the land, leading to wars between the Orange Free State and the Basotho people in 1858 and 1865; Moshoeshoe was forced to sign away much of his western lowlands.

The Road to Independence

In 1868 the British government annexed Basutholand and handed it to the Cape Colony to run in 1871. After a period of instability, the British government again took direct control of Basutholand in 1884, although it gave authority to local leaders.

Lesotho's existence is attributable to a quirk of history and fortuitous timing. In the 1880s, locals resented direct British rule – it was seen as an infringement on Basutholand's freedom and sovereignty. Ironically, British occupation secured the future independence of Lesotho: at the precise moment when the Union of South Africa was created, Basutholand was a British Protectorate and was not included in the Union.

In 1910 the advisory Basutholand National Council was formed from members nominated by the chiefs. In the mid-1950s the council requested internal self-government from the British; by 1960 a new constitution was in place and elections were held for a legislative council. The main contenders were the Basutholand Congress Party (BCP; similar to South Africa's African National Congress), and the conservative Basutholand National Party (BNP) headed by Chief Leabua Jonathan.

The BCP won the 1960 elections, then paved the way for full independence from Britain (achieved in 1966). However, at the elections in 1965 the BCP lost to the BNP and Chief Jonathan became the first prime minister of the new Kingdom of Lesotho, which allied itself with the apartheid regime across the border.

Big Brother

Stripping King Moshoeshoe II of the few powers that the new constitution had left him did not endear Jonathan's government to the people and the BCP won the 1970 election. After his defeat, Jonathan suspended the constitution, expelled the king and banned all opposition political parties. Jonathan changed tack, distancing himself from South Africa and calling for the return of land in the Orange Free State that had been stolen from the original Basutholand. He also offered refuge to ANC guerrillas and flirted with Cuba. South Africa closed Lesotho's borders, strangling the country.

Jonathan was deposed in 1986 and the king was restored as head of state. Eventually agitation for democratic reform rose again. In 1990

King Moshoeshoe II was deposed by the army in favour of his son, Prince Mohato Bereng Seeisa (Letsie III). Elections in 1993 resulted in the return of the BCP.

In 1995 Letsie III abdicated in favour of his father, Moshoeshoe II was reinstated and calm was restored after a year of unrest. Less than a year later he was killed when his 4WD plunged over a cliff in the Maluti Mountains. Letsie III became king for the second time.

A split in the BCP saw the breakaway Lesotho Congress for Democracy (LCD) take power. The 1998 elections saw accusations of widespread cheating by the LCD, which won by a landslide. Major tensions arose between the public service and the government; the military was also split over the result.

Following months of protests, the government appeared to be losing control. In late September 1998 it called on the Southern African Development Community (SADC) treaty partners, Botswana, South Africa and Zimbabwe, to help restore order. Troops, mainly South African, invaded the kingdom. Rebel elements of the Lesotho army put up strong resistance and there was heavy fighting in Maseru.

The government agreed to call new elections, but the political situation remained tense with the spectre of South African intervention never far away. Political wrangling delayed the elections until May 2002. The LCD won again and Prime Minister Mosisili began a second – and peaceful – five-year term.

The 2007 elections were highly controversial. A newly formed All Basotho Convention (ABC) party accused the LCD party of manipulating the allocation of seats. National strikes followed and several ministers were allegedly attacked by gunmen. There was an assassination attempt on ABC's leader, Tom Thabane, and many people were detained and tortured.

Lesotho Today

Lesotho ranks among the region's poorer countries, and has few natural resources other than water and gem diamonds. During the last century the country's main export was labour – approximately 60% of males worked, mainly in mining, in South Africa. In the late 1990s, the restructuring of the South African gold-mining industry, mechanisation and the closure of some mines resulted in huge employment losses. Meanwhile, the Lesotho

LESOTHO

economy – under transformation due to a rapid growth of the textile industry – also collapsed as a result of Chinese competition and changes to international agreements. These days, it is hoped that economic initiatives, such as the Economic Partnership Agreement (EPA), signed with the EU in 2007 to create free trade zones, will help revive the local business sector. Meanwhile, the spectre of HIV/AIDS is high but has stabilised in recent years – the infection rate (adult prevalence) is estimated at 24%.

The political situation is currently calm, although the elections of 2012 may bring tensions to the fore once again.

CULTURE

Traditional Basotho culture is central to the lives of the local people. It focuses on a belief in the power of ancestral spirits, and includes various customs, rites and superstitions. The community chief is respected and revered, and family is an important social unit. Music plays a vital part in the lives of the Basotho.

Cattle occupy an important role in traditional culture, with cattle ownership being a critical indicator of wealth and status. Shepherds, once revered, are today among the poorest males. The Basotho blanket, worn proudly by many in rural areas, reflects one's status in the community, according to the quality, material and design of the blanket itself.

Most Basotho in rural communities live in *rondavels*, round huts with mud walls (often decorated) and thatched roofs.

Poverty and death are ever present in Lesotho. Life for many people is incredibly harsh, and most try to eke out a living on the land or through subsistence agriculture, especially livestock; unemployment rates currently stand at about 45%. Education is not compulsory.

The citizens of Lesotho are known as the Basotho people. Most are southern Sotho and most speak Sesotho (Southern Sotho). The melding of the Basotho nation was largely the result of Moshoeshoe the Great's 19th-century military and diplomatic triumphs; many diverse subgroups and peoples have somehow managed to merge into a homogeneous society. Maseru, with 175,000 people, is the largest town.

Around 80% of the population is Christian (mainly Roman Catholic, Anglican and Episcopal). The remaining 20% live by traditional Basotho beliefs. There are churches throughout the country, many of which were (and continue to be) built by missionaries.

Good-quality tapestry and rug weaving is practised around the country, especially near Teyateyaneng and on the fringes of Maseru. Basotho hat baskets and grass and clay products can also be found.

FOOD & DRINK

You won't be writing home about the food in Lesotho – it's not bad, but it's not great, either. Staples include maize (often in the form of *mealie pap*, a type of maize porridge), as well as some vegetables and pulses. Maseru boasts a decent selection of restaurants serving a range of local and foreign foods, but outside the capital, you'll usually have to take what you're given.

ENVIRONMENT

Lesotho's western border is formed by the Mohokare (Caledon) River. The eastern border is the rugged Drakensberg Range, and high country defines much of the southern border. All of Lesotho is over 1000m in altitude, with peaks reaching 3000m in the centre and east of the country.

There are serious environmental concerns about the controversial Highlands Water Project, a series of dams on the Senqu (Orange) River in Lesotho, which provides water and electricity to South Africa and income to Lesotho. Several communities have been displaced (though compensation has been given) and some of the country's most fertile land has been flooded; it's already in short supply as only 10% is suitable for agriculture. Ironically, many people, especially in the drought-ridden lowlands, do not have easy access to water.

Overgrazing and soil erosion is an ongoing issue; dongas – massive eroded gullies caused by 19th-century agricultural practices – are throughout the landscape.

MASERU

pop Maseru District 430,000

Ever-expanding, bustling Maseru has a modest array of modern amenities and few sights, but it's a useful place for visiting the tourist office and stock up on supplies before heading into the highlands.

MASERU

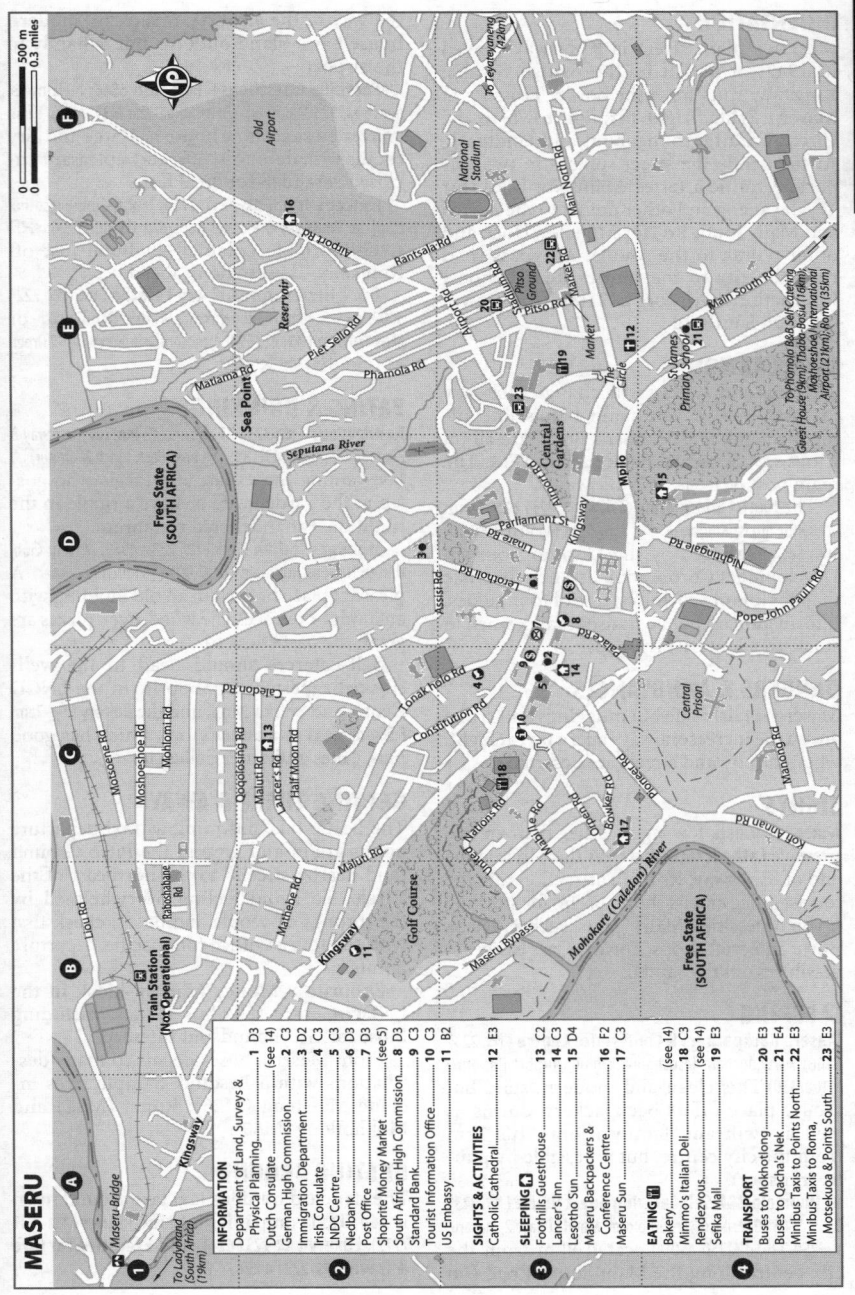

500 m
0.3 miles

To Teyateyaneng (32km)

Old Airport

National Stadium

Airport Rd

Rantsala Rd

Pitso Ground

Pitso Rd

22

20

Market Rd

12

19

Main North Rd

Main South Rd

St James Primary School

21

15

To Promola B&B Self Catering Guest House (9km); Thaba-Bosiu (16km); Mohale's Hoek (76km); Moshoeshoe International Airport (21km); Roma (35km)

Reservoir

Sea Point

Piet Salo Rd

Matlama Rd

Phamola Rd

Seputana River

Free State (SOUTH AFRICA)

Central Gardens

The Circle

Mpilo

Market

16

13

Mohloli Rd

Moshoeshoe Rd

Qoqolosing Rd

Maluti Rd

Lancer's Rd

Half Moon Rd

Mabile Rd

Caledon Rd

Assisi Rd

Lerotholi Rd

Linare Rd

Parliament St

Kingsway

3

1

6

8

2

9

5

14

4

10

18

17

11

Constitution Rd

Tonakholo Rd

Airport Rd

Pope John Paul II Rd

Nightingale Rd

Palace Rd

Pioneer Rd

Bowker Rd

Orpen Rd

Central Prison

Koh Annan Rd

Manong Rd

Mathebe Rd

Baobabane Rd

Lirou Rd

Mosehoe Rd

Kingsway

Train Station (Not Operational)

Maseru Bridge

To Ladybrand (South Africa) (19km)

Golf Course

National Rd

Kingsway

Maluti Rd

Maseru Bypass

Mohokare (Caledon) River

Free State (SOUTH AFRICA)

INFORMATION	
Department of Land, Surveys & Physical Planning..............	1 D3
Dutch Consulate.............(see 14)	
German High Commission...........	2 C3
Immigration Department..............	3 D2
Irish Consulate............	4 C3
LNDC Centre............	5 C3
Nedbank............	6 D3
Post Office............	7 D3
Shoprite Money Market...........(see 5)	
South African High Commission...	8 D3
Standard Bank............	9 C3
Tourist Information Office............	10 C3
US Embassy............	11 B2

SIGHTS & ACTIVITIES	
Catholic Cathedral............	12 E3

SLEEPING	
Foothills Guesthouse............	13 C2
Lancer's Inn............	14 C3
Lesotho Sun............	15 D4
Maseru Backpackers & Conference Centre............	16 F2
Maseru Sun............	17 C3

EATING	
Bakery............	(see 14)
Mimmo's Italian Deli............	18 C3
Rendezvous............	(see 14)
Sefika Mall............	19 E3

TRANSPORT	
Buses to Mokhotlong............	20 E3
Buses to Qacha's Nek............	21 E4
Minibus Taxis to Points North......	22 E3
Minibus Taxis to Roma,............	23 E3
Motsekuoa & Points South......	

LESOTHO

ORIENTATION

Maseru's main street is Kingsway (paved in 1947 for a visit by the British royals). Kingsway runs from the border crossing at Maseru Bridge right through town to the Circle, a traffic roundabout and landmark. At the Circle the street splits into two important traffic arteries: Main North Rd (for Teyateyaneng and other points to the north) and Main South Rd (for Mohale's Hoek and other points to the south). A bypass road rims the city to the south. Moshoeshoe I International Airport is 21km from town, off Main South Rd.

INFORMATION

The top-end hotels will change currency (at poor rates). The main banks, including Nedbank and Standard Bank, are all on Kingsway; Standard Bank has an ATM. The main post office is on Kingsway.

The **tourist information office** (☎ 2231 2427; tourist info@ltdc.org.ls; Kingsway; ⏰ 8am-5pm Mon-Fri, 8.30am-1pm Sat), managed by the Lesotho Tourism Development Corporation, is a helpful office that has lots of brochures, lists of tour guides, information on public transport and, when in stock, free Maseru city maps.

DANGERS & ANNOYANCES

Maseru is fairly safe but muggings and crime are on the increase; always take a taxi at night, when the city and streets are deserted.

SIGHTS

Maseru boasts few sights other than an impressive **Catholic cathedral** near the Circle at the end of Kingsway. Its main attractions are the tourist office and its shops, useful for stocking up on necessities. Many sights, such as Thaba Bosiu and craft shops, however, are easily accessible from the capital.

SLEEPING

Maseru Backpackers & Conference Centre (☎ 2232 5166; www.durham-lesotholink.org.uk; Airport Rd; dm/r M100/320) This clean and modern, staid but secure place offers backpackers' dorms as well as twin and family rooms. It's 3km from the city centre, but accessible by public transport.

Phomolo B&B Self Catering Guest House (☎ 2231 0755, 5805 0012; baso@ilesotho.com; Matala Phase 2, Maseru, s M250-320, d M350-450) Located 9km from the city centre along the Main South Road (on the way to the airport), this clean, modern house has a bland outlook, but is handy to the airport.

Foothills Guesthouse (☎ 5870 6566; melvin@xsi net.co.za; 121 Maluti Rd; s/d incl breakfast M340/480) This converted sandstone house has large and airy rooms with decor c 1960s, and a pleasant enclosed verandah for breakfasts.

Lancer's Inn (☎ 2231 2114; lancers-inn@ilesotho. com; cnr Kingsway & Pioneer Rd; s/d/tr US$66/79/96; 🖭) A comfortable colonial-era hotel just off Kingsway – best to book ahead.

For glitzier options, try **Lesotho Sun** (☎ 2224 3000; www.suninternational.com; r M1105; 🖭 🖵 🖳) or **Maseru Sun** (☎ 2231 2434; maseru@sunint.co.za; 12 Orpen Rd; r from US$130; 🖭 🖳).

EATING & DRINKING

Rendezvous (☎ 2231 2114; Lancer's Inn, cnr Kingsway & Pioneer Rd; mains M37-85; ⏰ breakfast, lunch & dinner) A fave among the expats and locals who gossip in the garden cafe or have a tipple in the traditional chandeliered restaurant.

Mimmo's Italian Deli (☎ 2232 4979; Maseru Club, United Nations Rd; mains M30-80; ⏰ lunch & dinner) A pleasant place housed in an old building with an outdoor terrace. The wood-oven pizzas are great; the pasta, less so.

Self-caterers should head to the well-stocked supermarket Shoprite in the LNCD Centre and Sefika Mall; and the **bakery** (⏰ 7am-8.30pm) next to Lancer's Inn, which has good pies, cakes and other delicacies.

GETTING THERE & AWAY

The hectic bus and minibus taxi departure points are in and around the Pitso Ground (and nearby streets) to the northeast of the Circle. To avoid feeling overwhelmed by the throngs of people and buses, check first with the tourist office for specific departure points.

Shoprite's 'Money Market' kiosk in the LNDC Centre sells bus tickets, including those for Greyhound and Intercape.

From Maseru, buses depart to many destinations within Lesotho. Sample fares include Mafeteng (M25), Roma (M12) and Mokhotlong (M80).

GETTING AROUND

The standard minibus taxi fare around town is M4. Taxi companies include **Planet** (☎ 2231 7777), **Luxury** (☎ 2232 6211) and **Executive Car Hire & Travel** (☎ 2231 4460).

ACTIVITIES ON HIGH

Pony Trekking

Lesotho's tough and sure-footed little Basotho ponies can take you to some remote and awesome places in the highlands. The main pony centres are Semonkong Lodge (below), Malealea Lodge (p898) and Trading Post Guest House (below). In some cases, the villagers provide the ponies and act as guides, contributing significantly to the local village economy.

Walking

Lesotho's high country offers some of the most spectacular walking in southern Africa. The crest of the Drakensberg Range, and rugged mountains in the south and east make for wilderness experiences reminiscent of the Tibetan plateau. Only experienced walkers should cover this area, and in a party of at least three people. For details on walks see *A Backpackers Guide to Lesotho*, by Russell Suchet, available locally and in South Africa for US$6.50.

For camping in or near a village, always ask permission from the village chief, and offer to pay a small fee.

AROUND MASERU

THABA-BOSIU

Moshoeshoe the Great's mountain stronghold, Thaba-Bosiu, about 16km east of Maseru, was first occupied in 1824 and played a pivotal role in the consolidation of the Basotho nation. The name Thaba-Bosiu, meaning Mountain at Night, may be a legacy of the site being first occupied at night, but many legends exist.

At the mountain's base is a **visitors information centre** (admission M10; ☼ 8am-5pm Mon-Fri, 9am-1pm Sat), where you can organise an official guide to accompany you on the short walk to the top of the mountain.

Good views from here include those of the **Qiloane Hill** (inspiration for the Basotho hat), along with the remains of fortifications, Moshoeshoe's grave and parts of the original settlement.

A smart new complex – with accommodation – was being constructed near the visitors centre at the time of research.

Mmelesi Lodge (☎ 5886 1116; s/d/tr M360/400/500) offers well-organised *rondavels*, about 2km before the visitors information centre.

SOUTHERN LESOTHO

ROMA

Getting to Roma is half the fun, as it is reached through a spectacular gorge south of Maseru. After that there's not a lot to do, but this university town features attractive sandstone buildings. Trading Post Guest House can point you in the right direction for activities.

Trading Post Guest House (☎ 082 773 2180; www. tradingpost.co.za; campsite per person M75, dm M125, r per person M175, s incl half board M375; ☒) is in a trading post that has been operated since 1903 by the Thorn family. Accommodation includes garden rooms, *rondavels* and the original sandstone homestead, with shared kitchen, set in a lush garden. A self-contained cottage sleeps six for M400. Breakfasts/dinners are available (M55/95). Pony trekking, hiking, 4WD trails and other action adventures can be arranged. There are even *minwane* (dinosaur footprints) nearby.

Minibus taxis run throughout the day to/from Maseru (M18, 45 minutes).

SEMONKONG

This place is as beautiful as its name. The Maletsunyane Falls are a 90-minute walk from Semonkong (Place of Smoke). They are more than 200m high and are at their most spectacular in summer. For a thrilling descent, Semonkong Lodge offers abseiling (per person in a group of one/two/three or more M850/750/700).

The remote 122m-high Ketane Falls are an exciting day's drive (30km) from Semonkong, or a four-day return horse ride from Malealea Lodge (see p898).

our pick **Semonkong Lodge** (☎ 2700 6037, 6202 1021; www.placeofsmoke.co.ls; campsite per person M70, dm/ s/d M110/330/560, rondavel s/d M385/600) The enchanting Semonkong has an excellent restaurant, and offers village tours, a pub crawl on the back of a donkey, hiking and pony trekking.

Buses between Maseru and Semonkong (M100) leave from both places in the morning, and arrive in the late afternoon.

MORIJA

Morija is a tiny town with a big history. **Morija Museum & Archives** (☎ 2236 0308; www.morijafest.com; admission M10; ⏲ 8am-5pm Mon-Sat, noon-5pm Sun), the best museum in Lesotho, has Basotho ethnographic exhibits. It also hosts the annual Morija Arts & Cultural Festival. Near the museum is **Mophato Oa Morija** (☎ 2236 0219; mophato@leo.co.ls; dm M60), an ecumenical conference centre that is sometimes willing to accommodate travellers. **Morija Guest House** (☎ 6306 5093; www.morijaguesthouses.com; r per person without bathroom M170-200) offers a range of excellent sleeping options – with views to match.

Minibus taxis run throughout the day between Maseru and Morija (M13, 45 minutes, 40km).

MALEALEA

Shortly before reaching Malealea is the Gates of Paradise Pass. A plaque announces 'Wayfarer – pause and look upon a Gateway of Paradise'. This says it all – about the region, village and the lodge. The breathtaking mountains feature caves with San paintings, and you can enjoy a well-organised pony trek, hikes on foot and fascinating village visits, including stops at a museum, a *sangoma* (witch doctor) and a reclaimed donga.

Malealea Lodge (☎ in South Africa 082 552 4215; www.malealea.co.ls, www.malealea.com; campsite per person M70, dm M120-140, r per person M200-250) was part of the original Malealea Trading Store established in 1905. These days it's a very friendly, well-run visitors' lodge. As well as comfortable rooms – *rondavels* or huts – there's a neat camping ground. Meals (breakfast/lunch/dinner E60/70/100) are available, with prior notice. There are also self-catering facilities and a small village shop with basic supplies. Maps of walks in the area are available, too.

Regular minibus taxis connect Maseru and Malealea (M30, 2½ hours, 83km). Otherwise, from Maseru or Mafeteng, catch a minibus taxi to the junction town of Motsekuoa (M13, two hours), from where there are frequent connections to Malealea (M18, 30 minutes).

QUTHING

Quthing, the southernmost town in Lesotho, is often known as Moyeni (Place of the Wind).

The town was established in 1877, abandoned three years later and then rebuilt at the present site.

The town comprises Lower Quthing and Upper Quthing, the former colonial administrative centre, with good views overlooking the dramatic Senqu (Orange) River Gorge. There are minibus taxis between Lower and Upper Quthing.

About 1.5km off the highway, 5km west of Quthing, is the intriguing **Masitise Cave House Museum** (☎ 5879 4167; admission by donation), built into a San rock shelter in 1866 by Reverend Ellenberger. Ask for the key from the local pastor in the house next to the church. There are San paintings nearby.

Between Quthing and Masitise there is a striking twin-spired sandstone church, part of the **Villa Maria Mission**.

Probably the most easily located of the dinosaur footprints in Lesotho are close to Quthing and are believed to be 180 million years old. To get to them, go up the Mt Moorosi road from Quthing until you reach the pink building.

At Qomoqomong, 10km from Quthing, there's a good gallery of **San paintings**; ask at the General Dealers store about a guide for the 20-minute walk to the paintings.

Fuleng Guest House (☎ 2275 0260; r per person M250-300), in Upper Quthing, offers excellent-value rooms, plus a friendly local experience. **Moorosi Chalets** (☎ in South Africa 082 552 4215; www.malealeatours.com/destinations/lesotho/mount-moorosi.html; campsite per person M70, rondavel per person M200, huts without bathroom per person M120, self-catering house per person M140) is part of a community program that has awesome activities, ranging from village stays to fishing. It is located 6km from Mt Moorosi village; take the turn-off to Ha Moqalo 2km out of the village towards Qacha's Nek.

Minibus taxis run daily between Quthing and Maseru (M60, 3½ hours) and Qacha's Nek (M70, three hours).

EASTERN LESOTHO

QACHA'S NEK

This pleasant town was founded in 1888 as a mission station near the pass (1980m) of the same name. It has an attractive church, colonial-era sandstone buildings and California redwoods.

HIGHLAND PARKS & RESERVES

Lesotho is blessed with some of the most remote and spectacular national parks and reserves in South Africa. Sure, they might lack lions and elephants, but they pack a punch when it comes to nature and beauty. **Lesotho Northern Parks** (☎ 2246 0723) handles all accommodation bookings for Bokong Nature Reserve, Ts'ehlanyane National Park and Liphofung Cave Cultural Historical Site.

Sehlabathebe National Park

Lesotho's first national park is remote and rugged – and that's its main attraction. Hiking (and horse riding from Sani Top or the uKhalamba-Drakensberg; see p1045) is the main way to explore the waterfalls and surrounding areas. Bookings are through the **Ministry of Tourism, Environment and Culture** (☎ 2231 1767, 2232 6075; New Postal Office Bldg, 6th fl, Kingsway, Maseru).

Camping throughout the park or staying at the **Sehlabathebe Park Lodge** (☎ bookings 2231 1767, 2232 6075; campsite per person M30, r per person M80) are the only accommodation options. Bring all food. A 4WD is usually required to cover the 12km between the entrance and lodge.

To get there and away, a daily bus connects Qacha's Nek and Sehlabathebe, departing from Qacha's Nek at around noon and Sehlabathebe at 5.30am (M40, five hours). The bus terminates in Mavuka village, near the park gate. From here, it's about 12km further on foot to the lodge. If you're driving, the main route into the park is via Quthing and Qacha's Nek. The road from Qacha's Nek is unpaved but in reasonable condition, and negotiable at most times of the year in 2WD. You can arrange to leave your vehicle at the police station in Paolosi village while you're in the park.

Keen walkers can hike the 10km up the escarpment from Bushman's Nek in KwaZulu-Natal. From Bushman's Nek to the Nkonkoana Gate border crossing takes about six hours. Horses can also be arranged through **Khotso Trails** (☎ in South Africa 033-701 1502; www.khotsotrails.co.za) in Underberg.

Bokong Nature Reserve

This **reserve** (adult/child M10/5, campsite M40, basic 4-person hut M250; ☽ 8am-5pm) is located at the top of the 3090m Mafika-Lisiu Pass, near the Bokong River. The park is home to Afro-alpine wetland sponges and an impressive waterfall. There are a number of day walks, a visitors centre and an overnight camping ground. Guides (per person M20) and pony trekking (from M100) can be arranged.

Ts'ehlanyane National Park

Deep in the rugged Maluti Mountains, this 5600-hectare **national park** (admission per person/vehicle M40/10, campsite from M50) protects a beautiful, high-altitude, 5600-hectare patch of rugged wilderness. Excellent day walks, a challenging 39km hiking trail to Bokong Nature Reserve, and pony trekking (per half/full day M300/350) are on offer.

Lesotho's smartest accommodation, **Maliba Mountain Lodge** (☎ in South Africa 031-266 1344; www.maliba-lodge.com; d per person incl full board from R2990) is also here.

Liphofung Cave Cultural Historical Site

San rock art is the main attraction of this 4-hectare **reserve** (adult/child M25/10, campsite M40, r per person M250), just off the main Butha-Buthe–Oxbow road. There are also horse trails (M50 per hour), a **cultural centre** (☽ 8am-5pm Mon-Fri) and a small craft shop.

Sleeping options include **Letloepe Lodge** (☎ 2295 0383; www.letloepelodge.co.ls; dm/s/d incl breakfast from M140/285/420), a 'palace below the clouds' with lofty prices; or the cheaper but modest **Anna's B&B** (☎ 2295 0374; annasb&b@leo.col.ls; s M100-150, d M180-280).

Minibus taxis go from Qacha's Nek to Maseru via Quthing (M100, six hours). A daily bus runs between Maseru and Qacha's Nek (M100, nine hours); and another, between Qacha's Nek and Sehlabathebe National Park, departing around noon (M30, five hours).

SANI TOP

Sani Top sits atop the steep Sani Pass, the only dependable road into Lesotho through the Drakensberg range in KwaZulu-Natal (4WD only). This astoundingly rocky, winding and steep (with 30-degree gradients!) road carves its way in a truly stunning fashion, offering stupendous views on clear days and unlimited hiking possibilities. These include **Hodgson's Peaks** (3257m), 6km south of Sani Top, from where you get views over Sehlabathebe National Park and down to KwaZulu-Natal; and the long and strenuous hike to **Thabana-Ntlenyana** (3482m), the highest peak in southern Africa (there's a path, but a guide is advisable).

On the edge of the escarpment at a lofty 2874m, **Sani Top Chalet** (☎ in South Africa 033-702 1158; www.sanitopchalet.co.za; campsite per person M80, dm M150, rondavel s/d R650/1000) resembles an old-fashioned ski chalet. It has cosy *rondavels*, backpacker lodgings and excellent meals. Pony trekking can be arranged with advance notice.

For details on reaching Sani Top from KwaZulu-Natal, see p1045. To reach the top of Sani Pass from Mokhotlong or anywhere in Lesotho by public transport takes patience. A minibus taxi runs daily from Mokhotlong via Sani Top down to Underberg (South Africa) and back (five hours). Note: ask around for border times as they change and allow enough time at either end.

MOKHOTLONG

Mokhotlong (Place of the Bald Ibis) is 270km from Maseru and is the first major town north of Sani Pass. It has an appealing Wild West feel to it, with locals – sporting Basotho blankets – on their horses.

Molumong Guesthouse & Backpackers (☎ in South Africa 033-394 3072; molumong@worldonline.co.za; campsite per person M60, dm/d M100/220) is a rustic lodge and former colonial trading post, about 15km southwest of Mokhotlong. It's a basic (electricity free) self-catering stay, so bring your own food. Pony trekking is available.

Twelve kilometres south of Mokhotlong on the road to Thaba-Tseka, you'll find **St James Lodge** (☎ in South Africa 033-326 1601; stjames guestlodge@yahoo.com; dm/d M125/350), housed in an old stone building on a working mission. It's self-catering, and offers pony trekking and scenic walks.

In town, the **Senqu Hotel** (☎ 2292 0330; s M260-320, d M320-380) is 2.5km from the buses at the western end of town. Nearby **Grow** (☎ 2292 0205; dm R70), a Lesotho-registered development office, has basic dorms and a simple kitchen.

Regular public transport runs to/from Butha-Buthe (M55, six hours), Maseru (M80, eight hours), Linakaneng (for Molumong Guesthouse & Backpackers) and Sani Top.

NORTHERN LESOTHO

TEYATEYANENG

Referred to as 'TY', Teyateyaneng (Place of Quick Sands) has been developed as the craft centre of Lesotho. Tapestry workshops include **Helang Basali Crafts** at St Agnes Mission, **Setsoto Design**, **Hatooa Mose Mosali** and **Elelloang Basali Weavers**.

Blue Mountain Inn (☎ 2250 0362; s/d M560/675; ☒) has rooms and a restaurant.

LERIBE

Leribe (also known as Hlotse) is a busy regional market hub. It served as an administrative centre under the British, as witnessed by the few old buildings slowly decaying in the leafy streets. The main sight is the crumbling **Major Bell's Tower** near the market, a government storehouse (1879).

The good **Leribe Craft Centre** (☎ 2240 0323; ☒ 8am-4.30pm Mon-Fri, 9.30am-1pm Sat) sells a range of high-quality mohair goods. There is a set of **dinosaur footprints** a few kilometres south of Leribe at Tsikoane village. Take the small dirt road to the right at the Tsikoane Primary School, towards some rocky outcrops. At the church, ask the way to the *minwane*, 1km up the mountainside.

Only stay at **Leribe Hotel** (☎ 2240 0559; Main St; s/d M395/510, meals M85) if you're desperate; this colonial relic, with a modern entrance, has seen better days.

LESOTHO DIRECTORY

ACCOMMODATION

Accommodation prices and standards are on par with the country's rocky passes – high and occasionally a little rough, although there is a range of comfort standards. The only five-star accommodation can be found in international-style hotels in Maseru and a new lodge in Ts'ehlanyane National Park (see the boxed text, p899). The rest of the country offers lodges of all standards, B&Bs, rough-and-tumble hotels and very basic Agricultural Training Centres.

PRACTICALITIES

■ Lesotho's electricity is generated at 220V. Appliances have three round pins as used in South Africa.

■ Lesotho uses the metric system.

ACTIVITIES

The main options in Lesotho are hiking and pony trekking (see the boxed text, p897).

BOOKS

An interesting history book on Lesotho is *A Short History of Lesotho* by Stephen Gill. Poignant Basotho accounts include *Singing Away the Hunger* by Mpho Matsepo Nthunya et al, and *Shepherd Boy of the Maloti* by Thabo Makoa.

BUSINESS HOURS

Government offices From 8am to 4.30pm weekdays; lunchbreak from 12.45pm to 2pm.
Post offices From 8am to 4.30pm weekdays and 8am to noon Saturday.
Shops Generally 8am to 5pm weekdays (8.30am to 1pm Wednesday) and 8am to 1pm Saturday.

CLIMATE

Come prepared. The climate in Lesotho is notoriously changeable: temperatures can plummet to near 0°C (even during summer – late November to March), rivers flood (most of Lesotho's rain falls between October and April) and thick fogs can delay you. During the dry season, water can be scarce. If hiking, bring your own food, sleeping bag, rain wear, sunscreen, warm clothing, a torch and water-purification tablets.

DANGERS & ANNOYANCES

Keep off high ground during electrical storms and avoid camping in the open. In the highlands, school children and herd boys may request 'Sweets! Sweets!'; responding to this encourages begging.

On the last Friday of the month, when many people are paid and some of them get drunk, things can get boisterous and occasionally aggressive.

EMBASSIES & CONSULATES

Lesotho has diplomatic representation in South Africa (Pretoria and Johannesburg;

see p1062). A number of countries have representation in Maseru:
Germany (Map p895; ☎ 2233 2292; c/o Alliance Française Bldg, cnr Kingsway & Pioneer Rd, Maseru)
Ireland (Map p895; ☎ 2231 4068; Tonakholo Rd, Maseru)
Netherlands (Map p895; ☎ 2231 2114; Lancer's Inn, cnr Kingsway & Pioneer Rd, Maseru)
South Africa (Map p895; ☎ 2231 5758; 10th fl, Lesotho Bank Tower, Kingsway, Maseru)
USA (Map p895; ☎ 2231 2666; http://maseru.usembassy .gov; 254 Kingsway, Maseru)

EMERGENCY

Ambulance (☎ 2231 2501)
Fire (☎ 115)
Police (☎ 2231 9900)

HOLIDAYS

As well as the Christian religious holidays noted in the main Directory chapter (p1140), the principal public holidays in Lesotho are the following:
New Year's Day 1 January
Moshoeshoe Day 11 March
Independence Day 4 October
Boxing Day 26 December

INTERNET ACCESS

At the time of research internet access was available in Maseru only.

MAPS

The **Department of Land, Surveys & Physical Planning** (Map p896; ☎ 2232 2376; Lerotholi Rd, Maseru; ☺ 9am-3pm Mon-Fri) sells good topographic maps. The tourist office has free maps of Maseru city.

MONEY

The unit of currency is the loti (plural: maloti; symbol: M), made up of 100 lisente. The loti is fixed at the value of the South African rand; rands are accepted everywhere in Lesotho, but maloti are not accepted back in South Africa. The only currency-exchange banks (including Nedbank and Standard Bank) are in Maseru.

POST

Post offices are open from 8am to 4.30pm weekdays and 8am to noon Saturday. Delivery is slow and unreliable.

TELEPHONE

The telephone system works reasonably well. Lesotho's area codes are already incorporated into their numbers. Lesotho's country code is ☎ 266; to call Lesotho from South Africa, dial the prefix ☎ 09 266. To call South Africa from anywhere in Lesotho, dial ☎ 00 27 and then the South African area code and phone number. Omitting the zero off the area code ☎ 082 and ☎ 083 numbers generally denote South African mobile phone numbers, so dial 00 82 and the number.

VISAS

Citizens of most Western European countries, the USA and most Commonwealth countries are granted an entry permit (free) at the border or airport. The standard stay permitted is two weeks and is renewable by leaving and re-entering the country or by application to the **Director of Immigration & Passport Services** (☎ 2232 3771, 2232 1110; PO Box 363, Maseru 100).

Visa requirements change, so first check with an embassy. Pretoria is the place to obtain visas for other African countries. Vaccination certificates are required if you've recently been in a yellow-fever area.

TRANSPORT IN LESOTHO

GETTING THERE & AWAY
Air

Lesotho's Moshoeshoe I International Airport is 21km from Maseru. **South African Airways** (SAA; ☎ in South Africa 011-978 5313; www.flysaa.com) flies daily between Maseru and Johannesburg for around US$150 one way. The airport departure tax is M50.

Land

All Lesotho's borders are with South Africa. Most people enter via Maseru Bridge (open 24 hours). Other main border crossings include Ficksburg (open 24 hours), Makhaleng Bridge (open 8am to 4pm) and Sani Pass (open 6am to 6pm, but ask around, as times change), however, these often have long queues.

Intercape (www.intercape.co.za) offers bus services to a changing timetable between Bloemfontein and Maseru (from M240, 1¾ hours). Daily minibus taxis also run between Bloemfontein and Maseru (M50, two hours). Another option is to head from Bloemfontein to Botshabelo (M35, one hour), from where you can catch a connection to Maseru (M20, 1½ hours). After your passport is stamped at the border, you'll need to catch a car taxi (called a four-by-one) from the Lesotho border to the Maseru taxi rank, from where you can organise other connections.

Other useful connections include a daily minibus taxi between Mokhotlong (Lesotho) and Underberg (South Africa) via Sani Pass; and several minibus taxis daily between Qacha's Nek (Lesotho) and Matatiele (South Africa; 45 minutes).

At least three buses run weekly between Johannesburg and Maseru (six to seven hours); and daily minibus taxis between both Johannesburg and Ladybrand (16km from the Maseru Bridge border crossing) and Maseru. Leaving Maseru, you'll need to go to the South African side of Maseru Bridge to catch the bus.

GETTING AROUND

A good network of slow, no-frills buses and faster minibus taxis access many towns. These leave when full; no reservations are necessary. You'll be quoted long-distance fares on the buses but it's best to just buy a ticket to the next major town, as you might be stuck waiting for the bus to fill up again while other buses leave before yours.

Madagascar

One look at a map of Africa, and you can imagine how Madagascar was ripped away from the coast of Mozambique some 165 million years ago. Isolated ever since, Madagascar's plants and animals have evolved into some of the weirdest forms on the planet. Nowhere else can you see over 70 varieties of lemur, including one that sounds like a police siren, the world's biggest and smallest chameleons, and the last stomping ground of the now-extinct elephant bird (*Aepyornis*), the largest bird that ever lived. Extraordinary plants include forests of twisted, spiny 'octopus' trees, bottle-shaped baobabs, pristine rainforests and vanilla, the orchid that has become a household name. Not for nothing is Madagascar regarded by the WWF as one of the world's most important conservation priorities.

And the people are no less interesting: arriving here some 2000 years ago along the Indian Ocean trade routes, they grow rice in terraced paddies, and speak a language that has more in common with their origins in Southeast Asia than with the African continent. Their culture is steeped in taboo and magic, imbuing caves, waterfalls, animals and even some material objects with supernatural attributes. Hill peoples live in traditional multistoreyed brick houses with carved balconies and, in some areas, dance with their dead ancestors in the 'turning of the bones' ceremony, the *famadihana*.

Throw in a dash of pirate history, coastlines littered with shipwrecks, great regional cooking, some of the world's longest place names, and unfailingly polite and friendly people, and you'll experience a refreshing take on the overused 'unique' tag.

FAST FACTS

- **Area** 587,401 sq km
- **ATMs** In all major towns
- **Budget** US$45 to US$211 per day
- **Capital** Antananarivo (often 'Tana' for short)
- **Languages** Malagasy, French
- **Money** Malagasy ariary; US$ = Ar2090, €1 = Ar2942
- **Population** 20.6 million
- **Seasons** Wet (November to March), dry (May to October), hot (October to April)
- **Telephone** Country code ☎ 261; international access code ☎ 00
- **Time** GMT/UTC + 3
- **Visa** One-month, single-entry visa US$84; issued on arrival

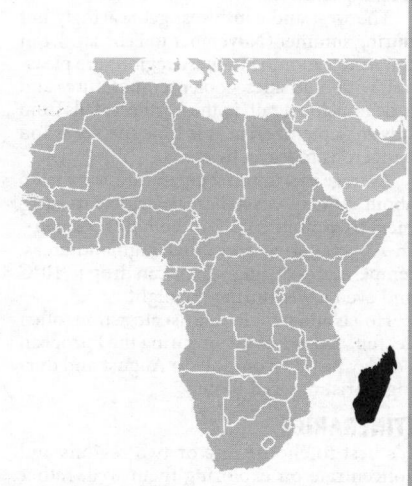

HIGHLIGHTS

- **Réserve Spécial de l'Analamazaotra** (p923) Wake to the eerie cries of indris as the sun burns the mist off the rainforest-covered hills.
- **Île Sainte Marie** (p925) Dive among coral canyons, marvel at humpback whales or laze on soft, white beaches in this tropical paradise.
- **Parc National de l'Isalo** (p920) Cool off under a waterfall while watching the sandstone cliffs turn red at sunset.
- **Antananarivo** (p909) Tuck into the country's finest dining at this most un-African of cities.
- **Parc National de Ranomafana** (p919) Encounter lemurs, chameleons and colourful birds in primeval forest criss-crossed with tumbling steams.

HOW MUCH?

- **Cup of coffee** US$1.90
- **Seafood feast** US$7.60
- **National park admission, including a guide** US$19
- **100km taxi-brousse ride** US$2.80
- **A zebu** US$190

LONELY PLANET INDEX

- **1L petrol** US$1.17
- **1.5L bottled water** US$1.20
- **Bottle of Three Horses Beer** US$1.40
- **Souvenir T-shirt** US$13.80
- **Sambos (samosas)** US$0.15

CLIMATE & WHEN TO GO

Any time of year is fine for a visit except from December to March, when heavy rainfall in many areas can make some roads all but impassable, and when there's a high risk of cyclones in the east and northeast. In general, the best time to travel in most areas is April and October/November. The coolest time to travel anywhere in Madagascar is during the dry season (ie the winter months, May to October), but during this time the *hauts plateaux* (central highlands; which include Antananarivo) can get cold and windy, with freezing showers.

The west and southwest get searingly hot during summer (November to February), but the winter months in these regions are pleasant, with blue skies, cooler temperatures and little rain. Most rain in the northeast falls from July to September; at this time the sea is too dangerous to travel by boat.

Average maximum temperatures vary from about 30°C in coastal areas (higher in summer) to around 25°C on the *hauts plateaux*. In Antananarivo and other highland areas, temperatures during winter can drop to 10°C and even lower during the night.

Hotels and popular tourist attractions often get full, and prices go up during the European holiday period from July to August and during Christmas and Easter.

ITINERARIES

It's best to choose one or two regions and concentrate on exploring them well, rather than trying to fit too much into one visit. Here are a few suggestions.

- **One Week** Spend the first day and evening enjoying the sights and sampling great cuisine in the capital, Antananarivo (p909). Then, take a two-day trip south through the *hauts plateaux*, taking in Antsirabe (p916), Ambositra (p916) and Ambalavao (p919), and stopping at whichever town takes your fancy. Along the way, you can admire the scenery, and do some walking and souvenir shopping at some of the country's finest woodcarving outlets. Head back to Tana, then wend your way east to Andasibe (p922) and the Réserve Spécial de l'Analamazaotra (p923) for a two-night stay in the rainforest, where you'll be woken by the hooting calls of indris.
- **Two Weeks** For the best of both worlds – national parks and beaches – spend a day and night in Antananarivo (p909) and take a trip through the *hauts plateaux* towns to Fianarantsoa (p918) to see rare bamboo lemurs in the rainforest at Parc National de Ranomafana (p919). Drive down to Toliara (Tuléar; p920) for a taste of the tropics, then fly back to Tana and travel eastwards for two nights at Andasibe's Réserve Spécial de l'Analamazaotra (p923), then fly over to Île Sainte Marie (p925) from Toamasina and spend a few days lazing on a beach, snorkelling or whale-watching. From there, take a boat back to Toamasina (p923) and travel by

> **YELLOW-FEVER VACCINATION CERTIFICATE**
>
> If you have just arrived from a country where yellow fever is present, you may be asked for a yellow-fever certificate upon arrival at immigration.

taxi-brousse (bush taxi) to Tana, or fly back.

- **One Month** With a month you can indulge in whatever takes your fancy by lingering in any or all of the previous locations. Add a few days to explore Toliara (Tuléar; p920) and Mangilly (p922) and finish off with some adventuring on Canal des Pangalanes (p923) near Toamasina.

HISTORY

Archaeological evidence suggests that Madagascar was uninhabited until about 2000 years ago, when the first Indo-Malayan settlers arrived in coast-hugging craft that skirted the Indian Ocean. They brought traditions with them, such as planting rice in terraced paddies, Southeast Asian food crops, and linguistic and musical roots that were buried in the subcontinent. The migration accelerated in the 9th century, when the powerful Hindu-Sumatran empire of Srivijaya controlled much of the maritime trade in the Indian Ocean.

European Arrival & Colonisation

Portuguese sailors named the island Ilha de Sao Lourenço, but like subsequent British, Dutch and French fleets they failed to establish a base here. European and North American buccaneers had notably more success, making Madagascar (and especially Île Sainte Marie) their base in the Indian Ocean during the 17th century.

Powerful Malagasy kingdoms developed with the growth of trade with European merchants. Most powerful of all were the Merina of the central highlands, whose chief, Ramboasalama, acquired the weaponry to subdue neighbouring tribes. His son Radama became king in 1810 and, sniffing the winds of fortune, entered diplomatic relations with the British in 1817 and allowed hundreds of Christian missionaries to enter the Merina court. However, his widow and successor, Ranavalona I, nicknamed 'The Bloodthirsty', passionately disliked all things *vahaza* (foreign); she persecuted the missionaries and ordered the execution of tens of thousands of her Malagasy subjects using barbarous and ingenious methods.

In 1890 the British handed Madagascar over to the French in exchange for Zanzibar. The French captured Antananarivo in 1895 and turned the island into an official colony in 1897. The French suppressed the Malagasy language; however, they constructed roads, expanded the education network and abolished slavery. Resentment of the French colonial presence grew in all levels of society, and Nationalist movements had developed by the 1920s. Strikes and demonstrations culminated in a revolt in 1947, which the French suppressed after killing an estimated 80,000 people and sending the rebel leaders into exile.

Nationalism & Independence

By 1958 the Malagasy had voted in a referendum to become an autonomous republic within the French community of overseas nations. Philibert Tsiranana became Madagascar's first president, and allowed the French to keep control of most of Madagascar's trade and industry. Tsiranana was forced to resign in 1972 and was succeeded by army general Gabriel Ramantsoa.

The socialist Ramantsoa made friends with China and the USSR, closed down the French military bases and collectivised the farming system, which led to an exodus of French farmers. The economy took a nosedive and Ramantsoa was forced to resign. His successor, Richard Ratsimandrava, lasted just one week before being assassinated by rebel army officers. They were almost immediately routed by Ramantsoa loyalists, and a new government headed by Admiral Didier Ratsiraka came to power.

The Ratsiraka years were characterised by more socialist reforms, but a debt crisis in the early 1980s forced him to abandon the reforms and obey the International Monetary Fund. In 1989 Ratsiraka was dubiously 'elected' to his third seven-year term, sparking riots that left six people dead. People were still demanding his resignation by 1991, and the ensuing demonstrations brought the economy to a standstill. In 1992 the Malagasy voted in a referendum to limit the presidential powers. General elections were held that year, and Professor Albert Zafy thrashed Ratsiraka, ending his 17 years in power.

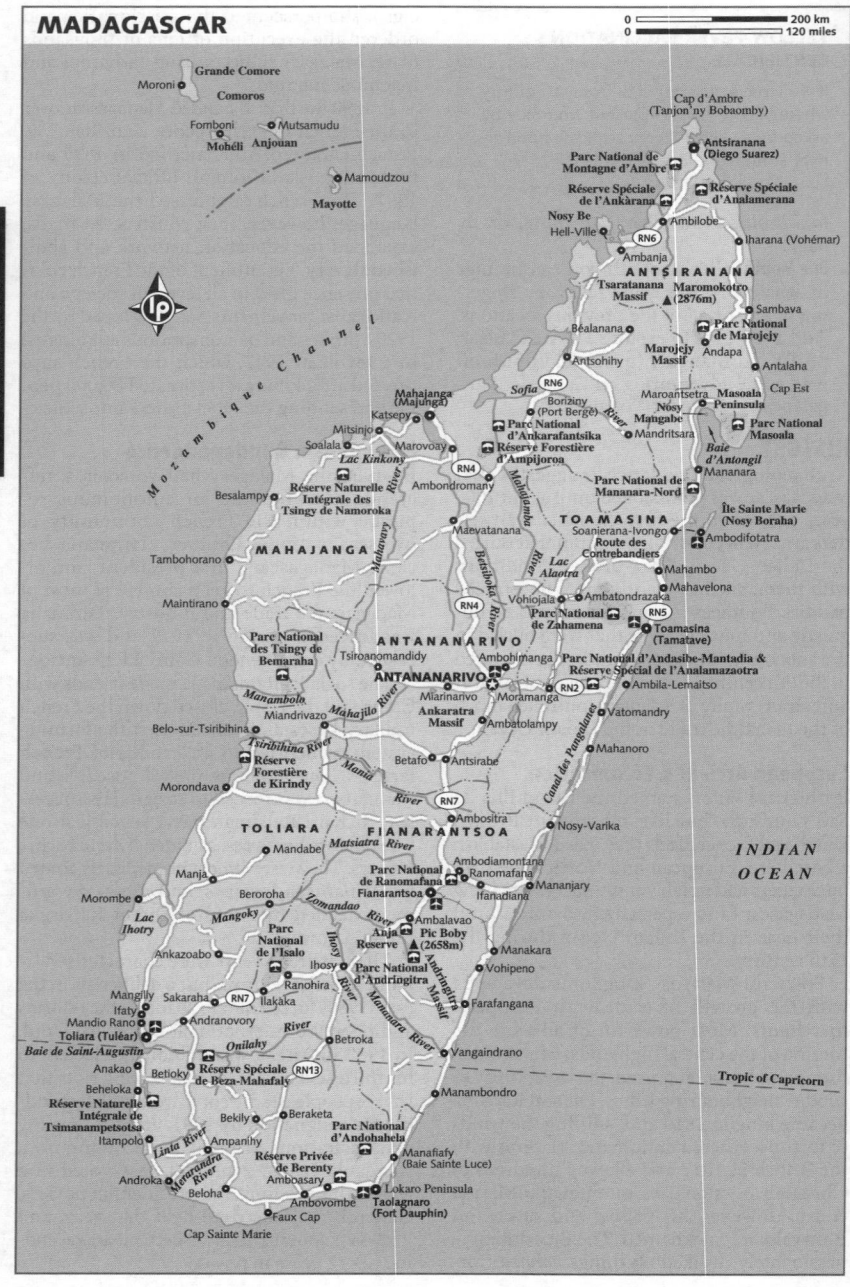

MADAGASCAR

0   200 km
0   120 miles

Moroni

Grande Comore

Comoros

Fomboni   Mutsamudu

Mohéli   **Anjouan**

Mamoudzou

Mayotte

Cap d'Ambre
(Tanjon'ny Bobaomby)

**Parc National de
Montagne d'Ambre**   Antsiranana
(Diego Suarez)

**Réserve Spéciale
de l'Ankàrana**   **Réserve Spéciale
d'Analamerana**

Nosy Be   Ambilobe
Hell-Ville   RN6   Iharana (Vohémar)
Ambanja

ANTSIRANANA
Tsaratanana   Maromokotro
Massif   ▲(2876m)   Sambava

Bealanana   **Parc National
de Marojejy**
  Marojejy   Andapa
Antsohihy   **Massif**   Antalaha

Mozambique Channel

Boriziny   Maroantsetra   **Masoala**   Cap Est
Sofia   (Port Bergé)   Nosy   **Peninsula**
Mahajanga   RN6   Mangabe   **Parc National
(Majunga)**   River   Masoala
Katsepy   **Parc National
d'Ankarafantsika**   Mandritsara
Mitsinjo   **Réserve Forestière**   *Baie
d'Ampijoroa**   d'Antongil*
Soalala   Marovoay   RN4   Mananara
Lac Kinkony   Ambondromamy   **Parc National de
Mananara-Nord**

**Réserve Naturelle
Intégrale des
Tsingy de Namoroka**   Maevatanana   Île Sainte Marie
(Nosy Boraha)
Besalampy   **MAHAJANGA**   Ambodifotatra

Tambohorano   *Lac*   Mahambo
  Alaotra   Mahavelona
Maintirano   RN4   Vohijala   Ambatondrazaka
  Parc National de   RN5
  Zahamena   **Toamasina**
  (Tamatave)
**Parc National
des Tsingy de
Bemaraha**   **ANTANANARIVO**   **Parc National d'Andasibe-Mantadia &
Réserve Spéciale de l'Analamazaotra**
  Tsiroanomandidy   Ambohimanga   Ambila-Lemaitso
Manambolo   **ANTANANARIVO**
Belo-sur-Tsiribihina   Miarinarivo   RN2   Vatomandry
Miandrivazo   **Ankaratra**   Moramanga
Mahajilo   **Massif**
  Ambatolampy   Mahanoro
**Réserve
Forestière
de Kirindy**   *Mania*   Betafo   Antsirabe
Morondava   *River*   RN7

Tsiribihina River

TOLIARA   **FIANARANTSOA**   Ambositra   Nosy-Varika
  Matsiatra River
Mandabe

*INDIAN
OCEAN*

Morombe   **Parc National
de Ranomafana**   Ranomafana
Manja   Beroroha   **Fianarantsoa**   Mananjary
Mangoky   Ifanadiana
Zomandao
  River   Ambalavao
Ankazoabo   **Parc
National
de l'Isalo**   **Pic Boby**
  ▲(2658m)   Manakara
*Lac
Ihotry*   Ihosy   **Anja
Réserve**
  Ihosy   **Parc National
d'Andringitra**   Vohipeno
Mangily   Sakaraha   RN7   Ranohira   *River*   Farafangana
Ifaty   Ilakaka
Mandio Rano   Andranovory
Toliara (Tuléar)   *Onilahy*   *River*
Baie de Saint-Augustin   Betroka
Anakao   Betioky   Betroka   Vangaindrano
  Réserve Spéciale   RN13
Beheloka   **de Beza-Mahafaly**   Tropic of Capricorn

**Réserve Naturelle
Intégrale de
Tsimanampetsotsa**   Bekily   Berakata   Manambondro
Itampolo   *Linta River*
  Ampanihy   **Parc National
d'Andohahela**
  **Réserve Privée
de Berenty**   Manafiafy
Androka   *Manandra River*   (Baie Sainte Luce)
  Ambovombe   Ambosary   Lokaro Peninsula
Beloha   **Taolagnaro
(Fort Dauphin)**
  Faux Cap
Cap Sainte Marie

Years of communist-style dictatorship and economic mismanagement made it hard for Zafy to ignite the economy and gain the trust of the people. He was eventually impeached for abuse of constitutional powers. Elections were called in 1996 and Ratsiraka surprised everyone by scraping by with a victory.

In the first round of the 2001 general election, Marc Ravalomanana, a dairy businessman, claimed victory, but Ratsiraka refused to accept the vote. Ravalomanana and his supporters mounted mass protests and a general strike at the beginning of 2002. A month later Ravalomanana went ahead and declared himself president anyway, sparking off clashes between rival supporters that nearly brought Madagascar to civil war. Bridges were bombed, and Ratsiraka's supporters blockaded Antananarivo, cutting off its fuel and food supply for weeks.

The Supreme Court held a recount of the votes and declared Ravalomanana the winner. When the US recognised Ravalomanana as the rightful president, Ratsiraka fled in exile to Paris. Ravalomanana's 'I Love Madagascar' party sealed its popularity at parliamentary elections in December 2002. The new president set about reforming the country's ruined economy, and announced salary increases for politicians in an effort to stamp out corruption. His government generally made the right noises to the World Bank, which, along with France and the US, pledged a total of US$2.3 billion in aid.

Ravalomanana had moved away from French colonial influence on the country, restoring the Malagasy language and traditions. Under his leadership, main roads were repaired and maintained, and tourism promoted by the declaration of new national parks. However, he also sold around a third of the country's arable land to a South Korean company to grow food for Koreans.

Madagascar Today

In January 2009, political unrest developed into violence and Ravalomanana was forced to resign in March. Thirty-four-year-old former mayor of Antananarivo and opposition leader, Andry Rajoelina, too young to become president himself but with the support of the military, took power and set up transitional bodies to govern the island, with the promise of elections in 2011. The African Union expelled Madagascar, saying that Ravalomanana's ousting was not democratic. The EU and G8 nations suspended nonhumanitarian funding, which resulted in serious repercussions for a country where around 70% of the population lives on less than US$1 a day.

The results of the political upheaval are apparent in a substantial fall-off in tourism, the abandonment of the Korean land deal and the collapse of the dairy industry as Ravalomanana's companies are investigated for tax fraud; all of which leave many people out of work.

At the time of research, the international community had persuaded Rajoelina to hold elections in October 2010. The country was stable with no political unrest evident, and the people eager to welcome back visitors.

CULTURE

Your first impression of the Malagasy is likely to be of a polite but reserved people. The concept of *fihavanana*, which means 'conciliation' or 'brotherhood', is enshrined in society; confrontation is avoided and compromises are sought. Politeness in general is very important to the Malagasy, and impatience or pushy behaviour is regarded as shocking.

The Malagasy do not consider themselves Africans. As far as the citizens of 'La Grande Île' are concerned, they are just that – an island people.

Despite independence, French culture remains influential and the French language continues to be widely spoken.

The family is the central tenet of Malagasy life, including departed ancestors. At *famadihana* (literally, 'the turning of the bones') exhumation ceremonies, people may line up for a photograph with the shroud-wrapped bodies of dead family members laid out neatly in the foreground. There's also a complex system of *fady* (taboos) that must be respected.

The Malagasy home, as the centre of the extended family (ancestors are included), is furnished with care and attention, regardless of how poor the household may be. Custom dictates that furniture, doors and windows should all be astrologically aligned and placed in specific parts of the building.

It's still common to find sacred offerings left at the base of baobab trees, beside forest waterfalls or in front of royal tombs. Family outings, usually accompanied by a picnic, to a beautiful spot of family or tribal significance, are a popular leisure activity.

MADAGASCAR

MALAGASY BLOGOSPHERE

Madagascar has a thriving blogging community that provides an interesting look at what's going on in the country. Antananarivo resident, **Lalatiana Rahariniaina** (http://ariniaina.wordpress.com), blogs in English about politics, people, life and aspects of culture such as circumcision and *famadihana*.

Lalatiana is also coordinator of **FOKO** (http://foko-madagascar.org), which comprises a group of bloggers from all over Madagascar. Its mission statement argues 'When often biodiversity and lemurs are in the spotlight, FOKO wants to focus on the Malagasy people and make them a crucial factor in their unique and threatened environment. FOKO's goal is to help the Malagasy people improve their quality of life without destroying the forest'.

Madafan (www.madafan.com) is another blog with fascinating tourism-related articles on surfing, hiking, lemur-spotting and conservation.

Time and dates have an influence on Malagasy lifestyle. One example of this is seen in the belief in *vintana* (destiny), which influences the dates of parties held to mark circumcisions, marriages or reburials. Friday, which is associated with nobility, is considered a good day to hold a celebration.

People

The Malagasy people are officially divided into 18 ethnic groups, whose boundaries are roughly based on old kingdoms. The main groups are Merina (27%), Betsimisaraka (15%), Betsileo (12%), Tsimihety (7%), Sakalava (6%), Antaisaka (5%) and Antandroy (5%), with a number of smaller groups making up the remainder. Also important is the distinction between Merina highlanders and so-called *côtiers*. Literally, *côtiers* refers to those from the coast, but really means any non-Merina groups.

Traditional Malagasy culture is rooted in reverence and respect for ancestors. While Madagascar's population still adheres to traditional beliefs, many belong to the Roman Catholic and Protestant churches. A small proportion is Muslim (around 7%). Evangelical Christian churches have become popular in recent years, but even among Christians there is generally great respect and reverence for traditional rituals.

Personal adornment and fashion are hugely important to the Malagasy, and men and women alike take great care with their appearance. Hats are the most beloved of all fashion items, and may be worn cocked jauntily over one eye or with the brims demurely turned down to shade the face.

Arts & Crafts

Textiles have always played a huge part in Malagasy society, with some types of cloth even being imbued, it is believed, with supernatural powers. The Merina used cocoons collected from the wild silkworm to make highly valued textiles called *lamba mena* (red silk). Worn by the aristocracy in life and death, *lamba mena* were also used in burial and reburial ceremonies. Ask at the Centre Culturel Albert Camus (p910) in Antananarivo for details of textile exhibitions.

Handmade paper is made in Ambalavao, where you can visit the Antaimoro factory Fabrique de Papier Antaimoro (p919).

Ambositra (p916) is the centre for wood-carving and marquetry.

FOOD & DRINK

You won't go hungry in Madagascar – eating is a real joy and prices are extremely cheap by Western standards. Rice is the staple and is often accompanied by a stew made from beef, fish, chicken, duck or vegetables. Favourite dishes include *romazava* (beef-and-vegetable stew) and *ravioto* (pork stew with manioc), with *mi sao* (fried noodles with vegetables or meat) or a satisfying *soupe chinoise* (clear noodle soup with fish, chicken or vegetables) the most usual alternatives. Restaurants normally also serve excellent French cuisine, from simple zebu *steack frites* (steak and chips), to *paté de foie gras* (goose liver paté) and *magret de canard* (duck breast). Western staples such as pizza and pasta are easy to find, too. Green peppercorn or vanilla-flavoured sauces are common.

French restaurants rarely cater for vegetarians, but local *hotelys* (Malagasy eateries that serve mainly inexpensive rice dishes and snacks) can usually whip up some noodles, soup or rice and greens. Seafood fans are in for a treat – every menu in coastal areas features cheap lobster, prawns or squid dishes together with a fish of the day.

The most popular local-brand beers are Three Horses Beer (known as THB) and Gold, but the alcoholic speciality is *rhum arrangé* – rum flavoured with fruits or spices. A taste of Malagasy wine is something you probably won't want to repeat, but imported French and South African wines are served in better restaurants.

ENVIRONMENT

Madagascar split from the African land mass around 165 million years ago and has been in its present position for about 100 million years. The island measures 1600km long and up to 570km wide, and the 5000km-long coastline is sprinkled with small islands, including Île Sainte Marie to the east.

Madagascar can be divided geographically into three parallel north-south zones, each with its own ecosystem: the west consists of dry spiny desert or deciduous forest; the central highlands, known as the *hauts plateaux*, have now been mostly deforested; and the eastern zone is rainforest. The coasts are marked by alternating mangrove forests and long, sweeping sandy beaches, with coral reefs offshore. The 2876m volcanic Maromokotro peak is Madagascar's highest point. All but the island's southern tip lies north of the Tropic of Capricorn.

Madagascar's unique wildlife is today among its biggest tourist drawcards and its imminent disappearance is one of the most pressing global conservation issues. Over the last thousand years many large animals, including giant lemurs, have been hunted to extinction.

Madagascar's best-known mammals are the lemurs, which include sifakas and the indri, mouse and ring-tailed lemurs, the incredible aye-aye and noisy black-and-white lemurs. Humpback whales migrate past Madagascar's shores from June to October.

Madagascar has 209 breeding bird species, of which about 57% (120 species) are endemic – the highest proportion of any country in the world. These include the diverse vanga shrikes, couas and various species of ground roller.

Chameleons are the best known of Madagascar's reptiles, and include the world's largest and smallest species. Other reptiles include frogs, geckos, harmless snakes such as the tree boa, the potentially dangerous Nile crocodile and strikingly marked tortoises.

The country's flora is no less diverse, with some 6000 species. These range from the bizarre plants of the spiny desert to magnificent rainforest trees, from huge baobabs to delicate orchids, of which vanilla is, perhaps, the most famous.

Only 10% of Madagascar's original rainforests remain. The country's big environmental issues are deforestation and the consequent erosion caused by 'slash-and-burn' farming. Today a wasteland of invasive, sun-loving grass covers more than 80% of the island. It supports very few native animals and plants, and even people have a tough time living on this fragile landscape.

Madagascar has more than 14 national parks. By visiting one, you are economically helping village residents: 50% of park admission fees are returned to villagers to build wells and small dams, buy vegetable seeds, help with tree nurseries and build schools.

ANTANANARIVO

pop 1.9 million

Madagascar's seemingly unpronounceable capital (commonly shortened to 'Tana') is like no other in Africa. Cobbled streets wind up steep, rocky hills past narrow houses with painted shutters to soaring church spires and grand edifices, recalling European rather than African cities.

HISTORY

Antananarivo was originally known as Analamanga (Blue Forest), and is believed to have been populated by the Vazimba people. In 1610 a Merina king, Andrianjaka, conquered the Vazimba and named his new settlement Antananarivo (Town of the Thousand) after the garrison he stationed there. Andrianjaka built his own *rova* (palace) on the highest of Antananarivo's hills and founded the Merina dynasty.

In 1895 the French captured Tana, renaming it Tananarive and using it as a seat of government. They built two great staircases, and drained swamps and paddy fields to create the present-day Analakely area. After independence, the city's name reverted back to Antananarivo.

ORIENTATION

Ivato airport, which serves both domestic and international routes, lies 19km from the centre of Antananarivo.

Central Antananarivo can be roughly divided into Haute-Ville (Upper Town) and Basse-Ville (Lower Town). The broad Ave de l'Indépendance runs from the train station towards the crowded main market area of Analakely, with a steep staircase leading to Place de l'Indépendance in the rather quieter Haute-Ville. Another staircase, directly opposite, leads to the busy district of Ambondrona. Narrow streets lead further uphill past several churches to the queen's *rova*.

INFORMATION
Bookshops
The best place to pick up English-language magazines is from the street vendors in Place de l'Indépendance.

Librairie de Madagascar (Map p912; ☎ 020-22 224 54; 38 Ave de l'Indépendance) Sells maps, guidebooks (in French) and dictionaries (French-English and Malagasy-English).

Cultural Centres
Alliance Française d'Antananarivo (off Map p911; ☎ 020-22 208 56; aftananarive@alliancefr.mg; Lalana Seimad, Andavamamba) Offers French- and Malagasy-language courses, and sponsors various cultural events.

Centre Culturel Albert Camus (Map p912; ☎ 020-22 213 75; ccac@wanadoo.mg; 14 Ave de l'Indépendance; ☺ 10am-1pm & 2-6pm Tue-Sat) Sponsors an extensive program of concerts, dance and film. The centre has a library and exhibition hall.

Emergency
Ambulance (☎ 020-22 200 40)
Espace Medical 24-hour clinic (☎ 020-22 625 66)
Fire (☎ 18)
Police (Map p912; ☎ 17; Lalana Karija)

Internet Access
Cyber-Paositra (☺ 8am-3.30pm Mon-Fri, 9-11am Sat) Basse-Ville (Map p912; paositra@dts.mg; Araben'ny 26 Jona 1960; per min Ar50); Haute-Ville (Map p912; Place de l'Indépendance; per min Ar50) Both main post offices have good internet centres.

Outcool Web Bar (Map p912; Lalana Andrianary Ratianarivo; per min Ar50; ☺ 9am-11pm Mon-Sat, 3.30-9pm Sun) Discounts apply for longer surfing times.

Teknet Group (Map p912; Arabe Ramanantsoa; per 45min Ar2000; ☺ 8am-6.30pm Mon-Sat, 2.30-6.30pm Sun) Also has fax and printing services.

Medical Services
Centre Hospitalier de Soavinandriana (Hôpital Militaire d'Antananarivo; Map p911; ☎ 020-22 397 51; ☺ 24hr) Has X-ray equipment and stocks most basic drugs and medicines. It employs several French doctors.

Clinique des Sœurs Franciscaines (Clinique et Maternité St-François; Map p911; ☎ 020-22 610 46; Lalana

Dokotera Rajaonah, Ankadifotsy) Has X-ray equipment and is well run and relatively clean.

Pharmacie Metropole (Map p912; ☎ 020-22 200 25; Lalana Ratsimilaho; ☺ 8am-noon & 2-6pm Mon-Sat) Antananarivo has many good, well-stocked pharmacies. This is one of the best and is conveniently located near Hôtel Colbert.

Money
All banks listed here exchange cash and travellers cheques.

Bank of Africa (BOA) Basse-Ville (Map p912; Ave de l'Indépendance; ☺ 8am-3.30pm Mon-Fri); Haute-Ville (Map p912; Place de l'Indépendance; ☺ 8am-3.30pm Mon-Fri) ATMs accept Visa cards. Both branches provide cash advances on MasterCard.

BFV-SG Basse-Ville (Map p912; Ave de l'Indépendance; ☺ 8am-4pm); Haute-Ville (Map p912; Arabe Ramanantsoa; ☺ 8am-4pm) The branch on Arabe Ramanantsoa has an ATM; both branches change travellers cheques (Amex only) and do advances on Visa cards.

BMOI (Map p912; Place de l'Indépendance; ☺ 8am-4pm) Has an ATM that accepts Visa cards.

BNI-CL Basse-Ville (Map p912; Araben'ny 26 Jona 1960; ☺ 8am-4pm); Basse-Ville (Map p912; Kianja 19 Mey 1946; ☺ 8am-4pm) Gives advances on Visa cards. The branch on Araben'ny 26 Jona 1960 has an ATM.

Socimad Bureau de Change (Map p912; Lalana Radama I; ☺ 8am-noon & 2-5pm Mon-Fri, 8-11.15am Sat) Gives cash advances on Visa cards.

MCB (Map p912; Lalana des 77 Parlementaires Français; ☺ 8.30am-4pm) Gives cash advances on both Visa and MasterCard.

Post & Telephone
There are public telephones for domestic and international calls at both post offices, as well as plenty dotted around town. You can buy phonecards from any shop or kiosk.

Paositra Basse-Ville (post office; Map p912; Araben'ny 26 Jona 1960; ☺ 7am-5pm Mon-Fri); Haute-Ville (main post office; Map p912; Lalana Ratsimilaho; ☺ 7am-5pm Mon-Fri, 8-11am Sat) Poste restante is sent to the main post office (which is located near the Hôtel Colbert). The Basse-Ville branch is closed on Saturday.

Tourist Information
L'Office Nationale de Tourisme de Madagascar (Map p912; ☎ 020-22 661 15; www.madagascar-tourisme .com; 3 Lalana Elysée Ravelomanantsoa; ☺ 8.30am-5.30pm Mon-Fri) Friendly but fairly clueless staff and very limited printed information.

Travel Agencies
For listings of agencies offering trips within Madagascar, see p934. If you're travelling

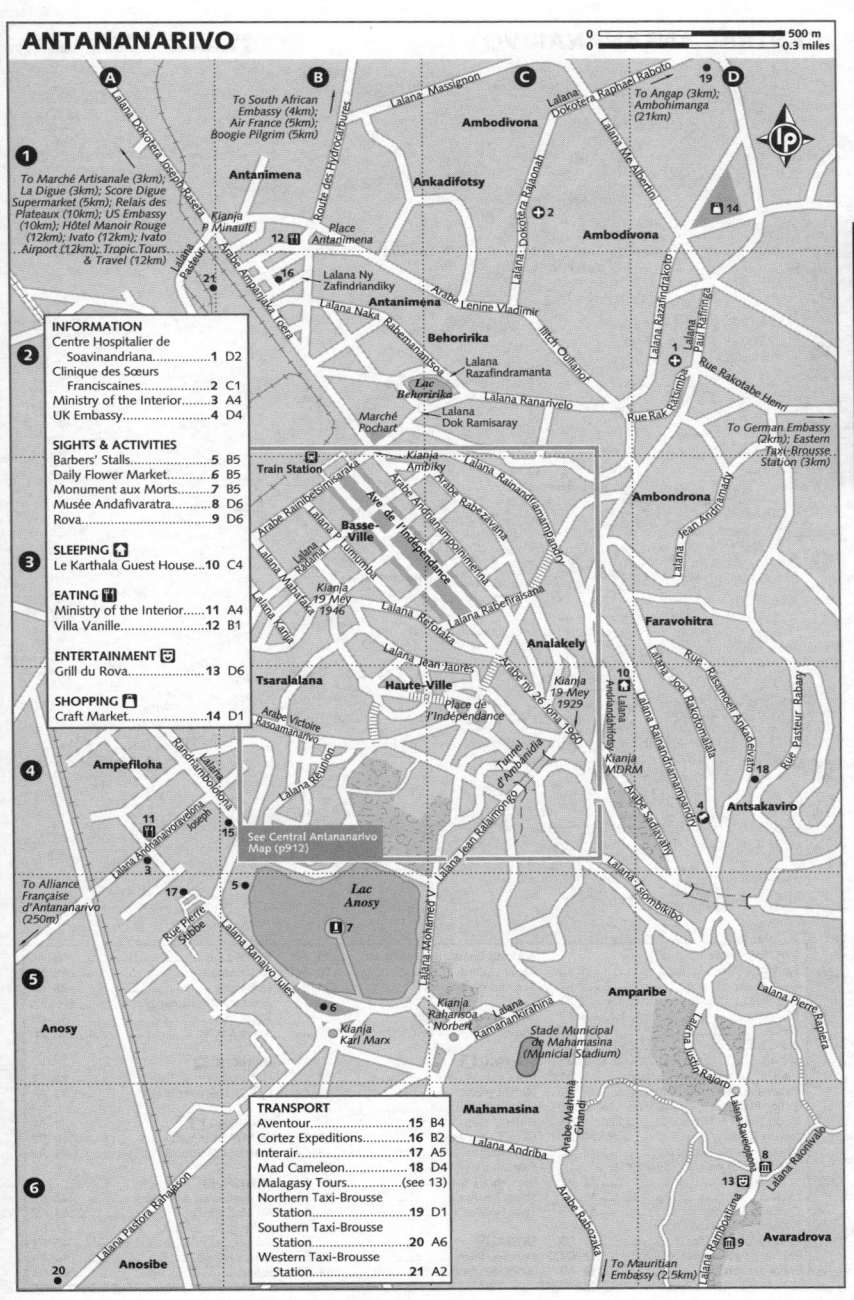

ANTANANARIVO

MADAGASCAR

INFORMATION
Centre Hospitalier de Soavinandriana......1	D2
Clinique des Sœurs Franciscaines......2	C1
Ministry of the Interior......3	A4
UK Embassy......4	D4

SIGHTS & ACTIVITIES
Barbers' Stalls......5	B5
Daily Flower Market......6	B5
Monument aux Morts......7	B5
Musée Andafivaratra......8	D6
Rova......9	D6

SLEEPING
Le Karthala Guest House...10	C4

EATING
Ministry of the Interior......11	A4
Villa Vanille......12	B1

ENTERTAINMENT
Grill du Rova......13	D6

SHOPPING
Craft Market......14	D1

TRANSPORT
Aventour......15	B4
Cortez Expeditions......16	B2
Interair......17	A5
Mad Cameleon......18	D4
Malagasy Tours......(see 13)	
Northern Taxi-Brousse Station......19	D1
Southern Taxi-Brousse Station......20	A6
Western Taxi-Brousse Station......21	A2

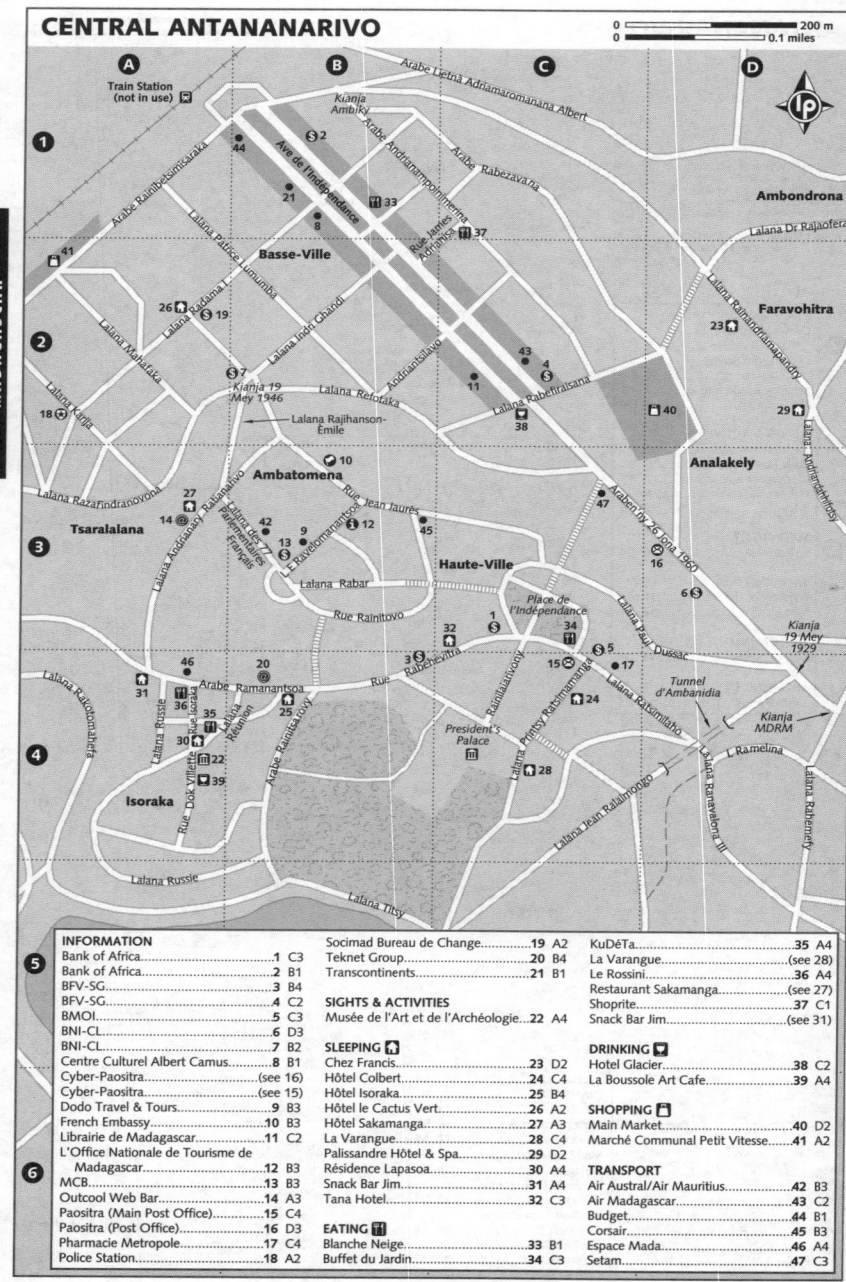

CENTRAL ANTANANARIVO

outside the country, the following agencies sell air tickets and package holidays:

Dodo Travel & Tours (Map p912; ☎ 020-22 690 36; www.dodotraveltour.com; Lalana Elysée Ravelomanantsoa)

Transcontinents (Map p912; ☎ 020-22 223 98; transco@dts.mg; 10 Ave de l'Indépendance) This company also has a branch in the Hôtel Colbert (p914).

Tropic Tours & Travel (off Map p911; ☎ 020-22 580 75; tropic@tropic-tours.net; Rte de l'Aéroport, Ivato)

DANGERS & ANNOYANCES

Tana is probably safer than most African cities of comparable size. It is not safe to take public transport at night, especially between the city centre and the airport, so take a taxi if you go out. If you do walk, go in a group and take a torch – in much of the city there are no street lights.

SIGHTS

The **Rova** (Queen's Palace; Map p911; Lalana Ramboatiana) crowns the highest hill overlooking Lac Anosy. Gutted in a fire in 1995, it was being restored at the time of research and was not open to the public. The Rova is a stiff 4km walk from central Antananarivo, or an easy taxi ride (Ar5000).

Housed in a magnificent burgundy baroque palace a few hundred metres downhill from the Rova, the **Musée Andafivaratra** (Map p911; admission Ar5000; ☉ 9am-5pm) is filled with furniture, portraits and memorabilia that bring the stories of the Merina monarchs to life. English-speaking freelance guides hang around here, and are full of anecdotes about the bloody history of the Merina kings and queens. They'll be asking for around Ar3000 per person once the Rova is open again (they can't show you round the Rova during restoration), but you really don't need a guide for the museum.

The **Musée de l'Art et de l'Archéologie** (Map p912; ☎ 020-22 210 47; Rue Dok Villette; admission free, donations welcome; ☉ 9am-4.30pm Tue-Sat) is worth popping into to see grave decorations from the south (known as *aloalo*), an extensive exhibition of musical instruments, and talismans and objects used for sorcery.

Lac Anosy (Map p911) is an easy downhill walk from Haute-Ville; the lake is at its most beautiful in October, when the surrounding jacaranda trees are covered in purple blossom. The **Monument aux Morts** (Monument to the Dead; Map p911), a WWI memorial erected by the French, is a large golden angel on an island connected to the shore by a causeway. There's a **daily flower market** (Map p911) just opposite the end of the causeway and a neat little row of **barbers' stalls** (Map p911) on the lake's western shore.

SLEEPING

The capital offers most types of accommodation, or you can stay near the airport at Ivato if you have an early flight to catch. Hotel prices usually don't include breakfast.

Budget

Hôtel Manoir Rouge (☎ 020-22 441 04; www.madatana.com, in French; dm Ar15,000, d with/without bathroom Ar39,000/29,000) Within walking distance of the airport, this long-running budget option is for those arriving late or departing early. Rooms are clean and the service friendly. Food is also available (mains Ar10,000).

Snack Bar Jim (Map p912; ☎ 032 56 696 96; Arabe Ramanantsoa; d Ar25,000) This Malagasy snack bar also has a few clean rooms available several storeys up, on the rooftop. There are fantastic views and rooms have internal showers, but the toilets are shared.

Chez Francis (Map p912; ☎ 020-22 613 65; hotel chezfrancis@moov.ma; Lalana Rainandriamapandry; from d Ar34,500) Up high above the city, this is a good choice, which offers clean, spacious rooms with a hot shower but shared toilets. The more expensive rooms have great views over Tana.

Le Karthala Guest House (Map p911; ☎ 020-22 248 95; fax 020-22 272 67; le_karthala@yahoo.fr; Lalana Andriandahifotsy; d incl breakfast Ar47,000) A friendly, family-run B&B with a pretty garden courtyard. Rooms are large and very well furnished, with bathrooms. Malagasy meals (Ar9500) are available with advance notice in the evenings.

Hôtel Isoraka (Map p912; ☎ 020-22 355 81; 11 Arabe Ramanantsoa; d with/without bathroom Ar50,600/20,600) One of the best budget places, it's up in trendy Isoraka, with its range of good restaurants nearby.

Midrange

Hôtel Sakamanga (Map p912; ☎ 020-22 358 09; www.sakamanga.com; Lalana Andrianary Ratianarivo; d Ar45,000-162,500) One of the best midrange choices, though room prices vary wildly. Advance bookings are advised. Airy, bright rooms with wooden floors all have TV, phone and bathroom; the pricier rooms have garden

MADAGASCAR

views. The bar and restaurant (see Restaurant Sakamanga, right) are great places to meet travellers of every stripe.

Hôtel le Cactus Vert (Map p912; ☎ 020-22 624 41; lecactusvert@moov.mg; 15 Lalana Radama I; d Ar75,000) Rooms are a bit characterless, but have a full-sized bath and a safe, and some have TV. The restaurant has a good reputation (mains Ar13,500).

ourpick Résidence Lapasoa (Map p912; ☎ 020-22 611 40; corossol@malagasy.com; 15 Lalana Réunion; d Ar112,500-150,000; 🖵) A fine Isoraka choice, with spotless, wood-appointed rooms, all with TV and some with minibar, four-poster bed and some with balcony. There's free internet use for guests, when it works. The top-notch KuDéTa restaurant (right) is attached.

Relais des Plateaux (off Map p911; ☎ 020-22 441 22; relaisdesplateaux@wanadoo.mg; d Ar225,400; ✂ 🍴) Newest and nicest of the Ivato hotels, this place offers spacious rooms with TV, minibar and safe, and tiled bathrooms with powerful hot shower. Meals are available (mains Ar15,000). Some English is spoken and airport transfers can be arranged.

Top End

La Varangue (Map p912; ☎ 020-22 273 97; www.tana-hotel.com; 17 Lalana Printsy Ratsimamanga; d/studio Ar160,000/450,000) This highly recommended boutique hotel is tucked down a cobbled lane near the President's Palace. Rooms feature minibar, coffee-making facilities, TV and phone. It has a fine restaurant (opposite), too.

Tana Hotel (Map p912; ☎ 020-22 313 20; www.tana-hotel-madagascar.com; 4 Rue Rabehevitra; d Ar235,000-455,000; ✂ 🍴 🖵) A smart, new, business hotel in a central location. Malagasy touches blend well with the modern decor. The rooms include TV, safe, phone and minibar.

Hôtel Colbert (Map p912; ☎ 020-22 202 02; colbert@moov.mg; Lalana Printsy Ratsimamanga; r Ar245,000-840,000; 🅿 🍴 🍴) Cheaper rooms lack the luxury promised by the flashy lobby, but this standout choice offers great service and a host of facilities, including a stunning spa, bars, a patisserie, two restaurants and a business centre. The rooms also include TV, safe, phone and minibar.

Palissandre Hôtel & Spa (Map p912; ☎ 020-22 605 60; www.hotel-palissandre.com; 13 Lalana Andriandahifotsy; s & d Ar399,000-614,000; 🍴 🍴) An elegant, quiet hotel where the spacious bedrooms all offer understated comfort. More expensive rooms overlook bustling Analakely, and hotel fa-

cilities include free internet use for guests, spa, bar and a restaurant with log fire. Room facilities include minibar, TV, phone and safe.

EATING

Tana is well served for eateries and it's worth splurging while you're in the capital. Others will have the same idea, so book ahead on Friday and Saturday nights. The best place to find cheap *hotelys* and stalls serving simple Malagasy fare is along the western end of Arabe Ramanantsoa or around the main market at Analakely. Tana's many gleaming *salons de thé* (tea rooms) serve pastries, cakes, coffee, tea and hot chocolate, breakfasts and, in many cases, wonderful ice cream.

Blanche Neige (Map p912; ☎ 020-22 206 59; 15 Ave de l'Indépendance; cakes Ar2000; 🕑 Tue-Sat) Among the better *salon de thés* in which to indulge. But it isn't open in the evening.

Snack Bar Jim (Map p912; Arabe Ramanantsoa; rice dishes Ar3500; 🕑 breakfast, lunch & dinner) A convenient *hotely* in the city centre, serving patisserie and delicious rice or noodle dishes.

Buffet du Jardin (Map p912; ☎ 020-22 338 87; Place de l'Indépendance; snacks from Ar5500; 🕑 7am-10pm) A pleasant umbrella-shaded stop for breakfast or a beer, next to the gardens.

Restaurant Sakamanga (Map p912; ☎ 020-22 358 09; Lalana Andrianary Ratianarivo; mains Ar12,000; 🕑 breakfast, lunch & dinner) Like its namesake hotel, this place is usually busy and reservations are advised on Friday and Saturday. Bistro-style food includes excellent grilled seafood and zebu meals. Daily Malagasy specials are chalked up on a blackboard and a set lunch is Ar9900.

ourpick KuDéTa (Map p912; ☎ 020-22 281 54; www.kudeta.mg; 16 Lalana Réunion; mains Ar14,000; 🕑 lunch & dinner) A very stylish bar-restaurant next to Résidence Lapasoa, with chic decor, friendly English-speaking staff and excellent fare. Bookings are essential for Friday and Saturday nights.

Le Rossini (Map p912; ☎ 020-22 342 44; cnr Arabe Ramanantsoa & Rue Isoraka; mains Ar16,000; 🕑 lunch & dinner) This is a lovely place for a splurge, with crisp napery and silver cutlery. No Italians in sight, though; the menu offers French and Malagasy favourites with French and South African wines.

Villa Vanille (Map p911; ☎ 020-22 205 15; Place Antanimena; mains Ar17,000; 🕑 lunch & dinner) A classy establishment, though rather out of the way, the menu in this old colonial villa features dishes from Mauritius and Réunion, as well as Madagascar. In the high season, there are nightly musical performances.

La Varangue (Map p912; ☎ 020-22 273 97; varangue@moov.mg; 17 Lalana Printsy Ratsimamanga; mains Ar22,000; ☺ lunch & dinner Mon-Sat) A very classy, if small, restaurant in the hotel of the same name. The menu mostly features French cuisine, with a few local touches, and reputedly offers the best French food in Madagascar.

There's a **Shoprite supermarket** (Map p912; ☺ 7.30am-7pm Mon-Sat) at Analakely in Basse-Ville, and another **branch** (☺ 7.30am-7pm Mon-Sat) next to Carlton Hotel near Lac Anosy. You can also buy fresh vegetables, meat and fish at the daily main market (Map p912) by the pavilions at Analakely.

DRINKING

La Boussole Art Café (Map p912; ☎ 020-22 358 10; 21 Dok Villette; ☺ lunch & dinner) A trendy bar-restaurant set among the chic shops and galleries of Isoraka, this is the place to be seen. Oh, and the food (mains Ar16,000) is good, too.

Hôtel Glacier (Map p912; Araben'ny 26 Jona 1960) A popular place with cheap drinks that gets jumpin' on weekends.

ENTERTAINMENT

Grill du Rova (Map p911; ☎ 020-22 627 24; Lalana Ramboatiana, Avaradrova; mains Ar12,000; ☺ lunch & dinner Mon-Sat, lunch Sun) A stylish restaurant-cabaret that showcases Malagasy jazz and traditional music. There are performances every Sunday and Friday at sunset, and musical soirees on the first and third Wednesday of each month.

SHOPPING

The markets in central Tana are great places to browse and buy. The **main market** (Map p912; ☺ daily) is found in the pavilions at Analakely, opposite the bottom of the stairs leading up to Haute-Ville. It's a packed, teeming place, selling every fruit, vegetable, fish or meat product you could imagine. The Marché Communal de Petit Vitesse (Map p912) is a similar, but smaller, market on the tracks west of the train station.

For crafts, the Marché Artisanale (off Map p911) is Tana's best-known market, found on a bend in the road about 2km south of the Score Digue supermarket in the suburb of La Digue. There's another, smaller, craft market (Map p911) at Andravoahangy, about 1.5km northeast of the northern end of Ave de l'Indépendance.

GETTING THERE & AWAY
Air

For details of international flights from Ivato airport, see p931. See relevant city sections for details of domestic flights. The following is a list of domestic and international airline offices in Tana.

Air Austral/Air Mauritius (Map p912; ☎ 020-22 359 90; www.airaustral.com, in French; Lalana des 77 Parlementaires Français)

Air France (off Map p911; ☎ 020-23 230 23; fax 020-23 230 41; Tour Zital, Rte des Hydrocarbures, Ankorondrano)

Air Madagascar (Map p912; ☎ 020-22 222 22; www.airmadagascar.mg; 31 Ave de l'Indépendance)

Corsair (Map p912; ☎ 020-22 633 36; www.corsairfly.com; 1 Rue Rainitovo Antsahavola)

Interair (Map p911; ☎ 020-22 224 06; fax 020-22 624 21; Galerie Marchand nosy) In the Carlton Hotel.

Car & Motorcycle

Car-rental agencies in Tana all handle rentals for use throughout the country; drivers are obligatory. Rates usually include driver, insurance and unlimited mileage, but don't include petrol. Recommended agencies:

Budget (Map p912; ☎ 020-22 611 11; 4 Ave de l'Indépendance)

Razafimahaleo Harizaka (☎ 034 03 957 78; md4exploration@yahoo.com) There's no office; just phone.

You can also rent cars through most of the tour operators listed on p910. See also p933 for general information on car rentals and rates.

Taxi-Brousse

Taxis-brousses (bush taxis) leave from Tana to almost everywhere in Madagascar, departing about every hour to Antsirabe, Fianarantsoa and Toamasina. See the individual town entries for more details.

There are four main *gares routières* (bus stations), all with a chaotic selection of minibuses, cars and buses.

Eastern taxi-brousse station (off Map p911; Gare Routière de l'Est) At Ampasampito, about 3.5km northeast of the city centre. *Taxis-brousses* to Moramanga en route to Toamasina cost Ar8000.

Northern taxi-brousse station (Gare Routière du Nord; Map p911) In Ambodivona, about 2km northeast of the city centre, this is the station for transport to points north. To get here take the Malakia bus 4 or a taxi (Ar4000).

Southern taxi-brousse station (Gare Routière du Sud; Map p911; Lalana Pastora Rahajason) At Anosibe About 1.5km southwest of Lac Anosy. Provides transport to all points south, as well as to some points on the east and west coasts. There are regular departures to Antsirabe, Fianarantsoa, Toliara and Fort Dauphin. To get there take the Fima bus 10 or a taxi (Ar4000).

Western taxi-brousse station (Gare Routière de l'Ouest; Map p911) About 400m northwest of the train station. Has *taxis-brousses* to Ivato and the airport.

GETTING AROUND

Ivato airport is 19km from the city centre. Taxis to/from Ivato airport should cost about Ar27,000. Most tour companies and many hotels can arrange a transfer for a fee.

It's usually no problem to walk between hotels and restaurants, except at night, when it's best to take a taxi; taxis are also recommended if you are visiting places in the suburbs.

There are a few large buses and many minibuses available for getting around Antananarivo. Fares cost Ar100 to Ar300, but it's often quicker to walk to places nearby. Otherwise, you'll never have much difficulty finding a taxi, even late at night. Taxis don't have meters, so agree on the price before you climb in. Fares around town start at Ar4000 and are more expensive at night.

CENTRAL HIGHLANDS

The *hauts plateaux* are a vast area of rolling hills interspersed with terraced valleys of rice paddies, the picture of rural tranquillity. It's a very scenic region, easily reached from Antananarivo, and features some of the country's most interesting and attractive towns. The main ethnic groups in the region are the Merina and Betsileo.

ANTSIRABE
pop 500,000

Antsirabe (pronounced 'ant-sira-*bay*') makes an ideal day trip from Tana or a base for excursions into the surrounding countryside. Its origins as a 19th-century spa town are reflected in elegant facades and wide boulevards.

The most convenient internet access is at **First In Cyber** (near the cathedral, Rue Stavanger; per min Ar30; ⏱ 8.30am-7.30pm Mon-Sat). There are banks along Rue Jean Ralaimongo that can change cash and travellers cheques, and have ATMs.

Don't miss a visit to the **thermal baths** (Station Thermale; Lac Ranomafana, west of Ave de l'Indépendance; ☎ 020-44 480 19; ⏱ 7am-1pm & 3-6pm, closed mid-Jun–end Jul). In an impressive setting, the Centre Nationale de Cranothérapie & de

Thermoclimatisme offers a range of massage treatments, jacuzzis and a hot pool. **Rando Raid Madagascar** (☎ 032 04 900 21; randoraidmadagascar@yahoo.fr; opposite L'Arche Restaurant, Rue Stavanger; push/mountain bikes per day Ar15,000/20,000) organises tours, horse riding and hiking. It also hires motorbikes, good quality mountain bikes and quad bikes.

With charming round bungalows and upstairs rooms overlooking a lake and green lawns where you can pitch a tent, it's not surprising that **Green Park** (☎ 020-44 051 90; greenparktsara@yahoo.fr; Rue Labourdonnais; campsites per tent Ar6000, d & bungalow Ar31,000) is the best choice in town. Lots of mozzies, though! The **Imperial Hôtel** (☎ 020-44 483 33; yuenkev@yahoo.fr; Grand Ave; r from Ar33,500) is pure grunge, but just serviceable. The more expensive renovated rooms are better, and there's a cybercafé in the lobby, but for the price you'd be better off shopping around. **Hôtel des Thermes** (☎ 020-44 487 61; sht@moov.mg; d/ste Ar130,5500/231,000; 🖥 🏊) is a sprawling 19th-century place boasting an enormous swimming pool and tennis courts. Service is attentive and efficient, and although clean and spacious, the motel-style rooms are rather dated. The restaurant is closed, but breakfast is served.

Mirvana Restaurant (opposite BNI Bank, Rue Jean Ralaimongo) provides a good start to the day with excellent coffee and croissants. **L'Arche** (☎ 032 02 479 25; Rue Stavanger; mains Ar7500; ⏱ lunch & dinner Mon-Sat) serves tasty but unadventurous French food and sometimes features live music. Round the corner is **Ristorante Italiano Saraband** (☎ 032 44 173 07; Rue Jean Ralaimongo; pizzas Ar8000; ⏱ lunch & dinner). You'll be a target for hustlers if you sit outside, but the food is good.

Taxis-brousses leave from the northern *taxi-brousse* station heading to Tana (Ar8000), Ambositra (Ar7000) and Fianarantsoa (Ar15,000).

Pousse-pousses (rickshaws) are the main form of local transport. Trips start at Ar2000 and a short city tour should be about Ar5000. Antsirabe is ideal for bike riding.

AMBOSITRA
pop 28,000

Widely touted as the arts-and-crafts capital of Madagascar, Ambositra (pronounced 'am-*boosh*-tr') is a great place to shop for carved wooden souvenirs and marquetry work. Prices are cheaper than in Tana, and you can arrange to visit the woodcarvers at work, both in town and in nearby Zafimaniry villages. The best

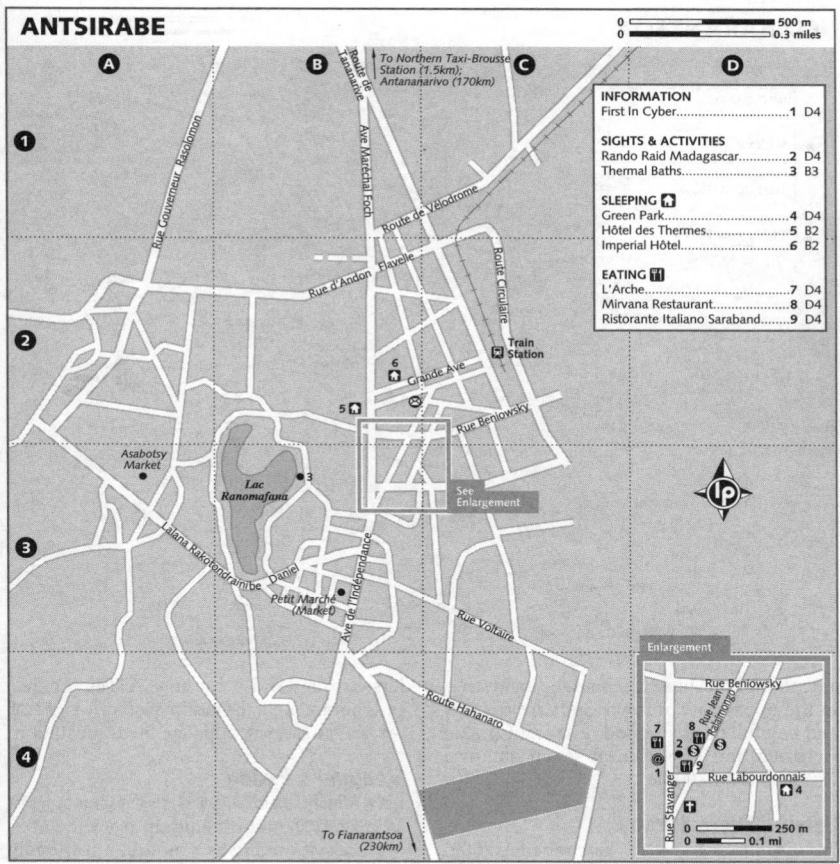

ANTSIRABE

| 0 | 500 m |
| 0 | 0.3 miles |

INFORMATION	
First In Cyber...............................1	D4

SIGHTS & ACTIVITIES	
Rando Raid Madagascar................2	D4
Thermal Baths...............................3	B3

SLEEPING	
Green Park....................................4	D4
Hôtel des Thermes........................5	B2
Imperial Hôtel..............................6	B2

EATING	
L'Arche...7	D4
Mirvana Restaurant.......................8	D4
Ristorante Italiano Saraband........9	D4

MADAGASCAR

To Northern Taxi-Brousse
Station (1.5km);
Antananarivo (170km)

Route de Tananarive
Ave Maréchal Foch
Route de Vélodrome
Rue d'Andon Flavelle
Route Circulaire
Rue Gouverneur Rasoloson
Train Station
Grande Ave
Rue Beniowsky
Asabotsy Market
Lac Ranomafana
Lalana Rakotondraibe Daniel
Petit Marché (MarkeD)
Ave de l'Indépendance
Rue Voltaire
Route Hahanaro
See Enlargement

To Fianarantsoa (230km)

Enlargement

Rue Beniowsky
Rue Jean Ralaimongo
Rue Labourdonnais
Rue Stavanger

| 0 | 250 m |
| 0 | 0.1 mi |

souvenir shops are in the upper (southern) part of town, near the Grand Hôtel.

Hikes into the countryside are popular and can be organised through **Tsangatsanga Maison des Guides** (☎ 032 04 621 28; lamaisondesguides.ambositra@ yahoo.fr) for Ar30,000/40,000 for a half-/full-day hike. It has an office near the Grand Hôtel.

Sleeping & Eating

Grand Hôtel (☎ 020-47 712 62; Rue du Commerce; dm Ar10,000, d with/without bathroom Ar25,000/19,000) Rooms here are a bit dark with a medieval feel, but that's in keeping with the overall ambience. It's in a great location near the craft shops, and the large dining room has a convivial atmosphere at lunch time. It can organise hikes and offers free bikes.

Hôtel Mania (☎ 020-47 710 21; toursmania@moov. mg; d Ar26,000) This brightly painted three-storey place has clean, comfortable rooms and great views from the top-storey balcony. It's not as manic as the gate would have you believe; Mania is the name of the nearby river.

our pick **Motel Violette** (☎ 020-47 713 43, 033 11 392 10; hotel-violette@moov.ma; d Ar28,000, bungalow for 2 from Ar40,000) This is the best choice, just north of town, with good views. Spick and span bungalows across the road feature traditional furnishings, zebu-design bedheads and some have a bathtub. The restaurant (three-course menu Ar16,000) has live music.

Prestige Hôtel (☎ 020-47 710 84; Rue Madiolahatra; d with/without bathroom Ar35,000/18,000) The Prestige is

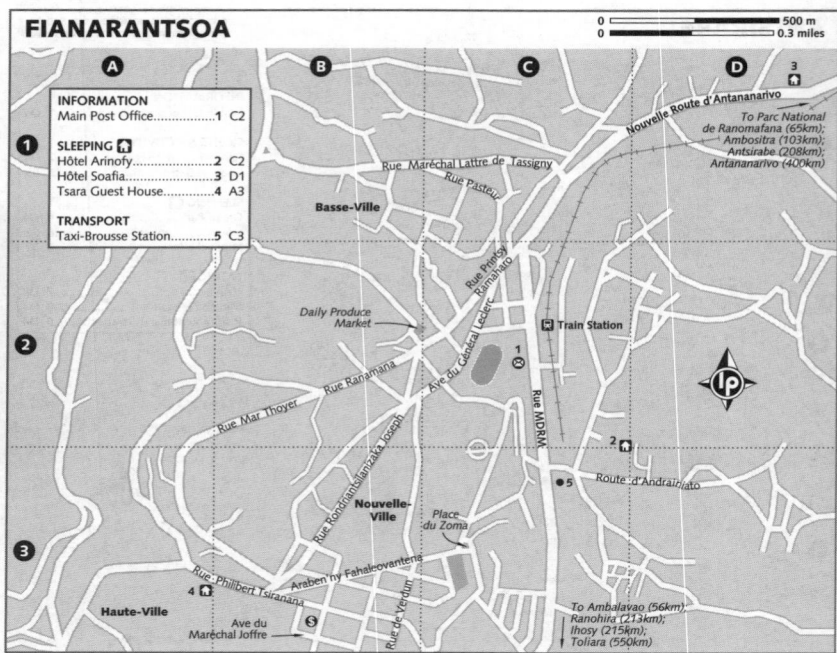

FIANARANTSOA

INFORMATION	
Main Post Office................1	C2
SLEEPING	
Hôtel Arinofy.....................2	C2
Hôtel Soafia......................3	D1
Tsara Guest House............4	A3
TRANSPORT	
Taxi-Brousse Station..........5	C3

MADAGASCAR

a rambling hotel tucked behind the main street in the upper part of town. Staff are friendly and helpful, there's a good restaurant (menu Ar10,000) and it's possible to set up your own tent here (Ar10,000).

Getting There & Away

Taxis-brousses travel to Antsirabe (Ar7000) and Tana (Ar15,000), and leave from the northern *taxi-brousse* station, 2km north of the fork in the main road. *Taxis-brousses* to Fianarantsoa cost Ar7000 and leave from the southern *taxi-brousse* station.

FIANARANTSOA
pop 144,225

The name Fianarantsoa can be translated as 'Place Where Good is Learned', but call it Fianar and you won't be misunderstood. This sprawling, hilly town lies in the agricultural heart of the *hauts plateaux,* surrounded by wine-, tea- and rice-growing villages. It makes a good base for exploring the region and Parc National de Ranomafana (opposite).

All the banks lining the main street in Nouvelle-Ville exchange money and travel-

lers cheques and most have ATMs. There's internet access in the **main post office** (per min Ar30; 7am-9pm Mon-Sat), opposite the train station.

Sleeping & Eating

Hôtel Arinofy (020-75 506 38; d with/without bathroom Ar25,600/23,600) A stiff climb up from the *taxi-brousse* station, this is a modest but friendly and well-kept place with great views over town. Rooms on the upper floor are best, with hot water and views. When the hotel is full, you can pitch a tent for Ar12,000.

Tsara Guest House (020-75 502 06; www.tsaraguest. com; r Ar40,300-115,300) This exceptionally stylish place with a beautiful garden was once a church. The cheaper rooms have shared bathroom but are spotless, and there are incremental degrees of luxury as you move up the price scale, like TV, endless hot water and valley views. It's relaxed and friendly.

Hôtel Soafia (020-75 503 53; soafia.hot@moov.mg; d Ar57,400-62,000, studio Ar67,400-72,400;) This Chinese-style place on the northern edge of town is down-at-heel, but offers a vast swimming pool, tennis courts, disco, shops and sauna. The wood-panelled rooms are cavernous, and have baths, antique replica telephones, TV and fridge.

All hotels have restaurants of varying standard. Pick of the bunch is the restaurant at Tsara Guest House (opposite), which offers the finest dining (mains Ar14,500) in town and a few vegetarian choices.

Getting There & Away
From the **taxi-brousse station** (Rue MDRM), there are plenty of *taxis-brousses* daily between Fianar and Ambositra (Ar7000), Antsirabe (Ar10,000), Tana (Ar15,000), Ranohira (Ar12,000) and Toliara (Ar15,000).

PARC NATIONAL DE RANOMAFANA
The 43,549-hectare park is a superb tract of rainforest that offers great birdwatching and lemur spotting. The park was declared to protect the rare golden bamboo lemur, discovered in 1986, and 11 other lemur species call it home. The weather is best between July and October.

The park entrance and **Angap office** (⏰ 7am–4pm) are at Ambodiamontana village (ask to be dropped here if arriving by *taxi-brousse*). **Permits** (1/2/3/4 days Ar25,000/37,000/40,000/50,000) are compulsory and are available at the Angap office. At the park entrance you must hire a guide (Ar5000Ar to Ar35,000 per person, depending on trail length and group size) to explore the trails. Take a night walk (Ar20,000 per person, one to two hours) and see if you can spot where the sportive lemurs hang out!

The most convenient accommodation option for those arriving by *taxi-brousse* is the basic **Rianala Gîte** (☎ 033 09 532 14; dm Ar12,000), right by the park entrance. **Hôtel Domaine Nature** (☎ 033 05 588 61; domnatrnmf@gmail.com; d/ste Ar87,500/120,000; 🛏), about 3km downhill from the park entrance, offers roomy cabins, perched on the hillside above the roaring river, with hot shower, mosquito net and minibar. There's a good restaurant (mains Ar16,000) here serving the local speciality, crayfish.

A 15-minute walk down from the park entrance is **Setam Lodge** (☎ 033 09 872 92; www.setam-madagascar.com; bungalow for 2 Ar130,000), a comfortable, pleasant option. The restaurant serves good meals (three-course menu Ar35,000) and Angap guides can be arranged. Look out for the enormous yellow comet moths here, after which the lodge is named.

Ranomafana is about three hours by *taxi-brousse* (Ar5000) from Fianarantsoa along a good road.

AMBALAVAO
pop 26,000
The picturesque little town of Ambalavao (New Valley) is famous for the production of *lamba arindrano*, which are scarves in dusky, vegetable-dye colours woven from hand-spun wild silk. Its narrow streets are lined with Betsileo architecture and every Wednesday the country's biggest zebu market (held just outside the south side of town) cranks up. The town's greatest attraction is **Fabrique de Papier Antaimoro** (admission free), which makes the famous Antaimoro paper. You can take a free tour of the factory and there's a shop selling fine souvenirs.

Anja Reserve (admission Ar7000, mandatory guide per 2hr per 2 people Ar8000) is a delightful reserve sporting ring-tailed lemurs. It's 12km south of Ambalavao and is run by local guide **Adrien** (☎ 032 48 479 30). All proceeds go towards job creation and conservation education in the community. Adrien is based at the Hôtel au Bougainvillées (below) and also runs hikes into the Parc National d'Angringitra further south.

Hôtel aux Bougainvillées (☎ 020-75 340 01; auxbougainvilléesambalavao@gmail.com; d/chalet Ar30,000/60,000) is in the grounds of the paper factory and comprises brightly painted two-storey chalets. The good restaurant (mains Ar10,000) is popular with tour groups.

At the clean **Tsienimparihy Hôtel Restaurant** (☎ 020-75 341 28; hoteltsienimpari@yahoo.fr; d Ar25,000) rooms all have toilet and hot water, and there's a patisserie-restaurant (mains Ar6000). It's opposite the main market on the southern side of town.

Ambalavao is 56km south of Fianar, to where a *taxi-brousse* will cost Ar2000. Connections to points further north and south can be made at Fianar.

SOUTHERN MADAGASCAR

Apart from the fairly well-maintained RN7, roads in the rural south can be rough and ready, but those who meet the challenge of independent travel in these parts will be amply rewarded by the world's weirdest vegetation, scenic sandstone massifs and the last stomping grounds of the elephant bird, the largest bird that ever lived.

RANOHIRA

The little town of Ranohira is the most convenient base for exploring Parc National de l'Isalo (right). The Angap office, where you can get permits and hire guides, is next to the Hotel Berny in central Ranohira. **Momo Trek** (☎ 033 14 685 46; momo_trek@yahoo.fr), based at Chez Momo (below), organises one- to five-day hikes into the park, including guiding, cooking and camping equipment. Hikes start at Ar165,000 per person per night, excluding the park permit fee.

All hotels listed here have restaurants. On the western side of RN7, 1km from Ranohira, so within walking distance of town, the **Les Toiles de l'Isalo** (☎ 033 11 025 25; www.hotel-toiles -isalo.com; campsite Ar5000, bungalow with/without bathroom Ar50,000/40,00) resort-restaurant complex offers simple thatched wooden bungalows. The restaurant (three-course menu Ar16,000) specialises in grilled zebu meat and does a damned fine job of it, too.

At **Isalo Ranch** (☎ in Antananarivo 020-26 011 11; info@isalo-ranch.com; campsite per person Ar8000, d bungalow with/without bathroom Ar75,000/50,000; 🏊), half a kilometre further south, clean thatched bungalows are somewhat spartan for the price. However, there's a reasonable dining room serving Malagasy meals, and a superb swimming pool where you can enjoy sunsets over the Isalo Massif. It's about 5km south of town, but there are free daily transfers into Ranohira at 7.30am.

Chez Momo (☎ 033 08 806 61; d bungalow without bathroom Ar20,000, d/tr bungalow Ar35,000/40,00) is the friendliest budget option in Ranohira, with thatched mud-brick bungalows with mosquito nets.

The eccentric stone manor **Hôtel Berny** (☎ 032 05 257 75; hotel.chezberny@gmail.com; d budget/ main Ar40,000/50,000) features rather cold, dingy budget rooms, but the new building is airy and comfortable, with good views.

our pick **Hôtel le Jardin du Roy** (☎ in Antananarivo 020-22 351 65; www.hotel-isalo.com; d €95; ✂ 🏊), located near the park's southern border, is carved out of the living rock and is one of the country's finest top-end hotels. It's in a brilliant setting, hidden among the sandstone, and offers fine dining, a massage centre, tennis and horse riding. Its sister hotel next door, Relais de la Reine, was closed at the time of research.

Taxis-brousses depart daily from Ranohira for Toliar (Ar15,000).

PARC NATIONAL DE L'ISALO

The flat, grassy plains of the *hauts plateaux* near Ranohira are abruptly broken by towering sandstone massifs sculpted by wind and water into gorges and craggy bluffs. It's one of the country's most spectacular regions, perfect for overnight hikes, rock-hopping along cool canyons and spotting lemurs. It's best to visit during the cooler months (April to October), when walking is more comfortable. The Bara people used to bury their dead in caves high up on cliff faces, and some areas remain *fady*.

One-/two-day national-park permits cost Ar25,000/37,000 per person per day and are available at **Angap** (🕑 6.30am-5pm) next to the Hôtel Berny in Ranohira (left). Official guides are compulsory for visits to the park and fees depend on the length of each hike. All trails start and finish in Ranohira, and range from one to seven days in length. Overnight hikes can be organised through Chez Momo (left) and more upmarket hotels, such as Isalo Ranch (left) and Hôtel le Jardin du Roy (left).

Some popular day-walk destinations are **Canyon des Singes**, **Piscine Naturelle**, where you can take a plunge in the cool water, and **Natural Window**, where you can watch the sun rise or set through a large, square hole in the rock.

TOLIARA (TULÉAR)
pop 101,661

Languid, tropical Toliara is the largest town in the south and Madagascar's major west-coast port. It's a hot, humid place, where *pousse-pousses* are the main form of transport and nobody's ever in a great hurry. Many visitors use it as the hub for the seaside villages around Mangilly (p922) and Anakao (opposite).

Information

There are several good internet cafes around town, all offering access for Ar30 per minute. Try along Blvd Philibert Tsiranana.

All banks exchange money and travellers cheques; there's an ATM at BFV-SG. The post office is located on Blvd Gallieni.

Staff at the new **Office Régional du Tourism de Tulear** (☎ 032 02 137 82; 🕑 8.30am-noon & 3-6pm), near the central market, is helpful for hotels and local tours.

Sights & Activities

Arboretum d'Antsokay (☎ 032 02 600 15; www.ant sokayarboretum.org; admission Ar10,000) is a botanical garden, located 12km southeast of Toliara, showcasing Madagascar's extraordinary arid-country vegetation. You'll need your own vehicle to visit. The restaurant is recommended.

The picturesque seaside village of **Anakao** south of town can only be reached by boat and makes a popular excursion for a few days.

There's windsurfing, snorkelling offshore at the little island of Nosy Ve and hikes to sand dunes littered with fragments of elephant bird eggs. **Safari Vezo** (☎ 020-94 413 81, 020-94 410 54; Rue Marius Jatop) can arrange boat transfers to Anakao (return Ar110,000) that take around an hour. There are plenty of accommodation options and places to eat in Anakao.

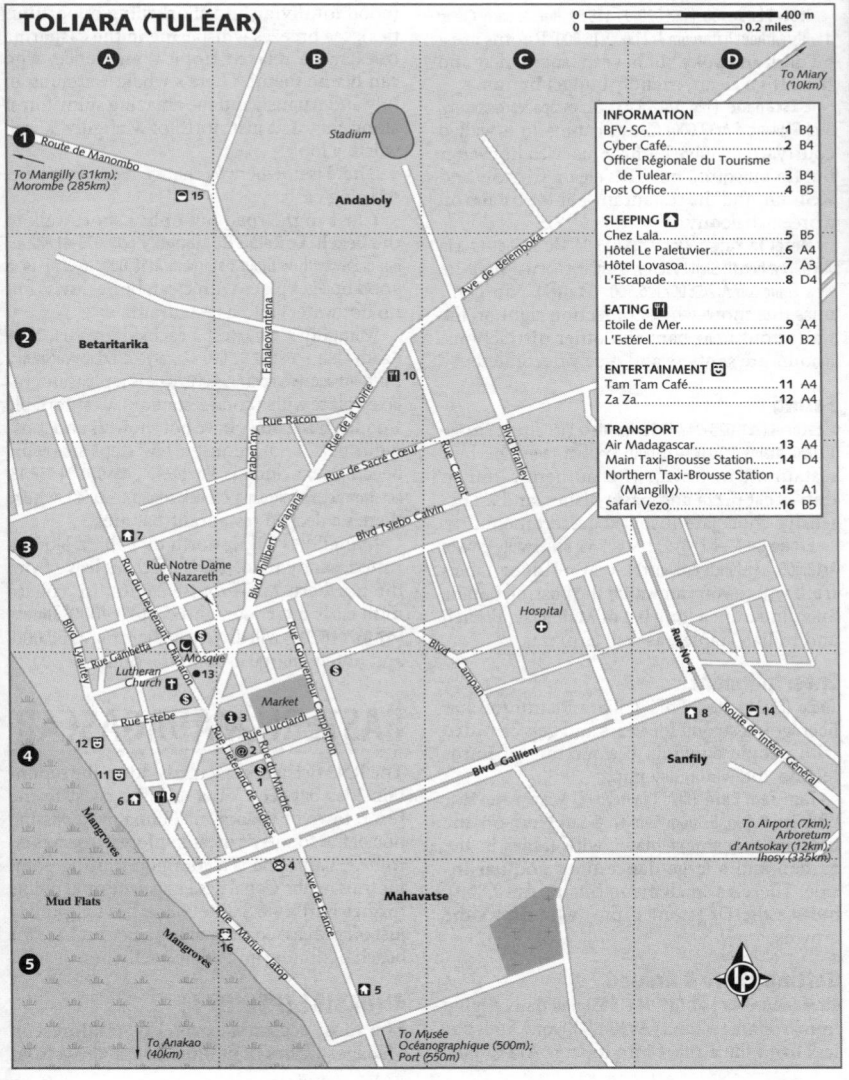

TOLIARA (TULÉAR)

INFORMATION	
BFV-SG	1 B4
Cyber Café	2 B4
Office Régionale du Tourisme de Tulear	3 B4
Post Office	4 B5

SLEEPING 🏠	
Chez Lala	5 B5
Hôtel Le Paletuvier	6 A4
Hôtel Lovasoa	7 A3
L'Escapade	8 D4

EATING 🍴	
Etoile de Mer	9 A4
L'Estérel	10 B2

ENTERTAINMENT 🎭	
Tam Tam Café	11 A4
Za Za	12 A4

TRANSPORT	
Air Madagascar	13 A4
Main Taxi-Brousse Station	14 D4
Northern Taxi-Brousse Station (Mangilly)	15 A1
Safari Vezo	16 B5

MADAGASCAR

Sleeping

There's a good choice of hotels in Toliara if you're laying over between trips up or down the coast.

Chez Lala (☎ 020-94 434 17; Ave de France; d without bathroom Ar15,000, d with/without hot water Ar21,000/19,000) In a handy location for boats to Anakao, with super-clean rooms and bathrooms, and decent food in the attached restaurant.

Hôtel Lovasoa (☎ 020-94 418 39; Rue de Sacré Cœur; d with/without bathroom Ar21,000/16,000) Rooms are a bit dark and poky but have mosquito nets and fans. It's a clean, friendly budget option.

L'Escapade (☎ 020-94 411 82; escapade@moov.mg; Blvd Gallieni; d Ar33,000) Clean cabins in a walled courtyard all have bathrooms with hot water but no mosquito nets. It's clean, friendly and well run, and the restaurant-bar is upstairs on a breezy balcony.

Hôtel le Palétuvier (☎ 020-94 440 39; hotelpaletuviertul@yahoo.fr; Blvd Lyautey; d without hot water/with sea view & air-con Ar26,500/126,500; ✗ P) You can't miss this snow-white confection right on the waterfront near bars and other distractions. Rooms are spotless and nicely decorated.

Eating

L'Estérel (☎ 020-94 441 92; Rue de la Voirie; pizza Ar8000-10,000, mains Ar10,000-16,000; ☽ 9am-1am) The best restaurant in town, with authentic Italian thin-crust pizza and pasta dishes, and an extensive chocolate-inspired dessert menu.

Etoile de Mer (☎ 032 02 605 65; Blvd Lyautey; mains Ar12,000; ☽ lunch & dinner) Great outdoor tables from where you can watch the passing parade and dine from a long list of Malagasy, French and Indian staples, as well as pizzas.

Entertainment

Za Za (Blvd Lyautey) This Toliara institution has been going strong for years and gets crowded with people dancing to a mixture of Euro-techno and Malagasy pop.

Tam-Tam Café (Blvd Lyautey; ☽ 5.30pm-2am Mon, Wed, Thu & Sun, 5.30pm-5am Fri & Sat) New on the block is this smart place, with tables in the garden and a large dance floor and bar inside. There's a small menu (mains Ar10,000), but it's the DJ (from 11pm) who draws the crowds.

Getting There & Around

Air Madagascar (☎ 020-94 415 85) has daily flights from Toliara to Tana (Ar354,000, one hour). A taxi from the airport into town is Ar15,000.

The main *taxi-brousse* station is at the eastern end of town. Several *taxis-brousses* leave daily for Tana.

MANGILLY

Most travellers visit the quiet coastal village of Mangilly (and nearby Ifaty and Mandio Rano) to sit under a palm tree on a white sandy beach. And with coral reefs just offshore (good for diving and snorkelling opportunities), sea breezes whispering in the casuarina trees and a relaxed tropical ambience, who can blame them? There's whale-watching in July and August, and the amazing spiny forest along the road just north of Mangilly is well worth a look.

There is nowhere to change money up here, so bring cash.

Close to the road but only a short walk to the beach, **Le Relais de Mangilly** (☎ 020-41 822 48; bungalow with/without bathroom Ar18,000/16,000) is a good budget place with clean bungalows (but no hot water) and a restaurant.

Mangilly's smartest beachside resort, **Ifaty Beach Club** (☎ 032 02 600 47; ifatybeachclub@moov.mg; 2-person bungalow from Ar94,000; ☒) is a pleasant, relaxed place with a good restaurant. Comfortable wooden bungalows have hot showers and mosquito nets, and are just a few steps from the beach. Next door is **Vovotelo** (☎ 020-94 937 18; hotelvovotelo@simicro.mg; bungalow from Ar97,000), where there's a decked restaurant-bar area.

Mangilly is 31km north of Toliara along a rutted, sandy road. *Taxis-brousses* leave from the northern *taxi-brousse* station in Toliara until early afternoon and cost Ar4000. **Jonasy** (☎ 032 04 689 89) will drive you there for Ar50,000, and hotels charge around the same.

EASTERN MADAGASCAR

The RN2 twists spectacularly down the mountainsides between Tana and the coast to the resort town of Toamasina (Tamatave), passing one of the country's great rainforest reserves en route. Toamasina is a common starting point for trips on the Canal des Pangalanes and points further north. Île Sainte Marie lies temptingly just off the east coast, making a perfect base for beach bumming and related activities.

ANDASIBE (PERINET)

The most accessible parcel of rainforest in Madagascar lies only three hours' drive from the capital. There are actually two reserves: the **Réserve Spécial de l'Analamazaotra** (often called Perinet, after the now-defunct train station) and the less accessible **Parc National d'Andasibe-Mantadia**. Both feature excellent lemur spotting and birdwatching. The highlights are the indris, which greet the dawn with hoots that can carry up to 2km through the forest canopy. They co-exist happily with 40 groups of diadem sifakas, who've been relocated from another forest destroyed by cobalt mining. October to March is best for amphibians and reptiles; birdwatching is at its peak from September to December. In winter, lemurs head for bed early, around 3pm, so make sure you do a morning walk.

About 1.5km from the junction with the main Antananarivo–Toamasina road (RN2) is **Analamazaotra Forest Station**. It's administered by the Association Mitsinjo ('protect the future') and provides jobs and education for local communities. **Forest walks** (per person 2-3hr/4-5hr day walk Ar20,000/30,000, 1½hr night walk Ar12,000) are on offer and prices include both a permit and a guide. You can pitch a tent here for Ar5000 and there's a shop and restaurant (though the latter was closed when we visited).

To visit the reserves you must purchase a permit from the **Angap office** (permits per person 1-/2-/3-/4-day permit Ar25,000/37,000/40,000/50,000), which has a brand-new interactive exhibition – how does the size of your hand compare with an indri's? The office is an easy 2km-long walk from the main Antananarivo–Toamasina road (RN2). The office can arrange a professional **guide** (per person 1-/2-/3-/4-day/night walk Ar15,000/25,000/35,000/50,000/10,000); a guide for a one- to two-hour indri-watching circuit costs Ar10,000 per person.

You can pitch a tent next to the Angap office for Ar5000 (be warned: it can rain at any time of year, especially in the wet season), where there's also **le Forestier** restaurant (mains 5000-7000Ar; ☽ breakfast & lunch). There's a new tented **camp** (tents 2-3 people Ar40,000) in the Angap grounds.

Feon-ny Ala (☎ 033 05 832 02; r without bathroom Ar21,000, bungalow Ar49,000) is a great place to stay, a couple of hundred metres from the main Antananarivo–Toamasina road (RN2). Here, thatched bungalows have toilet, hot shower and mosquito nets but no heating – snuggle up under the blankets and let the indris wake you. The good riverside restaurant (mains Ar9000) is open all day.

Andasibe is 142km east of Tana along the RN2. *Taxis-brousses* (Ar8000, three hours) can drop you at the park turn-off, from where it's an easy walk to Feon-ny Ala and the Angap office. If you're coming from Toamasina, a *taxi-brousse* costs Ar17,000 and takes five hours.

TOAMASINA (TAMATAVE)

In Toamasina you can soak up the elegant decrepitude of a faded colonial port. It's also the jumping-off point for the Canal des Pangalanes, Île Sainte Marie (p925) and the remote northeast corner of the country.

Information

Banks along Blvd Joffre will change cash and travellers cheques. BNI-CL, BMOI and BFV-SG all have ATMs. The main post office can be found on Araben'ny Fahaleovantena.

Cyber Sky (upstairs next to Hôtel Eden, Blvd Joffre; per hr Ar1800; ☽ 8am-7pm) The best place for internet access.

Librairie GM Fakra (Blvd Joffre) Sometimes has a few magazines and newspapers in English, plus town maps.

Sights & Activities

Parc Zoologique Ivoloina (☎ 020-53 012 17; admission 10,000Ar; ☽ 9am-5pm), a small captive-breeding facility for lemurs, is 13km north of town. It's a lovely, tranquil spot, where small bands of semi-wild lemurs roam the grounds and pose for great photo opportunities.

Touring the **Canal des Pangalanes** in a *pirogue* (traditional canoe) is high on most visitors' lists of things to do, whether for a day or longer, more adventurous trips. A day trip will provide a fascinating glimpse of life in the riverside villages, while longer tours can include white sandy beaches and wildlife parks. Trips depart from the Gare Fluviale. **Calypso Tours** (☎ 032 40 247 78; calypsotour@netcourrier.com; Blvd Joffre), based in the Hôtel Eden (below), specialises in trips on the canal, with day trips per person costing from Ar70,000, including breakfast in the hotel, transfers and guides.

Sleeping

Hôtel Eden (☎ 020-53 312 90; Blvd Joffre; d with/without bathroom Ar21,000/16,000) Offers basic rooms without mosquito nets, but it's in a handy location and is a good place for organising trips to the canal.

Hôtel Generation (☎ 020-53 321 05; generationhotel@moov.mg; Blvd Joffre; s/d Ar55,000/65,500; ☒) The spacious rooms all have hot shower, TV, fridge and mosquito nets, and get more expensive the higher up you go.

MADAGASCAR

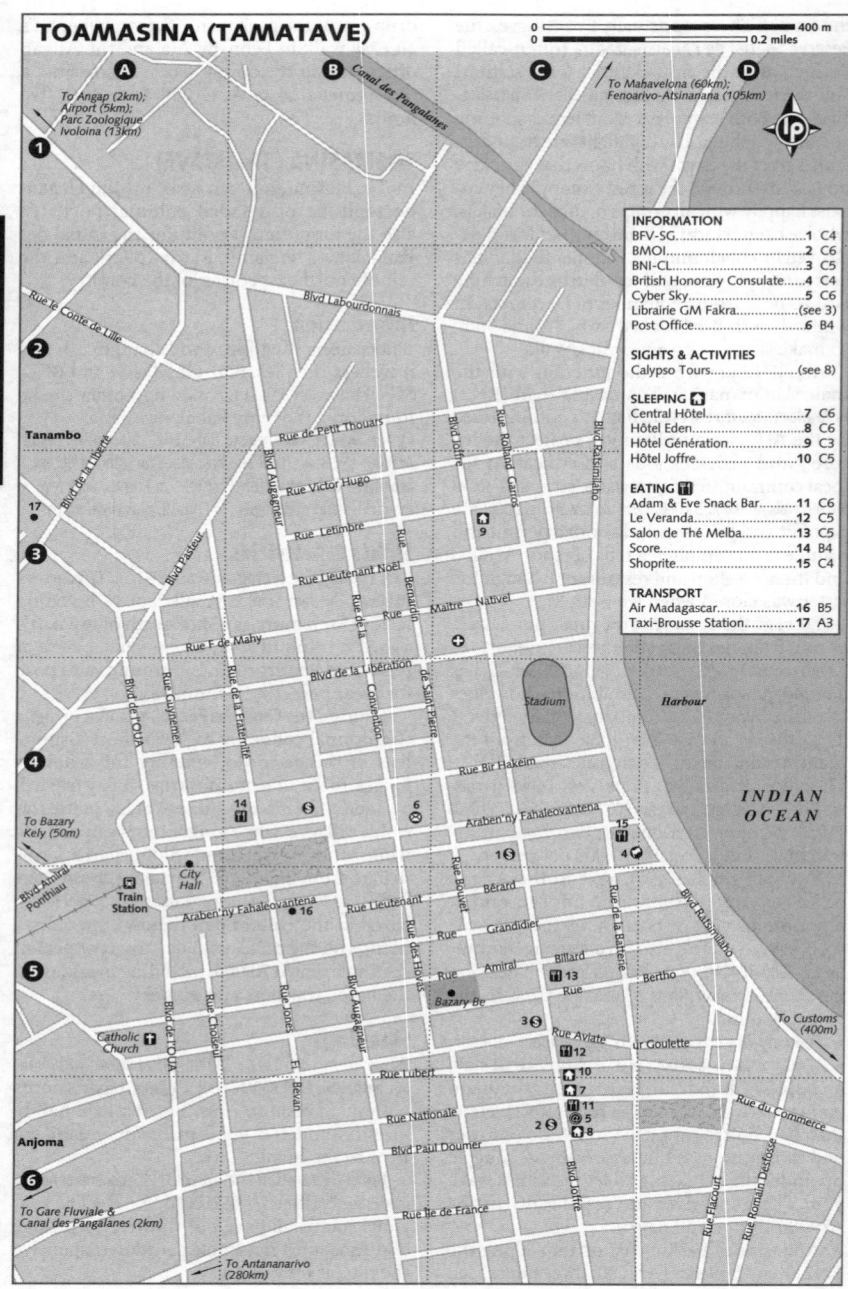

TOAMASINA (TAMATAVE)

0 — 400 m
0 — 0.2 miles

To Angap (2km);
Airport (5km);
Parc Zoologique
Ivoloina (13km)

Canal des Pangalanes

To Mahavelona (60km);
Fenoarivo-Atsinanana (105km)

INFORMATION
BFV-SG.....................................1 C4
BMOI...2 C6
BNI-CL.......................................3 C5
British Honorary Consulate.....4 C4
Cyber Sky..................................5 C6
Librairie GM Fakra..............(see 3)
Post Office................................6 B4

SIGHTS & ACTIVITIES
Calypso Tours.......................(see 8)

SLEEPING
Central Hôtel............................7 C6
Hôtel Eden................................8 C6
Hôtel Génération.....................9 C3
Hôtel Joffre............................10 C5

EATING
Adam & Eve Snack Bar..........11 C6
Le Veranda.............................12 C5
Salon de Thé Melba...............13 C5
Score.......................................14 B4
Shoprite..................................15 C4

TRANSPORT
Air Madagascar......................16 B5
Taxi-Brousse Station..............17 A3

Rue le Conte de Lille

Blvd Labourdonnais

Tanambo

Rue de Petit Thouars

Rue Victor Hugo

Rue Letimbre

Rue Lieutenant Noël

Rue F de Mahy

Blvd de la Libération

Rue Bir Hakeim

Araben'ny Fahaleovantena

Stadium

Harbour

**INDIAN
OCEAN**

To Bazary
Kely (50m)

City Hall

Araben'ny Fahaleovantena

Train
Station

Rue Lieutenant

Rue Bérard

Rue Grandidier

Rue Billard

Rue Amiral

Bazary Be

Rue Aviate

Rue Bertho

To Customs
(400m)

Catholic
Church

Rue Lubert

Rue Nationale

Blvd Paul Doumer

Rue du Commerce

Anjoma

To Gare Fluviale &
Canal des Pangalanes (2km)

To Antananarivo
(280km)

Rue Île de France

Hôtel Joffre (☎ 020-53 323 90; hotel.joffre@moov.ma; Blvd Joffre; r Ar46,000-85,000; 🖳) Probably the best place in town because of its lovely verandah, with a bar opening onto the street. Rooms come with TV, but unfortunately the holey mosquito nets and reluctant trickle of hot water let it down.

Central Hôtel (☎ 020-53 340 86; d Ar53,500) Not as slick as Hôtel Joffre next door but commendable. Rooms have four-poster beds, mosquito net, TV, safe and hot water. Its restaurant, Le Veranda, is up the road (see below).

Eating
Salon de Thé Melba (☎ 033 14 041 84; Blvd Joffre; coffee Ar1500, ice cream Ar3300) Serves tired patisserie but good coffee, fresh juices (try the *corossol*!) and ice cream.

Adam & Eve Snack Bar (☎ 020-53 334 56; Blvd Joffre; mains Ar7000; 🕒 Tue-Sun) The place to enjoy a good selection of halal snacks, drinks and ice cream while watching the streetside goings on.

our pick **Le Veranda** (☎ 020-53 334 35; Blvd Joffre; mains Ar16,500; 🕒 lunch & dinner Mon-Sat) Central Hôtel guests and nonguests alike tuck into a fine selection of French and Malagasy dishes or the daily specials.

Self-caterers have a choice of either Shoprite or Score supermarkets.

Getting There & Away
Boats for the Canal des Pangalanes leave from the Gare Fluviale. Daily flights are available with **Air Madagascar** (☎ 020-53 323 56) from Toamasina to Tana (Ar274,000) and to Île Sainte Marie at the same price.

Buses leave daily for Tana (from Ar15,000).

ÎLE SAINTE MARIE (NOSY BORAHA)
If romantic tales of swashbuckling buccaneers in lush tropic isles entice, then don your skull-and-crossbones neckerchief and head for Île Sainte Marie. The slender, 57km-long island lies 8km off the northwestern coast of Madagascar. Beach hotels take up much of the southwestern coastline, but there's plenty to do for more active types, from diving to cycling, motorcycling and walking.

Humpback whales visit from June to September, and a whale-watching boat trip is a highlight. It can rain at any time of year, but avoid visiting from December to March when there are violent cyclones.

The island's only town, Ambodifotatra, is clustered around its harbour. You probably won't want to stay here, but there's everything you need to plan your visit.

Information
Bank of Africa (Map p927) Handles cash, travellers cheques, cash advances on Visa cards and has ATM facilities. Found near the harbour on Ave La Bigorne.

BFV-SG (Map p927) Near the harbour on Ave La Bigorne. It handles cash, travellers cheques, cash advances on Visa cards and has ATM facilities.

Cyber Corsaire (Map p927; ☎ 020-57 403 59; Ave La Bigorne; per 10min Ar600; 🕒 8.30am-noon & 2-6pm Mon-Sat) Internet access.

Office Régionale de Tourisme Sainte Marie (Map p927; ☎ 032 50 923 16; Ave La Bigorne) This excellent office has information about all activities on the island. Near the harbour.

Sights & Activities
South of Ambodifotatra, just over the causeway, lies the eerie, overgrown **Cimetière des Pirates** (Pirates' Cemetery; Map p926). It can only be reached on foot at low tide, or by *pirogue*. Guides hang about here, but can't expect more than Ar5000 per person. True, one grave does bear a skull-and-crossbones and the big black marble tomb in the centre could be that of William Kidd (buried sitting upright for his sins), but there's not much evidence that all the graves belong to pirates. If you find any buried treasure, let us know!

The best **diving** is from July to December and there are some good sites in the north of the island. **Le Lémurien Palmé Dive Centre** (Map p927; ☎ 032 04 816 56; www.lemurien-palme.com; per dive incl equipment €35; Ambodifotatra) organises boat and diving trips and is recommended. Snorkelling gear is available from all the hotels.

Endemika (Map p926; admission Ar5000; 🕒 8am-noon & 2-5pm Mon-Sat), half-way between Ambodifotatra and the airport, is a small private zoo and botanical garden and a great place to spend an afternoon away from the beach.

Sleeping & Eating
Along the road leading south from Ambodifotatra to the airport are lots of hotels and bungalows, all set on the beach. The following are our favourites. All have restaurants and can arrange whale-watching in season and fishing expeditions.

La Bigorne (Map p927; ☎ 020-57 401 23; Ave Angleterre; bungalows Ar30,000-40,000) If you need to stay in

MADAGASCAR

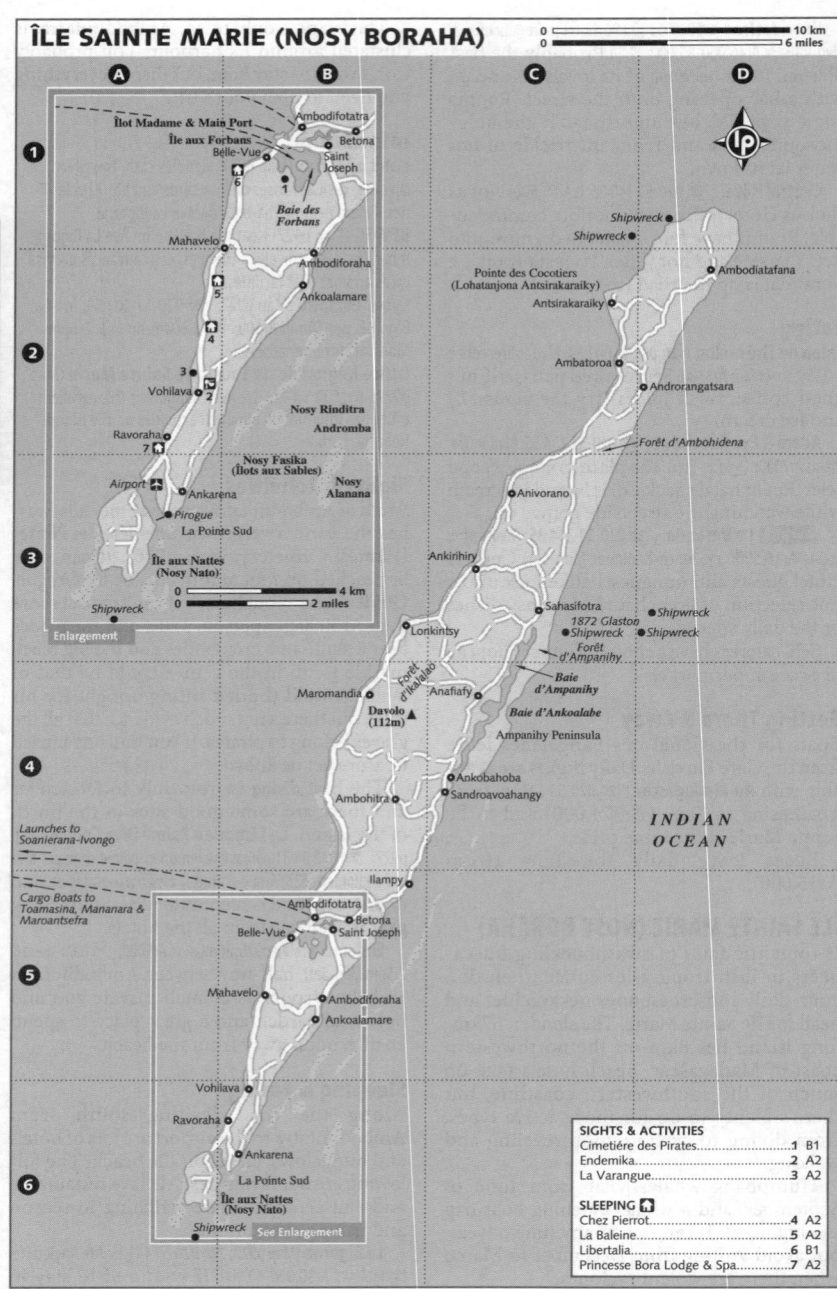

ÎLE SAINTE MARIE (NOSY BORAHA)

| | 0 | 10 km |
| | 0 | 6 miles |

Îlot Madame & Main Port
Île aux Forbans
Belle-Vue
Ambodifotatra
Betona
Saint Joseph
Baie des Forbans
Cimetière des Pirates
Libertalia
Mahavelo
Ambodiforaha
Ankoalamare
La Baleine
Chez Pierrot
Endemika
La Varangue
Vohilava
Ravoraha
Princesse Bora Lodge & Spa
Airport
Ankarena
Pirogue
La Pointe Sud
Île aux Nattes (Nosy Nato)
Nosy Rinditra
Andromba
Nosy Fusika (Îlots aux Sables)
Nosy Alanana
Shipwreck

Enlargement

| 0 | 4 km |
| 0 | 2 miles |

Shipwreck
Shipwreck
Pointe des Cocotiers (Lohatanjona Antsirakaraiky)
Antsirakaraiky
Ambodiatafana
Ambatoroa
Androrangatsara
Forêt d'Ambohidena
Anivorano
Ankirihiry
Sahasifotra
1872 Glaston
Shipwreck
Shipwreck
Shipwreck
Forêt d'Ampanihy
Lonkintsy
Forêt d'Ikidian
Anafiafy
Baie d'Ampanihy
Maromandia
Davolo (112m)
Baie d'Ankoalabe
Ampanihy Peninsula
Ankobahoba
Sandroavoahangy
Ambohitra
INDIAN OCEAN

Launches to Soanierana-Ivongo
Cargo Boats to Toamasina, Manarara & Maroantsefra
Ilampy
Ambodifotatra
Betona
Saint Joseph
Belle-Vue
Mahavelo
Ambodiforaha
Ankoalamare
Vohilava
Ravoraha
Ankarena
La Pointe Sud
Île aux Nattes (Nosy Nato)
Shipwreck   **See Enlargement**

SIGHTS & ACTIVITIES	
Cimetiére des Pirates	1 B1
Endemika	2 A2
La Varangue	3 A2

SLEEPING	
Chez Pierrot	4 A2
La Baleine	5 A2
Libertalia	6 B1
Princesse Bora Lodge & Spa	7 A2

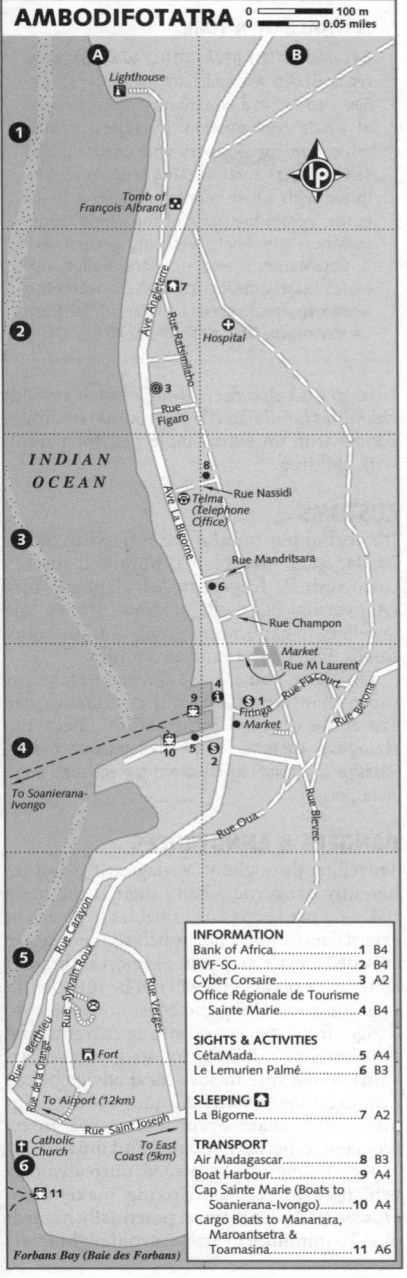

AMBODIFOTATRA

Ambodifotatra, head for La Bigorne, the best choice in town. The bungalows have mosquito nets and fans, and there's a good French restaurant (mains Ar7000 to Ar29,000) on the verandah in the garden.

La Baleine (Map p926; ☎ 020-57 401 34; www.hotel-la-baleine.com; bungalows with/without bathroom Ar50,000/30,000) There's not much beach, but the bungalows have nets and are good value.

Chez Pierrot (Map p926; ☎ 034 01 035 61; chezpierrot@moov.mg; bungalows Ar60,600). Another good-value option, with bungalows set in a neat garden with plenty of shade.

our pick **Libertalia** (Map p926; ☎ 020-57 903 33; www.lelibertalia.com; bungalows per person incl half board Ar79,000, 2-person bungalows Ar84,500) Grab your snorkelling gear and head out along the jetty to your own private island – this is a laid-back, friendly place with an excellent restaurant. Bungalows come with fans and mosquito nets; there's a shop and massage centre. Bikes are available, too.

Princesse Bora Lodge & Spa (Map p926; ☎ 032 07 090 48; www.princessebora.com; d incl half board per person high/whale-watching season from Ar295,000/375,000; ☒) This is the ultimate in luxury. Exquisite bungalows and family units are sensitively placed around the beach and pool, and there are plenty of activities on offer.

Getting There & Away

AIR

Daily flights are available with **Air Madagascar** (☎ 020-53 323 56) from Île Sainte Marie to Tana (Ar354,000), via Toamasina.

BOAT

The most reliable service is run by **Cap Sainte Marie** (Map p927; ☎ 020-57 404 06; www.cap-sainte-marie.com; Ambodifotatra harbour). Trips from Ambodifotatra to Toamasina cost one way/return Ar100,000/175,000 and depart at 6am daily. The journey includes an hour-long boat trip to Soanierana-Ivongo followed by a 2½-hour bus trip to Toamasina.

MADAGASCAR DIRECTORY

ACCOMMODATION

It's usually possible to find a decent, relatively clean room (with bathroom) from about US$20 (from Ar44,354), less with shared facilities. Single rooms are rare and you'll often

MADAGASCAR

MADAGASCAR

have to pay for a double. Prices are usually higher during the high season, ie between June and August and around Christmas, New Year and Easter. Prices quoted in this book are high-season prices, unless otherwise indicated. It's best to make advance reservations during the high season.

ACTIVITIES

Top spots for lemur spotting and birdwatching include Parc National de Ranomafana (p919) and Réserve Spécial de l'Analamazaotra (p923). Parc National de l'Isalo (p920) is excellent for hiking.

Madagascar is a good country for cycling and bicycles can be rented in many places, although for long-distance trips you'll need to bring your own bike from home. For additional information, check out **Madagascar on Bike** (www.madagascar-on-bike.com).

The waters around Mangilly (p922) and Île Sainte Marie (p925) are ideal for diving. Companies in every dive spot offer internationally recognised diving courses and many places offer a *baptême* ('try dive'). Dive centres close when conditions are unfavourable; check when that is in the area of your choice.

BUSINESS HOURS

Offices, post offices and banks Normally open from 8am to 4pm Monday to Friday and from 8am to 11am on Saturday.
Restaurants Most restaurants are open from noon to 2pm for lunch and from about 6.30pm to 10pm for dinner.
Shops Most shops close from noon to 2pm, but are open until 6pm or 7pm Monday to Friday and 8am to noon on Saturday.

CHILDREN

Madagascar is not an easy place to travel with young children, so junior travellers are a fairly rare sight. Disposable nappies are available in Antananarivo's supermarkets, but are

---

> **PRACTICALITIES**
>
> - Weights, measures and road distances use the metric system.
>
> - Electricity is 220V AC (use European two-round-pin plugs).
>
> - Daily newspapers include *Midi Madagasikara*, *Madagsacar Tribune* and *L'Express de Madagascar* (all in French).
>
> - Radio and TV programming is all in French.

> **A WHALE OF A TIME**
>
> **CétaMada** (Map p927; ☎ 032 40 889 37; www.cetamada.org; Ambodifotatra harbour; ☼ 5am-5pm Mon-Sat) is a community project aimed at whale conservation. Members provide education for skippers and children, and sell products such as raffia baskets embellished with whale motifs made by artisans in less accessible parts of the island. Some members run whale-watching excursions.
>
> CétaMada's president, Henri Bellon, operates hugely informative **whale-watching boat-trips** (per person 4hr Ar80,000-100,000) from **La Varangue** (Map p926; ☎ 032 40 889 37).

---

hard to find elsewhere. Many hotels provide *chambres familiales* (family rooms) or double rooms with an extra single bed for parents with children.

CUSTOMS

It's forbidden to take the following out of Madagascar: live plants, mounted insects, tortoiseshell, fragments of elephant bird (*Aepyornis*) eggshell, precious stones and jewellery in export quantities, antique coins, fossils, funerary art and antiquities.

Officially, you are not allowed to take any more than Ar400,000 out of Madagascar. For more detailed information, check out **Malagasy customs** (www.iatatravelcentre.com/MG-Madagascar-customs-currency-airport-tax-regulations-details.htm£currency).

DANGERS & ANNOYANCES

Travelling throughout Madagascar is not inherently dangerous. Petty theft is the main risk – do not keep your valuables in a pack or external money belt, and watch your pockets in crowded areas. Carry your passport with you at all times (a photocopy will not be sufficient).

Some areas along the coast are subject to danger from sharks and strong currents, and the shoreline might be infested with sea urchins. Make sure to seek local advice before heading into the water. Mosquitoes are ubiquitous and malaria occurs here – wear insect repellent, especially at dawn and dusk.

A combination of crowded, unroadworthy vehicles and reckless driving makes *taxi-brousse* (bush taxi) travel potentially hazardous. To minimise the risks, avoid night travel if possible.

EMBASSIES & CONSULATES

All enquiries for Canada should be addressed c/o Canadian High Commission, PO Box 1022, Dar es Salaam, Tanzania. The following embassies are all located in Antananarivo.

France (Map p911; ☎ 020-22 214 88; 3 Rue Jean Jaurès, Ambatomena, Antananarivo). There are also representatives in Diego Suarez, Majunga and Toamasina.

Germany (off Map p911; ☎ 22 238 02; 101 Rue Pasteur Rabeony, Ambodiroatra, Antananarivo)

Mauritius (off Map p911; ☎ 22 321 57; Rte Circulaire Anjahana, Antananarivo) South of the centre.

South Africa (off Map p911; ☎ 020-22 433 50; Lot IZO 68 bis, Ankorondrano, Antananarivo)

UK (Map p911; ☎ 020-22 273 70, Antananarivo) There's also an honorary consulate near the port in Toamasina.

USA (off Map p911; ☎ 020-22 212 57; Ivato, Antananarivo)

EMERGENCY SERVICES

Fire ☎ 18
Police ☎ 17

FESTIVALS & EVENTS

Many of these dates change yearly, so enquire at the tourist office for exact times.

Alahamady Be The low-key Malagasy New Year in March.

Santabary The first rice harvest held in April/May.

Fisemana A ritual purification ceremony of the Antakàrana people in June.

Famadihana Literally the 'turning of the bones'; these reburial ceremonies are held especially from June to September.

Sambatra Circumcision festivals held by most ethnic groups between June and September, and in November and December in the southwest.

FOOD

The budget restaurants as listed in this chapter are usually food stalls or small Malagasy *hotelys* that serve mainly rice dishes or snacks for under €2 (about Ar5000). Midrange restaurants generally serve plain French food, including staples such as *steack frites* (steak and chips), costing about Ar7500 to Ar9000 for a main course. Top-end restaurants serve French *haute cuisine,* which might include goose-liver paté or duck breast for around Ar14,000 per main course.

For more information, see p908.

GAY & LESBIAN TRAVELLERS

Homosexual practices are illegal in Madagascar for persons under 21 years of age. Homosexuality is not openly practised, and there are no organisations catering to gay and lesbian travellers. Overt displays of affection – whether among couples of the same or opposite sex – are culturally inappropriate.

HOLIDAYS

Accommodation and flights are often harder to organise during French school holidays; see http://about-france.com/school-holidays.htm for details.

Government offices and private companies close on the following public holidays; banks are generally also closed the afternoon before a public holiday.

New Year's Day 1 January
International Women's Day 8 March; a holiday for women only
Insurrection Day 29 March; celebrates the rebellion against the French in 1947
Easter Monday March/April
Labour Day 1 May
Ascension Thursday (40 days after Easter) May/June
Pentecost Monday (51 days after Easter) May/June
National Day (Independence Day) 26 June
Assumption Day 15 August
All Saints' Day 1 November
Christmas Day 25 December

INTERNET ACCESS

Fast and reliable email facilities (including some post offices) are available in most major towns. Prices start at about Ar30 per minute, but may be higher in remote areas.

LEGAL MATTERS

The use and possession of marijuana and other recreational drugs is illegal in Madagascar. If you're arrested, ask to see a representative of your country. Madagascar is strict in enforcing immigration laws, so don't overstay your visa. The legal age of consent for heterosexual sex is 15 years. The government has an active campaign against sex tourism to prevent hotels allowing nonguests in rooms.

MAPS

Official maps produced by Foiben Taosarintanin'i Madagasikara (FTM) are available at bookshops in Antananarivo and major towns for about Ar12,000. The maps are fairly dated but generally accurate, and more than adequate for visiting the country. FTM also produces street maps of the provincial capitals.

MADAGASCAR

MONEY

The Malagasy currency is the ariary. Outside major towns, you might be quoted prices in the old Malagasy franc – beware! Euros are sometimes accepted in major cities; and US dollars and euros are sometimes accepted in Antananarivo, major cities and tourist areas.

There are ATMs in Antananarivo and other major towns, but they only accept Visa cards.

Credit cards are rarely accepted, except at some upmarket hotels, at Air Madagascar offices and at some larger travel agencies. The most useful card is Visa, with MasterCard also accepted in a minority of places. Visa and MasterCard can also be used at some banks to obtain cash advances (in ariary). Major banks change travellers cheques and cash in major currencies.

The currency-exchange counter at Ivato airport has exchange rates that are just as good as those at the banks, and is usually open for international flight arrivals.

POST

There are post offices in all major towns and the postal service is generally reliable. Sending a letter to Europe costs Ar1500, and Ar2100 to Australia and the USA. Postcards are slightly cheaper.

SHOPPING

Madagascar offers a fantastic variety of handicrafts and souvenirs. Ambositra (see p916) in the central highlands is the shopping capital of Madagascar, with dozens of shops selling carvings and marquetry. Ambalavao (see p919) is known for its production of silk and handmade Antaimoro paper.

If you want to leave your purchasing until you're a taxi ride away from the airport, a good place to shop is the Marché Artisanale (p915) in Antananarivo. Bargaining hard is expected – start from 50% of the price and work upwards.

Bear in mind that embroidery and raffia do far less environmental damage than wooden products, which are often carved from endangered tropical hardwoods.

Don't go home without a packet of sweet-scented vanilla pods (from around Ar5000)!

TELEPHONE & FAX

Faxes can be sent from telephone offices, post offices and from upmarket hotels. Some internet cafes also offer fax services.

The country code for Madagascar is ☎ 261. To call out of Madagascar, dial ☎ 00 before the country code.

The best way to dial internationally is with a *telecarte* (phonecard). Phonecard phones are scattered around all larger towns. Cards are sold at post offices, at green-and-gold Telma kiosks, and some shops and hotels. For international calls you will need at least 100 units. Calls can also be made from more upmarket hotels (at much higher rates). The rate for international calls is Ar870 per minute to most countries, but Ar4200 per minute to Australia and New Zealand. The international operator can be reached by dialling ☎ 10.

Landline numbers in Madagascar start with 020, followed by a two-digit area code (eg 22 for Tana) followed by a five-digit local number (usually given in the form of a three-digit then a two-digit number). If you are quoted a seven-digit number, add 020 before the number.

Mobile phones are in common usage in Madagascar. Mobile-phone prefixes are ☎ 030, 031, 032 and 033. If dialling a mobile phone number from abroad, omit the zero but add the country code. For calls to mobile numbers from within Madagascar, you will need to dial the zero.

TOURIST INFORMATION

Tourist offices in Madagascar can provide lists of hotels and guesthouses. Contact **L'Office Nationale de Tourisme de Madagascar** (Map p912; ☎ 020-22 661 15; www.madagascar-tourisme.com; 3 Lalana Elysée Ravelomanantsoa, Antananarivo; ⊗ 8.30am-5.30pm Mon-Fri) in the capital.

TRAVELLERS WITH DISABILITIES

Madagascar has few, if any, facilities for the disabled. Public transport is very crowded and unable to accommodate a wheelchair unless it is folded up. Travelling around by rental car is the best option. In Antananarivo and most of the provincial capitals you will find hotels with either lifts or ground-floor accommodation. There are very few bathrooms large enough to manoeuvre a wheelchair in, and almost none with any sort of handles or holds.

The following organisations provide information on world travel for the mobility impaired:

Mobility International USA (☎ 541-343 1284; www.miusa.org) Located in the USA.

National Information Communication Awareness Network (NICAN; ☎ 02-6285 3713; www.nican.com.au) Located in Australia.
Royal Association for Disability & Rehabilitation (☎ 020-7250 3222; www.radar.org.uk) Located in the UK.
Society for Accessible Travel & Hospitality (SATH; ☎ 212-447 7284; www.sath.org) Located in the USA.

VISAS

All visitors must have a visa to enter Madagascar. Visas can be arranged in advance at any Malagasy embassy or consulate for the equivalent of about US$84 (€60) for single entry. One-month, single-entry visas are available on arrival at Ivato airport in Antananarivo, but get an update on the situation before arriving without one. Visas are valid for up to three months from the date of entry and must be used within six months of the date of issue.

As long as you have not exceeded the normal three-month maximum, visas can be extended at the immigration office at the **Ministry of the Interior** (Map p911; ☎ 020-22 243 26) in Antananarivo or any provincial capital. You will need to supply between two to four passport-sized photos as well as a copy of your return air or boat ticket. A one-month extension costs US$42 (€30) and can take several days to process.

Visas for Onward Travel

Visas for travel to South Africa are available from its embassy in Antananarivo (see p929).

WOMEN TRAVELLERS

Most women should not feel threatened or insecure in any way when travelling in Madagascar. The most you can expect is some mild curiosity about your situation, especially if you are single and/or don't have children. Physical harassment and violent crime are very rare, and in fact male travellers face far more pestering from the hordes of prostitutes who frequent nightclubs.

TRANSPORT IN MADAGASCAR

GETTING THERE & AWAY

Immigration officials generally just check or issue your visa before letting you go on your way. See above for information about visa requirements.

Air

Intercontinental flights arrive at Ivato airport, 19km north of the Antananarivo city centre. Air Madagascar is the national carrier and is relatively efficient.

The following airlines fly to and from Madagascar:

Air Austral (UU; ☎ 020-22 359 90; www.airaustral.com, in French)
Air France (AF; ☎ 020-23 230 23; www.airfrance.com)
Air Madagascar (MD; ☎ 020-22 222 22; www.airmadagascar.mg)
Air Mauritius (MK; ☎ 020-22 359 90; www.airmauritius.com)
Corsair (SS; ☎ 020-22 633 36; www.corsairfly.com, in French)
Interair (D6; ☎ 020-22 224 06; www.interair.co.za)

AFRICA & THE INDIAN OCEAN

Madagascar is well connected with the Indian Ocean islands of Mauritius and Réunion, and is reasonably accessible from mainland Africa.

Once you're in Madagascar, **Dodo Travel & Tours** (Map p912; ☎ 020-22 690 36; www.dodotraveltour.com; Lalana Elysée Ravelomanantsoa), in Antananarivo, is a useful place to seek information about flights within this region.

The main hubs for flights to Madagascar are Johannesburg in South Africa and Nairobi in Kenya. There are flights three times a week between Johannesburg and Antananarivo (about €460 return) on Air Madagascar. Travel between Madagascar and Nairobi (about €500 return) generally works better if you purchase your ticket directly from Air Madagascar in Kenya or Madagascar.

Air Austral has regular flights between Réunion and Mauritius and Antananarivo (from €350 return) and Toamasina (from €370 return).

ASIA

Air Madagascar has recently commenced a direct route from Antananarivo to Guangzhou, China. Air Mauritius has flights several times weekly from Singapore and Hong Kong to Mauritius, and South African Airlines flies regularly to Johannesburg from both cities. There are regular connections from Mauritius on Air Austral to Antananarivo, and from Johannesburg you can also connect with an Air Madagascar or Interair flight to Antananarivo.

It's also easy to get flights on Kenya Airways from Hong Kong to Nairobi, from where you can connect to Madagascar.

AUSTRALIA & NEW ZEALAND

There are no direct flights servicing Australia and Madagascar; the shortest route is to travel via Mauritius. Air Mauritius has weekly flights connecting both Melbourne and Perth with Mauritius from about A$3000 return. From Mauritius there are regular connections on Air Austral to Antananarivo.

Alternatively, Qantas and South African Airways both have flights connecting Sydney with Johannesburg at around A$3600 return. From Johannesburg, you can connect with an Air Madagascar or Interair flight to Antananarivo. Try these agencies:

Flight Centre Australia (☎ 133 133; www.flightcentre.com. au); New Zealand (☎ 0800-233 544; www.flight centre.co.nz)
STA Travel Australia (☎ 1300 733 035; www.statravel. au); New Zealand (☎ 0508-782 872; www.statravel.co.nz)

EUROPE

The main European hub for flights to/from Madagascar is Paris. Air Madagascar and Air France fly three to four times weekly between Paris and Antananarivo. Prices from Paris usually start from about €950 return.

It's also possible to fly from many European capitals to Johannesburg (South Africa), Nairobi (Kenya), St-Denis (Réunion) or Mauritius, and from one of these cities to Antananarivo. The best connections are usually via Réunion or Mauritius, which are linked by Air Austral flights to Antananarivo (from €350 return), as well as by several flights weekly to other places in Madagascar. Contact one of the following agents to get you started:

Air Fair (☎ 0900-7717 717; www.airfair.nl, in Dutch) A well-respected Dutch travel agent.
Nouvelles Frontières (☎ 01-49 20 65 87; www. nouvelles-frontieres.fr) A good French option, with group tours to Madagascar.
STA Travel UK (☎ 0871-230 0040; www.statravel. co.uk); Germany (☎ 069-743 032 92; www.statravel.de, in German) International travel agent with plenty of other offices across Europe.
Trailfinders (☎ 0845-058 5858; www.trailfinders.com) Reliable UK travel agent with huge amount of experience.

USA & CANADA

The cheapest way to fly from North America to Madagascar is generally via Paris. It may work out cheaper to get separate tickets – one from North America to Europe and then a second ticket from Europe to Madagascar.

Another option is to fly from Atlanta or New York to Johannesburg, with a connection to Antananarivo. In the USA, the main travel agency specialising in Madagascar is **Cortez Travel** (☎ 800-854 1029; www.air-mad.com). It has information on good-value airfares and can book Air Madagascar flights. The following companies might also be able to help:

Cheaptickets (www.cheaptickets.com) A good source of online fares.
Flight Centre Canada (☎ 1 877 967 5302; www.flight centre.ca); USA (☎ 1877-233 9999; www.flightcentre.us) Contact it directly for fares.
STA Travel (☎ 800-781 4040; www.statravel.com) Good deals to Paris.

Sea

It's possible to travel to and from Madagascar by boat, but you will need plenty of time and determination. Travel is likely to be on cargo ships – unless you find a ride on a yacht as a crew member – so sleeping and eating conditions, combined with sometimes turbulent seas, can make it a rough trip.

Mombasa (Kenya) and the island of Zanzibar (Tanzania) are the main places to look for cargo boats to Madagascar. It's also sometimes possible to find passage on a yacht heading from South Africa, Réunion or Mauritius to Madagascar.

Tours

For a list of organised tour companies within Madagascar, see p934. Following are a few companies operating general interest tours to, and around, Madagascar from Australia, the UK and the USA.

Adventure Associates (☎ 02-8916 3000; www.adven tureassociates.com; Australia) Runs tours to Madagascar, combined with Réunion.
Cortez Travel (☎ 800-854 1029; www.air-mad.com; USA) Well-established operator for Air Madagascar flights and tours.
Manaca (☎ 866-362 6222; www.manaca.com; USA) Specialists in ecotourism and responsible travel.
Rainbow Tours (☎ 020-7226 1004; www.rainbow tours.co.uk; UK) Specialist and general-interest guided trips to Madagascar.
Reef & Rainforest Tours (☎ 01803-866965; www. reefandrainforest.co.uk; UK) Focuses on wildlife viewing.
Wildlife Worldwide (☎ 0845-130 6982; www.wildlife worldwide.com; UK) Wildlife tours.

GETTING AROUND
Air

The national carrier, **Air Madagascar** (Map p912; ☎ 020-22 222 22; www.airmadagascar.mg; 31 Ave de l'Indépendance, Antananarivo), has a pretty comprehensive and efficient network of domestic routes. Tickets are relatively inexpensive, and air travel is a good way of covering large distances and avoiding long road journeys.

If you have flown into the country on Air Madagascar, you qualify for up to 30% off domestic flights.

You can pay for tickets in ariary, euros or US dollars at the head office in Antananarivo and Air Madagascar offices in larger towns, but smaller offices may only accept ariary. The office in Antananarivo also accepts travellers cheques and credit cards.

The baggage allowance for most internal flights is 20kg.

RESERVATIONS & CHECK-IN

Air Madagascar flights are frequently full, so it's always worth booking as far in advance as possible.

While it's officially unnecessary to reconfirm your Air Madagascar tickets, it's best to check with the airline a few days in advance and again on the day of departure, as there are frequent last-minute schedule changes.

If you have checked-in baggage, be sure to keep your baggage-claim ticket until you are reunited with your luggage at your destination.

Bicycle

It may often be just as fast to travel by bicycle as by *taxi-brousse*. A mountain bike is essential. Carry spare parts, although inner tubes and other basic parts are sometimes available in larger towns. The terrain varies from very sandy to muddy or rough and rocky.

It's usually no problem to transport your bicycle on *taxis-brousses* if you want to take a break en route.

Although you are able to rent mountain bikes in many larger towns, including Toamasina, Antsirabe and Ambodifotatra on Île Sainte Marie, they are not normally in good-enough condition for long journeys.

Boat

On the northeast coast, cargo boats (sometimes called *boutres*) are the primary means of transport. Overloaded cargo boats, including passenger ferries, have capsized with significant loss of life. Always check for lifejackets and don't get in if the seas are rough or if the boat is overcrowded. Boat travel on the east coast

is generally unsafe during the rainy season between May and September and don't run during the cyclone season, December to March.

Bus

Buses run from Toamasina to Antananarivo, using the same stations as the *taxis-brousses*. However, *taxis-brousses* remain the main form of public road transport in Madagascar.

Car & Motorcycle

To drive in Madagascar you will need to have an International Driving Permit (IDP).

You'll find petrol stations of some kind in all cities and in most major towns. Spare parts and repairs of varying quality are available in most towns. Make sure to check the spare tyre of any car you rent before setting out.

To rent a car in Madagascar, you must generally be at least 23 years old and have held a driving licence for at least one year. Rental costs include insurance. Due to the often difficult driving conditions and road hazards, most rental agencies make hiring a driver obligatory with their vehicles. Prices average Ar150,000 to Ar200,000 per day for a 4WD, excluding fuel. For almost all destinations off the main routes a 4WD is advisable, and essential in the rainy season.

Motorcycles can be rented by the half-day or full day at various places in Madagascar, including Toliara and Île Sainte Marie (for use on the island only). At most places, they range from a Honda or Yamaha 125cc or 250cc to a tiny Peugeot *mobylette* (moped). Some places also rent motorcycles suitable for longer, rougher journeys, and provide support vehicles as well.

ROAD CONDITIONS

Less than 15% of the country's roads are paved, and many of those that are paved are badly deteriorated. Nonpaved roads are often exceptionally muddy, sandy or rocky.

Most accidents are caused by human failing (especially drunkenness) rather than by dangerous vehicles and roads. Delays are more common than accidents, so always factor in a few extra hours to allow for breakdowns or social calls en route.

ROAD RULES

Driving in Madagascar is on the right-hand side. The police occasionally stop vehicles and carry out random checks, in the hope of detecting any of the 1001 possible (and probable) infractions of the vehicle code. Occasionally foreigners will be asked for their passport, but as long as your visa is in order there should be no problem.

If you aren't used to local driving conditions, watch out for pedestrians, animals, broken-down cars and slow-moving zebu carts on the road. It is particularly hazardous to drive at night, as there is no lighting, so try to avoid it.

Hitching

Hitching is never entirely safe in any country in the world, and we don't recommend it. Traffic between towns and cities is thin, and most passing vehicles are likely to be *taxis-brousses* or trucks, which are often full. If you do find a ride, you are likely to have to pay about the equivalent of the *taxi-brousse* fare.

Local Transport
POUSSE-POUSSE

Brightly coloured *pousse-pousses* (rickshaws) throng some Malagasy towns and you'll probably be hounded by drivers looking for a fare. The *pousse-pousse* men need the work, not sympathy, though, as they rent their rickshaws and have to pay a daily amount to the owners. If you have heavy luggage, it's polite to hire two *pousse-pousses*. Tourist rates start at about Ar2000 and are always negotiable, so agree on a fare before you climb aboard. When it's raining, the price sometimes doubles.

TAXI-BROUSSE

Taxis-brousses are a part of daily life in Madagascar and you'll find it hard to travel independently around the country without wedging yourself into one at some point.

Fares for all trips are set by the government and are based on distance, duration and route conditions. Prices are the same for locals and foreigners. If you want to keep a large backpack with you in the vehicle, you'll need to pay for an extra seat.

The *taxi-brousse* system is relatively well organised once you get the hang of it. Upon arrival in a town, you may well be besieged by pushy but harmless touts, tugging at your luggage and yelling in your ear to try and win your custom.

Vehicles display the destination on their windscreen and fares are pinned up in the transport company offices that line the edges of the station.

Tours

Madagascar's many tour operators and free-lance guides offer mountain-bike excursions, 4WD circuits, wildlife-watching trips, walking tours, and cultural and historic tours.

An organised tour can be particularly valuable if you don't speak much French, as it can otherwise be hard to break the communication barrier with the fairly reserved Malagasy, who rarely speak English.

The rule of thumb for organised tours is to check as much as possible beforehand – including vehicles, camping equipment and even menu plans. Try to get all the details, agreed by both parties in advance, in writing.

Following is a list of some of the reliable Antananarivo-based companies that can arrange excursions throughout Madagascar. For details about foreign travel agencies, see p910.

Aventour (Map p911; ☎ 020-22 317 61; www.aventour-madagascar.com; Immeuble FIARO, Ampefiloha) A very efficient company that can organise countrywide tours, car rental and ticketing.

Boogie Pilgrim (off Map p911; ☎ 020-22 530 70; www.boogiepilgrim-madagascar.com; Île aux Oiseaux, Tsarasaotra, Alarobia) Adventurous ecotours and camps in several places in Madagascar, including the Canal des Pangalanes. English speaking.

Cortez Expeditions (Map p911; ☎ 020-22 219 74; www.air-mad.com; 25 Rue Ny Zafindriandiky, Antanimena) American-based agency offering a wide range of itineraries for individuals and groups.

Espace Mada (Map p912; ☎ 020-22 262 97; www.madagascar-circuits.com; 50 Arabe Ramanantsoa, Isoraka) Vehicles, guides and off-road excursions.

Mad Cameleon (Map p911; ☎ 020-22 630 86; www.madcameleon.com; Rue Rasamoeli Ankadivato) Offers a range of tours, some off the beaten track.

Malagasy Tours (Map p911; ☎ 020-22 356 07; www.malagasy-tours.com; 54 DN Ambohidraserika, Mahazo-arivo) Upmarket operator offering tours, hiking and trips along the Canal des Pangalanes.

Setam (Map p912; ☎ 020-22 324 31; www.setam-mg.com; 56 Araben'ny 26 Jona 1960, Analakely) Bicycle expeditions, orchid tours and *famadihana* ceremonies.

Train

At the time of writing the Malagasy rail system, known as the Réseau National des Chemins de Fer Malgaches (RNCFM), operated only the Fianarantsoa–Manakara line. Judging by the ambitious renovation of Tana station, though, plans are afoot to restore the Antananarivo–Toamasina and Antananarivo–Andasibe services.

Malawi

With Tanzania and Zambia's big-name national parks and Mozambique's glorious beaches on its doorstep, Malawi has often been left on the sidelines; and when ot *has* made a splash on the international scene it's usually been for its HIV/AIDS rate or grim poverty statistics, not for the beauty and diversity of its environment or for the friendliness of its people. That's a shame because this small strip of land has serious crowd-pleasing potential.

Slicing through the landscape in a trough formed by the Great Rift Valley is the third-largest lake in Africa – Lake Malawi. A shimmering mass of crystal water, its depths swarm with clouds of vivid cichlid fish, and its shores are lined with secret coves, pristine beaches, lively fishing villages and dark, forested hills.

It's not all about the lake, though. Suspended in the clouds in Malawi's deep south are the dramatic peaks of Mt Mulanje, criss-crossed with streams, waterfalls and walking trails. Head north and you'll find the wild wilderness of the Nyika Plateau, where you can hike through rolling grasslands to reach a colonial hilltop town. And whilet a safari in one of Malawi's parks won't quite deliver 'Big Five' excitement, you can get up close to some pretty impressive beasts without having to fight with other cars for the privilege.

Malawi is often described as 'Africa for beginners' and true to form its compact size and relative safety make it easy to get around. What's more, the legendarily helpful locals and stunning backdrops will make sure that you'll have a fantastic time doing so.

MALAWI

FAST FACTS

- **Area** 118,484 sq km
- **ATMs** In major cities
- **Borders** Tanzania, Mozambique, Zambia; all main border crossings are open from 6am to 6pm
- **Budget** US$20 to US$40
- **Capital** Lilongwe
- **Languages** English, Chichewa
- **Money** Malawi kwacha; US$1 = MK141, €1 = MK210
- **Population** 13.1 million
- **Seasons** Cool and dry (May to August), hot and dry (September to mid-November), hot and wet (mid-November to April)
- **Telephone** Country code ☎ 265; international access code ☎ 101
- **Time** GMT/UTC + 2
- **Visa** Free (for most nationalities) for 30 days; issued at point of entry

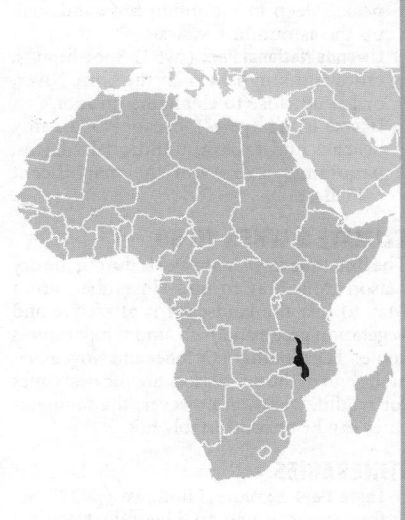

HOW MUCH?

- 100ml bottle of Nali (Malawi's own chilli sauce) US$1
- **Bottle of Malawi Gin** US$7
- **Folding bike** US$55
- **Bottle of wine** US$10 to US$15
- **Carving** US$10

LONELY PLANET INDEX

- **1L petrol** US$1.50
- **1.5L bottled water** US$2.50
- **Bottle of Kuche Kuche** US$1.50
- **Souvenir T-shirt** US$10
- **Plate of chips** US$1

HIGHLIGHTS

- **Lake Malawi** (p955) Soak up the sun in private coves, glide over glassy waters by kayak, or head beneath the surface and discover a world of impossibly brilliant fish.
- **Nyika National Park** (p944) Explore a sweeping, magnificent wilderness filled with antelope and zebra on foot, by bike or on horseback.
- **Mt Mulanje** (p952) Scramble up twisted peaks, sleep in mountain huts and soak up the astounding views.
- **Liwonde National Park** (p953) Spot hippos, crocs and kingfishers on the Shire River, or get up close to elephants on foot.
- **Likoma Island** (p947) Escape to dreamy beaches and explore traditional villages, panoramic walks and the magnificent cathedral.

CLIMATE & WHEN TO GO

The best time to visit Malawi is during the dry season from May to mid-November. From May to July the landscape is attractive and vegetation green and lush, and temperatures cooler. The months of October and November, at the end of the dry season, are the best times for wildlife viewing; however, the temperatures can be uncomfortably hot.

ITINERARIES

- **Three Days** Explore Lilongwe (p939) before going down to Liwonde National Park (p953) for two days of elephant and hippo spotting.
- **One Week** Head down from Blantyre (p948) to the woodland and streams of the Zomba Plateau (p952), then make for Mulanje (p952) for three or four days' hiking across the mountain's misty heights.
- **Two Weeks** Head north from Lilongwe (p939) and explore the wild spaces of Vwaza Marsh (p945) and Nyika Plateau (p944), and the colonial hilltop town of Livingstonia (p944). Then head for Nkhata Bay (p946) for some beachside frolics, before catching the *Ilala* ferry over to Likoma or Chizumulu Islands (p947). Charter a flight or wait for the *Ilala* to take you back to the mainland.
- **One Month** With more time on your hands you can take in all of the highlights above and add a few more: perhaps the southern beach resorts of Cape Maclear (p955) or Senga Bay (p947).

HISTORY

Since the first millennium, the Bantu people had been migrating from Central Africa into the area now occupied by Malawi, but migration to the area stepped up with the arrival of the Tumbuka and Phoka, who settled around the highlands of Nyika and Viphya during the 17th century, and the Maravi, who established a large and powerful kingdom in the south.

The early 19th century brought with it two significant migrations. The Yao invaded southern Malawi from western Mozambique, displacing the Maravi, while groups of Zulu migrated northward to settle in central and northern Malawi. This century also saw the escalation of the East African slave trade.

Enter the British

The most famous explorer to reach this area was Dr David Livingstone. He reached Lake Malawi in September 1859, naming it Lake Nyasa. His death in 1873 inspired a legion of missionaries to come to Africa, bringing the more 'civilised' principles of commerce and Christianity.

The early missionaries blazed the way for various adventurers and pioneer traders and it wasn't long before European settlers began to arrive in their droves. In 1889 Britain allowed Cecil Rhodes' British South Africa Company to administer the Shire Highlands, and in 1891 the British Central Africa (BCA) Protectorate was extended to include land along the western side of the lake. In 1907 the BCA Protectorate became the colony of Nyasaland.

Colonial rule brought with it an end to slave-traders and intertribal conflicts, but it also brought a whole new set of problems. As more and more European settlers arrived, more and more land was taken away from the locals and Africans were forced to pay taxes to the administration.

Transition & Independence

Not surprisingly, this created opposition to colonial rule and in the 1950s the Nyasaland African Congress (NAC) party, led by Dr Hastings Kamuzu Banda, began a serious push for independence. This came, after considerable struggle, in 1964, and Nyasaland became the independent country of Malawi. Two years later Malawi became a republic and Banda was made president, eventually declaring himself 'President for life' in 1971. He ruled for 30 years before his downfall and died three years later. Many achievements were made during his presidency but these were overshadowed by his stringent rule: banning of foreign press, imposition of dress codes and vendettas waged against any group regarded as a threat.

In June 1993, however, Banda agreed to a referendum that resulted in the introduction of a multiparty political system; at Malawi's first full multiparty election in May 1994, the victor was the United Democratic Front (UDF), led by Bakili Muluzi. On becoming president, Muluzi closed political prisons, permitted freedom of speech and print, and instituted several economic reforms. Muluzi was re-elected in May 1999 despite complaints of mismanagement and corruption at the highest government levels.

Malawi Today

In 2002, after failing to pass a bill that would have given him life presidency, Muluzi chose Bingu wa Mutharika as his successor, and in 2004 Mutharika duly won the election. Many thought he would simply follow in Muluzi's footsteps, but he soon declared his independence by quitting the UDF and setting up his own party, the Democratic Progressive Party (DPP). He set about stemming corruption, stepping up the fight against HIV/AIDS, attempting to attract greater foreign investment and introducing a hugely popular fertiliser subsidy program – all of which led to slow and steady economic growth. In 2009 Mutharika

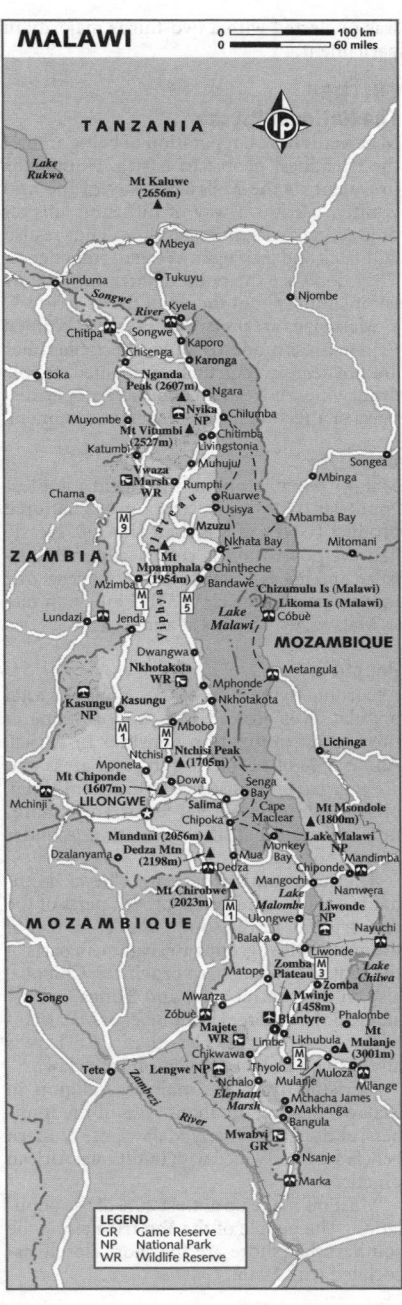

MALAWI

LEGEND
GR   Game Reserve
NP   National Park
WR   Wildlife Reserve

was re-elected with a two-thirds majority in parliament.

CULTURE
The National Psyche

Malawians have a reputation of being among the friendliest people in Africa. Humour is prevalent in the Malawian way of life and is often used as a way of diffusing tension or greeting a misunderstanding. They're also laid-back and lacking in Western impatience. They don't see the point of sweating over or complaining about the small things in life.

Malawians are pretty conservative. Women tend to dress modestly and respectable ladies are not seen in bars unaccompanied. Public drunkenness is frowned upon, as are open displays of affection between men and women.

Daily Life

Malawi remains one of the world's poorest countries, with a per capita gross national product (GNP) of less than US$250. Nearly half the population is chronically malnourished and life expectancy is only 43 years due in large part to the HIV/AIDS infection rate in Malawi, which runs at almost 12%.

People

According to the 2008 census, Malawi's total population is around 13.1 million – one of the highest population densities in Africa. About 85% of people live in rural areas and are engaged in subsistence farming or fishing, or work on commercial farms and plantations. Around half the population is under 15 years of age.

The main ethnic groups are: Chewa, dominant in the central and southern parts of the country; Yao in the south; and Tumbuka in the north. Other groups are: Nguni, in parts of the central and northern provinces; Chipoka, also in the central area; and Tonga, mostly along the lakeshore. The number of Malawians of European decent is less than 1%. There is also a small Indian population in Malawi.

Christianity is the majority religion in Malawi, making up about 75% of the numbers, although for many Malawians, Western beliefs are intertwined with traditional African practices.

Muslims make up almost 20% of the population. The people of the Yao tribe along the southern lakeshore are the most closely associated with Islam.

Arts & Crafts

Dance is an important social element across Malawi and most dances are rooted in traditional beliefs and customs. The most famous traditional dance is known as Gule Wamkulu, which reflects the traditional belief in spirits.

Poetry is very popular in Malawi: leading poets include Steve Chimombo, whose most highly acclaimed work is a complex poetic drama, *The Rainmaker*, and Jack Mapanje, whose poetry collection (*Of Chameleons and Gods*, published 1981) led to his imprisonment in 1987 and eventual release in 1991.

Most critics agree that Malawi's leading novelist is Legson Kayira, whose semiautobiographical *I Will Try* and *The Looming Shadow* earned him acclaim in the 1970s. Samson Kambalu's recent autobiography *The Jive Talker: or, how to get a British Passport* tells of his transition from schoolboy at the Kamuzu Academy to conceptual artist in London.

Home-grown contemporary music has become increasingly popular in Malawi, due largely to influential and popular musicians such as Lucius Banda, who performs soft 'Malawian-style' reggae, and the late Evison Matafale. Other reggae names to look out for are the Black Missionaries and Billy Kaunda.

Malawi is especially known for skilful woodcarvers and you'll see beautifully made wood and stone carvings, including walking sticks, chairs and coffee tables, in craft shops and markets all over the country.

FOOD & DRINK

Markets and bus stations usually harbour a collection of food stalls, where you can get tea with milk for around MK70 and a bread cake or deep-fried cassava for MK50, or a simple meal of beans or meat and *nshima* (maize porridge) for about MK150.

Local restaurants in small towns provide simple meals for around MK250. In cities and larger towns, cheap restaurants serve traditional food as well as chicken or fish with rice or chips for around MK400.

Most midrange hotels and restaurants serve European-style food, such as steak, chicken or fish, which is served with vegetables and chips or rice – usually around the MK700 mark.

In Blantyre and Lilongwe you can find restaurants serving Ethiopian, Indian, Korean, Chinese and Portuguese food. Main courses range from around MK700 to MK1500. More elaborate French and Italian cuisine is also available, and you'll also find several steak-houses. At most top-end establishments, main courses start from about MK1600.

Traditional beer of the region is made from maize; in Malawi this is commercially brewed as Chibuku. Malawi's local lager is called Kuche Kuche but most travellers (and many Malawians) prefer the beer produced by Carlsberg at its Blantyre brewery (the only one in Africa).

ENVIRONMENT
The Land

Pint-sized, landlocked Malawi is no larger than the US state of Pennsylvania. It's wedged between Zambia, Tanzania and Mozambique, measuring roughly 900km long and between 80km and 150km wide, with an area of 118,484 sq km.

Lying in a trough formed by the Rift Valley, Lake Malawi covers almost a fifth of Malawi's total area. Beyond the lake, escarpments rise to high rolling plateaus covering much of the country. Malawi's main highland areas are Nyika and Viphya in the north and Mt Mulanje in the south.

Malawi's main river is the Shire (pronounced 'shir-ee'); it flows out of the southern end of Lake Malawi, through Lake Malombe and then southward as the plateau gives way to low ground, to flow into the Zambezi River in Mozambique. In this area, the lowest point is a mere 37m above sea level.

Wildlife

Malawi has five national parks. These are (from north to south) Nyika, Kasungu, Lake Malawi (around Cape Maclear), Liwonde and Lengwe. There are also four wildlife reserves – Vwaza Marsh, Nkhotakota, Mwabvi and Majete. 16.4% of Malawi's land is protected.

Liwonde National Park is noted for its herds of elephant and antelope and is a good place to see hippos and crocodiles. Nyika National Park is renowned for roan antelopes and reedbucks; and you'll also see zebras, warthogs, jackals and possibly leopards. Nearby Vwaza Marsh is known for its hippos as well as elephants, buffaloes, waterbucks and other antelope. In southern Malawi, Lengwe National Park supports a population of nyalas – at the northern limit of their distribution in Africa.

Lake Malawi has more fish species than any other inland body of water in the world, with a total of over 600. Most of these are of the family *Cichlidae* – the largest family of fish in Africa – and 99% of these cichlids are endemic to the lake.

For birdwatchers, Malawi is rewarding; over 600 species have been recorded.

LILONGWE

pop 669,000

Lilongwe might be Malawi's capital but don't come expecting major attractions, great shopping or a happening music scene – compared to many other African capitals the city is a sleepy backwater. That being said, it has a quiet charm that makes it an enjoyable place to hang out for a day or two. The modern city centre and business hub is a dead loss in terms of atmosphere and activities, but the Old Town, where most tourists end up spending their time, has a friendly vibe.

ORIENTATION

Lilongwe is unusually spread out, and rather than one central business district it has two centres: City Centre and Old Town. City Centre is rather sterile with a handful of offices, banks and hotels. Three kilometres south, Old Town has a good range of places to stay, the bus station, the market and several restaurants, all in a condensed area easily covered on foot. The town is divided into Areas: the Old Town is comprised of Areas 1 to 4.

INFORMATION
Internet Access

Comptech Cyber Café (Mandala Rd; per min MK5) Fast internet connection, printing and photocopying, as well as Skype telephone service.

RSS Internet Cafe (Kamuzu Procession Rd; per min MK4.50) Offers quick access.

Medical Services

Adventist Health Centre (☎ 01-775456/680; Presidential Way) Good for consultations, plus eye and dental problems.

Medical Air Rescue Service Clinic (MARS; ☎ 01-795018, 794967, emergency line 794242; www.marsmalawi.com; Ufulu Rd, Area 43) Has an intensive care unit, a dental surgery, and offers laboratory tests for malaria, bilharzia and HIV among others. MARS also has road and air ambulances.

Money

Money Bureau City Centre (☎ 01-772239; Centre House Arcade, City Centre Shopping Centre); Crossroads

MALAWI

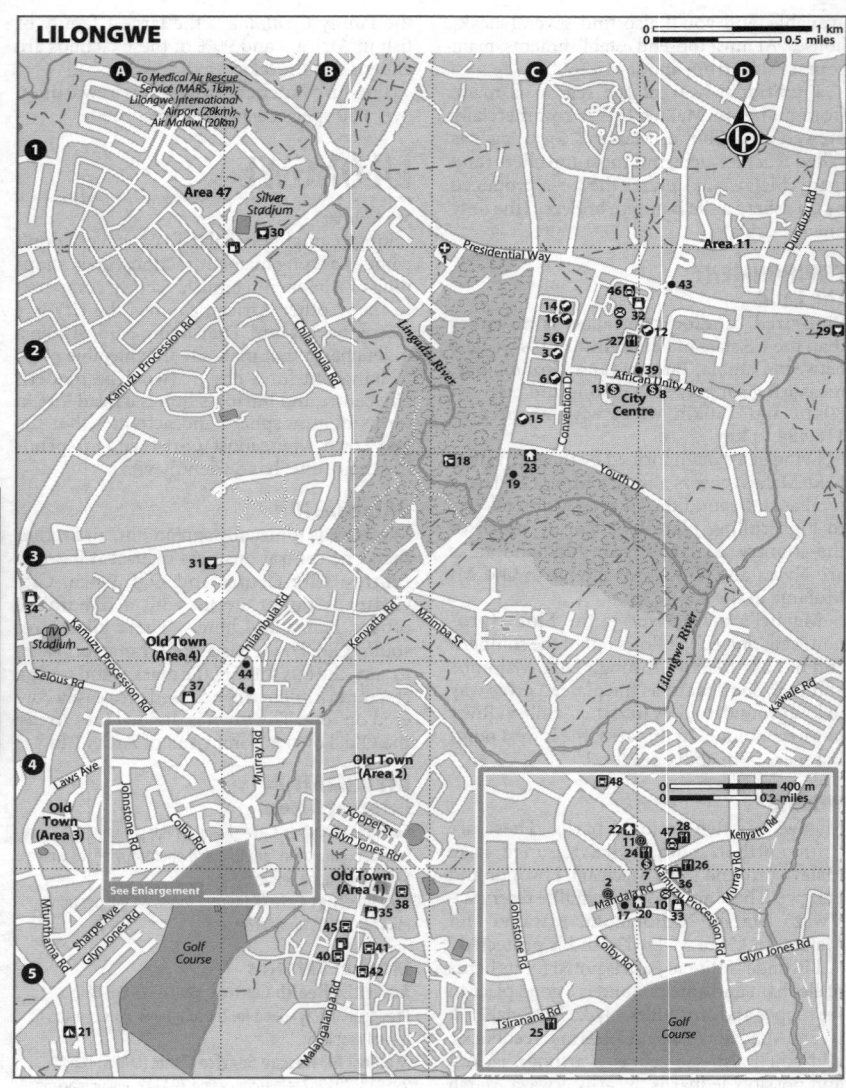

(☎ 01-750789; Crossroads Complex); Old Town (☎ 01-750659; Nico Shopping Centre, Kamuzu Procession Rd) Has good rates, doesn't charge commission and does cash advances on credit cards.

National Bank of Malawi City Centre (African Unity Ave); Old Town (Kamuzu Procession Rd) You can change money here and also get a cash advance on your Visa card.

Standard Bank City Centre (African Unity Ave); Old Town (Kamuzu Procession Rd) Offers the same facilities as National Bank of Malawi.

Post
Post office (Kamuzu Procession Rd, Old Town; ⏰ 7.30am-noon & 1-5pm Mon-Fri) Another office, with the same opening hours, is located next to the City Centre Shopping Centre.

INFORMATION		
Adventist Health Centre	1	C2
Comptech Cyber Café	2	C5
German Embassy	3	C2
Immigration Office	4	B4
Ministry of Tourism, Wildlife &		
Culture	5	C2
Money Bureau	(see 36)	
Money Bureau	(see 32)	
Money Bureau	(see 34)	
Mozambican Embassy	6	C2
National Bank of Malawi	7	D4
National Bank of Malawi	8	D2
Post Office	9	C2
Post Office	10	D5
RSS Internet Cafe	11	D4
South African High Commission	12	D2
Standard Bank	13	C2
UK High Commission	14	C2
US Embassy	15	C2
Zambian High Commission	16	C2

SIGHTS & ACTIVITIES		
Kibolo Safaris	(see 20)	
Land & Lake Safaris	17	C5

Lilongwe Nature		
Sanctuary	18	C3
Lilongwe Wildlife Centre	19	C3

SLEEPING		
Kiboko Town Hotel	20	D5
Mabuya Camp	21	A5
Mufasa Lodge	22	C4
Sanctuary Lodge	23	C3

EATING		
Ali Baba's	24	D4
Cappuccino's	(see 34)	
Don Brioni's Bistro	(see 20)	
Huts	(see 22)	
Korea Garden Restaurant	25	C5
Mamma Mia	(see 37)	
Metro Cash & Carry	26	D4
PTC Supermarket	27	C2
Shoprite	28	D4

DRINKING		
Chameleon Bar	29	D2
Chez Ntemba	30	B1
Harry's Bar	31	A3

SHOPPING		
City Centre Shopping Centre	32	C2
Craft Market	33	D5
Crossroads Complex	34	A3
Main Market	35	B5
Nico Shopping Centre	36	D5
Old Town Mall	37	A4

TRANSPORT		
AXA Ticket Office	(see 41)	
Buses to Dar es Salaam &		
Lusaka	38	B5
KLM & Kenya Airways	39	D2
Long Distance Minibuses	40	B5
Main Bus Station	41	B5
Minibuses to Zomba,		
Blantyre and Limbe	42	B5
South African Airways	43	D2
Sputnik Rent-a-Car	44	B4
Super Sink Buses	45	B5
Taxi Rank	46	C2
Taxis & Minibuses to City		
Centre	47	D4
Vaal Africa & Chita One (bus		
offices)	48	C4

Tourist Information

Ministry of Tourism, Wildlife & Culture (☎ 01-755499; Tourism House; ✆ 7.30am-5pm Mon-Fri, 8-10am Sat) The tourist office is located here, off Convention Dr, but information and advice is minimal.

DANGERS & ANNOYANCES

For years muggings were a serious problem around the Lilongwe Nature Sanctuary. Although the situation has improved in recent years, it's still not wise to walk around the area. If you're visiting the Lilongwe Wildlife Centre, take a taxi or a minibus.

During the day, it's fine to walk everywhere around the Old Town and City Centre, though it's much quieter at City Centre on the weekend so you should be on your guard. At night, Malangalanga Rd can be dangerous, and walking to Area 3 is not recommended. The bridge between Area 2 and Area 3 is a favourite haunt for muggers. If you arrive on a bus after dark, take a minibus or taxi to your accommodation.

SIGHTS & ACTIVITIES

The **main market** (Malangalanga Rd, Old Town) is a pocket of frenetic activity, with traders, market stalls and food vendors packed into a small area.

In between City Centre and Old Town and alongside the Lingadzi River is the 180-hectare **Lilongwe Nature Sanctuary**. Once one of the city's most popular attractions, the area had become neglected and run down. Luckily, a joint agreement between the Lilongwe Wildlife Trust and

the Department of National Parks and Wildlife is restoring the area to its former glory. Taking pride of place is the new **Lilongwe Wildlife Centre** (☎ 01-757120; www.lilongwewildlife.org; Kenyatta Rd; adult/child MK840/420; ✆ 8am-4pm Mon-Fri, 8am-noon Sat), an animal rescue and educational facility.

TOURS

Land & Lake Safaris (☎ 01-757120; www.landlake.net; Mandala Rd) Well-established and knowledgeable company organising tours for all budgets in both Malawi and Zambia.

Kiboko Safaris (☎ 01-751226; www.kiboko-safaris.com; Mandala Rd) Specialises in budget camping safaris throughout Malawi and Zambia, although it also has 'luxury' options for softies.

SLEEPING

Mabuya Camp (☎ 01-754978; www.mabuyacamp.com; Livingstone Rd; campsite per person US$4, dm US$6, d/tw US$18; 🅟 🖳 🛜) If you're looking for Lilongwe's liveliest backpacker spot, you've found it. This place buzzes with a happy mixture of solo travellers, overlanders and volunteers. There are dorms and a double in the main house, as well as chalets and plenty of campsites in the garden.

Sanctuary Lodge (☎ 01-775200/201/202; www.thesanctuarylodge.net; campsite per adult/child US$9/6, s/d incl breakfast from US$125/175; 🖳 🛜 🅟) Just outside the city's nature sanctuary, this peaceful ecolodge is encased in 8 hectares of woodland along the Lingadzi River. Made from environmentally friendly building materials, it has cool and

MALAWI

quiet stone chalets, and a campsite with *braai* (barbecue) sites and hot showers.

Mufasa Lodge (☎ 0999-071665; www.mufasamalawi. com; Kamuzu Procession Rd, Area 4; dm from US$8.50, tw without bathroom US$32, tw/d US$40 ☐ ☎) This is a fantastic new addition to Lilongwe's budget scene. It may not have a pool or large gardens but who needs them when you have a balcony with city views, spacious bathrooms and a home-away-from-home atmosphere. You can choose from doubles, singles or dorms, and there's an excellent self-catering kitchen.

Kiboko Town Hotel (☎ 01-751226; www.kiboko -safaris.com; Mandala Rd; s/d incl breakfast from US$48/ 58; ☐ ☎) Location wise, Kiboko can't be beat. It's in the heart of Mandala Rd, a mere skip away from Old Town's banks, shops and internet cafes. The rooms aren't bad either – four-poster beds and comfy bed linen are complemented with jazzy African prints, and they all have scrupulously clean bathrooms.

EATING

For self-caterers there's a Shoprite and a Metro Cash & Carry in Old Town and a PTC Supermarket at City Centre.

Cappuccino's (Crossroads Complex; cappuccino MK280, dishes MK1200-1600; ☎ 7.30am-6pm Mon-Fri, 8am-6pm Sat) There's a small terrace overlooking the mall, a collection of magazines for browsing, and a limited menu of English breakfasts, salads, wraps and sandwiches.

Ali Baba's (☎ 01-755224; Kamuzu Procession Rd; dishes MK500-900; ☎ 8am-9pm Mon-Fri, 10am-8pm Sun) Ever popular fast-food spot serving burgers and wraps as well as sturdier plates of curries and stews.

Korea Garden Restaurant (☎ 01-753467; starters MK500-700, mains MK1000-2200; ☎ breakfast, lunch & dinner) Flavoursome Korean favourites such as *bulgogi* and *kimchi* are on offer at this poolside restaurant within the Korea Garden Hotel.

Huts (☎ 01-752912; off Kamuzu Procession Rd; mains from MK750; ☎ noon-1.30pm & 6.15-9.30pm Mon-Sat) Come here for your fix of tandoori and *tikka masala*. The food here is filling, tasty and great value.

Don Brioni's Bistro (☎ 01-756998; Mandala Rd; mains from MK800; ☎ lunch & dinner) Long-time favourite Don Brioni's is a laid-back Italian-style bistro that fills up with an energetic mix of tourists and locals each evening. The food here is excellent and comes in hefty portions.

Mamma Mia (☎ 01-758322; Old Town Mall; mains from MK1400; ☎ lunch & dinner) The spaghetti and massive pizzas are the main event here but it also does a wide selection of seafood and steaks.

DRINKING & ENTERTAINMENT

Chameleon Bar (Four Seasons Centre, Presidential Way; ☎ 11am-midnight Mon-Sat, to 10pm Sun) This place is popular with Malawians and expats and puts on regular live music and DJ nights. It has an enticing cocktail menu and tables outside at which to enjoy them.

Harry's Bar (☎ 01-757979 ☎ 6pm-late) Harry's is an institution. The owner is a mine of information on the Malawian music scene and the bar is the place to come if you want to get the low-down on local bands and DJs

Chez Ntemba (Area 47; ☎ 6pm-late) Part of the Congolese nightclub chain that has branches across southern Africa, this is Lilongwe's most fun night out. Hordes of sweaty bodies pack the place out to dance to DJs and live bands with a totally African flavour.

SHOPPING
Malls

Nico Shopping Centre (Kamuzu Procession Rd) Has a bookshop, travel agency and pharmacy.

Crossroads Complex (Kamuzu Procession Rd) Houses banks, a hotel, minigolf and a variety of upscale shops.

City Centre Shopping Centre (off Independence Dr) Contains shops, travel agents, restaurants, a bank and a post office.

Old Town Mall (off Chilambula Rd) This small mall has a couple of bookshops and craft stores.

At the time of writing a new shopping centre was being constructed behind the Nico Shopping Centre and opposite Shoprite. It is due to open in late 2010.

Markets

The city's main market is by the bus station. There's also a craft market outside the Old Town post office, where vendors sell everything from woodcarvings to basketware.

GETTING THERE & AWAY
Air

Airlines with offices in Lilongwe include:
Air Malawi (☎ 01-700811; Kamuzu International Airport)
KLM & Kenya Airways (☎ 01-774227; City Centre)
South African Airways (☎ 01-772242, 770307; Capital Hotel, City Centre)

Bus

AXA City Trouper and commuter buses leave from the main bus station, where you'll find its ticket office. Destinations from the main bus station include Mzuzu (MK1200, five hours), Blantyre (MK700 to MK1400, four hours), Nkhata Bay (MK900, five hours) and Monkey Bay (MK1000, six hours).

AXA executive buses leave from outside the PTC supermarket in City Centre before stopping at the immigration office on Murray Rd and making their way to Blantyre. A ticket between the two cities costs MK3100.

A number of other bus companies including Coachline and Zimatha also leave from the main bus station at similar rates and times. Super Sink buses depart for Mzuzu from the Caltex petrol station next to the bus station between 7am and 8am (MK1000, six hours).

Long-distance minibuses depart from behind the main bus station to nearby destinations, such as Zomba (MK1200, four to five hours) and Limbe (MK1000, three to four hours).

Vaal Africa (☎ 0999-200086) leaves from the Total petrol station in Old Town for Johannesburg on Tuesdays and Saturdays at 6am (one way MK14,500, 17 hours).

Chita One (☎ 0999-45453/0999-22221) leaves for Johannesburg on Wednesdays and Sundays at 6am from near the Old Town Mall (one way MK15,500, 27 to 29 hours).

Zambia–Botswana Coach (☎ 0999-405340) leaves from Devil St for Lusaka on Tuesdays and Fridays at 6am (MK6000, 12 hours). Kob's Coach leaves the same days, same price, same location at 5.30 am. The Taqwa Coach departs from Devil St at 7pm on Saturdays, Sundays and Tuesdays for Dar es Salaam (MK8000, 27 hours), continuing on to Nairobi (MK14,000).

GETTING AROUND
To/From the Airport
Lilongwe International Airport (Kamazu) is 21km north of the city. A taxi from the airport into town costs MK2000.

Bus
From Old Town, local minibuses (marked Area 12) leave from either the bus rank near the market, or next to Shoprite. They then head north up Kenyatta Rd to reach City Centre. The fare between the two centres is MK80.

Taxi
The best places to find taxis are the main hotels. There's also a rank on Presidential Way, just north of City Centre Shopping Centre. Taxis also congregate outside Shoprite in Old

Town. The fare between Old Town and City Centre is about MK1000.

NORTHERN MALAWI

Northern Malawi is where ravishing highlands meet hippo-filled swamps, where vast mountains loom large over empty beaches, and where colonial relics litter pristine islands and hilltop villages. It is Malawi's most sparsely populated region, and the first taste many travellers get of this tiny country after making the journey down from East Africa.

KARONGA
pop 34,000
In the surrounding dry and dusty country, Karonga is a relaxed little town with wide streets, wandering cattle and shop fronts straight out of a western; you can almost see the tumbleweed rolling down the street.

It's the first and last town on the road between Malawi and Tanzania and has some good facilities, including the only bank north of Mzuzu.

Sleeping
Mufwa Lakeshore Lodge & Camping (☎ 01-362390, 0999-778451; campsite per person MK700, s/d without bathroom MK1200/2100, self-contained s/d MK2500/3800) A lodge overlooking the lake with a large, green lawn might sound like a good thing but in reality the owners don't make much of it. Bland and basic are the watchwords for the rooms here. The property can be difficult to find – there is no identifying sign and it's set back from the road; the turn-off is located after the National Bank of Malawi.

Safari Lodge (☎ 01-362340; s/d MK3000/3750) On the road to the lake, this place has spacious rooms but as with many places in this town they are a bit run-down.

Safari Lodge Annex (☎ 01-362340; standard/exec/chalet MK4500/4800/6500) Just around the corner from Safari Lodge is its much more attractive and better-endowed sister. There are solid-brick chalets here with large bathrooms and separate sitting areas, as well as a pretty garden.

Getting There & Away
Buses and minibuses run between Karonga and Mzuzu (MK800, 3½ to 4 hours). If you're heading north, minibuses and *matola* (unofficial public transport vehicles) travel to the Songwe border crossing (MK230, 45 minutes).

MALAWI

MALAWISAURUS AND OTHER ANIMALS

Karonga has the proud title of Malawi's 'fossil district'. Karonga's most famous discovery? The Malawisaurus (or Malawi lizard) – a fossilised dino skeleton found 45km south of the town. It's thought that the scaly one lived between 140 million and 100 million years ago during the cretaceous period, and was a hulking 30 long, 14ft high and weighed in at around 11,000kg. You can check out the skeleton (or a copy of it anyway) at the **Culture and Museum Centre Karonga** (CMCK; ☎ 01-362579; www.palaeo.net/cmck; ☼ 8am-5pm Mon-Sat, 2-5pm Sun).

It's 200m across the bridge to the Tanzanian border. Taxis direct to the Tanzanian border cost MK500 and leave from the main bus station.

LIVINGSTONIA

After two failed attempts at establishing a mission at Cape Maclear and at Bandawe the Free Church of Scotland moved its mission 900m above the lake to the village of Khondowe. Called Livingstonia after Dr David Livingstone, this isolated hilltop haven provides a fascinating glimpse into Malawi's colonial past, and the mixture of old architecture, wide, dusty tree-lined streets and panoramic views is quite beguiling.

Sights & Activities

The absorbing **museum** (admission/photos MK250/100; ☼ 7.30am-5pm) in the Stone House (the original home of Dr Laws and now a national monument) tells the story of European arrival in Malawi and the first missionaries.

The nearby mission church, dating from 1894, has a beautiful stained-glass window featuring David Livingstone with his sextant, his medicine chest and his two companions, with Lake Malawi in the background.

About 4km from town the impressive **Manchewe Falls** thunders 125m into the valley below. Follow a small path behind the falls and there's a cave where, as the story goes, local people hid from slave-traders a hundred years ago. Allow an hour going down and 1½ hours back up. Alternatively, if you're walking to/from Chitimba, you can visit on the way.

The more adventurous can go abseiling or try out a gorge swing. For more details, contact Mushroom Farm (below).

Sleeping

our pick **Mushroom Farm** (☎ 0999-652485; www.themushroomfarmmalawi.com; campsite per person MK640, tent from MK800, s/d from MK4000) Drive in to this sustainable bush retreat from the Livingstonia road and the views will hit you smack in the face. Camping spots with their own little fire pits teeter at the cliff edge and stunning rooms include a wood-and-thatch double completely open at the front, and a cob hut that looks as if it could house a hobbit. It's roughly 10km up the escarpment road and is signposted on the left.

Stone House (☎ 01-368223; campsite per person MK600, r per head MK1400, laundry MK200) Sleeping in Dr Laws' old house – complete with creaky wooden floorboards and pieces of original furniture – is probably the most atmospheric way to spend the night in Livingstonia. There's a verandah with outrageous views over the escarpment and wholesome meals are available.

Getting There & Away

From the main north–south road between Karonga and Mzuzu, the road to Livingstonia turns off at Chitimba, forcing its way up the escarpment in a series of acute hairpin bends. Drivers should attempt this only in a 4WD, and only if there's been no rain. There's no bus, and you'll wait a very long time if you're hitching.

The alternative is to walk up: it's about 15km, and steep, so it takes around four hours from Chitimba if you follow the road.

NYIKA NATIONAL PARK

At 1800m above sea level the Nyika Plateau – the main attraction of Malawi's **Nyika National Park** (per person/car US$5/2; ☼ 6am-6pm) – feels decidedly different from the rest of Malawi: think Yorkshire moors meets the Black Forest. Gently sloping hills, broad valleys and grasslands are met by sporadic pockets of thick pine trees and gin-clear streams; and in the mornings the air is cold and crisp and the landscape enveloped in fine blue mist.

With 3200 sq km of expanse you can quite easily spend the day hiking in the hills without happening upon another soul – except for the animals that is. Plenty of zebras, bushbucks and roan antelopes roam this domain, and you may also spot hyenas and leopards. If you're a twitcher, more than 400 species of bird have been recorded here. There are around 200 species of orchid alone growing on the plateau, and after the wet season the landscape bursts into life in a blaze of wildflowers.

It can get surprisingly cold on the Nyika Plateau, especially at night from June to August, when frost is not uncommon. Log fires are provided in the chalets and rooms, but bring a warm sleeping bag if you're camping.

Sleeping

Wilderness Safaris (www.wilderness-safaris.com) won the tender to run the park's tourist concessions in 2009. In late 2009 Chelinda Camp reopened; Chelinda Lodge was due to reopen in mid-2010.

Camping Ground (campsites per person US$10) About 2km from the main Chelinda Camp, this camp is set in a secluded site with vistas of the plateau's rolling hills. The site has permanent security, clean toilets, hot showers, endless firewood, and shelters for cooking and eating.

Chelinda Camp (☎ 01-771393; www.wilderness-safaris. com; full board per person per night from US$237) Chelinda Camp is a series of self-catering stone bungalows tucked into the forest. All of them have huge stone fireplaces, sitting rooms and fully equipped kitchens for self-caterers.

Chelinda Lodge (☎ 01-771393; www.wilderness-safaris. com) This cluster of log cabins sitting in a clearing of pine trees looks like something out of a Bavarian fairytale. When renovations are finished, luxury bathrooms, log fires and gourmet dinners should be the order of the day.

Getting There & Away

The main Thazima gate is in the southwest of the park, 54km from Rumphi; to Chelinda Camp it's another 55km. The road is dirt after Rumphi and in fair condition as far as Thazima gate. In the park the tracks are rough and really only suitable for 4WD vehicles or 2WD vehicles with high clearance. Fuel is available at Chelinda but in limited supply, so it's best to fill up before you enter the park.

VWAZA MARSH WILDLIFE RESERVE

This 1000-sq-km reserve is not on the mainstream tourist track but with its compact size, and plentiful buffalo, elephant and hippo, it shouldn't be overlooked. Like many of Malawi's parks, poachers have hit Vwaza hard in the past but animal numbers are still reasonably healthy. As well as a plethora of antelope –

puku, impala, roan and kudu, to name a few – there are around 2000 buffalo, 300 elephants and 500 hippos. Vwaza's birdwatching is also excellent, and this is one of the best places in Malawi to see waders, including storks and herons. There are few predators, but occasionally a lion or leopard is spotted.

The best time of year to visit is in the dry season. Just after the rainy season the grass is high and you might go away without seeing anything.

Sleeping

At the time of writing, the government was in charge of park accommodation, but had just awarded the tourism concession to a private company, so prices are sure to change. Ask on the ground for further information.

Kazuni Camp (campsite per person US$6, chalet s/d with shared bathroom US$10/20) Has simple, rustic chalets with clean sheets and mosquito nets. They are separated by a decent stretch of bush, so you still get a sense of privacy and wilderness while being within a camp. You must bring food, and there are cooking stations with barbecues.

Lake Kazuni Safari Camp (huts US$30) Consists of low-key grass and brick chalets with bathrooms, in a fantastic position overlooking the floodplains. There's a restaurant sitting underneath the acacia trees.

Getting There & Away

If you're travelling by public transport, first get to Rumphi (reached from Mzuzu by minibus for MK400 or public bus for MK250). From Rumphi there are plenty of *matola* travelling to and from the Kazuni area and you should be able to get a lift to the main gate for around MK500 to MK700. Otherwise buses and minibuses to Mzimba might drop you at Kazuni village, which is about 1km from the park gate.

By car, head west from Rumphi. Turn left after 10km (Vwaza Marsh Wildlife Reserve is signposted) and continue for about 20km. Where the road swings left over a bridge, go straight on to reach the park gate and camp after 1km.

MZUZU
pop 120,000

Compact, friendly Mzuzu is the largest town in northern Malawi and serves as the transport hub for the region. It has banks, shops, a post office, supermarkets, pharmacies, petrol

MALAWI

stations and other facilities, which are especially useful if you've come into Malawi from the north.

Internet access is available at the **City Cyber** (per 10 min MK100; ☾ 8am-5pm Mon-Fri, to 4pm Sat) or at **Postdotnet** (per 30 min MK200; ☾ 8am-5pm Mon-Fri, to 12.30pm Sat), both on Boardman Rd.

Sleeping & Eating

Mzoozoozoo (☎ 0888-864493; campsite MK300, dm MK800, d MK1400) The town's most popular backpacker haunt has a selection of dorms and rooms in timber bungalows. Meals are available from around MK700, and it's an excellent place to collect up-to-date information for your onward journey.

Flame Tree Guesthouse (☎ 01-310056, 0999-511423; campsite per person MK500, s/d incl breakfast MK3000/3800) Spotless units centre round a shady garden and all of them have a little piece of verandah to call their own. The neat lounge has DSTV and a book exchange. Dinner (meals start at around MK800, and include curries, steak and chips, and chicken) is available if ordered in advance.

CCAP William Koyi Guest House (☎ 01-931961; Boardman Rd; campsite per person MK350, dm MK500, r with /without MK2500/950) Quiet and good-value option for budget travellers. The church owns it so it's generally safe and secure, though that means there's no booze and you'll have to act in a respectful fashion.

Mimosa Court Hotel (☎ 01-312833/609; s/d MK8000) This is an excellent midrange choice – large bright corridors open up into scrupulously clean bedrooms, with plenty of wardrobe space and funky art on the walls. The welcome is warm and it's in a great location right in the centre of town.

Obrigado (Boardman Rd; snacks/meals from MK50/300; ☾ 6am-9pm) Soak up your beer with a mixed plate of samosas and gizzards, or tuck into a plate of offal and chips in this large outdoor cafe and beer garden. Fountains, trees and an enormous zebra statue accompany your meals.

A1 Restaurant (St Denis St; mains around MK900; ☾ 11.45am-2pm & 6-10pm; Ⓥ ☏) A large selection of vegetarian dishes as well as chicken *tikka masala* and other Indian restaurant standbys are served within these bright purple walls.

Getting There & Away

Buses go to a number of destinations, including Lilongwe (MK1000 to MK1200, five to seven hours) and Karonga (MK800, four hours). Minibuses go to Lilongwe (MK1300, five hours) Nkhata Bay (MK350, one to two hours), Karonga (MK800, three to four hours) and the Tanzanian border (MK1200, four hours).

The **Taqwa bus** (☎ 0999-670468), originating in Lilongwe, travels between Mzuzu and Nairobi on Tuesdays and Sundays (MK15000) calling at Songwe for the border (MK1500), Mbeya (MK3500) and Dar es Salaam (MK8000). You should report to the bus station at 11.30pm for a midnight departure.

NKHATA BAY

Nkhata Bay has quite a different feel from its beachside rivals. Get out of town, look back at the houses crawling up the lush hillside and you could almost be in St Lucia. The centre of gravity is a small town centre, nestled into a gully with the bay to the east and a gentle rise of dense forest to the west. It's a busy clutch of markets, craft stalls and wandering backpackers.

Information

There's nowhere to change money so make sure you cash up in Mzuzu or Lilongwe. Alternatively, some of the lodges accept credit cards, US currency and travellers cheques for payment. Internet access is available at **Aqua Africa** (per min MK12; ☾ 10am-4pm Mon-Sat).

Activities

Monkey Business (☎ 01-252365) on Chikale Beach operates fully inclusive kayak excursions. If you want to learn scuba diving, **Aqua Africa** (☎ 01-352284; www.aquaafrica.co.uk) offers a number of different diving options, from five-day PADI Open Water courses for US$310 to casual day dives for US$40.

Sleeping & Eating

Mayoka Village (☎ 01-352421; www.mayokavillage. com; per person campsite/dm/traditional mud hut US$3/4/5, chalet without bathroom s/d US$8/16, chalet s/d US$25/50) A rambling collection of chalets and beach huts, including bathrooms with huge stone baths, and back-to-basic reed huts near the water. Life revolves around the buzzing waterfront bar, which serves excellent food and has been the scene of many a raucous party.

Big Blue Star (☎ 01-352316; campsite per person US$3, dm/s/d without bathroom US$5/10/20) A large, busy and friendly place near the centre of town.

You can either camp or stay in colourful red-, yellow- and green- striped dorms and reed huts. Social life comes courtesy of the lively bar, where you can get chatting with one of the many locals who hang out here.

Njaya Lodge (☎ 01-352342; www.njayalodge.com; campsite/bandas per person US$7/12, chalets US$20, family cottages per person from US$28) This is the furthest lodge from town and often one of the quietest, but that's no bad thing. A selection of huts and chalets is hidden in fertile hillside grounds, and there's an open restaurant and bar area overlooking the lake.

Malawian Time (plate MK350, set meal incl soup & dessert MK750; ☺ 8am-6pm) This one is different. You can order plates (a small selection of different dishes on one platter) or larger set meals of beautifully presented Malawian/Japanese food, including croquettes, meatballs with peanuts, and sandwiches. There's an open kitchen at the front of the cafe with a couple of outdoor tables, and the dining room at the back is half restaurant, half cool craft shop.

Kaya Papaya (mains from MK600; ☺ 7am-late, food served to 9pm) It's hard to miss this bright-purple place. Downstairs is a little garden with brightly patterned deck chairs to chill out in and upstairs is an expansive open deck where you can order food and look down on the day-to-day business of the town. The Thai dishes here make a good alternative to the norm and there's a bar that stays open until the last person leaves.

Getting There & Away

All buses and minibuses go from the bus stand on the main road. AXA buses run to Mzuzu (MK300, two hours), and minibuses run to Nkhotakota (MK700, five hours), Chintheche (MK300, one hour) and Mzuzu (MK350, one to two hours). To reach Lilongwe, the quickest option is usually to go to Mzuzu and transfer. Many travellers also come or go on the *Ilala* ferry (see p959).

LIKOMA & CHIZUMULU ISLANDS

Bobbing in lucid azure water and blessed with stunning views out over to the mountain ranges of their nearest neighbour, Mozambique, these islands are perfect hideaways, with nothing much to do here except lounge in blinding white coves and soak up slow and friendly village activity. If you want to visit both islands, transport links make it best to go to Chizumulu first.

Sights

On Likoma, the huge Anglican **Cathedral of St Peter**, built by missionaries between 1903 and 1905, should not be missed. You can climb the tower for spectacular views.

Sleeping

Mango Drift (☎ 0999-746122; mailmangodrift@gmail.com; campsite/dm per person US$3/5, chalet s/d without bathroom US$10/15) Stone, reed and thatched chalets are basic but have nets, power points and lockboxes to stash your valuables. They are spread across a beautiful beach on the western side of the island. There's a bar under a mango tree, and clean hot showers.

Wakwenda Retreat (☎ 0999-348415; campsite/dm US$3.50/6, r from US$14) Smack bang on a postcard-perfect beach, this is utter chill-out material. The sizeable bar is constructed around a massive, hollow baobab tree, and the shaded lounge area is often the focus of lazy activity, such as snorkelling (free gear), and goat barbecues.

Kaya Mawa (www.kayamawa.com; per person chalets all inclusive US$350) The ideal place for a romantic retreat – Flintstones style. Chalets are carefully constructed around a rocky bay – there are stone baths, walls made from slabs of existing granite, and rock faces used as shower screens.

Getting There & Away

Nyassa Air Taxi (☎ 01-761443; www.nyassa.mw) provides charter flights to Likoma. The more of you there are, the cheaper it is per person. For example a one-way flight from Lilongwe to Likoma Island ranges between US$320 and US$210 per person depending on how many people are travelling.

The *Ilala* ferry (see p959) serves Likoma and Chizumulu twice a week. There are daily dhow ferries between Likoma and Chizumulu costing around MK200 per person. The trip can take anything from one to three hours depending on the weather.

Heading south, the *Ilala* sails to Metangula on the Mozambican mainland. Local dhows also sail to Cóbuè for MK250.

SENGA BAY

Sitting at the eastern end of a broad peninsula that juts into the lake from Salima, Senga Bay is the closest beach resort to the capital, with a range of accommodation to suit all budgets. The town lacks a real heart and resorts

MALAWI

MALAWI'S LAKE OF STARS

Since 2004, Lake Malawi's sandy shores have been regularly rocking to international DJs and local pop acts. Organised by a British club promoter, the three-day **Malawi Lake of Stars festival** (www.lakeofstars.org) is held every September/October at different locations around the lake – think miniature Glastonbury with heat and flip-flops instead of mud and wellies. All kinds of acts have taken to the stage, from Malawian reggae superstars the Black Missionaries to English folk musicians.

---

are spread over a distance of about 10km, so without wheels you'll need to make use of local bicycle taxis.

Sights & Activities

As a break from lazing on the beach, you can go windsurfing or snorkelling, take a boat ride or learn to dive. You could also take a trip out to nearby **Lizard Island** to see its population of giant monitor lizards and its cormorant colony. Alternatively, you can go hiking in the nearby **Senga Hills**.

Sleeping & Eating

Wamwai Beach Lodge (☎ 0888-709999; campsite/dm per person MK300/1500, d & tw MK4500) The wide verandah that wraps around this charming bungalow is a fantastic spot to chill and look out at the fishing boats from the local village. Inside are several homey rooms, a fantastic, airy dorm and a dining room – all decked out in plenty of wood and bright local fabrics.

Steps Campsite (campsite per person MK1000) This place combines beautiful views and a clean white sandy beach with excellent facilities – there's a volleyball pitch, clean hot showers, individual power points and round the clock security. A raised, circular bar provides the focal point of the campsite and makes a lovely spot for sundowners.

our pick **Safari Beach Lodge** (☎ 01-263143, 0999-365494; www.safaribeachlodge.net; s/d MK11,900/16,100) A quick scramble up the hill reveals a row of gorgeous stone huts perching cliff side. They all have wide balconies overlooking the lake, and separate, open-air bamboo-and-rock showers (watch out for the soap-stealing baboons). Follow a path down to a private beach where you'll find kayaks, snorkels and

a swing for two – a perfect spot for its regular Saturday barbecues. The lodge is 1km off the main road.

Red Zebra Cafe (waffles MK450, mains MK850-1200; ⏰ 7am-10.30pm) Black-and-white pictures of rock legends and an eclectic soundtrack of laid-back summer tunes set the scene here, and if you tire of lounging on the beach, a table on the verandah of this vibey cafe is a good alternative. Daily offerings are scribbled on the blackboard and include grills, stews, curries and waffles. Things kick off on weekend evenings and live bands occasionally put in an appearance.

Getting There & Away

First get to Salima. To reach Salima from Lilongwe, it's easiest to take a minibus (MK450, one hour). There are also minibuses to Nkhata Bay (MK900, six to seven hours) and Mzuzu (MK1000, seven to eight hours). From Salima, local pick-ups run to Senga Bay (MK200), dropping you in the main street. If you're travelling to/from Cape Maclear, consider chartering a boat (around US$180).

SOUTHERN MALAWI

This is the most developed and densely populated part of Malawi, home to the country's commercial capital and two of its major industries – sugar and tea. Visitors are drawn by the chance to scale mountains and watch wildlife in an incredibly beautiful and diverse landscape.

BLANTYRE

pop 661,000

Welcome to the oldest settlement in Malawi and the country's commercial and industrial hub. During the week the streets are alive with office workers, hawkers and shopkeepers. It has the best and most diverse choice of restaurants in the country, a national museum, and a fascinating library and archives where you can get to grips with the country's history. To the east Blantyre joins its more sedate sister city of Limbe.

Orientation

Blantyre's city centre is compact, with most places of importance to travellers within easy walking distance. The main street is Victoria Ave; along here are several large shops, banks and currency-exchange bureaus. To the east is Haile Selassie Rd, which contains many smaller shops. At the northern end of Victoria Ave is the landmark Sunbird Mount Soche Hotel.

Information
INTERNET ACCESS
E Centre Internet Café (cnr Victoria Ave & Independence Dr; per min MK4.50; ⏱ 8am-5pm Mon-Sat, 9am-4pm Sun)
Icon Internet Café (off Livingstone Ave; per min MK5) High speed internet access.

MEDICAL SERVICES
Mwaiwathu Private Hospital (☎ 01-822999; Chileka Rd; ⏱ 24hr) For private medical consultations or blood tests, this hospital, east of the city centre, is good. A consultation is US$10; all drugs and treatment are extra.
Seventh Day Adventist Clinic (☎ 01-820006; Robins Rd) For medical or dental problems, this clinic charges US$10 for a doctor's consultation and US$10 for a malaria test.

MONEY
There are branches of the National Bank of Malawi and Standard Bank on Victoria Ave, both of which can change cash and travellers cheques and have 24-hour ATMs. **Victoria Forex Bureau** (☎ 01-821026; www.victoriaforex.com) usually has more competitive rates and doesn't charge commission.

POST
Main post office (Glyn Jones Rd, Blantyre; ⏱ 7.30am-5pm) Has poste restante.

TOURIST INFORMATION
Immigration office (Government Complex, Victoria Ave) If you need to extend your visa, Blantyre has an immigration office.
Tourist office (☎ Regional Tourism officer 0888-304362; 2nd fl, Government Complex, Victoria Ave; ⏱ 7.30am-5pm Mon-Fri) This small office in the Department of Tourism stocks a few leaflets, sells maps of Malawi (MK500) and can offer enthusiastic, though not always helpful, advice.

Sights & Activities
Blantyre's most magnificent building is the red brick **CCAP Church**, officially called St Michael and All Angels Church. Built in the late 19th century, it's an impressive feat of elaborate brickwork topped with a grand basilica dome.

The **National Museum** (Kasungu Cres; admission MK200, ⏱ 7.30am-5pm) is of the small and dusty variety, with a number of not particularly well-laid-out exhibits documenting the country's history. It's midway between Blantyre and Limbe.

Mandala House (☎ 01-871932; Mackie Rd; ⏱ 8.30am-4.30pm Mon-Fri, to 1pm Sat) is the oldest building standing in Malawi and was built back in 1882 as a home for the managers of the Mandala Trading Company. Inside the house is a cafe (p951), an art gallery and the **Society of Malawi Library & Archive** (⏱ 9am-noon Mon-Fri, also 6-7.30pm Thu) which contains journals, books and photographs, some dating as far back as the 19th century.

Tours
Jambo Africa (☎ 01-823709/835356; www.jambo-africa.com; Sunbird Mount Soche Hotel, Glyn Jones Rd) Offers a wide range of tours and services including day tours in and around Blantyre.

Sleeping
Doogles (☎ 01-821128; Mulomba Pl; campsite/dm/chalets without bathroom US$3/5.50/16, d US$21; 🖳 🐾) A popular backpacker spot with dorms in the main house as well as self-contained chalets in the garden. There's plenty of space for pitching tents, as well as a swimming pool and a lively bar that's open to the general public. Be warned that the dorms in the main house are right behind the bar so can get pretty noisy.

Hostellerie de France (☎ 01-869626; www.hostellerie-de-france.com; cnr Chilomoni Ring Rd & Kazuni Close; studio/r/apt from US$40/50/100; 🐾 🖳 🛜) You'll find everything you need here, from dorms to executive doubles to apartments and studios, and there are discounts for long stayers.

Pedro's Lodge (☎ 01-833430; www.pedroslodge.com; 9 Smythe Rd, Sunnyside; s/d US$70/100; 🐾 🍽 🖳 🛜) Book in advance to stay at this small, family-run guesthouse where you'll immediately feel welcome. Eight clean comfortable rooms with DSTV look out onto a small swimming pool and lush green lawn.

Sunbird Mount Soche Hotel (☎ 01-620588; mount-soche@sunbirdmalawi.com; Glyn Jones Rd; s/d US$140/170; 🅿 🍽 🖳 🛜 🐾) This is a popular business hotel and is bursting with the requisite facilities. It's perhaps not such a good deal for tourists, though; the rooms are looking rather tired and aren't great value. If you do stay, plump for a room at the back; they have balconies with grand views over the hills.

Protea Hotel Ryalls (☎ 01-820955; ryalls@proteamalawi.com; 2 Hanover Ave; s/d US$215/245; 🐾 🖳 🛜) Ryalls is the oldest established hotel in Malawi. It opened in 1922 and was a legendary stop for travellers on the route from the Cape to Cairo. The hotel is full of old-fashioned flair

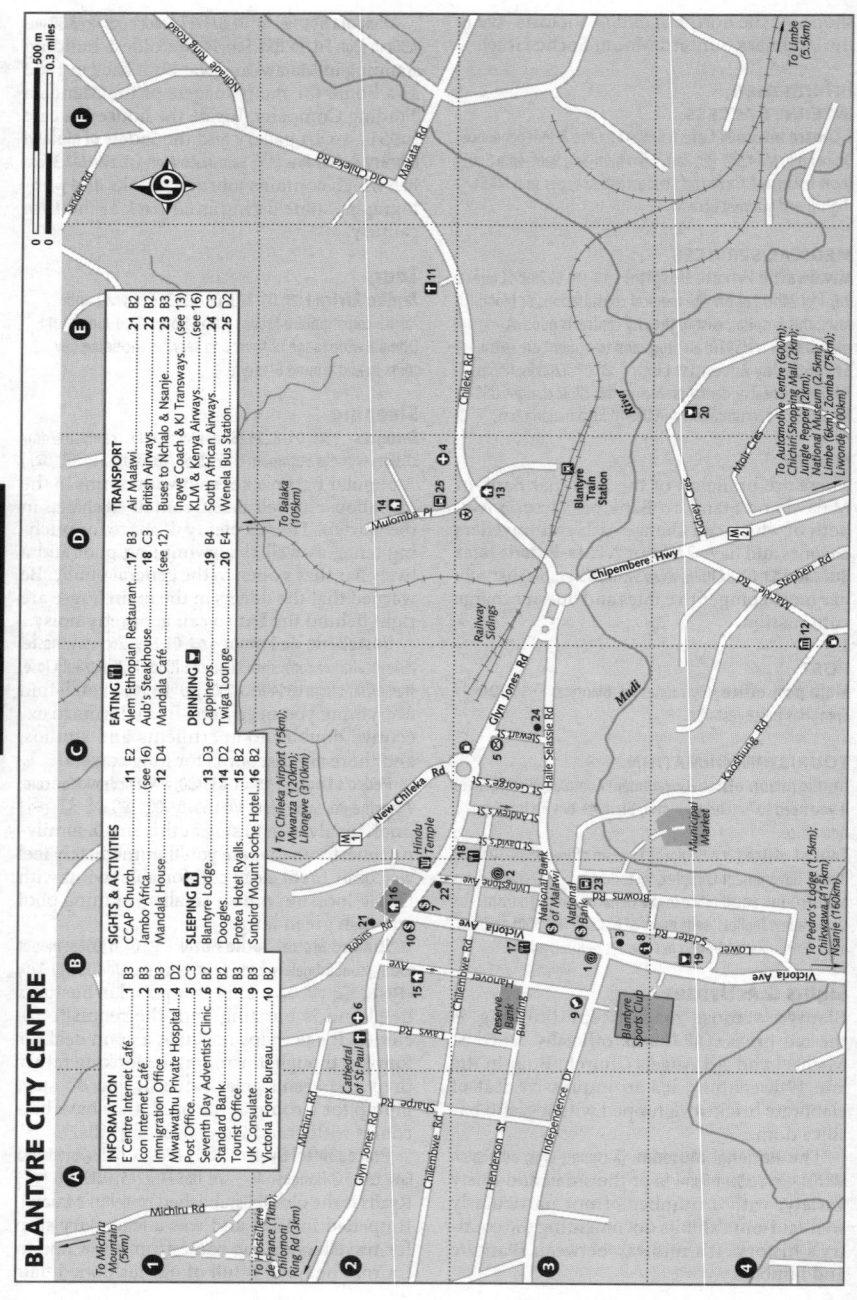

BLANTYRE CITY CENTRE

INFORMATION
E Centre Internet Café	.1 B3
Icon Internet Café	.2 B3
Immigration Office	.3 B3
Mwaiwathu Private Hospital	.4 D2
Post Office	.5 C3
Seventh Day Adventist Clinic	.6 B2
Standard Bank	.7 B2
Tourist Office	.8 B3
UK Consulate	.9 B3
Victoria Forex Bureau	.10 B2

SIGHTS & ACTIVITIES
CCAP Church	.11 E2
Jambo Africa	(see 16)
Mandala House	.12 D4

SLEEPING
Blantyre Lodge	.13 D3
Doogles	.14 D2
Protea Hotel Ryalls	.15 B2
Sunbird Mount Soche Hotel	.16 B2

EATING
Alem Ethiopian Restaurant	.17 B3
Aub's Steakhouse	.18 C3
Mandala Café	(see 12)

DRINKING
Cappineros	.19 B4
Twiga Lounge	.20 E4

TRANSPORT
Air Malawi	.21 B2
British Airways	.22 B3
Buses to Nchalo & Nsanje	.23 B3
Ingwe Coach & KJ Transways	(see 13)
KLM & Kenya Airways	(see 16)
South African Airways	.24 C3
Wenela Bus Station	.25 D2

and the plush rooms and communal areas are plastered with black-and-white photographs telling tales of old.

Eating

Alem Ethiopian Restaurant (☎ 01-822529; Victoria Ave; dishes MK300-800; ☒ 8am-5pm Mon-Sat) Delicious *injera* (sour millet pancake) and *doro wot* (chicken with hot-pepper sauce) are on the menu here, but you can also have a plate of bland old chicken and chips or beef stew if you so desire.

Aub's Steakhouse (☎ 0999-960628/0999-966507; Livingstonia Bldg, Chilembwe Rd; starters MK650-1000, mains MK1750-2300; ☒ noon-2pm & 7-10pm Mon-Sat; ☒ ☒ ☒) Mosey on down here and you'll be rewarded with a meat-, cheese- and carb-laden menu, all served up in the shadow of cowboy hat-, saddle- and horseshoe-adorned walls. For the faint hearted there are 'ladies' or 'low-carb' portions.

Jungle Pepper (☎ 0888-826229, 0999-826229; www.junglepepperpizza.com; pizzas MK1100-1400; ☒ 10.30am-2.30pm & 4.30-8.30pm) This popular takeaway pizza shop shares a big shaded courtyard at the Chichiri Shopping Mall with a number other fast-food joints. Toppings veer towards the exotic, such as mango chicken. You can also buy pizza by the slice for MK400.

our pick **Mandala Cafe** (Mackie Rd; light meals MK1200; ☒ 8.30am-4.30pm Mon-Fri, to 12.30pm Sat; ☒ ☒) Sit on a breezy stone terrace or in the garden at a table fashioned from a tree trunk at this chilled cafe in the grounds of Mandala House (p949). Regulars love the freshly brewed coffee and homemade 'cakes of the day' (MK500).

Drinking

Cappineros (☎ 0999-939260; Victoria Ave) A lively, friendly pub with a large beer garden that puts on regular music and theme events. It's next to the Kairo International Casino. Look for the sign – it's down the drive.

Twiga Lounge (☎ 0999-966507; Uta Waleza Centre, Kidney Cres) This bar and nightclub is popular with young Malawian professionals who come here to down cocktails and dance to the country's top DJs.

Getting There & Away

AIR

Blantyre's Chileka Airport is about 15km north of the city centre.

Airline offices in Blantyre include **Air Malawi** (☎ 01-820811; Robins Rd; ☒ 7.30am-4.30pm Mon-Fri, 8am-noon Sat), **KLM & Kenya Airways** (☎ 01-824524; Sunbird Mount Soche Hotel), **British Airways** (☎ 01-824333/519; Livingstone Towers, Glyn Jones Rd) and **South African Airways** (☎ 01-820627; Nico House, Stewart St).

BUS & MINIBUS

Blantyre's Wenela bus station is east of the centre on Mulomba Pl. National Bus Company and AXA City Trouper buses run from here to Lilongwe (MK1200, four hours), Mzuzu (MK2000, nine to 10 hours), Monkey Bay (MK890, five to six hours) via Zomba (MK350, 1½ to two hours), Mulanje (MK400, 90 minutes) and Karonga (MK2800, 14 hours).

AXA Executive buses depart from the Automotive Centre at Ginnery Corner, where you'll also find its ticket office, and call at the Chichiri Shopping Centre and the car park outside Blantyre Lodge before departing from the city. They leave twice daily to Lilongwe (MK3100, four hours).

Long-distance minibuses go from the bus station in Limbe. Routes include Zomba (MK390, one hour) and Mulanje (MK450, 70 minutes).

The car park outside Blantyre Lodge is the pick-up and drop-off point for long-distance bus companies headed for Jo'burg. **Ingwe Coach** (☎ 01-822313) goes to Jo'burg at 8.30am on Tuesdays and Sundays (MK15,000, 25 hours). **KJ Transways** (☎ 01-914017) leaves for Jo'burg on Tuesdays and Saturdays at 7am (MK13,500, 25 hours).

Getting Around

TO/FROM THE AIRPORT

A taxi from the airport to the city costs around MK2000, but agree on a price with the driver first. If your budget doesn't include taxis, frequent local buses between the Wenela bus station and Chileka Township pass the airport gate. The fare is MK100.

BUS

Blantyre is a compact city, so it's unlikely you'll need to use public transport to get around, apart from the minibuses that shuttle along Chipembere Hwy between Wenela bus station and Limbe bus station. The one-way fare is MK80.

TAXI

You can find private-hire taxis at the Sunbird Mount Soche Hotel or at the bus stations. A taxi across the city centre is around MK500;

MALAWI

between the city centre and Wenela bus station costs from MK600; and from Blantyre to Limbe costs around MK1200.

MT MULANJE

A huge hulk of twisted granite rising from the surrounding plains, Mt Mulanje towers over 3000m high. The mountain is covered in dense green valleys, and rivers drop from sheer cliffs to form dazzling waterfalls. The locals call it the 'Island in the Sky' and on misty days (and there are many of those) it's easy to see why – the mountain is shrouded in a cotton-wool haze, its highest peaks bursting through the cloud to touch the heavens.

For hikers, it's worth remembering that Mulanje is a big mountain with notoriously unpredictable weather. Even during the dry season, it's not uncommon to get rain, cold winds and thick mists, which make it easy to get lost. Between May and August, periods of low cloud and drizzle can last several days and temperatures drop below freezing.

Information

Hiking on Mt Mulanje is controlled by the **Likhubula Forestry Office** (PO Box 50, Mulanje; ⊙ 7.30am-noon & 1-5pm), at the small village of Likhubula, about 15km from Mulanje town. Entry fees are MK100 per person, vehicle entry is MK200 and the forestry office car park costs MK100 a day.

Also good for information is the **Mulanje Infocentre** (☎ 01-466466/506; infomulanje@malawi.net) based at Chitakale Trading Centre, on the corner of Phalombe Rd. It carries a good selection of books and maps and also rents out sleeping bags (MK500 per day), thermal sleeping pads (MK250 per day) and tents (MK700 per day). It can also arrange mountain guides and porters.

Activities

There are about six main hiking routes up and down Mulanje. The three main ascent routes go from Likhubula: the Chambe Plateau Path (also called the Skyline Path), the Chapaluka Path and the Lichenya Path. Other routes, more often used for the descent: Thuchila Hut to Lukulezi Mission; Sombani Hut to Fort Lister Gap; and Minunu Hut to Lujeri Tea Estate. A guide is not mandatory, but hikers need to register with the Likhubula Forestry Office before starting out.

Sleeping

At the foot of Mt Mulanje is Mulanje town, which has several places to stay. At the village of Likhubula, about 15km from Mulanje town, are a couple more options.

CCAP Guesthouse (Likhubula; campsite MK800, chalets per person MK2000) At the CCAP Mission, after the reserve gates, with cosy rooms, self-catering chalets and camping.

Likhubula Forest Lodge (☎ 01-467737; campsite per person MK900, s/d without bathroom bed & breakfast MK5000/7300, s/d incl half board MK6800/10,800, s/d incl breakfast MK5800/8200, half board MK7700/11,800, whole lodge MK36,000) At Likhubula, after the reserve gates, this lodge has simple clean rooms including two with bathroom.

Limbani Lodge (☎ in Mulanje town 01-466390; standard r MK1000, s/d VIP with fan MK3000/3500) This lodge has poky miserable standard rooms down a long, dark corridor, but the VIP rooms are light, with plenty of room and small kitchenettes. Take the turn-off opposite the bus station near the school for the blind.

On the mountain there are several **forestry huts** (camping per adult/child MK400/200, huts per adult/child MK700/350). Each is equipped with benches, tables and open fires with plenty of wood. You provide your own food, cooking gear, candles, sleeping bag and stove, and a caretaker chops wood, lights fires and brings water, for which a small tip should be paid. You can only camp near the huts when they are full.

Getting There & Away

AXA buses go between Mulanje town and Blantyre (MK400, 90 minutes), as do minibuses (MK450, 70 minutes). The dirt road to Likhubula turns off the main sealed Blantyre–Mulanje road at Chitikale, 2km west of the centre of Mulanje town; follow the signpost to Phalombe. If you're coming from Blantyre on the bus, ask to be dropped at Chitikale. From here, irregular *matola* run to Likhubula (MK150). Alternatively, you can walk (10km, two to three hours).

ZOMBA
pop 87,300

The capital of Malawi from 1891 until the mid-1970s, Zomba's past is still much in evidence, and the town's gently sloping hills are home to a number of faded old colonial beauties, including the impressive State House. East of the main road is the town's friendly commercial centre, with a market, banks and currency-exchange bureaus.

Rising some 6000ft behind the town, Zomba Plateau is a gorgeous highland paradise – Malawi style. Criss-crossed by streams, lakes and tumbling waterfalls, and covered in pine forest and patches of woodland, you half expect Little Red Riding Hood to come skipping out from between the trees – except here she'd be hiding from leopards, not the Big Bad Wolf.

The plateau can be explored on driveable tracks by car or on foot on the numerous winding paths and trails that ring and cross the mountain. There's no bus up here, so you'll have to hitch or take a taxi (around MK1500).

Sleeping & Eating

Forest Campsite (campsite per person MK400) An aptly named spot with toilets and wood-fired hot showers all among large pine trees. It's fantastic in the sunshine but feels a bit spooky on misty days – and of those there are plenty.

Ndindeya Motel (☎ 01-525558; s/d/executive MK1850/2350/2950) A good budget option right in the heart of the action and a short walk from the bus station. Large rooms are spread out across two rambling, bright buildings and all rates include breakfast.

Annie's Lodge (☎ 01-527002; Livingstone Rd; standard/superior/executive/apt MK6995/8995/11,195/16,995; ☐ ☎) Annie's jumble of faded colonial buildings hides a selection of perfectly modern rooms, with DSTV, air-con and large bathrooms.

ourpick Ku Chawe Inn (☎ 01-514237; r superior/deluxe US$80/110; ☐) Perched on the hillside like a mist-soaked Tuscan palace, red-brick Ku Chawe Inn is by far the nicest place to stay around these parts. After a hard day of hiking you can head back to your room, sink into a comfy chair and enjoy the astounding views from massive windows, perhaps toasting your feet by the warmth of your own stone fireplace.

Tasty Bites (Kamuzu Hwy; dishes from MK500; ☺ 8am-8pm Wed-Mon) Flavoursome Pakistani curries, *shwarmas,* samosas and Indian tea are all on the menu along with more standard meals such as burgers and steaks. The large dining room has a noticeboard with information about the local area and beyond.

Getting There & Away

Zomba is on a main route between Lilongwe and Blantyre. AXA buses run to/from Zomba and Lilongwe (MK1000, five to six hours), Blantyre (MK350, 1½ to two hours) and Liwonde (MK200, one hour). Minibuses go every hour or so to Limbe (MK390, one hour) and also leave to Lilongwe (MK1200, four to five hours) and Liwonde (MK250, 45 minutes).

LIWONDE

Straddling the Shire River, the small town of Liwonde is one of the gateways to Liwonde National Park. The river divides the town in two; to the east you'll find the main bus stations, the market, supermarkets and the train station. West of the river are several tourist lodges.

Shire Camp (☎ 0884-327794; campsite per person MK1000, chalet incl breakfast MK3500) An excellent budget choice with a fabulous setting bang on the river. You can either pitch a tent in its campsite or bed down in one of its kooky thatched chalets. Shire Camp is on the river's north bank. Take the dirt road on the right just before the National Bank.

Hippo View Lodge (☎ 01-542822, 542255; www.hippoviewlodge.com; s/d superior MK8900/13,800, s/d VIP MK11,400/17,300, chalet MK35,000; ☒ ℗ ☐ ☎) Turn right down the dirt road just before the National Bank and look out for the two hippos flanking the road just before the entrance. Set in sprawling, flower-filled grounds right next to the river this is the classiest and best-equipped joint in town.

Getting There & Away

Lakeshore AXA buses pass by Liwonde on their way up to Mangochi but most drop passengers at the turn-off and not in the town itself so you're better off using minibuses, which run regularly from Zomba (MK250, 45 minutes), Limbe (MK500, three hours) and Mangochi (MK450, two hours). You can also get a minibus to the Mozambique border at Nayuchi (MK850).

LIWONDE NATIONAL PARK

Though small in stature **Liwonde National Park** (per person car US$5/2) tops the list in visitor numbers and is Malawi's number-one wildlife destination. The Shire River dominates the 548-sq-km park – a wide, meandering stretch lined by thick undergrowth and tall, statuesque palms. Surrounding it are floodplains, woodland and parched scrub. Unsurprising then, that the park is prime hippo- and croc-spotting territory, and a favourite stomping ground for the abundant elephants.

MALAWI

Waterbucks are also common near the water, while beautiful sable and roan antelopes, zebras and elands populate the surreal flood plains in the east. Black rhinos are protected within a separate enclosure and there's a rich and colourful array of birdlife.

Sleeping

Places to stay in Liwonde remain open all year; you can reach them by boat even if rain closes some of the park tracks.

Chinguni Hills Lodge (☎ 0888-838159; www.chinguni. com; per person campsite/dm/tented chalet/main lodge without bathroom US$5/10/15/20, per person r/tent US$30/40; 🐘) Chinguni Hills lies in the south of the park, built in what was the old park warden's house. There are rooms in the main house as well as walk-in safari tents, a pool, a large viewing deck, dorms and a separate campsite.

Njobvu Cultural Village (☎ 0888-623530, through Mvuu Camp reception 01-542135; www.njobvuvillage.com; r per person US$6, incl full board & activities US$30) Sitting near the park's Makanga Gate, Njobvu offers visitors a rare opportunity to stay in a traditional Malawian village, sleeping in mud-brick huts. During the day you are invited to take part in the villagers' daily lives. All proceeds go directly to the community.

Mvuu Camp (☎ 01-771393/153; campsite per person US$10, all inclusive chalets per person US$250 🐘) Managed by **Wilderness Safaris** (www.wilderness -safaris.com), this camp is deep in the park's north on the banks of the river. Stone chalets have tented roofs, swish interiors and verandahs overlooking the river. There's also a swimming pool, which has helpful steps for hippos to get in and out.

Mvuu Wilderness Lodge (☎ 01-771393/153; all inclusive chalets per person US$400; 🐘) A short distance upriver from Mvuu Camp, this intimate lodge is full of romantic bush atmosphere. Sumptuous safari tents have huge beds and private balconies overlooking a waterhole. Need room service? Beat on the in-room drum.

Getting There & Away

The main park gate is 6km east of Liwonde town. There's no public transport beyond here. From the gate to Mvuu Camp is 28km along the park track (closed in the wet season), and a 4WD or high-clearance vehicle is recommended for this route.

Another way in for vehicles is via the dirt road (open all year) from Ulongwe, a village

between Liwonde town and Mangochi. This leads for 14km through local villages to the western boundary. A few kilometres inside the park is a car park and boat jetty, where a watchman hoists a flag to arrange a boat from Mvuu Camp to come and collect you.

For those without wheels, the best option is to get any bus or minibus between Liwonde town and Mangochi and get off at Ulongwe, where local boys wait by the bus stop and will take you by bicycle to the park gate (MK600).

MONKEY BAY

This small port is hidden behind the Cape Maclear headland. The town itself isn't particularly interesting but there are a couple of good places to stay should you end up here for a night or two. Monkey Bay has a market and a supermarket but no ATM or money exchange.

Sleeping

Mufasa Rustic Camp (☎ 0999-258959; campsite per person MK450) At just 400m from the harbour this beautiful beach spot offers hot showers, camping and rooms, and is electricity free. The owners arrange pickups from the *Ilala* Ferry by tuk-tuk.

Venice Beach Backpackers (campsite per person MK500, dm MK1120, s/d without bathroom MK2400/3200, r MK4000) This place, about 1.5km from the main road, is a worthy alternative to the lodges at Cape Maclear. There's a very clean stretch of beach, a chilled beach bar and a two-storey thatched building housing a selection of dorms and doubles as well as a top-floor viewing deck with plenty of hammocks.

Getting There & Away

From Lilongwe, AXA buses go to Monkey Bay, usually via Mua and the southern lakeshore (MK1000, five to six hours). You're probably better off going by minibus to Salima (MK450, one hour), from where you might find a minibus or *matola* going direct to Monkey Bay.

From Blantyre take the bus that travels via Liwonde (MK890, five to six hours). You could also go by minibus (MK1000, four to five hours), but you'll need to leave early and you might have to change at Mangochi.

From Monkey Bay, a *matola* ride to Cape Maclear should cost MK300. Although not far away, it can take forever to get there and you could have to wait hours for a *matola* departure.

CAPE MACLEAR

Cape Maclear sits on a long finger of golden beach at the southern end of Lake Malawi, shielded by granite hills and thick green bush, with the alluring Domwe and Thumbi Islands anchored offshore in a glassy blue bay. It's one of southern Africa's legendary backpackers hang-outs and the kind of place where plans are forgotten as you sink into a daily rhythm of sunbathing and snorkelling.

Sights & Activities

Much of the area around Cape Maclear, including several offshore islands, is part of **Lake Malawi National Park** (per person/car US$5/1), one of the few freshwater aquatic parks in Africa, and designated a Unesco World Heritage Site back in 1986. The park headquarters are just inside the gate where you'll also find a **Visitor Centre**, which doubles up as a small **museum and aquarium** (7.30am-noon & 1-5pm Mon-Sat, 10am-noon & 1-4pm Sun).

Guides registered with the Cape Maclear Tour Guides Association can organise a number of half- and full-day trips involving snorkelling. For example, trips to Thumbi Island will cost around US$30 per person. If you prefer to go snorkelling on your own, many places rent gear (rates start at about US$5).

Otter Point, around 1km from the National Park headquarters, is a small peninsula that is popular with snorkellers and more so with fish.

For diving, go to **Kayak Africa** (0999-942661; www.kayakafrica.net) or **Danforth Yachting** (0999-960077/960770; www.danforthyachting.com). Both offer PADI open-water courses for around US$300, as well as casual dives for experienced divers.

Sleeping

Malambe Camp (0999-258959; campsite per person MK450, dm MK700, standing tent MK800, hut MK1000) Choose from simple huts constructed from reed mats, permanent tents (with proper beds inside) or a large, light, reed dorm. There's also space for camping, spotless showers and toilets, a self-catering kitchen, barbecues and a bar.

Mufasa Backpacker Lodge Cape Maclear (0999-374631; www.mufasamalawi.com; campsite US$3.50, dm US$10, r US$23, f US$40;) Another top budget choice, with neat twins, doubles and dorms grouped around a cosy courtyard restaurant. There are hammocks to swing in and a thatched chill-out area right on the water.

Gecko Lounge (01-599188, 0999-787322; www.geckolounge.net; dm US$10, d US$55, chalet US$80;) Gecko is one of the best places to stay in Cape Maclear. Jaunty orange thatched huts contain a dorm, double rooms and self-catering chalets, all with solid beds, fans, nets and wooden lockboxes, which are large enough to stash all your valuables. Hammocks and cane pods swing from the trees, and there's an attractive bar-lounge right on the water that hosts regular parties and live music.

our pick Kayak Africa (www.kayakafrica.net, www.wilderness-safaris.com) Tour operator Kayak Africa own two incredibly romantic lodges just offshore Cape Maclear on deserted Domwe and Mumbo Islands. Domwe Island Adventure Camp (US$50 per person including kayak and snorkelling gear) is the smaller and most rustic of the two, with furnished safari tents sharing ecoshowers and toilets, as well as a beautiful, staggered open-air dining area. Mumbo Camp (US$180 per person including meals, kayak and snorkelling gear) has tents with bathrooms on wooden platforms, tucked beneath trees and above rocks, all with decks and outrageous views.

Eating & Drinking

Thomas's Grocery Restaurant and Bar (dishes from MK400) Meals are the usual fish or chicken and chips or *nshima,* with the odd nod to backpackers in the way of pasta and burgers. Seating is outdoors and is a suitable place to watch the village go by.

Mgoza Restaurant and Bar (dishes MK700-1000; 10am-late) Come here for a relaxed beer or cocktail. Inside is slinky, low, Moroccan-style seating, outside are cosy seats in the grass, and upstairs there's a viewing deck perfect for sundowners.

Boma/Hiccups Pub (dishes MK700-1000; noon-late) Sit in a window seat or at tables out on the street to watch the village action, enjoy tasty food in the courtyard restaurant at the back, or pull up a bar stool at the English-style bar. There's a DJ booth up in the eaves and a 1st-floor dance floor that gets packed at the weekends.

Getting There & Away

By public transport, first get to Monkey Bay, from where a *matola* should cost MK300. If you're driving from Mangochi, the dirt road to Cape Maclear (signposted) turns west off the main road, about 5km before Monkey Bay.

MALAWI

Be warned, however, that it's a bumpy ride and unless you're in a 4WD or high-clearance vehicle, it'll be slow going.

From Cape Maclear, if you're heading for Senga Bay, ask around about chartering a boat. It will cost around US$180. *Matola* leave for Monkey Bay from around 6am in the morning on a fill-up-and-go basis and take about an hour (MK300). From there you can get onward transport.

MALAWI DIRECTORY

ACCOMMODATION

In almost every town there is a council or government rest house. Prices vary from as little as US$2 up to around US$8 per double, but conditions vary from bare and basic to disgusting. In national parks and along the lakeshore, many places offer camping for around US$3 to US$10.

You'll find backpacker hostels all over the country. Prices range from US$5 to US$10 for a dorm, to US$10 to US$15 per person for a double or triple with shared facilities, to around US$30 for a room with bathroom. Camping at hostels is about US$3 to US$8.

Midrange hotels and lodges range from about US$40 to US$90 per double, including taxes, usually with private bathroom and breakfast, sometimes with air-con.

Standard top-end hotels in the big cities and at beach resorts range from US$100 to US$250 for a double room, with in-room facilities such as private bathroom, TV, air-con and telephone.

ACTIVITIES

Lake Malawi is one of the best freshwater diving areas in the world – and one of the cheapest places to learn how to dive. Places where you can hire scuba gear and learn to dive include Nkhata Bay, Cape Maclear, Likoma Island and Senga Bay. Kayaking is available at Cape Maclear and Nkhata Bay.

The main areas for hiking are Nyika and Mulanje. Other areas include Zomba, and various smaller peaks around Blantyre. Mulanje is Malawi's main rock-climbing area, with some spectacular routes (including the longest in Africa).

The main area for horse riding is the Nyika Plateau, which lends itself perfectly to travel on horseback. If you prefer nonanimated transport, Nyika's hilly landscape and good

---

PRACTICALITIES

■ Malawi's main newspapers are the *Daily Times,* the *Malawi News,* and the *Nation.* The *Chronicle* is a smaller publication but with a strong independent voice.

■ Malawi's national radio station is the Malawi Broadcasting Corporation. Commercial stations include Capital FM.

■ Television Malawi was launched in 1999 and consists mostly of imported programs, news, regional music videos and religious programs. International satellite channels are available in most midrange and top-end hotels.

---

network of dirt tracks are also great for mountain biking.

BOOKS

Day Outings from Lilongwe and *Day Outings from Blantyre,* both published by the Wildlife Society of Malawi, are highly recommended. They are well written and researched, and include suggestions on places to visit, things to see and local walks in the region.

Venture to the Interior, by Laurens van der Post, describes the author's 'exploration' of Mt Mulanje and the Nyika Plateau in the 1940s, although in reality this was hardly trailblazing stuff.

BUSINESS HOURS

Banks 8am to 3.30pm Monday to Friday.
Offices 8am to 5pm Monday to Friday.
Post and telephone offices 7.30am to 5pm Monday to Friday.
Restaurants Breakfast 7am to 10am, lunch noon to 2pm, dinner 6pm to 9.30pm.
Shops 8am to 5pm Monday to Friday and Saturday morning. In smaller towns, shops and stalls are open most days but keep informal hours.

DANGERS & ANNOYANCES

Reports of travellers being robbed in Lilongwe, Blantyre and the resorts of Cape Maclear and Nkhata Bay have increased. However, incidents are still rare compared with other countries, and violence is not the norm.

Potential dangers while at Lake Malawi include encountering a hippo or crocodile, but for travellers the chances of being attacked are extremely remote.

EMBASSIES & CONSULATES
The following countries have diplomatic representation in Malawi:

Germany (☎ 01-772555; Convention Dr, City Centre, Lilongwe)

Mozambique Lilongwe embassy (☎ 01-774100; Convention Dr, City Centre, Lilongwe); Limbe consulate (☎ 01-843189; 1st fl, Celtel Bldg, Rayner Ave, Limbe)

South Africa (☎ 01-773722, sahe@malawi.net; Kang'ombe Bldg, City Centre, Lilongwe)

UK Lilongwe High Commission (☎ 01-772400; off Kenyatta Rd, City Centre, Lilongwe); Blantyre Consulate (Hanover Ave, Blantyre)

USA (☎ 01-773166; Convention Dr, City Centre, Lilongwe)

Zambia (☎ 01-772590; Convention Dr, City Centre, Lilongwe)

HOLIDAYS
Public holidays in Malawi:

New Year's Day 1 January
John Chilembwe Day 15 January
Martyrs' Day 3 March
Easter March/April – Good Friday, Holy Saturday and Easter Monday
Labour Day 1 May
Freedom Day 14 June
Republic Day 6 July
Mother's Day October – second Monday
National Tree Planting Day December – second Monday
Christmas Day 25 December
Boxing Day 26 December

MONEY
Malawi's unit of currency is the Malawi kwacha (MK). This is divided into 100 tambala (t).

Bank notes include MK200, MK100, MK50, MK20, MK10 and MK5. Coins include MK1, 50t, 20t, 10t, 5t and 1t.

At big hotels and other places that actually quote in US dollars you can pay in hard currency or kwacha at the prevailing exchange rate.

Standard Bank and National Bank ATMs are the best bet for foreigners wishing to draw money from their home account. Standard Bank accepts foreign Visa, MasterCard, Cirrus and Maestro cards. National Bank ATMs only take Visa cards.

You can use Visa cards at many large hotels and top-end restaurants, though there may be a surcharge of around 5%.

POST
Post in and out of Malawi is a bit of a lottery. Some letters get from Lilongwe to London in three days, others take three weeks. Post offices in Blantyre and Lilongwe have poste restante services.

TELEPHONE
Malawi does not have area codes, but all landline numbers begin with ☎ 01, so whatever number you dial within the country will have eight digits. Telephone calls within Malawi are inexpensive; around MK50 per minute depending on the distance. Calls to mobiles within Malawi cost around MK70 per minute.

Mobile phone prefixes are ☎ 0888 or ☎ 0999 and the two major networks are TNM and Zain. SIM cards are readily available. They cost around MK700 and include a small amount of airtime. You can buy top-up cards from street vendors, at supermarkets and petrol stations, and they cost anything from MK35 to MK2800 depending on how much airtime you need.

TOURIST INFORMATION
There are tourist information offices in Blantyre and Lilongwe but you're much better off asking for advice from your hostel or hotel, or from a travel agency. Outside Malawi, tourism promotion is handled by UK-based **Malawi Tourism** (☎ 0115-982 1903; fax 0115-981 9418; www. malawitourism.com).

VISAS
Visas are not necessary for citizens of Commonwealth countries, the USA and most European nations (except Switzerland). Visas are limited to 30 days, although extensions are easy to get. You can get visa extensions at immigration offices in Blantyre or Lilongwe or at regional police stations. It's straightforward and free.

TRANSPORT IN MALAWI

GETTING THERE & AWAY
Air
Kamuzu International Airport (LLW; ☎ 01-700766), located 21km north of the Lilongwe city centre, handles the majority of international flights to the country. Flights from South Africa, Kenya, Zambia and Tanzania also land in Blantyre at **Chileka International Airport** (BLZ; ☎ 01-694244). The country's national carrier is Air Malawi.

AIRLINES FLYING TO/FROM MALAWI

Air Malawi (QM; ☎ 01-820811/773680; www.airmalawi.com) has a decent regional network, with flights heading to Dar es Salaam, Johannesburg, Nairobi, Lusaka and Harare from Blantyre and Lilongwe.

South African Airways (SA; ☎ 01-620617/772242; www.flysaa.com) flies twice weekly between Blantyre and Jo'burg, and five times weekly between Lilongwe and Jo'burg (with connections to Durban, Cape Town etc).

Kenya Airways (KQ; ☎ 01-774227/624/524; www.kenya-airways.com) flies four times per week to/from Nairobi and six times a week to/from Lusaka.

Ethiopian Airways (ET; ☎ 01-771002/771308; www.flyethiopian.com) flies four times a week from Addis Ababa.

Land

MOZAMBIQUE

South

The quickest way to reach Mozambique south of the Zambezi is to take a minibus to the Mozambique border crossing at Zóbuè (*zob*-way; MK500) and then a minibus to Tete (US$2), from where buses go to Beira and Maputo. You could also get a Blantyre–Harare bus to drop you at Tete and then get a bus to Beira or Maputo. See p979 for information on the Dedza border post, 85km southeast of Lilongwe.

Central

If you are heading for central Mozambique, there are several buses per day from Blantyre to Nsanje (MK850), or all the way to the Malawi border at Marka (*ma*-ra-ka; MK900). It's a few kilometres between the border crossings – you can walk or take a bicycle taxi – and you can change money on the Mozambique side. From here pick-ups go to Mutarara, Nhamilabue and Vila de Sena.

North

There are three border crossings from Malawi into northern Mozambique: Muloza, from where you can reach Mocuba in Mozambique, and Nayuchi and Chiponde, both of which lead to Cuamba in Mozambique.

Regular buses run from Blantyre, via Mulanje, to Muloza (MK750). From here, you walk 1km to the Mozambique border crossing at Milange, from where it's another few kilometres into Milange *vila* (town) itself. From Milange there's usually a *chapa* (pick-up or converted minibus) or truck about every other day in the dry season to Mocuba, where you can find transport on to Quelimane or Nampula.

Further north, minibuses and *matola* run a few times per day between Mangochi and the border crossing at Chiponde (MK800). It's then 7km to the Mozambique border crossing at Mandimba and the best way to get there is by bicycle taxi (US$2). Mandimba has a couple of *pensãos* (inexpensive hotels), and there's at least one vehicle daily, usually a truck, between here and Cuamba (US$4).

The third option is to go by minibus or passenger train from Liwonde to the border at Nayuchi (MK850). You can then take a *chapa* from the Mozambique side of the border to Cuamba.

SOUTH AFRICA

There are a number of bus companies running services from Lilongwe to Jo'burg, including **Vaal Africa** (☎ 0999-200086) and **Chita One** (☎ 01-622313/829879), both of which have offices near Old Town Mall. From Blantyre, try **Ingwe Coach** (☎ 01-822313) – buses depart from the car park outside Blantyre Lodge.

TANZANIA

Three buses a week (Tuesday, Saturday and Sunday) depart from Devil St in Lilongwe for Dar es Salaam. These buses also pick up and drop off in Mzuzu and Mbeya and are handy for going between northern Malawi and southern Tanzania.

If you're going in stages, buses and minibuses run between Mzuzu and Karonga (MK800, three to four hours), from where you can get a taxi to the Songwe border crossing (MK500). It's 200m across the bridge to the Tanzanian border crossing.

Once you're on the Tanzanian side of the border, minibuses and bicycle taxis travel the 5km distance to Kyela, from where you can get a bus to Dar es Salaam.

ZAMBIA

There are four direct buses per week (two on Tuesday and two on Friday) between Lilongwe and Lusaka (MK6000), also departing from Devil St – the journey takes at least 12 hours. Regular minibuses run between Lilongwe and Mchinji (MK400). From here, it's 12km to the border. Local shared taxis shuttle between Mchinji and the border post for around MK200 per person, or MK1000 for the whole car.

From the Zambian side of the border crossing, shared taxis run to Chipata (US$2), which is about 30km west of the border.

Lake
MOZAMBIQUE

The Lake Malawi steamboat *Ilala* (see below) stops at Metangula on the Mozambican mainland. If you're planning a visit, you must get your passport stamped at the immigration post in Chipyela (the main village) on Likoma Island.

Another way to get to the Mozambican lakeshore is to take a dhow (local sailing boat) from Likoma Island to Cóbuè.

GETTING AROUND
Air

Air Malawi (☎ 01-772123, 753181, 788415; www.airmalawi. com) operates regular domestic flights between Lilongwe and Blantyre (one way MK12,000).

Nyassa Air Taxi (☎ 01-761443; www.nyassa.mw) provides charter flights to airstrips around the country in five- and seven-seater aircraft.

Boat

The **Ilala ferry** (☎ 01-587311; ilala@malawi.net) chugs passengers and cargo up and down Lake Malawi once a week in each direction. Travelling between Monkey Bay in the south and Chilumba in the north, it makes 12 stops at lakeside villages and towns in between. The whole trip, from one end of the line to the other, takes about three days. The official schedules are detailed in the table (only selected ports are shown).

Northbound port	Arrival	Departure
Monkey Bay	-	10am (Fri)
Chipoka	1pm	4pm (Fri)
Nkhotakota	midnight	2am (Sat)
Metangula	6am	8am (Sat)
Likoma Island	1.30pm	6pm (Sat)
Nkhata Bay	1am	5am (Sun)
Ruarwe	10.15am	11.15am (Sun)
Chilumba	5pm (Sun)	-

Southbound port	Arrival	Departure
Chilumba	-	1am (Mon)
Ruarwe	6.45am	8am (Mon)
Nkhata Bay	12.45pm	8pm (Mon)
Likoma Island	3.15am	6.15am (Tue)
Metangula	noon	2pm (Tue)
Nkhotakota	5.30pm	7.30pm (Tue)
Chipoka	3.30am	7.30am (Wed)
Monkey Bay	10.30am (Wed)	-

The *Ilala* has three classes. Cabin class was once luxurious and the cabins are still in reasonable condition. The spacious 1st-class deck is most popular with travellers, due largely to the sociable bar. Economy covers the entire lower deck and is dark and crowded, and engine fumes permeate from below.

Reservations are usually required for cabin class. For other classes, tickets are sold only when the boat is sighted.

SAMPLE ROUTES & FARES

All of the following sample fares are from Nkhata Bay.

Destination	Cabin (US$)	1st class (US$)	Economy (US$)
Likoma Island	35	20	7
Metangula	50	35	8
Monkey Bay	111	65	15

Bus & Minibus

Malawi's main bus company is **AXA Coach Services** (☎ 01-876000; agma@agmaholdings.net), which operates three different classes. Executive buses provide a luxury nonstop service with air-con, TV and toilet. Services operate between Blantyre and Lilongwe twice a day.

AXA Luxury Coach and City Trouper services are the next in line. These buses have air-con and reclining seats as well as TVs, but don't have toilets. They ply the route between Blantyre and Karonga, stopping at all the main towns with limited stops elsewhere.

Lastly there are the country commuter buses. These buses have the most extensive network but they are also the slowest. Commuter buses are handy for backpackers as they cover the lakeshore route.

There are several other private bus companies that operate around Malawi, including Coachline and Zimatha. Most of these operate on a fill-up-and-go basis.

There are also local minibus services around towns and to outlying villages, or along the roads that the big buses can't manage. All of these operate on a fill-up-and-go basis.

In rural areas, the frequency of buses and minibuses drops dramatically – sometimes to nothing. In cases like this, the 'bus' is often a truck or pick-up, with people just piled in the back. In Malawi this form of transport is called a *matola*.

Car & Motorcycle

The majority of main routes are good-quality sealed roads, though off the main routes road are sometimes potholed, making driving slow, difficult and dangerous. Secondary roads are usually graded dirt and also vary in condition. Rural routes are not so good, and after heavy rain they are often impassable, sometimes for weeks. Several of the lodges along the lakeshore have poor access roads that need a 4WD. The same goes for the country's national parks and wildlife reserves.

Rental companies in Malawi include:

Avis (☎ in Lilongwe 01-756103/756105, in Blantyre 01-892368) Also has offices at Lilongwe and Blantyre airports and at some large hotels.

Sputnik Rent-a-Car (☎ 01-761563; www.sputnik-car-hire.mw; Lilongwe)

You need a full driver's licence (International Driving Permit is not necessary) and companies normally require a minimum age of 23 and two years' driving experience.

Train

Trains run every Wednesday between Blantyre and Balaka (MK500), but passengers rarely use them as road transport on this route is quicker and cheaper. The service of most use to travellers is the twice-weekly train service (Tuesday and Saturday) between Limbe and the Mozambique border at Nsanje (MK800).

Mozambique

Mozambique is one of the continent's insider tips, with long, stunning beaches, excellent diving and snorkelling, and magical offshore islands. Explore the crystal-clear depths around the Bazaruto Archipelago. Slip silently on a dhow through azure waters or laze under the palms in the Quirimbas Archipelago. Paint your face with *musiro* or watch the silversmiths at work on historical Ibo Island. Take an off-beat safari in the wilds of Gorongosa National Park. Wander along cobbled streets past whitewashed colonial-era buildings on Mozambique Island. Sip a cafe espresso at one of Maputo's lively sidewalk cafes (or maybe a *caipirinha* at one of its jazz bars). And dance the night away to the country's trademark *marrabenta* music.

Throughout the country (and in contrast to its more straight-laced neighbours, all of which are former British colonies or protectorates), Mozambique's modern face reflects a unique fusion of African, Arabic, Indian and Portuguese influences. Its cuisine is spicier, its rhythms more tropical and its pace more laid-back.

If you're inclined to something tamer, stick to the south, where roads and transport links (especially with neighbouring South Africa) are good and accommodation options abound. For more adventure, cross over the Zambezi into the wild north, one of Africa's last frontiers. Getting around here takes time, but the coastal panoramas and the islands, the sense of space and the sheer adventure of travel make the journey well worthwhile.

FAST FACTS

- **Area** 800,000 sq km
- **ATMs** In all major towns
- **Borders** Malawi, South Africa, Swaziland, Tanzania, Zambia and Zimbabwe
- **Budget** US$30 to US$150 per day
- **Capital** Maputo
- **Languages** Portuguese and 20-plus African languages
- **Money** Metical nova família; US$1 = Mtc25, €1 = Mtc45
- **Population** 21 million
- **Seasons** Dry (May to November), wet (December to April)
- **Telephone** Country code ☎ 258; international access code ☎ 00
- **Time** GMT/UTC +2
- **Visa** US$20 to US$70 for 30 days; issued at most border posts for US$25

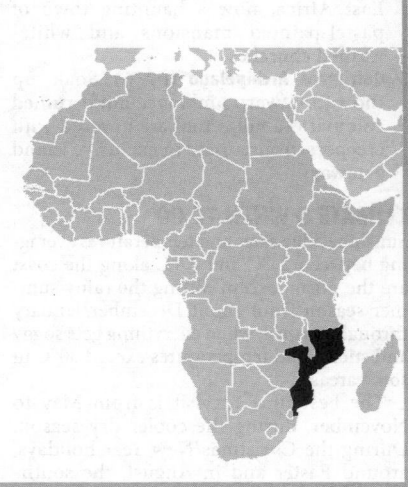

MOZAMBIQUE

HOW MUCH?

- **Plate of grilled prawns** US$12
- **Single-day dive** US$45
- **Short taxi ride** US$4
- **Day dhow safari** from US$40
- **Maputo–Inhambane bus fare** US$14

LONELY PLANET INDEX

- **1L petrol** US$1.20
- **1.5L bottled water** US$1.20
- **2M beer** US$1.60
- **Souvenir T-shirt** US$12
- **Plate of xima and sauce** US$2

HIGHLIGHTS

- **Maputo** (p965) Explore lively sidewalk cafes, pumping salsa bars, flame-tree-lined streets, and dynamic art and cultural scenes.
- **Bazaruto Archipelago** (p972) Swim and snorkel in a quintessential tropical paradise with turquoise waters full of colourful fish.
- **Tofo** (p971) Stroll past white sand dunes and dive with manta rays in this party-time town.
- **Mozambique Island** (p974) Delve into the past in the former capital of Portuguese East Africa, now a haunting town of pastel-painted mansions and white-washed churches.
- **Quirimbas Archipelago** (p976) Soak up Ibo's time-warp ambience amid ruined colonial-era villas that are covered with creepers, or luxuriate in exclusive island getaways.

CLIMATE & WHEN TO GO

Sunshine, blue skies and temperatures averaging between 24°C and 27°C along the coast are the norm, except during the rainy summer season from about December/January through to April, when everything gets soggy and sticky, and temperatures exceed 30°C in some areas.

The best time to visit is from May to November, during the cooler dry season. During the Christmas/New Year holidays, around Easter and in August, the south-

ern resorts fill up; advance bookings are recommended.

ITINERARIES

- **One Week** In the south, spend several days enjoying Maputo's (p965) vibe before heading to Inhambane (p970) and Tofo (p971), or on to Vilankulo (p971) and the Bazaruto Archipelago (p972).
- **Two Weeks** Follow the one-week itinerary then continue north to Nampula (p974) and divide your remaining time between Mozambique Island (p974) and Pemba (p976), Ibo or elsewhere in the Quirimbas Archipelago (p976).
- **One Month** Follow the previous itineraries, but now with time for all the options mentioned, plus a detour to Gorongosa National Park (p973) en route north. Alternatively, from Nampula take the train west to Cuamba (p975), then continue on to Lichinga (p975) and Lake Niassa (p975).

HISTORY

While Europeans were still struggling in the Dark Ages, the light of the ancient world had already fallen on Mozambique. From the 9th century AD, Mozambique's coast was part of a chain of civilised merchant kingdoms, visited by ships from as far afield as India, Arabia and Persia. Following the monsoon winds, they came to buy slaves, ivory, gold and spices. Muslim merchants intermarried with African families, and set up trading posts along the coast.

Sailing onto this scene came the first Europeans – Portuguese explorers such as Vasco da Gama. These 15th-century buccaneers pursued their trade interests with raids on coastal towns, and constructed forts to protect themselves from their English and Dutch rivals. In the 17th century, the Mozambican interior was divided into huge agricultural estates, nominally under the Portuguese crown but in fact run as private fiefdoms with their own slave armies.

In the late 19th century, Portugal and other European powers began a political arm wrestle for Africa. Britain began to eye Mozambique, and Portugal reacted by strengthening its previously lax colonial control. The country was so wild, however, that the government had to lease large areas of land to private firms, which soon became

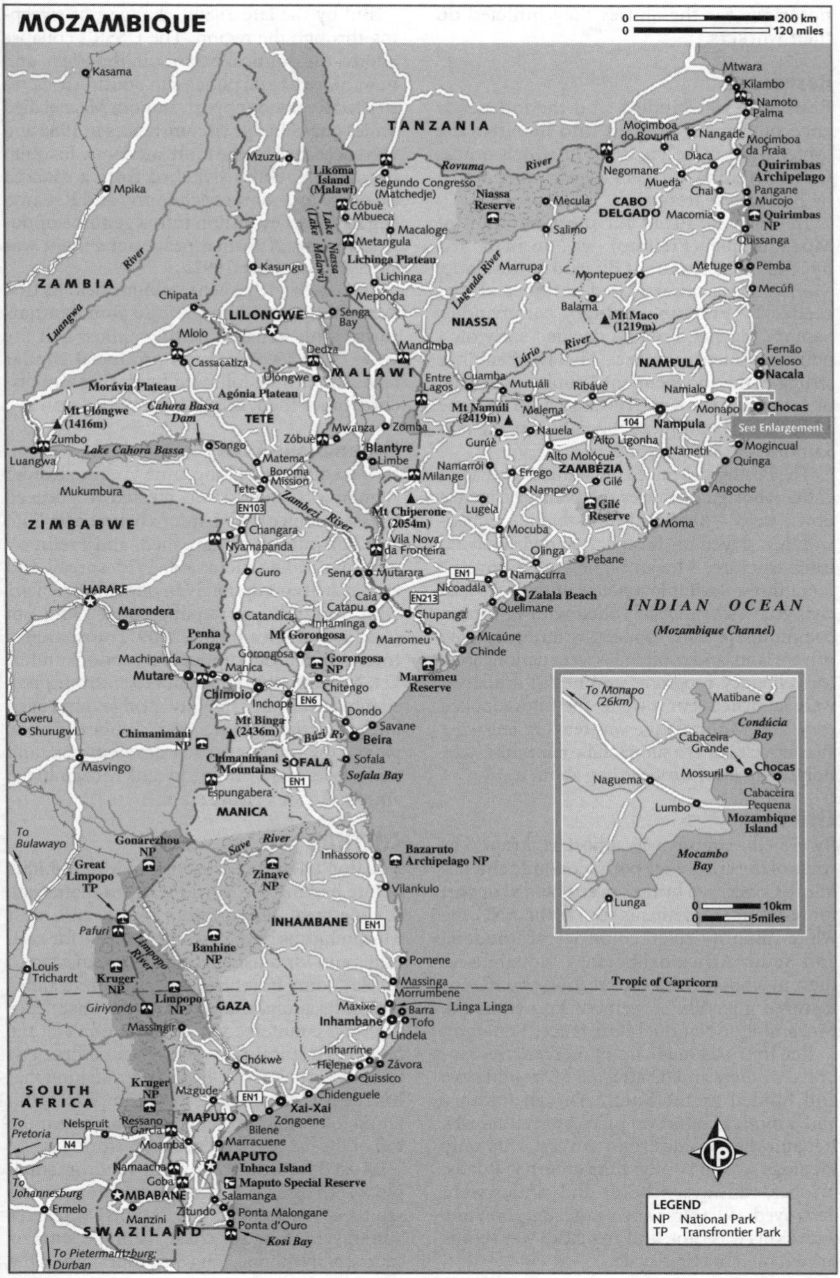
MOZAMBIQUE
0 200 km
0 120 miles
TANZANIA
ZAMBIA
MALAWI
ZIMBABWE
SOUTH AFRICA
SWAZILAND
INDIAN OCEAN
(Mozambique Channel)
Kasama
Mtwara
Kilambo
Namoto
Palma
Moçimboa do Rovuma
Nangade
Moçimboa da Praia
Mzuzu
Likoma Island (Malawi)
Rovuma
River
Negomane
Diaca
Quirimbas Archipelago
Segundo Congresso (Matchedje)
Mueda
Mpika
Niassa Reserve
Chai
Pangane
Cóbuè
Mecula
CABO DELGADO
Mucojo
Mbueca
Macomia
Quirimbas NP
Lake Niassa (Lake Malawi)
Macaloge
Salimo
Metangula
Quissanga
Lichinga Plateau
Kasungu
River
Lugenda River
Marrupa
Metuge
Pemba
Lichinga
Montepuez
ZAMBIA
Mecúfi
Chipata
Meponda
Luangwa
Senga Bay
Balama
LILONGWE
NIASSA
Mt Maco (1219m)
Mlolo
Mandimba
Lúrio
River
Fernão Veloso
Dedza
Cassacatiza
NAMPULA
Nacala
Ulongwe
MALAWI
Entre Lagos
Cuamba
Morávia Plateau
Mutuáli
Ribáuè
Namialo
Agónia Plateau
Mt Namúli (2419m)
Chocas
Mt Ulóngwe (1416m)
Cahora Bassa Dam
Malema
Monapo
TETE
104
Nampula
See Enlargement
Mwanza
Zomba
Zumbo
Zóbuè
Nauela
Alto Ligonha
Lake Cahora Bassa
Songo
Blantyre
Gurúè
Mogincual
Luangwa
Matema
Limbe
Alto Molócuè
Nametil
Quinga
Boroma Mission
Namarrói
ZAMBÉZIA
Milange
Errego
Mukumbura
Tete
Gilé
Nampevo
Angoche
Zambezi River
EN103
Mt Chiperone (2054m)
Lugela
Gilé Reserve
ZIMBABWE
Moma
Changara
Mocuba
Vila Nova da Fronteira
Nyamapanda
Olinga
Pebane
Guro
Sena
Mutarara
EN1
Namacurra
Nicoadala
HARARE
Caia
EN213
Zalala Beach
Catapu
Quelimane
Marondera
Chupanga
Catandica
Inhaminga
Penha Longa
Mt Gorongosa
Marromeu
Micaúne
Gorongosa
Chinde
Machipanda
Gorongosa NP
Marromeu Reserve
Manica
Mutare
Chimoio
Chitengo
Inchope
EN6
Gweru
Dondo
Shurugwi
Mt Binga (2436m)
Savane
Chimanimani NP
Búzi Rv
Beira
Sofala
Masvingo
Chimanimani Mountains
SOFALA
Sofala Bay
EN1
Espungabera
MANICA
To Bulawayo
Gonarezhou NP
Save River
Inhassoro
Bazaruto Archipelago NP
Great Limpopo TP
Zinave NP
Vilankulo
Pafuri
INHAMBANE
EN1
Limpopo River
Banhine NP
Pomene
Louis Trichardt
Kruger NP
Massinga
Tropic of Capricorn
Morrumbene
Limpopo NP
GAZA
Maxixe
Linga Linga
Giriyondo
Barra
Inhambane
Tofo
Massingir
Lindela
Inharrime
Chókwè
Helene
Závora
Quissico
SOUTH AFRICA
Kruger NP
Magude
Chidenguele
EN1
Xai-Xai
MAPUTO
Zongoene
To Pretoria
Nelspruit
Ressano Garcia
Bilene
N4
Marracuene
Moamba
MAPUTO
Namaacha
Inhaca Island
Goba
Maputo Special Reserve
To Johannesburg
MBABANE
Salamanga
Ermelo
Manzini
Zitundo
Ponta Malongane
Ponta d'Ouro
SWAZILAND
Kosi Bay
To Pietermaritzburg; Durban
To Monapo (26km)
Matibane
Condúcia Bay
Cabaceira Grande
Mossuril
Chocas
Naguema
Cabaceira Pequena
Lumbo
Mozambique Island
Mocambo Bay
Lunga
0 10km
0 5miles
LEGEND
NP National Park
TP Transfrontier Park

notorious for the abuses they inflicted on their workers.

Resistance

Resistance was kindled, and the independence movement erupted into life after the 'Mueda Massacre' in 1960, in which peacefully protesting villagers were gunned down by Portuguese troops.

In 1962 the Front for the Liberation of Mozambique (Frelimo) was formed, led by the charismatic Eduardo Mondlane. Mondlane was assassinated in 1969 and succeeded by Frelimo's military commander, Samora Machel. Frelimo decided early on a policy of violent resistance. Finally, after bitter struggle, the independent People's Republic of Mozambique was proclaimed on 25 June 1975, with Frelimo as the ruling party and Samora Machel as president.

The Portuguese pulled out virtually overnight –after sabotaging vehicles and pouring concrete down wells – and left Mozambique in chaos with few skilled professionals and virtually no infrastructure. Mozambique's new government threw itself into a policy of radical social change. Ties were established with European communist powers, cooperative farms replaced private land, and companies were nationalised. Mass literacy programs and health initiatives were launched. For a while, the future looked rosy, and Mozambique was fêted in left-wing Western circles as a successful communist state. Bob Dylan even wrote a song about it.

Civil War

By 1983 the country was almost bankrupt. The roots of the crisis were both economic and political. Concerned by the government's support for resistance movements such as the ANC, the white-minority-ruled countries of Rhodesia and South Africa deliberately 'destabilised' their neighbour with the creation of a manufactured guerrilla movement known as the Mozambique National Resistance (Renamo).

Renamo was made up of mercenaries, co-opted soldiers and disaffected Mozambicans, and funded by the South African military and a motley collection of Western interests. Renamo had no desire to govern – its only ideology was to paralyse the country. Roads, bridges, railways, schools and clinics were destroyed. Villagers were rounded up, anyone with skills was shot, and atrocities were committed on a massive scale.

But by the late 1980s, change was sweeping through the region. The USSR's collapse altered the political balance in the West, and new, more liberal policies in South Africa restricted Renamo support. Samora Machel died under questionable circumstances in 1986 and was succeeded by the more moderate Joaquim Chissano. Frelimo switched from a Marxist ideology to a market economy, and Renamo began a slow evolution into a genuine opposition party. A formal peace agreement was signed in October 1992.

In October 1994 Mozambique held its first democratic elections. Frelimo won, but narrowly, with Renamo netting almost half the votes. The 1999 election produced similar results, this time followed by rioting and discord. Since then, things have settled down.

Mozambique Today

In December 2004 long-time Frelimo insider Armando Guebuza was elected to succeed Chissano. Since then, tensions between Frelimo and Renamo have sharpened, and Frelimo's dominance has increased. Widespread and entrenched corruption is an ongoing problem, with Mozambique ranking equal 130th out of 180 countries in the 2009 Transparency International Corruption Perceptions Index. Yet, Mozambique continues to enjoy unprecedented peace and stability. Bridges have been built over the Rovuma and Zambezi Rivers, paving the way for further development, and most observers continue to rank Mozambique among Africa's rising stars.

CULTURE

You don't need to travel long in Mozambique before hearing the word *paciência* (patience). It's the great Mozambican virtue, and most Mozambicans have it in abundance – for each other and for outsiders. You'll be expected to display some in return, especially in dealings with officialdom, and Western-style impatience is always counterproductive. But don't let the languid, tropical pace sway you completely: underlying it is a rock-hard determination that has carried Mozambique from complete devastation following two decades of war to near the top of the list of Africa's success stories.

Most Mozambicans work tending small plots with cassava and other crops, and you'll see these *machambas* (farm plots) wherever you travel. Along the coast, fishing is a major source of livelihood. Yet while tourism and the economy are booming, life continues to be a struggle for many. HIV/AIDS (with infection rates over 20% in some areas) and malaria also take a heavy toll.

People

There are 16 main tribes, including the Makua and Makonde in the north and the Shangaan in the south. Although Mozambique is relatively free of tribal rivalries, there has long been an undercurrent of north–south difference, with geographically remote and independent-minded northerners often feeling neglected by the upwardly mobile denizens of powerhouse Maputo.

Once suppressed under the Marxist regime, religion now flourishes and most villages have a church, a mosque, or both. About 35% of Mozambicans are Christians, about 25% to 30% are Muslims – mostly in the north and along old trading routes – and the remainder follow traditional animist beliefs.

Arts & Crafts

Mozambicans are superb dancers, and experiencing the rhythms and moves is a chance not to be missed. Along the northern coast, watch for the Arabic-influenced *tufo,* and for the masked *mapiko* dancing of the Makonde.

Marrabenta is Mozambique's national music, and features a light, upbeat guitar-driven style and distinctive beat. New-generation groups to watch out for include Kapa Dêch and Mabulu, which fuses *marrabenta* rhythms with hip hop.

Among the most famous musical traditions are the Chopi *timbila* (marimba) orchestras, which are best seen around Quissico, north of Xai-Xai.

The late José Craveirinha (1922–2003) is Mozambique's greatest poet, and his work, including *Poem of the Future Citizen,* is recognised worldwide. The best-known contemporary author is Mia Couto, whose works include *Voices Made Night* and *Every Man is a Race.*

Mozambique's most famous painter is Malangatana, whose art is exhibited around the world. Makonde carving traditions flourish in the north.

FOOD & DRINK

Along the coast, tuck into a plate of giant *camarões* (prawns) or *lagosta* (crayfish), washed down with a cold Dois M (2M, Mozambique's favourite lager). Elsewhere the options include *xima* (maize porridge), *frango grelhado* (grilled chicken) and *matapa* (peanut and cassava-leaf stew). Freshly baked rolls are available everywhere.

Larger towns have restaurants, and many have sidewalk cafes where you can enjoy a light meal while watching the passing scene. For cheap local-style fast food, try the stalls *(barracas)* at markets, which offer plates of *xima* and sauce for about US$2.

Major towns all have supermarkets for self-catering.

ENVIRONMENT

A wide coastal plain rises to mountains and plateaus on the borders with Zimbabwe, Zambia and Malawi. Three of Africa's major rivers (the Zambezi, the Limpopo and the Rovuma) flow through Mozambique.

Mozambique has six national parks: Gorongosa (which is easy to reach and has rebounding wildlife populations), Limpopo (part of the Great Limpopo Transfrontier park, which also includes South Africa's Kruger), Banhine, Zinave, Bazaruto (famed for its corals and dugongs) and Quirimbas (encompassing northern offshore and coastal areas, and known for its diving).

Wildlife reserves include Niassa Reserve and Maputo Special Reserve; for hiking head to Chimanimani.

MAPUTO

pop 1.5 million

With its Mediterranean-style architecture, flame-tree-lined avenues, sidewalk cafes and waterside setting, Maputo is easily one of Africa's most attractive capitals. *Jellaba*-garbed men gather in doorways to chat, while colourfully clad women hawk seafood and spices at the massive Municipal Market and banana vendors loll on their carts in the shade. There are museums, shops and markets galore – don't miss spending time here before heading north.

ORIENTATION

Many businesses, the train station, banks, the post office and some budget accommodation are in the low-lying *baixa,* on or near Av 25 de Setembro, while embassies and most better hotels are about a 20-minute walk uphill from here in the city's more staid upper section, especially in and around the Sommerschield diplomatic and residential quarter. At the

MOZAMBIQUE

northern end of the seaside Av Marginal, 7km from the centre, are Bairro Triunfo and Costa do Sol, with a small beach (not good for swimming) and several places to sleep and eat.

INFORMATION
Bookshops
Livraria Europa-América (☎ 21-494692; 377 Av 24 de Julho) Next to the geology museum, with maps, English-language books and magazines.

Cultural Centres
Centro Cultural Franco-Moçambicano (☎ 21-314590; www.ccfmoz.com; Praça da Independência) Art exhibitions, music and dance performances, films, theatre and more.

Internet Access
Mundo's Internet Café (Av Julius Nyerere; per hr Mtc50; ☉ 8.30am-9pm Mon-Sat, 10am-4pm Sun) Next to Mundo's restaurant.
Pizza House Internet Café (Av Mao Tse Tung; per hr Mtc40; ☉ 8am-10pm) Upstairs at Pizza House (opposite).
Teledata (cnr Av 24 de Julho & Rua das Malotas; per hr Mtc30; ☉ 7.30am-8pm Mon-Fri, 9am-7pm Sat) Just west of Av Vladimir Lenine.

Medical Services
Clínica de Sommerschield (☎ 82-305 6240, 21-493924/5/6; 52 Rua Pereira do Lago; ☉ 24hr) Just off Av Kim Il Sung, with a lab and a doctor on call. Advance payment required (meticais, rand, dollars or Visa card).
Farmácia Capital (☎ 82-301 4055; ground fl, Franca Centro Comercial, cnr Avs 24 de Julho & Amilcar Cabral; ☉ 24hr)
Swedish Clinic (☎ 21-492922, emergencies 82-300 2610; www.indevelop.se/maputo.asp; 1128 Av Julius Nyerere)

Money
There are 24-hour ATMs all over town, including at the airport.
Millennium BIM (cnr Avs Mao Tse Tung & Tomás Nduda)
Standard Bank Headquarters (Praça 25 de Junho); branch (Av Julius Nyerere) Opposite Hotel Avenida.

Post & Telephone
Main post office (Av 25 de Setembro; ☉ 8am-6pm Mon-Sat, 9am-noon Sun) Talk-and-pay service is available 8am to 5pm weekdays (Mtc1 per impulse).

Travel Agencies
Dana Agency (☎ 21-484300; travel@dana.co.mz; 1170 Av Kenneth Kaunda) Domestic and international flight bookings.

Dana Tours (☎ 21-495514; info@danatours.net; 1170 Av Kenneth Kaunda) Midrange and upmarket travel arrangements countrywide.

DANGERS & ANNOYANCES
Walking around central Maputo during daytime hours is generally safe, and most tourists visit the city without mishap. However, be vigilant when out and about, avoid isolating situations and avoid the areas between Av Patrice Lumumba and Av 25 de Setembro, between Av Friedrich Engels and Av Marginal, and Av Marginal between Praça Robert Mugabe and the Southern Sun hotel.

Always carry your passport or a notarised copy (see Dangers & Annoyances, p977).

SIGHTS & ACTIVITIES
The artists at **Núcleo de Arte** (☎ 21-492523; www. africaserver.nl/nucleo; 194 Rua da Argélia; ☉ 10am-5pm Mon-Sat) turn arms into art, as AK-47s and other weapons are welded into moving sculptures. They're on display (along with other artwork) in the gallery and adjoining garden.

The **National Art Museum** (☎ 21-320264; artemus@tvcabo.co.mz; 1233 Av Ho Chi Min; admission Mtc20; ☉ 11am-6pm Tue-Fri, 2-6pm Sat, Sun & holidays), located just to the west of Av Karl Marx, showcases a collection of paintings and sculptures by Mozambique's finest contemporary artists.

The domed **train station** on Praça dos Trabalhadores was designed by a pupil of Gustave Eiffel (of Tower fame) and has been well restored with a coat of pistachio-green paint, potted plants and several old locomotives. Inside, to the left at the end of the platform, is **Kulungwana Espaço Artístico** (☎ 21-333048; kulungwana@clubnet.co.mz; ☉ 10am-5pm Tue-Fri, 10am-3pm Sat & Sun), with a small art gallery.

Between the mid-19th century Portuguese **fort** (Praça 25 de Junho; admission free) and the train station, in the oldest part of town, is the **National Money Museum** (Museu Nacional da Moeda; Praça 25 de Junho; admission Mtc20; ☉ 9am-noon & 2-5pm Tue-Thu & Sat, 9am-noon Fri, 2-5pm Sun) with exhibits of local currency ranging from early barter tokens to modern-day bills.

At the nearby **Municipal Market** (Mercado Municipal; Av 25 de Setembro) stalls overflow with fruits, vegetables and spices. On Praça da Independência, check out **City Hall**, the spired **Cathedral of Nossa Senhora de Conceição** and the **Iron House**.

SLEEPING
Budget & Midrange

None of Maputo's backpackers has a sign – just a house number.

Fatima's Place (☎ 82-414 5730; www.mozambiquebackpackers.com; 1317 Av Mao Tse Tung; campsites per person Mtc200, dm Mtc300, d Mtc750-1100) In the upper part of town, it has an outdoor kitchen-bar, cramped camping, and a mix of rather borderline rooms.

Base Backpackers (☎ 21-302723, 82-452 6860; thebasebp@tvcabo.co.mz; 545 Av Patrice Lumumba; dm/d Mtc220/600) The popular Base has a central location, kitchen, backyard bar, terrace and *braai* (barbecue) area overlooking the port in the distance. Via public transport from 'Junta', take a 'Museu' *chapa* (minivan) to the final Museu stop, from where it's a short walk.

Hoyo-Hoyo Residencial (☎ 21-490701; www.hoyohoyo.odline.com; 837 Av Francisco Magumbwe; s/d US$40/55; P X) In the upper part of town, it has good-value, no-frills rooms and a good restaurant.

Residencial Palmeiras (☎ 21-300199, 82-306 9200; www.palmeiras-guesthouse.com; 948 Av Patrice Lumumba; s/d US$55/70; P X 🛜) A converted residence in a convenient, central location near the British high commission, it has quiet, good-value rooms and a small garden.

Mozaika (☎ 21-303939; www.mozaika.co.mz; 769 Av Agostinho Neto; s/d Mtc2000/2750; P X 🛜 🛖) There are eight bright, well-equipped rooms around a walled garden courtyard, plus a bar.

Hotel Terminus (☎ 21-491333; www.terminus.co.mz; cnr Avs Francisco Magumbwe & Ahmed Sekou Touré; s/d from Mtc2000/2900; P X 🖥 🛜 🛖) Three-stars-plus in the upper part of town, this place has small, spiffy rooms around a tiny garden, plus a restaurant.

Top End

Hotel Cardoso (☎ 21-491071; www.hotelcardoso.co.mz; 707 Av Mártires de Mueda; s/d from US$140/155; 🖥 🛜 🛖) Opposite the Natural History Museum, with good service, recently renovated rooms and views over the water and port.

Hotel Polana (☎ 21-491001; www.serenahotels.com/mozambique/polana/home.asp; 1380 Av Julius Nyerere; s/d from US$265/290; P X 🖥 🛜 🛖) In a prime location on the cliff top, it has rooms in the elegant main building or in the more modernist 'Polana Mar'. There's a large pool and lovely gardens, and weekend dinner buffets are also available.

EATING

Pizza House (☎ 21-485257; 601/607 Av Mao Tse Tung; light meals Mtc100-200; 🕑 6.30am-10.30pm) Come for pizzas, sandwiches and meals in this popular streetside restaurant favoured by locals and expats alike.

Piri-Piri Chicken (Avenida 24 de Julho; meals from Mtc150) A long-standing place with grilled chicken (with or without piri-piri) and prawns, plus a good local vibe.

Restaurante Costa do Sol (☎ 21-450038; Av Marginal; meals from Mtc200; 🕑 11am-10.30pm Sun-Thu, 11am-midnight Fri & Sat; P) Another Maputo classic, this art-deco seafood restaurant on the beach draws the crowds on weekend afternoons.

O Escorpião (☎ 21-302180; Feira Popular, Av 25 de Setembro; admission Mtc20, meals from Mtc200; 🕑 lunch & dinner; P) Another Maputo institution, with hearty Portuguese fare.

Mundo's (☎ 21-494080; www.mundosmaputo.com; cnr Avs Julius Nyerere & Eduardo Mondlane; meals Mtc200-350; 🕑 8am-midnight; P) This place features chicken wings, nachos, burgers, pizzas, all-day breakfasts, wraps, salads, panini, smoothies and desserts.

Gelati (Av Julius Nyerere) Cool, smooth Italian gelato next to Xenon cinema.

There are dozens of sidewalk cafes where you can get pastries and light meals, and watch the passing scene. Try **Náutilus Pastelaria** (cnr Avs Julius Nyerere & 24 de Julho; X) or **Surf** (Jardim dos Namorados, Av Friedrich Engels; snacks from Mtc50) with garden seating.

For self-catering try **Shoprite** (Av Acordos de Lusaka) or **Mercado Janeta** (cnr Avs Mao Tse Tung & Vladimir Lenine).

DRINKING & ENTERTAINMENT
Pubs & Clubs

La Dolce Vita Café-Bar (822 Av Julius Nyerere; 🕑 10am-late Tue-Sun) A sleek tapas and late-night place near Xenon cinema, with live music on Thursdays.

Rua d'Arte (ruadarte@gmail.com; ; Rua Travessa de Palmeira) Drinks and dancing opposite the Municipal Market.

África Bar (☎ 21-322217; www.africabar.blogspot.com; 2182 Av 24 de Julho; admission Mtc50; 🕑 from 5pm Wed-Sun) A long-standing spot with jazz on Thursdays.

Coconuts Live (☎ 21-322217; Complexo Mini-Golfe, Av Marginal; admission disco/lounge Mtc200/free; 🕑 disco Fri & Sat, lounge Wed-Sun) A weekend disco, plus a chill-out lounge.

MOZAMBIQUE

CENTRAL MAPUTO

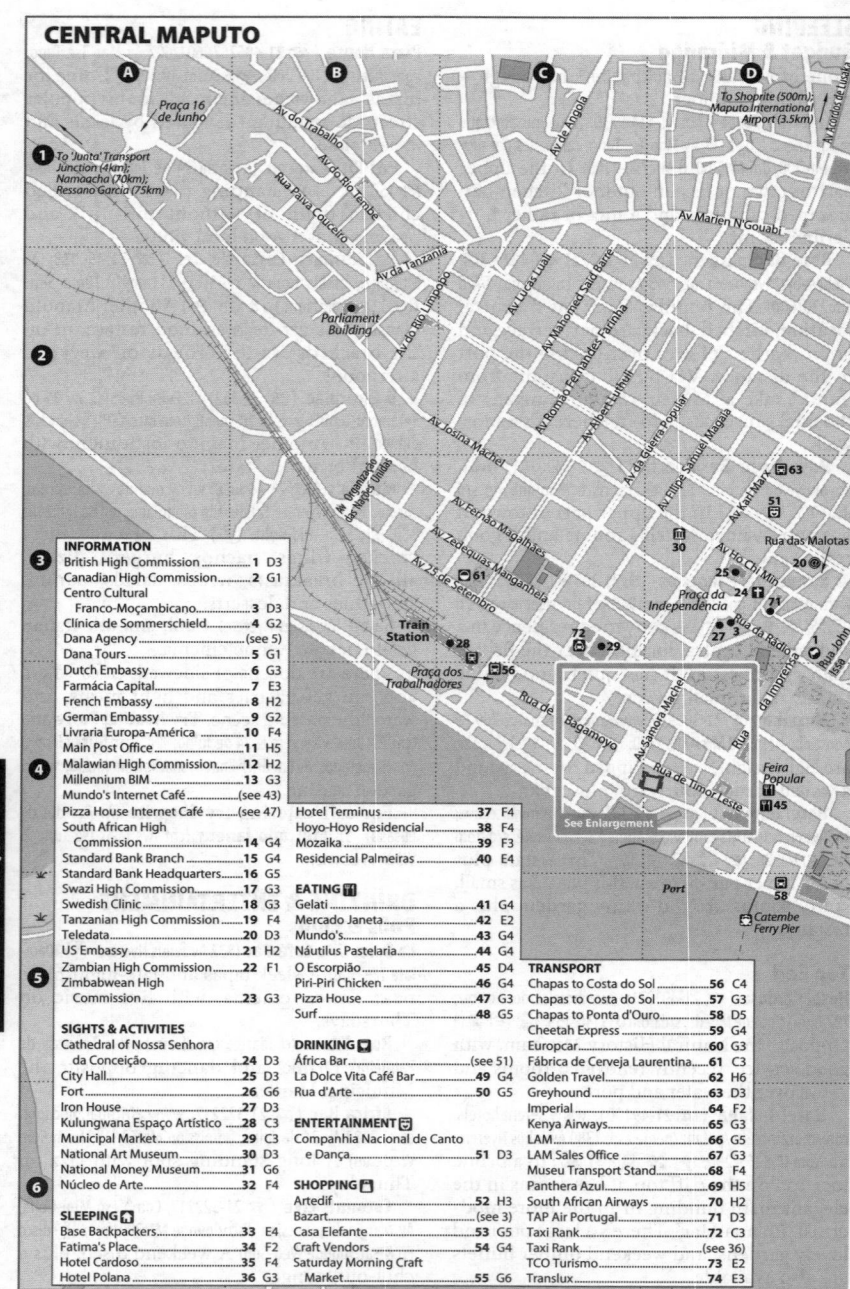

MOZAMBIQUE

INFORMATION
British High Commission	1	D3
Canadian High Commission	2	G1
Centro Cultural Franco-Moçambicano	3	D3
Clínica de Sommerscheild	4	G2
Dana Agency	(see 5)	
Dana Tours	5	G1
Dutch Embassy	6	G3
Farmácia Capital	7	E3
French Embassy	8	H2
German Embassy	9	G2
Livraria Europa-América	10	F4
Main Post Office	11	H5
Malawian High Commission	12	H2
Millennium BIM	13	G3
Mundo's Internet Café	(see 43)	
Pizza House Internet Café	(see 47)	
South African High Commission	14	G4
Standard Bank Branch	15	G4
Standard Bank Headquarters	16	G5
Swedish Clinic	18	G3
Tanzanian High Commission	19	F4
Teledata	20	D3
US Embassy	21	H2
Zambian High Commission	22	F1
Zimbabwean High Commission	23	G3

SIGHTS & ACTIVITIES
Cathedral of Nossa Senhora da Conceição	24	D3
City Hall	25	D3
Fort	26	G6
Iron House	27	D3
Kulungwana Espaço Artístico	28	C3
Municipal Market	29	C3
National Art Museum	30	D3
National Money Museum	31	G6
Núcleo de Arte	32	F4

SLEEPING
Base Backpackers	33	H4
Fatima's Place	34	F2
Hotel Cardoso	35	F4
Hotel Polana	36	G3
Hotel Terminus	37	F4
Hoyo-Hoyo Residencial	38	F4
Mozaika	39	F3
Residencial Palmeiras	40	E4

EATING
Gelati	41	G4
Mercado Janeta	42	E2
Mundo's	43	G4
Náutilus Pastelaria	44	G4
O Escorpião	45	D4
Piri-Piri Chicken	46	F4
Pizza House	47	G3
Surf	48	G5

DRINKING
África Bar	(see 51)	
La Dolce Vita Café Bar	49	G4
Rua d'Arte	50	G5

ENTERTAINMENT
Companhia Nacional de Canto e Dança	51	D3

SHOPPING
Artedif	52	H3
Bazart	(see 3)	
Casa Elefante	53	D3
Craft Vendors	54	G4
Saturday Morning Craft Market	55	G6

TRANSPORT
Chapas to Costa do Sol	56	C4
Chapas to Costa do Sol	57	G3
Chapas to Ponta d'Ouro	58	D5
Cheetah Express	59	G4
Europcar	60	G3
Fábrica de Cerveja Laurentina	61	C3
Golden Travel	62	H6
Greyhound	63	D3
Imperial	64	F2
Kenya Airways	65	G5
LAM	66	G5
LAM Sales Office	67	G3
Museu Transport Stand	68	F4
Panthera Azul	69	H5
South African Airways	70	H2
TAP Air Portugal	71	D3
Taxi Rank	72	C3
Taxi Rank	(see 36)	
TCO Turismo	73	E2
Translux	74	E3

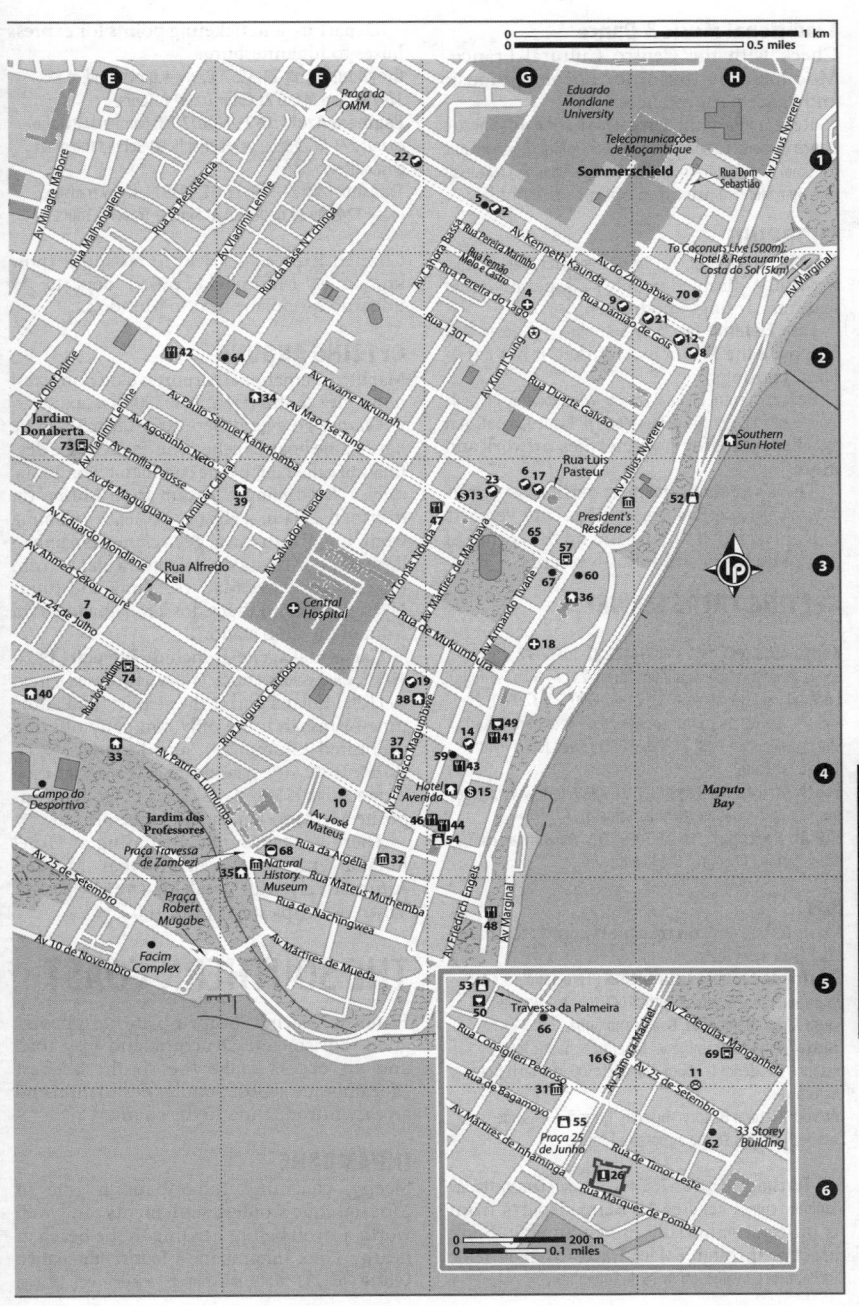

MOZAMBIQUE

Traditional Music & Dance

Check with the Centro Cultural Franco-Moçambicano (p966) for upcoming music and dance performances.

Rehearsals of the **Companhia Nacional de Canto e Dança** (National Company of Song & Dance; http://myspace.com/cncdmoz; Cine Teatro África, 2182 Av 24 de Julho; ☾ rehearsals 8am-3pm Mon-Fri) are often open to the public.

SHOPPING

Artedif (Av Marginal; ☾ 9am-2.30pm Tue, 9am-3.30pm Wed-Mon) A disabled people's cooperative that features carvings and basketry.

Casa Elefante (Av 25 de Setembro; ☾ closed Sun) Opposite the Municipal Market, it has *capulanas* (sarongs).

Bazart (Centro Cultural Franco-Moçambicano, Praça da Independência; ☾ 10am-7pm Mon-Fri, 10am-3pm Sat) An excellent place for crafts, textiles, artwork and more.

There's a **Saturday morning craft market** (Praça 25 de Junho; ☾ about 8am-1pm Sat), plus craft vendors in front of Hotel Polana and on the corner of Avs 24 de Julho and Julius Nyerere.

GETTING THERE & AWAY
Air

Kenya Airways (☎ 21-483144/5, 82-303 5931; sales@kenya-airways.co.mz; Aquarium Travel, 252 Av Mao Tse Tung)
LAM central reservations (☎ 21-468000, 21-326001, 21-465074; www.lam.co.mz; cnr Avs 25 de Setembro & Karl Marx); sales office (☎ 21-490590; cnr Aves Julius Nyerere & Mao Tse Tung)
South African Airways (☎ 21-488970/3; www.flysaa.com; Av do Zimbabwe, Sommerschield)
TAP Air Portugal (☎ 21-303927/8; www.flytap.com; Hotel Pestana Rovuma, 114 Rua da Sé)

Bus

Maputo has several transport stands for *chapa* and bus services:
Fábrica de Cerveja Laurentina ('Feroviario', cnr Avs 25 de Setembro & Albert Luthuli) *Chapas* to Swaziland, South Africa, Namaacha, Boane and Goba.
'Junta' (Av de Moçambique) Maputo's chaotic long-distance bus depot is about 7km (Mtc300 in a taxi) from the centre.
Museu (Natural History Museum, Praça Travessa de Zambezi) *Chapas* to the airport and Junta.

TCO Turismo's (☎ 82-768 4410; Jardim Donaberta, Av Vladimir Lenine) service to Beira departs from its office at 4am daily except Sunday. Book direct or through **Golden Travel** (☎ 21-309421/2; Rua Baptista Carvalho, off Av 25 de Setembro).

Departure and ticketing points for express buses to Johannesburg:
Greyhound (☎ 21-355700; www.greyhound.co.za; 1242 Av Karl Marx) At Cotur Travel & Tours.
Panthera Azul (☎ 21-302077/83; panthera@tvcabo.co.mz; 273 Av Zedequias Manganhela) Behind the main post office.
Translux (☎ 21-303825, 21-303829; www.translux.co.za; 1249 Av 24 de Julho) At Simara Travel & Tours.

Cheetah Express' services to Nelspruit (now known as Mbombela; p979) departs Av Eduardo Mondlane next to Mundo's.

GETTING AROUND

Maputo International Airport is 6km northwest of the city centre (from Mtc300 in a taxi).

Chapas go everywhere (from Mtc5). Some have name boards; otherwise listen to the destination called out by the conductor. For 'Junta' catch a *chapa* going to 'Jardim' from 'Museu' (in front of the Natural History Museum). Coming from 'Junta' into town, get a *chapa* heading to 'Museu'. For Costa do Sol, take a *chapa* from the corner of Avs Mao Tse Tung and Julius Nyerere, or from Praça dos Trabalhadores (in front of the train station).

Car-rental agencies include **Europcar** (☎ 21-497338; www.europcar.co.mz; 1418 Av Julius Nyerere), next to Hotel Polana and at the airport (and at the time of research the only company offering unlimited kilometres); and **Imperial** (☎ 21-465250, 82-300 5180; imperialmaputo@hotmail.com, info@interrent.co.mz; 1516 Av Mao Tse Tung), diagonally opposite Mercado Janeta and at the airport.

There are taxi ranks, including at Hotel Polana and at the Municipal Market. Alternatively, call a **tuk-tuk** (☎ 84-410 0001). Town taxi trips start at Mtc100.

THE SOUTHERN COAST

Fantastic beaches, heaped plates of prawns, good tourism infrastructure, and easy road and air access make the southern coast Mozambique's most popular destination and an easy introduction to the country.

INHAMBANE

Sleepy, charming Inhambane is one of Mozambique's oldest settlements, and well worth a stroll before heading to the beach at nearby Tofo. Inhambane's **Tourist Information Centre** (☎ 293-56149; info@inhambane-info.net; Litanga

Agência de Viagens), at the entrance to the central market, has city info, walking tours, dhow trips and more.

Pensão Pachiça (☎ 293-20565; www.barralighthouse. com; Rua 3 de Fevereiro; dm/s/d US$15/25/40) is a waterfront backpackers with spotless dorms and doubles, a restaurant-bar and a rooftop terrace. Go left from the ferry jetty for about 300m.

Verdinho's (Av da Independência; meals from Mtc200; ☺ closed Sun; ☜) has gourmet salads, burgers, continental dishes and indoor and outdoor seating.

Small motorised passenger boats (Mtc12.50, 25 minutes) and slower dhows (Mtc5) operate from sunrise to sundown between Inhambane and Maxixe.

Buses to Maputo (Mtc350, seven hours) and *chapas* to Tofo (Mtc15, one hour) depart from behind the market. For northbound transport, go to Maxixe.

TOFO

Tofo has long been legendary on the southern Africa holidaymakers' circuit, with its azure waters, sweeping white sands, rolling breakers and party atmosphere. The closest ATMs and banks are in Inhambane.

For diving contact **Diversity Scuba** (www. diversityscuba.com) or **Tofo Scuba** (www.tofoscuba.com). For surfing and yoga, head to **Turtle Cove** (www. turtlecovetofo.com) in nearby Tofinho.

Sleeping & Eating

Fatima's Nest (☎ 82-414 5730; www.mozambiqueback packers.com; campsites per person Mtc150; dm Mtc300; d tent or hut without bathroom from Mtc650) A makeshift budget travellers' haunt just north of town on the beach.

Bamboozi Beach Lodge (☎ 293-29040; www.bam boozibeachlodge.com; open/closed hut per person Mtc300/350; dm Mtc330; d & tr chalets Mtc2000-3000; ☒) Good dorm beds, basic reed huts and rustic chalets are all set among the sand dunes about 3km north of town.

Annex of Aquático Ocean Lodge (☎ 82-857 2850; www.aquaticolodge.com; tr US$68) Five attached self-catering rooms – each with one double and one twin bed – are directly on the beach next to Tofo Scuba. Good location and good value.

Casa Barry (☎ 293-29007; www.casabarry.com; d reed casita Mtc1800, 4-person chalets/cabanas Mtc4920/5600) On the beach at the southern end of town, it has well-equipped sea-facing self-catering chalets, basic reed huts to the back (no sea views or breezes) and a restaurant.

Waterworks Surf & Coffee Shop (light meals from Mtc100; ☺ 7am-5pm Tue-Sun) All-day breakfasts and light meals next to Diversity Scuba in the town centre.

Tofo Scuba (www.tofoscuba.com; light meals from Mtc150) Salads and other fresh, crunchy food – a good bet for vegetarians.

Casa de Comer (meals Mtc240-300; ☺ 9am-10pm Wed-Mon) Mozambique-French fusion cuisine in the town centre.

Getting There & Away

Chapas to Inhambane depart from about 5am, and there's sometimes a direct bus to Maputo at 4.30am (Mtc400, 7½ hours).

MAXIXE

Maxixe is the place to get off the bus and onto the boat if you're heading to Inhambane, across the bay. **Stop** (☎ 293-30025; N1; meals from Mtc125; r/ste Mtc900/1500; ☺ breakfast, lunch & dinner; ☒), at the jetty, has meals and rooms.

Buses to Maputo (Mtc300, 6½ hours) depart from the bus stand by the Tribunal from 6am. *Chapas* to Vilankulo (Mtc175, 3½ hours) leave from Praça 25 de Setembro, a few blocks north.

VILANKULO

Vilankulo is Mozambique's foremost holiday destination, and the gateway for visiting the Bazaruto Archipelago. During holidays it's overrun with 4WDs, but otherwise it is a very quiet town.

Tourist information (www.vilankulo.com; ☺ 9am-noon & 1-4pm Mon-Fri, 8am-noon Sat) is at the *município* in the town centre. **Sail Away** (☎ 293-82385; www.sailaway.co.za), near the old Dona Ana hotel, offers day and overnight dhow safaris. For diving, try **Odyssea Dive** (www.odysseadive.com; Baobab Beach Backpackers).

Sleeping & Eating

Baobab Beach Backpackers (campsites per person Mtc150) You can pitch a tent here.

Complexo Turístico Josef e Tina (☎ 82-965 2130; www.joseftina.com; campsites per person Mtc150, d hut without bathroom Mtc800, r Mtc1200) Basic reed huts in a large garden, plus a few no-frills rooms.

Zombie Cucumber (www.zombiecucumber.com; dm Mtc280, chalet d Mtc850; ☒) Comfy hammocks, a garden and bar, meals on order and lots of local info.

Na Sombra (☎ 293-82429; Bairro Mukoke; s/tw/ d/q with shared bathroom Mtc280/350/380/530) Tiny,

MOZAMBIQUE

no-frills rooms with fans near Millennium BIM. The good Restaurante Monica is next door.

Palmeiras Lodge (☎ 293-82257; www.smugglers. co.za; dm per person US$16; cottage d US$105; 🏊) Just in from the beachfront road, it has a large self-catering 'dorm' and lovely, whitewashed stone-and-thatch cottages in lush, green grounds. Continental breakfast is included, but there's no restaurant.

Smugglers (☎ 293-82253; www.smugglers.co.za; r with/without bathroom US$71/50, family cottage US$143; 🅿 ⊠ 🖳 🖳) A reliable midrange bet with rooms around lush gardens, and a restaurant serving up hearty pub fare.

Luxus (☎ 82-851 1301; s/d Mtc1500/2000; ⊠) Spotless, modern rooms in a small shopping mall opposite Taurus Supermarket.

Casa Rex (☎ 293-82048; www.casa-rex.com; s/d from US$140/220; 🅿 ⊠ 🛜 🖳 🏊) A lovely, upmarket getaway in peaceful, manicured gardens.

Complexo Âncora Seafood Restaurant/NY Pizza (☎ 293-82444; pizzas & meals Mtc150-250; 🕑 closed Tue; 🛜) Serves pizzas and continental fare overlooking the water, and also has upmarket rooms.

Other eating options include **Bar Ti'Zé** (meals from Mtc75), with local grills near the bus stand, **Café Moçambicano** (Av Eduardo Mondlane; pastries from Mtc15) opposite Barclay's, and **Vilanculos Backpacker** (Complexo Alemanha; meals Mtc100) for local cuisine.

For self-catering try **Taurus Supermarket** (Av Eduardo Mondlane), diagonally opposite Millennium BIM near the end of the tarmac road.

Getting There & Away

Buses to Maputo and Beira depart around 4am from the main road near Padaria Bento. To Chimoio, take a Beira bus to Inchope junction (Mtc500 from Vilankulo), then a minibus from there.

BAZARUTO ARCHIPELAGO

The Bazaruto Archipelago – much of which is a **national marine park** (adult/child Mtc200/100) – is a diver's paradise and a quintessential Indian Ocean retreat, with turquoise and jade waters, pristine coral reefs and white sand dunes.

There is no budget accommodation on the islands. If you have a limited budget, try arranging an island dhow cruise or visiting in the off-season for special deals. If cost is no object, try the intimate **Benguerra Lodge** (www.benguerra. co.za; Benguera Island; r per person incl full board from US$590; 🖳 🏊) or **Azura** (www.azura-retreats.com; Benguera Island; r per person incl full board from US$775; ⊠ 🖳 🏊).

CENTRAL MOZAMBIQUE

Central Mozambique doesn't draw the tourist crowds, but it's a convenient transit zone for travel to/from Malawi and Zimbabwe. Among its attractions are lovely Gorongosa National Park, hill landscapes and hiking.

BEIRA
pop 436,000

Mozambique's second-largest city is as famed for its steamed crabs and prawns as for its tawdry nightlife. A decent **beach** (at Makuti, 5km out of town) and a few well-preserved colonial buildings are the major attractions, but it's primarily of interest as a transport hub.

Sleeping & Eating

Rio Savane (☎ 23-323555; campsites per person US$10, 4-person barracas US$15 plus per person US$8, self-catering bungalows d/q US$50/100) About 40km north of town on the Savane River, it has camping, simple huts and self-catering chalets. Take the Dondo road past the airport to the signposted turn-off. Continue 35km to the estuary, where there's secure parking and a boat (until 5pm) to the camp.

Pensão Moderna (☎ 23-329901; Rua Alferes da Silva; d with/without bathroom Mtc980/750) No-frills rooms near the cathedral – overall, a reasonable budget bet.

Jardim das Velas (☎ 23-312209; jardimdasvelas@ yahoo.com; 282 Av das FPLM, Makuti Beach; d/f US$75/85; ⊠) Well-equipped doubles just back from the beach near the lighthouse, plus several family rooms. Very popular. There are no meals.

Beira Guest House (☎ 23-324030; 1311 Av Eduardo Mondlane; s/tw Mtc2300/2550; ⊠ 🖳 🛜) A quiet, shady, residential style B&B with well-appointed rooms and breakfast.

Café Riviera (Praça do Município; snacks & light meals from Mtc70) Plump, pink sofas inside, and outdoor tables overlooking the *praça*, for watching the passing scene.

Clube Náutico (Av das FPLM; meals from Mtc200, plus per person entry Mtc20) Seafood grills by the beach.

For self-catering, there's **Shoprite** (cnr Avs Armando Tivane & Samora Machel).

Getting There & Away

Buses leave from Praça do Maquinino to Chimoio (Mtc150, three hours), Vilankulo (Mtc550, 10 hours) and Maputo (Mtc1300, 16 hours). TCO buses to Quelimane (Mtc690, nine hours) depart from their office on Rua dos

Irmãos Roby in Bairro dos Pioneiros, 1km north of the centre, at 5am Monday, Wednesday and Friday. TCO to Maputo departs at 4am daily except Saturday (Mtc1300, 15 hours).

Otherwise, take a *chapa* to Inchope (Mtc100), 130km west of Beira at the N6–N1 junction, and try your luck with passing buses there.

GORONGOSA NATIONAL PARK

This **park** (www.gorongosa.net; adult/child/vehicle Mtc200/100/200, payable in meticais only; May-Nov), once one of southern Africa's premier wildlife areas, is on the rebound. It's worth visiting as much for its modest but improving wildlife-watching opportunities as for its lovely panoramas.

Arrange vehicle rental and guides, plus hikes on nearby Mt Gorongosa, at **park headquarters** (23-535010; travel@gorongosa.net), where there's also a **campsite** (per person Mtc210), a restaurant and nice **rondavels** (s/d Mtc2250/2990).

Explore Gorongosa (www.exploregorongosa.com; s/d all-inclusive US$500/800) runs walking safaris and canoe trips.

Head 43km north from Inchope to Nota village, then 17km east to the park gate, or take a *chapa* to Vila Gorongosa (25km further north) and arrange a pick-up from there in advance with park staff.

CHIMOIO

pop 239,000

Chimoio sits on the edge of scenic country near the Chimanimani Mountains. For info on hiking – you'll need to be self-sufficient and go with a guide – contact the excellent **Mozambique EcoTours** (www.mozecotours.com) or Pink Papaya backpackers.

The recommended **Pink Papaya** (82-555 7310; http://pinkpapaya.atspace.com; cnr Ruas Pigivide & 3 de Fevereiro; dm/s/d Mtc270/500/650;) is friendly and helpful, with rooms and dorms (no camping). With the bus stand to your right and train station to your left, walk straight, then take the fourth right into Rua 3 de Fevereiro; continue one block to Rua Pigivide.

Hotel-Residencial Castelo Branco (251-23934, 82-522 5960; Rua Sussundenga; s/d Mtc1850/2000;), just off Praça dos Heróis, caters mostly to business travellers.

Elo 4 (Av 25 de Setembro; meals from Mtc200) has pizzas and Italian dishes, and there's a **Shoprite** (N6).

Buses depart at 4am from the train station to Tete (Mtc350, six hours) and Maputo (Mtc900, 10 hours). For Vilankulo, take the Maputo bus to Pambara junction. *Chapas* to Beira (Mtc150,

three hours) and the Machipanda border run throughout the day.

TETE

Tete's reputation as one of the hottest places in Mozambique discourages visitors, but it's a useful transport hub. Pass the time sipping a cold drink at a riverside bar. About 150km northwest is Cahora Bassa dam and lake – a prime angling destination.

The scruffy **Campismo Jesus é Bom** (campsites per person Mtc100) is just over the bridge (north) and 300m to your right.

Rooms at **Prédios Univendas** (252-22670; Av Julius Nyerere; s/d from US$25/35;) are simple, clean and spacious. On the river, 20 minutes' walk from town, **Motel Tete** (252-22345; N103; r Mtc2000;) has riverside views and a restaurant.

Le Petit Café (Centro Comercial Fatima, cnr Avs Julius Nyerere & Liberdade; snacks from Mtc50; closed Sun;) has light meals and snacks. Opposite is **Pino's Restaurant** (Clube de Chingale, cnr Avs Julius Nyerere & Liberdade; pizzas & Italian meals from Mtc180).

Chapas for Zóbuè (Mtc70, two hours) and Nyamapanda (Mtc100, two hours) depart from along Av 25 de Junho. Transport to Chimoio (Mtc350, six hours plus) departs from Prédio Emose near Univendas.

QUELIMANE

pop 193,000

Friendly, compact Quelimane is convenient for a break on the journey north. **Zalala beach** is an hour's drive away through the coconut plantations.

Hotel 1 de Julho (cnr Avs Samora Machel & Filipe Samuel Magaia; tw with/without bathroom Mtc850/500;), near the old cathedral, has no-frills rooms and a *pastelaria*. **Hotel Rosy** (24-214969; cnr Avs 1 de Julho & Paulo Samuel Kankhomba; s/d Mtc850/1000;), near the old mosque, is still budget but better. **Hotel Flamingo** (24-215602; www.hflamingo. com; cnr Avs Kwame Nkrumah & 1 de Julho; s/d Mtc1550/1900;) has midrange rooms with full breakfasts, and a restaurant.

The riverside **Gani** (Náutica; Av Marginal; meals Mtc180) has good meals and good vibes. It's at the eastern end of town, at the curve to Av Maputo.

Piscina (Rua Filipe Samuel Magaia; meals Mtc180;) is popular for evening drinks.

The Mecula line to Nampula departs at 4.30am (Mtc350, 10 hours) and vehicles go daily to Milange (Malawi border) – all from the northern end of Av Eduardo Mondlane ('Romoza'). *Chapas* to Zalala (Mtc30) leave

MOZAMBIQUE

GOING GREEN

Here's a sample of what's happening in Mozambique (in addition to the GreenDex listings, p1216):

- **Ibo Eco School** (www.iboecoschool.be) gives Ibo Island children a good start in their crucial early years. It also takes volunteers.

- Feliciano dos Santos and his renowned band, **Massukos** (www.massukos.org), have received international acclaim for their work promoting social change and sanitation awareness.

- Teatro dos Oprimidos spreads social awareness messages on HIV/AIDS and malaria.

- Community tourism initiatives in Quirimbas National Park are training locals to be bird guides, and establishing community-run campsites, homestay programs and a tourist information centre.

from the *capuzínio*, 1km from town on the Zalala road. TCO to Beira (Mtc690, nine hours) departs at 5am on Tuesday, Thursday and Saturday from their ticket office at Zambézia Travels, diagonally opposite Hotel Chuabo.

NORTHERN MOZAMBIQUE

Northern Mozambique is one of the continent's last wild frontiers, offering adventure travel and island luxury. Other highlights include magical, time-warped Mozambique Island, stunning beaches and the unspoilt Swahili culture of the Quirimbas Archipelago.

NAMPULA
pop 471,000

Nampula – a crowded city with a hard edge – is the jumping-off point for visiting Mozambique Island (right).

The **National Ethnography Museum** (Av Eduardo Mondlane; admission Mtc100; ☽ 9am-5pm Tue-Fri, 2-5pm Sat & Sun) has English explanations and a mask collection.

Hotel Brasília (☎ 26-212127; 26 Rua dos Continuadores; s/d/tw Mtc700/750/960; ☒), near Shoprite and a 20-

minute hike from the bus and train depots, has budget rooms and a restaurant.

Residencial da Universidade Pedagógica (840 Av 25 de Setembro; s/tw Mtc800/1000), next to Hotel Milénio, has simple, clean rooms and breakfast. **Residencial Expresso** (☎ 26-218808/9; Av Independência; s/d from Mtc1450/1750; ☒ ☒) has spotless rooms with fridge and TV.

The more upmarket **Hotel Milénio** (☎ 26-218877; hotelmilenio@teledata.mz; 842 Av 25 de Setembro; tw/d/ste Mtc1950/1850/2500; ☒ ☒), near Mecula bus terminal and 10 minutes' walk from the train station, has an Indian-Chinese restaurant.

There's a supermarket in the Girassol hotel complex on Av Eduardo Mondlane.

Mecula buses depart for Pemba (Mtc250, seven to eight hours) and Quelimane (Mtc350, 11 hours) at 5am from the **Mecula garage** (Rua da Moma), off Av 25 de Setembro.

To Mozambique Island (Mtc120, three to four hours), get a *tanzaniano chapa* from the Padaria Nampula transport stand east of the train station between 7am and 10am. Be sure it's going direct, otherwise you'll need to change at Monapo.

Trains to Cuamba (2nd/economy class Mtc332/132, 10 to 12 hours) leave daily except Monday at 5am. Buy tickets the day before between 2pm and 5pm.

MOZAMBIQUE ISLAND

Tiny reed houses and pastel-coloured colonial mansions rub shoulders among the palm trees on tiny Mozambique Island (Ilha de Moçambique), the former capital of Portuguese East Africa. It's haunting, magical and a must-see.

The island is attached to the mainland by a 3.5km causeway. *Chapas* and buses arrive at the southern tip of the island, from where it's a short walk north through the *makuti* (reed) town to the old colonial stone town.

Sights

Wander through the *makuti* town as it's waking up, with cocks crowing in the narrow streets. After a breakfast of spicy *bhajias* (fried Indian-style vegetable pancakes) from the food market, walk into the stone town as the museums open.

The bright red **Palace and Chapel of São Paulo** (adult/child Mtc100/25; ☽ 9am-4pm) has been impeccably restored, with opulent furniture, tapestries and sinister portraits of colonial grandees. Adjoining are a **Maritime Museum** (closed at the time of research), the **Church of the Misericórdia** and the **Museum of Sacred Art**, which are all included in the entry price.

The massive Portuguese **Fort of São Sebastião** (closed for renovations at the time of research) is best visited in the late afternoon, when it's bathed in golden light.

Dominating the island's southern tip is the whitewashed **Church of Santo António**, overlooking fishermen repairing their nets on the sand.

Sleeping

Casuarina Camping (☎ 82-446 9900; casuarina09@ hotmail.com, helenaabelali@gmail.com; campsites/r per person Mtc150/700, entry per vehicle Mtc120) On the mainland opposite Mozambique Island, it has a beachside camping area and bungalow-style rooms.

Amakuthini (Casa de Luis; ☎ 82-436 7570; dm Mtc300, s/d without bathroom Mtc350/700) Quite basic, but an island institution, it has a friendly owner and a tiny courtyard. It is near the green mosque.

Residencial Amy (Av dos Heróis; d Mtc450) It's near the park, with basic, dark rooms, most without exterior windows. Breakfast costs extra.

Patio dos Quintalinhos (Casa de Gabriele; ☎ 26-610090; www.patiodosquintalinhos.com; s/d without bathroom US$25/30, d/q US$50/67, d ste with air-con US$62;) Opposite the green mosque and very nice, it has Italian-Mozambican fusion design, a rooftop terrace and help with excursions.

Mooxeleliya (☎ 26-610076; flora204@hotmail.com; d with/without air-con Mtc1500/750, family r Mtc1500;) Offers large, very good high-ceilinged rooms (avoid the musty family rooms) and breakfast. It's near the Church of the Misericórdia.

Casa Branca (☎ 26-610076; flora204@hotmail.com; Rua dos Combatentes; r with/without bathroom Mtc1000/750) Simple, spotless rooms (one with bathroom), plus sea views, breakfast and a kitchen.

O Escondidinho (☎ 26-610078; ilhatur@teledata.mz; Av dos Heróis; r Mtc1000-1950;) Spacious, high-ceilinged rooms, some with bathrooms, plus a good French-Mozambican restaurant.

Eating & Drinking

O Paladar (market; meals from Mtc100) Offers local meals – place your order in the morning.

Café-Bar Âncora d'Ouro (meals from Mtc150; closed Tue) Opposite the Church of the Misericórdia, it has soups, muffins, and homemade ice cream.

Relíquias (meals Mtc160-230; closed Mon) Near the museum, it has delicious prawn curries and other dishes.

Bar Flôr de Rosa (5pm-midnight Wed-Mon) Has espressos, pasta and a great rooftop sundowners terrace.

Getting There & Away

Transport departs from the bridge. Direct *tanzaniano chapas* to Nampula (Mtc120, three hours) leave between 3am and 5am; ask your hotel to arrange a pick-up. To Pemba, take the 4am *tanzaniano* to Namialo, and – with luck – connect there with the Mecula bus from Nampula.

CUAMBA

Lively Cuamba is a convenient stop en route to/from Malawi. **Pensão São Miguel** (271-62701; r with/ without bathroom Mtc800/500, with air-con Mtc1000;), 10 minutes' walk from the train and bus stations, has small, clean rooms and a restaurant.

Transport leaves from Maçaniqueira market south of the railroad tracks. Trains to Nampula (2nd/economy class Mtc332/132, 10 to 12 hours) depart at 5am daily except Monday.

LICHINGA

This low-key town with jacarandas and pine groves is a hub for travel to/from Lake Niassa and Malawi.

Ponto Final (271-20912; Av Filipe Samuel Magaia; s without bathroom Mtc650, d with hot water Mtc1000) has budget accommodation and a restaurant. **Residencial 2+1** (82-381 1070; Av Samora Machel; s/d Mtc1200/1500) is clean, efficient and central, and has a restaurant.

Hotel Girassol Lichinga (271-21280; www. girassolhoteis.co.mz; Rua Filipe Samuel Magaia; s/d from Mtc2000/2300;) has huge rooms, satellite TV and a restaurant.

Transport departs early from next to the market, including to Cuamba (Mtc350, eight hours), Metangula (Mtc120, 2½ hours) and the Rovuma River (Mtc500, six hours).

LAKE NIASSA

The tranquil Mozambican side of Lake Niassa (Lake Malawi) sees a small but steady stream of adventure travellers.

Chuwanga Beach Hotel (Catawala's; Chuwanga Beach; campsites per person Mtc150, d Mtc400) has bungalows on the sand 8km north of Metangula. The more upmarket **Mbuna Bay** (82-536 7782; www. mbunabay.ch; s/d incl full board in bush bungalow US$125/190, in beach chalet US$165/250) is about 15km south, and also on the lakeshore.

In Cóbuè, **Khango Beach** (☎ in Malawi 88-856 7885, in Mozambique 265-856 7885; r without bathroom per person Mtc200; ℗)) has reed bungalows on the sand, while **Mira Lago** (Pensão Layla; r without bathroom Mtc200; ℗)) has rooms with solar-powered lighting in the village centre.

The highlight is **Nkwichi Lodge** (www.manda wilderness.org; s/d incl full board US$375/580), a wonderful waterside retreat 15km south of Cóbuè, with handcrafted chalets, bush walks, boating, squeaky white sands and snorkelling. It's highly recommended and well worth a splurge. Advance bookings are essential.

Daily *chapas* connect Metangula and Lichinga (Mtc120, 2½ hours), and Metangula and Cóbuè (Mtc150, four hours). For Chuwanga Beach, take a Cóbuè *chapa* to the junction and walk.

The *Ilala* ferry (p980) goes to Metangula and Likoma Island (Malawi), from where you can arrange transfers to Cóbuè and Nkwichi. Mozambique visas are issued in Cóbuè. Immigration is on the hill near the antenna. The local boat, *Dangilila*, goes weekly between Metangula and Cóbuè (Mtc150), stopping on demand, including at Nkwichi Lodge and Mbuna Bay.

PEMBA

Sunny Pemba's centre of action is Wimbi (Wimbe) beach, 5km down the coast. **Kaskazini** (☎ 272-20371; www.kaskazini.com; Pemba Beach Hotel, Av Marginal, Wimbi beach) has heaps of information on the town and the Quirimbas islands, and can organise transport and excursions. **CI Divers** (☎ 272-20102; www.cidivers.com; Complexo Náutilus, Av Marginal, Wimbi beach) does diving. For crafts there's the excellent **Artes Maconde** (☎ /fax 272-21099; artesmaconde@tdm.co.mz; Town Centre Av 25 de Setembro; Wimbi beach Pemba Beach Hotel; Wimbi beach At CI Divers).

Sleeping & Eating

Pemba Magic Lodge ('Russell's Place'; ☎ 82-686 2730, 82-527 7048; www.pembamagic.com; Wimbi Beach; camping per person US$8, dm US$15, rental tent per person US$15, chalet d US$60; ☞) About 3.5km beyond Complexo Náutilus along the beach-road extension, with camping (but no self-catering), rental tents, chalets, a bar-restaurant and lots of overlander travel info.

Pemba Dive & Bushcamp (Nacole Jardim; ☎ 82-661 1530; www.pembadivecamp.com; campsites per person US$10, dm US$20, d/q chalet US$100/140) Offering camping and chalets, plus a beachside bar

and *braai* area, it's 10 minutes from town (Mtc200 in a taxi), behind the airport on the bay.

Pensão Baía (cnr Ruas 1 de Maio & Base de Beira; d with/without bathroom Mtc600/500) Spartan budget rooms in the town centre.

Wimbi Sun Residencial (☎ 82-318 1300; wimbisun@teledata.mz; 7472 Av Marginal; r/ste Mtc1250/1600; ⌗)) Spacious, soulless rooms diagonally opposite Complexo Náutilus. Breakfast costs Mtc150 extra.

Residencial Regio Emilia (☎ 272-21297, 82-928 5510; residencial.reggio.emilia@gmail.com; 8696 Av Marginal; r US$80; ℗ ⌗ ☞) Simple, lovely rooms and self-catering chalets in green, quiet grounds, and (soon) a restaurant.

Complexo Náutilus (☎ 272-21520; nautiluscas@teledata.mz; Av Marginal; s/d/q bungalows Mtc2500/3000/3500; ⌗ ⌷) A good beachside setting, indifferent management and closely spaced stone bungalows.

Pemba Dolphin (Av Marginal; seafood grills from Mtc180) on the beach, and **Restaurante Rema** (Av Marginal; meals from Mtc120), opposite, have meals. In town, try **Pastelaria Flôr d'Avenida** (☎ 272-20514; Av Eduardo Mondlane; meals from Mtc100) or the nice **Locanda Italiana** (☎ 272-20672; Rua Geronimo Romero; meals Mtc250; ⌚ from 5pm Mon-Sat) in the *baixa*.

Getting There & Away

Mecula buses go daily at 5am to Nampula, Moçimboa da Praia and Mueda, and every other day to Nacala (all Mtc250), from its office 1.5km from the centre on the small street behind Osman's supermarket. For Mozambique Island, continue to Nampula and get onward transport from there the next day. To get to Wimbi beach from town, there's a bus from town or taxis (Mtc150) from near Mcel.

Safi Rentals (☎ 82-380 8630, 82-684 7770; www.pembarentacar.com) has reliable car rentals for very reasonable prices.

QUIRIMBAS ARCHIPELAGO

Ancient wooden sailing dhows take fisherman around the remote and beautiful Quirimbas Archipelago, including sleepy Ibo, with its crumbling colonial mansions and centuries of history. Many of the islands are part of **Quirimbas National Park** (adult/child Mtc200/100). **Fim do Mundo Safaris** (☎ 82-511 6925, 82-304 2908; www.fimdomundosafaris.com) has liveaboard trips on a handcrafted dhow for

US$120 per person, plus day sails and sail-dive excursions.

Budget sleeping options include **Campsite do Janine** (Ibo Island; campsites per person Mtc150), next to Ibo Island Lodge; **Tikidiri** (Airfield Rd, Ibo Island; s/tw Mtc150/300), opposite the old cemetery, with stone-and-thatch bungalows with nets, bucket baths and local-style meals; and **Matemo Community Campsite** (campsites per person about Mtc100; Matemo Island). Get an update from Kaskazini in Pemba (opposite).

Miti Miwiri (☎ 26-960530, 82-543 5864; www.mitimiwire.com; Ibo Island; dm US$15, d US$50-80) and **Cinco Portas** (www.cincoportas.com; Ibo Island; d US$60-100; 🏊) are both lovely, atmospheric places. More upmarket is **Ibo Island Lodge** (www.iboisland.com; Ibo Island; s/d incl half board US$360/560), near the dhow port.

Kaskazini in Pemba arranges charter flights, speedboats, dhows and vehicle transfers. Alternatively, there's a **transfer service** (☎ 82-724 4437; jorickv@gmail.com; Ibo Island) offering Pemba–Tandanhangue transfers (US$200 per vehicle or US$30 per person if the vehicle is going anyway), motorboat transfers from Tandanhangue to Ibo (US$30 per boat) and reasonably priced island-hopping services (dhow or motorboat) around the archipelago.

A *chapa* departs daily at 4am from Pemba's Paquitequete fish market to Quissanga and on to Tandanhangue village (Mtc200, four to five hours), from where public dhows go to Ibo (Mtc100/10 with/without motor, one to six hours) at high tide. There's parking at Gringo's Place, next to Tandanhangue port.

MOÇIMBOA DA PRAIA

This one-horse port town is the last major stop between Pemba and the Tanzanian border. **Pensão-Residencial Magid** (☎ 272-81099; Av Samora Machel; r without bathroom Mtc350), downhill from the transport stand, and **Complexo Miramar** (Complexo Natasha; ☎ 272-81135/6; r Mtc1000) on the water have no-frills accommodation. **Hotel Chez Natalie** (☎ 272-81092; natalie.bockel@gmail.com; campsites per person Mtc300, 4-person chalets Mtc1800), 2.5km from town on the estuary, has spacious chalets and camping. **Restaurante Estrelha** (Av Samora Machel) has meals.

Pick-ups to the Rovuma ('Namoto') border via Palma depart from the top of town between 2.30am and 3.30am (Mtc300, four hours). The Mecula bus to Pemba departs at 4.30am sharp.

MOZAMBIQUE DIRECTORY

ACCOMMODATION

There are many campsites along the southern coast. The cheapest hotels – called *pensões* – start at around US$12. Backpacker places, found especially in the south, are better value; dorm beds average US$11. There are midrange options in all major towns, and for top-end travel, there are some idyllic island lodges. When quoting prices, many establishments distinguish between a *duplo* (twin beds) and a *casal* (double bed).

Around Christmas, Easter and during August, the southern coast fills up and peak pricing applies; advance bookings are recommended.

Except as noted, listings in this chapter include private bathroom.

ACTIVITIES

The best places for arranging dhow safaris are Ibo (for sailing around the Quirimbas Islands; see opposite) and Vilankulo (to the islands of the Bazaruto Archipelago; see p971).

There are diving and snorkelling operators all along the coast, notably at Tofo (p971), in Vilankulo (for the Bazaruto Archipelago) and on Ibo Island.

BOOKS

Kalashnikovs and Zombie Cucumbers: Travels in Mozambique by Nick Middleton and *With Both Hands Waving – A Journey Through Mozambique* by Justin Fox are highly entertaining travelogues full of historical snippets.

BUSINESS HOURS

See p1136 in the Africa Directory chapter for standard business hours. Banks open from 8am to 3pm Monday to Friday.

DANGERS & ANNOYANCES

Mozambique is generally safe, but there are some areas and situations where caution is warranted.

Thefts and robberies are the main risks: watch your pockets in markets, avoid isolating situations, and don't carry a bag or otherwise give a potential thief reason to think you have anything of value.

MOZAMBIQUE

More likely are simple hassles, such as underpaid authorities in search of bribes. You're required to carry your passport or (better) a notarised copy at all times. If stopped by the police, remain polite, but don't surrender your documents – insist on going to the nearest police station *(esquadrão)* instead.

Land mines – a legacy of the war days – are still a risk in some areas, although the four northern provinces (from the Zambezi River to the Rovuma) have been declared free of known mined areas. To be on the safe side, stick to well-used paths and seek local advice before wandering into the bush.

EMBASSIES & CONSULATES

The following are in Maputo; most are open from 8.30am to 3pm Monday to Friday. The closest Australian representation is in South Africa.

Canada (☎ 21-492623; www.canadainternational. gc.ca/mozambique/index.aspx; 1138 Av Kenneth Kaunda)
France (☎ 21-484600; www.ambafrance-mz.org; 2361 Av Julius Nyerere)
Germany (☎ 21-482700; www.maputo.diplo.de; 506 Rua Damião de Gois)
Malawi (☎ 21-492676; 75 Av Kenneth Kaunda)
Netherlands (☎ 21-484200; www.hollandin mozambique.org; 324 Av Kwame Nkrumah)
South Africa (☎ 21-490059, 21-491614; consular@ tropical.co.mz, sahc_cs@satcom.co.mz; 41 Av Eduardo Mondlane)
Swaziland (☎ 21-491601; swazimoz@teledata.mz; Rua Luís Pasteur)
Tanzania (☎ 21-491051; Av Mártires de Machava) Near corner of Av Eduardo Mondlane.
UK (☎ 21-356000; http://ukinmozambique.fco.gov.uk; 310 Av Vladimir Lenine)
USA (☎ 21-492797; http://maputo.usembassy.gov; 193 Av Kenneth Kaunda)
Zambia (☎ 21-492452; 1286 Av Kenneth Kaunda)
Zimbabwe (☎ 21-490404, 21-486499; 1657 Av Mártires de Machava)

EMERGENCIES

There are no nationwide emergency numbers, and even city-based fire and police numbers rarely work. If you are in trouble, try seeking help from your hotel or embassy. For Maputo-based emergency medical treatment, see p966.

FESTIVALS & EVENTS

The Chopi **Timbilas Festival** is held sporadically around August in Quissico, in southern

---

PRACTICALITIES

■ Weights, measures and road distances use the metric system.

■ Electricity is 220–240V AC, 50Hz (use South African–style two- or three-round-pin plugs).

■ For English-language news see www. poptel.org.uk/mozambique-news.

■ Radio Mozambique and TVM (TV) have occasional English programming.

Mozambique, and the **Mozambique Jazz Festival** (www.mozjazzfest.com) is held around April in Maputo. Also in Maputo is the **Cedarte National Art & Crafts Fair** (www.cedarte.org.mz, in Portuguese), held annually in December, and the **Maputo International Music Festival** (www.maputomusic.com).

HOLIDAYS

New Year's Day 1 January
Heroes' Day 3 February
Women's Day 7 April
Labour Day 1 May
Independence Day 25 June
Victory Day 7 September
Revolution Day 25 September
Christmas/Family Day 25 December

INTERNET ACCESS

All larger towns have internet cafes, often at the local TDM (telecom) office and often very slow. Rates average Mtc1 per minute. Broadband connections are becoming more frequent, and many midrange and upmarket hotels and eateries have wireless.

MONEY

Mozambique's currency is the metical (plural – meticais) nova família. Note denominations include Mtc20, Mtc50, Mtc100, Mtc200, Mtc500 and Mtc1000, and coins include Mtc1, Mtc2, Mtc5 and Mtc10.

All major towns have ATMs, mostly accepting Visa cards, but not always MasterCard. Useful ones include Millennium BIM (Visa and MasterCard), Standard Bank (Visa and MasterCard), Barclay's (Visa) and BCI (Visa).

You can change US dollars cash at most banks (though not at most Millennium BIM branches) without paying commission, and South African rand are widely accepted in southern Mozambique. Travellers cheques can be changed only with difficulty, only at a Standard Bank (original purchase receipt required) and for a high commission.

TELEPHONE

Provincial area codes must always be dialled, with no initial zero. The cheapest international dialling is with TDM's prepaid Bla-Bla Fixo card, sold at telecom branches everywhere. Mcel (prefix 82) and Vodacom (prefix 84) are the mobile providers and have shops and vendors countrywide where you can buy SIM-card starter packs (less than US$2) and air time. Mozambique mobile numbers have no initial zero – 82 numbers with an initial zero are in South Africa, and require the South Africa country code.

VISAS

Visas are required by all visitors except citizens of South Africa, Swaziland, Zambia, Tanzania, Botswana, Malawi, Mauritius and Zimbabwe. Single-entry visas (only) are available at most major land and air entry points (but not anywhere along the Tanzania border) for US$25 for one month. Your passport must be valid for at least six months, and have at least three blank pages. Multiple-entry visas should be arranged in advance.

Visas can be extended at immigration offices in all provincial capitals.

Visas for Onward Travel

Visas for neighbouring countries are available at most borders except Tanzania. Tanzania visas cost US$50 plus two photos and are issued within 24 hours from the Tanzania high commission in Maputo (see opposite), which is open from 8am to 11am for visa applications.

TRANSPORT IN MOZAMBIQUE

GETTING THERE & AWAY
Air

Linhas Aéreas de Moçambique (LAM; ☎ 21-468000, 21-490590; www.lam.co.mz) links Johannesburg (South Africa) with Maputo and Beira; Dar es Salaam (Tanzania) with Pemba and Maputo; and Lisbon (Portugal) with Maputo. Other connections include the following (see p970 for Maputo-based airlines):

Air Travelmax (☎ in South Africa 011-701 3222) Johannesburg's Lanseria to both Inhambane and Vilankulo.
Kenya Airways (☎ 21-320337/8; www.kenya-airways. com) Nairobi to Maputo.
Pelican Air Services (☎ in South Africa 011-973 3649; www.pelicanair.co.za) Johannesburg to Vilankulo via Nelspruit, with connections to the Bazaruto Archipelago.
SAAirlink (☎ 21-495483; www.saairlink.co.za) Johannesburg to Beira and Durban to Maputo.
South African Airways (☎ 21-488970; www.flysaa. com) Johannesburg to Maputo.
TAP Air Portugal (☎ 21-303927/8; www.flytap.com) Lisbon to Maputo.

Land

All overland travellers must pay an immigration tax of US$2 or the local currency equivalent. Most borders are open from 6am to 6pm.

MALAWI

There are at least eight border crossings, with only the main ones covered here.

To/From Blantyre

For the Zóbuè crossing between Blantyre and Harare (Zimbabwe), vehicles depart Blantyre for the border via Mwanza, connecting in Mozambique with *chapas* to Tete.

The Milange crossing is convenient for those heading to Quelimane and Mozambique Island, with regular buses from Blantyre via Mulanje to the border. Once across, daily vehicles service Mocuba, then Quelimane and Nampula.

Mandimba is convenient for Cuamba and northern Mozambique. There's frequent transport on the Malawi side to Mangochi, where you can get minibuses to Namwera and Chiponde. Once in Mozambique, vehicles go daily from Mandimba to Cuamba and Lichinga.

To/From Lilongwe

From the Dedza border post, 85km southeast of Lilongwe, *chapas* run along the sealed route to Tete via Ulongwé. Otherwise, go in stages via Moatize. Arrange your Mozambique visa in advance.

SOUTH AFRICA
To/From Johannesburg

Large 'luxury' buses go daily between Johannesburg and Maputo (US$30 to US$35, nine hours) via busy **Lebombo/Ressano Garcia**

MOZAMBIQUE

(☽ 6am-10pm), which is now a one-stop border. It's recommended to organise your Mozambique visa in advance if travelling by bus. Most companies will take you without one, but if lines at the border are long the bus may not wait. If you get stuck, take a *chapa* the remaining 90km to Maputo. Companies include the following:

Greyhound (☎ in South Africa 083-915 9000; www.greyhound.co.za)

InterCape Mainliner (☎ in South Africa 021-380 4400; www.intercape.co.za)

Panthera Azul (☎ in South Africa 011-618 8811/2; panthera@tvcabo.co.mz)

Translux (☎ in South Africa 011-774 3333; www.translux.co.za)

Cheetah Express (☎ 82-410 1213, 21-486 3222; cheetahexpress@tdm.co.mz) goes daily between Maputo and Nelspruit (Mtc660 one way).

To/From Kruger National Park

Neither of the borders between Mozambique and South Africa's Kruger park – **Giriyondo** (☽ 8am-4pm Oct-Mar, 8am-3pm Apr-Sep), west of Massingir, and **Pafuri** (☽ 8am-4pm), in northeastern Kruger – is accessible via public transport, and both require a 4WD on the Mozambique side. You'll need to pay entry fees for Kruger and for Limpopo park (Mtc200/100 per adult/child).

Other Routes

Between Durban and Maputo, **Panthera Azul** (☎ in Durban 031-309 7798) has buses via Namaacha and Big Bend in Swaziland (Mtc810, 8½ hours) three times weekly.

The **Kosi Bay border post** (☽ 8am-4pm) is 11km south of Mozambique's Ponta d'Ouro. There's no public transport on the Mozambique side, and you'll need a 4WD. Coming from South Africa you can leave your vehicle at the border and arrange a pick-up in advance with Ponta d'Ouro hotels. To/from Maputo there are direct *chapas* several times weekly between Ponta d'Ouro and Maputo's Catembe ferry jetty; otherwise, go in stages via Zitundo and Salamanga.

SWAZILAND

There are daily minibuses to Maputo via **Lomahasha/Namaacha** (Mtc50; ☽ 7am-8pm), which take 1½ hours.

The quieter border at **Goba/Mhlumeni** (☽ 7am-6pm) is good for drivers.

TANZANIA

Pick-ups depart Mtwara (Tanzania) daily at 6.30am to the Kilambo border post, and on to the Rovuma River, crossed – adventurously or dangerously, depending on your perspective and water levels – via dugout canoe. Once across, pick-ups go to the Mozambique border post (4km further) and on to Moçimboa da Praia (Mtc300, four hours).

Further west, the Unity Bridge (at Negomane) should be finished within the lifetime of this book. Meanwhile, still further west, there's a vehicle bridge and passport/customs posts at Segundo Congresso, with road links (and public transport) north to Songea and south to Lichinga.

ZAMBIA

The main crossing is at Cassacatiza, northwest of Tete. *Chapas* go daily from Tete to Matema, from where there's sporadic transport to the border, and then daily vehicles to Katete (Zambia), and on to Lusaka or Chipata.

ZIMBABWE

The main crossings are at Nyamapanda (on the Harare–Tete–Blantyre route), and at Machipanda (on the Harare–Beira route). *Chapas* go from Tete to Changara (Mtc90, 1½ hours) and on to Nyamapanda, where there are vehicles to Harare.

From Chimoio *chapas* go to Manica and the border. Take a taxi to Mutare for Zimbabwe transport.

Boat
MALAWI

The *Ilala* ferry stops at Metangula (but no longer Cóbuè) weekly on its way up Lake Malawi via Likoma Island (Malawi). Mozambique visas are issued at Cóbuè. Slow sailing boats also go between Likoma Island, Cóbuè and Metangula.

GETTING AROUND
Air

Linhas Aéreas de Moçambique (LAM; ☎ 21-468000; www.lam.co.mz) links Maputo with Inhambane, Vilankulo, Beira, Chimoio, Quelimane, Tete, Nampula, Lichinga and Pemba.

Car & Motorcycle

You will need a South African or international driving licence (as well as your home country licence) to drive in Mozambique, plus the vehicle registration papers, a temporary import permit (available at most borders) and third-party insurance. Driving on the beach, driving without a seatbelt (all vehicle occupants), driving while using a mobile phone, driving without two red hazard triangles and a reflector vest, and turning without indicating are all illegal.

While main roads in the south, and from Beira to the Zambezi River, are fine with a 2WD, you will need a 4WD for most other areas. Petrol (*gasolina*) supplies are unreliable away from main towns, especially in the north. Diesel (*gasóleo*) supplies are more regular. Carry an extra jerry can and tank up at every opportunity.

Hitching

Despite the potential dangers (see p1161), hitching is often the only transport option in rural areas. Modest payment is expected.

Local Transport

Machibombos (buses) are the best option for getting around on main routes. Elsewhere, overcrowded, wildly careening *chapas* (minibuses) connect smaller towns daily. Always take a bus if there's a choice.

Most routes are covered by freelancers, except in the north, where there's Grupo Mecula. 'Express' services are slightly more expensive, but faster and more comfortable.

All transport leaves early (between 3am and 6am), and often on time.

MOZAMBIQUE

Namibia

Wedged between the Kalahari and the South Atlantic, Namibia enjoys vast potential and promise as one of the youngest countries in Africa. A veritable hidden gem, Namibia remains very much a frontier realm for intrepid travellers to discover. Here you will find the oldest rust-red desert in the world, quintessential African landscapes teeming with wildlife, extraordinarily blue skies stretching above vast open horizons, and silent spaces where emptiness and desolation can quickly become overwhelming. Namibia is also a photographer's dream, boasting wild seascapes, rugged mountains, lonely deserts, colonial cities and nearly unlimited elbow room.

A predominantly arid country, Namibia can be divided into four main topographical regions: the Namib Desert and coastal plains in the west, the eastward-sloping Central Plateau, the Kalahari along the borders with South Africa and Botswana, and the densely wooded bushveld of the Kavango and Caprivi regions to the northeast. This defining geography fosters one of the largest animal congregations on the planet, alongside one of the lowest human population densities – a rare combination that yields unequalled opportunities for wildlife-watching.

FAST FACTS

- **Area** 825,000 sq km
- **ATMs** Found in most large towns around the country
- **Borders** Angola, Botswana, South Africa, Zambia, Zimbabwe – all accessible overland except Zimbabwe, which has no direct border crossing with Namibia
- **Budget** Budget US$30 to US$50, midrange and top-end US$75 to US$125
- **Capital** Windhoek
- **Languages** English, Afrikaans, German, Owambo, Herero, Nama, Damara
- **Money** Namibian dollar; US$1 = N$7.41; €1 = N$10.64
- **Population** 2.1 million
- **Seasons** Long rainy season (January to April), dry season (May to September), short rainy season (October to December)
- **Telephone** Country code ☎ 264; international access code ☎ 00
- **Time** GMT/UTC +2
- **Visa** None required for citizens of Australia, New Zealand, France, Germany, the UK, Ireland, Canada or the USA

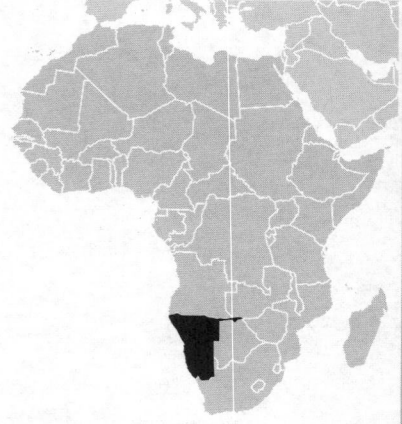

HIGHLIGHTS

- **Sossusvlei** (p995) Watch the sun rise from the tops of flaming red dunes on the edge of ephemeral salt pans.
- **Etosha National Park** (p1000) Go on a self-drive safari in one of the continent's premier wildlife venues.
- **Swakopmund** (p992) Get your adrenaline fix at the extreme-sports capital of Namibia.
- **Fish River Canyon** (p1005) Test your endurance on a five-day hike through one of the world's largest canyons.
- **Opuwo** (p999) Have a face to face encounter with the Himba, one of Namibia's most iconic peoples.

CLIMATE & WHEN TO GO

Namibia's climatic variations correspond roughly to its geographical subdivisions. In the arid central Namib Desert, summer daytime temperatures may climb to over 40°C, but can fall to below freezing during the night. Rainfall is heaviest in the northeast, which enjoys a subtropical climate, and reaches over 600mm annually along the Okavango River. The northern and interior regions experience 'little rains' between October and December, while the main stormy period occurs from January to April. The best time to go is between May and September.

ITINERARIES

- **Three Days** Namibia's number-one tourist highlight is the expansive sand sea of the Namib. If you have only a few days to visit, this is where you'll want to focus. From Sesriem (p995), spend a day hiking through the dunes, or arrange for a scenic flight from the beach town of Swakopmund (p992).
- **One Week** Combine a visit to the Namib with a safari through Etosha National Park (p1000), one of the continent's most distinctive safari experiences. Splurge on a hire car, and get ready for some hair-raising, self-driven good times.
- **One Month** With a month to explore the country, you can hire a 4WD or use a reputable safari company and see the best of the country: in addition to the sights listed above, you could also hike the Fish River Canyon (p1005), visit the Himba in Opuwo (p999) and go on an expedition along the Skeleton Coast (p997) or through Khaudom Game Reserve (p1004) in the Kalahari.

HISTORY
Pre-Colonial Period

The first agriculturalists and iron workers of definite Bantu-speaking origin in southern Africa belonged to the Gokomere culture. They settled the temperate savannah and cooler uplands of Zimbabwe and were the first occupants of the Great Zimbabwe site, in the southeastern part of modern-day Zimbabwe, where a well-sheltered valley presented an obvious place to settle. Cattle ranching became the mainstay of the community and earlier hunting-and-gathering San groups either retreated to the west or were enslaved or absorbed.

At the same time the San communities were also coming under pressure from the Khoi-Khoi (the ancestors of the Nama), who probably entered the region from the south. The Khoi-Khoi were loosely organised into tribes and raised livestock. They gradually displaced the San, becoming the dominant group in the region until around 1500.

During the 16th century, the Herero arrived in Namibia from the Zambezi Valley and occupied the north and west of the country. As ambitious pastoralists, they inevitably came into conflict with the Khoi-Khoi over the best grazing lands and water sources. Eventually, given their superior strength and numbers, nearly all the indigenous Namibian groups submitted to the Herero.

NAMIBIA

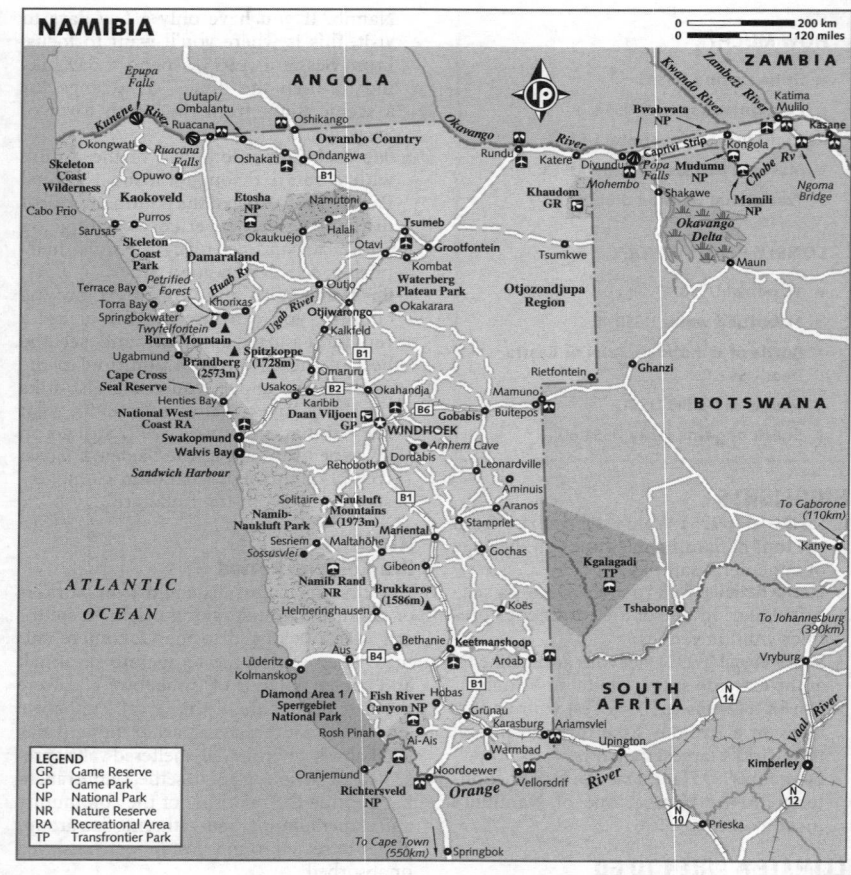

NAMIBIA

LEGEND
GR Game Reserve
GP Game Park
NP National Park
NR Nature Reserve
RA Recreational Area
TP Transfrontier Park

By the late 19th century, a new Bantu group, the Owambo, settled in the north along the Okavango and Kunene Rivers.

Colonial Period

Because Namibia has one of the world's most barren and inhospitable coastlines, it was largely ignored by European nations until relatively recently. The first European visitors were Portuguese mariners seeking a route to the Indies in the late 15th century, but they confined their activities to erecting stone crosses at certain points as navigational aids.

It wasn't until the last-minute scramble for colonies towards the end of the 19th century that Namibia was annexed by Germany (except for the enclave of Walvis Bay, which

was taken in 1878 by the British for the Cape Colony). In 1904 the Herero launched a rebellion and, later that year, were joined by the Nama, but the rebellions were brutally suppressed.

The Owambo in the north were luckier and managed to avoid conquest until after the start of WWI, when they were overrun by Portuguese forces fighting on the side of the Allies. Soon after, the German colony abruptly came to an end when its forces surrendered to a South African expeditionary army also fighting on behalf of the Allies.

At the end of WWI, South Africa was given a mandate to rule the territory (then known as South West Africa) by the League of Nations. Following WWII, the mandate was renewed by the UN, who refused to sanction the annexation of the country by South Africa.

Undeterred, the South African government tightened its grip on the territory, and in 1949 it granted parliamentary representation to the white population. The bulk of southern Namibia's viable farmland was parcelled into some 6000 farms owned by white settlers, while indigenous families were confined by law to their 'reserves' (mainly in the east and the far north) and urban workplaces.

Nationalism & the Struggle for Independence

Forced labour had been the lot of most Namibians since the German annexation. This was one of the main factors that led to mass demonstrations and the development of nationalism in the late 1950s. Around this time, a number of political parties were formed and strikes organised. By 1960 most of these parties had merged to form the South West African People's Organization (Swapo), which took the issue of South African occupation to the International Court of Justice.

The outcome was inconclusive, but in 1966 the UN General Assembly voted to terminate South Africa's mandate and set up a Council for South West Africa (in 1973 renamed the Commission for Namibia) to administer the territory. At the same time, Swapo launched its campaign of guerrilla warfare. The South African government reacted by firing on demonstrators and arresting thousands of activists.

In 1975 the Democratic Turnhalle Alliance (DTA) was officially established. Formed from a combination of white political interests and ethnic parties, it turned out to be a toothless debating chamber, which spent much of its time in litigation with the South African government over the scope of its responsibility.

The DTA was dissolved in 1983 after it had indicated it would accommodate members of Swapo. It was replaced by the Multiparty Conference, which had even less success and quickly disappeared. And so control of Namibia passed back to the South African–appointed administrator-general.

The failure of these attempts to set up an internal government did not deter South Africa from maintaining its grip on Namibia. It refused to negotiate on a UN-supervised program for Namibian independence until the estimated 19,000 Cuban troops were removed from neighbouring Angola. In response, Swapo intensified its guerrilla campaign.

In the end, however, it was neither the activities of Swapo alone nor the international sanctions that forced the South Africans to the negotiating table. The white Namibian population itself was growing tired of the war and the South African economy was suffering, making sustaining the war financially difficult.

The stage was finally set for negotiations on the country's future. Under the watch of the UN, the USA and the USSR, a deal was struck between Cuba, Angola, South Africa and Swapo, in which Cuban troops would be removed from Angola and South African troops from Namibia. This would be followed by UN-monitored elections held in November 1989 on the basis of universal suffrage. Swapo collected a clear majority of the votes but an insufficient number to give it the sole mandate to write the new constitution.

Independence

Following negotiations between the various parties, a constitution was adopted in February 1990. Independence was granted the following month under the presidency of the Swapo leader, Sam Nujoma. Initially, his policies focused on programs of reconstruction and national reconciliation to heal the wounds left by 25 years of armed struggle. In 1999, however, Nujoma had nearly served out his second (and constitutionally, his last) five-year term, and alarm bells sounded among watchdog groups when he changed the constitution to allow himself a third five-year term, which he won with nearly 77% of the vote.

In August 1999, a separatist Lozi faction in the Caprivi Strip launched a coup attempt – which was summarily put down by the Namibian Defence Force. In December of the same year, the Caprivi Strip suffered a spate of violent attacks on civilians and travellers, which were rightly or wrongly blamed on Unita sympathisers from Angola (see p851 for information on this group). These attacks destroyed tourism in the Caprivi Strip, but since Angola signed a peace accord in April 2002, the region is slowly starting to come back to life.

Namibia Today

In 2004 the world watched warily to see if Nujoma would cling to the office of power for a fourth term, and an almost audible sigh of relief could be heard all over Namibia when he

NAMIBIA

announced that he would finally be stepping down in favour of his chosen successor, Hifikepunye Pohamba. Like Sam Nujoma, Pohamba is a Swapo veteran, and swept to power with nearly 77% of the vote. He leaves behind the land ministry where he presided over one of Namibia's most controversial schemes – the expropriation of land from white farmers to be make available to black citizens.

Since Pohamba took power, Namibia has profited considerably from the extraction and processing of minerals for export. Rich alluvial diamond deposits alongside uranium and other metal reserves put the country's budget into surplus in 2007 for the first time since independence. Compared to other sub-Saharan countries, Namibia has one of the highest per capita GDPs, though this statistic masks one of the world's most unequal income distributions.

CULTURE

On a national level, Namibia is still struggling to attain a cohesive identity. History weighs heavy on generations who grew up during the struggle for independence. As a result, some formidable tensions endure between various social and racial groups. Although most travellers will be greeted with great warmth and curiosity, some people may experience unpleasant racism or apparently unwarranted hostility (this is not confined to black/white relations but can affect travellers of all ethnicities as Namibia's ethnic groups are extremely varied).

Most Namibians still live in homesteads in rural areas and lead typical village lives. Villages tend to be family and clan based and are presided over by an elected *elenga* (headman). The *elenga* is responsible for local affairs, everything from settling disputes to determining how communal lands are managed. He in turn reports to a senior headman, who represents a larger district comprised of several dozen villages. This system functions alongside Namibia's regional government bodies and enables traditional lifestyles to flourish side by side with the country's modern civic system.

People

Namibia's population in 2009 was estimated to be 2.1 million. This figure takes into account the effects of excess mortality due to AIDS, which became the leading cause of death in Namibia in 1996. With approximately two people per sq km, Namibia has one of Africa's lowest population densities, with an annual population growth rate of 2.3%, according to the World Health Organization (WHO) in 2006.

The population of Namibia comprises 11 major ethnic groups. The majority of people are Owambo (50%), with the other ethnic groups each making up a relatively small percentage of the population: Kavango (9%), Herero/Himba (7%), Damara (7%), Caprivian (4%), Nama (5%), Afrikaner and German (6%), Baster (6.5%), San (1%) and Tswana (0.5%).

Arts & Crafts

Although Namibia is still developing a literary tradition, its musical, visual and architectural arts are fairly well established. The country also enjoys a wealth of amateur talent in the production of material arts, including carvings, baskets and tapestry, along with simple but resourcefully designed and produced toys, clothing and household implements.

FOOD & DRINK

Traditional Namibian food consists of a few staples, the most common of which is *oshifima*, a doughlike paste made from millet, and usually served with a stew of vegetables or meat. As a foreigner you'll rarely find such dishes on the menu, however, as most Namibian restaurants serve a variation on European-style foods, like Italian or French, alongside an abundance of seafood dishes

ENVIRONMENT

Despite its harsh climate, Namibia has some of the world's grandest national parks, ranging from the world-famous wildlife-oriented Etosha National Park to the immense Namib-Naukluft Park, which protects vast dune fields, desert plains, wild mountains and unique flora. There are also the smaller reserves of the Caprivi region, the renowned Skeleton Coast Park and the awe-inspiring Fish River Canyon, which ranks among Africa's most spectacular sights.

Facilities in Namibian national parks are operated by the semiprivate Namibia Wildlife Resorts (opposite). When booking park campsites or accommodation by phone, fax or email, include the following information: your passport number; the number of people in your group (including the ages of any children); your full address, telephone/fax number or email address; the type of accommodation required; and dates of arrival and departure (including alternative dates).

Bookings may be made up to 12 months in advance, and fees must be paid by credit card before the bookings will be confirmed. Camping fees are good for up to four people; each additional person up to eight people will be charged extra. In addition, parks charge a daily admission fee per person and per vehicle, payable when you enter the park. Booking ahead is always advised for national parks. While you may be able to pick up accommodation at the last minute by just turning up at the park gates, it isn't recommended (especially for Etosha and Sossusvlei).

WINDHOEK

☎ 061 / pop 230,000

Largely influenced by its German colonial heritage, Windhoek's architecture is colourful and inspiring, and there are a few streets in the capital where colonial styling still radiates. Neobaroque cathedral spires, as well as a few seemingly misplaced German castles, punctuate the skyline, and complement the steel and glass high-rises that emerged from Namibia's rapid growth and development. Indeed, Windhoek is an extremely well-heeled city that stands in marked contrast to the desolate hinterlands that serve as Namibia's main tourist drawcards.

ORIENTATION

Central Windhoek is bisected by Independence Ave, where most shopping and administrative buildings are concentrated. The shopping district is focused on the pedestrian-only Post St Mall and the nearby Gustav Voigts Centre, Wernhill Park Centre and Levinson Arcade. Zoo Park, near the main post office, provides a green lawn and shady lunch spots.

INFORMATION

Internet Access

Virtually all hotels and hostels now offer cheap and reliable internet access, with wi-fi becoming increasingly the norm. If you're out and about, internet cafes can be found in every mall in the city.

Medical Services

Rhino Park Private Hospital (Map p988; ☎ 225434; Sauer St) Provides excellent care and service, but patients must pay up front.

Windhoek State Hospital (Map p988; ☎ 303 9111) An option for those who are short of cash but have time to wait. Located just off Harvey Rd.

Money

Major banks and bureaux de change are concentrated around Independence Ave, and all will change foreign currency and travellers cheques and give credit-card cash advances. First National Bank (FNB) and Standard Bank's ATM systems handle Visa and MasterCard.

Post & Telephone

The modern **main post office** (Map p990; Independence Ave) can readily handle overseas post. It also has telephone boxes in the lobby, and is located next door to the **Telecommunications Office** (Map p990; Independence Ave), where you can make international calls and send or receive faxes.

Tourist Information

Namibia Tourism Board (Map p990; ☎ 290 6000; www.namibiatourism.com.na; 1st fl, Channel Life Towers, 39 Post St Mall) The national tourist office can provide information for places all over the country.

Namibia Wildlife Resorts (NWR; Map p990; ☎ 285 7200; www.nwr.com.na; Erkrath Bldg, Gathemann's Complex, Independence Ave; 🕒 8am-3pm Mon-Fri) Books national park accommodation and hikes.

Windhoek Information & Publicity Office (Map p990; ☎ 290 2058; www.cityofwindhoek.org.na; Post St Mall) This friendly office answers questions and distributes local publications, including *What's On in Windhoek*.

Travel Agencies

Cardboard Box Travel Shop (Map p990; ☎ 256580; www.namibian.org) Attached to the backpacker hostel of the same name (see p989), this recommended travel agency can arrange both budget and upmarket bookings all over the country.

Chameleon Safaris (Map p990; ☎ 247668; www.chameleonsafaris.com) Likewise attached to a backpacker hostel of the same name (see p989), this travel agency is also recommended for all types of safaris around the country.

DANGERS & ANNOYANCES

Windhoek is generally safe by day, but avoid going out alone at night. Don't make yourself a target by walking around with a backpack or expensive camera, and never leave anything of value visible in a rented vehicle. Windhoek's townships are generally safer than those in South Africa, but use caution and try to take a local guide if you visit.

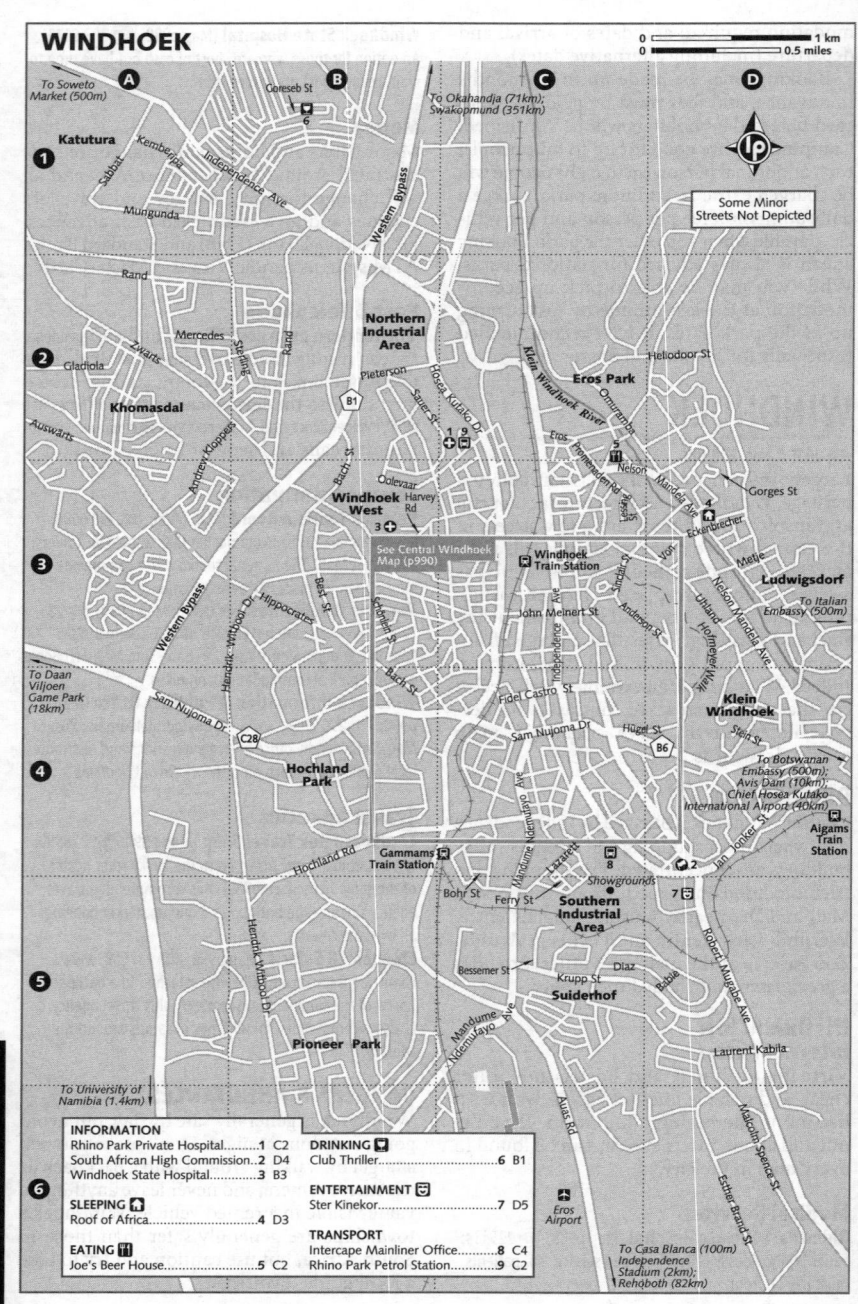

WINDHOEK

INFORMATION	
Rhino Park Private Hospital	1 C2
South African High Commission	2 D4
Windhoek State Hospital	3 B3

SLEEPING 🏠	
Roof of Africa	4 D3

EATING 🍴	
Joe's Beer House	5 C2

DRINKING 🍷	
Club Thriller	6 B1

ENTERTAINMENT 🎬	
Ster Kinekor	7 D5

TRANSPORT	
Intercape Mainliner Office	8 C4
Rhino Park Petrol Station	9 C2

SIGHTS

The whitewashed ramparts of the **National Museum of Namibia** (Map p990; ☎ 293 4437; Robert Mugabe Ave; admission by donation; ☺ 9am-6pm Mon-Fri, 10.30am-12.30pm Sat & Sun), Windhoek's oldest surviving building, date from the early 1890s. The building houses the historical section of the State Museum, and exhibits focus mainly on Namibia's independence struggle.

At the affiliated **Owela Museum** (State Museum; Map p990; ☎ 293 4358; 4 Lüderitz St; admission by donation; ☺ 9am-6pm Mon-Fri, 10.30am-12.30pm Sat & Sun), the exhibits focus on Namibia's natural and cultural history. The most interesting part of this museum is the big AIDS-awareness display at the entrance.

The heart of the Windhoek shopping district is the bizarrely colourful **Post St Mall** (Map p990). At the eastern end is a display of Gibeon meteorites; the rest of the mall is lined with vendors selling curios, art, clothing and other tourist items, mostly from Zimbabwe.

The **National Art Gallery** (Map p990; ☎ 231160; cnr Robert Mugabe Ave & John Meinert St; admission free; ☺ 9am-5pm Tue-Fri, 9am-2pm Sat) features work by local artists in various mediums, some of which is for sale. It also houses a permanent collection of works reflecting Namibia's history and nature.

Around Windhoek

The beautiful **Daan Viljoen Game Park** (per person N$40, per vehicle N$10; ☺ sunrise-6pm) sits in the Khomas Hochland about 18km west of Windhoek, though, unfortunately, it was being juggled between owners at the time of research. Once operated under the jurisdiction of Namibian Wildlife Resorts, the property is currently under private ownership and is no longer open to overnight guests. However, there are rumours circulating that a much-needed face-lift is underway, and that the campsite and resort will reopen in the years to come.

To get to Daan Viljoen, take the C28 west from Windhoek; Daan Viljoen is clearly signposted off the Bosua Pass Hwy, about 18km from the city.

SLEEPING

Cardboard Box Backpackers (Map p990; ☎ 228994; www.cardboardbox.com.na; 15 Johann Albrecht St; campsite N$40, dm N$80, r from N$220; ☐ ☒) Centred on a dreamy swimming pool that fronts a fully stocked bar, backpackers have a tough time leaving this oasis of affordable luxury,

though no one seems to be bothered in the slightest.

Chameleon Backpackers Lodge & Guesthouse (Map p990; ☎ 244347; www.chameleonbackpackers.com; 5-7 Voight St; campsite N$50, dm from N$90, r from N$325; ☐ ☒) This well-matched rival to the Cardboard Box caters to a slightly more subdued crowd, offering luxurious African-chic rooms with private bathrooms and spic-and-span dorms at shoestring prices.

Puccini House (Map p990; ☎ 236355; www.puccini-namibia.com; 4-6 Puccini St; s/d without bathroom N$215/360, s/d/tr N$385/450/630; ☐ ☒) The closest budget option to the city centre is conveniently located near the Wernhill Park Centre, yet retains its intimate atmosphere with only 14 rooms and a very welcoming management.

Roof of Africa (Map p988; ☎ 254708; www.roofofafrica.com; 124-126 Nelson Mandela Ave; s N$595-895, d N$795-1095; ☒ ☐ ☒) A pleasant haven located about 30 minutes by foot from the city centre, Roof of Africa has a rustic barnyard feel, offering well-designed rooms of varying price and luxury that attract laid-back travellers looking for a quiet retreat from the city.

Villa Verdi (Map p990; ☎ 221994; www.leadinglodges.com/villaverdi.htm; 4 Verdi St; s N$670-815, d N$1080-1340; ☒ ☐ ☒) This utterly unique Mediterranean-African hybrid features whimsically decorated rooms complete with original paintings and artsy finishing.

Hotel Heinitzburg (Map p990; ☎ 249597; www.heinitzburg.com; 22 Heinitzburg St; s/d from €150/230; ☒) This is Windhoek's most royal B&B option – quite literally – as it's located inside Heinitzburg Castle, which was commissioned in 1914 by Count von Schwerin for his fiancée, Margarethe von Heinitz.

EATING

Café Zoo (Map p990; ☎ 223479; Zoo Park, Independence Ave; coffee N$10-15, light meals $25-50) A storied Windhoeker cafe that is part of a long line of cafes stretching back nearly a century, this sheltered spot beneath a giant rubber tree on the edge of Zoo Park is just lovely for a cappuccino accompanied by a light meal.

Sardinia's Pizzeria (Map p990; ☎ 225600; 39 Independence Ave; dishes N$20-50) An energetic restaurant that sells decent pizza by the slice and other classic Italian dishes, as well as strong coffee and sugary gelato.

Gourmet (Map p990; ☎ 232360; Kaiserkrone Centre, Post St Mall; mains N$40-70) Tucked away in a nondescript courtyard just off of Post St Mall, this

NAMIBIA

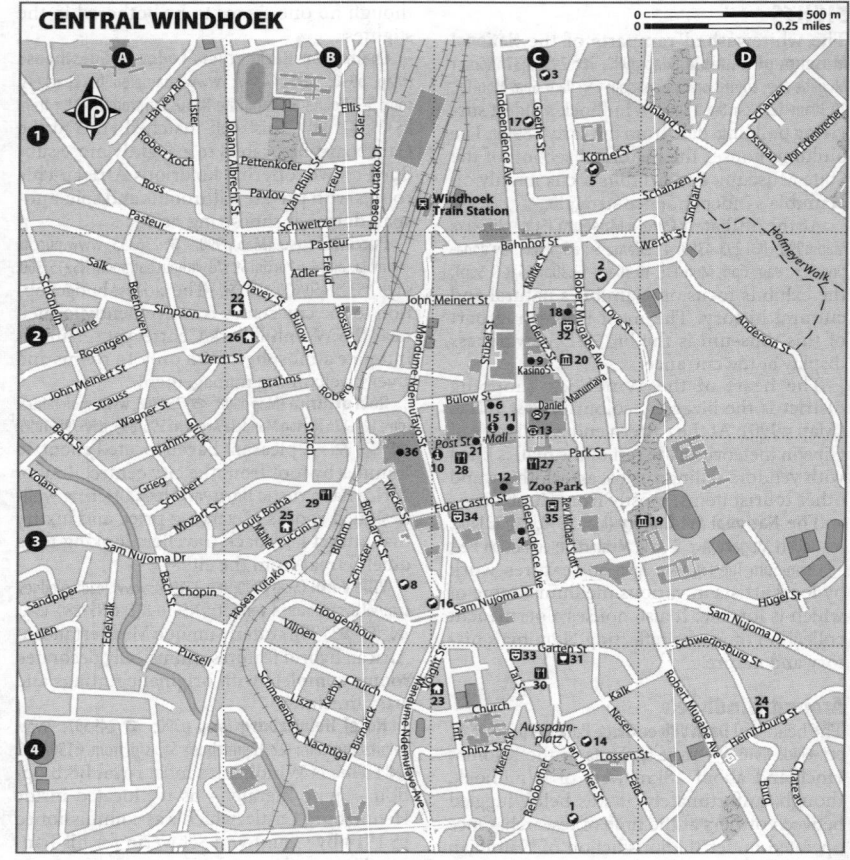

CENTRAL WINDHOEK

NAMIBIA

ANYONE FOR ZEBRA?

A legendary Windhoek institution that is something of an obligatory stop for foreign visitors, **Joe's Beer House** (Map p988; ☎ 232457; Green Market Sq, 160 Nelson Mandela Ave; beers N$10-30, mains N$50-100; ☺ 5pm-late) is where you can indulge (albeit with a little guilt...) in flame-broiled fillets of all those amazing animals you've seen on safari! Seriously. We're talking huge cuts of zebra tenderloin, ostrich skewers, peppered springbok steak, oryx medallions, crocodile on a hotplate and the house speciality, sliced and marinated kudu.

---

alfresco bistro has one of the most comprehensive menus you've ever seen.

nice (Map p990; ☎ 300710; cnr Mozart St & Hosea Kutako Dr; mains N$65-110) The Namibian Institute of Culinary Education – or 'nice' for short – operates this wonderfully conceived 'living classroom', where apprentice chefs can field test their cooking skills.

DRINKING

Club Thriller (Map p988; Katutura; ☎ 11pm-late) Lies in a rough area, but beyond the weapons' search at the door, the music is Western and African and the atmosphere upbeat and relatively secure. Admission charges vary.

Wine Bar (Map p990; ☎ 226514; 3 Garten St; ☺ 5.30-11pm) Wine Bar occupies a historic mansion on a quiet side street, and strives to satiate your palate with one of the city's best wine selections, paired with Mediterranean-style tapas.

ENTERTAINMENT

National Theatre of Namibia (Map p990; ☎ 237966; www.namibiatheatre.org) Located south of the National Art Gallery (p989), the national theatre stages infrequent theatre presentations; for information see the Friday edition of the *Namibian*.

Ster Kinekor (Map p988; ☎ 249267; Maerua Park Centre, off Robert Mugabe Ave) This place shows recent films and has half-price admission on Tuesdays.

Warehouse Theatre (Map p990; ☎ 225059; Old South-West Brewery Bldg, 48 Tal St) A delightfully integrated club staging live African and European music and theatre productions. Admission prices vary.

Windhoek Conservatorium (Map p990; ☎ 293 3111; Fidel Castro St) The conservatorium occasionally holds classical concerts.

GETTING THERE & AWAY
Air

Chief Hosea Kutako International Airport, located about 40km east of the city centre, serves most international flights into and out of Windhoek. **Air Namibia** (☎ 299 6333; www.airnamibia.com) operates daily flights between Windhoek and Cape Town and Johannesburg, as well as twice-weekly flights to/from Frankfurt. (Flights to London had been suspended at the time of writing.) Several airlines also offer international services to/from Maun (Botswana) and Victoria Falls (Zimbabwe).

Eros Airport, immediately south of the city centre, serves most domestic flights into and out of Windhoek. Air Namibia offers occasional flights to/from Katima Mulilo, Lüderitz, Ondangwa, Rundu, Swakopmund/Walvis Bay and Tsumeb.

Coming from Windhoek, make sure the taxi driver knows which airport you are going to.

Other airlines with flights into and out of Windhoek include the following:
British Airways (☎ 248528; www.ba.com)
Lufthansa (☎ 226662; www.lufthansa.com)
South African Airways (☎ 237670; www.flysaa.com)

Bus

From the main **long-distance bus terminal** (Map p990), at the corner of Fidel Castro St and Rev Michael Scott St, the **Intercape Mainliner** (www.intercape.co.za) runs to/from Cape Town, Johannesburg, Victoria Falls and Swakopmund, serving a variety of local destinations along the way.

Local *combis* (minibuses) leave when full from the Rhino Park petrol station and can get you to most urban centres in Namibia. However, these routes do not serve the vast majority of Namibia's tourist destinations, which are located well beyond major population centres.

Car & Motorcycle

Windhoek is the crossroads of Namibia – the point where the main north–south route (B1) and east–west routes (B2 and B6) cross – and all approaches to the city are extremely scenic, passing through beautiful desert hills. Roads are clearly signposted and those travelling between northern and southern Namibia can avoid the city centre by taking the Western Bypass.

Train

Windhoek train station has a **booking office** (☎ 298 2175; 🕓 7.30am-4pm Mon-Fri), where you can reserve seats on any of the country's public rail lines. Routes are varied, and include overnight trains to Keetmanshoop, Tsumeb and Swakopmund, though irregular schedules, lengthy travel times and far better bus connections make train travel of little interest for the vast majority of foreign travellers.

GETTING AROUND

Collective taxis from the main ranks at Wernhill Park Centre follow set routes to Khomasdal and Katutura and, if your destination is along the way, you'll pay around N$5 to N$10.

With private taxis from the main bus terminals or by radio dispatch, fares are either metered or are calculated on a per kilometre basis, but you may be able to negotiate a set fare per journey. Plan on N$25 to N$50 to anywhere around the city.

If you're arriving at Chief Hosea Kutako International Airport, taxis typically wait outside the arrivals area. It's a long drive into the city, so you can expect to pay anywhere from N$250 to N$300 to Windhoek, depending on your exact destination. For Eros Airport, fares are much more modest at around N$30 to N$50, though in all instances you're going to need to negotiate hard.

CENTRAL NAMIBIA

Central Namibia is defined by the barren and desolate landscapes of the Namib Desert. The Nama word 'namib', which inspired the name of the entire country, rather prosaically means 'vast dry plain'. Although travellers to Namibia are often surprised by the lushness of the Kalahari, the soaring sand dunes of the Namib rarely disappoint.

SWAKOPMUND

☎ 064 / pop 25,000

Often described as being more German than Germany, Swakopmund is a quirky mix of German-Namibian residents and overseas German tourists, who feel right at home with the town's pervasive *Gemütlichkeit*, a distinctively German appreciation of comfort and hospitality. With its seaside promenades, half-timbered homes and colonial-era buildings, it seems that only the wind-blown sand and the palm trees distinguish Swakop from holiday towns along Germany's North Sea and Baltic Sea coasts. The city has recently reinvented itself as the adventure-sports capital of Namibia, and now attracts adrenaline junkies dying for a fix. Whether you slide down the dunes on a greased-up snowboard, or go against your survival instincts by hurling yourself out of a Cessna, Swakop has no shortage of gut-curdling activities to choose from.

Information
BOOKSHOPS
CNA bookshop (Hendrick Witbooi St) Sells popular paperbacks.
Die Muschel Book & Art Shop (☎ 402874; Hendrick Witbooi St) Esoteric works on art and local history are available.
Swakopmunder Buchhandlung (☎ 402613; Sam Nujoma Ave) A wide selection of literature from various genres.

EMERGENCY
Ambulance (☎ 405731)
Fire brigade (☎ day 402411, after-hours pager 405544)
Police (☎ 10111)

INTERNET ACCESS
Swakopmunder I-Café (cnr Tobias Hainyeko St & Sam Nujoma Ave; per hr N$15; 🕓 7am-10pm Mon-Sat, 10am-10pm Sun)

MEDICAL SERVICES
Bismarck Medical Centre (☎ 405000; Bismarck St) For doctors' visits, see the recommended Drs Swiegers, Schikerling, Dantu and Biermann, all at this centre.

MONEY
Bureau de Change (Sam Nujoma Ave; 🕓 7am-7pm daily) The most convenient option for changing money. Charges no commission to change travellers cheques – the catch is that you'll need the slips verifying proof of purchase.

POST
Main post office (Garnison St) Also sells telephone cards and offers fax services.

TOURIST INFORMATION
Namib-i (☎ 404827; www.namibi.org; Sam Nujoma Ave; 🕓 8am-1pm & 2-5pm Mon-Fri, 9am-noon & 3.30-5.30pm Sat, 9.30am-noon & 3.30-5pm Sun) This tourist information centre is a very helpful resource. In addition to helping you get your bearing, it can also act as a booking agent for any activities and tours that happen to take your fancy.

Namibia Wildlife Resorts (NWR; ☎ 204172; www.
nwr.com.na; Woermannhaus, Bismarck St; � 8am-1pm &
2-5pm Mon-Fri) Like it's big brother in Windhoek (p987),
this office sells Namib-Naukluft Park and Skeleton Coast
permits, and can also make reservations for any NWR-
administered property in the country.

Sights

Swakopmund is Namibia's main beach resort
but, even in summer, the water is never warmer
than around 15°C (the Benguela Current sweeps
upwards from Antarctica). Swimming in the sea
is best in the lee of the **Mole** sea wall.

At the lagoon at the Swakop River mouth,
you can watch ducks, flamingos, pelicans,
cormorants, gulls, waders and other birds.
North of town you can stroll along miles and
miles of deserted beaches stretching towards
the Skeleton Coast. The best surfing is at
Nordstrand or 'Thick Lip' near Vineta Point.

A fascinating short hike will take you across
the Swakop River to the large **dunes** south of
town. The dune formations and unique vegetation are great for solo exploring.

Activities

Swakopmund is one of the top destinations in
southern Africa for extreme-sports enthusiasts. Although filling your days with adrena-
line-soaked activities is certainly not cheap,
there are few places in the world where you
can climb up, race down and soar over towering sand dunes.

Most activity operators don't have offices in
town, which means that you need to arrange
all of your activities through either your accommodation provider or the Namib-i tourist
information centre (opposite).

Alternatively, you can stop by Outback
Orange (right). Although it specialises in
quad biking, the friendly staff members are
more than happy to phone a few operators
for you.

CAMEL RIDING

If you want to live out all your *Lawrence of
Arabia*–inspired Saharan fantasies, visit the
Camel Farm (☎ 400363; ☟ 2-5pm), adjacent to
Okakambe Trails.

HORSE RIDING

Meaning 'horse' in the local Herero and
Oshivambo languages, **Okakambe Trails**
(☎ 402799; www.okakambe.iway.na) specialises
in horse riding and hiking through the

desert (prices vary). Located 12km east of
Swakopmund on the D1901.

QUAD BIKING

Outback Orange (☎ 400968; www.outback-orange.com;
42 Nathaniel Maxuilili St; 1-/2hr N$250/395) offers stom-
ach-dropping tours on quad bikes (motorcy-
cle-style 4WDs) through the enormous dune
field adjacent to Swakop.

SAND BOARDING

Sand boarding with **Alter Action** (☎ 402737; lie
down/stand up N$340/550) is certain to increase your
heart rate while going easy on your wallet (it's
by far the cheapest trip in town). If you have
any experience snowboarding or surfing, it's
highly recommended that you have a go at the
stand-up option.

SCENIC FLIGHTS

One of the most reputable light-plane operators in Namibia, **Pleasure Flights** (☎ 404500;
www.pleasureflights.com.na; Sam Nujoma Ave) has been
offering scenic aerial cruises for more than 15
years. Prices vary.

SKYDIVING

Ground Rush Adventures (☎ 402841; www.skydiveswa
kop.com.na; tandem jump N$1900, camcorder/professional
video N$450/850) provides the ultimate rush, and
skydiving in Swakopmund is sweetened by the
outstanding dune and ocean backdrop.

Sleeping

Desert Sky Backpackers (☎ 402339; dsbackpack
ers@swakop.com; 35 Lazarett St; campsite/dm/r per person
N$50/60/160; ☐) This centrally located back-
packers' haunt is an excellent place to drop
anchor in Swakopmund.

Dunes Lodge (☎ 463139; www.dunes.com.na; 12
Lazarett St; campsite per person N$50, dm N$110, r from
N$300; ☐ ☒) The Dunes Lodge is an upmar-
ket backpackers featuring a number of attractive perks, including an indoor pool and
billiards table, as well as traditional backpacker amenities.

Villa Wiese & Duendin Star (☎ 407105; www.villa
wiese.com; Windhoeker St; dm/s/d N$115/330/385; ☐)
Villa Wiese and the nearby Duendin Star are
friendly and funky guest lodges occupying
historic colonial mansions, complete with
vaulted ceilings, rock gardens and period
furniture.

Schweizerhaus Hotel (☎ 400331; www.schw
eizerhaus.net; 1 Bismarck St; s/d from N$510/850; ☐)

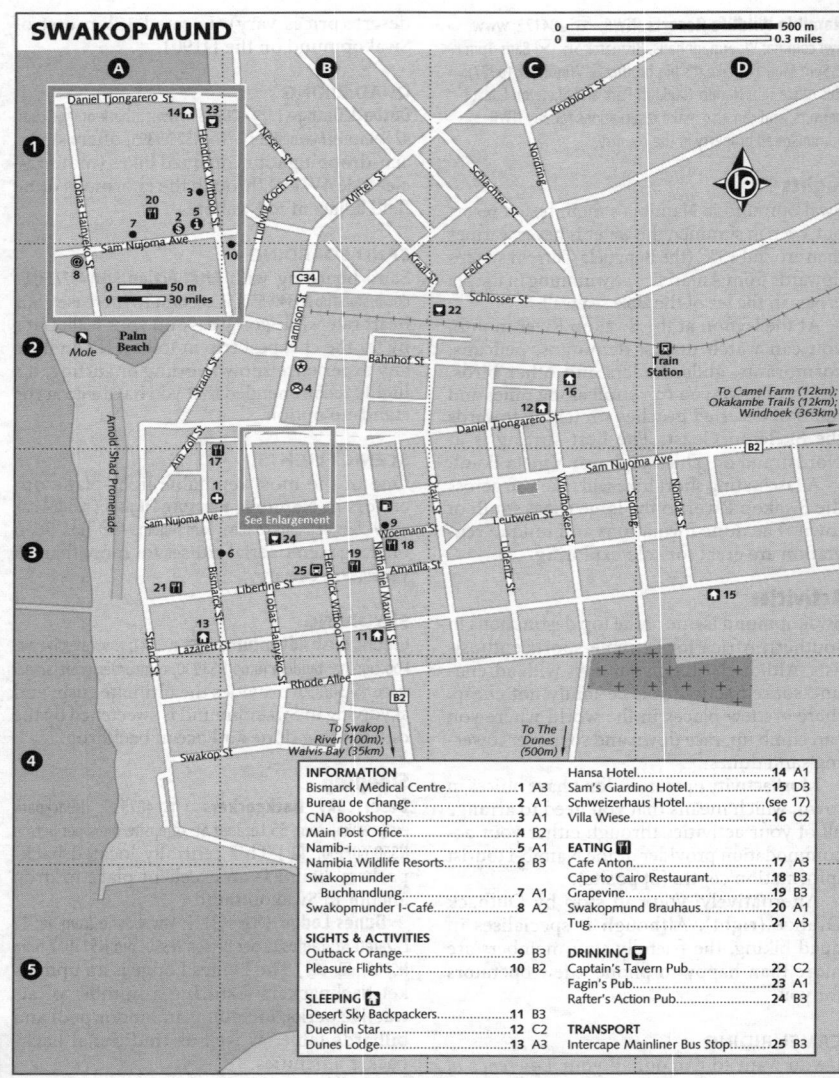

The Schweizerhaus Hotel is a class act with comfortable rooms that benefit from spectacular views of the beach and the adjacent lighthouse.

Sam's Giardino Hotel (☎ 403210; www.giardino.com.na; 89 Lazarett St; s/d from N$900/1150; ☒) A slice of central Europe in the desert, Sam's Giardino Hotel mixes Swiss and Italian hospitality and architecture, while emphasising fine wines, fine cigars and relaxing in the rose garden.

Hansa Hotel (☎ 400311; www.hansahotel.com.na; 3 Hendrick Witbooi St; s/d from N$1230/1730; ☒) Swakopmund's most established upmarket hotel bills itself as 'luxury in the desert', and offers individually decorated rooms with lofty ceilings and picture windows that are tasteful and elegant.

Eating

Cafe Anton (☎ 402419; 1 Bismarck St; light meals N$35-65) This much-loved local institution, located in Schweizerhaus Hotel (p993), serves superb coffee, apple strudel and other European delights.

Swakopmund Brauhaus (☎ 402214; 22 Sam Nujoma Ave; mains N$60-90) This excellent restaurant and boutique brewery offers one of Swakopmund's most sought-after commodities, namely authentic German-style beer.

Cape to Cairo Restaurant (☎ 463160; 7 Nathaniel Maxuilili St; mains N$60-95) This popular tourist restaurant serves a wide variety of dishes from across the African continent.

Tug (☎ 402356; mains N$75-125) Housed in the beached tugboat *Danie Hugo* near the jetty, the Tug is something of an obligatory destination for any diner in Swakopmund.

Grapevine (☎ 404770; Libertine St; mains N$80-155) True to its moniker, the emphasis at this upmarket bistro is on the fruit of the vine, and you'll be allotted plenty of time to select your vintage from the veritable novel of a wine list.

Drinking & Entertainment

Fagin's Pub (Hendrick Witbooi St) This extremely popular, down-to-earth watering hole is reminiscent of a US truckies' stop, complete with jocular staff, faithful clientele and evening videos of your day's adrenaline-fuelled activities.

Rafter's Action Pub (cnr Tobias Hainyeko & Woermann Sts) At Rafter's, it's a safe bet that the music is always pounding, the strobes are always flashing and everyone is strutting their stuff on the dance floor, regardless of the time of night.

Captain's Tavern Pub (2 Schlosser St) This upmarket tavern attracts highbrow clientele and sometimes features live music.

Getting There & Away

AIR

Air Namibia (☎ 405123; www.airnamibia.com.na) has several flights a week between Windhoek's Eros Airport and Walvis Bay, from where you can easily catch a bus or taxi to Swakopmund.

BUS

There are several weekly buses between Windhoek and Swakopmund (from N$180, five hours) on the **Intercape Mainliner** (www.inter

cape.co.za). You can easily book your tickets in advance online.

Also consider **Town Hopper** (www.namibiashuttle.com), which runs private shuttle buses between Windhoek and Swakop (N$220), and offers a door-to-door pick-up and drop-off service.

Finally, *combis* run this route fairly regularly, and a ride between Windhoek and Swakopmund shouldn't cost more than N$100. Swakopmund is also a minor public transportation hub, serving various regional destinations, including Walvis Bay by *combi*, with fares averaging between N$15 and N$30.

CAR

Swakopmund is about 400km west of Windhoek on the B2, the country's main east–west highway.

TRAIN

Trans-Namib (☎ 061-298 2175) operates night trains (from N$75), though they're not very convenient or popular, especially given the ease of bus travel.

NAMIB-NAUKLUFT PARK
☎ 063

This is the Namibia of picture books and movies, and it does not disappoint. The park is best known for Sossusvlei, a huge ephemeral pan set amid infamous towering red dunes that leave you speechless at first glance. The dunes are part of the Namib Desert, which stretches more than 2000km along the coast from Oliphants River in South Africa all the way to southern Angola. The Naukluft portion of the park is not as well known, but the craggy peaks here are almost as impressive as the dunes themselves.

Campsites must be booked in advance at the NWR office in Windhoek (p987) or Swakopmund (p992). Permits for Sesriem–Sossusvlei and Naukluft hikes must be booked in the office in Windhoek.

There is no public transport to the area; you will either need to have your own vehicle or be part of an organised tour.

Sesriem & Sossusvlei

Despite being Namibia's number-one attraction, Sossusvlei still manages to feel isolated. Hiking through the dunes, part of the 32,000-sq-km sand sea that covers much of western

NAMIBIA

Namibia, is a sombre experience. The dunes, which reach as high as 325m, are part of one of the oldest and driest ecosystems on earth. The landscape here is constantly changing: colours shift with the light, and wind forever alters the dunes' shape. If you can, visit Sossusvlei at sunrise when the colours are particularly breathtaking.

Sesriem is the gateway to Sossusvlei. Here you can pick up your park permit (which is needed to get to Sossusvlei). There is also a small food shop, a camping ground and the Sossusvlei Lodge. If you want to view the dunes at sunrise, you must stay at the camping ground or the lodge, and drive the 65km from Sesriem to Sossusvlei (on a sealed road). The park gate opens at sunrise and closes at sunset.

On the way from Sesriem, you'll pass Dune 45, the most accessible of the red dunes along the Sossusvlei road. It's a good place to take a photo (or 20) and is marked with a sign on the left side of the road driving towards Sossusvlei.

Unless you have a 4WD vehicle, you will have to park at the 2WD car park before you reach Sossusvlei. At the car park, either hike the last 4km into the pan or take one of the shuttles (US$10 round trip). Unless you have plenty of water and good walking shoes, the shuttle service is worth the hefty fee; the driver will stay with you and take you on guided hikes. Ask to be taken to Dead Vlei. The walk is stupendous and you will feel as if you have reached the ends of the earth.

With the exception of the upmarket Sossus Dune Lodge, the **Sesriem Camp Site** (campsite N$300, plus per person N$150) is the only accommodation inside the park gates – staying here guarantees that you will be able to arrive at Sossusvlei in time for sunrise. Given its popularity, you must book in advance at NWR and arrive before sunset or the camp staff will reassign your site on a stand-by basis; anyone who was unable to book a site in Windhoek may get in on this nightly lottery.

If money is no object, then splash out at the brand-new and ultra-exclusive **Sossus Dune Lodge** (☎ 061-285 7200; www.nwr.com.na; s/d US$600/835, full board from extra N$2300/3600; ☒), which is also administered by NWR. Constructed entirely of local materials, the lodge consists of elevated bungalows that run alongside a curving promenade, and face out towards the silent desert plains.

Naukluft Mountains

The Naukluft Mountains, which rise steeply from the gravel plains of the central Namib, are characterised by a high plateau bounded by gorges, caves and springs cut deeply from dolomite formations. The Tsondab, Tsams and Tsauchab Rivers all rise in the massif, and the relative abundance of water creates an ideal habitat for mountain zebras, kudus, leopards, springboks and klipspringers. In addition to wildlife-watching, the Naukluft is home to a couple of challenging treks and unofficial campsites that open up this largely inaccessible terrain.

The lovely **Waterkloof Trail** is a 17km anticlockwise loop that takes a total of about seven hours to complete, and begins at the Naukluft (Koedoesrus) campsite, located 2km west of the park headquarters.

The 11km **Olive Trail**, named for the wild olives that grow alongside it, begins at the car park 4km northeast of the park headquarters. The walk runs clockwise around the triangular loop and takes four to five hours.

Off-road enthusiasts can now exercise their machines on the national park's 73km **Naukluft 4WD Trail**. It begins near the start of the Olive Trail and follows a loop near the northeastern corner of the Naukluft area.

The Naukluft is best reached via the C24 from Rehoboth and the D1206 from Rietoog; petrol is available at Büllsport and Rietoog. From Sesriem, 103km away, the nearest access is via the dip-ridden D854. For specific information head to the NWR office in Windhoek (see p987).

NORTHWESTERN NAMIBIA

For 4WD explorers, Namibia is synonymous with the Skeleton Coast, a formidable desert coastline engulfed by icy breakers. Seemingly endless stretches of foggy beach are punctuated by rusting shipwrecks and flanked by wandering dunes. As you move inland, the sinister fogs give way to the wondrous desert wildernesses of Damaraland and the Kaokoveld. The former is sparsely populated by the Damara people, and is known for its unique geological features; the latter is known as one of the last great wilderness areas in southern Africa, as well as the home of the oft-photographed Himba people.

SKELETON COAST

The term 'Skeleton Coast' is derived from the treacherous nature of the coast – a foggy region with rocky and sandy coastal shallows – which has long been a graveyard for unwary ships and their crews. Early Portuguese sailors called it *As Areias do Inferno* (The Sands of Hell), as once a ship washed ashore, the fate of the crew was sealed.

Although it has been extrapolated to take in the entire Namib Desert coastline, the Skeleton Coast actually refers to the coastal stretch between the mouths of the Swakop and Kunene Rivers. For our purposes, it covers the National West Coast Recreation Area and the Skeleton Coast Park (including the Skeleton Coast Wilderness). These protected areas stretch from just north of Swakopmund to the Kunene River, taking in nearly 2 million hectares of dunes and gravel plains to form one of the world's most inhospitable waterless areas.

National West Coast Recreation Area

A 200km-long, 25km-wide strip from Swakopmund to the Ugab River, the National West Coast Recreation Area makes up the southern end of the Skeleton Coast. It's extremely popular with anglers and wildlife-watchers alike, and it's convenient to visit since you don't need to arrange a permit in advance, unlike other destinations along the Skeleton Coast.

Most visitors head for the **Cape Cross Seal Reserve** (per person N$45; ☾ 10am-5pm), where the seal population has grown large and fat by taking advantage of the rich concentrations of fish in the cold Benguela Current. The sight of more than 100,000 seals basking on the beach and frolicking in the surf is an impressive sight to behold.

Along the salt road that heads up the coast from Swakopmund, you will find several bleak beach campsites set up mainly for sea anglers. Sites at Myl 14, Jakkalsputz, Myl 72 and Myl 108 cost N$30 per person. (Myl means 'mile' – which is the distance from Swakop.)

Skeleton Coast Park

At Ugabmund, 110km north of Cape Cross, the road passes into the **Skeleton Coast Park** (per person/vehicle N$80/10). UK journalist Nigel Tisdell once wrote in the *Daily Telegraph*, 'If hell has a coat of arms, it probably looks like the entrance to Namibia's Skeleton Coast Park', and the description is fitting.

Accommodation is available at **Torra Bay** (campsite per person N$50; ☾ Dec & Jan only) and **Terrace Bay** (s/d N$950/1400, 8-person beach chalet N$3200). Both resorts must be booked ahead of time at the NWR office in Windhoek (p987) or Swakopmund (p992). If you are staying at either resort, you must pass through the Ugabmund gate before 3pm or the Springbokwater gate before 5pm.

No day visits to the park are allowed, but you can obtain a transit permit to pass between Ugabmund and Springbokwater. To transit the park, you must pass the entry gate before 1pm, and exit through the other gate before 3pm the same day. Note that transit permits aren't valid for Torra Bay or Terrace Bay.

Skeleton Coast Wilderness Area

The Skeleton Coast Wilderness, stretching between the Hoanib and Kunene Rivers, makes up the northern third of the Skeleton Coast. This section of coastline is among the most remote and inaccessible areas in Namibia, though it's here in the wilderness that you can truly live out your Skeleton Coast fantasies. Since the entire area is a private concession, you're going to have to part with some serious cash to visit.

If your budget stretches far enough, the **Skeleton Coast Wilderness Camp** (☎ 061-274500; www.wilderness-safaris.com, 4-/5-day trips per person from US$2500/3000) offers mind-blowing activities, including viewing desert elephants along the Hoarusib River, ocean fishing, dune climbing, hiking through the Clay Castles and basking in veritable isolation.

Access is restricted to fly-in trips operated by Wilderness Safaris.

DAMARALAND

The territory between the Skeleton Coast and Namibia's Central Plateau has traditionally been known as Damaraland, after the people who make up much of its population. Although it's not an officially protected area, its wild open spaces are home to many desert-adapted species, including giraffes, zebras, lions, elephants and rhinos. In addition to its sense of freedom, the region is rich in both natural and cultural attractions, including Brandberg, Namibia's highest massif, and the rock engravings of Twyfelfontein.

NAMIBIA

Spitzkoppe

☎ 064

The 1728m **Spitzkoppe** (Groot Spitzkoppe village; per car/person N$10/50; ☼ sunrise-sunset), is one of Namibia's most instantly recognisable landmarks, and rises like a mirage above the dusty pro-Namib plains of southern Damaraland.

Spitzkoppe Rest Camp (☎ 530879; www.nacobta. com.na; Groot Spitzkoppe village; campsite/bungalow per person N$35/100) is an excellent community-run camp that includes a number of sites that are dotted around the base of the Spitzkoppe and surrounding outcrops.

Under normal dry conditions, a 2WD is sufficient to reach the mountain. Turn northwest off the B2 onto the D1918 towards Henties Bay, then after 1km turn north on the D1930. After 27km (you will actually pass the mountain) turn southwest on the D3716 until you reach Groot Spitzkoppe village; here you turn west into the site.

Brandberg

☎ 064

The Brandberg (Fire Mountain) is named for the effect created by the setting sun on its western face, which causes the granite massif to resemble a burning slag heap. Its summit, Königstein, is Namibia's highest peak at 2573m.

Its best-known attraction, the gallery of rock art in **Tsisab Ravine**, features the **White Lady of the Brandberg**. The figure, which isn't necessarily a lady (it's still open to interpretation), stands about 40cm high and is part of a larger painting that depicts a bizarre hunting procession. In one hand, the figure is carrying what appears to be a flower or possibly a feather. In the other, the figure is carrying a bow and arrows. However, the painting is distinct because 'her' hair is straight and light coloured – distinctly un-African – and the body is painted white from the chest down.

At the **Brandberg White Lady Lodge** (☎ 684004; www.brandbergwllodge.com; camping per person N$50, bungalow/chalet from N$300/450), campers can pitch a tent along the riverine valley, all the while taking advantage of the lodge's upmarket facilities, while lovers of creature comforts can choose from rustic bungalows and chalets. From the C35, Uis-to-Korixas section, take the D2359 for 27km, following signs for the lodge.

Twyfelfontein

At the head of a grassy valley, **Twyfelfontein** (per person N$50; ☼ sunrise-sunset) is one of the most extensive galleries of rock art in Africa. The original name of this water source in the Aba-Huab Valley was /Ui-//Ais (Surrounded by Rocks), but in 1947 it was renamed Twyfelfontein, meaning 'doubtful spring', by European settler D Levin, who deemed its daily output of 1 cu metre of water insufficient for life in the harsh environment. The 6000-year-old petroglyphs here were executed by cutting through the hard patina covering the local sandstone. Guides are available (plan on N$10 as a tip), but the route is easy and you can usually walk alone.

The **Aba Huab** (☎ 697981; www.nacobta.com.na; campsite per person N$50, A-frame from N$300) is an attractively perched campsite beside the Aba Huab riverbed, immediately north of the Twyfelfontein turn-off. Pricier sites have electricity. The camp is a member of Nacobta, a collective of various organisations that aims to foster increased community-based tourism.

Over the hill from Twyfelfontein, the **Twyfelfontein Country Lodge** (☎ 374750; www.namibia lodges.com; s/d from N$1150/1730; 🖵 🔀 🏋) is an architectural wonder that is embedded in the red rock. The lodge boasts stylish rooms, an immense and airy elevated dining room, and a good variety of excursions throughout Damaraland.

KAOKOVELD

☎ 065

The northwest corner of the country represents Namibia at its most primeval. The Kaokoveld is a vast repository of desert mountains that is crossed only by sandy tracks laid down by the South African Defence Force (SAFDF). It is one of the least developed regions of the country, and is often described as one of the last true wildernesses in southern Africa. It is also home to the Himba, a group of nomadic pastoralists native to the Kaokoveld, who are famous for covering their skin with a traditional mixture of ochre butter and herbs to protect themselves from the sun.

There's no public transport anywhere in the region and hitching is practically impossible, so the best way to explore Kaokoveld is with a well-outfitted 4WD vehicle or an organised camping safari. In the dry season, the routes from Opuwo to Epupa Falls, Ruacana to Okongwati (via Swartbooi's Drift)

THE HIMBA

Even if you've never heard of the Himba prior to visiting Namibia, you'll quickly become enamoured with them. An ethnic group numbering not more than 50,000 people, the Himba are a seminomadic pastoral people that are closely related to the Herero, yet continue to live much as they have for generations on end.

The women in particular are famous for smearing themselves with a fragrant mixture of ochre, butter and bush herbs, which dyes their skin a burnt-orange hue, and serves as a natural sun block and insect repellent. As if this wasn't striking enough, they also use the mixture to cover their braided hair, which has an effect similar to dreadlocks. And of course, it is also worth mentioning that they tend to shun Western clothes, preferring to walk around bare-breasted, with little more than a pleated-animal skin covering their unmentionables.

---

and Sesfontein to Purros may be passable to high-clearance 2WD vehicles, but otherwise, you'll need a 4WD.

Opuwo
☎ 065

In the Herero language, Opuwo means 'the end', which is certainly a fitting name for this dusty collection of concrete commercial buildings ringed by traditional *rondavels* and huts. While first impressions are unlikely to be very positive, a visit to Opuwo is truly one of the highlights of Namibia, particularly for anyone interested in interacting with the Himba people. As the unofficial capital of Himbaland, Opuwo serves as a convenient jumping-off point for excursions into the nearby villages, and there is a good assortment of lodges and campsites in the area to choose from.

INFORMATION
At **Kaoko Information Centre** (☎ 273420; ⏰ 8am-6pm) KK and Kemuu, the friendly guys at this information centre (look for the tiny, tiny yellow shack), can arrange visits to Himba villages, in addition to providing useful information for your trip through the Kaokoveld region.

SIGHTS & ACTIVITIES
Meeting Himba people and learning about them and their culture (see the boxed text, above) through village visits is the main activity in the area. Be sure to treat the Himba people you meet with the appropriate respect (see the boxed text, p1000), just as you would anyone in your home country. There are a few ways to go about this: you can either join an organised tour through your accommodation, stop by the Kaoko Information Centre (above) or find an independent guide somewhere in Opuwo.

SLEEPING
Kunene Village Rest Camp (☎ 273043; www.nacobta.com.na; campsite per person N$40, s/d hut N$140/170) This amenable community-run rest camp has well-groomed campsites with adequate facilities, as well as basic thatched huts with shared bathrooms. Follow the signposted turn-off from the government housing project at the edge of town, en route to Sesfontein.

Ohakane Lodge (☎ 273031; www.natron.net/tour/ohakane/lodge.html; s/d N$450/800; ❄ ▨) This well-established and centrally located lodge sits along the main drag in Opuwo, and has fairly standard but fully modernised rooms.

Opuwo Country Hotel (☎ 061-374750; www.namibialodges.com/opuwo.html; campsite per person N$125, s/d N$1234/1748; ❄ ▨ ▨) This enormous thatched building lords elegantly over the town below. Accommodation is in a small handful of exclusive bungalows facing out across the valley towards the Angolan foothills, though most of your time here will be spent soaking your cares away in the infinity pool.

EATING
Food is available in Opuwo's hotels (see above) or, for self-caterers, there's an OK grocer in town.

GETTING THERE & AWAY
The marvellously paved C41 runs from Outjo to Opuwo, which makes Himbaland accessible even to 2WD vehicles. Although there is a temptation to speed along this long and lonely highway, keep your lead foot off the pedal north of the veterinary control fence as herds of cattle commonly stray across the road. If you're heading deeper into the Kaokoveld, be advised that Opuwo is the last opportunity to buy petrol before Ruacana or Sesfontein.

RESPECTING THE LOCAL CULTURE

All throughout Opuwo, you will see Himba people in traditional attire wherever you go – they will be walking the streets, shopping in the stores and even waiting in line behind you at the supermarket! However tempting it might be, please do not sneak a quick picture of them as no one appreciates having a camera unwillingly waved in front of their face.

If you would like to have free reign with your camera, visiting a traditional village – if done in the proper fashion – can yield some truly amazing shots. Needless to say, a guide who speaks both English and the Himba language is essential to the experience.

Before arriving in the village, spend some time shopping for gifts – entering a village with food items will garner a warm welcome from the villagers, who will subsequently be more willing to tolerate photography. At the end of your time in the village, buying small bracelets and trinkets direct from the craftspeople is also a greatly appreciated gesture.

Finally, don't be afraid to ask lots of questions with the aid of your translator, and spend some time interacting with the Himba rather than just photographing them. Showing respect and admiration helps the Himba reinforce their belief that their tradition and way of life is something worth preserving.

ETOSHA NATIONAL PARK

Covering an area of more than 20,000 sq km, Etosha National Park ranks as one of the world's greatest wildlife-viewing venues. Its name, which means 'Great White Place of Dry Water', is inspired by the vast greenish-white Etosha Pan, an immense, flat, saline desert covering over 5000 sq km that, for a few days each year, is converted by the rains into a shallow lagoon teeming with flamingos and pelicans. However, it's the surrounding bush and grasslands that provide a habitat for Etosha's diverse wildlife. Although it may look barren, the landscape surrounding the pan is home to 114 mammal species, as well as 340 bird species, 16 reptile and amphibian species, one fish species and countless insects.

Orientation & Information

Only the eastern two-thirds of Etosha are open to the general public; the western third is reserved exclusively for tour operators. Etosha's three main entry gates are Von Lindequist (Namutoni), west of Tsumeb; King Nehale, southeast of Ondangwa; and Andersson (Okaukuejo), north of Outjo.

Visitors are encouraged to check in at either Von Lindequist Gate or Andersson Gate (King Nehale Gate is frequently closed), where you must purchase a permit costing N$80 per person plus N$10 per vehicle per day. The permits are then to be presented at your reserved rest camp, where you pay any outstanding camping or accommodation fees.

Although fees are normally prepaid through the NWR office in Windhoek (p987), it is

sometimes possible to reserve accommodation at on of the gates. However, be advised that the park can get very busy on weekends, especially during the dry season – booking ahead is recommended.

Sleeping

Advance booking for the NWR-run camps listed below is mandatory. Although it is sometimes possible to reserve a space at either of the park gates, it's best to contact the NWR office in Windhoek well in advance of your visit.

Okaukuejo Rest Camp (camping per person/site N$100/200, s/d from N$800/1300, chalet from N$900/1500; ⛺ 🍽) Pronounced 'o-ka-kui-yo', this is the site of the Etosha Research Station, and functions as the official park headquarters and main visitors centre. The Okaukuejo water hole is probably Etosha's best rhino-viewing venue, particularly between 8pm and 10pm, though you're almost guaranteed to spot zebra, wildebeest, jackals and even elephants virtually any time of day.

Halali Rest Camp (camping per person/site N$100/200, s/d from N$800/1300, chalet from N$900/1500; ⛺ 🍽) Etosha's middle camp, Halali, nestles between several incongruous dolomite outcrops. The best feature of Halali is its floodlit water hole, which is a 10-minute walk from the rest camp, and is sheltered by a glen of trees with huge boulders strewn about. Like Okaukuejo, there is a very well-serviced campsite here, in addition to a fine collection of luxury chalets that make for a wonderfully relaxed night of sleep despite being deep in the middle of the African bush.

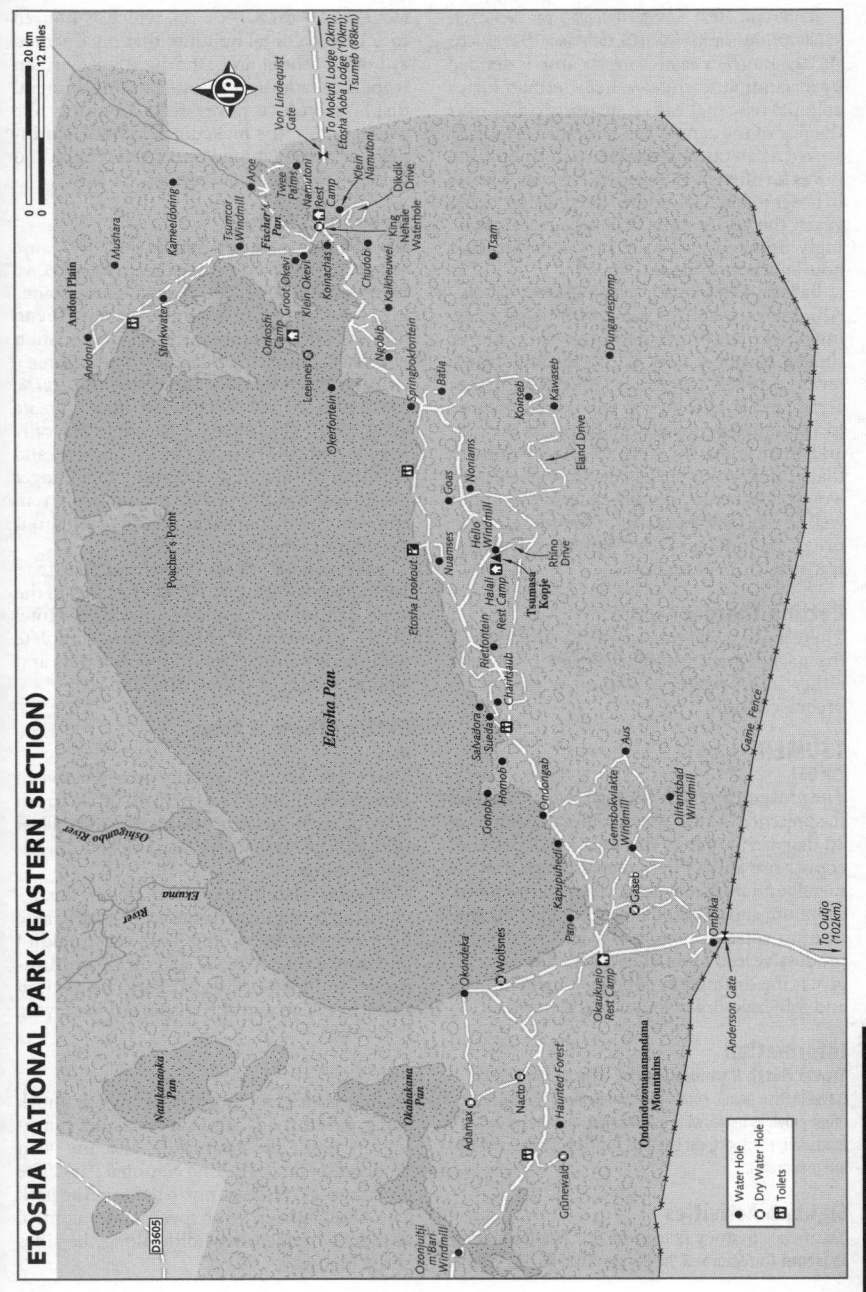

ETOSHA NATIONAL PARK (EASTERN SECTION)

Water Hole
Dry Water Hole
Toilets

NAMIBIA

Namutoni Rest Camp (camping per person/site N$100/200, s/d from N$1400/1800, chalet from N$2000/3000; ⊠ ⊠) Etosha's easternmost camp is defined by its landmark whitewashed German fort, a colonial relic that casts a surreal shadow over the rest of the camp. The structure originally served as an outpost for German troops, but it was fortified in 1899 by the German cavalry in order to quell Owambo uprisings. In recent years, the entire interior has been painstakingly updated and now serves as Etosha's boutique accommodation.

Onkoshi Camp (s/d from N$5500/9000; ⊠ ⊠) Although it requires some serious purchasing power, the brand-new Onkoshi Camp at Etosha National Park is the shining crown jewel of NWR's Premier Collection. Upon arrival in Namutoni, you will be chauffeured to a secluded peninsula on the rim of the pan, and then given the keys to one of only 15 thatch and canvas chalets that rest on elevated wooden decks, and occupy exclusive locations well beyond the standard tourist route. Room prices include activities, entrance fees and transfers from Namutoni.

Getting There & Away

There's no public transport into and around the park, which means that you must visit either in a private vehicle or as part of an organised tour.

TSUMEB

☎ 067

The prosperity of this mining town is based on the presence of 184 known minerals, including 10 that are unique to this area. Its deposits of copper ore and a phenomenal range of other metals and minerals (lead, silver, germanium, cadmium and many others) brought to the surface in a volcanic pipe, as well as Africa's most productive lead mine (the world's fifth largest), give it the distinction of being a metallurgical and mineralogical wonder of the world.

Information

Travel North Namibia Tourist Office (☎ 220728; travelnn@tsu.namib.com; 1551 Omeg Allee) This friendly office provides nationwide information, arranges accommodation, transport, car hire and Etosha bookings, and has internet access.

Sights & Activities

Tsumeb's history is told in the **Tsumeb Mining Museum** (cnr Main St & 8th Rd; admission N$15; ☼ 9am-

noon & 3-6pm Mon-Fri, 3-6pm Sat), which is housed in a 1915 colonial building that once served as both a school and a hospital for German troops. In addition to outstanding mineral displays (you've never seen anything like psittacinite!), the museum also houses mining machinery, stuffed birds, and Himba and Herero artefacts and weapons.

Sleeping & Eating

Mousebird Backpackers & Safaris (☎ 221777; www.mousebird.com; 533 4th St; campsite per person N$125, dm N$185, s/d from N$390/420; ⊠) Tsumeb's long-standing backpacker spot continues to stay true to its roots, offering economical accommodation without sacrificing personality or character.

Travel North Namibia Guesthouse (☎ 220728; http://natron.net/tnn/index.htm; Sam Nujoma Dr; s/d N$350/480; ⊠ ⊠) Situated adjacent to the tourist office, which is also run by the husband and wife duo of Johann and Regina, this budget guesthouse has airy private rooms on offer, in addition to customisable safaris throughout the whole of northern Namibia.

Makalani Hotel (☎ 221051; www.makalanihotel.com; 3rd St; s/d from N$420/610 ⊠ ⊠ ⊠) Located in the town centre, the upmarket Makalani Hotel exudes a positively Caribbean vibe, complete with shady palms, tranquil (pool) waters and vibrant shades of yellow, blue and red.

Getting There & Away

BUS

There are several weekly buses between Windhoek and the Travel North office (from N$350, six hours) on the **Intercape Mainliner** (www.intercape.co.za). Book your tickets in advance online.

Combis also run up and down the B1 with fairly regular frequency, and a ride between Windhoek and Tsumeb shouldn't cost more than N$200. If you're continuing on to Etosha National Park, be advised that there is no public transportation serving that route.

CAR

Tsumeb is an easy day's drive from Windhoek along paved roads, and serves as the jumping-off point for Namutoni and the Von Lindequist Gate of Etosha National Park. The paved route continues north as far as the park gate, though keep your speed under control as there's frequently wildlife along the sides of the highway.

TRAIN
Trans-Namib (☎ 061-298 2175) operates trains on Monday and Wednesday between Windhoek and Tsumeb (from N$175), though very limited early morning and late night departures are inconvenient for most.

WATERBERG PLATEAU PARK
Waterberg Plateau Park takes in a 50km-long, 16km-wide Etjo sandstone plateau, looming 150m above the desert plains. Rainwater is absorbed by the sandstone layers and percolates through the strata until it reaches the southwest tilting mudstone, forming an aquifer that emerges in springs at the cliff base.

Around this sheer-sided 'lost world' is an abundance of watering holes that support a mosaic of lush trees and rare wildlife. In addition to the standard complement of African herbivores, the park protects rare and threatened species, including sable and roan antelopes, white and black rhinos and even wild dogs.

Information
Waterberg Plateau Park (per person/vehicle per day N$80/10, game drive per person N$450) is accessible by private vehicle, though visitors must explore the plateau either on foot, or as part of an official game drive, which is conducted by NWR.

Activities
From April to November, the four-day guided **Waterberg Wilderness Trail** operates every second, third and fourth Thursday of the month. The walks, which are led by armed guides, accommodate groups of six to eight people. They begin at 2pm on Thursdays from the visitors centre and end early on Sunday afternoon. They cost N$100 per person and must be pre-booked through NWR in Windhoek. There's no set route, and the itinerary is left to the whims of the guide.

A four-day, 42km unguided hike around the figure-eight **Waterberg Unguided Hiking Trail** begins at 9am every Wednesday from April to November. It costs N$50 per person, and groups are limited to between three and 10 people. Book through NWR in Windhoek (p987).

Sleeping
The Waterberg Resort must be booked in advance through NWR in Windhoek (p987). The Waterberg Wilderness Lodge is privately owned and accepts walk-ins, though advanced reservations are recommended given its popularity.

Waterberg Resort (campsite N$100, s/d N$650/1000, s/d chalet from N$800/1300) At Waterberg, campers can pitch a tent in any number of immaculate sites (complete with power points) scattered around hot-water shower blocks, *braai* (barbecue) pits and picnic tables. If you're looking for a bit of bush luxury, try one of the well-designed newly constructed chalets.

Waterberg Wilderness Resort (☎ 687018; www.waterberg-wilderness.com; campsite N$120, s/d incl half board from N$1070/2100; ✖ ▣ ▣) Despite its former life as a cattle farm, the property has been painstakingly transformed by the Rust family through repopulating game animals and allowing nature to return to its pregrazed state. The main lodge rests in a sun-drenched meadow at the end of a valley, where you'll find red sandstone chalets adorned with rich hardwood furniture.

Getting There & Away
Waterberg Plateau Park is only accessible by private car – motorcycles are not permitted anywhere within the park boundaries. From Otjiwarongo, it's about 90km to the park gate via the B1, C22 and the gravel D512. While this route is passable for 2WD vehicles, go slow in the final stretches as the road is torn apart in several spots. If you have a high-clearance 4WD (and a bit of extra time on your hands), you might want to leave or arrive on the particularly scenic D2512, which runs between Waterberg and Grootfontein.

NORTHEASTERN NAMIBIA

Known as the 'Land of Rivers', northeastern Namibia is bounded by the Kunene and Okavango Rivers along the Angolan border, and in the east by the Zambezi and the Kwando/Mashe/Linyanti/Chobe River systems. Although Windhoek may be the capital, northeastern Namibia, which is the country's most densely populated region, is undeniably its cultural heartland.

RUNDU
☎ 066
Rundu, a sultry tropical outpost on the bluffs above the Okavango River, is a major centre

of activity for Namibia's growing Angolan community. Although the town has little of specific interest for tourists, the area is home to a number of wonderful lodges where you can laze along the riverside and spot crocs and hippos doing pretty much the same.

Sights & Activities

Take a stroll around the large **covered market**, which is one of Africa's most sophisticated informal sales outlets. From July to September, don't miss the fresh papayas, sold straight from the trees. Alternatively, head for the **Khemo Open Market**, where you can shop for both African staples and Kavango handicrafts.

Sleeping & Eating

Situated on the banks of the Okavango, about 20km from Rundu's town centre, is the **N'Kwazi Lodge** (☎ 255467; nkwazi@iafrica.com.na; campsite per person N$110, s/d N$520/590), a tranquil and good-value riverside retreat. The owners, Valerie and Weynand Peyper, are active in promoting responsible travel, and have begun a partnership with a local school.

The newest lodge in the Rundu area, **Sarasungu River Lodge** (☎ 255161; www.sarasunguriverlodge.com; campsite per person N$70, s/d/tr N$445/620/830; 🖳) occupies a secluded riverine clearing, with thatched chalets and an inviting landscaped pool.

Hakusembe Lodge (☎ 257010; www.natron.net/hakusembe; campsite per person N$80, chalet per person incl half board from N$880; 🍽 🖳) Has eight luxury chalets (one of which is floating) decked out with safari prints and locally crafted furniture.

A popular stop with passing motorists is **Ozzy's Beer House** (☎ 256723; meals N$35-60), which has plenty of kilojoule-loaded meals to fuel hungry drivers, as well as ice-cold draught beer if you're retiring in Rundu for the night.

Getting There & Away

There are several weekly buses between Windhoek and Rundu (from N$365, seven hours) on the **Intercape Mainliner** (www.intercape.co.za). Book your tickets in advance online.

Combis connect Windhoek and Rundu with fairly regular frequency, and a ride shouldn't cost more than N$200. From Rundu, routes fan out to various towns and cities in the north, with fares costing less than N$30 a ride.

KHAUDOM GAME RESERVE

☎ 066

Exploring the largely undeveloped 384,000-hectare Khaudom Game Reserve is an intense wilderness challenge that is guaranteed not to disappoint. Meandering sand tracks lure you through pristine bush and across *omiramba* (fossil river valleys), which run parallel to the east–west Kalahari dunes. With virtually no signage, and navigation largely based on GPS-coordinates and topographic maps, few tourists make the effort to extend their safari experience beyond the secure confines of Etosha.

In order to explore the reserve by private 4WD vehicle, you will have to be completely self-sufficient, as petrol and supplies are only available in towns along the Caprivi Strip. Water is available inside the reserve, though it must be boiled or treated prior to drinking. As a bare minimum, you will need a GPS unit, a proper topographic map and compass, as well as lots of common sense and genuine confidence and experience in driving a 4WD.

Wildlife viewing is best from June to October when herds congregate around the water holes and along the *omiramba*. November to April is the richest time to visit for birdwatchers, though you will have to be prepared for a difficult slog through muddy tracks.

In the past, NWR administered two official campsites in the park, though after one too many episodes of elephants gone wild, it decided to close down shop. The remains of the camps are still present, and you're still encouraged to camp there (the alternative is pitching a tent in the bush), though once again we need to stress that you must be completely self-sufficient before visiting Khaudom.

Sikereti Camp is located in a shady grove of terminalia trees, though full appreciation of this place requires sensitivity to its subtle charms, namely isolation and silence.

Khaudom Camp overlooks an ephemeral water hole, and is somewhat akin to the Kalahari in miniature.

From the north, take the sandy track from Katere on the B8 (signposted 'Khaudom'), 120km east of Rundu. After 45km you'll reach the Cwibadom Omuramba, where you should turn east into the park.

From the south, you can reach Sikereti Camp via Tsumkwe. From Tsumkwe, it's 20km to Groote Döbe and another 15km from there to the Dorslandboom turning. It's then 25km north to Sikereti Camp.

KATIMA MULILO
☎ 066

Out on a limb at the eastern end of the Caprivi Strip lies remote Katima Mulilo, which is as far from Windhoek (1200km) as you can get in Namibia. Once known for the elephants that marched through the village streets, Katima is devoid of wildlife these days – apart from the hippos and crocodiles in the Zambezi – though it continues to thrive as a border town and minor commercial centre.

Located behind the Engen petrol station, **Mukusi Cabins** (☎ 253255; camping N$50, s/d from N$300/350; ☒) has a good range of accommodation, from simple rooms with fans to small but comfortable air-con cabins.

Caprivi River Lodge (☎ 253300; www.capririver lodge.info; camping per person N$50, s N$305-800, d N$445-1075; ☒ ☒) offers options to suit travellers of all budgets, from a grassy campsite and rustic chalets with shared bathrooms to slightly more luxurious wooden cabins with private bathrooms.

Book your tickets in advance online for the **Intercape Mainliner** (www.intercape.co.za) bus service between Windhoek and Katima Mulilo (from N$350, 17 hours, several weekly).

Combis regularly connect Windhoek and Katima (N$225). From Katima, to nearby towns and cities in the north, fares cost up to N$30.

SOUTHERN NAMIBIA

The deserts of southern Namibia sparkle beneath the sun – quite literally – as they're filled with millions of carats of diamonds. Since the Germans first unearthed vast treasure troves resting beneath the sands, much of the region has been dubbed the *Sperrgebiet* (Forbidden Area). Following the recent declaration of Namibia's newest national park, this virtually pristine biodiversity hot spot is now open to the general public for the first time in more than a century.

FISH RIVER CANYON NATIONAL PARK
☎ 063

Nowhere else in Africa will you find anything quite like Fish River Canyon. Despite the seeming enormity of this statement, the numbers don't lie: the canyon measures 160km in length and up to 27km in width, and the dramatic inner canyon reaches a depth of 550m. Although these figures by themselves are impressive, it's difficult to get a sense of perspective without actually witnessing the colossal scope of the canyon. In order to do this, you will need to embark on a monumental five-day hike that traverses half the length of the canyon, and ultimately tests the limits of your physical and mental endurance.

Information
The main access points for Fish River Canyon are at Hobas, near the northern end of the park, and Ai-Ais, near the southern end. Both are administered by NWR. Accommodation must be booked in advance through the Windhoek office (p987). Daily park permits, N$80 per person plus N$10 per vehicle, are valid for both Hobas and Ai-Ais.

The **Hobas Information Centre** (☒ 7.30am-noon & 2-5pm) at the northern end of the park is also the check-in point for the five-day canyon hike. Packaged snacks and cool drinks are available here, but little else.

Sights
From Hobas, it's 10km on a gravel road to the **Hikers' Viewpoint** (start of the hiking route), which has picnic tables, *braai* pits and toilets. Just around the corner is a good overview of the northern part of the canyon. The **Main Viewpoint**, a few kilometres south, has probably the best – and most photographed – overall canyon view. Both these vistas take in the sharp river bend known as Hell's Corner.

The **hot springs** (per person N$15; ☒ 9am-9pm) at Ai-Ais (Nama for 'scalding hot') are beneath the towering peaks at the southern end of Fish River Canyon National Park. Although the 60°C springs have probably been known to the San for thousands of years, the legend goes that they were 'discovered' by a nomadic Nama shepherd rounding up stray sheep. They're rich in chloride, fluoride and sulphur, and are reputedly therapeutic for sufferers of rheumatism or nervous disorders. The hot water is piped to a series of baths and jacuzzis as well as an outdoor swimming pool.

Activities
The five-day **Fish River Hiking Trail** (per person N$100) from Hobas to Ai-Ais is Namibia's most popular long-distance walk – and with good reason. The magical 85km route, which follows

the sandy riverbed past a series of ephemeral pools, begins at Hikers' Viewpoint and ends at the hot-spring resort of Ai-Ais.

Due to flash flooding and heat in summer months, the route is open only from 1 May to 30 September. Groups of three to 30 people may begin the hike every day of the season, though you will have to book in advance as the trail is extremely popular. Reservations can be made at the NWR office in Windhoek (p987).

Sleeping

Accommodation inside the national park must be prebooked through the NWR office in Windhoek (p987).

Hobas Camp Site (campsite N$50, plus per person N$20; 🔲) Administered by NWR, this pleasant and well-shaded camping ground near the park's northern end is about 10km from the main viewpoints.

Ai-Ais Hot Springs Resort (camping per person/site N$20/50, flats from N$600; 🔲) Also administered by NWR, amenities include washing blocks, *braai* pits and use of the resort facilities, including the hot springs.

Fish River Guest Farm (☎ 683005; www.canyonna turepark.com; r without bathroom per person from N$250) Located near the eastern rim in the Canyon Nature Park concession off of the C12, this historic farmhouse serves self-catering hikers of all skill levels.

Grande View Lodge (☎ 683005; www.canyonna turepark.com; r per person from N$1550; 🔲 🔲) Perched on the western rim in the Canyon Nature Park concession along the D463, the Grande View is by far the most luxurious lodge in the region.

Getting There & Away

There's no public transport to Hobas or Ai-Ais, but hitching is fairly easy during the hiking season from 1 May to 30 September. Thanks to South African holiday traffic, the best-travelled route to Ai-Ais is via two turn-offs, one 36km north of Noordoewer and the other 30km south of Grünau. Once in Ai-Ais, plenty of holidaymakers head for the viewpoints around Hobas, thus facilitating hitching between Ai-Ais, Hobas and the beginning of the Hikers' Viewpoint trail head.

LÜDERITZ

☎ 063

Before travelling to Lüderitz, pause for a moment to study the country map and appreciate the fact that the town is sandwiched between the barren Namib Desert and the wind-swept South Atlantic coast. As if Lüderitz' unique geographical setting wasn't impressive enough, its surreal German art nouveau architecture will seal the deal. Something of a colonial relic scarcely touched by the 21st century, Lüderitz might recall a Bavarian *dorfchen* (small village), with churches, bakeries and cafes. Indeed, the local community is proud of the town's unique heritage, and travellers often find they're greeted in Lüderitz with a warm smile and a cold pint.

Information

Lüderitz Safaris & Tours (☎ 202719; ludsaf@ africaonline.com.na; Bismarck St; ☯ 8am-1pm & 2-5pm Mon-Fri, 8am-noon Sat, 8.30-10am Sun) Provides reliable tourist information, organises visitor permits for the Kolmanskop ghost town (p1008), books seats on the schooner *Sedina*, which sails past the Cape fur seal sanctuary at Diaz Point and the penguin colony on Halifax Island, and sells curios, books, stamps and phonecards.

Namibia Wildlife Resorts (NWR; ☎ 202752; Schinz St; ☯ 7.30am-1pm & 2-4pm Mon-Fri) This local office can help with national-park information.

Sights

Lüderitz is chock-a-block with colonial buildings, and every view reveals something interesting. The curiously intriguing architecture, which mixes German Imperial and art nouveau styles, makes this bizarre little town appear even more otherworldly.

The **Lüderitz Peninsula**, much of which lies outside the Sperrgebiet, makes an interesting half-day excursion from town.

Tours

With the exception of the Kolmanskop ghost town, allow at least five days to plan any excursion into the Sperrgebiet, as tour companies require time to fill out all the relevant paperwork and acquire all of the necessary permits.

In addition to Lüderitz Safaris & Tours (above), the following tour companies are recommended:

Coastways Tours Lüderitz (☎ 202002; www.coast ways.com.na) This highly reputable company runs multiday self-catering 4WD trips deep into the Sperrgebiet.

Ghost Town Tours (☎ 204033; www.ghosttowntours. com; Goerke Haus) This company operates day trips to Kolmanskop, Elizabeth Bay and other sights in the Sperrgebiet.

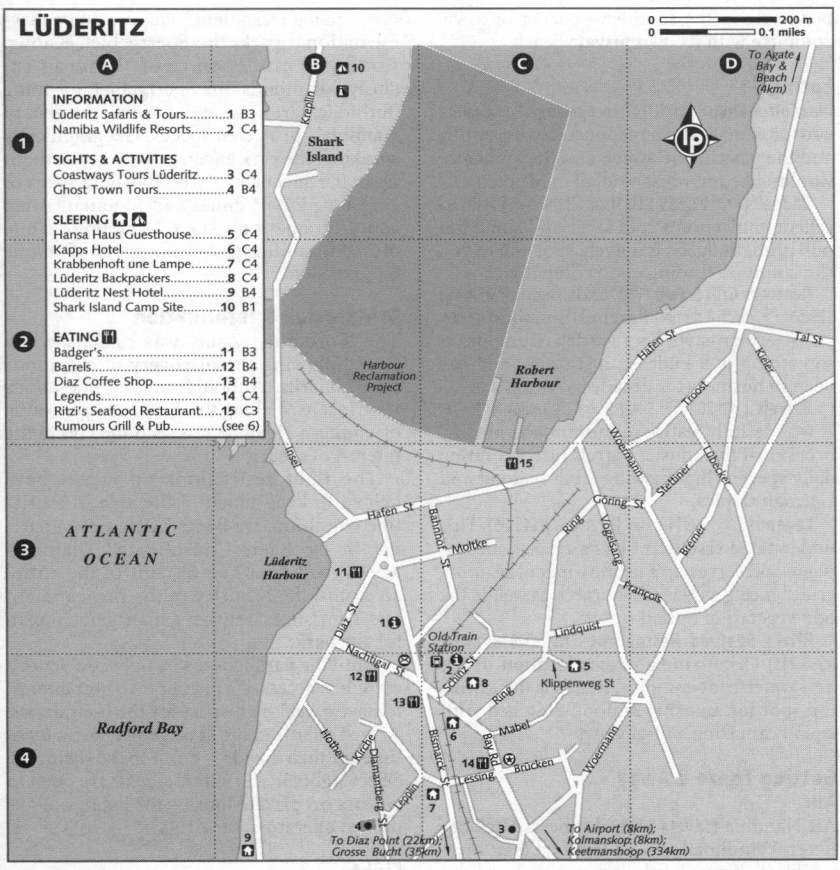

LÜDERITZ

0 _____ 200 m
0 _____ 0.1 miles

Sleeping

Shark Island Camp Site (day entry N$40, camping per person/site N$20/50, 6-person bungalow N$450, lighthouse N$850) This is a beautifully situated but aggravatingly windy locale.

Lüderitz Backpackers (☎ 202000; www.namib web.com/backpackers.htm; 7 Schinz St; campsite/dm/d N$115/145/365) Housed in a historic colonial mansion, this friendly place is the only true backpacker spot in town – the vibe is congenial and low-key, and the friendly management is helpful in sorting out your onward travels.

Krabbenhoft une Lampe (☎ 202674; info@klguest house.com; 25 Bismarck St; s/d from N$150/250) One of the more unusual sleeping options in town, the Krabbenhoft is a converted carpet factory

that now offers a number of basic rooms and self-catering flats upstairs from a weaver.

Hansa Haus Guesthouse (☎ 203581; mcloud@africa online.com.na; Klippenweg St; s/d from N$200/400) This imposing hilltop home, which dates back to 1909 and is presently splashed out in regal blues and rich woods, boasts dramatic sea views and quiet surroundings.

Kapps Hotel (☎ 202345; pmk@mweb.com.na; Bay Rd; r per person from N$225) This is the town's oldest hotel, dating back to 1907, though a recent renovation has managed to retain the historical ambience while adding a touch of modernity.

Lüderitz Nest Hotel (☎ 204000; www.nesthotel.com; 820 Diaz St; r per person from N$580;) Lüderitz's oldest upmarket hotel occupies a jutting

NAMIBIA

peninsula in the southwest corner of town, complete with its own private beach.

Eating

Diaz Coffee Shop (☎ 203147; cnr Bismarck & Nachtigal Sts; snacks & meals N$10-30) The cappuccinos are strong and the pastries are sweet, and the ambience wouldn't be out of place at all in Munich.

Badger's (☎ 202855; Diaz St; meals N$20-45) An excellent choice for a cold lager and some hot pub grub, Badger's is a lively spot where you can count on finding good company.

Rumours Grill & Pub (☎ 202655; Bismarck St; meals $25-55; ☽ lunch & dinner) Part bustling sports bar, part German-style beer garden, Rumours is something of a Lüderitz institution and has been in business for decades.

Barrels (☎ 202458; 5 Natchtigal St; mains N$35-75) A wonderfully festive restaurant accented by occasional live music, Barrels offers rotating daily specials highlighting fresh seafood and German staples.

Legends (☎ 203110; Bay Rd; mains N$45-85) This understated restaurant has a relaxed atmosphere and serves up a healthy mix of seafood, grilled meats, pizzas and burgers, as well as the odd vegetarian option or two.

Ritzi's Seafood Restaurant (☎ 202818; mains N$85-215) Occupying a choice location in the new waterfront complex, Ritzi's is the town's top spot for amazing seafood matched with equally amazing sunset views.

Getting There & Away

AIR
Air Namibia travels several times a week between Windhoek and Lüderitz, at least once weekly to/from Swakopmund and at least twice weekly to/from Walvis Bay. The airport is 8km southeast of town.

BUS
Somewhat irregular *combis* connect Lüderitz to Keetmanshoop, with fares averaging around N$175. Buses depart from the southern edge of town at informal bus stops along Bismarck St.

CAR & MOTORCYCLE
Lüderitz and the scenery en route are worth the 334km trip from Keetmanshoop via the tarred B4.

SPERRGEBIET NATIONAL PARK

Although it's been off-limits to the public for most of the last century, in 2008 the Namibian government inaugurated its newest national park, the Sperrgebiet. Known worldwide as the source of Namibia's exclusive diamonds, the Sperrgebiet, meaning 'forbidden area', is set to become the gem of Namibia's protected spaces. Geographically speaking, the park encompasses the northern tip of the Succulent Karoo Biorne, an area of 26,000 sq km of dunes and mountains that appear dramatically stark, but represent one of 25 outstanding global 'hot spots' of unique biodiversity.

Orientation & Information

The 'Forbidden Zone' was established in 1908 following the discovery of diamonds near Lüderitz. Although mining operations were localised along the coast, a huge swathe of southern Namibia was sectioned off in the interest of security.

The tight restrictions on access have helped to keep much of the area in a pristine condition. De Beers Centenary, a partner in De Beers Consolidated Diamond Mines, will continue to control the entire area until the Ministry of the Environment and Tourism establishes a management plan for the park.

Until the park loosens its tight restrictions on public access, it's in your own best interest to have a healthy respect for the boundaries. Armed guards in the Sperrgebiet have a lot of time on their hands – don't make their day. Select sights in the national park are open to visitors on private tours – for listings of approved operators, see p1006.

Sights

Named after an early Afrikaner trekker, Jani Kolman, whose ox wagon became bogged in the sand here, **Kolmanskop** was originally constructed as the Consolidated Diamond Mines (CDM) headquarters. By 1956, the town was totally deserted and left to the mercy of the shifting desert sands. Today, Kolmanskop has been partially restored as a tourist attraction, and the sight of decrepit buildings being invaded by dunes is simply too surreal to describe.

You can turn up at any time and you're not required to arrive as part of an organised tour, though you do need to purchase a permit (costing N$40) in advance through either NWR in Lüderitz (p1006) or a local tour operator.

NAMIBIA

Sleeping

There are no tourist lodges within the national park and bush camping is strictly forbidden. While it is likely that some form of accommodation will be constructed in the years to come, your best option in the meantime is to base yourself in Lüderitz (see p1007).

Getting There & Away

Do not attempt to access the Sperrgebiet in a private vehicle as you will be inviting a whole mess of trouble. The only exception to this statement is Kolmanskop, which can be accessed if you have a sturdy 4WD along with the necessary permits.

NAMIBIA DIRECTORY

ACCOMMODATION

Namibia is well equipped for travellers wanting accommodation of all price ranges – you can find backpacker accommodation in most places, camping areas throughout the country, midrange hotels and a healthy smattering of posh safari lodges. Quality is extremely high, and even budget lodges usually provide internet access, a pool, a bar and laundry facilities. Many hotels also serve meals and run travel centres.

ACTIVITIES

Namibia is an outdoor enthusiast's dream. There are endless opportunities for hiking and camping. Swakopmund (p992) is the adrenalin capital of the country with everything from skydiving to sand boarding.

BUSINESS HOURS

Cafes Open all day long, closing in the early evening.
Restaurants From around 10.30am to 11pm Monday to Saturday, usually with a break between lunch and dinner.
Shops Open from 8am to 1pm and 2.30pm to 5pm Monday to Friday. In the winter, when it gets dark early, some shops open at 7.30am and close at around 4pm. Lunchtime closing is almost universal. On Saturday, most city and town shops open from 8am to 1pm.

DANGERS & ANNOYANCES

Theft isn't particularly rife, but take care walking alone at night, conceal your valuables in Windhoek and other towns around the country, and don't leave anything in sight inside a vehicle. Take the same precautions at campsites in towns – although there's no problem at campsites in national parks (not

---

PRACTICALITIES

- The metric system is used for weights, measures and road distances.

- Electricity is 220V to 240V AC, 50Hz and uses South African–style two- or three-round-pin plugs.

- For English-language news, see www.namibianews.com.

- The Namibian Broadcasting Corporation (NBC) operates nine radio stations broadcasting on different wavebands in 12 languages.

---

from humans anyway; just watch out for the monkeys).

East of Lüderitz, do not enter the prohibited diamond area, mainly south of the road to Keetmanshoop; well-armed patrols can be overly zealous.

EMERGENCIES

Ambulance and fire brigade (☎ 211111)
Crime report (☎ 290 2239) Twenty-four-hour phone service.
National police (☎ 10111)
Police (☎ 228328)

EMBASSIES & CONSULATES

All of the following representations are in Windhoek:

Angola (Map p990; ☎ 061-227535; 3 Dr Agostino Neto St; ◷ 9am-1pm Mon-Fri)
Botswana (off Map p988; ☎ 061-221941; 101 Klein Windhoek; ◷ 8am-12.30pm Mon-Fri)
Canada (Map p990; ☎ 061-251254; Ste 1118, Sanlam Centre, 154 Independence Ave; ◷ 8am-12.30pm Mon-Fri)
Finland (Map p990; ☎ 061-221355; 5th fl, Sanlam Centre, 154 Independence Ave; ◷ 9am-noon Mon, Wed & Thu)
France (Map p990; ☎ 061-229021; 1 Goethe St; ◷ 8.30am-12.30pm & 2-5pm Mon-Thu, 8.30am-12.30pm Fri)
Germany (Map p990; ☎ 061-273100; 6th fl, Sanlam Centre, 154 Independence Ave; ◷ 9am-noon Mon-Fri)
Italy (off Map p988; ☎ 061-228602; cnr Anna & Gevers Sts, Ludwigsdorf; ◷ 8.30am-12.30pm & 2-5pm Mon-Thu, 8.30am-12.30pm Fri)
Kenya (Map p990; ☎ 061-226836; 5th fl, Kenya House, 134 Robert Mugabe Ave; ◷ 9am-12.30pm & 2-5pm Mon-Fri)
Malawi (Map p990; ☎ 061-221391; 56 Bismarck St, Windhoek West; ◷ 8am-noon & 2-5pm Mon-Fri)

South Africa (Map p988; ☎ 061-205 7111; RSA House, Jan Jonker St, Klein Windhoek; ☒ 8.15am-12.15pm Mon-Fri)
UK (Map p990; ☎ 061-223022; 116A Robert Mugabe Ave; ☒ 8am-1pm & 2-4pm Mon-Thu, 8am-noon Fri)
USA (Map p990; ☎ 061-221601; http://windhoek.usem bassy.gov; 14 Lossen St; ☒ 8.30am-noon Mon, Wed & Fri)
Zambia (Map p990; ☎ 061-237610; cnr Sam Nujoma Dr & Mandume Ndemufayo Ave; ☒ 8am-1pm & 2-4pm Mon-Fri)
Zimbabwe (Map p990; ☎ 061-228134; Gamsberg Bldg, cnr Independence Ave & Grimm St; ☒ 9am-12.30pm & 2-3pm Mon-Fri)

HOLIDAYS

Resort areas are busiest over both Namibian and South African school holidays, which normally occur from mid-December to mid-January, around Easter, from late July to early August and for two weeks in mid-October.

New Year's Day 1 January
Independence Day 21 March
Good Friday March or April
Easter Sunday March or April
Easter Monday March or April
Ascension Day April or May (40 days after Easter)
Workers' Day 1 May
Cassinga Day 4 May
Africa Day 25 May
Heroes' Day 26 August
Human Rights' Day 10 December
Christmas Day 25 December
Family/Boxing Day 26 December

INTERNET ACCESS

Internet access is available at backpackers hostels, internet cafes and hotels in larger towns, and also at several tourist offices and remote lodges.

MAPS

The Shell *Roadmap – Namibia* is the best reference for remote routes and has an excellent Windhoek map. Shell also publishes the *Kaokoland-Kunene Region Tourist Map* (N\$15), depicting routes and tracks in the area. It's available at bookshops and tourist offices.

MONEY

The Namibian dollar (N\$) is divided into 100 cents, and is pegged to the South African rand, which is also legal tender in Namibia, at a rate of 1:1. This can be confusing, given that there are three sets of coins and notes in use, all with different sizes: old South African, new South African and Namibian. Namibian notes

come in denominations of N\$10, N\$20, N\$50, N\$100 and N\$200, and coins in values of 5, 10, 20 and 50 cents, and N\$1 and N\$5.

POST

Overseas airmail post is normally faster than domestic post, and is limited only by the time it takes an article to reach Windhoek (which can be slow in the outer areas).

TELEPHONE

Namibian area dialling codes all have three digits that begin with ☎ 06. When phoning from abroad, first dial the country code (☎ 264), followed by the area code without the leading zero.

Phonecards are sold at post offices and retail shops.

VISAS

No visas are required for visitors from Australia, New Zealand, France, Germany, the UK, Ireland, South Africa, Canada or the USA, all of whom receive entry for an initial 90 days for free.

Visa Extensions

Extensions on the initial 90-day visa are available from the **Ministry of Home affairs** (Map p990; ☎ 061-292 2111; mlusepani@mha.gov.na; cnr Kasino St & Independence Ave; ☒ 8am-1pm Mon-Fri) in Windhoek. It's usually free to extend your visa; however, you are at the mercy of the immigration official. Another way of extending your visa is to simply leave the country for a few days and then return.

Visas for Onward Travel

Visas for the following neighbouring countries can be obtained in Windhoek, unless otherwise stated. See p1009 for embassy and consulate information.

Angola Travellers must apply for a visa in their home country (usually limited to fly-in visas for arrival in Luanda) or attempt to secure an overland visa from the Angolan consulate in Oshakati, northern Namibia. Visas cost US\$75 for 30 days.

Botswana No visa is required by citizens of most Commonwealth countries (including Australia and the UK), EU countries (except Spain and Portugal), Israel, Norway, South Africa, Switzerland and the USA. On arrival you'll get a 30-day entrance stamp.

South Africa No visa is required by citizens of most Commonwealth countries (including Australia and the UK), most Western European countries, Japan and the

USA; they'll be issued with a free entry permit on arrival, valid for a stay of up to 90 days. If you aren't entitled to an entry permit, you'll need to get a visa (also free) before you arrive.

Zambia Visas take one day to process, and the price varies according to nationality. Note that they're available at the border for considerably less.

Zimbabwe Visas take one day to process, and the price varies, though they're available at the border for most nationalities.

TRANSPORT IN NAMIBIA

GETTING THERE & AWAY
Air
Most international flights into Namibia arrive at Windhoek's **Chief Hosea Kutako International Airport** (WDH; ☎ 061-299 6602; www.airports.com.na), 42km east of the capital. Shorter-haul international flights may also use Windhoek's in-town **Eros Airport** (ERS; ☎ 061-299 6500), although this airport mainly serves internal flights and light aircraft.

The main carrier is **Air Namibia** (☎ 061-299 6000; www.airnamibia.com.na), based in Windhoek, which flies routes to southern Africa, as well as long-haul flights to Frankfurt. Reservations are best handled via the internet or telephone.

The following airlines also fly to and from Namibia:

British Airways (☎ 061-248528; www.ba.com)
Lufthansa (☎ 061-238205; www.lufthansa.com)
South African Airways (☎ 061-237670; www.flysaa.com)
TAAG Angola (☎ 061-226625; www.taag.com.br)

Land
To bring a foreign-registered vehicle into Namibia, you must purchase a US$10 road-use tax certificate at the border.

ANGOLA
There are three border crossings between Namibia and Angola: at Ruacana–Calueque (open 6am to 10pm); Oshikango–Namacunda (8am to 6pm); and Nkurenkuru–Cuangar (the crossing at Rundu; open 7am to 5pm). Travellers need an Angolan visa permitting overland entry, which is best obtained at the Angolan consulate in Oshakati, as the embassy in Windhoek tends to only give visas for air travel into Luanda. At Ruacana Falls, you can briefly enter the border area without a visa; just sign in at the border post.

BOTSWANA
The most commonly used border crossing is located at Buitepos–Mamuno, between Windhoek and Ghanzi, although the border post at Mohembo–Mahango is also popular. The only other real option is the crossing at Ngoma Bridge across the Chobe River. The Mpalila Island–Kasane border is only available to guests who have prebooked accommodation at upmarket lodges on the island.

Drivers crossing the border at Mahango must secure an entry permit for Mahango Game Reserve at Popa Falls. This is free if you're transiting, or US$3 per person per day plus US$3 per vehicle per day if you want to drive around the reserve (which is possible in a 2WD).

SOUTH AFRICA
The **Intercape Mainliner** (☎ in South Africa 0861-287 287; www.intercape.co.za) service from Windhoek to Cape Town runs four times weekly. Travelling between Jo'burg and Windhoek involves a connection in Upington.

If you're driving, there are border crossings at Noordoewer, Vellorsdrif, Ariamsvlei and Klein Menasse–Aroab.

ZAMBIA
A new kilometre-long **bridge** (⊙ 7am-6pm) spans the Zambezi between Katima Mulilo and Wenela, providing easy access to Livingstone and other destinations in Zambia. If you're heading to the falls, the road is now tarred all the way to Livingstone and is accessible by 2WD vehicle, even in the rainy season.

ZIMBABWE
There's no direct border crossing between Namibia and Zimbabwe. To get there you must take the Chobe National Park transit route from Ngoma Bridge through northern Botswana to Kasane/Kazungula, and from there to Victoria Falls.

GETTING AROUND
Air
Air Namibia (www.airnamibia.com.na) has an extensive network of local flights operating out of **Eros Airport** (ERS; ☎ 061-299 6500) in Windhoek. There are regular flights to Tsumeb, Rundu, Katima Mulilo, Lüderitz, Swakopmund/Walvis Bay and Oshakati/Ondangwa.

Car & Motorcycle

The easiest way to get around Namibia is by road, and an excellent system of sealed roads runs the length of the country from the South African border at Noordoewer to Ngoma Bridge on the Botswanan border and Ruacana on the Angolan border in the northwest. Similarly, sealed spur roads connect the main north–south routes to Buitepos, Lüderitz, Swakopmund and Walvis Bay. Elsewhere, towns and most sites of interest are accessible on good gravel roads. C-numbered highways are well maintained and passable to all vehicles, and D-numbered roads, although a bit rougher, are mostly (but not always) passable to 2WD vehicles. In the Kaokoveld, however, most D-numbered roads can only be negotiated with a 4WD.

For a compact car, the least-expensive hire companies charge US$40 to US$60 per day (the longer the hire period, the lower the daily rate) with unlimited kilometres. Hiring a 4WD vehicle opens up remote parts of the country, but it can get expensive at an average of US$80 to US$120 per day. Most companies include insurance and unlimited kilometres in their standard rates, but some require a minimum hire period before they allow un-limited kilometres.

It's cheaper to rent a car in South Africa and drive it into Namibia, but you need permission from the hire agency and paperwork to cross the borders. Drivers entering Namibia in a foreign-registered vehicle must pay a N$70 road tax at the border.

It's probably best to deal with one of these major car-hire companies:

Avis (www.avis.com) Offices in Windhoek, Swakopmund, Tsumeb and Walvis Bay, as well as Chief Hosea Kutako International Airport.

Budget (www.budget.co.za) Another big agency with of-fices in Windhoek and Walvis Bay, as well as Hosea Kutako International Airport.

Imperial (www.imperialcarrental.co.za) Offices in Wind-hoek, Swakopmund, Tsumeb, Lüderitz, Walvis Bay and at both Hosea Kutako International Airport and Eros Airport.

Triple Three Car Hire (www.iml.com.na/333) A competitive local car-hire firm with offices in Swakopmund and Walvis Bay.

Hitching

Hitching is possible in Namibia, but it's ille-gal in national parks, and main highways see relatively little traffic. It's reasonably safe and fairly common, though it's still always a risk (see p1161). Truck drivers generally expect to be paid per 100km, so agree on a price before climbing in. Your best options for lifts are Windhoek backpackers lodges, where you can post notices about rides.

Local Transport

Namibia's bus services aren't extensive. Luxury services are limited to the **Intercape Mainliner** (☎ 061-227847; www.intercape.co.za), which has scheduled services from Windhoek to Swakopmund, Walvis Bay, Grootfontein, Rundu and Katima Mulilo. You're allowed only two items of baggage, which must not exceed a total of 30kg. Fares include meals.

There are also local *combis* (minibuses), which depart when full and follow main routes around the country. From Windhoek's Rhino Park petrol station, they depart for dozens of destinations.

Tours

Namibia's public transport system will get you to population centres, but not the sites most visitors want to see: the Skeleton Coast, Damaraland, the Kaokoveld, the Kunene River, Fish River Canyon, Sossusvlei, the Naukluft and so on. Therefore, even those who'd normally spurn organised tours may want to consider joining an inexpensive par-ticipation safari, or a more luxurious option.

Cardboard Box Travel Shop (Map p990; ☎ 061-256580; www.namibian.org) This friendly agency offers bookings (including last-minute options) for all budget sa-faris; lodge, safari, car-hire and transport bookings; national parks bookings; good advice; and other travel services.

Chameleon Safaris (Map p990; ☎ 061-247668; www.chameleonsafaris.com) This budget safari company is geared to backpackers and does a range of good-value safaris.

Crazy Kudu Safaris (☎ 061-222636; www.crazykudu.com; Windhoek) One of Namibia's friendliest and most economical safari companies, Crazy Kudu does a variety of package trips around the country, as well as custom safaris to the Okavango Delta, Victoria Falls, Fish River Canyon and Kaokoland for the best possible price.

Kaokohimba Safaris (☎ 061-222378; www.kaoko-namibia.com) Kaokohimba organises cultural tours through Kaokoland and Damaraland and wildlife-viewing trips in Etosha National Park. A highlight is Camp Syncro, in remote Marienflüss.

Okakambe Trails (☎ 064-402799; www.okakambe.iway.na) With Okakambe, you can ride on horseback along the Swakop River to a moon landscape; it also organises a good variety of longer riding trips.

Outside Adventures (☎ 061-245595; www.namibia-adventures.com) These folks run excellent day tours from Windhoek: brewery tours, mountain biking in Daan Viljoen, Arnhem Caves, Katutura township, and tours to see cheetahs, leopards and rhinos on private reserves in the capital area.

Turnstone Tours (☎ 064-403123; www.turnstone-tours.com) Turnstone runs 4WD camping tours around Swakopmund, including Sandwich Harbour and Damaraland.

West Coast Safaris (☎ 061-256770; www.westcoast.demon.nl) The company runs camping participation safaris averaging one week in length to a variety of destinations, including Kaokoland, Etosha, Damaraland, Bushmanland and the Waterberg Plateau.

Wild Dog Safaris (☎ 061-257642; www.wilddog-safaris.com) This friendly operation runs Northern Namibia

Adventures and Southern Swings, and Etosha or Sossusvlei circuits, as well as longer participation camping safaris and accommodated excursions.

Trains

Trans-Namib Railways (☎ 061-298 2032; www.transnamib.com.na) connects some major towns, but trains are extremely slow – as one reader remarked, moving 'at the pace of an energetic donkey cart'. In addition, passenger and freight cars are mixed on the same train, and trains tend to stop at every post, which means that rail travel isn't popular and services are rarely fully booked.

South Africa

South Africa has always been a country that has made headlines. When apartheid crumbled and Nelson Mandela walked free – just three months after the Berlin Wall was torn down – it was a pivotal, hopeful moment in history, which spread hope around the world in a way rarely seen since.

Like the rest of the continent, Africa's southernmost nation is capable of worming deep into travellers' imaginations. Indeed, with South Africa's mix of epic landscapes, healthy travelling scene, and vibrant cultures and people such as the Xhosa and Zulu, relatively accessible tastes of Africa are on tap here. Whether you head into a national park on a wildlife-spotting mission, sample some home brew in a township *shebeen* (local bar), or hike through landscapes such as the Drakensberg, this mind-bogglingly diverse country rewards travellers' exploratory efforts.

Once you've recovered from all that, or from adrenalin-pumping activities such as the world's highest bungee jump, reflect on it all over a bottle in the Winelands, a *braai* (barbecue) in the wilderness, a beach session on the Wild Coast, or a tour of Cape Town's galleries. Whatever you choose, it will probably be, as South Africans like to say, *lekker* (tasty).

FAST FACTS

- **Area** 1,233,404 sq km
- **ATMs** Found in cities and most towns
- **Borders** Botswana, Lesotho, Mozambique, Namibia, Swaziland, Zimbabwe
- **Budget** US$35 to US$70 a day
- **Capitals** Pretoria (administrative), Bloemfontein (judicial) and Cape Town (legislative)
- **Languages** English, Afrikaans, Ndebele, Xhosa, Zulu, Northern Sotho (Sepedi), Southern Sotho (Sesotho), Venda, Tswana, Swati and Tsonga
- **Money** Rand; US$1 = R7.4, €1 = R11
- **Population** 49 million
- **Seasons** Cape Town: cold and wet (May to August), sunny and warm (September to May); Durban and Johannesburg: dry (May to September), wet (October to April)
- **Telephone** Country code ☎ 27; international access code ☎ 00
- **Time** GMT/UTC +2
- **Visa** Free 90-day entry permits issued on arrival to citizens of most Commonwealth countries (including Australia and the UK), most Western European countries, Japan and the USA

HOW MUCH?

- **Bottle of red wine** US$7 to US$11
- **Car hire per day** US$27 to US$40
- **Mango** US$0.40 to US$1
- **Township tour** US$47
- **Surfboard** US$400

LONELY PLANET INDEX

- **1L petrol** US$1.10
- **1.5L bottled water** US$2.20
- **Can of Black Label beer** US$1
- **Souvenir T-shirt** US$9.40
- **Roasted mealie (corn)** US$0.30

HIGHLIGHTS

- **Cape Town** (p1021) Marvel at the city's majestic setting and take a tipple tour of the area's wineries.
- **Kruger National Park** (p1046) Don some khaki and join the rangers on a safari of the most involving kind – on foot.
- **Drakensberg Mountains** (p1044) Hike the peaks of Royal Natal National Park's sublime Amphitheatre.
- **Wild Coast** (p1036) Choose between a hammock and the beach at one of the laid-back hostels.
- **Kgalagadi Transfrontier Park** (p1060) Become hypnotised by the vast and beautiful expanses of the Kalahari.

CLIMATE & WHEN TO GO

South Africa has a temperate climate compared with most African countries, and can be visited comfortably any time. Winter (June to September) is cooler, drier, and ideal for hiking and outdoor pursuits. Because vegetation is less dense, and thirsty animals congregate around water sources, winter is also the best time for wildlife-watching.

Summer (late November to March) brings rain, mists and – in the lowveld – some uncomfortably hot days. Along the Indian Ocean, conditions are sultry and tropical, with high humidity.

More of a consideration than weather are school holidays. From mid-December to January, waves of vacationers stream out of the cities, with foreign visitors adding to the crush.

The absolute peak is from Christmas to mid-January, followed by Easter. Accommodation in tourist areas and national parks is heavily booked, and prices can more than double.

Spring (mid-September to November) and autumn (April and May) are ideal almost everywhere. Spring is also the best time to see vast expanses of the Northern Cape carpeted with wildflowers.

ITINERARIES

- **Two Weeks** Touching down in Johannesburg, spend a few hours at the moving Apartheid Museum (p1049) before heading northeast to safari showpiece Kruger National Park (p1046). The teeming wildlife here will undoubtedly hold you captivated for several days. From Kruger, head south into KwaZulu-Natal, where the dramatic valleys and peaks of the Drakensberg Mountains (p1044) provide an endless array of excellent hikes. Head up Sani Pass (p1045) to the Lesotho border for breathtaking views before returning to the throbbing heart of the country to get a taste of township life in Soweto (p1049).
- **One Month** After a few days in Cape Town (p1021) and a trip to the top of Table Mountain (p1022), tear yourself away from the wonderful Mother City and head to the fertile valleys of the Winelands, with a night or two in Stellenbosch (p1031), then continue the wine tour along scenic Route 62 through the Little Karoo to ostrich-mad Oudtshoorn (p1032). Make your way south to the Garden Route, joining the N2 near arty, lagoon-side Knysna (p1033) and Plettenberg Bay (p1033), a relaxed beach town. Be sure to stop at Tsitsikamma National Park (p1034) along the coast. Move northeast through the striking Wild Coast (p1036), before spending a day or so on the beach in Durban (p1037). Head west to the Drakensberg (p1044) or northeast to President Zuma's birthplace, Zululand (p1043); or hit the park-packed Elephant Coast, where the wilderness areas include iSimangaliso Wetland Park (p1043) and Hluhluwe-iMfolozi Park (p1043), before returning to Durban or heading to Jo'burg for the flight home.

HISTORY

Rock art suggests that, possibly as early as 40,000 years ago, nomadic San hunter-gatherers

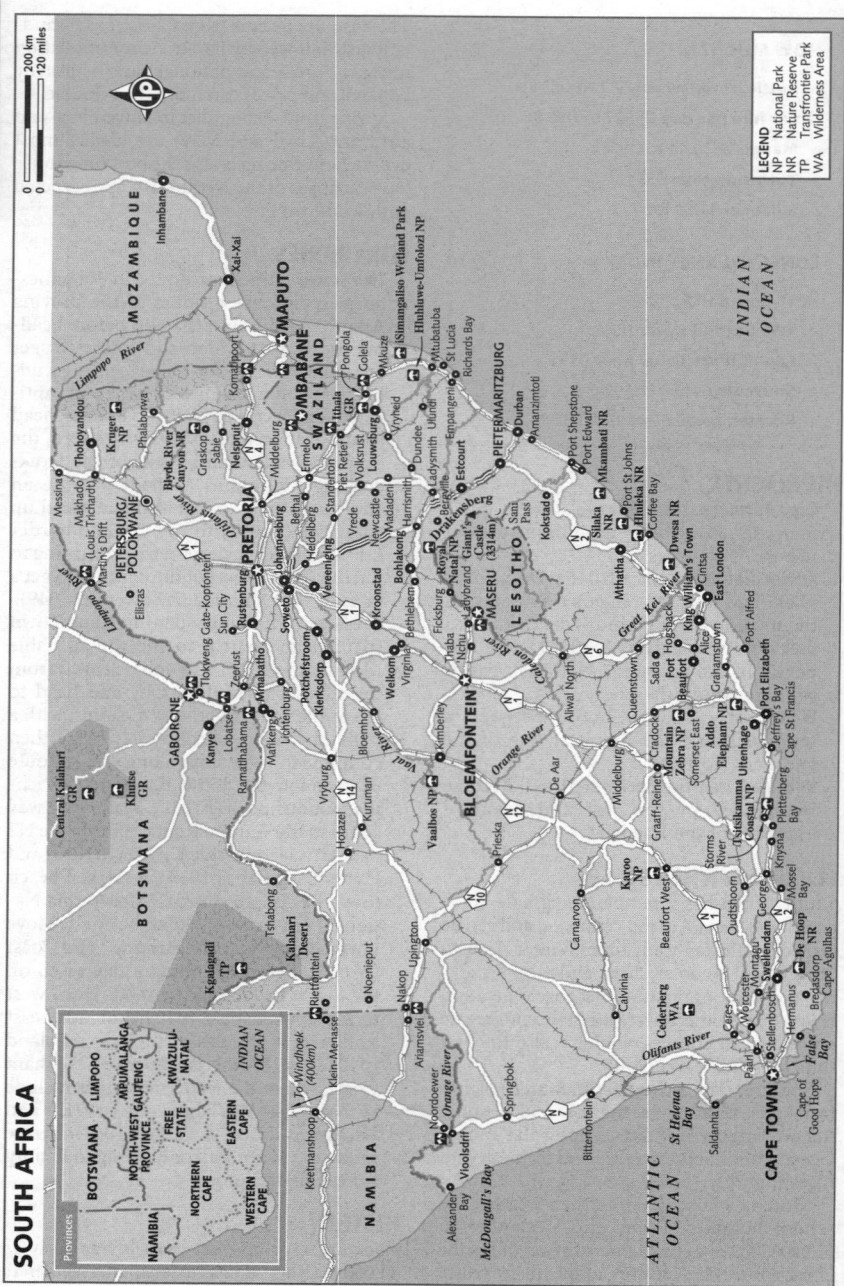

SOUTH AFRICA

0 ——— 200 km
0 ——— 120 miles

LEGEND
NP National Park
NR Nature Reserve
TP Transfrontier Park
WA Wilderness Area

Provinces

NAMIBIA

BOTSWANA

NORTH-WEST PROVINCE LIMPOPO MPUMALANGA

GAUTENG FREE STATE KWAZULU-NATAL

NORTHERN CAPE

EASTERN CAPE

WESTERN CAPE

INDIAN OCEAN

were living in the area that is now South Africa. The next arrivals were Bantu-speaking tribes who, by the 11th century, had settled the northeast and the east coast and, by the 15th century, most of the eastern half of South Africa. These tribes were pastoral but had trade links throughout the region. They were Iron Age peoples, and the smelting techniques of some tribes were not surpassed in Europe until the Industrial Revolution.

The Dutch East India Company established the first European settlement in South Africa at the Cape of Good Hope in 1652. The settlers developed a close-knit community with their own dialect (Afrikaans) and Calvinist sect (the Dutch Reformed Church). Slaves were imported from other parts of Africa and Southeast Asia.

Over the next 150 years, the colonists spread east, coming into violent contact with the Bantu tribes. In 1779 the eastward expansion of the Boers (Dutch-Afrikaner farmers) was temporarily halted by the Xhosa in the first Bantu War.

Further Boer expansion was hastened after the British annexed the Cape in 1806. The abolition of slavery in 1833 was regarded by the Boers as an intolerable interference in their affairs, and led to migration across the Orange River three years later. This became known as the Great Trek.

Pressure on the Bantu from both the Boers and the British caused political and social changes among the tribes of the Natal area, resulting in the rise of the Zulu king, Shaka, in the early 19th century. His policy of total war on neighbouring tribes caused immense suffering and mass migration in a period known as the *difaqane* (forced migration).

The Boers came into this chaos in search of new lands, and the British were not far behind them. The Zulu were eventually defeated, but relations between the Boers and the British remained tense – particularly after the formation of the Boer republics of the Orange Free State and the Transvaal.

Diamonds were discovered in 1867 at Kimberley, followed by the discovery of gold in 1886 on the Witwatersrand in Jo'burg. The Boer republics were flooded with British business and immigrant labourers, which created resentment among Boer farmers.

The British imperialist Cecil Rhodes encouraged a rebellion among the heavily taxed – but nonvoting – English-speaking miners in the Transvaal, with a view to destabilising the Boer republics and encouraging British intervention. The resulting tensions led to the Second Anglo-Boer War (1899–1902).

The war ended with the defeat of the Boer republics and the imposition of British rule over the whole country. Britain had pursued a scorched-earth policy to combat Boer guerrillas, destroying homes, crops and livestock. During this time more than 26,000 Afrikaner women and children died in the world's first concentration camps.

Independence & Apartheid

In 1910 the Union of South Africa was created, which gave political control to the whites. Inevitably, this prompted black resistance in the form of strikes, and political organisations were formed. Despite the moderate tone of these early resistance groups, the government reacted by intensifying repression.

The Afrikaner National Party won the election in 1948. It went even further in excluding nonwhites from having any political or economic power, and the security forces brutally enforced its laws. Violence was a routine method of reaction to any opposition or protest. The suppression of black resistance ranged from the Sharpeville massacre of 1960 and the shooting of high-school students in Soweto in 1976, to the forcible evacuation and bulldozing of entire urban areas like Cape Town's District Six, and the systematic torture – even murder – of political activists such as Steve Biko.

One of the most important organisations to oppose the racist legislation was the African National Congress (ANC). As it became obvious that the white rulers were unwilling to undertake even the most cosmetic reforms, guerrilla warfare became the preferred option for the ANC. In the early 1960s, many ANC leaders were arrested, charged with treason and imprisoned for long periods; the most famous of those was Nelson Mandela.

The system of apartheid was entrenched even further during the early 1970s by the creation of the so-called black homelands of Transkei, Ciskei, Bophuthatswana and Venda. These were, in theory, 'independent' countries. With the creation of the homelands, all black people within white-designated South Africa were deemed foreign guest-workers and as such were without political rights. Any black person without a residence pass could be 'deported' to a homeland.

Meanwhile, South Africa was becoming an isolated case in the face of successful liberation struggles in Angola, Mozambique and Zimbabwe, which brought Marxist-leaning governments into power. As a result, a war psychosis came to dominate government thinking, and resulted in the invasion of southern Angola by the South African Defence Force. The South African government also gave encouragement to counter-revolutionary guerrilla groups in both Mozambique and Angola, and refused to enter into genuine negotiations for the independence of Namibia.

The international community finally began to oppose the apartheid regime, and the UN imposed economic and political sanctions. The government made some concessions, including the establishment of a farcical new parliament of whites, 'coloureds' (people of mixed race) and Indians – but no black people.

The 'reforms' did nothing to ease sanctions. After the 1989 elections the new president, FW de Klerk, instituted a program that was aimed not only at dismantling the apartheid system, but also at introducing democracy. The release of political prisoners on 11 February 1990 (including Nelson Mandela), the repeal of the Group Areas Act (which set up the homelands), and the signing of a peace accord with the ANC and other opposition groups all opened the way for hard-fought negotiations on the path to majority rule.

The Post-Apartheid Era

The country's first democratic elections took place in 1994, and across the country at midnight on 26–27 April, 'Die Stem' (the old national anthem) was sung and the old flag was lowered. A new rainbow flag was raised and the new anthem, 'Nkosi Sikelele i Afrika' (God Bless Africa), was sung.

In the first democratic election in the country's history, the ANC won 62.7% of the vote; 66.7% would have enabled it to rewrite the interim constitution. The National Party won 20.4% of the vote, enough to guarantee it representation in cabinet. Nelson Mandela was made president of the 'new' South Africa.

In 1999, after five years of learning about democracy, the country voted in a more 'normal' election. Issues such as economics and competence were raised and debated.

There had been some speculation that the ANC vote might drop with the retirement of Nelson Mandela. However, the party's vote

increased to the point where it came within one seat of the two-thirds majority that would allow it to alter the constitution. The National Party lost two-thirds of its seats, losing its official opposition status to the Democratic Party. Thabo Mbeki, who had taken over the ANC leadership from Nelson Mandela in 1997, became president.

While Mbeki was viewed with less affection by the ANC grassroots than the beloved 'Madiba' (Mandela), he was a shrewd politician, maintaining his political pre-eminence by isolating or co-opting opposition parties. He led the ANC to a decisive victory in the 2004 national elections, with 70% of the votes, and the party today continues its dominance in political life.

Yet it was not all plain sailing. Mbeki's effective denial of the AIDS crisis invited global criticism, and his failure to condemn the forced reclamation of white-owned farms in neighbouring Zimbabwe unnerved both South African landowners and foreign investors.

South Africa Today

Mbeki's nemesis Jacob Zuma, an ANC veteran whose theme song is the Zulu protest anthem 'Umshini Wami' (Bring Me My Machine Gun), became president in 2009. A controversial figure, Zuma was assured of electoral victory when corruption charges against him, relating to a US$4.8 billion arms deal, were dropped shortly before the polls opened, due to claims that the evidence had been tampered with by his opponents. Zuma initially had a strong following, with people seeing the Zulu polygamist as more of a common man's champion than academic Mbeki. In his first state-of-the-nation speech, he promised to create 500,000 new jobs by the end of 2009 ('2380 jobs a day for the rest of the year!' responded the Sowetan newspaper). In July 2009, union strikes sparked violent expressions of general discontent with continuing deprivation in the townships; echoing xenophobic riots that had targeted economic immigrants from other African countries in May 2008.

Although the 2010 World Cup is set to lessen the blow of South Africa's first recession in 17 years, the ANC still faces major challenges in areas such as crime, economic inequality, education and, importantly, HIV/AIDS. South Africa has the highest number of cases of the disease, with an estimated 5.7 million people affected, and despite the efforts of AIDS activists and NGOs, the scourge threatens to eclipse all of the country's other problems.

In many ways the real work of nation building is only just beginning. While the political violence that threatened to engulf the country in the early 1990s has for the most part disappeared, racial and cultural divisions remain entrenched. Monuments, museums and other cultural heritage sites paying tribute to black South Africans and other previously excluded groups have been springing up across the country and filling a long-vacant gap. Yet many have served to reignite old tensions, and debate continues on all sides about which version of history is the 'real' one.

However, as the push to make the 2010 World Cup a success demonstrates, along with the united support for athlete Caster Semenya – whose gender was questioned following her victory in the 800m at the 2009 World Championships in Athletics – the spirit of the 'rainbow nation' extends well beyond the country's flag.

CULTURE

More than a decade has passed since South Africa's first democratic elections, and the country is still finding its way. While the streets pulsate with the same determination and optimism that fuelled the liberation struggle, the beat is tempered by the sobering social realities that are the legacy of apartheid's long years of oppression and bloodshed. Freedom also has brought with it a whole new set of challenges.

Unemployment, crime and HIV/AIDS – the leading cause of death in South Africa – are the top concerns of most South Africans today, and the nation is fast becoming a society divided by class rather than colour. The gap between rich and poor is vast – one of the highest in the world, according to World Bank statistics. Manicured suburbs rub shoulders with squalid townships where clean drinking water is a scarce commodity. Violent crime has reached unacceptably high levels, and a generation that saw almost daily brutality and uncertainty during its formative years is now coming of age. Although the formal racial divisions of apartheid have dissolved, shadows and old ways of interacting remain, and suspicions and distrust still run high.

Many middle-class and wealthy families live behind razor wire in heavily secured homes, and spend their leisure time in equally fortified shopping centres. The lingering sense of fear and loss, connected with the passing of the old regime, may be less common, but it has been replaced by gloomy predictions about the government and the future.

Life is very different for the millions of South Africans who are still living in poverty. Tiny matchbox houses are home to large extended families, clean drinking water remains a luxury in some areas, and health facilities are not uniformly available. Yet, township life is considerably more vibrant and informal than in middle-class malls. People gather on street corners and in *shebeens*. Weddings are big events, and frequently spill onto the streets with plenty of dancing. Unfortunately, funerals are becoming one of the most common gatherings in South Africa; on weekends, cemeteries are routinely crowded with mourners.

While crime continues to grab headlines and undermine South Africa's reputation as a tourism destination, it's important to keep it in perspective. The slowly and often fitfully emerging new South Africa is a unique and refreshing place to visit, offering a rare chance to experience a nation that is rebuilding itself after profound change.

It is only since 1994, with the ANC's commitment to build a nonracial 'rainbow nation', that there has been any significant degree of collaboration and peace between the races. During the apartheid era, the government attempted to categorise everyone into one of four major groups – easily enough said, perhaps, but disastrous to implement. The classifications – as African (at various times also called 'native' and 'Bantu', and sometimes now also 'black'), coloured, Asian or white – were often arbitrary and highly contentious. They were used to regulate where and how people could live and work, and became the basis for institutionalised inequality and intolerance.

These times are slowly fading into history, although discrimination based on wealth is threatening to replace racial discrimination. Yet the apartheid era's catch-all classifications continue to be used.

Most of the 'coloured' population lives in Northern and Western Cape Provinces. Cape Malays, who are mostly Muslims, are South Africans of long standing. Although many were brought to the early Cape Colony as slaves, others were political prisoners from the Dutch East Indies. Most South Africans of Indian descent live in KwaZulu-Natal.

Limpopo, Mpumalanga and the Free State are the Afrikaner heartlands. People of British descent are concentrated in KwaZulu-Natal and Western and Eastern Cape Provinces.

The Zulu have maintained the highest-profile ethnic identity; about 24% of South Africans speak Zulu as a first language, and the Inkatha Freedom Party wants an autonomous Zulu state. The second-largest group, the Xhosa, is found mostly in Eastern and Western Cape. They have traditionally formed the heart of the black professional class and been influential in politics (numerous figures in the apartheid struggle, including Mandela, were Xhosa). About 18% of the population uses Xhosa as a first language. Other major groups include the Basotho, the Tswana, and the distinct Ndebele and Venda peoples.

FOOD & DRINK

Before the end of apartheid, the Africans had their *mealie pap* (maize porridge), the Afrikaners their biltong (dried strips of salted meat), and the Indians and Cape Malays their curries. Today, culinary barriers are falling and a simmering *potjie* (pot) of culinary influences awaits the visiting gastronome, described by the well-known foodie writer Lannice Snyman as 'a bit of black magic, a dash of Dutch heartiness, a pinch of Indian spice and a smidgin of Malay mystery'.

Perhaps more than anything else, it's the *braai* (barbecue) – an Afrikaner institution that has broken across race lines – that defines South African cuisine. The Afrikaner history of trekking led to them developing portable food. Staples include rusks (hard biscuits) for dunking; dried fruit; and boerewors, where meat is preserved with spices and vinegar, also found dried *(droëwors)*. The most famous example of Cape cuisine, a fusion of Malay and Dutch influences (the former introducing tastes from Madagascar and Indonesia), is *bobotie* (curried-mince pie topped with savoury egg custard, served on a bed of yellow rice with chutney).

Since it made its debut in 1659, South African wine has had time to age to perfection, and is both of a high standard and reasonably priced. Dry whites are particularly good, while popular reds include pinotage (a local cross of pinot and *cinsaut*, which was known as hermitage). However, beer is the national beverage. The world's largest brewer, SAB Miller, is based in Jo'burg, so there's no shortage of brands, with Amstel the favour-ite. Windhoek, made in Namibia, is a crisp premium lager.

Tap water is generally safe in South Africa's cities. However, in rural areas (or anywhere that local conditions indicate that water sources may be contaminated), stick to bottled water and purify stream water.

ENVIRONMENT

South Africa spreads over 1,233,404 sq km – five times the size of the UK – at the tip of the African continent. On three sides, it's edged by a windswept and stunningly beautiful coastline, winding down the Atlantic seaboard in the west, and up into the warmer Indian Ocean waters to the east.

Much of the country consists of a vast plateau averaging 1500m in height, known as the highveld. To the east, extending along the coast and into Kruger National Park, is the lowveld, while to the northwest is the low-lying Kalahari basin. The dramatic Drakensberg Escarpment marks the point where the highveld plummets down towards the eastern lowlands.

South Africa is home to one of the most magnificent groupings of wildlife on the planet. It boasts the world's largest land mammal (the African elephant), as well as the second-largest (white rhino) and the third-largest (hippopotamus). It's also home to the tallest (giraffe), the fastest (cheetah) and the smallest (pygmy shrew). You probably have a better chance of seeing the Big Five – the black rhino, Cape buffalo, elephant, leopard and lion – in South Africa than anywhere else. There's also the opportunity to see a lesser-known 'Little Five' – the rhinoceros beetle, buffalo weaver, elephant shrew, leopard tortoise and ant lion – if you're looking for a challenge.

The best time for wildlife-watching is the cooler, dry winter (June to September), when foliage is less dense and animals congregate at waterholes, making spotting easier. Summer (late November to March) is rainy and hot, with the animals more widely dispersed and often difficult to see. However, the landscape turns beautiful shades of green around this time, and birdlife is abundant.

South Africa's 800-plus birds include the world's largest bird (the ostrich), its heaviest flying bird (Kori bustard), and smallest raptor (pygmy falcon). Birdwatching is good year-round, with spring (September to November) and summer the best.

South Africa is the world's third-most biologically diverse country. It's also one of Africa's most urbanised, with more than 50% of the population living in towns and cities. Major challenges for the government include managing increasing urbanisation and population growth, while protecting the environment. The picture is complicated by a distorted rural-urban settlement pattern – a grim legacy of the apartheid era – with huge population concentrations in townships that generally lack adequate utilities and infrastructure.

Land degradation is one of the most serious problems, with about one-quarter of South Africa's land considered to be severely degraded. In former homeland areas, years of overgrazing and overcropping have resulted in massive soil depletion. This, plus poor overall conditions, is pushing people to the cities, increasing urban pressures even further.

Water is another issue. South Africa receives an average of only 500mm of rainfall annually, and droughts are common. To meet demand, all major South African rivers have been dammed or modified. While this has improved water supplies to many areas, it has also disrupted local ecosystems and caused increased silting.

National Parks & Reserves

South Africa has close to 600 national parks and reserves, collectively boasting spectacular scenery, impressive fauna and flora, excellent facilities and reasonable prices. The majority of the larger wildlife parks are under the jurisdiction of **South African National (SAN) Parks** (☎ 012-428 9111; www.sanparks.org), except for those in KwaZulu-Natal, which are run by **Ezemvelo KZN Wildlife** (☎ 033-845 1000; www.kznwildlife.com). Several other provinces also have conservation bodies that oversee areas within their boundaries. Other useful contacts include **Cape Nature** (☎ 021-426 0723; www.capenature.org.za) in Western Cape and **Komatiland Forests Eco-Tourism** (☎ 013-754 2724; www.komatiecotourism.co.za) in Mpumalanga and Limpopo.

All South African national parks charge a daily entry (conservation) fee, though amounts vary. One way to save is to purchase a **Wild Card** (www.wildinafrica.com) online or at the parks. The version of the card for foreign tourists, which is valid for a year, gives you unlimited entry into any of the parks and reserves in the Wild Card system (R940/1640/2210 per adult/couple/family). If you're planning more

than five days in one of the more expensive parks such as Kruger, it's worth buying.

In addition to its national parks, South Africa is also party to several transfrontier parks joining conservation areas across international borders, and private wildlife reserves also abound. However, in total, less than 8% of South African land has been given protected status. The government has started teaming up with private landowners to bring private conservation land under government protection, with the goal of ultimately increasing the total amount of conservation land to over 10%.

CAPE TOWN

☎ 021 / pop 3.1 million

Prepare to fall in love, as South Africa's 'Mother City' is an old pro at capturing people's hearts. And who wouldn't swoon at the sight of magnificent Table Mountain, its summit draped with cascading clouds, its flanks coated with unique flora and vineyards, its base fringed by golden beaches? Few cities can boast such a wonderful national park at their heart or provide the range of adventurous activities that take advantage of it.

Accentuating this natural majesty is the Capetonians' imaginative flair. From the Bo-Kaap's brightly painted facades to the contemporary Afro-chic decor of the city's guesthouses, restaurants and bars, this is one good-looking metropolis.

Counterbalancing these splendid assets are some obvious flaws. One academic has gone as far as to dub this the world's most unequal city; comparing the mansions of Constantia with the shacks of Crossroads, you'd be tempted to agree. However, Capetonians don't lack charity or compassion, and it's a multicultural city where everyone has a fascinating, sometimes heartbreaking story to tell.

ORIENTATION

Cape Town's commercial centre, known as the City Bowl, lies to the north of Table Mountain and the east of Signal Hill. The inner-city suburbs of Gardens, Oranjezicht and Tamboerskloof are all within walking distance of the City Bowl. Near to Signal Hill, Green Point and Sea Point are densely populated seaside suburbs.

Cape Town sprawls quite a distance to the northeast (this is where you'll find the beachside Bloubergstrand district and the enormous Canal Walk Shopping Centre). To the south, skirting the eastern flank of the mountains and running down to Muizenberg at False Bay, are leafy and increasingly rich suburbs, including Observatory, Newlands and Constantia.

On the Atlantic Coast, exclusive Clifton and Camps Bay are accessible by coastal road from Sea Point or through Kloof Nek, the pass between Table Mountain and Lion's Head. Camps Bay is a 10-minute drive from the city centre and can easily be reached by public transport.

INFORMATION
Bookshops
The main mass-market bookshop and news-agent is CNA, with branches around the city.
Clarke's Bookshop (Map pp1026-7; ☎ 021-423 5739; www.clarkesbooks.co.za; 211 Long St, City Bowl)
Exclusive Books Waterfront (Map pp1024-5; ☎ 021-419 0905; Victoria Wharf); Gardens (Map pp1026-7; ☎ 021-426 2977; Lifestyles on Kloof, Kloof St)

Internet Access
Cape Town is one of Africa's most wired cities. Most hotels and hostels have internet facilities and you'll seldom have to hunt far for a wi-fi network or internet cafe. Rates are pretty uniform at R20 per hour. There is a handful of cafes in and around Lifestyles on Kloof (see Bookshops) and access is available at Cape Town Tourism's City Bowl office (see Tourist Information; per hour R10).

Medical Services
Groote Schuur Hospital (Map pp1024-5; ☎ 021-404 9111; http://capegateway.gov.za/gsh; Main Rd, Observatory)
Netcare Christiaan Barnard Memorial Hospital (Map pp1026-7; ☎ 021-480 6111; www.netcare.co.za; 181 Longmarket St, City Bowl)
Netcare Travel Clinic (Map pp1026-7; ☎ 021-419 3172; www.travelclinics.co.za; Room 1107, 11th fl, Picbel Parkade, 58 Strand St, City Bowl; ☼ 8am-4pm Mon-Fri)

Money
Money can be changed at the airport, at most commercial banks and at Cape Town Tourism (right).

There are ATMs all over town.
American Express City Bowl (Map pp1026-7; ☎ 021-425 7991; Thibault Sq); Waterfront (Map pp1024-5; ☎ 021-419 3917; V&A Hotel Mall, Waterfront)
Rennies Travel (Map pp1026-7; ☎ 021-423 7154; 101 St George's Mall, City Bowl) The local agent for Thomas Cook.

Post
Post office (Map pp1024-5; ☎ 021-421 4551; Upper fl, Victoria Wharf, Waterfront; ☼ 9am-7pm Mon-Fri, 9am-4pm Sat, 10am-2pm Sun)

Tourist Information
Cape Town Tourism (www.capetown.travel; City Bowl (Map pp1026-7; ☎ 021-487 6800; cnr Castle & Burg Sts, City Bowl; ☼ 8am-5.30pm Mon-Fri, 8.30am-1pm Sat, 9am-1pm Sun; Waterfront Map pp1024-5; ☎ 021-408 7600; Clock Tower Centre; ☼ 9am-6pm Oct-Mar, 8am-5pm Apr-Sep) books accommodation, tours and rental cars. The City Bowl branch offers a **Computicket booth** (☎ 083-915 8000; www.computicket.com), which is a booth where you can buy tickets for everything from concerts and films to buses and flights, a free phone for ordering *rikkis* (local shared taxis), and advice on Cape Nature reserves and national parks. The Waterfront office is shared with **Western Cape Tourism** (☎ 021-405 4500; www.thewesterncape.co.za; ☼ 9am-7pm).

DANGERS & ANNOYANCES
Cape Town is one of Africa's most relaxed cities, which can instil a false sense of security. Paranoia is not required, but common sense is. There is tremendous poverty on the peninsula and the 'informal redistribution of wealth' is reasonably common. The townships on the Cape Flats have an appalling crime rate; unless you have a trustworthy guide or are on a tour, they are not places for a casual stroll.

While the city centre is generally safe to walk around, always listen to local advice on where to avoid. At night, there is safety in numbers; stick to the main thoroughfares.

Swimming at any of the Cape beaches is potentially hazardous, especially for those inexperienced in surf. Check for warning signs about rips and rocks and only swim in patrolled areas.

SIGHTS & ACTIVITIES
Table Mountain National Park
Covering some three-quarters of the peninsula, **Table Mountain National Park** (www.sanparks.org /parks/table_mountain) stretches from flat-topped Table Mountain to Cape Point. For the vast majority of visitors the main attraction is the 1086m-high mountain itself, the top of which can easily be accessed by the **Cableway** (Map pp1024-5; ☎ 021-424 8181; www.tablemountain.net; adult one way/return R74/145, child R38/76; ☼ 8.30am-7pm Feb-Nov, 8am-9.30pm Dec & Jan), which runs every 10/20 minutes in high/low season. The hours of

operation we have listed are averages, as the times change monthly; check the latest information when you are in Cape Town.

The views from the revolving cable car and the summit are phenomenal. The Cableway doesn't operate when it's dangerously windy, and there's little point going up if you are simply going to be wrapped in the cloud known as the 'tablecloth'. The best visibility and conditions are likely to be first thing in the morning or in the evening.

Hikers can take advantage of 300-plus routes up and down, but bear in mind that the mountain is more than 1000m high, conditions can become treacherous quickly and it's easy to get lost. Unprepared and foolhardy hikers die here every year. **Abseil Africa** (Map pp1026-7; ☎ 021-424 4760; www.abseilafrica.co.za; Long St, City Bowl), among other companies, offers guided hikes up Table Mountain (R195).

There are two main multiday trails, both of which come with guides and portering services. The three-day **Table Mountain Trail** proceeds from the Waterfront to Kirstenbosch Botanical Gardens; the six-day, five-night **Hoerikwaggo Trail**, which stretches 97km from Cape Point to the upper cable-car station on Table Mountain, can also be tackled in two-day sections.

If you don't have your own transport, *rikki*s (see p1031) will drop you at the cable car from the city centre for R30; a nonshared taxi will cost around R60.

Robben Island & Nelson Mandela Gateway

Prisoners were incarcerated on **Robben Island** (off Map pp1024-5; ☎ 021-413 4220; www.robben-island. org.za; adult/child R180/90; ☒ ferries from Waterfront 9am, 11am, 1pm & 3pm) from the early days of the VOC right up until 1996. Now a museum and Unesco World Heritage Site, it is one of Cape Town's most popular attractions.

While we heartily recommend going to Robben Island, a visit here is not without its drawbacks. Most likely you will have to endure crowds and being hustled around on a guided tour, that at a maximum of two hours on the island (plus a 30-minute boat ride in both directions) is woefully short.

The standard tours include a walk through the old prison, as well as a 45-minute bus ride around the island with commentary on the various places of note. If you're lucky, you'll have about 10 minutes to wander around on your own. We recommend heading straight to

the prison's A-section to view the remarkable and very moving exhibition *Cell Stories*. In each of the 40 isolation cells is an artefact and story from a former political prisoner.

Tours depart from the **Nelson Mandela Gateway** (Map pp1024-5; admission free; ☒ 7.30am-9pm) beside the Clock Tower at the Waterfront. Even if you don't plan a visit to the island, it's worth dropping by the museum here. Make bookings through the website, Nelson Mandela Gateway or Cape Town Tourism (opposite) in the city. At holiday times all tours can be booked up for days.

City Bowl

The commercial heart of Cape Town, City Bowl is squeezed between Table Mountain, Signal Hill and the harbour. Immediately to the west is the Bo-Kaap, the Waterkant is to the north, and Zonnebloem (once known as District Six) lies to the southeast.

DISTRICT SIX MUSEUM

If you see only one museum in Cape Town, make it the **District Six Museum** (Map pp1026-7; ☎ 021-466 7208; 25A Buitenkant St; adult/child R15/5; ☒ 9am-2pm Mon, 9am-4pm Tue-Sat), which most township tours stop at. This emotionally moving museum is as much for the people of the now-vanished neighbourhood as it is about them. Prior to the forced evictions of the 1960s and 1970s some 50,000 people of all races lived in the area.

You can also arrange a **walking tour** (per person R50, 10 people minimum) of the old District Six.

LONG STREET

Whether you come to browse the antique shops, secondhand bookshops and streetwear boutiques, or to party at the bars and clubs that crank up at night, a stroll along Long St is an essential element of a Cape Town visit. The most attractive section, lined with Victorian-era buildings with wrought-iron balconies, runs from the junction with Buitensingel St north to around the Strand.

Green Point & Waterfront

Cape Town's prime Atlantic Coast suburbs start at the Waterfront, from where you'll depart for Robben Island (left). Near here you'll also find the bold new Green Point Stadium.

VICTORIA & ALBERT WATERFRONT

Commonly referred to as just the **Waterfront** (www.waterfront.co.za), this tourist-orientated

SOUTH AFRICA

CAPE TOWN

INFORMATION
American Express **1** E1
Cape Town Tourism .... (see 4)
Exclusive Books **2** E1
Groote Schuur Hospital **3** H4
Post Office .... (see 2)
Western Cape Tourism **4** E1

SIGHTS & ACTIVITIES
Lower Cableway Station **5** D4
Nelson Mandela Gateway **6** E1
Upper Cableway Station **7** D5
Waterfront Boat Company **8** E1

SLEEPING
Ashanti Lodge **9** E3
Cape Grace **10** E1
One & Only **11** E1
Sunflower Stop **12** D1
Villa Zest **13** E2

EATING
Arnold's **14** D3
Café Sofia .... (see 14)
Wakame **15** D1
Willoughby & Co .... (see 2)

DRINKING
Asoka **16** D3
La Med **17** B4

ENTERTAINMENT
Green Dolphin **18** E1
Mercury Live & Lounge.................. **19** E3

ATLANTIC
OCEAN

Mouille
Point

Beach Rd

15

Green Point

Three
Anchor
Bay

Rocklands
Bay

Three
Anchor
Bay

M
6

Western Blvd

12

High Level Rd

Beach Rd

Main Rd

High Level Rd

Sea
Point

M
6

Boat Bay

Signal Hill Rd

Signal
Hill

Sea
Point

Fresnaye

Tamboerskloof

Kloof Nek Rd

14

Kloof St

16

Victoria Rd

Bantry
Bay

No 1

Clifton

Lion's
Head
(669m)

Gardens

No 2

No 3

No 4

M
6

Kloof Nek

17

Round House

Kloof Rd

Tafelberg Rd

Camps
Bay

5

Whale
Rocks

Camps Bay

Table
Mountain
(1073m)

7

Pipe Track

Bakoven
Bay

Bakoven

M
62

Camps Bay Dr

Rontree

Klein-Koeël
Bay

Kasteelpoort

Oudekraal

Back
Table

Twelve Apostles

Woodhead
Reservoir

To Llandudno (5km);
Sandy Bay (6km);
Hout Bay (10km);
Kommetjie (20km)

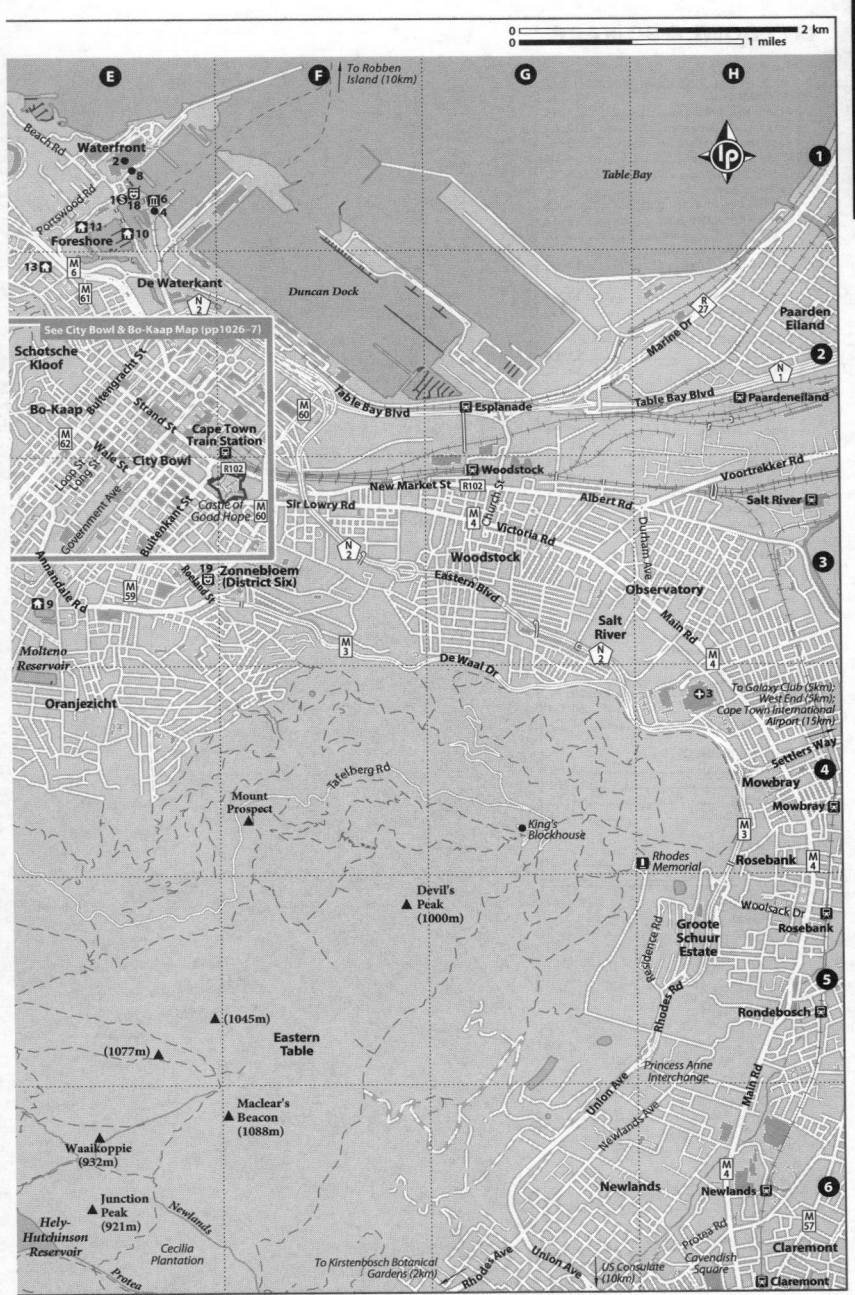

0 ————————— 2 km
0 ————————— 1 mile

E **F** To Robben
Island (10km) **G** **H**

1

Beach Rd
Waterfront
2 8
19 6
18 4
Foreshore 11 10
13 M6
M61
De Waterkant N7

Portswood Rd
Table Bay

Paarden
Eiland

R27

2
N
Paardeneiland

**Schotsche
Kloof**

See City Bowl & Bo-Kaap Map (pp1026–7)

Duncan Dock

Table Bay Blvd
Esplanade

Table Bay Blvd
Marine Dr

Voortrekker Rd

Salt River

Bo-Kaap Buitengracht St
M62 Strand St
Wale St **City Bowl**
Loop St Long St
Government Ave
Annandale Rd Buitenkant St

M60 **Cape Town
Train Station**
R102

New Market St
R102
Woodstock
Sir Lowry Rd
Church St
Albert Rd
Durham Ave

**Castle of
Good Hope** M60

19 **Zonnebloem
(District Six)** N2
M59

M3

Victoria Rd
Woodstock
Eastern Blvd

**Salt
River**
N2

Observatory

Main Rd
M4

3

Oranjezicht
9
Molteno
Reservoir

De Waal Dr

C3 To Galaxy Club (5km);
West End (5km);
Cape Town International
Airport (15km)

Settlers Way
Mowbray

4
M3
Mowbray

Tafelberg Rd
**Mount
Prospect**

King's
Blockhouse

Rhodes
Memorial
Rosebank
M4

Rosebank

Residentia Rd

5
Rondebosch

**Devil's
Peak
(1000m)**

Woolsack Dr

**Groote
Schuur
Estate**

Rhodes Rd

(1045m)

(1077m)
**Eastern
Table**

**Maclear's
Beacon
(1088m)**

Princess Anne
Interchange

Union Ave
Newlands Ave

Main Rd

Rondebosch

**Waaikoppie
(932m)**

**Junction
Peak
(921m)**

Hely-
Hutchinson
Reservoir

Newlands

Cecilia
Plantation

Protea

To Kirstenbosch Botanical
Gardens (2km)

Rhodes Ave Union Ave

US Consulate
(10km)

Protea Rd
Newlands
M4
Newlands

Cavendish
Square

6
M57

Claremont

Claremont

CITY BOWL & BO-KAAP

INFORMATION
American Express	1	F2
Botswanan Consulate	2	G1
Cape Town Tourism	3	E3
Clarke's Bookshop	4	D5
Dutch Consulate	5	E2
Exclusive Books	6	B6
French Consulate	7	C6
German Consulate	8	F2
Mozambican Consulate	9	E3
Netcare Christiaan Barnard		
Memorial Hospital	10	D3
Netcare Travel Clinic	11	F3
Rennies Travel	12	E3
UK Consulate	(see 2)	

SIGHTS & ACTIVITIES
Abseil Africa	13	C5
District Six Museum	14	F5

SLEEPING
Cape Diamond Hotel	15	F4
Daddy Long Legs	16	D4
Grand Daddy Hotel	17	E3
Hippo Boutique Hotel	18	B6
Long Street Backpackers	19	D5
St Paul's Guesthouse	20	C5
The Backpack	21	B5
Urban Chic	22	D4

EATING
Birds Café	23	D3
Bizerca Bistro	24	G2
Noon Gun Tearoom & Restaurant	25	C1
Nova	26	B5
Rick's Café Américain	27	B6
Royale Eatery	28	C5

DRINKING
Fireman's Arms	29	E1
Julep Bar	30	D5
Waiting Room	31	C5

ENTERTAINMENT
Artscape	32	H2
Hemisphere	33	F3
Old City Hall	34	F5
Zula Sound Bar	35	D5

TRANSPORT
Bus Terminus	36	G3
Golden Acre Terminal	37	G4

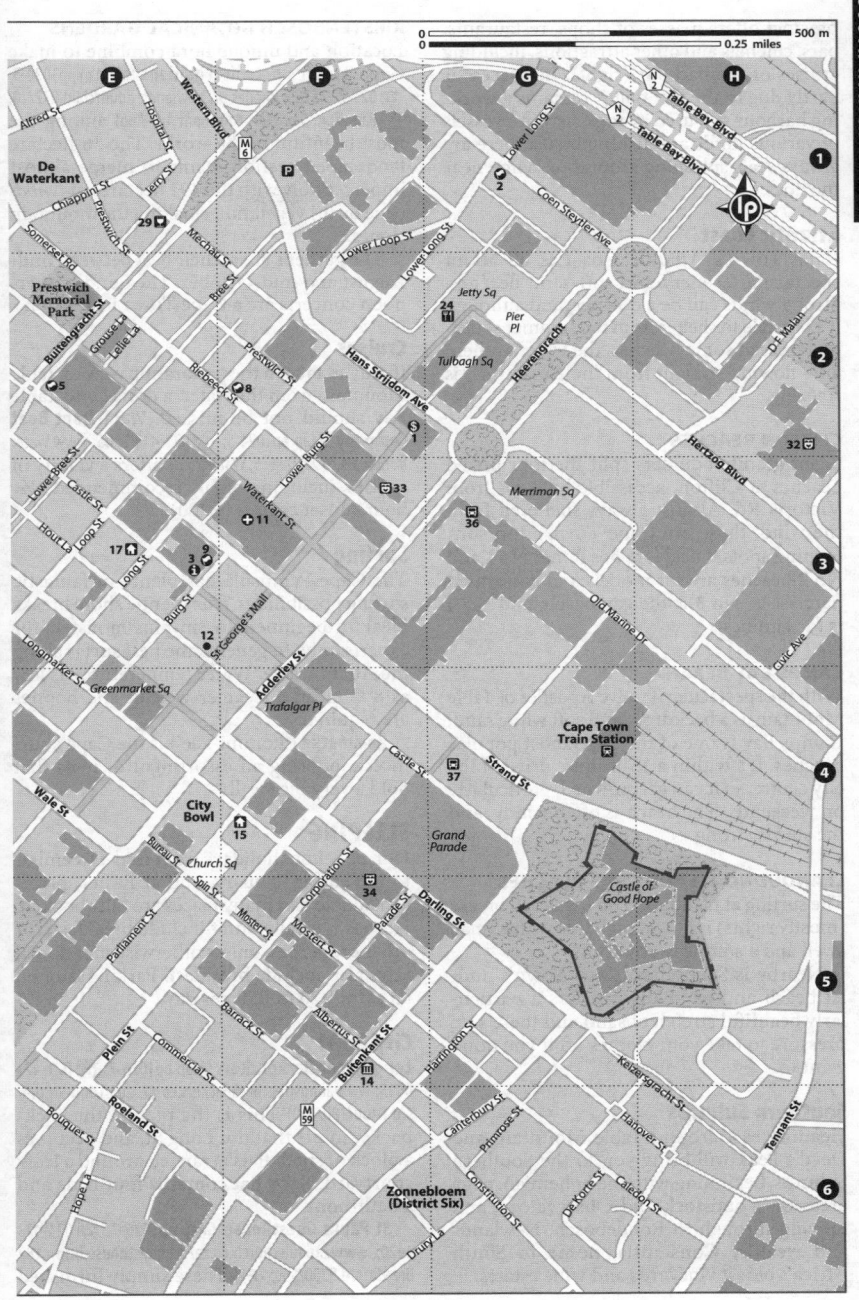

precinct offers masses of shops, restaurants, bars, cinemas and other attractions, including cruises of the harbour (right). Its success is partly due to the fact that it remains a working harbour still used by tugs, harbour vessels of various kinds and fishing boats; there are always seals splashing around or lazing near the docks.

Atlantic Coast

Cape Town's Atlantic Coast is all about spectacular scenery and soft-sand beaches. Strong winds can be a downer, and although it's possible to shelter from the summer southeasterlies at some beaches, the water at them all – flowing straight from the Antarctic – is freezing.

CLIFTON BEACHES

Giant granite boulders split the four linked beaches at Clifton, accessible by steps from Victoria Rd. Almost always sheltered from the wind, these are Cape Town's top sunbathing spots. Local lore has it that No 1 and No 2 beaches are for models and confirmed narcissists, No 3 is the gay beach, and No 4 is for families.

CAMPS BAY BEACH

With the spectacular Twelve Apostles of Table Mountain as a backdrop, and soft white sand, Camps Bay is one of the city's most popular beaches. It's within a 15-minute drive of the city centre, so it can get crowded, particularly on weekends. The beach is often windy, and the surf is strong.

LLANDUDNO & SANDY BAY BEACHES

The surfing at Llandudno on the beach breaks (mostly rights) is best at high tide with a small swell and a southeasterly wind.

Nearby is Sandy Bay, Cape Town's nudist beach and gay hang-out. It's a particularly beautiful stretch of sand and there's no pressure to take your clothes off if you don't want to.

Southern Suburbs

Heading east around Table Mountain and Devil's Peak will bring you to the Southern Suburbs, beginning with the bohemian, edgy areas of Woodstock and Observatory, and moving through to Rondebosch, Newlands and wealthy Constantia, home to South Africa's oldest vineyards and wine estates.

KIRSTENBOSCH BOTANICAL GARDENS

Location and unique flora combine to make Cape Town's **botanical gardens** (off Map pp1024-5; ☎ 021-799 8783; Rhodes Dr, Newlands; adult/child R32/10; ☻ 8am-7pm Sep-Mar, 8am-6pm Apr-Aug) among the most beautiful in the world. The 36-hectare landscaped section seems to merge almost imperceptibly with the 492 hectares of *fynbos* (fine bush) vegetation cloaking the mountain slopes.

The gardens are at their best between mid-August and mid-October. The Sunday afternoon concerts are a Cape Town institution.

Cruises

If only to take in the panoramic view of Table Mountain from the water, a cruise into Table Bay should not be missed. **Waterfront Boat Company** (Map pp1024-5; ☎ 021-418 5806; www.waterfrontboats.co.za; Quay 5, Waterfront) offers a variety of cruises, including highly recommended 1½-hour sunset cruises (R200).

Surfing

The Cape Peninsula has plenty of fantastic surfing possibilities, from gentle shore breaks ideal for beginners to 3m-plus monsters for experts only. In general, the best surf is along the Atlantic side. Water temperatures as low as 8°C mean a steamer wetsuit and booties are required.

Kommetjie ('kommi-kee') is the Cape's surf mecca, offering an assortment of reefs that hold a very big swell.

SLEEPING

During school holidays from mid-December to the end of January, and at Easter, prices can double and many places are fully booked. Hostels typically don't include breakfast; for other properties, unless otherwise mentioned rates also include breakfast. Parking is often an extra R20 to R50 per day.

City Bowl

Long Street Backpackers (Map pp1026-7; ☎ 021-423 0615; www.longstreetbackpackers.co.za; 209 Long St; dm/s/d R100/180/250) This is the pick of the backpacker joints that dot Long St, and occupies a block of small flats arranged around a leafy courtyard. Each flat contains four beds and a bathroom.

St Paul's Guesthouse (Map pp1026-7; ☎ 021-423 4420; www.stpaulschurch.co.za/theguesthouse.htm; 182 Bree St; s/d R300/500; Ⓟ) These simply furnished rooms, set around a vine-shaded courtyard, are a quiet alternative to a hostel.

Cape Diamond Hotel (Map pp1026-7; ☎ 021-461 2519; www.capediamondhotel.co.za; cnr Longmarket & Parliament Sts; s/d excl breakfast from R825/1090; P ⬛) This good-value hotel has kept features of its art-deco building, including the wood-panelled floors. It's short on natural light but there's a rooftop jacuzzi with a view of Table Mountain.

Daddy Long Legs (Map pp1026-7; ☎ 021-422 3074; www.daddylonglegs.co.za; 134 Long St; r R945, apt from R1045; ⬛ ⬛) A stay at this boutique-hotel-cum-art-installation is anything but boring. Thirteen artists were given free rein to design the boudoirs of their dreams, with results ranging from a bohemian garret to a hospital ward!

Urban Chic (Map pp1026-7; ☎ 021-426 6119; www.urbanchic.co.za; cnr Long & Pepper Sts; s/d from R1233/1369; P ⬛ ⬛) Rooms with fabulous floor-to-ceiling views towards Table Mountain feature at this stylish boutique hotel. Its Gallery Café is one of Long St's more polished watering holes.

our pick Grand Daddy Hotel (Map pp1026-7; ☎ 021-424 7247; www.daddylonglegs.co.za/grand-daddy.html; 38 Long St; r/ste R1500/2000; P ⬛ ⬛) Daddy Long Legs' sister operation takes creativity to new heights with its rooftop trailer park of penthouse suites, made from vintage Airstream trailers and decorated with themes including the John and Yoko bed-in. The regular rooms and Daddy Cool bar are also stylish.

Gardens

Ashanti Lodge (Map pp1024-5; ☎ 021-423 8721; www.ashanti.co.za; 11 Hof St; campsites R75, dm/s/d without bathroom R140/300/420, r R600; P ⬛ ⬛) One of Cape Town's premier party hostels. For something quieter, opt for the excellent rooms with en suites in two heritage-listed houses around the corner.

The Backpack (Map pp1026-7; ☎ 021-423 4530; www.backpackers.co.za; 74 New Church St; dm/s/tw without bathroom R145/440/650, dm/s/d R270/550/800; P ⬛ ⬛) Cape Town's longest-running backpackers sits at the boutique end of the hostel spectrum, with stylish dorms and rooms, a buzzy vibe, fantastic staff and Fair Trade accreditation.

Hippo Boutique Hotel (Map pp1026-7; ☎ 021-423 2500; www.hippotique.co.za; 5-9 Park Rd; r/ste excl breakfast R1290/2200; P ⬛ ⬛ ⬛) This boutique property offers spacious, stylish rooms featuring kitchenettes, computers and music systems. Larger suites have mezzanine-level bedrooms and funky theme designs.

Green Point & Waterfront

Sunflower Stop (Map pp1024-5; ☎ 021-434 6535; www.sunflowerstop.co.za; 179 Main Rd, Green Point; dm R120, r with/without bathroom R490/400; ⬛ ⬛) Set far enough back from Main Rd to offer tranquility, this sunny, spacious hostel near Green Point Stadium has a lounge, poolside bar and *braai*, and attractive en-suite rooms.

Villa Zest (Map pp1024-5; ☎ 021-433 1246; www.villazest.co.za; 2 Braemar Rd, Green Point; s/d from R1290/1590; P ⬛ ⬛ ⬛) A few doors from St John's Waterfront Lodge backpackers, this Bauhaus-style home's lobby is decorated with '60s and '70s groovy electronic goods, from Polaroid cameras to View-Masters. The seven individual rooms also pull off Austin Powers flourishes, with bold retro furniture and wallpaper-covered walls.

Cape Grace (Map pp1024-5; ☎ 021-410 7100; www.capegrace.com; West Quay, Waterfront; s/d from R5590/5750; P ⬛ ⬛ ⬛) Clint Eastwood and the *Invictus* cast reportedly loved this Waterfront stalwart. With its winning combination of antiques and hand-painted decor, the luxurious hotel provides a unique sense of place and Cape Town's history.

One & Only (Map pp1024-5; ☎ 021-431 5800; www.oneandonlyresorts.com; Dock Rd, Waterfront; r/ste from R6900/7900; P ⬛ ⬛ ⬛) The latest peacock feather in the cap of South African hotel magnate Sol Kerzner is a 131-room colossus that dominates even the showy Waterfront, with 41 suites on an artificial island and a Gordon Ramsay restaurant, Maze.

EATING
City Bowl & Around

Long St has many great places to eat, plus fantastic street life. Head to the Bo-Kaap to sample authentic Cape Malay dishes in unpretentious surroundings.

Birds Café (Map pp1026-7; ☎ 021-426 2534; 127 Bree St; mains R50-60; ⏱ 8am-4pm) The sophisticated rustic style (think milk-bottle-crate seats in a grand old Dutch building) matches the artisan food, including homemade pies, strudels and chunky scones.

Royale Eatery (Map pp1026-7; ☎ 021-422 4536; 279 Long St; mains R60-70; ⏱ noon-11.30pm Mon-Sat) The Royale does gourmet burgers grilled to perfection; for something different, try the Big Bird ostrich burger. Downstairs is casual and buzzy while upstairs is a restaurant.

Noon Gun Tearoom & Restaurant (Map pp1026-7; ☎ 021-424 0529; 273 Longmarket St; mains R65-80;

10am-10pm Mon-Sat) High on Signal Hill, this is a fine place to sample Cape Malay dishes such as *bobotie*.

our pick **Bizerca Bistro** (Map pp1026–7; ☎ 021-418 0001; Jetty St; mains R105) Run by a French chef and his South African wife, this fantastic bistro's atmosphere is contemporary and friendly. Expertly prepared dishes such as butternut pumpkin gnocchi and braised pig's trotter are bursting with flavour.

Gardens

Kloof St offers the best dining selection in Gardens.

Arnold's (Map pp1024–5; ☎ 021-424 4344; 60 Kloof St; mains R50–100; 8am-late) With a neighbourhood feel (customers greet the boss like old friends), Arnold's has a covered streetfront beer garden and a good breakfast menu.

Rick's Café Américain (Map pp1026–7; ☎ 021-424 1100; 2 Park Rd; mains R70–100) Popular with everyone from backpackers to models, Rick's evokes the famous nightclub in *Casablanca*. Tagines and tapas, steaks and seafood are on the menu.

Café Sofia (Map pp1024–5; ☎ 021-426 0801; 60 Kloof St; mains R89–109) Pinstripe wallpaper and customers plugged into laptops are a backdrop for tapas, meze, sangria and cocktails at this branch of the small chain.

Nova (Map pp1026–7; ☎ 021-422 3585; 70 New Church St; mains R95–135; 7-10pm Mon-Sat) Chef Richard Carstens, who dabbles in molecular gastronomy, is tickling Capetonian tastebuds with this elegant venture, at the same address as the cocktail and pizza joint Relish. Dishes include tempura prawns with prawn ravioli and a scoop of apple ice cream.

Waterfront & Around

The Waterfront's many restaurants and cafes have ocean views, although it's essentially a giant tourist trap. Better value and a less touristy dining experience are available a short walk away in Green Point and Mouille Point; closer to City Bowl is the Waterkant's Cape Quarter complex.

Willoughby & Co (Map pp1024–5; ☎ 021-418 6115; ground fl, Victoria Wharf, Waterfront; mains R60–100; noon-11pm) Huge servings of sushi are the standout in the good-value menu at this casual eatery-cum-fishmongers, commonly acknowledged as one of the Waterfront's best eateries.

Wakame (Map pp1024–5; ☎ 021-433 2377; cnr Beach Rd & Surrey Pl, Mouille Point; sushi R40, mains R75–100) Tucking into Wakame's salt-and-pepper squid or sushi platter, while gazing at the glorious coastal view, is a wonderful way to pass an afternoon. On the 2nd level it specialises in dim sum.

DRINKING

our pick **Waiting Room** (Map pp1026–7; ☎ 021-422 4536; 273 Long St, City Bowl) Climb the narrow stairway beside Royale Eatery to find this hip bar, complete with retro furniture and DJs spinning funky tunes. Head even higher and you'll reach the roof deck, perfect for admiring the city lights.

Julep Bar (Map pp1026–7; ☎ 021-423 4276; Vredenburg Lane) Occupying a former brothel, this hidden gem, a favourite with local hipsters, will set you apart from the riff-raff on nearby Long St.

Fireman's Arms (Map pp1026–7; ☎ 021-419 1513; 25 Mechau St, Waterkant) A traditional pub that's been here for eons; check out its memorabilia including colonial-era flags.

La Med (Map pp1024–5; ☎ 021-438 5600; Glen Country Club, Victoria Rd, Clifton) Sinking a sundowner and munching pizza at this alfresco bar with a killer view of the Twelve Apostles is a Cape Town ritual. Keep an eye out for the easily missed turn-off, between Clifton and Camps Bay.

Asoka (Map pp1024–5; ☎ 021-422 0909; 68 Kloof St, Gardens) There's a party going on at this Buddhist-themed preclub bar with a wooden deck overlooking Kloof St.

ENTERTAINMENT

Live Music

The **Cape Town Philharmonic** (☎ 021-410 9809; www.cpo.org.za) leads the way on the Mother City's classical music scene, performing mainly at **Old City Hall** (Map pp1026–7; Darling St), the performing arts complex **Artscape** (Map pp1026–7; ☎ 021-410 9800; www.artscape.co.za; DF Malan St, Foreshore) and the Waterfront.

Green Dolphin (Map pp1024–5; ☎ 021-421 7471; Waterfront; cover R30–35) There's a consistently good line-up of artists at this upmarket jazz venue and restaurant.

West End (off Map pp1024–5; ☎ 021-637 9132; http://superclubs.co.za; Cine 400 Bldg, College Rd, Rylands Estate, Athlone; cover R30; 5pm-4am Fri & Sat) Mainstream jazz is the name of the game here. One of Cape Town's top venues, it attracts a well-heeled clientele and top performers.

Mercury Live & Lounge (Map pp1024–5; ☎ 021-465 2106; www.mercuryl.co.za; 43 De Villiers St, Zonnebloem; cover R20–50) This long-running rock venue plays host to top South African bands and overseas visitors. The sound quality is good and there's a DJ bar below and the Shack bar next door.

Nightclubs

The major nightclubs are concentrated in the City Bowl around Long St and in the Waterkant. Cover charges vary between R30 and R60. The big nights are Wednesday, Friday and Saturday.

Galaxy Club (off Map pp1024-5; ☎ 021-637 9132; College Rd, Rylands Estate, Athlone) Next to the West End jazz club, this legendary Cape Flats dance venue is where you can get down to R&B, hip hop and live bands with a black and coloured crowd.

Hemisphere (Map pp1026-7; ☎ 021-421 0581; 31st fl, ABSA Centre, Riebeeck St; 10pm-3am Thu-Sat) This stylish club atop the ABSA Centre offers twinkling views of the city. It's velvet-rope-and-glamour-model stuff, so dress to the nines.

Zula Sound Bar (Map pp1026-7; ☎ 021-424 2442; 194 Long St, City Bowl) Funky venue that hosts an interesting range of events, including live bands, DJs, comedy (Mondays), acoustic musicians (Tuesdays) and open-mic poetry (last Wednesday of the month).

GETTING THERE & AWAY

Cape Town International Airport (off Map pp1024-5; ☎ 021-937 1200; www.airports.co.za) is 20km east of the city centre, approximately 20 minutes' drive depending on traffic.

In addition to **South African Airways** (SAA; ☎ 0861-359 722; www.flysaa.com), three budget airlines operate out of Cape Town: **Kulula.com** (☎ 0861-444 144; www.kulula.com), **Mango** (☎ 0861-162 646; ww5.flymango.com) and **1time** (☎ 0861-345 345; www.1time.aero), all flying to the major South African cities. For a list of international airlines serving South Africa, see p1064.

Greyhound, Intercape, SA Roadlink and Translux bus lines operate out of Cape Town. Their booking offices and main arrival and departure points are at the Meriman Sq end of Cape Town train station (City Bowl).

All trains, including Shosholoza Meyl's recommended tourist- and premier-class services to destinations including Jo'burg (see p1067), leave from the **central train station** (Map pp1026-7; Strand St). Be prepared for queues at the **booking office** (☎ 021-449 4596; 7.30am-4.55pm Mon-Fri, 7.30-10.30am Sat).

GETTING AROUND

Backpacker Bus (☎ 021-439 7600; www.backpackerbus. co.za) picks up from accommodation in the city and offers airport transfers from R150 per person. Expect to pay from R200 for a nonshared taxi.

For local bus services, the main station is the **Golden Acre Terminal** (Map pp1026-7; Grand Pde). From here **Golden Arrow** (☎ 0800-656 463; www. gabs.co.za) buses run, most useful for getting down the Atlantic Coast from the city centre. A tourist-friendly alternative is **City Sightseeing Cape Town** (☎ 021-511 6000; www.city-sightseeing.com; adult/child R120/60).

Minibus taxis cover most of the city with an informal network of routes, and are a cheap way of getting around.

A cross between a taxi and a shared taxi, **rikkis** (☎ 0861-745 547; www.rikkis.co.za; 6.30am-2am Mon-Thu, 24hr service 6.30am-2am Fri-2am Mon) offer shared rides most places around the City Bowl, and down the Atlantic Coast to Camps Bay, for R15 to R30. They are not the quickest option, as there is usually a degree of meandering as passengers are dropped off.

Consider taking a nonshared taxi at night or if you're in a group. Rates are typically R10 to R12 per km. Call **Marine Taxi** (☎ 021-434 0434) or **Unicab Taxis** (☎ 021-447 4402).

Metrorail (☎ 0800-656 463; www.capemetrorail. co.za) commuter trains are a handy way to get around, although there are few (or no) trains after 6pm.

AROUND CAPE TOWN

WINELANDS

The Boland, stretching inland and upwards from Cape Town, isn't South Africa's only wine-growing region, but it's certainly the most famous. Its name means 'Upland', a reference to the dramatic mountain ranges that shoot up to over 1500m, on whose fertile slopes the vineyards form a patchwork. Lively student-town Stellenbosch offers the most activities.

Stellenbosch

☎ 021 / pop 220,000

South Africa's second-oldest European settlement, established on the banks of the Eerste River in 1679, Stellenbosch wears many faces. At times it's a rowdy joint for Stellenbosch University students; at others it's a stately monument to colonial architectural splendour. But mostly it's just plain busy, as Capetonians, wine farm workers and tourists descend on its museums, buzzing markets, quality hotels and varied eating and nightlife options.

There are too many good wineries in the area to list all of them, so it's sometimes best to drive around and stop on a whim. We do, however, recommend **Villiera** (☎ 021-865 2002; Koelenhof; tastings free; ☺ 8.30am-5pm Mon-Fri, 8.30am-3pm Sat), which produces excellent Méthode Cap Classique wines and works with black-owned M'hudi Wines. The long-established **Easy Rider Wine Tours** (☎ 021-886 4651; Stumble Inn, 12 Market St) offer good value for a full-day trip at R350, which includes lunch and all tastings.

Lively and welcoming **Stumble Inn** (☎ 021-887 4049; www.stumbleinnstellenbosch.hostel.com; 12 Market St; dm R90, r without bathroom R250; ☐ ☒) is split over two old houses, one with a pool and the other with a pleasant garden. **De Oude Meul** (☎ 021-887 7085; www.deoudemeul.com; 10A Mill St; s/d incl breakfast R700/900; ☒), above an antiques shop in the centre of town, is very good and reasonable for the price. Comfortable, country-style **Stellenbosch Hotel** (☎ 021-887 3644; www.stellenbosch. co.za/hotel; cnr Dorp & Andringa Sts; s/d R795/1090; ☒) has a variety of rooms, some with four-poster beds.

Popular **Beads** (☎ 021-886 8734; cnr Church & Ryneveld Sts; mains R50-100; ☺ breakfast, lunch & dinner) has outside seating and a menu featuring 10 salads, *bobotie* and the recommended chicken pot with pineapple chutney. **Moyo** (☎ 021-809 1137; Spier Estate, Lynedoch Rd; buffet R225) is a lot of fun, with roving musicians and dancers, and alfresco dining in tents and up in the trees in the middle of a wine estate.

Long-distance bus services charge high prices for the short sector to Cape Town and do not take bookings. You're better off using **Backpacker Bus** (☎ 021-439 7600; www.backpackerbus. co.za), which charges R80 to R210 per person and picks up from accommodation.

Metrorail trains (see p1031) run to/from Cape Town (1st/economy class R12/7.30, about one hour). To be safe, travel in the middle of the day.

THE GARDEN ROUTE

The Garden Route is perhaps South Africa's most internationally renowned destination after Cape Town and Kruger National Park, and with good reason. Within a few hundred kilometres, the range of topography, vegetation, wildlife and outdoor activities is breathtaking. Roughly encompassing the coastline from Mossel Bay in the west to just beyond Plettenberg Bay in the east, it caters to all kinds of travellers and all manner of budgets.

You can hike and cycle in old-growth forests, commune with elephants, monkeys and birds, slide through a tree canopy, chill out on superb white beaches and canoe in lagoons. The towns most commonly used as bases are Knysna and Plettenberg Bay.

Places are described from west to east. Most travellers visit Oudtshoorn while traversing the Garden Route so, although this town is technically in the Little Karoo, we've included it in this section.

OUDTSHOORN
☎ 044 / pop 85,000
That Oudtshoorn thinks of itself as the ostrich capital of the world is no overstatement. These birds have been bred hereabouts since the 1860s, and at the turn of the 20th century, fortunes were made from the fashion for ostrich feathers. Oudtshoorn boomed, and the so-called 'feather barons' built gracious homes and other grand edifices.

The town still turns a pretty penny from breeding the birds for meat and leather. The ostriches also pay their way with tourists – you can buy ostrich eggs, feathers and *biltong* all over town – but more importantly Oudtshoorn is a great base for exploring the different environments of the Garden Route, Little Karoo and Great Karoo. The latter areas are respectively the southern and northern sections of a vast, semi-arid plateau, where stunning sunsets and starscapes can be seen from eccentric little towns.

Sights & Activities
On Grant McIlrath's (the so-called 'Meerkat Man of Oudtshoorn') **meerkat experience** (☎ 082-413 6895; admission R600; ☺ from sunrise on sunny days), at a natural burrow a few kilometres west of town, you will get to see up close how these curious, highly intelligent creatures communicate and live. No children under 10 are admitted.

If you're heading north to the Cango Caves or Cango Ostrich Farm, carry on driving and take the **Swartberg Pass** all the way to Prince Albert, then return via the **Meiringspoort Pass**. Both are engineering masterpieces, and halfway down the latter is a waterfall and small visitor centre.

Sleeping & Eating

Oasis Shanti (☎ 044-279 1163; www.oasisshanti.com; 3 Church St; campsites per person R40, dm R70, d without bathroom from R200; 🖥 🛋) A bit of a hike from the town centre, this friendly hostel occupies a large house with a *braai* and pool, and shady camping spots.

Backpackers Paradise (☎ 044-272 3436; www.backpackersparadise.net; 148 Baron van Rheede St; campsites per person R50, dm R90, r from R240; 🖥 🛋) In a large old house, this lively hostel has a separate dormbed annexe and free ostrich-egg breakfasts. There's an adventure centre attached.

Oakdene Guesthouse (☎ 044-272 3018; www.oakdene.co.za; 99 Baron van Rheede St; s/d R495/790; 🌊 🛋) Elegant cottage furniture, wooden floors, ostrich eggs and quality linen make each room special. There are lush gardens and a great pool.

Kalinka (☎ 044-279 2596; 93 Baron van Rheede St; mains R80-160; 🌙 dinner Mon-Sun) Kalinka is Russian and little touches of her heritage show in the imaginative menu at this stylish, upmarket restaurant.

Jemima's (☎ 044-272 0808; 94 Baron van Rheede St; mains from R85; 🌙 lunch Mon-Fri, dinner Mon-Sun) With a small menu specialising in traditional Cape fare, Jemima's is set in an attractive old house and garden.

Getting There & Around

Intercape (☎ 0861-287 287; www.intercape.co.za) serves Jo'burg (R532, 14½ hours, daily) and Cape Town (R238, eight hours). Cheaper **City to City** (☎ 021-449 3333; www.translux.co.za) runs to Jo'burg and to Mossel Bay (R90, two hours, daily), from where you can get to multiple destinations.

The Baz Bus (p1066) stops at George, from where you can arrange a transfer to Oudtshoorn with Backpackers Paradise (R50).

KNYSNA

☎ 044 / pop 54,000

Perched on the edge of a serene lagoon and surrounded by forests, Knysna's (pronounced '*ny*-znah') sylvan setting, gay-friendly vibe, good places to stay, eat and drink, and wide range of activities make it the major stop on the Garden Route. But if you're after something quiet and undeveloped, you should look elsewhere, particularly in high season.

Regulated by **SAN Parks** (☎ 044-302 5600; www.sanparks.org; Thesen Island), although much of it is privately owned, Knysna Lagoon (13 sq km) opens up between two sandstone cliffs, known as the Heads. There is a lookout on the eastern

head, and a cruise is a good way to appreciate the lagoon. The **Featherbed Company** (☎ 044-382 1697; www.featherbed.co.za; Waterfront) has several vessels, including the **John Benn** (adult/child R120/50; 🌙 departs 12.30pm & 5pm in winter, 6pm in summer). Snorkelling and scuba diving can be organised at **Hippo Dive Campus** (☎ 044-384 0831; the Heads).

Highfield Backpackers (☎ 044-382 6266; www.highfieldsbackpackers.co.za; 2 Graham St; dm R90, d without bathroom from R250; 🖥 🛋) feels a little like a B&B and has attractive doubles. Laid-back **Island Vibe** (☎ 044-382 1728; www.islandvibe.co.za; 67 Main St; dm R100, r without bathroom R270, s/d R224/320; 🖥 🛋) has a bar and a great view from the deck. Knysna's most imaginatively designed guesthouse is **Inyathi Guest Lodges** (☎ 044-382 7768; www.inyathi-sa.com; 52 Main St; d incl breakfast R620), with accommodation in uniquely decorated timber lodges – some with Victorian bathtubs, others with stained-glass windows.

Popular **Caffé Mario** (☎ 044-382 7250; Waterfront; mains R50-100; 🌙 breakfast, lunch & dinner) is, like 34 South, a superb lunch option in the Knysna Quays centre. **Knysna Oyster Company** (☎ 044-382 6941; Thesen Island; 6 oysters from R46, mains R80; 🌙 tours 10am-4.30pm Mon-Sat) grows its own oysters in the lagoon; you can take a tour of the processing plant and have an oyster tasting at its restaurant afterwards.

PLETTENBERG BAY

☎ 044 / pop 34,000

Plettenberg Bay, or 'Plett' as it's more commonly known, is a resort town through and through, with mountains, white sand and crystal-blue water making it one of the country's top local tourist spots. As a result, things can get very busy and somewhat overpriced, but the town retains a relaxed, friendly atmosphere and does have good-value hostels.

Those wanting to try surfing can take a lesson through the **International Surf School** (☎ 082-636 8431; 3½hr lessons R350), which caters to all levels of surfers.

Our choice for best budget option in town is the award-winning **Nothando Backpackers Hostel** (☎ 044-533 0220; www.nothando.com; 5 Wilder St; dm R120, r with/without bathroom R365/320; 🖥). There's a great bar area with satellite TV, yet you can still find peace and quiet in the large grounds. In the suburbs west of the town centre, beachfront **Periwinkle Guest Lodge** (☎ 044-533 1345; www.periwinkle.co.za; 75 Beachy Head Dr; d incl breakfast from R2024) offers individually decorated rooms, all with great views.

Lookout (☎ 044-533 1379; Lookout Rocks; mains R75; ☻ breakfast, lunch & dinner) is a great place for a simple meal on the beachfront deck and perhaps views of dolphins or whales.

TSITSIKAMMA NATIONAL PARK AREA

This **park** (adult/child R80/40) protects 82km of coast between Plettenberg Bay and Humansdorp, including an area 5km out to sea. Located at the foot of the Tsitsikamma Range and cut by rivers that have carved deep ravines into the ancient forests, it's a spectacular area to walk through. Several short day walks give you a taste of the coastline.

The main information centre for the national park is Storms River Mouth Rest Camp, 68km from Plettenberg Bay and 8km from the N2. The camp, which is open 24 hours, is 2km inside the park from the gate.

The 42km **Otter Trail** (☎ 012-426 5111; www. sanparks.org; per person R560) is one of South Africa's most acclaimed hikes, hugging the coastline from Storms River Mouth to Nature's Valley. The walk, which lasts five days and four nights, involves fording a number of rivers, and gives access to some superb stretches of coast. Book through **SAN Parks** (☎ 012-426 5111). The trail is usually booked up one year ahead, but there are often cancellations, so it's always worth trying.

Storms River Mouth Rest Camp (☎ 012-428 9111; www.sanparks.org; campsites/forest huts/family cottages R195/295/950) offers forest huts, chalets, cottages and 'oceanettes'; all except the forest huts are equipped with kitchens, bedding and bathrooms. Another good option is **Tsitsikamma Falls Adventure Park** (☎ 042-280 3770; www.tsitsikamma adventure.co.za; Witelsbos; per person incl breakfast from R220), a family-run guesthouse near a beautiful waterfall, about halfway between Nature's Valley and Jeffrey's Bay.

Greyhound, Intercape and Translux buses run along the N2, and the Baz Bus (see p1066) stops at Nature's Valley.

STORMS RIVER
☎ 042

Storms River is an odd little hamlet with tree-shaded lanes, a few places to stay and an outdoor centre. From the N2 the Storms River signpost points to this village, which lies outside the national park. The turn-off is 4km east of the turn-off to the national park (which is signed as Storms River Mouth, or 'Stormsriviermond' in Afrikaans).

Most activities on offer are organised by **Storms River Adventures** (☎ 042-281 1836; www.storms river.com; Darnell St), including a tree canopy slide (R395), 'woodcutter's journey' and forest tractor ride (R175 with lunch).

The world's highest bungee jump (216m) is at the **Bloukrans River Bridge** (☎ 042-281 1458; www.faceadrenalin.com; per jump R590), 21km west of Storms River.

If you're after a post-bungee rest, try **Dijembe Backpackers** (☎ 042-281 1842; www.dijembebackpackers. com; cnr Formosa & Assegai Sts; campsites R60, dm R110, d with/ without bathroom R310/270; 🖳), or **Ploughman's Rest** (☎ 042-281 1726; www.ploughmansrest.co.za; 31 Formosa St; s/d incl breakfast R350/600), a friendly B&B.

The Baz Bus stops at Storms River; otherwise buses and minibus taxis could drop you at Bloukrans River Bridge or Tsitsikamma Lodge, 2km away from town on the N2.

SUNSHINE COAST

The Sunshine Coast – the stretch of shoreline between the Garden Route and the Wild Coast – is best known for the surfing mecca of Jeffrey's Bay. We have also included the mystical mountain hamlet of Hogsback in this section because, although it's not actually on the coastline, it's often visited from East London.

JEFFREY'S BAY
☎ 042 / pop 25,000

Once a sleepy seaside town, 'J-Bay' is now one of the world's top surfing destinations. Boardies from all over the planet flock here to ride waves such as the famous Supertubes, once described as 'the most perfect wave in the world'. June to September are the best months for experienced surfers, but novices can learn year-round.

Development is raging at a furious pace, with shopping in the myriad clothing stores almost overtaking surfing as the main leisure activity, but the local board-waxing vibe remains. The biggest surf crowd comes to town every July for the Billabong Pro championship.

Rustic **Peggy's Place** (☎ 042-293 2160; pegjbay@ yahoo.com; 8A Oribi St; campsites/dm/d R40/70/200) is justifiably loved by readers, while J-Bay's most popular backpackers is surf and party spot **Island Vibe** (☎ 042-293 1625; www.islandvibe.co.za; 10 Dageraad St; campsites/dm/d R60/90/200), 500m south of the city centre. **Lazee Bay** (☎ 042-296 2090; lazeebay@worldonline.co.za; 25 Mimosa St; d incl breakfast R400; 🖳), one of J-Bay's best guesthouses, up on a hill above Da Gama Rd, is memorable for its funky decor and great sea views. **Supertubes Guesthouse** (☎ 042-293 2957; supertubes@agnet.co.za; 6/10/12 Pepper St; s/d incl breakfast from R550/760; ⚇ ▯) provides luxurious accommodation, right in the prime surfing spot.

A great sea view complements superb fresh fish and a good selection of salads at **Kitchen Windows** (☎ 042-293 4230; Diaz Rd; mains R36-50), one of the town's best eateries. **Die Walskipper** (☎ 082-800 9478; Marina Martinique; seafood platters R155; ☽ lunch & dinner Tue-Sat, lunch Sun), specialising in seafood, and crocodile and ostrich steaks, is just metres from the lapping sea at the Marina Martinique beach.

The Baz Bus (see p1066) stops daily at hostels in both directions. Travelling to Cape Town costs R950 (12 hours). **J-Bay Sunshine Express** (☎ 082-449 5735) runs door-to-door to/from Port Elizabeth (R175).

PORT ELIZABETH
☎ 041 / pop 1.5 million
Downtown 'PE', like many South African city centres, has long been run-down and full of fast-food chains and cheap stores. The more upmarket shops, bars and restaurants are found in suburban shopping centres such as the Boardwalk.

However, the run-down face of Port Elizabeth will hopefully change with the new **Nelson Mandela Bay Stadium**, built for the 2010 World Cup. The city also has some of the Eastern Cape's best bathing and surfing beaches.

Lungile Backpackers (☎ 041-582 2042; www.lungile backpackers.co.za; 12 La Roche Dr; campsites/dm/d without bathroom R60/100/240, r R320; ▯ ⚇), Port Elizabeth's most popular backpackers, is contained in an airy Swiss-style home minutes from the beachfront. The family-run **Chapman Hotel** (☎ 041-584 0678; www.chapman.co.za; 1 Lady Bea Cres, Brookes Hill Dr; s/d incl breakfast R580/785; ⚇ ▯ ▯), overlooking the sea south of the city centre, is an upmarket choice with great views. The many self-catering flats along the beachfront include **Langerry Holiday Flats** (☎ 041-585 2654; www.langerry.co.za; 31 Beach Rd; 1-/2-bedroom flats from R290/500).

Most of Port Elizabeth's best cafes are in the Boardwalk casino complex in Summerstrand, at the far end of Beach Rd. The atmosphere is a bit artificial, but you can at least sip a cappuccino in peace away from the beachfront's plastic fast-food joints. Large, airy deli-bistro **34 South** (☎ 041-583 1085; The Boardwalk, Marine Dr; deli dishes R25 per 100g, mains R80; ☽ 10am-10pm) has

a menu including lots of fish dishes, curries and sandwiches.

There are daily flights to Jo'burg, Durban and Cape Town on a number of airlines.

Port Elizabeth has regular bus connections to the major South African cities, including Cape Town (R250, 12 hours), Durban (R380, 13 hours) and East London (R140, four hours). The Baz Bus (see p1066) runs daily to Cape Town (R1110 one way – hop-on, hop-off). J-Bay Sunshine Express (see left) runs to/from Jeffrey's Bay and other coastal areas.

HOGSBACK
☎ 045 / pop 1500
Located, improbably, 1300m up in the beautiful Amathole Mountains, Hogsback makes you half expect to meet a hobbit. Locals might tell you the village inspired JRR Tolkien, who came here on childhood holidays from Bloemfontein. Its English climate (four distinct seasons), organic food and mind-boggling views of mountains and forested valleys in all directions make it an eco-destination *par excellence*.

There are great walks, bike rides and drives in the area. Be prepared for rain at any time, and in winter for temperatures that can drop to -1°C.

Away with the Fairies (☎ 045-962 1031; www. awaywiththefairies.co.za; Hydrangea Lane; campsites/dm/d R55/95/325; ⚇) is a delightful backpackers with terrific views. Alternatively, **Granny Mouse House** (☎ 045-962 1259; www.grannymousehouse.co.za; 1 Nutwoods Dr; per person incl breakfast/incl dinner R325/425; ⚇) has rooms in an old wattle-and-daub house, plus a self-catering garden cottage.

The easiest way to get to Hogsback without a car is by shuttle bus from Sugarshack Backpackers (below) in East London or Buccaneer's Backpackers (p1036) in Chintsa.

EAST LONDON
☎ 043 / pop 980,000
East London is the country's only river port, situated on a spectacular bay that curves round to huge sand hills. Queenstown Park (containing the zoo) is pretty, and the beaches and surf are excellent, but there's not a lot to keep you here. The city is a good base for moving on to holiday spots along the Sunshine or Wild Coasts.

With the beach just metres away, the surf's always up at lively **Sugarshack Backpackers** (☎ 043-722 8240; www.sugarshack.co.za; Eastern Esplanade, Eastern Beach; campsites/dm/d without bathroom R50/80/190; ▯). Surfboard hire and lessons are available.

SOUTH AFRICA

East London Backpackers (☎ 043-722 2748; www.elbackpackers.co.za; 11 Quanza St; dm/s/d R70/110/200; 🖥 🐾) has spacious and clean chilling areas and dorms, a *braai* area and plunge pool. **White House** (☎ 043-740 0344; www.thewhitehousebandb.co.za; 10 Whitthaus St, Gonubie; s/d incl breakfast R495/595; 🐾) is a stylish guesthouse with glass windows for panoramic views of cliffs and sea.

Imbizo (☎ 043-722 0155; 22 Currie St; mains R55) is a fun place to sample genuine African cuisine, including Xhosa and Shona dishes. A perfect cross-section of East London life frequents **Smokey Swallows** (☎ 043-727 1349; 20 Devereux Ave; mains R80-120), which stages live jazz.

Translux, Greyhound and Intercape have daily buses to Port Elizabeth (from R110, three hours), Durban (from R250, 8½ hours), Cape Town (from R340, 19 hours) and Jo'burg/Pretoria (R310, 13½ hours). The Baz Bus (see p1066) passes through en route between Port Elizabeth and Durban.

WILD COAST

With its green rolling hills, rugged cliffs plunging into the sea, remote coves sheltering sandy beaches, and a history of shipwrecks and stranded sailors, the aptly named Wild Coast is a place for adventure and intrigue. Stretching for 350km from East London to Port Edward, the area is dotted with tiny Xhosa settlements and the occasional holiday resort or backpacker hostel.

You may hear some people refer to the area as the 'Transkei', which was the name of the apartheid-era homeland that once covered this part of the country. The name 'Transkei', however, stills bears the stigma of an area once known for its crime rate and extreme poverty, so locals prefer the term Wild Coast.

CHINTSA
☎ 043 / pop 2000
Heading up the N2, the sea spray starts to hit your face at an unspoilt stretch of whitesand beach called Chintsa, 38km from East London. Chintsa comprises two small, pretty villages, Chintsa East and Chintsa West. It's definitely the best place on this part of the coast to hang out for a few days (or weeks).

Something of a rarity, **Buccaneer's Backpackers** (☎ 043-734 3012; www.cintsa.com; Chintsa West; campsites/dm/d incl breakfast R55/110/395; 🖥 🐾), or 'Bucks', is a sort of all-inclusive holiday resort for back-

packers offering every imaginable outdoor activity. The dorms and rooms are comfortable, and safari tents (R200) and cottages (for four R750) are available.

COFFEE BAY
☎ 047 / pop 600
This once-remote hamlet is today a commercialised backpackers' playground, with two busy hostels and a couple of more upmarket hotels. The village itself is a fairly scruffy place, but the surrounding scenery is dramatic, with a beautiful kilometre-long beach in front of towering cliffs.

The more hippified backpackers is **Bomvu Paradise** (☎ 047-575 2073; www.bomvubackpackers.com; campsites/dm/d without bathroom R60/90/170), which offers yoga instruction, organic meals and drum sessions. The dorms and rooms are comfortable and funky, and the staff efficient and friendly. Across the road, **Coffee Shack** (☎ 047-575 2048; www.coffeeshack.co.za; campsites/dm/d without bathroom R70/110/260; 🖥) has a definite party vibe. **Ocean View Hotel** (☎ 047-575 2005; www.oceanview.co.za; s/d incl half board R910/1400; 🍴 🖥 🐾) has good-quality, chalet-style rooms, with a deck overlooking the ocean.

A minibus taxi from Mthatha to Coffee Bay costs R25 (one hour). The backpacker hostels meet the Baz Bus (see p1066) at the Shell Ultra City, 4km south of Mthatha.

AROUND COFFEE BAY
There are a number of hotels and resorts along the stretch of coast from the Great Kei River to Coffee Bay, including the now legendary **Bulungula Backpackers** (☎ 047-577 8900; www.bulungula.com; campsites per person/dm/d without bathroom R60/100/250). Renowned for its stunning location, community-based activities and ecofriendly ethos, it's 40% owned by the local Xhosa community, which runs tours including horse riding, hiking and canoeing. There's a mellow vibe, and the beach parties take place well away from the main camp. Xhosa-style *rondavels* (round huts with conical roofs) serve as quarters.

Bulungula is two hours' drive southwest of Coffee Bay; phone ahead to get directions or to arrange pick-ups from locations including Mthatha (R60).

PORT ST JOHNS
☎ 047 / pop 2100
Deliciously laid-back Port St Johns has long been a magnet for hippy types and, more

recently, film crews. This idyllic little town on the coast at the mouth of the Mzimvubu River has tropical vegetation, dramatic cliffs, great beaches, no traffic jams and absolutely no stress. Many travellers succumb to the famous 'Pondo Fever' and stay for months.

Four kilometres from the town centre, **Amapondo Backpackers** (☎ 047-564 1344, 083-315 3103; www.amapondo.co.za; Second Beach Rd; campsites/dm/d without bathroom R50/100/250) is a beautiful and peaceful hostel with a great view of an idyllic beach. **Jungle Monkey** (☎ 047-564 1517; www.jungle monkey.co.za; 2 Berea Rd; campsites/dm/r without bathroom R50/100/250, log cabin R270; 🖳) has the 'party hostel' routine nailed, while its sister next door, Island Backpackers Lodge, is more upmarket. A favourite with movie crews, **Outspan Inn** (☎ 047-564 1057; www.outspaninn.co.za; s/d incl breakfast R325/590; self-catering per person R195; 🖳) has comfortable rooms set around a garden.

Most backpacker places will pick you up from the Shell Ultra City – where the Baz Bus (see p1066) stops, just outside Mthatha – for around R60, but it's essential to book ahead. There are also regular minibus taxis to Port St Johns from there (R40, two hours).

KWAZULU-NATAL

Rough and ready, smart and sophisticated, rural and rustic, KwaZulu-Natal is as eclectic as its cultures, people and landscapes. It has its metropolitan heart in the port of Durban and its nearby historic capital, Pietermaritzburg. The beaches along this coast attract visitors wishing to soak up the sand, sea, surf and sun, and to the north is Zululand, home to some of Africa's most evocative traditional settlements and cultural sites. The region also boasts alluring national parks and isolated, wild coastal reserves. The province's border in the far west, the World Heritage–listed uKhahlamba-Drakensberg Park, features awesome peaks, unforgettable vistas and excellent hiking opportunities.

DURBAN
☎ 031 / pop 3.5 million

Stretching along a swath of butter-yellow sand, South Africa's third-largest city offers a lively, if slightly tacky, prepackaged seaside holiday. The beachfront, with its stretch of highrise hotels and snack bars, remains a city trademark, and the city centre, peppered with some grandiose colonial buildings and art-deco architecture, throbs to a distinctly

African beat. Home to the country's largest concentration of people of Indian descent, Durban also boasts the sights, sounds and scents of the subcontinent. While the beachfront is still a favourite spot, many visitors, wary of the city's reputation for crime, base themselves in the suburbs, which are chock-a-block with accommodation, malls, funky bars and stylish eateries.

Information
INTERNET ACCESS
Most accommodation has wi-fi and/or a computer for guest use, and **Europa** (☎ 031-312 1099; 167 Florida Rd, Morningside) cafe offers wi-fi access. Another option is **Cityzen** (☎ 031-303 9169; 161 Gordon Rd, Morningside; per hr R20; 🕒 8am-midnight).

MEDICAL SERVICES
Entabeni Hospital (☎ 031-204 1300; 148 South Ridge Rd, Berea)
Umhlanga Hospital (☎ 031-560 5500; 323 Umhlanga Rocks Dr, Umhlanga) Handy to the north coast and north Durban.

MONEY
There are banks with ATMs and change facilities across the city – including Standard Bank, FNB and Nedbank.
American Express (☎ 031-202 8733; FNB House, 151 Musgrave Rd, Musgrave)
Rennies Foreign Exchange Central Durban (☎ 031-305 5722; ground fl, 333 Anton Lembede/Smith St); Musgrave Centre (☎ 031-202 7833; Shop 311, Level 3, Musgrave Centre, Musgrave Rd; 🕒 9am-5pm Mon-Fri, 9am-1pm Sat)

TOURIST INFORMATION
Durban Tourism (www.durbanexperience.co.za, www.durban.gov.za) Tourist Junction (see below); airport (☎ 031-408 1000; Arrivals Hall; 🕒 7am-9pm)
Tourist Junction (☎ 031-304 4934; 160 Monty Naicker Rd/Pine St; 🕒 8am-4.30pm Mon-Fri, 9am-2pm Sat) The main tourist information centre for Durban and the region houses the offices of Durban Tourism, Ezemvelo KZN Wildlife (www.kznwildlife.com), SAN Parks Reservations (www.sanparks.org) and Zulu Kingdom.
Zulu Kingdom (KZN Tourism; www.zulu.org.za) Tourist Junction (see above); uShaka Marine World (☎ 031-337 8099; 🕒 9am-9pm)

Sights
If you dip into the city's summer surf and sun, you have a playground of more than 6km of warm-water beaches (protected by the requisite shark nets). The 'Golden Mile' Beaches

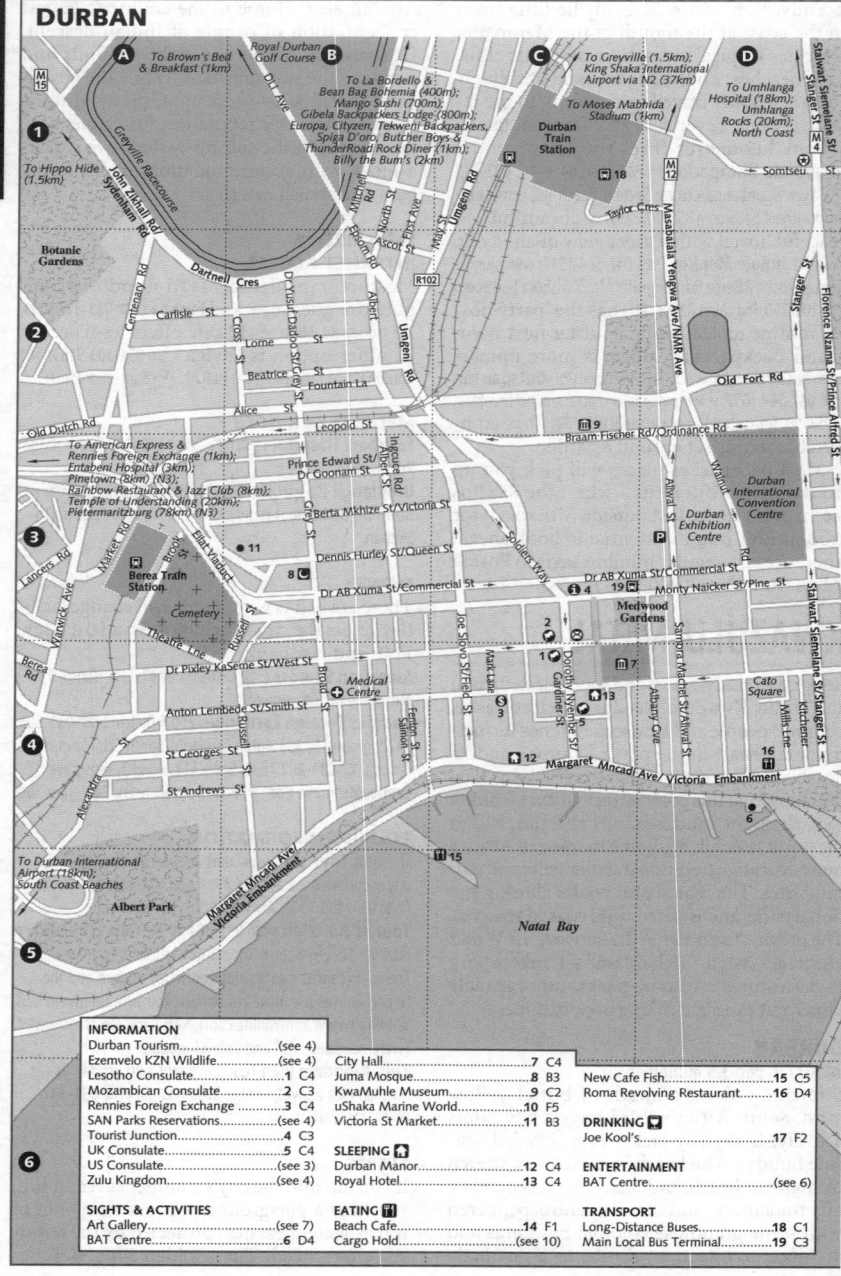

DURBAN

SOUTH AFRICA

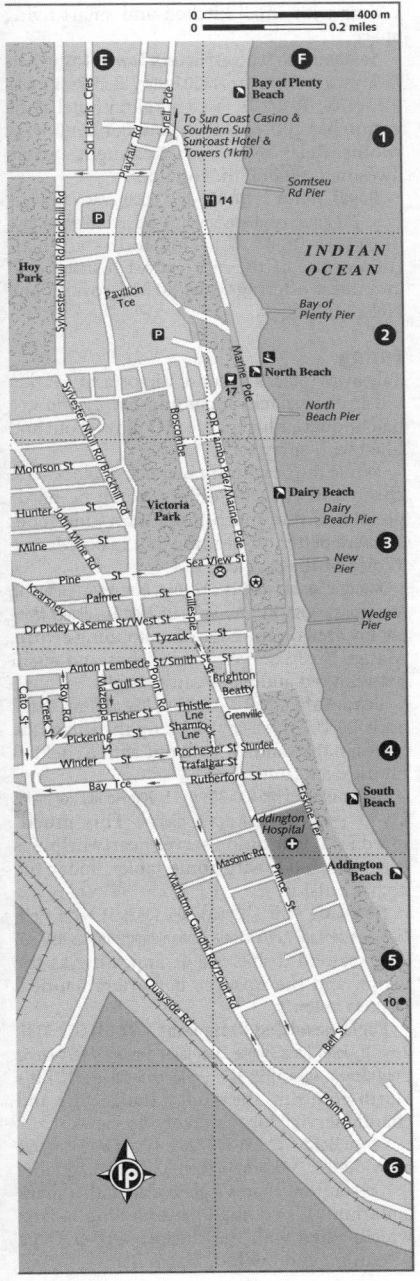

run from Blue Lagoon (at the mouth of the Umgeni River) to **uShaka Marine World** (☎ 031-368 6675; www.ushakamarineworld.co.za; Addington Beach, the Point; Wet'n'Wild adult/child/senior R79/62/62, Sea World R104/70/70, combination R152/100/100; ⏰ 9am-5pm) on the Point. But Durban's beachfront ain't for everyone; to some, its bars and restaurants and hectic holiday atmosphere are garish and tacky.

A planned promenade will link the beachfront near the glitzy, nouveau-art-deco **Sun Coast Casino** (☎ 031-328 3000; www.suncoastcasino.co.za; Snell Pde) to the new **Moses Mabhida Stadium**, with shops and cafes near the base of the stadium. A **cable car** will ascend to a viewing platform at the top of the 2010 World Cup stadium's 105m-high arch.

On Margaret Mncadi Ave/Victoria Embankment, the **BAT Centre** (☎ 031-332 0451; www.batcentre.co.za; 45 Maritime Pl) is a colourful bohemian arts centre housing art-and-craft shops, artists' studios and a bar-restaurant, all cut through with a lively trans-Africa theme.

Dominating the city centre is the opulent 1910 Edwardian neo-baroque **City Hall** (☎ 031-311 2137; Anton Lembede/Smith St). Upstairs is the **Art Gallery** (☎ 031-311 2264; City Hall; admission free; ⏰ 8.30am-4pm Mon-Sat, 11am-4pm Sun), an outstanding collection of contemporary South African works, especially Zulu arts and crafts.

The **KwaMuhle Museum** (☎ 031-311 2237; 130 Braam Fischer/Ordinance Rd; admission free; ⏰ 8.30am-4pm Mon-Sat, 11am-4pm Sun) has powerful displays on the 'Durban System', the blueprint of apartheid policy.

The big **Juma Mosque** (☎ 031-306 0026; cnr Dennis Hurley/Queen & Dr Yusuf Dadoo/Grey Sts; ⏰ 9am-4pm Mon-Fri, 9-11am Sat) is the largest in the southern hemisphere; call ahead for a guided tour.

At the western end of Berta Mkhize/ Victoria St, **Victoria St Market** (☎ 031-306 4021; Berta Mkhize/Victoria St; ⏰ 6am-6pm Mon-Sat, 6am-4pm Sun) offers a rip-roaring subcontinental shopping experience, with 160-plus stalls selling Asian wares. Note that most Muslim shops close between noon and 2pm on Friday, and watch your wallet.

Temple of Understanding (☎ 031-403 3328; Bhaktieedanta Sami Circle, Chatsworth; ⏰ 10am-1pm & 4-7.30pm), 20km south of Durban, is the southern hemisphere's biggest Hare Krishna temple.

Sleeping
Despite the hotel-lined beachfront promenade, much of Durban's good-value

THE SIGNS THEY ARE A-CHANGIN'

In 2007–08 Durban's municipal council controversially renamed many of the city's streets to reflect a 'new South Africa'; debate still rages over the changes. Many streets are now labelled twice: with the old sign – with a red line through it – as well as the new one.

Some new street names are awaiting the rubber stamp. We have provided, where possible, both the new and former street names; the old names, which many people still use, are listed second.

accommodation is in the western and north-western suburbs.

Hippo Hide (☎ 031-207 4366; www.hippohide.co.za; 2 Jesmond Rd, Berea; dm/s/d without bathroom R95/190/240; ⓅⓁⓐ) This friendly, cosy hide pulls in the punters with its choice of huts and rooms. It's a lengthy saunter to the beach or cafes, but staff help organise outings.

Tekweni Backpackers (☎ 031-303 1433; www.tekwenibackpackers.co.za; 169 Ninth Ave, Morningside; dm/s/d without bathroom from R105/220/300; ⓅⓁ) This old dog 'keeps on keeping on', attracting party animals who like raucous, gregarious surrounds. Its friendly staff are in the know about the nightlife on nearby Florida Rd.

Gibela Backpackers Lodge (☎ 031-303 6291; www.gibelabackpackers.co.za; 119 Ninth Ave, Morningside; tw without bathroom incl breakfast R150/300/400; ⓅⓁ) Become a flashpacker at this hostel, a tastefully converted 1950s Tuscan-style home with sparkling surfaces and rooms neat enough to pass an army major's inspection.

La Bordello (☎ 031-309 1001; www.beanbagbohemia.co.za; 18 Lilian Ngoyi/Windermere Rd; s/d incl breakfast from R450/650) Continuing the arty vibe of the adjoining cafe-bar Bean Bag Bohemia (opposite), this boutique hotel offers Moroccan-style rooms in a former brothel.

Durban Manor (☎ 031-366 0700; www.durbanmanorhotel.com; 93-96 Margaret Mncadi Ave/Victoria Embankment; s/d incl breakfast R520/750; ⓅⓍ) Housed in the former Durban Club, an opulent colonial-era landmark with large rooms, Durban Manor now has a more African flavour.

Brown's Bed & Breakfast (☎ 031-208 7630; www.brownsguesthouse.co.za; 132 Gladys Mazibuko/Marriot Rd, Essenwood; s/d incl breakfast R550/900; ⓅⓍⓐ) The chic interior attracts even chic-er guests who enjoy the fantastic views and 'suites' – spacious

rooms with small kitchen and smart living space.

Southern Sun Suncoast Hotel & Towers (☎ 031-314 7878; www.southernsun.com; 20 Battery Beach Rd; s/d from R1600/1700; ⓅⓍⓐⓖ) This glitzy hotel at the casino has 100-plus sleek and contemporary rooms. Relax over a spa treatment and an awesome vista on the top floor.

Royal Hotel (☎ 031-333 6000; www.theroyal.co.za; 267 Anton Lembede/Smith St; s/d incl breakfast from R1800/3000; ⓅⓍⓁ) This four-star institution, one of the city's most historic and swankiest offerings, has hosted royalty and Nelson Mandela.

Eating

Takeaway places around Victoria St Market sell Indian snacks including *bunny chow*, a half or quarter loaf of bread hollowed out and filled with curry stew.

While the beachfront is chock-a-block with cheap and cheerful diners, you'll be hard-pressed to find much more than junk food. You are better off heading to uShaka Marine World or the casino.

Mango Sushi (☎ 031-312 7054; Avonmore Centre, 9th Ave; mains & sushi R15-70; Ⓨ lunch Mon-Fri, dinner Mon-Sat) Located on the edge of a shopping centre, Mango Sushi serves Thai dishes and sushi between red and black canvas walls.

Beach Cafe (☎ 031-332 8302; Bay of Plenty Beach; snacks R30-45; Ⓨ 7am-6pm) Soak up the sun at the tables in the sand, or chill out with a cocktail on the deck (until 8pm).

Spiga D'oro (☎ 031-303 9511; 200 Florida Rd; mains R35-70; Ⓨ breakfast, lunch & dinner) This much-loved local institution serves hearty helpings of Italian food, with some tables under the arches outside.

New Cafe Fish (☎ 031-305 5062; 31 Yacht Mole, Margaret Mncadi Ave/Victoria Embankment; mains R50-75) The seafood dishes are as appealing as the views, and the upstairs bar offers nautical baskets aplenty.

Roma Revolving Restaurant (☎ 031-332 3337; 22nd fl, John Ross House, Margaret Mncadi Ave/Victoria Embankment; mains R55-150; Ⓨ lunch & dinner; Ⓧ) It's worth enduring the stodgy Italian fare and chaotic service for the revolving views.

Cargo Hold (☎ 031-328 8065; uShaka Marine World; mains R70-125; Ⓨ lunch & dinner) This high-quality fish restaurant shares a glass wall with a shark aquarium. It's on the Phantom Ship, a faux wreck, along with the cheaper Upper Deck restaurant and outdoor Shark Bar.

Butcher Boys (☎ 031-312 8248; 170 Florida Rd; mains R95-125; ☺ lunch & dinner; ☒) This carnivore's paradise attracts business people and the 'in' set to its stylish surrounds with creative cuts and combos.

Drinking

The best options are found in the suburbs.

Bean Bag Bohemia (☎ 031-309 6019; 18 Lilian Ngoyi/ Windermere Rd) This hip cafe-bar and restaurant is adorned with mosaics, chandeliers and gothic decor.

ThunderRoad Rock Diner (☎ 031-303 3440; 136 Florida Rd) This grungy bar has open-mic nights on Tuesdays and live music at weekends.

Billy the Bum's (☎ 031-303 1988; 504 Lilian Ngoyi/ Windermere Rd, Morningside) Attracting Durban's upwardly mobile set, this reliably raucous suburban cocktail bar has DJs on Friday and Saturday.

Joe Kool's (☎ 031-332 9698; Lower OR Tambo/Lower Marine Pde, North Beach; ☺ 10am-late Fri, Sat & Sun) This beachfront nightspot serves a cocktail of cold beer, big-screen TV, dance music and feisty crowds. If leaving at night, grab one of the taxis outside.

Entertainment

BAT Centre (☎ 031-332 0451; www.batcentre.co.za; 45 Maritime Pl) This venue offers performances including poetry (5pm to 7pm Wednesday and Thursday) and jazz (Friday evening and Sunday afternoon). Grab a taxi to/from the centre at night.

Rainbow Restaurant & Jazz Club (☎ 031-702 9161; 23 Stanfield Lane) In Pinetown, 8km west of the centre, Rainbow is considered the centre of the jazz scene, and is still the preferred local haunt.

Getting There & Away

King Shaka International Airport, 35km north of the city, is set to open shortly before the 2010 World Cup. Several airlines link Durban with South Africa's main centres.

The popular, backpacker-orientated Baz Bus (see p1066) serves Durban.

Long-distance buses leave from the bus stations near the Durban train station. It's safest to enter from Masabalala Yengwa/NMR Ave, not Umgeni Rd. The major companies have daily departures to destinations including Jo'burg (from R200, eight hours), Cape Town (from R510, 22 to 27 hours), Port Elizabeth (R395, 15 hours), Pietermaritzburg

(from R160, one hour), Gaborone (R345, 15½ hours) and Maputo (R400, 15 hours).

Some long-distance minibus taxis running mainly to the South Coast and the Wild Coast region of Eastern Cape leave from around the Berea train station. The areas in and around the minibus taxi ranks are unsafe and extreme care should be taken if entering them.

Durban train station is huge; use the Masabalala Yengwa/NMR Ave entrance, 1st level. Even hardy travellers report feeling unsafe on the local inner-city and suburban trains. In contrast, tourist-class, long-distance **Shosholoza Meyl** (☎ 0860-008 888; www. shosholozameyl.co.za, www.premierclasse.co.za) services are recommended, including the Saturday service to Jo'burg and the Friday service to Cape Town.

Getting Around

The **Airport Shuttle Bus** (☎ 031-465 1660) links Durban International Airport with the city, and will likely provide the same service for King Shaka. Some hostels run their own taxi shuttle services.

The **Durban People Mover** (☎ 031-309 5942; www.durbanpeoplemover.co.za) is a useful shuttle-bus service that operates along three routes within the city (with more planned). Day passes (R15) and single-journey tickets (R4) can be purchased on the buses, which run daily between 6.30am and 11pm.

The main bus terminal and information centre for inner-city and metropolitan buses is on Dr AB Xuma/Commercial St.

A taxi between the beach and Florida Rd, Morningside, costs about R30.

AROUND DURBAN

The South Coast is a 160km-long string of seaside resorts and suburbs running from Durban to Port Edward, near the Eastern Cape border. There's a bit of a *Groundhog Day* feel about the mass of shoulder-to-shoulder getaways along the N2 and Rte 102, albeit a pleasant one. The region is a surfers' and divers' delight (the latter because of the Aliwal Shoal), and in summer there ain't much room to swing a brolly. The stunning **Oribi Gorge Nature Reserve** (☎ 039-679 1644; www.kznwildlife.com; admission R10, campsites R66, 2-bed chalets R130; ☺ 6am-6pm summer, 7.30am-4.30pm winter), inland from the industrial town of Port Shepstone, provides beautiful forest walks,

SOUTH AFRICA

SOUTH COAST DIVING

The highlight of this strip is the Aliwal Shoal, touted as one of the world's 10 best dive sites. It's named after the wrecked ship, the *Aliwal*, which ran aground on the reef in 1849, and other ships have since met a similar fate here. Today, the shoal's ledges, caves and pinnacles are home to wrecks, rays, turtles, 'raggies' (ragged-mouth sharks), tropical fish and soft corals.

Operators including **2nd Breath** (☎ 039-317 2326; www.2ndbreath.co.za; cnr Bank St & Berea Rd, Margate) offer day dives and four-day courses with dives, equipment hire and air-tank refills. Rates for the latter range from R2000 to R2500. Always speak to other travellers about their experiences as safety standards vary.

eating and accommodation options. Nearby Margate is the claustrophobic holiday hub.

The stretch of coast from Umhlanga Rocks north to the Tugela River is a profusion of upmarket timeshare apartments and retirement villages, with some pleasant beaches. The section from Zimbali, slightly north of Umhlanga, to the Tugela is known as the Dolphin Coast because of the bottlenose dolphins that favour the area. The region is home to a fascinating mix of peoples: the descendants of colonialists, indentured labourers from the Indian subcontinent and French Mauritian sugar-cane growers, plus colourful Zulu cultures.

PIETERMARITZBURG
☎ 033 / pop 457,000
Billed as the heritage city, Pietermaritzburg's (usually known as PMB) grand historic buildings house museums and refurbished hotels. By day, KZN's administrative and legislative capital is vibrant: its large Zulu community sets a colourful flavour and the Indian community brings echoes of the subcontinent to its busy streets. A large student population adds to the city's vitality.

Pietermaritzburg is where you need to book most of the accommodation and walks for Ezemvelo KZN Wildlife parks and reserves. The **Ezemvelo KZN Wildlife Headquarters** (☎ 033-845 1000; www.kznwildlife.com; Queen Elizabeth Park, Peter Brown Dr; ☯ 8am-4.30pm Mon-Fri, 8am-12.40pm Sat) is a long way northwest of the town centre.

Sleeping & Eating
Prince Alfred Street Backpackers (☎ 033-345 7045; www.chauncey.co.za; 312 Prince Alfred St; per person R120; P 🖳) This bright place, with multicoloured mosquito-net extravaganzas and ethnic adornments, is handy to the centre and offers gourmet cuisine.

Sleepy Hollow (☎ 033-342 1758; www.wylderide. co.za; 80 Leinster Rd; campsite R60, dm/s/d R100/125/250) In the student precinct, this rambling, mint-coloured 1940s abode has a cosy, preloved feel, and offers rafting and cycling.

Smith Grove (☎ 033-345 3963; www.smithgrove.co.za; 37 Howick Rd; s/d R350/500) This renovated Victorian home offers B&B comforts with decorated, individually styled rooms.

Briar Ghyll (☎ 033-342 2664; www.bglodge.co.za; George MacFarlane Lane; s/d R495/650) This stunning historic home has large, luxurious rooms, stylish antique interiors and miles of green lawn, trees and birdlife.

Butchery (☎ 033-342 5239; www.thebutchery.co.za; 101 Roberts Rd; mains R46-70; ☯ noon-late) The name says it all – steaks of every type, racks of drying biltong, and wall-to-wall wine racks. Vegetarians are also catered for.

Eaton's on Eighty (☎ 033-342 3280; 80 Roberts Rd, Clarendon; mains R70-130; ☯ lunch Wed-Fri, dinner Tue-Sat) Mellow and romantic, Eaton's draws a slightly older and sedate crowd, but the menu (which leans towards seafood) is contemporary fusion.

Getting There & Away
SAAirlink (☎ 033-3869 2861; www.saairlink.co.za), with an office at the airport, flies to Jo'burg daily (high season R1130).

Greyhound/Citiliner, Translux/City to City, Luxliner and Intercape offer similar prices depending on the level of onboard services. Destinations offered include Jo'burg (from R140, six to seven hours), Pretoria (R200, seven to eight hours), Port Elizabeth (R320, 15 hours) and Durban (from R160, 1½ hours).

Underberg Express (☎ 033-701 2750, 086-111 4924; www.underbergexpress.co.za) offers a daily service to Durban Central (R130) and King Shaka International Airport. The Baz Bus (see p1066) travels between Durban and Pietermaritzburg three times a week.

KWAZULU-NATAL RESERVES

Hluhluwe-iMfolozi Park

☎ 035

These magnificent twin **reserves** (☎ 035-550 8476; www.kznwildlife.com; adult/child R90/45; ⊙ 5am-7pm Nov-Feb, 6am-6pm Mar-Oct), covering 96,000 hectares in a low-risk malarial area, are good places to spot 'the Big Five'. They are best visited in winter, when the animals range widely without congregating at water sources, although summer visits can be rewarding in the open savannah country areas.

One of iMfolozi's main attractions is its (seasonal) trail system in a special 24,000-hectare wilderness area. The **Base Trail** (3 nights/4 days R3080) is, as the name suggests, at a base camp. On the **Primitive Trail** (4 nights/5 days R2300), you carry equipment, and help prepare the food (provided), and hikers must sit up in 1½-hour watches during the night.

The signature resort on the Hluhluwe side, with stupendous views, is **Hilltop Camp** (☎ 035-562 0848; rest huts/chalets per person R276/550, 2-bed units incl full board per person R466). Morning and night wildlife drives (R200 per person) from here are very popular. Try one of the private and sedate bush lodges for more peace and quiet.

The main entrance, Memorial Gate, is 15km west of the N2, about 50km north of Mtubatuba.

iSimangaliso Wetland Park

☎ 035

This Unesco World Heritage Site stretches for 200 glorious kilometres, from the Mozambican border to Maphelana, at the southern end of Lake St Lucia. With the Indian Ocean on one side, and a series of lakes on the other (including Lake St Lucia), the 328,000-hectare park protects five distinct ecosystems, featuring everything from offshore reefs to woodlands, dolphins to zebras.

Ecotour operators offer birding, boat tours and whale-watching, canoeing, hiking, horse riding, turtle tours and wildlife-watching.

In St Lucia Estuary itself, you can camp at three sites run by **Ezemvelo KZN Wildlife** (☎ 033-590 1340; www.kznwildlife.com; Pelican St) for around R70 per person.

Occupying a series of sprawling buildings, **BiB's International Backpackers** (☎ 035-590 1056; www.bibs.co.za; 310 MacKenzie St; campsites R75, dm R115, d R245, self-catering d R315; P 🖳 🛋) offers a busy bar, a huge kitchen and organised fun. Owned by a tour-company operator, **Hornbill House**

(☎ 035-590 1162; 43 Hornbill St; s/d incl breakfast R475/750; 🖂 🛋) is a pleasant place to nest, with homey B&B comforts, pool and deck.

The Baz Bus (see p1066) drops backpackers in St Lucia Estuary several times a week.

Sodwana Bay

☎ 035

Spectacular **Sodwana Bay** (adult/child R20/15; ⊙ 24hr) is bordered by lush forest on one side, and glittering sands on another. Popular activities include guided walking and birding trails, winding through coastal forest and grassland, and serious deep-sea fishing. The diversity of underwater seascapes and marine flora and fauna makes it one of South Africa's diving capitals.

Ezemvelo KZN Wildlife (☎ 033-590 1340; www.kznwildlife.com; campsites per person R60-90, 5-bed cabins per person R330) has hundreds of campsites and cabins within the park in coastal forest. One of the outfits offering accommodation and dive packages, **Coral Divers** (☎ 035-345 6531; www.coraldivers.co.za; Sodwana Bay; tents per person R160, cabin d with/without bathroom from R640/520; 🖳 🛋) is a factory-style operation with cabins and a large dining-area-cum-bar.

Drivers should turn off the N2 at Hluhluwe village heading to Mbazwana, and continue about 20km to the park. Minibus taxis ply this route.

ZULULAND

Dominated by the Zulu tribal group, President Zuma's birthplace offers a fascinating historical and contemporary insight into one of the country's most enigmatic, and best-known, cultures. Intense poverty and all the social problems that come with it are still commonplace.

Eshowe

☎ 035 / pop 15,000

Situated around a beautiful indigenous forest and surrounded by green rolling hills, Eshowe has a rural, rough-and-tumble atmosphere, but the suburbs are leafy and quiet. It is well placed for exploring the wider region, and offers decent attractions and accommodation options.

The **Fort Nongqayi Museum Village** (☎ 035-473 3474; Nongqayi Rd; adult/child R25/5; ⊙ 7.30am-4pm Mon-Fri, 9am-4pm Sat & Sun), based around the fort built by the British in 1883, includes access to attractions including the Zululand Historical Museum.

In the forest where the 19th-century Zulu ruler King Shaka is said to have hidden his wives when war approached, the 125m-long

Dlinza Forest Aerial Boardwalk (☎ 035-474 4029; adult/child R25/5; ⌚ 6am-6pm Sep-Apr, 7am-5pm May-Aug) offers great views of the canopy and prolific birdlife. This is the start of the three-day Prince Dabulamanzi Trail through nature reserves and rivers.

The whitewashed **George Hotel & Zululand Backpackers** (☎ 035-474 4919; www.eshowe.com; 38 Main St; dm R100, s/d incl breakfast R295/395; 💻 🍴) has a colonial feel. The hotel's own beer brand flows on Friday night in particular; also on tap are the owner's 101 activities.

Minibus taxis connect to Empangeni (R40, one hour), the best place to catch taxis deeper into Zululand, and Durban (R70, 1½ hours).

Shakaland

☎ 035

Created as a set for the telemovie *Shaka Zulu*, the slightly Disney-fied **Shakaland** (☎ 035-460 0912; Nandi Experience R285; ⌚ displays 11am & noon), 14km north of Eshowe, includes a Zulu dance performance and the cultural Nandi Experience, named after King Shaka's mother.

You can stay on-site or with renowned 'white Zulu' Barry Leitch at **Simunye Zulu Lodge** (☎ 035-450 3111; www.simunyelodge.co.za; per person from R1100), where guests meet local Zulu and learn about their traditional and contemporary culture.

THE DRAKENSBERG

The tabletop peaks of the uKhahlamba-Drakensberg range, which form the boundary between South Africa and the mountain kingdom of Lesotho, offer some of the country's most awe-inspiring landscapes. This vast 243,000-hectare sweep of basalt summits and buttresses is so recognisably South African that it's become a tourist-brochure cliché. If any landscape lives up to its airbrushed, publicity-shot alter ego, it is the jagged, green sweep of the Drakensberg.

The Drakensberg (or the 'Berg', as it's often called) is usually divided into three sections, although the distinctions aren't strict.

The northern Drakensberg incorporates the Royal Natal National Park near the Free State border. Harrismith and Bergville are sizeable towns in this area.

The central Drakensberg's main features include the Giant's Castle area and, to the northwest, Cathedral Peak Nature Reserve. Estcourt and Winterton are towns adjacent to the central Drakensberg.

The southern Drakensberg, which runs down to the Wild Coast area of the Eastern Cape, is packed with wilderness areas and hiking trails, as well as the Sani Pass route into southern Lesotho.

In general, you must book all **Ezemvelo KZN Wildlife** (☎ 033-845 1000, 031-304 4934; www.kznwildlife.com) accommodation in advance. Other information offices:

Central Drakensberg Information Centre (☎ 036-488 1207; www.cdic.co.za; ⌚ 9am-6pm) This helpful private enterprise is based in the Thokozisa complex, 13km outside Winterton on Rte 600.

Okhahlamba Drakensberg Tourism (☎ 036-448 1557; www.drakensberg.org.za; Tatham Rd, Bergville; ⌚ 9am-4.30pm Mon-Fri, 9am-1pm Sat) Covers the northern and central Drakensberg; not particularly helpful.

Southern Berg Tourism (☎ 033-701 1471; www.drakensberg.org; Clocktower Centre, Old Main Rd, Underberg; ⌚ 8am-4pm Mon-Fri, 9am-1pm Sat & Sun) Has the useful *Southern Drakensberg Pocket Guide*.

There's no single road linking all the main areas of interest, so you're better off selecting one (or a few only) places rather than spending most of your time behind a wheel in search of sights. On public transport, a daily Greyhound bus stops at Estcourt and Ladysmith, where you can pick up minibus taxis into the Drakensberg, and **Underberg Express** (☎ 086-111 4924; www.underbergexpress.co.za) links Underberg with Durban, Pietermaritzburg and Kokstad; you must book in advance.

ROYAL NATAL NATIONAL PARK

☎ 036

Spanning out from some of the range's loftiest summits, the 8000-hectare **Royal Natal National Park** (☎ 036-438 6310; www.kznwildlife.com; adult/child R30/15; ⌚ 5am-7pm) has a presence that far outstrips its relatively meagre size, with many of the surrounding peaks rising as high into the air as the park stretches across. With some of the Drakensberg's most dramatic and accessible scenery, the park is crowned by the sublime Amphitheatre, an 8km wall of cliff and canyon where the Tugela Falls drop 850m in five stages. Looming up behind is Mont-aux-Sources (3282m), so called because the Tugela, Elands and Western Khubedu Rivers rise here; the last eventually becomes the Senqu (Orange) River and flows to the Atlantic.

The park's **visitors centre** (8am-12.30pm & 2-4.30pm) is about 1km in from the main gate. There's also a shop selling basic provisions.

The park is renowned for its excellent day walks, including the **Tugela Falls** (eight to nine hours return for fit hikers), which takes in the Amphitheatre. The hike involves climbing chain ladders; avoid cloudy days in summer.

Accommodation at the park's main camp, **Thendele** (033-845 1000; chalets per person R360-420), includes two-bed chalets. You can camp at beautiful **Mahai** or rustic **Rugged Glen Nature Reserve** (both 036-438 6303; campsites per person R80). There are also several places outside the park, including **Amphitheatre Backpackers** (036-438 6675; www.amphibackpackers.co.za; campsites R55; dm R85, d R240-280;), 21km north of Bergville.

CENTRAL BERG

036

Crowned with some of the Drakensberg's most formidable peaks – including Giant's Castle Peak (3312m), the Monk's Cowl (3234m) and Champagne Castle (3377m) – the central Berg is a big hit with hikers and climbers. But with dramatic scenery aplenty, this beautiful region is just as popular with those who prefer to admire their mountains from a safe distance.

A beautifully photogenic area in the shadow of the ramparts of Cathedral Peak, the **Cathedral Peak Nature Reserve** (036-488 8000; www.kznwildlife.com; adult/child R25/13; 6am-6pm) includes the Bell (2930m), the Horns (3005m) and Cleft Peak (3281m).

Obtain instructions and times regarding hikes, including that to Cathedral Peak, at the **park office** (036-488 8000; Didima Camp), which sells permits for the 4WD-only scenic drive up Mike's Pass (R50 per person) and arranges guides.

Boasting the Monk's Cowl and Champagne Castle peaks, **Monk's Cowl** (036-468 1103; www.kznwildlife.com; adult/child R30/15; 6am-6pm) is another stunning slice of the uKhahlamba-Drakensberg Park for hiking and climbing. The **park office** (036-468 1103; campsites per person R74), 3km beyond Champagne Castle Hotel, takes bookings for camping and overnight hiking (adult/child R40/20).

Inkosana Lodge (036-468 1202; www.inkosana.co.za; campsite R100, dm R150, d with/without bathroom R500/400, 2-person thatched rondavels with/without bathroom R500/400;), one of the best backpackers hostels in Africa, boasts an indigenous garden and excellent cuisine, and heaps of activities and walks are on offer.

Rising up to Injasuti Dome (3409m), **Giant's Castle** (036-353 3718; www.kznwildlife.com; adult/child R25/13; 5am-7pm) is one of the Drakensberg's loftiest sections; even its lowest point sits at 1300m above sea level. It's a rugged, remote and popular destination, with huge forest reserves to the north and south, and Lesotho's barren plateau over the escarpment to the west.

There are several accommodation centres inside the reserve, as well as trail huts and caves for hikers.

SOUTHERN DRAKENSBERG WILDERNESS AREAS

Best accessed from the pleasant towns of Himeville and Underberg, the southern Berg boasts one of the region's highlights: the journey up to Lesotho over the Sani Pass. It is renowned as a serious hiking area, offering a smorgasbord of wilderness areas and some great walks, including the fabulous Giant's Cup Trail.

The **Mkhomazi Wilderness Area** (033-266 6444; www.kznwildlife.com; adult/child R25/13; 6am-6pm) is one of the few places where you can hike for days without seeing anyone else.

The park office of **Garden Castle** (033-701 1823; adult/child R20/10, campsites per person R46, huts per person R60; 6am-6pm) is 30km west of Underberg; carry on along the road past Khotso Horsetrails. This reserve incorporates beautiful **Bushman's Nek Valley**, dominated by Rhino Peak (3051m), sandstone buttresses, rock-art sites, and a long day walk.

The drive up the **Sani Pass** is a trip to the roof of South Africa: a spectacular ride around hairpin bends into the clouds to the kingdom of Lesotho. At 2865m, this is the highest pass in the country, and the vistas (on a clear day!) are magical. There are hikes in almost every direction, and inexpensive horse rides are available. Amazingly, this is also the only road link between Lesotho and KwaZulu-Natal. You need a passport to cross into Lesotho. The border is open daily from 6am to 6pm, but check beforehand; times alter.

At the bottom of the pass you can sleep at the **Sani Lodge** (033-702 0330; www.sanilodge.co.za; campsites R60; dm/d without bathroom R90/240, 2-bed rondavel R360), which offers a range of fabulous tours and activities and insider tips about the region, as well as picking up guests from Himeville or Underberg.

Without doubt, the **Giant's Cup Trail** (68km, five days and five nights), running from Sani Pass to Bushman's Nek, is one of the nation's great walks. Early booking through **Ezemvelo KZN Wildlife** (☎ 033-845 1000; www.kznwildlife.com) is advisable.

MPUMALANGA

Unassuming Mpumalanga (Place of the Rising Sun) adheres to a quieter pace of life. This inland province is where the plateaus of the highveld begin their spectacular tumble onto the lowveld plains at the dramatic Drakensberg Escarpment. Many travellers zip through on their way to Kruger National Park, but it's well worth setting aside a few days to explore the historic towns, roaring waterfalls and some of the country's best hiking trails.

KRUGER NATIONAL PARK

Kruger is one of South Africa's national symbols, and for many visitors, the park is *the* 'must-see' wildlife destination in the country. Little wonder: in an area the size of Wales, enough elephants wander around to populate a city, giraffes nibble on acacia trees, hippos wallow in the rivers, leopards prowl through the night and a multitude of birds sing, fly and roost.

The park has an extensive network of sealed roads and comfortable camps, but if you prefer to keep it rough, there are also 4WD tracks, and mountain-bike and hiking trails. Even when you stick to the tarmac, the sounds and scents of the bush are never more than a few metres away. And, if you avoid weekends and holidays, or stay in the north and on gravel roads, it's easy to travel for an hour or more without seeing another vehicle.

Southern Kruger is the most popular section of the park, with the highest animal concentrations and the easiest access. Kruger is at its best in the far north. Here, although animal concentrations are somewhat lower, the bush setting and wilderness atmosphere are all-enveloping.

Information

Accommodation can be booked through **SAN Parks** (☎ 012-428 9111; www.sanparks.org), which has offices in Pretoria (p1055) and Durban (p1037), or through tourism offices in Mbombela (Nelspruit) and Cape Town.

Except in the high season and on weekends, bookings are advisable but not essential.

Day or overnight entry to the park costs R160/80 per adult/child. Bicycles and motorcycles are not permitted to enter the park. During school holidays you can stay in the park for a maximum of 10 days, and at any one rest camp for five days (10 days if you're camping). Visitor numbers are restricted, so arrive early in the high season if you don't have a booking. Opening times for the 10 entry gates vary slightly with the season.

Activities

Although it's possible to get a sense of Kruger in a day, the park merits at least four to five days, and ideally at least a week. There are four short **drives**, all averaging about four hours, and costing R460 per vehicle plus a R100 refundable deposit. Better than the drives are guided morning and afternoon **bush walks** (morning/afternoon per person R310/240), possible at many camps and some gates.

Kruger's three-day **wilderness walking trails** are done in small groups (maximum eight people), and guided by highly knowledgeable, armed guides. The walks are not particularly strenuous, covering about 20km per day at a modest pace. Trails cost R3120 per person, including accommodation in rustic huts, food and equipment; they depart on Wednesday and Sunday afternoon, and should be booked in advance.

Sleeping & Eating

Most visitors stay in one of the park's 12 rest camps. These offer camping, plus a range of huts, bungalows and cottages (self-catering or sharing cooking facilities), as well as shops, restaurants and other facilities. Several of the camps have satellite camps, which are located a few kilometres away, and are much more rustic, with only an ablutions block, kitchen and *braai* area.

Huts (two people from around R315) are the cheapest option, with shared ablutions and communal cooking facilities; bungalows (two people from around R670) range from simple to luxurious; cottages (up to four people about R1240), the next step up, usually have a living area.

Some camps also offer safari tents (about R350, with bathroom and kitchen about R780), all of which are furnished, and have a refrigerator and fan.

For those with tents or caravans, camping (campsites from R150) is available at many rest camps.

There are also five bushveld camps (smaller, more remote clusters of self-catering cottages without shops or restaurants; up to four people from R1035) and two bush lodges (up to four people from R2100), which are set in the middle of the wilderness, and must be booked in their entirety by a single group.

At the opposite end of the spectrum, there's luxurious accommodation in the private reserves bordering Kruger to the west. Another possibility is to stay outside the park in Hazyview or Mbombela (Nelspruit).

Getting There & Around

SAAirlink and its affiliates link Jo'burg (R900 to R1600, one hour), Cape Town (R2020, 2¼ hours) and Durban (from R1100, 1½ hours) with Mpumalanga Kruger International Airport near Mbombela (Nelspruit; for Numbi, Malelane and Crocodile Bridge Gates); it also serves Kruger Park Gateway Airport in Phalaborwa (2km from Phalaborwa Gate) and Hoedspruit Eastgate Airport (for Orpen Gate).

Mbombela (Nelspruit) is the most convenient large town near Kruger, and is well served by buses and minibus taxis to/from Jo'burg. Numbi Gate is about 50km away, and Malelane Gate about 65km away. Phalaborwa, right on the edge of the park, is a handy gateway for northern and central Kruger.

Most visitors drive themselves around the park, and this is the best way to experience Kruger. **Avis** (☎ 013-735 5651; www.avis.co.za) has a branch at Skukuza Rest Camp, and there is car rental from the Mbombela (Nelspruit), Hoedspruit and Phalaborwa airports.

MBOMBELA (NELSPRUIT)

☎ 013 / pop 235,000

As part of a nationwide drive to reflect the 'new South Africa', the city's name officially changed from Nelspruit to Mbombela in 2009. Mbombela, Mpumalanga's largest town and provincial capital, sprawls along the Crocodile River Valley in the steamy, subtropical lowveld. There are some decent shopping malls, good accommodation and excellent restaurants, making it a reasonable stopover on your way elsewhere.

A little far from town, but still the city's best hostel, the well-run **Funky Monkey Backpackers** (☎ 013-744 1310; www.funkymonkeys.co.za; 102 Van Wijk St; campsites per person R40, dm R130, d or tw without bathroom R600; 🖳 🖀) occupies a spacious house. A slightly more upscale option is **Old Vic Travellers Inn** (☎ 013-744 0993; www.krugerandmore.co.za; 12 Impala St; dm R100, d without bathroom from R260, s/d R240/360, self-catering house 1-7 people R320-740; 🖳 🖀), which has self-catering facilities or meals on request, and tents for rent. Quiet, well-maintained **Auberge Guest Lodge** (☎ 013-741 2866; www.aubergeguestlodge. com; 3 de Villiers St; s/d incl breakfast from R350/520; 🖳 🖀) has a plant-filled courtyard and comfortable rooms.

Jock & Java (☎ 013-755 4969; Ferreira St; mains R30-100; ☽ breakfast, lunch & dinner), a rambling pub and separate tearoom, is set in large lawns.

Mbombela is well served by buses and minibus taxis from Jo'burg, and flights to Cape Town, Durban and Jo'burg from the airport. **City Bug** (☎ 013-753 3392; www.citybug.co.za) operates a weekly shuttle to Durban (R520 one way), and a four-times-daily shuttle between Mbombela and OR Tambo International Airport (R320 per person).

BLYDE RIVER CANYON

The Blyde River's spectacular canyon is nearly 30km long and one of South Africa's most impressive natural features. Much of it is rimmed by the 26,000-hectare **Blyde River Canyon Nature Reserve** (admission per person R20), which snakes north from Graskop, following the escarpment and meeting the Blyde River as it carves its way down to the lowveld. Most visitors drive along the edge of the canyon, with stops at the many wonderful viewpoints, but if you have the time, it's well worth exploring on foot.

Heading north from Graskop, look for **God's Window** and **Wonder View** (on Rte 534), two viewpoints with amazing vistas and batteries of souvenir sellers. At God's Window take the trail up to the rainforest (300 steps). The Blyde River Canyon starts north of here, near **Bourke's Luck Potholes** (on Rte 532), bizarre cylindrical holes carved into the rock by whirlpools.

Forever Blyde Canyon (☎ 0861-226 966; www.for everblydecanyon.co.za; campsites R55, plus per person R95, 2-/4-person self-catering chalets R405/585, 2-/4-person deluxe chalets from R720/900; 🖀 🖟) is a rambling resort with a range of accommodation, restaurant, bar, supermarket, and six hiking routes.

GRASKOP

☎ 013 / pop 2000 / elev 1450m

A useful base for exploring the Blyde River Canyon, compact little Graskop is one of the

SOUTH AFRICA

area's most appealing towns. The nearby views over the edge of the Drakensberg Escarpment are magnificent.

Dutch-run **Graskop Valley View Backpackers** (☎ 013-767 1112; www.yebo-afrika.nl; 47 de Lange St; campsites per person R60, dm R85, s/d from R175/225, self-catering rondavel R290; 🖾 💽) has a variety of rooms, plus *rondavels*, tent sites, a self-catering flat, and adventure tours on offer. Another option is **Autumn Breath** (☎ 013-767 1866, 082-877 2811; autumnbreath@cfmail.co.za; Louis Trichardt St; s/d incl breakfast from R210/360), a quaint B&B with a charming restaurant.

The minibus taxi stand (Hoof St) is at the southern end of town, with daily morning departures.

GAUTENG

Fast, booming and a cabaret of contradictions, Gauteng (pronounced 'how-teng') is South Africa's smallest province, yet accounts for 34% of its gross domestic product (GDP), and 10% of the GDP of the whole of Africa. The laid-back, friendly atmosphere of Pretoria, the country's administrative capital, belies its turbulent past under the Boers and the apartheid regime. Some 50km away down the M1 motorway is Johannesburg, the provincial capital and third-largest city on the continent. Jo'burg is a sprawling, Orwellian conurbation of opulent suburbs set alongside some of the country's starkest urban poverty.

JOHANNESBURG
☎ 011 / pop 5.7 million

Jo'burg, also known as Jozi, is a rapidly developing city at the forefront of South Africa's development. The city centre is smartening up and Newtown, with its theatres, restaurants, museums and jazz clubs, is a lively cultural hub.

Jo'burg is the country's corporate capital and a thriving black middle class has risen up – in both the suburbs and the famous township of Soweto, which is attracting tourist dollars and investment. However, the city still bears the scars of past oppression and segregation. The glitzy shopping malls and exclusive restaurants found in affluent suburbs are down the road from desperately poor townships.

Jo'burg's notorious crime rate is another symptom of persisting inequalities, and it can make the city seem like an intimidating sprawl to first-time visitors. Although the tourist haunts of the northern suburbs are relatively safe areas, this is certainly a town where you should be on your guard.

That said, Jo'burg is a friendly, unstuffy city, worth tackling if only to take in the excellent Apartheid Museum. From bohemian Melville to the buzz of Newtown and the country's biggest township, Soweto, the City of Gold is increasingly cosmopolitan and confident about its future.

Orientation
OR Tambo International Airport (ORTIA) is 25km northeast of the city centre. The large city centre, laid out on a straightforward grid, is dominated by office blocks; after shops close, it becomes a virtual ghost town. Redevelopment of the Newtown cultural precinct at the northwestern edge of the city is at the core of an effort to clean up central Jo'burg. North of the centre, a steep ridge runs west–east from Braamfontein across to the dangerous suburb of Hillbrow. Northeast of the centre is the equally dangerous Yeoville.

The northern suburbs of big houses and big fences are predominantly white, middle- and upper-class, and where most travellers stay. Sterile shopping malls form the centre of most social life. The inner-suburban restaurant enclaves of Melville, Greenside, Parkhurst and Norwood make a refreshing change.

The black townships ring the city and present a stark contrast to the northern suburbs. Conditions within them range from the stereotypically suburban to the appalling. The main township is Soweto (opposite), but other big townships such as Alexandra surround the city in all directions.

Information
EMERGENCY
AIDS line (☎ 0800-012 322)
Fire (☎ 10111)
Police (Map p1052; ☎ 10111; Headquarters, Main Rd)
Rape Crisis Line (☎ 011-806 1888)

INTERNET ACCESS
Most sleeping options have internet facilities, charging anything from R20 to R60 per hour, and many offer free wi-fi. Most malls have an internet cafe, and wi-fi hotspots are increasingly prevalent in Melville.
Jetline.com (Map p1050; ☎ 011-726 1520; Shop 63, Campus Square Centre, Melville; per hr R40; 🕔 8.30am–5pm Mon-Fri, 9am–noon Sat) Also has a branch at Rosebank Mall.

MEDICAL SERVICES

Rosebank Clinic (Map p1050; ☎ 011-328 0500; 14 Sturdee Ave, Rosebank; ☽ 7am-10pm) A private hospital in the northern suburbs, with casualty, GP and specialist services.

MONEY

There are banks with ATMs and change facilities at every commercial centre. American Express and Rennies Travel (an agent for Thomas Cook) have branches at the airport and in major malls.

POST

Post office (Map p1050; ☎ 011-726 8505; Campus Square Centre, Melville; ☽ 8am-5pm Mon, Tue, Thu & Fri, 9am-5pm Wed, 8am-1pm Sat)

TOURIST INFORMATION

Gauteng Tourism Authority (Map p1052; ☎ 011-639 1600; www.gauteng.net; 1 Central Pl, cnr Jeppe & Henry Nxumalo Sts, Newtown; ☽ 8am-5pm Mon-Fri) The tourist body's headquarters in the Newtown cultural precinct provides basic information and brochures.

Johannesburg Tourism Company (Map p1050; ☎ 011-214 0700; www.joburgtourism.com; ground fl, Grosvenor Cnr, 195 Jan Smuts Ave, Parktown North; ☽ 8am-5pm Mon-Fri) A private endeavour; covers Jo'burg.

South African Tourism (Map p1050; ☎ 011-895 3000; www.southafrica.net; Bojanala House, 90 Protea Rd, Sandton; ☽ 8am-5pm Mon-Fri)

Dangers & Annoyances

Pay careful attention to your personal security in Jo'burg. Daylight muggings in the city centre and other inner suburbs, notably Hillbrow, do happen, and you must be constantly on your guard. Park Station's surroundings are notorious, including the pedestrian underpasses leading out of the station. You'd be crazy to walk the streets at night; if you arrive after dark and don't have a car, catch a taxi.

Crime is a big problem, but it is important to put things in perspective: remember that most travellers come and go without incident and that much of the crime afflicts parts of the city you would have little reason to stray into. It's when using ATMs that you're most vulnerable. Seek local advice, listen to it and remain aware of what's going on around you.

See p1062 for more advice.

Sights & Activities

CITY CENTRE & NEWTOWN

The area retains its edgy atmosphere, but regeneration projects in Newtown to the west

and university-oriented Braamfontein to the northwest are gradually helping to boost confidence in the heart of the city.

To view Jo'burg from on high, take the lift to the **Top of Africa** (Map p1052; ☎ 011-308 1331; 50th fl, Carlton Centre, 152 Commissioner St; adult/child R10/8; ☽ 9am-7pm). The entrance is via a special lift one floor below street level.

Rejuvenation has made Newtown the most appealing section of the downtown area. Surrounded by museums, eateries and the Market Theatre Complex (see p1053), Newtown's cultural precinct, which occupies **Mary Fitzgerald Square** (Map p1052), is the best place to focus on.

Overlooking the square, **Museum Africa** (Map p1052; ☎ 011-833 5624; 121 Bree St; admission free; ☽ 9am-5pm Tue-Sun) has several excellent exhibitions, covering diverse aspects of South Africa.

CONSTITUTION HILL

Inspiring **Constitution Hill** (Map p1052; ☎ 011-381 3100; Kotze St; tours adult/child R22/10; ☽ 9am-5pm Mon-Fri, 10am-3pm Sat) is one of the city's most important attractions. Built within the ramparts of the **Old Fort**, which dates from 1892 and was once a notorious prison, the development focuses on South Africa's new **Constitutional Court**, a very real symbol of the changing South Africa, with cases heard in all 11 official languages.

SOUTHERN SUBURBS

The **Apartheid Museum** (Map p1050; ☎ 011-309 4700; cnr Gold Reef Rd & Northern Parkway, Ormonde; adult/child R40/25; ☽ 10am-5pm Tue-Sun) remains one of South Africa's most evocative museums, using film, text, audio, exhibits and live accounts to provide a detailed insight into the architecture, implementation and eventual unravelling of apartheid.

SOWETO

Housing up to five million people (according to local estimates), Soweto is one of the world's most infamous townships, and a tour must not be missed. The 120-sq-km conurbation has received a face-lift in recent years, and some of its suburbs are looking downright affluent. Others remain as sad as any other ghetto in the developing world, with miles of cardboard-and-tin shacks with no plumbing. It might seem odd, even voyeuristic, to treat these places as a tourist attraction, but to get an appreciation of South African reality, you have to visit them. It's also a way

SOUTH AFRICA

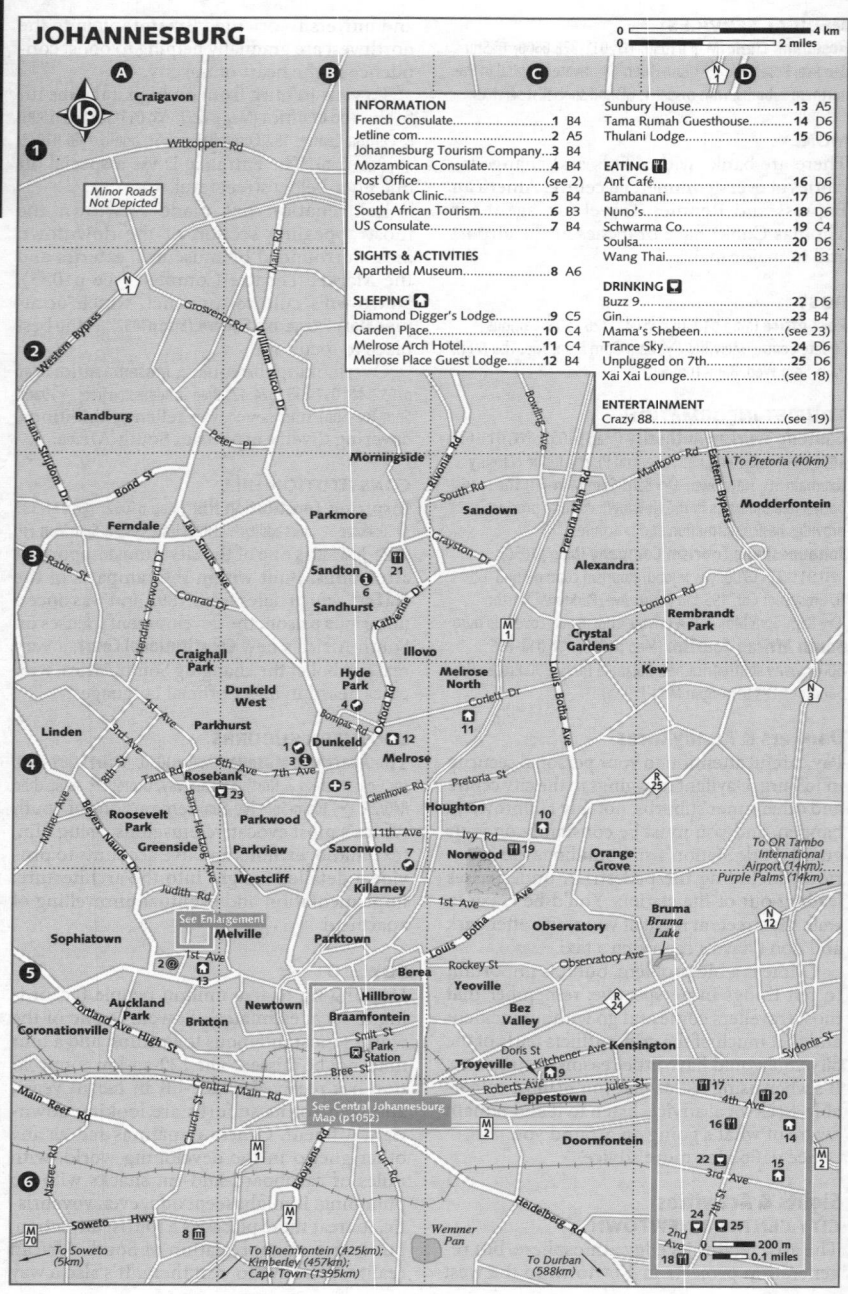

JOHANNESBURG

0 ————— 4 km
0 ————— 2 miles

INFORMATION
French Consulate..........................1 B4
Jetline.com.................................2 A5
Johannesburg Tourism Company...3 B4
Mozambican Consulate.................4 B4
Post Office...............................(see 2)
Rosebank Clinic..........................5 B4
South African Tourism..................6 B3
US Consulate.............................7 B4

SIGHTS & ACTIVITIES
Apartheid Museum.......................8 A6

SLEEPING 🏠
Diamond Digger's Lodge.............9 C5
Garden Place...........................10 C4
Melrose Arch Hotel...................11 C4
Melrose Place Guest Lodge........12 B4

Sunbury House..........................13 A5
Tama Rumah Guesthouse..........14 D6
Thulani Lodge.........................15 D6

EATING 🍴
Ant Café.................................16 D6
Bambanani.............................17 D6
Nuno's...................................18 D6
Schwarma Co..........................19 C4
Soulsa...................................20 D6
Wang Thai..............................21 B3

DRINKING 🍷
Buzz 9...................................22 D6
Gin......................................23 B4
Mama's Shebeen....................(see 23)
Trance Sky.............................24 D6
Unplugged on 7th....................25 D6
Xai Xai Lounge.......................(see 18)

ENTERTAINMENT
Crazy 88..............................(see 19)

of supporting local, black-owned businesses directly.

Two recommended tour companies are **Jimmy's Face to Face Tours** (☎ 011-331 6109; www.face2face.co.za), offering a 'Soweto by Night' package including dinner and *shebeens* as well as the usual minibus tours; and Soweto Backpackers' **Soweto Bicycle Tours** (☎ 011-936 3444; www.sowetobicycletours.com), which get you onto the streets with local guides in a way you can't do by bus. Alternatively, contact the **Soweto Tourism and Information Centre** (☎ 011-945 3111; Walter Sisulu Sq, Kliptown; ◷ 8am-5pm Mon-Fri).

Sleeping

our pick **Soweto Backpackers** (☎ 011-936 3444; www.sowetobackpackers.com; 10823 A Pooe St, Orlando West, Soweto; campsites R65, dm/s/d without bathroom R95/150/250) One of Gauteng's best hostels, offering a warm welcome, a garden with a bar and nightly bonfires, dinners and heaps of activities.

Diamond Digger's Lodge (Map p1050; ☎ 011-624 1676; www.oneandonly.co.za; 36 Doris St, Kensington; dm/d without bathroom R80/200, d R300; P 🖳 🛄 🐾) It's slightly worn and gloomy in places, but makes up for it with city views, a variety of dorms and doubles, and a range of facilities.

Purple Palms (off Map p1050; ☎ 011-393 4393; www.purplepalms.co.za; 1 Boompeiper Ave, Kempton Park; dm/s/d without bathroom R100/250/400, d R450; P 🛄 🐾) In a quiet suburb near the airport, this self-described 'flash-packers' has clean, well-equipped rooms and a garden bar.

Sunbury House (Map p1050; ☎ 011-726 1114; peterharris@telkomsa.net; 24 Sunbury Ave, Melville; s/d incl breakfast from R250/350; P 🛄 🐾) There's a down-to-earth vibe at this characterful guesthouse, where hearty breakfasts are served in a wood-floored dining room around a shared table.

Tama Rumah Guesthouse (Map p1050; ☎ 011-482 7611; www.tamarumah.co.za; 88 4th Ave, Melville; s/d incl breakfast from R520/730; P 🛄 🐾) African art and crafts decorate the rooms, which are dotted around pretty gardens with plenty of space to sit out in the sun.

Thulani Lodge (Map p1050; ☎ 011-482 1106; www.thulanilodge.co.za; 85 3rd Ave, Melville; s/d/tw incl breakfast R580/760/760; P 🛜 🐾) Comfortable, spacious rooms and a cosy lounge with wi-fi. Within staggering distance of 7th St.

Garden Place (Map p1050; ☎ 011-485 3800; 53 Garden Rd, Norwood; s/d R799/899; P 🖳 🛄 🐾) This leafy property offers options such as self-catering studios and luxury cottages, as well as a free shuttle service to nearby malls.

Melrose Place Guest Lodge (Map p1050; ☎ 011-442 5231; www.melroseplace.co.za; 12A North St, Melrose; s/d incl breakfast R995/1400; P 🖳 🛄 🐾) With a great spot between Rosebank and Sandton, this country-styled place has quiet rooms with private entrances and a tree-filled garden.

Melrose Arch Hotel (Map p1050; ☎ 011-214 6666; www.africanpridehotels.com; 1 Melrose Sq, Melrose Arch; s/d incl breakfast from R2800/3600; P 🖳 🛄 🐾) This ultramodern masterpiece is bursting with features such as rooms with 20 choices of mood lighting, and a Sherlock Holmes–style library bar.

Eating

Unfortunately for those without cars, most of the best places are scattered around the northern suburbs (often in malls). Grant Ave in Norwood has a string of cafes and restaurants that has grown into an east Jo'burg version of Melville's hip 7th St.

NEWTOWN

Nikki's Oasis (Map p1052; ☎ 011-838 9933; 138 Bree St, Newtown; mains R50) Traditional South African favourites such as mutton *potjie* and Western fare are served to a jazz soundtrack, and local musicians play some weekends.

Gramadoela's (Map p1052; ☎ 011-838 6960; Market Theatre Complex, Bree St, Newtown; mains R70-130; ◷ lunch & dinner Tue-Sat, dinner Mon; 🐾) This decades-old institution brims with curios and character, and international celebs have tried its African and Cape Malay cuisine.

MELVILLE, NORWOOD & GREENSIDE/ROSEBANK

Not far from Melville, around the junction of Gleneagles and Greenway Rds in Greenside/Rosebank, is a variety of restaurants, including sushi, Indian, Portuguese and tapas.

Ant Café (Map p1050; ☎ 011-726 2614; 7th St, Melville; mains R35-50; ◷ lunch & dinner) Light lunches, four types of spaghetti and 14 types of thin-crust pizza draw the local intelligentsia in their droves to this bohemian den.

our pick **Schwarma Co** (Map p1050; ☎ 011-483 1776; 71 Grant Ave, Norwood; mains R35-115; ◷ 10am-11pm) A popular place for a Middle Eastern fix; excellent quality ingredients are used in the delicious, filling *schwarma* and kebab platters.

Bambanani (Map p1050; ☎ 011-482 2900; 85 4th Ave; mains R40-75; ◷ 7.30am-10pm) This trendy hangout caters for families with its rear garden and play area, and the menu features tapas and Middle Eastern food.

SOUTH AFRICA

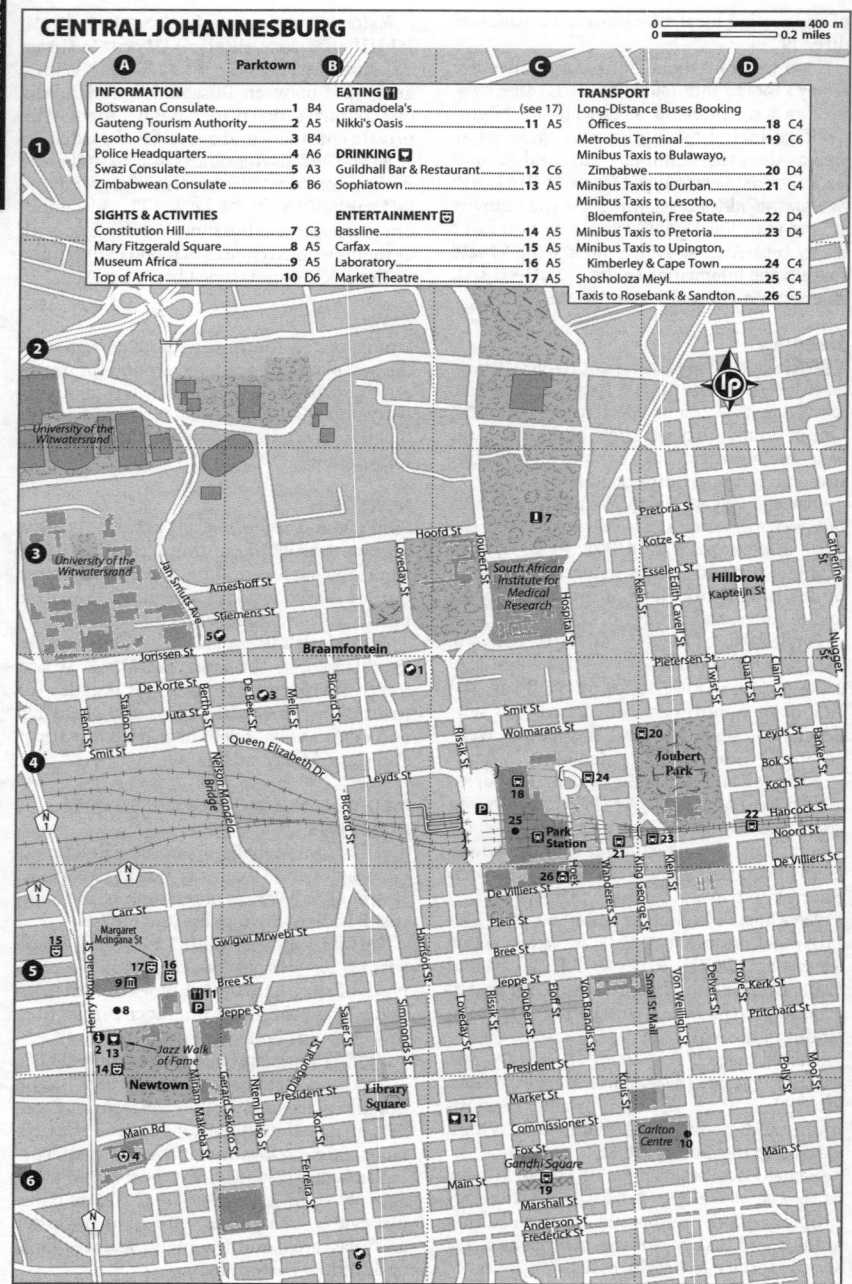

CENTRAL JOHANNESBURG

0 ——————— 400 m
0 ——————— 0.2 miles

INFORMATION
Botswanan Consulate.........................**1** B4
Gauteng Tourism Authority..............**2** A5
Lesotho Consulate...............................**3** B4
Police Headquarters............................**4** A6
Swazi Consulate....................................**5** A3
Zimbabwean Consulate.......................**6** B6

SIGHTS & ACTIVITIES
Constitution Hill...................................**7** C3
Mary Fitzgerald Square.......................**8** A5
Museum Africa.......................................**9** A5
Top of Africa.......................................**10** D6

EATING 🍴
Gramadoela's...............................(see 17)
Nikki's Oasis..**11** A5

DRINKING 🍷
Guildhall Bar & Restaurant..............**12** C6
Sophiatown...**13** A5

ENTERTAINMENT 🎭
Bassline..**14** A5
Carfax..**15** A5
Laboratory..**16** A5
Market Theatre....................................**17** A5

TRANSPORT
Long-Distance Buses Booking
   Offices...**18** C4
Metrobus Terminal..............................**19** C6
Minibus Taxis to Bulawayo,
   Zimbabwe...**20** D4
Minibus Taxis to Durban....................**21** C4
Minibus Taxis to Lesotho,
   Bloemfontein, Free State............**22** D4
Minibus Taxis to Pretoria..................**23** D4
Minibus Taxis to Upington,
   Kimberley & Cape Town................**24** C4
Shosholoza Meyl..................................**25** A5
Taxis to Rosebank & Sandton...........**26** C5

Nuno's (Map p1050; ☎ 011-482 6990; 3 7th St, Melville; mains R50-100; ⏰ 8am-1am) Dishes such as the Godfather pizza and the puttanesca are worth the wait at this Mozambican restaurant, as is the espresso.

Soulsa (Map p1050; ☎ 011-482 5572; 16 7th St, Melville; mains R90; ⏰ breakfast, lunch & dinner Tue-Sun; 🔧) With its mezzanine floor and small Zen garden, Soulsa's food is suitably creative, offering vegetarians interesting brunch and dinner choices.

Drinking

Much of the nightlife is in the northern suburbs, particularly around Melville, Greenside and Rosebank. The area around the cultural precinct in Newtown also has a few decent places.

CITY CENTRE & NEWTOWN

Guildhall Bar & Restaurant (Map p1052; ☎ 011-833 1770; 88 Market St, Marshalltown) Established in 1888, this wood-panelled, dimly lit bar serves pub grub upstairs.

our pick Sophiatown (Map p1052; ☎ 011-836 5999; 1 Central Pl, cnr Jeppe & Henry Nxumalo Sts, Newtown) Overlooking the Jazz Walk of Fame, this 'township chic' bar-restaurant has live music on Fridays and Saturdays.

MELVILLE

Unplugged on 7th (Map p1050; ☎ 011-482 5133; 8 7th St) This open-fronted bar offers amusingly named cocktails and DJs at weekends.

Xai Xai Lounge (Map p1050; ☎ 011-482 6990; 3 7th St) This Mozambican bar will transport you far from suburban Jo'burg, thanks to the Laurentina beer and the beach scenes on the walls.

Trance Sky (Map p1050; ☎ 011-726 2241; 7th St) With table football in the window, there's normally a party going on at this bar, popular with the black community.

Buzz 9 (Map p1050; ☎ 011-726 2019; 9 7th St) Funky multilevel bar with cosmically decorated banisters and a large menu of potent cocktails.

GREENSIDE/ROSEBANK

Gin (Map p1050; ☎ 011-486 2404; 12 Gleneagles Rd) House and hip hop keep the crowd happy at this bar, part shabby Caribbean shack, part gallery.

Mama's Shebeen (Map p1050; ☎ 082-965 2640; 18 Gleneagles Rd) From the outside seating under a corrugated awning to the Bo-Kaap Blues cocktails, Mama's is a nod to township cool.

Entertainment

LIVE MUSIC & NIGHTCLUBS

Bassline (Map p1052; ☎ 011-838 9145; 10 Henry Nxumalo St, Newtown; admission R60-170) A fantastic venue, Bassline hosts major local and international acts. It's known for jazz and blues, but you'll also catch world music, hip hop and rock.

Crazy 88 (Map p1050; ☎ 011-728 8417; 1st fl, 114 William Rd, Norwood) Hosts bands, DJs and comedians from around the country. It's all here: house, hip hop, rock and jazz; chilled-out Sunday sessions; and fancy dress parties on Fridays and Saturdays.

Carfax (Map p1052; ☎ 011-834 9187; 39 Pim St, Newtown; admission R70) Local and international DJs play house and hip hop to an eclectic crowd at this popular converted factory space.

THEATRES

Market Theatre (Map p1052; ☎ 011-832 1641; www. markettheatre.co.za; 56 Margaret Mcingana St) Has three live theatre venues as well as galleries, a cafe and Kippie's Jazz International.

Laboratory (Map p1052; ☎ 011-836 0516; 60 Margaret Mcingana St) An offshoot of the Market Theatre, it showcases community talent, with free shows every Saturday at 1pm.

Getting There & Away

AIR

South Africa's major international and domestic airport is **OR Tambo International Airport** (ORTIA; ☎ 011-921 6262; www.airports.co.za). For more information, including international flight connections, see p1064.

All regular flights to national and regional destinations with South African Airways and its subsidiaries can be booked through the airline, which has offices in ORTIA's domestic and international terminals.

Smaller budget airlines, including Kulula .com, 1time and Mango, also link Jo'burg with major destinations.

BUS

A number of international bus services leave Jo'burg from the Park Station complex (Map p1052) for Botswana, Lesotho, Malawi, Mozambique, Namibia, Swaziland, Zambia and Zimbabwe.

The main long-distance bus lines (national and international) also depart from and arrive at the Park Station transit centre, in the northwest corner of the site, where you will also find their booking offices.

Translux/City to City, Greyhound, SA Roadlink and Intercape service major and minor destinations. With the exception of City to City buses, which commence in Jo'burg, all services that are not heading north commence in Pretoria. Destinations include Cape Town (R450, 19 hours), Durban (R210, eight hours), Mbombela (Nelspruit; R200, five hours), East London (R320, 15 hours) via Bloemfontein (R190, seven hours), and Plettenberg Bay (R385, 18 hours).

Baz Bus (see p1066) picks up from hostels in Jo'burg.

MINIBUS TAXI

The majority of minibus taxis already use the new road-transport interchange in Park Station, over the train tracks between the Metro Concourse and Wanderers St. Because of the risk of mugging, it is not a good idea to go searching for a taxi while you have your luggage with you.

You can also find minibus taxis going in the direction of Kimberley, Cape Town and Upington on Wanderers St near Leyds St; Bulawayo taxis at the northern end of King George St; Pretoria, Lesotho, Bloemfontein (and other Free State destinations) taxis on Noord St; and Durban taxis near the corner of Wanderers and Noord Sts. Take extreme care waiting in these areas; you should ideally be accompanied by a local.

TRAIN

Shosholoza Meyl (☎ 0860-008 888, 011-774 4555; www. shosholozameyl.co.za, www.premierclasse.co.za; Park Station) offers tourist- and premier-class services, with sleeper compartments. These trains are a recommended way of travelling to destinations such as Cape Town.

Getting Around

ORTIA is located about 25km east of central Jo'burg in Kempton Park. The 24-hour **Airport Shuttle** (☎ 0861-748 8853; www.airportshuttle.co.za) charges R310 to R390 for most destinations in Jo'burg; book a day in advance if possible. Most accommodation will collect you from the airport; most hostels do so for free.

Gautrain (www.gautrain.co.za) is set to link Park Station and Pretoria, stopping en route at Rosebank, Sandton and ORTIA.

Taxis operate meters (if the meter works). It's wise to ask a local the likely price and agree on a fare at the outset. From the taxi rank at

Park Station, a taxi to Rosebank should cost around R80.

Metropolitan Bus Services (Metrobus; Map p1052; ☎ 011-375 5555; www.mbus.co.za; Gandhi Sq) runs services covering 108 routes in the Greater Jo'burg area. Fares work on a zone system, ranging from zone one (R6.50) to zone eight (R16).

If you take a minibus taxi into central Jo'burg, be sure to get off before it reaches the end of the route and avoid the taxi rank – it's a mugging zone. Fares differ depending on routes, but Rte 5 will get you around the inner suburbs and city centre, and Rte 9 will get you almost anywhere.

There has been a very serious problem with violent crime on the metro system. The Jo'burg–Pretoria metro line should also be avoided.

PRETORIA
☎ 012 / pop 1.65 million

Though only 50km from Jo'burg, South Africa's administrative centre is slower and more old-fashioned than its rough and tumble sister city, and many travellers feel safer here. It's also a handsome place, home to gracious old buildings, including the stately Union Buildings, and leafy suburbs. The wide streets are lined with a purple haze of jacarandas in October and November.

Culturally, Pretoria feels more like an Afrikaner-dominated country town than a capital city. Its bars and restaurants are less cosmopolitan than Jo'burg's. It was once at the heart of the apartheid regime, and its very name was a symbol of oppression, but today it's the base of the same black president who was inaugurated here in May 2009.

Information
INTERNET ACCESS
Most accommodation offers internet facilities and wi-fi; **4 in Love Internet Café** (☎ 012-362 5358; 1077 Burnett St; per hr R10; ⏰ 9am-7pm Mon-Fri, 9am-6pm Sat, 10am-5pm Sun) is a cheaper alternative.

MEDICAL SERVICES
Hatfield Clinic (☎ 012-362 7180; 454 Hilda St) A well-known suburban clinic.
Pretoria Academic Hospital (☎ 012-354 1414; Dr Savage Rd) The place to head for in a medical emergency.

MONEY
There are banks with ATMs and change facilities across town.

American Express (☎ 012-346 2599; Brooklyn Mall; ☯ 9am-5pm)

POST
Main post office (Church Sq; ☯ 8.30am-4.30pm Mon-Fri, 8am-noon Sat)

TOURIST INFORMATION
The fairly useless **Tourist Information Centre** (☎ 012-358 1430; www.tshwane.gov.za; Old Nederlandsche Bank Bldg, Church Sq; ☯ 7.30am-4pm Mon-Fri, 9am-3.30pm Sat) offers leaflets and a map.

The head office of **SAN Parks** (☎ 011-428 9111; www.sanparks.org; 643 Leyds St, New Muckleneuk; ☯ offices 7.45am-3.45pm Mon-Fri, 8am-12.15pm Sat, call centre 7.30am-5pm Mon-Fri, 8am-2pm Sat) handles park and reserve bookings and inquiries.

Dangers & Annoyances
Although Pretoria is safer and more relaxed than Jo'burg, crime is a problem, particularly in the city centre and Sunnyside. Restaurants and other businesses are mostly found in safer Hatfield and Brooklyn. Avoid the centre after dark and be on guard at the weekend when there are fewer people about.

Sights & Activities
The looming **Voortrekker Monument & Museum** (☎ 012-326 6770; Eeufees Rd; adult/child R32/12, vehicle R13; ☯ 8am-6pm Sep-Apr, till 5pm May-Aug) is hallowed turf for many Afrikaners. Built between 1938 and 1949 to commemorate the Battle of Blood River (1838), during which some 500 Boers defeated approximately 12,000 Zulus, it remains a powerful symbol of the 'White tribe of Africa' and their historical relationship to South Africa.

The monument is 3km south of the city, clearly signposted from the M18 or the N14.

Nearby, **Freedom Park** (☎ 012-361 0021; Koch St, Salvokop; admission free; ☯ tours 9am, noon & 3pm) is a dramatic new hilltop memorial to people, local and international, who sacrificed their lives in the name of freedom.

Church Square is the heart of Pretoria, surrounded by imposing public buildings. In the centre is a statue of Paul Kruger (president of the Boer republics during the 1899–1902 Anglo-Boer War) and, a short walk away, Kruger's former residence is now the **Paul Kruger House Museum** (☎ 012-326 9172; 60 Church St; adult/child R25/10; ☯ 8.30am-4.30pm Mon-Fri, 9am-4.30pm Sat).

About 1km north of the city centre are the **National Zoological Gardens** (☎ 012-328 3265; cnr Paul Kruger & Boom Sts; adult/child R45/30; ☯ 8.30am-5.30pm),

a pleasant spot to spend an afternoon. The highlight is probably the cable car that runs up to the top of a hill overlooking Pretoria.

Sleeping
Backpackers are well served in Hatfield, and along with Arcadia and Brooklyn, the area is the best place to start looking for midrange B&B options.

1322 Backpackers International (☎ 012-362 3905; www.1322backpackers.com; 1322 Arcadia St, Hatfield; dm/s/d without bathroom from R90/150/230, r R350; P ⚌ ⚌) A friendly hostel with comfortable dorm beds, a guesthouse-standard double in the main house, and log cabins in the garden.

Pretoria Backpackers (☎ 012-343 9754; www.pretoriabackpackers.net; 425 Farenden St, Clydesdale; dm R110, s/d without bathroom R200/280; P ⚌ ⚌) This large, well-equipped hostel has a lounge and bar, a travel desk offering tours, and several small cabins.

That's It (☎ 012-344 3404; www.thatsit.co.za; 5 Brecher St, Clydesdale; s/d incl breakfast R370/500; P ⚌ ⚌ ⚌) Owned by a friendly young couple, That's It boasts a wraparound verandah overlooking a garden, a sofa-filled *lapa* (circular thatched building), and meals are available.

B' Guesthouse (☎ 012-344 0524; www.bguesthouse.co.za; 751 Park St, Arcadia; s/d R440/660; P ⚌ ⚌) A pretty house with a cosy lounge and wine cellar, dinners available, and rooms with private entrances and patios.

Court Classique (☎ 012-344 4420; www.courtclassique.co.za; cnr Schoeman & Beckett Sts, Arcadia; s/d from R1220/1300; P ⚌ ⚌ ⚌) This is an excellent top-end choice: the rooms are comfortable suites, complete with kitchenette, lounge and patio or balcony.

Eating
The best eateries are in Hatfield, Brooklyn and New Muckleneuk, generally concentrated along a few streets.

Café Riche (☎ 012-328 3173; www.caferiche.co.za; 2 Church St; mains R40-75; ☯ 6am-6pm) This historic bistro is popular with tourists and visiting dignitaries.

Blue Crane (☎ 012-460 7615; cnr Boshiff & Melk Sts; mains R40-80; ☯ breakfast, lunch & dinner; ⚌) Offering Afrikaner dishes as well as the usual steak and seafood, this restaurant overlooks a lake that is the breeding site for its namesake.

Café 41 (☎ 012-342 8914; Eastwood Village, cnr Eastwood & Pretoria Sts; mains R40-110; ☯ breakfast, lunch & dinner) An attractively designed bistro-style

SOUTH AFRICA

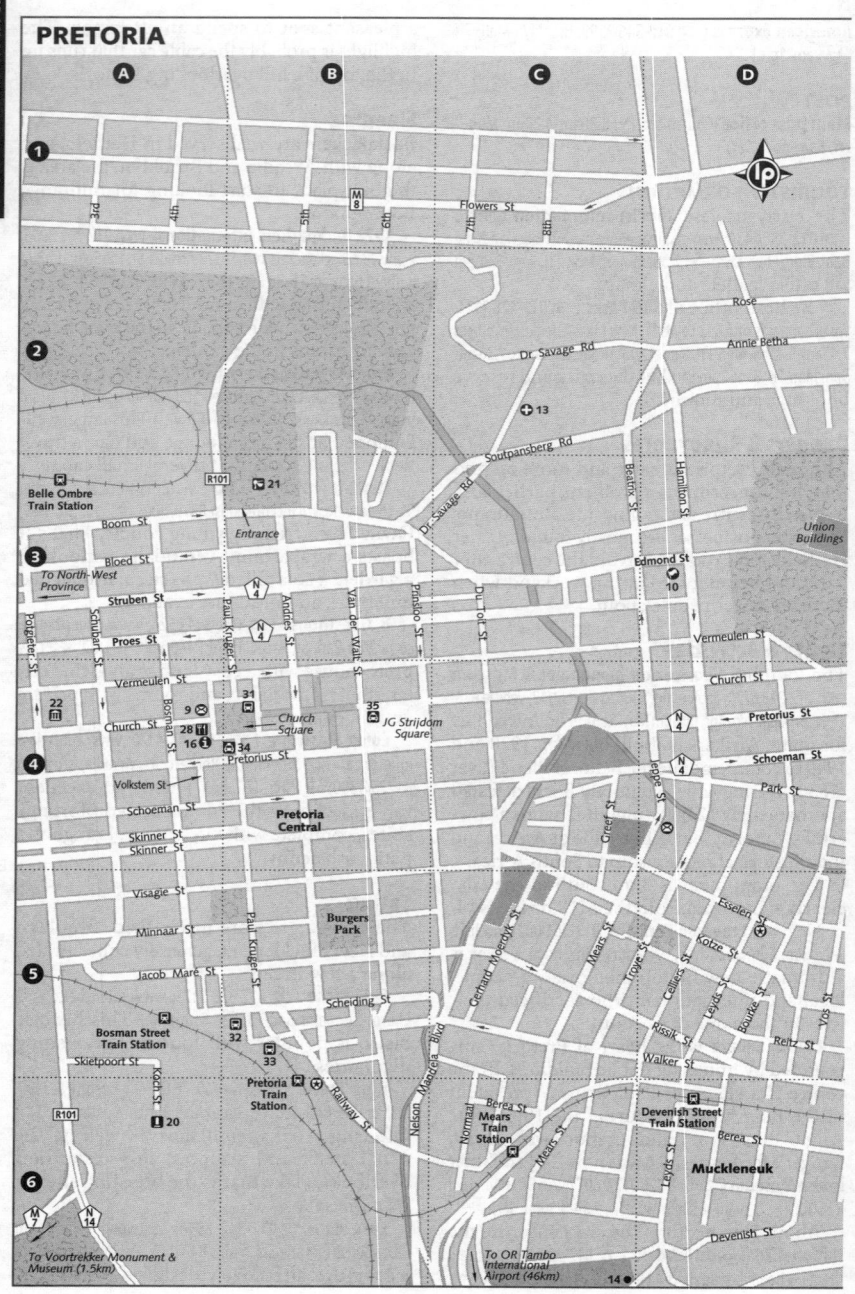

PRETORIA

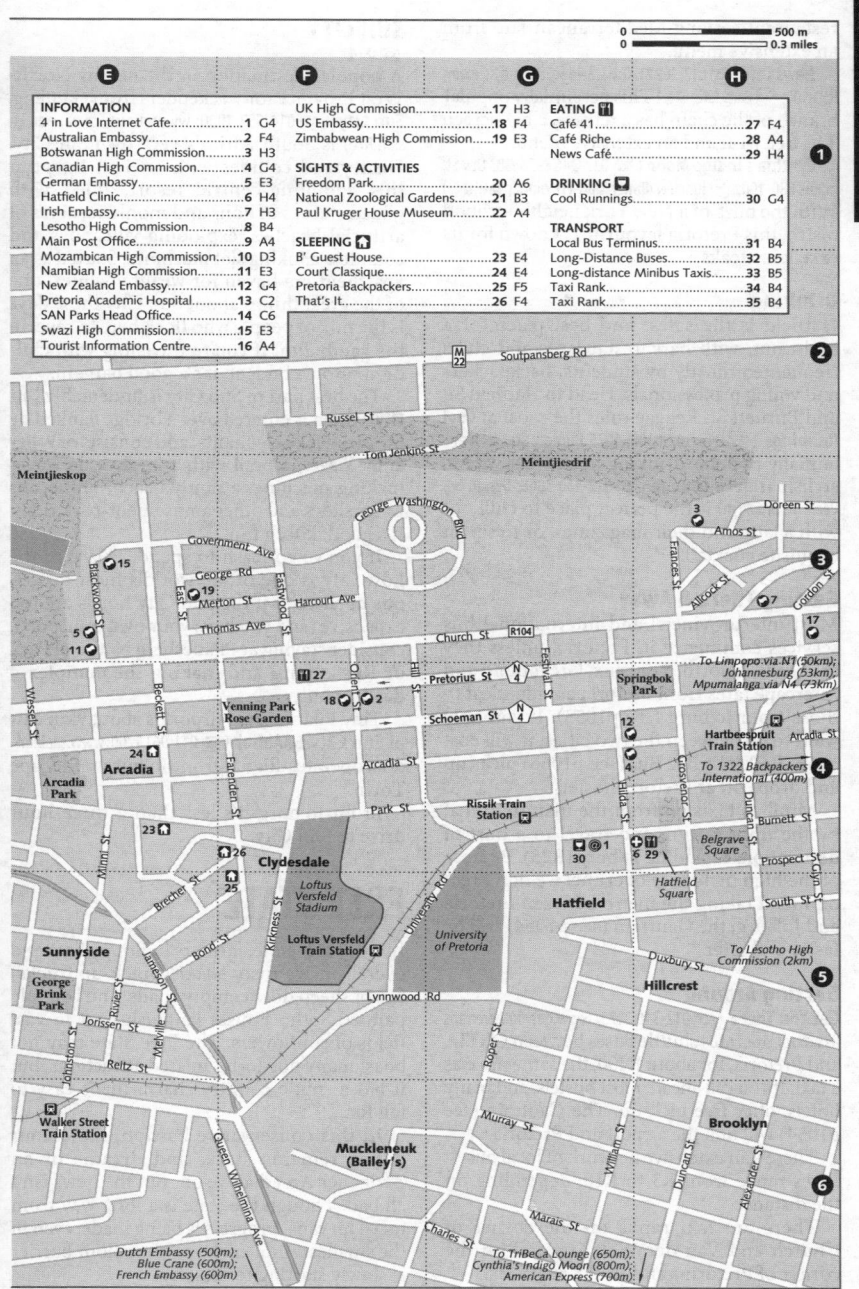

0 — 500 m
0 — 0.3 miles

INFORMATION
4 in Love Internet Cafe.....................1 G4
Australian Embassy...........................2 F4
Botswanan High Commission............3 H3
Canadian High Commission..............4 G4
German Embassy................................5 E3
Hatfield Clinic...................................6 H4
Irish Embassy....................................7 H3
Lesotho High Commission................8 B4
Main Post Office...............................9 A4
Mozambican High Commission........10 D3
Namibian High Commission.............11 E3
New Zealand Embassy......................12 G4
Pretoria Academic Hospital..............13 C2
SAN Parks Head Office.....................14 C6
Swazi High Commission...................15 E3
Tourist Information Centre...............16 A4

UK High Commission........................17 H3
US Embassy......................................18 F4
Zimbabwean High Commission........19 E3

SIGHTS & ACTIVITIES
Freedom Park....................................20 A6
National Zoological Gardens............21 B3
Paul Kruger House Museum.............22 A4

SLEEPING
B' Guest House.................................23 E4
Court Classique................................24 E4
Pretoria Backpackers........................25 F5
That's It..26 F4

EATING
Café 41..27 F4
Café Riche..28 A4
News Café...29 H4

DRINKING
Cool Runnings..................................30 G4

TRANSPORT
Local Bus Terminus..........................31 B4
Long-Distance Buses.........................32 B5
Long-distance Minibus Taxis............33 B5
Taxi Rank...34 B4
Taxi Rank...35 B4

Soutpansberg Rd

Russel St

Tom Jenkins St

Meintjiesdrif

Meintjieskop

George Washington Blvd

Government Ave

George Rd

Eastwood St

Blackwood St

East St

Merton St

Harcourt Ave

Thomas Ave

Doreen St

Amos St

Frances St

Allcock St

Gordon St

Church St   R104

Wessels St

Beckett St

Venning Park
Rose Garden

Oleo St

Hill St

Pretorius St

Festival St

Springbok
Park

To Limpopo via N1 (50km);
Johannesburg (53km);
Mpumalanga via N4 (73km)

Schoeman St

Arcadia St

Hartbeespruit
Train Station

Arcadia St

To 1322 Backpackers
International (400m)

Arcadia
Park

Farenden St

Arcadia

Park St

Rissik Train
Station

Hilda St

Crosvenor St

Burnett St

Belgrave
Square

Prospect St

Clydesdale

Loftus
Versfeld
Stadium

University Rd

Hatfield
Square

South St

Mitton St

Brecher St

Hatfield

Sunnyside

Kirkness St

Loftus Versfeld
Train Station

University
of Pretoria

Hillcrest

To Lesotho High
Commission (2km)

George
Brink
Park

Rivier St

Lameson St

Melville St

Bond St

Lynnwood Rd

Duxbury St

Jorissen St

Johnston St

Reitz St

Roper St

Walker Street
Train Station

Murray St

Brooklyn

William St

Duncan St

Alexander St

Queen Wilhelmina Ave

Muckleneuk
(Bailey's)

Marais St

Charles St

Dutch Embassy (500m);
Blue Crane (600m);
French Embassy (600m)

To TriBeCa Lounge (650m);
Cynthia's Indigo Moon (800m);
American Express (700m)

restaurant serving Mediterranean fare from an extensive menu.

News Café (☎ 012-362 7190; Hatfield Sq, Burnett St; mains R50-100; ☽ 8am-late; ☒) This perennially popular branch of the chain has a terrace, a big-screen TV, free wi-fi and an extensive menu.

Cynthia's Indigo Moon (☎ 012-346 8926; 283 Dey St; mains R80-100; ☽ lunch & dinner Mon-Fri, dinner Sat; ☒) With the buzz of a New York neighbourhood bistro, this Pretoria favourite is known for its excellent steaks.

Drinking

Hatfield is the safest and best place for a night out, with bars, restaurants and clubs frequented mostly by students, backpackers and young professionals. Head to Hatfield Sq and Burnett St. Reggae rules the roost at **Cool Runnings** (☎ 012-362 0100; 1075 Burnett St), a perennially popular drinking haunt. Elsewhere, stylish **TriBeCa Lounge** (☎ 012-460 3068; Design Sq, Veale St, Brooklyn) is the perfect place to chill out with a latte and their magazines, or to sip an exquisite cocktail.

Getting There & Away

Most interprovincial and international bus services commence in Pretoria, unless they are heading north. Translux, Greyhound and Intercape fares from Pretoria are identical to those from Jo'burg (see p1053). If you only want to go between the two cities, it will cost about R60. The Baz Bus (see p1066) picks up and drops off at Pretoria hostels.

Minibus taxis go from the main terminal by the train station and travel to a host of destinations including Jo'burg (R25). Because of the high incidence of crime, we don't recommend taking the metro between Pretoria and Jo'burg; the Gautrain (see p1054) will be faster and safer.

Getting Around

Get You There (☎ 012-346 3175; www.getyoutheretransfers.co.za) operates shuttle buses between ORTIA and Pretoria, for about R400, the same price as a taxi. If you call ahead, most hostels, and many hotels, offer free pick-up. The Gautrain (see p1054) will link the airport and Pretoria.

There's an extensive network of local buses. Fares range from R5 to R10, depending on the distance.

There are taxi ranks on the corner of Church and Van der Walt Sts, and on the corner of Pretorius and Paul Kruger Sts.

SUN CITY
☎ 014

A popular destination in the nearby North-West Province for weekenders from Gauteng, **Sun City** (☎ 014-557 1000; www.suncity.co.za; admission R70) is South Africa's very own Sin City. Disneyland collides with ancient Egypt at this gambling-centric resort, filled with gilded statues of lions and monkeys, acres of artificial beaches, exploding volcanoes and countless clinking slot machines. Started as an apartheid-era haven for wealthy whites, one of the great things about Sun City these days is the mix of people who flock here to revel in the gaudy fun. If you're travelling with children or on a budget, it's a good bargain.

The best part of Sun City is undeniably **Lost City**, which is entered over a bridge flanked by life-sized fake elephants, and consists of **Valley of the Waves**, a pool with a large-scale wave-making machine, a sandy beach, numerous water slides and other amusement-park rides. It's good, kitsch fun.

If you've got cash to spend, Palace of the Lost City is one of the world's most luxurious hotels, but if the Sun City hotels are too expensive (and you have your own transport), consider staying at Pilanesberg National Park or Rustenburg and making the complex a day trip only.

Tiny Pilanesberg Airport is about 9km east of Sun City. **SAAirlink** (☎ 011-961 1700; www.saairlink.co.za) operates flights from Jo'burg and Cape Town.

From Jo'burg it's less than a three-hour drive to Sun City.

FREE STATE

In this rural state, farmers in floppy hats and overalls drive rusty *bakkies* (pick-up trucks) full of sheep down empty roads, and brightly painted Sotho houses languish next to vast fields of sunflowers. The Free State may not boast many not-to-be-missed attractions, but it has a subtle country charm that's easy to fall for.

In this conservative bastion, the colour divide remains stark, and dreams of an Afrikaner Arcadia live on. But the news isn't all bad. Though the state is a long way from racial nirvana, progress is being made; even in the smallest rural enclaves, the colour barrier is slowly starting to dissolve.

BLOEMFONTEIN

☎ 051 / pop 645,000

Both the state capital and South Africa's judicial capital, Bloem (as the locals call it) is a spunky, progressive university town. When school's in session, nightlife is raging. There's no real reason to go out of your way to visit Bloemfontein, but it has a few interesting sights if you do pass through.

Commemorating the 26,000 women and children who died in British concentration camps during the 1899–1902 Anglo-Boer War, the **National Women's Memorial** depicts a bearded Afrikaner, setting off on his pony to fight the British, bidding a last farewell to his wife and baby, who are to perish in one of the camps. It's a powerful image and one still buried in the psyche of many Afrikaners.

Sleeping & Eating

Odessa Guesthouse (☎ 084-966 0200; odessa@telkomsa.net; 4 Gannie Viljoen St; s/d from R280/380; 🖥 🐾) For Ukrainian hospitality in the Free State, check out Odessa. Readers give the multilingual guesthouse rave reviews for friendly hosts.

Ansu Guesthouse (☎ 051-436 4654; ansugh@gmail.com; 80 Waverley Rd; s/d R350/400; 🐾) The modern rooms are light and airy, and open onto a leafy garden with a gazebo and tennis court by the pool.

Hobbit Boutique Hotel (☎ 051-447 0663; www.hobbit.co.za; 19 President Steyn Ave; r incl breakfast R900; 🍴 🖥 🐾) Inspired by JRR Tolkien, who was born in Bloem, the charming, old-world Hobbit, comprising two 1921 houses, is the winner of numerous awards.

Jazz Time Café (☎ 051-430 5727; Waterfront; mains R40-100; 🕘 9am-late) This hip rooftop bar-restaurant and venue, above NuMetro cinema, has an interesting menu featuring big, American-style sandwiches.

Bella Casa Trattoria (☎ 051-448 9573; 31 President Steyn Ave; mains R50-80) This popular Italian trattoria is a cheerful, family-friendly place with courtyard seating.

Drinking & Entertainment

As a university town, Bloemfontein has a good range of places to drink, party and listen to live music. Second Ave, particularly around Kellner St, bustles with revellers in the evening and competes for the nightlife scene with the Waterfront, which also has a cinema. Long-standing bar and live-music venue **Mystic Boer** (☎ 051-430 2206; 84 Kellner St) is decorated with psychedelic pictures of long-bearded Boers.

Getting There & Away

A number of airlines fly to Bloem from Cape Town or Jo'burg. **STA Travel** (☎ 051-444 6062; laudep@statravel.co.za; Mimosa Mall) can organise flights.

Translux, Greyhound, SA Roadlink, Intercape and Interstate run daily buses to Durban (R200, nine hours), Jo'burg/Pretoria (R150, five hours), Port Elizabeth (R230, nine hours), East London (R240, seven hours) and Cape Town (R380, 10 hours).

Minibus taxis leave from opposite the train station and head to Maseru, Lesotho (R45, three hours).

Shosholoza Meyl (☎ 0860-008 888; www.shosholozameyl.co.za, www.premierclasse.co.za) trains run weekly to/from Cape Town, Durban and Kimberley, and more frequently to/from Jo'burg, Port Elizabeth and East London.

NORTHERN CAPE

Covering nearly a third of the country, the vast and sparsely populated Northern Cape is South Africa's last great frontier. This is a land of stark contrasts, where the red sands of the Kalahari drift towards the Atlantic Coast, and the plains of the Upper Karoo collide with sun-scorched Namakwa's lunar landscape, famous for its spring wildflowers. Lions stalk prey across crimson plains in remote Kgalagadi Transfrontier Park at dawn; in the evening, big orange-ball sunsets set the stage for bright starry nights.

KIMBERLEY

☎ 053 / pop 171,000

An old diamond town with a chequered past, Kimberley is also the capital of the Northern Cape and definitely worth a few days' pause. Step inside one of the atmospheric old pubs with their dark smoky interiors and you'll feel you've been transported to the rough-and-ready diamond heyday of the late 19th century.

The hour-long tours of the world's largest hand-dug hole, the **Big Hole** (☎ 053-830 4417; West Circular Rd; admission R70; 🕘 8am-5pm, tours on the hour), start with a film on Kimberley's mining legacy, followed by a visit to the viewing platform, jutting out over the 800m gaping chasm. The coolest part of the tour is the simulated mining experience, and the partial reconstruction of Kimberley's 1880s mining camp is a surreal place for a stroll.

In a former jail, **Gum Tree Lodge** (☎ 053-832 8577; cnr Hull St & Bloemfontein Rd; dm from R100, s/d R120/240; 🐾)

offers large, basic self-catering flats with shared ablution facilities. Award-winning **Heerengracht Guesthouse** (☎ 053-831 1531; www.kelesedi.co.za; 42 Heerengracht St, Royldene; r incl breakfast R400-1200; ⊠ ⚐) has tasteful rooms on grassy grounds. In original late-19th-century diamond-rush buildings, rooms are perfectly Victorian down to the door-knobs at **Australian Arms Guesthouse** (☎ 053-830 4402; Big Hole Complex; r incl breakfast R800; ⊠).

Step back into Kimberley's mining hey-day at **Star of the West Hotel** (☎ 053-832 6463; North Circular Rd; mains R40-50; ⚑ breakfast, lunch & dinner), an atmospheric city staple that serves up hearty pub grub.

There are regular flights to Jo'burg and Cape Town on SA Express and SAAirlink. Three bus lines, including Translux, serve Jo'burg/Pretoria (R170, seven hours, daily) and Cape Town (from R360, 12 hours, daily). Minibus taxis service these and more local destinations.

UPINGTON
☎ 054 / pop 53,000
On the banks of the Senqu (Orange) River, orderly and prosperous Upington is a good place to catch your breath at either end of a long Kalahari slog. Wide boulevards slightly cluttered with supermarkets and chain stores line the centre of town, but on the side streets, lazy river views and endless rows of date palms create a calm and quiet atmosphere, perfect for an afternoon stroll (if the heat is not too stifling).

Die Eiland Holiday Resort (☎ 054-334 0286; tour ism@kharahais.gov.za; campsites R100, r from R200; ⚐), the best budget option, offers a range of huts, bungalows and shaded camping spots on tran-quil grounds adjacent to the eastern bank of the river. Right on the river with small but comfortable rooms is the **Affinity Guesthouse** (☎ 054-331 2101; www.affinityguesthouse.co.za; 4 Budler St; s/d R380/480; ⊠ ⚐).

SAAirlink (☎ 011-961 1700; www.saairlink.co.za) flies to/from Jo'burg and Cape Town. Buses run to Jo'burg and Pretoria (R360, 10 hours, daily), Windhoek (Namibia; R350, 12 hours, four times weekly) and Cape Town (R320, 10½ hours, four times weekly).

KGALAGADI TRANSFRONTIER PARK
A visit to the other-worldly **Kgalagadi Transfrontier Park** (☎ 054-561 0021; www.sanparks.org; adult/child R140/70), in your own vehicle or on a tour, is more than worth the effort it takes to get there. The scenery in this magical place is phenome-nal. Kgalagadi is the result of a merger between the former Kalahari-Gemsbok National Park in South Africa and the Mabuasehube-Gemsbok National Park in Botswana, forming one of Africa's largest protected wilderness areas, and the continent's first multinational park.

Visitors are restricted to four gravel/sand roads. Make sure to take one of the roads linking the rivers for unobstructed views of the empty expanses of the Kalahari. Visitors must remain in their cars, except at a small number of designated picnic spots.

The best time to visit is in June and July, when the days are coolest (below freezing at night) and the animals have been drawn to the bores along the dry riverbeds.

Inside the park there are three rest camps and seven luxury wilderness camps. All can be booked through **SAN Parks** (☎ 012-428 9111; www.sanparks.org). All rest camps have **campsites** (per 2 people R130, extra person R42) without electricity and with shared ablutions facilities. The camps also have a range of huts, bungalows and cot-tages. The wilderness camps, though much more expensive, give you the opportunity to really get off the beaten path.

The drive from Upington to Twee Rivieren gate is 250km, with about 60km on dirt roads.

SPRINGBOK
☎ 027 / pop 15,000
Springbok sits in a valley surrounded by harsh rocky hills that explode with colour in flower season. Outside of flower season there's little to see or do, although the town's remoteness and the desolate landscape are alluring. The nights are dramatically quiet, and with little light pol-lution, the stars are brilliantly bright.

Backpackers can shack up in dorm beds in the barn at cosy **Cat Nap Accommodation** (☎ 027-718 1905; Voortrekker St; dm R80, r from R400; ⊠), set in a spacious old house. **Annie's Cottage** (☎ 027-712 1451; annie@springbokinfo.com; 4 King St; r incl breakfast R600-1600; ⚐) has 10 lovely rooms and a quaint pool and garden area.

The simple, small **Godfather Restaurant** (☎ 027-718 1877; Voortrekker St; mains R25-50) serves everything from meat to sandwiches, and has a fun bar.

Intercape has four-times-weekly buses to Cape Town (R350, 7½ hours) and Windhoek (Namibia; R450, 12 hours) that leave from opposite the Springbok Lodge near the *kopje* (small hill). **VIP Taxis** (☎ 027-851 8780) operates a weekday taxi to/from Upington.

SOUTH AFRICA DIRECTORY

ACCOMMODATION

Whatever your budget, you'll generally find high standards, often for significantly less than you would pay for the equivalent in Europe or North America. Prices for a double room in this chapter are: budget – less than R400; midrange – R400 to R1000; top end – more than R1000. In Cape Town and some other more expensive places on the South Coast, these ranges move upward.

The main budget options are camping, backpackers hostels, self-catering cottages and community-run offerings such as homestays. The main caveat is that there aren't enough places in this category; away from tourist areas, sometimes the best budget option is camping.

Midrange accommodation is particularly good value, especially for B&Bs. Expect a private or semiprivate bathroom and a clean, comfortable room. Self-catering accommodation at national parks, usually in the midrange category, also tends to be good value.

At the top end, South Africa boasts some of the best wildlife lodges on the continent, as well as classic guesthouses and superb hotels. Places at this level offer all the amenities you would expect for prices that are similar to, or slightly less than, those you would pay in Europe or North America.

There are significant seasonal price variations, with rates rising steeply during the December–January school break, and again around Easter, when room prices often double and minimum stays are imposed. Advance bookings are essential during these times. Conversely, you can get some excellent deals during the winter low season, which is also the best time for wildlife-watching.

Minimum charges often apply at accommodation options in national parks and nature reserves, and at private reserves and lodges.

ACTIVITIES

Thanks to South Africa's diverse terrain and favourable climate, almost anything is possible – from ostrich riding to the world's highest bungee jump, and more standard activities like canoeing, kayaking, rafting, mountain biking, rock climbing, whale-watching and wildlife-viewing. Good facilities and instruction mean that most activities are accessible for anyone, whatever their experience level.

Diving

To the west, the main dive sites are around the Cape Peninsula, known for its many wrecks and giant kelp forests. To the east, the main area is the KwaZulu-Natal north coast where – particularly around Sodwana Bay – there are beautiful coral reefs and the chance to see dolphins, and sometimes whale sharks. There are several sites off the Eastern Cape coast near Port Elizabeth, and many resort towns along the Garden Route have diving schools.

The best time to dive the KwaZulu-Natal shoreline is from May to September, when visibility tends to be highest. Along the Atlantic seaboard, the water is cold year-round, but is at its most diveable, with many days of high visibility, between November and January/February. Strong currents and often windy conditions mean that advanced divers can find challenges all along the coast.

Hiking

South Africa is wonderful for hiking, with an excellent system of well-marked trails varied enough to suit any ability. Some trails have accommodation, ranging from basic camping areas to huts with electricity and running water, and all must be booked well in advance. Many trails have limits as to how many hikers can be on them at any one time.

Ezemvelo KZN Wildlife (☎ 033-845 1000; www.kznwildlife.com) controls most trails in KwaZulu-Natal. Elsewhere, trails are administered by **South African National (SAN) Parks** (☎ 012-426 5000; www.sanparks.org) or the various Forest Region authorities. To find out about local hiking clubs, contact **Hiking South Africa** (☎ 083-535 4538; www.hiking-south-africa.info).

Surfing

Most surfers will have heard of Jeffrey's Bay, but South Africa offers myriad alternatives, particularly along the Eastern Cape coast from Port Alfred northeastwards. The best time of the year for surfing the southern and eastern coasts is autumn and early winter (from about April to July).

For more information check out **Wavescape** (www.wavescape.co.za) and **Zig Zag** (www.zigzag.co.za), South Africa's main surf magazine.

SOUTH AFRICA

PRACTICALITIES

■ South Africa uses the metric system for weights and measures.

■ Access electricity (220–250V AC, 50Hz) with a three-pin adaptor (South Africa has a unique version with large, round pins), which is easy enough to find. Upmarket accommodation sometimes has European-style sockets.

■ Best weekly: *Mail & Guardian*. Best daily: the *Sowetan*. Others to look for: the *Sunday Independent*; the *Sunday Times*; the Johannesburg *Star*; and *Business Day*. Check out *Getaway* magazine for travel news.

■ Tune the TV to SABC for the news (SABC3 is mostly English). M-Net offers US films and series; e-TV carries alternative programs.

■ SABC radio broadcasts in 11 languages. BBC's World Service is available on some FM and AM stations.

BUSINESS HOURS

Banks 8.30am to 3.30pm Monday to Friday, 8.30am to 11am Saturday; many foreign-exchange bureaus open later
Businesses & shops 8.30am to 5pm Monday to Friday, 8.30am to 1pm Saturday; many supermarkets open later and also 9am to noon Sunday
Cafés 8am to 5pm
Government offices 8am to 4.30pm Monday to Friday
Restaurants 11.30am to 2.30pm and 7pm to 10pm

If an eatery has a closing day, it's usually Sunday or Monday. Exceptions to the above are noted in specific listings.

DANGERS & ANNOYANCES

Crime is the national obsession and, apart from car accidents, it's the major risk that you'll face in South Africa. However, try to keep things in perspective, and remember that despite the statistics and newspaper headlines, the majority of travellers visit the country without incident.

The risks are highest in Jo'burg, followed by some townships and other urban centres. Daylight muggings are common in certain sections of Jo'burg, and the city's metro train system has had a problem with violent crime.

In Jo'burg, and to a lesser extent in the other big cities, carjacking is a problem. The carjackers are almost always armed, and people have been killed for their vehicles. Stay alert, keep windows wound up and doors locked, and keep your taste in cars modest. If you're waiting at a red light after dark and you notice something suspicious, it's standard practice to check the junction is clear, and run the light.

If you get a failed transaction or anything irregular happens while making a payment

with a card, retrieve your card as quickly as possible and do not try the procedure again.

If arriving at ORTIA, ideally keep valuables in your hand luggage and vacuum-wrap your baggage, as items are sometimes pilfered from bags before they reach the carousel.

See p1138 for more advice.

EMBASSIES & CONSULATES

Most countries have their main embassy in Pretoria, with an office or consulate in Cape Town (which becomes the official embassy during Cape Town's parliamentary sessions). Some countries also maintain consulates in Jo'burg and Durban.

South Africa is a gold mine for travellers hunting for visas for other African countries.

The following list includes some of the more important embassies and consulates; most are open in the mornings only for visa services, usually between 9am and noon.

Australia Embassy in Pretoria (Map pp1056-7; ☎ 012-423 6000; www.australia.co.za; 292 Orient St, Arcadia)

Botswana High Commission in Pretoria (Map pp1056-7; ☎ 012-430 9640; 24 Amos St, Colbyn); Cape Town (Map pp1026-7; ☎ 021-421 1045; 13th fl, Metropolitan Centre, City Bowl); Jo'burg (Map p1052; ☎ 011-403 3748; 2nd fl, Future Bank Bldg, 122 De Korte St, Braamfontein)

Canada High Commission in Pretoria (Map pp1056-7; ☎ 012-422 3000; www.dfait-maeci.gc.ca/southafrica; 1103 Arcadia St, Hatfield)

France Embassy in Pretoria (off Map pp1056-7; ☎ 012-425 1600; france@ambafrance-rsa.org; 250 Melk St, New Muckleneuk); Cape Town (Map pp1026-7; ☎ 021-423 1575; www.consulfrance-lecap.org; 78 Queen Victoria St, Gardens); Jo'burg (Map p1050; ☎ 011-778 5600; 191 Jan Smuts Ave, Rosebank)

Germany Embassy in Pretoria (Map pp1056-7; ☎ 012-427 8900; www.pretoria.diplo.de; 180 Blackwood St, Arcadia); Cape

Town (Map pp1026-7; ☎ 021-405 3000; www.kapstadt. diplo.de; 19th fl, Triangle House, 22 Riebeeck St, City Bowl)
Ireland Embassy in Pretoria (Map pp1056-7; ☎ 012-342 5062; 1st fl, Southern Life Plaza, 1059 Schoeman St)
Lesotho High Commission in Pretoria (Map pp1056-7; ☎ 012-460 7648; 391 Anderson St, Menlo Park); Jo'burg (Map p1052; ☎ 011-339 3653; 76 Juta St, Indent House, Braamfontein); Durban (Map pp1038-9; ☎ 031-307 2168; 2nd fl, Westguard House, cnr Dr Pixley KaSeme/West St & Dorothy Nyembe/Gardiner St)
Mozambique High Commission in Pretoria (Map pp1056-7; ☎ 012-401 0300; 529 Edmond St, Arcadia); Jo'burg (Map p1050; ☎ 011-336 1819; 18 Hurlingham Rd, Illovo); Cape Town (Map pp1026-7; ☎ 021-426 2944; 10th fl, Pinnacle Bldg, 8 Burg St, City Bowl); Durban (Map pp1038-9; ☎ 031-304 0200; Room 520, 320 Dr Pixley KaSeme/West St); Mbombela (Nelspruit) (☎ 013-752 7396; 43 Brown St)
Namibia High Commission in Pretoria (Map pp1056-7; ☎ 012-481 9118; www.namibia.org.na; 197 Blackwood St, Arcadia)
Netherlands Embassy in Pretoria (Map pp1056-7; ☎ 012-425 4500; www.dutchembassy.co.za; 210 Queen Wilhelmina Ave, New Muckleneuk); Cape Town (Map pp1026-7; ☎ 021-421 5660; www.dutchconsulate.co.za; 100 Strand St, City Bowl)
New Zealand Embassy in Pretoria (Map pp1056-7; ☎ 012-342 8656; Block C, Hatfield Gardens, 1110 Arcadia St)
Swaziland High Commission in Pretoria (Map pp1056-7; ☎ 012-344 1910; 715 Government Ave, Arcadia); Jo'burg (Map p1052; ☎ 011-403 7372, 011-403 2036; 6th fl, Braamfontein Centre, 23 Jorissen St)
UK High Commission in Pretoria (Map pp1056-7; ☎ 012-421 7600; http://ukinsouthafrica.fco.gov.uk; 255 Hill St, Arcadia); Cape Town (Map pp1026-7; ☎ 021-405 2400; Southern Life Centre, 8 Riebeeck St, City Bowl); Durban (Map pp1038-9; ☎ 031-572 7259; FWJK Court, 86 Armstrong Rd, La Lucia Ridge)
USA Embassy in Pretoria (Map pp1056-7; ☎ 012-431 4000; http://southafrica.usembassy.gov; 877 Pretorius St, Arcadia); Cape Town (Map pp1024-5; ☎ 021-702 7300; 2 Reddam Ave, Westlake); Jo'burg (Map p1050; ☎ 011-644 8000; 1 River St, Killarney); Durban (Map pp1038-9; ☎ 031-304 4737; 29th fl, Durban Bay House, 333 Smith St)
Zimbabwe High Commission in Pretoria (Map pp1056-7; ☎ 012-342 5125; zimpret@lantic.net; 798 Merton St, Arcadia); Jo'burg (Map p1052; ☎ 011-838 2156; admin@ zimbabweconsulate.co.za; 17th fl, 20 Anderson St)

HOLIDAYS

New Year's Day 1 January
Human Rights Day 21 March
Good Friday March/April
Easter Sunday March/April
Easter Monday March/April
Family Day 17 April
Constitution or Freedom Day 27 April
Workers' Day 1 May
Youth Day 16 June

Women's Day 9 August
Heritage Day 24 September
Day of Reconciliation 16 December
Christmas Day 25 December
Day of Goodwill 26 December

INTERNET ACCESS

Internet access is widely available. Accommodation often offers a computer with access and most towns have an internet cafe. Costs average R30 to R40 per hour. Many accommodation options, cafes and eateries have wi-fi, often for free. Branches of PostNet normally have a few terminals.

MONEY

South Africa's currency is the rand (R), which is divided into 100 cents. The coins are one, two, five, 10, 20 and 50 cents, and R1, R2 and R5. The notes are R10, R20, R50, R100 and R200. There have been forgeries of the R200 note, and some businesses are reluctant to accept them.

The best currencies to bring are US dollars, euros or British pounds in a mixture of cash and travellers cheques, plus a Visa or MasterCard for withdrawing money from ATMs.

ATMs are widespread, both in the cities and beyond, but stash some cash if visiting rural areas and be wary of scams.

Credit cards are widely accepted, especially MasterCard and Visa. Nedbank is an official Visa agent, and Standard Bank is a MasterCard agent; both have branches nationwide.

Because South Africa has a reputation for scams, many banks abroad automatically prevent transactions in the country. Particularly if you plan to use a credit card here, inform your bank of your travel plans before leaving home.

Keep at least some of your exchange receipts as you'll need these to convert leftover rand when you leave.

TELEPHONE

South Africa has good telephone facilities. Local calls are inexpensive (about R1 for three minutes), whereas domestic long-distance calls (from about R2 per minute) and international calls (from R7 per minute to Europe) are pricier. Phonecards are widely available. There are also private phone centres where you can pay cash for your call, but at double the rate of public phones. International calls are cheaper between 8pm and 8am Monday to Friday, and over the weekend. For reverse-charge calls, dial ☎ 0900.

The mobile-phone network covers most of the country, and there are GSM and 3G digital networks.

TOURIST INFORMATION

The main government tourism organisation is **South African Tourism** (☎ 011-895 3000, 083-123 6789; www.southafrica.net), which has a helpful website with links and news of upcoming events.

For more details on individual provinces, there are provincial tourism organisations, of varying quality. Additionally, almost every town in the country has a tourist office – often private entities, surviving on commissions.

Provincial tourist offices:

Eastern Cape Tourism Board (☎ 043-701 9600; www.ectourism.co.za)

Free State Tourism Board (☎ 051-447 1362; www.dteea.fs.gov.za)

Gauteng Tourism Authority (☎ 011-639 1600; www.gauteng.net)

KwaZulu-Natal Tourism Authority (☎ 031-366 7500; www.kzn.org.za)

Limpopo Tourism Board (☎ 015-290 7300, 0860-730 730; www.golimpopo.com)

Mpumalanga Tourism Authority (☎ 013-759 5300; www.mpumalanga.com)

North-West Province Parks & Tourism Board (☎ 018-397 1500, 0861-111 866; www.tourismnorthwest.co.za)

Northern Cape Tourism Authority (☎ 053-832 2657; www.northerncape.org.za)

Western Cape Tourism Board (☎ 021-426 5639; www.tourismcapetown.co.za)

TRAVELLERS WITH DISABILITIES

South Africa is one of the best destinations on the continent for disabled travellers, with an ever-expanding network of facilities catering to those who are mobility or vision impaired. **South African National (SAN) Parks** (☎ 012-426 5000; www.sanparks.org) has a detailed and inspirational overview of accommodation and trail accessibility for the mobility impaired at all its parks.

Another helpful initial contact is the **National Council for Persons with Physical Disabilities in South Africa** (☎ 011-726 8040; www.ncppdsa.co.za).

VISAS

Visitors on holiday from most Commonwealth countries (including Australia and the UK), most Western European countries, Japan and the USA don't require visas. Instead, you'll be issued with a free entry permit on arrival, valid for a stay of up to 90 days.

If you aren't entitled to an entry permit, you'll need to get a visa (R425 or US$47 or €43) before you arrive. These aren't issued at the borders, and must be obtained at a South African embassy or consulate, found in most countries (see http://tinyurl.com/ydzbg8d for a list of South Africa's overseas missions). Allow at least a month for processing; for more information, visit the **Department of Home Affairs website** (www.home-affairs.gov.za).

Visas for Onward Travel

Many nationalities don't require a visa to enter Lesotho for up to two weeks, Swaziland for up to 60 days, Namibia for up to 90 days, and Botswana for up to 30 days. For Mozambique, it's cheaper to pick up a visa on the border (R180 for a one-month, single-entry visa) than using the same-day service available at offices such as the consulate in Mbombela (Nelspruit). Zimbabwe visas should be available at the border for most nationalities, although given the country's volatility, it may be worth applying at the High Commission in Pretoria.

If you'll be arranging your visa in advance: Zimbabwean visas take at least a week to issue in South Africa; those for Namibia take two to three days; and those for Botswana take between four and 14 days. Nonexpress Mozambique visas take one week.

See the relevant country chapters for more details.

TRANSPORT IN SOUTH AFRICA

GETTING THERE & AWAY

Air

The major air hub for South Africa, and for the surrounding region, is **OR Tambo International Airport** (ORTIA; ☎ 011-921 6911; www.airports.co.za). **Cape Town International Airport** (CPT; ☎ 021-937 1200; www.airports.co.za) receives numerous direct flights from Europe, and is becoming an increasingly important gateway. **Mpumalanga Kruger International Airport** (MQP; ☎ 013-753 7500; www.kmiairport.co.za), near Mbombela (Nelspruit) and Kruger National Park, handles several regional flights, as will King Shaka International Airport when it replaces Durban International Airport in 2010.

National airline **South African Airways** (SAA; airline code SA; ☎ 0861-359 722, 011-978 5313; www.flysaa.com) has an excellent route network and safety record. In addition to its international routes, it operates regional flights together with its subsidiaries **SAAirlink** (☎ 011-961 1700; www.saairlink.co.za) and **SA Express** (☎ 011-978 9900; www.flysax.com).

Other international carriers flying to/from Jo'burg include the following:

Air France (AF; ☎ 0861-340 340; www.airfrance.co.za)

British Airways (BA; www.britishairways.com) Jo'burg (☎ 011-441 8400); Cape Town (☎ 021-936 9000) Also serves Cape Town.

Cathay Pacific (CX; ☎ 011-700 8900; www.cathay pacific.com)

Egyptair (MS; www.egyptair.com.eg) Jo'burg (☎ 011-880 4360); Cape Town (☎ 021-390 2202)

Emirates Airlines (EK; ☎ 0861-364 728, 011-303 1951; www.emirates.com)

Kenya Airways (KQ; ☎ 011-571 8832, 011-928 8529; www.kenya-airways.com)

KLM (KL; ☎ 0860-247 747, 011-881 9696; www.klm.com) Also serves Cape Town.

Lufthansa (LH; ☎ 0861-842 538; www.lufthansa.com) Also serves Cape Town.

Qantas (QF; ☎ 011-441 8550; www.qantas.com.au)

Singapore Airlines (SQ; www.singaporeair.com) Jo'burg (☎ 011-880 8560); Cape Town (☎ 021-674 0601) Also serves Cape Town.

Virgin Atlantic (VS; ☎ 011-340 3400; www.virgin -atlantic.com) Also serves Cape Town.

Land

See opposite for information about visa requirements for onward travel to South Africa's neighbouring countries.

BOTSWANA

From Jo'burg/Pretoria, **Intercape** (☎ 0861-287 287; www.intercape.co.za) runs daily buses to Gaborone (from R170, 6¾ hours). A less safe and comfortable alternative is one of the minibuses that run throughout the day between Jo'burg and Gaborone (about R200, 6¾ hours) via Mafikeng (North-West Province). In Jo'burg, departures are from Park Station. To do the trip in stages, take a bus from Jo'burg to Mafikeng, from where there are direct minibuses over the border to Lobatse (1½ hours) and Gabarone (2½ hours).

LESOTHO

Big Sky Coaches (www.bigskycoaches.co.za) runs daily buses between Bloemfontein and Maseru Bridge (R40, three hours), with express weekend services. Via minibus taxi, the quickest connections are from Bloemfontein to Botshabelo (R35, one hour), and then from there to Maseru (R20, 1½

hours). There are also daily minibus taxis and at least three buses weekly between Jo'burg and Maseru (six to seven hours).

Other useful connections include a daily minibus taxi between Mokhotlong (Lesotho) and Underberg (South Africa) via Sani Pass; and several taxis daily between Qacha's Nek (Lesotho) and Matatiele (South Africa; about R20, 45 minutes).

MOZAMBIQUE

Several large 'luxury' buses, including Greyhound, Intercape and Translux, run daily between Jo'burg/Pretoria and Maputo via Mbombela (Nelspruit) and Komatipoort (R180 to R300, eight to nine hours). Intercape also has a three-times-weekly service from Durban to Maputo (R210), via stops in KwaZulu-Natal and Swaziland.

Alternatively, the **Baz Bus** (☎ 021-439 2323; www.bazbus.com) links Jo'burg/Pretoria, Mbombela (Nelspruit) and Durban with Mbabane (Swaziland), from where you can get a minibus taxi to Maputo.

Shosholoza Meyl (☎ 0860-008 888, 011-774 4555; www.shosholozameyl.co.za) runs a daily (except Saturday) train linking Jo'burg and Komatipoort via Pretoria and Mbombela (Nelspruit; economy class only, 11 hours). Trains in both directions travel overnight. Once at Komatipoort, you can change to the Mozambican train to Maputo (economy class only, five hours), but it's much quicker to take a minibus (1½ hours).

NAMIBIA

Intercape (☎ 0861-287 287, 021-380 4400; www.intercape.co.za) runs four times weekly between Cape Town and Windhoek (from R540, 21 hours) via Springbok. The **Trans-Namib** (☎ in Namibia 061-298 2657; www.transnamib.com.na/Starline.htm) 'StarLine' train runs twice weekly between Upington and Keetmanshoop (Namibia; 12½ hours), 12 hours southeast of Windhoek by train.

SWAZILAND

The best connections are on the **Baz Bus** (☎ 021-439 2323; www.bazbus.com), which runs from Jo'burg/Pretoria to Mbabane via Mbombela (Nelspruit), and from Swaziland down the KwaZulu-Natal coast to Durban.

Minibus taxis run daily between Jo'burg (Park Station), Mbabane and Manzini (R160, four hours), and between Manzini and Durban (R140, eight hours).

ZIMBABWE

Greyhound (☎ 083-915 9000; www.greyhound.co.za) runs buses from Jo'burg/Pretoria to Harare via Limpopo and Bulawayo. On both the north-bound and southbound services, passengers can get on but not disembark before the bus crosses the border.

GETTING AROUND
Air

In addition to being the international flagship carrier, **South African Airways** (SAA; ☎ 0861-359 722, 011-978 5313; www.flysaa.com) is the main domestic carrier, with an extensive network of routes. Its subsidiaries, **SAAirlink** (☎ 011-961 1700; www.saairlink.co.za) and **SA Express** (☎ 011-978 9900; www.flysax.com), also service domestic routes.

Domestic fares aren't cheap; one way to save significantly is to book online. Other airlines flying domestically:

1time (☎ 0861-345 345; www.1time.aero) No-frills flights linking Jo'burg, Cape Town, Durban, East London, George and Port Elizabeth. Also offers car rentals.

Comair (☎ 011-921 0222; www.comair.co.za) Operates British Airways flights in southern Africa, and has flights linking Cape Town, Durban, Jo'burg and Port Elizabeth.

Kulula.com (☎ 0861-444 144; www.kulula.com) No-frills flights linking Jo'burg, Cape Town, Durban, George and Port Elizabeth. Also offers hotel bookings and car rentals.

Mango (☎ 0861-162 646; ww5.flymango.com) No-frills flights linking Jo'burg, Cape Town, Durban and Bloemfontein. Also offers car rentals and hotel bookings.

Bus

Buses in South Africa aren't the deal that they are in many other countries. However, together with the less-appealing minibus taxis, they're the main form of public transport, with a reliable and reasonably comfortable network linking all major cities. Note that many long-distance services run through the night; travellers should take care of their valuables and women might feel more comfortable near the front of the bus.

An alternative to the standard bus lines is the **Baz Bus** (☎ 021-439 2323; www.bazbus.com), catering almost exclusively to backpackers and travellers. It offers hop-on, hop-off fares and hostel-to-hostel service between Cape Town and Jo'burg via the Northern Drakensberg, Durban and the Garden Route. It also has a loop from Durban via Zululand, Swaziland and Mbombela (Nelspruit; near Kruger National Park) to Jo'burg. Point-to-point fares are more expensive than on the other major lines, but

can work out more economically if you take advantage of the hop-on/hop-off feature. It's also worth checking out its travel passes (one/two/three weeks R1300/2300/3100).

The Baz Bus is a convenient option, and it has a strong presence in South Africa's hostels, but using it consigns you to a backpacker bubble. It's worth giving some thought to whether you want your trip to take that form.

Along with the main long-distance bus operator **Translux** (☎ 011-774 3333, 0861-589 282; www.translux.co.za), **Greyhound** (☎ 083-915 9000; www.greyhound.co.za), **Intercape** (☎ 0861-287 287, 021-380 4400; www.intercape.co.za) and **SA Roadlink** (☎ 011-333 2223; www.saroadlink.co.za) have services connecting the major cities. In partnership with Translux, no-frills **City to City** (☎ 011-774 3333, 0861-589 282; www.translux.co.za) has taken over the routes that once carried people between the homelands and the cities during the apartheid regime.

Prices rise during school holidays; all lines offer student and senior-citizen discounts, and Intercape has backpacker and ISIC discounts. Inquire about travel passes if you'll be taking several bus journeys, and always check with the bus companies to see if they are running any specials, which can sometimes save you up to 40%.

For the main lines, reservations should be made at least 24 hours in advance, and as far in advance as possible during peak periods. It's sometimes possible to get a seat at the last minute, but don't count on it. You can buy tickets for the major companies at branches of Shoprite/Checkers supermarkets and **Computicket** (☎ 083-915 8000; www.computicket.com).

Car & Motorcycle

South Africa is ideal for driving, and away from the main bus and train routes, having your own wheels is the best way to get around. If you're in a group, it's also often the most economical. Most major roads are in excellent condition, and off the main routes there are interesting back roads to explore.

Cars drive on the left-hand side of the road in South Africa. You can use your driving licence from your home country if it is in English (or you have a certified translation) and it carries your photo.

Petrol costs around R8 per litre. There is no self-service; an attendant will fill up your tank for you, clean your windows and ask if your oil, water or tyres need checking. If they do check your oil etc, tip them between R2 and R5. Along main routes there are plenty of petrol stations, many open 24 hours.

South Africa has a horrific road-accident record, with the annual death toll around 10,000 (although some estimates place it at over 15,000). The N1 between Cape Town and Beaufort West is considered to be the most dangerous stretch of road in the country. The main hazards are your fellow motorists, particularly minibus taxi drivers, who often operate under pressure on little sleep. Animals and pedestrians on the roads are another hazard, especially in rural areas such as the Wild Coast.

HIRE

Car rental is relatively inexpensive in South Africa. Rates start at about R200 per day, including insurance and 200km free per day (unlimited mileage in some cases); rental of a 4WD starts below R900 per day.

All the car-rental companies accept major credit cards, and most do not accept debit cards. Local operations are often less expensive; the budget domestic airlines and backpackers' hostels can also arrange good deals. Alternatively, try booking and prepaying through one of the international providers before coming to South Africa.

Abba (☎ 011-917 3037; www.abbacarrental.co.za)

Around About Cars (☎ 0860-422 4022; www.aroundaboutcars.co.za)

First Car Rental (☎ 011-230 9999; www.firstcarrental.co.za)

Tempest (☎ 011-552 3900; www.tempestcarhire.co.za)

Xpress Car & Van Rental (☎ 0861-116 000; www.xpressrental.co.za)

Local Transport

BUS

Cape Town, Jo'burg, Pretoria and several other urban areas have city bus systems. Fares are cheap, and routes, which are signposted, are extensive. Services usually stop running early in the evening, and there aren't many buses on weekends.

MINIBUS TAXI

Minibus taxis run almost everywhere – within cities, to the suburbs and to neighbouring towns. They leave when full and, happily, 'full' in South Africa isn't as cramped as it is in many neighbouring countries. Most accommodate 14 to 16 people. Driving standards and vehicle conditions often leave a lot to be desired, and there are many accidents. Things have settled down following a spate of gangster-style shoot-outs between rival companies, but minibuses in some areas and on some routes are still considered unsafe; reports of muggings and other incidents remain a regular feature. Terminals such as the one at Jo'burg's Park Station are notorious mugging zones. In cities such as Cape Town, minibus taxis are a handy and popular way to get around during daylight hours, but always seek local advice on lines and areas to avoid.

TRAIN

South Africa's **Shosholoza Meyl** (☎ 0860-008 888, 011-774 4555; www.shosholozameyl.co.za, www.premierclasse.co.za) offers regular services connecting major cities, with 'premier-', 'tourist-' and economy-class trains available. Premier class is a luxurious experience, offering a more affordable alternative to the country's premium lines. Tourist class is highly recommended – a scenic and secure, albeit sometimes slow, way to travel.

On overnight journeys such as Jo'burg–Cape Town, tourist-class fares include a sleeping berth (with a small additional charge for bedding hire). Couples are normally given two-berth coupés; single travellers and larger groups are put in four-berth compartments. If you are travelling alone and you want a coupé to yourself, you could buy two tickets. Meals and drinks are available in the dining car, or in your compartment.

Economy class does not have sleeping compartments (with the exception of the Jo'burg–East London service) and is not a comfortable or safe option for overnight travel.

Tickets must be booked at least 24 hours in advance (you can book up to three months in advance). Bookings can be made by phone (not as simple as it sounds, as you have to deposit the payment in Shosholoza Meyl's bank account and fax the deposit slip) or at train stations. Timetables can and do change.

Some sample fares: premier class Durban–Jo'burg R750 to R1100; tourist class Cape Town–Jo'burg R350; economy class Jo'burg–Musina (Messina) R110.

Swaziland

Embedded between Mozambique and South Africa, the kingdom of Swaziland is one of the smallest countries in Africa. What the country lacks in size, however, it makes up for in its rich culture and heritage, and relaxed ambience. With its laid-back, warm and personable people and relative lack of racial animosities, it's a complete change of pace from its larger neighbours.

Visitors can enjoy rewarding and delightfully low-key wildlife-watching, stunning mountain panoramas, adrenaline-boosting activities and lively traditions. Swaziland also boasts superb walking and high-quality handicrafts.

Overseeing the kingdom is King Mswati III, one of three remaining monarchs in Africa. The monarchy has its critics but, combined with the Swazis' distinguished history of resistance to the Boers, the British and the Zulus, it has fostered a strong sense of national pride, and local culture is flourishing. This is exemplified in its national festivals: the Incwala ceremony and the Umhlanga (Reed) dance.

The excellent road system makes Swaziland easy to access and navigate. Accommodation includes a decent network of hostels, family-friendly hotels and upscale retreats. Many travellers make a flying visit on their way to South Africa's Kruger National Park, but it's well worth lingering here if you can.

FAST FACTS

- **Area** 17,365 sq km
- **ATMs** In Mbabane and Manzini
- **Borders** Mozambique, South Africa
- **Budget** US$30 to US$60 per day
- **Capital** Mbabane
- **Languages** English, Swati
- **Money** Lilangeni; US$1 = E7.57, €1 = E10.66
- **Population** 900,000
- **Seasons** Wet (October to March), dry (May to August)
- **Telephone** Country code ☎ 268; international code ☎ 00
- **Time** GMT/UTC +2
- **Visa** Not required for most nationalities

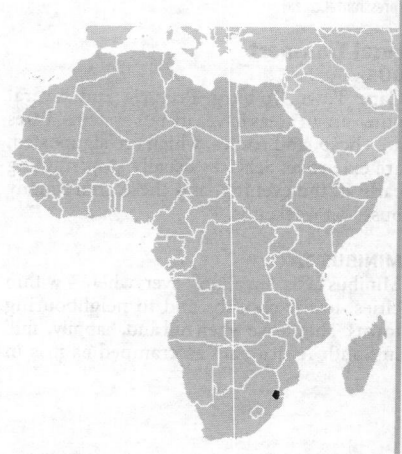

HOW MUCH?

- **Traditional dance** US$15
- **Internet per hour** US$3.30
- **Coffee** US$1 to US$2
- **Batik hanging** US$10
- **Basket** US$5

LONELY PLANET INDEX

- **1L petrol** US$0.90 (but fluctuates)
- **1L bottled water** US$0.90
- **Bottle of beer** US$1 to US$2
- **Souvenir T-shirt** US$10
- **Barbecued maize** US$0.50

HIGHLIGHTS

- **Mkhaya Game Reserve** (p1076) Spot black rhinos in the wild, one of Africa's great wildlife experiences.
- **Ezulwini and Malkerns Valleys** (p1074) Revel in a royal experience in the regal heartland of Swaziland and splurge on some handicrafts.
- **Usutu River** (p1076) Shoot the rapids or drift down the river through stunning gorges on a white-water rafting trip.
- **Malolotja Nature Reserve** (p1078) Hike in this tantalising area of genuine, unspoilt wilderness.
- **Mlilwane Wildlife Sanctuary** (p1074) Cycle or meander in the wilderness and relax in its bargain lodges.

CLIMATE & WHEN TO GO

The rainy season, from October to March, sees torrential thunderstorms, especially in the western mountains, and temperatures on the lowveld are very hot, often over 40°C; in the high country the temperatures are lower and in the dry season, May to August, it can get cool. Winter nights on the lowveld are sometimes very cold.

Try to avoid visiting rain-soaked Swaziland during the wet season (December to April). The best time to visit is in May, June or October, but bring something warm.

ITINERARIES

- **One Week** A half-day in Mbabane (p1072) is plenty to get your bearings. Spend two days poking around the pretty Ezulwini and Malkerns Valleys (p1074), including Lobamba (p1074), and make a trip into the relaxing Mlilwane Wildlife Sanctuary (p1074). If you have time and you want to see rare black rhinos in the wild, continue east to the stunning Mkhaya Game Reserve (p1076).
- **Two Weeks** Do the one-week itinerary, plus view wildlife at the extensive Hlane Royal National Park (p1076) and Mlawula Nature Reserve (p1077). On your circular route back to Mbabane, take a detour to the remote Bulembu, then Piggs Peak (p1077) for its handicrafts, and hike in Malolotja Nature Reserve (p1078), an unspoiled wilderness area.

HISTORY

In eastern Swaziland archaeologists have discovered human bones dating back 110,000 years, but the ancestors of the modern Swazi people arrived relatively recently.

During the great Bantu migrations into southern Africa, one group, the Nguni, moved down the east coast. A clan settled near what is now Maputo in Mozambique, and a dynasty was founded by the Dlamini family. In the mid-18th century, increasing pressure from other Nguni clans forced King Ngwane III to lead his people south to what is now southern Swaziland. The next king, Sobhuza I, withdrew under pressure from the Zulus to the Ezulwini Valley, which today remains the centre of Swazi royalty and ritual. When King Sobhuza I died in 1839, Swaziland was twice its present size. Trouble with the Zulu continued, although the next king, Mswazi (or Mswati), managed to unify the whole kingdom. By the time he died in 1868, the Swazi nation was secure. Mswazi's subjects called themselves Swazis, meaning 'people of Mswazi', and the name stuck.

European Interference

The arrival of increasing numbers of Europeans from the mid-19th century brought new problems. Mswazi's successor, Mbandzeni, inherited a kingdom rife with European carpetbaggers – hunters, traders, missionaries and farmers, many of whom leased large expanses of land.

The Pretoria Convention of 1881 guaranteed Swaziland's 'independence' but also defined its borders, and Swaziland lost large

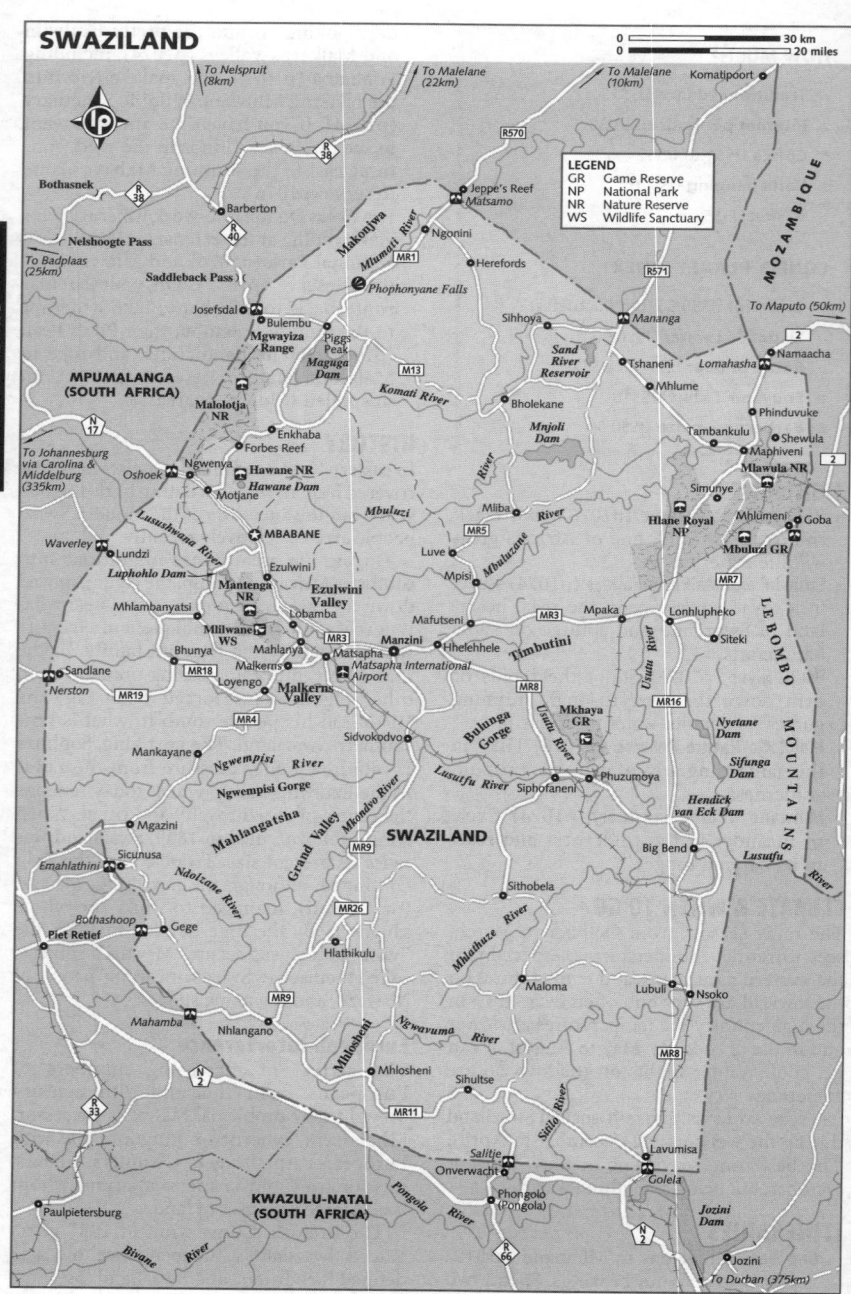

chunks of territory. 'Independence' meant that both the British and the Boers administered their various interests in Swaziland: the result was chaos. The Boer administration collapsed with the 1899–1902 Anglo-Boer War, and the British took control of Swaziland as a protectorate.

During this time, King Sobhuza II was only a young child, but Labotsibeni, his mother, acted as regent until her son took over in 1921. Labotsibeni encouraged Swazis to buy back their land, and many sought work in the Witwatersrand mines (near Johannesburg) to raise money.

Independence

In 1960 King Sobhuza II proposed the creation of a legislative council, composed of elected Europeans, and a national council formed in accordance with Swazi culture. The Mbokodvo (Grindstone) National Movement pledged to maintain traditional Swazi culture but also to eschew racial discrimination. When the British agreed to elections in 1964, Mbokodvo won a majority and, at the next elections in 1967, won all the seats. Swaziland became independent on 6 September 1968.

The country's constitution was largely the work of the British. In 1973 the king suspended it on the grounds that it did not accord with Swazi culture. He also dissolved all political parties. Four years later the parliament reconvened under a new constitution that vested all power in the king. Sobhuza II, at that time the world's longest-reigning monarch, died in 1982. In keeping with Swazi tradition, a strictly enforced 75-day period of mourning was announced by Dzeliwe (Great She-Elephant), the most senior of his hundred wives. Only commerce essential to the life of the nation was allowed.

Choosing a successor wasn't easy – Sobhuza II had fathered more than 600 children, thereby creating hundreds of potential kings. Prince Makhosetive, born in 1968, was finally chosen and crowned King Mswati III in 1986.

Swaziland Today

The king continues his role as absolute monarch. Following his predecessor's style, Mswati III dissolved parliament in 1992 and Swaziland was again governed by a traditional tribal assembly, the Liqoqo. Since then, democratic reform has begun with the drafting – albeit restrictive – of a constitution. Despite the increasing agitation for faster change, many reformers propose a constitutional king in a democratic system of government.

In September 2008 the king and government were criticised over the country's lavish 40:40 celebrations, which jointly marked the king's 40th birthday and the Swazi nation's 40 years of independence from Britain.

Swaziland has one of the world's highest HIV infection rates, although in recent years it has stabilised; around 26% of the adult population is HIV positive and the average life expectancy is currently 37 years. Figures vary widely, but it's predicted that tens of thousands of children have lost either one or both parents to the disease.

CULTURE

Swazis have an extremely strong sense of identity and pride. Social and cultural cohesion is maintained by a system of age-related royal regiments. Boys graduate from regiment to regiment as they grow older. This minimises the potentially divisive differences between clans, while emphasising loyalty to the king and nation.

The nonconfrontational, good-humoured and religious Swazis dislike embarrassment of any kind. Although there is widespread dissatisfaction with the lack of progress in their country's current socioeconomic climate, they tend to dislike outsiders meddling in internal political and social affairs and cultural practices. Despite constant controversy around the king, he represents the symbolic head of the Swazi family and, as such, he is generally highly regarded – disrespect for him can be interpreted as a lack of respect for the identity of the Swazi themselves.

As in other parts of Africa, the extended family is integral to a person's life. While polygamy is permitted and exists, it is not always practised. Traditional marriage allows for the husband to take a number of wives, although many Swazis also follow Western marriage conventions, rejecting polygamy but permitting divorce.

Many people in rural areas continue to live in the traditional beehive huts in homestead arrangements.

Schooling is not compulsory, with the rate of attendance decreasing due to social circumstances, particularly due to the HIV/AIDS epidemic.

People
Almost all people are Swazi (although there are about 70 distinct subgroups). The rest are Zulu, Tsonga-Shangaan and European. The dominant clan is the Dlamini – it's kind of the equivalent of having the name 'Smith' in anglophone countries, and you'll meet your fair share of them all over the country.

Around 70% of the population is Zionist (a mix of Christianity and traditional indigenous worship), with Roman Catholics, Anglicans and Methodists making up the balance. Muslims, Baha'i and Jewish faiths have small followings, too.

Arts & Crafts
Swaziland's handicrafts include jewellery, pottery, weapons and implements. Woven grass wares, such as *liqhaga* (grass-ware 'bottles') and mats, are popular, as are wooden items, ranging from bowls to knobkerries.

Dance and music are an integral part of Swazi cultural festivals. The *sibhaca* is a vigorous foot-stamping dance performed by males.

FOOD & DRINK
Swaziland isn't a gourmet's paradise, but you won't eat too badly. Tourist areas of the Malkerns and Ezulwini Valleys feature good international dishes and seafood. In more-remote areas, African staples, such as stew and pap (also known as *mealie meal*), are common.

RINGING IN CHANGES – NEW TELEPHONE NUMBERS

At the time of going to print, Swaziland announced changes to its telephone system.

As of 1 April 2010 all mobile (cell) numbers in Swaziland will have a prefix of ☎ 7. Previously all MTN mobile numbers in Swaziland would have started with ☎ 6, as in ☎ 602 0261; this number will now be ☎ 7602 0261.

Landline numbers will also be changing – all landline numbers will be prefixed with a ☎ 2. The implementation date for landlines is yet to be confirmed.

In this chapter, we've used the old system for landline numbers and the new system for mobile-phone numbers.

ENVIRONMENT
Swaziland has a wide range of ecological zones, from montane forest in the northwest to savannah scrub in the east. Western Swaziland is highveld, consisting mainly of short, sharp mountains; the centre and east of the country are plains, where plantations of sugar cane dominate the landscape. Further east, the harsh Lebombo Mountains form the border with Mozambique.

Conservation can come from the most unlikely sources. The monarchy reserved some areas for hunting; these preserve the remnants of indigenous flora (including 14% of the recorded plant life in southern Africa) and reintroduced animals (including elephants, warthogs, rhinos and lions) in parks such as Hlane Royal National Park, Mlilwane Wildlife Sanctuary and Mkhaya Game Reserve (these fall under the banner of 'Big Game Parks').

Swaziland has about a third of the non-marine mammal species in southern Africa.

Environmental issues include overgrazing of cattle, soil erosion, illegal hunting (see the boxed text, p1077) and the loss of certain indigenous plants sought for natural medicines.

MBABANE

pop 60,200
Swaziland's capital, Mbabane (pronounced mba-*baa*-nay), is pretty nondescript and there isn't that much to see or do here. It's in a pleasant setting in the Dlangeni Hills. These make Mbabane cooler than Manzini, which is one reason why the British moved their administrative centre here from Manzini in 1902. The adjacent Ezulwini and Malkerns Valleys have plenty of attractions.

ORIENTATION
Mbabane is a little disjointed. The main street is Gwamile St, but most things are available in Swazi Plaza, off Western Distributor Rd, and The Mall on Plaza Mall Dr.

INFORMATION
Internet access is available in a few places in town, including The Mall. Banks with ATMs include First National Bank, Nedbank and Standard Bank; these are in Swazi Plaza.
Mbabane Clinic (☎ 404 2423; St Michael's Rd) Medical service.

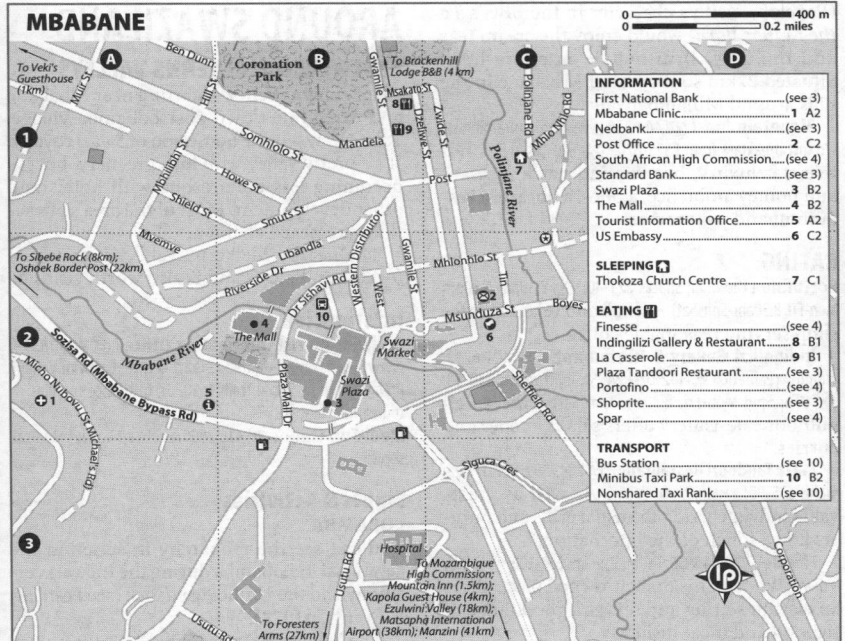

MBABANE

| 0 | 400 m |
| 0 | 0.2 miles |

INFORMATION

First National Bank	(see 3)
Mbabane Clinic	**1** A2
Nedbank	(see 3)
Post Office	**2** C2
South African High Commission	(see 4)
Standard Bank	(see 3)
Swazi Plaza	**3** B2
The Mall	**4** B2
Tourist Information Office	**5** A2
US Embassy	**6** C2

SLEEPING

Thokoza Church Centre	**7** C1

EATING

Finesse	(see 4)
Indingilizi Gallery & Restaurant	**8** B1
La Casserole	**9** B1
Plaza Tandoori Restaurant	(see 3)
Portofino	(see 4)
Shoprite	(see 4)
Spar	(see 4)

TRANSPORT

Bus Station	(see 10)
Minibus Taxi Park	**10** B2
Nonshared Taxi Rank	(see 10)

Post office (Msunduza St)

Tourist information office (☎ 404 2531; www.welcometoswaziland.com; Shop 2, Cooper Centre, Sozisa Rd; ⏲ 8am-4.45pm Mon-Thu, 8am-4pm Fri, 9am-1pm Sat) Operated by the Swaziland Tourism Authority, this office provides free maps and brochures on hotels, restaurants and entertainment. These include the tourist bible *What's Happening in Swaziland* and the smaller *What's on in Swaziland*.

DANGERS & ANNOYANCES

Mbabane is becoming unsafe at night, so don't walk around by yourself. Take precautions in the streets even during the day – muggings are on the increase.

SIGHTS & ACTIVITIES

There's not really much to see in Mbabane.

Eight kilometres northeast of Mbabane is **Sibebe Rock** (admission E30), a massive sheer granite dome hulking over the surrounding countryside; the area is managed by the local community.

SLEEPING

Good-value places to crash tend to be slightly out of the central area.

Thokoza Church Centre (☎ 404 6681; Polinjane Rd; s/d without bathroom E181/218, with bathroom E216/253) Fittingly monastic in nature, these small clean rooms might convert you to Mbabane. Turn left at the police station and head up Polinjane Rd for 500m; take a taxi at night (E30 from Swazi Plaza). Breakfast is included.

Veki's Guesthouse (☎ 404 8485; www.swazilodgings.com/vekis; 233 Somhlolo Rd; s/d E270/400, apt from E350) This nondescript but friendly place has homey, clean rooms decorated with animal-print decor. Rooms have cable TV; meals are available on request.

Kapola Guest House (☎ 404 0906; s/d incl breakfast E350/650) This comfortable abode's massive porch overlooks greenery; it has busy rooms and simple meals on request (E30 to E65). It's about 5km from Mbabane beside the MR3; watch for the wall painted with flags.

Brackenhill Lodge B&B (☎ 404 2887; www.brackenhillswazi.com; Mountain Dr; s/d E450/660) Located 4.5km north of Mbabane, this attractive place in tranquil gardens has a range of rooms. Ring for directions.

Foresters Arms (☎ 467 4177; www.forestersarms.co.za; r incl half board from E480) Audrey Forbes-Hamilton

(Penelope Keith's character in the BBC's *To the Manor Born*) would enjoy the cream teas and the cosy, British-style interiors here. Situated 27km southwest of Mbabane in the hills around Mhlambanyatsi.

Mountain Inn (☎ 404 2781; www.mountaininn.sz; s/d incl breakfast from E525/670; ☒ ☐ ☒) It's not five-star luxury, but this inn has a pleasant and homey ambience, a pool, a library, a restaurant and panoramas.

EATING

Portofino (The Mall; snacks E21-40; ☒ 8.30am-5.30pm Mon-Fri, 8.30am-5pm Sat) A small and relaxed coffee shop serving reasonable coffee.

Indingilizi Gallery & Restaurant (☎ 404 6213; indingi@realnet.co.sz; 112 Dzeliwe St; light meals E30-50; ☒ 8am-5pm Mon-Fri, 8.30am-1pm Sat) This small outdoor cafe-gallery offers salads, crêpes and curries.

Plaza Tandoori Restaurant (☎ 404 7599; Swazi Plaza; mains E35-90; ☒ lunch & dinner) As well as great-value Indian curries, the usual grills and burgers add a touch of the international.

Finesse (☎ 404 5936; The Mall; mains E60-100; ☒ lunch & dinner Mon-Sat) This French-owned place offers an elegant setting and serves a good range of seafood and meat dishes.

La Casserole Restaurant (☎ 405 0778; Gwamile St; mains E65-100; ☒ lunch & dinner) This long-standing, friendly place serves international cuisine, including pizzas. It also offers a few vegetarian dishes, plus a good wine selection.

For self-catering, there are: **Shoprite** (Swazi Plaza) and **Spar** (The Mall).

GETTING THERE & AWAY

Minibus taxis to South Africa (mostly northbound) leave from the minibus taxi park near Swazi Plaza, where you'll also find buses and minibus taxis to destinations within Swaziland. Any vehicle heading towards Manzini or Matsapha passes through the Ezulwini Valley, although most take the bypass road, as opposed to the valley's minor and more-scenic routes. Nonshared taxis to the Ezulwini Valley cost from E80, more to the far end of the valley (from E100) and still more at night. To Matsapha International Airport, expect to pay from E150.

GETTING AROUND

Nonshared taxis congregate near the bus station by Swazi Plaza. At night you can usually find one near the City Inn on Gwamile St.

AROUND SWAZILAND

EZULWINI & MALKERNS VALLEYS

The Ezulwini Valley – starting near Mbabane and extending down past Lobamba village, 18km away – is the homeland of Swazi royalty. It's a pretty valley with lush greenery, but it's becoming less picturesque with hotels and other development. Most of the area's attractions are near Lobamba.

The nearby Malkerns Valley is renowned for its handicrafts and is also worth visiting.

Information

Ezulwini Tourist Information Office (☎ 416 1834; www.swazi.travel; Mantenga Craft Centre, Ezulwini Valley) Privately run by Swazi Trails (p1076), this office supplies tourist information.

Medi-Sun Clinic (☎ 416 2800; Ezulwini Valley) Medical service.

Sights & Activities
LOBAMBA

You can see the monarchy in action at the **Royal Kraal** in Lobamba during the Incwala ceremony and the Umhlanga dance (see Festivals & Events, p1078).

The **National Museum** (adult/child E25/15; ☒ 8am-4.30pm Mon-Fri, 10am-4pm Sat & Sun) has some interesting displays on Swazi culture and a traditional beehive village. The ticket price also allows you to enter the **memorial to King Sobhuza II**, the most revered of Swazi kings.

Next to the museum is the **parliament**, which is sometimes open to visitors.

Nearby, in Ezulwini Valley, is **Mantenga Nature Reserve** (☎ 516 1178; admission E150; ☒ 7am-6pm), where you can visit a 'living' Swazi cultural village, and see a *sibhaca* dance and the Mantega Falls; it also has accommodation (opposite).

MLILWANE WILDLIFE SANCTUARY

This beautiful and tranquil **private reserve** (☎ 528 3943; www.biggameparks.org, www.mlilwane -wildlife-sanctuary.com; admission E25; ☒ 6.30am-5.30pm summer, 6am-6pm winter) was created in the 1950s by conservationist Ted Reilly.

While it doesn't have the drama or vastness of some of the South African parks, the reserve is easily accessible and worth a visit. Its terrain is dominated by the precipitous Nyonyane (Little Bird) peak, and there are some fine walks in the area. Animals include zebras, giraffes, warthogs, antelopes, crocodiles, hippos and a variety of birds, including black eagles.

Activities include horse rides (one to three hours costs E120; fully catered overnight trips E1085), mountain biking (E95 per person per hour) and game walks (E50 per person per hour).

Sleeping

WITHIN THE SANCTUARY

Book the following through the **Big Game Parks office** (☎ 528 3943/4; www.biggameparks.org).

Sondzela Backpackers (IYHF) Lodge (campsite per person E45, dm E80, s/d without bathroom E155/220, s/d rondavel E170/240) This place needs a bit of a touch up, but its delightful gardens and a hilltop perch in Mlilwane provide a perfect setting.

Mlilwane Wildlife Sanctuary Main Camp (campsite per person E60, s/d hut E315/450) This homey camp is set in a scenic wooded location 3.5km from Mlilwane's entry gate, complete with simple thatched huts – including traditional beehive huts.

OUTSIDE THE SANCTUARY

Malandela's B&B (☎ 7605 2598, 2528 3448; www.malandelas.com; r per person incl breakfast E180; ⊜) Along the MR27, this place offers stylish, ethnic-African rooms, a pool and a sculpture garden.

Mantenga Nature Reserve (☎ 516 1178; mnr@africaonline.co.sz; beehives E80, s/d safari tents incl breakfast E430/585) This reserve has safari tents, offering soft 'safari' adventure in stylish canvas comfort. There's a good on-site restaurant.

Good budget hostels in the valleys include:

Legends Backpackers Lodge (☎ 416 1870; legends@mailfly.com; campsite per person E45, dm E90, d without bathroom E220; 🖳)

Swaziland Backpackers (☎ 528 2038; campsite per person E45, dm E80, d without bathroom E200; 🖳 🕾)

Lidwala Backpacker Lodge (☎ 550 4951; www.all-out.org; campsite R50, dm E90, safari tent per person ER220)

Eating & Drinking

Guava Café (☎ 416 1343; snacks E50-90, light meals from E30; ⊙ 9am-5pm Tue-Sat, 10am-5pm Sun) Great for light meals; a gallery attached.

Malandela's Restaurant (☎ 528 3115; mains E45-80; ⊙ lunch & dinner Mon-Sun) Part of the Malandela's complex (above), this is one of the best restaurants in the region.

Quatermain's (☎ 416 3023; Gables Shopping Centre; mains E50-100; ⊙ lunch & dinner) This restaurant has an extensive menu. Arrive hungry.

Woodlands Restaurant (☎ 416 3466; mains E75-143; ⊙ lunch & dinner; Ⓥ) Good vegetarian and international cuisine served on a shady verandah.

It's in the Ezulwini Valley, near the Ezulwini craft market.

The Calabash (☎ 416 1187; mains E80-130; ⊙ lunch & dinner) Specialises in German and Swiss cuisine.

Entertainment

You'll rave about House on Fire, a fantastically decorated cultural and entertainment space at the Malandela complex (see left).

Getting There & Away

A minibus-taxi trip up the Ezulwini Valley from Mbabane costs E15 (35 minutes). Take a Manzini-bound bus from Mbabane, and make sure the driver knows you want to get off in the valley. Even some nonexpress buses aren't keen on stopping.

Nonshared taxis from Mbabane cost from E80 and up to double this as you head down the valley.

If you're driving from either Mbabane or Manzini, take the Ezulwini Valley/Lobamba exit off the bypass road to the MR103.

NGWEMPISI GORGE

The **Ngwempisi Gorge** (☎ 7625 6004), 30km south of the Malkerns Valley, is one of the country's few remaining untouched environments, with beautiful natural forests and the Ngwempisi River. Adventure seekers will love the Ngwempisi Hiking Trail, a community-run 33km trail in the Ntfungula Hills off the Mankayane road. You can spend two to three days exploring the area and sleep en route in several atmospheric huts. It's recommended you take a **local guide** (per day E50, plus per hiker E10).

Horseshoe Estate B&B (☎ 7606 1512; r per person E150) is near the trail entrance and offers accommodation. It can also arrange hikes.

MANZINI

pop 55,000

Manzini is the country's commercial and industrial centre. Central Manzini isn't large, but it feels like a different country from easygoing rural Swaziland. A hint of menace pervades; be careful both at day and night as muggings are common.

Manzini's main drawcard is its colourful **market** (cnr Mhlakuvane & Mancishane Sts; ⊙ closed Sun). The upper section is packed with handicrafts. **Kaphunga Homestead Swaziland Cultural Tours** (☎ 7604 4102; wozanawe@realnet.co.sz, www.swazilive.com/myxo/html) runs highly recommended

SWAZILAND

GO WILD!

Wildlife Drives

For wildlife drives, the Big Game Parks reserves organise good-value tours. Mkhaya offers Land Rover day trips (per person E475, minimum two people, includes lunch). These trips must be pre-booked through **Big Game Parks** (☎ 528 3943/4; www.biggameparks.org). Set arrival and departure times are 10am and 4pm. Hlane has a two-hour sunrise/sunset drive (per person E190, minimum two people). Mlilwane offers a shorter game drive (per person E165, minimum two people). Check the website for the latest activities on offer, as these do change.

White-Water Rafting

One of Swaziland's highlights is white-water rafting on the Usutu River. In sections, you'll encounter Grade IV rapids, which aren't for the faint-hearted, although even first timers with a sense of adventure should handle the day easily.

Swazi Trails (☎ /fax 2416 2180; www.swazitrails.co.sz; Mantenga Craft Centre, Ezulwini Valley) offers full-half-day trips for E750/650 per person, including lunch and transport, for a minimum of two people. Trips run from the Ezulwini Valley.

---

village visits and overnight stays (E550 to E720) to Kaphunga, 55km southeast of Manzini.

A casual affair, **Myxo's Backpackers** (☎ 7604 4102; www.swazilive.com/myxo/html; campsite E45, dm/d without bathroom E90/200) is located 5km northeast of Manzini and 1km off the main road. **Tum's George Hotel** (☎ 505 8991; www.tgh.sz; cnr Ngwane & Du Toit Sts; s/d incl breakfast from E680/890; ✷ ▣) is Manzini's fanciest and priciest hotel.

Manzini's elegant choice for dining, **Gil Vincente Restaurant** (☎ 505 3874; Ngwane St; mains R30-100; ⏲ lunch & dinner Tue-Sun) has smart decor and international cuisine and is located down from Tum's George Hotel.

A nonshared taxi to Matsapha International Airport costs around E50. The main bus and minibus taxi park is at the northern end of Louw St, where you can also find some non-shared taxis. A minibus-taxi trip to Mbabane costs E15 (35 minutes). Minibus taxis to Mozambique leave from the car park next to KFC up the hill.

MKHAYA GAME RESERVE

This top-notch **private reserve** (☎ 528 3943/4; www.biggameparks.org, www.mkhaya-game-reserve.com), off the Manzini–Big Bend road near the hamlet of Phuzumoya, was established in 1979 to save the pure Nguni breed of cattle from extinction. Its focus expanded to antelopes, elephants, and white and black rhinos. The reserve's name comes from the *mkhaya* (knobthorn) tree, which abounds here.

You can't visit or stay in the reserve without booking in advance, and even then you can't

drive in alone; you'll be met at Phuzumoya at a specified pick-up time, usually 10am or 4pm. While day tours can be arranged, it's ideal to stay for at least one night.

our pick **Stone Camp** (s/d incl full board E1650/2700) has a smart, slightly colonial feel; it's well worth the layover. Accommodation is in rustic and luxurious semi-open stone and thatch cottages (a proper loo with a view!). The price includes wildlife drives, walking safaris, park entry and meals; it's excellent value compared to many of the private reserves near Kruger National Park in South Africa.

HLANE ROYAL NATIONAL PARK

With white rhinos, antelope species, elephants and lions, **Hlane Royal National Park** (☎ 528 3943; www.biggameparks.org, www.hlane-national-park.com; admission E25; ⏲ 6am-6pm) offers wonderfully low-key wildlife-watching. There are guided walking trails (E75 per person), two-hour wildlife day drives (E145 to E155 per person; minimum two people), a cultural village tour (E50 per person; minimum four) and mountain bike rentals (per two hours E120).

our pick **Bhubesi Camp** (cottage E350-460) is the pick of the spots: it overlooks a river about 10km from Ndlovu Camp; accommodation is in tasteful, four-person, self-catering cottages.

Ndlovu Camp (campsite per person E40, 8-person cottage per person E220, s/d rondavel from E295/410) is a pleasant and rustic fenced-off camp, with no electricity, a communal area and a restaurant. Book for both through the **Big Game Parks office** (☎ 528 3943/4; www.biggameparks.org).

Minibus taxis from Simunye will drop you at the entrance to Hlane (E5; 7km from Simunye).

MLAWULA NATURE RESERVE

This tranquil **reserve** (☎ 383 8885; www.mlawula.com; adult/child E25/12; ⏱ 6am-6pm), where the lowveld plains meet the Lebombo Mountains, boasts antelopes, hyenas and crocodiles, plus rewarding birdwatching. You can bring your own mountain bike. Walking is a highlight, too, with hikes from two to nine hours in length.

There's tented accommodation at **Sara Camp** (s/d E150/300) and **Siphiso camping ground** (campsites per person E60). **Mapelepele Cottage** (cottage from E500) is self-catering and sleeps up to eight people. At the time of research, booking arrangements were changing; ring the reserve's reception office for booking details.

PIGGS PEAK

This small, gritty town is the centre of Swaziland's logging industry. Tragically, much of the forested area – pine plantations – were destroyed by forest fires in 2007. The town was named after a prospector who found gold here in 1884.

As well as its scenery, including the **Phophonyane Falls** about 8km north of town, this area is known for its handicrafts. Check these out at the Peak Craft Centre, just north of Orion Piggs Peak Hotel & Casino, where you'll find **Likhweti Kraft** (☎ 437 3127), a branch of **Tintsaba Crafts** (☎ 437 1260; www.tintsaba.com), which sells sisal baskets, jewellery and many other Swazi crafts. There are also numerous craft vendors along the road up from Mbabane.

An interesting detour from Piggs Peak is to wind your way 20km through scenic plantation country to the historic and very pretty town of **Bulembu**, a former asbestos mining centre and later a ghost town. The town's current investors run a community tourism project (based on Christian principles) to bring the town back to life, including renovating many corrugated iron houses and art deco buildings. Warning: asbestos (chrysotile) dumps exist around the village.

Sleeping

Jabula Guest House (☎ 437 1052; www.swaziplace. com/jabulaguesthouse; s/d incl breakfast E295/445; 🛏) The best B&B in Swaziland, whose delightful owner runs small, neat rooms in a pretty, residential setting. Follow the signs.

Phophonyane Lodge & Nature Reserve (☎ 437 1319; www.phophonyane.co.sz; s/d safari tent incl breakfast from E650/920, s/d cottage incl breakfast from E860/1300; 🛏) This stunning hideaway – in a nature reserve of lush indigenous forest on the Phophonyane River – is one of the best places to stay in Swaziland. Ring ahead for directions (you can usually arrange to be collected from Piggs Peak).

RHINO WARS

In 1965 white rhino were re-established in the kingdom after an absence of 70 years. That was the easy part. Since then there has been an ongoing battle to protect them from poachers. At the forefront of this battle has been Ted Reilly and a band of dedicated hand-picked rangers.

This defence wasn't easy, especially as the poachers had received hefty financial backing from crime syndicates supplying rhino horn to the lucrative Asian market. Poaching escalated in the late 1980s, and there were determined efforts to change rhino-poaching laws in Swaziland. Rhinos were dehorned and confined to enclosures for their own protection. After Hlane Royal National Park was attacked in January 1992 by poachers with AK47s, the rangers armed themselves. With the rhinos dehorned at Hlane, the poachers shifted to Mkhaya Game Reserve. The battle commenced.

In April 1992 there was a shoot-out between rangers and poachers at Mkhaya, and some poachers were captured. Another shoot-out occurred at Big Bend, in which two poachers were killed while selling their freshly poached horns. While the Swazi courts deliberated over action against the rangers, another rhino, the majestic bull Mthondvo, was killed for his horn in 1992. The young king, Mswati III, intervened, and the poaching of rhinos came to a halt. The rangers, however, still wait with their rifles at the ready. You can help: your presence at any one of the big wildlife parks assists in rhino conservation.

In 1996 the Taiwanese government donated money to purchase six black rhinos; a gesture of good faith that was welcomed with open arms. The black rhinos, which were relocated from parks in KwaZulu-Natal, are breeding well.

SWAZILAND

DETOUR

If you have time, it's worth taking a detour to the community-run **Nsangwini Rock Art Shelter** (☎ 7637 3767; per person R25). The paintings are under a small, but impressive, rock shelter, which is perched over the Komati River. The cave was believed to be that of the Nsangwini Bushmen. Nsangwini is signed from the main Piggs Peak road and the Maguga Dam loop road. Follow a dirt road for 7.5km; parking is available at the small reception hut. A local guide will take you on the slightly steep and rocky walk (15 minutes down, 20 minutes up) and will give a brief explanation.

Accommodation is also available at **Bulembu** (☎ 437 3888, 7602 4577; www.bulembu.org; per person from E240).

Getting There & Away
The minibus taxi stand is next to the market at the top end of the main street, with several vehicles daily to Bulembu (E8, 30 minutes) and Mbabane (E20, one hour).

The stretch of dirt road running west from Piggs Peak to Bulembu can be boggy when wet. The road to Barberton (Mpumalanga) has recently been paved.

MALOLOTJA NATURE RESERVE
This beautiful middleveld/highveld **reserve** (☎ 442 4241; www.malolotja.com; adult/child E28/14; ⏰ 6am-6pm) is a true wilderness area, with terrain ranging from mountainous and high-altitude grassland to forest and lower-lying bushveld.

It's an excellent walking destination, with around 200km of hiking trails, and an ornithologist's paradise, with over 280 species of birds.

Basic brochures outlining hiking trails are available for free at reception, where you can arrange a permit as well. For all longer walks, you'll have to bring whatever food you'll need, as well as a camp stove, as fires are not permitted outside the base camp. Wildlife drives can be arranged with advance notice.

Accommodation consists of **camping** (main camp/trail per person E70/50), either at the well-equipped (but infrequently used) main site or along the overnight trails (no facilities), and self-catering wooden **cabins** (adult/child E230/115, minimum E400). At the time of research, Hawane

Resort had formed a joint-venture project with Swaziland National Trust; prices may have increased on those quoted here.

The entrance gate for Malolotja is about 35km northwest of Mbabane, along the Piggs Peak road (MR1); minibus taxis will drop you at the entrance.

SWAZILAND DIRECTORY

ACCOMMODATION
Many of the country's hotels and lodges are geared towards South African tourists and are pricey, but there are some good B&B-style options. Nearly all designated campsites in Swaziland are in national parks and reserves. If you intend to camp in rural areas, always ask permission from the local people first.

ACTIVITIES
Swaziland's wildlife reserves offer some excellent walking, mountain biking and birdwatching. In the rainy season, white-water rafting is at its best (see the boxed text, p1076).

BUSINESS HOURS
Banks Open 8.30am to 3.30pm Monday to Friday (some also open 9.30am to 11am Saturday).
Offices and shops Open 8am to 5pm Monday to Friday.
Restaurants and cafes Hours vary from 8am to midnight depending on outlet.

EMBASSIES & CONSULATES
See p1080 for details on getting visas for onward travel.
Mozambique (off Map p1073; ☎ 404 3700; Princess Dr, Mbabane)
South Africa (Map p1073; ☎ 404 4651; PO Box 2507, The Mall, Mbabane)
USA (Map p1073; ☎ 404 6441; http://mbabane.usembassy.gov; Msunduza St, Mbabane) Be sure to check its opening hours; hours for visas are limited.

FESTIVALS & EVENTS
Colourful ceremonies (and traditional dress, which is still commonly worn) underline the Swazis' unique identity.

The following two major festivals are held near Lobamba in the Ezulwini Valley. Ask at the tourist office in Mbabane for exact dates. Photography is not permitted at the Incwala ceremony but is at the Umhlanga dance.
Incwala ceremony Held sometime between late December and early January. Swaziland's most sacred ceremony,

SWAZILAND

OFF THE BEATEN TRACK

Several excellent community tourism projects operate in Swaziland. Options include the following:

Shewula Mountain Camp (☎ 7603 1931, 7605 1160; www.shewulacamp.com; dm/r E90/260), a community-owned camp in the Lebombo Mountains, is 36km by dirt road (15km as the crow flies) northeast of Simunye. You can camp or stay in basic *rondavels*, with shared bathrooms and self-catering facilities. Local meals can also be arranged (breakfast/lunch/dinner costs E35/50/65 and must be booked in advance), as can guided cultural walks to nearby villages, plus nature and birdwatching walks (guided walks cost E30 per person).

The newer **Mahamba Gorge Lodge** (☎ 7617 9880; s/d E250/350, day visit E10), near Nhlangano, has received good reports for its clean, modern stone chalets and wonderful walks through the nearby gorge, where there are nesting eagles (guided walks cost E50 per person).

Contact the Mbabane tourist information office (p1073) or Ezulwini Tourist Information Office (p1074) for more information.

celebrating the New Year and the first fruits of the harvest in rituals of thanksgiving, prayer, atonement and reverence for the king. As part of the festivities, the king grants his people the right to consume his harvest, and rains are expected to follow the ceremony.

Umhlanga (Reed Dance) A great spectacle in August or September, performed by unmarried girls who collect reeds for the repair and maintenance of the royal palace. It is something like a week-long debutante ball for marriageable young Swazi women and is a showcase of potential wives for the king. On the sixth day they perform the reed dance and carry the reeds they have collected to the queen mother. Princesses wear red feathers in their hair.

HEALTH

Malaria is a minor summer risk in the northeast near Mozambique, with the country hoping to be declared malaria free by 2015. Bilharzia is present – be aware of the symptoms. Tuberculosis (TB) is widespread and care should be taken in sharing confined spaces with infected persons.

For more information on these potentially deadly diseases, see the Health chapter, p1164.

PRACTICALITIES

■ The *Times of Swaziland* (www.times. co.sz) and *Swazi Observer* are the country's English-language daily newspapers.

■ Electrical plugs have three large round pins, as used in South Africa.

■ Swaziland uses the metric system.

HOLIDAYS

As well as religious holidays in the Africa Directory chapter (p1140), the principal public holidays in Swaziland are the following:

New Year's Day 1 January
King Mswati III's Birthday 19 April
National Flag Day 25 April
King Sobhuza II's Birthday 22 July
Umhlanga (Reed Dance Day) August/September
Somhlolo (Independence Day) 6 September
Incwala Day December/January (dates vary each year)

INTERNET ACCESS

Internet facilities are found in Mbabane and a couple of places in the Ezulwini and Malkerns Valleys.

MAPS

Topographical maps (1:50,000) are available from the **Ministry of Public Works** (☎ 404 6267; Mhlambanyatsi Rd, Mbabane), although these maps have not been reprinted for years while the office is digitising new data. The Swaziland Tourism Authority (see the Mbabane tourist information office, p1073) also has hiking maps of most popular hiking spots, including Shewula, Mlawula, Sibebe, Mlilwane, Mantenga, Mahamba, Ngwepisi and Malolotja.

MEDIA

There are two English-language daily newspapers: the *Times of Swaziland* (www.times. co.sz) and the *Swazi Observer* (www.observer. org.sz). The former is an independent, and frequently courts the wrath of government and royalty; the latter is owned by the 'nation' and toes a conservative line.

MONEY

The unit of currency is the lilangeni; the plural is emalangeni (E). It is tied in value to the South African rand. Rands are accepted everywhere and there's no need to change them. Emalangeni are difficult to change for other currencies outside Swaziland.

Only a few ATMs accept international credit or debit cards. The most convenient are at banks in Swazi Plaza, Mbabane, and inside the Royal Swazi Hotel's casino in the Ezulwini Valley.

TELEPHONE

Swaziland's code is ☎ 268. To call overseas from Swaziland, use the code ☎ 00 plus a country code. The best way to make international calls is with phonecards available from post offices and shops. See p1072 for more information on Swaziland's phone numbers.

TOURIST INFORMATION

Swaziland's main tourist information office is in Mbabane (p1073). Privately run by Swazi Trails (see the boxed text, p1076), the Ezulwini Tourist Information Office (p1074) also supplies tourist information. The websites of **Swaziland National Trust** (www.sntc.org.sz) and **Big Game Parks** (www.biggameparks.org) offer some parks' information.

VISAS

Most nationalities don't need a visa to visit Swaziland. Those who do can obtain them in advance from the **Swaziland high commission** (☎ in South Africa 012-344 1910; 715 Government Avenue, Arcadia) in Pretoria. Anyone staying for more than 30 days must apply for an extension of stay. If staying for longer than 60 days, you must apply for a temporary residence permit from the **Chief Immigration Officer** (☎ 404 2941; PO Box 372, Mbabane), whose offices are in the Ministry of Home Affairs.

Visas for Onward Travel

Visas for Mozambique are available at the borders, but it's cheaper to arrange them in advance at the Mozambican high commission (p1078) in Mbabane or Nelspruit (South Africa). Allow 24 hours.

DEPARTURE TAX

A departure tax (E50) is levied at Matsapha International Airport.

TRANSPORT IN SWAZILAND

GETTING THERE & AWAY

Air

Swaziland's main airport is Matsapha International Airport, northwest of Manzini. (Schedules and tickets often refer to the airport as Manzini.) **Swaziland Airlink** (☎ 518 6155; www.saairlink.co.za) flies daily between Swaziland and Johannesburg (R770).

Land

BUS & MINIBUS TAXI

Generally speaking, Manzini has the main international transport rank for transport to Jo'burg, Durban and Mozambique. Less frequent departures are in Mbabane for the northern destinations of Gauteng and Mpumalanga (South Africa).

Mozambique

The main border crossing between Swaziland and Mozambique is at Lomahasha–Namaacha (open 7am to 8pm). The border crossing between Mhlumeni and Goba is open 7am to 6pm. Enquire at one of the tourist offices about bus services from Mbabane to Maputo (Mozambique). Minibuses between Maputo and Manzini depart daily in the morning via the Namaacha–Lomahasha border crossing (E40, 1½ hours); if entering Swaziland, some continue on to Manzini (E50, 3½ hours). See also p980.

South Africa

The main border crossings with South Africa are Josefsdal–Bulembu (open 8am to 4pm); Oshoek–Ngwenya (open 7am to 10pm); Emahlathini–Sicunusa (open 8am to 6pm); Mahamba (open 7am to 10pm); and Golela–Lavumisa (open 7am to 10pm).

The **Baz Bus** (☎ in South Africa 021-439 2323; www.bazbus.com) runs from Jo'burg/Pretoria to Durban via Mbabane and Malkerns Valley three times a week, and from Swaziland down the KwaZulu-Natal coast to Durban.

Minibus taxis run daily between Jo'burg (Park Station), Mbabane and Manzini (E160, four hours) and between Manzini and Durban (E140, eight hours). On many routes, you'll need to change minibuses at the border. Most long-distance taxis leave early in the morning.

GETTING AROUND
Bus & Minibus Taxi

There are a few infrequent (but cheap) domestic buses, most of which set off from and terminate at the main stop in the centre of Mbabane. Generally you'll find minibus taxis are the best public transport, although they often run shorter routes. There are also nonshared (private hire) taxis in some of the larger towns.

Hitching

Hitching is never entirely safe in any country, and we don't recommend it. But in some parts of Africa there is often simply no other option to grabbing lifts on trucks, 4WDs, trucks or whatever vehicle happens to come down the road first. Travellers who decide to hitch should understand that they are taking a small but potentially serious risk.

SWAZILAND

Zambia

Zambia, with its dreamy African landscapes and astonishing density of wildlife, fits perfectly into a trip around the wider region. Its unique appeal is its rough edge: Zambia is not set up for independent tourism and travel here is challenging – crumbling infrastructure, little signage and long distances between major towns make it one big adventure.

What makes it worthwhile is the stunning landscapes and the concentration and variety of wildlife. A fact you'll become acutely aware of when you watch a grunting hippo haul itself onto a grassy bank under a blood-red sunset, or admire a fish eagle as it swoops across glassy waters while you canoe the Zambezi River. South Luangwa, one of the best national parks on the continent, and monstrous Kafue National Park, classic African safari territory, epitomise the country's riches. And then there's Victoria Falls, the dazzling waterfall that is truly one of the greatest spectacles in Africa.

So if you like your travel easy and your wilderness neatly bundled into a homogenised and Westernised version of Africa, then much of Zambia may not appeal. But if you enjoy a raw edge and few tourists, then you're in the right country.

ZAMBIA

FAST FACTS

- **Area** 752,614 sq km
- **ATMs** Only in main cities
- **Borders** Angola, Botswana, Democratic Republic of Congo, Malawi, Mozambique, Namibia, Tanzania, Zimbabwe
- **Budget** US$30 to US$40 per day
- **Capital** Lusaka
- **Languages** English, Bemba, Lozi, Nyanja and Tonga
- **Money** Zambian kwacha; US$1 = ZK4410, €1 = ZK6221
- **Population** 12 million
- **Seasons** Cool and dry (mid-April to August), hot and dry (September to mid-November), hot and wet (mid-November to mid-April)
- **Telephone** Country code ☎ 260; international access code ☎ 00
- **Time** GMT/UTC +2
- **Visa** US$50 for 30 days; issued at point of entry

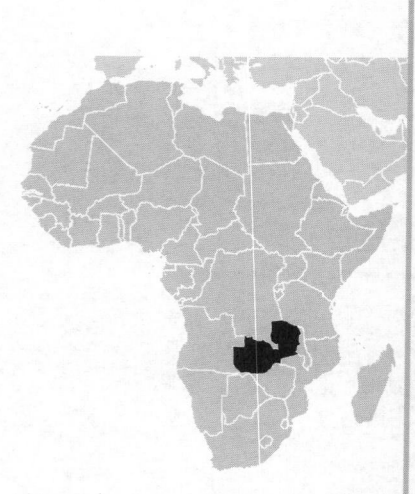

HOW MUCH?

- **Small wood carving** US$12
- **Bunch of bananas at roadside** US$1
- **Traditional dance** US$10 to US$20
- **Walking safari** US$45
- **Batik** US$13

LONELY PLANET INDEX

- **1L petrol/diesel** US$1.30/1
- **1L bottled water** US$3
- **Bottle of Mosi lager** US$1.50
- **Souvenir T-shirt** US$15
- **Sausage, nshima & veg street snack** US$2

HIGHLIGHTS

- **South Luangwa National Park** (p1091) Identify the incredible diversity of winged, hoofed and furred creatures along the majestic landscapes of Zambia's premier park.
- **Lower Zambezi National Park** (p1095) Gaze in awe at elephants strolling along the bank, teeming hippos in the river, and fish eagles soaring overhead, all while canoeing or fishing on the river.
- **Lake Kariba** (p1095) Boat or fish, or just sunbathe at a resort along one of the world's largest artificial lakes.
- **Victoria Falls** (p1098) Gaze at the magnificent, thundering waters, then get your adrenalin fix with a daredevil activity in the gorge below.
- **Northern Zambia** (p1093) Get lost in Zambia's land of adventure, the immense untamed north, with rarely another tourist in sight.

CLIMATE & WHEN TO GO

There are three seasons: the dry season (mid-April to August), when temperatures drop at night, but the landscape is green and lush; the hot season (September to mid-November), the best time to see wildlife as flora is sparse; and the wet season (mid-November to mid-April), ideal for birdwatching.

ITINERARIES

- **One week** With only one week, hit one of *the* major attractions of southern Africa:

Victoria Falls (p1098) or South Luangwa National Park (p1091).

- **Two weeks** You will have time for the great Victoria Falls (p1098), as well as one or two of the national parks – probably South Luangwa (p1091) or Lower Zambezi (p1095).
- **Three weeks** With extra time and money, go to Victoria Falls (p1098), South Luangwa National Park (p1091), a lodge on the Lower Zambezi (p1095) and the Copperbelt province (p1094). If you are travelling to/from Tanzania or Malawi, or have even more time up your sleeve, you can explore northern Zambia (p1093), including the Kalambo Falls (p1093) and Shiwa Ng'andu (p1094).

HISTORY

Zambia was originally inhabited by hunter-gatherer Khoisan people. About 2000 years ago Bantu people migrated from the Congo basin and gradually displaced them. From the 14th century more immigrants came from the Congo and, by the 16th century, various dispersed groups consolidated into powerful tribes and nations, with specific territories and dynastic rulers.

The first Europeans to arrive were Portuguese explorers, following routes established many centuries earlier by Swahili-Arab slave traders. The celebrated British explorer David Livingstone travelled up the Zambezi in the early 1850s in search of a route to the interior of Africa. In 1855 he reached the awesome waterfall that he promptly named Victoria Falls.

Livingstone's work and writings inspired missionaries to come to the area north of the Zambezi; close on their heels came explorers, hunters and prospectors searching for whatever riches the country had to offer. In 1890 the area became known as Northern Rhodesia and was administered by the British South Africa Company, owned by empire-builder Cecil John Rhodes.

At around the same time, vast deposits of copper were discovered in the area now called the Copperbelt. Although the indigenous people had mined there for centuries, large European-style opencast pits were now being dug. The main sources of labour were the Africans who had to earn money to pay the new 'hut tax'; in any case, most were driven from their land by the European settlers. In 1924 the colony was brought under direct British control.

ZAMBIA

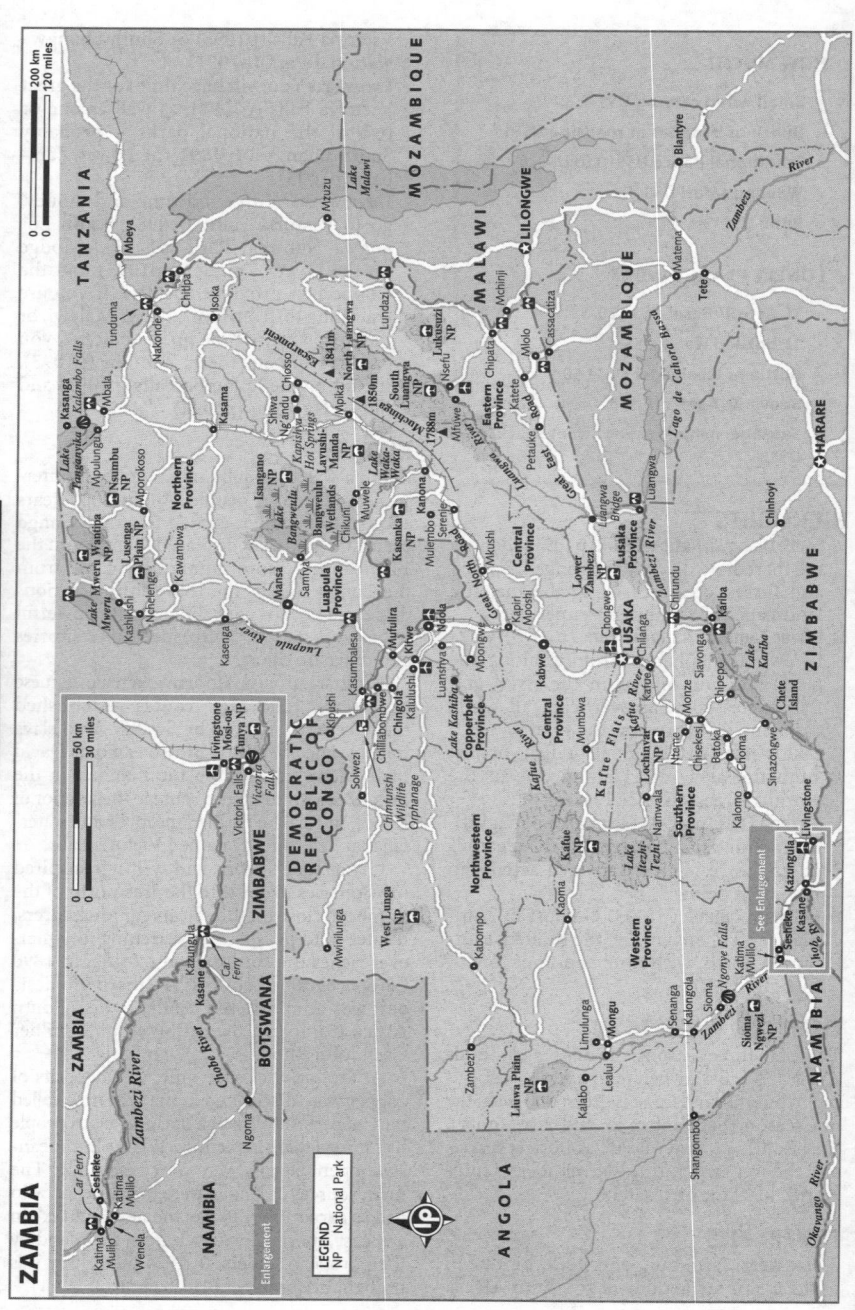

Nationalist Resistance

Meanwhile, African nationalism was becoming a more dominant force in the region. The United National Independence Party (UNIP) was founded in the late 1950s by Dr Kenneth Kaunda, who spoke out against the federation. Northern Rhodesia became independent in 1964, changing its name to Zambia. Kaunda became president and remained so for the next 27 years, largely because in 1972 he declared UNIP the only legal party and himself the sole presidential candidate.

Over the years, however, government corruption and mismanagement, coupled with civil wars in neighbouring states, left Zambia's economy in dire straits, and violent street protests were quickly transformed into a general demand for multiparty politics. Full elections were held in October 1991, and Kaunda and UNIP were resoundingly defeated by Frederick Chiluba and the Movement for Multiparty Democracy (MMD). Kaunda bowed out gracefully, and Chiluba became president.

With backing from the International Monetary Fund (IMF) and the World Bank, financial controls were liberalised to attract investors. But austerity measures were also introduced – and these were tough for the average Zambian. Food prices soared, inflation was rampant and state industries were privatised or simply closed, leaving many thousands of people out of work.

By the mid-1990s, the lack of visible change gave Kaunda the confidence to re-enter the political arena. He attracted strong support but withdrew from the November 1996 elections in protest at MMD irregularities. Chiluba won a landslide victory and remained in firm control – sometimes too firm. There was much speculation that the elections were rigged. However, most Zambians accepted the result, in the hope that at least the country would remain peaceful.

Zambia Today

Although Chiluba tried to amend the constitution to enable himself to run for a third term, he was unsuccessful. In 2001 Levy Mwanawasa, the new MMD leader, was elected Zambia's third president. Mwanawasa led an anticorruption drive and supported an (eventually unsuccessful) investigation into alleged charges of corruption and misappropriation of funds against Chiluba. In a separate case, the High Court in Britain ruled that Chiluba and four of his aides conspired to rob Zambia of about US$46 million.

Because Zambia was deemed a Heavily Indebted Poor Country, most of its US$7 billion international debt was eliminated in 2005. However, the country still suffers from high unemployment, a rapid population growth rate, a tragic HIV/AIDS pandemic, and an ineffectual government. In 2008 President Mwanawasa died in Paris, where he was seeking treatment for a stroke he suffered earlier in the year. Rupiah Banda narrowly won an election victory and was sworn in as president, although Michael Sata, the main opposition candidate, alleged fraud.

CULTURE

On a day-to-day level, the biggest issues on the table for most Zambians are high unemployment and the HIV/AIDS pandemic, with urban prevalence of the disease as high as 30%. HIV/AIDS has had an unexpected effect on the population, including a new population of street kids, who live in roadside sewers. There are also funeral processions on a daily basis – the disease has claimed enough lives to lower the average life expectancy to about 40 years. The population density is about 15 people per sq km, making Zambia one of the most thinly populated countries in Africa. But since almost 45% of Zambians live in urban centres, compounds designed for 50,000 now house over 150,000.

One social issue often discussed on the radio is cohabitation rather than marriage. The argument is that many Zambians feel that this will rock the foundations of their traditional values and therefore be the beginning of the end of society.

Soccer is always a topic on the minds of Zambians, whether it be domestic, within Africa, or the 2010 World Cup to be held in South Africa.

People

Tribal groups are (in order of size) the Bemba, the Tonga, the Nyanja, the Ngoni, and the Lozi. While most descendants of the original white settlers have moved away, one can still find a few, mostly farmers and business types. Indians and Pakistanis have long been a part of the mix, so don't be surprised to hear them proudly call themselves Zambians.

The majority of Zambians are Christians (75%), though others are Muslims and Hindus (24%) or animists (1%).

ZAMBIA

Arts & Crafts

Zambia has a thriving contemporary art scene. One of the country's most famous and respected painters is the late Henry Tayali, whose works have enjoyed a popular following among ordinary folk, and have inspired many other Zambian painters.

Other internationally recognised artists include Agnes Yombwe, who works with purely natural materials and uses traditional ceramics and textile designs in her striking sculptures.

Zambian artistry includes skilfully woven baskets from Barotseland (Western Province) and Siavonga, malachite jewellery from the north, and woodcarvings and soapstone sculptures from Mukuni village near Livingstone.

All of Zambia's tribal groups have their own musical traditions. The Lozi are famous for the large drums played during the remarkable Ku'omboka ceremony (see p1099); the Bemba are also renowned drummers.

The most notable traditional dance is the *makishi*, which features male dancers wearing masks of stylised human faces, grass skirts and anklets.

Contemporary Zambian musicians who have achieved international fame include Larry Maluma, who blends traditional Zambian beats with reggae, and had just released *Tusekelele* (Let's Celebrate) at the time of writing.

FOOD & DRINK

The national dish is unquestionably *nshima*, a bland but filling porridge-like maize dish. It's eaten with your hands and is always accompanied by a 'relish', such as beans or vegetables (in inexpensive eateries), or chicken or fish (in slightly better restaurants).

If you like lagers, the local beer, Mosi, is good. Traditional 'opaque' beer made from maize is sold commercially in cardboard cartons; make sure you shake the carton before drinking.

ENVIRONMENT

Landlocked Zambia is one of Africa's most eccentric legacies of colonialism. Shaped like a contorted figure of eight, its borders do not correspond to any tribal or linguistic area.

The diversity of animal species in Zambia is huge. The rivers support large populations of hippos and crocs, and the associated grasslands provide plenty of fodder for herds of zebras, impalas and pukus (antelopes common in Zambia, but not elsewhere), which in turn attract predators, so most parks contain lions,

leopards, hyenas and cheetahs. The other two big drawcards – buffalo and elephants – are also found in huge herds in the main national parks. Bird lovers can go crazy in Zambia, where about 750 species have been recorded.

Zambia boasts 19 national parks and reserves, and 34 game-management areas (GMAs). After decades of poaching, clearing and generally bad management, many are difficult to reach and others don't contain much wildlife. Since 1990, however, with the help of international donors, several of Zambia's parks have been rehabilitated and the wildlife protected by projects that also aim to give local people some benefit from conservation measures. Zambia's parks are well known for walking safaris, and some, particularly South Luangwa, have a great diversity of wildlife.

LUSAKA

☎ 0211 / pop 1.3 million

In this part of the world, all roads lead to Lusaka. Like it or not, there's no easy way of bypassing Zambia's capital, with its mishmash of dusty tree-lined streets, bustling African markets, Soviet-looking high-rise blocks and modern commerce. If that doesn't sound appealing, it's because Lusaka does not easily lend itself to superlatives. It's certainly an easy enough place to spend time, though, with a genuine African feel, a cosmopolitan populace, some excellent restaurants and quality accommodation options. It's a good spot to let loose, too – the expat bars and the homegrown nightclub scene will see you through to the wee hours.

ORIENTATION

The main street, Cairo Rd, is lined with shops, cafes, supermarkets, travel agencies, banks and bureaux de change. To the north is the major traffic circle and landmark, the North End Roundabout; to the south is the South End Roundabout. East of Cairo Rd are the wide jacaranda-lined streets of the smarter residential suburbs and the area officially called Embassy Triangle. West of Cairo Rd are 'compounds' (read 'townships').

INFORMATION
Emergency
Ambulance (☎ 992)
Police (☎ 991; Church Rd)

Internet Access

Wireless internet is now all over Lusaka. Look for the 'I Spot' sign.

Microlink I Zone (Arcades Shopping Centre, Great East Rd; per min ZK200) Reliable, fast internet access, plus wireless facility.

The Computer Lab (☎ 238375; Nkwazi Rd; per min ZK150) High-speed internet cafe – the best in the city centre.

Medical Services

Good options include the private clinics **Care for Business** (☎ 256731; Addis Ababa Rd) and **Corpmed** (☎ 222612; Cairo Rd), behind Barclays Bank. For evacuations, both clinics work with **Specialty Emergency Services** (☎ 273303; www.ses-zambia.com).

Money

Along Cairo Rd, Barclays Bank, Indo-Zambian Bank, Stanbic Bank and Standard Chartered Bank have branches with ATMs. There are also banks with ATMs at the Manda Hill and Arcades shopping centres (off Great East Rd).

Fx Foreign Exchange (Cairo Rd; ☺ 8am-4pm Mon-Fri, 8am-noon Sat) Changes cash only; has at least three branches along Cairo Rd.

Zampost Bureau de Change (cnr Cairo & Church Rds; ☺ 8am-5pm Mon-Fri, 8am-12.30pm Sat) Inside the main post office.

Post

Main post office (cnr Cairo & Church Rds; ☺ 8am-5pm Mon-Fri, 8am-12.30pm Sat)

Tourist Information

Zambia National Tourist Board (☎ 229087; www.zambiatourism.com; Century House, Cairo Rd; ☺ 8am-1pm & 2-5pm Mon-Fri, 9am-noon Sat) The head office has friendly enough staff, but information is limited to Lusaka and its environs.

Travel Agencies

Bush Buzz (☎ 256992; www.bush-buzz.com; 4169 Nangwenya Rd; ☺ 9am-5pm Mon-Fri, 9am-1pm Sat) This agency is especially popular for trips to Kafue and Lower Zambezi national parks.

Voyagers (☎ 253082; www.voyagerszambia.com; Suez Rd) Perhaps the most popular agency in Zambia, it arranges flights, hotel reservations and car hire.

DANGERS & ANNOYANCES

As in most African cities, pickpockets take advantage of crowds, so be alert in the markets and bus stations and along the busy streets immediately west of Cairo Rd. At night, most streets are dark and often empty, so even if you're on a tight budget, take a taxi. The corner of Church Rd and Cairo Rd, and around the railway line, are currently hot spots for pickpockets and local thugs.

SIGHTS & ACTIVITIES

Though there's not much to see, the downstairs galleries in the **National Museum** (Nasser Rd; adult/child US$2/1; ☺ 9am-4.30pm) offer a snapshot of Zambia, both past and present. Highlights are the displays of contemporary Zambian paintings and sculpture.

Check out **Henry Tayali Visual Arts Centre** (☎ 254440; Showgrounds; admission free; ☺ 9am-5pm Mon-Fri, 10am-4pm Sat & Sun) if you're in the mood for local contemporary art. It's a small collection but well worth a look. There are scenes of everyday Zambian rural life as well as abstract pieces. If you're keen on buying something, you can pick up an oil painting for between ZK1 million and ZK2 million. Ask about the nearby studio for working artists.

Town Centre Market (Chachacha Rd; ☺ 7am-7pm) is chaotic and, frankly, malodorous, but fascinating. It's pretty relaxed and probably a good first venture for visitors unfamiliar with African markets.

SLEEPING

Chachacha Backpackers (☎ 222257; www.chachachasafaris.com; 161 Mulombwa Close; campsite per person ZK27,500; dm ZK66,000, r without bathroom ZK137,500; ☐ ☒) It's unsurprising that this fairly relaxed hostel (that's also a good spot for meeting independent travellers) is so popular with young backpackers.

Kuomboka Backpackers (☎ 222450; kvkirkley@zamtel.zm; Makanta Close; dm ZK45,000, d without bathroom ZK125,000) Accommodation is around one big main building in this labyrinthine place; there are three dorms, each with 10 beds and low ceilings, which feel a bit cramped, especially when they get crowded.

Zamcom Lodge (☎ 251811, 097-8953019; doreen@zamcom.ac.zm; Church Rd; d ZK250,000-300,000; ☒ ☒) The spick-and-span rooms in this motel-style complex are devoid of charm, but they also have no dirt or mosquitoes. Rooms are simple but good value for what you get and the lodge is in a great location. Room 20 is the best double.

our pick **Fairview Hotel** (☎ 222604; www.fairview.co.zm; Church Rd; s/d ZK312,000/339,000; ☒ ☐ ☒) The Fairview is an old-style hotel, with dated rooms that could really do with sprucing up (and a few repairs). It's a very friendly, convivial place to stay, though, and there's

LUSAKA

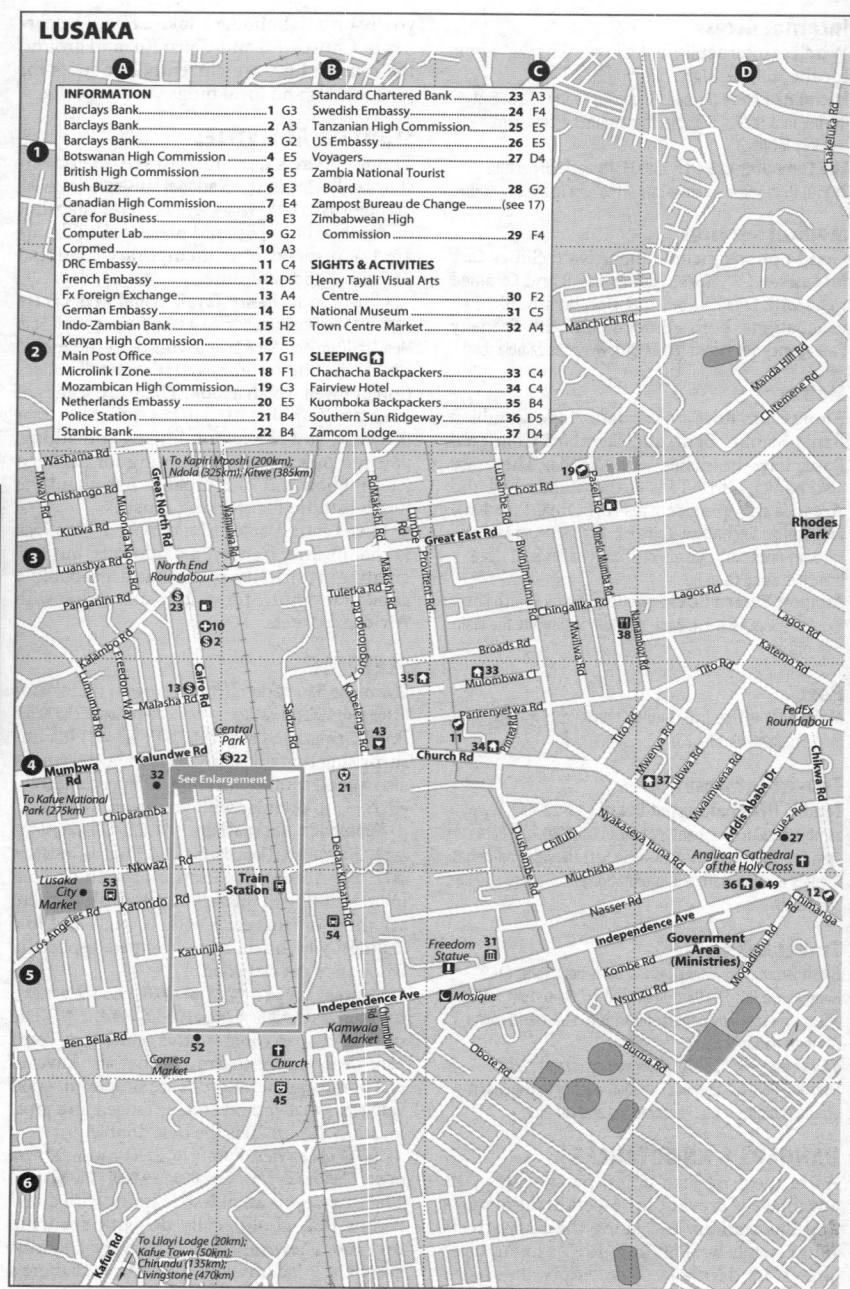

INFORMATION

Barclays Bank	1	G3
Barclays Bank	2	A3
Barclays Bank	3	G2
Botswanan High Commission	4	E5
British High Commission	5	E5
Bush Buzz	6	E3
Canadian High Commission	7	E4
Care for Business	8	E3
Computer Lab	9	G2
Corpmed	10	A3
DRC Embassy	11	C4
French Embassy	12	D5
Fx Foreign Exchange	13	A4
German Embassy	14	E5
Indo-Zambian Bank	15	H2
Kenyan High Commission	16	E5
Main Post Office	17	G1
Microlink I Zone	18	F1
Mozambican High Commission	19	C3
Netherlands Embassy	20	E5
Police Station	21	B4
Stanbic Bank	22	B4
Standard Chartered Bank	23	A3
Swedish Embassy	24	F4
Tanzanian High Commission	25	E5
US Embassy	26	E5
Voyagers	27	D4
Zambia National Tourist Board	28	G2
Zampost Bureau de Change	(see 17)	
Zimbabwean High Commission	29	F4

SIGHTS & ACTIVITIES

Henry Tayali Visual Arts Centre	30	F2
National Museum	31	E5
Town Centre Market	32	A4

SLEEPING

Chachacha Backpackers	33	C4
Fairview Hotel	34	C4
Kuomboka Backpackers	35	B4
Southern Sun Ridgeway	36	D5
Zamcom Lodge	37	D4

ZAMBIA

To Kapiri Mposhi (200km);
Ndola (325km); Kitwe (385km)

Washama Rd
Chishango Rd
Great North Rd
Mway Rd
Kutwa Rd
Luanshya Rd
Panganini Rd
North End Roundabout
Musonda Ngosa Rd
Kabanana Rd
Freedom Way
Lumumba Rd
Malasha Rd
Cairo Rd
Saizu Rd

Great East Rd
Chozi Rd
Libande Rd
Makishi Rd
Lunde Rd
Provident Rd
Paseli Rd
Oneza Rd
Bwinjimfumu Rd

Rhodes Park

Manchichi Rd
Manda Hill Rd
Chitemene Rd

Tuleteka Rd
Chingalika Rd
Lagos Rd
Lagos Rd
Katemo Rd
Tito Rd

Broads Rd
Mulombwa Cl
Mwilwa Rd
Namboer Rd

FedEx Roundabout

Parirenyetwa Rd
Church Rd
Chindolo Rd
Mwenya Rd
Libwa Rd
Tito Rd

Mumbwa Rd
Kalundwe Rd
Central Park

To Kafue National Park (275km)
Chiparamba
Nkwazi Rd
Lusaka City Market
Katondo Rd
Katunjila

Train Station

Dedan Kimathi Rd
Chilubi
Muchisha
Muaiinwela Rd
Addis Ababa Dr
Suez Rd
Chikwa Rd

Anglican Cathedral of the Holy Cross

Chimanga Rd
Mogadishu Rd

Nasser Rd
Independence Ave
Government Area (Ministries)

Freedom Statue
Nyakaseya Ituna Rd

Independence Ave
Mosque
Kombe Rd
Nsunzu Rd

Ben Bella Rd
Comesa Market
Church
Kamwaia Market
Chibumbu Rd
Obote Rd
Burma Rd

Kafue Rd

To Lilayi Lodge (20km);
Kafue Town (50km);
Chirundu (135km);
Livingstone (470km)

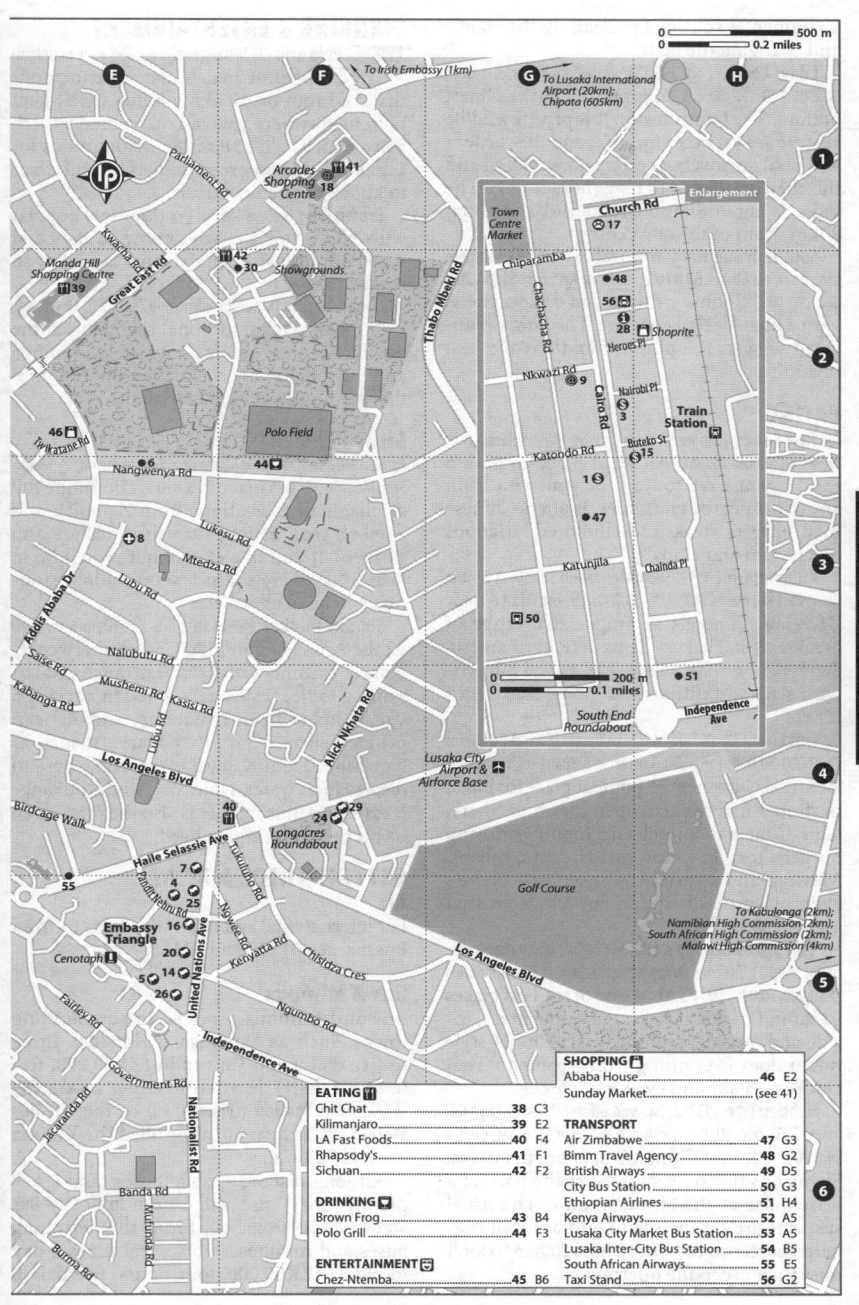

ZAMBIA

EATING 🍴
Chit Chat..**38** C3
Kilimanjaro...**39** E2
LA Fast Foods.......................................**40** F4
Rhapsody's...**41** F1
Sichuan..**42** F2

DRINKING 🍷
Brown Frog..**43** B4
Polo Grill..**44** F3

ENTERTAINMENT 🎭
Chez-Ntemba.......................................**45** B6

SHOPPING 🛍
Ababa House...**46** E2
Sunday Market............................(see 41)

TRANSPORT
Air Zimbabwe......................................**47** G3
Bimm Travel Agency.......................**48** G2
British Airways....................................**49** D5
City Bus Station..................................**50** G3
Ethiopian Airlines.............................**51** H4
Kenya Airways.....................................**52** A5
Lusaka City Market Bus Station....**53** A5
Lusaka Inter-City Bus Station.......**54** B5
South African Airways.....................**55** E5
Taxi Stand..**56** G2

a regimental routine for cleaning the rooms and changing the beds.

Lilayi Lodge (☎ 279024; www.lilayi.com; s/d from US$105/120; ✖ ✦) This is one of Lusaka's finest options. The bungalows in this private wildlife reserve are very comfortable, and the gardens and pool are lovely. It offers horse riding and the chance to learn to play (horse) polo. The lodge is about 8km off Kafue Rd and about 20km south of the city centre.

Southern Sun Ridgeway (☎ 251666; res@southern sun.co.zm; cnr Church Rd & Independence Ave; s/d US$180/200; ✖ ⊗ ✦) Rooms are what you'd expect here, with a high level of comfort. The newly renovated wing is the plushest and has the best furniture.

EATING

LA Fast Foods (Longacres Roundabout, Haile Selassie Ave; meals ZK20,000-50,000) An ideal place to grab a meal if you have to wait for your visa from any of the nearby embassies. It offers Chinese food, burgers, steaks and a hundred variations of 'chicken and chips'.

Kilimanjaro (☎ 255830; Manda Hill Shopping Centre, Great East Rd; mains ZK25,000-50,000; ⊗ breakfast & lunch; ▣ ⊗ Ⓥ) There's an impressive range of breakfasts and bakery items here, even muesli. Sandwiches, rolls, salads, pastas and burgers, with scores of different combos, feature for lunch.

Chit Chat (☎ 097-7774481; 5A Omelo Mumba Rd; mains ZK30,000-50,000; ⊗ noon-3pm Mon, 8.30am-midnight Tue-Sat, Sun hours variable; ⊗) A popular place for lunch or dinner in a relaxed, open-air atmosphere, Chit Chat has an eclectic menu featuring burgers, tortilla wraps, salads, pasta, kebabs, Mexican and a variety of breakfasts. There's even playground equipment and a grassed area for kids.

our pick **Rhapsody's** (☎ 256705/6; www.rhapsodys. co.za; Shop 41, Arcades Shopping Centre, Great East Rd; mains ZK30,000-70,000; Ⓥ) This is one of the best places to eat in Lusaka. It has huge eating areas, inside and outside, and the international-style menu does everything from steaks to Thai chicken, salads and even *nasi goreng*!

Sichuan (☎ 253842; Showgrounds, off Nangwenya Rd; mains ZK35,000-50,000; ⊗ lunch & dinner Mon-Sat, dinner Sun; Ⓥ) The best Chinese restaurant in Lusaka, Sichuan is bizarrely situated at the back of a warehouse at the Showgrounds. The usual suspects are on the menu and are well prepared in record time from the kitchen – don't miss their crocodile offerings.

DRINKING & ENTERTAINMENT

our pick **Polo Grill** (2374 Nangwenya Rd; ⊗ 8am-midnight) A large, open-air bar, under an enormous thatched roof overlooking a huge, well-kept polo field (where you can occasionally catch a live match) – it's all rather incongruous for Lusaka, but is an exceedingly pleasant place to knock back a few Mosis.

Brown Frog (Kabelenga Rd; ⊗ 11am-11pm) Popular with NGO workers who come to dance at weekends, this British-style pub is a bit of an institution.

Chez-Ntemba (Kafue Rd; admission ZK20,000; ⊗ till late Wed, Fri & Sat) This traditional nightclub in the downtown area usually blasts out loud rumba and the folk in here shake their booties until the wee hours on weekend nights.

SHOPPING

Ababa House (cnr Addis Ababa Dr & Twikatane Rd; ⊗ 9am-5pm Mon-Sat) This place is a smart boutique full of imaginative creations from Zambian and Zimbabwean artists, furniture makers and weavers. If you're a chocoholic, you'll be in heaven, as there's also a shop selling handmade Belgian chocolates.

Sunday market (Great East Rd; ⊗ 10am-6pm Sun) At the Arcades Shopping Centre, this weekly market features Lusaka's best range of artisanal goodies, especially wooden carvings, curios made from malachite, and African prints. Sellers from other markets, such as Northmead and Kabwata, also come here to display their wares. Note that, while the range is extensive, this market is also the priciest, so be prepared to bargain hard.

GETTING THERE & AWAY
Air

For international and domestic flights to/from Lusaka, see p1102 and p1103.

Bus & Minibus

Bus and minibus services to surrounding towns, such as Siavonga (ZK45,000, three to five daily) and Chirundu (ZK30,000, five to seven daily), leave from either **Lusaka City Market Bus Station** (Lumumba Rd) or the **City Bus Station** (off Chachacha Rd), also called the Kulima Towers Station.

All long-distance public buses (and a few private ones) use the **Lusaka Inter-City Bus Station** (Dedan Kimathi Rd). From this terminal, buses and minibuses go several times a day to Ndola (ZK65,000, four hours, five daily),

Livingstone (ZK100,000, seven hours, at least seven daily) and Chipata (ZK115,000, eight hours, eight daily). Heading west, 10 buses per day go through Kafue National Park and on to Mongu (ZK115,000, seven hours). Tracking northeast, buses make a beeline for Kasama (ZK130,000, 14 hours, four daily) and Mpulungu (ZK150,000, 18 hours, four daily).

Train

The *Zambezi Express* travelling to Livingstone (economy class ZK40,000, 14 hours), via Choma, leaves Lusaka at 11.50pm on Monday and Friday and no longer has 1st or sleeper class. Tickets are available from the reservations office inside the **train station** (btwn Cairo Rd & Dedan Kimathi Rd). Get there early and be prepared to hustle and bustle. Slow, 'ordinary' trains to Ndola (standard class ZK25,000, 12 hours), via Kapiri Mposhi (ZK17,000, eight hours), depart Tuesday and Saturday at 1.20pm.

GETTING AROUND

Local minibuses run along Lusaka's main roads, but there are no route numbers or destination signs, so the system is difficult to work out. The standard fare is ZK2000 to ZK3000. Official taxis can be identified by the numbers painted on the doors and their colour – light blue. They can be hailed along the street or found at ranks near the main hotels and markets.

EASTERN ZAMBIA

KATETE
☎ 0216
About 90km from Chipata and 500km from Lusaka, Katete is a small town just south of the Great East Rd. On the main road, 4km west of Katete, **Tikondane Community Centre** is a grassroots initiative that works with local villages. Among its many activities, it focuses on adult and child education, and agricultural initiatives, and trains home-based carers for AIDs victims. Tikondane also accept volunteers to work at its centre and on its projects (see www.tikondane.org for details). Consider staying at its **Guest House** (Tiko Lodge; ☎ 252122; Great East Rd; s without bathroom ZK60,000, d bathroom ZK90,000, tr ZK105,000). The simple rooms here come with beds, and a small chair and table. They are cool inside and monastic in size and feel. It's simple digs but very good value for the price. An internet cafe and further guest accommodation is planned.

CHIPATA
☎ 0216
Chipata is a large busy town and, despite its size, has a rural feel – it's the primary urban space in the district. There are some decent and affordable accommodation options, making it a very useful stop between Zambia and Malawi (30km from the border), as well as a launching pad into South Luangwa National Park. There are petrol stations and banks with ATMs along the main road. The lodges (below) are definitely the best places to eat.

Sleeping

our pick **Dean's Hill View Lodge** (☎ 221673; dean mitch@zamtel.zm; campsite ZK25,000, dm ZK50,000, tw per person ZK50,000) This lodge is a great little place run by an affable British chap. It features upstairs dorms, twin rooms and camping, a nice big sloping garden, spacious and spotless shared bathrooms and grand views over Chipata and the hills. Coming from Lusaka, take the first right after the welcome arch, just before the Total petrol station.

Mama Rula (☎ 097-790226; mamarula@iwayafrica. com; campsite US$8, dinner bed & breakfast per person US$75; 🖳 🖳) There's a huge grassy garden campsite here with a large bar that's very popular with the overland crowd. Next door is the B&B, which has some lovely, cosy rooms; each one is themed a little differently. It's a great place to stay and is located 4km out of Chipata along the Mfuwe Rd to South Luangwa.

Ndanji Lodge (☎ 097-6656460; r with/without bathroom ZK120,000/100,000) If you prefer more of a guesthouse vibe, then this locally run place makes an excellent choice. Rooms are reasonably basic, but have a homely feel, reflecting the rest of the house. It's a friendly spot and meals are available, although self-catering is also possible, as they will let you use their kitchen.

Getting There & Away

Several bus companies in Lusaka offer services to Chipata (see opposite). See p1093 for details about travelling between Chipata and South Luangwa National Park.

SOUTH LUANGWA NATIONAL PARK
☎ 0216
For scenery, variety of animals, accessibility and choice of accommodation, **South Luangwa** (admission per Zambian-registered vehicle/non-Zambian-registered vehicle/person ZK15,300/US$15/US$25;

6am-6pm) is the best park in Zambia and one of the most majestic in Africa. Impalas, pukus and buffalo wander on the wide open plains; leopards, of which there are many in the park, hunt in the dense woodlands; herds of elephants wade through the marshes; and hippos munch serenely on Nile cabbage in the Luangwa River.

The focal point is **Mfuwe**, a village with shops, a petrol station and a market. About 1.8km further on is **Mfuwe Gate**, the main entrance to the park, where a bridge crosses Luangwa River and several cheaper lodges, camps and campsites are set up. Most of the park is inaccessible between November and April (especially February and March), so many lodges close at this time.

Activities

Unlike other parks in Zambia, boat trips are not available in South Luangwa, but all lodges and camps run excellent day and night **wildlife drives** (all year) and some have **walking safaris** (June to November). These activities are included in the rates charged by the upmarket places, while the cheaper lodges and camps can organise activities at short notice. A three-hour morning or evening wildlife drive normally costs around US$40, and the evening drive in particular offers the chance to spot an elusive leopard.

Sleeping & Eating

our pick **Flatdogs Camp** (☎ 246038; www.flatdogs camp.com; campsite US$7.50, safari tent US$35-40, chalet US$50; 🖳 🐾) This large camp has great facilities and a wide choice of affordable accommodation, and is very popular. The safari tents are our favourites, perched right on the river's edge, with outside tables and chairs for enjoying the view. The chalets are enormous and surprisingly luxurious, with large, mosaic-tiled bathrooms and self-catering facilities – very good for families or small groups (up to six). Number 4 is the best, with a brilliant upstairs deck overlooking the river.

Croc Valley (☎ 246074; crocvalleycamp@iwayafrica. com; campsite/dm/chalet US$7.50/25/50; 🐾) Set under a tangle of trees on a large grassy area, this place is probably the best deal for budget travellers, with backpacker rooms that are surprisingly good value and very comfortable. (If you're on the bone-crunching minibus from Chipata, try asking the driver to take you straight here

instead of Mfuwe village.) The chalets have a vogue look, with sunken bathrooms; safari tents sitting under thatched roofs are also a good option. There's a bar-restaurant and plenty of hammocks and shaded chill-out spots.

Wildlife Camp (☎ 246026; www.wildlifecamp-zambia. com; campsite/safari tent/chalet US$10/40/60; 🐾) If you want a classic safari-camp atmosphere, without breaking the bank, this place is ideal. A spacious, secluded spot, about 5km southwest of Mfuwe village, the chalets here sleep up to three people. The safari tents and spacious campsite are well situated, with their own bar and pool, and perfect sundowner views. The camp operates in association with the Wildlife & Environmental Conservation Society of Zambia, so you know that part of your money is going directly into conservation and development projects.

our pick **Kawaza Village** (www.kawazavillage.co.uk; day visits US$25, s incl full board US$70) This enterprise is run by the local Kunda people and gives tourists the opportunity to visit a real rural Zambian village while helping the local community. The village has four *rondavel* huts (each sleeps two) reserved for visitors, and there are open-air reed showers and long-drop toilets. Visitors are encouraged to take part in all aspects of village life, such as learning how to cook *nshima* and other traditional foods, attending local church services and visiting local schools.

Kapani Lodge (☎ 246015; www.normancarrsafaris. com; ste US$550) The most famous of the top-end lodges is this classic Luangwa camp built by Norman Carr in Lupande Game Management Area. The 10 thatched cottages and large circular houses all have private verandahs and are set among neat lawns and colourful gardens overlooking a beautiful green lagoon frequented by birds and weed-munching hippos. Accommodation is among the most comfortable and roomy of the smaller camps in and around South Luangwa. The lodge runs highly rated walking safaris, usually to and between four smaller rustic bush camps, ideal for experiencing the African bush. Rates are all-inclusive and the lodge is open year-round.

All the lodges, camps and camping grounds provide meals. There are also a couple of basic eateries in Mfuwe village. **Cobra Resthouse** (Mfuwe village; meals ZK14,000) offers cheap Zambian stews, burgers and breakfasts.

Getting There & Away

Most people reach South Luangwa by air. Mfuwe (Masumba) airport is about 20km southeast of Mfuwe Gate and is served by chartered flights from Lusaka and, occasionally, from Lilongwe (Malawi). **Proflight** (☎ 0211-271032; www.proflight-zambia.com) offers regular flights between Lusaka and Mfuwe every day for US$250 one way.

To get to Mfuwe Gate and the surrounding camps from Chipata, you need a 4WD high-clearance vehicle. In the dry season the dirt road is usually poor and the drive takes about three hours. In the wet season, however, the drive can take all day (or be impassable), so seek advice before setting off.

Minibuses leave when very full one or two times a day from Chipata and Mfuwe village. Fares are squarely priced for foreigners (about US$8). You'd be wise to offer some extra kwacha to the minibus driver to take you on to one of the campsites near Mfuwe Gate.

NORTHERN ZAMBIA

MPULUNGU
☎ 0214

Resting at the foot of mighty Lake Tanganyika, Mpulungu is a crossroads between eastern, central and southern Africa. As Zambia's only international port, it's the terminal for the ferry across the lake to Tanzania. Don't be tempted to swim in the lake because there are crocs.

Nkupi Lodge (☎ 455166; campsite per person ZK40,000; chalet from ZK80,000) By far the best place for independent travellers. This shady campsite and lodge is a short walk out of town and has plenty of soft, grassy earth for erecting tents, as well as a number of *rondavels*, including a huge self-contained number with fresh stone floors and a large comfy bed.

New Harbour Inn (☎ 0978-571331; r from ZK80,000) A simple, friendly place, just a short walk from the centre of town, this small inn has rooms in little cottages in the grounds. They are large, clean and simple, with separate sitting areas, large fans, satellite TV and huge tiger-face rugs. There's a small restaurant, too.

Most buses'/minibuses' schedules tie in with the Lake Tanganyika ferry. To/from Lusaka, Juldan Motors depart at noon daily (ZK130,000, 13 hours), via Kasama (ZK50,000,

three hours) and Mbala (ZK10,000, one hour). Minibuses also depart from near the BP petrol station in Mpulungu for Mbala (ZK15,000, 50 minutes).

AROUND MPULUNGU

About 40km northwest of Mbala, and along the border between Zambia and Tanzania, is the 221m-high **Kalambo Falls** (adult/child/car US$3/2/3, campsite US$10). Kalambo is the second-highest single-drop waterfall in Africa; from spectacular viewpoints near the top of the falls, you can see the Kalambo River plummeting off a steep V-shaped cliff cut into the Rift Valley escarpment down into a deep valley, which then winds down towards Lake Tanganyika. There is a campsite here, with stunning views out over the Rift Valley. Facilities are basic (there's only a long-drop toilet), but there is a caretaker. The best way for travellers without a car to get here is from Mpulungu. One option is a thrice-weekly taxi boat that serves villages along the lakeshore east of Mpulungu.

MBALA
☎ 0214

Mbala is a small town perched on the edge of the Great Rift Valley, from where the road north drops over 1000m in less than 40km down to Mpulungu and Lake Tanganyika. All buses/minibuses travelling between Mpulungu and Kasama stop in Mbala.

The **Moto Moto Museum** (admission US$3; 🕒 9am-4.45pm), about 3km out of town, showcases a huge and fascinating collection of artefacts, focusing on the cultural life of the Bemba people of the surrounding area.

The best place to stay in town is **Makungo Guest House** (s/d ZK40,000/45,000). Rooms are clean and good value and are centred on a courtyard that also doubles up as a minibus garage. The guesthouse is about 100m off the main road; take the turning opposite the fuel station.

KASAMA
☎ 0214

Kasama is the capital of the Northern Province and is the cultural centre of the Bemba people. With its wide leafy streets and handsome old tin-roofed colonial houses, it is the most appealing of the northern towns. Places to stay include the **Thorn Tree Guesthouse** (☎ 221615, 096-951149; www.thorntreesafaris.com; 612 Zambia Rd; r per person from US$30), near the Heritage Centre, which

ZAMBIA

offers comfortable rooms in lush and colourful gardens; and the **Kalambo Guest House** (☎ 222221; Luwingu Rd; s/d from ZK50,000/60,000), where the welcome is warm and there are spotless rooms.

SHIWA NG'ANDU
☎ 0214

The vast estate of **Shiwa Ng'andu** (www.shiwa ngandu.com; tours US$20; ☻ 9-11am Mon-Sat, 10-11am Sun) was established in the 1920s by British aristocrat Stewart Gore-Brown. At its heart is **Shiwa House**, a splendid English-style mansion as described in *The Africa House* by Christina Lamb (see p1099).

Kapishya Hot Springs is about 20km west of Shiwa House, but still on the Shiwa Ng'andu estate. The setting is simply marvellous – a blue-green steaming lagoon surrounded by palms – and the springs are bathwater hot. It is possible to stay next to the springs at **Kapishya Lodge** (☎ 0211-229261; www.shiwasafaris.com; campsite/chalet per person US$10/90, d incl B&B per person US$130), and rather grand accommodation is also available at **Shiwa House** (bookings through Kapishya Lodge; d per person incl full board from US$350) itself.

To reach Shiwa House, head along the highway by bus (or car) from Mpika for about 90km towards Chiosso. Look for the signpost to the west, from where a dirt road (13km) leads to the house. Kapishya Hot Springs and the Lodge are a further 20km along this track. There is no public transport along this last section, but vehicle transfers are available from the Great North Rd turn-off.

SAMFYA

Perched on the western shore of Lake Bangweulu, about 10km east of the main road between Mansa and Serenje, you'll find Samfya. This small trading centre and lake-transport hub is small enough to get to know people and large enough to have rest houses, restaurants and bars. Just outside town is the majestic, sandy **Cabana Beach**, but stay away from the water – it may look inviting but it's full of crocs.

Samfya Sun and Sand Resort (s/d ZK90,000/110,000) has basic thatch huts on the beach, a restaurant and camping. **Samfya Beach Hotel** (campsite per person ZK40,000, r ZK120,000) has a pretty good location, but the rooms are poky with basic bathrooms and the food isn't much cop.

Samfya is regularly served by minibuses from Serenje (ZK60,000, four to five hours). Buses between Lusaka and Mpulungu go via Serenje.

THE COPPERBELT

NDOLA & KITWE
☎ 0212

These two towns lie at the heart of the industrial Copperbelt region and, although they're not tourist attractions in themselves, you might find yourself passing through on the way to Chimfunshi Wildlife Orphanage.

In Ndola, the far more pleasant of the two towns, the **New Ambassador Hotel** (☎ 097-7773909, 374396; President Ave; s/tw/d ZK100,000/130,000/210,000; ▯ ☎) is the best value in town. Try to get a light and airy room on the 3rd floor; some of these have great views. Or else try the grandiose **New Savoy Hotel** (☎ 611097; savoy@zamnet.zm; Buteko Ave; s/d/ste incl breakfast ZK425,000/475,000/545,000; ✕ ▯ ▣) in the centre of town.

In Kitwe, **Mukwa Lodge** (☎ 224266; www.mukwa lodge.co.zm; 26 Mpezeni Ave; s/d incl breakfast ZK500,000/600,000; ✕ ▣) has gorgeous rooms with stone floors that are beautifully furnished – the bathrooms are as good as you'll find in Zambia.

From Lusaka fast buses head to Ndola (ZK65,000, four hours, five daily) and on to Kitwe (ZK70,000, five hours). Slow 'ordinary' trains to Ndola and Kitwe, via Kapiri Mposhi, depart twice weekly.

CHIMFUNSHI WILDLIFE ORPHANAGE

On a farm 70km northwest of Chingola is this magnificent **chimpanzee sanctuary** (chimfunshi wildlife@iwayafrica.com; day visit adult/child project area ZK50,000/25,000, orphanage ZK25,000/10,000; ☻ 9am-3pm), home to nearly 100 adult and young chimps confiscated from poachers and traders in neighbouring Democratic Republic of Congo and other parts of Africa. It's the largest of its kind in the world. This is not a natural wildlife experience, but it's still fascinating to observe the chimps as they feed, play and socialise.

Visiting the sanctuary provides much-needed income and your entry fees go directly into helping it remain financially viable. Do not come, though, if you're sick in any way; the chimps can easily die of a disease like the flu. Visitors can stay at the **campsite** (per person US$10) or in the **self-catering cottage** (per person US$25, whole cottage US$200). Note that, at the time of writing, accommodation was about to undergo a serious overhaul.

By car, take the Solwezi Rd for about 43km northwest from Chingola, then turn right at the signposted junction and follow it for 18km to the orphanage. It's then a further 12km to the project area. A new, much better road is currently being graded (it's about 20km off the main road straight to the project area), and is 55km from Chingola and well signposted.

SOUTHEASTERN ZAMBIA

SIAVONGA

☎ 01

Siavonga is the main town and resort along the Zambian side of Lake Kariba. Just a few kilometres from the massive Kariba Dam, Siavonga is a quiet, low-key village. From here you can arrange boat trips on Lake Kariba and canoeing safaris on the Zambezi River.

A visit to the dam wall is a must while you're here – most lodges organise boat trips, otherwise you can take your own wheels (make sure you get a stamped pass to the dam wall at Zambian immigration). The lodges organise activities in and around the lake.

our pick Eagles Rest (☎ 511168; www.eaglesrest resort.com; campsite per person ZK40,000, chalet ZK200,000; ❄ ⬛) has the only campsite around town. It's the best-value place in Siavonga, with large, spacious chalets that boast stone floors, a double and a single bed, and great decking outside. The food here is excellent, too. Eagles Rest also has the greatest variety of activities, including a two-hour sunset cruise (ZK60,000) and a boat trip and village tour (from ZK265,000 per person).

The rooms at **Zefa Lodges** (☎ 511480; r ZK250,000-400,000; ❄) are of a high standard. Spotlessly clean and with plenty of space, rooms 1 to 6 are probably the best, and the Exec and VIP options are huge. It's on the road down to Eagles Rest. Rates are negotiable when it's quiet.

Minibuses from Lusaka (ZK45,000, three hours, three to five daily) leave when bursting to capacity for Siavonga and the nearby border.

LOWER ZAMBEZI NATIONAL PARK

Zambia's newest **national park** (admission per person/vehicle US$25/15; ⏱ 6am-6pm) covers 4092 sq km along the northwestern bank of the Zambezi River, opposite the Mana Pools National Park in Zimbabwe. This is now one of Zambia's premier parks, with a beautiful flood plain alongside the river, dotted with acacias and other large trees, and flanked by a steep escarpment on the northern side, covered with thick *miombo* woodland.

The best wildlife viewing is on the flood plain and along the river itself, so boat rides (about US$30) are a major feature of all camps and lodges. Seeing groups of elephants swim across the river could be the highlight of your trip.

The main entrance is at Chongwe Gate along the southwestern boundary, though there are gates along the northern and eastern boundaries for hardy travellers.

Sleeping

Community Campsite (campsite US$5) A basic place a few kilometres before Chongwe Gate. It's mainly set up for travellers with their own vehicles. It's run by local people, and the modest profits are put back into the community.

our pick Kiambi Safari (☎ 097-718 6106; www.kiambi.co.za; campsite US$19, chalet per person incl full board from US$139; ❄ 🛜 ⬛) This well-run operation at the confluence of the Zambezi and Kafue Rivers has a smattering of affordable accommodation options. Tented chalets here are a soothing, airy option – elevated and very comfy.

Mvuu Lodge (☎ in South Africa 012-660 5369; www.mvuulodge.com; campsite US$20, safari tent US$160, safari tent incl full board from US$210) Mvuu has comfortable tented rooms overlooking the Zambezi River, with balconies and sandy outdoor fireplaces that are lit outside your tent every night. There's superb decking overlooking the river that makes for a perfect spot for a sundowner, with grunting hippos below.

Sausage Tree Camp (☎ in Lusaka 0211-845204; www.sausagetreecamp.com; d per person incl full board US$895; ⏱ May–mid-Nov; ⬛) Overlooking the Zambezi, deep inside the national park, Sausage Tree is exclusive and slightly unconventional. Traditional safari decor is rejected in favour of cool and elegant Bedouin-style tents, completely rebuilt in 2008, each in a private clearing, with minimalist furniture, cream fabrics and vast open-air bathrooms that continue the North African theme.

Getting There & Away

There's no public transport to Chongwe Gate (and you need a high-clearance 4WD to visit independently), nor anything to the eastern and northern boundaries, and hitching is very difficult. Most people visit the park on an organised tour, and/or stay at a lodge that offers wildlife drives and boat rides as part of the deal.

ZAMBIA

SOUTHWESTERN ZAMBIA

LIVINGSTONE
☎ 0213

The historic town of Livingstone, named after the famous first European to set eyes on Victoria Falls, sprang to life following the construction of the Victoria Falls Bridge in 1904. For the remainder of the 20th century, it was a quiet provincial capital until the political and economic troubles in Zimbabwe deflected tourists. It then had to lift its game and a mass of renovations and construction commenced. Livingstone is now the preferred base for backpackers visiting Victoria Falls.

Unless you stay on the Zambezi riverfront, though, you are not staying in a natural setting, but in an African border town: not much to look at, but fun. It has excellent (read: roomy, cheap and well-organised) hostels, all with bar-restaurants, as well as wi-fi, and the full gamut of Vic Falls activities can be organised within.

Orientation
Several establishments are located along the Zambezi, but most are along – or just off – Mosi-oa-Tunya Rd, 11km from the falls.

Information
Barclays Bank (cnr Mosi-oa-Tunya Rd & Akapelwa St)
Cyber Post (216 Mosi-oa-Tunya Rd; internet per hr US$4)
Livingstone General Hospital (☎ 321475; Akapelwa St)
Police (☎ 320116; Maramba Rd)
Post office (Mosi-oa-Tunya Rd)
Standard Chartered Bank (Mosi-oa-Tunya Rd)
Tourist Centre (☎ 321404; Mosi-oa-Tunya Rd; ☽ 8am-1pm & 2-5pm Mon-Fri, 8am-noon Sat)

Dangers & Annoyances
When travelling to and from the falls, take a blue taxi for US$10. There have been muggings, even on bicycles.

Sights & Activities
One of the most popular sights is **Livingstone Island**, in the middle of the Zambezi River at the top of the falls, so you can literally hang your feet off the edge. A trip to the island costs about US$45 and can be arranged at your hotel or hostel.

African Culture, Language and Meals Experiences (☎ 323432; www.adventure-africa.com; 559 Mokambo Rd), which can be organised through Fawlty Towers, are good-value African experiences at Ngoma Zanga with a meal, singing, drumming and dancing.

Mukuni Village (admission US$3; ☽ dawn-dusk) is a 'traditional' Leva village that welcomes tourists on guided tours. Although the village can be inundated with tourists at times, the admission fee does fund community projects.

The **Capitol Cinema** (Mosi-oa-Tunya Rd), located quite close to the Jollyboys, caters for travellers with films, live shows and screenings of major football matches. Flyers with programs are distributed at hostels.

The stately **Livingstone Museum** (Mosi-oa-Tunya Rd; adult US$2) contains a collection of David Livingstone memorabilia and historic maps dating back to 1690.

The hotels and backpacker lodges are one-stop shops for arranging ongoing travel and day- and overnight trips, as well as all your adrenalin activities. Tour operators and accommodation facilities work together to help you plan.

Sleeping
Staying in town means being able to walk to the bars and restaurants; the riverfront allows relaxation in seclusion along gorgeous stretches of the Zambezi, and, when near the falls, views to the top of the falls. Downriver, away from the falls, where the Zambezi River opens up more, you can view wildlife without even leaving your hotel.

TOWN CENTRE
Livingstone Backpackers (☎ 323432; www.adventure-africa.com; 559 Mokambo Rd; campsite US$3, dm from US$5, r US$20; ☒) It's Fawlty Towers Mark II only new, and bigger, cheaper and better than before. It has a bar, climbing wall, pool, hot tub, snazzy open-air living room, satellite TV and self-catering. Good for groups of overlanders or individual travellers.

Jollyboys Backpackers (☎ 324229; www.backpackzambia.com; 34 Kanyanta Rd; campsite US$6, dm from US$6, d from US$25; ☒) The sunken lounge, observation tower, pool, restaurant-bar and satellite TV have been installed by fun-loving owners. At night, for security reasons, no nonguests are allowed.

Fawlty Towers (☎ 323432; www.adventure-africa.com; 216 Mosi-oa-Tunya Rd; s/d incl half board US$25/45;

LIVINGSTONE

ZAMBIA

) Has undergone renovations and been upgraded to a guesthouse, with wi-fi, a great pool and garden, a hip bar and an on-the-pulse vibe, via owner, Richard Sheppard, a campaigner for bringing back budget travel. Its restaurant-bar Hippos (p1098) is *the* hot nightspot in town.

ZigZag (☎ 322814; www.zigzagzambia.com; Mosi-oa-Tunya Rd; s/d/f US$45/70/90; ) Motel-style rooms with pool, huge garden, air-con, wi-fi and great cakes! Home of ZigZag Coffee House.

ZAMBEZI RIVERFRONT
Budget
Jungle Junction Bovu Island (☎ 323708; www.jungle junction.info; campsite per person US$10-15, hut per person US$20-30; ) For hippos, hammocks and harmony: an island in the middle of the Zambezi for travellers who simply want to hang out and lounge beneath palm trees, or fish. Meals cost US$7 to US$12.

Midrange
Zambezi Waterfront (☎ 320606; www.safpar.net /waterfront; campsite per person US$10, s/d tent per person US$30/20, s/d incl breakfast per person from US$125/110, f US$200; ) Accommodation includes luxury tents, riverside chalets and family suites. A highlight is the beer garden right on the Zambezi River.

Natural Mystic Lodge (☎ 324436; www.natural mysticlodge.com; s/d from US$85/95; ) The atmosphere is way more rustic than at some of the more upmarket lodges, though it makes for a peaceful retreat. It's 20km from Livingstone and 30km from the falls. Transfers are usually provided.

Top End

Chundukwa River Lodge (☎ 324452; info@maplanga. co.za; campsite per person US$10, hut per person US$125; Ⓟ Ⓢ) This simple but rustic lodge consists of thatched huts perched directly on the water. Sightings of elephants and hippos from the rooms are commonplace. There is a cooling plunge pool right on the riverbank and yummy, Zambian-style home cooking.

Tongabezi Lodge (☎ 323235; www.tongabezi.com; cottage/house per person US$430/530; Ⓟ ☒ Ⓢ) Here you'll find sumptuous spacious cottages and open-faced 'houses', with trees as part of the structure and private dining decks. Guests are invited to spend an evening on nearby Sindabezi Island (US$350 per person per night), selected by the *Sunday Times* as the best remote place to stay in the world.

Eating & Drinking

Funky Munky (216 Mosi-oa-Tunya Rd; snacks & mains US$5) This laid-back bistro is a popular backpackers' hang-out and prepares baguettes, salads and pizzas in a comfortable setting.

Olga's (cnr Mosi-oa-Tunya & Nakatindi Rds; mains US$5-10) A fab new pizza place.

Ngolide (Mosi-oa-Tunya Rd; mains US$5-10) For Indian tandoori or spicy chicken; popular with the locals and tourists.

Fez Bar (Kabompo Rd; mains US$6) Moroccan-inspired, it serves tasty meals by day, then gets rocking at night.

Hippos (Limulunga Rd; mains US$6) This raucous but newly renovated bar-restaurant at the back of Fawlty Towers is housed underneath a soaring two-storey thatched roof.

Ngoma Zanga (Mosi-oa-Tunya Rd; meals US$25) For an 'African experience' without being tacky: excellent African food, plus dancing, drumming and singing performances.

Getting There & Away

AIR

Proflight Zambia (☎ 0211-271032; www.proflight -zambia.com) connects Livingstone to Lusaka, Botswana and Namibia. **South African Airways** (www.flysaa.com) and **British Airways** (www.british airways.com) both have daily flights to/from Johannesburg, with fares starting at US$450 return.

BUS & MINIBUS

RPS (Mutelo St) has two buses a day to Lusaka (seven hours); **CR Carriers** (cnr Mosi-oa-Tunya Rd & Akapelwa St) has four a day (seven hours). Buses to Sesheke (five hours) leave at 10am from Mingongo bus station. Buses direct to Mongu (ZK51,370, nine hours) leave Maramba Market at midnight.

For travel to Botswana, crossing the Zambia–Botswana border at Kazungula, see p1102. For travel to Namibia, crossing the Zambia–Namibia border at Katima Mulilo, see p1102. For travel into Zimbabwe, see p1103.

HITCHING

To hitch to Livingstone from Kazungula (Botswana) and Katima Mulilo (Namibia), try at petrol stations.

TRAIN

The *Zambezi Express* leaves Livingstone for Lusaka (15 hours), via Choma, on Tuesday, Thursday and Sunday at 7pm. Book at the **train station** (☎ 320001).

Getting Around

TO/FROM THE AIRPORT

Livingstone Airport is 6km from town, US$10 by taxi.

CAR & MOTORCYCLE

Hemingways (☎ 320996; www.hemingwayszambia.com; Mosi-oa-Tunya Rd) has new Toyota Hi-Lux campers, fully kitted. Based at ZigZag (p1097).

COMBIS & TAXIS

Combis (minibuses) run regularly along Mosi-oa-Tunya Rd to the Victoria Falls Zambian border (US$0.50, 15 minutes). Blue taxis cost US$10.

MOSI-OA-TUNYA NATIONAL PARK

The park is divided into the Victoria Falls World Heritage National Monument Site and Mosi-oa-Tunya Game Park.

Victoria Falls World Heritage National Monument Site

The **entrance** (admission US$10; ☺ 6am-6pm), near the Zambian border post, has a visitors information centre just inside, then paths lead to different viewpoints. You can walk – with caution – along the Zambezi River, watching it flow to the top of the falls.

View the **Eastern Cataract** close up: it's a hair-raising walk across the **footbridge** through swirling clouds of mist, to the **Knife Edge**. If the water is low you'll get magnificent views of the falls and the yawning abyss below. If not, you will be nicely drenched by spray! Take the steep track to the riverbank to see the **Boiling Pot** – a huge whirlpool.

On the Zimbabwean side, the park is open in the evenings around full moon for viewing the amazing **lunar rainbow**. Tickets cost an extra US$10.

Mosi-oa-Tunya Game Park

Upriver from the falls, and only 3km southwest of Livingstone, is a tiny **wildlife sanctuary** (admission US$10; ☉ 6am-6pm), with rhinos, zebras, giraffes, buffalo, elephants and antelopes.

MONGU

☎ 0217

The largest town in Barotseland and the capital of the Western Province, Mongu is on high ground overlooking the flat and seemingly endless Liuwa Plain. This is a low-key town, with plenty of activity on the streets, but it doesn't feel as hectic as other Zambian towns. Around the **harbour** is a fascinating settlement of reed-and-thatch buildings, where local fishermen sell their catch, and passenger boats take people to outlying villages.

Mongu really comes alive once a year when thousands of people flock here for the **Ku'omboka ceremony**, held in March or early April. This colourful ceremony takes place when the king of the Lozi people moves from his dry-season palace out on the plains to his wet-season palace on higher ground. The king is transported to higher ground on a decorated river barge. The wet-season palace is at **Limulunga**, about 15km north of Mongu, where you'll find a museum containing exhibits about the Lozi people and the Ku'omboka ceremony.

Lyambai Hotel (☎ 221138; Lusaka Rd; r ZK80,000-100,000) has seen better days, but this beat-up place does have character, shade, sublime views over the flood plain and friendly staff; or try **Crossroad Guesthouse** (☎ 221649; Lusaka Rd; r ZK100,000; ⊠), with its clean rooms.

A daily bus operates between Livingstone and Mongu (ZK120,000, 10 hours) via Sesheke, Kalongola and Senanga, but you're advised to break up this horror journey in Senanga. Minibuses and pick-ups leave on a fill-up-and-go basis from near the Caltex filling station in

Mongu for Senanga (US$4.50, three hours), from where minibuses head to Sesheke.

ZAMBIA DIRECTORY

ACCOMMODATION

There isn't a great range of budget accommodation on offer in Zambia. The widest choice is in Livingstone, but Lusaka also has a couple of backpackers' hostels. However, there are plenty of cheap local guesthouses throughout the country. Most towns will also have one or two midrange accommodation options, with rooms with private bathrooms going for around ZK150,000 to ZK350,000 per double. All national parks have expensive privately operated lodges and 'camps', which will set you back between about US$250 and US$800 per person per night. These rates usually include all meals, drinks and activities, such as wildlife drives.

In this chapter, we've generally listed high-season prices (from June to September) for all accommodation.

ACTIVITIES

Companies in Livingstone (p1096) offer a bewildering array of activities, such as white-water rafting, river boarding and bungee jumping. The less adventurous may want to try some hiking and horse riding. Canoeing is also a great way to explore the Zambezi River and can be arranged in Siavonga (or Kariba in Zimbabwe).

Many tour companies in Livingstone offer short wildlife drives in Mosi-oa-Tunya National Park near Victoria Falls, while companies in Lusaka and Livingstone can also arrange longer wildlife safaris to more remote national parks.

BOOKS

The Africa House, by Christina Lamb, tells the story of Stewart Gore-Brown and his grand plans for a utopian fiefdom in a remote part of Zambia during the 1920s. His mansion at Shiwa Ng'andu is still standing (see p1094).

Although it's more a personalised selection of observations on wildlife and humans, *Kakuli*, by Norman Carr, also raises deeper issues and suggests some practical solutions to current conservation problems. The author spent a lifetime working with animals and people in the South Luangwa National Park.

Challenging the effectiveness of aid in Africa, Zambian-born Dambisa Moyo explodes the

ZAMBIA

PRACTICALITIES

- The *Daily Times* and *Daily Mail* are dull, government-controlled rags. The independent *Post* (www.postzambia.com), featuring a column by Kenneth Kaunda, continually needles the government.

- The monthly *Lowdown* magazine (www.lowdown.co.zm; ZK5000) has useful information for visitors such as restaurant reviews and lists of upcoming events in the capital, as well as handy adverts for package deals for lodges around Zambia.

- Both of the Zambian National Broadcasting Corporation (ZNBC) radio stations can be heard nationwide; they play Western and African music, as well as news and chat shows in English.

- Televisions use the PAL system.

- Electricity supply is 220V to 240V and 50Hz, and plugs are of the British three-prong variety.

- The metric system is used in Zambia.

---

myths in *Dead Aid*, arguing that aid is actually a major cause of poverty.

DANGERS & ANNOYANCES

Generally, Zambia is very safe, though in the cities and tourist areas there is always a chance of being targeted by muggers or con artists. As always, you can reduce the risk considerably by being sensible.

EMBASSIES & CONSULATES

The following countries have embassies or high commissions in Lusaka. The British High Commission looks after the interests of Aussies and Kiwis as the nearest diplomatic missions for Australia and New Zealand are in Harare (Zimbabwe). Most consulates are open from 8.30am to 5pm Monday to Thursday and from 8.30am to 12.30pm Friday, though visas are usually only dealt with in the mornings.

Botswana (Map pp1088–9; ☎ 0211-250555, fax 0211-253895; 5201 Pandit Nehru Rd)

Canada (Map pp1088–9; ☎ 0211-250833, fax 0211-254176; 5119 United Nations Ave)

Democratic Republic of Congo (Map pp1088–9; ☎ 0211-235679, 0211-213343, fax 0211-229045; 1124 Parirenyetwa Rd)

France (Map pp1088–9; ☎ 0211-251322, fax 0211-254475; 74 Independence Ave, Cathedral Hill)

Germany (Map pp1088–9; ☎ 0211-250644; 5209 United Nations Ave)

Ireland (off Map pp1088–9; ☎ 0211-291298; 6663 Katima Mulilo Rd)

Kenya (Map pp1088–9; ☎ 0211-250722; 5207 United Nations Ave)

Malawi (off Map pp1088–9; ☎ 0211-265764, fax 0211-260225; 31 Bishops Rd, Kabulonga)

Mozambique (Map pp1088–9; ☎ 0211-220333, fax 0211-220345; 9592 Kacha Rd, off Paseli Rd, Northmead)

Namibia (off Map pp1088–9; ☎ 0211-260407/8, fax 0211-263858; 30B Mutende Rd, Woodlands)

Netherlands (Map pp1088–9; ☎ 0211-253819, fax 0211-253733; 5208 United Nations Ave)

South Africa (off Map pp1088–9; ☎ 0211-260999, 26D Cheetah Rd, Kabulonga)

Sweden (Map pp1088–9; ☎ 0211-251711, fax 0211-254049; Haile Selassie Ave)

Tanzania (Map pp1088–9; ☎ 0211-227698, fax 0211-254861; 5200 United Nations Ave)

UK (Map pp1088–9; ☎ 0211-423200; http://ukinzambia.fco.gov.uk/en; 5210 Independence Ave)

USA (Map pp1088–9; ☎ 0211-250955; http://zambia.usembassy.gov; cnr Independence & United Nations Aves)

Zimbabwe (Map pp1088–9; ☎ 0211-254006, fax 0211-254046; 11058 Haile Selassie Ave)

HOLIDAYS

During the following public holidays, most businesses and government offices are closed:

New Year's Day 1 January
Youth Day Second Monday in March
Easter March/April – Good Friday, Saturday & Easter Monday
Labour/Workers' Day 1 May
Africa (Freedom) Day 25 May
Heroes' Day First Monday in July
Unity Day First Tuesday in July
Farmers' Day First Monday in August
Independence Day 24 October
Christmas Day 25 December
Boxing Day 26 December

INTERNET ACCESS

There are internet centres in Lusaka, Livingstone and most towns. Access at internet centres is cheap – about ZK150 to ZK200 per minute – but irritatingly slow at times. Wireless is becoming more common.

LANGUAGE

Of the 70 languages and dialects spoken in Zambia, seven are recognised by the government as official 'special languages'. These include Bemba (mainly spoken in the north); Tonga (in the south); Nyanja (in the east), which is similar to Chichewa spoken in Malawi; and Lozi (in the west).

As a lingua franca, and the official, national language, English is widely spoken across Zambia.

MONEY

Zambia's unit of currency is the kwacha (ZK), sometimes listed as 'ZMK', 'k' or 'kw', and is considered fairly stable. Some businesses in Zambia quote prices in kwacha and others in US dollars (US$) – most lodges and camps in and around national parks, for example, quote prices in US dollars. We have followed local convention in this chapter.

In the cities and larger towns, you can change cash and (sometimes) travellers cheques at branches of Barclays Bank and Standard Chartered Bank. Larger branches have ATMs that accept Visa cards. Foreign exchange offices are easy to find in all cities and larger towns.

POST

Postcards and normal letters (under 20g) cost ZK2700 to send to Europe and ZK3300 to the USA, Canada, Australia and New Zealand. Sending international letters from Lusaka is surprisingly quick (three or four days to Europe), but from elsewhere in the country it's less reliable and much slower.

TELEPHONE

Public phones operated by Zamtel use a token, available from post offices (ZK500) or local boys (ZK1000) hanging around phone booths. These tokens last three minutes but are only good for calls within Zambia. Phone booths operated by Zamtel use phonecards (ZK5000, ZK10,000, ZK20,000 or ZK50,000), available from post offices and grocery shops; these phonecards can be used for international calls. But it's often easier to find a 'phone shop' or 'fax bureau', from where all international calls cost about ZK12,000 per minute.

Mobile Phones

MTN, Celtel and Zain (best coverage) all offer mobile (cell) phone networks. If you own a GSM phone, you can buy a SIM card for around ZK8000 without a problem, and top-up cards are widely available. Numbers starting with ☎ 095, ☎ 096, ☎ 097 and ☎ 099 are mobile phone numbers.

TOURIST INFORMATION

The **Zambia National Tourist Board** (ZNTB; www. zambiatourism.com) has two international offices: in the **UK** (☎ 020-7589 6655; zntb@aol.com; 2 Palace Gate, Kensington, London W8 5NG) and in **South Africa** (☎ 012-326 1847; zahpta@mweb.co.za; 570 Ziervogel St, Hatfield, Pretoria). The official ZNTB website is outstanding and provides links to dozens of lodges, hotels and tour agencies.

VISAS

All foreigners visiting Zambia need visas but, for most nationalities, tourist visas are available at major borders, airports and ports. But it's important to note that you should have a Zambian visa *before* arrival if travelling by train or boat from Tanzania.

Citizens of South Africa and Zimbabwe can obtain visas on arrival for free. For all other nationalities, tourist visas are issued on arrival, and the prices have been standardised, with most nationalities paying US$50 for single entry (up to one month), US$80 for double entry (up to one month), and US$160 for multiple entry (up to three months). Note that only a single- or double-entry visa is available from Lusaka airport.

Visas for Onward Travel

It's always best to visit any embassy or high commission in Lusaka between 9am and noon from Monday to Friday. For embassy contact details, see opposite.

Visas for Zimbabwe, Malawi, Tanzania and Botswana are easy to obtain on arrival at the borders of these countries for most visitors. However, if you're travelling by train or boat to Tanzania, check with the Tanzanian high commission in Lusaka about whether you need a visa beforehand. If so, three-month visas cost about US$50 (depending on your nationality). You cannot obtain a visa for Namibia at the border; tourist visas are either free or cost US$50, depending on your nationality, in Lusaka. For Mozambique, single-entry visas (only) are available at most major land and air entry points for US$25 for one month.

TRANSPORT IN ZAMBIA

GETTING THERE & AWAY

Air

Zambia's main international airport is in Lusaka, though some international airlines fly to the airports at Livingstone (for Victoria Falls), Mfuwe (for South Luangwa National Park) and Ndola. The major domestic and international carrier was Zambian Airways, but it suspended operations in early 2009 citing high fuel costs, although it has been speculated that its high debt was the real reason.

Zambia is well connected with southern Africa. **Zambezi Airlines** (www.flyzambezi.com) flies to regional destinations, such as Johannesburg in South Africa (from Lusaka and Ndola), and Dar es Salaam in Tanzania. **South African Airways** (www.flysaa.com) is the major regional airline, flying regularly to Lusaka from its hub in Jo'burg; it also connects with the rest of the region and continent.

Air Malawi (www.airmalawi.com) connects Lusaka with Lilongwe three times a week, and with Blantyre twice a week; while **Air Zimbabwe** (www.airzimbabwe.com) also flies to Lusaka from Harare on the way to Nairobi.

Land

Zambia's main borders are open from 6am to 6pm, except for those at Victoria Falls, which closes at 8pm, and Chirundu, which closes at 7pm.

BOTSWANA

Several minibuses leave Livingstone every day for the terminal used by the pontoon ferry to Kazungula (ZK20,000, 35 minutes). The pontoon carries small cars/large cars/non-Zambian, registered vehicles for ZK20,000/ZK40,000/US$20, while foot passengers pay ZK4000. From the Botswanan border, minibuses regularly leave for Kasane.

A quicker and more comfortable (but more expensive) way to reach Botswana from Zambia is to cross from Livingstone to Victoria Falls (in Zimbabwe), from where shuttle buses head to Kasane. From the **Lusaka Inter-City Bus Station** (Dedan Kimathi Rd), there are buses to Gaborone (ZK180,000, 22 hours, three weekly), via Kasane and Francistown.

> **DEPARTURE TAX**
>
> The departure tax for all international flights is US$20. The departure tax for domestic flights is US$8. These taxes are *sometimes* included in the price of your airline ticket – if not they must be paid at the airport (in US dollars only).

MALAWI

Direct buses between Lusaka and Lilongwe are infrequent and slow, so it makes sense to do this trip in stages. From the BP petrol station on the main street in Chipata, regular minibuses (ZK20,000) run the 30km to the border. Once you've passed through Zambian customs, it's a few minutes' walk to the Malawian entry post, from where you can get a shared taxi to Mchinji for around MK300 per person, followed by a minibus to Lilongwe.

MOZAMBIQUE

There is no cross-border public transport between Zambia and Mozambique and the only common border leads to a remote part of Mozambique – you'll need to do the trip to Tete in stages via Katete, Cassacatiza (the border) and Matema. Note that this is a remote border crossing and most travellers, therefore, chose to visit Mozambique from Lilongwe in Malawi.

NAMIBIA

Buses (and several minibuses) leave Livingstone for Sesheke (ZK45,000, two hours, two or three daily). The bus may terminate in Sesheke or continue another 5km across the new bridge to Zambian immigration. From the Namibian side, it's a 5km walk to Katima Mulilo, from where minibuses depart for other parts of Namibia.

Alternatively, cross from Livingstone to Victoria Falls (in Zimbabwe) and catch a shuttle bus to Windhoek (Namibia).

SOUTH AFRICA

For South Africa, City to City has buses leaving every day for Johannesburg (ZK300,000, 26 hours, one daily). Trans Africa, however, is far more comfortable, with services to Jo'burg (ZK360,000) three times a week. All buses between Lusaka and Jo'burg travel via Harare, Masvingo and Pretoria.

TANZANIA
Boat
The MV *Liemba* leaves from Mpulungu harbour every Friday, arriving in Kigoma (Tanzania) on Sunday. Fares for 1st, 2nd and economy class are US$60/45/35. Visas can be issued on the ferry and cost US$50.

Bus
Services to Dar es Salaam from Lusaka (ZK250,000, 27 hours, six weekly) aren't very reliable. Alternatively, walk across the border from Nakonde, and take a minibus from Tunduma to Mbeya in Tanzania.

Train
The Tazara railway company usually operates two international trains per week between Kapiri Mposhi (207km north of Lusaka) and Dar es Salaam. The 'express train' leaves Kapiri Mposhi at 5.15pm on Tuesday, while the 'ordinary train' leaves Kapiri Mposhi at 5.15pm on Friday. The journey time for both trains is 48 hours; fares are ZK237,000/198,000/145,000 in 1st/2nd/3rd class (1st and 2nd class are sleeping compartments) on the express train and ZK187,000/151,000/125,000 on the ordinary train. A discount of 50% is possible with a student card.

ZIMBABWE
To Zimbabwe, take any bus going to South Africa. If you're travelling from Siavonga, take a minibus or charter a car to the border, and walk (or take a shared taxi) across the impressive Kariba Dam to Kariba, from where buses leave daily to Harare.

GETTING AROUND
Air
Zambia's main domestic airports are located at Lusaka, Livingstone, Ndola, Kitwe, Mfuwe, Kasama and Kasaba Bay, though dozens of minor airstrips throughout the country cater for chartered planes.

There is a plethora of charter services in Zambia, but only one airline offering scheduled flights. **Proflight Zambia** (www.proflight-zambia.com) has filled the domestic gap since Zambian Airways went out of business and is flying regularly (up to two or three times daily) from Lusaka to Mfuwe (for travellers heading to South Luangwa National Park), Lower Zambezi, Livingstone (for Victoria Falls) and Ndola.

Bus & Minibus
Distances are long, buses are often slow and many roads are full of potholes, so travelling around Zambia by bus or minibus can exhaust the hardiest of travellers, even those who do like a good butt massage.

All main routes are served by ordinary public buses, which run on a fill-up-and-go basis or have fixed departures (these are called 'time buses'). 'Express buses' are faster – often terrifyingly so – and stop less often, but cost about 15% more. In addition, several private companies run comfortable European-style express buses along the major routes. Many routes are also served by minibuses, which only leave when full. In remote areas the only public transport is often a truck or pick-up.

Car & Motorcycle
Cars can be hired from international and Zambian-owned companies in Lusaka, Livingstone, Kitwe and Ndola, but renting is expensive. For example, **Voyagers/Imperial Car Rental** (www.voyagerszambia.com/imperialrates.htm) charges from US$43 per day for the smallest vehicle, plus US$0.32 per kilometre (less per day for longer rental periods). Add to this insurance (from US$26 per day), VAT (17.5%) and petrol. Other companies, such as **4x4 Hire Africa** (www.4x4hireafrica.com), rent old-school Land Rover vehicles, unequipped or fully decked out with everything you would need for a trip to the bush, with prices for an unequipped vehicle starting at about US$120 per day.

Most companies insist that drivers are at least 23 years old and have held a licence for at least five years. You can drive in Zambia using your driving licence from home as long as it's in English.

While most main stretches of sealed road are OK, beware of potholes. Most gravel roads are pretty good, though they also suffer from potholes. If you're travelling outside of the urban centres, you'll need a 4WD.

NB: most rental companies do not insure their vehicles in Zambia.

Tours
Tours and safaris around Zambia invariably focus on the national parks. Since many of these parks are hard to visit without a 4WD vehicle, joining a tour might be your only option anyway. Most Zambian tour operators are based in Lusaka (p1087), Siavonga (p1095) and Livingstone (p1096).

ZAMBIA

Train

The Tazara trains between Kapiri Mposhi and Dar es Salaam in Tanzania (see p1103) can also be used for travel to/from northern Zambia. While the Lusaka–Kitwe service does stop at Kapiri Mposhi, the Lusaka–Kitwe and Tazara trains are not timed to connect with each other, and the domestic and international train terminals are 2km apart.

Zambia's only other railway services are the 'ordinary trains' between Lusaka and Kitwe (p1091), via Kapiri Mposhi and Ndola, and the 'express trains' between Lusaka and Livingstone (p1098).

On the 'express train' between Lusaka and Livingstone, a 'sleeper' is a compartment for two people; 1st class is a sleeper for four; 2nd ('standard') class is a sleeper for six; and 3rd class (economy) is a seat only. Sometimes these trains will only have economy or standard class available – just a seat. On the 'ordinary train' between Lusaka and Kitwe, 'standard' class – the only class – is also just a seat.

Zimbabwe

Zimbabwe continues to dip in and out of international headlines, often creating an unclear but daunting vibe for prospective visitors. In 2008 the economy collapsed and there was a cholera outbreak that killed around 4000 people. But in 2009 many Zimbabweans dared to dream (again) when Robert Mugabe's 29-year-old regime formed a unity government with the opposition.

Today, the cholera has abated, the economy has dollarised and, at least in the urban areas, things are easier and the people happier.

There remain, of course, more than enough reasons for the world's media to focus on the fall of Zimbabwe (not least of all the government). However, tourists will experience something worlds apart from outside perceptions. From the absolute wilderness of Mana Pools National Park, the five-star and adrenalin options at Victoria Falls and the mountains looking over Mozambique, to the serenity of the capital, Zimbabwe is an extraordinary place to visit. It remains one of southern Africa's most beautiful and – right now – untouristed countries. It is the path less travelled and history in the making.

Zimbabwe is no longer as dirt cheap as it once was, but it's not expensive either and its recording-breaking inflation stories are consigned to history. Whether you overland, arrange it all through a tour operator or figure it out for yourself, a country of charm, beauty and intrigue awaits.

FAST FACTS

- **Area** 390,580 sq km (slightly larger than Germany)
- **ATMs** Currently not used
- **Borders** South Africa, Botswana, Zambia, Mozambique
- **Budget** US$150+ per day, more if on safari
- **Capital** Harare
- **Languages** English, Shona, Ndebele
- **Money** The US dollar is now used legally throughout Zimbabwe
- **Population** 13 million (official, though up to three million Zimbabweans are thought to have emigrated since 2001)
- **Seasons** Cool and dry (May to October), warm and wet (November to April)
- **Telephone** Country code ☎ 263; international access code ☎ 00
- **Time** GMC/UTC +2
- **Visa** 90 days (US$30 for most nationalities), issued at point of entry

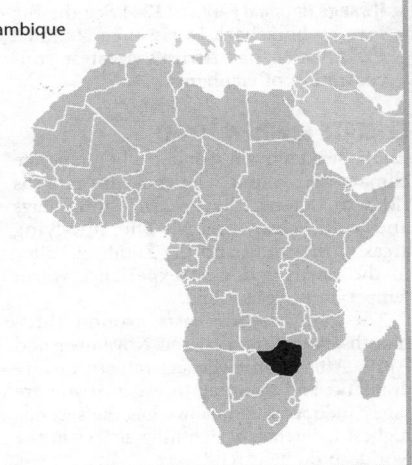

HOW MUCH?

- **Soapstone sculpture** US$2-200
- **Safari** US$50-350
- **Wooden carving** US$1-100
- **Steak** US$7
- **Sunscreen** US$7

LONELY PLANET INDEX

- **1L petrol** US$1.20
- **1L bottled water** US$0.80
- **Bottle of beer** US$3
- **Souvenir T-shirt** US$20
- **Plate of chips** US$1

HIGHLIGHTS

- **Victoria Falls** (p1124) Literally dive into Africa: adrenalin sports, stunning nature and five-star African dining and accommodation.
- **Mana Pools National Park** (p1119) Visit Africa's only national park that allows un-guided walking safaris (with lions); canoe the Zambezi – as far as Mozambique if you like; or volunteer for the Mana Game Count – first full moon in September.
- **Harare** (p1110) Check out the not-to-be-missed HIFA (Harare International Festival of the Arts), held annually in the last week of April.
- **Hwange National Park** (p1124) See the Big Five by horseback in Hwange National Park, which has Africa's greatest concentration of elephants.

CLIMATE & WHEN TO GO

Zimbabwe enjoys a wonderfully temperate climate year-round. The cool, dry months (May to October) have warm, sunny days and cold, clear nights. The low-lying areas of the south and the Zambezi Valley to the north and west experience warm temperatures year-round.

The rainy season lasts around three months, sometime between November and April. Afternoon electrical rainstorms are dramatic, and stunning to watch if you are safely indoors – Zimbabwe has the second-highest incidence of lightning strikes in the world, so do be careful.

Winter, consisting of several dry months, is the best time for wildlife viewing because animals tend to congregate at the diminishing waterholes, making the creatures easier to find.

ITINERARIES

- **One to Two Weeks** Base yourself in one or two places – eg Victoria Falls (p1124) for falls, river and bush, and then Hwange National Park (p1124) and Bulawayo (p1121) for Matobo National Park. Or take in Harare (p1110) before wandering through the Eastern Highlands (p1119).
- **Three Weeks** Spend longer at (and around) the places mentioned above, and add in Nyanga National Park (p1119), Kariba (p1118) or Mana Pools National Park (p1119).
- **One Month** Fly from Johannesburg, South Africa, to Victoria Falls for a few days, then on to Hwange National Park for a safari far from the madding crowds. Then fly to Harare and take a road trip to the Bvumba Mountains (p1119) overlooking Mozambique.

HISTORY

For general information on African history, see p27.

Beginnings of Nationalism

Conflicts between black and white in Zimbabwe came into sharp focus after the 1922 referendum in which the whites chose to become a self-governing colony rather than join the Union of South Africa. In 1930 white supremacy was legislated in the form of the Land Apportionment Act.

Poor wages and conditions eventually led to a rebellion, and by the time Southern Rhodesia, Northern Rhodesia and Nyasaland were federated, in 1953, mining and industrial concerns favoured a more racially mixed middle class as a counterweight to the radical elements in the labour force.

Two African parties soon emerged – the Zimbabwe African People's Union (ZAPU) under Joshua Nkomo, and the Zimbabwe African National Union (ZANU).

Ian Smith & the War for Independence

In 1964 Ian Smith took over the Rhodesian presidency and began pressing for independence. The British prime minister, Harold

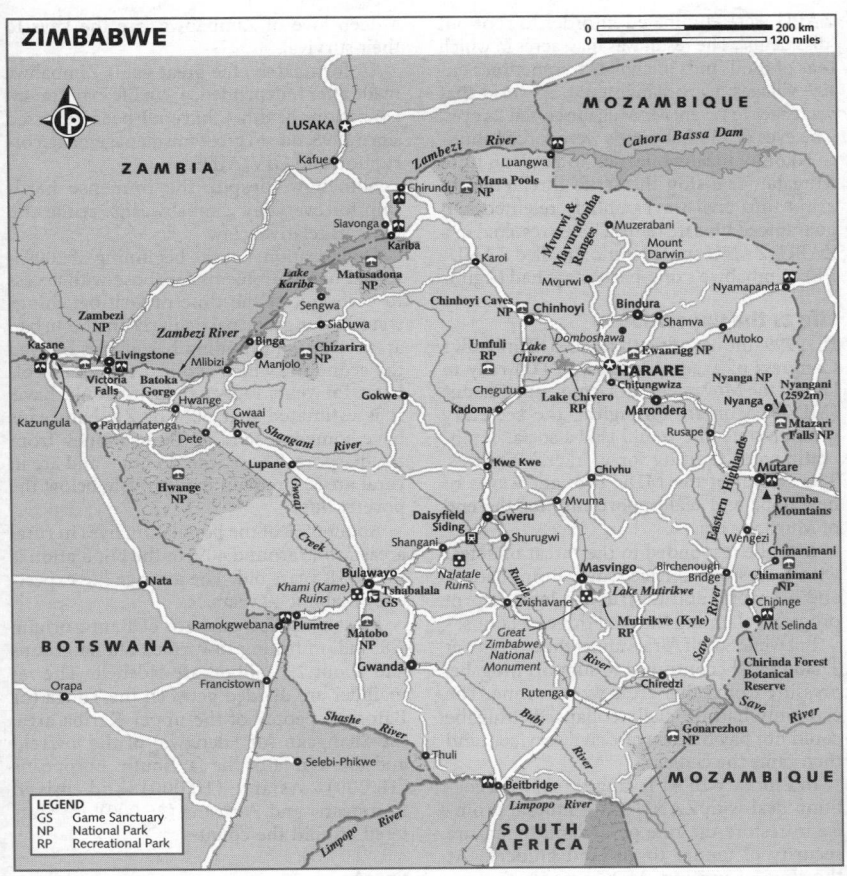

ZIMBABWE

LEGEND
GS	Game Sanctuary
NP	National Park
RP	Recreational Park

Wilson, argued for conditions to be met before Britain would agree: guarantee of racial equality, course towards majority rule, and majority desire for independence. Smith realised the whites would never agree, so in 1965 he made a Unilateral Declaration of Independence.

Independence

On 10 September 1979, delegations met at Lancaster House, London, to draw up a constitution favourable to both the Patriotic Front (an alliance between ZANU and ZAPU) of Nkomo and Robert Mugabe, and the Zimbabwe-Rhodesian government of Abel Muzorewa and Smith. Mugabe, who wanted ultimate power, initially refused to make any concessions, but after 14 weeks the Lancaster House Agreement was reached. It guaranteed whites (then 3% of the population) 20 of the 100 parliamentary seats.

Soon after, the economy soared, wages increased, and basic social programs – notably education and healthcare – were initiated. However, the initial euphoria, unity and optimism quickly faded: a resurgence of rivalry between ZANU (run mostly by Shona people) and ZAPU (mostly by Ndebele) escalated into armed conflict, and Nkomo was accused of plotting against the government. Guerrilla activity resumed in ZAPU areas of Matabeleland, and Mugabe deployed the North Korean–trained Fifth Brigade in early 1983 to quell the disturbances. Villagers were gunned down and prominent members of

ZAPU were eliminated in order to root out 'dissidents'. The result was massacres in which tens of thousands of civilians, sometimes entire villages, were slaughtered. A world that was eager to revere Mr Mugabe closed its eyes. The eyes of Zimbabweans were forced shut.

Nkomo, meanwhile, fled to England until Mugabe (realising the strife threatened to erupt into civil war) publicly relented and guaranteed his safe return. Talks resulted in a ZAPU–ZANU confederation (called ZANU-PF). Zimbabwe's one-party state had begun.

Life as the Opposition

In 1999 thousands attended a Zimbabwe Congress of Trade Unions (ZCTU) rally to launch the Movement for Democratic Change (MDC). Morgan Tsvangirai, the secretary general, stated he would lead a social democratic party fighting for workers' interests. The arrival of the MDC brought waves of new hope and real opportunity for the end of Mugabe's era.

Mugabe responded to the threat of defeat with waves of violence, voter intimidation, and a chaotic and destructive land reform program, claiming the next three elections.

But while South Africa under then-president Thabo Mbeki continued to support Mugabe, pressure from other areas was growing. The economy had officially collapsed, Mugabe could not pay his army or civil service…and then came the cholera.

In February 2009, Tsvangirai signed a coalition deal with ZANU-PF, a mutual promise to restore the rule of law and to 'ensure security of tenure to all land holders'. At the time of writing, MDC was in government with Mugabe's party, but was largely impotent. But with the 'dollarisation' of the economy, life in urban areas had become easier – supermarkets were full of local and imported food, albeit with prices similar to those in the West. Life in rural areas, however, remains extremely arduous.

CULTURE

Whether black, white or in between, Zimbabweans have a philosophical stoicism reminiscent of bygone eras. In Zimbabwe, the southern African expression to 'make a plan' can be defined as: if it's broke, fix it. If you can't fix it, live with it, or change your life (overnight if need be). This kind of mental strength and generosity, combined with a deep love of Zimbabwe, are the keys to their survival.

Unfortunately, the great gains Zimbabwe made after independence – in life expectancy, education, health – have all been reversed since 1998, due to gross mismanagement, corruption and HIV/AIDS.

Somehow, despite the immense hardship for everyday Zimbabweans, crime still remains relatively low.

Dollarisation – at the beginning of 2009 – solved many problems for those with access to cash. So, at the time of writing, things were looking up, particularly in the urban areas. Diaspora funding has always buoyed the economy, which avoided economic collapse for years longer than it should have. It is estimated that 60% of Zimbabweans have someone sending them money from the diaspora. Those who do not – and are in rural areas – remain dangerously below the poverty line.

About 65% of the population lives in rural areas, while around 40% of the population is under 18 years old. The average life expectancy is about 40 years.

Most Zimbabweans are of Bantu origin; 9.8 million belong to various Shona groups and about 2.3 million are Ndebele. The remainder are divided between the Tonga (or Batonga) people of the upper Kariba area, the Shangaan (or Hlengwe) of the lowveld and the Venda of the far south. Europeans (18,000), Asians (10,000) and mixed Europeans and Africans (25,000) are scattered around the country.

Sport

For a long time Zimbabwe punched well above its weight in sport, due largely to good administration and a dreamy climate for getting outdoors. They did well in football (soccer), constantly upset heavyweights in cricket, produced some cracking tennis players and won Olympic gold.

However, Zimbabwe's sporting teams have followed the same trajectory as the country's economy.

Religion

The majority of Zimbabweans are Christian, although traditional spiritual beliefs and customs are still practised – especially in rural areas, where merciless economic times are leading to an increase in faith (and fraud).

Arts & Crafts

Zimbabwe's festivals, fairs and streetside stalls, live music and poetry, dance, art, and sculpture are great expressions of Zimbabwean ideas and a wonderful way for visitors to meet the locals and learn about their lives. It seems like all Zimbabweans are creative in some way – whether they bead, embroider, weave, sculpt or carve. The household handicrafts made from recycled items are really the answer to ecotourism souvenir shopping, if not the future for interior decorating!

'Zimbabwe' means 'great stone house'. Stone sculpture most often represents the people of Zimbabwe to the outside world; a contemporary force guided by an ancient cultural heritage. The talent in this craft has led to years of contributions to major exhibitions worldwide, and critical acclaim.

For information on music in Africa, see p43.

Literature

Easy to find before you travel and most contemporary, *Mukiwa* (A White Boy in Africa) and its sequel, *When a Crocodile Eats the Sun*, by Peter Godwin, are engrossing books following the life of a small boy who witnesses the death of his neighbour by guerrillas, the beginning of the end of white rule in Africa and, eventually, life as an adult journalist in the beginning of the economic and political downward spiral.

Since independence, Zimbabwean literature has focused on the struggles to build a new society. *Harvest of Thorns*, by Shimmer Chinodya, on the Second War for Independence, won the 1992 Commonwealth Prize for Literature. Another internationally renowned writer, Chenjerai Hove, wrote the war-inspired *Bones*, the tragic *Shadows* and the humorous *Shebeen Tales*.

FOOD & DRINK

If you are eating in Victoria Falls, you can have a five-star fine-dining experience of ostrich, warthog, crocodile tail and various members of the antelope family. Otherwise, cafes and restaurants in all the big towns serve Western dishes. The staple for locals is *sadza*, a white maize meal made into either porridge or something resembling mashed potato. The locals are crazy about it – they eat it with tomato-based relishes or meat and/or gravy. Generally restaurants are good, and a meal will cost US$5 to US$30.

The tap water in Zimbabwe is not safe to drink, but bottled mineral water, fruit juices and soft drinks are widely available.

Tea and coffee are grown in the Eastern Highlands. Cafes and restaurants in the cities serve espresso coffee in all its forms – either local or imported beans – while, quirkily, some establishments, especially away from the main cities, serve either instant coffee or chicory! If you are a coffee connoisseur, check when ordering. Nyanga tea is also good and available throughout the country.

The religious majority aren't big drinkers, but *chibuku*, sold in large brown plastic containers ('*scuds*'), is popular with men. The beer you will more commonly see is lager, which is always served cold. The domestically brewed lagers – Zambezi and Bohlinger's – are really good.

ENVIRONMENT

Landlocked Zimbabwe is roughly three times the size of England. It lies within both tropics and consists of highveld and middleveld plateaus, 900m to 1700m above sea level. A low ridge, running northeast to southwest across the country, marks the divide between the Zambezi and Limpopo–Save River systems.

There are few countries better placed than Zimbabwe from which to view and study the stars – because Zimbabwe lies in low latitudes, 97% of the celestial sphere of the stars is available for observation.

Wildlife

The Big Five and most of the animals highlighted in the Wildlife chapter (see p55) are found in Zimbabwe. The number of elephants is almost at plague proportions, with Hwange said to have the most out of any park in the world.

Zimbabwe is also great for fishing: the rivers, dams and lakes are home to 117 species of fish. Anglers love the fight put up by the powerful tigerfish: there is no more fierce-looking freshwater fish. Its common name comes from the lateral stripes along the body and its large, sharp, protruding teeth – it is also related to the piranha. To take this beast on fly is every fisherman's dream.

The ubiquitous Msasa tree is the mascot for Zimbabwe, but in the town centres zillions of jacarandas and fire trees bloom

ZIMBABWE

between September and November, creating a riot of purple mixed with red. All year round, bougainvillea twist over bushes and huge mature trees. Gardens host succulent tropical flowers and palms, and, thanks to the English and their love of gardens, ubiquitous roses and stunning gardens remain one of the more pleasant colonial legacies.

National Parks

Most of Zimbabwe's national parks are – or contain – Unesco World Heritage Sites. With the current paucity of tourists, you will have the parks and reserves to yourself – or feel as though you do. Close to 20% of Zimbabwe's surface area is protected – or semiprotected – in national parks, privately protected game parks, nature conservancies and recreational parks.

Park entry fees range from US$5 to US$20 per day, and you can book your accommodation through tour operators or the National Parks & Wildlife Zimbabwe (NPWZ) offices. See p1113 for information about booking lodges and campsites run by NPWZ.

Environmental Issues

If you're interested in learning about Zimbabwe's ecological problems, contact **Wildlife & Environment Zimbabwe** (www.zimwild.org) or **Conservation Task Force** (www.zctf.mweb.co.zw), or marufu@forestry.co.zw for information on forestry issues.

If you want to help out physically, have a genuine Zimbabwean experience and a lot of fun, volunteer for the **Mana Pools Game Count** (bushpig@mango.zw), which is held over the weekend of the first full moon in September.

HARARE

☎ 04 / pop 2 million

Harare has enough sights and activities to keep visitors satisfied for a day or two. It is a very laid-back city, its best attractions being natural, though the live music, craft and interiors are also excellent. The town centre has high-rise office buildings ranging from cool to wacky, and some downtown madness at the edges comprising a huge bus station on one side and bargain Asian-goods shopping on the other.

ORIENTATION

The city is compact and easy to get around on foot. If you have time, spend some in town: shopping in and around Robert Mugabe St is hectic, with Indian fabric shops, cheap shoes and clothes shops, and outlets for car spares.

INFORMATION
Bookshops

To be honest, there were no longer any good bookshops at the time of writing, but you could buy secondhand books at Avondale markets.

Avondale Bookshop (Map p1111; King George Rd) Opposite Avondale Shopping Centre – sells a few locally written books.

Emergency

Avenues Clinic (Map pp1112-13; ☎ 251180/99; cnr Mazowe St & Baines Ave) Recommended by expats.
Medical Air Rescue Service (MARS; ☎ 727540)
Police station (Map pp1112-13; ☎ 733033; cnr Inez Tce & Kenneth Kaunda Ave)
Trauma Centre (Map p1111; ☎ 700666/815; Lanark Rd, Belgravia) Also recommended by expats.

Internet Access

Wireless internet access is available at several cafes around the northern suburbs, such as Italian Bakery, CeeCees, Cork Road and Arundel Spar Café (24 hours).

One Stop Internet Café (Map pp1112-13; 60 Speke Ave)
Quick N Easy Internet Shop (Map pp1112-13; ☎ 799224/5; Linquenda House, cnr First St & Nelson Mandela Ave)

Internet Resources

African Encounter (www.africanencounter.com) A good travel agent for bus timetables, hiring cars and internal and domestic flights.
Twin Arts (www.twinarts.co.zw) For what's on in Zimbabwe, particularly arts, music and dance; also festivals, shopping, bushwalking and links to NGOs.
ZWNews (ironhorse@zwnews.net) Email with subject as 'subscribe' for a free online subscription for daily news coverage about Zimbabwe from around the world.

Media

Zimbabwe's media is heavily controlled. The state runs the radio stations and the lone TV station, which broadcasts national news (mainly government propaganda), international news and music programs in English, Shona and Ndebele. The state also owns the only daily newspaper, the *Herald*.

ZIMBABWE

HARARE

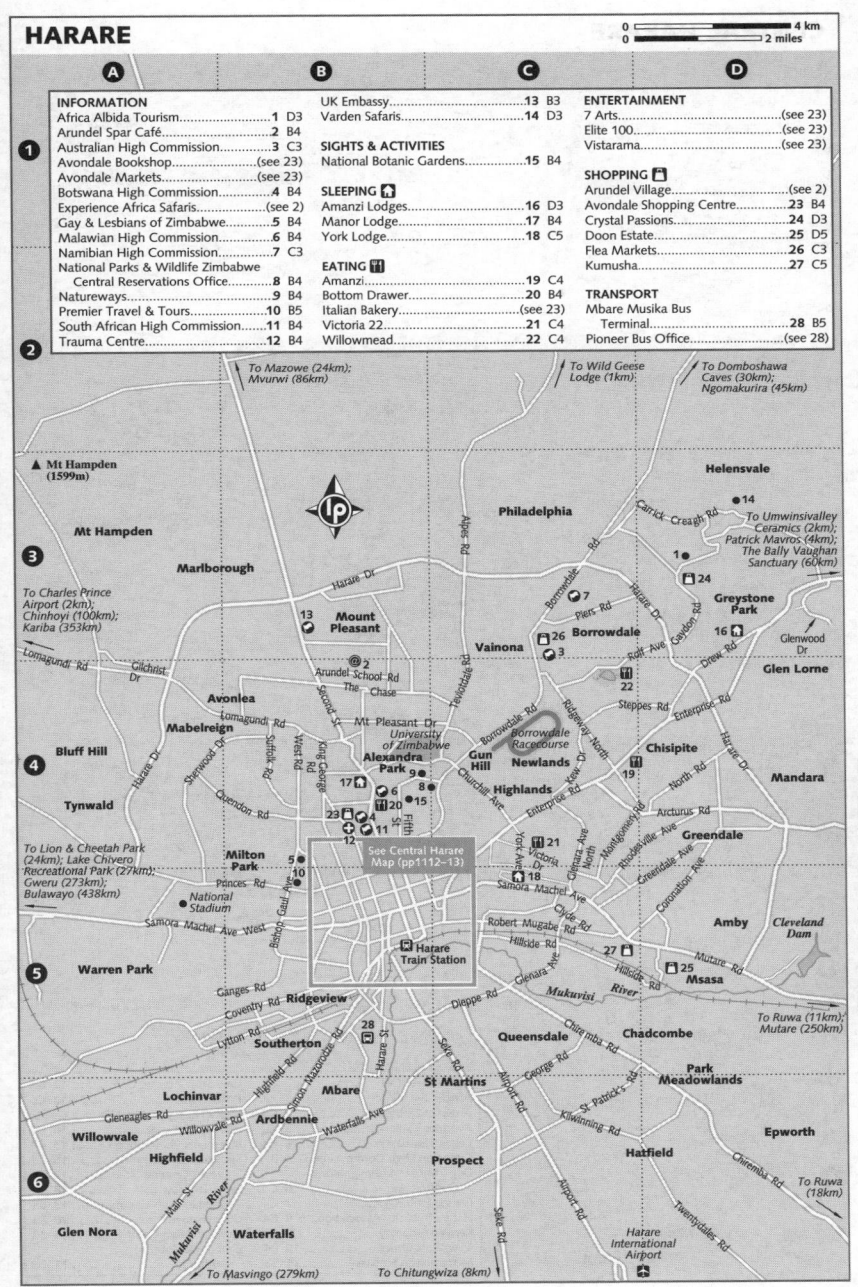

0 — 4 km
0 — 2 miles

INFORMATION
Africa Albida Tourism........................**1** D3
Arundel Spar Café...............................**2** B4
Australian High Commission...........**3** C3
Avondale Bookshop.....................(see 23)
Avondale Markets.........................(see 23)
Botswana High Commission...........**4** B4
Experience Africa Safaris................(see 2)
Gay & Lesbians of Zimbabwe.........**5** B4
Malawian High Commission............**6** B4
Namibian High Commission............**7** C3
National Parks & Wildlife Zimbabwe
  Central Reservations Office.........**8** B4
Natureways..**9** B4
Premier Travel & Tours.................**10** B5
South African High Commission....**11** B4
Trauma Centre................................**12** B4

UK Embassy......................................**13** B3
Varden Safaris..................................**14** D3

SIGHTS & ACTIVITIES
National Botanic Gardens...............**15** B4

SLEEPING 🛏
Amanzi Lodges.................................**16** D3
Manor Lodge....................................**17** B4
York Lodge.......................................**18** C5

EATING 🍴
Amanzi..**19** C4
Bottom Drawer................................**20** B4
Italian Bakery.............................(see 23)
Victoria 22..**21** C4
Willowmead......................................**22** C4

ENTERTAINMENT
7 Arts...(see 23)
Elite 100..(see 23)
Vistarama......................................(see 23)

SHOPPING 🛍
Arundel Village.............................(see 2)
Avondale Shopping Centre...........**23** B4
Crystal Passions..............................**24** D3
Doon Estate....................................**25** D5
Flea Markets....................................**26** C3
Kumusha...**27** C5

TRANSPORT
Mbare Musika Bus
  Terminal......................................**28** B5
Pioneer Bus Office......................(see 28)

ZIMBABWE

CENTRAL HARARE

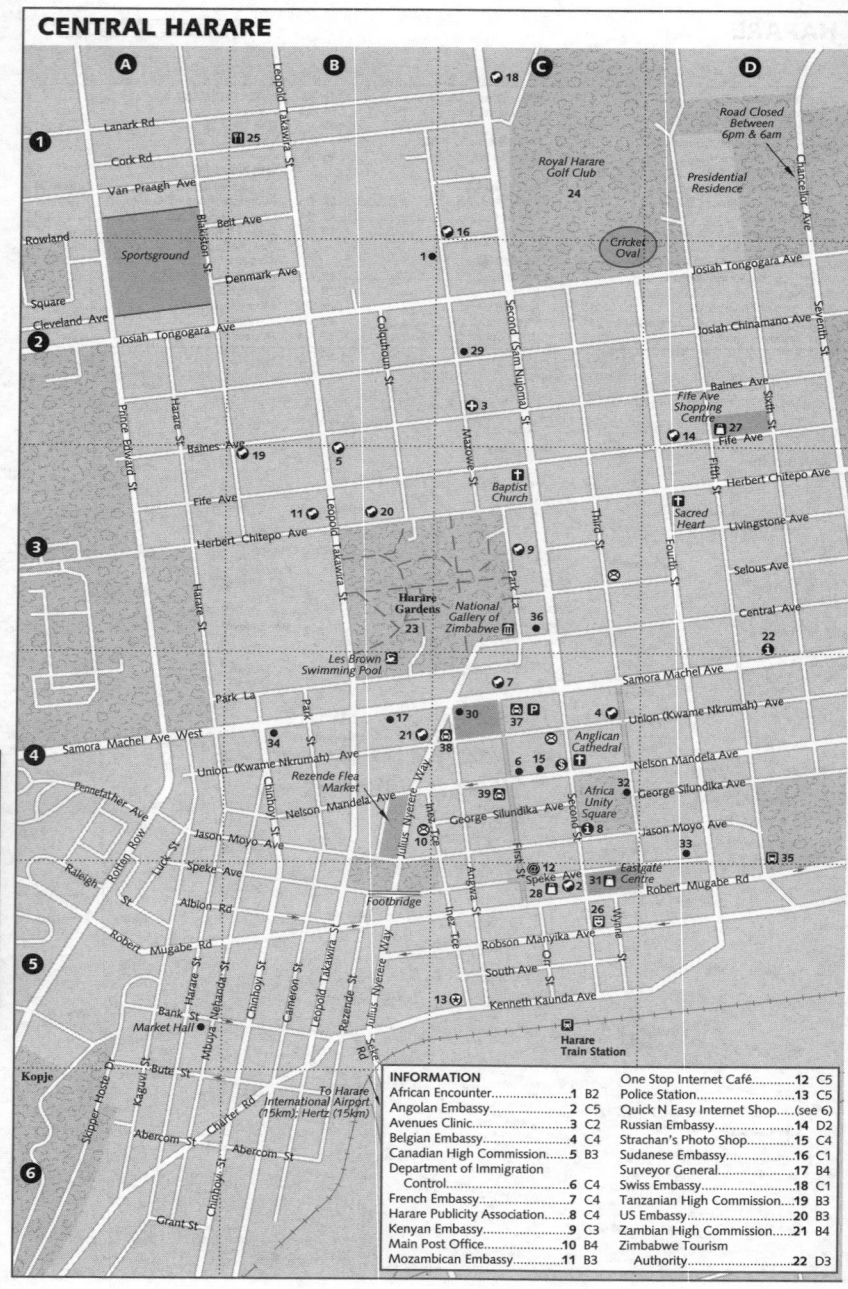

ZIMBABWE

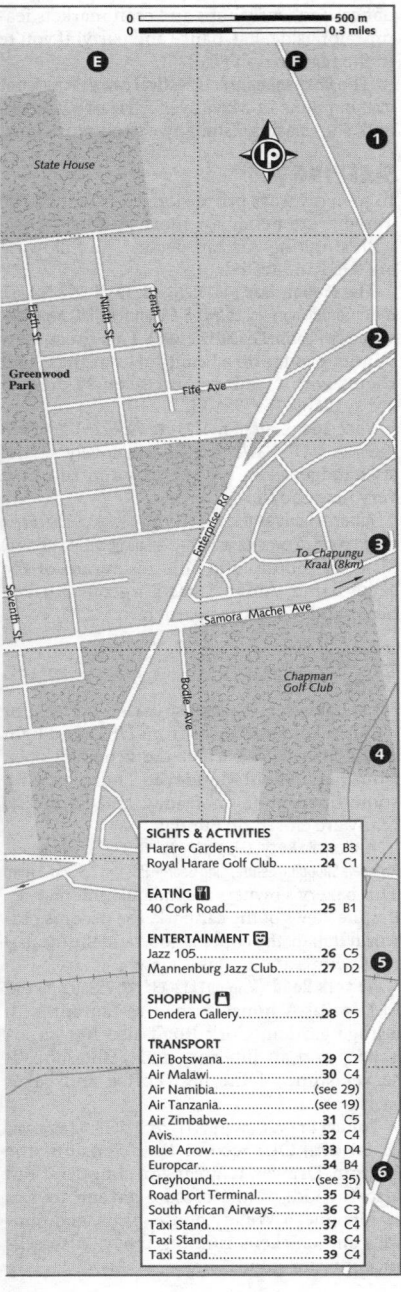

Some balance comes through Friday's *Independent* (a very good read) and the *Zimbabwean* (which comes out of London from Zimbabweans living there).

Money
Zimbabwe, at the time of writing, was calling itself a 'multicurrency economy', meaning it was 'officially' accepting sterling, rand, pula and US dollars. The reality was that the US dollar, and to a lesser extent the rand, were the ones being accepted.

Change for cash is a BIG problem so have plenty of small notes.

Post
Main post office (Map pp1112-13; Inez Tce; 🕑 8am-4pm Mon-Fri, to 11.30am Sat)

Telephone
Telephone booths are long gone, so take a phone with international roaming or use internet/telephone centres around First St in town, or your hotel.

Tour Operators
You can book directly with a tour operator once you know what they have to offer (check with tourist information for an idea of what each does offer):
Africa Albida Tourism (Map p1111; 🕿 885200; fax 860106; www.africaalbidatourism.com; Greystone Park Shopping Centre, Gaydon Rd)
Natureways (Map p1111; 🕿 /fax 744133/744159; www.natureways.com; 8 Kirkwood Rd, Alexandra Park)
Varden Safaris (Map p1111; 🕿 861766; www.varden safaris.com; 160 Gaydon Rd, Greystone Park)

Tourist Information
Department of Immigration Control (Map pp1112-13; 🕿 791913; 1st fl, Linquenda House, cnr Nelson Mandela Ave & First St) To extend your visa, contact this office.
Harare Publicity Association (Map pp1112-13; 🕿 752577-9, 781810, 775622; hhem@africaonline.co.zw)
National Parks & Wildlife Zimbabwe central reservations office (NPWZ; Map p1111; 🕿 706077; fax 726089; national-parks@gta.gov.zw; cnr Borrowdale Rd & Sandringham Dr; 🕑 8am-4pm Mon-Fri) For information and accommodation bookings relating to national parks and reserves.

Travel Agencies
African Encounter (Map pp1112-13; barry@africanen counter.org) Also does backpacking and overland bookings for more than two people.

Experience Africa Safaris (Map p1111; ☎ 301494/369185/369136, 011 603613; skype belinda. whitaker; belinda@xafricasafaris.com; Shop 37, Arundel Village, Quorn Ave, Mount Pleasant) The best travel agent in Zimbabwe.

Premier Travel & Tours (Map p1111; ☎ 704781-6, 91 306481, 011 605244; fax 738754; info@premier.co.zw; 24 Cleveland Ave, Milton Park) Has a mailing list you can join for news and updates for your planning phase.

DANGERS & ANNOYANCES

Bag snatching, pickpocketing and carjacking are on the rise in Zimbabwe, as are robberies at bars and nightclubs. Be careful in cars by keeping your windows up and your bags – including handbags – in the boot or, if that's not possible, safely wedged under your feet.

None of the internal political hostilities are directed at visitors, though this should not tempt you to openly espouse your political views (particularly if they are critical of President Mugabe – this is a crime). Nonetheless, despite the way Zimbabwe is featured in foreign press, the country is safe for visitors.

SIGHTS

In a city of extraordinary gardens, the 58-hectare **National Botanic Gardens** (Map p1111; Fifth St; admission US$5; ☼ dawn-dusk) has suffered some neglect. Most Zimbabwean species are represented, as well as specimens from southern Africa. It has an outdoor cafe.

ACTIVITIES

Go on a personal meet-the-sculptors tour; learn about the latest cutting-edge sculptures being produced in Zimbabwe today; meet the artists and their families and watch them work – you can even buy directly from the artists. Based in Harare, **Zimsculpt** (☎ 912 907758; www. zimsculpt.com; costs on demand; ☼ Nov-May) can offer you this rare opportunity.

The most famous of the seven golf courses around Harare is the internationally acclaimed **Royal Harare Golf Club** (Map pp1112-13; ☎ 702920; Fifth St; ☼ 6am-6pm). Guests are welcome for a temporary membership fee of US$12.

FESTIVALS & EVENTS

Harare International Festival of Arts (☎ 300119; www.hifa.co.zw), held in the last week of April, is on par with many international festivals. Embassies bring out international acts: opera, classical music, jazz, soul, funk, theatre and dance; and workshops and craft markets feature alongside. Eat, dance and party! If you're in the region, don't miss it.

The **Chimanimani Arts Festival** (www.chimanimani. com) happens in May, over Africa Day weekend, showcasing Zimbabwe's top musicians.

SLEEPING

In so many ways private lodges, from US$100 a night, are better for most visitors – cosy, with stunning African decor. The following are tried and tested.

The Manor (Map p1111; ☎ 332193/4, 912 604263; chelmsfordmanor@zol.co.zw; 8 Chelmsford Rd, Avondale; s/d incl half board US$100/120; 🏊) This great, new boutique lodge on a beautiful estate has eight rooms with facilities. Three-course dinners are available for US$35.

York Lodge (Map p1111; ☎ 746622; 1 York Ave, Newlands; s/d US$130/170) This is a lovely safari-style lodge set in the suburbs and run by a very nice couple.

Amanzi Lodges (Map p1111; ☎ 480880, 913 275786; www.amanzi.co.zw; 1 Masasa Lane, Kambanji; s/d US$185/280) Sister of the hip and chic restaurant of the same name, Amanzi has gorgeous African decor and a stunning garden.

EATING
Cafes

Most cafes serve espresso-based coffees for US$1, cakes and snacks from US$4 and light meals from US$7. Cafes are generally open from 9am to 5pm Monday to Thursday, with some open later on Friday and Saturday. Many are closed on Sunday.

Italian Bakery (Map p1111; ☎ 339732; ground fl, Avondale Shopping Centre, King George Rd; ☼ 7.30am-11pm) This bakery's owners are Italian-Ethiopian so, despite views of the car park, the decor is old-world Italian, the coffee is good and the meals – rolls, wraps and pastas – tasty.

40 Cork Road (Map pp1112-13; ☎ 253585; 40 Cork Rd, Belgravia) A house-turned-restaurant with a huge garden, Cork Road also has an art gallery and an interiors and plant shop. It serves some of the best coffee and cakes in Harare.

Bottom Drawer (Map p1111; ☎ 745679; 12 Maasdorp Rd, Belgravia) Off Second St Extension, the Bottom Drawer is great for shoppers, but also for kids – lots of cute garden toys, a trampoline, a Wendy house, birds, and bunnies and chickens running freely. Also sells nice interior goods.

Restaurants

Restaurants are open for lunch or dinner, but most are closed on Sundays.

Willowmead (Map p1111; ☎ 776429; Rolf Ave; lunch US$10) For breakfast or lunch, or coffee, tea and cakes. Adjoins a lovely fresh fruit and vegetable market; only open til late afternoon.

Wild Geese Lodge (☎ 860466; 2 Buckland Lane, off Alpes Rd; meals US$15) For Sunday roasts, with views across the grassy highveld and wildlife. Accommodation is also available in nine private thatched suites.

Amanzi (Map p1111; ☎ 497768; 158 Enterprise Rd, Highlands; dinner US$40) Set in a stunning former colonial house with African decor and an amazing garden, Amanzi has delicious international food and a great vibe. You can also buy a painting from a local artist on the way out. A must.

Victoria 22 (Map p1111; ☎ 776429; 22 Victoria Rd, Newlands; dinner US$40) A favourite of well-heeled locals, Victoria 22 is pretty formal (for Harare standards), with choices within a set menu of four delicious courses.

ENTERTAINMENT

For information on entertainment options, check the weekly listings in the *Standard* and the *Herald* or online at www.twinarts.co.zw.

Jazz 105 (Map pp1112-13; ☎ 722516; cnr Second St & Robson Manyika Ave) A local haunt with live Afro jazz on Sunday and Wednesday evenings.

Mannenburg Jazz Club (Map pp1112-13; ☎ 730902; Fife Avenue Shopping Centre, The Avenues) Live performances every night except Sunday. See notices and signs around town about events.

Elite 100, Vistarama and 7 Arts cinemas, are all located at the Avondale Shopping Centre; the **Goethe Institute** (Map p1111; ☎ 796836; 51 Lawson Ave, Milton Park), run by the German Society, often has events such as documentary screenings and feature films.

SHOPPING

The Avondale markets (Map p1111) are situated on top of the old car park at Avondale Shopping Centre and sell carvings, beaded jewellery and other crafts. You could also check out the Sunday flea markets (Map p1111) at Sam Levy's Village, behind the shops – although these days there are fewer crafts available.

Doon Estate (Map p1111; Harrow Rd, Msasa) Not to be missed, Doon Estate has a number of fabulous shops – including Art Mart, which is stocked with the work of dozens of local artisans and crafters. Veldemeers (more commonly known as the Belgian chocolate shop), also here, has to be experienced to be believed. Its novelty chocolates make great presents.

Kumusha (Map p1111; ☎ 446944; 2 Coronation St, Msasa) A must to check out for sublime, hand-made Zimbabwean furniture and household goods for interiors and exteriors.

Umwinsivalley Ceramics (off Map p1111; ☎ 883959) Along the Umwinsidale Rd, set on the top of a hill overlooking a valley, this is a workshop, gallery and shop specialising in hand-painted china. You can watch the artists at work, but the view alone is worth the trip.

Patrick Mavros (off Map p1111; ☎ 860131; www. patrickmavros.com) Follow the signposts to the studio and gallery at the end of Haslemere Lane, 1km off the Umwinsidale Rd. Set atop a spectacular hill, overlooking a picture-perfect valley complete with wildlife, a visit is a must; it sells designer silverware from jewellery to tableware and whimsical items.

Crystal Passions (Map p1111; ☎ 882466; www. ourcrystalpassion.com; 24 Newbold Rd, Greystone Park) Extraordinary hand-cut and polished Zimbabwean stones and crystal jewellery for fashion and healing. Get something bespoke or buy 'off the rack'. Open Wednesday afternoon and Saturday morning or by appointment only.

Dendera Gallery (Map pp1112-13; Speke Ave) Dendera has the best of Zimbabwean and African craft: masks, baskets, textiles, wooden carvings and paintings.

GETTING THERE & AWAY

Air

All international and domestic airlines use the Harare International Airport, 15km southeast of the city centre. Charter flights and other light aircraft operate out of Charles Prince airport, 2km northwest of Harare.

For details about international flights to and from Harare, see p1130.

Air Zimbabwe (Map pp1112-13; ☎ 253752; Eastgate Centre) operates flights to/from Bulawayo (US$140/250 one way/return, 45 minutes) and Victoria Falls (US$230/375 one way/return).

Bus

City Link Express is a new company that departs from Harare to Bulawayo daily at 7.30am, arrives in Bulawayo at 1pm, departs Bulawayo the same day at 2pm and arrives at 7.30pm in Harare. For more details contact **African Encounter Travel** (reservations@african encounter.org). It's both a tour operator and a travel agent.

Other bus companies servicing Harare include the following:

Blue Arrow (Map pp1112-13; ☎ 729514; barrow@ africaonline.co.zw; Chester House, Speke Ave)

Greyhound (Map pp1112-13; ☎ 720801; Road Port Terminal)

Pioneer Bus (Map p1111; ☎ 795863/0531; Mbare Musika Bus Terminal)

Train

The train station (Map pp1112–13) is near the corner of Kenneth Kaunda Ave and Second St. There are services from Harare to Bulawayo (sleeper US$10, nine hours, 9pm) and Mutare (US$6, 8½ hours, 9.30pm), and from Bulawayo to Victoria Falls (sleeper US$11, 8pm). Check with travel agents if you're going by train for the latest information.

GETTING AROUND
To/From the Airport

Taxis from Harare International Airport cost US$30 to town, the inner suburbs or 30km in any direction. For Charles Prince airport, book through tour operators and they will provide transfers.

Bus

Most bus companies have both local buses (chicken buses), which depart from Mbare Musika bus terminal (Map p1111) but are currently too dangerous to recommend, and luxury coaches.

Express or 'luxury' buses operate according to published timetables. They mainly leave from Road Port Terminal (Map pp1112–13) in town, which is where international services and buses for destinations within Zim – Bulawayo, Mutare, Gweru etc – leave from, or from designated pick-up points at hotels such as Holiday Inn/Rainbow Towers.

Car

Car rental companies in Harare include **Avis** (Map p1111; ☎ 796409/10; Third St) and **Europcar** (Map p1111; ☎ 750622/4; carhire@europcar.co.zw; 19 Samora Machel Ave).

Fuel is currently freely available, costing US$1 to US$1.10 per litre for petrol and US$0.85 per litre for diesel. Contact tour operators such as African Encounter for current prices and availability.

Taxi

Taxis are safe, and most reliable taxis are booked through your hotel front desk. Most are metered – charging between US$1 and US$2.50 for 1km – and travel within a 40km radius of Harare. Always take a taxi at night, rather than walking. There are taxi stands on the corner of First St and Nelson Mandela Ave; on Samora Machel Ave near First St; on Union Ave between Angwa St and Julius Nyerere Way; and in front of large hotels.

Official services include **Rixi Taxi** (☎ 753080-2), **AA Taxi** (☎ 704222) and **AI Taxi** (☎ 706996/8, 703334).

AROUND HARARE

Most places listed in this section can be visited on day trips from the capital (note that you'll need to hire a car or take a taxi, as buses are overcrowded and unsafe), but don't travel the roads in and out of Harare after dusk – they become too dangerous, with bad potholes and eroding edges, little to no lighting, bad drivers and people walking on the streets.

THE BALLY VAUGHAN SANCTUARY

In the Enterprise Valley, 60km from Harare, this **wildlife sanctuary** (off Map p1111; ☎ 601131, 912 592944/11, 912 264160; www.ballyvaughan.co.zw; Shamva Rd; admission US$3; ⏰ 9am-5pm Tue-Sun) is an orphanage/refuge run on donations. Help feed predators and meet the biggest lions in Africa. Also has a volunteer program.

LION & CHEETAH PARK

This **park** (off Map p1111; admission per adult/vehicle US$15/3; ⏰ 8am-5pm) sits on a private estate 24km west of Harare off the road to Bulawayo. There are no cheetahs, but certainly lots of lions. You can do 'self-drive safaris' and visit the Kiosk – a zoo, really, with baboons, crocodiles, hyenas and a 300-year-old tortoise.

ROCK ART

Domboshawa Caves (off Map p1111; ☎ 790044; admission US$4; ⏰ 6am-6pm), 30km northeast of Harare, is known for its prehistoric rock paintings – its name means 'Red Rock' in Shona. A well-marked 15-minute walk takes you across a rock range with stunning 360-degree views to the caves where the paintings are.

Ngomakurira (off Map p1111; ☎ 790044; admission US$2; ☼ 6am-6pm) offers even more spectacular rock paintings, which are especially photogenic in the afternoon.

Both sites make a half-day trip. For Domboshawa, drive or take a taxi 20 minutes north along Borrowdale Rd to Domboshawa village. Watch carefully for the turn-off, or ask the locals – then it's 1km in from the main road. For Ngomakurira, follow the same directions, but go 15km further to Ngomakurira village (45km north of Harare). The entrance is 2km in from the main road.

IMIRE SAFARI RANCH

Located 105km east of Harare, and built on a farm where indigenous wildlife – including black rhinos and elephants – were once hunted to clear for farming, **Imire** (☎ 912 522201, 243072, 022-2094; www.imiresafariranch.com) now conserves Zimbabwean wildlife. It's renowned for breeding and releasing black rhinos into Matusadona National Park and for providing orphan elephants a home.

From Harare, travel 70km on the Mutare Rd and turn right 3km before Marondera at the Imire signpost. After 2.5km (at another Imire signpost) turn left, then drive for another 40km; at the Sable Lodge turn-off, 800m past the Imire butchery, turn left. The lodge is 1km further up the road.

LAKE CHIVERO RECREATIONAL PARK

This 5500-hectare park is 32km southwest of Harare; it spreads around the 57-sq-km **Lake Chivero**. Take a picnic and day-trip from Harare, or spend the weekend. Rhinos, ostriches, zebras and giraffes may be seen – do a self-drive safari. You can't hire boats and you should avoid swimming: crocs and bilharzia bugs lurk.

National Parks Accommodation (lodges with 2/4/5 beds US$2/3/4, chalets with 1/4/5 beds US$1/2/3; ☒), on the northern shore of the lake, has a swimming pool – which may or may not have water in it – and *braai* (barbecue) pits. The views are stunning.

Admiral's Cabin (☎ 062-2309; birdpark@mango. zw; campsite per person US$3, chalets per person incl breakfast US$12) offers clean accommodation right near the lake, with an attached bar and restaurant.

NORTHERN ZIMBABWE

The major attractions in this part of the country are the Matusadona National Park on the eastern section of Lake Kariba, Kariba's islands and Mana Pools National Park. The Mavuradonha Mountains and Chinhoyi Caves are also fascinating.

Activities

You can safari in this area by houseboat, canoe, walking, hiking or driving in Mana Pools and/or Matusadona National Parks. These activities will be included in your accommodation price, but you will still need to pay park admission fees. Transfers can be arranged from Victoria Falls, Harare or Lusaka.

HOUSEBOAT SAFARIS

Houseboats are an amazing way to do a safari. You get the fun of a houseboat (including having the lake to yourselves, or at least feeling as though you do), plus in Matusadona National Park you get to observe animals, particularly elephants, at close range. The two top houseboat companies in Zimbabwe to book through are **Rhino Rendezvous** (☎ 04-745644/2; rhino ren@mweb.co.zw) and **Marineland Harbour** (☎ 2237; bookings@marineland.co.zw).

MIDDLE ZAMBEZI CANOE SAFARIS

Adventurous residents and visitors describe canoe trips down this awesome wilderness route as one of the best things they've ever done. Several companies run canoe trips between Kariba and Kanyemba (on the river junction with Zimbabwe, Zambia and Mozambique).

Canoe Safari Operators

Some tour operators for canoe safaris include transport to and from Kariba or Harare and visas (if required), so check, because these things can be a movable feast in Zimbabwe. Rates include transport from the booking office, guides, canoes, food and tented accommodation, but do not include admission fees to Mana Pools National Park. The high season is about July to October.

For classic tented-camp safaris to hiking or canoe trails (lower end), aim for guide James Varden of Natureways (p1113).

ZIMBABWE

Goliath Safaris (goliath@africaonline.co.zw) is more expensive and exclusive, but very popular – as the owner/guide, Stretch Ferreira, is an iconic character and great guide.

Classic Africa Safaris (xclusive@africaonline.co.zw) is also exclusive and a bit pricey, but has a really special owner/guide.

Wilderness Safaris (www.wilderness-safaris.com) also operates in this area.

Getting There & Away

The best way to get here is to hire a car; otherwise, some lodges or luxury camps can provide transfers from Harare. There are no buses or trains from Harare.

CATS (☎ 04-332141/2; info@centralair.co.zw) does reasonably priced charters from Kariba or Harare to Mana and back. You can fly from Victoria Falls to Matusadona on a charter flight operated by Bumi Hills Safari Lodge (right) – you don't have to stay there to book it. You will land at Bumi Hills airstrip, where your tour operator will collect you.

Getting Around

Kariba Ferries occasionally runs a ferry service between Kariba at the eastern end of the lake and Mlibizi at the western end. During high seasons (December–January, Easter, and June–July) there is a regular, weekly ferry service for cars and passengers. This service was being revamped at the time of writing and availability of services can be checked at www.afrizim.com/Travel_Guides/Houseboats/Info/Kariba-Ferry.asp.

KARIBA

☎ 061 / pop 15,000

The small town of Kariba is spread out along the steep lakeshore, with lovely views and elephants often coming through.

The main road leads to the **dam wall**, which straddles the Zimbabwe–Zambia border. Walk or drive across it, checking the spectacular view. Tell the Zambian or Zimbabwean immigration officials you're there, to avoid paying extra visa fees.

The main object of stopping in Kariba is to board a houseboat, to meet a boat transfer to one of the islands, or to meet a 4WD transfer to Matusadona or Mana Pools National Parks or the Lower Zambezi for a canoeing safari. Most camps in the Matusadona will offer a boat transfer over the lake if clients arrive in Kariba town.

Sleeping & Eating

For something stunning, just out of Kariba, further along the lake, there are a number of three-bedroom, self-catering houses (lodges), all booked through **Trish** (☎ 3127, 2225; baobab@zol.co.zw). **Nzou Lodges** (Charara; per night for 6 people US$120-180; ☒) and **Wild Heritage** (Charara; per night for 6 people US$160-200; ☒) have a cook/housekeeper on duty and private pools. **Cerruti Lodges** (Charara; per person US$35-55) is also lovely. But, for each, you need to be self-sufficient with a car and, perhaps, a boat.

For self-catering lodges, buy food at Spar Supermarket in Kariba or bring food from Harare, as Kariba is not well stocked.

MATUSADONA NATIONAL PARK & THE ISLANDS ON LAKE KARIBA

Matusadona is a beautiful national park situated on the shores of Lake Kariba, the third-largest artificial lake in the world, covering an area of over 5000 sq km.

The following accommodation is best booked through Harare-based travel agents before you travel to Zimbabwe, or through a travel agent in Harare, such as **Experience Africa Safaris** (☎ 04-301494/69185; belinda@xafrica safaris.com; Shop 37, Arundel Village, Quorn Ave, Mount Pleasant).

Musango (www.musangosafricamp.com; per person US$260-300) is the most popular (permanent) 'tented' camp in Kariba because of its location, good guiding and abundant wildlife.

Spurwing Island (www.spurwing.co.zw; ☒) is a good lodge for kids as it has a pool and babysitters and is safely fenced.

Rhino Island Safari Camp (☎ 04-753901-5, 0912 205000; rhino.safari.camp@mail.com) is wonderful – very remote and very wild.

Bumi Hills Safari Lodge (www.xafricasafaris.com; per person around US$200) is newly renovated and sits on the shoreline over at Bumi, up in the hills, overlooking the lake.

Classic Africa Safaris (www.classicafricasafaris.com; per person for 3 nights around US$1775) sets up luxury tented camps as per your booking.

Maronga Tented Camp (www.xafricasafaris.com; per person around US$350) is also a newly renovated, permanent camp. It sleeps 12 and is set at the bottom of the mountain range along the Maronga River. Here you can track black rhinos on foot or do boating, fishing, canoeing and wildlife drives.

There is also a National Parks campsite at Tashinga.

MANA POOLS NATIONAL PARK

This magnificent 2200-sq-km **national park** (admission US$15; ☺ 6am-6pm) is a Unesco World Heritage Site. Its magic stems from its remoteness and pervading sense of the wild and natural. This is one park in Zimbabwe where you're guaranteed to see plenty of hippos, crocs, zebras, antelope and elephants, and almost guaranteed to see lions, and perhaps some painted dogs.

What sets Mana Pools apart from just about any other safari park in the world is that nowhere is fenced in, so there can be elephants strolling by while you have breakfast. You're also allowed to walk around without a guide, as you can see for miles around. But beware, this is about personal responsibility: wild animals are incredibly dangerous…and fast.

You can also fish and canoe on the Zambezi flood plain, and you should book excursions to the famous Chitake Springs in advance.

EASTERN HIGHLANDS

Few travellers to Zimbabwe expect to find anything like the Eastern Highlands, but once they discover them, they can't get enough. The narrow strip of mountain country that makes up Manicaland province consists of a number of national parks, pine forests, botanical gardens, rivers, dams and secluded getaways. The province's capital, Mutare, is the country's third-largest city.

It's possible (and much cheaper) to take the train to Mutare; however, it's best to hire a car in Harare or organise a trip through a tour operator.

BVUMBA MOUNTAINS

☎ 020

Just 28km southeast of Mutare, the Bvumba (pronounced 'vumba') Mountains are cool, forested highlands with deep, dense valleys; yet the meadows, apple orchards, country gardens and teahouses seem to recreate British country life.

Sights

The sprawling 1558-hectare **Bunga Forest Botanical Reserve** (admission free) is a rare pocket of forest that has not been (nor can be) chopped down or burnt off. There are no facilities, but the 39 hectares that straddle the main road to the botanical gardens feature some ill-defined and overgrown hiking tracks, with plenty of butterflies, chameleons and birds to keep you company.

Activities

Even if you can't tell a putter from a wedge, don't miss out on a round of **golf** at the Leopard Rock Hotel, with its superb grounds and breathtaking vistas. The European PGA ranked it the second-toughest course in the world. There is a dress code: shirts with collar.

Twitchers can do a two-hour birdlife walk with **Seldomseen Farm** (☎ 68482). Keep your eyes peeled for a buff-spotted fluff tail or stripe-cheeked bulbul.

Sleeping & Eating

Ndundu Lodge (☎ 63777; www.ndundu.com; Bvumba Rd; campsite per person & dm US$5; s/d US$10/14) Ten minutes' walk from Bvumba Botanical Reserve. Ndundu's enthusiastic owners have mapped out great walking and bike trails (for free) through the Bvumba.

Genaina Lodge (☎ 68177; s/d/cottages US$100/140/200) Located 24km along Bvumba Rd from Mutare, Genaina has tiny, private, thatched cottages and a sometimes-open gallery of African artefacts. Serves breakfast and lunch.

Inn on the Vumba (☎ 67449; s/d US$100/140; ⚡) At the start of Bvumba Rd, 5km from Mutare. Has five cottages and two family rooms. Great for kids, with a swimming pool and playground.

Leopard Rock Hotel (☎ 60192; s/d US$150/200) Once a favourite of English royalty and one of Zimbabwe's grand old dames, the Leopard Rock is at the end of the Bvumba Rd. Although it reeks of glory from another era, it is still fancy and luxurious – with stunning views across to Mozambique.

NYANGA NATIONAL PARK

☎ 029

The 47,000-hectare **Nyanga National Park** (admission US$10; ☺ 6am-6pm) is a geographically and scenically distinct enclave in the Eastern Highlands.

The **Rhodes Hotel**, with its tropical verandah and well-kept gardens overlooking the Nyanga Dam, was once the home of Cecil

ZIMBABWE

Rhodes. It's worth a visit for a meal or drink or to admire the gardens.

World's View (admission US$4) is perched atop the Troutbeck Massif on a precipice above Troutbeck. It's located 11km up a winding, steep road from Troutbeck – follow the signposts.

The flat-topped and myth-shrouded **Nyangani** (2592m) is Zimbabwe's highest mountain. From the car park 14km east of Nyanga Dam, the climb to the summit will take you two hours. Note that the weather can change abruptly, and mists wipe out the view.

Sleeping & Eating

The stunning National Parks Lodge here is now under management with a private company, though NPWZ (p1113) will be able to assist you with booking it.

Inn on Rupurara (☎ 3021/4; rupurara@innsofzimbabwe .co.zw; s/d incl full board US$110/140) A beautifully appointed hotel of African-style bungalows with verandahs. Ask for views overlooking the valley to Rupurara Mountain (Bald Man's Head), not the 'water views' as the water is more like a pond.

Troutbeck Inn (☎ 8305; zimsuncro@zimsun.co.zw; s/d US$140/156) A very English-style inn with a lake, lovely views, roaring fires and hearty English food, including high tea. Good for families, with swings etc for the kids.

CHIMANIMANI

☎ 026

Chimanimani village, 150km south of Mutare, is enclosed by green hills on three sides and opens on the fourth side to the dramatic wall of the Chimanimani Mountains. Even if you're not going to Chimanimani National Park, the tiny village is certainly worth visiting for its serenity and scenery.

There are information notice boards at the Chimanimani Hotel, Blue Moon Bar and Msasa Café. Be careful about muggings while walking in more remote areas.

There are guides available in the village for mountain hikers, and local Doug, who can be contacted through Kweza Lodge, is the most knowledgable guy around regarding the mountains.

Sleeping, Eating & Drinking

Unfortunately most of the farms that used to host lodges and hotels have been

taken over by war veterans and no longer offer accommodation.

Kweza Lodge (☎ 3351, 3030, 912 101283; d US$10) A clean and cosy lodge with incredibly friendly and helpful managers. Offers horse riding. It is located 1.2km west of the village.

Frog & Fern (☎ 2294; d US$15) It's very hard to contact this hotel opposite the Kweza Lodge, but it's worth it for its three pretty stone lodges or the Round House, which sleeps six. It's very comfortable, with great views of the mountains.

Chimanimani Hotel (☎ 2511; s/d incl full board US$75/100; 🏊) In the village, this place is very nice. It's surrounded by pleasant gardens, a pool and a casino, which is still open. Ask for a room with mountain views.

Msasa Café (mains around US$10; 🕑 8am-5pm Mon-Sat) This place is the best spot in the village for eating out. It offers a wide variety of meals from *sadza* to tortillas. Do warn the owner, Daphne, in advance, however, if you want dinner.

For a cheap drink, and a long chat with some locals, head to Blue Moon Bar.

CHIMANIMANI NATIONAL PARK

A hiker's paradise, **Chimanimani National Park** (admission US$10; 🕑 6am-6pm), 19km from Chimanimani village, is really beautiful. The northern end of the park, called **Corner**, is still very wild and unspoiled, but the road there is not good.

To go hiking, you must sign in and pay park fees at Mutekeswane Base Camp, at the entrance. The road ends here and the park is then only accessible on foot.

THE MIDLANDS & SOUTHEASTERN ZIMBABWE

Geographically, the Midlands are known as the highveld, while the warmer, lower-lying southeast is the lowveld. At the transition of the two regions is the town of Masvingo. Nearby are Lake Mutirikwe and Great Zimbabwe. The lowveld's finest attraction is the wildly beautiful – but often ignored – Gonarezhou National Park.

You must only do this by private vehicle, either one you have hired personally, or via a tour operator.

GREAT ZIMBABWE

☎ 039

The greatest medieval city in sub-Saharan Africa, **Great Zimbabwe** (admission US$20; 6am-6pm) provides evidence that ancient Africa reached a high level of civilisation. As a religious capital, this city dominated a realm that stretched across eastern Zimbabwe and into modern-day Botswana, Mozambique and South Africa.

For more information about the site, try to find a *Great Zimbabwe* booklet (US$6) at the main gate or *A Trail Guide to the Great Zimbabwe National Monument* from bookshops around Zimbabwe. Alternatively, arrange a two-hour guided tour (about US$12 per person) at the **main gate** (☎ 7055) or the information centre at the start of the walking trails.

Sleeping & Eating

Great Zimbabwe is the best base for visiting the ruins and Lake Kyle.

Great Zimbabwe Campground (☎ 7055; campsite per person & dm US$3, s/d rondavels US$10/15) This camp, run by National Museums & Monuments, is inside the main gate within sight of the Hill Complex. Watch out for thieving baboons and monkeys.

Lodge at the Ancient City (☎ 7205; per person incl breakfast US$180) Beautifully designed individual African lodges set among recreated 'ruins' to blend beautifully with the landscape and the concept of the place. A treat worth indulging in.

Inn on Great Zimbabwe (☎ 64879; iogz@innsofzimbabwe.co.zw; per person incl breakfast US$180) This tranquil place on a wooded hill above Lake Mutirikwe, 6km east of Great Zimbabwe, is good value. Comfortable but dated decor, though, like everywhere, it lacks some life due to a lack of visitors!

GONAREZHOU NATIONAL PARK

Virtually an extension of South Africa's Kruger National Park, **Gonarezhou National Park** (admission US$20; 6am-6pm May-Oct) also borders Mozambique. So, in late 2002 the relevant authorities in Zimbabwe, South Africa and Mozambique created the **Great Limpopo Transfrontier Park**, a 35,000-sq-km park across the three countries (which has no boundaries). This was a kind of prototype park, which has been deemed successful enough that another will be created in the west of Zimbabwe, taking in Botswana and Zambia.

Although some roads in the park are passable to 2WD vehicles, most are rough and require a 4WD – especially in the south. From November to April there's no access to the national park camps at Chipinda Pools, Mbalauta and Swimuwini.

Sleeping

The costs of camping range from US$20 to US$50 per person, while chalets at Swimuwini cost about US$70. Book at NPWZ in Harare (p1113) or Bulawayo (p1123).

Pamushana (☎ +27 21 683 3424; www.singita.com; s/d incl full board $US800) Zimbabwe's uberluxurious lodge (Michael Douglas and Catherine Zeta-Jones are two past guests) is situated on its own private concession, called Malilangwe. Pamushana is nonprofit and dedicated to protecting and saving endangered species of wildlife. Millions of dollars have been poured into the research of many species of wildlife. The property is also actively involved in helping the local community: it employs hundreds of local villagers, has built schools and feeds thousands of local children in need.

WESTERN ZIMBABWE

With three of the country's major attractions – Victoria Falls and Hwange and Matobo National Parks – western Zimbabwe is an excellent place to spend a majority of your time in Zimbabwe.

BULAWAYO

☎ 09 / pop 1 million

With its wide streets and colonial buildings, Zimbabwe's pretty second city was originally called Gu-Bulawayo (Killing Place), because of the executions undertaken on Thabas Indunas (Hill of Chiefs) under Mzilikazi. Bulawayo makes a good base for those heading out on trips to nearby attractions, such as the Khami Ruins and Matobo National Park, as well as a starting point for adventures to Hwange National Park and/or Victoria Falls.

Information

BOOKSHOPS

Kingston's (91 Jason Moyo St) Sells maps and a few local novels.

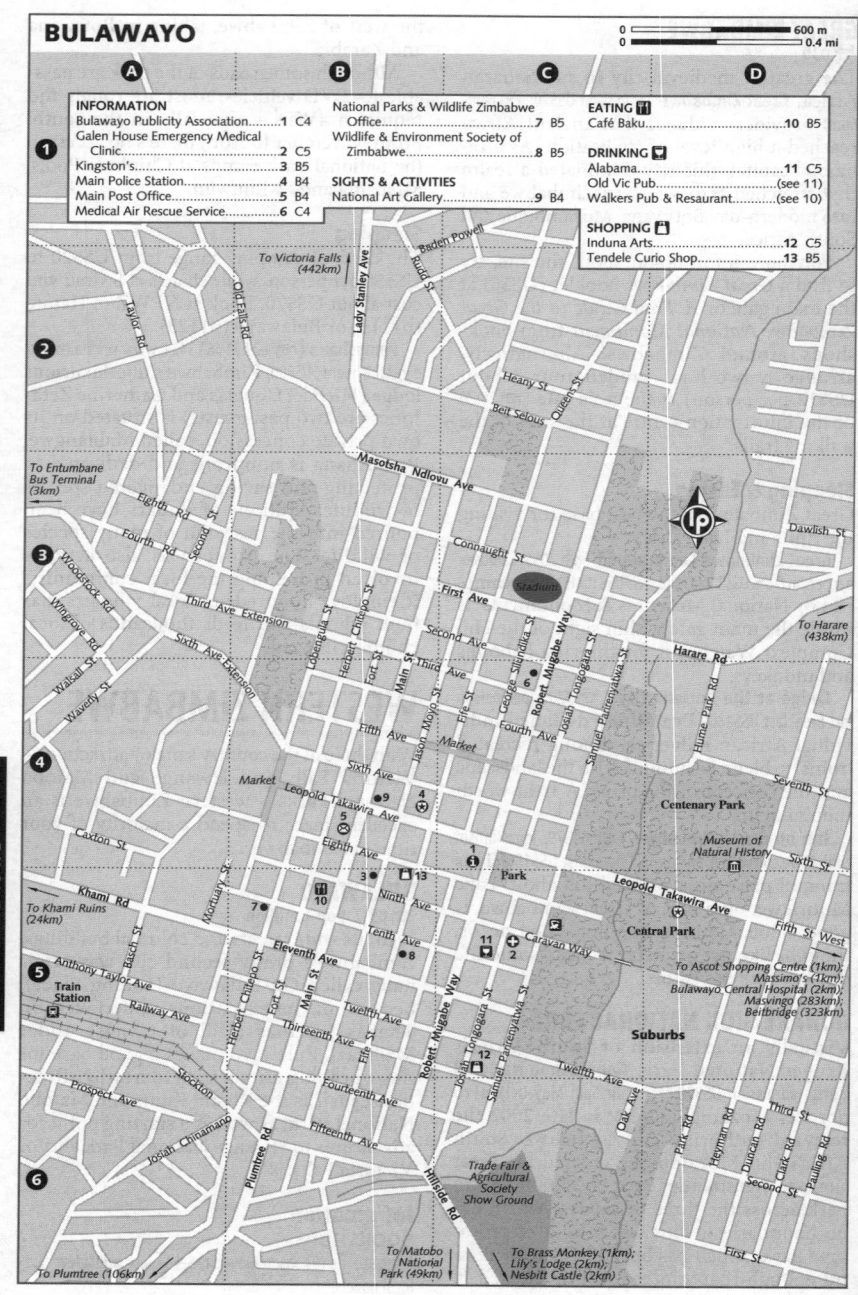

BULAWAYO

0 — 600 m
0 — 0.4 mi

INFORMATION
Bulawayo Publicity Association..........**1** C4
Galen House Emergency Medical
　Clinic..**2** C5
Kingston's..**3** B5
Main Police Station...........................**4** B4
Main Post Office................................**5** B4
Medical Air Rescue Service................**6** C4

National Parks & Wildlife Zimbabwe
　Office...**7** B5
Wildlife & Environment Society of
　Zimbabwe.....................................**8** B5

SIGHTS & ACTIVITIES
National Art Gallery...........................**9** B4

EATING 🍴
Café Baku..**10** B5

DRINKING 🍷
Alabama...**11** C5
Old Vic Pub....................................(see 11)
Walkers Pub & Resurant...................(see 10)

SHOPPING 🛍
Induna Arts.......................................**12** C5
Tendele Curio Shop...........................**13** B5

ZIMBABWE

EMERGENCY

Main police station (☎ 72516; cnr Leopold Takawira Ave & Fife St) For emergencies contact this office or the smaller office in Central Park.

Medical Air Rescue Service (MARS; ☎ 60351; 42 Robert Mugabe Way) For ambulance services.

MEDICAL SERVICES

Bulawayo Central Hospital (☎ 72111) The most accessible public hospital; near the Ascot Racecourse, off St Lukes Ave.

Galen House Emergency Medical Clinic (☎ 540051; cnr Josiah Tongogara St & Ninth Ave) This privately run clinic is better than the central hospital.

POST

Main post office (☎ 62535; cnr Eighth Ave & Main St; ☒ 8am-5pm Mon-Fri, to 11am Sat)

TELEPHONE

Telephone booths are long gone, so take a phone with international roaming or use internet/telephone centres or your hotel.

TOUR OPERATORS

Adventure Travel (☎ 66775)
Black Rhino (☎ 246448)
Driving You Wild (☎ 64868/9)
Eco Logical Africa (☎ 61189/9559, 888790, 91 2239729, +27 82 8284514; www.ecologicalafrica.com) Has 28 years of professional wilderness-guiding experience, plus charter flights.
Southern Comfort (☎ 281340)
Touch The Wild (☎ 888968/9088)
UTC (☎ 61402, 74701)

TOURIST INFORMATION

Bulawayo Publicity Association (Map p1122; ☎ 60867; www.arachnid.co.zw/bulawayo; ☒ 8.30am-4.45pm Mon-Fri, 8.30am-noon Sat)

National Parks & Wildlife Zimbabwe (NPWZ; ☎ 63646; cnr Herbert Chitepo St & Tenth Ave; ☒ 8am-4pm Mon-Fri) Takes accommodation bookings for Matobo National Park.

Wildlife & Environment Society of Zimbabwe (☎ 77309; 105 Fife St)

Dangers & Annoyances

Bulawayo is more laid-back than Harare, but massive increases in unemployment and general desperation mean it's not nearly as safe as it once was. Avoid walking alone anywhere at night.

Sights

The **National Art Gallery** (☎ 70721; Douslin House, cnr Main St & Leopold Takawira Ave; admission US$0.20; ☒ 9am-5pm Tue-Sun) is set in a beautiful, hundred-year-old colonial building and has temporary and permanent exhibitions of contemporary Zimbabwean sculpture and paintings. There's also a souvenir shop, a cafe and studios where you can see artists at work.

Sleeping

Lily's Lodge (☎ 245356; nyararai@excite.com; 3 Masefield Rd, Malindela; r US$30) This large house is frequented by locals. Lily organises traditional evenings with food and dancing for guests.

Nesbitt Castle (☎ 282726/735/736; www.nesbitt castle.co.zw; Percy Ave, Hillside; s/d US$120/190) Built by an eccentric Englishman as his home, this place is quite surreal in its decor. Each of the eight guest rooms is totally different – a great place for a decadent and romantic interlude. The food is good too.

Eating

Café Baku (☎ 883809; Bulawayo Centre, Main St; snacks from US$3; ☒ to late) This small, trendy cafe serves coffee, cakes and sandwiches.

Massimo's (Ascot Shopping Centre; mains around US$15) The Italian cuisine and the decor are authentic: red-and-white checked plastic table cloths and good pasta. Its host is eccentric.

Entertainment

Most Bulawayo pubs and clubs are fairly laid-back.

Old Vic Pub (☎ 881273; Bulawayo Rainbow Hotel, cnr Josiah Tongogara St & Tenth Ave) Exudes an Anglo-Zimbabwean atmosphere.

Alabama (Bulawayo Rainbow Hotel, cnr Josiah Tongogara St & Tenth Ave; ☒ Wed-Sun) A pleasant, casual bar with live jazz most evenings.

Walkers Pub & Restaurant (☎ 69527; Bulawayo Centre, Main St) Good for a drink.

Shopping

Bulawayo is a good place for art and craft galleries selling local jewellery, textiles, carvings, paintings and artefacts.

Tendele Curio Shop (☎ 52391; 90 Fife St)
Induna Arts (☎ 69179; 121 Josiah Tongogara St)

Getting There & Around

City Link Express is a new bus company that departs Harare for Bulawayo daily at 7.30am and arrives in Bulawayo at 1pm. The

ZIMBABWE

return service departs Bulawayo at 2pm and arrives in Harare at 7.30pm. For more details you can contact **African Encounter Travel** (reservations@africanencounter.org).

Trains run daily between Bulawayo and Victoria Falls (see p1126) and Harare (sleeper US$10, nine hours, 9pm).

Try **Rixi Taxi** (☎ 261933) and **Skyline** (☎ 470502) for getting around town. Agree on a price before setting out.

HWANGE
☎ 081

Hwange (sometimes still pronounced Wankie) is a stopover town along the road between Bulawayo and Victoria Falls and a gateway to Hwange National Park. Arrange everything either before you travel, or in Harare or Victoria Falls.

HWANGE NATIONAL PARK

The 14,651-sq-km **Hwange** (admission per day US$15; ☼ about 6am-6pm) is the largest and most wildlife-packed park in Zimbabwe. It's home to some 400 species of birds and 107 types of animals, including one of the largest numbers (30,000) of elephants in the world. The best time for wildlife viewing is July to October, when animals congregate around the 60 waterholes or pans (most of which are artificially filled by noisy, petrol-powered pumps).

When the rains come and the rivers are flowing, successful viewing requires more diligence, because the animals spread out across the park, seeking a bit of trunk or antler room. Most visitors will only see a fraction of this park, though wildlife viewing is good throughout.

Access is possible in any sturdy vehicle between May and October, but seek advice if driving a 2WD during the wet season. And always consult a ranger (at any of the three camps) about road conditions before heading off too far into the park, regardless of what sort of vehicle you're driving.

If you stay at Hwange Main Camp, you can book guided safaris in vehicles, through either individual operators that hang around outside the main office, or the nearby Hwange Safari Lodge. At Sinamatella and Robins camps the only options available are guided walks with the national parks rangers – drive yourself.

Sleeping & Eating

Miombo Lodge (www.africanencounters.com) Located right on the border of Hwange National Park, 300km from Bulawayo and 180km from Victoria Falls, Miombo offers budget accommodation and is a perfect base for wildlife drives into the park. The campsite is fully equipped for independent travellers, overlanders and groups.

Hwange Safari Lodge (☎ 750; fax 337; s/d incl meals & activities US$180/220; ☒) On a massive private estate within the Sikumi Forest Area, this place looks more like a motel than a lodge – though all rooms thoughtfully overlook a popular waterhole. There's a restaurant/bar (also open to nonguests) and a swimming pool. Tours and activities are also available to the public.

Ivory Lodge (☎ 243954, 11 438 162; skype sabeena. mckop26; www.campamalinda.com; per person US$255) The Ivory boasts six luxurious tree-house-style suites set in a teak forest. Loads of elephants here: sometimes herds of 100 drift around the stilted platforms.

Hide Safari Camp (☎ 04-498835; www.thehide.com; head office Triton Centre, 176 Enterprise Rd, Chisipite, Harare; per person incl full board US$275) One of the best safari camps in the country. Named after the artificial hiding points for viewing elephants close-up, it has good guides, lovely accommodation and good food.

Varden Safaris (☎ 04-861765; www.riding-in-hwange. com; per person incl full board US$325) Varden offers horse-riding safaris in Hwange. Explore winding animal trails, acacia canopies and open *vleis* or swim in muddy pans as elephants do. Only for experienced riders who will experience a combination of luxury tented camps, mobile tented camps and fine bush cuisine.

Waterbuck's Head (meals US$10) A charming bar/restaurant right outside the main gate and rangers office at Hwange Main Camp.

VICTORIA FALLS
☎ 013

Designed for tourism, Victoria Falls' neat streets – lined with eateries, bars and craft markets – are all walkable.

Isolated in terms of the rest of Zimbabwe, it manages to avoid the problems that plague other parts of the country, and being entirely dependent on tourism, locals work hard to ensure that all visitors take away positive memories of this stunningly beautiful destination.

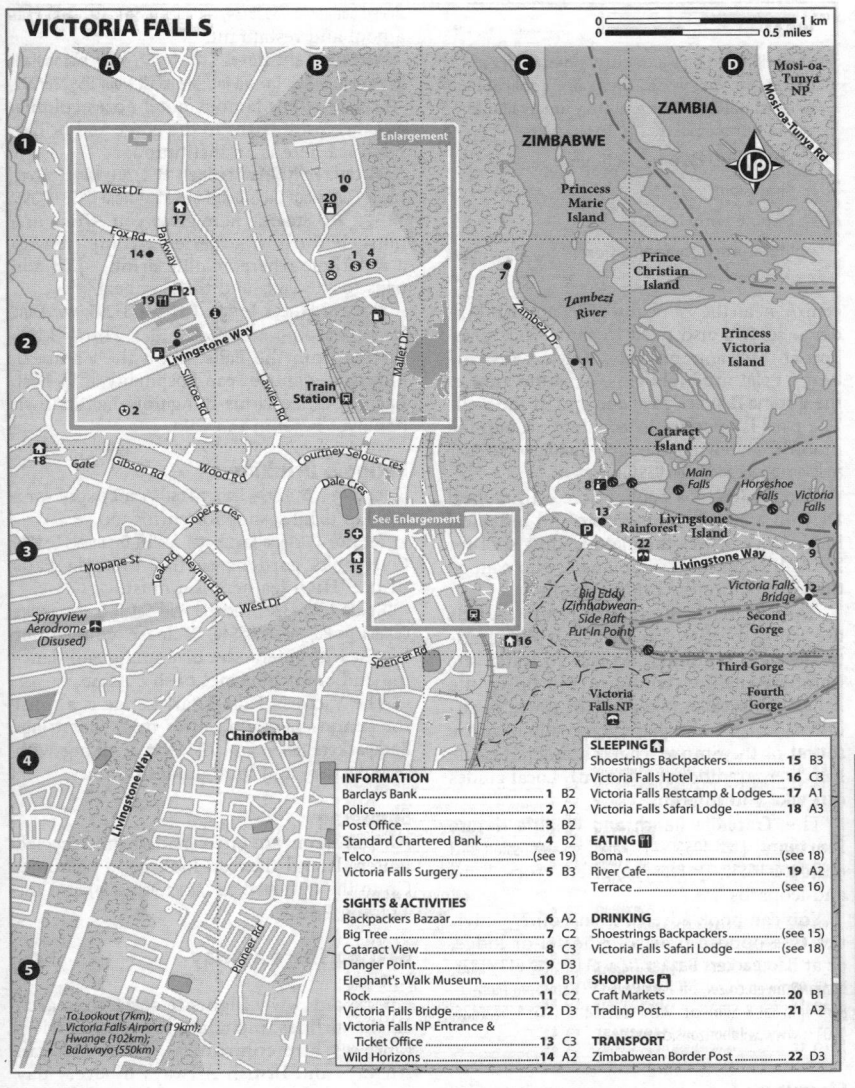

VICTORIA FALLS

INFORMATION	
Barclays Bank	**1** B2
Police	**2** A2
Post Office	**3** B2
Standard Chartered Bank	**4** B2
Telco	(see 19)
Victoria Falls Surgery	**5** B3

SIGHTS & ACTIVITIES	
Backpackers Bazaar	**6** A2
Big Tree	**7** C2
Cataract View	**8** C3
Danger Point	**9** D3
Elephant's Walk Museum	**10** B1
Rock	**11** C2
Victoria Falls Bridge	**12** D3
Victoria Falls NP Entrance & Ticket Office	**13** C3
Wild Horizons	**14** A2

SLEEPING	
Shoestrings Backpackers	**15** B3
Victoria Falls Hotel	**16** C3
Victoria Falls Restcamp & Lodges	**17** A1
Victoria Falls Safari Lodge	**18** A3

EATING	
Boma	(see 18)
River Cafe	**19** A2
Terrace	(see 16)

DRINKING	
Shoestrings Backpackers	(see 15)
Victoria Falls Safari Lodge	(see 18)

SHOPPING	
Craft Markets	**20** B1
Trading Post	**21** A2

TRANSPORT	
Zimbabwean Border Post	**22** D3

ZIMBABWE

Information

Barclays Bank (off Livingstone Way)
Medical Air Rescue Service (MARS; ☎ 44764)
Police (☎ 44206; Livingstone Way)
Post office (off Livingstone Way)
Standard Chartered Bank (off Livingstone Way)
Victoria Falls Surgery (☎ 43356; West Dr)

Dangers & Annoyances

At dawn and dusk lions, elephants and warthogs may roam the streets – so take taxis at these times.

Sights & Activities

The entrance to **Victoria Falls National Park** (admission US$20; 🕑 6am-6pm) is 1km from the town

---

VISAS

You will need a visa to cross sides from Zim to Zam or vice versa. These are applicable to most nationalities and they are available at the border posts.

- Day visit US$20 for 24 hours
- Single entry US$50
- Double entry US$80
- Multi-entry on application

---

centre, near the Zimbabwean/Zambian border – so you also need to show your passport at these entrance gates. **Cataract View** and **Danger Point** are highlights, as is the view of the **Victoria Falls Bridge** at the end of the walk. The park is open in the evenings around full moon for viewing the **lunar rainbow** (tickets in addition to park admission US$10).

The **Big Tree** is a baobab tree on Zambezi Dr with a 20m circumference and historical importance: it was the main trading spot for Zimbabweans and Zambians – who canoed the river before the bridge was built.

Coming back along the road towards the Falls, the first broad, clear path leads to **The Rock**, a wonderful place to watch the Zambezi rushing wildly to the lip of the Falls. The **Lookout**, 8km out of town, is another local secret, where you really hear the sound of the Smoke That Thunders (as the Falls were traditionally known). Local guides can take you to both.

The **Crocodile Ranch and Wildlife Nature Sanctuary** (☎ 40509-11; Parkway; admission incl guided tour US$10; ⏲ 8am-5pm) offers crocs, lions and leopards.

You can book adrenalin and other activities (see opposite) at your hostel or lodge, or at **Backpackers Bazaar** (Map p1125; ☎ 013-45828; bazaar@mweb.co.zw; off Parkway; ⏲ 8am-5pm Mon-Fri, 8am-4pm Sat & Sun) or **Wild Horizons** (☎ 44571/426, 42013; www.wildhorizons.co.zw).

Sleeping

Shoestrings Backpackers (☎ 40167; 12 West Dr; campsite per person/dm/d US$6/9/35; P ⏝) Shoestrings is popular for overlanders and independent travellers. Has a fun bar at night.

Victoria Falls Restcamp & Lodges (☎ 40509-11; www.vicfallsrestcamp.com; cnr Parkway & West Dr; campsites/dm/fitted dome tents US$10/11/60, s/d chalets with

shared bathroom US$25/34, cottages US$67; P ⏝) Has a pool and restaurant.

Victoria Falls Hotel (☎ 44751; www.victoriafalls hotel.com; Mallet Dr; s/d incl breakfast from US$216/232; P ⏝ ⏝) This famous hotel oozes colonial elegance, with lawns to the gorge and bridge. High tea here is an institution.

Victoria Falls Safari Lodge (☎ 43201; www.vfsl.com; Squire Cummings Rd; s/d incl breakfast from US$315/395; P ⏝ ⏝) Staying here gives you Africa in a nutshell: the bush experience complete with a waterhole where wildlife drink – just add trips to the Falls and the Zambezi.

Matetsi Water Lodge (☎ 04-731295; www.and beyond.com; per person US$435; ⏝) Thirty kilometres from the Falls, upon the Zambezi, Matetsi is Zimbabwean hospitality at its best. Each uberluxurious bungalow has its own pool, yet is set in the wild.

Eating & Drinking

River Cafe (☎ 42994; Trading Post) A nice spot for a meal or drinks; shop for curios too.

Terrace (Victoria Falls Hotel, Mallet Dr; meals US$20) Overlooks gardens to the Victoria Falls Bridge. High tea here is a must.

Boma (☎ 43201; Victoria Falls Safari Lodge, Squire Cummings Rd; meals US$40) Release your inner tourist with interactive drumming and dancing and enjoy gourmet bush cuisine.

The Victoria Falls Safari Lodge is a must for sundowners and, after that, **Shoestrings Backpackers** (drinks from US$3) for drinking with backpackers and local guides off duty.

Shopping

African items are often made from recycled materials and they do look good at home. Go to the **craft markets** (Adam Stander Dr) and the Trading Post.

Getting There & Away

AIR

Check out www.flightsite.co.za to search all the airlines, including low-cost carriers (and car hire companies). South African Airways and British Airways fly every day to Johannesburg, for around US$320 return. Air Namibia flies to Windhoek for around US$530 return.

TRAIN

The *Mosi-oa-Tunya* train leaves Victoria Falls daily at 6.30pm for Bulawayo (12 hours). Make a reservation at the station

ticket office (☎ 44391; ☽ 7am-noon & 2-4pm Mon-Fri, to 10am Sat & Sun).

Getting Around

TO/FROM THE AIRPORT
Victoria Falls Airport is 20km from town. Catch a taxi (US$20 each way).

CAR & MOTORCYCLE
When planning your trip, find out what the situation is with petrol availability, as this is an issue that has cycles all of its own.

TAXI
A taxi around town costs about US$10.

ZAMBEZI NATIONAL PARK
This **national park** (admission US$10; ☽ 6am-6.30pm) consists of 40km of Zambezi River frontage and a spread of wildlife-rich forest hosting sable antelope, warthogs, lions and elephants. Tour operators offer wildlife drives, guided hikes and fishing expeditions.

ZIMBABWE DIRECTORY

ACCOMMODATION
Zimbabwe's tourism industry has almost collapsed in terms of backpackers and DIY travellers, but top-end and regional travellers have kept coming – so infrastructure remains some of the best in the region. Victoria Falls has five-star food, accommodation and service as well as access to well-organised activities. Elsewhere, while some lodges and hotels have closed, just as many are being built or renovated. Those that have been riding the slide remain, offering stunning locations, good amenities and friendly service. Surviving the collapse of the tourism sector clearly means they have something good.

National Park Accommodation
Zimbabwe's national park accommodation provides the chance to stay in the best locations in Zimbabwe, indeed some of the best places in Africa. The NPWZ in Harare (p1113) is very efficient, or you can book through travel agents. Due to a lack of funds, many lodges and camps went out to private tender for management, and are doing better than before.

Reservations for national park accommodation are available through the NPWZ offices in Harare and Bulawayo (p1123).

ACTIVITIES
Victoria Falls is the epicentre of activities in southern Africa. The adventurous can get their adrenalin pumping with white-water rafting, helicopter rides, gorge swings and bungee jumping. There and elsewhere, it's all about natural features: river cruises, walks along the Falls, luxury tented camps and classic driving safaris, hiking in the cool Eastern Highlands, horse riding and wildlife viewing in national parks, canoeing safaris on the Zambezi River, houseboating on Lake Kariba, and fishing or golfing almost anywhere.

BOOKS
Guidebooks & Coffee-Table Books
Journey from the Depths of Zimbabwe, the Stone Sculptures is a stunning book that captures the ever-important sculpture work of Zimbabwean artists. Buy online from www.zimsculpt.com or at the National Art Gallery in Harare.

Great Zimbabwe Described & Explained, by Peter Garlake, reveals the history, purpose and architecture of the ancient ruins at Great Zimbabwe.

The Painted Caves – An Introduction to the Prehistoric Art of Zimbabwe, also by Peter Garlake, is a detailed guide uncovering major prehistoric rock-art sites in Zimbabwe.

The Painted Hills – Rock Art of the Matopos, by Nick Walker, covers the revealing and interesting rock art of the Matopos.

History & Politics
Where We Have Hope, by Andrew Meldrum, is a good overview of postindependence Zimbabwe, up to 2003. It's not beautifully written, but Meldrum has some good insights.

Mugabe, by Colin Simpson and David Smith, is a biography of the Zimbabwean president tracing his controversial rise to power.

The Struggle for Zimbabwe: The Chimurenga War, by David Martin and Phyllis Johnson, is a popular history of the Second Chimurenga, the tragic war that led to independence.

BUSINESS HOURS
Very little is open on Sundays.
Shops and restaurants Generally open from 8am to 1pm and 2pm to 5pm Monday to Friday, and from 8am to noon on Saturday.

ZIMBABWE

CHILDREN

Zimbabwe is a great place to travel with kids. You should organise your tour through a travel agent who can tailor your trip and all accommodation to suit your needs and wants; for example, some safari operations won't take children, but travel agents will know not only who does, but who caters best.

CUSTOMS REGULATIONS

Visitors may import a maximum of US$350 in nontrade items, excluding personal effects. Travellers over 18 years of age can also import up to 3L of alcohol, including 1L of spirits.

DANGERS & ANNOYANCES

Zimbabwe is nowhere near as dangerous as foreign media makes out, but crime is on the rise. Carjacking and smash-and-grabs are the current dangers. Although the number of incidents and degree of violence are a far cry from Johannesburg and other cities, it is a reality. Drivers should avoid stopping at traffic lights at night, lock all doors, lock all valuables in the boot and keep the windows up.

EMBASSIES & CONSULATES

The following embassies and high commissions are based in Harare.

Angola (Map pp1112-13; ☎ 04-790070; www.projectvisa. com; Doncaster House, 26 Speke Ave)

Australia (Map p1111; ☎ 04-852471/70566; www. zimbabwe.embassy.gov.au; 1 Green Close, Borrowdale)

Belgium (Map pp1112-13; ☎ 04-700112/943; www. diplomatie.be/harare; 5th fl, Tanganyika House, 23 Third St/Union Ave)

Botswana (Map p1111; ☎ 04-794645/7/8; www. embassiesabroad.com/embassies-of/Botswana; 22 Phillips Ave)

Canada (Map pp1112-13; ☎ 04-252181-5; www.harare. gc.ca; 45 Baines Ave)

France (Map pp1112-13; ☎ 04-703216; www.amba france-zw.org; First Bank Bldg, 74-76 Samora Machel Ave, Greendale)

Kenya (Map pp1112-13; ☎ 04-704820, 704833, 704937; kenhicom@africaonline.co.zw; 95 Park Lane)

Malawi (Map p1111; ☎ 04-798584; emba@embamoc. org.zw; 42-44 Harare St, Alexandra Park)

Mozambique (Map pp1112-13; ☎ 04-253871;152 Herbert Chitepo Ave)

Namibia (Map pp1112-13; ☎ 04-885841; 69 Borrowdale Rd)

Norway (☎ 04-252426; www.norway.org.zw; 5 Lanark Rd, cnr Sam Nujoma St, Belgravia)

Russia (Map pp1112-13; ☎ 04-701957/8; russemb@ africaonline.co.zw; 70 Fife Ave)

South Africa (Map p1111; ☎ 04-753147-9; dhacon@ mweb.co.zw; 7 Elcombe Ave)

Sudan (Map pp1112-13; ☎ 04-700111; www.sudan iharare.org.zw; 4 Pascoe Ave, Belgravia)

Switzerland (Map pp1112-13; ☎ 04-703997/8; 9 Lanark Rd, Belgravia)

Tanzania (Map pp1112-13; ☎ 04-721870; tanrep@icon. co.zw; Ujamaa House, 23 Baines Ave)

UK (Map p1111; ☎ 04-772990; www.britishembassy. gov.uk/zimb; cnr Norfolk Rd & Second St Extension)

USA (Map pp1112-13; ☎ 04-250593/4; www.usembassy. state.gov/zimbabwe; Arax House, 172 Herbert Chitepo Ave)

Zambia (Map pp1112-13; ☎ 04-773777; zambians@ africaonline.com; 6th fl, Zambia House, 48 Union Ave)

For any embassies not listed here, go to www.embassiesabroad.com/embassies-in /Zimbabwe to find addresses and contact details.

FESTIVALS & EVENTS

HIFA – Harare International Festival of Arts (☎ 04-300119; www.hifa.co.zw) Held annually in the last week of April.

Chimanimani Arts Festival Held in May – the Saturday/ Sunday of Africa Day weekend -- and sees Zimbabwe's top musicians perform.

Bulawayo Music Festival Mid-June.

Mana Game Count First full moon in September at Mana Pools National Park.

GAY & LESBIAN TRAVELLERS

Homosexual activity for men is illegal and officially punishable by up to five years in jail (though penalties are invariably not nearly as severe); lesbianism is not illegal.

Contact **Gays & Lesbians of Zimbabwe** (☎ 04-741736/0614; www.galz.co.zw; 35 Colenbrander Rd, Milton Park, Harare) for information about gay and lesbian clubs and meeting places in Zimbabwe.

HOLIDAYS

During the following public holidays, most government offices and other businesses are closed.

New Year's Day 1 January
Independence Day 18 April
Workers' Day 1 May
Africa Day 25 May
Heroes' Day 11 August
Defence Forces' Day 12 August
National Unity Day 22 December
Boxing Day 26 December

INTERNET ACCESS

There are internet centres in all the main cities and towns. Internet access is US$2 per hour.

LANGUAGE

The official language of Zimbabwe is English. It's used in government, legal and business proceedings, but is the first language for only about 2% of the population. Most Zimbabweans speak Shona (mainly in the north and east) or Ndebele (in the centre and west). Another dialect, Chilapalapa, is actually a pidgin version of Ndebele, English, Shona and Afrikaans, and isn't overly laden with niceties, so most people prefer you sticking to English.

MAPS

Hotels are the best place to find any decent tourist maps. More detailed maps of the cities and national parks are available from the **Surveyor General** (Map pp1112-13; Samora Machel Ave, Harare).

MONEY

Since 'dollarisation', Zimbabwe is now very easy to go to again, but it's nowhere near as cheap as it once was. Several years ago a main at a good restaurant cost the equivalent of US$3 to US$5; the same meal would cost a visitor the equivalent of US$7 to US$25 now, as everything is imported.

In 2009 Zimbabwe became a 'multi-currency' economy, meaning it was 'officially' accepting sterling, rand, pula and the US dollar. In practice, US dollars and, to a lesser extent, rand are the accepted currencies.

ATMs

At the time of writing, ATMs were not being used due to the 'multicurrency' situation.

Tipping

Some restaurants automatically add a 10% service charge to the bill; if so, no tip is required, though any tip is hugely appreciated.

Travellers Cheques

Don't take travellers cheques to Zimbabwe. You can use a credit card, or use cash.

PHOTOGRAPHY & VIDEO

Take your digital camera or flash card to **Strachan's Photo Shop** (Map pp1112-13; 66 Nelson Mandela Ave, Harare) for uploading photos or printing.

POST

Sending letters and postcards by surface mail to Europe and the UK costs US$0.80; it costs US$1.10 to the rest of the world.

TELEPHONE

You can make international calls from your hotel or lodge. It is impossible to buy a SIM card in Zimbabwe; it's best to put mobile (cell) phones on international roaming.

If calling from overseas, the country code for Zimbabwe is ☎ 263, but drop the initial 0 for area codes. The international access code from within Zimbabwe is ☎ 00.

TOURIST INFORMATION

The **Zimbabwe Tourism Authority** (Map pp1112-13; ☎ 04-758730; www.zimbabwetourism.co.zw; 55 Samora Machel Ave, Harare; 8am-4.30pm Mon-Fri) has general tourist info. There are Publicity Associations in Harare, Bulawayo, Victoria Falls, Kariba, Masvingo and Nyanga. Some have little more to offer than a smile.

VISAS

With a few exceptions, visas are required by nationals of all countries. They can be obtained at your point of entry. Single-/double-entry visas cost US$30/45 (and can be issued upon arrival); multiple-entry visas (valid for six months) cost US$55, but are only issued at Zimbabwean diplomatic missions. British citizens pay US$55/70 for single/double entry.

Visas for Onward Travel

Harare is one of the best places in southern Africa to pick up visas for regional countries. Requirements constantly change, but nearly all require a fee (US dollars) and two passport-sized photos.

Visas for Zambia, Namibia, Malawi and Botswana are easy to obtain on arrival in those countries for most visitors, so there's no need to obtain them in advance. In theory South Africa is easy too, though huge queues make it best to obtain a visa in advance.

ZIMBABWE

INTERNATIONAL FLIGHTS FROM ZIMBABWE			
Destination	One way (US$)	Return (US$)	Duration
Johannesburg (South Africa)	227	339	1½hrs
Gaborone (Botswana)	572	906	1½hrs
Windhoek (Namibia)	716	962	2½hrs
Maputo (Mozambique)	468	767	1½hrs
Lilongwe (Malawi)	999	1112	1hr
Lusaka (Zambia)	729	956	50 min
Dar es Salaam (Tanzania)	1154	1888	2½hrs
Nairobi (Kenya)	1070	1274	3½hrs

TRANSPORT IN ZIMBABWE

GETTING THERE & AWAY
Air

Some international flights arrive in Harare, and there are also direct flights between Victoria Falls and Johannesburg.

Airlines with services to/from Zimbabwe:

Air Botswana (Map pp1112-13; ☎ 04-793795/228/229; Travel Plaza, Harare)

Air Malawi (Map pp1112-13 ☎ 04-752563)

Air Namibia (Map pp1112-13; ☎ 04-732094/5; Travel Plaza, Harare)

Air Tanzania (Map pp1112-13; ☎ 04-752537/8)

Air Zimbabwe (Map pp1112-13; ☎ 04-253751/2; Eastgate Centre)

South African Airways (Map pp1112-13; ☎ 04-794511/2/6/47/83; SCC House, Harare)

Air France, British Airways, Cathay Pacific, KLM and Lufthansa can all be reached by calling ☎ 04-703880.

Land

Most of Zimbabwe's border posts are open from 6am to 6pm with the exception of Beitbridge (to South Africa, open 24 hours) and Victoria Falls (to Zambia, open 6am to 10pm). Other border posts are located at Plumtree and Kazungula (Botswana), Kariba and Chirundu (Zambia), and Mutare and Nyamapanda (Mozambique).

If you're driving a rented car or motorcycle from Zambia, you need a letter from your rental company stating that you are permitted to enter Zimbabwe.

GETTING AROUND
Air

Air Zimbabwe has one flight per day between Harare and Bulawayo (US$140/250 one way/return) and Harare and Victoria Falls (US$230/375 one way/return). There's a domestic departure tax of US$5. Air Zimbabwe no longer flies to Hwange or Kariba, but agents can organise charter flights.

Bus & Minibus

Zimbabwean minibuses (or combis) are no longer recommended to travellers as they get neglected and overused, break down frequently and are prone to horrible accidents.

Car & Motorcycle
DRIVING LICENCE

All foreigners can use their driving licence from their home country for up to 90 days in Zimbabwe, as long as it's written in English. However, given the growing propensity of police to illicit bribes, it's best to ensure you also have an International Driver's Licence.

FUEL

The cost of petrol ranges from US$1 to US$1.10 per litre.

HIRE

The minimum driving age required by rental companies varies, but is usually between 23 and 25 years. The maximum age is normally about 65 years.

It's important to note that most collision damage waiver (CDW) insurance policies do not cover 2WD vehicles travelling on rough roads in national parks, especially in Mana Pools National Park.

ROAD HAZARDS

Zimbabwe has some awful drivers and rarely any functioning street lights, so many residents make a rule of not driving outside the major towns after dark. The roads are also badly decaying, with eroding edges and potholes everywhere. In cities speeding drunk drivers tend to ignore red lights, so you should slow right down at every 'robot' – even if it's green – then proceed with caution.

Hitching

Hitching is not recommended for travellers, because of safety issues, yet is an official means of transportation for the masses in Zimbabwe.

Private operators in *bakkies* (pick-up trucks) charge the same as buses, usually about US$0.50 or US$1 to US$3 for longer trips.

Travel Agents/Tour Operators

Travel agents are invaluable for booking rental cars and safaris, and for local knowledge. You can get on mailing lists while in the planning stages and/or get travel agents to organise tailor-made safaris around the region, taking in the best locations. Trips can include safari lodges, tented camps, walking, canoeing and horse-back safaris. Zimbabwe is so diverse and it is easy to get around – you can do it all in one holiday.

Train

Connecting Harare, Bulawayo, Mutare and Victoria Falls, all major services travel at night, and sleeping compartments with bedding are available, which is lucky as the trains are very slow. Timetables are unreliable and trains are not recommended as safe or pleasant for tourists, yet some backpackers have also given positive feedback. Consider it another moveable feast, with no absolutes.

ZIMBABWE

Africa Directory

CONTENTS

Pan-continental information of a practical nature is briefly outlined in this Africa Directory. For more specific details, turn to the Directory sections towards the end of each country chapter.

ACCOMMODATION

In the country chapters, we sometimes list accommodation options in three categories – budget, midrange and top end. Of course, not all the places you'll be visiting will have accommodation choices that span this range. In many rural areas you'll find budget homestays only, while in certain national parks there's little available besides expensive luxury lodges.

Prices in this book are given for accommodation with a private bathroom, unless otherwise stated. If you're staying somewhere for a few nights, or at a quiet time, consider asking for discounts: some hotels will work out a deal, others will remain immoveable, but it's always worth a try.

Camping

A tent usually saves you money, and can be vital in some national parks or wilderness areas. However, it's not essential for travel in Africa, as many campsites have simple cabins, with or without bedding and cooking utensils. Official campsites, of varying quality and security, allow you to pitch a tent, as do most backpackers' hostels.

'Wild' camping is sometimes OK if you're in a place where no one will find you (or no animals trip over you). In rural areas, if there's no campsite, you're usually better off pitching your tent near a village. Seek permission from the village chief first, and you'll probably be treated as an honoured guest and really get under the skin of Africa.

Homestays

In rural areas you can sometimes arrange informal 'homestays' simply by politely asking for somewhere to bed down and get a dish of local food, in return for a payment. Do not get carried away with bargaining – pay a fair fee, normally the cost of a cheap hotel.

Hostels

Lodges and hostels aimed squarely at backpackers line the popular routes from Nairobi to Cape Town, although elsewhere in Africa they're less common. Most have beds in a

---

BOOK YOUR STAY ONLINE

For more accommodation reviews and recommendations by Lonely Planet authors, check out the online booking service at www.lonelyplanet.com/hotels. You'll find the true, insider low-down on the best places to stay. Reviews are thorough and independent. Best of all, you can book online.

dorm, as well as double or twin rooms. Backpackers' hostels are good places to get information on stuff to do or onward transport, and they also offer a range of cheap safaris and tours. A potential downside is that you'll be surrounded by fellow travellers, rather than the Africans you came to meet.

Hotels

Africa has numerous hotels, B&Bs and guesthouses, ranging from no-frills establishments and spotless family homes, to sky's-the-limit dens of luxury. Under the 'hotel' category you could also be bedding down at a guesthouse, rest house, *pensao* (in Mozambique) or *campement* (in West Africa). The latter is a simple rural hotel, often with a campsite attached. In West Africa (especially Burkina Faso), watch out for B&Bs that go by the names of '*chambres d'hôtes*' or '*maisons d'hôtes*'. A cheap local hotel in East Africa is called a *gesti* or lodgings, while *hoteli* is Swahili for basic eating place.

In cheaper local hotels, it's rare to get a private bathroom and you can forget air-conditioning. Other 'extras' like a fan or mosquito net usually increase the price. Africa has a huge choice of midrange hotels, and standards can be high, especially in privately run (as opposed to government-run) places. At the top end of the range, you'll find international chain hotels with all the trimmings, or boutique hotels with interior-design flair, delicious food and a great atmosphere.

ACTIVITIES

For those energetic types keen to enjoy the outdoors or work up a sweat, there's a great choice in Africa. This section gives an overview; see the individual country chapters for more inspiration.

Adrenalin Pumping

If you want to get the blood pumping, you'll find white-water rafting, bungee jumping, jet boating, microlighting (a cross between a hang glider and an ultralight aircraft) and abseiling at Victoria Falls – billed as the adventure hub of Africa. All these and more can be arranged on both the Zambian (p1096) and Zimbabwean (p1124) sides.

Swakopmund (p992) in Namibia is coming to rival Victoria Falls as southern Africa's adventure-sports capital. South Africa also offers a broad range of extreme activities.

PRACTICALITIES

Electricity

Most countries use a 220/240V current, but some mix 110V and 240V. Some (eg Liberia) still use mostly 110V. Generally, in English-speaking countries, sockets are the British type. In Francophone parts of Africa they're the Continental European two-pin variety. South Africa has yet another system. In some countries you'll find whatever people can get hold of. And if all that hasn't put you off, power cuts and surges are part of life in many African countries.

Weights & Measures

Metric units (metres, kilograms, litres etc) are officially used in most African countries.

In East Africa, head for Jinja in Uganda (see the boxed text, p831), the 'Vic Falls of East Africa', with adrenalin activities galore at nearby Bujagali Falls.

You can also raft and kayak on white water, or canoe on more gentle stuff, in Ethiopia (p699) and Swaziland (see the boxed text, p1076).

Cycling

Long-distance travel by bike is a great way to see Africa, but it's only for a hardy few; see p1156 for some pointers. For shorter trips, you can often hire bikes by the day or week, and tour some wonderful areas. Our favourites for relaxed peddling include Malawi, Uganda and the Cape region of South Africa. If you've got your own wheels, legs of steel and a sense of adventure, mountain bikers will love the ancient trails through Morocco's Atlas Mountains, the Fouta Djalon plateau in Guinea, rural Madagascar and the mountain tracks of Ethiopia.

For inspiration, see the excellent website of the **International Bicycle Fund** (www.ibike.org /africaguide).

Diving & Snorkelling

The east side of Africa is where you strap on goggles, snorkels or tanks, and slip into paradise. Egypt's Red Sea (p97 and p102) is one of the world's premier diving destinations, while Sudan (p208), Kenya (p725), Mozambique (p971 and p972) and Tanzania, especially Zanzibar (p781), have some of the finest reefs

in the Indian Ocean. And then there's Lake
Malawi (p956), with idyllic diving and dive
schools. In West Africa, the waters close to
Dakar (p486) are a possibility, while São Tomé
& Príncipe (see the boxed text, p626) are bril-
liant underwater destinations.

Hiking
South Africa has a huge network of well-
organised hiking trails, with Table Mountain
National Park (p1022), Tsitsikamma National
Park (p1034) and the Drakensberg area
(p1044) especially appealing options. Namibia
has some desert specials, including the classic
Fish River Canyon (p1005). Tiny Lesotho (see
the boxed texts, p897 and p899) also has some
terrific hiking trails.

In East Africa, a classic African hike is to
the summit of Mt Kilimanjaro (p789), the
'roof of Africa'. Less frequented are the hikes
in Tanzania's Usambara Mountains (p787).
Across the border, Mt Kenya (p715) is lower
than Kilimanjaro but more pleasing to the eye.
In Uganda the remote Rwenzori Mountains
(p835) are a more serious proposition, while
Mt Elgon (p830) is beautiful and the trails
rarely busy.

West Africa is home to some of the continent's best hiking, with Mali's dramatic
Dogon Country (p412) a journey into another
world and the pick of a very fine crop. Other
terrific hikes include: climbing Mt Cameroon
(p289) or through the Mandara Mountains
(p300); Burkina Faso's Sindou Peaks (p272);
Guinea's Fouta Djalon (see the boxed text,
p371); and Togo's Kpalimé area (see the boxed
text, p529).

At the top of the continent, you could hike
for months through the Atlas Mountains of
Morocco (see p183), while the Rif Mountains
near Chefchaouen (p153) are also terrific.

Skiing
Skiing and snowboarding in Africa? Surely
not. But yes, this activity is available during
winter in the high mountains of South Africa
and Morocco. For a new take on the experience, head for the dunes of Swakopmund in
Namibia (p993) and go sandboarding – it's
just what it says, and easier than the alpine
variety. The landing is softer too. Make sure,
however, that your operator follows basic
environmental guidelines before signing up.
Boarding over vegetation, using chemicals or
disturbing nesting birds are all no-nos.

Surfing
Get off the bus in South Africa and get your
baggy shorts on. Jeffrey's Bay (p1034) is classic Surfville RSA, but there are other options
on the south and east coasts, with some of
the best and least-crowded waves in the
world. For more information, turn to p1061.
Neighbouring Mozambique (p971) and
southern Madagascar are also pretty good,
while at the other end of Africa, the Atlantic
swell produces good breaks on the coast of
Morocco (see p189).

West Africa's Atlantic coastline is also an
increasingly popular destination for surfers,
partly for its waves and because you may just
have the breaks to yourself. In general terms,
the waves off Senegal and Gambia are best
during the European winter, while the coast
from Sierra Leone to Cameroon offers the
best conditions during the European summer.
Some of the possibilities include Dakar (p486)
in Senegal, Busua (p349) in Ghana and Côte
d'Ivoire (p312 and p312); *Sliding Liberia,* an
award-winning documentary on surfing in
Liberia, is definitely worth tracking down.

For wider coverage of surfing in Africa,
check out **Low Pressure** (www.lowpressure.co.uk).

Wildlife Safaris
Africa's many national parks, reserves and
conservation areas are some of the most beautiful places on the planet, and home to a bewildering variety of wild animals – watch lions
stalk their prey, see wildebeest and zebras
migrating, or track gorillas through rainforest. Wherever you go, a safari to see Africa's
wildlife will undoubtedly be a major highlight
of your trip.

Information on the safari scene in every
country is given in the individual chapters. See
also the Africa's Wildlife chapter (p55).

ORGANISED SAFARIS
Vast distances (some parks are bigger than
small European countries) and the unpredictable nature of large animals usually mean you
need a vehicle to visit the national parks, so
in countries like Kenya and Tanzania it's the
norm for visitors to join an organised safari.
There are options to suit all budgets, starting
from around US$100 per day for a basic all-
inclusive experience. Doing things yourself
(taking the bus, using your own tent, carrying
your own food) is rarely cheaper, and is a lot
more complicated. Public transport rarely goes

into parks, and even if it does, you still need to rent a vehicle or arrange lifts to tour the park itself. And the main expense – park entry fees – has to be paid however you get there.

In many places throughout East and southern Africa, including Tanzania and Mozambique, it's possible to organise multi-day bushwalking safaris or multiday canoe safaris in wildlife areas, usually also with community and/or cultural components. Such safaris are widely considered the future of safari tourism.

If you want to team up and share the costs of a safari, companies in Nairobi (Kenya), Arusha (Tanzania) and Kampala (Uganda) will help you find other travellers. Some have regular departures where you can just rock up, pay, and head for the wilds the next day. Many safari companies also take bookings in advance via email.

One factor that can make or break a safari is the driver. A good driver is a guide too, and can turn even the most mundane trip into a fascinating one; a driver's experience in spotting animals and understanding their behaviour is paramount. A bad driver does just that – drive. Always try to meet your driver-guide before booking a safari, to gauge their level of knowledge and enthusiasm.

Tips are an important part of the income of safari employees, so if your driver-guide and cook have given good service, tip them around 10% of the total cost of your safari (ie about 5% for the driver, 5% for the cook). If the service has been poor, tip less, and explain why.

If you're offered a ridiculously cheap deal by a safari company, think again. Anything less than the norm may compromise in quality – vehicles break down, food is substandard, park fees are dodged or fuel is skimped on, meaning your driver won't take detours in search of animals.

The best way to avoid the sharks and find good guides is to get advice from other travellers who've recently returned from a safari, so ask around before you go or once you arrive.

DIY SAFARIS

In some countries there's less of an organised safari set-up, and the usual way of doing things is to get to the park under your own steam, stay at a lodge or campsite (either inside the park, or just outside to save on park fees), then arrange activities on the spot to suit your budget and interest. You can join walking safaris, wildlife-viewing drives, boat trips or visits to nearby villages – all normally for a half day or full day, although longer options may also be available. National parks where this is possible include Liwonde (Malawi; p953), Kruger (South Africa; p1046), Gorongosa (Mozambique; p973) and South Luangwa (Zambia; p1091). Note that doing things this way can cost more than fully organised trips, but generally you're paying for a more exclusive experience.

BOOKS

We have covered the best in travel literature (p16) about Africa and the best African novels (see p17 and the boxed text on p39) elsewhere in the book.

For those interested in nonfiction, *In the Footsteps of Mr Kurtz* (2000), by Michela Wrong (author of the Africa & Development chapter of this book), is the definitive account of corruption and misrule in Africa, chronicling the Mobutu dictatorship in Zaïre (now the Democratic Republic of Congo).

King Leopold's Ghost (1998), by Adam Hochschild, is set in Congo and presents a devastating indictment on colonialism in Africa.

We Wish to Inform You that Tomorrow We Will be Killed with Our Families (1998) is Phillip Gourevitch's searing account of the Rwandan genocide and its aftermath as the consequences rippled out across Central Africa.

The Gates of Africa – Death, Discovery and the Search for Timbuktu (2003), by Anthony Sattin, is an elegantly written account of Europe's fascination with Africa, and the scramble to reach the continent's most elusive city.

You won't want it in your backpack, but the two-volume *African Ceremonies* by Carol Beckwith and Angela Fisher is one of the most beautiful photographic works on Africa.

BORDER CROSSINGS

In a continent of around 50 countries, there are a lot of borders, and a whole lot more border posts. Sometimes the process is quick and straightforward, but at other times it can take several hours to get through the queues at immigration or customs desks (even assuming that your visas and paperwork are in order), not to mention possible checks of medical certificates, or a detailed search of your luggage.

At all times remember that patience and politeness will see you through. Getting shirty with a person in uniform is one sure-fire way for 'discrepancies' to be discovered, and delays to be even longer.

Throughout this book (see the Transport sections of individual country chapters) we have listed the main border-crossing points – usually those on more-frequented roads and transit routes. Smaller or less formal border crossings are often used by locals, but may not be able to process your papers, may have little public transport and could involve a long and pointless detour.

Don't forget that there's usually a border post on each side of the border crossing (ie one belonging to each country). Sometimes the border posts are just 100m apart, such as at the Namanga crossing between Kenya and Tanzania; sometimes they can be 100km apart, with a 'no-man's land' in between, such as those on the route between Algeria and Niger. If you're catching a bus 'to the border', check exactly how far it goes. Does it take you just to the first border post (from where you have to walk or take a taxi to the second one)? Or does the bus go across the border all the way to the second border post, before you have to change to onward transport?

Although they're rare, it's also worth watching out for new border crossings. For example, it's now possible for travellers with their own 4WD to travel between Songea (Tanzania) and Lichinga (Mozambique), which opens up new possibilities in southern Tanzania and northern Mozambique. Further east, the 'Unity Bridge' over the Rovuma River is scheduled to be finished in late 2010 and will become the main border crossing between the two countries.

BUSINESS HOURS

Across Africa, official places like embassies, tourist offices, shops and travel agencies open from around 8am or 9am to around 4pm or 5pm, Monday to Friday (although most embassies are only open to the public during the morning – so that's when you need to apply for visas), and sometimes on Saturday mornings as well. In Islamic countries, most offices (including banks and shops) close on Fridays, but may open on Saturdays and/or Sundays.

Smaller shops and market stalls rarely keep strict business hours at all. When there

are customers around, the shopkeepers are behind their counters ready to serve, and when everyone is asleep in the heat of afternoon, they're snoring round the back. In most cities, many shops and supermarkets stay open until late in the evening and on Saturdays too, although only the largest are open on Sundays.

In East and southern Africa, shops and offices close for an hour or so around noon. In North, West and Central Africa, the noon break can be two to four hours long, and businesses may stay open until 7pm or 8pm, sometimes later. Places like phone and internet cafes keep much longer hours.

Banks in most countries are open from Monday to Friday from 8am or 9am to around 2pm or 3pm. Some banks will even shut at noon.

In Islamic countries, many businesses shut up shop at lunchtime and don't reopen during the Islamic fasting period of Ramadan.

Most cafes and smaller restaurants offer lunch from around noon to 2pm (for locals it's the main meal of the day) and dinner in the evening from around 5pm to 7pm. Larger restaurants catering for more affluent locals and tourists keep the same lunch hours, but open later in the evening, usually from around 7pm to 10pm or later. Many restaurants open all day.

Throughout this book, we don't repeat main opening hours for every place listed unless it has 'unusual' habits – such as a restaurant that opens for lunchtime only, or a bar that doesn't serve drinks until midnight.

CHILDREN

Travelling with kids in Africa might sound like a nightmare but in fact many families find an African holiday is a rewarding and thrilling experience. While some posh hotels and camps ban kids under a certain age, some higher-end safari lodges run special wildlife-watching programs for kids, and babysitting services are pretty widely available in midrange and top-end hotels. On the whole, Africans adore children, and wherever your kids go they will be assured of a warm reception and a host of instant new friends. Indeed, your children have a big advantage over the rest of us – having yet to acquire the stereotypes about Africa to which the rest of us are exposed, their first impression of the continent is likely to be the warmth and friendliness of the people.

Outside the main cities, you can pretty safely assume that disposable nappies won't be available, so bring everything you need with you. Child car seats, high chairs in restaurants and cots in hotels are rare except in top-end hotels in tourist areas.

For general advice on travelling with children, check out Lonely Planet's *Travel with Children*.

CLIMATE

Africa experiences huge climatic variation. Watch out for the wet or rainy seasons, which can turn dirt roads into rivers and curtail travel to remote regions. Just as uncomfortable can be the searing hot season in some countries, which can make moving around during the day nigh on impossible. For advice on the best times for travelling in Africa, see p15.

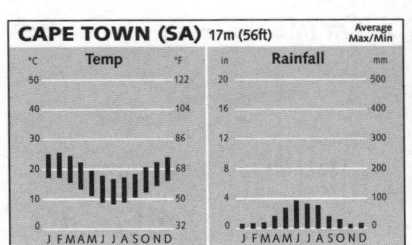

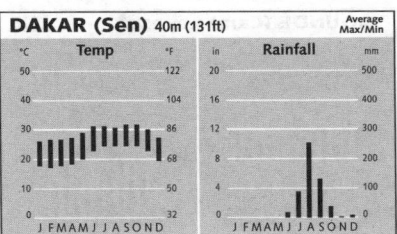

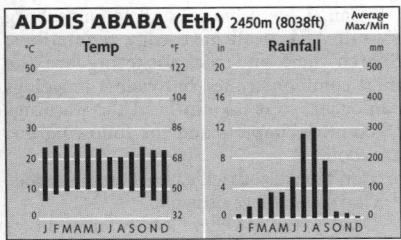

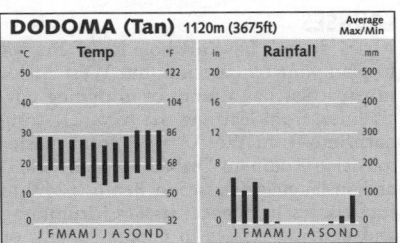

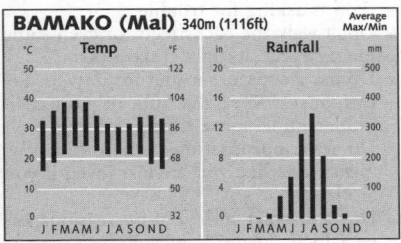

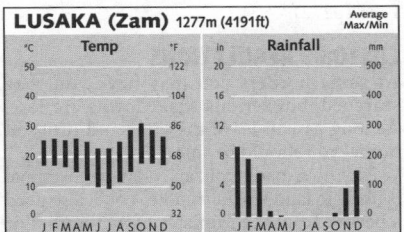

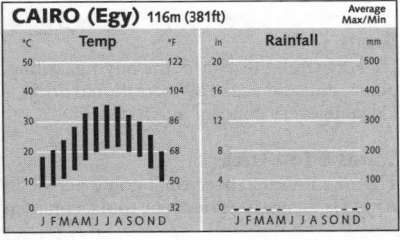

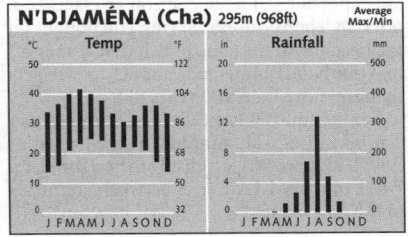

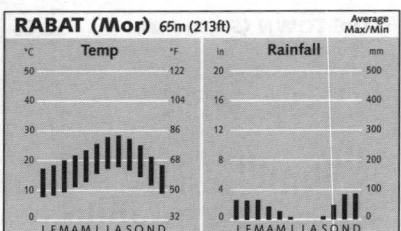

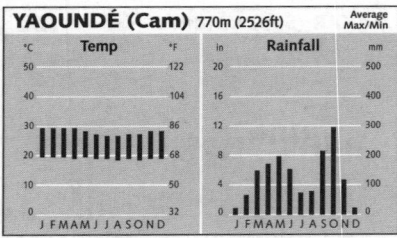

COURSES

Africa doesn't have a whole lot of courses to plan your trip around, but West Africa in particular has a range of intriguing possibilities, from learning the *kora* (21-string harp/lute from West Africa) from master musician Toumani Diabaté in Mali (p403) or Fon-language classes in Benin (p249) to surf classes in Senegal (p486), drumming and dancing classes in Ghana (p356), or percussion and cooking courses in Burkina Faso (p272).

CUSTOMS REGULATIONS

At some borders you may have your bag searched, but serious shakedowns are rare. As long as you leave the guns and drugs at home, you should be fine.

Anything made from an endangered animal is likely to land you in trouble. You'll also need a permit from the Ministry of Antiquities or a similar office in the relevant country if you are exporting valuable cultural artefacts (no, not that 'ebony' hippo carving you bought on the beach with the shoe polish that comes off on your hands). It usually applies to artefacts that are more than 100 years old.

Some countries limit the local currency you can take in or out, although a small amount (say, US$20 worth) is unlikely to be a problem. You can carry CFA francs between countries in the CFA zones.

A few countries have restrictive exchange regulations, and occasionally you may need to fill in a declaration form with details of your dollars or other 'hard' currencies.

DANGERS & ANNOYANCES

It's worth remembering that the overwhelming majority of travellers return home without encountering any of the following problems while in Africa. That said, it's always important to be aware of potential problems and keep your wits about you.

Crime

The vast majority of Africans are decent, hard-working people who want from you only respect and the chance to make an honest living; given the extreme poverty levels, robbery rates are incredibly low. Even so, you need to be alert on the streets of some cities. Nairobi (Kenya) is often called 'Nairobbery', Lagos (Nigeria) is not for the faint-hearted, while Dakar (Senegal), Abidjan (Côte d'Ivoire) and Johannesburg (South Africa) all have edgy reputations. Snatch-theft and pickpocketing are the most common crimes, but violent muggings can occur, so it pays to heed the warnings in country chapters and the following dos and don'ts:

- Don't make yourself a target on the streets. Carry as little as possible.
- Don't wear jewellery or watches, however cheap. Strolling with a camera or iPod is asking for trouble.
- Don't walk the backstreets, or even some main streets, at night. Take a taxi.
- Do use a separate wallet for day-to-day purchases. Keep the bulk of your cash hidden under loose-fitting clothing.
- Do walk purposefully and confidently. Never look like you are lost (even if you are!).
- Do be discreet with your possessions, especially in dorms. Keep your gear in your bag.

Drugs

It's very straightforward: the buying, selling, possession and use of all recreational drugs is illegal in every country in Africa.

Scams & Con Tricks

The main annoyance you'll come across in Africa is the various hustlers, touts, con men and scam merchants who always see tourists as easy prey. Although these guys are not necessarily dangerous, some awareness and suitable precautions are advisable, and should help you deal with them without getting stung. See the boxed text, p1140, for advice.

War Zones

Going to a war zone as a tourist is, to put it bluntly, bloody stupid. Sure, you'll get deep under the skin of the continent, and may even get to understand something about anarchy and suffering. But unless you're there to help out with a recognised aid agency and are qualified to do so, you'll be no help to anyone, and you'll quite likely get yourself kidnapped or killed.

Things change fast in Africa, so be aware that just because a place is listed in this book there's no guarantee that it's secure. Likewise, places we list as dangerous might become safe. The message here is to keep yourself up to date with what's happening on the ground. For a place to start, check out news websites such as bbc.co.uk or see the boxed text, below.

EMBASSIES & CONSULATES

In the Directory section of each country chapter we list embassies of neighbouring states and other useful countries (UK, Australia, US etc). In this book, the term 'embassy' often includes consulates and high commissions; for practical purposes they're pretty much the same thing.

If you need to find an embassy of an African country in your own country (to obtain visas before you go), it's easy to find them on the web.

EMERGENCIES

Generally speaking, emergency services in most African countries are not what you'd be used to at home. For example, if you're robbed or attacked, don't count on the police to respond quickly (or at all) when you dial an emergency number. However, you'll have to visit the police to report the offence – otherwise your insurance won't be valid – so expect an all-day form-filling process. Likewise, if you're sick or injured, don't waste time phoning an ambulance – get a taxi straight to a hospital or clinic. And if you want a private medical service or an English-speaking doctor, ask for directions at an embassy or a top-end hotel.

FESTIVALS & EVENTS

Whether it's a music festival or a traditional cultural celebration, planning your trip around a special event is a great idea. Have a look at the boxed text on p17 for inspiration, or check out the listings at www.whatsonwhen.com. Remember, though, that accommodation, flights and even souvenirs can skyrocket in price when there's an event on – booking far in advance is advisable.

GAY & LESBIAN TRAVELLERS

African societies are conservative towards gays and lesbians; same-sex relationships are a cultural taboo, and there are very few openly gay communities. Officially, homosexuality (male, female or both) is illegal in many African countries, even attracting the death penalty in Mauritania, Nigeria, Sudan and a few other areas. Although prosecutions rarely occur, discretion is key and public displays of affection should generally be avoided, advice

---

LATEST TRAVEL ADVICE

Lonely Planet's website (www.lonelyplanet.com) contains information on what's new, and any new safety reports, as well as reports from other travellers recounting their experiences while on the road.

Most governments have travel advisory services detailing terrorism updates, potential pitfalls and areas to avoid. Remember, however, that most government travel advisories can overstate the risks somewhat and you should read carefully through the reports to see when actual incidents occurred.

Australian Department of Foreign Affairs & Trade (☎ 1300 139 281; www.smartraveller.gov.au)

French Ministère des Affaires Étrangères Européennes (www.diplomatie.gouv.fr/fr/conseils-aux -voyageurs_909/index.html, in French)

UK Foreign & Commonwealth Office (☎ 0845-850 2829; www.fco.gov.uk)

US Department of State (☎ 202-647-4000; www.travel.state.gov)

SURVIVING SCAMS

Dud Sounds
You buy CDs from the market, but back at the hotel you open the box and it's got a blank CD inside, or music by a different artist. The solution: always listen to the CDs first.

Phone Home
You give your address to a local kid who says he wants to write. He asks for your phone number too, and you think 'no harm in that'. Until the folks back home start getting collect calls in the middle of the night. And when it's the kid's big brother making false ransom demands to your worried ma and pa, then things can get serious. Stick to addresses, and even then be circumspect.

Police & Thieves
Local drug salesmen are often in cahoots with the police, who then apprehend you and conveniently find you 'in possession', or just tell you they've seen you talking to a known dealer. Large bribes will be required to avoid arrest or imprisonment. To complicate things further, many con artists pose as policemen to extort money. Insist on being taken to the police station, and get written receipts for any fines you pay.

Take a Tour
A tout offers to sell you a tour such as a safari or a visit to a local attraction, and says he can do it cheaper if you buy onward travel with him too. You cough up for bus/ferry/plane tickets, plus another tour in your next destination, only to find yourself several days later with your cash gone and your reservations nonexistent. Best to pay only small amounts in advance, and deal with recommended companies or touts only.

Welcome, Friend
You're invited to stay for free in someone's house, if you buy meals and drinks for a few days. Sounds good, but your new friend's appetite for food and beer makes the deal more expensive than staying at a hotel. More seriously, while you're out entertaining, someone else will be back at the house of your 'friend' going through your bag. This scam is only likely in tourist zones – in remote or rural areas you'll more often than not come across genuine hospitality.

---

which applies to both homosexual and heterosexual couples. Cape Town is widely seen as Africa's most gay-friendly city, with a thriving club scene and a welcoming vibe.

An excellent website to get the low-down on local laws and attitudes to homosexuality is the South African–based **Behind the Mask** (www.mask.org.za), which has detailed information on each country. **Global Gayz** (www.globalgayz.com) and **Afriboyz** (www.afriboyz.com/Homosexuality-in-Africa.html) are also worth checking out.

HOLIDAYS

Public holidays such as Independence Day or President's Day are listed in the country chapters. The other main holidays are Christmas and Easter in the largely Christian countries, while in Muslim countries the main events are Eid al-Moulid, the birthday of the Prophet Mohammed; Eid-al-Fitr, marking the end of Ramadan; and Eid al-Adha (also called Eid

al-Haj, Eid al-Kebir or Tabaski), which commemorates Abraham's readiness to sacrifice his son on God's command, and coincides with the end of the pilgrimage to Mecca. Spellings may vary from country to country, and since the Islamic year has 354 or 355 days, these holidays fall about 11 days earlier each year in the Western calendar. During public holidays you can expect most businesses (apart from hotels, restaurants and tourist attractions) to close. To check the dates of Islamic holidays, go to www.bbc.co.uk/religion/tools/calendar/faith.shtml?muslim.

INSURANCE

Travel insurance to cover theft and illness is essential. Although having your camera stolen by monkeys or your music player eaten by a goat can be a problem, the medical cover is by far the most important aspect because hospitals in Africa are not free, and the good ones aren't cheap. Simply getting to a hospital can be expensive, so ensure you're covered for ambulances (land and air) and flights home.

Some insurance policies forbid unscheduled boat or plane rides, or exclude dangerous activities such as white-water rafting, canoeing, or even hiking. Others also don't cover people in countries subject to foreign office warnings. Others are more sensible and understand the realities of travel in Africa. Ask your flight agent or search on the web, but shop around and read the small print to make sure you're fully covered.

INTERNET ACCESS

Africa is firmly in the grip of the internet revolution, and with every passing year the distance of the average traveller from a decent online connection gets shorter. There are cybercafes in most capitals and major towns (there's even one in Timbuktu!), while many hotels and hostels also offer this service; midrange and top-end hotels increasingly offer wifi access for those carrying their own laptops. Expect to pay anything from US$1 to US$5 per hour, although wi-fi access is often free.

Be warned though – although things are improving, many connections are excruciatingly slow, with ancient PCs that are prone to crash just as you've finished that laborious round-robin email to your entire mailing list (tip: write it in a word-processing program and then copy it across). Uploading photos to your blog site or emailing attachments can prove arduous, not to mention expensive.

MAPS

For continental coverage, you can't go wrong with Michelin maps of Africa – No 741 North & West, No 745 North-East and No 746 Central & South. The detail is incredible, given the limitations of scale (1:4,000,000). Buy them before you leave home. Even so, expect a few discrepancies, particularly with regard to roads, as rough tracks get upgraded and smooth highways become potholed disasters.

For these and other African maps in the UK, try **Stanfords** (☎ 020-7836 1321; www.stanfords. co.uk; 12-14 Long Acre, Covent Garden, London, WC2E 9LP, UK), the world's largest supplier of maps. They also have stores in Manchester and Bristol. In France, **IGN** (☎ 01 43 98 80 00; www.ign.fr; 107 rue de La Boétie, 75008, Paris, France) sells its sheet maps at stores in Paris and Dijon.

MONEY

Throughout this book, we have quoted prices in local currencies in those countries where the currency and inflation are stable. For everywhere else, we've quoted prices in US dollars to ensure that the prices in this book remain current. However, it's important to remember that prices invariably increase – whatever prices we quote, they should always be regarded as guidelines, not guaranteed costs. We outline travel costs in the Getting Started chapter, and give more specific details in the country chapters.

ATMs

Along with email, the automated teller machine (ATM) is the greatest invention for travellers since the airplane, and in many (but by no means all) African countries you can draw local cash as you go with a credit or debit card. At the time of writing, there were no ATMs in São Tomé & Príncipe, Guinea-Bissau, Eritrea,

---

WHEN TO STORM THE EMBASSY

If you get into trouble on your travels, it's important to realise what your embassy can and can't do to help. Remember that you're bound by the laws of the country you are in, and diplomatic staff won't be sympathetic if you're jailed after committing a crime locally, even if such actions are legal at home.

In genuine emergencies you might get some assistance, but only if other channels have been exhausted. For example, to get home urgently, a free ticket is exceedingly unlikely – the embassy would expect you to have insurance. If all your money and documents are stolen, staff might assist with getting a new passport, but a loan for onward travel is way out of the question.

On the more positive side, some embassies (especially US embassies) have notice boards with 'travel advisories' about security or local epidemics. If you're heading for remote or potentially volatile areas, it might be worth registering with your embassy, and 'checking in' when you come back.

Somalia, Liberia, Niger and Zimbabwe, while ATMs worked only with local accounts in Sudan, Rwanda and Burundi. Guinea and Mauritania only had one ATM each; the use of credit cards should be avoided in Nigeria; and there are plans for ATMs compatible with international cards in the Central African Republic and Equatorial Guinea. Visa is the most widely (and often only) accepted card. For more information, see the individual country chapters. Charges can be low and exchange rates are usually good.

The downside for travellers in Africa is that although numbers are on the rise, ATMs are still located mostly in capitals and major towns, and even then not in every country, plus there are usually daily withdrawal limits. What's more, due to dodgy phone lines, they frequently malfunction, so you'll still need a pile of hard cash as backup.

Always keep your wits about you when drawing money out, as ATMs are often tar-geted by thieves. Try to visit them in busy areas during daylight hours, and stash your money securely before you move away.

Bargaining

Visitors may be used to things having a fixed value, but in Africa they're often worth whatever the seller can get. Once you get the hang of bargaining, it's all part of the fun. Hagglers are rarely trying to rip you off, so there's no point getting all hot and bothered about it. Decide what price you're prepared to pay and if you can't get it, simply decline politely and move on. While honing your bargaining skills can be satisfying, try to keep a sense of proportion – have you just wasted half an hour of your time arguing over a price difference that is worth a packet of chewing gum back home? By the same token, paying the first price asked may make it that much more difficult for the next person who comes along. See the boxed text, below, for tips.

THE FINE ART OF BARGAINING

Everyday Goods

Market traders selling basic items such as fruit and vegetables may raise their prices when they see a wealthy foreigner (that's you), so some minor bargaining could be called for, as long as you know the price that locals pay. But away from cities or tourist areas, many sellers will quote you the local price. It's important not to expect everybody to rip you off. If nothing else, thinking this way will ruin your trip.

After a couple of days in a new country (when you'll inevitably pay too much a few times) you'll soon learn the standard prices for basic items. But don't forget that these can change from place to place – a soft drink in a remote village can cost significantly more than what you'll pay in a city.

Souvenirs

At craft and curio stalls, where items are specifically for tourists, bargaining is very much expected. The vendor's aim is to get the highest price. Your aim is to get a good deal.

Some vendors may ask a price four (or more) times higher than what they're prepared to accept. You decide what you want to pay, and your first offer might be half this or even less. The vendor may feign outrage, while you plead abject poverty. Then the vendor's price starts to drop, and you make better offers until you arrive at a mutually agreeable price.

And that's the crux – mutually agreeable. You often hear travellers moaning about how they got 'overcharged' by souvenir sellers. But when things have no fixed price, nobody gets overcharged. If you don't like the price, it's simple: don't pay it.

And Finally...

Something to remember when bargaining is your own self-respect. Souvenir sellers normally give as good as they get, but if their 'final' price is close to what you're prepared to pay, consider accepting it. Buying food in markets, the same might apply; some travellers will happily spend US$100 on white-water rafting, then sternly barter with an old lady selling bananas to save a truly minuscule amount. It's worth being relaxed in such situations. You'll avoid stress, and most locals need that money more than you do.

Black Market

In countries with controlled exchange rates, you can get more local money for your hard currency by dealing with unofficial money-changers on the so-called black market, instead of going to a bank or bureau. This helps with costs, but it's illegal and sometimes dangerous – think twice before you do it.

However, you may have to resort to unofficial methods if you're stuck with no local cash when banks and exchange offices are closed. Hotels or tour companies may help, although rates are lousy. Try shops selling imported items. Be discreet though: 'The banks are closed, do you know anyone who can help?' is better than a blunt 'D'you wanna change money?'.

Even in countries with free exchange rates (and therefore no black market), money-changers often lurk at borders where there's no bank. Although illegal, they operate in full view of customs officers, so trouble from this angle is unlikely.

There's more chance of trouble from the moneychangers themselves, so make sure you know the exchange rates, and count all local cash carefully, *before* you hand over your money. Watch out for old or folded notes. A calculator ensures you don't miss a zero or two on the transaction. And beware of 'Quick, it's the police' tricks, where you're panicked into handing over money too soon. Use common sense and you'll have no problem, but it's best to change only small amounts to cover what you'll need until you reach a reliable bank or exchange office.

Credit Cards

Credit or debit cards are handy for expensive items such as tours and flights, but most agents add a hefty 10% surcharge. It's therefore usually cheaper to use your card to draw cash from an ATM, if they exist. If there's no ATM, another option is to withdraw money from a local bank using your card, but be warned – this also incurs a charge of around 5%, and can be an all-day process, so go early.

Before leaving home, check with your own bank to see which banks in Africa accept your card (and find out about charges). Debit cards are generally less hassle than credit cards for longer travels, provided, of course, that you have money in your account.

Throughout Africa, cards with the Visa logo are most readily recognised, although MasterCard is accepted in many places. Whatever card you use, don't rely totally on plastic, as computer or telephone breakdowns can leave you stranded. Always have cash or (less helpful) travellers cheques too.

To avoid credit-card fraud, always make sure that you watch the transaction closely and destroy any additional transaction slips that are produced, whether innocently or otherwise.

Currencies

Whether you're carrying cash or travellers cheques, or both, give some thought to the currency you take before you leave home. This will depend on the countries you visit. In East and southern Africa, by far the most readily recognised international currency is the US dollar (US$). Also accepted are euros (€), UK pounds (UK£) and South African rand (ZAR). Currencies from other European countries or Canadian dollars may occasionally be accepted, but don't count on it.

Many countries in West and Central Africa use a common currency called the Communauté Financière Africaine franc (usually shortened to CFA – pronounced 'say-eff-aah' in French), and here the euro is much more readily recognised by banks and bureaus. US dollars or other currencies are often not accepted at all. There are actually two CFA zones: the West African (or Banque Centrale des Etats de l'Afrique de l'Ouest) zone, which includes Benin, Burkina Faso, Côte d'Ivoire, Guinea-Bissau, Mali, Niger, Senegal and Togo; and the Central African (or Banque des Etats de l'Afrique Centrale) zone, which includes Chad, Cameroon, Central African Republic, Congo, Gabon and Equatorial Guinea.

The CFA is pegged at exactly 655.957 to one euro. If you're changing cash euros into CFA that's usually the rate you'll get (although there will be charges for travellers cheques); however, some out-of-the-way places may offer a little less.

Technically, you should be able to exchange West African CFA for Central Africa CFA and vice versa at a rate of one-to-one, but in reality you'll pay a bit over or under the odds, depending on the rates – and especially if you're dealing with traders at remote border posts a very long way from the nearest bank.

In non-CFA West African countries, the handiest currencies for travellers are euros and US dollars. It's the same for North Africa, where UK pounds are also accepted in some places.

Wherever you go, remember to carry a mix of large and small denominations. In many countries US$100 bills get you better rates, but note that the US changed the design of the US$100 bill in the mid-1990s and old-style US$100 notes, and sometimes other denominations, are not accepted at many places that don't have a light machine for checking watermarks; they'll often ask for the dollars with the 'big head'. Smaller denominations (cash or travellers cheques) can be handy if you need to change money to last just a few days before leaving a country.

Exchanging Money

You can exchange your hard cash or travellers cheques into local currency at banks or foreign-exchange bureaus in cities and tourist areas. For cash, bureaus normally offer the best rates, low (or no) charges and the fastest service, but what you get for travellers cheques can be pitiful – if they're accepted at all. Travellers cheques are more readily accepted at banks, but while rates may be OK, the charges can be as high as 10% or 20% – plus you'll often spend a lot of time queuing.

Travellers Cheques

You've a difficult choice to make when deciding to bring travellers cheques. On the one hand, they're secure – ATMs sometimes don't work and cash, unlike travellers cheques, cannot usually be replaced if lost. At the same time, many countries simply don't accept travellers cheques, and in those that do it's rare to find a bank that will change them outside of capital (or other major) cities, commissions can be prohibitive and they're often a pain to deal with. If you decide to bring travellers cheques, never make it your sole source of money. Check each individual country chapter for the situation.

When exchanging travellers cheques, most banks also check the purchase receipt (the paper you're supposed to keep separate) and your passport, so make sure you have these with you. You can sometimes pay for items such as safaris and activities directly with travellers cheques, but most operators add a surcharge – usually 10%, but sometimes up to 20%, because that's what banks charge them.

PHOTOGRAPHY

A simple point-and-shoot is fine for mementos of people, landscapes, market scenes and so on, but for better-quality shots, especially of animals, you'll need a zoom lens, and maybe an SLR camera with changeable lenses. It's also worth taking a couple of spare batteries with you and charging them whenever you have a reliable electricity source for those times when you're travelling in remote areas. For the same reasons, take extra memory cards and a cleaning kit. Africa's extremes of climate, especially heat, humidity and very fine sand can also take their toll on your camera, so always take appropriate precautions; changing lenses in a dust-laden wind is, for example, a recipe for disaster.

If you buy a new camera for your trip, get used to its workings at home – otherwise you could find yourself lurching around in a safari bus frantically reading the manual. Useful photographic accessories might include a small flash, a cable or remote shutter release, a sturdy tripod and a cleaning kit. Absolutely essential is a good padded bag, containing at least one desiccation sac, and sealed to protect your camera from dust and humidity. Avoid leaving your camera on the floor of buses or cars, as the jolting could well destroy the delicate inner workings of the lens.

Many internet cafes now offer to put your pictures on CD for you – a good idea is to get the CD copied at the same time, perhaps posting one home, to avoid the risks of files corrupting or the disc being damaged. Count on taking more photos than you expect to.

For more advice, Lonely Planet's *Guide to Travel Photography* is an excellent resource, full of helpful tips for photography while on the road. For more specific advice, Lonely Planet also publishes *Wildlife Photography* and *People Photography*.

POST

With the advent of email, few travellers use post these days, but if you do want to send a letter to a lover left behind, or a postcard to your granny, it's always better doing this from a capital city. From some countries, the service is remarkably quick (just two or three days to Europe, a week to the USA or Australia). From others it really earns the snail-mail tag, but it's still more reliable than sending stuff from really remote areas.

If your granny wants to reply, you can use the poste-restante service at any post office where mail is held for collection. Letters should be addressed clearly with surname underlined and in capitals, to '(Your Name), Poste Restante, General Post Office, Lusaka, Zambia' (for example). In French-speaking countries, send it to 'Poste Restante, PTT', then the name of the city.

To collect mail, you need your passport, and to pay about US$0.50 per item. Letters sometimes take a few weeks to arrive, so have them sent to a town where you'll be for a while, or will be passing through more than once – although in some places mail is only held for a month, then returned to the sender.

For sending home those carved rhinos from Kenya, or that beautiful cloth you bought in Mali, you'll need parcel post. Price, quality and speed vary massively from place to place, and courier companies can sometimes be more reliable than government postal services and not always a lot more expensive – see the individual country chapters for more details.

SOLO TRAVELLERS

Travelling alone in Africa is, for the most part, an exciting and liberating experience. Being on your own allows unbeatable flexibility and total immersion in the culture of the country you're travelling in.

Africans everywhere are incredibly sociable, so if you're looking for someone to chat to, you'll never be short of new friends eager to make your acquaintance. In some areas, fellow travellers can be easy to find, either at hostels or during those long waits at bus stations, although it depends how far off the beaten track you travel. And it's usually easy to make friends with local guides or hotel staff.

On the downside, prices for single occupancy in many African hotels are often not much less than for a double or twin room, and organised trips such as safaris can be prohibitively expensive if you're doing them on your own – you might have to wait around until a group comes along that you can attach yourself to. Travelling on your own might be regarded as rather bizarre by locals, but it's unlikely to be any more dangerous than being in a couple or group, even for solo women.

TELEPHONE & FAX

In most capital cities and major towns, phone connections are good. Thanks to satellite technology, it's often easier to make an international call than to dial someone 20km up the road. Rates vary from country to country, ranging from US$5 to US$15 for a three-minute call to Europe, the USA or Australia. Many cybercafes now offer dirt-cheap internet-connected phone calls, but the quality of the line depends on the quality of the internet connection – if it's a dial-up connection as opposed to ADSL, it's unlikely to be worth the effort.

In each country chapter we give further details, and in the Fast Facts boxes at the beginning of each chapter we give the country code and the access number for international calls.

Bureaus

To call long distance or even locally, you're usually better off at a public-phone bureau than a booth in the street. In each city, there's normally a bureau at the main post office, plus numerous privately run bureaus where rates can be cheaper and the service faster. At most bureaus you can also send or receive faxes.

Mobile Phones

Mobile (cell) phones are almost universal in Africa, with connection rates, call rates and coverage becoming better at a galloping rate, although you're unlikely to have coverage in remote rural areas. You can buy local SIM cards just about everywhere in Africa where there's mobile coverage. Some local companies also offer rates for international calls that work out cheaper than using landlines.

To check whether your phone will work in the African countries you plan to visit, contact your network provider. Ask about charges as well – and don't forget that if anyone rings you while you're overseas, the bulk of the cost goes on *your* bill.

Phonecards

In some countries you can buy phonecards that let you dial a local number, enter a PIN, and then make cheap international calls. You can also buy scratchcards to top up mobile phones, and phonecards to use in public booths instead of coins.

TIME

Africa is covered by four time zones, from UTC (formerly GMT) in the west to UTC +3 in the east (see Map p1159). Crossing from Chad to Sudan there's a two-hour difference, but elsewhere it's one hour or none at all. At borders where there's a one-hour time difference (eg Malawi–Tanzania), some have their opening and closing hours coordinated to avoid problems, but others don't – try to plan your travels at these crossings to avoid getting caught in no-man's land after you've been stamped out of one side, only to discover that the other side is already closed.

TOILETS

There are two types of toilet in Africa: the Western style, with a bowl and seat (common in most midrange or top-end hotels and restaurants); and the African style, a hole in the floor that you squat over. You might even find a combination of the two, with a Western-style toilet bowl propped over a hole in the floor. Standards vary tremendously, from pristine to those that leave little to the imagination as to the health or otherwise of the previous occupant. In our experience, a noncontact hole in the ground is better than a filthy bowl to hover over any day.

In rural areas, squat toilets are built over a deep hole in the ground and called 'long-drops'; the crap just fades away naturally, as long as the hole isn't filled with too much other rubbish (such as tampons – these should be disposed of separately). Toilet paper is OK – although you'll need to carry your own. In Muslim countries, a jug of water or hosepipe arrangement is provided for the same task. The idea is that you use your left hand to wipe, then use the water to wash your hand. This is why it's a breach of etiquette in many countries to shake hands or pass food with the left hand.

Some travellers complain that African toilets are difficult to use, but it only takes a little practice to accomplish a comfortable squatting technique, and you'll soon become adept at assuming the position in one swift move, while nimbly hoiking your trouser hems up at the same time so they don't touch the floor.

TOURIST INFORMATION

Much of Africa isn't geared for tourism, and decent tourist offices are rare. Some countries have a tourist-information office in the capital, but apart from a few tatty leaflets and vague advice from the remarkably little-travelled staff, you're unlikely to get much. Notable exceptions (such as South Africa) are listed in the country chapters. Tour companies, hotels and hostels are often better sources of information.

TRAVELLERS WITH DISABILITIES

There are more people with disabilities per head of population in Africa than in the West, but wheelchair facilities are virtually nonexistent. Don't expect things like wheelchair ramps, signs in Braille, or any other facilities that are available in tourist areas in other parts of the world. Most travellers with disabilities find travel much easier with the assistance of an able-bodied companion, or with an organised tour through an operator that specialises in arranging travel for those with disabilities. Safaris in South Africa and diving holidays in Egypt are both easily arranged with companies like these.

A final factor to remember, which goes some way to making up for the lack of facilities, is the friendliness and accommodating attitude of the African people. In the majority of situations, they will be more than happy to help if you explain to them exactly what you need.

Before setting out for Africa, travellers with disabilities should consider contacting any of the following organisations, which may be able to help you with advice and assistance:

Access-able Travel Source (☎ 303-232 2979; www.access-able.com; PO Box 1796, Wheatridge, CO, USA) Has lists of tour operators offering tours for travellers with disabilities.

Accessible Travel & Leisure (☎ 0145 272 9739; www.accessibletravel.co.uk) Claims to be the biggest UK travel agent dealing with travel for those with disabilities. The company encourages independent travel.

Disability Online (www.disabilityonline.com) A large database of links and resources for disabled travellers.

Endeavour Safaris (www.endeavour-safaris.com) Focuses on southern Africa.

Epic Enabled (www.epic-enabled.com) Trips in southern Africa for people with disabilities.

Mobility International USA (☎ 541-343 1284; www.miusa.org; 132 East Broadway, Suite 343, Eugene, OR, 97401, USA)

Royal Association for Disability & Rehabilitation (RADAR; ☎ 020-7250 3222; www.radar.org.uk; 12 City Forum, 250 City Rd, London, EC1V 8AF, UK) Publishes a useful guide called *Holidays & Travel Abroad: A Guide for Disabled People.*

Society for Accessible Travel and Hospitality (☎ 212-447 7284; www.sath.org; 347 5th Ave, Suite 610, New York, NY, 10016, USA)

Tourism for All (☎ 0845 124 9971; www.tourismforall.org.uk; Shap Rd Industrial Estate, Shap Road, Kendal, Cumbria, LA9 6NZ, UK)

EXTRA VISA REQUIREMENTS

A few countries demand a *note verbale* (letter of recommendation) from your own embassy before they issue a visa. This is generally no problem as your embassy will be aware of this, but be prepared to fork out yet more cash. It'll say: 'This letter is to introduce Mr/Ms [name], carrying [British/French] passport No [1234]. He/she is a tourist travelling to [Chad]. Please issue him/her with a tourist visa. All assistance you can give would be most appreciated.' Or: 'Par la présente, nous attestons que Mr/Ms [Name] est titulaire de passport [Britannique/Française] No [1234]. Il doit se rendre au [Tchad] pour faire le tourism. Toute assistance que pourrait lui être accordée serait appréciée.'

Australians travelling in Africa have only eight of their own embassies on the entire continent, so it's handy to obtain a letter of introduction from the Passports section of the Department of Foreign Affairs & Trade before you leave home.

Some countries have other arcane requirements. For Libya, you'll only get a visa if you have a prior booking with a Libyan tour operator, and a paper confirming this in Arabic. For more details see the Visas section of each country Directory.

VISAS

For a short trip through Africa you might get all your visas before you leave home. For a longer trip, it's easier to get them as you go along. Most countries have an embassy in each neighbouring country, but not all, so careful planning is required. Some visas are valid from when they are issued, so you may have to enter the country pretty soon after getting them. On other visas you say when you plan to enter the country and arrive within a month of that date. Sometimes it's convenient (and relatively cheap) to get several visas in one place – South Africa or Kenya, for example.

Prices vary widely, but you can expect to pay US$10 to US$50 for standard one-month single-entry visas, and up to US$200 for three-month multiple-entry visas. If you want to stay longer, extensions are usually available for an extra fee.

Rules vary for different nationalities: for example, British and Aussie citizens don't need advance visas for some southern African countries; French citizens don't need them in much of West Africa; Americans need them nearly everywhere. The price of a visa also varies according to nationality (lucky Irish-passport holders seem to be able to get free visas in dozens of countries!), and where you buy it. In some of Africa's more, ahem, *informal* countries, you'll also be factoring in the mood/corruption level of the person you're buying it from.

Most visas are issued in 24 or 48 hours – and it always helps to go to embassies in the morning – but occasionally the process can take a week or longer (such as for Sudan or Angola). You may have to show you have enough funds to cover the visit, or prove that you intend to leave the country rather than settle down and build a hut somewhere. (This could be an air ticket home, or a letter from your employer stating you're expected to return to work on a specified date.) For most visas you also need two or three passport photos, so take what you'll need, although you can get new supplies from photo booths in most capitals. Some embassies ask for a photocopy of your passport data page, so it's always worth carrying a few spare copies.

A final note: if you have Israeli stamps in your passport, they may prove problematic when you enter Algeria, Libya and Sudan. Israeli border officials may stamp a piece of paper, which you can then remove, but if you're travelling overland your Egyptian entry-point can still be a giveaway.

Specifics on visas are given in each country chapter, but regulations can change so it's always worth checking before you enter the country. For general details see lonelyplanet.com, which also has links to other visa sites.

Regional Visas
WEST AFRICA

If you're travelling in West Africa, ask about a Visa des Pays de l'Entente, a multicountry visa that covers travel in Benin, Burkina Faso, Côte d'Ivoire, Niger and Togo (however, at the time of writing the visa was not available in Benin or Togo, but you should be able to enter the country with it in Togo). Before you go rushing off to your nearest West African embassy to ask for this visa, remember that it's only obtainable *within* these five West African countries, which means that first you must obtain a visa for the first of these countries and, once there, apply at the immigration or visa extension office in the capital city. To get the Visa des Pays de l'Entente, which is valid for two months, you'll need to take along CFA25,000 and up to two passport photos. It usually takes a couple of days for the visa to be issued.

The Visa des Pays de l'Entente is only valid for one entry into each country, which makes it ideal for overlanders, but less so for those who plan to visit countries more than once. To further complicate matters, Benin and Togo border guards have been known to refuse to recognise the visa.

EAST AFRICA

After a 2009 agreement between regional governments, a new regionwide East African tourist visa was due to come into effect sometime in 2010. If or when it does, it will cover Tanzania, Kenya, Uganda, Rwanda and Burundi. For more information, see the boxed text, p737.

VOLUNTEERING

There are very few openings for ad-hoc volunteer work in Africa. Unless you've got some expertise, and are prepared to stay for at least a year, you're unlikely to be much use anyway. What Africa needs is people with skills. Just 'wanting to help' isn't enough. In fact, your presence may be disruptive for local staff and management, prevent locals from gaining employment, or cause a drain on resources.

For formal volunteer work, which must be arranged in your home country, organisations such as Voluntary Service Overseas (VSO; in the UK) and the Peace Corps (in the US) have programs throughout Africa where people, usually with genuine training (eg teachers, health workers, environmentalists), do two-year stints. Similar schemes for 'gap-year' students (between school and university) tend to be for shorter periods, and focus on community-building projects, teaching or scientific research. Almost all these projects require an additional financial donation, which may be raised by sponsorship and fundraising in your home country.

For information on volunteering in Morocco, see p192, while volunteering options in Sudan are covered on p211.

If you've got a genuine interest in volunteering in Africa, the following websites can provide more information:

Australian Volunteers International (www.austra lianvolunteers.com.au)
Coordinating Committee for International Voluntary Service (www.unesco.org/ccivs)
Earthwatch (www.earthwatch.org)
Frontier (www.frontier.ac.uk)
Global Volunteer (www.globalvolunteers.org)
Idealist.org (www.idealist.org)
International Volunteer Programs Association (www.volunteerinternational.org)
Intervol (www.intervol.org.uk)
Lattitude (www.lattitude.org.uk)
Peace Corps (www.peacecorps.gov)
Project Trust (www.projecttrust.org.uk)
Raleigh (www.raleighinternational.org)
Voluntary Service Overseas (VSO; www.vso.org.uk)
Working Abroad (www.workingabroad.com)
Worldwide Experience (www.worldwideexperience.com)
Worldwide Volunteering (www.worldwidevolunteer ing.org.uk)

WOMEN TRAVELLERS

It's no use pretending otherwise – women travelling in Africa (alone or with other women) will occasionally encounter specific problems, most often harassment from men. North Africa can be particularly tiresome from this perspective, although Libya is generally better than Tunisia or Egypt. And in places where an attack or mugging is a real possibility, women are seen as easy targets, so it pays to keep away from these areas (they're often listed in the individual country chapters, but talk to people on the ground to get the latest situation).

But don't panic! On a day-to-day basis, compared to many places, travel in Africa is relatively safe and unthreatening, and you'll meet friendliness and generosity – not to mention pure old-fashioned gallantry – far more often than hostility or predatory behaviour. Many men are simply genuinely curious as to why on earth a woman is out travelling the world rather than staying at home with the babies, so keep an open mind and try not to be too hostile in the face of endless questions. Remember also that half of the authors who worked on this book are women and many of them travelled alone and lived to tell the tale.

Having said that, when it comes to evening entertainment, Africa is a conservative society and in many countries 'respectable' women don't go to bars, clubs or restaurants without a male companion. However distasteful this may be to postfeminist Westerners, trying too aggressively to buck the system could lead to trouble.

Because of these attitudes, it can be hard to meet and talk with local women. It may require being invited into a home, although since many women have received little education, unless you have learnt some of the local language, communication could be tricky. However, this is changing to some extent because a surprising number of girls go to school while boys are sent away to work. This means that many of the staff in tourist offices, hotels or government departments are educated women, and this can be as good a place as any to try and strike up a conversation. In rural areas, a good starting point might be teachers at local schools, or staff at health centres.

Some expatriates you meet may be appalled at the idea of a female travelling alone and will do their best to discourage you with horror stories, often of dubious accuracy. Others will have a far more realistic attitude. When you are on the road, the best advice on what can and can't be undertaken safely will come from local women. Use your common sense and things should go well. It's also worth remembering that, as a solo female traveller, you might be best to pay a little extra for midrange hotels where the surroundings may make you feel more comfortable – many of the cheapest hotels in African towns rent rooms by the hour.

PHOTOS FROM HOME

Female backpackers may be regarded with a mixture of bewilderment and suspicion in places unused to tourists, especially if alone. You should be at home rearing families or tending the crops, not engaged in frivolous pastimes like travel, the thoughts sometimes go. To show you do have a home life, you could carry photographs of family or friends, or even a mythical husband (unless you've got a real one, of course). Photos of yourself at work sometimes do the same trick.

Sexual Harassment

Unwanted interest from male 'admirers' is an inevitable aspect of travel in Africa, especially for lone women. This is always unpleasant, but it's worth remembering that although you may encounter a lewd border official, or a persistent suitor who won't go away, real harm or rape is very unlikely. If you're alone in an uneasy situation, act cold or uninterested, rather than threatened. Stick your nose in a book, or invent an imaginary husband who will be arriving shortly. If none of this works and you can't shake off a hanger-on, going to the nearest public place, such as the lobby of a hotel, usually works well, or you could try asking for help from local women in a public place. If the problem still persists, asking the receptionist to call the police usually frightens them off.

POSITIVE VIBES Amy Marsh

Much advice for women travellers concentrates on negative aspects, reinforcing the stereotypical view that it's really only men who can do 'adventurous' things in Africa. The following observations form a refreshing and very welcome antidote:

I'm a 22-year-old white female, and I spent three months in Senegal, Mali, Niger, Benin, Ghana, Côte d'Ivoire and Guinea, travelling mostly alone, eating street food and sleeping in the most cockroach-laden hotels. I always wore a skirt and covered my hair, but often found myself surrounded by men, especially young men – often simply because men are more likely to be in a situation to interact with foreign travellers. Just the sheer numbers can be daunting! It was a lengthy learning process – understanding how to recognise innuendos, separate nice boys from those with ulterior motives, and generally how to raise the red flags at the appropriate time.

Eventually, though, I did learn, and felt very comfortable going solo. I went to Agadez, and hiked 100km through the villages of the Fouta Djalon. Wherever I went, people took excellent care of me. Fellow bus passengers brought me coffee or got my passport back for me from awkward border guards. They brought me home, showed me around, and gave me unlimited supplies of manioc and bananas. Once I'd learnt how to react, it seemed that locals knew I'd been travelling for a while, and I certainly found it increasingly easy and enjoyable to be in Africa.

Part of the reason for the interest is that local women rarely travel long distances alone, and a single foreign female is an unusual sight. And, thanks to imported TV and Hollywood films (and the behaviour of some tourists), Western women are frequently viewed as 'easy'.

What you wear may greatly influence how you're treated. African women dress conservatively, in traditional or Western clothes, so when a visitor wears something different from the norm, she will draw attention. In the minds of some men this is provocative. In general, look at what other women are wearing and follow suit. Keep your upper arms, midriff and legs covered.

Sanitary Protection

You can buy tampons and pads in most cities and major towns from pharmacies or supermarkets. Prices are about the same as in Europe (from where they're imported) but you seldom have choice of type or brand. They're rarely found in shops away from the main towns, so you might want to bring supplies if you're spending a lot of time in remote areas.

WORK

It's hard for outsiders to find work in most African countries, as high unemployment means a huge number of local people chase every job vacancy. You will also need a work permit, and these are usually hard to get as priority is rightly given to qualified locals over travellers. You're unlikely to see many jobs advertised, so the best way to find out about them is by asking around among the expatriate community.

Transport in Africa

CONTENTS

'Nothing in Africa is adjacent to anywhere.'
James Cameron, Point of Departure: Experiment in Biography (*Grafton Books, 1969*)

GETTING THERE & AWAY

Getting yourself into Africa can be as simple as booking a direct-flight ticket from a major European hub, or as adventurous as hitching a lift on a car ferry then jumping onto a cargo truck. However you choose to do it, it pays to put aside some research time in advance to make sure you don't blow unnecessary bucks or time. Flights, tours and rail tickets can be booked online at www.lonelyplanet.com/travel_services.

AIR

The bulk of air traffic with Africa is to and from Europe, but there are a handful of direct flights between Africa and North America, the Middle East and Asia. A few flights link Australia with Africa, and there are flights between South Africa and Brazil, Chile and Argentina. Many North American travellers pass through a European 'hub' en route to Africa. For Australasian travellers it's often cheaper to pass through a Middle Eastern and/or Asian hub before arriving, but these flights often pass through a European hub as well.

Wherever you're coming from, the main thing to remember is that flying into one of Africa's main hubs is going to be your cheapest option. Flights to the hubs can cost peanuts from Europe, and once you're there the national carriers of the various countries can easily transport you to other destinations across Africa. These extra flights are known as 'add-ons' and are often best booked in conjunction with your main international ticket through a decent travel agent at home (tip: flights with add-ons or multiple stops are still almost always best booked with a real live reservations agent rather than through a website).

The main gateway into East Africa is Nairobi (Kenya), although Dar es Salaam (Tanzania) is also busy. Johannesburg (South Africa) is the southern African hub offering the most options (flights arrive from the Americas, Asia and Australasia as well as Europe) and biggest bargains – also look out for cheap deals into Cape Town (South Africa). In West Africa, Dakar (Senegal), Accra (Ghana) and Lagos (Nigeria) are the busiest gateways. In North Africa, flying into Casablanca (Morocco) or Cairo (Egypt) is the cheapest option. If you're travelling from Europe, Tunis (Tunisia) is often the cheapest African city in which to arrive. However, it's surrounded by Algeria and Libya, which can make for tricky onward overland travel (see those chapters for details).

Tickets

Wild climatic variations across Africa, and differing holiday seasons in the northern and

---

THINGS CHANGE...

The information in this chapter is particularly vulnerable to change. Check directly with the airline or a travel agent to make sure you understand how a fare (and ticket you may buy) works and be aware of the security requirements for international travel. Shop carefully. The details given in this chapter should be regarded as pointers and are not a substitute for your own careful, up-to-date research.

southern hemispheres, means that it's tricky to pin down the cheapest times to fly to Africa – get the low-down on costs from a travel agent well in advance. Using mile-wide brush strokes it could be argued that flying from June to September or around Christmas (a 'peak season' that can last from November to March if you're coming from Australasia) is going to hit your budget hardest. But you don't need generalities if you've a well-defined trip in mind.

If you're planning a big trip consider open-jaw tickets, which allow you to fly into one city, then out of another, and can save you cash, time and hassle. All manner of combinations are available, enabling some great overland journeys: think about a ticket into Cairo and out of Cape Town (fares from here can be amazingly cheap), or into Nairobi and out of Cape Town, or even into Dakar and out of Cape Town. Even if you're not travelling so far, it can be helpful – flying into Dakar and out of Bamako, for example.

Another handy way of flitting around the continent is stopovers. Many flights to Africa stop at least once before arriving at the main destination, and on some tickets (sadly not always those at the cheapest end of the spectrum) you'll have the chance to get off; on some happy occasions taking advantage of these stopovers can effectively save the cost of an internal flight. For example, a Kenya Airways flight from London to Addis Ababa (Ethiopia) goes via Nairobi, allowing you to explore Kenya first. If you're coming from North America or Australia, a stopover in Europe can be handy if you need to pick up an obscure visa in Paris.

Jumping on a charter flight can sometimes save you a bundle if you're travelling from or via Europe, especially if you pick something up at the last minute. The main drawback is that short-date returns are common, but there is sometimes some flexibility.

It's not rocket science, but take your time, shop around, double-check all restrictions and date- or route-change penalties on your ticket, look out for credit-card surcharges and book well in advance. A couple of hours on the internet should give you an idea of the most useful travel agents; talk to as many as possible. Remember that although websites are great for straightforward return tickets, they cannot tell you about little add-ons and short cuts or custom-build itineraries from a cluster of domestic and regional flights.

If you're under 26 or a student you'll occasionally be able to turn up some juicy deals.

CLIMATE CHANGE & TRAVEL

Climate change is a serious threat to the ecosystems that humans rely upon, and air travel is the fastest-growing contributor to the problem. Lonely Planet regards travel, overall, as a global benefit, but believes we all have a responsibility to limit our personal impact on global warming.

Flying & Climate Change

Pretty much every form of motor travel generates CO_2 (the main cause of human-induced climate change) but planes are far and away the worst offenders, not just because of the sheer distances they allow us to travel, but because they release greenhouse gases high into the atmosphere. The statistics are frightening: two people taking a return flight between Europe and the US will contribute as much to climate change as an average household's gas and electricity consumption over a whole year.

Carbon Offset Schemes

Climatecare.org and other websites use 'carbon calculators' that allow jetsetters to offset the greenhouse gases they are responsible for with contributions to energy-saving projects and other climate-friendly initiatives in the developing world – including projects in India, Honduras, Kazakhstan and Uganda.

Lonely Planet, together with Rough Guides and other concerned partners in the travel industry, supports the carbon offset scheme run by climatecare.org. Lonely Planet offsets all of its staff and author travel.

For more information check out our website: lonelyplanet.com.

ONE WAY, NO WAY

One-way tickets to Africa are rarely a good idea. For the most part, immigration regulations forbid (or at least discourage) entry to people with one-way tickets; you need to show that you have a ticket out of Africa, although this seems a little perverse considering you can get a ferry to Africa and travel overland through the continent before picking up a one-way flight back home (these tickets tend to cost about half of the usual return fare).

There are many specialist student travel agents, but many 'normal' travel agents offer student fares, just as student travel agents can serve older travellers. **STA Travel** (www.statravelgroup.com) has hundreds of potentially useful offices and affiliates around the world, but service can vary and it's vital that you shop around. Travel agents that recognise the **International Student Identity Card** (ISIC; www.isic.org) scheme are another possibility – the contact details of thousands of agents are available on its website.

Reputable online agencies for scheduled carriers include:

Airtreks (www.airtreks.com)
Atrapalo (www.atrapalo.com in Spanish)
eBookers (www.ebookers.com)
Expedia (www.expedia.com)
Expedia (Germany) (www.expedia.de, in German)
Kayak (www.kayak.com)
Opodo (www.opodo.com)
PlaneSimple (www.planesimple.co.uk)
Rumbo.es (www.rumbo.es in Spanish)
STA (www.sta.com)
Travel.com.au (www.travel.com.au)
Travelocity (www.travelocity.com)

INTERCONTINENTAL (RTW) TICKETS

On the cheapest round-the-world (RTW) tickets Nairobi and Johannesburg are the usual stops, but stopping in these major hubs will cut down your options once you leave the continent. If you want more stops within Africa look at the Global Explorer or oneworld Explorer RTW tickets offered by the **oneworld alliance** (www.oneworldalliance.com). Coming from Europe with British Airways and Air France can get you to a variety of interesting African destinations, but flights within Africa are limited.

The trick with RTW tickets is to decide where you want to go first and then talk to a travel agent, who will know the best deals, cunning little routes and the pitfalls of the various packages. If you're departing the UK, you could also try the handy interactive route planner at www.roundtheworldflights.com.

Americas

There are only a handful of direct flights to Africa from North America. **Delta** (www.delta.com) flies from New Cork to Accra (Ghana), while **Royal Air Maroc** (www.royalairmaroc.com) connects Casablanca (Morocco) with New York and Montreal. **EgyptAir** (www.egyptair.com.eg) flies into Cairo (Egypt) from New York and Montreal, while **South African Airways** (www.flysaa.com) flies New York–Johannesburg (South Africa); the latter also flies between Johannesburg and São Paulo (Brazil) if you're coming from South America. South African Airways and Royal Air Maroc have the best onward connections within Africa.

Just because these flights are direct, however, doesn't mean that they're necessarily the cheapest options and 'through' ticketing via Europe is a popular option. Sometimes it even works out more economically to buy a ticket to Europe, then a separate ticket to Africa.

lonelyplanet.com (www.lonelyplanet.com) Includes links to a US RTW fare generator from Airtreks.
OneTravel.com (www.onetravel.com) Comprehensive North American fare generator.
STA Travel (☎ 800-781-4040; www.statravel.com) The biggest student/under-26 flight agent in North America.
Travel Cuts (☎ 1-866-246-9762; www.travelcuts.com) Canada's primary student and discounted travel agent.

Australasia & Asia

The only direct flights between Australia and Africa are those operated by **Qantas** (www.qantas.com.au) or **South African Airways** (www.flysaa.com), who both fly between Johannesburg and Perth or Sydney. Another option is to Johannesburg from Sydney or Perth via Mauritius with **Air Mauritius** (www.airmauritius.com). If Johannesburg doesn't work for you, flying via the Middle East with **Emirates** (www.emirates.com) greatly increases your options, with connections from Dubai to Cairo, Tripoli, Tunis, Casablanca, Abidjan, Accra, Lagos, Khartoum, Addis Ababa, Nairobi, Dar es Salaam, Johannesburg and Cape Town.

In Australia and New Zealand, the following are reputable agencies:

Flight Centre Australia (☎ 133 133; www.flightcentre.com.au); New Zealand (☎ 0800 243 544; www.flight centre.co.nz)

Ninemsn (http://travel.ninemsn.com.au) Good internet booking engine.

STA Travel Australia (☎ 134 782; www.statravel.com.au); New Zealand (☎ 0800 474 400; www.statravel.co.nz)

From Asia, **EgyptAir** (www.egyptair.com.eg) flies into Cairo from a host of cities, including Bangkok, Singapore and Beijing. **Kenya Airways** (www.kenya-airways.com) flies from Bangkok and Hong Kong to Nairobi. **Singapore Airlines** (www.singaporeairlines.com) connects Singapore and Johannesburg.

Europe

The choices for flying to Africa from Europe are almost endless.

As a general starting point, national airlines almost always fly into their former colonies, which means that **Air France** (www.airfrance.com), **British Airways** (www.ba.com) and **TAP Air Portugal** (www.flytap.com) together cover many capital cities throughout Africa from Paris, London and Lisbon respectively. Of the other European airlines, **KLM** (www.klm.com), **Lufthansa** (www.lufthansa.com) and **SN Brussels Airlines** (www.flysn.com) have extensive African networks, while **Swiss** (www.swiss.com) also flies into a few African cities.

Of the numerous African airlines that fly to/from Europe, **Royal Air Maroc** (www.royalairmaroc.com) flies from many European cities into dozens of African ones via its Casablanca hub, as does **Afriqiyah** (www.afriqiyah.aero) via Tripoli. **Ethiopian Airlines** (www.flyethiopian.com) and **Kenya Airways** (www.kenya-airways.com) are also worth considering, not least for their terrific pan-African connections from Addis Ababa and Nairobi respectively.

Charter airlines are another possibility. Heaps of other charter flights leave for Africa from across Europe. From the UK and France charter flights leave for the Gambia, Morocco, Tunisia, Egypt and Kenya. Charter flights to Senegal, Mali, Burkina Faso, Togo and Benin also leave from France between November and May. **Point Afrique** (www.point-afrique.com in French) offers well-priced flights to these and other Saharan countries from Paris and Marseille. Italy is a good place to look for cheap charters to Zanzibar (Tanzania) and Mombasa (Kenya).

Reputable European travel agencies include:

Africa Travel Centre (☎ 0845-450 1520; www.africatravel.co.uk; UK) Experienced UK operator offering flights and tours.

Airfair (☎ 0900 7 717 717; www.airfair.nl in Dutch; Netherlands)

Barcelo Viajes (www.barceloviajes.com in Spanish; Spain)

Connections (☎ 070 23 33 13; www.connections.be; Belgium)

CTS Viaggi (☎ 06-4411166; www.cts.it in Italian; Italy)

Nouvelles Frontières (☎ 01 49 20 65 87; www.nouvelles-frontieres.fr in French; France) Also in Belgium and Switzerland.

STA Travel (☎ 069-743 032 92; www.statravel.de in German; Germany) Also has offices in other countries.

Trailfinders (☎ 0845-058 5858; www.trailfinders.co.uk; UK)

Voyageurs du Monde (www.vdm.com in French; France)

Indian Subcontinent

There is plenty of traffic between Mumbai (Bombay) in India and East Africa and flights to and from Nairobi can be pretty darn cheap. **Ethiopian Airlines** (www.flyethiopian.com; Addis Ababa) and **Kenya Airways** (www.kenya-airways.com; Nairobi) have a number of direct flights to/from Mumbai. A number of Middle Eastern carriers – such as **Emirates** (www.emirates.com) via Dubai, **Gulf Air** (www.gulfair.com) via Bahrain, and **Qatar Airways** (www.qatarairways.com) via Doha in Qatar – service North and East Africa.

LAND & SEA

If you're setting off on an overland adventure from Europe you could drive, fly or even get the train to southern Europe. Once you've reached your port of choice in southern Europe, towering car ferries, sleek powerful 'fast ferries' and hi-tech catamarans ply the routes across the Mediterranean. A cheaper (but less comfortable) option is to go by bus. **Eurolines** (www.eurolines.com) runs a huge European network that includes Morocco.

Alternatively, head overland through the Middle East, where Africa's only land border divides Israel and Egypt in the Sinai – the continuing troubles in Israel and the Palestinian Territories mean that the direct route via Rafah is closed to foreigners, so make your way via the Eilat–Taba border crossing on the Gulf of Aqaba. However, note that if your passport has an Israeli stamp in it you won't get into countries such as Libya, so if this is going to be a problem take the (car and passenger) ferry from Jordan.

Egypt & Sudan

There are daily ferries and a catamaran between Nuweiba in Sinai (Egypt) and Aqaba (Jordan), which is a stone's throw from Eilat (Israel). For more details, see p123. Other boats also ply the routes between Suez (Egypt) and Jeddah (Saudi Arabia) and between Hurghada (Egypt) and Duba (Saudi Arabia).

There are regular ferry services between Suakin (Sudan; just south of Port Sudan) and Jeddah (Saudi Arabia). For more details, see p212.

If you're a real adventurer you could hunt down some informal cargo and local boat traffic; there's this kind of traffic from Mokha (Yemen) to Djibouti. For more details, see p657.

Morocco

The three main companies propelling travellers across the Strait of Gibraltar from Spain to Morocco are **Trasmediterránea** (www.trasmedi terranea.es), **EuroFerrys** (www.euroferrys.com) and **FRS** (www.frs.es). The main routes run to Melilla (one of Spain's North African enclaves) from Almería and Málaga; Nador from Almería; Tangier from Gibraltar, Tarifa and Algeciras; and Ceuta (another Spanish enclave on the Moroccan coast) from Algeciras. All routes usually take vehicles as well as passengers, and most services increase in frequency during the summer months, when other routes are sometimes added. For more details, see p193.

Longer-haul ferries that operate as part of the **Cemar** (www.cemar.it) network also sail to Tangier from Genoa (Italy) and Sète (France).

Tunisia & Algeria

Compagnie Tunisienne de Navigation (CTN; www.ctn. com.tn) runs ferries from Marseille (France) and Genoa (Italy) to Tunis (Tunisia). A host of other companies also offer services from Italy to Tunis (Genoa is a year-round departure point; summer services leave from La Spezia, Napoli and Trapani).

For Algeria, **Trasmediterránea** (www.trasmediter ranea.es) runs ferries from Almería in southern Spain to Ghazaouet (Algeria), and you might also find services to Oran (Algeria) from Almería or southern France.

GETTING AROUND

Travelling around much of Africa often requires time, patience and stamina. African public transport *sometimes* leaves and arrives roughly on time (off-the-beaten-track transport is more unreliable), but there are few interesting places that you cannot reach without your own car, even if you have to wait for a few days. It's also worth remembering that some of your most memorable and enjoyable travel experiences will take place en route between places – in Africa, the journey is the destination.

AIR

Africa's internal air network is pretty comprehensive and can save you considerable time and hardship on the roads; certainly flying over the Sahara, Democratic Republic of Congo (DRC) and the often difficult Chad and southern Sudan can be a good idea. Always check flight details carefully (many tickets are flexible), but be prepared for delays, cancellations and bureaucratic pantomimes, especially when travelling on state-owned enterprises. Don't expect to be put up in a four-star hotel should your flight get canned.

If you're serious about taking a few African flights, consider sorting it out when booking your main ticket. Any half-decent travel agent should be able to book a host of 'add-on' African flights and possibly find fares that allow a little flexibility. These add-ons are often sold at a discount overseas, so forward planning can save you a small fortune. See p1151 for more tips on buying African plane tickets.

Airlines with extensive African networks from their hub cities include **Ethiopian Airlines** (www.flyethiopian.com; Addis Ababa), **Kenya Airways** (www.kenya-airways.com; Nairobi), **Royal Air Maroc** (www. royalairmaroc.com; Casablanca), **South African Airways** (www.flysaa.com; Johannesburg), **Afriqiyah** (www.afriqi yah.aero; Tripoli), **Air Sénégal International** (www. air-senegal-international.com in French) and **Interair** (www.interair.co.za).

Air Passes

Air passes are something of a misnomer. All products purporting to be Africa air passes are just cheapo deals on domestic and transcontinental flights available to travellers flying into Africa with certain airlines.

BRINGING YOUR BIKE

You could cycle all the way into Africa or you could save your legs for Africa's rough roads and stick your wheels in the hold of a plane. There are two ways of doing this: you could partially dismantle your bike and stuff it into a large box or just simply wheel your bike to the check-in desk, where it should be treated as a piece of baggage (although you might need to take the pedals off, turn the handlebars sideways and wrap it in cardboard and/or foam). Don't lose too much sleep about the feather touch of baggage handlers – if your bike doesn't stand up to air travel it won't last long in Africa.

Some airlines don't include sports equipment in the baggage allowance; others may charge around US$50 extra because your bike is not standard luggage size; others, however, will take it without hassles.

These schemes operate on a tailor-made basis – routes are usually divided into price bands or sectors and you pick 'n' mix to make an itinerary. Most schemes are fairly limited and usually dictate that your flights include an arrival or departure at one or two hubs. The airlines mentioned in this section won't always offer the cheapest flights into Africa, but if you're planning to take a few African flights some 'air pass' schemes offer great value in the long run – the best offer savings of well over 50% on domestic and continental fares.

The 'Africa Airpass' scheme run by **Star Alliance** (www.staralliance.com) allows flights on South African Airways to 30 destinations across Africa if you fly in on a member carrier.

KLM (www.klm.com) offers a Passport to Africa, which hooks into the African network of Kenya Airways. It allows for between three and 12 African flight coupons in combination with intercontinental travel on KLM, Northwest Airlines or Kenya Airways.

BICYCLE

Cycling around Africa is predictably tough but rewarding. Long, hot, gruelling journeys are pretty standard, but you'll be in constant close contact with the peoples and environments of the continent and will get to visit small towns and villages that most people just shoot through. In general, the more remote the areas you visit, the better the experience, but you've got to be fully prepared. A tent is standard issue, but remember to ask the village headman where you can pitch a tent when camping near settlements in rural areas.

Touring bikes aren't the best choice for Africa, a continent not exactly blessed with smooth tarmac roads. Adapted mountain bikes are your best bet – their smaller 660mm (26in) wheel rims are less likely to be misshaped by rough roads than the 700mm rims of touring bikes, and mountain-bike frames are better suited to the rigours of African travel. Multipurpose hybrid tyres with knobbles on their edges for off-road routes and a smooth central band for on-road cruising are useful in Africa, but your tyre choices (along with the types of components, number of spares and the like) should depend on the terrain you want to tackle.

You may encounter the odd antelope or zebra while cycling, but motorists are more of a threat to cyclists than rampaging wildlife. Cyclists lie just below donkeys on the transport food chain, so if you hear a vehicle coming up from behind, be prepared to bail out onto the verges. That said, many of Africa's roads are pretty quiet. Be very cautious about cycling in busy towns and cities.

The heat can be a killer in Africa, so carry at least 4L of water and don't discount the possibility of taking a bus, truck or boat across some sections (bikes can easily be transported).

The **International Bicycle Fund** (IBF; www.ibike.org/africaguide) has a handy guide to cycling in Africa by country, although information for some countries is limited and out of date.

BOAT

Lakes Malawi (p959), Tanganyika (p813), Kariba (p1095) and Victoria (p813) in southern and East Africa all have ferries operating on them. There are even more fantastic river journeys to be had along the Niger (see the boxed text, p412), Congo (p574) and Nile (p112 and p117). Boat trips may also be possible on the Senegal, Gambia and Zambezi Rivers.

MASTER THE SAHARA

Chris Scott's www.sahara-overland.com is an excellent place to start planning any trans-African routes, and his books *Sahara Overland* and *Adventure Motorcycling Handbook* are highly recommended reading. *Sahara Handbook* by Simon Glen is also well worth reading. All these books will give you a better background than we can do here.

On simple riverboats you'll be sat on mountains of cargo, the bows of the craft sitting just above the water line, but on some major river routes large ferries and barges are used. Generally speaking, 3rd class on all ferries is crammed with people, goods and livestock, making it hot and uncomfortable. Happily there's usually a better way: at a price, cabins (semiluxurious and otherwise) with bar and restaurant access can be yours.

The most important coastal ferry service is that between Dar es Salaam and Zanzibar (p777). There are also some services along the West African coast, especially in Sierra Leone (p518) and Guinea-Bissau (p386). There are also ferries between Limbe (Cameroon) and Calabar (Nigeria; p479).

A more romantic alternative is to travel by small Arabic-style dhow sailing vessels that ply the Indian Ocean coast. The easiest place to organise this is in Mozambique, where you can sail to and around the Quirimbas Archipelago (p976). Similar to dhows are feluccas (see p112 and p117), the ancient sailing boats of the Nile.

Pirogues (traditional canoes) and *pinasses* (motorised canoes) are staples of travel on remote waterways where small, diesel-powered (and often unreliable) pontoon-style car ferries are not available. They're especially common in the rivers of West Africa. Not many ferries or boats take vehicles, but you can get a motorbike onto some.

Seafaring travellers might be able to hitch a lift on cargo boats down the West African coast, up the east coast of Madagascar (p933) and on the Red Sea, but this will take some work.

Travelling by boat can sometimes be hazardous in Africa. For the most part you can forget about safety regulations, lifeboats or life-jackets, and overloading is very common. To make matters worse, on some ferries the 3rd-class passengers are effectively jammed into the hold with little opportunity for escape.

CAR & MOTORCYCLE

Exploring Africa with your own wheels takes some doing, but is a wonderful way to see the continent. The easiest way to enter Africa with your own car or motorcycle is to cross from southern Europe to Morocco or Tunisia aboard a car ferry and then take it from there. The obvious main barrier to travelling this way is the Sahara, but it can be crossed with careful planning. At the time of writing, most trans-Saharan routes were off limits to travellers due to simmering rebellion and banditry, although the Western Sahara route (from Morocco to Mauritania via Dakhla) was considered safe, while the Route du Hoggar (from Algeria to Niger) remains open if not always recommended. Other potential barriers to getting around Africa by car or motorcycle include the cost of hiring a barge to transport your vehicle from Egypt into Sudan, and war and/or the nonexistent roads of the Democratic Republic of Congo. For a multitude of other options and inspiring tales from those who've made overland trips past, present and future, check out the website of the **Africa Overland Network** (www.africa-overland.net) or, for motorcyclists, **Horizons Unlimited** (www.horizonsunlimited.com).

If you're keen to begin in East or South Africa, it can be expensive to ship your vehicle all the way to Mombasa or Cape Town – it may work out cheaper to fly there and purchase something once you arrive. South Africa in particular is a pretty easy place to purchase a car – either from a dealership or from a fellow traveller who has finished with it. Handily, cars registered in South Africa don't need a *carnet de passage* for travel around southern Africa, but you will need to have an international driving licence, your home licence, vehicle insurance and registration, and you will have to get a new set of plates made. The **Automobile Association** (www.aasa.co.za) in South Africa offers vehicle check-ups, insurance and travel advice.

Travelling around Africa by motorcycle is popular among hard-core motorcyclists, but road conditions vary greatly. Remember also that many drivers (particularly truck drivers) are either unaccustomed or disinclined to

TRANSPORT IN AFRICA

Road Distances (km) & Time Zones

	Abidjan (Côte d'Ivoire)	Accra	Addis Ababa	Asmara	Bamako	Banjul	Bujumbura	Cairo	Cape Town	Conakry	Cotonou	Dakar	Dar es Salaam	Djibouti City	Gaborone	Harare	Kampala
Accra (Ghana)	560																
Addis Ababa (Ethiopia)	6710	6150															
Asmara (Eritrea)	6510	5950	1060														
Bamako (Mali)	1160	1710	6860	6670													
Banjul (The Gambia)	2490	3210	8200	8010	1340												
Bujumbura (Burundi)	7090	6530	2980	4040	8190	9530											
Cairo (Egypt)	7800	7240	3270	2210	7950	9290	6250										
Cape Town (South Africa)	8900	8340	8830	9890	9320	10660	6000	12250									
Conakry (Guinea)	1700	2260	7780	7580	920	1230	8780	8870	10600								
Cotonou (Benin)	910	360	5790	5600	2020	3360	6170	6880	7990	2610							
Dakar (Senegal)	2790	3350	8280	8090	1420	300	9610	9290	11420	1530	3360						
Dar es Salaam (Tanzania)	8120	7570	2510	3560	9580	10910	2070	5770	5280	10860	8250	11690					
Djibouti City (Djibouti)	7620	7060	910	1210	7780	9110	3890	3420	9740	8690	6710	9200	3420				
Gaborone (Botswana)	8600	8040	6300	7350	10020	11330	3460	9570	1500	10300	7680	11440	3780	7210			
Harare (Zimbabwe)	8220	7670	5150	6200	9330	10670	2310	8560	2530	9920	7310	10750	2630	6060	1150		
Kampala (Uganda)	6520	5970	2230	3280	7630	8970	760	5500	6750	8550	5610	9050	1600	3140	4220	3060	
Khartoum (Sudan)	5550	4990	1720	960	5710	7040	4700	2250	10700	6630	4640	7040	4230	2170	8170	7020	3950
Kigali (Rwanda)	7430	6880	2750	3800	8380	9720	230	6020	6230	9130	6360	9810	2300	3660	3700	2540	520
Lagos (Nigeria)	1030	480	5670	5480	2140	3480	6050	6760	7860	2730	120	3560	8120	6590	7560	7190	5500
Libreville (Gabon)	3580	3030	6760	6020	4690	6030	3830	7300	5480	5280	2670	6120	5900	7670	5180	4800	4540
Lilongwe (Malawi)	8450	7900	4180	5240	8880	10220	1840	7450	3490	10150	7540	10310	1670	5090	2120	970	2590
Lomé (Togo)	760	200	5950	5760	1870	3220	6330	7040	8150	2460	160	3290	8400	6870	7840	7470	5770
Lusaka (Zambia)	7740	7190	4810	5870	8850	10190	1830	8080	3010	9440	6830	10270	1990	5720	1640	480	2580
Malabo (Equatorial Guinea)	2220	1660	6450	5640	3430	4770	4790	6730	6600	4710	2100	5540	6860	6550	6300	5930	4230
Maputo (Mozambique)	9550	9000	6810	7850	10980	12290	4460	10080	1900	11250	8960	12400	3910	7720	960	1650	4710
Maseru (Lesotho)	9290	8740	7000	8700	10720	12030	4380	10270	1170	11000	8380	12140	4200	7910	700	1560	4920
Mbabane (Swaziland)	9310	8760	7020	8070	10740	12050	4300	10290	1690	11020	8400	12160	4130	7930	720	1400	4940
Nairobi (Kenya)	7180	6630	1570	2620	8290	9670	1530	4840	5630	8880	6270	9710	940	2480	4090	2940	660
N'Djaména (Chad)	3010	2450	3700	3170	3500	5170	4500	4300	7820	4080	2100	4500	5150	4610	7770	6610	3550
Niamey (Niger)	1570	1390	5470	5270	1410	2240	6070	6550	9020	2320	1040	2740	6920	6380	8720	8350	5320
Nouakchott (Mauritania)	2800	3360	8510	8320	1650	870	9840	9610	10030	2100	3670	570	10890	9430	11670	10980	9280
Ouagadougou (Burkina Faso)	1070	970	5970	5770	900	2240	6580	7050	9100	1820	1120	2240	7420	6880	8800	8430	5820
Rabat (Morocco)	5000	4910	8660	8470	3580	3530	9510	4590	12450	4810	4470	3270	10110	9580	12160	11570	8010
São Tomé (São Tomé & Príncipe)	3010	2450	7080	6060	3750	5200	4150	7150	5800	4450	1830	5280	6220	6970	5500	5120	4860
Tripoli (Libya)	6260	5090	5410	4350	4940	6280	7560	2140	11080	5850	4560	6080	8410	5560	11020	9860	6810
Tunis (Tunisia)	4960	4860	6170	6760	4800	6180	8310	2900	11840	5710	4440	5330	9160	6320	11780	10620	7020
Windhoek (Namibia)	7430	6880	6460	7520	8540	9890	3480	9730	1460	9900	7290	9970	3635	9740	1160	2030	4230
Yaoundé (Cameroon)	2650	2100	5280	5280	3760	4410	4430	6370	6240	4350	1740	5180	6500	6190	5940	5570	3870

taking two-wheeled transport into consideration. Motorcyclists, especially those with newer model bikes, should also, where possible, be self-sufficient in parts.

Carnets

A *carnet de passage* (sometimes known as a *triptyque*) is required for many countries in Africa, with the notable exceptions of Morocco, Algeria and Tunisia. A *carnet* guarantees that if you take a vehicle into a country, but don't take it out again, then the organisation that issued the *carnet* will accept responsibility for payment of import duties (up to 150% of its value). *Carnets* can only be issued by national motoring organisations;

Road Distances (km) & Time Zones

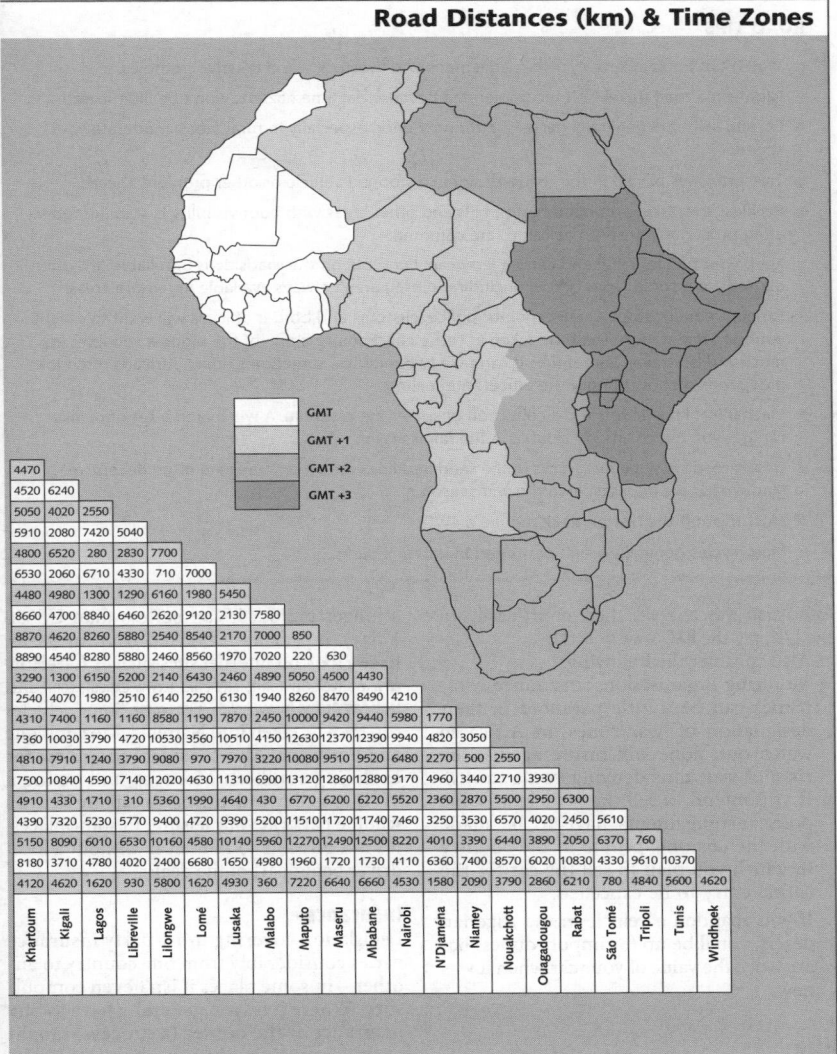

Legend: GMT · GMT +1 · GMT +2 · GMT +3

Khartoum	Kigali	Lagos	Libreville	Lilongwe	Lomé	Lusaka	Malabo	Maputo	Maseru	Mbabane	Nairobi	N'Djaména	Niamey	Nouakchott	Ouagadougou	Rabat	São Tomé	Tripoli	Tunis	Windhoek
4470																				
4520	6240																			
5050	4020	2550																		
5910	2080	7420	5040																	
4800	6520	280	2830	7700																
6530	2060	6710	4330	710	7000															
4480	4980	1300	1290	6160	1980	5450														
8660	4700	8840	6460	2620	9120	2130	7580													
8870	4620	8260	5880	2540	8540	2170	7000	850												
8890	4540	8280	5880	2460	8560	1970	7020	220	630											
3290	1300	6150	5200	2140	6430	2460	4890	5050	4500	4430										
2540	4070	1980	2510	6140	2250	6130	1940	8260	8470	8490	4210									
4310	7400	1160	1160	8580	1190	7870	2450	10000	9420	9440	5980	1770								
7360	10030	3790	4720	10530	3560	10510	4150	12630	12370	12390	9940	4820	3050							
4810	7910	1240	3790	9080	970	7970	3220	10080	9510	9520	6480	2270	500	2550						
7500	10840	4590	7140	12020	4630	11310	6900	13120	12860	12880	9170	4960	3440	2710	3930					
4910	4330	1710	310	5360	1990	4640	430	6770	6200	6220	5520	2360	2870	5500	2950	6300				
4390	7320	5230	5770	9400	4720	9390	5200	11510	11720	11740	7460	3250	3530	6570	4020	2450	5610			
5150	8090	6010	6530	10160	4580	10140	5960	12270	12490	12500	8220	4010	3390	6440	3890	2050	6370	760		
8180	3710	4780	4020	2400	6680	4980	1720	1730	4110	6360	7400	8570	6020	10830	4330	9610	10370			
4120	4620	1620	930	5800	1620	4930	360	7220	6640	6660	4530	1580	2090	3790	2860	6210	780	4840	5600	4620

they're only issued if it's certain that if ever duties arose you would reimburse them. This means you have to deposit a bond with a bank or insure yourself against the potential collection of import duties before getting a *carnet*.

You don't need to prearrange a *carnet* for many West and southern African countries (most southern African countries will issue a Temporary Import Permit at the border, which you must buy), but if you're driving through Africa, you're going to need a *carnet*, which sadly doesn't exempt you from the bureaucratic shenanigans encountered at numerous borders. If you're starting in South Africa, you can get one from the **Automobile**

ROAD TIPS

- Watch out for kamikaze cyclists, pedestrians and livestock – and massive potholes.

- Night-time road travel isn't recommended because daytime hazards won't be illuminated.

- Driving skills are generally nerve-shatteringly poor, especially in rural areas; moderate your speed.

- Tree branches placed in the roadway signal a stopped vehicle or other problem ahead.

- Reckless overtaking on blind bends, hills and other areas with poor visibility is standard operating procedure; head-on collisions are common.

- Keep your fuel tank full and carry a jerry can. Fuel sold on the roadside is unreliable (it's often diluted), and some types of fuel (including diesel) aren't always available in remote areas.

- Expect frequent stops at checkpoints; police, customs and border officials will want to see all your documentation. The time taken at these checkpoints is one of the biggest variables in much African travel. Sometimes it can take two minutes, sometimes hours. Africans often joke it depends on how hungry the officers are feeling.

- Mechanical knowledge and a collection of spares are essential. A winch and a set of planks can get you out of muddy trouble in the rainy season.

- Desert roads may be just tracks in the sand; red lines drawn on maps are often deceptive. Many roads are impassable in the wet season.

- Most trips off the beaten track require a 4WD.

- Motorcycles generally aren't permitted in national parks.

Association (www.aasa.co.za) there pretty easily. In the UK, try the **RAC** (www.rac.co.uk).

Also consider the following:

- Motoring organisations' insurance companies can be a little paranoid in their designation of 'war zones' in Africa so watch out; none will insure against the risks of war, thus denying you a *carnet*.

- If you intend to sell the vehicle at some point, arrangements have to be made with the customs people in the country in which you plan to sell the car for the *carnet* entry to be cancelled.

- If you abandon a vehicle in the Algerian desert, you'll be up for import duties that are twice the value of your car when it was new.

Hire

Hiring a vehicle is usually only an option to travellers over 25. For the most part, vehicle hire is a fairly expensive option (2WD vehicles commonly cost over US$75 a day in sub-Saharan Africa; you're looking at over US$100 a day for a 4WD) and rental can come with high insurance excesses and bundles of strings. On a brighter note, car hire in South Africa can be a real bargain (if you hire for a longer period, it can be less than US$30 a day), especially if booked from overseas; have a look on internet sites such as **Travelocity** (www.travelocity.com), **Expedia** (www.expedia.com) and **Holiday Autos** (www.holidayautos.com). Some vehicles can then be taken into Namibia, Mozambique and Botswana. Also consider hiring a car for exploring southern Morocco and taking a 4WD (possibly with driver) to explore Kenya's wildlife parks at your leisure. In some places, it's not possible to rent a car without a local driver being part of the deal.

Insurance

Legislation covering third-party insurance varies considerably from one country to another – in some places it isn't even compulsory. Where it is, you generally have to buy insurance at the border (a process fraught with corruption), but the liability limits on these policies are often absurdly low by Western standards; this means if you have any bad accidents you'll be in deep shit, so it's a smart plan to insure yourself before heading out. If you're starting from the UK, one company highly recommended for insurance policies and for detailed information on *carnets* is **Campbell Irvine** (☎ 020-7937 6981; www.campbellirvine.com).

HITCHING

Hitching is never entirely safe in any country, and we don't recommend it. But in some parts of Africa it's a recognised form of transport – there is often simply no other option than grabbing lifts on trucks, 4WDs, lorries or whatever vehicle happens to come down the road first. Whatever vehicle you jump on to, you'll generally have to pay. One exception might be in more developed countries, such as Ghana, Kenya, Morocco, South Africa, Tunisia and Zimbabwe, where there are plenty of private cars on the road and it's possible to hitch for free.

Travellers who decide to hitch should understand that they are taking a small but potentially serious risk. People who do choose to hitch will be safer if they travel in pairs. Remember that sticking out your thumb in many African countries is an obscene gesture; wave your hand vertically up and down instead.

LOCAL TRANSPORT
Bus

Bus travel is the way to go where there's a good network of sealed roads. International bus services are pretty common across the continent, and in the wealthier African states you may get a choice between 'luxury' air-con buses with movies (the trashy Hollywood/Bollywood variety) on tap and rough old European rejects with nonfunctioning air-con and questionable engineering. In some countries you just get the latter. Out in the sticks, where there are very few or no sealed roads, ancient buses tend to be very crowded with people, livestock and goods; these buses tend to stop frequently, either for passengers or because something is broken.

Minibus

Small minibuses take up the slack in many African transport systems. All too often they are driven at breakneck speed and crammed with close to 30 people when they were designed for 18 (there's always room for one more), with a tout or conductor leaning out the side door. The front seat is the most comfortable, but thanks to the high number of head-on collisions in Africa, this seat is called the 'death seat': how many old bus drivers have you seen? (If you do see one, be sure to choose his bus!) These minibuses are known by different names across the continent (*matatus* in Kenya, *dalla-dallas* in Tanzania, *tro-tros* in Ghana, *poda-podas* in Sierra Leone), names that are, confusingly, pretty interchangeable for shared taxis and bush taxis. Minibuses usually only leave when very full (a process that may take hours), and will stop frequently en route to pick up and set down passengers. Minibuses are also the favourite prey of roadblock police, who are not averse to unloading every passenger while they enter into lengthy discussions about paperwork and 'fines' that may need paying.

Shared Taxi

Shared taxis are usually Peugeot 504s or 505s or old spacious Mercedes saloons (common

---

BUS SURVIVAL TIPS

- Bus station touts are there to drum up business and work on commission; they're occasionally a pain but they can be very helpful.
- When using bush taxis keep your options open; hold on to your money until departure.
- Sitting on a camping mat or towel can ease the pain of African roads.
- Drinking more means peeing more – hydration must be balanced with bladder control.
- When travelling on dirt roads use a scarf to keep dust from your nose and mouth.
- That baby may look cute – but let it onto your lap and it WILL pee…
- Carry your passport at all times – getting through roadblocks without it can be expensive and complicated.
- Try to book your bus or minibus ticket in advance.
- Addressing questions to the driver directly is a social no-no – the conductor is the social hub of the journey, while the driver is the quiet achiever.
- If you have a choice as to your seat (more likely on buses), opt for what will be the shady side.

in North Africa). They should definitely be considered where they are found (which is not everywhere). Your average shared taxi is certainly quicker, more comfortable (if a little crowded) and less of a palaver than taking a bus or minibus, although many shared taxis are driven by lunatic speed freaks. They cost a little more than the corresponding bus fare, but in most cases once the vehicle has filled up (usually with nine to 12 people, packed in sardinelike) it heads pretty directly to the destination without constant stops for passengers. You should expect to pay an additional fee for your baggage in West Africa, but usually not elsewhere. Motorcycle taxis can also be convenient, if dangerous.

'Bush taxi' is something of a catch-all term and is used slightly differently across the continent. Basically, a bush taxi is any multiperson mode of public transport that isn't a bus.

TOURS

Overland truck tours did much to open up cheap travel in Africa, blazing trails where no tourist had boldly gone before. Today there are a huge number of overland trucks chugging around East and southern Africa (Arusha in Tanzania and Nairobi in Kenya are common starting points), but fewer range across West Africa. There are a number of trucks heading all the way from London or Istanbul to Cape Town, a trip that can last seven months.

Truck tours don't suit everyone, but a truck and its staff can take away many of the hassles of travelling in Africa (something you'll appreciate if you're crossing through tricky areas such as Nigeria, Chad and Sudan), and if you get on well with your fellow travellers it can be a real laugh.

There are, of course, downsides: you don't always get time to explore a place in depth, and sightseeing can end up being a terrible rush; cliquey and racist attitudes can mean it's much harder to meet locals or even other travellers; getting stuck with a bunch of drunken morons or anal retentive types for weeks on end might send you crazy; many campsites won't let overland trucks in; if you're used to travelling independently, having to leave decisions to someone else can be very hard; some trucks take up to 30 passengers; and group chores and vehicle security can be a pain. Remember also that once you've committed money to the communal food kitty, you won't get it back, even if you want to leave the tour before the end.

Whatever you decide, go through company brochures with a fine-tooth comb and always ask what you're required to do (on most tours you'll have to do the washing up at least), how many people are on the truck (loads of people equals cheaper prices) and how much flexibility there is. It's probably best to start with a shorter trip to see how truck life suits you before you commit to a six-month trip.

The truck tour business is dominated by British companies (see the following list), but they often have representatives in North America and Australasia (check out the websites for more information).

Acacia Expeditions (☎ 020-7706 4700; www.acacia -africa.com) Concentrates on East and southern Africa.

African Trails (☎ 01580-761171; www.africantrails. co.uk) Truck tours through much of Africa, including West and North Africa.

Dragoman (☎ 01728-861133; www.dragoman.com) West Africa, plus the Cairo to Cape Town route.

Keystone Journeys (www.keystonejourneys.com) One of few companies to go through West Africa as well as elsewhere.

Kumuka (☎ 1800 517 0867; www.kumuka.co.uk) Adventurous overland truck tours to East and southern Africa.

Oasis Overland (☎ 01963-363400; www.oasisover land.com) Runs overland truck tours through Africa and the Middle East.

TRAIN

Where available, travelling by train is a wonderful way to get around Africa. Even the shortest rail journey can be a classic

---

AFRICA'S TOP TRAIN JOURNEYS

- Dakar (Senegal) to Bamako (Mali; p504) – an African epic that could take anywhere between 48 hours and one week.

- Mauritania's iron-ore train (Mauritania; see the boxed text, p440) – one of the world's longest trains.

- Nampula to Cuamba (Mozambique; p974) – a southern African classic through northern Mozambique.

- Yaoundé to N'Gaoundéré (Cameroon; p304) – like crossing a continent with rainforests en route.

- Asmara to Nefasit (Eritrea; see the boxed text, p668) – a spectacular slice of colonial history.

experience, full of cultural exchange, amazing landscapes and crazy stations where all kinds of food, drinks and goods are hawked at train windows. Train travel is safer and usually more comfortable than travelling by road, although outside southern and North Africa the trains are often very slow. Long delays aren't uncommon. Second-class fares weigh in about the same as or less than the corresponding bus fare.

More expensive (but still negligible by Western standards) are sleeping compartments and 1st-class or 2nd-class carriages, which take the strain out of long journeys and occasionally allow you to travel in style – some high-class train carriages are like little wood-panelled museums of colonialism. It's worth noting that in many countries male and female passengers can only sleep in the same compartment if they buy the tickets for the whole compartment (four or six bunks), and even then you might be asked for evidence that you're married!

The flip side of train travel is that security and sanitation facilities on trains can be poor, especially in 3rd class, which, although novel and entertaining at first, soon becomes simply crowded and uncomfortable. Keep an eye on your baggage at all times and lock carriage doors and windows at night.

TRUCK

In many out-of-the-way places, trucks are the only reliable form of transport. They may primarily carry goods, but drivers are always keen to supplement their income, so there's usually room for paying passengers. Most folks are stuck up on top of the cargo, but

---

OVERLANDING ON THE CHEAP

Because most people prefer to travel north to south, overland truck companies sometimes drive empty trucks back from South Africa's Cape Town, Victoria Falls and Harare, and will sometimes transport travellers back up to Arusha (Tanzania) or Nairobi (Kenya) for negotiable knock-down prices, with a pleasant two-day stop by Lake Malawi sometimes thrown in. Ask around in backpackers' hang-outs in the departure towns for tips on when these trucks may be leaving.

---

a few more expensive spots are often available in the cab. Sitting high and exposed on top of a truck chugging through the African landscape can be a great experience; just take heavy precautions against the sun, wrap up against dust and bring a carry mat or similar to cushion yourself against uncomfortable cargo (you could find yourself sitting on top of a car engine for hours on end!). Also remember that trucks are even slower than buses.

On many routes you'll be able to wave down a truck, but lifts can often be arranged the night before departure at the 'truck park' – a compound or dust patch that you'll find in almost every African town of note. 'Fares' are pretty much fixed – expect to pay a little less than an equivalent bus fare, and make sure to agree on the price before climbing aboard. If the journey is going to take more than one night or one day, bring your own food and water.

Health Dr Caroline Evans

CONTENTS

As long as you stay up to date with your vaccinations and take some basic preventive measures, you'd have to be pretty unlucky to succumb to most of the health hazards covered in this chapter. Africa certainly has an impressive selection of tropical diseases on offer, but you're much more likely to get a bout of diarrhoea (in fact, you should bank on it), a cold or an infected mosquito bite than an exotic disease such as sleeping sickness. When it comes to injuries (as opposed to illness), the most likely reason for needing medical help in Africa is as a result of road accidents – vehicles are rarely well maintained, the roads are potholed and poorly lit, and drink driving is common.

Health care in Africa is varied: it can be excellent in the major cities, which generally have well-trained doctors and nurses, but it is often patchy off the beaten track. Medicine and even sterile dressings and intravenous fluids might need to be purchased from a local pharmacy by patients or their relatives. The standard of dental care is equally variable, and there is an increased risk of hepatitis B and HIV transmission via poorly sterilised equipment. By and large, public hospitals in Africa offer the cheapest service, but will have the least up-to-date equipment and medications; mission hospitals (where donations are the usual form of payment) often have more reasonable facilities; and private hospitals and clinics are more expensive but tend to have more advanced drugs and equipment as well as better-trained medical staff.

BEFORE YOU GO

A little planning before departure, particularly for pre-existing illnesses, will save you a lot of trouble later on. Before a long trip get a check-up from your dentist and from your doctor if you have any regular medication or chronic illness, eg high blood pressure and asthma. You should also organise spare contact lenses and glasses (and take your optical prescription with you); get a first-aid and medical kit together; and arrange necessary vaccinations.

It's tempting to leave it all to the last minute – don't! Many vaccines don't take effect until two weeks after you've been immunised, so visit a doctor four to eight weeks before departure. Ask your doctor for an International Certificate of Vaccination (otherwise known as the yellow booklet), which will list all the vaccinations you've received. This is mandatory for the African countries that require proof of yellow fever vaccination upon entry, but it's a good idea to carry it anyway wherever you travel.

Travellers can register with the International Association for Medical Advice to Travellers (IAMAT; www.iamat.org). Its website can help travellers to find a doctor who has recognised training. Those heading off to very remote areas might like to do a first-aid course (contact the Red Cross or St John's Ambulance) or attend a remote medicine first-aid course, such as that offered by the Royal Geographical Society (www.wildernessmedicaltraining.co.uk).

If you are bringing medications with you, carry them in their original containers, clearly labelled. A signed and dated letter from your physician describing all medical conditions and medications, including generic names, is also a good idea. If carrying syringes or needles be sure to have a physician's letter documenting their medical necessity.

How do you go about getting the best possible medical help? It's difficult to say – it really depends on the severity of your illness or injury and the availability of local help. If malaria is suspected, seek medical help as soon as possible or begin self-medicating if you happen to be well off the beaten track (see p1168).

INSURANCE

Find out in advance whether your insurance plan will make payments directly to providers or will reimburse you later for overseas health expenditures (in many countries doctors expect payment in cash). It's vital to ensure that your travel insurance will cover the emergency transport to get you to a hospital in a major city, to better medical facilities elsewhere in Africa, or all the way home, by air and with a medical attendant if necessary. Not all insurance covers this, so check the contract carefully. If you need medical help, your insurance company might be able to help locate the nearest hospital or clinic, or you can ask at your hotel. In an emergency, contact your embassy or consulate.

Membership of the African Medical and Research Foundation (Amref; www.amref. org) provides an air-evacuation service in medical emergencies throughout some African countries, as well as air ambulance transfers between medical facilities. Money paid by members for this service provides grassroots medical assistance for local people.

RECOMMENDED VACCINATIONS

The World Health Organization (www.who. int/en) recommends that all travellers be covered for diphtheria, tetanus, measles, mumps, rubella and polio, as well as for hepatitis B, regardless of their destination. Planning to travel is a great time to ensure that all routine vaccination cover is complete. The consequences of these particular diseases can be severe, and outbreaks of them do occur.

According to the Centers for Disease Control and Prevention (www.cdc.gov), the following vaccinations are recommended for all parts of Africa: hepatitis A, hepatitis B, meningococcal meningitis, rabies and typhoid, and boosters for tetanus, diphtheria and measles. A yellow-fever vaccination is not necessarily recommended for all parts of Africa, although the certificate is an entry requirement for a number of countries (see p1172).

MEDICAL CHECKLIST

It is a very good idea to carry a medical and first-aid kit around with you, to help yourself in the case of minor illness or injury. The following is a list of items you should consider packing.

- Acetaminophen (paracetamol) or aspirin
- Acetazolamide (Diamox) for altitude sickness (prescription only)
- Adhesive or paper tape
- Anti-inflammatory drugs (eg ibuprofen)
- Antibacterial ointment (eg Bactroban) for cuts and abrasions (prescription only)
- Antibiotics (prescription only), eg ciprofloxacin (Ciproxin) or norfloxacin (Utinor)
- Antidiarrheal drugs (eg loperamide)
- Antihistamines (for hay fever and allergic reactions)
- Antimalaria pills
- Bandages, gauze, gauze rolls
- DEET-containing insect repellent for the skin
- Iodine tablets (for water purification)
- Oral rehydration salts
- Permethrin-containing insect spray for clothing, tents and bed nets
- Pocket knife
- Scissors, safety pins, tweezers
- Sterile needles, syringes and fluids if travelling to remote areas
- Steroid cream or hydrocortisone cream (for allergic rashes)
- Sunblock
- Thermometer

If you are travelling through a malarial area – particularly an area in which falciparum malaria predominates – consider taking a self-diagnostic kit that can identify malaria in the blood from a finger prick.

ONLINE RESOURCES

There is a wealth of travel health advice on the internet. For further information, the Lonely Planet website at www.lonelyplanet. com is a good place to start. The World Health Organization publishes a superb book called *International Travel and Health,* which is revised annually and is available online at no cost at www.who.int/ith. Other websites of general interest are MD Travel Health at www.mdtravelhealth.com, which provides complete travel health recommendations for every country, updated daily, also at no cost; the Centers for Disease Control and Prevention at www.cdc.gov; and Fit for Travel at www.fitfortravel.scot.nhs.uk, which has up-to-date information about outbreaks and is very user-friendly.

It's also a good idea to consult your government's travel health website before departure, if one is available:

Australia (www.smartraveller.gov.au/tips/travelwell.html)
Canada (www.phac-aspc.gc.ca/index-eng.php)
UK (www.nhs.uk/nhsengland/Healthcareabroad/pages/Healthcareabroad.aspx)
USA (www.nc.cdc.gov/travel)

FURTHER READING

- *A Comprehensive Guide to Wilderness and Travel Medicine* by Eric A Weiss (1998)
- *How to Stay Healthy Abroad* by Richard Dawood (2002)
- Lonely Planet's *Healthy Travel Africa* by Isabelle Young & Tony Gherardin (2008)
- Lonely Planet's *Travel with Children* by Brigitte Barta et al (2009)
- *The Essential Guide to Travel Health* by Jane Wilson-Howarth (2009)
- *Travel in Health* by Graham Fry (1994)

IN TRANSIT

DEEP VEIN THROMBOSIS (DVT)

Blood clots can form in the legs during flights, chiefly because of prolonged immobility. This formation of clots is known as deep vein thrombosis (DVT), and the longer the flight, the greater the risk. Although most blood clots are reabsorbed uneventfully, some might break off and travel through the blood vessels to the lungs, where they could cause life-threatening complications.

The chief symptom of DVT is swelling or pain of the foot, ankle or calf, usually but not always on just one side. When a blood clot travels to the lungs, it can cause chest pain and breathing difficulty. Travellers with any of these symptoms should immediately seek medical attention.

To prevent the development of DVT on long flights you should walk about the cabin, perform isometric compressions of the leg muscles (ie contract the leg muscles while sitting), drink plenty of fluids, and avoid alcohol.

JET LAG & MOTION SICKNESS

If you're crossing more than five time zones you could suffer jet lag, resulting in insomnia, fatigue, malaise or nausea. To avoid jet lag try drinking plenty of fluids (nonalcoholic) and eating light meals. Upon arrival, get exposure to natural sunlight and readjust your schedule (for meals, sleep etc) as soon as possible. Antihistamines such as dimenhydrinate (Dramamine) and meclizine (Antivert, Bonine) are usually the first choice for treating motion sickness. Their main side effect is drowsiness. A herbal alternative is ginger (in the form of ginger tea, biscuits or crystallised ginger), which works like a charm for some people.

IN AFRICA

AVAILABILITY & COST OF HEALTH CARE

Most drugs can be purchased over the counter throughout Africa, without a prescription. Many drugs for sale within Africa might be ineffective – they might be counterfeit or might not have been stored under the right conditions. The most common examples of counterfeit drugs are malaria tablets and expensive antibiotics, such as ciprofloxacin. Most drugs are available in capital cities, but in remote villages you will be lucky to find a couple of paracetamol tablets. It is strongly recommended that all drugs for chronic diseases be brought with you from home. Also, the availability and efficacy of condoms cannot be relied upon – bring all the contraception you'll need. Condoms bought in Africa might not be of the same quality as in Europe, North America or Australia, and they might have been stored in too hot an environment. Keep all condoms as cool as you can.

There is a high risk of contracting HIV from infected blood if you receive a blood transfusion in Africa. The BloodCare Foundation (www.bloodcare.org.uk) is a useful source of safe, screened blood, which can be transported to any part of the world within 24 hours.

The cost of health care might seem very cheap compared to first-world countries, but good care and drugs might be not be available. Evacuation to good medical care (within Africa or to your own country) can be very expensive indeed. Unfortunately, adequate – let alone good – health care is available only to very few residents of Africa.

INFECTIOUS DISEASES

It's a formidable list but, as we say, a few precautions go a long way...

Cholera

Cholera is usually only a problem during natural or artificial disasters, eg war, floods or earthquakes, although small outbreaks can also occur at other times. Travellers are rarely affected. It is caused by a bacteria and spread via contaminated drinking water. The main symptom is profuse watery diarrhoea, which causes collapse if fluids are not replaced quickly. An oral cholera vaccine is available in the USA, but it is not particularly effective. Most cases of cholera could be avoided by close attention to good drinking water and by avoiding potentially contaminated food. Treatment is by fluid replacement (orally or via a drip), but sometimes antibiotics are needed. Self-treatment is not advised.

Dengue Fever (Break-Bone Fever)

Found in Sudan, Cameroon, Democratic Republic of Congo (DRC), Senegal, Burkina Faso, Guinea, Ethiopia, Djibouti, Somalia, Madagascar, Mozambique and South Africa. Dengue fever is spread through the bite of the mosquito. It causes a feverish illness with headache and muscle pains similar to those experienced with a bad, prolonged attack of influenza. There might be a rash. Mosquito bites should be avoided whenever possible. Self-treatment: paracetamol and rest.

Diphtheria

Found in all of Africa. Diphtheria is spread through close respiratory contact. It usually causes a temperature and a severe sore throat. Sometimes a membrane forms across the throat, and a tracheostomy is needed to prevent suffocation. Vaccination is recommended for all travellers, particularly those likely to be in close contact with the local population in infected areas. More important for long stays than for short-term trips. The vaccine is given as an injection alone or with tetanus, and lasts 10 years. Self-treatment: none.

Ebola & Marburg Viruses

Found throughout Central Africa (especially Congo, the Democratic Republic of Congo and the Central African Republic), in Sudan and in Uganda. These viruses cause haemorrhagic fever, which is usually fatal. The route of infection is not clearly known, although eating bushmeat is generally considered a common cause of Ebola. Both diseases are rare in travellers, although at least one traveller in Uganda is believed to have contracted the Marburg virus after visiting caves. Self-treatment: none.

Filariasis

This is found in most parts of West, Central, East and southern Africa, and in Sudan in North Africa. Tiny worms migrating in the lymphatic system cause filariasis. The bite from an infected mosquito spreads the infection. Symptoms can include localised itching and swelling of the legs and or genitalia. Treatment is available, but self-treatments are not.

Hepatitis A

Found in all of Africa. Hepatitis A is spread through contaminated food (particularly shellfish) and water. It causes jaundice and, although it is rarely fatal, it can cause prolonged lethargy and delayed recovery. If you've had hepatitis A, you shouldn't drink alcohol for up to six months afterwards, but once you've recovered, there won't be any long-term problems. The first symptoms include dark urine and a yellow colour to the whites of the eyes. Sometimes a fever and abdominal pain might be present. Hepatitis A vaccine (Avaxim, VAQTA, Havrix) is given as an injection: a single dose will give protection for up to a year, and a booster after a year gives 10-year protection. Hepatitis A and typhoid vaccines can also be given as a single-dose vaccine, hepatyrix or viatim. Self-treatment: none.

Hepatitis B

Found in all of Africa. Hepatitis B is spread through infected blood, contaminated needles and sexual intercourse. It can also be spread from an infected mother to the baby during childbirth. It affects the liver, causing jaundice and occasionally liver failure. Most people

HEALTH

recover completely, but some people might be chronic carriers of the virus, which could lead eventually to cirrhosis or liver cancer. In particular, those visiting high-risk areas for long periods or at social or occupational risk should be immunised. Many countries now give hepatitis B as part of the routine childhood vaccination. It is given singly or can be given at the same time as hepatitis A.

A course will give protection for at least five years. It can be given over four weeks or six months. Self-treatment: none.

HIV

Present in all of Africa. HIV, the virus that causes AIDS, is an enormous problem throughout Africa, but is most acutely felt in sub-Saharan Africa. The virus is spread through infected blood and blood products, by sexual intercourse with an infected partner, and from an infected mother to her baby during childbirth and breastfeeding. It can be spread through 'blood to blood' contacts, such as with contaminated instruments during medical, dental, acupuncture and other body-piercing procedures, and through sharing used intravenous needles. At present there is no cure; medication that might keep the disease under control is available, but many countries in Africa do not have access to it for their own citizens, let alone for travellers. If you think you might have put yourself at risk of HIV infection, a blood test is necessary; a three-month gap after the exposure and before testing is required to allow antibodies to appear in the blood. Self-treatment: none.

Leishmaniasis

Found in North Africa. This disease is spread through the bite of an infected sandfly. It can cause a slowly growing skin lump or ulcer (the cutaneous form) and sometimes develop into a serious life-threatening fever with anaemia and weight loss. Dogs can also be carriers of Leishmaniasis. Sandfly and dog bites should be avoided whenever possible. Self-treatment: none.

Leptospirosis

Found in West and southern Africa; in Chad, Congo and DRC in Central Africa; in Algeria, Morocco and Sudan in North Africa; and in Ethiopia and Somalia in East Africa. It is spread through the excreta of infected rodents, especially rats. It can cause hepatitis and renal failure, which might be fatal. It is unusual for travellers to be affected unless living in poor sanitary conditions. Leptospirosis causes a fever and sometimes jaundice. Self-treatment: none.

Malaria

Endemic in Central, East, West and southern Africa; slight risk in North Africa (except for Sudan, where the risk is significant). The risk of malarial transmission at altitudes higher than 2000m is rare. The disease is caused by a parasite in the bloodstream spread via the bite of the female Anopheles mosquito. There are several types of malaria; falciparum malaria is the most dangerous type and the predominant form in Africa. Infection rates vary with season and climate, so check out the situation before departure. Unlike most other diseases regularly encountered by travellers, there is no vaccination against malaria (yet). However, several different drugs are used to prevent malaria, and new ones are in the pipeline. Up-to-date advice from a travel health clinic is essential as some medication is more suitable for some travellers than others. The pattern of drug-resistant malaria is changing rapidly, so what was advised several years ago might no longer be the case.

Malaria can present in several ways. The early stages include headaches, fevers, generalised aches and pains, and malaise, which could be mistaken for flu. Other symptoms can include abdominal pain, diarrhoea and a cough. Anyone who develops a fever in a

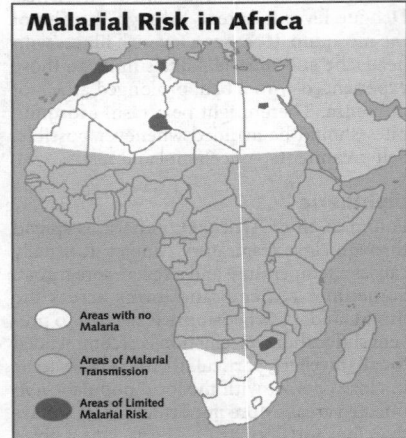

Malarial Risk in Africa

Areas with no Malaria

Areas of Malarial Transmission

Areas of Limited Malarial Risk

THE ANTIMALARIAL A TO D

A Awareness of the risk. No medication is totally effective.

B Bites – avoid at all costs. Sleep in a screened room, use a mosquito spray or coils, sleep under a permethrin-impregnated net at night. Cover up at night with long trousers and long sleeves, preferably with permethrin-treated clothing. Apply appropriate repellent to all areas of exposed skin in the evenings.

C Chemical prevention (ie antimalarial drugs) is usually needed in malarial areas. Expert advice is needed as resistance patterns can change, and new drugs are in development. Not all antimalarial drugs are suitable for everyone, particularly people with depression or epilepsy; children; or pregnant women. Most antimalarial drugs need to be started at least a week in advance and continued for four weeks after the last possible exposure to malaria. No drug is 100% effective, but protection of up to 95% is achievable with most drugs, as long as other measures have been taken.

D Diagnosis. If you have a fever or flulike illness within a year of travel to a malarial area, malaria is a possibility, and immediate medical attention is necessary.

---

malarial area should assume malarial infection until a blood test proves negative, even if you have been taking antimalarial medication. If not treated, the next stage could develop within 24 hours (particularly if falciparum malaria is the parasite): jaundice, then reduced consciousness and coma (also known as cerebral malaria) followed by death. Treatment in hospital is essential, and the death rate might still be as high as 10% even in the best intensive-care facilities.

Many travellers are under the impression that malaria is a mild illness, that treatment is always easy and successful, and that taking antimalarial drugs causes more illness through side effects than actually getting malaria. In Africa, this is unfortunately not true. Side effects depend on the drug being taken. Doxycycline can cause heartburn and indigestion; mefloquine (Larium) can cause anxiety attacks, insomnia and nightmares, and (rarely) severe psychiatric disorders; chloroquine can cause nausea and hair loss; and proguanil can cause mouth ulcers. Side effects are not universal, and can be minimised by taking medication correctly, eg with food. Also, some people should not take a particular antimalarial drug, eg people with epilepsy should avoid mefloquine, and doxycycline should not be taken by pregnant women or children younger than 12.

People of all ages can contract malaria, and falciparum malaria causes the most severe illness. Repeated infections might result eventually in less serious illness. Malaria in pregnancy frequently results in miscarriage or premature labour. Adults who have survived childhood malaria have developed immunity and usually only develop mild cases of malaria; most Western travellers have no immunity at all.

Immunity wanes after 18 months of nonexposure, so even if you have had malaria in the past and used to live in a malaria-prone area, you might no longer be immune. One million children die annually from malaria in Africa.

If you decide that you really do not wish to take antimalarial drugs, you must understand the risks, and be obsessive about avoiding mosquito bites. Use nets and insect repellent, and report any fever or flulike symptoms to a doctor as soon as possible. Some people advocate homeopathic preparations against malaria, such as Demal200, but as yet there is no conclusive evidence that this is effective, and many homeopaths do not recommend their use.

If you are planning a journey through a malarial area, particularly where falciparum malaria predominates, consider taking stand-by treatment. Emergency stand-by treatment should be seen as emergency treatment aimed at saving the patient's life and not as routine self-medication. It should be advised only if you will be remote from medical facilities and have been advised about the symptoms of malaria and how to use the medication. Medical advice should be sought as soon as possible to confirm whether the treatment has been successful. The type of stand-by treatment used will depend on local conditions, such as drug resistance, and on what antimalarial drugs are being used before stand-by treatment. This is worthwhile because you want to avoid contracting a particularly serious form such as cerebral malaria, which affects the brain and central nervous system and can be fatal in 24 hours. As mentioned on p1165, self-diagnostic kits, which can identify malaria in the blood from a finger prick, are also available in the West.

The risks from malaria to both mother and foetus during pregnancy are considerable.

HEALTH

Unless good medical care can be absolutely guaranteed, travel throughout Africa when pregnant – particularly to malarial areas – should be discouraged unless essential. Self-treatment: see stand-by treatment if you are more than 24 hours away from medical help.

Meningococcal Meningitis

Found in all areas of Central, West and East Africa; only in Sudan in North Africa; and only in Namibia, Malawi, Mozambique and Zambia in southern Africa. Meningococcal infection is spread through close respiratory contact and is more likely in crowded situations, such as dormitories, buses and clubs. Infection is uncommon in travellers. Vaccination is recommended for long stays and especially towards the end of the dry season, which is normally from June to November. Symptoms include a fever, severe headache, neck stiffness and a red rash. Immediate medical treatment is necessary.

The ACWY vaccine is recommended for all travellers in sub-Saharan Africa. This vaccine is different from the meningococcal meningitis C vaccine given to children and adolescents in some countries, and it is safe to be given both types of vaccine. Self-treatment: none.

Onchocerciasis (River Blindness)

Found in all of Central, West and East Africa; Sudan in North Africa; and Malawi in southern Africa. This is caused by the larvae of a tiny worm, spread by the bite of a small fly. The earliest sign of infection is intensely itchy, red, sore eyes. Travellers are rarely severely affected. Treatment in a specialised clinic is curative. Self-treatment: none.

Poliomyelitis

Found in all of Africa. Generally spread through contaminated food and water. It is one of the vaccines given in childhood and should be boosted every 10 years, either orally (a drop on the tongue) or as an injection. Polio can be carried asymptomatically (ie showing no symptoms) and can cause a transient fever. In rare cases it causes weakness or paralysis of one or more muscles, which might be permanent. Self-treatment: none.

Rabies

Found in all of Africa. Rabies is spread by receiving the bites or licks of an infected animal on broken skin. It is always fatal once the clinical symptoms start (which might be up to several months after an infected bite), so postbite vaccination should be given as soon as possible. Postbite vaccination (whether or not you've been vaccinated before the bite) prevents the virus from spreading to the central nervous system. Animal handlers should be vaccinated, as should those travelling to remote areas where a reliable source of postbite vaccine is not available within 24 hours. Three preventive injections are needed over a month. If you have not been vaccinated you will need a course of five injections starting 24 hours or as soon as possible after the injury. If you have been vaccinated, you will need fewer postbite injections, and have more time to seek medical help. Self-treatment: none.

Rift Valley Fever

Found in Kenya. This fever is spread occasionally via mosquito bites. The symptoms are of a fever and flulike illness, and it is rarely fatal. Self-treatment: none.

Bilharzia (Schistosomiasis)

We can't say this strongly enough: be extremely wary of paddling or swimming in freshwater lakes or slow-running rivers anywhere in Africa because of the danger of bilharzia. This disease is spread by flukes (minute worms) that are carried by a species of freshwater snail. The flukes are carried inside the snail, which sheds them into slow-moving or still water. The parasites penetrate human skin during paddling or swimming and then migrate to the bladder or bowel. They are passed out via stool or urine and could contaminate fresh water, where the cycle starts again. There might be no symptoms. There might be a transient fever and rash, and advanced cases might have blood in the stool or in the urine. A blood test can detect antibodies if you might have been exposed, and treatment is then possible in specialist travel or infectious disease clinics. If left untreated the infection could cause kidney failure or permanent bowel damage. It is not possible for you to infect others. Self-treatment: none.

Bilharzia can be a problem in the following countries:

Central Africa Central African Republic, Chad, Congo, DRC, Equatorial Guinea, Gabon, São Tomé & Príncipe
East Africa All countries
North Africa Egypt, Sudan
Southern Africa All countries
West Africa All countries

Trypanosomiasis (Sleeping Sickness)

Found in most of West, Central, East and southern Africa; only in Sudan in North Africa. Spread via the bite of the tsetse fly. It causes a headache, fever and eventually coma. There is an effective treatment. Self-treatment: none.

Tuberculosis (TB)

Found in all of Africa. TB is spread through close respiratory contact and occasionally through infected milk or milk products. BCG vaccination is recommended for those likely to be mixing closely with the local population. It is more important for long stays than for short-term stays. Inoculation with the BCG vaccine is not available in all countries. It is given routinely to many children in developing countries. In some countries, for example the UK, it is given to babies if they will be travelling with their families to high-risk areas of TB, and to previously unvaccinated school-age children if they live in areas of higher TB risk (eg multiethnic immigrant populations). The BCG gives a moderate degree of protection against TB. It causes a small permanent scar at the site of injection, and is usually given in a specialised chest clinic. It is a live vaccine and should not be given to pregnant women or immunocompromised individuals.

TB can be asymptomatic, only being picked up on a routine chest X-ray. Alternatively, it can cause a cough, weight loss or fever, sometimes months or even years after exposure. Self-treatment: none.

Typhoid

Found throughout all of Africa. Typhoid is contracted through food or water contaminated by infected human faeces. The first symptom is usually a fever or a pink rash on the abdomen. Sometimes septicaemia (blood poisoning) can occur. A typhoid vaccine (typhim Vi, typherix) will give protection for three years. In some countries, the oral vaccine Vivotif is also available. Antibiotics are usually given as treatment, and death is rare unless septicaemia occurs. Self-treatment: none.

West Nile Fever

Found in Egypt. This rare disease is spread via mosquito bites. The symptoms are fever and flulike illness; it is very occasionally fatal. Self-treatment: none.

Yellow Fever

Travellers should carry a certificate as evidence of vaccination if they have recently been in an infected country, to avoid any possible difficulties with immigration. For a full list of these countries visit the World Health Organization website (www.who.int/wer) or the Centers for Disease Control and Prevention website (www.cdc.gov/travel.htm). There is always the possibility that a traveller without a legally required, up-to-date certificate will be vaccinated and detained in isolation at the port of arrival for up to 10 days or possibly repatriated.

Yellow fever is spread by infected mosquitoes. Symptoms range from a flulike illness to severe hepatitis (liver inflammation), jaundice and death. The yellow fever vaccination must be given at a designated clinic and is valid for 10 years. It is a live vaccine and must not be given to immunocompromised or pregnant travellers. Self-treatment: none.

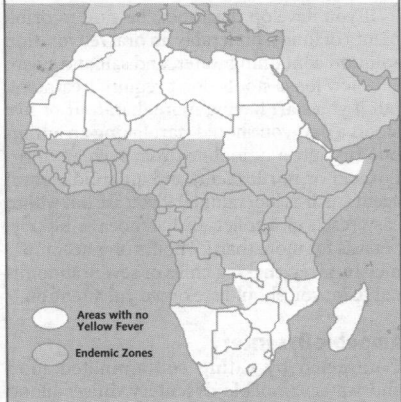

Yellow Fever Risk in Africa

Areas with no Yellow Fever

Endemic Zones

TRAVELLERS' DIARRHOEA

Found in all of Africa. Although it's not inevitable that you will get diarrhoea while travelling in Africa, it's certainly very likely. Diarrhoea is the most common travel-related illness – figures suggest that at least half of all travellers to Africa will get diarrhoea at some stage. Sometimes dietary changes, such as increased spices or oils, are the cause.

To help prevent diarrhoea, avoid tap water unless you're sure it's safe to drink (see p1173). You should also only eat fresh fruits or vegetables

HEALTH

MANDATORY YELLOW FEVER VACCINATION

The following list is a guide only. Please check with your doctor and the embassy of the country to which you are travelling for the most recent requirements.

Central Africa Mandatory in Central African Republic (CAR), Congo, DRC, Equatorial Guinea and Gabon, and recommended in Chad.

East Africa Mandatory in Rwanda and Uganda; it is advised for Burundi, Ethiopia, Kenya, Somalia and Tanzania.

North Africa Not mandatory for any areas of North Africa, but Algeria, Libya and Tunisia require evidence of yellow fever vaccination if entering from an infected country. It is recommended for travellers to Sudan, and might be given to unvaccinated travellers leaving the country.

Southern Africa Not mandatory for entry into any countries of southern Africa, although it is necessary if entering from an infected country.

West Africa Mandatory in Benin, Burkina Faso, Cameroon, Côte d'Ivoire, Ghana, Liberia, Mali, Niger, São Tomé & Príncipe and Togo, and recommended for The Gambia, Guinea, Guinea-Bissau, Mauritania, Nigeria, Senegal and Sierra Leone.

---

if cooked or peeled, and be wary of dairy products that might contain unpasteurised milk. Although freshly cooked food can often be a safe option, plates or serving utensils might be dirty, so you should be highly selective when eating food from street vendors (make sure that cooked food is piping hot all the way through).

If you develop diarrhoea, be sure to drink plenty of fluids, preferably an oral rehydration solution containing water, and salt and sugar.

A few loose stools don't require treatment, but if you start having more than four or five stools a day, you should start taking an antibiotic (usually a quinoline drug, such as ciprofloxacin or norfloxacin) and an antidiarrheal agent (such as loperamide) if you are not within easy reach of a toilet. If diarrhoea is bloody, persists for more than 72 hours or is accompanied by fever, shaking chills or severe abdominal pain, you should seek medical attention.

Amoebic Dysentery

Contracted by eating contaminated food and water, amoebic dysentery causes blood and mucus in the faeces. It can be relatively mild and tends to come on gradually, but seek medical advice as soon as possible if you think you have the illness as it won't clear up without treatment (which is with specific antibiotics).

Giardiasis

This, like amoebic dysentery, is also caused by ingesting contaminated food or water. The illness usually appears a week or more after you have been exposed to the offending parasite. Giardiasis might cause only a short-lived bout of typical travellers' diarrhoea, but it can also cause persistent diarrhoea. Ideally, seek medical advice if you suspect you have giardiasis, but if you are in a remote area you could start a course of antibiotics.

ENVIRONMENTAL HAZARDS
Heat Exhaustion

This condition occurs following heavy sweating and excessive fluid loss with inadequate replacement of fluids and salt, and is particularly common in hot climates when taking unaccustomed exercise before full acclimatisation. Symptoms include headache, dizziness and tiredness. Dehydration is already happening by the time you feel thirsty – aim to drink sufficient water to produce pale, diluted urine. Self-treatment: fluid replacement with water and/or fruit juice, and cooling by cold water and fans. The treatment of the salt loss component consists of consuming salty fluids, as in soup, and adding a little more table salt to foods than usual.

Heatstroke

Heat exhaustion is a precursor to the much more serious condition of heatstroke. In this case there is damage to the sweating mechanism, with an excessive rise in body temperature; irrational and hyperactive behaviour; and eventually loss of consciousness and death. Rapid cooling by spraying the body with water and fanning is ideal. Emergency fluid and electrolyte replacement is often also required by intravenous drip.

Insect Bites & Stings

Mosquitoes might not always carry malaria or dengue fever, but they (and other insects) can cause irritation and infected bites. To avoid these, take the same precautions as you would for avoiding malaria (see p1169). Use DEET-based insect repellents, although these are not the only effective repellents. Excellent clothing treatments are also available; mosquitoes that land on treated clothing will die.

Bee and wasp stings cause real problems only to those who have a severe allergy to the stings (anaphylaxis.) If you are one of these people, make sure you carry an 'epipen' – an adrenalin (epinephrine) injection, which you can give yourself. This could save your life.

Sandflies are found around the Mediterranean beaches. They usually only cause a nasty itchy bite but can carry a rare skin disorder called cutaneous Leishmaniasis (p1168). Prevention of bites with DEET-based repellents is sensible.

Scorpions are frequently found in arid climates. They can cause a painful sting that is sometimes life-threatening. If stung by a scorpion, take a painkiller. Medical treatment should be sought if collapse occurs.

Bed bugs are often found in hostels and cheap hotels. They lead to very itchy, lumpy bites. Spraying the mattress with crawling insect killer after changing bedding will get rid of them.

Scabies is also frequently found in cheap accommodation. These tiny mites live in the skin, particularly between the fingers. They cause an intensely itchy rash. The itch is easily treated with malathion and permethrin lotion from a pharmacy; other members of the household also need treating to avoid spreading scabies, even if they do not show any symptoms.

Snake Bites

Basically, avoid getting bitten! Do not walk barefoot, or stick your hand into holes or cracks. However, 50% of those bitten by venomous snakes are not actually injected with poison (envenomed). If bitten by a snake, do not panic. Immobilise the bitten limb with a splint (such as a stick) and apply a bandage over the site, with firm pressure – similar to bandaging a sprain. Do not apply a tourniquet, or cut or suck the bite. Get the victim to medical help as soon as possible, when antivenom can be given if needed.

Traditional Medicine

At least 80% of the African population relies on traditional medicine, either because they can't afford conventional Western-style medicine, because of prevailing cultural attitudes and beliefs, or simply because (in some cases) it works. It might also be because there's often no other choice: a World Health Organization survey found that although there was only one medical doctor for every 50,000 people in Mozambique, there was a traditional healer for every 200 people.

Although some African remedies seem to work on malaria, sickle cell anaemia, high blood pressure and some AIDS symptoms, most African healers learn their art by apprenticeship, so education (and consequently application of knowledge) is inconsistent and unregulated. Conventionally trained physicians in South Africa, for example, angrily describe how their AIDS patients die of kidney failure because a *sangoma* (traditional healer) has given them an enema containing an essence made from powerful roots. Likewise, when traditional healers administer 'injections' with porcupine quills, knives or dirty razor blades, diseases are often spread or created rather than cured.

Rather than attempting to entirely stamp out traditional practices, or simply pretend they are not happening, a positive first step taken by some African countries is the regulation of traditional medicine through the creation of healers' associations and by offering courses on such topics as sanitary practices. Although it remains unlikely that even a basic level of conventional Western-style medicine will be made available to all the people of Africa any time soon (even though the cost of doing so would be less than the annual military budget of some Western countries), traditional medicine will almost certainly continue to be practised widely throughout the continent.

Water

Never drink tap water unless it has been boiled, filtered or chemically disinfected (such as with iodine tablets), except in South Africa. Never drink from streams, rivers and lakes. It's also best to avoid drinking from pumps and wells – some do bring pure water to the surface, but the presence of animals can still contaminate supplies.

HEALTH

Language

CONTENTS

Africa's myriad ethnic groups speak several hundred local languages, many subdivided into numerous distinct dialects. The people of Nigeria, for example, speak around 500 languages and dialects according to the Ethnologue report, while even tiny Guinea-Bissau (population 1.4 million) has around 20 languages. Consequently, common tongues are essential, and several are used. These may be the language of the largest group in a particular area or country, such as Hausa, or a language that has spread beyond its original geographical boundaries due to trade, such as Swahili. The former colonial languages (French, English and Portuguese) also serve well as common languages. In some areas, the common tongue is a creole – a combination of African and European languages.

WHO SPEAKS WHAT WHERE?
Algeria
Official language: Arabic. Various Berber languages and French are also spoken, but very little English.

Angola
Official language: Portuguese (the first language of much of the population, especially in Luanda). At least some Portuguese is needed to get by in Angola. In the villages various Bantu languages predominate.

Benin
Official language: French, but many in the tourist industry speak reasonable English. Fon and Yoruba are the main indigenous languages in the south; Bariba and Dendi are spoken in the north.

Botswana
Official language: English. Tswana (also known as Setswana) is the principal spoken language; it's the first language of about 90% of the population.

Burkina Faso
Official language: French, which is spoken by almost everyone. The major African languages are More, Dioula, Gourma, Fulfulde and Lobi.

Burundi
Official languages: Kirundi and French, although Swahili can be useful. English isn't common, but a few people in Bujumbura can speak it.

Cameroon
Official languages: French and English, but English is rarely heard, except in larger towns in the far west of the country.

Central African Republic (CAR)
Official language: French, though Sango is known as the national language and is spoken by most people. Originally a trading language along the Oubangui River, Sango is, however, the mother tongue of few. Very little English is spoken.

Chad
Official languages: French and Arabic, but there are more than 120 local languages. The main ones include Sara, spoken primarily in the south, and Turku (often referred to as Chadian Arabic), in the north.

Congo
Official language: French. The main African languages spoken in Congo are Lingala and Munukutuba.

Côte d'Ivoire

Official language: French. Major African languages include Baoulé and Agni in the south; Mande, Malinke and Senoufo in the north; and Dioula, the language of trade.

Democratic Republic of Congo (DRC)

Official language: French. Lingala, spoken in Kinshasa and along the rivers, is the language of trade. Other major spoken languages are Swahili, Tshiluba and Kikongo.

Djibouti

Official languages: French and Arabic. Afar and Somali are also spoken. Few speak English outside Djibouti town.

Egypt

Official language: Arabic. English and, to a lesser extent, French are widely understood in the cities. Spoken Egyptian Arabic differs from other Arabic varieties (for more details, get a copy of Lonely Planet's *Egyptian Arabic* phrasebook).

Equatorial Guinea

Official languages: Spanish and French. Local languages such as Fang and Bubi are widely spoken, as is Creole English (Pidginglis) on Bioko Island.

Eritrea

Main languages: Arabic (common in coastal areas) and Tigrinya (used widely in the highlands). Each of the nine ethnic groups speaks its own language: Afar, Bilen, Bedawi, Kunama, Nara, Arabic, Saho, Tigre and Tigrinya. Amharic, a legacy of Ethiopian rule, is also still widely spoken. English is also surprisingly useful, not least because during the war most families had at least one member abroad, and most returnees from Western Europe or North America speak it fluently.

Ethiopia

Official language: Amharic (spoken predominantly in the central highlands and to the north). Tigrinya is spoken in the northern areas and Oromo in the south. Amharic is probably understood in most of the main cities (see the Amharic section on p1181). English is the language of schools and many people manage more than a smattering. Arabic is spoken in parts of the east and west. There are almost as many indigenous languages (from a variety of families: Semitic, Cushitic, Nilotic and Omotic) as there are peoples.

Gabon

Official language: French. In the interior there are many local languages spoken, including Fang and Punu.

The Gambia

Official language: English. Indigenous languages include Wolof (the main trading language), Mandinka and Pulaar (Fula).

Ghana

Official language: English. Hausa is the language of trade in the north. There are around 70 African languages spoken in Ghana, including Akan, Dagbani and Ga.

Guinea

Official language: French, widely spoken in all large towns and the less remote rural areas. The main indigenous languages are Susu, Malinke and Pulaar (Fula).

Guinea-Bissau

Official language: Portuguese, but Crioulo is the common tongue. Many other regional indigenous languages are spoken (mainly Wolof), and French is widely understood.

Kenya

Official languages: English and Swahili. There are many major tribal languages, including Kikuyu, Luo and Kikamba. Although English is spoken by most people in Kenya, a working knowledge of Swahili is useful, especially outside urban areas and in remote parts of the country (see the Swahili section on p1184).

Lesotho

Official languages: Southern Sotho (Sesotho) and English. For the all-important greetings, see the Southern Sotho section on p1183.

Liberia

Official language: English. Major indigenous languages spoken in the country include Kpelle, Bassa and Kru.

Libya

Official language: Arabic. All road, shop and other public signs are in Arabic, so some working knowledge of the language is extremely useful. Outside Tripoli and Benghazi, where some English or Italian is spoken, few people speak a foreign language. The exceptions are Ghadhames and Ghat, where some older people speak French.

Madagascar

Official languages: Malagasy, French and English. Malagasy is the everyday spoken language while French is often used for literary, business and administrative purposes, and in more upmarket sectors of the tourism industry. English is taught in schools, but it's uncommon outside the middle- to top-range hotels and restaurants in Tana, Nosy Be and Île Sainte Marie. For a few key Malagasy phrases, see the Malagasy section on p1183.

Malawi

Official language: English, which is very widely spoken. All the different ethnic groups in Malawi also have their own language or dialect. The Chewa are the dominant group and Chichewa is the national language, widely used throughout the country as a common tongue.

Mali

Official language: French, but Bambara is the most widely spoken tongue (especially south of Mopti). Other indigenous languages spoken in various areas of Mali are Fulfulde, Songhai and Tamashek (a Tuareg language). The Dogon language is spoken in a relatively compact area, but there are around 60 dialects.

Mauritania

Official language: Arabic. The Moors speak an Arabic dialect known as Hassaniyya, whereas the Africans of the south speak Pulaar (Fula), Soninke and Wolof.

Morocco

Official language: Arabic. Arabic and French are taught in schools and French is important in university education and commerce. Darija (spoken Moroccan Arabic) is different from the Arabic you hear in the Middle East (for more details on Arabic in Morocco, get a copy of Lonely Planet's *Moroccan Arabic* phrasebook).

Various Berber dialects are spoken in the countryside, particularly in the mountains. Spanish is spoken in former Spanish-held territory (particularly the north) and some English is spoken in the main tourist centres.

Mozambique

Official language: Portuguese. There are numerous indigenous languages, all belonging to the Bantu language family. Outside southern resorts and areas bordering Zimbabwe and Malawi, English is not widely spoken.

Namibia

Official language: English, but the most widely spoken European language is Afrikaans (first language of more than 100,000 people of diverse ethnic backgrounds). German is also widely used and, in the far north, many people speak Portuguese. As a first language, most Namibians speak either a Bantu language, such as Owambo and Herero, or a Khoisan language, including Nama and Damara dialects which are characterised by various 'click' sounds that make them difficult to pronounce for nonnative speakers and require quite a bit of practice.

Niger

Official language: French. Each ethnic group has its own language, but the main spoken languages are Hausa (see the Hausa section on p1182), Djerma, Fulfulde and Tamashek (a Tuareg language).

Nigeria

Official languages: English and French (the language of commerce for most of the region). The main indigenous languages are Hausa (see the Hausa section on p1182), Yoruba, Igbo, Edo and Efik.

Rwanda

Official languages: French, English and Kinyarwanda (the most widely spoken language). Some French will be enough in most areas, though English isn't far behind as the major European language, especially in Kigali. You'll also find Swahili useful in some areas.

São Tomé & Príncipe

Official language: Portuguese. Portuguese-based creoles are also widely spoken.

Senegal

Official language: French. Many Senegalese speak at least two indigenous languages. Some of the native tongues spoken as a first language by a significant proportion of people are: Diola (also called Jola), in the Casamance region; Pulaar (Fulfulde), mainly in the north and south; Futa Fula (also known as Fuuta Jalon), in the east; Malinke, in the northeast; Mandinka, in the south; Wolof (spelt *ouolof* in French), in central areas, north and east of Dakar, and along the coast. Wolof is the most widely spoken African language in Senegal.

Sierra Leone

Official language: English. There are also around 15 indigenous tribal languages, including Mende, Limba and Temne. The usual spoken language is Krio, which has its roots in English and various African tongues.

Somalia

Official language: Somali. English is widely used in the north but Italian dominates in the south. Written Somali is a very new invention and there are many variations – Hamar and Xamar, for example, both refer to Mogadishu (which can also be spelled Moqdishu). Somali is written using the Roman alphabet. Arabic script is only used for religious purposes.

South Africa

Official languages (listed in order of spoken predominance): Zulu, Xhosa, Afrikaans, Northern Sotho (Sepedi), English, Tswana, Southern Sotho (Sesotho), Tsonga, Swati, Venda and Ndebele. Most people speak Afrikaans, English or both, as well as their mother tongue. Xhosa and Zulu both use a variety of 'click' sounds, which are difficult for non-native speakers to reproduce without practice.

Sudan

Official languages: Arabic and English. Arabic is the lingua franca spoken almost everywhere and the mother tongue of about half the population, mainly in the north and centre). There are more than 100 languages spoken in Sudan. Nilotic and Nilo-Hamitic languages are spoken in the south, and Darfur is spoken in the western province of the same name. English is also widely spoken.

Swaziland

Official languages: Swati and English. Swati is similar to Zulu (see the Swati section on p1185).

Tanzania

Official languages: Swahili and English. Many local African languages are also spoken. Outside the larger towns and cities, fewer people speak English than in comparable areas of Kenya, so a smattering of Swahili is useful (see also the Swahili section on p1184).

Togo

Official language: French. Many people working in the tourism industry in Lomé also speak passable English. The main indigenous languages are Ewe, Kabye and Mina.

Tunisia

Official language: Arabic (the language of education and government), but almost everyone speaks some French. English speakers are uncommon outside the main tourist centres.

Uganda

Official language: English (spoken by most Ugandans). The other major languages are Luganda and Swahili (see the Swahili section on p1184), though the latter isn't spoken much in Kampala.

Zambia

Official language: English (widely spoken across the country, even in quite remote areas). There are about 35 different ethnic groups, all with their own language. Main groups and languages include Bemba (in the north and centre), Tonga (in the south), Nyanja (in the east) and Lozi (in the west).

Zimbabwe

Official language: English. Most people in Zimbabwe speak Shona or Ndebele as their first language.

EUROPEAN LANGUAGES

FRENCH

Visitors to West and Central Africa will find that a working knowledge of French is more or less essential. English is not widely spoken and you'll find yourself struggling if you don't have at least the basics in French. There are a number of other countries, such as Algeria, Burundi, Djibouti, Rwanda and Tunisia, where French will come in very handy.

African French varies quite widely from French elsewhere, and while you may sometimes find it hard to understand other people, you should have no difficulty making yourself understood. For a more in-depth guide to the language, pick up a copy of Lonely Planet's *French* phrasebook.

Though we have used the polite 'you' form *(vous)* in the following phrases, the informal form *(tu)* is much more common in Africa; you'll hear *s'il te plaît* more than *s'il vous plaît* (which may be considered impolite in France unless used between good friends). If in doubt, in Africa it's always safe to use the polite *vous* form (when dealing with police, border officials or older people). Where both forms are given in this section, the polite form is indicated by 'pol' and the informal by 'inf'.

Greetings & Civilities

Hello./ Good morning.	Bonjour./Salut. (pol/inf)
Good evening.	Bonsoir.
Good night.	Bonne nuit.
Goodbye.	Au revoir. (pol)
	Salut./A bientôt. (inf)
How are you?	Comment allez-vous? (pol)
	Ça va? (inf)
Fine, thanks.	Bien, merci.
What's your name?	Comment vous appelez-vous? (pol)
	Comment tu t'appelles? (inf)
My name is ...	Je m'appelle ...
Please.	S'il vous plaît. (pol)
	S'il te plaît. (inf)
Thank you (very much).	Merci (beaucoup).
You're welcome.	De rien.
Excuse me.	Excusez-moi.
I'm sorry.	Pardon.

Useful Words & Phrases

Yes./No.	Oui./Non.
Do you speak English?	Parlez-vous anglais?
I understand.	Je comprends.
I don't understand.	Je ne comprends pas.
How much is it?	Ça coûte combien?

When does the ... leave/arrive?	À quelle heure part/arrive le ...?
boat	bateau
bus	bus
train	train

Where's ...?	Où est ...?
a bank	une banque
the market	le marché
the post office	la poste
a public telephone	une cabine téléphonique

Where are the toilets?	Où sont les toilettes?
I want to go to ...	Je veux aller à ...
Go straight ahead.	Continuez tout droit.
Turn left/right.	Tournez à gauche/droite.

Do you have any rooms available?	Avez-vous des chambres libres?
I'd like a single room.	Je cherche une chambre à un lit.
I'd like a double room.	Je cherche une chambre double.

Food & Drink

bill	l'addition
breakfast	le petit déjeuner
lunch	le déjeuner
dinner	le dîner

banana	banane
beer	bière
bread	pain
chicken	poulet
fish	poisson
meat	viande
potatoes	pommes de terre
vegetables	légumes

Health

Where's the (nearest) ...?	Où est ... (le/la plus proche)?
doctor	le médecin
hospital	l'hôpital
pharmacy	la pharmacie

I feel dizzy.	J'ai des vertiges.
I feel nauseaous.	J'ai des nausées.
diarrhoea	la diarrhée
medicine	le médicament
sanitary napkins	des serviettes hygiéniques

LANGUAGE

EMERGENCIES – FRENCH

Help!	*Au secours!*
There's been an accident!	*Il y a eu un accident!*
I'm lost.	*Je me suis égaré/e.* (m/f)
Leave me alone!	*Fichez-moi la paix!*
Call ...!	*Appelez ...!*
a doctor	*un médecin*
the police	*la police*

Numbers

1	*un*
2	*deux*
3	*trois*
4	*quatre*
5	*cinq*
6	*six*
7	*sept*
8	*huit*
9	*neuf*
10	*dix*
11	*onze*
12	*douze*
13	*treize*
14	*quatorze*
15	*quinze*
16	*seize*
17	*dix-sept*
18	*dix-huit*
19	*dix-neuf*
20	*vingt*
21	*vingt-et-un*
22	*vingt-deux*
30	*trente*
40	*quarante*
50	*cinquante*
60	*soixante*
70	*soixante-dix*
75	*soixante-quinze*
80	*quatre-vingts*
90	*quatre-vingt-dix*
95	*quatre-vingt-quinze*
100	*cent*
200	*deux cents*
1000	*mille*
2000	*deux mille*
1,000,000	*un million*

PORTUGUESE

English isn't widely spoken in African countries with colonial links to the Portuguese, which means that in Angola, Guinea-Bissau and Mozambique at least some Portuguese is essential. For a more comprehensive guide to the language, get a copy of Lonely Planet's *Portuguese* phrasebook.

Note that Portuguese uses masculine and feminine word endings (usually '-o' and '-a' respectively); eg a man will say *obrigado* and a woman *obrigada* for 'thank you'. The differences are indicated in this section by the abbreviations 'm' and 'f' respectively.

Greetings & Civilities

Good morning.	*Bom dia.*
Good afternoon.	*Boa tarde.*
Good evening.	*Boa noite.*
Goodbye.	*Adeus.*
How are you?	*Como está?*
I'm fine, thank you.	*Estou bem, obrigado/a.* (m/f)
What's your name?	*Como se chama?*
My name is ...	*Chamo-me ...*
Please.	*Por favor.*
Thank you.	*Obrigado/a.* (m/f)
Excuse me.	*Desculpe.*

Useful Words & Phrases

Yes.	*Sim.*
No.	*Não.*
I don't understand.	*Não compreendo.*
I don't speak Portuguese.	*Não falo Português.*
Could you help me?	*Desculpe, podia ajudar-me?*
How much is it?	*Quanto custa?*
cheap	*barato*
(very) expensive	*(muito) caro*
When does the ... leave/arrive?	*A que hora chega/parte o ...?*
boat	*barco*
bus	*bus/machibombo*
truck	*chapa/chapa-cem*
plane	*aviaõ*
train	*comboio*
airport	*aeroporto*
(bus) stop	*paragem*
station	*estação*
ticket	*bilhete*
Where's ...?	*Onde é ...?*
the bank	*o banco*
a hotel	*um hotel/uma pousada*
the post office	*o correio*
a public phone	*um telefon público*
the police	*a policia*
the tourist office	*o posto de turismo*

LANGUAGE

How do I get to ...?	Como é que se vai para ...?
Is it near?	É perto?
Is it far?	É longe?
Go straight ahead.	Vá em frente.
on the left	à esquerda
on the right	à direita

Do you have a ... available?	Tem algum ... disponível?
double-bed room	quarto com cama de casal
double room	quarto duplo
single room	quarto simples

bathroom/toilet	casa da banho
bucket of (hot) water	balde de agua (quente)
shower	chuveiro

Food & Drink

breakfast	pequeno almoço
lunch	almoço
dinner	jantar

bill	quanto
market	mercado
menu (a set meal)	menu
menu (list)	cardápio
I'm a vegetarian.	Sou vegetariano/a. (m/f)

beer	cerveja
mineral water	agua mineral
tea	chá
water	aqua

bread	pão
chicken	frango/galinha
eggs	ovos
fish	peixe
fruit	fruta
meat	carne
potatoes	batata
rice	arroz
salt	sal
steak	bifel
sugar	açúcar
vegetables	legumes

Health

| I'm sick. | Estou doente. |
| I've been vomiting. | Tenho estado a vomitar. |

I feel ...	Estou ...
feverish	com febre
nauseous	com naúseas

EMERGENCIES – PORTUGUESE

Help!	Socorro!
Call a doctor!	Chame um médico!
Call the police!	Chame a polícia!
Go away!	Deixe-me em paz!
	Vai-te embora! (inf)
I'm lost.	Estou perdido/a. (m/f)

Where's the (nearest) ...?	Onde fica ... (mais próximo/a)?
doctor	o médico
hospital	o hospital
pharmacy	a farmácia

condoms	preservativos
sanitary napkins	pensos higíenicos
sunblock	protector do sol

Numbers

1	um
2	dois
3	três
4	quatro
5	cinco
6	seis
7	sete
8	oito
9	nove
10	dez
11	onze
12	doze
13	treze
14	catorze
15	quinze
16	dezasseis
17	dezassete
18	dezoito
19	dezanove
20	vinte
21	vinte e um
30	trinta
40	quarenta
50	cinquenta
60	sessenta
70	setenta
80	oitenta
90	noventa
100	cem
1000	mil
1,000,000	um milhão

LANGUAGE

REGIONAL LANGUAGES

See the 'Who Speaks What Where?' section on p1174 for information on the countries in which these regional and indigenous languages are spoken.

For additional languages that are not covered in this section (Afrikaans, Shona, Wolof, Xhosa, Yoruba and Zulu), get a copy of Lonely Planet's *Africa* phrasebook.

AMHARIC

Amharic word endings vary according to the gender of people you're speaking to, which is indicated in this section by the abbreviations 'm' (said to a man) and 'f' (said to a woman). Note that *gn* is always pronounced as the 'ni' in 'onion'. For a more comprehensive guide to the language, pick up a copy of Lonely Planet's *Ethiopian Amharic* phrasebook.

Greetings & Civilities

Hello./Goodbye.	teanastellen
How are you?	dehna neh/nesh? (m/f)
(response)	dehna
OK.	eshi
Please.	ebakeh/ebakesh (m/f)
	ebakon (pol)
Thank you.	amesegenallo

Useful Words & Phrases

Yes.	owo
No. (not true)	ie
No. (not available)	yellem
tomorrow	nege
tomorrow morning	nege twat
I want ...	afellegallo ...
I don't want ...	alfellegem ...
What is it?	minduno?
How much is it?	sint no wagaw?
That's expensive.	wedd no
Do you have anything cheaper?	rekash alle?
Where are you going?	wadyet te-hedaleh?
Where's the ...?	yeat ... no?
Which is the road to ...?	ye ... mengad yet no?
left	gra
right	kagn
main road	wanna menged

Food & Drink

I'm a vegetarian.	sega albellam
One tea, please.	ante shai ebakeh/ebakesh (m/f)
coffee	buna
milk	wetet
soda water	ambo wuha
tea	shai
water	wuha
banana	mooz
bread	dabbo
bread-like pancake	injera
egg	encular
raw minced meat and herbs	kitfo
saucy stew	wat
vegetables with bread	atkilt-b-dabbo

Numbers

1	and
2	hulett
3	sost
4	arat
5	amest
6	sedest
7	sebat
8	sement
9	zeteny
10	asser
11	assra and
20	haya
21	haya and
25	haya amist
30	salassa
31	salassa and
40	arba
50	hamsa
60	selsa
70	seba
80	semanya
90	zetena
100	meto
1000	and shi

ARABIC

While written Arabic (MSA or Modern Standard Arabic) is universally understood by literate speakers of all Arabic dialects, the spoken language is subject to considerable variation – eg 'camel' is *gamal* in Egypt but *jamal* in Sudan. The phrases included in this section should be understood in most of the Arabic-speaking regions in Africa. For a more detailed guide to Arabic for travellers, get a copy of Lonely Planet's *Egyptian Arabic*, *Moroccan Arabic*, or *Middle East* (which also covers Tunisian Arabic) phrasebooks. Even if you don't have the time or inclination to learn Arabic, you should at least take the time to familiarise yourself with some of the numerals.

Greetings & Civilities

Madam	*lalla*
Sir	*mansoor*
Sir (pol)	*sidi*
Greetings.	*salaam aleikum*
(response)	*wa aleikum as-salaam*
Thank you.	*shukran*
You're welcome.	*afwaan*

Useful Words & Phrases

Yes.	*naam*
No.	*ley*
How much?	*kem?*
I don't speak Arabic.	*ma-atkallam arabi*
Do you speak ...?	*tatkallam ...?*
	wash kt'aref ...? (in Morocco)
English	*ingleezi*
French	*faransi*
camel	*jamal*
market	*souq*
mountain	*jebel*
river bed	*oued/wadi*
sand	*ramia* (*ramla* in Egypt/Sudan)
bread	*khobz* (*a'aish* in Egypt/Sudan)
coffee	*gahwa*
fork	*mtaka*
knife	*mus* (*sekkin* in Egypt/Sudan)
spoon	*tobsi*
tea	*atai*
water	*mey/ma*

HAUSA

Dialectal variation in Hausa is not extreme so the phrases included in this section will be universally understood, and will prove useful in Benin, Burkina Faso, Côte d'Ivoire, Gabon, Niger, Nigeria and northern Ghana. Some knowledge of numbers in Hausa is particularly useful.

The Hausa greetings don't translate literally into their English equivalents. *Ranka/ Ranki ya dade* means 'may your life be long' and is said to seniors or those deserving of respect. *Sannu* (literally: 'gently') is the universal greeting.

Greetings & Civilities

Greetings. (said to man/woman)	*ranka/ranki ya dade*
Hello.	*sannu*
(response)	*yauwaa sannu*
Good morning.	*eenaa kwanaa*
(response)	*lapeeyaloh*
Good evening.	*eenaa eenee*
(response)	*lapeeyaloh*
Goodbye.	*sai wani lookachi*
Please.	*don allaah*
Thank you.	*naa goodee*
Sorry.	*yi hakurii*
How are you?	*inaa gajiyaa?*
I'm fine.	*baa gajiyaa*
What's your name?	*yaayaa suunanka?*
My name is ...	*suunaanaa ...*

Useful Words & Phrases

Yes.	*ii*
No.	*aa'aa*
Do you speak English/ French?	*kanaa jin ingiliishii/ faransancii?*
I speak only English.	*inaa jin ingiliishii kawai*
I understand.	*naa gaanee*
I don't understand.	*ban gaanee ba*
Can you help me, please?	*don allaah, koo zaa ka taimakee ni?*
Leave me alone!	*tafi can!*
Where's ...?	*inaa ...?*
Is it far ...?	*da niisaa ...?*
left	*hagu*
right	*daama*
straight ahead	*miiKee sambal*
How much is this?	*nawa nee wannan?*
That's too expensive.	*akwai tsaadaa ga wannan*

Food & Drink

chicken	*dantsako*
cola nut	*goro*
eggs	*kwai*
fish	*kifi*
food	*abinchi*
meat	*nama*
milk	*madara*
okra	*guro*
onions	*albasa*
rice	*shinkafa*
salt	*gishiri*
water	*ruwa*

LANGUAGE

Numbers

1	*d'aya*
2	*biyu*
3	*uku*
4	*hud'u*
5	*biyar*
6	*shida*
7	*bakwai*
8	*takwas*
9	*tara*
10	*gooma*
11	*gooma shaa d'aya*
12	*gooma shaa biyu*
13	*gooma shaa uku*
14	*gooma shaa hud'u*
15	*gooma shaa biyar*
16	*gooma shaa shida*
17	*gooma shaa bakwai*
18	*gooma shaa takwas*
19	*gooma shaa tara*
20	*ashirin*
30	*talaatin*
40	*arba'in*
50	*hamsin*
60	*sittin*
70	*saba'in*
80	*tamaanin*
90	*casa'in*
100	*d'arii*
1000	*dubuu*
1,000,000	*miliyan d'aya*

MALAGASY

Note that the pronunciation of Malagasy words can differ from their written form (and phrases may seem shorter in the spoken language), as the unstressed syllables in a word are often dropped, so make sure you listen carefully to the locals.

Greetings & Civilities

Good day. (any time)	*Salama.*
Good night.	*Tafandria mandry.*
Goodbye.	*Veloma./Manorapihaona.*
See you soon.	*Vetivety.*
See you later.	*Mandram pihaona.*
Bon voyage!	*Tongava soa!*
How are you?	*Manao ahoana ianao?*
I'm fine.	*Salama tsara aho.*
Very well, thank you.	*Tsara fa misaotra.*
What's your name?	*Iza no anaranao?*
My name is ...	*... no anarako.*
Thank you (very much).	*Misaotra (indrindra).*

Useful Words & Phrases

Yes.	*Eny.*
No.	*Tsia.*
Do you speak English?	*Miteny angilisy ve ianao?*
Do you understand?	*Azonao ve?*
I (don't) understand.	*(Tsy) Azoko.*
Cheers!	*Ho ela velona!*
Help!	*Vonjeo!*
How much is it?	*Ohatrinona?*
Do you have vegetarian food?	*Manana sakafo tsy misy hena ve ianareo?*
Where's the market?	*Aiza ny tsena?*
Where are the toilets?	*Aiza ny trano fivoahana?*

SOUTHERN SOTHO

Greetings are an important social ritual in Lesotho, so it's useful to know some. If you think the person you are greeting is older than you, use 'mother/father'; if they are younger, use 'sister/brother'.

Greetings, father.	*Lumela ntate.*
Peace, father.	*Khotso ntate.*
Greetings, mother.	*Lumela 'me.*
Peace, mother.	*Khotso 'me.*
Greetings, brother.	*Lumela abuti.*
Peace, brother.	*Khotso abuti.*
Greetings, sister.	*Lumela ausi.*
Peace, sister.	*Khotso ausi.*
Thank you.	*Kea leboha.*

There are three ways to say 'How are you?' in Southern Sotho (the first option in each pair listed below applies to one person, and the second to a group of people). All of the following questions and responses are interchangeable.

How do you live?	*O phela joang?/ Le phela joang?*
How did you get up?	*O tsohele joang?/ Le tsohele joang?*
How are you?	*O kae?/Le kae?*
I live well.	*Ke phela hantle./ Re phela hantle.*
I got up well.	*Ke tsohile hantle./ Re tsohile hantle.*
I'm well.	*Ke teng./Re teng.*

When parting, use the following phrases:

Go well.	*Tsamaea hantle./ Tsamaeang hantle.*
Stay well.	*Sala hantle./Salang hantle.*

LANGUAGE

SWAHILI

Swahili has become the lingua franca of Tanzania (though educated people still speak English). Much the same is happening in Kenya, though English is far more entrenched there. Swahili is also useful in parts of Uganda, eastern DRC, Malawi and Zambia, especially in rural areas where the locals are unlikely to speak any English or French.

Concentrate in particular on the all-important greetings (remember to exchange them before asking for help or information), and then on numbers (very useful when negotiating with market vendors, taxi drivers etc). For a more detailed guide to the language, get a copy of Lonely Planet's *Swahili* phrasebook.

Greetings & Civilities

Jambo is pidgin Swahili, used to greet tourists who are presumed not to understand the language. There are two possible responses, each with different connotations: *Jambo* (Hello, now please speak to me in English) and *Sijambo* (Things aren't bad, and I'm willing to try a little Swahili).

If people assume you can speak a little Swahili, greetings may involve the following exchanges:

How are you?	*Hujambo?* (to one person)
	Hamjambo? (to several people)
I'm fine.	*Sijambo.*
We're fine.	*Hatujambo.*

The word *Habari* (meaning 'news') can also be used for general greetings. Among other similar greetings, you may hear *Salama* instead of *Habari*, or *Habari* may be dropped altogether.

How are you?	*Habari?*
What's the news?	*Habari gani?*
Good morning.	*Habari za asubuhi?*
Good day.	*Habari za leo?*
Good afternoon.	*Habari za mchana?*
Good evening.	*Habari za jioni?*
(including night)	
Good night.	*Usiku mwema.*
Goodbye.	*Kwa heri.*

Useful Words & Phrases

Yes.	*Ndiyo.*
No.	*Hapana.*
Excuse me.	*Samahani.*
Please. (if asking a big favour)	*Tafadhali.*
Can you help me, please?	*Tafadhali, naomba msaada.*
Thank you (very much).	*Asante (sana).*
What's your name?	*Jina lako nani?*
My name is …	*Jina langu ni …*
Do you speak English?	*Unasema Kiingereza?*
Do you speak Swahili?	*Unasema Kiswahili?*
I understand.	*Naelewa.*
I don't understand.	*Sielewi.*

When does the … leave?	*… inaondoka saa ngapi?*
bus	*Basi*
minibus	*Daladala* (Tanzania)
	Matatu (Kenya)
train	*Treni*

I'd like to hire a …	*Nataka kukodi …*
bicycle	*baisikeli*
car	*gari*
motorcycle	*pikipiki*

I want to go to …	*Nataka kwenda …*
Is it near?	*Ni karibu?*
Is it far?	*Ni mbali?*

Go …	*Kata/Pita/Chukua …*
left	*kushoto*
right	*kulia*
straight ahead	*moja kwa moja*

Where's the …?	*… ni wapi?*
bank	*Benki*
market	*Soko*
pharmacy	*Duka la dawa*
police station	*Kituo cha polisi*
post office	*Posta*
telephone centre	*Mahali pa kupiga simu*

guesthouse	*gesti*
hotel	*hoteli* (also means 'restaurant')
Do you have a room?	*Je, kuna nafasi ya chumba hapa?*
How much is it?	*Ni bei gani?*
That's very expensive.	*Ghali sana.*

Food & Drink

Is there a restaurant near here?	*Je, kuna hoteli ya chakula hapo jirani?*
I'm a vegetarian.	*Nakula mboga tu.*

EMERGENCIES – SWAHILI

Help!	*Nisaidie!*
It's an emergency.	*Ni jambo la haraka.*
Call a doctor!	*Muite daktari!*
Call the police!	*Muite polisi!*
Go away!	*Toka!*
I'm lost.	*Nimepotea.*

bananas	*ndizi*
beef	*ng'ombe*
bread	*mkate*
chicken	*kuku*
egg(s)	*(ma)yai*
fish	*samaki*
food	*chakula*
goat	*mbuzi*
meat	*nyama*
milk	*maziwa*
rice	*mchele*
salt	*chumvi*
vegetables	*mboga*
water	*maji*

Health

Where can I find a doctor/hospital?	*Naweza kupata daktari/hospitali wapi?*
I'm sick.	*Niko mgonjwa.*

diarrhoea	*harisha/hara/endesha*
fever	*homa*
headache	*umwa kichwa*
medicine	*dawa*
nausea	*tapika*
sanitary napkins	*Kotex*
vomiting	*tapika*
water purifier	*chombo cha kusafishia maji*

Numbers

1	*moja*
2	*mbili*
3	*tatu*
4	*nne*
5	*tano*
6	*sita*
7	*saba*
8	*nane*
9	*tisa*
10	*kumi*
11	*kumi na moja*
12	*kumi na mbili*
20	*ishirini*
21	*ishirini na moja*
22	*ishirini na mbili*
30	*thelathini*
40	*arobaini*
50	*hamsini*
60	*sitini*
70	*sabini*
80	*themanini*
90	*tisini*
100	*mia moja*
200	*mia mbili*
300	*mia tatu*
1000	*elfu*
10,000	*elfu kumi*
100,000	*laki*
1,000,000	*milioni*

SWATI

Tonal quality (the raising and lowering of pitch on certain syllables) plays a part in Swati and there are some 'click' sounds to master, but people will be pleased with your attempts to speak their language.

Greetings & Civilities

Yebo is also a casual greeting. It's customary to greet everyone you meet. Often you'll be asked *U ya phi?* (Where are you going?).

Hello.	*Sawubona.* (to one person)
	Sanibona. (to several people)
How are you?	*Kunjani?*
I'm fine.	*Kulungile.*
Goodbye.	*Sala kahle.* (literally: 'stay well')
	Hamba kahle. (literally: 'go well')
Please.	*Tsine.*
I thank you.	*Ngiyabonga.*
We thank you.	*Siyabonga.*

Useful Words & Phrases

Yes./No.	*Yebo./Ha.*
Sorry.	*Lucolo.*
Do you have ...?	*Une ... yini?*
How much?	*Malini?*
Is there a bus to ...?	*Kukhona ibhasi yini leya ...?*
When does it leave?	*Isuka nini?*
morning/afternoon	*ekuseni/entsambaba*

Also available from Lonely Planet:
Africa phrasebook

LANGUAGE

The Authors

ANTHONY HAM   Coordinating Author, Libya & Mali

Anthony's love affair with Africa began on his first trip to Niger, when he fell irretrievably in love with the people and landscapes of the Sahel and Sahara. Since then, he has returned many times, visiting every Sahelian and Saharan country as he seeks out stories about the people and wildlife of West and North Africa. He loves nothing better than finding a remote corner of the Sahara and spending nights around the campfire with his Tuareg friends. In addition to Lonely Planet's *West Africa, Africa, Libya* and *Algeria* guides, Anthony writes for numerous newspapers and magazines around the world. When he's not in Africa, Anthony lives in Madrid with his wife and daughter.

KATE ARMSTRONG   Lesotho & Swaziland

Kate was bitten by the African bug when she lived and worked in Mozambique, and has returned to southern Africa frequently. For this edition she coaxed her wheels for hundreds of kilometres over Lesotho's remote mountainous passes in a 2WD (and learnt more about catalytic converters than she ever intended) and danced her way through Swaziland. Kate is continually humbled by the generosity of the local Swazi and Basotho people. When she's not eating, hiking and talking her way around parts of Africa, Europe and South America, her itchy feet are grounded in Sydney, where she is a freelance writer.

JAMES BAINBRIDGE   South Africa

Pictured here on Lion's Head in Cape Town, James was lucky enough to visit the rainbow nation twice in the space of six months for Lonely Planet. He explored the north while coordinating *South Africa, Lesotho & Swaziland,* then updated the South Africa chapter of *Southern Africa,* catching President Zuma's inauguration and driving a few thousand kilometres in the process. The London-based journalist's writing about Africa has appeared in publications including the *Guardian, Songlines* world-music magazine, Lonely Planet's *West Africa,* and the previous edition of this book.

LONELY PLANET AUTHORS

Why is our travel information the best in the world? It's simple: our authors are passionate, dedicated travellers. They don't take freebies in exchange for positive coverage so you can be sure the advice you're given is impartial. They travel widely to all the popular spots, and off the beaten track. They don't research using just the internet or phone. They discover new places not included in any other guidebook. They personally visit thousands of hotels, restaurants, palaces, trails, galleries, temples and more. They speak with dozens of locals every day to make sure you get the kind of insider knowledge only a local could tell you. They take pride in getting all the details right, and in telling it how it is. Think you can do it? Find out how at **lonelyplanet.com.**

THE AUTHORS

TIM BEWER
Central African Republic, Congo, Democratic Republic of Congo, Sierra Leone & Uganda

While growing up, Tim didn't travel much except for the obligatory pilgrimage to Disney World and an annual summer week at the lake. He's spent most of his adult life making up for this, and has visited more than 60 nations, including 22 in Africa. After university he worked briefly as a legislative assistant before quitting Capitol life in 1994 to backpack around West Africa. It was during this trip that the idea of becoming a freelance travel writer and photographer was hatched, and he's been at it ever since. The half of the year when he isn't shouldering a backpack somewhere for work or pleasure he lives in Khon Kaen, Thailand.

STUART BUTLER
Sudan, Chad & Ethiopia

With £200 in his pocket and three months to spare, English-born Stuart first hit Africa after hitchhiking across Europe and into Morocco in the early '90s. As soon as he arrived he knew Africa was for him, and he has since returned numerous times travelling through every region in the continent and over half the countries. Updating Ethiopia for this book involved covering old, and much loved, ground. Sudan was an unexpected surprise and shot quickly towards the top of his favourite countries list, and Chad – well that was an experience! When not in Africa he lives on the beautiful beaches of southwest France.

JEAN-BERNARD CARILLET
Burkina Faso, São Tomé & Príncipe, Djibouti, Eritrea & Somaliland, Puntland & Somalia

A Paris-based journalist and photographer, Jean-Bernard is a die-hard Africa lover who never misses an opportunity to explore the dark continent. He has travelled the length and breadth of the continent for nearly 20 years now, from the desolate landscapes of Djibouti and the remote corners of the Sahel to the buzz of Jo'burg and the markets of Addis Ababa. For this book he has crossed weird borders, sipped dozens of macchiatos, met leading artists, and got up close and personal with truck-sized elephants. In addition to Lonely Planet's *Africa*, *West Africa* and *Ethiopia & Eritrea* guides, Jean-Bernard writes for various newspapers and magazines around the world.

PAUL CLAMMER
Morocco, Mauritania & Nigeria

Once a molecular biologist, Paul has long since traded his test tubes for a backpack and the vicarious life of a travel writer. Overlanding in Africa was his first significant travel experience, and he has returned to the continent many times since, including a stint working as a tour guide in Morocco. For this book, Paul sampled the nightlife of Lagos, slept under desert stars in Mauritania and – on his 100th visit – still found a new part of the Fez medina to get lost in.

THE AUTHORS

LUCY CORNE
Angola

Lucy graduated with a degree in journalism but soon swapped the news desk for a backpack, and hasn't stopped moving since. She has penned several guidebooks and writes regularly on her three greatest passions – travel, food and beer. Despite visiting more than 40 countries, she still hasn't quite got the hang of it and was delighted to travel through Angola without leaving her camera on a bus, her money belt under a pillow, or falling off any horses. This is her first book for Lonely Planet.

EMILIE FILOU
Benin & Togo

Emilie first travelled to West Africa aged eight to visit her grandparents, who had taken up a late career opportunity in Mali. More visits ensued, including an epic family holiday in Togo and Benin, the highlight of which was the beautiful and amusingly named Grand Popo ('big poo' in French – simply hilarious when you're aged 10). Emilie pursued her interest in Africa at university where she studied geography and did her dissertation on health-care provision for nomadic people in Niger. For this book she has crossed borders, visited national parks and zoomed across Benin and Togo's cities, all aboard the dreaded *zemi-johns* (motorcycle taxis) – she is glad to be alive to tell the tale.

MATTHEW D FIRESTONE
Burundi, Egypt, Kenya, Namibia & Rwanda

Matt is a trained biological anthropologist and epidemiologist, who is particularly interested in the health and nutrition of indigenous populations. His first visit to sub-Saharan Africa in 2001 took him deep into the Kalahari, where he performed a field study on the traditional diet of the San. Unfortunately, Matt's promising academic career was postponed due to a severe case of wanderlust, though he has relentlessly travelled to more than 50 countries in search of a cure. Matt is hoping that this book will help ease the pain of other individuals bitten by the travel bug, though he fears that there is a growing epidemic on the horizon.

MARY FITZPATRICK
Tanzania & Mozambique

Mary is from the USA, where she spent her early years in Washington, DC – dreaming, more often than not, of how to get across an ocean or two to more exotic locales. After finishing graduate studies, she set off for several years in Europe. Her fascination with languages and cultures soon led her further south to Africa, where she has spent the past 15 years living and working all around the continent, including in Tanzania and Mozambique. When not travelling, she sates her wanderlust by writing, and has authored and co-authored numerous other Africa guidebooks.

KATHARINA LOBECK KANE
The Gambia, Guinea, Guinea-Bissau & Senegal

Over the last decade, Katharina has earned enough bush-taxi miles to tour the entire continent at least a dozen times. Ever since the seductive tremor of a Fula flute first lured her to West Africa in 1997, she hasn't been able to spend more than a few months without a stint in Africa. A year of PhD research in Guinea was followed by work visits to dozens of countries on the continent, usually clutching a camera and voice recorder, to dig up gems of the local music scenes. When London threw her out in 2005, she moved to Senegal. Katharina currently works as a writer, radio presenter and project manager from Dakar and Berlin.

ADAM KARLIN
Cameroon & Botswana

A trip to South Africa at age 20 was Adam's first real independent travel experience, and he has been locked in a long relationship with the mother continent ever since. Fast forward eight years, and Adam has worked on five Africa titles for Lonely Planet. He's slept in Moroccan mud castles, been charged by a pissed-off elephant in Botswana, briefly arrested in Cameroon (a shout out to the Wum police department) and found heaven in sacred forests on the Kenyan coast. All in a day's work and, for Adam, there are few places as rewarding in which to work or travel, or both.

NANA LUCKHAM
Malawi

Born in Tanzania to a Ghanaian mother and an English father, Nana started life criss-crossing Africa by plane and bumping along the roughest of roads. She first made it to southern Africa in 1994 when she spent six months living in Zimbabwe. After several years as an editor and a UN press officer she got into travel writing full time, and has hauled her backpack all over Africa researching guidebooks to destinations such as Algeria, Kenya, South Africa and Benin. She was thrilled to return to Malawi (the scene of her very first Lonely Planet assignment) for this book.

TOM MASTERS
Algeria, Niger & Liberia

Long a fan of places most people do their best to avoid, Tom was a natural choice to cover three of Africa's least visited nations, all now largely peaceful and safe after decades of troubles. Travelling through the Sahara in Algeria and Niger is an experience that he won't quickly forget, while crossing Liberia as it gradually gets back on its feet was one of the most exciting journeys imaginable. Tom lives in Berlin and more of his work can be seen on www.mastersmafia.com.

THE AUTHORS

ALAN MURPHY
Zambia

Alan remembers falling under southern Africa's ambient spell after bouncing around in the rear of a *bakkie* (pick-up truck) on the way from Jo'burg airport in 1999. Since then he's been back several times working for Lonely Planet, including this trip to Zambia. Whether watching elephants crossing a river, tracking lions in the bush, glimpsing elusive wild dogs or chuckling at the clownish behaviour of curious baboons, he finds wildlife-watching exhilarating. The logistical difficulties of getting around Zambia hit home, though, when he got told: 'go down the track and then take a right at the turn-off where the sign has fallen down.' This trip was one big adventure, made even more enjoyable by a 4WD named Bessie and a travelling companion named Smitzy.

HELEN RANGER
Madagascar

Captivated by indris and giraffe-necked weevils on her first visit to Madagascar in 1999, Helen relished the chance to return to the Big Red Island. Arriving shortly after a political crisis, she often found herself the only traveller on the road. But the Malagasy never fail to charm and the country is a fascinating repository of weird and wonderful animals and plants. Helen spent most of her life in Cape Town, but now lives in Fez; there's something about Africa that she can't tear herself away from. She has contributed to Lonely Planet's *Fez Encounter*, *South Africa, Lesotho & Swaziland* and *Cape Town*. Helen will have to go back to Madagascar again – she hasn't seen an aye-aye yet.

NICOLA SIMMONDS
Zimbabwe

Nicola has worked in and backpacked around Indonesia, India, Sri Lanka, Europe, Japan and Central and South America. She then lived in Angola and Zimbabwe for seven years (with her husband and, eventually, three kids), mastering water shortages, African bureaucracy and out-of-control economies, so covering Zimbabwe post 'dollarisation' was nothing but joy. She has just spent a year in Sri Lanka and is currently figuring out where to go next…

KATE THOMAS
Côte d'Ivoire, Ghana, Equatorial Guinea & Gabon

Kate has been based on the continent ever since finding herself on a press trip to West Africa while working for a national British paper. Two months after returning from that trip, she packed her bags for Liberia, where she spent a couple of years writing about everything from food and fashion to hospitals and mental health. Since then she's watched mountain gorillas in the Democratic Republic of Congo, bused her way from Accra to Dakar, danced about architecture in Guinea-Bissau and read her way through Equatorial Guinea's literary greats. Kate also writes for news and arts media, taking every opportunity to champion the good stuff coming out of Africa.

DONNA WHEELER   Tunisia

Donna had long gazed at the Mediterranean's African shore from France and Italy and, with this chapter, was thrilled to finally be able to experience the Maghreb first hand. Apart from indulging her fish couscous obsession and poking around the Punic and Roman ruins she'd been dreaming about since high school Latin classes, she was also excited to discover a contemporary Tunisia that is every bit as intriguing and vibrant as its historical counterpart. After many years working as an editor, digital producer and content strategist, Donna is now a full-time travel writer, specialising in art, design, history and food. This is her fourth title for Lonely Planet.

CONTRIBUTING AUTHORS

Jane Cornwell is an Australian-born, UK-based journalist, author and broadcaster, who wrote the African Music chapter. After graduating with a Masters degree in anthropology, she left for London where she worked, variously, at the Institute of Contemporary Arts and for Peter Gabriel's Real World company. She currently writes about arts, books and music – most notably world music – for a range of UK and antipodean publications, including the *Times*, *Evening Standard* and *Telegraph* newspapers, *Songlines* magazine and the *Australian* newspaper. She travels about the planet regularly, interviewing world musicians.

Dr Caroline Evans wrote the Health chapter. Caroline studied medicine at the University of London, and completed General Practice training in Cambridge. She is the medical adviser to Nomad Travel Clinic, a private travel-health clinic in London, and is also a GP specialising in travel medicine. She has been an expedition doctor for Raleigh International and Coral Cay expeditions.

Michela Wrong, who wrote the Africa & Development chapter, has spent the last 14 years reporting on Africa. She is author of the award-winning *In the Footsteps of Mr Kurtz*, which traces the rise and fall of the dictator Mobutu, and *I Didn't Do It for You*, about the tiny nation of Eritrea.

Behind the Scenes

THIS BOOK

This is the 12th edition of Lonely Planet's all-Africa title. The 1st edition, then called *Africa on the Cheap*, was written by Geoff Crowther in 1977. Geoff subsequently wrote, then became the coordinating author for, the next five editions of *Africa on a Shoestring*, before handing over the reins to Hugh Finlay, who coordinated the next four editions. As the scope of the book grew, so did the need to share the load. This edition was ably coordinated by Anthony Ham.

This book was commissioned in Lonely Planet's Melbourne office, and produced by the following:
Commissioning Editors Sasha Baskett, Stefanie di Trocchio, Will Gourlay, Shawn Low
Coordinating Editor Katie O'Connell
Coordinating Cartographer Mark Griffiths
Coordinating Layout Designer Yvonne Bischofberger
Managing Editor Liz Heynes
Managing Cartographer Alison Lyall
Managing Layout Designer Sally Darmody
Assisting Editors Sarah Bailey, Nigel Chin, Helen Christinis, Laura Crawford, Jessica Crouch, Peter Cruttenden, Trent Holden, Robyn Loughnane, Kristin Odijk, Stephanie Pearson, Angela Tinson, Gina Tsarouhas, Branislava Vladisavljevic
Assisting Cartographers Birgit Jordan, Valentina Kremenchutskaya, Andy Rojas, Andrew Smith, Brendan Streager
Assisting Layout Designers Jacqui Saunders, Carlos Solarte
Cover Research Naomi Parker, lonelyplanetimages.com
Internal Image Research Jane Hart, lonelyplanetimages.com
Project Manager Chris Girdler

Thanks to Lucy Birchley, Ross Butler, Lisa Knights, Rebecca Lalor, Annelies Mertens, Adrian Persoglia, Kalya Ryan, Glenn van der Knijff

THANKS
ANTHONY HAM

In Mali, Ogomono Saye and Azima Ag Mohamed Ali were wise and wonderful travel companions. Special thanks also to Baba Mahamane, Karen Crabbs, El-Mehdi Doumbia (In-a-Djatafane), Toumani Diabaté (Bamako), Vieux Traoré (Bamako) and Menidou Keita (Ibi). In Libya, *bari kelorfik* to Hakim Saleh Ashour, my companion and close friend on so many Libyan trails. Thanks also to Brahim, Najib,

Dr Mustafa Turjman, Muawia Wanis and Hussein Founi, and to my wonderful co-authors and editors Stefanie di Trocchio, Shawn Low and Errol Hunt. And a special dedication to Jan, Marina and Carlota, three much-loved generations of my family with whom I hope to share future African trails.

KATE ARMSTRONG

Many thanks to all the travellers who helped me along the way, especially the Australian Volunteers and Peace Corps. In Swaziland, a zillion thanks to Darron Raw, plus Mike Richardson and Benita; in Lesotho a massive thanks to Darren Elder, plus Di Jones and Stephen Gill. Thank you once again to Rose, Camilla and Carlos for their kindness; Peter Bendheim and Jenny Govender of Durban Tourism.

JAMES BAINBRIDGE

Many thanks to the helpful folk at the accommodation I crashed at – notably in Cape Town, Durban, Jo'burg and Soweto. Cheers also to Evelien Klokman for helping to set things up in Kruger for myself and the three French musketeers; to Julian and Nina for nights out in Jo'burg; to Eric in Port Edward for all your anecdotes; to Sam, Eva, Carmen and everyone I 'chillaxed' with on the Wild Coast; to Prudence for dinner and getting lost with me on Lion's Head; to Leigh-Robin for showing me Camps Bay, even if it was 3am; and to Chanelle (aka DJ Charm) at Cape Town Tourism for your encyclopedic knowledge of the Mother City's club scene. Finally, another shout out to everyone who helped me in Limpopo in 2008.

TIM BEWER

I owe debts of gratitude to many people, especially the following: John and Carolyn Jost, Daïmgar Maxime, Louis Sarno and, for the second time in as many countries, the entire Toldé family in Central African Republic. Hugue Mpassi, Valentin Ngouiri, Stephane Rebeye and Hilde van Leuwe in Congo; Tapani Aho, Léonard Chihenguza, Alain 'Alesh' Chirwisa, Alex Clement, Mumbere 'Praida' Kabaraza, Sekombi Katondolo, Serge Moka, Robert Mwinyihali, Jupiter Ngungu, Rosmarie Ruf, Oggi Saidi, Ms Stella, Tom Thamba, Richard Tshombe and Chris Vanden Hengel in DRC; Edward Aruna, Bimbola Carrol, Edleen Elba, Alieya

Kargbo, Alhaji Siaka and David Zeller in Sierra Leone; John Friday, Suni Magyar, Cam McLeay, Simon Musasizi, Dennis Ntege, Ralph Schenk, Richard Smith, Godfrey Pule Thomson, Richard Tooro, Anne-Marie Weeden, and Debbie Willis in Uganda. My apologies to anyone I forgot. Finally, as always, it was a pleasure working with Stefanie di Trocchio, Anthony Ham, Shawn Low and everyone else in Lonely Planet land.

STUART BUTLER

In Ethiopia I would like to thank Abraham for his driving, Tania and Cheru for their knowledge of all things Ethiopian, and Dawoud Sulayman in Gonder and the Simiens. In Sudan I'm indebted to Mohamed Sulaiman, Joseph Asaad and Hasan Mutaz for superb driving. and in Chad I am grateful to Mousa at Tchad Evasion. I'd also like to thank fellow Lonely Planet scribes Paul Clammer, Tim Bewer, Jean-Bernard Carillet, Dean Starnes and Anthony Ham for advice and help on all three countries and finally to Heather for everything she does (and for coping so well whilst heavily pregnant when I was off in the African bush again).

JEAN-BERNARD CARILLET

A huge thanks to everyone who helped out and made these African trips an enlightenment, including Guillaume, Maurice, Alain, Christophe, Xav, Gerard, Dominique, Simon, Mickael, Nicolas, Laure, Salifou, Hama, Princess Abiba, Princess Mehret, Olivia, Kader, Jerome, Lucien, Irene, Moko, Fernand, Bassirou, Luis, Carlos, Solomon, Tedros, Thomas, Adriano, Said, Shabeelle, David, Nico, Bruno, Vicente, Dominique, Abdurazak, Ermano and all the people I met on the road – you're all so charming. At Lonely Planet I'm grateful to Stefanie for her trust and support. The carto and design team also deserve a huge thanks for their input. It's been a pleasure to work with Anthony, who shares the same passion for Africa. And finally, thank you to my daughter Eva, who I hope will share sooner or later my travel and journalism bug.

PAUL CLAMMER

Number one thanks – for myriad reasons – to Mal and Awoba (and BB!) in Lagos. It literally couldn't have happened without you both. In Nigeria, thanks also to Summer and Nazih, Ridwan Siddiqi, David Ehrhardt, and Peter Jenkins of Pandrillus. In Mauritania, thanks to Christine and Sven for the brilliant trip to Ben Amira, Just and Cora in Atar, and Chris Kirkley in Nouakchott. In Morocco, thanks to Helen Ranger, Mike and the Clock crew in Fez, and Barakat Naim in Marrakesh. Finally, thanks as always to Jo, especially for her patience when visas were looking dubious.

LUCY CORNE

Enormous thanks to Nancy Gottlieb for her invaluable help both before and during the trip and to Rosa de Carvalho Malaquias for her crucial assistance with visas. Thanks also to my fiancé, Shawn Duthie, for keeping me sane when nothing went as planned and to Anthony Ham for never tiring of my endless questions. Finally I'd like to thank the Angolan people, who jumped cheerfully to our aid at every turn in the absence of any tourist information offices.

EMILIE FILOU

In Togo, I am hugely indebted to Ram Shriyan and his family for their heartfelt welcome. Thanks to Jean-Marie Lascaux, Eric Miens and the Henrys for their insight. In Benin, thank you to Rikke Offenberg, Sarah Christoffersen, Marie Heuts and Mireia Idiaquez for their hospitality. Thanks also to Hélène Verwaerde in Nati for her friendship and useful introductions. Back home, I'd like to thank Adolfo for his daily calls and apologise for the grey hair I've given him. And finally, thank you to my grandparents Pauline and Gilbert Tanguy for being such an inspiration: ce livre est pour vous.

MATTHEW D FIRESTONE

To my wonderfully supportive parents, thank you so much for always sticking by my side, through both the highs and the lows. To Kim and Aki, thank you both for finally taking the trip out to Namibia, and experiencing the country that I love so much. To my editor Stef, thank you for all the guidance and support you've shown me throughout this project. And to Anthony, thank you for coordinating another strong and solid edition of the Africa tome.

KATHARINA LOBECK KANE

It's hard to squeeze in the helping hands and minds of four countries into a few lines. First of all, apologies to Jules and Ishema for travelling on my own so much that I'm now too tired for family holidays. Coming home after each long trip has been fabulous. In Senegal: special thanks go to Cherif Bodian, PJ, Haidar, Elise, Marcel, Ursula, Jean-Jacques Bancal and Muriel, Ines Gontek, Alpha and Doba, Mwana, Julien, Romuald, Laure, Jean-Paul, Clara and Jean Pierrot, Stef and Baba. In Gambia: Geri and Maurice, Tomm, Lamine, Mark and Jayne, James, Peter and Malang, Deepa and Jess Tyrell. In Guinea-Bissau: Miguel, Solange and team, Diego,

Joseph and Martha. In Guinea: Telivel and Billy, Gerhard, Lama Foutah, Boubacar, Soundioulou, Cellou, Stefan and Mamadi, Marie-Claude, Diams Diallo, Solo, Peter, El Hadj Dioulde Ba and Salimatou.

ADAM KARLIN

Thank you to the Africans who have made a far place home: Shakes Mcithi, Yazir Henry, Nkululeko Booysen, Mwange Chege, Adamou Youmo Kopit, Mbouombouo Aramiyahou, Sally Collins, Emma De Villiers, Gordon Mackay, Jonathan Percale and many, many others. Thank you to those who introduced me to Africa or have helped me there from afar: Ben Spatz, Vijay Rajendran, Matthew Cochrane and the entire UW CHID program, especially my dear, departed friend and mentor James Clowes. Thank you all fellow authors, with particular shout outs to Kate Thomas for her friendship and Anthony Ham for his guidance. To our readers: *sahle kahle*.

NANA LUCKHAM

In London, thanks as ever to Patrick Smith for his pre-departure advice and contacts, and to the folks at Malawi Tourism. Thanks also to Gilbert at Njaya Lodge in Nkhata Bay, Patrick Jere at Mwabvi Wildlife Reserve, Ackson Kasonde, Benson Nkoma, Nancy Tembo, and to Patrick and Jona from Budget Safari for their kindness, good humour and company in northern Malawi and Zambia.

TOM MASTERS

In Algeria thanks to Nathan Eddy for his company and good humour. Big thanks to Chloe and

Christian Lowe in Algiers for their hospitality and Lamine Lansari, Elramiz, Mubarak and Mohammed of Tarakeft in Tamanrasset for an awesome trip to the Sahara. In Niger thanks to Douglas de Carvalho, Céline, Moussa and Turbo. In Liberia, thanks to Adam, Meredith, Dana and Cristy in Monrovia, Jeffrey and Soso in Harper.

ALAN MURPHY

Firstly I'd like to thank Smitzy, my travelling companion – his curiosity, incisive observations on the road and help with research were invaluable. Thanks, mate. Francis, a reliable taxi driver in Lusaka helped with research, especially public-transport information. Thanks to the many lodge owners in and around national parks who provided me with loads of useful information. Thanks also to Elke at Tikondane for taking me into a local village and helping me understand some of the challenges faced by Zambians. Lastly, thanks to the Zambian people we met, who were warm, friendly and unfailingly helpful.

HELEN RANGER

Thanks to Lonely Planet for sending me back to this fascinating country, to Stefanie di Trocchio, Anthony Ham, and to everyone in Melbourne for their support. In Fez, Hitesh Mehta provided inspiration. In Madagascar, *misaotra indrindra* to driver Jocelyn Raveloson who negotiated the Hauts Plateaux road with skill and made a good translator, to Lalatiana Rahariniaina in Tana, and to the ever-obliging Niaina Patrick Randriamboavonjy in Toamasina, who all made my life that much easier. And *merci mille*

THE LONELY PLANET STORY

Fresh from an epic journey across Europe, Asia and Australia in 1972, Tony and Maureen Wheeler sat at their kitchen table stapling together notes. The first Lonely Planet guidebook, *Across Asia on the Cheap*, was born.

Travellers snapped up the guides. Inspired by their success, the Wheelers began publishing books to Southeast Asia, India and beyond. Demand was prodigious, and the Wheelers expanded the business rapidly to keep up. Over the years, Lonely Planet extended its coverage to every country and into the virtual world via lonelyplanet.com and the Thorn Tree message board.

As Lonely Planet became a globally loved brand, Tony and Maureen received several offers for the company. But it wasn't until 2007 that they found a partner whom they trusted to remain true to the company's principles of travelling widely, treading lightly and giving sustainably. In October of that year, BBC Worldwide acquired a 75% share in the company, pledging to uphold Lonely Planet's commitment to independent travel, trustworthy advice and editorial independence.

Today, Lonely Planet has offices in Melbourne, London and Oakland, with over 500 staff members and 300 authors. Tony and Maureen are still actively involved with Lonely Planet. They're travelling more often than ever, and they're devoting their spare time to charitable projects. And the company is still driven by the philosophy of *Across Asia on the Cheap*: 'All you've got to do is decide to go and the hardest part is over. So go!'

fois to Henri Bellon on Île Sainte Marie for sharing his passion for hump-back whales.

NICOLA SIMMONDS

There are four people I want to keep thanking: James Elder, my husband, for his endless help covering for me while I was gone and; Justine Smith for donning her backpack and joining me on the road – and off the Falls!; the world's best travel agent: Belinda at Experience Africa Safaris in Harare; and, finally, Richard Sheppard of Fawlty Towers, Livingstone, who's on a passionate crusade to bring back budget travel so more and more people will come to Africa for 'the experience of their lifetime' – his words.

KATE THOMAS

Thanks to so many, including Aminata Soumahoro, Hortense Gnogono, Franck Kodjo, Ben Mpeck, Ben Clayton, Alain, all at Côte d'Ivoire Tourisme, Key Tugbe Toe, Daniel Oblie, John James, Jeff Simpson, Nico Colombant, Tristan and Tiggy, Olivier Asselin, Ross Mytton, Christian and Linda (who postponed their dinner date to chase that bus); Shelby Grossman, Adam Lifshey, Dave Jean, Daniel Riba, Belinda Jones, Demba Aloraco, Betty Chale, Rosa and Linda, Emmanuelo Gorala, Benito Auriales. At Lonely Planet, Stefanie, Shawn, Katie, Anthony, Rebecca and my fellow author Adam; all at Voice of America Dakar; and, lastly, to my good friends all over this beautiful corner of Africa.

DONNA WHEELER

Thanks to my Tunisia coauthors Emilie Filou and Paul Clammer, who were a true pleasure to work with and contributed much to this chapter, and to Anthony Ham for calm and wise coordinating. In Paris, thanks to the charming Chris Brasher for making the 20e feel like home and for stocking my iPod with the perfect research soundtrack. In Tunisia, thanks to Naceur and Nedra; Turkia and Moncef Gharbi, and Amel and Patrick Marguier for hospitality beyond the call of duty, and to Jan Demeulemeester, Bart, Machteld and family for the kindness and company. Lastly, much gratitude goes to my family Joe, Rumer and Biba Guario, for your constancy and love.

OUR READERS

Many thanks to the travellers who used the last edition and wrote to us with helpful hints, useful advice and interesting anecdotes:

Helmut Ablinger, Karen Adler, Frank Adventures, Emilie Alary, Amy Anderson, Kristin Ask, Lee Balot, John Beechen, Roger Bjelland, Jorgen Borg, Chris Bramall, Brecht, Phil Brooks, Amy

Brummit, Georg Caspary, Jarret Cassaniti, Mali Chic, Nathan Collett, Julie Collinsworth, Rebecca Conroy, Jack Cooper, Josh Coppersmith Heaven, Grigorios Delichristos, Manuel Faure, Gianni Filippi, John Fioretta, Devin Foxall, Kitty Frey Hopkins, John Frith, Kostas Gabriel, Nancy Gill, Eyal Ginzburg, Alessandro Golinelli, Brandon Gough, Kate Hendry, Sue Hunt, Stuart Hurlbut, Michael Jankulak, John Jeyes, Jan Joubert, Marinus Kasteleijn, Hakon Kavli, Moroesi Koali, Klaus-Peter Kownatzki, Michal Kozok, Kevin Krol, Richard Kuziara, Marie Estelle Lamy, Pieter Lein, Melanie Lemahieu, Alexia Liakounakou, James Lindsay, Erik Lorentzen, N M, Ragnhild Mæhre, Kmetova Marie, Koos Remmert Marinus, Grant McCall, Sarah McCombe, Taniya Morris, Jack Mui, Melissa Mullan, Marietjie Myburg, Szymon Myslinski, Anne Nagel, Joan Oberg, Michael Pearson, Rui Pereira, Niomie Perera, Lesley Pickering, Thomas Preinl, Julie Ranger, Russell Roark, Sandra Rutjes, Miguel Santos, Michael Schenk, Lucre Schoorlemmer, Paolo Serafini, Brook Silva-Braga, Danielle Steenman, Ann Stoughton, Bill Stoughton, Robert Swanepoel, Jesse Tawil, Katie Timmins, Jaenny Van Zyl, Heino Von Wiellígh, Paolo Votino, Paul Watson, M'Basen Wazir, Alan Weltzien, Luzia Werder, Kari Westersund, Jeffrey & Lindsay Wicharuk, Amaya Williams and Paul Wren.

ACKNOWLEDGMENTS

Many thanks to the following for the use of their content:

Globe on title page ©Mountain High Maps 1993 Digital Wisdom, Inc.

Index

000 Map pages
000 Photograph pages

INDEX

INDEX

INDEX

GreenDex

The following attractions, activities, tours, accommodation and restaurants have been selected by Lonely Planet authors because they demonstrate a commitment to sustainability. Our criteria for inclusion in the GreenDex covers environmental (minimising negative environmental impacts and, where possible, making positive contributions), social or cultural (respecting culture and traditions and fostering authentic interaction and greater understanding between travellers and hosts) and economic (providing financial benefits for the host community and operating on the principles of fair trade) issues. For more tips about travelling sustainably in Africa, turn to the Responsible Travel chapter (p54). We want to keep developing our sustainable-travel content. If you think we've omitted someone who should be listed here, email us at talk2us@lonelyplanet.com.au. For more information about sustainable tourism and Lonely Planet, see www.lonelyplanet.com/responsibletravel.

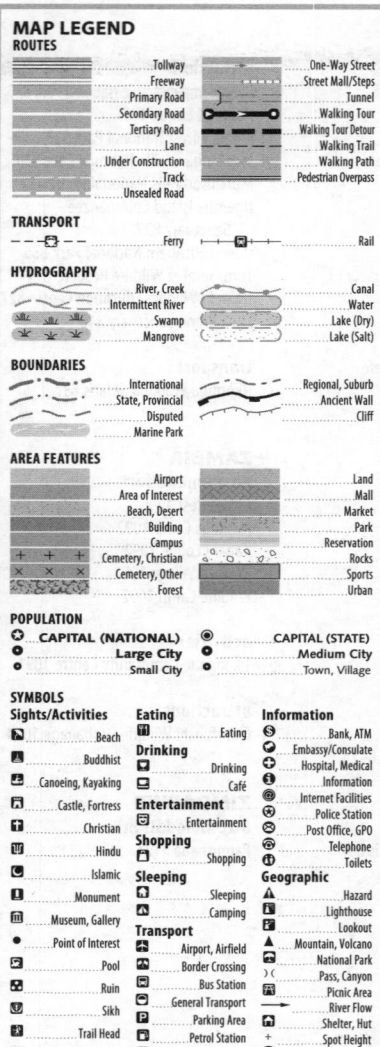

MAP LEGEND

ROUTES

- Tollway
- Freeway
- Primary Road
- Secondary Road
- Tertiary Road
- Lane
- Under Construction
- Track
- Unsealed Road
- One-Way Street
- Street Mall/Steps
- Tunnel
- Walking Tour
- Walking Tour Detour
- Walking Trail
- Walking Path
- Pedestrian Overpass

TRANSPORT

- Ferry
- Rail

HYDROGRAPHY

- River, Creek
- Intermittent River
- Swamp
- Mangrove
- Canal
- Water
- Lake (Dry)
- Lake (Salt)

BOUNDARIES

- International
- State, Provincial
- Disputed
- Marine Park
- Regional, Suburb
- Ancient Wall
- Cliff

AREA FEATURES

- Airport
- Area of Interest
- Beach, Desert
- Building
- Campus
- Cemetery, Christian
- Cemetery, Other
- Forest
- Land
- Mall
- Market
- Park
- Reservation
- Rocks
- Sports
- Urban

POPULATION

- ◉ **CAPITAL (NATIONAL)**
- ◎ **CAPITAL (STATE)**
- ● **Large City**
- ● **Medium City**
- ○ Small City
- ○ Town, Village

SYMBOLS

Sights/Activities
- Beach
- Buddhist
- Canoeing, Kayaking
- Castle, Fortress
- Christian
- Hindu
- Islamic
- Monument
- Museum, Gallery
- Point of Interest
- Pool
- Ruin
- Sikh
- Trail Head
- Zoo, Game Reserve

Eating
- Eating

Drinking
- Drinking
- Café

Entertainment
- Entertainment

Shopping
- Shopping

Sleeping
- Sleeping
- Camping

Transport
- Airport, Airfield
- Border Crossing
- Bus Station
- General Transport
- Parking Area
- Petrol Station
- Taxi Rank

Information
- Bank, ATM
- Embassy/Consulate
- Hospital, Medical
- Information
- Internet Facilities
- Police Station
- Post Office, GPO
- Telephone
- Toilets

Geographic
- Hazard
- Lighthouse
- Lookout
- Mountain, Volcano
- National Park
- Pass, Canyon
- Picnic Area
- River Flow
- Shelter, Hut
- Spot Height
- Waterfall

LONELY PLANET OFFICES

Australia (Head Office)
Locked Bag 1, Footscray, Victoria 3011
☎ 03 8379 8000, fax 03 8379 8111
talk2us@lonelyplanet.com.au

USA
150 Linden St, Oakland, CA 94607
☎ 510 250 6400, toll free 800 275 8555
fax 510 893 8572
info@lonelyplanet.com

UK
2nd fl, 186 City Rd,
London EC1V 2NT
☎ 020 7106 2100, fax 020 7106 2101
go@lonelyplanet.co.uk

Published by Lonely Planet
ABN 36 005 607 983

© Lonely Planet 2010

© photographers as indicated 2010

Mixed Sources
Product group from well-managed forests and other controlled sources
www.fsc.org Cert no. SGS-COC-005002
© 1996 Forest Stewardship Council